ENCYCLOPEDIA OF WORLD ART

Vol. XII
RENAISSANCE – SHAHN

ENCICLOPEDIA
UNIVERSALE
DELL'ARTE

Sotto gli auspici della Fondazione Giorgio Cini

ISTITUTO PER LA COLLABORAZIONE CULTURALE
VENEZIA–ROMA

ENCYCLOPEDIA
OF
WORLD ART

McGRAW-HILL BOOK COMPANY
NEW YORK, TORONTO, LONDON

ENCYCLOPEDIA OF WORLD ART: VOLUME XII

Paper for plates and text supplied by Cartiere Burgo, Turin — Engraving by Zincotipia Altimani, Milan — Black-and-white and color plates printed by Tipocolor, Florence — Text printed by "L'Impronta," Florence — Binding by Stabilimento Stianti, San Casciano Val di Pesa, Florence — Book cloth supplied by G. Pasini e C., Milan

Printed in Italy

Library of Congress Catalog Card Number 59-13433
19469

INTERNATIONAL COUNCIL OF SCHOLARS

Mario SALMI, University of Rome, President

† Marcel AUBERT, Membre de l'Institut; Director, Société Française d'Archéologie, Paris, Vice President
† Ernst KÜHNEL, Director, Islamic Section, Staatliche Museen, Berlin, Vice President
† Amedeo MAIURI, Accademico dei Lincei, Naples, Vice President
Gisela M. A. RICHTER, Honorary Curator, Metropolitan Museum of Art, New York City, Vice President
Giuseppe TUCCI, University of Rome; President, Istituto Italiano per il Medio ed Estremo Oriente, Rome, Vice President

Alvar AALTO, Architect, Helsinki
Jean ALAZARD, University of Algiers
Andrew ALFÖLDI, University of Basel; Institute for Advanced Study, Princeton, N.J.
† Carlo ANTI, University of Padua
Sir Gilbert ARCHEY, Auckland, New Zealand
A. S. ARDOJO, Jakarta, Indonesia
Bernard ASHMOLE, Emeritus Professor, Oxford University
Jeannine AUBOYER, Curator in Chief, Musée Guimet, Paris
† Ludwig BALDASS, Director, Kunsthistorisches Museum, Vienna
Sir John Davidson BEAZLEY, Oxford University
† Bernard BERENSON
W. BLAWATSKY, Institute of Archaeology, Academy of Sciences of the USSR, Moscow
† Albert BOECKLER, Staatsbibliothekar, Munich
Axel BOËTHIUS, formerly, University of Göteborg and Director, Swedish Institute, Rome
† Helmut T. BOSSERT, University of Istanbul
Cesare BRANDI, University of Palermo
† Henri BREUIL, Membre de l'Institut; Collège de France, Paris
Peter H. BRIEGER, University of Toronto
Joseph BURKE, University of Melbourne
A. W. BYVANCK, University of Leiden
Guido CALOGERO, University of Rome
Alfonso CASO, Tlacopac, Mexico
† Carlo CECCHELLI, University of Rome
Enrico CERULLI, Accademico dei Lincei, Rome
Jean CHARBONNEAUX, Inspecteur général honoraire des Musées de France, Paris
† Gino CHIERICI, Superintendent of Monuments, Pavia
Fernando CHUECA Y GOITIA, School of Architecture; Director, Museum of Contemporary Art, Madrid
Giuseppe COCCHIARA, University of Palermo
George CŒDÈS, Membre de l'Institut; Honorary Director, Ecole Française d'Extrême-Orient, Paris
Paul COLLART, Director, Swiss Institute, Rome
W. G. CONSTABLE, formerly, Museum of Fine Arts, Boston
Paolo D'ANCONA, University of Milan
† Sir Percival DAVID, London
Guglielmo DE ANGELIS D'OSSAT, University of Rome
Otto DEMUS, University of Vienna
Paul DESCHAMPS, Membre de l'Institut; Honorary Curator in Chief, Musée des Monuments Français, Paris
Prince DHANINIVAT, Honorary President, Siam Society, Bangkok
Adrian DIGBY, Keeper of the Department of Ethnography, British Museum, London
† Einar DYGGVE, Director, Ny Carlsberg Foundation, Copenhagen
Gustav ECKE, Curator of Chinese Art, Honolulu Academy of Arts; University of Hawaii
Vadime ELISSEEFF, Director, Musée Cernuschi; Director of Studies, Ecole Practique des Hautes Etudes, Sorbonne, Paris
A. P. ELKIN, University of Sydney
Richard ETTINGHAUSEN, Freer Gallery of Art, Washington, D.C.
Bishr FARÈS, Institut d'Egypte, Cairo
† Paul FIERENS, Curator in Chief, Musées Royaux des Beaux-Arts de Belgique, Brussels
Giuseppe FIOCCO, University of Padua; Director, Istituto di Storia dell'Arte, Fondazione Giorgio Cini, Venice
Pierre FRANCASTEL, Director of Studies, Ecole Practique des Hautes Etudes, Sorbonne, Paris
† Giuseppe FURLANI, University of Rome
Albert GABRIEL, formerly, Director, Institut Français d'Archéologie, Istanbul
O. C. GANGOLY, Calcutta
Antonio GARCÍA Y BELLIDO, University of Madrid
Alberto GIUGANINO, Vice President, Istituto Italiano per il Medio ed Estremo Oriente, Rome
Albert Rex GONZALES, Director, Museo de La Plata, Argentina
L. Carrington GOODRICH, Professor Emeritus of Chinese, Columbia University, New York City
Lloyd GOODRICH, Director, Whitney Museum of American Art, New York City
André GRABAR, Membre de l'Institut; Ecole Practique des Hautes Etudes, Sorbonne, Paris; Collège de France, Paris

ABBREVIATIONS

Museums, Galleries, Libraries, and Other Institutions

Antikensamml.	— Antikensammlungen
Antiq.	— Antiquarium
Bib. Nat.	— Bibliothèque Nationale
Bib. Naz.	— Biblioteca Nazionale
Brera	— Pinacoteca di Brera
Br. Mus.	— British Museum
Cab. Méd.	— Cabinet des Médailles (Paris, Bibliothèque Nationale)
Cleve. Mus.	— Cleveland Museum
Conserv.	— Palazzo dei Conservatori
Gall. Arte Mod.	— Galleria d'Arte Moderna
IsMEO	— Istituto Italiano per il Medio ed Estremo Oriente
Kunstgewerbemus.	— Kunstgewerbemuseum
Kunsthist. Mus.	— Kunsthistorisches Museum
Louvre	— Musée du Louvre
Medagl.	— Medagliere
Met. Mus.	— Metropolitan Museum
Mus. Ant.	— Museo di Antichità
Mus. Arch.	— Museo Archeologico
Mus. B. A.	— Musée des Beaux-Arts
Mus. Cap.	— Musei Capitolini, Capitoline Museums
Mus. Civ.	— Museo Civico
Mus. Com.	— Museo Comunale
Mus. Etn.	— Museo Etnologico
Mus. Naz.	— Museo Nazionale
Nat. Gall.	— National Gallery
Öst. Gal.	— Österreichische Galerie
Pin. Naz.	— Pinacoteca Nazionale
Prado	— Museo del Prado
Rijksmus.	— Rijksmuseum
Samml.	— Sammlung
Staat. Mus.	— Staatliche Museen
Staatsbib.	— Staatsbibliothek
Städt. Mus.	— Städtisches Museum
Tate Gall.	— Tate Gallery
Uffizi	— Uffizi Gallery
Vat. Mus.	— Vatican Museums
Vict. and Alb.	— Victoria and Albert Museum
Villa Giulia	— Museo di Villa Giulia

Reviews and Miscellanies

AAE	— Archivio per la Antropologia e la Etnologia, Florence
AAnz	— Archäologischer Anzeiger, Berlin
AAV	— Archivo de Arte Valenciano, Valencia
AB	— Art Bulletin, New York
AbhAkMünchen	— Abhandlungen der Bayerischen Akademie der Wissenschaften, Munich
AbhPreussAk	— Abhandlungen der preussischen Akademie der Wissenschaften, Berlin; after 1945, Abhandlungen der Deutschen Akademie der Wissenschaften zu Berlin, Berlin
ABIA	— Annual Bibliography of Indian Archaeology, Leiden
ABMAB	— Anales y Boletín de los Museos de Arte de Barcelona
ABME	— Ἀρχεῖον τῶν Βυζαντινῶν Μνημείων τῆς Ἑλλάδος, Athens

AC	— Archeologia Classica, Rome
ACCV	— Anales del Centro de Cultura Valenciana, Valencia
ActaA	— Acta Archaeologica, Copenhagen
ActaO	— Acta Orientalia, Leiden, The Hague
AD	— Antike Denkmäler, Deutsches Archäologisches Institut, Berlin, Leipzig
AE	— Arte Español, Madrid
AEA	— Archivo Español de Arqueología, Madrid
AEAA	— Archivo Español de Arte y Arqueología, Madrid
AEArte	— Archivio Español de Arte, Madrid
AErt	— Archaeologiai Értesitö, Budapest
AfA	— Archiv für Anthropologie, Brunswick
AfO	— Archiv für Orientforschung, Berlin
AfrIt	— Africa Italiana, Bergamo
AGS	— American Guide Series, U.S. Federal Writers' Project, Works Progress Administration, Washington, D.C., 1935–41
AIEC	— Anuari de l'Institut d'Estudies Catalans, Barcelona
AIEG	— Anales del Instituto de Estudios Gerundenses, Gerona
AJA	— American Journal of Archaeology, Baltimore
AM	— Mitteilungen des deutschen archäologischen Instituts, Athenische Abteilung, Athens, Stuttgart
AmA	— American Anthropologist, Menasha, Wis.
AmAnt	— American Antiquity, Menasha, Wis.
AN	— Art News, New York
AnnInst	— Annali dell'Instituto di Corrispondenza Archeologica, Rome
AnnSAntEg	— Annales du Service des Antiquités de l'Egypte, Cairo
AntC	— L'Antiquité Classique, Louvain
AntJ	— The Antiquaries Journal, London
AnzAlt	— Anzeiger für die Altertumswissenschaft, Innsbruck, Vienna
AnzÖAk	— Anzeiger der Österreichischen Akademie der Wissenschaften, Vienna
APAmM	— Anthropological Papers of the American Museum of Natural History, New York
AQ	— Art Quarterly, Detroit
ArndtBr	— P. Arndt, F. Bruckmann, Griechische und römische Porträts, Munich, 1891 ff.
ARSI	— Annual Report of the Smithsonian Institution, Bureau of Ethnology, Washington, D.C.
ArtiFig	— Arti Figurative, Rome
ASAtene	— Annuario della Scuola Archeologica Italiana di Atene, Bergamo
ASI	— Archivio Storico Italiano, Florence
ASWI	— Archaeological Survey of Western India, Hyderabad
AttiCongrStAMed	— Atti dei Congressi di Studi dell'Arte dell'Alto Medioevo
AttiDeSPa	— Atti e Memorie della Deputazione di Storia Patria
AttiPontAcc	— Atti della Pontificia Accademia Romana di Archeologia, Rome
Atti3StArch	— Atti del III Convegno Nazionale di Storia dell'Architettura, Rome, 1938
Atti5StArch	— Atti del V Convegno Nazionale di Storia dell'Architettura, Florence, 1957

AZ	— Archäologische Zeitung, Berlin
BA	— Baessler Archiv, Leipzig, Berlin
BABsch	— Bulletin van de Vereeniging tot bevordering der kennis van de antieke Beschaving, The Hague
BAC	— Bulletin du Comité des Travaux Historiques et Scientifiques, Section d'Archéologie, Paris
BAcBelg	— Bulletin de l'Académie Royale de Belgique, Cl. des Lettres, Brussels
BACr	— Bollettino di Archeologia Cristiana, Rome
BAEB	— Bureau of American Ethnology, Bulletins, Washington, D.C.
BAER	— Bureau of American Ethnology, Reports, Washington, D.C.
BAFr	— Bulletin de la Société Nationale des Antiquaires de France, Paris
BAmSOR	— Bulletin of the American Schools of Oriental Research, South Hadley, Mass.
BArte	— Bollettino d'Arte del Ministero della Pubblica Istruzione, Rome
BAT	— Boletín Arqueológico Tarragona
BBMP	— Boletín de la Biblioteca Menéndez Pelayo, Santander
BByzI	— The Bulletin of the Byzantine Institute, Paris
BCH	— Bulletin de Correspondance Hellénique, Paris
BCom	— Bullettino della Commissione Archeologica Comunale, Rome
BCPMB	— Boletín de la Comision Provincial de Monumentos de Burgos
BCPML	— Boletín de la Comision Provincial de Monumentos de Lugo
BCPMO	— Boletín de la Comision Provincial de Monumentos de Orense
Beazley, ABV	— J. D. Beazley, Attic Black-figure Vase-painters, Oxford, 1956
Beazley, ARV	— J. D. Beazley, Attic Red-figure Vase-painters, Oxford, 1942
Beazley, EVP	— J. D. Beazley, Etruscan Vase-painting, Oxford, 1947
Beazley, VA	— J. D. Beazley, Attic Red-figured Vases in American Museums, Cambridge, 1918
Beazley, VRS	— J. D. Beazley, Attische Vasenmaler des rotfigurigen Stils, Tübingen, 1925
BEFEO	— Bulletin de l'Ecole Française d'Extrême-Orient, Hanoi, Saigon, Paris
BerlNZ	— Berliner Numismatische Zeitschrift, Berlin
Bernoulli, GI	— J. J. Bernoulli, Griechische Ikonographie, Munich, 1901
Bernoulli, RI	— J. J. Bernoulli, Römische Ikonographie, I, Stuttgart, 1882; II, 1, Berlin, Stuttgart, 1886; II, 2, Stuttgart, Berlin, Leipzig, 1891; II, 3, Stuttgart, Berlin, Leipzig, 1894
BHAcRoum	— Bulletin Historique, Académie Roumaine, Bucharest
BICR	— Bollettino dell'Istituto Centrale del Restauro, Rome
BIE	— Bulletin de l'Institut de l'Egypte, Cairo
BIFAN	— Bulletin de l'Institut Français d'Afrique Noire, Dakar
BIFAO	— Bulletin de l'Institut Français d'Archéologie Orientale, Cairo
BIFG	— Boletín de la Institución Fernán González, Burgos
BInst	— Bullettino dell'Instituto di Corrispondenza Archeologica, Rome
BJ	— Bonner Jahrbücher, Bonn, Darmstadt
BM	— Burlington Magazine, London
BMBeyrouth	— Bulletin du Musée de Beyrouth, Beirut
BMC	— British Museum, Catalogue of Greek Coins, London
BMCEmp	— H. Mattingly, Coins of the Roman Empire in the British Museum, London
BMFA	— Museum of Fine Arts, Bulletin, Boston
BMFEA	— Museum of Far-Eastern Antiquities, Bulletin, Stockholm
BMImp	— Bullettino del Museo dell'Impero, Rome
BMMA	— Bulletin of the Metropolitan Museum of Art, New York
BMN	— Boletín Monumentos Navarra
BMQ	— The British Museum Quarterly, London
BNedOud	— Bulletin van de Koninklijke Nederlandse Oudheidkundige Bond, Leiden
BPI	— Bullettino di Paletnologia Italiana, Rome

BRA	— Boletín de la Real Academia de Ciencias, Bellas Letras y Nobles Artes de Córdoba, Córdoba
BRABASF	— Boletín de la Real Academia de Bellas Artes de San Fernando, Madrid
BRABLB	— Boletín de la Real Academia de Buenas Letras de Barcelona
BRAH	— Boletín de la Real Academia de la Historia, Madrid
BrBr	— H. Brunn, F. Bruckmann, Denkmäler griechischer und römischer Skulptur, Munich
Brunn, GGK	— H. Brunn, Geschichte der griechischen Künstler, 2d ed., Stuttgart, 1889
Brunn, GK	— H. Brunn, Griechische Kunstgeschichte, Munich, I, 1893; II, 1897
BSA	— Annual of the British School at Athens, London
BSCC	— Boletín de la Sociedad Castellonense de Cultura, Castellón de la Plana
BSCE	— Boletín de la Sociedad Castellana de Excursiones, Valladolid
BSEAAV	— Boletín del Seminario de Estudios de Arte y Arqueología, Universidad de Valladolid
BSEE	— Boletín de la Sociedad Española de Excursiones, Madrid
BSEI	— Bulletin de la Société des Etudes Indochinoises, Saigon
BSOAS	— Bulletin of the School of Oriental and African Studies, London
BSPF	— Bulletin de la Société Préhistorique Française, Paris
BSR	— Papers of the British School at Rome, London
Cabrol-Leclercq	— F. Cabrol, H. Leclercq, Dictionnaire d'archéologie chrétienne et de liturgie, Paris, 1907
CAF	— Congrès Archéologique de France, Paris, 1841–1935
CahA	— Cahiers Archéologiques, Fin de l'Antiquité et Moyen-Age, Paris
CahArt	— Cahiers d'art, Paris
CAJ	— Central Asiatic Journal, Wiesbaden
CAUG	— Cuadernos de Arte de la Universidad de Granada
CEFEO	— Cahiers de l'Ecole Française d'Extrême-Orient, Paris
CEG	— Cuadernos de Estudios Gallegos, Santiago de Compostela
CIE	— Corpus Inscriptionum Etruscarum, Lipsiae
CIG	— Corpus Inscriptionum Graecarum, Berolini
CIL	— Corpus Inscriptionum Latinarum, Berolini
CIS	— Corpus Inscriptionum Semiticarum, Parisiis
Coh	— H. Cohen, Description historique des Monnaies frappées sous l'Empire Romain, Paris
Collignon, SG	— M. Collignon, Histoire de la sculpture grecque, Paris, I, 1892; II, 1897
Comm	— Commentari, Florence, Rome
Cr	— La Critica, Bari
CRAI	— Comptes Rendus de l'Académie des Inscriptions et Belles-Lettres, Paris
CrArte	— La Critica d'Arte, Florence
CVA	— Corpus Vasorum Antiquorum
DA	— N. Daremberg, N. Saglio, Dictionnaire des antiquités grecques et romaines, Paris, 1877–1912
Dehio, I–V	— G. Dehio, Handbuch der deutschen Kunstdenkmäler, Berlin, I, Mitteldeutschland, 1927; II, Nordostdeutschland, 1926; III, Süddeutschland, 1933; IV, Südwestdeutschland, 1933; V, Nordwestdeutschland, 1928
Dehio, DtK	— G. Dehio, Geschichte der deutschen Kunst, 8 vols., Berlin, 1930–34
Dehio-VonBezold	— G. Dehio, G. von Bezold, Die kirchliche Baukunst des Abendlandes, Stuttgart, 1892–1901
DissPontAcc	— Dissertazioni della Pontificia Accademia Romana di Archeologia, Rome
EA	— Photographische Einzelaufnahmen, Munich, 1893 ff.
EAA	— Enciclopedia dell'Arte Antica, Rome, I, 1958; II, 1959; III, 1960; IV, 1961
EArt	— Eastern Art, London
EB	— Encyclopaedia Britannica
'EEBΣ	— Ἐπετερίς Ἐταιρεία Βυζαντινῶν Σπουδῶν, Athens
'Εφημ	— Ἀρχαιολογικὴ Ἐφημερίς, Athens

EI — Enciclopedia Italiana, Rome, 1929 ff.

EphDR — Ephemeris Dacoromana, Rome

'Έργον — Tὸ 'έργον τῆς ἀρχαιολογικῆς ἑταιρείας, ed. A. K. Orlandos, Athens

ES — Estudios Segovianos, Segovia

ESA — Eurasia Septentrionalis Antiqua, Helsinki

Espér — E. Espérandieu, R. Lantier, Recueil général des Bas-Reliefs de la Gaule Romaine, Paris

EUC — Estudis Universitaris Catalans, Barcelona

FA — Fasti Archaeologici, Florence

FD — Fouilles de Delphes, Paris

Friedländer — Max Friedländer, Altniederländische Malerei, Berlin, 1924–37

Furtwängler, AG — A. Furtwängler, Antiken Gemmen, Leipzig, Berlin, 1900

Furtwängler, BG — A. Furtwängler, Beschreibung der Glyptothek König Ludwig I zu München, Munich, 1900

Furtwängler, KlSchr — A. Furtwängler, Kleine Schriften, Munich, 1912

Furtwängler, MP — A. Furtwängler, Masterpieces of Greek Sculpture, London, 1895

Furtwängler, MW — A. Furtwängler, Meisterwerke der griechischen Plastik, Leipzig, Berlin, 1893

Furtwängler Reichhold — A. Furtwängler, K. Reichhold, Griechische Vasenmalerei, Munich

FWP — U.S. Federal Writers' Project, Works Progress Administration, Washington, D.C., 1935–1941

GBA — Gazette des Beaux-Arts, Paris

GJ — The Geographical Journal, London

HA — Handbuch der Archäologie im Rahmen des Handbuchs der Altertumswissenschaft . . . , herausgegeben von Walter Otto, Munich, 1939–53

HABS — Historic American Buildings Survey, U.S. Library of Congress, Washington, D.C.

HBr — P. Herrmann, F. Bruckmann, Denkmäler der Malerei des Altertums, Munich, 1907

Helbig-Amelung — W. Helbig, W. Amelung, E. Reisch, F. Weege, Führer durch die öffentlichen Sammlungen klassischer Altertümer in Rom, Leipzig, 1912–13

HIPBC — A Handbook for Travellers in India, Pakistan, Burma and Ceylon, London, 1955

HJAS — Harvard Journal of Asiatic Studies, Cambridge, Mass.

Hoppin, Bf — J. C. Hoppin, A Handbook of Greek Black-figured Vases with a Chapter on the Red-figured Southern Italian Vases, Paris, 1924

Hoppin, Rf — J. C. Hoppin, A Handbook of Attic Red-figured Vases Signed by or Attributed to the Various Masters of the Sixth and Fifth Centuries B.C., Cambridge, 1919

HSAI — J. H. Steward, ed., Handbook of South American Indians, 6 vols., Bureau of American Ethnology, Bull. 143, Washington, D.C., 1946–50

IAE — Internationales Archiv für Ethnographie, Leiden

IBAI — Bulletin de l'Institut Archéologique Bulgare, Sofia

IFAN — Institut Français Afrique Noire, Dakar

IG — Inscriptiones Graecae, Berolini

ILN — Illustrated London News, London

IPEK — Ipek, Jahrbuch für prähistorische und ethnographische Kunst, Berlin

ITTM — Instituto Tello Tellez de Meneses, Palencia

JA — Journal Asiatique, Paris

JAF — Journal of American Folklore, Lancaster, Pa.

JAOS — Journal of the American Oriental Society, Baltimore

JAS — Journal of the African Society, London

JBORS — Journal of the Bihar and Orissa Research Society, Patna, India

JdI — Jahrbuch des deutschen archäologischen Instituts, Berlin

JEA — Journal of Egyptian Archaeology, London

JhbKhSammlWien — Jahrbuch der kunsthistorischen Sammlungen in Wien, Vienna

JhbPreussKSamml — Jahrbuch der preussischen Kunstsammlungen, Berlin

JHS — Journal of Hellenic Studies, London

JIAI — Journal of Indian Art and Industry, London

JIAN — Journal International d'Archéologie Numismatique, Athens

JISOA — Journal of the India Society of Oriental Art, Calcutta

JNES — Journal of Near Eastern Studies, Chicago

JPS — Journal of the Polynesian Society, Wellington, New Zealand

JRAI — Journal of the Royal Anthropological Institute of Great Britain and Ireland, London

JRAS — Journal of the Royal Asiatic Society, London

JRS — Journal of Roman Studies, London

JS — Journal des Savants, Paris

JSA — Journal de la Société des Africanistes, Paris

JSAH — Journal of the Society of Architectural Historians, Charlottesville, Va.

JSAm — Journal de la Société des Américanistes, Paris

JSO — Journal de la Société des Océanistes, Paris

KbNed — Kunstreisboek voor Nederland, Amsterdam, 1960

Klein, GrK — W. Klein, Geschichte der griechischen Kunst, Leipzig, 1904–07

KS — Communications on the Reports and Field Research of the Institute of Material Culture, Moscow, Leningrad

Lippold, GP — G. Lippold, Die griechische Plastik (W. Otto, Handbuch der Archäologie, II, 1), Munich, 1950

Löwy, IGB — E. Löwy, Inschriften griechischer Bildhauer, Leipzig, 1885

MAAccIt — Monumenti Antichi dell'Accademia d'Italia, Milan

MAARome — Memoirs of the American Academy in Rome, Rome, New York

MAF — Mémoires de la Société Nationale des Antiquaires de France, Paris

MAGWien — Mitteilungen der anthropologischen Gesellschaft in Wien, Vienna

Mâle, I — E. Mâle, L'art religieux du XIIᵉ siècle en France, Paris, 1928

Mâle, II — E. Mâle, L'art religieux du XIIIᵉ siècle en France, Paris, 1925

Mâle, III — E. Mâle, L'art religieux de la fin du moyen-âge en France, Paris, 1925

Mâle, IV — E. Mâle, L'art religieux après le Concile de Trente, Paris, 1932

MALinc — Monumenti Antichi dell'Accademia dei Lincei, Milan, Rome

Mattingly-Sydenham — H. Mattingly, E. Sydenham, C. H. V. Sutherland, The Roman Imperial Coinage, London

MdI — Mitteilungen des deutschen archäologischen Instituts, Munich

MdIK — Mitteilungen des deutschen Instituts für ägyptische Altertumskunde in Kairo, Wiesbaden

Mél — Mélanges d'Archéologie et d'Histoire (Ecole Française de Rome), Paris

Mem. Junta Sup. Exc. — Memoria de la Junta Superior de Excavaciones y Antigüedades, Madrid

MemLinc — Memorie dell'Accademia dei Lincei, Rome

MGH — Monumenta Germaniae Historica, Berlin

MIA — Material and Research in Archaeology of the U.S.S.R., Moscow, Leningrad

Michel — A. Michel, Histoire de l'art depuis les premiers temps chrétiens jusqu'à nos jours, Paris, 1905–29

MInst — Monumenti dell'Instituto di Corrispondenza Archeologica, Rome

MLJ — Modern Language Journal, St. Louis, Mo.

MnbKw — Monatsberichte über Kunstwissenschaft

MPA — Monumenti della pittura antica scoperti in Italia, Rome

MPiot — Fondation Eugène Piot, Monuments et Mémoires, Paris

MPontAcc — Memorie della Pontificia Accademia Romana di Archeologia, Rome

NBACr — Nuovo Bullettino di Archeologia Cristiana, Rome

NChr — Numismatic Chronicle and Journal of the Royal Numismatic Society, London

NedKhJb — Nederlandsch Kunsthistorisch Jaarboek, 1945ff.

NedMon — De Nederlandse Monumenten van Geschiedenis en Kunst, 1911 ff.

NIFAN — Notes de l'Institut Français d'Afrique Noire, Dakar

NR	— Numismatic Review, New York
NSc	— Notizie degli Scavi di Antichità, Rome
NZ	— Numismatische Zeitschrift, Vienna
OAZ	— Ostasiatische Zeitschrift, Vienna
OIP	— Oriental Institute Publications, Chicago
ÖJh	— Jahreshefte des Österreichischen archäologischen Instituts, Vienna
ÖKT	— Österreichische Kunsttopographie, Vienna
OMLeiden	— Oudheidkundige Mededeelingen van het Rijksmuseum van Oudheten te Leiden, Leiden
OpA	— Opuscola Archaeologica, Lund
OTNE	— Old Time New England; the Bulletin of the Society for the Preservation of New England Antiquities, Boston, Massachusetts, I, 1910
OudJb	— Oudheidkundig Jaarboek, Leiden
Overbeck, SQ	— J. Overbeck, Die antiken Schriftquellen zur Geschichte der bildenden Künste bei den Griechen, Leipzig, 1868; reprint, Hildesheim, 1958
Oxy. Pap.	— The Oxyrhynchus Papyri, by B. P. Grenfell, A. S. Hunt, H. I. Bell, et al., eds., London, 1898 ff.
ΠAE	— Πρακτικά τῆς ἐν Ἀθήναις Ἀρχαιολογικῆς Ἑταιριας, Athens
PEQ	— Palestine Exploration Quarterly, London
Perrot-Chipiez	— G. Perrot, C. Chipiez, Histoire de l'art dans l'Antiquité, Paris, I, 1882; II, 1884; III, 1885; IV, 1887; V, 1890; VI, 1894; VII, 1898; VIII, 1903; IX, 1911
Pfuhl	— E. Pfuhl, Malerei und Zeichnung der Griechen, Munich, 1923
Picard	— C. Picard, Manuel d'Archéologie, La Sculpture, Paris, I, 1935; II, 1939; III, 1948; IV, 1, 1954
PL	— J. P. Migne, Patrologiae cursus completus, Series Latina, 221 vols., Paris, 1844–64
PM	— B. Porter and R. L. B. Moss, Topographical Bibliography of Ancient Egyptian Hieroglyphic Texts, Reliefs and Paintings, 7 vols., Oxford, 1927–51, 2d ed., 1960 ff.
Porter	— A. Kingsley Porter, Romanesque Sculpture of the Pilgrimage Roads, Boston, 1923
Post	— Charles Post, A History of Spanish Painting, 10 vols., Cambridge, Mass., 1930 ff.
ProcPrSoc	— Proceedings of the Prehistoric Society, Cambridge
PSI	— Pubblicazioni della Società Italiana per la ricerca dei papiri greci e latini in Egitto, Florence, 1912 ff.
QCr	— Quaderni della Critica, Bari
RA	— Revue Archéologique, Paris
RAA	— Revue des Arts Asiatiques, Paris
RAAB	— Revista de la Asociacion Artístico-Arqueológica Barcelonesa, Barcelona
RABM	— Revista de Archivos, Bibliotecas y Museos, Madrid
RACr	— Rivista di Archeologia Cristiana, Rome
RArte	— Rivista d'Arte, Florence
RArts	— Revue des arts, Paris
RBib	— Revue Biblique, Paris
RCHS	— Records of the Columbia Historical Society, Washington, D.C., I, 1897
RE	— A. Pauly, G. Wissowa, Real-Encyclopädie der classischen Altertumswissenschaft, Stuttgart, 1894 ff.
REA	— Revue des Etudes Anciennes, Bordeaux
REByz	— Revue des Etudes Byzantines, Paris
REE	— Revista des Estudios Extremesios, Badajoz
REG	— Revue des Etudes Grecques, Paris
Reinach, RP	— S. Reinach, Répertoire des Peintures Grecques et Romaines, Paris, 1922
Reinach, RR	— S. Reinach, Répertoire des Reliefs Grecs et Romains, Paris, I, 1909; II and III, 1912
Reinach, RS	— S. Reinach, Répertoire de la Statuaire Grecque et Romaine, Paris, I, 1897; II, 1, 1897; II, 2, 1898; III, 1904; IV, 1910
Reinach, RV	— S. Reinach, Répertoire des Vases peints, grecs et étrusques, Paris, I, 1899; II, 1900
REL	— Revue des Etudes Latines, Paris
RendAccIt	— Rendiconti della R. Accademia d'Italia, Rome
RendLinc	— Rendiconti dell'Accademia dei Lincei, Rome
RendNapoli	— Rendiconti dell'Accademia di Archeologia di Napoli, Naples
RendPontAcc	— Rendiconti della Pontificia Accademia Romana di Archeologia, Rome
RepfKw	— Repertorium für Kunstwissenschaft, Berlin, Stuttgart
REthn	— Revue d'Ethnographie, Paris
RhMus	— Rheinisches Museum für Philologie, Frankfort on the Main
RIASA	— Rivista dell'Istituto Nazionale d'Archeologia e Storia dell'Arte, Rome
RIE	— Revista de Ideas Estéticas, Madrid
RIN	— Rivista Italiana di Numismatica, Rome
RlDKg	— Reallexicon zur deutschen Kunstgeschichte, Stuttgart, 1937 ff.
RLV	— M. Ebert, Real-Lexicon der Vorgeschichte, Berlin, 1924–32
RM	— Mitteilungen des deutschen archäologischen Instituts, Römische Abteilung, Berlin
RN	— Revue Numismatique, Paris
RNA	— Revista Nacional de Arquitectura, Madrid
Robert, SR	— C. Robert, Die antiken Sarkophag-Reliefs, Berlin, 1890 ff.
Roscher	— W. H. Roscher, Ausführliches Lexikon der griechischen und römischen Mythologie, Leipzig, 1884–86; 1924–37
RQ	— Römische Quartalschrift, Freiburg
RScPr	— Rivista di Scienze Preistoriche, Florence
RSLig	— Rivista di Studi Liguri, Bordighera, Italy
RSO	— Rivista degli Studi Orientali, Rome
Rumpf, MZ	— A. Rumpf, Malerei und Zeichnung (W. Otto, Handbuch der Archäologie, IV, 1), Munich, 1953
RUO	— Revista de la Universidad de Oviedo
SA	— Soviet Archaeology, Moscow, Leningrad
SAA	— Seminario de Arte Aragonés, Zaragoza
SbBerlin	— Sitzungsberichte der preussischen Akademie der Wissenschaften, Berlin
SbHeidelberg	— Sitzungsberichte der Akademie der Wissenschaften zu Heidelberg, Heidelberg
SbMünchen	— Sitzungsberichte der bayerischen Akademie der Wissenschaften zu München, Munich
SbWien	— Sitzungsberichte der Akademie der Wissenschaften in Wien, Vienna
Schlosser	— J. Schlosser, La letteratura artistica, Florence, 1956
Scranton, Greek Walls	— R. L. Scranton, Greek Walls, Cambridge, Mass., 1941
SEtr	— Studi Etruschi, Florence
SNR	— Sudan Notes and Records, Khartoum
SPA	— A Survey of Persian Art, ed. A. U. Pope and P. Ackerman, Oxford, 1938
SymbOsl	— Symbolae Osloenses, Oslo
Tebtunis	— The Tebtunis Papyri, B. P. Grenfell, A. S. Hunt, et al., eds., London, 1902 ff.
ThB	— U. Thieme, F. Becker, Künstler Lexikon, Leipzig, 1907–50
TitAM	— Tituli Asiae Minoris, Vindobonae, 1901–44
TNR	— Tanganyika Notes and Records, Dar-es-Salaam
Toesca, Md	— P. Toesca, Il Medioevo, 2 vols., Turin, 1927
Toesca, Tr	— P. Toesca, Il Trecento, Turin, 1951
TP	— T'oung Pao, Leiden
UCalPAAE	— University of California, Publications in American Archaeology and Ethnology, Berkeley
USMB	— United States National Museum, Bulletin, Washington, D.C.
Van Marle	— R. van Marle, The Development of the Italian Schools of Painting, The Hague, 1923–38
Vasari	— G. Vasari, Vite, ed. Milanesi, Florence, 1878 ff. (Am. ed., trans. E. H. and E. W. Blashfield and A. A. Hopkins, 4 vols., New York, 1913)
Venturi	— A. Venturi, Storia dell'Arte Italiana, Milan, 1901 ff.
VFPA	— Viking Fund Publications in Anthropology, New York
Vollmer	— H. Vollmer, Allgemeines Lexikon der bildenden Künstler des XX. Jahrhunderts, Leipzig, 1953
Warburg	— Journal of the Warburg and Courtauld Institutes, London
Weickert, Archaische Architektur	— C. Weickert, Typen der archaischen Architektur in Griechenland und Kleinasien, Augsburg, 1929
Wpr	— Winckelmannsprogramm, Berlin
WürzbJ	— Würzburger Jahrbücher für die Altertumswissenschaft, Würzburg
WVDOG	— Wissenschaftliche Veröffentlichungen der Deutschen Orient-Gesellschaft, Leipzig, Berlin

ZäS	— Zeitschrift für ägyptische Sprache und Altertumskunde, Berlin, Leipzig
ZfAssyr	— Zeitschrift für Assyriologie, Strasbourg
ZfbK	— Zeitschrift für bildende Kunst, Leipzig
ZfE	— Zeitschrift für Ethnologie, Berlin
ZfKg	— Zeitschrift für Kunstgeschichte, Munich
ZfKw	— Zeitschrift für Kunstwissenschaft, Munich
ZfN	— Zeitschrift für Numismatik, Berlin
ZMG	— Zeitschrift der deutschen morgenländischen Gesellschaft, Leipzig
ZSAKg	— Zeitschrift für schweizerische Archäologie und Kunstgeschichte, Basel

Languages and Ethnological Descriptions

Alb.	— Albanian
Am.	— American
Ang.	— Anglice, Anglicized
Ar.	— Arabic
Arm.	— Armenian
AS.	— Anglo-Saxon
Bab.	— Babylonian
Br.	— British
Bulg.	— Bulgarian
Chin.	— Chinese
D.	— Dutch
Dan.	— Danish
Eg.	— Egyptian
Eng.	— English
Finn.	— Finnish
Fr.	— French
Ger.	— German
Gr.	— Greek
Heb.	— Hebrew
Hung.	— Hungarian
It.	— Italian
Jap.	— Japanese
Jav.	— Javanese
Lat.	— Latin
Mod. Gr.	— Modern Greek
Nor.	— Norwegian
Per.	— Persian
Pol.	— Polish
Port.	— Portuguese
Rum.	— Rumanian
Rus.	— Russian
Skr.	— Sanskrit
Sp.	— Spanish
Swed.	— Swedish
Yugo.	— Yugoslav

Other Abbreviations (Standard abbreviations in common usage are omitted.)

Abh.	— Abhandlungen
Acad.	— Academy, Académie
Acc.	— Accademia
Adm.	— Administration
Ak.	— Akademie
Allg.	— Allgemein
Alm.	— Almanacco
Amm.	— Amministrazione
Ann.	— Annals, Annali, Annuario, Annual, etc.
Ant.	— Antiquity, Antico, Antiquaire, etc.
Anthr.	— Anthropology, etc.
Antr.	— Antropologia, etc.
Anz.	— Anzeiger
Arch.	— Architecture, Architettura, Architettonico, etc.
Archaeol.	— Archaeology, etc.
Archeol.	— Archeologia, Archéologie
Arqueol.	— Arqueología, etc.
attrib.	— attributed
Aufl.	— Auflage
Aufn.	— Aufnahme
B.	— Bulletin, Bollettino, etc.
b.	— born
Belg.	— Belgian, Belga, etc.
Berl.	— Berlin, Berliner
Bern.	— Berner
Bib.	— Bible, Biblical, Bibliothèque, etc.
Bibliog.	— Bibliography, etc.
Bur.	— Bureau
Byz.	— Byzantine

C.	— Corpus
ca.	— circa
Cah.	— Cahiers
Cal.	— Calendar
Cap.	— Capital, Capitolium
Cat.	— Catalogue, Catalogo, etc.
Cath.	— Cathedral
Chr.	— Chronicle, Chronik
Civ.	— Civiltà, Civilization, etc.
cod.	— codex
col., cols	— column, columns
Coll.	— Collection, Collana, Collationes, Collectanea, Collezione, etc.
Com.	— Comunale
Comm.	— Commentaries, Commentari, Communications, etc.
Cong.	— Congress, Congresso, etc.
Cr.	— Critica
Cron.	— Cronaca
Cuad.	— Cuadernos
Cult.	— Culture, Cultura, etc.
D.	— Deutsch
d.	— died
Diss.	— Dissertation, Dissertazione
Doc.	— Documents, etc.
E.	— Encyclopedia, etc.
Eccl.	— Ecclesiastic, Ecclesia, etc.
Ep.	— Epigraphy
Esp.	— España, Español
Est.	— Estudios
Et.	— Etudes
Ethn.	— Ethnology, Ethnography, Ethnographie, etc.
Etn.	— Etnico, Etnografia, etc.
Etnol.	— Etnologia
Eur.	— Europe, Europa, etc.
ext.	— extract
f.	— für
fasc.	— fascicle
Fil.	— Filologia
Filos.	— Filosofia, Filosofico
fol.	— folio
Forsch.	— Forschung, Forschungen
Gal.	— Galerie
Gall.	— Gallery, Galleria
Geog.	— Geography, Geografia, Geographical, etc.
Giorn.	— Giornale
H.	— History, Histoire, etc.
hl.	— heilig, heilige
Holl.	— Hollandisch, etc.
Hum.	— Humanity, Humana, etc.
Ill.	— Illustration, Illustrato, Illustrazione, etc.
Ind.	— Index, Indice, Indicatore, etc.
Inf.	— Information, Informazione, etc.
Inst.	— Institute, Institut, Instituto, etc.
Int.	— International, etc.
Ist.	— Istituto
J.	— Journal
Jb.	— Jaarboek
Jhb.	— Jahrbuch
Jhrh.	— Jahreshefte
K.	— Kunst
Kat.	— Katalog
Kchr.	— Kunstchronik
Kg.	— Kunstgeschichte
K.K.	— Kaiserlich und Königlich
Kunsthist.	— Kunsthistorische
Kw.	— Kunstwissenschaft
Lett.	— Letteratura, Lettere
Lib.	— Library
ling.	— linguistica, lingua, etc.
Lit.	— Literary, Literarische, Littéraire, etc.
Mag.	— Magazine
Med.	— Medieval, Medievale, etc.
Meded.	— Mededeelingen
Mél.	— Mélanges
Mém.	— Mémoire
Mem.	— Memorie, Memoirs
Min.	— Minerva
Misc.	— Miscellany, Miscellanea, etc.
Mit.	— Mitteilungen
Mnb.	— Monatsberichte
Mnbl.	— Monatsblätter
Mnh.	— Monatshefte

Mod.	— Modern, Moderno, etc.	Rl.	— Reallexikon
Mon.	— Monuments, Monumento	Rom.	— Roman, Romano, Romanico, etc.
Münch.	— München, Münchner	rv.	— reverse
Mus.	— Museum, Museo, Musée, Museen, etc.	S.	— San, Santo, Santa (saint)
Muz.	— Muzeum	S.	— Studi, Studies, etc.
N.	— New, Notizia, etc.	Samml.	— Sammlung, Sammlungen
Nac.	— Nacional	Sc.	— Science, Scienza, Scientific, etc.
Nachr.	— Nachrichten	Schr.	— Schriften
Nat.	— National, etc.	Schw.	— Schweitzer
Naz.	— Nazionale	Script.	— Scriptorium
Notit. dign.	— Notitia Dignitatum	Sitzb.	— Sitzungsberichte
N.S.	— new series	s.l.	— in its place
O.	— Oriental, Orient, etc.	Soc.	— Social, Society, Società, Sociale, etc.
Ö.	— Österreichische	Spec.	— Speculum
obv.	— obverse	SS.	— Saints, Sante, Santi, Santissima
öffentl.	— öffentlich	St.	— Saint
Op.	— Opuscolo	Sta	— Santa (holy)
Pap.	— Papers, Papyrus	Ste	— Sainte
Per.	— Periodical, Periodico	Sto	— Santo (holy)
Pin.	— Pinacoteca, Pinakothek	Sup.	— Supplement, Supplemento
Pr.	— Prehistory, Preistoria, Preystori, Préhistoire	s.v.	— under the word
Proc.	— Proceedings	Tech.	— Technical, Technology, etc.
Pub.	— Publication, Publicación	Tecn.	— Tecnica, Tecnico
Pubbl.	— Pubblicazione	Tr.	— Transactions
Q.	— Quarterly, Quaderno	trans.	— translator, translated, etc.
Quel.	— Quellen	Trav.	— Travaux
R.	— Rivista	Treas.	— Treasury
r	— recto	u.	— und
r.	— reigned	Um.	— Umanesimo
Racc.	— Raccolta	Univ.	— University, Università, Université, etc.
Rass.	— Rassegna	Urb.	— Urban, Urbanistica
Rec.	— Recueil	v	— verso
Recens.	— Recensione	Vat.	— Vatican
Rech.	— Recherches	Verh.	— Verhandlungen, Verhandelingen
Rel.	— Relazione	Verz.	— Verzeichnis
Rend.	— Rendiconti	Vf.	— Verfasser
Rép.	— Répertoire	Wien.	— Wiener
Rep.	— Report, Repertorio, Repertorium	Yb.	— Yearbook
Rev.	— Review, Revue, etc.	Z.	— Zeitschrift, Zeitung, etc.

NOTES ON THE ENGLISH EDITION

Standards of Translation. Contributors to the Encyclopedia, drawn from the outstanding authorities of over 35 different countries, have written in many languages — Italian, Spanish, French, German, Russian, etc. To ensure faithful translation of the author's thought, all articles have been translated into English from the original language, checked for the accuracy of technical terms and accepted English forms of nomenclature by English and American art historians, and correlated with the final editorial work of the Italian edition for uniformity and coherence of the over-all presentation. Naturally the McGraw-Hill Book Company assumes full responsibility for the accuracy and completeness of all translations. Those articles written in English appear in the words and style of the authors, within the bounds of editorial attention to consistency and stylistic and organizational unity of the work as a whole. Article titles are in most cases parallel to those in the Italian edition, though occasionally they have been simplified, as *Dravidian Art* for *Dravidiche Correnti e Tradizioni.*

New Features. Although generally the English-language edition corresponds to the Italian version, a small number of purely editorial changes have been made in the interest of clear English-language alphabetization and occasional deletions or amplifications solely in the interest of clarity. Three major differences between the two editions do exist, however:

A considerable number of cross-references have been added in many places where it was felt that relating the subject under consideration to other pertinent articles would be of value to the reader.

A more extensive article on the Art of the Americas was projected for Volume One of the English edition with an entirely new text and many plates in black and white and color. This article was designed to give the completest possible coverage within the existing space of some 100,000 words to a subject which, because of its interest to the English-speaking public, was entrusted to a group of well-known American scholars, each expert in his respective area.

Some 300 separate short biographies have been added to the English edition to provide ready access to data on the lives, works, and critical acceptance of certain artists identified with schools, movements, and broad categories of historical development that are treated in the longer monographic articles. These articles are unillustrated, but works of the artists are represented in the plates accompanying the longer articles.

Bibliographies. The bibliographies of the original Italian edition have been amplified at times to include titles of special interest to the English-speaking world and English-language editions of works originally published in other languages.

In undertaking these adaptations of the Italian text and preparing original material for the English edition, the publisher has been aided by the generous advice and, in many cases, collaboration of the members of the Editorial Advisory Committee.

CONTRIBUTORS TO VOLUME XII

Bianca Maria Alfieri, University of Rome
Margherita Alosi Catelli, University of Rome
Giulio Carlo Argan, University of Rome
Edoardo Arslan, University of Pavia
Rosario Assunto, University of Urbino
† Marcel Aubert, Membre de l'Institut; Director, Société Française d'Archéologie, Paris
Eleanor D. Barton, Sweet Briar College, Sweet Briar, Va.
Giacomo Bascapé, Università Cattolica del Sacro Cuore, Milan
Hermann Bauer, Munich
Hermann Baumann, Institut für Völkerkunde der Universität, Munich
Anna Maria Bisi, Scuola Archeologica Orientale, Rome
Anthony Blunt, Courtauld Institute of Art, London
Renato Bonelli, University of Palermo
Gabriella Bordenache, Institute of Archaeology, Academy of the Romanian People's Republic, Bucharest
Cesare Brandi, University of Palermo
Theodore M. Brown, University of Louisville, Ky.
C. J. de Bruyn Kops, Assistant Keeper, Department of Paintings, Rijksmuseum, Amsterdam
Piero M. Capponi, Rome
Marco Chiarini, Florence
Maurice E. Cope, The Ohio State University, Columbus
Anne Crookshank, Keeper of Art, Museum and Art Gallery, Belfast, Northern Ireland
Paul Deschamps, Membre de l'Institut; Honorary Curator in Chief, Musée des Monuments Français, Paris
Vladimir Dumitrescu, Institute of Archaeology, Academy of the Romanian People's Republic, Bucharest
Dario Durbé, Rome
Luitpold Dussler, Munich
Wayne Dynes, London
Frank Elgar, Paris
Robert Enggass, Pennsylvania State University, University Park, Pa.
James H. Farquhar, Salisbury, Rhodesia
Oreste Ferrari, Rome
Sydney J. Freedberg, Harvard University, Cambridge, Mass.
Jean Gabus, Director, Institut d'Ethnologie, Musée d'Ethnographie, Neuchâtel; University of Neuchâtel, Switzerland
Georges Gaillard, Sorbonne, Paris
Lloyd Goodrich, Director, Whitney Museum of American Art, New York City
José Gudiol, University of Barcelona; Director, Instituto Amatller de Arte Hispánico
Robert H. van Gulik, Netherlands Ambassador to Japan, Tokyo
Julius S. Held, Barnard College, Columbia University, New York City
Robert L. Herbert, Yale University, New Haven, Conn.
Henry-Russell Hitchcock, Smith College, Northampton, Mass.
Wilhelm Holmqvist, Superintendent, Historiska Museet, Stockholm
William I. Homer, University of Delaware, Newark, Delaware
Donelson F. Hoopes, Associate Curator, Department of Paintings and Sculptures, Brooklyn Museum
Michael Jaffé, King's College, Cambridge
Sten Karling, University of Stockholm
Hans Erich Kubach, Speyer
† Ernst Kühnel, Director, Islamic Section, Staatliche Museen, Berlin
Lionello Lanciotti, University of Rome
James Laver, London

Victor Lazarev, Presidium of the Academy of Sciences of the U.S.S.R., Moscow
Michael Levey, National Gallery, London
Eileen A. Lord, University of Bridgeport, Conn.
Fernanda de' Maffei, Rome
Alessandro Marabottini Marabotti, University of Messina
Giuseppe Marchini, Soprintendente alle Gallerie delle Marche, Urbino, Italy
Wilhelm Messerer, Munich
Domenico Mustilli, University of Naples
Peter Murray, Courtauld Institute of Art, London
Maria Ana Musicescu, Bucharest
Bernard S. Myers, formerly, The City College, New York City
A. M. Nagler, Yale University, New Haven, Conn.
Francesco Negri Arnoldi, Rome
Claus Nissen, Stadtbibliothek, Mainz, Germany
Enrico Paribeni, Soprintendenza, Foro Romano e Palatino, Rome
Amelia Pavel, Academy of the Romanian People's Republic, Bucharest
Gennaro Pesce, Soprintendente alle Antichità, Cagliari
Paul Phillippot, Vice Director, Centro Internazionale di Studi per la Conservazione e il Restauro dei Beni Culturali, Rome
Mircea Popescu, Institute of Art History, Academy of the Romanian People's Republic, Bucharest
Jean Porcher, Curator in Chief, Cabinet des Manuscrits, Bibliothèque Nationale, Paris
Elena Povoledo, Centro-Studi, Enciclopedia dello Spettacolo, Rome
Mario Praz, University of Rome
Antonio Priori, Rome
Robert Rosenblum, Princeton University
Paolo Rossi, University of Bologna
Eberhard Ruhmer, Munich
Marleigh Ryan, Columbia University, New York City
Luigi Salerno, Soprintendenza ai Monumenti, Rome
François Salet, Curator, Musée de Cluny, Paris
Margaretta M. Salinger, Metropolitan Museum of Art, New York City
Mario Salmi, University of Rome
Roberto Salvini, University of Trieste
Willibold Sauerländer, Kunstgeschichtliches Institut der Universität, Freiburg im Breisgau, Germany
Gian Roberto Scarcia, Accademia dei Lincei, Rome
Umberto Scerrato, Istituto Orientale, Naples
Hans Sedlmayr, Kunsthistorisches Seminar der Universität, Munich
Doris Stone, President of the Board of Directors, National Museum of Costa Rica
Giovanni Urbani, Istituto Centrale del Restauro, Rome
Licia Vlad Borrelli, Istituto Centrale del Restauro, Rome
Marie-Louise Vollenweider, Collonges-sous-Salève, France
† Martin Weinberger, Institute of Fine Arts, New York University
Allen S. Weller, University of Illinois, Urbana
Margaret Whinney, formerly, Courtauld Institute of Art, London
Christopher White, Assistant Keeper, Department of Prints and Drawings, British Museum, London
Ernest Will, University of Lille
Franz Winzinger, Regensburg, Germany
George Zarnecki, Courtauld Institute of Art, London
Bruno Zevi, University of Rome

ACKNOWLEDGMENTS

The Institute for Cultural Collaboration and the publishers express their thanks to the collectors and to the directors of the museums and galleries listed below for permission to reproduce works in their collections and for the photographs supplied.

The Institute also acknowledges the kind permission of H. M. Queen Elizabeth II to reproduce works belonging to the Crown.

AACHEN, Germany, Cathedral Treasury
AMSTERDAM, Rijksmuseum
AMSTERDAM, Het Toneel Museum
ANKARA, Archaeological Museum
ANTWERP, Musée Royal des Beaux-Arts
AREZZO, Italy, Museo Archeologico
ATHENS, National Museum
AUTUN, Musée Rolin

BAGHDAD, Iraq Museum
BARCELONA, Archivo Histórico
BARCELONA, Coll. Mateu
BARCELONA, Museo de Bellas Artes de Cataluña
BARI, Italy, Museo Archeologico
BASEL, E. Borowski Coll.
BASEL, Kunstmuseum
BEIRUT, Kettaneh Coll.
BERGAMO, Italy, Accademia Carrara
BERN, Coll. Merz
BERN, Schweizerische Theater-Sammlung
BERLIN, Kupferstichkabinett
BERLIN, Staatliche Museen
BESANÇON, France, Musée des Beaux-Arts
BOLOGNA, Archivio di Stato
BOLOGNA, Biblioteca Comunale dell'Archiginnasio
BOLOGNA, Pinacoteca
BOLOGNA, Coll. A. Simoni
BOSTON, Museum of Fine Arts
BOUCHES-DU-RHÔNE, France, Archives Départementales
BRUGES, Belgium, Musée Memling
BRUNSWICK, Germany, Herzog-Anton-Ulrich-Museum
BRUSSELS, Musées Royaux des Beaux-Arts
BRUSSELS, Musées Royaux d'Art et d'Histoire
BUFFALO, N.Y., Albright-Knox Art Gallery

CAGLIARI, Sardinia, Museo Archeologico
CAIRO, Egyptian Museum
CALCUTTA, Asutosh Museum
CALCUTTA, Indian Museum
CAMBRAI, France, Bibliothèque Municipale
CAMBRIDGE, England, Corpus Christi College
CAMBRIDGE, Mass., Fogg Art Museum
CHANTILLY, France, Musée Condé
CHICAGO, Art Institute
CLEVELAND, Museum of Art
COLOGNE, Wallraf-Richartz-Museum
COPENHAGEN, Nationalmuseet
CREGLINGEN, Germany, Herrgottskirche

DAMASCUS, National Museum
DELPHI, Greece, Archaeological Museum
DERBYSHIRE, England, Trustees of the Chatsworth Settlement
DRESDEN, Gemäldegalerie

EDINBURGH, National Gallery of Scotland
EL ESCORIAL, Spain, Escorial
ESSEN, Germany, Folkwang Museum

FAENZA, Italy, Museo Internazionale delle Ceramiche
FERRARA, Italy, Pinacoteca
FIESOLE, Italy, Museo Bandini
FLORENCE, Accademia
FLORENCE, Archivio di Stato
FLORENCE, Biblioteca Laurenziana
FLORENCE, Casa Buonarroti
FLORENCE, Fondazione Horne
FLORENCE, Museo Nazionale
FLORENCE, Museo dell'Opera del Duomo
FLORENCE, Museo di S. Marco
FLORENCE, Museo di Storia della Scienza
FLORENCE, Palazzo Vecchio
FLORENCE, Pitti
FLORENCE, Uffizi
FRANKFURT AM MAIN, Städelsches Kunstinstitut

GENEVA, N. Koutoulakis Coll.
GENOA, Palazzo Bianco
GENOA, Palazzo dell'Università
GRANADA, Spain, Palace of Charles V

THE HAGUE, R. H. van Gulik Coll.
THE HAGUE, Mauritshuis
HAMBURG, Kunsthalle
HAMBURG, Museum für Völkerkunde
HAMPTON COURT, England, Royal Colls.
HARTFORD, Conn., Wadsworth Atheneum

INNSBRUCK, Tiroler Landesmuseum Ferdinandeum

JAPAN, Coll. Kawai Senro
JERUSALEM, Israel, Museum of the Patriarchs
JERUSALEM, Israel, Reifenberg Coll.
JERUSALEM, Jordan, Palestine Archaeological Museum

KARLSRUHE, Germany, Landesmuseum
KASSEL, Germany, Staatliche Kunstsammlungen
KYOTO, National Museum

LILLE, France, Archives du Nord
LIVERPOOL, Walker Art Gallery
LONDON, Aberconway Coll.
LONDON, Courtauld Institute Galleries
LONDON, Goldsmiths' Hall
LONDON, Kenwood, The Iveagh Bequest
LONDON, Lambeth Palace Library
LONDON (Greenwich), National Maritime Museum
LONDON, National Portrait Gallery
LONDON, Royal Academy of Arts
LONDON, Science Museum
LONDON, Tate Gallery
LONDON, University College, Department of Egyptology Museum
LONDON, Wallace Coll.
LOS ANGELES, County Museum
LUGANO, Switzerland, Thyssen-Bornemisza Coll.
LYONS, Musée des Beaux-Arts

MADRID, Academia de S. Fernando
MADRID, Museo de América
MADRID, Museo Arqueológico Nacional
MADRID, Museo Etnológico y Antropológico
MADRID, Museo Lázaro Galdiano
MADRID, Prado
MADRID, Real Academia de la Historia
MAINZ, Germany, Gutenberg-Museum
MANCHESTER, England, Whitworth Art Gallery
MANTUA, Italy, Biblioteca Nazionale
MESSINA, Sicily, Museo Nazionale
MEXICO CITY, Coll. D. Olmedo Phillips
MEXICO CITY, Museo Nacional de Antropología
MILAN, Brera
MILAN, Castello Sforzesco
MILAN, Coll. Tordini
MILAN, Museo Nazionale della Scienza e della Tecnica
MILAN, Museo Poldi Pezzoli
MILAN, Museo Teatrale alla Scala
MOSCOW, A. S. Pushkin Museum of Fine Arts
MOSCOW, Tretyakov Gallery
MUNICH, Alte Pinakothek
MUNICH, Bayerisches Nationalmuseum
MUNICH, Bayerische Staatsbibliothek
MUNICH, Deutsches Museum
MUNICH, Staatliche Antikensammlungen
MUNICH, Theater-Museum

NAPLES, Museo di Capodimonte
NAPLES, Museo Nazionale
NAPLES, Museo Nazionale di S. Martino
NEUCHÂTEL, Switzerland, Musée d'Ethnographie, Coll. J. Gabus
NEW DELHI, National Museum of India
NEW HAVEN, Yale University Art Gallery
NEW YORK, Frick Coll.
NEW YORK, D. Heeramaneck Coll.
NEW YORK, R. Lehman Coll.
NEW YORK, Metropolitan Museum
NEW YORK, Museum of Modern Art
NEW YORK, Pierpont Morgan Library
NOVGOROD, U.S.S.R., Museum of Art and History
NÜRNBERG, Germany, Germanisches National-Museum

OLYMPIA, Greece, Archaeological Museum
OSLO, Kunstindustrimuseet
OSLO, Universitetets Oldsaksamling
OSLO, Viking Ship Museum
OTTERLO, Netherlands, Rijksmuseum Kröller-Müller
OXFORD, England, Ashmolean Museum
OXFORD, England, Bodleian Library
OXFORD, England, Pitt Rivers Museum
OTTAWA, National Gallery of Canada

PAESTUM, Italy, Museo Archeologico
PARIS, Archives Nationales

PARIS, Bibliothèque de l'Arsenal
PARIS, Bibliothèque Nationale
PARIS, Cabinet des Médailles
PARIS, Ecole des Beaux-Arts
PARIS, Louvre
PARIS, Mobilier National
PARIS, Musée de Cluny
PARIS, Musée Guimet
PARIS, Musée de l'Homme
PARIS, Musée des Arts Décoratifs
PARIS, Musée Rodin
PERUGIA, Italy, Galleria Nazionale dell'Umbria
PERUGIA, Italy, Musei Civici
PESARO, Italy, Museo Civico
PETERBOROUGH, England, Elton Hall, Proby Coll.
PHILADELPHIA, Museum of Art, Johnson Coll.
PIEŠTANY, Czechoslovakia, Museum
PLOVDIV, Bulgaria, Archaeological Museum
PRAGUE, National Gallery

RABAT, Morocco, Musée des Arts Marocains
RAVENNA, Italy, Museo Arcivescovile
RAVENNA, Italy, Pinacoteca dell'Accademia di Belle Arti
REIMS, France, Musée des Beaux-Arts
ROME, Accademia di S. Luca
ROME, Antiquarium Forense
ROME, Antiquarium Palatino
ROME, Archivio Vaticano
ROME, Biblioteca Casanatense
ROME, Capitoline Museum
ROME, Gabinetto Nazionale delle Stampe
ROME, Galleria Borghese
ROME, Galleria Nazionale
ROME, Galleria Doria Pamphili
ROME, Lateran Museums
ROME, Museo Barracco
ROME, Museo della Civiltà Romana
ROME, Museo Nazionale Romano
ROME, Museo di Palazzo Venezia
ROME, Museo di Villa Giulia
ROME, Osservatorio Astronomico
ROME, Palazzo dei Conservatori
ROME, Palazzo Farnese
ROME, Coll. A. Prampolini
ROME, Società Montecatini
ROME, Vatican Library
ROME, Vatican Museums
ROTTERDAM, Museum Boymans-Van Beuningen
ROUEN, France, Bibliothèque de la Ville

SAINT-GERMAIN-EN-LAYE, France, Musée des Antiquités Nationales
SANSEPOLCRO, Italy, Pinacoteca Comunale
SEATTLE, Art Museum
SEATTLE, Art Museum, Eugene Fuller Memorial Coll.
SEVILLE, Spain, Museo Provincial de Bellas Artes
SIENA, Italy, Palazzo Pubblico
SIENA, Italy, Pinacoteca
SINGAPORE, Raffles Museum
STOCKHOLM, Royal Armory
STOCKHOLM, Statens Historiska Museum
SYRACUSE, Sicily, Museo Archeologico

TARANTO, Italy, Museo Nazionale
TARQUINIA, Italy, Museo Nazionale
TEHERAN, Archaeological Museum
TEHERAN, Foroughi Coll.
TERVUEREN, Belgium, Musée Royal de l'Afrique Centrale
TOKYO, National Museum
TOULOUSE, France, Musée des Augustins
TRIER, Germany, Stadtbibliothek
TRIVANDRUM, Kerala, India, Picture Gallery
TURIN, Galleria Sabauda
TURIN, Museo Civico

VENICE, Biblioteca Marciana
VENICE, Ca' d'Oro
VENICE, Doges' Palace
VENICE, Galleria Internazionale d'Arte Moderna
VENICE, Museo Correr
VENICE, Scuola di S. Rocco
VERSAILLES, Palace
VICH, Spain, Museo Arqueológico Artístico Episcopal
VIENNA, Albertina
VIENNA, Kunsthistorisches Museum
VIENNA, Österreichische Galerie
VIENNA, Österreichisches Museum für Angewandte Kunst
VIENNA, Österreichische Nationalbibliothek
VITERBO, Italy, Museo Civico

WARSAW, U.S.S.R., Regional Museum of Local History

WARSAW, University Library
WASHINGTON, D.C., Folger Shakespeare Library
WASHINGTON, D.C., Freer Gallery of Art
WASHINGTON, D.C., National Gallery
WEILHEIM, Germany, Städtisches Museum
WINTERTHUR, Switzerland, Georg Reinhart Coll.
WINTERTHUR, Switzerland, Oskar Reinhart Coll.
WÜRZBURG, Germany, Mainfränkisches Museum

YORK, England, Yorkshire Museum

ZURICH, Kunsthaus

PHOTOGRAPHIC CREDITS

The numbers refer to the plates. Those within parentheses indicate the sequence of subjects in composite plate pages. Italic numbers refer to photographs owned by the Institute for Cultural Collaboration.

A.C.L., Brussels: 96; 98 (2); 99 (1, 3); 327 (2); 330; 333 (1, 2); 369 (3); 374 (2); 505

ALINARI, Florence: 1; 2; 3 (2, 3); 4 (2, 3); 6 (1, 2); 8; 9; 10 (2); 11 (1-3); 12 (1); 13 (1-3); 14 (1, 2); 16 (1-4); 17 (1, 2, 4); 18 (1-3); 19 (1, 3); 21; 22 (2, 3); 23; 24 (1, 2); *25*; 27 (1); 28 (1); 29 (1); 30 (1-3); 31 (2, 3); 33 (*1, 2,* 3); 34 (2); 37 (2); 38 (1-4); 39; 40 (4); 45 (1); 47 (1, 2); 48 (3); 50 (1, 2); 51 (1, 2); 52; 53 (1); 55 (1, 2); 56 (2); 57 (1-3); 58; 59 (1, 2); 63 (1, 2); 64; *66*; 67 (1, 2); 68 (1, 2); 69; 71 (1-3); 73; 77 (1-3); 78 (1-3); 79; 81 (2, 4); 83 (2); 84 (1, 3); 85 (1, 2); 89 (2); 90 (1, 2); 91 (1, 2); 92 (1, 2); 97; 98 (1); 121 (1, 2); 122 (2, 3); 127 (1); 130 (1); 131 (2); 132 (3); 166 (1); 172; 178 (1, 2); 179 (1); 180 (3); 181 (1, 5); 187 (2); 195 (1); 216; 219 (1-3); 220 (1, 3); 221 (2, 3); 222 (2, 3); 223 (1, 2); 235 (3); 252; 255 (2); 256 (1, 2); 257 (1, 2); 260; 261 (1, 3); 275 (2); 276 (2, 3); 277 (1-3); *281* (4); 283; 285 (2); 286 (1, 3); 288 (2); 289 (1, 2); 290; 291 (2, 3); 292 (1, 2); 294 (1, 2); 297; 298 (2); 299 (1); 300 (1-4); 301 (1); 304; 366 (1); 367 (4); 368 (2); 369 (1, 4); *370* (2); 371 (2); 372 (3); 373 (3); 375 (1-3); 376 (2); 377 (2); 378 (2); 379 (1); 387 (1, 2); 388 (2); 390 (3); 391; 418 (1); 419 (2); 421 (1); *480*; 487; 488 (4); 492 (1, 2); *497* (3); 498 (3); 501 (3); 502 (4); 503; 508; *509*; 511 (4); 517; 519; 520 (2, 3); 521 (*2*, 4, 5); 537 (1); 540 (1, 4); 564 (1-3)

ANDERSON, Rome: 3 (1); 4 (1); 5; 10 (1); 12 (2, 3); 20; 22 (1); 28 (4); 31 (1, 4); 32 (2); 34 (1, 3); 40 (1-3); 45 (2); 46 (2); 48 (1); 49 (1); 54; 56 (1); 60; 73; 74; 86 (2); 88 (1, 2); 89 (1); 156; 167 (2); 169 (4); 194 (2); 221 (1); 224 (1, 2); 259 (2); 261 (2); 291 (1); 302; 306; 327 (1); 334 (2); 372 (4); 375 (4); 377 (1); 393 (3); 507 (1)

ANNAN, Glasgow: 368 (3)

ANTIKVARISK TOPOGRAFISKA ARKIVET, Stockholm: 233 (1); 267 (1-3); 416 (3)

ARCHIVE DU SERVICE DES MÉTIERS ET ARTS MAROCAINS, Rabat: 359

ARTE E COLORE, Milan: *41*; *116*; *174*; *184*; *499*

BALZARINI, Milan: *154* (2)

BARSOTTI, Florence: 468 (3); 473 (2)

BEARD, H. R., Cambridge, England: 430 (2)

BEVILACQUA, Carlo, Milan: *461*

BIBLIOTHÈQUE NATIONALE, Paris: 175 (1, 2)

BILDARCHIV FOTO MARBURG, Marburg, Germany: 105; 106 (1); 162 (2); 163 (2, 3); 168 (2); 169 (3); 170 (1); 180 (4); 187 (1); 225 (2); 226 (2, 3); 228 (1-3); 229; 262 (2, 3); 265 (1); 278 (1, 2); 453 (1, 2); 495; 496; 518 (1, 2)

BONNOLI, Siena, Italy: 422 (1)

BORCHI, Faenza, Italy: 373 (4)

BREDOL-LEPPER, Ann, Aachen: 280 (2)

BROGI, Florence: 28 (3); 91 (3); 376 (1); 388 (3)

BUNDESDENKMALAMT, Vienna: 170 (3); 278 (3)

BURKHOLZ, Alfred, Würzburg, Germany: 460 (1)

CACCO, Venice: 72; 435 (1)

CAISSE NATIONALE DES MONUMENTS HISTORIQUES, Paris: 100 (2); 113 (2); 165 (1); 181 (4); 195 (2); 200 (2); 201 (1, 3); 205 (1); 206; 234 (1); 237 (1, 2); 238 (1); 240 (1); 269 (2); 285 (1); 379 (2); 464 (1); 465 (1); 484; 488 (1); 493 (3); 502 (3)

CALZOLARI, Mantua: 53 (2, 3); 82 (1)

CENTRE D'ÉTUDES MÉDIÉVALES, Poitiers: 201 (2)

CIEMMEFOTO: 449 (2)

COUNTRY LIFE, London: 108 (3)

COURTAULD INSTITUTE OF ART, London: 230 (1, 2); 231; 232; 235 (3); 266 (2); 279 (4); 483 (2)

CROSSLEY, F. H., Chester, England: 483 (2)

DE ANTONIS, Rome: 7; *42*; 76; 94; *120* (1); *147; 148*; 181 (3); *200* (1); *202* (1); *203*; 205 (2); *208*; *217*; *236* (1, 3); *238* (1, 3, 4); *240* (2); *241* (1, 2); *246* (1-3); *331*; *341*; *350* (1); *351*; *353* (2); *408* (1, 2); *417* (1); *536*; *550* (1, 2); *551* (1, 2); *552* (1-3)

DEMANEGA, Innsbruck, Austria: 459 (3)

DEPARTMENT OF ARCHAEOLOGY, GOVERNMENT OF INDIA, New Delhi: 523 (3)

DEPARTMENT OF PRINTS, UNIVERSITY LIBRARY, Warsaw: 312 (1)

DEUTSCHE FOTOTHEK, Dresden: 46 (3); *154* (1); 343 (1)

DEUTSCHES ARCHÄOLOGISCHES INSTITUT, Rome: 128 (1); 189 (2); 194 (1); 287 (1); *293*; 417 (2); 418 (2); 563 (2)

DINGJAN, A., The Hague: 344 (1)

DIRECTION GÉNÉRALE DES ANTIQUITÉS ET DES MUSÉES, Damascus: 193 (2); 197 (2)

DOMÍNGUEZ RAMOS, Madrid: 504 (3)

DRÄYER, Walter, Zurich: 498 (1)

ELSWING, Niels, Copenhagen: 233 (2, 3)

ENCICLOPEDIA DELLO SPETTACOLO, Rome: 423; 424; 429 (1, 2); 430 (3); 433; 434 (1-3); 438; 443; 444

FÉRRIZ, Madrid: 494

FERRUZZI, Venice: *95*

FIORENTINI, Venice: 49 (2); 83 (1); 122 (1); 179 (3); 516 (2); 538 (1, 2)

FLEMING, R. B. & Co., London: *342*

FORMAN, Prague: 497 (1)

FOTOCIELO, Rome: 222 (1)

FREEMAN, London: 547; 548

FRODL-KRAFT, Eva, Vienna: 163 (1); 168 (1); 169 (2)

GABINETTO FOTOGRAFICO NAZIONALE, Rome: 48 (2); 86 (1); 143 (4); 178 (3); 182 (4); 276 (1); 281 (3); 301 (2); 303 (1); 308 (3); 309 (2); 310 (1, 2); 311 (2); 368 (1); 377 (4); 502 (1)

GABINETTO NAZIONALE DELLE STAMPE, Rome: 435 (2)

GABUS, Neuchâtel, Switzerland: 355; 356 (1, 2); 357; 358 (1, 2); 360 (1, 2); 361; 362; 363 (1)

GIACOMELLI, Venice: 522 (2)

GIOVETTI: 279 (1)

GIRAUDON, Paris: 17 (3); 28 (2); 29 (3); *35*; 37 (3); *65*; *80*; 100 (1); 101 (1-3); 117 (2); 160; 165 (2); 176 (2); 196 (1, 2); 199; 200 (3); 202 (2); 204; 239; 242; 245; 287 (2); 313; *314*; 319 (1, 2); 320; 321 (1, 2); 372 (2); *380* (2); *406*; 451; 454 (1); 497 (4); 506 (2); 507 (2); 511 (2); 514; 524 (4, 9, 10); *535*; 540 (2); 554; 558; 559; 561; 563 (1); 566; 569 (2); 570 (1, 4)

GUNDERMANN, Würzburg, Germany: 149

HINZ, Basel: 110

CONTENTS · VOLUME XII

RENAISSANCE. The term "renaissance," when applied to the relationship of one civilization to a more ancient one that serves as its model, concerns not only the representational arts of a particular period and culture but also that culture's literature, philosophy, science, and even its politics and mores. Nor can the term be restricted to Italian culture and society, though these were indeed preeminent in the 15th and 16th centuries. The term is applicable in a general sense to all or almost all the European countries that experienced during that period a process of cultural, political and even religious renewal from which their modern forms emerged. This article deals essentially with the manifestations of this renewal in architecture and the representational arts — within the framework of culture generally — and with related theoretical and critical developments. It must be remembered that this process of cultural renewal had widely varying limits, durations, and periods of decline: it began in some countries when it was already at its height in others and came to an end in some places while it was in full flower elsewhere.

According to the traditional concept, to the etymology of the word, and to the statements made by its protagonists, the Renaissance was the resurgence of the spirit and of the forms of antiquity or, at the least, it was the consciousness of the inevitable relationship between present action and the meditated experience of the past; it was also the manifestation of a new concept of the world and of man's place in history. The articles to be consulted as necessary complements to this one are ANTIQUE REVIVAL, CLASSICISM, HUMAN FIGURE, HUMANISM, MANNERISM, PERSPECTIVE, and TREATISES, as well as the biographical articles on the major artists of the period, which of all the great cycles of human creative activity was the one most strongly characterized by the highest expression of individualism. The stylistic developments of the period were reflected in the minor arts of the Renaissance (see CERAMICS, ENAMELS, GLASS, GOLD- AND SILVERWORK, TAPESTRY AND CARPETS, and TEXTILES).

SUMMARY. I. The Italian Renaissance. Introduction (col. 1): *Changing concepts; Survey of styles.* Early Renaissance (col. 10): *Architecture; Sculpture; Painting.* High Renaissance (col. 69): *Architecture; Sculpture; Painting.* Late Renaissance (col. 98): *Architecture; Sculpture; Painting.* II. The Renaissance outside Italy (col. 121). Introduction. Spain: *Architecture; Sculpture; Painting.* Portugal: *Architecture; Painting and sculpture.* France. The Low Countries: *Architecture; Sculpture; Painting; Engraving.* Germany: *Architecture; Sculpture; Painting; Engraving.* England. Scandinavia. Eastern Europe.

I. THE ITALIAN RENAISSANCE. INTRODUCTION: *Changing concepts.* The spiritual and esthetic movement known as the Renaissance, and clearly distinct from the Middle Ages, emerged in Florence in 1410–20 as the fulfillment of a new artistic need. It was the result of a gradual development that had its source in the Humanism of the 14th century and the fascination and stimulus exerted by classical antiquity, whose forms had also been repeated in the art of the medieval period. Moreover, the representation of the physical world took on new aspects at the beginning of the *novus ordo* ("new order") because of a systematization that brought about artistic mastery

of concrete and measurable space by means of the laws of perspective. Thus, when the artists of antiquity represented objective reality, they interpreted it as the embodiment of the very ideals to which they aspired. The Romanesque and Gothic styles also contributed some elements to the Renaissance search for models (although the Gothic taste has often been erroneously regarded as antithetical to the Renaissance). The conscious inspiration toward concreteness — that is, toward a more assured and profound knowledge — must be related to the Humanist moral order, according to which individual man could make what he wished of his own life. This concept had also been reached on the spiritual level during the course of the Middle Ages in a long, laborious process aimed at reconciling classical and Christian thought; therefore, even in this particular aspect there is no sharp break between the Middle Ages and the Renaissance.

However, a very vital movement such as this could not possibly have remained static in its principles, which from the very beginning were applied in a variety of interpretations that corresponded to the different sensibilities of individual artists. So the movement developed, its many facets changing to reflect a diversity of personalities and tastes and, also, of influences from beyond the Alps. This has led to a division of the movement into early, High, and late Renaissance (the last is often confused with mannerism) within chronological limits that are inevitably only approximate.

The initial phase, which began in the second decade of the 15th century, lasted approximately until the end of that century, though a later date applies in some cases; the two later periods occurred during the 16th century. Prior to a study of the development of the Renaissance the history of the word should be traced, though its connotations do not correspond to the actual significance of its art (an anomaly that also arises in the case of the term "Gothic"). In this connection it is also necessary to state the positions assumed by art history and criticism.

The word "renaissance" implies the rebirth, the resurgence, of something that has disappeared. Since the 14th century there had existed in Florence an awareness of an artistic awakening brought about through the robust genius of Giotto, still deemed by some to have been the first pillar of the movement. Thus Dante (*Purgatorio*, Canto XI), taking a debate on moral issues as a starting point, refers to the repute of the great painter with regard to the then-eclipsed fame of Cimabue. In this Dante echoed the art masters and the scholars, not the common people; this view was confirmed by Petrarch (*De remediis utriusque fortunae*), who as a Humanist extolled Giotto, while as a poet (*Canzoniere*) he held Simone Martini to be the painter closer to his heart. That Giotto was appreciated only in the intellectual milieu was also affirmed by Boccaccio in the fifth tale of the sixth day in the *Decameron*, where in connection with Giotto's art he introduced the Aristotelian concept of naturalistic illusion; but he also stated that Giotto had "brought to light that art which had been buried for many centuries through the error of those who painted more to delight the eye of the ignorant than to please the intellect of the wise." These words outline the idea of a "revival," opposed to the medieval world before Giotto; at the same time they imply the scheme of an artistic evolution in a classicist sense: antiquity, followed by a decadent and shadowy period, and, finally, a modern era, which through an outstanding artistic personality rises to equal once more the achievements of antiquity. This second point of view was clearly expressed by Filippo Villani (*Liber de origine civitatis Florentiae . . .*), according to whom Giotto was "not only equal to the ancient painters but superior in art and intellect." What is meant by "ancient painters" is explained by Cennino Cennini (*Trattato della Pittura*, Milanesi, ed., Florence, 1859) in his definition of the master: "Giotto again transformed the art of painting from Greek to Latin and made it modern, and his art achieved a perfection that no one had ever equaled." Antiquity was Latinity; it was, in substance, Rome, which had maintained a spiritual continuity in the Middle Ages from Charlemagne onward, even for the Florentines of the 14th century (Dante, Giovanni Villani, Petrarch, and other minor figures). And Rome once more resumed its own inspirational and renewing function. The return to Latinity was accompanied by a rebellion against the Greek world — that is, against the Byzantine world — which until then had dominated the art of painting.

The same concept was repeated by Lorenzo Ghiberti in the second of his *Commentarii* toward the middle of the following century, when the early Renaissance was at its peak. After discussing the ancients and the decadence that had set in under Constantine the Great and Pope Sylvester I, he considered the "new art" and the "doctrine" of Giotto as a reaction to the "crudeness" of the Greeks — that is, of the Byzantines. But, in recalling that the "many disciples" of Giotto were "as gifted as the ancient Greeks," he seemed to value Hellenic antiquity above that of Rome. It must be remembered, however, that he was writing at the height of the Neo-Platonic movement and that his art was related to a medieval classicism of Hellenic grace.

Even before Ghiberti, however, Leon Battista Alberti made some memorable observations in the prologue of his treatise on painting (*Trattato della Pittura*; L. Mallé, ed., 1950), which was dedicated to Brunelleschi. He praised some contemporary Florentine artists for their "talent," which was such that they were not to be set below anyone ancient and famous in these arts. He no longer looked to the past, and modern art was to him not that of Giotto but, rather, the Florentine art of his own time. Furthermore, the concept of "antiquity" was defined by him as going beyond the Latinity of the 14th century; in fact, his treatises on architecture (*De re aedificatoria*, 1485), painting (*Della Pittura*, 1950), and sculpture (*Della Statua*, 1568) refer frequently to the Greek world as well as the Roman. To him antiquity consisted in both the Greek and Roman worlds. In yearning for an idealized beauty, as in some passages in his treatises on painting and sculpture, he originated the rhetorical concept of antiquity. Filarete's *Trattato di architettura* (1451–64) followed Alberti's; in it the author described an ideal city inspired by the Humanist spirit and conceived and named in honor of a prince. He wrote that his work deserved "to be in Latin and not in the vernacular." He thus seemed to seek a return to the Roman origins, championing the anthropomorphic theory of architecture and especially praising the "ancient methods of constructions" revived by Brunelleschi in opposition to the "modern custom," which, he added, "I believe that only a barbarian people could have brought into Italy." (The "modern custom" of which he writes is the Gothic style.) Antonio Manetti, in his *Vita di Brunelleschi* (E. Toesca, ed., Florence, 1927), tried to explain "how this ancient method of building was revived" by Brunelleschi, rediscoverer of antiquity, on the foundations of which architecture was renewed, in contrast with the modern "Germans." He then stressed the opposition to the northern Gothic (the Goths had destroyed the ancient style), an opposition reinforcing that held toward Byzantine art by 14th-century writers under the influence of Italian Humanism, which regarded the Gothic Middle Ages as decadent compared with ancient grandeur. At the same time the biographer declared that the imitation of the antique, like the Humanists' return to antiquity by means of the Latin language, was a return to the national tradition.

The affirmation of this artistic awakening thus seems to have been interpreted by 15th-century writers (with the exception of Ghiberti) as being fully independent of the tendencies of the 14th century. For the 15th century, as for the 16th, the return to antiquity by means of a modern idiom was stressed by writers, and in the second half of the 15th century the *novus ordo* became associated with the court milieu by Filarete, among others. Cristoforo Landino, in the preface to Dante's *Divina Commedia* (Florence, 1481), reiterated the concept — only partly correct — of Florentine unity and, after discussing the painting of ancient Egypt and Greece, later "extinguished," saw the beginning of the new style in Cimabue, "who rediscovered natural features," and attributed its continuance to Giotto and his followers up to the major artists of the 15th century.

This and other minor sources provided the foundation built upon by Giorgio Vasari, who, following Landino's example, places Cimabue's biography first in his *Vite*. Vasari pointed out that he wrote to please and to stimulate a fruitful emulation of the ancients, accepting the dual concept of reaction to the Byzantines and to the Germans (i.e., the Gothic world), though in fact he limited this reaction to architecture. In the letter of dedication to Cosimo I de' Medici in the first edition (1550) Vasari recalled his intention of writing about the lives of those who ". . . the arts of drawing being already extinct, have first of all revived them and after a time extended them, adorned them and finally led them to that level of beauty and majesty where they stand today." And at the end of the introduction, in the first and in the second edition (1568), he reaffirmed the concept and used the word "rinascita" (presumably coined in the 16th century), which later became widely accepted, particularly in France, and which Italy was also to adopt as "rinascimento."

According to Vasari, art follows the laws of nature, or better still, since human bodies are not reborn, those of the plant world that resurges with spring. The rebirth in Italian art, beginning with Cimabue, was a continuous, gradual progress that was actually an increasing technical refinement. Thus Giotto was great not in himself but in relation to his time; the cultural flowering that had begun about 1250 continued after Giotto as an artistic awakening, in which painting gradually developed because it drew inspiration not only from antiquity but also from nature; this concept was widespread in Florence from the 14th century and, according to Vasari, reached its height in Michelangelo, who was regarded as the greatest genius who ever lived and after whom came only decadence. Vasari divided artistic styles into the ancient (classicism), the old (the medieval), the new (starting with Cimabue), and the modern (from Leonardo onward).

In fact, among the various writers on the subject, only Alberti had sensed with acumen that Brunelleschi had given birth to an artistic idiom distinct from that which had preceded it. But Vasari's classification was universally adopted, despite the fact that in artistic historiography different points of view emerged in the analysis and judgment of Italian art. For, in the face of the asserted superiority of Florentine-Roman formalism, that is, the classicist ideal that was propounded by Vasari and others, there arose in Venice, within regional limits, the historiographic movement that was to be widely followed during the next two centuries, which recognized the potential of color in creating luminist and atmospheric effects.

Thus there emerged an attitude of opposition between the ancient — characterized mainly by painting based on design, typical of central Italy — and the modern — that is, painting based on color; this attitude later reappeared as a subject of greater debate in France, especially in the "querelle des anciens et des modernes" of the 17th century, which was to have widely felt repercussions in literature. Two critical trends predominated in the 17th century: According to the first, art is the representation of the Idea, a concept that originated with Lomazzo (*Idea del tempio della pittura*, Milan, 1590); this concept was taken up by Giovanni Pietro Bellori (*Le vite*, Rome, 1672), by Nicolas Poussin (*Correspondance*, C. Jouanny, ed., Paris, 1911) and by the Académie Française, founded in Paris in 1648 and transferred to Rome in 1655. The second critical trend exalts pictorial sensitivity in art; it was advocated in Venice by Marco Boschini (*Carta del navegar pitoresco*, Venice, 1660) and in Paris by Roger de Piles (*Dialogue sur le coloris*, Paris, 1673).

In historiography that is concerned mainly with painting, Vasari's scheme endures; but there is seldom a backward glance at the past and, moreover, retrospection seldom goes beyond the 16th century, the century even then identified with the Renaissance and the imitation of antiquity. In Rome favorable critical judgment, which in the 16th century had been awarded to Michelangelo, was in the 17th century accorded to Raphael, who was extolled by Bellori for beauty of form as opposed to vulgarity of color. Bellori (who appears as a forerunner of neoclassicism) considered as divine the idea, reason, and truth, in relation to antiquity, which to him is represented by Roman art.

Among the art historians who looked to the past, Francesco Scannelli of Forlì (*Il microcosmo della pittura*, Cesena, 1657), in a very broad outline of painting that considers the artists' personalities, barely touched on the northern masters of the 15th century and ignored the Tuscans. But he too exalted the 16th century, particularly Correggio and Raphael, and contrary to Vasari's opinion he held Raphael to be superior to Leonardo and Michelangelo.

In contrast, the Florentine Filippo Baldinucci (*Notizie de' professori del disegno*, Florence, 1681–1728), who saw himself as a European historiographer, is linked with Vasari not only by the division into "lives," which was by then standard, but also because, like Vasari, he began with Cimabue; he brought his predecessor up to date, covering the period from 1260 to 1670 and maintaining the superiority of the Florentines and Tuscans in the renewal of the arts. Also like Vasari, Baldinucci considered the Renaissance as existing not as it did in fact — that is, as a spiritual and artistic movement limited in time (14th–15th century and with basic characteristics of its own — but rather as a progressive renewal of art.

Instead, the identification of the Renaissance with the 15th century, which was supported by another 17th-century school of historiographers who also admired antiquity, favored the attempt made outside Italy to consider the Renaissance as a movement restricted to that century, placing in a secondary position or ignoring altogether what had been the first and major manifestation of the Renaissance — its art. Thus, Pierre Bayle (*Dictionnaire historique et critique*, Rotterdam, 1697) emphasized the moral decadence and the decline of freedom; Voltaire (*Essai sur les mœurs et l'esprit des nations*, 1756) insisted that the fine arts that had emerged in Italy from ruins and barbarism were not matched by a correspondingly high civic sense; finally, Johann Jakob Brucker (*Historia critica philosophiae*, 2d ed., Leipzig, 1766–67) saw in the Reformation a spiritual revival, which, however, was not accompanied by the return to ancient letters and philosophies that was typical of the Renaissance (this opinion was to be developed further by Jules Michelet and especially by Jacob Burckhardt). On the other hand, the Italians, such as Girolamo Tiraboschi (*Storia della letteratura italiana*, Modena, 1772), insisted that especially during the 16th century the return of the arts to their ancient dignity was the result of the support given by "splendid patrons." Winckelmann (*Gedanken über die Nachahmung der griechischen Werke in der Malerei und Bildhauerkunst*, Dresden, 1755) placed the foundations of art history in ancient times, and Goethe affirmed the parallel between the age of Pericles and that of Pope Leo X. In the 18th and 19th centuries the study covered not only the Renaissance and its representative historical figures but was also extended to the Middle Ages. Various contributions to art history were published, and they often contained sharply controversial elements of a partisan spirit. Luigi Lanzi (*Storia pittorica dell'Italia*, Florence, 1792) remained detached from these polemics, covering the period from the 13th century up to the end of the 18th in a vast work linked to Vasari on one hand and to Tiraboschi on the other. Lanzi took up and developed the concept of regional and local schools that had emerged in the 16th century and remains valid; he tended to divorce the early period of the Renaissance (i.e., the 15th century) from the flowering of the 16th century in order to link that early

period to the preceding century and the primitive painters. More or less arbitrary divisions were established by art historians from Johann Fiorillo (*Geschichte der zeichnenden Künste*, Göttingen, 1798–1808) to Seroux d'Agincourt (*Histoire de l'art par les monuments*, Paris, 1811–23), and the idea of a "risorgimento" was extended by Leopoldo Cicognara to the history of sculpture, beginning with the 11th century. Amico Ricci (*Storia dell'Architettura in Italia dal secolo IV al XVIII*, Modena, 1857–59) applied the same idea to the history of architecture; it is evident that the concept of the Renaissance, of which even the chronological limits had become blurred in the course of the centuries, does not emerge in the work of these scholars.

Outside Italy great philosophical emphasis was given to Brucker's controversial position and even more to the religious ideas of the romantic W. H. Wackenroder (*Herzensergiessungen eines kunstliebenden Klosterbruders*, Berlin, 1797) in connection with the development of those 19th-century artistic movements which exalted the primitives and, more particularly, the artists preceding Raphael. The Renaissance was unfavorably regarded (A. F. Rio, *De l'art chrétien*, Paris, 1841) because of its enduring identification with the 16th century as opposed to the Middle Ages, the spiritual and artistic values of which were penetratingly studied by John Ruskin, the moving spirit of the English pre-Raphaelite movement (*Works*, E. T. Cook and A. Wedderbur, eds., London, 1903–12).

Even in Italy, and often with a rhetorically superficial tone, the Renaissance was identified with the 16th century, the antique revival, corruption, and tyranny — that is, with entirely negative judgments. However, despite Michelet's impassioned romantic vascillations, his limitations and platitudes and notwithstanding his statement that the Reformation was the true Renaissance, he managed to grasp the spirit of the *novus ordo* in a heroic conception of history (*Histoire de France*, Paris, 1867), defining it as "la découverte du monde et la découverte de l'homme." This felicitous intuition was taken up again by Burckhardt (1860) one year after Georg Voigt's work on Humanism (cf. *Die Wiederbelebung der classischen Alterthums oder das erste Jahrhundert des Humanismus*, Berlin, 1880–81), which dealt with a movement connected with art of which Burckhardt had already proved his knowledge in *Cicerone* (1855), his excellent synthesis of Italian art.

After examining — in addition to art — the literature, the private and social life, the morals and religion (though not the religious life), the doctrines and politics of almost three centuries of Italian life, Burckhardt defined the Renaissance as an esthetic masterpiece that coincided with the discovery of man as a triumph of personality and individualism. This discovery was seen not as an abstract concept but rather in its various human manifestations. Nevertheless, Burckhardt's lofty conception was weighed down by the reservation that the sense of esthetic perfection and the beauty of forms of the Renaissance lacked the moral content of the Lutheran Reformation, the Germanic world's contribution to modern civilization. And even the Counter Reformation was underestimated as a mere moral reaction to the corruption of the Renaissance, in which religion had become a political instrument. Therefore it seems, on one hand, that the Renaissance remained connected exclusively with antiquity, and, on the other, that the Counter Reformation was considered to be in opposition to the Renaissance, which thus would end with the "classical" flowering preceding the Counter Reformation.

In literature, moreover, with the rise of positivism, other debatable distinctions were established — for instance, that of the 15th century as the century of erudition and the 16th century as the century of the true Renaissance (L. Settembrini, *Lezioni di letteratura italiana*, Naples, 1866–72). But Giosuè Carducci, who defended the 16th century in his *Discorsi letterari e storici* (Bologna, 1899), named Petrarch as the initiator of the Renaissance, which in his view occurred in all areas between the 14th and 16th centuries; this judgment is quite different from that expressed by Francesco De Sanctis (*Storia della letteratura italiana*, B. Croce, ed., Bari, 1912), who leaned toward Burckhardt in judging the Renaissance as a movement strictly limited to the court circles and dedicated to the discovery of antiquity that took place in the 15th century and extended into the following century.

Also a contributor to art historiography, G. B. Cavalcaselle (1864), who sought to establish an Italian artistic continuity, could not escape a preconceived idea of classicism; this was also true of the indefatigable French scholar of the Renaissance, Eugène Müntz (1889). Cavalcaselle clearly specified, however, that a new vision of art came into being in the 15th century with Brunelleschi. This contrasts with other historical concepts originating outside Italy, such as that expressed by H. Thode (1885), who dated the origins of the Renaissance from St. Francis of Assisi and the 13th century, basing his theory on Vasari's views (according to which the 13th century marked the origins of the artistic revival), on those of Emil Gebbart, who in his study of the life of the common people went back to the 12th century (*L'Italie mystique*, Paris, 1890), and on the revived religious values of a sense of humanity that inspired art. Later, G. Toffanin (*Storia dell'umanesimo*, Naples, 1933) was to exalt the civilization and freedom of the 13th century in contrast to the authoritarianism of the two following centuries, although he did recognize the importance of Renaissance values. Similarly and more specifically, another German scholar, H. von Geymueller, saw the beginning of the Renaissance in the cultural movement that was given impetus by Frederick II.

The study of the Middle Ages that extended to all of Europe, and especially to France, led L. Courajod (*Leçons professées à l'Ecole du Louvre*, Paris, 1899–1903) to minimize the role played by classical civilization in the formation of French art, to the advantage of the Celtic-Germanic and Oriental elements. He asserted the priority of Flemish art over the influence of the Italian discovery of antiquity.

Others (e.g., C. H. Haskins, *The Renaissance of the Twelfth Century*, Cambridge, Mass., 1927) extolled the French Latin civilization of the Middle Ages, with its realism and its individualism, qualities that were merely reelaborated by the Renaissance. It has been stated (J. Nordström, *Moyen âge et Renaissance*, Paris, 1933) that not only was the Renaissance a continuation of the Gothic tradition, but that the "true and genuine" Renaissance was that which occurred in France and in the Netherlands, and that this was to be regarded as the true Renaissance instead of the "false" one, of which Italy was merely the transmitting agent. This absurd, even grotesque, thesis was rightly refuted by E. Anagnine ("Il Problema del Rinascimento," *Nuova Rivista Storica*, XVIII, 1924, pp. 555–94).

Henri Focillon (*Art d'Occident: le moyen âge roman et gothique*, Paris, 1938) maintained that the West returned to the classical Mediterranean world during the Romanesque and Gothic Middle Ages, thus assigning a subordinate role to the Renaissance. According to some scholars a predominant civilizing function is therefore to be attributed to France and Flanders, to the detriment of Italy. This position is based on an arbitrary interpretation of the concept of the Renaissance, a result of the fact that outside Italy, since the beginning of the 16th century, the Renaissance had been identified with classicism.

A result of this arbitrary judgment was the extension of the term to refer to those medieval movements in which antiquity played a more or less predominant role (e.g., the Carolingian and the Ottonian movements and the "Palaeologian renaissance"). These were, rather, movements that were part of the highest medieval civilization — they might be defined as pseudo-Humanistic; their incorrect denomination has contributed to increasing confusion regarding the concept of the Renaissance (cf. Panofsky, 1960). The centuries-old conviction (mentioned above) that the Renaissance was merely the classical trend of that movement (cf. Wölfflin, 1899) has led, since the end of the 19th century, to a critical view of mannerism as detached from, or actually opposed to, the Renaissance. It should be added that the many unilateral and fragmentary studies of the subject have distracted from an over-all view of the problem; C. Gurlitt (*Geschichte des Barock-stils in Italien*, Stuttgart, 1887), the first scholar to pose the problem as such, saw in all mannerism the free assertion of individual feeling apart from all intellectualism, but he correctly continued to regard mannerism as a late Renaissance movement, as part of a single spiritual and esthetic trend that had consisted in change and reaction. It is an established fact that these reactions in art are related to various cultural trends. In this sense, Renaissance studies have been and are being imbued with freshness and a variety of inquiry, exploration, and clarification in the fields of philosophy (E. Garin, *Medioevo e Rinascimento, Studi e ricerche*, Bari, 1954) and history (F. Chabod, *Questioni di storia moderna*, Milan, 1951; W. K. Ferguson, *The Renaissance in Historical Thought*, Boston, 1948), as well as philology, literature, music, and science. But there persist variations and misunderstandings of the use of the term and of its chronological bounds, especially in the field of law. Since it is specifically art that is being considered here, it is not possible to go into detail regarding the various attitudes of contemporary art historiography. However, although it has been almost unanimously agreed that the beginnings of the Renaissance are to be placed in Florence in the early 15th century, some reference should be made to the more recent studies concerning the distinction between the heroic concept inspired by classicism and that inspired by realism (Weise, 1952), and, regarding classicism, the relationship between the artists and the Humanists (Chastel, 1959). But as regards the High and late Renaissance [and although Croce acknowledged the later period by entitling his collection of essays *Poeti e scrittori del pieno e del tardo Rinascimento* (Bari, 1945)] there is a tendency to insist, especially in the Anglo-Saxon world, on Michelangelo's anticlassicism in order to place him within the sphere of mannerism (which, in this author's opinion, began instead with the late Renaissance). And, again taking up the old concept that identified the Renaissance with classicism, some art historians insist on calling the late Renaissance a "counter-Renaissance" (H. Haydn, *The Counter-Renaissance*, New York, 1950), an expression used with broader meaning by E. Battisti (1962).

It has been mentioned that influences other than that of antiquity were active in the Renaissance; these were made up of medieval elements that were absorbed and reelaborated in the Renaissance style. The principal innovation consisted in the discovery through perspective of a space that was concrete and measurable as opposed to the intuitive and empirical space known during the Middle Ages and that which emerged from contemporaneous esthetic trends of north-central Europe. Furthermore, the aim at concreteness resulted in an alteration of the representational vision, in a new relation of light and color in accordance with a systematic preparation that led the men of the Renaissance to view art as a science rather than — as it is in fact — the interpretation and transfiguration of the real world based on the personality and sensitivity of the individual artist. As has been stated above, it is possible (always within the limits of specific periods) to apply the concepts classical and anticlassical, imaginary and realistic; but these correspond primarily to a human condition. Thus, once the general characteristics of the Renaissance have been established, it can be understood how it comprised personalities who looked alternately to a heroic, idealized, classical vision and to dramatic and fantastic expressions. Hence the need to subdivide the art of the Renaissance into three different phases, as F. Chabod has insisted should be done, in order to distinguish "diverse spiritual trends" within its sphere.

Survey of styles. The definition of the Renaissance as a free expression of an artistic and spiritual movement that emerged in Florence in the first decades of the 15th century is now almost universally accepted; from Florence, the movement spread to the rest of Italy, where local artists became earnest advocates of the new order. Throughout the evolution of this artistic movement, the traditions of antiquity and the Middle Ages were of prime importance. The contrast between the school of form and that of color, a contrast already evident in the Gothic period, was more manifest in the two artistic centers, Florence and Venice, than in other parts of Italy, where the two opposite approaches were more or less satisfactorily fused.

In Florence the highest moment of artistic flowering coincided approximately with the first half of the 15th century with the activity of the three leading protagonists, Brunelleschi, Donatello, and Masaccio, as well as masters such as Fra Angelico, Paolo Uccello, Domenico Veneziano, and Andrea del Castagno, in whom the influence of antiquity, when it was present, was always expressed with restraint and individuality. In Padua, Ferrara, Urbino, Milan, Venice, Naples, and Sicily (to mention only the principal centers and refer only to the major artists), the beginnings of the movement can be placed in the second half of the century, with the work of Mantegna, Cosmè Tura, Luciano Laurana, Vincenzo Foppa, the Bellinis, and Antonello da Messina, while Piero della Francesca appears as the *summus moderator*.

In Florence during the second half of the 15th century, the sense of freedom and of spontaneity was hampered by intellectualistic limitations imposed by the myth of antiquity, although the Florentine spirit strove to overcome them and the major artists succeeded in doing so. These limitations were mainly the result of an intensification of humanistic studies and of classical erudition that fostered an open reaction to the Middle Ages. It is understandable that the atmosphere best suited to a lofty culture was that of the courts, particularly, of course, the papal court. At mid-century, Rome — the center richest in ancient traditions — adhered more than any other to classic ideals and, as a result, became the goal of pilgrimages by worshipers of ancient art. Courtly tastes were also predominant in the other Italian seigniories, as well as in oligarchical Venice.

But it is precisely the case of Florence that gives rise to further reflections. The myth of antiquity was artificially continued there by the increasing predominance of the Medici family, who had by then turned the city into their own seigniory, disguised under a republican system. An idealized classicism was represented by such sculptors as the Rossellino brothers and Benedetto da Maiano. In painting, Ghirlandajo, with his many erudite references to antiquity, can be considered a classicist. Botticelli, the greatest Florentine painter of the period, depicted some classical subjects but certain sincerely religious aspects appear in his work as a reflection of Savonarola's reforms. Filippino Lippi and Piero di Cosimo introduced a topical freedom into their mythological subjects, and their work is free of cultural pedantry. Thus there existed in Florence an independence of spirit that can be called anticlassicism. Its earliest manifestations are found in Donatello, especially in his later period, in a dramatic, biting, harsh expressionism (derived also from contacts with the northern world) that coincides with that of the period of Andrea del Castagno; it was continued by Pollaiuolo, both as a sculptor and as a painter, whose works convey a vital sense of movement, and, above all, by the nonerudite works of Bertoldo di Giovanni, Michelangelo's teacher. Anticlassicism therefore had its origin in Florence in the early Renaissance, and became linked with the name of Michelangelo, whose work was of fundamental significance and had repercussions in the late Renaissance.

In the work of Verrocchio and of his pupil Leonardo, classicism was expressed through a remarkable selectivity in the choice of compact form and of expression. Both artists achieved aerial perspective through the soft chiaroscuro previously emphasized by Ghiberti and by Desiderio da Settignano. In central Italy, Raphael's graceful painting reflects these influences. Mantegna's foreshortened figures against the painted sky in the ceiling of the Camera degli Sposi in Mantua were succeeded by Correggio's gigantic images hovering in an open, atmospheric space. Other artists, especially in northern Italy, moved from a central perspective to new and more complex spatial effects. Thus the transition was effected from the first phase of the Renaissance to the second. But from what has been said it appears that the first phase concluded with the exaltation of classicism; therefore Bramante and Leonardo are placed at the head of the second phase of the Renaissance.

The existence of so many outstanding artists in the High Renaissance inevitably accentuated stylistic contrasts. However, a broader, more grandiose vision remained fundamental to the period as a whole: it was the beginning of the search for a scale attuned to superhuman proportions and to the monumentality of the architecture of ancient Rome. The more intimate and delicate ideal of the early Renaissance, so human in its dimensions, had been characterized by a Hellenizing tone.

The late Renaissance was based on certain premises, especially in Rome, that were the result of Michelangelo's preeminence, and it overlapped chronologically with the High Renaissance since it began in the first half of the 16th century, with artists such as Pontormo and Parmigianino, when the High Renaissance was at its peak. The late Renaissance ended in the second half of the century, except in some minor centers where it survived into the beginning of the 17th century. In the late Renaissance two tendencies prevailed: an anticlassicist trend, which was intensified and developed an imaginative freedom, but eventually lost the stylistic severity and spiritual fervor of its beginnings and declined into genre expressions such as those of Vasari; and a classicist trend, which ultimately degenerated into irrational picturesqueness.

Venice stood apart from the various elaborations, interpretations, and changes that took place in the rest of Italy. This great artistic center retained its remarkable, uniform, poetic accent, because of a sensible moderation in interpreting classicism and a Hellenic subtlety. Its lofty creative values were to become a vital source of inspiration for the modern world.

EARLY RENAISSANCE. *Architecture.* Filippo Brunelleschi was the initiator of the *novus ordo* in architecture; by applying the new science of perspective (based on the principles of Euclidean optics) he achieved the great Renaissance conquest discussed above: the definition of space, as opposed to the vague Gothic concept of space. In reaction to the Gothic he took up again the structural divisions of ancient architecture, beginning with his designs for reworking the Baptistery and other Florentine buildings of the Romanesque period.

Brunelleschi's innovation was of fundamental importance for the system of perspective it provided for sculptors and painters, especially Donatello and Masaccio. His individuality in the preparation of the wooden model (1418) of the dome of S. Maria del Fiore in Florence marked a decided departure from Gothic tradition, while the systematic research that led him to a consummate mastery of technical means enabled him to solve the problem — studied in vain by his predecessors — of the construction of the dome. He accomplished this without using centering or scaffolding. In order to make it compatible with the distinctly Gothic character of the construction, Brunelleschi created two cloistered vaults, one inside the other (the hollow between is partly occupied by stairs; II, FIG. 655), giving the outer shell a completely original aspect in the marble ribs rising to the lantern, emphasizing them with the contrasting color of the baked bricks that form the convex sections (II, PL. 365). However, when he was able to work unhampered by preexisting structures, Brunelleschi gave free rein to his genius and personal vision. In the façade on the ground floor of the Ospedale degli Innocenti (1419; II, PL. 366), he repeated familiar rhythms in new proportions and with a new spatial intensity disciplined by classical structural elements (Corinthian columns and wide, semicircular arches). In completing the Palazzo di Parte Guelfa (destroyed 1944), he created a fresh movement with the corner parastades, which should have been trabeated like the interior of the hall (later modified by Vasari; FIG. 11) in keeping with an arrangement that remained peculiar to Florence.

It was, however, especially in religious architecture that Brunelleschi manifested his highly personal style. The Old Sacristy of S. Lorenzo in Florence (PL. 1; II, PL. 368) served as a model for similar Renaissance chapels; its square plan was geometrically doubled and became rectangular in breadth in the Pazzi Chapel in the medieval church of Sta Croce (II, PLS. 367, 368), which was once the chapter hall of the friars (hence its iconography). The ribbed dome (I, PL. 417) recalls the ribbing of ancient edifices and is derived from 14th-century vaults. Moreover, an atmosphere of serenity prevails in the juxtaposition of *pietra serena* (a blue-gray stone) and whitewash, which is enlivened in the Old Sacristy by the chiaroscuro and delicate coloring of Donatello's reliefs and in the Pazzi Chapel by the vibrant glazed terra cottas of Luca della Robbia. Unlike Gothic churches, with their piers and vaults, S. Lorenzo (II,

Florence, Palazzo di Parte Guelfa, ideal reconstruction of the main hall [*from Rinascimento (La Rinascita), Florence, March 1951*].

PLS. 369, 370, FIG. 654) reverted to Early Christian and Romanesque schemes in the colonnades and timber roof, while the stilted arches above the columns can be traced back to late antiquity, to the Romanesque style, and to Arnolfo di Cambio, and the transept and the lateral chapels to local tradition (Sta Trinita); in the solemn longitudinal perspective — here, too, balanced between sandstone and whitewash — there is a vibrancy in the slender and tensile line that strengthens the pilasters and trabeations, and the whole is suffused with a subtle chiaroscuro, far removed from the decorative richness of Early Christian architecture and from the somberness of the Romanesque.

In the Church of Sto Spirito (II, PLS. 370, 371, FIG. 658), in which the Latin-cross plan was inspired by that of Siena Cathedral, the architect's design called for an exterior line that would have followed with a repeated semicircular movement the shape of the niches along the interior perimeter. This would have complemented the interior line and the greater height of the aisles. However, after Brunelleschi's death the exterior was completed on a less forceful rectilinear plan.

The same remarkable individuality was displayed in the complex plans for the octagonal church of S. Maria degli Angeli (II, FIG. 659), of a more intense chiaroscuro in the external niches and chapels, in which the ancient style is revived, and in the small tribunes under the drum of the dome of Florence Cathedral (II, PL. 364). The same may be said of the two secular buildings linked with Brunelleschi's name. The first, the Palazzo Pitti (II, PL. 372), in its powerful rusticated blocks echoes antiquity (wall of the Forum of Augustus, Rome) and the Middle Ages (the Palazzo Vecchio, Florence), disciplining these reminiscences in a geometric execution softened by detail. The second, the Palazzo Pazzi (now Quaratesi; II, PL. 373), was constructed by Giuliano da Maiano with two-light windows that were copied from the Palazzo Vecchio but have a Renaissance feeling in their details.

A change of style is evident in the art of Brunelleschi, who was increasingly absorbed by the study of antiquity but nevertheless aimed at combining Romanesque and Gothic structural and decorative elements. His constant ability to surpass the motifs that originally inspired him eventually led the artist to a poetic expression of his own, and above all to a freedom in interpreting classical forms that was to remain a virtue of the Florentines.

Although Leon Battista Alberti did not ignore the Middle Ages as a source of inspiration when he began his activity as an architect (a work designed in his youth, the Campanile of Ferrara Cathedral, is derived from French Romanesque models), his preference later turned to the Roman world, as is evidenced both by his written works and by the many quotations on his monuments. As a Humanist, Alberti sensed the beauty inherent in the superposition of architectural orders, which he applied in the Palazzo Rucellai in Florence (I, PLS. 54, 55). He was also aware of the firmness and grandeur of the triumphal arch, which he used in his plan for the façade of the Tempio Malatestiano (I, PLS. 51, 52). This was designed to culminate in a large dome inspired by that of the Roman Pantheon (this dome was later executed in the apse of the SS. Annunziata, Florence; FIG. 11), with volutes such as those in the façade of

a

b

c

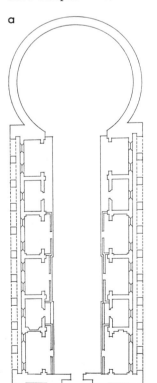 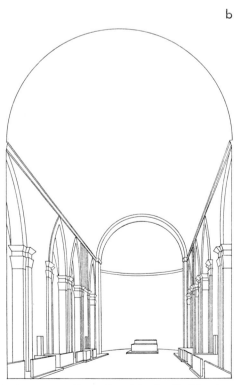 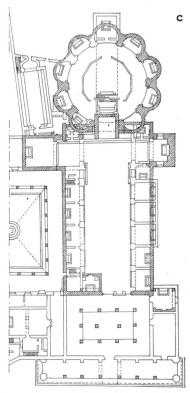

(a) and (b) Rimini, Tempio Malatestiano: (a) plan presumably projected by L. B. Alberti, according to M. Salmi (*from M. Salmi, Il tempio Malatestiano di Rimini, Atti della insigne Accademia Nazionale di S. Luca, Rome, 1951-52, Vol. I*); (b) perspective reconstruction of the interior based on Alberti's presumed project (*from Salmi, op. cit.*); (c) Florence, SS. Annunziata, reconstruction of 15th-century plan on the basis of present plan (*from O. Morisani, Michelozzo architetto, Turin, 1951*).

S. Maria Novella (I, PL. 53). He sought to reproduce the monumental sense of space of ancient thermae in the Greek-cross plan of S. Sebastiano in Mantua (I, PL. 56, FIG. 196) and, again, in the Latin cross of S. Andrea, also in Mantua (PL. 2; I, PL. 57, FIG. 204), which has a single nave, with transept and dome (present dome rebuilt by Juvara), and which tends in its plan and majesty to the *gravitas* of the 16th century. Alberti's treatise *De re aedificatoria* (1485) documents his feeling for antiquity in general and for Vitruvius in particular; he became the leading model for the writers of treatises on architecture who, during the 15th and 16th centuries, were to influence the changeable tastes of the Renaissance. Therefore, both as theorist and as artist, Alberti revived classical antiquity, which was identified with ancient Rome.

In Donatello's works of architectural decoration, which were always brilliantly inventive, he sometimes approached Brunelleschi's style (e.g., the marble tabernacle in Orsanmichele, Florence) and was, on occasion, extraordinarily original (tomb of the antipope John XXIII, PL. 16; III, PL. 13; Annunciation tabernacle in the Church of Sta Croce) and concerned with pictorial effects (singing gallery from Florence Cathedral; IV, PLS. 244, 247). At other times he showed a vigorously tense sculptural quality (doors of the Old Sacristy in S. Lorenzo).

The architecture of the early Renaissance was articulated mainly, but not exclusively, between the two great personalities of Brunelleschi and Alberti, champions of two different trends. In fact, that there were other architects working in Florence at that time is demonstrated by the new minor buildings — discreet and orderly, whitewashed, with doorways and arched windows in blue stone — that were being inserted, without excessive conflicts with medieval tradition, among the somber brown edifices of the 14th century. Some of the new constructions faithfully followed the trend set by Brunelleschi, represented in its most orthodox aspects by the master's favorite pupil, Andrea di Lazzaro Cavalcanti (Il Buggiano) in the Oratory of SS. Pietro e Paolo, known as the Cappella della Madonna di Piè di Piazza, and in the Cardini Chapel in S. Francesco, both at Pescia. Nevertheless, classicism was so strong in Florence that the Church of Sto Spirito was subjected after Brunelleschi's death to arbitrary alterations in his designs (see above), which provoked a violent protest from Giuliano da Sangallo.

A host of architects went out from Florence to spread the new style in other regions; they were almost always preceded by Florentine sculptors and, above all, painters. A clear distinction must, however, be made between those who were contemporary — or nearly so — with Brunelleschi and Alberti, and those who belonged to the younger generations; among the contemporaries of the masters, a further subdivision must be established between those who came to the Renaissance through a Gothic experience and the supporters of the new order.

Antonio Averlino, known as Filarete (1400–69), introduced the Renaissance to the court of Francesco Sforza in Milan; in the Tower of the geometric Castello Sforzesco at Porta Giovia, with its many recessed stories (reconstructed from old drawings), he created a rather laborious superposition of insufficiently elaborated elements, in a combination of Renaissance and Gothic styles that is also noticeable in the exterior of the Ospedale Maggiore (built 1456–65; PL. 3), which was designed with an arcade (now closed) that was later (1465) topped by Giuniforte Solari with a story of Gothic two-light windows. The Ospedale Maggiore was conceived by Filarete with exceptional magnificence; its eight internal courtyards (and a large central courtyard with the church at one end) with graceful superposed colonnades that were formerly adorned with graffiti, reveal the full impact of Brunelleschi's influence (FIG. 14). Filarete's measure as an architect is better given by the regular symmetrical plans and rather trite elevations in the drawings that illustrate his treatise on architecture (ca. 1461–64; dedicated 1465 to Piero de' Medici), in which he described an ideal town, Sforzinda, named in honor of Francesco Sforza (I, PL. 406; III, PL. 484). In the secular buildings designed by Filarete, the romantic nature of his fantasy inspired his picturesque adaptation of divisions typical of Alberti to superimposed architectural orders, with some Gothicizing elements. This trend

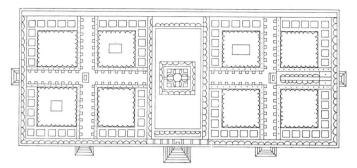

Milan, Ospedale Maggiore, plan according to project by A. A. Filarete in Codex Magliabecchianus (*from Tractat über die Baukunst, W. von Oettingen, ed., Vienna, 1896*).

toward the picturesque often led to the use of decorative effects in religious buildings, such as those that were intended to appear on the façade of Bergamo Cathedral, which was decorated with polychrome marbles, a work that undoubtedly had considerable influence on Lombard architecture of the early Renaissance. The secular buildings proposed in his treatise had some influence in the Veneto region and also in a building in Mantua, the *Domus Nova* (1480–84), built for the Gonzaga family by the Florentine Luca Fancelli near the Castello di San Giorgio. The treatise also had considerable value for the Renaissance vision of town planning.

The earlier works of Michelozzo (1396–1472) — an architect as well as a sculptor — were executed from about 1421 to 1436 and gave evidence of his links with the Gothic style: the mixtilinear arch in the façade of S. Agostino in Montepulciano (VIII, PL. 191); the ribbed vaults of the sacristy of Sta Trinita, Florence, of the church of the Monastery of S. Francesco (Bosco ai Frati) in the Mugello, of the church of the Castello di Trebbio, and of the apse in the church of the Monastery of S. Marco in Florence); and the projecting galleries and the battlements in the Castello di Trebbio and Villa Medici at Cafaggiolo (VIII, PL. 191) and, later, in the Villa Medici at Careggi (FIG. 21). His use of Gothic element spersisted even after the artist had adopted the ways of the Renaissance. Michelozzo favored massive and heavy effects (Chapel of the Novitiate in Sta Croce, the Annunciation edicule in the SS. Annunziata, both Florence), with some elements reminiscent of Brunelleschi in the library of the Monastery of S. Marco (FIG. 28), which Michelozzo designed, like a church, with three aisles, as if to emphasize the sacred nature of learning. He imparted similar sobriety to the Palazzo Medici-Riccardi (PL. 4; FIG. 14), relieving it on the facing, which is composed of rusticated ashlar on the ground floor and compact rows of two-light windows on the upper floors, crowned with a heavy cornice. The courtyard — a perfectly regular quadrangle (PL. 4) — acquires a solemn tone in the ground-floor colonnade; it is enlivened by graffiti and medallions in relief (partly inspired by ancient cameos) in the body of the piano nobile and is completed by an airy loggia. This extremely regular structure, later widely imitated, was repeated by Michelozzo himself when he remodeled the first courtyard of the Palazzo Vecchio (1454). But

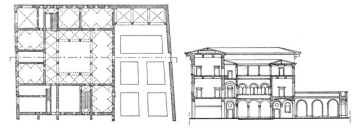

Florence, Palazzo Medici-Riccardi (architect, Michelozzo), plan of ground floor (*from E. Lundberg, Arkitekturens Formspråk, Italia 1420–1620, Stockholm, 1954*) and transverse section (*from B. Fletcher, A History of Architecture, New York-London, 1961*).

Michelozzo's style lost some of its individuality when the artist left Tuscany for Ragusa (now Dubrovnik, Yugoslavia) and Milan. In Ragusa, in 1464, he outlined the general idea for the reconstruction of the Palace of the Rectors — later executed by Giorgio da Sebenico — giving particular attention to the proportions of the colonnade, which faithfully followed the local building tradition. He again conformed to the local architectural style — in this case that of the Po Valley — in designing the Medici bank in Milan (known from a drawing by Filarete), in which the two-light ogival windows were a concession to the Gothic taste that was still very strong in that city, where the Cathedral was being built in Flamboyant Gothic style. Notwithstanding some Lombard additions the pure Renaissance aspects of the bank's splendid portal, with a trabeated arch, became a standard design in northern Italy (PL. 3). The Portinari Chapel in S. Eustorgio in Milan (PL. 3) repeated the plan and the structure of the ribbed dome of the Old Sacristy of S. Lorenzo in Florence. The chapel has a soaring elevation and is adorned with sculptural elements and with frescoes by Vincenzo Foppa, leader of one of the Lombard schools. The example of the Portinari Chapel was followed in Liguria, where the same scheme was used by an unknown Lombard in building the Church of S. Maria di Loreto in Finale Ligure.

Like Michelozzo, other Florentines were active outside their city. One of them was Pagno di Lapo Portigiani (1406–70), who had worked as a sculptor with Donatello and Michelozzo. In 1453 he went to Bologna where he gave a Florentine tone to the Casa Bolognini (now Isolani), begun two years earlier. The building is consonant with local tradition in its colonnades as well as in its height, which is limited to two floors, a typical feature of the Po Valley. Nevertheless, the two-light ogival windows show an assimilation of some Renaissance sculptural elements, which are also to be found in the cornice adorned with human heads, reminiscent of Donatello. The grace and elegance of the whole indicate that Portigiani was a rather timid artist, but one very close to Michelozzo. Portigiani had some following in Bologna, but he was soon surpassed because of his undistinguished artistic personality.

Another Florentine artist of even lesser prominence was Luca Fancelli, supposed author of the *Domus Nova* of the Gonzaga family in Mantua, in which Filarete's influence is clearly discernible. And even though he was the foremost architect of that city and worked on the churches of S. Sebastiano and S. Andrea and on one of the chapels in the Cathedral, his work was influenced sometimes by Alberti, at other times by Brunelleschi, so that, on the whole, he emerges as a rather colorless personality. By contrast, Bernardo Rossellino (1409–1464) resolutely followed his own inspiration. At a rather early date (1433–34) he built the upper portion of the Palazzo della Fraternità dei Laici in Arezzo using some Gothicizing elements (justified by the need to make the new portion compatible with the lower, Gothic floor), which he then repudiated in the mixtilinear arch bearing the relief of the Madonna della Misericordia. In the two lateral niches he expressed himself in a thoroughly Renaissance idiom, drawing steadily closer to Alberti's rules, which he was to interpret so successfully in Rome, where he supervised (1450) the construction of the Vatican Palace for the Humanist pope Nicholas V and the transformation of the old St. Peter's. Later, for Enea Silvio Piccolomini (Pius II; 1458–64), he transformed the Pope's home town of Corsignano, where the winding streets and most of the buildings were still predominantly Gothic, into a small Renaissance town, subsequently renamed Pienza in honor of the Pope. This transformation was effected by inserting a number of Renaissance palaces (e.g., that of Cardinal Francesco Gonzaga, now Palazzo Simonelli) into the old scheme and, more importantly, by creating the square around which the town's principal buildings are grouped: the Cathedral, the Palazzo Piccolomini, the bishop's palace, and the small Palazzo Comunale (FIG. 16; I, PL. 390; III, PL. 388). The square of Pienza is the first to have been created during the Renaissance by a single artist in accordance with a well-defined town-planning scheme; it was laid out in a spatial setting, with the clever expedient of making the two buildings facing either side of the Cathedral diverge away from

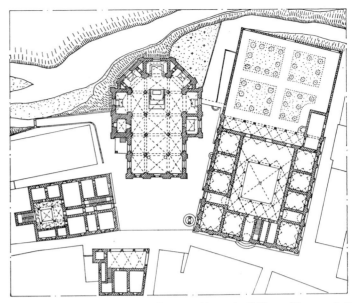

Pienza, plan of the monumental center (*from A. Schiavo, Monumenti di Pienza, Milan, 1942*).

it, to convey an illusion of greater space, and to bring into greater relief the façade of the church. Here the architect succeeded in prevailing over his patron's taste. But Pius II, recalling his trips to northern Europe (e.g., to participate in the Council of Basel), felt the fascination of Gothic architecture, particularly the *Hallenkirche* plan, which called for three aisles of equal height. The Cathedral, of rather limited dimensions, widens in a transept with a semioctagonal apse and three chapels and is divided into a nave and two aisles by clustered piers of equal height surmounted by stilted arches and a vaulted ceiling. The many-lighted windows of the gallery are Gothic in style. However, in the interior the Renaissance style predominates in the details (bases, capitals, stilted arches) and in the side windows, for Rossellino was mindful of Alberti's teachings and reworked the ancient style in materials of dazzling purity. Pius II himself prized the esthetic effects achieved in the Cathedral, which was flooded with light and so different from northern churches with their chiaroscuro; he wrote in his *Commentarii* (Rome, 1584) that when the sun shone, so much light came through the windows that the sacred building appeared to be a house not of stone but of glass. The façade is reminiscent of Alberti in its compactness, in its tripartite arrangement (but with a single, sloping roof that encompasses the nave and aisles), and in the severe simplicity that accentuates the monumental character of its structural members. The Palazzo Piccolomini, with its superposed orders reminiscent of the Palazzo Rucellai in Florence — though less slender because of the influence of Roman *gravitas* — was enriched with studied refinements that reveal the sculptor in Rossellino, refinements that extended to the graffiti of the equally monumental courtyard, in which the cross-mullioned windows are also of Roman derivation. The loggia opening onto the vast landscape of the Valle delle Orcia and Monte Amiata that was described and admired by Pius II, with its great colonnaded façade on three levels, acquires a Roman breadth, heralding the more complex and imposing Benediction Loggia that was inserted into the façade of St. Peter's in the Vatican.

The bishop's palace in Pienza, inspired by Rossellino and also exquisitely simple with its cross-mullioned windows, probably marks the beginning of the architectural activity of the Sienese Francesco di Giorgio. His hand is evident also in the Palazzo Piccolomini in Siena — in which, however, the Florentine influence is quite marked. Its mass recalls the buildings of the 14th century, although the regularity and rhythm of its vertical lines are clearly of the Renaissance.

In Rome, under the pontificate of Nicholas V, Alberti's influence prevailed. The palaces on the Capitoline hill were rebuilt (in 1451 three cross-mullioned windows were added to the Palazzo dei Senatori), the Apostolic Palace of S. Maria Maggiore was restored (since destroyed), and to the Vatican Palace (renovated in 1447) was added a new wing, completed in 1454 (during the pontificate of Alexander VI the addition was flanked with the Borgia Tower). The other wing, three-storied, with arched windows in the Florentine style on the ground floor and cross-mullioned windows on the upper floors, was crowned by a massive crenelation on corbels reminiscent of Michelozzo's archaizing style. The cross-mullioned windows in the courtyard of the papal palace of Pienza and in so many other later buildings were not at all similar. Those of the Vatican Palace may have been a Gothic touch demanded by the commissioning Pope. An experienced diplomat, he had participated with success in the Diet of Frankfurt, where he had seen the cross-mullioned windows of the Römerberg, a square noted for its Gothic edifices. It is also possible that, because of the apostolic dignity of the building, an effort was made to echo the similar windows of the Palace of the Popes in Avignon.

In Rome, in the oldest part of the Palazzo Venezia (1455; PL. 14), Cardinal Pietro Barbo (the future Pope Paul II) called for arched windows on the ground floor, cross-mullioned windows on the second floor, and a crenelated merlon in imitation of the new wing of the Vatican Palace. The proportions were subjected to the rules laid down by Alberti, which were also applied in the later enlargement of the building (1468–91). Moreover, the unfinished courtyard of the palace (VIII, PL. 205), for which many possible authors have been suggested, from Rossellino to Giuliano da Sangallo (who apparently did work on the palace from 1469 to 1474), perhaps echoes the Benediction Loggia of St. Peter's in the solemn superimposed arcades, reminiscent of the Colosseum and the Theater of Marcellus — reminiscences that seem to have been filtered through Alberti's ideals. During the sixth and seventh decades of the 15th century various sources testify to the great prestige enjoyed by Alberti in Rome and in all of Italy.

The Florentine Agostino di Duccio (1418–81), working as a sculptor, had decorated (1446–57) the interior of the Tempio Malatestiano in Rimini with his refined reliefs (see below). He repeated the monumental solemnity of the façade of the Tempio Malatestiano in the unfinished Porta S. Pietro in Perugia, with three arches and two projections that, in the semblance of towers, enclosed the single, ample barrel vault; however, the artist softened the general effect, resolving the problems of the structural articulations and decorative elements on the surface. Although Agostino di Duccio often seemed to strive for grandeur, he expressed his personal taste in the façade of the Oratory of S. Bernardino in Perugia (1457–61; VIII, PL. 191) by harmonizing architecture and sculpture in an original composition of lively polychromy, in which the white and red marbles blended to great effect with the dark-blue grounds (now faded to pale green).

In Rimini, Alberti had taken his inspiration for the façade of the Tempio Malatestiano from the Arch of Augustus in the same city. An anonymous artist, following his example, brought the same conception to the Arsenal gate (1457–60) in Venice, which repeats the scheme of a Roman triumphal arch, perhaps that of the Arch of the Sergi in Pulj (mod. Pola, Yugoslavia; PL. 285). This type remained confined to Venice and the Veneto region. Another example is the triumphal arch of Alfonso of Aragon in Naples (PL. 7), inserted between two towers at the entrance to the Castel Nuovo as a symbol of the power of the new ruler. Once ascribed to Alberti and later, because of its design, to Francesco Laurana, the arch was begun about 1455 and finished in 1466 by a certain Pietro (di Martino) da Milano. While it is true that an ancient source — similar to that of the gate of the Arsenal in Venice — can be discerned in the lower arch, the vertical course clearly recalls the arch built in Capua by Frederick II (known from a drawing), which represented a triumphal entrance to the kingdom of Apulia. This same concept was repeated in the arch in Naples with extreme classical redundance and with an alteration of the ancient proportions, which are weighed down by the excessive height of the relief

(illustrating the triumph of the Aragonese ruler) between the lower and upper sections as well as by the topmost part with niches, crowned by a curvilinear pediment in the manner of Donatello. These various elements form an eclectic whole that, through lack of restraint, betrays the prevailing Lombard taste. The dimensions of the relief mentioned above are, in fact, typical of the sculptural decorations of the Genoese portals designed by the Gaggini family of Lombardy, members of which made their way as far south as Sicily. The main credit for the work should probably be assigned to Pietro da Milano.

In the history of early Renaissance architecture the small town of Urbino gained prominence about the middle of the century. There, between 1449 and 1454 approximately, the Florentine Maso di Bartolomeo added a portal to the Gothic façade of S. Domenico; it is a very elongated, slender portal of late Gothic proportions, reminiscent of Ghiberti's pre-Renaissance style (Tabernacle of the Linaiuoli; Florence, Mus. di S. Marco), but the structure reveals an adherence to Alberti's tenets in its wealth of detail and is enriched with a lunette by Luca della Robbia. It is an example that was to bear modest fruit much later in Bologna (portal of the Church of the Madonna di Galliera) and in Aosta (Cathedral portal).

The impetus given by Federigo da Montefeltro, count, and, later, duke of Urbino, led to the building of the Palazzo Ducale, which Baldassare Castiglione, in Book I of The Courtier, praised as a "city in the form of a palace"; it is undoubtedly the noblest royal residence of the 15th century and a further demonstration of the way in which the Renaissance, after its beginnings in the trading republic of Florence, eventually asserted itself in the seigniories and became the heritage of princes. Among these, Federigo da Montefeltro was certainly the most cultured; he read the classics in the original and created a remarkable private library that is now one of the glories of the Vatican Library.

His palace was begun as the renovation of a medieval keep (the Castellare of the Montefeltros); the section built between 1454 and 1460 approximately had two floors in the nucleus facing S. Domenico and was intended to form one side of a regular courtyard. Its two-light windows in the manner of Brunelleschi were by Michele di Giovanni di Bartolo (known as Il Greco; formerly assistant to Maso di Bartolomeo) and Pasquino da Montepulciano. This section became known as the Palazzetto della Jole for a fireplace decorated with representations of the princess Iole and Hercules, clearly a nuptial allusion to the union between Federigo and Battista Sforza. The doors, corbels, and other interior ornamentation are somewhat eclectic in style, but they appear on the whole to be the result of a classicizing spirit. The figural elements are clearly reminiscent of Bernardo Rossellino, though they tend toward the geometric style through the influence of Piero della Francesca, who had painted The Flagellation of Christ for Urbino (XI, PL. 158).

The major and essential part of the Urbino palace is that begun in 1467 and designed by Luciano Laurana around the rectangular courtyard that was called for in the original plan (IX, FIG. 168); projecting from the center of its west façade, which terminates on either side in a slender tower, are three arched balconies that overlook the countryside (IX, PL. 96). The whole, originally crenelated, appears picturesquely fanciful owing to the irregularity of its external mass, although the façade is disciplined by nobly conceived windows similar to those of Piero's house in Sansepolcro. In the courtyard the ground-floor loggia and the pilasters and windows of the first story stand out against the pale brick; the pure geometric forms of these elements harmonize with the regular surfaces and endow the courtyard with a rigorously static quality that creates a luminous and still atmosphere. In this masterpiece Laurana took as his premises the Humanistic architecture of Alberti (whom he had met in Mantua) and the sublime rhythms of Piero della Francesca. Laurana's work appears, therefore, as the transposition to a correspondingly lofty architectural plane of the painting of the Sansepolcro master. This is also apparent in the interiors of the ducal apartment (IX, PL. 97), with their large embrasures and crystalline doors and windows, and also in the balconies of the west façade, one of which seems to imitate the loggia of Solomon's court as painted by Piero in the Arezzo frescoes. For a time the great painter did in fact inspire the artistic views of his very cultured patron. However, Federigo gradually turned to new esthetic contacts and acquired new tastes that are represented in the Urbino palace by the elegant decorative styles of the Florentines Domenico Rosselli and Francesco di Simone Ferrucci (who decorated the apartment of the duchesses that was built in the old Castellare). These artists ornamented the fireplaces and the doors with inlaid panels (X, PL. 437); their work, together with that of Francesco di Giorgio, can be seen in the Duke's *studiolo* (VIII, PLS. 80, 100; IX, PL. 97), also decorated with paintings by the Flemish artist Justus of Ghent and by Pedro Berruguete, a Spaniard.

Francesco di Giorgio (1439–ca. 1502) was a Sienese painter, sculptor, and architect. While he was engaged in building fortresses in the Marches, the artist also worked on the palace in Urbino, to which he added a second courtyard — known as the Pasquino Courtyard — of simple monumentality with its large barrel-vaulted arcades; the work was completed in only one wing, however, since building was discontinued in the Duke's death in 1482. Francesco di Giorgio is to be credited with the design of the entrance façade, but it was Ambrogio da Milano who ornamented its Laurana-inspired windows with a delightful decorative elegance, which he also imparted to the very ornate stairway with doors and portals, showing himself to be a consummate virtuoso and a follower of Pietro Lombardo (see below), whose influence is also apparent in the later Cappella del Perdono (II, PL. 337). Then, with the intervention of Gian Cristoforo Romano, the Palazzo Ducale was subjected to an even more exaggerated decorative treatment, completely antithetical to Laurana's art. It can be said that the artists represented in the Urbino palace form an exceptional group that synthesizes the many trends of the early Renaissance and that, among these, Luciano Laurana remains foremost for his lofty classicism. In fact, his design for the fortress of Rocca Costanza in Pesaro could not equal his accomplishment at Urbino; this was true also of Francesco di Giorgio, whose courtyard of the Palazzo Ducale in Gubbio is derived from that in Urbino but is clearly inferior to it.

In the meantime the evolution of architecture continued in Tuscany, which was described by Federigo da Montefeltro as "the fountain of architects"; the younger Tuscan artists were working at home and abroad. One of these, Bernardo Rossellino's brother Antonio (1427–79), who was primarily a sculptor, worked as an architect on the Chapel of the Cardinal of Portugal in the Florentine church of S. Miniato al Monte, completed about 1461. The plan is a short Greek cross of weighty proportions, recalling Alberti in the accentuation of the classical taste combined with color; it is, in other words, far removed from Brunelleschi's delicate contrasts between whitewash and bluish-gray stone. Several elements heighten the effect of the artist's outstanding achievement: the introduction in the vault of brilliant terra cottas by Della Robbia, the altarpiece (XI, PL. 182) and wall frescoes by the Pollaiuolos, the panels by Alesso Baldovinetti, the striking marble tomb executed by Rossellino himself (PL. 16), and the polychromy of the altar marbles, of the seats, and of the floor, which was paved in *opus Alexandrinum*. All of this reflected a profound change in the Florentine style, which was gradually acquiring clearer outlines, perhaps through the influence of the court style from the north. The change is also evident in Michelozzo's chapel in the Palazzo Medici-Riccardi, frescoed by Benozzo Gozzoli (1459; VIII, PL. 193) and graced with a panel, the *Madonna Adoring the Child*, by Fra Filippo Lippi (IX, PL. 146). Moreover, the outstandingly Florentine Martini Chapel in the Church of S. Giobbe in Venice, which has a vault decorated with Della Robbia's terra cottas and which contains a marble altarpiece by Antonio Rossellino, seems to demonstrate a continuity of culture and tastes destined to affect all aspects of art.

Another Florentine, Giuliano da Maiano (1432–90), originally a craftsman (in 1463 he received a commission to make some of the cabinets for the New Sacristy of the Cathedral of Florence; VIII, PL. 83), looked mainly to Brunelleschi for inspiration when he built, between 1459 and 1469, the Palazzo Pazzi (Quaratesi); later he turned to the classicizing schemes of Alberti. The modest Palazzo dello Strozzino (1462) in Florence echoes the Palazzo Pitti in its facing of rusticated ashlar. The Chapel of S. Fina (1468) in the Collegiata at San Gimignano recalls Brunelleschi in its proportions and Alberti in the structure of the vault and the decoration (which was taken as a point of departure by Benedetto da Maiano, Giuliano's brother, in the marble panel, whose pictorial quality was complemented by Ghirlandaio's frescoes; VI, PL. 179), following the richer example of the Chapel of the Cardinal of Portugal. Later, in 1470, Giuliano used the Brunelleschi-inspired rhythms on a grander scale in the cloister of the Benedictine Abbey (known as the Palazzo di Badia) in Arezzo; the scheme is that of other Florentine cloisters, with a ground-floor arcade and a loggia on the first story (cloisters of S. Lorenzo in Florence and of the Badia of Fiesole); but the greater spaciousness was definitely inspired by Alberti. In the Palazzo Spannocchi in Siena (PL. 4), designed by Giuliano, Alberti's style is also reflected in the smooth rustication, the elegant two-light windows, and the crowning cornice. Moreover, Giuliano's major achievement, Faenza Cathedral (1476–86), is reminiscent of S. Lorenzo in Florence in its external appearance as well as in the three-aisle plan with lateral chapels, and even in some details, such as the elongated windows. But in the interior structure, with an alternating sequence of piers and columns replacing the unbroken series of columns of Brunelleschi's churches, Giuliano adapted the new idioms to suit the architectural traditions established in the Po Valley during the Romanesque and Gothic periods. The massive supports and the vaults above the high trabeation are a departure from Brunelleschi's graceful curves and fragile elegance; their heavy lines harmonize with the gravity of the Lombard Romanesque style peculiar to the Po region. Later the artist worked in Recanati, in Prato, and in the Sanctuary of the Holy House in Loreto (1481), and then he went as far south as Naples. There, in the design of the Porta Capuana (1485), inspired by both Brunelleschi and Michelozzo, he attempted to emulate the monumentality of the earlier arch of Alfonso of Aragon. He worked on the villa at Poggioreale (1487–88; destroyed), which consisted of projecting structures at the corners of a square nucleus, which was faced with arcades on piers — unless these are additions made by Serlio when he illustrated the villa in Book VI of his *Regole generali di architettura* . . . (ms., Munich, Staatsbib.); there was also a courtyard with superposed arcades. In this work Giuliano arrived at a new conception, greatly influenced by antiquity. Although the villa at Poggioreale is no longer extant, there is a villa near San Potito that seems to resemble it closely. In Naples the far from unitary Palazzo Cuomo can be attributed to his influence if not actually to his design (Pane, 1937). Moreover, he is to be credited with the Piccolomini Chapel of the Church of Monte Oliveto in the monastic complex of S. Anna dei Lombardi in Naples, which repeats in its rich combination of sculptural and pictorial elements the above-mentioned Florentine examples. Thus Giuliano, who was again in Naples in 1490, had begun his work under the influence of Brunelleschi and finally assumed classicizing inflections; though not one of the major artistic personalities of the period, he is important historically as a propagator of the Renaissance.

Benedetto da Maiano (1442–97) worked with his brother Giuliano in Faenza, Loreto, Florence (Sala dei Gigli, 1476–81, in the Palazzo Vecchio), San Gimignano (Chapel of S. Fina, in the Collegiata; Chapel of S. Bartolo, in the Church of S. Agostino), and Rome (Carafa Chapel, in S. Maria sopra Minerva). He is the presumed author of the airy loggia on the façade of the small Gothic church of S. Maria delle Grazie in Arezzo (VIII, PL. 191); the church, with its contrasting effects, was intended to rise above a higher flight of steps than the present one so as to dominate in a very regular arcaded square — the first of the Renaissance — which was, however, only partially carried out and later closed (apparently in accordance with a design by Giuliano). Benedetto followed the taste of his patron Filippo Strozzi in the execution of the geometric mass of the Palazzo Strozzi in Florence (begun ca. 1490;

PL. 5; FIG. 21), with its massive, perfectly cut rustication seemingly pivoting on the ornate two-light windows, which are of imperfect proportions between the floors in order to create more spacious embrasures in the interior, especially in the rooms of the piano nobile. On the exterior, very vigorous effects of chiaroscuro were created in the high cornice by Simone del Pollaiuolo, known as Il Cronaca (1457–1508), sole author of the elegant courtyard (PL. 6), which on the level of the piano nobile is partially open, closed in part with cross-mullioned windows, and completed by a loggia; the tendency here was clearly to simplify and to impart to the structural members a vigor and a monumentality reminiscent of Rome, in opposition to the works of the colorless imitators of Brunelleschi. Il Cronaca was to follow the same line in the Palazzo Horne and in the Palazzo Guadagni (PL. 54), with one-light, round-arched windows, very regular dressed ashlar, and a loggia on the topmost story (a feature that was to be imitated repeatedly in Florence). In substance, Cronaca represented one phase of the sober, elegant purity peculiar to Florence; he also expressed this purity in

religious architecture, as in the Church of S. Salvatore al Monte (end of 15th cent.–1504; VIII, PL. 191, FIG. 392c). Built on a single-nave plan and roofed with plain beams (as was the earlier S. Maria Maddalena dei Pazzi), S. Salvatore al Monte repeated Brunelleschi's geometric divisions with noteworthy simplicity. Il Cronaca's style was to have repercussions well beyond the Florentine sphere.

Giuliano da Sangallo (1443–1516) reduced some of Brunelleschi's motifs to their sculptural essentials in S. Maria Maddalena dei Pazzi (begun in 1479) and in the quadriporticus that precedes it. In the slender structural members of S. Maria delle Carceri in Prato (1484–93; PL. 388; fig. in SANGALLO, q.v.; XIII, PL. 225) the plan may recall Alberti, as do the external marble facings, a reversion to Florentine-Romanesque picturesqueness also used by Sangallo in the Gondi Chapel of S. Maria Novella in Florence. The artist was also called to work outside his city. In Savona he built the Palazzo della Rovere for Pope Sixtus IV, with a façade veined by tall superposed pilaster strips, in which he interpreted Alberti's style with originality.

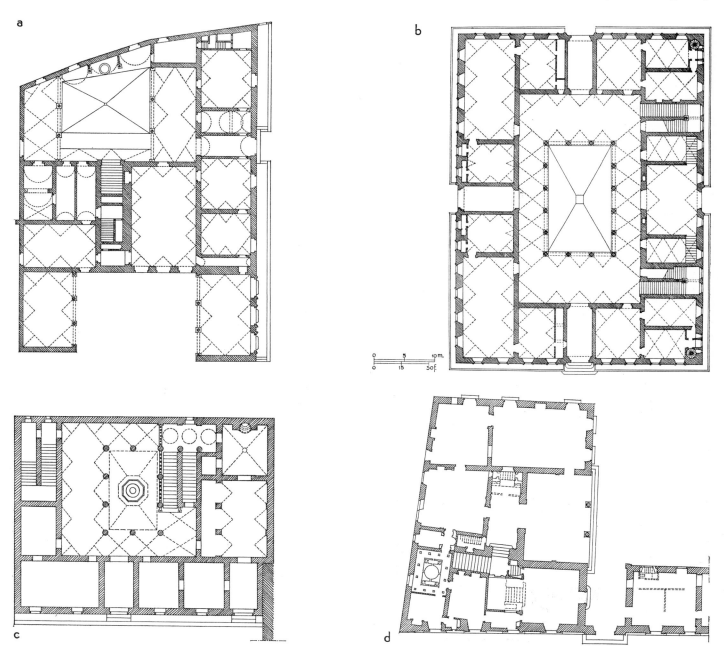

Tuscan civil architecture. (a) Careggi, Villa Medici (architect, Michelozzo), plan (from E. Lundberg, Arkitekturens Formspråk, Italia 1420–1620, Stockholm, 1954); (b) Florence, Palazzo Strozzi (architects, Benedetto da Maiano and Il Cronaca), plan (from A. Haupt, Architettura dei palazzi dell'Italia Settentrionale e della Toscana del sec. XIII al XVII, Milan, 1930); (c) Florence, Palazzo Gondi (architect, Giuliano da Sangallo), plan (from E. Lundberg, op. cit.); (d) Florence, Palazzo Pandolfini (architect, Raphael), plan (from G. Chierici, 1952–57).

In Loreto he provided the Sanctuary of the Holy House (1500) with a dome reminiscent of that of the Florence Cathedral but more restrained in the curve. He traveled to Rome, Naples, and even to Avignon and Lyons, acquiring a vast experience that had its beginnings in his first visit to Rome in 1465 and his confrontation of new problems related to antiquity; this experience was perfectly attuned to the Humanistic atmosphere of the court of Lorenzo de' Medici. (Although the Medicis were officially only private citizens, the term "court" is used here because the courtly atmosphere of their circle exalted the classicism which from the 16th century onward was to be identified with the true Renaissance, especially by historiographers outside Italy.) Probably a Roman nymphaeum or tomb — perhaps even an early Christian baptistery — was the prototype of the Sacristy of Sto Spirito (PL. 6; fig. in SANGALLO, q.v.), octagonal in shape, with semicircular and square niches, with interior structural members in two orders, and preceded by a vestibule (tentatively ascribed to Il Cronaca) with sculptured colonnades and an ornate barrel vault of classical inspiration that alters and enriches a scheme typical of Brunelleschi.

In the Palazzo Gondi in Florence (1490–94; PL. 388; FIG. 21; XIII, PL. 246), which was to have had two-light windows on two stories topped by a loggia as in the Palazzo Guadagni, Giuliano da Sangallo appears surprisingly timid. The rustication on the ground floor is not as powerful as that of the Palazzo Strozzi. Nonetheless, the artist achieved a subtle classical and courtly refinement, similar to that which he had previously attained in the Villa di Poggio a Caiano (ca. 1480–85; PL. 387; fig. in SANGALLO, q.v.), built for Lorenzo de' Medici. In this villa he used a continuous roof that eliminated the need for the corner towers and the battlements of medieval taste, introducing a new scheme for the use of rectangular windows and for the construction of country houses. Moreover, both the low arcade that serves as a basement and the pronaos (I, PL. 305), which is surmounted by a pediment and is similar to those of ancient temples, reveal a classical inspiration that is also apparent in the main hall with its barrel vault and stucco decorations. His contact with Rome (where Giuliano had created, among other things, the arcade of the Abbey of Grottaferrata) led him later to insert in the entablature of the pronaos a figural frieze in glazed terra cotta by Sansovino, contributing a picturesque touch that the artist was to use repeatedly in his later designs (1515) for the façade of S. Lorenzo in Florence. The purpose of these reliefs is clearly ornamental (courtyard of the Palazzo della Gherardesca, Florence), and their source is to be found in Roman triumphal arches. This trend was continued by Raphael.

The indefatigable Sangallo also submitted to Ferdinand II of Aragon, in 1488, the model for a royal palace, a plan known through the artist's sketchbook (Vat. Lib.). He designed a palace that for its vastness, imposing aspect, and magnificence would have been an exceptional example, at the end of the early Renaissance, of a residence worthy of a great ruler; it was conceived by the Florentine master on the basis of a pen-etrating, constant awareness of Roman imperial architecture. This same plan was elaborated by Sangallo for a palace that was to have been built in Florence for the Medici family after their return from exile. Like Politian, the artist expressed himself in the Italian idiom when continuing the tradition of Brunelleschi and in classical terms when investigating and re-creating antiquity, especially during his later period. Another interesting aspect of this great artist is his activity as a military architect. In the fortresses he built or reworked (Poggibonsi, Pisa, Sansepolcro, etc.) he never lost sight of the essential elements: the values of the mass and the technical innovations that made him a master of fortification architecture.

In Tuscany the greatest elaborator of Florentine tendencies was Ventura Vitoni (1442–1522) of Pistoia, who, after raising the dynamic elevation of the Church of S. Maria delle Grazie there, created his major work, the Church of the Madonna dell'Umiltà (also in Pistoia), in the shape of an octagon preceded by a vestibule, derived from the Sacristy of Sto Spirito in Florence but with a greater breadth in its amplified masses. Later, the church was covered by Vasari with a Michelangelesque dome.

Matteo Civitali (1436–1501) of Lucca imparted to the Shrine of the Holy Face (Tempietto del Volto Santo; 1474) in Lucca Cathedral the structural values of the Renaissance, combining them with graceful decoration and thus following the example of Bernardo Rossellino. However, next to the Palazzo Piccolomini in Siena, which was designed by Rossellino, the Sienese sculptor Antonio Federighi built a loggia (1462) that betrayed a lack of understanding of the new style and reverted instead to the Romanesque.

Another Sienese, Francesco di Giorgio, a painter and sculptor, showed equivalent genius as an architect. He earned an undisputed place in art history as a traveling artist who worked in Tuscany, in the Marches, and in Naples. In Milan his opinion was sought in the construction of the Cathedral, and there he came into contact with Leonardo da Vinci. In Pienza, through the work of Bernardo Rossellino, he became aware of Alberti's style and ideals; Alberti's influence, combined with the results of his study of ancient monuments, can be found in the Church of S. Bernardino in Urbino, a small edifice with one nave and three trefoil apses (the central apse was almost immediately replaced by a rectangular tribune) and a dome on a cylindrical drum, imitated by Giacomo Cozzarelli in the Church of the Osservanza, near Siena, which is in the Venetian tradition (cf. S. Michele all'Isola, Venice; VIII, PL. 198). In S. Bernardino, formerly attributed to Bramante, the geometric austerity of the masses reflects his designs both for the austere fortresses (Cagli, Sassocorvaro, etc.) he built in the Marches and for the Palazzo della Signoria in Iesi (1486). Still earlier, also in Urbino, where he lived in 1478, he had created the monumental arcades of the Pasquino Courtyard in the Palazzo Ducale (see above). However, his masterpiece is undoubtedly the Church of the Madonna del Calcinaio in Cortona (1485; PL. 8; FIG. 23), built on a Latin-cross plan, articulated on the

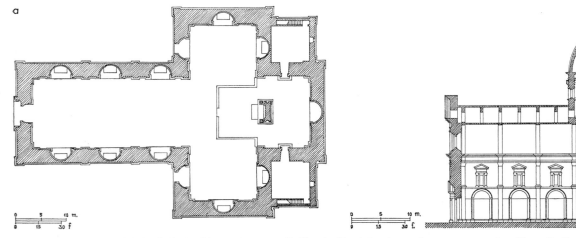

a   b

Cortona, the Madonna del Calcinaio (architect, Francesco di Giorgio Martini), plan and transverse section (*from R. Papini, Francesco di Giorgio Architetto, Florence, 1953*).

exterior by two superposed orders and relieved on the interior by semicircular chapels cut into the massive perimeter. This barrel-vaulted church of monumental proportions seems to have been inspired by the Church of S. Andrea in Mantua; it is outstanding for the elegance of its structural members, an elegance heightened by the fine play of light from the noble windows; the octagonal cloistered vault which rests on a high drum may be seen as the conciliation, in a Tuscan synthesis, of Gothic and Renaissance styles. The plan of this church was anticipated in the Badia of Fiesole (design ascribed to Cosimo I de' Medici); it is more or less contemporary with the Church of S. Maria del Sasso near Bibbiena, which is in the style of Sangallo. Nevertheless, the Church of the Madonna del Calcinaio became a model for other sanctuaries: the SS. Annunziata in Arezzo (by Bartolomeo della Gatta; completed by Antonio da Sangallo the Elder) and the Church of the Madonna dei Miracoli in Castel Rigone (1494).

The Gothic architectural tradition still bound most of the regions of Italy; reactions to the spread of the Renaissance, which had heretofore been centered almost exclusively in Tuscany, varied throughout the peninsula. Lombardy first responded to the new spirit through the work of the Solari family, as is evident in the Castello Sforzesco in Milan, which incorporated Filarete's tower; the massive towers at the sides of the castle were faced with diamond-cut rusticated blocks — the earliest instance of the use of this type of facing, which was to become widespread in Renaissance architecture. The Cortile della Rocchetta and the Ducal Court in the castle combine terra cotta and whitewash, thus linking the late Gothic that persisted in the churches (S. Maria delle Grazie, S. Pietro in Gessata, etc.) to the Renaissance. When the movement became independent, it expressed itself in the decorative forms proposed in Filarete's *Treatise on Architecture* (ca. 1461–64). However, at the same time, Milan's Cathedral, the work of Italian and foreign artists, was rising in Flamboyant Gothic style (VI, PL. 337), and the taste for decoration in delicate chiaroscuro and for fine detail was still firmly rooted. This taste was the heritage of the Lombards of the Renaissance, whose style was exuberant, aulic, and ostentatious — one in which the strictness of synthesis often disappeared in the predominance of detail. This trend first appeared, though tempered by a degree of compromise, in the art of the Gaggini family (see below) and later in the more refined brilliance of Giovanni Antonio Amadeo (1447–1522), displayed in the Cappella Colleoni in Bergamo (1470–75; PL. 9; FIG. 25) and in the lower section of the façade

shrine in the façade of S. Maria dei Miracoli in Brescia. When marble was not available for these painterly effects of chiaroscuro, Lombard artists used terra cotta, as in the overly ornate cloisters of the Certosa of Pavia. In secular architecture this trend is represented by the richly decorated, fragmented portals and by the columns and candelabra on the façades of buildings that were more or less ornate. The decoration was extended to courtyards (Palazzo Bottigella, presently the Convitto Gandini, in Pavia), where occasionally painting was also added. This was a style that not even Bramante could ignore during his stay in Lombardy. However, the personal taste of the Humanist Eliseo Raimondi created an exception in his palace (presently Palazzo Bellomi) in Cremona, with the aristocratic elegance of its rusticated ashlar and of the two superposed orders in the façade, which is reminiscent of both Alberti and Giuliano da Sangallo.

In the Veneto region, the graceful and flowery Loggia del Consiglio in Verona, ascribed to Fra Giovanni Giocondo (1433–1515), who also worked in Rome and in France, drew inspiration for its ground-floor arcade from the medieval *palazzi della ragione* (civic buildings of northern Italy). It is enlivened by an elegant polychromy, peculiar to the Veneto, that distinguishes it from the more sober Loggia della Gran Guardia (del Consiglio) in Padua. These aspects are distinct from those which remained typical of the architecture of Venice itself. Venice, faithful for centuries to a style that, for its predominance of voids over solids, had an exceptional lightness and a uniquely picturesque quality, clung tenaciously to the Flamboyant Gothic style, as demonstrated by the Foscari Arch (1457; XIII, PL. 238), by the courtyard of the Doges' Palace, and also — notwithstanding its sculptural character — by the loggia with ogival arches on the east side of the piano nobile of the Doges' Palace by the Veronese Antonio Rizzo (active 1463–98).

Pietro Lombardo of Carona (d. 1515) after completing his training in Florence, mainly as a sculptor, was active in the Veneto region. He worked in Padua as an architect, introducing into the old Gothic structures features that were derived from Donatello or, more generally, from the Renaissance. In Venice he created the style known as "Lombardesque," which made use of delicate chiaroscuro in ornamental sculpture and colored marble, but with a restraint and an equilibrium that are far more effective than the Lombard exuberance. Examples of his work in Venice are the Palazzo Dario and the façade of the Scuola Grande di S. Marco, in which a display of simulated perspectives is carried to extremes of virtuosity (VIII, PL. 198). Another of his works, S. Maria dei Miracoli (PL. 11; FIG. 26), is an intimate church in which, except for the crown that conceals the timbered barrel vault over the Alberti-inspired interior, the decorative division recalls that of the first two orders of the Florence Baptistery, which had also been Brunelleschi's earliest source of inspiration.

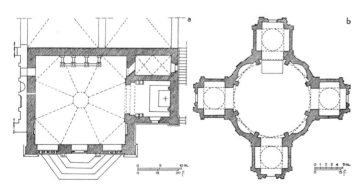

Religious architecture in Lombardy. (*a*) Bergamo, Cappella Colleoni (architect, G. A. Amadeo), plan (*from F. Malaguzzi Valeri, Gio. Antonio Amadeo, scultore e architetto lombardo, Bergamo, 1904*); (*b*) Crema, S. Maria della Croce (architects G. Battagio and G. A. Montanaro), plan (*from C. Baroni, 1941*).

of the Gothic Certosa of Pavia (begun 1481; PL. 10; VIII PL. 195), which has a splendid variety of inlaid marbles and sculptures that were created in part by the Mantegazza brothers, contemporaries of Amadeo.

The continued Lombard taste for ornamentation appeared in the marble decoration of Como Cathedral, by the Rodari family, particularly in the portals (VIII, PL. 187) and in the

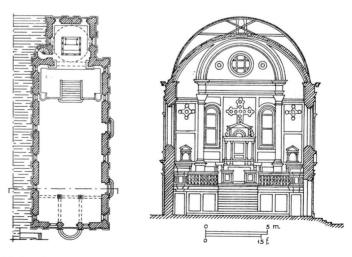

Venice, S. Maria dei Miracoli (architect, P. Lombardo), plan and transverse section (*from B. Fletcher, A History of Architecture, New York-London, 1961*).

The Procuratie Vecchie di S. Marco (ca. 1514) were executed by Guglielmo de' Grigi (or Bergamasco) and completed by Jacopo Sansovino with Bartolomeo Bon as the supervisor of works. The sequence of graceful arcades of the two superposed loggias seems to combine the rhythms of Filarete's cloisters in the Ospedale Maggiore in Milan — perhaps transmitted through the school of Pietro Lombardo — with the picturesque Venetian Romanesque architecture. A different dimension can be found in the work of Mauro Coducci of Bergamo, who was to complete the façade of the Scuola Grande di S. Marco in a more vigorous tone. In his work the picturesqueness and the color of Venice were allied to a strong sculptural quality derived from Alberti, which had been expressed by Coducci in the Palazzo Corner Spinelli (PL. 11), where, instead of loggias, there are solid walls of rusticated ashlar, piers, and two-light windows. This combination is particularly striking in the imposing Palazzo Vendramin Calergi (PL. 11), perfectly balanced in its arrangement on three floors, with each distinguished by the use of the architectural orders in the paired columns and pilasters, perhaps reflecting the influence of the Arsenal gate. Alberti's influence is equally apparent in the upper section of the façade of S. Zaccaria, the three-aisled church built (1444–65) by Antonio Gambello with some Gothic elements, as is evident in the ambulatory with radiating chapels. Its façade, rather trite and lacking in unity, is decorated with a high stylobate by Gambello and acquires monumental breadth from Coducci's curvilinear pediment between volutes, repeating the original design of the unfinished Tempio Malatestiano in Rimini as shown in a medal attributed to Matteo de' Pasti (I, PL. 52). This arrangement, which was repeated in various churches in and around Venice, was used also on the Dalmatian coast, in Emilia, and in Romagna. Coducci's style came even closer to Alberti's in the façade of S. Michele all'Isola in Venice, with its pristine facing, its lower order in ashlar, and its rather pronounced structural members (VIII, PL. 198). Though still elegant, Coducci's style seems less vigorous in the Church of S. Giovanni Crisostomo, built on an inscribed Greek-cross plan with three end chapels; this ichnography had come to the Western world from the Orient during the early Middle Ages and was at that time quite widespread in Venice. Various other 16th-century Venetian buildings show continued adherence to the early Renaissance taste.

In the late 15th century the predominant taste in Bologna was eclectic, receptive to various trends that often merged with the city's characteristic arcaded structures. These were almost always enlivened by the red tones of brick, sometimes discreetly complemented by sandstone, which predominates in a few rare exceptions that show the Florentine influence. Some of the major buildings reveal the influence of Lombard decorative elements, flowering on the façades of the Church of Corpus Domini (or La Santa), the former oratory of the Spirito Santo, and the Church of the Madonna di Galliera. These decorative motifs appear also in the Palazzo del Podestà, attributed to Aristotele Fioravanti, with its divisions based on ornate pilaster strips that echo Alberti's style, and in the Palazzo Ghisilardi (originally Casa Conoscenti; presently Palazzo Fava), designed by Giulio Montanari. A Florentine compactness is noticeable instead in the Palazzo Bevilacqua (1481–84; PL. 12) by Antonio (Marsilio) Infrangipani and Tommaso Filippi. The façade is without arcades and is faced in faceted, rusticated ashlar, which tends however to overwhelm the delicate lunette portal and the windows. The courtyard has a somewhat heavy elegance in the lower loggia and in the upper loggia with its double arcade corresponding to a comparatively frequent medieval survival. Some of the linear elements of this construction may derive from the interior decoration, mainly by Agostino di Duccio, of the Tempio Malatestiano in Rimini. This taste recurs again in the piers that divide S. Giovanni Evangelista in Parma (1510 on; VIII, PL. 200), by Bernardino Zaccagni the Elder, into three aisles, side chapels, and a vaulted and domed transept. In Emilia the style typical of the Po Valley, which remained constant, can be found in the Church of S. Pietro in Modena, divided into a nave and four side aisles, vaulted, and decorated with the terra cottas that are so widely used in that region.

In Ferrara, renovated under Ercole I d'Este according to the earliest known modern town-planning program, Biagio Rossetti (documented 1465–1516) was active. He was the author of, among other works, grandiose and airy churches such as S. Francesco (begun 1494), with colonnades marking a tripartite division, with vaults, side chapels, a transept, and an enlarged façade with volutes in the style of Alberti that are also found in the equally impressive church of S. Maria in Vado, to which the painter Ercole de' Roberti contributed. Rossetti also built the spacious church of S. Cristoforo, with a nave flanked with chapels and a broad transept, and added the imposing apsed tribune (1498) to the Romanesque Cathedral, accentuating it with arches on a monumental scale inspired by those of 5th- and 6th-century churches in Ravenna. Rossetti, who also had contacts with Bologna, was particularly active in the renovation of secular architecture, which he carried out with a rare sobriety, emphasizing the mass, in which red brick was combined with noble white arcades, with windows and portals of Istrian stone. He also worked on the palace (Palazzo Costabili) of Lodovico il Moro in Ferrara, with its courtyard in which the close-set arcades of the top-floor loggia contrast with the more widely spaced arcades of the solemn lower portico, and on the Palazzo Bevilacqua in Bologna (see above). Although Rossetti's assured style places him among the major architects of the Po Valley, his compromises with the Florentine Renaissance — and with Brunelleschi's style in particular — are clearly evident in Imola, Faenza, and Forlì. In the Biblioteca Malatestiana in Cesena (FIG. 28) a certain linearity is directly connected with Rimini, but the partition into aisles was derived from Michelozzo (Library of the Convent of S. Marco, Florence) and was to be used in other monastery libraries (S. Maria delle Grazie, Milan; S. Giovanni Evangelista, Parma; S. Domenico, Bologna; Monte Oliveto; and others in Ferrara and Perugia).

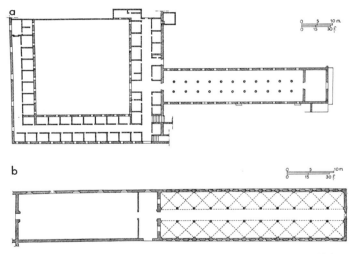

Renaissance libraries. (a) Florence, Museo di S. Marco, plan of Cloister of S. Antonino and library (*from O. Morisani, Michelozzo architetto, Turin, 1951*); (b) Cesena, Biblioteca Malatestiana, plan (*from L'Architettura, 40, 1959*).

As early as the Romanesque and Gothic periods the wandering Lombard masters had come down from the Alpine valleys, and during the Renaissance they continued their migrations into the peninsula, even to Sicily. They propagated the new movement, adding their own decidedly decorative and picturesque accents, which injected a touch of late Gothic into the new style. These wandering masters may be traced to the Po Valley, rather than to Lombardy alone (although in ancient times the term Lombardy indicated the entire Po Valley); in fact, the artists who spread their common style throughout peninsular Italy, although endowing it with stylistic nuances as yet undefined, were not only from Lombardy but also from the Veneto and Emilia and thus from the entire Po Valley.

With few exceptions — Turin Cathedral in particular — Piedmont remained securely attached to the Gothic style during the 15th century. Liguria, which had welcomed Lombard artists ever since the Romanesque period, had from about 1456 a kind of renaissance of its own, one which could be called pre-Amadean; weak and insignificant on the whole, it is expressed in the triumphal arch by Domenico Gaggini of Bissone in the Chapel of S. Giovanni (PL. 23) in Genoa Cathedral. In this work the architectural members are overwhelmed by the sculptural decoration and end in mixtilinear cusps; this betrays an uncertainty of expression also evident in other works by Gaggini's group (courtyard of the Villa Cambiaso in San Francesco d'Albaro), as well as in the Genoese portals ornamented by a high band of sculptural decoration, in which can be traced a subsequent change in style connected with contemporaries of Amadeo and of the Rodari family.

In 1463 Domenico Gaggini settled in Sicily, where he developed a type of architecture in full harmony with sculpture; this was a somewhat excessive trend that was to be continued by his son Antonello and his assistants. The delicate portal of the Church of the Annunziata in Palermo (with nave and side aisles and ogival arches; built after Domenico's death in 1491 by Gabriele di Battista) reveals the same spirit. Various chapels that were added to medieval Sicilian churches exemplify the characteristic aspects of this style, which was simultaneously architectural and sculptural. Nevertheless, the Gothic tradition remained firmly rooted in Sicily, especially in secular building. The Sicilian architect Matteo Carnevale created his masterwork in S. Maria della Catena in Palermo, with nave and two aisles and a portico, which continued the compromise between the local Gothic and the newly arrived Renaissance trends. This compromise was repeated to a greater or lesser extent in the various Italian regions in which local masters or craftsmen were active during the Renaissance. The only exception is Sardinia where, because of the Spanish domination, there was a flowering of late Catalan Gothic during the 15th and subsequent centuries that produced such remarkable structures as the Cloister of S. Domenico in Cagliari, the Campanile of Alghero Cathedral, and the Cathedral and the Church of S. Francesco in Iglesias.

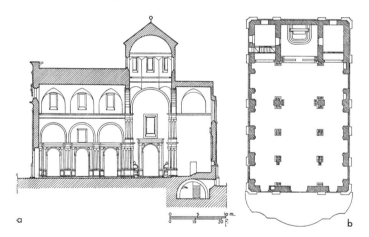

Palermo, S. Giorgio dei Genovesi. (a) Transverse section; (b) plan (from G. Spatrisano, 1961).

In southern Italy, Naples, which along with other localities in the Campania region had welcomed the Aragonese Gothic, became a center receptive to prevalently Lombard tendencies (profuse sculptural decoration appeared even in the triumphal arch of Alfonso of Aragon). In addition to Pietro da Milano, Domenico Gaggini also visited Naples in 1458, before he settled in Sicily. Moreover, early Renaissance trends continued in Naples, where they were slightly elaborated even into the 16th century (Church of S. Maria delle Grazie in Caponapoli); they are especially evident in the work of Tommaso Malvito of Como (Carafa Chapel of the Cathedral). However, notable instances of Alberti's persistent influence are found in the portal of the Church of S. Barbara in the Castel Nuovo and in the

Cappella Pontano (1492), inspired by Alberti's Shrine of the Holy Sepulcher (Florence, Pal. Rucellai; I, PL. 50). Moreover, Francesco di Giorgio's documented visits to Naples (1492–95, 1497) explain why many features of the Church of S. Caterina at Formello reflect Madonna del Calcinaio in Cortona as well as the presence of Florentine stylistic elements in the Church of S. Maria la Nova. As early as the 16th century Giovanni Donadio, an architect from Calabria known as Il Mormanno, was working in Naples on the construction of a number of princely buildings (mainly secular) that reflected both Tuscan traditions and derivations from Alberti; among these are the Palazzo Marigliano and, perhaps, the Palazzo Gravina (FIG. 30), which was executed by Francesco di Palma,

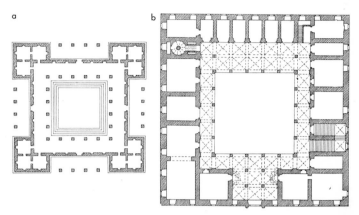

Domestic architecture in Naples. (a) Plan of destroyed villa at Poggioreale (architect, Giuliano da Maiano) according to Serlio; (b) Palazzo Gravina, plan without added rear wing (from R. Pane, 1937).

also called Il Mormanno, who in all likelihood succeeded Donadio in building the upper church of SS. Severino and Sosio. Donadio's hand is also apparent in a few monuments of the Calabria region (e.g., the Church of S. Michele in Vibo Valentia).

The Lombards were preceded by the Tuscans in the Marches. Among the monuments produced by the Tuscans, the courtyard of the late-15th-century Palazzo dell'Università (formerly Palazzo Ducale) in Camerino is faithful to Alberti's tenets; among the artists, Baccio Pontelli of Florence is credited with the Church of S. Maria delle Grazie in Senigallia. However, the Lombards, with their predilection for ornamental architectural styles, eventually prevailed. Always emphasizing the decorative element, they also dominated in regions firmly attached to their own local medieval traditions — for instance, in the Abruzzi (Palazzo dell'Annunziata in Sulmona) and in Apulia (Cathedral of Acquaviva delle Fonti).

It was inevitable that Florentine influences should reach neighboring Umbria; they were transmitted in forms similar to those used by the Maiano brothers in the former monastery and in some chapels of the Church of S. Pietro in Perugia, after Agostino di Duccio had built in that city the monuments mentioned above. Moreover, documents prove that Lombard artists (e.g., Gasparino di Antonio and Leone di Matteo) visited Perugia, where they created ornate two-light windows and a flowery balcony in the Palazzo del Capitano del Popolo.

In the portico in the façade of Spoleto Cathedral, created by Ambrogio da Milano (who also worked in Urbino) and by Pippo d'Antonio of Florence, the Lombard taste prevails. Rocco da Vicenza, another Po Valley artist who was also active in the Marches, worked in San Severino Marche on the so-called "S. Maria del Glorioso" (1519 onward), with a nave and two side aisles and columns on high pedestals. In Umbria he designed a ciborium for the Church of S. Maria Maggiore in Spello and built the Sanctuary of the Madonna of Mongiovino, in which his style is highly decorative, on an inscribed Greek-cross plan. Throughout the region, which was highly receptive to new influences and eclectic in their application, many examples of Lombard-inspired trends are to be found, some of them transmitted through Rome.

Classicizing tendencies, inspired by Alberti, were continued in Rome by Tuscan artists into the late 15th century. For example, both the Church of S. Maria del Popolo (VIII, PL. 205), which has been attributed by some to Meo del Caprino from Settignano, and the Church of S. Agostino (PL. 13) repeat in their façades, which have double orders of trabeated pilasters, the volutes on the façade of S. Maria Novella in Florence. But their interior plans consist of a nave and two side aisles divided by piers with a transept and a dome; this might suggest the introduction of influences from the Po Valley (the Church of S. Maria Maggiore in Città di Castello presents a similar though simplified structure) if it were not for the fact that

the windows (widely imitated in Rome and in Latium, Umbria, and the Marches) comparable to those of the Roman Porta dei Borsari in Verona. Subtle decorative refinements culminating in a rich balcony suggest that this is the work of the Lombard Andrea Bregno. The imposing courtyard (PL. 14), completed in the 16th century, with a portico and a superposed loggia and corner piers that reflect Laurana's influence, lacks the studied refinement of the exterior; its general tone is simplified and already tends toward the style of the High Renaissance. Most often cited as possible author of the courtyard is Bramante, the great master whose work marked the beginning of the second phase of Renaissance architecture.

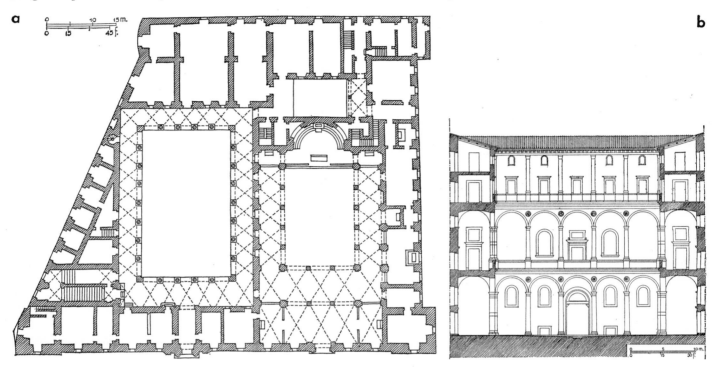

Rome, Palazzo della Cancelleria and S. Lorenzo in Damaso. (*a*) plan; (*b*) transverse section of palace courtyard (*after B. Fletcher, A History of Architecture, New York-London, 1961*).

Pienza Cathedral, by Rossellino, was also divided by piers and vaulted and that St. Peter's in Rome had been designed by Rossellino with a nave and four aisles divided by clustered piers that necessitated a vaulted roof, marking a clear break from Brunelleschi's Florentine churches. Besides, the two Roman churches differ considerably in appearance; the proportions of S. Maria del Popolo are somewhat heavy and broad; S. Agostino has, on the contrary, a marked vertical thrust. Very similar to the latter is the Cathedral of Turin (PL. 13), designed by Meo del Caprino. (The master from Settignano came to be in Turin because the archbishop of that city was Cardinal Domenico della Rovere, a nephew of Sixtus IV.) The Ospedale di Sto Spirito in Rome, commissioned by the same pope, is attributed to the Florentine Baccio Pontelli, who also worked in the Marches. Although this noble brick structure is on the whole typical of Pontelli, the artist reached a compromise in the two-light marble windows of Lombard style. Echoes of the style of Francesco di Giorgio are to be found in some Roman buildings (S. Aurea in Ostia, S. Pietro in Montorio); sometimes, as in the loggias on the façades of S. Pietro in Vincoli and SS. Apostoli, octagonal pillars of an obsolete Gothic taste were added.

By contrast, the Palazzo della Cancelleria in Rome, commissioned (ca. 1489–95) by Cardinal Raffaello Riario (FIG. 31), acquired a novel and highly outstanding aspect. Except for the ground floor with its high horizontal bands, the mass of the building has superposed orders and clearly reveals its origin in Alberti's style. Slender pilasters on high pedestals modify the effect, suggesting a Venetian variation that is confirmed by

Sculpture. At the beginning of the 15th century the Florentine guild Arte dei Mercanti di Calimala held a competition (judged in 1402) for the second pair of bronze doors for the Baptistery. The rules required that each competitor should model a relief in bronze of a single panel representing the Sacrifice of Isaac. The Tuscan goldsmiths and sculptors who participated were Filippo Brunelleschi, Lorenzo Ghiberti, Jacopo della Quercia, Francesco da Valdambrino, Niccolò di Piero Lamberti, Niccolò d'Arezzo, and Simone da Colle di Val d'Elsa. However, the beginnings of a Renaissance sculptural style cannot correctly be traced to the artistic results of this event — which was, nevertheless, strong evidence of Florentine civilization — even though Brunelleschi is the first-mentioned participant. Except for the last two artists named, the style of the competitors is well known and falls within the sphere of late Gothic; this is true of Lamberti, who was the most closely bound to the 14th century, and of Brunelleschi himself. The panels submitted by the two most outstanding competitors, Brunelleschi and Ghiberti, are extant and permit the formulation of a comparative judgment. Brunelleschi represented the Sacrifice of Isaac in a vigorous relief of uniform depth, in the tradition of the Florentine goldsmiths, showing himself to be extremely knowledgeable and skilled in the figural interpretation both of antiquity, as in the figure of the boy removing a thorn from his foot, and of the 14th century, as in the angel and the horse (II, PL. 363). In his low-relief treatment of landscape Ghiberti achieved a more pronounced chiaroscuro and a greater sense of space; in his figures he attained a sober balance and a fluidity that tends toward ornamental grace, corresponding to a more modern taste within the late Gothic style. He did not, however, ignore the inspiration of antiquity, as seen in the carefully modeled torso of Isaac (VI, PL. 169). Ghiberti won the competition and was commissioned to execute the work. The judgment seems to have been inspired, especially when it is remembered that in 1399 Brunelleschi had modeled two small statues for the altar of S. Jacopo in Pistoia Cathedral in which he demonstrated his continued adherence to the Gothic style, expressing himself in an idealized manner far removed from that feeling of rigorous, systematic concreteness which he was to display in his work as an architect.

In the first years of the century Nanni di Banco (1380–1421), a sculptor of noteworthy talent, evolved a powerful, simplified definition of form in an attempt to break away from typically Gothic expressions. He took up Arnolfo di Cambio's work with volume and also studied antiquity, as is clearly evident in his statues *The Four Crowned Saints* (III, PL. 391) in a large semicircular niche in Orsanmichele, Florence. However, in his last work, the cusp of the Porta della Mandorla (1414–21; VIII, PL. 184) in Florence Cathedral, the artist reverted to a late vision. Only Donatello, the first major sculptor of the Renaissance, with his amazing freedom of conception, displayed from the beginning an incisive physical and moral command of the subjects of his statues (PL. 15). Without considering his earlier works, it is possible to trace the development of Donatello's vision in a contrasting light and according to an ever-changing interpretation of antiquity (which Donatello saw mainly as Roman art) from his *St. George* (ca. 1416; IV, PL. 241) to the prophets from the Campanile of Florence Cathedral (IV, PL. 243), especially the prophet Habakkuk (1427–36). The artist was an innovator also in his reliefs; though not yet attempting a systematic solution, he posed the problem of central perspective in the scene that represents St. George rescuing the princess from the dragon (IV, PL. 242) on the tabernacle of Orsanmichele. The painterly effects introduced in this relief were perfected in subsequent stages that culminated in the lunettes in the Old Sacristy of S. Lorenzo (IV, PL. 246). Moreover, Donatello achieved a proportional relation of the figures to their surroundings, as in the *Feast of Herod* (IV, PL. 242) on the baptismal font in Siena and the scenes from the life of St. Anthony of Padua (1446–50; IV, PL. 251), in which there are intensely dramatic effects of light. Donatello's two-fold achievement in sculpture, both in the round and in relief, in relation to a culture stimulated by, and even derived from, Brunelleschi's rationalist spirit, has multiple aspects. Both the composure of the relief of the Annunciation in Sta Croce in Florence — as opposed to the exuberance of the putti in the singing gallery (1432–33; IV, PLS. 244, 247) — and the human quality of "the Gattamelata" in Padua (1444–47; IV, PL. 249) are relevant examples. The extreme intensity of the characterizations of Donatello's later works, which were of a profound and anguished spirituality, both in the round (*Judith and Holofernes*, IV, PL. 250; *Mary Magdalene*, III, PL. 211) and in relief (the pulpits in S. Lorenzo, IV, PL. 251), may be attributable to the influences of northern art, especially sculpture in wood, which must have penetrated into the Veneto region (as had works by German goldsmiths) and perhaps even as far as Florence; Florence's receptiveness to this art is demonstrated — some time later, it is true — by the statue of St. Rocco in the Church of the SS. Annunziata by the German Veit Stoss, a work that was noted by Vasari.

Donatello's unceasing creative activity extended over more than a half-century (he was eighty years old when he died on Dec. 13, 1466); he was animated by a vigorous naturalism and endowed with an exceptional wealth of human nuances. His signal artistic contribution was well received both in and outside Florence, primarily through his collaborators and pupils, each of whom according to his own temperament assimilated those aspects of the master that were most congenial to his own artistic personality. Outstanding among them was Michelozzo, with whom Donatello formed a collaboration (1423–33) that also included Pagno di Lapo Portigiani. In their work of that period Michelozzo's minor personality is easily distinguishable; his thoughtful temperament led him to restrain his expressive power even when attempting to approach the master's style, as

in the lunettes in S. Agostino in Montepulciano or in the figure of John the Baptist in SS. Annunziata in Florence. This is true also in the tomb of the antipope John XXIII (PL. 16), in the Brancacci monument (1426–28) in the Church of S. Angelo a Nilo in Naples, in which the edicule (derived, like the tomb, from a 14th-century Neapolitan scheme), enclosed within a mixtilinear arch that is still Gothic in its essence, undoubtedly was designed by Michelozzo; and in the dismantled monument to Bartolomeo Aragazzi — part of which is in the Cathedral at Montepulciano (III, PL. 391) and another portion of which is in the Victoria and Albert Museum in London. In this late work the sculptor best expressed his feeling for the classicism of the reliefs of the 1st century of our era (e.g., the touching scene in which Aragazzi takes leave of his family). In other works, especially in his representations of the Madonna and Child, it is possible to trace the variations in his style, oscillating between Donatello and antiquity. Classical influences emerge also in his decoration; in the Shrine of the Crucifix in S. Miniato al Monte (1447–48), gaily ornamented with inlays, he attempted to satisfy the courtly taste of the commissioner, Piero de' Medici, but the friezes of the Shrine of the Annunciation (1448–61) and the portal of the Medici bank in Milan (PL. 3), later enriched by a Lombard artist, were clearly inspired by ancient sources. The sculptor Michelozzo's artistic vision was merged with the serenity of that of Luca Della Robbia when, in 1446, together with Maso di Bartolomeo, they executed a bronze door for the New Sacristy of Florence Cathedral; in fact, Luca's art prevails in this work. Michelozzo's style remained, in substance, linked to a rather lofty classicism.

Instead, Isaia da Pisa, who followed him and who worked in Rome on the tomb of Pope Eugenius IV in the Church of S. Salvatore in Lauro (VIII, PL. 205), unimaginatively conformed to a scheme that was widely used in Rome as early as the Gothic period; he translated this scheme, which coldly imitated ancient forms, into the new idiom, creating a rectangular edicule that contains a sarcophagus bearing a statue of the Pope with the Madonna and angels in the background. Closer to Michelozzo's classicizing style than to Donatello's, Urbano da Cortona was active in Siena, where the monument of Cristoforo Felici in the Church of S. Francesco is attributed to him. Filarete, who returned to the Gothic in his work as a goldsmith, displayed a remarkable feeling for ancient forms in his work as a sculptor in the doors of St. Peter's in Rome (1445). The towering figures of Christ, the Madonna, and the two apostles reveal a rudimentary figural sense and a study of ancient sculpture that is apparent in the rather commonplace treatment of the drapery. Scenes representing the martyrdom of St. Peter and of St. Paul betray a badly assimilated classical erudition and a concern with details expressed in aspects of uncertain modeling, in a hackneyed chiaroscuro still very much in the Gothic taste. Even more heavy-handed are the disproportionate figures of the episodes representing the Council of Florence, which are treated as a frieze, and the raceme scrolls, copied from ancient decorations and encircling the two wings of the door, that are almost Romanesque in their starkness but with a late Gothic sensitivity in the modeling of the leaf motifs. To attract the curiosity of the less cultured observer to his compositions the artist interposed busts of Roman emperors, satyrs, bacchantes, and even episodes drawn from Ovid and Aesop. Filarete the classicist, far removed from Donatello's inspired art, merely documented a cultural phenomenon.

As Michelozzo had reached a compromise between classicizing tendencies and the free and spontaneous sculpture of Donatello, so other sculptors attempted to resolve the two ideals with substantially the same results that have previously been observed with Brunelleschi.

In Florence, Bertoldo di Giovanni (d. 1491), inspired by his master Donatello, displayed in his bronze *Crucifixion* (Florence, Mus. Naz.) an unrestrained linearity that is evident also in other of his works in flat relief, such as the *Pietà* in the same museum. Then, always mindful of Donatello, Bertoldo studied Roman reliefs, of which he gave a rather rhetorical and sketchy interpretation in the stucco decoration for the courtyard of the

Palazzo della Gherardesca, which he attempted to harmonize with the style of the architect, Giuliano da Sangallo. But he dramatically revived antiquity in rigorously compact forms — again taking his inspiration from 2d-century sarcophagi — in another bronze representing a battle scene (PL. 18), which in both the high relief and the freestanding portions displays the conflicting movement of masses. This constitutes Bertoldo's most original and most effective achievement; it could be termed an expression of anticlassicism and was undoubtedly valued as such by his pupil Michelangelo.

Agostino di Duccio was influenced by Donatello's dramatic intensity and, to a certain extent, by his sculptural values in the four reliefs illustrating scenes from the life of S. Gimignano that are now on a face of the Cathedral of Modena. However, he soon turned from Donatello's influence to a nervous linear style comparable to that of Bertoldo's earlier period. This is apparent at Rimini, where Agostino led the group of artists who decorated the interior of the Tempio Malatestiano. The chapel, containing the Arca degli Antenati e dei Discendenti and the reliefs illustrating the legend of St. Sigismund (PL. 18), formerly in the Chapel of the Reliquaries, are indications of the artistic stature of Agostino. In the other chapels and the interior, which is decorated with pilasters of a vibrant linear effect, the sculptor worked with great virtuosity, in *stiacciato* (III, PL. 302) relief and in the round, on the complex allegorical composition representing the planets, the signs of the zodiac, prophets and sibyls, and the arts and sciences.

His refined, linear decorative effects, enlivened by touches of blue and gold, have been interpreted as echoes of the Neo-Attic sculpture of the 1st century of the Christian era. However, Agostino may have intended to translate into the Renaissance idiom the flowing linearity that had been emphasized in late Gothic sculpture not only in northern Italy but also in Florence by Nanni di Banco and Ghiberti. A Madonna (Florence, Mus. Naz.) and the sculptures on the polychrome façade of the Oratory of S. Bernardino in Perugia — statues representing the three Franciscan virtues and St. Francis surrounded by a host of angels, statues of two saints and the Annunciation — and the high reliefs above the twin door tend toward a more substantial treatment within the same coherent idiom, using the same rhythms displayed in the surviving scenes from the façade of the Chapel of the Maestà delle Volte (Perugia, Gall. Naz. dell'Umbria) and in the sculptures in the Church of S. Domenico in the same city. In these works the influence of Donatello that was evident in the Modena reliefs is already greatly weakened.

Desiderio da Settignano had been fascinated by the painterly effects of Donatello's *stiacciato* reliefs and he imparted to the marble of his own works a gentle delicacy of outline and a gracefully flowing continuity of composition that were perfectly attuned to the various techniques utilized by Donatello. He worked in *stiacciato* relief (Panciatichi *Madonna*; Florence, Mus. Naz.), in high relief (putti heads in the exterior frieze of the Pazzi Chapel), and in the round (*Portrait of a Lady*; PL. 17). Desiderio's refinement and his sensuous decorative aspects, as in the tabernacle of S. Lorenzo (VIII, PL. 192), in which a Pietà in flat relief and two freestanding angels are enclosed in an impeccable architectural setting, derived from Bernardo Rossellino — that is, according to a classicizing scheme far removed from Donatello's brilliant freedom of invention. Moreover, in a decorative trend most probably derived from the Po Valley, slender candelabra and fantastic capitals exceed the strict Florentine architectural order. Earlier, in the tomb of Carlo Marsuppini in the Church of Sta Croce (PL. 16), Desiderio had repeated the scheme of Rossellino's monument to Leonardo Bruni in the same church. Of the two, it is in Desiderio's work that the artist dominates his materials with his usual delicacy, even in the separate details, and presents the whole composition in a diffused light that is very different from the dramatic contrasts of light on which Donatello insisted. In Florence at this time classicism had a number of staunch supporters. Only the Sienese Lorenzo di Pietro, known as Il Vecchietta (1412–80), remained faithful to Donatello's style, which he had been able to study in the baptismal font of the Baptistery in Siena. And he was clearly influenced by Donatello's sharply delineated mod-

eling when he conceived, for example, the funerary monument to Bishop Girolamo Foscari (1463–64), in S. Maria del Popolo in Rome, and to Mariano Sozzino Seniore (1467; Florence, Mus. Naz.). However, adhering to his native Sienese tradition, he tended, especially in religious themes, toward frail expressions alien to Donatello's vigorous compositions, insisting on a curving formal structure and on a spirituality that had nothing in common with Donatello's impetuosity, as in the bronze statue of the Risen Christ (1476; VIII, PL. 202) in S. Maria della Scala in Siena and in the relief of the Resurrection (New York, Frick Coll.).

Lorenzo Ghiberti's style, decidedly Gothic at the beginning of the 15th century, remained so in his second pair of doors for the Florence Baptistery and in the statues in Orsanmichele (VI, PL. 175); in these works the slender, aristocratic figures are imbued with spontaneity and freshness, instilling[1] new spirit into the idealized medieval classicism of Hellenic origin that had been inherited by the Byzantines and by the Sienese of the 14th century. This classicism, combined with linear rhythms, was the basis of Ghiberti's entrance into the new order. It is evident in the airy, ample rhythms of the episodes on the east doors of the Baptistery (1425–1452; VI, PLS. 172, 173), in which he displayed great talent (of which he was to boast in his *Commentarii*) in crowded reliefs of almost painterly effect. Though these reliefs lack a unitary vision, like those adorning some Roman triumphal arches, they are nevertheless endowed with a delicate and subtle chiaroscuro. This was, essentially, the tendency to which Brunelleschi also adhered as a sculptor; he expressed himself in a wholly Renaissance style in his crucifix in S. Maria Novella, Florence, a lofty idealization that was testified to by the comment that, according to Vasari, Donatello addressed to Brunelleschi: "You have represented the Christ. Mine is a common man."

From this renewed medieval classicism sprang the art of Luca Della Robbia, who emphasized in some of his works flowing harmonies that were inspired by Ghiberti (tomb of Bishop Federighi; IV, PL. 156), later departing from them in favor of a vigorously wholesome naturalism devoid of any realistic coarseness, as in the singing gallery of Florence Cathedral (1431–38; IV, PL. 157) and in his numerous glazed terra cottas. Luca's use of the enamel technique on terra cotta was the beginning of a flourishing activity that attained artistic status not only in his own work but also in that of his nephew Andrea and Andrea's son Giovanni, who augmented the variety of colors. Unfortunately, their followers later reduced it to a mere craftsmanship not always worthy of the art it once had been.

As a sculptor Bernardo Rossellino adhered even more closely to a structural classicism that was presumably derived from Alberti. An exception to this is one of his first works, the *Madonna della Misericordia* in the Palazzo della Fraternità dei Laici in Arezzo, which is placed within a Gothic mixtilinear arch. Outstanding among his many sculptures is the tomb of Leonardo Bruni (ca. 1444) in Sta Croce in Florence, which, as mentioned above, was taken as a model by Desiderio da Settignano and by other later sculptors. In this work the funerary architecture is disciplined within limits imposed by Renaissance structural elements, with ornamental refinements and figural representations that range from the serene statue of the deceased on the tomb (somewhat reminiscent of Ghiberti in its frontal section) to the large putti bearing the coat of arms that forms the finial. He also created a type of arcosolium tomb (later repeated and imitated) for the monument to Orlando de' Medici (1456) in SS. Annunziata in Florence. As for representational technique, the statues of the Madonna and St. Gabriel in the Church of S. Stefano in Empoli and the figures on the tomb of Beata Villana in S. Maria Novella in Florence and on the tomb of Beato Marcolino in Forlì (Pin. Com.) all display sturdy forms tempered with a measure of gracefulness.

Michele di Giovanni di Bartolo, known as Il Greco, creator of the Sala della Jole in the Palazzo Ducale in Urbino, resembled Rossellino in many ways; this similarity was later transmuted by the influence of Piero della Francesca in Il Greco's reliefs, with figures widely spaced on the marble mantelpieces and doorframes in Urbino. Another Tuscan, Domenico Rosselli (1439–ca. 1498), displayed a certain timidity and followed

Rossellino's style in work executed in the Marches, particularly in Urbino, where he created the fine decorations of the Sala degli Angeli. But he too felt the influence of the solemn rhythms of Piero.

Active in Forlì with Bernardo Rossellino was his brother Antonio, whose tomb of the Cardinal of Portugal (PL. 16), so original in its complete independence from the architecture of the chapel (with the exception of the polychromy common to both), seems almost a deliberate contrast with the plan of the tomb of Leonardo Bruni. In addition to a craftsmanlike skill in decoration this work displays a great poise in the Madonna and in the angels, which are endowed with an exquisite grace that was to find its full expression in the delicate images of Mino da Fiesole. Although this same idealized quality can be perceived in other Madonnas (Vienna, Kunsthist. Mus.; Berlin, Staat. Mus.) and in other angels (S. Clemente a Sociana, near Rignano sull'Arno), the figure of the cardinal foreshadows the marked tendency toward portraiture that was to be clearly defined in the bust of Giovanni Chellini (London, Vict. and Alb.) and in the ruthlessly objective bust of Matteo Palmieri (PL. 17).

Antonio later repeated the plan of the tomb of the Cardinal of Portugal in the monument of Mary of Aragon (ca. 1475) in the Piccolomini Chapel in the Church of Monte Oliveto (S. Anna dei Lombardi) in Naples. After Rossellino's death, the work was completed by Benedetto da Maiano (ca. 1485–88). However, the tripartite marble altarpiece is Antonio's; between statues of SS. James and John and the busts of two prophets, there is a relief with the Nativity (reminiscent of Filippo Lippi's Nativity scenes), in which a host of angels above the stable are executed with a bravura in the treatment of perspective that is inspired by Ghiberti and with a chiaroscuro that continues the earlier experiments of Florentine sculptors. This work remains the masterpiece of Antonio Rossellino, who concluded his activity with a rather heavy touch in the figures of the Madonna and Child (VIII, PL. 192) above the tomb of Francesco Nori (d. 1478) in Sta Croce, Florence. Previously, Antonio had collaborated with Mino da Fiesole in the circular pulpit of Prato Cathedral (1473), in which the highly original supporting pier was ornamented by Mino with four niches and as many saints in very low relief. The conception of the delicate structure was undoubtedly Mino's. Two of the five scenes in high relief around the pulpit (*The Beheading of John the Baptist, Herod's Feast*) are also by Mino; the other three (*The Assumption, The Stoning* and *The Funeral of St. Stephen*) are by Rossellino. Following Ghiberti's example the two sculptors strove to achieve a treatment of perspective previously realized in painting with a virtuosity that was echoed in Lombard artists of about the same period, perhaps as the result of direct contacts with Rossellino himself. In fact, Antonio Rossellino worked not only in Naples but also in Ferrara (tomb of Bishop Lorenzo Roverella, 1475, in the Church of S. Giorgio, executed in collaboration with Ambrogio da Milano) and in Venice (altarpiece in the Chapel of St. John in the Church of S. Giobbe); clearly, his was a fundamental role in the diffusion of Renaissance sculpture.

Mino da Fiesole is also important historically, although his sculpture, considered objectively, does not merit the praise lavished on it by modern critics in view of his many obvious uncertainties and inconsistencies. Following Rossellino's example, he modeled naturalistic busts such as those of Piero de' Medici (1453), and Rinaldo della Luna (1461; Florence, Mus. Naz.). He created the remarkably descriptive bust of Bishop Leonardo Salutati for the prelate's tomb in Fiesole Cathedral, placing it under the sarcophagus as if to give it autonomy. However, in this tomb the artist achieved a chiaroscuro similar to that of Desiderio da Settignano and more subtle than that of Rossellino; he also insisted on overly refined chromatic effects in his use of colored marble. In the tomb of Bernardo Giugni (ca. 1468) in the Church of the Badia in Florence, he strove to create an organic plan for funerary monuments, simplifying the design of the tomb of Leonardo Bruni. In this work, using red marble, he brought into striking relief a slender white personification of justice; all is neat and smooth (as in the tripartite altar for Dietisalvi Neroni in the

same church), with the Madonna between two saints, of a purity reminiscent of Angelico, within slender, elegant structural members. And here Mino obtained more effective results than in the altar — also tripartite but less consistent — of the Salutati Chapel in Fiesole Cathedral. He intensified the excessive refinements, which also appeared in the pulpit at Prato, in another altarpiece of the same year (1473) in the Vibi Chapel in S. Pietro, Perugia.

Like other Florentine artists, Mino went to Rome, where he remained from 1473 to about 1480; there he collaborated with Giovanni Dalmata on the monument to Pope Paul II (1475; fragments in the Vatican Grottoes). A drawing for this monument (Berlin, Kupferstichkabinett) repeats the scheme of the Giugni monument, but divides it into many scenes, perhaps by wish of Cardinal Marco Barbo, who had commissioned it and wanted it to include a vast sacred and allegorical repertory; the result was a trite chiaroscuro effect. Apparently the stronger personalities of Cardinal Barbo and of Giovanni Dalmata overwhelmed the mild Florentine artist; however, it is understandable that the monument should have been widely acclaimed, especially in Spain, which was still bound to the analytic late Gothic style diffused there by Italian sculptors. In Rome, Mino created other funerary monuments by varying the plan of the Bruni tomb (for instance, with the lunette not enclosed within an arch but independent and placed above the trabeation), as he did in the tomb of Cardinal Forteguerri in the Church of S. Cecilia in Trastevere, Rome — assuming that the reconstruction agrees with the original design. Also, he probably originated the monumental tomb design with simple trabeation or with a finial bearing the coat of arms, as in the tomb of Cardinal Riario in the Church of SS. Apostoli which was executed by one of Mino's followers with piers ornamented with niches, repeating details of the tomb of Paul II. While in Rome, Mino also adhered to the reduced design of the tomb of Pope Eugenius IV in S. Salvatore in Lauro, as, for instance, in the tomb of Giovanni Tornabuoni in S. Maria sopra Minerva, which displays ornamental refinements reminiscent of Desiderio da Settignano. Mino exerted considerable influence in Rome, especially on Lombard artists; one of these, Andrea Bregno (see below), had a style similar in its subtle refinements, although its Lombard exuberance was generally contrary to Mino's temperament. Upon his return to Florence, Mino again took up work (1481) on the tomb of Count Hugo in the Church of the Badia (PL. 16), which had been commissioned in 1469. He faithfully followed the original plan, patterned after that of the Giugni tomb, substituting a figure of Charity (VIII, PL. 192) for that of Justice; however, his style had become more overly refined in the figures, which are even more elongated.

The formal heaviness of Rossellino's later works is found in the work of minor artists, such as the eclectic and outdated Tommaso Fiamberti from Campione d'Italia (d. Cesena, 1524/25), who has been mistaken for Mino da Fiesole. Fiamberti worked in Tuscany (Madonna and Child in the Hermitage of Camaldoli), in the Marches, and in Romagna (Numai monument, in S. Maria dei Servi in Forlì), where he collaborated with other sculptors.

Rossellino's stylistic maturity cannot be dissociated from his contacts with Benedetto da Maiano, also an able ornamentalist and outstanding for his vigorous compositions, dense with figures. These contacts are evident in the bust of Pietro Mellini (1474; Florence, Mus. Naz.), comparable for its objective realism to that of Matteo Palmieri by Antonio Rossellino, and in the bust of Filippo Strozzi (PL. 17). Both were conceived on a broader scale than the portraits mentioned earlier. Another significant work by Benedetto is the polygonal pulpit in Sta Croce in Florence (1472–75). Pensile, like the pulpit by Buggiano (from a design by Brunelleschi) in S. Maria Novella, Florence, it is divided into five sections with scenes from the life of St. Francis set off by sturdy, ornate frames; compared with those of Rossellino and Mino da Fiesole, these scenes, in a sharp and skillful relief, have a much more solid construction and breadth. The altar-tomb of S. Savino (1474–76) in Faenza Cathedral, which expands the arcosolium plan created by

Bernardo Rossellino, is decorated with six reliefs with scenes illustrating the life of the saint that are in a somewhat contrasting chiaroscuro, quite different from the absolute formalism of the pulpit in Sta Croce. Hence the hypothesis of a collaboration with Rossellino seems tenable. The work of Benedetto da Maiano clearly reveals his search for a strengthening of figural values, and this explains his preference for a type of sculpture in which he could most easily satisfy this aim. Apart from the small freestanding Virtues in niches in the Sta Croce pulpit, of a stateliness that does not seem to be compatible with their modest size, he pursued his goal in his sculptures of a young St. John (a theme adopted previously by Donatello) and a figure of Justice above the double door between the Sala dei Gigli and the Sala dell'Udienza in the Palazzo Vecchio in Florence (VIII, PL. 192). The figure of Justice foreshadows the *Madonna dell'Ulivo* (1480) in Prato Cathedral, of a compact and regular pyramidal movement, with a density of mass also found in the figures in the extremely ornate altarpieces in the Chapel of S. Fina (1475) in the Collegiata (Cathedral) and in the Chapel of S. Bartolo (1473–95) in the Church of S. Agostino, both in San Gimignano. Falling chronologically between these two works, the tripartite altarpiece (1489) in the Mastrogiudice Chapel in the Church of Monte Oliveto (S. Anna dei Lombardi) in Naples has a grandiose but rather inflated Annunciation between the figures of the two St. Johns. Also outstanding among the many products of the Maiano workshop are the arcosolium tomb of Filippo Strozzi in the chapel of the same name in S. Maria Novella and an earlier group — another example of the artist's aims in sculpture — representing Cardinal Latino Malebranca Orsini crowning Ferdinand of Aragon (Florence, Mus. Naz.). This group, commissioned by that ruler in 1485, remained unfinished after the artist's death; it is noteworthy for the values of its mass, values which underline the fact that Benedetto da Maiano's expansive treatment of form foreshadows that characteristic of the second phase of the Renaissance.

Similar trends are also evident in sculptures by Matteo Civitali of Lucca, who was trained in Florence and who had a confidence in his craftsmanship that led him occasionally into superficiality. Civitali's style was close to that of Antonio Rossellino and even closer to that of Benedetto da Maiano (*Madonna della Tosse* in SS. Trinità, Lucca). In Lucca Cathedral Civitali repeated the design of the Bruni monument in his tomb for Pietro da Noceto (1467) and gave clear evidence of links to Benedetto da Maiano in the altar of S. Regolo, which is overelaborate and decorated with statues. However, he surpassed Benedetto's sculptural power in the statues (of Adam and Eve, Elizabeth, Zacharias, and the prophets Isaiah and Habakkuk) in the Chapel of S. Giovanni Battista in the Cathedral of Genoa.

In Siena, Vecchietta trained Francesco di Giorgio, who was thus indirectly influenced as a sculptor by Donatello's style. While retaining his own stylistic consistency, Francesco, who felt the influence of ancient art, attenuated Donatello's dramatic impact, abandoning his contrasts of light. His splendid bronzes (*Flagellation*, VIII, PL. 202; *Deposition*, PL. 18, containing the portraits of Federigo da Montefeltro and of his young son Guidobaldo) are in a sustained relief that is remarkably effective for its diffused chiaroscuro, in which it is possible to trace the influence of Ghiberti and perhaps even of Verrocchio and Pollaiuolo, and, as always, that of the Florentine milieu. Francesco's pupil, Giacomo Cozzarelli (1453–1515) never equaled his master's excellent command of chiaroscuro effects; he was nevertheless skillful, especially in his *St. John* in the Museo dell'Opera del Duomo in Siena and in the *Pietà* in the Church of the Osservanza near Siena.

The subtle chiaroscuro of Francesco di Giorgio recalls the work of Andrea del Verrocchio, whose training as a goldsmith is evident in the tomb of Piero and Giovanni de' Medici (1472; XIV, PL. 353), which is supremely aristocratic in taste, though its aims are almost exclusively decorative. However, when Verrocchio modeled the human figure (*Resurrection*; XIV, PL. 352) he used a soft line and alternated light and shadow, producing subtle pictorial effects. In freestanding sculpture he combined

this tendency with a highly individual feeling for composition that led to the creation of open and dynamic forms in perfect harmony with their surroundings (*Putto with a Fish*; XIV, PL. 355); this harmony was achieved by placing the human figure against realistic backgrounds (*The Doubting of Thomas*; XIV, PL. 358). Verrocchio, who was greatly influenced by antiquity, gave evidence of notable psychological insight in his portraits (*Bust of a Lady*, XIV, PL. 357; Colleoni monument, XIV, PL. 359); these works support the conclusion that he was undoubtedly a major figure in early Renaissance sculpture. Respected but surpassed by his pupil Leonardo da Vinci, Verrocchio had a less worthy successor in another pupil, Francesco di Simone Ferrucci from Fiesole, who combined ornamental and figural elements in his work. An extremely productive artist, Francesco popularized his master's style and works especially in Emilia (tomb of Alessandro Tartagni, 1477, S. Domenico, Bologna, one of the many imitations of the Bruni monument), in Romagna, in the Marches, and in Umbria.

In complete contrast with Verrocchio's mode of expression within the sphere of Florentine Renaissance sculpture was the style of Antonio del Pollaiuolo. Also trained in the goldsmith's art, which, like Verrocchio, he was never to abandon altogether, he worked alongside Verrocchio on the sumptuous altar of St. John (XI, PL. 184). The essential element in Pallaiuolo's art is the vibrant line that disciplines the planes, which are in sharp relief heightened by chiaroscuro, creating dynamic form and dramatic effects (*Hercules and Antaeus*; XI, PL. 179). Pollaiuolo displayed great vitality in portraiture and endowed the important works he executed in Rome (tomb of Sixtus IV; XI, PLS. 184, 186; tomb of Innocent VIII, reconstructed, in St. Peter's) with a contrasting light that contributes full stylistic uniformity to the creation of sculptural effects and a sense of movement that derived in part from Donatello. Unlike the classicizing sculptors, ranging from Ghiberti to Verrocchio, Pollaiuolo continued the freer and more spontaneous Florentine trend.

Like architecture, Renaissance sculpture was spread throughout Italy by Florentine and other Tuscan artists. Among the major artists, it was Donatello, the initiator of the new style in sculpture, who introduced it into the Veneto region; his influence was enthusiastically received in Padua, where his style was imitated in the fine terra-cotta altarpiece of the Ovetari Chapel in the Eremitani. This work, which was formerly attributed to one of his assistants, Giovanni da Pisa, is now recognized as the creation of Nicolò Pizzolo, who collaborated with Mantegna in the fresco cycle of the chapel. Donatello also had Bartolomeo Bellano from Padua among his many pupils. Bellano followed the master to Florence and worked with him on the pulpits in S. Lorenzo; then, an expert foundryman, he cast a large bronze statue of Paul II for Perugia (1466). Although the statue was destroyed in 1789, at the time of the French domination, on the basis of the artist's surviving works (*Madonna*, Amsterdam, Rijksmus.) it can be assumed to have reflected the ardor of Donatello's later efforts. After his return to Padua, Bellano's style was tempered, probably through the influence of Pietro Lombardo, in the relief *Miracle of the Mule* (Padua, S. Antonio, Treas.); however, in the ten bronze reliefs illustrating scenes from the Old Testament (1483–88), in the choir of S. Antonio, he reverted to an emotional and dramatic expressionistic style, which became gradually subdued in his last works (bronze panel with the Madonna, a putto, and two saints, Roccabonella monument in S. Francesco, Padua).

In Padua the examples of Donatello and of Bellano brought into favor the use of the smelting technique, which was applied to the small bronzes that responded to the aulic taste of the Renaissance. One of Bellano's pupils, Andrea Briosco, known as Il Riccio (d. 1532), was steeped in classical culture and dealt by preference with subjects evocative of antiquity, with a freshness of style comparable to that of Alexandrian art (PL. 502).

Giovanni Minelli de' Bardi of Padua (ca. 1460–1527) modeled powerful and realistic terra cottas (statues of Christ, St. Peter, and St. John; Padua, Mus. Civ.) that tend toward violent expressionism. The Florentine Niccolò Baroncelli (whose style in the door on the side of the Church of the Eremitani in Padua is a transitional one, between Gothic and Renaissance) eventually surrendered to Donatello's influence in the bronze statues of Christ Crucified, the Virgin, and St. John (1450–53) in Ferrara Cathedral, which have a powerful elemental form that is present to a lesser degree in the statues of St. George and St. Maurelio (1466) by Domenico di Paris of Padua. This artist's style is aulic, graceful, and notable for the decorative elements seen in high frieze (1467) in one of the halls of the Palazzo Schifanoia in Ferrara: putti playing musical instruments, personifications of the virtues, and scenes from the history of the Este family.

The highly dramatic quality that had its initial impulse in Donatello was given new accents in Bologna by Niccolò da Bari, known as Niccolò dell'Arca, who probably witnessed the constructions of the triumphal arch of Alfonso of Aragon in the Castel Nuovo in Naples. The explosive drama of his work, perhaps derived from the painter Ercole de' Roberti, is evident in the *Lamentation* in S. Maria della Vita in Bologna (PL. 19), where Niccolò displayed sculptural abilities comparable to those of Guido Mazzoni of Modena (see below). At first Niccolò combined elements reminiscent of Francesco Laurana and Verrocchio, perhaps assimilated through Francesco di Simone (*Madonna di Piazza*; Bologna, Palazzo Com.), and later added echoes of Burgundian and Flemish art (saints and an angel on the cover of the Arca in S. Domenico, Bologna, from which the nickname "dell'Arca" originated).

The artistic development of Agostino dei Fonduti of Crema was based on the Paduan figural tradition originated by Donatello and modified by currents of the Humanistic culture of that city. Agostino drew away from the dramatic intensity of Minelli toward an art that was equally concerned with form but more tranquil in spirit and probably influenced by Andrea Mantegna, as seen in the *Lamentation* (PL. 19) in S. Satiro in Milan. Also in S. Satiro, in the Baptistery, his vigorously modeled heads and putti are reminiscent of Bramante. It can be assumed that Agostino played a leading role in diffusing Mantegna's figural style throughout Lombardy, where engravings in that style were interpreted in marble (Palazzo Varesi in Lodi) and in wood (Sanctuary of S. Maria del Monte near Varese). In this author's opinion his influence is to be associated with the sculptural monumentality of the paintings of Guido Mazzoni (d. 1518), who was a powerful modeler with a heavy, incisive naturalistic style. Mazzoni's polychrome terra-cotta Nativity group (1485) in Modena Cathedral is a faithful sculptural interpretation of Mantegna's style, with some descriptive elaborations that heighten characterization. These elaborations are consciously overstated in his striking life-size representations of the Deposition (generally known as *compianti*, or "lamentations") that are found in Emilia (VIII, PL. 200), in the Veneto region, and even in Naples (Church of Monte Oliveto). Also in Naples Mazzoni modeled the bust of Ferdinand I with biting realism. His fame spread as far as France, where he created the tomb of Louis XII in the Abbey of St-Denis near Paris, a freestanding 16th-century monument, such as Michelangelo's for Julius II was originally to have been. Mazzoni's Lamentations, inspired by theatrical representations of the Mysteries, were often imitated during the 16th century in popular versions to be found in the countryside, especially in Piedmont, Lombardy, and Tuscany. Mantegna's later style, which tended increasingly toward classicism, undoubtedly inspired the bronze doors (1477) of the receptacle for St. Peter's chains in S. Pietro in Vincoli, Rome (PL. 24), which have been attributed to Cristoforo Foppa, known as Il Caradossa, who was highly praised as a goldsmith by contemporary sources. Mantegna's influence is even more evident in the compact bronzes by Pier Jacopo Ilario Bonacolsi, called L'Antico (1460–1528) (medallions representing the Labors of Hercules; Florence, Mus. Naz.).

The influence of Donatello in the Po Valley was eventually replaced by that of Mantegna. Nevertheless, in the second half of the 15th century a well-defined Lombard style also emerged there. Apparently among its exponents was another Mantuan artist, Sperandio, a sculptor, medalist, and painter who was responsible for the overloaded portal of the Church of Corpus Domini and the tomb of Pope Alexander V — Renaissance in style, but with some Gothic rhythms — in S. Francesco in Bologna.

In sculpture as in architecture the term "Lombard" includes variations of taste and nuances that are for the most part yet to be analyzed. One of these variations is associated with Donatello and with Padua. Although the style of the Mantegazza brothers, Cristoforo (d. 1482) and Antonio (d. 1495), remained basically Gothic, Lombard expressions of the late Gothic were developing elegant linear refinements and soft articulations of form that were alien to the Lombard temperament. In adopting the Renaissance style they created harsh, tortuous effects, contrasts of light, sharpness in the features and angular garments of their subjects, thus revealing indirect reflections of Donatello's style in addition to German influences; nevertheless, their work is not devoid of those aulic refinements which in the Lombard milieu were gradually annulling the formal structural values of the Paduan-Mantegnesque school.

There are examples of this in the Mantegazza brothers' reliefs in the base of the façade of the Certosa of Pavia (VIII, PL. 195), which were carved in collaboration with Amadeo, and in the overloaded *Lamentation* (PL. 19) of a very ornate tabernacle in the chapter hall.

The repetitious, detailed chiaroscuro that characterized the decorative elements in Lombard architecture is typical also of Giovanni Antonio Amadeo (ca. 1447–1522), the most celebrated of the Lombard sculptors. Basically Gothic in feeling, he was influenced only superficially by Donatello (possibly through Michelozzo) and then only in technique, in his ingenious use of *stiacciato*, or flat, relief; his rendering of figural elements was more studied than spontaneous. Revealing instances of this are the portal of the small cloister of the Certosa of Pavia, one of Amadeo's first works and one in which he tends toward Michelozzo's style, and the relief with the Madonna and Child (signed) in the seat of the Confraternity of the Misericordia in Florence. It is quite possible that Amadeo worked in Florence (although the relief mentioned does not constitute proof, as it may well have been transferred there from Lombardy), especially considering his later stylistic orientation toward the trends originated by Antonio Rossellino and Benedetto da Maiano. This would explain the serene image of Medea Colleoni (PL. 20), placed on a sarcophagus against a bicolor background within an ornate edicule in an attempt to reproduce that picturesque quality which abounds in the façade of the Cappella Colleoni in Bergamo.

In addition to Medea's tomb, the chapel contains that of her father Bartolomeo, a captain of the Venetian Republic, who is immortalized in Verrocchio's monument in Venice. Bartolomeo Colleoni's tomb is a far less organic unit. The marble bier on a long base supported by columns seems to be a second sarcophagus and is redundant; its reliefs are overloaded with figures and do not harmonize with the somewhat bare edicule that contains the equestrian statue of the *condottiere* by another artist. The perspective in the reliefs, which is not completely successful, reflects a style that is not yet fully realized, as is also evident in the overloaded decoration of the chapel's façade, in the portal, in the windows, and in the edicules, which are only superficially reminiscent of Donatello; in some slender statues that tend to geometric forms the influence of Antonio Rizzo (see below) is seen (Venturi, VI, p. 915). However, Amadeo was an eclectic artist; his images, only slightly formed and with sharply carved drapery, though less harsh than those of the Mantegazzo brothers, were to be presented later in compositions on a large scale in the Arca of S. Imerio in Cremona Cathedral, which can be traced to the influence of Rossellino rather than to that of the Po Valley, perhaps through Alberto Maffioli of Carrara, who worked on the Certosa in Pavia. These works retain their Lombard spirit, which survives even when the artist has eliminated some of the exuberant accents, as in the Arca of S. Lanfranco in the Church of the S. Sepolcro in Pavia. Both exuberance and harshness persisted, however, in Amadeo's collaborators and followers, among them, Tommaso Cazzaniga and Pietro da Rho; Tommaso Rodari of Maroggia (documented 1486–1526), notable for the quality and originality of his work, was one of a group that worked mainly in Como Cathedral and produced sharply angular sculptures.

In sculptural relief the Lombards often lacked unity of vision (as did Ghiberti in the third pair of doors for the Florence Baptistery). This is particularly evident in the work of Benedetto Briosco, who succeeded Amadeo in decorating the portal in the façade of the Certosa of Pavia (1501 onward) and created a feeling of perspective depth in his reliefs. This treatment of perspective may be derived from Gian Cristoforo Romano (son of Isaia da Pisa), who was a dedicated champion of antiquity; in fact a certain type of monumental sculpture in Rome, from the Arch of Titus onward — as was noted in connection with Ghiberti — conveys the same impression. Gian Cristoforo Romano, the author of a bust of Beatrice d'Este (Louvre) that was executed before her marriage to Lodovico il Moro, created the monumental tomb of Gian Galeazzo Visconti (1494–97) in the Certosa of Pavia, decorated with panoplies, medallions, coats of arms and festoons, in which he reveals an analytical view of the antique that is similar to Filarete's. (Work on the tomb was continued slowly by Benedetto Briosco and completed with mediocre statues by Bernardino da Novate. In it, Briosco softened the forms, tending away from the harshness of the Mantegazzo brothers and Amadeo; he gave the idealized figures a slender line and strove for a refined elegance.) An aristocratic and cultured artist, matchless as a cutter of gems, Gian Cristoforo Romano was esteemed at the courts of Milan and Mantua, where he was a favorite of Isabella d'Este. In Urbino, where he created portals with martial motifs similar to those of the Visconti monument, he was under the protection of Elisabetta Gonzaga, wife of Guidobaldo da Montefeltro; he is mentioned as a participant in the brilliant balls described by Baldassare Castiglione in *The Courtier*. His was, therefore, an aulic art, still of the 15th century even though it outlasted that century. This courtly style was also taken up at the end of the 15th century by Cristoforo Solari, known as Il Gobbo (d. 1527), who executed the marble tomb slabs of Lodovico il Moro and Beatrice d'Este, now in the Certosa of Pavia but originally intended for S. Maria delle Grazie in Milan, where they were to be placed under Bramante's dome. Solari rendered the physical mass of the figures with a measure of descriptive realism that is also evident in the statues executed by him for Milan Cathedral. A sensuous style attuned to the French taste (which exerted its influence after France conquered the duchy of Milan) is typical of Agostino Busti, known as Il Bambaja (1483–1548), who reduced sculpture to a micrographic game, with the result that in his work marble seems to have lost its essential characteristics and takes on the appearance of ivory or alabaster. This can be seen in the delicate figural reliefs of the dismantled tomb of Gaston de Foix (Milan, Castello Sforzesco). In the noble recumbent statue of the deceased undue emphasis on detail is avoided, although the work is modeled with extreme care.

Pietro Lombardo, who worked in Padua and Venice as an architect (see above), revealed a delicate temperament as a sculptor, especially in *stiacciato* and bas-relief, a technique he must have acquired in Florence through contacts with Desiderio da Settignano and Antonio Rossellino. His direct knowledge of Florence as an architect has already been mentioned. Among his sculptural works the tomb of Antonio Rosselli (PL. 21) is noteworthy; it follows the design of the Bruni tomb, with additional elements such as the two youths holding coats of arms, drawn from the Marsuppini tomb by Desiderio. True to the Lombard style, he overloaded his work and placed it within an edicule inspired by Michelozzo's portal for the Medici bank, an indication of his stylistic tendencies; he gave substance to his slender figures in a compositional pattern (e.g., in the lunette) that was probably derived from Mantegna. The artist tended in his very slight, almost *stiacciato* relief to an extreme delicacy approaching that of Giovanni Bellini, whose forms he was to imitate in his later work. In Venice, Lombardo's style developed even more ornamental tendencies and, at the same time, became more figural, especially in his tombs for the doges: for example, the tomb of Doge Pasquale Malipiero in the Church of SS. Giovanni e Paolo, in which

to the Renaissance structure is added a pavilion over the coffin, reminiscent of the Gothic but in doubtful taste; and the tomb of Jacopo Marcello in S. Maria Gloriosa dei Frari, where niches with statues were added to the Florentine scheme. Of these tombs, the most noble, the richest, and the most complex in its balanced relation of architecture and sculpture is that of Doge Pietro Mocenigo (1476–ca. 1480), also in the Church of SS. Giovanni e Paolo. In this work Lombardo reverted to the earlier, better proportioned scheme; the relief representing the Holy Women at the Sepulcher in the upper zone of the monument harmonizes perfectly with the impeccably restrained statues of Hellenicizing grace and of a form comparable to Rizzo's, especially in the static frontal figures that carry the doge's sarcophagus on their shoulders, repeating a 14th-century motif. In Lombardo's later period, only the statues of SS. Paul and Jerome (the latter is signed) in the Church of S. Stefano in Venice reveal a different attitude: a realistic tendency similar to that of the sculptors of his native region, with whom he may have had some contacts.

Generally, Lombardo and the minor artists close to him adhered to an idealized classicism closely related to that of painting. Notable among the works of these minor artists are the tomb of Doge Andrea Vendramin (d. 1478), in the Church of SS. Giovanni e Paolo, by Alessandro Leopardi, who cast Verrocchio's statue of Colleoni and who was assisted in this tomb by Pietro Lombardo's sons Antonio and Tullio, and the relief of the Madonna with Doge Leonardo Loredan and three saints by Giovanni Giorgio Lascaris, known as Pyrgoteles, in the Sala degli Scarlatti in the Doges' Palace. However, Lombardo and his sons retained superiority over their imitators and pupils in Venice. The style of the artist's sons evolved in the direction of an increasingly emphatic classicism. Antonio Lombardo's more limited personality attained facile, almost neoclassical results in the high relief *Miracle of the Newborn Child* in the Chapel of the Arca del Santo in Padua (PL. 22). In other reliefs (also representing miracles attributed to St. Anthony; I, PL. 306) Tullio revealed a less refined talent (e.g., in the double portrait in the Ca' d'Oro, Venice) and, sometimes, an almost romantic tone, as in the monument to Guido Guidarelli, a successful synthesis of classical form with sentiment (PL. 127).

Antonio Rizzo, presumably from Verona (active 1465–99), worked also in Lombardy, where traces of his style are to be found, and made his way to Venice after the Lombards Antonio and Paolo Bregno had emphasized Gothic forms there; his work displays a certain pomp and a Gothicizing composition in the tomb of Doge Francesco Foscari in S. Maria Gloriosa dei Frari, with slender statues that are, however, almost Renaissance in spirit. In the same church Rizzo built the tomb of Doge Nicolò Tron (1473 onward; VIII, PL. 198), a spectacular work of great originality, composed of a huge arch with pilasters in which tiers of niches are carved out to hold statues in accordance with the Lombard style. The image of the Doge stands between figures of Charity and Prudence in the lower order; the sarcophagus, above a plaque, is carved with another, recumbent statue of the deceased; and above that there is a row of statues in niches, surmounted by a lunette with the Resurrection. The composition is exceptional for its expanse, which entirely covers the high wall that supports it in the principal chapel of the church, and it achieves a monumental grandeur unparalleled in the early Renaissance. The statues, here too elongated in an attempt to attain ideal cylindrical volumes, have a restraint and rhythm comparable to some effects in the painting of Antonello da Messina (e.g., *St. Sebastian*; Dresden, Gemäldegalerie). Rizzo emphasized geometric form in the solid mass of his statue of Eve, executed together with the well-constructed but less felicitous representation of Adam for the courtyard of the Doges' Palace (PL. 22); both convey an impression of poised austerity quite opposed to the tormented figures found in Padua. In this restraint Rizzo was similar to Pietro Lombardo.

The history of the wandering masters of the Po Valley continued with Domenico Gaggini, who worked as an architect in the Chapel of S. Giovanni Battista (1456; see above) in the Genoa Cathedral; as a sculptor, he created the reliefs in perspective on the front of that same chapel (PL. 23). (After his departure for Naples and Sicily the reliefs were continued and completed in 1478 by his nephew Elia.) Beside the rather awkward reliefs, which are enclosed within raceme scrolls reminiscent of Filarete, statues of prophets — in a fluid style that echoes Ghiberti — stand in small superposed niches. Thus, also Gaggini, always with an archaicizing tone, looked to the earlier Florentine artists. His style is evident in the altarpiece of the Church of S. Lorenzo in Portovenere, a work divided in a manner similar to that used by Andrea Bregno in Rome. The fragile and timid forms of the altarpiece are of the type used in Genoa by Elia Gaggini and by other Lombard artists, with an obvious eclecticism in the sculptured lintels of portals (a typical example of which is the lintel of the portal in the Via degli Orefici, representing the Adoration of the Magi in a composition somewhat reminiscent of Masaccio).

In Naples, Domenico Gaggini met Pietro da Milano, who was working on the triumphal arch of Alfonso of Aragon, as well as sculptors from other regions who, in 1458, were engaged on the same undertaking. Among them were Isaia da Pisa, Antonio di Chellino (also from Pisa), Francesco Laurana, and Paolo Romano (two years earlier, Andrea dall'Aquila was also mentioned among these artists). As a result, the sculptures on the arch (two celebrative reliefs on the barrel vault, a relief representing Alfonso's triumph on the attic, and the statues of Virtues on the second attic) have been attributed variously to many artists and to the most diverse influences, including that of Burgundian art. It is impossible to trace Gaggini's hand in the reliefs with any certainty. The massive high reliefs were inspired by Roman examples, as had been those of Ghiberti and the Lombards, and they are perfectly compatible with the rhetorical and celebrative character evident in the architecture of the arch.

In Sicily, in addition to proving himself a skillful decorator, Gaggini also appeared as a mellowed, fluent sculptor of delicate Madonnas and saints (S. Francesco, Palermo; Arcivescovado, Syracuse). His son Antonello continued this style but amplified his father's figural manner, as for example in his nobly impressive *Annunciation* (Erice, Mus. Antonio Cordici). But not only the Lombards were working in Sicily; although Antonello Freri from Messina was similar to them in his delicate decoration of the transept of Catania Cathedral (in a taste that was to become widespread in Andalusian Spain), in his vigorous sculpture (tomb of Ferdinando d'Acuna, 1495, in the Chapel of S. Agata, Catania Cathedral), he favored the style of Francesco Laurana, who was in Palermo in 1468.

Laurana's familiarity with Gaggini's group (his work has, in fact, been mistaken for that of Gaggini) is indicated in the arch at the front of the Mastrantonio Chapel in S. Francesco d'Assisi, Palermo; the niches in the pilasters of this arch hold figures of prophets, evangelists, and doctors of the Church that are combined with a careful perspective. The *Madonna and Child* in the Church of the Crocifisso in Noto was created three years later (1471); it is as delicate as Gaggini's work, but it is notable for its more vigorous three-dimensional form. There is a geometrizing tendency in the face of the Madonna, probably a result of the influence of Antonello da Messina, whose brilliant talent was then beginning to be appreciated in his native island. However, like the *Madonna and Child* from S. Agostino (Messina, Mus. Naz.), this work is artistically inferior to Laurana's admirable busts of Eleanor of Aragon (XI, PL. 221) and Beatrice of Aragon (Berlin, Staat. Mus.), which are endowed with a profound spirituality and with a geometric synthesis that was to become supreme in the later bust of Battista Sforza (PL. 17). In his masterpiece Laurana did not indulge in superfluous modeling but remained instead within rigorous geometric limits, to which is added a spiritual impassivity related to the art of Piero della Francesca. Moreover, because the work was executed after the subject's death (1472), the sculptor was not bound by the requirements of realism and was thus free to achieve a sublime abstraction. Extremely active, Francesco Laurana had been in France after 1458; he had worked as a medalist there and returned there after his

visit to Urbino. But his stylistic development did not follow a direct course, and his contacts with the Lombards, with Antonello, and with Piero were followed by influences from French and Flemish art. This is evident in the relief on the altar of St. Lazarus in the Old Cathedral of La Major in Marseilles (1477–83), which was executed in collaboration with one of his Lombard successors, Tommaso Malvito of Como, who later worked in Naples as an architect and decorator in the Carafa Chapel of the Cathedral. The variety of Laurana's sources is confirmed by the imposing, though rather confused, *Bearing of the Cross* in the Church of St-Didier in Avignon (PL. 507). This last work was obviously inspired by the Flemish school in some of its portraitist details, notwithstanding the sharp contrast between the *stiacciato* background and the figures in very high relief — a contrast that recalls the reliefs on the arch of Alfonso of Aragon in Naples, although the work in Avignon is less vigorous.

Sculpture in southern Italy, primarily Lombard and decorative, often deteriorated into mere craftsmanship. Among the many artists active in the region Silvestro da Sulmona (Aquilano) and Mino (Dino) del Reame (Regno) are noteworthy. The former, son of Giacomo da Sulmona, known as L'Ariscola, was associated with the Neapolitan and Roman artistic circles. The tomb of Cardinal Amico Agnifili (1476–80) in Aquila Cathedral reveals some echoes of Antonio Rossellino acquired indirectly through the latter's work in Naples; in the tomb of Maria Pereira in the Church of S. Bernardino in Aquila, Silvestro adapted the scheme of the tomb of Paul II by Mino da Fiesole and Giovanni Dalmata, in a style fluctuating between Verrocchio and the Lombard school. Verrocchio's influence on Silvestro is noticeable also in the noble wooden statue of St. Sebastian (1475; Aquila, Mus. Naz. d'Arte Abruzzese). Lombard influences are best illustrated in the mausoleum of S. Bernardino (ca. 1505) in the Church of S. Bernardino in Aquila; many other artists participated in the execution of this work.

Mino del Reame worked in Naples, Montecassino, and Rome between 1463 and approximately 1477, and his work was often mistaken for that of Mino da Fiesole. His work has narrative aspects, as in the reliefs from the old ciborium now in the apse of S. Maria Maggiore in Rome, with elements of rhetorical magniloquence that were noted above in connection with the triumphal arch of Alfonso of Aragon in Naples. Moreover, the composition is reminiscent of Gaggini (e.g., *The Adoration of the Magi*) and demonstrates Mino's links with the Lombard school. This is affirmed also in an excessively ornate tabernacle (signed) in S. Maria in Trastevere, also in Rome. A similar celebrative purpose is evident in Mino's large tomb of Pius II in S. Andrea della Valle in Rome, previously attributed to the Lombard Andrea Bregno (1421–1506) and to one of his assistants (Venturi, 1908–40, VI, p. 959). In fact, the Lombard sculptors — or, rather, the Po Valley sculptors — were extremely active in Rome, where they decorated churches, creating rich altarpieces and ciboria, and conceived ornate tombs for prelates and dignitaries of the papal court. Most famous of these artists was Andrea Bregno (1418?–1506) from Osteno, who with his numerous pupils and followers created what can properly be termed an artistic industry. In the midst of so plentiful a production, it is difficult to identify individual artists because they were generally quite undistinguished and because many artists often contributed to a single work. Bregno attains fine sculptural effects in the recumbent statue of Cardinal Coca on the prelate's monument in S. Maria sopra Minerva, but he is notable mainly as an exquisite decorator. In the tombs of Cardinal Cristoforo della Rovere and Cardinal Giorgio Costa, both in S. Maria del Popolo, Rome, and in the monument of Archbishop Sopranzi in S. Maria sopra Minerva — the last two executed by his pupils — he followed the Florentine design of the tomb of Leonardo Bruni in Sta Croce, replacing the fluting on the pilasters with elegant candelabra motifs. The Bruni monument had been made known in Rome by Mino da Fiesole, who influenced Bregno while collaborating with the Lombard artist on the tomb of Cardinal della Rovere. Bregno undoubtedly appreciated Mino's figural refinements, though he retained a preference for ornamentation. The four saints in the niches of the altar executed by Bregno for S. Maria del Popolo are typically Lombard in conception and reveal a certain distinction and dignified restraint. The altar was commissioned in 1473 by Cardinal Rodrigo Borgia, who was to become Pope Alexander VI, at the beginning of Mino's Roman period. Bregno's fame spread as far as Tuscany, to Siena in particular, and between 1481 and 1485 he worked on the Piccolomini Altar in the Cathedral there; this altar, similar to that in Rome, though somewhat richer, is notable as an affirmation of the Lombard decorative taste in the Sienese milieu. The altar was later included in a larger, ornamental architectural framework that included niches containing statues by Michelangelo (1501–04). Bregno's presence in Siena had immediate repercussions: Neroccio de' Landi (1447–1500), a pupil of Vecchietta, who had derived from his master the typical structure of the minor Roman funerary monuments — that is, rectangular, with a solitary image of the deceased in an edicule — then enriched it with ornamentation, as in the tomb of Bishop Tommaso Piccolomini del Testa (1485) in Siena Cathedral.

In Rome, in the tomb of Cardinal Bartolomeo Roverella (1476–77) in S. Clemente, Giovanni Dalmata elaborated on the simple trabeated structure by inserting behind the sarcophagus bearing the figure of the deceased a niche with figures in high relief accompanied by lively decorative elements. Giovanni Dalmata, who was at the head of a group of artists who worked with him on the Roverella tomb, was called to Hungary in 1481 by Matthias Corvinus, and he introduced there the stylistic idioms of the Renaissance. In two high reliefs bearing the profiles of the sovereign and of Beatrice of Aragon (both Vienna, Hofmuseum) he showed himself to be a portraitist and, in the use of color, to have remained faithful to the Venetian tradition.

From the maze of Lombard sculptors in Rome, which was reduced to executing variations on existing formulas (mainly in the production of funerary monuments), emerged the artistic personality of Luigi Capponi of Milan. In an altar frontal in S. Gregorio Magno, illustrating episodes from the saint's life, Capponi delicately reiterated the style of Amadeo. However, while retaining some impeccable decorative elements in his Roman works, he amplified and simplified forms (relief with Leo I before St. John the Evangelist, in the Lateran Baptistery; *Crucifixion with the Virgin and St. John*, Church of S. Maria della Consolazione).

Among the many artists from other regions, a local sculptor, Paolo Romano (Taccone) from Sezze Romano, was also active in Rome. He attempted to revive the myths of antiquity in expressions connected ideally with those in the triumphal arch of Alfonso of Aragon in Naples, where he worked with Isaia da Pisa. His huge statue of St. Peter and the one of St. Paul by Mino del Reame (1461–62), which originally flanked the steps in front of St. Peter's and are now in the Palazzo della Radio Vaticana (formerly known as the Museo Petriano), are cold and coarse imitations of ancient sculpture, as is the statue of St. Paul (1463–64) on the Sant'Angelo bridge. In the same coldly classicizing style are the anonymous reliefs with the glories of the major apostles carved for the ciborium of Sixtus IV (I, PL. 306), which the Pope commissioned together with the statues of the Twelve Apostles (two ascribed to Mino da Fiesole, one to Giovanni Dalmata) and the busts of the evangelists and of the four doctors of the Church. The reliefs, produced by many different artists and varying widely in quality, contain an exalted echo of Roman monuments and ancient architecture, although these are represented in mistaken proportions. It is of little importance to distinguish the rather mediocre authors of the reliefs, which reveal a Roman-Lombard collaboration (it was at this time, 1480–81, that Bregno's workshop was executing the screen and the singing gallery of the Sistine Chapel; PL. 24). Of primary interest, however, is the prevailing influence of antiquity, which is evident even in the lack of unitary vision and which has its source in the Roman triumphal arch. Some classicizing tendencies in the reliefs acquired an academic tone that eventually reappeared on a much higher artistic level in the work of Gian Cristoforo Romano, who understandably

found a perfectly congenial atmosphere in the courts of Milan, Mantua, and Urbino.

The reliefs on the ciborium of Sixtus IV are significant because they were intended for the major church in Christendom; they prove, in fact, that in the field of sculpture the realistic trend originated by Donatello had been superseded in Rome by a trend toward idealized classicism. Notwithstanding some artistic compromises, the overwhelming effect of this second trend affected almost all of Italy, paralleling developments in early Renaissance architecture.

Painting. Masaccio was the initiator of Renaissance painting; but both in his native San Giovanni Valdarno and in Florence he lived in that late Gothic atmosphere whose principal exponent was Lorenzo Monaco. Nonetheless, in an eclectic spirit, Masaccio adopted some delicate and soft chiaroscuro effects of Emilian origin derived from Arcangelo di Cola da Camerino from the Marches; this chiaroscuro was endowed by Masaccio with a stirring, vibrant quality that created figural expressions of great clarity and luminosity. Within the new discipline of space defined in perspective (*The Trinity*, IX, PL. 345) man appears in Masaccio's paintings, as in Giotto's, with prevailingly sculptural qualities, but Masaccio's figures have a cohesive physical substance that is lacking in Giotto's works. Moreover, in achieving a moral characterization, the artist created not just types, but individuals, expressing himself dryly and emphasizing essentials. His style was tersely described by Cristoforo Landino as "pure and without ornamentation" (*La Divina Commedia di Dante Alighieri col commento*, Florence, 1481). Masaccio's style is therefore clearly distinct from the late Gothic style of Masolino, even in the paintings on which they collaborated (*The Virgin and Child with St. Anne*, IX, PL. 341; frescoes in the Brancacci Chapel of S. Maria del Carmine, Florence, IX, PLS. 347–350; a dismantled triptych from S. Maria Maggiore, Rome, IX, PL. 374). However, some medieval elements are present in his earlier works (triptych, Church of San Giovenale at Cascia di Reggello), which are also clearly distinguishable.

Although Masaccio died young he managed nevertheless to express his precocious genius in memorable works. However, unlike Donatello, he had no direct disciples. When, not yet twenty-seven, he died in obscurity in Rome, his death was lamented by Brunelleschi and (this author believes) also by the gentle Frate Giovanni da Fiesole, called Il Beato Angelico. Angelico's style, like Ghiberti's, had its beginnings in an idealized medieval classicism, the result of an apprenticeship under Lorenzo Monaco, and gradually rose to a level of spirituality; he produced truly unearthly Madonnas and saints, who are suffused with an abstract luminosity (PL. 28). Instead of remaining isolated in the silence of the cloisters, he studied Masaccio's perspective layouts and demonstrated a complete understanding of them (as, for instance, in the fragments of the predella depicting the *Marriage and Death of the Virgin*; Florence, Mus. di S. Marco); his awareness of other contemporary artists is also revealed in his prolific artistic activity in the Convent of S. Marco (I, PLS. 266, 272), the Chapel of S. Brizio in Orvieto Cathedral, and the Chapel of Nicholas V in the Vatican (I, PL. 270).

A number of Masaccio's contemporaries interpreted the new order according to their individual sensitivities. Among them was Paolo Uccello, whose beginnings were Gothic also, but whose enthusiastic study of perspective led him to spatial definitions that were of the Renaissance (e.g., *The Flood*, XI, PL. 37; *The Drunkenness of Noah*, Chiostro Verde, S. Maria Novella, Florence). He sought geometric solutions, defining human forms and objects within regular volumes, sometimes endowing them with monumental power, as in the equestrian portrait of Sir John Hawkwood (PL. 27) and in *The Battle of San Romano* (XI, PLS. 39, 42, 43), thus giving them inhuman and fantastic aspects. The art of this painter, who delighted in completing his figural compositions with unreal colors, eventually acquired a quality of fable in the predella illustrating the legend of the profanation of the Host (XI, PL. 44). During his second stay in the Veneto region (in Padua, about 1445; on his first visit he had remained in Venice from 1425 to about 1431), Paolo contributed to the diffusion of the Renaissance style in that area. Even in Florence there were those who felt his influence; among these was the Portuguese Giovanni di Consalvo, who probably painted the frescoes with scenes from the life of St. Benedict in the cloister of the Badia. But his extremely personal vision could not produce a following, nor did he have any pupils; in Florence, as well as Siena (e.g., Sassetta and Giovanni di Paolo), he left only the echoes of isolated solutions to problems of form and only traces of his peremptory perspective depth.

It can be assumed that Domenico Veneziano, who began his Florentine activity in the 1440s, was fascinated by the unusual artistic personality of Paolo Uccello, of whom he is reminiscent in the so-called "Carnesecchi Tabernacle" (IV, PL. 239). Veneziano's work also shows traces of his contact with the Florentine master of form, Andrea del Castagno; this is especially true of one of his later achievements, the fresco of John the Baptist and St. Francis in Sta Croce (IV, PL. 239). Nevertheless, Domenico brought to his work a uniquely personal poetic quality that transcends these influences of form: a new vision of color in relation to the concreteness of light, one different from Masaccio's, which resulted in a plein-air, or daylight, effect. The effects of perspective and light that he attained are evident in the altarpiece from S. Lucia dei Magnoli (IV, PLS. 233, 235) and in the five fragments of its predella (PL. 27; IV, PLS. 234, 238). In this work, moreover, the rendering of the elements — figures, backgrounds, and objects — acquired a particularly lofty tone. It is therefore noteworthy that in 1439 Piero della Francesca worked as assistant to this remarkable painter in the choir of S. Egidio, in Florence, on a cycle of frescoes (destroyed) to which Andrea del Castagno and Alesso Baldovinetti later contributed.

Piero, who had long been interested in perspective, on which he was to write a treatise, *De prospectiva pingendi* (1942), was fully aware both of Paolo Uccello's achievements in perspective and geometric studies and of the first Sienese experiments in this field (e.g., Domenico di Bartolo). Presumably he had contacts with Fra Angelico; he obviously knew the art of Donatello and Masaccio and was familiar with classical antiquity, of which some echoes are to be found in his work. But the luminist values of Domenico Veneziano remained fundamental for him and were amplified by him, especially in his later production, through his knowledge of Flemish painting. As a theorist of perspective and also as a mathematician, he imparted to his own pictorial vision a greater method and depth than had Paolo Uccello; furthermore, essential to his artistic evolution were the concepts of regulated beauty and dignity proclaimed by Leon Battista Alberti in a return to classicism. Thus Piero's solemn, impassive, and often impersonal humanity — its regular volumes combined with colors resplendent in a limpid morning light — was embodied within the framework of perspective discipline (PL. 26). This applies even in his earliest works, such as *The Flagellation of Christ* (XI, PL. 158), and in subsequent creations (Arezzo frescoes; XI, PLS. 159–161; Sansepolcro *Resurrection*) up to *The Nativity* (XI, PL. 165). In Piero's work the synthesis of form with color reached an apex of Hellenicizing classicism in the early Renaissance. Like Paolo Uccello, his approach was absolute; but, unlike Paolo's, Piero's art had an extensive influence because of the richness of his temperament and was interpreted in many ways in Tuscany, the Po Valley, the Marches, Umbria, and Latium, since he worked not only in Urbino and in his native town but also in Ferrara, Rimini, Rome, Arezzo, and Perugia.

The effects of Piero's artistic activity will be dealt with below; he has been mentioned in connection with a discussion of the Florentine milieu because he received his training in Tuscany, and particularly in Florence. In this city, the immediate results of Masaccio's example can be found in the art of Fra Filippo Lippi, especially in the values of form and composition evident in the work of his early period. Living as he did in the Florentine monastery of S. Maria del Carmine, he must have felt the impact of Masaccio's powerful achievements in the Brancacci Chapel frescoes and in the fresco of the *Sagra* (lost). This influence is especially notable in Filippo's figural

compositions (*Madonna of Humility*; Milan, Mus. del Castello Sforzesco), which are vigorous but occasionally somewhat unbalanced and imbued with a clear, orange tone, in a sort of compromise with the abstract colors of Fra Angelico and Lorenzo Monaco; the figures are placed against backgrounds conceived according to a still-intuitive perspective (PL. 35). Filippo Lippi was one of the first propagators of the Renaissance in Padua, which he visited in 1434. His exuberant temperament became more subdued about 1445, and the works of this period reveal a similarity to those of Fra Angelico; some of his intimate and touching Nativity scenes display subtle refinements of light and harmony of line that appear also in other panels as well as in the two cycles in Prato and Spoleto, which he painted in a narrative vein that foreshadowed Ghirlandajo's (IX, PLS. 145, 146).

Lippi and the other painters mentioned above represented the link in Florentine art between Masaccio and the following generations. Thus, from Domenico Veneziano sprang the art of Alesso Baldovinetti (1425–99), who was typically Florentine in his feeling for the values of design, which he often combined, through the influence of Paolo Uccello and, above all, of Piero della Francesca, with a broad vision of space and perspective; this vision was realized in his *Nativity* in the atrium of the SS. Annunziata (1460–62), in an *Annunciation* (VIII, PL. 194), and in a *Madonna and Child* (PL. 28), which, better than any of his works, reveals his delicate, subdued sensitivity. However, Baldovinetti did not fully grasp the luminist values of Veneziano's art, and his colors are generally rather dull and chalky; he carried out some technical experiments with color, but with negative results, as in the deteriorated *Nativity* in the SS. Annunziata and in similarly damaged frescoes of the apsidal chapel in Sta Trinita (1471 onward).

A pupil of Angelico, Benozzo Gozzoli (1420–98), did not possess his master's lofty spirituality, and his was a purely narrative art that extended into the Renaissance the superficial naturalism and the fablelike quality of northern late Gothic, that is, of Gentile da Fabriano and of Pisanello. An example is the lively decoration in the chapel of the Palazzo Medici-Riccardi, where Gozzoli painted *The Procession of the Magi* (VIII, PL. 193) and adoring angels next to Filippo Lippi's altarpiece *The Madonna Adoring the Child* (IX, PL. 146). He had previously illustrated in a rather superficial manner some scenes from the life of St. Francis in the Church of S. Francesco in Montefalco, then painted scenes from the life of St. Augustine in the Church of S. Agostino in San Gimignano (1463–65), and frescoed episodes from the Old Testament in rich compositions in the Camposanto in Pisa (1468–84; PL. 28). Another Florentine, Francesco Pesellino (1422–57), was very similar in style to Filippo Lippi, with whom he also collaborated in illustrating secular legends on the backs of armchairs and on wooden chests, in pleasing compositions still rooted in the late Gothic tendencies that had been inherited by the Renaissance and nourished especially by 14th-century literary sources, such as Petrarch's *Triumphs* and Boccaccio's *Decameron*. His paintings of sacred themes have a quiet grace that recalls Domenico Veneziano (though the formal aspects are reminiscent of Lippi; VIII, PL. 193); noteworthy examples of his work are the altarpiece of *The Holy Trinity* (London, Nat. Gall.) and a *Madonna and Child with Two Saints* (New York, Met. Mus.).

One of the masters of Florentine painting is Andrea del Castagno, whose art was based in particular on that of Lippi. Especially in frescoes, he created powerful figures disciplined by a skillful design made up of chiaroscuro that gave it substance, in an attempt to attain sculptural effects, and thus linking himself ideally with Masaccio and especially with Donatello. The structural character of his painting is evident even in his early works, such as the ceiling of the Chapel of S. Tarasio in S. Zaccaria in Venice (1442; I, PLS. 234, 235), an important manifestation of Tuscan style in the Veneto that was fully appreciated, however, only at a later time. Andrea's sculpturesque painting (frescoes from Villa Pandolfini; PL. 27; I, PL. 245) turned increasingly to the monumental with a pre-Michelangelesque breadth (*Christ on the Cross with the Virgin and SS. John, Benedict, and Romualdo*; I, PL. 240) and, particularly in his later period, emphasized powerfully dramatic effects (fresco of Niccolò da Tolentino; I, PL. 246) reminiscent of Donatello's later works.

Antonio and Piero del Pollaiuolo — Antonio in particular — continued that straightforward means of expression based on design and chiaroscuro, with an emphasis on harshness, sustained by a nervous line that endows the figures with dynamic power and a dramatic quality. Noteworthy among their works are the paintings depicting the Labors of Hercules (X, PL. 249; XI, PL. 181); the drawings for the embroidered vestments for use in the Baptistery of S. Giovanni, in which a grandeur of composition worthy of murals is achieved within a very limited space; and the altarpieces and portraits (PL. 29), in which the luminist rendering of the subject matter is derived from Domenico Veneziano but is even more emphatically realized.

As a painter, Verrocchio has been linked with both Baldovinetti and Donatello, although — while he was fully aware of their work, especially that of Donatello — he seems to have been affected primarily by various other experiences. His incisive linear quality represents an active, constructive element of form, which does not, however, result in particularly dynamic effects; it appears to be connected to the mellow chiaroscuro displayed by sculptors such as Ghiberti and Desiderio da Settignano, permitting a softening of the outlines and pointing the way for Leonardo's infinitely subtle gradations of light. It is notable that Leonardo has been suggested as author of one angel, part of the figure of the Redeemer, and the poetic background of Verrocchio's altarpiece *The Baptism of Christ* (XIV, PL. 356). Lorenzo di Credi (1459–1537) collaborated on a *Madonna and Child with Saints* in the Donato de' Medici Chapel in Pistoia Cathedral, commissioned from Verrocchio in 1478 and finished in 1485; he assimilated to a limited extent the structural character of Verrocchio's art and Leonardo's atmospheric innovations (VIII, PL. 194). Lorenzo later turned to refinements of a Flemish flavor (Flemish paintings and illuminated codices were extremely well received in Florence) with a technical virtuosity that softened the modeling and, by dwelling on detail, froze the spontaneity of inspiration. This tendency is evident in his *Annunciation* (Uffizi), *Madonna and Child* (Turin, Gall. Sabauda), and in altarpieces such as the *Adoration of the Shepherds* (Uffizi) and the *Baptism of Christ* (Fiesole, S. Domenico).

Even the minor Florentine artists expressed themselves in the new order with fascinating vivacity and clarity. Worthy of mention are Neri di Bicci, of an eclectic style and a good craftsman, and Cosimo Rosselli (1439–1507), presumably Neri's pupil, but superior to him in talent and sensitive to the influence of Baldovinetti and others. As a narrative painter, Rosselli can be placed between Gozzoli and Ghirlandajo; to attract the attention of more superficial observers, he even made use of the gold highlights typical of medieval art, as in his frescoes in the Sistine Chapel in the Vatican, which depict the Last Supper and episodes from the Passion. In the same chapel he produced two other compositions in collaboration with his pupil, Piero di Cosimo, but more in keeping with the simple spirit of Rosselli, who clearly had no intellectual pretensions, are his frescoes in the Chapel of the Miracle (1486) in S. Ambrogio, Florence, an effective rendering of a typical setting enlivened by portraits. Although in the second half of the 15th century Florentine painting was still centered mainly in Florence and part of Tuscany, it had attained such wide renown that when Pope Sixtus IV decided (1481–82) to decorate the chapel he had built in the Vatican, he called three fresco painters from Florence (Rosselli, Sandro Botticelli, and Domenico Ghirlandajo) in order that, in collaboration with Luca Signorelli, also a Tuscan, and with Perugino and Pintoricchio from Umbria, they might paint images of canonized popes and scenes from the Old and New Testament, in accordance with an old, firmly established iconographic tradition.

Well in advance of the other two major arts (architecture and sculpture), it was Florentine painting that spread the stylistic idioms of the Renaissance beyond Florence and Tuscany; in fact, as will be seen below, various schools of painting had already developed all over Italy. But, apparently, at the Pope's court, Florence and Tuscany were deemed to hold artistic supremacy, especially in mural decoration. Ghirlandajo, whose artistic roots are to be found in the work of Baldovinetti and Verrocchio, showed his preference for fresco as a medium even in his earliest work, expressing himself with a limpid clarity (scenes from the life of St. Fina, VI, PL. 179) in a style that was evidently amplified by his study of Masaccio's paintings (e.g., his representation of Christ calling SS. Peter and Andrew; VI, PL. 181). His compositions are vast and in deep perspective, and like Masaccio he filled them with portraits. Back in Florence, Ghirlandajo continued this trend, illustrating cycles of sacred legends and endowing them with a strikingly topical quality in a series of paintings in which the figural technique reflected the contemporary sculptures of Benedetto da Maiano (frescoes in the Sassetti Chapel of Sta Trinita and in the choir of S. Maria Novella; VI, PLS. 180, 182, 184).

Ghirlandajo's style, superficial and formal but quite pleasing in both his murals and panels, was made known through his many assistants and pupils, among them his own brothers Davide and Benedetto, as well as through Bartolommeo di Giovanni, Sebastiano Mainardi, Francesco Granacci, and even Michelangelo (with whom he had so little in common), whose practical father, Lodovico Buonarroti, had apprenticed him to Ghirlandajo. The art of Ghirlandajo was so successful precisely because, despite its superficiality, it was pleasant to look at. The panels painted by the master and by his workshop display considerable grace and elegance, often somewhat affected, combined with an over-refinement of details resulting from the objective Flemish realism with which the artist had come into contact. This is evident in the portraits (PL. 29) and, especially, in the altarpiece depicting the Adoration of the Shepherds in the Sassetti Chapel in Sta Trinita (VI, PLS. 182, 183). Some portions of this altarpiece were derived from the Portinari Altarpiece by Hugo van der Goes (ca. 1475; V, PL. 281), but Ghirlandajo never attained the chromatic transparencies of the Flemish master.

The essential value of the art of Sandro Botticelli, whose temperament was quite the opposite of Ghirlandajo's, is in the artist's interior vision — once considered morbid and decadent — that rises to lyrical heights in his use of the line as a means of expression (PL. 28). In this it is a refinement of Lippi's work, from which it derives. In Botticelli's painting, so solid in the vibrant youthful works inspired by Pollaiuolo and Verrocchio, and especially in the representation of religious subjects enclosed in tondos, the line is measured into regular rhythms; when illustrating the pagan themes that were cherished by the classical culture of Lorenzo de' Medici's circle, it achieves almost musical harmonies (*Pallas Subduing a Centaur*, II, PL. 329; *The Birth of Venus*, II, PL. 323; *Spring*, III, PL. 302). Botticelli revealed the essence of his figural approach in his frescoes in the Sistine Chapel (II, PLS. 326, 331) and for Villa Tornabuoni (Louvre), in which his line achieves effects of dramatic movement and of solemn monumentality. The same is true of the religious panels that were to express during his later period the mystic ardor resulting from the spiritual struggle aroused in him by Savonarola's preaching. In his manifestations of profound religious faith Botticelli reflects in art the crisis that Florence underwent after the death of Lorenzo the Magnificent, a crisis that was not merely historical and political, but also intellectual and artistic; it was, in other words, the crisis of classicism.

Signorelli, Perugino, and Pintoricchio were mentioned above as being among the painters of the Sistine Chapel. In this work they overcame all local and provincial tendencies, identifying themselves with the art of Tuscany, and that of Florence in particular; for this reason they will be considered at this point.

Initially the faithful pupil of Piero della Francesca, Luca Signorelli from Cortona learned from his master the careful organization of space in relation to the figures, which (after a Florentine apprenticeship that included contacts with Pollaiuolo) he endowed with a physical quality that is freely articulated in order to obtain concrete dramatic results (frescoes in the Sanctuary of the Holy House, XIII, PL. 35; *The Realm of Pan*, III, PL. 392). His style included luminist tendencies derived from some familiarity with Flemish painting and with that of the young Leonardo, especially in his easel paintings (Altarpiece of Sant'Onofrio, 1484; Perugia, Mus. dell'Opera del Duomo); his principal aim was to obtain sculptural effects. Since he was essentially a fresco painter, the essence of his style eventually emerged (after intermediate stages marked by his work in the Sistine Chapel and at the Abbey of Monte Oliveto Maggiore; XIII, PL. 35) in the series of mural paintings depicting the Antichrist, the Resurrection of the Body, the Damned, and the Blessed, for the Chapel of S. Brizio in Orvieto Cathedral (1499–1504; IV, PL. 179; VII, PL. 380; XIII, PLS. 36, 37). In these frescoes humanity is variously portrayed in the throes of violent passions, in aspects of great serenity, purified by redemption, or in the tragedy of eternal damnation; here he achieves a representational power of Dantesque awesomeness that was immediately perceived by Michelangelo, whose towering and heroic world seems to have its precedent in Signorelli's work, not only in the Orvieto frescoes but also in the tondo depicting the Holy Family (PL. 34), in which the adaptation of the three solemn figures to the round shape of the panel creates a notably compact figural intensity.

In the Sistine Chapel frescoes illustrating scenes from the life of Moses, Signorelli was assisted by Bartolomeo della Gatta (1448–1502), a fine painter and miniaturist from Florence. Having worked mostly in and around Arezzo, Bartolomeo was eclectic and sensitive to the influence of various painters, especially Piero della Francesca.

Pietro Vannucci, known as Perugino, from Città della Pieve, divorced himself completely from the artistic atmosphere of his native Umbria and turned to Tuscany, where he was a pupil of Piero della Francesca, whose poetic feeling for space influenced him and became fundamental in Perugino's compositions, with their broadly conceived perspective depth (PL. 34). These works were enriched by a Florentine graphic sense derived from Verrocchio, whose refined moderation Perugino approached in the small paintings with scenes from the life of St. Bernardino of Siena on the cupboard in which the saint's standard was stored in the Oratory of S. Bernardino in Perugia (1473; VIII, PL. 190). His achievement in the depiction of space in frescoes (*Christ Giving the Keys to St. Peter*, 1481–82, Sistine Chapel; XI, PL. 113; *Crucifixion*, 1493–96, Florence, S. Maria Maddalena dei Pazzi) can also be seen in Perugino's altarpieces (*Lamentation over the Dead Christ*, 1495, Pitti; *Madonna and Saints*, 1497, Fano, S. Maria Nuova), in which it is combined with a mellow chromatic impasto that can be found also in his portraits and in some of his secular paintings. Later the artist seemed to renounce his past achievements, placing his figures in the foreground and reverting to a medieval vision (altarpiece from the abbey at Vallombrosa; Florence, Uffizi). His painting, with its wistfully pathetic attitudes, was widely accepted and imitated not only in his native Umbria, in Latium, and Tuscany but also in northern Italy (e.g., by Galeazzo Campi in Cremona and Marco Meloni in Carpi).

Perugino inspired the style of Bernardino Pintoricchio (1454–1516), a skillful fresco painter who enlivened his compositions with clear, vivid colors and occasionally enriched them, as in the Borgia Apartments in the Vatican (1491–94; PL. 34), with gilded stuccoes. Since his youth, when he collaborated with his master Perugino in the scenes from the life of St. Bernardino, he had showed his chromatic preferences, combining them with fragile, delicate forms, which can best be seen in his small panels and in a polytych in the Lombard style, the *Madonna and Child Enthroned with the Young St. John* (1495; Perugia, Gall. Naz. dell'Umbria). But he never equaled Perugino's spatial sense in those large compositions rich in perspective canon, in which the figures appear in the foreground. Examples are the fresco cycle in the Bufalini Chapel in S. Maria in Aracoeli in Rome and the one with scenes from the life of the Virgin (1501) in the Baglioni Chapel in S. Maria Maggiore, Spello, in addition to the frescoes in the Vatican. Only in the series of scenes from the life of Pius II (1503–08) in the Piccolomini Library in Siena, which are organically conceived

within an arcaded architectural order, did he attain some spatial effects while retaining the illustrative character of the work, expressing himself gaily and fluently in a manner far removed from the solemnly historical approach of Mantegna.

Both Pintoricchio and Perugino were surrounded by many pupils and assistants, who were, with the exception of Raphael, inferior to them in talent. Among the many minor figures, Giovanni di Pietro, known as Lo Spagna (ca. 1450–1528), is noteworthy for his solid, wholesome painting, often enlivened in the frescoes by chromatic refinements. Although his painting revealed a knowledge of the art of the young Raphael, it remained essentially faithful to the taste of the early Renaissance (e.g., works in the Church of the Madonna delle Lacrime, Trevi, 1520, and in S. Giacomo, Spoleto, 1526–27).

To return to the Florentines, Filippino Lippi, a pupil of Botticelli, who is often mistaken in his very delicate youthful works for the master himself, reflected his master's linear style but proceeded toward a creative independence, that is, toward a liveliness and affinities with the warm, deep colors of the Flemish school as well as with Ghirlandajo, Piero della Francesca, and, later, Pintoricchio. The many individualistic aspects of his emotional and impulsive temperament are less evident in his panels than in his frescoes in the Brancacci Chapel in S. Maria del Carmine, Florence; in the Carafa Chapel of S. Maria sopra Minerva, Rome (PL. 29; IX, PLS. 148, 150); and in the Strozzi Chapel in S. Maria Novella, Florence (IX, PLS. 147, 148), in which he revealed an ever-increasing intensity in his interpretation of antiquity.

Piero di Cosimo (1462–1521) expressed himself with equal imaginative freedom, making himself artistically independent of his mediocre teacher Cosimo Rosselli at a very early period, even while collaborating with the latter on frescoes in the Sistine Chapel (*Pharaoh's Destruction in the Red Sea*). His contacts with Verrocchio are evident, and the vigor of his color reveals the influences of the young Leonardo and of Flemish art as well as those of Signorelli and Pintoricchio, whom he had met in Rome. However, Piero was not a fresco painter by choice; he preferred easel paintings, in which his imaginative talent is preserved. Although he did enliven his altarpieces with pictorial episodes of great spontaneity, in his portraits he detached himself with remarkable restraint from the superficially realistic interpretations of Ghirlandajo, as in portraits of Francesco Giamberti and of Giuliano da Sangallo (both Amsterdam, Rijksmus.), giving them an idealized tone instead, as in the portrait of Simonetta Vespucci (PL. 29). But the best of his art is to be found in those pagan works against which Girolamo Savonarola thundered at the time. Boccaccio's tales, the Old Testament, and Roman history, highly fashionable themes in Florentine paintings of the period, were replaced by Piero di Cosimo with mythological subjects (VIII, PL. 194) as a result of his orientation toward the classical. The artist displayed his poetic imagination in decorating panels for furniture of more limited dimensions, as in the panel illustrating the legend of Prometheus (Strasbourg, Mus. B.A.; Munich, Alte Pin.), in which Leonardo's influence is evident, and in an earlier series of small panels representing aspects of primeval life (*Return from the Hunt*, Met. Mus.; *A Forest Fire*, Oxford, Ashmolean Mus.; *The Fight Between the Lapiths and the Centaurs*, VIII, PL. 211). These were conceived in a tormented, obsessed fantasy reminiscent of the northern world and closer in inspiration to German than to Flemish art. One of Piero's undoubted masterpieces is the *Death of Procris* (London, Nat. Gall.), which depicts the tale with a sorrowfulness accentuated by the gloominess of the lagoon near which Cephalus's bride is killed by a fatal error. In the restlessness that characterized the early 16th century the best of Florence's young artists were to be attracted and stimulated by this eccentric and imaginative artist who was such an original interpreter of the Renaissance, which in Florence was always applied with intelligent freedom.

To complete the Florentine artistic milieu of the early Renaissance, some minor personalities must be discussed. Pier Francesco Fiorentino (1470–1500), following the example of Gozzoli and Baldovinetti, strove to achieve effects of wood inlay in his paintings, executed mainly in San Gimignano (*Ma-

donna and Child with Saints, 1494, in S. Agostino) and in other localities in the Val d'Elsa. Similar but somewhat superior, Jacopo del Sellaio (1441/1442–93) imitated Filippo Lippi's compositional style, repeating Lippi's preferred subjects. Although his original inspiration came from Lippi, Jacopo was sensitive to the most varied influences, up to his late, convulsive *Crucifixion with Saints* in the Church of S. Frediano in Cestello at Florence, a work that was inspired mainly by Botticelli. Both Francesco Botticini (1446–98), whose assurance in rendering forms was based on Andrea del Castagno (altarpiece with St. Monica and her companions, 1483, in Sto Spirito, Florence) and, later, Rosselli, approached Verrocchio's compactness and Botticelli's modulations of line (e.g., *Annunciation*, predella of the polyptych *Tabernacle of the Most Holy Sacrament*, 1489–91; Empoli, Gall. della Collegiata). Raffaellino del Garbo (1466–1524?) belonged to the circle of Botticelli and Filippino Lippi, but he had something of the manner of Ghirlandajo; he represents, with Raffaello de' Carli (b. 1470; who was influenced also by Lorenzo di Credi), the progress of the early Renaissance into the 16th century.

Outside Florence, the new style had been affirmed in painting as early as the 1440s in Siena — that is to say, in the only Tuscan center in which a late Gothic school of painting continued to be very active. Siena felt the renewal that had taken place, especially since during the third decade of the century Ghiberti and Donatello had wholeheartedly collaborated with Sienese artists on the baptismal font of the Church of S. Giovanni. And while two Gothic artists, Sassetta and Giovanni di Paolo (see above), were keenly interested in Paolo Uccello's geometric solutions, a young and spirited Sienese painter, Domenico di Bartolo (1400–45), displayed a Florentine spirit in his *Madonna and Child with Angels* (PL. 31), which is signed and dated 1433. In his complete and coherent composition Domenico created a sense of space by means of the relationship of the figures, accentuating in it the halo in perspective above the Virgin; he also drew close to Lippi in his clear, luminous colors. A year later, when executing a figure of the emperor Sigismund framed in an edicule, which was to be carried out in marble inlay for the Cathedral, he rigorously applied the norms of central perspective. Also because of the Florentine influence, his Madonnas acquired formal breadth (e.g., *Virgin and Child*, 1437; Philadelphia, Mus. of Art, Johnson Coll.), as did the series of frescoes (1443–44) in the so-called "Pellegrinaggio" of the Hospital of S. Maria della Scala, which depicts works of mercy and scenes from the history of the hospital (VIII, PL. 202). In these works breadth was combined with a precise and firm design, an insistent attention to detail that echoes the Gothic style (and Pisanello in particular), and a skillful treatment of perspective, which, however, was used in a purely decorative sense far removed from the solid figural and spatial achievements of the Florentines. This was the conclusion of the earliest and most memorable Renaissance period in Sienese painting.

Il Vecchietta, mentioned earlier as a follower of Donatello, strove for sculptural effects as a painter, thus tending away from Sassetta, from whom he derived his earliest style. About 1435, as part of Masolino's group, he went to Castiglione Olona to fresco the walls of the apsidal chapel of the Collegiata, together with the Florentine Paolo Schiavo. Il Vecchietta, who was experimenting with foreshortening and whose style was heavy with classicizing erudition in the fresco *Ladder of Paradise* (1441) in the Pellegrinaggio of the Hospital of S. Maria della Scala in Siena, evolved complicated one-point perspectives in his frescoes there in the Sala di San Pietro (1448), however without attaining in painting the coherence that he displayed in sculpture. Many of his other works show a gradual return to Gothic elements, as is clearly evident in an altarpiece in Pienza Cathedral depicting an Assumption of the Virgin (1461), which is irrational in its proportions and in the empirical distribution of the figures in space. Other Sienese painters favored dreamy, idealized images; this was true even of the greatest of them, Matteo di Giovanni (1435–95) from Sansepolcro. Influenced by Il Vecchietta (rather than by Domenico di Bartolo, as has often been maintained), his sharp chiaroscuro contrasts were aimed at achieving sculptural effects, as in the figures of SS.

Peter and Paul in panels from a triptych (Sansepolcro, Pin. Com.) that he executed in his youth. In his later period he toned down certain contrasts in the evocative images of many devotional paintings and altarpieces, but he often retained ornamental richness in the garments (the altarpiece *St. Barbara Enthroned*, 1479, S. Domenico, Siena), typical of 14th-century Sienese taste. Matteo di Giovanni drew his inspiration from the Florentines, and from Pollaiuolo in particular, in his violent renderings of the *Slaughter of the Innocents* (1481, Siena, S. Agostino; 1488, Naples, Mus. di Capodimonte; 1491, Siena, S. Maria dei Servi, PL. 31). The most spectacular interpretation of this subject, one imbued with classical elements, is that conceived for a large marble inlay in Siena Cathedral. Yet, even though he constantly attempted to achieve a more intense expression by straining the features of his figures realistically, their volumes are realized only superficially (VIII, PL. 202).

Of all the Sienese artists, Neroccio de' Landi (1447–1500) was the most firmly tied to the past in his use of line for stylizations ingenuously aiming at a greater spirituality (PL. 31); however, in an altarpiece of the Nativity (1475; Siena, Pin.), his rosy chiaroscuro acquired emphasis as a result of his collaboration with Francesco di Giorgio (X, PL. 84), who was certainly more concrete in his approach, though, like Il Vecchietta, he was somewhat incoherent as a painter and was imbued with Florentine influences that range from Pollaiuolo to Botticelli, and are often almost too obvious (*Nativity*, 1467, S. Domenico, Siena; *Coronation of the Virgin*, 1472, Siena, Pin.).

Other minor painters, such as Benvenuto di Giovanni and Girolamo di Benvenuto, tended toward a rendering of volume reminiscent of wood sculpture and derived from Il Vecchietta; this quality was brought up to date in Girolamo through the influence of Mantegna. This influence is evident also in some other painters and was probably assimilated through Girolamo da Cremona, an illuminator and painter who worked in Siena with Liberale da Verona in the 1580s, particularly on illuminations for the Cathedral's gradual (X, PL. 84). Of Pietro di Domenico and Guidoccio Cozzarelli, two more Sienese artists, the former was more eclectic in his limited activity, while the latter merely imitated his master Matteo di Giovanni faithfully and modestly. Giacomo Pacchiarotto (1474–1540) also followed Matteo's style at first, but he later drew closer to painters such as Perugino, who like Pintoricchio had worked in Siena, and Bernardino Fungai (1460–1516), whose style was derived from Perugino and also from Luca Signorelli, who worked in and around Siena.

Some painters felt only the superficial values of the new art, and certainly none of the moral ones, in their abundant production for individual patrons and for the churches of the widespread Sienese area. This production consisted almost exclusively in religious subjects, with the exception of some portraits, some painted wooden chests, and the panels (now dispersed) from the Palazzo del Magnifico in Siena. The panels portray famous figures of the past and allegorical compositions and represent practically the only trace of an early Renaissance Humanist culture in Siena. These artists still considered themselves, as they explained in their breve, or statement of purpose (G. Milanesi, *Documenti per la Storia dell'Arte Senese*, Siena, 1854), "revealers to gross men who know naught of letters, of things miraculous by virtue of the holy faith." Although in 15th-century Siena there were many men who were not "gross" and who did know of "letters" — Pius II, Lelio Sozzini, and others — nevertheless, the majority of the people were still linked to the medieval past, influenced by the preaching of the mystic St. Bernardino, who left a profound mark on Siena and who often appears in Sienese paintings as a symbol of faith, together with St. Catherine of Siena.

In following the development of art outside Tuscany, Filippo Lippi was mentioned as being in Padua in 1434, Andrea del Castagno in Venice in 1442, and Donatello in Padua from the end of 1444 to 1452, a period during which Paolo Uccello was also working there (he had been in Venice in 1425 and later, leaving some traces but without having had any immediate influence). These artists were the decisive proponents of Renaissance culture in Padua in reference to painting; this culture took shape in the fourth and fifth decades of the century, toward the end of which was to emerge Mantegna's outstanding personality. Admired above all were Lippi's massive figures, his light colors and orange skin tones, and his vitality; Andrea del Castagno's assured forms; Paolo Uccello's perspective and geometric treatment; and Donatello's solid sculptural material and neat linearity, though not the functional value of his dramatic line or the minute contrast of lights and shadows. New artists worked in close association with the by-then mature Francesco Squarcione (1394–1468), a strange and controversial man, tailor and painter, avid collector of paintings and especially of casts of ancient statues that were intended to serve as models for the many youths he wished to direct toward art, but, as a painter, completely lacking in consistent personality of his own. In fact, his polyptych with St. Jerome and other saints (VIII, PL. 197) is a forced experiment in Gothicism, close to the style of Dello Delli, and it recalls Lippi only chromatically. His signed *Madonna and Child* (PL. 32), which has an exceptionally fresh approach, reveals in the figure of the child an *élan* reminiscent of Donatello, perhaps absorbed indirectly through a similar composition by Filippo Lippi. The monochrome compositions in the portico next to S. Francesco in Padua (1452–60) seem to follow outmoded Florentine schemes. This unevenness indicates that he could not have been a very effective teacher. However, he inspired young artists, instilling in them an interest in the casts that he collected; for example, Andrea Mantegna might not have identified so wholeheartedly with his heroic world without that stimulus which moved him to sculptural interpretations. In fact, Mantegna, who was so prodigiously precocious that at eighteen years of age (1449), together with Nicolò Pizzolo (1421–53), he executed the first scenes and the vault decoration in the Ovetari Chapel of the Church of the Eremitani in Padua and had greatly admired Donatello's passionate art, nevertheless found a restraining element in the study of antiquity and took classical sculpture as a source of inspiration for his own work in that field. Mantegna also treasured the pictorial experience of the Tuscans: in connection with the monumental compositions in deep perspective of series of his later scenes from the lives of SS. James and Christopher (PL. 140; IX, PL. 324), the name of Piero della Francesca, who had worked in Ferrara about 1448, should be added to those of the Florentine artists mentioned above. Only Piero's monumentality, not his colors, were assimilated by Mantegna, whose aim was to give his figural compositions sculptural form through a strong graphic sense and use of chiaroscuro, conferring on them the heroic tone of ancient myths.

It is precisely this heroic tone that makes Mantegna's compositions valid as history, in accordance with the Humanist concept of rhetoric (cf. Leonardo Bruni, Poggio Bracciolini) that was inspired by Cicero, who had declared history to be the task of the orator. The paintings of the Camera degli Sposi in the Palazzo Ducale, Mantua, acquired a historical value (X, PL. 487), just as *The Triumph of Caesar* at Hampton Court (PL. 32; VII, PL. 268) constituted a romantically heroic interpretation of the Roman world and its *res gestae*, or military exploits; the task was facilitated by the fact that Gian Francesco Gonzaga had excelled in matters of warfare. A high ideal of faith was expressed in Mantegna's religious paintings, especially in the harshly portrayed *Dead Christ* in the Brera (IX, PL. 321).

In Padua, Ansuino da Forlì and Nicolò Pizzolo, who had frescoed the chapel of the Palazzo del Podestà (presently Palazzo Municipale), to which Lippi had contributed previously, were reminiscent of Lippi in their paintings in the Ovetari Chapel. Pizzolo's style, though very similar to that of Mantegna, is recognizable in the figure of God and in what little is left of the figure of St. James on the vault; Ansuino's hand is evident in a scene from the life of St. Christopher. Lippi's influence appears not only in the orange-hued complexions but also in the formal rhythms; the naturalistic festoons and vivacious putti were derived from Donatello. Such a similarity is also noticeable in Squarcione's pupils. Dario di Giovanni, author of the attractive *Madonna with Child and Saints* in the Church of S. Francesco in Schio, had a rather weak style as compared to that of Giorgio Schiavone as evidenced in the *Madonna and*

Child in Turin (PL. 33), with ornamental elements reminiscent of Lippi and a sharpness of line that recalls Donatello. Two of Schiavone's panels in Padua Cathedral follow the same lines, while softened aspects can be seen in his *Madonna and Child* in London (Nat. Gall.). Among the young artists of Squarcione's circle, Marco Zoppo (1433–78) sought to achieve metallic effects in an interpretation that presents some analogies with those of Cosmé Tura because both drew from the same Paduan sources and attempted to realize in their painting the hardness of minerals. This is more evident in Zoppo's *Dead Christ* (PL. 33) than in the noble triptych in the Collegio di Spagna in Bologna (VIII, PL. 197).

Padua attracted other minor artists who, often wavering between different styles, were influenced above all by the clearcut formal values that had emerged there as a result of Tuscan influence (though with a marked stylistic break). Among the names registered in the *fraglia* (guild) of painters in Padua is that of Giovanni Francesco da Rimini (d. before 1470), a wandering artist whose works appeared in Bologna and Umbria and who was influenced by a painter registered in the same guild, Girolamo di Giovanni da Camerino (documented 1449–90; VIII, PL. 203), who was later influenced by the styles of Piero della Francesca and Crivelli. Giovanni Boccati (active 1445–80; PL. 30), also of Camerino, was another guild member; he worked in his native region and in Perugia and came into indirect contact with the Tuscans and with Piero della Francesca. The two painters from Camerino had been preceded in the Marches by the Gothic Venetians, authors of elaborate polyptychs to which the local taste had remained attached. Like Giovanni Boccati, Girolamo di Giovanni also made his way into Umbria; his large polyptych from S. Francesco in Gualdo Tadino (Brera) and Boccati's polyptych in Belforte del Chienti are notable. It is understandable that some Paduan influence should have flowed indirectly into the work of Matteo da Gualdo (d. 1503), an Umbrian by assimilation, whose style was partly descended from the late Gothic style of Bartolomeo di Tommaso. This provincial art was in a local idiom but, despite its limitations, had the charm of sincerity and freshness.

In Padua, Antonio Vivarini from Murano (documented 1440–76) had been commissioned in 1449, together with Giovanni d'Alemagna (of Germany), to paint half of the Ovetari Chapel. Although the work of both collaborators was based on the late Gothic style, the Italian artist expressed himself with a soft, naïve innocence that had its origins in Masolino and contrasted with the German's persistent thorniness (polyptychs in S. Zaccaria in Venice). However, they completed the decoration of only four sections of the crossing vault (Giovanni died in 1450); theirs was a visible effort to adapt their art to the perspective innovations of the Renaissance and to Donatello's ornamental style, but it was marred by a discursive narrative and clumsy forms that lack a structural quality. Fortunately, Vivarini returned to the execution of sumptuous polyptychs, among them one in Bologna (1450; Pin. Naz.) painted in collaboration with his brother Bartolomeo (documented 1450–99). The latter had a clear vision of form, influenced by Mantegna and also, in its chromatic sensitivity, by Giovanni Bellini (VIII, PL. 197). The works of the two Vivarini brothers can be found in the Marches and even in Puglia (polyptychs by Antonio in the Church of the Assunta in Polignano a Mare and in S. Maria della Colonna in Rutigliano; altarpieces by Bartolomeo in Lecce, Mus. Prov., and in Bari Cathedral, 1476). Their works are also found in Lucania (panels with the Madonna and Child with saints by Bartolomeo in S. Francesco in Matera) and in Calabria (polyptych, also by Bartolomeo, 1477, in S. Bernardino in Morano Calabro).

Carlo Crivelli (ca. 1438–ca. 1495) was also trained in Padua but settled in the Marches in 1468. His painting, which continued the sumptuousness of the Byzantine and Venetian Gothic styles, dominated in the Marches; he emphasized the ornamental quality of the garments of saints and Madonnas by a lavish use of gold (reminiscent of the glowing work of the Lombard miniaturist Luchino Belbello of Pavia) in compositions abounding in festoons of fruit. But even in this decorative magnificence Crivelli showed an expressive power. His sorrowful Redeemers and his dramatic renderings of the Pietà, executed with a strong graphic sense, are clearly inspired by Donatello. Crivelli imparted an aristocratic grace to his Madonnas (*Madonna della Candeletta*; Brera) and a refined elegance to his stylized knights (PL. 42; *St. George*, Boston, Isabella Stewart Gardner Mus.), which he alternated with gruff saints. The artist created a mythical world of fantastic creatures (IV, PL. 170) for the panels of his polyptychs, with their splendid decoration — for example, that in Ascoli Cathedral (1473) and that from S. Domenico in Camerino (1482; Brera). The panel depicting the Annunciation (1486; London, Nat. Gall.), which is overloaded with aulic details, is an exception, as is the panel with the Coronation of the Virgin (1493; Brera), which has the dark tones of Cordoban leather. Crivelli, who followed an almost unvaried stylistic course, had a talented pupil in Pietro Alamanno (active 1466–98), who was more sensitive to color and more inclined to use refined aulic forms (*Madonna with Saints*; Collegiata, Cupra Marittima). Alamanno's work had a certain affinity with that of Andrea Delitio, whose decoration of the main chapel of Atri Cathedral shows the influence of artists from Umbria, the Marches, and southern Italy. Antonio da Fabriano (active 1450–85) is outstanding among the artists from the Marches; he combined some Tuscan accents (crucifix, 1452; Matelica, Piersanti Mus.) with elements derived from German and Flemish art. Francesco di Gentile (second half of 15th cent.), whose style was based on Antonio's, was also indebted to the Umbrians and to Crivelli (*Madonna with Two Saints*; Matelica, S. Francesco). Finally, Lorenzo d'Alessandro da San Severino (documented 1468–1503), who was perhaps a pupil of Girolamo di Giovanni, felt the influence of Crivelli and also that of the Umbrians, particularly Niccolò di Liberatore (see below).

The first phase of Renaissance painting was characterized in the Italian provinces by the use of harsh forms aimed primarily at achieving sculptural effects; and it was in the provinces that Paduan forms met with those evolved in Florence. In Montefalco, in Umbria, the rather wooden frescoes by Benozzo Gozzoli (completed 1452; Church of S. Francesco) eventually created an impetus in painting in Foligno, where Niccolò di Liberatore (da Foligno), also known as Niccolò Alunno (1430–1502) assimilated Gozzoli's influence in his earlier works, in which he used a dissonant, rather garish color scheme; he was later to draw away from this influence in favor of an insistent characterization and a decorative tendency that relates him to the Venetian painters, especially Crivelli. And it was Crivelli whom he imitated in his monumental polyptychs (PL. 30; *Madonna and Child with Saints*, 1471; Gualdo Tadino, Pin. Com.). His art was well received and spread to the Marches (*Madonna and Child with Saints*, polyptych, 1468; San Severino Marche, Pin. Com.; panels from a polyptych; Sarnano, S. Maria di Piazza). Instead, the mediocre production of Pierantonio Mezzastris (1430–1506) was limited to Foligno; Gozzoli's influence predominates in his work, and his style is similar to Alunno's.

Gozzoli's influence was felt also in Perugia by Bartolomeo Caporali (1420?–1505?), a painter and miniaturist whose rather heavy early style (*Madonna with Angels*; Perugia, Gall. Naz. dell'Umbria) later achieved greater fluency — after a period spent in Florence — under the influence of Baldovinetti (standard representing the Madonna of Mercy, 1482; Montone, Church of S. Francesco). His style was modified in his old age by echoes of Ghirlandajo (who worked in Umbria) and of Pintoricchio (frescoes, 1488; Montelabbate, Church of S. Maria). A more consistent and loftier artist was Benedetto Bonfigli (documented 1445–96), a collaborator of Caporali; while producing ornamental linear stylizations in the Gothic spirit, he carefully observed the style of Domenico di Bartolo (who painted a polyptych with the Madonna and saints in S. Giuliana in Perugia in 1438; presently Gall. Naz. dell'Umbria), of Angelico (also active in Perugia about that time), and of Gozzoli. He painted tranquil figures and Madonnas with delicate little angels (PL. 31) and, above all, banners with devotional images (banner of St. Bernardino, 1465; Perugia, Gall. Naz. dell'Umbria; cf. IV, PL. 209). Later, in the chapel formerly in the

Palazzo dei Priori (begun 1464; Perugia, Gall. Naz. dell'Umbria), he revealed his talent as a spontaneous and lucid narrator comparable to the more expert Carpaccio in his depictions of Perugia (his home town) in frescoes illustrating scenes from the lives of St. Louis of Toulouse and of St. Herculanus (VIII, PL. 203). This series is reminiscent of Lippi, who was to fresco the apse of Spoleto Cathedral (unfinished because of his death in 1469).

Fiorenzo di Lorenzo (1440–1522) was accorded an undeserved esteem during the 19th century as a result of the erroneous attribution to him of eight panels illustrating scenes from the life of St. Bernardino (VIII, PL. 190); these panels were the doors of the cabinet in which Bonfigli's standard was stored (see above). The scenes, probably conceived by Perugino, were executed by Perugino himself, Pintoricchio, and some minor Umbrian artists, among whom may have been Fiorenzo. This eclectic painter appears to have favored sharp forms that recall Niccolò Alunno and Bartolomeo Vivarini (VIII, PL. 203), strengthened by an indirect Mantegnesque influence (a *Madonna and Child* by Girolamo da Cremona, Perugia, Gall. Naz. dell'Umbria, seems to have influenced Fiorenzo), which were later subdued and softened by contacts with Pintoricchio and other artists (*Madonna and Saints*, polyptych; Perugia, Gall. Naz. dell'Umbria).

In northern Italy, Padua, where Renaissance art had been fostered by the above-mentioned group of Tuscans, gave impetus to the artistic activity of Cosmè Tura, the initiator and animator of early Renaissance painting in Ferrara. In fact, soon after the middle of the 15th century Bono da Ferrara collaborated with Mantegna and Ansuino da Forlì in decorating the Ovetari Chapel of the Church of the Eremitani in Padua with a fresco illustrating a scene from the life of St. Christopher (PL. 33). According to available documents, Bono painted for the Este family at Belfiore and at Casaglia between 1450 and 1452, with the collaboration of another Ferrarese artist, Galasso di Matteo Piva. Vasari states that Bono was inspired by the art of Piero della Francesca, whom he emulated in his compositions in Padua, in the monumentality and form of his figures and in the breadth of his hilly landscapes — that is, in the predominant characteristics of Florentine art. Bono's familiarity with Galasso tends to support the hypothesis that the *Allegory of Autumn* (PL. 33), so strongly reminiscent of Piero della Francesca, and a painting of two muses (Budapest, Mus. of Fine Arts) may well be ascribed to Galasso.

The work of Piero della Francesca in Ferrara (lost frescoes in S. Agostino and the Castello Estense) had a decisive influence on Ferrarese painters. After Piero, the Este family brought Mantegna and Rogier van der Weyden to Ferrara, where their influences were felt by Cosmè Tura about 1450; above all, in Padua, Tura developed a boundless admiration for Donatello, and became obsessed by the desire to give his painted figures the quality of bronze or marble. His tortured figures are often marked by suffering or dramatic passion and tend toward expressionism with a forceful exuberance that is typical of Emilia. From his youthful *Pietà* (PL. 36) to the organ doors from Ferrara Cathedral (XIV, PLS. 202, 203, 208), to the surviving fragments of the Roverella Altarpiece (XIV, PLS. 204–207) up to the *St. Anthony* (Modena, Gall. Estense), his style is always wholly committed and, except for a few fleeting echoes of Giovanni Bellini, is always consistent and faithful to his personal outlook. A substantial stylistic echo of this exceptional master, who became court painter to the Este family, can be found in the series of frescoes in the Palazzo Schifanoia (ca. 1469); hence the hypothesis that Cosmè Tura may have conceived their general outline.

Also active at Schifanoia was the second of the great Ferrarese artists, Francesco del Cossa, who in his representation of three months (*March, April, May*; PL. 37; IV, PLS. 1, 2, 3, 5) surpassed Tura's minor followers, such as the anonymous so-called "master of the wide-open eyes" (Longhi, *Officina ferrarese*, 1956), including the illustrators of the Bible of Borso d'Este (1455–61; X, PL. 83), the principal achievement of Italian illumination in the 15th century. Cossa was influenced by Cosmè Tura and by Piero della Francesca, whose solemn monumentality he sought to reproduce, as in the canvas commissioned for the Foro dei Mercanti (1474; Bologna, Pin. Naz.). He also felt the influence of the forms of Andrea del Castagno and Mantegna. However, his art has an individual, original quality in its harsh compositions and imaginative landscapes, which were attuned to the heavy Emilian rustic style. Cossa's work was echoed in a minor key by Leonardo Scaletti and with monumental vigor by the Modenese Bartolomeo Bonascia (*Pietà*; Modena, Gall. Estense). Paolo di San Leocadio from Reggio also followed Cossa's style at the beginning of his artistic activity, before he came to favor the Flemish style while working in Spain (*Madonna with a Knight of Montesa*; Prado). Other minor artists, especially in Bologna, were sensitive to Cossa's influence; among them was Baldassare d'Este, who painted in a somewhat more contemporary style (portrait of Borso d'Este; Venice, Coll. Cini).

Ercole de' Roberti was also close to Cosmè Tura in his *September* in the Palazzo Schifanoia, though he later drew closer to Cossa, whose composed monumentality he admired (PL. 37). Roberti was a man of restless temperament who was also open to influences from the Veneto. His emotional range went from lofty classical forms (altarpiece from S. Maria in Porto; PL. 156) to bursts of dramatic expression (predella in Dresden, Gemäldegalerie; and frescoes, known through fragments and copies, in Bologna Cathedral) always sustained by his brilliant poetic inspiration, which was manifested also in some poetic landscapes.

Similar to Cossa, to Ercole de' Roberti, and even to Marco Zoppo, in a style that combined outmoded elements and innovations, were Agnolo (1448–82) and Bartolomeo degli Erri (active ca. 1460) from Modena (*Coronation of the Virgin*, polyptych by Agnolo; Modena, Gall. Estense). Bartolomeo is outstanding for the terse quality of his narrative (in three altarpieces with scenes from the lives of St. Dominic, St. Vincent Ferrer, and St. Thomas Aquinas; formerly Modena, S. Pietro); he continued, in a new, restrained manner, the tradition of the fluently descriptive, spirited artists of the Gothic period in Emilia, starting with Niccolò da Bologna.

In Ferrara painting was later represented by Lorenzo Costa the Elder (1460–1535), who, having settled in Bologna in 1483, established there, after Cossa and Roberti, the robust forms of the Ferrarese school (*Madonna and Child*, 1488; PL. 38), with colors that became particularly vivid because of his contacts with Antonello da Messina and painters from the Veneto, as in his portrait of Giovanni II Bentivoglio, and his *St. Sebastian* reminiscent of Roberti (both Uffizi), and in monumental altarpieces in S. Petronio (1492) and S. Giovanni in Monte (1497), both in Bologna. Then, under the influence of the Bolognese Francesco Francia (1450–1517), Costa's painting became softer; its monumentality gave way to greater refinement as in the *Coronation of the Virgin* (1501; Bologna, S. Giovanni in Monte), two scenes from the life of St. Cecilia (VIII, PL. 201), and two paintings illustrating the court of Isabella d'Este (VIII, PL. 201) and the realm of the god Comus, inserted into silent landscapes; these works, together with paintings by Perugino and Mantegna, formerly decorated the *studiolo* of Isabella d'Este in Mantua. And it was in Mantua that Lorenzo Leombruno (1489–1517?) followed the path marked by Mantegna, Perugino, and Costa. Leombruno, a painter of frescoes as well as easel pictures, was to become Giulio Romano's collaborator.

In connection with Costa's more advanced period other minor artists should be mentioned, among them, Giovanni Chiodarolo of Bologna, whose decoration of the Oratory of St. Cecilia recalls Costa. Francesco de' Bianchi-Ferrari (1460–1510) of Modena in his later period softened his hard, wooden figures, which are reminiscent of Roberti and of German prints; he also showed some affinity to Gian Francesco de' Maineri (documented 1489–1504) from Parma, where Alessandro Araldi (1460–1528) also worked. Michele Coltellini (1480–1535/42) and Domenico Panetti (1460–1513) were active in Ferrara. The Bolognese Francesco (Raibolini) Francia (ca. 1450–1517), who started out as a goldsmith and drew his inspiration from Cossa and Roberti while remaining on an artistically inferior level, enlivened his work with a warm chromatic

brilliancy derived from the painters of the Veneto (*S. Stefano*; Rome, Gall. Borghese). Of a contemplative temperament, Francia favored languid forms in restrained compositions; moreover, he revealed an awareness of Perugino's work (altarpiece with the Madonna, saints, and donor; Bologna, Pin. Naz.) and on occasion produced overelaborate compositions (panel in S. Giacomo Maggiore; PL. 38).

Some variations in form and color in Francia's abundant production brought him closer to Costa with whom he worked in 1506 on the Oratory of St. Cecilia (VIII, PL. 201), and to the painters from Romagna in altarpieces executed by him not only in Emilia and Romagna but also in Tuscany (*Immaculate Conception*; Lucca, S. Frediano). However, his art was more effective in intimate paintings such as the *Madonna and Child in a Rose Garden* (IX, PL. 12), which reveals his simple and tranquil spirit.

Francia has an unusually numerous following (documents mention as many as two hundred pupils); however, his style was continued almost exclusively by his son Giacomo Raibolini. Of his many disciples, Timoteo Viti of Urbino (1469–1523), whose early training with Francia led him to repeat some of his master's compositional schemes, is distinguished from Francia by the luminosity of his colors, which were the result of the influence of Raphael (PL. 38). Only slight traces of Francia's style were continued in Bologna by Simone Spada (1482–1546) and in the work of two other painters who worked with Francia, Costa, and Chiodarolo on the Oratory of St. Cecilia: Cesare Tamaroccio (d. 1506) and Amico Aspertini (1475–1552), both of whom derived their style from the Tuscans (especially Filippino Lippi) and the Umbrians (especially Pintoricchio). A restless man, whose often overstated painting lacked a sense of balance, Aspertini left his mark in central Italy (Lucca, S. Frediano, frescoes in the Chapel of St. Augustine, 1508–09). Another Bolognese, Jacopo Ripanda (1490–1530) studied classical art, which he emulated with overwhelming erudition in his frescoes of scenes from Roman history in the Sala delle Guerre Puniche and the Sala della Lupa in the Palazzo dei Conservatori, Rome.

The Bolognese Antonio Pirri (d. 1511), creator of elegantly slender figures (*Visitation*; Milan, Mus. Poldi Pezzoli), who was in Naples in 1511, along with Ripanda represents an artistic variation that in some aspects is similar to the style of Francesco (ca. 1470–1531) and Bernardino Zaganelli of Cotignola in Romagna, whose art is in fact more complex and seems to be derived from that of Marco Palmezzano and enriched by Ferrarese and Bolognese influences. Of the two, Francesco attained much broader forms inspired by German engravings. The Zaganellis were followed by their compatriot Girolamo Marchesi (d. ca. 1550), who was later to produce affected imitations of Francia and Raphael. The figural force of Tuscan and Paduan art, by then weakened and adulterated, was, however, still strong in Melozzo da Forlì (1438–94), a pupil of Piero della Francesca, whose perspective he applied and developed, retaining his master's monumentality and luminosity but contributing a more human quality in his fleshy and occasionally rhetorical figures, which reveal contacts with the Paduan and Ferrarese schools. He executed two paintings in S. Marco in Rome (a three-quarter view of St. John the Evangelist and a frontal portrayal of St. Mark, lack the broad, expanded quality he was later to display); his *Annunciation* in the Pantheon shows vivid chromatic resemblances to Piero della Francesca. The fresco commemorating the inauguration of the Vatican Library (VII, PL. 274) achieves spatial depth by means of its central perspective and is animated by the varied and asymmetrical positions of the figures, among whom Pope Sixtus IV and the librarian Platina stand out in the foreground. Melozzo's aim was obviously to give the contemporary event a "historical" character in accordance with a concept derived from Alberti and developed by Mantegna.

The attribution of some other panels is still doubtful: the profile of Guidobaldo da Montefeltro (Rome, Gall. Colonna), and representations of the Liberal Arts (Berlin, Staat. Mus.; London, Nat. Gall.) have been ascribed, among others, to Justus of Ghent or to Pedro Berruguete, both of whom, like

Melozzo, worked for Federigo da Montefeltro. These artists decorated the *studiolo* of the Duke in the Palazzo Ducale in Urbino with 28 small panels in the Flemish taste portraying as many famous men (1476–77; the panels are now divided between the Louvre and the Palazzo Ducale, to which they were returned after the dispersion of the Barberini Collection in Rome). Another painting by Berruguete in the same building (formerly Coll. Barberini) clearly reveals echoes of Michelozzo in the broad conception of the portraits of the Humanist Duke absorbed in his reading, and his young son Guidobaldo with the ducal scepter.

Melozzo's outstanding creation is undoubtedly the fresco depicting the Ascension, which at one time decorated the vault in the apse of SS. Apostoli in Rome. The only surviving fragments of the work, now detached, are a blessing Christ, transferred to the staircase of the Palazzo del Quirinale, and the half-figures or heads of apostles, angel musicians (PL. 39), and cherubim (Vat. Mus.). An idea of the original composition can be had from a canvas by Bartolomeo della Gatta in the Church of S. Domenico in Cortona representing the Assumption of the Virgin; in the foreshortened apostles, arranged in a semicircle, and in some of the angels it reflects Melozzo's fresco, which must have been quite spectacular for its bold plan and daring foreshortening. The surviving fragments are evocative in themselves and suggest robust, rather worldly figures endowed with intense vitality and with an upward movement emphasized by foreshortening. The fresco, reminiscent of the great mosaic compositions in the apses of Roman and medieval basilicas, must have set up, in substance, an architecture of powerful figural volumes, disposed along a freely conceived semicircle within a unitary discipline of perspective and space. This constituted Melozzo's great innovation; this author believes that Raphael was influenced by it in his painting of the Dispute over the Holy Sacrament in the Vatican.

There is some rigidity in the angels and prophets that stand out from a faultless perspective design in Melozzo's frescoes in the Sacristy of S. Marco in the Sanctuary of the Holy House in Loreto. The heavy, discordant execution seems to be by someone other than Melozzo, who is, however, to be credited with the bold conception of the figures; the execution is therefore believed to be by Melozzo's pupil Marco Palmezzano (1456–1517) from Forlì, perhaps in collaboration with Raphael's father, Giovanni Santi (ca. 1435–94) from Urbino.

Monumental frescoes once decorated the dome and the lunette of the Feo Chapel in S. Biagio in Forlì, but they were completely destroyed in World War II. On the cornice of the illusionist coffered ceiling were painted monumental prophets (XI, PL. 99); the lunette depicted a miracle of S. Domenico della Calzada, generally ascribed to Marco Palmezzano. Compared to Melozzo, Marco's style was rather stiff; he often reduced his master's art to trite mannerisms, almost to craftsmanship, in numerous alterpieces and religious paintings, even though after Melozzo's death he sought inspiration in the painters of the Veneto. Melozzo was also imitated in some altarpieces (*Madonna with Saints*; Urbino, Palazzo Ducale) and in some frescoes (*Madonna and Saints*; Cagli, S. Domenico) by Giovanni Santi, who was, in turn, the teacher of Evangelista di Pian di Meleto, who was close to the young Raphael in Città di Castello. It was inevitable that Melozzo's influence should be felt also in Rome; in that city various painters felt the impact of his art, above all the very active Antoniazzo Romano (documented 1460–1508). Originally oriented toward Gozzoli, Antoniazzo assimilated Florentine and even Umbrian influences, but later became a faithful follower of Melozzo's style (*S. Illuminata with SS. Vincenzo and Nicola da Tolentino*; Montefalco, S. Francesco; *The Virgin with Pope Leo IX*; Dublin, Nat. Gall. of Ireland); he recaptured Melozzo's scope in frescoes in S. Giovanni Evangelista in Tivoli. Later, because of his excessively abundant production, his work became less monumental; this is evident, for example, in his frescoes illustrating the legend of the True Cross in the apse of Sta Croce in Gerusalemme in Rome, and, among his many panels, in the one depicting the Madonna and saints with members of the Rota (VIII, PL. 204).

Because of his kinship with the Umbrians, as well as with Antoniazzo, the anonymous Master of the Gardner Annunciation (VIII, PL. 190) should be mentioned here, along with Lorenzo da Viterbo (ca. 1437–70) who, in his noble frescoes of scenes from the life of the Virgin (VIII, PL. 204), in the Mazzatosta Chapel in S. Maria della Verità in Viterbo, generally followed the trend originated by Piero della Francesca and Melozzo da Forlì.

Farther north, Donato Bramante, as a painter, was especially sensitive to Melozzo's examples as a frescoist; this is evident both in the surviving fragments of frescoes portraying ancient philosophers, from the façade of the Palazzo dei Rettori in Bergamo (now in the Palazzo della Ragione), and in the sculpturesque men-at-arms set within large niches and vigorously composed, formerly in a hall of the Casa dei Panigarola in Milan (presently in the Brera). One of these figures, in a broadly conceived three-quarter view, allows a striking comparison with Melozzo's apostles and angels in the apse of SS. Apostoli.

Bramante was in Lombardy about 1477, and he found in the painting of that region those links with the Veneto — particularly Padua — that it is possible to trace also in sculpture. Vincenzo Foppa, master of the Brescia school, soon overcame the late Gothic survivals in his very early works in favor of a sure modeling enhanced by effects of light in stiffly draped figures that anticipate the style of the Mantegazza brothers and Amadeo. He also surpassed the Flemish influence, using a gray complexion tone that can be related to those leaden tones typical of Giovanni da Milano and thus gave life to a spontaneously natural art in which elements of Venetian origin are mingled with Tuscan elements in form and perspective (PL. 41). This is particularly evident in the frescoes, in which the colors are clearer than in the small paintings and altarpieces (V, PL. 359) and are suffused with a brilliant light, as in the series with scenes from the life of St. Peter Martyr in the Church of S. Eustorgio, Milan (V, PL. 358) and in two frescoes depicting the martyrdom of St. Sebastian (V, PL. 357) and the Madonna with the two St. Johns (1485; Brera).

Foppa had a strong influence over a vast area, having left works in the principal centers of his native region and in Liguria. In Savona, Ludovico Brea of Nice (ca. 1443–1523) collaborated with him in a polyptych in S. Maria di Castello (1490); generally, Brea's art was an attempt to reconcile Foppa's solid ways with Franco-Flemish styles of Provençal origin. The anonymous master of the Louvre *Annunciation*, erroneously identified as Carlo Braccesco, was influenced by Foppa, whose delicate colors he further softened and often enlivened with gold; this master also worked in Liguria, as did Luca Baudo (d. 1509) of Novara. Baudo tended away from the Piedmontese painters, who represented a fusion of two cultures, the Lombard and the Franco-Flemish (the latter produced some noteworthy works in Piedmont). This fusion led to the elegant and slender figures in the work of Defendente Ferrari from Chiavasso (documented 1511–35), creator of polyptychs and altarpieces (Avigliana, near Turin, Church of S. Giovanni), and a delightful narrator in scenes from the lives of SS. Crispino and Crispiniano in Turin Cathedral; Gerolamo Giovenone (documented 1480–1557) was close to his style. Even earlier than Ferrari, Giovanni Martino Spanzotti (documented 1480–1524), who lived in Vercelli and in Casale Monferrato, had revealed himself as an aulic and more refined painter in the triptych representing the Madonna with SS. Ubaldus and Sebastian (Turin, Gall. Sabauda) and as an incisive narrator, similar to the Lombards in his search for luminist effects (even effects of nocturnal light) in the noteworthy series of frescoes illustrating scenes from the life of Christ in S. Bernardino in Ivrea.

Another Piedmontese, Macrino d'Alba (Gian Giacomo de Alladio; ca. 1470–1528), who traveled through central Italy, is reminiscent, in his rather cold painting, of Filippino Lippi and Signorelli, Perugino and Pintoricchio (polyptych with the Madonna, two saints, and the Resurrection, 1495; in the Certosa of Pavia) and occasionally achieved truly monumental effects (altarpiece with the Madonna, angels, and saints, 1498; in Turin, Gall. Sabauda).

Foppa's luminism was continued in a poetic vein by the gentle Ambrogio da Fossano, known as Il Bergognone (ca. 1450–1523), who progressed from gray tones (*Crucifixion, St. Ambrose with Saints*, 1490, Pavia, Certosa) to more vivid and often warm colors [*Annunciation* (PL. 40), *Visitation, Adoration of the Magi, Presentation of the Child in the Temple* (1498–1500) in Church of the Incoronata, Lodi]; Foppa's figural style, however, was retained almost unchanged by Il Bergognone, only slightly amplified by this modest, monotonous artist, also an indefatigable fresco painter, up to his last work, *The Coronation of the Virgin* in S. Sempliciano, Milan. Il Bergognone's most poetic expressions are to be found in the backgrounds of his altarpieces (*Christ Bearing the Cross*; Pavia, Mus. Malaspina), in the predellas (scenes from the life of St. Ambrose; Turin, Gall. Sabauda), and in the small devotional paintings of Madonnas with Carthusian monks (VIII, PL. 196), in which some clear, silvery landscapes recall with great effectiveness the humid, gray aspect of those of Lombardy.

Bernardino Butinone (d. 1507) and Bernardo Zenale (data available until 1526) worked together on the spectacular altarpiece, resplendent with gold, in S. Martino in Treviglio (PL. 40), and on the decoration of the Chapel of S. Ambrogio in S. Pietro in Gessate, Milan (1489–93). Their work is easily distinguishable; the first by a harsh style related to various influences from the Flemish to the Ferrarese; the second by perspective methods derived from Bramante and by a figural treatment that is somewhat reminiscent of Mantegna.

It would be superfluous to dwell on the minor fresco painters of Lombard churches who reveal some connection with the artists of the Veneto, such as Donato da Montorfano, author of an undistinguished Crucifixion (1495) in the Refectory of S. Maria delle Grazie, Milan. Rather, mention should be made of the master glassmakers who worked mainly on the large stained-glass windows of Milan Cathedral in an illustrative style that is typically Lombard in its detailed narrative, attuned to contemporary illumination. Outstanding among them were Cristoforo (d. 1493), Jacopo (d. 1505), and Agostino de' Motti; to the latter have been attributed some frescoes (destroyed in World War II) in a chapel of S. Pietro in Gessate, in which traditional elements were combined with some echoes of Bramante. Lombardy's greatest artist, in the generation following Foppa's, however, was Bartolomeo Suardi, called Bramantino, who, with Foppa and Butinone, followed the Ferrarese school in the livid, metallic paintings of his early period, and who tended toward Bramante especially, as in the *Nativity* in Milan (VIII, PL. 196). Bramante's influence continued in Bramantino's later work (hence his nickname) and emerges in the monumental breadth and clear coloring that is evident, for example, in the *Pietà* in S. Sepolcro, Milan, and in the *Adoration of the Magi* (London, Nat. Gall.). In 1508 Bramantino traveled to Rome (documents of that year mention him as a painter in the Vatican), where his studies of the works of Piero della Francesca and Melozzo reinforced his own monumentality, as exemplified in the series of the months (Milan, Castello Sforzesco), executed from his cartoons in the tapestry factory at Vigevano for the marshal of France, Gian Giacomo Trivulzio. Bramantino continued these tendencies, inserting ancient edifices in his compositions (*Madonna with Saints*, Florence, Coll. Contini Bonacossi; *Holy Family*, Milan, Brera), which are often romantic (*Flight into Egypt*, Locarno, Church of the Madonna del Sasso).

Other Lombards, such as Vincenzo Civerchio of Brescia (1470–1544) and Agostino da Lodi (beginning of the 16th cent.), were eclectic in style and were influenced by the major personalities mentioned above. This eclecticism was extended to include the influences of Leonardo and Raphael by two artists from Lodi, Albertino and Martino Piazza, who worked in the first decades of the 16th century in a style that was still of the early Renaissance.

Andrea Mantegna, who was certainly the greatest master of form in Northern Italy, contributed even more impulse to the Renaissance in painting in the Veneto than he had in sculpture. In Padua, until the late 15th century and even beyond, after the disappearance of Francesco Squarcione's immediate followers, Mantegna's influence was felt not only by the mediocre Jacopo da Montagnana but also by Bernardo (Parenzano) Parentino (1437–1531), who, in contact with Ferrara and Verona, reduced Mantegna's spirit to a detailed graphic style with glassy transparency, both in his frescoes (cloister of St. Giustina, Padua) and in his panels [scenes from the lives of St. Anthony (IV, PL. 179) and St. Louis of France (Rome, Gall. Doria Pamphili)].

Earlier still, Mantegna and the Paduan school had been mainly responsible for leading the Venetian painters, especially Giovanni Bellini, to the Renaissance. It should be remembered that next to the frescoes by Andrea del Castagno in the main chapel of the old Venetian church of S. Zaccaria (of an earlier date, its ruins are next to the present church) were placed, as if with polemic intent, the graceful Gothic polyptychs of Antonio Vivarini and Giovanni d'Alemagna. But the stylistic values of Andrea's frescoes were taken up by Mantegna and by Nicolò Pizzolo of Padua (1421–53). Moreover, the Venetian Jacopo Bellini, a former pupil of Gentile da Fabriano, executed studies in perspective in his sketch books (Br. Mus.; Louvre, I, PL. 309) in which he was still inhibited by a certain scholastic timidity. The interest in archaeology demonstrated in these drawings is indeed far removed from Mantegna's truly Humanistic approach and would seem to be the product of a superimposed, only superficially assimilated culture, in view of Jacopo Bellini's family ties with the great master (Mantegna was his son-in-law). Nevertheless, those drawings give evidence of a certain trend. And Jacopo, a Gothic painter who was moving toward the Renaissance, must be credited with having established in Venice a narrative trend that was linked to a graphic means of expression — that is, to compositions that were often based on central perspective, in which the rigid and restrained figures are arranged parallel to the axis of the composition. Gentile Bellini, Jacopo's elder son, remained faithful to this rule in his canvases for the Scuola di S. Giovanni Evangelista (II, PL. 256) and the Scuola Grande di S. Marco (PL. 46). The painter reproduced his native Venice with precise diligence, also drawing human figures with such care as to show himself to be an accurate and incisive portraitist (II, PL. 251). His fame reached as far as the court of Mohammed II, who invited him to Constantinople in 1480 (cf. portrait of Mohammed II; London, Nat. Gall.). In the series for the Scuola di S. Giovanni Evangelista other minor artists collaborated with Gentile Bellini. Among them, Gentile's pupil Giovanni Mansueti (ca. 1470–1530; VIII, PL. 199) was rather weak throughout his abundant production, with a superficial narrative style tending toward the ornamental, as is also revealed in some scenes from the life of St. Mark (Venice, Gall. dell'Accademia; Brera; Vaduz, Liechtenstein Coll.). Lazzaro di Jacopo Bastiani (ca. 1470–1512) was influenced by Bellini in the series on which he collaborated with the master, but in other works, such as his compact altarpieces, he was a follower of Bartolomeo Vivarini, whose pupil he was and for whom he has often been mistaken. Another collaborator, Benedetto Diana (active 1482–1525), a pupil of Bastiani, retained the decorative uniformity of the series, though elsewhere he showed a freer style that was inspired by Dürer (*Assumption*; S. Maria della Croce near Crema).

Giovanni Carpaccio also worked on the series for the Scuola di S. Giovanni Evangelista. His work is reminiscent of that of Gentile Bellini but is endowed with a brilliant inventiveness and with a sense of composition and a delightful feeling for color that is lacking in the other painters mentioned in this context. Later, in other famous cycles — stories from the lives of St. Ursula (III, PLS. 73, 78), St. George, and hermit saints (PL. 46; III, PLS. 70, 71) — he gave a tonal significance to the relation between light and color, drawing closer to the style of Giovanni Bellini, whose influence is also evident in the composition of some of Carpaccio's monumental altarpieces.

Giovanni Bellini, trained by his father Jacopo, was deeply interested in the clear and compact compositional sense evident in the painting of Mantegna — who had come to represent the new order that had been proclaimed to the Tuscans — not because he wished to emulate its sculpturesque aspects, but because that approach to composition eventually led him to compose his own figures with a greater naturalness and freedom which gave them more emotional force. Moreover, following the example of Piero della Francesca, he perfected his use of color (II, PL. 258). But, when confronted with the brilliant colors of Antonello da Messina, Bellini transformed his art and through a pantheistic vision of creation arrived at a harmony of figures and landscapes (*Allegory of Souls in Purgatory*; Uffizi) with a sense of atmosphere that was the major achievement of Venetian painting in the 15th century (PL. 44; II, PL. 261).

Giovanni Bellini was not alone in feeling the influence of Antonello da Messina's style and some of his compositional schemes, which were widely diffused in the Venetian circle into which the Sicilian painter had been introduced. In his native Sicily, and presumably in Naples under the guidance of Colantonio, he had given substance to his painting with transparent colors that were derived more from his knowledge of Flemish and French art than of Spanish art — although the last was also represented in southern Italy. In fact, this author holds that the *Triumph of Death* from the Palazzo Sclafani in Palermo (Palermo, Gall. Naz. della Sicilia) is closely connected with Provençal art; so, too, in its vigorously expressionistic aspects, is the work of the anonymous Piazza Armerina Master, so named for a crucifix painted for the Cathedral of that city. In Naples, alongside Angelillo Arcuccio, whose archaizing style was open to Flemish influences, a number of more talented artists were active; among them were the so-called "Maestro di Capistrano" and, later, an unknown master who was creator of the altarpiece in the Church of SS. Severino e Sosio; Antonello rose above some painters who were notable for their figural approach to art and, overcoming the analytic Flemish quality perceptible in his early works, he achieved a synthesis of perspective and geometrically conceived volumes (*St. Sebastian*; I, PL. 316) as a result of his encounter with the poetic style of Piero della Francesca (perhaps in Ferrara). In regard to color, however, the two have nothing in common: Antonello's work was based on the full light of midday, while Piero's was a morning light, almost that of dawn. In Antonello's works and, later, in those of the Venetians, light acquired the warm intensity of high noon. His admirable portraits (PL. 43), so much more incisive psychologically than those of Gentile Bellini, were an inspiration to Giovanni Bellini as well as to Antonello's followers. The altarpiece painted by Antonello for the Church of S. Cassiano in Venice (I, PL. 318), with the figures framed in a large apse — a variation on the scheme of an altarpiece by Piero (XI, PL. 166) — served as a model for Giovanni Bellini, Carpaccio, and other, lesser, artists.

In Venice the art of painting, which had rediscovered the uses of color in the new order of the Renaissance, was to develop two distinct trends. The first and fundamental one, a synthesis of form and color, was derived, with some variations from Antonello da Messina, whse style was to be continued in Sicily by his son Jacopo (Jacobello; b. 1455) and by Antonello de Saliba (active 1480–1535). The second trend, with figures that are freer and more articulated and with softer colors, was originated by Bellini and tended toward the atmospheric transparencies of tonal painting.

The first of these trends had its major exponent in Venice in Antonio Vivarini's son, Alvise (ca. 1446–1505), the author of very clearly defined Madonnas (e.g., *Madonna*; Venice, Church of the Redentore) and of altarpieces in which he elaborated on Antonello's style, using monumental architectural settings, as in that representing St. Ambrose enthroned (PL. 45). This is Alvise's masterwork and was completed after his death by his pupil Marco Basaiti (ca. 1470–ca. 1530), a painter whose style later mellowed under the influence of Giovanni Bellini (*Calling of the Sons of Zebedee*, 1510; VIII, PL. 199). In the work of Jacopo de' Barbari (d. ca. 1516), another disciple of Alvise Vivarini, the figural solidity of the master was tempered by German influences (Dürer) that are also evident in his engravings. Jacopo had visited Germany and represents historically a contact with the northern world.

Bartolomeo Montagna (1450–1523) was from Lombardy but settled in Vicenza, where he founded a school; in the altarpiece from the Church of S. Michele (PL. 45) he expanded Antonello's style in a sculpturesque treatment sustained by light.

Indeed Montagna's severe style, geometrically flawless in his early works (*Madonna with John the Baptist and St. Onuphrius*; Vicenza, Mus. Civ.), tended toward compositions of greater breadth, warmed by colors and set against sunny landscapes in which traces of Bellini's style are also evident (*St. Paul, St. Jerome*; Milan, Mus. Poldi Pezzoli). Giovanni Buonconsiglio, known as Marescalco (1495–ca. 1537), was Montagna's pupil; he emphasized contrasts of light that heighten the dramatic tone of his art (X, PL. 504). Marcello Fogolino (active 1510–48) continued Montagna's style in Vicenza, adding some elements in the taste of the 16th century.

Cima da Conegliano (ca. 1459/60–1517/18) was another outstanding figure among the many painters from the Veneto; he based his early style on the work of Antonello and of Alvise Vivarini, whom he echoes in his altarpiece in Conegliano Cathedral (1493). He later followed various compositional schemes (*St. John the Baptist with Four Saints* in S. Maria dell'Orto; *Baptism of Christ* in S. Giovanni in Bragora; both Venice) and was subject to various influences, predominant among them that of Giovanni Bellini (Giambellino). Nevertheless his painting retained a very personal quality; his was an art of serene figures and pleasant hilly landscapes suffused with clear silvery colors (PL. 46; VIII, PL. 199).

Even the painters who had been most deeply affected by Antonello were eventually drawn to Bellini, whose influence was to prevail especially in Venice; Girolamo Mocetto (1458–1531) represents a perfect balance between the two trends. Among the artists whose styles were derived exclusively from Bellini, Vincenzo Catena (1470–1531) was closest to the master in his fine altarpieces, portraits, and *sacre conversazioni*, with half-figures at the side of the Virgin; he thus continued a scheme typical of Mantegna and of Bellini, which was monotonously repeated by another Bellini-inspired painter, Francesco Bissolo (active 1492–1554). Similar in style was Rocco Marconi (d. 1529). Marco Marziale (active 1489–ca. 1507) originally took Gentile Bellini as his model, but he also felt the influence of Giovanni Bellini, retaining an incisive metallic quality that links him with Cima da Conegliano and a certain harshness that distinguishes him from Gentile Bellini's more orthodox followers. Although these followers went beyond the 16th century stylistically and became aware of more advanced artistic personalities, they themselves did not adopt the spirit of the High Renaissance.

In the meanwhile provincial artists of the Veneto echoed the major masters of this large region, with varying degrees of adherence to local manners and styles. In Verona the S. Zeno Altarpiece by Mantegna (IX, PL. 322) had been slavishly imitated by Francesco Benaglio, who was surpassed by Francesco Bonsignori (1453–1519), an artist whose style showed Mantegna's influence as well as contacts with Giovanni Bellini and other minor artists. Domenico Morone (1442–after 1517) tended toward a narrative style after the example of Gentile Bellini (*The Triumph of the Gonzagas over the Bonacolsis*; VII, PL. 275); his work is also reminiscent of Mantegna and, in its warm color, of the Venetians. This is true also of a similar painter, Michele da Verona (1470–1536/44). Francesco Morone (1471–1529), son and pupil of Domenico, reelaborated similar elements and, while his tone was always rather provincial, it had a certain grace. Girolamo dai Libri (1474–1556), also a pupil of Domenico, displayed an eclectic and more varying style.

Earlier, Liberale da Verona (1445–ca. 1529), with his sinuous graphic style, created works reminiscent of Gothic survivals; he interpreted Mantegna's style with opulence, but without giving solid form to his figures. In this case the master's influence was strengthened by Liberale's contacts with Girolamo da Cremona. Liberale later felt not only the influence of the Bellini family but — having worked in Siena as a miniaturist — also drew some elements from the Tuscans. Gian Maria Falconetto (1458–1543), another itinerant Veronese, cannot be said to have profited much from his frequent visits to Rome, judging by his vacuous pictorial documents, which recall Mantegna and local styles.

Niccolò Giolfino (1476–1555), a disciple of Liberale, imitated his teacher and also expanded the traditional Veronese styles, recalling the Lombards in some of his harsh forms; the same tendencies can also be found, with more extensive exterior similarities, in another pupil of Liberale, Giovanni Francesco Caroto (ca. 1480–ca. 1555), whose work very closely resembles that of his brother Giovanni (1488–1566). As far as the Veneto is concerned, brief mention should also be made of Domenico di Candido and Gian Francesco da Tolmezzo, who represented in Carnia the late-15th-century provincial heritage of Mantegna's style.

Various echoes of Venetian painting are to be found in Lombardy, in Bergamo (then part of the Venetian Republic), in the work of Andrea Previtali (active 1502–28), who was faithful to the trend; and in the painters from Santa Croce (Francesco di Simone, Francesco and Girolamo da Santacroce) who were active during the 16th century.

The Milanese Antonio Solario, known as Lo Zingaro (beginning of the 16th cent.) was inspired by Giovanni Bellini and, above all, by Alvise Vivarini; he traveled through the Marches and as far as Naples where — enriched by Umbrian and Flemish influences — he painted a series of murals with scenes from the life of St. Benedict in the cloister of the Monastery of SS. Severino e Sosio. Andrea Solari (active 1493–ca. 1520) in his early period tended away from Alvise's training toward the influence of Bellini, which was then overcome in his later works by that of Leonardo da Vinci.

In Cremona, Boccaccio Boccaccino (1467–1525), also influenced by Alvise and connected with the city of Ferrara, retained the serene tone of the 15th century in his languid Madonnas, in *sacre conversazioni*, in altarpieces, and in the clear and luminous frescoes that decorate the apse (1506–08) and the nave (1515–18) of Cremona Cathedral; some of his compositions are derived from prints by Albrecht Dürer. Another Lombard, Bartolomeo Veneto (active 1502–ca. 1530), who declares himself to be half Venetian and half Cremonese in one of his Madonnas (1502; formerly Venice, Coll. Count Donà delle Rose), followed Giovanni Bellini in his sacred paintings; but as a portraitist he rose to more original achievements reminiscent of the Lombards.

The artistic circle of the Veneto included Emilia and Romagna. In Parma, Cristoforo Caselli, known as Il Temperelli (active ca. 1481–1521), who had patterned his style after Bellini, also revealed echoes of Antonello; these are also evident in the work of Filippo Mazzola (ca. 1460–1505). In Ravenna, Nicolò Rondinello (active ca. 1480–1500) created rather heavy imitations of Giovanni Bellini, presumably as a result of contacts with Palmezzano; Lattanzio da Rimini (documented 1495–1527) echoed with equal heaviness the later manner of the Venetian master.

In the history of the early Renaissance, therefore, the painting of the Veneto detached itself from the Florentine-Paduan mainstream, and ultimately achieved full autonomy. Moreover, it exerted a predominant influence on the Po Valley and was to initiate the High Renaissance with its refinement of color, far removed from those classicist excesses which, in Florence and in Rome, generated conflicting attitudes.

HIGH RENAISSANCE. *Architecture.* The work of Donato Bramante (see above) marked the beginning of the High Renaissance in architecture; as early as his Milanese period he turned toward the Humanist ideal of eurhythmy, partly because of his origins and background in Urbino. In Milan he became aware of the evocative power of such an imposing structure as S. Lorenzo, and there he came into contact with Leonardo. Some drawings by Leonardo (Paris, Inst. de France, Ms. B.25) reiterate his continued innovations in central-plan structures; in some of these drawings his ideas found their finest expressions.

Two works of Bramante's early period, the baptistery of S. Maria presso S. Satiro (PL. 47), with its extremely vertical lines and corner niches, and the nearby church, divided by piers into a nave and two aisles (1482–86; II, PLS. 339, 340, 344, FIG. 598) and crossed by a transept into which shallow niches are set, create an impression of movement. This is heightened in the church by the illusionistic perspective of the false choir, which repeats the lines of the barrel vault. The sculptural decoration was applied to the structural elements in accord with

traditional taste (II, PL. 338). The artist then turned to the monumental masses that had only been anticipated in the early Renaissance in the great architectonic spaces created by the Ferrarese Biagio Rossetti (ca. 1447–1516). It can therefore be assumed that Bramante played a leading role in the construction of Pavia Cathedral (1488; FIG. 70; II, PLS. 343, 344, FIG. 599), the plan of which was elaborated by Cristoforo Rocchi; it was executed with the collaboration of various artists, among them

Pavia, Cathedral, transverse section (*from C. Baroni, 1941*).

Giovanni Antonio Amadeo and Francesco di Giorgio. The Latin-cross plan of the Cathedral recalls that of the basilica at Loreto, but with basic alterations made necessary by the highly imposing proportions of the perimeter, dome, counterforts, and interior.

The tribune of S. Maria delle Grazie in Milan (begun 1492; II, PLS. 341, 342), with its calotte dome, encompasses a vast interior space, although the structural members seem too frail in relation to the expanse. On the exterior, these members are covered by Lombard ornamentation. In contrast, the large arch of the façade of the Cathedral of Abbiategrasso (1497; PL. 47), with superimposed paired columns and barrel vault emerging from the earlier, modest quadriporticus, is freer and tends toward a simplification of the mass that is evidence of Bramante's constant striving for a not yet fully attained monumentality — always within the sphere of classicism. The Roman creative atmosphere contributed decisively to the simplification of Bramante's style; it stimulated him to imitate the grandeur of the edifices of the imperial period, while spurring him to give his structural elements greater consistency by accentuating the chiaroscuro in widely varying works. For example, the Tempietto of S. Pietro in Montorio (1503; I, PL. 305; II, FIG. 602) displays the earliest modern use of the Doric order, combined with the lively chiaroscuro of the exterior niches, which were to have been echoed by corner trefoil niches (never executed) in order to achieve an effect of movement inspired by the architecture of the Romans. The cloister of S. Maria della Pace (II, PL. 345) aims by its harmonious proportions, its spatial volumes and structural elements, at an austere sculptural purity. Only later, in the Palazzo di Giustizia on Via Giulia (of which only the base remains) and in the House of Raphael (no longer extant), did the full power of the chiaroscuro emerge in the rusticated ashlar on the ground floor and in the single architectural order (Doric) on the first floor.

Bramante's boldly conceived project to connect the Vatican Palace with the villa on the Belvedere overcame the problems presented by an irregular, uneven terrain. Although he was ignorant of the fact that an Egyptian architect of the 17th dynasty had shaped a hill architecturally near Thebes to place the Temple of Deir-el-Bahri in a dominant position, certainly Bramante knew the town of Palestrina, where a steep elevation had been transformed into a monumental architectural complex that culminated in the Sanctuary of Fortuna Primigenia (VII, PL. 199). From the Cortile del Belvedere a progression of three levels connected by flights of steps climbs to the vertical mass of the large niche (II, PL. 346). The plan aimed at creating a contrast of masses similar to that already established in Abbiategrasso; it succeeded in this intent, with greater uniformity and a truly spectacular effect, in the contrast of the large vertical niche and the lateral elements. In the main body of the building, executed over a long period of time, the over-all effect was in part weakened by later modifications. The large niche of the Belvedere imitates the exedras of the nymphaea and thermae of the imperial age, even though the superimposed structural members retain a certain controlled elegance that weakens the sculptural effect, which, on the contrary, is quite evident in other works by Bramante (Tempietto of S. Pietro in Montorio; apse of S. Maria del Popolo, II, PL. 344).

For the new St. Peter's Bramante visualized a structure with a dome to rival that of the Pantheon, one that would rise above a barrel vault such as those favored in Roman imperial architecture; this exciting monumental concept was firmly supported by Pope Julius II. Conceived with a single interior architectural order and two exterior orders (cf. Caradosso's medal, which seems to illustrate the final version), the building would have constituted an example of perfect classicism and a peerless achievement of the principal Humanist esthetic aspiration of the early Renaissance, that is, to develop a building around an ideal vertical axis.

St. Peter's was to have been built as a Greek cross inscribed on a square plan, with four niched and domed cruciform chapels that would form four apses and interior ambulatories. From the center of this cross was to emerge a dome circled by an exterior colonnade. Towers were to be set at the corners of the square building. It was to have been an example, therefore, of a rigorously symmetrical and modeled architecture, organically unitary and eurhythmic in its cadences, its structural members, and its details, which can be assumed to have been extremely pure, an architecture far removed from the the timid applications of the inscribed Greek-cross plan realized by the Venetian early Renaissance.

Bramante's Lombard works had repercussions both in central-plan buildings with exuberant decorations on their reddish-toned facings [Church of the Incoronata in Lodi, begun 1488 by G. Battagio and G. G. Dolcebuono; S. Maria della Croce, in Crema, by Battagio and G. A. Montanaro (PL. 10; FIG. 25); S. Magno in Legnano, by Vincenzo Seregni] and in certain monumental divisions of basilican buildings, such as the trefoil apse of Como Cathedral (PL. 48) by Tommaso Rodari and the Milanese domes [e.g., the octagonal dome of S. Maria presso S. Celso by Dolcebuono (VIII, PL. 215); and that of S. Maria della Passione (PL. 48), of a much ampler breadth, with three chapels from a quadrilobate structure; Cristoforo Solari has been named tentatively as author of the last]. These and other Lombard buildings constitute various interpretations of Bramante's style by artists whose training was different and generally much inferior. Moreover, Bramante's Roman works were also imitated in Lombardy: the cloister of S. Abbondio in Cremona recalls that of S. Maria della Pace. Echoes of Bramante are also perceivable in some illustrations of Cesare Cesarino's translation of Vitruvius's De Architettura (1521). Lombard artists were often instrumental in spreading Bramante's influence to other regions.

In Piacenza, Bramante's influence was manifested by Alessio Tramello in the cruciform church of S. Maria di Campagna, as well as in the churches of S. Sisto and S. Sepolcro (FIG. 72), with small semicircular chapels running the length of both sides of the nave, in imitation of Pavia Cathedral. In Parma Bernar-

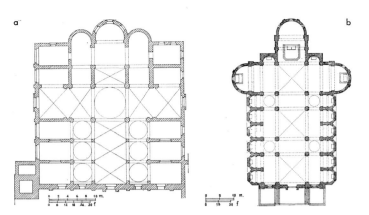

Religious architecture in northern Italy. (a) Venice, S. Maria Formosa (architect, M. Coducci), plan (from L. Angelini, Le Opere in Venezia di Mauro Codussi, Milan, 1945); (b) Piacenza, S. Sepolcro (architect, A. Tramello), plan (from Monumenti Italiani, Accademia d'Italia, pub., Rome, 1935).

dino Zaccagni the Elder and Giovan Francesco Zaccagni imitated Bramante in the quadrilobate Madonna della Steccata (VIII, FIG. 419), the plan of which is repeated by Cola da Caprarola, but with a different rhythm, in the Church of S. Maria della Consolazione in Todi (PL. 51; VIII, PL. 206, FIG. 419). (It is probable that both were derived from a common prototype, perhaps a drawing.)

In the Marches there are many central-plan buildings that recall Bramante's style (octagon of the Church of the Riscatto at Urbania and of S. Maria di Caspriano, between Camerino and Visso), which was spread by the Lombards who adorned the region with its typical portals. Notable among these is the Sanctuary of Macereto, near Visso, built on a complex octagonal plan with niches and a dome (under construction in 1527; finished in the second half of the century); this heavy, thickset edifice was conceived by Battista da Lugano (d. 1538). The later, imposing church of S. Maria delle Vergini in Macerata is also notable; on an inscribed Greek-cross plan, it was built after 1550 and once was attributed to Bramante himself. In L'Aquila, in the Abruzzi, the façade of S. Bernardino (1525–40) was executed by Cola dall'Amatrice, perhaps with the collaboration of Silvestro da Sulmona. It is rectangular, in accordance with a local tradition dating from the Romanesque period, and emulates Bramante's monumentality, with some reminiscences of Venetian style (particularly that of Mauro Coducci); this eclecticism was displayed by Cola in other buildings, especially in Ascoli Piceno.

Bramante's influence reached Venice, perhaps, through the mathematician Fra Luca Pacioli, who settled there after a sojourn in Milan. In religious architecture, traditional structural forms were adapted according to this new influence; in the Church of S. Salvatore (PL. 50), begun in the first years of the 16th century by Giorgio Spavento and finished by Tullio Lombardo, the succession of domes typical of the Greek-cross plan was interpreted in a monumental spirit clearly reminiscent of Bramante. The motif, used earlier in the Gothic church of S. Antonio in Padua, was applied in S. Salvatore with a different flow in the sequence of the three domes and especially in the slender piers that support them. And the Venetian model was to be given a much more monumental expression in the Church of S. Giustina in Padua (PL. 50), which was designed (1517) by Andrea Moroni of Bergamo, modified (1521) by Alessandro Leopardi, and later continued and finished by Vincenzo Scamozzi. In addition to expressions of the widespread, rather superficially assimilated influence of Bramante, there were individual interpretations by various artists with marked personalities and styles that were close to the master. Among these was Bramantino, whose paintings of classical buildings reveal an admiration for antiquity that is perfectly attuned to the works of Bramante in Rome. Bramantino's one surviving architectural creation is the Trivulzio Chapel; built on a square plan, with interior niches, it is placed against the façade of the Church of S. Nazaro Maggiore in Milan (FIG. 73). This chapel represents a convergence of esthetic concerns in its interpretation of Bramante's style in a romantic northern manner by means of the very high elevation marked by superimposed structural members on the exterior, to which a classic pronaos was to have been added.

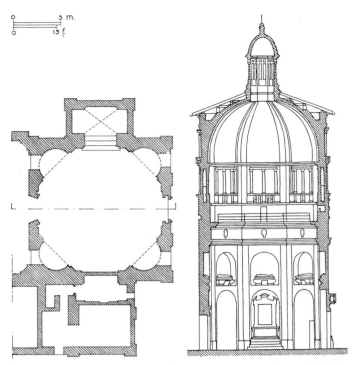

Milan, S. Nazaro Maggiore, Trivulzio Chapel (architect, Bramantino), plan and transverse section (*from C. Baroni, 1941*).

Two trends emerged from Bramante's Roman period: one tended toward painterly ideals; the other, Florentine in taste, moved toward sculptural ideals, always within the sphere of the inspiration provided by antiquity.

Raphael, who in architecture was Bramante's disciple, was also his successor in the construction of St. Peter's in Rome, where his collaborators were Giuliano da Sangallo and Fra Giovanni Giocondo. Although Raphael transformed the plan of the basilica into a Latin cross, apparently to comply with religious requirements, his work in the Cortile di San Damaso, also in the Vatican, is in perfect harmony with Bramante's pure forms.

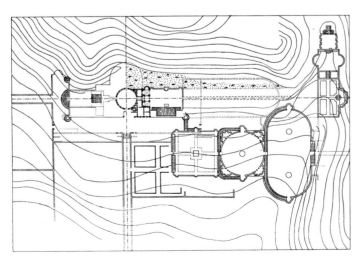

Rome, Villa Madama, plan of the building complex according to the project by Raphael (*from H. Geymüller, Raffaello Sanzio studiato come architetto con l'aiuto di nuovi documenti, Milan, 1884*).

With the assistance of Giovanni da Udine, Raphael decorated the loggias with stuccoes and ornamental paintings inspired by Nero's Golden House, by then already reduced to a hive of grottoes — hence the term "grotteschi" was applied to this kind of decoration. Echoes of Bramante also appear in the Villa Madama, built in the manner of Raphael, with clear divisions marked by pilasters and niches and decorated with frescoes by Giovanni da Udine, joined by a series of courtyards and loggias connected to an Italian garden (PL. 51; FIG. 73).

Raphael achieved a more subtle chiaroscuro in the façade of the Palazzo Vidoni (formerly Caffarelli), which repeats the scheme of Bramante's House of Raphael. Instead, the Palazzo Branconio dell'Aquila (ca. 1515; destroyed) inaugurated a wholly original trend in façades in its chiaroscuro contrasts, of a subtle painterly quality, between the solids and voids of the ground floor and mezzanine, above all those of the first-floor windows and the niches and stuccoes by Giovanni da Udine. Raphael's design (1516–20) for the Palazzo Pandolfini in Florence (FIG. 21), executed by Giovanni Francesco da Sangallo, acquired in the harmonious windows spaced between whitewashed walls a sculptural effect that is different but typical of the Florentine atmosphere.

Among Raphael's religious buildings, the small central-plan church of S. Eligio degli Orefici (ca. 1509; VIII, FIG. 419) is less interesting than the Chigi Chapel of S. Maria del Popolo (XI, PL. 436, FIG. 235), which has a dome on a cylindrical drum similar to that of S. Bernardino in Urbino. The arcaded and niched interior of the Chigi Chapel is enlivened by polychrome marble facings, against which stand two pyramidal tombs and some statues. The chapel represents an important innovation in the picturesque, one that was to have vast repercussions. Close to Raphael, and following Bramante's style, a large group of artists created works with a feeling of picturesque charm. Among these was the Florentine Giovanni Angelo Montorsoli (ca. 1507–63), probable author of the long, sober Palazzo Doria Pamphili in Genoa, with an airy loggia and with fresco decorations by one of Raphael's followers, Perino del Vaga, who may also have influenced the architecture of the building.

Baldassare Peruzzi, who worked in his native Siena, was active also in Carpi in the Emilia region (1514–22), where he designed the Cathedral (XI, FIG. 274), the Church of S. Niccolò, and the façade of the Old Cathedral ("La Sagra"), creating in the first two of these structures impressively proportioned forms of Bramantesque breadth. It was in Rome, however, that Peruzzi left the most individual imprint of his art, which aimed at achieving a linear framework and a chiaroscuro without strong projections, in the villa of Agostino Chigi, later renamed the Farnesina by its new owners, the Farnese family (XI, PL. 120, FIG. 273); it is animated by elegant pilasters superposed on pale brickwork and, in the façade overlooking the garden, by an airy and rhythmic ground-floor loggia between two projecting bodies. Compared to the Farnesina, the Palazzo Massimo alle Colonne (PL. 52; XI, PL. 121, FIG. 275), a town house, shows a more intense picturesque chiaroscuro in its convex façade with rusticated ashlar. The Doric order is used in the courtyard, which has trabeated and superposed loggias of great scenographic effect; the same order is applied on a reduced scale to the façade. Peruzzi's contribution to scenography is notable (Salone delle Prospettive in the Farnesina, which recalls the school of Urbino; XI, PL. 118), and included a treatise (*Taccuino senese*; Siena, Bib. Com., S. IV, 7), which was used extensively by Sebastiano Serlio.

At this point reference should be made to Gian Maria Falconetto (1468–1535), mentioned above as a mediocre painter of the early Renaissance, who was overly fascinated by classical antiquity. Among contemporary artists he most admired Raphael and his refinement; Falconetto adapted this refinement, with a light, painterly touch, to his predominating classical erudition. His work includes the portal of Villa Benvenuti (formerly Corner) in Este, with small niches inspired by those in the Arch of Janus in Rome; the Odeon and the Loggia (PL. 49; FIG. 75) built for Alvise Corner in the Palazzo Giustiniani in Padua, and the Porta S. Giovanni (1528) and the Porta Savonarola (1530), also in Padua.

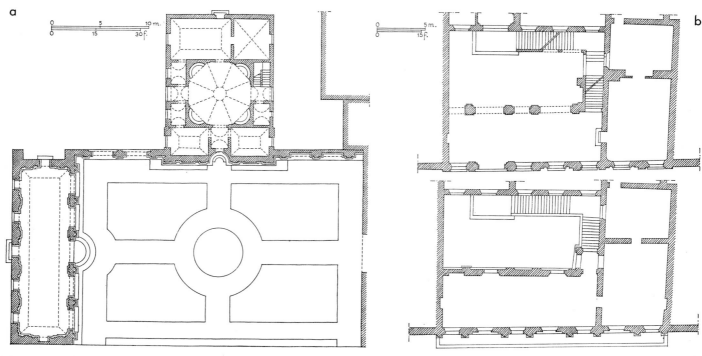

Domestic architecture in northern Italy. (*a*) Padua, Palazzo Giustiniani (architect, Falconetto), plan of the Loggia and Odeon (*from A. Haupt, Architettura dei Palazzi d'Italia settentrionale, Milan, 1930*); (*b*) Verona, Palazzo Bevilacqua (architect, Sanmicheli), plan of first and second stories (*from L'Architettura, 56, 1960*).

The names of Bramante and Raphael arise again in connection with Andrea Contucci (ca. 1470–1529), known as Sansovino after his birthplace (Monte San Savino). Primarily a sculptor, he also created exuberant decorations in the Lombard vein, which was the basis of the classicist trend in High Renaissance sculpture. Though he did adhere to Bramante's design (1509) for the marble facings of the Holy House in the Sanctuary at Loreto, he does not appear to have been a continuator of the master in his work on the Palazzo Apostolico and on the project for the vast atrium it was to form in front of the basilica, on which Antonio da Sangallo the Younger later worked. When working alone in his later period, Sansovino substantially reduced his forms, as in the elegant portico of S. Maria in Domnica in Rome and in the Doric portal of S. Giovanni Battista and the simple cloister of S. Agostino, both at Monte San Savino. It is this author's opinion that Sansovino did not contribute in an exceptional measure to the architectural training of his pupil Jacopo d'Antonio Tatti (1486–1570), who was also known as Sansovino. Jacopo left his native Florence for Rome and later

went to Venice (1527), where he held a preeminent position both as sculptor and as architect. He brought to Venetian architecture a touch of the Tuscan feeling for essentials, though this was always blended with local tradition in his churches (S. Fantin and S. Francesco della Vigna, in which the original nave and two aisles were later reduced to a single nave), where his style remained somewhat cold. It was, in fact, in secular architecture that he excelled.

In Venice, Pietro Lombardo and Mauro Coducci had already created delicate contrasts of light and shadow combined with picturesqueness. Sansovino accepted the Venetian manner enthusiastically and followed traditional schemes in the Palazzo Corner (Ca' Grande; FIG. 75) with its uninterrupted rows of windows in the first and second floors reminiscent of Coducci; decorations were, however, replaced with a strong chiaroscuro. The Palazzo della Zecca (1537–45) was extremely severe in its original plan, of only two floors, to which a third was later added, following the example of Roman buildings.

Sansovino turned his decorative talent to painterly effects

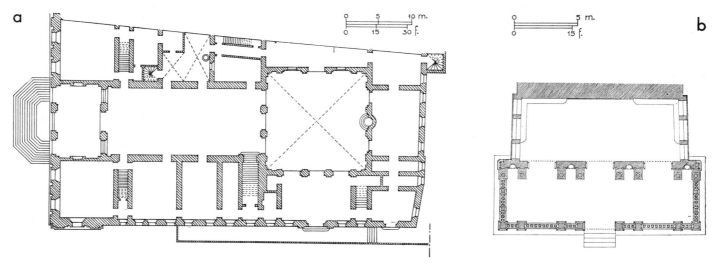

Venice. (*a*) Palazzo Corner, plan of ground floor; (*b*) Loggetta of the Campanile of S. Marco (architect, J. Sansovino), (*from F. Sapori, Jacopo Tatti detto il Sansovino, Rome, 1928*).

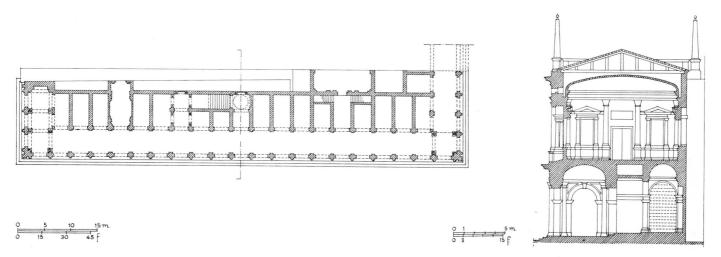

Venice, Libreria Vecchia di S. Marco (architect, J. Sansovino), plan of ground floor and transverse section (*from B. Fletcher, A History of Architecture, New York-London, 1961*).

in the Loggetta (PL. 56; FIG. 75) of the Campanile in Piazza S. Marco, which he profusely decorated with sculptures. His masterwork is the Libreria Vecchia di S. Marco (FIG. 77), admired by Palladio as "the richest and most ornate edifice" since ancient times. In this work a carefully achieved equilibrium results in a rhythmic discipline of the structural members, which are endowed with a solidity previously unknown in Venice: the stately Doric and Ionic orders mark intervals between the exuberant decorations (victories, friezes, and a crowning balustrade) and create a harmonious blend of modeling and color.

Of the architecture tending toward picturesqueness within the sphere of the classicist trend, that which felt the substantial value of the basic masonry structures established itself in Florence, thus continuing a centuries-old tradition. In the Palazzo Uguccioni by Mariotto di Zanobi Folfi and in the Palazzo Bartolini Salimbeni and the Palazzo Guadagni by Baccio d'Agnolo (1462–1543; PL. 54) the designers attempted to animate the façades by means of the architectural orders, following a graceful Raphaelesque inflection of Bramante's style, and Baccio d'Agnolo imparted considerable grace to the slender campanile of Sto Spirito; but these are exceptions. After Baccio had displayed sober vigor in a religious building — the single-nave church of S. Giuseppe — he reverted to the use of solid masonry in the Palazzo Rosselli del Turco (formerly Borgherini), as did Domenico di Baccio d'Agnolo in the Palazzo Niccolini. The Church of S. Paolino in Lucca is the work of a sculptor, Baccio da Montelupo (Bartolomeo Sinibaldi), who conceived it as a Latin cross of a height harmonizing with some aspects of earlier local architecture and of a compactness which, like the Romanesque buildings in the same city, emphasized the beauty of the fine stone used.

From the restrained atmosphere of Tuscan purity and clarity emerged Antonio Giamberti (1455–1534), brother of Giuliano da Sangallo and known as Antonio da Sangallo the Elder, whose major achievement falls within the sphere of Bramante's influence. In the loggia opposite that of the Ospedale degli Innocenti in Florence he conformed to Brunelleschi's scheme and retained a 15th-century elegance, which he went beyond, however, in the broader proportions of the loggia facing the Palazzo Comunale (formerly Del Monte) in Monte San Savino. In the building opposite, with rustication on the ground floor and pilasters on the first floor marking the intervals between the windows, the obvious adherence to Bramante's well-known arrangement of the House of Raphael is rather timidly expressed. In some of the fine buildings that he executed in Montepulciano — the Avignonesi, Contucci, Cocconi (Del Pecora), and Cervini palaces (PL. 389; XIII, PL. 237) — Antonio da Sangallo abandoned the architectural orders in favor of solid stone facing with smooth rusticated ashlar, into which portals and windows are inserted with a clearly sculptural intent; like most Florentine

artists, he tended toward simplification. Thus, when Antonio da Sangallo the Elder added lateral aisles to the Latin-cross plan of SS. Annunziata in Arezzo, he connected unadorned structural elements to a trabeated vestibule derived from Roman thermal architecture or, better still, from the presbytery of the Early Christian church of S. Salvatore in Spoleto. The tendency toward simplification then led him to emulate Bramante in works that found their most solemn expression in the Church of S. Biagio (1519–26; PLS. 55, 389; fig. in SANGALLO, q.v.; III, PL. 390), next to a rectory with superposed loggias, of which the second, with double lights, is derived from Bramante.

The Greek-cross plan of this church, reminiscent of S. Maria delle Carceri in Prato by Giuliano da Sangallo and with two superimposed orders like its prototype, is notable in its geometric elevation, dominated by a soaring dome that was to have been flanked by two bell towers (only one was built) echoing those conceived by Bramante for St. Peter's in Rome. And the feeling of gracefulness is replaced by the gravity of the 16th century, which is also sustained by the material used (travertine), especially in the interior, where the powerful barrel vaults of the crossing from which rises the dome rest on massive Doric orders (PL. 55).

This building helps to explain the artistic evolution of Antonio Cordiani, known as Antonio da Sangallo the Younger (1483–1546), a nephew of Antonio da Sangallo the Elder. A link between the two artists is represented by the fortress at Civita Castellana, where Antonio the Elder was responsible for the courtyard, comparable to that of the palazzo built by Bramante in Loreto. Sangallo the Younger, who started out as a craftsman, was both a building contractor and an artist. That he combined a practical activity with an artistic one is clearly evident in his drawings (IV, PL. 187), as well as in his many varied works, among them the powerful examples of military architecture, including — in addition to the fortress at Civita Castellana — the Fortezza da Basso in Florence (1534–35); the fortifications and the Porta Sto Spirito (1537–44) in Rome; the Rocca Paolina in Perugia (1544; destroyed); and other fortifications for the cities of Florence, Piacenza, Castro, and Orvieto, where the double ramp of the Pozzo di S. Patrizio goes deep down into the rock to reach the spring that used to supply the city with water.

As architect of religious buildings Sangallo the Younger designed S. Maria di Loreto in Rome (1507; fig. in SANGALLO, q.v.) as a perfectly geometric cube marked by pilasters and articulated by shallow niches; it generates an impression of movement in the structural members of the octagonal upper section and in the dome, on which rests the richly decorated lantern (1582) by Jacopo del Duca. The interior is more unitary, with two orders and corner niches inspired by Roman thermae. In connection with this church a project was developed, but never executed, for the renovation of S. Marco in Florence on a central plan that would replace the basilican one. The Church of Sto

Spirito in Sassia, in Rome, is a basilican edifice; its interior struc-
ture repeats Florentine models, with a single nave covered by
a timbered ceiling, and its lateral chapels are not rectangular
but semicircular, as in Roman churches of the 15th century.
The architecture is lively but the decoration is restrained.
A scheme derived from Bramante prevails in the façade, with
its two orders. Apart from minor works, such as the austere
Cappella Paolina in the Vatican, Antonio da Sangallo the
Younger, succeeding Raphael (1520) in the construction of St.
Peter's (assisted by Peruzzi, who died in 1536), conceived
an elaborate project, for which the model survives (X, PL. 102),
in which the basic cross was to be lengthened by a complicated
projection flanked by two bell towers that were inspired by the
Church of S. Biagio in Montepulciano and employ motifs from
Bramante's original plan. Moreover, the excessively cluttered,
fragmented facing with three orders lacking in proportions and
the double gallery encircling the dome, which together with
the very heavy lantern would inevitably have stifled the thrust,
indicate that the challenge was beyond the artist's capacities
— given as he was to analysis rather than to synthesis.

Instead, for the Church of S. Tolomeo at Nepi, a less ambitious undertaking, Sangallo achieved, in a second elaboration
of the façade, a uniformity that is totally lacking in his plan for
St. Peter's. The artist's interest was always drawn to secular
rather than religious architecture: the three-storied Palazzo Baldassini, which was to serve as model for many of the Roman
buildings of the 16th and 17th centuries, is full of vigorous relief
in the strongly emphasized quoins, in the portal and windows,
and in the rhythmic arcades of the superposed galleries of the
courtyard, which has two orders — Doric and Ionic — and in
which the adherence to Bramante's style is particularly marked.
Bramante's influence is even more manifest in the façade of the
Palazzo del Banco di Sto Spirito with its rusticated ground floor
and heavy trabeated pilasters continued on the two upper floors
(PL. 390); this concept is evident also in the design for the façade of Palazzo della Zecca in Castro. The most original and
remarkable expression of Sangallo's talent is undoubtedly the
Palazzo Farnese (PL. 56; FIG. 80). The motif of the third-story
windows in the powerful façade of the Roman building has a
precedent in an earlier design for a ducal palace, perhaps intended
for the town of Castro. Sangallo's work on the Palazzo Farnese
began in 1515 for Cardinal Alessandro Farnese; when the
prelate became Pope Paul III in 1534, he decided to have his
residence enlarged. The palace then acquired its unitary, monumental character; the Bramantesque divisions were abandoned,
and exceptional sculptural relief was created in the succession
of windows and in the quoins and the rusticated portal. The
effect is strengthened by the imposing cornice by Michelangelo,
who also designed the severe central window that opens onto
a balcony. In this work Sangallo insisted on a monumental
Roman application of Florentine styles, which were also used
in the vestibule (PL. 55), where motifs from the vestibule of the
Sacristy of Sto Spirito and from the Cardini Chapel in S.
Francesco at Pescia are given a 16th-century breadth in the division into three aisles that are flanked by Bramantesque niches.
The rhythmic "gravitas" of ancient Roman monuments (in this
case, especially that of the Theater of Marcellus) is echoed in
the three stories of the courtyard; the top story was the work
of Michelangelo (he also collaborated on the ground floor of the
rear façade), who replaced Sangallo's static rhythms with his
own dynamic ones. While taking into consideration Sangallo's
personal contribution, it must be admitted that he followed in
substance the course traced by Bramante, remaining on the
path of classicism but representing a distinct type that is Florentine in origin and of an eminently sculptural character.

Inevitably, a number of artists gravitated around Sangallo;
some of them belonged to his own family, which was truly a
dynasty, the "setta sangallesca" so colorfully described by Vasari, to which Michelangelo was fiercely hostile. Among his
many followers were Sangallo's brother, Battista, known as
Il Gobbo; Francesco (Giuliano's son), known as Il Margotta;
Bastiano, known as Aristotile; Giovanni Francesco; and Nanni
di Baccio Bigio.

Michelangelo, who was to dominate the century, personi-

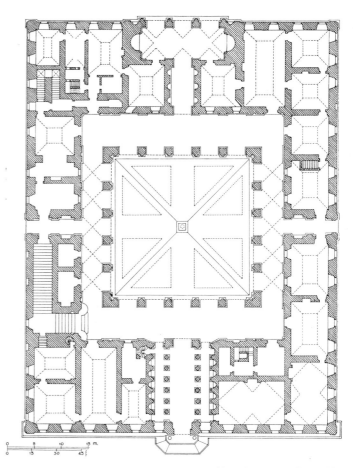

Rome, Palazzo Farnese, plan of ground floor (*from P. Letarouilly, Edifices
de Rome Moderne, London, 1930*).

fied that current which was opposed to the classical trend.
To him, sculpture was a means of obtaining dramatic effects,
even in architecture, on which he left an impressive mark,
though only in a later stage of his many-faceted activity. His
architectural experience began — as far as is known — with
the competition ordered by Leo X for the façade of the Church
of S. Lorenzo in Florence (I, PL. 406). Previously, for the tomb
of Julius II in St. Peter's, Michelangelo had conceived a parallel-
epiped with minimal, almost schematic, structural members
to connect the sculptures that were to have been the principal
elements in the monumental complex (IX, FIG. 881). And even
on the ceiling of the Sistine Chapel (II, PL. 291) the painted
architecture was expressed in simplified geometric schemes
that provide a background for the monumental figures.

For the façade of S. Lorenzo, which Michelangelo conceived
independently of the interior arrangement, he visualized a
great rectangular wall divided into five sections, with the central
part emphasized by a pediment and two extremities, in order
to create a contrast of masses. To justify the dramatic tension,
the artist placed on the lower Corinthian order the weight of
the very high pedestal that forms part of the upper order; this
is also evident in the wooden model by Baccio d'Agnolo (Florence, Casa Buonarroti). On the façade, sculpture was to have
been used to heighten the contrasting esthetic effect, with statues and marble and bronze reliefs, as shown in a clay model
(1518; lost). The façade of S. Lorenzo was never executed;
however, next to the apse of the church the artist later built
the New Sacristy (1520–34) for Pope Clement VII. While
repeating the plan of Brunelleschi's Old Sacristy, Michelangelo
accentuated its vertical thrust. To increase the tension, he
weighted down the structure with a deeply coffered dome topped
by a high lantern (IX, FIG. 892); the whitewashed walls were
enlivened by superposed structural members and windows
framed in somber sandstone, as if to confer an austere, funereal

tone on the building that was to become the mausoleum of the Medicis. In the walls of the chapel, the doors and the niches above them — of pure-white marble — were decorated with motifs derived from antiquity, adapted in their details to suit an original sculptural expression; and while they contrast with the darker stone structural elements of the edifice, the marble of which they are made harmonizes with the two tombs opposite each other, in which figural elements prevail. When architecture was not bound to sculpture Michelangelo sought effects of movement and of even more intense contrast, as in the vestibule of the Biblioteca Laurenziana in Florence (IX, PL. 540), started in 1523 and completed by Vasari (1552) after Michelangelo's departure for Rome. The vestibule is very high and vertical in feeling, with paired columns set into the walls and dividing the walls into panels; there are rectangular edicules with curvilinear pediments, tablets, and high windows that admit light from above, creating a striking contrast between the dark stone and the whitewashed surfaces. The general impression is one of restless movement culminating in the strongly projecting staircase, built by Vasari from a design by Michelangelo. In the long library (IX, FIG. 903), the pilasters, panels, and the ceiling, in addition to accentuating the perspective effect, generate an intense, uninterrupted sculptural feeling that is attuned to the design of the pavement of bicolored terra cotta and to the ornamentation of the large windows. Against the architectural framework of the walls, the heavy portals on the short sides acquire greater relief; on the exterior, the windows and the end brackets have an even stronger sculptural feeling.

Unlike Bramante, who had created a flow of calm classical rhythms in the courtyard of the Belvedere, Michelangelo produced in the fortifications of S. Miniato (1528–30) in Florence a striking ensemble of powerful, dynamically contrasting masses clinging to the slopes of the hill; the dramatic impact of this creation is better shown by the remarkable drawings preserved in the Casa Buonarroti than by the scarce remains. This contrast of architectural elements is also to be found in those sections of the Palazzo Farnese for which Michelangelo was responsible. In Rome, where he gave a new architectural aspect to the Piazza del Campidoglio (begun 1546), Michelangelo echoed the arrangement of the buildings around the central square of Pienza in the two lateral buildings — the Palazzo dei Conservatori (IX, PL. 542) and Palazzo dei Musei — which diverge from right angles with respect to the central Palazzo Senatorio in order to achieve a feeling of greater spaciousness (IX, FIG. 907). The massive front of the Palazzo Senatorio, scanned by pilasters rising on two floors and soaring high on an unadorned podium that contrasts with the double staircase, is markedly distinct from the two lateral buildings, uniform in their single order, but possessing striking chiaroscuro contrasts in the arcades, which create deep zones of shadow, and in the strongly projecting windows.

During his long stay in Rome Michelangelo constantly expressed himself with original innovations, from the studies for the Church of S. Giovanni dei Fiorentini (1550–59), in which he insisted on a central plan, to those (in collaboration with Tiberio Calcagni) for the Sforza Chapel in S. Maria Maggiore, whose oval shape anticipated some of his later works; and from the Porta Pia's powerful structural members (IX, PL. 542) to the Church of S. Maria degli Angeli, built over the Baths of Diocletian. Michelangelo's principal architectural undertaking, which occupied him from 1547 to the time of his death, was St. Peter's. While generally retaining Bramante's ichnographic scheme, he gave it a more compact and concentrated organic character in the perimeter (from which the towers were eliminated), marked by a huge single order of trabeated Corinthian pilasters with superposed, contrasting windows and niches (IX, PL. 541).

The dome, set among four lesser ones, was at first conceived as hemispherical with a double calotte, like that of Florence Cathedral, resting on a drum with paired columns and tabernacle windows. However, in the execution it was tapered by the use of stilted arches, and was given a sense of movement by the ribs and oculi that punctuate the exterior; it ends in a heavy lantern created by Giacomo della Porta after the master's death (1564).

If it can be said of Michelangelo the architect that he was anticlassical, that is, that he was in opposition to the classicizing trend, this does not imply that he was not of the Renaissance; within the sphere of this artistic movement — specifically, its intermediate phase — Michelangelo availed himself, also in the field of architecture, of the stimulation and inspiration of antiquity, which he interpreted through the originality of his own genius.

Sculpture. The classical trend in sculpture began with Leonardo, who, following his teacher Verrocchio, articulated and inserted the human figure into the surrounding atmosphere; this is evident not in any monumental works but in drawings and small bronzes attributed to him (equestrian statue; Budapest, Mus. of Fine Arts), where, although he strove for contrasting effects, he created a modulated chiaroscuro, as he did also in studies for the equestrian statues of Francesco Sforza (1483–98) and Gian Giacomo Trivulzio (1511–13; cf. IX, PL. 118).

In Florence, Giovan Francesco Rustici (1474–1554) elaborated some of Leonardo's qualities: intense chiaroscuro effects that aimed at creating perspective depth (glazed high relief of *Noli me tangere*; Florence, Mus. Naz.) and delicate modeling, together with physical features characteristic of the master's work (bronze group with John the Baptist; PL. 57). He translated into sculpture an episode derived from Leonardo's *Battle of Anghiari*, known through various copies painted by Rustici himself (Florence, Mus. Naz., Pal. Vecchio; Louvre). Rustici, who worked in France, was instrumental in spreading the Renaissance in that country.

Among the Florentines, Baccio da Montelupo (1469–1535) followed the style of Benedetto da Maiano, but his figures, with their flowing and ample draperies, have a more intense spirituality (bronze statue of St. John the Evangelist, 1515; Florence, Orsanmichele); in contrast, Benedetto da Rovezzano (1474–1552), in the reliefs on the monument to St. Giovanni Gualberto (1505–13; now divided in Florence between the Mus. Naz. and the refectory of S. Salvi), displayed a vigor typical of the 16th century, although slightly dispersive and disordered; it appears in fact as a somewhat superficial development of the dynamic tendencies of Bertoldo di Giovanni (PL. 18). Benedetto, who also contributed to spreading the Renaissance in France and England (1525), combined relief with an ornamental style of Lombard origin (tomb of Oddo Altoviti, 1507; Florence, SS. Apostoli) that had previously been introduced in Tuscany, where Andrea Ferrucci (1465–1526), although faithful to traditional styles, was one of the artists who combined them with figural elements (altar in Fiesole, Cath.).

Niccolò Tribolo (1500–50), who worked with Andrea Sansovino, was in Rome in 1524, where he took as his model the scheme of Sansovino's monuments in the Church of S. Maria del Popolo (see below), broadening it in the monument of Adrian VI in the Church of S. Maria dell'Anima. This is not, however, the most striking work of this artist, whose style tended toward the painterly and who showed a marked preference for secular sculpture. Imbued with motifs derived from ancient myths, he was extremely sensitive to idealized beauty, as in the Fountain of the Labyrinth in the Villa della Petraia (PL. 57) and in the fountain of the Villa di Castello, on which he may have collaborated with Pierino da Vinci; these fountains are masterfully inserted into the surrounding landscape. Tribolo also created fine landscapes in his designs for various gardens (at the Villa di Castello, VIII, PL. 431; Boboli Gardens, VIII, PL. 429, FIG. 1089). Tribolo, who was at one time Michelangelo's assistant, did not have his master's gigantic vision, although he sensed Michelangelo's dramatic values, if only superficially (sections of the lateral portals in Bologna, S. Petronio). Another sculptor, Silvio Cosini (ca. 1495–1547), inserted figural elements in the new style into outdated schemes (altar in the Sanctuary of Montenero, near Livorno, 1530). Giovanni Angelo Montorsoli (1507–63) acquired an assurance in his art from his teacher Ferrucci and he drew from Michelangelo, whom he assisted occasionally, some touching figural accents (altar in Bologna, S. Maria dei Servi, 1556–61); however, his efforts were devoted mainly to decoration. In this he was inspired by Tribolo's example, but he contributed a redundant richness of his own in the Fountain of Orion (1550) in Messina and the Fountain of Neptune (1557; PL. 57).

The Florentine sculptors went on to spread the Renaissance outside their native city: Cosini in Padua, Baccio da Montelupo in Bologna, and Tribolo and Montorsoli in Bologna and in Sicily. It is noteworthy that in the 16th century the Renaissance was carried across the Alps by Pietro Torrigiani (1472–1528), among others. In his youth a fierce opponent of Michelangelo, Torrigiani showed himself to be a vigorous and exuberant sculptor and modeler in London (tomb of Henry VII and Elizabeth of York, Westminster Abbey) and in Seville (*Madonna and Child*; *St. Jerome*; both, Mus. Provincial de Bellas Artes), where he died.

Other minor Tuscan artists, such as Lorenzo di Mariano Fucci (Il Marrina), Antonio Barile, and Bartolomeo Neroni (Il Riccio), working in wood or marble, introduced to Siena some decorative elements of a Lombard flavor. Lorenzo and Stagio Stagi worked in Pisa, in Pietrasanta, and along the Versilian coast. Outstanding among these artists was Andrea Sansovino (see above), in whom the transition from early to High Renaissance was marked by animated and lively forms that were derived from the Pollaiuolo brothers (two sculptural groups, of which one is glazed, in Monte San Savino, Church of S. Chiara), combined with a decorative taste of Lombard origin that is also evident in his compositions (altar of the Sacrament; Florence, S. Spirito) and probably resulted from contacts with Andrea Bregno and with the Roman school.

Andrea Sansovino, a balanced and thoughtful artist, tended toward figural sculpture, as in the *Christ and St. John* (1501–05) above the main portal of the Baptistery in Florence, in his harmoniously conceived and idealized nudes, and in the statues executed for the chapel in Genoa Cathedral (1504; continuing the work of Matteo Civitali): a *Madonna* and a *John the Baptist*, the latter also strongly idealized. A feeling of rather weighty poise is conveyed by the *Madonna, Child, and St. Anne* (1512) in S. Agostino in Rome, inspired by Leonardo, while in the two complex tombs of cardinals Ascanio Sforza (IV, PL. 455) and Girolamo Basso della Rovere in S. Maria del Popolo, Rome, the sculptor brought up to date and monumentalized some Lombard schemes, combining decoration with a flawless sculptural technique that echoes antiquity even in the postures of the deceased, which recall the recumbent figures on Etruscan cinerary urns.

As mentioned above, Bramante's design for the Sanctuary of the Holy House in Loreto was executed by Sansovino, who enriched it, decorating it with vigorous sculptural reliefs — perhaps slightly overabundant and overly descriptive — with scenes from the life of the Virgin, such as the Annunciation (PL. 58). It was precisely his fuller vision, strong in its sound and idealized sense of form, that placed Sansovino at the center of the classical trend of the High Renaissance, of which he was an eminent exponent. Two of the reliefs begun by Sansovino in Loreto were completed by other artists: the *Nativity* by Baccio Bandinelli and the *Marriage of the Virgin* by Raffaele da Montelupo (Sinibaldi; ca. 1505–66); the *Translation of the Holy House* is entirely by Tribolo. Tribolo collaborated with the Emilian Domenico Aimo (Il Varignana), with Raffaele da Montelupo, and with Francesco da Sangallo (Il Margotta; 1494–1576) in the scene of the Death of the Virgin. Francesco da Sangallo was inspired by the sculpture of Sansovino (*Madonna, Child, and St. Anne*, Florence, Orsanmichele; tomb of Bishop Angelo Marzi Medici, 1546, Florence, SS. Annunziata), but he strained his material to the utmost in his search for characterization by means of minute details.

In Rome, Lorenzo Lotti (Lorenzetto; 1490–1541) followed Sansovino's style in his heavy *Madonna and Child* above Raphael's tomb in the Pantheon, executed in collaboration with Raffaele da Montelupo, who worked with Sansovino at Loreto and who was later to come into contact with Michelangelo, without, however, reacting artistically to the experience. Lorenzetto rose above mediocrity in his elegant statues in S. Maria del Popolo, Rome (*Elias*; *Jonah*, PL. 59), executed after designs by Raphael.

In Naples and southern Italy the classicizing trend and the taste for decoration in the Lombard style continued, together with an intense activity that was attuned to new fashions, although it emphasized craftsmanship, especially in altars and in marble funerary monuments. In Naples the classicizing trend was represented by the Spaniards Bartolomé and Diego Ordóñez and by Girolamo Santacroce. In the region of Emilia the 15th-century sculptural styles were continued but updated. The outstanding artists here were the Ferrarese Alfonso Lombardi (ca. 1487–1537; *Death of the Virgin*, Bologna, Oratory of S. Maria della Vita) and the Modenese Antonio Begarelli (ca. 1499–1565), author of the *Madonna and Child with the Infant St. John* (Modena, Mus. Civ.), as well as of a spectacular *Deposition* (Modena, S. Francesco). Terra-cotta sculptures in a genre spirit flourished everywhere, and were especially appreciated when combined with painting, as in the very large and evocative group of scenes of the Passion at Sacro Monte near Varallo, by Gaudenzio Ferrari (IV, PL. 212).

Sansovino was in Rome at the height of the artistic activity during the reign of Pope Julius II. Under the influence of Raphael, decorative values were emphasized and the Roman technique of white stucco in low relief of slight chiaroscuro effect was revived. It has been seen that, following ancient models, this elegant ornamentation was combined with pictorial decorations, for example, by Giovanni da Udine (1487–1564), who used it lavishly in his Roman works (Vatican Logge and Villa Madama; PL. 51; XIII, PL. 285), and in the Castle of Spilimbergo, near Udine. Sansovino's disciple, Jacopo Sansovino, drew from the classicizing trend — first at Florence from Andrea del Sarto, later at Rome from his teacher Andrea Sansovino — the grace and refinement that he realized with a formal power typified by his slender *Bacchus* (III, PL. 391), *St. James* (Florence, Cath.), *Madonna del Parto* (Rome, S. Agostino), and *St. James* (Rome, S. Maria di Monserrato). In 1527 Jacopo Sansovino settled in Venice, where antiquity was interpreted in the Greek tradition and where he found survivals of the 15th century in the reliefs of Pietro and Tullio Lombardo, as well as in figural and other small bronzes by Alessandro Leopardi, Francesco da Sant'Agata, Vittore Gambello, and Maffeo Olivieri. However, Jacopo Sansovino recognized the genius of Titian and turned to a painterly style in his elegant *Madonna and Child with the Infant St. John* (PL. 59) and in the refreshingly spontaneous statues of the Loggetta of the Campanile in Venice (PL. 56). In the huge figures on the Scala dei Giganti of the Doges' Palace (VIII, PL. 198) he strove to express his matured experience as a sculptor. He also endeavored to emulate and surpass his contemporaries in the technique of bronze casting — an activity intensely cultivated in Venice — as in his dramatic bronze reliefs in the apse of S. Marco illustrating five scenes from the life of St. Mark, in the statues of the Evangelists on the balustrade, and in the reliefs on the sacristy door, in which a striking spirituality emerges through the precise modeling and the accentuated luminism (VIII, PL. 214). In the admirably sculptured reliefs on the sacristy door the influences of Donatello and Ghiberti and the spatial achievements of Sansovino are merged with the Venetian light and color.

Michelangelo was first trained as a painter by Domenico Ghirlandajo, then as a sculptor by Bertoldo di Giovanni in the "school" in the garden founded by Lorenzo de' Medici to induce young artists to the stimulating study of antiquity. But from the time of his first reliefs (Florence, Casa Buonarroti) Michelangelo showed in his sculptural works, along with some echoes of Donatello, his characteristic monumentality of form (*Virgin of the Stairs*; IX, PL. 524) and dramatic contrasts (*The Battle of the Lapiths and the Centaurs*; IX, PL. 525). These characteristics were immediately afterward tempered in Rome (1496) by the influence of classic sculpture, which Michelangelo imitated in compositions that hint at potential movement, as in the *Bacchus* (Florence, Mus. Naz.), and by the tendency toward idealization, as in the *Pietà* in Rome (IX, PL. 526). In this work the idealized tone is evident in the very pure nude form of Christ, which stands out against the sinuous draperies of the Madonna's robe. The idealized, truly immaculate Madonna contrasts with the touchingly sorrowful one in the Church of Notre-Dame in Bruges (ca. 1501). In his *David* (1501–04; VII, PL. 383) the proportions are gigantic, the modeling is powerful, and the statue expresses a conscious pride that recalls Donatello's *St. George*; it further reveals a psychological insight suited to the physical grandeur, which exalts the Biblical hero who was repeatedly portrayed by 15th-century Florentine artists as a symbol of intelligence and freedom opposed to brute force and tyranny.

In other works, such as the tondos in London (Royal Acad. of Arts) and Florence (1505; IX, PL. 525), the "unfinished" (*non finito*) quality is a conscious stylistic element, used by Michelangelo for its effects of chiaroscuro and luminism. Michelangelo visualized his art as the liberation of form from shapeless matter, from which the human figure would emerge "per forza di levare." Notable examples of this view are the statues in the Accademia in Florence: *St. Matthew* (ca. 1504; IX, PL. 529), and the dramatically expressive *Prisoners*, the so-called "Boboli Slaves" (1532–34; I, PL. 381), intended for the monumental tomb of Pope Julius II. Other pieces, now scattered, also intended for the projected tomb of Julius II, were executed over a long period of time, for example, the Louvre *Slaves* (IX, PL. 529), in which the contrast of mass in the figures straining for release and the painful torment they express indicate the extent to which Michelangelo was influenced by the discovery of the *Laocoön*. This same contrast was developed in the *Victory* (Florence, Palazzo Vecchio), also for the tomb of Julius II and endowed with a more intense articulation that follows a spiral, serpentine movement. But one of the four principal statues intended for the Pope's tomb, the colossal *Moses* (1515–16), which was the only one that was actually completed and, after a long odyssey, collocated in S. Pietro in Vincoli in Rome, is outstanding for its extreme sculptural force as well as for its powerfully vital form; moreover, it reveals a moral loftiness that is given concreteness by what is known as Michelangelo's seething temperament (*terribilità*).

The Medici tombs commissioned by Clement VII (1520–34) are quite distinct architecturally from those in the New Sacristy of S. Lorenzo in Florence. The statues form triangular units: Lorenzo di Piero de' Medici, duke of Urbino, is placed between the statues of *Dawn* (PL. 60) and *Evening* (IX, PL. 531); Giuliano di Lorenzo de' Medici, duke of Nemours — this statue is said to have been executed with the collaboration of Montorsoli — between *Day* and *Night* (IX, PLS. 530, 531). The allegories, which allude to the passage of time and to the sorrowful earthly pilgrimage, reflect Michelangelo's tormented spirit in their contrasting attitudes and in their "unfinished" quality. Among his other works, the three renditions of the Pietà — a theme to which Michelangelo persistently returned as a synthesis of human suffering — are notable for their lofty spirituality. The one in the Accademia in Florence was frontally conceived (to conform with the shape of the marble block from which it was carved) and brings into full relief the gigantic, limp figure of Christ. The *Deposition* in the Cathedral in Florence (PL. 517; IX, PL. 526), intended by Michelangelo for his own tomb, is more complex in its triangular composition, which permits observation from several points of view because of the contrasting plan of the figures and the variety of the workmanship (Tiberio Calcagni, a Florentine pupil who also worked in Rome, collaborated on the figure of Mary Magdalene), where the "unfinished" quality is used to achieve remarkable nuances. In the two ghostly, elongated figures of the *Rondanini Pietà* (IX, PL. 532) the "unfinished" quality renders perfectly the annulment of physical energy in favor of a greater elevation of the spirit. The sculptor, initiated in the classical vision of serene beauty, endowed man with a heroic quality, sustaining physical monumentality by sculptural tension of a sorrowful spirituality that attains an absolute sublimity.

Painting. Leonardo da Vinci can be said to have been the first painter of the High Renaissance, even though more than half his activity, as an artist and as a scientist dedicated to an unceasing quest for solutions to the most varied problems, occurred within the 15th century. This indefatigable artist aimed at a deeper understanding of all fields of human knowledge, but he was above all a painter and it is precisely in painting that he created an entirely new vision.

Leonardo conceived of the human figure as being constructed and set in the atmospheric space, but, although he accepted Verrocchio's unerring formalism, he turned away from his master's solid modeling in painting. He replaced it with a soft chiaroscuro that subdued or eliminated the outlines, a *sfumato* painting that was blended with light. Light is, in fact, another basic element in Leonardo's style; it is a very soft light, often that of dusk. In his compositions Leonardo shifted his perspective from linear to aerial. Fascinated by chiaroscuro, he considered color as a noble but not essential ornament, and his paintings — aside from the unfinished ones in which chiaroscuro produces effects of contrast, as in the *St. Jerome* (IX, PL. 115) and *The Adoration of the Magi* (IX, PL. 117) — are often suffused with subdued colors that create almost a monochrome effect. Leonardo tended to idealize his figures and to dispose them classically in balanced compositions and with a harmony of masses; the finest example of this is the *Last Supper* (1495–97; PL. 61; IX, PL. 125).

The artistic representation of reality in his drawings distinguishes Leonardo the artist from Leonardo the scientist. The scientist rendered with the utmost precision the plant and animal worlds and the many various instruments he invented, while the artist lyrically transfigured the visible world by means of his atmospheric chiaroscuro (IV, PL. 268; IX, PLS. 118, 119).

Leonardo's long artistic activity began with the execution of the figure of an angel and with the completion of the figure of Christ and the distant, poetic landscape in Verrocchio's *Baptism of Christ* (XIV, PL. 356). His career continued with the *Annunciation* (IX, PL. 116), depicted against a view of the Florentine countryside, and the unfinished *Adoration of the Magi* (IX, PL. 117), based on a broadly conceived pyramidal composition. Leonardo's sojourn in Milan (1483–99) led to refinements in his use of chiaroscuro modeled by light. This is evident in his first version of the *Virgin of the Rocks* (IX, PL. 121) — very different from his second interpretation of the subject (cf. IX, PL. 120), executed in part by his disciple Ambrogio di Predis — with its charming atmosphere heightened by the contrasting light of sunset that throws into relief the rocky landscape, rich with grass and flowers, where even inanimate objects seem endowed with a soul. In that noble, primordial landscape the four figures are set in pyramidal order. The *Last Supper* has almost completely disintegrated because of the painting technique used and because of careless past restorations. The figures of the apostles are arranged in balanced, compact groups of threes in freely dramatic poses. The light plays on them in various ways, creating a contrast with the frontal figure of Christ, who represents divine serenity in contrast with human passions.

During Leonardo's second visit to Florence (1501–06) he created such compositions as the cartoon of *The Virgin and Child with St. Anne and the Infant St. John* (IX, PL. 123), with its outlines in *sfumato*; this theme was taken up again later in *The Virgin and Child with St. Anne* (IX, PL. 122) with a much more complex articulation, although again within a pyramidal scheme, and with a more profound and refined spirituality in the faintly smiling faces. The linked composition of this painting was anticipated by the much more complex and contrasting one of the *Battle of Anghiari* (or the *Fight for the Standard*), conceived as a wild tangle of horsemen and foot soldiers on various planes, which was to be placed opposite Michelangelo's *Battle of Cascina* in the Salone dei Cinquecento in the Palazzo Vecchio in Florence. The original is lost, because it was executed in a technique (probably encaustic) that was not resistant, but is known to us through the master's detailed drawings as well as through a number of copies (IX, PL. 119). The *Gioconda* (or *Mona Lisa*; IX, PL. 126) was also created in Florence; the model's pose (including the full bust and the hands) became a model for High Renaissance portraits. Around the poetic rendering of the enigmatic figure, a similarly poetic landscape is a nostalgic echo of the silent and misty Lombard landscape.

From Leonardo's later period, the *John the Baptist* (IX, PL. 124) represents an artistic testament in its extreme simplification of painting as a synthesis of light and shade. Thus the luminous half-figure of the saint emerges as an apparition from the dense, brown-toned background. Along with the artist's achievements in the technique of painting, the perfection of his composition made him a master of classicism and, as such, the initiator of High Renaissance painting.

Leonardo's influence was extremely widespread and decisive for the classical trend because of his almost Hellenic idealization and because of the architectonic balance of his compositions. The first traces of the master's influence in Florence (see above) are evident in some painters still bound to an early Renaissance vision. Leonardo's long Milanese sojourn gave rise to a group of Lombard followers, who, inevitably, interpreted the master only superficially or partially. Ambrogio di Predis (ca. 1455–1522), pupil and collaborator of Leonardo, gave greater density and a darker tone to Leonardo's chiaroscuro (PL. 62) and excelled in portrait painting, such as the portrait of Gian Galeazzo Sforza (formerly Milan, Coll. Porro). Giovanni Antonio Boltraffio (1467–1516; VIII, PL. 196), highly sensitive to color, infused greater warmth into Leonardo's *sfumato* and achieved, particularly in his rendering of fabrics, chromatic combinations of courtly splendor (*Madonna and Child*, Milan, Mus. Poldi Pezzoli), while maintaining, like the good Lombard he was, close contacts with the gentle Il Bergognone (Ambrogio da Fossano). Further removed in time — and in quality — was the following generation of Lombard artists, who worked in the first decades of the 16th century. Among them were Giovanni Pedrini (Giampietrino); Marco d'Oggiono; and Cesare da Sesto, who was more talented than the first two and who tempered Leonardo's influence in drawings that were closer to Raphael (altarpiece depicting the Baptism, Milan, Coll. Molfetta). Later, Andrea Solari, who had contacts with Leonardo and the Flemish school, softened his basically Venetian style to the point of affectation (*The Virgin with the Green Cushion*; VIII, PL. 211). Bernardino Luini (ca. 1485–1532), although still bound to the local trends of the 15th century and particularly reminiscent of Bramantino in some of his compositional aspects, was influenced by Leonardo's idealized painting (PL. 62). This combination of influence is evident in his frescoes, for example, those from the Villa della Pelucca (Brera), among which is included the scene of St. Catherine received into Heaven, and in his altarpieces and devotional panels, such as the *Madonna of the Rose Garden* (Brera).

Gaudenzio Ferrari (1480–1546), from Valduggia, near Borgosesia, also a sculptor, at first worked in a 15th-century style that was perhaps patterned after that of Macrino d'Alba (Gian Giacomo de Alladio), but he later drew inspiration from various cultural sources. His vivid colors were softened into chiaroscuro as a result of his contacts with Leonardo's school. Moreover, he felt the influence of Bramantino's monumentality and, especially in frescoes (PL. 63), turned to decorative rhythms that expanded Gothic ones, achieving more highly developed volumes; his work also shows echoes of other artists, such as Perugino and Dürer. However, the various influences he assimilated were always elaborated by him and expressed in his own exuberant, original idiom, as, for example, in the crowded compositions of Sacro Monte at Varallo (1523; IV, PL. 212), combined with terra-cotta groups in a genre spirit, and again in the representations of Mary Magdalene and the Crucifixion (1530–32) in the Church of S. Cristoforo in Vercelli. Ferrari also worked in Lombardy, at Milan, at Como, and at Saronno in the Sanctuary of the Madonna dei Miracoli (where Luini was also active); the dome of the Sanctuary is crowded with figures by Ferrari (1535–36). Ferrari's art was continued by the faithful, although modest and rather colorless, Bernardino Lanino (ca. 1511–ca. 1582) and by the Piedmontese mannerists, such as Guglielmo Caccia (Moncalvo, ca. 1568–1625).

Another Piedmontese, Sodoma (Giovanni Antonio Bazzi; 1477–1549), from Vercelli, was much influenced by Leonardo. Sodoma settled in Siena about 1500. His soft style is shown in the frescoes (1503–04) of the Church of S. Anna in Camprena, near Pienza, illustrating scenes from the lives of Christ, the Virgin, St. Anne, and St. Benedict, and in the frescoes (1505–08) in the Abbey of Monte Oliveto Maggiore depicting scenes from the life of St. Benedict. In Siena, Sodoma's style became enriched with Tuscan and Umbrian elements, as in frescoes of scenes from the life of St. Catherine in S. Domenico (PL. 63). Also

noteworthy are Sodoma's frescoes in the Farnesina, Rome, and paintings in Pisa Cathedral.

Although some achievements of Venetian and Emilian painting also are related to Leonardo's new vision, the artist was essentially a Florentine, and as such was primarily a master of form. Thus his art leads back to Florence, where the predominant trend was a classical one promoted mainly by two artists: Fra Bartolommeo (Baccio della Porta) and Andrea del Sarto.

Fra Bartolommeo (1475–1517) emulated Ghirlandajo's symmetrical compositions in his fresco of the *Last Judgment* (1499–1501; Florence, transferred from S. Maria Nuova to the Mus. di S. Marco). He used bright, rather discordant silvery hues, revealing some chromatic similarities with Piero di Cosimo, as, for instance, in *The Vision of St. Bernard* (1506; VIII, PL. 209). He was extremely skilled in the use of perspective, which he combined with increasingly monumental figures, with a chiaroscuro that was shaded in imitation of Leonardo (whose influence also is evident in the pyramidal compositions of some of his renderings of the *Holy Family*, e.g., Rome, Gall. Naz.), and with vivid colors that became even brighter after his sojourn in Venice (1508). Fra Bartolommeo later tended away from the execution of altarpieces — usually of a high artistic level — (*Sacra Conversazione*, 1509, Lucca, Cath.; *Pietà*, in which two figures emphasize a vertical line, Florence, Pitti) toward large religious compositions (PL. 64; *God the Father with St. Catherine of Siena and the Magdalen*, 1509, and the *Madonna della Misericordia*, 1515, both, Lucca, Pin. Naz.; *Annunciation*, 1515, Louvre), in which sheer technical ability prevailed over the artist's innate painterly sense, which can be appreciated instead in his small paintings, of a perfection that is almost Flemish (small diptych representing the Annunciation, the Nativity, and the Circumcision; Uffizi), and particularly in his drawings. In his later works — slightly reminiscent of Michelangelo — the artist lapsed into rhetorical expressions.

Mariotto Albertinelli (1474–1515), who collaborated with Fra Bartolommeo and came under the latter's influence in his large *Annunciation* (1510; Florence, Acc.), painted with brilliant, enameled colors that appear consistently in his work, from the youthful *Annunciation* (1497; Volterra, Cath.) to the *Madonna and Child* (PL. 67), and from the well-balanced *Visitation* (Uffizi) to other works in which the compositional schemes are more traditional than those of Fra Bartolommeo.

Another disciple of Fra Bartolommeo, the Dominican Fra Paolino, from Pistoia, produced paintings that appear wooden and weak; in contrast, an eclectic, exuberant Sienese artist, Girolamo del Pacchia (1477–1533), allied himself with the Florentine trend — and Albertinelli in particular — as is evident in his *Annunciation* and *Visitation* (1518; both, Siena, Pin. Naz.). Initially an adherent of the provincial ways of his home town (represented by Bernardino Fungai, Giacomo Pacchiarotti, and others), he soon acquired the broader scope of 16th-century art, which had its exponents in Sodoma, Raphael, and Andrea del Sarto.

Andrea del Sarto, defined by Vasari as the "flawless" painter, was preeminently classical. But while his art, based on that of Piero di Cosimo, tended toward an orderly beauty in its successive phases, which came under various influences, he achieved poetic expressions of his own by means of his painterly instincts and some atmospheric effects of Leonardesque origin [in landscapes with scenes from the life of S. Filippo Benizzi (1509–10; I, PL. 251) and in interiors such as that in *The Birth of the Virgin* (1514; I, PL. 250)]. In some spontaneous portraits, such as his *Portrait of a Young Girl* (Uffizi) and the *Portrait of a Sculptor* (I, PL. 247), these values persist. His monochrome frescoes with their faceted forms in the Cloister of the Scalzo (1512–24; I, PLS. 257, 258) are original interpretations of Leonardo's chiaroscuro. Andrea created pyramidal compositions that aimed at greater coherence and breadth than those of Fra Bartolommeo, such as the Louvre *Charity* (painted for Francis I, who invited Andrea to France), and he also produced monumental frescoes: *The Last Supper* in the Convent of S. Salvi (1519; I, PL. 259) and the so-called "Madonna del Sacco" (1525; I, PL. 255), in which he surpassed Fra Bartolommeo. Andrea eventually became sensitive also to the influence of Michelangelo and of antiquity, which is evident in cold, reasoned compositions that are notable for their great dignity. He also excelled as an illustrator of sacred legends, and was one of the group that decorated a room for Pier Francesco Borgherini in Florence with panels (now dispersed) illustrating scenes from the life of Joseph (I, PL. 254); the group included Francesco Granacci, Bachiacca, and Pontormo.

The varied Florentine environment included minor artists who were more or less connected with and fascinated by the great masters — from Leonardo to Raphael — and who were receptive also to the influence of Andrea del Sarto and Michelangelo. As concerns easel paintings, the most traditional of these artists was Francesco Granacci (1469–1543), who trained with Michelangelo at Ghirlandajo's school; he combined his master's teachings with the youthful example of his fellow student (*Madonna and Child with the Infant St. John*; Dublin, Nat. Gall. of Ireland), in a style that was later broadened by the influence of Leonardo (*Assumption*; Florence, Acc.) and even by the superficial imitation of Pontormo (panels from an altar in S. Apollonia; Florence, Acc.); throughout his activity Granacci retained a measure of classicism.

Bachiacca (Francesco Ubertini, 1494–1557) also derived his art from a 15th-century painter, Perugino; he was later influenced by Raphael and Michelangelo, evolving a pleasantly descriptive style (scenes from the life of Joseph, from the Borgherini panels; Rome, Gall. Borghese). He painted graceful figures (*Baptism of Christ*, London, Launders Coll.; *Mary Magdalene*, Florence, Pitti) and executed tasteful decorations (cartoons for tapestries, 1549–53; Uffizi).

The more vigorous Ridolfo (1483–1561), son of Domenico Ghirlandajo, was orphaned at an early age and trained by his uncle David. He combined Ghirlandajo's graphic sense with the chiaroscuro of Leonardo, from whom he also derived some of his vivid colors (frescoes in the Cappella dei Priori in the Palazzo Vecchio, Florence; 1514), which were transmitted through the art of Fra Bartolommeo, Mariotto Albertinelli, and, finally, Raphael; this is especially true of his portraits (*Portrait of a Lady*, 1508; Florence, Pitti) and the compact altarpieces to which he transferred the narrative quality generally reserved by the Florentines for secular themes decorating pieces of furniture such as *cassoni* and chair backs (scenes from the life of St. Zanobi, 1510; Florence, Acc.).

A later group comprised other painters such as the uninspired Giovannantonio Sogliani (1492–1544), rather mediocre and harsh in his expressions, whose art derived at first from Lorenzo di Credi and then reflected echoes of Albertinelli and Fra Bartolommeo (*St. Dominic Fed by Angels*, Florence, Mus. di S. Marco; *The Last Supper* and *The Washing of the Feet*, Anghiari, Collegiata). Domenico Puligo (1492–1527) was close to Andrea del Sarto and Fra Bartolommeo in the shaded chiaroscuro of his gentle Madonnas and his altarpieces (*Deposition*; Anghiari, Collegiata). Similar to Puligo in his gentle timidity, Andrea Piccinelli (Andrea del Brescianino; ca. 1485–1545) was from Brescia but was active in Siena. From that environment, as well as from the Florentine masters and from Raphael (*Coronation of the Virgin*; Siena, Church of SS. Pietro e Paolo), he drew his inspiration. So did Franciabigio (Francesco di Cristofano; 1482–1525), a disciple of Albertinelli, who collaborated with Andrea del Sarto in the Cloister of the Scalzo. Franciabigio felt the influence of Raphael (*Madonna del Pozzo*, PL. 67; *Madonna and Child*, Rome, Gall. Naz.) and excelled in portraiture (two male portraits; Berlin, Staat. Mus.); in his frescoes he favored rather scenographic effects, as in the *Triumph of Caesar* (1521) in the Villa di Poggio a Caiano, near Florence.

Giuliano Bugiardini (1475–1554) appears excessively mechanical and calculating in his *Martyrdom of St. Catherine* (Florence, S. Maria Novella), which was inspired by various sources. Previously, he had been attracted by the work of Albertinelli (tondo with the Holy Family; Turin, Gall. Sabauda), tending away from Piero di Cosimo — after whom he had initially patterned his style — but he always retained a rather superficial grace (*John the Baptist*, Bologna, Pin. Naz.).

Raphael was the loftiest exponent of the classical trend in central Italy. Influenced by his origins in Urbino (where the teachings of the timid Timoteo Viti were augmented by the example of Piero della Francesca), he occupied himself with the concepts of space and equilibrium even in such balanced youthful works as the *Three Graces* (Chantilly, Mus. Condé); during his Umbrian period (1500–04), the teachings of Perugino reinforced Raphael's interest in these concepts. An apt example is *The Marriage of the Virgin* (1504; XI, PL. 423), which, derived compositionally from Perugino's interpretation of the theme (Caen, Mus. B. A.), achieves a fusion of space and form that is lacking in the model; the work has a sublime nobility and is notable for its effects of pure color and light. This masterful art, which soon acquired unmistakable characteristics, was united to Raphael's prodigious capacity for assimilating various influences. During the artist's Florentine period (1504–08) his art expanded in its spatial vision, in its composition, and in the atmospheric refinement that emulated Leonardo's softness [*Madonna of the Goldfinch*, Uffizi; *Madonna del Prato* (XI, PL. 425); *La Belle Jardinière* (PL. 65)], and these became essential components of Raphael's style. Moreover, in Florence, the artist's inspiration was intensified and extended to portraits that evoke Leonardo in their composition and pose (e.g., those of Angelo Doni and Maddalena Doni; both, Florence, Pitti). The search for stronger forms in the *Deposition* (1507; IV, PL. 314) reveals the influence of Michelangelo, and the composition evokes the influence of ancient art; these elements were strengthened during Raphael's Roman period (1508–20), during which he was intensely active until his premature death.

The last phase of Raphael's activity was characterized by an even greater breadth and by an opulent beauty, in which the purity and grace of the Umbrian and Florentine periods, which convey an impression of genuine moral soundness, were superseded by a serene and earthly vitality, achieved by means of colors that were richer and more vivid because of the Venetian influence introduced into Rome by Sebastiano del Piombo (*Madonna of Foligno*, 1511–12; XI, PL. 434). Characteristic of the artist's work during this period are some broadly conceived compositions that result in scenographic effects (*Sistine Madonna*; XI, PL. 433). Raphael's production was extremely varied and included portraits, easel paintings representing widely differing subjects, and frescoes. In his portraits, he emphasized the physical peculiarities of his subjects even while idealizing them, capturing the essence of their personalities, as in the portraits of Count Tommaso Inghirami (Boston, Isabella Stewart Gardner Mus.) and Baldassare Castiglione (Louvre). He applied his gift for portraiture also to his official paintings, such as that representing Pope Leo X with cardinals Giulio de' Medici and Luigi de' Rossi (XI, PL. 428).

The themes of his frescoes, especially those in the Vatican Stanze, which exalt historical events and doctrinal concepts that demonstrate the continuity of the Church, provided the artist with opportunities to express his stylistic ideals. Thus, in the Stanza della Segnatura (1509–11; I, PL. 307; III, PL. 209; IV, PL. 230; XI, PL. 426) the broad but serene forms are suffused with a limpid and clear color; in the Stanza d'Eliodoro (1511–14; XI, PLS. 426, 427, 430) the color is animated by warm tones and occasional luminist contrasts that intensify the impression of movement. In the Stanza dell'Incendio (1514–17; XI, PLS. 429, 430), the prevailing classicism emphasizes the influence of Michelangelo in the nudes, consistently sustained by a monumental scope, even though some sections were carried out by assistants (Giovanni Francesco Penni, Giulio Romano, Perino del Vaga). Finally, in the Sala di Costantino (1517–25) an agitated and ostentatious expression — made heavy through the intervention of his pupils — heralds a further step in stylistic development, which was to be continued by Raphael's disciples after his death in 1520.

Raphael's Roman years were highly productive — from the frescoes in the Farnesina (ca. 1511 and 1517; III, PL. 392; X, PL. 250) to those in S. Maria della Pace (XI, PL. 432), S. Agostino, and the Vatican Logge (XI, PL. 431), on which Giovanni da Udine and Perino del Vaga collaborated. Among the stuccoes and the *grotteschi* in the Logge appear episodes from the Old and New Testaments with scenes of great illustrative spontaneity, in which the master's unitary conception emerges despite the rather overstated execution by his pupils. His various collaborators (among them Penni, Romano, and Polidoro da Caravaggio) tended away from Raphael's rhythms, adapting them to their own modes of expression and forming a well-defined current within the late Renaissance period. In Raphael's harmonious art, the Humanist order of the Renaissance, with its spatial rhythms and idealization of the human figure, combined the grace of the 15th century with the compositional sense that is typical of the High Renaissance and was often given substance by Venetian color.

However, in Raphael's later period, his vision was altered by a change in figural emphasis; this can be seen in the large altarpiece of *The Transfiguration* (XI, PLS. 434, 435), which was unfinished because of his death. This work brings into sharp relief the contrast between the exaltation of the divine and the earthly drama of the human condition. Nevertheless, this change in emphasis is much more noticeable in his pupils. Raphael's school, almost without exception, followed the path of the late Renaissance (Baldassare Peruzzi, however, adhered to the still classic trend in his Roman and Sienese paintings); but even in the new figural exuberances and virtuoso expressions, his followers retained the rhythms of Raphael, whose art was widely diffused — mainly through the faithful copies engraved by Marcantonio Raimondi (ca. 1480–ca. 1534; IV, PL. 425).

In the Veneto, Giorgione (Giorgio da Castelfranco; ca. 1477–1510) pursued elegant Hellenic idealizations and led early Renaissance painting, with its concise forms, to a new synthesis of perspective and form, with soft, light, atmospheric colors that are far removed from Leonardo's, which were based on design and chiaroscuro. Giorgione's close links with the early Renaissance are evident in the altarpiece at Castelfranco Veneto (VI, PLS. 185, 188), in which the color and the tranquil light achieve a sense of nobility. However, *The Three Philosophers* (VI, PLS. 190, 191), one of whom is said to represent Copernicus, has a mysterious new fascination, particularly in the landscape in which the three meditative figures are placed; in this work Giorgione continued that total vision of reality that had characterized the Venetian early Renaissance. Giorgione's preference for secular subjects was attuned to the Humanistic atmosphere that flourished in Venice.

In *The Tempest* (VI, PLS. 186, 187), Giorgione's enigmatic masterpiece that represents a landscape at sunset, vibrating under flashes of lightning, the artist reproduces a fearful aspect of nature with an almost romantic sensitivity. In his *Judith* (VI, PL. 193), Giorgione achieved an expression of beauty suffused with melancholy that was to appear again in the *Sleeping Venus* (VI, PL. 195), a resplendent image of serene harmony in a tranquil landscape. By reason of his spiritual and esthetic attitudes and, above all, because of his painterly innovations, Giorgione was the first High Renaissance painter in Venice and the Veneto region.

Titian (Tiziano Vecellio; 1477–1576), an instinctive painter endowed with an exuberant temperament, soon surpassed his teacher Giovanni Bellini and tended toward the style of Giorgione (with whom he collaborated on the frescoes on the façade of the Fondaco dei Tedeschi in Venice), devoting himself almost exclusively to easel paintings. In these he varied his technique by means of washes of color to achieve either solid forms or light, evanescent effects. His colors are consistently warm and sensual. Throughout Titian's long and successful career his art underwent evident stylistic changes, but it always evokes a vital humanity of vast breadth and action. His religious paintings — from *The Assumption* (III, PL. 310; IV, PL. 276) and the *Pesaro Madonna* (XIV, PL. 96) to the later *Martyrdom of S. Lorenzo* in the Jesuit church of S. Maria Assunta in Venice (notable for the tragic power of its luminist contrasts, produced by torchlight) and the *St. Sebastian* (Leningrad, The Hermitage), which the artist painted against a somber landscape (cf. also PL. 94) — all reveal his inexhaustible creative imagination and those stylistic changes that are evident also in his portraits and secular paintings. It is interesting to note the clearly modeled forms of *The Man with a Glove* (Louvre), the atmospheric fluidity of the unfinished canvas portraying Pope Paul III between the cardinals Alessandro and Ottaviano Farnese (Naples,

Mus. di Capodimonte), and the painterly fluency of the portrait of Jacopo Strada (Vienna, Kunsthist. Mus.). Notable also is the stylistic similarity among *The Man with a Glove*, *The Concert* (Florence, Pitti), and the *Flora* (XIV, PL. 90), and also among the other two portraits mentioned above and the *Tarquin and Lucretia* in Vienna (XIV, PL. 101), which is of a later and especially successful period and in which the dynamic contrast of light and shade strengthens the dramatic action. An example of Titian's solid but joyously lively painting can be found in two canvases linked to the taste of the times: the youthful *Bacchanal* (XIV, PL. 93), painted for Alfonso d'Este, and the *Sacred and Profane Love* (XIV, PL. 94). In contrast, the *Danaë* (1545/46; Naples, Mus. di Capodimonte), the *Venus of Urbino* (PL. 66), and the *Venus with Cupid and Music* (Madrid, Prado) are in a freer style.

With his vast production and his chromatic formulas — always crowned with exceptional results — Titian represents the triumph of warm, vibrant, brilliant color, and his great success and popularity in Venice are understandable. Nevertheless, many other painters, including some from other artistic centers, collaborated actively in the Venetian school of color.

Titian was imitated in mediocre works by his brother Francesco Vecellio and his style was continued also by his son Orazio. Among his followers, Palma Vecchio (Jacopo Negreti; 1480–1528), of Bergamasque origin, approached the style of Giovanni Bellini in his own compact chromatic compositions. But he also followed Giorgione's and Titian's new conquests, and distinguished himself by his refreshing, vibrant, silvery tonality, almost an echo of the limpid atmosphere of his native mountains (XIII, PL. 213). He created a healthy, robust humanity, typified by his florid and opulent feminine figures (PL. 68), both in allegories (*Judith*; Uffizi) and in portraits (*Portrait of a Woman*; Berlin, Staat. Mus.). He was a lucid portraitist (*Portrait of a Poet*; London, Nat. Gall.) and a highly esteemed painter of religious subjects, as in his various depictions of the *Sacra Conversazione* and his altarpieces (*Madonna Enthroned with an Angel and Saints*; Vicenza, S. Stefano). Outstanding among this type of work, because of its fervor and Titianesque warmth, is the altarpiece of St. Barbara in S. Maria Formosa in Venice, which is generally considered to be his masterpiece.

Among Palma's followers was Cariani (Giovanni de' Busi, 1485/90–1547; PL. 68), whose style is reminiscent of Bellini. He worked in Bergamo in a fascinating and frankly provincial style that can be seen in some intimate paintings of secular subjects (*Lot and His Daughters*; Milan, Castello Sforzesco). Like other Bergamasque artists, he used colors with silvery tones, related to the metallic ones of the Venetian Lorenzo Lotto.

Lotto (ca. 1480–1556), whose starting point was in the precisely modeled figures of Alvise Vivarini, concluded his activity with a style based on a soft painterly technique reminiscent of Titian (*Gentleman with Gloves*, Brera). His restless personality is evident in one of his works, the *St. Jerome in the Wilderness* (Louvre), set in a harsh landscape that is in keeping with the austerity of the holy hermit. Lotto later traveled as far as Rome, and the influences of many artists — from Raphael to Fra Bartolommeo — can be seen in the many works he left in Bergamo and in the Marches (IX, PLS. 210–212). His boldness of form and his luminist effects were always sustained by a fervid and brilliant imagination (PL. 72).

Sebastiano del Piombo (ca. 1485–1547) left his native Venice to settle in Rome (where he was appointed to the office of the *piombo*, or seal, hence his surname). He was instrumental in introducing the Venetian style into the Roman artistic environment. Formed artistically in the tradition of Bellini and Cima da Conegliano, he was soon influenced by the atmospheric effects of Giorgione's color (altarpiece of S. Giovanni Crisostomo, ca. 1510). He strove for monumental effects in original compositional schemes that were strengthened by a sound graphic sense and by a Titianesque opulence, which he achieved in the large canvas of *The Death of Adonis* (PL. 537); this work hinted at the murky luminism that he was to develop later. In Rome (1511) he decorated the Farnesina with frescoes illustrating pagan myths in resplendently colored scenes that, despite their greater fullness of form, have something of Giorgione's romantic spirit, which is evident also in Sebastiano's portraits, such as the melancholy *Sick Man* (Uffizi). His contacts with Raphael, more obvious in other portraits (e.g., that of Cardinal Antonio Ciocchi del Monte Sansovino; Dublin, Nat. Gall. of Ireland), were eventually overshadowed by the influence of Michelangelo, perceptible in the imposing, haughty portrait of Pope Clement VII (1526; PL. 540) and, to an even greater extent, in sacred paintings. The *Pietà* (PL. 75) represents the loftiest fusion of Michelangelo's powerful sculptural form — in the two leadenly solemn figures — with Venetian color, which lends a tragic, almost sinister aspect to the somber nocturnal landscape. Notable among his other works are the somewhat dispersive *Transfiguration* and the monumental *Flagellation* (1517–25; PL. 537), both in S. Pietro in Montorio, Rome, and the severe *Birth of the Virgin* (begun 1532, finished by Francesco Salviati) in S. Maria del Popolo, Rome.

Giovanni Antonio da Pordenone (1483–1539) left his native Friuli to travel widely in the rest of Italy. He left his mark in Umbria, Lombardy, and Emilia, as well as in his own region. As a result of his wanderings, Pordenone assimilated influences of Giorgione, Titian, Palma Vecchio, Raphael, and Michelangelo. These various figural influences were intensified by his impetuous and uneven temperament in works of inexhaustible fervor and of vivid, fiery color. Pordenone's temperament is evident mainly in his frescoes. The fresco depicting the Madonna and Child with two saints and Pantesilea Baglioni in the parish church in Alviano, near Orvieto, marks one of the various stages of his artistic evolution, as do the frescoes (1520) in Treviso Cathedral portraying Augustus and the sibyl, God the Father and angels, and the Adoration of the Magi; frescoes with scenes from the Passion (1521–22), among them a spectacular, disordered *Crucifixion* (IX, PL. 302), and a *Lamentation* (PL. 71) in Cremona Cathedral, where Pordenone also painted a pensive *Madonna Enthroned* (1522); frescoes in S. Maria di Campagna in Piacenza (1529–31), with prophets, evangelists, saints, and scenes from the life of the Virgin; and frescoes in the Franciscan church in Cortemaggiore, near Piacenza, representing God the Father with angels, prophets, and doctors of the church. The increasingly intense but also superficial figural impetus in the works mentioned is also evident in some of Pordenone's rather rhetorical altarpieces (*Annunciation*, Murano, S. Maria degli Angeli). Apart from some influences of other schools — the organ shutters in S. Rocco in Venice (1528) recall the Roman environment — Pordenone, who worked in Venice only in his later period, always remained on the fringes of the Venetian school. In his exuberant, tumultuous, dramatic power, he is the antecedent of the late Renaissance current that was to develop around Tintoretto.

The works of Bernardino Licinio (ca. 1489–before 1565), probably from Poscante, near Bergamo, have occasionally been attributed to Pordenone. Licinio readily assimilated the style of more talented painters (among them Bonifazio Veronese); the best of his production is represented by portraits to which he imparted a wholesome, prosaic tone, such as the *Portrait of a Lady* in Milan (Castello Sforzesco). In addition to Licinio, and almost contemporaneously, two other painters, one from Verona, the other from Treviso, drew diverse inspirations from Venetian sources. The first, Bonifazio Veronese (Bonifazio di Pitati; 1487–1553), combined his initial training under Palma Vecchio with the influences of Giorgione and Titian, turning their splendid colors to effects of a joyfully sensuous chromatism in religious paintings and, above all, in compositions reflecting the carefree and sumptuous life of Renaissance Venice, set against the pleasant hills of the Venetian countryside, as in *The Finding of Moses* (PL. 69) and *The Rich Man's Feast* (VIII, PL. 213). The second painter was Paris Bordone (1500–71), a follower of Titian, whose mellow colors he assimilated in paintings such as *The Venetian Lovers* (Brera), of a sentimental tone reminiscent of Giorgione, as well as in decorative portraits and in rather spectacular religious and secular subjects (VIII, PL. 213). Bordone's showy painting ended in an often rhetorical display of practical virtuosity.

Titian was also imitated in Padua by Girolamo del Santo and Domenico Campagnola. In Verona, however, the local tradition was continued by Cavazzola (Paolo Moranda; 1486–1522), a pupil of Domenico Morone, whose art achieved a 16th-century breadth. The Caroto brothers (Giovanni, 1488/95–1563/66; Giovanni Francesco, ca. 1480–1555) retained early Renaissance characteristics, despite the fact that both lived to a ripe age and were influenced even by Raphael (especially Giovanni Francesco, who had visited Rome). In contrast, another Veronese artist, Il Moro (Francesco Torbido; ca. 1486–1561), whose early training was with Liberale da Verona and who openly admired Giorgione and Titian, felt the influence of Raphael, to which he added his admiration for Michelangelo; he was influenced by, and well within the taste of, the High Renaissance.

The artistic environment of Brescia was also nurtured mainly by Venice, although its roots were undoubtedly in the Lombard tradition of Vincenzo Foppa.

Giovanni Girolamo Savoldo (ca. 1480–ca. 1548) was an aristocratic, refined painter who came from Brescia but received his first training in Florence. He then settled in Venice, where he was influenced by the poetic effects of Giorgione's nocturnal light in contrast with shadows, which he interpreted with a palette rich in the subtle, silvery grays of Lombard origin (PL. 70; *Adoration of the Shepherds*, formerly Milan, Coll. Crespi Morbio; *St. Matthew*, Met. Mus.). Nevertheless, the compositional scheme of his imposing altarpiece (Brera), with its admirable landscape background, seems to echo Fra Bartolommeo. And his various Nativities (outstanding among them is that in Terlizzi, S. Maria della Nova) reveal, although only in their composition, some details of Florentine origin.

Il Romanino (Girolamo Romani; ca. 1484–ca. 1566) was trained in his native Brescia by Floriano Ferramola, a local artist who was very sensitive to color. Il Romanino later drew closer to Giorgione's art, interpreting it with vivid colors in the large *Madonna Enthroned* (VIII, PL. 216) and in the altarpiece in S. Francesco in Brescia. He created a warm style of his own, shaded with greenish tones, which was similar to Titian's (frescoes with scenes from the life of Christ; PL. 71). Il Romanino was a very talented and sumptuous decorative painter; the occasional unevenness of his style is a result of the influences of Lotto and Palma Vecchio, in addition to those of Giorgione and Titian; some of his harsh touches derive from Dürer's engravings. Il Romanino also worked in Trento (frescoes in the Castle of the Buonconsiglio, 1530–31) and in the neighboring valleys. In addition to excellent portraits, he produced many religious paintings, among them a *Mystic Marriage of St. Catherine* in the parish church of Calvisano, near Brescia; a nobly impressive and original composition of his later period representing SS. Faustinus and Jovita raising the reliquary of the Cross above kneeling worshipers (Brescia, Pin. Civ. Tosio Martinengo); the *Marriage of the Virgin* in the Church of S. Giovanni Evangelista in Brescia; and various paintings in the Corpus Domini Chapel in the same church (*The Raising of Lazarus, Christ in the House of Levi, St. John*, and *St. Matthew*). Of his last group of works, the *St. Matthew* is notable for the fantastic nocturnal illumination that prefigures Caravaggio. A highly productive artist, Il Romanino was surrounded by many assistants, disciples, and followers, among them Altobello Meloni and Gian Francesco Bembo from Cremona, who collaborated with him on the frescoes in Cremona (Cath.); Callisto Piazza from Lodi; Francesco Prato from Caravaggio; and the Cremonese Giulio Campi, more talented than the others and influenced by Titian.

In the Corpus Domini Chapel in S. Giovanni Evangelista at Brescia, the altarpiece depicting the Deposition is by Fanone (Vincenzo Civerchio); *The Gathering of the Manna, SS. Mark and Luke*, and, above the altar, the lunette depicting the Last Supper (1521) are by Moretto da Brescia (1498–1554), the best-known painter of the Brescia school. His was a serene, thoughtful, honest temperament and his neat formalism was sustained by the skill and the assurance of his design (PL. 71; VIII, PL. 216). Although he did draw from Venetian sources, he was nevertheless linked with the Lombard world by his use of color, characteristically silver-gray. His artistic expression retains its individuality while showing the influences — which he assimilated and surpassed — of Il Romanino, Savoldo, Lotto,

Titian, and of German engravers. The large *Adoration of the Shepherds* (Brescia, Pin. Civ. Tosio Martinengo) is Moretto's major work, but some of his paintings in Brescia are also noteworthy: the *Assumption* (1526; Old Cath.); *S. Margherita da Cortona with SS. Francis and Jerome* (S. Francesco); altarpieces (S. Clemente; Pin. Civ. Tosio Martinengo); and an *Ecce Homo* and an *Angel* (both, Pin. Civ. Tosio Martinengo) that are exceptional for their luminism.

Moretto, himself an expert portraitist (IV, PL. 27), initiated into the art of painting and portraiture Giovanni Battista Moroni (ca. 1525–78) from Bergamo, who became his best pupil. Although mediocre as a painter of altarpieces, Moroni was a subtle and perceptive portraitist. Adopting his teacher's limpid, silvery hues, and combining them with an instinctive, unaffected style that was admired by Titian, Moroni painted such well-known portraits as the *Portrait of a Gentleman* (1554; Milan, Pin. Ambrosiana), those of Bernardo Spino and of Pace Rivola Spino (both, Bergamo, Acc. Carrara), the half-figure portraits of Antonio Navagero (1565; Brera) and of an unknown man (London, Nat. Gall.), and the so-called "Titian's Schoolmaster" (XI, PL. 218).

In the region of Emilia, the city of Ferrara had maintained its contacts with the Venetian school of painting during the early Renaissance. During the High Renaissance, Titian received commissions from Alfonso d'Este, duke of Ferrara, and his works, displayed in the palaces of the Este family, constituted a stimulating example for the Ferrarese artists, foremost among whom was Dosso Dossi (Giovanni di Lutero; ca. 1479–1542), who continued into the 16th century the spirit of fable and chivalry typical of the Ferrarese court from the Gothic period onward, both in poetry and in the representational arts.

Dosso drew from the styles of Giorgione and Titian, contributing a greater intensity in the concreteness of his color, which often became more sensuous and brilliant with the sparkle of infinitesimal lights, in clearly perceptible echoes of Flemish art. Dosso's painting also was close to that of Il Romanino; that they had direct personal contacts is indicated by the fact that the periods in which they both worked on the decoration of the Castle of the Buonconsiglio in Trento overlap by one year, Dosso having worked there in 1531–32 and Il Romanino in 1530–31. In his secular paintings (e.g., *Nymph and Satyr*; Florence, Pitti) he translated a world of fable into the 16th century, giving it full expression in his *Circe* (PL. 73), in which the crowded landscape, animated by brilliant luminist touches, has its poetic equivalent in the verses of Lodovico Ariosto's *Orlando Furioso*. In the chromatic sphere, Dosso's art was also related directly to that of Raphael; especially in religious paintings it aims at a strong relief and sculptural effects, to the detriment of perspective, thus tending away from the poetic tone that he achieved in his mythological and allegorical paintings (VIII, PL. 212). Thus, the painter transformed his altarpieces into monumental compositions for the spacious Ferrarese churches, as in the spectacular polyptych with the Madonna and saints (Ferrara, Pin. Naz.).

Dosso's brother Battista (d. 1548) was even more influenced by Raphael (Lodovico Dolce, in *Dialogo della pittura intitulato l'Aretino*, Venice, 1557, even suggested that Battista was Raphael's pupil), and also undoubtedly absorbed some Flemish influences. The brothers occasionally collaborated, as in the *Adoration of the Shepherds* (1536; Modena, Gall. Estense).

Ferrara boasted other painters, such as Ortolano (Giovanni Battista Benvenuti), Garofalo (Benvenuto Tisi), and Lodovico Mazzolino. In his major work, *The Deposition* (Rome, Gall. Borghese), Ortolano (1488–1525) applied the deep, vivid colors of Dosso Dossi to solemn, rather outmoded forms. Garofalo (1481–1559) has undeservedly enjoyed greater fame than his Ferrarese contemporaries. Originally taking his inspiration from the outmoded style of the mediocre Domenico Panetti, which he broadened in his frescoes (Ferrara, Palace of Lodovico il Moro), Garofalo executed panels and canvases composed with a sure graphic sense and enriched by a warm coloring reminiscent of, although less intense than, that of Dosso. Noteworthy among his works is the *Slaughter of the Innocents* (1519; Ferrara, Pin. Naz.). Clearly, Garofalo was influenced by the

forms of Raphael, whose illustrative quality he emulated both in religious works (VIII, PL. 217; *The Calling of Peter*, Rome, Gall. Borghese) and in secular paintings (*Picus Transformed into a Woodpecker*, Rome, Gall. Naz.).

Lodovico Mazzolino (ca. 1478–1528), who was the most outmoded of all the Ferrarese painters of the period, based his early work on the firm figural concepts of Ercole de' Roberti and of the young Lorenzo Costa, to which he gave a detailed and harsh expression that was influenced by German engravings. But his color, under the influence of Dosso Dossi, acquired a violent, dissonant brilliance in his paintings (usually of small dimensions), in which the figures are often disposed against light-colored, complex architectural backgrounds (VIII, PL. 201; *Christ Disputing with the Doctors*, London, Nat. Gall.; *Sacra Conversazione*, in a precious, very ornate frame carved by Garofalo, Turin, Gall. Sabauda).

Girolamo da Carpi (1501–56) is said to have been one of Garofalo's pupils; he is, at any rate, closely connected to both Garofalo and Dosso Dossi and should therefore be included in the Ferrarese school (*Adoration of the Magi*, 1530; Bologna, S. Martino). He also felt the influence of Raphael and of Parmigianino, both of whom were widely known in Emilia.

An important contribution to the art of the time was made by Correggio (Antonio Allegri; ca. 1494–1534). In his earliest works he retained the compositional rhythms of the 15th century, reminiscent of Costa and Mantegna, only slightly enlivened by a graceful figural animation, as in the *Madonna of St. Francis* (1515; Dresden, Gemäldegal.), which, like some of his other youthful works, combines an atmospheric chiaroscuro of Leonardesque origin with a metallic, intense color that endows his forms with fluent movement and is indicative of a refinement innate in this artist's temperament. Correggio created subtle idealizations best expressed in his secular subjects, such as *Leda and the Swan* (PL. 567) and *Danaë* (Rome, Gall. Borghese), and also in small religious compositions, such as the *Madonna Adoring the Child* (Uffizi). The same sensitivity is evident in his altarpieces, in which space is created by the figures themselves by means of the compositional schemes and foreshortening. The diagonal arrangement and atmosphere of sensual abandon anticipate the baroque manner and contribute to the formation of an intense, freely conceived style independent of tradition. It is possible to follow the development of Correggio's art from the *Madonna of St. Sebastian* (Dresden, Gemäldegal.) through the *Madonna of St. Jerome* (III, PL. 474) and the *Madonna della Scodella* (III, PL. 468) up to the *Adoration of the Shepherds* (III, PL. 475), in which the nocturnal light seems to emanate from the Christ Child. The progress of Correggio's painting is also clearly evident in the more monumental mural paintings. The painted vault of the Camera di San Paolo (1519; III, PL. 465), with its figural ovals set at intervals and the soft monochrome of the lunettes, brilliantly evokes not only Mantegna and Leonardo but also Raphael, in the clearly symbolic, complex figures of the myth of Diana. The artist showed a broader figural concept in his bold *Christ in Glory* (1520–22; III, PL. 470). In a whirl of clouds in the immensity of the sky, the figures of the apostles are spaced around a foreshortened view of Christ, like satellites around a star. The images moving in full aerial perspective are reminiscent of Michelangelo in their monumental aspects. The decoration of the dome of the Cathedral in Parma (1526–30) is a much more crowded, complex, and agitated composition, which, by means of some architectural elements, accentuates the illusionistic feeling of space while creating a greater figural fusion, a choral harmony in the fiery figures, in vibrant movement around the Virgin received into Heaven (III, PLS. 471, 472). The double circle of figures among the clouds seems to herald baroque decoration, which was, however, to lack the prodigious atmospheric modulations of this great forerunner.

Many artists worked in Parma within Correggio's circle: Correggio's son Pomponio Allegri, Francesco Maria Rondani, Girolamo Mazzola-Bedoli (IX, PL. 301), and the Sienese, Michelangelo Anselmi. But the true continuer of Correggio's style was Parmigianino (see below), who interpreted Correggio's art with originality outside the local environment, and who very successfully inserted himself into the subsequent esthetic movement of the late Renaissance.

The unique genius of Michelangelo (1475–1564) dominated the world of High Renaissance painting. His known production begins with the representation of the *Holy Family* (or Doni Tondo; IX, PL. 527), in which the artist's personality appears to be fully formed; some scholars date it 1503 or 1504, others 1506, and it may even be later. Along with fresco techniques, he had learned from Ghirlandajo neatness of design and the effects of chiaroscuro. The gigantic figures of the evangelists conceived by Ghirlandajo for the vault of the choir of S. Maria Novella in Florence probably inspired Michelangelo to emulate their towering proportions and thus gave rise to his typically monumental conception. But whatever he absorbed from Ghirlandajo's teachings he always expressed in a much loftier spirit, endowing his figural world with a heroic quality and a forceful vitality derived from Luca Signorelli, as well as other minor influences. In the Doni Tondo the figural grouping is of superhuman stature, with the Virgin's vibrant upward movement in her proud contemplation of the Child setting off an interrelation of rigorously outlined forms in a serpentine movement that fills the perspective depths of the vast space, shattering the limits of the calm, geometric compositions typical of the contemporary classicizing styles. The color also is new; it is fluid in relation to the light, detached from tonal attempts to evoke a contingent reality; color acquires an intellectualist quality that contributes effectively — as it would in later works — to intensify design and chiaroscuro, that is, the artist's firm sculptural vision, which is also suggested by the nudes in the background.

The lost painting depicting the battle of Cascina is known through engravings by Marcantonio Raimondi and Agostino Veneziano; with its nude figures in motion, it was a translation into painting, in a finished composition, of the relief of *The Battle of the Lapiths and the Centaurs* (IV, PL. 525). This work marks the beginning of the glorification of man (the constant aim of the Florentines) through the nude figure. Next, Michelangelo created the Biblical world of the frescoes on the ceiling of the Sistine Chapel (1508–12; II, PL. 291; III, PL. 312). In the immense vault of the chapel, he used grayish tones that are admirably effective in representing, amid primordial landscapes, the origins of life — culminating in the creation of Adam (IX, PLS. 528, 535) — a life soon beset by suffering in the exodus of humanity vainly attempting to save itself from the flood. The stories, suffused with the mystery of myth, stand out from the geometrically conceived architectural elements between balanced nudes that glorify the physical strength of man; the towering figures of prophets and sibyls between pillars decorated with straining caryatids in the form of putti form a complex ideological system. These figures are echoed in the triangular sections of the vault by minor personages, arranged in a hierarchic order to represent the light of intellect connected with Biblical events and, more generally, with man's sorrowful destiny on earth. The sculptural power, intensified by color, bursts forth in the projecting elements and in the gestures of those solemn, thoughtful, and melancholy figures, giving dramatic expression to their tense aspiring to eternity.

Twenty-four years elapsed between Michelangelo's illustration of the beginnings of humanity and his representation of its epilogue in the frescoes of the Last Judgment (1536–41; IX, PLS. 533, 536), during which period he was also intensely active as an architect and sculptor. Michelangelo used the entire end wall of the Sistine Chapel to depict, in a way that overcame the symmetrical divisions of the 15th century, a dense crowd of figures who are no longer arranged according to the orderly hierarchy observed in the ceiling; the figures seem to move slowly in connected groups: the elect rising toward the eternal contemplation of God; the damned descending to meet their eternal doom, condemned by the irrevocable gesture of Christ in judgment (XIII, PL. 470), near whom stands the Virgin, looking touchingly young, anxious, and dismayed. The scene is dominated by angels bearing the instruments of the Passion, recalling the sacrifice of Christ. Lower in the composition, against the vast expanse of arid and desolate landscape, Charon, who ferries the souls across the Styx, and Minos, around whom

they crowd, represent the transition from the earthly to the eternal (IV, PL. 179; IX, PL. 536).

In the ceiling of the chapel Michelangelo had manifested a tendency away from the classical trend of the High Renaissance in the freedom of composition of the original painted architectural motifs and in the lively contrasting relief of the figures. But an over-all discipline prevails, subordinate, among other things, to the architectural structure of the chapel. The spectacular representation of the Last Judgment shows an extreme independence of composition that was carried over, in other aspects, to the two large compositions of the Pauline Chapel, also in the Vatican (1542–ca. 1550). *The Conversion of St. Paul* (IX, PL. 537), with only a sober hint of landscape, has a circular movement that seems to emanate from Christ and the figures surrounding him to the two divergent groups, outside any regular cadence, and illuminated by an oppressive, unreal light. However, the figures possess a psychological definition of their own, from the astonished onlookers to the Apostle himself, a figure who is inspired by Hellenistic sculpture and who, despite his closed eyes, conveys the impression that his soul is already open to revelation. In *The Crucifixion of St. Peter* the men lifting the cross create a feeling of toilsome movement surrounding the powerful figure of the Apostle while the empty space opposite involves the spiritual participation of the sorrowing groups, endowed with touches recalling classical sculpture (IX, PL. 534); the group of half-figures in the foreground appears cut off, in an echo of German styles.

Michelangelo drew his inspiration from antiquity, or, rather, from those aspects of it that were most congenial to his own personality, while his expressionism reveals his appreciation of the art that was developing beyond the Alps, an art with which he came into contact presumably by means of engravings. He reelaborated all these elements in his sublime painting, which represents the highest achievement of the High Renaissance and which, at least as concerns its external aspects, was to become the fundamental basis of one of the trends of the late Renaissance.

LATE RENAISSANCE. *Architecture.* During the late Renaissance, which was a unitary movement despite its varied tendencies, architecture developed as the focal point of reactions and adherences to the classicizing trend of Bramante and Raphael and to the anticlassical trend of Michelangelo. As the continuation of a longstanding Renaissance tradition, the classicizing trend was, inevitably, more readily and widely understood and interpreted. However, as early as the first half of the 16th century the signs of a reaction had appeared; these were evident even among Raphael's followers, and were manifested also in architecture. Giulio Pippi, known as Giulio Romano (1499–1546), was one of these disciples of Raphael; after the Sack of Rome, he settled in Mantua, where Baldassare Castiglione introduced him into the court of the Gonzagas. There he diffused Bramante's and Raphael's styles with notable originality, as in the unadorned, very large courtyard of the Palazzo Ducale (PL. 53) and in the long east façade of the Palazzo del Te, in which he accentuated the movement that is produced by the deep chiaroscuro contrasts of this building. In the Palazzo del Te, Giulio Romano gave free rein to his imagination — in the west façade, in the solemn courtyard, in the hemicycle at the end of the garden, and in the interiors decorated with his own frescoes and with heavy stuccoes by Francesco Primaticcio (PL. 53; VIII, PL. 428, FIG. 417e; IX, FIG. 463f). In various other buildings he used rustication as an expression of nature (Palazzo di Giustizia, Mantua). Even in one of his more restrained constructions, the two-story house that he designed for himself on a plan derived from Bramante, the artist manifested a reaction to High Renaissance rhythms (as in the portal, in which the pediment breaks through the string molding into the upper order of arcades in which edicule windows are recessed). It is notable that in the same period the sculptor Leone Leoni (1509–90) from Arezzo achieved effects of fantasy in his house in Milan in the weighty structural members and the colossal caryatids that earned the building the name of *Casa degli Omenoni* ("house of the big men"; PL. 91).

Giulio Romano's last architectural work was the reconstruction of Mantua Cathedral, which is laid out in a nave and four aisles divided by columns, reminiscent of Early Christian basilicas; in this work the artist again strove for contrasts, both in the rich, flat ceilings of the central nave and of the two outside aisles, alternated with the barrel vaults of the intermediate aisles, and in the very slight elevation of the side aisles compared to that of the nave.

A stream of activity that tended toward the harmony of Bramante and of Raphael developed from a vision particularly attuned to the period in which the new city of Sabbioneta was created because of the stimulus and personal intervention of Prince Vespasiano Gonzaga (d. 1591). Imbued with classical culture and a student of Vitruvius, the prince himself conceived a very regular plan of the town, with two city gates, straight streets, and a number of squares (VIII, FIG. 559). In the central square he built his own palace, in which the classical plan is enlivened by painterly touches that attenuate its rhythms (ca. 1560). He built a second palace, the Palazzo del Giardino (1580–84), on the parade ground and decorated it with frescoes, tapestries, and precious art objects; he later completed it with a long gallery, arcaded on the ground floor, decorated with murals depicting mythological scenes and with ancient sculpture (most of which are now in Mantua, Palazzo Ducale). These buildings overlooked a garden in the Italian style with grottoes, fountains, statues, and two small temples dedicated to Diana and to Venus. Sabbioneta also had a theater (FIG. 100; IV, PL. 188); designed by Vincenzo Scamozzi on an elongated plan, it was once adorned with frescoes and is an impressive structure opening onto three streets. Thus, in the small town of Sabbioneta the poetic evocation of antiquity promoted by the classicizing trend of Rome found a northern expression characterized by an independent interpretation that can be defined as romantic, rather than anticlassical, in the buildings and in the illusionist effects of the paintings, all in the idiom of the late Renaissance.

As a result of the initiative of another small court, that of the Rovere family, the Villa Imperiale at Pesaro had been enlarged much earlier (1529–30) by Girolamo Genga (1476–1551) from Urbino, who was also a painter, open to the influences of Perugino, Signorelli, Lotto, and Raphael. The villa at Pesaro recalls the Villa Madama in a weighty and scenographic interpretation in which Genga evokes the late Renaissance manner. Genga later executed the Church of S. Giovanni Battista in Pesaro (1543 onward) in a similar style; it has a single nave flanked by chapels and is built on an animated and contrasting plan with a monumental, though rather disordered, elevation.

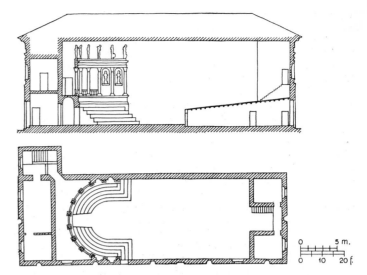

Sabbioneta, theater (architect, V. Scamozzi), transverse section and plan (*from L'Architettura, 5, 1956*).

Late Renaissance style had its theorist in Sebastiano Serlio (1475–1554), a Bolognese perspectivist and author of a treatise on architecture (1537–51). An "extraordinary" volume was published posthumously (Lyon, 1557). He furthered the interest of classicism in his third volume, on Roman antiquities (1540). In his work, Serlio presented examples of houses in their various parts and furnishings, mainly in a fantastic and bizarre style inspired generally by Venetian architecture. Later, Serlio tended toward a more marked and carefree picturesqueness and whimsy in the "extraordinary" volume, which provides examples of doors of mixed rustication with several orders.

The Neapolitan Pirro Ligorio (ca. 1510–83), especially in the Casino of Pope Pius IV (PL. 89; VIII, PL. 429; IX, PL. 313), on which he lavished stuccowork by Rocco di Montefiascone, strove for that chiaroscuro which Polidoro da Caravaggio and Maturius da Firenze had already achieved in painting in the façades of buildings in Rome (cf. IX, PL. 311). Giulio Mazzoni continued this style in the façade of the Palazzo Spada; Annibale Lippi also adopted it, using Roman reliefs in the garden façade of the Villa Medici (ca. 1580; IX, PL. 312). Also in Rome, later in the 16th century, a festive decoration was applied to

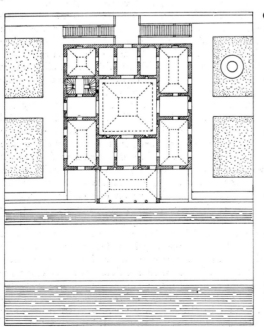

a

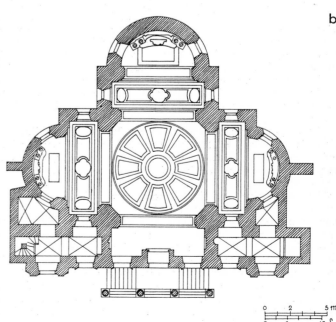

b

V. Scamozzi, (*a*) Padua, Villa Dondi dell'Orologio, plan according to the architect's project (*from F. Barbieri, Vincenzo Scamozzi, Vicenza, 1952*); (*b*) Salzburg, Church of St. Erhard, plan (*from R. Kurt Donin, V. Scamozzi, Innsbruck, 1948*).

the courtyard of the Palazzo Mattei by Domenico Fontana. In the early 17th century, the highly ornate façade of the Villa Borghese (later modified) with two towers, was built by Jan van Santen, who was known as Giovanni Vansanzio. In this feature it echoed Villa Medici, which can be considered as the culminating of the picturesque overrefinement of the late Renaissance, rather than as a baroque expression. Pirro Ligorio applied Bramantesque architectural discipline to the landscape of the Villa d'Este at Tivoli, adapting it to create surprising scenographic effects and an animation that arises from architectural details, from the landscape, and from a new element: water, which is mastered and made to form new esthetic expressions in waterworks, cascades, basins, and fountains (VIII, PL. 432; IX, PL. 313). The picturesque dominates in the Villa d'Este without, however, lapsing into fantastic extremes. The blending of architecture into the surrounding landscape is one of the most notable achievements of Galeazzo Alessi (ca. 1512–72) from Perugia, who worked mainly in Genoa. In order to take full advantage of the varied beauty of the hills that descend steeply to the sea, he enriched his buildings (Villa Cambiaso, FIG. 101; Villa Pallavicino delle Pe-

rito in Sassia, increasing it to three orders (he was not alone at the time in doing so).

In Umbria, with Giulio Danti, Alessi worked on the final construction of the soaring dome of S. Maria degli Angeli at Assisi, adapting a design by Vignola. Alessi's sojourn in Milan left an impression on architects there; Vincenzo Seregni, for example, recalled Alessi's architectural and decorative rhythms in the Palazzo dei Giureconsulti. In Bologna, while Antonio Morandi was designing buildings of wooden linearity, Giacomo da Vignola (1507–73) began his activity as an architect. Better known until modern times for his treatise on architecture (1562), Vignola originally patterned his work on that of Serlio, as in the analytic and picturesque Palazzo dei Banchi in Bologna. His architectural idiom attained poetic expressions in the geometrically conceived and severely harmonious Church of S. Andrea in Via Flaminia (1554; I, PL. 305), which was attuned to the taste of the Counter Reformation. This taste was to find its full expression in the Church of the Gesù in Rome (begun 1568), which was built with a single extended nave, transept, and dome and was clearly inspired by the Church of S. Andrea in Mantua; the transept was intentionally given

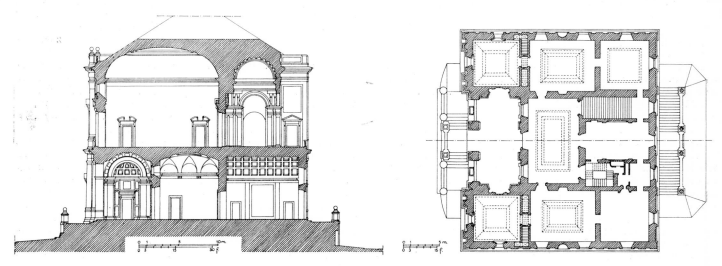

Genoa, Villa Cambiaso (architect, G. Alessi). *Left*: transverse section *(from A. Haupt, Architettura dei palazzi dell'Italia settentrionale. . . , Milan, 1930)*; *right*: plan *(from G. Chierici, 1952–57)*.

schiere; Palazzo Cambiaso; and Palazzo Parodi) with airy arcades, connecting them to flights of steps and splendid gardens in a freely picturesque interpretation that led him away from his principal sources, Michelangelo and Sangallo. In the Church of S. Maria Assunta di Carignano (VIII, FIG. 419e) Alessi used the central plan with an articulation and soaring quality that are clearly derived from those sources, but he combined them with a softened sculptural quality — a subdued development of the structural members — that echoes Raphael.

Alessi also played a fundamental role in the urban development of Genoa, where the Via Nuova (mod. Via Garibaldi), laid out in 1561 by Bernardino da Cabio, was graced with splendid town houses; some of these gaily decorated buildings are the work of artists such as Giovanni Battista Castello, known as Bergamasco, and Rocco Lurago. Alessi, whose style was continued in Genoa by Domenico Ponzello and Bernardo Spazio, built the Palazzo Marino (now Palazzo Municipale) in Milan for the Genovese merchant Tommaso Marino. The exterior of the building is richly decorated with rusticated ashlar and superimposed orders, in a constrast of surface motifs that is, however, rather stiffly executed (IX, FIG. 463d, e); the particularly elaborate courtyard (PL. 91) has stuccoes that recall trite Roman models. To satisfy the elaborate taste of the Lombards, Alessi crowded the façade of S. Maria presso S. Celso (1568; VIII, PL. 215; IX, FIG. 471c) with structural elements and changed the clearly defined scheme of the High Renaissance Roman façades, such as that of Sangallo in Sto Spi-

limited development in order to emphasize the length of the nave and to give greater relief to the dome, from which light streams down through the windows in the drum, leaving in shadow the chapels along the nave. The result was a particularly sober church, before the superimposition of the baroque style made it theatrically elaborate. The façade (IX, PL. 312) conveys a powerful feeling of mass that is linked with the elements in two orders dominated by the portal, executed with the collaboration of Giacomo della Porta. In the façade of S. Maria dell'Orto, Rome, Vignola created a contrast between the mainly linear conception and the sculptural intent of the projecting portal. And earlier still, the organic link between portal and balcony was made evident in the façade of the Villa Giulia, built in Rome for Pope Julius III, decorated with restraint also in the garden façade, which overlooks an elliptical courtyard (PL. 89; VIII, FIG. 1087). The Palazzo Farnese in Caprarola, which Sangallo had originally designed in the pentagonal shape of a small fortress, was reworked by Vignola and given a neat facing of superimposed orders retaining the geometric feeling of the structural elements (I, PL. 388; IX, FIG. 465). The slopes that are transformed into terraces and the circular courtyard, where slender, airy arcades create deep shadows, contribute to this sense of solidity. In this work, Vignola created a perfect balance between powerful structures (in this he was obviously influenced by ancient Roman architecture) and decorative elements in which he interpreted his own rules for the architectural orders with great originality (cf. IV, PL. 191).

Other architects also emphasized the effectiveness of variously expressed masses. The Florentine Bartolomeo Ammanati (1511–92) collaborated on the second courtyard of the Villa Giulia, and executed the loggia of the nymphaeum (XIII, PL. 238); he placed figural elements at intervals, perhaps an echo of Michelangelo's style enriched by Venetian influences. In the courtyard of the Palazzo Pitti (PL. 88), which is of a late Renaissance taste, he combined superimposed architectural orders and rustication (recalling Brunelleschi's façade), retaining a compact, organic architectural unity. The fourth side of the courtyard forms a setting for the Boboli Gardens.

In many of Ammanati's buildings in Florence heavy masonry prevails, with contrasts provided by projecting elements (e.g., Palazzo Firenzuoli, formerly Giugni; Palazzo Riccardi-Manelli, formerly Grifoni). He used this style also in the south wing of the Palazzo della Prefettura (formerly Palazzo della Signoria) in Lucca, with its high arcade. In the imposing Collegio Romano (1578) in Rome, Ammanati concentrated his esthetic effects in the structure and in the impression of movement generated, more than by the slight projection of the central section, by the two portals and the shadows created by the numerous windows. This building, which seems to reflect the austere spirit of the Jesuit Order for which it was created, was Ammanati's last work. Earlier, in the Ponte Sta Trinita in Florence (1567–69; destroyed during World War II, later faithfully reconstructed) Ammanati had followed a scheme by Michelangelo, creating a masterpiece of rhythmic harmony in the cadences of the three elliptical arches between solid piers and the wide, gentle curve of the parapet (XIII, PL. 265).

In Rome, Giacomo della Porta (1537–1602), a disciple of Vignola, whom he succeeded in many important works, intensified the contrasting rhythms that had been typical of Sangallo in the façade of Sto Spirito in Sassia and also of one of the Sangallo's imitators, Guidetto Guidetti, in S. Caterina dei Funari; these intensified contrasts are evident in his work as early as the façade of the Madonna dei Monti (IX, FIG. 471). In the façade of the Church of the Gesù, Porta also emphasized contrasts to achieve sculptural effects by pairing the pilasters and by imparting greater relief to the portal with its double pediment, to the central window, and to the string courses linking the two orders. And while he showed a decorative tendency (also evident in the façade of S. Paolo alle Tre Fontane), which lightened the heavy geometry of the octagonal church of S. Maria Scala Coeli, he built the churches of S. Atanasio and Trinità dei Monti with contrasting and soberly vertical lines.

Porta had also been influenced by Michelangelo. The tension of the structural elements in the façade of S. Luigi dei Francesi (PL. 90), its division into five sections, and its comparatively modest pediment, recalls Michelangelo's model for S. Lorenzo in Florence (cf. I, PL. 406). The architect later worked on the Capitoline hill complex (1564–94) and, as Vignola's successor, supervised the completion of St. Peter's, raising the curve of the small domes as well as of the principal one, thus altering Michelangelo's original design (IV, PL. 193; IX, PL. 541). In the massive Palazzo della Sapienza (1579; now the Archivio di Stato), with its long, roughly elliptical courtyard, he attempted to blend the styles of Michelangelo and Vignola. In the Villa Aldobrandini in Frascati (1598–1604), he used to full advantage the scheme of the architectural mass blending with the surrounding landscape. The villa rises high above graceful staircases; its narrow central section projects from the lateral ones, which are topped by a broken pediment. Following this model, many sumptuous villas, such as the Villa Mondragone by Flaminio Ponzio, also in Frascati, were built in the Alban hills near Rome.

During the late Renaissance, architecture based on the disposition of masses was taken up by Domenico Fontana (1543–1607), who, during the pontificate of Sixtus V, was the leading town planner of the city of Rome. He designed straight streets and broad squares for the city, marked by tall obelisks and fountains. One of these fountains, the Acqua Felice, which is architectural in character, was designed by Fontana himself; its design was later repeated on a more monumental scale by Flaminio Ponzio, during the early baroque period, in the fountain of the Acqua Paola (VIII, PL. 207). In religious architecture Fontana continued in his monumental conceptions the use of regular divisions culminating in a soaring dome, as in the Sistine Chapel of S. Maria Maggiore (IX, FIG. 473). The chapel is faced with marbles and decorated with frescoes that show Raphael's influence and it is enriched by the tombs of Pius V (XI, PL. 450) and of Sixtus V (V, PL. 326), conceived by Fontana himself as esthetic elements essential to the chapel, in the center of which rises a tall tabernacle.

Fontana succeeded Ponzio and Mascherino in the construction of the imposing Palazzo del Quirinale, but he alone was responsible for the geometrically conceived Lateran Palace (PL. 90), which surpassed the Palazzo Farnese in size, and for the exterior loggia at the end of the transept of the adjoining basilica, in which he used Vignola's schemes with great originality. In Naples, traces of his style remain in the Palazzo Reale, in the central section with its three superimposed orders, later partly modified and enlarged by Luigi Vanvitelli.

A type of architecture which was based on the inspiration of Sangallo and Michelangelo and which was influenced by Vignola was continued in Lombardy by Pellegrino Tibaldi, known as Il Pellegrino (1527–96) from Puria di Valsolda, near Como. Pellegrino designed the Collegio Borromeo in Pavia (1564; IX, FIG. 467) and the courtyard of the Palazzo Arcivescovile in Milan, using rusticated ashlar that suggests affinities with Sanmicheli. In the Gothic Cathedral of Milan, he ornamented the crypt, the choir, and the baptistery with decorative sculptural elements, while in the Church of S. Fedele (PL. 91) and in the heavy rotunda of S. Sebastiano, also in Milan, he made full use of strongly projecting members. In Novara, he renovated the church of S. Gaudenzio in a sustained, coherent style, in which the monumental masses are enlivened by a strong chiaroscuro; the same bold equilibrium is evident in Tibaldi's paintings (see below). In his reconstruction of S. Lorenzo in Milan, begun after 1574, Martino Bassi, who was influenced by Tibaldi and Alessi, retained the imposing central body of the Early Christian church. A monumental trend with classicizing aspects, foreshadowed in the superimposed trabeated loggias (destroyed) of the façade of the Villa La Simonetta in Milan — designed by Domenico Giuntalodi (1505–60) of Prato for Ferrante Gonzaga — flourished in Milan in the early 17th century, as a continuation of the late Renaissance style, in the courtyard of the Seminario Vescovile designed by Aurelio Trezzi and in the two monumental courtyards of the Palazzo del Senato by Fabio Mangone.

Tuscan architects drew mainly on Sangallo and Michelangelo for inspiration. In the Loggia di Mercato Nuovo in Florence, Giovanni Battista del Tasso (1500–55) adapted 15th-century schemes in a contemporary spirit that is manifested in the projecting structural members and the massive, compact corner piers that are decorated with edicules. The lively, much-discussed, and overly criticized Giorgio Vasari (1511–74) from Arezzo was a talented and eclectic architect. His decorations of the Salone dei Cinquecento and his design for the ducal apartments in the Palazzo Vecchio showed an aulic refinement that elaborated his sources with great taste and originality. His admiration for Michelangelo did not preclude his assimilation of Raphael's influence in ornamental fantasies. However, it was Michelangelo's influence that prevailed in the animated chiaroscuro contrasts of the rather tritely conceived structural members of the Uffizi (IX, PL. 312, FIG. 470). Vasari, of a very different temperament from that of the master, planned the building between the imposing mass of the Palazzo Vecchio and the Loggia della Signoria as an elegant scenographic setting leading to the banks of the Arno. Michelangelo's constant influence derives from Vasari's devotion to the master, a devotion that is confirmed by his writings and by the fact that Vasari completed the staircase of the Biblioteca Laurenziana, following Michelangelo's instructions. Vasari's refined elegance is evident also in the small loggia adjoining the Palazzo dell'Arte della Seta. He gave an unadorned and relatively modest elevation to the Loggia del Pesce (reconstructed) and to the corridor of the Uffizi; he conceived a similarly simple, though imposingly monumental elevation for the Palazzo delle Logge in Arezzo. In his renovation of the Palazzo dei Cavalieri (formerly Palazzo degli Anziani) in Pisa, Vasari used a rhythmical succession of windows and imparted animation in the double flight of stairs (recalling that of Michelangelo in the Palazzo dei Senatori, Rome), and in the graffiti, of a subdued chiaroscuro effect that is typical of the Tuscan Renaissance tradition. This subtle chiaroscuro is distinct from the intense sculptural effects of Roman chiaroscuro and is in opposition to the Venetian use of color, in marble facings and frescoes, to create effects of light and shade. In his renovation of the Church of SS. Flora e Lucilla in Arezzo, Vasari sought to introduce into Tuscany, on a reduced scale, the characteristic structure of Venetian churches — that is, a nave and two aisles elaborated by colonnades, piers, vaults, and domes.

Giovan Antonio Dosio (1533–1609), a Florentine who also spent some time in Rome, brought his own great vigor to the Raphaelesque harmony that inspired him in the Palazzo Larderel (formerly Giacomini) and in the Niccolini Chapel in the Church of Sta Croce (1578), both in Florence, which recalls the style of Fontana in its divisions and polychrome marble facings. Earlier, in the austere Gaddi Chapel in S. Maria Novella, Dosio had shown a tendency to draw closer to Michelangelo.

Also in Florence, Bernardo Buontalenti (1536–1608) introduced elements of fanciful inventiveness into an architecture that considered the masonry as a fundamental value. He expressed his fancy in his decorations for festivals, theatrical settings, and even fireworks (hence his nickname Delle Girandole, or "of the Catherine wheels"). He introduced whimsy into the architecture of the Casino Mediceo (now Palazzo della Corte d'Appello), decorating the portal and the windows with festoons, masks, and shells (IX, FIG. 463g), while displaying an organic unity that was lacking, for instance, in the architecture of Federico Zuccari. The latter attempted a bizarre treatment of form in his Roman house on the Via Gregoriana (IX, PL. 314); these efforts were undoubtedly more successful than those in his house in Florence, on what is now the Via Giusti. Buontalenti and Zuccari developed those elements which in Michelangelo's imagination had a determining, tormented expressive value, and which in them were reduced merely to a bizarre ornamental style.

Buontalenti had also shown individual qualities in the design of the Villa Medici-Demidoff in Pratolino (1569–81; destroyed); the villa was set in a large garden (viridarium), which had curved and rectilinear flights of steps. Similar flights of steps were reconstructed on the basis of Buontalenti's precise drawings in the Villa di Artimino at Artimino, a typically Tuscan structure in the loggia and the overhanging roof. The lateral projections of this villa, while reminiscent of ancient towers, create a new solemn movement; the loggia, with its reduced trabeation, achieves a tension (also perceptible in the loggia of the Fortezza di Belvedere, Florence) that echoes Michelangelo in emphasizing the mass. Mass is dominant also in the rear part of the Palazzo Vecchio (1588–92), so firm in the rustication framing its large windows. The artist's inventiveness later found expression in the Grotto in the Boboli Gardens (VIII, PLS. 430, 431), a return to nature in architecture, where Michelangelo's so-called "Boboli Slaves" (Florence, Accademia) had been placed as caryatids; in the octagonal tribune of the Uffizi (1574–81), with its ceiling decorated with shell motifs, he turned elements from the natural order into sources of light and color. Buontalenti developed fanciful echoes from Michelangelo in the Porta delle Suppliche at the Uffizi, with its broken pediment, and in the flight of steps formerly in the choir of Sta Trinita (now in S. Stefano; XIII, PL. 241), which in its projections and recesses is a capricious creation of form in space distinctly different from Michelangelo's staircase in the Biblioteca Laurenziana. Buontalenti's façade of Sta Trinita lacks balance between the upper and lower sections; the architect overcame this imbalance in his model for the façade of S. Maria del Fiore (Florence, Mus. dell'Opera del Duomo), in which the three orders were carefully studied in their proportions, in the strongly projecting elements, and in the decorative style.

Santi di Tito (1536–1603) was a thoughtful architect who was of the same environment, but possessed rather limited capabilities. The brilliant sculptor Giovanni Bologna, known as Giambologna (1529–1608), turned to architecture in his later period. He combined a sculptural quality with an inspiration derived from Michelangelo, evident in the subtle chiaroscuro effects of his strong structural design that is emphasized and animated by the colors of paintings, as in the Chapel of S. Antonino in S. Marco, Florence, which has frescoes by Passignano and canvases by Alessandro Allori, Il Poppi, and Giovanni Battista Naldini. Later, in the Chapel of the Madonna del Soccorso in SS. Annunziata, sculpture (executed in part by Pierre Franqueville and Pietro Tacca) prevails over the paintings of Giacomo Ligozzi, Il Poppi, and Passignano.

Florence, which was unsuited to the baroque, fostered a late Renaissance architectural style that continued into the early 17th century. The Palazzo Nonfinito by Ludovico Cardi, known as Il Cigoli (1559–1613), conveys a feeling of noble dignity that is perceptible also in the many other examples of this type.

In the Veneto two masters emerged: the Veronese Michele Sanmicheli (1484–1559) and Andrea Palladio (1508–80) from Vicenza; the first was closely connected to Roman influences, especially that of Antonio da Sangallo the Younger, from whom he acquired, as a military architect, a technique that he adapted locally in the fortifications of the Lido of Venice, Padua, Verona, and the Greek islands, commissioned by the Venetian Republic. Where esthetic considerations demanded, he ennobled the stark fortifications, as at the city gates of Verona, by means of low, squat arrangements, with regular intervals marked by strongly projecting structural members (e.g., the Porta Nuova, and especially, the Doric Porta Palio; PLS. 392, 393). Sanmicheli followed the classicizing trend in religious architecture in a painterly style derived instinctively from his Venetian origin, and directly from his study of antiquity; a noteworthy example of this is the Petrucci Chapel, striking for its effects of light, which forms the substructure of S. Domenico in Orvieto. Sanmicheli's originality is evident in the heavy octagonal mass of Montefiascone Cathedral, with its corner towers; Carlo Fontana retained the earlier scheme in his reconstruction. In Verona, to which he returned in 1527, Sanmicheli followed Sangallo, making his forms lighter and giving them greater articulation and grace in religious buildings: the elegant, restrained Pellegrini Chapel in S. Bernardino; the dome of S. Giorgio in Braida; the noble church of the Madonna di Campagna; and in impressive secular buildings.

Designing various buildings in Verona on the model of buildings of the Po Valley type, with only two stories (the same model used by Bramante for the House of Raphael), Sanmicheli repeated the division in two orders with rich structural members accentuating the chiaroscuro (Palazzo Canossa, PL. 391; Palazzo Pompei, VIII, FIG. 417f). A typical example of this is the Palazzo Bevilacque (PL. 92; XIII, PL. 234), where the alternating large and small arches between the architectural orders create contrasting effects that are consistently used with a restrained dignity that can be also seen in Venice in the Palazzo Cornaro-Mocenigo, in which Serlio's influence is evident. In the three stories of the Palazzo Grimani (PL. 393; VIII, FIG. 425b) the contrast between solids and voids of different dimensions is strictly contained within the regular rhythms of the orders, that is, within their projecting elements.

Andrea Palladio became an architect after training as a craftsman (between 1524 and about 1540 he worked as a stonemason). In Padua, influenced by Giangiorgio Trissino and the Paduan Humanist circles, he began his study of antiquity. Palladio visited Rome (1541), made drawings of ancient monuments, and wrote a treatise in four volume (I Quattro Libri dell'Architettura, Venice, 1570; XI, PLS. 351–353). He had contacts with Serlio and with Giulio Romano, and he was interested in antiquity, not as the object of esthetic contemplation but as a romantic, archeological study that was to lead him to build the Convento della Carità in Venice in the form of an ancient house and to create the Teatro Olimpico in Vicenza on ancient models (PL. 425; IX, PL. 312, FIG. 465).

In Vicenza, Palladio gave to the city its definite aspect. He used somewhat heavy but harmonious forms in the superimposed arcades of the Palazzo della Ragione, the so-called "Basilica" (XI, PL. 29, FIG. 65). Later, in a series of two-story buildings (Palazzo Thiene, now Banca Popolare, XI, FIG. 67; Palazzo Porto Colleoni; Palazzo Porto-Barbaran, I, PL. 406; XI, PL. 30), he adapted Bramante's schemes for the use of architectural orders to create effects of chiaroscuro; in the Palazzo Chiericati (1536; XI, PL. 30, FIG. 67d), in which the central body and the white colonnades contrast with the soft shade of the loggias, he achieved results later matched by Paolo Veronese in his paintings.

Another painterly effect is evident in the Palazzo Valmarana (XI, PL. 30, FIG. 67c), with its single order, a result of Michelangelo's influence; the same effect was intensified in the Loggia del Capitanio (XI, PL. 35). This type of architecture, based on a harmonious beauty, in the villas of wealthy Venetian families was made to blend with the landscape around Vicenza and Treviso and the Brenta River. Palladio's style tended toward a broader development in his use of arcades (Villa Barbaro, now Volpi, in Maser; XI, PLS. 33, 35, FIG. 75) and sometimes of curved colonnades and huge rectangular esplanades; this harmony of architecture and its surroundings foreshadowed the baroque (plan for the Villa Trissino in Meledo) and was characterized in Palladio by elevations with columns and pediments. Palladio's many villas have been classified in two groups: temple-villas, with a single order (e.g., Villa Badoer, now Cagnoni, in Fratta Polesine; Villa Emo Capodilista in Fanzolo, XI, FIG. 75g); and *palazzo*-villas, with two orders (Villa Pisani, now Placco, in Montagnana; Villa Cornaro in Piombino Dese). Palladio achieved an ideal of harmonious beauty in Villa Capra, called "La Rotonda," built near Vicenza for Paolo Almerico (1552; XI, PL. 31, FIG. 69); it was designed on the central plan used in 15th-century churches and later taken up by Bramante and Michelangelo in St. Peter's. In this villa, four pronaoi are set into the square nucleus which was to have a true dome.

In Venice Palladio applied his serene art to religious architecture. An early example is the Church of S. Giorgio Maggiore (1565; XI, PL. 34, FIG. 72), with its strikingly white interior divided by colonnades and its deep presbytery suffused with luminous shade; on the façade the central body is in relief, projecting from the wings on either side. The Chiesa del Redentore (1577; XI, PLS. 34, 35, FIG. 72) has a front of limited dimensions that widen in the central body; the single interior space is flanked by chapels and acquires greater complexity in the arrangement of the transept and the presbytery, which are united in a single space.

Palladio's architecture was inspired by that classicizing style which had originated with Raphael, and had flourished in the late Renaissance. This style reached its culmination in Palladio's work, which can be called its terminal point.

It has been stated by some scholars that the Teatro Olimpico in Vicenza (1580) was designed by Palladio in his old age and was inspired by ancient structures. However, that it also corresponded to new, contemporary tastes and cultural interest is shown by the much less monumental theater built in the Uffizi for the Medicis by Buontalenti; by Scamozzi's theater in Sabbioneta; by that of the Farnese family in the Palazzo della Pilotta in Parma, for which Giovanni Battista Aleotti (1546?–1636) drew his inspiration from Palladio's theater. The Teatro Olimpico, with its three divergent perspectives, facing the elliptical cavea, does indeed recall ancient models. Like many other works by Palladio, it was completed by Vincenzo Scamozzi (1552–1616). Scamozzi faithfully followed the rules of classicism but never displayed individual genius. The rules stated in his *Dell'Idea dell'Architettura universale* (Venice, 1615) were occasionally applied by him with a cold neoclassical approach (Villa Verlato at Villaverla) that was the result of a balance of architecture, chiaroscuro, and color typical of the Venetian environment. The theater in Sabbioneta, the *palazzo* built for Francesco Trissino near the Vicenza Cathedral (1577), and the Procuratie Nuove in Venice (1586; VIII, PL. 214), in which Scamozzi followed the example of Sansovino, are examples of this.

Of all the late Renaissance architects, Palladio is outstanding not only for having brought the classicizing trend to its culmination, but also for his architectural achievements in the scenographic taste, which were later interpreted and elaborated in the baroque style, and for original aspects of his classicism, which became part of the neoclassic trend of the 18th and 19th centuries and which influenced architecture outside Italy, especially in England and North America (cf. BAROQUE ART; NEOCLASSIC STYLES).

Sculpture. The two poles of the late Renaissance were the classicism that persisted through the myth of Raphael and the anticlassicism of Michelangelo; nevertheless, in the field of sculpture these two opposing currents were often reconciled, especially in central Italy, where artists found their stimulus and inspiration predominantly in the Roman milieu. However, a continuation of classicism combined with an extreme refinement can be traced in the work of Benvenuto Cellini (1500–71), a former goldsmith who carried over into the major art of sculpture the love of detail he displayed in his highly ornate but rather inconsistent enameled saltcellar of Francis I (VI, PL. 269). Thus he applied to sculpture an expert virtuosity — combined with his stylized interpretation of Sansovino's classical idealization that seems, through contact with Primaticcio, to echo Parmigianino — in the lithe *Nymph of Fontainebleau* (IX, PL. 307) and in the frail *Narcissus* (1548, PL. 84) sculptured for the Boboli Gardens, in which the weary pose already hints at a rather decadent style. Cellini's depiction of Perseus with the head of Medusa (1548–54; XIII, PL. 469) in the Loggia della Signoria in Florence, regarded as his masterwork for its elegance of form, assumes through its arrangement a certain articulation in space; in the somewhat swollen modeling it reveals a slight hint of Michelangelo, which is at once superseded by the emphatic, refined sensuality of the details and of the frail base decorated with elegant statuettes of mythological gods and with a scene depicting Perseus freeing Andromeda, in which the great variety of planes recalls Ghiberti's reliefs. In the bust of Cosimo I de' Medici (1545–58; Florence, Mus. Naz.) the detail is overwhelming. An attempt at synthesis is seen instead in his bust of Bindo Altoviti (Boston, Isabella Stewart Gardner Mus.). A remarkable example of idealization is provided by the marble *Christ* (1562) in the Escorial, a work of which Cellini was always justly proud. An adventurous man, Cellini the artist nevertheless enlivened classicism with a pseudo-Alexandrian subtlety, sustained by a deliberate, reflective intellectualism, far removed from Cellini the autobiographer, who was so spontaneous — not to say impulsive — in his outspoken Tuscan expressiveness. A meeting point between the writer and the artist is represented, however, by the conscious insistence on anecdote and detail apparent in his autobiography, which can be related to the constant, minute formalism noticeable in his work as a goldsmith and as a sculptor.

Cellini remained practically untouched by the influence of Michelangelo. This was not the case however with other Florentines. Pierino da Vinci (1530?–53), who retained Tribolo's grace and a measure of soft chiaroscuro modulation, eventually adopted a formal, monumental style (e.g., in the low-relief stucco portraying the death of Count Ugolino; Florence, Mus. Naz.), as did Vincenzo Danti (1530–76) from Perugia, whose artistic formation took place in Rome and, above all, in Florence, who displayed a certain similarity to Pierino da Vinci (relief with Moses and the brazen serpent). Later, in the allegorical group *Honor Conquers Deceit* (IX, PL. 307) he decisively followed Michelangelo's style, and in the three statues representing the beheading of John the Baptist above the south door of the Baptistery, he adopted extremely elongated forms and elegant, balanced rhythms, turning to aspects typical of the middle of the century.

Baccio Bandinelli (1493–1560) was trained by Giovan Francesco Rustici (1474–1554; PL. 57) and therefore absorbed an essentially Leonardesque tradition that was later perturbed by Michelangelo's heroic aggrandizement, which as imitated by Bandinelli became merely an exterior gigantizing. A pertinent example is the *Hercules and Cacus* (1530); together with Michelangelo's *David* it flanked the main door of the Palazzo Vecchio and certainly did not benefit by the comparison. Even when Bandinelli attenuated his gigantizing tendency, as in the altar for Florence Cathedral (the colossal figure of God the Father is in a cloister of Sta Croce, and the group of Adam and Eve is in the Mus. Naz.), the forms remained devoid of vitality, hard, and artificial. Instead, a kind of vitality animates the work that remains Bandinelli's outstanding achievement, the *Bacchus* (1547) in the Pitti, a statue which is perfect in its equilibrium and harmonious in its classicizing cadence. Some of Baccio's qualities are shown to best advantage in the reliefs of the choir screens for Florence Cathedral, which portray nude or elegantly draped figures (IX, PL. 307) that reveal a progress toward a refined, aulic virtuosity; this is more clearly apparent in the small bronzes that were to meet with great success in Florence during the 16th century, such as those in the *studiolo* of Francesco I de' Medici in the Palazzo Vecchio.

The tombs of the Medici popes Leo X and Clement VII in the main chapel of S. Maria sopra Minerva in Rome, with statues placed within a monumental architectural setting, were designed by Bandinelli, who simplified the scheme of the tombs realized by Andrea Sansovino in the early 16th century; however, they cannot be considered masterpieces. Just as Bandinelli was an uneven artist, so was his pupil Bartolomeo Ammanati (1511–92), who nevertheless displayed greater sensitivity to painterly refinements in the Virtues on the Benavides tomb in the Church of the Eremitani in Padua, perhaps as a result of his familiarity with Jacopo Sansovino during their collaboration on the Biblioteca Vecchia di S. Marco (Biblioteca Marciana) in Venice. In Rome, with fluent linearism, Ammanati, working from designs by Vasari, executed the marble tombs of Cardinal Antonio del Monte and of his brother Fabiano (1553) in the Church of S. Pietro in Montorio with a fluent linear style. Here, the mediocre puffy putti of the balustrade are in some respects reminiscent of the sturdy little telamones painted by Michelangelo on the ceiling of the Sistine Chapel. And Michelangelo's influence again emerges in two of Ammanati's Florentine works: the statue of Victory, formerly in the tomb of Mario Nari in the Church of SS. Annunziata and now in the Giardino dei Semplici, and the figure of Neptune that statically dominates the fountain in Piazza della Signoria (VIII, PL. 210). The latter gigantic statue could in no way bring out Ammanati's most notable quality, the pictorial intention, which instead is apparent in the lively bronze figurines set in the colored marble basin of the fountain, representing nymphs, fauns, and rivers; these were executed by a number of collaborators, among them Vincenzo Danti and Giambologna. The variety of the material employed accentuates the coloristic approach, while the elegant, elongated figures, similar to those of Cellini, fittingly represent the sensualistic, aulic Florentine taste of the late 16th century.

At an earlier date, the Sienese painter Domenico Beccafumi (ca. 1486–1551) had attempted a number of sculptural experiments and had modeled in bronze the candelabra-bearing angels in Siena Cathedral, achieving effects of painterly luminism fully attuned to his style in painting. But the Florentine milieu was even then the most fertile, and in Florence various sculptors openly followed Bandinelli's style or, at any rate, were influenced by him: Domenico Poggini (1520–90) expressed himself with unusual analytical refinement (busts of Virginia Pucci Ridolfi and Francesco I de' Medici; both, Florence, Mus. Naz.); Vincenzo de' Rossi (1525–87) executed animated groups (those depicting the labors of Hercules, begun 1568; Palazzo Vecchio) with an emotional and changeable spirit that on occasion attained a high artistic level (he also worked in Rome; statues of SS. Peter and Paul in the Cesi Chapel in S. Maria della Pace); and, finally, Giovanni Bandini, known as Giovanni dell'Opera (ca. 1540–98) adhered more closely to Bandinelli's style but showed less refinement than the other followers in his activity as a sculptor (PL. 84; a Pietà in Urbino Cathedral; an allegorical figure of Architecture on Michelangelo's tomb in Sta Croce). Considerable talent and ability were later displayed by the Lorenzi brothers, Battista (1527–94) and Stoldo (1534–83). In Florence, Battista Lorenzi executed the statue of Painting and the bust of Michelangelo for the master's tomb in Sta Croce.

In Pisa, where he died, he left, among other works, the large bronze chandelier, in the Cathedral, which tradition links with Galileo, one of whose scientific theories is said to have been inspired by it. Stoldo Lorenzi is to be credited with the picturesque fountain of Neptune in the Boboli Gardens (VIII, PL. 431), a bronze angel in Pisa Cathedral, and an Annunciation and a group representing Adam and Eve with saints — partly carried out in collaboration with Annibale Fontana — in the Church of S. Maria presso S. Celso in Milan, where Stoldo spread Tuscan styles and fashions.

Valerio Cioli (1529–99), who was in Rome with Raffaello da Montelupo (Sinibaldi), contributed the statue of Sculpture to Michelangelo's tomb; however, his best work is seen in the lively bronzes, such as the "Morgante" (X, PL. 137) and satyrs (Florence, Mus. Naz.) and in the statues of genre figures (VII, PL. 384), usually intended for the decoration of gardens.

In the more advanced aulic environment, a special role was played by Giambologna (1529–1608), who was born in Flanders, and, after the almost ritual visit to Rome, settled in Florence in 1553. His artistic expression leaned toward Tribolo's style, which he interpreted, however, with refreshing spontaneity and originality, at times achieving perceptive naturalistic solutions also in relation to the use of light — for instance, in the sculptures of birds from the grotto of the Villa di Castello (Florence, Mus. Naz.) — which was, perhaps, the result of the surviving stimulus from the Flemish school of Antwerp. At other times he achieved graceful stylizations, as seen in some beautifully finished statuettes and in the famous statues of Venus of which there are examples in the Museo Nazionale and the Buontalenti Grotto (cf. VIII, PL. 430) of the Boboli Gardens in Florence and at the Villa Medicea della Petraia near Florence. The lively conception of the last-mentioned statue, which portrays Venus in the act of drying her hair, is completed by the figures of four cupid-satyrs climbing the basin fountain; the whole is in an ensemble of sensualistic, aulic, originality. In this and other works Giambologna's awareness of Cellini's work can often be perceived, and especially so in his *Mercury* (1580) in the Museo Nazionale in Florence; in this work Giambologna surpassed Cellini in the lightly soaring composition and in the vibrant impression of movement he managed to convey. Earlier, Giambologna had created a remarkable bronze model for a statue of Neptune (IX, PL. 308), that was rather coldly realized in the famous Neptune fountain in Bologna — a work that is nevertheless superior to Ammanati's work of the same subject in Florence. In the Fountain of the Ocean in the Boboli Gardens, Tribolo's precedents inspired Giambologna's three symbolic figures of the Rivers, a play of volumes in motion, which are set into the space so as to afford multiple views and, by irrationally endowing the forms with great lyricism, are contrary to the unifying aims of the 15th century's perspective rationality. (See also the colossal "Apennine" for Villa Demidoff at Pratolino, VIII, PL. 430; model, PL. 498). This is even more apparent in a famous and very dramatic group by Giambologna, in which the figures create a spiral movement, that was originally called *The Three Ages* (1580–83) and later designated *The Rape of the Sabines* by the historian Raffaello Borghini (1541–ca.1588).

Meanwhile, in the noble bronze statues (PL. 84) from the Grimaldi Chapel of S. Francesco di Castelletto at Genoa, now part of the university of that city, Giambologna combined virtuosity with a degree of naturalness; in the reliefs, on the other hand, he remained rather dispersive. In Florence, this facet of the artist's personality was intensified in the reliefs in the Chapel of S. Antonino in the Church of S. Marco and in the Chapel of the Madonna del Soccorso in SS. Annunziata (partly carried out by pupils).

The indefatigable Giambologna also created, with restrained movement and a remarkable sobriety of form, the equestrian monument to Cosimo I de' Medici (commissioned 1587) in Piazza della Signoria and that to Ferdinand I (1608), which was executed in collaboration with his pupil Pietro Tacca (1577–1640), who erected it in Piazza della Santissima Annunziata.

The endeavors of many younger artists were derived from Giambologna. The aforementioned Pietro Tacca from Carrara continued his teacher's style into the 17th century with the same brilliantly restrained modeling; it suffices to compare Bandini's mediocre marble statue of Ferdinand I in the monument to the Grand Duke with Tacca's four bronze Moors on the base.

One of Giambologna's slightly older pupils, Pierre Franqueville (Pietro Francavilla; 1553–1615) from Cambrai, instead retained his northern aloofness. He collaborated with the master in Genoa and then worked mostly on official statues, as well as the statue of Spring, one of the ornamental figures representing the seasons on the Bridge of Sta Trinita in Florence. Of these statues, that of Winter is by Taddeo Landini (ca. 1550–96), a Florentine who had settled in Rome, where he produced the four lithe youths that decorate the Fountain of the Tortoises (Fontana delle Tartarughe; VIII, PL. 206). The statues of Summer and of Autumn on the famous Florentine bridge are by Giovanni Battista Caccini (1556–1612), who was endowed with a marked painterly sense and was master to Pietro Bernini; the latter soon afterwards worked in Rome and in Naples, where his son Gian Lorenzo, the first of the great baroque sculptors, was born. In fact the Tuscans continued to be quite active in southern Italy also. In Naples, there was Michelangelo Naccherino (1550–1622), who was trained by Bandinelli and also followed the work of Giambologna; in Sicily, where Montorsoli had lived for a time, Francesco Camilliani (d. 1586), also a Florentine and a pupil of Bandinelli, settled at Palermo (cf. VIII, PL. 225). In Messina, Andrea Calamech (1514–1579) from Carrara rose from mere craftsmanship to the production of an eclectic type of sculpture that occasionally attained a late Renaissance elegance, which can also be seen in works by his son Francesco and his nephews.

Two Lombard artists, Giovanni Giacomo (d. 1555) and Guglielmo (d. 1577) della Porta from Porlezza, near Lugano, had contributed, together with Niccolò da Corte (d. 1552), to the decoration of Genoa Cathedral, with statues (Altar of the Apostles) and reliefs (bases of the baldachin in the Chapel of S. Giovanni Battista; PL. 23). In Rome, Guglielmo created the tomb of Pope Paul III (Farnese) in St. Peter's (VIII, PL. 208; IX, PL. 365), a monument that underwent an extensive elaboration; it was inspired by Raphael in the use of polychrome marble, and by Michelangelo's Medici tombs (cf. IX, PL. 530) in the statues of Justice and Prudence that flank the imposing portrayal of the seated figure of the Pope; this work would often serve as a model for papal tombs in the baroque period. Also in Rome, a large group of artists — most of them from Lombardy — later followed the path toward a rather decadent classicism in reliefs that recall those of Roman triumphal arches, notwithstanding a greater vivacity of conception. In S. Maria Maggiore reliefs of this type were introduced into the polychrome marble setting of the tombs of Pius V (XI, PL. 450) and Sixtus V — by Giovanni Antonio Paracca (known as Valsolda; d. after 1642), Egidio della Riviera (Gillis van den Vlietz; d. 1602), and others; here the scheme repeats with some modifications that of Bandinelli's tombs for the Medici popes Clement VII and Leo X in S. Maria sopra Minerva (see above). The same architectural scheme was followed for the tombs of Clement VIII and Paul V in S. Maria Maggiore; they were, however, carried out on a more sumptuous scale and decorated with reliefs executed in part by Camillo Mariani (1556–1611), Pietro Bernini (1562–1629; see also VIII, PL. 208), Francesco Mochi (1580–1654), and Stefano Maderno (ca. 1576–1636) — that is, by artists who were tending toward the new baroque ideals or were decisively following them already.

Leone Leoni (1509–90) from Arezzo worked in Venice in his early period and later in Rome and in Milan (PL. 91), where he died. He is notable for his masterly bronzes, which display a firm, poised naturalism that is especially striking in busts and in statues that in many cases adorn funerary monuments, as well as for his medals. His assured Italian concept of form was enlivened by a touch of Flemish analytical objectivity resulting from his trips abroad. For Milan Cathedral, Leoni created the tomb of Gian Giacomo Medici (VIII, PL. 45), and for the Church of the Incoronata at Sabbioneta in Lombardy the central statue for the tomb of Vespasiano Gonzaga (PL. 85). As court sculptor and medalist to the Holy Roman emperor

Charles V (statue portraying the Emperor restraining Fury; Prado) he worked in Brussels and Augsburg; later, in Spain, he created, among other works, statues of Prince Philip II, Empress Isabella, and Maria of Portugal, as well as a number of busts (all in the Prado). Following his example, his son Pompeo (1533–1608) became an artist to the Spanish court and executed, along with many tombs of princes and cardinals the solemn, spectacular monuments of Charles V and Philip II in the Escorial, each of which includes four larger-than-life-size bronze statues (PL. 102).

In Milan the various authors of statues for the Cathedral, such as Annibale Fontana and Angelo Marini, were for the most part expert technicians in marble sculpture. Among them was the above-mentioned Stoldo Lorenzi, who offers a fine example of the restrained Florentine solidity. In the Cathedral choir stalls Pellegrino Tibaldi contributed a vital feeling of movement, which he passed on to his collaborators, Gian Andrea Biffi (d. 1631) and Francesco Brambilla the Younger (d. 1599).

In Venice the art of Jacopo Sansovino, by turning the solid Tuscan sense of form toward the painterly, had in a sense anticipated the style of the late Renaissance. One of his disciples, Tiziano Minio (1517–52), expressed himself with remarkable grace in the reliefs of the baptismal font of the Basilica of S. Marco and in those of the small loggia of the bell tower. Other minor artists, such as Girolamo Campagna, Nicolò Roccatagliata and the Paduan Tiziano Aspetti, displayed the innate refinement of the traditional Venetian sensibility. It was precisely in the Venetian region that the Tuscan concept of formal was reasserted by Danese Cattaneo (1509–73) from Colonnata near Carrara, a pupil of Sansovino in Rome whose art was perfected by his Florentine experience. Cattaneo excelled in portraiture, in which he not only rendered with great accuracy the physical features of his subjects but also brought out their inner personality, as in the portrait of Lazzaro Bonamico (XI, PL. 221) and in the portrait of Cardinal Pietro Bembo (1547) in the Basilica of S. Antonio in Padua.

Alessandro Vittoria (1525–1608) from Trento attained a similar synthesis of his outstanding ability by using his material to full advantage — through a search for chiaroscuro and chromatic effects — with the Venetian distinction in the execution of penetrating noble portraits, such as those of Doge Nicolò da Ponte and Pietro Zen in the collections of the Seminario Patriarcale and that of Marcantonio Grimani in the Church of S. Sebastiano in Venice. It is true that he achieved such brilliant results only by overcoming his native mountain harshness, which is still evident in his representation of John the Baptist (1542) in the Church of S. Zaccaria in Venice. In Venice, in 1547, he became acquainted with Palladio, for whose Villa Barbaro at Maser (near Treviso) he executed stucco decorations (VIII, PL. 434; XIII, PL. 181), and through subsequent artistic contacts he attained a refinement reminiscent of Parmigianino, which is noticeable in the decoration of the ceilings of the stairway of the Libreria Vecchia di S. Marco and the Scala d'Oro in the Doges' Palace (XIII, PL. 282). However, he always retained a passionate vitality in his religious statues, such as the stucco Evangelists in S. Giorgio Maggiore and the fervent St. Jerome in the Church of S. Maria Gloriosa dei Frari (PL. 86); this vitality was combined with a measure of calmness, in the spirit of Paolo Veronese, in four statues representing the Seasons (1565–76) at the Villa Pisani (now Placco) in Montagnana.

Vittoria's role in late Renaissance sculpture is practically equivalent to those of Palladio and Veronese in architecture and painting, respectively. Like them, he concluded the Renaissance with an art far removed from excesses and attuned to a sound naturalism. Instead, one of Vittoria's disciples, Camillo Mariani from Vicenza, who worked in Rome alongside sculptors who were tending to the baroque, was even more obvious in his pictorial accents reminiscent of Veronese, as in the white stucco statues in S. Bernardo alle Terme (PL. 86; II, PL. 164; XIII, PL. 284), which indicate a clear link between the Venetian culture and that of central Italy.

Painting. In the study of the late Renaissance, scholars have always favored painting as a subject for particular research.

The artistic manifestations in this field in central Italy took two forms: the *bella maniera* (beautiful style) of Raphael; and the tormented figural power of Michelangelo, a constant source of energy and lyrical contributions, erroneously considered as being anti-Renaissance by those who identify the Renaissance as a whole with its better-known, classicistic trend. The term "mannerism," which has been variously defined, cannot — however it may be interpreted — be stretched to cover the whole late Renaissance period. On the contrary, it can be stated that the term does not correspond to a conceptual need and, given the positive meaning with which it is currently endowed, it cannot even lead to a clarification of the esthetic phenomena connected with it by art criticism.

Michelangelo was the greatest genius of the period; even during his lifetime the impact of his lyrical power was felt in Tuscany, falling within an anticlassicistic category of a poetic quality that gradually declined in the second half of the 16th century.

In Florence, within the sphere of the sculptural-linear vision, always fundamental for that center, form was combined with color as understood by Michelangelo: an abstract strengthening of form itself, apart from any reference to factual reality. The style of Pontormo (Jacopo Carucci; 1494–1557) was more in harmony with that of his first master, Piero di Cosimo, than with that of Andrea del Sarto, to whom he was also close in his early period. Pontormo soon departed from Andrea's soft chiaroscuro that is evident in Pontormo's youthful works, such as the *Visitation* (Florence, SS. Annunziata). In the frescoes of the Villa di Poggio a Caiano (IV, PL. 201), depicting Pomona and Vertumnus, the images tend toward distortion, but the ornamental arrangement shows an original figural vision at work. Pontormo's designs are fluent (IV, PL. 274; IX, PL. 289), although often frozen into chromatic masses of a violent, abstract luminosity. Later his figures had a tormented and sensitive quality, as in the *Deposition* (IX, PL. 288), whose compact, uninterrupted grouping of figures was inspired by Michelangelo, as shown by their vigorous linear fluency, and whose outlines are represented by limits of clearly defined color, almost devoid of shadows. That Pontormo was inspired by Dürer's engravings is revealed in the *Visitation* (Carmignano, parish church), the Passion fresco cycle (Certosa of Galluzzo, near Florence), and the *Supper at Emmaus* (PL. 77). Pontormo strove to achieve a greater freedom of expression, which was to result in hallucinated, stylized images and ever brighter and more violent colors.

Pontormo, who was also an excellent portrait painter (XI, PL. 218), occasionally revealed a certain intolerance for precision in the rendition of his subjects, and in some of them he again hinted at distortion. Even in portraiture he expressed his temperament in the contraposition of chromatic violences or by keeping to somber, gloomy colors. The artist eventually attempted to find, if not total contentment, at least an outlet for an evident inner anxiety, always manifest in his many easel pictures, reverting to a weighty, towering, figural quality inspired by Michelangelo in the drawings for the frescoes of the choir in S. Lorenzo in Florence, which concluded his pictorial activity. These compositions, almost certainly endowed with a striking, dramatically tormented quality (outstanding among them are the scenes depicting the flood and the resurrection of the body), must have been far removed from any refined ornamental attractiveness, and probably reflected the artist's own torment. This may explain why they were eventually whitewashed.

Another restless personality, Il Rosso (Giovan Battista di Jacopo; 1495–1540; PLS. 76, 77; XI, PL. 370), also represented the anticlassicistic trend in his astonishing, original compositions peopled by hallucinated figures totally distinct from any accepted canons of beauty, and whose striking effect is sustained by the use of discordant colors. He strongly opposed the tradition tracing back to Fra Bartolommeo and Andrea del Sarto, even in his youthful, restless *Assumption* (Florence, SS. Annunziata), and transformed the faceted planes typical of Andrea into violent luminist contrasts. Particularly in the *Deposition* (1521; Volterra, Pin. Com.), which renewed the iconography established in Florence by Filippino Lippi and Perugino, he turned to dra-

matic effects and formal distortions, accentuated by the sweeping application of the iridescent colors and by the abstract light effects.

Even when he had to compose altarpieces on already familiar schemes [*Madonna with John the Baptist and St. Bartholomew* (1521; Villamagna, Pieve); *Marriage of the Virgin* (1523; Florence, S. Lorenzo); *Madonna with Saints* (1522; Florence, Pitti)], Il Rosso revealed, through the irrationality of his stylizations, the fiery colors employed, and the fantastic luminism, both his personality and his preference for Michelangelo, whose cartoons for the battle of Cascina he imitated in the nudes in *Moses and the Daughters of Jethro* (IX, PL. 290). In 1524, in Rome, his contacts with Michelangelo and Raphael led him to temper his exuberance with more compact figural aspects (frescoes in S. Maria della Pace). Moreover, his familiarity with Parmigianino, which resulted in reciprocal influences, together with the example of Raphael, caused Il Rosso to assimilate, if not Parmigianino's grace, at least that sense of rhythm which the latter so deeply felt; this is evidenced by the complex *Resurrection* in Città di Castello (Cath.) and by the crowded *Deposition* in Sansepolcro (S. Lorenzo).

This acquired art, which to some extent fettered his innate poetics gifts, Il Rosso took with him to France and he enriched it there with original, bizarre inventiveness in his frescoes for the Gallery of Francis I in the Château at Fontainebleau (PL. 100), placed among stuccoes of Roman overtones. But the Emilian style that by then prevailed at Fontainebleau, directed toward a courtly elegance, could not blend with Il Rosso's independent spirit, which again broke through in the dramatic *Pietà* (IX, PL. 291).

Remarkable esthetic results were achieved by the Sienese Domenico Beccafumi (1485–1551), who at first was influenced by the soft chiaroscuro modulations of Raphael and of Sodoma, but soon turned to the Florentines, as is evident in the iridescence and the chromatic disintegration in the altarpiece depicting St. Catherine receiving the stigmata and in its predella (painted ca. 1512) in Siena (Pin.). His artistic vision never reached Il Rosso's hallucinating extremes. Beccafumi's production was always rather uneven as a result of the influences he assimilated from various artists. Michelangelo's influence was felt in his early period and manifested itself particularly in later years, for example, in his painting of Moses, and in the pavement with scenes from the life of Moses (both in Pisa Cathedral), and the floor with scenes from the Old Testament in Siena (VIII, PL. 86). Like the Florentines, he also painted frescoes (ceiling of the Sala del Concistoro in the Palazzo Pubblico, Siena, 1529–35), panels (IX, PL. 295), and religious paintings, and he decorated furniture, all with a fluid and vibrant brushstroke, as in *Deucalion and Pyrrha* (PL. 77) and *Scipio's Continence* (Lucca, Pin. Naz.).

Bronzino (Angelo di Cosimo di Mariano; 1503–72; PL. 79) was a disciple of Pontormo. An assured designer, with a temperament opposite to the vibrant one of his teacher, Bronzino painted static and polished forms in cold, marblelike colors, thus creating a sort of faultless neoclassicism. Bronzino was attracted by Michelangelo's monumentality, and his influence is apparent especially in the frescoes (stories from the Old Testament, ca. 1555–64, Florence, Chapel of Eleanor of Toledo in Palazzo Vecchio; *Martyrdom of S. Lorenzo*, 1565–69, Florence, S. Lorenzo); in the altarpieces (*Resurrection*, Florence, SS. Annunziata; *Christ in Limbo*, Florence, Mus. dell'Opera di Sta Croce); in the designs for the Medicean tapestry factory (tapestries illustrating stories of Joseph, now divided between Palazzo Vecchio in Florence and Palazzo del Quirinale in Rome); and in the mythological paintings (*Venus, Cupid, Folly, and Time*; IX, PL. 292). Bronzino achieved a high artistic level in his portraits, where the attentive, perceptive rendition of reality alternates between spontaneous aspects derived from Pontormo, as in the portrait of Laura Battiferri (Florence, Palazzo Vecchio), and vigorous construction, as in the portraits of Ugolino Martelli (Berlin, Staat. Mus.) and Giannettino Doria (Rome, Gall. Doria Pamphili). Bronzino's numerous portraits of the polished, brilliant members of the Medici family are dignified and restrained; outstanding among these are the portraits of Cosimo I de' Medici (XI, PL. 225), his wife Eleanor of Toledo (IX, PL. 296), and their son Ferdinand (Uffizi).

Bronzino's careful formalism represented in Florence the most valid point of contact with the more advanced generations, whose work displayed the eclectic emergence of superficial and vacuous echoes of Michelangelo, idealized Raphaelesque styles, and, above all, particularly as concerns frescoes, Bronzino's hedonistic aulic refinements.

Florence also continued to lead in fresco painting; among the artists who excelled in this field was Francesco Salviati (1510–63), who derived his style from Andrea del Sarto and Pontormo. Salviati's ability in composition and elegant fluency of design are shown in the frescoes of the Sala dell'Udienza in Palazzo Vecchio, depicting Camillus and Peace symbolically burning weapons (1544), whose chromatic clarity is also present in his paintings of allegorical and religious subjects and in solid portraits. Giorgio Vasari decorated the Salone dei Cinquecento in Palazzo Vecchio of Florence (cf. II, PL. 28; VIII, PL. 102). In the decoration of the ducal apartments in Palazzo Vecchio (PL. 78) and in the frescoes of his house in Arezzo, Vasari avoided the dispersive characteristics of large decorations and achieved an atmosphere of intimacy combined with refinement, despite the occasional unevenness in the execution. Such unevenness was due to the intervention of various collaborators, among them Jan van der Straet (Stradano) from Bruges, who contributed in spreading the Flemish taste in Florence. Other fresco painters in Florence were Alessandro Allori (1535–1607), who decorated a corridor in the Uffizi, and Bernardino Poccetti (1548–1612), who did some of the frescoes in S. Marco (I, PL. 463) and in S. Lorenzo in the Certosa of Galluzzo.

Frescoes and altarpieces do not, however, represent the best of Florentine painting, although they do reveal the continuation of a traditional dignified style; cases in point are Santi di Tito (1536–1603; VIII, PL. 209), Jacopino del Conte (1510–98), Allori (IX, PL. 293), and Jacopo da Empoli (Jacopo Chimenti; ca. 1554–1640), who, although they did feel the need for renewal, were unable to give it practical expression. In fact, it was only in the 17th century that Giovanni da San Giovanni (1592–1636) and others were to bring their art up to date in the direction of color. During the late Renaissance, although Giacomo Ligozzi (1547–1626; PL. 480) came to Florence from Verona and brought with him the essence of Venetian color and Florentine palaces were gradually enriched with paintings from Venice and from the Veneto region, the city of Florence remained alien to the school of color.

The best of Florentine painting is to be found in small works done for the nobility, particularly those in the *studiolo* of Francesco I de' Medici in Palazzo Vecchio (VIII, PL. 103), designed by Vasari and decorated by artists who were his assistants or followers. Here a complex cultural outlook was expressed in a narrative and descriptive tone combined with the fluent style of Andrea del Sarto (which was long appreciated and imitated), with Michelangelo's grandiose forms, and with Flemish refinements, harmonizing with bronze statuettes modeled in the spirit of Giambologna. Among the painters who decorated the *studiolo* Girolamo Macchietti (PL. 78) and Mirabello Cavalori (PL. 78) are outstanding for their elegance and refinement.

The Roman artistic circle was the most active during this period because of the decisive stimulus given by Michelangelo and Raphael and the uninterrupted influx of vital artistic contributions that adapted the expression of those masters (from ca. 1523 to 1527) to the late Renaissance style. Among the many artists active in Rome, Parmigianino (Francesco Mazzola; 1503–40) soon became prominent. During his stay in Rome, Parmigianino, whose art was originally modeled on that of Correggio, strove to reconcile his art with Raphael's rhythms, in an original idiom typified by fluent design and soft, flaxen colors enlivened by vibrant lights, with a grace marked by very elongated forms of an anticlassical tone. Examples of his style are the frescoes with religious subjects in S. Maria della Steccata in Parma and the brilliant ones illustrating the legend of Diana and Actaeon, with putti and beautiful ornamental motifs, in Sanvitale Castle at Fontanellato. The later developments in Parmigianino's art, up to his superlative stylizations, are best

followed in his panels, from the *Vision of St. Jerome* (XI, PL. 45) to the *Madonna and Child, the Infant St. John, the Magdalen, and St. Zacharias* (PL. 49) up to the so-called "Madonna dal Collo Lungo" (XI, PL. 81). In their close adherence to reality, the portraits bear a lively imprint of naturalness, occasionally intensified by the set pose, as in the so-called "Antea" (XI, PL. 50), and they are rich in formal and psychological nuances, as in the *Young Woman in a Turban* (Parma, Gall. Naz.), the self-portraits (Uffizi; X, PL. 388), and the portraits of the knight of Calatrava (Lovere, Gall. dell'Acc. Tadini), Malatesta Baglioni (Vienna, Kunsthist. Mus.), and Gian Galeazzo Sanvitale (XI, PL. 47).

During this time Raphael's *bella maniera* was being disseminated throughout Italy by his numerous disciples. Of these, the Florentine Il Fattore (Giovan Francesco Penni) moved to Naples, and another Florentine, Perino del Vaga (IX, PL. 293), to Genoa; Raffaello dal Colle worked in the upper Tiber Valley region and in the northern Marches and Giovanni Udine in Venice and in the Veneto. Polidoro da Caravaggio and Maturino da Firenze remained in Rome, where they decorated façades of palaces (IX, PL. 311) in a Raphaelesque style but added themes inspired by antiquity; in S. Silvestro al Quirinale they painted landscapes, also based on classical models, in a style that later became widespread. As mentioned earlier, Marcantonio Raimondi made engravings of Raphael's paintings, and his prints were instrumental in spreading the master's style and works.

One of Raphael's altarpieces, the *Ecstasy of St. Cecilia* (PL. 367), made a profound impression on a number of minor artists in Emilia and Romagna, such as Innocenzo da Imola, Girolamo Marchesi, and Bagnacavallo (Bartolomeo Ramenghi). In Emilia, Raphael's style was continued in an original manner, particularly by the younger generation, who combined it with influences of Correggio and Parmigianino. Two exceptions stand out in the persons of the Ferrarese Scarsellino (Ippolito Scarsella; VIII, PL. 217), still tied to local tradition by the mellow colors of his elegant figures; and the Modenese Niccolò dell'Abate (PL. 81; IX, PLS. 299, 301), whose fiery color reveals echoes of Dosso Dossi, although it also shows some measured traces of Correggio (frescoes in Palazzo dell'Università, formerly Poggi, in Bologna; VIII, PL. 217), and who gave concrete form to various fables in poetic scenes (frescoes in Palazzo Zucchini in Bologna) inspired by the writings of Ariosto. Il Rosso, Niccolò dell'Abate, and Primaticcio introduced the art of the Renaissance to the court of Francis I in France.

Pellegrino Tibaldi, after his activity in Rome, worked in Ancona (frescoes in the Loggia dei Mercanti), Ferrara, and Bologna, where he painted some frescoes with bold perspectives in the Palazzo dell'Università (IX, PL. 298; XI, PL. 100) and in the Poggi Chapel in the Church of S. Giacomo. Although his reelaborations of Raphael and of Michelangelo were far from faultless and his pompous style tended to emphasize the athletic aspects of the figures, the results were not devoid of a certain grandeur, much appreciated later in Spain, where Tibaldi executed some frescoes in the Library and the Lower Cloister of the Escorial.

In Bologna in the second half of the 15th century Bartolomeo Passarotti, a skillful painter of altarpieces, distinguished himself for his solid qualities as a portraitist (IX, PL. 297), Bartolomeo Cesi exalted color in his frescoes, and Prospero Fontana and his daughter Lavinia developed their typically narrative painting. Both Orazio Samacchini, who also revealed some affinity with the Tuscans, and Lorenzo Sabatini, who worked in the Pauline Chapel and the Sala Regia (IX, PL. 294) in the Vatican, showed a predilection for Raphael.

Pictorial styles in Romagna and in Emilia were uneven, owing to local traditions and the influence of the major masters. In Reggio Emilia, Lelio Orsi (Lelio da Novellara; 1511–87) combined the style of Correggio and his school with that of Michelangelo, painting in an insistent, agitated, and occasionally stormy linear idiom, perhaps resulting from the study of northern engravings, adapted to bold stylizations and enriched by luminist effects, as in the *Martyrdom of St. Catherine of Alexandria* (IX, PL. 301). In Parma, Bertoia (Giacomo Zanguidi; 1544–74) produced precious and refined works (detached frescoes preserved in Parma, Gall. Naz.).

In Liguria a number of artists who worked in the style of Perino del Vaga were active, and some Sienese artists worked with them. Luca Cambiaso (1527–85; IX, PL. 302) from Moneglia was the greatest Genoese painter of the century. He was trained by his father and Giovanni Battista Castello. His frescoes in the Villa Imperiale and Palazzo Parodi in Genoa are outstanding. Cambiaso was influenced by various masters, including Michelangelo, but he preferred Correggio, and created fascinating modulations of light, especially nocturnal effects (*Adoration of the Child*, Brera; *Christ before Caiaphas*, Genoa, Palazzo Bianco).

Marcello Venusti (1515–79) from Como was initially trained by Pier Francesco Sacchi and then by the Campi brothers from Cremona, that is, in the Lombard environment. He then went to Rome, where he interpreted Michelangelo with great sensitivity when he did not copy the great master outright. The Milanese Giovanni Paolo Lomazzo produced some remarkable treatises (*Trattato dell'Arte della Pittura*; Milan, 1584; *Idea del Tempio della Pittura*, Milan, 1590), but was a mediocre painter.

Worthy of particular mention is a group of artists from Cremona, headed by the Campi brothers (Giulio, Antonio, and Vincenzo), whose father Galeazzo was himself a painter and a modest pupil of Boccaccio Boccaccino. Giulio (ca. 1505–72; IX, PL. 302) displayed great eclecticism in assimilating the styles of Giulio Romano, Correggio, and, above all, Parmigianino. Giulio frescoed S. Margherita in Cremona. S. Sigismondo in Cremona was entirely decorated by members of the Campi family, including Giulio's cousin, Bernardino Campi (1522–1590/95). Bernardino was trained in Mantua by Ippolito Costa and was influenced by Parmigianino's style in the elongated images of his altarpieces, but in his frescoes in S. Sigismondo his style was closer to Giulio Romano's. Giulio Campi's brothers, Antonio (d. ca. 1591) and Vincenzo (1536–91), worked in Cremona and Milan. Antonio was a sculptor, architect, and painter, as well as a historian of his native city. He worked as a painter in the churches of S. Sigismondo and S. Pietro al Po in Cremona, and collaborated with Vincenzo in decorating the Church of S. Paolo in Milan. Vincenzo painted a fresco with ten prophets in Cremona Cathedral, but revealed a greater talent for portraits and, as a result of Flemish inspirations, for genre paintings and still lifes (VI, PL. 69; XIII, PL. 198).

Giulio Romano's art was very influential in northern Italy. The artist went to Mantua from Rome in 1527. Although Romano departed from the style of Raphael in other types of painting, his easel pictures retained the master's rhythmic sensibility. Romano used dazzling, fiery colors both in easel paintings and in the frescoes of the Palazzo del Te in Mantua; the frescoes often bring to mind Michelangelo's monumentality but display on the whole a somewhat gaudy decorative taste. In the Palazzo del Te, the Sala dei Cavalli with its ample divisions, the Sala di Fetonte (PL. 53), the Sala di Cesare, and, especially, the Sala di Psyche (PL. 82) and the Sala dei Giganti (IX, PL. 298) represent the many significant aspects of Romano's striking painting. Primaticcio adorned the Palazzo del Te with stuccoes in the classicizing style, but later, in France, the style of this highly imaginative Mantuan artist became anticlassical.

Giulio Romano's trend (but it was not the only one) continued in Sabbioneta, at the court of Vespasiano Gonzaga, specifically in the mythological scene in the Galleria degli Antenati in the Ducal Palace and, through the work of Fornarotto from Mantua, in the Gabinetto di Diana of the same palace, where Bernardino Campi also painted a fresco. In the Palazzo del Giardino, Campi also decorated the Gabinetto di Venere with slender, flowing figures (executed with the collaboration of Fornarotto and a local painter, P. M. Pesenti) and the Sala degli Specchi with fanciful landscapes. The decoration of the Palazzo del Giardino was continued by other Paduan fresco painters. Giovanni and Cherubino Alberti from Sansepolcro and Pesenti completed the frescoes in the Galleria degli Antichità in 1590. The Alberti brothers were familiar with Raphael's style through the works of Raffaello dal Colle; they traveled in Italy and became acquainted with the work of Beccafumi, Correggio, and Paolo Veronese, and also with the perspective methods of Giulio Romano at Mantua. These precedents contributed in stimulating the two brothers to achieve bold illusionist perspectives in Rome, such as those in the Sagrestia dei Canonici in the Lateran (XI, PL. 100), the Sala Clementina in the Vatican, and S. Silvestro al Quirinale (XI, PL. 97). In some of their spatial achievements they even anticipated the excesses of the baroque artists, but their vision is less organic, the composition is stiffer, and the painting is more arid.

The Alberti brothers serve as a reminder that the Tuscans, well represented, among others, by the Florentine Mirabello Cavalori, were also established in the Marches. On the other hand, two artists from the Marches, Taddeo (1529–66) and Federico (ca. 1540–1609) Zuccari from Sant'Angelo in Vado, worked in Rome; they combined Raphael's rhythms with inventiveness and whimsy in the Sala Regia in the Vatican and the Palazzo Farnese at Caprarola (IX, PL. 310). Federico completed the decoration (begun by Vasari) of Brunelleschi's dome in S. Maria del Fiore in Florence in a rather pedestrian manner. In the Sala del Maggior Consiglio of the Doges' Palace in Venice he portrayed the German emperor Frederick Barbarossa before Pope Alexander III. He also worked in the Escorial in Spain. He was the author of a treatise entitled *L'Idea de' scultori, pittori e architetti* (2 vols., Turin, 1607).

On a higher artistic level was the work of Federico Barocci (ca. 1528–1612) from Urbino. Taking Bartolomeo Genga and Giovanni Battista Franco as a point of departure, he went on to express himself in a sensitive style of Correggio-like grace, adopting a delicate, pastel-like chiaroscuro, sustained by light, soft, iridescent colors (PL. 81; IX, PL. 303). The animated composition and the placement of figures in his religious paintings were inspired by Correggio and Raphael, and the pietism evident in these paintings was in keeping with the spirit of the Counter Reformation, which was to continue in some of the paintings of the 17th century. Barocci had considerable success not only in his own region but also in Rome (*Visitation* and *Presentation of the Virgin in the Temple*, Chiesa Nuova), in Umbria (*Deposition*, 1569, Perugia, Cath., reelaborating, with almost baroque ardor, Il Rosso's *Deposition* in Volterra), and in Tuscany (*Madonna del Popolo*, 1575–79, Uffizi, from the Pieve di S. Maria in Arezzo, whose crowded composition became a standard model for Florentine artists). Barocci's art was continued in the Marches by his disciples and imitators, and his style was echoed in Romagna, Umbria, and Tuscany, at Siena in particular.

In Rome, it cannot be said that the local painters, or more accurately those from Latium, enjoyed any artistic preeminence. Girolamo Siciolante (1521–ca. 1580) from Sermoneta and Scipione Pulzone (ca. 1550–1598) from Gaeta were influenced, on the one hand, by the styles of Raphael and Sebastiano del Piombo and, on the other, by Tuscan and Emilian trends. They produced a merely narrative art, more effective in some solid, objective portraits than in religious paintings: Siciolante's portrait of Francesco II Colonna (Rome, Gall. Naz.); Pulzone's portraits of Cardinal Ricci (IX, PL. 297) and Paul III (XI, PL. 452). Cavalier d'Arpino (Giuseppe Cesari; 1568–1640) also displayed an eclectic late Renaissance culture; he excelled in mural decoration, for example, the dome of St. Peter's (cf. X, PL. 192) and the Olgiati Chapel in S. Prassede (IX, PL. 303). But the leading role was played by those industrious artists from various Italian regions and from artistic centers of northern Europe, who considered Rome the supreme goal of an artistic pilgrimage. As mentioned earlier, Rome welcomed Parmigianino and Il Rosso; then, still within Michelangelo's lifetime, Daniele da Volterra (VIII, PL. 208; IX, PL. 294), so close to Michelangelo in his *Deposition* in the Church of Trinità dei Monti; Salviati [frescoes in the Palazzo Farnese (VII, PL. 268; IX, PL. 294)]; and Vasari [frescoes in the Salone dei Cento Giorni in the Palazzo della Cancelleria (XIII, PL. 355) and in the Sala Regia in the Vatican (IX, PL. 294)], who worked in collaboration with Lorenzo Sabatini.

The oratory of S. Giovanni Decollato was decorated by Salviati (IX, PL. 309); Jacopino del Conte, who was much more remarkable as a portraitist; Giovanni Battista Franco (IX, PL. 300) and Pirro Ligorio, whose painting was inspired by Raphael; and Jacopo Zucchi. Zucchi's work in Florence was influenced by Flemish minuteness, but in another of his Roman works, the frescoes in the apse of the Church of Sto Spirito in Sassia, there is a gigantic breadth derived from Michelangelo. More traditional in tone was the work of two other Tuscans from Pomarance near Volterra: Niccolò Circignani (1517–96) and his pupil Cristoforo Roncalli (1552–ca. 1626). Circignani displayed a watered-down Raphaelism, as in the dome of S. Pudenziana and the frescoes in S. Stefano Rotondo (XI, PL. 452). Roncalli, whose work was more advanced, also worked in Naples (altarpiece of St. Agnes in S. Filippo) and in Loreto (frescoes and a *Crucifixion* in the Sanctuary of the Holy House). Pellegrino Tibaldi worked in Rome (Sala del Consiglio in Castel Sant'Angelo); so did Girolamo Muziano (1528–92) from Brescia, who was in Rome by 1560, where he left works of vast breadth sustained by northern colors (e.g., the *Resurrection of Lazarus*, Vatican Mus.). Federico Zuccari, Raffaellino da Reggio (Raffaello Motta), Livio Agresti, Cesare Nebbia, and Marco da Siena (Marco dal Pino) collaborated in decorating the Oratory of S. Lucia del Gonfalone in Rome in a rather overloaded style, following a tendency which, combined with perspectivism, was fully expressed by the Alberti brothers.

In southern Italy individual artists worked in a wide variety of styles. In Campania, Andrea da Salerno (Andrea Sabatini), the most closely linked with the High Renaissance, displayed echoes of Cesare da Sesto, Fra Bartolommeo, and Raphael; a leading role was played by such painters as Giovanni Bernardo Lama and Giovan Filippo Criscuolo. Raphael's influence, combined with Venetian elements, can be seen in the work of Girolamo Imparato and Fabrizio Santafede, from both of whom Ippolito Borghese derived his style. Belisario Corenzio continued to work in the traditional idiom. Marco da Siena, whose training began in Siena but was completed in Rome, spread in Campania and even in Apulia his overstated painting, fluctuating between Raphael's grace and Michelangelo's monumentality.

In Sicily, Girolamo Alibrando from Messina followed the style of Cesare da Sesto; Vincenzo da Pavia (Il Romano), who worked in Palermo, drew his inspiration from the Lombards; Antonello Riccio's work in Messina imitated that of Polidoro da Caravaggio. They were all overshadowed by the strong artistic temperament of the Tuscan Filippo Paladino, from Val di Sieve, who spread throughout the island the formal, courtly elegance of the refined contemporary Florentines.

The height of poetic expression was attained particularly by the Venetian circle, faithful to an approach based on color rather than one based on line and chiaroscuro, typical of the painting of peninsular Italy.

Among the major Venetian names is that of Tintoretto (Jacopo Robusti; 1518–94), of whom Paolo Pini said in 1548 that his aspiration was the fusion of "Michelangelo's draftsmanship and Titian's colors." However, while his figural world often follows grandiose patterns, the powerful vitality of the personages — often portrayed in dramatic movement — is expressed in the Venetian tradition, that is, not according to a sculptural ideal but rather in terms of color combined, sometimes quite unrealistically, with striking effects of fitful light and violent contrasts; this light is essential to the imaginative, anticlassical vision of the master. Tintoretto's production was prodigious and imposing; he painted large religious and secular canvases, small concentrated paintings illustrating mythological tales and Biblical scenes, and portraits. Outstanding among the portraits are those of Jacopo Soranzo (XIV, PL. 77) and Antonio Cappello (Venice, Acc.). In the development of his style, the earlier works are more clearly drawn and have vigorous, sharp colors (*Cain and Abel*, Venice, Acc.; *The Last Supper*, XIV, PL. 81). These were followed by works of a more rarefied tone (the Doge Girolamo Priuli receiving the sword and the scale, on the ceiling of the square hall of the Doges' Palace; *The Marriage at Cana* in the sacristy of S. Maria della Salute). In Tintoretto's next works a vibrant luminism prevails over colors that become increasingly dark and gloomy (*Deposition*, 1592–94; *Last Supper*, 1594; *Gathering of the Manna*, 1594; all, Venice, S. Giorgio Maggiore). Tintoretto also painted some great cycles in Venice: the Scuola Grande di S. Marco (1548–68), with scenes from the life of the saint, now divided between the Accademia in Venice (XIV, PL. 80) and the Brera in Milan (XIV, PL. 83);

the Church of S. Rocco (1549–67); and especially the Scuola di S. Rocco (1567–87; PLS. 93, 372; XIV, PLS. 86–88). Finally, there is the huge *Paradise* (1588) in Venice (Sala del Maggior Consiglio of the Doges' Palace). Tintoretto's numerous pupils, including his children Domenico and Marietta, spread his mannerist style outside the Veneto, but not his art, which was too individual to be subject to imitation.

To some extent, this also applies to Bassano (Jacopo da Ponte; ca. 1517–92). His articulate, painterly style has a crisp touch derived from Parmigianino; in some of his work, with its chromatic splendor, he resembles Bonifacio Veronese (e.g., *Rest on the Flight to Egypt*; II, PL. 238). Starting around 1550, Bassano followed Tintoretto's style (*Baptism of Lucilla*; II, PL. 245); some of his stylizations are reminiscent of El Greco (small *Adoration of the Magi*, Rome, Gall. Borghese). He also painted genre subjects (II, PL. 239; VI, PL. 69). His sons Francesco (II, PL. 243), Leandro (a good portraitist; II, PL. 243), and Gerolamo (II, PL. 244) continued their father's style, especially in genre paintings and portraits, but their work was superficial and often a facile imitation.

At this time Venice was crowded with artists, among them El Greco, who found in the city, in the work of Titian, Bassano, and Tintoretto, the principal sources for the later expression of his genius. Lo Schiavone (Andrea Meldolla; d. 1563; PL. 82), from Zadar, basically patterned his art after Titian's but also was influenced by Parmigianino in his lithe, very elongated forms (*Adoration of the Magi*, Milan, Bib. Ambrosiana) and by Tintoretto's luminism. He was therefore well within the late Renaissance sphere, in which he evolved his spontaneous decorative vein, more evident in the organ shutters, back rests, and wooden chests that he decorated than in his altarpieces.

Palma Giovane (Jacopo di Antonio Palma; 1544–1628) closely followed Titian and Tintoretto in the easily accessible style of the many works he painted in Venice and in the Veneto (PL. 83; VIII, PL. 214), as well as in various locations throughout the peninsula. While Titian's style was being continued by a number of imitators, an academic trend connected with central Italy was developed in the city by, among others, Giulio Licinio, Giovanni de' Mio (Giovanni Fratino), and the Tuscan Giuseppe Salviati (Giuseppe Porta). These three artists collaborated with Lo Schiavone, Giovanni Battista Franco, G. Battista Zelotti (VIII, PL. 214), and Paolo Veronese in painting a series of allegories in the Sala Maggiore of the Biblioteca Vecchia di S. Marco in Venice (1556–57).

Paolo Veronese (Paolo Caliari; 1528–88), a pupil of Antonio IV Badile, seems to synthesize the late Renaissance on a highly poetic level; but, instead of concluding this phase, he opened new paths for it, especially in relation to decorative painting. In Mantua, with Giulio Romano's work on the Palazzo del Te, decorative painting had attained grandiose and rhythmic spaces in accordance with the canons of the Roman schools, with a formalism of sculptural relief that had been much appreciated in Verona. In fact, Verona had always set a high value on form, nourished by Giotto's art in the Gothic period, strengthened by Mantegna's trend during the early Renaissance, and continued in the 16th century both by Badile and by the painters with whom Veronese collaborated.

Form, clearly defined and composed, linked to tendencies of the central and Mantegnesque early Renaissance, completed by new spatial layouts and by a familiarity with the painting of Parma and of Brescia, is the basis of Paolo Veronese's painting; it is sustained by tonal colors, pure and clear, that are neither Titian's vivid colors nor Tintoretto's light-fragmented ones. In Venice and in the Veneto, as well as in his native city of Verona, Paolo Veronese excelled in compositions displaying great decorative talent, surpassing by their spaciousness and airiness the Roman-Mantuan vision. In addition to the sumptuous allegorical paintings on the ceiling of the Sala del Consiglio dei Dieci in the Doges' Palace in Venice (1553) and to the paintings in the Church of S. Sebastiano in Venice (1555–56), Veronese decorated a number of villas, such as the Villa Barbaro at Maser (ca. 1564), with paintings of architectural structures in the style of Palladio, fresh landscapes, and figures that reveal the happy spontaneity of a serene temperament (VIII, PL. 102; XIII, PL.

351; XIV, PLS. 343, 345, 346). He also painted a number of large canvases, such as the *Feast in the House of the Pharisee* (Turin, Gall. Sabauda), the *Marriage at Cana* (Louvre), and the *Last Supper* — later retitled the *Feast in the House of Levi* (XIV, PL. 348). These canvases, where the multiple views often surpass the perspective as a whole, display a spirit of opulent grandeur expressed in the spacious architectural structures and in the rich robes that reflect the Venetian atmosphere of magnificence (X, PL. 507). The grandeur is combined, moreover, with a tasteful refinement that is also noticeable in the full-length portraits, such as *Count Giuseppe da Porto with his son Adriano* (XIV, PL. 344), which also reveal some echoes of the Brescia school in their warm, homely character.

Together with remarkable painterly refinements, comprising among other things his justly famous luminous tones, Veronese displayed exquisite attention to detail (cf. X, PL. 493), as in the small canvas of *Mars and Venus* (Turin, Gall. Sabauda, Coll. Gualino), vibrant with shimmering light, and deep nocturnal effects in a sorrowful, elegiac tone, as in the *Pietà* (Brera). Simultaneously the artist painted ample, airy compositions (XIV, PL. 341; *Mystic Marriage of St. Catherine* in the Church of S. Caterina, Venice). It could be said that some of his canvases, including those representing secular scenes (*The Family of Darius before Alexander*, PL. 83), almost anticipated Tiepolo by the free layout of the compositions and the lilting colors, as did the allegories painted on the ceilings of the Doges' Palace (XIV, PL. 350).

Veronese's style was continued, in a modest way, by his brother Benedetto, his son Carlo, and his nephew Alvise dal Friso (Luigi Benfatto). With Paolo Veronese the Renaissance concludes, but his art, by its felicitous blending, or, rather, synthesis, of the schools of form and of color bore its principal fruits during the 18th century, in the rococo style.

Mario SALMI

II. THE RENAISSANCE OUTSIDE ITALY. INTRODUCTION. The problem of the Renaissance outside Italy lies in the absorption in other countries of the new ideas evolved in Florence, Venice, and Rome, and the grafting of them onto local traditions, which were, in most cases, forms of late Gothic. This process follows different patterns in different countries. In some cases — Hungary, France, and Spain, for instance — Italian artists traveled to these countries, sometimes staying only a short time, as Masolino did in Hungary, but sometimes, like Il Rosso and Primaticcio in France, settling there permanently and establishing schools that were absorbed into the art of the adoptive country. In other cases the process was reversed, as when artists such as Dürer and Jan Gossaert (Mabuse) crossed the Alps to study Italian painting and the monuments of antiquity and carried back their lessons to hand on to their compatriots. Generally speaking, the influence was from Italy outward, but in certain instances it was reciprocal. Hugo van der Goes's Portinari Altarpiece profoundly influenced Florentine art; Italian painting as a whole was transformed by the influence of the new Flemish method of oil painting; the Spaniard Pedro Berruguete and the Fleming Justus of Ghent established themselves as painters to the court of Urbino; and Dürer's works inspired Marcantonio Raimondi's engravings of Raphael's compositions and were frequently used as models by Italian painters in the first half of the 16th century.

Commercial, dynastic, and political ties between countries played an essential part in the diffusion of the new art. King Sigismund I of Poland introduced Italian artists to Kraków after seeing their work at the court of his brother, King Ladislas II of Hungary. Charles VIII and Louis XII of France were dazzled by what they saw in Italy during their campaigns, which, although disastrous politically, played a major part in the creation of the French Renaissance. Italian merchants and bankers trading with the Low Countries had their portraits painted by local artists. The Holy Roman emperor Charles V, Francis I of France, and Henry VIII of England vied with each other and with the Italian princes as patrons of the arts, and attempted to lure the finest Italian artists to their courts.

The invasion of foreign countries by Italianism in the arts was generally accompanied by parallel movements in other fields. The new learning created a body of Humanists who were consciously international and who did much to transmit from one country to another ideas that came primarily from Italian centers of learning. The effect of religious movements was also important, but was highly complicated. Before the Reformation split Europe into two opposed camps, Catholicism, like Humanism, was an international and unifying force. However, once the states of northern Europe had broken with Rome, religious differences impeded the spread of ideas from the Mediterranean to Protestant countries; but this was not an insuperable barrier, for some Italian states, such as Venice, maintained diplomatic relations with these countries and remained, particularly for England, an important link with Italian culture.

The assimilation of Renaissance art in northern countries was slow and sometimes even painful, particularly when there existed a strong local tradition of Gothic architecture or naturalist painting. Such traditions were not receptive to the influences of the methods of Brunelleschi and Masaccio or those of Bramante and Raphael. It can be said, in fact, that the true principles of Renaissance art were almost never fully understood outside Italy. What appealed to the French invaders of Lombardy was not Michelozzo's Portinari Chapel in S. Eustorgio or Bramante's S. Maria delle Grazie, both in Milan, but the fretted polychromy of the Certosa of Pavia or the Cappella Colleoni in Bergamo; the Italianate style of decoration, which was to have such a success in northern Europe in the second half of the 16th century, was derived from Italian mannerism rather than from the Renaissance. In fact, the works executed by non-Italian artists in the 15th and 16th centuries that are based on a real understanding of the principles of the Italian Renaissance are notably few: in architecture, Pedro Machuca's Palace of Charles V in Granada, Diogo de Torralva's Cloister of the Monastery of Christ in Tomar, Portugal, and one or two buildings by Philibert Delorme; in painting, the works of Pedro Berruguete (which were executed in Italy) and some of Dürer's paintings executed after his second visit to Venice; in drawing, portraits by Jean Clouet. Otherwise the Italian styles that northern artists found congenial were in the first phase those current in Lombardy, in which a strong element of the Gothic survived, and in the second phase those invented by the mannerists, who in certain respects were reacting against the High Renaissance.

The Renaissance outside Italy is not limited to these few examples. The exploration of the visible world by 15th-century Flemish painters was not inspired by the lessons of antiquity or by contemporary Italian currents, but was in itself a major contribution to artistic development subsequent to the Middle Ages and it can be properly considered an important aspect of the Renaissance. The art of Dürer and Hans Holbein the Younger, although unlike that of Raphael, embodies the Humanist principles that inspired the greatest artistic achievements of the High Renaissance in Italy. Many northern artists did not fully understand the principles of Raphael and Bramante, but they learned from them as much as was compatible with the traditions of their own countries, producing works of high quality that belong to the main current of European art in the 16th century. It may be that "Renaissance" is not the most appropriate term to describe their art, but they certainly believed that they had brought to their own countries the best of what they had seen in Italy, and they felt they were imitating the great painters and architects of southern Europe.

No satisfactory term has been found to describe the style of decoration and architecture that was almost universally employed in northern Europe in the second half of the 16th century. This style originated in Fontainebleau but was greatly modified in the Low Countries, whence it was transmitted to other countries, mainly by means of engravings. Late-19th-century art historians termed it "Renaissance," an obvious misnomer; it has recently been fashionable to call it mannerist, a term that is equally unsatisfactory, since, properly speaking, mannerism could only occur in centers that had passed through a Renaissance phase and where artists were partly developing out of the Renaissance and partly reacting against it. In most northern countries architectural styles went directly from late Gothic to the phase under discussion.

It could be argued that in certain countries, notably England and France, the art of the High Renaissance was not fully understood until the early 17th century, and then only in architecture. Inigo Jones created a style based on that of Palladio, but on precisely those features of Palladian architecture that are in accordance with the principles of the Renaissance, as opposed to those that may be regarded as mannerist. Although François Mansart never went to Italy, he studied Vignola's treatise on the orders and apparently drawings of buildings by Bramante and his contemporaries; his work (e.g., at Blois) can be regarded as paralleling in France Jones's achievement in England, although it derived from a different Italian source.

SPAIN. *Architecture.* The country in which the Italian Renaissance exercised the most profound influence and where its ideals were best understood was Spain. The two countries were linked by very close ties — political, ecclesiastical, and tommercial — and similarity of climate made it possible for ctalian architectural forms to be used in Spain with less adapta-Iion than was generally necessary in northern countries.

Nevertheless the first of the Spanish architectural styles influenced by Italy was as complete a negation of Renaissance principles as anything produced north of the Alps. This was the plateresque style. The term "plateresque" means "like silverwork" and was originally applied in the 16th century to describe the fretted decorative style of late Gothic architecture in Spain; later it was applied as a technical term to the mixed style of the early 16th century.

At the end of the 15th century a strong and inventive school of Flamboyant architecture flourished in Spain. To this architecture, which was marked by the fantasy of its forms, Spanish architects of the early 16th century applied decorative motifs borrowed from Lombardy, a part of Italy with which Spain was closely linked politically. In some cases architects were compelled to compromise because they were adding an element to an existing Gothic building. The most striking example of this is the central tower of the Cathedral of Burgos; the tower was begun in 1540 (VI, PL. 306), well after Machuca had established a true Renaissance style in Andalusia. The tower is Gothic in its vaulting and its external form, with crocketed finials, but is ornamented both inside and out with figures and decorative reliefs entirely Italian in derivation.

This particular combination of Gothic and Italianate elements is rare, though not unique, since it is paralleled in the door of the sacristy of Toledo Cathedral, designed by Alonso de Covarrubias in 1537. The more usual form of plateresque architecture is illustrated by a series of buildings erected in the early 16th century in Salamanca. The celebrated Casa de las Conchas, begun just before 1500 and finished in 1512, has something of the massive quality of a northern Italian 15th-century palace, and certain of its decorative motifs, including the shells from which it takes its name, are Italian in origin; however, the doors and the arches in the patio are late Gothic. The entrance to the university building in Salamanca, though consistently Italianate in detail, is, in its general disposition, and with every inch of surface covered by ornament, a continuation of the type of late Gothic decoration to be seen on the façades and screens of 15th-century churches throughout Spain.

Traces of Moorish influence add to the fantastic quality of some plateresque architecture. For instance, in the Chapel of the Annunciation in the Cathedral of Sigüenza, begun in 1515 in a predominantly Italianate style, several of the decorative motifs are taken directly from Mudejar woodwork, and the anteroom of the chapter house in the Cathedral of Toledo (1504–12), which consists mainly of Italianate woodwork and frescoes, incorporates an immensely elaborate Mudejar door executed at the same time and as part of the same scheme. Even more unusual is the mixture of styles in the buildings erected in Seville under Charles V (the Casa de Pilatos, the

Casa de Abades, and the pavilion of Charles V in the Alcázar gardens), in which Gothic balustrades appear between classic columns that support Moorish arches and Italianate shells decorate ceiling corners over walls covered with Arab tiles.

Meanwhile a tradition of architecture had been established in Spain that was based on a better understanding of the art of the Renaissance. The earliest manifestation of this new art appeared just before the end of the 15th century in a group of buildings designed by the architect Lorenzo Vázquez for various members of the Mendoza family, notably the Colegio de Sta Cruz at Valladolid (1491) and the Medinaceli Palace in Cogolludo (1492–95; XIII, PL. 123), both of which show a real feeling for mass and regularity of planning, as well as for Italianate decoration, although certain details, such as the forms of the windows and arches, are Gothic. It is not known whether the architect went to Italy, but the style of his works suggests that he had a knowledge of northern Italian architecture, probably that of Bologna.

By far the most notable building to be erected in Spain during the first half of the century was the Palace of Charles V in the Alhambra in Granada. This is the only known architectural work of Pedro Machuca, who began his career as a painter, an art for which he showed much less talent. The palace was begun in 1527, but the wooden model was not made until 1539 and the plans may have been altered later, perhaps even after the death of the architect in 1550, since work went on well into the 17th century. Nevertheless the main lines of the building must have been determined by Machuca.

The building has no precise parallel in Spain or in any other country. It consists of a square block enclosing a circular courtyard (PL. 102; FIG. 124). The outer façades, which were

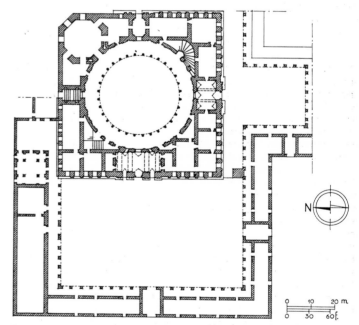

Granada, Palace of Charles V (architect, P. Machuca), plan (*from G. Kubler, M. Soria, 1959*).

probably the first part to be built, seem at first glance to be purely classical, since they are articulated with a single order over a rusticated ground floor, according to principles laid down by Bramante in Raphael's house in Rome, with another order introduced on the ground floor for the entrance doors. However, closer inspection shows that the disposition of the orders is irregular: the south side has Corinthian on the main floor, with Ionic on the ground floor in the entrance bay, whereas on the west front the main floor has Ionic with Doric below for the three bays of the entrance.

It is usually said that Machuca was trained in Florence, but both the palace and the surviving paintings suggest that he was more familiar with northern Italy and perhaps with

Rome. Even the exterior elevation, which is basically Bramantesque, borrows from Serlio, especially the use of circular windows and panels which are to be found in several designs of Book IV of Serlio's *Regole generali di architettura* (1st. ed., Venice, 1537), which Machuca no doubt knew. The rustication is similar to Giulio Romano's decoration of the courtyard of the Palazzo del Te in Mantua, and the arrangement of the entrance with three openings on the west side and one on the south is reminiscent of the same palace (VIII, PL. 428), although most of the detail of the triple bay on the west is in the style of Sanmicheli with Michelangelesque windows. The circular court is reminiscent of Antonio da Sangallo the Younger's plan for Caprarola, but its arrangement with two superimposed colonnades with flat entablatures — a great rarity at this date — seems to be based on Peruzzi's portico in the courtyard of the Palazzo Massimo alle Colonne in Rome (XI, PL. 121). The decoration is northern Italian rather than Florentine, particularly in the reliefs over the pediment and in the Palladian arch on the south entrance.

The palace is, therefore, an eclectic work, taking elements from many Italian sources, but it is nevertheless highly original in its total effect. On the exterior it combines a Bramantesque elevation with decoration which comes from the Lombardy plain, and within this shell it conceals the unexpected circular courtyard. Although the plan of the courtyard may be based on the design for Caprarola, it has a lightness and an elegance quite different from the castellated effect so marked in the Italian building as it was executed by Vignola and undoubtedly intended by Sangallo.

Machuca stands somewhat apart from his contemporaries in architecture as having a far more complete understanding of what had been taking place in Italian art, but two other names must be mentioned as typical of the inventive, though irregular, nature of Spanish architecture of the time: Alonso de Covarrubias (ca. 1488–1564) and Diego de Siloe (ca. 1495–1563). Neither is as sophisticated as Machuca in the use of Italian forms, but both show great invention in adapting these forms to local traditions. The work of Covarrubias in the Cathedral of Sigüenza and in the former Palace of the Archbishops of Toledo in Alcalá de Henares shows a sound knowledge of Italian structural and decorative conventions, but always includes a personal and Spanish element. In the sacristy of the Cathedral of Sigüenza Covarrubias inserted heads in the coffering of the vault; in the courtyard of the palace in Alcalá he used the curious imposts over the capitals that had been a regular feature of plateresque architecture since Vázquez used them in the Infantado Palace in Guadalajara. In the Alcázar and the Hospital of S. Juan Bautista (or de Afuera) in Toledo, which date from the 1540s, the style of Covarrubias had matured and the solecisms visible in earlier works had disappeared. In fact, the courtyard of the Alcázar would seem perfectly in place in an Italian town, and the bold plan of the hospital, with its two arcaded courts leading one into the other, was an advance on most Italian designs of this period.

Diego de Siloe began his career in Burgos, where, as a young man, he built the richly carved staircase, the Escalera Dorada 1519–28), in the Cathedral. In 1528 he moved to Granada, where he undertook the building of the Cathedral, the foundations of which had been laid a few years before. On a plan that is purely Gothic he raised a building that aimed at being "Roman," and although the conflict inherent in this attempt is apparent the result is a structure of great originality. The nave and four aisles (XIII, PL. 131), whose piers are Gothic in plan and Corinthian in their fluting and capitals, lead to a relatively small crossing that serves primarily as a prelude to the circular Capilla Mayor, a chapel designed for the perpetual adoration of the Sacrament to atone for the occupation of the city by the Moors. The plan of the chapel is based on the Church of the Holy Sepulcher in Jerusalem. To gain the height necessary for the various parts of the building, the architect was forced to use various devices that are quite contrary to Renaissance principles: high bases and elongated proportions for the bays of the nave, and five superimposed ranges of openings in the Capilla Mayor, reduced in appearance to three by the

fact that two pairs are linked by giant columns. Siloe's design was widely imitated in Andalusia, notably in the Cathedral of Málaga.

Even before his succession in 1556 Philip II showed an interest in architecture, and it was on his initiative that the Alcázar in Toledo was built. The great work of his reign, however, and the one that dominated Spanish architecture in the second half of the 16th century, was the construction of the Escorial, begun in 1562. It is impossible to distinguish, from what is known at present, the individual contributions of each of the two architects responsible for this vast undertaking, Juan Bautista de Toledo (d. 1567) and Juan de Herrera (1530–97), who succeeded him. There does not seem to be much conflict between their styles, and the palace must be regarded as a work of intimate collaboration.

It is usual in histories of Spanish architecture to explain the Escorial by pronouncing the name of Vignola, but this explanation is far from sufficient. It is true that both architects of the building show a fuller and more precise knowledge of the orders than their predecessors and that this knowledge was based on the study of Vignola's *Regole . . .* (1562), but nothing could be more remote from the grand and monumental simplicity of the Escorial than the thin, somewhat academic style of Vignola. In some parts of the palace, notably in the Court of the Evangelists (VII, PL. 221), certainly built by Juan Bautista de Toledo (see HERRERA, JUAN DE), a definite Italian source can be identified — in this case, the two lower orders of the courtyard of the Palazzo Farnese, built by Antonio da Sangallo the Younger — but neither Sangallo nor any other Italian architect of the 16th century conceived the idea of enlarging the simple Doric half-columns to the grand, majestic scale on which they are used in the main entrance façade of the Escorial (VII, PL. 223).

The Escorial is unique in its period both for its scale and for the novelty of its plan (FIG. 126). Nowhere in Europe

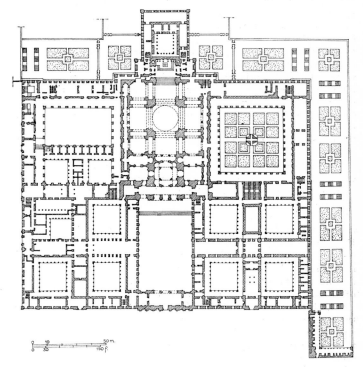

Escorial, plan of ground floor (architects, Juan Bautista de Toledo and Juan de Herrera). *(from G. Kubler, M. Soria, 1959).*

could one find before this date such a vast plan based on the most rigid simplicity, the church being the center of interest, with the king's palace behind it and the large courtyards of the monastery around and in front of it. It is often said that the plan represents the grid of St. Lawrence, to whom the monastery was dedicated, but this seems an insufficient explanation. The same has often been said of the various charterhouses dedicated to the saint, but they have neither the regularity nor the grandeur nor the centralization of interest that is so marked in the plan of the Escorial. A more plausible suggestion is that the plan is based on those of late Roman imperial palaces, such as that of Diocletian at Split, but it is very doubtful if these were known in the 16th century. It seems possible that the architects — and presumably the king — had a different idea in mind. During the 16th century great interest was shown in attempts to reconstruct the Temple of Solomon as described in the Bible, and it is not unthinkable that Philip II should have had in mind the great temple-palace of the Old Testament as a model for his own palace. The reconstruction of the temple devised by the Spanish Jesuit Juan Bautista Villalpando, and published in a celebrated commentary on Ezekiel (1596–1604), bears a striking resemblance to that of the Escorial, and although it was not published until later it may well embody ideas that were current half a century earlier, the more so as Juan Bautista Villalpando may belong to the same family as the architect Francisco de Villalpando (d. 1561), who worked for Philip II on the Alcázar in Toledo.

The church of the Escorial (XIII, PL. 131) has the form of a Greek cross within a square, with the addition of a choir at the east end and a gallery with monk's choir at the west. It belongs to that great family of churches which derived from Bramante's plan for St. Peter's in Rome, but the closest parallel is S. Maria di Carignano in Genoa, which was built by Galeazzo Alessi, one of the architects invited by Philip II to submit a design for the church at the Escorial. His plan may have been the basis of that used in building the church, and it is noteworthy that the very unusual arrangement of the drum of the dome, with alternate large and small openings, is also to be found in the Genoese church, although the Spanish architect added grandeur to his model by the substitution of Doric half-columns for Alessi's Corinthian pilasters. The splendid severity of the interior is also purely Spanish and is no doubt due to Herrera (VII, PL. 222).

One feature of Spanish architecture of the 16th century is particularly noteworthy. During that period architects seem to have shown an exceptional interest in the building of staircases, and they invented the three forms of staircase that were most widely favored in later periods. The staircase on a square plan around an open newel, which does not appear elsewhere in Europe until the 17th century, is to be found in fully developed form in the Hospital of Sta Cruz in Toledo and in the University of Salamanca, both built in the first quarter of the 16th century. The imperial staircase, frequently used in Genoese palaces from the very late 16th century onward and given monumental form by Longhena at S. Giorgio Maggiore in Venice in 1644, was introduced in the mid-16th century, when it is to be seen in the Alcázar in Toledo (1553). The third type of staircase is to be found in the Escorial and consists of one central flight dividing into two which turn back on themselves, all three flights being covered by a huge single vault. The Escalera Dorada at Burgos, mentioned above, is of an ingenious form — apparently unknown before this date, and little used until it was revived in Italy in the 17th century — consisting of two double flights addorsed to a wall, the whole forming a sort of diamond pattern in elevation.

With the conquest of the New World the Spaniards carried their art with them to the Western Hemisphere. Most of the surviving churches in Mexico and other conquered areas belong to what is usually, but perhaps improperly, called the baroque style; however, a few of the very early ones are in a variant of the plateresque style. A typical example is the church in Actopan (Mexico), with a fine coffered portal and Corinthian columns of almost Gothic elongation. The door to the Cathedral of Santo Domingo (West Indies), the first cathedral to be built in the New World, is even more curious in that it shows the false perspective effects employed by Antonio da Sangallo the Elder in the entrance to the Palazzo Farnese. In this instance an Italian motif seems to have traveled via Spain to the New World within a very few years. Toward the end of the century a more classical style was introduced. The nave of Guadalajara Cathedral (Mexico; begun 1571) reflects the style of Diego de Siloe in the Cathedral in Granada; the Cathedral by Claudio de Arciniega in Puebla, Mexico (II, PL. 163), with its severe Doric columns, approaches the manner of Herrera.

Sculpture. A few examples of Florentine sculpture appear to have reached Spain in the 15th century; they had little effect on local artists, however, and it was not until the early years of the 16th century that Italian influence penetrated deeply. The arrival of Italian works and of Italian sculptors then rapidly transformed the art of certain provinces in Spain.

The only major Italian sculptor who certainly visited Spain is Pietro Torrigiani, who came there from England about 1521 and died in Seville in 1528. The two works by him that survive in Spain, a *Virgin and Child* and a *St. Jerome* (both, Seville, Mus. Provincial de Bellas Artes), show that he was able to adapt his Florentine style to the religious feeling of Spain just as easily as he had harmonized it with the strong Gothic tradition in which he had been compelled to work in England (see below).

According to Vasari, Andrea Sansovino visited Spain as well as Portugal, and he may be the Andrés Florentín recorded as working on the high altar of the Toledo Cathedral about 1500. In any case the magnificent tomb of Cardinal Pedro Gonzáles de Mendoza (1495–1503) in the Cathedral shows the influence of his manner and may have been designed by him. The political and cultural link between Aragon and Naples was responsible for the existence of certain tombs erected in the north, notably that of Ramón de Cardona, viceroy of Naples, in the Church of Bellpuig. Genoa was another source of artists from whom tombs were commissioned by Spanish patrons, and the workshops of the Gaggini family and of Antonio Aprile supplied many examples, notably the fine monuments of Pedro de Ribera and his wife in the University Church in Seville. All these tombs follow the pattern set by the Mendoza tomb in Toledo. The Florentine Domenico Fancelli (1469–1519) began his career in Spain by designing a tomb on similar lines in Seville for Cardinal Hurtado de Mendoza, but in his later Spanish works he introduced a type of monument hitherto unknown in Spain, the freestanding altar-tomb with recumbent figure and reliefs on the sloping sides, a form based on Antonio Pollaiuolo's monument to Sixtus IV in the Vatican Grottoes. Fancelli's first use of this type was in the relatively simple tomb for Don Juan, only son of Ferdinand II and Isabella, in the Church of S. Tomás, in Avila (1511–13), but his later tomb of the Catholic Kings in the Royal Chapel in Granada (1514–17) is more complex in its forms and richer in its freestanding sculpture. This form of monument was much imitated by succeeding generations of Spanish sculptors.

In Castile and Aragon the new Italianate style was introduced partly through the intermediary of French artists. Felipe Vigarny (Vigarni), who was born about 1470 near Langres in Champagne, worked both in Burgos and in Toledo, where he died in 1543. He evolved a strange, emotional form of sculpture, with high-relief figures bursting out beyond the limits of 15th-century Italian architectural forms. Another Frenchman, Gabriel Joly (Joli; d. 1538), in his masterpiece, the high altar of the Cathedral in Teruel, of which only fragments survive, showed an understanding of the style of Michelangelo in the early Roman years that can only have been derived from direct knowledge. This forceful style is often combined with an intensity of feeling reminiscent of the late Gothic sculpture that he would have known in his native country.

The first Spanish sculptor to use the forms of the Italian Renaissance was Bartolomé Ordóñez (d. 1520), who spent much time in Naples, where he executed part of the altar of the Caraccioli in S. Giovanni a Carbonara (XIII, PL. 139). In Spain his principal work is the tomb of Joan the Mad and Philip I in the Royal Chapel in Granada, in which he goes beyond Fancelli in the direction of completely three-dimensional sculptural decoration.

It was with Alonso Berruguete (ca. 1488–1561) that Spanish sculpture took on real originality, and his work, in addition to being of very high quality, is significant as an anticipation of the baroque style (PL. 102). It appears that he spent the years

1508–17 in Italy, probably in Florence and Rome, and he returned to Spain deeply impressed, not by the tranquil style of Raphael's Stanze, but by the majesty of Michelangelo's Sistine Chapel and the tortured intensity of the late Filippino Lippi and, perhaps, of the very early Il Rosso. His earliest surviving work, the *Resurrection* in the Cathedral of Valencia, is primarily Michelangelesque in inspiration, but in the polychrome figures of the altarpiece for the Church of S. Benito (1527–32; Valladolid, Mus. Nac. de Escultura) he evolved a highly dramatic style, closer to what he had learned from Filippino and Il Rosso but marked by an almost grotesque intensity. More remarkably, he seems to have sensed the baroque tendencies which were latent in Roman art of the years when he was in Rome, but which were not developed in Italy until the 17th century. His *Transfiguration* (1543–48; XIII, PL. 141) embodies to a startling degree the principles of high baroque art in its mood, treatment of light and movement, and fusion of the three arts of sculpture, architecture, and painting into a single whole. That this was not a fortuitous instance is shown by his *Visitation* in the Church of S. Ursula, Toledo, and by the figures on the tomb of Cardinal Juan de Tavera in the Hospital of S. Juan Bautista in the same city, which are also almost baroque in their feeling and movement.

This "protobaroque" movement was continued for another generation by the sculptor Juan de Juni, a Frenchman who is first recorded in Spain in 1533 and who lived in Valladolid from 1541 until his death in 1577. His polychrome *Entombment* (XIII, PL. 141) owes much to northern Italian sculptural groups in the same medium, such as those by Giulio Mazzoni, whose work he may have known in France, but its sweeping movement brings it far closer to 17th-century sculpture. Even more completely baroque are certain smaller groups, such as those of *St. Matthew* (1540; León, Mus. de San Marcos) and *St. John the Baptist* (Salamanca, New Cathedral), both of which are rendered with a full baroque *contrapposto*, and his *Our Lady of Sorrows* (IV, PL. 210), which shows all the anguished intensity usually associated with 17th-century sculptors such as Juan Martínez Montañés. Equally surprising for its time is the architecture of Juni's altar in the Benavente Chapel of S. Maria de Mediavilla in Medina de Rioseco (1544–46), in which the side columns are canted outward in a manner usually thought to have been invented by Borromini.

As might be expected, this emotional style was not successful at the court of Philip II. The King preferred the art of Leone Leoni (1509–90) and his son Pompeo (ca. 1533–1608), who produced the huge statues for the high altar of the Escorial and the magnificent groups on either side of it representing the families of Charles V and Philip II (PL. 102). In their solemnity and severity they differ as sharply from the art of Berruguete and Juni as do the frescoes of the Escorial from the passionate mysticism of El Greco. The worlds of Toledo and Madrid were as different in sculpture as in painting.

Painting. Artistic contact between Italy and parts of Spain, particularly Catalonia, were already strong in the 14th century, and one painter, Ferrer Bassa (ca. 1290–1348), had, by midcentury, introduced a style of painting that clearly showed a knowledge of Sienese art. His principal work is a series of frescoes in the Monastery of Pedralbes near Barcelona (VI, PL. 374). In the 15th century Valencia replaced Barcelona as the artistic center of Spain, but the Catalan city produced two artists of importance, Jaime Huguet (active 1448–86) and Bartolomé Bermejo (active 1474–95), who, though Cordovan by birth, worked almost entirely in Catalonia. In his best works, such as the *St. George* (Barcelona, Mus. Diocesano), Huguet shows something of the breadth of Florentine monumental painting, combined with a Flemish observation of detail and a Spanish sense of decorative richness (cf. XIII, PL. 129). Bermejo was more completely dominated by Flemish influence, both in manner and in technique, and he was among the first artists to practice oil painting in Spain (cf. XIII, PL. 135). His most important surviving work is the *Pietà* in Barcelona Cathedral.

Painting in Valencia came under strong German influence, mainly through Andrés Marzal de Sax (active 1393–1410), who was probably, as his name indicates, of German origin. One of the most impressive works of this school is the huge Altarpiece of St. George (London, Vict. and Alb.), which combines a Spanish sense of decoration with rather brutal German naturalism. A manner strongly tinged with Flemish naturalism was introduced to Valencia by Luis Dalmau (active 1428–60), who was sent to Flanders in 1431 by Alfonso V of Aragon. His Altarpiece of the Councilors (1445; XIII, PL. 128) shows knowledge of Van Eyck's Ghent Altarpiece (V, PLS. 215, 216). Contact was also close between Valencia and Naples, which was ruled by the kings of Aragon; some Aragonese painters, notably Jaime Baçó (called Jacomart; ca. 1410–61), visited Italy and their styles were influenced by what they had seen.

With the union of the crowns of Aragon and Castile the artistic center again shifted, and the most original painter of the end of the 15th century, Pedro Berruguete (active ca. 1483–1503), worked mainly in Avila and Toledo (cf. XIII, PL. 129). His most important work, however, was the series of compositions executed for Federigo da Montefeltro in the Palazzo Ducale in Urbino.

Contact with Italy became closer as a result of the election in 1492 of the Spanish Pope, Alexander VI. He sent a number of Italian painters to Valencia, who, although they were second rate, brought a new kind of Italianism into Spain.

In the early 16th century Spanish artists seem to have visited Italy more frequently. Fernando Yáñez and Fernando de los Llanos (both active in Valencia from 1506 onward) brought to Valencia a knowledge of central Italian painting of the early 16th century, notably the styles of Fra Bartolommeo and Andrea del Sarto, together with some knowledge of the art of Leonardo. A generation later Luis de Vargas (1502–68) introduced the manner of Salviati and Vasari. It is, however, a notable fact that these contacts with Italy had no effect in secularizing Spanish art, which remained essentially religious throughout the 16th century.

Both Charles V and Philip II were ardent admirers of Italian, particularly Venetian, painting, and they accumulated the finest collection outside Italy of works by Titian, the greater part of which is still in the Prado. They did not, however, succeed in attracting to their court any of the great Italian painters — although both kings were painted by Titian during their travels in Italy and Germany — and for the decoration of the Escorial Philip II was compelled to call on artists of the second rank such as Luca Cambiaso, Federico Zuccaro, and Pellegrino Tibaldi, all of whom, however, rose to the occasion and produced some of their finest works for the palace. The most important Spanish artists employed by Philip II were Juan Fernández Navarrete (called El Mudo; ca. 1526–79), who painted altarpieces for the Escorial, and Alonso Sánchez Coello (1531–88; IV, PL. 27; IX, PL. 297), who adapted to Spanish court etiquette the style of portrait painting brought to Spain by the Dutch artist Anthonis Mor (IV, PL. 27; V, PL. 293; IX, PL. 297; XI, PL. 218).

The two most remarkable artists of the period worked independently of the court to all intents and purposes. Luis de Morales (active 1546–86), who painted mainly in Extremadura, expressed more fully than any other native artist the mysticism of the Spanish character (XIII, PL. 145), particularly in his paintings of an emaciated and grief-ridden Virgin supporting the dead body of Christ on which the streaming blood is often painted with almost frightening realism (PL. 102). It was, however, left to a foreigner, Domenico Theotokopuli, better known as El Greco (1541–1614), to give the most imaginative expression to this aspect of Spanish religious feeling. Born in Crete, and first trained in Venice, he moved to Rome in 1570 and went to Spain in 1577. He was profoundly influenced by the painting of Titian and Tintoretto, and was also affected by the art and religious atmosphere of Rome during his few years in that city. Soon after his arrival in Spain he obtained two commissions from Philip II: the so-called *Dream of Philip II* (VI, PL. 453), in fact an allegory of the Holy League, and the *Martyrdom of St. Maurice and the Theban Legion* (VI,

PL. 459). These were not received enthusiastically by the King, and El Greco withdrew to Toledo, where he devoted the rest of his life to producing those passionately felt religious works for which he is famous (VI, PLS. 451, 452; XIII, PL. 146), and which, although they never attained universal success, were greatly appreciated in the pious, even fanatical city in which he lived. Properly speaking, his art is outside the scope of this article, because it is one of the supreme forms of mannerism rather than of Renaissance art, but it marks the culmination of Italian influence in Spain and at the same time proves how completely a genius can transform a style to suit his own ends and the needs of the community for which he works.

PORTUGAL. *Architecture.* At the end of the 15th century Portuguese architecture reached an extreme of fantasy unattained even by flamboyant Gothic in the style called Manueline. The late Gothic system of vaulting became greatly complicated; columns were twisted like rope, and wall surfaces, voussoirs, and tracery were covered with decorative ornament with a richness reminiscent of Moorish styles.

It is not surprising that the visit of Andrea Sansovino to Portugal in the last decade of the 15th century should have had little influence on native architecture. The works that he executed in the country (Vasari) cannot be identified, but it is certain that his style was one that could not be wedded to Manueline Gothic.

About the year 1500, however, artists began to apply Italian ornament to Portuguese architecture, and produced such masterpieces as the Monastery of the Hieronymites (Jerónimos) in Belém, a suburb of Lisbon, and the Unfinished Chapels (Capelas Imperfeitas) in Batalha. The Belém complex was designed and executed by Diogo Boytac (active 1490–ca. 1528), probably French by birth, and the Spaniard João de Castilho (active 1517–ca. 1553). The church is late Gothic in plan and structure, save that the main crossing arches are round-headed; the tall Gothic columns are covered with arabesques and medallions purely Lombard in style. The same mixture is to be found in the cloisters, where cusped Gothic tracery fills openings decorated with Lombard candelabra.

The Unfinished Chapels in Batalha were begun by Mateus Fernandes I and probably continued by Boytac, who may also have built the magnificent Royal Cloister. The chapels, intended as a mausoleum for King Duarte and his family, consist of seven radial chapels around an octagon; the plan follows a basically Gothic scheme, but the ornament becomes increasingly Italianate as the walls rise. The huge door by Mateus Fernandes I that leads from the vestibule into the chapels marks an extreme point of Gothic fantasy, with a mixture of Italian and Gothic detail; it is characteristic of this work, and indeed of the best Manueline architecture, that even this profusion of decoration is controlled and ordered by the crisp and clear lines of the structure.

About 1525 Gothic forms tended to disappear. The church in the Monastery of Christ in Tomar is basically still a castellated medieval church, and although the decoration of its celebrated windows cannot be categorized stylistically, it could not have been created without the first hybrid phase of Manueline architecture. These windows are entirely unique in their motifs of naturalistic rope ornaments mixed with tree forms and representations of nautical instruments, particularly the armillary sphere, which was the symbol of Henry the Navigator. The principal architects of this period were the brothers Diogo (active 1510–31) and Francisco de Arruda (active 1510–47); Diogo was the architect of the Tomar monastery, and Francisco designed the grand and simple Tower of Belém.

As in Spain, Moorish elements survived in certain parts of Portugal, and the Royal Palace in Sintra bears clear traces of this influence in both architecture and decoration.

In the mid-16th century a more classical style was developed in Portugal, a style analogous to that of Herrera in Spain. The most distinguished architect of the period was Diogo de Torralva (d. 1566), who built the choir of the church in Belém (1551) and the cloister of the monastery in Tomar (begun 1557). The latter is one of the most personal interpretations of Italian High Renaissance architecture outside Italy, combining elements from Antonio da Sangallo the Younger with others taken from Pedro Machuca's palace of Charles V into a whole that has freedom of movement, regularity in design, and fine classical detail. Diogo de Torralva has also been credited with the little Church of the Conceição in Tomar, one of the purest Renaissance works in Portugal. This work faintly reflects the influence of Sansovino, to whom it has been attributed by some critics, but it must in fact be much later, since it is taken directly from Antonio da Sangallo the Younger's entrance to the Palazzo Farnese, ingeniously adapted to the form of a church with a nave and two aisles. The Cathedral of Leiria, built by Afonso Alvares between 1559 and 1574, is more strictly in the style of Herrera, as, curiously enough, is the work of the Bolognese Filippo Terzi, whose church of S. Vicente de Fora in Lisbon is the last important church built in Portugal before the baroque dominated (XIII, PL. 131).

Painting and sculpture. The enormous increase of wealth in Portugal in the late 15th and early 16th centuries attracted artists from many parts of northern Europe, particularly Flanders and France. The dominant influences in painting came from Flanders and continued into the second quarter of the 16th century, when Frei Carlos produced sensitive and individual variations on the style of Quentin Massys, who was known in Portugal through at least one important altarpiece (a panel is now in Lisbon, Mus. Nac. de Arte Antiga).

In the late 15th century Portugal produced one major painter, Nuno Gonçalves (active 1450–71), who is mentioned with admiration by 16th-century writers and whose works disappeared entirely until the rediscovery in the 1880s of his Polyptych of St. Vincent (XIII, PL. 126). This work shows a highly personal naturalism in the observation of human faces and an impressive simplification of form, with sharp edges and hewn surfaces reminiscent of late Gothic wood carving.

In sculpture the development of the Renaissance style followed a somewhat different path. The first artists to work on the church in Belém were still Gothic in style and partly Flemish in origin, but the arrival about 1517 of Nicolas Chanterene marked the first stage in the development of a style that can properly be called Renaissance. It has been suggested that Chanterene was a Walloon; whatever his birthplace, his training must have been purely French, for his figure sculpture reflects the tradition of Michel Colombe, and his decorative reliefs are equal to the finest sculpture of the Loire Valley in the early years of Francis I. His masterpiece, the altar in the chapel of the Royal Palace in Sintra, shows great decorative invention and astonishing skill in the handling of alabaster. His contemporary, Jacques Loguin (d. 1559), seems to derive his style from the same source, whereas another Frenchman active in Portugal, Jean de Rouen (João de Ruão; ca. 1495–1580), probably received his training by working on the Amboise tomb in the Cathedral of Rouen and developed a style that was slightly more northern in feeling, which he employed with success in the production of rather pedestrian religious images.

By far the most notable sculptor of the period, Filipe Udarte (Hodart; active 1522–34), belongs to an entirely different tradition. If, as is generally believed, he is French by birth, his art shows no traces of his national origin. The larger-than-life-size Apostles from a group representing the Last Supper (fragments in Coimbra, Mus. de Machado de Castro) are purely German in type and in the violence of their expressions. Udarte may have based his style on the engravings of Dürer, but his work suggests that he must have been trained in southern Germany before he came to the Iberian Peninsula. He is known to have worked in Spain on his way to Portugal.

FRANCE. Contact between Italy and southern France was close even as early as the 14th century, mainly because of the establishment of the papal court in Avignon from 1309 to 1377. As a result of the visit of Simone Martini (q.v.) to Avignon in the last years of his life, a school of painting that was deeply influenced by Sienese art came into existence there.

During the 15th century, however, Flemish influences prevailed in France; paintings such as the *Annunciation* of Aix (ca. 1445; V, PL. 394) and the Avignon *Pietà* (V, PL. 383) show an awareness of Flemish realism that is combined with Italian breadth in the treatment of the forms. Toward the end of the same century this tradition reached its finest expression in the paintings of the Master of Moulins (V, PL. 393).

In the middle of the 15th century direct Italian influence became apparent in the work of Jean Fouquet (ca. 1420–ca. 1480), who visited Rome in his youth and painted a portrait of Eugenius IV (lost). His paintings, particularly the *Virgin and Child* (V, PL. 361), show an abstract treatment of form, and his miniatures in the Book of Hours of Etienne Chevalier display a knowledge of 15th-century Italian architecture (V, PLS. 366, 367; X, PL. 84). He was also a keen student of perspective and was, in some respects, more advanced than his Italian contemporaries.

In architecture and sculpture no comparable manifestation of Italian influence emerged until the 16th century, although the arrival of Francesco Laurana in Provence, where he was invited by King René, led to the erection of a few isolated monuments in the Italian style, such as the Chapel of St. Lazarus in the Old Cathedral of La Major in Marseilles (1475–81).

With the beginning of the Italian campaigns, however, the situation changed completely. The invading armies of Charles VIII passed through Florence and went as far south as Naples, but this incursion did not have any permanent effect other than the importation into France of a few Italian artists. During the reigns of Louis XII and Francis I contact with Lombardy and Genoa was much more frequent, and an infusion of the northern Italian style became apparent in French art. This took two forms: first, the importation of purely Italian works, such as the great fountain from Genoa that was in Gaillon (1508; now in the Château of La Rochefoucauld) and Girolamo Viscardi's tomb of the dukes of Orléans, commissioned in 1502 by Louis XII (now in Saint-Denis); and second, the application of Italian decorative forms to late Gothic buildings, as in the entrance gate to the Château of Gaillon (1508) or in Hector Sohier's apse of the Church of St-Pierre in Caen (1528–45; V, PL. 391). Soon, however, the architects working for Francis I began to create personal syntheses of Italian and northern ideas. The spiral staircase of the Château of Blois (1515–24; IX, PL. 317), though medieval in its basic form, has an Italian monumentality that gives greater meaning to the delicate Lombard decoration that covers it. The Château of Chambord (PL. 101; V, PL. 398) is French and northern in its high-pitched roofs and fanciful chimneys, but is so lucid in its planning that the name of Leonardo has been invoked as its original designer, although without convincing evidence. The Château of Bury (1520; FIG. 134), which is now in ruins, was a typical example of French country houses of the period.

In some cases, notably in sculpture, the synthesis of northern and southern ideals was realized rapidly. The tomb of Francis II of Brittany in Nantes Cathedral (begun 1499) was a harmonious collaboration between the Italian Girolamo da Fiesole and the Frenchman Michel Colombe. In the four standing figures of Virtues, entirely by Colombe, is evident an understanding of the classical principles of the Italian Renaissance that was rarely found outside Italy at this date.

In painting, Jean Bourdichon (ca. 1457–1521), court painter to Louis XI and his two successors, freely copied and adapted Italian originals in the miniatures with which he illustrated Books of Hours for his royal patrons. The most original aspect of his art is the borders of naturalistic fruits and flowers that decorate the pages of these books and derive from a Flemish tradition. The principal portrait painter of this period, Jean Perréal (ca. 1455–1530), is known to have visited Italy and to have had contact with Leonardo, but what little survives of his painting shows almost no trace of this contact. Jean Clouet (active 1516–40; q.v.), one of the greatest French artists of this period, is not known to have crossed the Alps, but his chalk portraits show beyond doubt that he must have known Leonardo's drawings, and some of his few paintings, notably

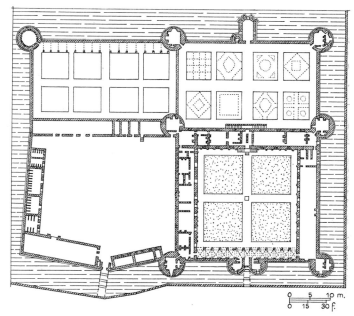

France. Château of Bury, plan of entire complex (*from B. Fletcher, A History of Architecture, New York-London, 1961*).

the portrait of Mme de Canaples (Edinburgh, Nat. Gall. of Scotland), recall Raphael's treatment of form.

The second stage of what may be called the Italian cultural invasion of France occurred in the years from 1530 onward, when a number of major Italian artists arrived in France and established their own style with little consideration for local traditions. Within a few years Il Rosso and Primaticcio (qq.v.) had created at Fontainebleau a stylistically original court art that could rival in quality those of Florence and Mantua. Their use of stucco decoration in high relief combined with painting (PL. 100; V, PL. 395) was an advance over anything previously executed in Italy, and probably influenced such Italian decorative schemes as that of the Sala Regia in the Vatican (IX, PL. 294). They invented the decorative motif known as strapwork, which was to be taken up throughout Europe, including Italy. The true extent of their achievement in painting has only recently become apparent through the uncovering of their work at Fontainebleau, which for a century had been completely obscured by drastic restoration. The influence of Italian decorators was intensified by the arrival about 1552 of Niccolò dell'Abate (PL. 81; IX, PLS. 299, 301), who brought with him from Bologna the latest style of Italian mannerism. The decorative style of Fontainebleau became widely known throughout Europe because of the engravings made of the decorations in the palace by Italians such as Antonio Fantuzzi and by Frenchmen such as René Boyvin.

Although there were few new developments in sculpture, in the district around Troyes a small school was started by Domenico del Barbiere, called in France Dominique Florentin, who came to France with Il Rosso in 1530, and after working at Fontainebleau settled in the Champagne region.

At this time French architecture was profoundly influenced by Sebastiano Serlio (q.v.), who, although responsible for few buildings in France — the Château of Ancy-le-Franc (ca. 1546) is the only one of his works to survive complete — was widely known through his *Regole generali di architettura* (1st ed., Venice, 1537), which became the standard textbook for French architects for many years. As a builder, Serlio was overshadowed by Philibert Delorme (ca. 1510–70), who, although influenced by the Italian, drew his main inspiration from what he himself had seen during his years in Rome (ca. 1533–36). Delorme combined a rare sense for monumental architecture with that technical skill which had distinguished late medieval architecture in France. The Château of Anet, begun in 1547 (PL. 101; IV, PLS. 163, 164), although traditional in plan, contains much magnificent and Italianate detail; its circular chapel (FIG. 135; IV, PL. 165) is an original well-understood design, based, however, on a study of Bramante's works in Rome. His monument to Francis I (begun 1547; IV, PL. 165) is an equally personal interpretation of a Roman triumphal arch.

During the last years of his life Delorme devoted much time to writing a treatise, *Le premier tome de l'Architecture de Philibert de l'Orme* (Paris, 1567), which was the most com-

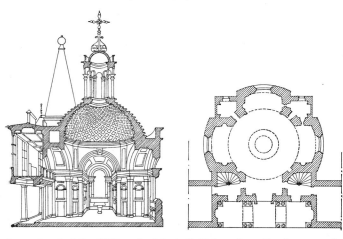

Anet, chapel of the Château (architect, P. Delorme), section in perspective and plan according to the design by Du Cerceau (*from A. Blunt, 1953*).

prehensive book of its kind produced in the 16th century; it propounds highly technical questions of structure in connection with stone vaults and wooden roofs, and at the same time treats the classical orders in detail. It also contains a wealth of miscellaneous learning and of personal experience, and it may be considered one of the foremost products of French Humanism. It was reprinted several times and widely read outside France; it is known, for instance, that Scamozzi owned a copy.

Delorme's contemporary, Pierre Lescot (ca. 1515–78; q.v.), was an architect of more limited talent; he is known for the Cour Carrée of the Louvre (begun 1546; V, PL. 396), which shows a brilliant use of the classical orders, combined with refined Italianate detail.

These two architects are paralleled in sculpture by Jean Goujon (ca. 1510–ca. 1565; q.v.), who, although he does not seem to have gone to Italy in his youth, absorbed many Italian ideas from Il Rosso and from Benvenuto Cellini, who spent the years from 1540 to 1545 in France. In the reliefs of water nymphs on the Fontaine des Innocents (1549; Louvre) he created a series of works almost Hellenistic in their combination of richness and elegance (cf. V, PL. 395).

French painters of the mid-16th century can be divided into two categories: those who simply imitated the Italian work at Fontainebleau, and those who, like François Clouet (ca. 1510–72), son of Jean Clouet, practiced a style of portraiture that was essentially Flemish in its method and, generally speaking, devoid of Italian influence (PL. 103; V, PL. 403; XI, PL. 225).

After the middle of the century the classicism of Delorme, Lescot, and Goujon, which brought their work very close in feeling to Italian art of the High Renaissance, gave place to an increasingly exaggerated form of mannerism. In painting, artists such as Antoine Caron (ca. 1520–ca. 1600) carried the ideas of Niccolò dell'Abate to an extreme, and architects such as Jacques Androuet Ducerceau (ca. 1520–ca. 1584) evolved a style dominated by great elaboration of detail and the fantastic breaking up of architectural form. Jean Bullant (active 1556–1578) alone among the major artists continued to show a real feeling for architectural as opposed to decorative forms. His porticoes in the Château of Ecouen are remarkable for their ingenuity and, in one instance, for a very grand and monumental use of colossal freestanding Corinthian columns.

Both Bullant and Ducerceau produced volumes on architecture; Bullant's treatise on the five orders was so highly specialized that it only had a limited circulation, but Ducerceau's *Les plus excellents Bastiments de France* (Paris, 1579; IV, PL. 163) and his other volumes did much to spread French taste throughout northern and central Europe.

In sculpture the religious works of Germain Pilon (ca. 1530–90; PL. 100) are among the most powerful expressions of the emotional atmosphere of the Counter Reformation. Their style shows a full awareness of certain types of Italian mannerism, but in a sense marks a further move toward the baroque.

Other arts flourished in France during this period. A school of engraving inspired by both Italian and German models played an important part in the country's artistic development, particularly that of book illustration. Jean Duvet (1485–ca. 1561) combined the iconography of Dürer with the technique of Marcantonio Raimondi to express a passionate and mystical feeling that, although highly personal, is almost medieval. The art of stained glass, like all other arts in France, underwent Italian influence, but produced a synthesis of northern and local principles. Guillaume (Guglielmo) de Marcillat was called to Italy by Julius II and executed stained-glass windows in Rome and Arezzo that are among the finest of the 16th century (XIII, PL. 179). The great tradition of enamel-making at Limoges experienced a revival (IV, PLS. 413–415), mainly under Italian influence. French artists successfully adapted designs from Italian engravings to their newly invented technique of enameling in black, gray, and white, and Limoges dishes of this kind remain among the most beautiful examples of the applied arts of the 16th century.

Anthony BLUNT

THE LOW COUNTRIES. *Architecture.* Although the Van Eycks and their followers were doing revolutionary work in painting, there was no comparable movement away from the Gothic in 15th-century architecture in Flanders. The first signs of awareness of a different style appeared early in the 16th century, and, as is common in the north, were manifested as new decorative motifs applied to basically Gothic designs. Even as late as the 1530s, in Malines, which was the headquarters of the regent's court, the architect of the House of the Salmon (V, PL. 332) applied a system of curiously proportioned orders to a tall, narrow façade with a steeply pitched roof, whose proportions are similar to those of many earlier buildings. After 1550, however, Gothic trends became less obvious, though verticals rather than horizontals were still dominant in design, and a better knowledge of classical forms (that came, perhaps, from France) was evident. This would seem to be the case in the façade added to the north transept of the Church of St-Jacques, Liège, in 1558, with its coupled orders superimposed on either side of the entrance. However, the work betrays its immaturity in the handling of the attic, and especially in the pair of tall columns, clumsily supported, that were inserted to provide emphasis at the center.

Because of the devastations of many wars, it is not easy to trace the development of architecture in Flanders and, indeed, little may have been built during the Wars of Religion in the last half of the 16th century. It is therefore remarkable that one major building, the Town Hall in Antwerp (PL. 99), has survived. This edifice was built by Cornelis II Floris de Vriendt between 1561 and 1565; it shows a conscious attempt to balance horizontals and verticals, a restrained and competent use of orders, both of pilasters and half-columns, and although the piling up of the center with its broken outline is an obviously northern feature it is not ill-adjusted to the mass of the building and the detail is good.

No building of equal importance was produced until after 1600. By then the prosperity of Holland was rising, and that of Flanders was diminishing. A style, which is termed "Renaissance" by Dutch art historians but which based its coarse strapwork detail on such mannerist pattern books as the *Architectura* (Antwerp, 1565) of Hans Vredeman de Vries, may be seen in numerous Dutch and some Flemish towns. With its curving gables, its naïve use of classical motifs, and its broken lines, it is a curiously mixed style, and is, in one sense, a regression from the relatively mature classicism of Cornelis II Floris de Vriendt. Its life, however, was both vigorous and long, and details taken from Vredeman de Vries can be traced beyond the mid-17th century.

Sculpture. The development of sculpture in the Low Countries is even more difficult to trace than that of architecture, for the destruction has been greater. The work of the 15th century was still Gothic, but the sweetness of the 14th century was replaced by a dramatic style derived from Claus Sluter (q.v.), who also had a strong influence on Flemish painting. An example from the end of the century, the tomb of Mary of Burgundy (1495–1502) in Notre-Dame in Bruges, is traditional in style and Gothic in decoration, but the bold modeling of the head, which must have been based on a portrait, and the treatment of the torso beneath the robes suggest a new sense of form.

The most notable sculpture undertaken for a Flemish patron in the early years of the 16th century in which Italian and northern elements are combined was produced outside Flanders. The series of tombs (I, PL. 385; IV, PL. 455) erected for the regent, Margaret of Austria, at Brou, begun in 1505, owes much to the German sculptor, Conrad Meit. She also employed Italian craftsmen, but they do not seem to have worked in Flanders. It was not until the 1530s that Italianate designs, generally Lombard in character, but probably of French derivation, began to be employed, for example, in the retable in the Church of Notre-Dame in Halle (Hal; 1533) by the Lorraine artist, Jean Mone, and in the mantelpiece in Bruges (1528–30; XIII, PL. 239) by Lancelot Blondeel and Guyot de Beaugrant. The overloaded character of the mantelpiece undoubtedly conformed to Flemish taste.

Before the middle of the century, however, Jacques Dubroeucq of Mons had brought back from Italy a deeper understanding of both Italian and antique sculpture, and the fragments that remain of his jube in Ste-Waudru, Mons (ca. 1535–50; PL. 99), are of exceptional quality. His pupil, Giambologna (q.v.), is perhaps the only great Italianizing Fleming, but his work hardly belongs to the story of Flemish art.

Cornelis II Floris de Vriendt, architect and engraver, also worked as a sculptor. His chief importance probably lies in his engraved designs of ornament, which did much to spread the Fontainebleau style; his work as a sculptor suggests that he himself had not assimilated the elegance of the style.

Owing to the Wars of Religion, little sculpture was produced in the last third of the century and undoubtedly much that existed was destroyed. After these conflicts, a somewhat heavy form of mannerism was still current in Flanders in the work of Hieronymus I Duquesnoy (II, PL. 170) and Jacob Colijn de Nole and in Holland in the workshop of Hendrik de Keyser and his sons (although the Virtues on his tomb of William the Silent in the New Church, Delft, still have something of Fontainebleau elegance).

Painting. In northern Europe it was only in Flanders that painters in the early 15th century turned away from the elegant charm of late Gothic painting and successfully explored new fields, evolving a style that was totally new. Their close attention to the fall of light, their development of transparent oil glazes, and their immense technical skill enabled them to achieve an illusion of reality in which every object had its place. Although scientific perspective, at that moment being explored in Florence, was unknown to them and they had no tradition of monumental art deriving ultimately from antiquity, they nevertheless exalted the dignity of man in an art that must be termed Renaissance.

Because of the lack of dated works from the first two decades of the 15th century it is impossible to say with certainty precisely how the new style was developed. It may well have appeared at about the same time in the workshops of the Van Eycks and Robert Campin (qq.v.), but if the *Heures de Turin* actually dates from about 1416 it follows that the first experiments in this style were made by artists associated with the Burgundian

court. Neither the *Birth of John the Baptist* in the *Heures de Turin* (V, PL. 283) nor the Master of Flémalle's (or Robert Campin's) Mérode Triptych (VI, PL. 66), a work of the 1420s, shows a complete control of figures in space. Both are, however, deeply concerned with the definition of form through the fall of light, and Campin, elsewhere profoundly influenced by the sculpture of Claus Sluter, also occupied himself with problems of weight and texture in figures and draperies. By 1434, Jan van Eyck, in the portrait of Giovanni Arnolfini and his wife (V, PLS. 222, 223), had overcome to a remarkable degree the difficulties left unresolved in the earlier works. The two figures in this painting, monumental in spite of their relatively small scale, stand convincingly in their room, surrounded by objects of everyday life. The perspective is not scientific because there is no single vanishing point, yet the effect of reality is astonishingly complete. Each object is rendered with great care (cf. the mirror detail); light, shadow, and reflected light are rendered with amazing subtlety, but the whole is never forgotten. This is not a representation of a series of individual objects separately seen but of an interior filled with light and atmosphere in which each object falls into place. Jan van Eyck painted on a smaller scale than Masaccio and used a different medium; he lacks the overwhelming grandeur and the broad and simple realization of form of the Italian, but in his conviction that form is defined by light he works toward the same end. No other Flemish painter of the 15th century surpassed Jan van Eyck's achievement in creating an illusion of total reality.

After the middle of the century the single vanishing point became common in painting, and in the Last Supper Triptych (1464–67; PL. 96) Dirk Bouts (q.v.) used both linear and aerial perspective. As with most painters after about 1460, his figures are more slender than the sculptural forms of Van Eyck. In paintings by Hans Memling of about 1480 (PL. 95) there is the same renewed interest in surface pattern that was being manifested in Florence at that time. Italianate decorative details such as putti and swags were used occasionally, derived presumably from objects seen in the houses of the Italian colony in Bruges.

The art of 15th-century Flemish painters was much prized by their Italian contemporaries (Michelangelo's condemnation of it was a 16th-century reaction). The Estes of Ferrara and the Medicis owned works by Rogier van der Weyden and Jan van Eyck; Justus of Ghent was entrusted with the commission, originally given to Piero della Francesca, for the altarpiece of the *Communion of the Apostles* (1473–74; Urbino, Gall. Naz. delle Marche), and Tommaso Portinari ordered from Hugo van der Goes the work known as the Portinari Altarpiece (ca. 1475; V, PL. 281; IX, PL. 10; X, PL. 509). These works, with their accurate rendition of lighting effects, brilliance of color, skillfully treated landscapes, and strong characterizations (especially notable in the shepherds in the Portinari Altarpiece), made a profound impression in Italy and were regarded as progressions far beyond the outmoded Gothic style.

The interest in character and in the precise appearance of a man led to a remarkable development of the portrait. The hieratic 14th-century type of profile or full-face portrait, almost always of a noble personage, was transformed by Jan van Eyck and his contemporaries to the three-quarter view and extended to sitters of many different social ranks. Van Eyck's so-called portrait of Cardinal Albergati (V, PL. 219) is an accurate appraisal of an aging face, in which the artist has succeeded in recording every tonal gradation of the soft, wrinkled skin. A similar mastery may be seen in the donor portraits in his larger works (V, PL. 218; VII, PL. 378) and in his only known portrait drawing (V, PL. 219). More than half his signed and dated works are portraits; all of them, except for the Arnolfini group, show the head against a dark ground (V, PL. 221; XI, PL. 217). Later portrait painters added architecture or landscape to the background of their works, thus giving a more complete account of the subject and his world. Jan van Eyck also almost certainly painted a half-length portrait group of the genre type, which no longer exists. Hans Memling, who was not inventive in his religious works, made a significant contribution to portraiture, for he seems to have originated the type showing the head against a background of an open landscape (PL. 95). Several such portraits appear to be of Italian sitters, and there can be little doubt of the influence they had in Italy itself. Still another type, which was to prove of importance throughout Europe, was developed by Quentin Massys (Metsys). His portraits of his Humanist friends Erasmus (PL. 98) and Petrus Aegidius (1517; Salisbury, Longford Castle, Coll. Earl of Radnor) show the scholars in their studies.

Throughout the 16th century Netherlandish artists continued to paint portraits of impressive dignity, but they did not make significant contributions to religious and historical painting. In portraits, the forms became more massive and the treatment broader; artists such as Anthonis Mor, who had a wide knowledge of European art, portrayed figures seated and, occasionally, full length (IV, PL. 27; V, PL. 293; XI, PL. 218). Until the end of the century portraiture was based on those principles of detailed observation of forms defined by light first exploited early in the 15th century by Jan van Eyck.

The keen interest in natural appearances that was characteristic of all Flemish art led, inevitably, to an extensive use of landscape. It appeared very early and, in the 15th century, always as a background, although often of equal or even greater interest than the figures (V, PLS. 216, 224, 282). Gradually the landscape came to dominate the compositions. Gerard David painted two altarpiece panels with landscapes in which no figures appear (V, PL. 286). The panoramic landscapes of Patinir, painted in the early 16th century, reflect the great increase in the knowledge of geography; they include figures and are narrative in theme, but the human element is subordinated to the landscape (PL. 378; V, PL. 296; IX, PL. 12).

By the beginning of the 16th century Flemish painting, at the time still largely untouched by Italian influence, was moving toward greater grandeur and simplicity. In Gerard David's *Crucifixion* (PL. 97), with its monumental figures starkly outlined against the sky, all irrelevant detail has been discarded, and the painting shows that refinement of form and technique typical of a High Renaissance picture. Massys' St. Anne Altarpiece (1509; Brussels, Mus. Royaux des B. A.) was planned on a grand scale and introduced a new range of color values that added a soft and glowing harmony to the design. Unfortunately, this phase was short-lived. The rise of the city of Antwerp, center both of trade and of the New Learning, the political changes that brought Flanders into the Holy Roman Empire and led to closer contacts with southern Europe, the growth of the book trade and the dissemination of engravings, especially those of Albrecht Dürer, contributed to a rising demand for paintings that were new in style and subject and that imitated, although never very successfully, Italian art. It is possible that Massys himself visited Italy; he certainly had some knowledge of the work of Leonardo and his followers. In his *Mary Magdalene* (V, PL. 284) he attained a fine balance between the old and the new, but in his later works he descended to a disagreeable sentimentality. Jan Gossaert, called Mabuse, was in Italy in 1508, but his drawings of antique sculpture prove that he hardly understood what he saw. About 1516 he began to create the "poesies" praised by Guicciardini — pairs of nudes, often based on classical themes (PL. 104) — but their proportions and their heavy limbs derive from Dürer's engravings (cf. IV, PL. 301) or works that the German sculptor Conrad Meit executed for the regent of the Netherlands rather than from Italian or antique sources. Bernart van Orley, the regent's painter, had some knowledge of the work of Raphael, possibly through Tommaso Vincidor da Bologna, of the school of Raphael, present in Brussels in connection with the weaving of the tapestries inspired by the Acts of the Apostles. Types derived from Raphael appear in Van Orley's paintings (V, PL. 287) but the significance of Raphael's composition was beyond his understanding.

No painter in 16th-century Flanders was able to assimilate Renaissance ideas and transform them into a national style. Much Italianate art was produced there, but it was always marked by a clumsiness of design or proportion that reveals only a superficial grasp of Renaissance art. More and more northern artists visited Italy and, especially, Rome (see ROMANISTS). The works they painted on their return show a wholesale borrowing of types and poses used indiscriminately and tangled into confused compositions. Many such examples could be cited; to an artist such as Michiel Coxie, for instance, who worked in Rome in the 1530s, the Raphaelesque was of more interest than the works of Raphael himself, and to Frans Floris de Vriendt, who was in Rome when the *Last Judgment* was unveiled, the Michelangelesque was overwhelming (PL. 98). Flemish painting of the 16th century often presented mannerist characteristics that were probably unconscious. They cannot have arisen as a conscious reaction against the calm lucidity of High Renaissance painting, but appear to be a naïve acceptance of current styles, jumbled together with little taste. Some mid-century artists, on the other hand, were obviously attracted by the elegant Fontainebleau style, known at first probably through engravings, but Flemish paintings in this manner are at once erotic and crude. Later in the 16th century the Venetian school and the work of Federico Barocci (PL. 81; IX, PL. 303) were to prove influential in Flanders, and artists such as Marten de Vos, Theodoor van Loon, and Otto van Veen could produce tolerable pastiches of the more sensual or sentimental aspects of Italian art. Their designs, however, are seldom memorable, for they added little of original worth, and it was left for Van Veen's great pupil, Rubens, to create a new art that was a synthesis of northern and southern trends.

The Flemings were more successful in their handling of Italian motifs in the realm of applied arts, where surface pattern and wealth of detail were not inappropriate and where monumental design was less necessary. Much of the tapestry designed (often by Italianizing painters) and woven at Brussels has a high decorative quality (XIII, PL. 401), and the combination of Italian decoration and figure designs is perhaps seen at its best in stained glass, notably in the windows of the Church of SS. Michel and Gudule in Brussels (XIII, PL. 176).

The two greatest painters of the century, Hieronymus Bosch (ca. 1450–1516) and Pieter Bruegel the Elder (ca. 1525–69; qq.v.), stand somewhat apart from the principal trends of Flemish painting. Bosch, who lived and worked at 's Hertogenbosch in North Brabant, created a style of great originality to express an esoteric mysticism that seems to have been widespread in this region. His paintings were later enthusiastically collected by Philip II of Spain. Bruegel went to Italy in 1552 and traveled as far south as the Strait of Messina. He returned from this journey profoundly influenced by the countryside he had seen, particularly in the Alps, and by the landscape painting of the Venetians. With elements drawn from both these sources he created a new concept of landscape painting in which nature is not merely the reflection of a human mood but has a grandeur of her own, which suggests that the artist was inspired by some sort of pantheism (cf. II, PL. 356). Unlike his contemporaries in Flanders, he never imitated the external forms of Italian art; nevertheless, the sculptural quality of his last figure paintings, such as the *Peasant Wedding* (II, PL. 361), surely derived from Bruegel's knowledge of the Italian art of the High Renaissance. Also in certain rare cases, such as the drawing of *Summer* (PL. 98), there are direct echoes of Michelangelo's *Last Judgment*, which Bruegel had probably seen in Rome.

Margaret WHINNEY

Engraving. Engraving plays a vitally important part in the art of the Low Countries in the late 15th and the 16th century, particularly as a vehicle for the transmission of Italian ideas. However, it is difficult to give a clear history of the first phase of its development because little is known about the nationalities and identities of the many engravers and designers of woodcuts, and it is often impossible to distinguish between an artist who worked in the Netherlands and one who worked on the Upper Rhine. The situation in general is, however, very similar to that in Germany (see below), but in assimilating Renaissance ideas the artists of the Netherlands lagged behind the German school by several decades.

The most important contribution to the woodcut technique usually credited to the Netherlands is the invention of the block book. This, it is reasonable to assume, was in use before the invention of movable printing type at mid-century, since, for the block book, illustration and text were cut on the same block. The books often went through several editions, the blocks being recut each time, so that the quality of each edition varies considerably. Among the earlier block books the most important are the *Exercitium super Pater Noster* and *The Apocalypse*, both of which were probably issued between 1430 and 1450. The *Ars moriendi* dates from about the middle of the century, and the *Biblia pauperum* from a decade or two later (VI, PL. 403). In all of these the illustrations are in the medieval tradition.

The predominant style in engravings by Netherlandish artists during the first half of the 15th century is Burgundian late Gothic, and it is not until the second half of the century that a new development emerges in the engraver's art. This was the contribution of the artist known as the Master of the Housebook or the Master of the Amsterdam Cabinet (active ca. 1480; VI, PL. 6). The site of his workshop has not been established and has been identified with areas ranging from Basel to the northern Netherlands; recent scholarship favors the latter. He was the first artist to use the dry-point technique. The subjects of his prints have, for the most part, a genre character deriving ultimately from the International Gothic style, but they are observed with a directness and wit that were entirely new.

At the turn of the 15th century there was little new in Netherlandish engraving. The prints of Master I. M. of Zwolle reflect the style of the paintings of Geertgen tot Sint Jans, and Alart Duhameel produced engravings inspired by Bosch's designs of fantastic satire. It was not until 1508 that a great Netherlandish engraver, namely Lucas van Leyden (1494–1533), emerged. His early works, which were apparently produced when he was only fourteen and are his most original inventions, show no trace of Italian influence but are the direct outcome of 15th-century northern art, principally German engraving and Netherlandish painting. In the middle of his career, Lucas was noticeably influenced by Dürer's engravings — and it must be remembered that Dürer's visit to the Netherlands took place in 1521. A few years later, according to Karel van Mander (*Het Schilder-Boeck*, Haarlem, 1604), Lucas went on a journey with Gossaert. Whatever the accuracy of this statement, the Romanist style of Gossaert's paintings and his few engravings can be detected in the engravings of Lucas, for example, *The Poet Vergil Suspended in a Basket* (IX, PL. 216). Apart from the forms of the figures and draperies, there is a self-consciousness that was conspicuously lacking in his earlier work. All traces of originality disappeared from his engravings about 1529, when he came into contact with the prints of Marcantonio Raimondi. Lucas slavishly copied the Raphaelesque figures, the classical compositions, and the cold regularity of the burin work of the Italian reproductive engraver. It should be added that Raimondi returned the compliment and copied and adapted one or two of Lucas's landscape backgrounds.

Other Netherlandish engravers of the time, such as Allart Claesz. and Cornelis Massys, took the German "Little Masters" as their models. A more Italianizing artist was Lambert Zutman (Suavius), who worked in Liège in the middle of the century; he studied the work of both Lucas van Leyden and Jacopo de' Barbari. Maerten van Heemskerck (PL. 307; X, PL. 207) and Frans Floris de Vriendt both worked in an Italian mannerist style, using the Raimondi tradition of line engraving. Cornelis II Floris de Vriendt was a more important engraver; his series of plates of ornaments and grotesques had great influence on 16th-century decoration.

All originality in the use of woodcut and engraving in the Netherlands in the 16th century disappeared with Lucas van Leyden. It was the age of the reproductive engraver — Cornelis Cort produced about 200 engraved copies of 16th-century Italian paintings — and the medium, instead of earning recognition as an art form in its own right, was of greater importance

as a vehicle by means of which knowledge of the various schools of painting and decoration was spread throughout Europe. The Netherlands led in publishing reproductive engravings, which by this time had replaced woodcuts as book illustrations. The publishing houses of Cock, Galle, and Passe were among the most productive in Europe. Particular attention was given to Italian art, and an increasing number of Netherlandish artists went to Italy; Cort remained there for the rest of his life and set up a school of engraving in Rome that, in its turn, was to influence Italian engravers for half a century.

Christopher WHITE

GERMANY. *Architecture.* There was no Renaissance movement in German architecture comparable to that in painting and sculpture. Bavaria was the only part of the Holy Roman Empire in which there was some real understanding of Italian principles. The Residenz in Landshut, built by Duke Ludwig X between 1537 and 1542, was planned and decorated by architects and painters from Mantua and has the air of a palace by Giulio Romano transplanted to a Bavarian valley. The Castle of Trausnitz, on a hill above Landshut, contains some Italianate architectural elements dating from a few years earlier, along with grotesque decoration in the manner of Friedrich Sustris, dating from the end of the 16th century. In Munich the Residenz was largely rebuilt in the late 16th and the early 17th century. The Antiquarium of the Residenz, begun in 1569 by Wilhelm Egckl, though un-Italian in its broad, low barrel vault, is covered with fine grotesques (PL. 105), and the imperial staircase (1611–19) in the Residenz shows an exceptionally pure use of the Doric order.

In church architecture the two most important monuments of the period in southern Germany are the Church of St. Michael in Munich and the University Church in Würzburg. The plan of St. Michael, built between 1583 and 1597, shows an attempt to adapt that of the Church of the Gesù in Rome to northern conditions, and the huge barrel-vaulted nave is a truly original invention (VI, PL. 138). The University Church, planned by the Fleming Georges Robin and begun in 1586, is remarkable for its superimposed classical arcades, of a kind otherwise unknown in Germany at that time.

Direct Italian influence scarcely penetrated the rest of Germany. An exception is the Ottheinrichsbau (begun 1556) in the Castle of Heidelberg, where the detail is purely Italianate and the huge Atlantes flanking the entrance show a true understanding of contemporary northern Italian sculpture. The design as a whole has a regularity that relates it to Italian Renaissance buildings, but the surface is loaded with decoration in a manner that would have seemed barbarous to Italian eyes (VI, PL. 138).

Architects in other parts of the Empire drew their inspiration from the Low Countries, and the decorative motifs designed by Cornelis II Floris de Vriendt and others gained great popularity. In many German towns tall houses survive with high-pitched gables, Gothic in form, but covered with broken and fanciful decoration based on these borrowed elements but employed with a fantasy unknown in the Low Countries. This decoration was carried to its extreme by Wendel Dietterlin in his *Architectura* (Nürnberg, 1593), which enjoyed great popularity and was widely used as a pattern book until well into the 17th century.

The last important building to be erected before architectural activity was cut off by the Thirty Years' War was the Town Hall in Augsburg, built by Elias Holl between 1615 and 1620. The exterior, tall and massive in its proportions, is German, although the detail is maturely classical, and the great Golden Hall in the interior shows an intimate knowledge of Venetian ceiling decoration of the late 16th century.

Scarcely any architecture from this period survives in Austria. The Schweizertor in the Vienna Hofburg, erected by Ferdinand I, brother of Charles V, in 1552, and those parts of Schloss Ambras near Innsbruck built by Archduke Ferdinand II of Tyrol from 1564 onward reveal a knowledge of contemporary Italian work, but in both the borrowed elements are mixed with northern features. In the Schweizertor the caryatids and scrollwork are Flemish in origin; in Ambras the ornament is used with a quite un-Italian profusion, and although much of the detail of the Spanish Hall is fine, the proportions are those of a northern European gallery (VI, PL. 138).

Sculpture. Of the three great German sculptors active in the early 16th century, two — Veit Stoss and Tilman Riemenschneider — although touched by the art of Italy, remained essentially Gothic artists and so have no place in this article. The third, Peter Vischer the Elder of Nürnberg (ca. 1460–1529; q.v.), marks the transition from the Middle Ages to the Renaissance. Most of his early work, such as the Monument of Archbishop Ernest in the Cathedral of Magdeburg (finished 1495), is wholly Gothic in conception and execution, but the sculpture of the so-called "Bough Breaker" (*Der Astbrecher*; Munich, Bayerisches Nationalmus.) has much in common with the naturalism of Antonio Pollaiuolo and suggests that engravings by him had reached Nürnberg. St. Sebald's Shrine (1508–19) in the Church of St. Sebald in Nürnberg is completely late Gothic in design, but the figures of the Apostles have a calmer aspect and fuller, more flowing draperies than most German sculpture of the period. This is usually explained as a return to 13th-century German sculpture (Strasbourg or Bamberg), but it seems also to imply a knowledge of Florentine work of the early 15th century, particularly that of Ghiberti. Vischer's King Arthur, made for the tomb of Maximilian I in Innsbruck (1513; VI, PL. 133), is still a medieval paladin, but the freedom of pose and treatment of the features could not have been achieved without some knowledge of what had taken place in Italy in the late 15th century. This statue has an affinity with the ideals of the early Renaissance that is completely lacking in the other, more fantastic figures in this memorable ensemble, in which the dazzling skill of German bronze casters is spurred to its highest achievements by the complexity of the designs provided by the artists.

With Peter Vischer's sons Renaissance elements became dominant in the sculpture of the time. The reliefs of Peter Vischer the Younger (1487–1528; VI, PL. 139) and the statues of his brother Hans (1489–1550) are the equivalent in sculpture of Dürer's most classicizing engravings, which must have been a direct source of inspiration to these artists.

Meanwhile a school of great importance had sprung up in Augsburg under the protection of the Fugger family. Hans Dauher (Daucher; ca. 1485–1538), Hans Schwarz (ca. 1492–after 1527), and Loy Hering (ca. 1484–after 1554) specialized in a kind of low relief, cut in a very fine stone, that imitated painting or engraving in that the artists introduced effects of space and perspective and even details of landscape in the manner of the so-called "Danube school." They also produced many portrait medallions in profile or three-quarter view that were directly influenced by Italian medals; in addition to a large number of medallions, Christoph Weiditz (before 1517–1572) made a few life-size busts that are reminiscent of Italian 15th-century works of the same kind.

In southern Bavaria and in Salzburg Hans Leinberger (active 1513–28) and the unidentified Master J. P. (traceable 1521) created pictorial reliefs based on the style of the Danube school. A peculiar example of this style is the pair of reliefs (Munich, Bayerisches Nationalmus.) by Hans Aesslinger of Munich (active 1552–67); these are direct copies of Raimondi's engravings of the *Massacre of the Innocents* and the *Judgment of Paris*.

Perhaps the most versatile sculptor of the early 16th century was Conrad Meit (ca. 1480–ca. 1550), who was born in Worms but worked in many parts of northern Germany and outside the country. His small statuettes in boxwood and alabaster are the counterpart of Dürer's nudes, and his portrait busts, also usually in boxwood, combine vigorous naturalism with a breadth of form rare in German sculpture. His most important commission was the designing of the monuments of the house of Savoy at Brou, undertaken in 1526–32 for Margaret of Austria (I, PL. 385; IV, PL. 455); unfortunately, it is difficult

to determine his exact share in the work. The four recumbent statues, two of Margaret of Austria and two of her husband, Philibert of Savoy, are, however, generally accepted as being of his invention, and they represent one of the most impressive examples of the synthesis of northern expressiveness with Renaissance monumentality. The head of the naked figure of Philibert, almost impossible to see through the Gothic arches that hide it, seems to be a direct imitation of an ancient head of Augustus.

In the second half of the century most German sculpture conformed to the style of court mannerism current in Europe. Alexander Colin (1527–1612) brought it from Flanders to Heidelberg and Innsbruck; Wenzel Jamnitzer (1508–85; IX, PL. 308) used it mainly in Nürnberg; and Hubert Gerhard (1540/50–1620) employed it on a monumental scale in Munich (PL. 106; VI, PL. 141). The most accomplished sculptor was the Dutchman Adriaen de Vries (ca. 1550–1626), who worked in northern Germany, in Augsburg, and for the Emperor Rudolf II in Prague (VI, PL. 139; IX, PL. 308).

Anthony BLUNT

Painting. From about 1495 to about 1545 painting in Germany flowered briefly but intensively; then, because of religious and political stresses, it faded rapidly. The stimulus that produced this brief period of intense activity came largely — but by no means entirely — from Renaissance Italy, and its impact was heightened by the genius, both intellectual and technical, of one artist, Albrecht Dürer (q.v.). His achievement was enormous, but although his influence was great it was not completely overwhelming. Several of his contemporaries and successors explored slightly different fields, proving themselves painters of high quality and often of supreme originality. This sequence of great individual painters in Germany within so brief a period was, for its time, unparalleled outside Italy. To a great extent their work reflected the subjective character of German culture, for it was the expression of intense personal emotion that divided each artist from his fellows. In this intensity of expression German painting far outstripped contemporary work in Flanders, for although it drew on Italy for inspiration, it added much of its own, transmuting what it borrowed into a national art. In contrast, the great majority of 16th-century Flemish artists were content with superficial imitation.

Dürer's life-long search for the principles of human proportions, which led him to a deep consideration of the nature of beauty, his studies in perspective (that lodestar of Renaissance theorists), his immense curiosity about the visible world, his profoundly religious temperament, and his unique control of hand and eye raise him to the stature of the great Italians and set him above all northern artists. His influence was most widely felt through his woodcuts and engravings (see below) rather than through his drawings and paintings.

The crucial event in Dürer's life as far as his painting is concerned was his second visit to Venice in 1506. Before that time his studies in perspective and also his feeling for landscape had been combined in paintings of hard brilliance, for example, the Paumgärtner Altarpiece (IV, PL. 299) and the *Adoration of the Magi* (IV, PL. 295). After this visit his sense of color mellowed and his feeling for monumental design grew (IV, PLS. 296, 300), culminating after his return in the grand conception of the *Adoration of the Trinity* (PL. 109), perhaps the most completely High Renaissance design created north of the Alps. His greatest paintings are of religious subjects, but his ability as a portraitist, in both painting and drawing (IV, PLS. 292, 293, 302), must not be overlooked. In his portraits the influence of Flanders, especially after his journey there in 1519, was greater than that of Italy. Dürer's achievement was at once vast and profound, for he grasped the spirit of Renaissance art but transformed it so that his style was at once both personal and northern. It is not surprising that lesser artists borrowed his forms, although they usually misunderstood their meaning. Moreover, they lacked his intellectual discipline and also, generally, his first-hand knowledge of Italy; so, like Hans

Baldung-Grien in his *Death Kisses a Maiden* (IV, PL. 468), they twisted Dürer's classical proportions into a restless, expressive art more nearly related to the Gothic past.

The greatest of Dürer's contemporaries, Matthias Grünewald (q.v.), rose to great artistic heights by totally different means. The Isenheim Altar has no reference to classical or Italian art, and its *Crucifixion* is among the world's great dramatic masterpieces of emotional painting (IV, PL. 180; VII, PLS. 85-89, 91, 92). Nevertheless, the setting of the figures firmly in space, the remarkable realism of the draftsmanship (above all of the hands), and the splendid radiance of color, controlled and directed to heighten emotion and add coherence to the design, proclaim it a Renaissance rather than a Gothic painting.

Lucas Cranach the Elder (q.v.), who was of the same generation as Grünewald and Dürer, was much influenced by the latter in his woodcuts; his contribution as a painter is more personal. His early religious pictures, probably produced in Vienna, show an exceptional interest in Austrian landscape. After his move to Wittenberg in 1505 he produced two very different kinds of subjects: portraits (IV, PLS. 43, 46), sometimes decorative and almost always distinguished, including probably the earliest known life-size full-length portraits; and erotic nudes (IV, PLS. 40, 44). Since most of the nudes have classical names they must to some degree be regarded as related to Renaissance ideals. However, these figures bear no relation to Dürer's serious art, with its amply built nudes; the sloping shoulders and high, small breasts of Cranach's nudes mark them as a frivolous continuation of Gothic forms. Eroticism, which may well be an inevitable result of mistaken notions of antiquity, especially when these are bred in an atmosphere of religious and social stress, is a fairly common ingredient of 16th-century German and Swiss painting, and is sometimes combined with a morbid feeling for the macabre (IX, PLS. 255, 257) and often with an interest in fantastic architecture and landscape.

Indeed, apart from the art of Dürer and the general development of portraiture, the major contribution of central European painters was in their attitude to landscape. The mysterious and emotional vision of forests, of tree branches silhouetted against a sunset, have seldom been more vividly expressed than in the work of Albrecht Altdorfer (q.v.). The paintings and above all the drawings of Altdorfer (PL. 107; I, PL. 66) and other masters of the Danube school combine a feeling for organic growth with a superb sense of decorative design. The artists may have lacked the scientific curiosity and the immense patience of a Leonardo or a Dürer, but their expressive art has a validity of its own and was to prove a source of inspiration to Italian painters such as Domenico Beccafumi and Tintoretto.

The last German painter to make an original contribution was Hans Holbein the Younger (see HOLBEIN). Almost a generation younger than Dürer, he absorbed Renaissance ideas more easily, perhaps at first through the influence of his fellow citizen in Augsburg, Hans Burgkmair the Elder (q.v.; PL. 106), one of the few German artists whose work shows direct Italian influence independent of Dürer. Holbein's subject paintings, both religious and classical, show an increasing control of monumental design that was strengthened by his study of Raphael's works during a visit to France in 1524. Unfortunately, by the time he reached full maturity, patronage in Germany and Switzerland was dwindling because of the upheavals following upon the Reformation, and he sought work in England. There he found little scope for monumental painting, and only his talent as a portraitist was appreciated (VII, PLS. 303, 304, 306). In his best portraits he combines an Italian sense of volume with a northern precision of detail and great mastery of technique (PL. 110); but his last works for the English court are detached and frozen in style. His work in England can also serve as an illustration of one aspect of German Renaissance art to which little space can be given, though it deserves much more — namely, decorative design. Like many of his fellow artists, he had an intimate knowledge of the techniques of the goldsmith, and his designs for goldsmiths' work and jewelry

indicate not only a repertoire of purely Renaissance motifs but also a sureness in their application; these objects must have been of great beauty and probably were an important medium for disseminating Renaissance ideas.

Margaret WHINNEY

Engraving. Although the practitioners of the arts of woodcut and engraving were two distinct groups before the advent of Dürer, the developments of the two media are closely related. Both made their appearance at the beginning of the 15th century, and they may reasonably be assumed to have been one of Germany's contributions to the history of art and were almost as important as movable type was in the history of printing. (For the history of the origins and techniques of woodcuts and engravings see ENGRAVINGS AND OTHER PRINT MEDIA.)

In the 15th century a great number of woodcuts were made representing incidents from the Passion or figures of saints, and they were either sold or given away to pilgrims at shrines. They were probably executed by the monks themselves, or at any rate were produced in the monasteries. Many were based directly on the works of art in the shrine, and they adumbrate in a crude way the idea of the print as a reproductive process.

Woodcuts were also used for playing cards, of which only a very small number has survived. Playing cards are known to have been introduced into Germany by 1377, and they were probably being printed from wood blocks by the beginning of the next century. Though woodcut cards probably preceded engraved cards in date, examples of the latter are the earliest to have survived. The earliest existing packs of woodcut cards cannot be dated earlier than the mid-15th century. The design was determined by conventional patterns, though individual cutters altered or embellished them according to changes in taste.

During the 15th century the most significant use of the woodcut was for book illustration. Its earliest form was the block book, but with the invention of movable type its use spread rapidly, and by the end of the century woodcut illustrations in printed books were in very wide use. Editions were lavishly illustrated, such as the *Schatzbehalter* (1491) and the *Nürnberg Chronicle* (1493), both published in Nürnberg. Until the end of the 16th century woodcut remained almost the only means of illustrating books.

Most of the German engravings of the 15th century are anonymous, but, unlike the woodcuts, their style is sufficiently clear for them to be arranged in groups based on a certain central work or on the initials with which some of them were signed. The status of engravers was much higher than that of the designers of woodcuts; instead of being classed as craftsmen, they were probably considered equal to painters and sculptors. Even if the artistic ability of the engravers was higher and their originality more apparent, the impact of the Renaissance on their art was no greater than it was in the case of the woodcut. Contemporary painting and manuscript illuminations were generally dominant influences, if not direct models.

The earliest date on a metal engraving, 1446, is to be found on one of a Passion series by an artist known as the Master of 1446. The Master of the Playing Cards, however, whose stylistic characteristics locate him in northern Germany, must have been active at a slightly earlier date. As the name implies, his main activity was designing playing cards, which have a marked International Gothic style. The types and style are comparable to some of Pisanello's drawings.

A slightly younger engraver, the Master E. S., a number of whose prints are dated 1466 and 1467, was a more important and more prolific artist. His sphere of activity was Strasbourg or nearby, and he was probably trained in a goldsmith's shop, since his *œuvre* includes a number of designs for metalwork, such as patens. His early work is in the International Gothic style of the Master of the Playing Cards, but, as he increased in technical proficiency, so he used a style more closely deriving from Flemish painting, probably communicated to him via contemporary German painting rather than by direct contact. But even with a touch of Flemish realism, he is an artist of the

Gothic world, for whom the ideas of the Renaissance never existed. The plate of his most ambitious print, the *Einsiedeln Madonna* (Bartsch 35; 1466), reached Italy, where it was extensively reworked by an anonymous Umbrian engraver.

Martin Schongauer (q.v.) was the first engraver whose name is known and, more significantly, was the first who was active also as a painter. He must have had some connection with a goldsmith's shop; his magnificent engraving of the *Censer* (Bartsch 107) demonstrates a knowledge of the goldsmith's craft. Most of his life was spent in Colmar, and he may have been trained in the workshop of the Master E. S. His early works show the same penchant for Flemish art, although in Schongauer's case it is known that he actually saw examples of it, because he copied Rogier van der Weyden's Last Judgment Altarpiece (XIV, PL. 414). Although the types and draperies in his works are still essentially Gothic in form (PL. 454), there is a new sense of the dignity of man. The setting of Gothic ruins, frequently used in his early works, was later replaced by a more austere background that enhances the impact of the subject. Schongauer was the first German engraver to achieve an international reputation, particularly in Italy. Vasari recognized the importance of his contribution to the history of engraving and recounts that a number of his prints reached Italy. He adds that the young Michelangelo was so impressed by Schongauer's engraving of *The Temptation of St. Anthony* (Bartsch 47; IV, PL. 427), a print of Gothic fantasy, that he made a copy of it.

It was Dürer who raised both the woodcut and the engraving to the same status as painting and sculpture. His technical virtuosity was such that he succeeded in giving to the woodcut the finesse of an engraving and to the engraving the tonal range of a grisaille. Equally important were the different uses to which he put both media. Up to this time books had almost always been commissioned by wealthy patrons, and the artist was limited to supplying designs, which were cut by a professional craftsman under the supervision of the printer. Dürer not only made the designs for his *Apocalypse* cycle (Bartsch 61–75; IV, PL. 467) and cut them on the wood block but he published the work himself, demolishing the conception, which was still prevalent in Germany, of the artist as a mere craftsman.

His woodcuts are mainly of religious subjects; the later ones are more humanistic than the earlier ones. The subjects of his engravings are far more adventurous. In his religious subjects there is a greater preoccupation with the pictorial content than with the narrative, and this interest may be directly related to Dürer's contacts with Italy. The nonreligious subjects of the engravings include nature scenes, such as *The Monstrous Sow of Landser* (Bartsch 95); mythological subjects, which he was the first to treat in Germany; allegorical scenes, of which the most important is the *Melencolia I* (III, PL. 203); and genre scenes, for example, *The Bagpiper* (Bartsch 91). The intermediate subjects, like *The Four Witches* (Bartsch 15; 1497) and *Nemesis* (Bartsch 77), are of particular interest as evidence of Dürer's impassioned ambition to discover the underlying principles of Renaissance art and recreate them in a personal way.

Although the technical aspect of Schongauer's influence was all-important in the formation of Dürer's engraving technique, the younger artist's interests were soon absorbed by the South rather than the North. Two visits to Italy and probable contacts with Jacopo de' Barbari in Germany gave Dürer the stimulus and knowledge that makes him the first Renaissance artist of the North. In 1494 Dürer made two drawings after engravings by Mantegna, whose technique and style were to have an important influence on his first graphic work after his return from Italy. Evidence of his acquaintance with Mantegna can be seen both in woodcuts such as *The Four Horsemen* (Bartsch 64), from the *Apocalypse*, and in engravings such as the *Hercules* (Bartsch 73). Dürer's contact with Jacopo de' Barbari was more important, not only for its influence on his style but also for the effect it had on his theoretical studies. The similarities in the engravings of both artists are complicated by the fact that none of Barbari's prints are dated. It seems unlikely that the influence was entirely one-sided, but it is clear that Dürer learned much from the Italian and did not

hesitate to say so. There is an obvious similarity of pose between Dürer's *Four Witches* and Barbari's *Victory and Fame* (Bartsch 18). The classical prototype of this group is the Three Graces, but characteristically Dürer has altered the subject and given it a slightly sinister tone. There is a similar close relation between Dürer's and Barbari's engravings of *Apollo and Diana* (PL. 107). Dürer's print marks the beginning of his preoccupation with theories of proportion. The pose of Barbari's Apollo was copied by Dürer in a drawing, and later adapted to the pose of Adam in his engraving of *Adam and Eve* (1504; IV, PL. 301).

Theoretical interests were of particular concern in Dürer's engraved work up to the time of his second visit to Venice. His experiments in constructed figures were seen in the *Nemesis* of 1501–02, designed according to a Vitruvian canon of proportion, and above all in the *Adam and Eve*, a study in classical *contrapposto*. In later years these interests were largely confined to his various treatises on art theory. The woodcuts of 1525 (Bartsch 146, 149) illustrate his method of drawing the human figure with a perspective apparatus.

Another related interest was the theory of perspective, the practical application of which can be seen most clearly in the engraving of *The Nativity* (1504; Bartsch 2). In 1505 he made a special journey to Bologna to "learn the secret art of perspective." Shortly before leaving Nürnberg he had been studying the anatomy of the horse, and his two engravings of this subject (Bartsch 96, 97), both dated 1505, show the practical application of this research. Inspiration from Leonardo's Sforza horse is clearly indicated (see IX, cols. 217–19).

After his second visit to Italy Dürer tended to consider his engravings less as spokesmen of his theoretical studies. He may well have felt, when he left Nürnberg in 1505, that his engravings were becoming too much exercises in theory, and it is significant that in Italy he should have turned to the least theoretical school of painting. The luminism of Venetian painting made a deep impression on him. In the woodcuts the concluding scenes of the cycles representing the Life of the Virgin and the Large Passion show an astonishing increase in range of tone. The engraving of *Knight, Death, and the Devil* (1513; IV, PL. 297) and the *Adam and Eve* of 1504 are set against similar backgrounds, but the strong tonal contrast between setting and ground figures in the earlier work is transformed in the later one into a tonal uniformity. The *St. Jerome in His Study* (1514; Bartsch 60) is an accurate observation of light in a room and is eloquent testimony both to Dürer's awareness of the qualities of Venetian painting and to his ability to express them in a personal manner.

The greater monumentality that Dürer must have noticed in the later work of Giovanni Bellini was undoubtedly in his mind when he experimented with the new medium of dry point in 1512 with the *St. Jerome by the Pollard Willow* (Bartsch 59) and the *Holy Family* (Bartsch 43). In later years he achieved a Michelangelesque austerity in engravings such as the *Virgin with the Child in Swaddling Clothes* (Bartsch 38) and in the woodcut of the *Last Supper* (1523; Bartsch 53).

At the end of his life Dürer made a number of engraved portraits, including those of Melanchthon, Cardinal Albrecht von Brandenburg, Frederick the Wise, and Erasmus (IV, PL. 301).

Dürer's influence was extensive in Europe. Artists in the Netherlands and Germany were aware of his work, and Vasari had already noted the influence of his prints on Italian artists. Raimondi copied no less than 74 of Dürer's prints; Andrea del Sarto and Pontormo must have known them because they both borrowed compositions. Dürer, by synthesizing German and Italian ideals, created a Renaissance style in Germany that was more or less accepted for the rest of the century.

Hans Baldung-Grien (q.v.), an artist of originality, who, although influenced by Dürer, cannot in any sense be called a follower, took the pictorial possibilities of prints a step further by his use of chiaroscuro woodcuts, for which he used variously colored grounds. His subject matter was more concerned with secular fantasy, such as witches (IX, PL. 257) and allegorical nudes (IX, PL. 255), than with Renaissance mythology and allegory. The *Horse and Groom* (Bartsch 2), one of his few engravings, owes much to Dürer's *Small Horse* (Bartsch 96) although it is less of an exercise on the geometric proportions of the horse.

Lucas Cranach the Elder was also influenced by Dürer, but his works have a more homely and idyllic character than Dürer's. Both the *Fall of Man* (Bartsch 1), a woodcut of 1509, and the *Penance of St. John Chrysostom* (IV, PL. 45), an engraving, were inspired by engravings of the same subjects by Dürer. Cranach's woodcut and engraved portraits of Luther were widely diffused.

More typical were the so-called "Little Masters," who managed to steer a middle course between the influence of Dürer and an interest in Italian art. Albrecht Altdorfer started his work as an engraver in a style close to that of Jacopo de' Barbari (e.g., *The Temptation of the Hermits*; PL. 107). His later work shows the influence of Dürer, but it always remained picturesque; for example, his nudes of Venus, Neptune, and Hercules are not austere studies in proportion but show the gods in a homely setting.

Of the remaining "Little Masters" — Berthel and Hans Sebald Beham, Georg Pencz, and Heinrich Aldegrever — all but the last were active in Nürnberg. The Italianate flavor of Aldegrever's mannerist figures (PL. 107) probably came indirectly from Italy via the Netherlands, perhaps through Bernart van Orley. Barthel Beham's prints give evidence of a much closer contact with Italian art (he died on a journey to Italy in 1540). His engraving of *Apollo and Daphne* (Bartsch 25) is based very closely on Raimondi's work, but his other engravings, in nearly all of which a nude figure predominates, show a more personal style. His brother, Hans Sebald, did not visit Italy but worked in a similar vein, and his *œuvre* includes four engravings of a horse designed according to rules of proportion and heads of a man drawn on the same principles. All these masters excelled in designing panels with grotesques or with figures in the style of antique friezes.

Virgilius Solis based his style on that of the "Little Masters." The subjects of his engravings include popular allegories, genre scenes, and costume plates, which show a tendency toward naturalism.

Dürer's successors lacked the intellectual curiosity necessary to comprehend the artistic theory underlying the art of the Italian Renaissance. For the most part they were content with adapting the purely decorative aspect of Italian and antique art to their own indigenous style.

Christopher WHITE

ENGLAND. The impact of the Renaissance was not as strong in England as it was in those countries that had more direct contact with Italy. Indeed, it would be difficult to prove that there was any real appreciation of Renaissance art in England until the early 17th century.

In the first half of the 16th century there were Humanists in England who were intimate friends of Erasmus and were themselves no mean scholars, but their interest lay more in the Greek of the New Testament than in classical literature. It is significant that in Sir Thomas More's *Utopia* the arts, except for music, play little part. Good craftsmanship, however, was well regarded by More for its moral value; and it follows therefore that for many years decoration was to be the main field in which Renaissance design was reflected. Later in the century, even though Castiglione's *Il Cortegiano* was translated into English in 1561 and Italian manners became a code of behavior (often exaggerated, as may be seen in Shakespeare's earlier plays), there was still little interest in Renaissance art. A few English patrons visited Italy; some, such as Sir Philip Sidney, were sufficiently impressed by Italian artists to have their portraits painted by them. More patrons visited France. However, these journeys do not seem to have resulted in intelligent patronage in England itself. Hardly any English artists are known to have traveled. Many foreign artists worked in England, the most accomplished being Pietro Torrigiani, Federico Zuccaro, Anthonis Mor, and Hans Holbein the Younger; they did not found any schools, although Mor and

Holbein left some mark on English portraiture. The less-skilled Netherlandish artists who settled in England during the Wars of Religion were to have a deeper effect on English taste.

English art of the 16th century was provincial in character. Except for the miniaturist Nicholas Hilliard, very few English-born artists rose above the level of craftsmen. Although masons, carvers, and plasterers knew and used foreign engraved ornament and reliefs of classical subjects, probably taken from Flemish engravings, were occasionally inserted in chimney pieces, the range of understanding was limited. Painting was confined almost exclusively to portraiture. Even before the establishment of Protestantism there seems to have been little demand for religious art, and there was none after it. Some wall paintings have survived, none of noteworthy quality; and the few history paintings that exist or are known through copies seem to be extensions of the tournament roll rather than monumental compositions. Very little sculpture, with the exception of tomb sculpture, was commissioned, although a few garden ornaments, with crude and timidly conceived classical figures, are recorded in drawings.

Only architecture had any real vitality, and the English passion for building country houses led to the evolution of a style in which symmetry, proportion, and the massing of parts were consciously displayed. The degree of assimilation of the classical idiom varied greatly and, for the most part, English houses present a hybrid architecture in which classical and Gothic motifs are combined. Some knowledge of Italian and French architectural treatises certainly existed among English patrons late in the century, but it is significant that no English edition of Vitruvius appeared, and the first translation of Serlio, published in 1611, was made from the Dutch. The single English treatise, John Shute's *First and Chief Groundes of Architecture* (1563), written and illustrated by an otherwise unknown painter who had visited Italy, is a naïve compilation of information drawn from Vitruvius, Philander, and Serlio, and shows a simple approach to the magic of ancient geometry, a love of legend, and pride in the lavish use of technical terms. The plates illustrate the classical orders and suitable personifications of each, which could be used as caryatids. However, since the book is now exceedingly rare, it seems probable that few copies were printed, and therefore its use must have been restricted.

Although in the last two-thirds of the 16th century English art suffered from the lack of that court patronage which was so crucial a factor in the development of the arts in France and elsewhere, the reign of Henry VIII (1509–47) fostered activities that might have led to closer links with Continental art. The King and his chief minister, Cardinal Wolsey, no doubt emulating Francis I of France and Cardinal d'Amboise, employed Italians, some of whom had already worked in France. Their chief works are the tomb of Henry VII (1512–18) in Westminster Abbey by Pietro Torrigiani and some terra-cotta decoration, executed mainly by Giovanni II da Maiano, at Wolsey's great house at Hampton Court (VI, PL. 430). It is noteworthy that even an accomplished Florentine such as Torrigiani was to some extent affected by the strength of Gothic tradition in the north, for although Henry VII's tomb itself is purely Italian the effigies with their long unbroken draperies are far more Gothic. It cannot be claimed that these Italians established a school; nevertheless, the putti on Henry VII's tomb were clumsily imitated by English craftsmen for many years and some examples of terra-cotta decoration with Italianate motifs survive in southern and eastern England, although the actual patterns seem to have come via France. Similar ornament appears in woodwork, one of the finest examples being the screen and stalls given to King's College Chapel in Cambridge (itself a royal foundation) by Henry VIII between 1533 and 1536 (PL. 108). The nationality of the creators of this work is unknown. A different kind of Renaissance influence may be seen in the stained-glass windows in the same chapel, which are possibly Flemish in design and have motifs borrowed from Dürer. There is, however, no evidence that Renaissance architecture, apart from decoration, had any impact on England during the reign of Henry VIII. The great undertaking of the last years of his reign, the palace of Nonsuch (demolished), was a fantastic turreted building; it was decorated with stucco reliefs made by artists who had worked at Fontainebleau.

Renaissance influence was also felt in portraiture, and some of Hans Holbein's finest work was done for English patrons. His life-size group of Sir Thomas More and his family (1527) is now recorded only in drawings and copies. His masterly technique is evident in the double portrait, *The Ambassadors* (1533; VII, PL. 304), although, like most of his later works, it is more rigid in design. His influence, except on the art of the portrait miniature, which he seems to have learned from Flemings in England, was rather less than might have been expected.

After the 1540s English art became increasingly provincial. Direct Italian influence was almost nonexistent; contacts with France continued, but on a diminished scale. Except in architecture, the main channels of Renaissance ideas were Flemish engravings and Flemish and Dutch refugee artists. Although the history of painting is still somewhat confused and fluctuations of style are evident, there was a progression from the comparative solidity of the figure, as shown, for instance, in the portrait of the Earl of Surrey (1546; Sussex, Parham, Hon. Clive Pearson Coll.) by the Fleming Guillaume Scrots, to the unsubstantial costume pieces of the end of the century, in which the elaborate decoration of the dress is of far more interest to both painter and patron than the structure of the body (VI, PL. 432). Such painting is a feeble form of mannerism, far weaker than mid-century cosmopolitan court portraiture, such as the portrait of Mary Tudor by Anthonis Mor (V, PL. 293). Nevertheless, these resplendent Elizabethan images were an effective form of decoration in a great hall or long gallery, and so are consistent with the English love of rich detail. Only the miniaturists Nicholas Hilliard and Isaac Oliver the Elder produced works that were lively and original. Hilliard, who knew something of French court portraiture, had a beautiful and delicate sense of line (VI, PL. 434; X, PL. 93); Oliver, a Fleming, modeled more heavily.

Much of the portraiture of the later part of the 16th and early 17th centuries was the work of mediocre Netherlandish artists. The same is true of sculpture. The tombs made by refugee sculptors are conservative in design, with recumbent effigies cut with fair competence, usually set under straight or arched canopies supported on Corinthian colonnettes. Although the architectural setting of such tomb sculpture is Renaissance, the general conception owes little to Italy, and is indeed a simple transformation of Gothic patterns. Strapwork decoration of the Flemish type is often found on tombs, and figures prominently in the ornate chimney pieces of the period, where it is often combined with grotesque herms (PL. 108). A few other tomb types — busts in roundels and figures leaning on one elbow — appeared before the end of the 16th century, and in the early 17th century were developed with greater naturalism and finer technique by Nicholas Stone (VI, PL. 432), whose training in the studio of Hendrik de Keyser helped to raise his art above the provincialism of that of his contemporaries.

Architecture presents a more interesting study. The English aristocracy and merchant classes were truly devoted to building, and the English medieval tradition of good masonry provided them with men who knew their craft and could on occasion adapt classical forms with adequate skill. Longleat House (1567–80; FIG. 151) has a fully coordinated design in which pilasters are used as accents with discretion and refinement, horizontals and verticals are carefully balanced, and, although the relation of window to wall is completely unclassical, it is nevertheless a conscious factor in the whole. The plan is traditional in that a series of rooms are ranged irregularly around one large and two small courtyards; the entrance to the great hall, its main axis parallel to the façade, is an awkward one through the screen at one end. There was in this design no sense of a symmetrical plan related to a symmetrical façade, but the plan of Wollaton Hall (1580–88; VI, PL. 430) was based on an engraving from Serlio, and the hall is at the center of the house. Its designer, Robert Smythson, manifested both here and in Hardwick Hall (1590–97; VI, FIG. 819) an ability to achieve an effect by the massing of parts that proclaims him an architect of notable talent. In other houses sky lines are broken by curved gables, an effect closely paralleled in the Low Countries and derived from the pattern book of Hans Vredeman de Vries. In all English houses, large and small, there was by the end of the century a marked tendency toward external symmetry, although this may have been a natural development rather than an importation from abroad. A number of Jacobean structures, both houses and university buildings, made use of the French motif of superimposed orders in a center piece or gateway (PL. 108); the proportion may be correct, but the detail is generally crude and its origin should be sought in Flanders rather than in France. The tendency to symmetry continued into the Jacobean period, as can be seen in the plan of Chastleton House (1603–14; FIG. 151).

In spite of its vitality, English architecture retained its conservative character, and there was no true understanding of Renaissance principles before the time of Inigo Jones (1573–1652; q.v.). This architect's work after 1616 displays not only a wide knowledge of 16th-century Italian architecture and an ability to handle classical forms but also marks the emergence of the architect as an artist and not a mere craftsman; at last English buildings were to present a unity of design totally lacking in the previous century, when patrons, masons, and a host of different craftsmen all had their share in the creation and decoration of a house. Although the hybrid style, often with a gabled sky line, was to persist far into the 17th century, Jones's buildings for the court brought a mature knowledge of Renaissance principles to England. His life coincides with the rise of the baroque on the continent, but Jones looked

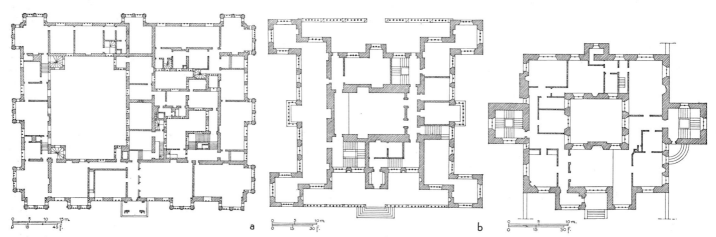

Plans of English buildings of the 16th and 17th centuries. (*a*) Longleat House (Wiltshire), 1567–80 (architects, J. Thynne, R. Smithson); (*b*) Wollaton Hall (Nottinghamshire), 1580–88 (architects J. Thorpe, R. Smithson); (*c*) Chastleton House (Oxfordshire), 1603–14 (*from J. Summerson, 1963*).

o 16th-century Italy and to antiquity for inspiration; he remains, therefore, one of the last architects of the Renaissance rather than one of the first of the baroque.

Margaret WHINNEY

SCANDINAVIA. Italian influences reached Scandinavia through Germany, Flanders, and France. In the late Middle Ages Scandinavian architecture had been closely linked with that of northern Germany through the activities of the Hanseatic League, and this connection continued into the 16th century and even later.

In Denmark there are traces of Italianate decoration that date to about the mid-16th century (e.g., the gables of the Castle from Hesselagergård, built ca. 1550), but it was not until the reign of Frederick II (1559–88) that a fuller awareness of what was happening in other parts of Europe became apparent. In Kronborg Castle in Helsingør (Elsinore), rebuilt for the king between 1575 and 1585 by two Flemish architects, Hans van Paeschen and Anthonis van Opbergen, some understanding of Renaissance principles of symmetry is evident, although the detail is naturally Flemish rather than Italian (PL. 111). This mixed style was continued into the reign of Christian IV (1588–1648) and can be seen in Rosenborg Castle (1606–17) in Copenhagen and in the Copenhagen Exchange, the design of which is based on the Arsenal at Danzig, but which has purer classical details in its doors and a spire composed of twisted dragons' tails that is almost oriental in character and is unparalleled in the art of the period.

In Sweden the Italianate style arrived a generation later, in a somewhat purer form. The door and the well in the Castle of Kalmar, designed about 1570 by Dominikus Parr (Pahr), who was probably of French origin and who came to Sweden through northern Germany, are classical but have a French rather than an Italian flavor. At the Castle of Vadstena, enlarged in the 1590s, the Italian sculptor Pietro della Rocca executed a door in pure Italian style, but a style that was outdated by three-quarters of a century.

EASTERN EUROPE. The expansion of Italian Renaissance ideas toward the east followed a somewhat different pattern. Dalmatia, which had been under Venetian domination during the entire span of the 15th and 16th centuries and which had a largely Catholic population, was naturally much affected by Italian influences. These came mainly from Venice, but, in a few cases, such as the Orsini Chapel in the Cathedral of Trogir (Traù; begun 1468), the designers were Florentine. A number of important buildings were designed by artists born in Dalmatia of Italian parentage, such as Giorgio Orsini (Giorgio da Sebenico), who was the author of the greater part of the Cathedral of Šibenik (1441–ca. 1536; FIG. 153), which is still mainly Gothic in the interior but which follows the Venetian 15th-century style on the exterior (XIII, PL. 76). He also executed Michelozzo's design for the rebuilding of the Palace of the Rectors in Dubrovnik, Yugoslavia (begun 1462).

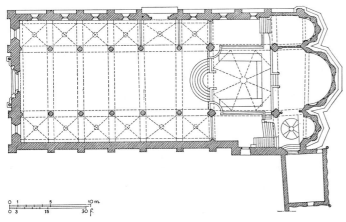

Šibenik (Yugoslavia). Cathedral, plan (from D. Frey, Der Dom von Sebenico, Vienna, 1913).

Dalmatian-born artists established reputations in Italy itself; notable among them were the various members of the Laurana family, prominent architects and sculptors of the 15th century, and Andrea Meldolla (Lo Schiavone), who played a considerable role in 16th-century Venetian painting (PL. 82).

In other parts of the Balkans the Byzantine tradition continued and was hardly affected by Italian influence until the Turkish invasion put a stop to Christian building activities.

A strong fusion of Byzantine and Italianate elements did, however, occur in Russia. During the reign of Ivan III (1462–1505) Italian architects were called to Moscow, where they built a great part of the Kremlin. Marco Ruffo and Pietro Antonio Solari (Solario) built the Granovitaya Palace (1487–91) which shows fine Italianate columns around the windows, well-understood rustication, and a symmetry of design previously quite unknown in Russia (PL. 112). Aristotele Fioravanti built the Cathedral of the Dormition (or the Assumption) in the Kremlin (1475–79; XIII, PL. 58) and created the first example of those hybrid churches, Byzantine in plan and Italianate in detail, that were to become standard in Russia until late in the 17th century. The Cathedral of the Annunciation, built in the Kremlin by Russian architects (1484–90), is a further step in the fusion of the two elements, which reaches its finest expression in the Cathedral of the Archangel Michael, designed by an Italian, Aloisio (Alevisio Novi) in 1505 (PL. 112; XIII, PL. 58). Roundheaded niches enclosing shells, used on the exterior of this building, remained popular until the Muscovite style was displaced by the Italian baroque style at the end of the 17th century.

Italian Renaissance art seems to have been known and understood in Hungary from a very early time. Masolino worked in Hungary in the 1420s for the condottiere Filippo Buondelmonti degli Scolari, but his visit does not seem to have borne fruit. King Matthias Corvinus (r. 1458–90) had an appreciation of Italian art which appears to have been unique outside the peninsula in the 15th century. Partly through his queen, Beatrice, daughter of Ferdinand I, king of Naples, Matthias was in direct contact with the great centers of artistic production in Italy and received as a present from Lorenzo de' Medici two bas-reliefs by Verrocchio representing Alexander the Great (Washington, Nat. Gall.) and Darius (known from the copy in Berlin, Staat. Mus.). The manuscripts commissioned by the king from Italian artists are of the highest quality, and from the few surviving fragments of the decoration of his palace it is clear that the sculptors whom he attracted to his court were of similar excellence. Too little of this period survives for it to be possible to say how much influence his example exercised, but the chapel built for Archbishop Tamás Bakócz in the Cathedral of Esztergom by the Florentine Andrea Ferrucci (1519), although the only work of its kind to survive, was probably not unique in its day. In certain other fields, notably in pottery, fine work in the Italian manner was produced locally; whether by Hungarian or southern artists is not clear.

The example of Matthias Corvinus was taken up in Poland, when Prince Sigismund, future king of Poland, visited his brother Vladislas, successor to Corvinus on the throne of Hungary, and saw what had been achieved in Buda. As a result of this visit, which took place shortly before 1500, some of the Italian artists working in Hungary were taken into the service of the Polish royal family. Later a more direct contact with Italy was established by the marriage of Sigismund I with Bona Sforza of Milan.

Among the earliest surviving works executed by these artists are two of primary importance, both in Kraków, which was the capital of that time. The first is the royal castle on the Wawel hill, with an exceptionally large courtyard of three stories, rebuilt by the Florentine Francesco della Lora in 1507 and finished in 1536 by another Florentine artist, Bartolommeo Berecci. The second is the Sigismund Chapel in the Cathedral, planned in 1516–17 and executed between 1519 and 1533. Berecci was in charge of a large workshop of builders and sculptors engaged on this building, and the most outstanding of his collaborators were two sculptors: Giovanni Maria Mosca of Padua and Giovanni Cini of Siena.

Although the builders and sculptors in the royal service were Italians, the painters were almost exclusively German. The most notable among them were Hans von Kulmbach (in Kraków from 1514) and Hans Dürer (in Kraków 1529–34), son of Albrecht Dürer.

Until the middle of the 16th century Renaissance art in Poland was confined mainly to the capital and was sponsored by the court, the aristocracy, and the higher clergy, while in the rest of the country late Gothic was still the dominant style. In the second half of the century the new style spread over many regions and was by then supported also by the lesser gentry and prosperous merchants. Foreign artists continued to come to Poland in great numbers and, although Italians predominated, Germans and artists from the Low Countries increased in numbers. Among the native artists who distinguished themselves working in the Renaissance style was Jan Michałowicz, a talented sculptor.

At this time the High Renaissance style gradually gave way to a style usually called mannerism, which was composed of Flemish and Italian elements. This highly ornamental manner suited Polish taste better than that of the High Renaissance, no doubt because it had certain affinities with late Gothic. Indeed, in the greater part of Poland — as in Germany — this style succeeded the Gothic style without any intervening Renaissance phase. The measure of its popularity is that it penetrated into even the most remote parts of the country, developed regional schools, and lasted well into the 17th century.

Anthony Blunt

Sources. A complete collection of references to sources may be found in Schlosser. See bibliog. for LEONARDO DA VINCI for his writings. Essential materials include: L. Ghiberti, I Commentarii (ca. 1450, ed. O. Morisani), Naples, 1947; A. Averlino (Filarete), Trattato di architettura (ca. 1461–64, ed. W. von Oettingen), Vienna, 1890; B. Facio, De viribus illustribus (ca. 1457, ed. L. Mehus), Florence, 1745; L. B. Alberti, De re aedificatoria, Florence, 1485; L. B. Alberti, Della pittura (ed. L. Mallé), Florence, 1950 (Eng. trans., J. R. Spencer, New Haven, 1956); L. B. Alberti, De statua (It. trans. by C. Bartoli), Venice, 1568; Francesco di Giorgio Martini, Trattato d'architettura civile e militare (after 1482, ed. C. Saluzzo), Turin, 1841; Piero della Francesca, De prospectiva pingendi (ed. G. Nicco Fasola), Florence, 1942; F. Colonna, Hypnerotomachia Poliphili, Venice, 1499; L. Pacioli, De divina proportione, Venice, 1509; S. Serlio, Regole generali di architettura VII libri, Venice, 1537–51 (complete ed. by G. D. Scamozzi, Venice, 1584); P. Pino, Dialogo di pittura, Venice, 1548; G. Vasari, Le Vite, Florence, 1550 (2d ed., 1568; mod. ed. by G. Milanesi); J. Barozzi da Vignola, Regole delli cinque ordini d'architettura, Venice, 1562 (2d ed., 1570); R. Borghini, Il Riposo, Florence, 1584; G. P. Lomazzo, Trattato dell'arte della pittura, Milan, 1584; A. Palladio, I quattro libri dell'architettura, Venice, 1570; V. Scamozzi, Dell'idea dell'architettura universale, Venice, 1615.

Bibliog. The following selection from the rich bibliography of the Renaissance should be completed by reference to the numerous theoretical, historical, and biographical articles relating to various aspects of the subject, particularly those mentioned below.

a. General works: J. C. Burckhardt, Der Cicerone, Basel, 1855 (Eng. trans., Mrs. A. H. Clough, London, 1908); J. C. Burckhardt, Die Kultur der Renaissance in Italien, Basel, 1860 (Eng. trans. S. G. C. Middlemore, 3d rev. ed., London, New York, 1950); J. A. Crowe and G. B. Cavalcaselle, A New History of Painting in Italy, London, 1864 (2d ed., R. Langton Douglas and G. de Nicola, 6 vols., London, 1903–14; It. trans., Storia della pittura in Italia, 11 vols., Florence, 1875–1908); J. C. Burckhardt, Geschichte der Renaissance in Italien, Leipzig, 1867; H. Thode, Franz von Assisi und die Anfänge der Kunst der Renaissance in Italien, Berlin, 1885 (4th ed., Vienna, 1934); H. Wölfflin, Renaissance und Barock, Munich, 1888; E. Müntz, Histoire de l'art pendant la Renaissance, 3 vols., Paris, 1889–95; H. Wölfflin, Die klassische Kunst, Munich, 1899 (Eng. trans., 2d ed., New York, 1953); Venturi, VI–XI, Milan, 1908–40; A. Schmarsow, Gotik in der Renaissance, Stuttgart, 1921; G. J. Hoogewerff, De entwikeling der italiaansche Renaissance, Zutphen, 1922; F. Landsberger, Die künstlerischen Probleme der Renaissance, Halle, 1922; W. von Bode, Die Kunst der Frührenaissance in Italien, Berlin, 1923; E. Panofsky, Idea, Leipzig, Berlin, 1924 (2d ed., Berlin, 1960); F. Antal, Studien zur Gotik im Quattrocento, JhbPreussKSamml, XLVI, 1925, pp. 3–32; A. Chiappelli, Arte del Rinascimento, Rome, 1926; P. Schubring, Die Kunst der Hochrenaissance in Italien, Berlin, 1926; M. Dvorák, Geschichte der italienischen Kunst im Zeitalter der Renaissance, 2 vols., Munich, 1927–29; D. Frey, Gotik und Renaissance, Augsburg, 1929; J. von Schlosser, Künstlerprobleme der Frührenaissance, 3 vols., Vienna, 1929–34; A. Haseloff, Begriff und Wesen der Renaissancekunst, Mitt. kunsthist. Inst. in Florenz, III, 1931, pp. 373–92; H. Wölfflin, Die Kunst der Renaissance: Italien und das deutsche Formgefühl, Munich, 1931 (Eng. trans., A. Muehsam and N. A. Shatan, The Sense of Form in Art, New York, 1958); A. Stokes, The Quattrocento: A Different Conception of the Italian Renaissance, London, 1932; A. Meyer-Weinschel, Renaissance und Antike, Reutlingen, 1933; T. Hetzer, Die schöpferische Vereinigung von Antike und Norden in der Hochrenaissance, Neue Jhb., XXXVIII, 1935, pp. 239–305; P. Lavallée, ed., Art italien des XVe et XVIe siècles (Ecole nat. supérieure des beaux-arts), Paris, 1935 (cat.); P. Johansen, Renaissance: Entwicklung der künstlerischen Probleme in Florenz-Rom von Donatello bis Michelangelo, Leipzig, 1936; H. Hoffmann, Hochrenaissance, Manierismus, Frühbarock, Zurich, Leipzig, 1938; M. Wackernagel, Der Lebensraum des Künstlers in der florentiner Renaissance, Leipzig, 1938; E. Panofsky, Studies in Iconology: Humanistic Theories in the Art of the Renaissance, New York, 1939 (repr. 1962); Atti del secondo Convegno nazionale di studi sul Rinascimento, Florence, 1940; M. L. Gengaro, Umanesimo e Rinascimento, Turin, 1940; W. Paatz, Italien und die künstlerischen Bewegungen der Gotik und der Renaissance, Römisches Jhb. für Kg., V, 1941, pp. 163–222; M. Salmi, Firenze, Milano e il primo Rinascimento, Milan, 1941; M. Salmi, L'arte italiana, II: L'arte gotica e l'arte del primo Rinascimento, Florence, 1942; M. Salmi, L'arte italiana, III: Dal medio Rinascimento ai tempi moderni, Florence, 1942 (4th ed., 1957); M. Salmi, Civiltà fiorentina del primo Rinascimento, Florence, 1943; P. O. Kristeller, Humanism and Scholasticism in the Italian Renaissance, Byzantion, XVII, 1944–45, pp. 346–74; G. J. Hoogewerff, Vlaamsche kunst en Italiaansche Renaissance, Amsterdam, 1947; A. von Salis, Antike und Renaissance, Erlenbach-Zurich, 1947; M. Salmi, La "Renovatio Romae" e Firenze, Rinascimento, I, 1950, pp. 5–24; L. Venturi, Arte e Rinascimento, I, 1950, pp. 115–24; W. K. Ferguson, The Interpretation of the Renaissance: Suggestions for a Synthesis, J. H. of Ideas, XI–XII, 1951, pp. 483–95; P. Francastel, Peinture et société, Lyon, 1951; G. Weise, Die spätgotische Stilströmung in der Kunst der italienischen Renaissance, Bib. d'humanisme et Renaissance, XIV, 1952, pp. 99–116; D. Frey, Kunst und Weltbild der Renaissance, Studium Generale, VI, 1953, pp. 416–23; W. Paatz, Die Kunst der Renaissance in Italien, Stuttgart, 1953; Il Rinascimento: Significato e limiti (Atti III Cong. int. sul Rinascimento), Florence, 1953; G. Weise, Renaissance und Antike, Tübingen, 1953; R. Bacchelli et al., Il Quattrocento (Libera cattedra di storia della civiltà fiorentina, 2), Florence, 1954; F. Bérence, La Renaissance italienne, Paris, 1954; A. Chastel, Fin du Moyen-âge et Renaissance: Architecture et sculpture, RArts, IV, 1954, pp. 53–60; F. Chabod et al., Il Cinquecento (Libera cattedra di storia della civiltà fiorentina, 3), Florence, 1955; E. Panofsky, Iconography and Iconology: An Introduction to the Study of Renaissance Art, Meaning in the Visual Arts, Garden City, N.Y., 1955, pp. 26–54; W. Sypher, Four Stages of Renaissance Style, New York, 1955; E. Battisti, Il concetto d'imitazione nel Cinquecento da Raffaello a Michelangelo, Comm, VII, 1956, pp. 86–104; Il mondo antico nel Rinascimento (Atti V Conv. int. di studi sul Rinascimento), Florence, 1956; F. Adama van Scheltema, Die Kunst der Renaissance, Stuttgart, 1957; H. Kauffmann, Italienische Frührenaissance, Cologne, Opladen, 1957; F. Saxl, Lectures, 2 vols., London, 1957; P. d'Ancona and M. L. Gengaro, Umanesimo e Rinascimento, 4th ed., Turin, 1958 (bibliog.); F. Chabod, Machiavelli and the Renaissance (trans. D. Moore), London, 1958; G. Francastel, Le style de Florence (Le Quattrocento), Paris, 1958; A. Del Vita, Rapporti e contrasti fra artisti nel Rinascimento, Arezzo, 1958; E. Wind, Pagan Mysteries in the Renaissance, London, 1958; A. Chastel, Art et humanisme à Florence au temps de Laurent le Magnifique, Paris, 1959; E. Battisti, Rinascimento e Barocco, Turin, 1960; E. F. Jacob, ed., Italian Renaissance Studies, New York, London, 1960; E. Panofsky, Renaissance and Renaissances in Western Art, 2 vols., Stockholm, 1960; E. Panofsky, La prospettiva come forma simbolica, Milan, 1961; E. Rosenthal, Changing Interpretations of the Renaissance in the History of Art, in T. Helton, ed., The Renaissance, Madison, Wis., 1961, pp. 53–75; E. Battisti, L'antirinascimento, Milan, 1962. See also bibliogs. for ANTIQUE REVIVAL; CLASSICISM; HUMAN FIGURE; HUMANISM; MANNERISM; MINIATURES AND ILLUMINATION; PROPORTION.

b. Architecture: (1) *General*: A. Haupt, Palastarchitektur von ober Italien und Toscana vom XIII. bis XVII. Jahrhundert, 6 vols., Berlin, 1886–1922; H. Willich and P. Zucker, Die Baukunst der Renaissance in Italien, 2 vols., Potsdam, 1914–29; J. Baum, Baukunst und dekorative Plastik der Frührenaissance in Italien, Stuttgart, 1920; G. Gromort, Histoire de l'architecture de la Renaissance en Italie, 2d ed., Paris, 1922; C. Ricci, L'architettura del Cinquecento in Italia, Turin, 1923; D. Frey, Architecture of the Renaissance from Brunelleschi to Michelangelo, The Hague, 1925; W. J. Anderson and A. Stratton, The Architecture of the Renaissance in Italy, 5th ed., New York, London, 1927; G. K. Lukomski, I maestri dell'architettura classica, Milan, 1933; E. Michalski, Das Problem des Manierismus in der italienischen Architektur, ZfKg, II, 1933, pp. 88–109; G. Giovannoni, Saggi sull'architettura del Rinascimento, 2d ed., Milan, 1935; G. Sepe, Rilievi e studi dei monumenti antichi nel Rinascimento, Naples, 1939; R. Zürcher, Stilprobleme der italienischen Baukunst des Cinquecento, Basel, 1947; R. Wittkower, Architectural Principles in the Age of Humanism, London, 1949 (3d ed., 1962); G. Chierici, Il palazzo italiano dal secolo XI al secolo XIX, 3 vols., Milan, 1952–57; A. Chastel, Travaux sur l'architecture italienne de la Renaissance, Bib. d'humanisme et Renaissance, XVII, 1955, pp. 359–75; W. Lotz, Die ovalen Kirchenräume des Cinquecento, Römisches Jhb. für Kg., VII, 1955, pp. 7–99; W. Lotz, Das Raumbild in der italienischen Architekturzeichnung der Renaissance, Mitt. kunsthist. Inst. in Florenz, VII, 1956, pp. 193–226; G. Soergel, Untersuchungen über den theoretischen Architekturentwurf von 1450–1550 in Italien, Cologne, 1958; R. Bonelli, Da Bramante a Michelangelo: Profilo dell'architettura del Cinquecento. Venice, 1960. See also bibliogs. for ALBERTI, LEON BATTISTA; ARCHITECTURE; BRAMANTE, DONATO; BRUNELLESCHI, FILIPPO; LAURANA, LUCIANO; MICHELANGELO BUONARROTI; PALLADIO, ANDREA; PERUZZI, BALDASSARE; SANGALLO, GIULIANO AND ANTONIO DA; SANMICHELI, MICHELE; TOWN PLANNING; VIGNOLA, GIACOMO DA.

(2) *Florence and Tuscany*: C. Stegmann and H. von Geymüller, Die Architektur der Renaissance in Toskana, 11 vols., Munich, 1855–1908; W. and E. Paatz, Die Kirchen von Florenz, 6 vols., Frankfurt am Main, 1940–54 (full bibliog.); C. Brandi, L'architettura fiorentina del Rinascimento, in R. Bacchelli et al., Il Quattrocento (Libera cattedra di storia della civiltà

fiorentina, 2), Florence, 1954, pp. 177–204; M. Gosebruch, Florentinische Kapitelle von Brunelleschi bis zum Tempio Malatestiano und der Eigenstil der Frührenaissance, Römisches Jhb. für Kg., VIII, 1958, pp. 63–191. (3) *Venice and the Veneto*: L. Cicognara, A. Diedo, and G. Selva, Le fabbriche e i monumenti cospicui di Venezia, 2d ed., 2 vols., Venice, 1856–57; P. Paoletti, L'architettura e la scultura del Rinascimento a Venezia, 4 vols. in 2, Venice, 1893–97; G. Berti, L'architettura e la scultura a Venezia attraverso i secoli: Il Rinascimento, Turin, 1916; E. Miozzi, Venezia nei secoli: La Città, 2 vols., Venice, 1957. See also the systematic annual bibliog. in Arte veneta, Venice, 1947 ff. (4) *Lombardy*: T. V. Paravicini, Die Renaissance Architektur der Lombardi, Dresden, 1878; P. Portaluppi, L'architettura del Rinascimento nell'ex-Ducato di Milano (1450–1500), Milan, 1914; C. Terrasse, L'architecture lombarde de la Renaissance (1450–1525), Paris, Brussels, 1926; C. Baroni, Documenti per la storia dell'architettura a Milano nel Rinascimento e nel Barocco, Florence, 1940; C. Baroni, L'architettura lombarda da Bramante al Richini, Milan, 1941. See also the systematic annual bibliog. in Arte lombarda, Milan, 1955 ff. (5) *Emilia*: G. Gozzadini, Note per studi sull'architettura civile in Bologna dal secolo XIII al XVI, Modena, 1877; F. Malaguzzi Valeri, I 'architettura a Bologna nel Rinascimento, Rocca San Casciano, 1899; L. Sighinolfi, L'architettura Bentivolesca in Bologna e il Palazzo del Podestà, Bologna, 1909. (6) *Piedmont and Liguria*: M. Labò, Studi d'architettura genovese, L'Arte, XXIV, 1921, pp. 139–51, XXV, 1922, pp. 70–75; C. Nigra, Torri, castelli e case forti del Piemonte dal 1000 al secolo XVI, Novara , 1937; V. Viale, Gotico e Rinascimento in Piemonte, Turin, 1939 (cat.); L. Mallé, Le arti figurative in Piemonte dalle origini al periodo romantico, Turin, 1962. (7) *Rome*: P. Letarouilly, Les édifices de Rome moderne, 2d ed., 3 vols., Paris, 1868–74 (repr., 4 vols., London, 1928–30); H. Strack, Baudenkmäler Roms des XV.–XIX. Jahrhunderts, Berlin, 1891; L. von Pastor, Die Stadt Rom am Ende der Renaissance, Freiburg im Breisgau, 1916; G. Giovannoni, Case del Quattrocento a Roma, Arch. e arti decorative, V, 1926, pp. 241–59; A. Proia and P. Romano, Roma nel Rinascimento, 12 vols., Rome, 1933–41; L. Crema, Roma e l'oriente nell'architettura del Rinascimento, Roma, XIV, 1936, pp. 539–57; P. Tomei, L'architettura a Roma nel Quattrocento, Rome, 1942; G. Giovannoni, Il quartiere romano del Rinascimento, Rome, 1946; G. Gasbarri, Gli sviluppi dell'Oratorio romano nel Cinquecento, S. romani, IV, 1956, pp. 539–57; T. Magnuson, Studies in Roman Quattrocento Architecture, Stockholm, 1958; M. Salmi, Roma nell'architettura del primo Rinascimento, S. romani, IX, 1961, pp. 245–52; G. Urban, Die Kirchenbaukunst des Quattrocento in Rom. Römisches Jhb. für Kg., IX–X, 1961–62, pp. 73–287. (8) *Latium, the Marches, Umbria, and Abruzzi*: P. Laspeyres, Die Kirchen der Renaissance in Mittelitalien, Berlin, Stuttgart, 1882; P. Laspeyres, Die Bauwerke der Renaissance in Umbrien, Berlin, 1883; D. Gaspari, Fortezze marchigiane e umbre del secolo XV, Foligno, 1886; I. C. Gavini, Storia dell'architettura in Abruzzo, 2 vols., Milan, Rome, 1927–28; L. Serra, L'arte nelle Marche, II: Il periodo del Rinascimento, Rome, 1934; U. Tarchi, L'arte del Rinascimento nell'Umbria e nella Sabina: Architettura civile dal principio del secolo XV a tutto il secolo XVIII, Milan, 1942; M. Zocca, Sistemazioni urbanistiche del Rinascimento nel Lazio, Palladio, VII, 1943, pp. 40–50; M. Salmi, Piero della Francesca e il Palazzo Ducale di Urbino, Florence, 1945; R. Papini, Francesco di Giorgio architetto, 3 vols., Florence, 1946; M. Salmi, Il Palazzo Ducale di Urbino e Francesco di Giorgio, S. artistici urbinati, I, 1949, pp. 9–56; P. Sanpaolesi, Aspetti dell'architettura del Quattrocento e Francesco di Giorgio, S. artistici urbinati, I, 1949, pp. 137–70; P. Rotondi, Il Palazzo Ducale di Urbino, 2 vols., Urbino, 1950–51; P. Zampetti, Il Santuario di Macereto ed altri edifizi a pianta centrale del secolo XVI, Urbino, 1957. (9) *Naples and Campania*: A. De Rinaldis, Forme tipiche dell'architettura napoletana nella prima metà del Quattrocento, BArte, N.S., IV, 1924–25, pp. 162–83; R. Pane, Architettura del Rinascimento a Napoli, Naples, 1937. (10) *Southern Italy, Sicily, and Sardinia*: G. V. Arata, L'architettura arabo-normanna e il Rinascimento in Sicilia, Milan, 1914; C. Aru, Un primo documento per la storia dell'architettura in Sardegna nel Rinascimento, Cagliari, 1931; C. Shearer, The Renaissance of Architecture in Southern Italy, Cambridge, 1935; E. Maganuco, Architettura plateresca e del tardo Cinquecento in Sicilia, Catania, 1938; A. Giuliana-Alaimo, Architetti regi in Sicilia, I, Palermo, 1952; G. Martelli, Chiese monastiche calabresi del secolo XV, Palladio, N.S., VI, 1956, pp. 41–53; G. Samonà, L'architettura in Sicilia dal secolo XIII a tutto il Rinascimento, Atti VII Cong. naz. Storia arch. (1950), Palermo, 1956, pp. 155–72; F. Meli, M. Carnelivari e l'architettura del Quattrocento e del Cinquecento in Palermo, Rome, 1958; G. Spatrisano, Architettura del Cinquecento in Palermo, Palermo, 1961.

c. Sculpture: (1) *General*: L. Cicognara, Storia della scultura dal suo risorgimento in Italia sino al secolo di Canova, 3 vols., Venice, 1813–18 (2d ed., 7 vols., Prato, 1823–25); W. von Bode, Die italienischen Bronzestatuetten der Renaissance, 2 vols., Berlin, 1906 (Eng. trans., 3 vols., London, 1908–12); J. von Schlosser, Werke der Kleinplastik in der Skulpturensammlung des Allerhochseten Kaiserhauses, I, Vienna, 1910; F. Goldschmidt and E. F. Bange, Die italienische Bronzen der Renaissance und des Barock, 2 vols., Berlin, 1914–22; L. Planiscig, Piccoli bronzi italiani del Rinascimento, Milan, 1930; G. Nicodemi, Bronzi minori del Rinascimento italiano, Milan, 1933; A. Riccoboni, Roma nell'arte: La scultura nell'evo moderno dal Quattrocento ad oggi, Rome, 1942; W. R. Valentiner, Studies of Italian Renaissance Sculpture, London, 1950; H. Landais, Les bronzes italiens de la Renaissance, Paris, 1958; J. Pope-Hennessy, Italian Renaissance Sculpture, London, 1958; J. Pope-Hennessy, Italian High Renaissance and Baroque Sculpture, 3 vols., London, 1963. See also bibliogs. for DELLA QUERCIA, JACOPO; DELLA ROBBIA, LUCA; DONATELLO; GHIBERTI, LORENZO; ITALIAN ART; MICHELANGELO BUONARROTI; POLLAIUOLO, ANTONIO AND PIERO; VERROCCHIO, ANDREA DEL.

(2) *Florence and Tuscany*: W. von Bode, Denkmäler der Renaissance-skulptur Toskanas in historischer Anordnung, 12 vols., Munich, 1892–1905; P. Schubring, Die Plastik Sienas im Quattrocento, Berlin, 1907; W. von Bode, Florentiner Bildhauer der Renaissance, 2d ed., Berlin, 1910 (Eng. trans., J. Haynes, 2d ed., New York, 1928); F. Gébelin, Scultori fiorentini del Quattrocento, Novara, 1941; G. Galassi, La scultura fiorentina del Quattrocento, Milan, 1949; E. Carli, Scultura lignea senese, Milan, 1951; E. Cecchi, La scultura fiorentina del Quattrocento, Milan, 1956. (3) *Venice and the Veneto*: P. Paoletti, L'architettura e la scultura del Rinascimento a Venezia, 4 vols., in 2, Venice, 1893–97; L. Planiscig, Randglossen zu Venedigs Bronzeplastik der Hochrenaissance, JhbKhSammlWien, XXXIV, 1917, pp. 1–24; L. Planiscig, Venetianischen Bildhauer der Renaissance, Vienna, 1921. See also the systematic annual bibliog. in Arte veneta, Venice, 1947 ff. (4) *Lombardy*: F. Malaguzzi Valeri, Leonardo da Vinci e la scultura, Bologna, 1922; H. Lehmann, Lombardische Plastik im letzten Drittel des XV. Jahrhunderts, Berlin, 1928; S. Vigezzi, La scultura lombarda dell'Antelami all'Amedeo, Milan, 1928; S. Vigezzi, La scultura lombarda nel Cinquecento, Milan, 1929; C. Baroni, Problemi della scultura manieristica lombarda, Le Arti, V, 1942–43, pp. 180–90; E. Arslan, Appunti sulla scultura lombarda del Quattrocento, Atti Conv. di studi per i rapporti scientifici e culturali italo-svizzeri, Milan, 1956, pp. 322–27. See also the systematic annual bibliog. in Arte lombarda, Milan, 1955 ff. (5) *Emilia*: F. Malaguzzi Valeri, Contributo alla storia della scultura a Bologna nel Quattrocento, RepfKw, XXII, 1899, pp. 279–99; I. B. Supino, La scultura in Bologna nel secolo XV, Bologna, 1910. (6) *Rome*: X. Barbier de Montault, Les tabernacles de la Renaissance à Rome, Arras, 1879; L. Motta-Ciaccio, Scultura romana del Rinascimento, L'Arte, IX, 1906, pp. 165–84, 345–56, 433–41; E. Steinmann, Studien zur Renaissanceskulptur in Rom, Mnh. für Kw., I, 1908, pp. 633–37, 963–74; G. Davies, Renascence: The Sculptured Tombs of the 15th Century at Rome, London, 1910; A. Paolucci, Monumenti sepolcrali della seconda metà del Quattrocento a Roma, Roma, X, 1932, pp. 525–42; A. Grisebach, Römische Porträtbüsten der Gegenreformation, Leipzig, 1936; J.-J. Gloton, Les obélisques romains de la Renaissance au Néo-Classicisme, Mél, LXXIII, 1961, pp. 437–69. (7) *Latium, the Marches, Umbria, and Abruzzi*: L. Serra, L'arte nelle Marche, II: Il periodo del Rinascimento, Rome, 1934; P. Rotondi, Sculture e bozzetti lauretani: Contributi alla scultura italiana del Cinquecento, Urbino, 1941; M. Chini, Silvestro Aquilano e l'arte in Aquila nella II metà del secolo XV, Aquila, 1954. (8) *Naples and Campania*: A. Muñoz, Studi sulla scultura napoletana del Rinascimento, BArte, III, 1909, pp. 55–73, 82–101; L. Planiscig, Ein Bildhauer am Hofe Alfons I von Neapel, JhbKhSammlWien, N.S., VIII, 1934, pp. 65–78; O. Morisani, Saggi sulla scultura napoletana del Cinquecento, Naples, 1941; O. Ferrari, Per la conoscenza della scultura del primo Quattrocento a Napoli, BArte, XXXIX, 1954, pp. 11–24. (9) *Southern Italy, Sicily, and Sardinia*: G. Di Marzo, I Gagini e la scultura in Sicilia, 2 vols., Palermo, 1880–83; C. Matranga, Scultura e pittura a Palermo dal XII al XIX secolo, Palermo, 1911; M. Accascina, Sculptores habitatores Panormi: Contributi alla conoscenza della scultura in Sicilia nella seconda metà del Quattrocento, RIASA, N.S., VIII, 1959, pp. 269–313; A. Franco, L'opera di un ignorato scultore salentino del Rinascimento, Lecce, 1960; M. Sánchez Reguira, Antonello Gagini y la escultura siciliana de los siglos XV y XVI, Goya, 42, 1961, pp. 396–401.

d. Painting: (1) *General*: L. Lanzi, Storia pittorica dell'Italia, Bassano, 1789 (and later eds.); J. A. Crowe and G. B. Cavalcaselle, A History of Painting in North Italy . . ., 2 vols., London, 1871 (2d ed., T. Borenius, 3 vols., New York, London, 1912); W. Friedländer, Die Entstehung des antiklassischen Stils in der italienischen Malerei um 1520, RepfKw, XLVI, 1925, pp. 49–86; Van Marle, X–XIX; N. Pevsner, Die italienische Malerei vom Ende der Renaissance bis zum ausgehenden Rokoko, Potsdam, 1928; C. Ricci, La pittura del Cinquecento nell'Alta Italia, Verona, 1928; B. Berenson, The Italian Painters of the Renaissance, Oxford, 1930 (2d ed., London, 1952); B. Berenson, Italian Pictures of the Renaissance, Oxford, 1932; M. Salmi, Lorenzo Ghiberti e la pittura, Scritti di storia dell'arte in onore di Lionello Venturi, I, Rome, 1956, pp. 223–37; M. Salmi, La miniatura italiana, Milan, 1956; I. Bergström, Revival of Antique Illusionistic Wall-painting in Renaissance Art, Göteborg, 1957; D. Formaggio and G. Basso, La miniatura, Novara, 1960 (Eng. trans., P. Craig, New York, 1962); F. Russoli, La pittura del Rinascimento, Milan, 1962; S. Sandström, Levels of Unreality (Figura, N.S., IV), Stockholm, 1963. See also bibliogs. for ANDREA DEL CASTAGNO; ANDREA DEL SARTO; ANGELICO; ANTONELLO DA MESSINA; BELLINI; BOTTICELLI, SANDRO; CARPACCIO, VITTORE; CORREGGIO; COSSA, FRANCESCO DEL; DOMENICO VENEZIANO; FOPPA, VINCENZO; GHIRLANDAJO, DOMENICO; GIORGIONE; ITALIAN ART; LEONARDO DA VINCI; LIPPI, FILIPPO AND FILIPPINO; LOTTO, LORENZO; MANTEGNA, ANDREA; MASACCIO; MASOLINO; MICHELANGELO BUONARROTI; PAINTING; PAOLO UCCELLO; PARMIGIANINO; PIERO DELLA FRANCESCA; RAPHAEL; ROBERTI, ERCOLE DE'; SEBASTIANO DEL PIOMBO; SIGNORELLI, LUCA; TINTORETTO; TITIAN.

(2) *Florence and Tuscany*: B. Berenson, The Florentine Painters of the Renaissance, 3d ed., New York, London, 1909; E. Jacobsen, Sodoma und das Cinquecento in Siena, Strasbourg, 1910; H. Voss, Die Malerei der Spätrenaissance in Rom und Florenz, 2 vols., Berlin, 1920; J. Alazard, Le portrait florentine de Botticelli à Bronzino, Paris, 1924; B. Berenson, Quadri senza casa: Il Quattrocento senese, Dedalo, XI, 1930–31, pp. 626–46, 735–67; B. Berenson, Quadri senza casa: Il Quattrocento fiorentino, Dedalo, XII, 1932, pp. 512–41, 665–702, 819–53; F. M. Perkins, Pitture senesi, Siena, 1934; B. Berenson, Drawings of the Florentine Painters, rec. ed., 3 vols., Chicago, 1938; G. Fiocco, La pittura toscana del Quattrocento, Novara, 1941; L. Becherucci, Manieristi toscani, Bergamo, 1944 (2d ed., 1949); K. Clark, Florentine Paintings: 15th Century, London, 1945; G. Nicco Fasola, Pontormo o del Cinquecento, Florence, 1947; J. Pope-Hennessy, Sienese Quattrocento Painting, London, 1947; R. G. Mather, Documents Mostly New Relating to Florentine Painters and Sculptors of the 15th Century, AB, XXX, 1948, pp. 20–65; C. Brandi, Quattrocentisti senesi, Milan, 1953; L. Becherucci, Momenti dell'arte fiorentina del Cinquecento, in F. Chabod et al., Il Cinquecento (Libera cattedra di storia della civiltà fiorentina, 3), Florence, 1955, pp. 159–83; C. Brandi, I cinque anni cruciali per la pittura fiorentina del Quattrocento, S. in onore di M. Marangoni,

Pisa, 1957, pp. 167–75; S. J. Freedberg, Painting of the High Renaissance in Rome and Florence, 2 vols., Cambridge, Mass., 1961 (bibliog.). (3) *Venice and the Veneto*: B. Berenson, The Venetian Painters of the Renaissance, New York, London, 1894; L. Venturi, Pittura veneziana (1300–1500), Venice, 1907; L. Testi, La storia della pittura veneziana, 2 vols., Bergamo, Venice, 1907–15; R. Longhi, Piero dei Franceschi e lo sviluppo della pittura veneziana, L'Arte, XVII, 1914, pp. 198–221, 241–56; D. von Hadeln, Venetianische Zeichnungen der Hochrenaissance, Berlin, 1925; D. von Hadeln, Venetianische Zeichnungen des Quattrocento, Berlin, 1925; D. von Hadeln, Venetianische Zeichnungen der Spätrenaissance, Berlin, 1926; S. Bettini, La pittura friulana del Rinascimento e Giovanni Antonio da Pordenone, Le Arti, I, 1938–39, pp. 464–80; L. Coletti, La crisi manieristica della pittura veneziana, Convivium, II, 1941, pp. 109–26; E. Arslan, La pittura e la scultura veronese dal secolo VIII al XVII, Milan, 1943; H. Tietze and E. Tietze-Conrat, The Drawings of the Venetian Painters in the 15th and 16th Centuries, New York, 1943; R. Pallucchini, La pittura veneziana del Cinquecento, Novara, 1944; R. Longhi, Viatico per cinque secoli di pittura veneziana, Florence, 1946; R. Longhi, Calepino veneziano, Arte veneta, I, 1947, pp. 79–90, 185–94, II, 1948, pp. 41–55; L. Coletti, Pittura veneta del Quattrocento, Novara, 1953; P. Erlanger, Venetian Painting from Bellini to Veronese (trans. M. A. Bera), London, 1953; A. Chastel, La mosaique à Venise et à Florence au XVe siècle, Arte veneta, VIII, 1954, pp. 119–30; M. Salmi, Aspetti della cultura figurativa di Padova e di Ferrara nella miniatura del primo Rinascimento, Arte veneta, VIII, 1954, pp. 131–41; G. Nicco Fasola, Il manierismo e l'arte veneziana del Cinquecento, Atti XVIII Cong. int. Storia dell'arte, Venice, 1955, pp. 291–93; T. Pignatti, Pittura veneziana del Quattrocento, Bergamo, 1957; G. Delogu, Pittura veneziana dal XIV al XVII secolo, Bergamo, 1958; C. Gould, The 16th Century Venetian School, London, 1959; T. Pignatti, Pittura veneziana del Cinquecento, Bergamo, 1959. See also the systematic annual bibliog. in Arte veneta, Venice, 1947 ff. (4) *Lombardy*: F. Malaguzzi Valeri, Pittori lombardi del Quattrocento, Milan, 1902; P. Toesca, La pittura e la miniatura nella Lombardia dai più antichi monumenti alla metà del Quattrocento, Milan, 1912; R. Longhi, Cose bresciane del Cinquecento, L'Arte, XX, 1917, pp. 99–114; C. L. Ragghianti, Studi sulla pittura lombarda del Quattrocento, CrArte, VIII, 1949, pp. 31–59, 288–300; C. Baroni and S. Samek-Ludovici, La pittura lombarda del Quattrocento, Messina, 1952; A. Bombelli, I pittori cremaschi dal 1400 ad oggi, Milan, 1957; Arte lombarda dai Visconti agli Sforza, Milan, 1959; A. Ottino della Chiesa, Pittura lombarda del Quattrocento, Bergamo, 1959. See also the systematic annual bibliog. in Arte lombarda, Milan, 1955 ff. (5) *Emilia*: G. Campori, I pittori degli Estensi nel secolo XV, Atti Deputazione di storia patria, Prov. modenesi e parmensi, 3d Ser., III, 1886, pp. 525–85; C. Grigioni, Per la storia della pittura in Cesena nel primo quarto del secolo XVI, Rass. bib., XVI, 1913, pp. 3–14; R. Buscaroli, La pittura romagnola del Quattrocento, Faenza, 1931; A. Venturi, La pittura del Quattrocento nell'Emilia, Verona, 1931; F. Filippini, Notizie di pittori fiorentini a Bologna nel Quattrocento, Florence, 1933; F. Filippini, Pittori ferraresi del Rinascimento in Bologna, Comune di Bologna, XX, 9, 1933, pp. 7–20; R. Longhi, Officina Ferrarese, Rome, 1934 (2d ed., Florence, 1956); G. Grigioni, La pittura faentina dalle origini alla metà del Cinquecento, Faenza, 1936; B. Nicolson, The Painters of Ferrara, London, 1950; G. Forghieri, La pittura a Modena dal XIV al XVIII secolo, Modena, 1953; M. Salmi, Arte e cultura artistica nella pittura del primo Rinascimento a Ferrara, Rinascimento, IX, 1958, pp. 123–39; M. Salmi, Echi della pittura nella miniatura ferrarese del Rinascimento, Comm, IX, 1958, pp. 88–98; M. Salmi, Riflessioni sulla civiltà figurativa di Ferrara nei suoi rapporti con Padova durante il primo Rinascimento, RArte, XXXIV, 1959, pp. 19–48; M. Salmi, Pittura e miniatura a Ferrara nel primo Rinascimento, Milan, 1961; M. Salmi, Schifanoia e la miniatura ferrarese, Comm, XII, 1961, pp. 38–51. (6) *Piedmont and Liguria*: S. Weber, Die Begründer der Piemonteser Malerschule im XV. und zu Beginn des XVI. Jahrhunderts, Strasbourg, 1911; A. M. Brizio, La pittura in Piemonte dall'eta romanica al Cinquecento, Turin, 1942; L. Mallé, La pittura piemontese del '400 e '500, B. Soc. piemontese di archeol. e belle arti, N.S., VI–VII, 1952–53, pp. 76–131; R. Carità, Ipotesi sul primo Cinquecento piemontese, BArte, XL, 1955, pp. 237–43; N. Gabrielli, Rappresentazioni sacre e profane nel Castello di Issogne e la pittura nella Val d'Aosta alla fine del Quattrocento, Turin, 1959; L. Mallé, Le arti figurative in Piemonte dalle origini al periodo romantico, Turin, 1962. (7) *Rome*: J. Klaczko, Rome and the Renaissance: The Pontificate of Julius II (trans. J. Dennie), London, New York, 1903; R. Lanciani, The Golden Days of the Renaissance in Rome from the Pontificate of Julius II to that of Paul III, London, Cambridge, Mass., 1906; E. Rodocanachi, La première Renaissance: Rome du temps de Jules II et de Léon X, Paris, 1912; H. Voss, Die Malerei der Spätrenaissance in Rom und Florenz, 2 vols., Berlin, 1920; E. Rodocanachi, Histoire de Rome: Une cour princière au Vatican pendant la Renaissance: Sixte IV, Innocence VIII, Alexandre VI Borgia, 1471–1503, Paris, 1925; U. Boncompagni-Ludovisi, Roma nel Rinascimento, 4 vols., Albano Laziale, 1928–29; U. Gnoli, Facciate graffite e dipinte a Roma, Il Vasari, VIII, 1936–37, pp. 89–123, IX, 1938, pp. 24–49; S. J. Freedberg, Painting of the High Renaissance in Rome and Florence, 2 vols., Cambridge, Mass., 1961 (bibliog.). (8) *Latium, the Marches, Umbria, and Abruzzi*: B. Berenson, Central Italian Painters of the Renaissance, New York, London, 1909; W. Bombe, Geschichte der Peruginer Malerei bis zu Perugino und Pintoricchio, Berlin, 1912; E. Jacobsen, Umbrische Malerei des XIV., XV., XVI. Jahrhunderts, Strasbourg, 1914; O. Fischel, Die Zeichnungen der Umbrer, Berlin, 1917; A. Bertini Calosso, Le origini della pittura del Quattrocento e miniatori nell'Umbria, Spoleto, 1925; G. Rossi, La Rinascenza dell'arte attorno a Roma, BArte, XIV, 1920, pp. 97–114, 185–232; U. Gnoli, Pittori nel Piceno, Macerata, 1925; W. Bombe, Urkunden zur Geschichte der Peruginer Malerei im 16. Jahrhundert, Leipzig, 1929; F. Fiocco, I pittori marchigiani a Padova nella prima metà del Quattrocento, Atti Reale Ist. Veneto, XCI, 2, 1931–32, pp. 1359–70; A. Colasanti, Die Malerei des XV. Jahrhunderts in den italienischen Marken, Berlin, Florence, 1932; F. Savini, Gli affreschi quattrocenteschi di S. Domenico e i miniatori teramani del Trecento e del Quattrocento, Abruzzo teramano, 3, 1932; L. Serra, L'arte nelle Marche, II: Il periodo del Rinascimento, Rome, 1934; E. Carli, Per la pittura del Quattrocento in Abruzzo, RIASA, IX, 1942, pp. 164–211; C. Gamba, Pittura umbra del Rinascimento, Novara, 1949; P. D'Ancona, Il secolo XV: Maestri toscani e umbri, Milan, 1953; U. Tarchi, L'arte del Rinascimento nell'Umbria e nella Sabina, Milan, 1954. (9) *Naples*: L. Serra, La pittura napolitana nel Rinascimento, L'Arte, VIII, 1905, pp. 340–54; W. Rolfs, Geschichte der Malerei Neapels, Leipzig, 1910; F. Nicolini, L'arte napolitana del Rinascimento, Naples, 1925; N. Catanuto, Contributi alla pittura napolitana del Rinascimento: Influsso ispano-fiammingo, Reggio Calabria, 1934; F. Bologna, Roviale spagnolo e la pittura napoletana nel Cinquecento, Naples, 1959. (10) *Southern Italy, Sicily, and Sardinia*: H. Janitschek, Zur Charakteristik der palermitanischen Malerei der Renaissance Zeit, RepfKw, I, 1876, pp. 353–74, III, 1880, pp. 144–55; G. Di Marzo, La pittura in Palermo nel Rinascimento, Palermo, 1899; E. Mauceri, La pittura in Siracusa nel secolo XV, Rass. d'arte, X, 1910, pp. 23–27; C. Matranga, Scultura e pittura a Palermo dal XII al XIX secolo, Palermo, 1911; W. Biehl, Der Meister von Castel Sardo: Ein Beitrag zur Geschichte der sardischen Malerei im 15. und 16. Jahrhundert, Mitt. kunsthist. Inst. in Florenz, II, 1912–17, pp. 118–48; E. Mauceri, Caratteri dell'arte siciliana del Rinascimento, Rass. d'arte antica e moderna, VI, 1919, pp. 210–22; C. Aru, La pittura sarda nei secoli XV e XVI, Atti X Cong. int. di Storia dell'arte, Rome, 1922, pp. 263–69; C. Aru, La pittura sarda nel Rinascimento, Cagliari, 1924; G. Libertini, Notizie intorno alla pittura del Cinquecento a Catania, Arch. storico per la Sicilia orientale, XXVII, 1931, pp. 374–89; F. Meli, Problemi di pittura siciliana nel Quattrocento, Palermo, 1931; A. Giuliana-Alaimo, Pittori sconosciuti o poco noti del Quattrocento siciliano, Palermo, 1953; S. Bottari, La cultura figurativa in Sicilia, Messina, 1954; S. Bottari, La pittura del Quattrocento in Sicilia, Messina, Florence, 1954; A. Frangipane, La Calabria e le arti del Rinascimento, Brutium, XXXVII, 1958, 1–2, pp. 11–13, 3–4, pp. 3–4; M. G. Paolini, Note sulla pittura palermitana tra la fine del Quattrocento e l'inizio del Cinquecento, BArte, XLIV, 1959, pp. 122–40; R. Salinas, Il Rinascimento in Sardegna, B. Centro di Studi per la Storia dell'Arch., XVII, 1961, pp. 137–56; C. Maltese, Arte in Sardegna dal V al XVIII secolo, Rome, 1962 (bibliog.).

e. The Renaissance outside Italy: (1) *General*: G. Glück, Die Kunst der Renaissance in Deutschland, der Niederlanden, Frankreich . . . , Berlin, 1928; O. Benesch, The Art of the Renaissance in Northern Europe, Cambridge, Mass., 1947 (bibliog.). (2) *Spain and Portugal*: M. Gómez-Moreno, Las águilas del renacimiento español, Madrid, 1941; J. M. Azcárate and F. Chueco Goitia, Ars Hispaniae, XI–XII, Madrid, 1947–62; R. dos Santos, A esculptura en Portugal, 2 vols., Lisbon, 1948–50; R. dos Santos, O estilo manuelino, Lisbon, 1952; G. Weise, Die spanischen Hallenkirchen der Spätgotik und der Renaissance, Tübingen, 1953; G. Weise, Die Plastik der Renaissance und des Frühbarock im nordlichen Spanien, I, Tübingen, 1957; J. Camón Aznar, La arquitectura y la orfebrería españolas del siglo XVI, Madrid, 1959; G. Kubler and M. Soria, Art and Architecture in Spain and Portugal and their American Dominions, 1500–1800, Harmondsworth, 1959; E. E. Rosenthal, The Cathedral of Granada: A Study in the Spanish Renaissance, Princeton, 1961. See also bibliog. for SPANISH AND PORTUGUESE ART. (3) *France*: P. Vitry, Hôtels et maisons de la Renaissance française, 3 vols., Paris, 1910; F. Gébelin, Les châteaux de la Renaissance, Paris, 1927; L. Hautecoeur, Histoire de l'architecture classique en France, I, Paris, 1943; G. Ring, A Century of French Painting, 1400–1500, London, 1949; A. Blunt, Art and Architecture in France, 1500–1700, Harmondsworth, 1953; S. Béguin, L'école de Fontainebleau: Le maniérisme à la cour de France, Paris, 1960; A. Denieul-Cormier, La France de la Renaissance, Grenoble, 1962. See also bibliogs. for DELORME, PHILIBERT; FOUQUET, JEAN; FRENCH ART; LIMBOURG; MANNERISM; MINIATURES AND ILLUMINATION. (4) *Flanders*: Friedländer; J. Lavalleye, Les quatres époques de l'art flamand, Antwerp, Paris, 1947; E. Panofsky, Early Netherlandish Painting: Its Origins and Character, 2 vols., Cambridge, Mass., 1953; M. J. Friedländer, From Van Eyck to Bruegel: Early Netherlandish Painting (trans. M. Kay), London, 1956. See also bibliogs. for BOSCH, HIERONYMUS; BRUEGEL, PIETER, THE ELDER; EYCK, HUBERT AND JAN VAN; FLEMISH AND DUTCH ART; MANNERISM; MEMLING, HANS; WEYDEN, ROGIER VAN DER. (5) *Germany*: P. Kristeller, Kupferstich und Holzschnitt in vier Jahrhunderten, 4th ed., Berlin, 1922; A. M. Hind, History of Engraving and Etching, London, 1923; C. Horst, Die Architektur der deutschen Renaissance, Berlin, 1928; Dehio, DtK, III, 1931; A. M. Hind, An Introduction to a History of Woodcut, 2 vols., Boston, London, 1935; H. Weigert, Geschichte der deutschen Kunst, Berlin, 1942; F. Winkler, Altdeutsche Tafelmalerei, 2d ed., Munich, 1944; E. Panofsky, Albrecht Dürer, 3d ed., Princeton, 1948; A. M. Hind, Processes and Schools of Engraving, 4th ed., London, 1952; E. Buchner, Das deutsche Bildnis der Spätgotik und der frühen Dürerzeit, Berlin, 1953; L. Lans, Die Malerei und Graphik der Renaissance in Deutschland, Dresden, 1958. See also bibliogs. for CRANACH, LUCAS THE ELDER; GERMAN ART; GERMANY; GRÜNEWALD, MATTHIAS; HOLBEIN; LOCHNER, STEFAN; PACHER, MICHAEL; RIEMENSCHNEIDER, TILMAN; SCHONGAUER, MARTIN; STOSS, VEIT. (6) *England*: H. A. Tipping and C. Hussey, English Homes, II, 1, III, 1–2, London, 1922–27; M. Jourdain, English Decorative Plasterwork of the Renaissance, London, 1926; A. T. Bishop, Renaissance Architecture of England, New York, London, 1938; F. Saxl and R. Wittkower, English Art and the Mediterranean, Oxford, 1948; G. Reynolds, English Portrait Miniatures, London, 1952, pp. 22–29; M. Whinney, Renaissance Architecture in England, London, 1952; E. Auerbach, Tudor Artists, London, 1954; J. Buxton, Elizabethan Taste, London, 1963; E. Mercer, English Art 1558–1625, Oxford, 1963; J. Summerson, Architecture in Britain 1530–1830, 4th ed., Harmondsworth, 1963, pp. 1–82; E. K. Waterhouse, Painting in Britain, 1530–1790, 4th ed., Harmondsworth, 1963, pp. 1–31. See also bibliog. for GREAT BRITAIN, ART OF. (7) *Czechoslovakia*: E. Šamánková, Architektura české renesance (Czech Renaissance Architecture), Prague, 1961. (8) *Hungary*: A. de Hevesy, La Bibliothèque du Roi Matthias Corvin, Paris, 1923; L. Palinkás, Il Rinascimento ungherese, Budapest, 1942. See also bibliog. for HUNGARY. (9) *Po-*

land: S. Lorentz, The Renaissance in Poland, Warsaw, 1955; Z. Dmochowski, The Architecture of Poland, London, 1956, pp. 169–244; J. Zachwatowicz, Polish Architecture up to the mid-19th Century, Warsaw, 1956; Studia renesansowe (Renaissance Studies), 2 vols., Wrocław, 1956–57. (10) *Russia*: A. Eliasberg, Russische Baukunst, Munich, 1922; D. R. Buxton, Russian Mediaeval Architecture, Cambridge, 1934; G. H. Hamilton, The Art and Architecture of Russia, Harmondsworth, 1954.

Illustrations: PLS. 1–112; 30 figs. in text.

RENI, GUIDO.

RENI, GUIDO. Italian painter of the Bolognese school (b. Bologna, Nov. 4, 1575; d. Aug. 18, 1642). Guido Reni's father was a musician and apparently was eager for his son to study music. Reni early showed an exclusive interest in art, however, and about 1584 he was apprenticed to the Fleming Denys Calvaert, who had established a teaching studio in Bologna. At about the age of twenty Reni broke with Calvaert and came under the influence of the Carraccis (q.v.). He engraved Annibale Carracci's *St. Roch Giving Alms* (Dresden, Gemäldegal.) and copied portions of Raphael's *Ecstasy of St. Cecilia* (Bologna, Pin. Naz.); he also copied the latter painting in full for S. Luigi dei Francesi in Rome. His earliest important commissions for altarpieces in churches of Bologna date from 1595 to 1598. In 1598 he won the competition for a painted memorial to celebrate Clement VIII's presence in Bologna, an achievement that focused attention on him. In December, 1599, he was elected to the Consiglio della Congregazione dei Pittori (painters' confraternity) in Bologna, and thereafter his career was divided in activity between Bologna and Rome.

He is first recorded as being in Rome in 1602, but had possibly gone there about 1600. He was probably back in Bologna by January, 1603, when a memorial service was held there for Agostino Carracci; Reni engraved the funerary decorations displayed. He is again recorded in Rome in April, 1607. In the following year Paul V commissioned him to fresco three scenes from the life of Samson for the Vatican (Sala delle Nozze Aldobrandini; largely repainted) and an additional three frescoes for another room. Reni was introduced into the papal circle by Cardinal Scipione Borghese, who took the painter into his service in 1608. He executed the frescoes in the Chapel of S. Andrea, adjacent to S. Gregorio Magno, for the Cardinal in 1608–09. In 1610 he was working for Paul V in the Cappella dell'Annunciata in the Palazzo del Quirinale, with Francesco Albani and Giovanni Lanfranco among his assistants. In 1611–12 Reni was back in Bologna, where he painted the *Samson Victorious* (Bologna, Pin. Naz.). Apparently he was suddenly recalled to Rome by Paul V early in 1612, when he received a final payment for the Quirinale frescoes. His famous *Aurora* fresco for Cardinal Borghese's Casino (VIII, PL. 218) was painted in 1613–14. Later in 1614 he returned to Bologna, where he completed the frescoes begun earlier at S. Domenico. In 1616–17 he painted his altarpiece, with the Assumption, for S. Ambrogio in Genoa, a work that was much acclaimed before it left Bologna.

Reni's contact with the Gonzaga court in Mantua began in 1617, and from then until 1621 he executed a series of Hercules subjects for the Duke of Mantua (e.g., II, PL. 194). In 1620 he worked in the Cathedral in Ravenna. He traveled to Naples in 1622 to paint in the Cathedral, but the contract was not satisfactory and he left abruptly for Rome. He was in Rome yet again in 1627 and probably also in 1632. He passed the rest of his life, fully occupied with commissions, in Bologna.

Reni's work was very famous during his lifetime and later, but was subjected to adverse criticism in the 19th century (especially through Ruskin's attacks). Modern scholarship has rejected from his *œuvre* many poor copies and derivations, and his reputation is again high; the merit of his pale late pictures (e.g., *Lucretia, Cleopatra*; Rome, Palazzo dei Conservatori, Pin. Capitolina) is particularly emphasized. Reni's own concept of art and of the artist's place was lofty. In his devotion to "ideal" beauty and his poetic reworking of many classical subjects there is perhaps some nostalgia for the Renaissance. (See also IV, PL. 430.)

BIBLIOG. C. C. Malvasia, Felsina pittrice: Vite de' pittori bolognesi, 2 vols., Bologna, 1678 (2d ed., Bologna, 1841); C. Gnudi and G. C. Cavalli, Mostra di Guido Reni, 3d ed., Bologna, 1954 (cat.); C. Gnudi and G. C. Cavalli, Guido Reni, Florence, 1955 (bibliog.).

Michael LEVEY

RENOIR, PIERRE AUGUSTE.

RENOIR, PIERRE AUGUSTE. French painter (b. Limoges, Feb. 25, 1841; d. Cagnes-sur-Mer, Dec. 3, 1919). Renoir's father, a tailor, left shortly after the birth of Auguste and settled in Paris in the Rue d'Argenteuil. The boy's elementary-school music master was Charles Gounod, who tried to direct his pupil's talents toward music. But the boy revealed such a gift for drawing that his parents apprenticed him to a porcelain factory in the Rue du Temple, where he painted plates. Attracted to painting, he made frequent visits to the Louvre. When the factory closed, Renoir worked for some time for his elder brother, an engraver of medals, for whom he decorated fans. He subsequently found employment with a purveyor of stores for missionaries, decorating wall hangings with religious subjects for chapels.

In 1857 Renoir painted his first known work, a portrait of his grandmother (Paris, Chanel Coll.), and in 1862 he decided to take up painting seriously. He enrolled at the Ecole des Beaux-Arts, in Gleyre's studio.

There he met Claude Monet, Sisley, and Bazille; he shared a small studio with Bazille in the Rue de la Condamine. With his three comrades, he often painted in the forest of Fontainebleau, where he met Narcisse Diaz, who had some influence upon the young man. At the Salon of 1864 Renoir exhibited *Esmeralda*, an academic work that he later destroyed. In spite of the intervention of Corot and Daubigny, one of his *Landscapes with Two Figures* was refused at the Salon of 1866. He was rejected again the following year. In 1868 he was successful with *Lise* (Essen, Folkwang Mus.), a work that revealed a surprising assurance. It is notable that at the age of twenty-five he was capable of painting the delicious *Mlle Romaine Lancaux* (Cleveland, Mus. of Art), the first of the many remarkable child portraits produced with such tenderness and delicate workmanship during his long career.

Renoir had acquired his sure touch as the result of a combination of events and influences. Among these was his admiration for Courbet, and even more for Manet whose pictures were then creating a scandal but were being enthusiastically acclaimed by the group of young painters at the Gleyre studio and at the Académie Suisse (Pissarro, Guillaumin, and Cézanne). Certain features of *Lise* and of *The Painter Sisley and His Wife* (1868; PL. 113) recall the style of Manet's *Déjeuner sur l'herbe* (VII, PL. 416), just as the *Bather with the Griffon* (1870; Paris, Coll. Pellerin) and the *Odalisque* (1870; PL. 113) owe something, respectively, to Courbet and Delacroix, while Renoir's landscapes, *The Park at Saint-Cloud* (1867; several versions) and *Barges on the Seine* (1869; Louvre), are related to those of Corot. Also, the fact that Renoir lived in very close association with the impressionists (see IMPRESSIONISM) should not be overlooked. Bazille (1869; PL. 113) was Renoir's constant companion until his death in 1870 in the Franco-Prussian War. Renoir often painted with Monet; he even shared with him the motif of *La Grenouillère* (1868–69), of which he was to paint three variations (Winterthur, Oskar Reinhart Coll.; Stockholm, Nationalmus.; Hamburg, Mme Esther Behrens Coll.). Renoir was to accompany Monet to Argenteuil in 1873, a memorable date in the history of impressionism.

In 1870 Renoir was called to military service at Bordeaux. He painted the portrait of his superior officer, *Captain Darras* (Dresden, Gemäldegal.), and also of *Mme Darras* (New York, A. Lewisohn Coll.). Having returned to Paris under the Commune, he accomplished an enormous amount of work — views of Paris; landscapes in the Île-de-France; the portrait of *The Henriot Family* (1871) and *The Breakfast* (1872; both, Merion, Pa., Barnes Foundation) — all bearing the imprint of the artist's strong personality. It was at this time that he discovered the richness of form bathed in light, the volumes enveloped in a fluid and transparent atmosphere, and the harmonious throb of evanescent color in which light and dark tones are blended by means of a softness of shading and an incredible lightness of touch.

Renoir was beginning to be appreciated at this period. Duret bought his pictures. He caught the interest of Durand-Ruel. Caillebotte, the first patron of the impressionists, became his friend. His financial difficulties at an end, Renoir moved from the Left Bank and rented a vast studio in Rue Saint-Georges. He sent seven canvases to the first impressionists' exhibition at Nadar's in 1874, among them *The Opera Box* (London, Courtauld Inst. Gall.), in which he equaled the treatest masters of scholarly painting, and *The Dancer* (Washington, D.C., Nat. Gall.). In this last picture, painted at the side of Claude Monet, as in the flickering and vaporous light effects of his landscapes and plein-air scenes, the tenets of impressionism are clearly evident. However, his portraits and interiors, in which the forms are more modeled and the colors more distinct, have none of these impressionist effects. Renoir was to continue painting in both these styles until 1883 (the end of his impressionist period), sometimes delicately blending his touches, sometimes using finely separated brush strokes, and occasionally employing both techniques in the same work. He came to diverge sharply from Monet and drew closer to Manet in style, as, for example, in *The Maid at the Duvals* (1875; New York, Stephen C. Clark Coll.), *The Little Girl in a Pinafore* (1875; Philadelphia, Henry P. McIlhenny Coll.), and the *Portrait of a Model* (1876; Louvre). Other portraits dating from 1876 show a more impressionist treatment: *Girl Reading* (Louvre), *Victor Choquet* (PL. 117; another portrait of the same subject is in Winterthur, Oskar Reinhart Coll.), and *Mlle Charpentier in Blue* (Costa Rica, Mme G. Tournon Coll.). Renoir had at his command such rich and varied resources that he could use all techniques with the same brilliance; here is a painter who combined the manners of Titian, Rubens, Watteau, and Manet.

About this time the impressionists met with some serious disappointments. They were systematically rejected at the Salon and were derided the first time they exhibited at Nadar's. In 1875 they suffered another setback: a sale of 70 pictures organized by Monet, Sisley, Berthe Morisot, and Renoir at the Hôtel Drouot was a commercial disaster. Renoir, however, obtained some commissions and was supported and encouraged by the Henriot family, the collector Choquet, and, later, by the Charpentiers and the Daudets. In 1876 he painted two major works: *Anna* (Moscow, Mus. of Mod. Western Art), a nude executed with dazzling skill, and the celebrated *Moulin de la Galette* (Louvre), a rustic scene animated by a large crowd grouped in bluish chiaroscuro where juxtaposed spots of shadow and sun form sharp contrasts. The same lighting effect is to be found in *The Swing* and *Torso of a Woman in the Sun* (both, Louvre). Immediately after completing these plein-air paintings, Renoir tried to reproduce the atmosphere of a theater interior in *The First Outing* (*La Première Sortie*, 1880; VII, PL. 432). The second exhibition of the impressionists, held in 1876 at Durand-Ruel's in Rue Le Peletier, was received even more badly than the first.

Fun-loving and sociable, Renoir took great pleasure in the company of the writers, artists, and political figures whom he met in the salon of Mme Charpentier, the wife of the publisher. It was from this sophisticated circle that he took a number of his models, such as the actress Jeanne Samary, of whom he did a dazzling portrait in 1877 (Paris, Théâtre Français Coll.). He sent it to the third exhibition of the impressionists in a group of 20 paintings, among which were the portraits of Mme Georges Charpentier (PL. 117), of one of her daughters, of Sisley (Chicago, Art Inst.), and of Mme Henriot (New York, David M. Levy Coll.). The following year he painted the large group portrait, *Mme Charpentier and Her Children* (PL. 114), which, although conventional, is remarkable for its details. In 1879 the Salon finally accepted the two paintings that he submitted.

Always entranced by the freshness and grace of childhood, he painted the exquisitely lively portraits of the little Cahen d'Anvers girls (1880; Paris, private coll.) and the Grimpel sisters, one with a blue ribbon and the other with a red ribbon

(1880; both, Paris, F. Javal Coll.); in the same year he also painted the daughters of the diplomat Paul Bérard (*Thérèse Bérard*, New York, private coll.; *Marthe Bérard*, São Paulo, Art Mus.), who often had the artist as a guest at his estate in Wargemont. No one before Renoir had succeeded in reproducing with such a delicate, caressing touch the bloom of a child's skin, the innocence of a glance, the soft, fluffy mass of hair, and the shimmer of material or a luminous gleam lightly catching a bodice or a skirt.

In the meantime, Renoir did not neglect landscape painting, working in Pourville, Berneval, Croissy, and Châtou, where, in 1879, he painted the *Boating Party at Châtou* (Washington, D.C., Nat. Gall.) and, in 1880, the famous *Luncheon of the Boating Party*, which he finished in 1881 (VI, PL. 77; another version is in Chicago, Art Inst.). In the latter work he demonstrated that he was capable of depicting the carefree atmosphere of a Seine-side restaurant and of individualizing each figure with a gesture and attitude that fixes it in the quivering architecture of the picture; he artfully depicts the blazing summer light filtering through the canvas awning above the heads of the lunching boaters.

During this period Renoir kept himself at a distance from the impressionists, no longer exhibiting with them but continuing to send works to the Salon. Moreover, he was frequently away from Paris. In 1881 he spent the spring in Algeria, the summer with the Bérards at Wargemont, and the autumn in Italy. He liked Venice and brought back a number of paintings he had done there. Since he did not care much for architecture, Florence and Rome interested him only for the masterpieces in their museums. Raphael, especially, aroused his enthusiasm, and he admired the frescoes in Pompeii. In Naples he painted the *Blonde Bather* (Oslo, J. P. Stang Coll.), in which he brought together the influences of Raphael and Titian. On Jan. 13, 1882, in Palermo, he "dashed off" a portrait of Wagner (Louvre) in a half-hour. On his return to France he stayed for three weeks at L'Estaque to work beside Cézanne; here Renoir painted *Rocky Crags at L'Estaque* (Boston, Mus. of Fine Arts). He caught pneumonia, and to regain his health he again visited Algeria, where several paintings were produced. He was back in Paris in May, 1882, and agreed to participate in the seventh exhibition of the impressionists. He submitted 25 pictures, including the *Luncheon of the Boating Party*. The following year he painted *By the Seashore* (XI, PL. 228). It was during this same year that he undertook a new technique in three paintings: *The Dance at Bougival* (*Le Bal à Bougival*, PL. 115), *The Dance in the Country*, and *The Dance in Town* (both, Paris, Durand-Ruel Coll.). After the blaze of impressionism evident in the beach scenes he had painted in Guernsey in September, 1883, Renoir seemed to be striking out in a new direction. It was then that what might be called his "harsh period" began.

Although he remained a close associate of Claude Monet — the two painters had traveled together to Marseilles and Genoa and, on their return, had paid a visit to Cézanne at L'Estaque — Renoir had divorced himself from the impressionists. Everything divided him from them: his curiosity about the human being, and particularly about woman; his pagan, almost animal love of life; his admiration of the classic masters of whom he felt himself to be the worthy heir, an admiration confirmed by seeing the Raphaels in the Vatican and the frescoes in Pompeii and by his reading of Cennino Cennini's *Il libro dell'arte* (late 14th cent.), which fell into his hands by chance in 1883. He was no innovator, but a very intelligent and sensual man who could strike a balance between instinct and reason, between an effervescent sensitivity and a thorough knowledge of his craft, who was just as hostile to the stanch solidity of the naturalist painters as to the impressionists' delicate dilutions.

Hence Renoir was to find, or to believe he had found, a response to his unrest in the Florentines, in the Flemish painters, and in Ingres. Merely to imitate nature, however, was not enough for Renoir. But classicism taught him that light is not an end in itself and that it must, of necessity, be subordinated to drawing and composition. So the artist who had just executed with masterly ease the *Luncheon of the Boating Party* and the *Blonde Bather* began to temper the brilliance of his palette and to paint in acid colors, reducing his drawing to the point of dryness in a series of such disappointing works as *The Umbrellas* (1883; London, Nat. Gall.) and *Afternoon of the Bérard Children at Wargemont* (1884; Berlin, Nationalgal.). Happily, he was not slow in finding himself again. Although Pompeian mannerism manifests itself in the refined delineation of the *Grandes baigneuses* (1884–87; Philadelphia, C. S. Tyson Coll.), based on the *Bathing Nymphs*, a bas-relief by François Giradon, Renoir's work reveals daring distortions.

During this period Renoir moved from one studio to another, traveled, and frequented Parisian society. At La Roche-Guyon in 1885 he received Cézanne, who, in turn, invited him to Provence in 1888 and again in 1889. Though he refused to exhibit in the eighth and last impressionist show in 1886, he rejoined the group when Durand-Ruel invited them to New York in the same year. After the *Girl with a Cow and a Ewe* (U.S.A., S. W. Sykes Coll.) and *Young Girls Playing Shuttlecock* (Minneapolis, Minn., Inst. of Arts), two mediocre paintings of 1887 that ended Renoir's "harsh period," there followed the *Child with a Cat* (Paris, Mme Ernest Rouart Coll.) and the *Little Blonde Bather* (Oslo, Nasjonalgall.), which show a freer and far more subtle treatment. The landscapes along the Seine from 1889 are still rather cold, but *Mount Sainte-Victoire* (Merion, Pa., Barnes Foundation), which also dates from 1889, is painted in quite a different style, one by no means far from Cézanne's.

At last Renoir decided to abandon a linear discipline that was hardly suited to his real nature. He gave up sharp delineation, precise brush strokes, and dryness of color for a veiled calligraphy, a diffused light, and a much less articulated form, executed with glossy, opalescent material. In this manner he painted a number of bathers and girls in summer dresses, sitting by the sea or lying in the green grass of the countryside. He took advantage of the various holidays he spent in Essoyes, where his wife was born, and in Mézy, at Berthe Morisot's home, and of his trips to Brittany and the south of France to produce some splendid landscapes. There are some intimate paintings too: *The Music Lesson* (1891; Lyons, Mus. B. A.); *Young Girl Reading* (1892; Paris, Durand-Ruel Coll.), *Berthe Morisot and Her Daughter* (1894; Paris, Mme Ernest Rouart Coll.), and *Jean Renoir Playing with Gabrielle and a Little Girl* (1898; New York, Mrs. H. H. Jonas Coll.). Jean, his second son, was born in 1894, eight years after Pierre, the eldest of Renoir's children. Gabrielle Renard, a cousin of Mme Renoir, who helped with the housework, posed for him many times, as did Jean, and, after 1901, his youngest son, Claude (known to the family as "Coco").

The death of Caillebotte, who had made Renoir the executor of his will, marked the beginning of involved arrangements to have the State accept the collection bequeathed to it by this generous and loyal friend of the impressionists. In 1895 Renoir visited the south of France, Brittany, London, and the Netherlands. This was the year of the *Calvary of Tréboul, Road from Versailles to Louveciennes* (several versions of both paintings exist), *Bay of Douarnenez* (Paris, Durand-Ruel Coll.), *Caillebotte Children* (Paris, Mme Chardeau Coll.), and the large canvas, *The Artist's Family* (Merion, Pa., Barnes Foundation), which he painted in his Montmartre studio at the Château des Brouillards and exhibited the year after at Durand-Ruel's.

This was an extraordinarily productive period for Renoir. It was interrupted in 1897, the year he created the admirable *Sleeping Bather* (PL. 118), when, at Essoyes, where he went every summer, he broke his arm in a house he was to buy shortly afterward. There, as in Berneval, and later in Cagnes-sur-Mer, he was to paint many landscapes in a rippling and fleecy style.

Unfortunately, his troubles with his health were only beginning. Stricken with rheumatoid arthritis, he sojourned repeatedly on the Côte d'Azur. In 1903, at the apex of his career, he settled in Cagnes-sur-Mer for the winter. Safe from all material cares, surrounded by friends and admirers, he nonetheless had to break many ties which were dear to him in order to concentrate his efforts on fighting a cruel illness. The cures had no effect. His crises became more acute. Gradually the arthritis took hold of all his limbs. He returned each summer

to Essoyes and to Paris, from which he was never able to tear himself away for long, enduring his sufferings with heroic optimism. Throughout this trying period his work attained a monumental scope and a carnal power reminiscent more of Rubens than of Raphael, as in *Le Lever* (1899, Merion, Pa., Barnes Foundation), *The Sicilian Girl* (1899; Oslo, J. P. Stang Coll.), the succession of bathers and sumptuous Venuses, the chubby-cheeked children built up with the ochers and vermilions of the artist's bucolic dreams — all in the pink of health!

At the second Salon d'Automne in 1904 an entire room was dedicated to Renoir. The reception was triumphal. But as the artist's fame was growing, his health was worsening. Now he suffered not only from arthritis but also from dyspepsia, a hernia, and bronchitis. However, in 1910 his health was sufficiently better to allow him to paint a series of portraits and even to visit Munich. Two years later he was stricken by a violent attack of arthritis and soon both legs were paralyzed; from then on, in order to paint, it was necessary to tie the brush to his gnarled fingers. With indomitable courage and without losing any of his mastery, he attempted in his landscapes, nudes, and still lifes to reconcile form and light within a harmonious composition, not giving them equal prominence, but letting each bring out the intensity of the other. Intoxicated by color, he still felt the need for full, dense volumes. And it is because he could only suggest weight and mass in his paintings that this cripple of seventy embarked upon a career as a sculptor. Confined to his chair, he directed the work of a young assistant whose hands he guided with the aid of a long stick. In this manner he created the *Kneeling Washerwoman* and the *Victorious Venus* (both, Cagnes-sur-Mer, Renoir Mus.), two masterpieces of modern sculpture that the artist endowed with youth and vigor at a time when he had lost both.

In the paintings of his last period Renoir had come a long way from the dry outlines of his "harsh" manner and from the sinuous brushwork and the opalescent color that characterized his work from 1890 to 1900. The paintings seem to be permeated by the influences of the Venetians and Rubens. The forms spread out, and their blurred contours go beyond the internal structure, which tends to dissolve into the mass. The dominant colors are vermilion, madder red, and brown. To these are added cobalt blue, emerald green, ocher, white, and ivory black. Among the most significant canvases in this generous, opulent manner are the *Judgment of Paris* (1908; Oslo, Halvorsen Coll.), *Gabrielle with Jewelry* (1910; Geneva, private coll.), the portraits of Mme Durand-Ruel (1911; Paris, Durand-Ruel Coll.) and Mme Durieux (1914; New York, Stephen C. Clark Coll.), and those female nudes in which Renoir accentuated the soft roundness and the ruddiness of their flesh.

While Renoir was thus celebrating the joys of life, further misfortunes befell him. His sons Pierre and Jean were mobilized in 1914. Seriously wounded at the front, Jean was sent to a hospital in Gérardmer. Mme Renoir rushed to his bedside; upon her return, on June 28, 1915, she died. Renoir's bereavement, the war, his immobility, increasing sufferings — none of these could break his will or diminish his frenzy for work, his lyrical impulses, and the agility of his spirit. The aging invalid had restored the Venus of the ancients to the Mediterranean shores, albeit in the guise of fat and heavy matrons or beneath the silks and velvets of the portraits of Mme Durieux and Mme de Galéa (Paris, Mme de Galéa Coll.), and this defiance of human capacities is a source of wonder. It is impossible not to marvel that a man so afflicted physically, already dead to himself, can yet be driven by an insatiable desire for perfection and Dionysian joy.

It is true that the last works of Renoir, charged though they are with sensual spirit, reveal signs of weakness. The bathers and odalisques of his last years are not of the same quality as the *Blonde Bather* of 1882 (Oslo, J. P. Stang Coll.), *Bather Standing in the Water* of 1888 (Cleveland, Ohio, Ralph M. Coe Coll.), or *Sleeping Bather* of 1897 (PL. 118), those superb nudes whose youthful grace, pure beauty of form, harmony of proportion, and radiant freshness of color never fail to arouse admiration. The purplish, heavily jowled mask that his models have after 1900 cannot compare with the charming faces of young girls such as *Mlle Charpentier in Blue* (1876), *Irene Cahen d'Anvers* (1880; Zurich, Coll. of the late E. Bührle), and many others. The portrait of Mme Durieux (1914) is much inferior to the portrait of another actress, Jeanne Samary (1879; Moscow, A. S. Puskhin Mus. of Fine Arts), which is radiant with all the charm the artist could communicate. Still lifes such as *Strawberries* (1908; Paris, Philippe Gangnat Coll.) and *Roses* (1917; Paris, private coll.) are minor works compared to *Femme demi-nue couchée: La Rose* (1873; Louvre) or *Bouquet in Front of a Mirror* (1876; Paris, Robert de Rothschild Coll.). In his old age Renoir overdid swollen forms, purplish tones, blurred and overladen compositions, and human types monotonously repeated in identical settings. Not a precursor of modern painting, he takes his place with the masters of all time.

Terrible afflictions had not darkened his character; he bore them without complaint for fear of distressing the people around him. Up to the end he wanted only to share his delight in painting and his love of life. In 1917 he painted the *Odalisque* (Merion, Pa., Barnes Foundation), *Bathers* (PL. 116), and *Vollard as a Torero* (New York, W. P. Chrysler, Jr., Coll.). In August, 1919, after spending a few weeks at Essoyes, he went to Paris to see his portrait of Mme Georges Charpentier (PL. 117), which the State had just purchased, hanging in the Louvre. Wheeled through the museum galleries in his invalid's chair, he stopped in front of Veronese's *Marriage at Cana*, which he was able to see *en cimaise* as he had so often wished to do. This last glimpse of him is that of an old man, already chilled by the approach of death, scanning with secret pride the works of the illustrious painters who are his peers.

On Renoir's tomb at Cagnes-sur-Mer might well have been written a saying of his that expresses his fundamental intentions: "The earth as the paradise of the gods, that is what I want to paint."

BIBLIOG. C. Mauclair, L'impressionnisme: Son histoire, son esthétique, ses maîtres, Paris, 1904 (repr. under the title Les maîtres de l'impressionnisme, Paris, 1923; Eng. trans., P. G. Konody, The French Impressionists, London, 1903); O. Mirbeau, Renoir, Paris, 1913; A. Vollard, La vie et l'œuvre de Renoir, Paris, 1918 (3d ed., 1938; Eng. trans., New York, 1925); L'amour de l'art, II, Feb. 1921 (special no.); G. Rivière, Renoir et ses amis, Paris, 1921; T. Duret, Renoir, Paris, 1924 (Eng. trans., M. Boyd, New York, 1937); A. André, Renoir, Paris, 1928; J. Meier-Graefe, Renoir, Leipzig, 1929; L. Delteil, Le peintre-graveur, XVII: Pissarro, Sisley, Renoir, Paris, 1932; L'art vivant, IX, July 1933 (special no.); C. Roger-Marx, Renoir, Paris, 1933; W. Grohmann, ThB, s.v.; A. C. Barnes and V. De Mazia, The Art of Renoir, New York, 1935; W. Pach, Queer Thing, Painting, New York, 1938; G. Bazin, Renoir, Paris, 1939; T. Duret, Histoire des peintres impressionnistes, 4th ed., Paris, 1939; L. Venturi, Les archives de l'Impressionnisme, 2 vols., Paris, 1939; J. Rewald, History of Impressionism, New York, 1946 (2d ed., 1961; bibliog.); J. Rewald, ed., Renoir: Drawings, New York, 1946; P. Haesaerts, Renoir sculpteur, Brussels, 1947 (Eng. trans., New York, 1947); C. Renoir, Souvenirs sur mon père, Paris, 1948; J. Baudot, Renoir, ses amis, ses modèles, Paris, 1949; M. Raynal, Renoir, Geneva, 1949 (Eng. trans., Cleveland, Ohio, 1950); W. Pach, Renoir, New York, 1950; M. Drucker, Renoir, Paris, 1955 (bibliog.); F. Fosca, Renoir: L'homme et son œuvre, Paris, 1961; J. Renoir, Renoir, My Father (trans. R. and D. Weaver), Boston, 1962; D. Rouart, The Unknown Degas and Renoir, New York, 1964.

Frank ELGAR

Illustrations: PLS. 113-118.

REPRODUCTIONS.

REPRODUCTIONS. The making of reproductions is one of the most significant phenomena in the history of art. The usual purpose is to produce objects corresponding in some way to the originals, in order to document them or to spread appreciation of their artistic, historical, cultural, and representational values. This wide range of functions reflects the various ways that interest in art has been expressed in different periods. For additional discussion of the nature and values of reproductions, see ART.

SUMMARY. Relationship between reproductions and originals (col. 167). Purposes of reproductions (col. 169): *Utilitarian purposes; Esthetic purposes; Educational purposes.* Techniques of reproduction (col. 174). Historical background (col. 174): *Antiquity; The modern period.*

RELATIONSHIP BETWEEN REPRODUCTIONS AND ORIGINALS. The significant relationship between a reproduction and an original is determined by the disparity between the artist's and the reproducer's intentions: the creation of a work of art as opposed to the creation of a work that is fundamentally subordinate and comparative. A difference in intention also underlies the distinction between reproductions and both forgeries and plagiarized works, which are intended as total substitutes for the originals (see FALSIFICATION AND FORGERY). It is possible, of course, that a forgery may serve as a reproduction once its falsification has been recognized or that a reproduction executed as such can be circulated as the original; modern copyright law therefore establishes norms that authorize reproductions and guard against their fraudulent use.

Reproductions form a general category to which copies, graphic renderings, photographs, and so on are subordinate. A copy, for example, is a reproduction executed in the same art form, although different materials and dimensions may be used; a copy of a sculpture must therefore be another sculpture. Even the most objectively faithful reproduction can never be an exact duplicate of its model, considering the total phenomenology of the latter; identical repetition of the creative process that generated the work is obviously impossible. Esthetic theory and critical practice held until fairly recently that the original work of art had no specific esthetic quality or inimitable objective reality simply by virtue of its being the direct product of an individual creator. This view still has some currency; there is a tendency to believe that reproductions are esthetic objects of an artistic quality essentially similar to that of the original, although of a lower order (Dufrenne, 1953).

Any thoroughgoing analysis of the relationship between original and reproduction hinges partly on the definition of "original," which varies according to the art form. In poetry only the first draft can be considered the original, and then only in a philological sense; the written text reproduced through literal transcription is merely a medium for the poetic content. Music notes written on the staff are analogous; the actual execution of a piece of music differs, however, as it cannot really be considered a reproduction and can itself be reproduced through recordings.

In the manual and visual arts the esthetic value of the work may be so closely bound up with its objective realization in a material object that only this object can be considered the original. In this field, however, other definitions should also be examined. Prototypes and art products derived from prototypes fall into this category: in architecture the design rather than its execution is, strictly speaking, the original (see DESIGNING), yet the execution may also be so considered. Similarly, if we disregard the factor of historical authenticity, any reconstruction of the kind made in restorations can achieve the artistic value of the original if the copy is executed with absolute fidelity to the design. In engraving and media requiring the use of a mold (e.g., metalwork, porcelain) the term "original" should, again, technically be applied only to the plates and molds (or rather to the models of these plates and molds). Nonetheless, all the prints or copies that the artist originally meant to produce are termed "original." It is common practice, in fact, to destroy plates and molds in order to prevent the production of additional copies that are not essentially different from the first prints.

Using the theoretical justifications for regarding certain art products derived from prototypes as originals, some specialists contend that when the original model of an industrial product is adopted as an international criterion and is conceived of as a general form or design that the machine simply produces in thousands, each object conserves intact the quality of being original. In this case the esthetic distinction between original and copy is canceled. The desire to invent forms of artistic production that eliminate the bond between the esthetic value of a work of art and its objective uniqueness, "to offer a solution to the conflict between art as quality and production as quantity," is particularly pressing in the modern era. One such solution is Jean Fautrier's attempt in 1949 to produce "originaux multiples" in painting (J. Paulhan, *Les débuts d'un art universel*, Gal. Billiet-Caputo, Paris, 1950).

Just as the concept of "original" acquires different meanings that in turn condition its relationship to "reproduction," so the latter term assumes different definitions according to the changing meanings of "original." This article will be limited to a general consideration of reproductions as both esthetically and empirically different from original works of art, whether the latter are considered such because of their specific nature or because they have been so acknowledged by history.

PURPOSES OF REPRODUCTIONS. A systematic analysis of the various reasons that have determined the making of reproductions of works of art since very remote times reveals three basic purposes: utilitarian, esthetic, and educational. From a study of these it is possible to place the phenomenon in historical perspective. Working within the frame of a historically determined civilization, the maker of reproductions inevitably shows his particular viewpoint or that of his group or period toward the original work reproduced, as well as the reasons for selecting one work rather than another or only one part of a work. Any single reproduction is therefore a historical document providing information about a particular cultural approach, critical attitude, or fashion in taste.

Utilitarian purposes. Essentially extraneous to art, utilitarian purposes behind the making of reproductions may specifically consider the esthetic quality of the original or may disregard it. An example of a work chosen primarily because of its intrinsic esthetic qualities is an illustration on a travel poster or folder; here the reproduction explicitly recalls the work of art but uses it as a means of attracting tourists. Similar examples are reproductions of famous works on coins, medals, and stamps designed to celebrate the artist's anniversary or an episode connected with the work represented. Direct reference to the esthetic quality of the art object is also displayed in travelers' sketches and photographs, picture post cards, and souvenirs. A reproduction may also serve as an ornament to embellish objects and interiors (e.g., furniture, boxes, jewelry, ceramics, porcelain), in which the practical value is prized rather than the intrinsic artistic quality of the work.

More often the reasons for reproducing a particular work have nothing whatever to do with the fact that it is art: interest is centered on subject matter, and concern for esthetic character becomes irrelevant. The most familiar examples of this class of reproduction, from antiquity on, have been the innumerable copies of religious paintings and sculptures as objects of devotion. Reproduced for the sole purpose of evoking a feeling of veneration, they manifest no particular concern for purely artistic qualities. When a certain work of art itself becomes an object of worship because of the thaumaturgic virtues attributed to the image, as in the case of the 14th-century *Madonna* by Montano d'Arezzo in the sanctuary at Montevergine near Avellino, the copyist's inevitable concern with the individuality of the painting is subordinated to nonesthetic considerations (i.e., the reproduction is not only a reproduction of the image of the Madonna but, rather, of that particular venerated image).

This category also includes reproductions based on the exemplary character of images represented in the original. When certain works become so completely identified with their subject that they can be treated as prototypes for every illustration of that subject (e.g., the Pantocrator, the Virtues, the Madonna Hodegetria, the Virgin enthroned), they are reproduced in order to hand down the meaning of certain concepts as they are expressed in particular images and to perpetuate those models that are assigned the status of prototypes. Reproductions of this type are therefore of major importance in iconography and iconology (q.v.), especially in the study of medieval art.

A great number of historical monuments and paintings have been reproduced for the sole purpose of preserving the memory of the model. These reproductions often become the expression of cultural attitudes. They may appear as a mark of prestige attending political success not only because of the circumstances giving rise to their manufacture but also because the reproductions are circulated among specific social groups. For example, numerous portraits of individuals who were famous or regarded as such in antiquity were circulated in copies during the Humanistic and neoclassical periods because

of a revived veneration for the culture of the ancient world. A more recent example may be seen in the reproductions of patriotic scenes made during the period when the concept of the nation and the sentiment of nationalism took root.

Still other reproductions that concentrate on the subject matter rather than on the esthetic aspect of their models are illustrations in books of biography, history, travel, costume, and so forth. A reproduction may also be made because of the special significance the original has acquired in the course of time, rather than because of its specific esthetic content: A certain monument has become the symbol of a city or an institution; replicas of the monument on seals, emblems, coins, medals, trademarks, and commercial advertising evoke an immediate association with the particular city or institution.

Esthetic purposes. In the Middle Ages painting and sculpture were considered *artes mechanicae*; the esthetic distinction between the original and a copy of any product of the *artes mechanicae* was blurred, even though the obvious dependence of copy on original could not be ignored. Drawing on all the skill he could command, the copyist tried to give his product the expressive potential of the original, and the spectator felt that he was deriving the same esthetic satisfaction from the copy as from the original. The production and use of copies for such purposes constitutes one of the most important aspects of the phenomenon with which we are dealing. The greatest number of examples of this occurred in antiquity, particularly in Rome, but the practice is still widespread. It documents the origin and persistence of preferences for particular works of art and is the chief concern of historians of taste. It is equally important to students of collections and museums, as is clearly revealed in the inventories of ancient collections, where the presence of numerous copies (recognized as such in most cases) is justified by the desire to possess particularly significant "exempla" of the various arts, thus creating a sort of ideal museum (see MUSEUMS AND COLLECTIONS).

During the early Middle Ages practically no reproductions were made for purely esthetic reasons. Admiration for ancient monuments, which flourished particularly in certain secular groups such as the Carolingian court and later the court of Frederick II, encouraged artists to draw inspiration from antiquities and even to imitate them in some fashion as a concomitant of the ethical and political ideals then current; but what resulted cannot strictly be called reproductions. Even the famous copies of earlier models in the codex of Cosmas Indicopleustes (copy of Cosmas Indicopleustes, *Christian Topography*, Rome, Vat. Lib., Ms. Vat. gr. 699; 11th-cent. copy, Florence, Bib. Laurenziana, Ms. Plut. 9.28), or in the Joshua Roll (Rome, Vat. Lib., Ms. Palat. gr. 431, modeled on an ancient Alexandrian prototype; II, PL. 447), or even in the treatise *De Universo* by Rabanus Maurus (Montecassino, Archivio dell'Abbazia, ms. 132), which seem to be the expression of a more explicitly nostalgic tribute to Hellenistic art than other copies, can only be explained by an interest in the iconography of the originals. The same is true of the Vercelli Cathedral frescoes reproduced in a 13th-century illuminated scroll (Vercelli, Bib. Cap.).

An interest in the purely artistic value of certain prototypes may have motivated their reproduction for decorative purposes; examples include the famous Romanesque reliefs from Sorrento (Rome, Mus. Barracco; Sorrento, Mus. Correale) derived from Eastern models, the lower part of the fresco in S. Maria di Foro Claudio, Ventaroli, representing an Islamic textile, and the friezes on the bronze doors by Barisanus of Trani (IX, PL. 508), copied from Byzantine ivories. These are obviously cases of the appropriation of a general repertory of forms, however, and do not necessarily imply an explicit reference to a definite and highly prized prototype.

In the Gothic period the drawings in Villard de Honnecourt's *Livre de portraiture* (ca. 1235) reproducing plans and details of contemporaneous buildings and ancient bronzes testify to the author's admiration for them as works of art and not merely his use of them as illustrative material. This reveals an entirely new attitude, which Vasari was later to attribute to Donatello and Brunelleschi at the time of their presumed period of study in Rome. Another proof that ancient art was highly admired in this period is seen in the intensive production of ivory and gold objects representing sculptured monuments of antiquity. During the Renaissance this resurgence of interest in the purely esthetic qualities of works of art led to a great increase in reproductions. As demand grew, the creators of the originals themselves were called upon to satisfy it, and with increasing frequency they or their pupils produced the replicas. A replica, which is autographic, is not essentially different from a copy, since it too is dependent on the original.

This demand for copies was partly responsible for the fresh impulse given to certain techniques of artistic production (e.g., the use of stucco and terra cotta) that made the process of reproduction easier. Florentine workshops produced great numbers of stucco reproductions of works by Benedetto da Maiano, Desiderio da Settignano, and Antonio Rossellino. As for terra cotta, the Della Robbia workshop itself soon specialized in the mass production of copies of its most popular models. A great increase in the fabrication of small bronze statues resulted from the fact that they readily lent themselves to the imitation and reproduction of classical originals, and they were often executed by artists with very distinctive styles. Examples are the many versions of Marsyas produced in the Pollaiuolo workshop; Bertoldo di Giovanni's *Battle Scene* (PL. 18), where certain parts of an ancient sarcophagus in the Camposanto of Pisa are reproduced; and the bronze *Sacrifice* relief by Riccio (Andrea Briosco) on the tomb of Marc'Antonio della Torre, which so faithfully imitates a marble relief depicting the sacrifice of Marcus Aurelius that it includes a figure which in the marble is part of an adjacent scene (Riccio relief, Louvre; tomb and copy of Riccio relief, Verona, S. Fermo Maggiore; original marble *Sacrifice of Marcus Aurelius*, Palazzo dei Conservatori, Rome). Then there are Pier Jacopo Alari Bonacolsi's bronze copy of the *Apollo Belvedere* (PL. 122; III, PL. 383) and *Venus felix* (Naples, Mus. di Capodimonte), as well as Guglielmo della Porta's *The Boy Hercules Strangling Snakes* (Naples, Mus. di Capodimonte), derived from an ancient copy of a Hellenistic original now in Florence (Mus. Arch.). These small Renaissance bronzes were widely reproduced in turn by further castings from studio copies (e.g., Giambologna's statues, which were often made in different sizes). There were also numerous reproductions of contemporaneous statues such as Michelangelo's *Moses* and *Pietà* (Nanni di Baccio Bigio copy, PL. 122; original, IX, PL. 526), and Bernini's bust of Pope Gregory XV.

Eventually engraving came to be considered the ideal medium for reproduction (see ENGRAVINGS AND OTHER PRINT MEDIA). Vasari called it "a very remarkable process, by means of which the world has been able to see the Bacchanalia, the battle of the sea monsters, the Deposition from the Cross, the Burial of Christ and the Resurrection, with Longinus and St. Andrew, all works of Mantegna, as well as styles of all the artists who have ever lived" (Vol. II, London, 1963, pp. 107-08). On the engraving the name of the original artist who "invenit" or "sculpsit" was often explicitly indicated — not only when the fame of the original left no doubt as to its author, but also when few people were familiar with it (as with engravings of drawings). This demonstrates that the engravings were presented as reproductions of works that the engraver had not himself created but which he admired and wanted to make available to others (IV, PL. 425, Raimondi's engraving of Raphael's *Lucretia*; IV, PL. 432). New engraving techniques were developed so that the specific qualities of an original painting could be faithfully reproduced, and a special attempt was made to render pictorial effects such as the subtle variety of tonal relationships, the precise and gradual shading of colors into a broad range of tints, and later even a certain density and mellowness of hue through the silk-screen process. All of this contributed to the general improvement in quality of reproductions, which were coming to be considered as good as or better than the originals and capable of fully satisfying the most exacting connoisseurs. Extremely significant was Vasari's praise of the copy of Raphael's portrait of Pope Leo X rendered by Andrea del Sarto for Pope Clement VII (original Raphael, Florence, Pitti Palace; copy, 1524-25, Naples, Mus.

di Capodimonte). Clement sent the copy to Federico II Gonzaga instead of the original he had promised; and, as Vasari relates, not only Federico was taken in, but Giulio Romano, the artist who had collaborated with Raphael on the original, was also fooled.

The continuous effort to capture the intrinsic esthetic quality of the original and not merely its surface led to numerous refinements of reproduction techniques. It became possible to render not only an impersonal appreciation of the original work but also the specific interpretation of the copier. The distinction between imitative and interpretive reproductions became sharper. A comparison of two etchings of the same monument or picture by different artists (e.g., Marcantonio Raimondi's copy of Raphael's *Parnassus* and the version two centuries later by Giovanni Volpato) demonstrates how differently each artist employed the available techniques in order to render his personal vision of the artistic values in the model.

The more closely the motives for reproducing works of art were linked to an appreciation of the esthetic qualities of the original, the more strikingly did the reproductions bear the imprint of their modest author's personality; reproductions began to be valued because of their own artistic quality rather then their fidelity to the model. Later, even in reproductions where mechanical processes were employed, an attempt was immediately made to produce a work that was more than a banal and lifeless facsimile of the original. This was particularly true of reproductions of architecture, sculpture, and three-dimensional objects, although it also applied to painting. In photography (q.v.), through lighting from a certain angle, use of a particular perspective, framing of a detail, or employment of one or another system of developing and printing, an attempt was made to express the photographer's personality and to bring out the esthetic qualities he had appreciated in the original (PL. 127). This resulted in the proliferation of "artistic" photographs. Even if one denies the possibility of a photograph achieving esthetic independence of its subject and serving as an independent substitute for the original (which André Malraux assumes is possible when he proposes the *musée imaginaire*), the fact remains that unless a photograph is considered in some sense an interpretation of the original — and thus esthetically independent in a sense — it cannot really serve as a means of perusing the original or of appreciating its esthetic values.

From an awareness of the unique relationship of the work of art to the copyist in the act of making a copy motivated by artistic appreciation, the growth of another phenomenon can be traced — that is, the making of reproductions in which the copyist's artistic sensitivity has reached such a high point that not only are his critical and creative faculties brought into play but what he has produced has a marked esthetic validity and originality. Copies of this sort represent a branch of reproduction that can be considered a kind of criticism. They are phenomenologically different from those which concern us here and properly belong to the area of art history proper. Examples of real excellence include Rubens's reworkings of Titian and Caravaggio (PL. 125), Delacroix's copies after Rubens, Degas's copies of Pontormo and Ingres, and Picasso's copies of Manet and Velázquez.

Topographical-view painting (*vedutismo*) has certain similarities to the above-mentioned type of reproduction. Only in its more commonplace manifestations was it narrowly illustrative. Along with a concern for scrupulous objective fidelity to the model went the expression of the author's point of view and his personal reaction to the monument or the place reproduced. Topographical-view painting, from its very beginnings in the etchings of Nicolaus Beatrizet (Beatricetto), Antonio Salamanca, Etienne Du Pérac, Willem Blaeu, and the Sadelers, as well as in the paintings of Paul Brill and Pieter Saenredam (V, PL. 307; XI, PL. 451), tended to identify itself with landscape painting (see LANDSCAPE IN ART), and the distinction between the "real" view and the "imaginary" view was purely nominal. Even if the original purpose of Piranesi (IV, PL. 438), Van Wittel (IX, PL. 18), Canaletto, Bellotto (IX, PL. 18), and the artists mentioned above was the simple depiction of monumental sites, this soon became subordinated to an interest in the intrinsic esthetic value of the work of art.

Educational purposes. Reproductions in this group are made with the specific aim of facilitating the teaching, study, and criticism of works of art. Like the reproductions in the preceding group, they are essentially motivated by an interest in the work of art as such. The making of a copy can be a means of coming to know the original; this method of teaching artists has been employed for centuries. As far back as the time of Cennino Cennini's *Libro dell'arte* (14th cent.) there has been expressed the idea that such an exercise is a useful introduction to actual artistic creation. Cennini points out that it serves both to refine the pupil's technique and to stimulate the development of his own artistic gifts. In the neoclassical period artistic creation was believed to depend on a set of formal rules; this implied that in the effort to copy ancient models the apprentice would absorb their esthetic quality.

Reproductions may also be executed to make the originals better known. Theoretically any reproduction may serve this end, regardless of its original purpose; the function is common to all. There is, however, a growing category of reproductions deliberately designed to facilitate the acquisition of a knowledge of art; reproductions are, in fact, among the most commonly employed instruments in the study of art history and criticism (e.g., PL. 124). This group includes illustrations for treatises on the history of art (PLS. 123, 126; cf. III, PLS. 93–95) and teaching materials such as photographs, color reproductions, slides and small models (q.v.), as well as plaster architectural models and casts for sculpture that render the formal values more accurately than photographs. Reconstructions of ruined monuments and unexecuted projects that re-create particular civilizations (PL. 128) are often collected in special educational exhibitions or preserved in museums such as the Musée des Monuments Français in the Palais de Chaillot, Paris.

The student may refer to reproductions to refresh his image of the original work; to examine morphological traits that have escaped him owing to inaccessibility, poor illumination, or poor state of preservation of the original; and to discover and relate similarities of form in different works and thus recognize stylistic parallels. The value of reproductions as tools of analysis and connoisseurship was recognized by Bernard Berenson. "Photographs, photographs, photographs! In our work we can never have enough of them," he declared.

Reproductions also advance the study of art history by preserving the likenesses of works destroyed or scattered, such as the Giorgione and Titian frescoes that once adorned the Fondaco dei Tedeschi (German Exchange) in Venice; these had been described and praised by art students up to about the middle of the 18th century, but they were not really known until Antonio Maria Zanetti made engravings of them in 1760. It is also possible to imagine the appearance of Michelangelo's *Battle of Cascina* and Leonardo's *Battle of Anghiari*, both lost, because copies and preliminary sketches of parts of the originals are available. An additional aid in recreating the Leonardo work is provided by the Rubens version (IX, PL. 119). It is possible to make an educated guess as to the composition of Masaccio's *Sagra del Carmine* in the cloister of S. Maria del Carmine, Florence, through those of Michelangelo's early drawings which are said to reproduce figures from that lost fresco. Examples of this kind can be multiplied endlessly. Other works have been changed or restored and can only be imagined in their original form with the aid of early copies. An example of this is Marcello Venusti's 1549 copy of Michelangelo's *Last Judgment*, which was made before Daniele da Volterra draped Michelangelo's nudes (Venusti copy, Naples, Mus. di Capodimonte).

It is chiefly because copies and reproductions are themselves documents that they are so valuable to art historians. Frequently they have transmitted themes formulated within a particular culture, thus disseminating knowledge, influencing taste, and promoting artistic movements. Even when such diffusion was due mainly to the fact that the originals were in circulation and the artists themselves traveled about (as they have in the modern period), without the help of reproductions certain works could not have become so familiar. For example, the homogeneous figural language of the International Gothic style throughout Continental Europe during the late Gothic period would have been difficult to achieve without extensive trade in commercially produced miniatures and ornaments of gold and ivory, which diffused certain styles and served as a link with the works of art that inspired them. Similarly, many offshoots of mannerism, especially the "Romanism" of northern Europe, derived their formal characteristics from Raphael, Michelangelo, and the first Italian mannerists whose works were often known at first hand but which were only really studied and analyzed later in the etchings of Raimondi, Giorgio Ghisi, Giulio Bonasone, and Gian Giacomo Caraglio.

TECHNIQUES OF REPRODUCTION. The specific purpose of a reproduction has a decisive effect on the degree to which it must correspond to the original, on the way it is executed, and on the development of the techniques invented to serve it. When reproductions are made by purely mechanical means such as the plaster cast (PL. 128), pantography, and photography, there seems to be no connection between the function and the technique employed. But even here the process is not one of totally passive duplication; the product obtained reveals in some way its purpose as well as the personality and taste of the operator.

The distinction already mentioned between "reproduction" as the general term and "copy" as the specific one is relatively unimportant as far as the intrinsic worth of the product is concerned; a drawing of a painting or sculpture may render some of its qualities far more effectively than an extremely accurate copy or even a fresh version. As has been indicated, a copy that merely mirrors the original can be distinguished from an interpretive copy only on the basis of the executor's intention and his concern with particular aspects of the model, artistic or otherwise. The same criterion can be used to distinguish between a copy that mirrors and a new version of the original; the latter, when it is not a mere exercise in virtuosity, implies a fresh reinterpretation of the values of the model so that the esthetic emotion aroused by the original becomes the impulse for a new creative act, which generates a new and original work of art.

Oreste FERRARI

HISTORICAL BACKGROUND. *Antiquity.* The basic conception of art in the ancient world was probably very different from Aristotle's authoritative postclassic definition in the *Poetics*: All art is imitation. This conception helps to explain how repetition or imitation (both voluntary and automatic) of forms, themes, or entire works of art did not imply any lowering of standards on the part of the Greek artist or impoverishment of esthetic expressiveness. Subjective or, rather, egocentric criteria that make total originality a basic principle were as alien to the ancient world as they were to the Byzantine and medieval tradition in the West. What the reverence for established and glorious traditions clearly implied was a continuous, unbroken advance in the footsteps of predecessors and masters, without upheaval or revolution. Consequently, when new ideas did appear they gushed forth spontaneously, sincerely, and irrepressibly. Artists were not hampered by the notion that in imitating, reinterpreting, or copying earlier works they were lowering themselves. The miraculously instinctive balance between discipline and freedom, so basic to Hellenic genius, was thus expressed in prodigious achievements.

Undoubtedly the destruction and decay of holy images and the need to replace them spurred the change from this attitude to one that actively encouraged the systematic production of completely accurate copies. P. Zancani Montuoro's observations on the *Madonna of the Pomegranate* in the church at Capaccio Vecchio, near Paestum, show the survival of certain fundamental aspects of the Heraion at Paestum, beginning with contemporaneous repetitions (*Heraion alla foce del Sele*, Rome, 1951–54, I, p. 17). One of the oldest and most dramatic examples of repetition for religious reasons can be found in the story of the Palladium, the statuette of Pallas believed to be of divine origin and said to exist simultaneously in Argos, Athens, Samothrace, Ilium Novum, other Hellenic cities, and Rome.

From the beginning of the Palladium story in poem cycles, mention is made of a perfect copy of a prodigious image that was indistinguishable from the original except that the latter fell from the sky and had a supernatural character. The copy was shown to the faithful while the original was jealously guarded in the temple recesses to prevent sacrilegious theft. In the intricate story of the stealing of true and false images, divine intervention and miracles come into play and bring about the recognition of the original statue. The very ambiguities of the story imply the existence of perfect duplicates, as does the frequent cropping up of Palladiums, each with its plausible story of theft by some hero such as Diomedes, Aeneas, or Damophon, and each with its claim to be the only true Palladium of divine origin.

The small bronzes, gems, coins, and especially terra-cotta statuettes that one encounters in Greek art are not so much copies and replicas as reflections of a great holy image or a famous votive work of art. These show what the individual deities looked like and indicate the most popular holy places. The production of votive terra cottas is particularly interesting because it illuminates the singular relation tha. apparently existed between original creation and copy in the ancient world. From a purely mechanical starting point such as the mold, through a process of modification, transformation, and invention, new and vital creations were achieved.

E. Langlotz (*MdI*, LXXI, 1956, pp. 149-52) maintains that in the limited number of reproductions of the Tyrannicides at our disposal it is possible to distinguish the face of Aristogeiton as rendered by Antenor (6th cent. B.C.) from the same face as rendered by Kritios. If one accepts this opinion the work by the later artists Kritios and Nesiotes (5th cent. B.C.; III, PL. 347) would be an essentially unchanged version of that of Antenor which had been carried away from Greece by the Persians. Similar problems of copies almost contemporaneous with their originals are presented by the statue of Penelope found in Persepolis, which one is obliged to assume had other archetypes in the Greco-Roman world. Although uncommon, examples of rather faithful contemporaneous copies can be seen in the small bronzes in the severe style such as the *Girl with a Dove* from Thessaly in Berlin. Casts from the modern era seem to have been the source of the various facsimiles in Rimini (Mus. Civ.), Leningrad (The Hermitage), and Modena (statuette of Apollo, Mus. Estense). There is only a very limited number of reproductions of painted vases. Some of the bowls with women's heads by Sakonides and Hermogenes can be considered facsimiles; the twin oinochoae by the Mannheim Painter in the Museo di Villa Giulia, Rome, and in the British Museum are outstanding examples of conscious and meticulous repetition.

In certain late Hellenic periods it became common to consider a copy an entirely acceptable substitute for an original creation. When Ptolemy took Bryaxis' statue of Serapis from Sinope to Alexandria he placed next to it a copy of the kore which had flanked the great sculpture originally. In the Alexandrian world the definitive indexing of great literary works in the library and the cataloguing of early art masterpieces in the museum encouraged a nostalgic contemplation of an unattainable past that gradually numbed the creative impulse. Hence copies of an official character could still be found in Pergamum and Delos as late as the Hellenistic period. In the Roman era the springs of free creativity gradually ran dry and were replaced by facile and accurate mechanical copying. The innovation introduced by the Roman epoch was not the execution of copies but rather their industrialized mass production, brought about by the enormous demand for art works to decorate public buildings, villas, and sumptuous palaces of the increasingly prosperous and resplendent empire (PL. 121).

Another factor contributing to Rome's easy abandonment of creativity was its indifference to the simple and organic form consecrated by Greek art. What interested Roman artists most were portraits and individual faces, probably because of an extreme attachment to family traditions and a need to glorify the imperial dynasties. The body simply served as a support for the head, and the secret of its disciplined harmony was

lost. Consequently a highly individualized head, perhaps depicting a subject of advanced years, was arbitrarily attached to the idealized body of a youth, generally a copy of an original Greek statue from one of the great periods (IV, PL. 313). Such was the fate of elderly emperors as well as beautiful heroes like Antinous (III, PL. 386) and Polydeuces, whose heads frequently crown the bodies of famous statues of Apollo and Dionysos.

Lucian tells of the mechanical techniques, especially plaster casts, that were commonly employed by copyists. This explains the activity of flourishing schools situated in peripheral localities such as Aphrodisias and Ephesus, where it is impossible to imagine the existence of numerous works of art that could have served as archetypes. Whether we accept G. M. A. Richter's hypothesis (1951) on the use of a "pointing machine" or assume that simpler systems were employed, the essential almost mechanical fidelity of the innumerable Roman facsimiles is beyond dispute. There is evidence that schools of copyists operated on a large scale, especially in Athens, in the Campania, in Rome, and in many cities of Asia Minor and the Greek islands. But it is difficult for us to evaluate the production of bronze statues, which were destroyed all over the ancient world so that the material could be re-used in other ways. On the basis of the numerous bronzes found in Herculaneum in the Villa of the Papyri (XI, PL. 189) and some exceptional discoveries such as the one at Piraeus it can be assumed that the production of bronzes developed in the same way as that of the marble industries.

Scholars have repeatedly questioned the value of copies as source material in the study of the history of Greek sculpture. There is no doubt, as the major specialist in the field, G. Lippold, points out (1951), that one of the most serious problems in the history of ancient art is the evaluation of copies. While copies of ancient paintings, as far as one can tell from mural frescoes and Greco-Roman mosaics, are too blurred and unclear a reflection of their models to afford a true appreciation of the originals, marble copies are a totally different matter: greater correspondence to the original was guaranteed by the very material and process employed. In the extremely rare cases where it is possible to examine and compare original and copy, as in the case of the korai of the Erechtheion and the copies of them made during the periods of Augustus (Forum of Augustus) and Hadrian (PL. 120), the copies contribute considerably to an appreciation of the appearance of the originals. Although Greco-Roman copies illuminate a very small segment of ancient art and are restricted to certain anthology pieces from the middle classic periods, the information furnished by them cannot be completely rejected without distorting the picture of the evolution of Greek art.

Enrico PARIBENI

The modern period. As previously suggested, any historical investigation of reproductions becomes a fragmentary listing of examples unless the method includes a definition of the term and an analysis of purposes. A distinction must be drawn between reproductions explicitly executed as such and reproductions made for other reasons. A true history of this subject should deal only with those reproductions made with complete awareness of the objective relationship between reproduction and original.

In the modern world this awareness became obvious beginning with the Gothic period, as has been indicated in the work of Villard de Honnecourt (ca. 1235). In the earlier Middle Ages it was much less clear. Reproductions of ancient depictions in medieval codices previously mentioned apparently were not made simply for the sake of reproducing certain intrinsically interesting objects (E. Panofsky, *Studies in Iconology*, New York, 1939). They really belong in a history of the survival and reappearance (often by means of copies) of certain formal and iconographic motifs in the Middle Ages, as well as of certain subjects represented in ancient art. As has been noted, the medieval artist made no basic distinction between originals and copies and did not consider making copies as an activity theoretically or practically different from other artistic pursuits.

Even when the reproduction of images followed a specific model more closely, as did copies of the Madonna Hodegetria or the Pantocrator, the results cannot really be considered reproductions; they were more the development of a theological idea in figural form rather than a repetition of the formal characteristics of the model regarded purely as an object.

The phenomenon took a very different form from the early Renaissance on. The idea of a work of art being "intellectual property" began to develop as a result of the new notion of creative genius (A. Hauser, *Sozialgeschichte der Kunst und Literatur*, II, Munich, 1956; Eng. ed., *The Social History of Art*, London, 1951). The maker of a copy, regardless of his purpose, became aware that his activity was reproducing and that his rights were different from the creator's as far as "intellectual property" was concerned. Proof of the enormous difference between the attitudes of the medieval craftsman and the Renaissance artist is the fact that in most reproductions of the later period, reference to the original is not only detailed but almost always explicit. In the workshops, for example, when the pupils made copies of a work by their master, often under his personal supervision, it was absolutely clear that they were doing an exercise and that their reproduction of the model in no way implied an appropriation of the teacher's "intellectual property." The same attitude is often expressed by artists' biographers, beginning with Vasari, who always regard a young artist's imitations of his master's work as altogether distinct from the young artist's creations, even when they are stylistically very similar to the master's.

It is extremely significant that the theoretical as well as pragmatic distinction between original works and reproductions became most apparent in the middle of the 15th century. This was a time of great creative fervor in societies such as the Florentine, which had achieved extremely high levels of artistic culture. A constantly growing demand for art objects stimulated the production of copies, even though this demand could be largely supplied by original works. The making of reproductions tended to take on a definite character and hence became a specialized activity, although the products had to serve a wide variety of purposes. The field became subject to the economic laws governing craft production, which were more and more sharply distinguished from genuine artistic production. Finally, with the important invention of engraving and the reintroduction of the techniques of stuccowork, stamped ceramics, and bronze smelting, the process of reproduction became industrialized. Copying gradually became a profession in itself, with the copyist specializing in certain artists' works or in certain styles. This led to the formation of particular repertories; some works were copied more than others because of esthetic appeal, prevailing taste, decorative or illustrative value, and so forth. But these reasons do not fully explain the popularity of individual pieces. There are specific explanations for the widespread reproduction of highly prized paintings such as Rogier van der Weyden's *Pietà* (Escorial, Spain), Leonardo's *Virgin of the Rocks* (IX, PLS. 120, 121), the lost *Martyrdom of St. Peter Martyr* by Titian, and Raphael's Madonnas. But unless historical factors connected with the professional specialization and commercial organization of copyists are considered, it cannot be explained why equally famous paintings such as Botticelli's *Primavera* (III, PL. 302) and Giorgione's *Tempest* (VI, PL. 186) were not reproduced until very recently.

On the threshold of the modern era, when the making of reproductions developed into a specialized large-scale activity, the process lost all trace of fortuitousness and became closely linked to the historical milieu. The copyist's effort to have his activity recognized as a separate art often engendered a sort of complacent virtuosity, as in the well-known case of Luca Giordano, who actually signed the copies he did in his youth (e.g., *The Miracle of the Lame Man*, a pastiche of various engravings by Dürer; formerly Munich, Nemeš Coll.). This attitude originated with the esthetic theories of late-16th-century eclecticism but manifested itself most clearly in the baroque period, a result of the development of a serious interest in the artistic tradition. Obviously it was bound to end in self-contradiction, since the very virtuosity of the copyist encouraged a tendency to attach esthetic value to the copy itself, raising it to the level of a creative version. The first outstanding examples occur in the 17th century with Rubens, Annibale Carracci, Giordano, and others, but the phenomenon still exists. Even when such a high level of artistry was not attained, the making of copies was not regarded as a purely imitative and routine craft; increased understanding of its character led to a greater stress on the interpretation of the esthetic qualities of the original. This emphasis also derived from the relationship between the technique of the copyist and the morphological traits of the original. Many copies made during the late Renaissance and baroque periods were characterized by this relationship, as is well illustrated by Longhi (1960) when he points out that while a noncontemporaneous copy of the "realistic" painting of Caravaggio "continues to transmit... the mental, almost moral, situation " of the original and thus brings it closer, enabling us to place it in a larger context, copies of nonrealistic paintings done with absolute formal accuracy do not necessarily communicate the artistic spirit of the original. A striking example of a noncontemporaneous copy of a "realistic" painting is the neoclassical *Flagellation* by Vincenzo Camuccini, from Caravaggio (coll. of Camuccini family).

Beginning with the middle of the 16th century a concern for richer documentation began to make itself felt. This was the result of a historiographical interest largely due to the publication of Vasari's *Lives*. The interest was encouraged by improvements in engraving techniques that made large-scale manufacture of marketable reproductions feasible. There were also, of course, some interpretive versions of originals (cf. E. Panofsky, *Meaning in the Visual Arts*, New York, 1955, for observations on the interpretation of Gothic art in the art of the late Renaissance). Very often the concern for documentation grew out of the pursuit of other aims, such as a desire to promote the cult of ancient civilizations that characterized the methodical collection of engravings of Roman statues and monuments by Philippe Thomassin, Antoine Lafréry (X, PL. 158), Francesco Villamena (PL. 305), Giacomo Lauro, and the Sadeler family.

The belief that primitive painting and sculpture were particularly edifying examples of religious art encouraged their diffusion for pietistic purposes with Counter Reformation overtones (e.g., pen-and-wash copies by Francesco Cavazzoni of Madonna figures in Bologna churches, 1608; now Bologna, Bib. Com. dell'Archiginnasio; see Previtali, 1960). But in response to a continually increasing interest in historical accuracy, particularly felt in the 18th century, attempts were made to provide reliable critical documentation, as shown by Luigi Crespi's collection (recorded by Giovanni Gaetano Bottari) of copies of altarpieces in the Bolognese churches (Previtali, 1960) and by illustrations prompted by excavations, restorations, and the first real monographs on art works. Along with developments in historiography and an expanding cultural interest in art there was an increase in the systematic execution of reproductions. That typically 18th-century Enlightenment phenomenon, the young aristocrat's educational grand tour of Europe, also played a role in the publication of collections such as those of Giuseppe Vasi, Richard Saint-Non, Giovanni Francesco Venturini, and Piranesi.

In the 19th century the conception of a copy as an accurate but lifeless transcription of its original gradually lost its hold. By the end of the century the execution of reproductions became an organized industry providing a wide range of illustrative material. It was then that the first specialized commercial photographic enterprises (Bulloz, O. Böhm, Alinari, Anderson, etc.) appeared, as did the first archives of reproductions, far more scientifically organized than similar undertakings of the romantic period (e.g., Musée des Monuments Français, Paris) and intended to provide authoritative centers of reliable documentation. Particularly since World War II, the most important international cultural organizations, with UNESCO in the lead, have shown their interest in these archives by supporting them.

Oreste FERRARI

BIBLIOG. *The esthetic problem of the relation between reproductions and original works of art*: B. Croce, La poesia, 3d ed., Bari, 1943, pp. 186, 349; C. Brandi, Carmine o della pittura, Florence, 1947, pp. 62–70; G. Morpurgo-Tagliabue, Il concetto dello stile, Milan, 1951; A. Malraux, Le musée imaginaire de la sculpture mondiale, Paris, 1952; M. Dufrenne, Phénoménologie de l'expérience esthétique, I, Paris, 1953, pp. 72–80; E. Gilson, Painting and Reality, New York, 1957, pp. 64–73.

The philological problem of the same relation: M. Prunetti, Avvertimenti per distinguere i quadri originali dalle copie, Florence, 1822; M. J. Friedländer, Der Kunstkenner, Berlin, 1919; E. Wind, Zur Systematik der künstlerischen Probleme, Z. für Ästhetik und allg. Kw., XVIII, 1925, pp. 438–86; M. J. Friedländer, On Art and Connoisseurship (trans. T. Borenius), London, Boston, 1942; C. Kennedy, The Selection of Copy for Illustrations, AB, XLIII, 1961, pp. 47–51.

Historical aspects: J. von Schlosser, Zur Kenntnis der künstlerischen Überlieferung im späten Mittelalter, JhbKhSammlWien, XXIII, 1902, pp. 279–338; E. Panofsky and F. Saxl, Classical Mythology in Mediaeval Art, Met. Mus. S., IV, 1932–33, pp. 228–80; J. Adhémar, L'estampe et la trasmission des formes maniéristes, in Le triomphe du Maniérisme, Amsterdam, 1955 (cat.), pp. 34–36; K. E. Maison, Copies and Interpretations in Painting, Apollo, LXVIII, 1958, pp. 99–103; W. Züchner, Über die Abbildung (Wpr. 115), Berlin, 1959; R. Longhi, Un originale del Caravaggio a Rouen e il problema delle copie caravaggesche, Paragone, XI, 121, 1960, pp. 23–36; K. E. Maison, Themes and Variations, London, 1960; G. Previtali, Le prime interpretazioni figurate dei "primitivi," Paragone, XI, 121, 1960, pp. 15–23.

Antiquity: *a. General*: A. Furtwängler, Über Statuenkopien im Alterthum, AbhAkMünchen, XX, 1896–97, pp. 525–88; G. Lippold, Kopien und Umbildungen griechischer Statuen, Munich, 1923; G. Becatti, Attikà: Saggio sulla scultura attica dell'Ellenismo, RIASA, VII, 1940, pp. 7–116; C. M. Olmstead, A Greek Lady from Persepolis, AJA, LIV, 1950, pp. 10–18; G. Lippold, Antike Gemäldekopien, AbhAkMünchen, N.S., XXXIII, 1951; G. M. A. Richter, Three Critical Periods in Greek Sculpture, Oxford, 1951; G. M. A. Richter, Ancient Italy, Ann Arbor, Mich., 1955, pp. 34–88. *b. Copies of vases*: E. von Merklin, Antiken des R. Museo Artistico Industriale in Rom, RM, XXXVIII–XXXIX, 1923–24, pp. 71–137. *c. The Korai of the Erechtheum*: S. Aurigemma, Lavori nel canopo di Villa Adriana, BArte, XXXIX, 1954, pp. 327–41; G. Q. Giglioli, Le copie romane delle "cariatidi" dell'Eretteo nel "Porticus" del foro di Augusto, RM, LXII, 1955, pp. 155–59.

*   *

Illustrations: PLS. 119–128.

RESTORATION AND CONSERVATION.

As an activity dealing with extending the life of a work of art and restoring its appearance, restoration and conservation represent a fundamental aspect of culture and of historico-artistic studies. It has always existed as a practice and technique of the craftsman and artist (see ART; PAINTING; TECHNIQUES). Differences of opinion have existed regarding the esthetic and historical requirements dictating alterations, additions, removals, and changes on architectural monuments and works of art. In modern times, with the development of criticism and scientific techniques, conservation and restoration have taken on new dimensions. Specialized institutes and museum laboratories are beginning to cope successfully with preventing the harm caused by destructive agents. Greater awareness on an international level is also contributing to the salvaging of many monuments of man's cultural heritage (see PRESERVATION OF ART WORKS). The following article discusses the historical evolution of the concept of restoration and conservation as well as the restorative and conservational techniques that have been applied to the various categories of art works according to well-articulated principles.

SUMMARY. Concept of restoration (col. 179). General problems (col. 180): *The material of the work of art; The problem of lacunae; Restoration dependent on historical requirements: Restoration dependent on esthetic requirements.* Painting on movable supports (col. 184): *Restoration of the supports; Cleaning; Reintegration.* Other techniques (col. 187): *Mural painting; Sculpture; Metals; Wood; Ancient ceramics; Mosaics.* Principles of architectural and urban restoration and conservation (col. 194). Conservation of architectural monuments (col. 197). Restoration institutes and laboratories.

CONCEPT OF RESTORATION. By restoration is generally meant any operation that aims to put back into effective order a product of human activity. It is possible to have a restoration related to industrial articles and one related to works of art. In the former case, restoration amounts to repairing an object or to restoring it to its original state, with an emphasis on its proper functioning. In the latter case there is a qualitative difference, and functional restoration (as in architecture) is secondary or concomitant. The primary concern is the work of art as such, and restoration depends upon the recognition or nonrecognition of the work of art (see ESTHETICS). Therefore, the quality and form of the restorative process is closely connected with this recognition. A work of art, although differing from all other human products, always maintains its characteristic of being produced by man. Both as a work of art and a man-made product it presents two requirements: the esthetic requirement (its artistic merit) and the historical one, which reflects its emergence as a human product at a certain time and in a certain place. In addition, the fact of its being acknowledged in a certain time and place confers upon the work of art a second historical aspect that is gradually transmitted through time.

At this point, restoration of an art work may be defined as the methodological recognition of a work of art in its physical form and in its esthetic-historical duality, with a view to its transmission to the future.

From this definition it follows that restoration, like the more general process of preservation (which is preventive restoration), concerns mainly the material form in which the image is manifested. However, the physical means on which the transmission of the image depends are not separated from the image but are coexistent with it. Despite this coexistence of material and image, some of the physical means are subservient and act as a support — canvas, panel, or wall for a painting and foundations for architectural structures.

If, then, the condition of a work of art is such that its preservation requires the sacrifice or the substitution of certain parts of it, the operation should be carried out according to esthetic requirements. However, the historical requirements must also be taken into consideration, not only those arising from the actual creation of the work but also those stemming from its subsequent history, beginning at the time of its completion and extending to the time and place in which it was consciously recognized.

The balancing of these requirements, which are often opposed, brings about the second principle of restoration: it must aim to reestablish the potential unity of a work without committing artistic forgery or historical falsification and without obliterating every trace of the work's existence in time.

GENERAL PROBLEMS. *The material of the work of art.* If only the material of the work of art is restored, this material must be considered as serving the manifestation of the image. The material, therefore, illustrates a division between appearance and structure. An example is the case of a painting on a panel which is so worm-eaten that it no longer gives sufficient support. The paint is the apparent material, and the panel is the structural material. But the distinction may be much smaller, since the picture was painted on a panel and acquired particular characteristics that could disappear if transferred to another support. Therefore, the distinction between appearance and structure becomes very subtle and a rigid separation cannot be maintained.

Another example is a building razed by an earthquake; because of the many surviving elements and because of authentic evidence it lends itself to a facsimile reconstruction. In this case the appearance does not depend on the surface of the stones but on the stones themselves. The interior walls may be changed in order to guard against future seismic accidents as well as the interior arrangement of the columns (if there are any), or the beams. Such was the case in the reconstruction of the Church of S. Pietro in Alba Fucense. The opposite was true in the reconstruction of Temple E in Selinunte; here the drums of the columns lay on the ground for more than a thousand years and deteriorated differently than if they had remained in place. It became impossible to give the surviving parts of the monument their original appearance. In fact, the parts of the drums lying on the ground were corroded and of a different color than the parts exposed to the air and sun, and they could not be used to reconstruct a column's monolithic unity, even though the structure seems to appear like the ancient one (VII, PL. 53).

In fact, even the structure had to be drastically altered with reinforced concrete, so that neither the esthetic nor the historical requirements were satisfactorily met. In this case it might have been better to preserve the remains of the temple in the state in which it had been transformed by time.

Many destructive and lamentable errors have been committed because the material of a work was not investigated in the dual terms of appearance and structure. It is an illusion to regard as identical the uncut marble of a given quarry and marble from the same quarry that has been made into statues. While both marbles have an identical chemical composition, the marble of the statue has undergone a radical transformation by becoming the medium of an image. Between its existence as marble and its existence as an image an irreparable break has occurred. The fact that the material may be the same is not enough to authorize the completion of an unfinished or damaged monument, since it would become a historical as well as an esthetic falsification. On this basis the reconstruction of the Stoa of Attalus in Athens with the same marble as was used in the original was perhaps an error; the 19th-century reconstruction in brick of several spans of the Colosseum (PL. 290), which was intended to guarantee the stability of the original surviving parts, gives proof of a straightforward intervention that is faithful to the historical requirements involved, although esthetically the difference in color is too marked. However, Valadier's solution for the missing parts of the Arch of Titus (PL. 131) may be considered perfect since the added sections harmonize in color with the surviving parts despite the use of different materials (e.g., travertine instead of marble).

The material of a work of art is never entirely uniform, even if the work is of a homogeneous material (wood, marble, bronze); it must be investigated as to structure and appearance before a restorative operation can be projected and executed.

The problem of lacunae. In a work of art a lacuna (gap) is an interruption in the representational context, similar to that in a text which has not been completely transcribed. The lacuna in an art work differs from that in a text in that it assumes an importance of its own as a negative element. The gap has a shape and may also have a color if it constitutes an absence of material (i.e., a detachment of the pictorial layer or of the marble covering on an architectural structure). The lacuna, with its shape and color, tends to intrude and forces the remaining parts of the image to recede into the background. In order to prevent the distortion and depreciation of the image a dull, neutral shade was used to prevent the lacuna from emerging into the foreground and to mute it. This was an honest but empirical and inadequate expedient as a remedy. It was easy to object that there is no neutral shade and that any supposedly neutral tone influences the color arrangement of a painting in which each isolated color has value only in relation to the whole scheme. A solution had to consider the spatial context of the painting.

It was, therefore, not a question of eliminating the lacuna or of shading its edges (the worst possible solution and one that blurs the entire surviving painting), but it was necessary to choose a shade in relation to the entire color scheme that made the lacuna recede. While there is no hope of eliminating a gap, it can be prevented from intruding and projecting forward. Honesty and suitability in the choice of a method often suggest simple and adequate solutions such as the exposure of the original canvas or wood surface in a painting, of the wall or rough plaster in a fresco, and of the warp of a tapestry or carpet.

Restoration dependent on historical requirements. While restoration depends on the harmonization of historical and esthetic requirements, special problems deriving from both factors must be considered so as to determine how far this balance can be effected without becoming arbitrary or abusive. For historical purposes the first stage to be considered is the ruin, an extreme case where the monument itself is reduced almost to a mere trace of its original material. Its condition is not confined to its present form but refers also to the past and to the future, for which the object must be saved as evidence of human activity. A ruin, therefore, is anything that documents human history but that has become different and almost unrecognizable compared to its original state. According to this definition even natural objects can sometimes be classified as ruins. For example, the dry trunk of Torquato Tasso's oak near the church of S. Onofrio in Rome should be preserved for the future as though it were a wooden sculpture.

Restoration as applied to a ruin can obviously consist only of strengthening and preserving the material. This is not always obvious when a work of art has not quite deteriorated to a ruined stage or when, on the contrary, its surviving elements redeem it from being termed a ruin and permit restoration beyond that of pure preservation. It is debatable, for example, whether the church of S. Chiara in Naples should not have been preserved as a ruin instead of being given a shape it never had. This church in its marvelous 18th-century re-creation (not restoration) was completely destroyed in World War II bombardments and rebuilt as an Angevin Gothic church with serious and irreparable mutilations. If the church had been preserved as a ruin it would certainly have remained an evocative and infinitely richer monument than that created by the additions.

The crucial problems in terms of the historical requirement are, first, the preservation or removal of additions and, secondly, the preservation or removal of later reconstructions. While in most instances a ruin has only historical value, in the case of additions and reconstructions the problem is also an esthetic one. From the historical point of view, the additions and interpolations to an art work are further evidence of human activity and of progress in time. In this sense the addition does not differ essentially from the original core and has the same right to preservation. On the other hand, a removal destroys a document, leads to the obliteration of a historic transition important to the future, and contributes to a falsification of data. It therefore follows that the preservation of an addition should be considered a rule and that of a reconstruction an exception. This is entirely contrary to 19th-century practice and to the advice of the ever-present defacers (e.g., the recent so-called "restoration" of the Church of S. Domenico in Siena).

There is, however, a case in which the addition found on a work of art is not necessarily the product of human activity. This is the alteration or coating called the patina. The patina is not a romantic concept imposed in the 19th century on the taste for old painting, but was already an idea expressed and defined in the 17th century by Filippo Baldinucci in his *Vocabolario toscano dell'arte del disegno*; it found fertile ground in the artists' workshops and studios. Patina was identified even before the 17th century, and artists knew of it as one of the changes that the passage of time caused in the material of an art work. In Greek painting and sculpture, for example, the intentional toning down of colors and surface glare is attested by certain historically documented procedures, such as the *atramentum* of Apelles (q.v.) and the process of ganosis used on marble statuary.

In considering the legitimacy or illegitimacy of the patina from the historical point of view, it must be recognized that in the process of restoration the removal of patina as the evidence of history is a way of falsifying art works: the materials, thus deprived of their age, are forced to acquire a freshness, a sharp edge, and a new aggressiveness that will only belie the true age of the work. Therefore, conservation of the patina — that special dimming which the material acquires over a period of time and which becomes an evidence of passing time — is not only desirable but imperative.

Restoration dependent on esthetic requirements. From an esthetic point of view a ruin can only be treated as such, and the process of restoration must only preserve it and never add to it. However, when considering the problem of conserving or removing additions and reconstructions, the temptation to retouch them can be very strong since they are most frequently found on vital works. Esthetically speaking, additions should be removed, but the situation is reversed when the problem calls for historical considerations. However, most of the time the contradiction is more seeming than real. In fact, removal of an addition is obligatory only in the case where an addition was applied without reworking the pictorial, sculptural, or architectural whole, where the addition is only an irreverent intrusion resulting from crude utilitarian aims or whims of fashion (PL. 136).

Wherever an addition or modification has been performed in a way that reestablishes the previous context, or when it represents a grafting designed to reconcile two theoretically discordant elements, conservation is equally imperative in terms of both esthetic and historical requirements. The façade of the Church of S. Maria in Cosmedin (I, PL. 394) in Rome is a case in point; the exquisite reworking of the 18th century was later completely annulled. This is even more true of the interior of St. John Lateran, which was so marvelously conceived by Borromini. There are also countless examples of modest, provincial Romanesque or Gothic buildings that were often transformed from the Renaissance to the end of the 18th century into outstanding monuments, sometimes of great architectural value.

Nor can additions or reconstructions always be removed from paintings or sculpture. For instance, the *Madonna* by Lippo Dalmasio in the Church of the Madonna del Baraccano in Bologna was repainted and completed by Francesco del Cossa (q.v.), and the *Madonna* of Bordone by Coppo di Marcovaldo in the Church of S. Maria dei Servi in Siena, was partly repainted about fifty years later by a student of Duccio di Buoninsegna. In sculpture there is the example of the pulpit by Nicola Pisano (the Cathedral of Siena), part of which was redone with elaborate additions by Riccio (X, PL. 322). The decoration of the Tempietto del Volto Santo in the Cathedral of Lucca is as much a part of the image as the merlons on the Tomb of Cecilia Metella in Rome or on the Arch of Augustus in Rimini. In all these cases the new and fascinating hybrid works that have resulted have every claim to respect from the esthetic standpoint, and the removal of the additions would be sheer folly from the esthetic as well as the historical standpoint.

There is no doubt that a reconstruction, because of its arbitrary and imaginative elements, should be eliminated provided its elimination leads to a *quo ante* state. Unfortunately such restoration is almost never possible in architecture or sculpture, since the remodeling alters the details of the old context. The removal of the remodeling will leave the work with a new defacement that is often more offensive than the remodeling itself. This can also be said of the established practice (until the 19th cent.) of completing mutilated ancient statues with added pieces. To apply these new pieces, the old break had to be cut off, evened, or fitted at the joint; when the added pieces are removed the mechanical cut is exposed and constitutes a new mutilation, whereas before it was easy to cancel mentally the remodeling or addition.

Such is the case with the *Apollo Belvedere* (Vat. Mus.; III, PL. 383); it would also apply if the pieces added by Thorvaldsen were to be removed from the pediment statues from the Temple of Aegina (Munich, Staatliche Antikensammlungen). It was also a grave error to recompose, except in the casts, the *Laocoön Group* (PL. 130) according to a version supposedly closer to the original conception; the group as it appeared prior to the last intervention was accepted in the 16th century by everybody from Michelangelo to Montorsoli and had acquired an established place in art history.

When considering patina the only case in which it might theoretically be preserved from a logical esthetic standpoint is when the modification of the excessively bright color has been explicitly foreseen by the artist; yet it would be a great error to preserve the patina only in such rare exceptional cases. The problem of conserving the patina should be resolved on the basis of the individual work, and the key to the solution is provided by the material. Assuming that the image is transmitted through the characteristics of the material and that the function of the material is to transmit the image to the viewer, the material itself should never dominate but be subordinate to the image. The patina, from the esthetic point of view, is that imperceptible and impalpable muting imposed by time on the material, which is compelled to maintain a more modest status within the image. For this reason conservation of the patina becomes legitimate. Also in architecture it is possible to indicate the particular cases in which the patina constitutes not only the subduing of the material but actually a sense of color. For more than four centuries this contribution by time to the beauty of monuments has been recognized and acknowledged by poets and painters who have drawn inspiration from the patina of the ages. Yet only recently the costly and disrespectful washing of the Colosseum in Rome was performed in an attempt to destroy the patina.

There is also great danger and difficulty involved in the removal of the patina from a painting. Here the patina is so uniformly attached to the varnish and glazing that the painting, if treated rashly, will be ruined on the principle that everything which medium-strength solvents can remove should be considered an illegitimate coating for old paintings. The objections raised — unfortunately in vain — to the ruinous cleaning performed on some of the greatest masterpieces of Italian and Flemish painting in London serve to point out the irreparable damage that empiricism cloaked in false scientific claims can produce in restoration.

Cesare BRANDI

PAINTING ON MOVABLE SUPPORTS. *Restoration of the supports.* Operations of a strictly preservative nature that protect from natural and accidental deterioration the materials contributing to the physical make-up of the work of art play a major role in restoration. In painting on movable supports (canvases, panels, etc.), these operations are aimed primarily at insuring the functional efficacy of the supports and of the various preparatory strata. In fact, the damage to which every painting is mostly exposed consists of the detachment and peeling of the paint film resulting from its defective adherence to the ground and of the decay (or defect) of the support's material. The three causes may develop independently, but more often they are interrelated.

The poor adhesion of the paint film to the ground and of the ground to the support is generally caused by natural aging of the adhesive substances in the color and in the ground. The typical color media (egg tempera, glue tempera, oil) gradually lose their elasticity, while the glues of the ground (generally animal glues, very diluted and mixed with inert substances like gesso [calcined gypsum]) decompose under the action of atmospheric humidity. Where these conditions exist in a painting, the normal occurrences to which every movable object is exposed (impacts, vibrations, etc.), and even the differences in thermal expansion among the various materials, may be sufficient to cause detachment and peeling of the paint from the ground or of the latter, together with the color, from the support. In many cases, additional causes of detachment are the glues and varnishes that have been superimposed at various times on the color surface, often with the intention of stopping peeling but with completely opposite effects.

A simple defect in adhesion between the various layers of a painting can be repaired by using various technical means to make suitable adhesive substances penetrate below the color surface. For paintings on canvas the normal procedure used is rebacking or relining (in use since the 18th century). Relining consists of the application, with various kinds of adhesives, of one or more new canvases to the back of the original canvas. The adhesives used in temperate climates are usually made of combinations of flour and animal glues mixed with organic plasticizers (molasses) and antidecay substances (alum, phenol). The new canvas is attached to the original, with heat so that the adhesive penetrates to the ground of the color surface. In Continental or particularly humid climates the most frequently used adhesive is composed of a mixture of beeswax and organic resin in variable proportions. The operation of relining can be facilitated by the use of special apparatuses such as the hot table (R. Sneyers, *BICR*, 13, 1953, pp. 9–10) and others that allow the two canvases to be glued in a vacuum (R. E. Straub, *Maltechnik*, 1, 1958, p. 70).

In cases where the canvas is so closely woven that the adhesive cannot penetrate the back of the color the so-called "transfer of color" procedure is used. This consists of the total removal of the original canvas, which is substituted by one or more canvases of the type commonly used for backing.

In order to aid the preservation of large paintings undergoing relining or transfer it is indispensable that the frame on which the new canvas is mounted is perfect. To control and correct the expansions and contractions that the canvas's support undergoes (due to variations in temperature and humidity), automatically expanding frames regulated by springs are used (R. Carità, *BICR*, 19–20, 1954, pp. 131–54).

In paintings on panels the problem of the adhesion of the paint film to the underlying layers and to the support is made more difficult by the nature of the support, which is particularly sensitive to every variation of temperature and humidity. Expansion and contraction of the wood are the main causes of the extreme fragility of panel paintings. The pictorial surface and the ground not only lose their original adhesion in the course of time, but also undergo a gradual decrease in elasticity and plasticity. On the other hand, these characteristics remain unchanged more or less indefinitely in the wood. This difference in reaction causes the blistering and flaking of the paint to which panel paintings are particularly susceptible. In less serious cases this difficulty is repaired by injecting adhesive substances below the color surface (properly treated animal glues, vinyl resins, or mixtures of wax and resin that are made to penetrate deeply with the aid of infrared heat [P. Philippot and R. Sneyers, *Les Primitifs Flamands*, III, Antwerp, 1953, p. 89]). To reduce the natural movement of wood, changes are made in the structure of the entire support. The oldest and most frequently adopted process is so-called "cradling" (parquetry) that consists of applying on the back of the board a series of slats that tend to limit the movement of the wood to one horizontal place. The traditional cradling consists of a series of fixed wooden slats glued to the back in the same direction as the grain of the panel and of another group of sliding wooden slats arranged at right angles to the grain and inserted in the slots made for them in the fixed parts; to this process the Istituto Centrale del Restauro (Rome) has recently contributed new methods of cradling with flexible metallic parts (PL. 142; R. Carità, *BICR*, 25–28, 1956, pp. 101–31).

The National Gallery in London and the Intermuseum Laboratory in Oberlin, Ohio, prefer to tackle the problem of reducing the natural movement of the wood with the radical, so-called "semitransfer" method. This consists of decreasing the board to about one-fourth of its original thickness and applying to the back of the reduced board various layers of inert material (such as balsa) cemented together with fine fiberglass cloth permeated with polyester resins. This system offers the advantage of more or less completely isolating the remaining wood and, consequently, of reducing the movement to limits that do not jeopardize the stability of the painted surface and the underlying layers. It is a great disadvantage, however, that the original wooden support, aside from being deprived of its specific function (insofar as it is a historical product), no longer exists as an integral part of the painting.

In order to preserve the wooden support as a whole the Istituto Centrale del Restauro has recently worked out a procedure of transferring paint that does not require destruction of the support itself. The painting is protected by a thin, tightly woven cotton cloth, whose perfect adhesion to the pigment is insured by an acrylic resin such as paraloid. A thin film of wax is then added, and this acts as a separating agent between the cotton cloth and the next layer of epoxy resin that covers the entire surface and acts as a reinforcement. Then the painting is floated in a tub of water, with the protected part above the surface. Within a few days the humidity passes through the thickness of the panel and reaches the preparatory layers (ground), which are so softened that they no longer adhere to the panel. The paint and ground can then be easily detached from the support, an operation facilitated by the elasticty given to these layers by the superimposed protective layers. In the successive stages of the operation the painted layer and the support are treated separately. The wooden support is dried by heat while clamped between metal bars that prevent its bending or warping.

In this way the entire panel remains flat and at the same time undergoes an almost permanent plastic change that prevents it, once exposed to normal environmental conditions, from warping as before. Finally, a fiberglass cloth (first coated by the same resin) is attached by means of a paraloid (mixed with titanium white and pumice powder) to the surface designated to receive the painted layer. At the same time the back of the painted layer is freed from all preparatory residues. A thin film of rabbit glue, of the type traditionally used in gypsum (gesso) base preparations, is spread over the exposed color, and a fine film of epoxy resin is added to make the surface perfectly level. To this is glued, with a rubber base adhesive, a tightly woven and smooth linen or cotton cloth. At this point the painted layer can be glued to the panel; this is done with a mixture of wax and natural resin between the surface of the fabric (joined to the layers on the back of the paint) and the paraloid surface (covering the panel). The process is complex because it is necessary to resort to solutions that will make future interventions possible or that will not seriously endanger preservation of the painting. In the solution described, the paint can again be removed from the panel. The fiberglass and paraloid layers have two functions: to isolate the color from expansion and contraction which the panel may develop on the surface (for now, to avoid warping, it will have been properly cradled); and to create (by the addition of titanium white and pumice powder to the paraloid) a surface suitable for receiving the adhesive layer of wax and resin.

With the procedure described here, the stability of the pictorial layer, which is the major restoration problem of panel paintings, can be completely assured. Obviously such a drastic and difficult solution should be used only in the extreme cases when normal preservation measures prove to be inadequate. In fact, there is a current tendency among the principal museums of the world to establish restoration laboratories and extend their activities to such an extent as to negate the sound principle by which a work of art should first of all be placed in conditions that will make restoration unnecessary. It would be desirable if each museum were to arrange its collection of panel paintings in a special section where temperature and humidity are kept constant and in no way affect the wood.

Cleaning. The old practice of retouching and revarnishing paintings originated the restorative operation commonly called cleaning. This is the removal from the original surface of all additions and superimpositions not properly belonging to it (i.e., that cannot be traced to the author of the work). Accepting this premise, it is necessary to make a basic distinction. The gaps in a painting, whatever their cause and origin, even if inherent in the structure of the painting itself (because of the craquelure, or network of fine cracks, that occurs in the color and the ground with the contraction of their respective media or because of the movement of the supports), cannot be considered original elements desired by the creator of the painting. And yet, respect for the work's originality, which is the basis of restoration as it is understood today, prescribes that these lacunae remain visible; when, for reasons of size or appearance, they affect the appearance of the work, they must be disguised but not hidden, remaining always is some way distinguishable from the original. The lacunae are nothing more than tangible evidence of a work's age. An old painting that does not in some way show traces of wear and decay is self-contradictory: it is not old but new. The same can be said of the patina, that thin transparent layer of yellowish, brownish, grayish color which in time forms on every kind of painting and which on paintings on movable supports is composed of varnish and atmospheric fogging. (The patina on frescoes is caused by the latter and by carbons and silicons produced by the change in the component materials of the fresco itself — lime, sand, etc.) The patina is also a tangible evidence of the work's age. Removing the patina in the course of cleaning is as senseless as hiding the craquelure of the old color. The claim of those who advocate complete cleaning is based on the absurd conviction that a restorative operation can bring the work of art back to a state of timelessness. Actually, a completely cleaned painting does not strike one as being in the state in which it was when it left the hands of the painter because one immediately interprets that unseemly clearness of color as only another sign of the wear and tear of time, a kind of damage resulting from excessive cleaning.

Several other arguments can be added to this fundamental one. The use of varnish since classical antiquity and the Middle Ages is documented in many known sources: Pliny, *Naturalis historia*, xxv; an 8th-century manuscript in the library in Lucca, *Compositiones ad tingenda musiva, pelles, etalia* ...; Heraclius, *De coloribus et artibus Romanorum*; Theophilus, *Diversarum artium schedula* (10th cent.?); Cennini, *Trattato* (15th cent.); and a 15th-century treatise from Bologna, *Segreto per colori*. As a matter of principle it can therefore be assumed that the patina of the large majority of paintings is composed completely or in part of the original varnish. There is no reason not to consider this varnish a material used by the artist for specific pictorial effects. The fact that the varnish has changed (i.e., darkened) with time is not in the least a determining factor for its removal. The real colors have also changed, but no one considers removing or substituting them. The patina's preservation is also a safety measure affecting the integrity of the colors, which in a painting are not applied as a body but as glazes. Finally, the more thoroughly a painting is cleaned the more apparent become its probable damages. Such cleaning inevitably reveals the need for extensive restoration and is thus less respectful to the original.

Both the technique and the means used in cleaning vary with the nature of the painting, as well as with the superimposed elements to be removed. Solvents which do not impair tempera paintings are petroleum ethers, toluene, xylene, oil of turpentine, dipentene, amyl acetate, cellosolve, and dimethylformamide. These may also be used on oil paintings, with a preference for polar solvents mixed with water or diluted with other solvents such as alcohol, acetone, pyridine, and morpholine. It is clear that the removal of retouchings from an oil or tempera painting cannot be performed without risks to the original. Therefore, it is necessary to keep the cleaning under careful manual control.

Reintegration. In modern restoration the practice of retouching has gradually lost importance, and today it is justifiably discredited, at least in theory. Respect for the original implies that any retouching be limited to the lacunae that disturb a work's appearance. Most of the time it is sufficient to make a gap clearly noticeable as such and not as a splash of color or a form interfering with the painting's effect. In cases where this is impossible, it is legitimate to turn to other solutions, provided they are based on two fundamental principles — that the addition is immediately recognizable, and that a minimum of material is used so that it can be removed later without damage to the original. One of the systems used is that of applying water color in separate vertical strokes to the gap (PL. 140). This system has the advantage of approximating the original while remaining distinguishable from it. Because of the nature of water color, which can be applied only to the white ground of the plaster, the inpainting cannot pass over the gap's edges.

Scientific research is being conducted in practically every area of restoration and aims at extending the knowledge of the materials used in the art work and in the various restorative operations. Chemical analysis of old paints and color media has become very important, and research in this area has required new impetus from recent analytical techniques (see TECHNIQUES).

Giovanni URBANI

OTHER TECHNIQUES. *Mural painting.* The deterioration of mural paintings is caused by damages in the support and on the pictorial surface. These changes are brought about by the infiltration and condensation of humidity and by corrosion from external factors such as atmospheric conditions, insects, salt deposits, the growth of roots, molds, and lichens. All these can cause the disintegration of the support and the subsequent detachment of the paint film, which gradually flakes, crumbles, or runs.

Restoration comprises many activities, from cleaning a surface and reattaching flaking sections to detaching an entire mural from its original support and placing it on a new one (PLS. 139, 144). Cleaning is done by mechanical means as well as with grease-removing substances such as trichloroethylene and butylamine. Sometimes it is necessary to rid the mural of later repainting and of poor restorations. The results often make unexpected salvaging possible. Among the more notable examples of such restoration is the cleaning of the Giotto frescoes in the Bardi Chapel of Sta Croce in Florence.

When the solidity and stability of a mural are not irremediably jeopardized, restoration is limited to reinforcement by injections of casein or other glues through the cracks into the support and to the application of fixatives to the paint surface. A restorative practice that consisted of protecting a mural's danger zones by means of metal clamps secured in gesso was begun in the mid-17th century (between 1640 and 1677) and remained in use until the beginning of the 20th century. Giovanni Francesco Rossi was the first to employ this method to reinforce the frescoes of the Carraccis in the Palazzo Farnese, Rome, where the plaster had swelled because of water penetration (G. P. Bellori, *Descrizione delle pitture di Raffaello*, Rome, 1751, p. 196 ff.; M. Cagiano de Azevedo, *BICR*, 7–8, 1951, pp. 99–100). Such clamps were later fixed in cement, which also served to secure the endangered edges of the frescoes.

When a mural cannot be restored by these methods the remedy is removal. There are many ways of detaching a mural; the oldest is "a massello," which consists of detaching the painting (after having protected its surface) together with its entire support. The first example is probably the removal in Naples (completed Oct. 5, 1507) of "a piece of wall on which was painted a fresco of St. Anne with her daughter the Virgin and the Infant Jesus. With great care this was cut out from the former palace of Troiano Caracciolo, prince of Melfi" (C. Celano, *Notizie*, Naples, 1758, p. 271) and was placed above the main altar of the Church of the Annunziata (M. Cagiano de Azevedo, *BICR*, 1, 1950, pp. 44–45).

In the *Vite* Vasari mentions the removal of a Madonna by Spinello Aretino from the now-demolished Church of S. Stefano in Arezzo, which took place shortly after 1550. The operation was executed by the citizens of Arezzo, who "cut the wall around it (the Madonna) and ingeniously bound and carried it into the city and placed it in a small church to honor her." Vasari also tells of the transfer (in 1564) of a St. Jerome by Ghirlandajo and of a St. Augustine by Botticelli into the Church of Ognissanti in Florence. In 1566, because of the destruction of the choir of Sta Croce, another famous fresco with John the Baptist and St. Francis (formerly considered the work of Andrea del Castagno but now attributed to Domenico Veneziano) was removed (F. Bocchi, *Le bellezze della città di Fiorenza*, Florence, 1591, p. 154). As recent restorative work has shown, Piero della Francesca's fresco of the Resurrection (now Sansepolcro, Pin. Com.) must have been removed from its original site (Procacci, 1958, pp. 15–17). A short time after its discovery in 1604–05 and its on-the-spot restoration by Federico Zuccari, the so-called "Aldobrandini Wedding" (VI, PL. 57) was detached by sawing the picture from the wall; it was then supported on oak beams and moved (B. Nogara, *Le Nozze Aldobrandine*, Milan, 1907, p. 2).

One can assume that this technique was already known in ancient times. In fact, Pliny and Vitruvius mention that many murals were transported from Greece to Rome at a time when the rage for collecting Greek art spurred the Romans to appropriate the ancient masterpieces wholesale. Such removals were accomplished by cutting away the plaster and protecting the part to be detached with a wooden framework (Pliny, op. cit., XXXV, 173; Vitruvius *De Architectura*, II, viii, 9). After the painting was detached it was often put into a new pictorial context, as many discoveries in Pompeii and Herculaneum demonstrate (A. Maiuri, *BArte*, XI, 1938, pp. 481–89; *RendLinc*, VII, i, 1940, p. 140 ff.; M. Cagiano de Azevedo, *BICR*, 9–10, 1952, p. 55).

This type of rather rudimentary removal involving the destruction of the entire wall bearing the painting is still used in special cases; more frequently only the plaster ground is detached and sometimes only the pictorial layer (a process called stripping). The earliest removals of this type date to the first half of the 18th century. One of the first to use this method was Alessandro Maiello, who, in 1720, transferred to panel a tempera painting by Giovanni Battista Caracciolo (called "Battistello") from the Church of S. Giuseppe in Naples (De Dominici, *Vite*, 1844, III, p. 62). Maiello and Niccolò di Simone were noted for transferring wall paintings to canvas provided they were painted in oil (De Dominici, *Vite*, 1843, II, p. 312). During the Bourbon excavations in Pompeii and Herculaneum many murals were removed to embellish the royal collections. The system used by the French sculptor Josef Canard (Canarte) was still limited to removing the mural with all the plaster. The detached murals were often covered with various kinds of varnishes to revive the colors, but these were always damaging (M. Cagiano de Azevedo, *BICR*, 1950, pp. 40–41). During the first half of the 18th century an Italian, Riario, brought to France the procedure for transferring murals to canvas. Almost at the same time, Jean Michel Picault, in Paris, transferred many murals to canvas, keeping to himself the technique he employed. Antonio Contri of Ferrara stripped pictures from walls and applied them to canvas, a technique he developed in 1725 (G. Baruffaldi, *Vite di pittori e scultori ferraresi*, Ferrara, 1844, I, pp. 39–40, 189–92, II, pp. 347–57). This technique was used only on small paintings. Leopoldo Cicognara mentions that in Florence in 1787 the painter Sante Pacini transferred a Cennino Cennini painting with rather unfortunate results. Giacomo Succi (Baruffaldi, op. cit., I, pp. 39, 336), Antonio Boccolari (Baruffaldi, op. cit., I, p. 393), and Giuseppe Rizzoli (Baruffaldi, op. cit., II, p. 435) worked in the first half of the 19th century. In 1842, two equestrian portraits — one of Niccolò da Tolentino by Andrea del Castagno (I, PL. 246), the other of Sir John Hawkwood by Paolo Uccello (PL. 27) — were detached from the walls of the Cathedral in Florence. Some years later Andrea del Castagno's frescoes of Famous Men and Women were removed from the Villa Pandolfini near Florence (now in the Cenacolo di S. Apollonia, Florence; I, PL. 245).

The techniques of these early removals, even though they were often cloaked in mystery, were not very different from those still in use. These consist of protecting the surface of the mural with canvas coated with glue; when this is dry, and the cohesion between the protective canvas and the paint film is greater than that between the paint and its support, the mural is detached with the aid of long metal scalpels. When it is necessary to detach frescoes (the technique most commonly used in murals) from a support that has not deteriorated too much, the preferred system is to preserve several millimeters of plaster on the back of the paint film. This is done for two reasons: the first is based on a principle of restoration according to which the state of the paint should never be disturbed at close quarters; the second, which is peculiar to fresco painting because the paint penetrates several millimeters of the underlying plaster, involves removing only the paint film, so the brightness of the painting is slightly weakened. In addition to the canvas covering, the surface of the painting is also protected by resting the picture on a wooden panel. The back, cleaned and reduced, is then supported by a wooden or metal frame that is often reinforced with wire netting joined permanently to the frame by mortar.

Numerous Roman wall paintings have been removed by this system: those from the large hall of the Villa of Livia in Prima Porta (VII, PL. 208), from the House of the Griffins (XIII, PL. 276), and from the House of Livia on the Palatine Hill. This work was done by the Istituto Centrale del Restauro and confirmed information from ancient sources in regard to the nature of the plaster (three layers of rough plaster and three of finer plaster containing marble dust), the hatching on vaults that served as ground for murals, the insulation against humidity by means of tiled walls supporting the plaster, and so on. The discovery of the signs marking the end of the day's work on the back of the murals proved beyond doubt that these were frescoes and settled the question of the technique of Roman wall paintings.

In the case of some medieval frescoes — the painting cycle in the Camposanto in Pisa, that by Masolino and his collaborator

in the Chapel of St. Catherine in S. Clemente, Rome (X, PL. 484), and some of the frescoes in the Lower Church of S. Francesco (Assisi) — removal has salvaged the underlying sinopias, which are valuable for their intrinsic qualities and because they reveal the artist's creative procedure.

In the 18th and 19th centuries the new supports for detached frescoes were made of gesso, which, however, decayed rapidly under humid conditions. At the beginning of the 20th century cement replaced the gesso. However, the use of cement is not advisable because of its excessive rigidity and weight; cement also prevents future interventions, and its alkaline and nitrate deposits, which its hygroscopicity brings to the color surface, slowly cause the mural to darken.

The transfer of only the paint film (stripping), which is done in cases where the plaster is completely crumbling and which seems to have been the discovery of 18th-century "magicians," is accomplished by using a strong glue to make the cloth adhere to the paint. One or more layers of canvas, which function as a new support, are glued to the back. Sometimes rigid supports (wood) are used; the use of asbestos has been discouraged because it is a pliable material and sensitive to humidity.

The transfer of Etruscan tomb paintings presents a very special problem (PL. 137). In the large necropolises of Tarquinia, Orvieto, and Chiusi the tombs are dug into tufa several meters below ground level. The paintings were done almost directly on the smoothed walls, separated from them only by a thin lime whitewash. The environment is almost always saturated with humidity since water penetrates from the surrounding terrain and condensation forms because of dry air currents that enter from outside. This condition, together with other factors (centuries of neglect, damage by animals, roots, etc.), made the detachment of many paintings necessary. Water-soluble glues could not be used, but shellac (a resin soluble in alcohol) was effective as an adhesive, and many paintings could be detached from the tombs. Alcohol was used to remove the shellac from the painted surfaces, and the separate panels, glued on canvas, were supported on expandable wooden or metal frames that accommodated the slightest movement of the painting and canvas. The separate walls were then joined to each other to reconstruct the inside of a tomb within a museum. Today, shellac is used as an adhesive whenever humidity prevents normal glues from drying.

Another special type of restoration is that which has salvaged some murals partially destroyed by bombardments during World War II, such as the frescoes by Lorenzo da Viterbo in the Mazzatosta Chapel of S. Maria della Verità in Viterbo (VIII, PL. 204), those by Mantegna and his students in the Ovetari Chapel of the Church of the Eremitani in Padua (PL. 140), and those of the Camposanto in Pisa. The minute remaining fragments were reduced to equal thickness. By following a photographic reproduction of the design of the lost fresco the pieces were fitted into place on a support of stretched canvas that was prepared with calcium caseinate and held on a metal frame. The numerous gaps were integrated with water colors in hatched inpainting. The lost image was thus recomposed, a task that had seemed impossible; the water color hatching maintained the distinction between original and integrated parts.

Sometimes more than one layer of fresco was executed on the same wall at different periods. Modern technological advances in the field of restoration have made it possible to remove these paintings by separating one layer from the other. In this way pictorial sections that would otherwise remain invisible have been salvaged.

Since ancient times various preparations have been used to brighten the color and protect painting surfaces, from "concoctions" applied in the 18th century to the paintings in Pompeii and Herculaneum (M. Cagiano de Azevedo, op. cit., pp. 40–41) to the oils, resins, and waxes used in the following centuries. All of these were materials that alter with time and were often fertile ground for molds and lichens. The current tendency is to leave the surface free and, when necessary, to use shellac or new synthetic products that have already been tested. Among the latter are carbowax, a synthetic wax, and paraloid and acresin, both methacrylates.

Sculpture. When restoration work is limited to repair and reinforcement the problem of restoring sculptures of marble, stone, and other materials is much less complicated than that of pictures. The statue is soaked to a saturation point in silicate base substances or more recently in silicon or methacrylate base substances.

Since ancient times there has been no lack of information dealing with the restoration of sculpture. In the 2d century B.C., Damophon of Messene restored Phidias's *Zeus* of Olympia because the ivory pieces forming the unclothed parts of the body did not adhere to the wooden core. In 160 B.C. Damophon also reworked the gold facing covering parts of Phidias's *Athena Parthenos*, which had been stolen by Lachares in 296. Aristandros of Paros, great-grandson of the famous Skopas, restored (ἐπεσ-χεύασεν) two statues by Agasias in Delos (*BCH*, VIII, 1884, pp. 143–44; *BCH*, XXXI, 1907, p. 458). Avianus Evander restored the head of Artemis by Timotheos in the Temple of Apollo on the Palatine Hill (Pliny, *op. cit.*, XXXVI, 32).

Ancient restorations have been found on the *Ephebus of Subiaco*, on the *Idolino* (G. Lippold, *Kopien und Umbildungen*, Munich, 1923, pp. 30, 101, 126), and on the Farnese Bull; according to certain authorities, the Pentelic marble figures on the west pediment of the Temple of Zeus in Olympia are part of a Greek or Roman restoration.

During the Renaissance, restoration was interpreted more as "remodeling" than "repairing." The restorers identified themselves with the ancient sculptors, often superimposing their own personality on those of the ancients and taking liberties that might seem arbitrary if they had not been some of the greatest artists of the time: Cellini, Michelangelo, Verrocchio, and Donatello. The most famous 16th-century restoration was done in 1532–33 by Giovanni Angelo Montorsoli on the *Laocoön Group* (PL. 130). The statue had been found in January, 1506, in the Baths of Titus, and it is possible that several parts had already been integrated by Sansovino. The prime importance of this restoration is that the *Laocoön* became an important factor in the formation of 16th- and 17th-century taste, and for centuries represented a basis of comparison in the taste of restoration.

In the 18th century the sculptor Augusto Cornacchini redid the arms of the sons, destroying Sansovino's restoration. These arms and the arm of Laocoön that was remodeled by Montorsoli were removed in 1796 after the group was moved to Paris under Napoleon's orders. In Paris, it was fitted with plaster parts that the sculptor François Girardon (q.v.), at the end of the 17th century, had based on the limbs restored by Sansovino and Montorsoli. When the *Laocoön* was returned to Rome in 1815 the arms by Cornacchi were put back as well as the arm by Montorsoli, which, however, had been made of terracotta and was then remade in marble. Slight alterations gave the group a pronounced neoclassical aspect.

A critical study was made by E. Vergara Caffarelli (1954) on the cast of the *Laocoön* in the Museo dei Gessi of the University of Rome; the complete revision made in 1960 by F. Magi (PL. 130) on the original in the Vatican, where he disassembled and carefully examined the individual pieces of which it was composed (including an arm of the figure of the father found by L. Pollak), has now brought the *Laocoön* as close as possible to the original concept. It has been useful to summarize the main steps in the history of the *Laocoön* because this statue represents an "epitome" of how the taste of the time can have an impact on restoration when the work to which it applies has had such a strong effect on esthetic sensibility. Many other ancient works of art have undergone similar, if less involved and spectacular, experiences.

In Venice, in 1587, Alessandro Vittoria and Domenico dalle due Regine restored the Grimani marbles "so they no longer seemed the same" (G. Valentinelli, *Marmi scolpiti nel Museo Archeologico della Marciana a Venezia*, Prato, 1866, p. xii). Often ancient fragments of different origin were combined to form a "pastiche" (the most extravagant example being the façade overlooking the garden in the Villa Medici, Rome). The principal restorer of the baroque period was Alessandro Algardi (q.v.), restorer of the Ludovisi collection and the

Hercules and the *Hydra* in the Capitoline Museum, for example, who changed ancient statues according to baroque taste. In the 17th century, François Girardon "slimmed" the Venus given to Louis XIV by the city of Arles because it seemed too fat for the current taste. However, there were many discordant voices among the experts who appealed to more scholarly criteria of restoration, and among the artists, some of whom were hostile to any type of integration. Canova (q.v.) refused to restore the Parthenon marbles. Thorvaldsen (q.v.) did not have the same scruples, and in 1812 he was assigned the task of restoring some sculptures from Aegina. He fitted these works to his own neoclassical taste, often tampering with them to adapt the breaks to new pieces and flattening the surfaces that seemed to him too protuberant.

Toward the mid-18th century Bartolomeo Cavaceppi worked in Rome, and his fame spread beyond Italy. He worked with discretion, but many of his restorations seem arbitrary. Though there are some later examples, the period of remodelings ended at the beginning of the 20th century with the restorations in Knossos, which were primarily concerned with architecture and painting. In modern times scholarly research and historical investigation, on the one hand, and the formulation of a philosophical basis for the criteria of restoration, on the other, have prevented the romantic interpretation that in past centuries permitted many arbitrary interventions on ancient works of art. Integration is now carried out only when it is necessary to join two close fragments, and the material used makes the integration evident. Respect for the history of some art works and their restorations, which in themselves have become a history of taste, has brought about modifications that reestablish the original appearance. These modifications are no longer done on the work itself but on plaster casts (PL. 138).

Metals. From a technical point of view the problem of restoring metal objects is much more difficult. Metals are subject to corrosion, in other words, to the loss of their metallic properties with the formation of mineral incrustations. Corrosion is produced by a series of chemical and electrochemical reactions caused by atmospheric agents (primarily oxygen in the air), by the acidity of the soil in which the objects are found, by humidity, and by other factors. Alloy metals are more susceptible to corrosion than others. Among the alloys, bronze has been preferred since protohistoric times as a material for sculpture and small objects because of its ductile characteristics.

Corrosion makes the surface of the metal porous. Salts lodge in the cracks and set off a series of chain reactions that can cause the total disintegration of the metal. Sometimes after preliminary development the mineralization stops, inhibits further changes, and forms a thick patina on the metal.

Even in ancient times the vulnerability of metal was known. From ancient sources dealing with patina it is apparent that the shellac, oils, waxes, and pitches that were applied to bronzes had a protective as well as an esthetic function (M. Cagiano de Azevedo, *BICR*, 9–10, 1952, pp. 58–9). Pliny (op. cit., XXXIV, 21) explicitly states that bronze objects were preserved by treating them with oil and diluted pitch; the Leiden papyrus (Berthelot, 1888, pp. 28–45) supplies other remedies of this sort.

For many centuries the restoration of metallic objects was connected with the mysterious formulas of alchemist-restorers. Actually, because of chemical and physical changes in the material, this type of restoration can be begun only after careful laboratory analysis. Only with the aid of technological science was the problem of restoring metals, bronze in particular, really faced. First the object is analyzed and examined on or below the surface by means of X-ray diffraction or fluorescence, ultrasonic and acoustical waves, and emission or gamma-ray spectrometers. Extensive research has been carried out in this field at the Istituto Sperimentale dei Metalli Leggeri of the Montecatini Company in Novara and in the laboratories of the British Museum, of the Institut Royal du Patrimoine Artistique in Brussels, and of the Musée Historique Lorrain in Nancy.

There are two main methods of restoration: mechanical and reduction methods. Often these two must be combined to achieve proper results. The mechanical methods consist of cleaning the surface with mechanical instruments. The reduction methods can be by physical, chemical, or electro-chemical means. The chemical methods use solvents from the mildest, distilled water to dissolve the soluble salts, to various kinds of acids such as Rochelle salts, oxalic acid, or even an electric arc that reduces the oxides to metals. The principal electrochemical means are various types of electrolytes that vary with the composition of the electrolytic bath. Immersion in an electrolytic bath is the most potent method of cleaning, but it can be used only when the metal still retains much of its consistency. However, this method presents a serious drawback that is noticeable even in the mildest forms, like autoelectrolysis or the use of buffers, for it deprives the object of its patina — both the applications made in ancient times and the changes that have occurred over a period of time. Both of these contribute to the integrity of the object and to its history. Until a few decades ago, it was the popular custom (in certain museums it still is) to use electrolytic reduction to clean bronzes and then to apply a new artificial patina. Today mechanical methods or mild chemical reduction that preserves the old patina is preferred, and the more drastic electrolytic procedure is used only in extreme cases.

Sometimes wax is used to protect the cleaned surface, but with time it yellows and in humid conditions may facilitate the growth of microorganisms. Therefore synthetic waxes or methacrylates, which are less susceptible to molds and more resistent to atmospheric agents, are preferred. An ideal condition that is seldom feasible, however, would be the conservation of the object in a vacuum. Instead of plaster and other kinds of materials used elsewhere for integrating gaps and patching, the Istituto Centrale del Restauro in Rome prefers to use a metallic stucco soluble in toluol that solidifies quickly and takes on a color which does not clash with that of the metal (PL. 143).

Wood. The ancients knew of the susceptibility of wood to attack from so-called "woodworms" and other insects, and to splitting because of atmospheric variations. In fact, they chose the most solid plants and the most suitable wood, and their statues were impregnated with special oils through special openings as an aid to preservation. This information is supplied in great detail by ancient sources (collected in M. Cagiano de Azevedo, *op. cit.*, pp. 53–4). The old practice of periodically immersing the wooden statue of Hera of Samos in a bath may have been dictated, aside from ritual purposes, by rudimentary preservation measures. In some portraits found in Fayum a special technique has been noted for leaving free the individual wooden panels that formed the support for the picture (XI, PL. 214). This method was a distant predecessor to movable cradling.

Today various safeguards are used to preserve wooden objects. First they are disinfected against attack by fungi with fungicides and against attack from woodworms by sterilization through fumigation, spraying, and impregnation with poisonous gases. Then consolidation is achieved by impregnations with wax or synthetic materials (generally methacrylates). If the wood is saturated with humidity — as is often the case with remains of ships or objects excavated from damp soil — the wood must be freed from water by gradually dehumidifying the environment, thus avoiding an abrupt change that might cause warping, splitting, or destruction of the object. The water lodged in the pores of the wood can be replaced with a liquid such as alum dissolved in water, which prevents the contraction of the wood; or the wood can be brought to a rigidity that prevents further warping by baths of alcohol and ether followed by soaking in a polyvinyl resin (experiments performed at the laboratories of museums in Zurich and Copenhagen, and of the British Museum). If the objects are too large to be transported to a laboratory they are protected against atmospheric agents by gradually acclimatizing them to the new conditions through very slow dehumidification and then saturation with silicate, resin, or methacrylic solutions.

Ancient ceramics. Because of the fragility of the material and the high value placed on some ceramic objects even in

ancient times, traces of ancient restorations consisting of bronze clamps have been discovered on Greek vases found in Italy (PL. 129). In the 18th and 19th centuries pottery was restored according to the principles of the time: both pertinent and spurious fragments were adapted to the same vase by means of a damaging filing process and then glued with fish or other glues; or the gaps were disguised with skilled replacements painted in plaster.

Today, substances such as shellac or other synthetic resins, which are not soluble in water and consequently not sensitive to humidity, are used to glue the fragments. The lacunae are filled either with plaster (left in its natural color or tinted) or, as in the restorations carried out in the Istituto Centrale del Restauro, with a mixture of marble dust, powdered brick, alabastrine plaster, and hydraulic lime and are kept at a different level from that of the original pieces.

Mosaics. Restoration of mosaics (q.v.) presents no special problems. Cleaning of the tesserae is done with ordinary solvents, and removal follows the same criteria discussed in reference to frescoes. The glues, mortars, and supports must of course be stronger because of the mosaics' greater weight. Large mosaics are usually removed in sections and then recomposed. Recently the Istituto Centrale del Restauro removed a Roman mosaic of about 230 sq. ft. in Cologne. The central section of about 160 sq. ft. was removed in one piece by winding it around a roller. Then the mosaic was spread out on a large board to facilitate improvement of the back and the application of a solid frame.

Licia VLAD BORRELLI

PRINCIPLES OF ARCHITECTURAL AND URBAN RESTORATION AND CONSERVATION. Architectural restoration is a modern concept that stems from a new approach to the monuments of the past. The fundamental principle of restoration, which was the basis of successive doctrines in the 19th century, is to return an architectural work to its well-defined historical context and, at the same time, to treat it in such a way as to make it once more alive and real as a valid part of the modern world. In the modern sense of the term, architectural restoration can be studied only from the decree of 1794, in which the French National Convention proclaimed the principle of preserving monuments. Different ways of maintaining respect for an architectural work were subsequently developed. Chronologically, the first idea of restoration was based on the principle of recomposing the structures by using their original parts or reproductions of them without making great distinctions between the two. In the first three decades of the 19th century restorations on monuments of classical antiquity were executed on the basis of this criterion, especially in Rome.

Between 1830 and 1870, in France, every monument was regarded as a "stylistic unit" which incorporated and cancelled out the individual characteristics of the work. The task of restoration was to recreate this stylistic unity. This in turn led to reconstructions, remodelings, and even additions based only on stylistic analogies to other monuments, and to alterations in the name of stylistic consistency. This so-called "stylistic" restoration is identified with the name of Viollet-le-Duc (q.v.; 1814–79), a historian and theorist of architecture, restorer of many French cathedrals, and the most outstanding advocate of "medievalism" whose pronouncements are still cited as rules (e.g.: "To restore a building means to restore it to a state of completeness that may never have existed.") Today, the severe judgment passed on the principles and methods of stylistic restoration should be revised.

In the mid-19th century "romantic" restoration developed, side by side with stylistic restoration, from the English movement that tried to replace extensive intervention with a religious respect for the monument in the form in which it was found. This concept was the result of an attitude that conferred on the past and the works it produced an autonomous value in relation to the present. It generated a passionate desire for sincerity, an almost morbid love for the monument, and consequently a repugnance for human intervention, which was considered brutal and sacrilegious. Romantic restoration regarded preservation with fatalistic renunciation. The monument must remain as it is, untouched and nothing must be done to prevent its breaking down and falling into ruin. John Ruskin was the outstanding advocate of this position. To him, restoration understood as preservation was a falsehood, because in substituting the ancient stones the monument is destroyed and only a model of the old building is obtained. In response to the demand for prolonging the life of an architectural work he maintained that restoration and abandonment were both equivalent to destruction. "Look the necessity full in the face, and understand it on its own terms. It is a necessity for destruction. Accept it as such, pull the building down, throw its stones into neglected corners, make ballast of them, or mortar, if you will; but do it honestly, and do not set up a lie in their place."

Two new concepts arose almost simultaneously in the decade from 1880 to 1890: "historical" restoration, advocated and applied by Luca Beltrami, was still dependent upon the criteria of broad and innovating intervention; the other was based on advances in scholarship and the conviction that each monument is a distinct and separate entity. This led to abandonment of the practice of using (by analogy) similar elements from other monuments and of considering every claim to personal inventiveness a falsification. The restorer defined as an "artist–re-creator," who sought to identify himself with the original architect, was replaced by the "historian-archivist," who based his activity exclusively on established evidence ranging from documents in archives to paintings, and from thorough analysis of the monument to the literary texts of its time.

As early as 1883, Camillo Boito had already stated the fundamental principles of restoration in its modern sense, which can be summarized in the following points: (1) monuments have a value not only for architectural study but as evidence of the history of peoples and nations and therefore must be respected since any alteration is deceptive and leads to mistaken deductions; (2) monuments should be strengthened rather than repaired, repaired rather than restored, and additions and renovations should be avoided; (3) if the additions are indispensable for reasons of stability or other absolutely necessary reasons, they should be executed on the basis of certain data and with different characteristics and materials, while maintaining the current appearance of the building; (4) additions made at various times must be considered part of the monument and maintained except when they cause concealments or alterations.

This doctrine spread very slowly. Only in 1931, at the International Conference on Restoration in Athens, were its principles accepted, recommending constant maintenance and reinforcement of the monuments and advocating the use of the most modern technical means and construction methods. In 1932, G. Giovannoni reworked, modernized, and extended this doctrine. In the new theory, inappropriately called "scientific" restoration, the salient feature was conservation; thus, elements having artistic or historical characteristics belonging to any period must be preserved, without allowing the desire for stylistic unity and the return to the primitive form to interfere in the exclusion of some to the disadvantage of others.

Practical factors were placed on the same level as creative acts, and the concept of art and architecture was a strictly empirical one. Scientific restoration, which should instead be called scholarly restoration, proved inadequate in 1943–45 when it became necessary to deal with the consequences of war damages. The extent of the damage made this method inapplicable. The scholarly position, which considers the monument as historical evidence but ignores its artistic value, was generally declared unacceptable.

A more modern theory assigns preemince to the work's artistic value as compared to its other aspects and characteristics, which must be considered subordinate. If architecture is art and, consequently, the architectural work a work of art, restoration must recognize the value of a monument and determine the presence or lack of artistic quality in it. Secondly, restoration must recover the work of art by restoring and freeing it.

Every operation should be subordinated to the aim of re-establishing and preserving the expressive meaning of the work, since the goal is the liberation of its true form. When a monument has been mutilated or destroyed it is impossible to recover it.

This approach determines the criteria to be followed and represents a reversal of the scholarly method. It declares the need to eliminate superimpositions and additions (even if outstanding and of documentary value) that undermine the architectural integrity (PLS. 132–135); and it upholds the legitimacy of reconstructions (provided they are absolutely valid and not substantial) in which missing parts are replaced so as to restore the authentic appearance. By this definition restoration must depend on a critical sense since an exact awareness of the action being performed and complete control of its results must be present during the entire operation. When the ability to retrace the image is hampered by destruction or visible obstacles, imagination must be used to recompose the missing parts or reproduce the hidden ones. Restoration as a critical process and restoration as a creative act are, therefore, linked by a dialectic relationship in which the former defines the conditions that the latter must adopt as its basic premises. This system of concepts called "critical" restoration recognizes the value that culture assigns to the monument, admits the need to restore to it that force and meaning which time and events have consumed, and adjust itself to the requirements of the new culture and of artistic appreciation.

In critical restoration there are two different and opposing tendencies: that of maintaining a respectful attitude toward the work as seen in its present form; the other of taking the initiative and responsibility for direct intervention that will change the form in order to increase the value of the monument. The first tendency corresponds to the evaluation of the building as documentary evidence. The second stems from an attempt to achieve that quality of form which corresponds to the contemporary architectural ideal. The second position is the logical consequence of the first and inevitably goes beyond it. Both recognize the historical and formal value of the work, and if the one stresses the evaluation of the monument as it is found, the other emphasizes the need for intervention, superimposing the present on the past in an effort to fuse the old and the new in a true unity.

The transition from the traditional concept of the architectural work as a single and isolated building to the modern one of architecture as a creation with a continuity in time, constantly growing and never finished, marks the discovery of the formal and historical values of the ancient world. This process has evolved slowly and sporadically since the last decade of the 19th century, and the focus of architectural studies has gradually shifted from the principal monuments to their surroundings (i.e., the visual background), to less important monuments, to small and modest buildings, to the more exceptional building complexes, and has finally come to include the entire ancient city. Consequently, restoration as a critical operation examines the entire urban environment and the complete ancient city. The aim is to capture from the complexity of the environment the major and dominant tendency, often one of a nonartistic value. Every real and actual "environment" interpreted in the architectural and figurative sense must be singled out and defined. To achieve this a study should be made in successive stages: (1) a scholarly study that includes a reconstruction of the chronological stages, of the constructive periods, and of the diverse building changes, achieved by examining documents, by a metric survey and analysis of the buildings' structure, and by a stylistic definition and comparative dating of the buildings and their parts; (2) an intuitive recollection of all these premises as the true history of the city; and (3) an artistic, literary, and historical evaluation of the figural complex.

Thus the restorer finds he must add to the aims of conserving or restoring the image those of maintaining the appearance of the city. These may be complex environmental forms, such as a habitual view long established by tradition or a panoramic profile that recalls the history of the city and its transformations to modern life; or they may be simple environmental forms, buildings lacking any artistic value but so closely bound up with the city's past that they become "representative" forms which are full of significance (a church, a bell tower, a castle, a bridge, a civic tower, a public building, etc.). Historical as well as artistic criticism must be used to answer the question of whether these "entities" should be considered essential to the city and whether, in case of total or partial destruction, they should be rebuilt to restore to the urban environment its integrity of form and function.

In this broad framework restoration must operate within the scope of policies and provisions of the civic plan as a whole, which in turn must define the historical center as an organism characterized by its own well-defined function in the life of a city. On this level restoration cannot ignore social and economic factors.

Within the framework of this concept, and to provide for its workability, the decade from 1953 to 1962 was devoted to the study of the technical, legal, and economic aspects of restoration in the context of town planning (q.v.). With absolute respect for the conservation of the ancient city in its present form the following criteria were adopted: to consider the historical center within the framework of the city plan in order to give it a fixed and specific function within the city and a relationship to the size, coordination, and location of the other zones and city services; to enable the ancient city once more to fulfill functions in keeping with its size and building structure and in harmony with its environment by transferring elsewhere all or almost all of the managerial, commercial, and financial offices in order to relieve congestion; to insure that the historical center may permanently retain the businesses and activities that determine its character and to make it the ideal center and "heart" of the city by preventing its decline; to abandon the policy of restrictions and the consequent repression and passive defense in favor of an active and programmed policy of full intevention designed to achieve wholesome reclamation of historical centers by means of a large-scale restorative operation extended to the entire ancient centers; and, finally, to classify such an operation as a program of town and regional planning and, therefore, an integral and essential part of the general plans for municipal, district, and regional development.

However, the obstacles are very great: the high cost of the operation, which is never economically profitable; the lack of legal instruments suitably coordinated with economic and municipal legislation; the absence of government agencies possessing the necessary power and cultural and technical competence to plan and execute the projects for preservative reclamation. In addition, there is the presence of residential communities that are haphazardly and discordantly super-imposed on the historical centers, ignoring, changing, or destroy-ing, for their own practical needs, the structure and form of the ancient city. The continuity that should connect the past to the present is broken, since with rare exceptions the inhabitants of the ancient sections are generally insensitive to the historical factors in their environment. An environment is nonexistent unless it is inhabited, full of life, of changing forms, of individual and group activities; but this life must be in direct rapport, in agreement and harmony with the building environment. This does not occur, and the reason lies in the very nature of contemporary civilization, which has absorbed almost all human energy in the manifestations of practical and economic life, depriving man of the need and capacity for understanding the formal values of architecture and the urban environment. This is why urban restoration remains an incomplete activity that stops at the stages of preservative reclamation and critical restoration and excludes the work of recreating the host com-munities.

Renato BONELLI

CONSERVATION OF ARCHITECTURAL MONUMENTS. The conser-vation of man's heritage is of greater concern than ever before since the rate of decay of architectural monuments has accelerated in recent years. Age and the whims of man have always taken their toll, and the natural corrosive elements (wind, sun, frost, rain, sand, humidity, sea-borne salts, jungle vegetation, lichen, bird droppings) have over the centuries caused great damage to the temples, palaces, churches, and outdoor sculpture that throughout the world give evidence of man's civilized spirit. But the industrial age has added its own destructive forces. As early as 1646, Londoners petitioned Parliament to ban coal from Newcastle because the fumes were considered to be especially harmful. The burning of coal and oil in factories, and the exhaust from automobiles (and motorboats in the case of Venice) have caused a pollution of the atmosphere that is as destructive to stone as it is to humans. Industrial fumes release sulphur compounds into the air that are converted into oxides of sulphur; in combination with water (rain, fog) highly corrosive sulphuric acid is produced; soot and dust particles settling on the monuments absorb the acid and the stone begins to crack, chip, and crumble. In addition to air-borne dangers, monuments are also threatened by the constant en-croachments of an expanding society: the construction of dams, highways, pipelines, new buildings, and the growth of cities has brought about the total or partial destruction of many monuments.

Fortunately there are numerous preventive and restorative measures that can be used to preserve the crumbling stone monuments although few advances have been made in finding adequate treatments that will enable the stone to resist the formation of corrosive chemical agents. (In experiments conducted at the Institute of Fine Arts at New York University the deterioration of limestone objects has been reduced by immersing them in a colorless liquid composed of water, barium hydroxide, and urea, with promising results under laboratory conditions.) Rescue operations are often hampered by high costs, impracticability, and lack of trained personnel. On the positive side are the public interest and concern, the increasing involvements of government agencies, and the active cooperation of international organizations (foremost of which is UNESCO and its International Campaign for Monuments launched in 1964).

Conservation falls into several major categories: immediate remedies in situ; removal either of the endangered object or of its threat; legislation and private intervention; and protection which includes active excavation and restoration or the main-tenance of the status quo.

It is now felt that stone monuments and statues can best be preserved by periodic washing with water in a fine spray, although the operation is costly. In France, André Malraux, Minister of Cultural Affairs, instituted a campaign for washing public buildings in Paris, with striking, though highly debated results. Repair work needs to be carried on continuously, and stone, wooden, or brick parts must frequently be replaced. On the Acropolis, splinters of stone are constantly put back and cracks are filled with cement. To conserve stone or marble, silicic acid, synthetic resins, or melted beeswax are sometimes brushed or sprayed onto the surface.

In extreme cases, when erosion is threatening to deface sculptures, reliefs, capitals, or columns, the original is removed to an inside location (usually a museum) and a copy replaces the damaged part. Many statues adorning French cathedrals have been saved in this manner. An even more drastic removal must be resorted to when rising rivers or the construction of dams threaten to submerge a monument. A most spectacular example is that of the temples in Nubia which have been raised from the water to a safe site some 200 ft. above their original location. The huge ruins (250 acres) of Mohenjo Daro, the great capital of the Indus River Valley civilization (4th mil-lennium B.C.), are being destroyed by water from the Indus River. The government of Pakistan, with the help of three UNESCO missions (1956, 1961, and 1964), has taken steps to pump away the water and permanently protect the site.

When industrial air pollution is the major culprit, the easiest, though not always most practical solution is to ban the offensive industries to the outskirts of a town. The British antipollution acts, aimed at coal fires, will hopefully decrease pollution.

Legislation of various kinds aims to protect movable and immovable monuments (see PRESERVATION OF ART WORKS).

A recent example is the Chinese People's Republic, where a Cultural Relics Administration has been set up under the Ministry of Culture. Between 1956 and 1959 approximately 86,000 art objects and monuments were classified for preservation. Under government order, repairs, excavations, and collections are undertaken, and personnel is trained to carry out the work. In most countries private organizations and the initiative of private individuals play a major part in the conservation of buildings.

Finally, the most general of all conservation is the over-all protection of sites, an activity that can extend to many different fields. The unique features of living and growing cities can be protected. Carcassonne in France was restored in the 19th century and looks today as it did in the Middle Ages. Venice, however, is in dire need of restorative and conservational measures as the level of its buildings is slowly sinking under the water; the exhaust and water currents resulting from motorboat traffic and the weight of the buildings on weakening wooden supports have created a desperate situation that can only be remedied by large-scale operations.

Conservation of an uninhabited site is most often an easier task. Angkor Wat in Cambodia, capital of the Khmer Empire (9th–13th cent.), has undergone restoration of its stone monuments, which had eroded over five centuries of disuse. In Turkey the government resettled an entire village in a new town in order to restore the ancient site of Aphrodisias (3d cent. B.C.). The Soviet Union has made an open-air museum of wooden architectural monuments at Kizhi, on an island in Lake Onega (XIII, PL. 63). Colonial Williamsburg, capital of Virginia from 1699 to 1779, is a remarkable example not only of the restoration of old buildings but of the rebuilding of houses, shops, and streets into a complete 18th-century town; some 600 extraneous buildings were totally eliminated, 80 were repaired and restored, some 300 were reproduced on the original sites, and 50 gardens were laid out. Historical accuracy was the guiding principle in the re-creation of an entire town and its way of life.

* *

RESTORATION INSTITUTES AND LABORATORIES. Institutes specializing in the preservation and restoration of art works and supplied with suitable scientific equipment have been set up only recently, although scientists had already studied the objects discovered after the first excavations in Pompeii and the archaeological remains found in Egypt during the Napoleonic campaigns. The quality and diversity of this material led archaeologists and art historians to call upon the knowledge of well-known scientists, such as Jean Antoine Chaptal (1756–1832), Sir Humphry Davy (1778–1829), Louis Nicolas Vauquelin (1763–1829), Alexandre Brongniart (1770–1847), Karl Sigismund Kunth (1788–1850), Etienne Geoffrey Saint-Hilaire (1772–1844), Pierre André Latreille (1762–1833), Albert Landerer (1816–93), Michael Faraday (1791–1867), and Philipp Emanuel von Fellenberg (1771–1844).

This early form of collaboration was more concerned with the study of the materials than with their preservation, and the techniques employed were still rudimentary. Definite progress was made with the introduction of the microscope by Max von Pettenkofer (1818–1901) and of microchemical techniques that made it possible to reduce to a minimum the samples of materials to be analyzed. A. Eibner, Max Doerner (1870–1939), and A. P. Laurie devoted their lives to the technological study of painting with the aid of laboratory methods.

In 1888 the first museum laboratory was created in what is now the Staatliche Museen in Berlin. During the period between the two world wars this example was followed by many other countries: the British Museum was equipped with a laboratory (1919); a little later the Egyptian Museum in Cairo; the Louvre (1925); the Fogg Museum of Art at Harvard University, Cambridge, Mass.; the Museum of Fine Arts in Boston (1927); the Metropolitan Museum in New York (1930); the National Gallery in London (1931); and the Courtauld Institute at the University of London (1933). In 1938, the Doerner Institut, affiliated with the Staatsgemäldesammlungen of Munich, was founded.

Soon afterward, independent institutions were founded: the Laboratoire Central des Musées de Belgique, which in 1958 became the Institut Royal du Patrimoine Artistique; the Istituto Centrale del Restauro (Rome, 1939); the Istituto di Patologia del Libro (Rome, 1938); the Laboratorio di Restauro of the Museo e Gallerie Nazionali di Capodimonte in Naples; the Istituto Statale d'Arte per la Ceramica "Gaetano Ballardini" in Faenza; the Istituto Sperimentale dei Metalli Leggeri in Novara, which is also interested in archaeological metallurgy; the Laboratory of the National Museum of India in New Delhi (1938); and the National Research Institute of Cultural Properties in Tokyo. A survey conducted in 1955 by the International Council of Museums (ICOM) and published in 1960 by the International Centre for the Study of the Preservation and Restoration of Cultural Property in Rome mentioned 133 institutions: 3 in Africa, 30 in the Americas (almost all in the United States), 13 in Asia, 85 in Europe, and 2 in Australia. In Europe and the United States the majority of institutions handle the preservation of paintings; however, the Research Laboratory of the British Museum has been concerned with the problems of the preservation of archaeological objects for over thirty years.

The rapid development of new countries, which are often repositories of an extremely rich archaeological patrimony but are exposed to the unfortunate effects of a tropical or subtropical climate, presents a serious problem that UNESCO and ICOM, in collaboration with the International Centre for the Study of the Preservation and Restoration of Cultural Property, are now trying to remedy by creating regional centers devoted to the training of specialists and to the study and application of modern conservation methods. In general, a conservation service needs the technical equipment to analyze and examine works with all possible physical and microchemical methods (see TECHNIQUES). The radiocarbon dating of archaeological objects by the carbon 14 test involves the use of very expensive equipment and therefore is used only in a few American and European laboratories: the British Museum, the Research Laboratory for Archaeology and the History of Art at Oxford University, the Nationalmuseet in Copenhagen, the Istituto di Fisica at the University of Pisa, and the Institute of the History of Material Culture in Leningrad.

The problem of training conservation specialists has become particularly urgent, and various institutions have organized special courses for this purpose. Among them are the Istituto Centrale del Restauro in Rome, the Istituto Statale d'Arte per la Ceramica in Faenza, the Institut Royal du Patrimoine Artistique in Brussels, the Institute of Archaeology and the Courtauld Institute at the University of London, the Institute of Fine Arts at New York University, the Akademia Sztuk Pieknych (Academy of Fine Arts) in Warsaw, and the University of Toruń, Poland.

Paul PHILLIPPOT

BIBLIOG. *Periodicals*: Technische Mitt. für Malerei (later Maltechnik), Munich, 1884 ff.; Mouseion, Paris, 1926–46 (later Museum, Paris, 1948 ff.); B. Mus. Royaux des Beaux-Arts, Brussels, 1928 ff.; Fogg Art Mus., Technical S. in the Field of the Fine Arts, Cambridge, Mass., 1932–42; B. Ist. di Patologia del Libro, Rome, 1939 ff.; Ochrona Zabytkow, Warsaw, 1947 ff.; B. Ist. Centrale del Restauro, Rome, 1950–59; S. in Conservation, London, 1952 ff.; B. Laboratoire du Mus. du Louvre, Paris, 1956 ff.; B. Inst. Royal du patrimoine artistique, Brussels, 1958 ff.

Exhibition catalogues of the Istituto Centrale del Restauro: Mostra dei dipinti acquistati dallo Stato per la R. Pinacoteca di Siena, Rome, 1942; Mostra dei dipinti di Antonello da Messina, Rome, 1942; Mostra dei frammenti ricostituiti di Lorenzo da Viterbo, Rome, 1946; V Mostra di restauri, Rome, 1948; VI Mostra di restauri, Rome, 1949; Mostra di dipinti restaurati, Rome, 1953.

General works: M. Berthelot, Collection des anciens alchimistes grecs, 4 vols., Paris, 1888; G. Secco Suardo, Il restauratore di dipinti, 4th ed., Milan, 1927; R. Mancia, L'esame scientifico delle opere d'arte e il loro restauro, Milan, 1936 (2d ed., 2 vols., 1944–46); M. Cagiano de Azevedo, Il gusto nel restauro delle opere d'arte antiche, Rome, 1948; L. Borrelli, Restauro e restauratori di dipinti in Francia dal 1750 al 1860, B. Ist. Centrale del Restauro, 3–4, 1950, pp. 71–84; P. Marot, A propos d'un tableau du Musée historique lorrain: Recherches sur les origines de la transposition de la peinture en France, Annales de l'Est, I, 1950, pp. 241–83; M. Cagiano de Azevedo, Conservazione e restauro presso i Greci e i Romani, B. Ist. Centrale del Restauro, 9–10, 1952, pp. 53–60; A. Prandi, La fortuna del

Laocoonte dalla sua scoperta nelle Terme di Tito, RIASA, N.S., III, 1954, pp. 78-107; E. Vergara Caffarelli, Studio per la restituzione del Laocoonte, RIASA, N.S., III, 1954, pp. 29-69; R. J. Gettens and B. M. Usilton, Abstracts of Technical Studies in Art and Archaeology, 1943-1952, Washington, D.C., 1955; H. J. Plenderleith, The Conservation of Antiquities and Works of Art, London, New York, 1956; U. Procacci, ed., Mostra di affreschi staccati, Florence, 1957 (cat.); U. Baldini and L. Berti, eds., II Mostra di affreschi staccati, Florence, 1958 (cat.); U. Procacci, La tecnica degli antichi affreschi e il loro distacco e restauro, Florence, 1958; P. Gaudel, Bibliographie der archäologischen Konservierungstechnik, Berlin, 1960; F. Magi, Il ripristino del Laocoonte, MPontAcc, 3d Ser., IX, 1960, pp. 1-59; Repertoire des laboratoires de musée et ateliers de restauration, Rome, 1960; G. Morandi, ed., Conversazioni su l'etica del restauro, Milan, 1961; G. Piva, L'arte del restauro, Milan, 1961; U. Procacci, Sinopie e affreschi, Milan, 1961.

Architectural restoration: C. Daly, L'archéologie aux prises avec l'architecture, Rev. d'arch., VI, 1845-46, cols., 273-85; A. Didron, Vandalisme et mouvement archéologique: Les architectes et les archéologues, Ann. archéol., 1846, pp. 46-50; J. Ruskin, The Seven Lamps of Architecture, London, 1849; E. Viollet-le-Duc, Entretien et restauration des cathédrales, Rev. d'arch., IX, 1851, cols. 3-17, 113-20, 209-17; E. Viollet-le-Duc, Dictionnaire raisonné de l'architecture française du XIᵉ au XVIᵉ siècle, VIII, Paris, 1869; J. Stevenson, Architectural Restoration, London, 1877; C. Boito, I restauratori, Florence, 1884; C. Boito, I nostri vecchi monumenti: Conservare o restaurare?, Nuova Antologia, LXXXVII, 1886, pp. 480-506; C. Boito, Questioni pratiche di Belle Arti, Milan, 1893; L. Beltrami, Il restauro dei monumenti e la critica, Il Marzocco, VI, 49, 1901, p. 1; F. Rückert, Les origines de la conservation des monuments en France, Paris, 1913; P. Léon, Les monuments historiques: Conservation, restoration, Paris, 1917; G. Giovannoni, Questioni di architettura, 2d ed., Rome, 1927; La conservation des monuments d'art et d'histoire, Athens, 1931; G. Giovannoni, Vecchie città ed edilizia nuova, Turin, 1931; A. Pica, Attualità del restauro, Costruzioni-Casabella, XVI, 182, 1943; R. Pane, Il restauro dei monumenti e la chiesa di S. Chiara a Napoli, Aretusa, I, 1944-45, pp. 68-79; G. Giovannoni, Il restauro dei monumenti, Rome, 1945; A. Annoni, Scienza ed arte nel restauro architettonico, Milan, 1946; E. Lavagnino et al., Offese di guerra e restauri al patrimonio artistico dell'Italia, Ulisse, I, 1947-48, pp. 123-240; M. Zocca, Il restauro dei monumenti e la sistemazione delle zone ambientali, in Urbanistica ed edilizia in Italia, Rome, 1948; R. Musatti, Il restauro come critica d'arte, Lo spettatore it., II, 1949, pp. 103-06; A. Dillon, Del restauro, Palermo, 1950; S. Muratori, Vita e storia delle città, Rass. critica d'arch., III, 11-12, 1950, pp. 3-52; R. Pane, La restauration des monuments historiques depuis la guerre, Museum, III, 1, 1950, pp. 36-48, 78-89; A. Pica, Italiam reficere, Spazio, 3, 1950, pp. 21-32; P. Léon, La vie des monuments français: Destructions et restaurations, Paris, 1951; C. Perogalli, Monumenti e metodi di valorizzazione, Milan, 1954; C. Perogalli, La progettazione del restauro monumentale, Milan, 1955; A. Barbacci, Il restauro dei monumenti in Italia, Rome, 1956; G. De Angelis d'Ossat et al., Difendiamo il patrimonio artistico, Ulisse, V, 1957-58, pp. 1325-1493; Attualità urbanistica del monumento e dell'ambiente antico (Atti Cong. int. Triennale), Milan, 1958; Difesa e valorizzazione del paesaggio urbano e rurale (Atti VI Conv. naz. di Urbanistica, Lucca, 1957), Rome, 1958; R. Bonelli, Architettura e restauro, Venice, 1959; L. Crema, Monumenti e restauro, Milan, 1959; R. Pane, Città antiche ed edilizia nuova, Naples, 1959; Congrès international des architectes et techniciens des monuments historiques (1957), Paris, 1960; L. Grassi et al., Il restauro architettonico, Milan, 1961; Salvaguardia e risanamento dei centri storico-artistici (Atti del Convegno di Gubbio, 1960), Turin, 1961; R. E. Straub, ed., Über die Erhaltung von Gemälden und Skulpturen, Zürich, Stuttgart, 1963; G. Thomson, ed., Recent Advances in Conservation: Contributions to the IIC Conference (Rome 1961), London, 1963.

* *

Illustrations: PLS. 129-144.

REYNOLDS, SIR JOSHUA. English painter (b. Plympton, Devonshire, July 16, 1723; d. London, Feb. 23, 1792). His father, Samuel, was a clergyman and master of the Plympton Grammar School; his mother, Theophila Potter, was the daughter of a clergyman. While still a boy in his father's school, Joshua showed a great interest in painting. He was only twelve when he painted his first portrait, that of the Reverend Thomas Smart. His earliest readings on art included the theoretical writings of Jonathan Richardson the Elder and an English translation of *Perspectiva pictorum et architectorum*, a manual on perspective by Andrea Pozzo. Joshua's father came to realize his son's artistic inclinations and in 1740 apprenticed him for four years to Thomas Hudson, one of the best-known portrait painters in London. Joshua remained with Hudson for only three years. He then came back to Plympton and began to work on his own as a portrait painter. Toward the end of 1744 he returned to London, where he probably attended the St. Martin's Lane Academy, founded and directed by William Hogarth. His first important work, the portrait of Captain John Hamilton, dates from 1746. Soon he was back in Devon, where he remained until 1749. In that year Commodore Augustus Keppel invited the painter to travel on his boat to Algiers. After disembarking at Minorca Reynolds fell from a horse, an accident that forced him to remain on the island for five months. He finally reached his true destination, Rome, in the early months of 1750. He remained there two years. On his way back to England he visited Florence, Bologna, Parma, and Venice, making notes on the artistic monuments, and also stayed a month in France. At the beginning of 1753 he established himself in London with an assistant, Giuseppe Marchi, whom he brought back from Italy and employed permanently as a drapery painter. Reynolds's success was immediate. In a short time he became not only the most fashionable and best-paid portrait painter in London but also the greatest authority in the field of art and one of the outstanding personalities in English intellectual circles. A friend of Dr. Johnson and a founding member of The Club, which included among its members Oliver Goldsmith, Edward Gibbon, and the actor David Garrick, he coupled his work as an artist with a substantial literary activity which culminated in the famous *Discourses*. He was one of the leading figures in the founding of the Royal Academy of Arts (1768), of which he was president, with a short interruption, from its inception until 1791.

In the last period of his life, cultural and didactic interests prevailed over his artistic activities. After 1768 his output of portraits was less prolific and their quality less outstanding, a situation that can partly be explained by failing sight and his intention of providing in these paintings a model of the "grand style" for the use of young artists. In 1781-82 he visited the Low Countries, assembling a vast body of notes. On his return he revealed a renewed simplicity and directness in his portraits, though he was plagued by ill-health and painted little in the last ten years of his life.

Reynolds's painting, so famous in his own day, has subsequently been viewed, perhaps rather harshly, as an outstanding example of representational "literature," weighed down by an oratorical tone, a superficial and eclectic classicism, and an excessive deference toward the tastes and demands of the public. A more careful evaluation of the artist's writings, which reveal the social aims he assigned to art and how they could be attained, and a study of the various phases of his work indicate that a modification of this severe judgment is overdue. His portraits can be considered mainly examples of an art keyed to the society in which he worked and lived. Their motifs are constant and recurring; while observing certain limits of decorum, they tend to emphasize the more attractive or impressive aspects of a sitter. Reynolds shows little interest in further investigation, for his art is rather the outcome of great technical skill; the various temporary and superficial influences do not contribute to a coherent stylistic development. After 1770, his painting becomes more academic and adheres to conventional formulas, selected with obvious eclecticism. Taken as a whole, Reynolds's art has a definite program but is sufficiently flexible to meet the changing requirements of contemporary taste. This program was complex: esthetically, its purpose was the formation of an English school of painting equal in quality to those of the Continent; the distinguishing mark of this school was what came to be called the "grand style," which resulted from a careful and balanced choice among the various trends of European painting, especially those of 16th- and 17th-century Italy. On the social level it attempted not only to extol the British ruling class but also to define its "historical" characteristics. As a whole it aimed to give to English taste both a classical and modern direction, free from subservience to rules and based instead on a clear, critical evaluation. In this sense, Reynolds was the first to perceive and declare that art was above all an aspect of culture.

The works of the period preceding Reynolds's journey to Italy do not go beyond the limits of traditional English portrait painting, but fluctuate between Hudson's conventional and accomplished painting and Hogarth's domestic realism. The first indications of that strength and sense of drama which are distinctive qualities of the art of Reynolds are visible only in a few early pictures, notably the portrait of Captain John Hamilton (1746; London, Duke of Abercorn). The same Hamilton appears again in a group portrait of the family of Richard Eliot (1746; Port Eliot, Earl of St. Germans). This portrait is still conceived within the tradition of the "conversation piece," but with a carefully planned composition that gives it unusual dignity. In this period the prevalent influence, both in the rendering of the figures and the use of color, is perhaps that of Anton van Dyck and of William Gandy (ca. 1660–1729), an English painter.

Reynolds's experiences during his Italian visit are described in his notes (Leslie and Taylor, 1865). In Rome he praised Raphael's balance and the beauty of his forms and admired Michelangelo's greatness. However the painters of the Bolognese school (Carracci, Guido Reni, Guercino) aroused his main interest and were most beneficial to his own artistic development. In Venice Reynolds's notes became more personal, analytical, and critical. In comparison with the paintings of Raphael and Michelangelo, those of the Venetian masters appeared to him poorer in ideas and more decorative. Here his criticism seems more direct, for by regarding one type of art as essentially decorative, religious and ideological differences tend to disappear and every problem can be reduced to a choice of the most effective means of achieving the desired end. His analyses of Tintoretto's paintings, seen as elaborate constructions of masses of light and shadow, are perhaps early examples of art criticism based on technical and visual aspects. The change in the orientation of taste in English art, which until the middle of the century was essentially determined by Dutch and Flemish influences, is undoubtedly due to Reynolds's Italian experience.

Aside from a few caricatures executed in Rome in the style of Pier Leone Ghezzi (III, PLS. 422, 423), which seem to confirm the existence of a Hogarthian phase in Reynolds's art, no pictures are known to have been painted by Reynolds during his Italian period. It seems likely that he preferred to give his observations as written critical comments rather than in drawings or copies. The first paintings after his return to London show various influences, mainly those of the Bolognese and Roman painters of the late 17th century. In the portrait of the Honorable Augustus Keppel (1753–54; PL. 147), which brought him his first great success, it is already clear that for Reynolds the formal themes of previous periods, whether of Van Dyck or the Italian and French painters, were all part of a repertory to be used according to the demands of the subject. His real aim was to find a new method of presenting the figure as the major theme of a painting. The problem was to render natural, or at least immediately acceptable, an image that was composed, artificial, and full of allusive references — such as the Keppel portrait, which represents a naval officer in full uniform making a gesture of command on the shore of a stormy sea, a reference to an escape from a shipwreck in 1747. One realizes immediately that the uniform, which is peculiarly unsuited to the situation, is present primarily as an indication of rank, while the background suggests the scene of the sitter's achievements, and the gesture refers not to a specific action but to one normal to a naval officer. The determination of the "moral" character was to become the dominant motif of this heroic type of portrait in which the formula of baroque historicoreligious or hagiographic painting was adapted to a social theme. Reynolds's avowed purpose was to transform portrait painting from a subordinate genre to one belonging to the "grand manner," from "face" painting to "historical" painting. For Reynolds the central problem was the building up of an image by means of all the elements that could qualify the subject as a historical personage. The painting itself became essentially a means of presenting a theme and was, so to speak, superimposed upon a previous choice of the appropriate type, gesture, dress, background, and other attributes. Thus, the execution of the painting could be left partly to skilled assistants whose task was to develop the design of the master in much the same way as the plans for a building are developed from an architect's sketches. In Reynolds's art it is useless to pose questions of space, volume, light, tone, and color; the scale of values established by the artist is primarily related to the importance and to the necessity of giving more or less emphasis to the component parts of the image.

The processes by which the individual figure is made "historical" can be reduced to two: (1) the merging of the individual characteristics, traits of physiognomy, dress, and landscape into an image which has a general value and interest; (2) allegory. Though indirectly, the first process raises the question of beauty, and here Reynolds drew on his experiences with Italian classical art. Beauty, as Reynolds understood it, was a balance of values, a harmony that was to be sought in the generic nature of the image. It did not derive from a canon, but moved from the particular to the general through the deliberate elimination of individual traits. Since the significance that the individual acquires in the heroic portrait coincides with his position in a given historical situation, beauty was a social rather than a natural quality for Reynolds. This, incidentally, is the origin of the difference between Reynolds's conception of the identity between society and history and Gainsborough's theory of the identity between society and nature. Side by side with this generalization of "historical" beauty, which as such is always connected with the art of the past, Reynolds used forms of allegory likewise derived from Italian art but with some new elements. Through this process (consisting of drawing similarities between the person portrayed and images from classical mythology or Christian iconography) the portrait's subject is represented as the personification of an idea or a virtue. In such paintings the clothes, the poses, and the settings, in which ancient and modern motifs are often fused, show that the process of allegorization occurs in Reynolds's paintings by analogy, similitude, or allusion; it is as if the painter wished to indicate that in the person portrayed ancient and eternal values were incarnated or lived again as contemporary values of the society to which he belonged.

In the history of English painting, wherein problems of iconography and representation have aroused comparatively little interest, Reynolds stands out as a fertile innovator in portraiture and in an iconography that aims to provide the portrait (usually considered merely an objective or flattering presentation of an individual) with the dignity, the exemplary nature, and the complexity of a historical painting. In the simplest type of portraits, in which the praise of social virtues still leaves room for an intimate quality, the sitter is presented directly without significant gestures and allegorical attributes; the relationship between the subject and his surroundings is expressed through the figure alone. This brings about an intensification in light and color that is rarely based upon direct observation but is used to bring out the character and psychological vitality of the sitter. Among the portraits of this type, undoubtedly some of the best that Reynolds produced, are those of Lady Caroline Keppel (1757–59; London, Kenwood, Iveagh Bequest), Lady Anne Lennox (1757–59; London, Nat. Gall.), Nelly O'Brien (1760–62; London, Wallace Coll.), Emma Gilbert (1762; formerly Earl of Mount Edgcumbe; destroyed), Dr. Samuel Johnson (1772; London, Nat. Gall.), Wang-ytong (1776; Kent, Knole, Lord Sackville), and Lavinia, Countess Spencer (1782; Northamptonshire, Althorp, Earl Spencer).

Among his heroic portraits are those of Peter, later 1st Earl Ludlow (1755; Bedfordshire, Woburn Abbey, Duke of Bedford), Captain Robert Orme (1756; London, Nat. Gall.), Captain Winter (1759; Townhill Park, Lord Swaythling), John, 1st Earl Ligonier (1760; London, Tate Gall.), Wilhelm, Count Schaumburg-Lippe (1764–67; London, St. James' Palace), Colonel John Hayes St. Leger (1778; Buckinghamshire, Waddesdon Manor), and George Augustus Eliott, Lord Heathfield (1788; London, Nat. Gall.). Another type is the large official portrait depicting the subject in ceremonial dress, such as the paintings of William Augustus, Duke of Cumberland (1758–60; Derbyshire, Trustees of the Chatsworth Settlement), the Earl and Countess Waldegrave (1759; Earl Waldegrave), Frederick, 5th Earl of Carlisle (1769; Yorkshire, Castle Howard, Trustees of Hon. Geoffrey Howard), and Frederick, Duke of York (1788; London, Buckingham Palace). Reynolds's allegorical portraits often employ formal elements borrowed from Italian art. In this group are the portraits of Lady Anne Fermor as Diana (1753–54; London, Lady Mary Crichton), Kitty Fisher as Cleopatra (1759; PL. 148), Lady Elizabeth Keppel (1761–

62; Bedfordshire, Woburn Abbey, Duke of Bedford), the actor Garrick between Comedy and Tragedy (1760–61; Rushbrooke, Lord Rothschild), Mary Chaloner, Mrs. Hale, as Euphrosyne (1762–64; Yorkshire, Harewood House, Earl of Harewood), Mrs. Abington as the Comic Muse (1764–65; Buckinghamshire, Waddesdon Manor), Lady Sarah Bunbury sacrificing to the Graces (1765; PL. 145), Miss Morris as Hope nursing Love (1769; Calne, Wiltshire, Bowood Park, Marquess of Lansdowne), Elizabeth, Duchess of Manchester, with her son, as Diana and Cupid (1769; Kimbolton, Duke of Manchester), the daughters of Sir William Montgomery adorning a term of Hymen, called "The Three Graces" (1773–74; VI, PL. 443), and Sarah Siddons as the Tragic Muse (1784; San Marino, Calif., Huntington Art Gall.).

Another group of portraits is associated with Christian iconography, especially with the theme of the Virgin and Child. Examples are the portraits of Lady Cathcart and her daughter (1755; Trustees of late Earl Cathcart), with obvious derivations from Parmigianino, and those of Mrs. Joseph Martin and her son (1761–62; Overbury Court, R. Holland Martin), Lady Harewood and her daughter (1762–64; Yorkshire, Harewood House, Earl of Harewood), Mrs. Richard Hoare and her son (1767–68; London, Wallace Coll.), Mrs. Crewe as St. Genevieve, a work somewhat in the manner of Correggio (1772; London, Marquess of Crewe), Lady Melbourne and her son (1773; formerly Panshanger, Lady Desborough), Master Wynn as the infant John the Baptist, which is reminiscent of Francesco Furini (ca. 1774; Wynnstay, Sir H. L. Watkin Williams Wynn), Mrs. Sheridan (?) as St. Cecilia (1775; Wynnstay, Sir H. L. Watkin Williams Wynn), and Miss Frances Isabella Gordon (*Heads of Angels*; 1787; London, Nat. Gall.). Close to these in spirit are the few Reynolds paintings that are not portraits: *John the Baptist* (ca. 1776; London, Wallace Coll.), *The Infant Samuel* (1776; PL. 146), *Nymph and Cupid* ("The Snake in the Grass"; 1784; London, Tate Gall.), and the designs for windows in the chapel of New College, Oxford.

On occasion Reynolds could paint sensitive and appealing portraits of women and children without reference to classical or religious themes, though at times with some action indicated to reveal character. Characteristic of these are the pictures of Lady Caroline Keppel (1757–59; London, Kenwood, Iveagh Bequest), Countess Spencer and Lady Georgiana Spencer (1759–61; Northamptonshire, Althorp, Earl Spencer), Lady Mary Bruce (1765–67; Sussex, Goodwood House, Duke of Richmond and Gordon), Mrs. Abington as Miss Prue in *Love for Love* (1771; Northamptonshire, Wakefield Lodge, Lord Hillingdon), Miss Jane Bowles (1775; London, Wallace Coll.), Mrs. Carnac (ca. 1778; PL. 145), Diana, Viscountess Crosbie (1779; San Marino, Calif., Huntington Art Gall.), Lady Caroline Howard (1779; Washington, D.C., Nat. Gall.), Lavinia, Viscountess Althorp (1782; Northamptonshire, Althorp, Earl Spencer), Georgiana, Duchess of Devonshire, and her daughter (1786; Derbyshire, Trustees of the Chatsworth Settlement), and Mrs. Braddyll (1788; London, Wallace Coll.), as well as *The Age of Innocence* (1788; PL. 146).

Reynolds also painted many portraits of lawyers, churchmen, and men of letters. In these paintings flattery was not important and the artist concentrated his attention on rendering the dignity and composure of the sitter, and on faithfully reproducing his features. Among these are the various portraits of Samuel Johnson (1756–57, London, Nat. Portrait Gall.; and 1770, London, Nat. Gall.), Horace Walpole (1756; London, Marchioness of Lansdowne), Laurence Sterne (1760; London, Marchioness of Lansdowne), Archbishop Richard Robinson (1763–64; Oxford, Christ Church), Edmund Burke (1767–69; Milton Park, Earl Fitzwilliam), David Garrick in the role of Kiteley (1768; Windsor Castle), William Robertson (1772; Edinburgh, Scottish Nat. Portrait Gall.), Joseph Baretti (1774; Melbury House, Earl of Ilchester), Archbishop William Markham (1778; Oxford, Christ Church), John Hely Hutchinson (1778; North Mymms Park, Mrs. W. S. M. Burns), and Joshua Sharpe (1786; Cowdray Park, Viscount Cowdray). To these must be added the fairly large group of self-portraits, among which those in the National Portrait Gallery (1753)

and in the Royal Academy (1773) are particularly important (PL. 146).

In his constant desire to free the portrait from the limitations regarded as natural Reynolds tried to invest some of his paintings with a narrative quality or to present an animated group of figures linked by feeling or action, as in the group portraits of Paul Cobb Methuen and Christian Methuen (1759; Chippenham, Wiltshire, Corsham Court, Lord Methuen), the children of Edward Holden Cruttenden (1763?; New York, Marshall Field), Amabel and Mary Jemima York (1760; Cleveland, Mus. of Art), Charles James Fox with Lady Sarah Bunbury and Lady Susan Fox Strangways (1761–64; Melbury House, Earl of Ilchester), the Penn family (1763–64; Tempsford Hall, Mrs. R. Wynne), Henry Fane with Inigo Jones and Charles Blair (1766; New York, Met. Mus.), Lord Thomas Sydney and Colonel John Dyke Acland as archers (1770; Tetton House, Mrs. Mervyn Herbert), David Garrick and his wife (1773; Apley Park, Major Arthur Foster), the family of George, Duke of Marlborough (1778; Oxfordshire, Blenheim Palace, Duke of Marlborough), and the Society of Dilettanti (I and II; 1777–79; London, Society of Dilettanti).

Reynolds was extremely sensitive to changes in public taste and to the work of painters who influenced it, and he could not fail to react to the presence of Ramsay and, after 1774, of Gainsborough. His relations with the latter were particularly complex. Though it is true that the professional rivalry between them led to friction in the Royal Academy, it is also true that each had a profound respect for the other. The dying Gainsborough summoned Reynolds to ask his opinion of his last paintings; and Reynolds dedicated to Gainsborough's memory one of the *Discourses*, a brilliant critical essay in which, though warning young painters of the dangers of imitating Gainsborough's style, he paid a moving tribute to his genius. It would be incorrect to speak of a direct influence of Gainsborough on Reynolds; nevertheless, Reynolds's interest in Gainsborough's portraits is demonstrated by his growing tendency to place figures in an open landscape, the colors of which blend with those of the figure. This tendency, already evident in the portrait of Thomas Lister, the so-called "Brown Boy" (1764; Swinton Park, Viscountess Swinton), grew stronger with the years and culminated in the grandiose compositions of figures and landscape that began in 1774, the very year Gainsborough moved to London. Among such paintings are the portraits of the Countess of Bellamont (ca. 1774; formerly Bath House, Lady Ludlow), Jane Fleming, Countess of Harrington (1775; Yorkshire, Harewood House, Earl of Harewood, and 1777–79; San Marino, Calif., Huntington Art Gall.), Lord Althorp (1776; Northamptonshire, Althorp, Earl Spencer), Mrs. R. B. Lloyd (1776; Rushbrooke Hall, Lord Rothschild), Catherine Moore, Lady Bamfylde (1777; London, Nat. Gall.), Lady Frances Marsham (1777; London, Baroness Burton), Lady Elizabeth Delmé and children (1777; Washington, D.C., Nat. Gall.), John Musters (1777–80; Boston, Mus. of Fine Arts), Colonel George Coussmaker (1782; New York, Met. Mus.), and Lady Selina Skipwith (1787; New York, Frick Coll.).

In the final phase of Reynolds's activity, particularly after his visit to the Low Countries, some Dutch and Flemish influence appeared in his style — notably that of Rubens. The brushwork becomes more nervous, the composition freer, and a greater predilection for sharp contrasts of black and white is noticeable. Gainsborough's influence seems to have become stronger in this period, as shown by the Arcadian nature of the sitters' costumes and of the settings in the portraits of the young Catherine Pelham-Clinton (1781; Salisbury, Wiltshire, Longford Castle, Earl of Radnor) and Lady Gertrude Fitzpatrick as Sylvia (1787; Boston, Mus. of Fine Arts). But in the choice of colors, the arrangement of the composition, and the technique it is possible to find evidence of Reynolds's careful study of the paintings of Frans Hals.

One of the most original aspects of Reynolds's art, particularly in his later period, is his choice and juxtaposition of colors. (Unfortunately the lavish use of varnish glazes and at times bitumen has caused a serious deterioration in the colors.) In accordance with his theories Reynolds paid much attention to the general color scheme, which was often based on a wide range of dark tones; within the limits of this general scheme he aimed at grouping his colors according to contrast and variety, and he frequently achieved effects of great liveliness and modernity, particularly in the juxtaposition of black with pure white, silver, gray, and pale pink.

The most important writings by Reynolds are the *Discourses* (15 in all), comprising his annual addresses as president of the Royal Academy. Reynolds does not set out to construct a theory of art, but rather to guide the artistic formation of young painters through the study of previous artistic achievements. His essays are interesting examples of art criticism directed toward a didactic end. Of particular importance is his theory — probably formulated in opposition to Gainsborough's ideas — that art is not the product of divine inspiration but depends on cultural experience guided by reason. For Reynolds, an artist who shared the rationalistic orientation of English culture, art is the product of criticism. An artist can succeed in developing a perfect standard of judgment and a valid art only after acquiring an ability to discriminate and choose the best values from the vast area of tradition. Like his painting, the *Discourses*, in their chronological sequence, reveal the changes in his views in relation to the general evolution of English culture.

Bibliog. J. Reynolds, Discourses Delivered at the Royal Academy, London, 1769–91; E. Malone, ed., The Works of Sir Joshua Reynolds, 2 vols., London, 1797 (new ed., R. R. Wark, San Marino, Calif., 1959); E. Edwards, Anecdotes of Painters, London, 1808; J. S. Northcote, Memoirs of Sir Joshua Reynolds, 2 vols., London, 1813–15; E. Wheatley, Descriptive Catalogue of All the Prints from Portraits, London, 1825; W. Cotton, Sir Joshua Reynolds and His Works, London, 1856; W. Cotton, A Catalogue of the Portraits Painted by Sir Joshua Reynolds, London, 1857; C. R. Leslie and T. Taylor, Life and Times of Sir Joshua Reynolds, 2 vols., London, 1865; E. Hamilton, A Catalogue Raisonné of the Engraved Works of Sir Joshua Reynolds, London, 1874; E. Chesneau, Joshua Reynolds, Paris, 1887; C. Phillips, Sir Joshua Reynolds, London, New York, 1894; A. Graves and W. V. Cronin, A History of the Works of Sir Joshua Reynolds, 4 vols., London, 1899–1901; W. Armstrong, Sir Joshua Reynolds, London, New York, 1900; F. Benoit, Les portraits de Reynolds, Rev. de l'art ancien et moderne, XVI, 1904, pp. 229–48; R. Davies, Reynolds, London, 1913; F. W. Hilles, ed., Letters of Sir Joshua Reynolds, Cambridge, 1929; E. Wind, Humanitätsidee und heroisiertes Porträt in der englischen Kultur des 18. Jahrhunderts, Vorträge der Bib. Warburg, IX, 1930–31, pp. 156–229; C. H. Collins Baker and M. R. James, English Painting, London, 1933; J. Steegmann, Sir Joshua Reynolds, London, 1933; ThB, XXVIII, s.v. (bibliog.); L. Greenway, Alterations in the Discourses of Sir Joshua Reynolds, New York, 1936; F. W. Hilles, The Literary Career of Sir Joshua Reynolds, Cambridge, 1936; E. K. Waterhouse, A Review of Reynolds, BM, LXX, 1937, pp. 105–12; E. Wind, Borrowed Attitudes in Reynolds and Hogarth, Warburg, II, 1938–39, pp. 182–85; E. K. Waterhouse, Reynolds, London, 1941; W. J. Hipple, General and Particular in the Discourses of Sir Joshua Reynolds: A Study in Method, J. of Aesthetics and Art Criticism, XI, 1952–53, pp. 231–47; E. K. Waterhouse, Painting in Britain: 1530 to 1790, London, 1953; A. Gwynne-Jones, The Life and Works of Sir Joshua Reynolds, J. Royal Soc. of Arts, CIV, 1955–56, pp. 793–807; M. L. d'Otrange-Mastai, Simplicity and Truth: Reynolds, Painter of Childhood, Apollo, LXV, 1957, pp. 201–05; D. Hudson, Sir Joshua Reynolds: A Personal Study, London, 1958; J. Steegmann, Some Reynolds Problems, AQ, XXI, 1958, pp. 246–56; S. Lövgren, Joshua Reynolds, Figura, N.S., I (Idea and Form), 1959, pp. 153–80; G. Boas, Sir Joshua Reynolds as Arbiter of Taste, GBA, LVIII, 1961, pp. 93–108; E. C. Elliott, Reynolds and Hazlitt, J. of Aesthetics and Art Criticism, XXI, 1962–63, pp. 73–79; A. L. Baldry, Sir Joshua Reynolds, London, n.d. [ca. 1905].

Giulio Carlo Argan

Illustrations: pls. 145–148.

RHODESIA, ZAMBIA, and MALAWI. Rhodesia (formerly Southern Rhodesia), Zambia (formerly Northern Rhodesia), and Malawi (formerly Nyasaland) are surrounded by the Congo (formerly Belgian Congo), Tanziana (formerly Tanganyika), Angola, Bechuanaland, South Africa (formerly Union of South Africa), and Mozambique. Rhodesia, Zambia, and Malawi are inhabited by Bantu peoples, whose contemporary artistic production is very limited. The numerous rock paintings and the archaeological complex of Zimbabwe are outstanding. Although contact with Western civilization, which began with British colonization in 1890, inaugurated a period of considerable economic expansion, it has nevertheless failed so far to give rise to artistic trends of any importance.

Summary. Prehistory and archaeology (col. 208): *Rock paintings; Ruins; Terracing and slave pits; Pottery and figurines.* Modern native art (col. 211): *Rhodesia; Zambia; Malawi.* Modern period (col. 212). Centers (col. 213).

Prehistory and archaeology. *Rock paintings.* Much of the territory is characterized by large, bare granite rock formations with so-called caves, which are really ledges with overhanging rocks. These have provided the setting for many pictures of animals, wild and domestic, and of hunting, battle, and dance scenes. Protected from the weather by overhanging ledges, most are in a good state of preservation and the color is excellent. Some paintings show one or two superimpositions, an indication that they were made at different periods. Some are drawn in outline; others are shaded in. They reveal a remarkable feeling for mass and movement and some knowledge of perspective.

There have been many theories about the dating and attribution of these paintings, but it now seems certain that they were executed by Bushmen in a period that cannot easily be determined and that may range from the Neolithic age to recent decades (see paleo-african cultures). Many rock paintings have been found throughout Rhodesia, Zambia, and Malawi; particularly important are those of the Bambata cave (Matopos Hills, Rhodesia), discovered by N. Jones in 1917. The presence of a large variety of implements, deeply buried in the cave, suggests that this was one of the oldest settlements in this part of Africa. The numerous engravings of imprints of men and animals (at Sunga Road, Wankie dist., Rhodesia) also deserve mention.

Ruins. Early Portuguese records mention stone buildings and frequently refer to Zimbabwe. The ruins stretch in a wide belt from the Limpopo River along the eastern side of Rhodesia to the Zambesi. There is definite evidence that they are connected with similar ruins in the northern Transvaal, and further exploration may reveal that they are distributed over a much wider area. The best-known ruins are those of Zimbabwe near Victoria (Fort Victoria), Khami near Bulawayo, Dhlo-Dhlo, and Nalatali.

In 1905 MacIver made a brief but scientific survey of the ruins, which has been the basis for all succeeding work. Hall (1902), who attributed great age to Khami, considered that it was of later construction than Zimbabwe and that there had been four successive occupations dating back to A.D. 915. He thought that the original builders and subsequent occupiers were probably of African stock. His theory of successive occupations, based on varying styles of wall construction, types of weapons and pottery, and the presence or absence of gold, lacks sufficient evidence, however, to satisfy modern archaeologists. MacIver (1906), Caton-Thompson (1931), Schofield (1948), and Robinson (1959) are all agreed about the culture being of African origin, but this does not necessarily mean Bantu origin. A wooden lintel found in the Zimbabwe ruins some years ago was subjected to the carbon 14 test and its age has been set as 1361 years. If this tree was felled specifically for a lintel at Zimbabwe, then Zimbabwe was built between A.D. 471 and 711. There are, however, other factors that could alter this date in either direction.

Terracing and slave pits. In the northeastern section of Rhodesia are remains of ancient terracing and possibly of an irrigation system. The area, which occupies the eastern slopes of the plateau, is well-watered, and it is possible that at some period it maintained a fairly dense agricultural population, probably non-African. Who these people were, what happened to them, and what connection they had with the ruins remains as much a mystery as the ruins themselves.

In this area are found the so-called "slave pits," which are roughly circular in shape although a few are more or less square. The bottom of the pit is about 3 to 4 feet below ground level and is unpaved; the sides are built of undressed stone. The narrow entrances to the pit — there is often more than one — are walled in stone and are partly covered with stone slabs overlaid with soil and grass. It would seem that the pits were used either

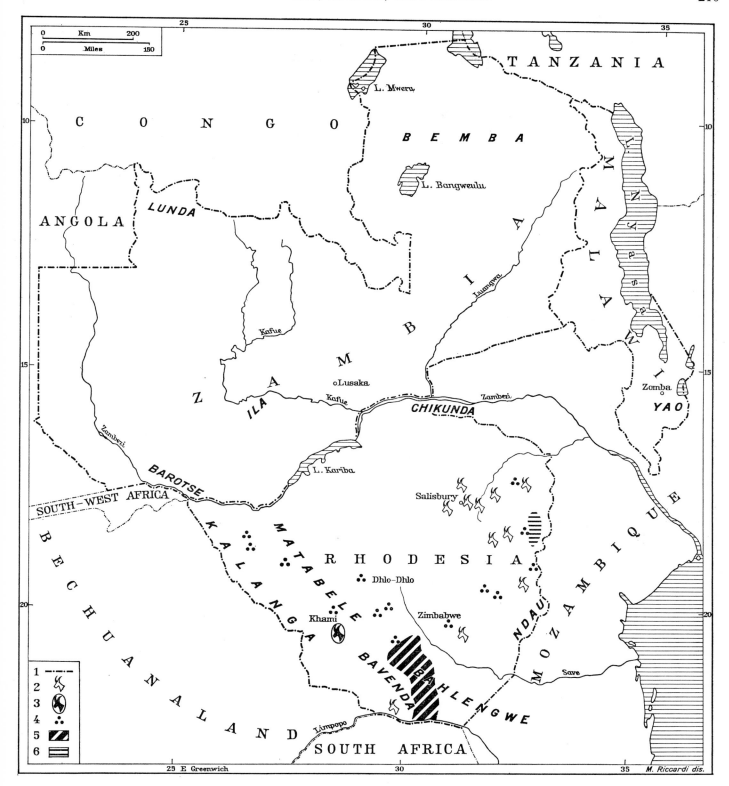

Rhodesia, Zambia, and Malawi, distribution of principal archaeological sites and ethnic groups with artistic production (boldface italic). *Key:* (1) Political boundaries; (2) isolated rock art monuments; (3) area with high concentration of rock art; (4) isolated archaeological centers; (5) area with high concentration of archaeological ruins; (6) area of terracing and "slave pits" (Inyanga complex).

as human habitations or as pens for animals, although there is no trace of the roof timbers that would have been necessary as protection against wild animals or heavy rainfall. Some theorists have suggested that they were reservoirs that collected water by the uphill passage and discharged it through the downhill passage to the terraces referred to above. An examination of the location of some of the pits and passages, however, does not support this view. Neither does it favor the theory that the pits

were used by slave dealers — hence the term slave pits — to house slaves during overnight halts.

Pottery and figurines. The pottery found in Rhodesia has been variously classified. Schofield (1948) has classed pottery found at Gokomere and Zimbabwe as R1 and considers that the pottery found at Khami has affinities with both the M1 and M2 types from Mapungubwe and Bambandyanalo in the Limpopo

Valley. Other types found have been classified as R2. Summers (1958) and Bernhard (1961), who have carried out work at Inyanga, have found what is termed Ziwa pottery, types Z1 and Z2. Schofield considered Ziwa ware a borderline case, because of the many instances where pot shapes show a strong affinity to type R2. Bernhard thinks it can be safely classed as R1, since the Ziwa was a Bush-Boskop culture, whereas the people of the ruins were Bantu-speaking Negro immigrants who settled in the region not earlier than the late 11th century.

Geometric designs, engraved in bands or panels, filled in with contrasting colors — buff, red, and black — are the original forms of decoration. Black was always burnished with graphite, and animal blood used for the reds. Polychrome band and panel decoration occurs at Zimbabwe and Schofield has included this in his type R3, which he attributes to the Rozwi period of dominance in Rhodesia during the 18th and 19th centuries. At Khami the polychrome type of decoration occurs throughout the ruins. At Dhlo-Dhlo polychrome pottery is also found.

Figurines of animals and humans, in clay and soapstone, have been found in various places. Clay figurines occur in the lower levels of the hill on which the "Acropolis" at Zimbabwe is located, while soapstone statuettes occur in the upper levels. The most famous are the Zimbabwe birds (Von Sicard, 1943). Von Sicard found a soapstone human figurine in the Belingwe district which he termed a fertility doll. Schofield considers that clay figurines of humans and animals are connected with initiatory ceremonies and adduces evidence from Zambia in support of this view.

Beads, gold, and ornaments have been found at Zimbabwe and Khami. At Gokomere some fine specimens of stone implements and weapons have been discovered.

MODERN NATIVE ART. The area covered by Rhodesia, Zambia, and Malawi was subject to migrations and raids, which created unsettled conditions not conducive to the development of any specialization. Moreover, because of the savanna type of vegetation and the climate, the tribes were nomadic cattle owners rather than settled agriculturists. The tribes only established themselves in the area when the migrations and raids were brought to a standstill by European settlement over the last 70 to 200 years.

As a result of these conditions, the type of arts and crafts existing today is the same as it was before the Europeans arrived, and is found over an eastern-central area extending from the Ciskei in South Africa to the borders of Ethiopia.

The articles manufactured by the Africans are determined by their needs, the available natural resources, their tools, and foreign introductions such as beads. Their needs are simple and limited. Articles fall into three classes: utilitarian, ceremonial, and religious or mystical, the ceremonial and the religious often being indistinguishable.

With the exception of iron and copper the raw materials are unprocessed. They include soft woods for drums and ebony and other hard woods for smaller articles; calabashes, gourds, grasses, and fibers for domestic purposes; clay for pots, which are made with the coil method; metals for personal decoration, weapons, and tools; and soapstone for figurines. The only tools are the hoe, knife, ax, and adze. There are no looms, spinning wheels, or potters' wheels.

There is a high degree of uniformity in design and decoration. The basis of decorative design is the triangle or the open V, and the hatchings made by comb or grasses follow the main lines of this basic design. It is found on pots, in wood- and metalwork, mats, baskets, and beadwork. In pottery one or more bands often supplement the main design, which is usually on the shoulder or the upper neck. The bands are incised with the open V design, or a small square, rectangle, or circle, or merely slanting lines. All designs on clay or metal are incised, while in calabashes and woodwork effects are achieved by incision, peeling, and marquetry. There is a basic square design for mats and some types of baskets. The snake pattern appears in some rock paintings and in decorative work, and may have a religious significance.

In pottery the clays are usually gray or red, and the colors — black, red, and yellow — are mixed with fat and applied after firing. Burnishing is done with a smooth stone. Bright colors are much used in beadwork. In fiberwork the pattern is usually black or brown.

It is difficult to distinguish between the arts and crafts of the different tribes. Generally tribes living on a subsistence economy have to be self-sufficient and hence the same products are found in varying degrees of craftsmanship all over the area and are similar to those in contiguous territories.

Rhodesia. In the eastern districts the Arabs and Portuguese have had an influence on the handicrafts of the Ndau (Vandau) and Bahlengwe, as can be seen in products of ivory, metal, and wood (II, PLS. 130, 131). In the southeast, bordering the Transvaal, the Bavenda work in iron and copper and produce anthropomorphic and zoomorphic statuettes whose rough modeling recalls the paliform style. They also carve wooden dishes with zodiacal motifs. In the southwest, particularly among the Kalanga, the wild animal skin blankets (karosses) are outstanding. The work of the Matabele is similar to that of the Zulu from whom they originated.

Zambia. The Ila are experts at ivory turning, iron smelting, and smithing, producing 12 varieties of spears, hoe heads, iron bullets, 3 varieties of axes, razors, tongs, adzes, billhooks, bells, and fishhooks. They are not skilled woodworkers. The Barotse (Lozi) work in iron, clay, and wood (II, PL. 131). The decoration and workmanship are of a high order, and there is a great variety in the design of articles and in the materials used. Their outstanding work is the royal barge of the Barotse king. The Lunda are skilled blacksmiths, and make good raffia mats, baskets, and dugout canoes. The Bemba crafts, with the exception of wood carving, are poorly developed and decoration is of a low order, being limited to the simplest geometric designs.

Malawi. The Yao (Wayao), as a result of Arab influence, build square houses, which have decorated exterior and interior walls, and in some cases roofs decorated with figures of birds. They also execute interesting clay reliefs, which are connected with initiation rites, and manufacture bark cloth. The Maravi are smelters of iron and forge hoes, adzes, axes, spears, needles, arrowheads, and bracelets. The Chikunda are skilled metalworkers, having been trained as goldsmiths by the Portuguese.

James H. FARQUHAR

MODERN PERIOD. With British colonization, started in 1890 by the British South Africa Company founded by Cecil Rhodes, a period of notable economic expansion began and a program of public works was undertaken — such as the Selous Road (1890), a major highway guarded by small garrison forts that linked the chief commercial centers of the region — and cities such as Salisbury (1890), Bulawayo (1893), and Livingstone (1905) were founded. Their growth is now controlled by modern town-planning criteria. Many other centers, for example, Fort Victoria, Fort Jameson, and Fort Rosebery, grew up around armed garrisons.

Blantyre, the main trade and industrial center of Malawi, has many administrative and religious buildings, of which the Scottish Mission Church is particularly noteworthy. Bulawayo is laid out on a rectangular plan, with a large market square in the center and extensive parks; some of the administrative buildings are particularly interesting, such as the Post Office, the Town Hall, the Museum, and the Matabeleland War Memorial. Livingstone is built on a checkerboard plan. Its most important architectural structures are the Roman Catholic and Protestant churches, the synagogue, the administrative buildings, and the Rhodes-Livingstone Museum, which contains a collection of native art and handicrafts. Lusaka, the capital of Zambia, has developed greatly in the last 30 years, with the construction of many government buildings and modern living quarters. Salisbury, the capital of Rhodesia, is a typically colonial city: it developed around a fort erected in 1890 and is built on a checkerboard plan. The most recent buildings are of an international type. The National Museum, built in 1957, is noteworthy.

Francesco NEGRI ARNOLDI

CENTERS. Zimbabwe. The chief features of the ruins at Zimbabwe or Great Zimbabwe are a main enclosure subdivided by high, freestanding walls, partially or entirely artificial platforms for small buildings, narrow passages and doorways, and conical towers of probable phallic significance (XI, PL. 26). The presence of drains indicates knowledge of how to deal with surface floodwater, elementary sanitation, or the use of the enclosures as animal pens. Zimbabwe seems to have been the center of the culture. There are three main portions (XI, PL. 25): the so-called "Temple," which is a large elliptical enclosure, the "Acropolis" on a neighboring granite hill, and the "Valley of Ruins," with its scattered remains of low buildings, the use of all of which is undetermined.

Stone walls may be divided into two main classes: retaining walls, 4 to 10 feet in height or mere curbs; or freestanding walls varying considerably in height and thickness, sometimes battered and sometimes stepped back. Both classes occur together. Wall stones are blocks of granite either square or triangular, 6 to 12 inches long and 3 to 6 inches thick. They were roughdressed on one or more sides by knapping, the hammer probably being made from dolomite boulders. At Zimbabwe blocks could be split from exfoliating sheets on the granite hill formations. At Khami they were formed from boulders. The blocks were laid in courses (without mortar) of dressed and sized blocks and the core was filled with rubble-waste. Very rarely stones were used to tie the wall into its filling. Line and level were not observed and the wall would follow the slope of the ground and avoid natural obstacles. Capping of a wall was done with flat stones and *daga* (clay, often wrongly called cement, though the presence of silicates gave it great strength). Natural rocks in many cases were used to anchor walls. In the "Acropolis" good examples of this are found in the narrow approaches between boulders and in the walls built on the edges of precipices. Some of these walls have truncated conical turrets and small upright monoliths.

Slabs of blue-colored dolomite were introduced probably for decoration, as it contrasted with the gray-white of the granite. Other decoration was carried out by laying only alternate blocks, setting stones obliquely, or by herringbone or chevron pattern. Occasionally designs are inscribed on the stones and have a decorative, a ritual, or other meaning.

James H. FARQUHAR

BIBLIOG. J. T. Bent, The Ruined Cities of Mashonaland, London, 1892; R. N. Hall and W. G. Neal, The Ancient Ruins of Rhodesia, London, 1902 (2d ed., 1904); D. R. MacIver, Mediaeval Rhodesia, London, 1906; E. de Renty, La Rhodesia, Paris, 1907; H. H. Fyfe, South Africa Today, with an Account of Modern Rhodesia, London, 1911; E. W. Smith and A. M. Dale, The Ila-speaking Peoples of Northern Rhodesia, 2 vols., London, 1920; E. T. Jollie, The Real Rhodesia, London, 1924; N. Jones, The Stone Age of Rhodesia, London, 1926; G. Caton-Thompson, The Zimbabwe Culture: Ruins and Reactions, Oxford, 1931; L. Cripps, Rock Paintings of Southern Rhodesia, Nada, XVIII, 1941, pp. 25–35; H. Wieschoff, The Zimbabwe-Monomotapa Culture in South-east Africa, Menasha, Wis., 1941; E. Paterson, The Nature of Bantu Art, Nada, XIX, 1942, pp. 41–57; H. von Sicard, The Bird in the Zimbabwe Culture, Ethnos, VIII, 1943, pp. 104–14; J. F. Schofield, Primitive Pottery, Cape Town, 1948; N. Jones, The Prehistory of Southern Rhodesia, Cambridge, 1949; M. Tew, The Peoples of the Lake Nyasa Region, London, 1950; M. McCulloch, The Southern Lunda and Related Peoples of Western Central Africa, London, 1951; W. H. Whiteley, Bemba and Related Peoples of Northern Rhodesia and East Central Africa, London, 1951; V. W. Turner, The Lozi Peoples of North-western Rhodesia, London, 1952; M. A. Jaspan, The Ila-Tonga Peoples of North-western Rhodesia, London, 1953; M. Trowell, Classical African Sculpture, London, 1953; M. Trowell and K. P. Wachsmann, Tribal Crafts of Uganda, London, New York, 1953; R. W. King and J. de Smidt, The Rhodesias and Nyasaland, Cape Town, 1954; W. Schmalenbach, African Art, London, New York, 1954; Musée National à Salisbury, Rhodesie, Arch. d'aujourd'hui, XXVIII, 70, 1957, p. xi; W. W. Battiss et al., The Art of Africa, Pietermaritzburg, 1958; R. F. H. Summers, Inyanga: Ancient Settlement in Southern Rhodesia, London, 1958; K. R. Robinson, Khami Ruins, Cambridge, 1959; R. F. H. Summers, ed., Prehistoric Rock Art of the Federation of Rhodesia and Nyasaland, Salisbury, 1959; M. Trowell, African Design, London, 1960; F. O. Bernhard, The Ziwa Ware of Inyanga, Nada, XXXVIII, 1961, pp. 84–92.

* *

Illustration: 1 fig. in text.

RIBERA, JUSEPE (JOSÉ) DE. Spanish painter and etcher (b. Játiva, Valencia Province, 1591; d. Naples 1652). Ribera was the son of a shoemaker. Almost nothing is known of his early life and very little of his mature personality. As a youngster, he went to the city of Valencia, where some speculate that he was the pupil of Francisco Ribalta. Possibly in 1616, following stays in Lombardy, Parma, and Rome, he established himself in Naples, then a part of the Spanish kingdom, and married Caterina Azzolino, daughter of a painter.

After a lapse of over a decade (Ribera spent some of this time in Rome), the names of seven children born to them are entered in Neapolitan baptismal records of 1627 to 1636.

Ribera's commissions came chiefly from the various Spanish viceroys of Naples and the Church. His interest in dramatic realism, acquired in his native Spain, would have conditioned him to become a member of the *tenebrosi* as a follower of Caravaggio (q.v.). The strong sense of corporeality resulting from this style must have been a factor in his acceptance of influences from the Carraccis and Guercino (qq.v.) when the subject called for softer or more ephemeral qualities. Within the frame of reference of Spanish art, it can be said that his impersonal objectivity is like that of Velázquez, while his sentimental interpretations, executed with amorphous luminosity, are comparable to Murillo's.

Ribera was an accomplished etcher, working in a painterly style with delicate precision. In his paintings his brush stroke was bold and vigorous, and he used a very heavy impasto to aid in giving the illusion of sculpturesque mass. In both art forms, Ribera revealed skill as a draftsman, dependence on the model, a tendency to static composition, and a provocative psychological range in themes. Assigned to his early period (ca. 1620–ca. 1634), despite the illegibility of the final digit in the date, his most famous painting, *The Martyrdom of St. Bartholomew* (1630 or 1639; II, PL. 192; VII, PL. 386), is composed on Caravaggio's "pinwheel" plan and renounces static qualities for violent action that projects a strong sense of brutality even though the flaying has not yet begun.

A possible connection has been seen between the appointment of the Count of Monterey as viceroy and Ribera's change of style and content in his middle period (ca. 1635–ca. 1639). The Count's taste ran to the Venetian school. He commissioned the *Immaculate Conception* (1635; Salamanca, church of the Augustinian convent). The change is startlingly clear in this work: the entire scene is flooded with light; the movement is soaring and graceful; the mood is one of triumphant joy in majestic grandeur; and the palette has changed from the somber to the radiant.

During the 1640s, severe economic distress in Naples culminated in street riots. As a consequence of the social disorder, the character of Ribera's commissions changed during his late period (ca. 1640–52), and he painted many solitary penitential saints. In executing these works, he reverted to his former Caravaggesque manner and to employing common types as models. Rare among the individual representations were a few group compositions, such as *The Holy Family with St. Catherine* (XIII, PL. 155). These late works are characterized by a dignified pathos poetically personified in realistic figures of serene deportment; the result is profoundly mystical.

Perhaps because he had been the favorite of a series of viceroys, he was taunted with having an "extinct fame." In addition, his health began to fail and he had difficulty collecting payment for his work. Nevertheless, he continued to paint until the year of his death. He signed and dated the majority of his works, sometimes identifying himself as a member of the Academy of St. Luke in Rome and generally designating his nationality. Probably because of this fact, he was nicknamed "Lo Spagnoletto" ("the little Spaniard").

BIBLIOG. A. L. Mayer, Jusepe de Ribera (Lo Spagnoletto), Leipzig, 1923; E. du Gué Trapier, Ribera, New York, 1952.

Eileen A. LORD

RICHARDSON, HENRY HOBSON. American architect (b. St. James Parish, La., Sept. 29, 1838; d. Brookline, Mass., Apr. 27, 1886). The first of the triumvirate of major American architects of the last hundred years — the other two being Louis Sullivan and Frank Lloyd Wright (qq.v.) — Richardson was the second American to study at the Ecole des Beaux Arts. His architecture, however, rarely echoed that of Second Empire Paris, to which he proceeded after graduation from Harvard, studying first at the Ecole and then, when his funds ran out, working for Théodore Labrouste. Returning to America after the Civil War, in October, 1865, he first settled in New York, but early in 1874 he moved to Brookline, Mass., so that he should be considered a Boston rather than a New York architect. His fame, however, was national, and several of his major buildings were erected in Buffalo, Chicago, Pittsburgh, Cincinnati, and even in Wyoming.

To his contemporaries Richardson's architecture, so enormously influential in the 1880s, was "Richardsonian Romanesque"; to posterity it is just "Richardsonian." In the formation of his personal style influences from the High Victorian architects of England were even more important than those from 12th-century France and Spain that were so marked in Trinity Church, Boston (designed 1872; built 1873–77; I, PL. 84), the major work that first made his reputation. This English inspiration is evident in various forms from the early years of his rapid development in his Unity Church, Springfield, Mass. (begun November, 1866), in the greatly superior Grace Church, Medford, Mass. (begun the following year), in which he first used glacial boulders for walling, in the State Hospital, Buffalo, N.Y. (designed 1870; built 1872–77), in the Hampden County Courthouse, Springfield, Mass. (1871–73), in the Andrews house, Newport, R.I. (1872), and in the Cheney Block, Hartford, Conn. (1875–76).

By the late 1870s his mature personal style was fully formed. His masonry buildings, culminating in the Allegheny County Courthouse and Jail in Pittsburgh (1884–88; I, PL. 83) and the Marshall Field Wholesale Store in Chicago (1885–87; I, PL. 84; now unfortunately demolished), were characteristically built of rock-faced random ashlar in granite, brown sandstone, or a combination of the two. As his practice grew larger in what should have been the middle rather than the terminal years of his life, Richardson's personal style was successfully adapted to such various new needs as small railway stations, public libraries, and commercial buildings and grew ever simpler and more regular. His city houses, notably the Glessner house in Chicago (1885–87), were closely related to his more monumental work; but his wooden houses, beginning with the Bryant house (1880) in Cohasset, Mass., were among the foremost examples of what has been called the "shingle style."

A reformer rather than a programmatic innovator, his influence reached Sullivan and Wright at a crucial moment owing to his great Chicago works begun a year before his death. Thus, despite the reaction coincident with his death that was led by his former assistants Charles Follen McKim and Stanford White and that brought about an academic revival of Renaissance and colonial forms in the eastern states, his work led to that of the Chicago school of the 1890s, and its influence is still evident.

Of the 80 or so works by Richardson that have not yet been mentioned, the following surviving examples should be noted: Brattle Square (now First Baptist) Church, Boston, 1870–72; Sherman house, Newport, R.I., 1874–75; Winn Library, Woburn, Mass., 1877–78; Sever Hall, Harvard University, Cambridge, Mass., 1878–80; Ames Monument, near Cheyenne, Wyo., 1879–80; Ames Gate Lodge, North Easton, Mass., 1880–81 (I, PL. 83); Crane Memorial Library, Quincy, Mass., 1880–83 (I, PL. 85); Austin Hall, Harvard University, Cambridge, Mass., 1881–83; Stoughton house, Cambridge, Mass., 1882–83.

BIBLIOG. M. G. Van Rensselaer, Henry Hobson Richardson and His Works, Boston, New York, 1888; H.-R. Hitchcock, The Architecture of H. H. Richardson and His Times, rev. ed., Hamden, Conn., 1961 (with bibliog. to 1961; new ed., Cambridge, Mass., 1966); H.-R. Hitchcock, H. H. Richardson as a Victorian Architect, Northampton, Mass., 1966.

Henry-Russell HITCHCOCK

RIEMENSCHNEIDER, TILMAN (Dill, Till, Thilman). German sculptor (b. ca. 1460 in Osterode, near Hildesheim, in the Harz Mountains, Saxony; d. Würzburg, 1531). He is first mentioned in Würzburg in December, 1483, when "Tylman Rymenschneyder from Osterode" was admitted as a journeyman painter into the guild of painters, sculptors, and glaziers of

Würzburg. In February, 1485, he became a citizen of Würzburg by marrying the widow of a goldsmith. In 1504 he was elected councilman, and from that time on he held various offices in the city government; several times he was elected a member of the Higher Council, and in 1520/21 held the office of burgomaster. His career reflects the rising social status of artists in a period when the great cities of southern Germany — Augsburg, Ulm, Nürnberg, Strasbourg — were full of the new ideas of Humanism. The social unrest that accompanied the early years of the Reformation drew the city of Würzburg into the confusion of the Peasants' War of 1524–25. A minority of the councilmen, Riemenschneider among them, were in sympathy with the peasants and opposed the bishop and other princes of the region who favored the use of force against the rebels. The council refused to mobilize municipal troops to fight the peasants and would not permit the concentration of other troops within the city walls. After the defeat of the peasants in 1525, Riemenschneider was placed on trial and even tortured, but he was soon released. This short but fearful experience does not seem to have broken his spirit, for immediately afterward he was at work again.

No trace of this violent episode is reflected in Riemenschneider's art, which shows a sense of harmony and balance rarely found in the work of his more forceful contemporaries of the late 15th century when, in the north as in Italy, vivacity of action and of characterization were generally considered to be most essential qualities. Nor can any vestige of Riemenschneider's North German origin be detected in his work. While he may have received his first training in that area, the style of his early work shows that he must have spent much time as a journeyman in the workshops of Alsace and Swabia, traveling from Strasbourg to Ulm where the busts of sibyls and, instead of prophets, classical savants (Cicero, Plato, Quintilian, Ptolemy; VI, PL. 129) that decorate the choir stalls of the Cathedral seem to have particularly attracted him. In the Ulm busts, one or more masters from the Upper Rhine (Strasbourg) collaborated with local masters; thus the balance and poise of the local Swabian tradition (e.g., Hans Multscher; cf. VI, PL. 129) were combined with a moderate acceptance of the bold movement and expression introduced by the Upper Rhenish masters. It is typical of Riemenschneider that his inclinations are all on the side of the local Ulm masters.

Riemenschneider's earliest documented work is the altarpiece of St. Mary Magdalene on the high altar of the parish church of Münnerstadt, 1490/92. The statue of the saint (in linden wood; 6 ft., 1 in. high) carried heavenward by angels, which was in the center of the shrine, is in Munich (Bayerisches Nationalmuseum); the large reliefs (Noli me tangere, Feast in the House of Simon) and the busts of the apostles from the predella are in Berlin (Staat. Mus.); and other parts are still in Münnerstadt. The composition of the altarpiece was based on engravings by Martin Schongauer (q.v.), which were widely admired and imitated in many parts of Europe in the last two decades of the 15th century because of the excellence of their composition and the expressiveness of their outlines. In contrast to others, Riemenschneider seems to have been fascinated more by the lyrical, melodious charm of the outline than by the expressive value. The limestone statues of Adam and Eve (1491/93; PL. 149) that once decorated the sides of the south portal of the Marienkapelle on the Marktplatz in Würzburg, in their suave, strongly lyrical style and undulating, swaying outline, are inspired by, if not actually derived from, Schongauer. The pictorial contrast in the head of Adam between shadowy masses (the wild confusion of hair) and surfaces spread out flat (the face) reveals great artistic sensibility. Three years later, in the marble monument (1496–99) of Rudolf von Scherenberg, bishop of Würzburg, in the Cathedral in Würzburg, a similar contrast is found in the head of the Bishop; the same style of portraiture is represented in the tombstone of Konrad von Schaumberg in the Marienkapelle, undocumented but stylistically unequivocal and dating from about 1502. On the basis of these works the tombstone of another knight in armor, Eberhard von Grumbach (d. 1487), can be attributed to Riemenschneider as his earliest (undocumented) work. Five years had passed since Riemenschneider had become a member of the Würzburg painters' guild. Evidently the young master had added to the Upper Rhenish–Swabian qualities that he brought to Würzburg some others of Franconian character, which are seen in the Grumbach monument.

After 1500, the modeling of groups and spaces in the large altarpieces slowly began to be more concentrated. In the Altar of the Holy Blood in the Jakobskirche, Rothenburg ob der Tauber, the shrine is filled with a group of the *Last Supper*, done in 1501/02; the reliefs on the wings and other parts were completed in 1504. The Altar of the Virgin in the Herrgotts-kirche of Creglingen, near Rothenburg, is more fully developed than the preceding altarpiece — perhaps Riemenschneider was influenced by the graphic art of Albrecht Dürer (q.v.) — and therefore can be dated 1505/10. The authenticity of the central group, *Assumption of the Virgin*, and of the *Annunciation* reliefs is unquestionable; other parts may have been done partly or wholly by assistants (PL. 496). The pictorial values which were developed to baroque proportions in the Creglingen altarpiece recede somewhat in the next work of importance, which is of a more tectonic nature: the marble sarcophagus (1499–1513) in the Cathedral of Bamberg for the founders of that church, the emperor Henry II (d. 1024) and his empress, Kunigunde. In 1519 the bishop of Würzburg, Lorenz von Bibra, who had commissioned the monument of his predecessor, Rudolf von Scherenberg, in 1496, ordered his own monument for the Cathedral in Würzburg; it was completed by 1522. In the marble relief figure, a turn toward the Renaissance is unmistakable. On the whole, the loss of pictorial vitality offsets by far any gain in monumental symmetry. The lime-stone frame uses in part Renaissance ornament, introduced by an assistant. Riemenschneider was happier in applying, under the influence of Dürer's later woodcuts and engravings, the new tectonic style to his statues of the Virgin and Child during the 1520s (PL. 150). In the limestone statue in Frankfurt am Main, simple horizontal divisions within the straight outlines of the figure produce pleasing effects of clear articulation and monumental balance. Dürer is not followed to the point where a contrast of directions seems, in appearance only, to challenge the balance of the parts by introducing a *contrapposto* movement. This group, dating from the early 1520s, has parallels in two wooden statues: one the model in the Dumbarton Oaks Collec-tion in Washington, D.C., for the life-size workshop piece of the *Madonna in the Rosary* (1522) in the Pilgrimage church near Volkach; the other published by T. Müller in *Die Kunst*, 1958, p. 328. Another prominent example of Riemenschneider's late style is the limestone relief of *The Lamentation* (1519–23) in the parish church at Maidbroon. Though Riemenschneider is still mentioned as working on this relief after his disastrous experience of 1525, it seems that the work he undertook at this time was only a base for the relief, with an inscription alluding to the suppression of the Peasants' War.

A very extensive workshop, in whose production several personalities can be distinguished, carried out the work of the master where he had not reserved the execution to himself as in the pieces listed above; to these must be added a small number of alabaster statuettes in the Louvre, in Cleveland, and in Bremen. His works were seen in many parts of Fran-conia and Swabia. However, in Nürnberg, where a more austere and powerful manner prevailed, a contemporary gold-smith called his faces "too childish"! Riemenschneider's altarpieces were sent to Thuringia and as far north as Lübeck. Then he was forgotten until the romantic movement of the early 19th century rediscovered him. His moderation in move-ment and expression appealed to the still half-neoclassical taste of the romantics, even more so the almost monochrome character of his altarpieces where the paleness of the white linden wood is rarely interrupted by a streak of color in an eyebrow, a lip, or a ribbon. (All the altarpieces, with the exception of the one at Creglingen, were either overpainted in later centuries or given a dark varnish.) Compared with the vigor and power of the sculpture by Michael Pacher and Veit Stoss (qq.v.), Riemenschneider's work appears to be lacking in forcefulness and conviction, but he makes up for

this, in the eyes of educated art lovers, by his superior "good taste." He is still better known than any other German artist of his time.

BIBLIOG. C. Becker, Leben und Werke des Bildhauers Tilman Rie-menschneider, Leipzig, 1849; E. Tonnies, Leben und Werke des Würz-burgischer Bildschnitzers Tilman Riemenschneider, Strasbourg, 1900; G. A. Weber, Leben und Werke des Bildhauers Tilman Riemenschneider, 3d ed., Regensburg, 1911; J. Bier, Tilman Riemenschneider, 2 vols., Würzburg, 1925–30; L. Schrade, Tilman Riemenschneider, 2 vols., Heidelberg, 1927; J. Bier, Tilman Riemenschneider: Ein Gedenkbuch, Augsburg, 1930; J. Bier, ThB, s.v. (bibliog. prior to 1934); T. Demmler, Die Meisterwerke von Tilman Riemenschneider, Berlin, 1936; L. G. Bachmann, Meister, Bürger und Rebell: Das Lebensbild Tilman Riemenschneiders, Paderborn, 1937; K. H. Stein, Tilman Riemenschneider im deutschen Bauernkrieg, Vienna, 1937; J. Bier, Riemenschneider's St. Jerome and His Other Works in Alabaster, AB, XXXI, 1951, pp. 226–34; M. H. von Freeden, Tilman Rie-menschneider, Leipzig, 1954 (2d ed., Munich, Berlin, 1959); J. Bier, Rie-menschneider as a Goldsmith's Model Maker, AB, XXXVII, 1955, pp. 104–12; K. Gerstenberg, Tilman Riemenschneider, 4th ed., Munich, 1955; G. Poensgen, Der Windsheimer Zwölfbotenaltar von Tilman Riemenschnei-der, Heidelberg, 1955; J. Bier, Riemenschneider und die Schaumünzen des Lorenz von Bibra, MJhb, 3d Ser., VII, 1956, pp. 95–110; J. Bier, St. Andrew in the Work of Tilman Riemenschneider, AB, XXXVIII, 1956, pp. 215–24; J. Bier, Riemenschneider's Use of Graphic Sources, GBA, L, 1957, pp. 203–22; J. Bier, Two Stone Reliefs from Riemenschneider's Workshop in Min-neapolis, Essays in Honor of H. Tietze, Paris, 1958, pp. 209–22; E. Redslob, Erfurt als künstlerische Heimat Tilman Riemenschneiders, Festschirft F. Winkler, Berlin, 1959, pp. 171–80; G. H. Schaeff, Erlebnis und Deutung: 4 Altäre Tilman Riemenschneiders, Rothenburg, 1959; W. D. Wixom, Two Lindenwood Sculptures by Tilman Riemenschneider, Cleve. Mus. B., XLVI, 1959, pp. 187–97; J. Bier, A "Pietà" by Tilman Riemenschneider, B. R.I. School of Design, XLVI, 3, 1960, pp. 1–12; J. Bier, Two Statues, St. Stephen and St. Lawrence, by Riemenschneider in the Cleveland Museum of Art, AQ, XXIII, 1960, pp. 214–27; K. Gerstenberg, Riemen-schneiders Sankt Georg in Stuttgart, Pantheon, XIX, 1961, pp. 88–93; J. Bier, Riemenschneider's Helpers in Need, BMMA, N.S., XXI, 1963, pp. 317–26.

Martin WEINBERGER

Illustrations: PLS. 149–150.

RIGAUD, HYACINTHE. French portrait painter (b. Per-pignan, July 18, 1659; d. Paris, Dec. 29, 1743). Rigaud's four years of study with Paul Pezet and Antoine Ranc in Montpellier were important primarily for introducing him to the portraits of Anton van Dyck (q.v.), on which he subsequently based his style. After another four years in Lyons, Rigaud arrived in Paris in 1681, entered the Académie Royale, and the next year was awarded the Prix de Rome for his *Cain Building the City of Enoch*. He declined on the advice of Charles Lebrun (q.v.), renouncing history painting and study in Rome for a career as a portraitist. Following the success of his portrait of Monsieur, the brother of Louis XIV, in 1688, he worked almost entirely at the court, unlike his good friend, the portrait painter Largillière (q.v.), who painted the *bourgeoisie* of Paris. Distinctions followed regularly for Rigaud, culminating with the Order of St. Michael and a pension from the King in 1727, and the directorship of the Académie in 1733. In 1710, when he was over fifty years old, Rigaud married Elizabeth de Gouy Le Juge, widow of the usher at the King's Grand Council. However, he had known her for some time (cf. his portrait of the Le Juge family, 1699; Ottawa, Nat. Gall. of Canada), and according to recently published documents he may have been the father of a son by her as early as 1685.

Rigaud was a methodical businessman, and from 1681 he kept a careful record of all his clients and the cost of their portraits (*Le livre de raison*); a second record of his payments to assistants was maintained from 1694 to 1726 (*Le livre de comptes*; Paris, Bib. de l'Inst. de France). From these it is known that he ran a large shop producing 30 to 40 portraits a year, copies as well as originals, and charged a higher fee for portraits with new poses and costumes than he did for those in which only the face was original.

Rigaud's paintings mark the full development of baroque state portraiture (see BAROQUE ART) in France and the triumph of the admirers of Rubens in their controversy with the Poussin-istes at the end of the 17th century. Although his mature work, like the parade portrait of Louis XIV (1701; Louvre), derives from Van Dyck's, it is more grandiose in design, richer in color, and stiffer in form. Later, in the playful pastoral portrait of Gaspard de Gueydan (1755; V, PL. 406), his style becomes more rococo. Rigaud himself owned eight paintings by Van Dyck, four by Rubens, and, more surprisingly, seven by Rembrandt. His admiration for the early work of Rembrandt is apparent in the naturalism and sensitive characterization of *The Artist's Mother* (1695; Louvre). Rigaud was indeed the first of a number of French artists of the 18th century to be indebted to Rembrandt.

BIBLIOG. J. Roman, Le livre de raison du peintre Hyacinthe Rigaud, Paris, 1919; A. Blunt, Art and Architecture in France, 1500–1700, Harmondsworth, 1954, p. 279 ff.; G. V. Gallenkamp, Rigaud's Group Portrait at Ottawa, Warburg, XXIII, 1960, p. 225 ff.

Maurice E. COPE

RIVERA, DIEGO (1886–1957). Mexican muralist, easel painter, and graphic artist, one of the founders of the Mexican mural movement and one of the so-called "big four" with José Clemente Orozco, David Siqueiros, and Rufino Tamayo (qq.v.). Between the ages of ten and sixteen he attended the Academia de San Carlos in Mexico City. His first exhibition in 1907 led to a European scholarship. From 1907 to 1922 Rivera remained abroad, where he absorbed various influences. His personal friendships in Paris (he knew Picasso, Braque, Gris, and Klee, among others, and even showed at the Salon des Indépendants) brought his early work within the cubist orbit on a high, colorful, and even lyrical level. By 1917 he had turned back toward the postimpressionists, particularly Gauguin and Cézanne. A meeting in 1920 with Siqueiros in Paris crystallized their mutual feeling about the need for a national and revolutionary art.

By the time Rivera returned to Mexico in 1922 the Revolution itself was over and a movement for the decoration of public buildings had already been launched. In the same year Rivera was commissioned to decorate the Anfiteatro Bolívar of the National Preparatory School; the result was an academic neoclassical allegory, *The Creation*, done in encaustic. Following some experience with the folk traditions of Mexico he began to decorate the Ministry of Education building, also in Mexico City, working in fresco (a technique that was then being revived by the members of the newly formed Syndicate of Technical Workers, Painters, and Sculptors) and in a new style reflecting a genuinely native subject matter. These murals (1922–30) were a direct reflection of the aims and aspirations of the Revolution and set the tone for the rest of Rivera's work, and for many artists they provided a kind of standard by which to measure their own accomplishments. Here, as later, Rivera's style expressed itself through large, bold areas of bright color, strongly outlined and solid but stylized forms, a deliberately restricted space in the modern sense, and a lyrical, even elegiac, quality of mood in his glorification of peasants and workers, who had become his main themes (XI, PL. 446). His next assignment, completed during the Ministry of Education project, was the decoration of the chapel in the National School of Agriculture at Chapingo near Mexico City (1926–27; I, PL. 145), a work generally acknowledged as Rivera's masterpiece. Such details as the monumental nude symbolizing the "sleeping earth" convey his lyrical expressiveness. In 1929 he began his murals in the Palacio de Cortés at Cuernavaca.

Between 1930 and 1934 Rivera was in the United States, where he did frescoes in San Francisco (e.g., California School of Fine Arts), Detroit (Institute of Arts), and New York City (the last, in Rockefeller Center, was destroyed as a result of disagreement with the sponsors). On Rivera's return to Mexico City the destroyed mural was reproduced in the Palacio de Bellas Artes. His murals in the Palacio Nacional (1929–35, 1944–50) represent various aspects of Mexican history, particularly that of the oppressed and the oppressors. Four panels painted for the Hotel Reforma in 1938 had to be removed because of their controversial nature. A large-scale mural for the Golden Gate International Exposition of 1939–40 in San Francisco was followed by a series in the Cardiological Institute of Mexico (1943). His 1948 mural *Dream on a Sunday Afternoon in the Alameda*, executed for the Hotel del Prado and perhaps

one of his best efforts, caused a furor as a result of one of Rivera's typical descriptive slogans (in this case derived from a famous writer of the Reform period), "God does not exist." Although damaged by excited mobs, the mural was ultimately repaired and reinstalled with a different slogan in 1960. Among the later works of the artist are the badly damaged painting in the tank of the Lerma Water Works (1951) and the unfinished mosaic and sculptured relief for the great stadium of University City on which he was working at the time of his death. To the very end his work was characterized by a certain blandness rather than emotional fire, a didactic and expository manner, a sophisticated sense of the decorative and of colorful narrative and detail, and an ability to arouse controversy.

BIBLIOG. B. S. Myers, Mexican Painting in Our Time, New York, 1956; B. Wolfe, The Fabulous Life of Diego Rivera, New York, 1963.

Bernard S. MYERS

RIŻĀ-I-ʿABBĀSĪ. Persian miniaturist at the court of Shah ʿAbbās I, recorded active 1618–34 but without doubt the leading personality of the Isfahan school (see MINIATURES AND ILLUMINATION) even earlier.

Still extant are both fully painted miniatures and more or less summary but extremely sure-handed brush sketches often enlivened by touches of color. His works show him to have been an outstanding observer of nature and of people in landscape and an excellent portraitist with an unusually fine sense of surface and line, a calligraphically lively brush stroke, and a sensitivity to color values. Especially characteristic of his work are the fringed or fanned-out ends of turbans and sashes. As backgrounds for his portraits he had a predilection for leafy bushes and reedlike grasses highlighted, in the colored miniatures, with gold wash.

Riżā-i-ʿAbbāsī, unlike any Persian painter before him, inscribed his miniatures and brush drawings not only with the exact date of execution but also with information about their *raison d'être*: the express wish of a patron, the visit of a friend, or the like. He almost invariably signed them *raqm-i-kamīna Riżā-i-ʿAbbāsī* ("drawing by the humble Riżā-i-ʿAbbāsī"). This stereotyped, calligraphically regular signature was comparatively easy to imitate and was often placed with fraudulent intent on works that were not his in order to give them currency under the name of the famous master.

The list below comprises the works considered unquestionably authentic; those in the first group bear the date (as shown), are signed, and are usually furnished with a further text. Works whose authenticity must be doubted on stylistic grounds, despite apparently reliable inscriptions, are omitted. (This list, although shorter than the less critical one compiled by R. Ettinghausen in 1934, includes several works not listed by him).

WORKS. Old man resting under a tree (PL. 152), A.H. 1031 (A.D. 1622). – Squatting youth with flask and beaker, A.H. 1032 (1623), Teheran, Gulistan Mus. (Kubičková, 1959, p. 43). – Shepherd with goat, sheep, and dog, A.H. 1033 (1624), Leningrad, State Lib. (Martin, 1912, II, pl. 159). – Youth with wine flask, A.H. 1034 (1625), formerly Homberg Coll. (Galerie Georges Petit, *Catalogue ... Collections de M. Octave Homberg*, Paris, 1931). – Standing youth with wine flask, A.H. 1037 (1627), Moscow, property of U.S.S.R. (Krachkovskaia, 1925, pl. IVb). – Lady with mirror and cushions, A.H. 1037 (1627), Teheran, private coll. (Kühnel, *SPA*, pl. 198). – Standing Europeans, A.H. 1037 (1628), Winchcombe, Glos., Sudeley Castle, S. Morrison Coll. (Sarre and Mittwoch, 1914, pl. 5). – Hunchback with bow (PL. 151), A.H. 1038 (1628), date and signature nearly effaced but still recognizable. – Lovers embracing (PL. 152), A.H. 1039 (1630). – Youth or girl in European hat carrying tray with cups, A.H. 1039 (1630), Teheran, Gulistan Lib. (Kubičková, pl. 42). – The dervish ʿAbd al-Muṭṭallīb, A.H. 1041 (1631), Leningrad, State Lib. (Martin, 1912, II, pl. 159). – Man with snakes and bearded spectator, A.H. 1041 (1632), formerly Paris, Demotte Coll. (Martin, 1912, II, pl. 158; Kühnel, 1923, pl. 85). – Lovers, A.H. 1041 (1632), Paris, Marquet de Vasselot Coll. (Kühnel, 1923, p. 79). – Meeting between Shah ʿAbbās and the Indian ambassador Khān ʿAlam, with two pages and a horse in the foreground, A.H. 1041 (1633), Leningrad, State Lib. The miniature bears a note in Riżā-i-ʿAbbāsī's hand, saying that it was executed for the celebrated physician Muḥammad Shamsā, from which Sarre and Mittwoch (1914) and others inferred that it depicted the latter with the shah; however, the Indian ambassador can be identified beyond question, and since he was at the Persian court in 1618–19, a drawing or study made at that time from life is no doubt the basis for the miniature. Apparently Riẓā's pupil Mu'īn copied the scene from two of the master's sketches, which he merely dated incorrectly. The whole composition in its present state is presumably a copy from the hand of the master. – Shepherd with goat and sheep, A.H. 1041 (1633), Sutherland Coll. (Binyon, Wilkinson, and Gray, 1933, pl. 11), an authentic but weaker version of the scene of the same title dated 1624, "made for an album." – Man with spindle (PL. 152), A.H. 1042 (1633), tinted drawing, also executed for the physician Shamsā. – European with dog, drinking wine, A.H. 1043 (1634), New York, Met. Mus. (Sarre and Mittwoch, 1914, pl. 6).

Of the many undated miniatures and drawings that bear the Riẓā-i-'Abbāsī signature, the majority are certainly apocryphal. The following, however, are of such quality and are so close stylistically to those already enumerated that their authenticity seems certain: Youth with album, London, Br. Mus. (Martin, 1912, II, pl. 110b), with long inscription saying that the miniature derives from a sketch by the painter Ustād Muḥammadī. – Youth reading a letter, formerly Paris, Jeuniette Coll. (Kühnel, 1923, pl. 78). – Several huntsmen, one mounted, by a stream, formerly Paris, L. Cartier Coll. (Kühnel, SPA, pl. 917a). – Maḥmūd, Beg of Georgia, Berlin, Staat. Mus. (Kühnel, 1957, pl. 4). – Double sheet, Youth and old man, New York, Met. Mus. (Dimand, 1958, pl. 20). – European with dagger and wine flask, Maidenhead (Eng.), Reitlinger Coll. (Kühnel, SPA, pl. 919).

There are also a number of brush drawings and sketches signed mashaqahu Riẓā ("Riẓā made this") or rāqimuhu Riẓā ("its draftsman is Riẓā") that so closely resemble the aforementioned authentic works of Riẓā-i-'Abbāsī in their concepts, surety and fullness of line, and other stylistic characteristics that they reveal the hand of that master. Because of their great liveliness and freshness one is inclined to group them before his period as "'Abbāsī" and thus classify them as early works. The most important of these are: Pilgrim to Mashhed, A.H. 1007 (A.D. 1598), Washington, Freer Gall. (Sarre and Mittwoch, 1914, pl. 1), with long inscription. – Youth with drinking cup, Paris, Marteau Coll. (Marteau and Véver, 1913, II, pl. 146). – Lady holding a chain, Boston, Mus. of Fine Arts (Marteau and Véver, 1913, II, pl. 156; Sakisian, 1929, pl. 167). – Peasant with horse, tying up faggots, Berlin, Staat. Mus. (Kühnel, 1957, pl. 1), exquisitely observed, signature small, perhaps a very early work. – Servant with horse, Anet Coll. (Marteau and Véver, 1913, II, pl. 134). – Lovers standing, Leningrad, State Lib., with inscription saying that the miniature was painted "in the palace at Herat," completely in the style of the works of the "'Abbāsī" period and related to the 1630 miniature of lovers embracing but signed only rāqimuhu Riẓā.

No works by Riẓā-i-'Abbāsī after 1634 can be documented. Two drawings in the so-called "Sarre album" (Sarre and Mittwoch, 1914, pls. 15, 16) dated 1638 and 1639 bear an inscription in a different hand together with an excellently forged signature of the master, as does a charming miniature in the British Museum (Death of the Scholar), which carries the indistinct date A.H. 1050 (A.D. 1640) in the hand of Mu'īn (see Kühnel, 1943). It must therefore be assumed that Mu'īn was correct, despite his notoriously unreliable dating, when he wrote, of an excellent portrait of his master (formerly London, Quaritch Coll.), that this work of 1673 derived from a sketch executed in 1635 "shortly before his death." In this very lifelike portrait, of which there is another version of 1676, Riẓā looks at least sixty years old; if 1635 is accepted as the year of his death, he could not therefore have been born much later than 1575. It is not known when he entered the service of the shah and, as a court functionary, was entitled to add to his name the honorary title of 'Abbāsī. In any case, since he apparently had no other first name, he was until then known merely as Riẓā.

There are also a small number of sheets which, on the basis of stylistic similarities, might be attributed to Riẓā but which are inscribed, by a different hand, Āqā Riẓā or mashaqahu Āqā Riẓā. There is, however, every reason to suppose that these inscriptions refer to Riẓā-i-'Abbāsī, who may well have been known to his contemporaries as Āqā Riẓā (roughly, "Lord Riẓā"), while refraining, out of modesty, from using this title himself. There is much evidence for this supposition: the brush drawing of a youth with a flower (formerly Martin

Coll.), whose attribution to Riẓā is uncertain, bears the attribution Āqā Riẓā 'Abbāsī (see Karabacek, 1911, pl. 7), and a sheet in Paris (Mus. des Arts Decoratifs), Teacher with girl pupil (see Sakisian, 1929, pl. 184), in Riẓā-i-'Abbāsī's style but definitely not by him, is inscribed rāqimuhu Āqā Riẓā 'Abbāsī. This suggested identification of Āqā Riẓā with Riẓā-i-'Abbāsī is sustained by Schulz (1914), Arnold (1921), and Kühnel (SPA), while Blochet (1926), Binyon, Wilkinson, and Gray (1933), Sakisian (1929) and Gray (1961) reject it; Ettinghausen (ThB) somewhat warily distinguishes between the two painters.

Iskandar Monshi, a source of historical information about this period, mentions Āqā Riẓā as the son of Maulānā 'Alī Aṣghar of Kashan, stating that he had a great reputation as a portrayer of single figures and enjoyed the favor of Shah 'Abbās but that in later years he tended to associate with wrestlers and dissolute persons and thus neglected his work. Qāḍī Aḥmad speaks of him more congenially and in more detail in his work of about 1600, Calligraphers and Painters, translated by Minorsky; he says that he himself was a pupil of Riẓā's father, 'Alī Aṣghar, and praises the young Āqā Riẓā as a "painter of the beautiful," unsurpassed in the elegance of his brushwork and the verisimilitude of his portraits and acclaimed and admired by other contemporary masters. Riẓā, according to Qāḍī Aḥmad, had been brought to the court by Shah 'Abbās, and the author predicted still greater success for him. In a later edition of the same work, about 1606, Qāḍī Aḥmad also mentioned that Āqā Riẓā had changed for the worse, owing to his athletic interests and unsuitable company, but emphasized that he still continued to enjoy an honored position at court.

The testimony of Qāḍī Aḥmad, together with the stylistic evidence previously discussed, justifies the assumption that Āqā Riẓā and Riẓā-i-'Abbāsī are in fact one and the same artist. It is possible that he fell temporarily from favor, but he was still using the honorary title of 'Abbāsī even after the death of Shah 'Abbās I in 1628 or 1629. He must have had a large workshop and many pupils in Isfahan. The most important of these pupils were Mu'īn, already mentioned several times, and his own son Muḥammad Shafī 'Abbāsī. The latter has left us further evidence for the identity of Āqā Riẓā on a drawing that he said was made after a sketch by Bihazād executed in 1619 by "the late Āqā Riẓā" and colored by him, Shafī, in 1654 (see Martin, 1912, I, pl. 39). There is reason to suspect that Shafī also finished other sketches by his father and signed them with a clever imitation of Riẓā-i-'Abbāsī's well-known signature. (Shafī himself later went to India, where he worked especially as a painter of birds and flowers.)

It is certain that the shah called upon Riẓā-i-'Abbāsī for other services. The remains of wall paintings in the 'Alī Qāpū and Julfa palaces in Isfahan and in the palace at Ashraf reveal his style, as do the figural tiled panels in the Chihil Sutūn at Isfahan and various brocades and velvets produced at that time in the imperial factories, whose designs were undoubtedly his or at least came from his workshop. It is safe to say that in the first decades of the 17th century he was the most influential artistic personality at the court of Isfahan.

SOURCES. Qāḍī Aḥmad, Calligraphers and Painters (ca. 1606, trans. V. Minorsky), Washington, 1959.

BIBLIOG. J. Karabacek, Riẓā-i 'Abbāsi, ein persischer Miniaturenmaler, SbWien, CLXVII, 1, Vienna, 1911; F. R. Martin, The Miniature Painting and Painters of Persia, India and Turkey from the 8th to the 18th Century, 2 vols., London, 1912; G. Marteau and H. Vever, Miniatures persanes, 2 vols., Paris, 1913; F. Sarre and E. Mittwoch, Zeichnungen von Riza Abbasi, Munich, 1914; P. W. Schulz, Die persische-islamische Miniaturmalerei, Leipzig, 1914; T. W. Arnold, The Riza Abbasi Manuscript in the Victoria and Albert Museum, BM, XXXVIII, 1921, pp. 59–67; E. Kühnel, Miniaturmalerei im islamischen Orient, Berlin, 1923; V. Krachkovskaia, Musulmanskoe isskustvo v sobranie Khanenko (Muslim Art in the Khanenko Collection), Zapiski Kollegii Vostokovedov, II, 1925, pp. 1–50; E. Blochet, Les enluminures des manuscrits orientaux — turcs, arabes, persans — de la Bibliothèque Nationale, Paris, 1926; T. W. Arnold, Painting in Islam, Oxford, 1928; T. W. Arnold and A. Grohmann, The Islamic Book, Paris, 1929; A. Sakisian, La miniature persane du XIIe au XVIIe siècle, Paris, Brussels, 1929; M. S. Dimand, A Handbook of Mohammedan Decorative Art, New York, 1930 (3d ed., 1958); L. Binyon, J. V. S. Wilkinson, and B.

Gray, Persian Miniature Painting, Oxford, 1933 (cat.); R. Ettinghausen, ThB, s.v.; E. Kühnel, SPA, III, pp. 1884–97; E. Kühnel, Der Maler Mu'īn, Pantheon, XXIX, 1942, pp. 108–14; E. Kühnel, Arbeiten des Riẓā 'Abbāsi und seiner Schule, Staatlichte Mus. Forsch. und Berichte, I, 1957, pp. 123–31; V. Kubičková, Persian Miniatures (trans. R. Finlayson-Samsour), London, 1959; B. Gray, Persian Painting, Geneva, 1961; E. J. Grube, Muslim Miniature Paintings, Venice, 1962 (cat.).

Ernst KÜHNEL

Illustrations: PLS. 151–152.

ROBERT, HUBERT. French landscape painter and architect (b. Paris, May 22, 1733; d. Paris, Apr. 15, 1808). Robert studied first under the sculptor Michel-Ange Slodtz and then, in 1754, went to Rome under the protection of the French ambassador to the Vatican, the future Duc de Choiseul. There he began the painting for which he was to become most famous — architectural scenes and ruins in the style of Giovanni Paolo Pannini and Giovanni Battista Piranesi. There is evidence that Robert visited the ancient city of Cora with Piranesi, and in 1760 he traveled to Naples and Paestum with his good friend Jean Honoré Fragonard and the Abbé de Saint-Non, making drawings for Saint-Non's *Voyage pittoresque dans . . . Naples et Sicile.* Following his return to Paris in 1765, Robert became particularly successful painting decorations for large homes and public buildings, among them the four ancient monuments of Provence for the Château of Fontainebleau (1787; now in the Louvre) and the four views of Norman cities (Le Havre, Rouen, Dieppe, and Gaillon) in the Palais Archiépiscopal in Rouen. He was also much admired in Russia and was invited there by Catherine the Great in 1782 and 1791. He declined these invitations but sent many paintings, including one of the artificial ruin in the park of Tsarskoe Selo (see MOSAICS), which he signed in Russian (1783; in the palace at Gatchina, near Leningrad), although he had first-hand knowledge neither of the building nor of the language.

In 1770 Robert was named designer of the king's gardens, and in 1775 he planned an immense artificial rock with caves for Versailles into which Girardon's *Bath of Apollo* and its subsidiary groups (V, PL. 407) were moved. During the French Revolution he was imprisoned, but in the following year, 1794, he was released and given a position with Fragonard and Pajou in the Conservatoire du Museum National that was comparable to the posts he had held since 1778. His project for installing skylights in the Grande Galerie of the Louvre to make it an effective picture gallery, an idea originally recommended to Louis XVI, was exhibited at the Salon de l'an V (1796) and later executed by the architect Jean Arnaud Raymond; his original painting of the scheme hangs in the Louvre.

Although Hubert Robert painted a variety of subjects, including rococo gardens and genre scenes, his fame rested so much on his paintings of architectural ruins that he was nicknamed "Robert des ruines." He was particularly fond of dramatizing his noble ruins by setting small rustic figures against them (V, PL. 423) or by silhouetting them against the sky or the lurid light of a destructive fire. His exaggerations of illumination and perspective, however, never lost the French restraint and lightness that distinguishes his work from Piranesi's (PL. 310).

Robert's obsession with the ephemeral nature of the works of man and the picturesqueness of ruins led him to paint not only the remains of ancient and medieval buildings but also the devastations of his own time. He recorded the burning of the Opéra (Paris, Mus. Carnavalet; Mus. de l'Opera), the uprooting of the gardens of Versailles for the replanting of 1775 (XI, PL. 150), the demolition of the houses on the Pont Notre-Dame (Louvre), and the Pont de Neuilly, the violation of the royal tombs in St. Denis, and the razing of the Bastille (last four subjects, Mus. Carnavalet). Indeed, Catherine the Great once remarked ironically that the Revolution was a blessing for Robert, since it provided him with "the most beautiful and the freshest ruins in the world." Even undamaged buildings seemed more interesting to him as potential ruins; in 1796, as a pendant for his project to improve the Grande Galerie, he exhibited a painting of the Louvre as an ancient ruined monument, with an artist seated amid the fallen stones sketching the *Apollo Belvedere* (palace at Tsarskoe Selo, near Leningrad).

BIBLIOG. C. Gabillot, Hubert Robert et son temps, Paris, 1895; P. de Nolhac, Hubert Robert, Paris, 1910; T. Leclère, Hubert Robert et les paysagistes français du XVIIIᵉ siècle, Paris, 1913; L. Réau, L'Œuvre d'Hubert Robert en Russie, GBA, 4th ser., XI, 1914, pp. 173–88; L. Réau, Histoire de la peinture française au XVIIIᵉ siècle, Paris, 1926, II, 46–53; P. Sentenac, Hubert Robert, Paris, 1929; Hubert Robert, Catalogue de l'Exposition au Musée de l'Orangerie, Paris, 1933; M. R. Michel, From the "Museum" to Musée du Louvre: Schemes and Transformations in connection with two paintings by Hubert Robert, BM, CV, 1963; J. Thuillier and A. Châtelet, French Painting from Le Nain to Fragonard, Geneva, 1964.

Maurice E. COPE

ROBERTI, ERCOLE DE'. Italian painter (b. Ferrara, between 1451 and 1456; d., 1496). In records and chronicles there appear two family names: Hercules de Grandiis (or Ercole di Giulio Cesare de' Grandi) and Hercules de Robertis (or Ercole d'Antonio de' Roberti). This fact led Barotti (1770) to assume the existence in Ferrara of two approximately contemporary painters, both named Ercole. Even in Bologna, where the young Ercole was primarily active, Malvasia (1686) and G. Achillini (*Viridario,* Bologna, 1513) supposed that there were two artists of this name. Since Filippini's work of 1917, however, there seems to be little doubt that Ercole de' Roberti and Ercole de' Grandi (his mother's name) were the same person. This is confirmed by a document of 1530 in which Ercole's son, the painter Girolamo, is referred to as "Hieronymus filius quondam Erculis de Robertis alias de Grandiis pictor." The determining factor in resolving the problem is undoubtedly the publication of all relevant documents by Bargellesi (1934).

The question of Roberti's birth date has not yet been settled. P. A. Orlandi (*Abecedario pittorico . . . ,* Bologna, 1704) gives the year as 1440; Ortolani (1941) as 1445; Longhi (1934) as about 1450; and Venturi (1890) as not before 1450–60. In a petition to Duke Ercole I of Este, dated March 19, 1491 (Modena, Arch. di Stato), the artist himself writes, "half the years of my life have gone by . . . ." If this approximate indication is assumed to be based on the biblical life span, Roberti must have been thirty-five or, at most, forty years old at the time, and, therefore, he must have been born between 1451 and 1456. In agreement with this supposition is the fact that he was still apprenticed to Francesco del Cossa (q.v.) not later than 1473–74 (Lamo, ca. 1560; Vasari, 1550) and did not appear as a "master" before 1479.

It seems that Francesco del Cossa took his pupil with him when he left Ferrara in 1470. Cossa's Griffoni Altarpiece in S. Petronio, Bologna, can be dated 1473; its predella (PL. 155) is attributed to Roberti by Vasari and Lamo, although it seems that Roberti only finished it. Another work of Cossa completed by Roberti was the S. Lazzaro Altarpiece for the church in Ferrara (formerly in Berlin; destroyed in 1945); the date of completion of this work must be assumed to be 1474. Hence Roberti must have returned to Ferrara at that time. Subsequently, he remained in Cossa's workshop in Bologna until the master's death in 1478.

At the beginning of 1479 Roberti intended to settle permanently in Ferrara. On Feb. 3, 1479, he opened a workshop together with his brother Polidoro and the goldsmith Giovanni di Giuliano da Piacenza, but he seems to have left his native city soon again. In 1480–81 Roberti painted an altarpiece for S. Maria in Porto, Ravenna (PLS. 154, 156), that is reminiscent of the S. Lazzaro Altarpiece. He was godfather to a son of Bartolomeo Garganelli (Gualandi, 1843–45) in Bologna in 1482 or 1483. Between 1482 and 1486 he was occupied with the completion of the frescoes, begun by Cossa, in the Garganelli Chapel in the Metropolitana (S. Pietro), Bologna, where the sculpture was executed by an artist called "Duca" — probably Antonio di Gregorio. The three panels depicting the Passion of Christ from S. Giovanni in Monte, Bologna (PLS. 154, 157) were also executed at this time. During the same period Roberti supposedly executed paintings in the Palazzo Bentivoglio in Bologna, the Chapel of St. Sebastian in the Church of S. Agostino, Cesena, and the scenes from Roman history in the Este castle in Sassuolo (Baruffaldi, 1844).

In 1486 Roberti returned to Ferrara where Duke Ercole I soon appointed him court painter to replace the aging and infirm Cosmè Tura (q.v.). In the same year he was paid for a small painting he had executed for Ercole's duchess, Eleonor of Aragon. In 1487 he painted a small panel for Ippolito d'Este. According to Fino il Volterrano, Roberti accompanied Cardinal Ippolito to Hungary in the same year.

On April 4, 1489, Roberti was paid for work done in a building of the so-called "secret garden" in Ferrara. In 1489–90 Roberti and the sculptor Domenico di Paris worked on the preparations for the wedding of the princess Isabella d'Este to Giovanni Francesco II Gonzaga. Roberti accompanied the princess to Mantua. In 1491 she commissioned a portrait of Duke Ercole I. The painting was still unfinished at Roberti's death in 1496 and was sent to Mantua in that condition. The portrait of the Duke in Modena (Gall. Estense), thought to be a copy of Roberti's portrait, can perhaps be identified with the "Retracto del quondam Ill.mo Ducha herculle" for which Dosso Dossi was paid on April 4, 1526. In 1491 Roberti executed decorations for Beatrice d'Este, the betrothed of Lodovico il Moro. On Dec. 30 of that year the artist received payment for a Madonna fresco commissioned by the duchess Eleonor for an oratory. During the autumn of 1492 he painted trumpet banners for Alfonso d'Este, whom he accompanied to Rome.

Several rooms, including a large loggia ("loggia grande"), were decorated under Roberti's direction for Eleonor of Aragon's so-called "secret garden" between 1492 and 1493. This work was paid for between April and August, 1492, and September and October, 1493. In 1493 Roberti also painted decorations in the Este residence of Belriguardo near Voghiera and produced a topographical map of Naples, Eleonor's native city.

During 1494 he was again at work for Ippolito d'Este. On Jan. 24 Clara Clavee of Valenza commissioned him to execute an altarpiece for the Church of Sto Spirito in Ferrara with the following scenes: an Annunciation in the main panel, an Adoration of the Magi with shepherds and a Presentation in the Temple in the predella, figures of four saints on the framing pilasters, and God the Father with the Holy Ghost in the form of a dove in the lunette. The frame was carved by Bernardino da Venezia (Cittadella, 1864). Also in 1494 Roberti painted a portrait of Alfonso d'Este for Isabella d'Este and executed several works for Alfonso himself.

Construction of the Church of S. Maria in Vado, Ferrara, was begun in 1495 under the direction of the architect Biagio Rossetti and the master of works Bartolomeo Tristani. According to Vasari, Antonio di Gregorio (mentioned above as "Duca") had returned with Roberti to Ferrara, where he was engaged as sculptor to work with Roberti. Like Tristani, he had to work from drawings already drafted by "M. Hercule di Grandi depintore" (Cittadella, 1864). Three years after Roberti's death, Antonio di Gregorio was called upon to execute the sculptured decoration for a memorial column to Duke Ercole I, according to a "designum . . . magistri herculis de Grandis pictoris" (Cittadella, 1864). In 1497, one year after Roberti's death, Fra Jacopo Foresti's work *De claris mulieribus* was published in Ferrara with woodcut illustrations of which several can be so closely linked to some of Roberti's extant paintings that he must be assumed to have designed at least a part of these illustrations.

The extent of Roberti's artistic influence was considerable, as is indicated by the number of works attributed to him that are probably the work of students and disciples, among whom are Lorenzo Costa the Younger, Lodovico Mazzolino, and, perhaps, Bernardo Parentino (Parenzano). A number of works with affinities to the school of Roberti are attributed by Longhi (1934) to Vicino da Ferrara, whom he identifies with Baldassare d'Este, an artist active during the last years of Tura's career. The esteem in which Roberti was held during his lifetime is reflected in the *Cronaca rimata delle imprese del duca Federigo d'Urbino* by Giovanni Santi (H. Holtzinger, ed., Stuttgart, 1897), in the eulogy pronounced by Michelangelo in 1494 and recorded by Lamo (ca. 1560), and in the praise of his patrons. Many chroniclers of the 16th–18th century held him in higher regard than all the other Ferrarese painters and considered him one of the major artists of the period. Numerous copies of his works were executed in the 15th and 16th centuries, especially of the frescoes of the Garganelli Chapel.

Among the few original works that have been documented, those that can be identified with works that have survived are the predella of the Griffoni Altarpiece (PL. 155); the S. Lazzaro Altarpiece; the altarpiece for S. Maria in Porto (PLS. 154, 156); a head of Mary Magdalene, the only remaining fragment of the frescoes from the Garganelli Chapel (Bologna, Pin. Naz.), and some preparatory drawings for the chapel (Berlin, Kupferstichkabinett; New York, Pierpont Morgan Lib.; Munich, Staat. Graphische Samml.); the panels depicting the Passion of Christ from S. Giovanni in Monte (PLS. 154, 157), with several preparatory drawings (Uffizi, Gab. di Disegni e Stampe; London, Br. Mus.); and the drawing of a rider (Budapest, Naz. Gall.), on the back of which a German legend dated 1569 claims it as Roberti's work. Of these the altarpiece for S. Maria in Porto is thoroughly documented; the other works mentioned are stylistically so consistent with it that the traditional attributions to Roberti must be accepted, with the exception of the predella of the Griffoni Altarpiece and the S. Lazzaro Altarpiece, which are not completely consistent stylistically and cannot be attributed entirely to Roberti, but must also be recognized as partly Cossa's.

The monumental altarpiece for S. Maria in Porto, however, is a touchstone of Roberti's style, a fusion of all the stylistic nuances that appear scattered among his other works. An elastic and richly detailed style and inventive draftsmanship characterize the simulated reliefs of 12 biblical scenes on the back and base of the throne. This style, which Roberti derives from Tura and Cossa, is also evident in the simulated reliefs in the S. Lazzaro Altarpiece and in the small Crucifixion scene in the background of the *Pietà* (PL. 157); there are single aspects of it in the predella of the Griffoni Altarpiece (PL. 155).

Some of the main figures in the altarpiece for S. Maria in Porto, especially the standing saint, Beato Pietro degli Onesti, on the right (PL. 156), present an angular, somewhat stiff and construed simplification in the style of the drapery. The sharply silhouetted fold of material along the left leg is typical. This stylistic nuance is even more marked in such works as the Passion panels of S. Giovanni in Monte and the copies of the Garganelli Chapel frescoes. The style of the Madonna's robe in the altarpiece for S. Maria in Porto differs, however, in the rounded lines, which have a Tuscan character; similar folds occur repeatedly in Roberti's later works.

The gestures of the tall, slender figures of the altarpiece for S. Maria in Porto are contained, expressing mood and emotion rather than action. Lively external movement appears only in the simulated reliefs. Although Roberti's color has a rich luminosity, the brilliant tones of his master Cossa are attenuated by him with shadows and delicate nuances of light. Cossa died in 1478; by the time of the altarpiece for S. Maria in Porto (1480–81) Roberti had already freed himself of Cossa's influence. On later occasions he completed works left unfinished by Cossa, but he did this with such freedom of style that Roberti's early period under Cossa's influence may be considered to have ended in 1478.

Between Cossa's death and Roberti's departure from Bologna in 1486 the free use in Roberti's own works of models taken from Mantegna, as well as copies from Mantegna attributed to Roberti, testify to the fact that he was studying the Mantuan master at that time. All Roberti's works in which his artistic expression is most personal and freest from the influences of Cossa and Mantegna can be assigned to his last period. Most of the works of this period (1486–96) have been lost, and are best authenticated in documents. After Roberti's return to Ferrara, where he was the leading master, he enjoyed unlimited authority and artistic freedom, and his radical "expressionism" found great favor.

In a chronological organization of Roberti's works, a drawing of St. Sebastian (New York, Lehman Coll.) belongs at the beginning of his early period (to 1478). The general composition and the landscape motifs indicate a painting by Cossa, reworked by Roberti in an uncertain technique that suggests a very early date — one shortly after 1470.

The drawing of John the Baptist (Vienna, Albertina, No. 392) can be clearly recognized as an early work when compared with

8. XII.E.W.A.

Roberti's later painting of the same subject (PL. 153). The drawing is similar in manner to the work of Tura and Cossa, especially in the treatment of the drapery.

Generally considered Roberti's earliest known painting is a large canvas of *St. Jerome*, from the Church of S. Girolamo in Ferrara (PL. 37). The pointed draperies are more dramatic than in the Vienna drawing. The finely modeled head, with a sad expression, prefigures the type of saint that Roberti preferred, as do the thin, long-fingered hands that do not really grip but seem to touch emptiness. The decorations of the triumphal arch, both in form and motif, are found repeatedly in Roberti's work and appear soon afterward on the walls of the salon in the Palazzo Paleotti, Bologna, and in the altarpiece for S. Maria in Porto.

On July 19, 1473, the woodcarver Agostino de' Marchi was paid for the frame of Cossa's Griffoni Altarpiece. A similar date can thus be assumed for the predella of the triptych (PL. 155). The general plan as well as many details of this work can be attributed only to Cossa; but several figures give evidence of Roberti's expressionist drawing technique, the deep melancholy of his mood, and the exalted pathos of movement and gesture typical of his work.

The portraits of Giovanni II Bentivoglio and his wife (PL. 158) were drawn by Cossa. Roberti modeled the heads of Cossa's basic drawing with restrained shadows and added a strip of landscape in the background that anticipates the landscape in the altarpiece for S. Maria in Porto. The most eloquent evidence of the collaboration of Cossa and Roberti, however, is the S. Lazzaro Altarpiece, which, during the 18th century, was attributed alternately to Roberti and Tura, but which Longhi in 1934 more justly recognized as a collaboration between Cossa and Roberti. Cossa must have painted the most important parts, working in his usual manner from the edges toward the center. The parts left to Roberti's execution are in a startlingly contrasting style. The two female saints have exaggeratedly narrow hands, and St. Apollonia's robes are arranged in the slightly curving lines that also appear in the painted reliefs of the altarpiece for S. Maria in Porto. In the similar reliefs on the throne of the S. Lazzaro Altarpiece appear landscapes typical of Roberti's style. The head of St. Jerome is reminiscent of the *St. Jerome* from Ferrara as well as of the figure of Beato Pietro degli Onesti in the altarpiece for S. Maria in Porto.

The chiaroscuro figure of a youth holding a staff (St. Jacob?; New York, Pierpont Morgan Lib.) is similar to the figures on the predella of the Griffoni Altarpiece and its style identifies it as a work of Roberti. The depiction of a lion — a fragment of a painting of St. Jerome (formerly Bergamo, Coll. Vernier) — is stylistically very close to the S. Lazzaro Altarpiece.

The *Madonna and Child* (formerly Milan, Coll. Canto) also can be assigned to Roberti's early period. The Madonna is very like the one in the altarpiece for S. Maria in Porto. The precise and angular style of the drapery is in the Ferrarese manner and is also found in the figure of St. Jerome in the S. Lazzaro Altarpiece.

The period of Mantegna's influence can be dated from 1478 to 1486. It is introduced by some drawings that are copies of unknown Mantegna models: four drawings on two sheets depict a soldier squatting on the ground and the lower part of a Madonna's robe (Windsor Castle, Royal Lib., no. 12795) and the heads of a Madonna and Child and the head of an old woman or possibly a warrior (Rotterdam, Boymans-Van Beuningen Mus., no. 574). Scattered among these sketches are details of ornaments and figures as well as free sketches of nude youths. The warrior's head and the squatting soldier reveal Mantegna's influence in their spareness of form. For the figure of a warrior in the *Crucifixion* in the Garganelli Chapel, Roberti took as his model a Hercules by Mantegna, a figure known from an etching (Hind, 1938, no. 20) and a drawing (London, Br. Mus.). The figure of St. Longinus from Mantegna's etching (Bartsch, XIII, 6) appears in Roberti's *Adoration of the Shepherds* (Paris, Wildenstein Coll.). Closely connected to the Mantegna copies are a drawing of a battle scene (Venice, Mus. Correr) and a dramatic small painting of St. Jerome doing penance (London, Barlow Coll.).

A number of smaller works are similar stylistically to the altarpiece for S. Maria in Porto. Among these a *Madonna and Child* (Ferrara, Coll. Vendeghini) and the *John the Baptist* (PL. 153) can be attributed to Roberti. A *St. Maurelius* (Mombello di Torino, Coll. Principe Pio Falcò), which is closely related to the altarpiece, has been attributed by Longhi to Vicino da Ferrara (Baldassare d'Este). The *John the Baptist* is one of Roberti's most powerful and expressive creations. The autumnal coloring of the twilight landscape, so close in mood to the harbor landscape of the altarpiece for S. Maria in Porto, dominates the whole painting and organically envelops the emaciated figure of the saint in meditation with its melancholy atmosphere. The style of the drapery — a mixture of Ferrarese and Mantegnesque elements — is characteristic; while the naked torso delicately glows with the red of the crepuscular sky, the drapery has an oppressive heaviness.

A cycle of seven small panels — *St. Petronius* (Ferrara, Coll. Vendeghini); *St. Apollonia* and *St. Michael* (PL. 37); *St. George, St. Catherine of Alexandria,* and *St. Jerome* (Venice, Coll. Cini); and *St. Anthony Abbot* (Rotterdam, Boymans-Van Beuningen Mus.) — originally must have decorated the frame of an altarpiece by Cossa (according to Longhi, the Griffoni Altarpiece). The *St. Petronius* is undoubtedly by Cossa, who would have left the execution of the more purely decorative work to his pupil. Even in such a small task as this Roberti's scrupulosity is evident. The difference in style in these panels indicates that Roberti began them while still under Cossa's supervision, that is, before 1478, and completed them at a later date. *St. George* and *St. Michael* have some of the elegance and elasticity of Tura and *St. Anthony Abbot* displays Cossa's powerful plastic qualities; *St. Catherine* and *St. Apollonia* have the grandeur and expressionist elements of the mature Roberti, freed from all influences. A half-figure of John the Evangelist (Bergamo, Acc. Carrara) should be assigned to this period because of the stage of its stylistic development, although its authorship is disputed because of affinities to the work of Lorenzo Costa the Younger.

Roberti executed frescoes (*Crucifixion; Death of the Virgin*) for the Garganelli Chapel in the Metropolitana, Bologna, and Cossa provided ceiling paintings and an Annunciation scene. Of Roberti's masterpiece from 1482 to 1486 all that remains are an original fragment — a head of Mary Magdalene (Bologna, Pin. Naz.) — and several original studies: the first, later altered, general layout for the *Crucifixion* (Berlin, Kupferstichkabinett, no. 615); the head of a lamenting woman, which, however, might have been intended for a *Massacre of the Innocents* (New York, Pierpont Morgan Lib.); and a group sketch on gridded paper with the figures of St. Longinus, a young knight, and a lamenting woman (Munich, Staat. Graphische Samml., no. 2144), previously believed to be a copy. There are several copies, apparently painted in the original size and partially substantiated as the work of Lorenzo Costa the Younger (Bologna, Metropolitana; Louvre; Sarasota, Fla., Ringling Mus.); another partial copy known from sources has not yet been found. The authenticity of two life-size portraits of donors (Hannover, Landesmus.) that Gamba (1915) held to be copies from Roberti is doubtful. For the rest, only enthusiastic descriptions by contemporaries remain, particularly Vasari's life of Roberti. It is possible with these clues to reconstruct the main parts of this monumental composition, which was removed at the latest in 1605 and carefully preserved but was lost in the course of the centuries except for the above-mentioned fragment. The copy of the *Crucifixion* in Bologna is the continuation toward the right of the section of the composition that Roberti's Munich sketch has handed down. The seamless transition leads to the figure of the lamenting woman who appears in both representations. The copy of the *Death of the Virgin* in Sarasota is the continuation toward the right of the section of the composition that is shown in the copy in the Louvre. Here too a figure, a lamenting apostle, appears in both cases.

The lower part of the *Crucifixion* was crowded with soldiers (some mounted) and a group of lamenting women who surrounded the fainting Virgin; in the upper part of the composition, John's coat was seized by a soldier as he attempted to flee.

On the right Mary Magdalene rushed in and on the left the mounted St. Longinus pointed his lance toward the crucified Christ, while a young squire attempted to stop him. On the far left soldiers cast lots for Christ's garment. Above these groups rose the three crosses. Soldiers on ladders were depicted in the act of breaking the legs of the thieves. The crosses, some lances, and the banner held by a rider on a rearing horse divided the expanse of sky.

The simpler composition of the *Death of the Virgin* began on the left with a portrait of the patron (Bartolomeo Garganelli) and a self-portrait of the artist. Eleven apostles stood by, some of them leaning over the Virgin's deathbed. In the foreground was a prostrate sinner. In the Sarasota copy the apostle on the far right looks up with arms outspread in a gesture of pathos to the figure of God the Father that appeared presumably at the upper right. The figures of two apostles at the lower right are missing. Appraisals such as that of Vasari emphasize the formal virtues as well as the many nuances and power of expression in both compositions. Whereas the compressed and crowded nature of the *Crucifixion* has a medieval quality, the simple and concisely articulated composition of the *Death of the Virgin* is classical and represents a northern Italian anticipation of the High Renaissance. In this work Roberti turned from a contrapuntal composition to a distinctly rhythmical one. Judging by the copies, the frescoes of the Garganelli Chapel must have been stylistically consistent with the Passion panels from S. Giovanni in Monte, which have been preserved and which were executed at the same time.

For the three Passion panels — *The Seizing of Christ* (PL. 154), *The Way to Calvary* (Dresden, Gemäldegal.), and the *Pietà*, with a Crucifixion scene in the background (PL. 157) — a number of preparatory studies exist (Uffizi, Gab. dei Disegni e Stampe, nos. 1444 E, 1444 F; London, Br. Mus., no. 542, a variant of the Liverpool *Pietà*; Berlin, Kupferstichkabinett, no. 5034, a copy, possibly, of another representation of the Dead Christ by Roberti). The original destination of this small Passion cycle has not been ascertained; however, in 1497 it served as the predella of the altarpiece for S. Giovanni in Monte by Lorenzo Costa the Younger.

From this period come two small, brilliantly colored paintings, a *Madonna* (Berlin, Staat. Mus.) and a *St. Michael* (Bologna, Pin. Naz.); two disputed panels with saints (Settignano, near Florence, Berenson Foundation); the drawing of a pagan sacrifice (Donnington, Eng., Gathorne-Hardy Coll.); a *St. Jerome* (Bologna, S. Petronio), begun by Cossa and finished by Roberti; and a large *Descent from the Cross* (Bologna, Pin. Naz., no. 4658), possibly drawn by Roberti and later painted by others or else a copy from Roberti. A *St. Sebastian* (Florence, Pitti), formerly attributed to Pollaiuolo, is a copy from Roberti. A number of portraits have been attributed to Roberti: the head of a boy (formerly Munich, Böhler Coll.), with a preparatory sketch of a girl's head on the back, attributed by Longhi; a very similar and poorly preserved boy's head (Paris, Mus. Jacquemart-André); the portrait of Francesco IV Gonzaga as a child (Washington, D.C., Nat. Gall.); and a bust of Giovanni II Bentivoglio (Bologna, Univ.) attributed by Longhi (1940). Stylistically these very expressive portraits lead into Roberti's last period.

From the artist's last period (ca. 1486–96) there are a number of studies of riders and soldiers (Rotterdam, Boymans-Van Beuningen Mus.; Donnington, Gathorne-Hardy Coll.; Budapest, Nat. Mus.), which, according to sources, may have some connection with the various secular subjects that Roberti executed as court painter to the Estes. Related themes appear in the illustrations for the *De claris mulieribus*; in three small paintings, *Hasdrubal's Wife*, *Brutus and Portia* (formerly Richmond, Eng., Cook Coll.), and *Lucretia* (Modena, Gall. Estense; generally believed to be a copy or the work of Guido Aspertini); in a battle scene (Pavia, Mus. Civ.); and in various scenes from the legend of the Argonauts (Padua, Mus. Civ.; Florence, Coll. Rucellai; Lugano, Thyssen-Bornemisza Coll.), of which only the work in Florence is considered by Longhi to be Roberti's.

The religious compositions that, to judge by their highly expressive character, probably belong to this last period are a drawing, *Massacre of the Innocents* (Louvre); a small *Last Supper* (PL. 157); a diptych consisting of an Adoration of the Child and a Pietà with St. Jerome and St. Francis (London, Nat. Gall.), whose authenticity is in doubt; and the small *Israelites Gathering Manna* (PL. 157), of which there are two copies, one a free variant in London by Boccaccio Boccaccino, Roberti's successor as the Este court painter, and the other an identical copy in Dresden that exhibits the same style as a copy of Roberti's *Abraham and Melchizedek* (formerly Florence, Bruscoli Gall.). According to sources, these two works formed part of the predella of an unknown altarpiece of which the *Last Supper* (PL. 157) may have formed the central panel.

Two undoubtedly authentic paintings of half-figures — a *Madonna and Child* (PL. 158) and the *Portrait of a Lady* (PL. 158), stylistically very similar to the portrait of Giovanni II Bentivoglio in Bologna — are, for their exceptional psychological insight and their formal originality, among the finest of Roberti's known works.

BIBLIOG. G. Vasari, Le vite de' più eccellenti pittori, scultori e architettori, Florence, 1550 (ed. C. Ricci, II, Milan, 1927, pp. 153–55; Vasari, III, pp. 131–40, 141–48); P. Lamo, La graticola di Bologna (ca. 1560, ed. G. Zanotti), Bologna, 1844; R. Borghini, Il riposo, Florence, 1584 (ed. A. M. Bisconi, Florence, 1730, p. 275); A. Superbi, Apparato de gli Hvomini Illustri, Ferrara, 1620, pp. 121–22; M. A. Guarini, Compendio historico dell'origine... di Ferrara, Ferrara, 1621, pp. 89, 127; A. Masini, Bologna perlustrata, Bologna, 1666, pp. 121, 290; C. C. Malvasia, Le pitture di Bologna, Bologna, 1686, pp. 44–45 (2d ed., C. Bianconi and M. Oretti, Bologna, 1782, p. 311); C. Barotti, Pitture e sculture... di Ferrara, Ferrara, 1770; G. Scalabrini, Memorie historiche delle chiese di Ferrara, Ferrara, 1773; C. Cittadella, Catalogo istorico de' pittori e scultori ferraresi, I, Ferrara, 1782, pp. 105–18; G. Gatti, Descrizione delle più rare cose di Bologna, Bologna, 1803, p. 15; M. Gualandi, ed., Memorie originali risguardanti le Belle Arti, V, Bologna, 1843, pp. 203–04, VI, Bologna, 1845, p. 192; G. Baruffaldi, Le vite de' pittori e scultori ferraresi, I, Ferrara, 1844, pp. 132–48; M. Gualandi, Tre giorni in Bologna, Bologna, 1850, p. 33; L. N. Cittadella, Notizie relative a Ferrara, Ferrara, 1864, pp. 583, 588–89; A. Venturi, Ercole de' Roberti, Arch. storico dell'arte, II, 1889, pp. 339–60; A. Venturi, L'arte a Ferrara nel periodo d'Ercole I d'Este, Bologna, 1890, pp. 78–103; J. A. Crowe and G. B. Cavalcaselle, History of Painting in North Italy (ed. T. Borenius), 2d ed., II, New York, London, 1912, pp. 241–47; Venturi, VII, 3, pp. 656–712; C. Gamba, Ercole ferrarese, Rass. d'arte, XV, 1915, pp. 191–98; F. Filippini, Ercole da Ferrara ed Ercole da Bologna, BArte, XI, 1917, pp. 49–63; G. Zucchini, La distruzione degli affreschi della cappella Garganelli, L'Arte, XXIII, 1920, pp. 275–78; F. Filippini, Ercole de Ferrara, Florence, 1922; B. Berenson, Italian Painters of the Renaissance, Oxford, 1930, pp. 268–71 (2d ed., London, 1952, pp. 162–64); N. Barbantini, Catalogo dell'esposizione della pittura ferrarese del Rinascimento, Ferrara, 1933, pp. 93–110; F. Filippini, Pittori ferraresi del Rinascimento in Bologna, Il Comune di Bologna, XX, 9, 1933, pp. 7–20; D. G. Fornasini, I Garganelli, Bergamo, 1933, pp. 25–27; O. H. Giglioli, Disegni inediti di Francesco del Cossa e di Amico Aspertini, BArte, XXVII, 1933–34, pp. 455–59; G. Bargellesi, Ercole di Ferrara, Riv. di Ferrara, II, 1934, pp. 399–413; G. Fiocco, Tre disegni dell'esposizione ferrarese del Rinascimento, L'Arte, N.S., V, 1934, pp. 230–45; G. Gronau, ThB, s.v.; R. Longhi, Officina ferrarese, Rome, 1934 (2d ed., Florence, 1956); A. Busuioceanu, Dipinti sconosciuti di Ercole Roberti e della sua scuola, L'Arte, N.S., VIII, 1937, pp. 161–82; A. M. Hind, Early Italian Engravings, I, London, 1938, pp. 225, 281; I. B. Supino, L'arte nelle chiese di Bologna, II, Rome, 1938; R. Longhi, Ampliamente nell'Officina ferrarese, Florence, 1940, pp. 8–13; S. Ortolani, Cosmè Tura Francesco del Cossa, Ercole de' Roberti, Milan, 1941, pp. 139–203; G. Zucchini, Un frammento degli affreschi di Ercole da Ferrara per la cappella Garganelli, Proporzioni, I, 1943, pp. 81–82; M. Davies, National Gallery Catalogues: The Earlier Italian Schools, London, 1951, pp. 356–59 (2d ed., 1961, pp. 458–61); B. Nicolson, The Painters of Ferrara, London, 1951, pp. 19–20; L. Coletti and T. Spini, La collezione Ottaviano Vernier, Bergamo, 1954, p. 30; C. Padovani, La critica d'arte e la pittura ferrarese, Rovigo, 1955; E. Ruhmer, Francesco del Cossa, Munich, 1959; M. Salmi, Ercole de' Roberti, Milan, 1960; E. Ruhmer, Ergänzendes zur Zeichenkunst des Ercole de' Roberti, Pantheon, XX, 1962, pp. 241–47.

Eberhard RUHMER

Illustrations: PLS. 153–158.

ROCOCO.

ROCOCO. The term "rococo" encompasses an art style that was characteristic of the 18th century in Europe, succeeding the baroque (q.v.) — to which it was related in certain aspects — and preceding the neoclassic style (q.v.). Its focal point was France, where it flourished in the first half of the century contemporaneously with the baroque and classic schools, and where it acquired the stylistic character and formal idiom that were determining factors in its diffusion throughout Europe, even in the countries in which very similar stylistic developments were taking place (e.g., the Germanic countries). The break with tradition is particularly apparent in architecture, where a new concept appeared according to which a building's form differed from the function for which it was destined. A new, not necessarily interdependent, relationship came into existence between exterior and interior. These factors formed the basis for the importance acquired by interior decoration and design (q.v.), in which decoration and furniture are conceived strictly as a unit. The minor arts — porcelain, silver, furniture, and mirrors — acquired a new preeminence. Even painting and sculpture, with a predominance of color and a choice of subject matter of a "pleasant" or "gallant" nature, seem to have adapted themselves to the refined lightness and to the lively interpretation of the social scene that are stylistic hallmarks of rococo art.

SUMMARY. Concepts of rococo art (col. 231): *Etymology of the term; Criticism.* French rococo (col. 236): *General aspects; Architecture and the decorative arts.* Phases of French rococo (col. 247): *Origins (1675–1715); Style Régence (1715–30); Style rocaille (1730–45); Style Pompadour (1745–64); Diffusion.* International rococo (col. 253): *Porcelain; Pastel, sketch, and capriccio; Mirror cabinets.* Regional forms (col. 256): *England; Spain; Italy; The German-speaking countries.* Historical significance (col. 268).

CONCEPTS OF ROCOCO ART. *Etymology of the term.* The word "rococo" in its present meaning denotes a particular phase of 18th-century art. Originally it was one of the terms used disparagingly in the classic age (see CLASSICISM) for "unclassical" styles such as Gothic, baroque, and rococo. Not until the 19th century, when the concept of style was no longer bound to value judgments and became an art-historical tool, did rococo — like Gothic and baroque — become a stylistic concept.

Etymologically the word "rococo" is related to *rocaille*. As early as the 17th century, *rocaille* was used for the shellwork in grottoes and gardens, *travail de rocaille* being the equivalent of *travail de coquille*. Rococo is thus often equated with *style rocaille*. Since, from the beginning, this style was considered to be a carry-over of Italian baroque into French classicism, it can be assumed that the ending -oco was used as an analogy to the Italian *barocco*. The word *rocaille* had been used as early as 1736 for that specific type of ornament, but the term "rococo" was first encountered in the supplement of 1842 to the *Dictionnaire de l'Académie Française*, which defined it as the commonplace term for the ornament, style, and design peculiar to the Louis XV and early Louis XVI periods. In 1828, Stendhal wrote: "May I whisper an aside? Bernini was the father of the bad taste designated in the studios by the somewhat vulgar name of *rococo*." (*A Roman Journal*, New York, 1957, p. 117). This equating of the rococo with Bernini and the baroque raised the criticism of the style that set in with its formation and continued in its biased point of view for a long time.

Criticism. Although Régence art was not considered by its contemporaries to be a revolutionary reaction to the art in the time of Louis XIV, it was generally acknowledged in the 1730s that an anticlassical current of art was making headway. French academicism was diffident of a new art that recalled the high baroque in the sense of Borromini or Bernini and conflicted with the current rules of taste in its exaggeration of the ornamental function. In 1754, in an attack on the new style, Charles Nicolas Cochin (Cochin the Younger; 1715–90) summarized the academic opinion when he stated that nothing had been produced since Meissonier that was not already present in the germ of his works. Cochin's satirical defense was followed in 1774 by a mention of the style in Jacques François Blondel's *Les amours rivaux*, in which some of the originators of the style are clearly recognizable and in which the very apt word "picturesque" appears. That picturesque is nothing other than baroque is evident in many vituperations from Diderot to the Saxon classicists. "Baroque is the ultimate in the bizarre," wrote Milizia in 1797, thereby repeating Diderot's opinion (*Encyclopédie*, 1751–65). The term "bizarre" had already appeared in an advertisement in the newspaper *Mercure de France* (1734) for Meissonier's book *Cinquième livre d'ornemens inventés*, which constituted the first new set of engravings of the rococo. Here were mentioned the extraordinary forms of fountains, waterfalls, ruins, shellwork, and bits of architecture, all producing bizarre and

picturesque effects. These adjectives characterize the rococo quite aptly and they are in agreement with the views expressed by the critics of classicism.

The new style neither developed theories of its own nor named itself. The best definitions came from the opposition. As well as in Paris, where the style originated and at the same time ran into the greatest opposition, the rococo came under fire in Germany, specifically in Saxony. In 1742, Reifstein declared that the wild and unnatural figures, the arbitrary and lawless combination of the natural with the unnatural being incorporated into buildings and monuments, constituted a disgrace to art and to the enlightened age. Originating in France, these forms spread over Germany via Augsburg and Nürnberg. In agreement, Boffrand in his *Livre d'architecture* (1745) bewailed the confused mixture of curved and straight lines, regretting that it was permitted in the name of genius. In Germany, the word *Grillenwerk* came into usage for the bizarre, the grotesque, and the asymmetry of the new ornamentation. Ornamental engravings from Augsburg, which disseminated the style, led to talk of the "bad Augsburg taste." Pastor Mertens in 1770 disparaged the love for curlicues, which in his opinion made some sculptures seem to have a stomach ache or to want to dance the minuet, instead of revealing the more serious meditations of the soul; this summarized the aversion of the classicists to the rococo in a Germany that was predominantly Protestant. The new ornament continued to be the target for attacks, and since a theory was lacking, it was measured by architectural standards that considered the beauty of architecture to lie in the impression of duration and strength it created on the observer. The new *Grillenwerk* was found to be the opposite, giving an impression of weak, delicate, and stuck-on material, incapable of supporting any weight or thrust but, on the contrary, retaining water and thereby accelerating its own disintegration (J. G. Fünck, *Betrachtungen über den wahren Geschmack*, 1747). Such attacks provide an important source for the interpretation of rococo ornament, since the rejection of a style often results in an acute characterization.

In France, the aversion to rococo soon led to a delimitation of the style. In his monograph *Louis David, son école et son temps* (1855) Etienne Jean Delécluze wrote that the expressions "Pompadour" and "rococo" were acceptable in reference to the fashion under Louis XV, when they had first been used by Maurice Quaï in 1796–97. At the same time, the word "rococo" was used more and more to designate this style, and it became part of German art-historical writing in which it was first systematically investigated. In A. von Zahn (1783) and Anton Springer (1867), the viewpoint is no longer biased, but it is still dependent on the previous limitations and interpretations of the style.

The first critical studies of the rococo were concordant in considering it a late phase of the baroque, an inheritance of the old viewpoint which saw the rococo as inspired by the Italian high baroque. As a result, rococo was generally thought of as the dissolution of the baroque. Shortly thereafter, following Jacob Burckhardt and his efforts to establish basic principles for a scholarly study of style successions, "rococo" became a generic term for the dissolution that occurred in the late phases, of all periods and styles. Thus there was seen to be a "rococo" in Romanesque, Gothic, and, later, even in ancient art. Historically, a similar stylistic designation was already found in German romanticism when Friedrich von Schlegel called picturesque exaggeration in late forms "Gothic." Even rococo with its *mode à la Pompadour* was disposed of as "Gothic" and therefore termed decadent. But the approach that searched for rules in the rise and fall of styles led to a scientific comprehension of the rococo. While for Gottfried Semper (1860–63) the rococo served as evidence for his theory of the origin of a style in the material, R. Dohme, C. Gurlitt, and particularly A. Schmarsow laid the necessary foundations for a more serious study by collecting material and by formal analyses. Common to all is the approach to the rococo as an antithesis. According to W. Lübke (ed. M. Semrau, 1907) the new rococo style is fundamentally nothing but another reaction of the baroque against the cold, severe forms of classicism. The results of such a view led to a recognition of

Principal European localities with rococo monuments. *Key:* (1) Modern national boundaries.

the traditions in which rococo was rooted and to an awareness of the dialectic of the rococo. In 1922 H. Rose (proceeding from Burckhardt and Wölfflin) attempted to transform into a general historical tool Wölfflin's opposition pair of Renaissance-baroque by establishing the fact that with the regressive evolution of the baroque in the 18th century the classical point of departure had again been attained. This attitude toward the rococo *sub specie finis*, which considered the style only from the baroque or classical point of view without recognizing its individual characteristics, was countered by the discovery of its purely esthetic value, primarily by the Goncourt brothers. It is significant that with impressionism just around the corner the bourgeois taste created a second rococo and rediscovered the antiabsolutist quality of the rococo in terms of a beautiful, worldly, nonmeta-

physical art. The accomplishment of the Goncourts was a feat of discovery. Their *L'art du XVIII*^{e} *siècle* (1873–74) is outstanding in its use of previously unknown sources. By stressing the esthetic values of rococo the way was paved for an approach that was to prove more fruitful than a schematizing into "basic principles." For the Goncourts had discovered the inner laws of the rococo: "Watteau renewed the quality of grace. It is no longer the grace of antiquity that we meet with in his art: a precise and tangible charm, the marble perfection of Galatea, the seductiveness — exclusively plastic — the material glory of a Venus. The grace of Watteau is grace itself. It is that indefinable touch that bestows upon women a charm, a coquetry, a beauty that is beyond mere physical beauty. It is that subtle thing that seems to be the smile of a contour, the soul of a form, the spiritual physiognomy of matter" (E. and J. Goncourt, *French 18th Century Painters*, trans. R. Ironside, London, 1948). This characterization was one of the first attempts to synthetize principles from rococo art itself. Charm, seductiveness, grace, and play became catchwords which art historians still use in their treatment of rococo.

Rococo art history of the first half of the 20th century is characterized by a continuation and refinement of 19th-century attempts at classification (above all by Rose and A. E. Brinckmann) and by the continuation of a connoisseurlike conception in the tradition of the Goncourts. This led to the first large monographs by A. Michel, P. de Nolhac, G. Wildenstein, and F. Ingersoll-Smouse, to mention only a few. L. Dimier's *Les peintres français du XVIIIe siècle* (1928–30) is a standard work on rococo painting, more informative than the Goncourts' book but offering few new points of view. The formalistic approach of the standard work on architecture, the third and fourth volumes of Hautecoeur's history of classical architecture in France (cf. 1951–52 ed.), hinders an explanation of the unique relationship of rococo architecture to French classicism. In this respect the small monograph on a single architect, such as that on François de Cuvilliés by W. Braunfels (1938), is more useful. It tersely presents the underlying principles of 18th-century architectural concepts. Historicocultural research has also been notably productive. Rococo as a fertile field for a study of mores has resulted in a large body of literature on the subject, starting with the Goncourt brothers. E. Fuchs, H. L. von Gleichen-Russwurm, and W. Hausenstein stressed the erotic sensation or the interest in ingenious wit; Mussia Eisenstadt's study on Watteau's *fêtes galantes* (1930) formed the starting point for a more general understanding of the background of a specific rococo iconology.

A new period in the study of the rococo began in 1949 with F. Kimball's book *Le style Louis XV: Origine et évolution du Rococo*. The availability of previously inaccessible material made it possible to follow the formation of the style from a central point, namely, interior decoration. In keeping with tradition, Kimball saw the rococo as a partial phenomenon of the baroque but simultaneously limited it to a single field, that of decoration. This viewpoint is justified by the actual development of rococo in the Parisian palaces of the nobility. Yet in his confusion of genesis and style, Kimball closed the door to the metamorphoses of the style, which shortly appeared throughout most of Europe. Particularly in Germany, a consideration of the term "rococo" for German and church art was strongly urged (W. Boeck). As B. Rupprecht (1959) pointed out, certain characteristics of church architecture in southern Germany can actually be called rococo. But this implies an understanding of the actual stylistic structural principles of the rococo.

Rococo as an all-inclusive phenomenon existed only in France. But forms, phases, and phenomena similar or analogous to rococo, proceeding from other basic premises, made a simultaneous appearance in other parts of Europe. A differentiation must therefore be made as follows: (1) French rococo in France and its offshoots in almost all European and certain overseas countries; (2) international rococo — rococo forms, motifs, themes, and textiles that spread throughout Europe, particularly the *rocaille*; (3) local or regional forms (*Sonderformen*) analogous to the rococo (e.g., in Venice, Turin, and Palermo), including the unique phenomenon of southern German church rococo that can be designated as *Sonderrokoko*, corresponding to the accepted concept of the German *Sondergotik*; and (4) the Régence and those stages which are comparable to the rococo within the late baroque. The Viennese Belvedere by Hildebrandt is unmistakably a Régence stage of the Viennese late baroque (cf. Hôtel de Noailles in Paris, finished by Lassurance in 1711; Hautecoeur III, 1951–52, fig. 90), but it is in no sense of the Régence. Similarly, Sanssouci in Potsdam is a rococo stage of the late baroque under Frederick the Great but is not really rococo (PL. 163; V, PL. 197; X, PL. 272). The church in Ottobeuren (XIII, PL. 254), despite a wealth of rococo motifs in its decoration, is a work of the south German late baroque, not of the *Sonderrokoko*.

The concept of rococo must be clearly defined: (1) Rococo is not a stylistic phase of the classic or the late baroque, neither in France nor elsewhere. Even where it grows out of the classic and late baroque, it remains hostile to these stylistic concepts. (2) Rococo was only one of the art movements of the 18th century. (3) Even in the first half of the 18th century, rococo was only one among other European styles (e.g., different types of late baroque, English classicism). (4) In France, under Louis XV, rococo was only one art current among others, although it was predominant between 1730 and 1750. It is a *Genos-Stil* (style tied to specific types) found only in some of the official state architecture in a few of the church buildings or appearing secondarily in their decoration. (5) Despite these limitations, rococo was in no way only a mode of decoration but a true style that formed complete works in a synthesis of all the arts (*Gesamtkunstwerk*). (6) The Régence stylistic phase must be regarded as the closest relation of the rococo. In France, this means that the rococo, in a broad sense, included the Régence and the rococo proper (in the narrower sense) and was thus more or less synonymous with Louis XV, though the stylistic period did not coincide exactly with his reign (1715–1774); and that the rococo in the narrower sense was just the second phase of art under Louis XV, from 1728/30 to 1745/50, which was called by contemporaries *style rocaille*.

FRENCH ROCOCO. *General aspects.* An attempt has been made to establish the unity of the rococo by means of a *modus* of beauty (E. Przywara). The beauty of the baroque is comparable to *pulchrum* and that of the rococo (including Régence) to *bellum*. *Pulchrum* is sensual magnificence, fame through richness and splendor. *Bellum* is self-contained beauty in the sense of pretty, delightful, charming, fine, gay, pleasing, exquisite, but also gallant and, above all, gracious and comely (*anmutig* in the double sense of the German word). *Bellum* is foreign to the Roman spirit. Both *pulchrum* and *bellum* are as opposed to καλον as real beauty is to ideal beauty. This defining of rococo by *bellum* is appropriate since it embraces those features which the general idea of rococo superficially arouses; but it is too general. More concrete concepts, differentiating it from late Hellenistic "rococo" for example and applicable only to 18th-century rococo, are needed.

One may attempt to establish the unity of rococo from architecture, specifically with the wall as a point of departure. Each architectural "system" has its own kind of wall. The form particular to Régence and rococo exteriors is as follows: the external planes consist of two, and only two, elementary architectural forms, namely, undecorated, slender semicircular or segmental arched openings (windows, doors, French windows), all of which are flatly framed or cut into the surface. (Openings with a straight lintel, considered too "hard," are only exceptionally permitted.) Between 1705 and 1750 this system appeared on innumerable *hôtels* and *maisons de plaisance*, in everchanging combinations of the two elements, but only rarely on church façades. Characteristic is the extreme flatness and quality of the large form (i.e., the surface). Sculpture in the round appears only as cartouches in a frame or as the crowning of a balustrade. On exteriors the most important element is the delicate grooving of the real stone or, on decorative buildings, of the imitation stone. This gives the wall an impression of being made of delicate, shingled plates that are liberated of weight by the many large openings, by the organization of the stories, and by the low-pitched roofs. Two-storied buildings whose stories seem to duplicate each other, as well as one-storied ones, are preferred by this system. According to J. F. Blondel, the proportion of ground floor to first floor should be 20:19. The delicate quiet surfaces are enlivened by the movable elements of outward-opening shutters (*jalousie, persienne*), the earliest of which were apparently first used between 1713 and 1718 in the Hôtel de Seignelay in Paris.

The old orders of columns were abolished — in itself a revolutionary event. Freestanding columns appear only exceptionally in buildings of a particular social status (e.g., the Palais Bourbon, Paris, which was the palace of a princess of royal blood), and their significance is that of rank, of an emblem. Occasionally, delicate pilasters decorated parts of the buildings: "On ne doit mettre d'ordres qu'aux avant-corps" (Briseux). The old and new Roman forms of engaged columns, emphasizing the three-dimensionality of the wall mass, were completely avoided. The gable motif was also relegated: J. F. Blondel advised against the "misuse" of the gable in private buildings. "Noble simplicité" was the ideal and was later taken over by neoclassicism. Yet, Régence and rococo buildings continued to be arranged and proportioned so that they could still adopt "orders."

The situation was more or less the same for the interior wall. Here, too, orders were permitted only in ceremonial rooms, such as the vestibule or the *chambre de parade*. On the wall they were replaced by a system of fine listel moldings that embraced double doors, windows, the flat, jutting mantelpieces with their mirrors, and the bed alcoves; this transformed the interior into a delicate framework of slender upright panels (*panneaux*). Generally the interiors were covered with paneling (*boiserie*) to the ceiling. The wood — mainly of hard oak — was transformed by the art of the joiners (*menuisiers*) into an ornament of such finesse and suppleness as to equal the most ductile stuccowork.

While in French exteriors ornament was permitted only sparingly here and there — on keystones, crowns, and fillers for wooden doorwings — the fillet molding of the inner walls was the basis from which and toward which the characteristic ornament of the Régence and rococo gravitated. This is best seen at the articulation points of the listels, as fillers for the panels, at the angle between the ceiling and wall — that is, preferably in transitions (V, PL. 421). While to a certain extent the principle "what is inside is outside" was true in the baroque, and while in English classicism the exterior determined the forms of the interior, in the Régence and the rococo there arose a previously unknown differentiation between exterior and interior. Although, through its large openings and reflections of the outside, the rococo interior communicated to a great extent with the exterior, the former is qualitatively different from the latter.

Only a limited role was conceded to large sculpture in this system. The *grandes machines* of monumental ceiling painting gave way to airy, tentlike ceilings. Wall painting was limited to decorative insertions, and "independent" easel paintings were accommodated on the walls of galleries and cabinets. Decorative painting dominated over autonomous painting. The place of sculpture, except for small pieces, was mostly in the open.

The appearance of this system, its renunciation of the old orders, was a radical break not only with the high Louis XIV style but also with older traditions established on the threshold of the Renaissance. With the rebirth of gods and heroes in art, the idea of the "great man" and of *pulchrum* became the central point of secular and, then, sacred art; the antique orders became architectural law, and the ceilings began to open up into heavenly vistas. This is also the reason why monumental ceiling painting that transcends the earthly sphere had to recede; for the rococo knew no real transcendance but only a revelation and enchantment of the earthly presence. Utilitarian ("low") elements of architecture, previously admitted only in cellars, climbed up into the upper stories, where they were "ennobled" and became part of the new spare elegance of airy, floating surfaces. Just as the *bellum* can hardly be considered a species of *pulchrum*, so Régence and rococo can hardly be considered a late phase of the baroque, the high Louis XIV style. This phenomenon of the rise and ennoblement of utilitarian forms as exemplified in architecture can be generalized. Forms, motifs, types, and attitudes which up to then had been considered "low" made their appearance everywhere. This can be observed in all the arts and on many levels.

In painting the ascendancy of a sensuous colorism over spiritual imagery, the victory of the Rubenists over the Poussinists, is well known. The gallant idyll, which had played a very minor part in 17th-century art, became the leading genre, and drew other themes in its wake. This is shown most clearly in iconology. Pan and Venus, whose domain is an elementary timeless sphere, eclipsed the old, great light-dispersing, order-establishing gods and replaced Apollo-Helios and Hercules. They became the new focal points not only of painting but of all the pictorial arts. A new repertory of motifs, in which the manifold attributes of these gods dominated, assumed pre-eminence in decoration and emblemistics, such as the syrinx and the shell. Pan became the leading figure of Régence art, and Venus of the rococo. Contemporaries were quite aware of this change of rule. In a ballet by Le Jay, performed in 1719, Apollo's hopes for a reform of Parnassus were thwarted when, through the ignorance of Midas (i.e., the plutocracy), Pan was preferred to the sun god. The statue of Cupid carving his bow from the club of Hercules (Bouchardon, 1739) is an allegorical self-portrait of the period. The "high" official ornament was universally superseded by a "low" form, that is, a species of grotesque.

The principle of the Régence and rococo garden was "faire céder l'art à la nature." This signified an increased importance of the "low" elements — unornamented lawns and a retrogression of architectural elements in landscape architecture (q.v.). In art history, under the impulse of the new esthetic of Jean Baptiste Dubos (1719), "sentiment" conquered "reason."

A single common denominator for Régence and rococo art was thus determined, namely, the rise of "low" elements over "high" ones. This common denominator was not a stylistic tendency such as the "movement and mass" (Wölfflin) of the baroque, but one that was literally revolutionary. The rise of "low" forms was primarily an artistic process and cannot be simultaneously taken as a sociohistorical factor. The new tendency took form during the late Louis XIV period in the royal palaces and pleasure buildings (*maisons de plaisance*) and particularly in the apartments of the younger generation. It was then adopted by the *hôtels* (private town houses) in Paris, still generally commissioned by the high nobility and not — as is often assumed — by the new nobility and the financiers.

This phenomenon can be followed far beyond the bounds of the pictorial arts, and even beyond art itself. Part of the same concept is the prevalence of the skip dances, popular in origin, over the stately step dances, the new importance of "low" wind instruments such as the syrinx, bagpipes, and jew's harp, and the heightened interest in the *comédie italienne*. In the historicocultural sphere there was a victory of the intimate over the official, comfort over dignity, that manifested itself in the new furniture forms (see FURNITURE) such as the chaise longue, *fauteuil*, *bergère*, commode (a name that speaks for itself), or in the promotion of the berlin, a light coach used as a state and even coronation carriage. Particularly pertinent is the importance attached to sensual love as the highest life force, allegorically legitimized by mythological examples. The victory of the skeptical-critical intellect over "high" speculative and contemplative reason and the victory of *bellum* over *pulchrum* are also part of the same concept.

In this turnover, which brought the "low" to the top and simultaneously ennobled it, the rococo was a revolution in the true meaning of the word. It is one of the great European revolutions in that chain of revolutions which once begun cannot be stopped.

The ennoblement of the shepherd, his transformation into a "berger galant," played a leading role. Two opposing worlds — the folk-natural and the royal-aristocratic, at times "divine" — are mirrored in the pastoral. The fact that a shepherd, Paris, won the wife of King Menelaus, while a shepherdess, Aphrodite, cast King Anchises under her spell, was an allegorical representation of the Arcadian principle that echoes in all pastoral poetry up to the gallant shepherd romances of the 18th century. In the paradisaical kingdom of love, position and rank are meaningless and give way to natural feelings and evaluations. Bucolic poetry was particularly fashionable at a time when the contrast between the rarefied court or city life and the healthy natural environment of the country was stressed. In the culture of an upper class secure in its social position in the Régence and rococo periods, Western pastoral art experienced its last incomparable bloom, and bucolic themes assumed a hitherto unknown diffusion. The gods of Olympus were only guests in Arcadia, for the lord of Arcadia was Pan; his was that timeless borderland between wilderness and farmland, the woods, pastures, and shores as they appear in the cartouches of Audran and Gillot and in the backgrounds of Watteau. It is a world of nymphs and satyrs, themes which — openly or in diguise — dominated the whole pictorial world of the Régence (the nymphlike became the feminine ideal); the hunt, the dance, and leisure were the favorite occupations of the time. In Watteau's work the world of Pan, with its dryads and oreads, trees and hills, nymphs and shepherds, merges with an idealized social life and with elements from the dream world of the theater; nature, art, and love fuse into a mystico-earthly paradise of eternal youth, gaiety, and glorified sensuality. The regent himself appeared at private festivities dressed as Pan, and it is as Pan that Nicolas de Largillière (q.v.) portrayed him. But the Arcadian world also appertains to Venus. The Aeneas saga that Antoine Coypel (q.v.) painted in the gallery of the Palais-Royal, the Paris residence of the regent, does not have the political significance of Tiepolo's Madrid frescoes; instead they glorify the son of the heavenly shepherdess. The regent had his wife's room decorated with pastoral scenes from the late Hellenistic pastoral romance *Daphnis and Chloe* and commissioned a French edition of the work under the title *Les amours pastorales de Daphnis et Chloé* (1718), illustrated with engravings from paintings which he himself had designed, which became one of the favorites of society. The "Aphrodite" Society, over which the regent presided, owned an immense estate near Montmorency with a pleasure palace with interiors that were decorated with painted shrubbery, artificial lawn carpets, and illusionistic tree domes, all of which were intended to simulate pastoral landscapes. All the arts and life itself took part in the creation of this Arcadian world. *Maisons de plaisance* and *pavillons d'amour* (V, PL. 421) were built and, in the sense of a *Gesamtkunstwerk*, were decorated with *boiserie*, tapestries, paintings, furniture, porcelains, textiles, and so on, to represent pastoral motifs and elements. The shepherd's play was the favorite theme in the theater, ballet, and opera. Rococo poetry coined the concept of the shepherds' little hour, which continued to be a designation for the hour of love, of the tender meeting.

The central figure of the *style rocaille* is a Venus that approaches the nymphlike ideal of the naiads. Her earthly paradise was the island of Cythera, which, since Watteau's *L'Embarquement pour Cythère* (XIV, PL. 403), had become a central concept of erotic imagination and idiom. Boucher painted a triumph of Venus (II, PL. 334), and her attributes — rocks, shells, coral, reed, water, foam, and waves — formed the arsenal of the early *rocaille* ornamental vocabulary. Its form of movement was a tumbling motion, and its colors a deep, cool sea-blue and foam-white, which, together with the rose of the shell interior and the iridescence of mother-of-pearl, provided a typical rococo color harmony; the enameled interior of the shell was close to the texture of porcelain. Rococo rooms are unthinkable without the mirror, also an attribute of Venus. In her realm all is transformed into charm and fragrance (F. G. Jünger).

It is necessary to attempt to explain the unity of rococo through its conception of light, for each true style has a specific relation to light. Rococo light is a transfigured, but earthly, sensuous light. The three physical means contributing to it are French windows, the whiteness of the rooms, and mirrors, as well as the particular sheen given to ordinary materials. French windows are characterized not only by a greater amount of light and tall, slender openings which come close to Gothic proportions, but primarily by the fact that they admit light to the room upward from the floor. In contrast, light from above practically never occurs and, where it does (in the octagon of the Palais-Royal), gives the impression of being a baroque survival. Light streaming in along the floor is a particularly earthly light that is transfigured by the mirrorlike smoothness of the parquet floors.

No less an innovation was the adaptation of the interior to the predominantly white color of the walls. This white was, in a way, materialized light that had become color. The warm white of the Régence and the cool white of the rococo were not colorless like the white of classicism, which was combined with gray, but was the lightest of all colors. After 1725–30, in the rococo proper, the white color was often replaced by light-hued tones containing a great deal of white (light blue, light yellow, pink, reseda, etc.). In the decoration of walls and furniture white was combined with a finely distributed gold (or silver) and became a materialized shimmer. White was the lightest of colors, gold the material of light, and the mirrors were both shimmer and illusion, increasing the effect of luminosity, and subtracting all remaining weight from the confines of the room (PL. 180). Further, the mirror transfigured the light, making it intangible and fantastic, yet without robbing it of its earthly character. In the large mirrors, which often filled whole walls, the interior fused with the exterior, and the earthly light attained the highest degree of luminosity. In mantelpiece mirrors (PL. 180) light became symbolically related to the element of fire (i.e., to Venus and Vulcan).

Many materials with particularly light-catching surfaces contributed to the luminosity of the mirror: the brilliantly polished parquets; the varnish of the furniture; the shiny iridescent silks or softly glowing velvets, used for both upholstery and dress; the milk-white gleam of porcelain, mother-of-pearl, and lacquer; and the moonlike shimmer of lead sculpture. The rococo was the age of splendor for brilliants, which were used everywhere: in pendants, necklaces, jacket and waistcoat buttons, hat brooches, shoulder clasps, watches, boxes, shoe buckles, rings, cane handles, and sword hilts and scabbards (PL. 181). The brilliant cut for diamonds was discovered in 1660, and thus the relationship of rococo to light is an inheritance from the time of the Sun King. But the rococo developed new, refined effects from this inheritance.

This luminism is also evidenced in the light fixtures of the rococo. The actual source of artificial light was solely the wax candle. The rococo was unique in its use of fixtures both on interior walls in the form of appliqués, girandoles, and in the center as hanging chandeliers or table candelabra. Importance was put on the effect produced by a relatively low-placed light source. Boffrand counseled a height of six feet, that is, not much over the height of a man's head, so as to avoid circles and hollows under the eyes. The aim was to lift all deep shadows by means of soft lighting, thus beautifying the objects illuminated and rejuvenating and enlivening the individual. A special role was played by the Venetian chandelier, with its countless cut-glass prisms, which at the least tremor transformed the flickering light of the candles and dispersed it in sparks of light. This luminism was the negation of everything dark or heavy. Dark corners, considered the acme of bad taste, were eliminated by rounding out the corners of the room. In staircases and balconies the massive balustrades were replaced by airy, transparent grills and wrought-iron railings (V, PL. 420).

This tendency to avoid darkness infiltrated every esthetic concept. The ideal of the rococo was an earthly paradise of eternal youth, gaiety, graceful beauty, and sensuality that negated death, sin, old age, infirmity, and loneliness. The whole of existence was conceived of as something light and gay, the harmony of which depended on the avoidance of ponderosity and the exclusion of pathos and darkness. This was valid for manners as well as language and art in all its manifestations. This ethos abhorred stilted eloquence and the blustering pedantry of the severeness of custom: simplicity, reticence, charm, intimation, and allusion were its ideals (Rouvier). Superficial intellect, even to the point of frivolity, was considered a social virtue.

This paradise is "transfiguration," the transposition of objects into a natural-supernatural clarity. Light and material are transfigured. It is easy to understand why silk — a light, cool fabric, both sensually and texturally provoking, with a sheen that seems disembodied from the material itself — should have been preferred above all other textiles. Much the same can be said for porcelain. The bliss of this earthly Elysium is enjoyed by all the senses — not only seen and heard, but felt, tasted, breathed. Distinction between the higher and lower senses vanishes. The arts of taste and smell — culinary arts and perfume — achieve a previously unheard-of rank and arrive at their greatest refinement. Since enjoyment is the bliss of the refined sensuality (*volupté*), the conflict between sensuality and the spirit ceases to exist. Divinely transfigured, refined sensuality — that is, the sublimation of the senses — becomes the ideal. Paradise is togetherness; there is no loneliness; its inhabitants are always numerous, a blessed folk. These are the themes in the paintings by Watteau and his followers. All the transfigured are rendered as closely as possible to an ideal. In an art which springs from an ethos such as this there can be no profound individual portraiture. The Régence and rococo are the golden age for the *portrait historié*, which transforms the subject, seen allusively, into the role of a god, goddess, or nymph (V, PL. 406). (The reverse of the coin are the "unmasking" portraits by Maurice Quentin de Latour [q.v.].) Existence in the earthly paradise guarantees eternal youth. The rococo shunned signs of old age in its paintings. The white wigs, already small in the rococo, paradoxically rejuvenate the wearers, conferring upon their complexions the bloom of youth. Winter — the death of nature — is now seen for the first time in all its gaiety as a world transformed by soft, white snow, in which cheeks glow with youth. Winter provides the new entertainment of dancelike ice skating (VI, PL. 76) and pleasure rides in feather-light sleighs. Even war is represented in its most idyllic aspects.

A world that so completely ignores the darker sides of life is a world of lighthearted play, and any definition of rococo must include the adjective "playful." Lighthearted play is par excellence child's play. Therefore, in both life and art the spheres of a child's life assume a hitherto unknown importance (as with Chardin; III, PLS. 214, 218), and children's games become adult amusements and are mirrored in paintings (the swing, blindman's buff). In the innumerable cupids, the child's world meets the erotic paradisaical world. Play is not only a subject of art, but art itself is conceived of and represents itself as play. A wedding of the arts is playfully achieved. In the rococo, as in no other *Gesamtkunstwerk*, the arts play within and with each other lightly, vivaciously, ingeniously. Rococo ornament takes the lead. In ornamental forms never-ending variations and surprising metamorphoses are "playfully" elicited. With but a few figures and rules the architect plays a game with unlimited possibilities, the results of which are taken lightly. The nobility, deprived of its most vital function and seeking a substitute in play (including games of chance), helped to diffuse this lighthearted art which crosses the confines between art and life. To a certain extent this historical situation recalls the "international style" of around 1400.

An ethos that denies death, sin, old age, and sickness is in itself no longer Christian; nor is it stoic but, rather, Epicurean. This evaluation of the rococo also helps to explain its interest in China — an attraction to a world which combined an unmetaphysical philosophy with a deeply refined and sensual culture. The Christian counterparts to the erotic sensuality of the Régence and the rococo and its worship of worldly love were the cults of the Sacred Heart of Jesus and the Immaculate Heart of Mary, both established late in the Louis XIV period. In 1675 St. Margaret Mary Alacoque experienced her vision of Lord Jesus; in 1681 Jean Eudes's *Le Cœur admirable de la Mère de Dieu* was published; and in 1689 Croisot's *Devotion du S. Cœur de Jésu*, which led the way to the popular cult of the Sacred Heart.

The greatest two publishing enterprises of the 18th century seem to embody the two opposite and contrasting poles of the rococo. Diderot's and D'Alembert's 35-volume encyclopedia (1751–65) is a compendium of the world of the Enlightenment. This was countered by the 1762 luxury edition of Jean de La Fontaine's *Contes et Nouvelles en vers*, financed by the "Fermiers Généraux"; with its illustrations by Charles Eisen, P. P. Choffard, and later Fragonard, it was a high point of the amorous and tasteful genre. Both works have something in common: a scholarly interest in natural phenomena, whether physics or love.

In illustrations for books by Ariosto, Boccaccio, A. H. de la Motte, Margaret of Navarre, Ovid, Rabelais, and Voltaire, and in Germany for books by C. F. Gellert and C. M. Wieland, the rococo was released from the bonds imposed on large-scale painting, and could "unmythologize" in the private sphere of book illustrations and engravings. Boucher, Fragonard, P. A. Baudouin (1723–69), A. C. P. Caylus (1692–1765), P. P.

Choffard (1730–1809), C. N. Cochin (1715–90), C. Eisen (1720–78), H. Gravelot (1699–1773), N. Lafrensen (1737–1807), J. M. Moreau le Jeune (1741–1814), the Saint-Aubins, and J. G. Wille (1715–1808) mirror the gradual transfer of love into bourgeois life until it reaches the sentimentalism of the end of the period that is best exemplified by Jean Baptiste Greuze (1725–1805). Baroque pathos has been translated into amorous ardor. Fragonard's *La chemise enlevée* (V, PL. 370), in which Cupid snatches away a girl's shirt, is perhaps the most telling example of this phenomenon. The baroque mythological precedent was, however, still noticeable. The allegorical attributes — Hymen's torch — still hark back to similar baroque representations with Amor and Venus, but here their function is that of providing an alibi. Venus has become a mere maiden. In the rape of the shirt the symbol and the symbolic event have become one, and there is no longer reference to an Olympian paradigm. The uncovering as such has become the subject of the picture: Amor becomes Libido, although still in the guise of Amor. Baroque elements continue to be present in other similar representations; the kiss, the bridal night, the surprise by the spouse, the bed as a setting are genetically to be understood as the dissolution of the baroque themes of "encounter," the earthly loves of Jupiter, Pan's pursuit of the nymphs, and the bed as a ceremonial place (PL. 176).

Pierre Antoine Baudouin's *Coucher de la mariée* (1767) indicates most strikingly the end of this baroque period. In a sumptuous chamber with classical décor and a ceiling fresco of cupids floating in heaven there is a four-poster bed. The bride is thrust into the bed by her companions, while she wipes a crocodile tear from her eyes. She is embraced by a man, but it is not clear whether it is the bridegroom or the lover from whom she is taking leave. The discrepancy between the classical space and the event is thoroughly savored by the painter. The theme harks back to the bacchantic processions, but there is no suggestion of a mythological event, but, rather, of a worldly reality taking place under a seeming Olympus. The effect is ironic. In art, mythology is banned. But the detail of a door slightly ajar, yet hidden by a screen, is significant. The ceremonial door of Louis XIV is shut off by an "intimate" piece of furniture (the screen). The capriccio has become an amorous joke. While Fragonard (q.v.) in his *Le Jet d'Eau* turned the depiction of Actaeon surprising the nymphs into a realistic scene, mythological qualities are still present. But it is no longer the theme, but the passion, which reveals them.

In rococo ornament, above all in ornamental prints, further revolutionary tendencies of the style are evident. The *rocaille* ornament can even be considered as having sprung from these trends. In J. Meissonier's *Livre d'ornemens* (1734), a set of relatively small ornamental prints, the *genre pittoresque* received its first full characterization. Shell shapes and other ornamental parts such as C arches crystallize into constructions, which, on the one hand, might be architecture or, on the other, pure ornament. The result is a special kind of counterplay. Before our eyes the ornament becomes an object in a picture; it appears in a landscape like a picturesque ruin, but then this quasi-architecture becomes once more pure ornamental form, representing nothing but form.

In its origin, this *forme rocaille* goes back to the grotesques of Jean Bérain (1640–1711) and Daniel Marot (1663–1752). In ornamental prints of the late Louis XIV period, strapwork design forms the frame of a small central picture, and the frame itself is gradually absorbed into the picture, thus assuming architectural and objective substance. With Meissonier and, most especially, Jacques de La Joue (de Lajoue; 1687–1761), the grotesque ornament becomes the subject of the picture. The *forme rocaille* is represented as a picturesque thing. But, just because it is not an object but an ornament, these prints document a particular kind of irony. Ornamental logic and pictorial logic come into conflict, interpenetrate, and result not in a separation of the two but rather in a clash that becomes a formal principle. All objects take on ornamental forms and become imaginative irreality; at the same time ornament as a reality volatilizes into something conceivable only in illustrations. In the *Livre nouveau de divers morceaux de fantaisie*

(La Joue, 1736) there exists a world of grotesques in which ornament and picture are mingled without neutralizing each other.

To the ambiguity between the ornamental and the pictorial is joined the ambiguity of size relationships. The *forme rocaille* teems with humans and putti. But are they real people in a giant ornament-architecture or are they dwarfs as in Jonathan Swift's *Gulliver's Travels*, which appeared in 1726? Are they pieces of garden scenery or table centerpieces? One cannot say. One is reminded of Voltaire's *Micromegas* (1752) and the inhabitant of Sirius who travels through the universe and, according to the inhabitants of the stars he encounters, alternately experiences immense size or smallness.

Thus the *rocaille* of the grotesque ornamental engraving — on which neoclassicism based its definition of *genre pitto-resque* — was "micromegalithic" in structure. A basic rule of the rococo was coined, namely, to produce artificially a counter-play within some form of reality. Complementing each other, changing, holding each other in suspension, the effect was one of irony, which is ultimately nothing but the result of the artist playing with the possibilities of art.

Architecture and the decorative arts. Even more than in the 17th century, Régence and rococo architectural theory cannot be separated from actual architecture. The architect is a *savant*. This is a far cry from the glorification of the geniuses who worked without rules. The theoreticians of the first half of the 18th century had only one ideal of taste, a requisite if one wished to be taken seriously. It is the theoretician's lot to deduce general rules for architecture from this ideal of "good" taste, which the individual could then vary according to his specific task. "Le gout réuni aux règles forme le bon architecte" (taste combined with rules makes a good architect; Blondel). The rules were woven into a system according to the laws of pure logic.

The center of gravity of this rational architectural thinking shifted to the interior and to the measured differentiation of the various requirements and purposes of a building. Already, in the "querelle des anciens et des modernes," the moderns were aware of the weak spot of classicism — neglect of the interior; after 1700 the voices which considered this an esthetic deficiency increased. Seventeenth-century works were criticized in that the interior did not fulfill the promises of the façade; in that the exterior failed to indicate clearly the purpose of the building; and in that the decoration did not correspond to the forms of architecture. Every 17th-century building was of the same solemn size and showed the same striving for absolute perfection. According to 18th-century theoreticians the works of François Mansart, François Blondel (the Older), and Claude Perault lacked unity as a whole as well as appropriateness.

In 1702 the expression *convenance* appeared for the first time. *Convenance*, or suitability, required a differentiation of structures and of rooms (according to their purpose). The 17th century was reproached as having been concerned merely with satisfying the taste of the ruling classes and because individuals were taken too little into consideration (Jombert, 1728). In the individual building the principle of *convenance* led to a differentiation of its parts. The sharp distinction between exterior and interior in the rococo kept faith with this principle. It would not have been suitable to decorate the exterior like the interior. The particular purpose of each room determined its form, size, proportions, and particularly its dimensions, character, and the themes of its decoration. This architectural ideal, a purely intellectual creation, brought about a good training of the senses for comprehending decorative values. Beauty did not exist outside of this appropriateness.

In the camp of the French architectural theoreticians it became clear that this new architectural ideal brought into being a new style, even a new art — the art of "distribution." In it the greatest achievements of the immediate past were discernable (Patte, 1765). In 1752 Blondel stated of his contemporaries that in the last fifty years the latter had invented a new art.

In the rococo, pictures, furniture, utensils, and so on, can be fully understood only in their original connection with the building or the room for which they were destined. An overdoor by Chardin or by Jean Baptiste Oudry indicates by its subject, its emblems or allegorical allusions, by form and format, even by its color harmony for what context it was painted. This is not true for a free, autonomous painting by the same painter.

Large-size ceiling painting declined. Too heavy both in form and color and transcending earthly space, the baroque principle of illusion was not sufficiently congenial to the rococo, which preferred allusion and sought more ingenious ways of crossing the boundaries. This also explains why an illusionistic lateral opening of individual wall panels is the exception in French rococo; it is found more often in projects of the ornamental print makers than in reality (Oppenord, Hôtel d'Assy; Meissonier, Hôtel Sartorinski, or Czartoriski). Where illusionistic painting still appeared, it shared the weightlessness, the luminosity, and the lightheartedness of decoration as a whole. On the wall, paintings appeared on overdoors, in the framed surfaces of panels, and as transitional ceiling corners. The wooden panels themselves might be painted or paintings on canvas might be set into the space (PL. 162). A characteristic innovation was the frameless picture placed in an empty surface framed by listel molding like the painted or carved cartouche of an ornament. This was the result of a growing independence of idyllic pictures in grotesque ornaments, from which panel painting had originated. With the utmost faithfulness to nature in details, this frameless picture shifted both materially and spiritually between near and far. The themes and pictorial content of these architecturally bound paintings were prescribed by the use of the particular room just as was the choice of emblems and ornament. It was considered particularly distinguished to have everything in a hunting lodge refer to the hunt, in a falcon house to falcons, and in a music room to music.

While tapestry (see TAPESTRY AND CARPETS) formerly served to cover the wall, in the rococo it became a wall painting framed with *boiseries* (PL. 177; V, PL. 416; XIII, PL. 413). Tapestry relinquished its own unique expressive possibilities (as did other branches of art) in order to be integrated better into the general decorative scheme of a room. Great improvements in weaving and dying techniques led to a previously unachieved delicacy of texture and color nuances. Ultimately, over a thousand different hues became available. While previously the weavers had transferred the cartoon into a coarse textile structure, they could now copy the most delicate shading of the model and were able to rival painting itself. In addition to the pictorial tapestries made on high-warp looms with vertical warp threads (as in Paris), or on low-warp looms with horizontal warp threads (as in Beauvais), the Savonnerie tapestries achieved importance in the 18th century. These were floor and wall carpets in a kind of tie technique woven on the high-warp loom; they acquired a velvetlike surface by the cutting of the front knots (French factories in Chaillot and Aubusson). In keeping with European taste, they replaced with their light colors the Oriental rugs (and their generally heavy tones), thus also integrating the floor coverings into the harmony of the room (Schönberger, 1958).

In sculpture, the effect of the most important works was usually planned for a given environment and lighting so that any transferal essentially changed the appearance of the object. The *hôtel* and *maison de plaisance* offered little room for large sculpture. Except for a few putti or trophies, sculpture vanished from the attics and balustrades. The gables were more often filled with heraldic than with figural representations, and the façades were devoid of large sculpture. A magnificent exception was Robert Le Lorrain's high relief of the Horses of Apollo over the portal of the stables of the Hôtel de Rohan (1740), constituting an unframed figural cartouche. In the interiors, large sculpture, generally in niches, was found only in the state halls or galleries (Hôtel de Toulouse) or as freestanding sculpture on the staircases. But they were most at home in gardens and fountains (E. Bouchardon's Fontaine de Grenelle, 1739). Lead with its soft sheen was a favorite material; its relation with the element of water was particularly desirable.

Primary among the objects closely bound to the architectural ensemble were chimney furnishings, with girandoles, andirons, and fire tongs often completely made of iron or bronze *rocaille* curlicues (PL. 181). In furniture (q.v.), *convenance* was the guiding principle as well. Size and expense of individual pieces of furniture depended on the use for which the room in question was designed. Adaptation went so far as a change of upholstery according to the seasons: velvet in winter, taffeta in summer. The large state rooms usually contained little furniture. Console tables — occasionally enormous — were stock pieces along the wall and continued the interior decoration (V, PL. 445). Chairs, armchairs, and wall sofas were placed in regular rows in front of the paneling (Kreisel). Within the ensemble, furniture and fireplaces had the strongest curves. The bodies of commodes or the backs and legs of armchairs and chairs showed the typical large curves as early as the Régence stage, while similar curves appeared in the *boiseries* only in small format. The great furniture designers of the period such as Charles Cressent (1685–1768) and Jacques Caffieri (1678–1755) were pupils of sculptors or sculptors themselves.

The singularity of the Régence and rococo garden is not easy to grasp (see LANDSCAPE ARCHITECTURE). As in the wall system, the basis was found in the rational geometry of the late Louis XIV garden as continued by Le Nôtre (VIII, PL. 438). According to the principle of having art yield to nature ("faire céder l'art à la nature"), *nature* was the man-made world of plants and *art* the stone steps, ramps, and statues. A clear, lucid layout lent charm to a garden and provided surprise and amusement. Smooth and copsed lawns (*boulingrins*: bowling greens) came to the fore, and bordered flowerbeds embodied the contrast, asymmetry, and complexity of the *rocaille* ornament (FIG. 266). In the rococo garden Venus became the iconographical center.

In addition to the arts bound to the *Gesamtkunstwerk* those independent thereof are found everywhere. In contrast to the furniture closely tied to the decoration of a room, single pieces, such as commodes, desks, and pendulum clocks (PL. 181), introduced a new note sometimes simply by means of the contrast of their brown veneer with the white and gold paneling. Since their position could be varied, they interrupted the severe spatial arrangement of the furnishings. Certain pieces, like the writing table of the master of the house, the lady's *poudreuse*, and the *trésor* (writing cabinet) in which documents and letters were kept, became expressions of the personal taste, fancy, and hobbies of the owner. These individual and intimate pieces of furniture, which barely touched the floor, were made by the cabinet maker, who even outside France often bore the title *ébéniste*. He was the sovereign of wood craftsmen, veneering or inlaying with precious woods (cayenne, satinwood, violet wood, rosewood, amaranth, palisander wood) and creating costly inlay work; the relief ornament of the showpieces was in fire-gilded bronze. These articles of furniture were extremely highly prized and often more was paid for them than for a great painting. Their type was created by the guild of Parisian *ébénistes*, founded in 1723.

Movable sculpture included the portrait bust and small pieces of various sizes and materials. Marble dominated in portrait sculpture; its natural heaviness was countered by making the skin seem to have the dull sheen of silk. Wooden sculpture played no part in France. Where it did appear, it usually imitated marble in its whiteness. Small sculpture was in lead or clay, later in *biscuit* (twice-fired, unglazed porcelain). The subjects came from intimate mythology, the pastoral, and the world of the theater (PLS. 171, 182). Contemporary paintings show this movable sculpture standing on console tables, mantels, and *étagères*. The art of precision modeling of reliefs embraced the art of the medalist. The refinement of the art of coinage (see COINS AND MEDALS) is noticeable in the work of the third and fourth decades of the 18th century. The zenith was reached in the middle of the century. The portrait medals of this time, in an extremely delicate and low relief like the most beautiful contemporary gold coins, rivaled the most elegant painted portraits. As gifts between sovereigns and the nobility, rococo medals went out into the world. In this field too, Paris, with its great tradition based on Jean Mauger (ca. 1640–1719) and Jean Duvivier (1687–1761), led the way.

The independent framed panel and easel painting, when not collected in picture cabinets, was placed according to the owner's taste and fancy either within or outside the wall panels. Though some of Watteau's painting is decorative, more often it is "independent" cabinet painting and small in size. Yet one of his masterpieces was the shop sign set outside the shop of the art dealer Gersaint (IV, PL. 29; XIV, PL. 404). The *Gilles* (XIV, PL. 407) must originally have been intended for the same purpose. Most of Chardin's pictures are independent paintings, with the exception of the overdoors with music instruments and similar elements (III, PL. 213). By contrast, the large state portraits by Hyacinthe Rigaud (q.v.), Nicolas de Largillière (q.v.; V, PL. 406), Jean Marc Nattier (V, PL. 415), and François Boucher (q.v.) were often closely tied to the interior decoration.

The single graphic sheet, the drawing, the individual engraving, and the mezzotint also belonged to the category of independent art (PL. 175). In them the improvisational genius of the rococo triumphed. The fine editions of books were at times part of the interior decoration with their homogeneous binding. The constituent parts — binding, title page, printed page, and illustrations — formed a small *Gesamtkunstwerk* in themselves (see GRAPHIC ARTS). For book art, particularly book illustration, the rococo was a golden age. Fine illustrations were particularly an achievement of the Parisian book illustrators. In this field, too, the weighty, the sober, and the pompous were driven out by the light, the gay, and the festive. Folio and quarto formats yielded to the elegant small octavo and duodecimo volumes. The Goncourt brothers called the 18th century the century of the vignette in contrast to the previous century of the frontispiece. In a hitherto unknown multiplicity the vignettes not infrequently crowded the text into a secondary role. Engraving almost completely replaced the woodcut. The illustrators' designs were executed by first-class engravers. The bindings — brown calf for ordinary books, red morocco for de luxe editions — were usually limited in decoration to an elegantly articulated frame of flower tendrils and palmettes with projecting cornerpieces that deviated into the center field (VI, PL. 420). A novelty was the leather mosaic binding that appeared in the Régence; only a few hundred examples are still extant, and in the 18th century they were already prized collector's items. Three families stand out among the many hundreds of Parisian bookbinders — the Padeloups, the Lemonniers, and the Deromes. These families were in most cases related to each other by marriage and handed down their traditions from generation to generation.

In the rococo the ornamental print acquired an exceptional importance. The representatives of the extremes of the *genre pittoresque*, Justin Aurèle Meissonier (1693–1750), Jacques de La Joue (1687–1761), Pierre Edme Babel (ca. 1720–75), and François de Cuvilliés (1695–1768), worked in a kind of exile. With the exception of Cuvilliés, they were generally excluded from official art activities and compensated by expressing their architectural ideas in grotesque ornamental prints. Through their bizarre imagination they lost contact with architecture and interior decoration. The *forme rocaille* of the ornamental print was not translatable into carving or stucco — at least not in France; in Germany, however, such a transferal did take place. The ornamentalists came all the closer to painting: Boucher produced the most exquisite pages of *rocaille*, and the influence of the ornamental print is undeniable in his paintings. La Joue transferred the *forme rocaille* to oil painting. This particular form of the ornamental print was not new; it had appeared already in the 16th century when the mannerist ornamental print had lost its connection with practical ornament. The innovation in the rococo was that these simple graphic sheets of grotesque ornamental motifs were looked upon with great suspicion by the classical opposition. Did they suspect that a revolution was in progress, a particularly dangerous one just because it came playfully on little velvet paws? Indeed this last exaggeration of fantasy was the swan song of Western ornament.

In the theater, beginning in 1680, two types of comedy dominated in Paris, the *comédie des mœurs* and the *comédie des surprises*. The Comédie Française and the Comédie Italienne were established in 1680. The importance of the *comédie italienne* was limited to France, and did not play an important artistic part in Italy, Germany, or England. Comic opera also flourished.

Little is known about stage sets. Jean Bérain's projects for the division of the stage into transverse spaces one behind the other still belong to the late Louis XIV period. But in his rejection of heavy light-and-space effects, Bérain prepared the way for Régence and rococo scenery (see SCENOGRAPHY). A fairly good picture of the former is found in Gillot's and Watteau's paintings, but it is not clear who was the leading stage designer of the Régence. What the early rococo sets were like can only be surmised from a few projects by La Joue. In 1737, Boucher appeared. He has been described as the most typically French designer of the rococo. Next to him G. N. Servandoni (1695–1766), who introduced Ferdinando Galli Bibiena's (1657–1734) and Juvara's (q.v.) *scena per angolo* into Paris, represented the French version of the Italian set designer. The theater in its turn influenced the subject matter of painting. Nowhere else in Europe were the paintings of theater subjects as well as portraits of actors and actresses of such high quality as in Régence and rococo France. Only England took up this tradition and continued it into the late 18th century.

PHASES OF FRENCH ROCOCO. *Origins* (1675–1715). The "querelle des anciens et des modernes" occurred between 1678 and 1701 and ended with the victory of the moderns. Between 1670 and 1690 the battle over the significance of color took place both within and outside the Académie Royale — the Poussinists versus the Rubenists, the latter taking the part of the moderns. In 1673 appeared *Dialogue sur le coloris* by Roger de Piles. Under Coypel (president of the Académie after Lebrun's death in 1690), the battle was already as good as won.

At this time the system of façade, which was to take the lead in the later phases, originated on smaller châteaux. It appeared first in 1674, on the Château du Val near Saint-Germain, which Hardouin Mansart (q.v.) built as a *retour de chasse* (hunting lodge) for Louis XIV, who sought rest and solitude in this simple house. Although far from recalling the *décor* of the theater (as does the Trianon), it heralds the small *maisons* that soon became fashionable (Hautecoeur, 1943, fig. 415). The same system was developed in two stories on the Château d'Issy of President Talon (1681, by P. Bullet). Nevertheless, 25 years were to pass before this system imperceptibly and encountering no resistance was to assert itself in countless Paris *hôtels*. 1699 was a decisive year. The Académie was reorganized, Roger de Piles was accepted, and Mansart became Surintendant des Bâtiments with Pierre Lepautre as his first designer; new activity began in Meudon, Marly, Versailles (IX, PLS. 319, 320), and Trianon. In the *appartements* for the King, the Grand Dauphin, and the young Duchesse de Bourgogne, Lepautre introduced a new decorative system for interiors, becoming a pioneer of the *style nouveau* and the "father of the rococo." Audran found new principles for decorative painting in the same commissions. Both Lepautre and Audran followed Bérain. In these works for the court, the baroque with its spatial and plastic dynamism was already replaced by a delicate movement of flowing lines and surfaces (F. Kimball).

After 1705, a new wall system appeared in many *hôtels* in the new quarters of the nobility in Faubourg Saint-Germain and Faubourg Saint-Honoré, particularly after Mansart's death in 1708. He was succeeded as royal architect by De Cotte. Yet neither De Cotte nor Gabriel Germain Boffrand (1667–1754) played a decisive part in this new development. De Cotte's domain was that of the large royal buildings. Boffrand's somewhat old-fashioned broad style was more suitable to Leopold's court sphere in Lorraine than to Paris. Between 1703 and 1720 he designed several large châteaux for Leopold (Lunéville, La Malgrange, Nancy) and, in Brussels, for the elector of Bavaria, Max Emanuel (the hunting lodge at Bouchefort, 1713). In Paris, where the colossal order still played a part (Hôtel Amélot de Gournay, 1712), Boffrand's buildings were just as out of date as J. S. Cartaud's (1675–1758) rural Château de Montmorency, begun in 1702 for the rich banker Pierre Crozat (1665–1740), a great art collector and the patron of Watteau. The standard buildings were Lassurance's Hôtel de Maisons and Hôtel d'Auvergne (both 1708), built according to a plan which was to remain unchanged throughout the first half of the century. Next to them stand the early works of Le Blond — Hôtel de Vendôme (1705–06, enlarged 1714–16), Hôtel de Clermont (1708–14), Maison Dunoyer (1708) — and somewhat later De Cotte's Hôtel de Lude (1710) and Hôtel d'Estrées (1713). Oppenord had not yet come into the limelight. René Frémin, author of *Mémoires critiques d'architecture* (1702), already propagated the new style in theory. Due to numerous casualties it is impossible to determine precisely just when and in which building the new form of exterior and interior decoration appeared together. In any case, Lepautre was the uncontested leader in interior decoration. Not until 1712 did François Antoine Vassé, full of new ideas, make his appearance. In painted decoration Audran was joined around 1700 by Gillot, and in 1707–08 by the young Watteau, who collaborated in Audran's atelier. In 1712 Watteau was accepted as an associate member (*agrégé*) of the Académie. In 1714 Le Blond went to Russia and did not return; with him went Nicolas Pineau (1684–1754). In 1716 Lepautre died. The subject of the ceiling in the Chancellerie d'Orléans (Paris, 1708) was the pictorial proclamation of these new convictions: the *amours* drive the great gods from Olympus. It must have seemed just as revolutionary as the performance of Beaumarchais's play *The Marriage of Figaro* at the Versailles court in 1784.

MAJOR ARTISTS. Jules Hardouin Mansart (1646–1708); Pierre Bullet (1639–1716); Jean Bérain (1637–1711); Pierre Lepautre (ca. 1648–1716); Claude Audran III (1658–1734); Pierre Lassurance (1655–1724); Alexandre Jean Baptiste Le Blond (1679–1719); Robert de Cotte (1656–1735); Claude Gillot (1673–1722); Jean Antoine Watteau (1684–1721).

Style Régence (1715–30). When in 1715, after the death of Louis XIV, Philippe II, duke of Orléans, an ardent collector and gifted amateur, assumed the regency for the five-year-old Louis XV, the constellation of architects, decorators, painters, cabinetmakers, and landscape architects that was to determine the style had already assembled. Oppenord (the family originated in Geldern), since 1712 *premier architecte de Monseigneur le Duc d'Orléans*, took the lead in architecture, Vassé (De Cotte's right hand) in decoration, Watteau in painting, and Nattier in portraiture (V, PL. 415). Cressent as court cabinetmaker for the regent initiated the new furniture style of the Régence. Cartaud also worked for the regent from 1715 on. The leading project was not the Paris residence of the young King in the Tuileries, but the regent's residence in the Palais-Royal, where, even before 1715, the great suite of rooms in the former Palais Brion and the Aeneas Gallery had been built and painted by Coypel. Oppenord built and decorated the large corner salon on the Rue de Richelieu and the private apartment of the Duchesse d'Orléans on the garden side. But the most up-to-date part was the series of small cabinets flanking the large rooms on the south side.

New to the regent, his mistresses, the members of the council, and the high officials, an outstanding role as patron was played by the rich financiers, such as the notorious Law and, above all, Pierre Crozat. His *hôtel*, built in 1704 (Rue de Richelieu 91–93), was designated by Brice as one of the most pleasing and singular houses in Paris. In the *galerie dorée*, which had aroused the ire of Louis XIV, was the marvelous art collection where Watteau had studied the Venetians. Crozat was also the regent's neighbor in his château (Montmorency), which had an orangery built by Oppenord (719). The buildings for the natural sons of Louis XIV represented in a certain sense a different direction. Their architects were De Cotte, Boffrand, Jumel, Mollet, the Italian Giardini, and Aubert. The most important building is the *hôtel* of the Duke of Toulouse (formerly Hôtel de la Vrillière; now Banque de France), in which the *galerie dorée* (PL. 162), retaining the *grisaille* ceilings by François Perrier, was decorated by Vassé beginning in 1719. It is almost the only room of the period in which large sculpture was used.

The height of the Régence was between 1717 and 1721. These years saw the creation of the late masterpieces by Watteau, among them *L'Embarquement pour Cythère* (XIV, PL. 403),

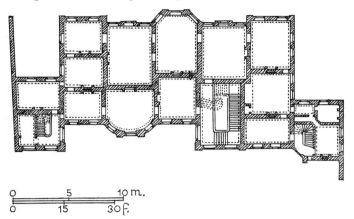

Paris, Hôtel de Matignon, ground plan (*from GBA, XIII, 1935*).

which brought him admission to the Académie (1721). Oppenord's career also culminated in these years. Little of his work remains — for example, the *salon* of the Hôtel d'Assy (1719). The great elegant court stables of the Duc de Bourbon (Condé) in Chantilly date from 1719, the *hôtels* de Noirmoutier and de

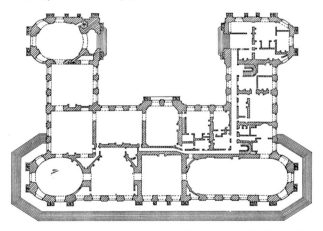

Paris, Palais Bourbon, ground plan (*from H. Courtant, Le Palais Bourbon au XVIIIe siècle, Paris, 1905*).

Matignon (FIG. 249) from 1720, both by Jean Courtonne (1671–1739), and the Palais Bourbon (FIG. 249) and the neighboring Hôtel de Lassay (FIG. 249) from 1720 and 1722, both begun by Giardini and completed by Lassurance, Gabriel, and Aubert. In 1719, appeared the *Reflexions critiques sur la poésie et sur la*

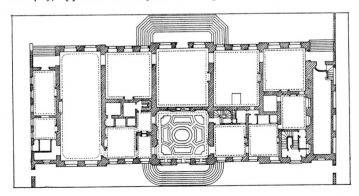

Paris, Hôtel de Lassay, ground plan (*from H. Courtant, Le Palais Bourbon au XVIIIe siècle, Paris, 1905*).

peinture by Abbé Dubos with the hypothesis that the laws of art are determined not by reason but by feeling. In 1722, the regent's court was transferred to Versailles; after his death in 1723 a certain stagnation set in.

The decorative system as formulated by Pierre Lepautre remained basically unchanged under the Régence. Italian elements were infused through Oppenord, Vassé, and particularly Bernard Toro (1672–1731). These were reminiscent not only of Borromini but of north Italian styles as well, and they were more evident in the ornamental print than in the interior decoration itself. The genius of this phase was Watteau. His work is far more significant than the consciously conventional Régence art. For him, ancient Olympus including its *amours* is present only as a parenthesis; the gods figure in his paintings only as stone statues or herms.

MAJOR ARTISTS. Gilles Marie Oppenord (1672–1742); Jean Courtonne (1671–1739); François Antoine Vassé (1681–1736); Jean Antoine Watteau (1684–1721); Jean Marc Nattier (1685–1766); Charles Cressent (1685–1768); Sébastien Slodtz (1655–1726); Jacques de La Joue (1687–1761).

Style rocaille (1730–45). After 1730, new protagonists appeared on the stage: Meissonier, Pineau (who had returned from Russia before 1728), and Boucher. They formed the "troika" of the rococo, just as Oppenord, Vassé, and Watteau had for the Régence. In the formulation of the new style, which manifested itself first in designs for goldsmith work, Meissonier had a certain lead. His art, heavily laden with Italian late baroque motifs (he was born in Turin), was more indicative of the state of his Portuguese and Polish patrons than of Parisian fashions (ornamental projects for Marshal Bielinski and his sister, the Princess Czartoryski). His only project for an entire house, Maison Bréthous, displayed heavy late baroque details in the traditional decorative system. It is significant that the house was designed not for Paris, but for Bayonne. His engravings, however (the first series appeared in 1734), exercised a strong influence, more enduring abroad than in France. Pineau was important for the discovery of the *genre pittoresque* and its acceptance in French interiors. Working together with the architect Jean Baptiste Lerouc, he designed and executed rooms, earlier than Meissonier, in which all the new discoveries were incorporated — *rocaille*, asymmetry, and contrast. More than Meissonier or anyone else he established the character and type of decorative ensemble that became predominant in France. The real innovations were to be found in the interior; the exterior had hardly anything new to offer. Between 1730 and 1735 the *genre pittoresque* was delineated in private buildings. Only after 1738 did it also penetrate into the apartments of the court. Nothing seemed very revolutionary at all, only an extreme lightness, delicacy, and naturalness in the play of new forms. Yet contemporaries immediately recognized the *style nouveau* in these works. The antechamber in the Hôtel de Matignon (by Pineau), a masterpiece of the new taste, dates from 1731, the Hôtel de Rouillé is from 1732, the gallery in the Hôtel de Villars from 1733, and the Grand Salon and the Salon Rouge in the Hôtel de Roquelaure from 1732 — all by Leroux and Pineau. From 1732 to 1737 Boffrand, who, approaching seventy, only now became fully connected with the new development, built the famous oval *salons* in the Hôtel de Soubise (PL. 162), with paintings by Natoire and reliefs by Jean Baptiste Lemoyne. In 1735 followed the Hôtel de Gontaud and the Hôtel de Mazarin, and in 1738 the Maison de Boutin.

In 1731 Boucher returned from Italy; he was accepted into the Académie in 1734, and joined the new current with his decorative paintings. His contemporaries were already aware that La Joue's designs belonged as much to the preceding reign as to the present one.

The revolutionary ideas of ornament as the pictorial expression of the concern with minute details and of the interchangeability of categories first appeared in the independent ornament of innumerable prints and in the engravings of the architectural treatises propagating the new style, and not in the dependent ornament of interior decoration. The titles alone of the following books are a reflection of the new preferences: Meissonier's *Livre de légumes* (1732 or 1733) and his *Cinquième livre d'ornements* (1734); La Joue's *Livre de cartouche* (after 1734); Babel's *Cartouches pittoresques* (probably after 1734); La Joue's *Livre nouveau de divers morceaux de fantaisie* (1736); Fraisse's *Livre des dessins chinois . . . de Perse, des Indes* (1735); Mondon's *Premier livre de forme rocaille et cartel* (1736); Babel's *Rocaille* (before 1740); Mondon's *Ornements chinois* (1736); Peyrotte's *Vases rocailles* (1743); C. A. Briseux's *Architecture moderne* (1727); *Architecture moderne*, released by the editor Jombert in 1728–29; J. F. Blondel's *De la distribution des maisons de plaisance* (1737–38); the fourth volume of Mariette's *Architecture française* under the title *L'architecture à la mode* (1738); and Briseux's *L'art de bâtir des maisons de campagne* (1743).

Chardin (q.v.) occupies a special place. His art with its still lifes, its domestic subjects, and its range of warm colors makes him seem a straggler of the Régence (like a Watteau of bourgeois idylls) carried over into colder times. Yet subtle threads bind his art with that of his time, even with Boucher. It is a high point in French 18th-century painting taken as a whole.

The fields of rococo art are the same as those of Régence. In the twenties they were enriched by pastel, which came from Italy, and in the thirties by porcelain from Germany. The relationships of these categories to each other within a formal system are outwardly similar. Their diversity can best be grasped through the contrasts between the paintings of Watteau and Boucher. In the latter, the color range is warmer, in the former it is cooler; in the forties, particularly with Latour (V, PL. 411) an ice-blue occasionally became the preferred color. The paint itself is looser in Watteau; in Boucher it is smoother, arriving at a porcelainlike firmness in his nudes (PLS. 569, 570). Watteau's dreamlike quiet gives way to Boucher's more lively movement, an academic baroque in miniature.

But there are more basic differences. Rococo did not believe in the possibility of a synthesis, an assimilation of opposites, in which the German late baroque passionately believed, as did also in its own way the Régence. Therein lies its inner skepticism. But the rococo did not reject an encompassing of opposites; rather, it enjoyed them esthetically. Therein lies its refinement and its "immorality." This is expressed on the most diverse levels of rococo forms, most characteristically in the *rocaille* ornament with its peculiar way of half detaching itself from its ground, simultaneously denying and affirming it, turning the rational components into irrational ones in an indecisive hovering between various meanings and dimensions. Compared with the rococo, the art of the Régence impresses one as being naïve, unself-conscious, and lyrical.

MAJOR ARTISTS. Nicolas Pineau (1684–1754); Justin Aurèle Meissonier (1693–1750); François Boucher (1703–70); Maurice Quentin de Latour (1704–88); Charles Joseph Natoire (1700–77); Nicolas Lancret (1690–1743); Jean Baptiste Siméon Chardin (1699–1779); Jean Etienne Liotard (1702–89).

Style Pompadour (1745–64). By 1737–38 admiration for the *style nouveau* was general. In 1742 Boffrand predicted that it would not last long. Toward 1745, just 10 years after its culmination, the *forme rocaille* was already meaningless in France. It did, of course, continue to appear even later, but it was no longer stylistically formative: it presented no new problems.

It is erroneous to conceive of the transition from rococo to classicism in the 1760s as a retrogressive formation in Wölfflin's terms (*Dreitakt*), but it is correct to consider the change of decoration in the late forties and fifties under this aspect. In exteriors as well, certain elements disappeared which had been considered obligatory for more than two generations. "Undifferentiated" arch forms vanished from both façades and panels and were replaced by straight lintels and plane surfaces. The delicate relief of the preceding stage was preserved, but it now appeared as the surface of a more massive substance. This transformation can be followed step by step on the many costly buildings for the *maîtresse en titre* of the king. Beginning in 1746, the following buildings were built for the Marquise de Pompadour: the Château de Crécy near Dreux (demolished in 1830), with paintings by Boucher; the Château de Champs en

Brie, still completely in the *genre pittoresque*; the Petit Château de La Celle (1747); the three hermitages at Versailles, Fontainebleau (both 1749), and Compiègne (1753–54); Bellevue (1748–50); her *hôtel* in Versailles; and the Hôtel d'Evreux in Paris. Her chief architect was Jean Lassurance II (1695–1755), his draftsman, Jeanson.

The architect called upon to make the change was Ange Jacques Gabriel (1698–1782), a member of the older rococo generation. After De Cotte withdrew in 1734, Gabriel became *premier architecte du roi*. Jacques Verberckt (1704–71), the leading decorator, continuously collaborated with him. The break with rococo is marked by Gabriel's main building of the Petit Trianon (V, PL. 421). Here he translated English Palladianism into French elegance in the new *noble simplicité* of this short, classic, late stage. But interior decoration still retained the delicate panel system, which in France was not superseded by Robert Adam's English system until 1770. With Fragonard (1732–1806; PL. 174) rococo iconographical elements (airy, fiery, forceful, and unexpected) reached into the new period.

Diffusion. From Paris, the new style of the Régence and the rococo soon spread to the provinces, throughout almost all of Europe, and even overseas and to the Orient. It was not a diffusion of single elements, motifs, and forms but rather of that symbiosis of categories described above. The restrained, sparing elegance of Parisian *hôtels* rendered them ideal for large *présidences* and abbey buildings in the French provinces. Abroad, the typically French *maison de plaisance* was preferred for small pleasure palaces: the "Bagatelles," "Sanssoucis," "Monbijous," "Monrepos," "Favorites," "Solitudes," "Ermitages" — all typical names. Their diffusion began early. Some examples of typically Régence forms are: the Hôtel de la Première Présidence (Rouen, 1717, by Jean Martin); in Switzerland, the Maison Lullin (Genthod, 1723, by Blondel); in Alsace, annexed to France since 1681, a *hôtel* at Andlau (1725–31), built on the French system but with non-French bay windows. De Cotte brought the style to Bonn in 1616–17 (Palais del Buen Retiro) and to Frankfurt (Palais Thurn und Taxis), Oppenord in 1720 to La Granja, Leblond and Pineau after 1714 to St. Petersburg, Cuvilliés after 1728 to the Rhineland and the Bavarian court. Next to these buildings, which propagated the totality of the style, apartments in the new French Régence and rococo fashion were installed in old-style castles throughout Europe.

The fact that there were art currents in France that from Louis XIV to Louis XVI continued untouched by Règence and rococo art is explained by the principle of *convenance*. Depending on the project, a level of style was chosen. The same architect carried out an "official" building in forms quite different from those used in a private *hôtel*. The first half of the 18th century was the time for great city-planning projects; monumental *places royales* sprang up everywhere. That church art should hardly have been touched by rococo art is self-evident when the basically unchristian quality of rococo is taken into consideration. Some of the decorative schemes can be seen in church furnishings (Orléans, stalls of the Cathedral, 1702–06; Paris, Notre Dame, altar by Vassé, 1712); but only these church furnishings and objects show *rocaille* influences. The simple elegance of arched doorways and segmental arched windows were used in only one or two isolated church façades. In contrast, Meissonier's famous project for the façade of St-Sulpice, a transposition of Domenico da Cortona's façade for S. Maria della Pace (Rome) into light, late baroque, displays rococo echoes only in the roof area. Like Guarini's design for Ste-Anne-la-Royale (under Louis XIV), this project also remained on paper. The *noble simplicité* of the rococo applied to a church is strikingly shown in designs of Giovanni Niccolò Servandoni (1695–1766, an exact contemporary of Meissonier) for the façade of St-Sulpice, which was built between 1733 and 1745. The interior decoration of the Hôtel de Soubise was created at the same time. Pineau's design for a church in Russia (Hautecoeur, 1951–52, III, fig. 70) comes closest to being a rococo church, both for the dominance of round and segmental arches as well as the emphasis on width, but the high dome is a baroque residue.

Together with this "official" architecture went "official" monumental sculpture, which existed side by side with the intimate but as a separate class. Nicolas Coustou's *Jules César* (1713 or 1722) displays completely different stylistic principles than the mythological portraits by Raoux or Nattier; Bouchardon's *Fontaine de Grenelle* (1739), his solemn, heavy statues for St-Sulpice, and Falconet's *Bronze Horseman* (Peter the Great) for St. Petersburg are stylistically distinct from the former's *Amor* and the latter's *Baigneuse* and *Madame de Pompadour as Venus* (PL. 171).

It is senseless to classify this "official" architecture, sculpture, and painting as Régence and rococo simply on chronological grounds. It is rather a Régence or rococo stage of the French classic. The fact that there was also a preference for the more secular *Hallenkirche*, with its spatial simplicity, absence of tension, and verticality, can perhaps be interpreted as analogous to the secular, spatial concept of the rococo. It is also noteworthy that at this stage several churches were planned in Gothic form (e.g., the alternate design for Notre-Dame-la-Novelle in Orléans, 1718, by Hénault, 1684–1723). It was not mid-century classicism that first rediscovered the Gothic (see NEO-GOTHIC STYLES).

Although Paris set the fashion in the first half of the 18th century, in the French provinces there existed currents of modern rococo motifs that were basically closer to the late baroque. Here the *corps de logis* of the *hôtels* sometimes had Borromini-like curving ground plans; here were to be found the despised colossal orders or heavy caryatids. This unconvincing mixture of heterogeneous elements was capable of producing works that actually seemed to anticipate the 19th-century baroque-rococo — for example, the famous Fontaine du Gros-Horloge in Rouen (1731; Hautecoeur, 1951–52, III, fig. 437).

INTERNATIONAL ROCOCO. To a great extent the style of the rococo was determined by what is today known as handicrafts (q.v.). Certainly of major importance among the determining factors was the ornament, which influenced the style and passed most easily beyond national boundaries. Not only were art objects, porcelains, and dishes imported and exported, but there was a brisk trade in ornamental devices. In Paris, Venice, Augsburg, Nürnberg, Munich, and London there existed publishing houses that dealt in nothing but ornamental prints used by craftsmen throughout Europe. Thus German porcelain borrowed motifs from the French ornamental print and Russian goldsmiths from Augsburg graphic art, while Watteau motifs appeared in the paintings on German lacquer cabinets. It soon became difficult to distinguish between a Spanish, Swabian, or Neapolitan *rocaille* ornament. It should be noted that this was true for the individual ornament but not of its place within the decoration. The objects from the porcelain factories of Meissen, Nymphenburg, Berlin, Chelsea, Capodimonte, Buen Retiro, Vienna, and Sèvres differed in stylistic nuances and national characteristics (PL. 182); but the elements which they have in common are more numerous. International rococo originated not in France but in Germany. It would, however, be senseless to speak of national characteristics in the light of this international phenomenon. The most important German porcelain artist, F. A. Bustelli (1723–63; PL. 182), was probably a native of Locarno and was one of the many peripatetic artists who appeared on the scene in this century.

In France, after the ban on the production of tableware in precious metals was partially lifted in 1721, gold and silver, for evident reasons, became the material which best satisfied the requirements for pomp of the nobility and emancipated *bourgeoisie*. It is indicative that one of the leaders of the *genre pittoresque*, Meissonier, was a goldsmith. The *forme rocaille* came into being through a direct contact with the art of the goldsmith rather than with the field of architecture. Meissonier's designs for gold or silver ware were often barely distinguishable from his graphic ornamental fantasies. As Meissonier executed orders for his ware from Poland and England, his ornament (particularly in graphic form) spread across Europe. In the international style the work of Paul de Lamerie (1712–51; PL. 181) in London can be distinguished from that of François Thomas Germain (1726–91) in Paris, but the underlying ornament is always the same,

whether classically simplified or imaginatively exuberant as in Germany. In the internationalization of the rococo an important part was played by the wandering artists, specialists in the individual art fields who spread similar forms throughout Europe. Perhaps the best-known example is the stuccoworkers from Wessobrunn. By the hundreds they left a small village in Bavaria, particularly in the 18th century, diffusing stucco *rocaille* ornament wherever they went. They worked in Berlin (Gigl and Landes), Amsterdam (Lidl), Orval (Gannebacher), Einsiedeln (Merk), St. Gallen (Gigl), Warsaw (Schaidhauf), and Paris (Schweiger and Vogl), not to mention the more circumscribed sphere of activity in southern Germany. This resulted in a somewhat uniform appearance of rococo interior decoration and movable art objects. On the negative side, this made-to-order decoration with its uniform stucco or carved wood motifs paid little attention to the individuality of the building. Ornament could be purchased like porcelain. In the meantime, the relationship between wall and decoration reached the point where the ornament was only an appliqué on a wall background.

Through the engagement of the most diverse artists extremely heterogeneous styles and phases were intermingled on and in the large buildings. In Berlin, the Frenchman Pesne painted ceiling *plafonds* in Palladian-style buildings. The most important architect of the so-called "Russian rococo," Bartolomeo Rastrelli (1700–71; XIV, PL. 237), Italian by birth and committed to the north Italian late baroque, used French elements (after De Cotte) for ground plans, motifs of the south German rococo (after Cuvilliés), and Austrian ones (after Hildebrandt), mingling the whole with a spirit of theatrical fantasy reminiscent of Bibiena. Thus, in Tsarskoe Selo a syncretistic architecture that evades any exact stylistic definition came into being. At the most it is rococo in the sense of a new international style.

Porcelain. G. Semper's thesis that the rococo began with porcelain is untenable. But the reverse is true: in porcelain the rococo found an extremely characteristic and suitable material, and the time was ripe for its discovery (by Johann Friedrich Böttger, 1708–09). If a style can be characterized by the discoveries and new fields it opens up, then for rococo first place goes to porcelain. The passion for small sculpture and tableware in porcelain — for the precious, the fragile, the exotic — had until then been satisfied by porcelain imported from China or by its imitations. But only a few years after the discovery of the formula of porcelain, a completely new type of small sculpture came into existence in addition to the costly tableware (PL. 510; III, PLS. 157, 159, 162). Small sculpture, which in Western art had always been made of the same material as large works — wood, clay, metal — now found its own material, which set absolute limits on the size. Until then, a relationship had existed between small and monumental sculpture; the smaller was bound to the larger either as a reduction or as a preparatory sketch, and usually the differences were only proportional. In the rococo, small sculpture was emancipated and became a field in its own right. From the outset a risk presented itself. Knickknacks and useless trifles were produced, and it is significant that the rococo has continued uninterruptedly into the present century in the production of porcelain figures and imitations.

The porcelain figurine became a souvenir, no longer meaningful in itself, but a sentimental object. The tendency toward such a loss of meaning was no doubt already present in the rococo itself. Porcelain sculpture is always unnaturalistic: it remains porcelain. At the same time, painting the porcelain enlivens the figure in a naturalistic sense (III, PL. 158). The porcelain group is a small object, like a *rocaille* ornament. It is also the essence of vivacity. These features mutually interact in a charming counterplay. The work of art is naturalistic, often to an extreme, but it is always "only" a work of art (XIII, PL. 374).

The influence of the "porcelainlike" was so great that in southern Germany, for example, garden sculptures in sandstone (Veitshöchheim, 1768, by Ferdinand Dietz) were painted *à la porcelaine* — that is, varnished shiny white and colored. This again paralyzed the lifelikeness, which was often exaggerated to the point of caricature. They were presented as being only porcelain, only art illustrations.

It is significant that in France the production of porcelain played a lesser role than in Germany, Italy, or England. Figural porcelain was soon limited to the so-called "biscuit" (III, PL. 159), which, dispensing with glaze, was considered "plus noble, d'un goût plus général." In the classicist reaction the porcelain figure even attained monumental qualities, and in such pieces the pretension to monumentality easily becomes ridiculous. Knickknacks had come into being.

Pastel, sketch, and capriccio. The technique of pastels was not a rococo discovery, but it became a favorite and typical medium of expression at this time. After its perfection in about 1700 by Joseph Vivien (1657–1734), it was used, above all, by Rosalba Carriera (1675–1757; X, PL. 497), Quentin de Latour (1704–88), Jean Baptiste Perroneau (1715–83; V, PL. 411) and Jean Etienne Liotard (1702–89; V, PL. 201). The characteristics of the pastel technique correspond to the rococo *Kunstwollen* (artistic intentions), the apparent ease and swiftness of the performance to artistic improvisation, its intermediate position between drawing and painting to the new popularity of the sketch, the "alive" quality of pastel to the penetrating representations and grasp of psychological features evident, above all, in portraiture. The colorfulness of pastel, which seems almost artificial, points to the rococo aim toward stylization. Results were achieved, similar to the colorfulness of porcelain, which again produced an interplay between naturalism and artificiality.

Many preparatory sketches, mostly in oil, for frescoes in southern Germany and Austria have been preserved. A closer perusal of these sketches has established (according to E. Bushart) that they are not necessarily preparatory stages for monumental painting but are often translations of a fresco into easel painting (with the necessary changes). This leads one to conclude that the nature of fresco in the rococo often comes close to being a reduction of an illusionistic structure, thus making such a translation easier. These "sketches" — often prepared later — document above all the new passion of the rococo for the sketch as an "autonomous work of art" (Bushart). The setting down of the first brilliant idea becomes the actual artistic manifestation. From Fragonard through Guardi and Maulbertsch, the sketchlike in painting became accepted as an independent artistic form. The drawings of Gabriel de Saint-Aubin (1724–80) are an extreme example of this tendency. The journalistic perfection of the sketch, the fixing of a situation, and the utilization of the unfinished announced a new epoch.

If one attempts to study Tiepolo's frescoes on the basis of their content, which, as in Würzburg, is facilitated by the existence of the original sketches, one soon runs into considerable difficulties. The baroque idea is clear, but its formulation is often bizarre, fantastic, and strange. Particularly in the border areas one encounters an informality of content that stands in opposition to the precise and detailed baroque iconology (PL. 179). Here Tiepolo's painting approaches the small paintings of his countryman Guardi, whose fantasies of picturesque landscapes with bizarre ruins and unreal combinations of heterogeneous elements (V, PL. 241) are capriccios, devices something like La Joue's *morceaux de fantaisie.*

On the ornament pages of Meissonier, La Joue, Babel, and Cuvilliés, as far as Guardi, the young Tiepolo, and even Piranesi in his early years, the capriccio is a characteristic art form of the rococo. Genetically it can be explained as the continuation of the earlier grotesque (see FANTASY). In this sense, the capriccio is an ornamentalization of the content. The ambivalence of the content, its multiple possibilities of meaning, are analogous to the micromegalithic structure of the *rocaille.* Like the *rocaille*, the capriccio continually changes meaning. This indecision as an artistic principle and the resulting interplay is a characteristic feature of the rococo.

Mirror cabinets. Following the example set by the Hall of Mirrors in Versailles (1678–84; V, PL. 409), large panels of mirror glass became part of the articulation of the wall and played an important role. At Versailles these mirrors served to enlarge the space in the sense of a multiple enfilade; somewhat

later, in the Galerie des Glaces in the Trianon (1706), or as Paul Decker formulated in the *Fürstlicher Baumeister* (1711–16), the intention was grotesque, somewhat similar to booths at a fair; in the rococo the mirror assumed a special meaning. France, however, no longer participated in this development, and large mirror ensembles, as in Meissonier's project for Bielinsky, remained a provincial exception. The French rococo (e.g., Oppenord) used the mirror as a framed wall unit, not for a total reflection of a room.

By contrast, in Germany there was a solid tradition of mirror cabinets. The most important examples are the cabinets in Pommersfelden (F. Plitzner, 1714–18), Schloss Merseburg (J. M. Hoppenhaupt I, ca. 1720), the main hall of the Amalienburg in the Nymphenburg park (Cuvilliés and Zimmermann, 1739; VIII, PL. 117), and that of the Würzburger Residenz (A. Bossi, 1741–45; PL. 180). An Italian example is that of the Royal Palace in Portici, now in the Palazzo di Capodimonte (VIII, PL. 108).

All these small rooms aimed at a particular effect; the concept of space was not only transformed and enchanted, but the mirror also projected the visitor into art itself. The festive life seemed multiplied by its mirror images and raised into another sphere. Since the room's only firm point of reference was the ornamental framing, and before and behind it there were no longer obligatory concepts, the ornament of the frame set the stage. As in the ornamental engravings of the *genre pittoresque*, the dimensions fluctuated and the picture in the mirror became "micromegalithic." The ornamental frame also became increasingly important. As a "scenario" for the mirrored image the ornament was overwhelmingly large.

REGIONAL FORMS (*Sonderformen*). Outside France, secular architecture and its related arts were modeled on the Château of Versailles. By the mid-18th century in France, the large palace as an all-embracing stage for absolutist ceremonial had become an anachronism, but the European princely courts began to use it as their example. The Royal Palace in Madrid (II, PL. 160), Blenheim Palace (VI, PL. 436), the Palazzo Reale in Caserta (near Naples), Nymphenburg in Bavaria, the Residenz in Würzburg (II, PL. 152), Schönbrunn and the two Belvederes in Vienna (II, PL. 158), the Zwinger and the Royal Palace in Dresden (II, PL. 155), the palaces in Stockholm and even Nancy, all raised the same monumental pretension, which of necessity led to the use of late baroque and classical building elements. At the same time the new decorative art of the rococo — the very essence of the modern — arrived from Paris, that is, from the Parisian *hôtels* of the nobility. Thus almost everywhere in Europe the result was a chimerical manifestation: requirements of state architecture conflicted with the modern style of the intimate and tastefully elegant rococo. An intimate art averse to all pomp and ambition swept like a conqueror through the countries, while architecture in no way corresponded to this style. The result of this situation differed from country to country. Sometimes, above all in England and Spain, rococo was limited to interior decoration in the form of imported merchandise. Sometimes, as in Germany, a true synthesis between large-scale architecture and *style moderne* was reached. In almost all cases this new style had to come to terms with a late baroque art which, however, had already reached a rococolike phase. (This makes 18th-century art difficult to interpret. If, contrary to F. Kimball, one considers the rococo not only as a style of French decoration of the Louis XV period but as a genuine style encompassing all the arts, then certain late baroque, rococolike phenomena outside of France must be summarized under this stylistic name.)

In church architecture the situation was different. In this field, it was not France but Italy (in the Catholic sphere) that continued to set the example. Similar to Versailles in the secular field, late baroque Italian church architecture was an anachronism in the religious sphere, conflicting with the rococo interior decoration that was invading church art. The late baroque pathos of interiors, influenced above all by northern Italy (Guarini), recast the unemotional art of the rococo into a pathetic mold. Only in Bavaria was a type of church evolved which, *sui generis*, can be called genuine rococo, since its architecture was conceived according to the new rococo principles.

(Whenever rococo elements made their way into the decoration of Protestant church interiors, occasionally combining with classicist space and wall interpretation of Protestantism, a synthesis resulted which seemed very modern. For here, as in French architecture, the wall was un-baroque, thus forming an appropriate background for rococo decoration.)

In reviewing the rococo outside of France it should be further noted that under the influence of the widely diffused treatises on theories of art, of the ornamental prints, the pattern pages, the many journeys abroad of artists, and the export and import of portable art objects, the rococo developed an internationalism hitherto unknown.

England. The rococo was almost unknown in England. This means only that the French influence was trifling, and that there was no individual development from a late baroque tradition which led to the formation of rococolike forms. Nevertheless, certain phenomena of 18th-century English art (see GREAT BRITAIN, ART OF) may be regarded as parallels to the Continental rococo. Architecture was characterized by a new great wave of Palladianism, which offhand does not seem to call forth a comparison with French rococo architecture; but in comparing Palladian buildings of the mid-century with those by Colin Campbell (d. 1729) one becomes aware of a new decorative note. William Chambers's (1726–96) Casino at Clontarf (Dublin, 1769) was no longer classical when contrasted with Campbell's Mereworth (Kent, 1723) or Lord Burlington's (1695–1753) Chiswick House (VI, PL. 441), both modeled on Palladio's "La Rotonda." The "antique" ingredients were used ornamentally. Composed within the context of an English garden, the architecture was more of a picture subject, the ornamental part of a larger picturesque ensemble in which the classicist aspect of the building was preserved.

In the transition from late baroque classicism to the classicism of Louis XVI the rococo stage was omitted. The façade of Robert Adam's (1728–92) Kedleston Hall consists of a wideset block of architecture, in front of which was set an antique triumphal arch to serve as entrance. A comparison with Jaime Bort Miliá's façade for the Cathedral in Murcia (1741–54) may seem absurd for many reasons. But both buildings have in common the use of a motive estranged from its purpose and converted into an applied façade, something like a giant ornament. In the Spanish example it is an exaggeratedly large niche, in Kedleston a triumphal arch. The effect is similar in both cases — architecture was erected from the picturesque point of view and thereby became ornamental. This can also be found in contemporaneous south German buildings. Neither example was rococo.

The closest England came to the rococo was in the sphere of the Neo-Gothic (q.v.). While Neo-Gothic elements can already be discerned in Wren (q.v.) and Vanbrugh (q.v.), the real pioneers of this style were William Kent (1684–1748), Batty Langley (1696–1751), and the amateurs Sanderson Miller (1717–80) and Horace Walpole (1717–97). The "modern Gothick" was essentially ornamental. As a decorative style the Neo-Gothic was best characterized in Walpole's Strawberry Hill, most of all in the library designed by John Chute (VIII, PL. 109). Tudor-Gothic elements combined to create a wall decoration that structurally differed little from the Continental rococo interior. The Gothic elements formed a framework that could just as well have consisted of *rocaille*. Exotic motives, such as *chinoiseries*, could also be used in the same way. This ornamental use of the Gothic as a bizarre exotic element constituted a special, typically English form of the rococo.

The relationship of English furniture to Continental rococo was also very similar (see FURNITURE). While the craftsmen Matthias Lock and H. Copland still remained for a while under the influence of the forms diffused by the ornamental prints (Cuvilliés), this rococo was again transformed into a specifically English form by Thomas Chippendale (1718–79), the most important cabinetmaker. His pattern book, *The Gentleman and Cabinet-Maker's Director* (1754), bears the subtitle: "a large collection of the most elegant designs of household furniture in the Gothic, Chinese, and Modern Taste." This coupling of "modern taste" (*style moderne*) and Neo-Gothic and exotic ornament defined the style (with interchangeable ornamental parts) as typically English. In English art, as on the Continent, there had always been a limited connection between the ornament and the ground on which it was placed.

England's special position led to a revolution that soon invaded the Continent. Unthinkable without French aid, it could, however, have come into being only in England, away from more traditional connections. Anthony Ashley-Cooper, Earl of Shaftesbury (1671–1713), can be considered the father of the esthetic enlightenment. Feeling as the source of perception, art as creation and not imitation, virtue as love of beauty and social order — to mention only a few of his maxims — were soon to be found with the French Encyclopedists and then again in the German *Sturm und Drang*. Rococo sentimentalism as well as a novel individualization had its roots in these concepts. The fact that 18th-century English painting offered a very uneven picture may depend on this individualization. The paintings of William Hogarth (1697–1764), Joseph Highmore (1692–1780), George Knapton (1698–1778), Bartholomew Dandridge (1711–51), Francis Hayman (1708–76), Allan Ramsay (1713–84), Thomas Gainsborough (1727–88), and Joshua Reynolds (1723–92) all seem superficially to present more or less the characteristics of the *style moderne*. But in most cases it is a "disguising" of a typically English style that has roots very deep in the past. In 18th-century England new picture types came into being, often in rococo vestment, which can be understood only in terms of their national peculiarity: caricature (see COMIC ART AND CARICATURE) and the related sociocritical painting (Hogarth and Rowlandson, 1756–1827), the "role portrait" (Reynolds), the child portrait (Reynolds, Gainsborough), the animal portrait (George Stubbs, 1724–1806), and the portraitized theater scene (Hogarth and Hayman). There was also a sentimental genre that soon influenced France (Greuze) and Germany. While Gainsborough alone often came close to the stylistic stage of Fragonard in French painting, the rococo form often seemed to be interchangeable with borrowings from Rubens, Van Dyck, Rembrandt, or Lorrain. It is just this exchangeability and disguise in art which constituted the essence of a style that introduced a new historical viewpoint into art.

The most original contribution of England to the European rococo may very well be Hogarth's *The Analysis of Beauty* (1753), a treatise in which the painter attempted to establish the elusive concept of taste. Although many elements stem from the mannerist art theory (Lomazzo), such as the idea of the serpentine line, or even go back to Alberti, whose *varietà* is to be found in the concept of the manifold, the work still presents an amateur's expression of the rococo, unlimited, however, by classicistic restrictions. His discussion of "the beauty of a composed intricacy of form" could regard all interior decoration. But it is particularly the transitory and tensile aspects of the rococo that are described by Hogarth. Beauty consists in continual change. Yet, seen from the viewpoint of ethos, Hogarth's world-view is the opposite of the rococo: in place of the earthly paradise the worthlessness of the world dominates, which, in the end, is bequeathed not to God, but to Chaos (*Finis*, painting of 1764).

Spain. Spain provides a model example of how rococo imported from France can coexist with an indigenous, late baroque tradition without having any real connections (see SPANISH AND PORTUGUESE ART). Side by side — but only side by side — is found a rococo court art introduced by the Bourbons, above all in interior decoration, but no real rococo architecture. The greatest architectural undertaking, the Royal Palace of Madrid (1738–64; II, PL. 160), begun by Filippo Juvara (1676–1736), belongs to the series of buildings modeled on Versailles. Northern Italian motifs mix with French classicism and result in a typical example of an anachronistic desire for emulation by a non-French absolutist power. In its relative smallness and refined simplicity, the palace of La Granja (1721–23), built for Philip V by Teodoro Ardemans (1664–1726), comes closest to being a rococo building, but at no point does it have French format. On the other hand, a Spanish peculiarity, the small pleasure houses for the princes (El Escorial, Aranjuez, and El Pardo) once again take up the tradition of the *bagatelles*; but these are already late 18th century.

A completely different picture is presented by church architecture. A disintegration of architectural form — a translation of architecture into ornament — had already manifested itself with José de Churriguera (1650–1723) and Francisco Hurtado (1669–1725). The Churrigueresque as a manifestation of baroque dissolution still characterized the mid-18th century and evoked forms that present an analogy to the rococo of other countries insofar as ornament is capable of taking over the function of architecture (PL. 169; see CHURRIGUERESQUE STYLE). The façade of Santiago de Compostela (by Fernando de Casas y Novoa, 1738; XIII, PL. 134) ultimately makes sense only as an ornament that has become monumental. The remodeling of the façade of the Cathedral of Gerona (1730–33) by Pedro Costa (1693–1761), which combined a medieval wall and a wheel window with a gigantic portal frame, enclosing the window like a gigantic ornament, is to be understood in the same way: ornament goes its own independent way while architecture's creative power weakens. The façade of the palace of Marqués de Dos Aguas in Valencia (1740; XIII, PL. 137), one of the main works of relief decoration in Spain, can be compared with the relief structure of the Asam house in Munich (1746; Egid Quirin Asam, 1692–1750). In both examples a native tradition led to light, graceful rococolike forms; yet that tradition was independent of France. The windows of the palace in Valencia are framed by exuberant *rocaille* forms — a rarity for Spain — but they are not, as supposed by scholars, derived from French forms but go back to German ornamental prints.

Spanish sculpture stands in the same relationship to the European rococo as its architecture. While, on the one hand, courtly elements are superposed on an indigenous late baroque, as in the work of Manuel Alvarez (1727–97), on the other hand, this late baroque with its typically Spanish realism usually predominated over the extra-Spanish influences. The acme of this sculptural realism was unquestionably reached in the processional groups and nativity figures of Francisco Zarcillo (1707–83). A synthesis of Neapolitan heritage and Spanish tradition seems to have resulted in an art that is far removed from courtly rococo sculpture. Such groups are also found in other countries. Neapolitan nativity scenes (especially by the Sammartino family), works by Antonio Maria Maragliano (1664–1741) in Genoa, and procession groups by Ignaz Günther in Bavaria indicate that an indigenous late baroque of a naturalistic manner forms as much a part of the 18th century as the courtly porcelain. On closer observation, the Neapolitan nativity groups are not so different from the Nymphenburg porcelain figures. After all, Günther also worked for the Bavarian court.

Only in painting did 18th-century Spain arrive at a European status, and not till very late, namely with Francisco José de Goya y Lucientes (1746–1828). As no other painter, he marked the end of the rococo and the beginning of a new period. His early work, the cartoons for the 46 tapestries which were executed from 1776 on in the Royal Tapestry Factory of Santa Barbara (Madrid), were the swan song of the rococo. The play in them has become a farce: death breaks into the porcelainlike charm of childish occupations (as in the accident of a craftsman), and the icy breath of winter is felt in the spring of a rococo arcadia. The late baroque iconology was also destroyed with Goya. The capriccio as a playful idea was converted into a destructive force in his graphic works, in which wit became an oppressive vision. The *Sleep of Reason* (VI, PL. 402), which in French ornamental prints shortly before was an artistic whim, a play of the imagination, became a nightmare. In the frescoes in the small church of San Antonio de la Florida in Madrid (1798), the long period of baroque dome paintings also came to an end. Here the fresco was no longer a celestial place. This was already apparent from the dark, gloomy, earthy colors, and from the earthly scenes on the ceiling. In order to recognize fully the revolutionary in

Goya one need only compare his paintings with the very similar ones of Ramón Bayeu (1746–93) or Mariano Salvador de Maella (1739–1819), which remained within conventional bounds. Mention must also be made of the *Bodegón* paintings of Luis Menéndez (Meléndez, 1716–80), a traditional, naturalistic still-life painter in the sense of Zurbarán, who at the same time arrived at a tasteful refinement in his Chardin-like concept of simple objects.

Italy. The diffuseness of mid-18th-century art was nowhere so clear as in Italy (see ITALIAN ART). Although there was no real rococo architecture in Italy, single elements of the rococo were to be found almost everywhere, both in interior decoration and in painting. The power of the baroque tradition was very strong. Italy, therefore, had a unique reaction to its baroque heritage. In landscape painting — which next to Tiepolo's large frescoes was Italy's greatest contribution to the rococo — the baroque tradition turned into a painted picture, and the baroque became the subject of a picture, a purely historical element.

At the same time, after 1700, when the grand tour climaxed the education of a gentleman, Italy documented her own baroque past in large paintings. From Luca Carlevaris (1665–1731), to Antonio Canal (Il Canaletto, q.v.), his nephew Bernardo Bellotto (1720–80), Francesco Guardi (q.v.), Giovanni Battista Piranesi (q.v.), and Giovanni Paolo Pannini (1691/2–1765) Italy regarded its cities as historical theater. The fact that there was no longer any real difference in their considerations of ancient and baroque buildings may have been the Italian way of demonstrating that a period was coming to a close. Actually, the newly built architecture of 18th-century Italy was already old. True, the villas and palaces did combine baroque elements with modern ones taken from the French *hôtels*, but Italian architecture on the whole was, like most of the German, an anachronism. The Palazzo Gallenga Stuart (formerly Antinori; 1758) in Perugia, by Francesco Bianchi; the Palazzo Madama in Turin (1718), with the façade by Filippo Juvara (VIII, PL. 226); the Palazzo Reale in Caserta (1752 on; I, PL. 389), by Vanvitelli; the Villa Pisani in Stra (1740), by Frigimelica; and the hunting lodge of Stupinigi (begun 1729; I, PL. 389), by Juvara — all were differentiated stylistically and by the influence played by the surrounding landscape. Common to all, however, was the late baroque ambition for official, massive architecture. The baroque wall articulation (Caserta) was often simplified under French influence and resulted in an already classically charming surface quality; or the ground plans became complex at the juncture of central buildings or round rooms with their wings (Stupinigi). But, for the most part, local late baroque tradition was little modified in the modern sense. Thus the great palacelike Villa Pisani went back to the Palladian type of villa, in which the central body with its three stories and engaged columns supported by caryatids in front stemmed from the high baroque, and only the sparing use of articulation, even of pillars, indicated the building to be from the 18th century. The large hall in this villa with Tiepolo's fresco and the rococo details in its decoration is not, however, a rococo room; it is a baroque room for formal ceremonies.

In smaller buildings Italy came closest to ground plans that were almost rococo. An example is the Villa Palagonia in Bagheria near Palermo (1715, by Maria Tommaso Napoli and Agatino Daidone). In ground plan this small pleasure palace is crescent-shaped with a central oval room. This resulted in intimate room shapes and purposely built spaces of the type that "loosened up" the architecture of the large official buildings. In both iconology and architecture this building was a capriccio. Villa Valguarnera (1715, built by the same architects), also in Bagheria, shows that the reduction of a baroque kind of architecture leads to an inversion of the meaning. An incurving façade receives a convex central body, a general practice in the 17th century; but in this relatively small capriccio it became an outright architectural parody.

While in Rome the formality of the baroque hindered the passage to rococo, which does not mean that there were no single rococo forms, in Piedmont a playful type of late baroque made its appearance. As in Genoa, it was not directly correspondent to the rococo but did contribute considerably to its formation (Carignano, S. Giovanni Battista, FIG. 261). The most important architect was Filippo Juvara (q.v.), born in Messina, who was also a stage designer. His basilica of the Superga (near Turin, 1717–31; II, PL. 140) was still a classical synthesis of Roman and northern Italian traditions. The façade

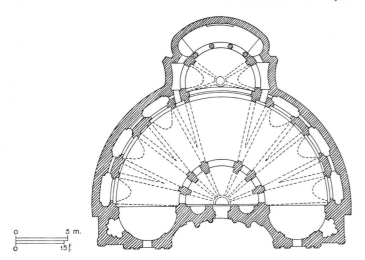

Carignano, Italy, S. Giovanni Battista, ground plan (*from EI, s.v. Rococo*).

of S. Cristina (Turin, 1715) and the interior of the Carmine church (Turin, 1732), as well as the façade of Palazzo Madama (1718; VIII, PL. 226), are original in their continuation of baroque principles, while in the interiors (above all, in Stupinigi, 1729 on) an imagination reigned in the ornamental articulation which justified its designation as *theatrum architectonicum*. Curving galleries, floating window openings, and pilasters ending in volutes carrying the vaulting present an ornamental dissolution of architecture which approaches that of the stage set. In a drawing of a stage set by Juvara (1728; Turin, Mus. Civico) the new tendencies become quite clear: the dissolution of the architectural in an ornamental *capriccio*. Juvara was less important for the rococo as an architect than he was as a draftsman. This imaginative exaggeration of the architectonic is at the base of the French *genre pittoresque* as manifested in the drawings of Meissonier (also of Piedmontese orgin) and La Joue; it is Italy's essential contribution to the rococo.

Another typically rococo revolution, which began in Italy, had to do with the *scena per angolo*. It was developed particularly in the Galli Bibiena circle (see SCENOGRAPHY). As early as 1703 Ferdinando Galli Bibiena (1657–1743) built a stage set in which the architecture no longer opened up before the spectator in a symmetrical and linear perspective, but, rather, the architecture was seen at an angle and gave the impression of an almost chance section of a larger complex. This system was perfected by his son Giuseppe (1696–1756). Toward the middle of the 18th century stage sets came into being which, apparently cut off from the auditorium, were nothing but a picture. The stage became a peep-show stage and signified the end of the baroque theater. There was no longer a community of stage and audience; the stage was kept at a distance as a work of art.

The 18th century and the rococo mark one of Venice's great periods. In certain aspects Venetian art bears some resemblance to that of England, which may in part depend on their similar position as maritime powers. Venice, like England, bypassed a late baroque of its own, and a Palladian constant lingered on into the 18th century; painting rose to an international rank. The other important contribution is Venice's rococo furniture (see FURNITURE). After Andrea Brustolon (1662–1732), the Remondini family from Bassano, in particular, made commodes, mirrors, and cradles, which in their heavy forms dif-

fered from the French but presented a popular variation of the *galant* type of furniture in their colorfulness and their *rocaille* decoration. To satisfy the great demand for show, richness and popular art were brought into a unique harmony in Venice, as attested by the projects of the young Piranesi for gondolas that consist of nothing but *rocaille* ornament (PL. 176). However, the monumental painting of Giovanni B. Piazzetta (PL. 183) and Tiepolo (q.v.) cannot be judged from a rococo point of view, since monumental painting can automatically be regarded as a late baroque phenomenon. But, simultaneously, Venice also developed a popular rococo painting. Not only the *vedute* appeared as a rococo form, but the capriccio also became an art form. The pastel was promoted to the *salon*, and the art of the *galant* book blossomed.

Just as south Germany produced local rococo forms in the field of church architecture, so Venice created local rococo painting. In Pietro Longhi (q.v.), his son Alessandro, Sebastiano Ricci (1659–1734; VIII, PL. 227), his nephew Marco (1676–1729), Canaletto, and Guardi (PL. 179), an outstanding gift of observation was joined to an equally rich imagination. As eyewitnesses, Guardi not only described a balloon ascension or the fire in the San Marcuola quarter and Longhi the exhibition of a rhinoceros (IX, PL. 185) or the Venetian *feste* and carnivals, but before the blazing buildings stands a human wall of cavaliers, enjoying the spectacle as in a theater, all dressed alike, anonymous, masked as for a carnival. It is characteristic of the rococo that although a realistic event is accurately presented, the whole picture is transposed out of this world as in a charade. The mask can actually be considered the symbol of the Venetian rococo. A "pictorial priapism" (as Greuze said of Saint-Aubin), inexorably greedy for ever-new motives, now preserves the baroque form, the ceremonial, only in form of the mask.

"And evenings they go to the theater and see and hear the daily life, artificially put together, prettily propped up, interwoven with fairy tales, set apart from reality by means of masks. But here again the people (*Volk*) is the base on which all rests: the spectators participate and the multitude fuses with the theater into a whole." Thus wrote Goethe in his Italian diary regarding the Venetian comedy. These words would be just as appropriate for the pictures by the young Tiepolo (Giovanni Domenico, 1727–1804), embracing both the popular quality of the Venetian rococo and the dissociation from reality existing in the artificiality of the play.

The German-speaking countries. The picture of 18th-century Germany changes from one princely court to another (see GERMAN ART). Common to almost all was the fact that at the beginning of the century the Italian influence — under which the prostrate art had slowly recovered — progressively decreased with the formation of a national art, which, in turn, was soon (at least in the court sphere) directed toward France. Long after the middle of the century the building of large palaces continued to be the leading architectural activity. But its relationship to French art was defined, limited for the most part to an adoption of individual decorative forms and the system of smaller *bagatelle* structures.

This complicated situation may to a certain extent be clarified by citing an example. The actual center of a German palace was the large *Treppenhaus* (staircase; PL. 167), which represented the artistic and ceremonial zenith. But such a staircase is in itself contrary to all principles of French rococo: it is the opposite of the intimate; it is not a tasteful, clear interior but, rather, a stage set, a meeting place. Rococo decorations for such staircases do exist however. Projects for Würzburg resolve the stair railing in *rocaille* forms — yet it can hardly be fortuitous that the largest staircase at Würzburg remained unfinished until the neoclassical period, after the completion of Tiepolo's frescoes. Thus the rococo was often limited to a French decorative fashion and was not a comprehensive formative principle. True rococo architecture generally existed only in the less important part of the large, ambitious palaces.

In Austria, Vienna with Johann Bernhard Fischer von Erlach (q.v.) had achieved a baroque art of its own. Thereafter, classical pathos for a long time dominated imperial architecture. The buildings of Johann Lukas von Hildebrandt (1668–1745), architect of Prince Eugene (Lower and Upper Belvedere, 1714, 1720, and later; II, PLS. 158, 159), at best exhibit an ornamental dissolution of the façade (window forms) and a less rigid ground plan, but this is more traceable to Italian influences (Genoa). Under Maria Theresa rococo arrived in Austria from Bavaria. In the matter of spatial solutions, however, Austria was eliminated from the stylistic phase of the rococo (B. Grimschitz). A few interiors remain from the time of Empress Maria Theresa in Schönbrunn, in the Hofburg in Innsbruck, and in the large monasteries such as Wilhering (1733; VI, PL. 152), either of a courtly and somewhat boring elegance or of a popular originality.

Bohemia's contribution to 18th-century art consisted above all in the development of a church architecture whose complicated wall structure and vaulting were to promote the formation of a rococo-type church in southern Germany. Leading architects were the Dientzenhofers (Christoph D., 1655–1722; Johann D., 1665–1725; Kilian Ignaz D., 1689–1751). Taken as a whole the art of Bohemia is late baroque.

Much the same thing happened in Saxony. The relatively early bloom of art under Augustus the Strong, elector of Saxony, resulted in Matthäus Pöppelmann's (1662–1736) Zwinger in Dresden (1711–22; II, PL. 155), a princely festive building that was novel as pavilion architecture but late baroque in its treatment of the architecture as a festive place.

Franconia, with its political mixture of small principalities, free imperial cities, and ecclesiastical states, presented a completely diverse picture from Austria and the electorates, and was also different in its art. The ruling house of the Schönborns, which provided the electors of Mainz and the prince-bishops of Bamberg and Würzburg, documented the architectural passion of the German late baroque. The Palace of Pommersfelden (VI, PL. 147), the Favorite in Mainz (by Maximilian von Welsch; built 1712–18), and the Würzburger Residenz (VI, PL. 147) are the major buildings. Above all in Würzburg a synthesis of many European trends was reached; as if combining the plans of the most famous European architects (De Cotte, Hildebrandt), Balthasar Neumann (q.v.) created from 1719 on a mirror of the manifold possibilities of the mid-18th century. Here, classical castle architecture united such elements as German staircases, intimate and pompous interior decoration after modern patterns, and a gigantic fresco by Tiepolo. On the other hand, in church architecture (Dientzenhofer, Neumann) the power of the rococo, which in the meanwhile had reached its zenith, becomes apparent. In the Sanctuary of Vierzehnheiligen (X, PL. 314) late baroque architecture was combined with a decoration (stuccoes by J. A. Feichtmayr; fresco by Giuseppe Appiani) in which the *rocaille* ornament assumed enormous proportions. The Nothelferaltar (Altar of the Miracle) by J. J. M. Küchel is a single monumental ornament, a piece of *rocaille* architecture.

In Westphalia, which had close links with the art of the Netherlands, Johann Conrad Schlaun (1695–1773), departing from completely different principles, arrived at a genuine rococo architecture. The hunting lodge Clemenswerth (1736–50), an arrangement of court buildings around a main pavilion, is a variation of the French *pavillon-bagatelle* architecture. Under Dutch influence and conditioned by the traditional brick building, elegance was united with an almost puritanical simplicity. The result corresponds to the French theoretical requirements of parsimonious delicacy. The only characteristic decoration consists of trophy festoons covering both stories of the pavilion. While in the Haus, Beck Schlaun returned to the ground plan of the Hôtel Matignon, in the incurving ground plan of Erbdrostenhof (Münster, 1753–57) he harked back to late baroque examples.

The greatest similarity to French style was found at the court of Hessen-Kassel. For three generations the Huguenot Du Ry family had determined city and court architecture. Sober moderation and protestant restraint prepared the way for a tasteful rococo. The castle Wilhelmstal (near Kassel), begun in 1753 by Simon Louis du Ry (1726–99) and decorated by Johann August Nahl (1710–81), is a typical offshoot of late Louis XV style. Latent classicism and a sparingly and taste-

fully applied *rocaille* decoration are combined in a harmonious balance.

In Bavaria, an almost megalomaniacal phase of large palace building (Nymphenburg, Schleissheim; VIII, PL. 439) ended with the death of Elector Max II Emanuel (1726). Thereafter, practically the only activity was the building of small pleasure buildings and the interior decoration of the palaces. The circumstances in which Bavaria took over the rococo are paradigmatic. François de Cuvilliés (1698–1768), born in Hennegau, at first served as court dwarf to Max Emanuel. Sent to Blondel in Paris for artistic training, he returned in 1724 and through his contact with the French ornamentalists was the first to use *rocaille* ornament in Germany. Although he was trained as an architect, his activity was mostly limited to interior decoration and small *maisons de plaisance*: the royal hunting lodge of Falkenlust (near Brühl, 1729); the Paradezimmer in the Residenz in Munich (1730–37); the Amalienburg in the park of Nymphenburg (PL. 166); and the Residenztheater in Munich (XIII, PL. 258). Notwithstanding his extraordinary talent, he had a difficult position as court architect; this was expressed, although never openly, by the conflict between monumental ambition and the more limited possibilities of the rococo. Cuvilliés then worked under Joseph Effner (1687–1745), also trained in Paris, who represented the Régence. Under Effner a style stemming from the decorative art of the late baroque with French Régence influences developed in Bavaria, which became similar to the French rococo. This is exemplified by the Asam brothers (Cosmas Damian A., 1686–1739 and Egid Quirin A., 1692–1750). Both studied in Rome; although they never went to France the Asams developed an ornament so close to the French contemporary decoration that the invention of rococo has even been attributed to them (II, PL. 154; XIII, PL. 297). Under suppositions that were extremely favorable to imports from France and yet restricted to interior decoration and *maisons de plaisance*, Cuvilliés in 1734 created the Amalienburg (FIG. 264),

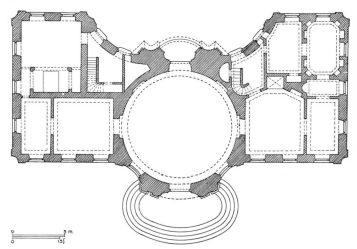

Munich, Nymphenburg park, ground plan of the Amalienburg (*from RDK, IV*).

a small royal hunting lodge for the electress, which can be considered one of the purest rococo buildings. One-storied, restrained, and modern according to French theory, the exterior hardly gives an idea of the overpowering impression of the interior, above all the central circular hall, in which the windows and mirrors alternate, encompassed by a decorative system which, although derived from French precedents, is unique. This was a decoration oriented not to contemporary French examples (Hôtel de Soubise) but to the ornamental print of the *genre pittoresque*. Cuvilliés's other buildings demonstrate this even more clearly. It is his and the German rococo's particular accomplishment to have enabled the *genre pittoresque*, which in France soon died in the restrictiveness of the printed page, to become applicable to decoration. With Cuvilliés the courtly rococo also overlapped into church architecture.

The architecture of the Rhineland must be considered together with that of Bavaria. Here the synthetic feature of German rococo is again apparent. Brühl Castle near Bonn was built by Clemens August, archbishop of Cologne, who was a Wittelsbach. Collaborators were the Westphalian Schlaun (1725 on), Cuvilliés from Munich, and the Franconian architect Neumann. The great staircase by Neumann (1740) is baroque in the use of paired columns and in the heavy sculpture and ceiling paintings by Carlo Carlone (1686–1775). The *rocaille* stuccowork and the light wrought-iron railing neutralize this impression. But it is above all the flat vault under the dome with openings all around it that changes the sense of the baroque layout. The architectural elements, dome, staircase, and state room have almost become elements of theatrical scenery.

The most important 18th-century building in Württemberg is the palace of Ludwigsburg, whose *corps de logis* was carried out (1724–33) by Donato Frisoni (1683–1735) after plans of Paolo Retti (1691–1748). The dependence on French example (as almost always in Württemberg) is unequivocal. While, on the one hand, it was derived from the Château de Montmorency, on the other, modern elements hardly conceivable without the French theory can be discerned in the single forms, such as the flat ornamental window framing. The staircase on the interior, however, is incongruous with this and stems from Austrian models.

The Prussian rococo is tied to the name of Frederick the Great. His preference for French language and philosophy and for the Watteau genre is well known. It is, therefore, all the more surprising that with his architect Georg Wenceslaus von Knobelsdorff (1699–1753) a Palladian classicism with late baroque tendencies should have been created. The intimate rococo interiors contrasted sharply with the heavy exterior wall elements. The palace of Sanssouci (1744–47; PL. 163) was for the most part designed by the King himself and was the source of an altercation between him and his architect, embodying their conflicting tastes. Due to its position on a hill, the single-storied structure seen from below seemed to sink down in its surroundings and was partly covered by the hill. While Knobelsdorff wanted to raise the foundation to arrive at a Belvedere type of building according to late baroque examples, the King put up with this defect to preserve the propriety of the building according to the French theory.

With the interior decorators J. August Nahl (1710–81) and Johann Christian Hoppenhaupt (died 1778), a unique style of decoration developed in Prussia. In contrast to south Germany it used the *rocaille* sparingly and left large wall areas free, with often nothing more than a light floral tracery drawn over the surface, as in the Blumenzimmer of Sanssouci, by Hoppenhaupt (after 1750) and the Goldene Galerie in Charlottenburg, by Knobelsdorff and Nahl (1740). The Prussian rococo tended to classical arcadian forms in contrast to the imaginative style of the German south.

Antoine Pesne (1683–1757) carried over the Watteau genre into monumental painting. Here, as in southern Germany, the Venetian influence is clearly discernable. Jacopo Amigoni (1675–1752) and Tiepolo worked in Bavaria and hardly a subsequent fresco was left untouched by the latter's work in Würzburg. Next to monumental painting the easel picture in Germany remained unimportant. The many altar pictures by the great fresco painters Johann Georg Bergmüller (1688–1762), Johann Wolfgang Baumgartner (1712–61), Matthäus Günther (1705–88), Johann Evangelist Holzer (1709–40), and Johann Baptist Zimmermann (1680–1758) lost in transparency because of the oil technique. An exception was Franz Anton Maulbertsch (1724–96; PL. 159), who together with Johann Wenzel Bergl (1718–89) embodied a rococo stage within late baroque Austrian painting. His small pictures transformed the sketch into a system and always harked back to monumental painting. Aside from the painting related to architecture, the art of portraiture remained either under the influence of French or English precedents (Georg Desmarées, 1697–1776, and Johann Georg Ziesenis, 1716–76) or else it indulged in a tempered realism typical of the bourgeois enlightenment (Anton Graff, 1736–1813; Daniel Nikolaus Chodowiecki, 1726–1801; Januarius Zick, 1730–97).

With Anton Raphael Mengs (1728–79) Germany finally produced her only international painter of the 18th century. But he destroyed the rococo.

In sculpture, Germany (particularly the south) countered the mythological sculpture of France with a religious sculpture, retaining, however, certain courtly *galant* elements (PL. 173). Characteristically marble was no longer used, but almost exclusively wood or stucco (excepting, of course, freestanding sculpture). With Ignaz Günther (1725–75), Joseph Anton Feichtmayr (1696–1770), Paul Egell (1691–1752), and Johann Baptist Straub (1704–84) the translation of the religious into sensual terms is almost always carried to the edge of triviality but never beyond (PL. 170). The interplay between theme and gallant exalted form is the artistic principle. The sources of the style are to be sought not in France but in Italy. Yet the best comparison is with *galant* French painting, particularly Fragonard, except that here the amorous is sublimated in a naïve yet refined manner. Yet, even with this vitalization and sensualization, the sculpture clearly shows that it is "only" art. Embellished in gold and white like porcelain, this form was not intended to create an illusion, as did late baroque sculpture, but attempted to be art.

In this, as in many other points, rococo came close to 16th-century mannerism. Mannerist elements also appeared in the proportions, in the artistic passion, in the contrast between the realistic and the rich embellishment. What is astonishing is the simultaneous popular appeal of this rococo.

The passage to the *capriccio* was completed in Franconia by Ferdinand Dietz (1709–77). His garden sculpture in Veitshöchheim (FIG. 266) is committed only to "whim." The great garden iconology is dissolved in play and travesty. The sculpture of the German rococo is a world of putti, which determine its nature. Through them the great themes are travestied or endeared (PL. 171).

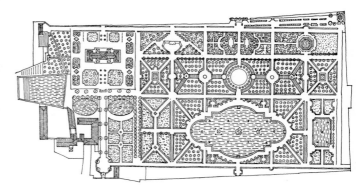

Veitshöchheim, Germany, plan of the gardens (1763–79), layout by J. P. Mayer.

While in France the court rococo barely achieved a synthesis with religious art, and in Italian church architecture the late baroque remained dominant, in south Germany a genuine rococo church architecture came into being. The premises were, on the one hand, an ornamental dissolution of the late baroque Italianizing architecture and, on the other, a carrying over of French rococo ornament of the *genre pittoresque* into church architecture. The Bavarian rococo church can be defined as a translation of ornamental thoughts into architecture (FIG. 267). As G. Dehio (1930) has pointed out, the rococo character of a building is not determined by the decoration alone, but principally by the relationship of the decoration to the architecture. In this ornamentalization, therefore, the nature of the architecture was completely transformed. The ground plans of churches by Dominikus Zimmermann (q.v.) at Steinhausen (PL. 167) and the Wies pilgrimage church (PLS. 161, 165; VI, PL. 153), which are oval areas with pillars, can be traced back to late baroque premises. In the same way the pilaster churches by Johann Michael Fischer (1692–1766), such as Osterhofen (1726) or Diessen (PL. 168), are related to the late

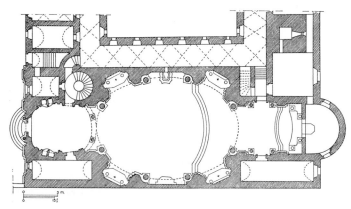

Weltenburg, Germany, Abbey Church (1717–21), ground plan, architect, C. D. Asam (*from RDK, III*).

baroque system of the Vorarlberg school of architecture. But such explanations of the sources are but little help in understanding such buildings. Their character is determined by the ornament, which has taken hold of the entire structure, and also by the fresco decoration. While ornament could replace architecture, as in the Gnadenaltar in Vierzehnheiligen or in the ceiling of the Wies pilgrimage church, architecture now began to repel ornament. It often seemed as if the *rocaille*

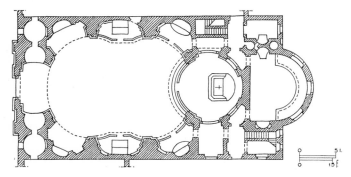

Munich, St. Anna am Lehel (1727–39), ground plan, architect, J. M. Fischer (*from RDK, II*).

exuberances were superficially laid onto an already neoclassically pure wall, and that this ornamentation could "slither off" at any moment (Pinder, 1933). Thus ornament and architecture began to separate; ornament became self-sufficient as a substitute for architecture, while architecture itself was again potentially antiornamental.

It was just this dialectic interplay which led to the unique creations of the Bavarian rococo church. In Zimmermann's Wieskirche this contrast between ornament and architecture was utilized to create theatrical effects of a completely new kind. Pairs of supports set into an oval space stand so far apart that the ambulatory hardly gives the impression of being one. At the same time, these supports have been degraded into pieces of stage scenery; they have become images of pillars, a major reason for this being that they carry practically no weight; a structural framework no longer runs along the abutments of these supports; the junction with the dome is dissolved in ornament which gives way to fresco; the choir of the church is curiously small, seemingly difficult to enter from the church area, as in a theater picture. That this removal of architecture to a picturelike theatrical plane is not a modern overinterpretation is evident in the significance of the inevitable fresco.

After Andrea Pozzo had devised the obligatory fresco system for the late baroque, in which the church was opened to the "sky" through illusionistic painting (II, PL. 172), southern Germany took over a system that had been formed in Venice (see PERSPECTIVISTS). In 1724–25, Tiepolo painted an allegory on

the might of rhetoric in the Palazzo Sandi. On the four sides of the fresco — that is, in the "sky" — the ground appears as the setting for an event. Jacopo Amigoni introduced this possibility to Germany. In 1725, in the cloister chapel in Ottobeuren, a small dome was painted with an encircling terrestrial scene. This tendency is shown in a large example — Franz Joseph Spiegler's (1691–1757) main fresco in the Abbey church of Zwiefalten (1751; cf. PL. 164). Under an apparition of Mary in the sky opening, the surrounding scenery includes the most famous pilgrimage places from Genazzano to Fourvière and Altötting — that is, historical places were painted in that area of the fresco where previously the church space itself had been illusionistically continued upward. This principle, whereby not only the earth but even the ocean and ships (Battle of Lepanto) were depicted on the ceiling, must have aroused the violent aversions of the neoclassicist, rational theorists. It also meant the destruction of the baroque system of the unifying and heightening function of the fresco. Historical places pictured on the ceiling — Golgotha, Mt. Gargano, the Areopagus — made the inner space of the church something other than the baroque illusionistic opening of the sky. When in addition, as in many churches, the story of the church itself was shown in a "terrestrial" fresco, then the context of the church building was decisively changed. It was no longer identical with the place of the fresco, as with Pozzo, but through imagery the church became a second Golgotha, Mt. Gargano, or Areopagus, or even repeated its own foundation. This was an attempt to legitimize historically the respective church through typological similarity. Enlightenment and irrational demonstration came together into a unique and individual style. But at the same time the fresco, an independent pictorial world of its own, left the sphere of architecture. B. Rupprecht (1959) has listed the main features of the southern German rococo church: (1) development of a central space, which is the only part of the structure that is esthetically satisfying; (2) the limits of this central area remain unclear, so that "blurred" types of areas come into existence, in which no architectural spatial concepts are engaged but, so to speak, only adjectival types of space sensations; (3) deformation, isolation, and removal of the traditional architectural forms occur (the observer is in any case kept at a distance from the usual individual architectural form); (4) a zone of ornamentation is inserted between the fresco and the architecture, becoming part of the architecture and the picture; and (5) the west end of the central area becomes the observer's vantage point, since the main frescoes are chiefly planned around it, and the pictorial order of the space as given by special layering and arch, pillar, and altar placement is most meaningful and richest when seen from the west.

The question remains as to how far these criteria can be covered by the definition of rococo as presented here. When the tension between the means becomes an end in itself and the categories of painting, architecture, and ornament elide and overlap as in the Bavarian rococo church, then it is genuine rococo. It has little to do with the French secular rococo architecture. But the fact alone that it sought out the extremes of *genre pittoresque* ornament and turned it into an architectural substitute is indicative. Nowhere in Europe did the rococo, which came from the courtly sphere, penetrate so deeply into church and folk art as in southern Germany. An electoral decree of 1770, which advocated classicism for church architecture, put an official end to this rococo just as the secularization of 1803 destroyed the magnificence of the monasteries and abbeys forever. But as late as the beginning of Biedermeier, in the 1820s, peasant furniture with *rocaille* ornament could still be found. In this the rococo proved itself to be the last style capable of penetrating all spheres of art. After its end came the plurality of styles of the 19th century.

HISTORICAL SIGNIFICANCE. Rococo as a stylistic entity is difficult to grasp with the conventional art-historical tools. Untenable delimitations such as those of Fiske Kimball thus came into being. Rococo is not a mere ornamental style but a style capable of suffusing all spheres of art. In this, however, art-historical analysis runs into difficulty. The basic features of rococo can hardly be grasped through a comparison of forms and their change. For rococo took over many form elements of the late baroque and surpassed them. While there was a formal tradition, the meaning of the forms was often basically different from those of the baroque. Gradually the encompassing baroque illusion became an illusionizing of art. In other words, rococo often turned art itself into the subject of a picture, whether in the ornamental print, where the ornament became the subject of the picture, or in the Bavarian rococo church, which can be experienced only as a picture. This phenomenon can be designated as "meta style" — "meta" because an influential intermediate member stands between the work of art and the observer. The arts represent themselves, they do not simply create. This was the closing of a great epoch. A formerly transcendental principle had become immanent. Not until near the end of the period did this find a theoretical formulation in German idealism. In a fragmentary essay of 1795 entitled *Baukunst* Goethe established that architecture, although in itself not an imitative art, must on its highest level necessarily become imitation. This was the poetical fiction of architecture.

The value of English landscape architecture must be examined from its effect as a picture. The gardens are the stage scenery of a picture that is meant to create a particular mood; they are, as it were, monuments to themselves. Thus the reception of the most diverse styles, which appeared above all in English gardens, becomes understandable. Gothic, Moorish, classical, and Chinese elements were ornamentally adapted in the rococo and applied to architecture. Disguises of architecture in which it "represented something" came into being. Walpole's Strawberry Hill seen from this point of view is a rococo building, coming close to the artificial ruins that were the rage. It is less architecture than the image of an architectural past. Other styles, the Gothic as well as the Chinese, could take over the role of ornament. Since this ornament had already become independent and the subject of a picture, this is quite logical. At the end of the rococo there are all kinds of pictures of art. Marie Antoinette's chalet in the Petit Trianon is just as little architecture as the Bavarian rococo churches are architecture in the narrow sense. They are pictures of a church, and the chalet is a picture of peasant life.

At the same time, the baroque stage via the *scena per angolo* became a peep-show stage with a picture of a theater in place of a true theater, which for the spectator unites action and observer. It would, however, be completely erroneous to interpret this as the end of naturalistic tendencies. True, the stage offered a cutout picture that destroyed the inherent reality, the baroque illusion. Goethe (*Frauenrollen auf dem Römischen Theater*) considered it particularly charming that in the theater the concept of imitation, the thought of art, remained alive and that only a kind of self-conscious illusion was achieved. With this characterization of the Italian theater, where the parts of women were still played by men, the poet presented us with an apt characterization of the waning rococo.

By subjecting art to the picture, this art of self-conscious illusion becomes a single, great contrast. The esthetic appreciation is once more intensified to the highest degree but the concept of beauty, just as the principle of baroque illusion had, becomes inverted. From theatrical representations the baroque had created a possibility of illusion and transcendency. In the rococo the esthetic appreciation lies in a recognition of the artificial, of the artistic. Rococo art obtains its beauty from the transitory. The everlasting dialectic interplay within the classes of art and changeability and tension as principles are the esthetic values of the rococo. A beauty of a kind that until then had been unknown in Western art was thus made possible, but a beauty of this kind was destructive to art itself.

Hans SEDLMAYR, Hermann BAUER

SOURCES AND LITERATURE PRIOR TO 1800. A. C. Daliver, Cours d'architecture, 2 vols., Paris, 1691 (German ed., L. C. Sturm, Augsburg, 1725); R. Frémin, Mémoires critiques d'architecture, Paris, 1702; L. Liger, Le jardinier fleuriste et historiographe, 2 vols., Paris, 1704; A. J. Dézallier d'Argenville, La théorie et la pratique du jardinage, Paris, 1709 (2d ed., 1728; Eng. trans., London, 1712); P. Decker, Kurfürstlicher Baumeister oder Architectura civilis, 3 vols., Augsburg, 1711–16; J.-L. de Cordemoy, Nouveau traité de toute l'architecture, 2d ed., Paris, 1714; S. Le Clerc, Traité d'architecture avec remarques et des observations, 2 vols., Paris, 1714; A. Palomino de Castro y Velasco, El Museo pictórico y Escala óptica, 3 vols., Madrid, 1715–24 (2d ed., 3 vols., 1795–97); L. C. Sturm, Vollständige Anweisung grosser Herrenpäläste ... nach dem heutigen Gusto schön und prächtig anzugeben, Augsburg, 1718; J. B. Dubos, Réflexions critiques sur la poésie et sur la peinture, Paris, 1719 (7th ed., 3 vols., Paris, 1770); N. Goldmann, Vollständige Anweisung aller Arten von regularen Prachtgebäuden nach gewissen Regeln zu ersinnen, auszuteilen und auszuzieren (enlarged ed. by L. C. Sturm), 21 vols., Augsburg, 1720–61 (imprinted 1721); A. Coypel, Discours prononcés dans les conférences de l'Académie Royale de peinture et de sculpture, Paris, 1721; L. C. Sturm, Vollständige Anweisung alle Arten von bürgerlichen Wohnhäusern wohl anzugeben, Augsburg, 1721; K. Lohmeyer, ed., Die Briefe Balthasar Neumanns von seiner Pariser Studienreise (1723), Düsseldorf, 1911; G. M. Oppenord, Œuvre, contenant différents fragments d'architecture et d'ornaments..., Paris, ca. 1725; J. Mariette, L'architecture française, 5 vols., Paris, 1727 (repr., I–III, Paris, Brussels, 1927–29); J. Marot, L'architecture françoise, new ed., Paris, 1727 (vol. 4 of preceding work); C. E. Briseux, Architecture moderne ou l'art de bien bâtir pour toutes sortes de personnes tant pour les maisons des particulières que pour les Palais, 2 vols., Paris, 1728; C. A. Jombert, Architecture moderne, ou l'art de bien bâtir pour toutes sortes de personnes, Paris, 1728 (2d ed., 2 vols., Paris, 1764); B. Langley, New Principles of Gardening, London, 1728; J. J. Schübler, Weitere Fortsetzung des gründlichen Unterrichts in der vollständigen Civil-Baukunst, Nürnberg, 1728; T. Corneille, Dictionnaire des arts et des sciences, 2d ed., 2 vols., Paris, 1731; J. J. Schübler, Perspectivische Belustigung und neue Versuche von kleinen Lusthäusern wie auch allerhand künstlichen Vogelbauern..., Nürnberg, 1732; J. H. Zedler, Grosses vollständiges Universal-Lexikon aller Wissenschaften und Künste, 64 vols. in 43, Halle, Leipzig, 1732–50; J. F. Blondel, De la distribution des maisons de plaisance et de la décoration des édifices en général, 2 vols., Paris, 1737–38; T. Temanza, Zibaldone di memorie storiche appartenenti a professori delle belle arti del disegno, Venice, 1739; J.-A. Piganiol de la Force, Description de Versailles et de toutes les autres belles maisons et châteaux des environs de Paris, 8 vols., Paris, 1742; G. Boffrand, Description de ce qui a été pratiqué pour fondre en bronze d'un seul jet la figure équestre de Louis XIV élevée par la ville de Paris dans la place de Louis le Grand, Paris, 1743; C. E. Briseux, L'art de bâtir des maisons de campagne, 2 vols., Paris, 1743–61; J. F. Penther, Ausführliche Anleitung zur bürgerlichen Baukunst, 4 vols., Augsburg, 1744–48; G. Boffrand, Livre d'architecture, Paris, 1745; A. J. Dézallier d'Argenville, Abrégé de la vie des plus fameux peintres, 3 vols., Paris, 1745–52 (2d ed., 4 vols., 1762); L. C. Sturm, Kurtze Vorstellung der gantzen Civil-Baukunst, Augsburg, 1745; C. Batteux, Les beaux-arts réduits à un même principe, Paris, 1746; De La Font de Saint-Yenne, Réflexions sur quelques causes de l'état présent de la peinture en France, The Hague, 1747; A. N. Dézallier d'Argenville, Voyage pittoresque de Paris, Paris, 1749; C.-A. Coypel, Dialogue ... sur l'exposition des tableaux dans le salon du Louvre en 1747, Paris, 1751; D. Diderot and J. d'Alembert, ed., Encyclopédie ou Dictionnaire raisonné des sciences, des arts et des métiers, 17 vols., Paris, Neuchâtel, 1751–65; L. Petit de Bachaumont, Essai sur la peinture, la sculpture et l'architecture, Paris, 1751; J.-F. Blondel, Architecture française, 4 vols., Paris, 1752–56 (repr. 1904); C. E. Briseux, Traité du beau essentiel dans les arts, 2 vols., Paris, 1752–55; J. Lacombe, Dictionnaire portatif des beaux-arts, Paris, 1752 (2d ed., 1759); B. Lépicié, Vies des premiers peintres du roi, depuis M. le Brun jusqu'à présent, Paris, 1752; G. Boffrand, Oeuvres d'architecture ... contenant les principaux bâtiments civiles, hydrauliques et mécaniques..., Paris, 1753; W. Hogarth, The Analysis of Beauty, London, 1753 (ed. J. Burke, Oxford, 1955); M. A. Laugier, Essai sur l'architecture, Paris, 1753; P. A. Orlandi, Abecedario pittorico (new ed. by P. Guarienti), Venice, 1753; G. Bottari, Raccolta di lettere sulla pittura, scultura ed architettura, 6 vols., Rome, 1754–83 (2d ed., 8 vols., Milan, 1822–25); T. Chippendale, The Gentleman and Cabinet-Maker's Director, London, 1754 (3d ed., 1762); G. A. Méhégan, Considérations sur les révolutions des arts, Paris, 1755; E. Héré, Recueil des plans, élévations et coupes tant géometrale à qu'en perspective des châteaux, jardins et dépendances que le roi de Pologne occupe en Lorraine, 2 vols., Paris, 1756; I. Ware, A Complete Body of Architecture, London, 1756; P. L. P. de la Guépière, Recueil d'architecture, Paris, 1758; J. F. de Neufforge, Recueil élémentaire d'architecture, Paris, 1758; A. A. Guillaumot, Dissertation sur l'architecture française, The Hague, 1762; A. R. Mengs, Gedanken über die Schönheit und den Geschmack in der Malerei, Zürich, 1762; H. Walpole, Anecdotes of Painting in England, 4 vols., Strawberry Hill, 1762–71; M. Dandré Bardon, Traité de peinture..., 2 vols., Paris, 1765; M. A. Laugier, Observations sur l'architecture, The Hague, 1765 (see also A. A. Guillaumot, Remarques sur un livre ... de M. l'abbe Laugier, Paris, 1768); P. Patte, Monuments érigés en France à la gloire de Louis XV, Paris, 1765; M. J. Peyre, Oeuvres d'architecture, Paris, 1765; P. F. Basan, Dictionnaire des graveurs anciens et modernes, Paris, 1767; P. Patte, Mémoires sur les objets les plus importants de l'architecture, Paris, 1769; M. Pilkington, The Gentleman's and Connoisseur's Dictionary of Painters from the Year 1250 to the Year 1767, London, 1770; C. F. Roland le Virloys, Dictionnaire d'architecture civile, 3 vols., Paris, 1770–71; J.-F. Blondel, Cours d'architecture, 9 vols., Paris, 1771–77; W. Chambers, A Dissertation on Oriental Gardening, London, 1772; P. G. Bergeret de Grancourt, Bergeret et Fragonard: Journal inédit d'un voyage en Italie 1773–74 (ed. M. A. Tornézy), Poitiers, 1895; G. L. Le Rouge, Détails des nouveaux jardins à la mode, 19 vols., Paris, 1776–87; J. M. Morel, Théorie des jardins, Paris, 1776; C. C. L. Hirschfeld, Theorie der Gartenkunst, 5 vols., Leipzig, 1779–85; J. C. Richard de St. Non, Voyage pittoresque ou déscription des royaumes de Naples et de Sicile, 5 vols., Paris, 1781–86; H. Walpole, Essay on Modern Gardening, Strawberry Hill, 1785; A. N. Dézallier d'Argenville, Vies des fameux architectes et sculpteurs depuis la Renaissance des arts, 2 vols., Paris, 1787; D. Diderot, Essais sur la peinture, Paris, 1796.

BIBLIOG. *a. General*: L. Dussieux, Les artistes français à l'étranger, Paris, 1852; E. and J. de Goncourt, Les maîtresses de Louis XV, 2 vols., Paris, 1860; G. Semper, Der Stil in den technischen und tektonischen Künsten, 2 vols., Munich, 1860–63; H. Destailleur, Notices sur quelques artistes français, architectes, dessinateurs, graveurs, Paris, 1863; H. Destailleur, Recueil d'estampes à l'ornementation des appartements aux XVIe, XVIIe et XVIIIe siècles, 2 vols., Paris, 1863–71; A. Springer, Der Rokokostil, Bilder aus der neueren Kunstgeschichte, Bonn, 1867, pp. 241–82; E. and J. de Goncourt, L'art du XVIIIe siècle, 2 vols., Paris, 1873–74 (Eng. trans., R. Ironside, French 18th Century Painters, London, 1948); A. von Zahn, Barock, Rokoko und Zopf, ZfbK, VIII, 1873, pp. 1–11, 33–44; D. Guilmard, Les maîtres ornementistes, Paris, 1881; R. Dohme, Barock- und Rokokoarchitektur, 3 vols., Berlin, 1884–92; R. Schumann, Barock und Rokoko, Leipzig, 1885; R. Dohme, Geschichte der deutschen Baukunst, Berlin, 1887; C. Gurlitt, Geschichte des Barockstils in Italien, Stuttgart, 1887; E. and J. de Goncourt, Madame de Pompadour, 2d ed., Paris, 1888; C. Gurlitt, Geschichte des Barockstils, des Rokoko und des Klassizismus in Belgien, Holland, Frankreich und England, Stuttgart, 1888; C. Gurlitt, Geschichte des Barockstils und des Rokoko in Deutschland, Stuttgart, 1889; O. Aufleger and K. Trautmann, Münchner Architektur des 18. Jahrhunderts, 2 vols., Munich, 1892; G. Hager, Die Bauthätigkeit und Kunstpflege in Kloster Wessobrunn und die Wessobrunner Stuccatoren Oberbayern (Arch. für vaterländische Geschichte, 48), Munich, 1894; P. Jessen, ed., Katalog der Ornamentstich-Sammlung des Kunst-Gewerbe-Museums Berlin, Berlin, 1894; E. Renard, Die Bauten der Kurfürsten Joseph Clemens und Clemens August von Köln, BJ, XCIX, 1896, pp. 164–240, C, 1896, pp. 1–102; W. Kick and B. Pfeiffer, Barock, Rokoko und Louis XVI aus Schwaben und der Schweiz, Stuttgart, 1897; A. Schmarsow, Barock und Rokoko, Leipzig, 1897; E. Molinier, Le mobilier au XVIIe et au XVIIIe siècle (Histoire générale des arts appliqués à l'industrie, III), Paris, 1898; E. F. Strong (Lady Dilke), French Painters of the 18th Century, London, 1899; G. Dehio, Die Kunst des 17. und 18. Jahrhunderts (Kunstgeschichte in Bildern, V), Leipzig, 1900; E. F. Strong (Lady Dilke), French Architects and Sculptors of the 18th Century, London, 1900; E. F. Strong (Lady Dilke), French Furniture and Decoration of the 18th Century, London, 1901; R. Graul, Das 18. Jahrhundert: Dekoration und Mobiliar, Berlin, 1905; P. Marcel, La peinture en France au début du XVIIIe siècle, Paris, 1906; E. Baumeister, Rokokokirchen Oberbayerns, Strasbourg, 1907; W. Lübke, Die Kunst der Barockzeit und des Rokoko (ed. M. Semrau), 13th ed., Stuttgart, 1907; K. Cassirer, Die ästhetischen Hauptbegriffe der französischen Theoretiker von 1650–1780, Berlin, 1909; A. Fontaine, Les doctrines d'art en France, Paris, 1909; S. Lami, Dictionnaire des sculpteurs de l'école française au XVIIIe siècle, 2 vols., Paris, 1910–11; W. Hausenstein, Rokoko, Munich, 1912; W. Pinder, Deutscher Barock, Königstein, Leipzig, 1912; C. Ricci, Baukunst und dekorative Skulptur der Barockzeit in Italien, Stuttgart, 1912; H. Vial, A. Marcel and A. Girodie, Les artistes décorateurs de bois: Répertoire alphabétique des ébénistes, menuisiers, sculpteurs, doreurs etc.... ayant travaillé en France aux XVIIe et XVIIIe siècles, 2 vols., Paris, 1912–21; H. Clouzot, L'ameublement français sous Louis XV, Paris, 1913; H. Popp, Die Architektur der Barock- und Rokokozeit in Deutschland und in der Schweiz, Stuttgart, 1913; G. Biermann, Deutscher Barock und Rokoko, Leipzig, 1914; A. E. Brinckmann, Stadtbaukunst des 18. Jahrhunderts, Berlin, 1914; P. Frankl, Die Entwicklungsphasen der neueren Baukunst, Leipzig, Berlin, 1914; F. Gysi, Die Entwicklung der kirchlichen Architektur in der deutschen Schweiz im 17. und 18. Jahrhundert, Aarau, Zürich, 1914; A. E. Brinckmann, Die Baukunst des 17. und 18. Jahrhunderts in den romanischen Ländern, Potsdam, 1915; M. Wackernagel, Die Baukunst des 17. und 18. Jahrhunderts in den germanischen Ländern, Potsdam, 1915; A. E. Brinckmann, Barockskulptur: Entwicklungsgeschichte der Skulptur in den romanischen und germanischen Ländern seit Michelangelo bis zum Beginn des 18. Jahrhunderts, Berlin-Neubabelsberg, 1917: P. de Nolhac, La décoration de Versailles au XVIIIe siècle, GBA, XIII, 1917, pp. 393–416; R. Sedlmaier, Grundlagen der Rokoko-Ornamentik, Strasbourg, 1917; P. Jessen, Der Ornamentstich, Berlin, 1920; H. Rose, Spätbarock, Munich, 1922; A. E. Brinckmann, Barock-bozzetti, 4 vols., Frankfurt am Main, 1923–25; A. Reichwein, China und Europa, Berlin, 1923; K. Borinski, Die Antike in Poetik und Kunsttheorie, II, Leipzig, 1924; R. Berliner, Ornamentale Vorgeblätter, 2 vols., Leipzig, 1925–26; H. Loubier, Der Bucheinband, 2d ed., Leipzig, 1926; W. Drost, Barockmalerei in dem germanischen Ländern, Wildpark-Potsdam, 1928; N. Pevsner and O. Grautoff, Barockmalerei in den romanischen Ländern, Potsdam, 1928; W. Pinder, Das Problem der Generationen, 2d ed., Berlin, 1928; M. Osborn, Die Kunst des Rokoko, Berlin, 1929; W. Slomann, Chinesische Möbel des 18. Jahrhunderts, Pantheon, III, 1929, pp. 142–48; C. Linfert, Die Grundlagen der Architekturzeichnung, Kunstwissenschaftliche Forsch., I, 1931, pp. 133–246; A. E. Brinckmann, Von Guarino Guarini bis Balthasar Neumann, Berlin, 1932; E. Michalski, Die Bedeutung der ästhetischen Grenze für die Methode der Kunstgeschichte, Berlin, 1932; T. Borenius, English Painting in the 18th Century, London, 1938; J. Huizinga, Homo ludens, Haarlem, 1938 (Eng. trans., R. F. C. Hull, New York, 1950); A. Lotz, ed., Katalog der Ornamentstichsammlung der staatlichen Kunstbibliothek Berlin, 2d ed., Berlin, 1939; H. Tintelnot, Barocktheater und barocke Kunst, Berlin, 1939; A. E. Brinckmann, Die Kunst des Rokoko, Berlin, 1940; P. Lavedan, Histoire de l'urbanisme: Renaissance et temps modernes, Paris, 1941; F. Kimball, The Creation of the Rococo, Philadelphia, 1943; O. Sirén, China and Gardens of Europe of the 18th Century, New York, 1950; F. Fosca (G. de Traz), Le XVIIIe siècle (de Watteau à Tiepolo), Geneva, 1952 (Eng. trans., S. Gilbert, New York, 1952); W. Mrazek, Ikonologie der barocken Deckenmalerei, Vienna, 1953; H. Ladendorf, Zur Wiederkehr des 16. Jahrhunderts im 18. Jahrhundert, Sb. der kg. Gesellschaft zu Berlin, V, 1956–57, pp. 3–4; A. Pigler, Barockthemen, 2 vols., Budapest, 1956; R. Stamm, ed., Die Kunstformen des Barockzeitalters, Munich, 1956; H. Müller, Natur-Illusion in der Innenraumkunst des späteren 18. Jahrhunderts, Göttingen, 1957; Europäisches Rokoko: Kunst und Kultur des 18. Jahrhunderts, Munich, 1958 (Eng. trans., M. D. Senft-Howie and B. Sewell, The Age of Rococo, Munich, 1958; cat.); A. Schönberger and H. Soehner, Die Welt des Rokoko, Munich, 1958 (Eng. trans., D. Woodward, London, New York, 1960); N. Powell, Second and Third Rococo, Mouseion: Studien aus Kunst und Geschichte für O. H. Förster, Cologne, 1960, pp. 240–43; H. Honour, Chinoiserie, London, 1961; H. A. Millon, Baroque and Rococo Architecture, New York, 1961; H. Bauer, Rocaille, Berlin, 1962; Manierismo, barocco, rococò: Concetti e termini (Convegno int., 1960), Rome, 1962.

b. France: H. Clouzot, Les meubles du XVIIIe siècle, Paris, 1922; R. de Félice, Le meuble français sous Louis XIV et la Régence, Paris, 1922; F. de Salverte, Les ébénistes du XVIIIe siècle, Paris, 1923 (4th ed., 1953); E. Hildebrandt, Die Malerei und Plastik des 18. Jahrhunderts in Frankreich, Wildpark-Potsdam, 1924; L. Réau, L'histoire de l'expansion de l'art français, 4 vols., Paris, 1924–33; L. Réau, Histoire de la peinture française au XVIIIe siècle, 2 vols., Paris, 1925–26; R. Lanson, Le goût du Moyen-âge en France au XVIIIe siècle, Paris, Brussels, 1926; R. Schneider, L'art français au XVIIIe siècle, Paris, 1926; M. Furcy-Raynaud, Les sculptures exécutées au XVIIIe siècle pour la direction des bâtiments du Roi, Paris, 1927; P. Ratouis de Limay and E. Dacier, Pastels du XVIIe et XVIIIe siècle, Paris, 1927; L. Dimier, Les peintres français du XVIIIe siècle, 2 vols., Paris, Brussels, 1928–30; A. Feulner, Französische Möbel in Deutschland, Pantheon, IV, 1929, pp. 406–12, VII, 1931, pp. 237–46, VIII, 1931, pp. 490–95; E. Kurzweg, Überblick über die Entwicklung der französischen Landschaftsmalerei im 18. Jahrhundert, Berlin, 1929; M. J. Ballot, Le décor intérieur au XVIIIe siècle à Paris et dans l'Île-de-France: Boiseries sculptées et panneaux peints, Paris, 1930; M. Eisenstadt, Watteaus Fêtes galantes und ihre Ursprünge, Berlin, 1930; C. de Peloux, Répertoire biographique et bibliographique des artistes du XVIIIe siècle français, 2 vols., Paris, 1930–41; F. de Salverte, Le meuble français d'après les ornemanistes, 1660–1789, Paris, 1930; L. Réau, G. Lundberg, and R. A. Weigert, L'art français dans les pays du Nord et l'art de l'Europe (XVIIIe-XIXe siècles), Paris, 1932; S. Rocheblave, L'âge classique de l'art français, Paris, 1932; A. Leroy, Histoire de la peinture française au XVIIIe siècle, Paris, 1934; P. de Nolhac, Peintres français en Italie, Paris, 1934; A. Teunissen, Meubles et sièges du XVIIIe siècle: Menuisiers, ébénistes, marques, plans et ornementation de leurs oeuvres, Paris, 1934; L. Gillet, La peinture de Poussin à David, Paris, 1935; S. Rocheblave, La peinture française au XVIIIe siècle, Paris, 1937 (Eng. trans., G. F. Lees, London, 1937); L. Benoist et al., Les peintres de fêtes galantes, le portrait et le paysage, Paris, 1938; P. Francastel, Les relations entre la France et la Pologne au XVIIe et XVIIIe siècles, La France et la Pologne, dans leurs relations artistiques, I, 1938, pp. 269–312, II, 1939, pp. 71–152; G. Wildenstein, La peinture française au XVIIIe siècle, Paris, 1938; L. Hourticq, La peinture française en XVIIIe siècle, Paris, 1939; E. Donnell, Juste-Aurèle Meissonier and the Rococo-Style, BMMA, XXXVI, 1941, pp. 254–60; F. Kimball, The Creation of the Style Louis XV, AB, XXIII, 1941, pp. 1–15; P. Verlet, Le Style Louis XV, Paris, 1942; E. de Ganay, Les jardins à la française en France au XVIIIe siècle, Paris, 1943; L. Hautecoeur, Histoire de l'architecture classique en France, II, Paris, 1943; P. Verlet, Le mobilier royale français: Meubles de la couronne consérvés en France, 2 vols., Paris, 1945–56; P. Florisoone, La peinture française: le XVIIIe siècle, Paris, 1948; E. de Ganay, Les jardins de France, Paris, 1949; F. Kimball, Le style Louis XV: Origine et évolution du Rococo, Paris, 1949; A. Marie, Jardins français classiques des XVIIe et XVIIIe siècles, Paris, 1949; J. Richardson, Some Notes on the Régence and the Beginnings of Rococo, Apollo, XLIX, 1949, pp. 9–11; L. Hautecoeur, Histoire de l'architecture classique en France, III–IV, Paris, 1951–52; E. Dacier, L'art au XVIIIe siècle: Régence, Louis XV, Paris, 1952; H. Junecke, Die "maisons de plaisance," Sb. der kg. Gesellschaft zu Berlin, I, 1952–53, pp. 26–28; H. Rommel, Die Entstehung des klassischen französischen Gartens im Spiegel der Sprache, Berlin, 1954; J. Nicolay, L'art et la manière des maîtres ébénistes français au XVIIIe siècle, Paris, 1955; P. Verlet, Les meubles du XVIIIe siècle, 2 vols., Paris, 1955; Connaissance des arts, Le XVIIIe siècle français, Paris, 1956; F. de Catheau, La décoration intérieure des hôtels parisiens au début du XVIIIe siècle, GBA, L, 1957, pp. 271–84; G. Martin-Mèry, Paris et les ateliers provinciaux au XVIIIe siècle, Bordeaux, 1958 (cat.); F. J. B. Watson, Louis XVI Furniture, London, 1960; I. Dennerlein, Die Gartenkunst der Régence und des Rokoko in Frankreich, Munich, 1961; C. Connolly and J. Zerbe, Les Pavillons: French Pavillions of the 18th Century, London, New York, 1962.

c. England: H. Cescinsky, English Furniture of the 18th Century, 3 vols., London, 1909–11; F. Lenygon, Furniture in England, 1660–1760, London, New York, 1914; F. Lenygon, Decoration in England, 1640–1760, 2d ed., London, 1927; G. Mourey, La peinture anglaise du XVIIIe siècle, Paris, 1928; K. Kimball and E. Donnell, The Creators of the Chippendale-Style, Met. Mus. S., I, 1929, pp. 115–54, II, 1929, pp. 40–59; E. Wind, Humanitätsidee und heroisierendes Porträt in der englischen Kultur des 18. Jahrhunderts, Vorträge der Bib. Warburg, IX, 1930–31, pp. 155–229; A. E. Richardson, Georgian England 1700–1820, London, 1931; G. M. Ellwood, English Furniture and Decoration, 1600–1800, 4th ed., London, 1933; J. Steegmann, The Rule of Taste from George I to George IV, London, 1936; B. S. Allen, Tides in English Taste 1619–1800, 2 vols., Cambridge, Mass., 1937; D. Frey, Englisches Wesen in der bildenden Kunst, Stuttgart, Berlin, 1942; J. Lees-Milne, The Age of Adam, London, 1947; J. Summerson, Architecture in Britain 1530–1830, Harmondsworth, 1953 (4th ed., 1963); E. K. Waterhouse, Painting in Britain 1530–1790, Harmondsworth, 1953; M. D. Whinney and O. Millar, English Art 1625–1851, London, 1953; F. J. B. Watson, English Villas and Venetian Decorators, J. Royal Inst. of Br. Architects, LXI, 1954, pp. 171–77; C. Hussey, English Country Houses, 3 vols., London, 1956–58.

d. Spain, Portugal, and their colonies: M. Lorente Junquera, La evolución arquitectonica en España en los siglos XVIII y XIX, Arte español,

XVI, 1946, pp. 74–79, XVII, 1947, pp. 102–10; P. Kelemen, Baroque and Rococo in Latin America, New York, 1951; R. C. Taylor, Rococo in Spain, Arch. Rev., CXII, 1952, pp. 8–15; D. Angulo Iñiguez, ed., Historia del arte hispanoamericana, III, Barcelona, 1956; G. Kubler, Arquitectura de los siglos XVII y XVIII (Ars Hispaniae, XIV), Madrid, 1957; G. Kubler and M. Soria, Art and Architecture in Spain and Portugal and Their American Dominions, 1500–1800, Harmondsworth, 1959; R. dos Santos, Historia del arte portugués, Barcelona, 1960.

e. Eastern Europe: V. Wagner, Czech Baroque, Prague, 1940; G. H. Hamilton, The Art and Architecture of Russia, Harmondsworth, 1954; K. Garas, Magyarországi festészet a XVIII. században (Hungarian Painting during the 18th Century), Budapest, 1955; V. Stech, Baroque Sculpture in Bohemia (trans. R. F. Samsour), Prague, 1959; A. Angyal, Die slawische Barockwelt, Leipzig, 1961.

f. Italy: G. Ferrari, Lo stucco nell'arte italiana, Milan, 1910; G. Chevalley, Gli architetti, l'architettura e la decorazione delle ville piemontesi nel XVIII secolo, Turin, 1912; A. Midana, L'arte del legno in Piemonte nel Sei- e Settecento, Turin, 1924; H. Voss, Die Malerei des Barock in Rom, Berlin, 1924; H. Voss, Studien zur venetianischen Vedutenmalerei des 18. Jahrhunderts, RepfKw, XLVII, 1926, pp. 1–45; G. Morazzoni, Mobili veneziani del '700, Milan, Rome, 1927; Il ritratto italiano da Caravaggio a Tiepolo, Bergamo, 1927 (cat.); G. Damerini, I pittori veneziani del Settecento, Bologna, 1928; N. Pevsner, Die italienische Malerei vom Ende der Renaissance bis zum ausgehenden Rokoko, Wildpark-Potsdam, 1928; G. Fiocco, La pittura veneziana del Sei- e Settecento, Verona, 1929; G. Natali, Settecento, 2 vols., Milan, 1929; G. Delogu, Pittori veneti minori del Settecento, Venice, 1930; A. E. Brinckmann, Theatrum novum Pedemontii, Düsseldorf, 1931; B. Brunelli and A. Callegari, Ville del Brenta e degli Euganei, Milan, 1931; A. Calabi, L'incisione italiana del '700, Milan, 1931; V. Moschini, La pittura italiana del Settecento, Florence, 1931; G. Delogu, La scultura italiana del Sei- e Settecento, 2 vols., Florence, 1933; L. Rosso, La pittura e la scultura del '700 a Torino, 1934; W. Arslan, Studi sulla pittura del primo Settecento veneziano, CrArte, I, 1935–36, pp. 18–97, 238–50; G. Delogu, L'architettura italiana del Sei- e Settecento, 2 vols., Florence, 1935; G. Zucchini and R. Longhi, Il Settecento bolognese, Bologna, 1935 (cat.); M. Goering, Italienische Malerei des 17. und 18. Jahrhunderts, Berlin, 1936; G. Lorenzetti, Le feste e le maschere veneziane, Venice, 1937 (cat.); R. Gallo, L'incisione nel Settecento a Venezia e a Bassano, Venice, 1941; R. Pallucchini, Gli incisori veneti del Settecento, Venice, 1941 (cat.); A. Ressa, L'architettura religiosa in Piemonte nei secoli XVII e XVIII, Torino, XXI, 7, 1941, pp. 5–22; K. Lohmeyer, Palagonisches Barock, Berlin, 1942; G. Lorenzetti, La pittura italiana del Settecento, Novara, 1942; V. Viale, La pittura in Piemonte nel Settecento, Torino, XXII, 6, 1942, pp. 3–22; M. Salmi, L'arte italiana, III, Florence, 1944; G. Fogolari, L'arte monumentale del Settecento italiano, Scritti d'arte, Milan, 1946, pp. 199–211; G. Delogu, Disegni veneziani del Settecento, Milan, 1947; V. Golzio, Il Seicento e il Settecento, Turin, 1950; M. Lanckoronska, Die venetianische Buchgraphik des 18. Jahrhunderts, Hamburg, 1950; G. Morazzoni, Stucchi italiani: Maestri genovesi dei secoli XVI–XIX, Milan, 1950; M. Pittaluga, Acquafortisti veneziani del Settecento, Florence, 1950; G. Policastro, Catania nel Settecento, Catania, 1950; V. Ziino, Contributi allo studio dell'architettura del '700 in Sicilia, Palermo, 1950; R. Pallucchini, La pittura veneziana del '700, 2 vols., Bologna, 1951–52; R. Bacchelli and R. Longhi, Teatro e immagini del '700 Italiano, Turin, 1953; A. M. Brizio, L'architettura barocca in Piemonte, Turin, 1953; M. Valsecchi, La pittura veneziana, Milan, 1954; D. Gioseffi, Pittura veneziana del Settecento, Bergamo, 1956; A. Blunt and E. Croft-Murray, Venetian Drawings of the 17th and 18th Centuries at Windsor Castle, London, 1957; G. Chierici, Il palazzo italiano dal secolo XVII al XIX, Milan, 1957; D. Donzelli, I pittori veneti del Settecento, Florence, 1957; R. Wittkower, Art and Architecture in Italy, 1600–1750, Harmondsworth, 1958; M. Levey, Painting in 18th Century Venice, London, 1959; R. Pane, Ville Vesuviane del Settecento, Naples, 1959; Il Settecento a Roma, 2d ed., Rome, 1959 (cat.; full bibliog.); R. Pallucchini, La pittura veneziana del Settecento, Rome, Venice, 1960.

g. German-speaking lands: J. L. Sponsel, Der Zwinger, die Hoffeste und die Schlossbaupläne zu Dresden, 2 vols., Dresden, 1909–24; M. Dvořák, Die Entwicklung der barocken Deckenmalerei in Wien, Vienna, 1920; M. Hauttmann, Geschichte der kirchlichen Baukunst in Bayern, Schwaben und Franken, 1550–1780, Munich, 1921; H. Schmitz, Kunst und Kultur des 18. Jahrhunderts in Deutschland, Munich, 1922; A. Feulner, Bayerisches Rokoko, Munich, 1923; H. Schmitz, Deutsche Möbel des Barock und Rokoko, Stuttgart, 1923; R. Sedlmaier and R. Pfister, Die fürstbischöfliche Residenz zu Würzburg, 2 vols., Munich, 1923; H. Popp, Die Architektur der Barock- und Rokokozeit in Deutschland und in der Schweiz, Stuttgart, 1924; P. Seidel, Friedrich der Grosse und die bildende Kunst, 2d ed., Berlin, 1924; M. Zweig, Zweites Rokoko, Vienna, 1924; A. Feulner, Kunstgeschichte des Möbels, Berlin, 1927; P. du Colombier, L'art français dans les cours rhénanes, Paris, 1930; G. Dehio, Geschichte der deutschen Kunst, III, Berlin, Leipzig, 1930; H. Sedlmayr, Österreichische Barockarchitektur, Vienna, 1930; K. Lohmeyer, Die Baumeister des rheinisch-fränkischen Barock, Vienna, Augsburg, 1931; M. Lanckoronska and R. Oehler, Die Buchillustration des 18. Jahrhunderts in Deutschland, Österreich und der Schweiz, 3 vols., Leipzig, 1932–34; A. Streichhan, Knobelsdorff und das friederitianische Rokoko, Burg bei Magdeburg, 1932; W. Pinder, Deutsche Barockplastik, Königstein im Taunus, 1933; R. Meyer, Hecken- und Gartentheater in Deutschland im 17. und 18. Jahrhundert, Emsdetten, 1934; G. Adriani, Die Klosterbibliotheken des Spätbarock in Österreich und Süddeutschland, Graz, Leipzig, Vienna, 1935; H. Keller, Das Treppenhaus im deutschen Schloss- und Klosterbau des Barock, Munich, 1936; L. Réau, Les relations artistiques entre la France et la Suisse au XVIIIe siècle, XIVe Cong. int. de l'art, II, Basel, 1936, pp. 146–53; W. Braunfels, François de

Cuvilliés, Würzburg, 1938; M. Kühn, Die Gärten Friedrich des Grossen, Brandenburgischer Jhb., XIV–XV, 1939, pp. 33–67; M. Goering, Deutsche Malerei des 17. und 18. Jahrhunderts, Berlin, 1940; N. Lieb, Münchner Barockbaumeister, Munich, 1941; H. Schnell, Die Wessobrunner Stukkatoren, D. Kultur im Leben der Völker, XVI, 1941, pp. 183–93; O. Fischer, Geschichte der deutschen Malerei, Munich, 1942; W. Hager, Die Bauten des deutschen Barock, 1690–1770, Jena, 1942; J. Brandis, Die Genesis des süddeutschen Muschelwerks, Frankfurt am Main, 1943; K. Ginhart, Die gesetzmässige Entwicklung des österreichischen Barockornaments, Kunstgeschichtliche S., Breslau, 1943, pp. 62–77; W. Pinder, Deutscher Barock, Königstein im Taunus, 1943; H. Landolt and T. Seeger, Schweizer Barockkirchen, Frauenfeld, 1948; E. Hempel, Geschichte der deutschen Baukunst, Munich, 1949; E. Bachmann, Anfänge des Landschaftsgartens in Deutschland, ZfKw, V, 1951, pp. 203–28; O. Fischer, Geschichte der deutschen Zeichnung und Graphik, Munich, 1951; H. Tintelnot, Die barocke Freskomalerei in Deutschland, Munich, 1951; G. Weise, Das Problem der Herkunft des Rokokomuschelwerks unter besonderer Berücksichtigung des barocken Kunstschaffens in Schwaben, Neue Beiträge zur Archäologie und Kunstgeschichte Schwabens J. Baum gewidmet, Stuttgart, 1952, pp. 217–24; A. Feulner and T. Müller, Geschichte der deutschen Plastik, Munich, 1953; H. Kreisel, Deutsche Spiegelkabinette, Darmstadt, 1953; N. Lieb, Barockkirchen zwischen Donau und Alpen, Munich, 1953; E. Redslob, Barock und Rokoko in den Schlössern von Berlin und Potsdam, Berlin, 1954; H. Kohlhausen, Geschichte des deutschen Kunstgewerbes, Munich, 1955; P. du Colombier, L'architecture française en Allemagne au XVIIIe siècle, 2 vols., Paris, 1956; W. Graf Kalnein, Das kurfürstliche Schloss Clemensruhe in Poppelsdorf, Düsseldorf, 1956; A. Reinle and J. Gantner, Kunstgeschichte der Schweiz, III: Die Kunst der Renaissance, des Barock und des Klassizismus, Frauenfeld, 1956; Rococo Art from Bavaria, London, 1956 (cat.); W. Fleischhauer, Barock im Herzogtum Württemberg, Stuttgart, 1958; N. Powell, From Baroque to Rococo: An Introduction to Austrian and German Architecture from 1580 to 1790, London, 1959; B. Rupprecht, Die bayerische Rokoko-Kirche, Munich, 1959; B. Grimschitz, R. Feuchtmuller, and M. Mrazek, Barock in Osterreich, Vienna, 1960; H. Bauer, Zum ikonologischen Stil der süddeutschen Rokokokirche, MJhb, 3d Ser., XII, 1961, pp. 218–40; Kurfürst Clemens August, Landesherr und Mäzen des 18. Jahrhunderts, Cologne, 1961 (cat.); W. Kurth, Sanssouci, Berlin, 1962.

* *

Illustrations: PLS. 159–184; 9 figs. in text.

ROCK ART. See AUSTRALIAN CULTURES; PALEO-AFRICAN CULTURES; PREHISTORY.

RODIN, AUGUSTE. Sculptor (b. Paris, Nov. 12, 1840; d. Meudon, Nov. 17, 1917). The artist came from a family of the *petite bourgeoisie*, and his school years were divided between a religious institute and the private school run by his uncle in Beauvais. An indifferent pupil, interested only in drawing, the boy made no progress. His father then sent him, although reluctantly, to the Ecole Impériale, which was to become the Ecole Nationale des Arts Décoratifs, also known as the Petite Ecole. Between 1854 and 1857, he studied there under two teachers of outstanding merit, Horace Lecoq de Boisbaudran for drawing and J. B. Carpeaux (q.v.) for modeling. Ashamed of his own ignorance, Rodin set himself a reading program of novelists and poets (Dante was his favorite) and registered for literature and history courses at the Collège de France. Strong-willed, hard-working, and fully conscious of his talents, he decided at the age of twenty to become a sculptor. Three times rejected by the Ecole des Beaux-Arts and forced to undertake tiresome decoration work in order to make a living, he did not lose heart. In 1862, Maria, his sister and confidante, died in the convent into which she had retired not long before. Rodin's grief was so profound that he in turn entered the order of the Pères du Saint-Sacrament (Fathers of the Holy Sacrament). Perceiving the artist's true vocation, the Father Superior dissuaded him from pursuing his novitiate; Rodin returned to his parents' home and started working again. During the day, he carried out decorations for public monuments; at night, he attended a course given by A. L. Barye (q.v.), the renowned sculptor of animal subjects.

The year 1864 marked a turning point in Rodin's life: he fell in love with a young seamstress, Rose Beuret, and entered the studio of Carrier-Belleuse, who was to exert a lasting influence on him. The first work Rodin submitted to the Salon, *The Man with the Broken Nose* (Louvre), was refused by the jury. In spite of this disappointment, of his poverty, of the daily struggle to ensure his own subsistence, that of Rose Beuret and of the son born to them in 1866, his energy and self-confidence were in no way affected. Models being too expensive, it was Rose who sat for a series of busts and "maternities." The artist also made terra-cotta portraits, which he then gave away in payment of services received. This was a period of apprenticeship and of groping, which came to an end with the Franco-Prussian war of 1870. Carrier-Belleuse proposed that Rodin participate, under his direction, in the decoration of the Bourse in Brussels. Rodin accepted. One year after their arrival in Belgium, Carrier-Belleuse quarreled with his pupil and returned to Paris. Rodin was engaged by the artistic director A. J. van Rasbourg to carry out the monumental groups and the caryatids that were to decorate the Bourse. The artist spent five years in Brussels, with an interruption in 1875 for a trip to Italy, where he "discovered" Michelangelo. "My liberation from academism was effected by Michelangelo," he was to say later.

Almost as though to confirm this statement, Rodin sculptured *The Age of Bronze* (1876; PL. 185), a superb statue of a standing man, which he exhibited at the 1877 Salon. The work was considered so nonconformist that it became the target of violent criticism. Nevertheless, it struck the public's imagination and was bought by the State for the Musée du Luxembourg. It was immediately followed by *Man Walking* (Paris, Mus. Rodin), a masterpiece of almost overwhelming expressive power.

Carrier-Belleuse, who appreciated the integrity and ability of his former pupil, invited him to work in the Manufacture de Sèvres, of which he was the artistic director. From 1879 to 1882, Rodin strove to renew the art of ceramics. Even when he no longer supplied the manufacture with models and patterns, he had many of his works executed in *grès* (stoneware). He also tried his hand at engraving between 1881 and 1886; his drypoints have the assurance and the incisiveness that also characterize his drawings (cf. IV, PL. 281).

At this stage, Rodin was beginning to enjoy a certain fame: the circle of his friends widened, and he was welcomed into the artistic and literary salons. But he had not yet overcome his financial difficulties. He was then forty; this was the time when a new love renewed and multiplied his creative faculties: in the youth and beauty of Camille Claudel, a student of modeling, he found the inspiration that Rose Beuret, the humble companion of his early struggles, could no longer supply. Camille became his collaborator and model, and he undoubtedly owed to her the most productive years of his career. In 1880, the French Government commissioned him to execute a monumental door for the Musée des Arts Décoratifs (models and preliminary drawings in Paris, Mus. Rodin). He called it the Gate of Hell in honor of Dante. Though he never finished it, certain details of this door — duly enlarged — were to inspire some of his most moving sculptures: *Three Shadows* (1880), *Crouching Woman* (1885), *The Kiss* (1886; PL. 186), *The Prodigal Son* (1885–88), and *The Thinker* (1888). If his *John the Baptist* (1880; PL. 185), *La Luxure* (1882), and *Fugit Amor* (1886) are added to the list, it can be said that never since Gothic times had the whole gamut of human feelings — sorow, anxiety, anguish, desire, voluptuousness, or simply virile strength — been rendered in marble or bronze with such passion and mastery. (Note: Various versions and casts of all the works of Rodin are preserved in the Musée Rodin, Paris).

The well-known group *The Bourgeois of Calais*, commissioned from Rodin by that municipality, required two years of strenuous work (1884–86) and was not installed until 1895. In 1889 he was entrusted with the monument to Victor Hugo, to be placed in the Panthéon in Paris, but he never finished it (model in Mus. Rodin, Paris). With the exception of the monument to Bastien-Lepage (1887), unveiled at Damvillers in 1889, and those to Claude Lorrain (1889; Nancy, Jardin de la Pépinière) and President Sarmiento (1895; commissioned by the city of Buenos Aires), none of Rodin's monuments went beyond the stage of sketches or models (e.g., monuments to Whistler, Napoleon, Eugène Carrière, Puvis de Chavannes). The fact is that the composition of groups was never Rodin's forte. He was more successful with his statue of Balzac (Paris, Mus. Rodin), for which he made several head studies (PL. 185) and full-length portraits. This statue is unquestionably a master-

piece; but it will be noted that the author of *La Comédie Humaine* is represented without the least allegorical or ornamental attribute. The statue had been commissioned from the artist in 1891 by the Société des Gens de Lettres: it stirred up such lively controversy that, at the last moment, the Société refused to honor its commitment. It was only in 1939 that this admirable work was put up at the Raspail-Montparnasse intersection in Paris. And yet, at the time when Rodin was suffering these rebuffs, his genius was unquestioned and his fame widespread. After 1900, all the great men of the time passed through his studio, to sit for a portrait or to meet this outstanding artist. Having acquired considerable wealth, he settled in 1897 in the Villa des Brillants, which he had bought, at Meudon; later, in 1908, he went to live in the Hôtel Biron, the future Musée Rodin. Surrounded by apprentices and collaborators such as Jules Desbois, François Pompon, Emile Antoine Bourdelle, and Charles Despiau, and by secretaries such as Rainer Maria Rilke, Charles Morice, and Mario Meunier, he worked all day long with youthful enthusiasm.

To those of Rodin's works that are universally known should be added his innumerable studies — sculptures, drawings, water colors — of dancers, of nude women in a variety of poses, of heads, torsos, legs, feet, and hands, sometimes carried out in the heat of improvisation, sometimes after long and careful thought. It was in his statuettes, so striking in their robust grace and vivacity, in their anecdotal details overflowing with life, and also in his busts of famous contemporaries, such as Henri Rochefort, Georges Clémenceau (PL. 185), George Bernard Shaw, and the Comtesse de Noailles, that Rodin revealed the breadth of his artistic power; on the other hand, it was in his monumental works that he had to admit his limitations. While he excelled in the portrayal of specific facets of life and in partial depiction of the whole, he seemed to hesitate, or even draw back, before a broad system of representation. He had no feeling for composition or for vast syntheses. He commands admiration for his genius combined with craftsmanship, for the vigor that sustained his inspiration, for his detailed analyses, and for the masterly way in which he enclosed his tremendous personality in a mere fragment. But it must be admitted that his impressionism was the end-product of the realistic tradition, the extreme consequence of the illusionist naturalism deriving from the Renaissance; Rodin was a reformer rather than a revolutionary, a modeler rather than a sculptor.

Immediately after Rodin's death, a reaction against his esthetics sprang up; his art was too individual to be transmitted. After him, his artistic idiom could go no further. It was in opposition to him, to his romanticism, and to his artistic methods that a type of sculpture evolved that constituted a return to the fundamental laws of sculpture. It is precisely because he gave rise to a need for new forms that Rodin has acquired such considerable importance. He defined his own role by stating: "I am a bridge joining the two banks; the past and the present."

Conscious that the end was approaching, the artist bequeathed his works to the State in 1916. On Jan. 29, 1917, he married Rose Beuret, whom he had never deserted notwithstanding his many liaisons; Rose died a fortnight later, and Rodin expired on Nov. 17 of the same year.

BIBLIOG. R. M. Rilke, Auguste Rodin, Berlin, 1903 (2d ed., Leipzig, 1913; Eng. trans., J. Lemont and H. Trausil, New York, 1945); J. Cladel, Auguste Rodin: L'oeuvre et l'homme, Brussels, 1908 (Eng. trans., S. K. Star, New York, 1912); A. Rodin, L'art: entretiens réunis par Paul Gsell, Paris, 1912 (rev. ed., 1951; Eng. trans., K. W. D. Fedden, Boston, 1912, repr. 1957); G. Coquiot, Rodin à l'Hôtel Biron et à Meudon, Paris, 1917; C. Mauclair, Auguste Rodin, Paris, 1918 (Eng. trans., C. Black, London, 1905); R. M. Rilke, Lettres à Rodin, Paris, 1928–34; J. Cladel, Rodin: Sa vie glorieuse, sa vie inconnue, Paris, 1936 (rev. ed., 1951; Eng. trans., J. Whitall, New York, 1937); A. Bourdelle, La sculpture et Rodin, Paris, 1937; S. Story, Rodin, New York, 1939 (2d ed., London, 1961); G. Grappe, Catalogue du Musée Rodin, 5th ed., Paris, 1944; J. Charbonneaux, Les sculptures de Rodin, Paris, 1949; A. Elsen, Rodin's Gates of Hell, Minneapolis, 1960; C. Goldscheider, Rodin: Sa vie, son œuvre, son héritage, Paris, 1962; C. Goldscheider, Rodin inconnu, Paris, 1962 (cat.); A. Elsen, Rodin, New York, 1963 (bibliog.); E. C. Geissbuhler, Rodin: Later Drawings, Boston, 1963.

Frank ELGAR

Illustrations: PLS. 185–186.

ROMAN ART OF THE EASTERN EMPIRE. The Romans always recognized the special place held in the Empire by the eastern provinces, which were ultimately to be united under the name *pars orientalis*. This identity and unity were chiefly due to one of the great events of the ancient world: the conquests of Alexander the Great, which resulted in the Hellenism (see HELLENISTIC ART) that the Romans found on the eastern shores of the Mediterranean and which they acknowledged as a culture superior to their own (see HELLENISTIC-ROMAN ART). Unity of language and civilization existed, but only to a certain degree. The ascendancy of Hellenism varied according to the region. It was more or less imposed or superimposed in countries such as Egypt — considered by the ancients as the oldest country in the world — and Syria, where Semitic civili-

zations, in their religious form at least, had struck such deep roots. It established itself earlier and more firmly in Macedonia, Asia Minor, and the barbarian lands bordering the old Greek colonies. Finally there was Greece itself, existing largely on memories of the past. Hellenistic unity was affirmed in the face of the Roman west on the one hand and in the face of ancient national diversities on the other. These two factors should be borne in mind in a study of the art of the Roman Empire in *pars orientalis*.

SUMMARY. Architecture (col. 279): *Town planning; Temples and sanctuaries; Arches and gates; Nymphaeums and libraries; Theaters, odeums, amphitheaters, and stadiums; Thermae; Basilicas; Palaces and houses; Funerary monuments; Orders and decoration; Building techniques.*

Principal cities and archaeological sites of the eastern provinces of the Roman Empire, with provincial subdivisions for the period between Augustus and Trajan (the inset shows Syro-Palestinian area). *Key:* (1) Boundaries of the Roman provinces.

Sculpture (col. 303): *Schools and artists; Portraits; Reliefs; Sarcophagi; Provincial styles; Sculpture of the late Empire.* Painting and mosaics (col. 309). Minor arts (col. 311).

ARCHITECTURE. *Town planning.* Our knowledge of the architecture of the eastern provinces of the Empire is seriously curtailed by lack of data on such great metropolises as Alexandria and Antioch in the early period, as well as Constantinople, Salonika, and Nicomedia in later times. On the other hand, with growing information we have an increasingly clear picture of Ephesus, capital of the province of Asia, and Corinth, capital of Achaia, as well as of many other towns of varying sizes in the rest of Asia Minor and Syria.

Clearly, then, the eastern provinces participated in the urban growth that characterized the history of the early Empire, and in fact boasted the most flourishing cities, outside Rome, a galaxy of metropolises that eclipsed those of the west in brilliance. It should be added that this urban growth, although interrupted by historical accidents as in Petra or Palmyra, did not suffer, on the whole, from the effects of the crisis of the 3d century as did its western counterparts. Thus its evolution continued unbroken through the history of the Byzantine world. These great cities commanded enormous prestige with their spacious avenues, interspaced by broad squares and imposing monuments, glittering with a profusion of marbles, forests of columns, and roofs scintillating with gold and bronze. Contemporary writings such as the *Antiochikos* of Libanius celebrated their beauty; in some instances their image was perpetuated in art, Antioch being preserved for us in the mosaic of the Yakto complex and Jerusalem in the Madaba Map (III, PL. 494). This splendor was a no doubt external, but nonetheless dazzling, triumph of the polis, and the *evergetes* (patrons) had never before been so numerous or so munificent. The emperors set the tone. Following Augustus, the Hellenophile Hadrian left his mark on many places. Nor did lesser personalities lag behind. In Syria, Herod the Great perpetuated his name in public monuments throughout the land as far as Antioch, and in Greece the name of Herodes Atticus was known thanks to his endowments in Athens, Delphi, and Olympia.

In Greece, with its small population and scanty resources, the Roman contribution could be limited to such propaganda gestures as the small monopteral temple of Rome and Augustus in front of the Parthenon, the Odeum of Agrippa in the center of the Agora, and such elaborate un-Hellenic embellishments as the ascent to the Acropolis, the Altis gates at Olympia, the entrances to the stadiums at Delphi and Olympia, and the propylaeum of Eleusis. There was, however, no lack of architectural complexes. The new Athens built by Hadrian near his Temple of Zeus Olympius has almost entirely disappeared, but there are more extensive remains of the group of buildings stretching along the east side of the Agora: the Roman forum dating from the time of Augustus (31 B.C.–A.D. 14), the "Tower of the Winds" by the Syrian architect Andronicus Cyrrhestes (VII, PL. 149), and, immediately beside it, Hadrian's Library. New cities were founded, such as Nicopolis in Epirus, and old cities thoroughly remodeled, such as Philippi in Macedonia or Gortyna in Crete, but these sites are still insufficiently explored. At present the Roman city in Greece about which there is most information is Corinth, which was reconstructed at the order of Julius Caesar. Its agora is still a classical Greek square surrounded by monuments, but among these is noteworthy, on the west side, a series of little temples raised on podiums. To the south, east, and north stand three basilicas, all Roman in style. There is also a monumental arch marking the end of the road from Lechaion, this being a colonnaded street in a style to be discussed below.

It is more difficult to form a clear impression of the Roman cities in Egypt, which included Antinoë (Antinoopolis), which was entirely conceived by Hadrian and was remarkable for its regular plan and its great thoroughfares in the form of a cross, and Hermopolis, probably built on a very similar plan. A comparison of papyrus records and the monuments would have been illuminating, had not both cities been almost completely destroyed.

Our knowledge of the great metropolises of the time is based above all on those in Asia Minor and Syria. Since the time of the Hellenistic kings, these two regions had possessed strong town-planning traditions of various derivations. The primary influence was that of Pergamum (mod. Bergama), tending to monumentality, to the arrangement of perspectives and panoramas, and to the organization of architectural masses by skillful terracing up the sides of the acropolis. In Pergamum, for example, even the Temple of Trajan fitted gracefully into the Hellenistic layout, its three porticoes dominating the theater. Terraced towns of the Roman epoch are not rare in Asia Minor; characteristic is the group of towns in Pamphylia and Pisidia known to the ancient world as Perga, Side, Cremna, Aspendus, Termessus, and Sagalassus. Everywhere are to be found the great arterial roads and monumental complexes that marked the layout of the metropolis. At Ephesus an extraordinary monumental quarter surrounded the port at the foot of the hills, which were terraced into residential areas.

A regular plan is to be found in Perga, where the two main avenues crossed in the center of the town — as was probably the case also in Nicaea (mod. İznik) in Bithynia — and in Cremna. This town was laid out on the checkerboard plan, which tradition attributes to Hippodamos (q.v.) of Miletus, and which has in fact survived in Miletus, Priene, Rhodes, and Cnidus (Knidos). This functional plan, the basic element of which was the insula, or block of buildings, was rather austere in tone and no doubt was not entirely in keeping with the spirit of Roman times. Apparently it no longer found favor with the imperial architects in Asia Minor. In Syria it was used in the ancient cities founded by the Seleucids, such as Antioch, Apamea, Beroea (mod. Aleppo), Laodicea ad Mare (mod. Latakia), and, exceptionally, in Damascus. Everywhere its original severity was modified by the introduction of the great novelty of the times: the colonnaded street. These streets were also a dominant feature in cities that attained their highest development in the imperial epoch: Petra, Philadelphia (mod. Amman), Gerasa (mod. Jerash), Samaria (mod. Sebastye), Bostra (mod. Bosra), Philippopolis (mod. Shahba), Palmyra, Heliopolis (mod. Baalbek), and Beirut.

The colonnaded street, which was often more than half a mile long and was crossed by colonnaded side streets or doubled or tripled by parallel streets, reveals a taste for ostentation entirely alien to the Greek checkerboard plan. Although A. von Gerkan (1924) affirms the contrary, this style was Roman in inspiration, if the term is used in a strictly chronological sense. The first colonnaded street was the one in Antioch, which tradition associates with the names of Herod and Tiberius. This early dating, which is confirmed by excavations in Antioch, is further confirmed in epigraphic documents from Attaleia (mod. Antalya) in Pamphylia and from Diocaesarea (Sepphoris) in Cilicia.

The principle of the colonnaded street is a simple one: a broad roadway running between raised sidewalks that are covered by a continuous arcade. The dimensions are impressive, 33–47 ft. for the roadway and 65–85 ft. for the over-all width. Sometimes shops opened onto the arcade (there is a well-preserved example at Apamea). The variations in detail are numerous. The order of the columns, although Corinthian for the most part, may also be Ionic (this is partly the case in Gerasa) or reveal curious combinations (Corinthian capitals and a frieze with metopes and triglyphs in Apamea). There were probably two-story arcades in Antioch; in Apamea and elsewhere the arcade was paved with mosaics; at Ephesus, on the street of late date known as the Arcadiane (Arcadian Way), provision was made for lighting at night.

It should be made clear that these streets were in no way tied to a rectangular plan; such a system may have occurred in a few towns as a survival of Hellenistic tastes or as a special isolated venture, as in the grandiose plan for Gerasa, but in general the greatest care was taken to avoid monotony. In the streets themselves, the colonnades were interrupted by arcades marking the entry of side streets (Apamea and Palmyra); arches were built across avenues (as in Bosra, Gerasa, Palmyra, and Damascus) to disguise or to accentuate the changes in direction inevitable over long distances. At important intersections more complicated devices were introduced: the tetrapylon, a four-fronted arch (in Laodicea ad Mare, Gerasa, Philippopolis, and Perga), or the tetrastyle peculiar to Syria, consisting of four clusters of four columns on a small circular plaza (Gerasa and Palmyra). Near the city gates the avenue broadened into an oval piazza, as in Palmyra and, on a reduced scale, in Perga. The example of the oval forum in Gerasa (PL. 190), built on a much larger scale, is of course quite different. The final result was sometimes unexpected, as in the case of streets blocked at their extremities, of which there are two examples in Ephesus and one in Gerasa, the street leading from the gate to the stadium. The street had become a monument in its own right, along with the other monuments beside it. Space was definitively controlled, even when it widened into squares, which were so numerous in these cities: there was at least one forum, and there were countless shrines, gymnasiums, and thermae.

In its ideal form the agora or forum was completely enclosed, in the shape of a court bordered by four porticoes. In Miletus, for example, a fourth portico was added to the northern agora at the end of the Hellenistic period. Nonetheless there were still three porticoes in Philippi and in Aphrodisias, in the porticoed court of Tiberius and the great agora. The colossal dimensions that had already made their appearance in Hellenistic times were characteristic of the period: the southern agora of Miletus measured 538 × 646 ft.; the agora in Ephesus, 525 ft. square; the forum in Palmyra, 561 × 275 ft.; that in Athens, 367 × 315 ft.; and the great agora of Aphrodisias, 672 × 394 ft. Also typical are the series of porticoed courts, for example in Aphrodisias, where one passed from the court of the thermae into the court of Tiberius and from there into the agora and the sanctuary of the goddess. Antioch in Pisidia also had twin forums of this kind connected by monumental passages — one dating from the time of Augustus, the other from that of Tiberius. The porticoes of the forums had either two or three aisles, and in a number of cities one of the porticoes was replaced by a basilica (see below).

The conception of the sanctuary as a porticoed court has well-known Hellenistic antecedents in Pergamum, Miletus, and Priene. This tendency was accentuated in the imperial period both for urban and extra-urban sanctuaries: the Temple of Trajan and the Aesculapium in Pergamum, the Temple of Serapis in Ephesus, the temples of Aphrodite in Aphrodisias, of Zeus in Aizani (mod. Çavdarhisar), and of Antoninus Pius in Sagalassus. But the most grandiose and fully planned examples are to be found in Syria. This is the country of the great court-sanctuaries that date from the very beginning of the Empire: the Temple of Bel in Palmyra (built by Tiberius), the Temple of Augustus in Samaria, the sanctuaries of Seia (Si'), and the Temple of Jerusalem (built by Herod). The sanctuaries of Baalbek (PL. 192) were constructed toward the end of the 1st century and in the 2d century, at the same time as the temple of Damascus, followed by the two great temples of Gerasa. The dimensions were on a colossal scale: the temple in Palmyra measured 672 × 689 ft. in its 2d-century form; in Damascus, the inner court of the temple measured 508 × 328 ft. and the outer court about 850 × 985 ft.; the rectangular court of the great sanctuary in Baalbek measured 443 × 377 ft., and its hexagonal court was 197 ft. along the central diagonal.

The construction of the porticoed court seems to have been an established convention, in the light of the great number of minor examples such as the Temple of Jove at Baetocaece (Hisn Sulayman) and the temples of Hisn Niha, Qal'at Faqra, Deir al-Qal'a, and others in Lebanon. The small round temple of Venus at Baalbek also had a peribolus, as has recently been established, while at Palmyra the Temple of Baal-shamin (Ba'al-shamîn) was built at the time of Hadrian's visit in the court of a sanctuary of local type. There is, in fact, good reason to believe that the traditional sanctuary in Phoenicia and western Syria included the court as an essential feature, and that here the altar, the cleansing basin, and also the tabernacle for the divine images were set up (as in the sanctuary of Khirbat el-Tannur in Jordan, the high places of Petra, etc.). Moreover, the porticoes here were not always mere promenades: the sumptuous exedras be-

hind the porticoes of the great sanctuary in Baalbek are sufficient proof of this.

Also noteworthy are the bathing establishments, of which a series of monumental examples has been preserved at Ephesus: the Gymnasium of Vedius (2d cent.), the thermae of the theater, and above all the harbor baths, where the immense triple-porticoed court of Verulanus (2d cent.; 656 × 787 ft.) — probably a xystus — stretched beside the palaestra, a court 295 ft. square.

The peristyle court was also a feature of private dwellings, so that the inhabitants of these towns were everywhere surrounded by colonnades, which stretched before them along the streets and squares and framed the monuments of the city or the surrounding space. They lived in a world of bounded and articulated perspectives. This principle was also known in the west, where, however, the greater use of curved lines and of the centrally planned building seems to have allowed more varied and subtle effects.

Temples and sanctuaries. The Empire provided considerable resources for architecture, so that some of the great buildings begun in the past were successfully completed during that period. The Didymaeum of Miletus was given its eastern colonnade with irregular bases and scrolled Ionic capitals decorated with protomas; the Temple of Zeus Olympius (VII, PL. 149) in Athens — one of the largest temples of the ancient world, with a stylobate measuring 354 × 141 ft. — was completed by Hadrian. He also undertook the construction of the great temple of Cyzicus (mod. Kapidagi), and during his reign the Temple of Zeus at Aizani was begun. Among the other great buildings of Asia Minor, the Temple of Rome and Augustus (dating from the beginning of the Empire) at Ankara (anc. Ancyra), the Temple of Trajan in Pergamum, and the Temple of Aphrodite at Aphrodisias (of doubtful date) should all be mentioned. Syria, too, was the site of some colossal building programs: the Temple of Bel in Palmyra, the Temple of Augustus in Samaria, the Sanctuary of Artemis (FIG. 288) and the Temple of Zeus at Gerasa, and the temples of Baalbek. Most remarkable, however, is the large number of sacred temples of lesser importance, some of which are located in outlying areas: the temples of the Pamphylian and Pisidian cities, temples in obscure sites in Lebanon, such as Antilibanus and Hermon, and temples in southern Syria (Auranitis) and northern Syria. It is in Greece that temples of the Roman period are rarest (cf., however, the little temples in Corinth). Almost nothing survives of the Roman contribution in Egypt. Building in the indigenous style certainly continued there (e.g., Trajan's pavilion in Philae), and monuments of hybrid style were also constructed (the temple of Philae dating from the time of Augustus).

There is some question as to which innovations were due to Roman influence in monuments in the classical tradition. According to a well-known thesis (Weigand, 1924–25) the principal features of the true Roman temple were the podium (which gradually replaced the stepped *krepis*), the cella without an opisthodome, and the placing of the building at the far end of the court of the sanctuary, as well as a symmetry governed by the rules of axiality and frontality. It is surprising to find a line of small temples with podiums on the eastern side of the agora in Corinth and to see that the Temple of Augustus in Samaria was an imposing peristyle building at the top of a monumental staircase, and that the Temple of Bel in Palmyra, which was originally built on a *krepis*, was later provided with a base in the form of a podium.

As might be expected, Asia Minor remained most faithful to the Hellenistic traditions. The two great temples at Ankara and Aizani (PL. 189) are Ionic pseudodipteral buildings with colonnades of 8 and 15 pillars; the cellas are laid out like that in the earlier Temple of Zeus Sosipolis by Hermogenes in Magnesia-on-the-Maeander: four prostyle columns in front of a deep pronaos and two columns *in antis* in the opisthodome; the same arrangement is used in the Corinthian pseudoperipteros in Cnidus. The temple of Aizani is set on a *krepis* that in turn rests on a terrace-podium. Another Corinthian pseudoperipteros on a *krepis* is the Temple of Domitian at Ephesus (8 and 13 columns), where the cella had four prostyle columns in the pronaos

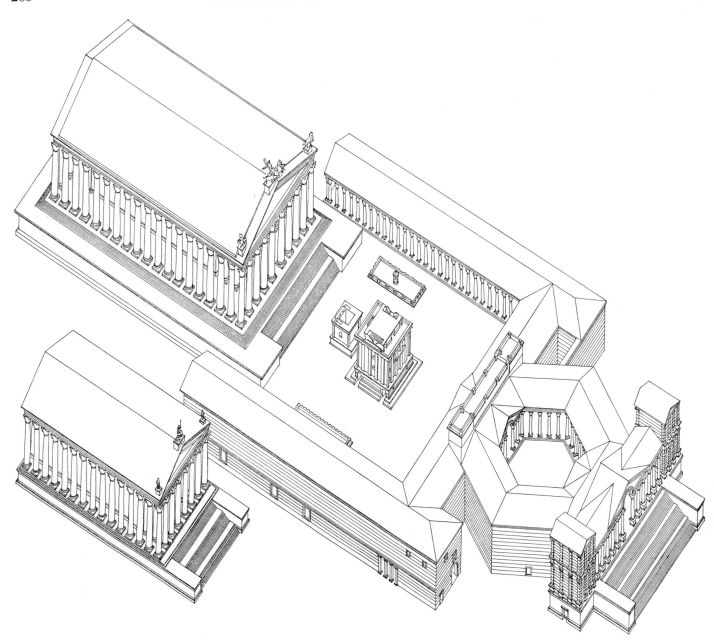

Baalbek, Sanctuary of Heliopolitan triad, axonometric plan (*from P. Collart and P. Coupel, L'autel monumental de Baalbek, Paris, 1951*).

and no opisthodome. On the same plan, but peripteral, again with a *krepis* as base, are the two Corinthian temples (6 and 11 columns), in Side and Sagalassus, both with a columned pronaos *in antis*; at Termessus there is an Ionic peripteros (6 and 11 columns), but the cella has been destroyed, as has that of the Ionic temple of Aphrodisias (8 and 13 columns).

The Roman temple conforming to the definition given above is well represented by the Temple of Trajan in Pergamum; it was a Corinthian peripteros (6 and 10 columns), had a cella without an opisthodome, and was raised on a podium that was reached by a monumental staircase. The Temple of Serapis in Ephesus was a colossal Corinthian prostyle with 8 columns along the façade on a raised podium. It had monolithic columns 46 ft. high and a door 19½ ft. wide with a three-piece lintel.

Along with these remarkable buildings existed a series of small prostyles, with four or six columns, which had a podium and flight of steps or were simply raised, as in Termessus, Sagalassus, Side, and Antioch in Pisidia. Undoubtedly there were many other examples, but the fact remains that Hellenistic traditions continued to be very strong in the country that contributed so largely to their creation.

Certain buildings or complexes that were sacred to particular divinities gave rise to original arrangements. At Pergamum the Aesculapium (FIG. 285), built in the 2d century, grouped a whole series of constructions around a large rectangular court; on the eastern side, the propylaea of Claudius Charax were set between the hall dedicated to Hadrian and the round temple of Zeus-Aesculapius; a second rotunda rose to the southeast, while on the northwest corner stood the theater. Again in Pergamum the group of buildings known as Kızıl Avlı or the Red Basilica, which was undoubtedly a Sanctuary of Serapis (PL. 188), reveals a completely eccentric plan: a large high hall, lighted by about ten windows, was placed between two symmetrical groups of buildings, in each case a rotunda between two rectangular rooms with a porticoed court in front. The Temple of Serapis in Miletus was built on a much less complex plan: a simple basilica with three aisles, a pronaos porch, and a bema opposite the entrance, against the back wall. At Ephesus the Mouseion (which was later to become the Council Church) consisted of a

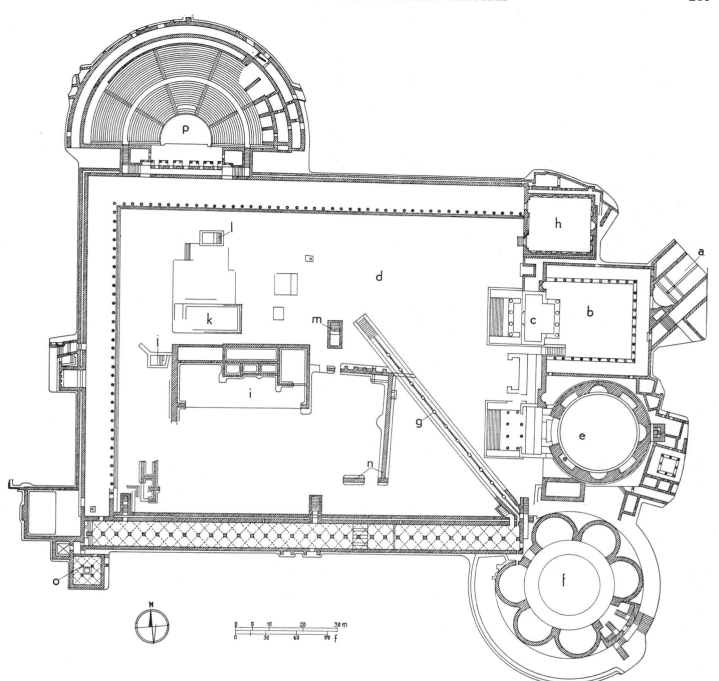

Pergamum, Aesculapium, reconstructed plan. (*a*) Sacred Way; (*b*) court of the propylaea; (*c*) Propylaea of Claudius Charax; (*d*) porticoed court; (*e*) Temple of Zeus-Aesculapius; (*f*) rotunda; (*g*) cryptoporticus; (*h*) hall (library?) consecrated to Hadrian; (*i*) enclosure for the sick; (*j*) fountain; (*k*) Temple of Aesculapius Soter; (*l*) basin for baths; (*m*) sacred spring; (*n*) Hellenistic walls; (*o*) *forica* (public lavatory); (*p*) theater (*from K. O. Dalman and H. Hanson, reproduced by Deubner, 1938*).

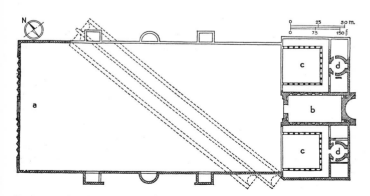

Pergamum, sanctuary (prob. of Serapis), known as Kızıl Avlı, reconstructed plan. (*a*) Square with tunnel of Selinus River underneath; (*b*) hall; (*c*) peristyles; (*d*) rotundas (*from L. Crema, L'architettura romana, Turin, 1959, p. 387*).

narrow three-aisled hall, 853 ft. long, flanked on the two short sides by two halls with apses; a long hall, of the same kind in which statues of the Muses have been found, was discovered in the Baths of Faustina at Miletus.

A series of temples dedicated to the worship of the emperor have already been mentioned. There was nothing original in their plan. One of them was the small temple of Hadrian at Ephesus (PL. 189), which consisted of a simple cella covered by a vault, with a deep pronaos in front. Other sanctuaries dedicated to emperor worship fall within the tradition of the classical and Hellenistic heroon. This seems to have been the case of the Caesareum in Antioch and that in Alexandria, which are known only from texts and are believed to have been similar to the one discovered at Cyrene (a porticoed court with a basilical hall on one of the sides; FIG. 287). It is certainly the case of Building M at Side, which was composed of three halls or exedras opening onto a peristyle court, the center one richly decorated with statues in niches. Similar halls are to be found in Ephesus adjoining the courts of several of the gymnasiums; these have been connected with emperor worship (e.g., the aula of the imperial cult in the Gymnasium of Vedius). There is also the monumental niche, which, in Aphrodisias, breaks the west side of the court of the thermae. Another noteworthy structure connected with emperor worship was recently discovered in Egypt: a hall of the late Roman castrum of Luxor, with a niche, decorated with a series of frescoes dating from the reign of Diocletian.

Buildings on a circular plan were not frequent in Asia Minor or elsewhere in the east. Examples are the Ionic monopteral temple of Rome and Augustus on the Acropolis in Athens and that of C. Babbius Philinus in the Corinth agora, as well as the monopteron in the Side forum. The round temple of Baalbek, which was possibly a Tycheum (2d–3d cent.; PL. 191; FIG. 288), was also built on a small scale. It was on a horseshoe plan, raised on a podium, with niches both inside and out; the little cella was fronted by two sets of four prostyle columns and surrounded by four others that were linked by concave architraves. But the most remarkable buildings are the two rotundas of the Aesculapium in Pergamum (FIG. 285), one of which (the Temple of Zeus-Aesculapius) was on a simple plan, probably domed, and very similar to the Pantheon in Rome, while the other was evidently covered with a wooden roof, was subdivided into six recesses in the shape of three-quarter circles, and was provided with underground bathing installations.

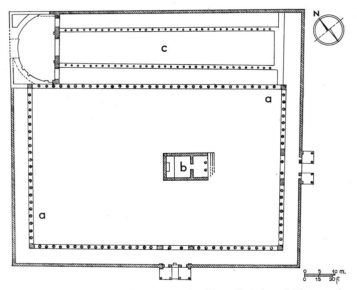

Cyrene, plan of Caesareum. (a) Peristyle; (b) small shrine of Dionysus (or intended for imperial cult?); (c) basilica (from Ward Perkins, 1948).

In Syria, Hellenistic traditions were clearly less strong. The result was, firstly, that during imperial times local religious custom conditioned the arrangement of buildings to a greater extent and, secondly, that Romanization was more rapid and complete.

It is no longer possible to form a clear idea of the nature of the Hellenistic temple, whether in Antioch, Hierapolis (Bambyce), or elsewhere. Only in the marginal region of Auranitis has a group of local sanctuaries survived, at Seia (1st cent.), as well as a temple in Greco-Oriental style at Suwaida. Perhaps the Temple of Bel at Palmyra (PL. 191), dedicated in A.D. 32, demonstrates certain aspects of the purest Hellenistic traditions, undoubtedly derived from the great center of Antioch. It is a Corinthian pseudodipteros of 8 and 15 columns, standing on a krepis of seven steps; two engaged Ionic half columns make the façades of the short sides resemble an opisthodome and a pronaos in antis. Finally, the arrangement of the peristyle columns as well as the capitals of the antas and the Ionic capitals of the short sides clearly recall Hermogenian models — all the rest, apart from the classical moldings, being a concession to Eastern practice. On the other hand, at Baalbek the presence of Rome

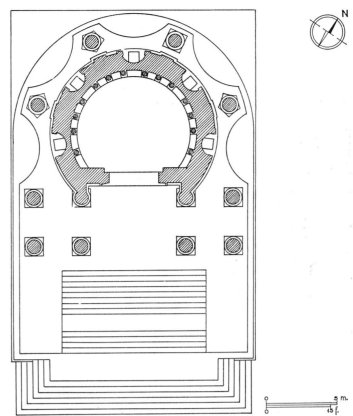

Baalbek, round temple, reconstructed plan (from T. Wiegand, ed., Baalbek II, Berlin, Leipzig, 1923).

in Syria manifests itself. While the temple of Palmyra rises in isolation in the center of a vast court, the great temple of Baalbek is placed on the axis and at the far end of its court, raised on an impressive podium. The small temple, which is almost entirely preserved, is likewise a Corinthian peripteros on a podium with a deep pronaos and no opisthodome. Very similar in conception are the two temples of Gerasa, the Temple of Artemis (FIG. 288), which is a Corinthian peripteros of 6 and 11 columns, and the Temple of Zeus with 8 and 12 columns, both dating from the middle of the 2d century.

Apart from these large buildings, well-preserved peripteral buildings are rare [the Temple of Helios at Qanawat (Roman Kanatha); Temple A at Hisn al-Safiri (Sfire)]. Otherwise the many temples of Lebanon and Syria share two or three simple types: a cella with two columns in antis ('Atil, Mushennef, Nebi Safa, Hibbariye, and Hebran); prostyle temples, usually with four columns (Sanamen, Temple A at Niha and at Hisn Niha,

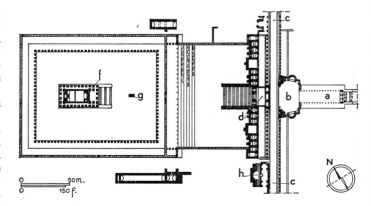

Gerasa, Sanctuary of Artemis, reconstructed plan. (a) Colonnaded approach; (b) east propylaea; (c) colonnaded street (cardo maximus); (d) west propylaea; (e) colonnaded temenos; (f) Temple of Artemis; (g) altar; (h) nymphaeum (from L. Crema, L'architettura romana, Turin, 1959, p. 397).

Baetocaece, Qasr Neba), sometimes with six (Qal'at Faqra, Musmieh), or with four prostyle columns and two columns in front of the antas (Deir al-Qal'a, Qasr Naus, Amman, the Temple of Baal-shamin at Palmyra). All these temples rise on a podium with a more or less monumental flight of steps leading up to it. Some variations may be observed: the Temple of Zeus at Qanawat has a prostyle with four columns and two *in antis*, and in the temple of Slem the antas have absorbed the volume of the two stairwells that lead up to the roof, framing a flight of steps and two successive pairs of columns.

Externally all these monuments are in the Greco-Roman style, i.e., they have a normal elevation, at least where their façades are concerned. Sometimes the decoration extends to the sides in the form of engaged columns (Baetocaece) or pilasters (Qasr Neba, Hisn al-Safiri, Mushennef, and Slem); on a small temple like the one in Dmer near Damascus the decoration is identical on all four sides. These buildings differ from those in Asia Minor in that their Greco-Roman facing is adapted to local traditions. A number of them were entirely or partially covered by terraces — undoubtedly for religious requirements — and the stairwells leading to the terraces were topped by square towers with merlons. These towers, particularly those in the towns of Decapolis in Jordan, can be seen pictured on coins, and the towers themselves are almost entirely preserved at Dmer. The existence of large stairwells together with other surviving features makes it possible to form a good impression of them elsewhere, especially at Palmyra and Slem. It is of course possible that these stairways, which are frequent in Syrian temples although their placing varies, met practical requirements and allowed access to the rooftops and pediments for purposes of maintenance. It is also possible that the windows that are sometimes to be found in the pediments (in Baalbek and Slem in Syria, and also in Ephesus in Asia Minor) must be considered in relation to these stairways.

The internal layout also gave rise to specifically Syrian or Syro-Phoenician plans. Almost all these temples had an adytum at the back of the cella, in other words an inner sanctuary, which contained the sacred image of the cult, and which, without actually concealing this image, rendered it inaccessible to the public. There are two ancient types. In the Temple of Bel in Palmyra, the adytum consisted of an adjoining room, with several steps leading up to it, which opened by means of a richly decorated but rather narrow bay onto the rest of the cella. This was the traditional layout in ancient Mesopotamia (cf. also the temples in Gerasa). The second type is to be found in Baalbek and elsewhere in Lebanon: a raised podium with a monumental staircase leading up to it supported a baldachin or tabernacle protecting the ritual statue. This was the Phoenician layout. Finally, in Auranitis the adytum was in the form of an apse on a square or semicircular plan, slightly raised and with a wide opening onto the cella, as in Qanawat, Slem, Sanamen, and Musmieh. The apse situated at the back of the cella has been considered a Roman invention; the fact that this form of adytum appears in the Temple of Baal-shamin in Palmyra in the 2d century may well confirm its Western origin. In these cases the apse is normally flanked by two lateral rooms, and this tripartite layout would seem to foreshadow Christian sacred buildings. The existence of the adytum must have stimulated the development of architectural decoration in the interior of the cella: such decoration is particularly well developed in Syrian temples.

The particular demands of Semitic cults also led to buildings that diverged more widely from classical models the farther removed they were from the great Hellenized centers, particularly in Nabataean country (Seia, Dat Ramm, Khirbat el-Tannur). One of the most striking examples is that of the Qaṣr Firun in Petra, which had a cella broader than it was long, a pronaos of four columns *in antis*, a complex two-storied adytum, and a terraced roof. The whole of Syria must have been covered with local types of sanctuaries like those discovered at Palmyra (Baal-shamin), Dura-Europos, and on the northwestern outskirts of Palmyra. The most important chamber of these sanctuaries is the banqueting hall, which can be identified by the couches on which the banqueters lay. The banqueting hall had penetrated into the Greek world before our era in the "Syrian" sanctuary

of Delos. There is also a series of such halls in the Sanctuary of Apollo Hylates in Cyprus (2d cent.). We know that this type of hall was the place of worship for the Mithraic cult, but although Mithraism originated on the borders of Syria and Cilicia, the only known Mithraeum in Syria is the one in Dura-Europos, which hardly differs from those of the West.

Judaism has left some original monuments (see JEWISH ART). Although the great temple built by Herod in Jerusalem is known only from texts, many of its features (such as its succession of courts, and its inner sanctuary) reveal points of contact with pagan temples. Galilee has preserved the even more important ruins of a dozen synagogues dating from the 2d and 3d centuries, such as those at Capernaum (VIII, PL. 334, FIGS. 909, 910) and Chorazin (Korazin). The sanctuary includes a porticoed court and a basilical hall in the Hellenistic tradition: a central nave, surrounded by a two-storied gallery with a colonnade, and with stone benches running along the walls. The synagogue at Dura-Europos (3d cent.) belongs to this type, although it is more renowned for its Parthian-style frescoes (VIII, PLS. 333, 335, 336).

In Syria the cleansing basins and altars form an indispensable part of the cult. Examples of the former are the two great basins of the sanctuary in Baalbek and the much more elaborate but poorly preserved basin in Palmyra. As for altars, in Palmyra there are the remains of an altar whose structure must have been similar to that of the Ara Pacis in Rome, and one should also mention in this connection the monumental altar of the Temple of Domitian in Ephesus, which is more in the tradition of the one in Pergamum. But it was Baalbek that possessed the most extraordinary altars: two tower altars are placed on the axis of the court of the great sanctuary. The smaller, which is in a poor state of preservation and whose structure is partly problematic, was accessible by means of a small, narrow staircase. The larger one (ca. 49 ft. wide and 59 ft. high) had two spacious flights of steps, which led up through successive landings to the terrace at the top. The building is remarkable for the richness of its sculptured ceilings.

Finally, the sacred theaters that were a feature of the Syrian sanctuaries should be mentioned. The one on Delos is still the earliest known example; it is of classical type — except for the absence of a stage — like those found in Roman Syria at Sahr, Tyre (Es Sur), and Gerasa [cf., too, the odeum of the Sanctuary of Artemis at Dura-Europos, where we also find *salles à gradins* (tiered halls) with the same function]. In the Sanctuary of Baal-shamin at Seia, it was the porticoed court that was used as a theater, according to an inscription — and probably this was often the case elsewhere.

Arches and gates. The triumphal arch is usually considered more typical of the western than of the eastern provinces; however an almost equal number of these monumental archways has so far been found in both areas, although the census, particularly for the east, is far from being complete or satisfactory. From present knowledge it would seem that the triumphal arch proper, corresponding to the isolated examples in the Roman Forum and at Benevento (X, PL. 154), Ancona, Orange (V, PL. 470), and elsewhere, is less frequent in the east, where the arch seems to have been more closely connected with the colonnaded street or conceived as a monumental entrance to the city itself and to its squares and buildings. There is no support for the view that the arch reached the east only at a late date and enjoyed only a brief vogue there. The arch at Philippi goes back to the time of Augustus, as does the gate of the Corinth agora and the one at Ephesus; the triple arch that joins the two squares of Antioch in Pisidia dates from the reign of Tiberius; an arch at Cyzicus dates from the time of Claudius; and one of the last great monumental arches of the Roman world is the Arch of Galerius in Salonika (PL. 198).

It is true that the east made no attempt to develop the more or less orthodox type represented by the Arch of Titus in the west, but used widely varying styles. There are, for example, the rather crude little arches — a mere passage surmounted by an attic story — in Philippi and Isauria (three arches at the entry to a square dating from the time of Hadrian, Marcus Aurelius, and Alexander Severus). An impression of massive simplicity is given by the Gate of Mithridates and Mazaeus in Ephesus: three equal arches, framed by pilasters and topped by an attic story, the central one set farther back than the other two. The gateway in the Corinth agora, which spanned the Lechaion roadway, is also impressive: there, a wide arch set between two pairs of pilasters and under a heavy attic story is flanked by two smaller arches leading to the colonnades lining the roadway. The triple arch seems in fact to have been more frequent in the east than in the west, a preference that may be largely explained by its close association with the street. Of course there are single-vaulted monumental arches at the entrance to some cities, as in Bosra, Gerasa (north gate), and Nicaea in Bithynia. Such an arch may also mark the entrance to a street, as in Korykos (mod. Korigos). In both these contexts, however, triple arches are also very frequently found. The two most famous are the one at Attaleia (mod. Antalya) in Pisidia (era of Hadrian) and the arch in Palmyra (PL. 190), which, by a trick of construction, disguised the change in direction of the main avenue (the arch had two separate façades constructed on diverging axes). There are other examples of triple arches in Hierapolis in Phrygia (between two towers, dating from the time of Commodus), at Diocaesarea (north gate), and at Antioch in Pisidia (Gate of C. Julius Asper, A.D. 212). The archway at Patara in Lycia with three equal vaults (2d–3d cent.) should also be mentioned, as well as the Arch of Plancia Magna (constructed between A.D. 117 and 122 behind the city gate in Perga), the arch at Anazarbus in Cilicia, and numerous others in Syria: in Damascus, Bosra, Gerasa, Jerusalem, and Petra (cf. also the triple gate of the Altis in Olympia, dating from the time of Nero).

In many cases the unity of the architectural decoration on the façades of these arches is maintained, as in the west, by the frame formed by the line of columns that bear the entablature and are surmounted by an attic story. But there are also cases where the façade is composed of two stories, as in Attaleia, probably in Bosra and Perga, and finally in Anazarbus, where the arch is remarkable for its curious decoration. The same principle is adopted in Athens in the Gate of Hadrian (PL. 187), where the arch of the gate is surmounted by a triple window on the upper story, in imitation of the Lesser Propylaeum in Eleusis or of an arch over a street in Ephesus. The design of the façades follows the architectural style of the times, particularly in the transition from the pilaster to the engaged column and the column on an isolated pedestal (cf. Attaleia, Anazarbus, Petra). A detail often found in the east deserves mention: it is the presence of little niches, with or without aediculas, that either flank the passages or surmount them. A very complex design is to be seen in the north gate of Gerasa, where the arch is flanked on both sides by a pair of columns, joined by a pediment and framing two superimposed aediculas (cf. a similar design in the Porta Maggiore in Rome; IV, PL. 199). These niches must have contained statues, a fact that also explains the occasional presence of consoles similar to the ones on street columns, as in Patara, Diocaesarea, and Bosra. At Perga and on the island of Thasos, among other places, remains of sculpture have been found. The eastern arch — and this is what distinguishes it particularly from the western arch — was rarely decorated with sculptured reliefs (cf. the isolated fragments at Antioch in Pisidia); following the sound traditions of Hellenism, the façade was treated as an architectural structure and not as a support for reliefs. It is interesting to note that at a late date the Arch of Galerius in Salonika (PL. 198) literally disappeared under its sculptural decoration, while the Arch of Janus (IX, PL. 35) in the Forum Boarium in Rome is nothing but a mass of niches.

The structure of the Arch of Galerius is very complicated: its three openings on the Egnatian Way are formed by two ranks of four piers; it was possible to pass through these ranks and walk laterally into the street leading to the Mausoleum of Galerius. A similar plan appeared at an even earlier date in Bosra at a crossroads, and in this connection the tetrapylons, or four-façaded arches, should be mentioned that were set in colonnaded streets, as in Gerasa, Philippopolis, Perga, and Laodicea ad Mare. An unusual tetrapylon is the one in the "Camp of Dio-

cletian" in Palmyra; it is a large square structure with three passages and a normal entablature on each face. Nothing certain is known about the top.

The arch, which finally became a feature of every important town, is considered to be a result of western influence. However, some monumental gates remained faithful to the traditions of Greek classicism. These are to be found particularly in the great centers of western Asia Minor. For example at Ephesus there is a series of monuments dating from the Hellenistic epoch to A.D. 200: first the western entrance to the agora with an Ionic colonnade on a parascenia plan; then, dating from the beginning of the Empire, the port gateway of the street that was to become the Arcadiane. This had three gates, the middle one with a straight lintel, the other two vaulted and set between four piers formed by four columns each. Finally, there is the south gate of the port, with two stories of Corinthian columns, built on a triangular plan with a concave façade. There are two other examples in Miletus: one is the port gate near the north agora, formed by two groups of eight columns arranged in two lines along a central passage; the other is the propylaea of the south agora (PL. 189), a *frons scaenae* of two stories set before three arched gates.

Nymphaeums and libraries. At Miletus the agora gate led to the city nymphaeum, just as in Ephesus the Gate of Mithridates and Mazaeus led to the Library of Celsus. Various nymphaeums and fountains, libraries and propylaea — these were the structures that broke the monotony of the lines of columns. The fountain was indispensable in the cities of hot countries and appeared in highly varied forms. First there was the little nymphaeum in Bosra, which stood at a crossroads and consisted of a large semicircular apse behind a prostyle façade of four columns. This apse acquired monumental proportions in Gerasa, where it stood beside the propylaea of the Sanctuary of Artemis, and was approached through an opening in the great colonnade. The same idea had been adopted by Herodes Atticus in the nymphaeum at Olympia in the form of a simple apse (VI, FIG. 925), and in Corinth in the fountain of Peirene in a more complicated cruciform plan (VI, FIG. 915). But the nymphaeum that was to become the glory of the cities of the period was the type with a large architectural façade. One of the largest known examples is that in Philadelphia (mod. Amman), which covered about 230 ft. on a horseshoe plan; at regular intervals the Corinthian colonnade was interrupted by three arches, which opened onto three semicircular niches in the back wall. The three niches were also a feature of the nymphaeum of Side. Another type had a façade with aediculas on several levels; it was probably preferred to the preceding type and was adopted in Miletus, Aspendus, Sagalassus, Termessus, and Ephesus. Like the gateway in Miletus, it was modeled on the *frons scaenae*.

This was the façade that the son of Celsus used in Ephesus for the library dedicated as a heroon to his father. The plan of the building followed the principle also found in Pergamum and, in a simpler form, in Hadrian's Library in Athens. Essentially it consisted of a large rectangular hall with the walls pierced by niches. Two superimposed galleries gave access to the tiered niches and in the back wall was a large apse for a statue of a god. The crypt with the sarcophagus of Celsus was in the basement under the library.

Theaters, odeums, amphitheaters, and stadiums. In the eastern provinces the building of theaters was part of urban development and it was by no means rare for a single city to have several theaters. In Greece, with very few exceptions (such as Nicopolis and Gortyna), theaters had been built since classical or Hellenistic times, first and foremost in Athens, where the Roman *pulpitum*, or stage, made its first appearance. In Asia Minor, too, several theaters were adapted to the fashion of the day, like those in Priene, Miletus, and Ephesus (PL. 188; VII, FIG. 299). Most of the new theaters benefited particularly from the technical developments of the period; their construction was no longer closely governed by the natural configuration of the site: following the western technique the cavea, or auditorium, could be partially raised on powerful substructures, as in Sagalassus, or completely built up, as in Side, Palmyra, Gabala (mod. Geble), and Bosra. There were internal corridors and staircases for access to the seats; often a covered gallery ran all round the upper section of the cavea (cf. Termessus, where the principal entrance was at the top; Perga, where there were arcaded galleries; Aspendus; and Bosra). In fact the theater was transformed, like the forum, into a closed monument; the cavea was joined to the *scaena*, or stage building, which rose as high as the top of the cavea. The theaters were spacious enough to hold a very large audience (Miletus: diam. ca. 460 ft., ca. 25,000 spectators; Termessus: ca. 215 ft.; Ephesus: 25,000 spectators; Sagalassus: ca. 320 ft.; Perga: ca. 370 ft., ca. 12,000 spectators; Side: ca. 390 ft., ca. 13,000 spectators; Aspendus: ca. 315 ft., ca. 7,000 spectators; Apamea: ca. 475 ft., the largest known theater apart from that in Autun; Bosra: ca. 330 ft.).

Theater layout underwent definitive transformations at the time of the Empire. In the Roman west the cavea and orchestra were semicircular in shape, in order to allow for the development of the action. The orchestra, having lost its function, was used to accommodate the ceremonial seats of the leading citizens; later it was transformed into a *conistra*, or sandy arena, for amphitheater games. The Roman layout was uniformly adopted in Syria, while in Asia Minor, where Hellenistic traditions were stronger, a cavea extending beyond a semicircle was the general rule. Only at Aspendus was the semicircular shape used. The device of the parascenia, which was often adopted for the stage building, made it possible to cover the stage; in this respect the theater at Aspendus provides a good counterpart in the east to the theater at Orange in the west.

The most intricate problems for the architect were undoubtedly those involved in the design of the *frons scaenae*, or back wall of the stage. The principle is that of an architectural façade of two or even three stories, serving as a frame for the doors leading onto the proscenium, which numbered three or five, depending on the design. The variations of this design are normally classified in three main types: (1) The back wall of the stage was straight, and the decoration consisted of a series of two-columned aediculas, which were repeated on two or three levels, framing the doors or small intermediary niches. This system is found in its purest form in Aspendus, Ephesus, Termessus, and Sagalassus in Asia Minor, in Philippopolis (mod. Shahba) in Syria (the small theater), in the Odeum of Herodes Atticus in Athens, and at Stobi in Macedonia. (2) The back wall had a large axial niche framing the principal door, or *porta regia*, while the rest of the wall was straight as in the preceding type. The curved niche had a two-columned *prothyron* in front of the door. The aediculas were again arranged on different levels. This is the design at Aizani, Miletus, Gerasa, and Laodicea ad Lycum. (3) The stage wall was subdivided into three large niches corresponding to three doors: this was the case at Palmyra (two flat niches and a third curved one), at Bosra, and at Corinth (three curved niches).

According to an already long-established theory (E. R. Fiechter, *Die baugeschichtliche Entwicklung des antiken Theaters*, Munich, 1914) the straight wall must be considered as of "eastern" or, more specifically, of Hellenistic inspiration, whereas the niched wall can be regarded as "western" or of Roman or Italian invention. Attempts have been made to establish very clearly defined geographic zones for the distribution of these types. But the straight wall was also used in the Theater of Marcellus in Rome, and the single niche was very widely used in the west and in North Africa; the three niches, it is true, seem to have been unknown in Asia Minor. There is an obvious interrelation between the three types described and also between their regions.

These splendid buildings were not devoted solely to intellectual pastimes. The ruling passion of the times for arena entertainments resulted in the transformation of the orchestra into a *conistra*, or arena, and in measures for the protection of the spectators in the cavea, which often consisted merely in isolating the cavea by a sufficiently high wall. The most radical transformation occurred in Corinth and Philippi, where the *pulpitum* was abolished and the arena encroached substantially on the proscenium. At Stobi in Macedonia the proscenium had never existed and there was direct access to the *conistra*

down steps leading from the doors of the *scaena*; in a later form these steps were separated from the *conistra* by a raised wall. The room communicating with the *porta regia* was a small sacellum dedicated to Nemesis.

One more special feature should be mentioned: the combining of the theater with a temple or chapel. There are early examples in the west of a temple placed at the top of the cavea and on the axis (Theater of Pompey); in the east the only example of this arrangement is in Philadelphia. As already mentioned, however, it was the east that introduced the theater into the sanctuaries of Syria.

Related to the theater was the odeum, which was essentially a closed hall reserved for a rather limited audience (a few hundred people). At Gortyna and on the island of Thasos the outer odeum wall still followed the curve of the cavea, but the rectangular plan was the rule elsewhere. In these halls, which were sometimes rather small, the tiers of seats for the audience were arranged in segments of circles (Cretopolis, Termessus, Cnidus), and the proscenium was restricted in size and soberly decorated. However, there were also more grandiose constructions such as the Odeum of Agrippa in the Athens Agora, dating from the beginning of the 1st century. Here the semicircular cavea was

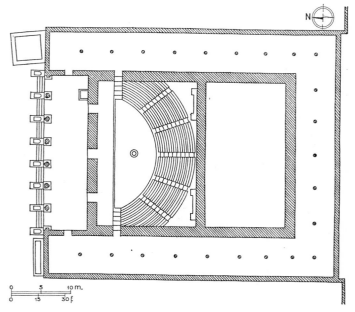

Athens, Agora, Odeum of Agrippa after its transformation in 2d century of our era, reconstructed plan (*from Thompson, 1950, p. 100*).

placed in a hall about 82 ft. square and was surrounded by raised galleries: this hall, which could contain an audience of a thousand, was reduced, no doubt for reasons of stability, when it was remodeled during the 2d century. The Odeum of Herodes Atticus in Athens also dates from the 2d century. This is in effect a small theater with a seating capacity of 5,000–6,000; it is not certain whether it was ever covered. Odeums of this type are to be found in Corinth (also built by Herodes Atticus), Epidaurus, Aphrodisias, and Ephesus.

The other monuments used for games and spectacles are less well known. The amphitheater — that typically Roman building — was undoubtedly less common in the east than in the west, which does not necessarily mean that bloody spectacles were any less popular in the east. In some cases stadiums as well as theaters could be adapted for these sports. Present knowledge hardly extends beyond a list of the known amphitheaters (Corinth, Sparta, Cyzicus, Nysa, Perga, Aspendus, Comara, Jerusalem, and Pergamum, the last having an almost circular plan). The same applies to circuses (Gortyna, Antioch).

The stadium, on the contrary, which was of Greek origin, is known from some very famous examples. Herodes Atticus had tiered marble seats installed in the Athens stadium; at Delphi and Olympia the stadiums had monumental entrances. Outside Greece the traditional type of stadium with one straight end is to be found in Ephesus, Perga, and Gerasa. Elsewhere the two ends were rounded, as in Aphrodisias and Laodicea ad Lycum. At Aizani (FIG. 295) the straight end was closed by the stage wall of the adjoining theater. The dimensions were usually very large (at Aphrodisias the arena measured ca. 750 ft. in length, and the one at Laodicea, ca. 1,245 ft.). As in the theaters there were sometimes substantial substructures under the stands (Aphrodisias and Perga).

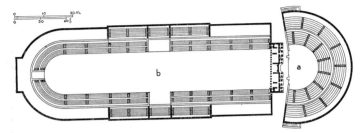

Aizani, theater and stadium, reconstructed plan. (a) Theater; (b) stadium (from L. Crema, L'architettura romana, Turin, 1959).

Thermae. There is no doubt that bathing establishments were no less popular in the eastern provinces than they were in the west. What is considered the chief invention of the Roman thermae, the combination of bath and gymnasium, seems to have been very generally accepted, and the technical problems appear to have been resolved in a similar manner. Even less is known about thermae than about triumphal arches, and this knowledge is confined to only a few places. Variations according to locality seem to have been considerable.

In the capital of the province of Asia, Ephesus, are the remains of four great bathing establishments, in addition to a fifth example dating from Byzantine times (the Baths of Scholastikia). They were all combined with a gymnasium, that is, the bath complex was flanked on one side by a spacious colonnaded court, which in turn was surrounded by various rooms. The public function of this part of the building is indicated by the presence of the chamber for emperor worship in this court. This has already been mentioned, as well as the fact that in the harbor baths the gymnasium is followed by a second enormous court, the porticoed court of Verulanus (probably a xystus).

A typical feature of these thermae in Ephesus is the fact that the gymnasium section, or area dedicated to physical and intellectual training, encroaches on the bathing area with a very large, elongated hall, which often assumes highly complicated forms: it is H-shaped in the Gymnasium of Vedius, where it lies between the gymnasium and the baths; in the

harbor baths it is a great oblong hall stretching the length of the building near the gymnasium with a swimming pool in the center; in the theater baths it has a [-shaped plan and lies beyond the bathing halls; in the east thermae a similarly planned hall contains the whole bathing establishment, which again adjoins the gymnasium. The main axis of the bathing halls is the same as in the west: *natatio*, frigidarium, tepidarium, caldarium. The great caldarium, a hall with large niches along the sides, may be placed axially or transversely, and is always flanked on both sides by a pair of subsidiary rooms, so that the complex has a transverse axis formed by these five juxtaposed rooms. This arrangement occurs in Aphrodisias and also in the Humei Tepe baths in Miletus, where these five rooms form the main body of the establishment (classified as *Reihentyp* by German archaeologists).

While Ephesus seems to have created a local type, the situation is more complex at Miletus. The small baths just mentioned adhere closely to the plan of the Greek gymnasium. In the Baths of Faustina (FIG. 296) the bathing halls are arranged in a ring and are flanked by a very long room (mouseion), similar to the ones in Ephesus. The Baths of Capito had two courts adjoining the thermae: one was a gymnasium and the other contained a large swimming pool. The rooms had an axial and symmetrical plan.

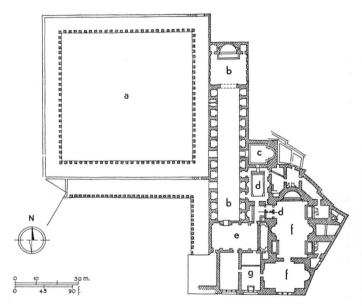

Miletus, Baths of Faustina, reconstructed plan. (a) Gymnasium; (b) Mouseion and apodypterium; (c) frigidarium (?), later used for water storage; (d) frigidariums; (e) tepidarium; (f) caldariums; (g) sudatorium (from Milet, I, 9, Berlin, 1928, p. 93).

A layout more akin to the "imperial" plan of the West is found in Alexandria Troas, Antioch, and undoubtedly elsewhere in Syria; but for this region knowledge is limited to a catalogue of the sites of the thermae.

As in the West, urban development in general and the construction of the thermae in particular made the building of large aqueducts necessary. What these works owed to Hellenistic tradition cannot yet be established with any certainty; it should be noted that in Antioch the name of the Roman architect Cossutius — who worked for Antiochus III (ruled 223–187 B.C.) — was engraved on one of the oldest conduits in the city, which he no doubt installed.

At the beginning of the Christian era, aqueducts were built in many places, among them Patras, Ephesus, Laodicea ad Lycum, and Jerusalem. Extensive ruins have been found, particularly in Ephesus, Anazarbus, and Aspendus, where there is a very remarkable pressure conduit (1st cent.). These aqueducts were similar in construction to those found in the west. When they ran overhead and crossed valleys, they were composed of several stories of arches.

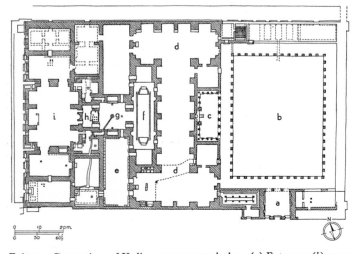

Ephesus, Gymnasium of Vedius, reconstructed plan. (a) Entrance; (b) gymnasium; (c) aula of the imperial cult, with base that probably supported statue of Antoninus Pius; (d) room for gymnastic exercises and games; (e) apodyterium; (f) swimming pool; (g) frigidarium; (h) tepidarium; (i) caldarium (from J. Keil, Ephesos, Vienna, 1955, p. 47).

Basilicas. Nothing is at present known about the origin of the Roman basilica. In the Corinth agora there are three basilicas built on the usual plan; they all consist of a hall with a central nave surrounded by a colonnaded gallery; the largest, stretching along the Lechaion roadway, has a deep vestibule and, at the other end, a tribune between two adjoining rooms. The southern basilica has three niches on one of its long sides opposite the entrance; the Basilica Julia is a simple oblong hall with an entrance on one of its long sides. In the 2d century Asia Minor introduced an entirely new concept. Not only did the basilica here occupy a whole side of the porticoed court of the forum, but it opened through a simple colonnade onto the central square — in other words, the fourth portico of the court was developed to form a hall with several aisles. This system was adopted in Cremna and especially in Smyrna (mod. İzmir), which had one of the most grandiose forums of the period. The basilica is of the type with a central nave surrounded by two-storied galleries; on the side of the square the upper gallery was separated by a partition from the rest of the hall. At Aspendus the basilica, which had several aisles, formed an isolated building. Among the other buildings connected with the forum should be mentioned a few examples of the bouleuterion in the form of a hall with tiered seats in the shape of a horseshoe or semicircle, as in Thasos, Corinth, and Palmyra. Little is known about the layout of the Capitol in the east, although there is evidence of the worship of Jupiter Capitolinus or the Capitoline Triad.

Palaces and houses. Although palaces existed in the east from a very early date, information on palace architecture in the imperial period is very scanty. Yet a man like Herod built a great many princely palaces, as well as castles and strongholds. Only the ground plan of the palace of Masada (El Sebbe, Metsada) has survived. This seems to conform to the old eastern formula of a complex of buildings centered on courtyards (VIII, cols. 905–06). Remains of the palace of Jericho have also been partially excavated: on one side there is a structure that resembles a gymnasium or palestra; on the other a large garden terrace with an exedra and pools. The so-called "palace" at Petra is still problematic.

The important complex of ruins of the Palace of the Dux at Dura-Europos, which must have been constructed at the beginning of the 3d century, yields fuller information. The building has a large peristyle court, which serves as an entrance, a peristyle house in Hellenistic style, and a series of reception rooms with terraces overlooking the Euphrates. This last part is related to the villa with porticoes and projecting wings found in the west and has affinities with the Palace of Diocletian in Spalato (mod. Split, Yugoslavia). Other features, especially the architectural group formed by the room with an axial apse between two pairs of lateral rooms, can be related to the *praetoria* of the military camps and particularly to the so-called "Sanctuary of the Standards" in the Camp of Diocletian in Palmyra (the camp that some scholars claim was the palace of the princes of Palmyra, but which appears to be of decidedly later date).

With such incomplete data it is not possible to define the part played by Syria in the development of the palace during the late Empire. The Diocletian palace in Antioch is only a memory, just as there is little known about the Palace of Philip the Arabian in Philippopolis, the city that bears his name. The same is true of other palaces, in Constantinople and Salonika, for example.

Information on domestic architecture is also very limited, chiefly because the documentation is widely dispersed and inadequately classified. Ruins of houses of the Roman period are frequently discovered, but the results are very seldom published (an example is the villa at Corinth). In Syria, however, the sites of Antioch and Palmyra have furnished a mass of useful data, to which further information from Baalbek and Byblos in Lebanon can be added. There it appears that the peristyle house in the Hellenistic tradition still persisted. Local types existed, naturally, as in northern Syria, where the villa was reduced to a single building with a galleried upper floor and a court in front.

Funerary monuments. Whereas classical and Hellenistic Greece was always poor in funerary monuments other than sculptured and painted steles, Asia Minor employed Greek artists at a very early date to design monumental tombs; thus it became the homeland of the mausoleum, which had considerable influence throughout the ancient world. Under the Empire there was a great variety of these monuments in the eastern provinces, although as far as it is possible to judge, the greater contribution in this field seems to have been made in the west.

The part played by regional and local traditions was decisive in funerary architecture. Thus, since earliest antiquity the hypogeum had been common in Egypt and Syria, but was more rarely found in Asia Minor. In the necropolises of Alexandria, dating from the imperial period, there are hypogeums of all sizes [Anfouchi, Hadra, Gabbari, El Meks (Mex)], in which the sculptured or painted decoration is of greater interest than the architecture. This is also true of certain Phoenician hypogeums (Tyre, Sidon, Masyaf in Syria). In Syria and Palestine there is a series of rock tombs with monumental façades, for example the tombs dating from the period of the kings around Jerusalem. Normally the façade has a columned porch bearing an entablature. Inside, a series of rooms is grouped around a vestibule-hall; at first the bodies were laid in loculi, but these were later replaced by the system of sarcophagi placed in an arcosolium. Tombs of the same kind are found in northern Syria (Frikya) and southern Syria (Auranitis). A large group of hypogeums exists in Palmyra. The façade is simply an austerely decorated door at the foot of the staircase leading down from ground level or from a funerary tower. Beyond the vestibule there is a single room or a group of chambers arranged in the form of a cross or a T. Painted or sculptured architectural decoration separates the high bays holding the loculi (e.g., the Tomb of Julius Aurelius Maqqai and that of the Three Brothers). At the ends of the chambers there are sometimes *kline* (couch) sarcophagi arranged in triclinium form (PL. 193). The famous tombs of Petra are cut out of the rock (PL. 193); they are more remarkable for their sculptured façades than for their interior layout (see below). The raised tombs are also of considerable architectural interest. In Syria and Anatolia they often consisted merely of sarcophagi placed side by side. For protective reasons these monuments were raised on pedestals with several steps, or on some other support, and were then covered. The necropolis at Termessus has an unusually rich selection of the different types of protective aediculas, of which the final elaboration was the funerary temple. The aedicula tomb is found in varying forms depending on its location. It does not always contain the sarcophagus or sarcophagi, which may be laid inside the podium, or even in a hypogeum. At Ephesus there is a Corinthian monopteron of this type with six columns and a conical roof ending in a tuft of acanthus, as well as an octagonal Corinthian monument on a square base, surmounted by a stepped pyramid; in both cases the funerary chamber is in the podium. In two neighboring regions, Commagene and northern Syria, a simple kind of aedicula was very widespread: this was a sort of tetrapylon on a podium, first with straight architraves (Assar), then with arches, in both cases covered by a pyramid ('Alif, Hassan-oglu, northern Dana, and Brad); at Cyrrhus the monument was hexagonal.

A more elaborate type is the tomb on the plan of a house. At Palmyra (cf. also the examples at Hatra) there is an obvious adaptation of the peristyle court. The building is completely closed on the outside, and its severity is tempered only by classical architectural decoration [Qasr el-Haye, the Tomb of A'ailami and Zebīda (or Aailamis and Zenobius), etc.]; in one case a prostyle colonnade gives the impression of a funerary temple. In western Syria as in Asia Minor, there developed rather early a form that was later to become quite widespread: this was a square building with a cruciform central plan, as a rule covered by a dome. At Kedesh (Qedesh) in Upper Galilee the arms of the cross were occupied by loculi; elsewhere there were arcosolium niches, which were to be definitively adopted, as in Scythopolis (mod. Beth Shan), Samaria (mod. Sebastye), and Philadelphia (mod. Amman). This type is also found in central Syria at Sednaya and Philippopolis, and, dating from a later period, at Hass and Ruweha in northern Syria. In Asia Minor the Tomb of Claudia Antonia Sabina at Sardis was a famous example, and to this may be added a newly discovered tomb at Side, which is probably of later date. Finally in Athens there is the Monument of Philoappos (PL. 187), of the family of the last kings of Commagene. This monument, built between 114 and 116, has a curved northern façade that would appear to be unique in its architectural and figured decoration. More ambitious isolated monuments were the mausoleum in Attaleia (1st cent.), which, like the Tomb of Caecilia Metella in Rome, had a cylindrical drum on a square ground floor; or the mausoleum on the island of Papanisi, probably dating from the 2d or 3d century, which had a pyramid above a circular funerary chamber set in a square ground floor; or the final grandiose example of the Mausoleum of Galerius in Salonika, an imposing domed rotunda with six rectangular niches surmounted by eight windows (diameter, ca. 80 ft.). Finally, there was the funerary temple. Side offers the best example of a funerary temenos with two courts, one leading into the other; in the second a prostyle temple was built with arcosolium niches in the interior (3d cent.).

The monument in the form of a temple constitutes a return to the mausoleum in its original classical form. But the mausoleum is in fact a complex monument, easily identifiable by its structure: a base with steps, usually a solid block for the ground floor, an upper floor with a real or engaged colonnade, and a pyramidal roof. It was in Syria — and not in Asia Minor — that the great Carian monument had a long development. The oldest examples go back to the Hellenistic period, for instance the Mausoleum of Chamrate at Suwaida (a single-storied structure, now destroyed) and the Hermel mausoleum in the Biqa region. While these two monuments had a solid block surmounting the burial chamber, others had an internal chamber, for example the vanished Mausoleum of C. Julius Sampsigeramus at Homs (anc. Emesa), and the so-called "Mausoleum of Diogenes" at Hass. Similar monuments are to be found in Serrin and Urfa (anc. Edessa). With the exception of Hass, which has a real peripteros on the upper story, only applied architectural decoration is found elsewhere. These Syrian mausoleums, with their simple, austere structure, their plan based on a square, their tall proportions, and their pyramidal tops, served as models outside their own country: their influence can be traced across the whole of North Africa and as far as Spain and Gaul.

There are indications that these tall mausoleums assumed a significance that the original model did not have: they are in fact steles, or vertical stone slabs. Not only in Suwaida and Hermel but also in Jerusalem ["Tomb of Absalom" (VIII, PL. 331) and "Tomb of Zechariah"] there are solid blocks cut from the rock indicating the presence of a hypogeum; the same is true in Petra, and texts clearly illustrate this primary function of the funerary tower in Palmyra. It must be borne in mind that these towers were transformed only at a late date into real burial places provided with loculi on several stories, and were originally no more than towers with an internal staircase, housing tombs in the basement. At first the towers were undoubtedly put to a practical use (perhaps as watchtowers), and a similar process of development seems to be evident in the towers of Auranitis, which are called "dovecots" in inscriptions. These towers — there are others, the Palmyra type at Dura-Europos and Halabiye, and a local type in Cilicia (Diocaesarea) — are all found in outlying regions; as monuments they may be considered as rustic substitutes for the other mausoleums of Roman Syria.

Another monument peculiar to Syria may also be included in the category of vertical stones: the distyle monument found in three places in the north of the country (Sermada, Sitt er-Rum, and Qatura, all 2d cent.). It has two columns or pillars joined by an entablature, without statues, urns, or any other objects, and simply marks the site of the tomb, which is constructed as a hypogeum. The origins of this type are still obscure.

Orders and decoration. In the choice of orders there was an increasing preference for the Corinthian, which prevailed almost exclusively in Syria, while the Ionic was more persistent in its place of origin, Asia Minor. There are also a few examples of composite capitals (e.g., the pronaos of the temple at Aizani) or even more hybrid combinations such as that of the Corinthian capitals with a frieze of Doric metopes (colonnades in Apamea). But "irregular" forms were less frequent than in the Hellenistic period; this fact has been analyzed in detail in Syria, where a new classicism seems to have arisen in the time of Augustus, especially in a great center like Antioch (adaptation of the Vitruvian capital). In any case, under the early Empire a uniform imperial style pervaded the whole of Syria and penetrated into peripheral areas like Auranitis and Palmyra; it was in architecture especially that these regions became most deeply Romanized.

In the elevation as a whole, certain characteristic features developed; the shafts of the columns were usually smooth; they were frequently placed on plinths; the frieze was reduced in height and became protuberant in outline. The decoration of foliated scrolls and acanthus leaves followed a well-known cycle, passing from the naturalistic carving of the beginning of the Empire to the rather stiff carving of the following centuries. In some places there are regional characteristics, which are often Hellenistic survivals. In Auranitis and Baalbek, for example, the meander occupied an unusual place in the decoration either in the cornice or the architrave. The friezes of the temple of Baalbek were supported by means of raised corbels surmounted by the forequarters of bulls and lions; raised corbels appear in the same position in a temple in Side and in the Temple of Trajan in Pergamum; earlier examples are those in the octagon at Ephesus. In Syria the intercolumniation of a façade or colonnade is often spanned by an arch, whose moldings continue without interruption those of the architrave of the colonnade. This "Syrian" arch, which is certainly of Oriental origin, was widespread throughout Asia Minor; but we also find there the independent arch, with the architrave interrupted above the intercolumniation. The arch, however, except in the case of the monumental arch, had a relatively limited place in the east. The existence of a colonnade with arches in the funerary temenos of Side has nonetheless recently been established. This is a pendant to the one built at the same time in the Severan forum in Leptis Magna.

Generally speaking, the development of ornamentation and moldings was toward uniformity and simplification. The difference between the Temple of Bel in Palmyra and the temples of Baalbek is striking in this respect. Syria, however, had some unusual decorative features that deserve mention, for example the decoration of the gates in Palmyra and Baalbek. The fasciae of the arches of these gateways are richly decorated. This seems to have been a Syrian tradition, since Asia Minor and the west have nothing really comparable; during the late Empire a very similar decoration was used on the gates of Diocletian's Palace in Spalato. Palmyra and Baalbek are also famous for their richly decorated ceilings, namely, those of the peristyles of temples and of the adytum in Palmyra and those of the monumental altar in Baalbek. The coffered ceiling, both decorated and undecorated, is essentially in the Greek tradition, and some examples dating from the late Empire are also known in Asia Minor (as in the Temple of Serapis in Miletus). In Syria the design is complicated and geometric: squares, rectangles, diamonds, triangles, and circles combine and intersect, as they also do in Roman mosaics. In this design animal and human figures occupy a limited place in Palmyra and in the Baalbek altar, but the ceilings of the so-called "Temple of Bacchus" in Baalbek are all covered with a geometric design in which busts of gods appear.

The inclusion of human or animal figures in architectural decoration occurs early in Greek art, but this does not help to solve the problem of their origin. In Asia Minor and Syria such motifs appear long before imperial times, for example, the famous feminine figure among the foliated scrolls of the Temple of Trajan in Pergamum, the one on the monumental arch of the baths at Aphrodisias, and, quite recently discovered, the one above the door of the cella of the Temple of Hadrian in Ephesus. There were also the atlantes, of which various related buildings provided monumental examples, such as the "Façade of the Captives" in the Corinth agora, the "Incantada" in Salonika, and the "Portico of the Giants" in Athens, which constituted the façade of the Odeum of Agrippa in its remodeled 2d-century form. Foliated scrolls with figures are found everywhere: on a beamed coffered ceiling in Palmyra, on the doors of the Temple of Bacchus in Baalbek, on the pilasters of the arch of the baths in Aphrodisias (Istanbul, Archaeol. Mus.). The latter closely resemble the famous pilasters of Leptis Magna, a similarity that has contributed to the assignment of an important role to the "Aphrodisias school" at a certain stage in the history of architectural decoration. These baths also had large brackets with the heads of mythological figures, and these 2d-century examples have precursors in the frieze of the Court of Tiberius, where the garland, in itself quite commonplace, rests on a row of heads, masks, gods, and heroes.

These problems of architectural influence still remain obscure, however. Baalbek provides a clearer instance. The city and the sanctuary underwent a great development as a result of the foundation of the Roman colony under Augustus. E. Weigand (1924) formulated the famous and substantially correct hypothesis that the two great temples there were Roman in type. This was confirmed more recently by a study of the altar ceilings; the connection between certain slabs and the Ara Pacis in Rome seems clear and there is good reason to believe that teams of craftsmen and overseers from Rome worked on them. Other slabs, however, give evidence of the adapting of motifs by local workmen. It should also be mentioned that, according to another recent study, the Ara Pacis itself has very close affinities with the decorative art of Pergamum.

A form of architectural decoration already mentioned, the *frons scaenae*, deserves special discussion. Unlike the classical and Hellenistic architects, those of imperial times seem to have had a strong dislike of bare walls. Any conspicuous wall tended to be given architectural decoration. Initially this was merely applied, then it was done in higher relief, and finally it was sometimes set in front of the back wall. Two elements prevailed in this decoration in varying degrees: the column, and the aedicula framing a niche. The development took place in the course of the 1st century; it seems that the Flavian period marked the final triumph of a decorative scheme that is of rather uncertain origin.

This decoration was applied extensively. It is found first of all on large external façades, as in the specific case of the *frons scaenae* of the theater, as well as in nymphaeums and other monuments: libraries (Ephesus), propylaea (agora of Miletus), various mausoleums (the Philopappos Monument in Athens, the tombs of Petra); the triumphal arch must also be mentioned in this context.

This type of decoration was then applied to interior walls. In Syria the walls of temple cellas were gradually invaded by architectural decoration; applied or projecting columns framed the aediculas, which were generally on two levels. A good example is the Temple of Bacchus in Baalbek. Occasionally niches arranged on several levels are also to be found on the wall of the pronaos, on both sides of the cella door. This type of decoration often adorns other chambers, for example, the exedras of the large court at Baalbek. At Ephesus and elsewhere, chambers dedicated to emperor worship have this decoration, and there are many other examples of its use (the atrium of the harbor baths in Ephesus, the propylaea of the sanctuary of Artemis at Gerasa, and the gate at Side).

The *frons scaenae* proper consists of aediculas on several levels. Two types can be distinguished. In the first the structural function of the decoration is maintained. In the theater of Aspendus (cf. also the nymphaeum of the same town) the decoration served to underline the position of the doors. The *porta regia* was surmounted by a large triangular pediment, which linked two aediculas; each end of the *scaena* was marked by a half pediment above the last aedicula. The propylaea in the Miletus agora had a similar decoration, clearly architectural in its composition. The second type of decoration was entirely different; it literally covered all the available wall space with a forest of small columns. Thus in the nymphaeum in Miletus and the Library of Celsus in Ephesus the aediculas are not set exactly one above the other, but those of the second level span the intervals between those of the first, while those of the third

are in alignment with those of the first level. Here architecture has given way to decoration.

A detailed study of this kind of decoration may be made from the rock façades of the tombs in Petra. Moreover, in Petra one can follow the development from indigeneous forms (tombs with rows of merlons, or with steps at the corners), which first incorporated features of classical architecture, particularly in the doors and at the corners, and were finally replaced by later forms. Here, too, one can follow the transition from features which still had an architectural function to those which were purely decorative. Thus the famous "el-Khazna" (PL. 193; VII, FIGS. 308, 309) — perhaps the tomb of king Aretas IV — has the façade of a Corinthian temple at ground level; the decoration grows fanciful on the upper story, with the small tholos placed between two structures bearing half pediments; this is perhaps based on the idea of a porticoed court surrounding a funerary tholos. Later one finds enormous façades weighed down under ranks of superimposed columns.

This imperial "baroque," which was the complete antithesis of the functional inspiration of Greek architecture, was the sign of an evolution that had reached its end, the product of a civilization that, at least in certain fields, was condemned to variations on a hackneyed theme.

Building techniques. The general development of Roman architecture is dominated by problems of building technique: certain programs could be executed only by means of special techniques. It is now necessary to define the place of the eastern provinces within this evolution.

As is well known, classical Greek and Hellenistic building was based almost entirely on the dry-masonry technique, and its problem was therefore one of stonecutting. Far from declining under the Empire, this technique even spread to new domains in Asia Minor, and especially in Syria, the traditional land of light building materials. Study of the "dead cities" in northern Syria has revealed what enormous success Greek-trained stonecutters achieved there; in peripheral regions and in remote villages there is still evidence of this refined technique, which finally won its independence: an individual style, very different in its sober decoration from that of the large towns of the period, established itself there in the first centuries of the Christian era. But during the imperial age stonecutters everywhere showed great skill and precision in the carving of large blocks, of stone, drums of columns, moldings, and decorative motifs.

This technique could be readily adapted to colossal structures, as is sufficiently proved by Baalbek, Palmyra, and other sites, but it was inadequate for solving certain roofing problems, particularly those of vaults and domes. The important role played by arches in the architecture of the eastern provinces has already been noted; that of the vault was certainly less important. In southern Syria, in Auranitis, a land poor in timber and rich in stone, the roof was often constructed by means of a series of arches joined by flat slabs of stone, not with a masonry vault. At the beginning of the Empire, in Corinth and Athens, the cryptoporticus of the basilicas and the Odeum of Agrippa had a horizontal roof, whereas in the west, where the system originated, vaulting was used. Later, in Asia Minor particularly, the vault was rather widely used in the building of theaters, stadiums, and thermae. J. Ward Perkins (1958), in a study devoted to these problems of building technique in Asia Minor during imperial times, has pointed out the slowness with which mortar masonry was introduced into these regions and the difficulties it always encountered there.

At the beginning of the Empire masonry with a facing of *opus reticulatum* is occasionally found, particularly in Cilicia — at Elaioussa (Sebaste) and Korykos — and in Syria — in Herod's buildings in Jericho and Samaria (mod. Sebastye) and the Mausoleum of C. Julius Sampsigeramus in Homs (anc. Emesa). It was a passing fashion, which can perhaps be attributed to the presence of teams of workers from Italy.

Later the vault developed, but the east proved incapable of making the cement-hard mortar that Italian masons produced with the help of pozzuolana. The mortar used in the east was usually of inferior quality with much stone filling, and the eastern architects preferred to cover the vault with fine stonework rather than simple masonry. The use of brick developed even more slowly; it became widespread only in the 3d century (cf. on this point the funerary temenos in Side, which must date from the time of Severus). Large domes were much rarer in the east than in the west: a monument such as the rotunda of the Aesculapium in Pergamum can be considered an imitation of the Pantheon in Rome. Vaults, domes, and brickwork — elements that were to characterize Byzantine building, particularly in Asia Minor — were not greatly favored by the imperial architects; it can be said that it was only with the decline of the west that these forms and techniques took firm and definitive root in the lands of the Hellenized east.

The same timidity or the same traditionalism is apparent in the conception of masses, volume, and planes. The eastern provinces have nothing to compare with those buildings so typical of the genius of the western architects, such as Hadrian's Villa near Tivoli (PL. 291; III, PL. 386) or the villa at Piazza Armerina in Sicily. In pomp and grandeur, on the other hand, the east can bear comparison with the west, for these two qualities, sometimes considered so typically Roman, were freely expressed in the architecture of the eastern Empire.

SCULPTURE. *Schools and artists.* The prestige of sculpture remained undiminished under the Empire: the Roman conquest contributed to the preservation of this great legacy of Hellenism in the old centers of Greece and Asia Minor, and to its diffusion throughout the other provinces of the east.

Of the Hellenistic "schools," one in particular appears to have been associated with the artistic education of Rome, the Neo-Attic school, whose influence during the 150 years preceding the Christian Era was decisive in definitively establishing the prestige of the great works of Hellenic classicism (see NEO-ATTIC STYLES). Throughout this period constant requests were addressed to the workshops and artists of Athens and the rest of Greece; from the eve of the Empire and its early years a whole series of names associated with more or less famous works has survived: Kleomenes, son of Kleomenes (pseudo-Germanicus; in the Louvre); Apollonios, son of Nestor ["Belvedere torso," (VII, PL. 367), boxer (VII, PL. 366)], Sosibios [marble amphora (X, PL. 264)], Pontios [rhyton (Rome, Palazzo dei Conservatori, Mus. Nuovo)], Salpion [crater (X, PL. 264)]. Tradition has preserved the names of other famous sculptors, such as C. Avianus Evander and Arkesilaos. These Athenians and Greeks shared the favor of the Romans with other artists no less Greek or Hellenized from southern Italy, especially Pasiteles, his pupil Stephanos, and the latter's disciple Menelaos. There are indications that this privileged position of Hellenic sculpture persisted under the Empire. From the Appian Way, for example, comes a caryatid attributed to the 2d century and signed by Kriton and Nikolaos (Rome, Torlonia Coll.). To the first of these sculptors, who declared himself Athenian, we owe a Mithras Tauroctonous, unique of its kind, dressed in a Greek tunic, which was discovered quite recently in a sanctuary in Ostia Antica (Mus. Ostiense). At about the same period another Greek named Demetrios produced another unusual figure of the same Persian god, this time portrayed standing, for the Mithraeum of Mérida in Spain (Mérida, Mus. Arqueológico). Finally, another famous name in this tradition is that of Zenodoros, Nero's favorite artist and the sculptor of the colossal Mercury of the Arverni.

The best known and most significant instance of all this artistic activity is the "school" of Aphrodisias. It arose at the very beginning of the Christian Era. A certain M. Cossutius of Aphrodisias, who is known from an inscribed base from Paros, must be associated with M. Cossutius Cerdo (Kerdon), and M. Cossutius Menelaos, a pupil of Stephanos, the disciple of Pasiteles. Possibly they were members of the same workshop managed by some Roman businessman dealing in works of art. (The conditions under which Greek artists came to work in Rome have been specifically recorded in the case of C. Avianius Evander.) The sculptors of Aphrodisias are known from their works and signatures during the first three centuries of our era and throughout the Empire: in Corinth, Olympia, Paros, Lyttos in Crete, Cyrene, Sorrento, and Rome. Their works were certainly exported in some cases, but more often they were undoubtedly created on the spot by itinerant sculptors. One of these, Zeno, who was buried in the capital, boasts in the epitaph of his funerary herm that he had passed through numerous cities in the course of his life and a number of Roman signatures suggests that this artist had a workshop on the banks of the Tiber. Certain Carian masters enjoyed imperial favor, for example, Aristeas and Papias, who produced a pair of centaurs mounted by Erotes for Hadrian's Villa near Tivoli (PL. 194; the Eros is lost), and, perhaps, the Antonianos who carved an Antinous as Sylvanus (Rome, Banca Romana, Palazzo Ruspoli).

It is certainly not possible to speak of an Aphrodisias "school" if this term supposes a coherent set of traditions and a common inspiration. The works that have come down to us are primarily eclectic, like those of the above-mentioned masters from Athens. The entire Greek heritage runs through them: that of the two great centuries of classicism first and foremost, but also the heritage of Pergamum and Rhodes; and throughout this period these traditions were used indiscriminately. Nothing shows more clearly that the artist of antiquity was very little concerned with originality. The groups of sculptures preserved in the eastern half of the Empire — and there are several important ones, but not from Aphrodisias, for example the Muses from the Baths of Faustina in Miletus (Istanbul, Archaeol. Mus.), the allegorical figures from the Library of Celsus in Ephesus, various statues from the gymnasiums and nymphaeums of Ephesus, the nymphaeum of Miletus, etc. — reveal the works of copyists and adapters, just as they do in Italy and the west. Their skill, which at times attained virtuosity, could not conceal the absence of true inspiration, and can only be described as eclectic and academic. The fame of such sculptors as Phidias, Polykleitos, and Praxiteles usually led sculptors under the Empire to sign their works, as they felt they were representations of the noblest art; but to us their works constitute the least vital part of all Roman art, while the more original creations of these centuries remain for the most part anonymous.

Portraits. These original creations are to be sought in certain specific fields: portraits, reliefs (mostly historical), and decorative sculpture.

As in the Hellenistic period, the portrait continued to enjoy unrivaled popularity, either for political reasons (statues honoring some public figure) or religious reasons (funerary statues), whether the models were illustrious personages such as the emperor and members of his family, officials of every rank, or private citizens. Today, as a result of discoveries, particularly in Corinth, Olympia, and Athens, a gallery of the portraits of emperors as conceived by the artists of the eastern half of the Empire could be assembled from Greece and western Asia Minor alone; and this collection would undoubtedly be more eloquent than the well-known and extensively studied series of portraits (Athens, Nat. Mus.) of the Athenian *cosmetes* (civic officials), which was not from the best workshops of the time. A study of such a collection would be the only way of thoroughly testing the generally accepted opinion that the Hellenized east had its own inspiration, characterized by the persistence of Hellenic idealism, which tended to temper the brutalities of Roman realism. So far this inquiry has been made in detail only for the 3d century (L'Orange, 1933) and still has to be undertaken for the early Empire. Moreover western realism was countered not only by Greek idealism but also by certain tendencies native to Asia Minor, notably a predilection and feeling for decorative line.

Reliefs. A fundamental distinction between the two halves of the Empire has also been made, more or less justifiably, in the field of reliefs. The notable Roman invention was the historical relief covering triumphal monuments, arches, and columns, and it now seems certain that this kind of relief held a much less important place in the east, at least during the early Empire. Timid attempts such as those of the arches in Antioch

in Pisidia are significant in this respect. There are only two notable examples: the Monument of Philopappos in Athens (PL.
187) and a triumphal monument of the 2d century (probably
to Marcus Aurelius), the remains of which were discovered at
Ephesus (PL. 194). On the first is depicted the entrance of a
consul on his chariot preceded by lictors, very similar to the one
on the Arch of Titus in Rome (VII, PL. 262); on the second,
the customary scenes of battle and sacrifice were combined with
allegorical representations: the apotheosis of the emperor borne
up to heaven on the chariot of Helios and preceded by the chariot
of Selene drawn by two deer. This set of panels shows a style
very different from that which was current in the capital at the
time and is a further indication of the persistence of the traditions of Hellenic classicism.

Before defining the main point of contrast between east and
west, one should try to distinguish the centers and workshops
of the eastern provinces. For the 2d century, in fact, there are
several groups of reliefs: in Athens itself there is the Dionysiac
cycle of the *pulpitum* of the Theater of Dionysos (apparently
dating from Hadrian's time; PL. 194); in Smyrna, the figures
of the twelve gods on the large panels from the agora; at Aphrodisias, a series of pedestals decorated with a gigantomachy; and
at Miletus, the reliefs of the Roman monument of the bouleuterion. Except for the last, which was characterized by a rather
dry local style, these monuments seem for the most part to be
characterized by a marked taste for the high relief that is almost
sculpture in the round, for airy, frontal composition, and for
softly rounded forms. This same style, in a rather loose and ornamental version, recurs in the decorative art of Aphrodisias,
which survives chiefly in the remains of the thermae: capitals
and frieze panels, pilasters with animated scrolls, and figured
corbels (Istanbul, Archaeol. Mus.). The affinity of subject
and style between these monuments and those recently discovered at Leptis Magna — in the Severan basilica — is immediately striking and archaeologists have not hesitated to attribute
the African works to what is still commonly termed the school
of Aphrodisias. Undoubtedly the problem is a far broader one,
both for mythological reliefs and for decorative sculpture. There
are other examples of decorative sculpture in Asia Minor itself
that deserve mention or comparison: apart from the well-known
pillar of Cyzicus (Istanbul, Archaeol. Mus.), there are those of
the Library of Celsus in Ephesus and the feminine figure in the
foliated scroll in the Temple of Hadrian, also in Ephesus, as
well as the pillar found in Rome itself. Although it is impossible
to distinguish a style peculiar to the statuary of Aphrodisias —
at least from the signed statues — may it not be possible to
define an ornamental style characteristic of that Carian center?
The known examples of decorative sculpture still require closer
examination, however, and even then may not provide enough
information for a final answer.

Sarcophagi. The problem of the workshops is crucial for
our knowledge of another form of decorative sculpture — the
sarcophagus. In the 2d century the sculptured sarcophagus
became extremely widespread throughout the Empire and remained so for about 200 years. Certain clear and simple characteristics make it possible to distinguish between the production of the eastern and western halves of the Roman world.
In keeping with Hellenic tradition, the east decorated the four
faces of the sarcophagus, and not just three as was the practice
in Rome; as a covering it used the *kline* with or without a reclining figure, or a ridged lid with scale ornamentation (PL. 195).
The architectural structure was always well defined.

In the east several series of sarcophagi can be distinguished
and attributed to particular centers with a fair degree of certainty.
Thus Greece, probably Athens, produced the sarcophagus in
the form of an empty *kline* with carved feet at the angles; a more
developed form replaced the feet with figures — atlantes framing
large mythological panels. Sometimes, as in the sarcophagi with
Erotes, this structure was missing.

The distinguishing feature of the workshops of Asia Minor
was that they evolved an architectural type of sarcophagus
with columns. The long sides were subdivided into three aediculas with small twisted columns and concave triangular

pediments decorated with Oriental-type shells; on the short
sides was depicted the gate of Hades. The lid took the form
of a *kline* with a reclining figure of the deceased, or that of a
ridged roof. Figures were set in sharp isolation between the
columns; everything was small-scale sculpture in the round and
the whole composition, even in detail, recalled the *frons scaenae*
that held such an important place in the architecture of the times.
Details of structure and technique have made it possible to distinguish at least two local series [one of them Lydian, the other
called the Sidamara type after the place of origin of the first
known example (II, PL. 465)], but it is impossible to locate the
workshops (Ephesus or Smyrna?) with any certainty. This type
underwent various developments, as in the sarcophagus with
five arched panels on the long sides, which was quite common
(it was adapted to the Labors of Hercules); and a series like the
sarcophagi found in Torre Nova in Minorca — large figured
panels between corner pilasters — has some connection with
this type despite a strong Attic influence.

Another type — the most widespread, no doubt because
of its simplicity — is the garlanded sarcophagus: this had Erotes
at the corners and on the long sides marking the sinuous rhythm
of the garlands. An Anatolian, or more exactly a Pamphylian,
center is undoubtedly the source of one of these variants; very
recently discoveries in the necropolis of Perga (31 sarcophagi
of this type) have substantiated this hypothesis. The possibility
of other centers, however, must be admitted and explored,
for example, Alexandria (Erotes on plinths) and perhaps a
Syrian center (bunches of grapes hanging from the garlands).

The great number of sarcophagi discovered, their type
and style, and the kind of marble used made it possible to define these series and to form an idea of the workshops that produced them. The question, however, is a complex one. Recently
attempts have been made to localize these workshops near well-
known marble quarries, especially those of Proconnesus (mod.
Marmara), but this does not seem to afford a satisfactory explanation of the differences of composition and style. A study of
the distribution of the sarcophagi found so far reveals the remarkable fact that the east exported its production to the western half of the Empire, to Italy, especially to Rome, and also
to Gaul (Trinquetaille, La Gayolle) and Spain. On the other
hand, the west had no such exports to the east, and this curious
fact clearly emphasizes the prestige enjoyed by the sculptors
from the Hellenized part of the Empire. Naturally exchanges
occurred within the eastern half, with Athens undoubtedly
playing a dominant role. How did these exchanges take place?
The works must sometimes have been completed in the original
workshops and then exported, in spite of the difficulty of trans-
porting an elaborately carved sarcophagus. Elsewhere there are
indications that the artists may have accompanied the partially
executed work and finished it at its final destination (e.g., the
carving of heads and portraits); alternatively, a part of the decoration may sometimes have been left in the rough and completed by local craftsmen. It is certain that Rome imitated Greek
and eastern works and installed eastern workshops in the capital
— as has been noted in the case of the sculptors from Aphrodisias. More exact knowledge of these workshops might provide
important information on all the sculpture of the imperial period. The creators of the figures of these eastern sarcophagi,
if they were not themselves the sculptors of the larger-scale
statuary, at least came under the influence of these sculptors
and showed a very similar style and technique.

Provincial styles. The eastern half of the Empire has proved
rich in reliefs and funerary steles: steles with standing human
figures in Athens and elsewhere, reliefs of banquet scenes and
horsemen almost everywhere, and reliefs with busts and heads
in Macedonia especially. Like the ex-votos, these works are for
the most part the products of provincial and popular art and
as such can be clearly distinguished from the works so far discussed. The distinction is a fundamental one and is valid for
the whole Empire, but it has been more particularly noted and
studied in certain provinces, for example, in the east, in Syria
and Egypt.

There is evidence that under the Empire the diffusion of

sculpture, at least in the form of honorary or funerary portraits and funerary reliefs, was as great in these countries as it was elsewhere in the Roman world. In Egypt the development that had begun in the Hellenistic period continued with very little modification, except perhaps for a decline in the number of purely Greco-Roman works: those that have been preserved can on the whole be more accurately defined as " Greco-Egyptian," although the proportion of Egyptian and Greek elements varies and is moreover sometimes difficult to determine. Sometimes an Egyptian statue, characterized by the column placed at its back, has something Greek in its face or draperies; sometimes a Greek model is treated in a more or less Egyptian manner. Hellenism always remained rather superficial in these works and western influence was practically nonexistent: only a few faces reveal a fair degree of Roman realism, such as the so-called "Caesar" in the Museo Barracco (2d century; PL. 197) and one or two heads from Heracleopolis. On the whole, Egypt produced nothing very original during the early imperial period, and its contribution to the development of the sculpture of the time lay rather in its exports of rare materials to the west: diorite, porphyry, and alabaster. It was only at a much later date that the Egyptian artists almost changed the evolutionary course of sculpture under the late Empire (see below).

Syrian sculpture under the early Empire reveals very similar characteristics. Some of the works are Greco-Roman in style and closely resemble those found elsewhere in the Empire. It would appear that first in Antioch, and then in the coastal cities and their hinterland, this type of sculpture predominated (Jupiter and Hygeia, Beirut, Nat. Mus.; goddess from Laodicea ad Mare, Damascus Nat. Mus., etc.). Greco-Roman-style bronzes were found in the same region (at Sidon particularly), as well as small pieces of sculpture for house interiors [Aphrodite from Restan (anc. Arethusa), Aspasia from Hama (anc. Epiphania)]. A provincial style of Syrian sculpture is also found, however, in several places inland, notably in the Hauran. Here an important collection was discovered: portrait heads, divine and mythological figures, and reliefs carved in rough black basalt. In the great majority of these cases there is no doubt that the model was Greco-Roman, although it was rendered with varying degrees of skill and fidelity. It is interesting to note the gradual shift toward increasingly stiff and frozen figures that are far removed from the ease and freedom of Greek sculpture. Finally, there is a quite distinct group of sculptures whose presence has also been noted in other provinces of the Empire: these are wholly primitive works, which owe practically nothing to the art of Greece and Rome. This was the phenomenon of the reawakening of primitivist tendencies in the provincial and popular arts of the Roman Empire.

Syria also provides the particularly interesting case of an art that recovered its independence from Hellenic influence; for while Egypt was renowned for its Greco-Egyptian works, there developed in Roman Syria a Greco-Oriental art that has been called Parthian art (q.v.), whose extension in time and space corresponded roughly to that of the Parthian empire. This art spread to the Roman territory of Palmyra, at least in sculpture and painting, at a time when architecture was becoming increasingly Romanized, and the Romans also encountered it in Dura-Europos during their occupation of this town, and even in Hatra. Palmyra, especially, produced works in a very unified style (PL. 196; XI, PLS. 54, 56); whether in funerary banquet scenes, busts on loculi plaques, ex-votos, or reliefs in the Temple of Bel, the city's workshops made only minor concessions to western models. Parthian art, which was governed by specific and rigid conventions, was far removed from Greek art, with its love of freedom and illusionistic effects. One of these conventions — the most original and striking in its illogicality — was the frontality of the reliefs and paintings: the figures participate in a common action, and whatever this action may be, are portrayed full face. The problem then arises of the influence that Parthian art exerted on the evolution of Greco-Roman art, both in Syria and beyond, particularly with reference to the profound transformations that art underwent under the late Empire. The final impression is that this influence was minimal; the direct connection which is thought to exist between certain

paintings in Dura-Europos and the panels of the Arch of Septimius Severus in Leptis Magna — and which has been disputed by some authorities — is an isolated case. Greco-Roman art developed organically rather than through external influences. However, it is quite possible that at a very late date this Parthian art or its derivatives had a considerable influence on the formation of Byzantine art. This possibility, though often recognized, has not yet been thoroughly explored.

Sculpture of the late Empire. It had been the task of the Hellenized east to provide artistic precepts for Rome and the west, and this it accomplished without losing its own individuality, and without crushing that of its disciples and emulators. Again in the 3d century, when Rome and the east almost fell before the barbarian invasion, it was the task of the Hellenized east to save the heritage of Hellas and transmit it to Byzantium. For the west the crisis of the 3d century resulted in a marked recession of the fundamental principles of Hellenism; elementary forces were released, and the friezes of the Arch of Constantine (VII, PL. 265; IX, PL. 54) reveal the temporary triumph of popular art tendencies. This return to very primitive formulas appears elsewhere as well. To the time of the Tetrarchy can be attributed the famous groups of emperors in red porphyry that today adorn St. Mark's in Venice (IX, PL. 56). These and other related porphyry statues, such as the two tetrarchs in the Vatican Library (VII, PL. 371), are far removed, in their abstract and intellectual conception, from the illusionistic effects of Greek art. In these statues, volume, geometrical line, and graphic design prevail over the realistic rendering of the body and facial features. The material used, porphyry, suggests a workshop in Egypt, and the fact that some of these sculptures were discovered in Egypt (Athribis) seems to confirm this hypothesis. This then is a case of a province imposing its law on the capital, a province quite prepared to repudiate an imported Hellenism.

These works were the product of an extreme and temporary reaction; classical moderation soon returned to temper the crudity of primitivism. Another official triumphal monument, the Arch of Galerius in Salonika (PL. 198; IX, PL. 49), built shortly before the Arch of Constantine in Rome, remains, in the style and composition of its scenes, very strictly within the tradition of the preceding centuries; only some of the heads of the sovereigns reveal a Tetrarchic heaviness. This arch marked the beginning of a new series of eastern triumphal monuments decorated with sequences of figured panels. In their subjects and composition the columns of Theodosius (ca. 386–94) and Arcadius (ca. 301–21; IX, PL. 58) in Constantinople, both practically destroyed, like the last known example, the Column of Marcianus (540–57), continue the tradition of the Arch of Galerius. They unite various tendencies: a picturesque vein in the Hellenistic tradition in the battle scenes and a hieratic inspiration more typical of the late Empire in the scenes where the emperor appears before the people. This inspiration is particularly striking in the reliefs on the base of the obelisk that Theodosius erected in Constantinople (II, PL. 467; VII, PL. 265; IX, PL. 57). Frontal presentation, symmetrical composition, parataxis, and hierarchic arrangement characterize these stone panels, which show the emperor and his sons watching circus games. The style of the figures is that of the period known as the "Theodosian renaissance" (IX, col. 111).

The sculpture workshops were, in fact, still fully active all through the 4th century and after, particularly in the east. The decline in sculpture that is considered one of the characteristics of the art of the late Empire was a slow process. The works that have survived, principally portrait heads or full-length statues, are sufficient proof that flourishing workshops existed in Greece (Corinth) and in Asia Minor, at Ephesus and Aphrodisias. A statue of Valentinian II from Aphrodisias (Istanbul, Archaeol. Mus.) recaptures the serenity and nobility of classical sculpture; the balanced pose, the full folds of the drapery, and the smooth round face enlivened by a smile are features that are found in other works dating from the Theodosian renaissance. Two other examples are undoubtedly more indicative of the imperial image as it existed at that time: the first is the Colossus of Barletta (IX, PL. 60), which was stolen from Constantinople during the Middle Ages and was subsequently found off the coast of Italy. It is uncertain whether it represents Valentinian I, Theodosius, or Marcianus, but in any case it shows the *dominus* in his terrifying omnipotence. The second example is the so-called "Barberini Diptych" (IX, PL. 85), which shows the emperor as defender of the faith; here too he can only be dubiously identified as Anastasius, Constantine, or Justinian. There are also two statues of magistrates from Aphrodisias (II, PL. 466; IX, PL. 59), which already denote the beginning of a new era; their bodies and draperies have lost the lifelike quality that animates the sculpture of Valentinian; the classical serenity has vanished from their faces, which, however, have become more than ever the essential part of the portrait. The ravaged and irregular features reveal the search for a characteristic ugliness expressive of personality. But it is the heads from Ephesus, also attributed to the 5th century, that, in their distorted volumes, the harsh lines of the features, and their distant and visionary gaze, give proof of the close of an era and the decisive triumph of another.

PAINTING AND MOSAICS. The eastern provinces had no equivalent of Pompeii and Herculaneum, even bearing in mind the particular case of Dura-Europos, and very little is as yet known about the development of painting in this part of the Empire. With a few exceptions, only minor examples have been preserved, these being mostly paintings in hypogeums. Only a few examples can be mentioned for Asia Minor. The post-Severan house of the consul Attalus in Pergamum has remains of a painted architectural decoration; at Ephesus, Smyrna, and Sardis there are tombs decorated with nature motifs: garlands, fruit, and birds combined in a form of decoration that seems to have been very widespread. In Syria the surviving monuments are both more numerous and more varied. The Phoenician coast seems to have been rich in tombs with painted decorations. There are several examples at Sidon with decorations of garlands, birds, vines, and grapes. The same motifs are found in a hypogeum in Tyre (Es Sur) where a painted ceiling divided into sections decorated with fruit, flowers, leaves, and the heads of the four winds in the corners has also been preserved. The hypogeum at Masyaf in Syria is richer in its decorations: on the sarcophagus cut from the rock the rape of Persephone is depicted; on the walls of the tomb there are other mythological scenes (2d and 3d cent.). The group of Pluto and Persephone appears again in Marwa in Jordan, and at Ashkelon (Ascalon) there is a bust of Persephone together with a Medusa head, a figure of Pan, and Erotes harvesting grapes. These examples supply little more than the documentation for a catalogue of motifs.

The necropolis of Palmyra also had painted tombs, some of which have long been famous, for example, the Tomb of the Three Brothers with its Victories standing on a globe, holding medallions with portraits of the deceased. But as in the case of sculpture, with only a few exceptions (e.g., the Tomb of Julius Aurelius Maqqai with the picture of Dionysus at the feast), these paintings really belong to Parthian art, as does the much more important group of paintings in Dura-Europos. The most important monuments of this city date from the time of the Roman occupation (166–260). They are the frescoes of the Temple of Bel (or the Palmyrene Gods; PL. 196), those of the Christian chapel or *domus ecclesiae*, those of the Mithraeum, and above all the cycles of the Synagogue (VIII, PLS. 333, 335–37). But the Roman occupation barely affected the evolution of the art, which showed no notable change from that of the preceding period. The Dura-Europos paintings are Parthian in style, and their Greek, or more particularly Hellenistic, elements, which are most apparent in the Synagogue frescoes, are explained by the fact that Parthian art is a Greco-Oriental art, in whose origins Hellenic influences played an outstanding part. But this development was outside the main trend of Greco-Roman art.

The special place of Palmyra and Dura-Europos can be clarified by a comparison with Egypt. In fact, that country offers, along with minor examples (hypogeum paintings as in Phoenicia and Asia Minor; paintings in the Temple of Pnepheros in Theadelphia), two remarkable monuments or groups

of monuments. The first are the frescoes that decorated the Temple of the Imperial Cult in the late Roman castrum of Luxor. These are large figured panels above a plinth decorated with mock inlay. The style of these lines of soldiers (period of the Tetrarchy) is very clearly Greco-Roman and quite distinct from that of the Synagogue paintings in Dura-Europos. The same thing can be ascertained from an examination of the extraordinary series of mummy portraits discovered chiefly in Fayum and Antinoë (PL. 197; IV, PL. 451). In the 1st century it became customary in some Egyptian centers to replace the mummy mask with portraits of the deceased painted on wooden panels. The chronological classification of these portraits, facilitated by such details as hair style, makes it possible to follow the development of styles in Roman art with its alternations of classical sobriety and imaginative exuberance. The scarcity of comparable examples in the west makes it possible to establish with certainty whether tendencies characteristic of the Hellenized east are present here. In any case this series of provincial works by minor artists provides striking evidence of the powerful influence of Hellenism in Egypt — an influence that the sculptural remains in no way reveal; this conclusion could probably be extended to other provinces of the East. Finally, it is not surprising to note that in the 4th century the primitivist tendencies, which in Egypt appear in sculpture, also appear in these portraits, thus beginning the transition to Coptic art (q.v.).

The history of mosaics (q.v.) in the eastern provinces is known with some accuracy only in the case of Syria. It is now well established that the more lavish houses had mosaic decorations, and, at least from the 2d century onward, mosaics with figures. Houses of this type are known in Palmyra, Philippopolis, Baalbek, Beirut, Byblos, Apamea — where over 2,000 sq. ft. of mosaics have been discovered in the porticoes of the colonnaded street — and especially in Antioch (IX, PL. 76; X, PL. 177). The long series of mosaics in that city has made it possible to study the whole subject, and establish a chronology (Levi, 1947), and the conclusions reached here seem to be borne out by the other sites mentioned. However, it is still difficult to form a complete and definite picture, the more so as there are considerable gaps in the documentation for the other eastern provinces and also for the west.

The range of subjects is very wide. Naturally mythological subjects appear frequently, a large number of them linked to the Dionysiac cycle, but there are also others of an epic and narrative nature: the Judgment of Paris (from Antioch; Louvre), the adventures of Zeus (Beirut), the Marriage of Thetis and Peleus (Philippopolis), and Achilles on Skyros (Palmyra). There are also a few more or less historical subjects: the eight sages around Calliope (Baalbek) and the childhood of Alexander (from Baalbek; Beirut, Nat. Mus.). Geographic or topographic subjects are sometimes found, for example the picture of Antioch in the border of the mosaic in the Yakto complex and that of Jerusalem in the Madaba Map (III, PL. 494). Allegorical themes (probably of magicoreligious inspiration) frequently appear: several mosaics show Ge (Gaia) with Karpoi and Horae, or else the Horae alone. A remarkable example is the mosaic from Philippopolis (Damascus, Nat. Mus.) showing Ge surrounded by a crowd of allegorical or mythological figures, among them Georgia, Triptolemos, and Prometheus and Protoplastos. Of a more intellectual nature are Philosophia, Eutekneia, and Dikaiosyne in another mosaic from Philippopolis (Damascus, Nat. Mus.), and Megalopsychia in the Yakto-complex mosaic. At a later date themes such as the hunt apparently enjoyed increasing popularity [Antioch (IX, PL. 73) and Apamea].

A study of the technique and style of these mosaics shows a development apparently similar to that which the fuller documentation in certain western provinces has made it possible to establish. The east, however, was to continue a development that in the west slowed down or stopped altogether at the beginning of the 5th century. Once again the transition to the Byzantine period occurred imperceptibly. At Antioch itself late mosaics (4th–5th cent.) are numerous; and mosaics of the same date and even later, up to the Arab conquest, are to be found in the rest of Syria on the Phoenician coast (Sidon) and in Palestine, in churches (Gerasa, Tabgha, etc.) and in synagogues (Beth Alpha; VIII, PL. 337). In this period there was a return to large compositions with geometrical decoration. Nevertheless, figured mosaics remained quite frequent, as recent discoveries have proved, for example, the mosaic of the months at Argos, and especially the decoration of the Great Palace of the Emperors in Istanbul (II, PL. 437; VII, PL. 372), probably dating from the 5th century, which is in the Hellenistic tradition. Its surviving fragments do not depict continuous scenes, but rather isolated motifs, which are often full of life. Hunting scenes are still popular, but there are also other scenes, such as two boys riding a camel, and a man being thrown from a bucking mule.

The art of mosaics would seem to be strictly Greek or Greco-Roman and one might suppose that it never spread beyond the Empire. In fact, at Palmyra itself, where it has been seen that painting and sculpture belong to the domain of Parthian art, the few great mosaics that are known at present are Greco-Roman in style. But recent discoveries in the city of Edessa, the capital of the little principality that formed a buffer state between the Romans and the Parthians, have revealed some mosaics in Parthian style in the hypogeums surrounding the town. One of these is the so-called "tripod mosaic" (scenes of sacrifice with incensing), and another shows a funerary banquet — both themes whose frequent appearance in Dura-Europos and Palmyra is well known. Inscriptions make it possible to ascribe these works to the 3d century. Another example of the influence of the Parthian-Sassanian world has come to light at Bishapur, the capital of Shapur I, in whose palace a room decorated with mosaics has been found (X, PL. 177). On one side there is a series of mythological heads unquestionably Hellenistic in style; they could have been created only by artists whom the Sassanian ruler brought back from his Syrian conquests. It is still impossible to establish whether the second series, representing female dancers, whose posture and whole style clearly proclaim their eastern origins, should be attributed to Syrian craftsmen or to Iranian artists newly initiated in Hellenistic culture. Nor is it possible to determine whether this kind of homage paid by the lords of Iran to a specifically Greco-Roman mosaic technique produced any other examples.

MINOR ARTS. The eastern provinces were the centers of certain industries, which had originated there in very remote antiquity. Syria was the terminal point of the caravan routes from Arabia, the Persian Gulf, Iran, and beyond. Under the Empire the famous Silk Route was often a political and economic storm center. Generally speaking, the east continued to be both the great market and the production center for luxury fabrics. Firsthand knowledge of these fabrics is today confined to the rather pitiful remains discovered at Dura-Europos and Palmyra and in Egypt, so that it is only the figure reliefs or paintings that convey a lifelike impression of the richness and art of the costumes of that period.

Syria, Phoenicia, and Egypt were also the countries that started the manufacture of glass, and they never lost this dominant position under the Empire, which, moreover, was one of the great periods of glass production. Techniques were already highly specialized, judging by the range of products: multicolored and millefiori glass, glass with painted figures and scenes (VI, PL. 220), with interlaminated gold leaf, with engraved decoration (for example, the famous *diatreta*), glass with molded and applied ornamentation. The originality, variety, and elegance of form and decoration of this glassware were always admirable. The workshops of Syria and Egypt had their own specialties, which are not always easily distinguishable. The motifs are only rarely realistic, for example, the Pharos of Alexandria depicted on the glass found in Begram (Kabul Mus.).

This development of the art of glass is all the more remarkable in that in a related field, that of terra sigillata, the east seems to have yielded first place to the west although it had initiated the west in this technique. In the workshop of Arezzo the names of artists from the east (M. Perennius Bargathes, M. Perennius Tigranus) give evidence of contacts. Under the Empire the eastern workshops confined themselves to a more sober decoration, but developed a new technique, that of high glaze using different colors, brown, green, and blue. (See also GLASS, VI, col. 370 ff., PLS. 220, 221.)

The working of precious metals goes back to ancient traditions in the east. Jewelry certainly enjoyed constant favor; but here again it is perhaps the sculptured busts of the women of Palmyra (PL. 196) that give us the best idea of the taste of the time and the variety of its jewels (rings, bracelets, necklaces, earrings, etc.).

Unfortunately, less precious metalwork dating from the early Empire has survived from the east than from the west. There are, however, numerous examples of precious plate, especially silverware, of a late date (4th cent. and later). Specialists in this field have tried to distinguish between the products of the various workshops in the principal centers: Alexandria, Antioch, and Byzantium. The era of daring and absolute themes, like that of T. Schreiber on the Alexandrian origin of this silverware (Die Alexandrinische Toreutik, *Abh. der Sächsischen Gesellschaft der Wissenschaften*, Philologische-historische Klasse, XIV, 1894), is by no means over and opinions vary with each fresh discovery. (See also GOLD- AND SILVERWORK.)

The remarkable finds at Begram, in Afghanistan, seem to illustrate very clearly the role of the Egyptian capital, if the curious plaster casts found there were indeed modeled, as has been very plausibly maintained, on pieces of silver. The Alexandrian origin of the entire find appears to be almost certain. The importance of the eastern workshops seems to be demonstrated in a more general way by the finds from the royal tomb in Bizye in Thrace (beginning of the Empire). These have their counterparts in Hildesheim and elsewhere in the west. Finally, the place of toreutics in Syria has become much clearer owing to the large find in the necropolis of Emesa. The visored helmet (PL. 197) with a foliated roundel and headband is in all probability of Syrian make, dating from the beginning of the Empire. Two other helmets of the same kind, discovered at Nawa in the Hauran, certainly of much later date (2d cent.), and very richly decorated with battle scenes and divinities, seem to demonstrate the persistence of this tradition.

There is also some evidence that in Syria, as in Egypt, the production of small bronzes was abundant. Egyptian subjects exported far afield, in the west as well as in the east (Begram), provide good indications of this. In Syria, particularly on the coast, there have been numerous finds of small bronzes, some of them clearly of local origin.

Finally, ivory carving, an art whose origins go very far back in the east but which seems to have been very little developed during the early Empire, was vigorously revived under the late Empire. A special feature of the art was the carving of diptychs, known as consular diptychs, which were produced in various centers.

BIBLIOG. *Architecture and town planning*: 1. *Town planning*: A. von Gerkan, Griechische Städteanlagen, Berlin, 1924; E. Fabricius and K. Lehmann-Hartleben, RE, s.v. Städtebau; F. Castagnoli, Ippodamo di Mileto e l'urbanistica a pianta ortogonale, Rome, 1956; R. Martin, L'urbanisme dans la Grèce antique, Paris, 1956. 2. *Triumphal arches*: E. Weigand, Propylon und Bogentor in der östlichen Reichskunst, Wiener Jhb. für Kg., N.S., V, 1928, pp. 71-114; H. Kähler, RE, s.v. Triumphbogen; G. A. Mansuelli, El arco honorífico en el desarrollo de la arquitectura romana, AEA, XXVII, 1954, pp. 93-178; M. Pallottino, EAA, s.v. Arco onorario e trionfale. 3. *Nymphaeums*: J. Hülsen, Das Nymphaeum (Milet, I, 5), Berlin, Leipzig, 1919; G. Lugli, Nymphaea sive musaea: Osservazioni sopra un gruppo di monumenti repubblicani in Italia in rapporto con l'architettura ellenistica, Atti IV Cong. naz. di S. romani, I, Rome, 1938, pp. 155-68; P. Mingazzini, Le grotte di Matermania e dell'Arsenale a Capri, AC, VII, 1955, pp. 139-63. 4. *Libraries*: G. Götze, Antike Bibliotheken, JdI, LII, 1937, pp. 225-47; C. Callmer, Antike Bibliotheken, OpA, III, 1944, pp. 145-93; F. Eichler, ed., Die Bibliothek (Forsch. in Ephesos, V, 1), Vienna, 1944. 5. *Theaters*: M. Bieber, The History of the Greek and Roman Theater, 2d ed., Princeton, 1961; A. Neppi Modona, Gli edifici teatrali greci e romani, Florence, 1961. 6. *Thermae*: T. Wiegand, 8. vorläufiger Bericht über die von den staatlichen Museen in Milet und Didyma unternommenen Ausgrabungen AbhPreussAk, 1924, 1, pp. 1-25; A. von Gerkan and F. Krischen, Thermen und Palästren (Milet, I, 9), Berlin, 1928; T. Wiegand, Gymnasien, Thermen und Palaestren in Milet, SbBerlin, 1928, pp. 250-54; D. Krencker et al., Die Trierer Kaiserthermen, I, Berlin, 1929; G. de Angelis d'Ossat, Tecnica costruttiva e impianti dei bagni, Rome, 1943. 7. *Façades of buildings*: H. Kohl, Kasr Firaun in Petra, Leipzig, 1910; H. Hörmann, Die römische Bühnenfront zu Ephesos, JdI, XXXVIII-XXXIX, 1923-24, pp. 275-345; H. Hörmann, Die Fassade des Apsidensaales im Heiligtum der Fortuna zu Präneste, RM, XL, 1925, pp. 241–79; H. Hörmann, Das Nymphäum zu Aspendos, JdI, XLIV, 1929, pp. 263–74; R. Naumann, Der Quellbezirk von Nîmes, Berlin, 1937. See also (3) and (5) above. 8. *Technique*: J. B. Ward Perkins, The Italian Element in Late Roman and Early Medieval Architecture, Oxford, 1947; J. B. Ward Perkins, Notes on the Structure and Building Methods of Early Byzantine Architecture, in D. Talbot Rice, ed., The Great Palace of the Byzantine Emperors: Second Report, Edinburgh, 1958, pp. 52–104. 9. *Relations between West and East*: J. B. Ward Perkins, Severan Art and Architecture at Leptis Magna, JRS, XXXVIII, 1948, pp. 59–80; G. von Kaschnitz-Weinberg, Die Baukunst im Kaiserreich (Römische Kunst, IV), Hamburg, 1963.

Sculpture: 1. *General*: G. Mendel, Musées impériaux ottomans: Catalogue des sculptures grecques, romaines et byzantines, 3 vols., Istanbul, 1912–14; R. Delbrück, Antike Porphyrwerke, Berlin, 1932; R. Delbrück, Spätantike Kaiserporträts von Konstantinus Magnus bis zum Ende des Westreiches, Berlin, 1933; H. P. L'Orange, Studien zur Geschichte des spätantiken Porträts, Oslo, Cambridge, Mass., 1933; J. Kollwitz, Oströmische Plastik der theodosianischen Zeit, Berlin, 1941; M. Floriani Squarciapino, La scuola di Afrodisia, Rome, 1943; H. P. L'Orange, Apotheosis in Ancient Portraiture, Oslo, Cambridge, Mass., 1947; R. Bianchi Bandinelli, Storicità dell'arte classica, 2d ed., Florence, 1950; H. Jucker, Vom Verhältnis der Römer zur bildenden Kunst der Griechen, Frankfurt am Main, 1950; G. Becatti, Arte e gusto negli scrittori latini, Florence, 1951; G. M. A. Richter, Three Critical Periods in Greek Sculpture, Oxford, 1951; J. M. C. Toynbee, Some Notes on Artists in the Roman World, Brussels, 1951; W. Sas-Zaloziecky, Die Kunst Ost- und Westroms im frühen Mittelalter, Das Münster, V, 1952, pp. 301–13; L. Budde, Die Entstehung des antiken Repräsentantionsbildes, Berlin, 1957; H. Kähler, Wesenzüge der römischen Kunst, Saarbrücken, 1958; G. von Kaschnitz-Weinberg, Zwischen Republik und Kaiserreich (Römische Kunst, II), Hamburg, 1961. 2. *Sarcophagi*: G. Rodenwaldt, Säulensarkophage, RM, XXXVIII–XXXIX, 1923–24, pp. 1–40; C. Morey, Roman and Christian Sculpture: The Sarcophagus of Claudia Antonia Sabina and the Asiatic Sarcophagi (Sardis, V, 1), Princeton, 1924; G. Rodenwaldt, Der Klinensarkophag von S. Lorenzo, JdI, XLV, 1930, pp. 116–89; G. Rodenwaldt, Sarcophagi from Xanthos, JHS, LIII, 1933, pp. 181–213; J. M. C. Toynbee, The Hadrianic School, Cambridge, 1934; G. Rodenwaldt, Gestalten in der Sarkophagkunst, JdI, LV, 1940, pp. 44–57; G. Rodenwaldt, Sarkophagprobleme, RM, LVIII, 1943, pp. 1–26; J. B. Ward Perkins, The Hippolytus Sarcophagus from Trinquetaille, JRS, XLVI, 1956, pp. 10–16; B. Kallipolitis, *χρονολογικῆ κατατάξες τῶν μετά μυθοκογικῶν παραστασεῶν ἀττικῶν σαρκοφαγῶν τῆς ρωμαικῆς ἐποχῆς*, Athens, 1958; J. B. Ward Perkins, Four Roman Garland Sarcophagi in America, Archaeology, XI, 1958, pp. 98–104.

Greece: 1. *General*: P. E. Arias, Civiltà romana: La Grecia nell'impero di Roma, Rome, 1940; A. Baccin, Aspetti dell'architettura romana in Grecia, Atti III Cong. naz. Storia Arch., Rome, 1940, pp. 131–42; V. Ziino, Riflessi architettonici italici in Grecia: Studi sul capitello, Atti III Cong. naz. Storia Arch., Rome, 1940, pp. 39–60; O. A. W. Dilke, The Greek Theater Cavea, BSA, XLIII, 1948, pp. 125–92. 2. *Athens*: P. Graindor, Athènes sous Auguste, Cairo, 1927; M. A. Sisson, The Stoa of Hadrian at Athens, BSR, XI, 1929, pp. 50–72; P. Graindor, Un milliardaire antique: Hérode Atticus et sa famille, Cairo, 1930; P. Graindor, Athènes de Tibère à Trajan, Cairo, 1931; P. Graindor, Athènes sous Hadrien, Cairo, 1932; A. von Gerkan, Die neronische Scaenae Frons des Dionysiostheaters in Athen, JdI, LVI, 1941, pp. 163–77; M. Santangelo, Il monumento di C. Julius Antiochos Philopappos in Atene, ASAtene, N.S., III–V, 1941–43, pp. 153–253; H. S. Robinson, The Tower of the Winds and the Roman Market-place, AJA, XLVII, 1943, pp. 291–305; A. W. Pickard-Cambridge, The Theatre of Dionysus in Athens, Oxford, 1946; J. Travlos, *Ἀνασκαφαὶ ἔρευναι παρὰ τὸ Ὀλυμπιεῖον ΠΑΕ*, 1949, pp. 25–43; U. Kahrstedt, Die Stadt Athen in der Kaiserzeit, MdI, III, 1950, pp. 51–67; H. A. Thompson, The Odeion in the Athenian Agora, Hesperia, XIX, 1950, pp. 31–141; J. Travlos, *Ἀνασκαφαὶ ἐν τῇ βιβλιοθήκῃ τοῦ Ἁδριανοῦ, ΠΑΕ*, 1950, pp. 41–52; I. C. T. Hill, The Ancient City of Athens: Its Topography and Monuments, London, Cambridge, Mass., 1953. 3. *Corinth*: T. L. Shear, The Roman Villa (Corinth, V, 1), Princeton, 1930; O. Broneer, The Odeum (Corinth, X), Princeton, 1932; R. Stillwell, The Theatre (Corinth, II), Princeton, 1952; S. Charitodinidis and R. Ginouvès, Bain romain de Zevgolatio près de Corinthe, BCH, LXXIX, 1955, pp. 102–20. 4. *Eleusis*: G. Libertini, I propilei di Appio Claudio Pulcro ad Eleusi, ASAtene, II, 1915, pp. 201–17; H. Hörmann, Die inneren Propyläen von Eleusis, Berlin, Leipzig, 1932. 5. *Kos*: L. Laurenzi, Nuovi contributi alla topografia storico-archeologica di Coo, Historia, V, 1931, pp. 603–26; A. Neppi Modona, L'isola di Coo nell'antichità classica (Mem. Ist. storico-archeol. di Rodi, I), Rhodes, 1933; L. Morricone, Frammento di bassorilievo arcaico di Coo, BArte, XXXV, 1959, pp. 1–5. 6. *Gortyna*: G. Porro, Il pretorio di Gortina, BArte, VII, 1913, pp. 349–60; A. Maiuri et al., Gortina (Creta), ASAtene, I, 1914, pp. 119–59; A. M. Colini, Gortina (1935), BArte, XXIX, 1935–36, pp. 360–64. 7. *Nicopolis*: A. Philadelpheus, Nicopolis, Athens, 1938; A. Baccin and V. Ziino, Nicopoli d'Epiro, Palladio, IV, 1940, pp. 1–17. 8. *Delphi and Olympia*: E. Curtius, ed., Olympia, 10 vols., Berlin, 1890–97; Ecole française d'Athènes, Fouilles de Delphes, Paris, 1902 ff.; Deutsches archäologisches Institut, Bericht über die Ausgrabungen in Olympia, Berlin, 1936 ff. 9. *Sculpture*: A. Conze, Die attischen Grabreliefs, 4 vols., in 6, Berlin, 1893–1922; P. Graindor, Les cosmètes du Musée d'Athènes, BCH, XXXIX, 1915, pp. 241–401; P. Johnson, The Sculptures 1896–1923 (Corinth, IX), Cambridge, Mass., 1931; G. Jacopi and L. Laurenzi, Monumenti di scultura del Museo archeologico di Rodi (Clara Rhodos, V, 2), Rhodes, 1932; R. Herbig, Das Dionysostheater in Athen, II: Die Skulpturen von Bühnenhaus, Stuttgart, 1935; A. Mühsam, Die attischen Grabreliefs in römischer Zeit, Berlin, 1936; F. Chamoux, Un portrait de Thasos: Lucius Caesar, MPiot, XLIV, 1950, pp. 82–96; F. Chamoux, Un portrait de Thasos: Jules César, MPiot, XLVII, 1953, pp. 131–47; E. B. Harrison, The Athenian Agora, I: Portrait Sculpture, Princeton, 1953; A. Mühsam, Attic Grave Reliefs from the Roman Period, Berytus, X, 1953, pp. 55–110; E. B. Harrison, New Sculpture from the Athenian Agora, Hesperia, XXIX, 1960, pp. 369–92. For sarcophagi, see above.

Macedonia and Constantinople: 1. *Salonika*: K. F. Kinch, L'arc de triomphe de Salonique, Paris, 1890; O. Tafrali, Topographie de Salonique, Paris, 1912; C. Diehl, M. Le Tourneau and H. Saladin, Les monuments chrétiens de Salonique, Paris, 1918, pp. 19–31; O. Tafrali, Thessalonique des origines au XIVe siècle, Paris, 1919; P. Perdrizet, L'"Incantada" de Salonique, MPiot, XXI, 1930, pp. 51–90; G. Daux, Chronique des fouilles en 1957: Salonique, trouvailles fortuites, BCH, LXXXII, 1958, pp. 759–61 (mausoleum of Galerius); L. Guerrini, "Las incantadas" di Salonico, AC, XIII, 1961, pp. 40–70. 2. *Philippi*: P. Collart, Philippes, ville de Macédoine, Paris, 1937. 3. *Stobi*: B. Saria, Das Theater von Stobi, AAnz, 1938, cols., 81–148; E. Dyggve, Le théâtre mixte du Bas-Empire d'après le théâtre de Stobi et les diptyques consulaires, RA, 1958, 1, pp. 137–57, 2, pp. 20–30. 4. *Constantinople*: K. O. Dalman, Der Valensaquädukt in Konstantinopel (Istanbuler Forsch., 3), Berlin, 1933; G. Bruns, Der Obelisk und seine Basis auf dem Hippodrom zu Konstantinopel (Istanbuler Forsch., 7), Berlin, 1935; D. Talbot Rice, ed., The Great Palace of the Byzantine Emperors, 2 vols., Edinburgh, 1947–58; G. Q. Giglioli, La colonna di Arcadio e Costantinopoli, Naples, 1952; G. Becatti, La colonna coclide istoriata, Rome, 1960; G. Becatti, EAA, s.v.

Asia Minor: 1. *General*: K. Lanckoronski, G. Niemann and E. Petersen, Städte Pamphyliens und Pisidiens, 2 vols., Vienna, 1890–92; Monumenta Asiae Minoris Antiquae, 8 vols., London, 1928–62. 2. *Antalya*: A. M. Mansel, Antalya bölgesinde araştirmalar (Researches in the Antalya Region), II, Ankara, 1949; H. Metzger, Catalogue des monuments votifs du Musée d'Adalia, Paris, 1952. 3. *Aphrodisias*: L. Crema, I monumenti architettonici Afrodisiensi, MAAccIt, XXXVIII, 1939, cols., 233–312; G. Jacopi, Gli scavi della Missione archeologica italiana ad Afrodisiade nel 1937, MAAccIt, XXXVIII, 1939, cols., 173–232; M. Floriani Squarciapino, La scuola di Afrodisia, Rome, 1943. 4. *Anazarbus*: P. Verzone, Città ellenistiche e romane dell'Asia minore: Anazarbus, Palladio, N.S., VII, 1957, pp. 9–25. 5. *Ankara*: D. Krencker and M. Schede, Der Tempel in Ankara, Berlin, Leipzig, 1936. 6. *Antioch in Pisidia*: D. M. Robinson, A Preliminary Report on the Excavations at Pisidian Antioch and at Sizma, AJA, XXVIII, 1924, pp. 435–44; D. M. Robinson, Roman Sculptures from Colonia Caesarea (Pisidian Antioch), AB, IX, 1926–27, pp. 5–69. 7. *Aspendus*: H. Hörmann, Das Nymphäum zu Aspendos, JdI, XLIV, 1929, pp. 263–74; J. B. Ward Perkins, The Aqueduct of Aspendos, BSR, XXIII, 1955, pp. 115–23. 8. *Ephesus*: Forschungen in Ephesos, Vienna, 1906 ff. 9. *Hierapolis*: Altertümer von Hierapolis, Berlin, 1904. 10. *Magnesia on the Maeander*: C. Watzinger, Magnesia am Meander, Berlin, 1904. 11. *Miletus*: Milet-Ergebnisse der Ausgrabungen und Untersuchungen seit dem Jahr 1899, Berlin, 1906 ff. 12. *Nicaea*: A. M. Schneider and W. Karnapp, Die Stadtmauer von Iznik (Nicaea), Berlin, 1938. 13. *Nysa*: Nysa ad Maeandrum nach Forschungen und Aufnahmen in den Jahren 1907 und 1909 (JdI, sup., X), Berlin, 1913. 14. *Pergamum*: Altertümer von Pergamon, Berlin, 1885 ff.; T. Wiegand, Zweiter Bericht über die Ausgrabungen in Pergamon, 1928–32: Das Asklepieion, AbhBerlAk, 5, 1932; O. Deubner, Das Asklepieion von Pergamon, Berlin, 1938. 15. *Priene*: T. Wiegand and H. Schrader, Priene 1895–98, Berlin, 1904. 16. *Sardis*: American Society for the Excavations of Sardis, Sardis, Leyden, 1910 ff. 17. *Side*: A. M. Mansel, Side, Berlin, 1962. 18. *Smyrna*: R. Naumann and S. Kantar, Die Agora von Smyrna, Kleinasien und Byzanz (Istanbuler Forsch., 17), Berlin, 1950, pp. 69–114. 19. *Tarsus*: H. Goldmann, Excavations at Gözlii Kule, Tarsus, I–II, 2 vols. in 4, Princeton, 1950–56.

Syria, Phoenicia, Palestine, Jordan: 1. *General*: E. Renan, Mission de Phénicie, 2 vols., Paris, 1864; M. de Vogüé, Syrie centrale: architecture civile et religieuse, 2 vols., Paris, 1865–77; H. C. Butler, Architecture and Other Arts (Am. Archaeol. Expedition to Syria in 1899–1900, II), New York, 1903; R. E. Brünnow and A. von Domaszewski, Die Provincia Arabia, 3 vols., Strasbourg, 1904–09; J. Jaussen and R. Savignac, Mission archéologique en Arabie, 3 vols., Paris, 1909–22; H. C. Butler, Ancient Architecture in Syria (Princeton Univ. Archaeol. Expedition to Syria in 1904–1905 and 1909, II), 2 vols., Leyden, 1919–20; C. Watzinger, Denkmäler Palästinas, 2 vols., Leipzig, 1933–35; B. M. Felletti Maj, Siria, Palestina, Arabia settentrionale nel periodo romano, Rome, 1950; H. T. Bossert, Altsyrien, Tübingen, 1951; G. Tchalenko, Villages antiques de la Syrie du Nord: Le massif du Bélus à l'époque romaine, 3 vols., Paris, 1953–58. 2. *Antioch*: G. Downey, A History of Antioch in Syria, Princeton, 1961. For other localities, see ISRAEL; JORDAN; LEBANON; SYRIA. 3. *Architecture and town planning*: H. Kohl and C. Watzinger, Antike Synagogen in Galilaea, Leipzig, 1916; A. von Gerkan, Griechische Städteanlagen, Berlin, Leipzig, 1924; A. Poidebard, La trace de Rome dans le désert de Syrie, Paris, 1934; J. Sauvaget, Le plan de Laodicée-sur-Mer (note complémentaire), B. d'ét. orientales, VI, 1936, pp. 51–52; D. Krencker and W. Zschietzschmann, Römische Tempel in Syrien, I, Berlin, Leipzig, 1938; R. Mouterde and A. Poidebard, Le limes de Chalcis, Paris, 1945; J. Sauvaget, Le plan antique de Damas, Syria, XXVI, 1949, pp. 314–58; E. Will, La tour funéraire de la Syrie et les monuments apparentés, Syria, XXVI, 1949, pp. 258–312; R. Amy, Temples à escaliers, Syria, XXVIII, 1950, pp. 82–136; E. Will, Le sanctuaire syrien de Délos, Ann. archéol. de Syrie, I, 1951, pp. 59–79; E. Frézouls, Recherches sur les théâtres de l'Orient syrien, Syria, XXXVI, 1959, pp. 202–27, XXXVIII, 1961, pp. 54–86; J. A. Hanson, Roman Theater-temples, Princeton, 1959; E. Will, L'adyton dans le temple syrien de l'époque impériale, Et. d'archéol. classique, II, 1959, pp. 136–45. 4. *Relations between West and East*: E. Weigand, Baalbek und Rom: Die römische Reichskunst in ihrer Entwicklung und Differenzierung, JdI, XXIX, 1914, pp. 37–91; E. Weigand, Baalbek: Datierung und kunstgeschichtliche Stellung seiner Bauten, Jhb. für Kw., 1924–25, pp. 77–99, 165–200; D. Schlumberger, Les formes anciennes du chapiteau corinthien en Syrie, en Palestine et en Arabie, Syria, XIV, 1933, pp. 283–317; H. Seyrig, Ornamenta Palmyrena antiquiora, Syria, XXI, 1940, pp. 276–328; M. Avi-

Yonah, Oriental Elements in the Art of Palestine in the Roman and Byzantine Periods, Q. of the Dept. of Ant. in Palestine, X, 1944, pp. 105–51, XIII, 1948, pp. 128–65, XIV, 1950, pp. 49–80; E. Will, De l'Euphrate au Rhin: étude sur quelques motifs ornementaux, Syria, XXXI, 1954, pp. 271–85. 5. *Sculpture*: H. Ingholt, Studier over Palmyrensk Skulptur, Copenhagen, 1928; M. Dunand, Mission archéologique au Djebel Druse: Le Musée de Soueida, Inscriptions et monuments figurés, Paris, 1934; H. Ingholt, Palmyrene Sculptures in Beirut, Berytus, I, 1934, pp. 32–43; H. Seyrig, Bas-reliefs monumentaux du temple de Bèl à Palmyre, Syria, XV, 1934, pp. 155–86; H. Ingholt, Five Dated Tombs from Palmyra, Berytus, II, 1935, pp. 58–120; M. Rostovtsev, Dura and the Problem of Parthian Art, Yale Classical S., V, 1935, pp. 155–304; H. Ingholt, Inscriptions and Sculptures from Palmyra, Berytus, III, 1936, pp. 83–128, V, 1938, pp. 93–140; H. Seyrig, Notes sur les plus anciennes sculptures palmyréniennes, Berytus, III, 1936, pp. 137–40; H. Seyrig, Sur quelques sculptures palmyréniennes, Syria, XVIII, 1937, pp. 31–53; N. Glueck, The Other Side of the Jordan, New Haven, 1940; R. B. Freeman, Nabataean Sculpture in the Cincinnati Art Museum, AJA, XLV, 1941, pp. 337–41; H. Seyrig, Sculptures palmyréniennes archaïques, Syria, XXVII, 1941, pp. 31–44; N. Glueck, The River Jordan, Philadelphia, 1946; S. and A. Abdul-Hak, Catalogue illustré du Département des antiquités gréco-romaines au Musée de Damas, Damascus, 1951; E. J. Parr, Recent Discoveries at Petra, PEQ, LXXXIX, 1957, pp. 5–16; E. Will, Art parthe et art grec, Et. d'archéol. classique, II, 1959, pp. 125–35; P. J. Parr, Nabatean Sculpture from Khirbet Brak, Ann. Dept. of Jordan, IV–V, 1960, pp. 134–36; D. Schlumberger, Descendants non-méditerranéens de l'art grec, Syria, XXXVII, 1960, pp. 131–66, 253–318; E. Will, L'art sassanide et ses prédécesseurs, Syria, XXXIX, 1962, pp. 45–63. 6. *Painting*: G. Cotenau, Mission archéologique à Sidon (1914): Caverne aux inscriptions, Syria, I, 1920, pp. 147–54, 198–205; D. Le Lasseur, Mission archéologique à Tyr (avril–mai 1921), III: Fouilles à Djel el-'Amad, Syria, III, 1922, pp. 14–26; G. Contenau, Deuxième mission archéologique à Sidon (1920): Tombe peinte de Bramieh, Syria, V, 1924, pp. 127–30; F. Cumont, Fouilles de Doura-Europos (1922–1923), Paris, 1927; J. Ory, A Painted Tomb near Ascalon, Q. Dept. of Ant. in Palestine, VIII, 1938, pp. 38–44; C. C. McCown, A Painted Tomb at Marwa, Q. Dept. of Ant. in Palestine, IX, 1939, pp. 1–30; F. Chapoutier, Les peintures murales d'un hypogée funéraire près de Massyaf, Syria, XXXI, 1954, pp. 172–211; C. H. Kraeling, The Excavations at Dura-Europos: Final Report, VIII, 1: The Synagogue, New Haven, 1956; C. H. Kraeling, Color Photographs of the Paintings in the Tomb of the Three Brothers at Palmyra, Ann. archéol. de Syrie, XI–XII, 1961–62, pp. 13–18, pls. I–XVI. 7. *Mosaic*: M. Dunand, Sondages archéologiques effectués à Bostan-ech-Cheikh, près Saida, Syria, VII, 1926, pp. 1–3; D. Levi, Antioch Mosaic Pavements, 2 vols., Princeton, London, 1947; E. Will, Une nouvelle mosaïque de Chahba, Ann. archéol. de Syrie, III, 1953, pp. 27–48; M. Avi-Yonah, The Madaba Mosaic Map, Jerusalem, 1954; M. Chehab, Mosaïques du Liban (BMBeyrouth, XIV–XV), 2 vols., Paris, 1957–59; M. Avi-Yonah, Israel: Ancient Mosaics (UNESCO World Art Series, 14), New York, 1960.

Egypt: 1. *General*: R. Paribeni, L'Egitto romano, Africa romana, Milan, 1935, pp. 207–18; P. Jouguet, La domination romaine en Egypte aux deux premiers siècles après Jésus-Christ, 1947. 2. *Alexandria*: A. Adriani, EAA, s.v., 3. *Antinoë*: E. Kuhn, Antinoopolis, Göttingen, 1913; E. Breccia, Il viaggio dell'imperatore Adriano in Egitto e ciò che resta della città di Antinoo, Atti IV Cong. di S. romani, I, Rome, 1938, pp. 119–24; H. J. Bell, Antinoupolis: A Hadrianic Foundation in Egypt, JRS, XXX, 1940, pp. 133–47. 4. *Hermopolis Magna*: G. Méautis, Une métropole égyptienne sous l'empire romain: Hermopoulis la Grande, Lausanne, 1918; S. Gabra et al., Rapport sur les fouilles d'Hermopoulis Ouest (Touna el-Gebel), Cairo, 1941; S. Gabra and E. Drioton, Peintures à fresques et scènes peintes à Hermopoulis Ouest (Touna el-Gebel), Cairo, 1954; G. Röder, Hermopolis 1929–1939, Hildesheim, 1959. 5. *Karanis*: A. E. R. Boak and E. E. Peterson, Karanis: Topographical and Architectural Report of Excavations during the Seasons 1924–28, Ann Arbor, 1931; D. B. Harden, Roman Glass from Karanis, Ann Arbor, 1936. 6. *Sculpture*: P. Perdrizet, Bronzes grecs d'Egypte de la Collection Fouquet, Paris, 1911; W. Weber, Die ägyptische-griechischen Terrakotten, Berlin, 1914; P. Perdrizet, Les terres-cuites grecques d'Egypte de la Collection Fouquet, Paris, Strasbourg, 1921; E. Breccia, Monuments de l'Egypte gréco-romaine, 2 vols., Bergamo, 1926–34; F. W. von Bissing, Ägyptische Kultbilder der Ptolemaier und Römerzeit (Der alte Orient, 34), Leipzig, 1936; P. Graindor, Terre-cuites de l'Egypte gréco-romaine, Antwerp, 1939; P. Gilbert, La valeur de la statuaire égyptienne aux époques grecque et romaine, Chronique d'Egypte, XXIX, 1954, pp. 14–28. 7. *Painting*: C. C. Edgar, Graeco-Egyptian Coffins, Masks and Portraits (Cat. gén. du Caire, 8), Cairo, 1905; P. Buberl, Griechisch-ägyptische Mumienbildnisse der Sammlung T. Graf, Vienna, 1922; C. Watzinger, Die griechisch-ägyptische Sammlung E. von Sieglin, I: Malerei und Plastik, Leipzig, 1923; E. Breccia, Monuments de l'Egypte gréco-romaine, I, Bergamo, 1926, pp. 110–14, pls. LVII–LIX (frescoes of the Temple of Pnepheros at Theadelphia); H. Drerup, Die Datierung der Mumienporträts, Paderborn, 1933; F. Cumont, Un dieu supposé syrien, associé à Hérôn en Egypte, Mél. Dussaud, I, Paris, 1939, pp. 1–9 (tablets of the Fayum); E. Coche de la Ferté, Les portraits romano-égyptiens du Louvre, Paris, 1953; U. Monneret de Villard, The Temple of the Imperial Cult at Luxor, Archaeologia, XCV, 1953, pp. 85–105.

Minor arts: 1. *Ceramics*: R. J. Charleston, Roman Pottery, London, 1955. 2. *Glass*: F. Neuburg, Glass in Antiquity (trans. R. J. Charleston), London, 1949. 3. *Gold- and silverwork*: H. Seyrig, Antiquités de la nécropole d'Emèse, Syria, XXIX, 1952, pp. 205–50 (helmet of Emesa); S. Abdul-Hak, Chronique des monuments historiques, Ann. archéol. de Syrie, IV–V, 1954–55, pp. 219–24 (helmets of Nawa). 4. *Objects from Begram*: O. Kurz, Begram et l'Occident gréco-romain, in J. Hackin, ed., Nouvelles recherches archéologiques à Begram (1939–1940), Paris, 1954, pp. 89–150. 5. *Textiles*:

R. Pfister, Textiles de Palmyre, 3 vols., Paris, 1934–40; R. Pfister, Nouveaux textiles de Palmyre, Paris, 1937; R. Pfister and L. Bellinger, The Excavations at Dura-Europos: Final Report, IV, 2: The Textiles, New Haven, 1945. 6. *Ivories*: R. Delbrück, Die Consulardiptychen und verwandte Denkmäler, Berlin, 1929; F. Volbach, Elfenbeinarbeiten der Spätantike und des frühen Mittelalters, Mainz, 1952; P. Metz, Elfenbein der Spätantike, Munich, 1962.

Ernest WILL

Illustrations: PLS. 187–198; 11 figs. in text.

ROMANESQUE ART

ROMANESQUE ART. Romanesque art flourished primarily in the 11th and 12th centuries, but continued in certain countries and regions into the 13th century. In the preceding centuries significant artistic movements had been largely localized, and their influences were usually only weakly exerted outside the cultural sphere in which they originated. This was the case with Celtic art, Anglo-Saxon art, and the art of the Carolingian and Ottonian periods (see PRE-ROMANESQUE ART). Romanesque art, however, based everywhere on an essential unity of purpose that was to become steadily stronger in the Gothic period (see GOTHIC ART), acquired a truly European character. This did not exclude the expression of various styles and tendencies in keeping with the traditions of the different countries and the different regions of those countries; the panorama of Romanesque art is extremely varied. It might be likened to a tapestry unified in design but tremendously enriched by varied motifs, characteristic of their individual lands of origin, merging to create a rich and complex pattern.

SUMMARY. Introduction (col. 316). I. Architecture. France (col. 318). *The early period (ca. 1000–ca. 1070): a. The northern provinces; b. The southern provinces. The mature French Romanesque style. The Holy Land. Abbeys. Civil architecture. Military architecture.* Iberian Peninsula (col. 338). *Catalonia. León. The pilgrimage churches. Portugal. The 12th century.* Italy (col. 353). *The 11th century. The 12th century.* Germany and Central Europe (col. 366). *The 11th and 12th centuries.* England (col. 378). Scandinavia (col. 381). II. Sculpture. France (col. 385). The Iberian Peninsula (col. 392). Portugal. Italy (col. 401). Germany and Central Europe (col. 407). Eastern Europe (col. 414). England (col. 416). Scandinavia (col. 417). III. Painting and illumination. France (col. 419). Spain (col. 431). Italy (col. 435). Germany and Central Europe (col. 446). England (col. 450). Scandinavia (col. 451). IV. Minor arts. France (col. 453). Spain and Portugal (col. 455). Italy (col. 458). Germany (col. 461). England (col. 463). Scandinavia (col. 464).

INTRODUCTION. At the end of the 10th century, after the establishment of the viking Rollo (Rolf, Hrolf, the Ganger) in one of the richest provinces of Gaul and the halting of the Norman and Magyar invasions (which had stifled the artistic and cultural movements of the 9th cent.), an architectural renaissance began to take shape in Europe. This revival was brought about by the advancement of feudal organization and the development of royal power, which gradually enforced peace and the security of persons and goods, and in part by the strengthening of papal authority and the revival of the religious orders. As the Cluniac monk Rudolf (Raoul) Glaber wrote, "Around the third year after 1000 A.D., over nearly all the earth, but especially in Italy and in the land of the Gauls, churches were being rebuilt. . . . In fact, it was as though the world, rousing itself and putting aside its decrepit old age, was donning the gleaming white vestiture of new churches. The faithful did not content themselves with rebuilding the cathedrals; they also restored the monastery churches and even the little village churches."

After the troubled times of the 10th century — the famine, the terror, the disasters resulting from the Norman and Magyar invasions — arts and letters gradually revived in the great abbeys, in the pilgrimage centers, and in the canonical churches. These were protected by the fortresses and stone keeps that had been erected throughout the Christian world in the great fiefs organized on the ruins of the Carolingian empire. In France the duchies of Normandy, Aquitaine, Gascony, and Burgundy and the counties of Flanders, Champagne, Anjou, Brittany, Toulouse, and Rouergue were grouped around the young Capetian monarchy. It was in these areas that Romanesque art flourished in the 11th century and the first half of the 12th century, and it was there that the sumptuous buildings were erected that, because of their large size and rich decoration of sculpture and paintings, scandalized certain moralists of the time (see IMAGES AND ICONOCLASM). From this movement of religious fervor and artistic revival Romanesque art emerged, derived from Carolingian (see CAROLINGIAN PERIOD) and Ottonian art (see OTTONIAN PERIOD), against a firm background of Roman traditions and permeated, during the late Middle Ages, with Oriental influences and, in some regions, with barbaric and Moslem influences.

The Romanesque church is a religious edifice dominated by the semicircular arch and covered with a wooden ceiling, or sometimes with barrel vaulting, with groin vaulting, or with domes. It leans heavily on the earth that supports it, and the stone of which it is constructed seems to identify itself with the soil from which it has emerged, with the atmosphere in which it is steeped. Structures of this type dominated the landscape of France in the 11th century and the first half of the 12th century, and in some regions until the end of the 12th century. They persisted in Germany until the 13th century, and even later in Italy and Spain.

Romanesque art holds a powerful attraction for the modern eye in its plenitude, in the solidity of its masses and the thickness of its walls, in its perfect adaptation to the country, the climate, and the soil in which it is so deeply rooted, and in its suitability to its purpose, the nobility of its composition, and the power of its execution. It might be said that the 11th century is the century of creations, inventions, experiments, trials and successes, the 12th is the century of epic poetry, *chansons de geste*, the flowering of the schools, and of concrete achievements expressing this grandeur, this epic enthusiasm.

The iconography of the period provides simultaneously religious, historical, doctrinal, and moral lessons; the scenes depicted always have hidden symbolic and allegorical meaning (see SYMBOLISM AND ALLEGORY), with plant, animal, and fantastic motifs, drawn from the traditional heritage of all peoples, that have value for their hidden meanings, as symbols of historical, religious, or higher moral truths (see MONSTROUS AND IMAGINARY SUBJECTS); even numbers have their own peculiar beauty and symbolic meaning (see PROPORTION).

Romanesque sculpture is both decoration and part of the building; it is perfectly wed to the contours of its setting, submitting to all the dimensions and curves of that setting. It relates, in picturesque and dramatic style, the lessons of the Gospels, the Apocalyptic visions, the miracles, the struggles against the powers of hell, portrayed in great sculptured pages in which the figures, heightened by light and shadow, stand out against the background in a manner somewhat reminiscent of the frescoes and mosaics of ancient basilicas.

This encyclopedic art was universal in the sense that it triumphed throughout the Christian world. In the 12th century that need for universality which inspired the vast medieval conception of man and his relationship to God and creation had already appeared. This universality is explained by the constant contacts among different countries, extending as far as Africa and the East, through commercial routes, crusades, pilgrimages, and artistic exchanges. Masons and artists moved about constantly from town to town and from workshop to workshop. But this art was also personal. Although the actual creators of the buildings are unknown and the churches seem to arise from the efforts of an entire community — indeed of an entire epoch — the personal and human quality so evident in this architecture must not be overlooked; even in buildings otherwise nearly alike, many details express the personality, the taste, the "presence" of the builder.

At the beginning of the 11th century, in southeast France, in Burgundy, in Franche-Comté, in the Meuse Valley, from the Moselle to the Rhine, as in northern Italy and Catalonia, Romanesque art uniformly reflects the characteristics favored by Carolingian builders: simplicity of the central plan and of its parts and simplicity of decoration. In other regions — in central, southern, and western France — the buildings, often larger, are vaulted and the interiors are less well lighted; in the Loire

Valley and in Normandy they are timbered and are full of light. Around these buildings are grouped families of churches having characteristics in common, often quite different from the churches in other regions. Such differences can be explained by previous local traditions, by the greater or lesser wealth of the region, by the climate and the quality of materials available, by the local influences of a particular religious order, or even by the preferences of an individual patron. In the 12th century, as these special characteristics became more distinct, church complexes became more differentiated and reached great artistic heights, not only in France but also in England, in Germany, in Spain, and in Italy.

The grandeur of concept and the multiplicity of the means of expression of these Romanesque architects must be recognized, as well as their unity of effort in erecting such solid, powerful, well-lighted buildings. At the same time, the diversity in their methods of solving problems must also be recognized in the various solutions for the establishment of volumes, the balancing of masses, and the distribution of sculptured decoration on both interior and exterior and in the setting aside of large bare walls for paintings in which beauty vies with the historical and mystical interest of the scenes and figures they represent.

Romanesque art, an art of force and of power, full of mystery, seems to have been created for meditation rather than for the expression of the joy and hope that was to burst out in the dazzling light and vitality of the Gothic cathedrals.

Marcel AUBERT

I. ARCHITECTURE. FRANCE. The limits of the period described as Romanesque in France are open to discussion; some aspects of French Romanesque art are merely extensions of Carolingian art, and other, original, elements survived in details of the early French Gothic churches. It is nevertheless legitimate to take as a starting point the year 1000 or, more precisely, the year 987, when the Capetian dynasty came to the throne of France. The concluding date of the Romanesque period varies from region to region. From the middle of the 12th century Gothic architecture was established in and around Paris, but in the other provinces it came very gradually and coexisted with Romanesque art during the second half of the 12th century and well into the 13th.

It is even more difficult to establish a geographic framework. What was France at the time of Hugh Capet's accession to the throne? What had France become at the end of the Romanesque period, in the reign of St. Louis? The boundaries of the kingdom had changed so much in the interval that to us any other framework than that of present-day France invites confusion.

The Romanesque era corresponded to the golden age of feudalism; and the territorial divisions of the feudal system roughly correspond to certain artistic divisions. Thus there existed not one French Romanesque architecture but many. Furthermore, the different provincial styles became distinct and were established only gradually. Initially, broad currents of interprovincial, even international exchanges flowed through the entire territory, and it was from them that Romanesque art originated and took shape. The activity and influence of monastic orders such as those of Cluny and Cîteaux knew no borders, further adding to the complexity of the artistic phenomena of the period.

Within the chronological and geographic framework thus indicated, it is possible to define the French Romanesque church from the point of view of structure and architectural style. It is, with almost no exceptions, a building with its choir oriented toward the east. The central plan is rare; the rectangular plan with a single aisle or, more often, a nave and two aisles predominates. The type having a nave and four aisles is exceptional. A transept frequently runs between the nave and the choir. But none of this was new; the plan of the Romanesque church was distinguished from that of preceding eras by several features, the first of which was the different structure of its two extremities. Except in the eastern part of France, there rarely appeared the two facing apses or transepts (characteristic of the

Carolingian and Ottonian periods) that create confusion as to the functions of the different parts of the buildings. A second distinguishing feature, in all the major examples of the Romanesque church, is the ambulatory with radiating chapels; these chapels are separate from one another, in contrast to those of the Gothic era, which are continuous.

In elevation, the French Romanesque church displays the traditional elements: rows of supports separating the aisles and bearing the great arcades; windows pierced in the sustaining wall to illuminate directly the central aisle, except in churches having three aisles of almost equal height. Above the side aisles there are often galleries opening onto the interior by means of arcades which mark a second level between the large arcades below and the windows or the vault above. The supports of the central aisle are sometimes columns, more often piers, which increase the intricacy of design in that for each supported element there is a corresponding supporting one in the pier rising along the wall as far as the springer of the main vault in such a way that the division of the masonry into bays is better defined than before. Upon consideration it becomes apparent that, compared with preceding eras, it is this articulation of the structure that represents the chief progress of the Romanesque period. In place of the large unbroken wall surfaces of the previous era, the Romanesque church presents a decidedly rhythmic arrangement, bay by bay and sometimes story by story, because of the bands that divide the elevation.

Finally, the French Romanesque building can be characterized by its type of roof. The wooden framework, uncovered or plastered, above the main aisle was prevalent in the northern provinces, but the church that was completely vaulted, the better to resist fire, was an innovation of fundamental importance peculiar to the southern provinces. The vaults used were of various kinds: the tunnel vault was either semicircular or pointed (in Burgundy and Provence); the series of transverse barrel vaults was exceptional; the half-barrel vault and the raking barrel vault were used over the side aisles; the groin vault was frequently used, even over the main aisle. The various types of vaults were usually marked or separated by transverse molded ribs descending to the supports and thereby reiterating the articulation of the structure even in its upper parts. The dome was also widely used in the Romanesque era and was of two types, according to whether the corners of the support were pendentives or squinches. The pendentives provide the dome with a circular base, the squinches with an octagonal one. The dome on squinches is therefore normally an octagonal cloister vault. In a number of provinces it is used at the crossing of the transept. Only rarely are cupolas on squinches found in a row over the main aisle; a row of cupolas on pendentives, however, covers many single-aisled churches. Among the types of Romanesque roofs should also be mentioned the rib vault supported by two ribs. It has now been established that this type was used in the Anglo-Norman area from the end of the 11th century.

The problem of the thrust of these heavy stone vaults was a formidable one; although it was easily solved in single-aisled churches by strengthening the walls, bay by bay, with external buttresses, this system could not be employed in churches having side aisles. In these, such buttresses, leaning against the walls sustaining the ceiling of the nave, would have crushed the vaults of the side aisles. From the standpoint of the solutions adopted, Romanesque churches can be divided into three main categories: those in which the main aisle is not vaulted, thus eliminating the problem; those in which it is vaulted but is framed by two lateral aisles of approximately the same height, so that the three vaults balance one another, the central aisle then being illuminated only indirectly; and those in which vaulting and direct lighting have been reconciled and in which the main aisle, higher than the side aisles, is covered with a vault supported only by the sustaining walls, which, however, the builders were not afraid to weaken by piercing them with windows.

Among the characteristics of French Romanesque architecture, mention should be made of the importance given to the crypts, which are, for the most part, subterranean (although

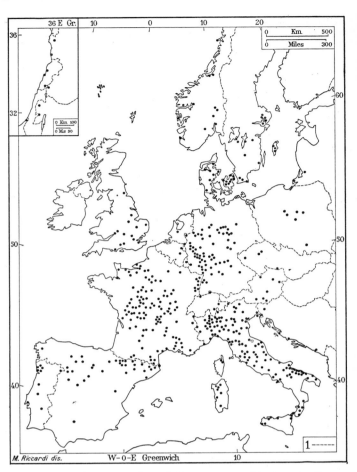

Distribution and concentration of Romanesque architecture in Europe. Key: (1) modern national boundaries.

the word *crypta* had previously been applied to any enclosed and vaulted space, whether above the ground or half-buried), and of the development of bell towers and steeples, which, in their number and size, go beyond the functional role of shelter for church bells and become symbols of power.

The early period (ca. 1000–ca. 1070): a. The northern provinces. Developments in the 11th century in the regions north of the Loire are not well known. Several churches founded by King Robert II the Pious (996–1031) display architectural features different from those of Carolingian times, which were characterized by cruder construction and roughly hewn stone, invariably embedded in mortar and with thick joints. Such features are found in the crypt of Notre-Dame-du-Fort at Etampes and the lower chamber of the Treasury of Saint-Benoît-sur-Loire.

The ambulatory with radiating chapels appeared at the beginning of the 11th century. Although the model might perhaps be found in the crypt of the Cathedral of Clermont-Ferrand, dedicated in 946, where the radiating chapels served as receptacles for relics, it was in the Loire region that the style was developed. Possibly this type of ambulatory was used in the raised choir of Notre-Dame-de-la-Couture, Le Mans, about the year 1000; it probably appeared in St-Martin of Tours in the same period, in St-Aignan of Orléans (where the crypt of the church of Robert the Pious is still preserved), and in Bishop Fulbert's Cathedral of Notre-Dame at Chartres and thereafter spread throughout northern France. The Cathedral of Rouen, consecrated in 1063, had an ambulatory with three radiating chapels; its crypt has been uncovered by excavations. A similar choir was added to the church of Vignory between 1049 and 1057. Much simpler plans, however, continued in favor, with flat *chevet* or with one or three apses.

The experiments conducted during this period concerning

the location of the steeples must also be considered. At the beginning of the 11th century a tower porch at the façade was used at St-Germain-des-Prés in Paris; it was the design of Abbot Morard (990–1014). That of Saint-Benoît-sur-Loire, magnificently powerful, could not have been the *turris* constructed by the abbot Gauzlin in the first years of the 11th century; it is no earlier than 1067. The towers erected over both sides of the choir, in the Carolingian tradition, indicate an influence from the countries of the Holy Roman Empire. At Morienval (near Compiègne) there are two towers which previously flanked a simple apse (as in St-Germain-des-Prés during the 11th cent.). The most usual place for the tower was at the crossing, where it often took the form of a lantern tower, hollow to the top and increasing the interior light. Such a tower apparently existed at St-Ayoul in Provins shortly after 1048.

The churches of this period rarely included columns as supports, except in the choir and at the *rond-point* of the ambulatory. The nave nearly always had rectangular piers supporting the great arcade by means of simple imposts. Examples of this are found in the Church of Notre-Dame, in Melun, founded by Robert the Pious; in St-Mexme, in Chinon (980–1007); and at Château-Landon. The great arcades, always semicircular, are most often filled with rubble in the center, with only the ribs being of masonry. The windows open in the wall above the arcades. From this period on, a second story was sometimes inserted between the arcades and the windows. Galleries were used at Montier-en-Der, a church whose nave has been attributed (surely erroneously) to Abbot Adson and dated to the end of the 10th century. An open arcade between the nave and the side aisles at Vignory does not seem to have been related to a plan for galleries.

These very simple and, as it were, "inarticulated" plans are well suited to the timbered naves which were the rule during this period and in this region. Even large aisles like those in the church of the Abbey of Beaulieu-lès-Loches, from about 1007, were timbered. Nevertheless, the first attempts at vaulting, made as early as the 11th century, particularly in the region of the Loire, should be pointed out. Barrel vaulting was used in the churches of Reignac and of Perrusson, in St-Jean-Baptiste in Langeais, and in St-Genest in Lavardin (ca. 1032–47). The last-named has, in its west tower, traces of a vault between the domical vault and the dome. Another church in Lavardin, St-Gildéric (1037–47; largely destroyed), showed the beginnings of a true dome on crude squinches. Groin vaulting was used from the beginning of the 11th century, without dividing ribs, as in the lower chamber of the Treasury of Saint-Benoît-sur-Loire, but examples of it are chiefly found in crypts such as that of the Cathedral of Auxerre, in which the plan is extended by an axial chapel. There, however, ribbed vaults led to the adoption of compound supports with engaged half columns. This crypt has been dated to about 1030–50. Such experiments led in the north to varied but strongly characterized styles.

Eastern France, which was politically subject to the Holy Roman Empire, followed the examples of Ottonian architecture. The most important building of this area, the Cathedral of Verdun, was built between 1049 and 1083 and is fairly well preserved. It includes two transepts and two opposing apses flanked by towers. The western apse has a flat *chevet*; the eastern one was rebuilt in about 1144. The Cathedral (begun 1015) built in Strasbourg by Bishop Wernher is known, from excavations, to have had a massive façade facing west with a porch and flanking towers, a columned nave, a continuous transept in the style of the early basilicas, and a choir reduced to an apse but framed by storied chambers. Similar features were found in the Cathedral of Metz, also known through excavations. The towers flanking the apse separated it from two apsidioles opening on the transept. At St-Maurice in Epinal there can be seen built into the middle of the rear wall of the transept a curious small exterior tower that recalls such Ottonian models as St. Michael of Hildesheim (X, PL. 455). The doubling of the apse and the transept, the frequent use of the columns as supports, the towers of the apse, the importance of the

massive west façade with platform chapel, the monumental grandeur of the transept — these are the many characteristics by which the 11th-century churches of eastern France were related to the architecture of the Holy Roman Empire.

Normandy, governed by its dukes with a strong hand, constructed, from the first half of the 11th century, buildings that revealed a coherent style. One of the oldest is the Abbey church in Bernay, partially destroyed but the plan of which can be reconstructed; it had an elongated choir with three aisles and three apses, a transept with opposing apsidioles, and a long nave with side aisles. Work on this church began before 1017. The choir was erected between about 1020 and 1028, the nave between about 1028 and 1040. The nave includes a true triforium at the second level; the south transept has a passage within the thickness of the wall, the first example of the Norman technique of the hollow wall. Since, between 1017 and 1028, Abbot Thierry simultaneously governed Bernay, Jumièges, and Mont-Saint-Michel, it is not surprising to find architectural similarities in the three places. At Mont-Saint-Michel the construction of the church undoubtedly began with the choir, in 1023; the nave, completed in 1063, remains. It shows the progress that had occurred; the compound piers consist of four half columns, that of the interior rising to the top of the wall. Notre-Dame of Jumièges (PL. 201) was the chief building of the duchy in the 11th century. It was probably begun as early as 1020 and was consecrated in 1067. The choir, reconstructed during the Gothic period, is known through excavations. It had an ambulatory without radiating chapels, but on the arms of the transept there opened two chapels. On the west side of the nave, almost entirely in ruins, the western façade, with two towers and a central tribune deriving from Ottonian models, remains. The nave consists of alternating columns and compound piers, the origin of which can be traced to the architecture of Lombardy or to that of the Holy Roman Empire. The galleries running along the arms of the transept are reminiscent of certain Ottonian models such as St. Michael of Hildesheim. The main aisle was timbered, but the side aisles and the galleries above them were groin-vaulted. There was a lantern tower over the crossing, and in the transept, at the level of the upper windows, a circular gallery. Thus it might be said that all the elements of Norman Romanesque architecture were to be found at Jumièges as early as the middle of the 11th century.

A consideration of the important buildings (many subsequently destroyed or greatly modified), such as the cathedrals of Avranches, of Coutances, of Rouen, and of Bayeux, can give an idea of the intense architectural activity of Normandy during the early Romanesque period.

Certain churches in the region between eastern France and Normandy must be considered separately, for they anticipated a style that was subsequently to spread to the south of the Loire. First of these is St-Remi of Reims, with 11th-century nave and transept (somewhat modified during the Gothic period) still standing. The church was begun by Abbot Airard, resumed by Abbot Thierry between 1039 and 1045, and completed by Abbot Herimar between 1045 and 1049. In addition to the galleries opening onto the nave through semicircular archways, and the façade, framed by two towers like that of Jumièges, St-Remi is characterized by its transept, which includes barrel-vaulted side aisles with three two-storied apsidioles on each arm. The side aisle was continued behind the north transept, an innovation of major importance. The development of the Cathedral of Orléans was also interesting; its plan, ascertained by excavations, included a relatively short nave that probably dates from the end of the 10th century. The transept included side aisles (doubled in the course of the following century) that continued to the back of the transept arms; and the choir, rebuilt at the end of the 11th century, had an ambulatory with radiating chapels. Of this series of churches, the most important one is certainly St-Martin of Tours, a great center of pilgrimages. This church, which was almost entirely destroyed during the French Revolution, also had a transept with side aisles, but scholars do not agree as to its dates. According to Lesueur (1949), the work was carried out by the treasurer, Hervé, from

Principal centers of Romanesque architecture in northwestern Europe and the Holy Land. *Key:* (1) modern national boundaries.

about 1003 to 1014; but various other scholars date it to the end of the 11th century. The transept had galleries behind the arms, in the Norman style. St-Remi of Reims, the Cathedral at Orléans, and St-Martin of Tours, all churches with wide transepts and galleries, seem to have played a dominant role in the development of the architectural type of the so-called "pilgrim roads."

b. The southern provinces. A style of architecture very different from that of the north developed in the Mediterranean region beginning in the 10th century. Puig y Cadafalch (1928) has called this style, somewhat imprecisely, "the first Romanesque art." An international style of Eastern origin, it took shape in Lombardy, from there spread to southern France and Catalonia, and later extended up the Rhone and Saône valleys to Burgundy and Lorraine. The construction and materials, consisting largely of stones broken with a hammer, were crude. The most constant characteristic of this style was its exterior decoration of "Lombard bands" — festooned cornices ascending to the top of the walls and returning from one point to another onto slender buttresses. The buildings are extremely varied and include timbered churches without transepts terminating in three apses, churches with barrel-vaulted naves, and large basilicas with transept and with domed crossings. St-Martin of Aimé in Savoy (ca. 1019) is of the first type; in it, the Lombard bands are replaced at the apse by arcading. The church of Arles-sur-Tech, which was probably originally timbered, was consecrated in 1046; it has three apses, all of them facing west. The second type is found at Saint-Martin-du-Canigou (XI, PL. 308) in the Pyrenees; the third style (of which S. María of Ripoll in Catalonia is the most famous example) is found in France in Quarante. This church, consecrated in 1053, has barrel vaulting over the main aisle, groin vaulting over the side aisles, and a dome on rectangular squinches over the crossing.

In the north, at Gigny, in Franche-Comté, the church was constructed at the same time as the church at Romain-môtier (Switzerland) built by St. Odilon, abbot of Cluny, and shows the influence of his great Burgundian abbey. St-Philibert of Tournus (XI, PL. 308) also reveals the influence of Cluny in the use of radiating chapels in the crypt. These chapels were built on the foundations of the church that was destroyed by fire in 1007 or 1008. St-Philibert, however, combined other elements through which it united southern and northern styles. The ground floor of the narthex was begun after 1007/1008, and the upper story of the narthex, consecrated to St. Michael, was built at the same time as the new nave, sometime before the death of Abbot Ardain in 1056. This narthex belongs to southern art by virtue of the use of cylindrical supports for the different types of vaults, and especially because of its exterior decoration of Lombard bands. The transept, not vaulted in the 11th century, was of the "low" type, which was found in Ottonian architecture (see OTTONIAN PERIOD, col. 876) but was essentially a southern characteristic. The apse included at the end of the 11th century an ambulatory with three radiating rectangular chapels; above the tall cylindrical columns of the nave, the transverse barrel vaults were begun at the end of the 11th century and were completed in the 12th century.

The influence of Tournus is seen again in certain Burgundian churches that stem from the first Romanesque art; an example is Chapaize, built in the 11th century and vaulted anew in the 12th century. It was, moreover, in upper Burgundy that northern forms, stemming from Carolingian traditions, and southern forms met. Begun in 1029 and consecrated in 1058, St-Etienne of Nevers (PL. 200) included two opposing apses and, undoubtedly, two transepts. The west apse and the crypt below it are still intact, as is the west transept, which was previously timbered and onto which platform apsidioles opened. The Church of St-Vorles, Châtillon-sur-Seine, displays more than any other the dualism then reigning in Burgundy. Constructed at the beginning of the 11th century (and subsequently modified), it possesses two transepts, the west transept forming a porch. This is a northern architectural feature, but the presence of a tower on a dome over the crossing and of

Lombard bands on the exterior give evidence of the strength of southern influences. The Abbey church, later the Cathedral, of St-Bénigne of Dijon was most probably the chief building of Burgundy in the 11th century. The church, which no longer exists, was built by Abbot William of Volpiano between 1002 and 1017. It included a choir with chapels of decreasing depth, a transept, and a nave with double side aisles. The system of alternating piers in the nave, which was probably timbered, may have served as a model for Norman churches. At the end of the choir, William of Volpiano built a large rotunda, three stories high, with a concentric passage. Of this, only the ground floor remains. This arrangement, known in pre-Romanesque art, is found in the churches of St-Pierre-le-Vif of Sens, St-Germain of Auxerre, and Flavigny.

The central and western regions display varied experiments rather lacking in unity. In Berry, the most noteworthy building is the church at Neuvy-Saint-Sépulcre, with a rotunda containing a side aisle in imitation of the Church of the Holy Sepulcher in Jerusalem; it dates in part from about 1045 and is modeled on the basilican plan. From the beginning of the 11th century, Poitou showed remarkable architectural activity. The Abbey church of Maillezais, of which the façade and the northern wall of the nave remain, was begun between about 1003 and 1015 and presents some unusual characteristics: a west façade with two towers in the Carolingian and Ottonian tradition, a two-storied elevation with groin-vaulted side aisles and galleries covered by transverse barrel vaults, and a windowless nave that was probably vaulted. This was a powerful and remarkably advanced synthesis of the northern use of the *Westwerk* and the southern style of vaults on a windowless nave, balanced by side vaults. St-Hilaire of Poitiers is much more closely related to northern than to southern architecture. Dedicated in 1049, it was built by an English architect, Walter Coorland, who, subsidized by Queen Emma of England (before 1044), built the large transept and the tower to the west of the north transept. This tower is in the same position as the tower of Chartres Cathedral, erected by Bishop Fulbert, who was also treasurer of the collegium of Poitiers. Except for the tower, which was groin-vaulted, the church was timbered. A second building program, perhaps completed by the time of the consecration in 1049, was responsible for the erection of a large nave with side aisles, the vaulting of the transept, and the construction of a west aisle that incorporated the tower into the church. It has been thought that Coorland continued working until at least 1049, a fact that would explain the Norman style of alternation that appears in the nave. The Abbey church of Charroux, almost entirely destroyed, was a building of exceptional splendor; probably it must be dated between 1017 and 1047. The nave with side aisles and the choir, of which one radiating chapel remains, were separated by an immense rotunda with three concentric aisles into which there opened two slanting apsidioles and onto which were grafted the two arms of a transept with side aisles and platform chapels. Of this rotunda, evidently inspired by the Church of the Holy Sepulcher, there remain the central piers, made up of four half columns supporting two levels of arcades. This central section was directly lighted by windows and was covered by a dome almost 100 ft. high.

The important church of Saint-Sever, in Landes, had probably not been completed by the time Abbot Gregory of Montaner died in 1072, but the remarkable arrangement of the choir had certainly been determined. Together with Châteaumeillant, in Berry, and La Charité-sur-Loire (in its original state), it is the finest example of the plan having seven apses of decreasing depth; in addition, the four end apsidioles are on two stories and are preceded by galleries that recall those of St. Michael of Hildesheim. They communicate through angular corridors, as in the Carolingian crypts of Saint-Philibert-de-Grandlieu (III, FIG. 99) and of St-Germain of Auxerre.

The mature French Romanesque style. Following the experiments of the first period, Romanesque architecture, by about 1070, seems to have been firmly established in France; its well-defined technical solutions, especially vaulting, and its different provincial styles were thenceforth fairly clearly marked.

French scholars have made great efforts to define the provincial "schools" without ever arriving at a uniform theory. The differentiation into schools, a useful but artificial device, cannot really mirror the changing and complex historical reality. Care must be taken to avoid considering the schools as artistic territories bounded by well-defined frontiers; the various "schools" that formed through the imitation of models (often difficult to identify) are spread over vast regions subject to diverse influences, and it is impossible to place their buildings within any formal scheme. The fairly clear distinction between a northern "timbered" zone and a southern "vaulted" zone is not so valid a guide as it was for the preceding period; vaulting came to be used throughout France, at least for large buildings, during the mature phase of the Romanesque.

In Normandy buildings were constructed that were admirable both for their size and for the nobility of their articulation. Following the Norman conquest, the Norman style took root in England (see GREAT BRITAIN), where it developed characteristic nuances. In Caen, Duke William, later known as the Conqueror, ordered the building of St-Etienne — the men's abbey — between 1064 and 1087; and his wife, Duchess Matilda, erected La Trinité — the women's abbey (PL. 201) — between 1062 and 1083. The former combines all the characteristics of mature Norman architecture. The piers of the nave (the choir was reconstructed in the 13th cent.) are grouped, with the half column facing the main aisle reaching to the top of the wall. The large arcades are semicircular. The second story is occupied by galleries opening onto the nave by means of arcades nearly as tall as those of the ground story. These galleries seem from the beginning to have been covered with half-barrel vaulting. Windows pierced at the third-story level abundantly light the great nave; the "thick wall" technique made it possible to place

with which it communicated only by a single door, and ending in an apse surrounded by a narrow gallery, has retained its original vaulting, consisting of two groin vaults and a half dome. This is also the case in St-Nicolas of Caen, built between about 1083 and 1093, a well-preserved example of a Norman church.

The church at Cerisy-la-Forêt seems to date from the same period as the three above-mentioned churches of Caen; in it the bays of the galleries of the nave have the same proportions as those of St-Etienne but are further divided by small columns. A high gallery runs behind the continuous arcades, of which there are three to each bay. The apse is lighted by three stories of windows, with galleries at the second and third stories, although this last feature was modified in the 14th century. This was an exceptional feature in Normandy (but one commonly found in England), where the apses generally have only two rows of superimposed bays. The well-preserved Church of St-Georges in Saint-Martin-de-Boscherville is not earlier than about 1125. A building with a triforium opening beneath the roof, its piers are not alternated, but it is possible that, two by two, the small engaged columns near the central aisle may have borne diaphragm arches to support the original timbering. The existence of such arches seems certain for St-Gervais of Falaise.

Other Norman churches do not have such marked characteristics. The Abbey church of Fécamp, built by Abbot Guillaume du Ros, had in 1106 an ambulatory with radiating chapels, of which two remain. The alternation of piers is found in Ouistreham as well as in Graville-Sainte-Honorine. The church of Secqueville-en-Bessin is one of the rare churches of Normandy that has not subsequently been vaulted; its arcades bear the geometric decoration that, favored by the architects of this province, flowered magnificently in the nave of Bayeux

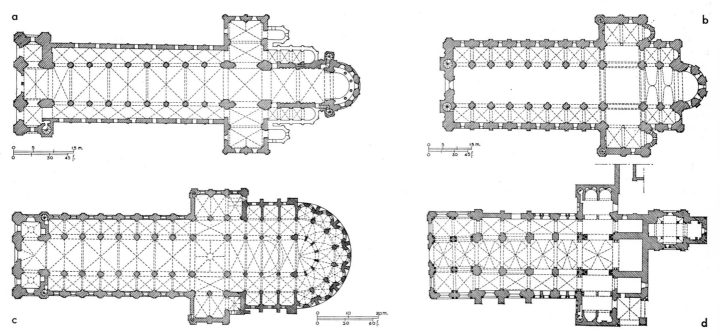

France. (a) Caen, Church of La Trinité, 1062–83, plan; (b) Boscherville, St-Georges, 1125, plan; (c) Caen, St-Etienne, 1064–87, plan (from E. Lundberg, 1950); (d) Le Puy, Cathedral, 12th century, plan (from A. Fikry, 1934).

a gallery in front of the windows. It is generally agreed that the central nave was originally covered with timbering; there is, however, a kind of alteration in the piers, suggesting groin vaults on a square plan, each one covering a double bay. The crossing of the transept was surmounted by a lantern tower with an octopartite rib vault; the transept was covered by oblong rib-vaulted bays. The façade, with two magnificent towers, might be called organic, in that its divisions correspond to those of the interior. La Trinité differs from St-Etienne in that it has no galleries but does have a blind arcade. The choir, originally flanked by apsidioles of decreasing depth,

Cathedral. The beautiful Abbey church of Lessay is of exceptional importance. Its choir, begun about 1080, was sufficiently advanced in 1098 for the founder to be buried there. The recent restoration has proved that the vaults on ogive ribs found there are integrally constructed from the top of the walls; it is possible, therefore, to conclude that they were being built in 1098, which would make them contemporary with the oldest ones known in the Anglo-Norman domain, those of Durham Cathedral.

The architecture of the north of France, including the region of Paris, can hardly be considered to constitute a Romanesque "school," in spite of all that has been said of it by various scholars. The characteristics found there are not sufficient to define a style. At best, one can point to the presence of pointed arches in the broad arcades, of diaphragm arches such as those across the main aisle at Courville and Cerny-en-Laonnois, and to the perforation of the upper windows along the axis of the piers, as, for instance, at Champlieu. The two-storied elevation nearly always remains inarticulated, and visible timbering is the rule. Completely vaulted churches are exceptional. The late-11th-century church at Saint-Loup-de-Naud has barrel vaulting, groin vaulting, and a dome on squinches and appears to be an imitation of the Abbey church of St-Pierre-le-Vif in Sens, to which this priory church was subordinate. The influence of Normandy on the architecture of northern France has been greatly exaggerated; it is clearly seen in the decoration but is little evident in the structure, except in the churches at Maule and Lillers. The latter church (ca. 1120–1135) is the largest building in the region. Hardly anything is known of the great masterpiece that St-Lucien in Beauvais (ca. 1095–1109) must have been. Emerging from the old Carolingian tradition, the architecture of northern France adopted Gothic methods of construction too rapidly to have had time to form a strongly characterized Romanesque school.

The east of France, by contrast, having been strongly influenced by Ottonian architecture, reveals a highly individual provincial art that differs little from that of the German Rhineland. France, however, has nothing to compare with the outstanding buildings of Germany. Of the characteristics of the Rhenish scoool, France retained the two-story elevation with direct lighting; the absence of an ambulatory; the choir ending in three apses or in a flat *chevet*, as in Murbach; the division of the main aisle into large square bays, each corresponding to two similar square bays in the side aisles; and, always, the alternation of supports. This type of structure, together with the massiveness of forms that is the dominant characteristic of the region of Alsace and Lorraine, raises a problem of roofing. It has perhaps been too hastily claimed that the original roofing was visible timbering, later replaced by groin vaults. The church at Champ-le-Duc is timbered, but it lacks those half columns ascending the height of the wall that appear everywhere else. It is not impossible that groin vaults, with a vault for each large square bay, might have constituted the original roofing in certain German churches (such as the Cathedral of Speyer), and that the same may have been true of such French buildings as the Cathedral of Saint-Dié and the Church of Notre-Dame in the same town. The latter has such vaults, but they have been reworked. Actually, the churches of Alsace and Lorraine were built rather late in the 12th century to have been originally vaulted with diagonal ribs; but the Romanesque style persisted in eastern France, as in Germany, until well into the 13th century. The buildings of this region are notable for their façades, which often have two towers (as in St-Léger in Guebwiller; PL. 226), sometimes built above a porch, as in Marmoutier. They are also remarkable for the size of their bell towers, which, in keeping with tradition, were placed along the choir; the church at Mont-devant-Sassey is a good example of this practice. In Murbach (PL. 226), the bell towers rise above the arms of the transept and accompany a monumentally impressive *chevet* pierced by two stories of windows. Finally, everywhere there are examples of the early Romanesque tradition, which was strongly established in this region, of using Lombard bands as exterior decoration, and there are occasional examples of communicating galleries.

Various influences converge at Berry, where there are churches of many different types, but where there are also markedly characteristic traits — the arcades on the exterior of the choir at Saint-Genou; the typical Berry arcade, the so-called *berrichon*, running along a transept narrower than the single nave found at La Berthenoux, Les Aix-d'Angillon, and Bommiers (where there is, in addition, a semicircle of *secretaria* between the apse and the apsidioles); the choir separated from its aisles by narrow arcades on columns at La Celle-Bruère, at Les Aix-d'Angillon, at Saint-Genou, and at Saint-Oustrille in Graçay. This is the most remarkable characteristic of the choir of the distinguished but difficult to classify church of Saint-Benoît-sur-Loire, built 1067/1080–1108. It is notable for its ambulatory with two radiating chapels, for its two transepts (the eastern one being the lower), for its blind arcading running unbroken above the large arcades, and for its windows opening under the barrel vaults. The main transept is of the same date, but its south arm has been reconstructed. The nave dates from the 12th and 13th centuries.

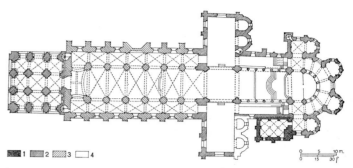

Saint-Benoît-sur-Loire (France), Abbey church, plan. *Key:* (1) 10th century; (2) 11th century; (3) 12th century; (4) later additions (*from K. J. Conant, 1959*).

The Loire region possesses some remarkable buildings, but they present no unity of style. These include the churches of Selles-sur-Cher; Saint-Aignan, related to Saint-Benoît in its three-storied elevation and its barrel vaulting over the early-12th-century choir; Chatillon-sur-Indre, with an arcaded nave and a pointed barrel vault, in the formula of southwestern France; and Le Ronceray at Angers, built 1088–1119, with a central barrel vault supported by transverse barrel vaults. The influence of this region is noticeable in Brittany, where, however, only buildings of little importance have survived.

The southwest, even taking into account the differences in details between Poitou and Aulnay-de-Saintonge, has, by contrast with the above-mentioned regions, remarkable stylistic unity. In the majority of churches the side aisles rise high enough to support the vault of the windowless nave; but the method of vaulting permits many variations. At Saint-Savin, where choir and transept date from about 1060 to 1075, as do the tower porch and the three western bays of the nave (the rest of the nave dating from about 1095 to 1115), the semicircular barrel vault of the main aisle is supported by lateral groin vaults. The same is true of Notre-Dame-la-Grande in Poitiers and of St-Pierre in Chauvigny. The aisles are covered by semicircular barrel vaults in the Saint-Jouin-de-Marnes church and by pointed barrel vaults in St-Hilaire and St-Pierre at Melle and in St-Pierre-de-la-Tour, at Aulnay-de-Saintonge, the finest building of this type. This buttressing by half-barrel vaults is also found at Parthenay-le-Vieux. A great number of churches of secondary importance conform to these models, making for great unity of style in the Romanesque architecture of southwestern France. This unity is also noticeable in the façades entirely covered by rich sculptural ornament at Notre-Dame-la-Grande, Echillais, Chandenac, Civray, and Aulnay-de-Saintonge (XIII, PL. 345).

At the center of the southwest region can be found a very different group of churches, having a single nave divided by piers into square bays, each covered by a cupola on pendentives. This was an imitation of the Byzantine and Cypriote buildings that were dispersed along the Cahors-Périgueux-Angoulême-Saintes axis, where the subsoil provided easily cut stone that made possible structural methods that dispensed with scaffolding and timber framework in a region lacking forests. The prototypes seem to have been St-Etienne-de-la-Cité, in Périgueux (built 1101–06, although the church, which was subsequently enlarged, retains only its western bay from this period); the church at Saint-Avit-Senieur, covered by domes, probably since 1117, although it was subsequently given pointed vaults; and the Cathedral at Cahors, begun about 1090 (although the large dome was not erected until after Bishop Geraud de

Cardaillac returned from the East in 1112). St-Front, Périgueux, entirely rebuilt in the 19th century, reproduces the Greek-cross plan of St. Mark's in Venice, which was itself an imitation of the Church of the Holy Apostles in Constantinople. The churches of Souillac and Solignac date from the same period. The Cathedral of Angoulême (V, PL. 378, FIG. 655) was begun by Girard de Blaye, about 1105, but it was not completed until much later. At the Church of Ste-Marie-

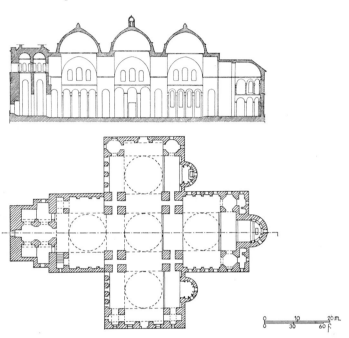

Périgueux (France), St-Front, 1120 and following centuries, longitudinal section and plan (*from B. Fletcher, A History of Architecture, New York, 1950*).

des-Dames in Saintes there is an 11th-century nave that was covered by cupolas in the 12th century, after the elimination of the side aisles. The fine nave of Fontevrault, in Anjou, appears to be both the most recent and the most isolated of the buildings of this type.

In the lower Auvergne is found a group of solidly constructed churches: Notre-Dame-du-Port in Clermont-Ferrand (FIG. 331), Issoire, Saint-Nectaire, Orcival, Saint-Saturnin. But, with the exception of the nave of Ennezat, which might date from the early 12th century, these buildings are not earlier than the

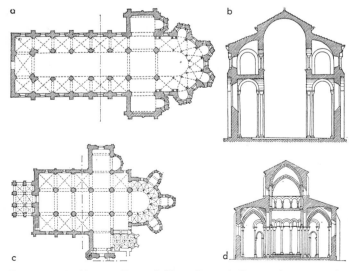

France. (*a, b*) Clermont-Ferrand, Notre-Dame-du-Port, 12th century, plan and section; (*c, d*) Paray-le-Monial, Notre-Dame, 12th century, plan and section (*from E. Lundberg, 1950*).

middle of the 12th century. Thus a distinctly Auvergnais style did not appear until the late Romanesque period. The nave, often preceded by a porch surmounted by two towers, is covered by barrel vaulting without transverse ribs over each bay; this vaulting is strengthened by the half-barrel vaults of the galleries. As in the southwest, there are no high windows. The dome on squinches at the crossing of the transept is supported by two half-barrel vaults, which are taken up, on the exterior, into a large oblong front supporting the central bell tower. Other, more simple churches (Glaine-Montaigut, Besse-en Chandesse, Volvic) have no galleries. The so-called *à copeaux* modillions, the triangular arches, and the decorative display contribute to the individuality of Auvergne churches.

The architecture of the Velay region is slightly related to Auvergne but lacks true unity. Its most beautiful building, the Cathedral in Le Puy (PL. 203; FIG. 328; V, PL. 377), cannot be included in any stylistic group. A church with nave and two aisles, it is covered in the center by a row of cupolas on squinches, a system found nowhere else but in Champagne and later used to alter the original part of St-Hilaire in Poitiers. Since the Cathedral is built on a mountain, the entrance is lower than the floor of the nave, which is entered by means of a stairway. The decoration, which is clearer evidence of Islamic influence than can be found elsewhere in France, adds still further to the originality of this building. Its tower, later reconstructed, is similar to that of the neighboring chapel of St-Michel d'Aiguilhe. Both of them are related to the towers of the southwest, of Brantôme, and of Limousin. These towers, square at the base, become octagonal at the pinnacle, with large gables over the bays. The models for these must be sought in the Limoges cathedral and in the Abbey church of St-Martial (destroyed). In addition to this type of tower, there are, in Limousin, several octagonal towers placed over crossings whose ribs are in the axis of the nave and the transept, as in Le Dorat. The powerful tower porches in Le Dorat and in Saint-Junien; the presence of cupolas on pendentives as in La Souterraine (often with a drum as at Saint-Léonard-de-Noblat); the barrel vaults, sometimes pierced at the base with small bays as in Le Dorat, in Beaulieu, and in Bénévent-l'Abbaye; the portals frequently polylobed or with arches extending the jambs — all these characteristics give the Limousin group a unity.

On the other hand, what has been termed the "school of Languedoc" hardly exists at all, so great is the diversity in that region. Such reminders of Carolingian architecture as the apses of the churches of Bourg-Saint-Andéol and La Garde-Adhémar and the west gallery of the Cathedral of Maguelone; the Mozarabic influence (see MOZARABIC ART) in the horseshoe minor apse of St-Just of Valcabrère; the constant reminders of early Romanesque art manifested in the use of Lombard bands; the plan with a single nave having large relieving arches along the walls, as in the Cathedral of Agde; the trefoil plan of the churches of Allenc and Saint-Martin-de-Londres; the presence of galleries at Alet — all these make it difficult to define a Languedoc style.

Outside of any regional category, a type of "pilgrimage church" developed along the roads that led to Santiago de Compostela, in Galicia. St-Martin of Tours and the Cathedral of Ste-Croix, Orléans, certainly played an important part in the development of this type, which seems to have come from the north. According to a recent theory, St-Martial of Limoges must have been built (1017–28) on the same plan, that is, with timber-covered galleries; but the fire of 1053 led to the barrel-vaulting of the west part, which had been spared, as well as to the lengthening of the church. It is undoubtedly in this way that the pilgrimage church became defined. The place of the church of St-Géraud of Aurillac in this definition must still be established; but Ste-Foy of Conques (PL. 200) is the first example of it that has survived. Begun between 1041 and 1052, completed in 1087, but reworked in the upper parts of the choir and the transept in the first quarter of the 12th century, Ste-Foy has an ambulatory with three radiating chapels, a relatively short nave with side aisles, and a transept. In elevation, the church has very high arcades and galleries vaulted in half barrels, which support the barrels on the transverse ribs of the nave. This formula, somewhat resembling that of the churches of Auvergne but undoubtedly of earlier date, was to blossom at St-Sernin in Toulouse (PLS. 199, 200). Begun around 1060, its main altar consecrated in 1096, and completed in 1118, with the addition of the porch and the west towers in the middle of the 12th century, this enormous church has double side aisles running the length of the nave and aisles running along the arms of the transept. Santiago de Compostela (PL. 213) was both the goal of the pilgrimages and the most beautiful building of the series. Recent excavations have established its dates: the ambulatory was built by the French architect Bernard between 1075 and 1088; the right side of the choir was built by the Spanish architect Esteban from about 1100 to 1128. The side aisles are simple at the nave, but they return upon themselves at the back of the arms of the transept, a feature more fully developed here than elsewhere. In all the churches of this type, the nave and the transept are wide in relation to the choir, which remained exiguous. This resulted from the necessity of receiving crowds of pilgrims.

In Provence, over a small area, early Romanesque architecture was replaced, late in the 12th century, by churches of a well-defined type. The influence of ancient buildings was of greatest importance in the blossoming of the Provençal style. The majority of churches have a single nave as at Le Thor, for example; others have narrow side aisles with vaults (half barrels at St-Trophime in Arles, rampant barrels at the Cathedral of Vaison-la-Romaine) supporting the central barrel vault, which is quite often pointed. This support, however, occurs low enough to permit the opening of windows under the vault at Arles and at St-Paul-Trois-Châteaux. In all these buildings, the supports, engaged along the length of the walls or separating the three aisles, are pillars with numerous projections and carry pointed arcades with double scrolls. The dome of the crossing, on squinches, is ribbed, as is the half dome of the apse, at Saint-Restitut, for instance. The walls are remarkably ornamented; all the decoration is in the early style. This influence is found even on the exterior, in pediments like those of Le Thor, at Notre-Dame-des-Doms in Avignon, and at Saint-Gabriel. Farther up the Rhone valley this influence is present everywhere, for example, in St-André-le-Bas and the Cathedral of St-Maurice in Vienne and in St-Paul and St-Martin-d'Ainay (PL. 205) in Lyons.

Farther north lies the region of what it is convenient to term the "Burgundian school." However, any more-than-superficial analysis will reveal the lack of unity of this "school." In addition to examples of early Romanesque art, there are buildings that seem to be derived from it. These have large arcades, and windows and groin vaults over the nave. The church of Anzy-le-Duc is one of the oldest examples of this style; moreover, the plan of this building, which contains an apse extended by a minor apse, was borrowed from that of St-Fortunat at Charlieu, which was barrel-vaulted. The groin-vaulting formula is found again at La Madeleine in Vézelay (PL. 204), where the nave (built 1120–40) was supported by iron tie beams, while the galleries, which are rare in Burgundy, support the nave in the narthex (1140–51) as in many churches of the style of St-Lazare of Avallon. The structure of the large Abbey church of Cluny (V, FIG. 653) was completely different; here were found tall pointed, decorative arches, and three windows to each bay under a pointed barrel vault 98 ft. high. This prodigious church, Cluny III, built by St. Hugh, was begun in 1088; the main altar was consecrated in 1095; the church was completed around 1113; and the vaulting was reworked after 1125. With its narthex, begun before 1113 but completed in the 13th century, the double side aisles of its nave, its two east transepts, its choir with ambulatory, and its seven towers, it was the largest church built during the Middle Ages. It was razed after the French Revolution, however, and nothing remains of it but the south arm of the large transept. A building so extraordinary had to serve as a model; its plan was followed at Lewes in England and its structure at Paray-le-Monial (PL. 202; FIG. 331; V, PL. 376), also built by St. Hugh. With variations in the number of windows and in the use of fluted pilasters all along the supports, the structure was also followed at La Charité-sur-Loire, at Notre-

Dame in Beaune, and in the Cathedral of Autun. The two groups, that of Vézelay and that of Cluny, have in common a boldness in the use of windows opening under an unbuttressed vault and an extremely rich decoration inspired by styles of antiquity.

The influence of the Burgundian style reached into neighboring provinces, notably Bourbonnais, at Saint-Menoux, St-Pierre in Souvigny, and (combined with the influence of Auvergne) Châtel-Montagne. It also reached Nivernais, although the beautiful Church of St-Etienne in Nevers (PL. 200), completed in 1097, cannot be included in any grouping; it is the only building in France having half-barrel-vaulted galleries, and, above, sustaining walls pierced by windows that seemingly weaken them under the large central barrel vault. Such boldness, which recalls that of Burgundy but which stems from a possibly earlier date, was the achievement of an architect of genius. The place of this building in French Romanesque architecture has never been defined exactly — its relationship to the earliest pilgrimage churches, which have the same structure except that they lack windows; its influence on the churches of Burgundy, which are well lit but lack galleries; and its influence on the churches of Auvergne, which were to borrow from it many decorative arrangements, particularly the use of triangular arches.

The Holy Land. The churches built by the Crusaders in the Holy Land, from the time of the founding of the kingdom of Jerusalem in 1099, adopted nearly all the Burgundian and Provençal styles. Most are Romanesque, since the defeat at Hattin in 1187 largely put an end to the activity of the Franks, at least in the realm of religious architecture. Many of the churches have been destroyed, some in modern times. Nearly always, these buildings preserve or reuse more ancient elements, Byzantine or even Roman, as on the four walls of the church of Quariet-el-Enab or the columns of the Cathedral of Ramès (Er Ramle). The plans are always very simple. The choir has three apses, often set into a flat wall. The only example of an ambulatory is that of the Church of the Holy Sepulcher in Jerusalem (FIG. 334), which has three radiating chapels; there, in the first half of the 12th century, the Crusaders joined a Romanesque church to the ancient rotunda of the Anastasis.

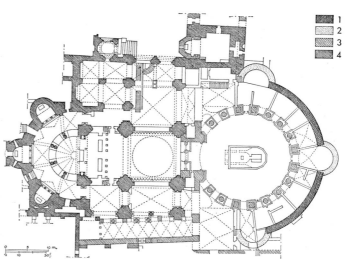

Jerusalem, Church of the Holy Sepulcher, plan. *Key*: (1) structures of the 4th century; (2) 7th century; (3) 11th century; (4) 12th century (*from K. J. Conant, 1959*).

Transepts are rarely found, although they exist (in not very outstanding form) at the Holy Sepulcher, at St. Anne in Jerusalem, and at Sebastye (anc. Samaria). The use of the pointed arch in the arcades and in the tracery of the windows shows the influence of the Arabs, who used such tracery before it was known in the West.

All the churches in the Holy Land are completely vaulted. In Syria, pointed barrel vaults similar to those of Provence were preferred over the nave. In Palestine, groin vaults in the Burgundian style were preferred. The barrel vault without windows is found in the Cathedral of Byblos, dating from about 1115, and in the east part of the beautiful Cathedral of Tortosa, built in the latter half of the 12th century and completed in the 13th century. More frequently, however, there are bays piercing the barrel vault to light the nave, as at St. John in Beirut, which is related to the churches of Limousin, and at the Cathedral of Ramès, which is notable for the width of its side aisles and for its Burgundian style. There are groin vaults over the Cathedral of Gaza, which is largely destroyed, and over the churches of Quariet-el-Enab and St. Anne in Jerusalem. The last-named building has a barrel-vaulted transept and, at the crossing, a lantern tower on pendentives. The Church of the Holy Sepulcher, the choir of which was perhaps originally (that is, before 1172) vaulted with diagonal ribs, also has such a lantern tower on pendentives at the crossing.

Abbeys. All the elements which characterize the Romanesque and are found in the churches of the secular clergy — cathedrals, collegiate churches and parish churches — are found also in those of the Benedictine abbeys. The Benedictines were the most important monastic order and the only one that had existed before the end of the 11th century. The Cistercian Order, founded in 1098 but whose surviving churches date from no earlier than about 1125, insisted on greater austerity; in its churches are found neither huge towers nor painted or sculptured decorations. Recent studies have brought to light the great variety of Cistercian buildings. The plan having a square *chevet* opening on a transept that is itself bordered with square chapels is today termed "Bernardian," because it seems to have been originated by St. Bernard at his abbey in Clairvaux in 1135 and imposed on the abbeys derived from it. But after 1154 the choir of Clairvaux was rebuilt with an ambulatory and a ring of adjoining chapels in order to increase the number of altars. Many other plans were used, notably that of the sanctuary having three apses, found in southern France, which testifies to the Cistercians' respect for local practices. The structure also varied: the beautiful church of Fontenay in Burgundy is vaulted with a pointed barrel supported by transverse barrels, but at the abbey churches of Le Thoronet and Sénanque, in Provence, the support is given by lateral half barrels, and at Silvacane by rampant barrels; the church of Les Vaux-de-Cernay, near Paris, adopts the Burgundian style of groin vaults; and in Périgord, the church of Boschaud Abbey conforms to the local use of domes on pendentives. Finally, the pointed vault appeared rather early but without changing the Romanesque character of such constructions as the nave at Pontigny.

In addition to the church proper, an abbey includes a cloister that runs the length of the nave. Some cathedrals — that of Le Puy, for instance — also have cloisters formed by four galleries, usually vaulted during the Romanesque era, either with barrel vaults as at Le Thoronet and Silvacane, or with half barrels, as at St-Trophime in Arles and at Montmajour, or with groin vaults. The galleries open onto the main courtyard by means of arcades supported on massive pilasters or on small columns as at Moissac (PL. 237) and at Saint-Bertrand-de-Comminges (PL. 206). To the east of the cloister opens the chapter room, sometimes provided with an apse, as at Jumièges and at Lessay, but most often rectangular in shape and opening onto the gallery by a door surrounded by two bays with arcades; sometimes it is groin-vaulted, as at Aubazine. Above extends the monks' dormitory, which communicates with the church. One of the most beautiful, that at Le Thoronet, is barrel-vaulted; the majority, however, were timbered. The refectory is situated on the side of the cloister opposite the church, near the lavabo. The one at Aiguebelle still displays its magnificent pointed barrel vault. In addition, the abbey includes a room where the monks gather to work; one of the oldest of these can be seen at Morthemer, under a semicircular barrel vault. Those of Noirlac and Aubazine are groin-vaulted. In addition to the kitchen, which is often set off by itself, as at Fontevrault, the abbey contains numerous other buildings — the almshouse, the infirmary, the storerooms, the barns, the workshops —

Romanesque examples of which remain at Breuil-Benoit, at Pontigny, and at Vauclair, as well as at Fontenay (V, FIG. 654), which has the most complete group extant in France.

Civil architecture. Very few Romanesque houses remain in France. Since the fortified walls of the city enclosed only a confined area, the height of houses had to be increased; from the 12th century on they had two stories, or even three, like certain houses in Cluny, and often their narrow façades faced the street. The St-Genès house in Thiers has a gable facing the street; other houses have a porch roof sloping toward the street. The cellars and the ground floor are groin-vaulted in certain houses in Arras, Rouen, Vézelay, and Provins. Each story contains few rooms, and each room can be partitioned by hangings. Heating was provided by fireplaces, of which there still remain some Romanesque examples at the château of Fougères, dating from the beginning of the 12th century; at the Chapter House of Le Puy; and at the leper hospital of Périgueux. The Romanesque period limited itself to straight staircases, inside or outside, in stone or, more often, in wood. The ground floor often served as a shop, with the door having a second opening, the lower part of which was closed off to form a counter. The windows were set below a straight lintel at the Saint-Livier house in Metz and under semicircular arches at La Chaise-Dieu; they were arranged side by side under an arcade at Cluny, at the Bishop's Palace in Auxerre, and at the town hall in Saint-Antonin. The palaces and town houses were merely larger developments of the private residence, with the number of rooms increased, as, for example, at the Bishop's Palace in Angers, dating from the beginning of the 12th century. There was always a private chapel in these palaces, often two stories high; the Bishop's Palace of Laon supplies an example that has retained the pure Romanesque structure.

The majority of towns in the Middle Ages developed in haphazard fashion. Although new towns were founded on a regular plan and town-planning statutes were framed during the Romanesque period, it was chiefly in the Gothic period (see GOTHIC ART) that this movement attained any importance. Streets were not paved until the reign of Philippe-Auguste (Philip II, 1180–1223). Although the Middle Ages did little more than maintain the Roman roads, they did see the construction of bridges through the efforts of religious communities and brotherhoods. Many of these bridges were destroyed during World War II. The oldest of them have narrow semicircular arches, as in Airvault, on abutments that frequently have cutwaters. The famous bridge of Avignon, built 1177–85 through the efforts of a simple shepherd, St. Bénézet, has four elliptical arches left, with a chapel in honor of its founder standing above the second pier. Although the communal movement had not yet been firmly established in the 12th century, some towns have a town hall dating from this time. That of La Réole, Romanesque in appearance, dates from the end of the 12th century; the ground floor, divided into two aisles, served as a covered market. The remains of a market made into a town hall in 1197 have come to light at Clermont-en-Beauvaisis.

Military architecture. In the military architecture of the early Romanesque period the ancient system of wooden fortifications was used; but nothing now remains of these. From the end of the 10th century, notably in Touraine, a region possessing good quarries, stone was used. The keep, dwelling place of the feudal lord and chief element in the defense of his castle, was first built on a rectangular plan. It could be entered only at the first story above the ground, by the aid of a ladder or a movable bridge. In 994 Fulk III Nerra, Count of Anjou, built the keep in Langeais; none of it was vaulted. In the 11th century this plan was followed at Beaugency, where the ground floor was divided into two barrel-vaulted aisles, and at Loches, where the walls were supported by semicircular buttresses, as at Montbazon; and in the 12th century, at Montrichard (1110–28), in Normandy at Falaise, and in many other regions (Chauvigny, Loudun, Pons, Huriel). The more logical circular plan was used from about 1040 at Fréteval and, at the end of the 11th century, at Mondoubleau; it blossomed magnificently in the 12th century at Châteaudun, which is vaulted with two domes, and in Laval; and it became the rule in the time of Philippe-Auguste. However, the variety of Romanesque keeps is limitless: that of Gisors, built in 1096–97 by William the Red (William II, King of England), is octagonal; that of Roudan (1105–37) is circular and is flanked by four turrets; the Tour Guinette of Etampes has a four-lobed plan; the so-called "Caesar's Tower" in Provins is an octagon with four turrets. The Castle of Niort is unusual in that it has two rectangular keeps joined by a closed courtyard. From the 11th century on, the keep was surrounded by a fortified enclosure tangential to it; at Gisors, for instance, there is such a keep at the top of an artificial earth mound. The keep of Loches (PL. 234) was provided with concentric defenses during the course of the 12th century. Thus, the large Romanesque and Gothic type of fortified castle had its origins. One of the most important is that of Arques-la-Bataille, rebuilt by Henry I of England (ca. 1123) in order to block the Dieppe-Rouen road. It includes a massive square keep surrounded by a fortified enclosure, which is flanked by round towers and extended by outworks. The same king had the original castle of Gisor surrounded by a vast wall; he also marked out the eastern and southern frontiers of his duchy of Normandy with a network of fortresses. In 1196, after the loss of Gisors, Richard the Lion-Hearted built, in Les Andelys, the Château-Gaillard in order to control the Paris-Rouen road. This castle, small but very strong, includes a buttressed keep surrounded by a fortified enclosure whose adjoining towers flank it strategically, a second surrounding wall, and isolated triangular outworks. Nevertheless Château-Gaillard was taken in an attack by Philippe-Auguste in 1204. The keep, built in the strongest part of the fortress and practically impregnable, was of no help to the garrison which had crowded together there and finally had to surrender. The Gothic age was to abandon this type of plan in order to situate the keep at the weakest point, thus making it cooperate in the defense of the whole.

Starting in Romanesque times, at least in the 12th century, military engineers were concerned with resisting the enemy by the marksmanship of the defenders and not merely by the strength of the masonry. Balistraria through which archers could shoot existed in the wooden castle of Puiset in 1111. In Ghent, at the castle of the Counts of Flanders (at that time French princes), overhanging turrets were contrived beneath true machicolation. At the keep of Château-Gaillard, the presence of machicolation is revealed by the large buttresses that rise the length of the high wall, starting from the base ramp. In the Holy Land, the Crusaders built a close network of fortresses the length of their immense frontier. These castles, which often made use of Byzantine constructions, were reconstructed during the 13th century by the Franks themselves, and later by the victorious Arabs. The most beautiful, Le Crac des Chevaliers, belongs to the Romanesque period only by virtue of the layout of its interior wall, doubled in the 13th century by gigantic ramps enclosing a gallery. Sahyun (Saône), the largest castle in Syria, is a composite; the Crusaders surrounded this Byzantine fortress with a wall having an enormous square keep in front of which a steep trench was dug out of the rock. Only a single projection of stone was retained as a support for the access bridge. Qal'at es-Subaybi, begun in 1130 and reconstructed by the Arabs; the Castle of Beaufort (Lebanon), built in 1139 on top of a protective wall 984 ft. high; and El Kerak (anc. Kir Moab), occupied only 1142–88 and related to Frankish architecture only by virtue of the lower sections of its walls, bear further witness to the talent of the military architects who came from France. Moreover, these architects made great advances as a result of contact with Greek and Armenian artisans; they developed the system of ramps at the base of the walls and, it seems, used brattices and machicolation earlier than these were used in the West.

The principles used in the fortification of castles were also applied to the fortification of towns, which were entirely surrounded by walls, but very few of these have been preserved from the Romanesque era. Although the walls of Carcassonne (V, FIG. 658) do not date from this period — they are both older and more recent — the castle, which is the last redoubt of the

city, is remarkable in its arrangements, dating from the middle of the 12th century: the system (later to become general practice) involves a door cut out between two towers, armed with portcullises, and set beneath the strategically arranged balistraria. The towers flanking the angles and faces of this rectangular castle are tall enough to dominate the neighboring curtain walls.

François SALET

IBERIAN PENINSULA. Shortly after the year 1000, when Romanesque art was developing in Western Europe, and particularly in France and Italy, Spain was languishing under one of the worst scourges of its history; from 981 until 1002 the incursions of al-Manṣūr had devastated the northern Christian states of the Iberian Peninsula, burning the towns and plundering the churches. Even more grievous than the material destruction was the outrage inflicted on Christianity by the Moslems when in 997 they reached Compostela, at the far end of Galicia, where the tomb of St. James had attracted pilgrims from all over the western world. The town was destroyed by fire and the basilica razed to the ground, but al-Manṣūr ordered the tomb to be spared and the church bells and the folding doors of the enclosure to be carried away to Córdoba on the shoulders of the Christian prisoners and used in the roofing of the mosque. The poverty of the Christian kingdoms after these raids is shown clearly in a document describing how the king of León, Alfonso V, had to restore in common materials such as pisé and bricks the Church of St. John the Baptist, which had been destroyed in his capital (see below).

Spain, however, although seriously impoverished, was able to draw from a more ancient tradition for the models that were to serve in the formation of Romanesque art. On her soil were preserved Visigothic constructions, great structures in ashlar; this technique, which had almost entirely disappeared elsewhere after the barbarian invasions, aroused great admiration at that time (several contemporary texts compared it with Gallic constructions). After the Moslem invasion, the small kingdom of Asturias (where the reconquest of Spain began) had erected in Oviedo, as far back as the 9th century, buildings that may well be considered forerunners of Romanesque architecture. Among these are S. María, Naranco (III, PL. 51), which has a barrel vault whose transverse arches rest on groups of engaged columns joined together by arcading on the interior walls and buttresses corresponding to them on the outside; S. Miguel de Lillo (of which only a fragment is preserved), which displays a skillful arrangement of longitudinal and transverse vaults alternating over the side aisles that flank the central barrel vault; and S. Cristina (Pola de Lena; XI, PL. 317), which is a perfect example of the organization of a building on a central plan.

In addition to these models, in the 10th century Mozarabic art (q.v.) had produced churches that were among the most advanced pre-Romanesque constructions. Few Christian buildings erected under the Moslem domination are known; the Christians were permitted to practice their religion in the existing churches, but not to build new ones. Without a doubt, some of the laborers used by the Moslems in building their mosques and palaces were Christians. Thus, when in the 10th century growing intolerance and persecutions compelled the Andalusian Mozarabs to leave Córdoba, they took with them Córdoban traditions and influences. Most of the Mozarabs settled in the recently reconquered regions, and in particular in the Duero Valley, near León; inscriptions there commemorate the foundation of monasteries by communities coming from Córdoba.

Mozarabic art links together Visigothic and Ommiad (see OMMIAD SCHOOLS) traditions. Its most striking feature is the horseshoe arch; but its influence is particularly felt in construction techniques, in which it utilized with great skill the structural disposition of stretchers and headers, made use of the composite pier with engaged columns, and combined different systems of vaulting. In a period in which technical decadence was almost general elsewhere in Spain, Mozarabic art offered many useful models in architecture and even more in sculpture.

Romanesque art, however, is a Western art, common to all the countries of Western Europe. The conditions that fostered its development in Spain were the result of the political climate in the Christian kingdoms of northern Spain and the growing relationships with their neighbors across the Pyrenees. After the death of al-Manṣūr his successors proved to be incapable of continuing his work; anarchy was rife in the Caliphate. The Christians, on the other hand, showed a tendency to unite; in the first third of the century, Sancho the Great, King of Navarra, grouped Aragon and Castile under his authority and thus acquired the title of *Rex hispanorum regum*. He introduced the Cluniac reform in Spain in the monasteries of San Juan de la Peña, in Aragon, San Salvador, at Leyre, in Navarra, and San Salvador, in Oña, Castile; he reorganized the pilgrimage to the tomb of St. James in Compostela and laid out the *camino francés*, which crosses Spain from the Pyrenees to Galicia. Sancho of Navarra maintained close relations with France; according to the testimony of Adémar de Chabbannais d'Angoulême, he exchanged gifts every year with the powerful duke of Aquitaine; according to Rudolf (Raoul) Glaber, he corresponded with Robert the Pious, King of France; in 1010, he was present at the feasts organized in St-Jean-d'Angély to celebrate the finding of the head of John the Baptist; he was also on friendly terms with the great Catalan prelate, Oliva.

Unfortunately, it is impossible to make an accurate appraisal of the contribution of these relations with the outer world to Spanish art under the reign of Sancho the Great, inasmuch as the numerous churches he restored after al-Manṣūr's raids have since been reconstructed. The only structures that remain are the tower of S. Pedro de Cardeña, near Burgos, and the crypt of the Palencia Cathedral. An almost contemporary document indicated that the reconstruction of the Palencia Cathedral was recommended by Ponce, Bishop of Oviedo and disciple of Abbot Oliva. It was dedicated to a saint held in great reverence in southern France, St. Antolín (St. Antoninus of Pamiers). Of the building consecrated in 1034 only the crypt — which extended the one built in the Visigothic age — remains. The Romanesque crypt, a simple rectangle terminated by an apse decorated by three arches, is covered by a barrel vault on transverse arches, entirely bonded in ashlar; the vault starts from a ledge close to the ground, for the underground structure lacks height and is devoid of buttresses. The comparison is inevitable with the S. Leocadia Chapel, which is the crypt of the Cámara Santa in the Oviedo Cathedral, built by Alfonso the Chaste at the beginning of the 9th century; this crypt is also covered by a low barrel vault, but is without transverse arches. However, Asturian art also furnished the model of the transverse arches, since they are found in Oviedo as early as the 9th century.

Spanish traditions persisted in Navarra under the successors of Sancho the Great. The Church of S. María de Nájera, founded by his son García in 1052 and consecrated by his grandson Sancho de Penalén in 1056, is known today only through a miniature, but its horseshoe arches clearly prove the survival of Mozarabic influences. A Navarrese building of the middle of the 11th century, San Salvador at Leyre, has been preserved, but for a long time historians were mistaken about its date. The Abbey of Leyre was one of the numerous monasteries founded in the 9th century in Navarra and Aragon under the Carolingian influences. When in 924 'Abd-ar-Raḥmān III destroyed Pamplona, the bishops took refuge in Leyre, which was off the roads usually followed by the Moslem incursions. The episcopal see of Pamplona was restored by Sancho the Great, but the bishops continued to be chosen from among the monks of Leyre; until 1076, the bishop of Pamplona was also the abbot of San Salvador. Sancho the Great introduced the Cluniac reform in the monastery and heaped great riches upon it. Situated in the neighborhood of the road that came from the Somport, Leyre soon became a halting place for the pilgrimage to Compostela. The *chevet* of the church, however, dates back to an earlier period than that of the development of Compostela art. That a solemn consecration took place in 1057 is known from the record of a donation made on that occasion by Sancho de Penalén and countersigned by the bishop-abbot of the monastery, by several other bishops, and by many lords. This text mentions a construction in an already advanced stage, which was the work not of the reigning king but of his father; perhaps it had been begun by his grandfather, Sancho the Great. The only part of the church that remains is the *chevet*. To neglect the 1057 document and take into account only the later consecration, which took place in 1098, leads to the error of the historians who assigned this building to a date no earlier than the end of the century and thus were forced to consider it a work behind the times. This hypothesis is hard to accept when the building in question is a royal monastery, not far from the capital, which was for a long time the political and religious center of the kingdom and which was located virtually on the pilgrimage route. The very coarse decoration seems to be particularly convincing in that respect; it could only be explained as having been a case of the re-use of elements of an earlier date, another unacceptable hypothesis in a building so rigorously constructed.

For the construction is magnificent. It is erected on two stories, the eastern side of the crypt being free because of the unevenness of the ground. The work is homogeneous, the product of a single uninterrupted outburst of creative energy, and must have been carried out in a rather short space of time. The masonry was very carefully handled, laid with sharply defined joints and made of a beautiful dark-red stone. It presents some unquestionable archaisms: the size of the stones is considerably larger here than that customary at the end of the century; the blocks are almost square; the disjunctions and the asymmetry of the joints, the irregular keying up of the arches, the off-centering of the intrados, the rough simplicity of the moldings are survivals of Mozarabic influences. No feature of specifically Romanesque decoration is apparent, either in the figures of the modillions or on the internal capitals. The beauty of the architecture lies in its vigor and grandiose sobriety.

The plan is composed of three apses preceded by a nave flanked by side aisles; only two bays were built. In the crypt (PL. 209) the nave is divided into two by a row of columns, which starts rather awkwardly from the middle of the curve of the apse. Other columns alternate with thick piers and divide each bay of the crypt into two. The two stories are barrel-vaulted on transverse arches supported by piers (in the crypt) and by engaged columns in the dosseret blocks of the walls. There are, however, no buttresses on the exterior.

Catalonia. At the northeast extremity of the Iberian Peninsula, the *Marca Hispanica* followed a very different artistic destiny. Its counts were vassals of the king of France, but this suzerainty had been only nominal since the time they had, in their own right, defended their independence against the incursions of the caliph's armies. They very readily, however, put their own troops at the disposal of the Moslems and found a personal profit in the internal fights of Arabic Spain. As a rule they had little to do with the other Spanish Christian sovereigns. The abbot Oliva, a friend and counselor of Sancho of Navarra, appears as an extraordinary exception. Catalonia, open wide onto the Mediterranean, turned in the opposite direction.

Catalonia, however, had not been completely unaware of Mozarabic art, but had received it under a different form from that of León. There was no Mozarabic colonization in the northeast of the Peninsula as there had been in the northwest. Moslem influence there was the result not of a popular movement but of individual contacts. It was through books that Córdoban civilization penetrated into the Catalonian monasteries, which transmitted Arabic science as well as part of their own ancient heritage to the West. It is known that the monk Gerbert (later Pope Sylvester II) was educated at Ripoll. In the artistic field, the Mozarabic constructions of Catalonia are not the work of an entire community of Andalusian monks transplanted to a Christian land, as in León, but of isolated artists — a sculptor in Ripoll, an architect in Cuxa. S. Miguel of Cuxa (on the northern slope of the Pyrenees) has many characteristics of Carolingian architecture. It is also the only Mozarabic church in Catalonia of noteworthy dimensions; the others are only modest country churches.

However, it is to Mozarabic tradition that an early building of the 11th century in Catalonia must be ascribed, one that was for a long time an enigma to archaeologists. This is S. Pedro de Roda (on Cape Creus, a spur of the Pyrenees overlooking the sea). Consecrated in 1022, the church of this monastery presents unusual characteristics in its plan with three elliptical apses; the main apse is encircled by an ambulatory devoid of chapels. The high barrel vault of the nave, reinforced by transverse arches, is abutted by the vaults of the side aisles. The piers (PL. 209) are of masonry, but monolithic columns are applied to them. The capitals and the bases are very close to the forms prevailing in the Caliphate; the similarity is so striking that these elements were formerly believed to have been earlier ones re-used. The masonry of the piers, however, shows an alternation of stretchers and headers characteristic of Córdoban constructions of the 10th century. The windows, very wide and with embrasures only on the outside, must have been trimmed with *claustra* (pierced slabs) of Moorish style. Finally, two pre-Romanesque shrines, found *in situ* in the altar of the crypt, confirm the early date of the construction.

Other scattered buildings belonging to this same period (from the beginning to the middle of the 11th century) also utilize the ashlar technique, undoubtedly favored by the fine quality of the materials available in the region. The Church of S. María, in Besalú, Gerona, which was the chapel of the castle of the local counts and also the collegiate church of a community of regular canons founded in 977, was reconstructed in the 11th century and consecrated in 1055. The nave, which fell into ruin during the 18th century, perhaps dated to a period slightly later than the date of this consecration; but the *chevet*, well preserved, is reminiscent of S. Pedro de Roda. The reconstruction is finely bonded; the blocks, of large size but of irregular proportions, have well-defined joints. The window of the apse is narrow (unlike those of S. Pedro de Roda) and has a double embrasure. The apsidal exterior is decorated by columns applied to the wall, which support large arches. The capitals and the bases belong to the Mozarabic style which was brought to Ripoll, was developed at S. Pedro de Roda, and was here more advanced.

These beautiful and interesting buildings remain, however, exceptions amidst the largely Lombard-influenced art of Catalonia. The great Catalan archaeologist, Puig y Cadafalch (1928), suggested the term "first Romanesque art" to indicate the interregional character of that art and its early development. Examples of this art are indeed as numerous in Catalonia as in Lombardy. However, the Lombard origin appears unquestionable; several documents certify that during the Romanesque era teams of Lombard masons crossed the Alps to work in other countries; their traces can be followed even beyond the Pyrenees. But the term "first" Romanesque art has been inexact since the study of the great buildings of many other regions, especially along the banks of the Loire, has revealed another form of Romanesque art of at least as early a date. "Mediterranean art" would be more precise if these Mediterranean forms were recognized in Burgundy and even beyond; but the ancient name "Lombard art" is still the best, if the traditional emigration of the Lombard masons is kept in mind. Extending over an immense territory, this uniform art is characterized by its great simplicity. The construction is of roughhewn blocks, flat and similar to bricks. Lombard art spread in the regions of dry limestone, which is easily broken; but its origins must be sought in the brick technique of Ravenna and even of Mesopotamia. An elementary, though typical, architectural decoration proves this: the so-called "Lombard bands" that decorate the wall with a dark line and are joined at the top by arched corbel tables that sometimes form niches. The cornices with saw-tooth motifs are also characteristic.

The earliest ancient churches, such as S. Pedro in Burgal, were undoubtedly covered with a simple wooden roof. Nevertheless, the use of the vault began early in Catalonia; two precise documents certify this for S. Esteban, Bañolas (957), and for S. María, Ripoll (977). A decisive novelty appears at S. Vi-

cente, Cardona, in the church of the castle, begun in 1019 and consecrated in 1040, in which a dome on squinches rises above the crossing (PL. 210), thus giving a center to the basilican plan. This model was followed in the church at San Llorens del Munt (1064), but became general in Catalonia only during the 12th century.

The most famous monastery of Catalonia is that at Ripoll in Gerona (FIG. 342), used as a tomb by the counts of Barcelona. Documents show that the Church of S. María was reconstructed and reconsecrated by each new generation: in 888 by Wilfred

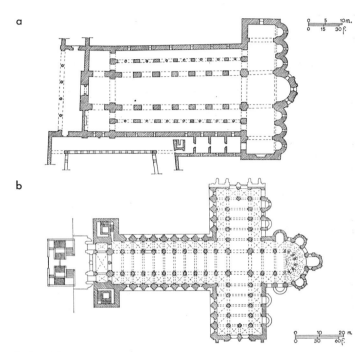

Spain. (*a*) Ripoll, S. María, 1020–32, plan (*from K. J. Conant, 1959*); (*b*) Santiago de Compostela, 11th and 12th century, plan (*from E. Lundberg, 1950*).

(Wifredus); in 935 (the record has not been preserved); in 977 by Count Oliva Cabreta; in 1032 by his son Oliva, Bishop of Vich and Abbot of Ripoll and Cuxa. It is known that the authority of this great prelate extended over several monasteries; he took an active part in the reconstruction and restoration of many churches and was often present at consecrations. In him can be seen the principal propagator of Lombard art in Catalonia. S. María of Ripoll (PL. 211) is an imposing construction, both for its size and for the richness of its plan; the wide transept onto which seven apses open directly and the double side aisles flanking the nave recall St. Peter's in Rome. It is surprising, however, to find in it forms that are behind the times; S. María has no transverse arches across the barrel vault of the nave, its piers preserve their mural form, and the crossing is not marked by a dome — this at the time when the more modest church of the castle of Cardona presented an example of perfect Romanesque organization. The total restoration that Ripoll underwent in the 19th century does not permit a clear vision of what the construction was in the 11th century, but the Mozarabic capitals, authentic fragments that belong to it, undoubtedly date from the 10th century. Had the abbot Oliva, struck by the beauty of these capitals that his father had had made by a Córdoban sculptor, wished to reemploy them when reconstructing the church? A more plausible explanation seems to be that in 1032 Oliva perhaps did not demolish the building consecrated in 977 as completely as the documents affirm but preserved part of it, at least in the nave and the side aisles.

Churches of Lombard style are innumerable and monotonous in Catalonia; the style extended into the 12th century. What are the features that separate it from the true Romanesque that was developed elsewhere? In plan, in elevation, and in vaulting the churches of the "first Romanesque art" are complete Romanesque churches; they lack only the ashlar walls and the monumental sculpture.

In the Pyrenees, in the kingdom of Aragon, there are to be found between Navarra and Catalonia a few peculiar buildings, undoubtedly preserved because of their isolated position in the mountains. A group of these has been studied not far from Jaca, between the Gállego and the Aragón rivers; they include Lárrede, San Juan de Busa, and Susín. Others probably exist. None of these buildings is dated; but whatever their exact age, which only the fortunate discovery of an inscription or a date concerning them could establish, they represent the survival of ancient Spanish traditions (ashlar walls, horseshoe arches) mingled with Lombard influences ("Lombard bands" and corbel tables, or forms that seem to derive from them). The rural character of these buildings, the simplicity of construction, and the absence of carved decoration make them interesting examples of Spanish art prior to the development of the great Romanesque art.

León. After so many early manifestations, still incomplete, however, in the various regions of Christian Spain, it is in León that one witnesses the decisive creation of Spanish Romanesque art.

According to the custom of the time, Sancho the Great on his deathbed (1035) divided his estates among his sons, thus running the risk of destroying his work of unifying the land. But the tendency to unity persisted; a grouping together, at least in part, was soon to take place around a different center. Ferdinand (Fernando) I, King of Castile, had married Sancha, sister of Bermudo, King of León. After Bermudo's death, his kingdom passed into the hands of his brother-in-law. Ferdinand, having thus become king of Castile and León, concentrated his efforts on the reconquest of Spain and won many victories, imposing tributes on the Moslem kings of Toledo, Badajoz, and Seville. The continual wars that drained the resources of Spain were undoubtedly a hindrance to artistic development and to the religious life of the country; but Spanish historians have rightly stressed the prominent part played by women in the development of art while the men were almost completely absorbed by the army. Documents reveal the names of founders and donors: Doña Mayor of Castile, the widow of Sancho of Navarra; the queens of Navarra — Stefania, Placencia, and Felicia; Sancha, the queen of León. The victories won were probably often the occasion for such munificence, offered in thanksgiving.

It was in answer to a request of Sancha that Ferdinand chose for his sepulcher the monastery where her ancestors, the kings of León, were buried — the Church of St. John the Baptist, in León. Ferdinand rebuilt the church (which after the Moslem raids had been restored in pisé and brick) in stone: FECIT ECCLESIAM HANC LAPIDEAM QUAE OLIM FUIT LUTEA ("This church, once of mud, he rebuilt in stone"), reads his epitaph. Having obtained from the Moslem ruler of Seville the relics of St. Isidore, he dedicated to the great Hispanic scholar this new building, which was solemnly consecrated on Dec. 21 or 22, 1063. The most eminent personalities of the Spanish church were present at the ceremony, as well as the Bishop of Puy, Pierre, who was probably passing through on a pilgrimage to Compostela. In the years that immediately preceded this consecration, the King and Queen had bestowed upon the monastery rich gifts (some of which have been preserved there), among them reliquaries and other objects in ivory and gold. Two years later, the King also had the relics of St. Vincent transferred from Ávila to León. Toward the end of 1065, as he was fighting in the region of Valencia, he suddenly fell ill and had to hasten back to his capital; before dying, he was able to celebrate Christmas in the sanctuary he had so munificently endowed. His widow finished the construction and died in 1067.

Only the vestibule, or narthex, which is that part known as the Kings' Chapel (Panteón de los Reyes; PL. 212), used solely for the entombment of princes, remains today of S. Isidoro, the church of Ferdinand and Sancha. The western and northern walls of the nave have also been preserved but are embodied in those of the 12th-century church. Their elevation, which bears the trace of the primitive vaults, and the foundations brought to light during the excavations help to visualize the building as it was in 1063, a structure similar to the Asturian churches of the 9th and 10th centuries (see PRE-ROMANESQUE ART), of small dimensions and without carved decorations. The Kings' Chapel, on the contrary, is an entirely Romanesque construction, supported by cruciform piers with engaged columns and carved capitals. There is a fundamental difference between the church, as its original appearance can be imagined, and the chapel, which appears as the first truly Romanesque building in Spain. It almost seems doubtful that the two parts of the building were erected at the same time; could it be that Ferdinand had spared the church of Alfonso V and built only the funeral chapel? The texts formally deny this, as does Ferdinand's epitaph (see above); moreover, the western and northern walls of the nave, in the 12th-century construction, can in no way be assigned to the building of the beginning of the 11th century. The facing in ashlar of medium size is the same as in the chapel; no resumption of the work is visible in the construction. One is led to conclude that Ferdinand first rebuilt the church with modest means, using local masons; the funeral chapel was then undertaken, following a far more ambitious plan, and was probably the work of a master mason from abroad. The tower porches, common in France from the middle of the 11th century (St-Hilaire-le-Grand in Poitiers and Saint-Benoît-sur-Loire), are in fact obvious models of the Kings' Chapel in León. This one, however, was not utilized as a porch because it was erected very close to the Roman walls of the city; between the walls and the two bays, which seem to respond to the primitive conception of the porch, there was not enough space for a façade. This is probably what led, during the construction, to the idea of adding a third bay that joins the church to the Roman walls. At the same time an open gallery was built along the north side of the chapel and the church, according to a custom that was widespread in Spain during the pre-Romanesque age. Local practices can also be recognized in certain features of the construction: the use of light tufa in the vaults, frequent in Asturian art; the calotte form into which the groins of the vault disappear. The general inspiration of the architecture, however, is French.

The first church of S. Isidoro was so archaic that it could not survive long at a time when architecture was renewing itself all over the western Christian world with exceptional speed and vigor. Even before the end of the 11th century, the daughter of Ferdinand and Sancha, Doña Urraca, undertook to enlarge it (HAEC AMPLIAVIT ECCLESIAM HANC, reads her epitaph). What actually took place, however, was not so much an enlarging as a reconstruction. Doña Urraca died in 1101, after having erected, on the east side of the church built by her parents, the *chevet* of a new church, its transept, and the east bays of its nave, flanked by side aisles, up to the junction point with the first church. Of Doña Urraca's work only the two bays of the nave and the side aisles joining the 12th-century transept remain. The main apse was demolished at the beginning of the 16th century and was replaced by a construction in late Gothic style. Even the lateral apses were rebuilt in the 12th century, as is proved by the foundations (brought to light in the course of excavations) of minor, narrower apses corresponding to the width of the side aisles; the resumption of the work is also evident over the entire height of the inner wall. The transept, opening through large multifoil arches, goes back only to the 12th century; as a matter of fact, the last piers of the nave bear, at the entrance to the transept and at the height of the capitals of the arcades, the trace of a capital (now entirely blunted), which seems to indicate that the side aisles extended up to the present site of the transept. However, the width of this transept is almost one and a half times that of a simple bay of the nave; perhaps there was a lower transept there, as is often found in Carolingian art. The pillars supporting the nave are alternating (PL. 212); the weaker originally had only two engaged columns, bearing the springers of the arcades; a third engaged column was added later, in order to support the trans-

verse arches of the side aisle; the one opposite it runs vertically
through the middle of the window opened in the outer wall.
The walls of these bays are so thin that it seems unlikely that
they were ever vaulted; Doña Urraca's church was covered by
a simple timbered roof.

Interrupted by the wars that troubled the beginning of
the 12th century, the construction was resumed only toward
1120 and finished in time for the consecration in 1149 by the
architect Petrus Deustamben, QUI SUPERAEDIFICAVIT ECCLESIAM
HANC, according to the epitaph engraved on his tomb in the
church itself. The building was raised and vaulted. The clerestory windows, which let the light directly into the nave between the large arcades and the vault, date from that time —
in fact, a few engaged columns still bear the trace of the earlier
capitals below the level of those that support the transverse
arches.

The pilgrimage churches. The complexity of S. Isidoro
clearly shows that Spanish Romanesque architecture was still
far from having found its definitive form. Foreign elements
and local ones mix with one another in faltering and imperfect
realizations. It was with the pilgrims that the French master
masons arrived; it is interesting to discover their traces at the
various halting places along the route. Unfortunately, although
the early dates of the Kings' Chapel at León are not in doubt,
the same cannot be said of other buildings, since the documents
that refer to them are too uncertain to assign them definitely
to the same period.

When in his will (1035) Sancho the Great divided his properties among his sons, he left to his natural son Ramiro only
a small mountain estate, Aragon; as Ramiro I, first king of
Aragon, he was able to establish his authority there only after
many years of struggles, in about 1054. The ancient episcopal
city of Huesca was still in the hands of the Moslems. Ramiro
established his capital in Jaca and founded a Cathedral there
(PL. 212; FIG. 345). Jaca, at the foot of the Somport, is the first
Spanish halting place of the pilgrimage to Santiago de Compos-

tela. Not far from it stands the monastery of San Juan de la
Peña, the first abbey in which Sancho the Great introduced
the Cluniac reform in 1025. A text dated 1063 describes the
Cathedral while it was being built; but this document, known
today through several copies of the end of the 11th and 12th
centuries, is not altogether conclusive. It seems safer to connect
the main part of the construction with a donation *ad opus* of
1094.

The simple plan includes a nave flanked by side aisles,
terminated by three apses; the transept is not predominant.
Composite piers alternate with columns; there are neither
engaged columns inside the walls nor buttresses outside. The
16th-century vault does not permit an analysis of the original
state of the roof. Above the crossing is a domical vault with
ribs of Moslem style; it is the most remarkable element of the
structure. The carved decoration, of great beauty, is discussed
below.

Near Jaca a monastery of nuns, Sta Cruz de la Serós, benefited by the bounties of Doña Sancha, King Ramiro's daughter, at the same time as the Cathedral. Farther south, the church
of the castle at Loarre (PL. 234), an advance post of King Sancho
Ramírez in his march toward Huesca, is magnificently built
in very regular masonry and with rich and elaborate decoration.

In Castile, far from Jaca but on the route of the pilgrimage,
stands the church of S. Martín, in Frómista (PL. 211). In her
will, dated 1066, Doña Mayor made it the object of a donation.
Sancho of Navarra's widow states that she started the construction of this church, but it is unlikely that this document refers
to the building that stands there today. In fact, as far as can
be seen in the too-radical restoration of the 19th century, this
church presents the most perfect example of Romanesque organization preserved in Spain: barrel vaults, transverse arches,
composite piers, buttresses, domed crossing. The whole building
is harmoniously proportioned, and the decoration is perfectly
suited to the construction. Frómista cannot have been erected
before Jaca or S. Isidoro of León.

Not only on the road to Santiago de Compostela do these
artistic creations exist; they are found wherever religious life
was intense. S. Domingo in Silos, the goal of a famous national
pilgrimage, included one of the most beautiful of Romanesque
cloisters. It is most regrettable that this church disappeared
almost completely in the 18th century. It had been restored
— probably rebuilt — by St. Dominic, who arrived in Silos
in 1041; it was enlarged after his death (1073), when it became
a shrine housing his relics. Its consecration took place in 1088,
perhaps even before it was finished.

The Cathedral of Santiago de Compostela (FIG. 342), the
masterpiece of Romanesque architecture in Spain, is fortunately
dated with certainty and is on the whole well preserved. Two
texts dating from the first half of the 12th century, the *Historia
Compostellana* (Madrid, 1765) and the Pilgrim's Guide that
constituted the fifth book of the *Codex Calixtinus*, indicated
that the Cathedral was begun in the year 1116 of the Spanish
era, that is to say, in A.D. 1078, on the site of an earlier basilica.
The *Historia Compostellana* even states the day, the fifth of
of the Ides of July. A dedication engraved on one of the posts
of the "silversmiths' door" (Puerta de las Platerías; PL. 249) records that date: ERA DCXVI V IDUS ILII. The interpretation of
this inscription has been subject to argument, but even if one
refuses to accept it, the testimony of the two historical sources
that date from only half a century later is sufficient. In any
event, the text of an agreement imposed in 1077 by King Alfonso VI on the bishop of Compostela and the abbot of the monastery of San Pelayo de Antealtares, which was close to the
Cathedral and upon whose territory the new construction was
to encroach, proves that works, probably of demolition and
embankment, had already been undertaken at that date and that
the plan of the *chevet*, with the inscription of the three eastern
chapels, was by then established. An inscription engraved
in the Chapel of the Saviour, only a fragment of which has
been preserved, seems even to indicate, if the proposed interpretation is correct, that the work had begun as early as 1075.

The *Historia Compostellana* gives very precise information
as to the building of the church. In 1088, Bishop Diego Pe-

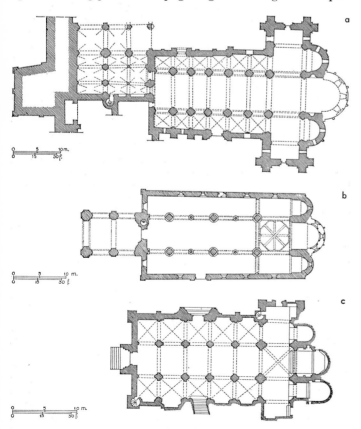

Spain and Portugal. (a) León, San Isidoro, 11th century, plan (*from K. J.
Conant, 1959*); (b) Jaca, Cathedral, end of 11th century, plan; (c) Coimbra,
Cathedral, 1130-85, plan (*from J. Gudiol Ricart, J. A. Gaya Nuño,
1948*).

láez was removed by the king and imprisoned for political reasons. The diocese, deprived of its bishop until 1094, went through a period of misery during which construction was certainly interrupted; it was resumed only in the very last years of the century by Diego Gelmírez, who governed the diocese as its vicar from 1096 and was appointed bishop in 1100 and later archbishop. A resumption can be noted in the construction between the semicircular part of the ambulatory and the straight part. The three farthest chapels (the axial one, which is quadrangular, and the other two, which are round) thus were built between 1078 and 1088; but they were not consecrated until 1105, at the same time as the last two chapels (which are polygonal) of the ambulatory and three of the apsidioles of the transept (the two of the southern arm and the first of the northern one). The division into two periods is as clear in the decoration as it is in the architecture.

It was only in 1112 that the part of the old basilica which had been preserved for religious services, and which occupied the whole crossing of the transept and part of the sanctuary of the new church, was demolished. Work on the Cathedral was delayed by a revolt of the inhabitants of Compostela, who in 1117 set fire to the Cathedral and drove Diego Gelmírez from the city. However, the main work was finished in 1122 or 1124.

The Cathedral of Santiago de Compostela is by far the largest Romanesque church in Spain (it is more than 296 ft. long) and the most complete. The nave, made up of twelve bays, is barrel-vaulted on transverse arches and flanked by groin-vaulted side aisles (PL. 213); over the side aisles, the galleries, with half-barrel vaults, abut the central barrel vault; the nave consequently has no direct lighting. A dome covers the crossing (modified over the centuries). The arms of the transept, each made up of six bays, forming a marked projection on the plan, are surrounded on three of their sides by aisles and galleries, thus prolonging the architectural scheme of the nave. Two apsidioles open in the eastern wall of each arm of the transept. The *chevet* is surrounded by an ambulatory with five radiating chapels.

Here can be recognized the plan, elevation, and vaulting methods of the great pilgrimage churches, the most perfect and best preserved of which is St-Sernin in Toulouse (PL. 199). It would be meaningless to try to establish which of the two, Santiago or St-Sernin, was built earlier. The two churches are almost contemporary, but neither is an original creation — they were both preceded by numerous examples, all of them French, and even the earliest of these, undoubtedly St-Martin of Tours, appeared only after many experiments. There are no antecedents of these forms in Spain. Galicia, where this masterpiece stands, is artistically the poorest of all the Spanish provinces, and Kingsley Porter rightly observed that the characteristic of pilgrimage art is that masterpieces spring out of an artistic desert.

There is no mystery about the heavy French influence in Santiago de Compostela; most of the pilgrims came from France. Moreover, Cluny dominated the main Spanish monasteries and occupied several episcopal sees, and in Santiago itself, a monk from Cluny, Dalmatius, was bishop in 1094 (he died the following year during a journey to France). The influence of Cluny on the Spanish church is clearly indicated by the abolition of the ancient Hispanic rite, known as the Mozarabic rite, which was replaced by the Galician or by the Roman rite by the Council of Burgos in 1080. At the same time the ancient script, called Visigothic or Mozarabic, gave way to the French hand. Relations among laymen were just as close, in the families of princes as well as among the throng of new settlers. The king of Castile and León, Alfonso VI, first married Agnes, the daughter of Guy Geoffroy d'Aquitaine, and then Constance, the daughter of the duke of Burgundy, Robert I, and niece of the abbot of Cluny, St. Hugh. A daughter of this second marriage, Urraca, married Raymond, the son of William the Great, Count of Burgundy; their son was Alfonso VII, King of Castile, León, and Galicia and Emperor of all Spain. Before becoming bishop of Compostela, Diego Gelmírez was Raymond's notary; he remained all his life on very friendly terms with the French

and played a dominant political role during the nonage of Alfonso VII. Raymond's brother and the uncle of Alfonso VII, Guy of Burgundy, became Pope Calixtus II; he raised the see of Compostela to the rank of metropolis and Diego Gelmírez to the dignity of archbishop.

The Pilgrim's Guide from the *Codex Calixtinus* introduces two master masons who at the beginning directed the building of Santiago: Bernard, the old "admirable master," and Robert, "with about fifty other stonecutters." These two names are foreign and confirm the French origin of their art. Only a few details of the architecture of Santiago are Spanish: the square chapel in the axis with its corner niches, the multifoil arches that decorate the outer story of the apse, and the "silversmith's façade." The sculpture, however, as will be seen later, originated in León and is profoundly Spanish.

The architecture of Santiago, imported into Spain, did not result in the founding of a school there. There is no other example of this model in Spanish Romanesque art. Only in Portugal (but on a much smaller scale) was the influence of the great sanctuary of Galicia manifested.

Portugal. The artistic development of Portugal during the Romanesque age in no way parallels that of Spain. The reconquest, which took place later in Portugal, did not allow the area to profit from the great creative impulse of the 11th century. It brought foreign knights, but Portugal did not experience, as did the north of Spain, the flow of pilgrims or the massive settlement of French colonists. Alfonso VI, whose daughter Urraca had married Raymond of Burgundy, married his illegitimate daughter, Teresa, to another Burgundian prince, Henri, who became Count of Portugal; his son, Affonso Henriques (1111–85), was the first king of Portugal. It was under his long reign that the most important buildings of Portuguese Romanesque art were built.

Until then Portugal had had only modest churches that faithfully reproduced the simplest pre-Romanesque model of the church having a nave without side aisles, prolonged by a quadrangular choir that was narrower and lower. The material poverty, the mediocrity of the technical means, and the coarseness of the granite, the only stone the north of the country offered, all contributed to the simplicity of these buildings. Among the earliest that have been preserved is the chapel of S. Miguel in the castle of Guimarães, where the future king Affonso Henriques, born in 1111 in that castle, was probably baptized. The little church called the Cedofeita, in Oporto, belonged to a monastery mentioned in a bull of Pope Calixtus II in 1120. Numerous rural churches were erected according to this model during the entire 12th century and undoubtedly even later. Churches with naves flanked by side aisles are exceptions, such as S. Salvador, in Travanca, or S. Pedro, in Rates, the latter rebuilt in 1152 by Queen Mafalda, the wife of Affonso Henriques. But these churches are not vaulted; even when the composite piers seem to point to a plan of vaulting, it was not carried out. The continuance of the simple wooden roof is a clear sign of the technical inadequacy of Portugal at that time.

This modest indigenous art remains quite distinct from that of the 12th-century cathedrals erected in the towns that were ancient episcopal sees restored by the reconquest. Cathedral art was an imported art; it borrowed nothing from local traditions and offered nothing to rural art.

Many Portuguese cathedrals have been carefully restored and freed from the baroque additions with which they were encumbered, but most of them had undergone such radical alterations that these restorations necessarily required a great deal of remodeling based on pure conjecture. At Braga, the piers and the arches of the interior and the carved doors of the façade are about the only remains of the Romanesque period. At Oporto only the original outline is preserved. Both these cathedrals were built during the first half of the 12th century. The Cathedral (Sé) of Lisbon (XIII, PL. 120), begun soon after the reconquest (1147), maintains, despite earthquakes, its Romanesque design, with ambulatory and radiating chapels; in the nave, the triforium with small arcades derives from a French model. The Old Cathedral (Sé Velha) of Coimbra is the best preserved and the most famous; probably erected between 1139 and 1185, it is this Cathedral which, more than any other in Portugal, follows the Santiago de Compostela model — not in plan, however, which does not offer, like the preceding churches, the splendid development of the ambulatory with the radiating chapels, for Coimbra has only three oriented and parallel apses, the two lateral ones being oddly asymmetrical. But the galleries that surmount the groin-vaulted side aisles and abut the barrel-vaulted nave derive from the pilgrimage churches; their large bays are characteristic. In addition to the Cathedral, there are in Coimbra, which was the site of many churches in the 12th century, S. Salvador and Santiago, which belong to the same period.

The Cathedral of Evora was begun in 1185 and consecrated in 1204. It has a barrel vault over the nave and groined vaults over the side aisles, but the triforium derives from a Burgundian Gothic model and all the arches are pointed.

These cathedrals were fortified. Modern restorations have given them a picturesque and a seemingly precise outline; but it is obvious that the details of the reconstruction cannot claim authenticity.

The 12th century. After the creative period of the end of the 11th century, Spanish Romanesque art entered a period of stagnation. It seems that Santiago de Compostela absorbed all the available energies during the first third of the 12th century. French influence increased in proportion to the re-population, which in many places included colonies of Franks, but the mediocrity of available materials prevented Romanesque art from developing in Spain as richly as it did in France.

The model most frequently followed was the Church of S. Isidoro of León. It was reproduced, as is natural, first in León itself, in the Church of S. María del Mercado (originally "del Camino"), then elsewhere in the region, as in the monastery of S. Pedro de las Dueñas. The constant features of this art, which rapidly tends to become monotonous, are the careful construction, the medium and regular ashlar walls, the windows with embrasures inside and outside and flanked by small columns, the cornices and imposts decorated with the same motifs, billet moldings, foliage scrolls, palmettes. This ornamental repertory is typical of León, as well as the foliage, the interlacing, and the monsters that decorate the capitals.

One of the most commonly found characteristics of Spanish churches is the portico, which usually flanks the southern side of the church. In pre-Romanesque art it was used to shelter the tombs; in the parochial churches it had a municipal function as the meeting place of the council. Examples may be found in Castile in Segovia, in Sépulveda, and in Soria. In the later examples this lateral portico is only the wing of a cloister. The cloisters themselves are numerous; for present purposes their major interest lies in their decoration.

It is, in fact, mainly in the decoration that outside contributions and novelties can be noted. In Ávila, the important Burgundian colony may have supplied masons and sculptors. S. Andrés, S. Pedro, and other examples, however, constantly repeat the simple model of the three parallel apses and the transept only slightly marked on the outside; this generalized type is primarily French, but Spanish features are not absent. One notices them in particular at S. Millán in Segovia (PL. 215), an imitation of the Cathedral of Jaca, but whose dome was much more directly derived from the Córdoban models: four arches, parallel two by two, rest in the middle of the sides of the basic square and cross each other, leaving an open square at the top. The rest of the church was covered with a wooden roof (destroyed) of Moorish influence.

The latter half of the 12th century received a second and far more decisive contribution from France — a new form of architecture, introduced by the Cistercian monks. The Cistercian churches properly belong to the Gothic style (see GOTHIC ART), but Romanesque art continued to survive in Spain long after the building of the first Cistercian church at Moreruela, erected between 1160 and 1168. Late Spanish Romanesque art adopted certain elements of the new style, often, however, giving them a Spanish touch and thus a particular character.

The last of the Romanesque churches of Ávila, S. Vicente (PL. 215; FIG. 350), the largest and most beautiful, throws diagonal ribs above its Romanesque piers in order to cover the nave; but this is only a juxtaposition of different forms — a new element had been imported but not yet assimilated.

The Cathedral of Zamora, which was built in a short space of time (1151–74), has groin-vaulted side aisles and a nave covered with diagonal ribs, with the arms of the transept barrel-vaulted. At the crossing, the lantern tower on pendentives includes a circular drum with 16 windows; the ribbed dome is formed by a framework of eight arches which cross at the center and bear 16 concave sections (*gallones*); the arches are offset

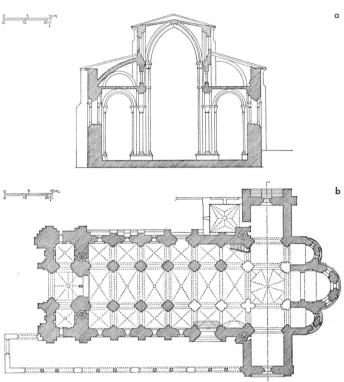

Ávila (Spain), S. Vicente, 12th century, (*a*) section; (*b*) plan (*from K. J. Conant, 1959 and from V. Lampérez, Romea II, 1930*).

on the outside by protruding cresting, which separates the convexities of the sections; four turrets at the corners are topped by small cupolas. The unmistakable Oriental character of these cupolas is reminiscent of certain Sicilian examples; but this is not merely Romanesque art colored by Arab influences — it is a complex and profoundly original composition in which the Gothic system of ribbing plays an important role.

The admirable creation of Zamora was repeated in the Old Cathedral of Salamanca in the famous Tower of the Gallo, more slender and more richly carved than its model; the tower of the Colegiata de S. María la Mayor, in Toro (PL. 214), however, is heavier. In the rest of its building, the Old Cathedral of Salamanca combines other varied elements — domical ribbed vaults, simple ribbed vaults — without ceasing to be Romanesque in its whole aspect.

The Arabic influence is also manifested in the construction in brick, which never ceased to be used in Spanish art, not only in popular art (because of its simplicity and low cost) but also in buildings of a certain importance. Among the numerous examples one is particularly striking: at Sahagún, close to the stone church of the famous Benedictine abbey of San Facundo, rose many brick churches, massive and imposing, parts of which have survived. Domes with intersecting ribs were used at the end of the 12th century in basilical-plan churches, over the crossing, as in S. Miguel de Almazán, and in churches with a centered plan, as at Torres del Río in Navarra, and in the Vera Cruz of Segovia. Finally, the pointed,

Principal sites of Romanesque architecture in Italy and Dalmatia. *Key*: (1) Modern national boundaries.

horseshoe, and intersecting arches of the cloister of S. Juan de Duero in Soria offer a most evocative picture of this penetration of Moslem art into Christian art.

Thus Spanish Romanesque architecture came to an end; from its Mozarabic forerunners through the Mudéjar phase, traditionally Spanish characteristics never ceased to give a personal touch to the art of the Peninsula. More apparent at the beginning of Romanesque architecture, they partially explain the precocity and the peculiarities of certain 11th-century buildings; but the French contributions, which had been prevalent from the beginning of the first period on the pilgrimage roads to Santiago de Compostela, gradually spread and threatened to suffocate the Spanish originality of the 12th century. That was when new Andalusian elements appeared and multiplied in late Romanesque art, already mingled with Gothic forms, thus giving birth to some of the most colorful creations of Spanish art.

Georges GAILLARD

ITALY. *The 11th century.* The first indications of a new style in Italian architecture date to the middle of the 10th century and primarily concern decorative, rather than structural, aspects such as the pilaster strips, which throughout the Middle Ages (beginning with the buttresses characteristic of late-4th-century architecture in Milan, of which a typical example is found in the Church of S. Simpliciano) characterized church exteriors. But in about 950 appeared the hints of the regular rhythm of small arches (at first coupled) on the apses that were to become a dominant element of Romanesque style, spreading from Catalonia to Germany. The oldest examples (S. Maria, Disentis; the Church of S. Maria, Amer; S. Pedro of Burgal; S. Cecilia of Monserrat, in Catalonia) are possibly of the 10th century, as is the vaulted apse of the Church of S. Ambrogio in Milan. About the year 1000, a typical treatment of the walls was large blind arcading (Church of S. Vincenzo at Galliano; Church of S. Giovanni of Vigolo Marchese; the towers of the Cathedral of Basel). This is perhaps the period in which these new ways of treating walls spread (through the work of the Lombards) in Germany, after they had appeared in Catalonia. In about 1025 there were already numerous examples of the extension of the use of small arches in the main body of the church. The principal buildings in northern Italy are the complex of Agliate (near Monza); the Church of S. Paragorio, Noli; the Abbey church of S. Giustina, Sezzadio; and the Church of S. Pietro (the Old Cathedral), Acqui. However, many other such churches of the 11th century can be cited in Piedmont (the Cathedral of Susa), in Tuscany (the parish church at Arliano), in Catalonia, in Burgundy, in Switzerland, and along the Rhine. It is very likely that the spread of increasingly refined exterior decorative trim was fostered by the stonecutters of Como, while the basilican style (Church of S. Vincenzo in Prato, Milan) or single hall (Church of S. Pietro al Monte, Civate) was still customary for the interior. It is, however, significant that the builders of Como did not use the vault until a later time, and therefore they were receptive to the varied ground plans, as is evident in the Church of S. Carpoforo, near Como (1020–40), in the Church of S. Eufemia (of the same period) on the Isola Comacina (in which the refined treatment of the complex profiles was already exceptional) and, in the second half of the century, in the Church of S. Benedetto, in Val Perlana, and in the Church of S. Abbondio at Como (PL. 219), with trusswork vaulting and nave and four side aisles.

The first attempts at rational organization in *ad oratorio* crypts as a space divided into square cells covered by vaults were possibly made in the Carolingian period. It is doubtful that these cells were in common use much before the year 1000 in Italy, at which time they were to be found in Lombardy (Agliate, Galliano, etc.) and in Piedmont (Cavour, S. Lorenzo, of 1037). Of a later period are the first examples of the division and covering of the lateral aisles with cross vaults (Church of S. Maria Maggiore at Lomello, ca. 1025), while the nave, covered by a trusswork roof, was spanned by transverse diaphragm arches. At the same time, the Romanesque pillar, which was square in section in the older monuments (Galliano),

was gradually evolving. Two half-columns were added to it (the Church of SS. Pietro e Paolo, Bologna, and the Church of S. Michele, Nonantola) and eventually it evolved into a four-lobed plan.

In the second half of the 11th century the architecture of cross vaults was finally born, most probably through the efforts of artisans from Milan. Famous monuments at Milan such as the Church of S. Lorenzo and the so-called Imperial Baths were most certainly studied by these builders, who, perhaps precociously, adopted the use of tunnel vaults over central spaces (parish church of Lenta and the Church of S. Maria of Rado in the Vercelli region; the former Church of S. Stefano at Milan, and the even older Church of S. Michele of Balocco, with an almost perfectly barrel-vaulted roof supported by arches on interior buttresses). Perhaps as early as the middle of the century there was already the vogue at Milan for simple non-ribbed cross vaults and domical cross vaults, of which there were echoes at the end of the century in the distant churches of the Vercelli and Novara regions (inspired by the rotunda of S. Lorenzo?), which were followed by cross vaults with square-section ribs.

In about 1080, the Romanesque in Milan was already fully developed. Otherwise it could not be explained (apart from other arguments) how, as early as the beginning of the 12th century, obviously Lombard-influenced churches bore the unmistakable characteristics of the architecture of Milan, as for example in Latium (at Anagni), in Aragon (Jaca; PL. 212), and elsewhere. The Church of S. Babila, Milan, contains an octagonal dome at the center, and in the Church of S. Ambrogio (ca. 1080; PL. 216; FIG. 355) women's galleries counterbalance the large central ribbed vaults. In this latter building, the most important of the Lombard Romanesque, a feeling of solemn maturity was achieved by the "alternate" system of construction (already established in northern Europe), which gives a subtle and regular alternation of dark and light areas to the whole, marked by the flawless rhythm of the supporting elements — which were repeated in the atrium. The octagonal dome, which appeared in Lombardy possibly at the end of the 10th century, became widespread in northern Europe at the beginning of the 11th century. In Lombardy walls did not tend to be thickened and solidified, as they did outside Italy, but were framed and characterized by the supporting elements. The walls achieved a new definition of space that was not to be overlooked by the Italian Gothic and was to constitute the essence of Tuscan Renaissance architecture. Other important buildings that developed the idiom of S. Ambrogio are the Church of S. Sigismondo, Rivolta d'Adda, consecrated in 1096, which has no galleries but has Romanesque apses; the badly damaged Church of S. Celso at Milan, of about 1100; and the Church of S. Savino at Piacenza, of about 1107.

The restoration, transformation, and new roofing of the crumbling Early Christian basilicas were great undertakings of the builders of Milan; one of the most memorable of these works was the dome which for four centuries crowned the rotunda of S. Lorenzo, added at about the same time as the large vaults thrown over S. Nazaro Maggiore, which in turn were followed by the vaults destined to change the appearance of the Church of S. Simpliciano (already divided, perhaps in the Lombard period, into aisles of equal height).

A type apart is represented in Milan by the Church of S. Sepolcro (1036), which was planned according to a trilobed scheme with two bell towers on the façade (this trilobed scheme was to become common, in the 11th and 12th centuries, in the churches of the Rhine).

Likewise, at the beginning of the 11th century, the barrel vault, common in Catalonia and Provence, is found somewhat differently applied in Lombardy and even more frequently in Liguria, in the basilican plan with high polygonal dome [church of the monastery of S. Fruttuoso, Portofino; the churches of S. Siro of Struppa and S. Andrea (destroyed), in Genoa; the Cathedral of Ventimiglia].

The influence of Lombard architecture was already widespread in all of Italy within the 11th century. Among the numerous works, of particular importance are the buildings

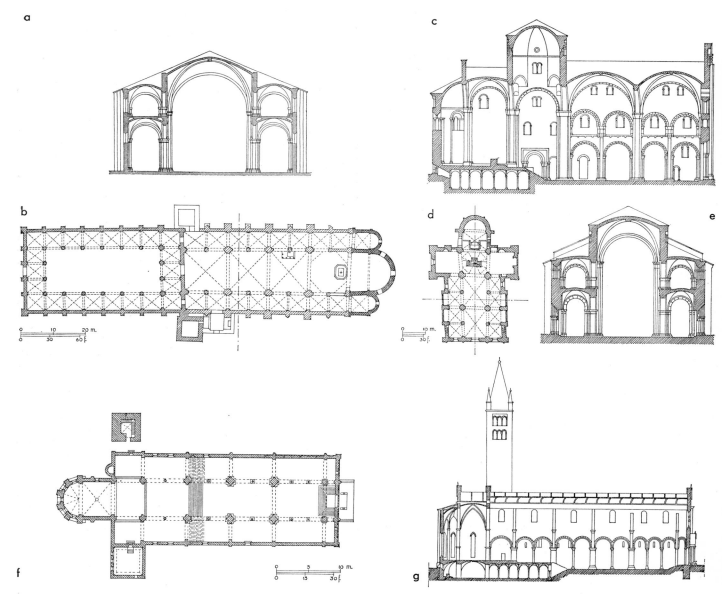

Italy. (*a, b*) Milan, S. Ambrogio, 10th and late 11th century, cross section and plan; (*c, d, e*) Pavia, S. Michele, 11th–12th cent., longitudinal section, plan, and cross section (*from E. Lundberg, 1950*); (*f, g*) Verona, S. Zeno Maggiore, 12th cent., plan and longitudinal section (*from W. Arslan, 1939*).

that show the early spread of ideas which undoubtedly had been established previously in Lombardy. At a very early date Tuscany was subject to the influences of Lombardy (the Church of S. Leonardo, Artiminio; parish churches at Arliano, Lammari, and Coreglia Antelminelli, in the area of Lucca). Strong Lombard elements are evident in the Cathedral of Carrara, in the Church of S. Maria, Impruneta (consecrated in 1060), and in the Church of S. Pietro Scheraggio, in Florence (1068). Characteristics of the Lombard style can also be seen in the eastern part of the Church of S. Pietro a Grado (1000–30), near Pisa, and in the Church of S. Sisto, Pisa. The Cathedral of Sovana, with its octagonal dome and ribbed vaults, was begun in 1073/85. Undoubtedly the plan of the Abbey church of S. Salvatore on Monte Amiata (consecrated in 1036) with its vast crypt and two façade towers was brought there by the builders of Lombardy. Northern European influences and Lombard workshops exerted their influence on the Church of S. Martino at Farfa and the Church of S. Pietro at Tuscania. Most certainly the Church of S. Maria at Bominaco (Abruzzi) is the work of Lombard stonecutters. The presence of the Lombards is particularly notable in that century in Terra di Bari. The wall structure of the oldest parts of the Church of S. Nicola at Bari, begun ca. 1087 (PL. 223), is, for the most part, of the Lombard style. In the second half of the 11th century, Lombard work-

shops were undoubtedly active in the building of the Abbey church of S. Maria di Colonna and the Church of Ognissanti at Trani, in the churches of S. Benedetto and S. Giovanni al Sepolcro, Brindisi, and in the Cathedral of Troia (PL. 223). In Calabria, the Church of S. Adriano in San Demètrio Corone is the work of Lombards.

In the second half of the 11th century, Cluny-type plans spread in Italy — from the simplest ones (nave with two side aisles, transept not protruding from the exterior, high octagonal tambour), of which the Church of S. Salvatore at Capo di Ponte (Brescia) and the Abbey church of Vertemate (Como) are outstanding examples, to the more complex Norman ones (deep central apse flanked by two minor ones, protruding transept with wings transformed into chapels). The Cathedral of Acqui, the churches of S. Fermo Maggiore and S. Lorenzo, in Verona, the Church of S. Giacomo, in Como, and the Church of S. Maria Maggiore, in Bergamo, offer the most outstanding examples of this peculiar structural development, which was contained, for the most part, within the limits of the century. In southern Italy, the best Romanesque of French influence appears in the semicircular ambulatory with three projecting chapels of the unfinished SS. Trinità in Venosa, which was certainly the work of craftsmen of French origin (ca. 1060; however, now some attribute a later date to it). In the 11th century, baptisteries once again took up Early Christian and Carolingian schemes (Galliano, Vigolo Marchese; Biella; Agliate) but added (in the cross-shaped sacellum of the Chapel of S. Benedetto at Civate) a maturity of form that was completely Romanesque.

South and west of the Apennines the old basilican module with columns still prevailed. The interior of the octagonal Baptistery of Florence (FIG. 357), with its double dome, was probably built over an Early Christian structure (of Milanese origin in style?); it was consecrated in 1059. An undeniable classical inspiration marks the colonnades of the churches of S. Miniato al Monte (built in 1018; PL. 221) and SS. Apostoli (prior to 1075), Florence, where the architecture does not express the contrast of force obvious in the buildings of Lombardy and where the surfaces are enlivened by brilliant marble facings.

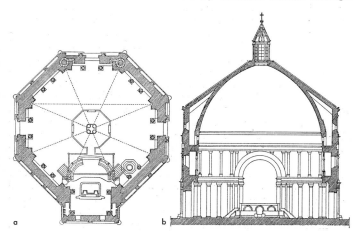

Florence, Baptistery, 11th century. (a) Plan; (b) section (from Nardini Despotti Mospignotti, Il duomo di S. Giovanni, oggi Battistero di Firenze, Florence, 1902).

The Basilica of Montecassino (consecrated in 1071, with a transept that does not protrude on the exterior, three apses and a large hall) was based on Roman models and became a model for churches throughout southern Italy, such as the Cathedral of Salerno (consecrated in 1084); and, in Apulia, the Cathedral of Taranto (founded 1071) and the original Church of S. Nicola at Bari (begun 1087) as well as certain other structures of the 12th century. The basilica based upon Early Christian and early medieval models also appeared frequently in the Po Valley and along the Adriatic slope during the 11th century. The Cathedral of Torcello (VIII, FIG. 424), the Church of S. Vincenzo in Prato, Milan, the Basilica of Pomposa (set against the atrium built by Mazulo, 1026; VIII, FIG. 410), the Church of S. Eufemia alla Giudecca and other 11th-century Venetian churches, the Basilica of Aquileia (reconstructed by Poppo in 1031), the Church of S. Giusto, in Trieste, and the parish church of San Lorenzo del Pasenatico in Istria are all products of an Early Christian revival; contact with Lombard early Romanesque is evident in the Church of S. Salvatore, in the Palazzo di Calchi at Ravenna. There is a notable difference between these basilicas, which,

thanks to a long tradition, were marked by an exceptionl equilibrium of volume and rhythm, and the coarse (and sometimes disproportionate) power of the 11th-century Romanesque structures in Lombardy and adjacent regions, as, for example, the Church of S. Giorgio, near Sant'Ambrogio di Valpolicella, on nonuniform supports; the Church of S. Severo, Bardolino; and other buildings in the early Romanesque style in the Po region.

Among the rare surviving nonreligious structures of the northern Italy of this period is the Palazzo della Ragione, Pomposa, which was probably modeled on the Palazzo dei Partecipazio (destroyed) in Venice.

Following the Norman conquest, in Calabria a building type predominated that was the same type (going back to Cluny II) as that established in northern Italy; however, earthquakes have destroyed the most important of these monuments. In 1062, Robert Guiscard began the Abbey church of S. Eufemia (Catanzaro); subsequently the Cathedral of Mileto was founded. It had a Cluny-type plan, and was supported by coupled columns (as in the Cathedral of Trani; FIG. 357; VIII, PL. 172). The Cathedral of Mileto was contemporary with the Cathedral of Gerace, which still stands, and the impressive S. Maria della Roccella (Catanzaro Marina) of about 1096, which has a Norman plan with a single aisle and large windows (now in ruins); and the Church of S. Giovanni Vecchio (1090–1100) near Stilo, which, with the Church of S. Maria of Tridetti, is one of the Calabrian basilican churches of the second half of the 11th century in which Byzantine elements are recognizable. These churches bear great similarity to certain churches of eastern Sicily (S. Filippo of Demenna, near Frazzanò, founded in 1090; S. Maria of Mili S. Pietro, ca. 1092; S. Pietro of Itala, founded in 1093), with domes on cylindrical drums and with friezes with interlaced arches on the sides. The Abbey church of Sant'Angelo (or S. Michele al Raparo) in Lucania is a type completely apart. It is of uncertain date and has barrel vaults over the nave, directly recalling the churches of Crete.

Indeed, Byzantine architecture is a fundamental element in many regions of Italy, and the central plan much used in Byzantium is very common. In addition to S. Marco in Venice (PL. 220), remodeled in 1053 by Domenico Contarini, there are the Church of SS. Vittore e Corona at Feltre (1096–1101); the Cathedral of S. Sabino of Canosa di Puglia (consecrated 1101), covered with a row of domes; the Church of S. Maria di Portonuovo, near Ancona, which combines Lombard, Norman, and Byzantine characteristics; the Church of S. Fosca at Torcello (VIII, PL. 174); and the old Cathedral of Arezzo, erected by one Maginardo, who was sent to Ravenna in 1026 to study the Church of S. Vitale.

The 12th century. Though Romanesque architecture seemed to have reached maturity in Lombardy by the last decade of the 11th century, in other areas it was only at the dawn of the 12th century that the new forms achieved a complexity and uniformity of expression unknown in the preceding decades. In Lombardy, churches inspired by the great models of the end of the 11th century, using a uniform or alternate system, must have been very numerous. Examining the progress of this ar-

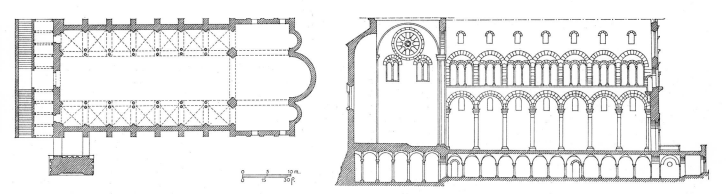

Trani (Italy), Cathedral, begun in 1097. *Left:* plan. *Right:* longitudinal section (from E. Lundberg, 1950).

chitecture at Milan, it should be noted that dome-shaped vaults were already widespread in the areas of Novara and Vercelli in the first decade of the 12th century (S. Pietro, Casalvolone, 1118–19; S. Giulio, Dulzago, 1118–48; San Nazzaro Sesia, 1125–30). However, in addition to this trend, which was concentrated in the cities of Lombardy and closely tied to the use of brick, there was the work of the stonecutters of Como who gave more importance to the stone walls than to the vaulting. The influence of these "masters of Como" (*magistri comacini*) appeared wherever cut stone was used for the construction of churches, whether they were of the basilican plan or had articulated supports and vaults. However, the ground plans were still varied; for example, the Church of S. Fedele at Como, of 1100–20 (albeit begun earlier), which has nave and side aisles that spread out into three lobes around the polygonal dome and women's galleries, undoubtedly re-creates an older plan. Originally the central nave was covered by a roof. The Church of S. Maria del Tiglio at Gravedona, which is of a later period, has a plan that is similar to the one of S. Fedele.

The great Lanfranco, who constructed the Cathedral of Modena (PL. 219; FIG. 359), was undoubtedly of the Lombard lake region. Contrary to what might have been expected — that is, a building in the Po style — he built a monument predominantly of stone. Constructed at the beginning of the 12th century without vaults and with simple transverse arches, this is the building in which Lanfranco fully achieved the Como ideal of the wall. The small arches, the galleries, the portals, and the buttresses create strong shadows which accentuate the sharp, plastic relief effects. Later on, the Cathedral of Ferrara (VIII, PL. 171; transformed in the 18th cent.) was inspired by the same principle. It has five aisles, a trusswork roof, transverse arches, and galleries along the sides. In the Po Valley, aside from the Milanese-style churches, two groups of buildings are notable; the group of churches at Pavia and the group of the cathedrals of Piacenza, Parma (VIII, PL. 171), and Cremona. At Pavia, the interior of the Church of S. Michele (FIG. 356) takes up the concept of the women's gallery used at Milan, but it differs because of its greater vertical force and because the wings of the transept are covered by barrel vaults. The wonderful sandstone façade (PL. 219) with two slopes (dating perhaps from as

Klosterrath; in the Church of Our Lady, Maastricht; and in the no longer existing Church of St. Mary at Utrecht). Single-gable façades and polygonal-domed transepts flanked by barrel vaults are found in other churches of Pavia, and also in the Church of S. Michele at Lomello. This plan was carried further in S. Giulio (Orta); in Novara (Cathedral, consecrated in 1132; destroyed); and in Vercelli (the Church of S. Maria Maggiore, of 1148; destroyed); it reached maturity in the *chevet* of the Cathedral of Parma (VIII, PL. 171). The Cathedral of Piacenza was erected in three periods, from about 1122 to 1150. It has a nave and two side aisles (with transept that does not project on the exterior) divided by massive circular pillars arranged in an alternate system of Anglo-Norman inspiration, which is also evident in the two towers planned for the façade, the projected six-sectioned vaults, and the false women's gallery (later transformed into a triforium). About 1140, the Cathedral of Parma, rebuilt after the earthquake of 1117, once again used the alternate system and the idea of towers on the façade. The Cathedral of Cremona, destroyed by the same earthquake, was planned in the fourth decade of the 12th century on the example of Piacenza (the transept is much later). At the end of the 12th century, the Cathedral of Piacenza had an exposed-beam roof which was replaced, in the 13th century, by six-sectioned vaults and polygonal dome modeled after contemporary buildings of the Île-de-France, thus constituting the sole example of its kind in the Po Valley (Romanini, 1951). Echoes of Norman characteristics of the first cathedral of Piacenza are found in other churches of the city. At the end of the century, the Baptistery of Parma (begun in 1196; PL. 220), with its octagonal plan and several stories of exterior architraved loggias hiding the "French style" dome, the work of Benedetto Antelami, was the most ingenious interpretation of the original principle of the Lombard polygonal dome. This structure opened one of the paths by which the French Gothic was to reach Italy and which, in this case, was to result in complexes that can already be considered "Gothic," for example, the interior of the Cathedral of Fidenza (formerly Borgo San Donnino) and the Church of S. Andrea, Vercelli (I, PL. 297). See GOTHIC ART.

For the most part, central plans were used only in baptisteries, which in Lombardy abandoned the Early Christian

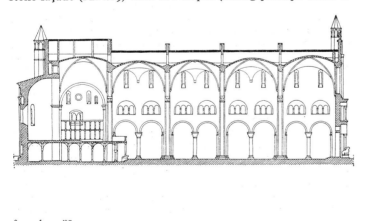
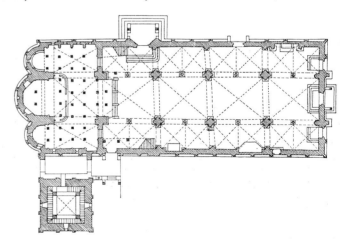

Modena, Cathedral, early 12th century. *Left*: longitudinal section; *right*: plan (*from L'Architettura, 27, 1958*).

early as the 11th century) presents, in the calm rhythm of empty and full spaces and in the novelty of the gallery running under the coping, an insurpassable model, which was to be imitated later in the narrower façade of the Church of S. Giovanni in Borgo (destroyed in 1811) and in the façade of the Church of S. Pietro in Ciel d'Oro (both, Pavia), which completed the reconstruction of an earlier building. The nave of the original S. Pietro in Ciel d'Oro was probably covered by oblong vaults similar to those that existed in the (destroyed) Church of S. Maria del Popolo (and in the Church of S. Stefano at Milan). S. Maria del Popolo had, in addition, the peculiarity of two false transepts (raised) in a longitudinal body (as at Cluny III; at

schemes that were common during the 11th century. In the Church of S. Maria del Solario at Brescia, the octagonal dome (ca. 1120), similar to that of the Baptistery of Agrate Conturbia, is set on a square base. The rotundas of S. Tommaso in Limine, Almenno, San Salvatore; S. Lorenzo, at Mantua; and the imposing Old Cathedral at Brescia (VIII, PL. 171) are all circular with interior pillars. However, the octagonal Baptistery of Cremona (begun in 1167) carries out a principle of construction similar to that of the Baptistery of Florence.

The Lombard workshops that were active in the new Romanesque style were also productive in the 12th century (more so than before) throughout Italy and in northern Europe; artisans from Como worked all over, building flawless brick walls designed for the most varied settings and spatial plans. It is clear that they were present in Bergamo (the apses of the Church of S. Maria Maggiore, 1137), in Verona, in Piedmont (at Asti, at Montechiaro, at Cortazzone, in the Val d'Ossola, etc.), and at Trento.

As far as the spread of the strictly Milan-Pavia building style is concerned, some examples outside the Lombardy-Emilia area are particularly interesting. In the Church of S. Flaviano, Montefiascone (FIG. 361), of which the lower part was by Lombard workshops and the upper part perhaps by local workers, there is repeated, at the beginning of the 12th century,

area) to numerous building projects, including the Church of S. Liberatore della Maiella, not before 1100, and the older parts of the superb Basilica Valvence (or Basilica of S. Pelino) at Corfinio, dated to 1104–24.

In the Terra di Bari, grandiose structures were fostered by the Lombard Romanesque, which contributed, in the second phase of construction of the Church of S. Nicola at Bari (PL. 223, FIG. 362), to the transformation of the basilica into a nave with Norman-style women's galleries and a façade flanked by two towers. Later on, in S. Nicola, the crossing was separated from the nave, and two other towers were added to the eastern part of the building, giving it a Rhenish character. The Cathedral

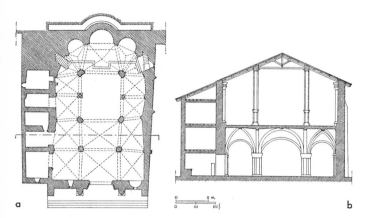

Montefiascone, S. Flaviano, early 12th century. (a) Plan of the lower church; (b) section (from L'Architettura, 29, 1958).

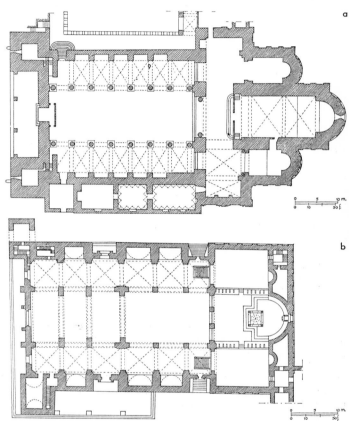

Italy. (a) Cefalù, Cathedral, founded 1131, plan; (b) Bari, S. Nicola, begun in 1087, plan (from K. J. Conant, 1959).

the alternate system with typical Lombard capitals. The Cathedral of Sovana (near Siena) is characteristically Lombard in character. The churches of Tarquinia (S. Maria di Castello, S. Giacomo, the Annunziata) have ribbed vaults supported by complex polystyle pilasters. The alternate system in the Cathedral of Anagni (1072–1102) shows an extremely early derivation from Lombard prototypes, as does the Church of S. Eufemia at Spoleto, of about 1100 (with its alternate system and women's galleries), which recalls the Church of S. Lorenzo, Verona. A more detailed study presents evidence of the presence of Lombard workmen in all of Italy, where these craftsmen were employed either independently or with local workers.

Works of these artisans were to be found in the area of Lucca as early as the beginning of the 12th century (the Church of S. Frediano at Lucca, founded in 1112, has a Pisa-type basilican interior, but the superb façade with its single architraved gallery has a severity which is completely Lombard); in the Garfagnana region of Pisa (the Church of S. Cecilia, founded in 1103); in the elaborate interior of the Pieve di S. Maria, Arezzo; in the area of Siena (Cuneo, the Church of S. Maria, consecrated in 1124), in the basilican parish churches of Casentino and Valdarno Superiore (at Gropina), and in the Abbey church of S. Antimo (with obvious French accents) near Montalcivo (PL. 221).

In the Marches a lively understanding of the Lombard-style Romanesque is found mixed with a certain freedom of imagination; this is very obvious in the squared façade of the Church of SS. Vincenzo and Anastasio at Ascoli Piceno and in the very different, later partitioning of the façade of the Church of S. Maria della Piazza at Ancona (VIII, PL. 176). In Umbria, at the end of the century the high presbyteries of Lombard inspiration gave way to basilican structures of Roman influence; and the decoration, by local stonecutters, became classicizing in style. The Cathedral of Todi (alternate system, with trusswork roofing), which is a unique example in Umbria, is dated to 1225–50. In the Marches and in the Abruzzi, the alternate system sometimes has a spirit that is distinctly Lombard (in the churches of the Ascoli region, in the wonderful Cathedral of Teramo). The very good stone of the Abruzzi attracted the Lombard stonemasons (more precisely, those from the Como

of Bitonto (1175–1200) and that of Molfetta (ca. 1180) were also inspired by this last phase. On the other hand, the Cathedral of Bari (after 1156) abandoned the more severe rhythmic pattern of S. Nicola and returned to the basilican system with false women's galleries. A cornice that went all around the interior over the arches was an example for a similar motif that was to appear at Ruvo (Apulia) and in the Cathedral of Siena. The Cathedral of Trani (begun in 1097; the aisles later than 1160; FIG. 357; VIII, PL. 172) is also derived from S. Nicola, but, as at Sens, the arches rest on twin columns and there is a triforium above them. This completely northern European vertical thrust was also passed on to the façade (which in the 13th century was to be imitated by that of Ruvo; VIII, PL. 172). Among the minor churches of Apulia that evidenced the greatest Lombard influence is the Church of S. Maria Amalfitana at Monopoli. In Sardinia the presence of Lombard workshops is deduced from the extraordinary purity of style in churches such as S. Maria del Regno, Ardara (1107), and, even admitting a Tuscan intermediary, S. Maria, in Uta, in the Cagliari zone. In the second half of the 12th century, churches with nave and side aisles of equal height in which the vaults rest on impost blocks of equal height (a vault type that was to be widely adopted in the Gothic style) were found in northern Italy (S. Bernardo,

Vercelli, 1164; S. Valeriano, Robbio; S. Simpliciano, Milan). Lombard artisans (from Milan, Como, and Pavia) were active outside Italy as well. The Grossmünster of Zurich (ca. 1160); the Cathedral of Chur (Coire), Switzerland; the Church of St. Arbogast at Oberwinterthur; the Cathedral of Basel (ca. 1185); the Church of St. Servatius of Maastricht (whose façade is reminiscent of the lost one of the Cathedral of Novara); the Cathedral of Quedlinburg (very similar to the Church of S. Abbondio at Como); the Cathedral of Nijmegen; the Cathedral of Lund, in Skåne, Sweden, founded in 1100 (and built by a certain Donatus); the Seo de Urgel, in Lérida, Catalonia, and many others are structures directly influenced by the Lombard style, in which the Lombard masters of wall construction were joined by stonecutters from the Po region. About 1160, artisans from Milan and Pavia introduced into northern Germany (the Cathedral of Havelberg, in Brandenburg) and into Denmark the use of brick construction, which spread in that area after that date (Clemmensen, 1922). The use of ribbed vaults of rectangular sections was found wherever the Lombards went, in Burgundy (where Lombard workers were already active in the 11th century), along the Rhine, in Provence, in Spain (Jaca), in Poitou, and in the Netherlands.

In Rome, the churches executed after original plans of the 12th century or remodeled at that time (S. Maria in Cosmedin; S. Clemente, VIII, PL. 176; S. Maria in Trastevere), even though they have different characteristics, conform to the basilican model which, from Genoa to Pisa to Montecassino, marked so much of religious construction west of the Apennine Mountains. In Rome, S. Maria in Trastevere repeats S. Maria Maggiore; however, the bell towers recall the Lombard tradition even though they have classical modulations. Pre-Renaissance classicism also inspired the marble workers (see COSMATI) who created marble liturgical furnishings, pavements, cloisters, and other more complicated architectural elements between the 12th and 13th centuries.

The Cathedral of Pisa (PL. 222; FIG. 364), founded in 1063, originally must have been a church with four aisles and the nave projecting beyond the transept, in imitation of the large Early Christian Roman basilicas; the transept and presbytery were enlarged, perhaps in 1089, on the model of Eastern sanctuaries to a church in which the nave does not extend beyond the transept. The church was consecrated in 1118. Later on it was extended by Rainaldus to the present façade, which was begun by Rainaldus (1120–25), continued by the master Gugliemo (1130–60), and finally completed by Biduinus (1170). Thus, in the hands of the masters of Pisa, the Lombard motif of the gallery underwent a complete change, and the severity of the Lombard-style façade was dissolved into light and color. However, the Como style, which in the Cathedral of Modena had already elaborated the beauty of the walls without concern for statics, on the exterior of the Cathedral of Pisa was accentuated and strengthened even more by the magnificence of the marble works. This was accomplished by blind arcading, of Early Christian origin, decorated with lozenges; and the interior, with false women's galleries, follows the same plan. The Church of S. Paolo a Ripa d'Arno (1148–65; VIII, PL. 178) is derived from the Cathedral of Pisa. The campanile of the Cathedral of Pisa, founded in 1173, represents the most ingenious interpretation of the principle of several levels of marble loggias applied to a round tower. The taste for this kind of polychromy was even more accentuated in the churches of Pistoia (S. Giovanni Fuorcivitas; VIII, PL. 178) and was later to become a determining factor in Guidetto da Como's façade for the Cathedral of Lucca (1204; VIII, PL. 178). Inseparable from Pisan-Luccan architecture is the 12th-century architecture of Liguria, where the solemn basilican type with bicolored walls prevails (Cathedral of S. Lorenzo, Genoa, rebuilt at the beginning of the 14th century) and where the high polygonal domes are reminiscent of Burgundy (S. Donato, Genoa) and towers with pyramidal spires and pinnacles and dormer windows prevail (common to the valleys of Piedmont, Dauphiné, and Vallese).

The architectural forms of Pisa were particularly widespread in the Capitanata, in Sardinia, and in Dalmatia. The Cathedral of Troia (PL. 223) was begun in 1093. S. Maria at Siponto,

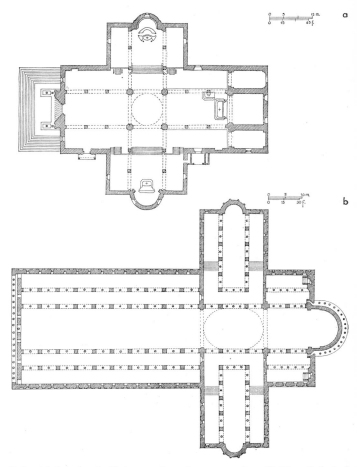

Italy. (a) Ancona, S. Ciriaco, 11th–12th century, plan; (b) Pisa, Cathedral, founded in 1063, plan (from K. J. Conant, 1959).

Apulia (with a central plan; VIII, PL. 178), was consecrated in 1117, and the Cathedral of Foggia (to which the Cathedral of Termoli in Molise is similar) is of 1179. Elements of Pisan-Luccan and Lombard origin are present in the Church of S. Chrysogonus at Zadar, Yugoslavia (begun in 1175). In Sardinia, echoes of the Cathedral of Pisa can be detected in the Church of S. Giusta at Oristano (1135–45; VIII, PL. 178), and in the similar Church of S. Antioco of Bisarcio — two single-apsed basilicas with vaults on the small aisles and large arcading on the exterior — and in the Church of S. Niccolò at Ottana (1140–60). However, from about 1170 on, very strong Pisan-Luccan characteristics appeared in the buildings of the northern part of Sardinia (S. Pietro of Sorres, which also bears resemblances to the Cathedral of Grosseto; the Trinità of Saccargia, of 1180–1200). In Corsica, more or less archaic Pisa-style forms are found at Mariana (La Canonica and S. Perteo) and in Nebbio (with Lombard accents as well).

The Byzantine role in 12th-century Italian architecture was of notable importance, particularly along the Adriatic coast. Even though there is uncertainty about placing the date of the Church of S. Maria of Portonuovo, near Ancona, in the 12th century (Krönig, 1938), Byzantine elements must be recognized in the Church of S. Vittore delle Chiuse, near Genga. This latter has an inscribed Greek-cross plan, eight cross vaults, a central dome, and five small apses. An almost identical scheme is found in the Church of S. Claudio al Chienti, near Macerata, which has two stair towers at the sides of the façade; noteworthy, too, in the Marches are the churches of S. Maria de "le Moie" at Maiolati and Sta Croce at Sassoferrato. The most complex elaboration of these central-plan schemes is represented at Ancona by the Church of S. Ciriaco (PL. 221; FIG. 364), which is a transformation of a basilican structure. In the Veneto, in addition to the numerous brick constructions in Lombard Romanesque style which are scattered everywhere (in the areas of Padua, Treviso, etc.; in the Venetian mainland) and have not yet been studied, there is also the presence of Byzantine style, which added to the brick walls elaborate arcading and niches (the Cathedral of Murano; Sta Sofia of Padua).

The architecture of Verona is one of the richest chapters in the Romanesque style of the Po region. Veronese architecture uses the alternate system but rejects the vaults; from alternating layers of tufa and brick it achieves a vivid bichromy, which gives the walls a character that is essentially Lombard (with small arches in the style of Como). This architecture, which reached its flowering between 1120 and 1140, also takes some of its forms from French art (apse of SS. Apostoli). The interior of the Cathedral, founded in 1139, was redone in the 15th century, but the remarkable apse still exists. The Church of S. Zeno (PL. 220; FIG. 355) follows the principle of free wall arrangement used in the cathedrals of Modena and Pisa, but in its façade achieves an exquisite color effect in harmony with the rose window. In addition to those at Verona, monuments that prove the activity of artisans from northern Europe are found in all of Italy. At about 1150, elements clearly derived from western France were used in the Abbey church of S. Fede of Cavagnolo (Turin); in the Church of S. Lorenzo of Montiglio (Alessandria), which has barrel vaults and very beautiful capitals; and at a later date, at Casale Monferrato in the atrium of the Church of S. Evasio, which has high cruciform pillars reminiscent of Poitou structures (where, however, the interlaced arches of the vaults recall Moslem examples).

Parallel to the spread of Lombard forms, some regions of Italy adopted the French use of barrel vaults and half-barrel lateral vaults (so common in the Auvergne). Beginning with the second half of the 12th century, the row of domes along the axis of the central aisle was a type of roofing that was to characterize some notable buildings. Thus, the churches of Ognissanti at Valenzano, S. Benedetto at Conversano (Bari), S. Francesco at Trani, and the Cathedral of Molfetta reveal, alongside Byzantine accents, important contact with the architecture of southern France. The churches of S. Margherita at Bisceglie (covered by a dome inserted in a barrel vault over a single nave), S. Pietro at Balsignano, and S. Lucia at Rapolla, Lucania, also witness to relationships to Dalmatian and eastern structures. However, the most elegant elaboration of the French principles can be seen at Lecce, in the beautiful Church of SS. Nicolò e Cataldo, completed in 1180, in which the central dome is harmoniously joined to the scheme of three aisles of equal height, which was typical of Poitou (Krönig, 1959). Also completely apart is the remarkable three-aisled Church of S. Sepolcro in Barletta (1180–1200) with the rectangular transverse bays customary in Burgundy and based on a principle originating in the Holy Land (ibid.). Toward the end of the 12th century the use of barrel vaults (tending, basically, to avoid the Lombard forcefulness in favor of a greater clarity of composition based upon the cross-vaulted bay) was also found in other regions of Italy. The three aisles of the Cathedral of S. Leo in the Marches (ca. 1200) are covered by barrel vaults. Examples can also be cited in Umbria and Latium (S. Silvestro at Bevagna; S. Pietro at Bovara, of the second half of the 12th century; and the later S. Sisto at Viterbo). It is possible that the Cathedral of Assisi was also of this type.

In southern Italy, the example of Venosa was followed in the cathedrals of Aversa and Acerenza; and the same motif is found in the Church of S. Antimo at Montalcino (PL. 221). However, at the end of the century, a new wave of French taste was to spread the Burgundian architecture imported by the Cistercians (see GOTHIC ART).

In the 12th century there penetrated into Campania, both directly and by way of the Normans, the taste for polychrome decoration with interlaced arches (which was to last into the 13th century) evident in the ground plan of the Cathedral of Caserta Vecchia (VIII, PL. 175), in the Castel Terracena (Palatium Terracenae) in Salerno, and in the cloister of Amalfi (PL. 224). In this region (Caserta Vecchia, Ravello) the ground plans of the churches are basilican with high polygonal domes.

The first important example of Norman architecture in Sicily is the Cathedral of Mazara del Vallo, founded in 1093 by Roger II. It follows the most complicated Cluny-type scheme (Bernay), with towers on the façade. In 1094 it was followed by the old part of the Cathedral of Catania. On the other hand, the Cathedral of Messina, which was constructed in the decade 1130–40, appears to be tied to the Benedictine type of ground plan. In the Cathedral of Cefalù (FIG. 362; VIII, PL. 173), founded in 1131, can be seen the solemn conclusion of Norman architecture in Sicily. The great apses (1140–45), decorated with interlaced archings that are undoubtedly of Norman origin (and the use of which spread from here throughout the island), and the transept (1160–70) derive their unusual energy from adherence to northern plans. The façade with two towers, perhaps the most monumental expression of this northern concept in Italy, is also ascribed to the 12th century (Schwarz, 1942–44). The Martorana (S. Maria dell'Ammiraglio) in Palermo, of a Byzantine plan but with Islamic pendentives, should be attributed to a more decisive Eastern influence which began to be felt about 1150; and purely Islamic domes also cover the Church of S. Giovanni degli Eremiti (1132). In the Cappella Palatina, Palermo (1140), there is a lively and magnificent fusion of Byzantine, Latin, and (in the ceiling decorations) Islamic elements, according to a principle that was carried out on a large scale in the Cathedral of Palermo (1170–85), which, after the type of the cathedrals of Trani and Mileto, has columns grouped in fours. The towers of the Cathedral of Palermo (like that of the Martorana) seem to be of French origin, but the abstract decorations once again are Islamic.

The Cathedral of Monreale (PL. 224; VIII, PL. 173), which is of the same epoch as that of Palermo, shows, in its proportions and in the existence of its quadriporticus, contacts (through Cava dei Tirreni) with the architecture of Campania, as do the magnificent cloister and the exterior polychrome decoration of arches, disks, and other abstract forms, which are similar to certain elements of the buildings of Salerno (and were later found at Palermo, Messina, and the Cathedral of Tropea).

In western Sicily many churches were undoubtedly built by architects who expressed a particular taste of their own in wall masses of extraordinary precision (masses reduced to quasi-geometrical elements), in the dressing of the walls, in the extrados of the domes, and in the stalactite squinches. This taste was derived from Fatimid architecture (albeit alongside Norman motifs). Examples of these churches are S. Giovanni dei Lebbrosi and S. Cataldo (ca. 1160) at Palermo, the Cathedral of Mazara del Vallo, and the SS. Trinità of Delia (1100–50), near Castelvetrano.

In addition to public buildings (the *broletto*, or courthouse, of Bergamo, 1182, and that of Brescia, ca. 1186) — with open portico on the ground floor in Lombardy, but with central courtyard at Verona (Palazzo del Comune) — the first private houses built of stone appeared during the 12th century in Florence (Palazzo Bezzoli in Piazza dell'Olio; the house and tower of the Saltarellis in the Chiasso del Buco), Rome (the house of Nicolò Crescenzi), Verona ("La Canonica" of S. Giovanni in Valle), and elsewhere (of less certain date), and they are undoubtedly the oldest in Europe. City walls were rebuilt in Genoa (1155–57; with half-round towers), Milan (1171), and Como (Porta Vittoria, 1192); as were the towers of the nobility (which established prestige) at Pavia, Bologna, and in Tuscany; and castles. The Castel Terracena of Salerno was completely perforated by loggias, as were the older Venetian palaces. In the palaces of the Norman kings (the Torre Pisana in the Palazzo Reale of Palermo; La Zisa, PL. 235; La Cuba, FIG. 367) distinctly northern European elements are combined, as in religious architecture, with Moslem elements.

Edoardo ARSLAN

GERMANY AND CENTRAL EUROPE. In the study of the Romanesque, the classifications "early" for the period from the end of the 10th century to 1070/80, "middle," or "high," till 1150, and "late" till the middle of the 13th century seem in many respects to be questionable; still they give an easily remembered

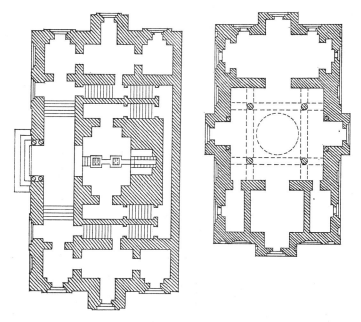

Palermo. *Left*: La Zisa, 12th century, plan. *Right*: La Cuba, 1180, plan (*from G. U. Arata. Architettura arabo-normanna e il Rinascimento in Sicilia, Milan, 1914*).

and for the most part appropriate framework for Central European Romanesque architecture. For a discussion of the early Romanesque style of this area see OTTONIAN PERIOD. In contrast to the early style, the middle Romanesque restricted the characteristic diversity of theme and redefined the shapes of space and mass of the flat-ceiling basilica to an articulated simplicity "classic" in its concept. On the other hand, with the complete vaulting of the high spaces — the choir, crossing, transept, and nave of the basilica — in individual Rhenish structures it advances toward solutions which lay the foundations for the whole of the development of the late Romanesque style. The flat-ceiling construction, however, prevailed in the area north of the Alps and east of the Meuse, with numerous adherents well into the 12th century. Stylistic and regional differences appear secondary here, although the arrangement of space does not seem to be uniform throughout the area.

In contrast to early Carolingian and Ottonian early Romanesque architecture (of which there are few well-preserved structures), middle Romanesque (and even more often, late Romanesque) architecture is represented by a large number of completely intact churches. In addition, there are secular constructions, such as castles, palaces, town fortifications, and dwelling houses, to be observed. The geographic range is also expanded; to the north the boundaries of Occidental art pushed beyond Jutland (Denmark) to Skåne (southern Sweden); in the east this art followed the expansion of Germanic colonization from the Elbe across the Oder to Bohemia. As was true in the early period, only scattered edifices with the Romanesque imprint were constructed outside the areas of colonization of the Germanic peoples in the Polish, Czech, and Hungarian domains.

In this middle, or "high," period, in addition to cathedrals, monastery churches, and collegiate churches, an increasing number of parish churches of considerable size were constructed, with the corresponding architectural display. The various ground plans and spatial types are, however, less differentiated according to their purpose. At this stage new monastic orders, principally the Premonstratensian and Cistercian, joined the old and the reformed Benedictine monasteries as builders. Their influence on the development of special architectural forms, nevertheless, seems to be widely overrated. For the present brief review it is enough to point out that the Cistercians offered a few plans for the arrangement of chapels at the transept and the choir, and in general omitted towers and crypts. (Crypts,

as a result of the raising of relics to the altars, were in general gradually abandoned.) Baptismal and castle chapels show preference for the central layout.

The flat-ceiling basilica is prevalent, with few exceptions, in the whole of Central Europe until about 1140, till 1170 in the northeastern countries, and till the end of the Romanesque period in the southeastern part of the territory. Even in the Rhineland some significant flat-ceiling constructions are found as late as 1200. The utilization of space, structural types, partial vaulting, and arrangement vary greatly in the different areas. In common they have, as it were, a "crystalline" consolidation; the walls, through jutting socles and cornices, through stepped framing of openings, through incorporation of structural members into the surfaces, become unequivocally powerful masses; the support is no longer a sector of the wall or an "antique" column with remnants of an organic-articulate life, but abstract sustaining members, square or round pillars; the space is a box, or consists of several adjoining boxes, and the tower is built up of cubic stories. The law of frontality, of axiality, of addition, controls the outer structure as well. The cushion capitals, in stressing the four semicircular faces, as a motif exemplify the fully abstract, clear norm, just as the surface articulation finds a means of delimiting areas by the use of horizontally connected pilaster strips and round arch friezes, without calling attention to the structural plan with pilasters and engaged columns. Architectural ornamentation is restrained, and is almost entirely limited to capitals, portals, and the apse.

The austere, at times even sober, but always monumental style of this architecture occurs in its most convincing form in the two regions which were closest to the Hirsau reforms of Benedictine monastery life — the Upper Rhine region and Lower Saxony; but it is not limited to buildings of the reform monasteries. The best-preserved churches are in the Upper Rhine district and in Swabia: Alpirsbach, Kleinkomburg, Gengenbach, and Schaffhausen (all of about 1100), all column basilicas; Maulbronn, dedicated 1178 (VI, PL. 123, FIG. 162), and Ilbenstadt (dedicated 1172) have a double alternating system of supports; Hecklingen has a simple alternating system; the Church of Our Lady (Liebfrauenkirche) in Halberstadt and the church in Talbürgel have piers; those in Hamersleben, Paulinzella, and Jerichow (a brick construction) have columns. The last three are from the middle of the 12th century. The cruciform plan with a square choir, square transept, and segregated crossing emphasize the late Romanesque standard in almost all of these churches. St. Godehard, Hildesheim, with its east and west choir, crossing tower, and the eastern choir ambulatory is a rather rare exception. Pairs of towers on the west or east, exceptionally on both ends (Halberstadt), are frequent. In Lower Saxony the preferred form is the western transept surmounted by an octagonal tower. The absence of crypts is almost general. There is a wide scope in variation of proportions from the broad layout of Kleinkomburg to the pronounced vertical design of Schaffhausen and St. Godehard.

Westphalia was less fruitful in this middle period; there the principal pier basilicas worth mentioning are Freckenhorst and the Abdinghofkirche, Paderborn. Along the Rhine the larger churches of this period were of vaulted construction; but there were a number of the flat-ceiling basilicas (principally in the Lower Rhine-Meuse district) which show an appreciable versatility of space arrangement and design. For instance, there is a group of galleried churches (St. Ursula in Cologne; the church at Dietkirchen, on the Lahn river). Another group is characterized by blind arcades on the upper inner walls (the church at Saint-Séverin-en-Condroz in Liège). There are simple pier churches even in the affluent capital of Cologne (St. Caecilien). In this region, rich in tradition, the architectural ideas of the early Romanesque live on, as can be seen in the cloverleaf choir of Klosterrath (Rolduc, near Maastricht), the three-towered *Westwerk* of Brauweiler, and the great *Westwerk* of Maria Laach (PL. 225).

The southeastern region, Swabia and Bavaria, at least in that part not directly connected with the Upper Rhine, remain attached throughout to the simple plan with three apses and no transept. In Austria the Gurk Cathedral is an example of an

Principal centers of Romanesque architecture in German territory and in Scandinavia. *Key:* (1) Modern national boundaries.

imposing pier basilica and Seckau one with column construction. In Bamberg (St. Jakob) and Würzburg (St. Burkard), in Mainfranken, there were in this period new constructions without any strong individual features.

The 11th and 12th centuries. In the 11th and 12th centuries stone vaulting of large spaces seemed to present such a fascinating problem in church construction that not only should its technical solution be considered one of the revolutionary events of the epoch but also the temptation arises to read into it an

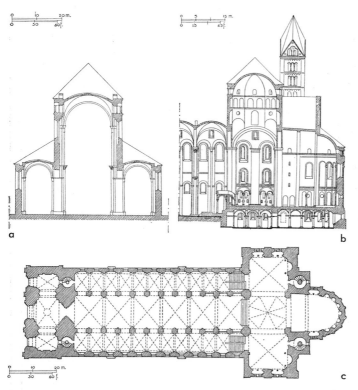

Speyer (Germany), Cathedral, 12th century. (*a*) Cross section; (*b*) longitudinal section on the apse; (*c*) plan (*from F. Klimm, Der Kaiserdom zu Speyer, Speyer, 1953*).

accomplishment or a denial of a basic ideological and political viewpoint, perhaps as in the struggle over lay investiture. In the Central European region the reconstruction of the Speyer Cathedral (PL. 225; VI, FIG. 159) under Emperor Henry IV between about 1080 and about 1106 was the turning point; in western Europe the Norman architecture of Durham and Caen and the Burgundian architecture of Cluny III had reached

about the same point. In Speyer the general ground plan is provided by the early Romanesque construction of about 1030–61 (VI, FIG. 159). The transept and choir were almost entirely rebuilt; the nave (PL. 225) was changed by vaulting the interior. It was here that the architectural system was founded which reigned for a century and a half throughout the architecture of Central Europe — the *gebundene* system, in which the two vaulted bays of the side aisles balanced the single bay of the nave, and every second pier was given a stronger reinforcement of engaged shafts, so forming a compound column; these reinforcements in the zone of the clerestory windows were tied in with longitudinal arches on the walls and transverse arches across the upper nave space. Between these arches were set groined vaults almost 90 feet high and with a span of almost 45 feet. Thus the square plan, on which the early Romanesque had already been built, became evident; the scheme is no longer buried in the ground plans, but controls through its round arches and its three-dimensional vaulting the whole of the space, since it is obviously built up from equal units. Thus, in contrast to the Italian constructions, the stepping and the lightness of the basilica are maintained. The arms of the transept are done in the same design, with the choir square only lightly differentiated by a barrel vault. Above the crossing a 150-ft.-high octagonal tower was constructed, open to the interior. The newly built walls of the transept and the apses use the leading motif of the early Romanesque nave — the high blind arcade on the interior as well as on the exterior. The strength of the walls was at the same time fully utilized and made visible in all parts of the construction, through the recessed niches in the apses and the crossing tower, through vaulted chapels to ground level in the transept and the choir, and through the dwarf galleries on the upper cornice, so that here the idea of a doubleshell hollow wall (*mur évidé*) was for the first time developed on a large scale. The upper part of the *Westwerk* and all six towers in their existent form are of the 12th century.

The reconstruction of the Speyer Cathedral was followed by that of the Cathedral of Mainz (PL. 225), which is the second of the very large Rhenish vaulted constructions. The eastern end and the nave have been retained in their main features: a transept with octagonal central tower and east apse, quite similar to that of Speyer, and the nave in the *gebundene* system (in which, however, the blind arcade ends below the level of the clerestory windows). The Abbey church of Maria Laach (PL. 225), founded in 1093, followed the example of this Cathedral with eastern and western transepts with three towers each; however, a large part of this construction was carried out first in the course of the 12th century. The vaulting was planned from the beginning as a special case: the quadrangular vaulted structure corresponds directly to the succession of the piers and the crossbeams (cf. the Burgundian Abbey church of Vézelay).

Subsequent to 1140, these first large towering vaulted structures generated what might be termed a "school" in the two groups of the Upper Rhine and Lower Rhine vaulted basilicas in the *gebundene* system. The first are concentrated in Alsace

a

b

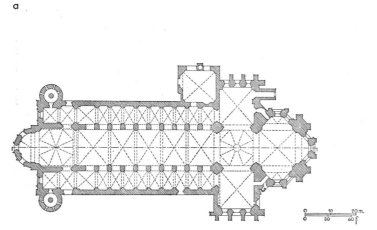

Mainz, Cathedral, 1009–1239. (*a*) Plan, (*b*) section (*from E. Lundberg, 1950, and from P. Metz, Dom zu Mainz, Augsburg, 1927*).

— in Neuwiller (SS. Peter and Paul), and in Sélestat (Schlettstadt), with offshoots toward the west in Saint-Dié (the Cathedral) and toward the north in Eberbach in Rheingau (PL. 226). Among the Lower Rhine examples Klosterrath, near Aachen, and the Abbey of Knechtsteden, near Cologne, are those with the most beautiful and most classically pure forms. In both groups the Speyer system is reduced to its simplest form but is often emphasized by a pronounced alternating system of supports (piers and column). In the Upper Rhine area another characteristic is the twin-tower façade with an open vestibule (Sélestat; Guebwiller, St-Léger; Lautenbach); in the Lower Rhine area the choir façades framing the three-story articulated apses with a pair of towers, as in Cologne, Bonn, Koblenz (XIII, PL. 254), and Maastricht, and with their dwarf galleries tie in to the examples of the Trier Cathedral *Westwerk* (X, PL. 459). The nave of the vaulted Abbey church in Brauweiler, with its niched triforium, already shows the three-story division as a principal motif of late Romanesque art.

One problem that scholars have not yet solved is represented by the early churches with flat-ribbed vaults in the *gebundene* system. Although this type of arch in the Upper Rhine area from Murbach (PL. 226) and Speyer to Worms (PLS. 228, 229) and Maulbronn (VI, FIG. 162) shows a continual development but is used preferably in the choir and transept, in Utrecht and Maastricht are found large vaulted edifices with the flat ribs and the corresponding inclined supports in the nave which, by means of a doubling or even a tripling of the transept, bring a powerful rhythm into the space arrangement. Both forms were present in the (no longer extant) northern Italian buildings of Novara and Vercelli (ca. 1130); the (destroyed) Church of Our Lady in Utrecht probably was constructed at about the same time, and the Church of Our Lady in Maastricht in about 1170.

Speyer and Goslar (St. Ulrich) introduced in about 1100 the series of the vaulted double chapels situated one directly over the other but connected by a central opening. The Cathedral of St. Godehard in Mainz, dedicated in 1137, points, as does Goslar, to the later typical use as a palace or castle chapel. Another form of central construction, the quatrefoil plan, is found, in about the middle of the 12th century, in the Chapel of All Saints in the Regensburg Cathedral cloister and the castle chapel (1151) of Schwarz-Rheindorf, near Bonn. The latter, with a double chapel related to the previously mentioned constructions and with a crossing tower and dwarf galleries, forms the starting point for the rich late Romanesque development in the Lower Rhine region.

Further directions of development that began early in the 12th century and were important for late Romanesque architecture emanate from the group of hall churches, or *Hallenkirchen*, of the area around Regensburg (Prüll, dedicated 1110) and from the flat-ceiling basilicas with vaulted east end found in the Lower Rhine region (Hochelten, dedicated 1129), in Lower Saxony (Königslütter, begun 1135), and also near and in Regensburg (Kastl, 1129; Prüfening, dedicated 1119).

The *Westwerke* belong to the most imposing and purest impression of middle Romanesque architecture. The most beautiful examples of the type of transept with central tower are the Abbey church of Marmoutier (Maursmünster), in Alsace, Minden, in Westphalia (both mid-12th century), and Havelberg, near Wellenberg; they demonstrate the gamut from the Rhenish wealth of articulation to the serrated massiveness of the eastern colonial lands. Gandersheim shows the Lower Saxony transept with lateral octagonal towers. Examples of the three-tower west ends are found in the Abbey church of Brauweiler, near Cologne (1141), and Freckenhorst in Westphalia (1129); twin-tower façades include, in addition to the above-mentioned Alsatian examples, St. Florin in Koblenz (ca. 1100). The east end of Murbach (remains of Abbey church), in Alsace, with its stepped and towered design is of a similar pure grandeur.

Late Romanesque architecture differentiates in its building program, its building types, and special regional developments and brings with it a great abundance of outstanding and personally influenced creations (particularly in the west). As was true of Ottonian architecture, in the Rhine regions the main interest is the exterior (though often there is much of interest in the interior) and the east and west groups; in Westphalia, however, many types of vaulted *Hallenkirchen* were produced, thereby introducing a most significant theme for German art history. The eastern regions only hesitantly went over to completely vaulted construction and held back from facing the problem of jointed and hollow walls and manifold articulated spaces. In so doing, they renounced the extraordinarily well-developed western possibilities for expression and persisted often in following the monumentality of the middle Romanesque.

Late Romanesque architecture experienced its richest development between 1150 and 1250 in the districts of the Lower Rhine and the Meuse. It shows its relationship with the other German art regions, particularly Westphalia, through its tightly clustered tower groups, its preference for mass (although admittedly lightened with articulation and perforation), and its narrow spaces stretched between two poles; but it does not deny its close relationship to the western regions of Central Europe; the multistoried articulation of the walls and its structural composition link it with the architecture of northwestern France.

The great trefoil of Gross St. Martin, Cologne (PL. 228), was designed originally with a dome; it was crowned in about 1200 with a gigantic crossing tower, which is reminiscent of the contemporaneous English *Westwerk* at Ely. For the storied construction of the apse the classic three-part division was used; and a highly ingenious system was developed for the wall leading over inner niches and galleries to the outer dwarf galleries, with increasing spatial volumes from bottom to top. Also in Cologne, St. Aposteln carried this idea, in about 1200, to perfection. In Roermond the Abbey church in Neuss and St. Quirinus continued the series of trefoil plans during the 13th century, but not without a manneristic exaggeration of the idea. Along with this cloverleaf plan, which signified the climax and synthesis of the cruciform basilica with its crossing tower and choir towers, the *Westwerk*, which since Carolingian times had been a preferred building form in Central Europe, found a new cultivation and development.

The *Westwerk* of the Abbey church of Maria Laach (the ground plan of which was already laid out by 1093), a cruciform construction with apse, central tower, and lateral turret staircases, was finished in about 1200. The *Westwerk* of the collegiate Church of Ste-Gertrude, Nivelles, with its similar silhouette (ca. 1170), increased the interior division of the space arrangement. Galleries and cupolas were multiplied, and for the first time there appeared a cruciform western choir, in which the great strength of the walls permitted further tower construction. This was richly elaborated through its inner twin-shell construction and the outer projection of the towers. These elements were apparently a mutually beneficial development of the trefoil construction.

In about 1200 the nave became part of this interesting development; the niched triforium, appearing as a prototype in the 11th century in Werden and in the 12th in Brauweiler, was taken up again in St. Andreas in Cologne; in St. Aposteln (dedicated 1219) it was reduced to a blind-arcaded triforium; it became a gallery triforium in Bonn and in Gross St. Martin in Cologne; and at the same time the rise of the nave was drawn into the vaulted construction of the *gebundene* system, as in the parish churches of Andernach, Neuss, Roermond, Sinzig, and Boppard and the Abbey church of Werden an der Ruhr. This sequence finally resulted in the four-story constructions with galleries and triforium, which certainly seem to be a logical expansion, although often in the course of its development the exchange of ideas with French builders is evident.

Just as the number of stories increased, the wall members were perfected, with the walls perforated and transformed into a sort of inwardly directed buttress system; thus the general spatial layout of the whole as well as the development of the other parts of the building, such as the apse and the tower, corresponded ever more to this comprehensive restructuring. In St. Aposteln the completion of the Ottonian flat-ceiling basilica with the western choir and transept resulted in a balanced design, one which further increased the Ottonian bipolar plan. St. Andreas and St. Kunibert, in Cologne, and the Cathedral (formerly Stiftskirche St. Georg) of Limburg an der Lahn (PL. 228;

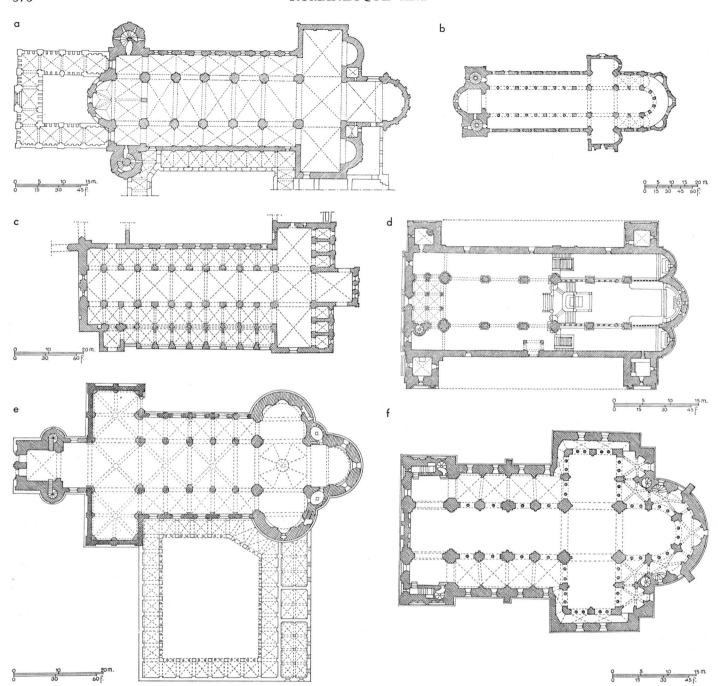

Central Europe. (*a*) Maria Laach, monastery church founded in 1003, plan; (*b*) Hildesheim, St. Godehard, 1133–72, plan; (*c*) Eberbach, monastery church, 1170–86, plan; (*d*) Pécs, Cathedral, 1150, plan; (*e*) Cologne, St. Aposteln, consecrated in 1219, plan; (*f*) Limburg-an-der-Lahn, St. Georg, 13th century (*from E. Gall, Dome und Kloster-Kirchen am Rhein, Munich 1956, and from E. Lundberg, 1950*).

VI, PL. 123) also belong to this series, in which all of the churches strive toward an increase in the tower groupings and to some extent emphasize the bipolarity despite the western portals. The surface articulation, especially on the *Westwerk* and the towers, follows with an increasing accumulation of registers in relief and single decorative forms. A congenial solution for the tower roof was found in the use of the four-sided pitched roof; the apse was transformed (possibly under the influence of the Trier-Lorraine prototypes) into a polygon, and began to resemble the tower with its gables and folded roof areas (Bonn, Cologne, Sinzig, among others). The openings, ever more richly decorated and more luxuriously framed, finally resulted in the windows in fan and palmette shapes that hint at the baroque structures of the 18th century.

The crowning activity of this extraordinarily rich and multi-form era of building can be seen in the so-called "Gralsbau"

(Grail house) of St. Gereon in Cologne, where a towerlike extended central construction, with galleries, corridors, and ribbed dome on compound supports, is built over the oval of a Roman ground floor with deep niches. Smaller similar examples are the centrally arranged castle chapel of Kobern on the Moselle and Vianden in Luxembourg.

If the over-all picture of the Lower Rhine region is varied and full of movement — historically as well as in the individual buildings — in the Upper Rhine region it is more unified and closed, more monumental. There the large form, the plastic mass, were held more important than the vertical articulation. The middle Romanesque reduction of the *gebundene* system is maintained, as in the Worms Cathedral (PLS. 228, 229), in Gueb-willer, Neuwiller, Rufach, Otterberg, and Eusserthal and in the Abbey church of Enkenbach (Ries). In the Mainz Cathedral the vaulting was renewed without any significant changes. Even when beamed construction gave way to the square-ribbed arches, as in St. Adelphi, Neuwiller, the wall of the nave remained without any division into stories. Basel Cathedral, as a follower of the older Grossmünster, is an exception with its galleries.

Imposing choir layouts, transepts, and *Westwerke* were given much more importance, as spaces as well as construction groups, than the nave. The Worms Cathedral is a prime example; on the east the transept, the right-angled choir, the octagonal crossing tower, and the round corner towers present a unified whole (about 1180); the west choir, with its polygonal apse, built about fifty years later, gathers together and intensifies the group in an unprecedented concentration toward the steeply rising choir

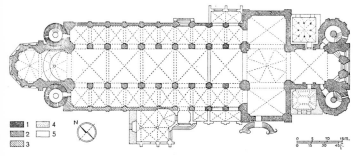

Worms, Cathedral, plan. *Key:* (1) construction of 1000–25; (2) of 1181; (3) of 1186–1200; (4) of 1200–25; (5) later additions (*from R. Kautzsch, Der Dom zu Worms, Berlin, 1938*).

tower, which itself is flanked with round towers. The framework, in which the dwarf galleries and masterly varied window forms play an important role, shows the typical strong plasticity of the Upper Rhine region. Not less impressive is the approximately contemporary *Westwerk* of Mainz Cathedral (completed in 1239), a cloverleaf construction with polygonal apses joined to gigantic transepts, with crossing surmounted, as in Worms, by an imposing tower open on the interior. In Strasbourg, where only the eastern sections of the Cathedral of Notre-Dame (built atop an Ottonian crypt) have retained its late Romanesque style, the transepts are transformed by four slim columns to a double-aisled hall, a space of sublime fantasy, distinguished by the famous sculptures on the double portals and on the "Piliers des anges" (VI, PL. 359).

The late Romanesque architecture of Westphalia clearly demonstrates a special regional development. Here also there is a group of vaulted basilicas in the *gebundene* system that tend in their shape and spatial arrangement to the broad and heavy (St. Patroklus, in Soest; the Osnabrück Cathedral). The double-choired Cathedral in Münster omitted the intermediate pillars, thereby achieving a tremendous space with hall-like breadth. A large number of small vaulted buildings in the district elaborate the late Romanesque *Hallenkirche* in various systems. The churches of Soest (St. Maria zur Hoehe), Billerbeck, and Legden are the loveliest of these. The series continued directly with the new constructions of the cathedrals of Paderborn and Minden, as well as the Abbey church of Herford, all of which utilized Gothic motifs. The origin of these *Hallenkirchen* is a much discussed problem of German art history, in which, for the period from the 13th to the 16th century, this type of church is the central theme of church architecture. Autochthonous origin and western French or northern Italian contributions and their elaboration are all part of the debate. In northern Westphalia, as far as Friesland, there is a large number of single-aisled vaulted buildings, some of which are magnificent. The *Westwerk* of St. Patroklus in Soest, a powerful tower rising out of a broad construction beneath it, shows Westphalian architecture at its most convincing in its union of monumental mass and contrasting articulation. The choirs of the cathedrals of Münster, Osnabrück, and Minden, on the other hand, adapt motifs of the Lower Rhine area with their two- and three-story wall divisions.

In northern, central, and southern Germany the regional character of late Romanesque architecture is less developed than in the Rhine regions and in Westphalia. In all these regions the flat-ceiling construction remained valid to the end of the Romanesque period. However, for the principal buildings the *gebundene* system prevailed almost generally. Lower Saxony and Thuringia were particularly conservative; in the Brunswick (Braunschweig) Cathedral (after 1170) and several subsequent buildings the *gebundene* system is found with pointed-arch cross vaulting, elsewhere throughout with ribbing, as in the Naumburg Cathedral and the Cistercian monastery churches of Loccum and Riddagshausen. The Magdeburg Cathedral choir stands alone with its two-story ambulatory and radial chapels, strongly influenced by the western Gothic but reconstructed magnificently in late Romanesque style. Twin-towered façades (Halberstadt) and *Westwerke* with towered construction, as in Brunswick, Goslar, and Arnstadt, are numerous. Brick construction and the use of irregular granite blocks strike a special note in Altmark, Brandenburg, and along the coast (vaulted basilicas in the *gebundene* system in Ratzeburg, Lehnin, and Lübeck). In Mecklenburg and Brandenburg, Rhenish, Westphalian, and Lower Saxon styles are all in evidence.

The architecture of central Germany is closely related to the architecture of the Upper Rhine region, being manifest in Hesse in the collegiate churches of Fritzlar and Gelnhausen (with magnificent three-towered eastern sections), in Mainfranken, Würzburg, and Bamberg, in Swabia and Middle Franconia as far as Ellwangen and Nürnberg, in the Cistercian churches of Arnsburg, Ebrach, and Bronnbach, and even as far as Bohemia (Eger). An especially fine construction is the double-choired Bamberg Cathedral, with the *gebundene* system in the nave, a richly articulated apse, and pairs of towers on the east and west.

Monastery and chapter buildings show throughout the typical plan with rectangular cloisters, as in Bonn, Millstatt, and Lilienfeld. The oldest example remaining in good condition is St. Simeon (Simeonkloster) in Trier, from the 11th century. Vaulted halls (chapter rooms, refectories, dormitories) are very impressive, as for example in Zwettl, Eberbach, and Maulbronn.

The Bavarian region, especially Alt-Bayern, is highly conservative; only a few distinguished buildings remain complete, as in Altenstadt and Regensburg (St. Jakob). In Austria there are the churches of St. Paul (Lavanttal), St. Maria, the so-called "Neukloster" church at Wiener Neustadt, the twin-tower façade of St. Stephen (Vienna), and among constructions of smaller size, a number of *kainer* (two-storied circular funerary chapels; Tulln, Mödling, Hartberg).

In military and civil architecture, the various types of dwellings and defense constructions, of which only rare and partial examples of earlier periods have survived, are represented in late Romanesque architecture in several well-maintained examples. The typical Hohenstaufen hill castle (see GERMANY), with its watchtower, palace, defense wall, and outer wall, generally constructed of magnificent ashlar, is found in relatively good condition in the ruins of Ortenberg in Alsace, in Trifel and Grafenstein in the Palatinate, on the Wildenburg in Odenwald, on Münzenberg in Hesse, and on Gutenfels on the Rhine. Palatinate buildings of the rulers are found in the ruins of Gelnhausen and Seligenstadt, and at many other sites. The growing importance of the towns is seen in the extensive fortifications of such cities as Cologne, where a late Hohenstaufen city wall more than five miles long was built with numerous fine fortified gates, of which three remain. City dwelling houses of stone with ornamented façades survive in Cologne, in Trier, and in other cities, and fortified dwelling towers of even earlier dates remain in Trier and Regensburg.

Hans Erich KUBACH

ENGLAND. The Norman conquest of England in 1066 provides a useful conventional date for the beginning of Romanesque art in England. In fact, however, during the reign of Edward the Confessor (1042–66), who was half Norman by blood and thoroughly Norman in upbringing and sympathies, the Romanesque style, especially in architecture, had already made inroads into Anglo-Saxon art. For instance, Westminster Abbey, dedicated in 1065, was a triple-apsed building of Norman inspiration, and the church at Sompting (ca. 1060) in Sussex was embellished with half columns and crude capitals of a vaguely

Corinthian design, both clearly derived from Normandy. There can be little doubt that even without the Norman conquest the Romanesque style would eventually have triumphed in England, but the process of its adoption would have been slow; in the event, however, once the Normans felt themselves secure in their new kingdom, they settled down to a gigantic work of reorganization that profoundly affected all fields of artistic activity.

The new Norman bishops and abbots set the pattern by rebuilding the majority of cathedrals and abbeys on Norman models. The king and his barons, as well as the Norman ecclesiastics, employed master masons from Normandy and elsewhere in most of their building enterprises, whether for castles or churches; but the Normans in England had far greater material resouces at their disposal than they had possessed in their own duchy. This, together with the desire to impress their conquered subjects, resulted in the English buildings being even larger than those in Normandy.

The two types of church that were in current use in the duchy, the triple-apsed constructions (as at Bernay Abbey) and those having an ambulatory (as at Rouen Cathedral), found numerous imitations in England. To the first type belonged the metropolitan church of England, Canterbury Cathedral, rebuilt by its first Norman archbishop, Lanfranc (ca. 1070), who was of Italian birth; St. Albans Abbey, built with reused Roman bricks by Abbot Paul of Caen (1077–88); Ely Cathedral (PL. 231; VI, PL. 425); Lincoln Cathedral (finished in 1092; VI, FIG. 503); and many others. The ambulatory plan was as popular as the apsidal and includes many cathedrals and abbeys of great importance, for instance, Winchester Cathedral (begun in 1079; PL. 230), Gloucester Cathedral (then an abbey, begun in 1089; VI, FIG. 504), and Norwich Cathedral (begun in 1096). Winchester (and its imitation, Ely, also) had stone galleries at the ends of the transept providing communicating passages between the tribunes and the upper stories of the chapels projecting on the east side of the transepts. All these churches, although closely linked with the Norman school across the Channel, differ from it not only in their far greater size but also in the greater solidity of their structure. In internal elevation, the majority of these buildings were three-storied, consisting of main arcade, gallery, and clerestory, usually with a wall passage in the thickness of the wall below the windows.

gives the impression of overwhelming solidity; even the elaborate system of moldings and decorative motifs does not conceal the massiveness of the walls and of the alternating compound piers and cylindrical shafts.

Durham must be considered the highest achievement of the Anglo-Norman school, the true successor of Jumièges Abbey. But not all Romanesque churches in England can be explained as a further development of the Norman school; the most striking in this respect is the group of churches in the west of England, with Gloucester Cathedral, Tewkesbury Abbey (PL. 232), and Pershore Abbey as the chief examples. Their massive cylindrical piers without any articulation, influenced by those of St. Philibert at Tournus (XI, PL. 308), contrast strikingly with the usual interiors, which were clearly divided into bays. Another departure from Anglo-Norman design was the division of the interior elevation into four stories (at Tewkesbury and Pershore), with the corresponding use of the colossal order carried up to the second story of the elevation. This method was further employed at Romsey Abbey (ca. 1120–40), Oxford Cathedral (ca. 1170–80; PL. 231), Glastonbury Abbey (ca. 1190; VI, PL. 310), and Jedburgh Abbey in Scotland. The façade of Tewkesbury, with its enormous recessed arch, suggests that whatever the principal origin of this school, it was capable of developing highly original ideas.

There are numerous other examples of departure from Norman models in the design of English churches. For example, Lewes Priory (dedicated ca. 1145), the mother house of the Cluniacs in England, was built on the model of Cluny III, thus introducing the double-transept plan, which was to become, during the Gothic period, a favorite English form for large churches; Canterbury Cathedral, rebuilt between 1096 and 1130, also had this plan. The other Cluniac priories in England, all of which survive only as ruins, were remarkable for their stress on allover surface decoration, which was in keeping with this order's love for lavish display. In contrast, the Cistercians, who first came to England in 1128, brought from Burgundy an austere type of church with a square east end and pointed arch, thus paving the way for the English Gothic style.

After the initial spectacular development, Anglo-Norman architects of the late Romanesque period showed little concern for structural improvements and concentrated on secondary

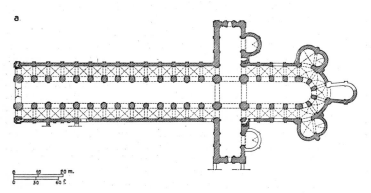

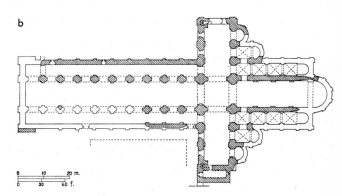

England. (a) Norwich, Cathedral, begun in 1096, plan; (b) Abbey of St. Albans, 1077–88, plan (from A. W. Clapham, English Romanesque Architecture, Oxford, 1930–34).

A special place in the history of Romanesque architecture, not only in England but in Europe as a whole, is occupied by Durham Cathedral (PL. 230), a building whose history is unusually well documented. Begun in 1093, the work proceeded rapidly from east to west; in 1133 it was finished. From the beginning the church was designed to be covered with ribbed vaults over the choir and aisles and eventually over the nave. Thus the choir of Durham (1104) had the earliest rib vaulting in Europe, but the invention made there was not exploited any further in England; in fact, the majority of subsequent Romanesque churches were covered with flat wooden roofs. The true possibilities of rib vaults were understood and developed not in England but in France. The interior of Durham (VI, PL. 425)

decorative motifs. The façades of churches in particular became a favorite field for enrichment. The screen façades, so characteristic a feature of the early Gothic cathedrals in England, originated in mid-12th-century Romanesque buildings, perhaps not without some influence from Aquitaine.

The most important surviving examples of secular buildings are castles, with square keeps. The earliest of these was William the Conqueror's "white tower" in the Tower of London. This keep contains a chapel, an austere aisled structure with barrel vaulting (ca. 1080). Good 12th-century examples of keeps survive at Rochester (PL. 235) and Corfe. In the second half of that century the round keep came into use (e.g., Orford, Conisbrough) as a result of the influence of the Crusaders' castles in the Holy Land. The living quarters of these castles were provided by halls, of which an aisled example from the end of the 12th century survives at Oakham.

The fire that consumed the choir of Canterbury Cathedral in 1174 is important in the history of English architecture, since the subsequent rebuilding of Canterbury was entrusted to a French master mason, William of Sens, who introduced into England the early Gothic style of northern France. The new style was not accepted readily in other parts of the country, however, and the last quarter of the century was a period of transition during which Gothic construction was gradually gaining ground; but Romanesque decoration persisted for some time (e.g., Glastonbury Abbey).

George ZARNECKI

SCANDINAVIA. Christian missionary activity began in the Nordic lands in about 800; shortly afterward the first churches, invariably of wood, began to be built. Pagan resistance was nevertheless strong. Christianity did not gain definite recognition in Denmark until 950, when King Harald Blaatand (Harold Bluetooth, 940–85) was baptized. In Gamla Uppsala the pagan temple famed from Adam of Bremen's description was still standing in 1100. Finland did not adopt Christianity until about 1200, the result of a Swedish war expedition. Remains of the church Harald had built in Jelling, Jutland, make it possible to reconstruct the form of a small stave church, about 36 ft. long and 20 ft. wide, with a small, square-ended choir about 6 ft. long. Other churches from this period in Scandinavia were of similar character. In building technique they adhered to the old native tradition evident, among other examples, in the house construction of the Viking period. In Denmark only fragments of stave churches have been preserved, but important remains of such churches have been found in Lund in Skåne. One of these, St. Mary Minor, was twice as large as the church in Jelling and was furnished with posts parallel to the walls in the nave and choir. It is obvious that although Continental stone churches were imitated, native stave technique was retained. Interesting remains of such a stave church from about 1000 have been found in Hemse in Gotland (now in Stockholm, Statens Historiska Mus.). Only one stave church in Sweden, that of Hedared, in the woods of Västergötland, has been preserved; it appears to have been built as late as 1200. Otherwise, by about 1100 most stave churches had been replaced by stone churches.

Stave churches survived longest in Norway, where they passed through the richest development. Of the hundreds of stave churches constructed there, only about 30 have been preserved. The earliest type, consisting of a small rectangular nave and a projecting straight-ended choir, is represented by the churches in Holtålen and Kinsarvik and also by the first church in Urnes (PL. 233). Still existing from this church are the keyhole-shaped portal, the corner posts, and a number of wall boards, all decorated with rich ornament consisting of slender entwined animal forms (X, PL. 438). The wooden posts with capitals bearing carved Romanesque animal figures of English type clearly show the constructor's attempt to approach stone architecture. The Norwegian stave churches erected in the 12th and 13th centuries were given basilican status and generally had a choir and apse. With their turrets, their dragon heads on ridgepoles, and their tarred, shingled walls, they appear as original elements in the European architecture of the Middle Ages. As a rule the portals (PL. 415) of the stave churches were intricately carved with elaborate ornament, the Nordic animal motifs dominating and the Romanesque elements being subsequently assimilated. Among the best-preserved examples of the stave church in its most highly developed form are those at Borgund, Hoprekstad, and Heddal. The latter (ca. 1150) has a magnificent portal.

The first stone churches began to be constructed in Scandinavia in the 11th century. None of these churches has survived intact, but important parts remain from the basilica with piers and wooden ceiling erected in Dalby in Skåne (ca. 1065). Triple-aisled basilicas devoid of towers and transepts were also built in Roskilde (Church of Our Lady, ca. 1080) and likewise in Tamdrup, Asmild, and Skarpsalling, Jutland. The latter has apses on the east of the choir as well as on the side aisles. In many places in Denmark, Sweden, and Norway single-aisled Romanesque country churches of the early type may be found, but in the majority of cases they appear to have been constructed not earlier than 1100.

Scandinavia's earliest churches in stone are based on influences from the Continent as well as from England. During the missionary period Scandinavia belonged to the archdiocese of Hamburg-Bremen, but in 1103 it became an independent archbishopric, with its center in Lund. In 1136 Sweden acquired an archbishopric in Uppsala, and in 1152 Norway was granted one in Trondheim. Besides the German mission, there was also English missionary work, connections with England having been kept alive since Viking times. Actually, considerable English influence asserts itself in the history of Northern art during the Middle Ages. It was of greatest and most permanent significance for Norway, but in Sweden and Denmark also it left important marks.

The first Cathedral of Lund was erected at the instigation of King Canute IV (ca. 1080). This edifice, which was located on the same site as the present-day Cathedral, is supposed to have been an edifice of Anglo-Saxon type with a single-aisled nave and a rectangular, straight-ended choir. Over the choir was probably a tower. When a new and larger cathedral was required the present great basilica was built (1103) with a crypt under the transept, choir, and apse and with two west towers. Worthy of note are the square chapels attached to the east side of the transept on each side of the choir. These and the occurrence of Norman scalloped capitals in the tower have given researchers studying the Cathedral (Cinthio, 1957) reason to surmise an influence from Flanders and Normandy. Formerly Lund Cathedral was considered to have been designed and executed by builders coming from Speyer and Mainz; but even if the plans for the church reveal influence from the west, it is evident that the actual workers came from the south. That they were Italians from Lombardy, and perhaps also from middle and southern Italy, is clear from the rich stone sculpture of high quality adorning the capitals, moldings, and portals. Contemporary documents speak of one Donatus as *architectus magister operis hujus*. After Donatus's death (ca. 1130), Regnerus appears as construction leader. During the time of the former, Como-Lombard ornamental features dominated; under the latter the capitals and moldings assumed a more classical, partly Byzantine style. The design of the chancel and apse with its blind arcade and crowning eaves gallery marks (ca. 1161) the end of the Romanesque building period of the Cathedral. The center aisle, which was constructed with a (later removed) gallery, without vaulting, was vaulted after a fire in 1234.

Lund Cathedral exercised great influence in Skåne as well as in Denmark, especially in Viborg Cathedral (choir finished in 1150), which was partly restored in the 19th century. It has a crypt under the choir only and lacks the wealth of decoration distinguishing Lund. Ribe Cathedral (PL. 233), its foundations laid before 1134, has no crypt. It was built of Rhenish tufa in close alliance with Rhenish architecture, as its rhythmically rich façade articulation especially bears witness. Noteworthy is the huge domical vault over the crossing; but the center aisle, even here, lacked vaulting originally.

In Roskilde, Sjælland (Zealand), at the end of the 11th century, foundations were laid on the site of an earlier church for a basilica with nave and two side aisles and two western towers and with a gallery for the royal family. The two-towered western section with gallery that distinguished Roskilde Cathedral is reflected in smaller size in the royal church of Tveje-Merløse in Sjælland. Other western structures characteristic of German architectural traditions may be found in several other places in Scandinavia. Foremost among them is the extension (ca. 1130) to the old church in Dalby, the lower part of which, with its cross vault borne by richly formed columns, remains. Here also the Lombard-schooled master stonemasons were active. A huge square tower with two flanking round towers was added to a stave church in Husaby (ca. 1100). Later a single-aisled stone church replaced the stave church. Mariakirken (the Cathedral, dedicated to Our Lady) in Visby, which was built in the beginning of the 12th century for the German merchants in this flourishing commercial city, was a triple-aisled basilica with transept and apses and also a west tower with side galleries of Rhenish-Westphalian type. A triforium faced on the nave. Other variations of this type are the first Cathedral of Linköping, the Abbey church of Vreta, St. Per in Sigtuna, and the Gamla Uppsala (Old Uppsala) Cathedral. In Denmark this type of Romanesque basilica is represented by Venge Church, Jutland, which was completed before 1166. Like those of St. Per in Sigtuna, the transepts, equipped with apses, are here isolated from the center aisle by narrow vaults and formed as special chapels. The richly articulated triumphal arch in Venge bears witness to the Anglo-Norman influence, as do the decorative motifs employed (roll and billet molding). Similar Norman features are present in Lime and in the Church of Our Lady (Vor Frue) in Aalborg, Jutland.

In Norway the English influence is dominant. The earliest stone churches preserved there are from the beginning of the 12th century. Among these are the stone church in Tingelstad, Mariakirken in Gran, and also certain churches of Vaernes and Alstahaug. In all these are found ornament of Norman influence, especially the star pattern of the "sunken star" type. Stavanger Cathedral (ca. 1130) has massive pillars with scalloped capital and typical Anglo-Norman forms, which also characterize the Romanesque nave in Mariakirken in Bergen. The foremost example of Anglo-Norman architecture, however, is the majestic transept that constitutes the oldest part of the present Cathedral of Trondheim. It was built (ca. 1150) upon the base of an earlier church, and was erected in two stages. The lower part is severe and distinctly English, while the upper part shows a richer articulation, of Continental character. A long choir adjoining the transept, terminated with an octagonal chapel over St. Olaf's grave, was planned by Bishop Eystein Erlandsøn, the widely traveled leader of building operations. However, these parts of the Cathedral were not constructed until the 13th century. On the north side of the choir the bishop placed a Lady chapel (finished about 1170), which, with its ribbed vaults and pointed arches, may be said to have inaugurated the Gothic style in Norway.

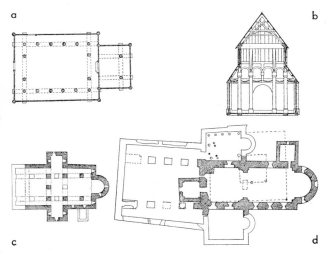

Scandinavia. (a, b) Urnes, wooden church, 12th century, plan and section (from E. Lundberg, 1950); (c) Sigtuna, S. Olaf, 1100–35, plan; (d) Gamla Uppsala, church, 1134–50, plan (from K. J. Conant, 1959).

In southern Norway in the 12th century basilicas were constructed, such as Gamle Akers, Ringsaker, St. Halvard's (Oslo), and the Hamar Cathedral, which, with their heavy round piers and east tower, suggest England, although the English features do not appear in pure form. German influence is also noticeable. The same is true for St. Olaf's Church in Sigtuna, a town situated on Lake Mälaren. Sigtuna was Stockholm's predecessor as commercial center and was also the bishop's see for a short time. St. Olaf's triple-aisled choir with apse, short-

ened nave, and narrow portal tapering toward the top have suggested to researchers the influence of both England and Byzantine Russia. As in the church ruins of Sigtuna, the partly preserved church in Gamla Uppsala is dominated by a heavy tower over the crossing. Churches with east towers occur frequently in eastern Sweden, where the church in Skåne constitutes one of the best examples. It has been established that this and other closely related churches have their forerunners in western Germany. However, the majority of the small Romanesque stone churches with square, straight-ended choirs erected during the 12th century in Västergötland may probably be attributed to the English missionary activity carried on in these regions. Here are also found portals of Anglo-Norman character with the chevron motif (Skalunda and Häggesled).

The round churches are particularly interesting. Though predominant on Bornholm (PL. 416), they also occur in various parts of Denmark (Bjernede and Torsager), Sweden (among others, Valleberga, Hagby, Vårdsberg, Solna, Bromma, Munsö), and occasionally in Norway (Tönsberg). Also used as strongholds, they often served for purposes of defense, as did a group of Romanesque churches in Småland and Öland. In certain cases, for example in Bjernede, the round church assumes the character of a fortress chapel. This is also true of the octagonal St. Heddinge and the double chapel in Ledøje, both in Sjælland, the latter church as well as Helgeands Church (Church of the Holy Spirit) in Visby carrying associations with Rhenish architecture (Schwarz-Rheindorf). Both these churches belong to the last quarter of the 13th century. The most original centrally planned church in Scandinavia is, however, Kalundborg Cathedral (PL. 233), whose exterior is dominated by five octagonal fortresslike towers. The plan consists of a square from which four outstretched arms terminate polygonally. The interior, however, does not create the same mighty impression; the cross vault in the center is supported by slender columns of granite with trapezoidal capitals. The foundations were laid in about 1170, and the building was erected in brick. The eastern European influence manifested here is evident in other forms in Visby, Gotland, in the Church of St. Lars, one of the town's many remarkable ruins. The almost-square central space suggests the Byzantine architecture that characterized medieval Russia (Visby had lively commercial relations with Novgorod in the 13th century).

The first Cistercian monastery was founded in Sweden in about 1140. The Abbey church in Alvastra, Östergötland, dedicated in 1185, closely follows the plan of Fontenay with its straight-ended chancel, as is true of Nydala in Småland and Roma in Gotland. The monks transported to Sweden not only monastery plans but also the masonry techniques and methods of vaulting currently prevailing in Burgundy; they became pioneers in Sweden in the field of architecture. Cistercian features characterize not only monastery cloisters (for example, Vreta in Östergötland) but also numerous parish churches near the monasteries, especially in Gotland's countryside, which became the center of an exceedingly lively ecclesiastical building activity and a consequent blossoming of the arts. The economic requirements were covered by the remunerative commerce with Russia and other countries around the Baltic Sea.

In Denmark the Cistercians did not have native stone at their disposal; they built in brick and took into their service master bricklayers and stonemasons from Lombardy. The abbey churches at Sorø and Ringstad (both built ca. 1160–70) follow a simple Cistercian plan, but the masonry and its details are excellent examples of brick architecture of the north Italian type. One of the reasons for the rapid spread of brick architecture in Denmark was, aside from the natural qualifications, the interest with which this new material was embraced by the Danish king Waldemar the Great, who began in 1162 to build a wall, the so-called "Danevirke," for the kingdom's defense to the south. For this it seems likely that he had help from workers summoned from Milan. From the end of the 12th century the majority of Danish churches were built of brick, the material used to complete Roskilde Cathedral and Løgum Monastery, two structures in which the Romanesque gradually merges into the Gothic. In Skåne the first brick church was in Gumlösa (1191), but brick construction did not reach the neighborhood of Stockholm until the beginning of the 13th century, when it was introduced by the Dominicans (Mariakirken, Sigtuna) in connection with an architecture that was in some respects already Gothic (Sko Abbey church and Strängnäs Cathedral).

Not until the beginning of the 11th century was the slaking of lime for mortar and the bonding of stone learned from missionaries and priests. This new technique was quickly claimed for fortifications and fortress towers, built partly to supplement wooden entrenchments and stone embankments and partly as new constructions. Fortresses consisted of towers with a girdle of outer fortifications, which also soon came to be built of masonry (Søborg, Sprogø, Tornborg, and Gurre, all in Sjælland). In several instances, the towered fortress was replaced (as early as the 13th century) by a larger stronghold surrounded by an encircling wall with wall towers and palace (Søborg, Kalmar). Occasionally the old tower was maintained inside the new walls (Stockholm). The earliest royal stronghold in Sweden of the type with an encircling wall and hall building was Näs, on Visingsö (ca. 1100). A few towers or keeps, so-called "kastaler," were built beside the churches in Gotland; one, called the "Gunpowder Tower," was erected in the beginning of the 12th century at the harbor in Visby as protection for the city. At the same time a wall around Visby was begun. The oldest section is incorporated in that part of the later (and considerably reinforced) wall which faces toward the sea.

Sten KARLING

II. SCULPTURE. FRANCE. After the almost complete abandonment during the period from the 5th to the 11th century of the portrayal of the figure in stone, a true revival of the art of sculpture took place in France at the beginning of the Romanesque period. It was slow to appear, inasmuch as the Porte Miégeville sculpture (ca. 1100; PL. 236) on the south side of the Church of St-Sernin, Toulouse, constitutes the first complete and well-defined example of a Romanesque portal adorned with figures.

The earliest testimonies to this revival are two marble slabs mounted as lintels for the façades of two neighboring churches in Roussillon — Saint-Génis-des-Fontaines and Saint-André-de-Sorède (Pyrénées Orientales). The lintel of the former is adorned with a figure of Christ in Majesty surrounded by angels. This central group is flanked by six Apostles placed at random under horseshoe arches; and over the lintel is carved an inscription of enormous importance for the history of sculpture, which states that the work was executed in 1019-20, in the time of King Robert II the Pious, the second of the Capetian dynasty. The lintel of St-André-de-Sorède is almost identical, and precisely the same decoration of scrolls frames the small figures. (The lintel of St-Génis-des-Fontaines is 6½ ft. long and 2½ ft. high.)

A certain number of capitals with roughly sculptured figures were executed in the 11th century in various regions, such as those of the crypt of St-Aignan, Orléans, of St-Bénigne of Dijon, and of the Church of St-Germain-des-Prés (Paris, Mus. de Cluny), as well as the figures sculptured in stone in Carennac (Lot) and Cruas (Ardèche).

Figures more freely detached from the mass, a more accentuated relief, and an abler distribution of design elements around the bells may be observed in the capitals of the porch of the Abbey church of Saint-Benoît-sur-Loire (Loiret); these undoubtedly date to the resumption of the work undertaken toward 1070 by the abbot Guillaume. The capitals of the church of Ronceray in Angers bear a certain resemblance to those of Saint-Benoît-sur-Loire (IV, PL. 178) and obviously belong to the same period.

To the 11th century also must belong the tiny tympanum (3½ ft. high and 6½ ft. wide) of the Church of St-Ursin (destroyed) in Bourges. Shown on three superimposed rows are the Labors of the Months representing the chores of the peasant, a staghunt, and some scenes from Aesop's *Fables*. In the hunting scene the sculptor has imitated a Gallo-Roman sarcophagus preserved at Déols in Berry.

A particularly interesting date for the history of Romanesque sculpture is that provided by the slab of the high altar of the Church of St-Sernin in Toulouse (PL. 236). In 1096 Pope Urban II, who was traveling through France to raise the First Crusade, consecrated the high altar of the Church of St-Sernin of Toulouse. This altar has been preserved in the transept of the church. An inscription indicates that it is the work of the sculptor Bernard Gilduin. It is a magnificent slab of marble hollowed into the shape of a basin and framed with semicircular lobes ornamented with stylized foliage. On the hollowed surface there is a bust of Christ framed by six horizontally placed angels. It is an imitation of the type of Gallo-Roman sarcophagus in which a bust of the deceased is closed in a medallion supported by two winged genii. This slab of the altar, accurately dated, is a monument of major importance for the history of figural sculpture at the moment when its revival, which until then had made only slow progress, was about to flower in Languedoc in a whole series of works of the same style.

The small figures of the altar bear a close resemblance to other sculptures of St-Sernin, in particular to the seven marble figures which constitute the earliest attempt at large-sized Romanesque figure sculpture that has survived. These sculptures undoubtedly adorned a portal that no longer exists, and represent Christ in Majesty (PL. 236) with four angels and two Apostles. In the latter the artist imitated to the best of his ability the funeral stele of some Gallo-Roman nobleman, but he was unable to conceal his difficulty in executing large figures. He timidly gouged the surface of the slab around a figure that he had barely outlined. It is generally recognized that these large low reliefs belong to the second half of the 11th century, and the few figured capitals that are to be seen in the chancel and the transept should be ascribed to the same period.

At St-Sernin there was a third innovation; the Porte Miégeville, with its figured capitals, its tympanum adorned with a depiction of the Ascension, its two large figures of St. Peter and St. James, and its corbel table supported by animated figures, opened the way to a new field of activity for French sculptors. Finished about 1100 or soon after, it was the first complete realization of a large Romanesque portal. Here the artist displayed greater boldness in freeing the figures from the mass, giving them a much deeper relief than in the seven figures previously mentioned.

In the same period as the Porte Miégeville, another workshop of sculpture was being set up at the Abbey church of St-Pierre in Moissac, in which the sculptures show many similarities to those of St-Sernin. It was from these two sites that the Languedoc school received its impulse (later to spread over a vast region). Moissac possesses two magnificent groups of sculpture, its cloister (PL. 237) and its portal. An inscription engraved on one of the piers of the cloister indicates that it was built in 1100 in the time of the abbot Ansquitil (1085-1115). Wide rectangular piers are placed at the corners and in the middle of its sides. On each of these piers is sculptured an inscription and a figure in low relief, in all, nine Apostles (PL. 237) and the abbot Durand. Durand, who was bishop of Toulouse as well as abbot of Moissac, died in 1072; he had consecrated the church in 1063. Between the piers stand columns, single or paired, crowned with capitals, some bearing ornamental sculptures, others, the more numerous, decorated with religious scenes. There are 76 in all.

The cloister of Moissac is the most complete and the richest in sculptures of the Romanesque period, and the Moissac portal (PL. 237) also has a place of foremost importance in Romanesque art. For the nobility of the attitudes and the spirituality of the figures, it seems comparable only to the Madeleine portal in Vézelay (V, PL. 376). The portal, placed on the south side of the porch leading to the church, has sculptures that are considerably more highly developed than those of the cloister; but they are the normal continuation and the affirmation of a style that the artists of the cloister had already tried to express. This portal must have been begun at the time of Ansquitil (ca. 1115) and finished by the abbot Roger (ca. 1151), whose statue can be seen at the top of a column on the right of the framework of the portal. The tympanum represents the appearance of Christ on the day of the Last Judgment as described in the Apocalypse.

It is the replica of a miniature in the famous "Apocalypse of Saint-Sever" (PL. 207), and must have been even more striking when its figures still glowed with the vivid painting and the gilding that originally covered them. Christ flanked by the symbols of the Evangelists is surrounded by the 24 Elders of the Apocalypse. The *trumeau* (PL. 238) is a masterpiece of ornamental composition; on its front panel, three lions and three lionesses stand out against a background of *rosaces* imitating those of the lintel. On the lateral panels two elongated figures occupy the entire height of the *trumeau*. The artist, disregarding the laws of anatomy, elongated the bodies to an extreme degree in order to cover the whole surface to be decorated. The lateral jambs, cut into a series of curves, are adorned with two high reliefs representing Isaiah and St. Peter. These, with their long supple bodies clad in clinging draperies, were later to be used as models at Souillac (Lot; PLS. 238, 239) and Beaulieu (Corrèze; V, PL. 377). The portal of Moissac influenced all the art of Languedoc profoundly. This style can be found again much farther north in the portal of St-Denis through the intermediary of the portal of Beaulieu.

Thus the style was set in Toulouse and Moissac that was to endure through the 12th century in Toulouse itself (in the cloisters of the churches of St-Etienne (PL. 238) and Notre-Dame, La Daurade, numerous capitals of which are preserved in the Musée des Augustins, Toulouse, so rich in Romanesque monuments), in the whole of the southwest of France, and even farther, beyond the Pyrenees in S. Isidoro of Léon and at Santiago de Compostela.

On the tympanum of the Cathedral of Cahors (Lot), where the *Ascension* (V, PL. 378) is one of the most moving sculptures produced by Romanesque art, at Carennac and Martel (Lot), at Collonges (Corrèze) and at Mauriac (Cantal), the style of the workshops of St-Sernin and Moissac is recognizable.

The artist who decorated the portal of Moissac was inspired by a miniature, but it was mostly through the imitation of figures in relief that the first Romanesque sculptors learned the techniques of their art; they imitated works of the Gallo-Roman period and sought models in ivory carvings and in altarpieces of gold, which were adorned with images in high relief. Many such altarpieces were created during the Carolingian period and later in the 11th and 12th centuries. Most of these works disappeared over the centuries, victims of greed for the precious metal; two that survived are the altar of S. Ambrogio in Milan (see CAROLINGIAN PERIOD, col. 120), dating from the beginning of the 9th century, and the altarpiece of the Cathedral of Basel (VI, PL. 263).

The tympanum of Carennac (Lot) is a faithful reproduction in stone of a metal altarpiece; the horizontal and vertical strips that divide the scene of Christ among the Apostles into various compartments represent the wooden crossbars onto which were fixed gold or silver-gilt leaves, and in the oval halo that surrounds the figure of Christ are recognizable representations of the precious stones that were set in the metal.

The Church of Ste-Foy in Conques (Aveyron) owed its fame to the relics of a young girl martyred in Agen at the beginning of the 4th century; these reputedly miracle-working relics attracted crowds of pilgrims who came from distant lands to venerate them. In the organization of its plan and its elevation, Ste-Foy belongs to the family of great pilgrimage churches that includes St-Sernin of Toulouse, St-Martial of Limoges (destroyed 1792), and Santiago de Compostela, although it seems to have been built a few years earlier than the others. Begun in the middle of the 11th century (replacing an earlier church), Ste-Foy houses the earliest examples of the goldsmith's art that France possesses, the major piece being a wooden reliquary covered with gold leaf and encrusted with precious stones (X, PL. 473), dating from the end of the 10th century. The church has more than 250 capitals, many of which bear figures, and an admirable tympanum representing the Last Judgment (V, PL. 377). The tympanum is decorated with 124 figures, accompanied by inscriptions, illustrating the joys of heaven and the torments of the damned. This complex is dominated by the figure of Christ Triumphant, blessing and condemning, surrounded by clouds and stars.

This tympanum, which probably can be dated between 1130 and 1140, therefore antedates that of Moissac by only a few years; but the two works differ fundamentally in spirit as well as in form. The Abbey church of Moissac was in the 11th and 12th centuries one of the main centers of theological debate and exegesis. It is not surprising, therefore, that its portal is illustrated with the Vision of St. John, one of the most mysterious texts ever conceived, while the Abbey of Conques, which opened wide its doors to veritable invasions of pilgrims, most of them illiterate, chose the more readily comprehensible theme discussed above. Of all Romanesque tympanums, that of Ste-Foy is the only one in which are preserved noteworthy traces of the paint that originally colored the sculptures. On the tympanum as well as on the capitals inside the church the figures are normally proportioned, as they are in the sculptures of Auvergne; there are none of the elongated silhouettes of Moissac, Beaulieu (V, PL. 377), and Burgundy (the tympanum of the Cathedral of Autun; PL. 240; VII, PL. 374). The artistic relations between Conques and Auvergne can easily be explained, since this church stood on one of the main pilgrimage routes to Santiago de Compostela — that starting at Le Puy.

During the Romanesque age, other regions besides Languedoc witnessed a flowering of the art of decorating the capitals and portals of churches with sculpture. It was particularly in Burgundy and in the Rhone Valley and in the regions of Berry, Poitou, and Saintonge that this art developed, but fine examples can also be found in other regions, especially in Roussillon.

Why was there such a wealth of sculptured works in these areas, while in others the art was little practiced or was entirely unknown? For certain regions, such as Île-de-France, the answer lies in the fact that Gothic architecture supplanted Romanesque at an early stage; for others the richness of resources provides an answer. Roussillon was rich in marble quarries, Languedoc and Burgundy supplied excellent materials, and Berry, Saintonge, and Angoumois offered a soft limestone that was easily worked. Auvergne, however, offered its sculptors only hard stone; there are very few carved portals there. The portal of the Church of Notre-Dame-du-Port in Clermont-Ferrand is made of arkose; although its design is very beautiful, the sculptor obviously had great difficulties in dealing with the figures that decorate it and consequently they lack character. However, the churches in Auvergne possess capitals with figures of good quality; for these, stone was imported from Berry.

Thanks to accurately dated monuments such as those of St-Sernin and Moissac, chronological precedence has always been given to the school of Languedoc; but it would seem that the revival of sculpture appeared in Burgundy as early as it did in Languedoc. The crypt of St-Bénigne of Dijon (XI, PL. 308) has archaic capitals that must date back to the time of the abbot William of Volpiano (1001–1017).

The enormous Abbey church of Cluny (begun 1088 by St. Hugh), with a nave 560 ft. long, two transepts, and superb belfries, was wantonly destroyed at the beginning of the 19th century; only the northern arm of the large transept remains. The slab of the high altar, consecrated by Pope Urban II on Oct. 25th, 1095, and the eight capitals that surmounted the columns of the ambulatory at the rear of the high altar have been preserved in the Musée du Farinier, originally the granary of the abbey. Remains of the tympanum of the portal, which, as in Moissac, was decorated with the figure of Christ among the Elders of the Apocalypse, were found in the course of an excavation directed by Kenneth Conant (1929–42). The capitals of the chancel are almost 3 ft. high; they are works of marvelous technique and high symbolic value, worthy of the scholars who were the monks of the great abbey that influenced the entire Christian world. Two of these capitals are decorated with figures representing the tones of the Gregorian music scale (PL. 240); on others can be seen the rivers and trees of Paradise and figures of women symbolizing the Seasons, the Virtues, and the Arts. The dating of these capitals has roused discussion; perhaps, as Aubert (1947) has suggested, they were executed between 1113 and 1118 under the abbot Pons de Melgueil.

The Cathedral of Autun was consecrated in 1132 by Pope Innocent II. Sculpture is abundantly represented there by numerous capitals (PLS. 240, 241) of varied iconography, by the large tympanum of the western portal, and by a fragment of the lintel of the north lateral portal (PL. 240), which shows the reclining figure of Eve leaning on one elbow and picking the forbidden fruit; on this fragment can be seen the demon's claw bending a fruit-laden branch toward Eve.

The large tympanum, signed by the sculptor Gislebertus, shows the dead rising from their tombs and the Last Judgment. Among the resurrected, two pilgrims can be noticed; each carries a satchel, one decorated with a shell, the other with a cross, showing that both have deserved heaven, the former for a pilgrimage to Santiago de Compostela and the latter for one to the Holy Land. Heaven is represented by a series of arcades into which angels lift the elect.

The artist has shown the hems of the robes as if they had been lifted by a gust of wind, a device used to fill in the empty spaces; another device characteristic of Burgundian art is the designing of excessively long and slender bodies (to fill the vertical spaces) with clinging robes adorned with fine, small pleats. These two devices are to be found at Anzy-le-Duc and Perrecy-les-Forges (Saône-et-Loire), at Saulieu (Côte-d'Or), at Vézelay and Avallon (Yonne), and at Donzy (Nièvre).

The Cathedral of Autun once possessed a monument of a period more recent than that of its portal and capitals. This was the tomb of St. Lazarus, executed between 1170 and 1189 by "the monk Martinus." It had (an unusual feature in Romanesque art) statues sculptured in the round, about 1½ ft. high (V, PL. 376). Several of these statues have been preserved (Autun, Mus. Rolin).

The *décor* of the nave and the narthex of the Church of La Madeleine in the Abbey of Vézelay, with its numerous capitals and three portals that give access to the nave, was carried out between about 1120 and 1150. On the central tympanum appears the figure of Christ sending the Apostles to preach throughout the world (PL. 242; V, PL. 376). The small figures grouped on the lintel and around the framing arch represent the nations to whom the messengers of Christ were to bring the Gospel; even the fabled peoples of distant countries — pygmies of central Africa, cynocephali of India — can be recognized. Here, as in Autun, but with greater skill and nobility, the artists have managed to give their figures an extraordinary vivacity of movement.

The art of Cluny, Autun, and Vézelay spread throughout Burgundy and the bordering regions: Orléanais (Saint-Benoît-sur-Loire; IV, PL. 178), Nivernais (Perrecy-les-Forges, Saint-Pierre-le-Moûtier, La Charité-sur-Loire, Donzy), Bourbonnais (Saint-Menoux, Souvigny), Berry, and also the Rhone Valley (the cathedrals of Lyons and of Vienne, Isère, the Church of St-André-le-Bas in Vienne).

Berry, in the center of France, was a crossroads of influences where elements of the schools of Burgundy, Auvergne, and Poitou were blended. In this region have been preserved many beautiful Romanesque churches adorned with the capitals of fine workmanship that were made possible by the soft limestone native to the area. Among these are the churches of Neuvy-Saint-Sépulcre, Saint-Genou, La Berthenoux, and Gargilesse (Indre); Neuilly-en-Dun, Chalivoy-Milon, Blet, and the Abbey church of Plaimpied (Cher). This last church holds the magnificent capital of the Temptation of Christ (PL. 247), one of the masterpieces of Romanesque art (this work is dealt with later, when the expansion of French art in Palestine at the time of the Crusades is examined).

Vézelay and Auvergne offered only very hard materials such as lava, granite, and arkose, all unsuited to works of sculpture; the artists therefore limited themselves to ornamental motifs, which sometimes achieve a magnificent decorative effect, as in the Cathedral of Le Puy. The naves of the main Romanesque churches in Auvergne, however, have rows of columns crowned with magnificent figured capitals cut in a soft limestone imported from Berry down the southern affluents of the Loire.

Gallo-Roman art (q.v.) had left a deep mark on Auvergne; monuments of antiquity were still numerous there in the 12th century, and Romanesque artists imitated them in their creations, using motifs such as centaurs, sirens, confronted genii, and winged

victories along with Christian themes. They often preserved the graceful sweep of the Corinthian capital, as in the capitals presenting four figures which, placed at the corners and with their heads deliberately enlarged, replace the volute of the antique capital; a pine cone hanging from the abacus replaces the central rosette. In other capitals the haloed heads of four angels, one on each side, replace the rosette, and their wings, raised at the corners, replace the volute. The churches possessing the most interesting series of figured capitals are those of Clermonte-Ferrand (Notre-Dame-du-Port), Saint-Nectaire, Issoire, Mozac (Puy-de-Dôme), and Brioude (Haute-Loire; St-Julien).

The soft-stone quarries of Poitou, Saintonge, and Angoumois explain the marvelous fertility in the development of sculpture there. The artists of that region did not use an architectural element particularly suited to the composition of a sculptured scene — the tympanum; but their portals bore four or more arch moldings (eight at Ste-Marie-des-Dames, in Saintes; V, PL. 378) which they decorated copiously with sculptures. Sometimes the figures are placed symmetrically along the arch molding and converge toward the keystone, where the main subject of the scene is located; thus there may be seen such compositions at that of the arch moldings of the western portal of the Church of St-Pierre-de-la-Tour in Aulnay de Saintonge (X, PL. 439; XIII, PL. 345). This church, so lavishly decorated both on the interior and the exterior, is certainly the flower of Saintonge sculpture. Sometimes the sculptors used yet another ornamental device; on a particular arch molding they placed rectangular voussoirs each decorated with the same small figure. Thus the Elders of the Apocalypse, all identical, with their *vielles* and their perfume jars, fill the voussoirs of the arch molding; instead of the 24 Elders, there are 31 figures on the south portal of the transept of the church in Aulnay de Saintonge and 53 on the portal of Ste-Marie-des-Dames, restored, in Saintes. This creates a somewhat monotonous impression of standardized production but is highly ornamental in effect when viewed from a distance. Certain of the iconographic subjects that have just been mentioned were particularly appreciated in southwestern France. Mention should also be made of the figure on horseback in high relief often found under one of the large arcades flanking the central portal — it represents Constantine, the first Christian emperor. There are about 15 of these in the region.

The artists of southwestern France decorated not only the archivolts of the portals but also the blind bays framing the entrance and the arcades of the upper story. Sometimes the whole surface of the façade was abundantly decorated as, for instance, in the Cathedral of Angoulême (Charente; V, PL. 378), which has been much restored, and in Notre-Dame-la-Grande of Poitiers (PL. 202).

Catalonia, which included Roussillon, was subject to the kingdom of France during the 11th and 12th centuries. The churches and cloisters of these regions were decorated with numerous sculptures, thanks to the marble quarries of the Pyrenees. Worthy of mention on the French side are the sculptures of the cloisters of Elne Cathedral (Pyrénées-Orientales); the low reliefs of the door of the abbot's residence and the capitals of the old Abbey of Saint-Michel-de-Cuxa; and the sculptures of the Abbey of Serrabone, of Arles-sur-Tech, and Boulou and Corneilla-de-Conflent (all in Pyrénées-Orientales). The departments bordering on Aude and Hérault also possessed good marble quarries. Noteworthy are the capitals of Rieux-Minervois (Aude), which recall those of Saint-Michel-de-Cuxa, and the basin of the fountain (Carcassonne, Mus. du Chateau Comtal) from the cloister of the Abbey of Lagrasse. The frieze of scrolls that decorates this basin must be compared to the one adorning the lintel, dated 1178, of the portal of the Cathedral of Maguelonne (Hérault). The large monasteries of Aniane, Saint-Guilhem-le-Désert and the fortified Cathedral of St-Pons-de-Thomières (Hérault) were also copiously decorated. The remains of these sculptures are dispersed in several museums. Particular mention must be made of the large figured low reliefs of the destroyed Abbey of St-Guilhem-le-Désert (some in the church, others in Montpellier, Mus. de la Soc. Archéol.).

The region of the Rhone basin with its monuments from antiquity offered Romanesque artists admirable models of architecture and sculpture. They did not fail to imitate them, as can observed in the friezes of the Cathedral of Nîmes, in Notre-Dame-des-Pommiers (Beaucaire), and also in the two buildings so characteristic of the Romanesque school of Provence: the church of Saint-Gilles-du-Gard and St-Trophime of Arles. There have been extensive discussions regarding the dates of execution and decoration of these buildings, but it would appear that Provençal art reached its full expression here only at the end of the 12th century.

The vast façade of St-Gilles (III, PL. 390) includes three portals, six tall columns rising from the ground and four small columns on plinths framing the central portal, large statues representing the Apostles and two archangels (PL. 246), magnificent cornices, and a frieze decorated with scenes from the life of Christ. The façade is not the result of a single uninterrupted creative act; interruptions as well as alterations took place during the course of the work, which must have been begun in about 1160. In 1179 work seems to have been suspended because of financial difficulties. Two statues of Apostles bear the signature "Brunus." It is known that this sculptor was in Nîmes between 1164 and 1175; he also appeared as witness in an act dated 1186, in which he was referred to as *Petrus Brunus, artifex in opere ligneo et lapidea*. Work was resumed between about 1185 and 1195, was again interrupted, and was resumed in about 1209. It seems that the frieze of the life of Christ and the lateral tympanums representing the Adoration of the Magi and the Crucifixion should be ascribed to the later periods. The crouching lions on the sides of the central portal are seen again at St-Trophime in Arles (PL. 245) and in the Cathedral of Embrun and in several other churches in the vicinity. These lions suggest a borrowing from the great Lombard school of sculpture.

The decoration of the cloister of St-Trophime of Arles (PL. 246; I, PL. 385) was begun about 1170 and was finished only in the 14th century. In the northern gallery (of earliest date), the piers are decorated with statues and low reliefs. On the pier of the northwest corner the image of S. Trophime can be recognized, and beneath his feet is carved the funeral inscription of one "Jourdain," a canon of St-Trophime, dated 1188. The sculpture is therefore of an earlier period (V, PL. 375). The façade of the church must date from the end of the 12th century or the beginning of the 13th (PL. 245). Although it is smaller in size, it presents amazing similarities to the façade of St-Gilles. The fore part with columns is decorated with statues and friezes in low relief; at the side of the portal four statues, their feet placed on lions, face one another, as in St-Gilles.

Like Toulouse, Avignon had splendid monuments in the 12th century. Many of the capitals from the cloister of the Cathedral of Notre-Dame-des-Doms are dispersed in several museums of France and the United States (Cambridge, Mass., Fogg Art Mus.), but similar ones can be found in Provence, particularly in the cloister of the former Cathedral of Vaison-la-Romaine (Vaucluse). The bells of these capitals include finely sculptured representations of broad, fleshy leaves forming spiral scrolls. Provence presents a belated school of Romanesque art, which continued into the early 13th century.

The northern provinces of France participated to a lesser degree in the great renewal of sculpture that began in the 11th century; good examples of Romanesque sculpture are seldom to be found in Normandy, in Brittany, in the Île-de-France, in Champagne, or in the east.

French art left its mark beyond its own frontiers; there were exchanges of influences with Italy and Spain. During the 11th century and at the beginning of the 12th many French knights crossed the Pyrenees to join the Spanish armies in the fight against the Moors. No sooner was a city liberated from the Moslems than a monk from Cluny or Conques established himself in the restored episcopal see, bringing monks from the two great abbeys to populate the priories founded in the reconquered lands. Thus French art penetrated into Spain (see below).

French art spread over the east coast of the Mediterranean, Palestine, and Lebanon; Syria also felt its influence. Following the First Crusade, a certain number of knights, with Godefroy de Bouillon and his brother Baudoin (Baldwin I, who became the first king of Jerusalem), Raymond de Saint-Gilles, Count of Toulouse, and Bohémond, Prince of Taranto, and his cousin Tancred, both of Norman origin, settled in these distant lands and founded a vast colony that was to survive in the Levant until 1291. Magnificent monuments, sumptuous palaces, and powerful fortresses were erected, as well as numerous religious buildings; churches, monasteries, and 20 cathedrals were built in styles that developed and were transformed just as in the West. Magnificent examples of these have been preserved, but few traces are left of sculptural decoration, since the Moslems often destroyed the sculptures decorated with figures.

The large portal of the Church of the Holy Sepulcher, Jerusalem, preserves a double carved lintel. One part illustrates scenes from the life of Christ; the other is decorated with inhabited scrolls reminiscent of the art of Toulouse. In this church and in several other religious monuments of Jerusalem, the capitals reflect the influence of Languedocian and Provençal art.

In Nazareth is to be found the most interesting example of the French art of the Holy Land that has been preserved. It consists of six pieces of sculpture, one of which is a stone block decorated with two heads, larger than life-size, of men with long beards (the block from which they project was never completed). The others are five large capitals with figures (PL. 247). The Cathedral of Nazareth was destroyed by the Moslems; the six sculptures, found in the course of excavations, had been designed to become part of a lateral portal that was never finished. They can be numbered among the masterpieces of Romanesque art. The evidence indicates that they are the work of a sculptor who had practiced his art in Burgundy and Berry. The architectural decoration that crowns the capitals, the concentric folds of the draperies on the protruding parts of the bodies, the clothing dotted with small holes, the tucked-up hems of the robes, the bristling hair of the demons, and the large halos of Christ and the Apostles recall the capitals of Autun, Vézelay, and other churches of Burgundy and Berry. But the most immediate and truly remarkable comparison that can be established is with a capital of Plaimpied (PL. 247) — the previously-mentioned Temptation of Christ. Every one of the above-mentioned details of the capitals of Nazareth can be found at Plaimpied; and the two demons of the Plaimpied capital, one with long fleece and the other with smooth skin, can be seen in Nazareth.

The period of the crusades, which kept the Christian world in turmoil for two centuries, in turn left its trace on the French art of the West in architectural monuments imitating the oldest Christian buildings of the Near East, in paintings and sculptures representing battles against the Moslems, in ornamental sculpture inspired by Oriental models, and in objects of gold wrought to house the relics that had been gathered in the Holy Land.

Romanesque art continued in certain regions until the end of the 12th century, but in the middle of the century a new art was developing in the Île-de-France, where builders using the vault on diagonal ribs were to create Gothic architecture. Sculpture, too, was about to be transformed; the stylized formulas cherished by Romanesque sculptors were soon to be abandoned for figures closer to nature and for the quieter and more serene attitudes of the Gothic.

Paul DESCHAMPS

IBERIAN PENINSULA. Romanesque sculpture in Spain was much more deeply influenced by native tradition than was architecture. Historians, however, have sometimes thought they could discern an anti-iconic tendency in the Iberian Peninsula, which Moslem influence would have intensified but which could be traced back, in Christian art, to the canon of the Council of Elvira (Iliberius), of about 300, forbidding the painting of sacred subjects on church walls. This hypothesis is contradicted, however, by more convincing testimonies from as early as the end of the 4th century; Prudentius composed in verses the inscriptions that were to accompany the scenes of the Old and New Testaments decorating the sanctuaries, and Visigothic Spain in particular is richer than any other Western country not only in decorative but also in iconographic sculptures. Even if one rejects the date — which, however, seems certain —

of the 7th century for San Pedro de Nave and Quintanilla de las Viñas, it is impossible to ignore the recent discoveries of a Córdoban capital decorated with the symbols of the Evangelists (Córdoba, Mus. Arqueol. Provincial) and the piers of El Salvador in Toledo, carved with Biblical scenes. But it was mainly Mozarabic ornamental sculpture (see MOZARABIC ART) that was the decisive influence in the emergence of the Romanesque capital.

The model of the Corinthian capital of antiquity was never entirely forgotten during the early Middle Ages. In Christian art it had degenerated to the point of becoming shapeless; but Moslem art in Córboda gave it a monumental renewal, elongating it, enlarging the volutes in order to give a firmer support to the corners of the abacus, simplifying the acanthus leaves and accentuating their curved ends, or sometimes merely squaring the outline. In short, the sculptors of the Caliphate of Córdoba created a new capital on the old model, one well suited to its function of supporting arches instead of an architrave (X, PL. 162).

A few well-preserved examples in Catalonia (in S. María of Ripoll, in S. Benito de Bages, Barcelona, in the crypt of the Vich Cathedral, etc.) are so like those of the Córdoba Mosque (X, PL. 162) that is it impossible to doubt their Andalusian origin and their date (about the middle of the second half of the 10th century). Historical documents agree on dating the consecration of Ripoll in 977 and that of S. Benito de Bages in 972. These capitals are so similar that they might have been imported to Catalonia from Córdoba, but they are of the local stone, so it is obvious that they were executed in Ripoll by an Andalusian artist. The bases of the columns have a characteristic outline — the scotia is almost vertical — and the comparison of certain fragments found in Ripoll with the bases in the Córdoba Mosque leaves no room for doubt.

It is not surprising to find Andalusian importation at Ripoll. Exchanges and journeys were frequent between Moslem and Christian countries; the Ripoll monastery library was rich in Arabic manuscripts, and Catalonian monasteries were highly receptive to Córdoban civilization. It is therefore not at all unlikely that Córdoban craftsmen worked in Ripoll, even though this was a matter only of an individual contribution, undoubtedly the work of a traveling artist or of a small team. On a given model a new evolution immediately began; Catalan artists reproduced Córdoban forms less rigorously, but they preserved their monumental aspects, accentuating the variable points of the capital. At the same time they created new ornaments by separating the elements of the acanthus leaf to form floral ornaments and palmettes. In Ripoll one can clearly distinguish on one hand the Andalusian model reproduced with great precision, true Ommiad capitals, and on the other hand examples of varied influences that can be called Mozarabic. Other more advanced examples can be found at Cornellá, in the Llobregat Valley, near Barcelona.

This tradition persists through the 11th century; it explains the precocity of the beautiful capitals of the monastery church of San Pedro de Roda (consecrated 1022) and of S. Maria in Besalú, Gerona (consecrated 1055). These capitals were not derived directly from the ancient Corinthian model, but from the Córdoban one; their height is superior to their breadth, the hollowing of the abacus is very pronounced, the detail of the acanthus leaves is not sculptured in the mass but is applied on the roughing out of the leaves, either in sunken beveling or by a flattened slight projection. Sometimes the curved end of the leaf thickens and forms a wedgelike protuberance; often the edges of the leaves form small arches. The design of the cutting out and ribbings gradually became more abstract and decorative.

At the same time the marble cutters of the Pyrenees were also inspired by Hispano-Moresque ornament. The technique of sculpture, much neglected in other areas, was preserved in the vicinity of the quarries; but the decorative repertory was borrowed from Mozarabic manuscripts — flower-shaped ornaments, palmettes, and undulating stems were to become models for the Romanesque capitals and abacuses.

These sculptures of the 10th century and the beginning of the 11th in Catalonia are of much interest for their precocity,

but were sporadic and had scarcely any continuation in that region. Lombard art, which at the time had invaded all the Mediterranean countries, ignored sculpture almost completely; cheap and rapid construction in coarse hammer-hewn stone gave foremost importance to ornamental painting, indispensable for concealing the poverty of the materials. Catalonia, which has preserved so many buildings and documents of the middle or the end of the 11th century, has nothing to show but a few isolated and mediocre sculptures. Undoubtedly the sculptors of capitals and the marble cutters of the Pyrenees had even then been attracted to the great center of Toulouse. It is in the south of France, in places such as Rieux-Minervois, that the continuation of the style of San Pedro de Roda and of S. María of Besalú is to be found.

In the northwest of the Peninsula the situation was different; instead of a few traveling artists, whole colonies and organized monastic communities arrived from Andalusia and settled in the Douro Valley. The art that these Mozarabs practiced was not a precise imitation but a reminiscence of that of Córdoba. This can be observed in the capitals of the monastery of Sahagún; in Santiago, Peñalba; in S. María, Lebeña; in S. Román, Hornija; and in S. Cebrián, Mazote. Nevertheless, the form preserves a monumental quality, the corners of the bell of the capital are strongly indicated, a thick relief is found at the end of the leaves, and the design of the acanthus leaves undergoes the same transformations; it is carved with the same technique of beveling, which deals with the surface of the stone obliquely and incises channels of a more or less deep and decided V-shape. The examples are much more numerous than in Catalonia. There, from Visigothic times, ashlar never ceased to be in favor; and there can be felt the preparation for the Romanesque.

The birth of Spanish Romanesque sculpture took place in Léon and can be explained by the historical reasons set forth earlier. The first building of Spanish Romanesque art was the sanctuary to which King Ferdinand transferred the relics of St. Isidore of Seville, a Doctor of the Spanish Church. The dates of the Church of S. Isidoro of León are given with great certainty by chronicles and inscriptions. Consecrated in 1063 and finished in 1067, the church proper was destroyed soon afterward and later rebuilt, but the original portico still exists and certainly dates from that period, since the main purpose of its foundation was its destined use as a funeral chapel (Pantéon de los Reyes; PL. 212). The architecture of this chapel is a French importation that entered Spain with the pilgrims to Santiago de Compostela, but the sculpture of the capitals is directly related to Mozarabic tradition. For the certainty of their early date and the originality of their forms, they can be considered the point of departure for the various series of capitals in the church rebuilt in the 12th century, whose influence permeated all Spanish Romanesque art.

The Corinthian capitals remain very close to the Mozarabic model. Although less rigorously squared, the hollowing of the abacus is carved very deeply, thus giving the bell of the capital an individual form and throwing into relief the protuberances of the corners and of the face; the stress lines are oblique in the prolongation of the arches and vertical in the axis of the column. They accentuate even more strongly the curved and thickened ends of the leaves, which become balls or pine cones. The cutting out of the acanthus leaves alternates and joins one leaf to another, forming flower-shaped designs, typical ornaments that also decorate the abacus.

Other capitals simplify the Corinthian scheme and preserve only a single row of large leaves. The modeling differs from one example to another; it is sometimes more freely carved, sometimes more stiffly, but always beveled. Later, instead of the sunken cutting-out, the decoration is superimposed on the surface of the leaves in fine, delicately modeled ribbons. A much more elaborate technique is seen in most of the capitals of St-Sernin of Toulouse, which are related to those of León but are undoubtedly of later date.

A second group of capitals abandons the Corinthian model, eliminating the acanthus leaf and covering the bell of the capital with scrolls, but with corners still strongly marked with human, animal, or monster heads. This capital takes on a very delicate and elaborate form in S. Isidoro (PL. 248) and in many other Spanish churches of the 12th century.

Capitals decorated with monsters also utilize the Corinthian scheme. The real Romanesque creation consists in forming, with the monsters themselves and with confronted quadrupeds and serpent-men, the architecture of the capital. A particularly convincing example is that of the confronted dragons at the corners, framing a little figure seated underneath; this composition decorated a capital of the open bay of the tribune above the 11th-century nave in León, and is almost exactly repeated at St-Sernin of Toulouse.

The iconographic scenes stand out either on a background of foliage or on a plain background. The figures take on a bold relief; the folds of the draperies are superimposed as though they were pressed flat; the faces are depicted in full round, creating an expressive and characteristic type.

One can observe in the Church of S. Isidoro, erected in various stages, that the tradition of this art continued until the middle of the 12th century. The Corinthian capitals differ only slightly from those of the 11th. The interlacings grow more intricate and embellish the original model; birds nest among the scrolls. Human figures and monsters crowd together in confused huddles, where the power of the relief, the brutality of the expression, and the baroquelike aspect of Spanish art are displayed with great originality (PL. 248). Soon, however, the need for organization, typical of Romanesque art, disciplined the compositions, but without depriving them of their savor; that was when masterpieces were born. The most frequently used theme is the squatting figure, man or monkey, which appeared as early as the 11th century in the niches of apses, and was often to be repeated elsewhere in the 12th century.

In S. Isidoro of León are also found the earliest sculptures. The western façade of the church being occupied by the Panteón de los Reyes, the main entrance is on the south side, facing the city. This portal (XIII, PL. 122) was built in the 12th century, but its reemployed sculptures date from the 11th. The Mystical Lamb is figured in the tympanum and the Sacrifice of Abraham on the lintel. Although it is carved in very low relief, the marble (of local origin) displays a rounded modeling, without the engraved features and the pinched folds typical of Languedoc sculpture. The full faces, with their broad chins and heavy hair, are similar to those of the slab of the altar of St-Sernin but are more expressive and varied.

The masterpieces of S. Isidoro are the two statues placed to the right and the left of the arch over the door: one depicts St. Isidore, whose name is given by an inscription, and the other perhaps St. Vincent, the other titular of the church; they are seated, seen from the front, immobile and monumental. The fluted folds of their garments are derived from the Visigothic sculpture of Quintanilla de las Viñas (XI, PL. 321); they are also typical of a work dated 1093, the sarcophagus of Alfonso Ansúrez from Sahagún, Zamora (PL. 248). In any event the very simply modeled forms of the rounded faces and enormous hands are very different from those of Toulouse, to which they have erroneously been related. The Toulouse sculptor, the descendant of the Pyrenean marble cutters, started from a drawing engraved on the smooth surface of a slab which he hollowed to form a basin, leaving aside the outlines of the figures with which he dealt later, accentuating them by surface modeling. The sculptor of León attached the block on three of its sides and in the three dimensions of space; he obtained a powerful form resulting from the roundness of the relief and the lack of details in the modeling.

The originality of this creation influenced Spanish Romanesque sculpture for a long period, but even in León other forms existed at that time; above the tympanum of the Lamb the signs of the zodiac and the group of musicians are finely modeled. The pilgrimage route also introduced foreign elements: the Toulouse style, which cannot be discerned in the Portal of the Lamb, is noticeable in the Portal of Forgiveness, which opens at the south end of the transept and dates from the 12th century. The tympanum, with three juxtaposed scenes (the Descent from the Cross, the Three Marys at the Sepulcher, and the Ascension)

and two statues, of St. Peter and St. Paul, framing it, is the expression in low relief of a complex tradition.

The centers of early Spanish sculpture were situated on the road of Santiago de Compostela. One of the oldest, after León, is undoubtedly Jaca, Huesca, in Aragon, at the foot of the Col de Somport. Its cathedral dates, if not, as was formerly believed, to 1063, at least to the end of the 11th century. The exterior decoration of the apse contains the usual elements, a cornice of billets and modillions decorated with sculptures; but the stretchers, small slabs separating the modillions, like metopes, are carved with rare delicacy; a lion, a basilisk, a bear, a dromedary, and dancers (snake charmers) form lively and picturesque motifs (PL. 212).

The motif of the tympanum of the western portal is a large chrismon flanked by two lions. Long inscriptions explain the symbolism of the chrismon (confused here with the sign of the Trinity) and of the lion, which spares the repentant sinner and triumphs over malevolent beasts. The style is that of the "metopes" of the apse, but harsher and more conventional.

The capitals of the nave and of the portals, cut from a hard stone with a very fine grain, follow the Corinthian model in the evolution begun in León, but at Jaca they acquired monumentality and at the same time a wonderful delicacy in the details. They are decorated with figures and are more innovating and complex (PL. 248); extraordinary compositions pile up in confused groups of men, lions, birds, and serpents. The sculptor, however, soon returned to quieter and often more symmetrical groupings. The imitation of ancient sarcophagi (a beautiful example of which still exists in Huesca) is particularly noticeable in the anatomical treatment, which is admirable; in the graceful children that look like cupids, in the confronted figures bearing the *imago clipeata*, and in the beautiful athletes striking proud postures. But an opposite characteristic also appears in these same capitals; next to the beauty of the nudes appear in exaggerated relief bloated faces with Gorgon hair of an almost expressionist ugliness that was to become a model for several other works of Spanish Romanesque sculpture.

The León tradition and the influence of Jaca spread all over Aragon. Other contributions seem to have come from Languedoc and the north of Italy. The sarcophagus of Doña Sancha (erected in a chapel of the cloister of Sta Cruz and transferred later to the museum in the Benedictine convent in Jaca) took its inspiration from Modena and Cremona. The tympanum of the Church of Santa Cruz de la Serós (near Jaca) and the three tympanums of S. Pedro el Viejo (Huesca) show the chrismon between two lions. The draperies are remarkable for the stylization of the folds. The copious and rich decoration of the church of the Castillo Carreres in Loarre, far from the route of the pilgrimages, is derived from León rather than from Jaca.

The sculpture of S. Martín of Frómista (Castile) combined even more harmoniously the repertory of Jaca and León. The beautiful golden limestone quarried in the area permitted a softer and more sensitive modeling. The lions and the wrestlers of Frómista lack the wild grandeur of those of Jaca, but their design is purer and constitutes a rare example of formal beauty in Romanesque sculpture.

It is impossible to establish a precise chronological order of the monuments that have just been cited; they are roughly contemporaneous, dating from the end of the 11th century or the beginning of the 12th. Their relationship, despite the physical distances involved, is typical of pilgrimage art. Itinerant workshops traveled from one sanctuary to another in both directions, carrying with them varied influences and making rapid exchanges. According to the remark, already cited, of Kingsley Porter (1923), the characteristic of pilgrimage art is to create masterpieces in an artistic desert.

It is in the basilica of the Apostle James in Galicia — Santiago de Compostela — that the various tendencies born in the great creative centers of León and Jaca and all along the road are best combined. Galicia did not supply any models and had but a modest artistic tradition; but the intense religious life created by the pilgrimage called forth works that, far from simply copying imported models, are among the most beautiful creations of Spanish Romanesque art.

The history of architecture furnishes the exact dates of the different parts of Santiago de Compostela. The building, begun from the *chevet* in about 1075, was interrupted in 1088. The three lower chapels and the ambulatory erected during these first ten years offer no reminiscence, in the decoration of the capitals, of the art of León. The angels carrying scrolls and the forktailed sirens vaguely recall Auvergne. At the junction point of the building, resumed in the last years of the century, two capitals, recently identified, represent the martyrdom of Ste-Foy and seem to be a copy of those of Conques. In the transept the damned soul hanged by demons was to become in turn a model for a scene of hell on the tympanum of Conques; this is a typical example of the two-way exchanges that went on among the basilicas along the pilgrimage route. From then on, almost all the capitals were exclusively ornamental. It was the León style that dominated, but in simplified form, undoubtedly because it was necessary to adapt to the coarseness of the granite so ill-suited to sculpture. Out of this very difficulty came a renewal of style; the almost rough-hewn forms, the crockets, and the leaves split through the middle produce a splendid monumental effect.

Of the three Romanesque façades which originally decorated the Cathedral and which are described in Aymery Picaud's Pilgrims' Guide (see above), only one remains — the one including the Puerta de las Platerías (PL. 249). This is where the main street of the city ends and where the silversmiths and sellers of medals and souvenirs for the pilgrims were installed. The *camino francés* led to the opposite end, hence the name Puerta Francigena, given to the north door of the transept. The Puerta de las Platerías, which faces the city, must have been badly damaged during the revolt of the inhabitants of Compostela in 1117. Hastily restored in the next few years, it displays a number of unmatched statues, reemployed and haphazardly placed. This disorder was increased by later restorations and during the demolition of the other two façades in the 17th and 18th centuries. Some fragments of their decoration were fitted into the façade of the Puerta de las Platerías, no doubt to replace sculptures destroyed by time: the group picturing the Expulsion of Adam and Eve had originally been on the north portal, and most probably certain figures of the Transfiguration scene had once decorated the main door. It is not known in what year the figure of Christ, which had always occupied the center of the upper part of the façade, was replaced; the one seen there today dates from the end of the 12th century and forms a contrast with its neighbors. But the contrasts among the sculptures of the beginning of the 12th century are scarcely less noticeable, though all of them are almost contemporaneous.

The iconographic program of the portal is complex and confused: "The wall from top to bottom and from right to left is magnificently carved with flowers, saints, beasts, birds, fishes, and other works," says the 12th-century Pilgrims' Guide. The upper part must have been devoted essentially to the series of the Apostles; the statues, of different sizes, no doubt originally fitted into the curves of the arches that open beneath them. At the right hand of Christ, St. James stands between two pruned trees, which the Pilgrims' Guide calls cypresses. These trees also frame the statue of St. James on the Porte Miégeville of St-Sernin in Toulouse, as they do many other statues of saints on the Puerta de las Platerías. The simple ornamental framework formed by the trees was borrowed from antique sarcophagi. These two representations of the Apostle, that of Compostela and that of Toulouse, have little else in common.

The left tympanum of the Puerta de las Platerías shows the Temptation of Christ and also contains the strange figure of the adulteress condemned by her husband to hold her lover's skull on her lap (this interpretation, from the Pilgrims' Guide, was perhaps a legend invented on the spot by the pilgrims to explain a fragmentary and incomprehensible sculpture). The right tympanum represents the Adoration of the Magi and, below, a miracle and some scenes from the Passion. Other reliefs, at the spandrels and jambs, would require a minute description. Widely varied styles mix and clash within the whole without the slightest attempt at harmony. The small figures decorating

the small marble columns of the splays under the arcading recall the Toulouse technique of stonecutting but are very Spanish in expression. The angel of the Temptation (left tympanum) offers a splendid example of the draperies with pressed folds seen particularly in Aragon; the figure of Christ is partly in the round; the demons of the same scene form two groups very different in technique and appearance — the first, in rounded modeling, is somewhat placid, the second is thin and nervous. The figures of the Passion (right tympanum) are for the most part small statues detached from the background; short and squat, with large heads, they recall Auvergne sculpture but are almost isolated cases in Compostela. In some the León style is evident in the bulging draperies formed by segments of concentric circles. The same style can be found in the larger statues on the right jamb of the left door (St. Andrew) and at the top left of the façade (three Apostles). The tendency, so characteristic of early León sculpture, to exaggerate the relief is here accentuated, as in Jaca, by features of expressive and individual ugliness. The woman holding the skull, with her swollen cheeks and thick locks, cannot be confused with any foreign work. The figure of the woman with the lion cub (on the right jamb of the right door), although it is executed with the same roundness and the same fullness of relief, has different proportions and more vigorous modeling.

From these different, often contrasting, qualities were born the masterpieces of Compostela sculpture — the figures of the Apostles at the top of the façade, representing St. Peter and St. Andrew, St. James the Greater between two cypresses, and below, another waist-length figure of St. James represented at the moment of the Transfiguration (which, however, because of an undecipherable inscription, was long mistaken for Abraham emerging from the tomb). On these sculptures, instead of bulging or pressed folds, the draperies show slight movement and let the light play over the large smooth surfaces of the marble. The figures are graceful and animated; the faces with their deeply molded features are highly individual.

It is not suprising that so vast an enterprise as Compostela attracted a great number of sculptors from the various centers of Romanesque art; they came from León, from Jaca, and even from Toulouse. The diversity of these artists and the difficulties of the work situation account for the incoherence and imperfections of the result. These diverse styles soon were blended and modified, however, to create the works characteristic of that great religious metropolis of the Western world.

The influence of Compostela was quickly felt throughout Spain, in, for instance, such a remote region as Santa Marta de Tera, Zamora, on the Portuguese border. Moreover, a significant document introduces one of the traveling artists of the *camino francés*: in 1101, a master mason from Santiago de Compostela, one Stephanus, was working at the Cathedral of Pamplona, the ruins of which are of pure Compostela style. The imitation is clumsier in the capitals and the statues that decorate the portal of the monastery of San Salvador da Leyre, the large Navarrese sanctuary, which, before the introduction of pilgrimage art had had (11th cent.) only an elementary and coarse decoration.

The 12th century proved to be a far less fruitful period for Spanish Romanesque art than the 11th; an exceptional creation, however, appeared in Castile, at Silos. The monastery of S. Domingo in Silos is not situated on the road to Santiago de Compostela but in a wild and isolated region southeast of Burgos. Its fame arose after the death of Abbot Domingo (1073), whose relics immediately began to attract pilgrims. These were at first buried in the cloister, but the multitude of visitors forced the monks to transfer them (1076) to the church, which was enlarged and rededicated in 1088. Only part of the southern transept remains; it gives onto the cloister through the so-called "Door of the Virgins." The strange capitals of its splays are decorated with brutal figures who are wrapped in cerements and who have enormous protruding eyes and faces that are almost caricatures in their ugliness.

The wonder of Silos is its cloister, whose capitals and reliefs are the work of an exceptional sculptor and his assistants. The work extended over three periods, which are fairly easy to identify, but the initial date of this creation has been a subject of dispute. Some scholars place it immediately after the death of Domingo; his epitaph, engraved on the abacus of a capital in the northern gallery of the cloister, would seem to prove that that part of the construction is earlier than 1076, the year in which the relics were transferred to the church. However, it may well be that this commemorative inscription was engraved later, just as in the 14th century a cenotaph was raised on the original site of the tomb. The end of the 11th century, more plausibly, was devoted to enlarging the church, a measure necessitated by the multitude of pilgrims; and the cloister could have been begun only in about 1100. The second period should be placed in the middle of the century, for a document of 1158 mentions that an important part of the income of the monastery came *ad opera claustri et domorum*. The sculptures of the third period are closely related to works of the end of the century, discussed below.

Emile Bertaux (1906) tried to justify the date of 1076 by recognizing an Arab influence in the capitals of Silos; the sculpture would appear to be the work of Moorish prisoners who worked at the monastery in Domingo's time. Certain motifs — pine cones and superimposed animals — are in fact characteristic. They could, it is true, have been derived from Eastern fabrics or ivories; but the technique of the stone sculpture at Silos seems itself to be directly related to ivory and gold sculptures. On the admirably sculptured bodies of the birds and quadrupeds, which follow the form of the bell of the capital, the surface modeling is made solely of small thin strokes, as delicately worked as in an engraving. In the more complex compositions of scrolls or groups of beasts, the relief is always flattened; the forms are sunk on a regular surface and achieve a general effect of smoothness. A comparison with the ivory casket of Silos (carved by Muḥammad Ibn-Zayan; Burgos, Mus. Histórico y Artístico) is particularly convincing. The finished form of these capitals, very different from the Corinthian style, consists of a lower part shaped like the frustum of a cone and an upper part in the form of a parallelogram, bordered at the top by a rectilinear abacus without hollowings. The hypothesis of a penetration of Moorish art and techniques should therefore not be discarded, even if the date is not as early as Bertaux thought.

The high reliefs decorating the corner pilasters of the cloister are also the result of a creative art. Nevertheless, they allow certain comparisons with Languedoc sculpture. Their location is the same as in the cloister of Moissac; the attitudes of the characters, with their crossed legs, and certain typical faces of angels are borrowed from Toulouse; but the ball-shaped capitals that support the framing arches come from León.

A certain archaism marks the two reliefs (the Ascension and Pentecost) at the southeast corner. The figures, in two close rows, are monotonous and the feet are in an unnatural position. At the northwest corner, the Doubting Thomas is more dynamic and more expressive; the Supper at Emmaus consists of three huge figures in very flat relief in which the clinging draperies are stylized in vast luminous surfaces and the faces are treated with the same simplicity. The scenes of the northeast corner, the Deposition (PL. 251) and the Entombment, are more carefully studied; the modeling of the draperies is subtler but is still very stylized, and the composition is most elaborate. The two reliefs at the southwest corner (the Annunciation and the Tree of Jesse), as well as certain capitals of the eastern gallery of the cloister, belong to another period.

Navarra is one of the regions of the Peninsula richest in Romanesque sculptures, but it is also one of those most dominated by French influence. It adopted the Aquitaine portal, with no tympanum and with elaborate arch molding (examples at Puente la Reina, Cirauqui, etc.); but the multifoil arch of these portals is evidently a vague reminiscence of Moslem art. Other churches of the area kept the tympanum decorated with a majestic scene such as an Apocalyptic vision or the Last Judgment. In Estella, the façade of S. Miguel is almost entirely covered with sacred figures and scenes; the forms are full but heavy. In the same town, which was a royal residence and a halting place for the pilgrims to Compostela, the cloister of S. Pedro de la Rúa is decorated with capitals that are remarkable for the harmonious composition of the ornaments and the elegance of the figures. The collegiate church of Tudela developed the sculptures of the archivolts to an extreme degree. S. María la Réal of Sanguesa adopts the column-statues of the Île-de-France, but the top of the façade is adorned, according to a typically Spanish custom, by statues under arcades, here placed in two superimposed rows; the spandrels themselves are strewn with a confused multitude of monsters. Finally, the early Romanesque cloister of the Pamplona Cathedral possessed an exceptional series of iconographic capitals, of which only a few examples remain (Pamplona, Mus. de la Diputación de Navarra).

Sculpture is rougher in Soria, where the portal of the Church of S. Domingo shows a Christ in Majesty on the tympanum, and where figures are placed following the radii of a semicircle on the voussoirs, along the lines of the Aulnay de Saintonge model. Moslem influence is very marked in the decoration of the churches of S. Juan de Duero and S. Juan de Rabañera; the capitals of the cloister of S. Pedro are but pale copies of those of Silos.

Even more rustic in the mountains of Aragon, Romanesque sculpture often takes on a popular form, as for instance in the small chapel of Santiago in Agüero. Even in the glorious monasteries of S. Juan de la Peña and S. Pedro el Viejo, in Huesca, where the iconographic series of the cloisters are richly developed, the heavy figures form a single block with the bell of the capital, to which they give a monumental beauty. The Toulouse cloisters undoubtedly inspired the artists, but the style is totally different. The costumes of the figures, particularly the headdresses and the wimples of the women, are typically Spanish.

Catalonia is certainly the richest region of the Peninsula in Romanesque architecture, but the first period, that of Lombard art, had not favored sculpture, which came to its flowering only in the 12th century. Catalonia, however, should be studied with Roussillon, where the Master of Serrabone and the Master of Cabestany produced their great works.

In the famous Monastery of S. María, in Ripoll, the façade of the church (PL. 250) has fortunately been preserved. Studded with sculptures, it seems to be the enormous page of a stone book the size of an arch of triumph. One finds there, in fact, developed on several tiers, the main themes of the Farfa Bible (Rome, Vat. Lib., Vat. lat. 5729) and the Bible of San Pedro de Roda (Paris, Bib. Nat., Ms. lat. 6), which originated from Catalan scriptoriums: God the Father Enthroned, the Elders of the Apocalypse, scenes from the Old Testament, the lives of SS. Peter and Paul, and fabled monsters. The unity of this vast composition leaves room for several styles: animals in the round at the base; typically Spanish stylization of both the flattened relief and the delicate modeling in the statues of the engaged columns of the portal; picturesque little rustic scenes, influenced perhaps by Italian models; the expressive rude strength of the figure of God, closely related to the one of Besalú. The portal of Ripoll is one of the most imposing creations of Romanesque art.

The Catalan cloisters are numerous and rich in sculptures. S. María de la Seo in Manresa and S. Benito de Bogea, near San Fructuoso, seem to be the oldest; Ripoll is related to the Abbey church of Elne; S. María of Estany introduced some exceptional forms. Special mention must be made of the cloisters of S. Pedro de Galligans (Gerona) and the Cathedral of Gerona for the harmony of their ornament, the beauty of the modeling of the figures, the nobility of the draperies, and (in the latter) the richness of the iconography. Provençal influence probably accounts for certain features, such as the friezes. Near Barcelona, the cloister of S. Cugat (San Cugat del Vallés) continues and enriches this series. Later the cloister of Tarragona combined this abundant iconography with a certain Cistercian austerity and with Moorish influences.

The end of the Romanesque period, which persisted through the 13th century in Catalonia, is in fact marked by an expansion of Mudejar forms: multifoil and intersecting arches, small domes, pierced slabs, carved tracery. The Old Cathedral of Lérida and the Church of S. María (Agramunt) offer the most beautiful examples of this art, which extended as far as Valencia, in the Portada del Palau of the Cathedral.

The same phenomenon had occurred, but with greater emphasis, in architecture in the west of Spain. It is noticeable in the portals of Zamora (XIII, PL. 117) and Toro and of S. Juan del Mercado in Benavente and S. Martín in Salamanca.

The southern regions of Old Castile had received their first models of Romanesque art from León; the French settlers brought new ones. From these different elements was born the rich (though somewhat monotonous) decorative art that came to be used all over the capitals, the portals, and the lateral porticoes of the churches. The most colorful such creations are found in remote places; they have a rustic touch at Sepúlveda, in the churches of El Salvador and Nuestra Señora de la Peña, and an amazing delicacy at Fuentidueña. This clearly proves that exterior influences are not all-important. They play an unquestionable part in the masterpieces of the second half of the 12th century in Spain, but that part has been exaggerated by historians. At Ávila, it is possible to follow the development of an original art in the statues of the south portal of S. Vicente (two saints and the Annunciation) and on the tomb of the martyrs inside the church. The western façade of the same church gives considerable space to a decoration of Burgundian origin, yet the figures do not lose their Spanish character because of this. The column-statues of the Cámara Santa at Oviedo are highly stylized, which distinguishes them from the art of the Île-de-France and relates them instead to the art of Ávila and to that of Compostela. To the same order of research belong the sculptures of Armentia (S. Andrés) in the Basque country and Carrión de los Condes (S. María del Camino) and Moarbes (S. Pedro) in Castile, as well as the reliefs and capitals of the last period at Silos.

The most splendid realization of this style of sculpture is found in the Pórtico de la Gloria, which replaced the Romanesque portal of the façade of Santiago de Compostela in 1088, according to an inscription dated and signed by one Master Matthew. This masterpiece no longer belongs to Romanesque art; Master Matthew led the way to a new period in which sculpture directly translated the appearance of reality. The Romanesque and Spanish features that he retained, however, prove the vitality and originality that characterized even the earliest works of Spanish Romanesque sculpture.

Portugal. Portugal was only very slightly influenced by Compostela. The poverty of the recently reconquered country was well matched by the coarseness of the local granite, which did not lend itself to finely modeled sculpture. The Agnus Dei, carved in flattened relief, decorates the tympanums of several portals of the beginning of the 12th century — S. Marthino (Cedofeita) in Oporto, Fonte Arcada, and others. Christ in Majesty appears on the tympanums of Bravães (San Salvador), S. Pedro of Rates, and others. Most of these sculptures retain a popular character, particularly evident at Bravães, in the figured columns. The beautiful limestone of Coimbra permitted a more delicate decoration and prompted a splendid series of ornamental capitals. S. Pedro of Rates, a royal foundation of the middle of the 12th century, has a beautiful series of capitals decorated with Romanesque monsters. S. Cristovão of Rio Mau displays figured capitals on which scenes of the Chanson de Roland have been recognized, but their style owes nothing to French influence. Funeral art was highly developed, as is evident in the scenes of the life of the deceased and of the funeral shown on the tomb of Egas Moniz at Paço de Sousa.

Georges GAILLARD

ITALY. Throughout the Romanesque period the most technically advanced regional school of Italian sculpture was undoubtedly the Lombard school, which had its centers at Milan, Como, and Pavia; it was the most traditional one and was, in a certain sense, autochthonous since it was directly derived from that modest pre-Romanesque sculpture (see PRE-ROMANESQUE ART) which often is called Langobard or barbarian, although essentially it evolved from the provincial late-Roman sculpture. It was in Lombardy, as early as the first decade of the 10th century, that the trend to figural sculptured decoration had shown clear signs of revival, notably in the capitals of the crypts of S. Savino (restored), Piacenza, and those of S. Maria del Popolo, Pavia. If the earliest date for the construction of S. Ambrogio in Milan is accepted (an argument persuasively sustained by many scholars; Cattaneo, 1890; Arslan, 1954) Romanesque sculpture in Lombardy had already appeared in relatively mature development before 1090 in a great number of capitals: in the aisles and later in the atrium of S. Ambrogio; in the next decade in those of S. Sigismondo, Rivolta d'Adda, and those of the churches of S. Eustorgio and S. Babila in Milan; and eventually those in the aisles of S. Savino. For the most part, all these are zoomorphic decorations in which bulls, horses, lions, and sometimes monstrous animals — drawn from the repertory of diverse Eastern traditions and remodeled to fit into the Romanesque framework — confront each other, rear, and are interlaced in compositions in which the rules of symmetry are blended with unbridled fantasy and imagination. The results are often humorous and keenly expressive. A highly developed sculptural sense is evident in the large bull figures set on a column in the portal of S. Ambrogio; their very heaviness expresses a sense of torpor. From time to time human figures appear. Sometimes they are archaizing (but not, for this reason, older) forms, as in the two reliefs of the Church of S. Celso or, outside this region, in the crucifixes of the parish church of Arbizzano and in the crypt of the Church of S. Zeno Maggiore in Verona. At other times, as in some capitals in Milan and elsewhere, the figure shows a more conscious adaptation of Roman provincial forms. In the reworked pulpit in S. Ambrogio (first decade of the 12th cent.) the difference between the monotonous relief of the Last Supper and the lively hunting scenes is obvious. Although the depictions in those scenes are subordinate to the architectural demands, a fierce naturalism animates the structure of the pulpit, showing that the work has no connection whatever with the art of Wiligelmo da Modena (q.v.; see below), whose influence some have tried to detect, but instead is closely connected with the sculpture of Como, which is best exemplified by the portal of the Church of S. Fedele and by sporadic works in the region of Bergamo (e.g., the tomb of St. Albert at the Abbey of Pontida, ca. 1095) and in the region of Milan (portal of S. Maria Assunta, Calvenzano), as well as in the Lombard lake region. Points of contact have been recognized, and justly so, between this group and Burgundy (tympanum of St-Fortunat, Charlieu), although at Como the taste for the monstrous and grotesque was more straightforward and folklike.

The sculpture of Como reached its peak in the ambo of S. Giulio, Orta (ca. 1118), where the artistic idiom is more reserved and nobler in tone, combining a sense of vitality with a spirit of quiet solemnity that, by adaptation rather than by direct descent, goes back to the Ottonian style. Although in Milan the taste for the fantastic was early exhausted, culminating in the crude reliefs of Porta Romana (1171; Castello Sforzesco), this vein was to reappear shortly afterward in the work of the Campionesi (q.v.). From about 1120 to 1130 Pavia was the scene of the flowering of the style influenced by Anselmo da Campione and his followers; in fact, it is difficult to accept the backdating proposed for a large part of the sculpture of Pavia to 1090-1110 (Arslan, 1943) because, even if the capitals of S. Pietro in Ciel d'Oro could have belonged to the earlier, 11th-century church, those of S. Giovanni in Borgo cannot be prior to about 1120 because of their similarity to the friezes of the façade of S. Michele. The main portal of S. Michele is, in turn, similar to the portal of S. Pietro in Ciel d'Oro (the later church, consecrated in 1132). In addition, the sharp and vigorous carving of the sculptures of the right portal of S. Michele is similar to that of the capitals of the cloister of the Church of S. Orso, Aosta, which are dated about 1133 (and are, therefore, the work of a master trained at Pavia).

The problems remaining to be clarified for the sculpture of Pavia are that of derivations from Armenia and that of the relationships — which may be reciprocal — with the sculpture of the western regions of France. The beautiful capitals of the Cathedral of Parma and some modest sculptures in the region of the Emilian Appennines and in the city of Bologna can be retraced to Pavia. In the sphere of Lombard sculpture, special place is reserved for the oldest panels of the bronze door of the Church of S. Zeno Maggiore in Verona. They are an expression of an uncultivated but vigorous art in an idiom that conforms to no rules but is striking in its expressive force. Lombard style was widespread; it appeared in various places throughout Italy and sporadically in France and Spain, was particularly notable in the Germanic and Scandinavian countries, and made its influence felt even in Hungary and Russia.

This development in Lombard sculpture in Emilia (capitals of the crypt in the Cathedral of Modena, 1099) was nipped in the bud by the emergence between 1100 and 1106 of the great art of Wiligelmo da Modena in the reliefs (PL. 255) and in the portal and (later) in some capitals of the façade of the Cathedral of Modena. On the façade his direct disciples executed the symbols of the Evangelists and a series of capitals in a style that tended toward refined, geometric simplifications; they also did capitals for the north side, and in a vividly episodic translation of the dramatic style of the master, the Porta dei Principi (restored) on the south side (all within the first decade of the 12th century). The spirited sculptor who about 1110 executed the foundation slab for the Cathedral of Cremona and what remains of a frieze with scenes from Genesis also belonged to the school of Wiligelmo; but the four great Prophets of the portal are the work of an artist influenced by him but of an older tradition related to the first Languedoc school. At Nonantola, the Christ enthroned between two angels and the symbols of the Evangelists (XIV, PL. 426), which were later arranged to form the lunette of the portal, are also derived from Wiligelmo and are the work of the same artist who sculptured, after 1122, the architrave of the left portal of the Cathedral of Piacenza. The work of the two sculptors of the door jambs of Nonantola showed a softening of forms traceable to Burgundian influence.

In Modena one of these two sculptors executed a series of capitals on the south side of the Cathedral, on the apse, and inside, in the women's galleries; the other is believed to have created the vigorously sculptured holy-water stoup depicting an exorcism (Modena, Mus. Civ.) and a charming Virgin and Child (Zurich, Kunsthaus). Contacts with Burgundy and the second Languedoc school were probably facilitated by the presence in Modena of a French-trained sculptor who executed in the dynamic style of Moissac the beautiful relief of Truth tearing out the tongue of Falsehood (PL. 255) and who, in a highly imaginative style similar to that of Vézelay and Autun, executed five capitals of the loggias on the sides and apse of the Cathedral and three in the women's galleries. There is great controversy about the date and subject of the Porta della Pescheria, which contains an episode from the Arthurian cycle in its archivolt (X, PL. 253). By some it is dated to the beginning of the 12th century and by others to the middle of the century or later. Analysis of the subject, however, and the forms of the names of the knights inscribed there indicate an earlier version of the legend than that which was made popular in 1135–40 by Geoffrey of Monmouth; further, a stylistic examination of the sculptures connects them with the circle of Wiligelmo's disciples, who were strongly influenced by the art of Burgundy. Thus the date of these sculptures is established at about 1125–1130. To the single creator of the portal, which describes in a painterly style an idyllic vision, must also be ascribed two capitals of the apses and two of the small side loggias, as well as the telamon from the portal (Modena, Mus. Estense). The last phase (about 1130–35) of the sculptural decoration of the Cathedral of Modena is represented by the "metopes" or antefixes (VIII, PL. 171) of the exterior buttresses of the central nave (Modena, Mus. del Duomo). This extraordinary work, by an artist trained more in the tradition of Cluny, Autun, and Nevers than in that of Wiligelmo, is highly original in that its artistic expression is based upon the representation of clear volumes in a calculated and suspended balance. Six exterior capitals and two in the women's galleries are also attributed to him; the holy-water stoups in the Church of S. Giorgio in Ganaceto and in the parish church of Rubbiano are of his workshop.

From about 1135 to 1150 Emilian sculpture was dominated by the work of Nicolaus (q.v.; X, PLS. 327, 328), which was influenced by the intermediate phase of the school of Toulouse as well as by the school of Wiligelmo. Among the works directly descended from the style of Nicolaus are the ambo in La Sagra of Carpi and the reliefs of artisans on the piers of the Cathedral of Piacenza. Here, in the figures of the keystone of the arch and those on the exterior of the large apsidal window, the ornate style of Nicolaus is modified and somewhat stiff. At first this modification was called the "reduced style" and was attributed to internal developments; but later it was connected with the sculpture of the Île-de-France. The true explanation, however, can probably be found in the revival of Provençal influence on the artisans of the school of Nicolaus.

To this "school of Piacenza" belong (from about 1150 to 1180) many other sculptures in the Church of S. Antonio, Piacenza; in Cadeo; in Castell'Arquato; and even (by the same artist as those in Castell'Arquato) the figures on the inside of the large apsidal window in La Sagra of S. Michele in Sant'Ambrogio (Susa Valley).

While this style was spreading to other regions, in about 1170 the activity of the Campionesi began in the Cathedral and in the campanile of Modena. Anselmo da Campione himself was undoubtedly the author of the reliefs and the telamons of the pontile (III, PLS. 17, 18). The origins of this refined and somewhat cold style can clearly be traced to Provence, especially to the cloister of Arles (PL. 246; V, PL. 375). The Porta Regia, the ambo, and other minor decorative works of the Cathedral of Modena show that the Campionesi were still active in the Cathedral at the beginning of the 13th century. This activity concluded with the pulpit completed by Enrico da Campione the Younger in 1322. A series of capitals from the Church of S. Vitale delle Carpinete and other pieces prove the activity of the Campionesi in Emilia during the 12th century, while other workshops of the same origin executed the figures of the Apostles (III, PL. 18) for the old Cathedral of Milan, the red marble altar of the Cathedral of Parma, and some sculptures in the Cathedral of Chur (Graubünden). Other works at Bologna, Verona, Mantua, and Ferrara represent, toward the middle of the 13th century, the last phase of the Campionesi school.

During this period the style of Benedetto Antelami (q.v.), based on Provençal premises, was developing in Parma (PL. 252). Later in its development, Antelami's art was strongly influenced by Chartres. The school of Antelami produced remarkable works in the first half of the 13th century, especially in Milan, in Ferrara (VIII, PL. 171), in Cremona, in Venice, in Trento, and in Bologna; and the Antelami style also spread to Tuscany and other areas of central Italy.

Tuscany did not contribute, as did its northern neighbors, to the forming of the Romanesque style; but after lagging behind until the first decades (and in certain areas until almost the middle) of the 12th century, Tuscany received outside influences. Thus, in the Abbey church of S. Antimo (PL. 221), consecrated in 1118, although the portal and various capitals show the influence of Pavia, other capitals actively interpreted Languedoc styles, especially those of Moissac. Lombard influences prevailed at Pienza and at Sovana, but toward the end of the century a relief of knights at Sansepolcro and the capitals of the Church of S. Lorenzo in Sovicille belatedly elaborated the styles of western France.

A school with its own characteristics emerged in Pisa, possibly about 1140, in the Cathedral workshop, then at work on the construction of the new façade (PL. 222). Although it has been shown (Sanpaolesi, 1956–57) that credit for remodeling is due less to Guglielmo (see below) than to Rainaldo, who did the ornamentation of the three portals and of the cornice under the first loggia, nevertheless it cannot be denied that the school was developed under the influence of Provençal sculpture. The lion of the main portal (whose corbel with a rampant lion within a braided medallion has its precedents in Saint-Gilles-du-Gard) was derived from Provence, as were the moldings of the large arches, the cornice with hunting scenes, and, more obviously, the heavy classicizing ornamentation of the columns flanking the door, which derive from St-Gilles, Beaucaire, and Vienne. Within the sphere of Rainaldo, but with renewed contacts with Provence (especially Arles), was developed the vigorous sculptural idiom of Guglielmo (said, though without evidence, to be from Innsbruck). Guglielmo did the ambo (dated 1159–62) in the Cathedral of Pisa, which was, after 1311, transferred to the Cathedral of Cagliari and there, in 1670, split into two parts (VIII, PL. 181). To a sculptural concept of form Guglielmo added a painterly intensity in the modeling of the folds. The composition has a slow rhythm of heavy forms and bestows on the representation a gravity that, however, does not exclude dissonances and elements of an almost expressionistic inspiration. Much of the sculpture in the Pisa and Lucca areas is derived from Guglielmo: the pulpit in Volterra, the rediscovered panels of the pulpit of Pistoia (III, PL. 19), and the architrave by the brothers Gruamonte and Adeodato in the Church of S. Andrea (Pistoia). The remarkable Biduinus, creator (1180) of the architrave of the portal of the parish church of San Cassiano a Settimo (near Pisa) and of various portals in Lucca, was a spiritual descendant of Guglielmo. Maestro Roberto, the author of the baptismal font in the Church of S. Frediano in Lucca (PL. 257), proved in his vivid and narrative style to be one of the major exponents of this trend, which undoubtedly was being carried forward in Pisa, in Lucca, in Pistoia, and in Volterra by Guglielmo — not, however, without occasional renewed contacts with Provence. It is true that these masters also drew inspiration and motifs from the monuments of antiquity still existing in Pisa and its environs, but it is also true that their manner of interpreting the antique was similar to that of the workers of Provence, who, in fact, gave the Tuscans their orientation to the classical world. Proof of this can be found in the font of the parish church of Calci (near Pisa). Here the motif of the series of figures under arches could have been directly derived from an antique sarcophagus, but in certain aspects it shows more marked traces of Arles than does the work of Guglielmo himself. Further proof of this can be found in the well-known statue of King David on the Cathedral façade, which is generally recognized as showing the direct influence of Provence. The capitals of the campanile of Pisa develop the same tradition (from 1175 on) with lively imagination; and in the Baptistery (founded 1154), along with the Provence-type columns of the portal, there are other columns, as well as jambs with beautiful Labors of the Months, and friezes on the architrave, all showing evidence of the work of artisans with Byzantine training. Byzantine-trained artists were also responsible for the portal of the Church of S. Michele degli Scalzi; however, their work must have begun about 1180, because similar Byzantine elements can be found in the work of Bonannus of Pisa, creator in 1180 of the bronze door (later destroyed) of the Cathedral, in 1186 of the bronze door of Monreale (PL. 257), and of the Porta di S. Ranieri in the Cathedral of Pisa (IX, PL. 508).

At Lucca, in the second half of the 12th century, the Provence-style tradition of Guglielmo was represented not only by the works of Biduinus and Maestro Roberto (PL. 257) and by various beautiful fragments such as the Samson (Lucca, Mus. Naz. di Villa Guinigi), the King on Horseback of the Museo Bardini (Florenze), and others but above all by the sculptured decoration of the capitals and of the historiated columns of the portico in the Lucca Cathedral (S. Martino; VIII, PL. 178). The same tendency was continued (ca. 1204) in the sculptured columns by Guidetto da Como and his associates in the loggias, but died out after 1211 in this master's work for the Cathedral of Prato and its small cloister. A Lombard workshop, which probably succeeded that of Guidetto, was responsible for the beautiful sculpture of St. Martin and the Beggar (VIII, PL. 181), the lunettes (PL. 256), and the friezes around the portals. The description of this workshop as "Lombard," however, is correct only if it is interpreted as meaning in the style of Antelami. The common Provençal substratum of the three trends (Guglielmo, Antelami, and Campionesi) explains the uncertainty of critics. The Antelami current ended with Guido Bigarelli da Como, who was possibly the creator of the main portal of the Church of S. Martino (Salmi, 1928) and certainly was responsible for the pulpit in the Church of

S. Bartolomeo in Pantano, Pistoia (III, PL. 19). Pisa influenced the scant figural sculpture in Florence (early-13th-cent. pulpit from S. Pietro Scheraggio, demolished, in the Church of S. Leonardo in Arcetri), while the Lucca Antelami sculpture influenced the lunettes of 1216 (by Marchionne) and 1221 (but both with Byzantine influences) in the Church of Pieve di S. Maria in Arezzo. The Labors of the Months in the archivolt (PL. 256) of this last church are in a purer Antelami style. The remarkable wooden Deposition in Volterra (ca. 1240) is also related to the Antelami current. It is, in fact, related to the activity in the Marches, in Tuscany, in Latium, and in Umbria of a wide circle of carvers. There were two distinct tendencies among these artists, one a Byzantinizing tendency, which reached its peak in the Madonna by the priest Martino (Berlin, Museen in Dahlem) of 1199, and the other a clearly Romanesque tendency originating from the Antelami style, which is represented by the wooden crucifix of Matelica (Matelica, Mus. Piersanti), the Madonna of Acuto (Rome, Mus. di Palazzo Venezia), the Deposition in Paris (Mus. de Cluny) and that of Tivoli (S. Lorenzo, PL. 258), as well as by the so-called "Madonna of Constantinople" in Alatri, with carved panels (PL. 273) that reveal contact with the Île-de-France.

In the Marches and Umbria monumental sculptures elaborated influences from the Campionesi (Fano) and Antelami (Ancona, Spoleto, Assisi), while in Rome and Latium the marbleworkers were dominant — from the plutei of the Cathedral of Ferentino, by Paolo di Cosma (1108–1110), to the mature works of the Cosmati (q.v.) and the Vassallettos, well into the 13th century. However, the few figured sculptures and the Easter candlestick (III, PL. 477) of S. Paolo fuori le Mura in Rome, signed by Niccolò d'Angelo and Pietro Vassalletto, reveal a classicizing idiom of Campanian origin undoubtedly influenced by Provence.

In Campania, in fact, classicism was not a miraculous resurgence from Magna Graecia (as some would have it) but is instead of Provençal origin, as Salvini (1954) has shown. The Provençal origin of a few single works had been indicated by others (Bologna, 1955; Cochetti, 1956). The Salerno altar frontal (PL. 281) is a problematic work. However one wishes to explain it, it still belongs to the 11th century and to a courtly idiom, somewhere between the Byzantine and Ottonian; thus the Aquitanian-Romanesque interpretation of F. Bologna must be rejected. Not only can the figures of pulpits (Cathedral of Salerno, the left pulpit, 1175, the right pulpit, ca. 1180; Sessa Aurunca PL. 259; VIII, PL. 175; Ravello PL. 259) and Easter candlesticks be traced, in their original execution, back to Arles, but also the archivolt of Sessa Aurunca, which is probably of the end of the 12th century, and the early-13th-century reliefs of the Church of S. Restituita in Naples seem to be derived from late Roman reliefs through the agency of the Romanesque sculpture of Provence. It is agreed that this figural sculptured art fits into a decorative system of Islamic origin similar (at least from the time of the right pulpit in Ravenna, which does not contain figures and is prior to 1150) to that of the Roman marbleworkers. The masterpiece of this genre is, without a doubt, the lectern of the pulpit at Salerno, in which the pictorial quality of the drapery is emphasized by a kind of frozen solemnity of form. In addition, there is the bronze door (damaged) of the Cathedral of Benevento. Probably of the 12th century, it is the work of a great artist who used Provençal principles but turned them to vigorous narration and an almost expressionistic tone. The relationships with Sicilian Romanesque sculpture, which also is derived from interpretations of Provençal models and often has a similar refined classical spirit, are not clear. The earliest Sicilian Romanesque work is probably the telamons of the tomb of Roger II (1154) in the Cathedral of Palermo; these, in stylistic origin, can be traced to Arles and Nîmes and have a sobriety of form comparable to that of the lectern of Salerno, yet they translate the decorative idiom of the Provençal sculptors into an expression of heroic impetus and fresh immediacy. The expressive force of the sharply modeled line in the capitals (ca. 1160) of the Cathedral of Cefalù (PL. 261) is no longer reminiscent of the art of Lombardy but is similar to the figures and reliefs of the Church of St-Maurice in Vienne, works of Provençal derivation (probably prior to 1152, which is the date of the latest works in the Church of St-André-le-Bas, in Vienne); and if the trite and freely narrative manner of some of the capitals of the cloister is reminiscent of Arles, the beautiful one of the griffins translates a motif of Islamic bronzes that had already appeared at Saint-Gilles-du-Gard. The Easter candlestick of the Cappella Palatina (VIII, PL. 173) shows a closer connection with the art of Campania. It is possibly later than the period of Roger II, but it too can be traced back over more or less direct paths to Provençal origins, as can the capitals in the cloister of Monreale, which are of the time of William II of Sicily (1172–89; PL. 261). The capitals of the cloister of Monreale are the work of a number of artisans and are similar in part to the depictions on the Salernitan pulpits, but at times they seem directly related to Provençal sources. And while the holy-water stoup of the church in Lentin is related to the archivolt of Sessa Aurunca, the portal of the Church of S. Maria Alemanna (Messina), which is commonly believed to have been built before the end of the 12th century, stands by itself, stemming in a direct line from the monuments of the western regions of France.

If the pulpits of Acceptus and the cathedra of Romualdo at Canosa di Puglia are attributed to a courtly idiom of Arabic and Byzantine descent, the Romanesque in Apulia can be considered to have had its beginnings with the cathedra of Bishop Elia in S. Nicola, Bari (PL. 269), a little before 1105. This work elaborated with great originality the styles of Languedoc and of Wiligelmo, as did the arch of Monopoli of 1107 and the powerful architrave (now in the sacristy of S. Nicola) that reflects the manner of the Portal of the Counts and the south portal (Porte Miégeville) at Toulouse (PL. 236). In the so-called "Tomb of Rothari" at Monte Sant'Angelo, the Languedoc concepts seem to be modified in a way that brings them closer to the sculpture of western France (Chauvigny, Bordeaux); but the portal of Trani (IX, PL. 508) is more obviously connected with Poitou. Arabic and Byzantine influences cannot be denied, especially in the ornamentation; however, the north portal of the Cathedral of Troia is obviously derived from Angoulême. The influence of Angoulême is also noticeable in the sculptures unearthed in the Cathedral of Foggia after a bombardment (this influence is so clear that it casts doubt upon the commonly ascribed date of ca. 1170). In the same way the sculptural decoration of the Church of S. Leonardo, in Siponte, Foggia (perhaps ca. 1130), is linked to schools of western France.

From the magnificent one at Troia (1119; PL. 260) to the less inspired ones by Barisanus of Trani (IX, PL. 508), the splendid series of bronze doors present difficult problems in the question of influences and relationships. Beginning with the pulpit of Troia (1169), Provençal characteristics, perhaps sometimes modified by way of Tuscany, spread in Apulia in the second half of the 12th century; typical is the portal of S. Maria Maggiore in Monte Sant'Angelo (1198) and those in the 13th-century cathedrals in Bitonto and Ruvo di Puglia (VIII, PL. 172), where unclarified Eastern and French influences complicate the problem. Also unclear is the relationship between the sculpture of Apulia and that of the Abruzzi, where pulpits were the most characteristic production (e.g., Cugnoli, Church of S. Stefano, 1166; Bominaco, Church of S. Maria, 1180). In these pulpits there was a characteristic fusion of Arab, Byzantine, and northern European motifs. There were also bronze and wooden doors and sculptured portals (such as that of the Church of S. Clemente a Casauria in Torre dei Passeri, ca. 1160, and that of the Church of S. Giovanni in Venere, near Fossacesia, ca. 1230) whose ornamentation, at least in part, indicates a Provençal origin.

Roberto SALVINI

GERMANY AND CENTRAL EUROPE. The sculpture of the late 11th, the 12th, and the early 13th centuries in the German-speaking lands and their eastern neighbors shows characteristics that diverge from those of the central regions of Romanesque art (southern France, northern Spain, and northern Italy). With few exceptions the German sculpture lacks completely the important characteristics of the Romanesque epoch — the decided orientation toward architectural sculpture and the corresponding formation of distinct schools of sculpture that concentrated on the specific tasks set by the figured portals, figured capitals, and façade decoration.

This divergence can be explained by the special historical conditions that influenced the development of Romanesque sculpture in the German-speaking territories, where stylistic patterns in great part remained under the influence of the artistic production of the preceding Ottonian period (q.v.), even beyond 1080. Hence there were often found in church interiors movable sculptured pieces that were unrelated to the construction itself. For example, most of the liturgical objects, choir screens, pulpits and altars, church portals, baptismal fonts, and tombstones may be traced back to the Ottonian period through existent sculptural works or via documentary records. Stylistically sculpture remained for a long time (in some cases well into the 13th century) closely allied to the applied arts, principally those of ivory carving and goldwork and, in lesser degree, illumination. Thus, in contrast to western and southern Europe, an art resulted that was strongly influenced by examples from the early Middle Ages. The loose connection with architecture and the close relationship to arts and crafts and also the great variety and diversity of the individual pieces of sculpture sometimes impede the investigation of German Romanesque sculpture.

True Romanesque architectural sculpture was brought into the German-speaking regions as a direct import. The few earlier attempts at architectural sculpture essayed in the 11th century and possibly as early as the end of the 10th century remained without successors. The architectural-sculpture cycles that appeared during the 12th and early 13th centuries in the Upper Rhine area, in the Alps, in the Danube districts, and especially in Saxony were almost entirely the result of a direct connection with one of the northern Italian sculpture workshops. The influence of French architectural sculpture, however, was absent except for a few unusual examples.

The period of Romanesque sculpture in the German-speaking regions corresponds to an era beginning with the waning of Ottonian art in the third quarter of the 11th century and lasting until the end of the penetration of the Gothic cathedral sculpture of northern France, which began after 1200 but which did not completely replace Romanesque sculpture until the middle of the 13th century.

During the 11th century, probably as early as 1000, isolated architectural-sculpture cycles are found in the German-speaking areas. They appear principally in the neighborhood of former Roman cities such as Cologne (anc. Colonia Agrippina) or Regensburg (anc. Reginum) and are manifestly in the tradition of provincial Roman art.

The *Westwerk* of the Church of St. Pantaleon in Cologne was decorated with large statues in niches (XI, PL. 313); the generally accepted date for these pieces is about the end of the 10th century, thus definitely assigning them to the pre-Romanesque era (Wesenberg, 1955). Certainly the so-called "Immunitätstor" in Xanten, which has reliefs representing SS. Victor and Gereon on either side of a large entrance niche, belongs to the 11th century. The whole composition indicates an origin in the prototypes of Roman castle gates, as does that of the double portal of St. Emmeram in Regensburg, for which the date of execution is known through an inscription from the period of Abbot Reginward (1048–60). Figured reliefs centered over the abutment depict Christ in Majesty flanked by SS. Emmeram and Dionysius (Denis).

These early beginnings of portal sculpture, inspired by Roman prototypes, have their parallels in France in the 11th century (Marcilhac in Languedoc and Azay-le-Rideau and Chinon in Touraine); however, although these works heralded the beginning of a rich development that was to continue throughout the 12th century in France, the German portal niches had no successors. In the French as well as in the German regions the early niche reliefs were allied to more ancient monuments, such as the tombstones of the Roman legionaries. From an artistic point of view, German statuary was of high quality up to about 1080 because of its close association with the contemporary applied arts; the Regensburg reliefs, for example, were probably derived partly from the local illumination and goldwork. A comprehensive cycle of reliefs with convex figures on concave, or basinlike, surfaces has been preserved in Brauweiler, though not in its original location. It probably originally formed part of an atrium built under the abbot Wolfhelm (1065-91), and owes its form and style as much to Roman stone sculpture as to the contemporary ivory carvings in the fashion of the Namur portable altar (W. Bader, 1937). Another series of niche reliefs, on the east towers of St. Mauritz in Münster, presumably derives from the time of the founding under Bishop Frederick of Meissen (1063-84).

In the 11th century architectural sculpture within the church itself seems to have existed only in one German province, Saxony. The Cathedral of Goslar (erected ca. 1050; demolished 1819) had a series of statues along both inner walls of the nave, a device that later became a regional tradition. In the early 12th century similar statues appeared in the collegiate church of Gandersheim and in the monastery church of Clus; toward the end of the 12th century the same arrangement appeared in St. Michael in Hildesheim (XIII, PL. 278), where eight stucco figures remain in the north aisle but it is assumed that originally all parts of the nave were decorated in this manner. A similar early-13th-century cycle in the monastery church in Hecklingen should be seen as an independent, Ottonian-derived form of Saxon interior statuary.

Movable sculpture or sculpture introduced into the interior of the church (rather than architectural sculpture) has been preserved in fairly large quantity in the German-speaking areas. Since research in this field has been incomplete and many questions of chronology remain to be answered, the works cited here are restricted to examples of fairly certain date. A relief depicting Samson from the Obermünster in Regensburg seems to be a fragment of a choir screen; a date of the first half of the 11th century has been proposed for it. In the Abbey church of Werden an der Ruhr there remain parts of a sarcophagus and tomb construction that include two standing images of priests, in niches, and 14 small enthroned figures in an arcade. This sculpture, apparently closely related in style to the sculpture of St. Moritz in Münster, was carved under the abbot Adalwig (1066-81) on the occasion of the raising of the remains of St. Ludger. An important early tomb construction with sculptured images is the slab and sarcophagus cover of the tomb of St. Bernward in Hildesheim. The slab bears a fine cross with the Agnus Dei and the symbols of the Evangelists; the gable-shaped cover shows a much coarser carving of busts of angels. That this work originated in the first third of the 11th century is certain, but the exact date is controversial. Extant figured tombstones that date from the end of the 11th century include the bronze plate in the Merseburg Cathedral of Rudolf von Schwaben, who died in 1080. It is carried out in very low relief and shows an attractive courtly elegance, neatly rendered. A stucco tomb in Enger has not been accurately dated but is undoubtedly of a slightly later date and probably is the tomb of Wittekind. Sculptures in the round of the Virgin Enthroned have been preserved from Ottonian times, for example, the wood carving thinly plated with gold (Essen, Cathedral Treas.), which because of stylistic similarities is attributed to the time of the rule of Abbesse Mathilde, 973-1011 (Panofsky, 1924). A similar wooden carving (plating lost) remains in Paderborn (Diözesanmus.) and is certainly from the time of Bishop Imad (1051-76).

A large number of carved wooden crucifixes, some of appreciable size, have been preserved from the Ottonian period. The most important example is one (Cologne, Cathedral Treas.) documented in the Thietmar Chronicles as a bequest of Archbishop Gero, who died in 976. Other crucifixes of the 11th century show their relationship to the Gero Cross (X, PL. 466) in their depiction of the hanging body, the arms pulled downward, and the bent knees. Among these are a piece probably made in Salzburg (Boston, Mus. of Fine Arts) and a cross from Birkenbringhausen (Marburg, Universitäts-mus.). There are other types, such as those that depict the Christ erect;

among these are the bronze crucifix in the Abbey church of Werden an der Ruhr and a crucifix from Münstereifel in the Liebighaus in Frankfurt am Main. Thus in the German-speaking regions an impressive series of 11th-century movable sculpture still exists. The crucifixes, in their artistic independence, are perhaps superior to such works as the Aribertus Cross (Milan, Cathedral Treas.) of the period about 1040.

Other important examples of movable relief sculpture are figured church doors. According to an inscription, the bronze doors of St. Michael, Hildesheim, were hung in 1015. The reliefs of these doors, which show scenes from Genesis and from the youth of Christ, are derived from the illuminations of Tours (see below). The bronze doors of the Augsburg Cathedral (IX, PL. 508) have not been dated with certainty but undoubtedly belong to the 11th century. The flat relief, the representation of single figures in rectangular fields, and the division of the door surface into panels indicate a Byzantine pattern, possibly from Venice. The wooden door of St. Maria im Kapitol, Cologne, belongs to the period before 1065. Its arrangement is related to Early Christian wooden doors such as those of S. Sabina in Rome (IX, PL. 83) and S. Ambrogio in Milan.

The broad influence of northern Italian architectural sculpture may be linked to the various geographic centers that developed, each independently, as a result of the immigration of northern Italian sculptors into Germany.

In the central Rhine regions, forms of the Lombard-Como architectural ornamentation appeared as early as 1100, during the reconstruction of the eastern part of the Speyer Cathedral under Henry IV. The window frames (PL. 262) on the south transept, with their richly ornamented motifs, are without precedent in Ottonian architecture. There is no doubt of their affinity to S. Abbondio in Como; this is shown by the individual designs — spiral tendrils and leaf motifs — as well as the flat treatment of the relief. Further, the antique type of capital ornamentation, no less unusual for Germany, is certainly influenced by the pulpit of S. Giulio in Orta. The architectural sculpture of the eastern part of the Cathedral of Mainz should be considered in direct relationship with Speyer and its Lombard origins. Details such as a centaur capital in Mainz repeat literally the motifs of the pulpit of S. Giulio; also allied to these are the architectural sculpture of the Abbey church of Maria Laach (especially the eastern parts, built ca. 1100) and that of Ilbenstadt (Hesse), which was constructed in the second quarter of the 12th century. Here, from the point of view of time and geography, is a closely related group to which can be ascribed the early stage of Romanesque architectural sculpture. Toward the end of the 12th century a new wave of Lombard motifs reached the central Rhine regions; this is especially evident in the decorations of the eastern part of the Cathedral of Worms, which include the animal figures on the sills of the choir windows, heads and pedestal figures in the same location, and the Daniel relief in the interior of the Cathedral, iconographically related to S. Fedele in Como. Closely related to the Worms Cathedral sculptures are works such as those at Frankenthal and Guntersblum; and the portals of Remagen, near Koblenz, and Grossen-Linden, near Giessen, can also be attributed to the Lombard current. The last two are characterized by tangentially arranged low reliefs on the portal arch, which is without tympanum or lintel (this portal type survived into modern times in local house construction). Prototypes could be the Castle Tirolo in Merano and S. Giovanni in Isola Gran Sasso (Abruzzi).

Motifs of northern Italian architectural ornamentation are common in 12th-century Alsatian architecture. The choir of the Abbey church of Murbach is so decorated; the Abbey church of St-Jean, Saverne (Zabern), has lions on the sills of the choir windows; and at Marmoutier (Maursmünster) there are the characteristic flat tendril decorations combined with the transalpine motifs of the cubic capitals in a manner similar to that of other German architectural schools. The Church of SS. Peter and Paul, Rosheim, shows a diversity of decor reminiscent of northern Italy — reliefs in the apse, animal figures on the outside. The Swiss Upper Rhine area adapted norther

Italian and French motifs and developed sculptured portals more thoroughly than other German regions. Modest beginnings that definitely show Italian influence are found in the first half of the 12th century in Murbach, in St-Jean, Saverne, and in Lautenbach. The designs are still essentially without figure decorations. The portal structure of the Abbey church of Andlau demonstrates its relationship to Emilian works such as S. Pietro in Nonantola (XIV, PL. 426) in the arrangement of its doorposts; but the sculptures, in very low relief with linear incised folds, were certainly not derived from the northern Italian style. Together with the sarcophagus of Bishop Adelog in the Church of St. Thomas in Strasbourg and the carvings of the cloisters of Eschau (Strasbourg Mus.), they seem to be the products of a school of sculpture allied to the local illumination. Other sculptures, however, were certainly derived from northern Italian, more specifically, Emilian models. These include the portal of the Abbey church of Petershausen (1173–80; although there, in addition to the Italian, the question of Burgundian influences also arises); the St. Gallus Portal in Basel (after 1185); and the portal of the Sigolsheim parish church, which may be compared to that of Basel. During a probably somewhat later stage the influence of Benedetto Antelami (q.v.) made itself felt, as in the portal of the church of Saint-Ursanne and the closely allied sculptures of the Freiburg Cathedral, which included the St. Nicholas Portal and the David relief. On the other hand the latest of the Upper Rhine portals, that of Egisheim, which was produced after 1235, turned again to the local illumination for inspiration, in the style of the *Hortus Deliciarum* of Herrad von Landsberg. It is interesting that, on an over-all quite low artistic level, the portal carvings that are independent of French and Italian influences and derive from graphic models show the finest work. This observation may be made of Romanesque sculpture in the whole of the German-speaking area. Other works in the Swiss region that should be mentioned are the statues of the Apostles in the Cathedral of Chur (Coire), which were strongly influenced by the Apostle panels of the Cathedral of Milan (III, PL. 18); and the so-called "Apostle" and "Vincentius" panels in the Basel Cathedral. These last, strongly reminiscent of Early Christian sarcophagus sculpture, occupy a completely isolated position in German Romanesque sculpture. Late research seems to have proved their relationship to northern Italian, and specifically to Campionesi (q.v.) sculpture, and further, that a sarcophagus, reworked in the Middle Ages, that belonged to the Cathedral of Mantua exercised a direct influence (Will, 1955; Francovich, 1952).

Brief mention should be made of the architectural sculpture of Swabia, which appeared late in the period but still utilized northern Italian motifs. All the examples are from the 13th century; all are predominantly ornamental sculpture in low relief on window framing and fill round arch friezes; most of the figures are crude. The most important Swabian edifices are the Church of St. Gallus in Brenz, St. Johannes in Schwäbisch-Gmünd, the monastery church of Faurndau, and the Walderich Chapel in Murrhardt.

In Bavaria and Austria, architectural sculpture as well as architecture itself shows a strong relationship to that of northern Italy. An outstanding example of this association is the so-called "Schottentor" of St. Jakob (founded by Scottish Benedictine monks) in Regensburg. Here the individual motifs — columns covered with tendrils, the braidlike ornament, the highly stylized human and animal figures — are directly dependent on the Campionesi movement, and the crude treatment of the folds, like the allover distribution of the decoration, can be traced to Pavia. It is further presumed that the portal composition may be linked to the portals of western France. A long series of Bavarian portal sculptures, for the most part of inferior quality, indicates the use of the Lombard design repertory by the local stonemasons. Such portals are to be found in Moosburg, Münchmünster, Altenstadt, Straubing (Church of St. Peter), Windberg (Abbey church), and Paring (Abbey church), among other locations. Although the "Schottentor" was created in the last decades of the 12th century, the other examples mentioned originated in the first half of the 13th.

Quite apart from these is the appreciably finer portal sculpture of the same era in Salzburg (portals of the Franciscan church, of the Church of St. Peter, and the tympanum in the Mus. Carolinum, Salzburg). Here again the influence of the Antelami school, brought in through Trento, is evident. The figures, in contrast to the Lombard ones, approach the naturalistic. The most important examples of the spread of the northern Italian style through the rest of Austria are the decoration of the apse in Schöngrabern (the rather crude sculptures are offshoots of the Lombard current; the apse decorated with figures has been related to western France), the ornamental parts of the principal door (*Riesentor*) of St. Stephan in Vienna (the ornamented column shafts), and the portal and cloister carvings of Millstatt, in Carinthia. The continued elaboration of Norman ornamental motifs is characteristic of Austrian architectural sculpture in the first half of the 13th century (Novotny, 1930).

With the exception of Speyer, Saxony is the most important district that fell under the influence of northern Italian sculpture. Saxon Romanesque architectural sculpture (almost all of which was produced in the 12th century) is both technically and artistically on a higher level than that of southern Germany.

Northern Italian motifs appeared for the first time in Saxony in about the year 1100 in the collegiate church in Quedlinburg. These motifs — wavelike tendrils with leaves and clusters of grapes — were borrowed from S. Abbondio in Como but in Quedlinburg were used only for the decoration of the interior of the church. The capital and abutment sculpture also derives from S. Abbondio. The modification of Italian motifs is more decisive than that of the contemporaneous Upper Rhine workshops. Italian themes such as the eagle capitals were transformed into abstract motifs in which the local motif of the cubic capital remained distinct. This process was carried further until in Hamersleben, founded in 1112, the Italian patterns were completely subjugated to the facets of the traditional cubic capitals. A new wave of Italian influence that originated in Ferrara, Verona, and Modena appeared in Königslutter, founded in 1135, where, in place of the cubic capitals, capital forms of a definite antique derivation were used. The apse in Königslutter is richly figured in a *décor* reminiscent of Ferrara and Verona and displays, in a manner unusual for Germany, a prideful inscription: HOC OPUS EXIMIUM VARIO CELAMINE MIRUM SC . . . ("this wonderful work, with its varied reliefs, [will be thought] extraordinary"). It is likely that there were Italian stonemasons collaborating on this construction, in which the technical quality of the rendering can be compared only with Speyer and Mainz. Numerous imitations of Königslutter (Braunschweig, Goslar, Hildesheim, Wunstorf, Landsberg bei Halle, and Hecklingen) show throughout a stiffening of the motifs and pattern first used in Königslutter with such freshness and brilliance.

Thus even an incomplete survey of architectural sculpture in the German-speaking regions demonstrates that virtually all of it is of Italian derivation. The accent is on decorative patterns, with figures adopted only exceptionally. The most important points of penetration — Speyer, Quedlinburg, Königslutter — result from the initiative of the imperial house acting as patron; regional expansion of the art spread from these nuclei. As already observed, the influence of French sculpture during the Romanesque period was negligible. In two southwestern monasteries (Alpirsbach and the previously mentioned Petershausen) there are figured tympanums in the Burgundian style. The architectural sculpture of Trier under Archbishop Albero of Montreuil (1131–52) is associated with the art of Lorraine. Verdun is especially important in this respect (Irsch, 1927), but other than this, French architectural sculpture shows its first real effect on German art history with the introduction of the Gothic style.

An original effort of German Romanesque art may be seen in the figural works (which in essence do not form a part of architectural sculpture) produced locally in the various districts in affiliation with the minor arts and painting. These works continued the traditions of the Ottonian period and occasionally attained a measure of formal perfection comparable to some of the finest western and southern European architectural sculpture. Some of the most important examples may be found in the Lower Rhine area, where during the whole of the 12th century stone sculpture of significant quality, derived from the art of the goldsmith and the ivory carver, was produced. The earliest of these is a screen relief, which has been moved from Gustorf to the Bonn Landesmuseum. Below a plain arcade there are scenes from the life of Christ. The date of origin is uncertain, but it was probably produced about the middle of the 12th century. A stylistic relation to one of the regional groups of ivory carvings is generally assumed. Some reliefs of Christ and the Virgin produced about 1174 were designed for Brauweiler and apparently were carved in a workshop near St. Pantaleon in Cologne. This workshop, which apparently was closely associated with the local goldsmiths and ivory carvers, brought out a whole series of significant works, among them a portal arch decorated with figures (Darmstadt, Landesmus.) from Brauweiler; the tombstone of Plectrudis in the Church of St. Maria im Kapitol, Cologne; remains of an abbot's throne in Siegburg (Cologne, Schnütgenmus.); a retable in the Abbey church in Brauweiler; and a Virgin in St. Maria im Kapitol that was originally designed as a relief. In one case this workshop was given a large commission: a tympanum for St. Pantaleon (Cologne, Kunstgewerkemus.). Other than this its commissions continued to be associated with nonmonumental art, and its style — delicate and full of movement and always in the form of high relief — was definitely a transposition of the language of the applied arts to stone sculpture (Bader, 1937; Beutler, 1958). Somewhat different in style but still related to the minor arts is the tympanum of St. Caecilien in Cologne (after 1174), which shows stiffer and flatter forms (Püttmann, 1955).

In Westphalia there are only a few scattered works worth mentioning. A large relief of the Descent from the Cross is carved in the rock wall of a hermit chapel at the Externsteine in the Teutoburger Forest; its style is crude but not without a certain power of expression. The traditional date of dedication of this work, 1115, is often considered by scholars to be too early. Certainly painting and the minor arts also furnished the stimulation for this completely isolated case (Gaul, 1954). A baptismal font dated 1129 and displaying reliefs of scenes from the life of Christ on its sides has been preserved in Freckenhorst; this work is so fine that it might be considered engraving rather than sculpture. It has been associated with related ivory carving and goldsmith's work. Closely allied to this are the tombstone of Reinheldis in Riesenbeck and the crucifix in Cappenberg, which is a masterpiece of wood carving from about 1225. Its sharp and elegant interpretation had its origin in a foundry workshop, as was demonstrated by a comparison with the Hildesheim baptismal font (IX, PLS. 167, 511; Hamann-MacLean, 1955).

In southern Germany a remarkable piece from the group of the Hirsau reformed monasteries is worthy of mention — a wooden lectern (PL. 262) supported by figures of the Evangelists, which are executed in a powerful, simple style close in feeling to the Zwiefalten illuminations of the middle of the 12th century (Gombert, 1950). Closely related to this is a fine wooden crucifix in Oberzell, on Reichenau. The Bamberg choir screen (PL. 262) is the most obvious translation into stone carving of a style developed in painting; it can be shown with the aid of the Aldersbach Codex (Munich, Staatsbib., Clm. 2599) that its rich rendering of garments derives at least indirectly from southern German painting. In this choir screen the style is certainly carried over in a form possessing great energy and even a certain turbulence (H. Möhle, 1927).

During the whole of the Romanesque period Saxony possessed a significantly independent sculpture. The preferred materials were stucco, bronze, and wood, and the work was principally limited to the decoration of church buildings. Constructed at the beginning of this period, the Church of the Holy Sepulcher (before 1130) in Gernrode has stucco figures in delicate relief, in the Saxon tradition of the 11th century. Three tombstones of abbesses in the collegiate church of Quedlinburg were executed after 1129 and show a stiffening and an impoverishment of the motifs of Gernrode. The rich decoration covering the surfaces of the figures is something new; but an even more compact mode of expression is shown in the stucco figures of the Gröningen galleries and the marble beatitudes from an ambo in the Magdeburg Cathedral. This heavy solidification of style appears in a crudely executed stucco altarpiece in the Erfurt Cathedral that is stylistically closely related to the work of a Magdeburg foundry shop. In the Cathedral of Magdeburg the tomb plaque of Archbishop Frederick of Wettin (d. 1152) leads all the individual forms back to a closed, generally cubical aspect; here the harshness of the Saxon Romanesque style appears in its consummate form. The bronze doors of the Cathedral of Novgorod (PL. 265), although produced by the same foundry, manifest a definite awkwardness in both technique and design. These can be dated 1152–54 (Goldschmidt, 1932). Apparently a bronze candelabrum in the Erfurt Cathedral is related to the same circle and was possibly executed by the "Wolframus scultetus" mentioned in a document of 1157. The famous Brunswick lion, however, seems instead to be the work of a local art group, differentiated from that of Magdeburg by a livelier style.

Toward the end of the 12th century, in the areas of Hildesheim and Halberstadt, sculpture with a new richness in the movement of the garments and a new vitality in the characterization of the physiognomy began to appear. It is probable that the stimulus of Byzantine minor arts brought about this sudden revolution, which was definitely a break with the older development, but a possible simultaneous contact with the southern German goldsmiths' art and the diversity of its design repertory should not be excluded. Representative of these stylistic innovations are the choir screen of St. Michael and the tympanums of St. Godehard in Hildesheim, and of the Liebfrauenkirche in Halberstadt. The remnants of the screens in Hamersleben may also be included in this group (Beenken, 1926). This style assumed an increased vivacity and fluidity of execution in the baptismal font of the Hildesheim Cathedral (IX, PL. 167); it later incorporated details of the Gothic design repertory, generating works of a rich, sometimes floridly luxuriant, eclecticism. Among examples of the later creations of this Saxon Byzantinism are the Golden Portal in Freiberg, the choir screen and the tomb of Dedo of Wettin in Wechselburg, and the tomb of Wiprecht von Groitsch the Elder in Pegau and that of Henry the Lion in the Brunswick (Braunschweig) Cathedral. Further, there are the numerous triumphal crosses in Halberstadt, Freiberg, Merseburg, Corvey, and Lausnits (see GERMANY, col. 213). A school of sculpture flourished in Saxony well into the 13th century and, despite its predilection for overly rich decoration and abundant curlicues, retained good craftsmanship. It was only with the penetration of the fully developed Gothic style — seen first in the west choir of the Naumberg Cathedral (II, PL. 289) — that an architectural sculptural cycle in the strict sense of the word came into being (Goldschmidt, 1915, 1924; Wennig, 1951).

EASTERN EUROPE. The spread of Romanesque sculpture into the eastern European countries may be traced through a few individual works in Hungary, Czechoslovakia, Poland, and certain areas of Russia.

In Hungary the remains of the ciborium of the Cathedral (St. Stephan) of Pécs — columns and panels decorated with plaited bands and tendrils — demonstrate a relationship with northern Italy, but with the Veneto rather than with the Como-Pavia region. The extensive and interesting cycle of figures in relief that remains on the west wall of the crypt of Pécs (late 12th cent.?) is usually thought of in connection with Modena; the portals of Gyula fehérvár and Horpacs are more probably late offshoots of the Lombard school. The most famous work of the Hungarian Romanesque, the great west portal of the Abbey church of Ják, shows a highly eclectic mixture of Lombard-Norman decorative motifs imported from Austria, with a figure style derived from the Bamberg choir screen; the apse also shows a juxtaposition of northern Italian and Norman influences — blind arcade friezes and lions. The chronological relationship to later Austrian works is controversial. A similar mélange of diverse motifs is shown in an advanced stage on the portals of the Abbey church of Lébény. Hungarian Romanesque sculpture, on a low artistic plane throughout, reveals a mixture of northern Italian styles, probably introduced via Dalmatia, with motifs from the neighboring Austrian and southern German regions (Gál, 1929; Dercsény, 1957; Entz, 1958).

There is little Romanesque sculpture of artistic significance in Czechoslovakia. The earlier works belong to the broad stream of northern Italian influence that spread over the whole of Central Europe. For example, there are the fragments of reliefs in Oldřis showing Christ giving a blessing, St. Peter, and a martyr (Kvet, 1959). Unmistakable northern Italian motifs are on the portal of the Church of St. Prokop, Zábŏr, built before 1200 (Schürer, 1929). The Church of St. Jakob at Kutná Hora has on its façade large sculptures in niches comparable to those of western France, at least in their disposition. Here, too, the date of origin is probably about 1200. During the 13th century the influences of the Italian school were replaced by influences from Saxony and Austria. In the relief of the tower of the Malá Strana bridge in Prague, which was constructed after 1257, the assertion of Saxon derivation may be suspect; however, the relation of the portal of Tišnovic to the Golden Portal of Freiberg is obvious, and the articulation points to a Saxon prototype of the style of the collegiate church of Helmstedt. The portal of the monastery church of Mnichovo Hradiště also shows a similar Saxon influence. The splendid great portal of Třebič and a more modest installation in Ilija, both showing Norman decorative motifs, belong to the Austrian current.

The most important work of Romanesque sculpture in Poland and Silesia is the bronze doors of Gnesen (mod. Ghiezno). The style is most nearly comparable to that of the Hildesheim Bernward doors (X, PL. 467); artistically they far surpass the Romanesque doors of Novgorod (PL. 265) and Verona. Originally Goldschmidt traced the style of the reliefs (representing scenes from the life of St. Adalbert) to Prague manuscripts; however, a derivation from the Meuse region now seems more likely. The date of execution is within the first half of the 12th century (Walickiego, 1959). Although these doors remain an isolated example of large sculptural work, there are other works related to the great migration of northern Italian motifs, for example, the fragments of the portal in Czerwińsk and the portal of the collegiate church of Tum, near Łęczyca, for which a direct connection with the northern-Italian-influenced Lund Cathedral has been proposed. One highly characteristic variation of northern Italian and Byzantine motifs is presented by the nave supports of the Premonstratensian church in Strzelno; they are decorated with small figures under tiered arcades. The tympanum of the Church of St. Vincent in Wrocław (Breslau) is derived from Saxon art despite the archivolt images, which in the period about 1200 had not yet appeared in Saxony. A direct French influence cannot be excluded, and must also be considered for the tympanum of the Cistercian Abbey church in Trezbnica (Trebnitz), which shows David and Bathsheba (Frey, 1935; Kalinowski, 1959).

In Russia, in the period of the late 11th and early 12th century, there was evidently an influx of western Romanesque art, especially that of the Lombard school, which made itself felt in two widely separated geographic areas. One is represented by Halicz (now Polish) in Galicia, where the Franciscan church shows unmistakable western European Romanesque forms. Much farther east, in Great Russia, the architectural sculpture of the region around Vladimir (the Church of the Intercession of the Virgin, Pokrov, before 1200; the Church of St. Dmitri, in Vladimir, first third of the 13th century; the Church of St. George, in Yuriev-Polski, after 1229) can best be explained by considering this area a meeting point of Byzantine, Iranian, and Western motifs. Details such as the human and animal masks under the supports, depicted in fully rounded form, seem unlikely to have been created without Lombard influence; further, certain documentary records indicate such an origin (Halle, 1929; Hamilton, 1954). Certainly the tapestrylike distribution of the sculptured decoration, which

during the course of the local development returned strongly to flat forms, is far removed even from such extreme European examples as S. Michele in Pavia (PL. 219).

Willibald SAUERLÄNDER

ENGLAND. At the time of the Norman Conquest there were two styles of stone sculpture current in England, one closely related to the manuscript painting of the Winchester school (and thus a late descendant of Carolingian art) and the other of Viking inspiration.

Builders of early Anglo-Norman churches at first paid little attention to local traditions of sculpture, introducing instead Norman sculptural decoration, which was extremely modest, being confined to geometric patterns and simple figure sculpture applied to capitals and arches and, toward the end of the 11th century, to tympanums as well. The decoration of the crypt in the castle chapel in Durham (ca. 1080) is typical of this early Romanesque style, for which close parallels exist in Normandy.

Toward the end of the 11th century, with a growing desire for richer decoration stimulated by the rapid development of sculpture on the Continent, Norman models were no longer sufficient and English sculptors looked for inspiration to local pre-Conquest art, reviving old Winchester motifs (e.g., capitals at Milborne Port) and looking back to the art of the viking settlers (e.g., lintels in Southwell Minster and Hoveringham and capitals in Norwich).

During the comparatively peaceful reign of Henry I (1100–35) many churches begun in the 11th century were completed and much attention was given to sculptural decoration; not only capitals but tympanums and even whole door frames were carved. The demand for sculpture led to the formation of numerous workshops and regional schools. The rebuilding of the choir of Canterbury Cathedral (dedicated 1130) marks the beginning of a vigorous style in sculpture in which foliage and grotesque motifs derived from contemporaneous manuscripts played a predominant part. Various stages in the development of this style are to be seen in Westminster Abbey, Reading Abbey (a royal foundation of 1121), Romsey Abbey (ca. 1130), Christchurch Priory (ca. 1140), and a number of smaller churches; its influence reached as far north as Durham (portal, ca. 1130).

Another distinct school existed in Northamptonshire (Barnack, 1124), specializing in church decoration and baptismal fonts. The rich decoration of Ely Cathedral owes much to this school but also incorporates some foreign, notably Italian, elements. That Italy played no small part in the development of English 12th-century sculpture is seen in the use of the figural columns in Durham (chapter house, ca. 1133) as well as on numerous baptismal fonts.

Italy was not the only country from which English sculptors sought inspiration; a school of sculpture came into being in the west of England, chiefly in Herefordshire, that owed its origin to a recorded journey of Oliver de Merlemond, founder of the 12th-century church of Shobdon, to Santiago de Compostela in about 1135. He must have had in his retinue a sculptor who, on his return to England, made use of the sketches he had made on the journey, for in Shobdon (and in a number of related churches, such as those in Kilpeck, Brinsop, and Stretton Sugwas), motifs derived from churches on the pilgrimage route are used side by side with Anglo-Norman and Viking decorative elements.

The influence of the Romanesque sculpture of Aquitaine became even stronger during the reign of Henry II Plantagenet (1154–89), under whose rule England was united with his vast possessions in France. A regional school in Yorkshire, which flourished in the third quarter of the century, was particularly indebted to Poitou; in southeastern England influence from Poitou was also strong, particularly in Rochester and Barfreston (PL. 266), but there it was combined with elements derived from the Île-de-France: in Rochester, for example, two column figures (ca. 1175, the earliest example in England) are incorporated into a doorway otherwise related to Notre-Dame-la-Grande in Poitiers.

Foreign influences on English sculpture of the 12th century were numerous and varied. The large reliefs in Chichester Cathedral (VI, PL. 428) seem to have been inspired by German art, while a relief with the Virgin and Child (ca. 1150) in York Minster is so Byzantine in character that it is tempting to see in it a copy of a Byzantine work brought to York by Archbishop William Fitzherbert (St. William of York, d. 1154) upon his return from an exile spent chiefly in Sicily. Strong Byzantine elements in the reliefs from a choir screen at Durham (ca. 1150) are derived from illuminations such as those of the Bury Bible (PL. 274). The importation of fonts and tombstones from the Tournai workshops introduced into England decorative motifs from that region of Europe.

During the second half of the 12th century the revolutionary developments in the field of sculpture in the Île-de-France were gradually penetrating into England; but as they were not properly understood at first, the French transitional forms were incorporated into purely Romanesque decorative schemes. Thus the façade of Lincoln Cathedral (ca. 1145), although it shows some knowledge of the Abbey of St-Denis, is entirely Romanesque. The column figures of Rochester were used as elements in a Romanesque framework, but those from St. Mary's Abbey in York (PL. 266) show a far better understanding of the transitional style; it has been shown that they were inspired by the classicizing sculpture of Sens.

The example of illumination was more important than the influence of transitional French sculpture in breaking the Romanesque tradition in England. The classical trend in late-12th-century illumination provided an interlude between the Romanesque and Gothic styles. The Christ in Majesty in St. Mary the Less in Durham and the decoration of the Lady Chapel in Glastonbury Abbey are examples of the corresponding development in sculpture. French-inspired Gothic sculpture, such as that decorating the façade of Wells Cathedral, thus followed not the Romanesque but a brief period of transition.

George ZARNECKI

SCANDINAVIA. The art of stone carving had reached a high level by the time Christianity arrived in the northern lands. The Jelling Stone (PL. 414) bears a runic inscription saying that it was erected by King Harald Bluetooth (ca. 940), who Christianized the Danes; it also bears the earliest representation of Christ created in Scandinavia. A similar representation of Christ was carved on a wooden baptismal font in Alnö in the north of Sweden as late as the end of the 12th century (X, PL. 136), showing the persistence with which the old Scandinavian style survived despite its adoption of Christian content.

In Norway in the 11th century decorative animal forms were used with foliage tendrils of Continental character, and the so-called "Dynna stone" (Oslo, Universitetets Oldsaksamling), which shows the Nativity, is the first sculpture with Christian significance in that country.

The rapid development of figure sculpture in southern and central Europe in the 12th century was soon echoed in Scandinavia, with the construction of the Cathedral of Lund initiating the development of Lombard and Byzantine forms. In the Cathedral's crypt, finished in 1131, two columns are decorated with large figure sculptures in scenes from the story of Samson. Among the elaborate decorations of Lombard origin in the upper body of the church there are mythical animals and figure reliefs as well as several large pieces of sculpture — lions and cherubs — originally intended for the Cathedral's west façade. A more severe, almost Byzantine, style characterizes a Christ in Majesty and an angel probably originally from a lectern (of ca. 1150) and later (1234) inserted into the west portal. The tympanum relief showing the Deposition in the south portal of Ribe Cathedral (ca. 1130) shows Spanish (Silos) and Italian (Parma) influences.

The sculptors who worked on the Cathedral of Lund during the first half of the 12th century exercised an important influence on native production. In Skåne the narthex of the Dalby Church, with its capitals and large baptismal font, bears witness to a bond with the decorative art of the Lund Cathedral. Palmettes and

mythical-animal motifs, decoratively stylized, were developed in simpler forms by local sculptors of Skåne, such as the master masons Martin, Karl, and the "Master of Skåne," the last being the creator of the baptismal fonts adorned with reliefs in Gumlösa (PL. 267) and Lyngsjö. Unknown masters made the slabs with effigies of bishops in the cathedrals of Lund and Ingelstorp; the latter are related to the façade sculptures on the Cathedral of Verona. Notable also are the granite reliefs of the portal of the church of Rydaholm in Småland. The abundant production of baptismal fonts, especially in Gotland, is remarkable; Gotland exported some of its production to Denmark, among other places. One master, who signed a font in Etelhem, Gotland, "Hegvald," was obviously acquainted with the stone sculpture of Lund, but his animated narrative reliefs and his folk figures are rooted in Scandinavian tradition. Closely related to Hegvald's work but with an almost Byzantine restraint of form is the work of the unknown master (the so-called "Magister Majestatis") whose most important creation is the baptismal font in the church in Tryde, Skåne (PL. 267). Associated with him is the master who achieved the most beautiful font in Gotland, that of the Barlingbo church. In this font (ca. 1150) the figures on the basin are English in style. Other workshops in Gotland worked in a drier, more decorative manner, just as on the mainland, until the 13th century, when the fonts ceased to be embellished. A later master, active at the end of the 11th century, was one "Sighraf," who signed the relief with figures ornamenting the baptismal font in the Aakirkeby church in Bornholm.

In Jutland the fonts as well as the decoration of church portals were usually in granite. Mythical animals and lions of Lombard type played a dominating role here (fonts in Munkbrarup and Tamdrup and also reliefs from the church of Øster Starup). Master Horder (d. 1175) worked in a more popularly decorative style (Vejlby church portal). In Norway, as in the western Swedish provinces, fonts of Anglo-Saxon type are to be found; one of the most impressive is from the church in Skjeberg (middle of the 12th cent.). Evidence of English influence can be seen in some reliefs from the church in Trondheim, which was the predecessor of the Cathedral of Trondheim, as well as the reliefs in the Lunner church. Contrasting with the crudity of these reliefs is the marble portrait head inscribed "Eystein Rex" (Bergen, Historisk Mus.). This, the earliest known royal portrait in Scandinavia, comes from the monastery of Munkaliv, near Bergen, founded by King Eystein (Øistein) Magnusson (r. 1103–22) between 1103 and 1110. Among the few sepulchral monuments with figural representations are the tombs at Husaby (in the stave-church graveyard) and Hällstad, the former the tomb of the so-called "tributary King Olaf," distinctly of Anglo-Saxon type, and also the stone sarcophagus from Botkyrka (near Stockholm), which has the form of a church with an apse and is signed by a "Master Karl" (perhaps the Karl from Skåne) and decorated with reliefs in Byzantine style and old Scandinavian animal ornament (PL. 415). The crude but expressive reliefs such as the Expulsion from Paradise from the Cathedral of Skara (ca. 1140) and the kindred reliefs in the nearby church of Forshem should also be mentioned. In a more sober, severe style the German (?) master stonecutter, Othelric, executed a tympanum for the church in Skälvum (ca. 1150).

Figure sculpture was not unknown to the pagan vikings, who carved images of their gods in wood. A few examples in wood, bronze, and horn have been preserved, all small in size. Even in Christian figure sculpture occasional associations with pagan themes can be perceived; but naturally the themes the missionaries brought with them and those executed by foreign artists for the larger churches were most important in the formation of style for the native production. The most beautiful of the 12th-century representations of the Virgin, for example, are the French-influenced sculptures from Urnes in Norway and Viklau in Gotland. The latter strongly influenced sculptures of the Virgin from the end of the 12th century and the beginning of the 13th in widely separated parts of Sweden (the most northern example is found in the Skelleteå church, Västerbotten). The Viklau Virgin (Stockholm, Statens Historiska Mus.), which has exceptionally well-preserved polychromy, is related to the sculpture on the west portal of Chartres; and although it was long regarded by scholars as a French import, it is now contended that it was executed in Gotland by a master who also created a number of beautiful triumphal crosses in Hemse, Väte, and other places. The most typical representations of the Virgin in the Scandinavian countries, including Iceland, clearly show a connection with western German sculpture. However, elements of English style also characterize numerous sculptures of the Virgin in Norway as well as in Sweden (Hall, the 12th-cent. church; Rö; and Träkumla, the late-12th-cent. church).

Triumphal crosses also show the different lines of development in Scandinavian Romanesque sculpture. An exceptional work is the noble figure of Christ in the church in Tryde, Skåne (ca. 1160), which in all probability reflects the triumphal cross of the Lund Cathedral (lost in a fire in 1234). A softer, more Rhenish style characterizes the crucifixes of Vitaby and Kvibille in southern Sweden. In contrast to these are the uncompromisingly severe figures of Christ in Hall, Gotland, and in Aasnaes in Denmark, and the grieving, bowed figures in the church in Danderyd, near Stockholm, and in Vänge, in Gotland. In Norway there are not only the older types of rigidly frontal crucifixes, among others the one at Grindaker from the beginning of the 12th century, but also expressively modeled crucifixes in Urnes and Giske.

Among other sculptures of remarkable quality are a head of a monk from the stave church at Urnes (Bergen, Historisk Mus.) and a figure of St. Olaf from Vaernes, also in the Bergen University museum. Elements of Romanesque style characterize Scandinavian figure sculpture far into the 13th century; however, this sculpture was stimulated by close contact with different art centers in Germany (Rhine areas, Westphalia, and Saxony) and England. Important workshops of English bias were found in Norway and in Stockholm in the beginning of the 13th century, of Rhenish influence in Denmark, and of Westphalian and Saxon influence in Gotland. Besides crucifixes and Madonnas, these workshops produced figures of popular saints, especially St. Olaf, which were sometimes inserted in folding shrines; examples of these from the 13th century have been preserved in the church of Dadesjö (Småland) among others.

Sten KARLING

III. PAINTING AND ILLUMINATION. FRANCE. From Early Christian times mural painting played a considerable role in the decoration of the churches of Gaul (where mosaics were little used), even during the period of about 500 years from the end of the barbarian invasions until the 11th century, during which figure sculpture had been abandoned. Thus, for at least seven centuries before the Gothic period, when the churches were lighted with the iridescent reflections of stained glass, paintings were the chief decoration of religious buildings (see CAROLINGIAN PERIOD; OTTONIAN PERIOD; PRE-ROMANESQUE ART).

Among the examples of painting that have survived from the early Romanesque period are those in a rock-cut church in Auvergne (similar to those in the monasteries of Cappadocia and in the chapels hewn out of living rock in Apulia, particularly in the region of Taranto) situated in the "Grottes de Jonas" in Saint-Pierre-Colamine (Puy-de-Dôme). These paintings of mediocre quality might be considered archaizing; however, it is believed that they can be dated somewhere about the year 1000. In the remains of the Cluniac priory church of Domène (Isère), founded about 1027 and consecrated in 1058, a fragment of a Crucifixion has survived. The apse of the chapel in the château at Allinges (Haute-Savoie) has retained all its decoration: Christ with the Virgin, St. John and some admirable seraphim, and below, four half-length figures of the Virtues, in rectangular frames. The ruined 11th-century church of Cortrat (Loiret) retains of its painted decoration only the intrados of the triumphal arch, with two angels holding a key supporting a medallion enclosing the Lamb.

In 1945, an important and vigorously executed pictorial composition was revealed during the restoration of the choir of the Church of St-Jean-Baptiste in Saint-Plancard (Haute-Garonne). In it can be recognized the Adoration of the Magi, the Crucifixion, the Ascension, and a Christ in Glory, framed by the Evangelists (who are shown dipping their pens in inkwells in the manner in which they are represented in Carolingian illumination; III, PL. 59) and their symbols. At one side there are painted inscriptions (taken from the *Carmen Paschale* of the 5th-century poet Coelius Sedulius) in praise of the Evangelists. The wide-eyed countenances and exaggerated lower eyelids recall such Coptic paintings as those in Bawit, Egypt (III, PL. 454), suggesting that the artist had seen Eastern Christian works. This group is difficult to date, since bases of comparison are lacking, but the archaic appearance of the paintings and the rendering of the inscriptions suggest a date of the second half of the 11th century.

On the ground floor of the bell tower of the collegiate church of St-Hilaire-le-Grand, in Poitiers — the part of the construction antedating the consecration of 1049 — there were four painted figures, one of which represented Fulbert, Bishop of Chartres and treasurer of this church; only one of these figures, who is shown wearing the lay costume of the mid-11th century, has survived. Also in Poitiers, the crypt of Notre-Dame-la-Grande is decorated with paintings dating from the second half of the 11th century. In the old Benedictine Abbey at Ligugé, near Poitiers, there remain traces of paintings showing Herod's Feast and Salome's Dance.

In Tours some magnificent figures of saints were discovered in 1938 on a pillar of the Charlemagne Tower of the old basilica of St-Martin, which was built in the mid-11th century. In the Church of St-Julien, also in Tours, the west wall of the nave (1080) is decorated with illustrations from the story of Moses. The Abbey of St-Julien had long been an artistic center; about 1029, in the large Abbey of Fleury (Saint-Benoît-sur-Loire), Abbot Gauzlin (1004–30) had the Church of St-Pierre decorated with frescoes by Odolric, a monk of St-Julien.

The largest group of works surviving from this period is in the gallery of the north transept of Le Puy Cathedral, one of the constructions of Bishop Pierre II (1050–73). The paintings covering the three walls of the gallery are excellently preserved and include a majestic St. Michael, 18 ft. high. This is the largest known figure in France painted during the Middle Ages. The saint is garbed in ceremonial Byzantine robes, including the *loron*, a long stole covered with golden plaques and precious stones; with his wings held high, his head erect, and his gaze steady, the archangel stands upright, trampling under his feet a dragon that he pierces with his lance. Skillfully arranged along the walls are other, smaller figures, scenes from the Old Testament, a magnificent peacock, and two confronted stags. The gallery of the south transept was also richly decorated, notably with paintings of Moses striking the rock, of Christ entering Jerusalem, and of the Last Supper. These paintings were destroyed during restorations in the middle of the 19th century, but sketches of them were made (Deschamps and Thibout, 1951, figs. 10–12). These paintings, by virtue of their style, their costumes, and their decorative frames, attest to an art completely different from that of the 12th century.

As at Le Puy, the gallery above the north arm of the transept of the Abbey church of Saint-Chef (Isère) is covered with paintings arranged harmoniously around a single theme: the Court of Heaven. At the top of the vault, Christ sits enthroned in an oval glory, and on the rampant vaults the Virgin is shown in a choir of angels. In the west segment there is a representation of a building crowned with a belvedere above which rises the Lamb, to illustrate the text of the Apocalypse: "The city has no need of sun or moon to shine upon it, for the glory of God is its light and its lamp is the Lamb." The city is the Heavenly Jerusalem, into which the angels introduce the elect, dressed in white. Mention must also be made of the paintings decorating the vault of the apsidal chapel of the crypt of the Cathedral of Auxerre, representing the Christ of the Apocalypse on a white horse and surrounded by four angels, also mounted. Painted during the time of Bishop Humbaud (1087–1114), this complex belongs to the early Romanesque period.

In the oldest surviving paintings the basic colors are red,

yellow, gray, black, and white; a little later there appeared a dark green, particularly in Le Puy. The 12th century was to see the appearance of richer palettes, with the basic colors diversified into tints and shades and mixtures of colors resulting in tonalities of mauve, various greens, and a coppery yellow. Blue was to appear rather late.

The masterpiece of French Romanesque painting is in the region of Poitou, at the Benedictine Abbey church in Saint-Savin-sur-Gartempe (Vienne). It extends into all parts of this vast building: the crypt, the pillars of the choir (decorated with large figures of saints), the columns of the nave (painted to imitate marble), its 141-ft.-long vault, the west porch, and the high gallery above it.

Prosper Mérimée revealed (1845) the majestic arrangement of this remarkable edifice, which holds a position of primary importance in the history of early French painting not only because of the vastness of the decorated surfaces (1356 sq. ft. in the vault of the nave), the unsurpassed talent of the artists, and the elegance of the skillfully contrasted colors, but also by virtue of the variety of iconographic subjects employed. In the crypt there are scenes of the martyrdom of St. Savinus and St. Cyprianus; in the porch there are extremely detailed scenes from the Apocalypse. In the gallery, above the bay opening onto the nave, there is a tympanum decorated with the Deposition, showing the Virgin resting her cheek on her Son's arm in a touching gesture; around this central scene there are episodes from the Passion, from the Entombment, and from the appearances of Christ after the Resurrection. Finally, on the semicircular vault of the nave, there is a vast composition setting forth, in four registers at a height of 42–50 ft., the main episodes of Genesis and Exodus. Henri Focillon (1938) has rightly called this church "the Sistine Chapel of Romanesque art." There is the solemn figure of God the Father creating the stars, the graceful Eve spinning, the Lord welcoming Noah as he leaves the ark, the Tower of Babel (PL. 208), the stories of Abraham, Joseph, and Moses; in all of them there is evidence of admirable talent and extraordinary virtuosity.

Much has been written about the frescoes at Saint-Savin-sur-Gartempe. Their dates of execution have been extensively debated, with some writers estimating that the work was carried on at intervals throughout the 12th century and attempting to distinguish the work of different ateliers in the different parts of the church. There is also the theory, however, that these differences were imposed on the artists by the lighting and by the location and the height of the walls and of the vaults in the various parts of the building; for, in spite of these differences, the methods of outlining the folds of garments, of shaping the faces, and of indicating light and shadow are alike throughout, as are the letters of the inscriptions, which are in the style of the late 11th–early 12th century. According to this theory the painters at Saint-Savin-sur-Gartempe worked rapidly, completing this vast undertaking in only a few years, at most a generation. (For discussion of dating and opinions, see Anthony, 1951.)

When, in 1940, bombardment started a fire in the Church of St-Jean in Château-Gontier (Mayenne), the whitewash covering some old frescoes fell off, disclosing in the transept a cycle of paintings, similar to that of the large vault of Saint-Savin-sur-Gartempe, showing in great detail scenes of the Creation and of the story of Noah. In one episode of the Creation Adam is shown receiving the "breath of life" from the Creator; in theme and style it is much like a painting from the Church of St. Saturninus at Osormort, Catalonia (Vich, Mus. Episcopal).

The largest number of examples of 12th-century painting have survived in western and central France — in Poitou, in Berry, in Touraine, and in the Loire Valley. In Poitiers, particular attention must be given to the decoration of the Baptistery of St-Jean and especially to the excellent equestrian figure of a Christian emperor (probably Constantine), whose gown is painted in an unusual mauve (PL. 269). Mention should also be made of the large composition decorating the vault of the choir of Notre-Dame-la-Grande, also in Poitiers, where frescoes in the semidome show the Virgin and Child surrounded by holy women, in the right bay Christ in Majesty between groups of the Apostles, and, above, the Lamb in a glory between large archangels who are introducing the elect to the Heavenly Jerusalem.

In Berry, the two most important groups are the paintings in the unvaulted choir of St-Martin in Nohant-Vicq (Indre) and the very different paintings in the choir (also unvaulted) of the church in Brinay (Cher).

At Nohant-Vicq, the figures are represented in tumultuous movement, as in the Entry into Jerusalem and the Kiss of Judas (PL. 268). The scenes are not arranged in chronological order (the Visitation is placed next to the Crucifixion of St. Peter), and the palette is reduced to three basic colors — red, yellow, and slate gray; in the faces, no attempt was made to show individuality. The work reveals a remarkable decorative sense and shows similarities to certain Catalan paintings, notably those of the Church of S. Juan in Bohí.

In contrast to the frescoes of Nohant-Vicq, those of Brinay are distinguished by a softness and harmony of tonality and a gentleness of spirit. They include a charming scene of shepherds celebrating the Nativity on their pipes; the Flight into Egypt, with the Virgin feeding the Child at her breast; expressively depicted angels approaching Christ to serve Him after the Temptation in the Desert; and a calm and dignified Marriage Feast at Cana. The serenity of Gothic art is anticipated here.

The admirable figure of the Virgin in Majesty in the apse of Palluau (Indre) was recently discovered. In Chalivoy-Milon (Cher), the Raising of Lazarus, the Expulsion of the Moneylenders from the Temple, and the Entry into Jerusalem may also be pointed out.

The paintings in the crypt of the Church of St-Nicolas in Tavant (Indre-et-Loire; PL. 269) have been widely discussed, and the skill of the artist and the animation of his figures have won praise. In 1945, in the choir of the same church, other scenes probably painted by the same hand were discovered beneath the whitewash. As in the crypt, the faces are violently highlighted in red ocher, and they have the same vigor of expression. In the semidome Christ in Majesty is depicted surrounded by the symbols of the Evangelists and by a choir of angels in procession. In the right bay there remain vestiges of scenes of the childhood of Christ. All these figures possess an extraordinary nobility. Certain details such as the design of the garments and, in particular, the folds in concentric curves (bourrelets) on the breasts of the figures show the close relation of these paintings to those of Poitou and Berry.

The Loire Valley saw the flowering of magnificent pictorial decorations, examples of which remain in Montoire-sur-le-Loir, Lavardin, Areines, Saint-Jacques-des-Guérets, Souday (all, Loir-et-Cher), and in Poncé-sur-le-Loir (Sarthe). The entire group found in this area presents obvious similarities. These works are characterized by a tone of sweetness and serenity, by attractive compositions on brilliant white backgrounds, and by luminous colors, especially the touches of limpid blue in the halos.

Of the Chapel of St-Gilles in Montoire-sur-le-Loir there remain only the three apses of the choir and the arms of the transept, the semidomes of which are each decorated with a central figure of Christ in Majesty. In the east apse, around the large figure of God the Father, the symbols of the Evangelists alternate with slender angels who seem to be revolving in mid-air (PL. 217).

The church of Poncé-sur-le-Loir (Sarthe) was once entirely painted, but the frescoes are greatly faded. The nave holds a painting of an episode drawn from folk tales of the First Crusade: St. George and some heavenly warriors carrying white standards and riding on white horses have descended from the clouds to come to the aid of the crusaders and repel the Saracens.

Cavalry battles representing the crusaders fighting against the infidels are found in other French churches, as in a church of the Knights Templar in Cressac (Charente), but there it is an authentic rather than a legendary event that is represented — the victory won in Syria in 1163 against the sultan Nūr ad-Dīn at the foot of Le Crac des Chevaliers (El Kerak) by crusaders from Angoumois, joined by Knights Templar and Hospitalers.

In Romanesque times Cluny was preeminent in the domain of the intellect and the arts; priories of the great Benedictine Abbey were spread over all France, as well as beyond its borders. Nothing remains of the frescoes that decorated the choir of the Abbey church, but the decoration of the chapel of the small priory of Berzé-la-Ville (Saône-et-Loire), a few miles south of Cluny, gives some idea of what Cluniac painting must have been. This chapel was entirely painted, but only faint traces remain on the walls of the nave. The marvelous decoration of the apse, however, has survived in surprisingly good condition. In the semidome there is a large figure of Christ in Majesty, 13 ft. high, surrounded by 16 other figures. Lower down, at the spandrels of the windows, there are half-length figures of Byzantine saints reminiscent of Theodora and her ladies-in-waiting in the mosaics of S. Vitale in Ravenna. In the left arcade is an episode from the life of St. Blaise, and in the right arcade, the torture of St. Vincent. At the base, half-length figures of Greek saints honored by the Cluniac Congregation appear from behind draperies. At the entrance to the choir are two standing figures wearing cowls and holding crosses; they are presumably the first abbots of Cluny. The abbots of Cluny maintained constant contact with the Benedictine monasteries of Italy. The illuminators and painters who worked for them no doubt accompanied them on their trips to Ravenna, to Rome, to Farfa, and to Montecassino, bringing back such ornamental motifs as the vases containing thorny acanthus and the deep tonalities that set the figures off in such strong relief.

Documents show that the great abbot St. Hugh, who governed Cluny for 60 years and who built the Abbey church, made frequent visits to Berzé-la-Ville between 1103 and 1109, the date of his death, and that he was interested in the building projects of the priory there. With the help of these texts, the Burgundian archaeologists Charles Oursel (1928), Jean Virey (1928), Fernand Mercier (1932), and Emile Magnien (1958) have concluded that the Chapel of Berzé-la-Ville was decorated toward the end of St. Hugh's life. Very different in character, yet both of high artistic quality, Berzé-la-Ville and Saint-Savin-sur-Gartempe can be considered the two peaks of Romanesque painting in France.

Catalonia is known to be rich in Romanesque painting. Roussillon (Pyrénées Orientales), which shares its language and tradition with Catalonia, also has preserved some paintings that are closely related to those of Catalonia. The best-preserved are in the Church of St-Martin-de-Fenollar in Maureillas (Pyrénées-Orientales). On the vault a figure of Christ is framed by the symbols of the Evangelists, who are represented as four flying angels. One of them, St. Matthew, holds a book; each of the others holds in his arms the forepart of an animal. They bear inscriptions taken from the *Carmen Paschale* by Coelius Sedulius (see above). The figure of Christ is set off against a blue background, and the figures that surround Him are thrown into relief on a yellow tone crisscrossed with red lines; the entire work gives the impression of a carpet shot through with iridescent hues. The walls are adorned by two zones with figures: in the lower, the Annunciation, the Nativity, the angel of the Annunciation to the Shepherds, and the journey of the Magi; above, the procession of the Elders of the Apocalypse. These paintings are composed of various colors, with the dominant note being a more or less intense brown; two shades of green and a yellow-orange are also used. Areas of dark red in the shape of a curvilinear triangle are applied to the lower part of the cheeks, giving the faces a fierce appearance. The paintings seem to date from the beginning of the 12th century.

In the same department (Pyrénées Orientales) there are remains of paintings in the church of Caseneuve (near Ille-sur-Têt), undoubtedly dating from the 11th century; at Saint-Michel-de-Cuxa (near Codalet), in the embrasures of the windows of the choir and of the nave there are vestiges of painted decorations consisting of the contiguous half circles so common in Carolingian and Romanesque times and the

medallion enclosing a bird with spread wings; there are also frescoes in the apse of Notre-Dame-du-Vilar in Villelongue-dels-Monts, which are related to the paintings in St-Martin-de-Fenollar. The frescoes of large figures of seraphim with white ocellated wings, discovered in 1954 at Ste-Marie in Arles-sur-Tech, must date from shortly before the consecration in 1157; in the church at Serrabone (near Boule-d'Amont), the remains of a Nativity and of a Deposition belong to the same period; and, finally, there is a beautiful fragment in Esperaza (Aude) and an important group discovered in 1956 in Vals (Ariège).

One of the most important discoveries of the Service des Monuments Historiques was made in 1957 in Brioude (Haute-Loire) in the fine Romanesque Church of St-Julien. The polychrome decoration of the six west pillars of the nave — square pillars divided into four engaged half columns — was found nearly intact. Here a vivid imagination combined representations of human figures, birds, and real and imaginary quadrupeds with an extraordinary variety of decorative motifs — fluting, hollow cubes, diamond shapes, folded ribbons, and half circles — using veritably the whole decorative repertory of Romanesque art. The palette is extremely rich: vermilion, pink, fiery yellow, gray, green, and violet are boldly combined.

Among the decorative elements favored during Romanesque times, there is often found (especially at the base of the apses) a characteristic decoration of the so-called *serviettes*, the upper borders of which are adorned with medallions framing birds or quadrupeds; these *serviettes* are representations of precious fabrics that bear the *pallia rotata* (medallions, often of gold thread, framing various animals). These painted medallions are found in the intrados of the arches (as in the Baptistery of St-Jean in Poitiers), in wide bands on a wall (as in the crypt of the Cathedral of Chartres), and decorating an entire vault (as in the Cathedral of Clermont-Ferrand).

In this brief survey of French Romanesque painting discoveries of late date have been deliberately emphasized; they undoubtedly anticipate others, for the last word has not yet been said concerning this vital, imaginative art.

Paul DESCHAMPS

During the Romanesque period illumination, or the art of illustration, was the most cultivated of pictorial styles, and it played a major role in determining the evolution of styles in stained glass, mural painting, tapestry, enamelwork, and even perhaps ivory carving and goldwork. Thus, in spite of its small production, this art is of major importance (see MINIATURES AND ILLUMINATION).

The book, the tool so essential to literary and artistic culture, was then exclusively in the hands of the clergy and especially of the monks, who, for the requirements of the liturgy and of public worship, made use of texts produced with a care and lavishness in keeping with the respect due them. This does not mean that illumination was practiced only by clerics, but rather that it was produced at their request, according to their wishes, and for a purpose they considered essential and which, more than any other, engaged their concern; the copying of these texts and the decoration of them was one of the chief occupations of the monks.

The fall of the Carolingian dynasty and the ensuing struggles, as well as the ruin brought about by the Norman and Saracen invasions, made the 10th century a dark period for the area that was to become France. Art, and especially pictorial art, was not to be revived until about the year 1000 and was to appear only little by little in divided and varied territories until about 1130 — as a series of local and ephemeral flowerings with only accidental links between them. After the Carolingian period a debilitated France had to learn from her less afflicted neighbors and had to borrow from the English, from the regions of the Meuse and the Rhine, and from the lands bordering the Mediterranean the elements of a renewal that was to produce, during the 12th century, harbingers of the great Gothic style. In a general way, it may be said that during the Romanesque period France assimilated influences from abroad, whereas during the following era, having achieved mastery through experience, she would herself export. It is the diverse currents of those influences and borrowings from the past and from abroad that are examined here.

Influences from the past, those of antiquity first of all, were constantly present through the writings in the monastic libraries. Some of these writings, illustrated with outline drawings, lent themselves perfectly to being copied many times over; in the forefront were the comedies of Terence and the works of Prudentius (348–410?) whose *Psychomachia* had a great success and still exists in many copies. Except that they were made in France in the 10th century, it is difficult to tell exactly where and when these were made, since they are faithful copies lacking distinctive styles. They have been attributed — but without great conviction — to Reims, to Saint-Amand, and to the Abbey of Fleury (Saint-Benoît-sur-Loire). Other examples of this style, which is imitative of both classical and late antiquity, are the treatises on astrology and cosmography by Hyginus Aratus (X, PL. 284), and Isidore of Seville. The drawings in these copies, more or less highlighted, scrupulously reproduced those of the originals throughout a whole series that continued to be executed until the 11th century (see ASTRONOMY AND ASTROLOGY). But the antique style passed the stage of simple copying and came to be applied to works of more current interest, such as a troper (Paris, Bib. de l'Arsenal, Ms. 1169) painted about the year 1000 for Bishop Gautier of Autun; and, in the north, the lives of saints, for which the illustrators found their artistic inspiration in pictures similar to those in the copies of Prudentius: the lives of St. Wandrille (Saint-Omer, Bib. Municipale, Ms. 764) and SS. Valery (Walaricus) and Philibert (Boulogne-sur-Mer, Bib. Municipale, Ms. 106) from the Abbey of St-Bertin at Saint-Omer; and the life of St. Quentin, from the beginning of the 12th century, preserved in the collegiate church of Saint-Quentin. In the same vein, it would seem, is the series of paintings executed for the Abbey of Saint-Maur-des-Fossés, near Paris, where two copies of the life of St. Maurus, patron saint of the Abbey, stem from the second half of the 11th century (Paris, Bib. Nat., Ms. lat. 3778; Troyes, Bib. Municipale, Ms. 2273). Other reminiscences are of the Merovingian and Carolingian periods, seen in a Bible (Paris, Bib. Nat., Ms. lat. 5) and a lectionary (Paris, Bib. Nat., Mus. lat. 5301) painted at the Abbey of St-Martial in Limoges toward the end of the 10th century. These volumes (the latter, at least) owe their decoration to various sources, chief of which appears to be a compilation of Gospels from Tours (Paris, Bib. Nat., Ms. lat. 260) dating from the begining of the 9th century, the motifs of which are combined with 8th-century zoomorphic elements and with figures that faithfully imitate those of contemporary Byzantine ivories. From Saint-Denis, near Paris, a superb missal (Paris, Bib. Nat., Ms. lat. 9436) from the middle of the 11th century appears to have been inspired by works painted in the time of Charles the Bald (r. 840-77), a fact that seems quite natural when one recalls that this sovereign had left his books to the Abbey (see CAROLINGIAN PERIOD). At the Abbey of St-Vanne in Verdun, in the first half of the 12th century, the four Evangelists and the initials of a manuscript of the Gospels (Verdun, Bib. Municipale, Ms. 43) are such faithful imitations of a volume decorated during the 9th century that they seem to have been reprinted from it. But these various residual influences were not intended to — and could not — assure the future: the support of living arts, of original and independent painters, was necessary, and this France was to find among her neighbors to the north and to the south.

From the beginning, these two opposing sources of inspiration, corresponding not only to different geographic situations but also to different political and social realities within France itself, divided a country whose political unification was not to be completed until the century of Philip II (r. 1180–1223). The art of painting mirrored the two wings of this diptych. In the north of France, English art, which was then so brilliant and original, exerted a profound influence on the area along the Channel coast, but the exchanges of personnel and the relationships between one abbey and another spread this

influence as far as Fleury (Saint-Benoît-sur-Loire) in the Loire region and Cîteaux in Burgundy. At St-Bertin, toward the end of the 10th century, an English painter decorated a collection of Gospels (Boulogne-sur-Mer, Bib. Municipale, Ms. 11) in which are combined motifs from both the Reims and Franco-Saxon styles of the Carolingian period (see III, cols. 111–114). Odbert, the abbot of St-Bertin (986–1007), who was an artist of marked personality and great talent, signed (along with his collaborators) an important Psalter (Boulogne-sur-Mer, Bib. Municipale, Ms. 20) in which the silver has oxidized, thus spoiling some beautiful paintings. He was also the author of a certain number of illustrations inspired to a degree by Carolingian art but even more by the English technique and manner, which he adroitly assimilated and combined with a great range of motifs taken from varied sources. This English style is particularly evident in his light and spirited drawing, in black or red, which distantly echoes the work of the Carolingian style of Hautvillers (near Reims) that so greatly inspired the English. This drawing is often set off against a background of blue-red or green and is sometimes bordered in the English manner. At Fleury some homilies on Ezekiel by Gregory the Great (Orléans, Bib. Municipale, Ms. 175) contain a large drawing, probably by an English painter (10th cent.); it is known that Abbon, the abbot from 988 to 1004, spent two years in England and brought books back from there. His successor, Gauzlin, was to receive manuscripts from Romsey and from Winchcombe. At Cîteaux, the third abbot was an Englishman from Sherborne, Stephen Harding (1109–33). He was to decorate or have decorated under his direction a Bible in four volumes (Dijon, Bib. Municipale, Mss. 12–15), the illustrations of which resemble contemporaneous English illuminations and are distinguished by their liveliness, their wit, and a sense of humor unique at that time. In addition, Harding painted (or ordered painted, though this is less likely since the style disappeared with his death) four volumes of the *Moralia in Job* of Gregory the Great (Dijon, Bib. Municipale, Mss. 168–70, 173). The example of Harding sums up perfectly the history of French Romanesque illumination in its early stages; foreign contributions enriched the impoverished art of France, but there were also local contributions (although these did not have a direct influence on subsequent artists) stemming from the presence or initiative of a particular abbot or artist. At Cîteaux itself, for example, a painter whose temperament was the opposite of Stephen Harding's was his immediate successor. This artist undoubtedly came from the south, which had an early influence on the painting of the north.

The first signs of original illumination appeared in the south in about the year 1000, at the same time as in the north, and first, it seems, in the region of Albi. Many details show that this southern art was related to the Byzantine East through the intermediary of southern Italy and even more that of Spain (see BYZANTINE ART). It is possible that Spain, because of the presence of Arabs on its soil, played a determining role, but this is not certain. As in sculpture (see above), there were exchanges between the two sides of the Pyrenees that make it impossible to establish precisely the direction of the trend or to settle once and for all the question of priority. From the beginning, the characteristic motif of the Romanesque illumination of southern France was a special filiform interlacing ending in large flat palmettes with lanceolate tips, the whole set off against a dark background of blue-red or dark green. Though remote in some details, it is clearly an imitation of a capital of the time of Justinian I (527–65) — that of Hagia Sophia in Istanbul or of S. Vitale in Ravenna (I, PL. 379; II, FIG. 793; XIII, PL. 233). The painter, by setting the motif off against a background, wanted to reproduce the effect of fretwork provided by undercut stone, and he may have been directly inspired by the art of the Arabs in Spain. Other palmettes, however, notably in the area around Narbonne, have spatulate endings and recall the illuminated manuscripts of Montecassino. Hence the immediate origin of the motif remains uncertain. Another motif, rarer but indicative of Byzantine origins, is the golden filigree found as early as the second half of the 11th century in a Psalter in Albi (Bib.

Municipale, Ms. 45). This motif can be compared only with that which borders the garments of the Eastern emperor Nicephorus III Botaniates (r. 1078–81) in a copy of the Homilies of St. John Chrysostom that belonged to the Emperor (II, PL. 489). Still another indication of Byzantine origins is the depiction of combats of animals and monsters set off against a dark background on the uprights of pilasters and the curves of arches. This decorative theme is well known from the famous examples in Moissac and Souillac (see above), and an 11th-century Greek marble provides a sculptured equivalent (Louvre). However, similar combats of animals, as well as representations of the hunt (whose origin is lost in the ancient Middle East), adorn various ivories, diptychs, oliphants, and caskets that might equally well have served as models, while the late-11th-century paintings of the Gospel Canons from Roussillon (Perpignan, Bib. Municipale, Ms. 1) seem a distant echo of the capitals with bull protomas from Susa (XIII, PL. 231). Thus the paths by which these influences were borrowed from the East are uncertain.

It is certain, however, that the famous copy of the *Commentary on the Apocalypse* of Beatus of Liebana (PL. 207), painted about 1050 in the Abbey of Saint-Sever in Gascony (not far from Auch), is the Gallic response to Mozarabic models (see MOZARABIC ART). The painter, Stephanus Garsia, retained the lively and animated design, the flat tones, the brilliant coloring, and the ardor of the Spanish models, but he mixed with them a sense of balance and a kind of discipline in which a vestige of the Carolingian tradition, so to speak, can be observed. In the same region of Auch, similarly animated figures of dancers, jugglers, and musicians illustrate a troper in the same Castilian tonalities and with the same lack of shading (e.g., Paris, Bib. Nat., Ms. lat. 1118). As in Albi and in Figeac (e.g., the Sacramentary of St-Sauveur; Paris, Bib. Nat., Ms. lat. 2293), filiform interlacing and the spiked acanthus relate the painting of Auch and of Saint-Sever to the whole of southern art. This is also true of Toulouse, unless, that is, one must attribute to the Abbey of St-Pierre of Moissac a copy of Josephus's *History of the Jewish War* (end of 11th cent.; Paris, Bib. Nat., Ms. lat. 5058) whose similarities to the contemporaneous sculpture of the Church of St-Sernin in Toulouse provide suggestive hints as to the origin of the latter (PLS. 236, 238). The two full-page illuminations that form the frontispiece of the *History of the Jewish War*, especially the figure on the right, correspond closely to the Toulouse marbles in many revealing details: the generally solid and massive appearance (even though Josephus and the two emperors are perfectly flat) achieved by a strictly schematized representation, the full faces and wide eyes with ardent expressions, low and tightly curled hair style, and flat nose. The marbles of St-Sernin recall the statues of saints and Apostles of the Moissac cloister and the similar figures adorning the manuscripts from the same region (Abbey of St-Martin in Agen, end of the 11th cent.). In front of Titus and Vespasian, presented with great stateliness in the manner of traditional iconography, Josephus, bent over as he runs, calls to mind in a simplified but accurate version one of those adoring angels leaning forward in three-quarter view that were produced in great quantity in Byzantium and which can be seen in a beautiful contemporaneous example at Sant'Angelo in Formia, near Capua. Historical links sufficiently explain these contacts of Languedoc with Spain and southern Italy. The pictorial groups of Albi and of Auch (or Saint-Sever), however, like those of the north, had only a local and temporary influence (unlike the groups of Toulouse, Moissac, and Agen, which had ramifications extending toward the center of France as far as Le Mans). Another southern branch, stemming from Catalonia and perhaps even from Beneventine Italy, followed a parallel route and reached Anjou, passing through Poitiers and Saint-Savin. In fact, one cannot understand the illuminated painting of the Abbey of St-Aubin in Angers (end of the 11th cent.) without considering its relationship to southern Catalonia. The Bible (Angers, Bib. Municipale, Mss. 3, 4), the Life of St. Aubin (Paris, Bib. Nat., Nouv. Acq. lat. 1390), and the Psalter (Amiens, Bib. Municipale, Ms. Lescalopier 2) clearly reveal this relationship as well as

the direct and natural contacts with the Toulouse branch. These influences, apparent even on rapid examination, should be studied not only stylistically, but also, as much as possible, chronologically and historically. The undeniable similarities between the Josephus of Toulouse (see above) and the Life and Miracles of St. Audomarus (Saint-Omer; X, PL. 71) can be explained historically too, by the presence, at the Abbey of Andres, near Arras, of monks from Charroux in Aquitaine. It must be remembered, however, that the stiff and fluted style of representation so characteristic of southern painting is not foreign to the art of the region of the Meuse River, as seen, for example, in Liège. Thus perhaps it may be advisable to extend into the extreme north of France the area of southern influence so clearly traceable from the Pyrenees to the Loire.

In the study of Mediterranean contributions to the art of the south, it is also necessary to note the possible influence of Lombardy (e.g., the manuscripts of Bishop Warmund, Ivrea, Bib. Capitolare) on certain southeastern illumination that was isolated in France in this early Romanesque period in the lectionary from the Abbey of Montmajour, near Arles (Paris, Bib. Nat., Ms. lat. 889). Some 11th-century Gospels from St-Sauveur in Aix-en-Provence (Bib. Méjanes, Ms. 7) also seem akin both to Roussillon (the Gospels of Perpignan, Bib. Municipale) and, by virtue of the initials, to Cluny (see below).

Like England and the Mediterranean countries, Germany (see below), especially the Rhenish provinces, inspired its eastern French neighbors. Its influence is found in the Abbey of St-Vanne in Lorraine, in the diocese of Verdun: the 11th-century Gospels (Verdun, Bib. Municipale, Ms. 52) and lectionaries (Verdun, Mss. 1 and 119) from there recall, by their classical elegance, the Egbert Psalter (X, PL. 464) and the Codex Egberti (Trier, Stadtbib., Cod. 24) executed for Egbert, Archbishop of Trier, about the end of the 10th century (see OTTONIAN PERIOD). The same is true of the Abbey of St-Martin in Metz, another tributary of Trier. Farther south, the friendship between Abbot Hugh of Cluny and the German king Henry IV undoubtedly explains the kinship between Ottonian art and the painting of Cluny. The best evidence of this is the manuscript rescued from the ruin of the famous abbey and taken to Parma (Bib. Palatina, Ms. 1650). History also explains the links in illumination between the German-speaking countries and Limoges. A magnificent late-11th- or early-12th-century Sacramentary from St-Etienne, the Cathedral of Limoges (Paris, Bib. Nat., Ms. lat. 9438), certainly relies for its iconography on Ottonian models, and its style evinces both German and southern French influences. This style is very different from that of the volumes executed in the neighboring Abbey of St-Martial, where another style, inspired by the East, is found — rigid, severe, and impassioned in tone. The direct relation between this Sacramentary and the enamels for which Limoges was famous from the 12th century on has already been mentioned; it is possible that Ottonian enamel-work gave rise to this Limoges technique.

Normandy and Paris occupy a special place in the field of illumination by virtue of the variety of influences to which they were exposed and the persisting difficulty in identifying the origin of those influences. The two principal groups in Normandy, that of Mont-Saint-Michel and that of lower Normandy, are unrelated to each other; the first group seems to be linked to England through certain decorative elements that recall the Winchester style, but it is difficult to relate the figures to English characteristics (e.g., the Arundel Psalter; VI, PL. 429; XI, PL. 315). Thus, until further investigations are made, perhaps in Anjou, the origins of the Mont-Saint-Michel style must remain obscure. In lower Normandy is found the first example of French exports. The Norman Conquest of England would be sufficient explanation for this, even if history did not indicate that William of Saint-Carilef (or Saint-Calais), Bishop of Durham, was exiled in Normandy (1088–91), where he stayed with his friend Odo (or Eudes), Bishop of Bayeux, and that he brought back from exile some illuminated manuscripts which he had his painters copy and which gave rise to a new style in England (see GREAT BRITAIN,

ART OF). Certain manuscripts preserved in Bayeux and in Durham reveal identical stylistic treatment; to this group is directly related a series of volumes (whose style also spread in England) executed in lower Normandy in the neighboring abbey churches of Saint-Evroult, Lyre, Préaulx, and La Croix-Saint-Leufroy. Historical links suggest Burgundian origins for this lower-Norman style, but this remains in the realm of speculation. In Paris the talented writer and painter Ingelard decorated, at the time of Abbot Adelard (ca. 1030–60), a lectionary and a Psalter (Paris, Bib. Nat., Mss. lat. 11751, 11550), in which the drawings, set off against green and blue-red backgrounds, seem to resemble the Carolingian art of Reims. But the talent of this Parisian artist hardly provides a basis for the exact determination of the origin of his art. Normandy and Paris, however, were the two groups that marked, by their relative independence and their originality, a kind of transitional period between the primitive and the mature styles.

The 12th century was, in a broad sense, the era of Romanesque maturity, in which France, previously a borrower, created its own style in illumination. Antiquity, however, was not forgotten; evidence of this is an interesting lectionary (Reims, Bib. Municipale, Ms. 294) given to the Cathedral of Reims (a city rich in the influences of antiquity) some time before 1096 by the provost Manasses. It is ornamented with initials taken from the classical repertory (undoubtedly from mosaics).

The south, so prolific until about 1100, was no longer the center of activity it had been, but nevertheless two important works originated there. A two-volume Bible painted in Limoges at about the beginning of the 12th century seems to sum up the essential character of previous southern production. Known as the "second Bible of St-Martial" to distinguish it from the first, which was produced in the 10th century (see above), it shows both the details and the general traits characteristic of the regions of Albi, Toulouse, and Auch. It was executed by an eminent artist who was not unfamiliar with neighboring Spain and had, perhaps, himself given some ideas to northern Italy. A French mastery is asserted here, one based on elements assimilated during the previous era but well enough established to absorb still further influences without losing its character and capable of influencing others. The links with Italy are obvious in certain characteristic details (for example, the supports of the columns) and seem to confirm what is known from other sources about the relations of Italy with southern France. The second great work of southern illumination is in Cîteaux, but it has no links with the art of Stephen Harding that immediately preceded it in that abbey (see above). The painter who executed the two volumes of the Commentaries of St. Jerome on the Prophets (Dijon, Bib. Municipale, Ms. 132) and the copy of the *Moralia in Job* of Gregory the Great now in Dijon (Bib. Municipale, Ms. 173) — which inherited them from Cîteaux — was imbued with the decorative traditions transmitted from Mozarabic Spain and southern France. The severe nobility of his work resembles that of the "second Bible of St-Martial," whose origins are the same. This artist also worked for the neighboring Abbey church of St-Bénigne (now the Cathedral of Dijon), which at just that time had frequent contact with the Spanish princes of Burgundian stock; the historical links thus confirm those revealed by stylistic comparisons (e.g., the St-Bénigne Bible, Dijon, Bib. Municipale, Ms. 2).

In this second period of the Romanesque era the north overtook the rest of France. Carrying on the activities of their predecessors, but in a totally different manner, painters whose style was that of the Meuse region worked at St-Bertin, where all English influence had totally disappeared. Nothing distinguished these painters as a group from their colleagues of Floreffe and Averbode in Flanders (see X, col. 638), with whom they shared characteristics of style and technique that extended as far as the Rhineland. These artists possessed particular mastery in drawing, as is shown by some magnificent specimens; the color, however, is heavier, occasionally destroying the spontaneity and vigor of the drawing. An exception is the Gospel Book (Boulogne-sur-Mer, Bib. Municipale, Ms. 14) of the Abbey of Hénin-Liétard (Pas-de-Calais), in which the coloring takes on a quality of warmth and a boldness that points to future Gothic splendors. The manuscripts of St-Bertin and those related to them were produced throughout the last two-thirds of the 12th century and were marked by the influence of Byzantium, especially in the decorative figures (sirens, centaurs, sphinxes, warriors, hunters) and illustrative themes, such as that of a woman (sometimes the Virgin) wearing the portrait of her son in a clipeus (an example of this is the Blacherniotissa; see III, col. 602).

The group of painters who worked for the abbeys of Anchin and Marchiennes in about the second half of the 12th century give evidence of remarkable virtuosity as draftsmen and colorists, which abilities they applied almost exclusively to the ornamented letter, using many ancient and Byzantine models. The *Enarrationes in Psalmos* of St. Augustine (Douai, Bib. Municipale, Ms. 250), painted at Anchin, provides a wealth of excellent examples. The activity of the Abbey of Corbie continued from about 1130 to 1170; a signed manuscript of St. Augustine's Commentary on the Epistles of St. Paul (Paris, Bib. Nat., Mss. lat. 11575–76) dated 1164 gives the name of the best of its painters, Felix. In general, however, the manuscripts executed at the Abbey are far from equaling in quality those of the other abbeys of northern France, particularly those of Saint-Amand.

The Abbey of Saint-Amand, near Tournai, has left a series of important manuscripts. This center had already distinguished itself in the Carolingian era and was still producing interesting works during the 11th century, but these productions bear no relation to the work, which began around the middle of the 12th century and continued into the second half of that century, inspired by Savalo and his successors (PL. 218). Savalo, a monk of Saint-Amand, was an imaginative artist whose firm and resolute drawing, characterized by full, somewhat heavy but powerful curves, reveals in numerous details his imitation of Islamic or Byzantine designs, no doubt known through ivory carving (Savalo himself was a sculptor in ivory). He signed, among other works, a Bible (Valenciennes, Bib. Municipale, Ms. 5), each of whose four volumes opens with a full-page painting of a carpet ornamented with scrolls of acanthus leaves obviously taken from the Arabic repertory. Savalo also illustrated in part a life of St. Amand (Valenciennes, Bib. Municipale, Ms. 500), which was completed, along with a fifth volume of the Bible, by a painter of whom nothing is known except that he brought to his painting those qualities that Savalo's lacked: movement and suppleness. These qualities were to be further developed by the apparently numerous artists who worked at Saint-Amand-en-Pevele, at Liessies, and elsewhere, in direct contact with the artists across the English Channel. Thus new ties with England were established, although it is not possible to ascertain clearly the details of this relationship.

The fact remains that, whatever the direction of the current linking the two sides of the Channel, the art of northern France as it was practiced in these abbeys is hardly distinguishable from that of Canterbury or of York (the Lambeth Bible, PL. 279; the Dover Bible, Corpus Christi College, Cambridge, Ms. 4; and the Psalter attributed to the York scriptorium in the Hunterian Museum, Glasgow, Ms. U.3.2.). In this art the imitation of 9th-century Byzantine painting and ivories is evident, even in the technique. Particularly revealing of this influence are the rope circles enclosing the shapes. Some of these artists are among the best representatives of French Romanesque painting. One of them illuminated a new life of St. Amand (Valenciennes, Bib. Municipale, Ms. 501), the third to be produced at the abbey (as far as is known). This artist retained the innovations made since the time of Savalo, bringing to them a greater suppleness and breaking away from excessive schematization; he handled daring colors with unequaled virtuosity, and his elegant compositions, whose figures seem to move in a luxurious and unreal world, brilliantly sum up the Romanesque age even while they herald the age that was to follow (see GOTHIC ART).

Romanesque illumination in the north, during this phase of maturity, is represented not only at St-Bertin, Corbie, Marchiennes, Anchin, Liessies (X, PL. 74), and particularly Saint-Amand; numerous manuscripts from various sources (not always exactly ascertainable) show that similar activity, though on a smaller scale and of varied origins, was also taking place at Cambrai, Cysoing, Clairmarais, and perhaps elsewhere. This work, however, was little more than the residuum of previous ages, interesting but scattered. The work of the future, whose beginnings can be traced at Saint-Amand, was to be more clearly defined by a group of varied yet homogeneous artists about whom there is still little information. They were certainly independent from one another but were nonetheless similar in their training. One of the regions in which they worked seems to have been that between Paris and Sens, and one of the centers was the Cistercian Abbey of Pontigny, although certain of these artists seem to have worked farther south, around Bourges and Lyons. Among the manuscripts decorated by them, none is more important than two series of Bibles that are related, sometimes closely, to Byzantine models. These include the Bible of Manerius (Paris, Bib. Ste-Geneviève, Mss. 8–10), named after the scribe of Canterbury; Bibles from Ste-Colombe in Sens (Bib. Municipale, Ms. 1) and from St-Germain-des-Prés (Paris, Bib. Nat., Ms. lat. 11535); and the Bibles of Souvigny (Moulins, Bib. Municipale, Ms. 1), of St-Sulpice in Bourges (Bib. Municipale, Ms. 3), of Clermont-Ferrand (Bib. Municipale et Univ., Ms. 1), and of Lyons (Bib. Municipale, Ms. 410), to name only a few. The first series, that of the Sens-Pontigny-Paris region, had branches as far as Clairvaux, despite the prohibition by St. Bernard of immoderate decoration of books and despite the unadorned style preferred by him. Links with England can be explained by St. Thomas à Becket's stay in Pontigny (1164). The second series, closer to Byzantine sources, has a number of points of contact with the first.

Since the style of these Bibles and their characteristic decoration quickly spread, it is possible to establish that, at the end of the 12th century and the beginning of the 13th, there evolved a sort of centralization, a preparation for the flowering throughout the entire French territory of the styles of the Île-de-France and Paris.

Jean Porcher

SPAIN. Romanesque painting in Spain is of two basic types, mural decoration and painting on wood (altar frontals, baldachins, and liturgical furnishings and objects). Favorite iconographic themes are the Pantocrator, the Agnus Dei, and the Blessing Hand (PLS. 244, 271). Representations of the Virgin Enthroned (PLS. 270, 271), of the Apostles, and of saints and prophets (XIII, PL. 127) are frequent, as are narrative scenes from the Old Testament and the Apocalypse and depictions of the damned in hell. Flora and fauna as decorative motifs also abound. Many Spanish pre-Romanesque monuments are decorated with archaic paintings in which the influence of illuminated manuscripts can be seen; but the mural painting of Spain was derived from a long tradition that had continued (although sporadically) from classical antiquity.

The most common technique in mural painting combined fresco and tempera; first the fresh, soft plaster was painted with solid colors, then the details and the outlines were done in tempera, with black and white used to obtain a suggestion of dimension. Color schemes were confined to those obtained with earth pigments: red, bister, yellow ocher, and green. By juxtaposing lampblack with chalk white or by mixing the two, a variety of hues, tints, and shades was obtained; occasionally, however, exotic colors are found, such as vivid red, carmine, blue, sharp green, and orange-yellow.

In the first quarter of the 12th century mural decoration achieved a remarkably high development in Spain; two main trends appeared that, despite many intermediate strains, were clearly differentiated. One, which appears to be of Byzantine origin, is distinguished by its structural severity, geometric design, decorative interpretation of physiognomic outlines, and the predominance of verticality and of the law of frontality. The other, with obvious influences from Carolingian art, derives from autochthonous illuminations and is characterized by an animated narrative style, free-flowing lines, and a tendency toward the fantastic. This last factor emerges in a particularly masterful way in works influenced by Mozarabic miniatures, which were exceptionally rich in depictions of fabulous fauna.

Three great painters of Catalonia belong to the first-mentioned trend: these were the masters of Tahull, Maderuelo, and Pedret. The masters of Tahull and of Maderuelo, after working in churches in the province of Lérida, in the area where it borders Aragon, went, respectively, to Aragon and to Castile. The Master of Tahull, one of the most important artists of Romanesque painting in Europe, decorated (1123) the Church of S. Clemente in Tahull (PL. 271) with forms of supreme clarity and expressiveness and with magnificent colors; later he decorated a lateral apse of the Cathedral in Roda de Isábena (Huesca). The Master of Maderuelo painted in the Church of S. María in Tahull (PL. 270), in a style very close to that of the Master of Tahull and of the same date, and after that he worked in the Hermitage of S. Baudilio (or Baudel; X, PL. 196), a Mozarabic edifice near Casillas de Berlanga (Soria), and in the nearby Church of the Holy Cross in Maderuelo (Segovia; VII, PL. 375). Frescoes removed from S. Baudilio are now in New York (Met. Mus., The Cloisters), in Boston (Mus. of Fine Arts), in Indianapolis (John Herron Art Mus.), in the Prado, and in private collections. The Master of Pedret worked in a region extending from Berga (Barcelona) to the Valley of Arán (Lérida); within his marked Byzantinism the ascendancy of the pictorial quality over schematic linearity is surprising. His figures are exquisitely drawn in brilliant colors, with carmine, vermilion, gray, green, and yellow predominating. This artist worked at Ager, Pedret, Esterri de Aneu, Tredós (fresco from the Church of S. Juan, now in Met. Mus., The Cloisters), and in the Monastery of S. Pedro de Burgal near Escaló.

In the pictorial works of the 12th century in Catalonia, most of which are preserved in the Museo de Bellas Artes de Cataluña in Barcelona, there are many artists of interest. Among these must be mentioned the very archaizing Master of Bohí, who in the Church of S. Juan in Bohí (Lérida) illustrated the prophecies of Daniel and the Stoning of St. Stephen with great liveliness, achieving striking lighting and spatial effects; the Master of the Last Judgment, who painted the naves of S. María in Tahull (PL. 272) with narrative scenes; the creator of the paintings from the apse of S. María de Mur (Boston, Mus. of Fine Arts); and the Master of Urgel, who decorated the church of S. Pedro, which is annexed to the Cathedral of Seo de Urgel (PL. 271), and whose influence may be seen in various churches and in panel paintings.

The second of the above-mentioned trends is represented in the eastern section of Catalonia during the second half of the 12th century in the work of the Master of Roussillon in L'Ecluse and in St-Martin-de-Fenollar (see above); in the work of the Master of Polinyá, which shows Italo-Byzantine influence; and in the work of the Master of Osormort, who worked in the districts of Vich and Gerona. The Master of Espinelvas decorated (last quarter of the 12th cent.) a lateral apse in S. María in Tarrasa dedicated to Thomas à Becket.

Aragon possesses few mural paintings dating from before 1200; the work of the Master of Tahull in Roda de Isábena (Huesca) has already been mentioned. In Castile some paintings of great interest exist, such as the afore-mentioned ones of Casillas de Berlanga and Maderuelo and also those of the Chapel of S. Pelayo de Perazancas and of the churches of Tubilla del Agua and San Estaban de Gormaz. In S. Baudilio at Casillas de Berlanga, the Master of Maderuelo worked with the Master of S. Baudilio, whose work was more Mozarabic than Byzantine in style. The famous hunting scenes and the figures of fantastic animals, executed in clear tones on backgrounds of vivid red, were painted by the Master of S. Baudilio.

In León the most complete series of Spanish Romanesque frescoes is found in the Panteón de los Reyes of S. Isidoro (PL. 243). These were executed during the reign of Ferdinand II (1157–88), who is depicted in one of the frescoes. These paintings show undeniable French influence. Gómez-Moreno (1934) demonstrated the stylistic affinity of these paintings with certain French illuminations that were in the library (destroyed by fire) of S. Isidoro; it is a style that is primarily characterized by its sense of life and movement, qualities that are directly opposite to the Byzantine hieratic tradition. French influence is even more evident in the above-mentioned frescoes of S. Pelayo de Perazancas.

In the last quarter of the 12th century a neo-Byzantine trend began, represented in Catalonia by the Master of Llussanés, one of the few Romanesque painters who executed both frescoes and panel paintings. During the same period a tendency toward free lines was developing in works such as those in the lateral apse of the Cathedral of Seo de Urgel (PL. 367) and the murals in the Tinell, or great hall, of the Palacio Real Mayor in Barcelona. In Aragon this trend produced an extraordinary mural decoration in the chapter house of the Convent of Sigena (seriously damaged in 1936). This work was executed by an artist who evidently was a foreigner — an Italian or an Englishman; it is stylistically related to English illuminations of the early 13th century.

The progress toward the Gothic is represented by a group of works in the province of Huesca — S. Miguel de Foces in Ibieca, S. Fructuoso in Bierge, Nuestra Señora del Monte in Liesa, S. Miguel in Barluenga, and the Cathedral of Roda de Isábena — and also the murals of Nuestra Señora de Cabañas near La Almunia de Doña Godina (Saragossa). Most of these works are of the 13th century and were executed in a combination of fresco and secco, with pigments mixed with linseed oil. In Navarra, also, works of this century are comparatively plentiful; of particular interest is the production of the Master of Artajona, who worked in the town of that name, in S. Pedro in Olite, and in Artaiz (paintings preserved in Pamplona, Mus. de la Diputación de Navarra), and in the apse of the convent church of Sigena (Huesca). To this same stylistic group belong the paintings in the Church of S. Juan Uncastillo. In Galicia the frescoes of the Church of S. Martín de Mondoñedo anticipate the transition to the Gothic style. In Castile and León the neo-Byzantine style of the 13th century is evident in only a few murals, among them the frescoes of the Monastery of S. Pedro de Arlanza (two sections in Met. Mus., The Cloisters), possibly the work of the master who decorated the chapter house at Sigena, and those of the Church of Vileña (Burgos). In León there are few examples of the style transitional to the Gothic, but the paintings (badly preserved) that completed the Panteón de los Reyes and those of the Capilla de los Quiñones in S. Isidoro should be mentioned, as well as the mural paintings of S. Pedro in Alcazarén (Valladolid) and those in the tower of the so-called "Casa de Hércules" in Segovia.

According to the identification of the artists and the geographical location of these paintings, it appears that the creators of these murals traveled constantly to places where the construction of churches and other buildings had been completed and decoration was to begin. The possibility is strong that some of them were foreigners who brought with them elements of the Byzantine style or of its Italian or French interpretations (see BYZANTINE ART). However, a common denominator does exist in these paintings — a Spanish spirit strongly impregnated with Mozarabic art (q.v.).

Panel paintings generally appear in the same regions as the frescoes, but are most widespread in Catalonia. The heavy panels, of rectangular shape for altar frontals (PL. 271) and square for baldachins, were covered with a coating of gesso and then painted over with egg tempera, producing a hard surface with the brilliant qualities of enamel. The palette included white, black, yellow ocher, red vermilion, carmine, green, burnt sienna, and two shades of blue, but the color harmony was usually based on simple, intense effects in which red and yellow predominated. The same influences, that is, the Mozarabic, the Byzantine, and the Carolingian, prevailed as are found in mural painting. The works were products of settled artists in local workshops, where religious images and furniture were also produced; the best known of these in Catalonia were in Seo de Urgel, Ripoll, Vich, and Lérida. Many of these works are now preserved in Barcelona (Mus. de Bellas Artes de Cataluña) and Vich (Mus. Episcopal). In Aragon groups having unified styles were formed in Huesca, around Sigena, and in the southern part of the region. During the 13th century the same developments occurred as in mural painting, but,

in addition, a technical innovation was introduced: the imitation of goldwork, achieved by a mixture of gesso paste with gold varnish and varnish. Altar frontals of carved wood or of polychromed gesso in relief appear frequently; the iconography resembles that of the frescoes, but representations of the Virgin (XIII, PL. 125) and the saints are more common. Exemplifying the style of Byzantine origin is the splendid baldachin from Ribas (PL. 244), whose influence can be seen in the altar frontals of Seo de Urgel, San Saturnino de Tabérnolas (Lérida), and Sagós (XIII, PL. 127). In Vich a group of altar frontals exists deriving from the illuminations of the local scriptorium (see below). The neo-Byzantine trend is represented by the work of the Master of Llussanés, who was mentioned in connection with wall painting at the end of the 12th century, and also by the master who worked at Valltarga (altar frontal, Barcelona, Mus. de Bellas Artes de Cataluña) and Oreilla in Roussillon (altar frontal *in situ* there). The transition to the Gothic style is illustrated in the paintings by the Master of Soriguerola (frontal in Barcelona, Mus. de Bellas Artes de Cataluña).

Aragonese examples include the altar frontal of Berbegal (Lérida, Mus. Diocesano) and the chest for vestments in the church of Daroca. Some Castilian examples are the large polychrome reliquary in the Archbishop's Palace in Astorga and a fragment of an altar panel with the figure of St. Paul in Ávila (Cath. Mus.). The transition to the Gothic style is shown in the magnificent representation of a funeral procession on the wooden sarcophagus of Sancho Saiz de Carillo from Mahamud, Burgos (Barcelona, Mus. de Bellas Artes de Cataluña), dating from the end of the 13th century. The life and emotion expressed within the schematized formula is extraordinary.

In Majorca the Master of Palma worked in the period of the late 13th–early 14th century; his style is related to that of the frescoes in the Tinell of the Palacio Real Mayor in Barcelona. Until the middle of the 13th century large sections of the regions of Estremadura, Andalusia, Murcia, and Valencia were under the dominion of Islam; therefore there is no Romanesque painting from these areas.

José GUIDOL

During the 11th century Spanish illumination, which had reached its highest expression in Mozarabic art, underwent a profound change after absorbing new elements, primarily from France, as a result of the spread of the Cluny influence and of the close relations between the kings of Navarra and the French sovereigns. The monasteries continued to be the centers of production, among them S. María in Ripoll (Catalonia) and the Benedictine Abbey at San Millán de la Cogolla (Old Castile). In Catalonia (the old Spanish March) new forms of a predominantly Western character arose, and the Carolingian minuscule, which gradually replaced the Mozarabic and Visigothic scripts, was diffused. Consequently there was a change in the decoration of the initial letters, which now became fantastic compositions with intertwined birds, leaves, human figures, and monsters, similar to those in fashion in French illumination.

The manuscripts dating from the beginning of the 11th century produced in the Spanish March (which included Vich) are far removed from the refined arabesques of the Mozarabic manuscripts. The Biblical scenes depicted are in freer and livelier forms, and the colors are less bright but more varied. Two surviving examples are the Bible of San Pedro de Roda (Paris, Bib. Nat., Ms. lat. 6; also known as the Noailles Bible), and the Farfa Bible (Rome, Vat. Lib., Vat. lat. 5729; also known as the Ripoll Bible). They were probably executed during the time that Abbot Oliva was bishop of Vich (early 11th cent.). Story cycles such as that of Tobias are illustrated for the first time in these Bibles. The iconographic motifs of widely varying origins (Carolingian, Ottonian, Islamic, and Coptic) lead to the assumption (Neuss, 1922) that the illuminators had older Bibles at their disposal and borrowed freely from them. A confirmation of this hypothesis appears to be provided by some resemblances to the much earlier Ashburnham Pentateuch (see X, cols. 132–33). The novelty of these codices lies in the decidedly Western character of the illuminations, which, although the work of several artists, are stylistically consistent and have a Romanesque quality that is clearly opposed to the decorative tendency bordering on the abstract typical of Mozarabic illuminations. Another contrast with Mozarabic illumination is provided by the depiction of architectural elements, executed with the particular sense of perspective that is found in the Ottonian codices.

During the 11th and 12th centuries the Mozarabic style was continued in many copies of the commentary on the Apocalypse by Beatus of Liebana, such as those of San Millán de la Cogolla (PL. 279), of Ferdinand I (Madrid, Bib. Nac., Ms. Vitrina 14.2), of Seo de Urgel (X, PL. 73), and of Silos (Br. Mus., Add. ms. 11695), and in some Bibles, such as the one in León (1162; S. Isidoro). The new stylistic movement had already become established in Léon with the Diurnal of Queen Sancha (1055; Santiago de Compostela, Bib. de la Univ.) and was continued in the Spanish March with St. Gregory's *Moralia in Job* (Gerona, Mus. Diocesano), the Evangelistary in Perpignan (Bib. Municipale), and the Venerable Bede's Homilies (Gerona, Mus. Diocesano). But even in those Beatus manuscripts that, according to Neuss (1922) are related to the "Apocalypse of Saint-Sever" (PL. 207) the artists accepted new elements. Thus, in the Bible signed by Martinus, in the Cathedral of Burgo de Osma (1086), initials of the Montecassino type and Byzantine-style touches in the figures appear. French influence is obvious in the Beatus Apocalypse of San Pedro de Cardeña, which is dispersed among various museums (Madrid, Mus. Arqueol. Nac.; Paris, Bib. Nat., Nouv. Acq. lat. 1366; etc.).

Spanish Romanesque miniature painting reached its full maturity in the 12th century. The *Libro de los Testamentos* (a collection of deeds and donations) in Oviedo (Cath. Archives) was compiled between 1126 and 1129. The figures and compositional sense of the magnificent full-page illustrations have the same abstract quality and inherent sublimity that are found in the frescoes, such as those in Seo de Urgel. The master responsible for the scenes from the Life of Christ in the Farfa Bible perhaps inspired the illuminator who in the 12th–13th century added some illustrations to the Avila Bible (Madrid, Bib. Nac.), which probably came from Sicily (cf. the scene of Doubting Thomas in both manuscripts). However, in the Avila Bible there is a strong emphasis on the miniatures themselves, resulting from the greatly enlarged figure of Christ in the various scenes. The lectionary from the Monastery of S. Domingo de Silos (Paris, Bib. Nat., Nouv. acq. lat. 2171) belongs to the same sphere. The Huesca Bible (Madrid, Mus. Arqueol. Nac.) was influenced mainly by French models.

Trans-Pyrenean influences are also apparent in two codices in Barcelona (Archivo de la Corona de Aragón): the *Liber Feudorum Maior* (Cod. 1), a chartulary begun in the reign of Alfonso II of Aragon (1162–96) and continued in the 13th century, and the *Liber Feudorum Ceritaniae*, containing copies of documents pertaining to Cerdagne, which was ordered by Alfonso II, carried on during the reign of Pedro II (1196–1213), and finished in 1241. In both books some of the scenes presage the Gothic style, as do the miniatures in the Beatus Apocalypse from Spain (2d half of 12th cent.–13th cent.; now in Manchester, John Rylands Lib., Ms. lat. 8) and in the *Libro de las Estampas* in León Cathedral (13th cent.).

ITALY. Romanesque painting in Italy presents a complicated and varied picture because of the geographic location of the Italian peninsula and because of its history. Venice and southern Italy were in direct contact with Byzantium and the East, northern Italy was open to influences from northern Europe, and central Italy, especially Umbria and Latium, in a certain sense remained immured in its ancient traditions. Thus different tendencies met and blended in works (often isolated) that, especially in the 11th century, are difficult to classify and date. The presence of Byzantine mosaicists and the renewal of influences from Byzantium made it difficult to overcome the Byzantine style.

In Lombardy and Piedmont some cycles of 11th-century frescoes can be considered a transition from the Ottonian to the Romanesque. The date of the first cycle, that in S. Vincenzo at Galliano, is certain. In 1007 the church was consecrated after its restoration by Aribertus of Intimiano (Ansaldi, 1949). The frescoes in the nave depict scenes from the lives of SS. Christopher and Margaret and Biblical scenes of Samson and of Adam and Eve. In the apse is the standing figure of Christ (XI, PL. 324) with kneeling figures of the prophets Ezekiel and Jeremiah and the Archangel Michael (PL. 254) behind Jeremiah. Below are scenes from the life of St. Vincent. (The fresco depicting Aribertus offering the model of the church to Christ was detached and removed to Milan, Pin. Ambrosiana.) The frescoes were executed by more than one painter and in the same period. The vigorous modeling of the faces, obtained by powerful contrasts of color and white highlights, the majesty of the figures contained within strong outlines, and the clothing that, although it reveals Byzantine influences in the way the folds are painted, has an unusual fullness and gives body to the figures, indicate artists who were familiar with Ottonian models, especially those of Reichenau. However, these artists were able to achieve a majesty in which the influence of Early Christian mosaics does not seem foreign and which in itself influenced the later frescoes of Saint-Savin-sur-Gartempe (PL. 208) in France (Francovich, 1955). Galliano constitutes a fixed reference point and, during the first half of the 11th century, are included within its sphere the less forceful frescoes in S. Fedelino at Novate Mezzola.

Of the same artistic koine, but of a different current, are the fragments in SS. Pietro e Orso in Aosta, which can be dated, on the basis of what Gabrielli (1944) reports, to the first quarter of the 11th century. Bologna (1962) suggests the end of the 10th century; Grabar (1949), the 12th century, comparing Aosta to Vich and to Bohí (this suggestion, however, does not seem acceptable for stylistic reasons). The scenes are powerful and expressive; and the figures, executed in thick, heavy colors, are wrapped in large cords simulating folds that, in their circular movement, create an almost sculptural effect. The faces are not elongated but round, and it is this fact perhaps that has led to the insistence that their derivation is from Münster (Bologna, 1962). However, the wide-open round eyes under deeply arched eyebrows and the rise of color in the cheeks also suggest a connection with Ottonian art in one of its typical Lombard interpretations. The paintings in Aosta, more provincial than those in Galliano, have an originality and narrative quality that can be considered Romanesque. It seems possible that the head of Eve, and other fragments in S. Maria di Castelvecchio in Mongrando, may be related to the paintings in Aosta because of the heavy and thick style of the short strokes.

The great cycle in S. Michele at Oleggio, built between 1050 and 1075, was painted by several artists. The scenes of saints in the central nave are reminiscent of Galliano, but their execution is more delicate and their color more mellow. It is primarily in the imposing figures of the deacons that the luminous highlights are subdued into gradual passages of color; and the artists of the Christ, of the delicate angels of the apses, and, above all, of the Last Judgment — which is very similar in iconography to that of the Gospel Book in Paris (Bib. Nat., Ms. gr. 74) — show that they were receptive to the new wave of Byzantine influence. Also in the Lombard school are the frescoes in S. Carlo in Prugiasco, Switzerland. They are probably from the middle of the 11th century (although some scholars consider them to be of a later date) and Christ and the apostles are executed with an abstract linear feeling similar to that of the Christ between two saints on the entrance door of S. Pietro al Monte in Civate. On the interior of this church the second notable Lombard cycle of the 11th century is found. The date of 1093 suggested for this cycle by Bognetti and Marcora (1957) seems to be the most likely one. The complex reveals a vigorous revival of Ottonian elements, especially in its iconography; but it has a completely new feeling, the result of a blending with Byzantine elements that are very different from those of the previously mentioned frescoes. The workmanship seems varied; the artist responsible for the scene of the angels killing the dragon (PL. 275) chose, in the Byzantine trend of his period, that particular transhumanized liveliness, while the artist responsible for Christ and for the Lamb appears to have been influenced by the very much older frescoes of Castelseprio (II, PL. 445), from which he derived the ecstatic Redeemer among towering green trees framed by the city wall with figures leaning over it. This theme was very common in Ottonian iconography and was derived from late-antique models. Civate seems to be the most "cultured" and therefore the most isolated of the Lombard cycles. Didactic and symbolic aims are linked together compactly and concisely in the appearance of choruses of angels grouped in threes, in the representation of the Trinity, in the theme of salvation and the defeat of evil promised by the prophetic visions of the Old Testament, in the realization of this theme in the figure of the Redeemer, in the Four Rivers of Paradise, and in the miracles performed by the saints. Related to the frescoes in Civate, but of inferior quality, are the frescoes in S. Giorgio in Como, dated 1084 by Toesca (1912).

Frescoes in Lombardy from the early part of the 12th century are scarce. The fragments in Milan (S. Ambrogio, S. Celso) and in Pavia (crypts of S. Giovanni Domnarum and of S. Eusebio) are tired and arid. Toward the end of the century in Piedmont, in the frescoes of the oratory of S. Siro next to the Cathedral in Novara, the plastic forms of the first Lombard Romanesque turned into sinous lines that, in the ease of composition of the scenes, already forecast the Gothic. The frescoes in S. Eldrado at Novalesa are of an excessively mannered style, and the extreme harshness of their lines reveals an eclecticism in which Byzantine elements derived from the neo-Hellenistic current are apparent. This current found its full expression at the end of the century in the Baptistery in Parma (I, PL. 414), where the figures, emphasized by dark outlines, are executed with lively combinations of color. The Virgin between SS. Peter and Paul, in the crypt of S. Vincenzo at Galliano, and probably the fragments of the saints in S. Fermo Maggiore in Verona are by a painter who followed the same trend.

In the late 13th or early 14th century an anonymous painter depicted at Rocca d'Angera scenes of the battle between the Visconti and the Torriani that were a prelude to the taste for secular decoration that was to spread increasingly in the Gothic period.

Ottonian influences are present in the surviving 11th-century wall paintings of the Veneto hinterland. Byzantine influences (but still in an Ottonian key) are found in the 11th century in the frescoes in the parish church at San Giorgio (near Verona) and seem to be more closely related to the art of Lombardy. Those of the Romanesque sacellum at Summaga have nothing to do with the often-invoked (Zovatto, 1957) but here nonexistent "Benedictine current." The 11th-century frescoes in S. Severo in Bardolino reflect the influence of the apocalyptic codexes of Reichenau; and it seems that the later rows of frescoes in S. Andrea at Sommacampagna with scenes from the lives of the saints must be ascribed to the same influence. However, all of these works, along with those of the 12th century described below, are, more than anything else, provincial echoes of diverse tendencies not necessarily blended to form a school or even an easily recognizable style. The lack of a precise direction is also evident in the apse frescoes (1st half of 11th cent.) of the Cathedral in Aquileia, where the Early Christian influence is obvious. However, the figures in the lower register of the apse reveal contacts with Byzantine painting. Christ and the Archangel Gabriel (12th cent.) in the Lower Church of S. Fermo Maggiore in Verona are similar, but in a minor degree, to the frescoes of Galliano; but the frescoes of the apostles are still in the Ottonian tradition. Contacts with Salzburg, perhaps by way of Alto Adige, are also noticeable in S. Fermo Maggiore in the Virgin and Child flanked by the personification of the Church. Among the other remains of frescoes in S. Fermo Maggiore the Christ Child also iconographically reflects fundamentally Byzantine traits. The frescoes in S. Pietro at Caldiero have a plasticity and vigor reminiscent of the Lombard school. Those in S. Maria at Bonavigo are of a rather pale and flat Byzantinesque style. The frescoes of the second layer

of the sacellum of SS. Nazaro and Celso in Verona (detached, now in Verona, Mus. Civ.) are of a rather high quality and show contacts with the wall paintings of Stift Nonnberg in Salzburg (PL. 278). The frescoes in the Baptistery at Concordia Sagittaria (1089–1105) are, on the other hand, connected to the courtly Byzantine trend.

Toward the end of the 12th century a new wave of Byzantine influence, which reflected formal aspects of the Byzantine-Macedonian current (frescoes at Nerezi, Yugoslavia, XIII, PL. 52; Magnani, 1960), penetrated into the Veneto. Examples of this are the frescoes in the crypt of the Cathedral in Aquileia (PL. 275), which were executed by various artists. However, in the scenes of the Passion, the principal artist captured a quality of dramatic expressiveness. The Crucifixion (13th cent.) in the sacellum at Summaga reflects this tendency, which is also present, but in a cruder form, in the frescoes of the parish church of the same town. Here the artist retained certain elements of the art of northern Europe. The artist who executed the Last Judgment (late 12th cent.) in S. Andrea at Sommacampagna had a more refined style, one that included Byzantine accents derived from Aquileia, but he blended them with iconographic schemes from northern Europe (Burgenfeld).

The 13th-century frescoes of the tower of S. Zeno Maggiore in Verona are eclectic and in part (especially in the French-style friezes) derived from miniatures. The frescoes in S. Maria di Gradaro in Mantua are attributed to an artist from Verona. These frescoes, similar to the Resurrection of Lazarus in S. Zeno Maggiore in Verona and to the frescoes of S. Giovanni in Valle (also in Verona), are of a Byzantine style which is harsh and rough but which already has some characteristics of the Gothic. The frescoes in S. Giovanni Decollato in Venice are from the end of the 13th century and are connected to the painting in the convents of Serbia. The Crucifixion fresco in S. Nicolò in Treviso contains hints of the Gothic and reveals some contact with Tuscany.

The mosaic decoration of S. Marco in Venice constitutes a special chapter in the history of painting in the Veneto during the Romanesque period in that it can be said to have remained an isolated, even if most coherent, phenomenon. From the first works begun, according to tradition, during the time of the doge Domenico Selvo (1071–84), only fragments remain. The cycles, dating from the 12th (PL. 277; IV, PL. 230; VIII, PL. 174), 13th (X, PL. 187), and 14th centuries, reveal the presence of Byzantine craftsmen who alternated and combined their talents with local artisans; the result is a "typically Venetian syncretism" (Demus, 1935) in which stylistic and iconographic elements of diverse origins converge (Ottonian influences have also been mentioned; Demus, 1935). In the small dome of the atrium, which is decorated with scenes from Genesis (II, PL. 286), there is clear evidence of the influence of miniatures of the type found in the Early Christian Cotton Genesis (Br. Mus., Cod. Cott. B.vi). An obvious example of this syncretism is the Last Judgment on the entrance wall of the Cathedral at Torcello (IV, PL. 463; 12th–13th cent.), which, although it retains typically Byzantine iconography, is still stylistically resolved in decorative and expressionistic terms that are local. The Byzantine forms in the apse of SS. Maria e Donato at Murano and in the apse of the chapel to the right of the altar in the Cathedral at Torcello are purer. The mosaics in S. Marco by the master who painted the scenes of the Passion (mid-13th cent.), which are perhaps the greatest expression of the Romanesque style in Venice, have a dramatic vitality that is emphasized by particularly subtle use of color. In all probability the remains of the decoration in the apse of the Cathedral in Ravenna (1112) and the mosaics in the Cathedral in Trieste (ca. 1200) can also be attributed to Venetian craftsmanship.

In the 12th and 13th centuries this same alternation of accents — with new characteristics which, however, are not connected among themselves — is found in the Alpine regions of Trentino and Alto Adige. Far from contact with the large cultural centers because of their geographic positions, they contained cycles that were often mediocre and at other times surprisingly refined, like that, for example, in the crypt of the Church of Monte Maria in Burgusio (1160) where the artist (perhaps a monk) revitalized, in very personal form, the Ottonian tradition of Reichenau. He elevated the abstract concept of Reichenau in the figure of Christ in the apse and in the figures of angels, which have almost become extremely stylized flowers that open their wings like petals around the glory of God. A very faint echo of the work of this artist can perhaps be found in the scene of the Traditio Legis in the castle chapel at Castel Appiano, where the frescoes were painted by an eclectic craftsman probably toward the end of the 12th century. Influences of Byzantine art, which came perhaps indirectly through Aquileia, can be seen here in the Annunciation, the Visitation, and the Foolish Virgins, which appear to be by the same artist who was responsible for the Last Judgment in Sommacampagna. The artist of the main apse, where there are representations of the Virgin and Child, reveals that he had contact with contemporary Lombard sculpture. Possibly drawn from illustrations of nonsacred books, the Foolish Virgins are of an elegance that recalls feudal courts and can be compared to some of the miniatures of the Salzburg school. The painting of a deer pursued by dogs and by a mounted hunter (perhaps the legend of Theodoric, a rare example of a painting of the period with a purely profane subject), which is on the façade of the chapel at Castel Appiano, is derived from Byzantine prototypes depicting the legend of St. Eustace (Paris, Bib. Nat., Ms. gr. 20, fol. 5v).

Within the sphere of Castel Appiano are the later frescoes in S. Margherita at Lana di Sotto, but unfortunately they have been so retouched that it is difficult to evaluate them. Other cycles, undoubtedly already of the 13th century, reveal a less cultivated and less open environment than the preceding one. Perhaps this is why they show much more original traits. For example, at Termeno the socle in S. Giacomo is decorated with extraordinarily violent imaginary monsters, although the movement in the figures of the Apostles, which are under the arches, is a faint echo of the Ottonian miniatures from Fulda (cf. X, PL. 465). The same monsters of Termeno are found again in the socle at the base of the oldest chapel in the Sanctuary of S. Romedio near Sanzeno. The fragmentary and very rough frescoes in S. Bartolomeo at Romeno are of a rather mediocre eclecticism in which Byzantine elements are interpreted with a certain coarseness, and the scene of the Magi foreshadows the cycle of the same period in S. Jacopo at Grissiano. Although the artist at Grissiano followed traditional models for the Christ in Majesty, in some other scenes, such as the Sacrifice of Abraham, he expressed himself with charming lyricism. The landscape — which is basically the traditional Ottonian one — extends and stands out against snow-covered mountains, at the base of which spring up very delicate white flowers. The figure of Abraham reveals Byzantine influences derived through Aquileia. The frescoes in the Church of the Beata Vergine in Bressanone are connected to Salzburg and are rather more expert and mannered.

The last expression of the Romanesque in this zone is to be found in the secular frescoes in the Castello dei Castelbarco at Avio (early 14th cent.; VII, PL. 271), where the representation of a group of archers (perhaps by a painter from Verona) in the guards' quarters already heralded the Gothic.

During the 11th and 12th centuries Rome and Latium were in a position, primarily for historical and political reasons, that can be considered isolated. Therefore, painting followed its own particular course and had nothing to do with the so-called "Benedictine current," which, as Francovich (1955) has shown, was nonexistent. A reconstruction of the stylistic evolution is not possible, owing to the destruction of many monuments, even though, from the point of view of iconography and the basic arrangement of the buildings, fidelity to themes widely used by the Early Christian world is evident. Nevertheless, from what remains, it can be seen that during the 11th century there were two different currents.

The first current appeared in 1011 in the stories of the martyrs (very much overpainted) in S. Urbano alla Caffarella in Rome (Toesca, Md, considers them to be of a later date), and it is characterized by figures sketched in subtle dark outlines but lacking depth because they are in light, uniform colors

that seem to be derived from Roman mosaics of the 9th century (e.g., the mosaics in the triumphal arch of S. Pudenziana in Rome).

The second current, which can be seen in the apse of S. Sebastiano al Palatino in Rome, prior to 1065 — Toesca (Md, p. 407) judges it to be of the 10th century — is characterized by heavier workmanship that tries to give the figure more depth by strong shapes. This is achieved primarily by means of vivacious colors of contrasting tones emphasized by highlights. As Toesca points out (Md p. 408) this current can be linked to the frescoes (7th–8th cent.) in S. Maria Antiqua (II, PL. 445; XI, PL. 327).

The first current found its greatest expression in the Lower Church of S. Clemente (after 1084; PLS. 276, 369). In these frescoes (cleaned in 1964) a perfect synthesis is achieved between the architecture of the setting and the figures, which are elongated, flexible, and very elegant in their dress and movements. The borders are highly refined, and include floral motifs, birds, and acanthus candelabra which often stand out like embroidery on backgrounds of Pompeian color and which always appear where some characteristics of this style are evident. This type of border is used in the frescoes of S. Elia in Castel Sant'Elia near Nepi, which were painted (according to Matthiae, 1961) by Johannes, Stephanus, and Nicolaus, presumably before 1085, but in any case certainly not later than the 11th century. These frescoes, although not directly influenced by S. Clemente, belong to the same stylistic tendency, especially the scene of Christ between SS. Peter and Paul in the apse (which iconographically recalls the one in SS. Cosma e Damiano in Rome) and the Elders of the Apocalypse (PL. 276). The work of the artist responsible for the apocalyptic scenes is inferior. The master who painted the Virgins and the Archangel Michael was steeped in Byzantine influences derived most probably from enamels of Constantinople, as may be seen by comparing these figures with those of the Pala d'Oro in Venice (IV, PL. 405). Echoes of the stylistic tendency, sometimes of S. Clemente and at others of Castel Sant'Elia, are noticeable in Rome in the frescoes of the oratory in S. Pudenziana (1073–85). They have bright colors and a line technique and highlights that reveal a harsher Byzantine influence; at the same time they have a more vigorous style. The same echoes can be found in the much more refined but very fragmentary frescoes in a chapel in the old part of the Lateran Palace; in the fresco, formerly on the portico, in S. Cecilia in Trastevere (which is perhaps a bit later); and in the frescoes from the Grotta degli Angeli at Magliano Romano near Nepi (now in the Loggia of the Palazzo Venezia, Rome). To this group can be added some frescoes in the nave of S. Pietro at Tuscania.

This style was continued in the 12th century, but with a broader acceptance of Byzantine influences whose origin is difficult to localize. There are, for example, fragments from S. Nicola in Carcere in Rome (1128; now in Vat. Mus.); frescoes in the apse of S. Pietro at Tuscania; and busts of the prophets in Sta Croce in Gerusalemme, which recall the bust of St. Clement flanked by donors in the Lower Church of S. Clemente. The motifs used in the borders in S. Clemente are found in all these frescoes.

The masterpiece of the period is the triptych of the Saviour (a large processional icon) in the Cathedral at Tivoli, in which the line technique used in the clothing of Christ and of the Elders in Castel Sant'Elia is changed in Tivoli into very light lines of gold. The scenes on the shutters of the triptych, however, are obviously derived from the school of S. Clemente, and they also repeat the architectural backgrounds of S. Clemente. The frescoes in the apse of S. Silvestro at Tivoli are also generally of this style. Executed by various artists (but all in the first half of the century) they reveal, especially in the legend of St. Sylvester, more accentuated Byzantine-style elements. However, in the figures of the Virgin and the saints on either side of her, the connection with the style of the triptych is evident.

This stylistic trend appears also in the mosaics of the period. The figures of the Virgin and of St. John that flank the Crucifix in the apse mosaic in the Upper Church of S. Clemente (1128;

X, PL. 194) are similar to, and perhaps precede, those of the triptych at Tivoli. But in S. Clemente the garlands of acanthus leaves populated with figures and animals are derived from Early Christian mosaics. The figures, outlined with thin lines, and the faces with large almond-shaped eyes are similar to those in the mosaics of S. Maria in Trastevere (1140; VIII, PL. 177), where there is also, in the drapery and in a special sumptuousness of color, an obvious search for a more realistic technique, and to those of S. Francesca Romana (1161). Reflections (primarily iconographic) of Roman painting are found toward the end of the 12th century at Spoleto in the frescoes under the ceiling in S. Paolo Intervineas. The crucifix by Alberto Sotio (1187; VIII, PL. 177) and the frescoes attributed to him in SS. Giovanni e Paolo at Spoleto are more imitative of the Byzantine.

At the end of the 12th century there was a sudden revival in Rome of the above-mentioned current found in S. Sebastiano al Palatino, which, during the 11th century, was always evident in the miniatures, for example, in the Bible in Perugia (Bib. Augusta, Ms. L. 59). In the great cycle of frescoes with scenes from the Old and New Testaments in S. Giovanni a Porta Latina (1191) in Rome, this trend returned in a more evolved form and showed more accentuated echoes of the Roman-Hellenistic tradition also in the landscapes of the background. It was also present in Umbria in the cycle in the church of the Abbey of S. Pietro in Valle at Ferentillo (1191–98), which was executed by various artists. In this cycle some of the scenes are marked by a greater Byzantine influence and others, such as the Creation of Adam and Adam Naming the Animals, show a more active realism.

The development of this effective beginning in Roman painting was perhaps obstructed by the Venetian mosaicists who were called to Rome in 1198 to decorate the apse of Old St. Peter's and in 1218 that of S. Paolo fuori le Mura. From the fragments remaining it is not possible to deduce what these mosaics were like, unless they are attributed to the same artists who executed the mosaic with the prophets flanking the empty throne in S. Maria of the Abbey at Grottaferrata. What is certain is that these mosaics contributed to the tendency to accept Byzantine-style elements in the local painting, as appears evident in the Last Judgment in the Vatican (VIII, PL. 177). Because of the signature this was erroneously attributed to painters from Nepi; it can be dated, because of its accentuated Byzantine-style elements, to the end of the 12th or the beginning of the 13th century (see bibliog. under *Sculpture*, Francovich, 1952). In the oratory of St. Sylvester preceding SS. Quattro Coronati (1246) in Rome this influence is emphasized in scenes that, although they recall the local tradition, are stiff, and the figures are like wooden mannequins, also because of their colors, which are almost opaque.

The artists of the provinces had a freer style, such as the First Master of Anagni, who painted the Elders of the Apocalypse in the crypt of the Cathedral and who was faithful to the tradition of the school of S. Clemente, and the master who painted the chapel of St. Gregory in the Monastery of S. Benedetto (or Sacro Speco) at Subiaco. However, the author of the frescoes in S. Niccolò at Filettino rigidly imitated the Byzantine style.

The painting of icons of Christ also continued along Byzantine lines, all more or less reproducing the same model: in Casape near Tivoli (parish church), Sutri (S. Maria di Capranica), and Trevignano Romano (S. Maria Assunta). There were also devotional images of the Virgin (often repainted in the Romanesque period, e.g., those in Rome in S. Francesca Romana and the Pantheon, the latter recently restored); many of these icons repeat the scheme of the so-called "Madonna of S. Luca" (Rome, S. Maria Maggiore, 13th cent.) or of the Madonna "Avvocata" (Rome, S. Maria in Campo Marzio and S. Maria in Aracoeli; Tivoli, S. Maria Maggiore; Vetralla, Cath., which is somewhat similar in style to that of the triptych at Tivoli).

Toward the end of the century a group of artists instilled new life into the worn-out Byzantine-type forms, animating them with a rigorous but realistic quality that in part had its prelude in the Third Master of Anagni (PL. 264). Among this group were Jacopo Torriti, who did the apse mosaics of S. Maria Maggiore (1295; VIII, PL. 177; X, PL. 188) and of S. Giovanni in Laterano (unfortunately totally restored; III, PL. 303); Filippo Rusuti, who created the mosaics on the façade of S. Maria Maggiore; and, at a very high level, Pietro Cavallini (q.v.), who did frescoes and mosaics in Rome and Naples. Cavallini's influence is clearly noticeable in S. Maria in Vescovio at Stimigliano; in the backgrounds with the figures of saints in the transept of S. Maria Maggiore in Rome; in the frescoes of the Roman school in the Upper Church of Assisi, which contributed so greatly to the formation of Giotto (q.v.); and in the frescoes by Conxolus in the Lower Church of the Monastery of S. Benedetto at Subiaco.

The loss of the mosaics (1071) commissioned from Byzantine artists by Desiderius, abbot of Montecassino, makes it impossible to establish an exact point of departure for the development of the painting of Campania in the 11th and 12th centuries. However, the importance of these mosaics is demonstrated by the sudden revival of a local painting activity. The surviving frescoes do not show strong ties among themselves, but they appear, in the general nature of their Byzantine quality, to depend upon common prototypes that were variously interpreted but do not belong to a real school.

The most notable cycle is that in the Church of Sant'Angelo in Formis (PL. 263; II, PL. 285). Because the figure of Desiderius (d. 1087) depicted in the apse has the aureole of the living, this cycle can be considered to have been executed in the second half of the 11th century. The artists responsible for this work have added to the Byzantine style a lively sense of color and an unusual sense of movement that have particular narrative strength. It does not seem, however, that there are any Ottonian elements in them (as Bologna, 1962, has proposed), and the only points of contact are with local miniatures like the *Vita Sancti Benedicti* (Vat. Lib., Vat. lat. 1202) and a few illuminations in Exultet rolls (see below) of the time of Desiderius. The frescoes in S. Pietro ad Montes near Caserta, as far as can be discerned from their present state, are more refined and have an almost courtly flavor. Other frescoes of the period, like those in S. Maria di Foro Claudio at Ventaroli, do not have the same narrative strength, and the figures are stiff and the Byzantine elements have become sterile and provincial.

Sporadic Byzantine influences, perhaps owing to a second wave coming from the East or to some wandering "Greek" artist, are also found in 12th-century frescoes. Those in the reconstructed portico of the Church of Sant'Angelo in Formis depict the Archangel Michael, the Virgin, and the lives of the anchorites. In the crypt of S. Maria del Piano near Ausonia the Virgin portrayed in the vault is a poor copy of the Virgin at Sant'Angelo in Formis. The frescoes in the crypt of the Church of the Annunziata at Minuto near Amalfi, in a grotto at Rongolise near Sessa Aurunca, and in the chapel of the Crocifisso at Cassino also show Byzantine influences.

Some of the works executed in Sicily during the 12th century — the mosaics of Monreale (II, PLS. 286, 457; X, PL. 193), Cefalù (II, PL. 456), Palermo (PL. 277; II, PLS. 457, 458; VIII, PL. 173), and Messina — are clearly Byzantine (see II, cols. 810–11). The painted wooden ceiling of the Cappella Palatina, the mosaics in La Ziza, and the mosaics in the room of Roger II (VIII, PL. 426) in the Palazzo Reale, all in Palermo, are related to the Arabo-Fatimid tradition and therefore cannot be considered to be by a local school (in fact, there do not seem to have been any local schools in Sicily). Influences of the Byzantine mosaics done in Sicily can be found, in harsh and crude forms, in the mosaic decoration of the Cathedral in Salerno, which was done by local artists.

Of noteworthy interest, although not of very high quality, are the frescoes in the crypt of S. Lucia (or Sta Trinità) in Brindisi and in the subterranean Church of S. Margherita near Melfi, which are of a votive nature and reflect, like those of the local churches (e.g., S. Maria del Casale near Brindisi with a fresco of the Last Judgment signed by Rainaldo da Taranto), the Eastern monastic influence.

The surviving cycles in the Abruzzi (which have still not been thoroughly studied) are remarkable. They are not related to each other. The cycle in S. Pietro ad Oratorium near Capestrano (very difficult to date), which Bologna (1962) considers to be within the sphere of the southern Italian influence, seems instead to show a certain provincialism that derives from Latium and also is not lacking in elements coming from the north. These northern elements are particularly noticeable in the series of saints under the arches. These are rigid, almost wooden, with large wide-open eyes reminiscent of Lombard sculpture. The racemose decoration is in the typical style of Benedetto Antelami. In the author's opinion, these frescoes belong to the end of the 12th century. The narrative liveliness of the frescoes in S. Maria di Ronzano near the Mavone river seem to be derived from miniatures (such as the scene of the Slaughter of the Innocents) or to interpret French sculpture from the area of Chartres (such as the Flight into Egypt). The frescoes in S. Pellegrino at Bominaco (1263) are not related to the Benedictine influence, as has been maintained up to now. They have an ease of composition that is closer to the Gothic. The frescoes in S. Maria delle Grotte (or ad Cryptas) near Fossa (1283) are stylistically similar to those in Bominaco but are inferior in quality. In the crypt of S. Giovanni in Venere near Lanciano the frescoes depicting Christ and four saints are permeated with Gothic elements, and those in the main apse have elements that are obviously Byzantine.

In the 12th century Tuscany distinguished itself in the production of panel paintings, altarpieces, which were derived from the medieval *icone*, and crucifixes. The first center to develop this kind of painting, which was probably tied to the presence of some monastic scriptoriums, was Lucca. The first monumental crucifixes were produced in Lucca, and later they also appeared in Umbria and the Marches. Their prototype was the crucifix of the Cathedral at Sarzana (III, PL. 306), signed by Gulielmus in 1138 (bust and head repainted in the 13th cent.). Shortly afterward the crucifixes in S. Michele in Foro, S. Maria dei Servi, and S. Giulia, all in Lucca, were made. In these works the iconographic type of the Christ is the Western one, alive, with eyes open, and sometimes crowned, the Christus Triumphans, which is also found in the later crucifixes in S. Frediano in Pisa and in the parish church at Rosano near Pontassieve, as well as in the crucifix in Florence (Acc.) and in the one by Alberto Sotio in Spoleto (1187; VIII, PL. 177). At the end of the 12th century the type of the Christ derived from Byzantine models, the Christus Patiens, in which Christ is depicted dead, with closed eyes, was introduced in Tuscany in the crucifix in Pisa (III, PL. 306).

The painters of the 13th century followed these two iconographic models. The Christus Patiens was preferred in Pisa and found its highest expression in the work of Giunta Pisano (d. 1255/67). In the crucifix in Assisi (PL. 276) and even more so in the one in S. Domenico in Bologna, both by Giunta, the bent form of the body of Christ almost becomes exaggerated. Enrico di Tedice (crucifix in Pisa; II, PL. 284) was a follower of Giunta, as was the Master of S. Francesco, who worked in Umbria (crucifix in Perugia, Gall. Naz. dell'Umbria). A combination of the two models is noticeable in the poorly executed crucifix by Berlinghiero Berlinghieri (Lucca, Pin. Naz.).

The most interesting aspect of these crucifixes is not so much the figure of Christ as the Passion cycle often depicted at the sides (VIII, PL. 179). In these scenes the artists both stylistically and iconographically revived old schemes and succeeded in instilling such passion and vitality into the narrative that in effect they discovered a new artistic expression. Scenes of the same type are also depicted on altarpieces with the figure of the Virgin or a saint at the center. There are numerous ones with the figure of St. Francis, in which the artists, freed from a preestablished iconographic tradition, found new accents. Examples are the altarpiece by Bonaventura Berlinghieri in Pescia (1235; VIII, PL. 181) and the altarpiece in S. Francesco in Pisa (1250-60) by an unknown artist whose style is similar to Giunta's. Connected to the stylistic circle of this last artist is the author of the altarpiece in S. Verano at Peccioli, with stories from the life of St. Nicholas of Myra (or Bari). In the altarpiece in Pisa (Mus. Naz.), with scenes from the life of St. Catherine, there is a renewed sense of color with broad highlights that shade into the other colors (a hint of this was already found in the work of Enrico di Tedice). This sense of color was to become the basic characteristic of painting of the Pisan school, while that of Lucca remained more arid and harsher. This new taste found its full expression in the work of the Master of S. Martino (late 13th cent.), who painted the altarpiece in Pisa (VIII, PL. 181) and the panel with St. Anne and the Virgin as a child (Pisa, Mus. Naz.). Carli et al. (1959) attribute the miniatures of the Exultet roles in Pisa (Mus. Naz.) to this master. This painter, in his use of color to absorb and reflect highlights, achieved a sense of realism that, along with the revived sense of the landscape, has an almost neo-Hellenistic flavor.

The other cities of Tuscany also followed the schools of Pisa and Lucca. In the *Madonna and Child Enthroned* (VIII, PL. 185; the date is disputable between 1221 and 1271, with the latter more likely) Guido da Siena retained marked Byzantine elements. Margaritone d'Arezzo (d. ca. 1290), in the *St. Francis* in Arezzo (Pin. Com.) and the *Virgin and Child* in S. Maria della Vertigine near Monte San Savino, had a crude but forceful and expressive style.

A revival occurred in Florence at the beginning of the 13th century when, in 1225, work was begun on the mosaics of the Baptistery (PL. 277; III, PLS. 12, 490; IV, PL. 177; X, PL. 188) under the direction of Jacopo, a Franciscan brother who was probably trained in the school of Venetian mosaicists (Salmi, 1930–31). But what still remains of the Byzantine in these mosaics was so changed by the impetuosity and ardor of the narration — even arriving, in the scene of Hell (attrib. to Coppo di Marcovaldo), at Bosch ante litteram — that it becomes sure evidence of a Romanesque style which by then had reached its peak and had found its precedents in the narrative ability of the painters of the stories on panels. The artists who worked on the mosaics of the dome of the Baptistery have been precisely identified by means of these panels. The Master of the Bardi S. Francesco, who painted the altarpiece with scenes from the life of St. Francis in the Bardi chapel in Sta Croce, acquired a new sense of volume. The Master of the Bigallo Crucifix created the crucifix in the Loggia del Bigallo and the altarpiece with scenes from the life of St. Zenobius that was in the convent of the Bigallo and is now in Florence (Mus. dell'Opera del Duomo). Coppo di Marcovaldo, the most notable of all, reduced the graphic Byzantine style to a kind of subtle luminous network that envelops his figures, which have unusual volume, as in the *Madonna and Child with Two Angels* (1261) in Siena (S. Maria dei Servi) and the *Madonna and Child Enthroned* in Orvieto (VIII, PL. 183), and which are animated by a violent dramatic pathos, as in the Crucifixion with stories of the Passion in San Gimignano (Pin.). Meliore di Jacopo (X, PL. 490) retained the harsh vivacity of Coppo. The figures of the Magdalen Master in the altarpiece of the Magdalen in Florence (Acc.) are suffused with melancholy. Cimabue (q.v.) was much influenced by Coppo, but his figures have a more human emphasis and a delicate sense of sweetness that foreshadowed the Gothic.

The production of illuminated manuscripts was resumed in the second half of the 11th century in some of the scriptoriums of the old Benedictine communities (Bobbio, Polirone, Farfa, Nonantola). Activity was concentrated mainly on copying older codices. Outstanding among these communities was Montecassino, which flourished under the rule of Abbot Desiderius (1058–87).

The codices illuminated in Montecassino (of which no basic study yet exists) are of different qualitative levels, but all are distinguished by their superb decorated initial letters. Interweaving bands of designs enclosed in borders outline the letters, which are decorated with interlaced plant and animal designs. The animal designs, among which the howling greyhound predominates (this animal is also found at Montecassino in two fragments of marble inlay from the time of Desiderius), are an intelligent mixture of Hiberno-Saxon and Moslem motifs, blended with a sensitivity that is distinctly Latin. These initials achieved their highest expression in the Homilies in

Montecassino (Ms. 99), executed by Brother Leo, and in the Lectionary of SS. Benedict and Maurice (III, PL. 8), both from the time of Desiderius.

During the rule of Desiderius depictions of the human figure — which rarely appeared in earlier codices and, when they did, were in a crude style — attained, by adopting Byzantine forms introduced in the mosaics of the Abbey, a rather high expressive quality that vied with the beauty of the illuminated initials. This is demonstrated by the above-mentioned Homilies (Ms. 99) and by another Homilies in Montecassino (Archivio dell'Abbazia, Ms. 98), which are decorated with elegant full-page pen figures (IV, PL. 265) that seem, in the grandiosity of the drawing, to be derived from wall compositions. Ties with the frescoes in Sant'Angelo in Formis (PL. 263) can be discerned in the Lectionary of SS. Benedict and Maurice. Because of its lively narrative style and the way in which the color is used to create the form, this Lectionary from Monte-cassino can justifiably be classified as Romanesque. Later codices, such as the *Chronicon Vulturnense* (Rome, Vat. Lib., Barb. lat. 2754), the *Chronicon S. Sophiae* (Rome, Vat. Lib., Vat. lat. 4939), a breviary (ca. 1099; Paris, Bib. Mazarine, Ms. 364), and the Register of Sant'Angelo in Formis (1107–16; Montecassino, Archivio dell'Abbazia, Regesto 4), are uninspired imitations of Byzantine elements, and they show signs of the decline of the scriptorium of Montecassino.

The most original production in southern Italy, including Montecassino and other monasteries of the same order (Cava dei Tirreni, Montevergine), is that of the long, illuminated rolls of parchment or vellum containing liturgical prayers for religious ceremonies. Most of these are Exultet rolls. They were unrolled over the back of the lectern as the Exultet was chanted; thus the figures are upside down in relation to the text (X, PL. 73). These rolls, which are difficult to date, range from the most refined, clearly imitative of the Byzantine, such as those in Bari (X, PL. 73), Troia (Bib. Capitolare), and Rome (Vat. Lib., Vat. lat. 3784, stylistically close to Ms. 99 in Monte-cassino; and Barb. lat. 592, XIII, PL. 343), to those that retain obvious influences of Campanian painting before the time of Desiderius (two Exultet rolls in Pisa, Mus. Naz.; Exultet I in Gaeta, Cath. Archives), to others that are cruder and in a folk idiom (VIII, PL. 175). However, even in this last type the artists gave a personal interpretation to the lines of the hymn for which there did not exist a traditional iconography. For example, there are illuminations for the gathering of the flocks, night, the lighting of the paschal candle, and the final blessing of prelates, princes, and commoners.

In southern Italy a special position was occupied by Sicily, where a school of illumination developed during the Norman domination that Buchthal (1955) places in Messina. The codices produced in Sicily, especially in the 12th century, have markedly Byzantine-style elements (full-page figure of the Virgin and Child on fol. 8or of Cod. 52 in Madrid, Bib. Nac.), but they are particularly distinguished by the characteristic ornamenta-tion of the initials with vine tendrils and palmettes (the latter often of a distant Sassanian derivation) that are strongly modeled and highlighted and are often enclosed in borders that outline the letter. The same Byzantine-style elements, but mixed with accents that already had a Gothic flavor, also exist in secular codices of the 13th century such as the *De arte venandi cum avibus*, composed for Frederick II and known from a copy in Rome (Vat. Lib., Pal. 1071) illuminated about 1260 for his son, King Manfred.

The so-called "Atlantic" Bibles were produced from the 11th century on in Rome and central Italy. These Bibles, which are very large in format, are written in Roman minuscule script and are rich in ornate initials and full-page illuminations for the most important parts of the text. The figural scenes are arranged in horizontal registers, as in the Pantheon Bible in Rome (Vat. Lib., Vat. lat. 12958), and in all probability reflect the influence of the type of Carolingian miniatures found in the Bible of S. Paolo fuori le Mura in Rome (III, PL. 61). The flat-toned coloring of the background of the registers (Salmi, 1956) is similar in both Bibles. The quality of the manuscripts is generally not very high. The figures,

often executed with broad areas of color, reflect influences from contemporaneous painting (Toesca, Md, II, pp. 1052 ff.), and the illuminators demonstrated a clarity of composition and a vitality, of classical origin, that helped them overcome the late-Byzantine graphic style (Bible in Perugia, Bib. Augusta, Ms. L. 59). Contacts with the scriptorium of Montecassino are clearly noticeable in the initials of the Evangelistary of Farfa (Rome, Bib. Vallicelliana, Ms. E. 16). In the "Atlantic" Bibles produced in the monasteries of Tuscany elements derived from Latium were blended with Byzantinizing styles, as in the Bible in Calci (1169; Bib. della Certosa), and with some elements of French derivation, as in the Bible in Montalcino (12th cent.; Mus. Civ.).

The production of illuminated manuscripts was much smaller in northern Italy. The codices of the 11th and 12th centuries show very disparate tendencies, and they are not of great artistic merit. Ottonian, or in any case northern European, influences predominated, especially in the older codices (11th-cent. missal in Trento, Cath.; late-11th-cent. Gospel Book in New York, Pierpont Morgan Lib., M. 492) and in the group of manuscripts attributed by Arslan (1934) to the school of Verona. In the Benedictine abbeys of Nonantola and Polirone northern European influences were interpreted in different ways: in the Evangelistary of Nonantola (12th cent.; Archivio della Badia) the outlines are rigid, reflecting Byzantine influences; in the Psalter from Polirone (PL. 279), with its violent colors, there is a greater freedom of composition and liveliness of narrative. Arslan rightly compares the style of the Psalter to the frescoes in S. Severo at Bardolino and points out influences from the miniatures of the Salzburg school. Ottonian influences also must have permeated Donizo's *Vita Mathildis* (Rome, Vat. Lib., Vat. lat. 4922; also known as the Canossa Codex), of which there are later copies such as the one in Lucca (Bib. Governativa, Ms. 2508), where Matilda is depicted on the frontispiece in the same manner as the German emperors were in the Ottonian codices. The work of northern Italy is enlivened by a narrative force that is emphasized by vivid colors, as in the Evangelistary written and illuminated by Isidoro (1170; Padua, Bib. Capitolare). In the epistolary written and probably illuminated by Giovanni da Gaibana (1259; Padua, Bib. Capitolare) the miniatures are very subtle and full of Byzantine elements, both iconographically and stylistically.

Beginning in the second half of the 13th century the schools in Emilia, particularly Bologna, specialized primarily in the decoration of juridical texts and other secular works, although the production of liturgical manuscripts, especially choir books, continued. Byzantine elements are still present, but French influence can be seen in the miniatures and the Gothic style is already apparent (see GOTHIC ART).

Fernanda de' MAFFEI

GERMANY AND CENTRAL EUROPE. Of the frescoes executed during the Romanesque period only a fraction are still extant. The dating of these works is thus often possible only with the help of contemporaneous illuminations. The present condi-tion of these paintings varies widely. The restorations and retouchings of the 19th century have been in part removed in recent years.

The artists used a blend of fresco and secco techniques; sketches, as some pentimenti prove, were made directly on the walls. The most important themes were Christ in Majesty surrounded by saints and the Virgin Enthroned, which were portrayed in the main apse; the remaining walls were decorated with representational or symbolic themes.

In the late 11th century the paintings that decorate the upper walls of the church at Burgefelden like a frieze were produced: a Last Judgment and, presumably, Biblical parables. The frescoes follow the great Ottonian traditions, but the elongated figures are firmer and bulkier. The fresco cycle in the *Westwerk* of the monastery church in Lambach (dedicated 1089) shows much more of the new Romanesque solidity of the individual figure, but Byzantine elements are also present. The Adoration of the Magi is depicted in the vault; the walls (first uncovered in 1956) are covered with scenes mainly from the youth, works, and parables of Christ, with particular emphasis on the theophany scenes and the evidences for Christ's divinity.

Frescoes belonging to the 12th century and which are characterized by a certain harshness of style are those in the apse (much retouched) of the church in Petersberg (1104–20), the apse of SS. Peter und Paul in Niederzell on Reichenau Island, and the Last Judgment on the outer wall of the apse of St. Georg in Oberzell, also on Reichenau Island. The frescoes of the church in Idensen, probably executed between 1120 and 1130, are of high quality. The tension typical of the 11th-century prototypes has been converted here into the Romanesque solidity.

The masterpieces of the Salzburg frescoes are the half-length figures of saints painted in the niches in Stift Nonnberg (ca. 1150; PL. 278). They show definite acquaintance with Byzantine models and are intensely expressive. Other frescoes belonging to the Salzburg school are found in Friesach (ca. 1130, 1140, and 1190) and in Frauenchiemsee near Munich (ca. 1160). The frescoes in the more remote Alpine districts show a variety of styles and are by no means all provincial. Dating from the 12th century are the frescoes in the Church of the Rosary at Maria Wörth, in St. Nikolaus at Matrei in Osttirol, and in the Chapel of St. John at Pürgg.

The earliest of the Regensburg works, and the one most closely related to Salzburg, is the fresco decoration of the east end of the Abbey church of Prüfening (ca. 1140). The walls of the forechoir are decorated with frescoes in horizontal registers, each of which contains a chorus of the blessed — single monumental figures in austere rows bound together by banderoles. Above this, in the vault, is the enthroned Ecclesia surrounded by painted architectural forms. The frescoes in the Chapel of All Saints in Regensburg (PL. 278), which were restored to their original form in 1955, date from about 1155 to 1164. They correspond to the mature phase of the Regensburg illuminations, whose miniatures have lively and supple figures. The principal themes in the Chapel of All Saints are the protection of the chosen according to the Apocalypse (VII, 4–8) and Christ in Glory. Other frescoes in the Regensburg style are found in the west choir (after 1166) of St. Emmeram in Regensburg, in the castle chapel in Donaustauf, on the piers of the crossing (ca. 1160) of the Abbey church in Prüfening, in SS. Peter und Paul (ca. 1180) in Perschen, and in the church in Karthaus-Prüll (Annunciation, ca. 1200).

The symbolic paintings of the Death and Resurrection of Christ in St. Aegidius of Kleinkomburg in Komburg near Schwäbisch-Hall are the most important of the remaining Swabian frescoes from the late 12th century.

One of the Rhineland masterpieces is the cycle of frescoes in the Lower Church of Schwarz-Rheindorf near Bonn (1151–56; restored to its original form in 1935). These paintings have a continuous deep blue and green background. The symbolism of the cardinal points is expressed by the Expulsion from the Temple and St. Michael in the west-oriented entrance, the Crucifixion in the north apse, the Transfiguration in the south apse, Christ in the main apse, and, in the vault preceding this, Mary as the symbol of the gate of Heaven. In the niches are the enthroned rulers, probably the four kingdoms of the earth. The destruction of the old Jerusalem and the building of the Heavenly Jerusalem are depicted on the four sections of the crossing. In the Upper Church are scenes based on themes from the Apocalypse (ca. 1170; PL. 278). Related to the style of the decoration of the Lower Church is that in the richly decorated vault of the chapter house (ca. 1174) in the Abbey church at Brauweiler near Cologne (restored to its original form in 1958–59); it shows the confirmation of the faith according to Hebrews (XI, 33–39), especially by the suffering of the martyrs. Further works of Rhineland painting are in the apse of the Abbey church at Knechtsteden near Düsseldorf (ca. 1162); in St. Martin (ca. 1150) at Emmerich (remains of the Seizing of Christ and of the Descent into Hell); and in the Baptistery (ca. 1227) of St. Gereon in Cologne.

In Lower Saxony the wall paintings of the main apse of St. Patroklus at Soest (before 1166) were destroyed in 1945; those in the apse of the northern aisle (ca. 1200) are still preserved. The agitated style characteristic of the end of the 12th century is seen in the paintings of the monastery church of Neuwerk in Goslar (Mary symbolizing the throne of Solomon; choruses of the blessed).

In Belgium the frescoes in the ruined monastery of St. Bavon at Ghent and those in the castle at Mons are related to the illuminations of the Mosan region, those of the Cathedral in Tournai principally to the illuminations of Arras. The frescoes in Tournai consist of the Crucifixion and the life of St. Catherine (ca. 1170) and the life of St. Margaret in the north transept (late 12th cent.).

Of the panel paintings executed in the 12th century one of the most important is the antependium (ca. 1180) from the Church of St. Walpurgis in Soest (Münster, Landesmus.). Christ is depicted enthroned and flanked by standing saints; the figures are full of austerity. The wooden painted ceiling of the Church of St. Martin in Zillis, Switzerland, dates from the mid-12th century. The ceiling is divided into 153 almost square panels; depicted are scenes from the Life of Christ and of St. Martin. In some of the panels there are fantastic animals.

In Swabia the Benedictine monastery at Hirsau was of particular importance in illumination, as it was also in monastic reform and architecture. The Passional in Stuttgart (Landesbib., Cod. bibl. fol. 56–58) from Hirsau incorporates Bavarian and Italian models. The legends of the saints are told through individual figures or scenes, more or less closely bound to the initials, in pen drawings with inks of various colors (only the grounds of the initials are colored). The precision of the form and of the narration and the humanity of the representations are new features. Characteristic of the Hirsau and Swabian style in these miniatures is the combination of dryness and exactness with imagination, lightness, and grace. The first volume of the Passional (ca. 1110–20) is, in the free movement and delicacy of the figures and scenes, the most delightful; it is one of the highest achievements in small format painting. In the second volume the voluminous figures resemble those of the Augsburg stained-glass windows (ca. 1130; cf. XIII, PL. 161). In the third volume the elongated forms, tense and more rigid, show correspondences with the figures on the lectern (ca. 1140–60) of the parish church in Freudenstadt.

The Zwiefalten scriptorium, at first quite provincial, combined, in the choir book for matins (1147; Stuttgart, Landesbib., Cod. theol. 4° 141), narrative scenes of the preceding type, with heavy-set figures, into full pages within a border. The monasteries at Gengenbach, Komburg, and Weingarten used the same type of color in their miniatures. The style of Gengenbach was similar to that of Hirsau and of the Guta-Sintram Codex from Marbach (Strasbourg, Grand Séminaire, Ms. 78). In the 12th century the Weingarten scriptorium continued the Ottonian models of Reichenau and the Mosan region in a style rich in contrasts, which was softened and consolidated about 1180 (frontispiece to the *Vita Gregorii*, Chicago, Art Inst., No. 44.704), and blossomed fully in the 13th century (Berthold Missal, X, PL. 73). In the scriptorium at Engelberg, Switzerland, lively historiated initials were created; the manuscripts produced here are more interesting for their drawings and calligraphy than for their miniatures.

Production was revived in Salzburg in the 12th century, first with Bibles, where at the beginning of each book framed miniatures were inserted on the written page. Here all is weighty, concise, serious, and powerful. The Bible in Michael-beuern (ca. 1130; Stiftbib., Cod. perg. 1), with its soft and voluminous figures and free narration, was followed by the Gebhardt Bible from Admont (ca. 1140–50; Vienna, Nationalbib., Ser. Nov. 2701–02) and the Book of Pericopes from Stift Nonnberg (PL. 279), with elongated figures, drawn features, tense movements, stronger relief effects, often symmetrically balanced compositions, and a restrained tension of new monumentality. Byzantine models, which had been influential in Salzburg since the 11th century, were interpreted in new ways, as can also be seen in the frescoed half-length figures in Stift

Nonnberg (PL. 278). This style, also used in drawings, became more vigorous, monumental, clear, and schematized around the middle of the century. The figures and pictures in the Antiphonary from St. Peter's in Salzburg (Vienna, Nationalbib.), whose parallels in frescoes are in Frauenchiemsee, are more compact and solid, and the miniatures, which were conceived as the more exalted form of art, are set among the more numerous drawings on a colored background. In the Prayer Book from Stift Nonnberg (ca. 1200; Munich, Bayerische Staatsbib., Clm. 15902), the sculptural quality, fullness of the garments, and new dignity of the figures foreshadow the 13th century. A number of smaller schools, above all in Austria, followed the example of Salzburg illumination. The Genesis from Millstatt (Klagenfurt, Landesmus. f. Kärnten, Hs. 6/19) can be considered as deriving from Salzburg rather than Regensburg.

The so-called "Bavarian monastery school" at first continued to use Ottonian models but in a livelier way. In some manuscripts from Weihenstephan near Freising and Passau the Salzburg forms are employed with an almost baroque effect. Hirsau influence is evident prior to about 1140 in the production of the Regensburg-Prüfening school; after that a stylistic phase related to Salzburg can be surmised from the mural painting of Prüfening and an Old Testament from Biburg near Abensberg (1147; Munich, Universitätsbib., 2° cod. ms. 28, Perg.). Between 1150 and 1200 a style derived partly from the Rhineland but mainly from Salzburg was predominant, whose outstanding feature was pen drawings of a ductile and elegant calligraphy. The figures are airy and fit easily into the composition; banderoles of ten form the structural framework. Although the scenes are depicted with a rich variety of composite solutions, they are worked out in a unified manner. The human figure, which in the illuminations of about 1150 was slim and graceful, became heavier about 1164 and then was depicted in a looser, more flowing manner.

The late-11th-century manuscripts produced in Bohemia are related to the Bavarian style but have a freshness of their own and an original iconography. The most important example is the Vyšehrad Evangelistary (Prague, Univ. Lib., Ms. XIV A13). The codices of the second half of the 12th century, such as the Ostrow Psalter (Prague, Lib. of the Metropolitan Chapter, Ms. A57 1/209), and the wall paintings are closely related to the Regensburg school. The manuscripts of the scribe Hildebertus, such as the copy of St. Augustine's *De Civitate Dei* in Prague (Lib. of the Metropolitan Chapter, Ms. A7), have more affinity with the art of the Mosan region. Less important schools existed in Würzburg and Fulda.

Book illumination revived in Saxony in the second half of the 12th century, and the works produced show influences from the Rhineland, from the Mosan region, and later from England; in their turn they influenced Scandinavia and perhaps Poland. The figures in the Hildesheim illuminations are severe, harsh, and monumental, as in the Ratmann Sacramentary or Missal of 1159 (Hildesheim, Cath. Treas., Ms. 37). Typological and New Testament scenes together form a unified pictorial system. Miniatures from Helmarshausen, in which elegant and strong figures are depicted on densely illustrated pages, combine a feeling for balanced composition with a great joy in ornamentation (Br. Mus., Landsdowne Ms. 381; Psalter, Baltimore, Walters Art Gall., W. 10). Certain aspects of Ottonian-Saxon art seem to have been revived; folk motifs have been transformed through the medium of the fine arts. The sumptuous manuscripts executed by the monk Herimann (e.g., Gospel Book in Brunswick, Herzog-Anton-Ulrich-Mus.) for Henry the Lion at times produce the effect of embroidery and have affinities with the stained glass by Master Gerlachus (XIII, PL. 160). That the effect of this art was not merely external is proved by the Hardehaus Evangelistary (Kassel, Landesbib., Ms. theol. fol. 59), much simpler but with pictures that are warmly human and tightly composed. The style of the late 12th century has greater movement and is pictorially richer, and this style became characteristic of the Saxon-Thuringian school of painting in the 13th century.

In the Lower Rhine region and probably in its main center, Cologne, several schools of illumination existed side by side in the 12th century. One, for example, closely followed the art of the Mosan region; another, with its more delicate and nervous drawing and lighter rendering of color, was allied with the Rhenish art of the preceding period. The extremely regular disposition of small, solid figures in the Lectionary of Archbishop Frederick (ca. 1130; Cologne, Erzbischöfliches Diözesan-Mus., Ms. fol. 59) and the delicate, flowing style of the Book of Pericopes in Paris (ca. 1150; Bib. Nat., Ms. lat. 17325) with its undulant and sinuous curves can be compared to the contemporaneous goldsmith's art of Cologne and to the frescoes in Schwarz-Rheindorf.

Important but so far relatively isolated works have survived from the Middle and Upper Rhine regions. In the Theofried manuscript (ca. 1105–10; Gotha, Thüringische Landesbib., Cod. I 70) the Ottonian style of Echternach was transformed into the Romanesque style. The slender, precise, and sharply drawn figures in the Prayer Book of St. Hildegard of Bingen (ca. 1190; Munich, Staatsbib., Clm. 935) seem to foreshadow the freer movement in space and the more corporeal figures of a *Speculum virginum* from Brohl near Andernach of the turn of the century (Bonn, Rheinisches Landesmus.).

The lively figures with heavy outlines in the strongly colored pictures of the Evangelistary from Speyer Cathedral (ca. 1197; Karlsruhe, Landesbib., Cod. Bruchsal 1) are related on the one hand to the goldsmith's art of the circle of Nicholas of Verdun and on the other to the more supple and rounded figures of the *Hortus deliciarum* of Herrad von Landsberg (only copies of this work survive). In the powerful miniatures that portray the visions of St. Hildegard of Bingen contained in the *Liber scivias* (ca. 1170, formerly Wiesbaden, Landesbib., Cod. 1) an exceptional creative force is revealed.

Wilhelm MESSERER

ENGLAND. Few Romanesque frescoes exist in England today. Dating from the earlier Romanesque period are some important, but badly preserved, wall paintings in Sussex (Church of St. Botolph at Hardham; Church of St. John the Baptist at Clayton; church at Coombes), Kent (St. Gabriel's Chapel in the crypt of Christchurch Cathedral in Canterbury), and Gloucestershire (Church of St. Mary at Kempley). The decoration of the Galilee Chapel in Durham Cathedral is the most outstanding work from the late 12th century, but it is very fragmentary. Master Hugo, the illuminator of the Bury Bible, was also a painter, and his style is reflected in the fragment of the fresco with St. Paul and the viper in St. Anselm's Chapel in Christchurch Cathedral in Canterbury.

English masters were also active on the Continent. The frescoes in the Chapel of St-Julien at Petit-Quevilly near Rouen in France are remarkably close in style and iconography to the Psalter of Henry of Blois and are presumably the work of an English painter. The frescoes in the chapter house of the monastery at Sigena in Spain, executed by itinerant English painters, are in a classicizing style that is akin to the style of the Westminster and Paris Psalters.

Soon after the Norman Conquest numerous books were brought from Normandy to England, for example, those that William of Saint-Carilef (d. 1096), bishop of Durham, gave to Durham Cathedral. Many Norman illuminators were employed in England. Thus the Norman style of illumination, characterized by decorated initials in which rich foliage was combined with human, animal, and grotesque figures, established itself in England, without, however, replacing the Winchester style (see X, col. 142), which continued to exist in a modified form well into the 12th century (see below).

In the first half of the 12th century a new, highly individual school of book decoration was evolved in the abbeys of Bury St. Edmunds and St. Albans. The masterpieces of this group are the St. Albans (or Albani) Psalter, the *Life of St. Edmund*, undoubtedly executed at Bury St. Edmunds, and the Bury Bible. Some scholars consider that all these manuscripts show influences from the Rhineland and the Mosan region. They have many full-page illustrations and beautiful decorated initials. In the *Life of St. Edmund* (New York, Pierpont Morgan Lib.,

M. 736) the Ottonian tradition is very strong, as can be observed in the scene depicting St. Edmund crowned by angels, but in other pages (VI, PL. 429) the Winchester style with its elongated and nervous figures is clearly echoed. The St. Albans Psalter (Hildesheim, Church of St. Godehard Treas.) displays strong Ottonian elements combined with Italo-Byzantine influences. It has been suggested that this Psalter is the work of an itinerant artist who had Italian training. The Byzantine elements are evident in the rather stiff figures and in the drapery; the compositions are well balanced and the borders of the pages are quite elaborate. The Bury Bible (PL. 274) is the most remarkable manuscript of the Bury St. Edmunds group. Here the Byzantine influence is even stronger. It was illuminated by Master Hugo, a secular painter of extraordinary gifts who was also a sculptor and metalworker. Hugo's work at Bury St. Edmunds coincided with the abbacy of Anselm (1121–48), previously abbot of S. Saba in Rome, who through his contacts with the Greek monasteries in southern Italy may have been influential in introducing Byzantine elements into English art. The colors in the Bury Bible are very bright; the stiff figures of the St. Albans Psalter have been transformed here into elegant but controlled forms, and the contours of the bodies are evident under the draperies.

In the middle of the 12th century the English taste for vigorous, exaggerated movement and decorative patterns led to changes in style that found expression in a group of manuscripts produced in Canterbury, where two scriptoriums, St. Augustine and Christchurch, were very active, and in Winchester. In the Lambeth Bible (PL. 279), illustrated in Canterbury, the local style and the new elements coming from the Continent were finally fused. The geometric decorative patterns predominate even in the figures, which are almost agitated in their movements and are detached from the grounds of solid color. Some scholars also assign the following works to the Canterbury scriptorium: a Gospel Book in New York (Pierpont Morgan Lib., M. 777) and two sections of a large Bible (New Testament in Baltimore, Walters Art Gall., W. 18; Old Testament in London, Br. Mus., Royal I, C.vii).

The new style that was developed in the Lambeth Bible was taken up by the Winchester school, which attained an outstanding position in the second half of the 12th century. Two of the most important manuscripts produced by the Winchester school are the Psalter of Henry of Blois (Br. Mus., Cott. Nero C.iv) and the Winchester Bible (Winchester, Cath. Lib.). In both these codices the historiated initials are elaborately decorated, often with interweaving scrollwork, and very bright colors are used. The figures themselves become a decoration because of the abstract way in which the folds are interpreted and draped around the elongated bodies. The Winchester Bible was illuminated by a number of artists. The most orthodox among them still worked in the style of the Lambeth Bible. At least two of the masters display an intimate knowledge of Byzantine art, probably that of Sicily. The leaf from a Bible in New York (X, PL. 73) may have been executed for the Winchester Bible. The quality of the illuminations in the Psalter of Henry of Blois is not as high as in those of the Winchester Bible, owing to the synchretism that resulted from the presence of so many different artists in the Winchester school. The assimilation of classical and Byzantine elements is perhaps the most original feature of this codex.

The Paris Psalter (Paris, Bib. Nat., Ms. lat. 8846), which is the last known copy of the Carolingian Utrecht Psalter (see III, col. 112), at that time in Canterbury, and the Westminster Psalter (Br. Mus., Royal 2, A.xxii) represent a similar assimilation of classical elements derived from Byzantine sources.

George ZARNECKI

SCANDINAVIA. Romanesque mural paintings have been preserved, although generally in a fragmentary state, in a number of parish churches in Denmark and Sweden, but these are only a fraction of what once existed. The loss of most of the frescoes of the Romanesque churches is due to reconstructions, fires, and, above all, to the addition of vaults during the Gothic period. Fragments of the paintings can be found between the vault and the roof. This is particularly true for the Romanesque paintings in the churches in Östergötland, Sweden. The frescoes were generally executed in a blend of fresco and secco techniques.

Among the earliest are the frescoes executed in Jutland, of which the best preserved are found in Todbjerg and Ørritslev. On the triumphal arch in the church at Ørritslev, Cain and Abel are portrayed with masklike faces and elongated figures; their garments are drawn in a calligraphic style. Closely connected with the frescoes at Todbjerg are the well-preserved fragments in the church at Finja in Skåne, Sweden, where a representation of the Last Judgment beside the triumphal arch is outstanding. The facial features and the muscles are strongly accentuated in a purely calligraphic manner, which together with the large eyes give the figures a frightening aspect. Similar elements characterize the frescoes in the apses of the churches at Vinslöv and Övraby, both in Skåne. Below the Christ in Majesty in Övraby are the standing figures of Mary, John the Baptist, and the apostles. The frescoes are executed in an archaic style, but they contain some manneristic elements of a later period. These paintings are related to German illuminated manuscripts (Fulda and Helmarshausen).

The frescoes of the church at Jelling in Denmark, of which only copies remain, and the beautiful Christ in Majesty in the church at Vä in Sweden have an elegance of a Byzantine type and are free from the provincialism evident in Övraby. In the church at Bjäresjö in Sweden the tunnel-vaulted chancel with an apse contains paintings that unfortunately have been much restored. Christ in Majesty is depicted in the apse; in the crown of the vault within a decorative framework is a Tree of Jesse, flanked by scenes from the Old and New Testaments arranged in registers. Near the triumphal arch are female personifications of the Virtues trampling the Vices. These frescoes, which stylistically and iconographically are related to French work, date from about 1200.

The wall paintings of the churches in Sjælland in Denmark — Jørlunde, Alsted, Hagested, Broby, and Fjenneslev — constitute a special group. Analogous works occur in Skåne (Lyngsjö and Asmundtorp). The frescoes of this group (1st half of 13th cent.) show influences of late Byzantine models, which probably were transmitted through western Germany. The Sjælland frescoes have borders with a meander pattern and other geometric designs.

The master who was active in the region around Ribe (e.g., at Vilslev) in Denmark about the same time had a more lively and dramatic style.

The nave of the church at Myresjö in Småland, the Swedish province north of Skåne, contains frescoes with scenes from the New Testament, divided by borders with vines and palmettes. In the church at Kaga near Linköping in Östergötland are frescoes on the chancel vault of the 12th century (Cain and Abel), as well as scenes from the infancy of Christ of an earlier date executed in a lively narrative style. The nave, decorated in the mid-13th century, preserves some vigorously drawn figures, among which are St. Olaf and someone who is thought to represent Sweden's first archbishop, Stefan (d. 1185). Among the best preserved Romanesque frescoes in Sweden are those above the vault in the church at Fornåsa in Östergötland, depicting the Passion of Christ; these are of a distinctly Byzantine character. Remarkably rich in color are the frescoes above the vaults in the church at Skönberga in Östergötland, seriously damaged but extensive.

The frescoes in the church at Garde (ca. 1150) in Gotland occupy an exceptional place in Scandinavian painting because of their pronounced Russo-Byzantine character. Other Romanesque frescoes in Gotland are found in Källunge, Kräklingbo (1211), and Mästerby (Virgin Enthroned, ca. 1200).

The Romanesque style lasted well into the 13th century in Scandinavia, as can be seen in the wooden ceiling of the church at Dädesjö in Småland, which is completely preserved and has never been repainted. Scenes from the lives of the Virgin Mary, of Christ, and of the Scandinavian missionary Stefan are depicted within circular borders. These paintings, which reveal affinities with those in western Germany, date from about 1270. The frescoes on the walls of the church were executed by the same artist who painted the ceiling: his name, Sigmund, appears in runic characters.

Few illuminated manuscripts of Scandinavian origin have survived. The quality of local production was relatively low, as attested by the Gospel Book from the Augustinian monastery at Dalby, Sweden (2d half of 11th cent.; Copenhagen, Royal Lib., Gl. Kongl. Saml. 1325, 4°), and a missal in Skara, Sweden (1100–50; Stiftsbibliotek). The so-called "Colbaz Annals" in East Berlin (ca. 1140; Deutsche Staatsbib.), containing some sketchy pen drawings, originated in Lund, Sweden. The Gospel Book in Uppsala (Univ. Lib., Cod. C.83), which has affinities with the illuminated manuscripts produced in Helmarshausen, also comes from Lund. A similar Gospel Book in Copenhagen (Royal Lib., Gl. Kongl. Saml. Thott. 20, 4°) was perhaps executed in Lund. The Gospel Book in Copenhagen (Nationalmus.) is from the monastery of Bosjö in Skåne. It has a magnificent binding with a cover of carved walrus tusk; the miniatures (ca. 1200) are of good quality and are stylistically similar to contemporaneous frescoes of Sjælland. The necrology in Copenhagen (1st half of 13th cent.; Univ. Lib., Cod. E. don. var. 52, 2°) from the Benedictine monastery of Naestved in Denmark, with illustration in the Saxon-Thuringian style, recalls Sigmund's frescoes in the church at Dädesjö.

Sten KARLING

IV. MINOR ARTS. FRANCE. One of the first French centers of gold- and silverwork was Conques, already active in the 10th century, where notable objects of the 11th and 12th centuries from the Abbey workshop are preserved in the treasury of the Church of Ste Foy. Among the early examples is the chest known as the reliquary of Pepin, which some scholars have tried to identify with Pepin of Aquitaine (817–38); however, in recent criticism (see *Les trésors des églises de France*, Paris, 1965, p. 296) it has been recognized as a work of about 1000 in which older pieces have been reused. Works from the end of the 11th century include the reliquary, or lantern, of St. Vincent, in the shape of a hexagonal tower with a conical roof and a quadrangular base; the portable altar of Ste Foy; another portable altar with an alabaster plaque; an object known as Charlemagne's A because its shape suggests the first letter of the alphabet; and the reliquary of Pope Paschal II (1099–1118), which contains a relic of the True Cross. All these objects are outstanding for the working of the embossed metal on a wooden core and for the profusion of cabochon stones, filigree, and, in some pieces (e.g., the portable altar with a central plaque of alabaster), the insertion of cloisonné enamels of obvious Byzantine imitation. Closely related to the production of the Conques workshop are three splendid reliquary busts of the 12th century: that of St-Chaffre in the church of Le Monastier (Haute-Loire); that of St. Baudime at Saint-Nectaire (PL. 379; the head and the hands of cast bronze led to this being erroneously classified in the past as a work of Limoges); and that of St-Césaire in the church of Maurs (Cantal). Each of these has a wooden core covered with a plating of precious metals, and the immobile stare and the richness of ornamentation recall the well-known statue of Ste Foy (X, PL. 473), a 10th-century product from the Conques workshop. The smaller Virgin reliquaries evidence the same type of workmanship; one of the most famous is that of the church of Orcival (12th cent.).

The second large center of French goldwork, but in a completely different style, arose at the Abbey of Saint-Denis at the time of Abbot Suger, who supplies ample information about the workshop in his account book of 1147. The goldsmiths of Saint-Denis — the "aurifabri lotharibgi," as Suger called them — came from the Rhenish-Mosan school.

The chief representatives of this school were Renier de Huy, Godefroid de Claire, who was also a native of Huy, and Nicholas of Verdun (q.v.). Renier made the baptismal font in Liège (V, PL. 319). Works attributed to Godefroid are the reliquary triptych in New York (Pierpont Morgan Lib.), the reliquary bust of St. Alexander (ca. 1145) in Brussels (Mus.

Royaux d'Art et d'H.), two enamel plaques in New York (Met. Mus.), and the triptych of the True Cross (ca. 1150) in Liège (Church of Ste-Croix). The enameled cross in London (Br. Mus.) and the reliquary chests of St. Mangold and St. Domitian in Huy (Notre-Dame) were made by Godefroid. The portable altar from Stavelot (IV, PL. 409) and the candlestick in Hildesheim (IX, PL. 167) belong to the same school.

Godefroid de Claire was the creator of the monumental cross (destroyed during the French Revolution) erected on the tomb of St. Denis. In Saint-Omer (Mus. B. A.) is the foot of a cross from the church of St-Bertin (1170–80), which is considered to be a copy, on a smaller scale, of the foot of the original cross on the tomb of St. Denis. Precious antique objects were mounted in Abbot Suger's workshop; extant examples are a porphyry vase in a gilded-silver eagle mounting (VI, PL. 263), the sardonyx vase of Eleanor of Aquitaine (Louvre), and a rock-crystal vase (PL. 282).

The greatest productivity in enamelwork at Limoges was reached during the 12th and 13th centuries, when this production gave rise to an export industry. According to Vasselot (in Michel, I, pt. 2a), this enamelwork may be divided into two groups: in one group the figures are executed in enamel and stand out against an all-gold background, with a marked projection of the heads of the figures (e.g., the manuscript cover with Christ in Majesty, IV, PL. 406); in the other group the background is executed in enamel with an infinite variety of decorative motifs (IV, PL. 408). According to Gauthier (1950), this second group appeared toward 1200. Among the objects produced in Limoges were reliquary chests in the shape of a simple house with a gable roof, such as the one with appliqué enamelwork in the church of Bellac (variously dated, but certainly one of the earliest known productions of this workshop); one with animal motifs in Washington (IV, PL. 408); and one with figural scenes in Sens (IV, PL. 408). Among the liturgical objects produced in Limoges are the Eucharistic doves in Paris (IX, PL. 164) and New York (Met. Mus., The Cloisters), altar cruets and basins (The Cloisters), and crosses (e.g., the one from Montmajour in the Louvre). A unique product of this workshop is the enameled copper tomb slab in Le Mans (IV, PL. 398).

The continuation of the same characteristics in all these objects (see Vasselot in Michel, I, pt. 2, p. 866) often makes dating difficult. Thus, for example, the pyx of the master G. Alpais, which was formerly considered to be from 1200–10, is now variously dated within the 13th century (IX, PL. 171).

Bronze sculptures were produced in the 12th century in Lorraine (IX, PL. 511) and the Mosan region. Sometimes the bronzes were gilded — for example, the allegorical figure of the Sea in London (Vict. and Alb.). The production of candelabra, sometimes enormous, like the seven-branched candelabra in Brunswick (IX, PL. 170) and in Reims (Mus. B. A.), continued. Outstanding examples of Mosan work of the early 13th century are the aquamanile in London (IX, PL. 164) and the arm reliquary and reliquary statuette of St. Stephen in New York (both Met. Mus., The Cloisters).

In the 13th century activity decisively passed from monastic to secular workshops; the goldsmiths formed a guild (see P. Le Roy, *Status et privilège du corps de marchands orfèvres-joyalliers de la ville de Paris*, Paris, 1759), and workshops opened on the Pont au Change in Paris. The goldsmiths then turned to the Gothic style, as is seen, for example, in the reliquary of St. Taurin (X, PL. 99), which is a miniature reproduction of Ste-Chapelle. Meanwhile, in Flanders, in the workshop of Hugo d'Oignies (IX, PL. 174) at Notre-Dame in Namur, there appeared new decorative accents in goldwork that also announced the Gothic style (see GOTHIC ART).

Fernanda de' MAFFEI

French production of ivories was scant during the Romanesque period. It is also difficult to distinguish the works of the shops in northern France from those of southern England because of the similarity in style, a similarity that is also noticeable in other fields of artistic endeavor. A group of works of certain French origin (for the most part fragmentary) is listed by Goldschmidt (1914–26, III). Among them are some 12th-century figures of the Elders of the Apocalypse (Lille, Mus. B. A.; Saint-Omer, Mus. B. A.) and the pastoral staff and tau staff in Florence (Mus. Naz.). The Elders of the Apocalypse are notable for a plastic force that links them to the sculpture of the period. The two staffs are noteworthy for their dense leaf decoration, which was also a characteristic of contemporaneous miniatures.

An "Ordenance du mestier des ouvriers de drap de soye de Paris" proves that silk was woven in Paris during the 13th century. Brocades with fleurs-de-lis, similar to those produced in Lucca, were depicted in the miniatures of the time. Fragments of this type of textile from the 13th century can be seen in Paris (Mus. de Cluny), Lyons (Mus. Historique de Tissus), and Berlin (Staat. Mus.). However, it is most likely that this art was practiced even before then if one attributes to France, as Falke (1913) does, the fragment of brocade with parrots, vine leaves, young hens, and hares found in the tomb of Leopold III, the Pious (d. 1136) at Klosterneuburg.

The first French stained glass (q.v.) was probably produced in Reims at the end of the 10th century, and a workshop is known to have existed at Cluny in the 11th century; yet it was not until the 12th century that the use of stained glass became widespread in France. Technically, this stained-glass work was characterized by a metal grating that was often unrelated to the contours of the composition.

The cathedrals of Le Mans (XIII, PLS. 159, 163), Poitiers (XIII, PL. 157), Angers, Chartres (XIII, PLS. 158, 162), Chalons-sur-Marne (XIII, PL. 158), and Strasbourg, the church in Le Champ (Isère), and La Trinité in Vendôme still preserve part of their Romanesque stained glass. The compositions in stained glass in western France are characterized by a vehement expressiveness that is typically Romanesque; in parts of the north — for example, in St-Remi in Reims (XIII, PL. 158) — the stained glass has a monumental style that heralds the Gothic.

About twenty mosaic pavements of various dates still exist in France. According to Stern (1962), the floor in St-Genès at Thiers (beginning of the 11th cent.), with medallions containing fantastic animals, is Romanesque. The pavement in St-Bénigne in Dijon contains Islamic elements. Another type of mosaic decorated with leaves, concentric arcs, animal figures, and other motifs common to the miniatures of the time is found in the Church of Sorde-l'Abbaye (Landes) and in the Church of St-Martin-d'Ainay in Lyons (with an inscription from the beginning of the 12th cent.). These mosaics are similar to those of the Cathedral of Lescar (Basses-Pyrénées), executed 1115–41, with scenes of animal combat that are of Hispano-Arabic origin. Other iconographic motifs, including Early Christian elements mingled with typically Romanesque imaginary animals, are found in the valley of the Rhone at Valence (Mus.), Die (town hall with a mosaic depicting the universe), and Lyons (Church of St-Jean). The mosaic in the monastery church of Gânagobie (Basses-Alpes) is dated 1122–24. In this mosaic, as in some mosaic floors in northern Italy, Romanesque and Eastern elements are blended. At St-Bertin in Saint-Omer *opus tessellatum* and *opus sectile* were used (1109); the tomb mosaic of William (d. 1109), son of Robert of Flanders (now in Saint-Omer, Mus. B. A.), is outstanding. The floors of St-Denis in Saint-Denis, St-Bertin in Saint-Omer, and St-Irénée in Lyons also prove that Romanesque floor mosaics were common. The pavement of the Church of St-Remi in Reims is known only from an 18th-century description. The pavement in the Chapel of St. Firmin in St-Denis, which was executed with the technique used in wall mosaics, recalls the style of northern France and the Mosan region. An elaborate work, it includes personifications of the months within octagons, as well as representations of people, among whom is the monk Albéric, who was probably the donor of the mosaic (1144–45).

* * *

SPAIN AND PORTUGAL. The casket of partly gilded repoussé silver made for the relics of St. Isidore (León, Mus. Arqueol. Provincial) can be dated about 1063, when these relics were brought from Seville. The casket is decorated with scenes from Genesis, images, inscriptions, and symbols of the Evangelists. Somewhat later, from about 1075, is the so-called "Arca Santa" of Oviedo Cathedral (PL. 280), larger than the reliquary of St. Isidore; it is also of repoussé silver with engraved work. The compositions, similar to those on antependiums, are bordered with decorative Kufic inscriptions, and there is a calvary on the lid. The beautiful reliquary casket of St. Eugenius (12th cent.) in Toledo Cathedral is made of repoussé silver sheets decorated with scenes from the life of the saint. The engraved and nielloed silver cross in Mansilla de la Sierra (Logroño) dates from 1109. The reliquary of the True Cross in Astorga Cathedral, which is in the shape of a cross with two crossarms, is decorated with filigree over gold; it is a work of the 12th–13th century and has some parallels in Portugal.

The finest of the chalices, made of onyx with gold mountings, was donated by Doña Urraca, daughter of King Ferdinand I, to the church of S. Isidoro in León (PL. 282); an opulent piece, it is exceptional for the beauty and quality of its decorations. No less notable are the chalice of gilded silver with filigree in S. Domingo de Silos, which dates from shortly after 1040, and another one from Celanova, known as the chalice of S. Rosendo (Orense, Mus. Diocesano), a 12th-century work of partly gilded silver with elegant decorations only on the stem. The cover of the Evangelistary of Queen Felicia (d. 1086), wife of Sancho Ramírez of Aragon, is incrusted with magnificent silver filigree and carbuncles; originally in the Cathedral of Jaca, it is now in New York (Met. Mus.). Also important are the covers of the Evangelistary in the collegiate church of Roncesvalles and the reliquary diptych of Bishop Gonzalo Menéndez (1162–75) in Oviedo Cathedral, with a calvary and the Pantocrator in engraved and nielloed silver on the outside and with figures of ivory on the inside, where there is also a border of filigree and carbuncles.

In Portugal, in addition to the crosses that are related to the reliquary of the True Cross in Astorga, an interesting group of Romanesque chalices is preserved. The most famous one, in Brage (Cath. Treas.), is of gilded and nielloed silver, with Mozarabic details, commissioned by Mendo Gonçalves (d. 1008) and his wife Doña Toda. A chalice commissioned by Geda Menediz in 1190, with a filigree stem, the Apostles on the cup, and the symbols of the Evangelists on the base, is preserved in Coimbra (Mus. de Machado de Castro). Of a uniform style, but with decorations only on the stem and base, are the chalice given by Queen Dulce to the Monastery of S. Maria in Alcobaça (Lisbon, Mus. Nac. de Arte Antiga) and the one presented in 1187 to the Monastery of S. Marinha da Costa by King Sancho I and Queen Dulce (Guimarães, Mus. Regional de Alberto Sampaio).

Closely related to the goldsmiths' work are the enamels, of which there are examples of high quality in the pieces that formed part of the 11th- or early-12th-century sepulchral urn of St. Dominic of Silos; one side of the cover is still in the Monastery of S. Domingo de Silos, and the front of the urn is in Burgos (Mus. Arqueol. Provincial). The front shows Christ in Majesty, with the Alpha and Omega and the symbols of the Evangelists in the center, and at the sides the Apostles are depicted under arches richly executed in champlevé enamels. On the cover are the Apostles with the Agnus Dei in the center. The urn was executed with a cold chisel on brown varnish (*vernis brun*), a technique related to that of Germanic goldwork. A work of equal excellence is the retable of enameled copper (12th cent.) preserved in the Sanctuary of S. Miguel de Excelsis near Pamplona. In the center within a mandorla are the Virgin and Child, and at the sides are two series of figures under arches — six Apostles above and the Three Kings, the Annunciation, and St. Joseph below; on the crown there are four minor pieces in the center, and on each side there are nine circular medallions of excellent workmanship, all in perfect condition. The fragments of a similar group, more closely related to the workshops of Limoges, are preserved in Orense Cathedral.

The Virgen de la Vega (12th cent.) in the New Cathedral of Salamanca is of gilded copper, with some parts of cast bronze, over a wooden core; the throne and footrest are decorated with enamels of great interest that appear to have been produced in a Spanish workshop. Similar to it, but inferior in quality, are the statues of the Virgin and Child from Husillos (Palencia, Bishop's Palace), in S. María in Ujué near Artajona, and in S. Clara in Huesca. Many small chests, such as those in Huesca Cathedral, S. Domingo de Silos, and Viseu Cathedral in Portugal, are decorated with enamels, as are the staffs in the cathedrals of Roda de Isábena and Cuenca, the covers of the Evangelistary of Tortosa Cathedral, and a number of liturgical objects.

Wrought iron was used for grilles during the Romanesque period. Fine examples of grilles with spiral motifs are found in the Cathedral of Jaca, in S. Vicente in Avila, in Oviedo, in Zamora, in the churches of S. María del Mercado and S. Isidoro in León, and in the Cathedral of Palencia. Other examples of the same type of metalwork, with decorations in which spirals are included, are the iron fitting on the doors of many Romanesque churches, braziers, candelabra, and small pieces of furniture.

The art of ivory carving was adopted by the Christian kingdoms of the Iberian Peninsula, possibly through Moslem or Byzantine influence, to which the Germanic influence of the Ottonian workshops was added later. An outstanding piece of Leonese production is the crucifix that Ferdinand I of León and his wife Sancha donated to the Church of S. Isidoro in León in 1063 (PL. 281). Other examples of Leonese work are the ivories decorating the reliquary caskets of John the Baptist and S. Pelayo (León, S. Isidoro); the casket of the Bienaventuranzas (Madrid, Mus. Arqueol. Nac.); the crucifix from Carrizo (León, Mus. Arqueol. Provincial); and some smaller pieces, among them a book cover with a varied iconography (Louvre), some plaques with scenes from the Passion (Oviedo, private coll.; Leningrad, The Hermitage; Met. Mus.), a St. Peter (Bryn Athyn, Pa., Pitcairn Coll.), a crucifix (Oviedo, Cath., Cámara Santa), two staffs (Vict. and Alb.; Roda de Isábena, Cathedral), and several plaques with Biblical themes in various museums and collections.

Although different in style, the two most important series of ivories from San Millán de la Cogolla perhaps denote the existence of another workshop in this Benedictine monastery. The casket of S. Millán was decorated with 22 plaques, which were carved between 1067 and 1070 by order of King Sancho IV of Navarra; 16 are still preserved in the monastery, and the others are in Madrid (Mus. Arqueol. Nac.), Leningrad (The Hermitage), Florence (Mus. Naz.), and Washington, D.C. (Dumbarton Oaks Coll.). The casket was made by Engelram and his son Rodolfo, undoubtedly Germans, who signed it and also portrayed themselves among the figures (this portrait is in the Dumbarton Oaks Coll.). The style, even though of an expressionist liveliness, nevertheless exhibits certain Peninsular characteristics. More related to the style of León are the five plaques (one in Vienna and four in the Monastery of San Millán de la Cogolla) from the reliquary casket of S. Felices (late 11th cent.). Other noteworthy examples of ivory carving are the pyx (ca. 1100) in S. Isidoro in León, with the Pantocrator on a background of gold filigree, and a crucifix with the right arm missing (12th cent.; Met. Mus.), which shows a relationship with contemporaneous wooden images.

Embroideries constitute an important field of Romanesque production in Spain, and outstanding among them is the so-called "Genesis of Gerona" (12th cent.; PL. 253). The composition, which is incomplete, consists of a circular arrangement of scenes from Genesis in the center, the Four Winds in the corners, and a border with the Months, the Seasons, and the Four Rivers of Paradise, all of a symbolic character and in a lively style, with a naturalness and decorative charm with which only the famous Bayeux tapestry can be compared. Similar in technique, but of a different style, are two works from Seo de Urgel: the so-called "standard of S. Odón" (12th cent.; Barcelona, Mus. de Bellas Artes de Cataluña), signed by Elisava, in a form typical of the standards and flags from the 11th and 12th centuries, and a relatively well-preserved frontal (Vict. and Alb.) with the Pantocrator, the apostles, and the symbols of the Evangelists in an arrangement similar to

that of frontals painted on wood. The miters of S. Ramón and S. Valero in the Cathedral of Roda de Isábena are embroidered on Moslem textiles. Two stoles in S. Isidoro in León are decorated with crosses and heraldic castles; according to the inscription, they were embroidered by Queen Leonor, wife of Alfonso VIII of Castile, in 1197–98.

José R. GUDIOL

ITALY. The few surviving examples of gold- and silverwork show continuing use of the techniques of enamelwork — both in cloisonné, in accordance with Byzantine practice, and in champlevé, in accordance with northern European custom — and of filigree, damascening, and niello. In addition, there was widespread use of molded embossed plates; and even in the 12th century works were made more colorful by mounting them with large cabochons, a continuation of barbarian practice. Enamelwork was especially popular in Milan, where the cover of the Evangelistary of Aribertus, archbishop of Intimiano (1018–45; Milan, Cath. Treas.), was made. The figural enamels show Byzantine influence; the precious stones and filigree are still barbarian in style. The 12th-century cover in Vercelli (Cath. Treas.) has figural enamels similar to those of western Germany and embossed busts of angels in roundels that are stylistically close to contemporaneous sculpture. In the so-called "Chiavenna pax" (Chiavenna, S. Lorenzo), of slightly later date and originally an Evangelistary cover, the artist achieved a dignified balance in the distribution of decorative elements.

Goldsmith's work was produced in Venice, where the Pala d'Oro of S. Marco (end of 11th cent.; IV, PL. 405), subsequently rearranged (1209, 1345), combines imported Byzantine enamels with locally made enamels, which are framed with precious stones, embossed plant decorations, and filigree. Venice was distinguished for its special way of working filigree, which was called *opus veneticum*. An example of this is the antependium (1195–1204) in the Cathedral of Cividale del Friuli. It is also known that the Holy Roman emperor Frederick II ordered his throne and crown in Venice.

The production of southern Italy was rich and distinctive. The famous altarpiece commissioned by Desiderius, abbot of Montecassino (1058–87), has disappeared. There still exists a remarkable group of objects made in Palermo under the Normans, such as the imperial garments adorned with enamels, filigree, and pearls (see the discussion of textiles below) and the splendid ceremonial sword (1133; Vienna, Schatzkammer der Wiener Hofburg). Also in the Schatzkammer is the sword of St. Maurice (late 12th cent.). The floral and geometric motifs of the enamels are linked stylistically to Moslem models; in fact, in the ceremonial sword there are even interlaced Arabic letters. In the works from Palermo the filigree, which is not twisted in the Venetian manner but arranged in spirals (i.e., circinate), is thickly set on the surfaces, and the stones are inset. However, the most characteristic feature of these objects is the use of beaded borders, which are almost always double and frame the individual motifs of both the filigree and the enamelwork. As in the embroidered textiles, echoes of the Byzantine, the Islamic, and even the barbarian worlds are blended with a highly developed taste. Similar to these works (in the use of circinate filigree, for example) are the cover of the Evangelistary of Archbishop Alfano (1173–82) in Capua (Cath. Treas.); the *staurotheke* in the Archbishop's Palace in Cosenza (II, PL. 485), now thought to date from the late 12th or early 13th century; the *staurotheke* in Naples Cathedral, of the late 12th century; and the *staurotheke* in Cava dei Tirreni (Abbey church of Trinità della Cava). However, in all these works the figural enamels, the embossed plant ornamentation, the type of frame, and the form of the cross itself indicate a direct dependence on the Byzantine, an influence that may have been transmitted by the lost altarpiece of Montecassino.

Connections with typically Norman works can be found in the cross in Velletri (Mus. Capitolare) and in the cross of the Guelph Treasure in Berlin (Kunstgewerbes Mus., Schloss Charlottenburg), which show a compromise between Lombard and Sicilian art. These two works have been variously dated between the mid-11th and 13th centuries. They may be, as Lipinsky (1957) believes, the work of a Lombard who emigrated to Sicily.

In the Italian production of embossed metalwork Byzantine influences and connections with the work of northern Europe alternate and overlay each other according to region. The reliquary in Zadar Cathedral, Yugoslavia, and the cover of the Evangelistary in Padua (Cath. Treas.) can be ascribed to the 11th-century and the Byzantine-style sphere of Venice. The silver cover with the Annunciation in Rome (Vat. Mus.) should be considered a copy of a Byzantine model (Toesca, Md). Ottonian echoes are noticeable in the figures on the verso of the cover of the Evangelistary of Aribertus and on the cover in Vercelli. The portable altar in Modena (Cath. Treas.), the almost identical one in the Guelph Treasure (Berlin, Kunstgewerbes Mus., Schloss Charlottenburg), and the reliquary in Genoa (S. Stefano) are Lombard works of the late 11th or early 12th century. The reliquary in S. Stefano has stone and filigree decoration and busts of angels in roundels, which are similar to those on the cover in Vercelli.

The masterpiece of Lombard gold- and silverwork is the 12th-century antependium in Città di Castello (IX, PL. 168). In this work the influence of contemporaneous sculpture is revealed in the plastic quality of the figures, which have a vague Ottonian ancestry, and the large bosses of the frame take the place of colored stones. The antependium in Cividale del Friuli is clearly a Byzantinizing work, especially in the framing, where busts in roundels alternate with panels of plant decorations. This Byzantine influence is even more evident in the central figures (under the arches) of the Virgin and angels, which reveal, however, an unusual sense of modeling under the close-set folds of their clothing. The modeling is even more apparent in the three side rows of saints, which show the influence of the sculpture of the Venetian hinterland. The gilded copper sheet of Adalpreto in Trento (Cath. Treas.), datable between 1156 and 1177, can probably be ascribed to Verona because of the clear connections with the figures on the sarcophagus of SS. Lucilio, Lupicino, and Crescenziano in Verona (S. Zeno Maggiore). The Cross of the Field in Brescia (Rotonda, or Old Cathedral) can be considered a work of the end of the 12th century. Although it shows some similarities, especially in the figure of Christ, to the antependium in Città di Castello, the facial types are much closer to the sculpture of the west portal of the Cathedral of Verona.

The late-13th-century reliquaries of Rab Cathedral, Yugoslavia, and Anagni (Cath. Treas.) still maintain some Byzantine accents, even though that of Rab approaches northern European iconographic schemes. The processional cross (1228) in Padua (Cath. Treas.) is also clearly Byzantinizing in style, but in the figure of the Virgin it shows obvious influence from the Rhenish workshops. This Rhenish influence is even more evident in the silver cover with Christ in Majesty in the treasury of S. Marco, Venice. The reliquary of S. Maria in Zadar, of rather high quality and perhaps made in Venice, can be dated to the end of the 13th century. Although it remains within the Byzantine sphere, it already has some Gothic elements.

Early indications of a flourishing goldsmith's art in Tuscany are the oldest parts of the Altar of St. James (begun 1287; Pistoia, Cathedral) and the reliquary bust of S. Galganus (late 13th cent.; Siena, Mus. dell'Opera del Duomo), both of which show clear connections with local sculpture but also contain Gothicizing elements.

Bronze was used particularly for the doors of churches, as well as for stationary and processional crosses, for censers, candelabra, and for other liturgical objects.

The masterpiece of Romanesque ivory sculpture is the Salerno altarpiece (PL. 281). If this work was executed in southern Italy, as it is believed to have been, it constitutes the sole evidence of a thriving Italian workshop in the Romanesque period. It has been dismantled and reassembled, and no longer retains its original 12th-century form. Goldsmith has suggested that it be reconstructed in the form of a cathedra, like the "throne of Maximian" (V, PL. 432). The small plaques, which are by a different hand, show a predominant Byzantine

influence, combined however with a Romanesque sense of form; the ornamentation is related in part to Arabic art, and the iconography shows some Spanish traits. A few scattered ivories (Florence, Mus. Naz.; Louvre) seem to be products of this workshop, which cannot be more specifically identified.

Some of the ivories in Ravenna (Mus. Naz.) and Florence (Mus. Naz.) are more decidedly Byzantine. They are characterized by harsher carving and by flattened relief. Many chess pieces were probably produced in southern Italy. The small, so-called "Siculo-Arabian" ivory chests, with Eastern-style pen designs, were probably executed in Sicily, and they are to be found in various museums and church treasuries.

The oldest examples of silk weaving are from southern Italy, particularly Sicily, where the first looms were probably put into operation by the Saracens in the 9th century. This typically Eastern industry — first Persia and then Byzantium enjoyed a monopoly of it — had its greatest flowering in Sicily during the time of the Normans, especially after the war with Greece (1146), when Roger II did not return prisoners skilled in the art of silk but ordered them to be taken to Palermo.

The workshop connected to the Norman court in Sicily was known by the Moslem name of tirāz or by the Greek one of ergasterion (as is known from a fragment in Hannover, Kestner-Mus.). These names are indicative of the two principal currents — the Islamic and the Byzantine — that were joined there. However, the original interpretation given to the characteristic motifs of the two different cultures (both of which, in so far as textiles are concerned, have their roots in the Sassanian tradition) gave Sicilian textiles a completely new aspect. The garments belonging to the Norman kings are embroidered with pearls, gold thread and paillettes, precious stones, and enamels; these include the coronation mantle of Roger II (1134; V, PL. 244), the alb of William II (1181; XIV, PL. 7), and Roger's dalmatic and William's coronation stole, shoes, and stockings (all, Vienna, Schatzkammer der Wiener Hofburg), to which the apparel of Henry VI and Frederick II must have been similar. To this group should be added the Coif of Constance and the antependium (restored in the 18th cent.), both in Palermo Cathedral, the bishop's miter (restored in the 15th cent.) in Linköping, Sweden (Mus.), the miter (restored in the 18th cent.) in Skara Cathedral, Sweden, and probably the miter with gold, coral, and pearls in Halberstadt (Cath. Treas.).

Although the weaving in these examples evidences Byzantine technique, the embroidered motifs of the decoration are linked to Fatimid art. The influence of Fatimid art is seen in the two lions, each devouring a camel, that entirely cover the mantle of Roger II (V, PL. 244) almost as if it were half of an enormous orb. The lions are separated by a very stylized palmette. Also Fatimid are the palmettes decorating the edges of the sleeves and the hem of the dalmatic. To these were added the clearly Islamic motif of ornamental script — in this case, Naskhi letters, which flow elegantly to form a border.

Another group of fabrics, in which the design is woven rather than embroidered, is exemplified by the lining of the cloak of Frederick II. Here serpentine dragons, intertwined to form lozenges, stand out on a gold background, and within these lozenges are figural scenes. There are also birds and trees of life in the form of three-leaf palmettes. The same kind of cloth was found in the tomb of Henry VI, and fragments are scattered throughout various European museums.

A third group of textiles, the so-called "exarentasmata," is more directly tied to Byzantine tradition, as shown by the cloth with griffins and birds within orbs in the reliquary of St. Potentien in Sens (Cath. Treas.) and by the fragment, also with orbs, in Hannover (Kestner-Mus.). To this group belong textiles that are iconographically different and that are sometimes difficult to distinguish from Spanish ones. The iconography comprises motifs popular in the East (e.g., the gazelle, hare, partridge, and peacock) and continues to follow the usual affronted arrangement of these figures, which are disposed in a freer composition instead of within orbs. Animals, affronted (cf. XIV, PL. 7) or addorsed, are repeated in horizontal rows. There are also alternating rows of different animals (birds and quadrupeds), as in the textiles discovered in the tombs of Henry VI and Constance in Palermo and in the tomb of St. Servatius in the parish church of Siegburg (the latter also has a row of two-headed eagles above a row of gazelles), while a vertical rhythm is suggested by the upward unwinding of stylized plant motifs that repeat the tree of life motif.

In the 13th century Sicilian production was notable for another type of embroidered textile. In the dossal in Assisi (Cath. Treas.) griffins and parrots, embroidered in burnished gold that stands out against the bright gold of the background, are enclosed within lobed frames. Similar in the embroidery technique are the dalmatic in Halberstadt Cathedral, in which centaurs shoot arrows at deer on a background strewn with stars, and the so-called "cope of Otto IV" in Brunswick (Cath. Treas.), which some authorities consider to be of English origin. On the cope, lions are scattered on a background of stars and crescent moons. The borders are decorated with angels bearing frankincense interspersed with the traditional Fatimid palmette. As correctly noted by Santangelo (1958), these fabrics repeat the decoration of the Siculo-Arabian ivory chests.

In Lucca the richness of the fabrics never depended upon embroidery, as it did in the Sicilian textiles, but rather upon the quality of the material used, often gold and silver thread. Notable examples are the fabrics covered with animals whose heads and wings are sprinkled with gold and silver, at first in a single color but later in contrasting colors. In these textiles the placement of the figures, often gazelles and birds (Siena, Mus. dell'Opera del Duomo; Rome, Mus. di Palazzo Venezia), repeats that of the fabric from the tomb of Henry VI. Orbed fabrics, which can perhaps be considered the oldest, are rarer. Among them, important noteworthy examples are those in the tomb of Bernardo degli Uberti (Florence, Sta Trinita) and in Marburg (Universitätsmus.), and perhaps the cope in Anagni (Cath. Treas.). Also in Anagni is an embroidered 13th-century antependium that shows Gothic influence.

In Italy, although floors decorated with religious scenes are extremely rare (Casale Monferrato, Cathedral; Bobbio, S. Colombano), those with nonreligious subjects are numerous. There are epic cycles (Trojan epic in Otranto, Cathedral), stories of the crusades (Ravenna, X, PL. 190), cycles inspired by classical mythology (the labyrinth with Theseus and the Minotaur in Pavia, S. Michele), representations of the year and months (Aosta, Cathedral; Pavia, S. Michele; Piacenza, S. Savino), the Liberal Arts (Ivrea, Palazzo del Seminario), the Virtues (San Benedetto Po near Mantua), and the struggle between the virtues and the vices (Crema, Cathedral). Mosaic decorations were sometimes derived from Eastern fabrics and depicted fantastic figures within circles (Caserta Vecchia, Cathedral; Pomposa, Abbey; Tremiti Islands, Abbey; Church of S. Maria del Patir near Rossano; Otranto, X, PL. 190).

In central and southern Italy opus Alexandrinum (differently colored marble tiles forming geometric patterns) was first used in 1071 in Montecassino. There are also fragments of floors of this type in the church at Sant'Angelo in Formis and in the cathedrals of Salerno (1153–81; presbytery), Terracina, and Caserta Vecchia. In Sicily floors of the same type include Moslem motifs (Palermo, Cappella Palatina; Monreale, Cathedral). In Latium the Cosmati (q.v.) reelaborated the decorative repertory in a way that was completely personal but also similar to that of late antiquity. In Campania marble tiles and genuine mosaics were alternated in lively contrasts of color. In Tuscany dichromatic tarsia (green and white) was used with designs drawn from fabrics or with representations of the year (e.g., in Florence, X, PL. 439).

Fernanda de' MAFFEI

GERMANY. In the Romanesque period there was a lively exchange of ideas between the goldsmith workshops of northern Germany and the Walloon valley of the Meuse (then German). During this time copper began to be used more frequently. In the works (ca. 1100) by Roger of Helmarshausen, especially the portable altar of SS. Kilian and Liborius in Paderborn (Cath. Treas.), the portable altar from Abdinghof Monastery in Paderborn (Franciscan church), and a book cover in Trier (Cath. Treas.), models of the Mosan region were transformed into an individual style, characterized by a narrative liveliness and concise graphic forms. The traditional techniques were employed by Roger in a new Romanesque manner. His style was continued in Saxony in the so-called "Weser school" up to about 1150, and still longer in illuminated manuscripts. In the St. Godehard and St. Epiphanius shrines (ca. 1132) in Hildesheim Cathedral this style was transformed into fuller and rounder forms; the taste for weighty forms is characteristically Saxon.

From about 1130 on the Rhenish workshops, especially in Cologne, were very active and often worked closely with those of the Mosan region. The main commissions were for portable altars and for reliquary shrines that tended increasingly to assume architectural forms. They were decorated with representational, narrative, and symbolical scenes. Chalices, censers, and other liturgical objects were also designed in architectural shapes (e.g., the bronze censer cover in the Br. Mus.). The works of the Eilbertus group, named after the goldsmith Master Eilbertus (probably ca. 1130–60; IX, PL. 168), were characterized by concisely delineated figures, often on an enameled ground, and were very detailed. The so-called "Fridericus group" (named after a goldsmith or donor) was active between about 1170 and 1190; their production is distinguished by curving lines in the tendril motifs, in the figures, and even in the niches and cupolas of reliquary shrines and by soft transitions from one enamel color to the other. The following works were executed by Rhenish artists under the direction of Mosan artists: the Heribert shrine (ca. 1170; Deutz, St. Heribert), the St. Anno reliquary in Siegburg (parish church), and the Three Kings reliquary (X, PL. 316), the last two with the collaboration of Nicholas of Verdun (q.v.). Frederick Barbarossa commissioned from a Rhenish or more westerly workshop (perhaps Aachen) the Aachen circular chandelier (ca. 1180; III, PL. 484), made by Master Wibert; the baptismal basin of the Emperor (engraved after 1155; Berlin, Kunstgewerbemus., Schloss Charlottenburg); and the head of the Emperor (between 1155 and 1171; Cappenberg, Abbey church), which is one of the first true portraits although it was in the form of a reliquary bust and probably was meant to be used as such.

In Saxony in the second half of the 12th century the very rare disk crosses (Met. Mus.) were produced in Hildesheim, and then, in Brunswick or Hildesheim, the goldwork of the so-called "Welandus group," most of whom worked for Henry the Lion. This group followed the style of the Rhenish Eilbertus group, but with a harsher expression of forms. A chalice and paten from Wilten (PL. 282) are decorated with scenes depicting the whole salvation story from Adam to the Redemption. In the Abbey church in Tremessen, Poland, is a chalice of Lower Saxony provenance. The later Saxon works display a lively movement and richness of lines resulting from English and Byzantine influence.

In contrast, in southern Germany only individual works are found. Noteworthy are another chalice in the Abbey church in Tremessen, Poland, probably of Middle Rhenish origin; the processional cross (1122–37) in the Abbey church of Zwiefalten; the reliquary chest from Gruol (Frankfurt am Main, Mus. f. Kunsthandwerk), perhaps made in Zwiefalten; the circular chandelier and antependium (ca. 1140–50) of Grosskomburg in Komburg near Schwäbish-Hall, probably made locally; and several chalices, especially the one (ca. 1200) from St. Peter's in Salzburg (Vienna, Kunsthist. Mus.).

Bracteates were widespread in Germany in the 12th century. The most important ones come from Saxony and Thuringia (III, PL. 408).

The ivory plaques of the so-called "Würzburg group," made in Franconia about 1090, although they follow Ottonian traditions and are inspired by Byzantine models, represent the distinct beginning of Romanesque art in the decisive separation of the figures from the background and in the complexity of the design. In the 12th century ivory carving was no longer as important as it had been in the early Middle Ages, partly because ivory was used for small or practical objects (hooks of bishops' crosiers, chess pieces, etc.) and partly because the art compared with monumental sculpture (crucifix in Bamberg, Cath. Treas.). In Cologne numerous works in ivory, walrus tusk, and bone were made, which were copied again and again. More important pieces were inserted in reliquaries, such as the Eltenberg Reliquary (VI, PL. 261) and the Dome Reliquary of the Guelph Treasure (Berlin, Kunstgewerbemus., Schloss Charlottenburg), and the contrast between the different materials was very effective. Among the most beautiful ivory plaques are those made about 1130 in Cologne, which are related to the somewhat earlier stucco sculpture of Gernrode and to the Gustorf screens. Characteristic features of this group are the union of firm and soft forms of sculptural density and of ornamental effect and the warmth of expression (PL. 281).

A new technique was introduced in textiles, that of half silk woven with a linen warp, which reached its highest level in the 13th century. The chief centers of textile art were the great merchant cities of Regensburg and Cologne. Numerous printed textiles have been preserved (the earliest probably from the 11th cent.), some with patterns in gold or silver. Often Oriental models were continued but executed in a free and lively, and at times monumental, style (XIV, PL. 10). Masterpieces of 12th-century textile art are the tapestries, which were produced in several German centers. Important Saxon examples have been preserved in Halberstadt (XIII, PL. 391) and Quedlinburg. In embroidery work both the old technique of gold embroidery and the new technique of colored embroidery on linen were used.

The most important stained glass from the early 12th century is the cycle in Augsburg Cathedral. The five prophets depicted (XIII, PL. 161), despite their monumental solidity and the severity of their frontal position, are vigorous and alive; the miniatures of the Passional in Stuttgart (Landesbib., Cod. bibl. fol. 56–58) from Hirsau show affinities with the Augsburg windows. The stained glass by Master Gerlachus (XIII, PL. 160), which stylistically is closely connected with the miniatures of Lower Saxony (Helmarshausen), is characterized by compact composition, dry drawing, and broad ornamental borders that are partly executed in a new technique in which the opaque areas were scratched out to expose the glass; this technique had widespread influence. Stained glass is preserved in Klagenfurt (XIII, PL. 161), Eisenach (Thüringer Mus.), Weimar (in the Mus. in Goethe's house), Darmstadt (Landesmus.), and Zurich (Schweizerisches Landesmus.). The animated style of the late 12th century was represented by the stained-glass windows from Ingelheim (formerly in Berlin; destroyed). The stained glass from Alpirsbach (Stuttgart, Württembergisches Landesmus.), which depicts Samson at the gate of Gaza, is similar to that of the Cathedral in Strasbourg; both date from about 1200.

The mosaic floors in the crypt of St. Gereon in Cologne, originally in the choir, date from the time of Archbishop Anno (1056–75). Represented are scenes from the lives of David and Samson. Mosaic was also used for the tomb of Abbot Gilbert (d. 1152) in Maria Laach (Bonn, Rheinisches Landesmus.).

Wilhelm MESSERER

ENGLAND. Of the surviving gold- and silverwork from the Romanesque period, the Gloucester Candlestick (ca. 1110; VI, PL. 252) of gilded bronze is one of the most notable pieces. It is of excellent workmanship and closely related to the illuminations of the early 12th century. In the Victoria and Albert Museum are two beautiful plaques in champlevé enamel on gilded copper, which were made in Winchester between 1150 and 1160. A number of English cathedrals have 12th-century screenwork; the finest example is the St. Swithin grille in Winchester. The Trivulzio candlestick (ca. 1200) in the Cathedral in Milan is sometimes attributed to England, but this attribution is far from convincing.

Exquisite works in ivory and, more often, whalebone were produced, as the surviving reliefs (VI, PL. 428), book covers, boxes, portable altars, and crosses show. The crosier head with

scenes from the Life of Christ and of St. Nicholas (ca. 1180; PL. 281) is an outstanding example of Romanesque carving. The Bury St. Edmunds cross (Met. Mus., The Cloisters), a superb example of Romanesque art, dates from the second half of the 12th century. The cross is carved from walrus tusk, and depicts eight scenes from the Old and New Testaments. There are over 60 inscriptions in Latin and Greek. Also from the 12th century are a carved ivory group of the Flight into Egypt (Met. Mus.), a fragment of a panel (Br. Mus.), and a set of chessmen found on the Island of Lewis (Br. Mus.).

The Bayeux tapestry (ca. 1080; VII, PL. 271; XIV, PL. 312), which, in spite of its name, was an embroidery, was probably made for Odo, bishop of Bayeux and half-brother of William the Conqueror. Although some scholars attribute it to Normandy, in this author's opinion it is undisputably the work of English craftsmen. It has recently been attributed with some justification to Canterbury.

The only extensive series of 12th-century stained glass surviving in England is found in Canterbury in Christchurch Cathedral (ca. 1190); it is of a transitional style. Unlike the manuscripts of the period, which reveal Byzantine influence, this stained glass shows French influence. The Tree of Jesse window in the Minster in York is of the late 12th century.

George ZARNECKI

SCANDINAVIA. Many gilded bronze weather vanes of the 11th century, such as those from Heggen, Norway (Oslo, Universitetets Oldsaksamling) and Söderala, Sweden (XIV, PL. 463), have zoomorphic ornamentation in the viking style. Other weather vanes, such as the gilded copper one from Tingelstad, Norway (Brandbu, Hadelands Folkemus.), are perforated in a typically Anglo-Saxon pattern.

Only fragments of the large reliquary chests containing the remains of St. Canute (d. 1086) and his brother, Benedict, remain in the Cathedral in Odense, Denmark. The decoration is similar to that of the gilded metal antependiums that still exist in numerous churches in Jutland. Some complete altars have also been preserved in Jutland; they consist of an antependium, a retable, and above the retable a freestanding crucifix within a semicircular frame. The most remarkable, those from Lisbjærg and Odder, both from 1150, are in Copenhagen (Nationalmus.). Other examples are in the churches at Sahl and Stadil. The crucifixes from Aaby and Tirstrup (both, Copenhagen, Nationalmus.) and a Virgin of bronze that was found in Randers fiord originally belonged to some altar furnishings. The style of the Virgin is reminiscent of Burgundian production.

The altars and antependiums of Jutland appear to have been executed in workshops in Aarhus, Ribe, and Schleswig during the late 12th and the early 13th century. These workshops, undoubtedly established by foreign masters, some of whom came from Cologne, were active for several generations, and therefore the production displays styles from different periods and of different origins.

The antependium and retable from Broddetorp in Sweden (Stockholm, Nationalmus.) closely resemble the Lisbjærg altar, but they may have been executed in Skara. Of a different type is the antependium in the church at Lyngsjö in Sweden, which depicts the Virgin surrounded by Old Testament figures. It is not as elaborately decorated as the Jutland antependiums, and its style, more severe and pure, demonstrates connections with Saxony. The Lyngsjö antependium was perhaps executed in Lund. Some bronze processional crosses with engraved figures of Saxon character may also have been made in Lund. The earliest of these crosses (Lund, Universitetets Historiska Mus.) dates from the late 11th century.

A number of Swedish reliquary chests are made in the form of rural houses with dragon heads at the ends of the ridge poles, for example, the gilded copper chest from Eriksberg (late 12th cent.; Stockholm, Nationalmus.). A dragon head of gilded bronze from Viborg Cathedral (Copenhagen, Nationalmus.) once probably adorned a reliquary chest. The reliquary chest from the Thomaskirke on the Filefjell in Norway (ca. 1230–

50; Bergen, Historisk Mus.), of gilded copper, is in the form of a stave church, but the figures of Christ, the Evangelists, and the apostles show Continental and Byzantinizing elements.

Many of the churches in the region around Lake Vetter (Vättern) in central Sweden have wrought-iron doors from the 12th century. The master of one of the most beautiful doors, that of the church at Rogslösa, has depicted Theodoric with a falcon and dog chasing a deer. A slightly younger master, by the name of Asmunder, mingles figures and ornaments in a more symmetrical composition. In this part of Sweden wrought iron of a similar type is also found on chests (Voxtorp and Rydaholm).

The so-called "Cross of Gunhild" (Copenhagen, Nationalmus.), named after the Danish princess who commissioned it, is a unique piece of work in walrus tusk (the figure of Christ has been lost). This cross, made shortly after 1079, is signed by Liutger, who perhaps learned his art in Cologne. That Byzantine ivory reliefs were known in Scandinavia as early as the 11th century is proved by a Crucifixion group in Copenhagen (Nationalmus.) with a runic inscription.

The textiles (11th cent.) in Överhogdal in northern Sweden are in the form of long friezes, as were the fragments of textiles (9th cent.) found in the burial ship in Oseberg, Norway. The Överhogdal textiles depict a church and belfry, horses, and other animals as well as scenes that have been interpreted as episodes from the *Volsunga Saga*. In a tapestry from Skog in Sweden (IV, PL. 176) a church and a detached wooden belfry and figures of animals, people, and demons are represented; the contents have been interpreted as a description of the conflict between Christianity and paganism. In the Baldishoel Tapestry from Norway (ca. 1180) the cycle of the seasons was depicted; two panels, the months of April and May (PL. 415), remain.

Stained-glass windows have been preserved in various churches in Gotland. A workshop was established at the beginning of the 13th century in Visby, and a window depicting St. Margaret in the church at Dalhem is proof of the Saxon influence on its style. This workshop existed for a long time, and gradually developed a more rustic style that turned in a Gothic direction. Its evolution can be followed in the stained glass in Barlingbo, Lojsta, and Alskog.

Sten KARLING

BIBLIOG. *General works*: C. Schnaase, Geschichte der bildenden Künste, 2d ed., IV, 2: Die romanische Kunst, Düsseldorf, 1871; V. Gay, Glossaire archéologique du Moyen-Age et de la Renaissance, 2 vols., Paris, 1882–1928; J. von Schlosser, Quellenbuch zur Kunstgeschichte des abendländischen Mittelalters, Vienna, 1896; Michel, I; A. Schmarsow, Kompositiongesetze in der Kunst des Mittelalters, 2 vols., Bonn, Leipzig, 1915–20; G. Schnürer, Kirche und Kultur im Mittelalter, 3 vols., Paderborn, 1924–29; R. Berger, Die Darstellung des thronenden Christus in der romanischen Kunst, Reutlingen, 1926; W. Molsdorf, Christliche Symbolik der mittelalterlichen Kunst, 2d ed., Leipzig, 1926; E. Mâle, Art et artistes du moyen âge, Paris, 1927; M. Hauttmann, Die Kunst des frühen Mittelalters, Berlin, 1929; G. Galassi, Roma o Bisanzio, 2 vols., Rome, 1930–53; J. Roosval, Romansk konst, Stockholm, 1930; J. Baum, Die Malerei und Plastik des Mittelalters, Berlin, Leipzig, 1933; F. Benoit, L'Occident médiéval du romain au roman, Paris, 1933; J. Baltrušaitis, Art sumérien, art roman, Paris, 1934; L. Bréhier, L'art en Occident du Ve au XIe siècle et l'art roman, in G. Huisman, ed., Histoire générale de l'art, II, Paris, 1938, pp. 45–147; D. Frey, Die Entwicklung nationaler Stile der mittelalterlichen Kunst des Abendlands, D. Vierteljahrsschrift, XVI, 1938, pp. 1–74; O. Lehmann-Brockhaus, Schriftquellen zur Kunstgeschichte des 11. und 12. Jahrhunderts für Deutschland, Lotharingen und Italien, 2 vols., Berlin, 1938; G. Haupt, Die Farbensymbolik in der sakralen Kunst des abendländischen Mittelalters, Dresden, 1941; W. Weisbach, Manierismus in mittelalterlicher Kunst, Basel, 1941; L. Bréhier, Le style roman, Paris, 1942; P. Francastel, L'humanisme roman, Rodez, 1942; J. Pijoan, El arte románico: Siglos XI y XII (Summa artis, IX), Madrid, 1944; R. Rey, L'art roman et ses origines, Paris, 1945; M. Schapiro, On the Aesthetic Attitude in Romanesque Art, Art and Thought, London, 1947, pp. 154–64; H. Schnitzler, Mittelalter und Antike, Munich, 1949; J. Evans, Cluniac Art of the Romanesque Period, Cambridge, 1950; A. Hauser, The Social History of Art, I, London, 1951; L. I. Ringbom, Graltempel und Paradises: Beziehungen zwischen Iran und Europa im Mittelalter, Stockholm, 1951; F. Adama van Scheltema, Die Kunst des Abendlandes, II: Die Kunst des Mittelalters, Stuttgart, 1953; R. W. Southern, The Making of the Middle Ages, London, 1953; F. P. Verrié, La vida de l'artista medieval, Barcelona, 1953; K. Erdmann, Arabische Schriftzeichen als Ornamente in der abendländischen Kunst des Mittelalters, Mainz, 1954; J. Baltrušaitis, Le moyen âge fantastique, Paris, 1955; J. Gudiol Ricart, Les peintres itinerants de l'époque romane, Cah. de civ. méd., I, 1958, pp. 191–94; O. Homburger, Zur Stilbestimmung der figürlichen Kunst Deutschland und des westlichen Europas im Zeitraum zwischen

1190 und 1259, Formositas romanica, Frauenfeld, 1958, pp. 29–45; R. Huyghe, Aux sources de l'esthétique occidentale et de l'art roman, B. Centre int. d'ét. romanes, I, 1959, pp. 3–7; W. Oakeshott, Classical Inspiration in Medieval Art, London, 1959; J. Panain, Le fantastique dans l'art du moyen-âge, Clermont-Ferrand, 1959; P. Bargellini, L'arte romanica (Belvedere, V), Florence, 1960; J. Puig i Cadafalch, L'art wisigothique et ses survivances, Paris, 1961; El arte románico, Barcelona, 1962 (cat.; bibliog.); M. Cagiano de Azevedo, L'eredità dell'antico nell'alto medioevo, Settimane di studio del Centro it. di s. sull'alto medioevo, IX, 1962, pp. 449–76; H. Schrade, Dämonen und Monstren: Gestaltungen der Bösen in der Kunst des frühen Mittelalters, Regensburg, 1962; H. Focillon, The Art of the West in the Middle Ages (trans. D. King), I, London, New York, 1963.

General works concerning individual countries: a. *France*: E. Mâle, L'art religieux du XIIe siècle en France, Paris, 1922; J. A. Brutails, La géographie monumentale de la France aux époques romane et gothique, Paris, 1923; R. Colas, Le style roman en France, Paris, 1927; C. Oursel, L'art roman de Bourgogne, Dijon, Boston, 1928; V. R. Markham, Romanesque France, London, 1929; L. Bréhier, L'art en France dès invasions barbares à l'époque romane, Paris, 1930; R. Crozet, L'art roman en Berry, Paris, 1932; E. Lambert, Caen romane et gothique, Caen, 1935; J. Adhémar, Influences antiques dans l'art du moyen-âge français (S. of the Warburg Inst., VII), London, 1939; V. Allègre, L'art roman dans la région albigeoise, Albi, 1943; L. Raymond and J. Hubert, Les origines de l'art français (N. E. de l'art fr., I), Paris, 1947; R. Crozet, L'art roman en Poitou, Paris, 1948; J. Evans, Art in Mediaeval France, London, New York, 1948; L. Lefrançois-Pillion, L'art roman en France, Paris, 1948; L. Réau and G. Cohen, L'art du moyen âge, Paris, 1951; L. Gischia and L. Mazenod, Les arts primitifs français, Paris, 1953; J. Ebersolt, Orient et Occident: Recherches sur les influences byzantines et orientales en France avant et pendant les Croisades, 2d ed., Paris, 1954; J. Gantner, M. Pobé and J. Roubier, Gallia romanica, Vienna, Munich, 1955 (2d ed., 1962; Eng. trans., M. Heynemann, London, 1956); La nuit des temps, La Pierre-qui-vire, 1955 ff.; A. Gybal, L'Auvergne: Berceau de l'art roman, Clermont-Ferrand, 1958; R. Crozet, Remarques sur les relations artistiques entre la France du Sud-Ouest et le Nord de l'Espagne à l'époque romane, Actes XIXe Cong. int. d'h. de l'art (1958), Paris, 1959, pp. 62–71; M. Aubert, L'art roman en France, Paris, 1961; J. Maire, L'influence des chemins de Saint-Jacques de Compostelle sur l'art roman en Poitou, Saintonge et Angoumois, Poitiers, 1961; R. Crozet, L'art roman, Paris, 1962; G. Richter, Romanisches Burgund, Stuttgart, 1962.

b. *Spain and Portugal*: Marqués de Lozoya, Historia del arte hispánico, I, Barcelona, 1931; M. Gómez Moreno, El arte románico español, Madrid, 1934; L. Torres Balbás, El arte de la alta edad media y del periódo románico en España, Barcelona, 1934; E. Camps Cazorla, El arte románico en España, Barcelona, 1935 (2d ed., 1945); A. de Lacerda, Historia de arte em Portugal, I, Porto, 1942; M. Gómez Moreno, El arte árabe español hasta los Almohades: Arte Mozárabe (Ars Hispaniae, III), Madrid, 1951; R. dos Santos, O Românico em Portugal, Lisbon, 1955; J. E. Cirlot, Romanesque Art: The Art Museum of Catalonia, New York, 1956; E. Junyent, Catalogne romane (La nuit des temps, 12–13), 2 vols., La Pierre-qui-vire, 1960–61; M. A. García Guinea, El arte románico en Palencia, Palencia, 1961; M. Durliat, L'art roman en Espagne, Paris, 1962; F. García Romo, De l'art mozárabe à l'art roman, L'information d'h. de l'art, VII, 1962, pp. 169–73.

c. *Italy*: G. Bertaux, L'art dans l'Italie méridionale, Paris, 1904; Venturi, III; G. Vitzthum and W. F. Volbach, Die Malerei und Plastik des Mittelalters in Italien, 2 vols., Wildpark-Potsdam, 1924; Toesca, Md; G. Panazza, L'arte medievale nel territorio bresciano, Bergamo, 1942; F. Kayser, Werdezeit der abendländischen Kunst: Frühchristliche und romanische Kunst in Italien, Freiburg im Breisgau, 1948; R. Longhi, Giudizio sul Duecento, Proporzioni, II, 1948, pp. 5–54; J. Alazard, L'art italien dès origines à la fin du XIVe siècle, Paris, 1949; H. Decker, Italia romanica, Vienna, 1958 (Eng. trans., J. Cleugh, Romanesque Art in Italy, New York, 1959); E. Lavagnino, L'arte medioevale, 2d ed., Turin, 1960; L. Mallé, Le arti figurative in Piemonte dalle origini al periodo romantico, Turin, 1962.

d. *Germany, Low Countries, Central Europe*: G. Dehio, Geschichte der deutschen Kunst, I, Berlin, Leipzig, 1919; P. Clemen, Belgische Kunstdenkmäler, I, Munich, 1923; J. Gantner, Kunstgeschichte der Schweiz, I, Frauenfeld, 1936; K. Ginhart, Die bildende Kunst in Österreich, II, Baden bei Wien, 1937; G. Dehio, Handbuch der deutschen Kunstdenkmäler (ed. E. Gall), 2d ed., Berlin, 1954 ff.; KbNed; J. Lejeune, Renaissance romane (XIe–XIIe siècles): Liège et l'occident, Liège, 1958; T. von Bogyay, Der Eintritt des Ungarntums in die christlich-europäische Kulturgemeinschaft im Lichte der Kunstgeschichte, Südost-Forsch., XVIII, 1959, pp. 6–26; P. Ganz, Geschichte der Kunst in der Schweiz von den Anfängen bis zur Mitte des 17. Jahrhunderts, Basel, 1960; Z. Świechowski, Zagadnienie odrodzenia romanizmu w Polsce (The Problem of the Renaissance in Polish Romanesque Art), B. h. sztuki, XXII, 1960, pp. 339–50; Dehio-Handbuch: Die Kunstdenkmäler Österreichs, 4th ed., Berlin, 1961; P. Baldass, W. Buchowiecki, and W. Mrazek, Romanische Kunst in Österreich, Vienna, 1962; S. Collon-Gevaert, J. Lejeune and J. Stiennon, Art roman dans la vallée de la Meuse aux XIe et XIIe siècles, Brussels, 1962.

e. *England*: O. E. Saunders, A History of English Art in the Middle Ages, Oxford, 1932; T. S. R. Boase, English Art 1100–1216, London, 1953; O. Lehmann-Brockhaus, Lateinische Schriftquellen zur Kunst in England, Wales und Schottland vom Jahre 901 bis zum Jahre 1307, 5 vols., Munich, 1955–60; City of Manchester Art Gallery, Romanesque Art c. 1050–1200 from Collections in Great Britain and Eire, Manchester, 1959 (cat.; rev. by G. Zarnecki, BM, CI, 1959, pp. 452–56).

f. *Scandinavia*: F. Beckett, Danmarks Kunst, I, Copenhagen, 1924; H. Aars et al., Norsk kunsthistorie, I, Oslo, 1925; L. Wennervirta, Finlands konst, Stockholm, 1926; H. Shetelig., ed., Nordisk kultur, XXVII: Kunst, Stockholm, 1931; V. Lorenzen, ed., Nordisk kultur, XXIII: Kirkebygninger og deres udstyr, Copenhagen, 1933; E. Lexow, Norges kunst, 2d ed., Oslo, 1942; A. Borelius, Konstens historia i Sverige, I, Lund, 1943;

H. Cornell, Den svenska konstens historia, I, Stockholm, 1944; A. Lindblom, Sveriges konsthistoria från forntid till nutid, I, Stockholm, 1944; A. Lindblom, Svensk konst från stenåldern til rymdåldern, Stockholm, 1960.

Architecture: general works: F. de Dartein, Etude sur l'architecture lombarde, 2 vols., Paris, 1865–82; Dehio-von Bezold; O. Stiehl, Der Backsteinbau romanischer Zeit . . . , Leipzig, 1898; H. von Gabelentz, Die kirchliche Kunst im italienischen Mittelalter, Strasbourg, 1907; C. Ward, Mediaeval Church Vaulting, Princeton, 1915; K. M. Swoboda, Römische und romanische Paläste, Vienna, 1919; P. Frankl, Die frühmittelalterliche und romanische Baukunst, Wildpark-Potsdam, 1926; P. Lavedan, Histoire de l'urbanisme, I, Paris, 1926; J. Puig i Cadafalch, Le premier art roman, Paris, 1928; H. Phelps, Die farbige Architektur bei den Römern und im Mittelalter, Berlin, 1930; D. Knopp and G. P. Jones, The Mediaeval Mason, Manchester, 1933; J. Puig i Cadafalch, La géographie et les origines du premier art roman, Paris, 1935; A. W. Clapham, Romanesque Architecture in Western Europe, Oxford, 1936 (2d ed., 1962); H. Stolper, ed., Bauen in Holz, Stuttgart, 1937; J. Evans, The Romanesque Architecture of the Order of Cluny, Cambridge, 1938; J. Bony, La technique normande du mur épais à l'époque romane, B. mon., XCVIII, 1939, pp. 153–88; F. Bandmann, Die Bauformen des Mittelalters, Bonn, 1949; E. Lundberg, Arkitekturens formsprak, III: Västerlandets medeltid, 600–1200, Stockholm, 1949; H. Focillon, L'an mil, Paris, 1952; A. Boëthius, Kejsarnas Rom och medeltidens städer, Göteborg, 1953; U. Günther, Der Vierungsturm bis zum Ende des romanischen Stils unter besonderer Berücksichtigung der deutschen Entwicklung, Darmstadt, 1953; H. E. Kubach, Die vorromanische und romanische Baukunst in Mitteleuropa: Literaturbericht 1950–1954, ZfKg, XVIII, 1955, pp. 157–98; H. Hahn, Die frühe Kirchenbaukunst der Zisterzienser, Berlin, 1957; J. Eisenwerth, Zisterzienser-Romanik, Formositas romanica, Frauenfeld, 1958, pp. 151–80; H. Peters, Dome und Kathedralen, Honnef, 1958; H. Busch and B. Lohse, Baukunst der Romanik in Europa, Frankfurt am Main, 1959; K. J. Conant, Carolingian and Romanesque Architecture 800–1200, Harmondsworth, 1959 (bibliog.); P. Heliot, Les antécedents et les débuts des coursières anglo-normandes et rhénanes, Cah. de civ. médiévale, II, 1959, pp. 429–43; P. Héliot, Saint-Etienne de Caen, Saint-Paul d'Issoire, la Cathédrale d'Osnabruck et les arcades murales dans l'architecture du Nord-Ouest de l'Europe (X^{e}–XIIIe siècles), Wallraf-Richartz-Jhb., XXI, 1959, pp. 41–74; E. R. Sunderland, Symbolic Numbers and Romanesque Church Plans, J. Soc. of Arch. Historians, XVIII, 1959, pp. 94–103; L. Torres Balbás, Naves de edificios anteriores al siglo XIII cubiertas con armaduras de madera sobre arcos trasversales, AEArte, XXXII, 1959, pp. 109–19; M. Aubert, La construction au moyen âge, B. mon., CXVIII, 1960, pp. 241–72, CXIX, 1961, pp. 7–42, 82–120, 181–209, 297–323; P. Héliot, Encore l'ordre colossal et les arcades murales dans les églises romanes, B. mon., CXVIII, 1960, pp. 31–36; P. Héliot, Les voûtes d'arête et les coupoles dans l'architecture romane, BAFr, 1960, pp. 148–50; O. Feld, Der Beitrag des Elsass zur Geschichte des Kreuzrippengewölbe, Cah. techniques de l'art, IV, 2, 1961, pp. 15-32; V. Gilardoni, Il romanico, Verona, 1963.

Architecture: works concerning individual countries. a. France: (1) *General*: V. Mortet, Recueil de textes relatifs à l'histoire de l'architecture et à la condition des architectes en France au moyen âge: XIe–XIIe siècles, Paris, 1911; R. Colas, Le style roman en France, Paris, 1927; F. Deshoulières, Au début de l'art roman: Les églises de l'XIe siècle en France, Paris, 1929; J. Vallery-Radot, Eglises romanes: Filiations et échanges d'influences, Paris, 1931; L. Lacrocq, Les églises de France: Creuse, Paris, 1934; F. Deshoulières, Elements datés de l'art roman en France, Paris, 1936; H. Reinhardt and E. Fels, Etude sur les églises-porches carolingiennes et leur survivance dans l'art roman, B. mon., XCVI, 1937, pp. 425–69; G. Plat, L'art de bâtir dès Romains à l'an 1100, Paris, 1939; M. Aubert, L'architecture cistercienne en France, 2 vols., Paris, 1943; M. Gieure, Les églises romanes de France, 2 vols., Paris, 1953–54; R. Ritter, Chateaux, donjons et places fortes, Paris, 1953; R. Crozet, Problèmes de méthode: Les théories françaises sur les Ecoles Romanes, B. Seminario de estudios de arte y arqueología, XXI–XXII, 1954–56, pp. 39–45; J. Hubert, Les églises à rotonde orientale, Frühmittelalterliche Kunst in den Alpenländen (1951), Lausanne, 1954, pp. 309–20; R. Chappuis, Géométrie et structure des coupoles sur pendentifs dans les églises romanes entre Loire et Pyrénées, B. mon., CXX, 1962, pp. 7–39. (2) *Single regions or monuments*: N. Thiollier, Architecture religieuse à l'époque romane dans l'ancien diocèse du Puy, Le Puy, 1900; E. Lefèvre-Pontalis, Saint-Hilaire de Poitiers, CAF, LXIX, 1903, pp. 361–405; C. Enlart, La cathédrale Saint-Jean de Beyrouth, Soc. nat. des ant. de France: Centenaire, 1804–1904, Paris, 1904, pp. 121–33; F. Deshoulières, Les églises romanes du Berry, B. mon., LXXIII, 1909, pp. 469–92; F. Deshoulières, Nouvelles remarques sur les églises romanes du Berry, B. mon., LXXXI, 1922, pp. 5–27; C. Enlart, Les monuments des Croisés dans le royaume de Jérusalem: Architecture religieuse et civile, 4 vols., Paris, 1925–28; R. Rey, La cathédrale de Cahors et les origines de l'architecture à coupoles d'Aquitaine, Paris, 1925; E. Gall, Die Abteikirche S. Lucien bei Beauvais, Wien. Jhb. für Kw., IV, 1926, pp. 59–71; L. M. Michon, L'abbaye de Jumièges, Paris, 1927; G. Chapeau, L'église abbatiale de Charroux, B. Soc. des Ant. de l'Ouest, 3d Ser., VIII, 1928–30, pp. 503–33; G. Lanfry, Fouilles et découvertes à Jumièges, B. mon., LXXXVII, 1928, pp. 107–37; C. Oursel, L'art roman de Bourgogne, Dijon, 1928; K. J. Conant, Mediaeval Academy Excavations at Cluny, Speculum, IV, 1929, pp. 3–26, 168–70, 291–302, 443–50, V, 1930, pp. 77–94, VI, 1931, pp. 3–14, XVII, 1942, pp. 563–65; H. Reinhardt, Hypothèse sur l'origine des premiers déambulatoires en Picardie, B. mon., LXXXVIII, 1929, pp. 269–88; J. Vallery-Radot, Les analogies des églises de Saint-Fortunat, de Charlieu et d'Anzy-le-Duc, B. mon., LXXXVIII, 1929, pp. 243–67; M. Aubert, La cathédrale de Metz, Paris, 1931; J. Hubert, Le Saint-Sépulcre de Neuvy et les pélerinages de Terre Sainte au XIe siècle, B. mon., XC, 1931, pp. 91–100; K. J. Conant, The Apse at Cluny, Speculum, VII, 1932, pp. 23–35; R. Crozet, L'art roman en Berry, Paris, 1932; J. Puig i Cadafalch, Saint-Martin du Canigou, Cah. d'h. et d'archéol., IV, 1932, pp. 237–43; H. Reinhardt, La cathédrale de l'evêque Wernher, B. Soc. des amis de la cathédrale de Strasbourg, II, 1932, pp. 39–64; G. Bazin, Le Mont-Saint-Michel, 2 vols., Paris, 1933; R. Crozet, La corniche du clocher de Saint-Hilaire de Poitiers, B. mon., XCIII, 1934, pp. 341–45; P. Deschamps, Les châteaux des Croisés en Terre Sainte, 2 vols. in 4, Paris, 1934–39; A. Fikry, Les influences musulmanes dans l'art roman du Puy, Paris, 1934; E. Maillard, Le problème de la reconstruction de Saint-Hilaire-le-Grand au XIe siècle, B. Soc. des Ant. de l'Oeust, 3d Ser., X, 1934–35, pp. 323–28; M. and C. Dickson, Les églises de l'ancien diocèse de Chalon, Mâcon, 1935; E. Lambert, Caen roman et gothique, Caen, 1935; J. Virey, Les églises romanes de l'ancien diocèse de Mâcon, Mâcon, 1935; P. Héliot, Lillers, CAF, XCIX, 1936, pp. 576–92; G. Lanfry, La crypte romane de l'XIe siècle de la cathédrale de Rouen, B. mon., XCV, 1936, pp. 181–201; F. Salet, La Madeleine de Vézelay et ses dates de construction, B. mon., XCV, 1936, pp. 5–25; J. Vallery-Radot, La limite méridionale de l'école romane de Bourgogne, B. mon., XCV, 1936, pp. 273–316; F. Anus, Etude sur la structure des églises à file de coupoles du Sud-ouest de la France, Les monuments historiques de la France, II, 1937, pp. 172–91; H. and D. Du Ranquet, Eglise de Ris, B. mon., XCVII, 1938, pp. 29–48; J. Vallery-Radot, L'église Saint-André-le-Bas de Vienne et ses rapports avec Saint-Paul de Lyon, Notre-Dame d'Andance et Notre-Dame de Die, B. mon., XCVII, 1938, pp. 144–72; M. Anfray, L'architecture normande, Paris, 1939; J. Bony, La technique normande du mur épais à l'époque romane, B. mon." XCVIII, 1939, pp. 153–88; L. Schürenberg, Der Dom zu Metz, Frankfurt am Main, 1940; J. Vallery-Radot, Les églises romanes du Rouergue, B. mon., XCIX, 1940, pp. 5–68; C. K. Hersey, The Church of Saint-Martin at Tours (903–1150), AB, XXV, 1943, pp. 1–39; E. Lambert, L'église Saint-Martin de Tours, BAFr, 1945–47, pp. 189–91; J. Vallery-Radot, Le domaine de l'école romane de Provence, B. mon., CIII, 1945, pp. 5–63; R. Crozet, L'art roman en Poitou, Paris, 1948; J. Hubert, Les dates de construction du clocher-porche et de la nef de Saint-Germain-des-Prés, BAFr, 1948–49, pp. 253–54; C. Perrat, L'église de Ris, BAFr, 1948–49, p. 123; F. Salet, La Madeleine de Vézelay, Melun, 1948; L. Grodecki, Le transept bas, A Cluny: Congrès scientifique, Dijon, 1949, pp. 265–69; F. Lesueur, Saint-Martin de Tours et les origines de l'art roman, B. mon., CVII, 1949, pp. 7–84; L. Grodecki, Les débuts de la sculpture romane en Normandie: Bernay, B. mon., CVIII, 1950, pp. 7–67; J. Hubert, Les dates de construction du clocher-porche et de la nef de Saint-Germain-des-Prés, B. mon., CVIII, 1950, pp. 69–84; M. Anfray, L'architecture religieuse du Nivernais au moyen-âge: Les églises romanes, Paris, 1951, pp. 62–98; M. Duchein, Note sur la chronologie de la collégiale du Dorat, B. Soc. archéol. du Limousin, LXXXI, 1951, pp. 258–67; P. Héliot, La Normandie et l'architecture romane du nord de la France, RA, XXXVII, 1951, pp. 60–70; J. Vallery-Radot, Le style et l'âge du clocher de Saint-André-le-Bas, B. mon., CIX, 1951, pp. 113–33; C. Connoué, Les églises de Saintonge, 4 vols., Saintes, 1952–59; E. Lambert, L'ancienne abbatiale de Saint-Remi de Reims, BAFr, 1952–53, pp. 91–93; R. Louis, Les églises d'Auxerre dès origines au XIe siècle, Paris, 1952; H. P. Eydoux, Les fouilles de l'abbatiale d'Himmerod et la notion d'un "Plan Bernardin," B. mon., CXI, 1953, pp. 29–36; P. Verzone, Les églises du haute moyen âge et le culte des anges, L'art mosan (1952), Paris, 1953, pp. 71–80; M. Aubert, L'église de Vignory, MAF, LXXXIII, 1954, pp. 165–69; K. J. Conant, Mediaeval Academy Excavations at Cluny, Speculum, XXIX, 1954, pp. 1–12; M. Duchein, Note sur la chronologie de la collégiale du Dorat, B. mon., CXII, 1954, pp. 95–98; E. Fels, La façade de la cathédrale de Strasbourg élevée par l'evêque Wernher au début du XIe siècle, BAFr, 1954–55, pp. 28–30, 79–80; E. Gall, Zur Frage der "Westwerke," Jhb. des römisch-germanischen Zentralmuseums in Mainz, I, 1954, pp. 245–52; G. Lanfry, L'abbaye de Jumièges: Plans et documents, Rouen, 1954; R. Louis, Fouilles exécutées dans la cathédrale Saint-Jacques-de-Compostelle, BAFr, 1954–55, pp. 152–53; R. Tournier, Les églises comtoises, Paris, 1954; P. Balme, Eglises romanes d'Auvergne, Clermont, 1955; G. Lanfry, L'alternance des piles de l'église Notre-Dame de Jumièges, Jumièges: Congrès scientifique du XIIIe centénaire, Rouen, 1955, pp. 489–92; C. Oursel, Saint-Bénigne de Dijon et Notre-Dame de Jumièges, Jumièges: Congrès scientifique du XIIIe centénaire, Rouen, 1955, pp. 493–98; J. Taralon, Jumièges, Paris, 1955; J. Vallery-Radot, Saint-Philibert de Tournus, Paris, 1955; J. Verrier, Cathédrale de Rouen, Les monuments historiques de la France, N.S., II, 1956, pp. 93–100; F. Lesueur, Saint-Aignan d'Orléans l'église de Robert le Pieux, B. mon., CXV, 1957, pp. 169–206; P. Mesplé, L'art roman décadent du Sud-Ouest, B. mon., CXV, 1957, pp. 7–22; Y. Bruand, Le château de Gisors, B. mon., CXVI, 1958, pp. 243–65; R. Crozet, Chauvigny et ses monuments, Poitiers, 1958; V. Froidevaux, L'abbatial de Lessay, Les monuments historiques de la France, N.S., IV, 1958, pp. 100–150; R. Grand, L'art roman en Bretagne, Paris, 1958; E. Lambert, Abbayes et cathédrales du Sud-Ouest, Paris, 1958; M. Rumpler, L'architecture religieuse en Alsace à l'époque romane dans le cadre du Bassin rhénan, Strasbourg, 1958; H. H. Hilberry, The Cathedral of Chartres in 1030, Speculum, XXXIV, 1959, pp. 561–72; M. Martinet, Influence de l'école romane auvergnate dans la partie septentrionale du diocèse de Moulins et dans le diocèse de Nevers, Clermont-Ferrand, 1959; B. Bligny, Les églises et les ordres religieux dans le royaume de Bourgogne aux XIe et XIIe siècle, Paris, 1960; R. Clair, L'église abbatale d'Hautecombe au XIIe siècle, B. mon., CXVIII, 1960, pp. 89–109; P. Héliot, L'ordre colossal et les ordres superposés de Saint-Etienne de Caen à Notre-Dame d'Amiens, RA, 1960, 1, pp. 183–202; A. Lapeyre, Des façades occidentales de Saint-Denis et de Chartres aux portails de Laon: Etudes sur la sculpture monumental dans l'Ile-de-France et les régions voisines aux XIIe siècle, Paris, 1960; J. Secret, Les façades à arcatures dans les églises romanes du Périgord, B. mon., CXVIII, 1960, pp. 89–109; C. D. Sheppard, Jr., An Earlier Dating for the Transept of Saint-Sernin, Toulouse, Speculum, XXXV, 1960, pp. 584–90; M. Vieillard-Troiekonroff, La cathédrale de Clermont du Ve au XIIIe siècle, CahA, XI, 1960, pp. 199–247; C. Daras, Les façades des églises romanes ornées d'arcatures en Charente: Leur origine, leur filiation, B. mon., CXIX, 1961, pp. 121–38; L. Chaigne, L'âme romane du Bas-Poitou, Deux-Sèvres, Vendée, Niort, 1962; J. and S. Hubie, Les mervielles de la Saintonge romane, Paris, 1962; E. M. Janet Le Caisne, Vézelay, Paris, 1962.

b. Spain and Portugal: (1) *General*: V. Lampérez y Romea, Arquitectura civil española de los siglos I al XVIII, I, Madrid, 1922; V. Lampérez y Romea, Historia de la arquitectura cristiana española en la edad media, 2d ed., 3 vols., Barcelona, Madrid, 1930; W. M. Whitehill, Spanish Romanesque Architecture of the 11th Century, London, 1941; J. Gudiol i Ricart and J. A. Gaya Nuño, Arquitectura y escultura románicas (Ars Hispaniae, V), Madrid, 1948 (bibliog.). (2) *Single regions or monuments*: J. Puig i Cadafalch, A. de Falguera, and J. Goday y Casals, L'arquitectura romànica a Catalunya, II–III, Barcelona, 1911–18; K. J. Conant, The Early Architectural History of the Cathedral of Santiago de Compostela, Cambridge, Mass., 1926; G. Gaillard, L'église et le cloître de Silos: Dates de la construction, B. mon., XCI, 1932, pp. 39–80; F. Hernández, San Miguel de Cuixá iglesia del ciclo mozárabe catalán, Arch. español de arte y arqueol., VIII, 1932, pp. 157–99; F. Iñiguez and R. Sánchez Ventura, Un grupo de iglesias del Alto Aragon, Arch. español de arte y arqueol., IX, 1933, pp. 215–35; J. Puig i Cadafalch and G. Gaillard, L'église Saint-Michel de Cuxa, B. mon., XCIV, 1935, pp. 353–73; J. Vieillard, La Guide du pèlerin de Saint-Jacques de Compostelle, Mâcon, 1938; P. David, A Sé Velha de Coimbra das origines ao século XV, Porto, 1943; J. M. Lacarra and J. Gudiol i Ricart, El primer arte románico en Navarra, Principe de Viana, V, 1944, pp. 1–54; G. Gaillard, Besalu, CAF, CXII, 1954, pp. 236–46; G. Gaillard, La Catalogne entre l'art de Cordoue et l'art roman, S. Islamica, VI, 1956, pp. 19–35; E. Tyrrell, Historia de la arquitectura románica del Monasterio de San Salvador de Leyre, Principe de Viana, XIX, 1958, pp. 305–35; F. Vásquez Saco, Iglesias románicas de la provincia de Lugo, B. Com. provincial de mon. h. y artisticos de Lugo, VI, 1958–59, pp. 262–70; M. A. García Guinea, La iglesia románica de Santa Eufemia de Cozuelos (Palencia), AEArte, XXXII, 1959, pp. 295–311; J. Pérez-Carmona, Arquitectura y escultura románica en la provincia de Burgos, Burgos, 1959; I. Villalonga y Casañes, Iglesia de San Miguel de la Seo de Urgel, Academia, IX, 1959, pp. 76–77; J. Guerra, Excavaciones en la catedral de Santiago, Ciencia tomista, LXXXVII, 1960, pp. 97–168; E. Kirschbaum, Die Grabungen unter der Kathedrale von Santiago de Compostela, RQ, LVI, 1961, pp. 234–54; R. Crozet, L'art roman en Navarre et en Aragon, Cah. de civ. médiévale, V, 1962, pp. 35–58.

c. Italy: (1) *General*: A. Ricci, Storia dell'architettura in Italia, I, Modena, 1857; C. Boito, Architettura del medioevo in Italia, Milan, 1880; R. Cattaneo, L'architecture en Italie du VIe au XIe siècle, Venice, 1890 (Eng. trans., I. Curtis-Cholmeley, London, 1896); C. Enlart, L'art roman en Italie: L'architecture et la décoration, Paris, 1924; C. Ricci, Romanesque Architecture in Italy, London, New York, 1925; G. C. Argan, L'architettura protocristiana, preromanica e romanica, Florence, 1936; H. Thümmler, Die Baukunst des XI. Jahrhundert in Italien, Römisches Jhb. für Kg., III, 1939, pp. 141–227. (2) *Single regions or monuments*: G. T. Rivoira, Le origini dell'architettura lombarda, Milan, 1908 (Eng. trans., G. McN. Rushforth, 2 vols., Oxford, 1910; 2d ed., 1933); P. de Truchis, L'architecture lombarde: ses origines: son extension dans le centre, l'est et midi de la France, CAF, LXXVI, 1909, pp. 204–42; U. Monneret de Villard, L'architettura romanica in Dalmazia, Milan, 1910; A. K. Porter, Lombard Architecture, 4 vols., New Haven, 1915–17; R. Kautzsch, Oberitalien und der Mittelrhein im 12. Jahrhundert, Atti X Cong. int. di storia dell'arte (1912), Rome, 1922, pp. 123–30; O. Stiehl, Backsteinbauten in Norddeutschland und Dänemark, Stuttgart, 1923; I. C. Gavini, Storia dell'architettura in Abruzzo, 2 vols., Milan, 1927–28; R. Krautheimer, Lombardische Hallenkirchen im XII. Jahrhundert, Jhb. für Kw., 1928, pp. 176–91; M. Salmi, L'architettura romanica in Toscana, Milan, 1928; P. Orsi, Le chiese basiliane della Calabria, Florence, 1929; R. Krautheimer, San Nicola in Bari und die apulische Architektur des XII. Jahrhunderts, Wien. Jhb. für Kg., IX, 1934, pp. 5–42; P. Verzone, L'architettura romanica nel Vercellese, Vercelli, 1934; C. Shearer, The Renaissance of Architecture in Southern Italy, Cambridge, 1935; P. Verzone, L'architettura romanica nel Noverese, 2 vols., Novara, 1935–36; R. Krautheimer, Die Doppelkathedrale in Pavia, in R. Salomon, Opicinus de Canistris, London, 1936, pp. 323–37; P. Verzone, S. Andrea di Vercelli e l'arte emiliana, B. storico-bibl. subalpino, XXXVIII, 1936, pp. 403–26; R. Bordenache, La SS. Trinità di Venosa, EphDR, VII, 1937, pp. 1–76; G. Chierici, Il duomo di Salerno e la chiesa di Montecassino, Rass. storica salernitana, I, 1937, pp. 96–109; E. Calandra, Breve storia dell'architettura in Sicilia, Bari, 1938; W. Krönig, Hallenkirchen in Mittelitalien, Kunstgeschichtliche Jhb. der Bib. Hertziana, II, 1938, pp. 1–142; M. Salmi, La genesi del duomo di Pisa, BArte, XXXII, 1938, pp. 149–61; H. Thümmler, Die Kirche S. Pietro in Tuscania, Kunstgeschichtliche Jhb. der Bib. Hertziana, II, 1938, pp. 263–88; W. Arslan, L'architettura romanica veronese, Verona, 1939; S. Bottari, Le chiese basiliane della Sicilia e della Calabria, Messina, 1939; S. Samonà, Il duomo di Cefalù, Rome, 1939; P. Verzone, La scuola milanese del secolo XI, Atti II Cong. naz. di storia dell'arch. (1937), Rome, 1939, pp. 87–96; P. Verzone, L'architettura dell'XI secolo nell'esarcato, Palladio, IV, 1940, pp. 97–109; E. Olivero, Architettura religiosa preromanica e romanica nell'archidiocesi di Torino, Turin, 1941; P. Verzone, L'origine della volta lombarda a nervature, Atti IV Cong. naz. di storia dell'arch. (1939), Milan, 1941, pp. 53–64; G. U. Arata, Architettura medievale in Sicilia, Novara, 1942; G. De Angelis d'Ossat, Le influenze bizantine nell'architettura romanica, Rome, 1942; U. Formentini, L'arte romanica genovese ed i "Magistri Antelami," Storia di Genova, III, Genoa, 1942, pp. 277–311; H. M. Schwarz, Die Baukunst Kalabriens und Siziliens in Zeitalter der Normannen, Römische Jhb. für Kg., VI, 1942–44, pp. 3–110; A. M. Romanini, Contributo alla conoscenza del romanico piacentino, Palladio, N.S., I, 1951, pp. 78–93; R. Delogu, L'architettura del Medioevo in Sardegna, Rome, 1953; W. Krönig, Toskana und Apulien: Beiträge . . . , ZfKg, XVI, 1953, pp. 101–44; P. Verdier, L'origine structurale et liturgique des transepts de nef des cathédrales de Novare et de Pavie, Arte del primo millennio (1950), Turin, 1953, pp. 354–61; E. Arslan, L'architettura romanica milanese, Storia di Milano, III, Milan, 1954, pp. 397–521; C. Ceschi, Architettura romanica genovese, Milan, 1954; A. M. Romanini, Die Kathedrale von Piacenza, ZfKg, XVII, 1954, pp. 129–62; S. Bottari, I rapporti tra l'architettura siciliana e quella campana nel Medioevo, Palladio, N.S., V, 1955, pp. 7–28; G. Panazza, Campanili romanici di Pavia, Arte lombarda, II, 1956, pp. 18–27; P. Sanpaolesi, La facciata della cattedrale di Pisa, RIASA, N.S., V–VI, 1956–57, pp. 248–394; D. de Bernardi Ferrero, L'architettura romanica nella diocesi di Biella, Turin, 1959; S. Casartelli, Quattro chiese benedettine del XII secolo in Monferrato, Atti IX Cong. naz. di storia dell'arch. (1957), Rome, 1959, pp. 301–30; W. Krönig, Contributi all'architettura pugliese del Medioevo, Atti IX Cong. naz. di storia dell'arch. (1955), Rome, 1959, pp. 39–66; W. Krönig, Frankreich und die romanische Architektur in Unteritalien, Actes XIXe Cong. int. d'h. de l'art (1958), Paris, 1959, pp. 92–99; M. C. Magni, Architettura romanica comasca, Milan, 1960; M. Marinelli, L'architettura romanica in Ancona, 2d ed., Rome, 1961; M. Salmi, Chiese romaniche della Toscana, Milan, 1961; M. Moretti, L'architettura romanica religiosa nel territorio dell'antica repubblica senese, Parma, 1962.

d. Low Countries: W. Randolph, The Churches of Belgium, London, 1919; M. Laurent, L'architecture et la sculpture en Belgique, Paris, Brussels, 1928; P. Rolland, Les églises paroissiales de Tournai, Brussels, 1936; Fr. Firmin, De Romaansche kerkelijke bouwkunst in West-Vlaanderen, Ghent, 1940; E. Rogge, Einschiffige romanische Kirchen in Friesland und ihre Gestaltung, Oldenburg, 1943; S. Brigode, Les églises romanes de la Belgique, 3d ed., Brussels, 1944; E. H. ter Kuile, De bouwkunst van de Middeleeuwen: De architectuur, Amsterdam, 1948; M. D. Ozinga, De romaanse kerkelijke bouwkunst, Amsterdam, 1949; H. E. Kubach, Die spätromanische Baukunst des Maaslandes, Das Münster, VII, 1954, pp. 205–16; L. Devliegher, De kerkelijke romaanse bouwkunst in Frans-Vlaanderen, B. Commission royale des mon. et des sites, IX, 1958, pp. 3–125; H. E. Kubach, Eine unbekannte romanische Kirche der Maasgegend, ZfKg, XXII, 1959, pp. 118–23; G. Gaillard, La cathédrale romane de Tournai: La nef, le transept, Inf. d'h. de l'art, VII, 1962, pp. 63–67.

e. Germany and Central Europe: (1) *General*: L. Gál, L'architecture religieuse en Hongrie du XIe au XIIIe siècle, Paris, 1929; P. Pühringer, Denkmäler der früh- und hochromanische Baukunst in Österreich, Vienna, 1931; L. Schürenberg, Der Anteil der südwestdeutschen Baukunst an der Ausbildung der salischen Stiles, ZfKg, VIII, 1939, pp. 249–80; E. Lehmann, Über die Bedeutung des Investiturstreits für die deutsche hochromanische Architektur, Z. d. Vereins für Kw., VII, 1940, pp. 75–88; P. Meyer, Schweizerische Münster und Kathedralen des Mittelalters, Zurich, 1945; E. Lehmann, Vom Sinn und Wesen des Wandlung in der Raumanordnung der deutschen Kirchen des Mittelalters, Z. für K., I, 3, 1947, pp. 24–43; E. Hempel, Geschichte der deutschen Baukunst, Munich, 1949; H. E. Kubach and A. Verbeek, Die vorromanische und romanische Baukunst in Mitteleuropa, ZfKg, XIV, 1951, pp. 124–48, XVIII, 1955, pp. 157–98 (bibliog.); H. P. Eydoux, L'architecture des églises cisterciennes d'Allemagne, Paris, 1952; H. Planitz, Die deutsche Stadt im Mittelalter, Graz, Cologne, 1954; R. Hamann and E. Lehmann, Corpus der romanischen Kunst Mitteldeutschlands, A: Architektur, Berlin, 1961 (bibliog.). (2) *Single regions or monuments*: H. Christ, Romanische Kirchen in Schwaben und Neckar-Franken von der Karolingerzeit bis zu den Cisterciensern, Stuttgart, 1925; K. H. Clasen, Die mittelalterliche Kunst im Gebiet des deutschordensstaates Preussen, Königsberg, 1928; J. Hecht, Der romanische Kirchenbau des Bodenseegebietes von seinen Anfängen bis zum Ausklingen, Basel, 1928; O. Linck, Vom mittelalterlichen Mönchtum und seinen Bauten in Württemberg, Augsburg, 1931; O. Gaul, Die romanische Baukunst und Bauornamentik in Sachsen, Magdeburg, 1932; R. Kautzsch, Der Meister des Westchors am Dom zu Worms, Z. d. Verein für Kw., I, 1934; pp. 1–15; R. Gabel, Die romanischen Kirchtürme Württembergs, Stuttgart, 1937; K. H. Clasen, Die mittelalterliche Bildhauerkunst in Deutschordensland Preussen, Berlin, 1939; R. Kautzsch, Der romanische Kirchenbau in Elsass, Freiburg im Breisgau, 1944; K. Wilhelm-Kästner, Der westfälische Lebensraum in der Baukunst des Mittelalters (Der Raum Westfalen, II, 1–2), Münster, 1947; H. Tintelnot, Die mittelalterliche Baukunst Schlesiens, Kitzingen, 1951; W. Meyer-Barkhausen, Das grosse Jahrhundert kölnischer Kirchenbaukunst, 1150–1250, Cologne, 1952; F. V. Arens, Rheinhessische Bauplastik um 1100 unter lombardischen Einfluss, Wandlungen christliche Kunst im Mittelalter, Baden-Baden, 1953, pp. 253–60; G. Bandmann, Die Werdener Abteikirche (1256–1275), Bonn, 1953; I. Hoefelmayr-Straube, Ják und die normannische Ornamentik in Ungarn, Freising, 1954; Z. Świechowski, Architektura na Śląsku do połowy XIII wieku (Architecture in Silesia to the Middle of the 13th Century), Warsaw, 1955; K. H. Clasen, Die Baukunst an der Ostseeküste zwischen Elbe und Oder, 2d ed., Dresden, 1956; L. Blondel, Architecture civile en Suisse à l'époque romane, Formositas romanica, Frauenfeld, 1958, pp. 181–93; E. Bock, Romanische Baukunst und Plastik in Württemberg, Stuttgart, 1958; E. Bock, Das Zeitalter der romanischen Kunst, mit besonderem Berücksichtigung der württembergischen Denkmäler, Stuttgart, 1958; G. Entz, Westemporen in der ungarischen Romanik, Acta h. artium. VI, 1959, pp. 1–19; A. Merhautová-Livorová, Cizí podněty a domácí tradice v románské architektuře severozápadních Čech (Indigenous Tradition and Foreign Influences in the Romanesque Architecture of Northwest Bohemia), Umění, VII, 1959, pp. 228–53; E. Vogt, Zur Baugeschichte des Fraumünster in Zürich, ZSAKg, XIX, 1959, pp. 133–63; M. Zadnikar, L'architecture romane en Slovénie, Cah. de civ. médiévale, II, 1959, pp. 469–72; M. Zadnikar, Romanska arhitektura na Slovenskem (Romanesque Architecture in Slovenia), Ljubljana, 1959; M. Kroh, Die spätromanischen Fensterformen im Kirchenbau des Rheinlandes, Mainz, 1960; C. Lapaire, Les constructions religieuses de Saint-Ursanne et leurs relations avec les monuments voisins, VIIe–XIIIe siècle, Porrentruy, 1960; K. Białoskórska, L'abbaye cistercienne de Wachock, Cah. de civ. médiévale, V, 1962, pp. 335–50; G. W. Holzinger, Romanische Turmkapellen in Westtürmen überwiegend ländlicher Kirchen im südlichen Teil des alten Erzbistums Köln, Aachen, 1962; H. E. Kubach, La tour de croisée de la cathédrale de Spire, Cah. techniques de l'art, IV, 1962, pp. 27–35; H. Wille, Die romanische Pfarrkirche St. Andreas in Hildesheim, Niederdeutsche Beiträge zur Kg., II, 1962, pp. 45–84; H. J. Mrusek, Drei deutsche Dome, Dresden, 1963.

f. England: E. S. Armitage, The Early Norman Castles of the British Isles, London, 1912; C. H. Moore, The Mediaeval Church Architecture of England, New York, 1912; F. Bond, An Introduction to English Church Architecture from the 11th to the 16th Century, London, 1913; E. S. Prior,

Eight Chapters on English Mediaeval Art, Cambridge, 1922; A. H. Thompson, The Cathedral Churches in England, London, 1925; A. W. Clapham, English Romanesque Architecture, 2 vols., Oxford, 1930–34; R. Palmer, English Monasteries in the Middle Ages, London, 1930; A. W. Clapham, Romanesque Architecture in England, London, 1950; H. Braun, An Introduction to English Mediaeval Architecture, London, 1951; L. F. Salzman, Building in England down to 1540, Oxford, 1952; R. A. Brown, English Mediaeval Castles, London, 1954; H. G. Leask, Irish Churches and Monastic Buildings, I: The First Phases and the Romanesque, Dundalk, 1955; G. Webb, Architecture in Britain: The Middle Ages, Harmondsworth, 1956 (bibliog.); G. H. Cook, English Collegiate Churches of the Middle Ages, London, 1959; E. Dyggve, Three Sanctuaries of Jelling Type, Lund, 1960; G. H. Cook, English Monasteries in the Middle Ages, London, 1961.

g. Scandinavia: H. Fett, Norges kirker i Middelalderen, Oslo, 1909; J. Roosval, Die Kirchen Gotlands, Stockholm, 1911; S. Curman, Bidrag till kännedom om cistercienserordens byggnadskonst, I, Stockholm, 1912; V. Lorenzen, De danske klosters bygningshistorie, 11 vols., Copenhagen, 1912–41; E. Ekhoff, Svenska stavkyrkor, Stockholm, 1914–16; J. Meyer, Domkirken i Trondhjem, Trondhjem, 1914; O. Rydbeck, Bidrag till Lunds domkyrkas byggnadshistoria, Lund, Leipzig, 1915; M. Clemmensen, La parenté entre les architectures en briques lombarde et danoises, Mem. Soc. Royale des Art du Nord, 1920–24, pp. 137–90; H. Cornell, Sigtuna och gamla Uppsala, Stockholm, 1920; E. Fischer, Västergötlands kyrkliga konst under medeltiden, Uppsala, 1920; B. Thordeman, Alsnö hus, Stockholm, 1920; M. Clemmensen, Slaegtskabet mellem lombardisk og dansk tetelstensarkitektur, Aarbøger för nordisk oldkyndighed, 3d Ser., XII, 1922, pp. 267–312; M. Clemmensen and V. Lorenzen, Kallundborg Kirke, Copenhagen, 1922; E. H. Wrangel, La cathédrale de Lund et l'influence italienne au XIIe siècle, Atti X Cong. int. di storia dell'arte (1912), Rome, 1922, pp. 131–34; O. Rydbeck, Lunds domkyrkas byggnadshistoria, Lund, 1923; J. Roosval, Den baltiska nordens kyrkor, Uppsala, 1924; H. Matthiessen, Middelalderlige Byer: Beliggenhed og Baggrund, Copenhagen, 1927; S. Anjou, Heliga korsets kyrka i Dalby, Göteborg, 1930; G. Boethius, Hallar: Tempel och stavkyrkor, Stockholm, 1931; C. M. Smidt, Cistercienserkirken i Løgum, Copenhagen, 1931; A. L. Romdahl, Linköpings domkyrka, Göteborg, 1932; C. G. Schultz, Nogle tidlig-romanske Landsbykirker, Aarbøger för nordisk oldkyndighed, 3d Ser., XXIV, 1934, pp. 195–236; E. Ekhoff and E. O. Janse, Visby stadsmur, Stockholm, 1936; E. Lundberg, Byggnadskonst i Sverige, I, Stockholm, 1940; R. Blomqvist, Tusentalets Lund, Lund, 1941; A. Roussell, Danmarks Middelalderborge, Copenhagen, 1942; V. Wanscher, Danmarks Arkitektur, Copenhagen, 1943; M. Mackeprang, Vore Landsbykirker, 2d ed., Copenhagen, 1944; O. Rydbeck, Lunds domkyrkas historia 1145–1945, Stockholm, 1946, pp. 7–139; V. Lorenzen, De gamla danske domkirker, Copenhagen, 1948; J. Roosval, Den gotländske ciceronen, 2d ed., Stockholm, 1950; G. Fischer, Norske kongeborger, Oslo, 1951; E. Lundberg, Visby kyrkoruiner och domkyrka, 2d ed., Stockholm, 1951; E. Moltke and E. Møller, ed., Roskilde Domkirke, I, Copenhagen, 1951; A. Tuulse, Borgar i västerlandet, Stockholm, 1952; A. Bugge, Norske stavkirker, Oslo, 1953 (Eng. trans., R. Cristophersen, Oslo, 1953); H. Langberg, Danmarks Bygningskultur, I, Copenhagen, 1955; A. Tuulse, Hossmo: En försvarskyrka med österns, Stockholm, 1955; E. Dyggve, Jellingkongernes Mindesmaerker, Kolding, 1956; E. Cinthio, Lunds domkyrka under romansk tid, Lund, 1957; T. Paulsson, Scandinavian Architecture, London, 1958; E. Gustafsson, Den romanska stenkyrkan i Atlingbo, Stockholm, 1959; H.-E. Lidén, Mariakirken: Romansk kirkebygningskunst i Bergen, Bergen, 1961; A. Tuulse, Der Kernbau des Doms zu Strängnäs, Stockholm, 1964.

Sculpture: general works: G. Clausse, Les marbriers romains et le mobilier presbytéral, Paris, 1897; A. K. Porter, Les débuts de la sculpture romane, GBA, LXI, 1919, pp. 47–60; A. K. Porter, Romanesque Sculpture of the Pilgrimage Roads, 10 vols., Boston, 1923; L. Bréhier, Les sculptures de routes de pélerinages, Rev. de l'art, XLV, 1924, pp. 127–33; F. de Mély, Signature de primitifs: De Cluny à Compostelle, GBA, X, 1924, pp. 1–24; L. Bréhier, L'homme dans la sculpture romane, Paris, 1927; J. Baltrušaitis, La stylistique ornementale dans la sculpture romane, Paris, 1931; R. Bernheimer, Romanische Tierplastik und die Ursprünge ihrer Motive, Munich, 1931; G. Pudelko, Romanische Taufsteine, Berlin, 1932; W. R. Valentiner, The Front Plane Relief in Mediaeval Art, AQ, II, 1938–39, pp. 155–72; J. C. Webster, The Labour of the Months in Antique and Mediaeval Art to the End of the 12th Century, Princeton, Chicago, 1938; U. Monneret de Villard, Per la storia del portale romanico, Mediaeval S. in Memory of A. Kingsley Porter, I, Cambridge, Mass., 1939, pp. 113–24; G. de Francovich, Viligelmo da Modena e gli inizi della scultura romanica europea, RIASA, VII, 1940, pp. 225–94; R. Wiebel, Die geistige Botschaft romanischer Bauplastik, Munich, 1940; J. Kühn, Mythologische Motive in romanischen Kirchen, Schaffhausen, 1945; H. Einem, Die Monumentalplastik des Mittelalters und ihr Verhältnis zur Antike, Antike und Abendland, III, 1948, pp. 120–51; J. Gantner, Romanische Plastik, 3d ed., Vienna, 1948; G. Gaillard, De la diversité des styles dans la sculpture romane des pélerinages, RArts, I, 1951, pp. 77–87; F. Kaempfer, Das Faltenprofil der mittelalterlichen Plastik, Wissenschaftliche Z. der Friedrich-Schiller-Univ. Jena, V, 1952–53, pp. 107–29; H. Leisinger, Romanische Bronzen: Kirchentüren im mittelalterlichen Europa, Zurich, 1956; R. Salvini, La scultura romanica in Europa, Milan, 1956; J. Baltrušaitis, La troisième sculpture romane, Formositas romanica, Frauenfeld, 1958, pp. 47–84; F. García Romo, Problemes actuales de la escultura románica, Rev. de ideas esteticas, XVI, 1958, pp. 17–40; W. Messerer, Das Relief im Mittelalter, Munich, 1959; C. D. Sheppard, Pre-romanesque and Romanesque Sculpture in Stone, AQ, XXIII, 1960, pp. 341–58; G. Weise, Vorbemerkungen zu einer Formengrammatik der vegetabilischen Grundmotive romanischer Kapitelldekoration, Das Werk des Künstlers: S. zur Iconographie und Formgeschichte H. Schrade, Stuttgart, 1960, pp. 72–100; W. Bech, Europäische Skulpturen des Mittelalters, Darmstadt, 1961 (cat.); H. Bosch and B. Lohse, Romanesque Sculpture, New York, 1964.

Sculpture: works concerning individual countries. a. France: (1) *General*: R. de Lasteyrie, Etudes sur la sculpture française du moyen-âge, MPiot, VIII, 1902, pp. 1–144; J. Jahn, Kompositiongesetze französischer Reliefplastik im 12. und 13. Jahrhundert, Leipzig, 1922; P. Deschamps, French Sculpture of the Romanesque Period, Florence, 1930; H. Focillon, L'art des sculpteurs romans, Paris, 1931; A. Gardner, Mediaeval Sculpture in France, Cambridge, 1931; L. Lefrançois-Pillion, Les sculpteurs français du XIIe siècle, Paris, 1931; L. Réau, Les sculpteurs français en Italie, Paris, 1945; M. Aubert, La sculpture française au moyen-âge, Paris, 1947; M. Durliat, La sculpture romane en Roussillon, 3 vols., Perpignan, 1948–52; J. Vanuxem, The Theories of Mabillon and Montfaucon on French Sculpture of the 12th Century, Warburg, XX, 1957, pp. 45–58; P. Pradel and E. Sougez, Sculptures romanes des Musées de France, Paris, 1958; G. Beaudequin, Les representations sculptées de l'Adoration des Mages dans l'ancien diocèse d'Autun à l'époque romane, Cah. de civ. médiévale, III, 1960, pp. 479–89; D. Jalabert, La flore romane bourguignonne, GBA, LV, 1960, pp. 193–208; V. H. Debidour, Le Bestiaire sculpté du moyen âge en France, Paris, 1961; M. Vieillard-Troiekouroff, Survivances mérovingiennes dans la sculpture funéraire du moyen âge, Art de France, I, 1961, pp. 264–69. (2) *Single regions or monuments*: L. Bréhier, Les chapiteaux historiés de Notre-Dame du Port (à Clermont-Ferrand), Rev. de l'art chrétien, LXII, 1912, pp. 248–62, 339–50; E. Mâle, L'influence de la miniature sur la sculpture du Languedoc au XIIe siècle, Actes XIe Cong. d'h. de l'art, II, Paris, 1921, pp. 455–63; P. Deschamps, L'autel roman de Saint-Sernin de Toulouse et les sculptures du cloître de Moissac, B. archéol., 1923, pp. 239–50, pls. XIX–XXVII; M. Aubert, Moissac: L'Abbaye et la cloître, CAF, XCII, 1929, pp. 494–525; K. J. Conant, The Iconography and the Sequence of the Ambulatory Capitals of Cluny, Speculum, V, 1929, pp. 278–87; M. Aubert, La Bourgogne: La sculpture, 3 vols., Paris, 1930; R. Rey and A. Auriol, La Basilique Saint-Sernin de Toulouse, Toulouse, Paris, 1930; P. Deschamps, La sculpture française en Palestine et en Syrie à l'époque des Croisades, MPiot, XXXI, 1931, pp. 91–118; P. Deschamps, Un chapiteau roman du Berry imité à Nazareth au XIIe siècle, MPiot, XXXII, 1932, pp. 119–26; M. Aubert, L'église Saint-Sernin de Toulouse, Paris, 1933; M. Aubert, L'église abbatiale de Cluny, CAF, XCVIII, 1935, pp. 503–22; R. Rey, La sculpture romane languedocienne, Toulouse, 1936; P. Quarré, La sculpture romane de la Haute-Auvergne: Décor des chapiteaux, Aurillac, 1938; M. Aubert, L'église des Conques, Paris, 1939; E. Mendell, Romanesque Sculpture in Saintonge, New Haven, London, 1940; P. Deschamps, Etude sur les sculptures de Sainte-Foy de Conques et de Saint-Sernin de Toulouse et leurs relations avec celles de Saint-Isidore de Léon et de Saint-Jacques de Compostelle, B. mon., C, 1941, pp. 239–64; M. Lafargue, Les chapiteaux du cloître de Notre-Dame la Daurade, Paris, 1941; J. Talobre, La reconstitution du portail de l'église abbatiale de Cluny, B. mon., CII, 1944, pp. 225–40; D. Jalabert, L'Ève de la cathédrale d'Autun: Sa place dans l'histoire de la sculpture romane, GBA, XXXV, 1949, pp. 247–74; M. Gouron, Saint-Gilles du Gard, CAF, CVIII, 1950, pp. 104–19; R. Hamann, Die Abteikirche von St. Gilles und ihre künstlerische Nachfolge, 3 vols., Berlin, 1955; M. Aubert, L'église d'Aulnay, CAF, CXIV, 1956, pp. 310–27; C. Bernouilli, Die Skulpturen des Abtei Conques-en-Rouergue, Basel, 1956, R. Crozet, L'abbaye aux Dames de Saintes, CAF, CXIV, 1956, pp. 106–18; M. Durliat, Christs romans: Roussillon, Cerdagne, Perpignan, 1956; R. and A. M. Oursel, Les églises romanes de l'Autunnois et du Brionnais: Cluny et sa région, Mâcon, 1956; M. Durliat, La sculpture romane en Cerdagne, Perpignan, 1957; Mme. Masdupuy, Du porche de Moissac au portail royal de Chartres, B. Soc. géog. de Toulouse, LXXVIII, 1959, pp. 245–51, 258–61, 269–71; G. Gaillard, Le chapiteau de Job aux Musées de Toulouse et de Pampelune, RArts, X, 1960, pp. 147–56; M. Gauthier, La Résurrection de Lazare dans l'art roman français, Lyons, 1960; D. Grivot and G. Zarnecki, Gislebertus: Sculpteur d'Autun, Paris, 1960 (Eng. trans., New York, 1961; rev. by F. Salet, B. mon., CXIX, 1961, pp. 325–43); M. Rumpler, Sculptures romanes en Alsace, Strasbourg, 1960; R. Lejeune, Le linteau d'Angoulême et la "Chanson de Roland," Romania, LXXXII, 1961, pp. 1–26; P. Mesplé, Toulouse, Musée des Augustins: Les sculptures romanes, Paris, 1961; W. Sauerländer, Art antique et sculpture autour de 1200, Art de France, I, 1961, pp. 47–56; P. Bouffard, Sculpteurs de la Saintonge romane, Paris, 1962; M. Durliat, Les chapiteaux et le portail de Saint-Michel de Lescure, Cah. de civ. médiévale, V, 1962, pp. 411–18; P. Quarré, Les sculptures du tombeau de Saint-Lazare à Autun et leur place dans l'art roman, Cah. de civ. médiévale, V, 1962, pp. 169–74; M. Rumpler, La frise dans la sculpture romane en Alsace, Cah. techniques de l'art, IV, 1962, pp. 37–49; W. Sauerländer, Skulpturen des 12. Jahrhunderts in Châlons-sur-Marne, ZfKg, XXV, 1962, pp. 97–124.

b. Spain and Portugal: (1) *General*: A. L. Mayer, Mittelalterliche Plastik in Spanien, Munich, 1922; P. Deschamps, Tables d'autel de marbre executées dans le Midi de la France, Mél. Lot, Paris, 1925, pp. 137–68; A. K. Porter, Spanish Romanesque Sculpture, 2 vols., Florence, 1928; G. Gaillard, Les débuts de la sculpture romane espagnole: Léon-Jaca-Compostelle, Paris, 1938; G. Gaillard, La sculpture romane espagnole, Paris, 1946; J. Gudiol i Ricart and J. A. Gaya Nuño, Arquitectura y escultura románicas (Ars Hispaniae, V), Madrid, 1948 (bibliog.); M. E. Gómez Moreno, Breve historia de la escultura española, 2d ed., Madrid, 1951. (2) *Single regions or monuments*: F. Hernández, Un aspecto de la influencia del arte califal en Cataluña, Arch. español de arte y arqueol., VI, 1930, pp. 21–49; J. M. Lacarra, La Catedral románica de Pamplona: Nuevos documentos, Arch. español de arte y arqueol., VII, 1931, pp. 73–86; G. Gaillard, L'église et le cloître de Silos: Dates de la construction, B. mon., XCI, 1932, pp. 39–80; G. Gaillard, Les chapiteaux du cloître de Santa Maria del Estany, GBA, X, 1933, pp. 139–57, 257–71; G. Gaillard, Premiers essais de sculpture monumentale en Catalogne aux Xe et XIe siècles, Paris, 1938; J. Puig i Cadafalch, L'escultura romànica a Catalunya, Barcelona, 1949; G. Gaillard, Besalu, CAF, CXII, 1954, pp. 236–46; G. Gaillard, La sculpture du XIe siècle en Navarre avant l'influence des pélerinages, B. mon., CXIII, 1955, pp. 237–49; J. M. Pita Andrade, Escultura románica en Castilla: Los maestros de Oviedo y Avila, Madrid, 1955; M. Schneider, Singende Steine, Kassel, 1955; G. Gaillard, Le Porche de la Gloire et ses origines espagnoles. Cah. de civ. médiévale, I, 1958, pp. 465–73; R. Crozet, Recherches sur la sculpture romane en Navarre et en Aragon, Cah. de civ. médiévale, II, 1959, pp. 333–40, III, 1960, pp. 119–27; J. M. Pita Andrade, Sobre los origines españoles del Pórtico de la Gloria, Cuadernos de estudios gallegos, XIV, 1959, pp. 131–37; A. Ruiz, Abadia de Santo Domingo de Silos, Burgos, 1960; O. Naesgaard, Saint-Jacques de Compostelle et les débuts de la grande sculpture vers 1100, Aarhus, 1962.

c. Italy: (1) *General*: M. G. Zimmermann, Oberitalische Plastik im frühen und hohen Mittelalter, Leipzig, 1897; P. d'Ancona, L'uomo e le sue opere nelle figurazioni italiane del medioevo, Florence, 1923; G. Sinibaldi, La scultura protocristiana, preromanica e romanica, Florence, 1935; G. de Francovich, Viligelmo da Modena e gli inizi della scultura romanica europea, RIASA, VII, 1940, pp. 225–94; G. de Francovich, La scultura medioevale in legno, Rome, 1943; R. Jullian, L'éveil de la sculpture italienne, I, Paris, 1945; G. H. Crichton, Romanesque Sculpture in Italy, London, 1954; R. Salvini, Wiligelmo e le origini della scultura romanica, Milan, 1956; R. Jullian, Les persistances romanes dans la sculpture gothique italienne, Cah. de civ. médiévale, III, 1960, pp. 295–305. (2) *Single regions or monuments*: H. von der Gabelentz, Mittelalterliche Plastik in Venedig, Leipzig, 1903; M. Wackernagel, La bottega dell'"Archidiaconus Acceptus," BArte, II, 1908, pp. 143–50; M. Wackernagel, Die Plastik des XI. und XII. Jahrhunderts in Apulien, Leipzig, 1911; F. Rupp. Inkrustationstil der romanischen Baukunst zu Florenz, Strasbourg, 1912; R. S. Loomis, The Story of the Modena Archivolt and Its Mythological Roots, Romanic Rev., XV, 1924, pp. 266–84; W. Biehl, Toskanische Plastik des frühen und hohen Mittelalters, Leipzig, 1926; T. Krautheimer-Hess, Die figurale Plastik der Ostlombardei, Marburger Jhb. für Kw., IV, 1928, pp. 231–307; M. Salmi, Romanesque Sculpture in Tuscany, Florence, 1928; L. Biagi, Nel chiostro di Monreale, L'Arte, XXXIV, 1931, pp. 468–85; A. Boeckler, Die Bronzetür von S. Zeno, Marburg, 1931; L. Biagi, La scultura del periodo normanno in Sicilia, L'Arte, XXXV, 1932, pp. 452–75; G. de Francovich, La corrente comasca nella scultura romanica europea, RIASA, V, 1935–36, pp. 267–305, VI, 1937–38, pp. 47–129; G. H. Gerould, Arthurian Romance and the Modena Relief, Speculum, X, 1935, pp. 355–76; L. Olschki, La cattedrale di Modena e il suo rilievo arturiano, Arch. romanicum, XIX, 1935, pp. 145–82; W. F. Volbach, Scultura medievale della Campania, RendPontAcc, XII, 1936, pp. 81–104; S. Bottari, I Mesi di Lucca, Le Arti, I, 1938–39, pp. 560–66; G. Nicco Fasola, Due pulpiti campani del XII e XIII secolo, L'Arte, XLI, 1938, pp. 3–25; M. Salmi, Maestri comacini e maestri lombardi, Palladio, III, 1939, pp. 49–62; P. Gazzola, La chiesa di S. Maria degli Alamanni in Messina, Palladio, V, 1941, pp. 207–21; G. Chierici, Le sculture della basilica di S. Michele Maggiore a Pavia, Milan, 1942; O. Lehmann-Brockhaus, Die Kanzeln der Abruzzen im 12. und 13. Jahrhundert, Römisches Jhb. für Kg., VI, 1942–44, pp. 257–428; W. F. Volbach, Oriental Influence in Animal Sculpture of Campania, AB, XXIV, 1942, pp. 172–80; E. Arslan, La pittura e la scultura veronese dal secolo VIII al secolo XIII, Milan, 1943; F. Schettini, La scultura pugliese dal secolo XII al secolo XIII, Bari, 1946; V. Martinelli, Bonanno Pisano scultore, Belle Arti, I, 1948, pp. 272–97; C. D. Sheppard, Jr., Iconography of the Cloister of Monreale, AB, XXXI, 1949, pp. 159–69; C. D. Sheppard, Jr., Monreale and Chartres, GBA, XXXV, 1949, pp. 401–14; F. Bologna and R. Causa, Sculture lignee della Campania, Naples, 1950 (cat.); E. Hutton, The Cosmati, London, 1950; C. D. Sheppard, Jr., A Chronology of Romanesque Sculpture in Campania, AB, XXXII, 1950, pp. 319–26; R. Salvini, I discepoli di Wiligelmo a Cremona, Comm, II, 1951, pp. 153–61; G. de Francovich, Benedetto Antelami e l'arte del suo tempo, 2 vols., Milan, Florence, 1952 (rev. by R. Salvini, L'Arte, XXIX, 1954, pp. 214–22); C. D. Sheppard, Jr., A Stylistic Analysis of the Cloister of Monreale, AB, XXXIV, 1952, pp. 35–41; A. Boeckler, Die Bronzetüren des Bonannus von Pisa und des Barisanus von Trani, Berlin, 1953; E. Arslan, La scultura romanica, Storia di Milano, III, Milan, 1954, pp. 525–600; S. Bottari, La cultura figurativa in Sicilia, Messina, Florence, 1954, passim; N. Rasmo, La scultura romanica nell'Alto Adige, Bolzano, 1954; E. Arslan, Note sulla scultura romanica pavese, BArte, XL, 1955, pp. 103–18; F. Bologna, Opere d'arte nel Salernitano dal XII al XVIII secolo, Naples, 1955; S. Bottari, Note sul Duomo di Monreale, Atti Convegno di s. ruggeriani, Palermo, 1955, pp. 269–75; L. Cochetti, Problemi della scultura romanica campana, Comm, VII, 1956, pp. 9–18; P. Sanpaolesi, La facciata della cattedrale di Pisa, RIASA, N.S., V–VI, 1956–57, pp. 248–394; L. Cochetti, La decorazione plastica del chiostro di S. Sofia a Benevento, Comm, VIII, 1957, pp. 17–26; H. Giess, Capitelli romanici a Montevergine, Comm, VIII, 1957, pp. 27–30; G. Marchini, Il Duomo di Prato, Milan, 1957; G. Capelli, I mesi antelamici nel Battistero di Parma, Parma, 1958; L. Cochetti Pratesi, Rilievi nella cattedrale di Sessa Aurunca e lo sviluppo dei marmorari "neocampani" nel XIII secolo, Comm, IX, 1958, pp. 75–87; C. D. Sheppard, Jr., The East Portal of the Baptistery and the West Portal of the Cathedral of Pisa, GBA, LII, 1958, pp. 5–32; G. P. Bognetti, Una rettifica epigrafica a proposito dei limiti cronologici dell'opera dell'Antelami, SbMünchen, 1959, 3, pp. 1–11; R. Salvini, Un inedito di scultura romanica piacentina, Arte antica e moderna, II, 1959, pp. 407–19; C. A. Willemsen and D. Odenthal, Apulia: Imperial Splendor in Southern Italy (trans. D. Woodward), London, New York, 1959; L. Cochetti Pratesi, Contributi alla scultura veneziana del Duecento, Comm. XI, 1960, pp. 3–21, 209–19, XII, 1961, pp. 12–30; O. Demus, The Church of San Marco in Venice: History, Architecture, Sculpture, Washington, 1960; K. Forster and L. von Matt, Benedetto Antelami: Skulpturen im Dom und am Baptisterium zu Parma, Du, XX, 228, 1960, pp. 2–48; A. Petrucci, Cattedrali di Puglia, Rome, 1960; M. Weinberger, Nicola Pisano and the Tradition of Tuscan Pulpits, GBA, LV, 1960, pp. 129–46; L. Cochetti Pratesi, Il candelabro pasquale della Cappella Palatina, Scritti di storia dell'arte in onore di M. Salmi, I, Rome, 1961, pp. 291–304; R. Salvini, Il chiostro di Monreale e la scultura romanica in Sicilia, Palermo, 1962. See also the bibliogs. for ANTELAMI, BENEDETTO; CAMPIONESI; COSMATI; NICOLAUS; WILIGELMO DA MODENA.

d. Low Countries: R. Ligtenberg, Die romanische Steinplastik in den nördlichen Niederlanden, The Hague, 1918; M. Laurent, Trois bas-reliefs romans de la Belgique méridionale, Oud-Holland, XLI, 1923–24, pp. 198–206; J. de Borchgrave d'Altena, Oeuvres de nos imagiers romans et gothiques . . . , Brussels, 1944; J. de Borchgrave d'Altena, La passion du Christ dans la sculpture en Belgique du XIe au XVIe siècle, Paris, Brussels, 1946; D. P. R. A. Bouvy, Middeleeuwsche beeldhouwkunst in de noordelijke Nederlanden, Amsterdam, 1947; L. Tollenaere, La sculpture sur pierre de l'ancien diocèse de Liège: L'époque romane, Louvain, 1957 (rev. by K.-A. Wirth, Kchr., XI, 1958, pp. 185–95).

e. Germany and Central Europe: (1) *General*: H. Beenken, Romanische Skulptur in Deutschland, Leipzig, 1924; E. Panofsky, Die deutsche Plastik des 11.–13. Jahrhunderts, Munich, 1924; H. Beenken, Schreine und Schranken, Jhb. für Kw., 1926, pp. 65–107; L. Gál, L'architecture religieuse en Hongrie, Paris, 1929; O. Schürer, Romanische Doppelkapellen, Marburger Jhb. für Kw., V, 1929, pp. 99–192; F. Novotny, Romanische Bauplastik in Österreich, Vienna, 1930; A. Feulner and T. Müller, Geschichte der deutschen Plastik, Munich, 1953; G. H. Hamilton, The Art and Architecture of Russia, Harmondsworth, 1954; E. Kluckhohn and W. Paatz, Die Bedeutung Italiens für die romanische Baukunst und Bauornamentik in Deutschland, Marburger Jhb. für Kw., XVI, 1955, pp. 1–120; H. P. Hilger, Romanik am Rhein, Cologne, 1959; E. Steingräber, Deutsche Plastik der Frühzeit, Königstein im Taunus, 1961; J. Zachwatowicz, Polska architektura monumentalna w 10 i 11 wieku (Monumental Architecture in Poland in the 10th and 11th Centuries), Kwartalnik arch. i urbanistyki, VI, 1961, pp. 101–31; J. Hawrot, Problematyka przedrománskich i románskich rotund bałkańskich, czeskich i polskich . . . (Problem of Pre-romanesque and Romanesque Circular Buildings in the Balkans, Czechoslovakia and Poland . . .), B. h. sztuki, XXIV, 1962, pp. 255–82. (2) *Single regions or monuments*: N. Irsch, Die Trierer Abteikirche St. Matthias und die trierisch-lotharingische Bautengruppe, Augsburg, 1927; H. Möhle, Die romanische Bildhauerschule des Bamberger Domes und ihre Beziehungen zur Malerei, Strasbourg, 1927; F. Halle, Die Bauplastik von Wladimir-Ssusdal, Berlin, 1929; A. Wentzel, Die Baugeschichte der Klosterkirche zu Trebitsch, Marburger Jhb. für Kw., V, 1929, pp. 353–419; A. Goldschmidt, Die Bronzetüren von Nowgorod und Gnesen, Marburg, 1932; D. Frey, Ein neu entdecktes romanisches Tympanorelief, Z. d. Verein für Kw., II, 1935, pp. 496–518; W. Bader, Die Benediktinerabtei Brauweiler, Berlin, 1937; E. Bachmann, Eine spätstaufische Bautengruppe im mittelböhmischen Raum, Brünn, Leipzig, 1940; W. Weisbach, Der Skulpturenschmuck der Basler Galluspforte, ZfSAKg, III, 1941, pp. 110–35; H. Gombert, Das Freudenstädter Lesepult, Das Münster, III, 1950, pp. 257–65; W. Wennig, Ein spätromanisches Triumphkreuz in Thüringen, ZfKw, V, 1951, pp. 17–28; A. Kippenberger, Der Kruzifixus aus Birkenbringhausen, Wallraf-Richartz-Jhb., XIV, 1952, pp. 41–44; E. Gaul, Neue Forschungen zum Problem der Externsteine, Westfalen, XXXII, 1954, pp. 141–64; R. Hamann-MacLean, Zur Zeitstellung und Herkunft des Cappenberger Kruzifixus, Westfalen, XXXIII, 1955, pp. 113–24; H. Püttmann, Das Tympanonrelief von St. Caecilien, Wallraf-Richartz-Jhb., XVII, 1955, pp. 43–61; R. Wesenberg, Die Fragmente monumentaler Skulpturen von St. Pantaleon in Köln, ZfKw, IX, 1955, pp. 1–28; R. Will, Répertoire de la sculpture romane en Alsace, Strasbourg, 1955; P. Schlopsnies, Die romanischen Backsteinportale nord-west Mecklenburgs, Wissenschaftliche Z. der technischen Hochschule Dresdens, VI, 1–3 (Festschrift E. Hempel), 1956–57, pp. 5–26; M. Walickiego, ed., Drzwi Gnieźnieńskie (Gniezno Cathedral Doors), 3 vols., Wrocław, 1956–59; D. Dercsényi, Zur 700-jährigen Feier der Kirche von Ják, Acta h. artium, IV, 1957, pp. 173–202; C. Beutler, Die Madonna von St. Maria im Kapitol in Köln, Kchr., XI, 1958, pp. 61–63; G. Entz, La Cathédrale de Gyulafehérvár (Alba Julia), Acta h. artium, V, 1958, pp. 1–70; Y. Balogh, L'art français et la sculpture de la Hongrie médiévale, Actes XIXe Cong. int. d'h. de l'art (1958), Paris, 1959, pp. 33–35; E. Doberer, Die ursprüngliche Bestimmung der Apostelsäulen im Dom zu Chur, ZfSAKg, XIX, 1959, pp. 17–41; L. Kalinowski, Influence de l'art français sur la sculpture médiévale en Pologne, Actes XIXe Cong. int. d'h. de l'art (1958), Paris, 1959, pp. 87–91; J. Kvet, L'art français et la Bohème à l'époque romane, Actes XIXe Cong. int. d'h. de l'art (1958), Paris, 1959, pp. 105–10; G. Robra, Mittelalterliche Holzplastik in Ostfriesland, Rautenberg, 1959; K.-A. Wirth, Nachrichten über Begräbnis und Grab Bernwards von Hildesheim, ZfKg, XXII, 1959, pp. 305–23; G. Troescher, Koblenzer Bildschnitzer in salischer und staufischer Zeit, Jhb. der Berliner Mus., III, 1961, pp. 18–37; R. Feuchtmüller, Die steinerte Bibel: Die romanische Kirche von Schöngrabern, Vienna, 1962; F. Mühlberg, Grab und Grabdenkmal der Plektrudis in St. Marien im Kapitol zu Köln, Wallraf-Richartz-Jhb., XXIV, 1962, pp. 21–97.

f. England: F. H. Crossley, English Church Monuments A.D. 1150–1550, London, New York, 1921; A. Gardner, English Medieval Sculpture, 2d ed., Cambridge, 1951; G. Zarnecki, English Romanesque Sculpture 1066–1140, London, 1951; G. Zarnecki, Later English Romanesque Sculpture 1140–1210, London, 1953; F. Saxl, English Sculptures of the 12th Century, London, 1954; G. Zarnecki, English Romanesque Lead Sculpture, London, 1957; P. A. Faulkner, Domestic Planning from the 12th to the 14th Centuries, Archaeol. J., CXV, 1958, pp. 150–83; G. Zarnecki, The Early Sculpture of Ely Cathedral, London, 1958; D. Talbot Rice, Essai de classification de la sculpture anglo-saxonne des Xe et XIe siècles, Cah. de civ. médiévale, III, 1960, pp. 195–207.

g. Scandinavia: L. Tynell, Skånes medeltida dopfuntar, 4 vols., Lund, 1913–21; C. R. af Ugglas, Gotlands medeltida träskulptur, Stockholm, 1915; J. Roosval, Dopfuntar i Statens Historiska Museum, Stockholm, 1917; E. Fischer, Västergötlands romanska stenkonst, Göteborg, 1918; J. Roosval, Die Steinmeister Gottlands, Stockholm, 1918; E. Wrangel, Lunds domkyrkas konsthistoria, Lund, 1923; W. Anderson, Romanesque Sculpture in South Sweden, Art S., VI, 1928, pp. 49–70; R. Blomqvist, Studier i Smålands romanska stenkonst, Lund, 1929; M. Rydbeck, Skånes stenmästare före 1200, Lund, 1936; R. Norberg, Bohuslänsk medeltida träskulptur, Göteborgs och Bohusläns fornminnesförenings tidskrift, V, 1939, pp. 3–52; M. Mackeprang, Danmarks middelalderlige Døbefonte, Copenhagen, 1941; V. Nyman, Ålands medeltida träskulptur, Årsbock Ålands odling, 1947, pp. 57–91; W. Holmqvist, Sigtunamästaren och hans krets, Situne Dei, VII, 1948; M. Mackeprang, Jydske Granitportaler, Copenhagen, 1948; A. Andersson, English Influence in Norwegian and Swedish Figure

Sculpture in Wood 1220–1270, Stockholm, 1949; V. Thorlacius-Ussing, ed., Danmarks Billedhuggerkunst, Copenhagen, 1950, pp. 9–80; M. Blindheim, Main Trends of East-Norwegian Wooden Figure Sculpture in the Second Half of the 13th Century, Oslo, 1952; A. Andersson, England-Norge-Sverige i 1200-talets plastik, Konsthist. Tidskrift, XXIV, 1955, pp. 41–56; A. Andersson, Madonnan från Gesäter och hennes Anförvander, Fornvännen, XLIX, 1955, pp. 156–76; B. C. Lange, Østnorske gravmonumenter fra tidlig middelalder, Viking, XIX, 1955, pp. 121–46; A. Andersson, Kristusbilden i Danderyd och de äldsta uppländska triumfkrucifixen, Stockholm, 1958; S. A. Hallbäck, Medeltida dopfuntar på Dal, Vänersborg, 1959; B. I. Larsen, Nesland-portales, Viking, XXIV, 1960, pp. 119–37; E. Cinthio, Der Dom zu Lund in romanischer Zeit, Arte lombarda, VI, 1961, pp. 178–89; E. Forssman, Medeltida träskulptur i Dalarna, Falun, 1961; A. Andersson, Viklaumadonnans mästare, Stockholm, 1962; Museum of National Antiquities Stockholm, Medieval Wooden Sculpture in Sweden, I, V (plates), Stockholm, 1964; C. A. Nordman, Medeltida skulptur i Finland, Helsinki, 1964.

Painting: general works: E. Steinmann, Die Tituli und die kirchliche Wandmalerei im Abendlande vom V. bis zum XI. Jahrhundert, Leipzig, 1892; D. V. Thompson, The Materials of Mediaeval Painting, New Haven, London, 1936; E. Hempel, Der Realitätscharakter des kirchlichen Wandbildes im Mittelalter, Kunstgeschichtliche Studien: Festschrift D. Frey, Breslau, 1943, pp. 106–20; E. W. Anthony, Romanesque Frescoes, Princeton, 1951; K. M. Swoboda, Geometrische Vorzeichnungen romanischer Wandgemälde, Alte und neue Kunst, II, 1953, pp. 81–100; G. de Francovich, Problemi della pittura e della scultura preromanica, Atti Centro it. di s. sull'alto medioevo, II, 1955, pp. 355–519 at 355; A. Grabar and C. Nordenfalk, Romanesque Painting from the 11th to the 13th Century, New York, 1958, pp. 23–130; L. Grodecki, Les origines de la peinture médiévale, Critique, XIV, 1958, pp. 1059–70; H. Schrade, Vor- und frühromanische Malerei, Cologne, 1958; W. Frodl, Zur Erforschung der Wandmalerei des Mittelalters, Zbornik za umetnostno zgdovino, N.S., V–VI (L. F. Stelè septuagenario oblatae), 1959, pp. 323–35; W. Schöne, Über den Beitrag von Licht und Farbe zur Raumgestaltung im Kirchenbau des alten Abendlandes, Evangelische Kirchenbautagung (Stuttgart, 1959), Berlin, 1961, pp. 89–154; Theophilus presbyter, Schedula diversarum artium (ed. and trans., C. R. Dodwell, The Various Arts), London, New York, 1961.

Painting: works concerning individual countries. a. France: (1) *General*: H. Focillon, Peintures romanes des églises de France, Paris, 1938; C.-P. Duprat, Enquête sur la peinture murale en France à l'époque romane, B. mon., CI, 1942, pp. 165–223, CII, 1943–44, pp. 5–90, 161–223; P. Deschamps, Combats de cavalerie et épisodes des Croisades dans les peintures murales du XIIe et XIIIe siècle, Orientalia christiana periodica, XIII, 1947, pp. 454–74; P. Deschamps and M. Thibout, La peinture murale en France: Le haut moyen âge et l'époque romane, Paris, 1951; R. de la Moussaye, Petit guide de fresques romanes en France, Paris, 1956; L. Brion-Guerry, Fresques romanes de France, Paris, 1958; P. H. Michel, La fresque romane, Paris, 1961. (2) *Single regions or monuments*: P. Merimée, Peintures de l'église de Saint-Savin, 5 vols., Paris, 1845; E. Maillard, L'église Saint-Savin, Paris, 1927; G. Plat, La Chapelle Saint-Gilles de Montoire, B. Soc. archéol. du Vendômois, LXVII, 1928, pp. 93–105; J. Virey, Saint-Hugues et la chapelle de Berzé, Cong. Assoc. bourguignonne des soc. savantes (1927), II, Dijon, 1928, pp. 302–07; F. Mercier, Les primitifs français: La peinture clunysienne en Bourgogne à l'époque romane, son histoire et sa technique, Paris, 1932; I. Yoshikawa, l'Apocalypse de Saint-Savin, Paris, 1939; M. Thibout, Découverte de peintures murales dans l'église de Château-Gontier, B. mon., CI, 1942, pp. 5–40; M. Thibout, Les grottes de Jonas et les peintures murales de leur chapelle, CahA, II, 1947, pp. 115–28; J. Zvěřina, Les peintures de la crypte de Tavant, Orientalia christiana periodica, XIII, 1947, pp. 675–93; J. Laffargue and G. Fouet, Peintures romanes: Vestiges gallo-romains à Saint-Plancard (Haute-Garonne), Toulouse, 1948; J. Verrier, Tavant, CAF, CVI, 1948, pp. 314–21; P. Deschamps, La date des peintures de Saint-Savin sur Gartempe, CRAI, 1949, pp. 73–80; P. Deschamps, Les peintures du choeur de Saint-Pierre-les-Eglises, CRAI, 1950, pp. 33–44; R. Louis, Les églises d'Auxerre des origines au XIe siècle, Paris, 1953; P. Ponsich, L'abbaye de Sainte-Marie d'Arles, CAF, CXII, 1954, pp. 347–77; M. Durliat, Arts anciens du Roussillon: Peinture, Perpignan, 1955; P. Deschamps, Les fresques des cryptes des cathédrales de Chartres et de Clermont et l'imitation des tissus dans les peintures murales, MPiot, XLVIII, 1956, pp. 91–106; P. Deschamps, Peintures murales préromanes et romanes récemment découvertes en France, Cah. de civ. médiévales, I, 1958, pp. 188–91; F. Enaud, Les peintures murales de Saint-Julien de Brioude, Mon. h. de la France, N.S., IV, 1958, pp. 178–86; E. Magnien, Le problème de la date des peintures murales de Berzé-la-Ville, Cong. int. d'ét. romanes, II–III, Paris, 1958, pp. 13–23; R. Storz, Zu den romanischen Wandmalereien in St.-Chef (Isère), Das Werk des Künstlers: S. zur Ikonographie und Formgeschichte H. Schrade, Stuttgart, 1960, pp. 108–25; M. Durliat, La peinture romane en Roussillon et en Cerdagne, Cah. de civ. médiévale, IV, 1961, pp. 1–14. *b. Spain and Portugal*: (1) *General*: J. Folch i Torres, Imitation de l'orfèvrerie dans les devants d'autels et les retables catalans de l'époque romane, GBA, III, 1930, pp. 248–56; C. R. Post, A History of Spanish Painting, I, Cambridge, Mass., 1930; W. W. S. Cook and J. Gudiol Ricart, Pintura e imaginería románicas (Ars Hispaniae, VI), Madrid, 1950 (bibliog.); R. dos Santos, O Românico em Portugal, Lisbon, 1955; W. W. S. Cook and J. Ainaud, Spain: Romanesque Paintings, Greenwich, Conn., 1957. (2) *Single regions or monuments*: J. Pijoan, Les pintures murals catalanes, 5 vols., Barcelona, 1907–21; G. Richert, La pintura medieval en España: Pinturas murales y tablas catalanas, Barcelona, 1926; J. Gudiol i Cunill, La pintura mitgeval catalana: Els primitius, I, Barcelona, 1927; C. L. Kuhn, Romanesque Mural Paintings of Catalonia, Cambridge, Mass., 1930; F. Soldevilla, Die Kunst Kataloniens, Vienna, 1937; Junta de Museus, Frontals romànics del Museu d'Art de Catalunya, Barcelona, 1944; J. Pijoan and J. Gudiol Ricart, Les pintures murals romàniques de Catalunya (Monumenta Cataloniae, IV), Barcelona, 1948; J. A. Gaya Nuño, La pintura románica en Castilla, Madrid, 1954; M. Durliat, Arts anciens du Roussillon: Peinture, Perpignan, 1955; W. W. S. Cook, La pintura mural románica en Cataluña, Madrid, 1956; J. Folch i Torres, La pintura románica sobre fusta (Monumenta Cataloniae, IX), Barcelona, 1956; J. Gudiol Ricart, Historia de la pintura en Cataluña, Madrid, 1956; A. Cruz Martín, Pinturas románicas del Panteón Real de San Isidore de León, 2d ed., León, 1959; L. Schreyer, Romanische Malerei, Wand- und Tafelmalereien Kataloniens aus romanischer Zeit, Bonn, 1959; O. Beyer, Romanik in Spanien: Die frühen katalanischen Kirchenbilder, Kassel, 1960; W. W. S. Cook, La pintura románica sobre tabla en Cataluña, Madrid, 1960.

c. Italy: (1) *General*: Van Marle, I; G. Vitzthum and W. F. Volbach, Die malerei und Plastik des Mittelalters in Italien, Wildpark-Potsdam, 1924; E. Sandberg-Vavalà, La croce dipinta italiana . . . , Verona, 1929; G. Ladner, Die italienische Malerei im 11. Jahrhundert, JhbKhSammlWien, N.S., V, 1931, pp. 33–160; R. Longhi, Giudizio sul Duecento, Proporzioni, II, 1948, pp. 5–54; E. B. Garrison, Italian Romanesque Panel Painting, Florence, 1949; E. B. Garrison, Studies in the History of Mediaeval Italian Painting, 4 vols., Florence, 1953–60; R. Oertel, Die Frühzeit der italienischen Malerei, Stuttgart, 1953; P. Francastel, ed., Histoire de la peinture italienne, I, Paris, 1955; E. Carli et al., Pittura italiana, I: Medioevo, romanico e gotico, Milan, 1959; A. Maiuri and L. Venturi, La pittura italiana dalle origini al secolo XIII, Lausanne, 1959 (Eng. trans., J. Emmons, New York, 1959); R. Oertel, Italienische Malerei bis zum Ausgang der Renaissance, Munich, 1960; F. Bologna, La pittura italiana dalle origini, Rome, 1962 (bibliog.). (2) *Single regions or monuments*: F. X. Kraus, Die Wandgemälde von S. Angelo in Formis, JhbPreussKSamml, XIV, 1893, pp. 3–21, 84–100; P. Toesca, Gli affreschi della cattedrale di Anagni, Gall. naz. it., V, 1897–1902, pp. 171–73; A. Baumstark, Wandgemälde in Sutri, Nepi und Civita Castellana, RQ, XVI, 1902, pp. 243–48; F. Hermanin, La grotta degli Angeli a Magliano-Pecorareccio, B. Soc. filologica romana, IV, 1903, pp. 45–55; F. Hermanin et al., I monasteri di Subiaco, I, Rome, 1904; A. de Waal, Das Oratorium unter der Kirche S. Maria in via Lata, RQ, XXI, 1907, pp. 1–6; P. Toesca, La pittura e la miniatura nella Lombardia, Milan, 1912; A. Muñoz, Il restauro della chiesa e del chiostro dei Santi Quattro Coronati, Rome, 1914; L. Fiocca, La chiesa di Santa Maria in Vescovio, Arte cristiana, III, 1915, pp. 368–75; C. R. Morey, Lost Mosaics and Frescoes of Rome of the Mediaeval Period, Princeton, 1915; J. Wilpert, Die römischen Mosaiken und Malereien . . . , 4 vols., Freiburg im Breisgau, 1916, passim; V. Pacifici, la chiesa di San Silvestro a Tivoli, Arte cristiana, IX, 1921, pp. 67–78; A. Busuioceanu, Un ciclo di affreschi del secolo XI: S. Urbano alla Caffarella, EphDR, II, 1924, pp. 1–65; G. Soulier, Les influences orientales dans la peinture toscane, Paris, 1925; G. Gerola, L'affresco della torre di S. Zeno a Verona, BArte, N.S., VII, 1927–28, pp. 241–59; L. Serra, L'arte nelle Marche, III: La pittura romanica, Rass. marchigiana, V, 1927, pp. 159–84; J. Garber, Die romanische Wandmalerei Tirols, Vienna, 1928; U. Nebbia, Rinvenimenti e restauro dell'antica decorazione absidiale dell'abbazia di Summaga, BArte, N.S., VIII, 1928–29, pp. 241–58; M. Salmi, I mosaici del Bel San Giovanni e la pittura del secolo XIII a Firenze, Dedalo, XI, 1930–31, pp. 543–70; E. Sandberg-Vavalà, Mediaeval Painting at Verona, Art S., VIII, 2, 1931, pp. 159–67; V. Lasareff, Early Italo-Byzantine Painting in Sicily, BM, LXIII, 1933, pp. 279–87; W. Arslan, Cenni sulle relazioni tra la pittura romanica d'Oltralpe e alto atesina, S. trentini di sc. storiche, XV, 1934, pp. 317–29; A. Morassi, Storia della pittura nella Venezia Tridentina, Rome, 1934; O. Demus, Die mosaiken von S. Marco in Venezia, Baden bei Wien, 1935; P. Bianconi, La pittura murale nel Canton Ticino, Bellinzona, 1936; P. Bianconi, La pittura murale nel Canton Ticino, Manuel XIVe Cong. int. d'h. de l'art, Basel, 1936, pp. 69–74; C. A. Isermeyer, Die mittelalterlichen Malereien der Kirche S. Pietro in Tuscania, Kunstgeschichtliche Jhb. der Bib. Hertziana, II, 1938, pp. 289–310; A. Medea, Gli affreschi delle cripte eremitiche pugliesi, Rome, 1939; L. Coletti, I primitivi, Novara, 1941; E. Arslan, La pittura e la scultura veronese dal secolo VIII al secolo XIII, Milan, 1943, passim; S. Bettini, Mosaici antichi di San Marco a Venezia, Bergamo, 1944; N. Gabrielli, Repertorio delle cose d'arte del Piemonte, I: Le pitture romaniche, Turin, 1944; F. Hermanin, L'arte in Roma dal secolo VIII al secolo XIV, Bologna, 1945; G. Panazza and C. Boselli, Pitture in Brescia dal Duecento all'Ottocento, Brescia, 1946 (cat.); P. L. Zovatto, Il Battistero di Concordia, Arte veneta, I, 1947, pp. 243–46; G. Ansaldi, Gli affreschi della Basilica di S. Vincenzo a Galliano, Milan, 1949; O. Demus, The Mosaics of Norman Sicily, London, 1949; A. Grabar, Les fresques d'Aoste et l'étude des peintures romanes, CrArte, VIII, 1949, pp. 261–73; G. Vigni, La pittura del Duecento e Trecento nel Museo di Pisa, Palermo, 1950; E. B. Garrison, Addenda ad Indicem, I–II, BArte, XXXVI, 1951, pp. 206–10, 293–304; O. Demus, Regensburg, Sizilien und Venedig, Jhb. ö. byz. Gesellschaft, II, 1952, pp. 95–104; O. Demus, Die sizilianischen Mosaiken, Venedig und der Norden, Atti VIII Cong. int. di s. bizantini (Palermo, 1951), II, Rome, 1953, pp. 131–35; W. Gaeta, La pittura a Spoleto nell'età romanica, Spoletium, I, 1954, pp. 11–28; R. Salvini, La pittura dal secolo XI al XIII, Storia di Milano, III, Milan, 1954, pp. 601–42; G. A. Dell'Acqua, Affreschi inediti del Medioevo lombardo, BArte, XL, 1955, pp. 289–97; O. Morisani, Bisanzio e la pittura cassinese, Palermo, 1955; C. L. Ragghianti, Pittura del Dugento a Firenze, Florence, 1955; G. Bognetti and C. Marcora, L'abbazia benedettina di Civate, Civate, 1957; P. Toesca and F. Forlati, Mosaici di S. Marco, Milan, 1957, pp. 5–31, 45; P. L. Zovatto, Gli affreschi romanici di Summaga, Il Noncello, VIII, 1957, pp. 3–36; J. Lafontaine, Peintures médiévales dans le temple dit de la Fortune Virile à Rome, Brussels, Rome, 1959; O. Demus, The Church of San Marco in Venice: History, Architecture, Sculpture, Washington, 1960; L. Magnani, Gli affreschi della basilica di Aquileia, Turin, 1960; Pitture murali nel Veneto e tecnica dell'affresco, Venice, 1960 (cat.); J. Wettstein, Sant'Angelo in Formis et la peinture médiévale en Campanie, Geneva, 1960 (bibliog.); G. Matthiae, Gli affreschi di Castel Sant'Elia, RIASA, N.S., X, 1961, pp. 181–226; T. Pignatti, Origini della pittura veneziana, Bergamo, 1961; O. Morisani, Gli affreschi di S. Angelo in Formis, Naples, 1962; L. Vayer, L'affresco absidale di Pietro Cavallini nella Chiesa di S. Maria in Aracoeli a Roma, Acta h. artium, IX,

1963, pp. 39–73; C. Segre Montel, Gli affreschi della cappella di S. Eldrado alla Novalesa, BArte, XLIX, 1964, pp. 21–40.

d. Germany, Low Countries, Central Europe: (1) *General*: C. Schnaase, Peintures murales du moyen âge en Allemagne et Hollande, Ann. archéol., VI, 1847, pp. 185–93; H. Janitschek, Geschichte der deutschen Malerei, Berlin, 1890; R. Borrmann, Aufnahmen mittelalterlicher Wand- und Deckenmalereien in Deutschland, 2 vols., Berlin, 1897–1928; K. Escher, Untersuchungen zur Geschichte der Wand- und Deckenmalerei in der Schweiz, Strasbourg, 1906; A. Stange, Deutsche romanische Tafelmalerei, MJhb, N.S., VII, 1930, pp. 125–81; O. Fischer, Geschichte der deutschen Malerei, 2d ed., Munich, 1943; B. Brenk, Die romanische Wandmalerei in der Schweiz, Bern, 1963. (2) *Single regions or monuments*: E. aus'm Weerth, Wandmalereien des christlichen Mittelalters in den Rheinlanden, Leipzig, 1880; J. Bethune de Villers, Anciennes peintures murales aux "Ruines de Saint Bavon" à Gand, Rev. de l'art chrétien, I, 1890, pp. 361–72; P. C. Heimann, Der Bildercyklus in der ehemal. oberen Vorhalle des Domes zu Hildesheim, Z. für christliche K., III, 1890, cols. 307–20; P. Keppler, Die Wandmalereien in Burgfelden bei Balingen, Archiv für christliche K., XI, 1893, pp. 1–6, 13–18; J. A. Endres, Romanische Deckenmalereien und ihre Tituli zu St. Emmeran in Regensburg, Z. für christliche K., XV, 1902, cols. 205–10, 275–82, 295–306; P. Clemen, Die romanischen Wandmalereien der Rheinlande, Düsseldorf, 1905; J. A. Endres, Romanische Malereien in Prüfening, Die christliche K., II, 1905–06, pp. 160–71; H. Schmitz, Die mittelalterliche Malerei in Soest, Münster, 1906; P. Buberl, Die romanischen Wandmalereien im Kloster Nonnberg und ihre Beziehungen zur Salzburger Buchmalerei und zur byzantinischen Kunst, Kunstgeschichtliches Jhb. der K. K. Zentralkommission, III, 1909, pp. 25–98; J. A. Endres, Die Wandgemälde der Allerheiligenkapelle zu Regensburg, Z. für christliche K., XXV, 1912, cols. 42–52; W. Neuss, Das Buch Ezechiel in Theologie und Kunst bis zum Ende des 12. Jahrhunderts, mit besonderer Berücksichtigung der Gemälde in der Kirche zu Schwarzrheindorf, Münster, 1912; P. Clemen, Die romanische Monumentalmalerei in den Rheinlanden, Düssedorf, 1916; H. Karlinger, Die hochromanische Wandmalerei in Regensburg, Munich, 1920; K. M. Swoboda, Der romanische Epiphaniezyklus in Lambach und das lateinische Magierspiel, Festschrift Schlosser, Leipzig, Vienna, 1927, pp. 82–87; A. Frh. von Reitzenstein, Romanische Wandmalereien in Frauenchiemsee, MJhb, N.S., IX, 1932, pp. 211–52; P. Schweinfurth, Byzantinisch-romanische Wandmalereien in Frauenchiemsee, Pamatki archeol., X, 1936, pp. 267–72; F. Graf Wolff Metternich, Die romanischen Monumentalmalereien in Schwarz-Rheindorff, Jhb, der rheinischen Denkmalpflege, XIV–XV, 1938, pp. 511–28; E. Poeschel, Die romanischen Deckengemälde von Zillis, Erlenbach-Zürich, 1941; W. Frodl, Die romanischen Wandmalerei in Kärnten, Klagenfurt, 1942; S. Hartwanger, Neuaufgedeckte romanische Wandmalereien in Kärnten, Ö. Z. für K. und Denkmalpflege, I, 1947, pp. 138–55; W. Frodl, Die romanischen Wandgemälde in Pürgg nach der Entrestaurierung, Ö. Z. für K. und Denkmalpflege, II, 1948, pp. 147–63; P. Rolland, La fresque tournaisienne, Brussels, 1948; L. Tondreau, Les fresques de la chapelle castrale de Mons, Rev. belge d'archéol. et d'h. de l'art, XIX, 1950, pp. 71–82; U. Rapp, Das Mysterienbild, Münsterschwarzach, 1952, pp. 133–40; D. Kluge, Neuentdeckte Wandmalereien des 12. bis 17. Jahrhunderts in Westfalen, Westfalen, XXXI, 1953, pp. 220–27; A. Verbeek, Schwarzrheindorf: Die Doppelkirche und ihre Wandgemälde, Düsseldorf, 1953; F. Dambeck, Die rückrestaurierten Fresken der Allerheiligenkapelle in Regensburg, Bericht des Bayerischen Landesamts für Denkmalpflege, 1955, pp. 35–40; W. Frodl, Die romanischen Wandgemälde in der Stiftskirche am Nonnberg in Salzburg, Ö. Z. für K. und Denkmalpflege, X, 1956, pp. 90–101; W. Jung, Die ehemalige Prämonstratenser-Stiftskirche Knechtsteden, Rating bei Düsseldorf, 1956; R. Ehmke, Der Freskenzyklus in Idensen, Bremen, 1958; R. Ehmke, Zum Stil und Bildinhalt der Wandmalereien von St. Luzius in Werden, Die Kirchen zu Essen-Werden (Kunstdenkmäler des Rheinlandes, 7), Essen, 1959, pp. 268–80; F. Goldkuhle, Zum heutigen Bestand und zur Technik der Wandmalereien in St. Luzius, Die Kirchen zu Essen-Werden (Kunstdenkmäler des Rheinlandes, 7), Essen, 1959, pp. 251–60; H. Beseler, Zu den Monumentalmalereien im Kapitelsaal von Brauweiler, Jhb. der rheinischen Denkmalpflege, XXIII, 1960, pp. 98–124; W. Glaise, Die Restaurierung der romanischen Wand- und Deckenmalereien im Kapitelsaal der ehem. Benediktinerabtei Brauweiler, Jhb. der rheinischen Denkmalpflege, XXIII, 1960, pp. 46–97; I. Rozványi-Tombor, A középkori Magyarország falfestés ornamentikája (Ornamental Elements in Medieval Hungarian Mural Painting), Müvészettörténeti ertesítö, IX, 1960, pp. 83–88; N. Wibiral, Die Freilegungsarbeiten im ehemaligen Westchor der Stiftskirche von Lambach, Ö. Z. für K. und Denkmalpflege, XIV, 1960, pp. 1–24; J. Philippe, Peintures murales de Belgique (XIIe–XVIe siècle): Les documents et les techniques, Ann. Inst. archéol. du Luxembourg Arlon, XCII, 1961, pp. 181–95; H. Schnitzler, Zum Spätstil der ottonischen Kölner Malerei, Festschrift H. R. Hahnloser, Basel, Stuttgart, 1961, pp. 207–22; R. Ehmke, Die romanischen Wandmalereien in der Pfarrkirche zu Neunkirchen-Sieg, Jhb. der rheinischen Denkmalpflege, XXIV, 1962, pp. 23–30.

e. England: E. W. Tristram, English Medieval Paintings, I: The 12th Century, London, 1944; M. Rickert, Painting in Britain: The Middle Ages, Harmondsworth, 1954; D. Talbot Rice, English Art 871–1100, Oxford, 1957.

f. Scandinavia: O. Rydbeck, Medeltida kalkmålningar i Skånes kyrkor, Lund, 1904; H. Fett, Norges Malerkunst i Middelalderen, Oslo, 1917; P. Nørlund and E. Lind, Danmarks romanske kalkmalerier, Copenhagen, 1944; E. Zahle, ed., Danmarks malerkunst, Copenhagen, 1947; R. Norberg, Nordisk medeltid, Tidens konsthistoria, III, Stockholm, 1950, pp. 91–121; B.G. Söderberg, Svenska kyrkomålningar från medeltiden, Stockholm, 1951; A. Borelius, Skånes medeltida monumentalmålei, Stockholm, 1954; R. Hauglid and L. Grodecki, Norway: Paintings from the Stave Churches, Greenwich, Conn., 1955; A. Borelius, Romanesque Mural Painting in Östergötland, Stockholm, 1956.

Miniatures and illumination: *a. General*: F. Saxl, ed., Verzeichnis astrologischer und mythologischer illustrierter Handschriften des lateinischen Mittelalters, 3 vols. in 4, Heidelberg, London, 1915–53; K. Loeffler, Romanische Zierbuchstaben und ihre Vorläufer, Stuttgart, 1927; M. R. James, ed., The Bestiary, Oxford, 1928; A. Watson, The Speculum Virginum with Special Reference to the Tree of Jesse, Speculum, III, 1928, pp. 445–69; S. H. Steinberg, Die Bildnisse geistlicher und weltlicher Fürsten und Herren, I, Leipzig, 1931; G. Haseloff, Die Psalterillustration im 13. Jahrhundert, Kiel, 1938; B. Smalley, The Study of the Bible in the Middle Ages, Oxford, 1941 (2d ed., 1952); P. d'Ancona and E. Aeschlimann, Dictionnaire des miniaturistes du moyen âge et de la Renaissance, 2d ed., Milan, 1949; E. A. van Moé, Illuminated Initials in Mediaeval Manuscripts (trans. J. Evans), London, Paris, 1950; F. Wormald, Some Illustrated Manuscripts of the Lives of the Saints, B. John Rylands Lib., XXXV, 1952, pp. 248–66; A. Grabar and C. Nordenfalk, Romanesque Painting from the 11th to the 13th Century, New York, 1958, pp. 131–206 (bibliog.); L. M. J. Delaissé, ed., Miniatures médiévales, Brussels, 1959. See also the bibliog. for MINIATURES AND ILLUMINATION.

b. France: S. Berger, La Bible française au moyen âge, Paris, 1884; A. Boinet, Un manuscrit à peintures de la bibliothèque de Saint-Omer, B. archéol. du Comité des trav. h., 1904, pp. 415–30; C. Oursel, La miniature du XIIe siècle à l'abbaye de Citeaux, Dijon, 1926; P. Lauer, Les enluminures romanes de la Bibliothèque Nationale, Paris, 1927; F. Mercier, Les primitifs français: La peinture clunysienne en Bourgogne à l'époque romane, Paris, 1931; A. Boutemy, L'illustration de la Vie de Saint Amand, Scriptorium, X, 1940, pp. 231–49; E. A. van Moé, L'Apocalypse de Saint-Sever, Paris, 1943; A. Boutemy, De quelques enlumineurs de manuscrits de l'abbaye de Corbie, Scriptorium, IV, 1950, pp. 246–52; Y. Deslandres, La décoration des manuscrits dans la région parisienne du IXe au début du XIIIe siècle (Ecole Nat. des Chartres, Diss.), Paris, 1950; J. Porcher, Les manuscrits à peinture en France du VIIe au XIIe siècle, Paris, 1954 (cat.); S. Schulten, Die Buchmalerei des 11. Jahrhunderts im Kloster St. Vaast in Arras, MJhb, 3d Ser., VII, 1956, pp. 49–90; J. Porcher, Byzance et la peinture romane française: La Bible de Souvigny, RArts, VIII, 1958, pp. 137–40; J. Porcher, L'enluminure française, Paris, 1959 (Eng. trans., J. Brown, New York, 1960; bibliog.); F. Masai, Les manuscrits à peinture de Sambre et Meuse aux XIe et XIIe siècles: Pour une critique d'origine plus méthodique, Cah. de civ. médiévale, III, 1960, pp. 169–89.

c. Spain and Portugal: R. Beer, Die Handschriften des Klosters Santa Maria de Ripoll, 2 vols., Vienna, 1907–08; A. Boinet, Notice sur un évangéliaire de la Bibliothèque de Perpignan, CAF, LXXIII, 1907, pp. 534–51; J. Pijoan, Les miniatures de l'Octateuch et les Bíblies romániques catalanes, Anuari Inst. estudis catalans, IV, 1911–12, pp. 475–507; W. Neuss, Das Buch Ezechiel in Theologie und Kunst bis zum Ende des 12. Jahrhunderts, mit besonderer Berücksichtigung der Gemälde in der Kirche zu Schwarzrheindorf, Münster, 1912; J. Pijoan, Miniatures españolas en manuscritos de la Biblioteca Vaticana, II: Vat. Lat. 3547, Cuadernos de trabajo de la escuela española de arquitectura y h. en Roma, II, 1914, pp. 1–4; W. Neuss, Die katalanische Bibelillustration, Bonn, Leipzig, 1922; A. Albareda, Els manuscrits de la Biblioteca Vaticana Reg. Lat. 123, Vat. Lat. 5730, i el Scriptorium de Santa Maria de Ripoll, Catalonia Monastica, I, 1927, pp. 24–71; W. Neuss, Eine katalanische Bilderhandschrift in Turin, Münster in Westfalen, 1929; G. G. King, Divagations on the Beatus, Art S., VIII, 1930, pp. 1–58; H. A. Sanders, Beati in Apocalipsin libri XII, Rome, 1930; J. Domínguez Bordona, Manuscritos con pinturas, 2 vols., Madrid, 1933; M. Churruca, Influjo oriental en los temas iconográficos de la miniatura española, Madrid, 1939; J. A. Marazuela, Un scriptorium español desconocido, Scriptorium, II, 1948, pp. 3–27; J. Gudiol i Cunill, La pintura mitgeval catalana, III, 3: Els Primitius, els llibres illuminats, Barcelona, 1954; P. Bohigas, La ilustración y la decoración del libro manuscrito en Cataluña: Periodo románico, Barcelona, 1960; J. Domínguez Bordona, La miniatura, Ars Hispaniae, XVIII, Madrid, 1962, pp. 43–97; J. Marqués Casanovas et al., ed., Sancti Beati a Liebana i Apocalypsin codex Gerundensis, Olten, Lausanne, 1962.

d. Italy: O. Piscicelli Taeggi, Paleografia artistica di Monte Cassino, Montecassino, 1876; P. Toesca, La pittura e la miniatura nella Lombardia, Milan, 1912; P. d'Ancona, La miniatura fiorentina, 2 vols., Florence, 1914; P. d'Ancona, La miniature italienne du Xe au XVIe siècle, Paris, 1925; J. P. Gilson, ed., An Exultet Roll (B. M. Add. Ms. 30377), London, 1929; P. Toesca, Miniature romane dei secoli XI e XII: Bibbie miniate, RIASA, I, 1929, pp. 69–96; B. Katterbach, Le miniature dell'Evangelario di Padova del 1170, Rome, 1931; M. R. Gabrielli, Un exultet cassinese dell'XI secolo, BArte, XXVI, 1933, pp. 306–13; B. Pagnin, Della miniatura padovana dalle origini al principio del secolo XIV, La bibliofilia, XXXV, 1933, pp. 1–20; D. M. Inguanez, Miniature cassinensi del secolo XI illustranti la vita di S. Benedetto, Montecassino, 1934; G. Castelfranco, Contributi alla storia della miniatura bolognese del '200, Bologna, XXII, 7, 1935, pp. 11–22; M. Avery, The Exultet Rolls of South Italy, II (pls.), Princeton, Oxford, 1937; W. F. Volbach, Le miniature del Cod. Vat. Pal. Lat. 1071 "De arte venandi cum avibus," RendPontAcc, XV, 1939, pp. 145–75; A. Barzon, Codici miniati: Biblioteca Capitolare della Cattedrale di Padova, 2 vols., Padua, 1950; P. Baldass, Disegni della scuola cassinese del tempo di Desiderio, BArte, XXXVII, 1952, pp. 102–14; P. Baldass, Die Miniature Zweier Exultet-Rollen, Scriptorium, VIII, 1954, pp. 75–88; Mostra storica nazionale della miniatura, Florence, 1954 (cat.); H. Buchthal, A School of Miniature Painting in Norman Sicily, Late Classical and Mediaeval Studies in Honor of A. M. Friend, Jr., Princeton, 1955, pp. 312–19; M. Salmi, La miniatura italiana, Milan, 1956 (bibliog.); F. Babudri, L'Exultet di Bari del secolo XI (Q. Arch. storico pugliese, 5), Bari, 1959; F. Dell'Oro, Il Sacramentario di Ariberto, Ephemerides liturgicae, LXXIV, 1960, pp. 3–35; J. Wettstein, Un rouleau campanien du XIe siècle conservé au Musée San Matteo à Pise, Scriptorium, XV, 1961, p. 234–39; M. L. Gengaro, Tra i più antichi codici latini della Biblioteca Ambrosiana, Arte lombarda, VII, 1962, pp. 17–28.

e. Low Countries: H. Liebrecht and A. Vincent, Histoire du livre et de l'imprimerie en Belgique des origines à nos jours, I, Brussels, 1923; J. Ladmirant, Un évangélaire du XIe siècle conservé au Grand Séminaire de Namur, Annales Soc. archéol. de Namur, XLI, 1934, pp. 29–42; G. J. Hoogewerff, De noord-nederlandsche schilderkunst, I, The Hague, 1936, pp. 18–39; A. W. Byvanck, La miniature dans les Pays-Bas septentrionaux,

Paris, 1937; A. W. Byvanck, De middeleeuwsche boekillustratie in l e noordelijke Nederlanden, Antwerp, 1943; S. Collon-Gevaert, Etude sur les miniatures mosanes prégothiques, Brussels, 1948; J. Philippe, L'Evangélaire de Notger et la chronologie de l'art mosan des époques pré-romane et romane, Brussels, 1956.

f. Germany and Central Europe: R. Durrer, Die Maler- und Schreiberschule von Engelberg, Anz. für schweizerische Altertumskunde, N.S., III, 1901, pp. 42–55, 122–76; S. Beissel, Ein Missale aus Hildesheim und die Anfänge der Armenbibel, Z. für christliche K., XV, 1902, cols. 265–74, 307–18; F. J. Lehner, Česka škola malířská XI. věku, I: Konunovačni Evangelistář krale Vratislava řečený Kodex Vyšchradský, Prague, 1902; H. J. Hermann et al., Beschreibendes Verzeichnis der illuminierten Handschriften in Österreich, 4 vols., Leipzig, 1905–11; P. Buberl, Über einige Werke der Salzburger Buchmalerei des 11. Jahrhunderts, Kunstgeschichtliches Jhb. der K. K. Zentralkommission . . . , I, 1907, pp. 29–60; G. Swarzenski, Die Salzburger Malerei von den ersten Anfängen bis zur Blütezeit des romanischen Stils, 2 vols., Leipzig, 1908–13; P. Buberl, Die romanischen Wandmalereien im Kloster Nonnberg in Salzburg und ihre Beziehungen zur Salzburger Buchmalerei und zur byzantinischen Kunst, Kunstgeschichtliches Jhb. der K. K. Zentralkommission . . . , III, 1909, pp. 25–98; R. Kahn, Hochromanische Handschriften aus Kloster Weingarten in Schwaben, Städel-Jhb., I, 1921, pp. 43–74; E. F. Bange, Eine bayerische Malerschule des 11. und 12. Jahrhunderts, Munich, 1923; A. Boeckler, Das Stuttgarter Passionale, Augsburg, 1923; E. Winkler, Die Buchmalerei in Niederösterreich von 1150–1250, Vienna, 1923; A. Boeckler, Die Regensburger-Prüfeninger Buchmalerei des 12. und 13. Jahrhunderts, Munich, 1924; A. Boeckler, Beiträge zur romanischen Kölner Buchmalerei, Mittelalterliche Handschriften: Festgabe zum 60. Geburtstage von H. Degering, Leipzig, 1926, pp. 15–28; H. J. Hermann, Die deutschen romanischen Handschriften der National-Bibliothek in Wien, Vienna, 1926; A. Friedl, Hildebert a Ewerwin, Romansti Maliri, Prague, 1927; H. Swarzenski, Vorgotische Miniaturen, Königstein im Taunus, Leipzig, 1927; A. Boeckler, Corveyer Buchmalerei unter Einwirkung Wibalds von Stablo, Westfälische Studien: Festschrift Bomer, Leipzig, 1928, pp. 133–47; K. Loeffler, Schwäbische Buchmalerei in romanischer Zeit, Augsburg, 1928; A. Boeckler, Abendländische Miniaturen bis zum Ausgang der romanischen Zeit, Berlin, Leipzig, 1930, pp. 78–89; K. Preisendanz and O. Homburger, Das Evangelistar des Speyerer Domes, Leipzig, 1930; E. Lutze, Studien zur fränkischen Buchmalerei im 12. und 13. Jahrhundert, Giessen, 1931; F. Jansen, Die Helmarshausener Buchmalerei zur Zeit Heinrichs des Löwen, Hildesheim, 1933; H. L. Keller, Mittelrheinische Buchmalereien in Handscriften aus dem Kreise der Hiltgart von Bingen, Stuttgart, 1933; K. M. Swoboda, Die Bilder der Admonter Bibel des 12. Jahrhunderts, Neue Aufgaben der Kunstgeschichte, Brünn, 1935, pp. 45–63; K. Weitzmann, Zwei Fuldaer Handschriften des 12. Jahrhunderts, Marburger Jhb. für Kw., VIII–IX, 1936, pp. 172–81; P. Buberl, Die Buchmalerei des 12. und 13. Jahrhunderts in Österreich, Die bildende Kunst in Österreich, II, Vienna, 1937, pp. 145–70; J. Schomer, Die Illustrationen zu den Visionen der hl. Hildegard als künstlerische Neuschöpfung, Bonn, 1937; A. Goldschmidt, A German Psalter of the 12th Century Written in Helmarshausen, J. Walters Art Gall., I, 1938, pp. 18–23; A. Boeckler, Zur Freisinger Buchmalerei des 12. Jahrhunderts, Z. d. Vereins für Kw., VIII, 1941, pp. 1–16; P. Buberl, RlDKg, s.v. Buchmalerei, II, 1948, cols. 1461–79; A. Boeckler, ed., Ars sacra: Kunst des frühen Mittelalters, Munich, 1950 (cat.); A. Boeckler, Deutsche Buchmalerei vorgotischer Zeit, Königstein im Taunus, 1952; A. Boeckler, Die Buchmalerei, Handbuch der Bibliothekswissenschaft, I, Stuttgart, 1952, pp. 249–387; A. Boeckler, Zur böhmischen Buchkunst des 12. Jahrhunderts, Konsthistorisk tidskrift, XXII, 1953, pp. 61–74; H. Menhardt, Die Bilder der Millstädter Genesis und ihre Verwandten, Beiträge zur alteren europäischen Kulturgeschichte, III, 1954, pp. 247–371; W. N. Lasarew, Die Malerei und die Skulptur der Kiewer Rus, Geschichte der russischen Kunst, I, Dresden, 1957, pp. 141–43; M. Harrsen, Central European Manuscripts in the Pierpont Morgan Library, New York, 1958; H. Swarzenski and J. Kvet, Czechoslovakia: Romanesque and Gothic Illuminated Manuscripts, Greenwich, Conn., 1959; B. Bruch, Die alte Bremer Dombibliothek: Ihre Geschichte und die hochromanische Buchmalerei in Bremen, Philobiblon, IV, 1960, pp. 292–353; P. Bloch, Das Steinfeld-Missale, Aachener Kunstblätter, XXII, 1961, pp. 37–60; F. A. Schmitt and E. J. Beer, ed., Das Evangelistar aus St. Peter, Basel, 1961; K. Weitzmann, Zur byzantinischen Quelle des Wolfenbüttler Musterbuches, Festschrift H. R. Hahnloser, Basel, Stuttgart, 1961, pp. 223–50; H. Voss, Studien zur illustrierten Millstätter Genesis, Munich, 1962.

g. England: M. R. James, ed., The Canterbury Psalter, London, 1935; R. Mynors, Durham Cathedral Manuscripts to the End of the 12th Century, Oxford, 1939; N. Gray, Jacob's Ladder: A Bible Picture Book from Anglo-Saxon and 12th Century English Mss., London, 1949; T. S. R. Boase, English Romanesque Illumination, Oxford, 1951; C. R. Dodwell, The Canterbury School of Illumination 1066–1200, Cambridge, 1954; M. Rickert, La miniatura inglese, I, Milan, 1959; N. R. Ker, English Manuscripts in the Century after the Norman Conquest, Oxford, 1960; O. Pächt, C. R. Dodwell, and F. Wormald, The St. Alban Psalter, London, 1960; F. Wormald, An English 11th Century Psalter with Pictures: Cotton Ms. Tiberius C. VI, Walpole Soc., XXXVIII, 1960–62, pp. 1–13.

h. Scandinavia: Greek and Latin Illuminated Manuscripts X–XIII Cent. in Danish Collections, Copenhagen, 1921; C. Nordenfalk, Romanskt bokmåleri i Skara stiftsbibliotek, Göteborgs högskolas årsskrift, XLVII, 20, 1941, pp. 1–31; C. Nordenfalk, Golden Books in Scandinavian Collections, Konsthistorisk Tidskrift, XXII, 1953, pp. 41–50; C. Nordenfalk, En medeltida bönbok fran Metz, Linköpings biblioteks handlingar, N.S., IV, 3, 1953, pp. 65–88; P. G. Hamberg, Kungabilder i svenska laghandskrifter, in Svenska arkeologiska samfundet, Proxima Thule: Sverige och Europa under forntid och medeltid, Stockholm, 1962, pp. 229–38.

Minor arts: *general works*: J. Labarte, Histoire des arts industriels au moyen âge et à l'époque de la Renaissance, 4 vols., Paris, 1864–66; E. Molinier, Histoire générale des arts appliqués à l'industrie, I–II, Paris, 1896–97; O. von Falke et al., Illustrierte Geschichte des Kunstgewerbes, I, Berlin, 1907; H. T. Bossert, ed., Geschichte des Kunstgewerbes aller Zeiten und Völker, V, Berlin, 1932; H. Swarzenski, Monuments of Romanesque Art, London, Chicago, 1954; H. Kohlhaussen, Geschichte des deutschen Kunsthandwerks, Munich, 1955; A. Bochnak and J. Pagaczewski, Polskie rzemiosło artystyczne wieków średnich (Industrial Arts in Medieval Poland), Krakow, 1959.

Gold- and silverwork and metalwork: *a. General*: See the bibliogs. for ENAMELS; GOLD- AND SILVERWORK; METALWORK.

b. France: H. Havard, Histoire de l'orfèvrerie française, Paris, 1896, p. 95; H. P. Mitchell, Some Enamels of the School of Godefroid de Claire, BM, XXXIV, 1919, pp. 85–92, 165–71, XXXV, 1919, pp. 34–40, 92–102, 217–21, XXXVI, 1920, pp. 18–27, 128–34, XXXVII, 1920, pp. 11–18; J. J. Marquet de Vasselot, Bibliographie de l'orfèvrerie et de l'émaillerie française, Paris, 1925; O. von Falke, Reiter-Aquamanilien, Pantheon, I, 1928, pp. 246–52, 557–64, II, 1929, pp. 426–30; H. Garnier, Le pied de la Croix de Saint Bertin exposé au Musée de Saint-Omer, B. Soc. d'ét. de la province de Cambrai, XXXII, 1932, pp. 216–29; J. Babelon, L'orfèvrerie française, Paris, 1946 (bibliog.); M. M. Gauthier, Emaux limousins champlevés de XIIe, XIIIe et XIVe siècles, Paris, 1950; P. Thoby, Les croix limousines de la fin du XIIe siècle au début du XIVe siècle, Paris, 1953; M. M. Gauthier, Les décors vermiculés dans les émaux champlevés limousins et méridionaux, Cah. de civ. médiévales, I, 1958, pp. 349–69; A. Beaufrère, Orfèvrerie et statuaire romane, Aurillac, 1959; R. Gaudilhon, Le trésor roman de la cathédrale de Châlon-sur-Marne, Bordeaux, 1959; M. M. Gauthier, Notes sur l'émaillerie de Limoges, B. Soc. archéol. et h. du Limousin, LXXXVIII, 1961, pp. 93–102; G. François-Souchal, Les émaux de Grandmont au XIIe siècle, B. mon., CXX, 1962, pp. 339–57.

c. Spain and Portugal: C. Davillier, Recherches sur l'orfèvrerie en Espagne, Paris, 1879; J. Ferrandis, Marfiles y azabaches españoles, Barcelona, 1928; W. L. Hildburgh, Medieval Spanish Enamels, London, 1936; Exposiçao da ourivesaria portuguesa dos séculos XII a XVII, Lisbon, 1940 (cat.); M. C. Ross, Esmaltes catalanes de los siglos XII–XIII, AEArte, XIV, 1940–41, pp. 181–84; J. Hernández Perera, Los esmaltes románicos y su origen español, Goya, II, 1955–56, pp. 297–303; R. dos Santos and I. Quilho, ed., Les trésors de l'orfèvrerie du Portugal, Paris, 1955 (cat.); J. Filgueira Valverde, El tesoro de la Catedral Compostelana, Santiago de Compostela, 1959; M. M. Gauthier, Esmaltes meridionales en la exposición internacional de arte románico en Barcelona y Santiago de Compostela, Goya, IX, 1961–62, pp. 400–07.

d. Italy: L. Gmelin, L'oreficeria medievale negli Abruzzi, Teramo, 1891; M. Abramich, Il tesoro del Duomo di Gorizia, Arte cristiana, IV, 1916, pp. 240–48; M. Salmi, L'oreficeria medievale nell'Aretino, Rass. d'arte, XVI, 1916, pp. 236–46; M. Salmi, Il tesoro del Duomo di Milano, Dedalo, V, 1924–25, pp. 267–88, 358–82; O. Grosso, Il reliquario di S. Stefano a Genova, Dedalo, VI, 1925–26, pp. 749–53; P. Guerrini, Oreficerie sacre medievali nelle chiese di Brescia, Per l'arte sacra, Jan.-Feb., 1925, pp. 18–24; O. von Falke, Romanisches Bronzgerät aus Verona, Pantheon, IX, 1932, pp. 165–67; M. Accascina, L'oreficeria italiana, Florence, 1934; A. Morassi, Antica oreficeria italiana, Milan, 1936; Y. Hackenbroch, Italienisches Email des frühen Mittelalters, Basel, 1938; A. Lipinsky, Goldene und silberne Antependien des Mittelalters in Italien, I: Aus romanischen Zeit, Das Münster, V, 1952, pp. 22–31, 194–205; I. Marchetti, Orafi senesi, Siena, 1953; F. Santi, Ritrovamenti di oreficerie medioevali in S. Domenico di Perugia, BArte, XL, 1955, pp. 354–58; G. Panazza, Il tesoro delle SS. Croci nel Duomo Vecchio di Brescia, Comm. dell'Ateneo di Brescia, CLVI, 1956, pp. 101–31; F. Rossi, Capolavori di oreficeria italiana dall'XI al XVIII secolo, Florence, 1956 (bibliog.); A. Lipinsky, Sizilianische Goldschmiedekunst im Zeitalter der Normannen und Staufer, Das Münster, X, 1957, pp. 158–86; G. Marchetti, L'oreficeria medioevale nel Friuli e i reliquiari di Pordenone, Il Noncello, IX, 1958, pp. 3–40; C. Oman, Two Siculo-Norman Silver Cups, BM, CI, 1959, pp. 350–53; A. Lipinsky, Gli splendidi gioielli della Corte Normanna in Sicilia, Arte figurativa, X, 1962, pp. 37–44.

e. Germany, Low Countries, Central Europe: O. von Falke and H. Frauberger, Deutsche Schmelzarbeiten des Mittelalters, Frankfurt am Main, 1904; O. Posse, Die Siegel der deutschen Kaiser und Könige von 751–1806, I, Dresden, 1909; A. Fuchs, Die Tragaltäre des Rogerus in Paderborn, Paderborn, 1916; J. Braun, Meisterwerke der deutschen Goldschmiedekunst der vorgotischen Zeit, 2 vols., Munich, 1922; O. von Falke, R. Schmidt, and G. Swarzenski, Der Welfenschatz, Frankfurt am Main, 1930; M. Laurent, Art rhénan, art mosan et art byzantin, Byzantion, VI, 1931, pp. 75–98; G. Swarzenski, Aus dem Kunstkreis Heinrichs des Löwen, Städel-Jhb., VII–VIII, 1932, pp. 241–397; F. Witte, Tausend Jahre deutscher Kunst am Rhein, I, II, V, Leipzig, 1932; O. von Falke, Die Inkunabeln der romanischen Kupferschmelzkunst, Pantheon, XVII, 1936, pp. 166–69; A. Herrmann, Zum Komburger Kronleuchter und Antependium, Z. d. Vereins für Kw., III, 1936, pp. 174–95; H. Klapsia, Der Bertholdus-Kelch aus dem Kloster Wilten, JhbKhSammlWien, N.S., XII, 1938, pp. 7–34; E. Meyer, Neue Beiträge zur Kenntnis der Kunst des Roger von Helmarshausen und seines Kreises, Westfalen, XXV, 1940, pp. 6–17; F. Mütherich, Die Ornamentik der rheinischen Goldschmiedekunst in der Stauferzeit, Würzburg, 1941; S. Collon-Gevaert, L'orfèvrerie mosane au moyen âge, Brussels, 1943 (bibliog.); E. Meyer, Der Kaiserstuhl in Goslar, Z. d. Vereins für Kw., X, 1943, pp. 183–208; H. Reiners, Die romanischen Reliquienschreine in St. Maurice im Wallis, Pantheon, XXXI, 1943, pp. 84–90; E. Meyer, Die Hildesheimer Rogerwerkstatt, Pantheon, XXXII, 1944, pp. 1–11; M. Bernhart, RlDKg, s.v. Brakteat, II, 1948, cols. 1099–1104; R. Schilling, Studien zur deutschen Goldschmiedekunst des 12. und 13. Jahrhunderts, Form und Inhalt: Festschrift für O. Schmitt, Stuttgart, 1950, pp. 73–88; H. J. Heuser, Das Niellokreuz von St. Trudpert, ZfKw, VI, 1952, pp. 27–46; R. Wallrath, Kathedrale und Kultgerät als Bildträger, Das Münster, VI, 1953, pp. 1–19; T. Rensing, Der Kappenberger Barbarossakopf, Westfalen, XXXII, 1954, pp. 165–83; E. Steingräber, Alter Schmuck, Munich, 1956 (Eng. trans., Antique Jewelry, New York, London,

1957); J. Weitzmann-Fiedler, Romanische Bronzeschalen mit mythologischen Darstellungen: Ihre Beziehungen zur mittelalterlichen Schulliteratur und ihre Zweckbestimmung, ZfKw, X, 1956, pp. 109–52, XI, 1957, pp. 1–34; W. Biehl, Die romanische Cimelien des Klosters Marienstern, Wallraf-Richartz-Jhb., XXI, 1959, pp. 209–13; H. Grundmann, Der Cappenberger Barbarossakopf und die Anfänge des Stiftes Cappenberg, Cologne, Graz, 1959; H. Schnitzler, Rheinische Schatzkammer, II: Die Romanik, Düsseldorf, 1959; V. Kovács, Romanische gravierte Bronzeschalen in Ungarn, Acta h. artium, VII, 1960, pp. 1–17; F. Kreusch, Zur Planung des Aacheners Barbarossaleuchters, Aachener Kunstblätter, XXII, 1961, pp. 21–36; T. Poklewski, Misy brązowe z XI, XII i XIII wieku (Bronze Basins of the 11th, 12th and 13th Centuries), Łódź, 1961; P. Skubiszewski, La patène de Kalisz, Cah. de civ. médiévales, V, 1962, pp. 183–91. See also the bibliog. for NICHOLAS OF VERDUN.

f. England: H. P. Mitchell, English Enamels of the 12th Century, BM, XLVII, 1926, pp. 163–70; T. Borenius and M. Chamot, On a Group of Early Enamels, Possibly English, BM, LIII, 1928, pp. 276–87; C. Oman, An 11th Century English Cross, BM, XCVI, 1954, pp. 383–84; C. Oman, English Church Plate, New York, London, 1957 (bibliog.).

g. Scandinavia: A. Romdahl, Roglösadörren och en grupp romanska smiden i de gamla Götalandskapen, Fornvännen, IX, 1914, pp. 231–45; T. Kielland, Norrsk guldsmedskunst i middelalderen, Oslo, 1926; E. Nørlund, Gyldne altre, Copenhagen, 1926; E. Lundberg, Järnbeslagna dörrar från romansk tid i Östergötland, Rig, X, 1927, pp. 49–60, XII, 1929, pp. 61–72; C. Nordenfalk, Konstantin den store i Skåne, Årsberättelse humanistiska vetenskapssamfundet i Lund, 1943–44, pp. 112–60; E. Cinthio, Frontalet i Lyngsjö, Lund, 1954; M. Blindheim, Brukrusifikset et tidlig-middelaldersk klenodium, Årbok univ. oldsaksamling (Oslo), 1956–57, pp. 151–93; A. Andersson, Thomas av Beckets skrin i Trönö kyrka, Hälsigerunor 1951,Lund, 1957, pp. 65–81.

Ivory and bone: A. Goldschmidt, Die Elfenbeinskulpturen aus der Zeit der karolingischen und sächsischen Kaiser, 4 vols., Berlin, 1914–26; W. F. Volbach, Mittelalterliche Elfenbeinarbeiten, Berlin, 1922; M. H. Longhurst, English Ivories, London, 1926; M. Gómez-Moreno, Los marfiles cordobeses y sus derivaciones, AEArte, III, 1927, pp. 233–43; A. S. Keck, A Group of Italo-Byzantine Ivories, AB, XII, 1930–31, pp. 147–62; P. B. Cott, Siculo-Arabic Ivories, Princeton, 1939; L. Grodecki, Ivoires français, Paris, 1947; G. Bovini, Gli avori del Museo Nazionale di Ravenna e del Museo Civico di Bologna, Felix Ravenna, 3d Ser., XX, 1956, pp. 50–80; W. S. Dale, An English Crosier of the Transitional Period, AB, XXXVIII, 1956, pp. 137–41; M. Bárány-Oberschall, Baculus Pastoralis; Keltisch-irische Motive auf mittelalterlichen beingeschnitzen Bischofsstäben, ZfKw., XII, 1958, pp. 13–36; W. F. Volbach, Les ivoires sculptés de l'époque carolingienne au XIIᵉ siècle, Cah. de civ. médiévale, I, 1958, pp. 17–26; E. von Phillippovich, Elfenbein, Brunswick, 1961.

Textiles: a. General: F. Michel, Recherches sur le commerce, la fabrication et l'usage des étoffes de soie, d'or et d'argent... pendant le moyen âge, 2 vols., Paris, 1852–54; M. Dreger, Künstlerische Entwicklung der Weberei und Stickerei, Vienna, 1904; A. F. Kendrick, The Sicilian Woven Fabrics of the 11th and 12th Centuries, Mag. of Fine Arts, I, 1905–06, pp. 36–44, 124–30; O. von Falke, Kunstgeschichte der Seidenweberei, 2 vols., Berlin, 1913; A. F. Kendrick, Catalogue of Early Woven Fabrics, Vict. and Alb. Mus., London, 1925 (bibliog.); H. d'Hennezel, Histoire du décor textile depuis le début de l'ère chrétienne jusqu'à nos jours, 3 vols., Lyons, 1928; H. Schmidt, Deutsche Seidenstoffe des Mittelalters, Z. d. Vereins für Kw., I, 1934, pp. 95–112; W. F. Volbach, I tessuti del Museo Sacro Vaticano, Vatican City, 1942; Stoffe medievali, Vatican City, 1943; A. C. Weibel, Two Thousand Years of Textiles, New York, 1952; R. Jaques, Deutsche Textilkunst, Krefeld, 1953; Probleme der mittelalterlichen Textilforschungen, Kchr., VIII, 1955, pp. 305–30; E. Flemming, Encyclopedia of Textiles, 2d ed., London, New York, 1958; H. J. Schmidt, Alte Seidenstoffe, Brunswick, 1958 (bibliog.); L. von Wilckens, Textilien in Westeuropa: Literatur von 1945–1961, ZfKg, XXIV, 1961, pp. 261–75.

b. Spain: A. Wittlin, The Development of the Textile Craft in Spain, Ciba Rev., II, 1939, pp. 699–726; P. Palol de Salellas, El bordado de Génesis de la Catedral de Gerona, Goya, II, 1955–56, pp. 166–76; F. L. May, Silk Textiles of Spain: 8th to 15th Century, New York, 1957; D. G. Shepherd, Two Medieval Silks from Spain, B. Cleve. Mus., XLV, 1958, pp. 3–7.

c. Italy: A. Venturi, Un drappo prezioso del secolo XIII nella basilica di S. Francesco d'Assisi, L'Arte, IX, 1906, pp. 216–18; P. Perali, Tovaglie e mantiglie di Perugia (sec. XIII–XVI) con segni e simboli magici, Augusta Perusia, I, 1907, pp. 65–71; R. Cox, Les soieries italiennes du moyen âge et de la Renaissance, Rev. de l'art ancien et moderne, XXX, 1911, pp. 409–20; E. Ricci, Ricami italiani antichi e moderni, Florence, 1925; A. Weixlgärtner, Die weltliche Schatzkammer in Wien: Neue Funde und Forschungen, JhbKhSammlWien, N.S., I, 1926, pp. 15–84; F. Podreider, Storia dei tessuti d'arte in Italia, Bergamo, 1928; L. Ciucci, L'arte della seta a Lucca, Como, 1930; L'antico tessuto d'arte italiano nella Mostra del Tessile Nazionale, Rome, 1938 (cat.); W. Arslan, La mostra dell'antico tessuto d'arte italiano, ZfKg, VIII, 1939, pp. 62–66; W. Reininger, The Textile Trades in Medieval Florence, Ciba Rev., II, 1939, pp. 957–73; G. de Francesco, Venetian Silks, Ciba Rev., III, 1940, pp. 1027–48; A. de Capitani d'Arzago, Antichi tessuti della Basilica Ambrosiana, Milan, 1941; G. Morazzoni, Le stoffe genovesi, Genoa, 1941 (cat.); U. Monneret de Villard, La tessitura palermitana sotto i Normanni e i suoi rapporti con l'arte bizantina, Misc. G. Mercati (S. i testi, CXXIII), III, Vatican City, 1946, pp. 464–89; U. Monneret de Villard, Il frammento di Hannover e la tessitura palermitana di stile bizantino, RIASA, N.S., II, 1953, pp. 162–70; A. Santangelo, Tessuti d'arte italiani dal XII al XVIII secolo, Milan, 1958 (bibliog.); C. G. E. Bunt, The World's Heritage of Woven Fabrics, I–III, Leigh-on-Sea, 1959–61 (Venice, Florence, Sicily, and Lucca); G. Tascione, San Leucio e l'arte della seta nel mezzogiorno d'Italia, Naples, 1961.

d. Germany and Central Europe: R. Jaques, Deutsche Textilkunst, Berlin, 1942; V. Trudel, Schweizerische Leinenstickereien des Mittelalters und der Renaissance, 2 vols., Bern, 1954.

e. England: H. Belloc, The Book of the Bayeux Tapestry, London, 1914; A. Levé, La tapisserie de la reine Mathilde dit la tapisserie de Bayeux, Paris, 1919; R. S. Loomis, The Origin and Date of the Bayeux Embroidery, AB, VI, 1923–24, pp. 3–7; E. Maclagan, The Bayeux Tapestry, London, 1949; F. Stenton, ed., The Bayeux Tapestry, London, 1957.

f. Scandinavia: H. Dedekam, Baldisholstaeppet, Oslo, 1918; E. Salvén, Bonaden från Skog: Undersökning av en nordisk bildvävnad från tidig medeltid, Stockholm, 1923; V. Sylvan, Bonaden från Skog, Fornvännen, XLIV, 1949, pp. 330–51.

Stained glass: A. Boeckler, Die romanischen Fenster des Augsburger Domes und die Stilwende von 11. zum 12. Jahrhundert, Z. d. Vereins für Kw., X, 1943, pp. 153–83; M. Aubert et al., Les vitraux de Notre-Dame et de la Sainte-Chapelle de Paris (Corpus vitrearum medii aevi, France, I), Paris, 1959; H. Wentzel, Zur Bestandsaufnahme der romanischen Chorfenster von St. Patroklus in Soest, Westfalen, XXXVII, 1959, pp. 92–103; J. Baldet, Le vitrail de la Crucifixion de la Cathédrale Saint-Pierre de Poitiers, Poitiers, 1960; A. van der Boom, De Kunst der Glazenier in Europa 1100–1600, Amsterdam, 1960; A. Andersson et al., Die Glasmalereien des Mittelalters in Skandinavien (Corpus vitrearum medii aevi, Scandinavia), Stockholm, 1964. See also the bibliog. for STAINED GLASS.

Mosaic pavements: J. Durand, Pavés mosaïques en Italie et en France, Ann. archéol., XV, 1855, pp. 223–31, XVII, 1857, pp. 119–27; E. Müntz, Etudes iconographiques et archéologiques sur le moyen âge, I: Les pavements historiés, Paris, 1887, pp. 1–63; E. Bertaux, L'art dans l'Italie méridionale, Paris, 1904, pp. 483–94; Toesca, Md, I, pp. 450–51, II, pp. 1081–85; H. Stern, Mosaïques de pavements préromanes et romanes en France, Cah. de civ. médiévales, V, 1962, pp. 13–33. See also the bibliog. for MOSAICS.

* *

Illustrations: PLS. 199–282; 26 figs. in text.

ROMANIA. The modern state of Romania — a kingdom from 1881 and the Romanian People's Republic since December 30, 1947 — was formed in 1859 by the union of the two autonomous principalities of Walachia and Moldavia and gained complete independence following the victorious war of 1877–78 against the Turks. In 1918, after the fall of the Austro-Hungarian Empire, the provinces of the former Hapsburg monarchy inhabited by Romanians (Transylvania, Crişana-Maramureş, part of the Banat, and the northern part of Moldavia) were also annexed. Exceptionally rich in ancient remains and monuments, Romania has preserved its Latin linguistic character from its colonization by Rome, despite the hiatus caused by later invasions (especially by the Slavs) in the early Middle Ages. Its art and culture are characterized by Slavic-Byzantine elements and, from the 19th century, by strong European influences.

SUMMARY. Cultural and artistic phases (col. 482): *Antiquity and early Middle Ages; Feudal period; Modern period.* Monumental centers (col. 493): *Bucharest; Argeş; Bacău; Braşov; Cluj; Dobruja; Hunedoara; Iaşi; Oltenia; Ploieşti; Suceava.*

CULTURAL AND ARTISTIC PHASES. *Antiquity and early Middle Ages.* Romania has been inhabited since Paleolithic times, but the oldest artistic manifestations go back to the Neolithic age, beginning about 5000 B.C. The Neolithic tribes of the Criş-Starčevo culture came across northeastern Yugoslavia after a series of successive migrations from continental Greece and Asia Minor and occupied almost all the territory of Romania. Toward the end of the 5th millennium tribes with a *Bandkeramik* culture arrived from Czechoslovakia, and at approximately the same time the tribes of the Hamangia culture reached Dobruja from the eastern Mediterranean. Subsequently, an entire series of other cultures of the middle and late Neolithic period developed in Romania as well as in the surrounding regions(Vinča-Turdaş, Boian, Precucuteni, Petreşti, Gumelniţa-Sălcuţa, Cucuteni, etc.). The Neolithic tribes lived in settlements, which were sometimes surrounded by protective moats. The houses were large and carefully constructed and almost always rectangular; some of the floors were formed by a kind of clay platform. Among the most characteristic objects left by them (apart from utensils of stone, bone, clay, and, slightly later, copper) are pottery and sculpture. The decorative motifs, incised, cut out, or painted, the elegance and precision of the decoration (especially the spiral meanders), and the harmonious line of the forms make Romanian Neolithic pottery one of the most outstanding expressions of its kind in Europe's Stone Age. The polychrome ceramics of the Cucuteni culture, in which the perfection of the forms and the harmony of the colors are combined with the skillful execution of various motifs, often covering the entire surface of the vases, are noteworthy (III, FIG. 199; IX, PL. 416,

FIG. 659; X, PL. 433). The sculpture is exceptionally rich. Almost all the clay statuettes (bone was rarely used and marble only occasionally) depict females, certainly related to the fertility cult and derived from prototypes of the western Asian and Aegean cultures. Most of them are stylized, but there are also more realistically modeled examples and numerous zoomorphic statuettes, as well as anthropomorphic and theriomorphic vases.

The end of the Neolithic age was marked by great disturbances and profound social transformations that took place simultaneously

artistic achievements. The clay female statuettes of the Gîrla Mare-Cîrna culture also give evidence of the Aegean-Mycenaean influence: certain features of their costumes can be recognized in the popular dress of today — a proof of continuity through many millenniums.

Toward the end of the Bronze Age the character of the economy changed, owing to the importance that livestock raising assumed. The settlements became predominantly temporary in character, and the material culture was less varied. Although recent studies have

Romania, chief sites of historical and artistic interest. *Key:* (1) National boundaries; (2) Neolithic centers and cultures, Bronze and Iron Ages; (3) Greek colonies; (4) Roman castra and cities; (5) centers of the period of migrations (4th–10th cent.); (6) centers with medieval and modern monuments.

with the penetration of seminomadic tribes from the east. At the same time the Indo-Europeanization of the local population also occurred (see EUROPEAN PROTOHISTORY).

Around 1700 B.C., under Mediterranean-Asian impulses, the Bronze Age began (see MEDITERRANEAN PROTOHISTORY). Its three principal phases are well documented by various cultures, among which are the Periam-Pecica, Otomani, Verbicioara, Monteoru, Vattina-Gîrla Mare-Cîrna, Wietenberg, and, at the end of the period, Noua. Along with the pottery (that of the Gîrla Mare-Cîrna and Wietenberg cultures is particularly noteworthy) there was an increase, from the end of the first period of the Bronze Age, in metal products, but a large part of the more noteworthy examples belongs to the final period and to the period of transition to the Iron Age. Under Mycenaean-southern European influences there was a return to the spiral decorative motif, and Mycenaean metal products (swords, ornaments, etc.) entered the country (see CRETAN-MYCENAEAN ART). Particularly in Transylvania, which was rich in copper and gold, the finely decorated weapons, utensils, and ornaments — for the most part of bronze but a good many of gold — are often outstanding

placed the beginning of the Iron Age at approximately 1200–1100 B.C., in Romania the working of iron did not begin until about 800 B.C. Between those dates the bronze products were of a high technical and artistic level, but the quality of the pottery declined completely. It now seems certain that in this period almost the entire territory began to be inhabited by Thracian tribes (although some linguists maintain that it is possible to speak of Thrace as early as the height of the Bronze Age), from whom, later, the Geto-Dacian tribes branched off north of the Danube and in Dobruja while the tribes south of the Danube constituted the Thracian population, which is well attested by literary sources.

Among the cultures of the first Iron Age, in addition to those that represent the continuation of an earlier tradition, are the Basarabi and Bîrsești-Ferigele cultures. The latter persisted until about 300 B.C. During the 6th century B.C., thanks to southern influences (whose focal point had been the Greek cities of Pontus), the first clay vases worked on the wheel appeared, but the technique became common north of the Danube only in the 3rd century B.C. with the second Iron Age (La Tène).

In the 7th–6th century B.C. there was an Illyrian influx in the southwest regions of Romania, and between the end of the 6th and the beginning of the 5th century the local population came in contact with the Scythians, who, it seems, only exerted a cultural influence. Nevertheless, at some time during the Hellenistic era, some Scythian tribes settled, at least in Dobruja, for a certain length of time, and even created small states governed by kings (whose names are preserved on a series of coins). The presence of these tribes in Dobruja justified the name of Scythia Minor that was later given to the province. The historic event which, however, had far more profound repercussions on the culture of the Geto-Dacian tribes was the Greek colonization of the western and northern coasts of the Black Sea. In fact, beginning about the mid-7th century B.C. the first Greek colonies settled on the Romanian coast of Pontus (Istria, Tomis, Kallatis) and intense trade exchange was established between the Thraco-Getic tribes of the inlying regions and the Greeks of the coastal cities. Thus Greek culture was rapidly diffused over the entire area of Dobruja and to the north and west of the Danube, even beyond the Carpathians. At the same time the flourishing trade between the Pontic colonies and the various production centers of the Aegean (the islands, the coasts of Asia Minor, Attica) promoted the economic development of the colonies themselves; in the 5th century Istria coined its own money and constructed many important public buildings. The passage of the Celts, on the other hand, left no visible mark on the local culture.

Toward the end of the 4th century and especially in the 3d century the Geto-Dacian tribes began to unite in alliances important enough to constitute a threat to the Pontic cities. In this precarious situation it was natural that the oligarchic regimes of the Greek cities should have entered into an alliance with a great political personality such as Mithridates VI Eupator (120–63 B.C.) as soon as he appeared on the political scene of Pontus. Mithridates was defeated by the Romans in 72–71 B.C., and the cities became part of the Roman protectorate which became permanent during the reign of Augustus with the victory of M. Licinius Crassus in 29 B.C. In A.D. 45 all of Dobruja, including the coastal cities, became part of the province of Moesia. In 86, after the division of the province into Moesia Superior and Inferior, Dobruja formed part of Moesia Inferior and then, at the time of Diocletian, it became part of Scythia Minor. During the 2d century the Greek cities joined in that confederation — κοινὸν τῶν Ἑλλήνων — of five or six cities (Pentapolis or Hexapolis), which may already have existed (although there is no proof of it) in an earlier period.

In the relative tranquillity assured by the Roman Empire the Pontic cities, particularly Tomis (Tomi), flourished again. Roads, urban and semiurban centers, and a whole series of castra along the limes of the Danube were constructed. As a result of the Roman domination, construction activities were stimulated and the Hellenistic artistic heritage was diffused. This was no longer limited to articles made in quantity (vases, weapons, furniture, etc.) but now it extended to include monuments of votive and funerary character.

Among the most representative discoveries of 4th-century B.C. Geto-Dacian art, with undeniable Scythian influences, are the gold helmet of Poiana Prahova (north of Bucharest) worked in repoussé, with apotropaic eyes on the forehead, sacrificial scenes on cheekpieces, and imaginary animals on the neckguard; the rich grave furnishings (beautiful vases, weapons, and harnesses of gilded silver) of a Geta chieftain at Hagighiol (Dobruja); and the repository of silver harnesses at Craiova (Oltenia). Among the pieces that are certainly Scythian is the bronze sword emblem of Medjidia and the caldron of Scorțaru (Muntenia). During the period between 100 B.C. and A.D. 100 such silver treasures were so generally spread over the entire territory inhabited by the Dacians that they became characteristic of that culture. The treasure of silver vases at Sîncrăeni (Translyvania) is particularly interesting.

During the second Iron Age the Geto-Dacians formed important tribal alliances and even established kingdoms under Dromichaetes (3d cent. B.C.), Burbista (mid-1st cent. B.C.), and Decebalus (d. 107 A.D.) who opposed the victorious Roman armies to the death. In this period the Geto-Dacian culture was profoundly influenced by contact with the Hellenistic and then the Roman cultures, and Greek goods and money were extensively circulated. Dacian silver money, based on the Macedonian types, was coined, and in the final period powerful citadels with stone walls and complex sanctuaries were constructed in some of the regions of Transylvania and even in Moldavia. The principal politico-military and religious center of the Dacians (ca. 100 B.C.–A.D. 100), was Sarmizegetusa (mod. Grădiştea Muncelului) in the Orăştie mountains of southern Transylvania. Trajan overthrew this city in two victorious campaigns (101–02, 105–06), conquering the vast region to the south and north of the Carpathians that constituted Dacia. On the site of ancient Dacian villages — Apulum, Potaissa, Napoca, Porolossum, Brobeta, Sucidava — Roman cities were built, while the new capital, Colonia Ulpia Traiana, located at some distance from the old Dacian capital, was connected with it by the

same name of Sarmizegetusa. The limes were reinforced by a whole series of castra and the wealth of the country — gold, salt mines, stone quarries, and hot thermal springs (Pagus Aquensis, mod. Călan; Germisara) — was methodically exploited. A recently discovered military diploma has made it possible to establish that already at the time of Hadrian's rule Dacia had been reorganized into Dacia Porolissensis, Apulensis, and Malvensis. The architectural and sculptural monuments of Dacia (which, unlike those of Moesia, had remained untouched by the intense centuries-old Greek influence) show a direct Italic influence. The invasions and attacks of the Germanic populations, as well as those of the free Dacians who lived beyond the frontier, led to Rome's abandonment of Dacia in 271 under the rule of Aurelian. Life continued at a much slower pace in the cities and rural centers.

Moesia, however, remained under Roman occupation for another three centuries. From the middle of the 3d century the entire province was exposed to attacks by migrating populations (Goths and Sarmatians). The minor centers were completely destroyed; the Pontic cities and the limes fortresses lived out their final phase between the 4th and 7th centuries and finally collapsed under the Slavo-Avarian attacks in the first decades of the 7th century. The powerful walls of isodomic blocks which enclosed cities and castra, residential houses and palaces, and the numerous Christian basilicas (those of Tropaeum Traiani and Tomis are particularly noteworthy) show the continuation of the Greco-Roman building tradition. But as yet there is no evidence of sculpture connected with the monuments of the new faith.

During the Roman occupation of Dacia, the free Dacians to the north, east, and southeast of the province continued to live in the traditional manner. In the middle of the 3d century, when the migrations of people from the east and northeast began, the peace of the entire region was completely disrupted. The most important archaeological document of this period is the 4th-century Petrossa treasure belonging to a Geta king (perhaps Athanaric), which originally consisted of over 25 solid gold pieces, some of which disappeared immediately after the discovery was made. The most important pieces are four enormous bird-shaped fibulas (V, PL. 58), two polygonal cups with modeled handles, an elegant oenochoë, collars (V, PL. 59), bracelets, a patera, and a large tray. Most of these have perforated surfaces decorated with semiprecious stones (cloisonné), and one necklace has an inscription in runic characters. The pieces are unequal in value and of various origins. Along with pieces produced in the Greco-Roman cities north of the Black Sea there are others, especially those decorated with semiprecious stones, which betray the influence of Iranian art.

Treasures of great artistic value have been discovered in Romania: the treasure of a Hunnic chieftain who had been buried under a tumulus at Conceşti (5th cent.; Leningrad, The Hermitage); the Petcheneg (?) treasure of Sînicolaul Mare (near Arad) of the 10th–11th century (V, PL. 96; VI, PL. 257); and work from Apahida (V, PL. 62). Along with these exceptional pieces, others more ordinary for daily use were discovered in a series of necropolises; these prove that the local culture developed forms which, although gradually influenced by the various migrating populations (Sarmatian, Germanic, Hun-Avarian, Slavic), still maintained, in an almost permanent way, their contact with the regions south of the Danube. After the penetration of the Slavs north and south of the Danube in the 6th–7th century (archaeologically documented on Romanian territory thanks to the recent discoveries in Suceava-Şipot, Sarăta Monteóru, Istria, Someşeni, and Hlincea), a gradual integration took place between the Slavs and the local population north of the Danube. Thus the formation of the Romanian people finally began to crystallize. The language was Neo-Latin (Romance), in structure, although it contained a great number of Slavic elements. This formative process finally came to an end in the 9th–10th century with the appearance of the Dridu culture, considered by some scholars to be the oldest Romanian culture.

It was in this period that the first Romanian and Slavic-Romanian political entities were established in Transylvania, before the arrival of the Hungarians. In Dobruja, where Byzantine rule continued intermittently until the 10th century, once heavily populated centers have been uncovered that had been constructed during the 9th to the 12th century on the ruins of some of the Roman fortresses of the Danube limes (Dinogetia, Capidava, etc.).

Gabriella BORDENACHE, Vladimir DUMITRESCU

Feudal period. Transylvania was incorporated in the 12th century into the Hungarian kingdom. The independent feudal states of Walachia and Moldavia were formed during the first half of the 14th century and waged lengthy victorious battles against the Tatars and against the feudal Magyar kingdom, which advanced claims to sovereign powers.

Walachia became consolidated under Mircea the Old (1386–1418) and Moldavia under Alexander the Good (1400–32). From the second half of the 14th century the Romanian states were engaged for centuries in fierce wars against the Ottoman Empire, and their struggle had wide repercussions in all Europe. The periods of relative tranquility and economic prosperity during the reigns of Stephen the Great in Moldavia (1456–1504) and of Radu the Great (1495–1508) and Neagoe Basarab (1512–21) in Walachia favored a considerable development in the arts.

In the first half of the 16th century the Romanian states, which had been a bulwark of Christianity, remained without support from other European nations and fell under Turkish domination. Consequently their natural development was halted, or at least retarded, for about three centuries. Michael the Brave (1593–1601) regained independence for Walachia and Moldavia; the subsequent reigns of Vasile Lupu (1634–53) in Moldavia and of Matei Basarab (1632–54) and Costantin Brîncoveanu (1688–1714) in Walachia represented the last period of flourishing artistic activity.

In the 18th century the Ottoman domination of Walachia and Moldavia and the presence of foreign princes as rulers of both states resulted in a more decided eastern influence. The peace of Kuchiuk-Kainarji (1774) opened the way to western trade in the Romanian state, and the Russian-Austrian-Turkish wars, fought in Moldavia and Walachia, paved the way for the increasing penetration of western influences that transformed society and its arts. Life in Transylvania, although the region had long been under Magyar and then Hapsburg rule, did not differ greatly from that in Walachia and Moldavia. Walachia and Transylvania maintained constant economic and cultural relations, but strong western influences were also evident.

The relations of the feudal Romanian states with the Orthodox Byzantine world and the Slavic-Byzantine Balkan countries on the one hand and with the western Catholic world on the other resulted in the superimposition of Byzantine, Romanesque, and Gothic elements on a vigorous popular art of pre- and protohistorical tradition. Romanian medieval art emerged from this background. The penetration of Byzantine and western influences had begun in the 10th century but, despite the unity of the ethnical substructure, the different historical conditions of the country produced aspects of civilization and culture which were accordingly different. This explains both the variations and the chronological discrepancies between the art of the three Romanian provinces of Transylvania, Walachia (mod. Muntenia and Oltenia), and Moldavia. Taken as a whole, Romanian medieval art still possessed stylistic unity as a consequence of the Orthodox religion, the common Slavic-Balkan cultural background, and permanent political and cultural relations maintained with the countries to the south of the Danube. Together with a feudal society, the forms of a cultured medieval art developed on a popular tradition dating from ancient times. The double contact with the Slavic-Byzantine culture, on the one hand, and that of the West on the other, created a complex artistic phenomenon in which a strong native tradition was combined and achieved a balance with artistic elements and movements from other countries, while still maintaining a development of its own.

During the penetration of various foreign influences the beginnings of this art were expressed in a period of experiments with selections of material as well as with stylistic idioms. Thus there are architectural elements of the Byzantine-Constantinople school in the oldest buildings extant (Church of St. Nicholas at Curtea de Argeş, 1352). In the same school the eastern decorative elements in painting and sculpture came by way of Serbia, such as the stone sculpture on the façade of the Cozia Monastery church, 1388. Western elements came via Hungary, for example, the tomb slab which is believed to have been used for the grave of the founder of the first dynasty of Romanian princes (the Basarab dynasty of Walachia) and the Gothic motifs in the doors and windows of Moldavian monuments.

In Transylvania two clearly distinguishable schools of art appeared — that of the Romanians, who formed the majority of the population, and that of the Magyar feudal class and the Saxon urban class, which had been settled in the 12th century by the kings of the Árpád dynasty. Particularly in the urban centers of Transylvania, which had become the extreme eastern boundary of Catholicism, the Romanesque, Gothic, Renaissance, and baroque styles successively constituted the predominant aspect of feudal and urban art although lagging in chronology when compared to developments in the West. For example, important Romanesque elements can be found in Cisnădioara (early 13th cent.) or in the Cathedral of Alba Iulia (2d half of 13th cent.); Cistercian Gothic elements in Cîrţa (mid-13th cent.) and Gothic ones derived from the school of the Parlers in the Black Church of Braşov (14th cent.); and Renaissance sculpture in the Lazonyius Chapel of the Cathedral of Alba Iulia. Few paintings have been preserved (Church of Bistriţa Năsăud, St. Bartholomew in Braşov, and Mălîncrav) since, beginning with the 16th century, the great majority of Magyars and Saxons adhered to the Reformation.

Among the most important creations of medieval art in Transylvania were the fortified churches constructed by the Saxon population between the 14th and 17th centuries as defense against the frequent Turkish attacks. The church-fortress, generally situated on high ground, is an architectural complex consisting of a large inner court surrounded by powerful walls (of more than one circumference at times) measuring up to 50 feet in height and from 10 to 12 feet in thickness, with a church at the center. Living quarters and deposits for arms and food were built in the walls, which were generally crenelated and reinforced with massive towers of three or four stories. The church itself was protected by crenellated fortifications in the nave, the choir, and the transept. Of the 300 church-fortresses mentioned in documents 200 have survived. The most important are Gîrbova (14th cent.), Vorumloc (15th cent.), Cisnădie (fortified in the 15th cent.), Biertan (16th. cent.), Cîlnic, Slimnic, and Prejmer.

Examples of architecture that combined military and civil functions were the strongholds erected in Transylvania from the 12th to the 14th century. Some are partially preserved, while others have been destroyed but are documented: frontier fortresses constructed by the Saxons (Sebeşel, Răşinari) or the Teutonic Knights (Feldioara, Codlea, destroyed by the Tatars in 1345); royal castra such as Deva (1269), which became an important citadel in the 15th century, Hunedoara in its first form, and Fagaras; and refuge strongholds for urban or rural communities (Biertan, Gîrbova). All these were built of stone and were similar in type to those of central Europe. At the beginning of the 18th century new strongholds, conceived according to more modern tactical requirements (e.g., Alba Iulia and the citadel of Arad), were built on the ruins of the old citadels.

In Transylvania the artistic activity of the predominantly Romanian population was particularly interesting. In spite of persecutions the Orthodox religion continued to influence the art forms, which retained elements of the popular tradition. Between the end of the 13th and the beginning of the 14th century contact was established between the Byzantine and western schools. The paintings in the churches of the Haţeg region are particularly significant: Sîntămăria-Orlea (mid-14th cent.), Ribiţa (1417), Crişcior (15th cent.), Strei (15th cent.), Cinciş (15th cent.), and others. These churches, in addition to containing Byzantine iconography with echoes of the western Catholic tradition, depicted the church founders in special local ways. The few princely dwellings of masonry also represent a synthesis between Byzantine art forms (predominant in the two principalities located beyond the Carpathians) and western art forms, which enjoyed the full support of the Transylvanian feudal and ecclesiastical hierarchy. During the 16th and 17th centuries, Walachian motifs penetrated sporadically but caused few changes. Beginning with the 18th century the Brîncoveanu style of painting from Walachia became widespread in Transylvania, where it assumed a markedly popular character with picturesque and typically regional accents.

In Walachia and Moldavia, the artistic development had a unified aspect even where it contained local characteristics. The oldest medieval masonry monuments of Walachia and Moldavia belong to the period in which the feudal states were formed and organized. In Walachia, the ruins of the churches of Turnu Severin and St. Nicoara at Curtea de Argeş (late 13th and early 14th cent.) go back to this period. They were constructed on a rectangular plan with one and three apses to the east respectively. The Church of St. Nicholas in Curtea de Argeş (1352), the oldest building of Byzantine type in Romania, is well preserved and belongs to a more advanced historical phase of Walachia. In the second half of the 14th century the church of the Monastery of Cotmeana (rectangular presbytery with barrel vault and three semicircular apses, one to the east and two lateral), with its decoration of brick and of enameled ceramic disks, is similar to the religious monuments of Bulgaria, which, in turn, were closely related to Byzantium (Mesambria, Tîrnovo). Cozia (1388) was the first monument in Walachia to have a three-apse plan similar in type to the Serbian churches in the Morava Valley; this style was followed in other buildings. Both St. Nicholas in Curtea de Argeş and the church in Cozia contain paintings that also demonstrate a relationship with the Byzantine-Balkan art of the Paleologus style. From the same period, some tombstones and the ornaments found in a tomb in the church of St. Nicholas in Curtea de Argeş, show un undeniable relationship between the court art of Walachia and the West.

In the second half of the 15th century, under Moldavia's Stephen the Great, a more organic synthesis of the different elements was achieved. In that period the medieval Moldavian style, the beginnings of which can perhaps be traced to the end of the 14th century and the period of Alexander the Good, was at the height of its development. The first citadels were constructed (Suceava, Neamţ, etc.) as well as the first masonry church buildings (St. Nicholas in Rădăuti, Holy Trinity Church in Siret, etc.). Illuminated manuscripts and sacred subjects in embroidery became widely used. Works such as the Four Gospels of 1429 (Oxford, Bodleian Lib.), a stole with religious scenes and portraits of Alexander the Good and his wife (lost), and the epitaph of Siluan (1437) at Neamţ, indicate the high level achieved during the formative period of the Moldavian style. However, as has already been mentioned, there was a harmonious synthesis in all the expressions of the period of Stephen the Great.

In architecture, original elements were grafted onto the Byzantine-type plans, whether rectangular or three-apsed. For example, the "Moldavian vault" appeared, based on the principle of reducing the space to be covered by gradually reducing the diameter of the dome with one or two series of superimposed and slanted arches; a western type of decoration with ornamental features on doors and windows in Gothic style was used, together with other, Byzantine-eastern elements (disks of enameled ceramics). Thus, innovations consisting of quite differing elements were assimilated in a unified, harmonious, and typically Moldavian form. Of the 40 churches attributed to Stephen the most noteworthy are Dolheştii Mari (before 1481) and Bălineşti (end of 15th cent.), both of rectangular plan; Voroneţ (1488), Hîrlău (1492), and Popăuţi (1496), all three-apsed; Borzeşti (1493-94), Războieni (1496), and Piatra (1497-98), with the so-called "mixed" plan, an original form derived from the combination of the two preceding plans.

In the 15th century Walachia was so disrupted by the continuous fighting against the Turks that no monuments have survived that show the evolution of architecture and painting. Two monuments of impressive proportions belong to the beginning of the 16th century: the church of the Monastery in Dealu (1500-02) and that of the Monastery in Argeş (1517); these possess rich sculptured stone decorations that clearly show an eastern influence (Armenian-Georgian and even simplified Moslem style). Similar decorations appear in the frontispieces of manuscripts and on tombstones. During the same period a number of more modest buildings in brick were constructed. Faithful to the plan and structure of the church of Cozia, they were adapted to the construction material and to the taste of the minor nobility, and by the end of the 15th century they determined the type of structure that became characteristic of the majority of Walachia's religious buildings. The decoration generally consisted of blind arcades placed on two levels which were divided by a broad stringcourse (composed of a torus between saw-teeth), while the facing presented a pleasant two color effect resulting from the alternation of crude bricks with whitewashed areas divided in rectangles by a regular sidewise insertion of the bricks. The most representative of these monuments are Căluiu (before 1521), the chapel of Cozia (1542), Curtea Veche in Bucharest (1559), Bucovaţ (ca. 1570), Tutana (1589), and Mihai Vodă in Bucharest (1589-91). Refined or rustic, monumental or modest, chapel or princely church, the works of the great 16th-century builders of Walachia, even in their great variety, are closely related to each other. They are the result of various attempts to assimilate the forms and structures diffused throughout the Balkans, and in the synthesis represented by each the possibilities of further solutions can be found. The selective choice of the various components — bound as it was to the Romanian use of materials and style — permits the grouping of the various monuments in a style characteristic of Walachia; in fact, the architectural style which developed in the 17th century was based on these monuments.

The Moldavian architecture of the 16th century continued the style of the previous century. An innovation appeared, however, which was to characterize the religious buildings: the esonarthex was transformed into a broad arcaded portico and the *camera mortuaria* became widespread in use. Some of the finest architectural monuments belong to this period: Probota and Humor (1530), Vatra Moldoviţii (1532), St. Demetrius in Suceava (1534-35), Slatina (1561), and Suceviţa (1582-84).

The frescoes and religious embroideries are important for their quality and expressive richness. Although faithful to Byzantine iconography, the Romanian craftsmen revealed great originality. In Moldavia the frescoes in Bălineşti (1493), which are almost completely preserved in an unaltered state, part of those of Pătrăuţi (1487), Voroneţ (1488), St. Ilie near Suceava (after 1488), and others, represent one of the most successful expressions of post-Byzantine art. The essential characteristics of this phase of Moldavian painting are its monumentality, the sobriety of its composition, the highly symbolic character of its iconography, and the attempts at characterization in the depiction of faces. This last element is also evident in the portraits of the founders (Stephen the Great in Voroneţ, the dignitary Ioan Tăutu in Bălineşti, and Luca Arbore in the church of Arbore). Yet each of these frescoes possesses various stylistic elements: the contour line, the shading of the colors, and the proportion and typology of the images. The Moldavian craftsman, while following the Orthodox iconography established in Byzantium in the 14th century, created an original pictorial style that reflected a new culture and a new artistic vison. About 1530 Moldavian painting acquired new stylistic characteristics: the scenes increased in variety and the compositions contained more figures and became more complex and dynamic in gesture. However, the most original medieval Romanian art was the mural paintings which, in the 16th century, completely covered the façades of the contemporary Moldavian churches and sometimes were applied even to those of an earlier period (Voroneţ, Humor, Vatra Moldoviţii, Arbore, and Suceviţa). The harmony of the colors, which retain their original freshness, the elegance of the design, and especially the thematic richness of the various compositions make this type of painting a unique phenomenon in European medieval art. The last church to be painted on the outside was that of the Monastery of Suceviţa (1601), founded by Prince Ieremia Movilă, and it was here that the first signs of the influence of Russian art appeared.

In Walachia, painting was limited to interiors and flourished in the 16th century. The small number of paintings preserved (undamaged or unretouched) make it difficult to define the characteristics of the school of Muntenia. The small church of the Hospital of Cozia (1543) has the best preserved paintings, and there are also interesting surviving examples in the church of the Tismana Monastery in Stăneşti and in the chapel of the Monastery of Bistriţa. Recent investigations show that during the reign of princes such as Radu the Great and Neagoe Basarab (protectors of the Orthodox religion in the Balkan countries that had fallen to the Turks) the art of Muntenia — especially painting — spread south of the Danube.

The rich collection of religious embroideries of the 15th and 16th centuries (Putna, Monastery; Bucharest, Nat. Mus.) completes the picture of an artistic activity that was exceptional in its originality and creativity.

During the 17th century Moldavian art showed signs of considerable renewal. In spite of strong foreign influence never wholly assimilated, architecture adhered to the traditional motifs in plan and structure. In addition to structural elements that were typically Muntenian, some large monuments (Dragomirna, 1609, Trei Ierarhi, 1639, the church of the Golia Monastery, 1660, and Cetăţuia 1672, all in Iaşi) introduced rich stone decoration which included eastern (Dragomira and Trei Ierarhi) and western (Colia) elements. In the following century neoclassic influences, which penetrated by way of Russia and Constantinople, basically modified Moldavian art.

In contrast to Moldavia, Walachia during the 17th century achieved a style that can be called Walachian. The first half of the 17th century was characterized by buildings that still reflected the style of the preceding century. Moldavian influences are visible in the Stelea Church of Tîrgovişte (1650), built by the Moldavian workmen of the reigning prince of Moldavia, Vasile Lupu. During this time Prince Matei Basarab and his nobles built extensively. The churches in Arnota (1633), Brebu (1650), and Gura Motrului (1633) are characteristic of this period. Toward the end of the century the building activities of Prince Şerban Cantacuzino and Constantin Brîncoveanu brought to full development the new style, which was characterized by rich stone decoration. In the 18th century decorative elements also became predominant in the field of applied arts. Baroque elements of western derivation, assimilated and adapted to the local style, appeared both in religious buildings, which were endowed with sumptuous furnishings (Cotroceni, 1678; Horezu, 1691-92; Antim, 1715; Văcăreşti, 1716-22), and in the residences of the reigning princes such as Potlogi, Mogoşoaia, and others.

Beginning with the second half of the 18th century, as a result of social and political transformations, the reigning princes and the nobility seem to have stopped founding cathedrals; this function was then assumed by town communities (corporations) and by peasant landowners. Thus, there were great transformations in esthetic concepts, which came to include more and more popular art motifs and forms. While less visible in architecture, the new tendencies were felt in many rural buildings in which painting was characterized by a folkloristic interpretation of the iconographic tradition. The paintings on often very modest monuments (St. Nicholas in Tîrgul-Jiu, 1810; the Church of Cartiu, 1817; the Church of Băltişoară, 1860) represented the end of a cultivated feudal court art and, at the same time, were a highly original expression of popular creativity. Local secular elements connected with the social life and problems of the villages were added to the traditional iconography. In such paintings the lack of compositional sense, the weakness of design, and the violence of the color pass unnoticed and attention centers of the nonconformity of the iconography, the sincerity and spontaneity of line, the expressive force, and the picturesque and ingenuous liveliness of the figures and scenes — all elements expressing the creative vigor of a people whose folk painting, in the period between the late 18th and the first half of the 19th century, constituted an experience as profoundly representative as that of the refined Moldavian painting of the 16th century.

Maria Ana MUSICESCU

Modern period. The changes that took place in the social structure of Romania at the beginning of the 19th century were responsible for a shift of interest toward secular art, which soon became the predominant art form. The Romanian painters' works of these early years were aimed at conquering the rudiments of a realistic art, and their awkwardness and naïveté are not without charm. For decades portraiture remained the dominant theme. Foreign painters such as Anton

Chladek (1794–1882), Niccolo Livaditti (1804–58), and Giovanni Schiavoni (1804), as well as the first of the Romanian secular painters who emerged from the ranks of church decorators, such as Eustatie Altini (1780–1815), Ion Balomir (b. 1794), and Nicolae Polcovnicul, devoted themselves to this art form. The interest gradually became broader with the artists' efforts to adhere to the ideas of social emancipation, independence, and national unity. C. Lecca's (1807–87) historical paintings, the first of their kind, were done in this spirit; others who worked in this direction were the Moldavian G. Asachi (1788–1869), an organizer of cultural activities and the first forms of art education, Ion Negulici (1812–51), Constantin Rosenthal (1820–51), Barbu Iscovescu (1815–54), and G. Tattarescu (1818–94).

Without doubt Theodor Aman (1831–91) was the major figure of this period. His historical paintings are filled with a sense of intense reality, while the portraits, genre paintings, and engravings show not only individual psychological characterization but also the social life and spirit of the times. Aman, together with Tattarescu, founded the School of Fine Arts.

Carol Pop de Szathmary (1812–85) was a talented water-colorist who chose rural life as his source of inspiration. At the time of Aman's death, the Romanian school of painting was already well established. This was largely due to the exceptional work of Nicolae Grigorescu and Ion Andreescu. Grigorescu (1838–1907), with his plein-air painting inspired by a great love for nature and man, was responsible for a change in the artistic style of the period. In landscapes, portraits, and large compositions dedicated to the 1877 War for National Independence (during this period he executed hundreds of sketches), he expressed his preferred themes: figures of all ages, the vibrant quality of light, and various aspects of the country. Ion Andreescu (1850–82), who was strongly influenced by Grigorescu, produced serious works of dramatic intensity.

In the second half of the 19th century sculpture also began to develop in Romania. The most outstanding sculptors of this period were Karl Storck (1826–87), Ioan Georgescu (1856–98), who produced more than 150 busts and statues in the classic style, and Stefan Ionuesc-Valbudea (1856–1918), whose works reflect a feeling of romantic revolt.

The political and social changes that modified the structure of the Romanian regions in the 19th century also influenced the field of architecture. In the first half of the century the neoclassic style predominated. This can be observed in such outstanding buildings as the Stirbey Palace (1820) and the Colentina-Tei Palace (1822), both in Bucharest, the Palace of the reigning princes in Iași, and the National Theater (1851) and University (1857–64) in Bucharest, both designed by A. Orăscu (1817–94).

In the last quarter of the century Ion Mincu (1852–1912) was the innovator of the movement that introduced traditional elements from popular architecture into architectural decoration. Examples of this trend can be seen in the Central School for Women and in the Bufet restaurant in Bucharest. Two other movements existed in this period: one inspired by Renaissance forms (Palace of Justice and Ministry of Agriculture in Bucharest) and the other by the French neoclassic style (Post Office in Bucharest by A. Săvulescu, 1847–1902).

The painter Ștefan Luchian (1868–1916), who had been strongly influenced by Grigorescu at the beginning of his career, initiated a new period of experimentation in painting. His warmth, pathos, and unusual color harmonies represent something genuinely new.

A strong social and realistic orientation is apparent in a series of drawings in the social protest style by such artists as Iosif Iser (1881–1958), Francisc Șirato (1877–1953), and Camil Ressu (1880–1962). This was continued during the period between World Wars I and II in the works of Iser, Ressu, Ștefan Popescu (1872–1948), Ștefan Dimitrescu (1886–1933), Dimitru Ghiață (b. 1888), and Jean Steriadi (1880–1956). Steriadi and Nicolae Tonitza (1885–1940) depicted the life of the common man and the Romanian city scene. Others who worked in the same tradition were Gheorge Petrașcu (1872–1949), Theodor Pallady (1871–1956), N. Dărăscu (1883–1959), Marius Bunescu (b. 1881), and Aurel Ciupe (b. 1900).

In sculpture, where portraiture was particularly developed, outstanding artists were D. Paciurea (1873–1932), Frederic Storck (1872–1942), Ion Jalea (b. 1887), Corneliu Medrea (b. 1889), and Oscar Han (b. 1891). Constantin Brancusi (1876–1957, q.v.), was one of the most original sculptors of 20th-century European art (V, PL. 128; XI, PL. 332).

In the graphic arts new tendencies also appeared. The etchings and drawings by painters such as Iser, Steriadi, Petrascu, and Popescu and by graphic artists such as Vasile Dobrian (b. 1912), Marcel Olinescu (b. 1896), Mircea Olarian (b. 1898), Henri Catargi (b. 1894), Jules Perahim (b. 1914), Vasile Kazar (b. 1913), and Béla Gy Szábo (b. 1905) prepared the ground for the energetic development of contemporary Romanian graphic art.

In architecture, in the period between 1900 and 1944, various schools existed. Some retained traditional forms that related directly to the Romanian landscape (Ion Mincu), while others adhered to the Neo-Gothic style and later to revivals of the French Renaissance. As a result, the large cities present an eclectic and mixed aspect. Some interesting buildings of this period with well-defined and elegant forms are by the architects Horia Creangă, Duiliu Marcu, and Horia Maicu.

Since the proclamation of the Romanian People's Republic, artistic activity has intensified both in the capital and in the provincial cities. Representatives of the older generation — the painters Iser, Ressu, Steiradi, Catargi, Bunescu, Ghiață, and the sculptors Jalea, Medrea, Han — have contributed greatly to shaping the new art and illustrating the new content while remaining within the tradition. The younger artists such as Corneliu Baba (b. 1906), Alexandru Ciucurencu (b. 1903), Stefan Szönyi (b. 1913), Brăduț Covaliu (b. 1924), Spiru Chintilă (b. 1921), Lucian Grigorescu (b. 1894), Eugen Popa (b. 1919), and Ion Placea (b. 1923), worked along similar lines. In sculpture, Boris Caragea (b. 1907), Ion Irimescu (b. 1903), Mac Constantinescu (b. 1900), Geza Vida (b. 1913), Ion Vlad (b. 1920), Gheorge Anghel (b. 1904), R. Ladea (b. 1901), Zoe Băicoianu (b. 1910), and Ovidiu Maitec (b. 1925) are active.

The development of contemporary graphic arts has been equally vigorous; advertising design, political cartoons, and book illustration are documents of contemporary life. Among the most important figures are Perahim, Kazar, Gheorge Ivancenco (b. 1914), Dobrian, Szabo, Ligia Macovei (b. 1916), Florica Cordescu (b. 1914), Corina Beiu Angheluță (b. 1919), Mariana Petrașcu (b. 1915), and Aurel Jiguidi; in caricature Iosif Ross (1899), Cik Damadian (b. 1919), Eugen Taru (b. 1913), Rik Auerbach (b. 1920), Adrian Lucaci (b. 1913); in advertising design Iosif Molnar (b. 1907), Iosif Cova (b. 1912), Val Munteanu (b. 1927), Nicolae Popescu (b. 1915); in book illustration Florica and Marcela Cordescu (b. 1914) and Aurel Stoicescu (b. 1920).

Architecture, city planning, monumental sculpture, and painting have been intensively developed and the creation of large architectural complexes has changed the face of the cities. This can be seen in the Congress Palace in Bucharest, the extensive housing developments in the capital and many other cities, the industrial complexes of Onești, Săvinești, and Sighișoara, the new industrial centers conceived as homogeneous urban units (Victoria in Transylvania), and the new buildings in the Black Sea bathing resorts (Mamaia, Eforie, Costinești, and Mangalia.)

Mircea POPESCU, Amelia PAVEL

BIBLIOG. *General*: A. Philippide, Originea Romînilor, I, Iassi, 1925; C. C. Giurescu, Istoria Romînilor, Bucharest, 1935 ff.; D. Onciul, Originile Principatelor Romîne, Bucharest, 1938 ff.; Istoria Romîniei, I–II, Bucharest, 1960–62 (III to be published; bibliog. for each chapter); C. Daicoviciu and others, Din istoria Transilvaniei, 11 vols., Bucharest, 1961.

Antiquity and early Middle Ages: B. Pick and K. Regling, Die antiken Münzen Nord-Griechenlands: Die antiken Münzen von Dacien und Moesien, 2 vols., Berlin, 1890–1910; G. Tocilescu, Fouilles et recherches archéologiques en Roumanie, Bucharest, 1900; G. Tocilescu, Monumente epigrafice și sculptural ale Muzeului Național din București, 2 vols., Bucharest, 1902–08; I. Weiss, Die Dobroudscha im Altertum, Sarajevo, 1911; I. Andriesescu, Contribuție la Dacia înainte de Romani, Iassi, 1912; C. Diculescu, Die Wandalen und die Goten in Ungarn und Rumänien, Würzburg, 1923; V. Pârvan, Începuturile vieții romane la gurile Dunării, Bucharest, 1923; D. M. Teodorescu, Cercetări arheologice în Munții Hunedoara, Cluj, 1923; V. Pârvan, Getica, Bucharest, 1926; V. Pârvan, Dacia: An Outline of the Early Civilizations of the Carpatho-Danubian Countries, Cambridge, 1927; I. Nestor, Der Stand der Vorgeschichtsforschung in Rumänien, Bericht der Römisch-Germanische Kommission, XXII, 1932, pp. 11–181; H. Schmidt, Cucuteni, in der oberen Moldau, Berlin, 1932; S. Ferri, Arte romana sul Danubio, Milan, 1933; H. Schroller, Die Stein und Kupferzeit Siebenbürgens, Berlin, Leipzig, 1933; V. Dumitrescu, L'art préhistorique en Roumanie, Bucharest, 1937; C. S. Nicolăescu-Plopșor, Le paléolithique en Roumanie, Dacia, VI–VII, 1937–40, pp. 41–107; R. Vulpe, Histoire ancienne de la Dobroudja, Bucharest, 1938; D. Berciu, Arheologia preistorică a Olteniei, Craiova, 1939; A. Prox, Die Schneckenberg-Kultur, Brașov, 1941; D. Popescu, Die frühe und mittlere Bronzezeit in Siebenbürgen, Bucharest, 1944; C. Daicoviciu, La Transylvanie dans l'antiquité, Bucharest, 1945; N. Bănescu, L'ancien Etat bulgare et les pays roumains, Bucharest, 1947; C. Daicoviciu, Așezările dacice din muntii Orăștiei, Bucharest, 1951; C. Daicoviciu, Cetatea dacică de la Piatra Roșie, Bucharest, 1954; V. Dumitrescu et al., Hăbășești: Monografie arheologică, Bucharest, 1954; R. Vulpe, Izvoare, Bucharest, 1957; O. Floca, Contribuție la cunoașterea tezaurelor de argint dacice, Bucharest, 1958; K. Horedt, Untersuchungen zur Frühgeschichte Siebenbürgens, Bucharest, 1958; D. M. Pippidi, Contribuții la istoria veche a Romîniei, Bucharest, 1958; D. Tudor, Oltenia romană, 2d ed., Bucharest, 1958; I. I. Russu, Limba traco-dacilor, Bucharest, 1959; D. M. Pippidi, Un nouveau document sur le Koinon pontique, BCH, LXXXIV, 1960, pp. 434–58; D. Berciu, Contribuții la problemele neoliticului în Romînia, Bucharest, 1961; C. and H. Daicoviciu, Sarmizegetusa, Bucharest, 1961; V. Dumitrescu, Necropola de incinerație din epoca bronzului de la Cirna, Bucharest, 1961; C. Danov, RE, s.v. Pontos Euxinos, sup., IX, 1962, cols., 866–1175.

Feudal period: Buletinul Comisiunii Monumentelor Istorice a Romîniei, Bucharest, 1908–45; N. Iorga and G. Balș, Historie de l'art roumain ancien, Paris, 1922; G. Balş, Bisericile lui Ştefan cel Mare, B. Com. Mon. Ist., XVIII, 1926, pp. 43–46; N. Ghica-Budeşti, Evolutia arhitecturii în Muntenia şi Oltenia, 4 vols., Vălenii de Munte, 1927–36; G. Balş, Bisericile moldeştioven din veacul al XVI-lea, B. Com. Mon. Ist., XXI, 1928, pp. 55–58; I. D. Stefănescu, Contribution à l'étude des peintures murales valaques (Orient et Byzance, III), Paris, 1928; I. D. Stefănescu, L'évolution de la peinture religieuse en Bucovine et en Moldavie, 2 vols., Paris, 1928; I. D. Stefănescu, L'évolution de la peinture religieuse en Bucovine et en Moldavie depuis les origines jusqu'au XIXᵉ siècle: Nouvelles recherches, 2 vols., Paris., 1929; H. Paul, Les églises de la Moldavie du Nord des origines à la fin du XVIᵉ siècle: Architecture et peinture, 2 vols., Paris, 1930; I. D. Stefănescu, La peinture religieuse en Valachie et en Transylvanie depuis les origines jusqu'eau XIXᵉ siècle, 2 vols., Paris, 1930–32; G. Balş, Bisericile moldoveneşti din veacurile XVII si XVIII, Bucharest, 1933; N. Iorga, Les arts mineurs en Roumanie, 2 vols., Bucharest, 1934; V. Roth, Die deutsche Kunst in Siebenbürgen, Berlin, Sibiu, 1934; Anuarul Com. Mon. Ist.: Secţia Transilvania, I-IV, 1936–39; G. Ionescu, Istoria arhitecturii romîneşti, Bucharest, 1937; I. D. Stefănescu, L'art byzantin et l'art lombard dans la Transylvanie, Paris, 1938; W. Horwath, Siebenbürgisch-sächsische Kirchenburgen, Sibiu, 1940; J. Balogh, Az erdélyi renaissance, I, 1460–1541 (The Transylvanian Renaissance), Cluj, 1943; Documente de arhitectura romînească (8 fasc. of pl.), Bucharest, 1952–62; Studii si cercetări de istoria artei, Bucharest, 1954 ff.; T. Gerevich, Erdélyi magyar müvészet (Hungarian Art in Transylvania), Bupadest, 1955; Scortă istorie e artelor plastice în România, I: Arta romînească în epoca feudală, Bucharest, 1957; Repertoriul monumentelor şi obiectelor de artă din timpul lui Ştefan cel Mare, Bucharest, 1958; Studii asupra terzaurului restitut de U.R.S.S., Bucharest, 1958; V. Vătăşianu, Istoriz artei feudale in Ţările Romîne, I, Bucharest, 1959 (full bibliog. to the early decades of the 16th cent.); N. Stoicescu, Repertoriul bibliografic al monumentelor feudale din Bucureşti, Bucharest, 1961; G. Ionescu, Istoria arhitecturi în Romînia, I, Bucharest, 1963 (bibliog.); G. and V. Sebestyen, Arcitectura Renasterii în Transilvania, Bucharest, 1963; S. Ulea, L'origine et la signification idéologique de la peinture extérieure moldave, Rev. roumanie d'h., II, 1963; pp. 29–71.

Modern period: G. Oprescu, Pictura romînească in sec. al XIX-lea, Bucharest, 1943; G. Ionescu, Relatare asupra istoriei arhitecturii romîneşti din cele mai vechi timpuri pînă in ziua de azi, Bucharest, 1954; G. Oprescu, Sculptura statuară romîneasca, Bucharest, 1954; S. si cercetări de ist. artei, Bucharest, 1954 ff.; I. Frunzetti and M. Popescu, ed., Scortă istorie a artelor plastice în Romînia, II, Bucharest, 1958, Artele plastice in Romînia după 23 August 1944, Bucharest, 1959; Cronica ilustrată a unei apuse, Bucharest, 1959; G. Oprescu, Nicolae Grigorescu, 2 vols., Bucharest, 1961; Architecture in the Rumanian People's Republic, Bucharest, 1964 (cat.).

MONUMENTAL CENTERS. Only the centers of major archaeological and artistic interest are listed here. They are grouped by region, in the order given in the summary. The capital is placed first.

Bucharest (Bucureşti). Capital of the Romanian People's Republic, it was previously the capital of Walachia and was mentioned for the first time in a document of 1459. An important transit center for commerce between Transylvania and the Balkans during the feudal period, it was at that time the permanent residence of the voivodes of Walachia. After the unification of Walachia and Moldavia in 1859, it became the capital of Romania in 1862 and developed rapidly under the influence of western countries, especially France. Among the oldest religious buildings is Curtea Veche (1559), formerly the church of the princes' residence, a three-apsed structure with a dome over the presbytery, once frescoed; the baroque portal is by Stefano Cantacuzino (1715). Mihai Vodă, a church constructed between 1589 and 1591 by the voivode Mihai Viteazul, is the most important monument of Muntenia from the second half of the 16th century. Completely restored in the interior, it had a three-apsed plan with a large tower over the cella and two small turrets over the spaces that flank the altar. Patriarchia, constructed in 1655, follows the style of the Monastery church of Curtea de Argeş with the addition of a small pilastered portico; it was once frescoed. Doamnei was founded in 1683 by Princess Maria, wife of the voivode Şerban Cantacuzino; the church has a three-apsed plan with a spherical vault over the cella, a bell tower (collapsed) over the pronaos, an entrance portico with stone columns topped by prismatic capitals, and fine frescoes of the same period. The façade of Fundeni Doamnei, constructed in 1699 by Mihail Cantacuzino, is covered with rich stucco decoration of eastern origin (geometrical and plant motifs, depictions of buildings). This type of decoration, which probably originated in Constantinople, was used for the first time in Walachia in Fundeni Doamnei. Kretzulescu, founded by a dignitary of the same name in 1722, and restored in 1935, is built on a three-apsed plan, with brick walls, a dome over the cella, and a bell tower over the pronaos; the beautiful frescoes in the entrance portico depict episodes from the Apocalypse. Among the most important public buildings of the 19th century are the Romanian Atheneum (1888), the National Bank building (1885), the Palace of Justice, and the Post Office (1900). The National Museum of Antiquities has a rich collection of antiquities from the first phase of the Paleolithic period to the late feudal period (18th cent.) and a numismatic collection. The National Museum contains feudal art, representative works of western painters, and Far Eastern art. Also

important are the Historical Museum of the City of Bucharest, the Folk Museum, an outdoor museum with buildings brought from all regions of the country, the Aman Museum, the Tattarescu Museum the Feudal Art Museum-Mogoşoaia, and the Zambaccian Museum.

On the outskirts are the Potlogi and Mogoşoaia palaces. The Potlogi Palace was constructed by Constantin Brîncoveanu, with richly decorated stuccoes in the eastern manner in the same style as those of Fundeni Doamnei. The Mogoşoaia Palace was constructed

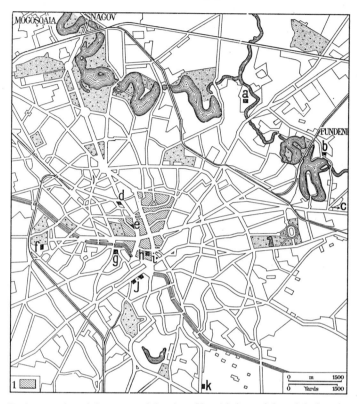

Bucharest, plan of the center of the city. Key: (1) Area of the original settlement. Principal monuments: (a) Plumbuita monastery; (b) Fundeni Doamnei church; (c) Mărcuţa monastery; (d) Ştirbey Palace-Art Museum; (e) Kretzulescu church; (f) Cotroceni monastery; (g) former Mihai Vodă monastery-State Archives; (h) Stavropoleos church; (i) Curtea Veche church; (j) Patriarcha and old metropolitan's palace; (k) Văcăreşti monastery.

in 1702 by the voivode Constantin Brîncoveanu; it has an elegant loggia on the west façade opening onto a lake and an east façade with a belvedere overlooking a large courtyard. The palace is a synthesis of baroque elements and eastern motifs. In front of the palace is a church on a rectangular plan. The palace houses a section of the Bucharest National Museum, and is rich in the art of the Brîncoveanu period.

BIBLIOG. V. Drăghiceanu, Curţile domneşti brîncoveneşti, II: Mogoşoaia, B. Com. Mon. Ist., II, 1909, pp. 149–64; N. Ghica-Budeşti, Evoluţia arhitecturii în Muntenia şi Oltenia, III-IV, Vălenii de Munte, 1933–36; G. Ionescu, Istoria arhitecturii romîneşti, Bucharest, 1937; N. Iorga, Istoria Bucureştilor, Bucharest, 1939; G. Ionescu, Bucureşti: Ghid istoric şi artistic, Bucharest, 1958; N. Stoicescu, Repertoriul bibliografic al monumentelor feudale din Bucureşti, Bucharest, 1961; R. Popa, Palatul şi muzeul de arta brîncoveneasca, Bucharest, 1962.

Argeş. Cozia. The church of the Monastery, founded by Mircea the Old (1388), has a three-apsed plan, similar in type to the Serbian churches of the Morava Valley; it has walls of stone and brick courses with engaged colonnettes and ornate windows. In 1706–07 an entrance portico supported on piers was added. In the pronaos are frescoes of the Paleologus style from the end of the 14th century. The chapel of the infirmary, which was constructed in 1542, is one of the most harmonious 16th-century monuments in Muntenia. Its slender forms are reminiscent of the Moldavian churches of the last two decades of the 15th century. Built on a three-apsed plan, it contains an outstanding group of well-conserved frescoes.

BIBLIOG. P. Antonescu, Mănăstirea Cozia, Bucharest, 1904; I. D. Stefănescu, La peinture religieuse en Valachie et en Transylvanie depuis les origines jusqu'au XIXᵉ siècle, I, Paris, 1930; G. Ionescu, Istoria arhitecturii romîneşti, Bucharest, 1937; V. Vătăşianu, Istoria artei feudale în Ţările Romîne, I, Bucharest, 1959.

Curtea de Argeș. One of the oldest cities of Walachia, it was the residence of the earliest voivodes. The former voivode palace and the Church of St. Nicoara are in ruins. The Church of St. Nicholas, which was still under construction in 1352, was built on the plan of an inscribed Greek cross, following the "Constantinople" variation, with irregular stones alternating with courses of three to five bricks; the well-preserved pictorial decoration (14th cent.) forms the most important group of Byzantine paintings in Romania, and is related in style to that of the Kariye Camii of Constantinople and to other paintings of the Paleologus period in the Balkan peninsula. The church of the Monastery of Argeș, founded by the voivode Neagoe Basarab, was completed in 1517; built on a three-apsed plan, it is the most ornate monument in Walachia. The pictorial decoration dates from about 1526; there are fine tombstones from the 16th century. Fragments of frescoes, removed when the church was restored at the end of the 19th century, are kept in the Bucharest National Museum. More recent ecclesiastical buildings include the Olari Church, Bradu Botușari, and Valea Danului.

BIBLIOG. L. Reissenberger, L'église du monastère épiscopal de Kurtea d'Argis en Valachie, Vienna, 1867; F. Jaffet, Die bischöfliche Klosterkirche von Curtea de Argeș, Berlin, 1912; V. Drăghiceanu and others, Curtea Domnească din Argeș, B. Com. Mon. Ist., X-XVI, 1917-23, pp. 9-73; V. Vătășianu, Istoria artei feudale în Țările Romîne, I, Bucharest, 1959.

Horezu. This is the largest monastic complex in Walachia. Founded by Constantin Brîncoveanu (1692) it includes a series of small churches: the chapel of the infirmary (1699), the Holy Apostles Church (1698), and St. Stephen (1703). The principal church, on a triple-apsed plan, has a dome over the presbytery. The circumference wall, with colonnaded porticoes on its interior, encloses a series of cells. The frescoes of the church are well-preserved and are the most important of the Brîncoveanu period; all 18th-century painting in Walachia derives from them. Restoration work was begun in 1960.

BIBLIOG. N. Iorga, Hirtii din arhiva mănăstirii Hurezului (S. și doc., XIV), Bucharest, 1907; B. Com, Mon. Ist., I-II, 1908-09, passim; I. D. Stefănescu, Contribution à l'étude des peintures murales valaques (Orient et Byzance, III), Paris, 1928; I. D. Stefănescu, La peinture religieuse en Valachie et en Transylvanie depuis les origines jusqu'au XIX⁰ siècle, II, Paris, 1932.

Bacău. **Neamț.** This monastic complex and that of Putna are the most important in medieval Romania, and Neamț is still a large cultural center today. It includes the Church of the Resurrection, from the period of Stephen the Great, with a bell tower of four stories, a smaller tower, monks' cells on two stories around the central court, and three small churches in the vicinity of the monastery. The Church of the Resurrection, on a triple-apsed plan, has a wall of dressed stone with a plinth of square blocks. Disks of enameled ceramics (green, yellow, brown) are inserted under the frame and on the windows; doors and windows have decorative Gothic elements. In the interior are fragments of frescoes of Stephen the Great and tombstones with the characteristic motif of Moldavia — the semi-palmetto superimposed on a sinuous raceme. It was restored in 1959-61. The fortress, mentioned for the first time in 1395, was probably constructed by Petru Mușat (1374-91) to defend the western frontier of Moldavia. Originally on a quadrangular plan with square towers reinforced at the angles by buttresses, then enlarged and adapted to newer military needs by Stephen the Great, it was later transformed into a monastery by the voivode Vasile Lupu (1634-35) to save it from the demolition ordered by the Turks. It was destroyed in 1718. In 1952-54 excavations and restoration work were carried out.

BIBLIOG. S. Balș and C. Nicolescu, Mănăstirea Neamț, Bucharest, 1958; Repertoriul monumentelor și obiectelor de artă din timpul lui Ștefan cel Mare, Bucharest, 1958; V. Vătășianu, Istoria artei feudale în Țările Romîne, I, Bucharest, 1959; N. Constantinescu, Date noi în legătură cu Cetatea Neamtului, S. și cercetări de ist. veche, XI, 1960, pp. 81-105.

Piatra Neamț. On Mount Bîtca Doamnei, about 1 mile to the northwest of the city, on the right bank of the Bistrița, excavations in 1961-62 revealed the ruins of a Dacian fortress of the 1st century. Its massive stone walls had been constructed with a technique different from that used in the Dacian forts of Transylvania. Inside the walls is a sanctuary with the typical alignment of drums of columns. Near the fortress are the remains of a castrum constructed of earth, used by the Romans during the siege of the citadel.

Brașov. **Bran.** Its castle was constructed in 1377 on the slopes of a hill by the Hungarian king Louis I to control the road connecting Brașov and Tara Bîrsei with Walachia. Today it houses a museum of regional folk art and ethnography.

BIBLIOG. V. Roth, Die deutsche Kunst in Siebenbürgen, Berlin, Sibiu, 1934; A. Husar, Dincolo de ruine, Bucharest, 1959; V. Vătășianu, Istoria artei feudale în Țările Romîne, I, Bucharest, 1959.

Brașov. Developed in the 12th-13th century, the city became in the 14th century one of the most important handicrafts, cultural, and commercial centers of Transylvania. Among its more interesting civil and ecclesiastical buildings is the Citadel of Stone, built in 1630 on an earlier wooden bastion, which is partially preserved. The Black Church, of the *Hallenkirche* type, is late Gothic, and was begun in the 14th century; the interior was restored after the fire of 1689; its portals have a richly sculptured decoration. It contains a fine collection of Oriental carpets from the 17th and 18th centuries. The Church of St. Bartholomew (1260), of Gothic-Cistercian style, was transformed after a fire in the second half of the 15th century; it has capitals using plant motifs. The city hall (about 1420) was constructed around a tower and is now very much altered. It is used as a city museum. The Church of St. Nicholas of Schei (Orthodox) is made of stone; it was built between the end of the 15th and the beginning of the 16th century on an earlier wooden church; in spite of numerous transformations it preserves frescoes of the 16th century. The church contains valuable medieval works of art.

BIBLIOG. N. Iorga, Brașovul și romînii (S. și doc., X), Bucharest, 1905; N. Iorga, Picturi și obiecte de artă din biserica Scheilor Brașovului, B. Com. Mon. Ist., XVII, 1925, pp. 8-11· V. Roth, Die deutsche Kunst in Siebenbürgen, Berlin, Sibiu, 1934; C. C. Muslea, Biserica sf. Nicolae din Scheii Brașovului, 2 vols., Brașov, 1938; V. Vătășianu, Istoria artei feudale în Țările Romîne, I, Bucharest, 1959.

Făgăraș. A citadel constructed in 1310 and rebuilt in the 17th century, Făgăraș belonged to those voivodes of Walachia who also bore the title of dukes of Făgăraș. It is one of the most impressive and famous rock fortresses of Transylvania. Although in ruins, its outer walls with angular towers, part of the rooms, and the ancient prison have been preserved.

BIBLIOG. A. Husar, Dincolo de ruine, Bucharest, 1959; V. Vătășianu, Istoria artei feudale în Țările Romîne, I, Bucharest, 1959.

Rîșnov. Initially a fortress built in the 14th century by the peasants of the region with a vast powerful outer wall, six towers, and dwellings for the population, it is in ruins. The outer wall and the fallen towers have been partially preserved.

BIBLIOG. A. Husar, Dincolo de ruine, Bucharest, 1959; V. Vătășianu, Istoria artei feudale în Țările Romîne, I, Bucharest, 1959.

Sibiu. A city recorded in the documents of the 12th century (Cibinium), it was from the beginning of the 14th century extremely important for its handicrafts and trade activities; in 1376 it possessed 19 guilds which practised 25 trades. From the beginning of the 15th century the importance of cultural life in Sibiu was demonstrated by the presence of public libraries, a print shop, schools, and a theater. The turreted walls were erected against the permanent danger of attack by the Turks. In 1699, following plans of Morando Visconti, new towers and bastions were raised, and a complex defensive system of lakes and canals was constructed. Among the city's important historical monuments is a Gothic church of the 14th century. The Bruckenthal Museum, installed in an imposing baroque palace of the second half of the 18th century, is the second most important art museum in the country; it contains representative works of western painting, folk art, applied arts, graphic arts, archaeology, and weapons. In the library are manuscripts, maps, music manuscripts, and coins.

BIBLIOG. V. Roth, Die deutsche Kunst in Siebenbürgen, Berlin, Sibiu, 1934; E. Schileru, Centenarul Muzeul Brukenthal, S. și cercetări de istoria artei, I, 1954, pp. 169-84; V. Vătășianu, Istoria artei feudale în Țările Romîne, I, Bucharest, 1959; N. Lupu and C. Irimie, Sibiu și împrejurimi, Bucharest, 1962.

Sighișoara. A city founded by the Saxons on the site of an old fort and mentioned in documents of 1298, it is medieval in appearance. Some of the towers are well preserved (towers of the Jewelers, Tailors, Butchers, Blacksmiths, and Dyers); they were built by the city's craft guilds after the Tatar invasions of the 12th century. The Clock Tower houses the historical museum of the city. The 14th-century *Bergkirche*, built originally on the basilica plan with three aisles, and transformed in 1483 into a *Hallenkirche* is noteworthy. The sculptured stone decoration, in Gothic style (Adoration of the Magi), is outstanding. There are fragments of frescoes, also Gothic, of the 14th century, and wooden chairs, sculptured and inlaid by Johann Reychmut in 1523.

BIBLIOG. V. Roth, Die deutsche Kunst in Siebenbürgen, Berlin, Sibiu, 1934 (full bibliog.); H. Ursu, Sighișoara et ses environs, Bucharest, 1944; V. Vătășianu, Istoria artei feudale în Țările Romîne, I, Bucharest, 1959.

Tilișca. At the eastern end of the Sebeș mountains, on the site of a Hallstatt settlement, a Dacian fortress was recently uncovered with the same defensive system as the previously known citadels (see Grădiştea Muncelului). The finds of this excavation are preserved in the Bruckenthal Museum of Sibiu.

Cluj. Căşeiu. The remains of an important Roman castrum on the northern limes of Dacia can still be seen. Built on a square plan (540 × 540 ft.) it has stone walls and on each side a door flanked by two semicircular bastions, with another bastion of the same shape between it and the corner. The corner itself is reinforced by a trapezoidal bastion. On the inside of the west wall there is a series of buttresses that probably supported a guard's round platform.

Bibliog. C. Daicoviciu, Notite arheologice şi epigrapice, Anuarul Cluj Inst. de s. clasice, I, 2, 1928–32, pp. 58–63; E. Panaitescu, Castrul roman de la Căşei, Anuarul Com. Mon. Ist., Secţia pentru Transilvania, II, 1929, pp. 321–42; E. Panaitescu, Le limes dacique, B. Section historique de l'Acad. romaine, XV, 1929, pp. 77–82; V. Christescu, Consideraţiuni asupra unei stele funerare de la Căşei, Rev. ist. română, II, 1932, pp. 267–88; V. Christescu, Istoria militară a Dacici Romane, Bucharest, 1937, pp. 63, 86, 91, 131, 133, 136–37, 183; D. Adamesteanu, EAA, s.v.

Cluj (Napoca). The site of an ancient Dacian center, it later became a flourishing Roman colony called Napoca. Mentioned as the residence of a courtier in 1173, destroyed by the Tatars in 1241, the city was slowly rebuilt; in 1316 it was given the status of *civitas.* Important in the Middle Ages as a trade, handicrafts, artistic, and cultural center, the city enjoyed royal privileges. In 1405 Sigismund of Luxemburg granted the city the right to build walls to enclose it. Over the centuries it became the most important urban center of Transylvania and is now one of the largest cities in Romania. The Church of St. Michael, late Gothic (mid-14th to 2d half of 15th cent.), is of the *Hallenkirche* type. The Reformed Church (called the church of Matthias Corvinus), formerly belonging to the Minorite Monastery, was begun in 1484 and finished a century later; it has a polygonal choir and decoration in flamboyant Gothic style. The library of the University possesses a collection of medieval manuscripts; the Museum of Archaeology of the Historical Institute contains Roman and medieval sculpture.

Bibliog. S. Pacsu, I. Pataki, and V. Popa, Clujul, Cluj, 1957; V. Vătăşianu, Istoria artei feudale în Ţările Romîne, I, Bucharest, 1959.

Moigrad (Παράλισσον, Παρέλισσον, Porolissum, Paralissum). Near this village, dispersed on hills, lie the ruins of Porolissum, a Dacian center, which, at the time of Trajan, was one of the most important border cities in Dacia. Excavations have traced the outline of the Dacian village area, fortified by a rampart and an inner moat, and a large crematory necropolis. The city gave its name to Dacia Porolissensis. At the time of Septimius Severus, Porolissum was elevated to the rank of a municipality. Two castra (one of which had been abandoned after the Marcomannic War) and the urban center have been excavated from Roman times. Among the monuments are the so-called "Terrace of the Sanctuaries" (which includes the Temple of the goddess Suria and Liber Pater, later replaced by the eastern deity Bel), the baths, a gymnasium, and an amphitheater. After Dacia was abandoned by the Romans, Porolissum declined. With the arrival of the Slavs (6th–7th cent.), who gave the name of Moigrad to the village, even the name of the ancient Daco-Roman center was lost.

Bibliog. A Buday, Porolissumból (Archaeological Research at Porolissum), Erdélyi Muzeum, XXV, 1908, pp. 337–48, XXVI, 1909, pp. 26–34; A. Buday, Porolissumból, Dolgozatok Erdélyi nemzeti muzeum (Cluj), II, 1911, pp. 70–105, V, 1914, pp. 67–94, VI, 1915, pp. 51–111; C. Daicoviciu, Neue Mitteilungen aus Dazien, Dacia, VII–VIII, 1937–40, pp. 299–366 at 323; A. Stein, Dacian nach dem Bruderkrieg im Hause des Severus, 1942; A. Radnóti, A dáciai limes a Meszesen (The Dacian Limes at Mt. Meszen), Archaeol. Ertesitö, 3d ser., V–VI, 1944–45, pp. 137–68; M. Moga et al., Traiul populaţiei Daco-Romane şi barbare la graniţa de vest a Daciei: Activitatea şantierului arheologic Porolissum, S. şi cercetări de ist. veche, I, 1950, pp. 131–35; M. Macrea, D. Protase and M. Russu, Şantierul arheologic Porolissum Materiale şi cercetări arheologice, IV, 1958, pp. 361–90, V, 1959, pp. 485–504; C. Daicoviciu, RE, s.v. Porolissum.

Dobruja (Dobrogea). Adamclisi (Tropaeum Traiani). Near this village are the ruins of a large trophaeum and a neighboring Roman city. Constructed, according to prevailing opinion, at the time of Trajan's rule to commemorate a great victory over the Dacians, the trophaeum (100 ft. high, 95 ft. in diameter) consisted of a cylindrical structure whose top part was decorated with a frieze (IV, PL. 111) and a denticulated parapet. This was covered by a conical roof under which the pedestal that supported the trophy was mounted. Next to the trophaeum the remains of a mausoleum, which does not seem to be of the same period as the triumphal monument, were found. The city, elevated to the rank of a municipality under

the Severus emperors, was destroyed in the 3d century, completely reconstructed in the 4th century by Constantine and Licinius, and destroyed at the time of the Slavo-Avarian invasions. Among the monuments of the late-Roman city are the circumference wall with two gates and heavy oval towers; a well-paved *via principalis*; six basilicas of which only one, conventionally called *forensis*, is of a secular nature; a cistern and a small catacomb basilica outside the walls. A local museum is being built to house the sculptured decorations of the trophaeum, which are now in the Bucharest National Museum of Antiquities.

Bibliog. *On the trophaeum*: G. Tocilescu, O. Benndorf, and G. Niemann, Das Monument von Adamklissi: Tropaeni Traiani, Vienna, 1895; E. Petersen, Sul monumento di Adamklissi, RM, XI, 1896, pp. 302–16; A. Furtwängler, Das Tropaion von Adamklissi, Munich, 1903; G. Cichorius, Die römische Denkmäler in der Dobrudscha, Berlin, 1904; F. Studniczka, Tropaeum Traiani, Leipzig, 1904; T. Antonescu, Le Trophée d'Adamclissi, Iassi, 1905; V. Pârvan, Getica, Bucharest, 1926, pp. 122–25; S. Ferri, Arte romana sul Danubio, Milan, 1933, pp. 372–78; S. Ferri, Nuovi documenti relativi al Trofeo di Traiano nella Mesia Inferiore, Ann. R. Scuola normale superiore di Pisa, N.S., II, 1933, pp. 369–75; R. Vulpe, Histoire ancienne de la Dobroudja, Bucharest, 1938, pp. 143–55; F. Bobu Florescu, Monumentul de la Adamklissi: Tropaeum Traiani, 2d ed., Bucharest, 1959. *On the city*: V. Pârvan, Cetatea Tropaeum, Bucharest, 1911 (repr. from B. Com. Mon. Ist., IV, 1911, pp. 163–91); R. Vulpe, Histoire ancienne de la Dobroudja, Bucharest, 1938, passim.

Capidava. A pre-Roman Getic village, on the eastern bank of the Danube, it was at first a simple military station for privileged soldiers and a customs post, and only later assumed the character of a town. A castrum (430 × 320 ft.) was installed here at the time of Trajan, destroyed by the Goths in 248, reconstructed during the reign of Aurelian, and at the end of the 4th and the beginning of the 6th century. From the 10th to the 11th century a small village was sheltered in the ruins of the Roman fortress. The powerful outer walls preserve the general form of the restorations made during the Aurelian period; seven outer towers of varying shapes (rectangular, oval, rectangular with rounded front) and a gate remain.

Bibliog. G. Florescu, R. Florescu, P. Diaconu, Capidava I, Bucharest, 1958, pp. 1–245 (bibliog.); D. Adamesteanu, EAA, s.v.

Constanţa (Τόμις, Τομύς, rarer, Τόμοι, Tomis, Tomi). A modern port on the Black Sea, it was founded by Constantine the Great as Constantiana on the site of ancient Tomis, a colony founded by Miletus probably at the end of the 6th century B.C. Of little importance during the archaic and classic periods, Tomis is mentioned in documents only in the 3d century B.C. After the conquest of Dobruja in 28 B.C. it accepted the protectorate of the Roman Empire. Ovid was exiled to Tomis and died there. Between A.D. 15 and 46 the *praefectus orae maritimae* resided at Tomis, as the Pontarch of the Pontic community (Pentapolis or Hexapolis) did later; in A.D. 46 it was included in the province of Moesia Inferior. After the reorganization of the Empire under Diocletian, Tomis was made the capital of the new province of Scythia Minor and, following the triumph of Christianity, became the seat of the bishopric. Excavations have brought to light a section of the outer wall from Justinian's period, imposing fragments of architecture, sculpture, epigraphs, and various necropolises from the Hellenistic to the late Roman period. A building of exceptionally large proportions is built on three terraces that are cut into the high coast on the sea; the first two terraces have a series of storehouses, the third a portico paved in polychrome mosaics (plant and geometric designs). Two large Christian basilicas with crypts (5th–6th cent.) document the importance of Tomis in this period. Among the numerous mosques remaining from the long Turkish domination (15th–19th cent., when the city was called Küstenja), the Hunchiar Mosque (mid-18th cent.) is outstanding. Constanţa is today a maritime city. It has an Archaeological Museum and a Museum of Modern Art.

Bibliog. B. Pick and K. Regling, Die antiken Münzen von Dacien und Moesian, II, 1, Berlin, 1910, pp. 587–917; D. M. Teodorescu, Monumente inedite din Tomi, B. Com. Mon. Ist., VII, 1914, pp. 180–92, VIII, 1915, pp. 6–20, 74–87, 186–89; V. Pârvan, Zidul cetăţii Tomi, Analele Acad. Romăne, 2d ser., XXXVII, 1915, pp. 415–50; R. Netzhammer, Die christlichen Altertümer der Dobruscha, Bucharest, 1918, pp. 15–112; E. Coliu, Un sarcophage à symboles à Tomis, Istros, I, 1934, pp. 81–116; R. Vulpe, Histoire ancienne de la Dobroudja, Bucharest, 1938, pp. 62–383 passim; I. Barnea, Creştinismul în Scythia Minor după inscripţii, S. teologice, VI, 1954, pp. 65–107; I. Barnea, Quelques considérations sur les inscriptions chrétiennes de la Scythe Mineure, Dacia, N.S., I, 1957, pp. 265–88; R. Vulpe, Tomi al tempo di Ovidio, S. romani, VI, 1958, pp. 629–48; G. Bordenache, Attività edilizia a Tomi nel II secolo dell'e. n., Dacia, N.S., IV, 1960, pp. 255–72; I. Stoian, Tomitana: Contribuţii epigrafice la istoria cetăţii Tomis, Bucharest, 1962; C. Canarache and others, Tezaurul de sculpturi dela Tomis, Bucharest, 1963.

Garvăn Bisericuța (Dinogeția). A late-Roman fortress (from the time of Diocletian to Constantine the Great) is located on a small island in the Danube (mod. Bisericuța) that faces the present rural center of Garvăn. Trapezoidal in form, with 3 doors and 14 towers in the shape of a horseshoe, the fortress was reconstructed many times between the 4th and the 6th centuries. It was abandoned toward the end of the 6th century when the boundary line was broken by Slavo-Avarian attacks. Three centuries later the Byzantine Empire installed a garrison in the abandoned fortress (in the period between John Zimisces and the Comneni), and exploited the wealth of the river and surrounding lakes. On the ruins of this last Byzantine level are the remains of poor dwellings and a small church of the 10th–12th century. The household goods that were recovered show evidence of relations with Byzantium and Kiev.

BIBLIOG. G. Ştefan, Dinogetia I, Dacia, VII–VIII, 1937–40, pp. 401–25; I. Barnea, Byzance, Kiev et l'Orient sur le Bas-Danube du Xᵉ au XIIᵉ siècle, Nouvelles études d'histoire, Bucharest, 1955, pp. 169–80; G. Ştefan, La Legio I Iovia et la défense de la frontière danubienne au IVᵉ siècle de notre ère, Nouvelles études d'histoire, Bucharest, 1955, pp. 161–67; D. Adamesteanu and G. Ştefan, EAA, s.v., Dinogetia; I. Barnea, Garvăn-Dinogetia, Bucharest, 1962.

Igliţa (Troesmis). A fortified center on the lower Danube, first Thraco-Getic, then Roman, in A.D. 46 it was included within Moesia province and in A.D. 86 in Moesia Inferior. Destroyed many times (in the 3d and 5th cent.) and reconstructed, it was finally permanently destroyed in the 6th century by the Slavo-Avarian attacks. Two distinct parts formed Troesmis — the old town and the canabae of the fifth Macedonian legion; both merged into a municipality at the time of Marcus Aurelius. Most of the epigraphical materials found at Troesmis are in the Louvre. The western walls of the fortress (built on the old Geta center) have been partially excavated.

BIBLIOG. E. Desjardins, Sur quelques inscriptions inédites de Valachie et de Bulgarie, AnnInst, XL, 1868, pp. 5–107 at 58; CIL, III, pp. 145, 999; G. Tocilescu, Monumente epigrafice şi sculpturali, Bucharest, 1902, pp. 56–82; V. Pârvan, Descoperiri nouă în Scythia Minor, Analele Acad. Române, Mem. secţiunii ist., 2d ser., XXXV, 1913, pp. 401–502; R. Vulpe, Histoire ancienne de la Dobroudja, Bucharest, 1938, passim; R. Vulpe, Canabenses e Troesmenses, S. şi cercetări de ist. veche, IV, 1953, pp. 557–82; A. Betz, RE, s.v. Troesmis.

Istria ('Ιστρος, 'Ιστρία, 'Ιστρίη, Histria). The village is about 5 miles from the ancient Milesian colony of Istros founded on the coast of the Black Sea in 657 B.C. (Eusebius-Hieronymus, Chronicon, ed. Helm, Berlin, 1956, p. 956b). The port was buried by sand, apparently at the end of the Hellenistic period. The imposing ruins

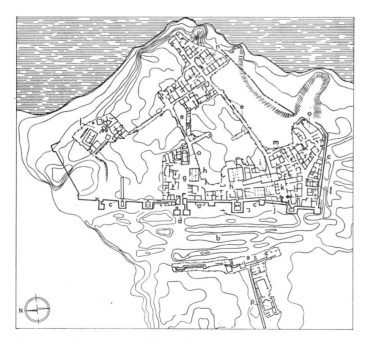

Istria, plan of the old city. (a) Hellenistic wall; (b) earthwork ramparts (6th–7th cent.); (c) late-Roman circumference wall (4th–6th cent.); (d) main gate; (e) streets of Byzantine-Roman period; (f) sacred area of the Greek city (5th–1st cent. B.C.); (g) square of Byzantine-Roman period; (h) public buildings of basilican type; (i) trade building; (j) square with portico; (k) Roman baths; (l) business district (5th–6th cent.); (m) residential district; (n) district with residential houses, domus type; (o) Christian basilicas; (p) Christian basilica outside the walls.

are on the banks of Lake Sinoe. Istria flourished during the archaic and classical periods; in the 3d century it entered a period of crisis caused by the incursions of the hinterland tribes who had united under the authority of local kings. Istria entered the zone of Roman influence in the 1st century B.C., had a temporary rebirth from the 2d to the 3d century until the Carpatho-Gothic attacks (in 238) finally destroyed the small Pontic city. The Slavo-Avarian attacks of the 6th–7th century put an end to its existence. Some of the more important monuments discovered are a sacred area from the archaic and classic periods (a so-called "Temple of Aphrodite," several altars, anathema bases, the remains of a small Hellenistic temple dedicated to Θεὸς Μέγας); four outer walls, two from the Greek period and two from the Roman, the last of which (3d–4th cent.) has towers and bastions on a rectangular plan and constitutes one of the most monumental walls to have survived; large buildings of the Roman and Roman-Byzantine city, including a small square surrounded by porticoes, baths, six basilicas, a zone of residential housing, and a section of smaller insula houses. The collection of epigraphs, ceramics, and sculpture is in the Bucharest National Museum of Antiquities, in the small museum near the ruins, and in the Constanţa Archaeological Museum.

BIBLIOG. V. Pârvan, Histria IV, Analele Acad. Române, 2d ser., XXXVIII, 1916, pp. 533–732; V. Pârvan, Histria, VII, Analele Acad. Române, 3d ser., II, 1923–24, pp. 1–132; V. Pârvan, Fouilles d'Histria, Dacia, II, 1925, pp. 198–248; S. Lambrino, Fouilles d'Histria, Dacia, III–IV, 1927–28, pp. 378–410; S. Lambrino, Histria romaine à la lumière des fouilles, REL, IX, 1931, pp. 77–83; M. Lambrino, La céramique d'Histria: Série rhodo-ionienne, Bucharest, 1938; L. Buzdugan et al., Originea şi desvoltara aşe-zărilor omeneşti depe literalul Mării Negre, I: Rezultatul săpăturilor de la Istria, S. şi cercetări de ist. veche, I, 1950, pp. 75–82; E. Condurachi et al., Cercetările arheologice efectuate in campania anului 1950 la Histria, S. şi cercetări de ist. veche, II, 1951, pp. 127–58; C. Calinescu et al., Săpă-turile arheologice din 1951 pe şantierul Histria, S. şi cercetări de ist. veche, III, 1952, pp. 231–80; E. Condurachi et al., Campania de cercetări arheo-logice dela Histria, S. şi cercetări de ist. veche, IV, 1953, pp. 90–152; Histria I: Monografie arheologica, Bucharest, 1954; G. Ştefan et al., Rezultatele cercetărilor arheologice pe şantierul dela Histria, S. şi cercetări de ist. veche, V, 1954, pp. 69–117; E. Condurachi, Der Beitrag der Münzfunde von Istros zur Kenntnis des Waren und Geldumlaufes an der unteren Donau im vorrömischen Zeitraum, Wissenschaftliche Ann., VI, 1957, pp. 289–304; E. Condurachi, Histria à l'époque du Bas-Empire d'après les dernières fouilles archéologiques, Dacia, N.S., I, 1957, pp. 245–64; E. Condurachi et al., Şantierul arheologic Histria, Materiale şi cercetări arheologice, IV, 1957, pp. 9–102; D. M. Pippidi, Contribuţii la istoria veche a Romîniei, Bucharest, 1958, pp. 13–213; D. M. Pippidi, Les fouilles d'Istros (1914–57), BCH, LXXXII, 1958, pp. 335–50; G. Bordenache and D. M. Pippidi, Le temple du Θεὸς Μέγας à Istros, BCH, LXXXIII, 1959, pp. 455–65; E. Condurachi, Histria, Bucharest, 1959; D. M. Pippidi, Der sogenannte Aphroditentempel zu Istros, Ethn.-archaeol. Forsch., VI, 1959, pp. 62–82; D. M. Pippidi et al., Raport asupra activitatii santierului Histria în cam-pania, Materiale si cercetari arheologice, V, 1959, pp. 283–328; G. Borde-nache, Histria alla luce del suo materiale scultoreo, Dacia, N.S., V, 1961, pp. 185–211; G. Bordenache, EAA, s.v. Histria.

Mangalia (Κάλλατις, Callatis). An important Doric colony of Heraclea Pontica, it was founded toward the end of the 6th century B.C. In 313 B.C. it took part in the revolt of the Pontic cities against Lysimachus; later it became the ally of Mithridates VI Eupator, and was conquered by Burbista toward 50 B.C.; in the Roman period it flourished. It was destroyed between the end of the 6th and the beginning of the 7th century by the Slavo-Avars. In the 10th century a village was built on the ruins of the Roman-Byzantine city. In the 13th and 16th centuries it was recorded as an important port under the new name of Mangalia. Its principal monuments are: walls of isodomic blocks from the late-Roman period, reconstructed on an outline of the 4th century B.C.; a fine basilica from the Roman-Byzantine period (5th–6th cent.) with a colonnaded atrium; and important Greek and Roman necropolises, both level and tumular. There is a local museum with architectural, sculptural, and epigraphic materials.

BIBLIOG. T. Sauciuc-Saveanu, Callatis, Dacia, I, 1924, pp. 108–65; II, 1925, pp. 104–47, III–IV, 1927–32, pp. 411–34, 435–82, V–VI, 1935–36, pp. 247–78, 279–319, VII–VIII, 1937–40, pp. 223–81, IX–X, 1941–44, pp. 243–347; T. Sauciuc-Saveanu, Callatis, L'archéologie en Roumanie, Bucharest, 1938, pp. 51–79; G. Bordenache, Antichità greche e romane nel nuovo Museo di Mangalia, Dacia, N.S., IV, 1960, pp. 489–509; C. Preda, Callatis, Bucharest, 1963; Vulič, RE, s.v. Kallatis; D. Adamesteanu, EAA, s.v. Callatis.

Pantelimon de Sus (Ulmetum). Near this rural center are the ruins of Ulmetum, a village probably founded at the time of Trajan and destroyed by the Avars at the end of the 6th century. In the 3d century, under pressure of the Goths, or perhaps in the 4th century, a castrum was constructed which underwent many restorations. Its remains — the boundary walls as well as the constructions contained within them — belong to the 6th century. It has the unusual shape of a section of a circle (ca. 460 × 530 ft.) with 13 outer towers of different shapes and sizes, 3 round, 4 semicircular, and 6 rectangular; on the inside there is an apsidal construction, which was perhaps the *praetorium*.

BIBLIOG. V. Pârvan, Cetatea Ulmetum, Analele Acad. Române, 2d ser., XXXIV, 1912, pp. 495–607, XXXVI, 1913, pp. 245–328, 329–40, XXXVII, 1915, pp. 265–304; R. Vulpe, Histoire ancienne de la Dobroudj, Bucharest, 1938, passim; I. I. Russu, Vicus Ultinsium, S. și cercetări de ist. veche, VIII, 1957, pp. 311–15.

Slava-Rusă (Ibida). Near this rural center are the remains of the outer walls, with numerous towers and three gates, of the Roman-Byzantine city of Ibida. Excavations have uncovered a basilica with a nave, two aisles, three apses, and some marble capitals.

BIBLIOG. R. Netzhammer, Die christlichen Altertümer der Dobrudscha, Bucharest, 1918, pp. 154–56; R. Vulpe, Histoire ancienne de la Dobroudja, Bucharest, 1938, passim; I. Barnea, Nouvelles considérations sur les basiliques chrétiennes de la Dobroudja, Dacia, XI–XII, 1945–47, pp. 221–41; R. Vulpe, Cercetările din sectorul Camena-Slava Rusă-Babadag, S. și cercetări de ist. veche, V, 1954, pp. 110–12; G. Bordenache, EAA, s.v. Ibida.

Hunedoara. Alba Iulia (Apulum). The Roman city of Apulum, first a municipality (Municipium Aurelium Apulense), then a colony (Colonia Aurelia Apulensis), was developed on an earlier Dacian center near the castrum where the *Legio XIII Gemina* was stationed. Abundant material from the Roman period has been found: figured polychrome mosaics, ceramics, glass, lanterns, votive and funerary reliefs, clay and bronze statuettes, huge imperial statues, and portrait statues. The new city, perhaps the seat of a Slavo-Romanian voivodate in the 9th and 10th centuries, is mentioned as a *civitas* in the 12th and 13th centuries. In 1599–1600 it was conquered by Mihai Viteazul, voivode of Walachia. In 1658 and 1661 it was devastated by the Turks. Beginning in 1699 (when the principality of Transylvania came under the rule of the House of Austria), Alba Iulia lost its cultural and political importance and became a small military center. Between 1714 and 1738 Charles VI of Austria ordered a powerful fortress to be erected on the site of the old Roman castrum and the medieval city. This imposing work of military art, reminiscent of the classical style, was designed by the Italian architect G. M. Visconti. The Roman Catholic Cathedral, built in 1246–1300 on an older Romanesque church, is one of the most outstanding medieval monuments of Transylvania; built on a basilica plan, it has a nave and two aisles with semicircular apses, a transept, two towers to the west, and a tower over the transept and the choir. The old Romanesque portal is now located on the south façade and there is a Gothic portal on the western façade. In 1512, a Renaissance chapel was added. On the inside are a Gothic altar of the 14th century, sarcophagi, and tombstones. The Library, called Batthyaneum, once a monastery which became a cultural institute in 1792, contains 1200 manuscripts and 530 incunabula. The Orthodox Cathedral (1921–22), built on the model of the princely church of Tîrgoviște, is surrounded by an open portico that contains the lapidary collection of the adjoining Alba Iulia Regional Museum.

BIBLIOG. I. Berciu, Alba Iulia, scurtă privire istorică, Alba Julia, 1943; G. Entz, La cathédrale de Gyulafehérvár (Alba Julia), Acta h. artium, V, 1958, pp. 1–40; V. Vătășianu, Istoria artei feudale în Țările Romîne, I, Bucharest, 1959; A. Popa and I. Berciu, Cetatea Alba Iulia, Bucharest, 1962; D. Adamesteanu, EAA, s.v. Apulum.

Bănița. On Dealul Cetății hill, near Petroșani, a fortress was recently excavated with imposing walls of stone blocks, a tower, and a monumental stairway. The citadel guarded the road that led from the plain south of the Carpathians toward the Dacian center of Sarmizegetusa.

Demuș. The village, about 11 miles from Sarmizegetusa, is famous for a small stone church (13th–14th cent.) with a form unique in Romania; it is built on the Greek cross plan with a semicircular apse and a small central bell tower supported by four pilasters. Roman material was reutilized in the outer wall facing as well as in the pavement. There are remains of a fresco from the 15th century.

BIBLIOG. V. Vătășianu, Istoria artei feudale în Țările Romîne, I, Bucharest, 1959.

Hunedoara. The castle, constructed in several stages on a rocky peak during the second half of the 14th century, has a very complex plan. Ceded in 1409 by the king of Hungary, Sigismund, to Voicu, a courtier, it became a powerful military fortress under Ioan de Hunedoara, son of Voicu. At the beginning of the second half of the 15th century the building was altered; the work was completed about 1480 under Matthias Corvinus. The Room of the Knights

has columns of red marble and Gothic vaults, the Diet Hall is restored, and the chapel has Gothic sculptured decoration; the north wing, constructed by Matthias Corvinus, has loggias with partly preserved frescoes, towers, bastions, and monumental stairs.

BIBLIOG. V. Vătășianu, Istoria artei feudale în Țările Romîne, I, Bucharest, 1959; O. Velescu, Castelul de la Hunedoara, Bucharest, 1962 (bibliog.).

Grădiștea Muncelului (Sarmizegetusa). South of the limes on the hills along the banks of the Apa Orașului that runs down from the Orăștie mountains are the ruins of an entire system of fortifications and citadels that can be dated as belonging to the period of maximum development of the Dacian state (ca. 100 B.C.–A.D. 100).

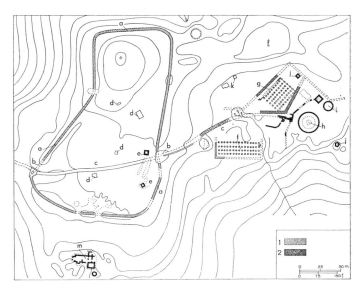

Grădiștea Muncelului, (Sarmizegetusa), plan. *Key:* (1) Dacian walls of phase I; (2) Dacian walls of phase II. Principal structures: (*a*) circumference walls; (*b*) gates; (*c*) ancient roads; (*d*) wooden huts; (*e*) Roman structures; (*f*) older large sanctuary; (*g*) later large sanctuary; (*h*) large round sanctuary; (*i*) small round sanctuary; (*j*) towers; (*k*) warehouses; (*l*) workshop; (*m*) Roman baths (*from C. and H. Daicoviciu, 1961*).

The river Apa Orașului constitutes the central axis of this fortified zone, which, starting from the village of Costești, terminates with the citadel of Sarmizegetusa at Grădiștea Muncelului, about 4,000 ft. above sea level. The other fortresses, called by Tacitus "castles on sloping mountains" and by Dion Cassius "mountains reinforced by walls," are those of Costești, Blidaru, and Piatra Roșie, which constitute a unique complex. To the east are the fortresses of Căpîlna and Tilișca (northwest of Sibiu), and much further to the south is the citadel of Bănița, near Petroșani. All these fortresses and the numerous isolated towers were destroyed by the Romans in A.D. 106, during the second Dacian war. For the temporary quartering of troops before the final siege of the capital of Decebalus, the Romans constructed a series of castra with earth ramparts all around the area.

The most important Dacian citadel was Sarmizegetusa at Grădiștea Muncelului, capital of the Dacian kingdom and residence of the Dacian kings. Its walls were reconstructed by the Romans for the use of the garrison. A sacred area, entered by means of a paved road about 330 ft. in length, indicates that Sarmizegetusa was also an important religious center of the Dacians. Many sacred buildings have been excavated including some, most characteristic of the Dacian civilization, constructed of four to six parallel rows of cylindrical bases supporting andesite columns which do not seem to have supported a roof. There are also other temples, some on rectangular plans but of smaller size, and others on a circular plan. A paved square among the sanctuaries, with lateral drainage canals, used probably for ceremonies and sacrifices, completes this monumental complex. Most of the material discovered at the site is kept in the Archaeological Museum of Cluj; the rest is in the National Museum of Antiquities in Bucharest.

Near the village of Costești, on a hill called Cetățuia, are the ruins of another Dacian fortress that blocked the northern approach toward the complex of fortifications which defended the capital of Sarmizegetusa. An earth rampart surrounded the oval platform on the hill's summit, while toward the east-southeast, behind the rampart, was a powerful wall built in the specifically Dacian technique of large blocks connected by beams, the spaces between filled with earth and stone, and furnished with three outer tower bastions. Isolated towers on the slope defended the approach to the fortress. A wooden palisade surrounded the platform behind the wall and on the highest point were two dwelling towers with the ground floor of stone and earth and the upper floor of wood. A stone stairway ran from the palisade up to the first dwelling tower. Two cisterns and four temples with rows of stone bases to support wooden columns have been excavated.

The second fortress that defended the approach to the capital is on Mount Blidaru (ca. 2,300 feet above sea level). It was equipped with two outer stone walls, built during successive periods. The older wall contained a large dwelling tower and towers at the corners; the second wall contained, in addition to the towers at the corner, a series of storage chambers for arms and provisions. Outside the walls was a cistern dug in the rock and made watertight with a wall covered by a thick layer of *opus signinum*.

In the western zone of the mountainous group of the Piatra Roşie (ca. 2,700 ft. above sea level), almost isolated among the surrounding mountains, is a fortress (ca. 330×150 ft.) with five interior towers. A wide paved street, alternating with series of stairs, gave access to the city. On the inside of the fortress the plinth of a rectangular building has been preserved. Later, a second wall was added in order to include some terraces and two towers which had originally been on the exterior. Two other towers completed the defensive system. The remains of a sanctuary with rows of column bases confirm the frequency of this type of construction in all the Dacian fortresses.

BIBLIOG. D. M. Teodorescu, Cercetări arheologice în munţii Hunedoarei, Cluj, 1923; V. Pârvan, Getica, Bucharest, 1926; D. M. Teodorescu, Cetatea dacă de la Costeşti, Anuarul Com. Ist., Secţia pentru Transilvania, II, 1929, pp. 265–98; D. M. Teodorescu, Cetatea dacă de la Grădiştea, Muncelulei, Anuarul Com. Mon. Ist., Secţia pentru Transilvania, III, 1930–31, pp. 45–58; C. Daicoviciu, Aşezările dacice din munţii Orăştiei, Bucharest, 1951; C. Daicoviciu, Cetatea dacica de la Piatra Roşie, Bucharest, 1954; H. Daicoviciu, Il tempio-calendario dacico di Sarmizegetusa, Dacia, N.S., IV, 1960, pp. 231–54; C. and H. Daicoviciu, Sarmizegetusa, Bucharest, 1961. See also the reports in S. şi cercetări de ist. veche, I–VI, 1950–55, and Materiale şi cercetări arheologice, III ff., 1957 ff.

Sarmizegetusa (Ulpia Traiana). Now a modern village, it was formerly called Grădişte. Nearby are the imposing ruins of Ulpia Traiana, capital of the province of Dacia, founded by Trajan between 108 and 110 with the rank of a colony. The original name was Colonia Ulpia Traiana Augusta Dacica. In Hadrian's time the name of Sarmizegetusa took the place of the older name and came to be preferred to it. The prosperity of Sarmizegetusa, which reached its peak at the beginning of the 3d century, continued even after the abandonment of Dacia, until the 4th century. The city was built on a rectangular plan (ca. 1,600×2,000 ft.), and had important public and private buildings some of which are: the remains of a Mithraeum, temples to the Syrian gods, to the goddess Nemesis, to Jupiter Dolichenus, especially the imposing *aedes augustalium*, as well as a forum in the style of Trajan's time. Outside the city excavations have uncovered an amphitheater, suburban and country villas, and several necropolises, in one of which is the circular mausoleum of the Aurelia family of the 2d century of our era. Part of the excavated material is preserved in the Archaeological Museum of Deva and part in the local Archaeological Museum.

BIBLIOG. C. Daicoviciu, Fouilles et recherches à Sarmizegetusa, Dacia, I, 1924, pp. 224–63, III–IV, 1927–32, pp. 516–56; C. Daicoviciu, Sarmizegetusa (Ulpia Traiana), Cluj, 1939; O. Floca, Săpăturile arheologice din jud. Hunedoara, S. şi cercetări de ist. veche, I, 1950, pp. 108–10; C. Daicoviciu, Sarmizegetusa et ses environs, Bucharest, 1955; C. and H. Daicoviciu, Ulpia Traiana, Bucharest, 1962.

Veţel (Micia). A Roman center of Dacia along the valley of the Mureş, it developed around a castrum (in the western limes) which first had walls of earth and later (Antoninus Pius) of stone. The excavations have uncovered a temple with three cellae built by the local Mauretanians to their gods (Mauretanian troops had been stationed in Dacia since Trajan's period). The inscriptions record a temple of Isis and baths.

BIBLIOG. C. Daicoviciu, Micia I: Cercetări asupra castrului, Anuarul Com. Mon. Ist., Secţia pentru Transilvania, III, 1930–31, pp. 3–43; O. Floca, Descoperiri arheologice în ţinutul Hunedoara, Sargetia, I, 1937, pp. 64–66; N. Gostar, Vamile Daciei, S. şi cercetări de ist veche, II, 1951, pp. 165–82; O. Floca, Cîteva monumente epigrafice si sculpturale din epoca sclavagistă romana, Materiale şi cercetări arheologice, I, 1953, pp. 755–72; M. Macrea, Une nouvelle inscription latine de Dacie datant du IVe siècle, Dacia, N.S., II, 1958, pp. 467–72; M. Fluss, RE, s.v. Micia; E. Dorutiu, EAA, s.v. Micia.

Iaşi. Iaşi (Jassy). Toward the middle of the 16th century it became the capital of Moldavia and is one of the oldest cities of the region (recorded in 1408). Today one of the most important urban centers of Romania, it possesses churches of great artistic and historical importance such as Trei Ierarhi (Three Saints), constructed by workmen from Constantinople in 1639 and restored in the 19th century by the Frenchman Jean Lecomte du Noüy; it was built on a three-apsed plan with a tower over the cella and pronaos, raised on a squared and stellate double base. The façades are completely covered by sculptured stone decoration, originally gilded with eastern-style motifs. The church of the Golia Monastery was built in 1660 on an earlier church from the end of the 16th century. The façades are completely different from those of the Moldavian type as they were inspired by Italian architecture of the 17th century; they are decorated by massive pilasters terminating in Corinthian capitals, a frieze with brackets and consoles, a classical frame, and large gabled windows. The church has a baroque portal with stone sculpture with plant motifs of eastern derivation. Among the monumental buildings of the 19th century are the former Administrative Palace, today the seat of the Historical Museum of Moldavia; the University with an important library; the National Theater; and many villas surrounded by large gardens.

BIBLIOG. N. A. Bogdan, Oraşul Iaşi, Iassi, 1913; G. Balş, Bisericile moldoveneşti din veacurile XVII si XVIII, Bucharest, 1933; G. Ionescu, Istoria arhitecturii romîneşti, Bucharest, 1937; E. Condurachi, Iassy et ses environs, Bucharest, 1944.

Hîrlău. The village is known for the Church of St. George, constructed in 1492 by Stephen the Great; it is built on a three-apsed plan with a presbytery dome on vaults of the Moldavian type. Its decorative elements are Gothic in style. There are well-preserved frescoes inside.

BIBLIOG. Repertoriul monumentelor şi obiectelor de artă din timpu lui Ştefan cel Mare, Bucharest, 1958 (bibliog.).

Oltenia. Celei (Sucidava). A Dacian center on the north bank of the Danube, it became later a Roman city of lower Dacia. At the time of Trajan a castrum with earth walls was constructed there and reinforced in the 3d century with a rampart and moat. Constantine the Great constructed a new fortress and joined it at Oescus with a bridge of stone and wood; today, the visible parts of the fortress are the outer wall with seven double towers of square and trapezoidal form; inside are buildings used as dwellings or stalls. In the 6th century the citadel of Constantine was restored and inhabited by a Byzantine garrison which was maintained there until the time of Maritius Tiberius, when it was destroyed by the Slavo-Avarian attacks; there is a secret well reached by means of an underground passage. Inside the citadel is a Christian basilica, the oldest church of Dacia, with an apse, diaconicon, and an ambo (5th–6th cent.).

BIBLIOG. D. Tudor, Sucidava I–II, Dacia, V–VI, 1935–36, pp. 387–422, VII–VIII, 1937–40, pp. 359–400, XI–XII, 1945–47, pp. 145–208; D. Adamesteanu, Luigi Ferdinando Marsigli: il primo archeologo della Romania, Roma, XX, 1942, pp. 492–500; D. Tudor, Sucidava IV, Materiale arheologice privind istoria veche R.P.R., I, 1954, pp. 693–742; D. Tudor, Oltenia romană, 2d ed., Bucharest, 1958, passim; D. Tudor, Le dépot de miroirs de verre doublé de plomb trouvé à Sucidava, Dacia, N.S., III, 1959, pp. 415–32; D. Tudor and E. Bujor, Die geheime Brunnenanlage von Sucidava, Dacia, N.S., IV, 1960, pp. 541–52.

Slăveni. Near the village are the ruins of an important castrum on the Aluta (Olt) River boundary, constructed at the time of Trajan and Hadrian, reconstructed under Septimius Severus, and apparently abandoned shortly after the fall of Philip the Arabian. The castrum, of rectangular shape (460×400 ft.), has surrounding walls constructed in brick and a fortification comprising four ramparts. The remains of a Mithraeum are also of interest.

BIBLIOG. D. Tudor, Oltenia romană, 2d ed., Bucharest, 1958, passim.

Turnu Severin (Drobeta, Drubeta). Turnu Severin stands on an important Roman urban center which in turn had been constructed on a Dacian village. At the time of Trajan (103–05) a large bridge was constructed, the work of the architect Apollodorus (two pylons survive, one on the northeast bank of the Danube and another on the southwest bank), as well as a castrum that defended the bridge. The city, built north of the castrum, grew rapidly and became a municipality during Hadrian's time and a colony under Septimius Severus. Monuments which have come to light include the baths and a construction which may have been the gymnasium. The castrum, rectangular in form (450×405 ft.), with walls of stone and lime, had its principal streets flanked by colonnaded porticoes; destroyed perhaps at the time of M. Antonius Gordianus III (r. 238–44), it was immediately reconstructed with walls of stone and earth. After the abandonment of Dacia, Drobeta was kept by the Romans. Constantine reconstructed the castrum on a typical plan of his period. At the time of Justinian, Drobeta, which was reoccupied after having been abandoned, received the name of Theodora. The Avar invasion brought an end to the Byzantine occupation. In the 13th century the Teutonic Knights constructed a castle on the ruins of the Roman-Byzantine city and remains of it can still be seen in the public garden. The Museum of the Iron Gates contains collections of works from the Paleolithic period to modern times. There is also an ethnographic section.

BIBLIOG. G. Tocilescu, Ms. Acad. R.P.R. 5131 and 5135; G. Florescu, Castrul roman de la Drobeta (Turnu Severin), Rev. istorică română, III, 1933, pp. 54–77; A. Bărcărilă, Une ville daco-romaine: Drobeta, L'archéologie en Roumanie, Bucharest, 1938, pp. 7–50; D. Tudor, Oltenia romana, 2d ed., Bucharest, 1958; passim; D. Adamesteanu and G. Florescu, EAA, s.v. Drobeta.

Ploieşti. Tîrgovişte. The second capital of Walachia beginning with the end of the 14th century, and residence of the Metropolitan of Walachia, it was an important cultural and commercial center during the entire feudal period. A great many monuments are preserved from the 13th to the 18th century. The church of the Monastery of Dealu was built by the voivode Radu the Great (1495–1508) on a three-apsed plan with a dome above the presbytery; the exterior is decorated with motifs of Armenian tradition, used for the first time in Walachia. The Palatine Church was constructed at the end of the 16th century, and is of unusually large proportions; it has an inscribed cross plan with an entrance portico of brick pilasters; the interior has a sculptured wooden iconostasis from the Brîncoveanu period. Near the church are the still imposing ruins of the voivode palace, the most impressive monument of Walachian civic architecture (14th–17th cent.), which is being restored. The Church of the Holy Emperors, built by Matei Basarab around 1650, is now in ruins; it has an iconostasis in masonry work with painted icons of the 18th century. The Stelea Church was built in 1650 by Moldavian workmen by order of the voivode Vasile Lupu; heavy buttresses of the Moldavian type flank the apses and the angles of the narthex; there is a Gothic portal and window. The museum contains a lapidary collection and sculpure from the 17th to the 18th century.

BIBLIOG. N. Ghica-Budeşti, Evoluţia arhitecturii în Mintenia şi Oltenia, I, IV, Vălenii de Munte, 1927–36; G. Ionescu, Istoria arhitecturii romîneşti, Bucharest, 1937; V. Vătăşianu, Istoria artei feudale în Ţările Romîne, I, Bucharest, 1959.

Suceava. Arbore. The Church of St. John (XIII, PL. 74) was constructed in 1502 by Luca Arbore on a rectangular plan with a semicircular apse to the east; there are fine frescoes on the interior walls, including the portraits of Luca Arbore with his wife and children; the exterior, of 1541, is also decorated with frescoes that are among the most important of their kind.

BIBLIOG. Repertoriul monumentelor şi obiectelor de artă din timpul lui Ştefan cel Mare, Nucharest, 1958 (bibliog.); V. Vătăşianu, Istoria artei feudale în Ţările Romîne, I, Bucharest, 1959.

Bălineşti. The Church of St. Nicholas, from the end of the 15th century, is rectangular in plan with a double apse. The bell tower is Gothic. The frescoes in the interior constitute the most important pictorial group from the period of Stephen the Great.

BIBLIOG. Repertoriul monumentelor şi obiectelor de artă din timpul lui Ştefan cel Mare, Bucharest, 1958 (bibliog.); V. Vătăşianu, Istoria artei feudale în Ţările Romîne, I, Bucharest, 1959.

Dragomirna. The Monastery, founded at the beginning of the 17th century, is grouped around a large church which has a rectangular plan with a polygonal apse to the west. The monastery complex is surrounded by high, heavy walls reinforced with towers. The façades and towers with stone decoration are eastern in character. There are frescoes in the cella and in the apse. The type of plan, the structure, the proportions, and the decorations constitute a prototype for 12th-century Moldavian art. A large collection of embroideries and illuminated manuscripts bound in silver is kept in the monastery.

BIBLIOG. G. Balş, Bisericile moldoveneşti din veacurile XVII şi XVIII, Bucharest, 1933; G. Ionescu, Istoria arhitecturii romîneşti, Bucharest, 1937; S. Ulea, Autorii ansamblului de pictură de la Dragomirna, S. şi cercetări de ist. artei, VIII, 1961, pp. 221–22.

Humor. The church, constructed in 1530, is 4 miles north of the village of Gura Humorului. There are fine frescoes on the interior and exterior, some Romanian icons of the 16th century, and sculptured tombstones.

BIBLIOG. G. Balş, Bisericile moldoveneşti din veacul al XVI-lea, B. Com. Mon. Ist., XXI, 1928, pp. 55–58.

Moldoviţa. The Monastery constructed by Petru Rareş in 1532 is composed of a heavy quadrangular wall with the monks' cells and the church in the center. With a three-apsed plan, a dome over the presbytery, and an entrance portico with five large arcades, the church is the last of its kind in Moldavia. The system of vaulting of the pronaos, similar to that of the oldest Armenian vaults, is exceptional. The portal and windows have Gothic stone decoration. The interior and exterior walls are decorated with frescoes from 1537. The church contains sculptured wooden furniture of the 16th century.

BIBLIOG. G. Balş, Bisericile moldoveneşti din veacul al XVI-lea, B. Com. Mon. Ist., XXI, 1928, pp. 55–58; I. D. Stefănescu, L'évolution de la peinture religieuse en Bucovine et en Moldavie, 2 vols., Paris, 1928; P. Henry, Les églises de la Moldavie du Nord..., Paris, 1930; G. Ionescu, Istoria arhitecturii romîneşti, Bucharest, 1937; S. Balş and C. Nicolescu, Mănaştire Moldoviţa, Bucharest, 1958 (bibliog.).

Probota (Monastery of). The church was constructed by the voivode Petru Rareş in 1532 on a three-apsed plan with a dome over the cella. Renaissance elements, such as frames and roundheaded arches, were added to the Gothic elements on the doors and windows. The frescoes — those on the exterior are barely visible — are from 1532; the frescoes on the vaults of the narthex are outstanding. There are fine tombstones of the 16th century.

BIBLIOG. G. Balş, Bisericile moldoveneşti din veacul al XVI-lea, B. Com. Mon. Ist., XXI, 1928, pp. 55–58; P. Henry, Les églises de la Moldavie du Nord..., Paris, 1930.

Putna. The Monastery, founded by Stephen the Great in 1466–69, was reconstructed in 1486. The restorations of 1756–60 and of 1902 have altered its original appearance. The museum contains Byzantine embroideries, manuscripts, silver, and Moldavian icons.

BIBLIOG. O. Tafrali, Le trésor byzantin et roumain du monastère de Poutna, Paris, 1925; Repertoriul monumentelor şi obiectelor de artă din timpul lui Ştefan cel Mare, Bucharest, 1958.

Suceava. The residential seat of the voivodes of Moldavia, it was first mentioned in 1388. The castle, constructed by Petru Muşat in the last third of the 14th century, is one of the most remarkable complexes of military and civil architecture of the Romanian feudal period. Religious buildings include the Church of St. George (1514–22); the Church of St. Demetrius (1534–35); and the Armenian monastery of Zamca (early 12th cent.). The museum contains examples of prefeudal and feudal art.

BIBLIOG. G. Diaconu, Observaţii cu privire la urmele vechiulu tîrg al Sucevei în vremea marilor asedii otomane şi polone din veacul al XV-lea, S. şi materiale de ist. medie, I, 1956, pp. 267–83; Repertoriul monumentelor şi obiectelor de artă din timpul lui Ştefan cel Mare, Bucharest, 1958; V. Vătăşianu, Istoria artei feudale în Ţările Romîne, I, Bucharest, 1959; M. Matei, Unele probleme în legătură cu inceputurile vieţii orăşeneşti la Suceava, S. şi cercetări de ist. veche, XI, 1960, pp. 107–24; N. Constantinescu, Precizări în legătură cu data construirii mănăstirii armeneşti Zamca-Suceava, S. şi cercetări de ist. artei, VIII, 1961, pp. 361–79; M. Matei, Zur Ausdehnung der Stadt Suceava im 14.–16. Jahrhundert, Dacia, N.S., V, 1961, pp. 521–32; M. Matei, Contribuţii arheologice la istoria oraşului Suceava, Bucharest, 1963.

Suceviţa. The church and Monastery date from 1582 to 1585 (XIII, PL. 74). The church is the last Moldavian one to have the façades completely covered with frescoes (1601). Rising in the middle of a large square courtyard surrounded by imposing walls with corner towers, the church is on the three-apsed plan, with a dome over the presbytery, and two small lateral entrance porticoes. The portal and windows are Gothic. It was restored in 1959–61. The museum contains art from the 15th to the 17th century.

BIBLIOG. M. A. Musicescu and M. Berza, Suceviţa: monografia artistica, Bucharest, 1957 (bibliog.); S. Ulea, Datarea ansamblului picturii de la Suceviţa, Omagiu lui G. Oprescu, Bucharest, 1961, pp. 561–66.

Voroneţ. The Church of St. George, constructed at the time of Stephen the Great, is a typical example of Moldavian feudal art. It has three semicircular apses and a dome over the cella. The windows and the portal have frames in Gothic style. The interior frescoes are from the 15th and 16th centuries, those of the exterior from 1547 (*Last Judgment* on the west wall).

BIBLIOG. Repertoriul monumentelor şi obiectelor de artă din timpul lui Stefan cel Mare, Bucharest, 1958; V. Vătăşianu, Istoria artei feudale în Ţările Romîne, I, Bucharest, 1959.

Gabriella BORDENACHE, Vladimir DUMITRESCU, Maria Ana MUSICESCU

Illustrations: 4 figs. in text.

ROMAN IMPERIAL ART. The artistic tradition of the Roman world, inasmuch as it differed from the traditions that preceded it in Italy (see ETRUSCO-ITALIC ART) and from the Hellenistic style that is so indelibly impressed upon it (see HELLENISTIC ART; HELLENISTIC-ROMAN ART), was determined chiefly by the homogeneous structure of the Empire, by the importance of Rome as its administrative and cultural center, by the ideals of the court, and by the energy and sometimes the personal tastes of the emperors. These factors produced a tradition of great importance, one that incorporated the basic concepts of classical and Hellenistic art and preserved them until the end of the ancient world; this tradition developed contemporaneously with other trends that reflected classical values to a lesser degree and even foreshadowed their disappearance, especially in provincial and popular production (see AFRICAN-ROMAN ART; DANUBIAN-ROMAN ART; GALLO-ROMAN ART; HISPANO-ROMAN ART; ITALO-ROMAN FOLK ART; ROMAN ART OF THE EASTERN EMPIRE). The tradition in question is essentially that which was dominant in the different aspects of official Roman art, or, more precisely, the art of the Roman Empire, which became known as imperial art. Its beginnings coincided with the reign of Augustus, while its decline can be traced to the spiritual and cultural crisis of the 3d century, when the late-antique artistic tradition appeared (see LATE-ANTIQUE AND EARLY CHRISTIAN ART).

SUMMARY. Roman imperial art (col. 507). Architecture (col. 508): *Architecture of the 1st century of the Christian Era: a. Materials and construction; b. City planning and forums; c. Temples and basilicas; d. Buildings for public spectacles; e. Bridges; f. Triumphal arches and city gates; g. Thermae; h. Private buildings; i. Monumental tombs. Later imperial architecture: a. Construction; b. City planning and forums; c. Basilicas and temples; d. Buildings for public spectacles; e. Triumphal arches and city gates; f. Thermae; g. Private buildings; h. Monumental tombs; i. Conclusion.* Painting and mosaics (col. 534). Sculpture (col. 540): *From the Augustan period to the end of the 1st century of our era. The later imperial period.*

ROMAN IMPERIAL ART. In the early centuries of Roman civilization, together with primitive and spontaneous expressions of local craftsmanship, many works of a more refined and elaborate kind were produced. The inspirations and the criteria that produced these objects seem to have been drawn first from Etruria, then from Greece — in particular from the western Greek world of southern Italy and Sicily, where art followed the Greek mainstream but had subtle peculiarities of its own (see GREEK ART, WESTERN). In about the 3d century B.C., when contacts with the Hellenistic world became close and Rome began to grow rich with the spoils of conquered cities, the Etrusco-Italico-Roman koine grew up, perhaps less homogeneous than is commonly supposed but undoubtedly held together by a common basis. New and more direct influences were derived from Greece and the East throughout the upheavals of the period from the second half of the 2d century B.C. to the death of Caesar, until, with the disappearance in Egypt of the last Hellenistic dynasty, Rome became the center and the sole ruler of the Mediterranean.

With the rise of the Empire, Rome became the magnet and the focal point of all the intellectual and artistic activity of the civilized world. Even in Greek literature it was more influential than any Greek city, including Alexandria, Athens, and Rhodes (these cities — especially the last two — remained flourishing centers of learning, while Athens was also the largest and most active market for works of figural art). Moreover, although Atticism did not originate in Rome, it truly and exclusively flourished there and, in spite of sometimes vigorous opposition, was long in the ascendant. By centralizing all the active creative forces in the figural arts and by combining them and blending them with local traditions, Rome was able to use art as the symbol of a political system. It has often been stated, not without foundation, that from the beginning of the Empire onward two distinct and homogeneous artistic movements can be distinguished, both operating in their own geographic spheres — areas that roughly correspond to the Latin-speaking and the Greek-speaking regions, which met at the junction of the Latin

province of Dalmatia and the Greek province of Macedonia; this became the political border of Rome and Byzantium after the division of the Empire. Certainly in regions such as Greece and Asia Minor, an ancient and glorious culture that had flourished for centuries could not disappear overnight, nor could it be suppressed without leaving some trace. In this context, some observations in the correspondence between Trajan and Pliny the Younger, who was legate in Bithynia in 111 and 112, have not been given the emphasis they perhaps deserve. When Pliny, who was not satisfied with some buildings, asked for architects from Rome, Trajan replied that every province had architects of skill and that many came from the provinces to exercise their profession in Rome (Pliny, *Epistolae*, X, xxxvii, 39–41). It should be added that, in the time of Nero, the sculptor Zenodorus, who created the colossal statue of Mercury in the capital of the Arverni in Gaul, was working in Rome; that a school of artists from Aphrodisias worked uninterruptedly for several centuries in Rome, and that one of them, Zenon, boasted that he had executed sculptures in various cities of the Empire (M. Squarciapino, *La scuola di Afrodisia*, Rome, 1943, pp. 15, 37); and that it was asserted of Novius Blesamus, who died in Rome, that his statues adorned not only the city but the whole world (*Corpus inscriptionum latinarum*, Berlin, 1886, VI, 23083).

Although Roman imperial art was subject to ideas and influences from all sides, it retained a homogeneous aspect; concepts were elaborated and new forms of art were realized in Rome, and their influence was transmitted to and assimilated by the more ancient local cultures in neighboring and distant provinces. It was only during the 3d century of the Christian Era, in the violent upheavals that shook the foundations of the Empire, when new modes of thought profoundly altered the essence and the ideas of Roman society, giving rise to what is now known as late-antique art, that Roman imperial art was to lose its expansionary and unifying vigor, thereby encouraging the affirmation of local art forms increasingly divergent from the official art of Rome. It is best, therefore, to limit the discussion of Roman imperial art to the first two centuries of the Empire, citing only exceptional examples of trends still active in the art of the capital during the succeeding period.

ARCHITECTURE. *Architecture of the 1st century of the Christian Era.* In the last century of the Republic the Greek style became prevalent in Rome, with the presence there of Greek architects and architects of Greek origin and with the widespread acceptance of Greek architectural schemes in basilicas (e.g., the Fulvia-Emilia, Aemilia, and Sempronia basilicas), theaters with large porticoes, private residences, streets lined with arcades, and especially the interplay of long views and theatrical perspectives obtained by setting structures on terraces of different heights. The Greek concepts of symmetry and eurythmy were adopted and were blended with the Roman sense of decoration, which was based not only on the harmony of single elements but also on the planned arrangement of a homogeneous whole.

a. Materials and construction. During this period Roman architecture clung to indigenous structural methods. The Greek custom of adding stone block to stone block, each one squared with minute precision, always remained more a sculptural than a structural technique; in Roman architecture, *opus caementicium* (rubblework), which was an amalgam of small stones and lime mortar used to enclose and cover over large areas, always provided the basic mass of the wall. On top of this were placed squared slabs of marble, but not before the 1st century B.C. (Pliny, *Naturalis historia*, XVII, 6), although some informants give an earlier date; more often the slabs were of tufa or travertine (*saxo quadrato*; Vitruvius, *De architectura*, II, viii, 4, 16), generally carefully cut. Only in Claudian times did the surface, with its coarse rusticated ashlar, contribute to creating more vivid chromatic effects; later this type of rustication seems to have been discontinued. In the facing of the curve of the arch, pentagonal blocks were used to assure a more solid link with the horizontal courses. In the Augustan period the uneven manner of facing with irregularly cut stones (*opus incertum*), described by Vitruvius (op. cit., II, vii, 1) as antiquated, was replaced by a system of more regular appearance consisting of small pyramidal blocks (tesserae) of tufa or limestone embedded in the central substance of the wall (*opus reticulatum*), which Vitruvius considered more refined but less durable than *opus incertum*. Outside Rome, in certain regions of Italy (e.g., Umbria and the Marches), in Gaul, and less often in Greece, walls were often faced with small blocks or cubes of stone placed in horizontal rows (*opus vittatum*). Facings of *opus testaceum* (fired bricks) and *opus latericium* (sun-dried bricks) did not appear before the time of Tiberius and the curtain walls of the Domus Tiberiana on the Palatine. Earlier, in structures that were in underground sites or subject to humidity, broken tiles with rounded fronts were used; in the time of Tiberius, triangular bricks with rounded faces (made by breaking in half square bricks, *laterculi besales*, about 8 in. wide) were added to these tiles. Toward the middle of the 1st century B.C., it became customary to impress the name of the potter's workshop (*figlina*) in the clay. The bricks used outside Rome were larger (those of the Porta Palatina in Turin may be considered an example of this, if a date in the early days of the Empire is correct for this structure). In other cities (e.g., Pompeii and Herculaneum) some buildings were made of alternate courses of bricks and small pieces of tufa (*opus mixtum*). At about the time of Nero the thickness of the bricks used for facing increased to about 1½ in. From the age of Domitian onward, bonding courses of large square tiles (*bipedales*) were introduced into the concrete at intervals of 3 ft., holding together the inner facings and forming a sort of framework on which the rest of the wall could be built without delay while the lower part hardened. At the same time, *opus vittatum* continued to be widely used over a long period; and *opus mixtum*, which in the curtain walls included elements of *opus reticulatum*, was used on a wider scale than in earlier times and was framed by brickwork.

Relieving arches became common in the construction of walls, not only above vaulted and architraved openings but also as part of the walls themselves. Their purpose was to ensure more solid construction and better internal articulation (although sometimes the reason for their use by the architect is not clear). From the Augustan period onward, this was the purpose of the series of arches placed radially around the central mass of a building (e.g., the Mausoleum of Augustus) and of reinforcements, which in some cases were extended outside the buildings, as in the theater at Augusta Praetoria (mod. Aosta). These supporting walls or buttresses were called *erismae* or *anterides* (Vitruvius, op. cit., VI, viii, 6).

With regard to vaults, the treatise of Vitruvius (the first six books of which have been dated 45–27 B.C., the remainder 10 years later) mentions, without much detail, only the barrel vault (Vitruvius, op. cit., V, x, 1) and, although in a somewhat obscure manner, possibly alsot hose rising on a circular or quadrangular base. The writer seems to refer to these in relation to the vaulted ceilings of the baths, which, he says (Vitruvius, op. cit., V, x, 3), should be built in masonry or, if this is not possible, in brickwork attached by an iron framework to the wooden roof trusses, so as to protect them from rot caused by the steam. The thermal hall at Baiae (mod. Baia), known as the Temple of Mercury, has been ascribed to the Augustan period. Not all scholars agree to this dating, but it is clearly confirmed by the construction of the walls and by the manner of their evolution in Campania. The hall is covered by a shallow dome made from wedge-shaped chips of tufa cut in different sizes, cemented with mortar and arranged radially so as to fit the curve of the vault. This recalls the earlier technique of false vaulting with projecting trapezoidal blocks; it certainly did not attain the boldness shown soon afterward in the use of rubblework for vaulting. Moreover, in the Augustan period there appeared the first examples of a cross vault, in a room of the House of the Cryptoporticus in Pompeii, which appears to have been rebuilt at this time, and of a sail vault, in a room of a house at Minori, near Amalfi, certainly no later than the early decades of the 1st century of our era. Vaulting was widely used in the Theater of Marcellus to cover the radially arranged rooms under the cavea.

In the Flavian age, rubblework was skillfully used in barrel-vaulting areas about 100 ft. in diameter, as, for example, in the Domus Flavia and the Palace of Domitian on the Palatine. There is evidence in the time of Domitian of attempts to lighten the vault by using lightweight materials (chips of peperino and scoriae of tufa). Occasionally arches of brickwork, joined by bricks, were inserted into the rubblework vault, perhaps to speed the building process; this can be seen in the barrel vaulting of the exterior corridor of the lower order of the Colosseum and in the corresponding one of the second order. However, in the second interior corridor on the second tier and in those above it, cross vaulting is used; this type of vaulting appears not only in the examples mentioned from the Augustan period but also in a small cruciform room in the Domus Aurea (Golden House of Nero).

The materials used in the construction of this time — rubblework and bricks — permitted the builder to curve the walls to enclose a greater interior space into which all the exterior decorations and columns had been transferred, giving positive value to what had previously been merely empty space. This tendency, initiated as early as the time of Augustus, developed into a truly formal use of space in the Flavian period, when the arrangement of the walls in geometric schemes to form circular and polygonal spaces, juxtaposed with quadrangles, relieved the uniformity and monotony; in the walls themselves, apses, niches, and aediculas surmounted by pediments of various kinds created a vivid chiaroscuro. These innovations are generally attributed to the architect Rabirius, designer of Domitian's Palace. In fact, he merely followed a long-established trend (cf. the vigorous design of the Domus Aurea; FIG. 522). During the Flavian period occurred the real emergence of that dynamic use of space which was long to be the chief characteristic of Roman architecture.

b. City planning and forums. The urban layout of Rome was unpretentious at the beginning of the Empire; the city had not yet been "embellished as the dignity of the Empire demanded" (Suetonius, *De vita caesarum, Divus Augustus*, XXVIII, 3). Julius Caesar had died before he could carry out the provisions of the law for "improvements of the city" (Cicero, *Epistolae ad Atticum*, XIII, 33a; Suetonius, op. cit., *Divus Julius*, XLIV, 1), which should have solved the problem of urban overcrowding that had arisen immediately after the Punic Wars. Augustus undertook the task and later said that he had found a city built of brick and left it made of marble (Suetonius, op. cit., *Divus Augustus*, XXVIII, 3). The fervor for building spread from Rome to the provinces.

Political and esthetic reasons induced Augustus to build a new forum (FIG. 511), planning it to correspond to the already existing Forum of Caesar (VII, FIG. 402); his forum extended to the flat area east of the Via Flaminia, the Campus Martius. Strabo, visiting Rome for the second time in 7 B.C., admired the beauty of its layout; according to the literature of the period his admiration was widely shared. Tradition, largely echoed by Roman writers (Suetonius, op. cit., *Tiberius*, XLVII; Tacitus, *Annales*, VI, xli, 1), accused Tiberius of having neglected the city; Claudius devoted himself to public works, while Nero, although he viewed the simplicity of the city almost as a personal affront (Suetonius, op. cit., *Nero*, XXXVIII) and might have undertaken its reconstruction after the fire of A.D. 64, confined himself to rebuilding the monumental area south of the forum and to the erection of his Domus Aurea. It was not until the Flavian emperors, particularly Domitian, who followed in the footsteps of Augustus and completed his work, that the center of the city was transformed; the Temple of Peace in the Forum of Peace (Forum of Vespasian), which was more a sacred precinct than a forum, was joined to the Forum of Augustus by the Forum of Nerva (Forum Transitorium), finished and inaugurated by that emperor (cf. FIG. 511).

Little is known of the cities founded during the early period of the Empire: Aosta and Turin (anc. Augusta Taurinorum; VIII, FIGS. 537, 541), with their axial layouts derived from the layout of Roman camps, introduced no new forms to city planning, although the rectangular arrangement of the streets was modified for practical reasons. As for other cities, it is difficult to reconstruct their appearance during this period because of subsequent alterations. Generally, new architectural ideas found expression in the forum, the square that increasingly resembled a precinct separate from the main part of the city, often sacred in character because of the temple that dominated it. The basic form was derived from the enclosed Hellenistic square, surrounded by arcades, such as those in Priene (VII, FIG. 311), Miletus, Assos, and other ancient Mediterranean

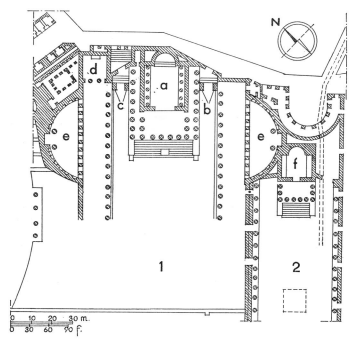

Rome, plan of the Forum of Augustus and of part of the Forum of Nerva, partially reconstructed. (1) Forum of Augustus: (*a*) Temple of Mars Ultor; (*b*) Arch of Germanicus; (*c*) Arch of Drusus; (*d*) hall of the "colossus of Augustus"; (*e*) hemicycles, originally with statues of famous men; (2) Forum of Nerva, also known as Forum Transitorium: (*f*) Temple of Minerva (*from G. Lugli, Roma antica, Il centro monumentale, Rome, 1946*).

cities; it was already evident in Caesar's Forum, which was long and rectangular, like that in Pompeii, but in the Forum of Augustus (FIG. 511), begun in 42 B.C. and completed forty years later, it found new expression. The wall of ashlar (*opus quadratum*), which was intended as a protection against fire, emphasized its isolation and gave it the appearance of a meeting place and, at the same time, functioned as a link with previously existing forums. This last characteristic had a precedent in the design of the squares in Pergamum (VII, FIG. 310). The two great exedras that opened beyond the porticoes at the sides of the forum were surmounted by attics decorated with caryatids and clipei; and the skillful arrangement of the colonnades to balance the lack of symmetry, possibly a result of difficulties encountered by Augustus in acquiring the land, created a greater feeling of space. Perspectives were carefully graduated, and the combination of straight lines and curves and the niches with statues of legendary heroes and famous generals provided variety within the rigid symmetry imposed by the temple at one end of the forum.

In the Flavian period, this desire for variety found wider expression: the Forum of Nerva had columns placed in front of the walls and entablatures that projected above each of them in such a way as to articulate the surface with calculated effect. Also built on the plan of the enclosed square were the forums — all dating from the Flavian period — of Brixia (mod. Brescia), Asisium (mod. Assisi), and Cambodunum (mod. Kempten, Germany; forum built after A.D. 70). This type of plan was not, however, used exclusively in the western empire; similar in character, though slightly modified, were the Roman agora in Athens, built in 10 B.C., which was used as a market, and the forum in Aphrodisias, which was of exceptional length com-

pared to its width and was surrounded by arcades (one of the longer sides dated from the Tiberian period). Even the agora in Corinth, while retaining its Hellenistic appearance after it was redesigned about 44 B.C., clearly showed Roman influence in the dramatic arrangement of the surrounding buildings (VI, FIG. 915).

Porticoes flanking the streets had appeared in Rome as early as republican times; later, they were used to enclose garden areas with scholas and semicircular or rectangular exedras, or to surround public buildings or temples; in this last case they assumed the character of temene, or sacred precincts.

c. Temples and basilicas. More monumental effects were attained in temples with the increased use of marble, although the old Etruscan style of temple persisted, built on a high podium with deep pronaos. Greek influence was evident in these temples, as early as republican times, in the predominance of the Corinthian among the orders used. In the Augustan period, rectangular and, less frequently, circular-plan temples took on more balanced and less ponderous proportions, with increased emphasis on vertical lines. The style of ornamentation also became less heavy, and while it lost some of the freshness of decoration of republican times, it gained a firmer and more detailed accuracy in modeling; this was later to be blurred by the desire for more elaborate chiaroscuro contrasts in the Flavian period.

Among the examples of rectangular temples in the Augustan age was the Temple of Castor and Pollux in the Roman Forum, restored by Tiberius in A.D. 7, enclosed by a portico and on a raised podium; another example, the Temple of Mars Ultor (FIG. 511), was octastyle, with no colonnade at the rear, where it was built against the wall bordering the Forum. The pseudo-peripteral Temple of Apollo Sosianus was built in 32 B.C. on a plan similar to that of the Temple of Apollo on the Palatine (FIG. 519); it was enclosed by a portico with statues of the Danaides. The temples of Jupiter and Juno on the Campus Martius and that of Diana on the Aventine (rebuilt by Augustus on the site of the ancient temple of the goddess; known from the *Forma Urbis*, which dates from the time of Septimius Severus) also were enclosed by porticoes. The Temple of Divus Julius, voted in 42 B.C. and dedicated in 29 B.C., had a quite different plan: it was pycnostyle, according to Vitruvius (op. cit., III, iii, 2), and hexastyle, with Ionic columns; the podium was very large, with a platform that served as a tribune for orators and had a niche in front, in which an altar of earlier date was inserted. Also unusual was the width of the cella of the Temple of Concord, restored by Tiberius in A.D. 10.

Examples of circular temples were those of Mars, built in 20 B.C. on the Capitoline, known from coins, and of Vesta (PL. 132), reproduced in some reliefs of the 1st century (Sorrento, Mus. Correale di Terranova; Palermo, Mus. Naz. Arch.). The temple dedicated to Vesta is probably not that believed to have been erected by Augustus on the Palatine, but the elegant shape of the Ionic columns and the roof, with its somewhat antiquated conical outline, would certainly tend to support its attribution to the Augustan period. The temple in the Forum Boarium, dating from the beginning of the imperial age, was also circular; built over an earlier structure, it stood on a marble step and had slender Corinthian columns (XIII, PL. 244).

No ruins of important temples have survived from the reigns of Tiberius and his immediate successors, with the exceptions of the temple built by Tiberius in the name of the deified Augustus and that begun by Agrippina and finished by Vespasian for the deified Claudius, built on an extensive, largely artificial terrace that has the rough ashlar walls characteristic of the Claudian age.

Religion sometimes inspired strange buildings, as, for example, the Iseum in the Campus Martius, built in 43 B.C., razed by Tiberius, reconstructed by Caligula, and finally restored by Domitian. If its appearance in the *Forma Urbis* reflects Caligula's reconstruction, it consisted of a large peristyle, of which two of the arches (one with three openings, the other square) formed the entrance. The temple itself was situated inside a semicircular portico; illustrations on coins show that it was surmounted by a semicircular pediment, a feature found again in a temple, dedicated perhaps to Mercury, that appears on a coin of Marcus Aurelius. Apart from the rich decoration found in some of the temples of the Flavian period (e.g., the peripteral hexastyle temple near the Temple of Apollo Sosianus; the temple in Via delle Botteghe Oscure, Rome, Flavian reconstruction; the Temple of Vespasian and Titus between the Tabularium and the Clivus Capitolinus; the Temple of Minerva in the Forum of Nerva), the principal characteristic of these temples is their importance as elements in monumental complexes of exceptional grandeur, with peristyles that were complements to the monumental and religious aspects of their architecture. A large portico, called a temple or portico of the gods, was used to enclose two small temples in the Campus Martius that were dedicated to Vespasian and Titus and the temple of an unknown divinity built probably by Domitian in the Orti dei Barberini on the Palatine. A semicircular portico enclosed the circular Temple of Bacchus, known from a coin of Antoninus Pius and perhaps similar in shape to the temple of the Flavian family on the Quirinal; both were works of Domitian. The Temple of Peace was the finest example of a monumental complex. The cella of this temple was apsidal at one end, like that of the Temple of Venus Genetrix (begun by Domitian and completed by Trajan), and those of the Temple of Minerva in the Forum of Nerva and the earlier Temple of Mars Ultor in the Forum of Augustus. The Temple of Peace was begun after the pacification of the east and finished in A.D. 75. In front there was a large portico that enclosed a garden with three buildings at one end; the central building was the temple, which was hexastyle and had columns larger than those of the colonnade from which it projected. This plan was followed elsewhere in buildings attributed to the same period, for example, in the Capitolium in Brescia, and in the so-called "Serapeum" in Pozzuoli (actually the *macellum*, or market). A strange subterranean edifice near Porta Maggiore, believed to have been used as a place of worship for mystery cults (a theory that seems to be confirmed by the wall decorations), also had a semicircular apse at one end (XIII, PL. 269). It consisted of a small anteroom, with a skylight in the ceiling that was the only source of light, and a hall divided into three vaulted aisles. Its dating to the early decades of the 1st century of the Christian Era is probably correct, judging from the type of masonry and the decorations.

Among the structures connected with religious worship, the great altars are notable. These were surrounded by an almost square marble precinct, elaborately sculptured on both sides; the Ara Pacis, which was built between 13 and 9 B.C., was apparently enclosed by a large portico, but this has not been definitely established. The altar (Ara pietatis Augustae) erected in A.D. 43 in honor of Augustus is presumed to have been similar in design. Monumental altars also were built elsewhere. Among them was that set up by Drusus at Lugdunum (mod. Lyons) in 12 B.C., dedicated to Rome and Augustus; those parts of the sculptured decoration that have survived from this altar are too meager to permit reconstruction of its architectural design. A round precinct surrounded the Sacellum Cloacinae in the Roman Forum, enclosing an altar and a statue of Venus.

The characteristics of religious architecture in Rome were strongly reflected in provincial architecture. The Temple of Augustus in Pietas Julia (mod. Pulj), with its unfluted Corinthian columns and its frieze richly sculptured with floral motifs, was notable for its strong vertical lines; so also was the temple in Assisi, in which columns on high bases were used to break up the unity of the steps that led to the pronaos. The great temple of Baalbek (anc. Heliopolis) was notable for the rich decoration of its epistyle; this temple, which was incorrectly attributed by ancient tradition to Antoninus Pius (J. Malalas, XI, 280, 8; from *Die Römische Kaisergeschichte*, Stuttgart, 1931) but should be considered as belonging to the Augustan period or slightly later, probably was pseudodipteral in form, with tall unfluted Corinthian columns. Similar decoration, in a different form, was to be found in the temple at Nemausus (mod. Nîmes), known as the Maison Carrée, probably rebuilt by Agrippa (XIII, PL. 245). This was similar to the Augustan temples in

the same emphasis on the perpendicular, evident also in the Temple of Augustus and Livia in Vienne (PL. 285), which was begun as pseudoperipteral and was continued as a peripteral building, notable for the depth of its pronaos. The Temple of Rome and Augustus in Ancyra (mod. Ankara), with its tetrastyle cella and pronaos and its distyle opisthodome with columns *in antis*, was more Hellenistic in style. An example of classical inspiration was the Ionic monopteron on the Acropolis in Athens, dedicated to Rome and Augustus, in which the decoration was directly influenced by the columns of the Erechtheion. The monumental grandeur characteristic of the architecture of the second half of the 1st century of the Christian Era was executed in a lively design, with a variety of decoration, in the great court in front of the temple at Baalbek (IX, FIG. 180), in the center of which the altar rose to a height of almost 60 ft. While the eastern taste is evident in the bronze facing of some of the exterior cornices of this temple, the inspiration was decidedly Roman in the interior sculptural decoration, notwithstanding the flatness of the relief. Also Roman in style were the aediculas in the interior walls of the Ionic prostyle temple at Beziza (Bziza), in Lebanon, while the pseudodipteral octastyle temple at Ephesus (mod. Selçuk), built in honor of Domitian, was a more direct continuation of the Hellenistic tradition.

As early as republican times the basilica had assumed the exterior form of a hall, rather long in proportion to its width and with an interior portico. This was the plan of the Basilica Aemilia, first rebuilt in 34 B.C. and again in A.D. 14 according to the original plan. A double row of columns in so-called "breccia Africana" and a single row of columns in cipolin marble stood on the side of the basilica opposite the forum; in front was a row of tabernae preceded by a portico. Similar in plan, though different in detail, was the basilica at Fanum Fortunae (mod. Fano) described by Vitruvius (*De architectura*, V, i, 6). In the basilica, behind a row of columns 50 ft. high that enclosed a central area, another row of columns 20 ft. high supported an open gallery; thus it resembled the Basilica Argentaria in the Forum of Caesar (VII, FIG. 402), and, just as in the latter the temple was built at the end, at Fano a sacellum dedicated to Augustus ended in an apse, in which the tribunal was set. Also different in shape, besides the Basilica Julia at Aquileia described by Vitruvius (op. cit., V, i, 4), was the Basilica Julia in Rome, rebuilt after the fire of A.D. 12 and dedicated by Augustus to his nephews. In this structure, the increase in width counteracted the tendency to length always present in the earlier type. Vaulted double aisles, topped by open galleries, surrounded the central area, which, according to some opinions, was uncovered; except on the side opposite the forum, where there was a row of rooms, the basilica opened in a series of arches flanked by pilasters, as is shown in the reproduction on the rostra balustrade (PL. 292). The most common type of Roman basilica, of elongated rectangular shape, was also widely diffused in the east. The best example is in Corinth (VI, FIG. 915), where three basilicas were built between the end of the 1st century B.C. and the middle of the next century, each of them with an internal peristasis; the third, larger than the others, had three rectangular niches in the wall opposite the entrance, with two columns placed in front of the largest, central niche.

d. Buildings for public spectacles. The motif of arcades on piers with engaged columns was known as early as the time of Sulla (e.g., the Tabularium; XIII, PL. 250); it reappeared later in superposed orders on the exteriors of theaters and amphitheaters, where it complemented the curve of the structures. Curved porticoes were in existence in Rome as early as the Flavian age. Of the Theater of Balbus in Rome, built in 13 B.C., only a few ruins have survived; however, the Theater of Marcellus, planned by Caesar and dedicated by Augustus to the memory of his nephew and son-in-law, has been largely preserved (PL. 284). By this time Roman theater design had already been established; the cavea was united to the *scaena* by means of the *tribunalia* and the passages underneath, and the *frons scaenae* was on a level with the top of the cavea, which rose directly from ground level and rested on a series of radial walls that were linked by sloping vaults with two passages between them under the *praecinctiones*. The lower series was barrel vaulted, while above, in order to reduce the outward thrust, small radial vaults rested on heavy transverse architraves, which were supported by corbels. Since only the two lower stories of the Theater of Marcellus have survived, details of the appearance of the third story are not known; the *summa cavea* may conceivably have had wooden seats. As is known from the *Forma Urbis*, the *frons scaenae* was rectilinear; so also were the reconstructed stage of the large theater at Pompeii, which was perhaps quite close in date to the Augustan period, and the stage of the theater at Volaterrae (mod. Volterra).

By the late Augustan period, the *frons scaenae* had become less static, as in the theater at Aosta, where the center of the wall projected in such a way as to contain the *porta regia*; this was recessed in the *frons scaenae* of the theater at Casinum (mod. Cassino), and even more so in the theater at Herculaneum, attributed to the time of Nero or perhaps a few decades later. The articulation seems even more pronounced in some other theaters where the central niche was flanked by side niches, as in those at Eugubium (mod. Gubbio), Verona, Neapolis (mod. Naples), and in the second reconstruction of the theater at Pompeii, built between A.D. 63 and 79; the same applies to some theaters in southern Gaul, the best-known example of which was the one in Arausio (mod. Orange). The attempt to enliven the appearance of the stage was perhaps motivated by a desire to exalt the emperor, either by a statue in the central niche or in person, as when Nero appeared on the stage as an actor. This trend originated in the Augustan period (along with the theater at Aosta, that at Leptis Magna, with three curved niches, belongs to this period) and was continued in later theaters, as in the Flavian theater at Sabrata; the model seems to have been imitated during this period especially in Italy, the western provinces, proconsular Africa, Tripolitana, Mauretania, and also in the Syrian provinces, although the theaters there seem to have belonged to a later date and were sometimes rectangular.

In the east, rectilinear *scaenae* apparently predominated, as, for example, in Athens, where the *scaena* seems to date from the time of Nero, and in Asia Minor, where the use of the high logeum persisted. However, examples were not lacking in this region of the influence of the western style: the *scaena* of the theater of Ephesus, which was perhaps rebuilt in the 3d century of the Christian Era, probably copied the earlier structure (which dated from A.D. 66, according to an inscription) and, in spite of the rectangular frontal of the *pulpitum*, showed Roman influence in the rich decoration of the front. This influence was even more pronounced in the reconstruction of the theater at Miletus, in which there was one niche, and in the one at Priene that had three niches; these examples in Asia Minor were probably earlier than the 2d century of the Christian Era.

In the large theater of Pompeii the remains of a tank can be seen in the orchestra; at the beginning of the imperial age these tanks were rectangular in shape. They were used probably to store perfumed water for spraying the theater (Pliny, *Naturalis historia*, XXI, xvii, 33), but they may have served other purposes; for instance, in Rome, Marcus Scaurus exhibited crocodiles in a theater (Pliny, op. cit., VIII, xl, 96). The theory that they were used for choreographic water spectacles is less likely, although it is known that such shows were in vogue in Antiochia (mod. Antakya), that Titus perhaps attended them, and that they were probably referred to by Martial (*De spectaculis liber*, XXVI).

In some African theaters, a temple was built at the top of the cavea, as at Leptis Magna, where the cavea was dominated by a prostyle hexastyle temple erected in A.D. 35–36 and dedicated to Ceres; a similar temple was built in the Theater of Pompey in Rome. In the theater of Vienne a small tetrastyle temple, dedicated perhaps to Apollo, was placed at the center of the topmost part of the cavea, and similar structures are known in the theaters of Cassino and Saepinum (mod. Sepino).

In the small theater of the Villa of Agrippa Postumus, on the island of Pianosa, and in another theater, part of a villa at Posillipo in Naples, the line of the cavea was broken at the center by a platform on which presumably stood a sacellum. It is possible, however, that its function was to hold seats of honor, as in the podium in the lowest cavea of the theater in Aosta. The theory that these platforms were used as *stibadia* for Dionysian banquets (a theory based on the increase in width of the podiums, perhaps determined by the curve of the cavea) is improbable, since no writings of the period are yet known to have connected them in any way with the cult of Dionysus.

Amphitheaters were similar in structure to theaters. In Rome, during the Republic and the Julio-Claudian dynasty, there were no amphitheaters built of stone; spectacles with gladiators were held in the forum, in accordance with ancient tradition. An example of a temporary wooden amphitheater, besides that of Caius Curio, was the amphitheater built by Caesar in 48 B.C. (*Dio's Roman History*, E. Cary, trans., London, New York, 1914–27, XLIII, xxii, 3); also mainly of wood with stone substructures were the amphitheater erected by Statilius Taurus in 29 B.C. on the Campus Martius and that built by Caligula near the Saepta Julia, subsequently abandoned and later completed by Nero.

In the early period of the Empire, several stone amphitheaters were built outside Rome; the one at Lucera, built by Manlius Vecilius Campus in honor of Augustus, was excavated partly out of the ground and partly out of the embankment formed by the excavated earth (this technique dates from the republican era and was used in the amphitheater at Pompeii, built shortly after the removal of the Sullan colony). Among amphitheaters contemporaneous with that at Lucera were those at Venusia (mod. Venosa), which differed from the others in its tiers supported by a radial substructure, and Syracusae (mod. Siracusa), where the structure was built in the first half of the 1st century of the Christian Era, half cut into rock and half built up in masonry, and where for the first time the arena had a rectangular pit for the stage apparatus and the cages of wild beasts. The amphitheater at Cassino was slightly later in date. Partly built into the mountain, it was bounded on its free side by a wall in *opus reticulatum* covered with plaster in which were three doors that, together with two arches, served as entrances. The amphitheater was constructed by the Roman matron Ummidia Quadratilla, mentioned by Pliny the Younger, and this would indicate a date about the middle of the 1st century of our era. In Spain, the amphitheater built in 8 B.C. in Augusta Emerita (mod. Mérida) lies partly in the slope of a hill; it is surrounded by a wall with 16 doors at various levels. In A.D. 32 the amphitheater in Interamna Nahars (mod. Terni) was built in concrete work faced with *opus reticulatum*; it was the first constructed entirely in masonry. Other amphitheaters excavated from the earth were the one at Aosta, which can be attributed to the Augustan age because of its massive rusticated ashlar blocks (very different from Claudian ashlaring, with its international play of tones), and those at Verona and at Pulj. In Pulj the lower order of the amphitheater was covered by the slope of the ground on the side toward the mountain. The caveas of the amphitheaters at Verona and Pulj rested on a system of radial walls connected by vaults; both opened to the outside, at Verona with a triple order of arcades that diminished in span toward the top, and at Pulj with a double order surmounted by an attic story with a row of square windows. The Pulj amphitheater appears to have been built on the side of a smaller one of the Augustan period; a coin found in the mortar used in the steps seems to indicate that the interior was finished in the age of Titus, while the great rusticated blocks on the exterior suggest the Claudian period as the most likely date for the start of construction. The amphitheater at Verona was probably slightly earlier.

The amphitheater in Rome (PL. 290), known as the Colosseum since the 8th century (more probably because of the proximity of the Colossus of Nero than because of its size), was begun by Vespasian, inaugurated in A.D. 80 by Titus, and completed by Domitian. Domitian added the *maenianum sum-*

mum, the final steps, and the highest exterior fascia, with tall, square windows; this fascia completes and unifies the movement of the façade, which consists of alternating solids and voids in the three stories, each with 80 arches, with engaged columns in the bottom order, Ionic in the middle, and Corinthian at the top. The four arches opposite each other on the transverse axes are on a larger scale, and what is presumed to be the main entrance was preceded by a vestibule that gave it the appearance of a triumphal arch; it was perhaps reserved for the emperor. The arena was separated from the cavea by a podium about 12 ft. high; the first two or three tiers had seats of marble, and two boxes in line with the lesser axis were reserved for the emperor and high officials. In its earlier stages the arena had no system of underground passages, or if it did, they were on a very small scale, but by the time of Domitian they had become very complicated. The travertine façade (which rose to a height of 157½ ft.), the proportions, and the structural details make this one of the most important works of Roman architecture. In it, the qualities of beauty (*venustas*), solidity (*firmitas*), and utility (*utilitas*), as prescribed by Vitruvius (*De architectura*, I, iii, 2), were fully achieved.

In Campania, during the Flavian period, an amphitheater, in which the underground passages were perhaps of a later date, was built at Pozzuoli; the amphitheater at Santa Maria Capua Vetere, which was built at the same time but was not completed until the following century, may have been constructed on the site of an older amphitheater, of which few traces remain.

e. Bridges. The arch was widely used in such works of civil engineering as aqueducts, bridges, and viaducts. In bridge-building, the preferred technique was to reinforce and multiply the piers; only rarely were arches with widened spans used, as in the unusual viaduct in Pont d'Ael in the Val de Cogne, with its double passage, the lower one covered and the upper one open. The bridge at Narni was built during the Augustan period; the width of each of its piers was equal to half the span of an arch. In the aqueduct known as the Pont du Gard (V, PL. 474), near Nîmes, the span of the topmost row of arches is much less than that of the two lower rows, a variation that creates a lively feeling of movement. The Puente de las Ferreras near Tarragona (XIII, PL. 265) is also of the Augustan age. Of a slightly later date, the bridge at Ariminum (mod. Rimini), which has elegant aediculas between the arches, was finished in A.D. 22. The style also spread to the eastern provinces; in the aqueduct at Ephesus, built between A.D. 4 and 14, two small arches in the upper row correspond to each large arch in the lower row. The aqueduct at Patrae (mod. Patras), which had two rows of arches of equal span, was also built in the 1st century of our era.

f. Triumphal arches and city gates. With the beginning of the Empire, freestanding arches were built to celebrate triumphs and important events. The functional character of the arch as a vaulted passage was still apparent in, for example, the Fornix Fabianus, erected in 121 and reconstructed in 56 B.C., but the purpose became increasingly commemorative. Under the Empire, these arches were composed of elaborate architectural members, with cornices that emphasized the junction of the impost of the arch with the piers and with three-quarter columns in the corners and columns or engaged columns, single or paired, on the façades. The arch at Rimini dates from 27 B.C. and replaced an arch that was purely functional; it has two engaged Corinthian columns on its façade, supporting two elements projecting from the ends of the entablature on which the pediment rests. More lively in appearance — and this has led some to give it a later date — is the Arch of the Sergi at Pulj (PL. 285), with paired engaged columns on each pier; like the arch at Rimini, it was richly ornamented with sculptural decoration in the spandrels of the arch. The arch in Aosta (25–23 B.C.), with tall unfluted Corinthian columns resting on a continuous base and a Doric frieze in the entablature, seems to have been inspired by the greater structural solidity of the earlier style, and this impression is reinforced by the disappear-

ance of the attic story. The rectangular niches on the piers contained sculptures or, as some scholars have suggested, paintings; they serve to relieve the monotony of the surface. The Arch of Augustus in Susa (9–8 B.C.), which has a fascia with reliefs commemorating the pact made by Augustus with the Cottii (VIII, PL. 230), is characterized by greater elegance and sense of proportion; only the corner columns have bases, and the archivolt rises on two slender pilaster strips. Between the Temple of Castor and that of Divus Julius in Rome was an arch with three openings; the central opening was vaulted and the lateral ones were trabeated (these seem to have been later additions rather than elements conceived as intrinsic parts of the arch). The Arch of Gallienus on the Esquiline hill, with three vaulted openings, of which the central one is higher, shows a similar lack of unity; the material (travertine) and technique indicate a date in the Augustan period. It can be said that a more unitary plan had been used earlier in the arch at Orange (V, PL. 470) if, as is commonly supposed, it is true that the arch dates from the pre-Augustan period and that the only addition in Tiberian times was the attic story. The faces of the arch have four columns that carry a false arch in the tympanum of the pediment, over an entablature; they reveal a strong Hellenistic influence, indicating an attempt to combine different styles and thereby confirming the attribution of the arch to the early years of the Empire.

Many quadrifrons arches of the Flavian period are known from reproductions on coins or reliefs. If, as has been proposed, the chamber in the attic story was intended as a tomb for the emperor, the Arch of Titus (PL. 131) had a funerary as well as an honorary character. Apart from the reliefs on the fascia in the entablature (PL. 291), the decoration was limited to the inside of the arch, thus preserving the simplicity, the balance, and the unity of the structural mass; at the inside and outside corners the piers were framed by engaged columns with Composite capitals — a style that was to gain increasing acceptance; only the strongly projecting corbel-like keystone of the arch and the decorative figures alongside introduced a more vigorous feeling of movement. The Arch of the Gavii in Verona, designed by the architect Lucius Vitruvius Cerdo, was similar in style; the façades were animated by the articulation of the bases of the columns, which, together with the pediment projecting over the attic, created the sense of energy characteristic of the Flavian epoch. The lateral vaults constitute secondary axes that recall the plan of the quadrifrons arch.

The arches at Rimini and on the Esquiline (see above) fulfilled the function of city gates. The Porta Venere at Hispellum (mod. Spello) has three arches; the larger (central) arch is framed by heavy Doric pilasters, and the arch is surmounted by an attic story with a covered loggia and arched windows. The loggia of the Porta Palatina at Turin has a double row of windows, the lower ones arched and the upper ones rectangular; the same is true of the Turin city gate, which has been incorporated into the Palazzo Madama. Also in Spello, the Porta S. Ventura has an archivolt flanked by two pilasters that carry the pediment. This is similar to the Porta Tiburtina, built in Rome in 5 B.C. to carry the channels of the Aqua Tepula, Aqua Marcia, and Aqua Julia and later incorporated into one of the gates of the Aurelian walls. A calculated play of light and dark is evident in the Porta Maggiore in Rome, with its two arches supporting the channels of the Aqua Claudia and Anio Novus. In Claudian times, city gates were embellished with architectural decorations, as, for example, in the Porta Paphia in Colonia Agrippinensium (mod. Cologne), dating from A.D. 50. This decoration, however, was evident also in some gates of a slightly earlier date, such as the one at Fano and the lower part of the Porta dei Borsari in Verona. The latter was given a new facing of white stone, quarried nearby, toward the second half of the 1st century (not in the time of Gallienus, as the inscription in his honor would suggest); its entablatures and small pediments — both curved and straight — give it some of the liveliness of Flavian architecture. Even closer to this style is the Porta dei Leoni, also in Verona, in which two twisted columns on high pedestals on the attic story flank each side of a large niche.

g. Thermae. Little is known of the thermae in the 1st century of the Empire. At Baia the thermal hall was perhaps used as the frigidarium. Next to it was a second thermal building, enclosed in a great rectangle spreading over three levels of terraces, the highest of which terminated in a semicircular exedra with a round tank in the center. The walls, which were faced in *opus reticulatum*, and the piers and arches with facings of tufa ashlar blocks tend to indicate a date for these thermae in the early imperial age, although numerous and radical alterations were carried out later. If the Baths of Agrippa (built in 19 B.C., when the Aqua Virgo aqueduct, which fed them, was completed), with their imposing hall, approximately 60 ft. square and ending in an apse, later reconstructed by Hadrian, were an example of an earlier layout, the original plan of the huge thermal complexes must be dated to the beginning of the Empire, confirming previous deductions from the baths at Baia. It was probably at this time that these buildings first became known

as "thermae" (*Pliny*, op. cit., XXXVI, 189). The admiration aroused by the Baths of Nero, as reflected in Martial (*Epigrams*, W. Ker, trans., London, New York, I, 1919, VII, 34), demonstrates that they already showed aspects of the monumental grandeur that was to become standard in later times. Few traces remain of the Baths of Nero and of those begun by Titus and completed by Domitian, but from plans made during the Renaissance it is clear that Nero's Baths exemplified the fusion of the Roman thermae with the Greek gymnasium. The Baths of Titus had a more compact plan in the axial arrangement of the three main halls (frigidarium, tepidarium, and caldarium), with the smaller rooms on either side.

h. Private buildings. Private building in Rome in the early period of the Empire has not left extensive traces; however, the interest of Augustus in this aspect of civil life is indicated by his instructions for the publication of a speech by Rutilius

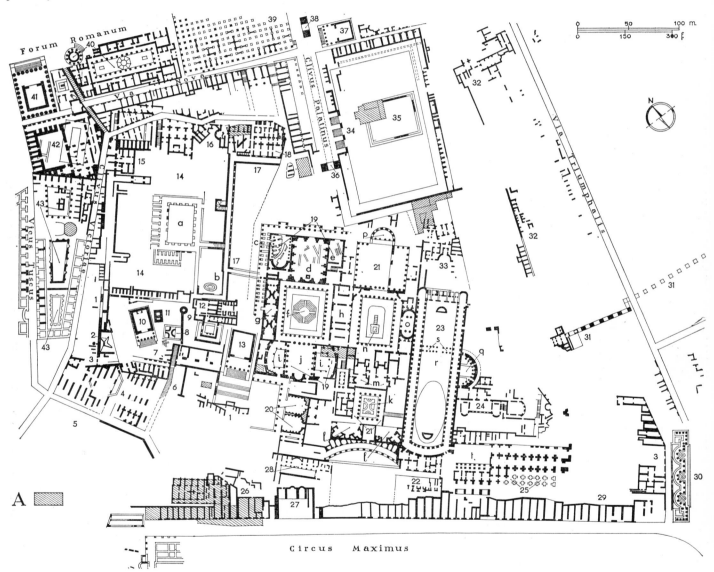

Rome, buildings of the Palatine and the area adjoining the Roman Forum, plan. *Key*: (A) constructions later than the Roman period. Principal monuments: (1) houses of republican period; (2) walls of "Roma quadrata"; (3) insulas of imperial period; (4) altar of an unidentified god; (5) Lupercal; (6) steps of Cacus; (7) tombs and sacellums of archaic period; (8) silos and walls of archaic period; (9) tholus-shaped tank; (10) Temple of the Magna Mater; (11) auguratorium; (12) House of Livia; (13) Temple of Apollo (known as the Temple of Jupiter Victor); (14) Domus Tiberiana: (*a*) central atrium; (*b*) *vivarium*; (15) remains of the Palace of Caligula; (16) remains of the House of Commodus; (17) Cryptoporticus of Nero with south wing added by the Flavians; (18) building from the age of Domitian; (19) Domus Flavia: (*c*) basilica; (*d*) so-called "royal hall"; (*e*) *lararium*; (*f*) peristyle; (*g*) nymphaeums and baths; (*h*) tablinum; (*i*) fountains; (*j*) triclinium; (20) libraries; (21) Domus Augustana: lower floor, (*k*) peristyle; (*l*) *diaeta*; (*m*) tablinum; upper floor, (*n*) peristyle with aedicula at center of impluvium; (*o*) nymphaeum; (*p*) exedra; (22) imperial box overlooking the Circus Maximus; (23) stadium or hippodrome; (*q*) exedra; (*r*) altar of the twelve gods; (*s*) medieval portico; (*t*) remains of façade built by Domitian; (24) Baths of Septimius Severus; (25) Severan substructures; (26) constructions under S. Anastasia; (27) Schola Praeconum; (28) Paedagogium; (29) tabernae opposite the Circus Maximus; (30) Septizonium; (31) Aqua Claudia; (32) houses of imperial period; (33) nymphaeum; (34) Pentapylon of Heliogabalus (?); (35) Temple of Caesar; (36) Arch of Domitian (or of Augustus); (37) Temple of Jupiter Stator; (38) Arch of Titus; (39) vestibule of the Domus Aurea; (40) Temple of Vesta and atrium of the vestals; (41) Temple of Castor and Pollux; (42) vestibule of the Domus Palatina; (43) Horrea Agrippiana (*after* G. Lugli, *Roma antica, il centro monumentale*, Rome, *1946*).

on the height of buildings, and by the Julian law that limited the height of façades to 70 ft. (Suetonius, *De vita caesarum, Divus Augustus*, LXXXIX, 2; Strabo, *Geografikon*, V, iii, 7–8), that is, to six or seven stories. Violations incurred the demolition of the floors that exceded the provisions of the law (Ulpianus, *Digesta*, XXXXIII, 24, 7). As early as the republican era houses were several stories high; this is known from a reference to events in 218 B.C. (Livy, *Ab urbe condita*, XXI, lxii, 3). It is unlikely, however, that houses rising straight from ground level were built to great heights; at the most, they might have been constructed so as to exploit the slope of the ground or artificial terraces (the limitation in height referred in fact to the façade). Thus Seneca's reference (*Epistolae morales*, XC, 8) to "these contrived dwellings of ours which rise story upon story" is more easily explained. The top floors were made of wood (Gellius, XV, 1, 2), and dividing walls (Plutarch, *Vitae, Crassus*, II, 4) as well as wooden lofts or pergolas (Suetonius, op. cit., *Divus Augustus*, XCIV, 12) were widely used.

After the fire of A.D. 64, Nero stipulated the use of building stone from Gabii and Alba Longa, more resistant to fire, and instructed that houses should be spaced at intervals of 10 ft.; he also suggested that houses should be built with porticoes in front (Tacitus, *Annales*, XV, xliii), thus giving impetus to new architectural forms. As buildings became higher, they naturally tended to open outward with windows and balconies (*maeniana*) and with stairs leading directly into the street; this was the origin of the multistoried tenement that came to be called an *insula*. The word was first used in this sense by Cicero (*Orationes, Pro Caelio*, VII, 17); originally it referred to the land on which the tenement was built, "isolated" from nearby structures. The traditional axial design of the *domus* did not disappear, although for some time it had been increasing in depth, with the peristyle and other rooms arranged around the atrium; however, the type was declining. Pliny the Younger referred to this design as the main characteristic of the ancient house ("after the manner of the ancients," Pliny, *Epistolae*, V, 6). At Pompeii and Herculaneum the transformation of the old style can be observed in some houses that are thought to belong to the middle of the 1st century of our era or to have been rebuilt at that time. The house usually opened onto terraces dug out of a hill [e.g., the terraces in Region VIII and in the House of Loreius Tiburtinus in Pompeii (VIII, PL. 425); the House of the Stags at Herculaneum]. Sometimes a feature of the older style, such as the tablinum, was eliminated (e.g., the House of the Vettii at Pompeii). Even the plan of the House of Livia on the Palatine (FIG. 519), which may or may not have been the house occupied by Augustus (the different stages of its construction have not yet been traced), was adapted to the slope of the terrain. The smaller rooms were grouped around the main enclosure, consisting of a quadruple portico, which rose where a tetrastyle atrium, perhaps part of an earlier structure, had been transformed into a vestibule. At Ostia — where the alterations are better seen in houses attributed to the 2d century — from the earliest times rows of shops were set into the house fronts, and sometimes arcades lined the main streets.

Outside Italy, evidence is limited to Gaul; the atrium was comparatively rare and its design in that region was apparently very elaborate, as in the Corinthian atrium of a house at Vaison-la-Romaine (V, FIG. 762), but elsewhere the most usual plan called for rooms arranged around the peristyle, of which there were sometimes two placed along the same axis. Less important houses had a court without columns in the center, following a plan that was closer to Greek architecture.

The building of residences in Rome found greater scope in the palaces of the emperor and in private villas. Beginning with Augustus, the emperors lived on the Palatine (FIG. 519), and magnificent palaces there are attributed to Tiberius, Caligula, Claudius, and Nero. The Domus Transitoria stretched as far as the Esquiline; a round hall from this structure has survived, with four wings that extend under the Temple of Venus and Rome. These palaces foreshadowed the monumental architectural scale of the Domus Aurea (FIG. 522) and the Domus Flavia.

The Domus Aurea, designed by the architects Severus and Celer (Tacitus, *Annales*, XV, xlii), had more the character of a villa than a palace, with its buildings interspersed with woods and gardens scattered over a vast area, so extensive as to provoke the sarcastic comments of Nero's contemporaries (Suetonius, *De vita caesarum, Nero*, XXXI, 1–2). The main building, in large part preserved beneath the thermae built by Trajan, appears to have been rectilinear in shape, its façade interrupted at the center by a polygonal recess, or court, onto which opened a large hall with a projecting front. The plan was, in fact, that of a villa without the portico that usually enlivened the façade. The wings on either side of the polygonal court had different plans: the west wing, mainly built along straight lines, was more or less uniform, while the east wing had more variety, in that the rooms were built around an octagonal hall

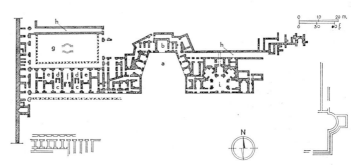

Rome, Domus Aurea, plan of the excavated zone. (*a*) Vestibule; (*b*) "hall of the gilded vault"; (*c*) cubiculum; (*d*) dressing-room; (*e*) chapel; (*f*) tablinum; (*g*) peristyle; (*h*) cryptoporticus; (*i*) octagonal hall (*from A. Boethius, 1960*).

covered by coved vaulting. This plan was much copied in subsequent architecture; it can be seen in the disposition of a series of square rooms around a hexagonal hall in a Roman villa, probably of the 1st century of our era, at Abicada in Portugal, and in some nymphaeums in the Domus Flavia, of even more complex design, with wall niches that were sometimes of two orders.

The palace complex built on the Palatine was divided into the Domus Augustana, the private residence of the emperor, and the Domus Flavia, which consisted of reception rooms and was intended for public affairs; it was completed by Domitian in A.D. 92. It had been designed by the architect Rabirius (Martial, *De spectaculis liber*, VII, lvi), to whom some scholars attribute the east wing of the Domus Aurea as well, because of the variety of movement in its walls and vaults and the deliberate calculation of effects of light. Both the Domus Augustana and the Domus Flavia generally follow the scheme of the *domus* type, with the rooms arranged around one or more peristyles. The Domus Augustana had no external façade, except for a large semicircular exedra that overlooked the valley in which lay the Circus Maximus. At the center of the Domus Flavia was the large so-called "Royal Hall," which was in a shallow apse; the other walls were articulated by niches with statues flanked by columns of colored marble. A theory that the hall was barrel-vaulted, with a coffered ceiling, has not yet been validated. The imaginative internal plan, in a closed and perfectly rectangular general scheme, denotes a great architect, one who adapted traditional features to provide original and sometimes novel architectural solutions.

By the beginning of the Empire, the Roman villa no longer had the appearance of a single structure that was at the same time a farm and a private residence. In the more important villas, the type of main building constructed on a terrace with nymphaeums and niches inside the walls was abandoned, and the villa consisting of scattered buildings of varying size and proportions became increasingly widespread; these were adapted to the conformation of the site, and the main part of the villa was broken up by separate tricliniums, often semicircular in shape; secluded pavilions (*diaetae*), often in the form of towers with one or two rooms; swimming pools; and promenades (*ambulationes*). A larger building was usually, although not always, erected in a central position dominating the entire complex; on its façade, a straight or curved portico was often prolonged by two wings at right angles. Sometimes, instead, a series of porticoes was used to enrich the façade and give unity to the architectural design. The terraced-villa type continued into the era of Domitian, as in his villa near Alba Longa in the Alban Hills, while the other, more dispersive type appeared in Nero's villa at Antium (mod. Anzio) and in the villa on the inlet of Val Catena on the island of Brioni Grande in Campania.

i. Monumental tombs. The architecture of monumental tombs was varied. The tumulus type, if not the most common, was certainly the most characteristic and was preceded by a long tradition. In this type the circular podium was surrounded by a ringwall, somewhat low in relation to the diameter; in the center was the burial cella, which was reached by a corridor. The most impressive example of the tumulus type is the mausoleum constructed by Augustus in the Campus Martius in 28 B.C. to hold the ashes of the members of his family. The outer perimeter wall, cylindrical in form, was faced with travertine and enclosed five concentric ringwalls that progressively augmented in height toward the center. The three inmost walls were notably closer to one another and contained two vaulted passages and the cella. In the center was a great column, out of which a small chamber had been cut; the column rose above the tumulus, bearing the statue of the emperor. The two outermost walls were linked by radial walls with niches and buttresses and were filled with earth from the tumulus (this was perhaps the only part of the structure that was covered with earth). Above the center of this base structure was a second perimeter wall about whose height there are various theories; it was built in masonry and supported the central column.

In other tombs the cylindrical podium was of greater height and importance, as in the mausoleums of L. Munatius Plancus and L. Sempronius Atratinus near Caieta (mod. Gaeta), built about 20 B.C., in both of which can be observed a marked tendency to increase the number of rooms accessible from the outside; probably, also, the roof line was broken up by architectural elements. In the Mausoleum of Plancus the perimeter wall was topped by cippi. This motif also appeared in the Tomb of Caecilia Metella, who was perhaps the wife of Crassus, Augustus' fellow consul in 30 B.C.; the cippi were later incorporated into the medieval building that was built over her tomb, in which the cylindrical perimeter wall rested on a square base.

Honorary monuments in the Augustan period were similar in plan to the funerary monuments. The so-called "Egelstein" trophaeum near Mogontiacum (mod. Mainz), alleged to have been the cenotaph erected to Drusus by his soldiers, is reduced to a shapeless ruin. Perhaps it resembled the trophaeum of Augustus built in 7-6 B.C. at La Turbie in Alpes-Maritimes (XIII, PL. 243), in which the main cylindrical body rested on a square podium and was encircled by an order of 24 Tuscan columns that supported the cone-shaped roof. Later, toward the Flavian period, the cylinder was embellished with exedras and niches of various sizes, as in the so-called "Mausoleo delle Carceri Vecchie," near Santa Maria Capua Vetere, and in the Catacomb of Priscilla on the Via Appia, in which the cylinder rests on a square base.

From the Augustan period onward, the problem of superposing volumes found a variety of solutions. The simplest appear in a tomb at Sarsina, near Forlì (IV, PL. 456), in a number of mausoleums in northern Italy (Aquileia), in the so-called "Tomb of Vergil" in Naples, and in the Tomb of the Istacidi at Pompeii. A more elaborate design was used in the Mausoleum of the Julii at Glanum (mod. Saint-Rémy-de-Provence; V, PL. 470), in which a tetrapylon with corner columns rested on a square podium; it was topped by a small round temple with a conical roof similar to that of a recently reconstructed mausoleum at Aquileia. An even more complex design is to be found in the tomb known as La Conocchia, near Santa Maria Capua Vetere, which dates from after the middle of the 1st century of our era.

Although the simple niche type of tomb was the most common and was used over a long period, as early as the 1st

century tombs sometimes took the form of a small temple or heroon, as in the tetrastyle Tomb of C. Lusius Storax, near Chieti. In the Augustan period there were instances of unique tombs, such as that in Rome of the baker M. Vergilius Eurysaces, which was a copy of his bakery set on a square base, and others derived from exotic models, such as the Pyramid of Caius Cestius (V, PL. 195); among others should be mentioned the Tomb of Porsena at Clusium (mod. Chiusi), known from the description of Varro in Pliny (*Naturalis historia*, XXXVI, xc, 3). Tombs of the exedra type with marble seats and columns were of little architectural or monumental interest. Equally simple in design were the columbariums, collective burial places, which had funerary niches, or loculi, in the walls. These have been found mainly in Rome and in the Campania region (especially along the Via Campana at Pozzuoli); they spread to other regions presumably in the second half of the 1st century. They had semicircular passages, preceded by or ending in a rectangular chamber [e.g., Bordj el-Aïn in Tunisia, Carmo (mod. Carmona) in Spain].

Noteworthy examples of funerary architecture outside the Italian world, besides the example at Saint-Rémy-de-Provence, are the tumulus tomb of the Lollii near Cirta (mod. Constantine), of the late 1st century, and the so-called "Tomb of Absalom," near Jerusalem (VIII, PL. 331), with its superposed volumes, which dates from the middle of the 1st century.

Later imperial architecture. The architectural concepts of the Augustan and of the Flavian period, the former more serene and more purely classical, the latter more dynamic and more sumptuous in its contrasts of light and shade, were transformed in the succeeding period and often achieved impressive effects. The two trends interacted, producing different results, while at the same time the classical ideal exercised a restraining influence on any tendency to excess. It was not until late in the 3d century, in the period of the Tetrarchy, that the equilibrium maintained by the classical ideal was lost and the two currents diverged. Before this occurred, however, a unitary style of Roman imperial architecture was to be diffused throughout the ancient world.

a. Construction. The use of brickwork in buildings became widespread; however, the bricks were no longer cut, and from the time of Trajan to that of the late Antonines, the consular date, together with the name of the owner of the workshop, was generally imprinted on them. Cornices and decorations were often of varicolored brickwork, and the intrados of the vaults were faced with brickwork in a technique that had been used previously in one of the vaults of the Domus Aurea and in various Flavian buildings. Lightweight materials were used in vaulting, especially near the keystone; in some instances cavities were introduced into the ribs, and rows of amphoras were inserted into the domes. The vertical thrust of the vault was increased; it rested on a fenestrated drum, which was sometimes polygonal, as in the so-called "Temple of Venus" at Baia.

b. City planning and forums. The construction of Trajan's Forum (I, PL. 323, FIG. 513) connected the center of Rome to the Campus Martius by creating an opening in the rocky spur that jutted out from the Quirinal toward the Capitoline hill. The work was entrusted to Apollodoros of Damascus (q.v.) and was inaugurated in A.D. 113 (*Dio's Roman History*, E. Cary, trans., London, New York, 1914-27, LXIX, 4). The entrance was in a convex wall that curved toward the Forum of Augustus; two great exedras, each preceded by columns and an ambulatory, opened on either side. The ambulatory led into a colonnaded rectangular area, in the middle of which stood the equestrian statue of the emperor. The Basilica Ulpia was opposite the entrance, occupying the site originally planned for a temple that was later built by Hadrian in honor of his adoptive father in the enclosed semicircular space behind the basilica; the temple opened onto a porticoed court with the Greek Library and Latin Library on either side and Trajan's Column in the center. The technique of graduating perspectives by means of colonnades, used earlier in a more restrained way, was here exploited to the full. It is clear, therefore, that Apollodoros, in spite of his eastern origin, was familiar with Roman architectural tradition. His plan extended to the slopes of the Quirinal, where an impressive complex of tabernae, known as Trajan's Market (I, PL. 323), was built on different levels. The two lowest levels were arranged in a large hemicycle following the curve of the exedra nearest the hill and terminating at either end in a semicircular building. Above this ran a street, known in the Middle Ages as the Via Biberatica, bordered by another complex of tabernae, also on different levels; at the end stood a great hall, roofed with six cross vaults (XIII, PL. 222), believed to be the Basilica Traiana mentioned by ancient writers (*Scriptores Historiae Augustae, Commodus*, II, 2). A slight similarity to the Forum of Trajan is perhaps recognizable in the forum of Velleia, in which the basilica stands on one of the shorter sides. Provincial forums at this time [e.g., those in cities of Gaul: Augusta Raurica (mod. Augst), Lugdunum Convenarum (mod. Saint Bertrand-de-Comminges)] always included temples, following the ancient plan; even in later times, in the age of the Severi, the forum of Leptis Magna conformed to this plan (FIG. 525), with a temple opposite the basilica finished by Caracalla in 216.

The urban layout of provincial cities was modeled after that of Rome. Gerasa (mod. Jerash) is notable in this connection. It was rebuilt by Pompey; colonnaded streets, many of them curved, were added only in Hadrian's time, and the Temple of Artemis was built on the main axis (VIII, FIG. 940). Colonnaded streets were used in African cities built along the lines of military camps, as in Thamugadi (mod. Timgad) and

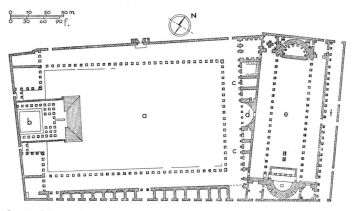

Leptis Magna, Severan forum and basilica, plan. (*a*) Forum; (*b*) temple, perhaps dedicated to the Gens Septimia; (*c*) tabernae; (*d*) apsidal entrance; (*e*) basilica; (*f*) vestibule (*after J. B. Ward-Perkins, JRS, XXXVIII, 1948, p. 62*).

Lambaesis (mod. Lambessa), both founded by Trajan; in cities of Asia Minor (e.g., Termessus, Miletus); and in Greece itself, in Corinth. Behind these colonnades rose buildings that were often imposing in appearance.

c. Basilicas and temples. The Basilica Ulpia was divided into five aisles by two double orders of columns and ended in exedras on its shorter sides, thus introducing a monumental interpretation of a feature that had appeared on a more modest scale in earlier rectangular buildings. The motif reappeared in provincial basilicas, such as those of Augusta Raurica, Alesia (mod. Alise Sainte-Reine), and Volubilis (mod. Qasr Faraoun); it was used also in the basilica at Leptis Magna (I, FIG. 87), which had three aisles, and in which the exedras were not screened by columns. The basilicas at Volubilis and Augusta Raurica were similar in plan. The older type of rectangular plan continued to be used, both in Italy (the basilica at Ostia, of the time of Trajan) and elsewhere (the long rectangular buildings at Tipasa and Sigus in Algeria — although it is not certain that these were used as basilicas). The plan persisted even later, and the basilica built in Rome by Alexander Severus

(*Scriptores historiae Augustae, Severus Alexander*, XXVI, 7) was perhaps of this type; the location of its ruins, however, has not been ascertained.

In the 2d century, temples were built on plans similar to those used in the Flavian period. The octastyle temple depicted on a coin of Trajan and the temple built by Hadrian in honor of Trajan, according to the design of Apollodoros of Damascus, in the area adjoining the forum (I, FIG. 513) were rectangular in shape and were raised on high podiums and surrounded by large precincts. The Temple of Hadrian, from which several imposing columns survive in the modern Piazza di Pietra in Rome, was erected in 145 in the center of a rectangular portico. The building was peripteral and octastyle, and the interior walls were articulated by engaged columns or pilasters on high bases that were decorated by reliefs with figures of the provinces (Rome, Palazzo dei Conservatori, Vat. Mus.; Naples, Mus. Naz.). The temple erected to Faustina in 141, dedicated also to her husband, the emperor Antoninus, after his death (161), was built on a high podium and is reminiscent of the temples of the Augustan age, with its deep pronaos and its elegant outline (PL. 294). The Temple of Venus and Rome (FIG. 526),

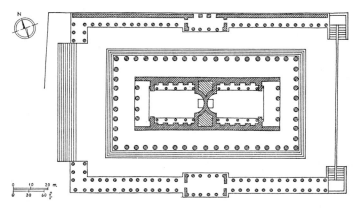

Rome, Temple of Venus and Rome, integrated plan (*from G. Lugli, Monumenti minori del Foro romano, Rome, 1947*).

designed and built by Hadrian, was peripteral and decastyle, and its two flanking apsidal cellas seem to recall, although somewhat vaguely, a Greek temple at Mantineia. The form in which it has survived is that of the reconstruction by Maxentius; if this form reproduces the previous plan, the criticism of Apollodoros that the cella was too large in proportion to the small space that surrounded it would seem fully justified, although his comments were ill-received by Hadrian (Dio Cassius, op. cit., LXIX, iv, 4).

The Pantheon (I, PL. 401) was built by Hadrian between 118/19 and 128 to replace that built by Agrippa (no evidence has yet been uncovered to prove that the original structure was circular in plan). In Hadrian's building, the hemispherical dome (XIII, PL. 224) was placed on a cylinder made of masonry and faced with brickwork, according to the method used in thermae. As in the thermae, the height of the dome was equal to its diameter, following the precepts of Vitruvius (*De Architectura*, V, x, 5). The concrete wall of the rotunda was divided into three zones of different composition, and on the exterior the base of the dome was covered with a series of steps; the dome itself was made of a lighter material which diminished in width toward the skylight and which was covered with gilded bronze plates (removed by the emperor Constans II in 663).

The dominant feature of the structure is the interior space, which achieves an independence of earlier religious architectural forms that was not feasible in the exterior plan because of cultural requirements. It is not clear whether the Pantheon was built as a heroon in honor of Mars and Venus, the protective deities of the imperial house, or whether the dome with its coffers and with alternating stars and rosettes was intended to suggest the vault of the sky. Certainly the alternation of semicircular and rectangular niches and the arches of the entrance and of the opposite niche breaks the continuity of the curving lines and the unity of the classical rhythm. The octastyle portico in gray granite (PL. 294) is of the same period as the wall of the rotunda, even though the stylistic and material connection may seem to be somewhat weak. The portico is divided into three aisles, following the basilican plan; the two side aisles end in apses. The portico serves as a façade dominating the square on which it stands; the rotunda itself must have been partly hidden by adjacent buildings such as the Saepta and the Basilica of Neptune.

Round temples different in shape from the Pantheon were by no means rare in Rome, and more were constructed in later periods, as, for example, the Temple of Serapis, built by Caracalla on the Quirinal hill, and the Temple of the Sun, built by Aurelian. Both were in the center of vast precincts, and in the walls of the precinct of the Temple of the Sun were niches and exedras. A round temple was built in the late Severan period at Ostia; it had a pronaos that was much wider than the cella and a portico on a lower level that was connected to the temple by a wide flight of steps. On the interior, seven curved niches alternated with seven rectangular ones. The Capitolium at Ostia had been built in the time of Hadrian, and numerous capitoliums rose in the 2d century in Italian and provincial cities. In some cases they took the form of three small adjacent temples on a single podium, as at Teate (mod. Chieti), where, however, one was notably smaller than the others. Some African capitoliums had similar plans; for example, in the one at Sufetula (mod. Sbeïtla) the central temple was larger than the other two, and perhaps the one at Cirta also was similar. In general, however, capitoliums were of the common type consisting of a single temple with three cellas, although not all such temples known in Africa are believed to have been dedicated to the Capitoline Triad.

In some regions of Greece and Asia Minor, the Greek tradition was continued in the temples; the Greek style was evident in the Olympieion in Athens, begun by the Roman architect Cossutius between 174 and 164 B.C. (after the Pisistratid building had been abandoned) and finished by Hadrian, and in the temple of Aizani in Phrygia, which was built not later than A.D. 125 and recalls in various details the temple of Ancyra. The so-called "Temple of Zeus-Asklepios" at Pergamum (FIG. 285), also in the eastern provinces, was inspired by the Pantheon; it was round and domed and had four curved niches alternating with four rectangular ones. The great apsidal hall in Pergamum, which was part of the sanctuary of the Egyptian deities, also revealed Roman influence. The same influence is evident at Baalbek in the sanctuary of the Heliopolitan Triad, where in the first half of the 2d century the great court and the entrance steps were completed; the propylaea and the hexagonal court were added later. The great court was surrounded by a rectangular enclosure in which there were rectangular and semicircular exedras and a colonnade, as in similar monuments in Rome. The niches in the walls of the smaller temple in the sanctuary complex, the so-called "Temple of Bacchus," which may have been dedicated to the Heliopolitan Triad, also recalled these monuments, as did the curving base and architrave of the small round temple (PL. 191). This has survived in its 3d-century form, a replica of the structure of the previous century.

In the European provinces (such as northern Gaul and the provinces on the Rhine and the Danube) earlier religious buildings were replaced by others, sometimes on a magnificent scale. Notable examples of these are the long rectangular hall that opens onto a colonnade in the Temple of Lenus Mars at Trier and the octagonal building, perhaps a temple, erected at Mainz in the 2d century; this building had wall niches and a precinct, also octagonal, that was decorated on the interior with pilasters.

d. Buildings for public spectacles. A large number of theaters were built from the 2d century onward, many of them by Hadrian (*Dio's Roman History*, E. Cary, trans., London, New York, 1914–27, LXIX, x); however, the changed character of the spectacles and the substitution of mimes and aquatic shows for the dramatic repertory brought about many alterations in the design of the orchestra and the stage. Moreover, it was in the theaters that gladiatorial combats and *venationes* took place in regions where amphitheaters were rare, as in Greece and the east (only three amphitheaters are known in Asia Minor: in Pergamum, in Cyzicus, and in Cilicia; the one in Corinth has not been conclusively identified). To accommodate these spectacles the first tiers of seats were removed and a parapet was erected either to protect the spectators or to hold the water tank (*colimbetra*), as in Corinth and, in the 3d century, in the Theater of Dionysus in Athens. Sometimes the theater was similar in plan to an amphitheater, with the difference that a block of seats was eliminated to make space for the addition of a simple structure for the stage; examples of such theaters are known in Gaul and at Verulamium in Britain. Amphitheaters were especially numerous in the west. The amphitheater at Santa Maria Capua Vetere was second in size only to the Colosseum; those at Nîmes and Arelate (mod. Arles; V, PL. 473) probably belong to the 2d century (in view of the movement in the external fascias, interrupted by the projecting entablatures), notwithstanding some outdated structural details. Amphitheaters were built in the frontier provinces, such as Pannonia [e.g., at Aquincum (mod. Budapest) and Carnuntum (mod. Petronell)]; and 25 were constructed in the African provinces.

During the 3d century, the exterior appearance of amphitheaters became more solid and severe, as in the Amphitheatrum Castrense in Rome. In the amphitheater at Thysdrus (mod. El Djem) in Africa, the exterior wall had no cornice but was enlivened by arches and half columns and parastades in shallow relief. In contrast, the *frontes scaenae* became increasingly elaborate (PL. 418). The rectilinear plan of the *scaena* persisted, especially in the eastern regions, and was continued also in some of the theaters in the west (e.g., the Severan reconstruction of the theater at Ostia; the theater at Thamugadi). It was used consistently in the odeums, notable among which is that built by Herodes Atticus in Athens about 175. However, the western type, with a central niche and rectangular exedras at the sides, appeared also in Greece (e.g., in Corinth) and Asia Minor (throughout Syria), with the exceptions of the theater of Philippopolis and the reconstruction of the theater of Miletus. Later, about the Severan period, the two exedras also became semicircular; this applied to the theater of Sabrata, in which three orders of columns framed the lateral openings of the wings in a vigorous design that stood out from the background wall (PL. 418). The same tendency can be noted in the elaborate ornamentation of the nymphaeums that often abutted on the outside of the wall bordering the stage in a manner supposedly influenced by eastern styles, and precisely, by those from Antioch. Some scholars hold that this theory is proved by the Theater of Pompey in Rome, although in fact the addition belonged to a rather late date. Comparable in design to the stage in Sabrata was the huge monumental structure, the septizonium (FIG. 519), built by Septimius Severus to screen the constructions at the southwestern end of the Palatine.

e. Triumphal arches and city gates. Commemorative arches, especially in the first half of the 2d century, followed the plan of the Arch of Titus. In the arch at Ancona, built in 115, bronze festoons (lost) added a contrasting touch to the sober and elegant design. The design of the arch at Benevento (X, PL. 154), begun by Trajan and completed by Hadrian, in which the sculptural decoration spreads across the faces of the piers and the attic story, also is of this type. In general, the basic structural masses of the many provincial arches are heavily emphasized, whether they have one opening [e.g., the arch at Bará, in Spain (VII, PL. 244), built in 102–07] or three [e.g., the arch at Medinaceli (anc. Ocilis?; XIII, PL. 243)]; in the last the vertical line of the piers is interrupted by a cornice with two niches in slight relief above it. During the 2d century, triple arches became as common as quadrifrons arches, which sometimes had unusual designs. The quadrifrons Arch of Marcus Aurelius at Tripoli had a cross-vaulted roof supported by four columns, and, on the exterior, a small octagonal stone dome.

At about the time of the Severi, sculptural decoration was extended to the structural members of the arch, as in that erected in the Forum Boarium by the *argentarii et negotiantes* in honor of Septimius Severus and his family, and as in the Arch of Septimius Severus in the Roman Forum, in which the sculptures appeared in large panels on its faces. The eight columns, supported by projecting bases decorated with sculpture, had by this time lost all character as frames for the openings; their purpose has been said to derive from that of the votive and honorary columns that were particularly common in the region of the Rhine Valley from the very beginning of the Empire. Like the sculptural decoration, they distract from the structural mass of the arch; this is evident in the quadrifrons Arch of Septimius Severus in Leptis Magna, in which projecting columns frame the arches and sculptural decoration appears even in the attic story.

The decoration of city gates also was considerably elaborated and was extended to the adjacent towers. The Porta Nigra at Augusta Treverorum (mod. Trier; V, PL. 471), with its solid, rusticated exterior, might seem to belong to the Claudian period, but the use of orders of engaged columns flanking the openings on the upper stories and in the towers is sufficient proof that it dates from the Severan age. Other gates were more soberly designed, as, for example, the north gate of Gerasa, built in the time of Trajan, and the elegant Gate of Hadrian in Athens (PL. 187), surmounted by a light, architraved attic derived from Greek models that was similar to the Propylaea of Eleusis, which date from Marcus Aurelius. In the Porta Gemina at Pulj, built in the reign of the Antonines, the arches were adorned by a thin cornice; this cornice was lost when the arches were incorporated into the gates of the wall built by Aurelian after 272.

f. Thermae. In the Baths of Trajan, begun by Domitian on a portion of the site of the Domus Aurea (Domitian's architect, Rabirius, perhaps contributed to them), a system of porticoes and gardens separated the bathing rooms, which were confined to the central building, from the rooms intended for physical exercise, study, and meetings, which were placed next to the surrounding wall. The bathing rooms were situated along two axes at right angles, and at their intersection was a large hall that was used more as a meeting place or ambulatory than as a tepidarium, as was at first believed. In the baths built by Hadrian, both those on the site of the Baths of Agrippa (built perhaps with the intention of preserving part of the existing structure) and those in the emperor's villa at Tivoli (PL. 291; FIG. 531), the plan seems to have been conceived with greater freedom. More symmetrical in design were the magnificent baths begun by Septimius Severus, inaugurated by Caracalla in 216, and finally completed by Heliogabalus and Alexander Severus (I, PL. 384; XIII, PL. 264). The huge square enclosure curves at either end into two imposing exedras that enclose two rectangular halls and an octagonal nymphaeum. At the center of the building used for bathing (FIG. 530) was a vast open swimming pool (*natatio*), open to the sky, and adjoining it was the most remarkable part of the construction, an enormous hall roofed with three cross vaults. In this hall the walls, with eight freestanding columns, carried the main thrust. For this reason, they were reinforced by other, normally disposed walls that functioned as buttresses and, at the same time, as links with adjoining rooms. Along the lesser axis of the hall lay the tepidarium, with one curving wall, which led to the caldarium, a round room covered by a graceful dome.

The general scheme of the Roman baths had been used as early as the 2d century in the baths at Trier (the so-called "Baths of Barbara") and in those at Leptis Magna, built in the time of Trajan. The baths at Baia (the so-called "Temple of Diana" and "Temple of Venus") were differently arranged because of topographic exigencies and the need to utilize the thermal waters. In the 3d century the new style spread to Africa, in the baths constructed at the time of Septimius Severus, and also to Asia Minor (e.g., Ephesus) and the *castella* on the limes of the Rhine region (e.g., Saalburg). In other places baths were more freely designed and closer in style to those of Hadrian's time, as, for example, at Thaenae (mod. Thyna) in Tunisia, where projections of the circular frigidarium extended along two axes at right angles, creating four rectangular rooms.

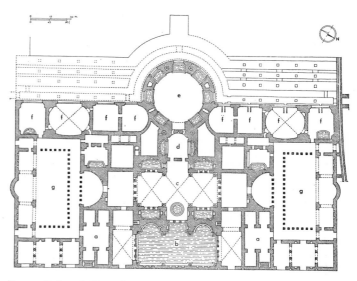

Rome, Baths of Caracalla, reconstructed plan of the thermal building. (*a*) Apodyterium; (*b*) *natatio*; (*c*) frigidarium; (*d*) tepidarium; (*e*) caldarium; (*f*) bathrooms; (*g*) "palaestra" (basilica?) (*from E. Brödner, Untersuchungen an den Caracallathermen, Berlin, 1951*).

g. Private buildings. The earlier style in private building persisted, and patrician houses, especially in the aristocratic quarters of Rome, were still built with rooms grouped around the peristyle, rather than around the atrium. This style endured also in the eastern provinces, as is evident in a house in Kos and in the cities of North Africa, where special modifications were made to adapt the style to climatic conditions by means of underground rooms and sunken peristyles [e.g., at Bulla Regia (mod. Hammam-Derradji)].

In Rome and other cities the insula, with apartments on several floors, each served by the same staircase, became widely used, as at Ostia. Wherever population density reached a high level, as in Rome, residential buildings became notably taller, so much so that Trajan was compelled to restrict the height of façades to 60 ft. (Sextus Aurelius Victor, *Epitome de Caesaribus*, XIII, 13); however, to judge from some remains (e.g., the five-storied building on the slopes of the Capitoline hill), the rule soon fell into disuse. There were two main types of insula. The first was narrow, with the rooms at the front; an example of this may be the Roman structure above which was built the Church of SS. Giovanni e Paolo on the Caelian hill in Rome, dating perhaps from the Severan age and drastically altered in the 4th century. The second type usually was built around a central court that provided a second source of light for the rooms. The building discovered under the Via Nazionale in Rome, perhaps of the 2d century but not known in any detail, may have been of this second type. At Ostia a large central room was sometimes located at the back of the court; it has been proposed, quite arbitrarily, that this may have been a deliberate approximation of the domus type. However, the function of the court was not to take the place of the atrium or the peristyle but to give light to the structures that surrounded it. The remains are too sparse to permit a progressive study of the evolution of the insula in the provinces.

Villas in Italy and the Empire, especially those in the border provinces, closely followed the style according to which the rooms were grouped around one or more peristyles. Sometimes the central peristyle was lengthened along the line of the main axis, as in the villa at Sirmione, built perhaps at the beginning of the 2d century; this has much movement in the façade, which is reminiscent of those of Flavian palaces. Villa façades were often adorned by porticoes, which sometimes extended into wings on either side; the villa at Nennig near Trier, of the 3d century, was of this type. Other villas, some of them near Rome, had plans that were more articulated and less uniform, as, for instance, the Villa of Settimio Basso (known as the Villa di Settebassi) on the Via Tuscolana and the Villa of the Quintilii on the

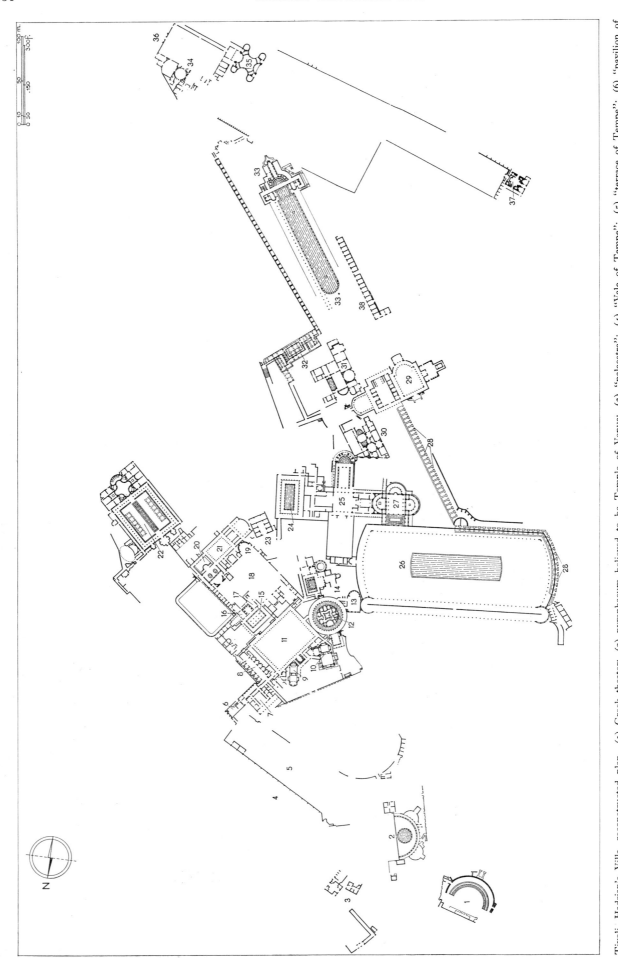

Tivoli, Hadrian's Villa, reconstructed plan. (1) Greek theater; (2) nymphaeum believed to be Temple of Venus; (3) "palaestra"; (4) "Vale of Tempe"; (5) "terrace of Tempe"; (6) "pavilion of Tempe"; (7) imperial triclinium; (8) *hospitalia*; (9) "Latin library"; (10) "Greek library"; (11) "court of the libraries"; (12) island nymphaeum (maritime theater); (13) "hall of the philosophers"; (14) baths; (15) cryptoporticus; (16) hall with nave and two aisles; (17) private library; (18) "palace" peristyle; (19) summer triclinium; (20) "palace" nymphaeum; (21) hall with Doric pillars; (22) courtyard known as Piazza d'Oro; (23) "barracks of the guards"; (24) quadriporticus with fishpond; (25) nymphaeum, formerly believed to have been a stadium; (26) "Poikile"; (27) building with three exedras; (28) "one hundred cubicles"; (29) vestibule; (30) great baths; (31) small baths; (32) "Praetorium"; (33) Canopus; (34) vestibule of the "academy"; (35) pavilion of the "academy"; (36) odeon; (37) tower of Roccabruna; (38) museum (*after R. Vighi. Villa Hadriana, Rome. 1958*).

Via Appia. Both consisted of large buildings, but in the first not all were of the same period. This type of villa, made up of separate buildings, found its most magnificent expression in the villa that Hadrian built between 118 and 138 near Tibur (mod. Tivoli; FIG. 531), incorporating the core of an older villa. The single buildings of this villa provided bold solutions to problems of design, proportion, and structure — solutions that seem to synthesize and exemplify all the previous achievements of Roman architecture. Although it is perhaps possible to distinguish four principal groups of buildings, joined by galleries and connecting elements of various kinds, the complex lacks an over-all visual unity, and in fact, it must be conceded that the villa constituted a reaction against neoclassical rationalism.

h. Monumental tombs. No important changes are evident in the design of tombs in relation to the preceding period. The mausoleum erected by Hadrian in 130 was tumulus-shaped, with the main cylindrical structure surmounted by an attic; this supported an embankment, from the center of which rose a high podium with a group of statues on top. The precinct, added to it by Antoninus Pius, gave the whole the appearance of a cylindrical monument resting on a square base, a plan that reappears in a mausoleum in Attaleia (mod. Antalya); this plan was also used in honorary monuments such as the trophaeum near the mouth of the Danube, which was probably built by Trajan. In its simplest form, without a base, the tumulus appeared in Rome in the so-called "Monte del Grano," and it continued to be used for a long time in the provinces of the limes. Tombs formed of superimposed geometric masses were even more common than previously; sometimes the upper part was pyramidal in shape, as in the tomb on the Via Appia attributed, perhaps incorrectly, to Geta. An example in brickwork has survived in Greece (on the island of Papanisi in the Aegean); its superstructure, however, was perhaps influenced by the pyramidal type of tomb known in Asia Minor.

Honorary and votive columns were built in Rome, and others, with sculptural decorations, were known along the Rhine (at Mainz) from the 1st century. At the beginning of the 2d century, columns were also used for funerary purposes. In the base of Trajan's Column, which is 100 ft. high, was deposited the golden urn containing the ashes of the emperor. The column erected in honor of Antoninus by his adopted sons Marcus Aurelius and Lucius Verus had a similar purpose, as is evident in the reliefs on the base. Columns as funerary monuments were common in Greece and above all in Syria during this period. In the evolution of this type of monument, the columns that were built in the center of funerary exedras at Pompeii and the cuspidated burial columns that were common along the Rhine (e.g., Neumagen) from the middle of the 2d century are notable.

After this time, the most widely used type of tomb had a rectangular or, less frequently, square burial chamber formed by one or more superimposed rooms; the walls came to contain arcosoliums instead of niches as the practice of interment became more common. The burial chambers were faced with brickwork in both red and yellow bricks, evidence of a deliberate pursuit of color effects that is emphasized in the stone cornice and frames and in the marble tombstones. These tombs were sometimes monumental in appearance, with the lower chamber more or less sunk in the ground and a stairway on the front that led to the upper room; the façade was elaborately ornamented (e.g., in Rome, the so-called "Sedia del Diavolo" and the Tomb of Annia Regilla). The façade sometimes resembled a pronaos, either with two columns between the piers (e.g., the Tomb of the Valerii on the Via Latina, where one descends from an open atrium to three underground rooms) or with four columns (e.g., the tomb that was transformed into the Church of S. Urbano alla Caffarella, near Rome).

If the mausoleum situated to the south of St. Peter's (next to the smaller one in which Maria, the daughter of Honorius, and Theodosius II were buried) can be dated correctly to the 2d century, then it is evident that this type, a dome on a circular base, appeared at that time, rather than in the post-Constantinian period. This would seem to be confirmed by the brickwork and by recent excavation. The design became more complicated

in the Severan age, as in the so-called "Temple of Portuno" near Ostia and in the tomb at the 9th milestone along the Via Appia, believed to be that of Gallienus because of an observation by Aurelius Victor (*Epitome de Caesaribus*, XL, 3); this type became common in the imperial mausoleums of later times.

Brickwork was not used extensively as facing in the provinces; there, structures were of stone and were mainly of the heroon type. However, Roman influence is evident in details, as in the great niche of the tomb built by Philopappos in Athens (114–16; PL. 187), which recalls the niche in the tomb of the poet Persius on the Via Appia.

i. Conclusion. With the upheavals of the 3d century that resulted in the Tetrarchy, the hegemony of Rome gradually declined until there occurred a cultural break that produced what is known as late-antique style; nevertheless, the vigor of Roman architecture was not exhausted, although it drew its inspiration chiefly from the past. The reconstruction of the Curia under Diocletian (IX, PL. 33) conformed to the rules prescribed by Vitruvius (*De Architectura*, V, ii) for proportion among height, width, and depth. In Diocletian's Palace at Spalatum (mod. Split), engaged columns framing arches were used on the façade facing the sea in an adaptation of what was by then an antique motif. The plan of the Baths of Diocletian (IX, PL. 37) imitated that of the Baths of Caracalla; the changes that were introduced did not give a sense of unity to the buildings or to the composition as a whole. The plan of the imposing central rooms of the baths reappeared in the basilica begun by Maxentius between 306 and 310 and completed by Constantine, who added to the apse at the end a second apse on the right side (IX, PL. 36). With the removal of the capital to Byzantium, the decline of Roman artistic influence was inevitable, and only the desire to flatter could have induced Constantine's panegyrist to extol a city again resplendent with monuments that surpassed those of antiquity (*Panegyrici Latini*, IV, 38). Not even these monuments were saved by the edicts promulgated between 364 and 458. The Porticus Maximae erected in 380 across the Campus Martius from the Circus Flaminius to the Aelian Bridge were to lead to the source of the new beacon of light, the basilica of the Apostle Peter.

PAINTING AND MOSAICS. Most of the evidence of painting in the imperial period comes from houses in the Campanian cities that were buried under the Vesuvian eruption of A.D. 79 (see HELLENISTIC ART, cols. 364–66). In decoration, it is known that at the beginning of the Empire the illusionistic style, which had the effect of enlarging rooms by the use of perspective so that these sometimes had the appearance of arcaded courts, had reached such a degree of elaboration as to arouse misgivings in the most impartial minds. An echo of this is found in the treatise of Vitruvius (*De Architectura*, VII, v), in the section written in the penultimate decade of the 1st century B.C.; a reference to the scene that Apatourios of Alabanda painted at Tralles makes it clear that this elaborate style originated in Asia Minor, but some features occasionally evident in paintings discovered in Italy seem to indicate that it may have been influenced by the styles of other regions, perhaps including southern Italy.

At the same time, Egyptian motifs were widely used and became even more evident in the manner of decoration usually known as Pompeian Style III (V, PL. 195), the oldest example of which is to be seen in the burial chamber of the Pyramid of Caius Cestius in Rome, of 13–12 B.C. In fact, these motifs were reproduced only superficially, with no real attempt to imitate the style. The principal characteristic of this kind of decoration, which was distinguished by its refinement of detail, was its renunciation of illusionistic perspective views and a return to the concept of the wall as a solid mass. Style III decorations were divided into three zones: the uppermost was usually white, painted with elegant and delicate architectural motifs that suggested spatial depth; the middle zone was wider; and the lowest was a painted wainscot in dark colors, often with slender arabesques. The middle zone was more complex; it was painted in luminous but cold colors and sometimes entirely in black. In the center, delicate architectural motifs surrounded the aedicula that served as a picture frame. This decoration was undoubtedly very costly because of the refinement of technique and the care with which the motifs were executed; it was, therefore, used mainly in the houses of the wealthy. It must have influenced the development of illusionistic painting, since in later examples of such painting unusual similarities to the delicate architectural motifs of Style III are clearly evident; this applies to some monuments attributed to the Tiberian age (e.g., the columbarium of Pomponius Hylas) and to the slender columns placed at several levels in a hall dedicated to Isis under the Domus Flavia, which dates from the time of Caligula.

Thus emerged the kind of decoration known as Style IV, in which illusionistic perspective, following the architectural trends of the Flavian period, was carried to its most extreme form. Style IV, with its sumptuous colors (vermilion, purple, yellow, pale blue), was utterly unrelated to the walls that it decorated and, instead, was aimed at creating a fantastic display of painted architectural elements — projections, recessions, niches containing statues (VII, PL. 214; VIII, PL. 93). It destroyed any sense of solidity in the walls, overloading them with decorative effects and often adding stucco ornamentation to the painted design; the motifs in stucco were made from molds or dies and not by hand as in the preceding period. While one can admire the richness of the style in its general effect, it cannot compare with the others either in refinement or in taste. Only in occasional examples can there be seen a tendency to subordinate the decoration to linear design and to replace architectural elements with plant motifs recalling delicate garden structures and pergolas. In various rooms of the Domus Aurea the decorations were executed in large panels against a white background (PL. 288; VII, PL. 215), a feature for which there were even earlier precedents, such as the panels in the columbarium of Hylas decorated with motifs of plants and birds and other animals.

The real flowering of Style IV occurred in the Flavian period; when the houses of Pompeii and Herculaneum were restored after the earthquake of A.D. 62 or 63, they were decorated in this style. A notable feature of its design was gradual elevation of the location of the central painting, which was also the main element of the decoration; when the room was barrel-vaulted this painting was placed in a lunette, otherwise it was placed on the ceiling. The origin of the new decorative style has been attributed by some scholars to the east; however, considering that Style IV assimilated many elements of Style III, the hypothesis of an evolution on Italian soil seems more likely. Furthermore, while painted decoration inspired by the *frons scaenae* was widely copied in the preceding period, it was even more frequently used in Style IV, as in the houses of the Gladiators, of Apollo, and of Pinarius Cerealis (PL. 418; I, PL. 409) at Pompeii. These paintings showed the elaborate *frontes scaenae* of the western type (see above).

From Rome and Italy decorative styles spread to the provinces. In Central Europe appeared a kind of panel decoration that was clearly inspired by Pompeian Style IV; examples are preserved at Aquileia, at Vindonissa (mod. Windisch), and in Britain. In the east, where Style II decoration was first successful, there are several examples in Greece and Asia Minor. However, decorations of Style III are also known in Delos and Priene (T. Wiegand and H. Schrader, *Priene*, 1895–98, Berlin, 1904, p. 318), and this fact must be considered in a study of the historical evolution of decorative styles.

The development of floor decoration in mosaic (q.v.) was analogous to that of painted wall decoration. By the beginning of the Empire, mosaic floors had had a long history and were widely used. Wall mosaics, often made with glass paste, also were common; examples are preserved at Pompeii, at Herculaneum (X, PL. 173), and in the Villa of Agrippa Postumus near Pompeii. Probably also of glass paste were the tesserae in the vaults of the "glass ceilings" mentioned by Pliny (*Naturalis historiae*, XXXVI, 189). In mosaics in *opus tessellatum*, the coloring, which had previously been based principally on the contrast between black and white tesserae, came to be more frequently elaborated by the addition of other colors; in mosaics in *opus vermiculatum*, which either formed the emblema in the center

of the floor or were laid in places less liable to wear, the old technique was still employed. The few mosaicists known by name, among them Dioskourides and Herakleitos, were of Greek origin. Designs followed the development of contemporaneous painting, which seems to have achieved less striking effects than did mosaic decoration. From the time of Style II onward, subjects of mosaic pictures were varied and often were mythological in theme. These pictures — especially those of mythological subjects — seem to have been of Greek inspiration and coloring. Roman subjects were rare and became more common only in decorations of Style III; so also the influence of Roman literary themes, which is sometimes vigorously upheld, seems doubtful. It should be remembered, also, that pictures and representations in mosaic, even when found in widely separated places, are often identical not only in subject and design but also in coloring and detail. It is therefore reasonable to suppose that they evolved from earlier archetypes; whether they were actual copies is debatable. The attribution to artists of a desire to create new forms in mural paintings in houses in Rome, in the cities of Campania, and in other places where such decorations have survived, is contradicted by conclusions that can be drawn from the scanty remains of ancient painting and of a literary tradition. Nevertheless, it cannot be denied that these artists showed remarkable skill and amazing technical experience. The difficulty lies in identifying the means that provided them with examples of the original compositions for use in their own works; these means were probably the pictures that had been imported from Greece by Rome and other Italian cities. That there existed books of plates or cartoons reproducing the originals in color is a hypothesis for which there is no proof; nor is there proof for the theory that artists made use of illustrated manuscripts, which existed as early as the Hellenistic period and of which a few late examples with reproductions of earlier works have survived.

In studying the chronological development of the art of decoration, it becomes clear that painting fully conformed to decorative trends. For example, the well-known wall painting from the House of Livia depicting Io guarded by Argos, surrounded by Style II decoration (PL. 288), is characterized by a delicacy of coloring and shading that both softens and emphasizes the figures in the diffused light that illuminates the scene. The picture with the same outline found in the Macellum of Pompeii (X, PL. 329), surrounded by Style IV decoration, is entirely different in its execution. Therefore, if there was an archetype — and in this case a famous picture by Nikias of Athens, who lived in the 4th century B.C., has been cited — it is clear that only the composition of the original group was preserved. A study of the Dionysiac wall painting in the Villa of the Mysteries at Pompeii (IV, PL. 168; VII, PL. 203; IX, PL. 246), a scene of which is reproduced in a mosaic found in Algeria dating from the 2d–3d century of our era, leads to the same conclusion; so also does an appraisal of the frieze in the Villa of Boscoreale (VII, PL. 192; X, PL. 481), in which the subject is probably not a religious scene, as has been alleged, but a group of members of the family of Antigonos II Gonatas. In this last frieze there are many sketchy areas that sometimes suggest the spontaneity of impressionism; in the other, however, the outlines of the figures are more carefully defined and emphasized by means of linear hatching. In both, the aim is to represent the figures as single entities or as isolated groups. This pursuit of sculptural definition in the figures applies also to other paintings included in Style II decoration, such as the so-called "Aldobrandini Wedding" (VI, PL. 57), in which mythical and historical personages are combined. The sculptural quality is more evident in the central group; the lateral groups show more pronounced linearity. This admixture of styles reappears in various paintings on white backgrounds from the Roman house at the Farnesina (I, PL. 299), in which the pure abstraction of Greek design is combined with an elegance that sometimes borders on affectation, while the solidity of the figures and the shading reveal an affinity with Neo-Attic sculpture. The same is true of the series of small pictures on marble discovered at Herculaneum, particularly that signed by Alexandros of Athens (X, PL. 266). These pictures are incorrectly called monochromes: only the preliminary drawings were monochromatic; the finished paintings were vividly polychromatic, with areas of solid colors, as is shown by a painting of the murder of the sons of Niobe and by two other paintings from Herculaneum, still unpublished, one of which also is signed by Alexandros.

In Style II landscape painting, space is marked by a sense of breadth that perhaps does not occur elsewhere in ancient painting. It should be stressed that at present only the works discovered in Italy show this complete mastery of free, unlimited space especially evident in the landscapes found in a house on the Esquiline (VII, PL. 180), known as the Vatican Odyssey landscapes, in which the Greek allegories and the inscriptions accompanying the figures prove that the pictures were the work of Greek artists. These landscapes are executed in an impressionistic style, with effects of light that accentuate the fleeting impression of the moment and reduce the evanescent figures to mere splashes of color. The long monochrome yellow frieze in the House of Livia on the Palatine is painted in the same style, with the contrasts of light and shade executed in variations of a single color; the frieze from the House of the Farnesina is similar but has figures in several colors (VII, PL. 207). This technique, which is so akin to modern impressionism, was probably that known as *compendiaria* painting and undoubtedly seemed extremely bold to contemporaries, who attributed its development to the Egyptians; its origins can, however, be traced through literary traditions to the actual beginnings of Hellenism.

The frieze from the House of the Farnesina, which belongs to the late stages of Style II, shows greater graphic precision than the other examples mentioned above. This quality is even more evident in the painting reproducing a garden from the Villa of Livia at Prima Porta near Rome (VII, PL. 208), in which the care devoted to the depiction of each single element, sometimes so meticulous as to seem contrived, demonstrates a deliberate pursuit of naturalism. The scene seems to be framed by a pergola with a projecting roof: this is a recent interpretation of the fragmentary upper part of the painting, which is attributed to the Claudian period, although this may seem doubtful when the work is compared with the scenes painted on a black ground in the Villa of the Mysteries at Pompeii, which are perhaps no later than the Augustan age. At this time motifs inspired directly by nature were introduced into the largely fanciful atmosphere of landscapes. This innovation, according to the tradition reported by Pliny (*Naturalis historiae*, XXXV, 116), was first introduced by a painter, Ludius, or Studius, at the time of Augustus.

With the flowering of Style III, outlines became sharper, and the figures, which were painted in single colors and divided into precisely defined chromatic areas, became more sculptural in their conception. These figures, generally of small size in relation to the whole, stand out against a background formed of rocks or architectural elements arranged in the manner of a stage setting. In landscape painting the rapid impressionistic technique was still employed, with certain limitations, and the painter relied chiefly on his own ability to render perspective, simplifying his task by representing the scene from above, almost as a bird's-eye view (IX, PL. 5).

This technique was to become even more common in the landscapes of a later period, which were bathed in brilliant light and sometimes illuminated by fantastic colors; these colors were used also in still lifes that contrast strongly with the naturalistic tones in those of the preceding period. Indeed, the predominant feature of paintings in decorative schemes of Style IV, apart from the more highly developed sense of space, was the effect of light reflecting on people and objects, and often this light was coordinated with the natural light that illuminated the room containing the paintings. The brilliant clarity of Style III became subdued, and the figures were often delineated by means of splashes of color that merged with one another in various ways and were enlivened by bright touches that created effects of light; just as the figures were built up by light effects, the composition of the picture as a whole also was dependent on them.

Any attempt to trace the development of painting between the Augustan period and the end of the 1st century of the Christian Era on the basis of facts deduced from the decoration must be subject to certain limitations. The decoration and the paint-

ing were not always the work of the same painter; in some cases the decoration was redone but the original painting was retained, while in other cases the painting was fitted into a wooden frame in the wall. It may be supposed, too, that the picture was originally an easel painting that was then adapted as a mural decoration. Finally, possible stylistic anticipations and, more frequently, stylistic lags must be taken into account.

It is obvious that the distinction made in an edict of Diocletian between a painter of pictures (*pictor imaginarius*) and a mural painter (*pictor parietarius*; *Corpus inscriptionum Latinarum*, III, Berlin, 1873, p. 830) must date from an earlier period. It is equally probable that painters worked in groups, associated in workshops, as is apparently confirmed by an inscription from Ostia (*Ephemeris epigraphica*, IX, 478). Apart from Ludius, or Studius, ancient tradition records at this period the names of Fabullus, or Amulius (*pictor floridus*, a floral painter; Pliny, op. cit., XXXV, 120), decorator of the Domus Aurea; Quintus Pedius, of noble birth, who dedicated himself to art because of a physical disability (Pliny, op. cit., XXXV, 21); Titidius Labeo, who was more of a dilettante than a painter, as perhaps can be said of Nero (Suetonius, *De vita Caesarum, Nero*, 52; Tacitus, *Annales*, XIII, iii) and of the copyist and restorer Dorotheus (Pliny, op. cit., XXXV, 91). More or less contemporaneous were the Venetian Turpilius, who was also more of a dilettante than a painter, and Publius and Artemidorus, who were both mentioned by Martial (*Epigrams*, W. Ker, trans., London, 1919, I, 109; V, 40). Among the painters working in Rome in the time of Vespasian were Cornelius Pinus and Attius Priscus, both named by Pliny, who described the second as "nearer in style to the artists of old days" (Pliny, op. cit., XXXV, 120). The only signature that survives (apart from that in graffito of Seleukos, not readily ascribable to the author of the decoration in the House of the Farnesina, and that of a painter named Sabinus, inscribed on a wall of the Villa of Agrippa Postumus at Boscotrecase, near Pompeii) is that of Lucius, who executed a painting of Narcissus, of inferior quality, in the Pompeian house of Octavius Quartio.

Although none of the surviving paintings were done by artists of the first rank, and while the painters generally were no more than craftsmen, it cannot be denied that this craftsmanship belonged to an artistic culture of the highest level and that some of these painters showed well-defined styles, on which modern criticism has rightly concentrated its attention. Thus it has been possible to identify a painter noted for firmly painted nudes and richly folded draperies executed with restrained coloring and to attribute to him the paintings from Herculaneum of Zeus with the young Eros whispering mischievously to him (Naples, Mus. Naz.) and of Herakles and the young Telephos (VII, PL. 193); the same painter, with the help of assistants and collaborators, painted other pictures found in the basilica at Herculaneum. At Pompeii, also, groups of paintings have been identified as belonging to individual painters. One of them executed the paintings in the atrium of the House of the Tragic Poet, the painting of Iphigenia in the House of the Citharist, and that of Mars and Venus in the same house; this painter, who used subtle psychological touches, seems to have mastered a broad formal technique that was characterized by delicacy of coloring and skillful light effects.

Outside the Italian world, fewer examples of painting have survived. The painting in a house at Vienne in Gaul would seem to correspond to the transition from Style III to Style IV; however, the lack of chronological data makes it impossible at present to trace the influence of Roman painting in the provinces.

From the end of the 1st century of our era, examples of painting became somewhat scarce even in Italy. In the few surviving decorative schemes, which date probably from the beginning of the 2d century, a more pronounced adherence to the structural shape is apparent, and the fantastic and elaborate motifs so common in the Flavian period are missing. Painted architectural settings became simple frames or interlaced motifs surrounding panels with human figures, animals, and plants. Even where architectural fantasies reappeared in the upper part of the wall, as in the house, which can be dated to A.D. 134, discovered on the site of the Villa Negroni in Rome, the feeling for space was lost. In general, decoration returned to those linear motifs noted in the preceding period and to the upward shift of the key element of the decorative scheme; this is evident in the paintings in a tomb at Caivano, near Naples. In the late 2d century, pictorial decoration was often combined with stucco: well-known examples of this are the tombs of the Valerii (VII, PL. 215) and of the Pancratii on the Via Latina and some tombs at Ostia.

Later, the renunciation of illusionistic spatial effects became more emphatic, even when architectural elements were used, as in the rooms believed to have belonged to the Paedagogium on the Palatine. At the same time, the decorations came to be framed by red or green fascias, at first narrow and later of larger dimensions. During the 3d century the evolution of painting styles terminated with the disappearance of all organic unity; only the heavy fascias remained as frames for the pictures.

In the 2d century the names of Roman painters appeared more frequently in burial inscriptions. Even emperors such as Hadrian (*Dio's Roman History*, E. Cary, trans., London, New York, 1914–27, LXIX, iii, 2; *Scriptores historiae Augustae, Hadrianus*, XIV, 8; Aurelius Victor, *Epitome de Caesaribus*, 14) and Marcus Aurelius, who was perhaps taught by Diognetos (*Scriptores historiae Augustae, Marcus Antoninus*, IV, 8), dabbled with some success in painting, and in this they were frequently imitated by their successors. The painter Hermogenes, denounced by Tertullian (*Adversus Hermogenem*, 11), appears from his name to have been Greek, as do the painters Eumelos (Philostratus and Nobius, *Lives of the Sophists*, W. Wright, trans., London, New York, 1922, 11, 5) and Aristodemos (Philostratus, *Imagines*, I, iii, 5), who were active in Rome at the time of Septimius Severus. Only much later, in the time of Valentinian, during the 4th century, a painter with a Roman name, Lucillus, is mentioned (Symmachus, *Epistolae*, 11, 2).

The pictures reproduced in mosaic in Hadrian's Villa indicate that painting in the 2d century was distinguished by greater density of color and by the increased solidity of its figures. In addition, the use of aerial perspective was largely discontinued, so that background figures shared equal prominence with those in the foreground. The possibility that the mosaics antedate the construction of the villa is disproved by the similarity to the rocky background in some of the reliefs of Trajan's Column. However, a landscape painting found in a building on the Via Appia that was undoubtedly constructed in the first half of the 2d century is evidence that illusionistic perspective was still used (PL. 301); in this case, its tenets seem to have been more correctly understood. The figures of heroines who were victims of illicit love, portrayed in the paintings discovered at Tor Marancia (Vat. Mus.), and the majority of the portraits from Fayum that date from the 2d century are decidedly classical in style; certain pictures from Ostia appear to be somewhat less traditional. The painting supposed to represent the return of Proserpina from Hades accompanied by Bacchus and Ceres, which is in a room under the Church of SS. Giovanni e Paolo in Rome (PL. 301), is attributed to the end of the century. The figures are painted in dense colors and modeled with sure, rather hard outlines. The same qualities are visible in the *imago clipeata* (Berlin, Staat. Mus.) that represents Septimius Severus and his family in the glass medallion in Brescia from the time of Julia Maesa, in a group of portraits from Fayum (PL. 197; IV, PL. 451; X, PL. 489; XI, PL. 214), and in various paintings in the Hypogeum of the Aurelii in Rome (III, PL. 305; VII, PL. 218). After the end of the 2d century, figures began to lose their solid sculptural quality in an anticipation of the abandonment of organic forms characteristic of the late-antique style.

The development of pictorial decoration spread from Rome to the provinces — from Germany and Gaul to Holland and Britain. Surviving examples are now reduced to fragments, but regional differences are distinguishable in the context of the general uniformity of style. In the eastern provinces, to judge by some paintings from Eleusis and Pergamum that belong to the 2d century of our era, the divergence from western tradition that took place in later times was not yet noticeable. The number of pictures discovered outside Italy that can be attributed with certainty to this period is small. The fragmentary painting from Augusta Vindelicorum (mod. Augsburg; Maximilianmus.), which

dates perhaps from the middle of the 2d century, shows notable imagination in the composition and exceptional sculptural quality in the representation of the figures; similar qualities exist in a painting of Apollo and the Muses in a modest sacellum excavated near Sparta.

After the end of the 1st century, mosaic became a predominantly Roman art; mosaicists often had Roman names, and Roman subjects were more widely used. The use of separately worked emblemas framed by bands of *opus tessellatum* was discontinued during the course of the 2d century, and the work was carried out directly on the site. From that time, artists using the *opus vermiculatum* technique worked side by side with those specializing in *opus tessellatum*; sometimes the floor was executed by a single artist, and thus a greater unity was achieved. In about the middle of the 2d century, or even earlier in some places (e.g., at Trier), workshops of mosaicists were formed throughout the Empire; their output was slowly emancipated from Italian styles, even though contacts with Italian workshops were never entirely broken. In mosaic, as in painting, western and eastern schools can be distinguished, each divided into local groups of varying affinities according to the geographic, cultural, and commercial links between the different parts of the Empire in which the workshops operated.

SCULPTURE. *From the Augustan period to the end of the 1st century of our era.* The abundance of sculptural works from this period marked a new phase in the history of ancient sculpture. Previously, the preference for Greek art shown by the cultured classes of Rome had been so emphatic as almost to stifle any response from the native tradition, which remained confined to portraits and reliefs.

There were few precedents for such reliefs in the classical style as those of the so-called "altar of Cn. Domitius Ahenobarbus" (VII, PL. 210). In a frieze from the Basilica Aemilia (PL. 286) that dates probably from between 55 and 34 B.C. and certainly from before the fire of 14 B.C., motifs typical of the local iconographic tradition reappear in some groups, and some realistic details in the same tradition can be seen in some of the heads; however, the predominant inspiration, the tendency to avoid overcrowding, and the rejection of spatial depth were inherited entirely from Greek models. It is possible that the frieze was the work of a Greek artist living in Rome.

Until the Augustan age, Greek and Roman elements had appeared side by side; the fusion of the two was only partially achieved in the Ara Pacis of Augustus, which was voted in 13 B.C. and consecrated in 9 B.C. Classical elements predominated in the work, however. It has been suggested that the frieze on the interior of the precinct that surrounded the altar illustrates in marble the temporary wooden enclosure (erected either for ceremonies or to contain the animals intended for sacrifice) and the ornamental festoons (VII, PL. 211). On the exterior, in the upper zones of the south and north sides, is a sculptural representation (PL. 286; VII, PL. 261) of the procession that accompanied the emperor to ceremonies; members of the imperial family, important officials of the state and Senate, and the people are represented in a somewhat idealized manner, with little reference to individual physical characteristics — hence still-unresolved difficulty in identifying them. The two entrances, which visibly emphasize the contrast between this monument erected in honor of peace and the Temple of Janus, are flanked by four panels. The panels on the west side represent Tellus accompanied by the Aurae Velificantes (III, PL. 488) and Rome seated above a bundle of weapons, together with Peace and Honor. The two panels on the east side represent the festival of the Lupercal and Aeneas making sacrifice to the penates (III, PL. 385). In the lower zone, on the four sides of the exterior, branches thick with leaves twine in elaborate spirals from a central acanthus plant. Swans with outspread wings stand on large branches while other animals, small reptiles, and birds move among the foliage (VII, PL. 211).

In this composition, historical and allegorical subjects are juxtaposed in a uniquely Roman manner. The intention was to celebrate the benefits of the new political stability, while the connection between the various subjects depended on the most elusive sequence of ideas. For example, the floral reliefs, which were mistakenly thought to have been imitations of eastern carpets, are symbolic of the beneficial power of peace over nature. The concept is repeated in the Tellus panel, in which Mother Earth lavishes copious gifts in honor of the emperor; this concept was to be reiterated constantly in Roman art. The reliefs that decorated the altar itself (the podium, which also had figural reliefs, has unfortunately been lost) are preserved only in the sides of the *mensa*, or altar. These reliefs are decorated with spiral motifs and fascias bearing the scene of a sacrifice. That this scene represents the annual sacrifice to Peace is evident in the presence of the vestals and ritually established victims (refuting recently expressed doubts about the traditional identification of the monument). Allegories and historical scenes are represented in Greek forms, with smoothly flowing lines. The figures, which were modeled out of rather than cut into the marble; the plant and animal motifs, which were carved in very low relief on the farthest planes and give atmosphere to the scene; the unity of the composition, achieved by the interplay of glances; and the actual cutting, which faceted rather than smoothed away the stone — all contributed new elements to the Greek style. The figures on the sides of the altar seem especially sharp and less elaborate in style. The sculptures of the Ara Pacis may be considered as expressions of a new Roman artistic style to which artists — whom a careful analysis may show to have been many — adapted themselves perfectly, even though they may have been Greeks and adherents of the Neo-Attic school (in the form under which it developed in Asia Minor and especially in Pergamum; see also HISTORICAL SUBJECTS, col. 476).

Several works of sculpture from this period have been compared to the Ara Pacis in the fusion of the background with the figural elements; among these works are the so-called "altar of the plane trees" (PL. 286) and the Grimani reliefs (Vienna, Kunsthist. Mus.; a later date has been suggested for these), which had a curved shape that was perfectly suited to their use as fountain decoration. Even in these reliefs the figures are not completely fused with the landscape, which seems pervaded, as so often in Hellenistic art, by a mysticoreligious sense; nevertheless, the feeling for nature and the realism of the plant motifs constitute a link between the reliefs and the floral decoration of the Ara Pacis.

Designs that are more frankly patterned on Greek models are to be seen in a large number of marble vases, candelabra, and *oscilla*; some of these sculptural works show similarities to archaic Greek art, although the modeling lacks the delicacy and grace of the original works. It is widely supposed that the emperor's personal taste determined the choice of models, but this has never been proved conclusively. The classical style was used in many works of a more or less artisan character, such as the vases in red terra sigillata from the factory at Arezzo (VII, PL. 216), the Campana slabs (X, PL. 435), the stuccowork exemplified by that in the Farnesina (IX, PL. 4; XIII, PL. 270), and, most importantly, the gem stones. The artists who executed these works apparently had Greek names, as, for example, Dioskourides, who was the official portraitist of Augustus (VI, PL. 38). Among the cameos attributed to him, the Evans Cameo (Met. Mus.) vibrates with the vivid effects of middle Hellenism, while the Strozzi Cameo (Br. Mus.) is colder and more academic. If the second is correctly attributed to the artist, a similar attribution must be given to the "Gemma Augustea" in Vienna (VI, PL. 39). In the latter work Augustus, seated next to the goddess Rome, is represented as being crowned by Oikoumene in the presence of Oceanus and Tellus, while Tiberius descends from the triumphal chariot (perhaps on the occasion of one of the two triumphs that took place in A.D. 7 and 12); at the bottom, Roman legionaries are raising a trophy and leading barbarian prisoners. As in a commemorative picture, allegories and historical references are combined.

Allegories were also represented in other objects, such as glass vases of different colors (e.g., white on a blue background). An example of this is the Portland Vase (cf. X, PL. 276), in whose decoration an allusion to the birth of Augustus among Roman divinities and mythical heroes has recently been seen.

A similar technique is used in a glass panel from Pompeii, decorated with a Dionysiac scene (PL. 295). The motifs mentioned above reappear in pieces of toreutics, in the bronze and silver vases, often gilded, found in various places and especially in the Campanian cities destroyed in A.D. 79 (VII, PL. 216). Two cups discovered at Boscoreale are decorated with plane-tree leaves, another two with intertwined olive branches; a cantharus (VII, PL. 315) from the same source is ornamented with spiral motifs resembling those of the Ara Pacis, and several silver vases from the House of Menander at Pompeii (Naples, Mus. Naz.) are decorated with plant motifs. Spiral lacustrine plants with fishes, crustaceans, and fishing Cupids (PL. 287) cover the surface of a crater that was cast and not embossed like the other vases mentioned. The vase vas found at Hildesheim, in Germany, with other silver vessels, and it has often been suggested that they belonged to the table service of the ill-fated Varus.

Mythological scenes decorate other silver cups such as two found at Hoby, in Denmark (XI, PL. 51), signed by the Greek Cheirisophos, whose name appears also in Roman letters. The cups were found with objects from the workshop of Gn. Trebellius, an artist of the Augustan age. Under the foot of one of the vases is scratched the name of the owner, Silius, who has been identified with the legate of Tiberius in Upper Germany. It is possible that the entire treasure was a gift of the Romans to a friendly chieftain of some of the barbarian peoples living in areas bordering the Empire. In the silver vase found at Ingolstadt in Bavaria (Munich, Glyptothek) a facial resemblance has been seen between one of the figures represented in a scene from the Trojan War and Augustus; even if the vase was worked in the time of Hadrian or Antoninus, as is believed, the design clearly belongs to the Augustan period.

In addition to Greek myths, historical scenes were also represented: in a cup from Boscoreale (Louvre) the figure of Victory pays homage to Augustus, who is seated on the *sella curulis*; on the other side, Augustus is seated on the *sella castrensis*, receiving the homage of the barbarians. A second cup is decorated with scenes of the triumph of Tiberius and a sacrifice performed by Tiberius. The relief, which is deeper in the central area, is very shallow in the background, and the whole composition is dominated, as in the frieze of the procession on the Ara Pacis, by an attempt to capture realistic expressions and details.

The various aspects of Augustan art are best observed in the many representations of the emperor; the imperial person became the principal theme of Roman portraiture. In order to explain the sameness of physical appearance of the images in works found in different places and regions, it has been asserted that Augustus was followed on his travels by artists who portrayed him according to the requirements of the moment, or that wax or clay models were sent to the provinces and there copied in marble and stone. However, this was probably true only of the emperors who succeeded Augustus. The numerous portraits of him — about 150 of them have been preserved and have attributions of varying plausibility — can be divided into two categories, with numerous modifications and overlaps. One category clearly reveals the heroic type of the Hellenistic dynastic portrait and the refinement of Neo-Attic modeling, as, for example, a portrait from Fondi (Naples, Mus. Naz.) and another in Boston (Mus. of Fine Arts). The other category reflects greater concern with recording naturalistic details and physical peculiarities, as in the firm, sober portraits of Chiusi (Mus. Civ.) and Ancona (Mus. Naz. delle Marche).

No other sculpture shows so fully the fusion of the various aspects and trends of Augustan art as the statue of the emperor discovered at Prima Porta (PL. 283). In this figure, the Polycletan rhythms of the Doryphoros (spear bearer) were transformed into a gesture of address, and this, together with the statue's stance and varied proportions, replaced the immobility of the model with a feeling of energy and movement. The decoration of the armor, in which a Roman figure, Mars or Tiberius, receives from the king of the Parthians the ensigns lost on the ill-fated day of Carrhae while divinities and human characters watch the scene, shows the same qualities as those already noted in smaller works of art in metal. The classical treatment of the hair, which was also inspired by the Polycletan model, contrasts with the shape of the face, with its hollow cheeks and slender chin. The balance between classical and realistic elements is so perfect that there is no suggestion of coldness or academicism.

This style influenced such later portraits as the statue of the emperor from Via Labicana (VII, PL. 370), which shows greater feeling for artistic refinement. In contrast, the Vatican head, which shows the emperor with the *corona spicea* as a member of the Fratres Arvales, to which he was appointed in the last year of his life, is entirely classical in style; in it, realistic elements have been overwhelmed by a strong hieratic feeling. Portraits of contemporaneous officials and private individuals were modeled on that of the emperor and often showed the same fluctuation between the two styles: for example, the portrait of Agrippa (Louvre) is pervaded with the pathos of Hellenistic baroque, while the one in the Six Collection in Amsterdam seems academic, and the Butrinto portrait is closer to the Italian style. Generally, portraits of women, especially those of Octavia and Livia, were classical in style. The same style appears in the late Augustan period in portraits of children, examples of which can be seen in the frieze of the Ara Pacis, where they are represented with a fresh and lively naturalism; this is true also of the Leningrad portrait (The Hermitage) identified by one scholar as the young Tiberius.

In other sculptures, particularly in the series on the altars dedicated to the *lares* by the *vicomagistri* after the religious reform of 7 B.C., the treatment is more summary. In some, as in the altar from the Vicus Sandalarius (Uffizi), which dates from A.D. 2, the figures seem isolated and self-sufficient, like statues against an undefined background. There are notable similarities among such sculptures as the relief in Ravenna (Mus. Naz.), in which Augustus is accompanied by two princes of the imperial house and by Venus, or Livia in the guise of the goddess; the relief of Avellino (Budapest, Mus. of Fine Arts), commemorating the battle of Actium and the subsequent visit of Germanicus in A.D. 18 (Tacitus, *Annales*, II, 3); the pedestal of Pozzuoli (Naples, Mus. Naz.), which supported a statue of Tiberius erected in A.D. 30; and the pedestal in Sorrento (Mus. Correale di Terranova). These works, which belong to the late Augustan or Tiberian period, show the diffusion of a classical style that stifled all sense of freshness and realism and also characterized most of the portraits of Tiberius.

Soon after this interlude, however, more lively elements reappeared, together with more elaborate and vigorous modeling, probably at about the time of Caligula or Claudius. In altars, cippi, and marble cinerary urns, the chromatic effect was sometimes heightened by the extravagance of the ornamentation. Even in glyptics similar tendencies can be seen, so that the attribution of the great "Paris cameo" (PL. 287) to the period A.D. 23–29 is probably correct, even if it was almost certainly reworked in the time of Hadrian or Antoninus, a period when apotheoses were more commonly represented. Sharper and more concise modeling was used in the Ara Pacis relief with the scene of the sacrifice and in the altars of the lares cult, suggesting the existence of a less cultivated and more popular current in the broad classical stream. Identical features appear in the figures of the relief (Vat. Mus.) that was found in Rome near the Palazzo della Cancelleria and perhaps formed part of a huge altar built in Tarentum (mod. Taranto). The ornamentation recalls that of the Augustan period in the precision of the intaglio, but the more inorganic and squat appearance of the figures (who represent a procession of *vicomagistri*) and the greater spontaneity in their postures reveal a decidedly popular characterization. This recurs, in spite of the generally classical style, in certain details of the reliefs supposed to be from the Ara Pietatis Augustae, which was voted in A.D. 22 and consecrated in 43, presently scattered among various collections and museums in Rome (Capitoline Mus., Villa Medici).

In the time of Nero, chromatic effects became even more vivid, especially in later portraits of the emperor, with their heroic attitudes and fanciful treatment of the hair (PL. 289).

The play of dark and light was used also in classically composed female portraits such as the bust of Agrippina (Rome, Capitoline Mus.). It was under the early Flavian emperors that the use of chromatic effects reached its climax: examples are the portraits of the banker Caecilius Jucundus from Pompeii (XI, PL. 211), of Vespasian (PL. 289), and of Titus (Rome, Capitoline Mus.), notable for their plastic energy. In female portraits (PL. 516) there is a strong contrast between the delicate shape of the face and the hair with its deeply drilled grooves; a typical example is the bust of Julia (Rome, Mus. Naz.). Vivid chiaroscuro, together with the soft and flowing treatment of the surface, is the dominant feature of the panels on the intrados of the Arch of Titus (VII, PL. 262; IX, PL. 161). In these panels, which celebrate the victory and triumph of Jerusalem, the figures suggest physical movement with their whole bodies, while the density of the crowds and the oblique postures of people, animals, and objects effectively create a feeling of continual movement, even though the composition is sometimes partially deprived of organic unity. This lack of unity is even more evident in the scenes of the Haterii reliefs (PL. 291; IV, PL. 454) that refer perhaps to the activities of a building contractor and to burial ceremonies; in contrast, the floral ornamentation in these reliefs is notably delicate.

The sense of color and spatial depth seem to have diminished in Domitian's time; later portraits of him were quite solidly modeled and closer to the classical style. Also definitely classical are the great reliefs discovered near the Palazzo della Cancelleria in Rome (Vat. Mus.). One of these (VII, PL. 262) represents the *profectio* or the *adventus* of Domitian (whose head was remodeled to resemble that of Nerva); in the others are shown the meeting between Vespasian and Domitian in Rome (not at Benevento) and the naming of the latter to the throne. These reliefs, which were the work of at least two sculptors, have in common their neutral background, the clean and precise modeling, and the almost total rejection of spatial effects, so that the figures sometimes seem arranged not in terms of depth but on planes of different height. Similar characteristics appear in other reliefs, as in those of Pozzuoli (Berlin, Pergamon Mus.; Philadelphia, Univ. Mus.), and for this reason they can be attributed with certainty to the time of Domitian and not to the succeeding period; the same applies to the frieze in the Forum of Nerva decorated with scenes illustrating the works of Minerva, with figures on a background occasionally enlivened by faint suggestions of landscape.

The sculptural production of the 1st century consisted of a series of concrete attempts to adapt the new ideals to classical forms, which had evolved over a long period, without rejecting local styles and traditions. Even in works executed by foreign artists, unexpected details peculiar to Roman sculpture often emerged. The sense of movement was not confined to Rome or to Italy but also extended to the provinces, to which Rome probably sent works of sculpture and sculptural models other than imperial portraits. The two reliefs discovered in Carthage form part of the Roman tradition. One (Louvre) represents Tellus, with the sun on one side and the moon on the other, against a background of landscape motifs; the other relief (Algiers, Mus. Stéphane Gsell), not conclusively demonstrated to be related to the first, shows Mars and Venus and a deified figure, possibly Caesar. The statuesque appearance of these figures would suggest that the relief belonged to the late Augustan or Tiberian period.

Local elements appear in some contemporary portraits from the northern regions of Italy; others remain completely within the imperial court tradition. In the sculpture that decorates the Arch of Augustus built at Segusium (mod. Susa) in about the first decade B.C. (VIII, PL. 230), the figures, which were taken from life with a certain liveliness of observation although executed somewhat roughly and frequently presented frontally, seem isolated from one another; for this reason they are thought to have been influenced by Greek art, which had for some time been widely diffused over the neighboring regions of southern Gaul. The evidence generally cited for this is that motifs from Greek art reappear in the reliefs that decorate the Mausoleum of the Julii in Saint-Rémy (anc. Glanum; V, PL. 470), in the sculpture on the arch of Carpentras (anc. Carpentorate; V, PL. 476), and in the rather flat ornamentation of festoons of oak leaves sculptured on the altar dedicated by Drusus to Rome and Augustus at Lyons in 12 B.C. The reliefs of the arch of Orange (it seems likely from recent research that both the attic and the decoration date from the 1st century of the Christian Era; V, PL. 470) reveal a more acute realism. These qualities can be observed also in the two small busts from Neuilly-le-Réal representing Augustus and Livia (Louvre); however, the antiquity of these busts is doubtful, and their inscriptions are definitely not of the period.

Many sculptures and busts of the imperial family that were found in Gaul reflect the classical trend in the art of the capital. Based on the classical style, if less elaborate, are the figures on the column in Mainz, which was dedicated to Jupiter and Nero in A.D. 65 (V, PL. 475) by two Gallic merchants of the Julian family, Priscus and Auctus. The sculptures are the work of two artists, a certain Samus, who was perhaps Greek, and Severus, who would seem from his name to have been a native of Gaul. Only rarely do the burial steles found in the regions bordering the limes of the Rhine and the Danube achieve the level of art; in general they show limited sculptural value.

As might be expected, the classical style persisted at length in Greece. Notable examples of this trend are the portraits of Augustus from the agoras of Athens and Corinth (Athens, Nat. Mus.; Corinth, Archaeol. Mus.); the latter was found with the statues of Gaius and Lucius Caesar (III, PL. 385). Some Greek sculptures reflect Roman stylistic elements, as do the harsh realism of the features in the heads of a relief from Athens (Berlin, Pergamon Mus.), a few Attic steles of the 1st century, and some portraits of the period.

Contemporaneously, the earlier style flourished in Asia Minor; typical examples are the portraits of Augustus and of other important figures, the festoons in the epistyle of the Temple of Augustus at Antioch in Pisidia, and the frieze of the agora at Aphrodisias (Istanbul, Archaeol. Mus.), which dates from the Tiberian period, although there are alleged to be naturalistic elements in some of the heads. Various sculptures from Egypt, such as the portrait of Augustus in Stuttgart (Württemburgisches Landesmus.) and the black-basalt statue in Cairo (Egyptian Mus.) that is probably another portrait of the emperor, reveal the influence of Pharaonic sculpture. Only in the faces was there some attempt to reproduce physical traits and imitate the refinement of neoclassical models; these refined elements are more evident in the group of three statues representing Augustus, Livia, and Tiberius (Copenhagen, Ny Carlsberg Glyptotek) that were found at Fayum (anc. Arsinoë). Particularly important examples of refinement of technique are some silver vases (Br. Mus.) that probably came from Egypt and a vase found in a tomb in Meroë, Nubia. These vases have been attributed to the workshops of Asia Minor and Egypt; they are decorated with ornamental motifs similar to those mentioned above as being widely used in Rome and with mythological scenes in which the figures often had the physical appearance of Julio-Claudian princes.

The later imperial period. It is commonly supposed that a new artistic expression that was fully emancipated from classical styles developed at the time of Trajan; this was only partly true, for none of the earlier developments had been repudiated. However, during this period there emerged some remarkable personalities, who succeeded in blending traditional styles and in giving life to their sculptural works. The reliefs of the Rostra balustrade in the Roman Forum, known as the "Anaglypha Traiani" (PL. 292), which have also been ascribed to the time of Domitian or Hadrian, were the work of a sculptor who succeeded in conferring a unitary aspect on two different scenes representing political achievements by means of the documentary precision with which he executed the buildings in the background. While delighting in capturing occasional details of figures or of their gestures, he used a modeling technique that drew away from, while not abandoning, the illusionistic and spatial tendencies common in the Flavian period. The same qualities appear in other works of sculpture, as in the

frieze of the Cupids from the Lateran (Rome, Vat. Mus.), which has acanthus scrolls at each end; the frieze of the Victories slaughtering a bull, perhaps from the Basilica Ulpia and divided among various museums in Italy and elsewhere; the decoration of the Temple of Venus Genetrix in the Forum of Caesar, which was rebuilt by Trajan; and the relief of the eagle with a solid wreath of oak leaves (X, FIG. 843, 21; Rome, SS. Apostoli).

The art of sculptural relief in Trajan's time found its highest expression in the spiral frieze of the 100-ft. column (III, PL. 329; VII, PL. 263; X, PL. 152; XIII, PL. 109) in the Forum of Trajan, which was equivalent in height to the cut made into the hillside to contain the Market of Trajan. Celebrative columns topped by statues had been known for some time in both Greece and Rome; in the 1st century of the Republic — according to tradition in 439 B.C. — the first of these monuments was erected in honor of the prefect of food supplies, Lucius Minucius. The votive column in Mainz of the imperial age has been mentioned above. Perhaps Trajan's Column had also an honorary significance at first and only later was adapted to be the emperor's tomb; it was then that the eagle at the top was replaced by the statue of Trajan, the interior staircase was built, and loopholes were made in the shaft to admit light. The shaft rises on a torus molding in the form of a laurel wreath above a cubed base decorated with bundles of weapons in very low relief, almost cut into the marble. The surface of the column is covered by a spiral band representing the Dacian campaigns of 101–02 and 105–06, divided into two episodes by a figure of Victory, who records the heroic deeds on her shield. The site once occupied by the column in the center of the court between the Greek and the Latin library and the actual form of the decoration suggest scrolls, or *volumina*, with continuous illustrations. (It is now alleged, however, that these scrolls took their form from the spiral reliefs, especially as the surviving examples belong to a comparatively late period.) The narration of the two wars, from the crossing of the Danube to the tragic suicide of Decebalus while being pursued by the Roman cavalry, unfolds steadily up to the last scene, in which herds of animals are depicted in an idyllic landscape, perhaps to emphasize the calm that follows war and bloodshed.

A number of scenes repeat themselves in fixed patterns, with constantly changing details. These patterns seem to be derived from an earlier pictorial tradition — the illustration of wars and triumphs — mentioned by writers of Roman times (Pliny, *Naturalis historia*, XXXV, 22); the oldest of these paintings recorded the triumph of Manius Valerius Maximus Messala over the Carthaginians and Hieron II of Syracuse in 264 B.C. What is probably a remnant of the triumphal paintings is to be seen in the fragment from a tomb on the Esquiline (Rome, Palazzo dei Conservatori), which refers perhaps to the Samnite Wars and is contemporaneous with the picture of Messala. The Esquiline fragment indicates that the narration in triumphal paintings was divided into separate episodes, while on the column these episodes follow one another in strict rhythm and with a sense of continuity. The description abounds with emotional and sentimental references, and the presence of the emperor among the soldiers of his army (PL. 293) is constantly emphasized, so that he becomes the real protagonist of the story. The flow of the architectural lines is not interrupted by the low reliefs, in which details are scarcely defined against the background; on the nearer planes the figures are more solid, and their sculptural quality is emphasized by the groove that outlines them, whether they are isolated or in groups. The composition of the landscape is dominated by the human figures, who are sometimes represented in inverted perspective, widely used in later works. In this way motifs that had already appeared in more spontaneous and unsophisticated expressions in provincial sculpture were raised to the level of art; however, the liveliness and the spatial depth that characterize the decoration of the column maintain it within the tradition of imperial art that preceded it, at the same time as there constantly appear such classical elements as heightened sculptural quality and idealization of figures such as the Danube or Night. The master sculptor, who must have had many assistants, judging from the stylistic differences in the individual scenes, represented the Greek tradition but must have matured in Roman surroundings. It would be too bold, perhaps, to identify him with Apollodoros of Damascus.

The same sculptor is supposed also to have been responsible for the great frieze of which four panels were used in the Arch of Constantine (PL. 292), while others are in Roman museums and fragments are in the Louvre and in Berlin (Staat. Mus.). The theory that this frieze once decorated the wall that enclosed Trajan's Forum is improbable, because the panels from the Forum were used in the Arch of Constantine, and the Forum remained intact until a date later than that of the construction of the arch. As on the column, the figure of the emperor appears often in the frieze, in which he is an ideal central figure on horseback, riding against the barbarians. The figures in high relief in the foreground, with their vivid chiaroscuro contrasts, contribute to the density of the composition. However, the use of very low relief, the groove that outlines the figures, and the repetition of identical details link the decoration with that of the column.

The works mentioned above have much in common, in matter and form, with the reliefs on the piers and on the intrados of the arch built in 114 at Benevento to commemorate the opening of the Via Traiana (IX, PL. 161; X, PL. 154). Single episodes in panels depict the benefits lavished on Rome, Italy, and the provinces, and while it might seem audacious to attribute the Benevento reliefs to the artist who was responsible for the sculptures of the column and the great frieze because of their less vigorous modeling and some rather uninspired details, it is clear that the work is close in style to that of the master. The Dacian figures on the Arch of Constantine can be ascribed to him with far more certainty. Also similar in style is the portrait of Trajan (Ostia Antica, Mus. Ostiense), which combines traditional sculpture with a feeling of spontaneous naturalism; this naturalism is also to be found in a number of contemporaneous anonymous portraits that would seem to recall the works of the late republican period in their emphasis on individual physical traits.

In the reliefs on the attic of the Benevento arch the figure of Hadrian appears twice, evidently to emphasize the legitimacy of the succession. The sculptural modeling of these figures was achieved with more artificial and contrived means; the figures of the gods welcoming the emperor as he receives the thunderbolt from Jupiter as a symbol of supreme power are undoubtedly derived from Greek figures. The fragment with the head of a lictor, which has been restored to one of the reliefs, also has obvious similarities to the portraits of Hadrian in the careful intaglio and the calligraphic rendering of the hair and beard (cf. PL. 297). It is highly probable, therefore, that these reliefs were done after the death of Trajan in 117 and are characteristic of Hadrianic art, which must have been greatly influenced by the personality of the emperor, in view of his artistic leanings and his spiritual affinity for the Greek cultural ideals. In one relief (Derbyshire, Trustees of the Chatsworth Settlement), representing the remission of the taxes, a subject known earlier in one of the "Anaglypha Traiani," the figures seem better spaced, with more classical definition. The new style is better seen in eight tondos (PL. 298; VII, PL. 212; IX, PL. 35), which perhaps once decorated the precinct wall surrounding an altar built by Hadrian and which were later used in the Arch of Constantine. On them are depicted scenes of hunts and sacrifices against backgrounds faintly suggesting landscapes, with figures of classical severity arranged in symmetrical groupings. The circular shape of these reliefs had a precedent in the *imagines clipeatae*, of which examples are known from the time of Trajan and perhaps earlier (in their turn, the *imagines clipeatae* can be compared with the round burial steles in the northeastern regions of the Empire and in certain provinces of the east).

The Greek taste is evident in the marble sarcophagi of the period; these became more numerous than the *kline*-shaped tombs of Trajan's time, of which there are few examples, because of the increased practice of interment. The ancient distinction between two types of tombs — the Greek, decorated on four sides, and the Roman, decorated only on the front and the two shorter sides — is still valid. In the second type, which was often decorated with Greek mythological subjects drawn from Greek pictorial prototypes and adapted to a particular symbolic meaning, the fusion of the various scenes into a single composition and the frequent reappearance of the main figures attest the influence of the Roman historical relief. The ornamentation of the Greek type of sarcophagus had a more sculptural quality and was more closely integrated with the architectural design of the whole. Those examples which clearly belong to the time of Hadrian, although discovered in Italy, seem to have been executed chiefly in the workshops of Athens, which was at that time particularly active artistically. Later, perhaps in the time of Antoninus, the flow of cultural influences from Asia Minor was intensified in Roman sarcophagi. Cippi, altars, and cinerary urns (e.g., that of Lucius Lucilius Felix; Rome, Capitoline Mus.; usually attributed to the 1st century of the Christian Era) were decorated at this time with elements of Greek origin, Victories, cupids, and masks supporting garlands or festoons of flowers and fruit.

To the various features in the portraits of Hadrian mentioned above, apart from portraits in the classical manner (e.g., the Ostia portrait, in which the treatment of the curls in the beard was patterned after Greek Archaic art), must be added those in a number of portraits (XI, PL. 215) found in Italy that abounded in naturalistic and psychological touches, by then the common basis of art in Rome (e.g., the portrait in the Uffizi). Better than anywhere else, the classicism fostered by Hadrian found concrete expression in the portraits of Antinous (III, PL. 386). The surviving likenesses (more than a hundred) of the emperor's favorite portray him after his death as a god (e.g., Apollo, Bacchus, Osiris). They were all inspired by Greek, and mainly Attic, models, but the idealized figure is endowed with such personal characteristics as a sullen expression, full lips, soft flesh, and broad shoulders, rendering the sculpture less purely classical. Both the academic relief in the Villa Albani, which represents him as Vertumnus, and the relief found near Lanuvium (Rome, Banco Romano, Palazzo Ruspoli), in which he is given the likeness of Sylvanus, show the same treatment. The latter work, inspired by the dignity of Attic steles of the 5th century B.C., was created by Antonianos of Aphrodisias, the city which from the beginning of the 1st century of the Christian Era had been the seat of a flourishing school of sculptors and decorative artists whose work was characterized by virtuosity of technique and eclecticism of form.

While there is no conclusive evidence, it is possible that some of the portrait types of Antinous were created by members of the school of Aphrodisias at the time when many of them, after the end of the Flavian period, moved to Rome. It is certain that these artists played a large part in the decoration of Hadrian's Villa at Tivoli, as is shown by the signatures on certain works. Other contemporaneous sculptures were also of eclectic inspiration, as, for example, the young Dionysus (Rome, Mus. Naz.), in which forms of Attic sculpture of the 5th century B.C. were fused with those of the 4th century, and some of the reliefs preserved in the Palazzo Spada in Rome, which represent various mythological scenes with a cold and academic severity. The Italian marble that was used in many of the works is evidence that Rome was one of the centers, possibly the most important one, of this classical revival.

Historical reliefs that can be dated to the time of Hadrian are rare; this scarcity has been attributed to the lack of military events during his reign — an explanation that is neither convincing nor entirely exact. However, Hadrian has been identified in two reliefs (Rome, Capitoline Mus.), one of which represents the apotheosis of an empress (PL. 298), perhaps Sabina, while the other shows the emperor reading a proclamation or perhaps the *laudatio* of the deceased (these two reliefs were reused in the decoration of an arch that was built at a later time on the Via Flaminia). In the same category is a third relief (also Capitoline Mus.), with the scene of the *adventus* of the emperor, and yet another in Rome (Coll. Torlonia), representing the submission of the barbarians. As in other sculptural works, the background is scarcely defined, spatial depth is slight, and the connection between the few figures is very tenuous. The motifs derived exclusively from the preceding style; only the winged female deity bearing the empress toward the sky in the apotheosis scene is a new feature. The design of the figures shows definite similarities to that of the figures in the upper part of the "Paris cameo," but the identification of the seated emperor with Hadrian, on the basis of which the cameo has been given the approximate date of 136, is highly implausible. The representations of the provinces (XIII, PL. 339) that adorned the temple dedicated by Antoninus Pius to Hadrian in 145 in the Campus Martius reveal stylistic analogies with Hadrianic sculpture; Hadrian's political idealism, according to which the provinces would have formed part of a peaceful and homogeneous world-state, seems to be embodied in the evident sculptural quality of the figures, which are isolated by grooves from the background, in the ethnic representation of the various symbolic personages, and, above all, in the nobility of the composition.

With the accession of Antoninus Pius, portraiture acquired a more vivid and colorful sculptural quality, as in the portraits of the emperor and his wife; in reliefs, Hadrianic motifs were again employed. The apotheosis of the imperial couple is represented on the front of the base supporting the column built in honor of Antoninus (IV, PL. 220); the sides of the base are perhaps more interesting and show the *decursiones* (contests that took place at imperial funerals; XI, PL. 84). The figures stand on rocky shelves in high relief against a smooth background. Although the impression of whirling movement is fully achieved, the naïve use of perspective hardly reconciles the suggestion of space with the traditional classical background. The two styles used on the base show that the classical style was slowly losing its force, although traces of it were seen again in the portraits of Marcus Aurelius, especially the more youthful ones. The later portraits, however, and those of his brother Lucius Verus (PL. 300) contributed to the development of elaborate chiaroscuro elements that reached a climax in the brilliant portrait of Commodus in the likeness of Hercules; in this, the flesh, which has the appearance of porcelain, contrasts with the dark areas of the deeply carved curls of hair (PL. 300).

A series of panels with scenes of battling giants, divided among various Roman museums, belongs to a style that originated in the Hellenistic baroque tradition; these may have come from a single composition of the time of Marcus Aurelius, although not all scholars agree on this. The same style characterizes other works of the period that are still to be studied. The eleven reliefs, of which three are in the Palazzo dei Conservatori in Rome (PL. 299) and eight decorate the attic of the Arch of Constantine, could hardly have belonged to the same monument (however, suggestions that other reliefs should be included in this group are of doubtful validity). The first three probably came from an arch built in 176 on the Clivus Argentarius to celebrate the triumph of Marcus Aurelius over the Germans and the Sarmatians; the style and the theme were directly inspired by the historical reliefs of the time of Trajan. Striking similarities have been pointed out between the figure of Marcus Aurelius on horseback in one of these reliefs and the statue of gilt bronze in the Piazza del Campidoglio in Rome (X, PL. 148); however, in contrast with the clear and balanced forms of the relief, in the statue the sense of rhythmic movement was replaced by a stationary rhythm, while the forms, including that of the massive and ponderous horse, are neither so pure nor so elegant. Most of the eight reliefs on the Arch of Constantine are generally similar to the panels in the Palazzo dei Conservatori, although some of them show more movement and greater surface articulation; however, the relief on the *lustratio* of the field is stylistically less organic in the representation of details, while the general effect is more expressionistic.

In this it resembles the reliefs on the Column of Marcus Aurelius (PL. 299; VII, PL. 264, col. 479; XIII, PL. 337) erected in the Campus Martius beside the Via Flaminia. Although it tapered less toward the top, the column seemed taller and more slender than that of Trajan because it rose on a base more than 9 ft. high. For this reason it was called the *columna maior*, although, in fact, the two columns are equal in height. The emphatic modeling of the reliefs, often cited as evidence of

indifference to the architectural design, was rather a result of the column's situation in a spacious area that was not so restricted as that which surrounded the Column of Trajan; the modeling was heightened by the strong light, which emphasized the projecting figures and their now-vanished coloring, more clearly illustrating the episodes in the *bellum germanicum et sarmaticum*. The narrative begins with the events of 172 and ends with those of 175, at least in the first part of the relief; some experts relate the second part, beginning with scene 55, to the events that took place between 177 and 180, although the representation of Commodus in the reliefs seems highly doubtful. Commodus appeared perhaps only in the base, in the scene of the submission of the barbarians, if the diagram of the relief in the restoration of Domenico Fontana is correct. As in Trajan's Column, the narrative is interwoven with conventional scenes and historical episodes; especially in the former, the link with the earlier monument is clear, although it may not be so close as is usually affirmed. The composition is executed in a rough, vividly expressive style, with slight landscape touches limited to those synthetic allusions indispensable to the description of the action. From this style derives a dissolution of organic form and a consequent modification of technique that included extensive use of the drill to cut the outlines and incise the details of the figures.

These sculptures seem to herald a new artistic style that was to be superimposed on the Hellenistic tradition and the sterile remnants of Roman classical style, replacing a visual form of art with one that was conceptual. The many stylistic differences in the execution of the reliefs imply that different sculptors were employed on them, but it is difficult to distinguish individual characteristics; some of the sculptors rose above the level of mere craftsmen. Nevertheless, the whole work leaves an impression of homogeneity that cannot be explained unless its execution was directed by a single artist. It would require a detailed analysis to demonstrate this unity and to disprove the theory that the artistic style changed in the later stages of the narrative. That this change corresponded to the development of the master artist's style during the execution of the work is quite impossible because of the short lapse of time between the beginning and the end of the work (inscriptions prove that the column was completed in 193). The emergence of a completely plain style, whose formal characteristics have been correctly described as belonging to the vernacular of ancient sculpture, as an official artistic language is not consistent with the idea of a group of artists working together spontaneously and collectively. Nor does it suffice to trace artistic precedents in previous manifestations of popular art or to cite the primitive quality in the figural sculpture of craftsmen working far from the cultured world of the capital, such as the sculptors of the monument at Adamclisi (anc. Tropaeum Traini; IV, PL. 111; XI, PL. 357), which has been proved to belong to the time of Trajan. It is equally inadequate to point out similarities with the Column of Trajan in certain details. Neither social conditions nor the much exaggerated personal taste of the emperor, which have also been proposed as explanations for the anomaly, provide a genuine solution unless the sculpture of the column was guided and conceived by a single artist.

In assessing the achievement of the hypothetical master sculptor, his faults must be recognized as well as his virtues; most obvious among his shortcomings are the limited technique, which sometimes becomes repetitious and monotonous, and the persistence of illustrative motifs that destroy the unity of the composition. However, it was he who created the new style and initiated the abstract treatment of the imperial figure (it should be noted that Marcus Aurelius is often represented in a frontal position flanked by two officials and separated from his army), which opened the way to the artistic achievements of late-antique portrait sculpture (cf. PL. 303). After the emperor's death other types of work continued to be produced (an example has been mentioned above in the portrait of Commodus), but the new style flourished in sarcophagi with battle scenes (PLS. 302, 303; also, e.g., the sarcophagus found in the Via Labicana, Rome, Mus. Naz.) and mythological scenes that actually consisted of realistic portraits (e.g., the sarcophagus of C. Junius Euhodus; Vat. Mus.) and, above all, in official monuments. The panels on the Arch of Septimius Severus with the scenes of eastern victories (VII, PL. 264) are divided into two parts by borders of rocks, against which stand out the schematic figures that unite the scenes into a single composition; the Arch of the Argentarii is notable for extensive drill-work and for more lively effects of light and shade in the highly modeled figures and in the overpowering ornamental decoration, but its shape was derived from eastern models, from the sacred gates.

As in the 1st century, later Roman art influenced that of the provinces of the Empire. A series of reliefs from the Rhine region represents native scenes and customs with brilliant touches and lively realism. In this region, as in the neighboring provinces of Gaul and in other western provinces, Roman rule fostered the influx of copies of sculpture, bronzes, and silverwork, while in some places there was a flourishing production of vases; these were made of terra sigillata and were less elegant imitations of those produced in the Arretine factories (III, PL. 138).

The reaction in Greece and in the eastern Mediterranean countries to the official art of Rome is of more interest than that in the west, which was so Romanized that the Latin style continued there in almost every region. Although Roman elements appear in certain Greek portraits, as in the heads of some Athenian *cosmetes* (civic officials), they are very rare in Asia Minor, where only figural subjects and designs from the Roman repertory were adopted; there they were transformed into fluid and refined expressions of Hellenistic forms, as in the reliefs of Ephesus (PL. 194), which perhaps commemorate the victories of Lucius Verus or Marcus Aurelius over the Parthians, and in other sculptural works. Even when artists of Asia Minor worked outside their own region, as on the Arch of Marcus Aurelius at Tripoli (I, PL. 414) and later on that of Septimius Severus at Leptis Magna (III, PL. 387; XI, PL. 358), their use of these forms did not vary. The calligraphic and linear style of the Palmyra steles can also be traced to remote eastern works. Obviously, Rome did not attempt to impose its own culture on the countries of the eastern Mediterranean basin. Greek writers, from Dio of Prusa and Plutarch to Dio Cassius Cocceianus, while proclaiming their loyalty to Rome, seem never to have been struck by the fear or suspicion that their native culture might be threatened, and the trepidation of Lucian and some others, springing from intellectual sources, was more imagined than real. Rome had drawn from the artistic forms of these provinces for so long that she represented no threat to their native styles. Only when Roman art ceased to model itself on Greek forms, which had by that time lost some of their vitality, did there occur the divergence between the eastern and western artistic currents, the evaluation of which is the main problem in the assessment of the art of late antiquity.

BIBLIOG. *Architecture: a. General*: E. B. Smith, Architectural Symbolism of Imperial Rome and the Middle Ages, Princeton, 1956; H. Drerup, Zum Ausstattungsluxus in der römischen Architektur, Münster, 1957; A. W. Byvanck, Le problème de l'art romain, BABsch, XXXIII, 1958, pp. 1–32; A. Grenier, Manuel d'archéologie gallo-romaine, III–IV, Paris, 1958–60; P. Chiolini, I caratteri distributivi degli antichi edifici, Milan, 1959; L. Crema, L'architettura romana, Turin, 1959; L. Crema, Significato dell'architettura romana (B. Centro di S. per la storia dell'arch., XV, sup.), Rome, 1959; H. Drerup, Bildraum und Realraum in der römischen Architektur, RM, LXVI, 1959, pp. 147–74; R. MacMullen, Roman Imperial Building in the Provinces, HJAS, LXIV, 1959, pp. 207–35; A. Boethius, The Golden House of Nero: Some Aspects of Roman Architecture, Ann Arbor, Mich., 1960; F. E. Brown, Roman Architecture, London, New York, 1961; G. M. Hanfmann, Roman Art, Greenwich, Conn., 1964; W. L. MacDonald, The Architecture of the Roman Empire, New Haven, 1965.

b. Technique and ornament: P. Hommel, Giebel und Himmel, Istanbuler Mitt., VII, 1957, pp. 11–55; M. Wegner, Ornamente kaiserzeitlicher Bauten Roms: Soffiten, Cologne, Graz, 1957; J. Fink, Die Kuppel über dem Viereck, Freiburg, Munich, 1958; L. Laurenzi, L'origine della copertura voltata e la storia della cupola, Arte antica e moderna, I, 1958, pp. 203–15; M. E. Blake, Roman Construction in Italy from Tiberius through the Flavians, Washington, 1959; E. Hansen, La "Piazza d'Oro" e la sua cupola (Analecta Romana Inst. Danici, I, sup.), Copenhagen, 1960; D. E. Strong, Some Early Examples of the Composite Capital, JRS, LX, 1960, pp. 119–28; H. Klingelhöfer, Römische Technik, Zürich, Stuttgart, 1961; F. Rakob, Litus beatae Veneris aureum: Untersuchungen am "Venustempel" in Baiae, RM, LXVIII, 1961, pp. 114–49.

c. Single monuments or edifices: P. M. Duval, Observations sur les amphithéâtres, particulièrement dans la Gaule romaine, Et. d'archéol. classique, I, 1955–56, pp. 65–73; F. Fasolo, La villa romana di Sperlonga detta di Tiberio, Q. Ist. di storia dell'arch., XIV, 1956, pp. 1–6; G. A. Mansuelli, Le ville del mondo romano, Milan, 1958; R. Staccioli, Sugli edifici termali minori, AC, X, 1958, pp. 273–78; A. van Buren, RE, s.v. Villa; G. Caputo, Il teatro di Sabratha e l'architettura teatrale africana, Rome, 1959; H. Drerup, Die römischen Villa, Marburger Winckelmannsprogramm, 1959, pp. 1–24; F. B. Florescu, Monumentul de la Adamklissi: Tropaeum Traiani, Bucharest, 1959; B. Forlati Tamaro, A proposito della datazione dell'arco di Orange e dell'arco dei Serpi a Pola, AC, XI, 1959, p. 92; J. A. Hanson, Roman Theater-temples, Princeton, 1959; G. A. Mansuelli, Il monumento augusteo del 27 a.C., Arte antica e moderna, II, 1959, pp. 363–91, III, 1960, pp. 16–39 (rev. by R. Chevalley, Latomus, XX, 1961, pp. 195–96); G. Tosi, Il palazzo principesco dell'arcaismo greco alla Domus Flavia, Arte antica e moderna, II, 1959, pp. 241–60; J. Balty, Etudes sur la Maison Carrée, Brussels, 1960; J. E. Skydsgaard, Den romerske villa rustica, Copenhagen, 1961; M. Wegner, Kapitelle und Friese vom Bogen der Sergier zu Pola, BJ, CLXI, 1961, pp. 263–76; R. Amy et al., L'Arc d'Orange (Gallia, XV, sup.), 2 vols., Paris, 1962; H. Finsen, Domus Flavia sur le Palatin: Aula Regia — Basilica (Analecta Romana Inst. Danici, II, sup.), Copenhagen, 1962.

d. Town planning: F. Castagnoli, Roma antica, in Topografia e urbanistica di Roma, Bologna, 1958, pp. 1–186; E. Nash, Pictorial Dictionary of Ancient Rome, 2 vols., London, New York, 1961–62.

Painting: a. General: Pfuhl, I, p. 18, II, p. 832; L. Curtius, Die Wandmalerei Pompejis, 1929 (2d ed., with added material by W. Klinkert, Hildesheim, 1960); P. Marconi, La pittura dei Romani, Rome, 1929; G. E. Rizzo, La pittura ellenistico-romana, Milan, 1929; C. M. Dawson, Romano-Campanian Mythological Landscape Painting (Yale Classical S., IX, XI), 2 vols., New Haven, 1944–50; F. Matz, Stilphasen der hellenistischen Malerei, AAnz, 1944–45, cols. 89–112; R. Bianchi Bandinelli, Storicità dell'arte classica, 2d ed., Florence, 1950, pp. 135, 155; W. Kraiker, Aus den Musterbuch eines pompejanisches Wandmalers, S. Presented to D. M. Robinson, I, St. Louis, 1951, pp. 801–07; G. Lippold, Antike Gemäldekopien, Munich, 1951; J. M. C. Toynbee, Some Notes on Artists in the Roman World, Brussels, 1951; K. Schefold, Pompejanische Malerei, Basel, 1952; A. Giuliano, Iscrizioni romane di pittori, AC, V, 1953, pp. 263–70; A. Maiuri, La peinture romaine, Geneva, 1953 (Eng. trans., S. Gilbert, New York, 1953); H. G. Beyen, Klassieke en Nieuwere Schilderkunst, Amsterdam, 1956; K. Schefold, Vorbilder römischer Landschaftsmalerei, AM, LXXI, 1956, pp. 211–31; F. Eckstein, Untersuchungen über des Stilleben aus Pompeji und Herculaneum, Berlin, 1957; K. Schefold, Die Wände Pompejis, Berlin, 1957; M. Borda, La pittura romana, Milan, 1958; A. M. Tamassia, La pittura nell'età di Augusto, Arte antica e moderna, I, 1958, pp. 319–33, II, 1959, pp. 17–36; C. C. van Essen, Compendiaria, BABsch, XXXV, 1960, pp. 90–91; M. Napoli, Pittura antica in Italia, Bergamo, 1960; M. Robertson, Greek Painting, New York, 1960; K. Schefold, Origins of Roman Landscape Painting, AB, XLII, 1960, pp. 87–96; Monumenti della pittura antica scoperti in Italia, III (in preparation).

b. Technique: O. Breitschedel, Zur Technik der römische pompejanische Wandmalerei, Munich, 1911; O. Dannenberg, Technik der pompejanischen Wandmalerei, AAnz, 1927, cols. 178–81; M. Cagiano de Azevedo, Il restauro degli affreschi della Casa di Livia, BArte, XXXV, 1949, pp. 145–49; S. Augusti, La tecnica dell'antica pittura parietale pompeiana, Pompeiana, Naples, 1950, pp. 313–54; W. Lepik-Kopaczyńska, Z zagadnień antycznej enkaustyki (On the Problem of Encaustic in Antiquity), Archeologia, VIII, 1956, pp. 65–75; W. Klinkert, Bemerkungen zur Technik der pompejanischen Wanddekoration, RM, LXIV, 1957, pp. 111–48; M. Cagiano de Azevedo, Tecniche della pittura parietale antica, B. Ist. centrale del restauro, XXXIII, 1958, pp. 9–16; W. Lepik-Kopaczyńska, Colores floridi und austeri in der antiken Malerei, JdI, LXXIII, 1958, pp. 79–90; S. Augusti, La tecnica della pittura murale di Ercolano, RendNapoli, XXXIV, 1959, pp. 15–19.

c. Particular periods and works: A. Mau, Geschichte der dekorativen Wandmalerei in Pompeji, Berlin, 1882; F. Wirth, Römische Wandmalerei vom Untergang Pompejis bis am Ende des III. Jahrhunderts, Berlin, 1934; H. G. Beyen, Die pompejanische Wanddekoration vom zweiten bis vierten Stil, 2 vols., The Hague, 1938–60; A. von Salis, Pompejanischer Beitrag, OJh, XXXIX, 1952, pp. 89–93; R. Bianchi Bandinelli, Continuità ellenistica nella pittura di età medio- e tardo-romana, RIASA, N.S., II, 1953, pp. 77–165; P. W. Lehmann, Roman Wall Paintings from Boscoreale, Cambridge, Mass., 1953; R. Bianchi Bandinelli, La composizione del Diluvio nella Genesi di Vienna, RM, LXII, 1955, pp. 66–77; R. Bianchi Bandinelli, Hellenistic Byzantine Miniatures of the Iliad, Berne, Olten, 1955; C. C. van Essen, Studio cronologico sulle pitture parietali di Ostia, BCom, LXXVI, 1956–57, pp. 155–81; K. Parlasca, Römische Wandmalereien in Augsburg, Munich, 1956; H. G. Beyen, Das stilistische und chronologische Verhältnis der letzten 3 pompejanischen Stile, Antiquity and Survival, II, 1957–58, pp. 349–72; H. G. Beyen, The Wall-decoration of the Cubiculum of the Villa of P. Fannius Synistor near Boscoreale in its Relation to Ancient Stage-painting, Mnemosyne, 4th Ser., X, 1957, pp. 147–53; J. Liversidge, Wall-painting in Roman Britain: A Survey of the Evidence, Antiquity and Survival, II, 1957–58, pp. 373–86; F. L. Bastet, De Datum van het Grote Hypogaeum bij de Porta Maggiore te Rome, Leiden, 1958; R. Herbig, Neue Beobachtungen am Fries der Mysterien-Villa in Pompeji, Baden-Baden, 1958; E. Simon, Die Fürstenbilder von Boscoreale, Baden-Baden, 1958; K. Weitzmann, Ancient Book Illumination, Cambridge, 1959; P. H. Blankenhagen, Paintings from Boscotrecase, RM, sup., VI, 1962, pp. 7–61.

d. Identification and attribution of paintings to individual artists: M. M. Gabriel, Masters of Campanian Painting, New York, 1952; C. L. Ragghianti, Personalità di pittori a Pompei, CrArte, III, 1954, pp. 202–38; M. M. Gabriel, Livia's Garden Room at Prima Porta, New York, 1955; L. Richardson, Pompeii: The Casa dei Dioscuri and Its Painters (MAARome, XXIII), Rome, 1955.

Mosaics: A. Blanchet, La mosaïque, Paris, 1928; M. E. Blake, The Pavements of the Roman Buildings of the Republic and Early Empire, MAARome, VII, 1930, pp. 7–159; M. E. Blake, Roman Mosaics of the 2d Century in Italy, MAARome, XIII, 1936, pp. 67–214; E. Pernice, Die hellenistische Kunst in Pompeji, VI: Pavimente und figürliche Mosaiken, Berlin, 1938; D. Levi, Antioch Mosaic Pavements, 2 vols., Princeton, 1947; D. Gioseffi, La terminologia dei sistemi di pavimentazione marmorea e una pagina della "Naturalis historia," RendLinc, 8th Ser., X, 1955, pp. 572–95; B. Pace, I mosaici di Piazza Armerina, Rome, 1955; G. Gullini, I mosaici di Palestrina, Rome, 1956; J. Lassus, Réflexions sur la technique de la mosaïque, Algiers, 1957; L. Foucher, Note sur des signatures de mosaïstes, Karthago, IX, 1958, pp. 129–36; H. Stern, Les origines de la mosaïque murale, BAFr, 1958, pp. 137–38; L. Foucher, Influence de la peinture hellénistique sur la mosaïque africaine aux IIe et IIIe siècles, Cah. de Tunisie, VII, 1959, pp. 263–74; G. V. Gentili, La villa Erculia di Piazza Armerina: I mosaici figurati, Rome, 1959; K. Parlasca, Die römischen Mosaiken in Deutschland, Berlin, 1959; H. Stern, Origine et débuts de la mosaïque murale, Et. d'archéol. classique, II, 1959, pp. 99–121; G. Caputo and A. Driss, Tunisia: Ancient Mosaics, Greenwich, Conn., 1962; J. M. C. Toynbee, Art in Roman Britain, London, 1962, pp. 196–205.

Sculpture: a. *General*: G.-C. Picard, Les trophées romains, Paris, 1957; P. Reutersward, Studien zur Polychromie der Plastik, Stockholm, 1958; M. Bieber, Roman Men in Greek Himation (Romani palliati): A Contribution to the History of Copying, Proc. Am. Philosophical Soc., CIII, 1959, pp. 374–417; G.-C. Picard, Les frises de la Via del Mare et les débuts de l'art triomphal romain, CRAI, 1959, pp. 131–32; A. Frova, L'arte di Roma e del mondo romano, Turin, 1961, pp. 173–338; D. E. Strong, Roman Imperial Sculpture, London, 1961; P. S. R. Payne, The Roman Triumph, London, 1962.
b. *Particular monuments and localities*: U. Scerrato, Un frammento dell'Arco di Traiano a Benevento, AC, V, 1953, pp. 215–21; J. M. C. Toynbee, The Ara Pacis Reconsidered and Historical Art in Roman Italy, Proc. Br. Acad., XXXIX, 1954, pp. 67–95; F. Magi, Sui rilievi della Cancelleria, BJ, CLV–CLVI, 1955–56, pp. 309–13; B. Brentjes, Zwei orientalische Motive auf der Marcussäule, Wissenschaftliche Z. der Univ. zur Halle, VI, 1956–57, pp. 673–77; A. W. Byvanck, Le problème des sarcophages romains, BABsch, XXXI, 1956, pp. 31–38; J. Guey and A. Audin, Les guirlandes de l'autel d'Auguste, B. Mus. Lyonnais, V, 1956, pp. 41–46, 56–62; P. Mingazzini, La datazione del rilievo di Praeneste al Vaticano rappresentante una bireme, RendPontAcc, XXIX, 1956–57, pp. 63–68; J. M. Salomonson, Chair, Sceptre and Wreath, Amsterdam, 1956; G. Pesce, Sarcofagi romani di Sardegna, Rome, 1957; J. M. C. Toynbee, The Flavian Reliefs from the Palazzo della Cancelleria in Rome, London, 1957; V. Tusa, Sarcofagi romani in Sicilia, Palermo, 1957; G. Daltrop, Die stadterömischen männlichen Privatbildnisse trajanischer und hadrianischer Zeit, Münster, 1958; J. J. Hatt, Les influences hellénistiques sur la sculpture gallo-romaine dans le Nord-Est de la Gaule, depuis le premier siècle jusqu'au milieu du IIe, Pub. Univ. de Dijon, XVI, 1958, pp. 71–74; M. Lawrence, Season Sarcophagi of Architectural Type, AJA, LXII, 1958, pp. 273–95; G. A. Mansuelli, Studi sull'arte romana dell'Italia settentrionale: La scultura colta, RIASA, N.S., VII, 1958, pp. 45–128; F. Matz, Ein römisches Meisterwerk: Der Jahreszeitenssarkophag Badminton-New York, Berlin, 1958; G. Bermond Montanari, Monumenti funerari atestini, RIASA, N.S., VIII, 1959, pp. 111–45; F. Braemer, Les stèles funéraires à personnages de Bordeaux, Paris, 1959; W. H. Gross, Zur Augustusstatue von Prima Porta, Nachr. Akad. der Wissenschaften in Göttingen, VIII, 1959, pp. 144–68; H. U. Instinsky, Kaiser Nero und die Mainzer Jupitersäule, Jhb. zur Mus. Mainz, VI, 1959, pp. 128–41; H. Kähler, Die Augustusstatue, Cologne, 1959; E. Simon, Der Augustus, Bremen, 1959; E. Thiemann, Adventus und Profectio: Beobachtungen an zwei Attikareliefs der Konstantinsbogens, RM, LXVI, 1959, pp. 192–95; C. C. Vermeule, Hellenistic and Roman Cuirassed Statues, Berytus, XIII, 1959–60, pp. 1–82; A. Adriani, Il vaso argenteo di Ingolstadt e un suo modello alessandrino, RM, LXVII, 1960, pp. 111–25; G. Becatti, La colonna coclide istoriata, Rome, 1960; G. Bruns, Was tut der Parther auf dem Panzer der Augustusstatue von Primaporta?, Theoria: Festschrift für W. H. Schuckardt, Baden-Baden, 1960, pp. 29–41; A. W. Byvanck, Le début des sarcophages romains, BABsch, XXXV, 1960, pp. 31–38; K. Hanell, Das Opfer des Augustus an der Ara Pacis, Op. Romana, II, 1960, pp. 31–123; F. Miltner, Ein Reliefplatte vom Tempel Hadrians in Ephesos, Schlern-Schriften, CCVI, 1960, pp. 93–97; V. Poulsen, Claudische Prinzen, Baden-Baden, 1960; D. Tsontchev, Contribution à l'étude de la sculpture romaine dans la province de Thrace, Hommages Hermann, Brussels, 1960, pp. 731–38; P. Veyne, Une hypothèse sur l'arc de Bénévent, Mél, LXXII, 1960, pp. 191–219; A. Giuliano, Il commercio dei sarcofagi attici, Rome, 1962; W. H. Gross, Julia Augusta, Göttingen, 1962; H. P. L'Orange, Ara Pacis Augustae: La zona floreale, Acta Inst. Romanum Norwegiae, I, 1962, pp. 7–16; V. Poulsen, Les portraits romains, Copenhagen, 1962; O. Vessberg, A Reconstruction Problem on the Arch of Benevento, Op. Romana, IV, 1962, pp. 159–64; C. C. Vermeule, Augustan and Julio-Claudian Court Silver, Antike Kunst, VI, 1963, pp. 33–40.

Domenico Mustilli

Illustrations: PLS. 283–304; 7 figs. in text.

ROMANISTS.

The appellation "Romanists" was originally used for those non-Italian painters in late-16th-century Rome who based their works on those of Michelangelo and Raphael and who drew inspiration from the ancient world. The term subsequently came to mean those who loved Rome and its monuments, its history, its culture, and its traditions, including the popular, many of which were disappearing or were destined to do so. In this sense it is also an expression of nostalgic enthusiasm for the grandeur and the picturesque aspects that Rome displays. The beginnings of the Romanists may be traced to the Renaissance and, specifically, to the Flemish Romanists of the 16th century (see FLEMISH AND DUTCH ART).

Not only was Rome the center of Christianity but, after the pontificates of Leo X and Julius II and the great undertakings of Michelangelo and Raphael, it became the center of world art. At that time, what exercised a fascination was not so much ancient Rome or its ideal reconstruction in the sense of classicism as the survival of the classical, in a ruined condition, within the modern city, a city, moreover, that seemed to have resurrected the classical spirit through the works of the Renaissance masters. Ever-present reminders of antiquity gleamed at various levels and blended into the modern city. Evidence of the past was ubiquitous — in the layout of the city, in the streets, the squares, the countryside, as well as in the toponymy, the dialect, the life of the aristocracy and the common people, and the authority vested in the popes for more than a thousand years. As the seat of the popes, Rome was the goal of pilgrimages and the center of devotion for all Europe. The papacy was not a hereditary monarchy but an elected power; through nepotism, it created a new Roman aristocracy, which from the 16th to the late 18th century developed the system of patronage to a spectacular degree.

At the beginning of the 16th century, the antiquarian trade and artistic activity reached heights maintained until the neoclassic era. Social life was notable for its spectacular feasts, theater, music, carnivals, markets, and fairs. Romans and foreigners lived side by side; the various "nations" had their own churches and districts; trades were grouped into guilds, and craftsmen assembled in streets or quarters which were named for their trades. Rome had become a capital that was both aristocratic and plebeian, shabby and cosmopolitan, bigoted and tolerant, a city both ancient and modern, conservative and radical, of Romans and foreigners, ascetics and libertines, forever oscillating between pagan past and Christian present, the city of the Inquisition and of good-natured indulgence.

From the 16th century on, the foreign artists who came to Rome for brief periods were numberless. The very history of Rome at the time was made mainly by foreigners; as was often the case also with the religious hierarchy, all the major artists came from outside the city, invited by the popes or by aristocratic patrons. The acceptance of immigrant ethnic groups by Romans themselves indicated an exceptional capacity for assimilating foreigners into a population that nevertheless remained compact and strongly individualistic. Artistically, the city was the home not only of classicism but also of romanticism, where an ideal concept of beauty coexisted with the realism of Caravaggio.

The Flemish Romanists viewed both the Italian style and the ancient in a general way that was influenced by their own northern sensitivity and mannerist taste. Michiel Coxie (1499–1592), who worked in Malines and Brussels, was a member of the Accademia di S. Luca in Rome. Coxie, who was mentioned by Vasari, painted frescoes in S. Maria dell'Anima in Rome. Pieter Coecke van Aelst (d. 1550) translated the treatises of Sebastiano Serlio, and was the teacher of Gillis van Coninxloo and other Flemish painters. Lambert Lombard was the leader of another school. Frans Floris de Vriendt, an imitator of Michelangelo (PL. 98), depicted allegories of the liberal arts and views of the Roman ruins in the style typical of this school. Marten de Vos was another leader and teacher. Others who should be noted include Heinrich van den Broeck (Arrigo Fiammingo; PL. 306), Adam van Noort, Otto van Veen (Vaenius), Bartholomaeus Spranger (PL. 122; IX, PL. 316), and Tobias Haecht (Verhaegt).

What attracted the Romanists was the idea they already had of Rome and its special character. Maerten van Heemskerck's "Sketchbook" was the most important of the sketchbooks depicting the Roman antiquities: ruins, fragments of gigantic statues, and temples transformed into churches (PL. 307; X, PL. 207). In these sketches the emphasis is on the picturesque disorder of the ruins rather than on an objective study of their form and their hidden canons of proportion. This scenographic style was developed in architecture by Pirro Ligorio and Carlo Maderno. The antiquities and ancient marbles were set into façades, assembled in trophies (PL. 308), or piled in picturesque disorder within "museum-gardens" (X, PL. 207). Ancient fragments were utilized as decorative elements in a new architectural style that drew its inspiration from both the symmetry and the casual disorder of nature, apparently following the medieval custom of using materials from earlier buildings. In this way, the ancient lived again in the modern. Borromini incorporated antique marbles in the monuments for the aisles of St. John Lateran in Rome. Piranesi (q.v.) composed picturesque trophies in the Church of S. Maria del Priorato and in the Piazza dei Cavalieri di Malta (PL. 308). Giovanni Paolo Pannini (IX, PL. 18) and Piranesi (PL. 316; I, PL. 309; IV, PL. 439; V, PL. 241) were exponents of this romantic taste for the picturesque. Romantic and neoclassic interpretations of Roman ruins culminate in the work of Henry Fuseli (J. H. Füssli), such as the drawing known as "the woman moved by the grandeur of ancient ruins" (PL. 308), a representation whose roots lie in the 16th-century vision of Maerten van Heemskerck.

Urban planning schemes were resumed by Sixtus V, and the face of the city gradually changed. Guidebooks (PL. 305), maps, and engravings were published, recording the phases of development of the city and illustrating the new buildings.

The myth of the Campagna Romana gave rise to the "heroic" or "ideal" or "classical" landscape. Whereas the views painted by some 16th- and 17th-century artists demonstrated a purely illustrative and topographical interest in the countryside of Latium and its monuments, another type of landscape painting developed, based on the Humanistic concept of the ideally beautiful, exemplified in the work of Annibale Carracci, Domenichino, Nicolas Poussin, Gaspard Dughet (G. Poussin), and Claude Lorrain (III, PL. 83; V, PL. 400; IX, PLS. 15, 204). For more than two centuries the Campagna Romana appeared in art as the surviving setting of the ancient world. The painters of the 17th and 18th centuries saw Tivoli and the hills around Rome as a countryside strewn with remnants of an ancient civilization and regarded the inhabitants and their customs as directly descended from the Latins.

Among the artists who painted views of Rome and the Campagna Romana were Jan Frans van Bloemen (PL. 310; IX, PL. 17), Andrea Locatelli (IX, PL. 17), Paolo Anesi, Paolo Monaldi, Bernardo Bellotto (XI, PL. 151), Canaletto, Pannini, Hubert Robert (PL. 310; V, PL. 423), Piranesi (I, PL. 410; IV, PL. 438), Charles-Louis Clérisseau, Claude Joseph Vernet (IX, PL. 22), Gaspar van Wittel (Vanvitelli; PL. 311; IX, PL. 18), J. R. Cozens, Fragonard, J. C. Reinhart, Jan Hackaert, and Adrien Manglard. A factor that contributed to the presence of foreigners in this group was the existence of the French Academy in Rome and, later, other national academies. Moreover, a study trip to Rome was considered essential by most European artists. This tradition of landscape painting ended at the beginning of the 20th century with the formation of the school of the "Twenty-five of the Campagna Romana," which included Enrico (Henry) Coleman and Duilio Cambellotti.

From the 17th century on, the popular and religious festivals that enlivened the city evoked the interest of the Bamboccianti (q.v.), who painted narrative scenes of the daily life of the common people. They were followed by countless painters and engravers, who depicted the Roman carnivals (PL. 309; II, PL. 94), the city squares with their vendors of tobacco and melons, and the picturesque costumes. Antonio Tempesta engraved these scenes, as did Giuseppe Vasi (IV, PL. 438; V, PL. 199), Giovanni Ottaviani, Luigi Rossini, F. Ferrari, Manglard, Philothée François Duflos, Anesi, Francesco Londonio, Richard de Saint-Non, N. Beatrizet (Beatricetto; PL. 307), and Bartolomeo Pinelli (PL. 312; IV, PL. 441). Especially among the neoclassicists, and Pinelli in particular, the Romans are shown as descendants, in physique as well as in customs, of the people of ancient Rome. Pier Leone Ghezzi caricatured the society of his time — the artists, patrons, priests, and innkeepers (III, PL. 422). The Roman artistic milieu was always

very lively, and foreign artists were an integral part of it. Poets and writers, notably Goethe (PL. 311) and Stendhal, kept diaries of their journeys and published their impressions of Rome.

Rome's decline as the capital of world art began in the 19th century. Impoverished aristocratic families sold their collections, and art patronage (q.v.) was conducted on a reduced scale. The city was modernized, new streets and suburbs were created, and embankments were constucted to contain the floodwaters of the Tiber; in the process many of the landmarks of Renaissance Rome were destroyed. Out of this activity emerged a renewed taste for "the vanished Rome." The water colors of Ettore Roesler Franz, engravings, drawings, and photographs have become precious historico-artistic documents.

Thus the interests of the Romanists have always encompassed the city's past as well as present life, and in their art they have created and preserved records of both. The Romanist movement tended to degenerate into provincialism, but it was also a phenomenon deeply rooted in the history of Rome and its complex and particular historical condition.

BIBLIOG. For the Flemish Romanists, see the bibliog. of FLEMISH AND DUTCH ART. On the ideal of Rome and the various aspects of the Romanists the bibliography is immense. See, as well as the bibliog. for ITALY (VIII, cols. 529–31), these works in particular: General: R. De Cesare, Roma e lo Stato del Papa: Dal ritorno di Pio IX al XX settembre, 2 vols., Rome, 1907; C. Bandini, Roma al tramonto del Settecento, Palermo, 1922; Atti Cong. naz. di s. romani, I–V, Rome, 1929–40; P. Romano, Campomarzio, 2 vols., Rome, 1938–39; P. Romano, Quattro, Cinque, Seicento romano: Voci del tempo, Rome, 1941; P. Paschini et al., Le grandi famiglie romane, 12 vols., Rome, 1942–60; C. Ceccarelli (Ceccarius), Bibliografia romana, Roma, 1945 ff. (basic); R. De Mattei, Labirinto romano, Florence, 1954; R. Giani, ed., Il Colombo romano, Rome, 1954; S. Negro, Album romano, Rome, 1956. Periodicals: Roma, 1923–44; Capitolium, 1925 ff.; L'Urbe, 1936–44, N.S. 1947 ff.; Strenna dei Romanisti, 1940 ff.; S. romani, 1953 ff.; Palatino, 1955 ff. Topography and toponymy: A. Rufini, Dizionario etimologico storico delle strade, piazze, borghi e vicoli della città di Roma, Rome, 1847; B. Blasi, Vie, piazze e ville di Roma nel loro valore storico e topografico, Rome, 1923; B. Blasi, Stradario romano, Rome, 1933; U. Gnoli, Topografia e toponomastica di Roma medievale e moderna, Rome, 1939; P. Romano, Roma nelle sue strade e nelle sue piazze, Rome, 1949; A. P. Frutaz, ed., Le piante di Roma, I–III, Rome, 1962. Town planning and monuments: See the bibliog. for ITALY (VIII, cols. 529–31). An early and a recent example of a historical study of one unit, Piazza Navona, may be cited: F. Cancellieri, Il mercato, il Lago dell'acqua vergine ed il Palazzo Panfiliano nel Circo Agonale, Rome, 1811; P. Romano and P. Partini, Piazza Navona nella storia e nell'arte, Rome, 1944. See also U. Barberini et al., Via del Corso, Rome, 1962 (bibliog.). Sketchbooks and views of Rome and the countryside: H. Egger, ed., Römische Veduten, 2 vols., Vienna, 1911–31; C. Hülsen and H. Egger, ed., Die römischen Skizzenbücher von Marten van Heemskerck, 2 vols., Berlin, 1913–16; A. Bartoli, I monumenti antichi di Roma nei disegni degli Uffizi di Firenze, 5 vols., Florence, 1914–22; M. Fischer, ed., Das römische Skizzenbuch von J. H. Füssli, Zurich, 1942; Palazzo Braschi, Mostra di vedute romane appartenenti alla raccolta del Barone Basile di Lemmerman, Rome, 1955 (cat.); Palazzo delle Esposizioni, Vedute Romane di Ippolito Caffi, Rome, 1957 (cat.). Foreigners in Rome: A. Bertolotti, Artisti subalpini a Roma, Turin, 1877; A. Bertolotti, Artisti belgi e olandesi a Roma, Florence, 1880; A. Bertolotti, Artisti lombardi a Roma, 2 vols., Milan, 1881; A. Bertolotti, Artisti modenesi, parmensi e della Lunigiana, Modena, 1882; A. Bertolotti, Artisti veneti in Roma, Venice, 1884; A. Bertolotti, Artisti bolognesi . . . in Roma, Bologna, 1885; A. Bertolotti, Artisti francesi a Roma, Mantua, 1894; F. Noack, Das Deutschtum in Rom seit dem Ausgang des Mittelalters, 2 vols., Berlin, Leipzig, 1927; Musée des arts décoratifs, Les artistes français en Italie de Poussin à Renoir, Paris, 1934 (cat.); L. Jannattoni, Roma e gli inglesi, Rome, 1945; L. van Puyvelde, La peinture flamande à Rome, Brussels, 1950; Palazzo dell'Esposizione, Italia vista dai pittori francesi del XVIII e XIX secolo, Rome, 1961; F. Spanu Satta, Memorie sarde in Roma: Prefazione di Ceccarius, Sassari, 1962. Academies and institutes: H. Lapauze, Histoire de l'Académie de France à Rome, 2 vols., Paris, 1924; Jumelage Paris-Rome, Les français à Rome résidents et voyageurs dans la ville éternelle de la Renaissance aux débuts du Romantisme, Paris, 1961 (cat.). Diaries, "avvisi," and journals: S. Infessura, Diario della città di Roma (new ed. by P. Tommasini), Rome, 1890; G. Gigli, Diario romano (1608–1670; ed. G. Ricciotti), Rome, 1958; L. Felici, Giornali romani del Sette e dell'Otticento, Palatino, IV, 1960, pp. 181–84, V, 1961, pp. 21–23, 64–66, 109–11, 144–46, 224–28, VI, 1962, pp. 31–33, VII, 1963, pp. 48–54, 130–35; C. D'Onofrio, Gli "avvisi" di Roma dal 1554 al 1605 conservati in biblioteche ed archivi romani (I–II), Palatino, VI, 1962, pp. 177–83, VII, 1963, pp. 18–23. The carnival and folk traditions: F. Clementi, Il Carnevale romano nelle cronache contemporanee, Rome, 1899; G. Zanazzo, Tradizioni popolari romane, 3 vols., Turin, Rome, 1907–10 (sup., ed. G. Orioli, 2 vols., Rome, 1960); A. G. Bragaglia, Le maschere romane, Rome, 1947. Ideals derived by painters from the Roman countryside: W. Friedländer, Claude Lorrain, Berlin, 1921; K. Gerstenberg, Die ideale Landschaftsmalerei, Halle, 1923. Vanishing Rome: Roma sparita dai quadri di Ettore Roesler Franz, I–III, Rome, 1931–36; S. Negro, Fotografia a Roma dal 1840 al 1915, Rome, 1953 (cat.).

Luigi SALERNO

Illustrations: PLS. 305–312.

ROMANO, GIULIO. Italian painter and architect (b. Rome, 1499; d. Mantua, 1546). Giulio Romano entered the workshop of Raphael (q.v.) at an early age, becoming, while still in his teens, one of the master's most important assistants. Of the frescoes in the Vatican Stanze begun under Raphael's direction, Giulio is usually assigned a major share in the execution of *The Battle of Ostia* and a considerably lesser role in the creation of *The Fire in the Borgo* (XI, PLS. 429, 430). Documents demonstrate that he played an important but unspecified part in completing Raphael's famous *Transfiguration*, which was unfinished when Raphael died in 1520 (XI, PLS. 434, 435). Beyond this there is little agreement. Whether the tensions that modern critics have found in the designs produced by Raphael's workshop during the last years of his life are the result of changes in Raphael's own style or represent new directions initiated by his pupils remains an unsolved question.

Only with the death of his teacher did Giulio emerge as an independent artist. He and Gianfrancesco Penni were considered Raphael's successors, and soon gained fame and affluence. In the four years that he was to remain in Rome Giulio produced a whole series of paintings in which he transmuted the style of Raphael into a mannered, highly personal idiom. The most notable of these are *The Holy Family* (Madrid, Prado), *The Martyrdom of St. Stephen* (Genoa, S. Stefano), and *The Holy Family with Saints* (Rome, S. Maria dell'Anima). For their settings Giulio drew heavily on the ruins of ancient Rome, transcribing them with almost archaeological accuracy but also emphasizing instability and dissolution.

In the fall of 1524 Giulio left Rome for Mantua, where he was to remain for the rest of his life, working first for Federico II Gonzaga, ruler of the small duchy, and, after the Duke's death in 1540, for his brother, Cardinal Ercole Gonzaga, who served as regent. For more than two decades, as director of a large workshop, Giulio dominated the artistic activity of the duchy both in architecture and in painting. Yet during this period he painted almost nothing and inferior artists executed his designs. Among the hundreds of frescoes and panels that were painted under his direction in the Palazzo del Te in Mantua between 1527 and 1535, the few that are by his own hand — notably a small number of ceiling panels in the Sala di Psiche (PL. 82) — are almost lost in a welter of mediocrity. What the visitor tends to remember are the cataclysmic effects of *The Fall of the Giants* (Sala dei Giganti; IX, PL. 298). Here the concept of a collapsing universe, surrounding the viewer on every side with visions of tumbling temples and falling boulders that crush the fleeing giants, is so powerful as to distract from Rinaldo Mantovano's coarse execution.

In architecture, where Giulio's ideas could be transmitted more accurately, his success is far greater. The Palazzo del Te (PL. 53; VIII, PL. 428) is his masterpiece. Though it is based on Vitruvius and Bramante, Giulio's classicism is full of subtle inversions and distortions, which must have delighted the sophisticated court. Gombrich (1934, 1935) has analyzed the principles of dynamic conflict that animate the various façades. While the famous slipped triglyphs of the courtyard (which are directly related to the instabilities in Giulio's paintings) form the most striking motif, the endless variations in the treatment of the rusticated surfaces and their relationship to the orders are also admirable. Equally sophisticated though smaller in scale are the façade of the Appartamento Estivale in the Palazzo Ducale in Mantua (1538–39) and Giulio's own house in Mantua (1544), both filled with intentional incongruities.

Under the regency of Cardinal Ercole Gonzaga, Giulio built churches instead of palaces. His work assumed a new sobriety, not without archaistic overtones. For the Cathedral of Mantua, which was completely rebuilt within its Romanesque shell (beginning in 1545), Giulio planned an Early Christian basilica, free of all the discords of his earlier style. Little more than a year after the reconstruction of the cathedral had begun he was dead.

Much of Giulio's work shows an attraction to the weird and bizarre as well as a propensity to compositional conflicts that is associated with mannerism (q.v.). A few of his buildings had a decisive influence on later 16th-century architects, notably Palladio, and many of his pictorial compositions would influence not only his own century but also the illusionistic ceiling painting of the baroque (see PERSPECTIVISTS). See also PL. 51; VIII, PLS. 206, 208; XIII, PL. 285.

BIBLIOG. S. Serlio, Tutte le opere d'architettura . . . (ed. G. D. Scamozzi), Vicenza, 1619; C. D'Arco, Notizie di Isabella Estense moglie a Francesco Gonzaga, Archivio storico italiano, 1845, App. II, pp. 319ff.; Vasari; A. Luzio, Federigo Gonzaga ostaggio nel Vaticano, Archivio di storia patria rom., IX, 1886, pp. 509–82; S. Davari, Descrizione del Palazzo del Te di Mantova di Giacomo Strada, Arte, II, 1899, pp. 248–53, 392–402; P. Carpi, Giulio Romano ai servigi di Federico II° Gonzaga, Atti e mem. della real acc. virgiliana, N.S., XI–XIII, 1918–20; E. Gombrich, Zum Werke Giulio Romanos, JhbKhSammlWien, N.S., VIII, 1934, pp. 79–104, IX, 1935, pp. 121–50; F. Hartt, Giulio Romano, 2 vols., New Haven, 1958 (review by J. Shearman, BM, CI, 1959, pp. 456–60).

Robert ENGGASS

ROMANTICISM. Romanticism in art was a movement that began about 1750 and continued throughout the 19th century. Developing from the culture of the Enlightenment, it found expression in its early stages in Piranesi, Goya, and English landscape architecture, the last emphasizing the picturesque, the exotic, and the characteristic irregularity of nature. The movement reached its high point in France with the work of Delacroix and the wave of enthusiasm aroused by the Revolution of 1830.

The main characteristic of romanticism was the mystique of nature, from which two artistic currents developed: the naturalistic, culminating in the work of Constable, and the visionary, exemplified by Turner. The latter current was informed by the idea of the sublime, deriving from those aspects of nature inspiring awe, terror, and majesty. Romanticism was a complex phenomenon, spreading to various European countries and America and bringing to each local flowering a profound emphasis on the mystical communion between artist and nature, individualism in thought and expression (as opposed to the restrictive formality of classicism), a reassertion of passion, sentiment, and the imagination, and a tendency toward the picturesque, the macabre, and the exotic.

SUMMARY. General considerations (col. 558). English-style gardens and the feeling for nature (col. 559). Romantic landscape painting in England (col. 560). The sublime (col. 561): *Piranesi. Interest in the Middle Ages* (col. 563). Fuseli and Blake and their influence (col. 563). Scandinavia and Germany (col. 565). Goya (col. 567). France (col. 568). The spread of romanticism (col. 572). Postromanticism (col. 574).

GENERAL CONSIDERATIONS. Romanticism in the Western world during the 18th and 19th centuries was a complex phenomenon impossible to reduce to a superficial formula, purely formal explanation, or manifestation of a timeless spiritual outlook (e.g., D'Ors's "eternal baroque," 1937). The most typical element of the romantic sensibility lies in that "mystique of nature" which Seillière (1932) has stressed; although not an adequate historical definition of romanticism, this constitutes its basic motif. On a historical level the forces that determined the major romantic phenomena between 1750 and 1900 at first seem to contradict romanticism. During this period there was a profound need to verify the achievements of the Enlightenment. A popular conception of Enlightenment philosophy as the pure predominance of abstract reasoning and intellect has often obscured the forceful impulse of 18th-century rationalism and of certain attitudes that were to have an important development in romanticism.

A movement of enormous complexity as well as force, the Enlightenment influenced the character of individual artists and various orientations of style, aided in the maturing of esthetic positions corresponding to specific political and social developments, and effected profound cultural changes in countries having little or nothing of the social bases from which the movement had developed in England and France. Notwithstanding its extreme richness and variety of trends, the Enlightenment was a deeply unifying force in European civilization, irreversibly establishing several basic points of modern thought as well as determining the great variety of romantic phenomena.

Aspects of 18th-century culture that fundamentally influenced romantic art were an awareness of history, a sense of the organic whole, and a heightened feeling for nature. These were born in close logical relationship to Pascal's "l'esprit de géometrie." The emphasis of the philosophers on clarity, rationality, and social commitment similarly gave rise to some of the most important social elements of romanticism, such as the emergence of national feeling and socialism. Only the perpetuation into the 19th century of the manifestations of the Enlightenment can explain most romantic art from Goya to Delacroix, from Constable to Corot, from Géricault to Daumier. The rise in the importance of dreams, the occult, night, the infinite, and nostalgia for exotic lands (all of which constitute such a significant part of the romantic imagination) was related from the 18th century onward to a concept of reason and a usually conscious need to explore the limits of the intellect. This is exemplified in Goya's famous caption: "The sleep of reason produces monsters" (VI, PL. 402). It was not mere chance that William Blake, the most extreme spokesman of European romanticism, acquired his training from Voltaire and the Libertines.

Romanticism emerges as the result of a concomitant expression of styles of widely assorted artistic origins, the variety and character of these styles having their roots in the culture of the Enlightenment. The common denominator in 18th- and 19th-century romantic phenomena can be defined as "the crisis of the enlightened conscience"; restlessness, emotionalism, and "pathetic" appeal to sentiment are undoubtedly the recurrent and characteristic traits of the romantic sensibility, as they are in all times of "crisis." These traits were gradually intensified to the point of exasperation as the 18th-century utopia, in the course of its advance, came into conflict with a social and historical reality to which it was deeply repugnant. It is precisely here, in a profound aspiration toward an unattainable ideal and not in any mysterious yearning of the soul for unknown places, that the romantic torment had its true source.

The Shaftesburian phase in European culture, based on the mystique of nature, produced two aspects of romanticism — the naturalistic and the visionary: a tendency to integrate sympathetic responses to nature into historic reality and the objective world and to draw from this integration the theme for an exploration of inner spiritual life. For an entire group of romantic artists these two aspects resulted in a kind of renovated classicism tinged by realism or in an acute dissociation of sensibility, easily subject to deterioration, where the work lost its character of tormented necessity in morbid complacency and estheticism. Here again romanticism appears as a continuation of the Enlightenment, with characteristics varying according to local cultural conditions and historical events.

Romanticism is traditionally subdivided into three chronological periods: the first comprises the phenomena that have been termed, in an unfortunate expression, "preromantic" (including Piranesi, Goya, and certain aspects of English and German art up to about 1820); the second is romanticism proper, with France as its center, up to the Revolution of 1848 and the decisive triumph of realism; the third includes the creative reassertion of romantic themes in the second half of the 19th century. This rather arbitrary subdivision may be replaced by the idea of an organic development expressed in different periods and countries in close relation to the complex historic situations of these countries.

ENGLISH-STYLE GARDENS AND THE FEELING FOR NATURE. The word "romantic" is not literary in origin, as is often claimed, but was introduced for the first time in connection with English-style gardens. The popularity of these gardens was widespread in England from the first decades of the 18th century, in response to a need for naturalness that developed simultaneously with the establishment of middle-class commercial life. From the beginning of the century a literature of adventure had developed that offered a picture of nature and an extreme immediacy of feeling, portraying the events of real life in a direct and detailed way. Daniel Defoe, using memoirs of underworld characters or books by travelers as a point of departure, gave impetus to this genre, of which Samuel Richardson, Henry Fielding, Tobias Smollett, and Laurence Sterne became the major exponents. In the 1798 edition of the *Dictionnaire de l'académie française*, the term "romantic" was explicitly used to describe those gardens and landscapes whose spirit approached that of the novels.

According to Jacques François Blondel (1705–74), romantic gardens tended "toward the beautiful simplicity of Nature," at the same time bearing characteristics of the exotic and the picturesque (the term was later defined by Uvedale Price as the continual variation of forms, colors, lights, and sounds; *An Essay on the Picturesque as Compared with the Sublime and the Beautiful*, London, 1794–98). "Romantic" was used in Blondel's sense by Jean Bernard Leblanc, who in *Lettres d'un Français sur les Anglais* (1745) wrote: "Many Englishmen try to give their gardens an air they call 'romantic,' that is, picturesque." In 1777 René Louis Girardin used the word similarly in his essay *De la composition des paysages sur le terrain*.

In contrast to the geometric rigor of the French-style gardens, with their regular pattern of flower beds and mirrors of water (made fashionable by André Le Nôtre), a livelier landscape architecture began to develop. Gardens displayed winding paths, irregular lawns, sloping banks, skillful intertwining of trellises and pergolas, Gothic ruins, Chinese pavilions, and artificial ponds and classical ruins as in the paintings of Claude Lorrain (II, PL. 200; IX, PLS. 203, 205, 206) or Salvator Rosa (XI, PL. 149). The appeal of the exotic, including an interest in the Middle Ages, was linked to the ideal of fidelity to nature and to its organic character; the exotic and the picturesque were the most superficially apparent results. Paradoxically, few phenomena in the history of art seem so unnatural today as some of the manifestations of English exoticism of this period. Specific examples are the famous Strawberry Hill (1750–90) in Middlesex, a rococo country house disguised as Gothic, built for Horace Walpole on the Thames; and the no-longer-extant Gothicizing structure of Fonthill Abbey (1795–1807; X, PL. 290) in Wiltshire, capriciously built by James Wyatt for the writer William Beckford. The latter structure is considered the extreme example of 18th-century English exoticism.

Despite the artificiality of these houses, they are expressions of a tendency that was among the liveliest and richest in cultural potential for the period. At a time when France and England appeared to the civilized world as unsurpassed models of culture, there began to grow in these countries a sense of a dimension of man different from that which was accepted in the West. This led to an increasing curiosity concerning cultures distant in time and space. Signs of this curiosity had already appeared in the 1600s in the representation of the "parts of the world" widely developed in decoration from Lebrun to Tiepolo; and in the interest in *chinoiserie* and motifs from India stimulated by colonialism and the Jesuit missions and commonly reflected in tapestries. Gradually there developed a skepticism concerning the superiority of the Western view of the world. The writings of the Abbot Dubos (*Reflexions critiques*, 1719), so admired by Voltaire, or works such as Montesquieu's *Lettres Persanes* (1721) and Swift's *Gulliver's Travels* (1726) mark extremely significant stages in this development.

The adjective "romantic," from its earliest usage, was accompanied by the idea of a free expansion and projection of individual feeling. "The romantic location should be calm and solitary so that the spirit may wholly abandon itself to the softness of a deep feeling," wrote Girardin (op. cit.). It was not by chance that Rousseau was to eulogize the English-style garden; this was the spirit of his *Rêveries du promeneur solitaire* (1782) and characterized his landscape description in *Julie, ou la nouvelle Héloïse* (1761). The English-style garden was to find greater artistic expression in landscape painting, which had an important development during the 18th century in England. (See also LANDSCAPE ARCHITECTURE; NEO-GOTHIC STYLES; PICTURESQUE, THE.)

ROMANTIC LANDSCAPE PAINTING IN ENGLAND. English landscape painting was initiated by Richard Wilson (1713–82; VI,

PL. 440). Still tied to the school of Claude Lorrain and an idealizing vision of the Roman countryside, Wilson was in certain respects the artistic figure corresponding to the elegiac poets of the 18th century. Landscape art emerged with its own original characteristics about 1760 in the work of Alexander and John Robert Cozens (1716–86 and 1762–99; VI, PL. 447), executed in the new technique of water color. In the same period, Francis Towne (1740–1816) and John Baptist Malchair (1731–1812), founder of the Oxford school, also won recognition in this medium. All the major English landscape painters of the last generation of the century — John Crome (1768–1821; VI, PL. 450), founder of the Norwich school; Thomas Girtin (1775–1802; VI, PL. 450); John Sell Cotman (1782–1842); and even John Constable (q.v.; PL. 317; IX, PL. 23) and Joseph Mallord William Turner (q.v.; PL. 317) — devoted themselves to water color, the use of which cannot be overestimated.

In their fragility, transparency, and spare purity of subject matter, water-color mountain landscapes captured the essence of a current taste. Their vogue began with the visits to the English lake district by the poet Thomas Gray and illustrator William Gilpin, and with Gilpin's landscapes (from 1782 on) of the lakes, Wales, and the Scottish Highlands. A light, rapid, and very easily handled technique, water color enabled the painter to achieve the richest subtleties while remaining direct and unpretentious; the medium was analogous in many ways to the humble and seemingly trivial vocabulary of everyday speech. Through water color, painters expressed their lyrical intuition of a presence diffused in the landscape and a mystical communion between artist and nature that was the true nerve ending of the romantic sensibility.

From this communion, as has been noted, stemmed the two fundamental aspects of romanticism, both clearly apparent in English landscape art: the naturalistic current culminating in Constable and the visionary trend in the art of Samuel Palmer (1805–81) and Turner. This ambiguity of possible results was already perceptible in embryo in the art of Alexander Cozens, who in *A New Method of Assisting the Invention in Drawing Original Composition of Landscape* (1785) refers to the famous passage in Leonardo's *Treatise on Painting* on the spots on walls, in which may be seen "an infinity of things which you will be able to reduce to their complete and proper forms" (see LANDSCAPE IN ART). Like the Chinese, Cozens advises the study of chance piles of stones, where the imagination may find a stimulus to the creation of new forms. According to Reynolds, Gainsborough used a similar method for his landscapes. While in Wilson the relationship between subjective sensibility and nature was still organized according to strict rules, in J. R. Cozens and later in Crome the subjective reaction determined the discovery of light and space. Taking this path, Girtin became the most delicate and inspired interpreter of atmospheric values, a true forerunner of the "completely poetic" landscape of Corot (VI, PL. 450). The figure of Constable is more complex. Judging Cozens to be one of the greatest geniuses to devote himself to landscape, Constable himself had a keener sensitivity to the scientific-naturalistic interests of the century. His submersion in nature, which was troubled and often colored by an innate dramatic impulse, ultimately expressed itself in a calm and sometimes minutely descriptive view that opened the way to realistic landscape with its tension between lyrical immediacy and the specific desire for an objective definition.

The results achieved by Turner, whose mood was similar to that of J. R. Cozens, were very different. An enthusiastic admirer of Claude Lorrain and Girtin, from whose schools he learned the technique of water color, Turner gradually made this technique an extraordinarily successful means of expression for visions that constantly tended toward the exceptional. His oil paintings, depicting fantastic sunsets, mysterious lighting, turbulent outbursts of nature, and picturesque and theatrical effects, are simple transfers of his early ideas in water color.

THE SUBLIME. It would be difficult to understand the art of Turner without comprehending the revolution of sensibility that was maturing contemporaneously in England under the banner of "the sublime." Contrary to "good taste" and all accepted canons, the sublime and "genius" had become, in late-17th-century France and England, a justification for a series of high-level artistic phenomena that could not be defined under the rigidity of classicist precepts. Longinus, in his essay *On the Sublime* (circulated in paraphrased form by Boileau), discussed the characteristics of a rhetorical form which, by boldness of content and force of style, could persuade a listener against his will and reason and arouse passions to a pitch of violence. Longinus acknowledged that such effectiveness of style could not be transmitted according to rule but was rather the natural gift of some erratic, stray genius particularly close to the sublimity of nature.

These themes suggest the release of energy confined by an overly severe rationalism and they increasingly attracted English culture. Voltaire, after studying the English empiricists and subjective idealists, used these very concepts in *Lettres philosophiques sur les Anglais* (1733) to justify the art of Shakespeare. The sublime was a disturbing problem for Voltaire, as the problem of Flemish and Dutch painting from Rubens to Rembrandt had been for classicist esthetics. Solitude, silence, the sense of infinity arising from certain landscapes, and an unleashing of the elements of nature were considered *sui generis* in art and not subject to the idea of beauty. According to Edmund Burke, the beautiful is that which is shapely, harmonious, and pleasing; the sublime is irregular, jagged, awe-inspiring. Sublime elements tend to overwhelm reason and "to fill the spirit with an agreeable horror"; insofar as they are capable of arousing the sense of a higher power, they do so in an uncontrollable and irresistible manner (*A Philosophical Enquiry into the Origins of Our Ideas of the Sublime and Beautiful*, 1756). Burke tried by means of an introspective study to give a scientific basis to the irrationality of the sublime and was the first to reveal in it the form of terror, which was destined to have success. In 1785 the anonymous author of the *Enquiry Concerning the Principles of Taste* wrote: "Where pure charm ends, the majesty of the sublime begins, composed of pain, pleasure, grace, and ugliness, so mingled that the mind no longer knows what name to give them, whether it should be pain, pleasure, or terror." The sublime is "the pinnacle of blessedness, bordering on horror, ugliness, madness: a height that causes the mind that dares look beyond it to go insane."

Piranesi. From the standpoint of the sublime, a special study should be made of the relation between English culture and the Italian artist and architect Giovanni Battista Piranesi (1720–78; q.v.), one of the major figures of preromantic Europe. A close friend of Robert Adam, Piranesi was noted by Coleridge and De Quincy for his depiction of terror and was much admired by Horace Walpole. The artist's *Carceri*, a series of prison etchings (PL. 316; IV, PL. 439), inspired *The Castle of Otranto* (1764) by Walpole, the first of the Gothic novels. Walpole later advised young artists to study Piranesi's "sublime dreams."

Piranesi presented a complexity attuned remarkably to 18th-century English culture. He was bound to his enlightened epoch not only by a delight in intellectual knowledge but also by the utopian boldness of his ideas and his ethical commitment to them. The polemic debate he fearlessly conducted in defense of the grandeur and magnificence of Rome was not purely literary; rather it was the defense of a modern ideal of life then becoming established in the most sophisticated Italian circles — an ideal that derived vigor from the social realities of disintegration and sharp contrast between splendor and misery (I, PLS. 309, 410; IV, PL. 438). This contrast is emphasized in Piranesi's art, where the magnificence of Roman monuments is set against the tattered beggars who populate the scenes. Also emphasized is the "pathetic" element emanating from the ruins, seen as a triumph of human intelligence in its struggle against the degradation of time.

In a letter of Mar. 27, 1778, the artist expressed indignation over the inertia of the Italians of his period; he eulogized England, adding that if he had to choose a homeland it would be London. Forced to leave Venice because he could find no position in keeping with his abilities, he saw England as the only country capable of understanding his far-reaching concepts. His great qualities as scholar and archaeologist, the outcome of a highly select humanistic tradition that no longer found a cultural outlet in Italy, produced the pathetic aspects of Piranesi's view — a nostalgia for the grandeur of Rome and a tendency toward the illogical, the enormous, the unlimited. The whole of his art, which was both hallucinatory and solemn, became an impressive document of this discrepancy. Piranesi's prison series seems an exemplification of Burke's ideas on the sublime. His Roman fantasies, in their nostalgia for a lost world, have a somewhat exotic fascination. It is quite understandable that these works should have so strongly attracted the attention of De Quincy; in speaking of the prison series (*Confessions of an English Opium Eater*, 1821) the writer imagined Piranesi eternally in the act of climbing an aerial ladder suspended above the abyss, until the endless ladder and the despairing artist were "lost in the upper gloom of the hall." (See also PLS. 176, 308, 316; V, PL. 241; X, PL. 267.)

INTEREST IN THE MIDDLE AGES. The romantic interest in the Middle Ages (see CRITICISM) had a clearly expressed history long before 1800, when it acquired the character of a religious and mystical revival, especially in Germany. In 1699, Jean François Félibien, in his *Dissertation touchant l'architecture antique et gothique*, noted the two-sided formation of French culture; and from that time on, the indigenous medieval movement was increasingly recognized and valued. It was, however, a curious idea of medievalism, extending well into the 16th century, and including the Gauls, the Druids, and the ancient Celts — just as in England the "Middle Ages" extended from early barbaric times to the Renaissance and included Chaucer, Shakespeare, Spenser, and Milton. This picturesque confusion was to be handed down in Chateaubriand's *Génie du Christianisme* (1802).

The term "national antiquities" was definitely established with the Musée National des Monuments Français (established by Alexandre Lenoir after the Revolution), which was used as a repository for precious objects to be saved from the destruction of religious buildings. The idea of national antiquities was to have a powerful effect on the romantic imagination. It already had a precedent in the publication of P. Pezron's *Antiquités de la nation et de la langue des Celtes* (1703) and was dealt with again extensively in works by S. Pelloutier (*Histoire des Celtes*, 1740–50), P. H. Mallet (*Monuments de la mythologie et de la poésie des Celtes*, 1756), J. Le Brigant (*Eléments de la langue des Celtes Gomérites ou Bretons*, 1779), and T. Malo Corret La Tour d'Auvergne (*Recherches sur la langue, l'origine et les antiquités des Bretons*, 1792). In some ways these works constitute a parallel to James Macpherson's alleged discovery in Scotland of the writings of the legendary Gaelic bard Ossian, adapted and reevaluated by Macpherson in *Fragments of Ancient Poetry . . .*; and the rediscovery by J. J. Bodmer in Germany of medieval texts such as the *Nibelungenlied* (1757); or, also in Germany, the exaltation by J. G. Herder of popular poetry. This type of interest has often been considered a process of negation of the culture of the Enlightenment and its "clear and distinct" ideas; in reality, however, it is a progressive historical substantiation of 18th-century principles and the point of departure for that cultural relativism which is one of the major "enlightened" conquests of our times.

FUSELI AND BLAKE AND THEIR INFLUENCE. The attraction to the Middle Ages and the sublime arose in England through the publication of *Night Thoughts* by Edward Young, a renewed interest in Shakespeare and Milton, the poems of Ossian, John Hervey, and Thomas Gray, and the Gothic novels of Ann Radcliffe and M. G. Lewis with their themes of tombs, moonlight, and ghosts. In English art the movement found its highest expression in two well-known personalities: Henry Fuseli (Johann Heinrich Füssli, 1741–1825; q.v.) and William Blake (1757–1827; q.v.), both of whom were writers, engravers, and painters. Fuseli was educated in Switzerland in the cultural environment stimulated by the writings of Jean Jacques Rousseau, Johann Kaspar Lavater, and Heinrich Hess — a milieu that nurtured the fertile seeds of Pietism and Christian Neopla-

tonism. In 1764 Fuseli moved to London and continued his literary career. From 1767, on the advice of Sir Joshua Reynolds, he devoted himself entirely to painting and in 1769 went to Rome for an eight-year stay. There he copied ancient statues and became passionately interested in Michelangelo, whose work embodied the then-current idea of the sublime; he returned to London (1779) by way of Switzerland. Fuseli was appointed a full member of the Royal Academy of Arts in 1790. At the suggestion of Antonio Canova he was made a member of the Accademia di S. Luca in Rome (1817).

Fuseli's character as an artist was formed by the contradiction between the incandescent content of his art and his cold linear drawing and classical, polished style. Though primarily a draftsman (e.g., illustrations for Dante's *Inferno* and the *Nibelungenlied*), he preferred fantastic subjects, nocturnal visions imbued with eroticism (*The Nightmare*, Frankfurt am Main, Goethe Mus.; Detroit, Inst. of Arts; pencil and wash, Zurich, Kunsthaus), scenes of witchcraft (*The Three Witches*, 1783; Zurich, Kunsthaus), and Shakespearean themes (*A Midsummer Night's Dream*, 1788; London, Tate Gall.). Numerous canvases were contributed to Boydell's Shakespeare Gallery. For the Milton Gallery he painted 47 illustrations for *Paradise Lost*. Fuseli's students included William Blake and Thomas Lawrence (1769–1830); the latter, strikingly different from Fuseli, at the beginning of the century (and with profitable contacts with French culture) continued the aristocratic tradition of portrait painting from Van Dyck to Reynolds.

Blake is undoubtedly one of the personalities of romanticism who best illustrates the transition from an esthetic position of materialistic extremism to a mystical vision tinged with magic and the occult (PL. 316). He was one of the first to become interested in the Gothic revival; while still a boy he sketched the tombs of Westminster Abbey. In the last decade of the 18th century the numerous forces upholding the creative value of the unleashing of emotions (as opposed to the banality of the current morality and religion) found an instrument in Blake. Other artists influenced by these forces were Mozart (in *Don Giovanni*, 1789) and Goya (in *Los Caprichos*, 1799; PL. 315; IV, PL. 440; V, PL. 241; VI, PL. 402). Blake found materials for the expression of his themes in texts such as the Bible, Ossian, Shakespeare, Milton, Dante (hundreds of sketches were devoted to the *Divine Comedy*), the literature of magic and the occult, which he studied in detail, and, above all, his visions, which he claimed made possible direct conversations with the saints (II, PL. 296). An innate tendency to symbolize drove Blake to break all the patterns of tradition; in Fuseli's Michelangelesque aspects Blake sought the most adequate means of rendering the absolute nature of his vision (X, PLS. 139, 252).

The illustrations for Blake's books, colored by a method of illuminated printing invented by him, give the impression of brilliant content in forms inadequate for its expression (VI, PL. 445). Often profound truths announced with disconcerting sincerity and power emerge from graphic compositions that bear the characteristics of a grotesque ingenuousness; from the academic standpoint of the time they seem childish and awkward. Blake's masterpieces were the series of illustrations (1795–97) for Young's *Night Thoughts* and for the Book of Job (I, PL. 309).

Samuel Palmer (1805–81), a student of Blake, showed many similarities to his master. Palmer was a landscapist with a keen sense of the microcosm. An impassioned reader of Young, he employed a technique of *gouache* and Chinese ink to render Young's sense of panic in the struggle between Light and Darkness. Another of the visionaries of early romanticism was John Martin (1789–1854), a famous illustrator of Milton. Characteristic of these artists, and much of contemporaneous English art, was the capacity for imaginary and almost surrealistic evocation, sometimes released by a simple exploitation of a naturalistic fact. A further example of this is found in the work of George Stubbs (1724–1806), a naturalist by profession. Stubbs was admirable for the fidelity with which he was able to render lifelike the anatomy and behavior of horses (PL. 316); he succeeded in transposing the animal to an unreal level by suggestive ambiguity of effects, influencing both Géricault and Delacroix.

James Ward (1769–1859), an admirer of Fuseli and Blake and a follower of the apocalyptic doctrine of Edward Irving, was the author of a huge composition (now lost) depicting the Battle of Waterloo. Ward was noted for his paintings suggesting a sense of panic in the universe, as were Alexander Runciman (1736–85), Edward Calvert (1799–1883), the eclectic John Flaxman (1775–1826; q.v.), Francis Danby (1793–1861), and John Varley (1778–1842), all directly tied to the influence of Blake and Fuseli. Runciman, a friend of Fuseli, painted the famous lost frescoes on the Ossianic theme. Danby, an Irishman, was a founder-member of the Old Water-Colour Society. Varley had a notable influence, especially on Palmer, and was a friend of Blake.

SCANDINAVIA AND GERMANY. At the end of the 18th century and the beginning of the 19th, interest in Michelangelo was not limited to England, where Fuseli and Blake were the major exponents of that aspect of romanticism. In Scandinavia, Asmus Jakob Carstens (1754–98) of Copenhagen was a connecting link between the artistic cultures of England and Germany. His fervent passion for Michelangelo, his love for Italy, where he lived in 1792–93, and his extensive reading (Dante, the Bible, Goethe, the Eddas, the *Nibelungenlied*, Plato) combined to produce a kind of impassioned romantic classicism that exerted a great influence on German romantic painting. Copenhagen was at this time an important center for several generations of artists, not only because such famous masters as Nicolai Abraham Abildgaard (1743–1809) and portrait painter Jens Juel (1745–1802) taught there, but also because of the attraction exerted by the epic world of sagas and war poems common to Germany and Scandinavia.

The Scandinavian contribution to German art was substantial. German painters drawn to the Danish masters included Philipp Otto Runge (a pupil of Juel), Caspar David Friedrich (q.v.), Karl Blechen, Georg Friedrich Kersting, and Bonaventura Genelli (1798–1868). Genelli, in whose painting the influence of classicism and Greek mythology combines with medieval and Shakespearian themes, was connected with Carstens. Johan Christian Dahl (1788–1857), a Norwegian, had enormous success in Saxony; a close friend of Friedrich, he contributed extensively to making Dresden an important center of romanticism. Writers gravitated toward Dresden, including Heinrich von Kleist, who founded an art journal there, and Ludwig Tieck, who lived in Dresden from 1819 to 1842. Artists such as Runge, Friedrich, Kersting, and Johann Friedrich Wilhelm von Müller lived and worked for many years in that city.

The various Nordic influences on German art should not obscure the basic structure of German romantic culture, which consisted essentially of elements of the Enlightenment. Even though the art that resulted was rather modest compared with the impressive achievements in literature and music, several artists made a particularly important contribution to the formation of a concept of nature which in literature as well as philosophy strongly characterized German culture: Carl Gustav Carus (1789–1869), a painter, physiologist, geologist, and naturalist, was also the author of *Nine Letters on Landscape-painting* (1831) and *Twelve Letters on the Life of the Earth* (1841). The ideas of Runge and Friedrich, as seen from their letters, show remarkable similarities to those of the scientists and thinkers of the time.

The foregoing artists, along with others, participated in the general tendency of the century to reimmerse natural science in that magical-symbolical medium from which it had emerged during the Renaissance. Recurring in their thinking were elements of tellurism, a species of animal magnetism propounded by Dietrich Georg Kieser; of structuralism, as applied to the human organism by the mathematician Giovanni Malfatti; of the violent state of nature proclaimed by the philosopher Henrik Steffens; and of the "Weltorganismus" of the German physiologist Karl Friedrich Burdach. This tendency to view natural sciences as more intimately connected with its medieval antecedents was fully documented in writings by Friedrich Wilhelm Joseph von Schelling, the naturalist and philosopher Gotthilf Heinrich von Schubert, Franz Xaver von Baader,

and Adam Karl August Eschenmayer; it found its highest expression in the works of Goethe. In P. O. Runge (1777–1810; PL. 318) the need for an intimate communion with nature assumed the aspect of a return to the pure and innocent spiritual state of childhood. He attempted to fuse all the arts in a single effect, an ideal later widely adopted by German romanticism up to Richard Wagner. Runge wanted the viewer to contemplate his works while listening to music and poetry. His premature death interrupted a cycle dedicated to the hours of the day, which at completion would have represented cosmic upheavals and the gradual triumph of the spirit over matter. Not only in his themes, but also in the quality of his imagination, Runge often suggests Blake.

The artist who most completely expressed the German romantic feeling for nature was Caspar David Friedrich (1774–1840), undoubtedly the major German landscape painter of the 19th century. Friedrich's interest in the faithful reproduction of nature, an objectivism carried to the most extreme consequences, also concerned Constable and the French landscapists of the 1830s. But profoundly different cultural conditions lent to Friedrich's analytical spirit a meditative, philosophical quality; his attempt to seize the vital principle of each tree, branch, and leaf produced an almost surrealistic effect because of a sense of the absolute reality of the inner vision (PL. 318; 1819, *Two Men Watching the Moon in the Mountains*, Dresden, Gemäldegal.; 1807, *The Cross on the Mountain*, Dresden, Gemäldegal.).

Ernst Ferdinand Oehme (1797–1855), another important German landscapist, produced work dominated by typical romantic themes such as Gothic peaks, bare trees, and nocturnal light. Also of interest is Karl Blechen (1798–1840), trained as a scenographer under Karl Friedrich Schinkel (1781–1841) and at first influenced by Schinkel's rather theatrical dramatic and medievalizing themes. Blechen radically changed his style after a long stay in Italy; and in landscapes of Naples, Amalfi, Capri, Sorrento, and the Roman countryside (e.g., studies of the Villa Borghese), he showed a rare sensibility and an almost impressionistic sense of immediacy. Georg Friedrich Kersting (1785–1847), a painter particularly linked to Friedrich, spent a period of apprenticeship in Copenhagen. There he painted a number of war pictures inspired by the Napoleonic Wars and later became one of the major exponents of *bourgeoise intimisme* in Germany. It was in the studio of Friedrich, of whom he painted an evocative portrait, that Kersting acquired the taste for rendering quiet, intimate interiors.

Runge and Friedrich present the concept of a universal and omnipresent spirit (as does Friedrich Hölderlin) rather than a deification of nature or a return to religion. In other German artistic circles, however, interest in the medieval and the Gothic had the characteristics of a return to the religious spirit of Catholicism. In *Outpourings of the Heart of an Art-loving Monk* (1797), Wilhelm H. Wackenroder, a young writer influenced by Vasari, and a member of the literary circle of Jena, meditated on Raphael, Michelangelo, and Fra Angelico. Wackenroder discovered Dürer, the beauty of Nürnberg, and German medieval art and launched a religious and patriotic campaign whose participants included the writer Friedrich von Schlegel (after his sensational conversion in Cologne Cathedral), Ludwig Tieck, Novalis, Clemens Brentano, and many other German men of letters. The Cologne Cathedral, which was begun in the Middle Ages but not completed until the romantic period, constituted a bridge between the past and present and lent substance to the myth, based on an archaeological misunderstanding, of Germany as the homeland of Gothic architecture. The celebration in honor of Dürer at the artist's house in Nürnberg in 1828 made this 15th–16th-century artist appear as the most complete expression of German medieval art.

The religious and mysticizing tendency of the period had its most obvious artistic expression in the German Neo-Gothic style and in the group of Nazarene painters who attempted to reinvigorate art by a return to the purity of the primitives (see PRE-RAPHAELITISM AND RELATED MOVEMENTS). They worked mainly in Rome, living an almost monastic life under the leadership of Johann Friedrich Overbeck (1789–1869; XI, PL. 299) in the deserted Monastery of S. Isidoro a Capo le Case. Connected with this group was Joseph Anton Koch (1768–1839), a Tirolese artist considered the initiator of romantic landscape painting in Germany. From his early years (before going to Rome, where he lived 45 years) and throughout the remainder of his life, Koch drew lyrical inspiration from the landscape of the Viennese Oberland. Franz Pforr, another member of the group, was a painter whose robust naturalism broke away from the ideal of beauty of the Nazarenes and was modeled on the early Italian Renaissance. Carl Philipp Fohr (1795–1818), a remarkable personality whose work was strongly influenced by Koch, reflected in a particularly effective way the powerful influence that Italy exerted on the German painters of the time, especially in the rendering of landscape. Fohr's work was imitative of Poussin, Claude Lorrain, and Rosa (qq.v.) with unmistakable touches of local color. Similar to the art of the Nazarenes in the genuineness of its religious feeling and moving spirituality was the work of the painter Maria Agatha Alberti (1767–1810). A sister-in-law of Ludwig Tieck, she tended the poet Novalis during the last hours of his life and ended her days in a Westphalian convent nursing typhus patients. She held an important place in German romanticism, exerting an influence on Runge.

Perhaps the most gifted of the Nazarene group was Peter Cornelius (1783–1867), an outstanding painter of frescoes on religious and philosophical subjects. His work was later continued by Wilhelm von Kaulbach and notably influenced Moritz von Schwind (1804–71), who learned fresco technique from Cornelius and executed enormous mural compositions in Munich, Hohenschwangau, and Vienna. This remarkable Austrian painter, whose circle included Franz Schubert, writers Franz Grillparzer and Nikolaus Lenau, and painters Leopoldo Kupelwieser (1796–1862), Johann Peter Krafft (1780–1856), and the Olivier brothers (Ferdinand, 1785–1841; Friedrich, 1791–1859), is particularly esteemed for work of more modest dimensions in the field of genre painting; his genre scenes were endowed with a feeling of delightful intimacy. Schwind also painted illustrations of fairy tales, in which he embodied their popular romanticism, Gothic bell towers, and the charm of the forest. His was the expression of a middle-class world that was ironically represented by Carl Spitzweg (1808–85) in another way — as tender and sly. Adrian Ludwig Richter (1803–84), noted illustrator of romantic books and popular songs, can, in a sense, be connected with these artists.

GOYA. While German painting held only a secondary place in the framework of romanticism, one of the high points of the entire movement was achieved in Spain in the work of Goya. At the outbreak of the French Revolution this superb artist, who was already forty-three and had achieved unparalleled fame, began to change his style. Up to that time his work had been essentially related to the rococo tradition of Tiepolo or Fragonard. The change became gradually more marked as the influence of the enlightened and liberal culture arriving from France and England was intensified.

A close relationship existed between *Los Caprichos* (published 1799; IV, PL. 440; V, PL. 241; VI, PL. 402) and the writings of Gaspar Melchor de Jovellanos, Juan Meléndez Valdés, Leandro Moratín, and Ramírez de Góngora, members of the circle of *Afrancesado* friends of Goya. The ideas of Rousseau, Jean François Marmontel, and Johann Heinrich Pestalozzi, placed in contact with an ethical world in Spain that was strongly bound to tradition, awoke a vivid imagination in Goya. This imagination drew on the deepest springs of the unconscious through an exaltation of the world of dreams and on several tendencies of contemporaneous culture then reaching Spain in the physiognomic theories of Lavater, the animal magnetism of Mesmer, and the visions of Swedenborg. Goya also had a thorough understanding of such literary figures as Novalis and Tieck. He collected Piranesi etchings, which epitomized all the trends of the century — classicism, seen in the scientific pictures; the delirious vision of an architectural imagination, which never ceased to obsess this age; and the baroque depiction of perspectives from the bottom upward, lending the building

or ruins a dizzy perpendicular aspect. In Goya, three centuries of the highest European artistic culture — from Titian to Velázquez to Rembrandt, through Piranesi, Gainsborough, and Reynolds — were mobilized to create a vision from which Venturi has said that modern painting descends, "as does ancient poetry from Homer." (See also PL. 315; VI, PLS. 391–402.)

FRANCE. During the years in which Blake in England, Friedrich in Germany, and Goya in Spain created their greatest masterpieces, artistic production in France developed profoundly original characteristics related to the social upheavals in that country. The ideas of Rousseau and Diderot that influenced the genre scenes of Jean B. Greuze in the form of bourgeois sentimentality (VI, PL. 77) were noticeable even in Fragonard's last period (V, PLS. 368, 373). Hubert Robert (1733–1808; q.v.; V, PL. 423), a friend of the artist G. P. Pannini, took his inspiration from contemporaneous events (*Destruction of the Houses of the Pont au Change in 1788*; Paris, Mus. Carnavalet) and later from the destructive acts of the Revolution (*The Destruction of the Bastille, 1789*; *Profanation of the Royal Tombs in St-Denis in October, 1793*; both Paris, Mus. Carnavalet). In his paintings of classical and Gothic ruins, Robert shows a subtle sense of the frailty of human works.

The cultural climate preceding the French Revolution of 1789 decisively influenced the work of Jacques Louis David (1748–1825; q.v.), a major exponent of the neoclassical movement. Neoclassicism was, in certain ways, an opposed tendency to romanticism. Although David, whose style was marked by a Roman austerity and theatrical grandeur, had much in common with the romantics in the force of his passion, he differed in his secure and almost stoic emotional control. Beginning with his *Oath of the Horatii* (painted and exhibited in Rome, 1785; I, PL. 307; V, PL. 424), David stamped the neoclassical movement with the civic dedication and intransigent rationalism that even today constitute its most important values.

Within the pre-Revolution climate in which David worked the political function attributed to a work of art mitigated the burden of energy and irrationality that arose from the culture of the Enlightenment itself and that provoked such widespread uneasiness in the European conscience. This partially explains the historic significance of neoclassicism. Yet neoclassicism remains essentially an episode, although an extremely important one, within the larger process — despite its artificial continuation in the Académie. In its most authentic values it corresponds to the period in which the triumph of the Jacobin utopia created absolute faith in the ideals of the Enlightenment. It was this faith that was translated by David into a truly remarkable realistic observation and, at his best, a sober naturalism.

Before long, the contradictions of the Napoleonic system spread within French culture those anxieties which in Europe had characterized the last two decades of the 18th century and which found their most favorable ground in artists of a particular temperament. Pierre Paul Prud'hon (1758–1823) was considered by the Goncourt brothers, Edmond (1822–96) and Jules (1833–70), as the last painter of the 18th century because of his delicately sensual melancholy. (To Delacroix, however, he seemed isolated.) Compared with David, Prud'hon represented a vein of exquisite refinement and Alexandrine grace, open to the romantic anxieties and the influence of *sensiblerie*. A friend of Canova, he was trained in the writings of Rousseau and Jacques Henri Bernardin de Saint-Pierre and became enamored of Leonardo and Correggio. Some of his works, such as the famous *Abduction of Psyche* (1808; Louvre) and *Justice and Divine Vengeance Pursuing Crime* (1808; Louvre), are among the masterpieces of 19th-century French painting. Napoleon had a particular fondness for Prud'hon (as he had for Ossian and Rousseau), in whose works the conqueror's practical rationalism found sentimental compensation. To satisfy this inclination, even Ingres, a classicist, adapted his style to paint the exquisitely romantic *Dream of Ossian* (1815; Montauban, Mus. Ingres) to decorate Napoleon's bedchamber in the Palazzo del Quirinale in Rome, a work that remains an outstanding example of the romantic picturesque. Ingres's delicate taste for the exotic and fondness for formal themes and solutions reveal contact with the Nazarenes. Paradoxically, his steady aspiration to a classical style in conflict with his sentimental inclination and almost morbid sensuality was typically romantic.

From 1808 onward, romantic themes with a religious feeling, spread by the works of Chateaubriand, were already found in the limited circle of the school of David: *The Burial of Atala* by Anne Louis Girodet-Trioson (1767–1824; PL. 319) is an example. The painter's sentimental and romanticizing tendencies clearly appear in a series of works beginning with *Endymion Asleep* (1792; Louvre), which is much closer to Prud'hon than to David. These same qualities are continued through Girodet-Trioson's Ossianic paintings, one of which was painted in 1801 for Napoleon's residence of Malmaison (see MYTH AND FABLE). Similar accents are found in François Gérard (1770–1837), who emulated Girodet-Trioson by contrasting the latter's *Endymion Asleep* with *Psyche Receiving Amor's First Kiss* (X, PL. 252). The languid and caressing glances of his *Comtesse Regnault de Saint-Jean d'Angély* (1798; Louvre) forecast Prud'hon's portraits of Empress Josephine (X, PL. 269) and Mme Récamier (IV, PL. 122).

The artist who best expressed the profound moral contradictions of the Empire (1805–14) was Baron A. J. Gros (1771–1835; PLS. 319, 320). In complying with the imperial directive to depict Napoleon's sensitivity to the tragic aspects of war, Gros emphasized a paradox to which French society was sensitive. Paintings such as *The Pesthouse at Jaffa* (1804; Louvre) or *Napoleon on the Battlefield at Eylau* (PL. 319) brought him enormous fame, not only for his representation of panoramic battle scenes conveying a feeling of immediacy but also for the humanitarian overtones and pervading sense of anxiety in these works. The effects were achieved in part through a sensitivity to color acquired from contact with Venetian painting, Rubens, and Van Dyck.

Gros's motifs were repeated in the following years with a note of high tragedy by Jean Louis André Théodore Géricault (1791–1824; q.v.). The art of Géricault, which began with the collapse of Napoleon's fortunes, expressed the profound spiritual conflict of a generation trained in the ideals of the Enlightenment and deeply disappointed by historical events. The entire period of the Restoration (1814–30) was marked by a gloomy intellectual pessimism accompanied by an overwhelming outburst of passion. This found fuel in Byronism and the sentimental participation in various struggles for national independence, which inspired many paintings by Géricault, Delacroix, and others. Géricault's *Raft of the Medusa* (PL. 314; VI, PL. 118), conceived and painted between 1818 and 1819 and exhibited the following year in England, began a trend of Titanism in France that found corresponding expression in Goya's *Executions of May 3, 1808* (VI, PL. 399) and in the last works of Beethoven. Géricault, unlike Byron, grew up in contact with doctors and naturalists; his work therefore reveals a rigor of rational training, a materialistic and almost stoical sense of nature, that makes him a precursor of realism.

French artistic culture during the Restoration was increasingly involved in European romanticism through various influences. Eugène Delacroix (q.v.), after admiring the atmospheric luminosity of Constable's landscapes, reworked a great part of his *Massacre at Chios* (IV, PL. 142) and repainted the background. This work, exhibited in the Salon of 1824, was one of the first manifestations of romanticism proper in France. Other European influences in France were the trips to England of Géricault (1820–21) and Delacroix (1825); Delacroix's friendship with Richard Parkes Bonington (q.v.); the diffusion of Goya's art in France, especially through his prints (some of which were copied by Delacroix); and the rapidly spreading admiration for German philosophy, literature, and music. The July Revolution of 1830, which deposed Charles X, marked a decisive date in the integration of French artistic culture into European romanticism. Delacroix's *Liberty Guiding the People* (PL. 313), painted to celebrate the event, is perhaps the finest product of the entire movement in France. Apparently the painting also marked the extinction of civic passion in Delacroix, for it was precisely at this time that he closed himself in aristocratic and splendid isolation. The rise to power of the commercial middle class under Charles's successor, Louis Philippe, seemed destined to crush any generous liberal impulses in France and to suppress the values placed on intellect and emotional sensitivity. Although Delacroix was politically committed to the moderate *juste-milieu* of Louis Philippe, he was culturally closer to the society of the Empire. Deeply repelled by every democratic or socialistic attitude, he found the resolution to his youthful impulses only in the world of the imagination. Long familiarity with Voltaire and the 18th-century writers lent him an interpretation of the world tinged with ancient Stoicism and a keen, yet humane, sense of the value of science. The latter led him directly to the discovery of the effects of pure and separate colors, a point from which the impressionists were to proceed.

Others equally disenchanted by the outcome of the July Revolution but nonetheless rooted in democratic ideals were Honoré Daumier (q.v.) and a separate group of artists who were to find their meeting place at the village of Barbizon near the forest of Fontainebleau. Daumier and the Barbizon school (also called "the school of 1830") gave rise to other principal lines of French art. The members of the Barbizon school sought compensation for their political disillusionments in the isolation of the forest and in direct contact with nature; they longed for an objectively strict reproduction of reality. Daumier, the realist, continued in his social satire the political battle he had started with his caricatures of the *juste-milieu* and Louis Philippe in the years 1830–35, but he was forced to interrupt his work because of the September Laws of 1835 restricting freedom of the press. Among the members of the Barbizon school, only Corot, who had little enthusiasm for anything other than painting, maintained his uninterrupted direction as a landscape painter from the second decade of the century until his death in 1875. This direction had its roots in the tradition of the classical landscape from Lorrain to Pierre Henri de Valenciennes (1750–1819), in the humble, spiritual landscape of the English painters, and in the Holland of Jan Vermeer and Jacob van Ruisdael.

Around the major figures in French romantic painting there was a large group of artists who spread and often vulgarized the new achievements. For example, exoticism (q.v.), which in Delacroix was a phenomenon of broad spiritual scope, often became in Alexandre Gabriel Decamps (1803–60) a simple tendency toward escapism and the picturesque. A brief stay in Smyrna was sufficient for Decamps to collect an enormous quantity of material from which he drew inspiration for countless paintings throughout his life. Decamps exhibited a rich sense of color, representing bazaars, odalisques, and the immense spaces of Africa, in a prevailingly narrative spirit. He was also the author of historical paintings, in particular the very famous *Defeat of the Cimbri* (1833; Louvre), considered one of the best French historical paintings after those of Delacroix. In his own time, however, Decamps was placed far below such mediocrities as the very celebrated Paul Delaroche (1797–1856), François Joseph Heim (1787–1865), Ary Scheffer (1795–1858), and Eugène Devéria (1805–65).

The Orient of Eugène Fromentin (1820–76) was marked by more realistic and direct impressions than Decamps's. Unfortunately Fromentin's abilities as a painter were not equal to his writing talents: he left an unforgettable literary work in *Les maîtres d'autrefois* (1876). Jules Robert Auguste (1789–1850), a friend of Géricault and Delacroix, also devoted his attention to the Orient, as did Alfred Dehodencq (1822–82), Prosper Marilhat (1811–47), and Adrien Dauzats (1804–68).

Théodore Chassériau (1819–56; q.v.), a student of Ingres, was the only French artist of his time to understand the significance of Delacroix, whom he recalls in his passionate impetus, taste for color, and genuine exoticism. Like Delacroix, Chassériau was attracted by large decorative projects; he completed a vast cycle of pictures for the Paris Cour des Comptes, which were lost during the Commune uprisings. Xavier Sigalon (1787–1837) died too young to fulfill his genius (*Athalia Butchering the Royal Children*, 1827; Nantes, Mus. B.A.). Louis Boulanger (1806–67) produced the noteworthy *Mazeppa* (ca. 1827; Rouen, Mus. B.A.). Between 1830 and 1840 works on literary subjects and historical scenes were executed by several painters with a certain talent for illustration that was often exercised in etching and lithography. Horace Vernet (1789–1863), Nicolas Toussaint Charlet (1792–1845), and Auguste Raffet (1804–60) were popular illustrators of the Napoleonic legend. Charlet was, in a sense, a counterpart to Béranger in poetry. Joseph Ferdinand Boissard de Boisdenier (1813–66), a friend of Baudelaire, is particularly remembered for *The Retreat from Russia* (1835; Rouen, Mus. B.A.), a painting inspired by Géricault. The works of Eugène Lami, Alfred Dedreux, Eugène Isabey (1804–86), Eugène Devéria, and Hippolyte Guillaume Sulpice Chevalier (known as Paul Gavarni; 1804–66) during Louis Philippe's July Monarchy and the Second Empire were of a worldly character. A lithographic designer of exceptional ability, Chevalier was one of the major 19th-century illustrators of magazines and newspapers — an honor he shared with Daumier.

The number of French landscapists was extremely large. Valenciennes and Claude Michallon (1751–99), the major representatives of historical landscape painting spanning the two centuries, were also authors of small realistic impressions which, like the work of the first English landscapists, show evidence of direct contact with nature. Following their example, between 1820 and 1840 Jean Joseph Xavier Bidauld (1758–1846), François Edouard Bertin (1797–1871), and Théodore Caruelle d'Aligny (1798–1871) attempted a renewal of the classical formula. In 1825–28 Corot made his first trip to Italy, planning to follow in the footsteps of Poussin and Valenciennes.

The true romantic landscape was achieved in France with the Barbizon school, around the figure of Théodore Rousseau (PL. 321), who first joined the group in 1832–33. It was then that this artistic center became animated. In some respects the forerunners of this school were Louis Gabriel Moreau the Elder and Georges Michel (1763–1843), the latter an impassioned connoisseur and restorer of Flemish and Dutch paintings, who depicted turbulent skies and dramatic views of the Paris suburbs in his compositions. Typically romantic in their treatment of nature were Paul Huet (1803–69), painter of flood scenes, sea storms, cataclysms, and forest landscapes; and Narcisse Diaz de la Peña (1807–76), a vivid colorist, painter of flowers, exotic scenes, and, above all, brilliantly hued underbrush. From 1848 Diaz worked with Rousseau and Jean François Millet (qq.v.) at Barbizon. Particularly close to Rousseau were Jules Dupré (1811–84), Constant Troyon (1810–65; PL. 321), and, from 1849, Millet. After a trip to Holland in 1846, Troyon became primarily a painter of animals; Jacques Raymond Brascassat (1804–67) and Rosa Bonheur (1822–99) also distinguished themselves in this genre.

About 1840 there was a tendency among some landscape painters to give a more drawn, Ingres-like character to the landscape ("ingreser la campagne," according to Baudelaire), which constituted a motif of the transition toward realism. Examples can be found in some of the works of Decamps, Troyon, Auguste Charles de Laberge (1807–42), François Louis Français (1814–97), and Louis Cabat (1812–93). About twenty years later a similar transition from Ingres-like drawing to realistic renderings characterized the landscapes of the Macchiaioli (q.v.), but with very different artistic results (PL. 322).

The contribution of French sculpture to romanticism was much more modest than that of painting. The *Orlando Furioso* by Jean Bernard Du Seigneur, known as Jehan (1808–66), though actually a very minor work, was the manifesto of romantic sculpture, as Victor Hugo's preface to *Cromwell* was for the theater. The work of Antoine Auguste Préault (1809–79), an outstanding sculptor and close friend of Daumier, was characterized by a violent and lyrical expressionism (*La Tuerie*, Chartres, Mus. Municipal; *La Famine*; *La Misère*). François Rude (1784–1855), another excellent sculptor, was particularly noted for *Le Départ des volontaires en 1792*, more commonly called *La Marseillaise*, the most beautiful relief of the Arc de Triomphe de l'Etoile in Paris. His masterpieces, in bronze, are the statue of Gaspard Monge at Beaune, the funerary statue of Godefroy Cavaignac in the cemetery of Montmartre, and the monument *The Awakening of Napoleon* at Fixin, near Dijon. Other significant sculptors of the period are the skillful medalist Pierre Jean David d'Angers (1788–1856) and the brilliant Antoine Louis Barye (1796–1875), who, in the wake of Géricault and Delacroix, depicted scenes of violent struggles between wild animals.

THE SPREAD OF ROMANTICISM. By the mid-19th century such great giants of French romanticism as Delacroix, Corot, and Daumier had no rivals of comparable stature in the rest of Europe. In Italy Purism was a movement of some cultural vitality; its best-known representative in sculpture was Lorenzo Bartolini (1777–1850), a student of David and a friend of Ingres. Connected with Bartolini were the Sienese Giovanni Dupré (1817–82), Vincenzo Vela (1822–91), and Pietro Tenerani (1789–1869; XI, PL. 303), who adhered to the Purist manifesto in 1843. The only artist of importance was Giovanni Carnevale (Il Piccio; 1806–73), an imaginative landscapist and painter of mythological subjects; although bound to the Lombardy tradition, he bears a certain similarity to Delacroix. Tommaso Minardi (1787–1871) produced a remarkable self-portrait (1807; Uffizi). In Milan, where French and German influences met, the work of Francesco Hayez (1791–1882) was a romanticism of subjects, including Mary Stuart, the two Foscaris, and Marino Faliero. In Spain the followers of Goya (Leonardo Alenza y Nieto, 1807–45; Rafael Esteve y Vilella, 1772–1847; Eugenio Lucas, 1824–70; Francisco Lameyer y Berenger, 1825–77) were no more than imitators.

English historical painting, despite some interesting technical qualities, assumed a rhetorical and declamatory tone in the works of Benjamin West (1738–1820; q.v.), John Singleton Copley (1738–1815; q.v.), James Northcote (1746–1831), and Daniel Maclise (1806–70), decorator of the new Houses of Parliament. The influence of Géricault is noticeable in David Scott (1806–49), who had some importance in the formation of the Pre-Raphaelite group and was in contact with the Nazarenes in Rome. David Wilkie (1785–1841), William Mulready (1786–1863), and the American Charles Robert Leslie (1794–1859) continued the English tradition of genre painting. Thomas Lawrence, the celebrated portrait painter (VI, PL. 446), exerted a certain influence on portraiture, a particularly cultivated genre. In Germany the school of Düsseldorf achieved European importance through the work of Karl Friedrich Lessing (1808–80), author of historical paintings inspired especially by the Reformation, and through that of Adrian Ludwig Richter of Dresden, who returned to popular tradition. The most outstanding artist of the Düsseldorf school was Alfred Rethel (1816–59), an able illustrator. Today the importance of this group is difficult to ascertain.

In Austria the Congress of Vienna (1815) made that city a fashionable international center. Miniature painting, which in France was influenced by Jean Baptiste Isabey (1767–1855), found expression in Austria with Moritz Michael Daffinger (1790–1849) and Ferdinand Georg Waldmüller (1793–1865), the latter a typical representative of the Biedermeier style. Landscape art, with its touches of naïve idyllic realism, was particularly successful in Austria, although of minor importance. Among the numerous Austrian landscape artists were Matthäus Loder (1781–1828), Jakob Alt (1789–1872), Franz Steinfeldi (1787–1868), Peter Fendi (1798–1842), Friedrich Loos (1797–1890), and Joseph Anton Koch.

Switzerland, which had produced Fuseli, was of great importance in the development of English romantic landscape painting. During the 18th and 19th centuries Switzerland also produced a considerable amount of its own landscape art. François Diday (1802–77), who discovered the magnificence of the Alps in the Bernese Oberland, was a painter of exceptionally fine mountain scenes. He acquired his training from the example of such predecessors as Pierre Louis de La Rive (1753–1817), Adam Töpffer (1766–1847), and Nicolas Fassin (1728–1811), who was the first in Switzerland to use models from Dutch art. Diday was followed by Alexandre Calame (1810–64), whose solemn Alpine peaks rise amid scenographic settings of fir trees and streams.

In Scandinavia, Christen Schjellerup Købke (1810–48) was an excellent Danish portrait painter endowed with a delightful sense of color. His compatriot Vilhelm Marstrand (1810–73) portrayed intimate scenes with great delicacy and was noted for his illustrations of *Don Quixote*. Among the Norwegians, Thomas Fearnley (1802–42) was a student of Johan Christian Dahl (see above).

Polish romantic painting was related to French historical and patriotic painting and derived from the influence of Jean Pierre Norblin de la Gourdaine (1745–1830), a Frenchman who settled in Poland. Piotr Michałowski (1800–55), a draftsman of considerable inspiration, took as his models the French painters Horace Vernet, Nicolas Toussaint Charlet, and Auguste Raffet. These same painters influenced many others including Jan Matejko (1838–93), considered the Polish national painter because of his renderings of scenes from Polish history, and Artur Grottger (1837–67), who also derived inspiration from the Austrian Moritz von Schwind and from the larger movement of French romanticism. Russia produced Karl Briullov (1799–1852), who achieved brief international fame for *The Last Days of Pompeii* (1828–30; Leningrad, Rus. Mus.), and Aleksandr Ivanov (1806–58), noted for his sincere religious feeling, especially in sketches and water colors; Ivanov was influenced by the Nazarenes. Aleksei Gavrilovich Venetsianov, among others, helped spread genre painting in Russia.

In the United States, the romantic period included some notable painters particularly distinguished in landscapes, members of the so-called "Hudson River school." Among them were Thomas Doughty (1793–1856), Asher B. Durand (1796–1886), and the most important, Thomas Cole (1801–48; q.v.). Romantic ideas of the picturesque and the sublime were fostered in American painting by Emerson's theories on nature, giving life to a landscape art that showed original characteristics. The primitive, virgin character of the American countryside was depicted with enthusiasm and a sense of its beauty and lyric quality (I, PL. 105). Some of Cole's paintings offer a fresh and faithful image of Connecticut and the White Mountains. Cole tended to lyricize nature mystically (*The Oxbow*, 1836; Met. Mus.), sometimes achieving — with increasing frequency in his last years — authentic and original symbolic compositions (*The Course of Empire*, 1836; New York, New-York Historical Soc.). His impassioned vision was akin in some aspects to that of Friedrich and John Martin, whom he admired greatly. American landscape art remained essentially bound to the influences of Crome and Wilson and to the sketches of Claude Lorrain (see IV, PL. 278; IX, PL. 204) and Salvator Rosa, although John Frederick Kensett (1818–72) and George H. Durrie (1820–63) were closer to 17th-century Dutch painting, and Washington Allston (1779–1843; q.v.) more allied to Poussin. (See AMERICAS: ART SINCE COLUMBUS.)

The spread of photography (q.v.), which corresponded perfectly to the taste of many American painters for objective reality, nourished the fashion for views, panoramas, and perspective illusionism. Panoramas like those of Henry Lewis (1819–1904) and John Banvard (1815–91) show the entire course of the Mississippi River. Also in vogue at this time was trompe l'oeil, including some remarkable works by John F. Peto (1854–1907) and William Harnett (1848–92). An imaginative inspiration that seemed to anticipate surrealism was displayed in the works of Edward Hicks (1780–1849; I, PL. 107), which have a quality reminiscent of Henri Rousseau. A preacher by profession, Hicks was convinced that painting should have an edifying and moralizing function. Erastus Salisbury Field (1805–1900), an authentic visionary attracted by Egyptian monuments and mysterious and imposing architecture, executed the *Historical Monument of the American Republic* (ca. 1876; Springfield, Mass., Mus. of Fine Arts, Morgan Wesson Memorial Coll.).

Another characteristic aspect of 19th-century American art was the depiction of Indians. Interest in the Indian was shared by Baudelaire, who praised the manner in which "these savages, with their beautiful postures and nimble movement, helped in the understanding of ancient sculpture." George Catlin (1796–1872) devoted his attention to the Indians with the enthusiasm of an ethnologist (I, PL. 107); he was also the author of a remarkable book called *Manners, Customs and Condition of the North American Indians* (1841). The work of Catlin was carried on by enthusiastic followers including James Otto Lewis (1799–1858), Charles Bird King (1785/6–1862), Alfred Miller (1810–74), and George Caleb Bingham (1811–97).

POSTROMANTICISM. In the work of the foregoing minor artists romanticism lost its central position during the first half of the 19th century, changing to a phenomenon of taste and custom or to a stale repetition of themes. During the second half of the century, however, there occured a genuine creative revival of romantic motifs. This was due to the spiritual discontent expressed in many quarters toward realism (q.v.), the esthetic solution to the romantic crisis provided by French culture. But the work of the realists Daumier and Courbet did not in itself resolve all the doubts of the time. Their approach was rather an expression of the recovery of middle-class society after the Restoration — a recovery that had its fundamental stages in the revolutions of 1830 and 1848. This realism was so permeated by new and irreconcilable contradictions, however, that toward the end of the century it led to an even more profound and painful crisis than that which had occurred toward the end of the 18th century.

The last period of Daumier's production, dominated by the lithographs of the Franco-Prussian War and in a sense symbolized by his *Don Quixote*, was extremely significant. The restless, vigilant eye of the great artist turned to a panorama of events and emotions betraying deep flaws in a society convinced that the solution to its problems lay in bourgeois democracy and the philosophy of positivism. These flaws were clearly apparent after the middle of the 19th century; they are reflected in a series of cultural events that occurred parallel to the blossoming of realism in its last phase and impressionism. Particularly indicative of the developments is the sculpture of Auguste Rodin (q.v.). In many ways Rodin was related to Daumier; like Daumier, he cast his roots in the titanic Michelangelesque influence that was a characteristic feature of early romanticism from Fuseli to Flaxman and Géricault. The content of Rodin's work, however, was very new. Its detachment from sentimental commitments led him to a deep introspection and to the exploitation of a dynamic force which as an outstanding draftsman he was able to transmit to sculptured forms. From this point of view, Rodin closed the 19th century in sculpture, opening the way to all the boldness of contemporary art.

Together with Rodin, such artists as Gustave Moreau (1826–98) and Pierre Puvis de Chavannes (1824–98; XI, PL. 305) today appear equally indicative of the spirit of the time. Moreau had a cultivated mind, was a lover of Oriental art (Byzantine, Persian, Hindu), and was heir to the sensual and sanguinary exoticism of Delacroix and Baudelaire, which was so entrenched in violently antirealist positions. Puvis de Chavannes was an artist of great purity of design, tending toward large decorations and the symbolic use of the image; he was one of the major creators of modern symbolism. A separate place should be assigned to Odilon Redon, a figure influenced by the esthetic ideas of Delacroix. Redon's refined work as a painter, draftsman, and engraver has a mysteriously and poetically literary character. He was a writer, musician, and enthusiast of the natural sciences and was able to suggest, through a flower or a face, an entire world of symbolic-religious association.

These spiritualistic tendencies of French culture had their counterparts in various sections of Europe, with characteristics determined by the specific artistic cultures. The most important European phenomenon was English Pre-Raphaelitism, begun by Dante Gabriel Rossetti in 1848. The Pre-Raphaelite group, which followed the example of the Nazarenes and proposed to rediscover original purity by a study of the primitives, was joined about 1860 by Edward Burne-Jones (XI, PL. 305), the critic John Ruskin, and William Morris (q.v.), the reviver of decorative arts. A phenomenon similar to Pre-Raphaelitism occurred in Germany in the painting of Hans von Marése and the Swiss artist Arnold Böcklin (q.v.). The latter had a strong artistic personality characterized by nostalgia for an imaginary antiquity conceived as a land in which every conflict is resolved (*Pan in the Bullrushes*, 1857, Munich, Neue Pin.; *Pan Frightening a Shepherd*, 1857, Munich, Schackgal.; *Triton and Naiads*,

1886; *Flora*, 1868–70, last two, Basel, Kunstmus.). At other times Böcklin achieved a melancholy evocation of the unconscious life as revealed in dreams (*Island of the Dead*, 1880, Met. Mus.).

Bibliog. *General*: T. Gautier, Histoire du Romantisme, Paris, 1874; L. Hautecoeur, Rome et la Renaissance de l'antiquité à la fin du XVIIIe siècle, Paris, 1912; J. Meier-Graefe, Entwicklungsgeschichte der modernen Kunst, 3 vols., Munich, 1914 (4th ed., 1924); A. Kuhn, Die neuere Plastik von 1800 bis zur Gegenwart, Munich, 1922; K. Gerstenberg, Die ideale Landschaftsmalerei: Ihre Begründung und Vollendung in Rom, Halle, 1923; C. Glaser, Die Graphik der Neuzeit vom Anfang des 19. Jahrhunderts bis zur Gegenwart, 2d ed., Berlin, 1923; H. Hildebrandt, Die Kunst des 19. und 20. Jahrhunderts, Wildpark-Potsdam, 1924; P. van Tieghem, Le Préromantisme, 5 vols., Paris, 1924–48; B. Knauss, Das Künstlerideal des Klassizismus und der Romantik, Reutlingen, 1925; G. Pauli, Die Kunst des Klassizismus und der Romantik, Berlin, 1925; L. Reynaud, Le Romantisme: Ses origines anglo-germaniques, influences étrangères et traditions nationales, le réveil du génie français, Paris, 1926; K. Scheffler, Die europäische Kunst im 19. Jahrhundert, 2 vols., Berlin, 1926–27; H. Focillon, La peinture au XIXe siècle: Le retour à l'antique, le Romantisme, Paris, 1927; H. Focillon, La peinture aux XIXe et XXe siècles: Du Realisme à nos jours, Paris, 1928; A. Neumeyer, Die Erweckung der Gotik in der deutschen Kunst des späten 18. Jahrhunderts: Ein Beitrag zur Vorgeschichte der Romantik, RepfKw, XLIX, 1928, pp. 75–123, 159–85; A. Neumeyer, Zum Problem des Manierismus in der bildenden Kunst der Romantik, ZfbK, LXII, 1928–29, pp. 184–88; L. Réau, L'art romantique, Paris, 1930; A. Rümann, Das illustrierte Buch des 19. Jahrhunderts in England, Frankreich und Deutschland, Leipzig, 1930; H. Tronchon, Romantisme et préromantisme, Paris, 1930; V. Husarski, Le style romantique, Brussels, 1931; E. Seillière, Le romantisme et la religion: Essai sur le mysticisme chrétien et le mysticisme naturiste, Paris, 1932; F. Antal, Reflections on Classicism and Romanticism, BM, LXVI, 1935, pp. 159–68, LXVIII, 1936, pp. 72–80, 188–92, LXXVII, 1940, pp. 130–39, LXXVIII, 1941, pp. 14–22; P. Colin, La peinture européenne au XIXe siècle: Le Romantisme, Paris, Brussels, 1935; E. d'Ors, Du Baroque, Paris, 1937; A. E. Addison, Romanticism and the Gothic Revival, New York, 1938; E. Wind, The Revolution of History Painting, Warburg, II, 1938–39, pp. 116–27; A. M. Brizio, Ottocento e Novecento, Turin, 1939; E. P. Richardson, The Way of Western Art 1776–1914, Cambridge, Mass., 1939; N. Pevsner, Academies of Art: Past and Present, Cambridge, 1940; L. Venturi, Peintres modernes, Paris, 1942 (Eng. trans., New York, 1947); M. P. Boye, La mêlée romantique, Paris, 1946; A. Comfort, Art and Social Responsibility: Lectures on the Ideology of Romanticism, London, 1946; K. Scheffler, Verwandlungen des Barocks in der Kunst des 19. Jahrhunderts, Vienna, 1947; U. Christoffel, Malerei und Poesie: Die symbolistische Kunst des 19. Jahrhunderts, Vienna, 1948; J. Barzun, Romanticism: Definition of a Period, Mag. of Art, XLII, 1949, pp. 243–48; E. H. Gombrich, Imagery and Art in the Romantic Period, BM, XCI, 1949, pp. 153–58; L. Réau, L'ère romantique: Les arts plastiques, Paris, 1949; P. Francastel, Peinture et société, Lyon, 1951; A. Hauser, The Social History of Art, 2 vols., London, 1951; M. Raynal, Le XIXe siècle: De Goya à Gauguin, Geneva, 1951 (Eng. trans., J. Emmons, London, New York, 1951); K. Lankheit, Das Freundschaftsbild der Romantik, Heidelberg, 1952; K. Scheffler, Das Phänomen der Kunst: Grundsätzliche Betrachtungen zum 19. Jahrhundert, Munich, 1952; F. H. Man, 150 Years of Artist's Lithographs (1803–1953), London, 1953; R. Zeitler, Klassizismus und Utopia: Interpretationen zu Werken von David, Canova, Carstens, Thorwaldsen, Koch, Stockholm, 1954; L. Eitner, The Open Window and the Storm-tossed Boat: An Essay in the Iconography of Romanticism, AB, XXXVII, 1955, pp. 281–90; P. Moreau, Le romantisme littéraire dans ses rapports avec les arts plastiques, Atti Cong. int. di lingue e letteratura moderna (1951), Florence, 1955, pp. 341–51; F. Baumgart, Geschichte der abendländischen Plastik, Cologne, 1957; G. Grundmann, Das Riesengebirge in der Malerei der Romantik, 2d ed., Munich, 1958; C. G. Heise, Grosse Zeichner des 19. Jahrhunderts, Berlin, 1959; J. Laran, J. Adhémar, and J. Prinet, L'Estampe, 2 vols., Paris, 1959; I. Babbitt, Rousseau and Romanticism, 5th ed., New York, 1960; K. Badt, Wolkenbilder und Wolkengedichte der Romantik, Berlin, 1960; M. Brion, Romantic Art, London, New York, 1960; W. Hofmann, Das irdische Paradies: Kunst im 19. Jahrhundert, Munich, 1960 (Eng. trans., B. Battershaw, New York, 1961); F. Novotny, Painting and Sculpture in Europe 1780–1880, Harmondsworth, 1960; N. Pevsner, Art and Architecture 1830–1870, in Cambridge Modern History, 2d ed., X, 1960, pp. 134–55; P. Courthion, Le Romantisme, Geneva, 1961 (Eng. trans., S. Gilbert, Geneva, 1961).

France: E. Chesneau, L'art et les artists modernes en France et en Angleterre, Paris, 1864; C. Baudelaire, Curiosités esthétiques (Oeuvres complètes, II), Paris, 1868; A. Moreau, Decamps et son œuvre, Paris, 1869; C. Clément, Prud'hon: Sa vie, ses œuvres et sa correspondance, Paris, 1872 (3d ed., 1880); A. Sensier, Souvenirs sur T. Rousseau, Paris, 1872; A. Sensier, Etude sur Georges Michel, Paris, 1873; E. de Goncourt, Catalogue raisonné de l'œuvre peint, dessiné et gravé de Prud'hon, Paris, 1876; C. Blanc, Les artistes de mon temps, Paris, 1877; P. Burty, Maîtres et petits maîtres, Paris, 1877; H. Jouin, David d'Angers, 2 vols., Paris, 1877; E. Chesneau, Peintres et statuaires romantiques, Paris, 1880; L. Gonse, Eugène Fromentin: Peintre et écrivain, Paris, 1880; J. Gigoux, Causeries sur les artistes de mon temps, Paris, 1885; B. Prost, Octave Tassaert, Paris, 1886; J. W. Mollett, The Painters of Barbizon, London, 1890; A. Dayot, Charlot et son œuvre, Paris, 1893; T. Thoré, Les salons (1844–68); Etudes de critique et d'esthétique, 3 vols., Paris, 1893; F. Benoit, L'art français sous la Révolution et l'Empire, Paris, 1897; P. Signac, D'Eugène Delacroix au néo-impressionnisme, Paris, 1899; L. Rosenthal, La peinture romantique, Paris, 1900; G. Lanoë and T. Brice, Histoire de l'école française du paysage depuis Poussin jusqu'à Millet, Paris, 1901; R. Muther, Ein Jahrhundert französischen Malerei, Berlin, 1901; H. Lemonnier, Gros, Paris, 1905; P. Lasserre, Le romantisme français, Paris, 1907 (2d ed., 1920); Mme. de Basily-Callimachi, J. B. Isabey: Sa vie, son temps, Paris, 1909; L. Hautecoeur, Le sentimentalisme dans la peinture française de Greuze à David, GBA, XLI, 1909, pp. 159–76, 269–86; A. Marie, Un imagier romantique: Célestin Nanteuil, Paris, 1910; C. Saunier, Un artiste romantique oublié: Monsieur Auguste, GBA, III, 1910, pp. 441–60, IV, 1910, pp. 51–68, 229–42; G. Séailles, Alfred Dehodencq: L'homme et l'artiste, Paris, 1910; H. Marcel and J. Laran, T. Chassériau, Paris, 1911; P. Dorbec, Les paysagistes anglais en France, GBA, VIII, 1912, pp. 257–81; P. A. Lemoisne, Eugène Lami, Paris, 1912; J. Locquin, La peinture d'histoire en France de 1747 à 1785, Paris, 1912; D. Mornet, Le romantisme en France au XVIIIe siècle, Paris, 1912; G. Pellissier, Le réalisme du romantisme, Paris, 1912; P. Dorbec, Les influences de la peinture anglaise sur le portrait en France (1750–1850), GBA, X, 1913, pp. 85–102; P. Marmottan, Le peintre Louis Boilly (1761–1845), Paris, 1913; L. Dimier, Histoire de la peinture française au XIXe siècle, Paris, 1914 (2d ed., 1926); L. Rosenthal, Du romantisme au réalisme, Paris, 1914; J. Calmette, François Rude, Paris, 1920; J. Locquin, Un grand statuaire romantique: Auguste Préault, La renaissance, III, 1920, pp. 454–63; R. Escholier, L'orientalisme de Chassériau, GBA, III, 1921, pp. 89–107; G. Wildenstein, Un peintre de paysage au XVIIIe siècle: Louis Moreau, Paris, 1922; A. Fontainas and L. Vauxcelles, Histoire générale de l'art français de la Révolution à nos jours, I, Paris, 1923, F. Calot, Le livre illustré du XIXe siècle, in Le livre français des origines à la fin du Second Empire, Paris, 1924, pp. 109–29; J. Guiffrey, L'œuvre de P. P. Prud'hon, Paris, 1924; G. G. Hartlaub, Gustave Doré, Leipzig, 1924; E. Hildebrandt, Malerei und Plastik des 18. Jahrhunderts in Frankreich, Wildpark-Potsdam, 1924; M. Sander, Die illustrierten französischen Bücher des 19. Jahrhunderts, Stuttgart, 1924; P. Dorbec, L'art du paysage en France: Essai sur son évolution de la fin du XVIIIe siècle à la fin du Second Empire, Paris, 1925; M. Gauthier, Achille et Eugène Devèria, Paris, 1925; A. Marie, Alfred et Tony Johannot, Paris, 1925; A. Marie, Le peintre-poète Louis Boulanger, Paris, 1925; C. Saunier, Barye, Paris, 1925; R. Escholier, Victor Hugo artiste, Paris, 1926; F. Ingersoll-Smouse, Joseph Vernet: Peintre de marines, 2 vols., Paris, 1926; R. Lanson, Le goût du moyen âge en France au XVIIIe siècle, Paris, Brussels, 1926; T. Silvestre, Les artistes français, 2 vols., Paris, 1926; H. Clouzot, Architectes, sculpteurs, décorateurs (Le musée romantique, 7), Paris, 1927; L. Benoist, La sculpture, romantique, 7), Paris, 1927; L. Benoist, La sculpture romantique, Paris, 1928; P. du Colombier, Decamps, Paris, 1928; J. Robiquet, L'art et le goût sous la Restauration, Paris, 1928; Le romantisme et l'art: Recueil de conférences faites à la Sorbonne, Paris, 1928; L. Rosenthal, L'art et les artistes romantiques, Paris, 1928; P. Schommer, L'art décoratif au temps du romantisme: Le style troubadour, Paris, 1928; H. Jacoubert, Le genre troubadour et les origines françaises du romantisme, Paris, 1929; A. Keim, La décoration et le mobilier à l'époque romantique, Paris, 1929; R. Schneider, L'art français au XIXe siècle: Du classicisme davidien au romantisme, Paris, 1929; P. Sentenac, Hubert Robert, Paris, 1929; J. Alazard, L'Orient, et la peinture française au XIXe siècle, Paris, 1930; W. Friedländer, Hauptströmungen der französischen Malerei von David bis Cézanne, I: Von David bis Delacroix, Leipzig, 1930 (Eng. trans., Cambridge, Mass., 1952); A. Monglond, Le préromantisme français, 2 vols., Grenoble, 1930; P. de Nolhac and G. K. Loukomsky, La Rome d'Hubert Robert, Paris, 1930; J. Robiquet, Le décore de la vie à l'époque romantique, Paris, 1930 (cat.); J. Alazard, L'exotisme dans la peinture française au XIXe siècle, GBA, VI, 1931, pp. 240–55; L. Bénédite, T. Chassériau: Sa vie et son œuvre, 2 vols., Paris, 1931; D. Jalabert, La sculpture française, Paris, 1931; H. Leblanc, Catalogue de l'œuvre complète de G. Doré, Paris, 1931; R. H. Wilenski, French Painting, Boston, 1931; R. Fry, Characteristics of French Art, London, 1932; P. Jamot, T. Chassériau, Paris, 1933; P. Lelièvre, Gros: Peintre d'histoire, GBA, XV, 1936, pp. 289–304; M. Kolb, Ary Scheffer et son temps, Paris, 1937; M. W. Brown, The Painting of the French Revolution, New York, 1938; E. Goldschmidt, Frankrigs Malerkunst, Copenhagen, 1938; P. Jourda, L'exotisme dans la littérature française depuis Chateaubriand, Paris, 1938; R. Jullian, L'œuvre de Puvis de Chavannes, GBA, XX, 1938, pp. 237–50; H. Clouzot, Le style Louis-Napoléon III, Paris, 1939; P. Francastel, Le style Empire (du Directoire à la Restauration), Paris, 1939; B. Dörries and U. Christoffel, Klassizismus in Frankreich um 1800, Munich, 1941; R. Escholier, La peinture française au XIXe siècle, 2 vols., Paris, 1941–44; L. Venturi, P. H. de Valenciennes, AQ, IV, 1949, pp. 89–109; L. Réau, Un siècle d'aquarelle: De Géricault à nos jours, Paris, 1942; K. Scheffler, Die grossen französischen Maler des 19. Jahrhunderts, Munich, 1942 (2d ed., 1949); J. J. Seznec, The "Romans of the Decadence" and Their Historical Significance, GBA, XXIV, 1943, pp. 221–32; U. Christoffel, Von Poussin zu Ingres und Delacroix: Betrachtungen über die französischen Malerei, Zurich, 1945; M. L. Dufrénoy, L'Orient romanesque en France, Montreal, 1946; M. Rose, G. Doré, London, 1946; B. Dorival, La peinture française, Paris, 1948; R. Huyghe and P. Jaccottet, Le dessin français au XIXe siècle, Lausanne, 1948; K. Clark, Landscape into Art, London, 1949; K. Berger, French Master Drawings of the 19th Century, New York, 1950; G. Levitine, Girodet-Trioson: An Iconographical Study, Cambridge, Mass., 1952; F. Daulte, Le dessin français de David à Courbet, Lausanne, 1953; C. O. Zieseniss, Les aquarelles de Barye, 2 vols., Paris, 1954; K. Berger, Le style du Poussin et le XIXe siècle, GBA, XLV, 1955, pp. 161–70; P. Francastel, La peinture française du classicisme au cubisme, Paris, 1955; F. Fosca, La peinture française au XIXe siècle, Paris, 1956; L. Hautecoeur and P. Jamot, La peinture au Musée du Louvre: Ecole française, XIXe siècle, 2 vols., Paris, 1956–57; G. Levitine, L'ossian de Girodet et l'actualité politique sous le Consulat, GBA, XLVIII, 1956, pp. 39–56; P. Francastel, Les grandes tendances de l'art européen au XIXe siècle, Cah. d'h. mondiale, III, 1957, pp. 909–40; I. Elles, Das Stilleben in der französischen Malerei des 19. Jahrhunderts, Zurich, 1958; F. Grappe, Prud'hon, Paris, 1958; C. Sterling and H. Adhémar, La peinture au Musée du Louvre: Ecole française, XIXe siècle, 4 vols., Paris, 1958–61; P. Grate, La critique d'art et la bataille romantique, GBA, LIV, 1959, pp. 129–48; J. Lindsay, Death of the Hero: French Painting from David to Delacroix, London, 1960; M. Z. Shroder, Icarus: The Image of the Artist in French Romanticism, Cambridge, Mass., 1961;

G. Bazin, P. H. de Valencienne, GBA, LIX, 1962, pp. 353–62; P. Guinard, Romantiques français en Espagne, Art de France, II, 1962, pp. 179–206; J. Leymarie, French Painting: The 19th Century (trans. J. Emmons), Geneva, 1962; J. Lethève and J. Adhémar, Delacroix et la gravure romantique, Paris, 1963 (cat.).

Austria: L. Hevesi, Österreichische Kunst im 19. Jahrhundert, 2 vols., Leipzig, 1903; E. H. Zimmermann, Das Alt-Wiener Sittenbild, Vienna, 1923; H. Tietze, Das vormärzliche Wien in Wort und Bild, Vienna, 1925; B. Grimschitz, Die österreichische Zeichnung im 19. Jahrhundert, Zurich, Vienna, Leipzig, 1927; B. Grimschitz, Maler der Ostmark im 19. Jahrhundert, Vienna, 1940; K. Ginhart, Die bildende Kunst in Österreich, VI: Von Ausgang des 18. Jahrhunderts bis zur Gegenwart, Baden bei Wien, 1943; K. Ginhart, Wiener Kunstgeschichte, Vienna, 1948; O. Benesch, Kleine Geschichte der Kunst in Österreich, Vienna, 1950; W. Buchowiecki, Geschichte der Malerei in Wien (Geschichte der Stadt Wien, N.S., VII, 2), Vienna, 1955; H. Schwarz, Salzburg und das Salzkammergut: Die künstlerische Entdeckung der Stadt und der Landschaft im 19. Jahrhundert, 3d ed., Vienna, 1958; E. Buschbeck, Romantik in Österreich: Malerei und Graphik, Salzburg, 1959 (cat.).

Belgium and The Netherlands: G. Vanzype, L'art belge du XIXe siècle, 2 vols., Paris, Brussels, 1923; G. Brom, Romantiek en Katholicisme in Nederland, I: Kunst, Groningen, 1926; P. Fierens et al., L'art en Belgique du moyen âge à nos jours, Brussels, 1939; F. M. Huebner, Die Kunst der niederländischen Romantik, Düsseldorf, 1942; J. Knoef, Tussen Rococo en Romantiek, The Hague, 1944; P. Fierens, L'art flamand, Paris, 1946; J. Knoef, Van Romantiek tot Realisme, The Hague, 1947; H. E. van Gelder and J. Duverger, eds., Kunstgeschiedenis der Nederlanden, II-III, Utrecht, 1955–56; Le romantisme au pays de Liège, Liège, 1955 (cat.); J. H. M. van der Marck, Romantische Boekillustratie in België, Roermond, 1956; P. K. van Daalen, Nederlandse beeldhouwers in de negenteinde, The Hague, 1957.

Scandinavia: K. L. Fernow, Leben des Künstlers A. J. Carstens: Ein Beitrag zur Kunstgeschichte des 18. Jahrhunderts, Leipzig, 1806 (2d ed. by H. Riegel, Hanover, 1867); C. A. Been, ed., Danmarks Malerkunst: Billeder og biografier, 2 vols., Copenhagen, 1902–03; G. Nordensvan, Schwedische Kunst des 19. Jahrhunderts, Leipzig, 1904; A. Aubert, Die norwegische Malerei in 19. Jahrhundert, Leipzig, 1910; Dänische Maler von Jens Juel bis zur Gegenwart, Düsseldorf, Leipzig, 1911; G. Nordensvan et al., Svensk konsthistoria, Stockholm, 1913; G. Nordensvan, Svensk konst och svenska konstnärer i 19de århundradet, 2 vols., Stockholm, 1925–28; S. Schultz, Dansk genremaleri, Copenhagen, 1928; H. Bramsen, Landskabsmaleriet i Danmark 1750–1875: Stilhistoriske hovedtræk, Copenhagen, 1935; C. Hintze, Kopenhagen und die deutsche Malerei um 1800, Würzburg, 1937; A. Kamphausen, A. J. Carstens, Neumünster in Holstein, 1941; O. Okkonen, Die finnische Kunst, Berlin, 1943; H. Cornell, Den svenska konsten historia, 2 vols., Stockholm, 1944–46; A. Lindblom, Sverige konsthistoria från forntid till nutid, III, Stockholm, 1946; E. Zahle et al., Danmarks malerkunst: Fra middelalder til nutid, 3d ed., Copenhagen, 1947; V. Thorlacius-Ussing, ed., Danmarks billedhuggerkunst fra oldtid til nutid, Cophenagen, 1950; Svenskt konstnärslexikon, Malmö, 1952 ff.; A. Durham, Painting in Norway, Stockholm, 1955.

Switzerland: D. Baud-Bovy, Les maîtres de la gravure suisse, Geneva, 1935; W. Hugelshofer, Schweizer Kleinmeister, Zürich, 1943; L. Fromer im Obersteg, Die Entwicklung der schweizerischen Landschaftsmalerei im 18. und frühen 19. Jarhundert, Basel, 1945; P. R. Wescher, Die Romantik in der schweizer Malerei, Frauenfeld, 1947; H. W. Lanz, Der Basler Maler Jacob Christoph Miville, Lörrach, 1954; A. Reinle, Kunstgeschichte der Schweiz, IV: Die Kunst des 19. Jahrhunderts, Frauenfeld, 1962.

Eastern Europe: *a. Poland*: T. Dobrowolski, Stattler a Michałowski (Stattler and Michałowski), Kraków, 1955; Warsaw Mus., Z epoki romantyzmu (The Romantic Period), Warsaw, 1955; J. Zanosiński, Malarstwo polskie okresu romantyzmu (Polish Painting in the Romantic Period), Warsaw, 1958 (cat.). *b. Czechoslovakia*: J. Neumann, Czech Classic Painting of the 19th Century (Eng. trans., I. Urwin), Prague, 1955. *c. Hungary*: B. Lazar, Ladislaus de Páal: Un peintre hongrois de l'école de Barbizon, Paris, 1904; I. Genthon, Az új magyar festészet története (History of the New Hungarian Painting), Budapest, 1934; K. Lyka, Magyar müvészet 1800–1850 (Hungarian Art 1800–1850), Budapest, 1939; L. von Balás-Piry, Die ungarische Malerei des 19. and 20. Jahrhunderts, Berlin, 1940; K. Lyka, Nemzeti romantika 1850–1867 (National Romanticism 1850–1867), Budapest, 1942; Ö. G. Pogany, 19th Century Hungarian Painting, Budapest, 1955; I. Genthon et al., Magyar müvészet: 1800–1945 (Hungarian Art: 1800–1945), Budapest, 1958 (bibliog.); L. Végvári, Katalog der Gemälde und Zeichnungen Mihály Munkácsys, Budapest, 1959. *d. Rumania*: G. Oprescu, Rumanian Art from 1800 to Our Days, Malmö, 1935; G. Oprescu, Grigorescu, Bucharest, 1961. *e. Serbia*: Dwa weka srpskoga slikarstwa (Two Centuries of Serbian Painting), Belgrade, 1943.

Germany: C. G. Carus, Neun Briefe über Landschaftsmalerei, Leipzig, 1831 (ed. K. Gerstenberg, Dresden, 1955); C. G. Carus, Zwölf Briefe über das Erdleben, Stuttgart, 1841 (ed. C. Bernouilli and H. Kern, Celle, 1926); H. A. Schmid, ed., Arnold Böcklin: Eine Auswahl der hervorragendsten Werke des Kunstlers, 4 vols., Munich, 1892–1901; H. von Tschudi, Ausstellung deutscher Kunst aus der Zeit von 1775–1875 in der königlichen Nationalgalerie Berlin (1906), 2 vols., Munich, 1906; L. Réau, Max Klinger, GBA, XL, 1908, pp. 265–88, 505–17; A. Aubert, Runge und die Romantik, Berlin, 1909; J. Meier-Graefe, Hans von Marées: Sein Leben und sein Werk, 3 vols., Munich, 1910; H. von Kleinmayr, Die deutsche Romantik und die Landschaftsmalerei, Strasbourg, 1912; R. Hamann, Die deutsche Malerei im 19. Jahrhundert, Leipzig, Berlin, 1914; F. H. Meissner, ed., Max Klinger, Munich, 1914; A. Aubert, C. D. Friedrich: Gott, Freiheit, Vaterland, Berlin, 1915; U. Christoffel, Die romantische Zeichnung von Runge bis Schwind, Munich, 1920; K. K. Eberlein, Deutsche Maler der Romantik, Jena, 1920; A. Quenzel, Der Maler Feuerbach, Leipzig, 1920; J. Justi, Deutsche Malkunst im 19. Jahrhundert: Ein Führer durch die Nationalgalerie Berlin, Berlin, 1921; H. Uhde-Bernays, Münchener Landschafter im 19. Jahrhundert, Munich, 1921; R. Oldenbourg and H. Uhde-Bernays, Die Münchener Malerei im 19. Jahrhundert, 2 vols., Munich, 1922; P. F. Schmidt, Biedermeier-Malerei: Zur Geschichte und Geistigkeit der deutschen Malerei in der ersten Hälfte des 19. Jahrhunderts, Munich, 1922; P. F. Schmidt, Die deutsche Landschaftsmalerei von 1750–1830, Munich, 1922; L. Zahn, Moritz von Schwind, Munich, 1922; A. Farinelli, Il romanticismo in Germania, 2d ed., Bari, 1923; C. Gurlitt, Die deutsche Kunst seit 1800, 4th ed., Berlin, 1924; H. Nasse, Deutsche Maler der Frühromantik, Munich, 1924; W. Wolfradt, C. D. Friedrich und die Landschaft der Romantik, Berlin, 1924; R. Hamann, Die deutsche Malerei vom Rokoko bis zum Expressionismus, Leipzig, Berlin, 1925; A. Rümann, Die illustrierten deutschen Bücher des 19. Jahrhunderts, Stuttgart, 1926; F. Noack, Das Deutschtum in Rom, 2 vols., Stuttgart, 1927; W. Weidmann, Der Maler Franz Krüger: Der Mensch und das Werk, Berlin, 1927; A. Feulner, Skulptur und Malerei des 18. Jahrhunderts in Deutschland, Wildpark-Potsdam, 1929; P. O. Rave, Deutsche Bildnerkunst von Schadow bis zur Gegenwart, Berlin, 1929; E. Waldmann, La peinture allemande contemporaine, Paris, 1930; F. Landsberger, Die Kunst der Goethezeit: Kunst und Kunstanschauung von 1750 bis 1830, Leipzig, 1931; H. Jerchel, Malerei der Romantik, Munich, 1932; L. Justi, Von Runge bis Thoma: Deutsche Malkunst im 19. und 20. Jahrhundert, Berlin, 1932; D. Verein für Kw., Schrifttum zur d. K., I–XIX, 1933–59; H. Karlinger, München und die deutsche Kunst des 19. Jahrhunderts, Munich, 1933; R. Weiss, Das Alpenerlebnis in der deutschen Literatur des 18. Jahrhunderts, Horgen-Zurich, Leipzig, 1933; K. Gerstenberg and P. O. Rave, Die Wandgemälde der deutschen Romantiker im Casino Massimo zu Rom, Berlin, 1934; W. Goldschmidt, Die Landschaftbriefe des C. G. Carus: Ihre Bedeutung für die Theorie der romantischen Landschaftsmalerei, Breslau, 1935; E. Schilling, Deutsche Romantiker-Zeichnungen, Frankfurt am Main, 1935; W. R. Deusch, Malerei der deutschen Romantiker und ihre Zeitgenossen, Berlin, 1937; L. Réau, La peinture romantique en Allemagne, Cah. du Sud, XXIV, special no., 1937, pp. 41–50; H. von Einem, C. D. Friedrich, Berlin, 1938; L. Grote, Die Brüder Olivier und die deutschen Romantik, Berlin, 1938; R. Benz and A. von Schneider, Die Kunst der deutschen Romantik, Munich, 1939; M. Goering, Deutsche Malerei des 17. und 18. Jahrhunderts: Von den Manieristen bis zum Klassizismus, Berlin, 1940; P. O. Rave, Karl Blechen, Berlin, 1940; C. D. Friedrich, Skizzenbuch aus den Jahren 1806 und 1818 (ed. L. Grote), Berlin, 1942; C. de Prybram-Gladona, C. D. Friedrich, Paris, 1942; A. von Schneider, Deutsche Romantiker-Zeichnungen, Munich, 1942; E. L. Schellenberg, Das Buch der deutschen Romantik, 2d ed., Bamberg, 1943; P. du Colombier, L'art allemand, Paris, 1946; J. H. Schmidt, O. Achenbach, 2d ed., Düsseldorf, 1946; A. Elsen, Carl Spitzweg, Vienna, 1948; H. Busch, Moritz von Schwind, Königstein, 1949; P. O. Rave, Deutsche Malerei des 19. Jahrhunderts, Berlin, 1949; B. Dörries, Zeichungen der Frühromantik, Munich, 1950; H. Geller and H. von Einem, Die Bildnisse der deutschen Künstler in Rom 1800–1830, Berlin, 1952; G. Glück, Moritz von Schwind und seine Vaterstadt Wien, Vienna, 1954 (cat.); L. Justi, and H. Weissgärber, Zeichnungen deutscher Meister von Klassizismus bis zum Impressionismus, Berlin, 1954; E. Bülau, Der englische Einfluss auf die deutsche Landschaftsmalerei im frühen 19. Jahrhundert, Freiburg im Bresgau, 1955; L. Dussler, Die Inkunabeln der deutschen Lithographie (1796–1821), 2d ed., Heidelberg, 1955; W. Hager, M. Imdahl, and G. Fiensch, Die Anfänge des deutschen Landschaftsbilde, Münster, Cologne, 1955; P. F. Schmidt, Philipp Otto Runge: Sein Leben und sein Werk, 2d ed., Wiesbaden, 1956; W. Hutt, Die Düsseldorfer Kunst und die demokratische Bewegung in der ersten Hälfte des 19. Jahrhunderts, Wissenschaftliche Z. der Martin-Luther-Univ. Halle-Wittenberg, VII, 1957–58, pp. 383–403; K. Kaiser, Deutsche Malerei um 1800, Leipzig, 1959; G. Berefelt, P. O. Runge zwischen Aufbruch und Opposition, 1777–1802, Uppsala, 1961; H. Geller, Deutsche Künstler in Rom, Rome, 1961.

Italy: A. R. Willard, History of Modern Italian Art, New York, 1898; H. Focillon, G. B. Piranesi, Paris, 1918; H. Focillon, G. B. Piranesi, Essai de catalogue raisonné de son œuvre, Paris, 1918; A. M. Hind, G. B. Piranesi: A Critical Study, London, 1922; E. Cecchi, Pittura italiana dell'8oo, Rome, 1926; U. Ojetti, La pittura italiana dell'8oo, Milan, Rome, 1929; M. Bernardi, A. Fontanesi, Turin, 1932; L. Vitali, Incisione italiana moderna, Milan, 1934; V. Mariani, Studiando Piranesi, Rome, 1938; A. M. Brizio, Ottocento e novecento, Turin, 1939 (2d ed., 1947); A. Dragone and J. Dragone Conti, I paesisti piemontesi dell'Ottocento, Turin, 1947; G. Briganti, A Fontanesi, Reggio Emilia, 1949 (cat.); A. Huxley and J. Adhémar, Prisons, London, 1949; H. O. Corfiato, Piranesi's Compositions, London, 1951; J. Anderson, Giant Dreams: Piranesi's Influence in England, Eng. Misc., III, 1952, pp. 49–60; G. Castelfranco et al., eds., Pittori italiani del secondo Ottocento, Rome, 1952 (cat.); R. Longhi, Paesisti piemontesi dell'Ottocento, Cat. Biennale di Venezia, XXVI, 1952, pp. 33–36; A. H. Mayor, G. B. Piranesi, New York, 1952; C. A. Petrucci, La caricatura italiana dell'Ottocento, Rome, 1954; H. Thomas, The Drawings of G. B. Piranesi, London, 1954; U. G. Vogt, G. B. Piranesi: Carceri, Zurich, 1958; C. Maltese, Storia dell'arte in Italia 1785–1943, Turin, 1960; M. Praz and L. Jannattonni, eds., Magnificenza di Roma nelle vedute di G. B. Piranesi, Milan, 1961; S. Salamon, G. B. Piranesi: Acqueforti e disegni, Turin, 1961 (cat.); M. Wackernagel, Romantik und Naturalimus in der italienischen Malerei des Ottocento, S. it., VI, 1961, pp. 106–13; M. Yourcenar, Le cerveau noir de Piranesi, Nouvelle rev. fr., IX, 1961, pp. 63–78.

Spain: J. F. Ráfols, El arte romántico en España, Barcelona, 1954 (bibliog.).

England: J. Knowles, The Life and Writing of H. Füssli, London, 1831; J. Ruskin, Modern Painters, London, 1843 (complete ed., 6 vols.,

London, 1888); A. Gilchrist, Life of William Blake, 2 vols., London, 1863 (repr. 1880, 1907); R. Gower, Sir David Wilkie, London, 1902, C. J. Holmes, Constable and His Influence on Landscape Painting, London, 1902; H. Ward and W. Roberts, Romney: A Biographical and Critical Essay, 2 vols., London, 1904; P. Berger, William Blake: Mysticisme et poésie, Paris, 1907 (Eng. trans., London, 1914); H. Cundall, A History of British Watercolour Painting, London, 1908 (2d ed., 1929); C. H. Collins Baker, Crome, London, 1921; L. Binyon, The Drawings and Engravings of William Blake, London, 1922; A. Dubuisson, Richard Parkes Bonington (trans. C. R. Hughes), London, 1924; R. Haferkorn, Gotik und Ruine in der englische Dichtung des 18. Jahrhunderts, Leipzig, 1924; D. Figgis, The Paintings of William Blake, London, 1925; E. W. Manwaring, Italian Landscape in 18th Century England: A Study Chiefly of the Influence of Claude Lorrain and Salvator Rosa on English Taste 1700–1800, New York, London, 1925; W. Wartmann, J. H. Füssli, Zürich, 1926 (cat.); A. Federmann, J. H. Füssli: Dichter und Maler 1741–1825, Zürich, Leipzig, 1927; W. T. Whitley, Art in England, 1800–1820, London, New York, 1928; W. T. Whitley, Artists and Their Friends in England, 1700–1800, 2 vols., London, New York, 1928; T. Wright, The Life of William Blake, 2 vols., London, 1929; O. Aubrat, La peinture de genre en Angleterre de la mort de Hogarth au Préraphaelisme, Paris, 1933; L. Binyon, English Watercolours, London, 1933; J. Piper, British Romantic Artists, London, 1942; K. Clark, English Romantic Poets and Landscape Painting, Mem. Manchester Literary and Philosophical Soc., LXXV, 1943, pp. 103–20; S. Colomb, L'art anglais, Paris, 1947; P. Ganz, Die Zeichnungen von Hans-Heinrich Füssli, Bern, 1947 (Eng. trans., F. B. Aikin-Sneath, New York, 1949); G. G. Hough, The Last Romantics, London, 1949; A. P. Oppé, Alexander and John Robert Cozens, London, 1952 (Cambridge, Mass., 1954); F. Antal, Fuseli Studies, London, 1956; C. P. Brand, Italy and the English Romantics, London, 1957; M. H. Grant, A Chronological History of the Old English Landscape Painters, 8 vols., Leigh-on-Sea, 1957–61; T. S. R. Boase, English Art 1800–1870, Oxford, 1959; G. Schiff, ed., Zeichnungen von J. H. Füssli, Zurich, 1959; F. Spar, Le style anglais, Paris, 1959; J. Mayne, English Romantic Water Colours, BMMA, N.S., XX, 1961–62, pp. 237–47. See also the bibliog. for PICTURESQUE, THE.

United States: J. T. Soby and D. C. Miller, Romantic Painting in America, New York, 1943 (cat.; bibliog.); E. P. Richardson, American Romantic Painting, New York, 1944; J. I. H. Baur, American Painting in the 19th Century; Main Trends and Movements, New York, 1953; F. M. Huebner and V. Pearce Delgrado, Die Maler der Romantik in Amerika, Bonn, 1953; E. P. Richardson, Painting in America, New York, 1956, pp. 138–266; B. Rowland, Popular Romanticism: Art and the Gift Books, AQ, XX, 1957, pp. 364–81; M. Brion, L'art romantique en Etats-Unis, Jardin des arts, 70, 1960, pp. 33–43; S. Hunter et al., Old and New Romanticism, Art in Am., XLVIII, 4, 1960, pp. 19–55; J. T. Flexner, That Wilder Image: The Painting of America's Native School from Thomas Cole to Winslow Homer, Boston, 1962; D. L. Smith, Romanticism and the American Tradition, Am. Artist, XXVI, 3, 1962, pp. 28–33.

Dario DURBÉ

Illustrations: PLS. 313–322.

ROMNEY, GEORGE. English portrait painter (b. Dalton-in-Furness, Lancashire, Dec., 1734; d. Kendal, Westmorland, Nov., 1802). Romney was the son of a cabinetmaker. He was apprenticed to Christopher Steele, a traveling portrait painter, between 1755 and 1757; at that time Romney established himself in Kendal, where he had a fairly prosperous trade in small portraits. In 1762 he left for London; here he broadened his style considerably, possibly as a result of his study of the collection of casts owned by the Duke of Richmond. In 1763 and 1765 he won awards at the Society of Arts. During the next few years he became steadily more popular as a portrait painter and exhibited with both the Free Society of Artists and the Incorporated Society of Artists. In 1764 Romney paid a short visit to Paris. In 1773 he left England and spent two years in Italy, mainly in Rome, studying antique sculpture and the work of Raphael. These studies had a major influence on the development of his style.

On his return to England in 1775 Romney rapidly became and remained for many years one of the most sought-after portrait painters in London; his patrons ranged from the Prince of Wales and members of the aristocracy to the literary and dramatic figures of the day. Second only to Sir Joshua Reynolds in popularity, Romney was, however, such a pathologically timid character that he never ventured to present himself for the honors of the Royal Academy of Arts and hence acquired an unmerited reputation as a recluse. In 1782 he met his "divine lady," Emma Hart, later Lady Hamilton, of whom he painted a great number of famous portraits in various character roles. Romney painted four pictures for John Boydell's Shakespeare Gallery between 1786 and 1791. These were among the very few subject pictures he finished, though he left thousands of

rough sketches that are of great interest. Unlike his public work, these sketches link Romney with the imaginative world of Henry Fuseli and William Blake. After 1796, ill health forced Romney to stop painting. His extreme hypochondria developed to the point of insanity in his last years, which were spent in Kendal.

Romney's best portraits are characterized by simplicity, good design, and charming color. Though they lack the deep penetration evident in the work of Reynolds, they have an unassuming dignity and a natural grace that place them in the history of English painting on a level below the great but well above the average.

REPRESENTATIVE WORKS. *Mr. and Mrs. William Lindow*, 1772, London, Tate Gallery. – *Mrs. Carwardine and Son*, 1775, Northamptonshire, Wakefield Lodge, Lord Hillingdon Coll.– *The Leveson-Gower Children*, 1776 (VI, PL. 443). – *Mrs. Robinson*, 1781, London, Wallace Coll. – *Lady Hamilton as a Bacchante*, ca. 1783, Mrs. Tankerville Chamberlayne Coll. – *Warren Hastings*, 1795, London, India Office Library.

BIBLIOG. W. Hayley, Life of George Romney, London, 1809; J. Romney, Memoirs of the Life and Works of George Romney, London, 1830; H. Ward and W. Roberts, Romney, 2 vols., London, 1904 (*catalogue raisonné*); A. B. Chamberlain, Romney, London, 1910; A. Crookshank, The Drawings of George Romney, Burlington Mag., XCIX, Feb., 1957, pp. 43–48.

Anne CROOKSHANK

ROSA, SALVATOR. Italian painter of the Neapolitan school [b. Naples, July 21(?), 1615; d. Rome, March 15, 1673]. His mother was the daughter of Vito Greco and the sister of Domenico Antonio Greco, both painters, and Rosa is recorded to have studied with his uncle at an early age. In October, 1632, Rosa's sister married Francesco Fracanzano and in the marriage documents Rosa is mentioned as a painter. In the following years he probably worked for some time under Ribera and then under Aniello Falcone.

Rosa's first known dated picture (*Battle Piece*, 1637; London, W. Mostyn-Owen Coll.) shows the strong influence of Falcone. The sources (e.g., Passeri, 1772) speak of a *Hagar and the Angel* that was noticed and acquired by Lanfranco, who arrived in Naples in 1634. Almost certainly Rosa left Naples in 1635 for Rome, where he stayed with his friend Mercuri, house steward (*maestro di casa*) to Cardinal Brancacci. After an illness Rosa returned to Naples; he is recorded there in October, 1638, and it was from Naples that he sent a *Tityus* (lost; engraved by Ferdinando Gregori) to the connoisseur and collector Niccolò Simonelli, then in Cardinal Brancacci's service. This was exhibited publicly in Rome, very probably in 1638. The Cardinal commissioned *The Doubting of St. Thomas* for his diocesan church in Viterbo (now in the Mus. Civ.), probably early in 1639. Rosa was in Rome that year and created a sensation by his satirical attack on Bernini at the carnival — the first public manifestation of his literary ability and his restless, antiofficial, nonconforming nature. Baroque Rome was not a sympathetic environment and in 1640 Rosa accepted an invitation to the Medici court in Florence, remaining there until 1649. During this period, which included visits to various parts of Tuscany, and also to Venice, Rosa met Donna Lucrezia, who was to become his wife in all but name (they were finally married in 1673).

In Florence Rosa's house was the center of a sophisticated circle, reflecting his interest in acting, music, and literature. It was at this time that he formed an intimate friendship with the poet Giovan Battista Ricciardi, to whom he sent a long series of letters that vividly document much of his work and his personal opinions. His first satire, *La Musica*, was written in 1640 and was soon followed by similar compositions on poetry, painting, and other themes. In 1649 he returned to Rome, where he settled despite invitations to the courts of Sweden (1652) and France (1665). Capricious in his attitude to patrons, he made particular use of the annual picture exhibitions in Rome to draw attention to his work. He was active as an engraver (IV, PL. 436), and about 1656 he executed the series of small engravings dedicated to the banker Carlo de Rossi, his chief patron. In 1664 his letters mention fatigue and eye trouble, and in the next two years his sight grew worse. During the period from September, 1669, until March, 1670, he did no painting at all.

Rosa began as a painter of landscapes (IX, PL. 16; XIV, PL. 183) and battles, but seems to have aspired early to paint subject pictures and to introduce personal and philosophic themes, somewhat as did Poussin, into his landscapes (e.g., *The Philosophers' Grove*, Pitti). More directly personal are subject pictures like the satirical *Fortuna* (London, Marlborough Fine Art), exhibited in Rome in 1659, and the pessimistic *L'Umana Fragilità* (XIV, PL. 186), possibly connected with the deaths of Rosa's son and brother in a plague in 1656. He occasionally treated fantastic subjects, as in his *Witch* (IX, PL. 256) and his *Temptation of St. Anthony* (Pitti). Nevertheless, he is still chiefly famous for his landscapes, which, along with his drawings, remain his finest work. He was a lonely, consciously revolutionary artist, outside the Roman baroque hierarchy, who perhaps never succeeded in fully expressing himself through his paintings, and who was probably always aware of this fact.

BIBLIOG. G. B. Passeri, Vite de' pittori, scultori ed architetti..., 1st ed. G. L. Bianconi, Rome, 1772, ed. J. Hess (Römische Forschungen, XI), Vienna, 1934; U. Limentani, Bibliografia della vita e delle opere di Salvator Rosa, Florence, 1955; L. Salerno, Salvator Rosa, Milan, 1963.

Michael LEVEY

ROSSELLINO, BERNARDO AND ANTONIO. Florentine artists (b. Settignano, d. Florence; Bernardo, sculptor and architect, b. 1409, d. Sept. 23, 1464; Antonio, sculptor, b. 1427, d. 1479). The Rossellino brothers were the sons of Matteo di Domenico Gamberelli. Bernardo may have worked briefly in Rome in 1433 and certainly did in 1451–53; the remainder of his life was centered in Florence, where he had an extremely active workshop that included his brother Antonio and younger members of the family.

The façade of the Palazzo della Fraternità dei Laici in Arezzo was one of Bernardo's early works (1433); then followed commissions for tabernacles in Florence and Arezzo (1435–36), work for the Cathedral in Florence (1441–44), and his most significant monument, the tomb of Leonardo Bruni in the Church of Sta Croce, Florence (1444–46/47). Bernardo's association with Leon Battista Alberti on the Palazzo Rucellai in Florence (1446–51) is clearly reflected in the later Palazzo Piccolomini in Pienza (1460–63), part of Bernardo's work for Pius II. Bernardo also designed the Cathedral in Pienza (1459–62; III, PL. 388). In his later years Bernardo served as the *capomaestro* for the Cathedral of Florence. Other examples of Bernardo's sculpture in Florence are the tabernacle in the Church of S. Egidio (1449) and the tombs of Beata Villana in S. Maria Novella (1451) and Orlando de' Medici in SS. Annunziata (1456–57).

Antonio Rossellino became increasingly important as a collaborator of Bernardo, assisting him in such work as the tomb of Beato Marcolino (1458; Forlì, Pin. Com.) and executing from Bernardo's designs the tomb of Filippo Lazzari (after 1464; Pistoia, S. Domenico).

Antonio's *Giovanni Chellini* (1456; Vict. and Alb.) is the first known example of his independent work as a sculptor and the first of his incisive portraits. Chellini's finely drawn features contrast sharply with those of the more vigorous *Matteo Palmieri* (1468; PL. 17). Antonio's most sensitive characterization is a part of his finest monument, the tomb of the Cardinal of Portugal in the Church of S. Miniato al Monte in Florence (1461–ca. 1466; PL. 16), placed in a specially designed chapel to which Luca Della Robbia, Antonio and Piero Pollaiuolo, and Alesso Baldovinetti all contributed. Similar in style is the tomb of Mary of Aragon in the Piccolomini Chapel in the Church of Monte Oliveto (S. Anna dei Lombardi) in Naples (1470 and later), which was completed after Antonio's death by Benedetto da Maiano. This same chapel also possesses one of the last and finest of Antonio's many reliefs, the *Na-*

tivity (1470s). Antonio's sculpture includes single figures such as the *St. Sebastian* (1460; Empoli, Gall. della Collegiata) and the *Young St. John* (1477; Florence, Mus. Naz.), and he may well be the author of various reliefs of the Madonna and Child although none of the many examples attributed to him is securely documented. However, Antonio and the Rossellino workshop undoubtedly helped to establish the popularity of these graceful, agreeably idealized images through such models as the Madonna and Child of the S. Miniato tomb and the relief above the tomb of Francesco Nori in Sta Croce, Florence (before 1478; VIII, PL. 192).

The work of Bernardo and Antonio Rossellino reveals a high level of technical accomplishment and the distinctly personalized styles of the artists. Bernardo's mastery of the contemporary architectural style, as well as the clarity and precision of form in his sculpture, made possible the harmonious blending of the two arts in the tomb of Leonardo Bruni, which established a model for monumental wall tombs that was followed for decades. Antonio, in turn, created one of the best variations of this model in his tomb of the Cardinal of Portugal, a more spacious composition that relied on a greater use of sculptural elements, carved with the easy elegance characteristic of Antonio's style. His freedom of handling is found in both individual figures and groups and in the lively and dexterous balance of surface and space in the *Nativity* relief.

BIBLIOG. Vasari, pp. 93–105; M. Tyskiewicz, Bernardo Rossellino, Florence, 1928; H. Gottschalk, Antonio Rossellino, Liegnitz, 1930; L. Planiscig, Bernardo und Antonio Rossellino, Vienna, 1942.

Eleanor D. BARTON

ROSSO, IL (GIOVANNI BATTISTA DI JACOPO). Italian painter of the Florentine school (b. Florence, 1495; d. Paris, 1540). Nothing is known about Il Rosso's earliest education. According to Vasari, he was impatient of any teaching, having "a certain contrary opinion of his own." About 1512 Il Rosso was briefly in the workshop of Andrea del Sarto, probably as an assistant rather than as a pupil. His contemporary, Pontormo (q.v.), who was also to become an innovator of the Florentine postclassical style, was in this workshop at the same time. Paintings have been attributed to Il Rosso that would date from as early as about 1513, but the earliest known pictures that are certainly by him do not antedate 1516 or 1517 (cf. XI, PL. 370). By 1518, when he painted an altarpiece for the Hospital of S. Maria Nuova in Florence, Il Rosso had achieved a novel personal style that quite opposed, or even inverted, the tenets of the then-current classical Florentine style. This assertion of a new style was contemporaneous with Pontormo's in his altarpiece for S. Michele Visdomini in Florence, but more extreme. By 1521 Il Rosso had defined his innovations quite explicitly and created in his *Deposition* in Volterra (Pin. Com.) and in his altarpiece in Villamagna masterpieces in his new style that are more radical and more striking in their formal and expressive novelty than the works in Pontormo's concurrent development.

Il Rosso's style is achieved by a kind of fragmentation and dissolution of the synthetic unities of classical painting: emotion tends toward abnormality; substance is replaced by faceted planes of light; colors become unreal and at times sharply dissonant. The paintings of 1521 affirm a new esthetic that is generally recognized as pertaining to the style of mannerism (q.v.), but as yet in an experimental phase in which there is a protest against classical values (in Il Rosso's case apparently deliberate) that is not characteristic of the later art of the *maniera*. In his subsequent paintings in Florence, in 1523 (and perhaps early in 1524), Il Rosso continued his progressive and often remarkably diverse searches for novelties of style. He did not relinquish his extreme position, yet in these works there are indications that he was more disposed than he was earlier to tolerate values that had their source in the classical tradition (such as ideas of grace and of the ornamental function of a work of art) provided that he could transform them and accommodate them within his new idiom. This tendency toward a partial reconciliation with classical values was accentuated during Il Rosso's residence in Rome between 1524 and 1527. His *Dead Christ with Angels* (Boston, Mus. of Fine Arts), painted in Rome about 1526, in effect achieves that kind of formal modification of classical precedents toward mannerist expressive ends that may be associated with the subsequent *maniera*.

Il Rosso fled from Rome after the Sack of 1527 and for nearly three years practiced his art in the provincial towns of Arezzo, Sansepolcro, and Città di Castello. Away from the atmosphere of Rome his art reassumed some of the diversity and eccentricity of expression that had characterized it earlier in Florence (*Deposition*, Sansepolcro, S. Lorenzo; *Resurrection*, Città di Castello, Cathedral). In 1530 Il Rosso went, by way of Venice, to the court of Francis I of France. As court painter to Francis from 1532 onward Il Rosso designed, supervised, and in part executed (with assistants recruited from Italy, France, and Flanders) two major decorative projects of great subsequent influence at Fontainebleau (PL. 100). At the French court his art became the most sophisticated expression of the *maniera*: precious, full of intellectual conceits, and at times bizarre, but powerful to a degree that the later exponents of the mannerist style only very rarely attained.

Il Rosso, with Pontormo, introduced the mannerist style into Florentine painting. His works are often more immediately striking than Pontormo's, but they are not of profounder interest. The very extremism of Il Rosso's art made it less influential than Pontormo's for the later course of Florentine mannerism. Il Rosso was, however, a major agent in the dissemination of the mannerist style outside Italy: in France and into those spheres of north European painting that were influenced by the style of Fontainebleau.

MAJOR WORKS. *Portrait of a Young Man*, ca. 1517 (Berlin, Mus. Dahlem). - *Assumption*, fresco, 1517 (Florence, SS. Annunziata). - Altarpiece for Hospital of S. Maria Nuova, 1518 (Uffizi). - *Deposition*, 1521 (Volterra, Pin. Com.). - *Madonna with John the Baptist and St. Bartholomew*, 1521 (Villamagna, Pieve). - *Man with a Helmet*, 1521-24 (Liverpool, Walker Art Gall.). - Dei altarpiece, 1522 (Florence, Pitti). - *Marriage of the Virgin*, 1523 (Florence, Church of S. Lorenzo). - *Moses and the Daughters of Jethro*, ca. 1523 (IX, PL. 290). - *Portrait of a Young Man*, ca. 1524 (Washington, D.C., Nat. Gall.). - *Creation of Eve, Temptation*, frescoes, 1524 (Rome, S. Maria della Pace). - *Dead Christ with Angels*, ca. 1526 (Boston, Mus. of Fine Arts). - *Deposition*, 1527-28 (Sansepolcro, S. Lorenzo). - *Portrait of a Young Man*, ca. 1528 (PL. 76). - *Resurrection*, 1528-30 (Città di Castello, Cathedral). - Pavilion of Pomona, frescoes, 1532-35 (Fontainebleau; destroyed). - Gallery of Francis I, frescoes and stuccoes, 1534-37 (PL. 100). - *Holy Family*, ca. 1532 (PL. 77). - *Pietà*, ca. 1535 (IX, PL. 291).

BIBLIOG. G. Vasari, Vite (ed. Milanesi, 1906), V, pp. 155-74; F. Goldschmidt, Pontormo, Rosso und Bronzino, Leipzig, 1911; H. Voss, Die Malerei der Spätrenaissance in Rom und Florenz, Berlin, 1920, pp. 182-89; W. Friedlaender, Die Enstehung des antiklassischen Stiles in der italienischen Malerei um 1520, RepfKw, XLVI, 1925, pp. 243-62 (Eng. trans., Mannerism and Anti-Mannerism in Italian Painting, New York, 1957); M. Roy, La Galerie de François I à Fontainebleau, in Artistes et monuments de la Renaissance en France, Paris, 1929, p. 226 ff.; K. Kusenberg, Le Rosso, Paris, 1931; K. Kusenberg, Autour du Rosso, GBA, 6th ser., X, 1933, pp. 158-72; L. Becherucci, Manieristi toscani, Bergamo, 1944; P. Barocchi, Il Rosso Fiorentino, Rome, 1950; F. Bologna et al., Fontainebleau e la maniera italiana (cat.), Florence, 1952; F. Hartt, review of Barocchi (1950), AB, XXXIV, 1952, pp. 63-69; E. Panofsky, The Iconography of the Gallery of François Ier at Fontainebleau, GBA, 6th ser., LII, 1958, pp. 113-90; E. Carroll, Some Drawings by Rosso Fiorentino, BM, CII, 1961, pp. 446-54; E. Carroll, The Drawings of Rosso Fiorentino (diss.), Harvard University, 1964; M. Hirst, Rosso: A Document and a Drawing, BM, CVI, 1964, pp. 120-26.

Sydney J. FREEDBERG

ROUAULT, GEORGES. French painter (b. Paris, May 27, 1871; d. Paris, Feb. 13, 1958). In 1881 Rouault received his first art lessons from his maternal grandfather, Alexandre Champdavoine, and then served an apprenticeship as a stained-glass painter with Tamoni and Hirsch, during which time he restored medieval windows (1885-90). His penchant for religious art was further extended by his training at the Ecole des Beaux-Arts, where, after studying first with Elie Delaunay (1890-92), he entered the studio of the more liberal Gustave Moreau, whose imaginative style and iconography stimulated Rouault's own mystical direction. Neo-Catholic literary influences were also essential to his formation. He was a friend of the writer Léon Bloy, who subsequently introduced him to the philosopher Jacques Maritain, who was to write an essay on the artist in 1924. Moreover, in 1901 Rouault had visited the Benedictine abbey at Liguge, where the converted Catholic writer J. K. Huysmans directed a neomedieval brotherhood of artists. Rouault exhibited frequently in Paris, first at the Salon des Artistes Français (1895-1901), and then at the Salon d'Automne (1903-08), where in 1905 his work was included with that of the Fauves. After his first one-man show at the Galerie Druet in 1910 his reputation increased; and in 1913 the contents of his studio were bought by Ambroise Vollard, who became his dealer in 1917 and whose heirs were obliged in 1947, after a trial, to return about 800 paintings to the artist. Of these, Rouault burned 315 canvases before a court official. From 1930 on, many Rouault exhibitions were held outside France, gaining him an international acclaim that was honored, in 1958, by a state funeral. In 1963 the artist's widow, Marthe Le Sidaner, donated a large group of his unfinished works to the state. Rouault's production comprises not only paintings, gouaches, water colors, tapestries, and enamels (IV, PL. 420), but also many prints in all media, generally for illustrated books. Of these, the most famous are the *Miserere* and *Guerre* series, executed in the 1920s but not published until 1948. He also designed the sets and costumes for Diaghilev's ballet *The Prodigal Son* (1929).

Although Rouault's earliest Biblical paintings of the 1890s (II, PL. 296) reflect the murky Rembrandtesque atmosphere of his master, Moreau, his style after 1902 was rapidly "modernized" until his broad washes, vigorous drawing, and intense colors could be identified with the Fauves. His subjects also changed from religious themes to figures often reminiscent of the pathetic outcasts in Picasso's early work — prostitutes, clowns, and lawyers — whom he treated as tragic metaphors of good and evil. Closer to German expressionists such as Emil Nolde than to his own French contemporaries, Rouault explored ostensibly coarse pictorial means to achieve emotionally forceful ends. The leading and color of medieval stained glass provided particular inspiration for the heavy, rugged drawing and vibrant luminosity of his mature work (V, PL. 125). Rouault's art represents a combination, rare in the 20th century, of elements conforming to modern pictorial taste with a revitalized interpretation of traditional Christian motifs that attests to the strength of his personal belief. His position, embracing both the modern and the conservative, was analogous to that of the French Neo-Catholic writers who inspired him.

WRITINGS. Souvenirs intimes, Paris, 1926; Correspondance de Rouault et de Suarès, Paris, 1960.

BIBLIOG. G. Charensol, Georges Rouault, l'homme et l'œuvre, Paris, 1926; L. Venturi, Georges Rouault, New York, 1940; J. T. Soby, Georges Rouault, New York, 1945; B. Dorival, Cinq études sur Georges Rouault, Paris, 1957; P. Courthion, Georges Rouault, 1962.

Robert ROSENBLUM

ROUSSEAU, HENRI. French painter (b. Laval, May 21, 1844; d. Paris, Sept. 2, 1910). The son of a poor family, Rousseau was educated at a *lycée* in his native city. After serving in the army he was employed as a lawyer's clerk; then in 1869 he became a clerk in the customs office, serving at a post on the outskirts of Paris (hence he is often referred to as Le Douanier Rousseau). He held this position until 1885, when he retired on a small pension, with the aim of following the career of an artist. Although he subsequently held a few minor posts, including one as a teacher of art, he devoted most of his time to painting until his death.

Although none of his pictures are extant that date from before 1880, Rousseau probably painted and drew from early childhood. He had no formal training, being too poor to afford art school. He thus began to paint in a "primitive," or folk, tradition; as he himself wrote, he "worked alone, without any master but nature and some advice from [Jean Léon] Gérôme and [Félix Auguste] Clément." He first showed his work before the public in 1886, at the Salon des Indépendants in Paris, to whose annual exhibitions he contributed almost every year until 1910. The themes of Rousseau's pictures were drawn from the life around him, but he also unleashed his imagination in creating (after 1890) exotic jungle landscapes populated by savages and wild animals.

The naïve, untutored style of Rousseau's paintings brought him ridicule from the critics and public; understandably, they found it hard to take his work seriously. But slowly, in the 1890s, the avant-garde painters began to admire his work, some for its innocent freshness, others for its bizarre and strange imagery; in both respects Rousseau could be regarded as a prophet because he violated the prevailing taste for realistic art. Picasso (q.v.), Guillaume Apollinaire, and their friends "discovered" him early in the 20th century and delighted to find in their midst one who was a real "primitive," both in personality and in his pictorial style; for several years Rousseau frequented the most sophisticated artistic circles in Paris. Apparently he considered himself a formidable rival of the great French artists of his day, unaware that even his friends sometimes poked fun at him.

Rousseau's style is typical of that of most untrained, naïve artists, who represent the world according to their idea of it, not according to the retinal image of what they see in nature. Although he was deeply involved in the life of the late 19th to the early 20th century, Rousseau's style had little in common with the highly developed language of representation in western art. His was a childlike ideographic style, in which the subject was portrayed in bright, slightly modeled planes of color; objects were usually represented in profile or in front view; and human and natural forms were drawn in a schematic manner, reflecting little understanding of their actual structure. In spite of these shortcomings, however, and in spite of his lack of technical facility, Rousseau's innate sense of pictorial design gave his paintings a distinctive charm that has appealed to a wide public, particularly to those who admire abstract and surrealist art.

MAJOR WORKS. *Myself, Portrait-Landscape*, 1890, Prague, Mus. of Mod. Art. - *War*, 1894, Paris, Louvre; XI, PL. 335. - *The Sleeping Gypsy*, 1897, New York, Mus. of Mod. Art. - *The Snake Charmer*, 1907, Paris, Louvre; XI, PL. 330. - *The Poet and His Muse*, 1909, Basel, Kunstmuseum; V, PL. 121. - *The Dream*, 1910, New York, Mus. of Mod. Art.

BIBLIOG. W. Uhde, Henri Rousseau le douanier, Paris, 1911; A. Basler, Henri Rousseau, Paris, 1927; A. Salmon, Henri Rousseau dit le Douanier, Paris, 1927; C. Zervos, Rousseau, Paris, 1927; P. Courthion, Henri Rousseau, le Douanier, Geneva, 1944; D. C. Rich, Henri Rousseau, New York, 1946; J. Bouret, Henri Rousseau, Neuchâtel, 1961; H. Certigny, La Vérité sur le Douanier Rousseau, Paris, 1961; D. Vallier, Henri Rousseau, Cologne, 1961 (English ed., 1962).

William I. HOMER

ROUSSEAU, THÉODORE (Pierre Etienne Théodore). French painter (b. Paris, 1812; d. Barbizon, 1867). Rousseau was artistically precocious, and began his formal training in painting at the age of fourteen under Charles Rémond; subsequently, he worked under Guillon Lethière. At an early age he painted landscapes out of doors, directly from nature — a radical departure from the traditional studio methods then practiced in France. At the beginning of his career, he also copied works by Claude Lorrain (q.v.) and the Dutch masters as a means of studying their styles. Rousseau's first landscape paintings, executed in the neighborhood of Paris (especially Fontaine-bleau) and in the Auvergne Mountains, depicted the wild, untamed aspects of nature. He painted these early pictures in a romantic spirit, employing free, vigorous brush strokes and intense colors that foreshadow the work of the Fauves (q.v.).

By the early 1830s Rousseau's prodigious talents had earned him a position of leadership among the young landscape painters of his generation. His abilities were also recognized by the noted painter Ary Scheffer and the writer Théophile Gautier,

and by the end of that decade he had become the favorite of a discriminating circle of aristocratic collectors. Rousseau's innovations in landscape painting made him a controversial figure, however, and after initial successes at the Salon his work was rejected between 1837 and 1847. Although he sold few paintings during this period, his art progressed steadily, and he was increasingly recognized as a prophet by his patrons and fellow painters.

During the 1830s Rousseau had traveled about France in search of remote landscape motifs of primitive, savage power; but, by the 1840s, his romanticism was tempered by a predilec-tion for more tranquil, pastoral subjects, which he found in the forest of Fontainebleau and at Barbizon, where he eventually settled (PL. 321; IX, PL. 22; XI, PL. 440). Rousseau's studio became a meeting place for the painters of the Barbizon school, and it was in this rural village that he developed a close friendship with Jean François Millet (q.v.). In the 1850s he finally won wide public acclaim, and by the time of his death in 1867 he was recognized as a central figure in the development of landscape painting in France. Rousseau's fame, like that of his contemporaries of the Barbizon school, has diminished over the years, but his best paintings are still of interest, both historically and as works af art. Historically, Rousseau must be recognized as one of the earliest and most successful plein-air painters in France and as an important precursor of im-pressionism.

MAJOR WORKS. *Descent of the Cattle*, 1835, Amiens, Mus. de Picardie. - *The Forest of Fontainebleau, Bas-Bréau (Le Vieux Dor-moir)*, 1836-37, 1867, Louvre. - *Valley of Tiffauge (Marais en Vendée)*, 1837-41, Cincinnati, Mus. - *Under the Birches (Le Curé)*, 1842-44, Toledo, Mus. - *Route dans la forêt de Fontainebleau, effet d'orage*, ca. 1860-65, Louvre.

BIBLIOG. A. Sensier, Souvenirs sur Th. Rousseau, Paris, 1872; A. Sen-sier, Etudes et croquis de Th. Rousseau, Paris, 1876; P. Burty, Maîtres et petits maîtres, Paris, 1877; J. W. Mollett, The Painters of Barbizon, London, 1890; W. Gensel, Millet und Rousseau, Bielefeld and Leipizig, 1902; P. Dorbec, Théodore Rousseau, Paris, 1910; R. L. Herbert, Barbizon Revisited, Mus. of Fine Arts, Boston, 1962.

William I. HOMER

ROWLANDSON, THOMAS. English painter and draftsman (b. London, 1756; d. London, Apr. 22, 1827). At school, in Soho Square, Rowlandson paid little attention to his studies but filled many sketchbooks with clever caricatures. Entered as a student at the Royal Academy of Arts, he was noted for his high spirits and the humor and facility of his draftsmanship. At the age of 16 he went to Paris to continue his studies, returning to England two years later. By 1777 he was settled in London as a portrait painter with a studio in Wardour Street and began contributing regularly to the Royal Academy exhibitions. But it soon became obvious that his real talent lay in the humorous delineation of scenes from social life.

A trip to Spithead in 1782 resulted in no less than 67 drawings. In these he demonstrated not only his grasp of landscape composition but also his power of depicting crowds. He never lost sight of individual characteristics, and his roistering sailors, rollicking girls, fine gentlemen, and beggars are brought to life with an economy of means, a calligraphic line of unfailing accuracy and verve. His most notable production in this period was the large drawing *Vauxhall Gardens* (1784), which was reproduced by Pollard and Jukes as an engraving that became widely popular in Rowlandson's day and remains a valuable contribution to English social history. The Prince of Wales (afterwards King George IV) commissioned several works by his pen. Book illustration seemed a natural outlet for Row-landson's talents. In 1809 the publisher Rudolph Ackermann started his *Poetical Magazine*, and the plates that Rowlandson contributed were later published in book form as *The Tour of Dr. Syntax in Search of the Picturesque*. Its two sequels, *The English Dance of Death* (1815-16) and *The Dance of Life* (1816), provide lively pictures of life in the Regency period. An aquatint like *The Surgery* (III, PL. 427) is both an excellent design and a vivid social comment; the same, but in a more specialized sense, can be said of *The Military Adventures of Johnny Newcome* (1815) and *The Adventures of Johnny Newcome in the Navy* (1818). For the magnificent production *The Microcosm of London* (1808) Augustus Charles Pugin (q.v.) supplied the architectural scenes and Rowlandson the *staffage* that brought them to life.

He is said to have been married in 1800 to a Miss Stuart of Camberwell, but nothing more is known of her, and there do not seem to have been any offspring. Although he earned considerable sums and even inherited a legacy of £ 7,000 (a sizable sum in those days) from a French aunt, he had no sense of economy and was a confirmed gambler. Many of his later drawings were done on the spot to meet a debt, and he sometimes adopted the rather doubtful expedient of producing a *contre-épreuve* (counterproof) by pressing another sheet of paper onto a drawing while it was still wet. But even in his most hurried works his special gifts are plainly discernible: his rapid, flowing notation is never perfunctory or meaningless, and the charm and the humor of his small figures are never lost. He was indeed a "mirror of the passing show" in a rumbustious period of English history.

BIBLIOG. J. Grego, Rowlandson the Caricaturist: A Selection from His Works, London, 1880, 2 vols.; A. P. Oppé, Thomas Rowlandson, New York, 1923; E. C. J. Wolf, Rowlandson and His Illustrations of Eighteenth Century English Literature, New York, 1946; F. G. Roe, Rowlandson, The Life and Art of a British Genius, London, 1947; A. Bury, ed., Rowlandson Drawings, London, 1950; B. Falk, Thomas Rowlandson, His Life and Art, London, 1950.

James LAVER

ROY, JAMINI. A contemporary Indian painter, Roy is among the most representative of modern Indian culture and certainly the most widely discussed for the quantity and originality of his work.

Born in 1887 in Beliatore, a small village in West Bengal, Roy showed an interest in art from a very early age. His father, a small landowner of modest means but of progressive spirit, sensed the boy's capacity and, although severely criticized by many members of his caste, sent his son to study at the Government School of Fine Arts in Calcutta, which was then the capital, at the age of sixteen. Anxious to master the secrets of the art that filled him with enthusiasm, the boy made rapid progress. He learned immediately the technique of Western painting, which was taught at the school, and at twenty-one he was already known for a large series of sketches that he was later to scorn. His rural scenes of this period are of almost no esthetic value; nonetheless, one finds in them the author's affectionate involvement with that small world to which, poor and without friends, he felt he belonged and in which perhaps he sought solace.

After some years, however, Roy realized that he had, in his own words, been working "like a blind tool, faithful to the established traditions." He judged his work as completely worthless because, although he had succeeded in painting skillfully any subject he undertook, he had as yet been unable to express himself as he truly desired. Undecided and unsure of himself as an insignificant provincial confronted by the acknowledged theories of the majority, he chose, almost against his will, to associate himself with the Bengal school. This artistic movement, fostered by Abanindranath Tagore (q.v.) and Nandalal Bose toward the end of the 19th century, was considered the leading school of the time (see ORIENTAL MODERN MOVEMENTS). First using the medium of water color and later also those of tempera and fresco, the two leaders of the movement proposed to paint scenes from real life. Their inspiration, however, was derived from the esthetic principles of the paintings of Ajanta (q.v.), from the miniatures of the Moghul and Rajput schools (qq.v.), and even from Chinese and Japanese ink painting. Although many of their works contained a dreamy and delicate grace, Tagore and Bose had not succeeded in freeing themselves completely from the European tradition instilled in them by a British education. Roy also fell into this ambiguous position, and for some time he allowed himself to be drawn into the sphere

of the school, painting portraits in an impeccable but equally academic style. In his work of this period, and above all in his manner of applying color, some critics have seen the influence, perhaps unconscious, of the American painter Whistler (q.v.). In the second half of the 19th century Whistler was renowned as a fine portrait artist who had drawn his inspiration not only from Courbet but also from the great masters of the past, such as Rembrandt and Velázquez.

Roy soon realized that he was being too faithful to traditions other than his own. In fact, he concluded, as he later declared, that one is not an Indian painter if he paints an Indian figure using European methods. He therefore decided to leave Tagore's movement, effecting a silent rebellion that led him to search laboriously, above all else, for a new form of individual expression. He sensed the necessity of reviving his country's artistic traditions, but in a more radical and profound way than had yet been attempted. These traditions had long been forgotten as a result of childlike dependence on everything European (actually, at that time India was completely dominated by England). He felt that he must seek independence from the West through his art. He was not concerned with the social problems of India; he did not believe in politics, nor did he adhere to the restoration movement of Rabindranath Tagore or, later, to that of Mohandas Gandhi. Instead, it was the folk culture, its forms and its myths, that interested him. He wished to draw near to the spirit of the people, to understand their traditions in order to interpret them and, at the same time, to respect their formal symbolism and decorative rhythms. Thus he discovered the whole poetic world, naïve and picturesque, that lived around him. Bengal is rich in folklore: its frequent religious ceremonies and the village festivals with their dances, songs, and processions have long given rise to a flourishing and lively popular art. Evidence of this can be seen in the abundant production of carpets, fabrics, toys, and the great variety of utensils created by the region's innumerable craftsmen. The objects have abstract or fanciful forms and are decorated with motifs taken from the animal and plant worlds and painted with vivid colors often boldly juxtaposed. Roy also studied with great interest the pata productions, those graceful, naïve works of the village painters, who for many generations have handed down from father to son the secrets of decorating the village temples, the religious objects, and the rolls of paper that are similar to Tibetan tankas. The last-mentioned works are inspired by epic or popular literature, and the subjects are adorned with geometric plant and animal motifs, usually symbolic or stylized in form, and are enhanced by the use of vivid colors — predominantly yellows, reds, blues, and blacks — in daring and brilliant arrangements. These local artists paint without artifice, not what they see but what they think they see or what they believe a thing must be. The rules of style or the conventions of perspective are not respected in their paintings; after all, psychological perspective almost always takes precedence over physical perspective in Indian art. In its designs gods or heroes are often larger in scale than the surrounding figures or mountains (including the Himalaya), even when the mountains are placed in the foreground. The painter's intention is to represent the power of the gods in relation to the surrounding world of nature. The beauty of these childlike compositions stems from their gay coloring and their freshness of treatment.

After a long period of trials and hesitations Roy concluded that he must totally adhere to the genuine character and tastes of his people and consequently renounce his technical skill of Western origin. He did not regret the many sacrifices that this would cost him, provided he could achieve the goal he had set for himself. His palette was reduced to only seven colors, which he himself learned to prepare by carefully grinding earth and local ingredients and mixing them, according to ancient formulas, with egg white and tamarind glue. He strove to find a specific style of his own, simplifying everything as much as possible. He employed simple lime for white, smoke black for black, indigo for blue, diluted river mud for all the gray tonalities, and so on. He applied the colors on canvases prepared beforehand with cow dung, following an ancient practice of his ancestors that he wished to bring back into esteem. His stroke became rapid and decisive; the colors were applied in a smooth and uniform manner — almost as though to remove any semblance of reality from his subjects — and then outlined with heavy dark lines. He reduced the details to a minimum, deliberately ignored perspective, and eliminated any hint of chiaroscuro or volume from his forms. The colors, only rarely in subtle gradations such as antique rose, golden yellow, turtledove gray, were placed in flat color areas boldly juxtaposed: green and red, black and blue, brown and red, with an occasional touch of white. For subject matter Roy drew fully from the life and activity of his people. He often depicted strange ritual dances, various Hindu divinities, scenes from the *Rāmāyaṇa*, scenes of rural life, figures of the faithful making offerings, male and female dancers, drum players, and young girls of the town. All India — the minute and the monumental, the mystic and the sensual — began to pulsate with life in his compositions, which had the fascination of a new yet ancient language. Roy did not seek human expression in his figures. On the contrary, he wanted to give them, as do the patas, a symbolic significance, to capture the universality of nature on canvas. Thus, all his trees were reduced to the universal tree, stripped of individual identity. His dancers were meant to symbolize only the dance. That is why his figures have faces that are stylized almost like masks: the oblong eyes are more prominent than the contours of the face; the eyebrows are united in a single stroke with the rigid lines of the nose; and the mouth is like a small flower or like an abstract seal set on the other vaguely mysterious features. The bodies have feline yet slightly rigid movements that vaguely resemble those of certain ancient Egyptian paintings. The postures are simplified to the maximum degree. In a certain sense, in this return to the joyous primitiveness of his country, Roy had been preceded by the female painter Sumayani Devi, who had also discovered popular painting and incorporated its pleasing gracefulness into her compositions, which are greatly admired in Calcutta. But Roy was not satisfied with reproducing only the themes: he wanted his paintings to express the spirit of the Indian people, to whom he now felt deeply attached. At the same time, however, knowing that he had found his true style, he also frequently touched on "heterodox" themes, seeking inspiration from the West. Therefore, he created typical figures of Christian saints and portraits of Christ that strangely resemble Byzantine paintings, with their huge almond-shaped eyes set in long, unreal, almost bewitching faces. According to a French critic it is precisely this resemblance to Byzantine works that demonstrates the authenticity of Roy's inspiration, since Byzantium had always constituted a melting pot and a bridge between the East and the West. In any case, the stylized features in the immobile faces are characteristic of Roy's latest work and recur in all his figures.

The work of the Indian artist has often been compared, in certain of its aspects, to that of Henri Matisse (q.v.), particularly in the drawing, which conveys an extreme immediacy and simplicity, as well as for the curved, decisive arabesque and the smooth and brilliant colors. Aside from these affinities, which may be regarded as secondary, it is apparent that Roy's work conserves precisely those characteristics which he had most firmly proposed to eliminate. Notwithstanding his initial intentions to repudiate everything Western, Roy was unable to forget his European education, and this foundation, though denied, remains evident in the stylistic substance of his work. In spite of himself, the gods, the dancing girls, and the bearers of offerings are seen in the manner of the postimpressionists and Pablo Picasso. In viewing his compositions one cannot help thinking that even his discovery of Bengal folklore was based on intellectual premises, just as the cubists' discovery of African sculpture was. Perhaps Roy himself is not aware of this latent contradiction, but it exists. And so, in the long run, he has found himself prisoner of his own inventiveness. His style has not developed, and his discovery, now become a formula, has crystallized into a merely decorative function. The generic character of his subjects and the mechanical repetition of the formal procedure have rendered his figures so stiff that now one can be distinguished from another only by some small detail — a veil covering the head, the flexing of a muscle — or by the variation of a color. What originally constituted the most genuine and original discovery of the artist has unfortunately become his limitation, the weak point that earns him the most adverse criticism. In spite of this, Roy's fame has spread beyond the boundaries of India, and more than a few critics consider him to be, with Amrita Sher-Gil, Maqbool Fida Husain, and George Keyt, among the country's most sincere and powerful personalities. Although he lives more or less in isolation and shrinks from contacts with other artists, many young people have been attracted to his way of thinking and painting. Among these are Sunil Paul, Sitesh Das Gupta, Manishi Dey, Sailoz Mukherjea, K. Sreenivasulu, and Sheila Auden. (The latter is perhaps closest to the Bengalese spirit, though she lacks the native impetus of Roy.)

From 1929 to 1936 Roy was assistant director of the Mayo School of Art (National College of Arts) in Lahore; during the next two years, still in Lahore, he taught art and held the office of president at Forman Christian College; then, from 1938 to 1947, he directed that city's School of Fine Arts. After the partition of the Punjab he went to Delhi where he became interested in the formation of the "Silpi Chakra" art society. Roy has sometimes been accused of commercializing his work for monetary gain. Actually, he is rather jealous of it and has often renounced easy earnings for the pleasure of keeping his work. Many of his paintings are now in the Baroda Museum and Picture Gallery, in the Sri Chitra Art Gallery of Trivandrum, in the Asutosh Museum of Calcutta, and in various Indian and European private collections. In fact, during and after World War II, Roy's work became known and appreciated by foreigners. Among his most typical compositions are *Gopīs in an Arbor* (PL. 323), *Radhika, Kṛṣṇa and Balaram, Pujari Women, Gaṇeśa and Pārvatī, Women of Bengal, Dancing Figure, Three Drum Players, Donors, Dancer, Three Women, Jesus and Joseph, Christ and Two Disciples, Christian Subject*, a scene from the *Rāmāyaṇa*, and *Santhal Dance*. Some of his paintings were in the Indian section of the 1952 Venice Biennale.

Despite the limitations mentioned above, Roy certainly offers an example of a searching and intense artistic life, and he will continue to hold an outstanding place in the cultural reawakening of modern India. (See also PL. 324).

BIBLIOG. Bishnu Dey and J. Irwin, Jamini Roy, JISOA, XII, 1944, pp. 99–128; J. Irwin, Jamini Roy and the Indian Tradition, Indian Art and Letters, XX, 1946, pp. 37–39; S. Suhrawardy, Jamini Roy, Mārg, II, 1947, pp. 65–77; P. R. Ramachandra Rao, Modern Indian Painting, Madras, 1953; W. G. Archer, India and Modern Art, London, New York, 1959, pp. 100–15; H. Goetz, India: 5000 Years of Indian Art, New York, London, 1959; M. Kaul, Trends in Indian Painting, New Delhi, 1961, pp. 190–92; G. Venkatachalam, Contemporary Indian Painters, Bombay, n.d.

Bianca Maria ALFIERI

Illustrations: PLS. 323–324.

RUBENS, PETER PAUL. The artist was born at Siegen, Westphalia, on June 28, 1577, to Maria Pypelinckx and Jan Rubens, and died in Antwerp on May 30, 1640. His father was born a Roman Catholic, but his name had appeared on a list of Calvinists. In 1568, after the Protestant counts of Egmont and Horn had been decapitated in Brussels, Jan (who had been an Antwerp alderman) fled to Cologne with his wife and four children. There he became agent and adviser to Anna of Saxony, second wife of William the Silent, prince of Orange. An unlucky pregnancy revealed Anna's relationship with Jan, for whom, however, she obtained some clemency from William. Jan was nevertheless under house arrest at Siegen when both Peter Paul and Peter's elder brother Philip were born.

Jan Rubens, *doctor utriusque juris*, taught Philip and Peter Paul himself. He died in 1587, after he had been allowed to return to Cologne. His widow then thought it prudent to settle with her four surviving children in Antwerp, where Philip and Peter Paul continued their classical education at the Latin school of Rombaut Verdonck. There Rubens befriended Balthasar Moretus, heir to the Plantin Press and a future patron. In 1590 a shortage of money and the need to endower Rubens's sister Blandina forced Maria to withdraw the young artist from school and to send him as page to the Countess de Lalaing. But he soon tired of courtly life and was permitted to turn to his real vocation. To learn the rudiments of his *dolcissima professione* he was first placed with his kinsman Tobias Verhaecht (Haecht), a painter of mannerist landscapes in the stale tradition of Joos (Jodocus) de Momper. Later Rubens was apprenticed for four years to Adam van Noort, an abler master, and subsequently to Otto Vaenius (van Veen), the most distinguished of the Antwerp Romanists. In Italy, Vaenius had been a specialist in emblems and an active admirer of Federico Barocci (Baroccio) and the strictly Roman tradition in painting. His culture in matters concerning art impressed Rubens, whose earliest independent works are said to have resembled the style of Vaenius. Male portraits painted by Rubens in this phase include the signed miniature of a young architect on copper (1597; New York, J. Linsky Coll.) and the life-size, three-quarter-length *Man with a Sword* on canvas (ca. 1598; New York, W. P. Chrysler, Jr., Coll.). During this period Rubens also studied the woodcuts of Tobias Stimmer's 1576 Bible (Sandrart, 1675–79) and those by H. Weiditz, the prints of Hendrik Goltzius (Goltz; 1558–1617), and engravings by or after masters of the Italian Renaissance (numerous copy drawings in the Louvre; Rotterdam, Mus. Boymans-Van Beuningen; etc.).

On May 9, 1600, with two years' seniority as a master in the Antwerp Guild of St. Luke, Rubens set out for Italy with Deodat del Monte, his first pupil and constant traveling companion for eight years, to study the works of ancient and modern masters. Reaching Venice in about a month, he soon had the good fortune to meet a gentleman in the service of Vincenzo I Gonzaga, duke of Mantua, and was offered employment in that duchy painting portraits, copies of Italian masterpieces, and perhaps landscapes; his senior contemporary Frans Pourbus the Younger was also to be installed in this capacity. On Oct. 5, 1600, Rubens was with the Gonzaga retinue in the Florence Cathedral for the marriage by proxy of Marie de Médicis, his future patron, to Henri IV of France.

From summer, 1601, to spring, 1602, Rubens was in Rome, recommended to Cardinal Alessandro Montalto by Duke Vincenzo, for whom he was to paint copies. There he painted (perhaps for the Cardinal) *The Lamentation over the Dead Christ* (PL. 327), whose composition was inspired by Giuseppe (Porta) Salviati, the lighting by Tintoretto, and the morphology by Vaenius. In Rome he also painted *Nero and Seneca* (London, private coll.), in which he gave flesh-and-blood life to Roman statuary. Through the Flemish agent Jean Richardot, Rubens obtained his first public commission: three altarpieces (now Grasse, Hôpital du Petit-Paris) for the crypt chapel dedicated to St. Helena in Sta Croce in Gerusalemme, Rome, which was the titular basilica of Archduke Albert of Austria, then consort to Infanta Isabella, regent of the Spanish Netherlands. By Dec. 13, 1601 (letter of Philip Rubens), the artist had found opportunities to see the sights of almost every Italian city of note.

From March, 1603, Rubens was away from Mantua for nearly a year on his first diplomatic mission (correspondence with Annibale Chieppio), entrusted by Vincenzo with costly presents to Philip III and the Spanish court. Thus he obtained his first view of the Hapsburg treasures in Madrid and the Escorial, which contained more than 70 works by Titian. Among the Titians he copied the head and shoulders from *Charles V after Muhlberg* (Rubens version, London, Seilern Coll.) and, full length with slight variations, the standing portrait of *Philip II in Armor* (Rubens version, Derbyshire, Trustees of the Chatsworth Settlement). The Mantuan gifts included Pietro Facchetti's copies of famous works by Raphael and others, which were intended for Philip III's court favorite, the Duke of Lerma. Two paintings, rain-sodden beyond repair on the journey, were promptly replaced by Rubens with the *Democritus* and *Heraclitus* (Wales, private coll.) of his own invention. His resourcefulness and tact in dealing with Iberti, the regular Mantuan agent at Valladolid, raised him in Vincenzo's estimation and prepared him for the diplomatic voyages of his later career.

His life-size *Duke of Lerma* (Madrid, Capuchin Fathers of Castilla), as captain-general of the Spanish cavalry, initiates his masterpieces of equestrian portraiture and inaugurates the baroque achievement in this genre. Its spectacular success produced another Lerma commission a decade later for an *Apostelado* (Prado) and a *Christ* (London, private coll.). Rubens's fruitful association with the banking patriciate of Genoa began with his return voyage from Spain to Mantua early in 1604 and his meeting with Nicolò Pallavicini, Vincenzo's banker. Soon afterward Rubens painted *Hercules and Omphale* (Louvre) and *Death of Adonis* (Amsterdam, Coll. P. de Boer) for Gian-Vincenzo Imperiale, another Genoese merchant.

By Trinity Sunday, 1605, he had finished his threefold decoration (*The Baptism of Christ*, Antwerp, Mus. Royal B.A.; *The Gonzaga Family in Adoration of the Most Holy Trinity*, Mantua, Palazzo Ducale; *The Transfiguration*, Nancy, Mus. B.A.) for the *cappella maggiore* of SS. Trinità, Mantua. This was his sole major work for the Mantuan court in eight years of service and established his first connection with the Company of Jesus of whose lay sodality he was to become a member. Nothing of his was actually ordered for the ducal gallery except portraits of court beauties. He became in effect curator of the gallery and supervised its arrangement with an architect, inducing the Duke to buy (1606) Caravaggio's rejected *Death of the Virgin* (Louvre) and negotiating the purchase of a Pomarancio for the Duchess's chapel. Before the end of 1605 Rubens's *Circumcision* was installed at Nicolò Pallavicini's expense on the high altar of S. Ambrogio in Genoa. During the last months of that year he obtained leave to reside in Rome for an extended period. There Rubens shared a house and two servants in Via della Croce (legal document of Aug. 4, 1606) with his brother Philip, then librarian to Cardinal Ascanio Colonna. Daily contact for almost two years with Philip, the most brilliant pupil of Justus Lipsius and a promising scholar in classical studies, added zest to Rubens's personal discovery of the antique world. The combined fruits of their learning were incorporated into the text and illustrations of the *Electorum Libri II* (Plantin Press, 1608).

During this second and longer stay in Rome, Rubens developed splendid means to portray the Genoese plutocracy, based on his study of Raphael, Titian, and Pordenone. His *Portrait of Brigitte Spinola Doria* (1606; Dorsetshire, Kingston Lacy, Bankes Coll.) and *Gian Carlo Doria on a Prancing Horse* (Naples, Coll. Doria d'Angri) are from this period. In 1607 he was summoned to accompany the Gonzaga court on a summer progress to Sampierdarena; but otherwise he was left largely to his studies, except for the discreet inspection, at Vincenzo's request, of the Palazzo Capo di Ferro (now Spada) as a possible residence in Rome for the young Gonzaga cardinal, and his own grave pleurisy in the summer of 1606 (almost the only recorded illness of his life). However, chronic arrears in his salary and the ambition to extend his reputation prompted him to seek the backing of a Genoese patron, the papal banker Monsignor Jacopo Serra, in obtaining the coveted commission for the high altarpiece of the Chiesa Nuova (S. Maria in Vallicella) in Rome. As a by-product of this he brought off at great speed (Mar. 9–June 7, 1608) another stupendous altarpiece, *The Adoration of the Shepherds*, for a sister congregation, S. Filippo in Fermo (now Pin. Com). However, the protracted difficulties of the Chiesa Nuova project still occupied him when Philip, already back in Antwerp, called him to their mother's deathbed in October, 1608. Rubens arrived too late to see his mother alive, but his first altarpiece on canvas for the Chiesa Nuova became her monument (Sept. 29, 1610). It had almost been completed by May 25, 1607, and had been offered in vain to Mantua; the work, which was later placed in St-Michel in Antwerp, is now in Grenoble (Mus. de Peinture et Sculpture).

Within a year of his return to the Netherlands, Rubens was "bound with golden fetters" (Sept. 23, 1609) to the service of the Hapsburg regents in Brussels and painted their portraits (Vienna, Kunsthist. Mus.). But he maintained contacts beyond the Alps and for years contemplated his return to reenter the milieu of the Italian painters. An *Adoration of the Magi* (PL. 327) was painted in 1609 for the Antwerp Town Hall. This large canvas was presented by the magistrates to Rodrigo Calderón, the Spanish ambassador, in September, 1612, and was extended and retouched by the artist in Madrid during his second diplomatic mission to Spain in 1628–29.

In October, 1609, Rubens married Isabella, daughter of Jan Brant, the Antwerp lawyer and Humanist. The artist's portrait of himself and his bride seated in the honeysuckle bower (PL. 325) is presumably of this date and was later to inspire Frans Hals. Rubens established himself within the next five years not only as a court portraitist but also, by designing a trilogy of altarpieces, as the leading painter of his country. The altarpieces were *The Raising of the Cross* (1610; PL. 327) for St. Walpurgis, Antwerp (now in Antwerp Cathedral), fully baroque though in triptych form and a mature criticism of his treatment of the theme in Sta Croce in Gerusalemme, Rome; the more classical *Descent from the Cross* (Sept. 7, 1611–Mar. 6, 1614) for the altar of the Arquebusiers in Antwerp Cathedral; and *The Conversion of St. Bavo* (PL. 328) for St.-Bavon, Ghent (now in Antwerp Cathedral). This last — although, like the other two, first conceived as a triptych (*modello* of 1612, London, Nat. Gall.) — was much modified to fit a single field and finally executed in 1623. Contemporaneous with these grand designs are the pendant portraits of Rogier Clarisse (San Francisco, De Young Mus.) and his wife, the latter authoritatively inscribed 1611. In these portraits Rubens showed his mature understanding of the paradigms of Titian and Raphael. On May 11, 1611, the artist sold his newly painted *Juno and Argus* (PL. 328), and on Apr. 27, 1612, he was paid 600 gulden for the *Resurrection* triptych in commemoration of Jan Moretus in Antwerp Cathedral.

In 1613 Rubens signed and dated the panel of *Jupiter and Callisto* (PL. 329), in which Jupiter assumes the guise of Diana. A year later he signed and dated at least four panels: *Venus Chilled* (Antwerp, Mus. Royal B.A.), *Susanna and the Elders* (Stockholm, Nationalmus.), *The Lamentation of Christ* (Vienna, Kunsthist. Mus.), and *The Flight into Egypt* (PL. 329), inspired by Adam Elsheimer (1574/8–1620), as well as his free copy on canvas of Parmigianino's *Cupid Cutting His Bow* (Munich, Alte Pin.). The date 1615 painted over the date 1613 indicates the span of time spent on the triptych of the *Doubting Thomas* (Antwerp, Mus. Royal B.A.) with the donor portraits of Nicolaes Rockox and Adriana Perez. After this 1612–15 phase, when Rubens's interest in bas-relief and studies of sculpture became most evident in figure composition, he very rarely signed and dated his paintings.

In 1613–14 Rubens was dean of the Antwerp Guild of Romanists, and on June 30, 1614, he presented them with a *SS. Peter and Paul* (*modello*, Brussels, Coll. F. M. Philippson). In 1614 he first contracted to decorate the new Jesuit church in Antwerp, which was then being planned. In 1617 six designs were composed for a suite of tapestries on the history of the consul Decius Mus (Vaduz, Liechtenstein Coll.). In 1617–18 Rubens painted the *Christ à la Paille* triptych for the funerary monument of Jan Michielsen in Antwerp Cathedral (now in Mus. Royal B.A.). The *Adoration of the Magi* triptych for the high altar of SS. Jean-Baptiste et l'Evangeliste, Malines, was painted 1617–19, and in 1618 he did a triptych for St-Gommaire, Lier (the central field, *Virgin Presenting the Child Jesus to St. Francis of Assisi*, now in Dijon, Mus. B.A.). Rubens also sold to Sir Dudley Carleton for 100 florins *The Dismissal of Hagar* (London, Grosvenor Coll.); on May 26, 1618, the artist wrote: "It is done on a panel because small things are more successful on wood than on canvas." The composition was in part inspired by the Stimmer Bible illustration. In February of that year Rubens was commissioned by the Fishermen's Guild of Malines to paint a triptych for their church, Notre-Dame-au-delà-de-la-Dyle. During 1619 he gave a quittance for 750 gulden to Jaspar Charles for *The Last Communion of St. Francis* (PL. 330), which he had painted for the altar of the saint in the Antwerp Church of the Recollects. He also dispatched to the Jesuit church at Neuberg a *Nativity* and a *Pentecost*, the latter executed entirely by his assistants, at the order of Count Palatine Wolfgang Wilhelm. Also in 1619 Rubens signed and dated the *Augustus*, the first in a series of 12 bust-length depictions of emperors (Berlin, Grunewald Castle) which were ordered from different

masters in the Low Countries. After sending a *modello* for approval to the heirs of Nicolò Pallavicini, he dispatched in 1619 *The Miracle of St. Ignatius* (PL. 377; *modello* in Dulwich, Alleyn's College of God's Gift), and in the 1620s he supplied "alcuni cartoni molto superbi" for tapestries to the order of other Genoese gentlemen.

On Mar. 29, 1620, Rubens signed his second contract with the Antwerp Jesuits, to sketch 39 compositions for execution by his assistants (Van Dyck being specially named) on large canvases to be set in the ceiling compartments of the side aisles and galleries of the Jesuit church. He had already provided alternative altarpieces for the high altar and was to add an *Assumption* for the Lady Chapel (all three altarpieces, with *modelli* for the first two, now in Vienna, Kunsthist. Mus.). In July, 1620, the Earl of Arundel's secretary reported that Rubens had made sketches for the group portrait *The Countess of Arundel and Her Attendants* (XI, PL. 220). In the same year *Le Coup de Lance* (Antwerp, Mus. Royal B.A.) was painted for the high altar of the Church of the Recollects in Antwerp at the charge of Burgomaster Nicolaes Rockox (grisaille sketch for this altarpiece, London, Nat. Gall.). On Aug. 6, 1621, Rubens drew *The Carmelite General Ruzzola* (Plymouth, Eng., City Mus. and Art Gall., Cottonian Coll.) in preparation for the seated portrait (Hampshire, Eng., Verdon-Roe Coll.). On Sept. 5, Jan Brueghel the Elder wrote a letter to his patron Cardinal Federigo Borromeo covering the dispatch of *The Madonna in the Garland* (Louvre) to Milan, in which he boasted the success of his own work as well as that of Rubens.

In 1622–23, commissioned by Louis XIII of France, Rubens supplied 12 *modelli* for designs to be incorporated into the *Life of Constantine* (Philadelphia, Mus. of Art), a tenture that was presented in part complete and in part in the form of cartoons to Cardinal Francesco Barberini; extra cartoons were commissioned by the recipient from Pietro da Cortona (Florence, Coll. Corsini). For six weeks early in 1622 and again in February, 1925, Rubens was in Paris working on 21 enormous canvases for the first gallery of Marie de Médicis, mother of Louis XIII, in Luxembourg Palace. These works comprised the artist's extensive cycle of political allegories (Louvre), which outdid in scale and significance the King's gift to the Roman cardinal. Rubens's portraits of Louis XIII (oil sketch of the head, Melbourne, Nat. Gall. of Victoria), his wife Anne of Austria, and Marie de Médicis (both, Prado) were initiated during the 1622 visit. [*The Reconciliation of Marie de Médicis with Her Son, with Mercury and Prudence* (X, PL. 251) was done after 1622.]

I Palazzi di Genova, a collection of ground plans and façades published in 1622, was Rubens's souvenir of the civilized modern architecture of Galeazzo Alessi and others. The Luxembourg Palace and the Jesuit church in Antwerp were featured among the more recent buildings that Rubens praised in his preface. Drawings for some of the engraved elevations of Genoese palaces show Rubens's own corrections and annotations (London, Royal Inst. of Br. Arch.).

In 1625 Rubens drew a head of the Duke of Buckingham (Vienna, Albertina) and within the year painted his elaborate equestrian portrait of the Duke (now destroyed; formerly Osterley, Middlesex). Buckingham was then in Paris to negotiate the marriage of Charles I, the Prince of Wales, to Henrietta Maria of France, and was accompanied by his Master of the Horse, the painter and agent Balthasar Gerbier. Rubens's letter of Jan. 10, 1625, records the *Self-portrait* (London, Royal Colls.) done for Charles, the only prince to be thus honored. The gift was not just a bid to secure the commission for the Whitehall ceiling in London, in which Rubens had professed his interest at least since 1621, but also a heartfelt compliment to "le prince le plus amateur de la peinture qui soit au monde" (correspondence with Valavez).

In 1624 Rubens was paid 1,500 gulden for painting a huge panel, *Adoration of the Magi* (PL. 333), for the high altar of the Abbey of St-Michel, Antwerp. The surmounting statues were also designed by Rubens (oil sketch depicting Tanchelm, New Rochelle, N.Y., C. O. Baer Coll.) and probably the marble tabernacle as well, the finished works carved by Johannes van

Mildert. Rubens also painted on a separate panel the portrait of Abbé Matthäus Yrsselius kneeling as donor (Copenhagen, Nationalmus.).

In 1625 he signed and dated the small *Flight of Lot* (Louvre). From 1626 to 1628 he provided for Infanta Isabella rapid oil sketches (Cambridge, Fitzwilliam Mus.), finished *modelli* (Prado; Winchcombe, Gloucestershire, Sudeley Castle), and finally — in large part by his own hand — full-scale cartoons (Sarasota, Fla., Ringling Mus.) for eight vast tapestries depicting the triumph of the Eucharist (Madrid, XIII, PLS. 408, 409). He also painted the *Assumption* (1626) for the high altar of Antwerp Cathedral and the *Madonna and Child Adored by Saints* (1628) for the high altar of the Church of St-Augustin in Antwerp, the largest (19 × 13 ft.) of all the altarpieces entirely by his own hand. In July, 1927, he visited Dutch cities and painters, including Hals and Terbrugghen, to control arrangements for the sale of prints from his designs.

The period of Rubens's most intense diplomatic activity was 1628–30. He had been involved in politics since 1621, which saw the end of the Twelve Years' Truce and the death of Archduke Albert of Austria, governor of the Spanish Netherlands. Rubens was appointed adviser to the widowed archduchess, Infanta Isabella, who at her husband's death became ruler of the Spanish Netherlands. With her support, Rubens sought to prolong peace in these provinces during the Thirty Years' War (1618–48). In 1624 the French ambassador wrote from Brussels: "Rubens is here to take the likeness of the Prince of Poland, by order of the Infanta. I am persuaded that he will succeed better in this than in his negotiations for the truce." This was a correct prediction, although Rubens and Gerbier were able to maintain a secret correspondence even after the fresh outbreak of war between England and Spain, which led to the Duke of Buckingham's disastrous expedition to Cádiz. Not until the assassination of the Stuart favorite on Aug. 23, 1628, was the way reopened for Rubens to negotiate peace on behalf of the sorely tried Spanish Netherlands. (He described Antwerp to Louis XIII's librarian as "languishing like a consumptive body, declining little by little.") Unfortunately, Don Gaspar de Guzmán, the count-duke of Olivares, court favorite of Philip IV, had persuaded his master to make a close pact with France to reconquer England for Catholicism. On Aug. 29, 1628, Rubens traveled in secret haste to Madrid. The papal nuncio reported his arrival: "It is considered certain that Rubens, the Flemish painter, is the bearer of a negotiation, for we hear that he often confers in secret with the Count-Duke and in a manner very different from that which his profession permits. They say that he left England a short time ago; and since he is said to be a great friend of Buckingham, it is believed that he comes with some peace treaty between the two crowns. Others think his main object is the truce of Flanders and that he has received this commission as one who enjoys the confidence of all that country."

During nine months in Madrid, Rubens took the one recorded holiday of his life — ten days with John of Braganza (later João IV of Portugal). At the Spanish court, besides negotiations and royal portraiture, he set himself to school again before Titian's masterpieces, revisiting the Escorial with Velázquez; Rubens's inventory of 1640 lists 21 copies after Titian, most of which he must have painted during these months in Madrid. Eventually Rubens overcame Philip IV's prejudice against him as a suitable negotiator, and he was named secretary of the Privy Council of the Netherlands to conduct a special mission to England. Hastening across France, he reported to Isabella in Brussels. News awaiting his return made his mission yet more urgent and difficult: England had made a treaty with France on Apr. 24, 1629, and Charles I wished to treat with Rubens as a plenipotentiary without waiting for the exchange of regular envoys. Rubens succeeded in laying the groundwork for the peace protocol (Nov. 15, 1630). For this he was knighted, and Cambridge University gave him an honorary degree. His painted proclamation of success in realizing his own "Project for the Cessation of Armes" was *The Blessings of Peace* (London, Nat. Gall.), which depicted Mme Gerbier's children. The children also appeared in *Mme Gerbier and Her Children* (Bayford House, Fremantle Coll.) and *Peace and War* (PL. 331).

In England, Rubens discussed painting with King Charles, who knew the Spanish royal collections, and spoke of projects for the Whitehall ceiling. He was struck by the beauty and peacefulness of the English countryside. The *Landscape with St. George* (1630; Buckingham Palace, Royal Colls.) was his private souvenir of the view of the Thames from his lodgings in York House, with the royal couple depicted in masquerade as patron saint and rescued princess. Politically, however, a general peace was far away. Rubens's letter of Mar. 12, 1638, adumbrates *The Horrors of War* (PL. 334), his last work for an Italian client, the Medicis. He identifies the figures of the allegory as "that grief-stricken woman clothed in black, with torn veil, robbed of all her jewels and other ornaments . . . the unfortunate Europe, who for so many years now has suffered plunder, outrage, and misery."

At his homecoming in 1630 Rubens was rewarded by the Archduchess with exemption from further diplomacy. "This favor I obtained with more difficulty than any other she ever granted me," he later wrote. "Now for three years I have found peace of mind, having given up every sort of employment outside my beloved profession." He began to reorganize the work of his studio, the material of which had been entrusted for two years to Willem Panneels. On Dec. 6, 1630, four years a widower, he married 16-year-old Helena Fourment, whose charms recur frequently in his later figure subjects. Helena's portrait as a bride is in the Alte Pinakothek in Munich.

Major altarpieces from Rubens's last decade done entirely by his own hand include the *Triptych of St. Ildefonsus* (PL. 326), commissioned by the Archduchess for St-Jacques-sur-Coudenberg, Brussels, and finished in early 1632 — a noble last work for her before her death on Dec. 1, 1633; an *Adoration of the Magi* (Cambridge, Eng., King's College) painted for the 25 nuns of the Convent des Dames Blanches de Louvain during the winter of 1633–34, reputedly in eight days; *The Mystic Marriage of St. Catherine* (Toledo, Ohio, Mus. of Art); *The Martyrdom of St. Livinus* (ca. 1635; PL. 333); *The Ascent to Calvary* for the Abbey of Afflighem (Brussels, Mus. Royaux B.A.), a troublesome commission lasting from 1634 to Apr. 8, 1637; and, at the end of his life, *The Crucifixion of St. Peter*, which was still in his possession when he died but which was bought eventually for the church of that saint in Cologne, as the banker Jabach had intended from the first. Contemporaneous with these commissioned works is the *Santa Conversazione*, featuring Rubens himself as St. George, which became the altarpiece of his funerary chapel in the artist's parish church, St-Jacques in Antwerp.

By Aug. 11, 1634, Rubens had ready in Antwerp for dispatch to London the nine great canvases to be fitted in the Venetian manner into the ceiling compartments of the Banqueting House in Whitehall — all but the ovals for the four corners, which were being extensively worked by his own hand. "I confess that I am, by natural instinct, better fitted to execute very large works than little curiosities," he had written to William Trumbull with this enterprise in mind (Sept. 13, 1621).

On Apr. 17, 1635, Cardinal Infante Ferdinand, successor to the Archduchess and brother of Philip IV, made his state entry into Antwerp. Thirty-six years prior to this, Rubens had assisted his master Vaenius to convert the city into a theater for the archdukes. In November, 1634, he mobilized every artist in Antwerp to paint arches and towers according to his designs, to be ready by the end of the first week in January. The decorations were intended to impress the new ruler with the poverty of the city. Their official record is the *Pompa Introitus Ferdinandi* (1642), with explanations by Caspar Gevaerts, the city historian, and engravings by Theodor van Thulden, one of Rubens's principal assistants. Many of the *modelli* on panels are still in existence (e.g., Leningrad, The Hermitage; Antwerp, Mus. Royal B.A.), as are a number of canvases from that period with larger-than-life-size figures (Vienna, Kunsthist. Mus.; Windsor, Royal Colls; Raleigh, North Carolina Mus. of Art; Uffizi, including the *Quos Ego* (Dresden, Gemäldegalerie) and the *Meeting after Nordlingen* (Vienna, Kunsthist. Mus.), which Rubens painted between Feb. 15 and mid-April, 1635, without further assistance than his own sketches (Boston, Fogg Art Mus.; New York, Mrs. S. Kramarsky Coll.). On Nov. 12, 1635, Rubens bought Het Steen, the château of Elewijt. Many of his grandest and most romantic interpretations of landscape date from the succeeding years, among them, *Landscape with Rainbow* (London, Wallace Coll.; see also PL. 332), *The Château de Steen* (London, Nat. Gall.), and *Landscape with Peasants Returning from the Fields* (IX, PL. 19).

In 1636, through the Cardinal Infante, Rubens was commissioned by Philip IV to supply decorations on themes from Ovid and other sources for the Torre de la Parada, the King's hunting box near Madrid. On Mar. 11, 1638, there were 112 paintings dispatched to Spain. Among Rubens's assistants on the large canvases were Van Thulden, Cornelis de Vos, Jacques van Eyck, J. P. Gouwi, and Thomas Willeboirts. Some works were by Rubens's own hand, such as the *Democritus*, the *Heraclitus*, the *Marsyas*, the *Vulcan*, and the *Mercury* (all, Prado). Before June 20 of that year, Rubens received a further contract for the Torre. But during the following month he was unable to work because of gout in his painting arm; by mid-October he had become very ill. In July, however, he sketched the *Triumphal Car to Celebrate the Battle of Calloo* (Antwerp, Mus. Royal B.A.). During 1639 he was able to work at intervals and to supervise. The *St. Augustine* and *The Martyrdom of St. Thomas* (Prague, Rudolfinum), ordered for the Church of St. Thomas by Countess Helena Martinitz in August, 1637, were ready by May, 1639; and by July 22 Rubens had made the sketches for 18 of the pictures for Philip IV. On Sept. 25, 1639, after a month free of gout, he was reported to be working on four large pictures for Philip: *The Meeting of Romans and Sabines, The Rape of the Sabines* (oil sketches of both, London, Weston Coll.), *Hercules*, and *Andromeda*. The crippling gout returned in the winter. In February, 1640, he was made an honorary member of the Accademia di S. Luca in Rome. On May 30, 1640, he died in his house in Antwerp.

The printed inventory of July 14, 1640, listing works of art for sale in Antwerp, included well over 300 paintings by himself or by other masters; the group included 17 by Adriaen Brouwer, 3 oils and 4 water colors by Pieter Bruegel, 3 by Lucas van Leyden, a pair by Jan van Eyck, and numerous examples by Van Dyck and others of Rubens's principal associates. Like Jan Pourbus, an earlier master in the Antwerp school, Rubens provided that his graphic material (including many drawings by or after other draftsmen, Italian as well as northern, often retouched by him, and numerous sheets worked entirely by his own hand) should not be dispersed while there remained a possibility that a son or son-in-law might make use of it as a painter. This immense wealth of material was not auctioned until August, 1657. Access to his drawings was later to benefit artists as diverse as Watteau and Pierre Boulle.

Though variously appraised, Rubens has never been a forgotten painter. The grandeur of his pictorial language served not only the Roman Catholic Church, of which he was always a devout member, and the princess, with whom he kept faith and gave his undivided loyalties, but also left him a central figure in European art. He has influenced significantly painters as assorted as Jacob Jordaens and Luca Giordano, Feti and Fragonard, Castiglione and Constable, Van Dyck, and Matthew Smith. Rembrandt owned Rubens's early *Hero and Leander* and was an ardent admirer. Renoir, second only to him as a painter of flesh, was seduced by his brushwork and mastery of warm color. Gainsborough and Cézanne each made copies from Rubens. Even if no painter in Paris before Delacroix, except Charles Lebrun, fully appreciated his achievement in the Medici Gallery of the Luxembourg Palace, the enthusiasm for his art among French and English romantic painters was to have a sensational effect. In the formation of the baroque style, Gian Lorenzo Bernini (q.v.), another seminal genius, was anticipated by Rubens in essential ways (see BAROQUE ART). The Jesuit professor Cornelissen van den Steen left Louvain University in late summer, 1616, for the Collegio Romano in Rome with first copies of his *Commentaria in Pentateuchum Mosis*; Bernini's earliest altar tabernacle, for S. Agostino in

Rome, adheres closely to the pattern of Rubens's title page for this book. The *modello* (Montpellier, Mus. Fabre) drawn by Rubens for his first altarpieces for Rome's Chiesa Nuova was then in that city and was probably available to Bernini; it was this *modello* which demonstrated for the first time how the actual path of light could appear as a palpable entity in the drama of composition. Certainly Bernini could see in the tribune of Rubens's Chiesa Nuova how the air ambient between the high altarpiece and the separate groups of saints ranged on either flank was laden with significance; there was an emotive relationship between elements spaced apart, but the whole formed a total work of art, to which spirit Bernini himself gave the fullest expression in his Cornaro Chapel in S. Maria della Vittoria (cf. II, PL. 273).

The sheer magnitude of Rubens's production has never been exceeded; it was the triumph of "la gran prontezza, e la furia del pennello" (Bellori, 1672) and of his powers as impresario. His career was marred only by ill health during the last 18 months — never by idleness or any lengthy distraction other than diplomacy. Even in the almost impossible tasks forced on Rubens as an amateur diplomat he had fair success. Once he had dispensed with the drudge of painting beauties for Vincenzo, frustrations in his professional life were rare; the priestly delays and difficulties in the Chiesa Nuova, in St-Bavon at Ghent, and at Afflighem are the signal exceptions. Of all his projects, only his work for Marie de Médicis's second gallery — the sketches and cartoons for *The History of Henri IV* — was left on his hands, and this was due to political events rather than to an unsatisfied client. Rubens always dealt openly and honorably. He graded the prices of work according to the degree of his personal participation in the products finished to his designs. There were contretemps only when clients such as Charles I were devious.

Though Rubens despaired politely that men and arts had fallen away even more rapidly from the second golden age of the High Renaissance than they had from the first of antiquity, he never lost his warm hold on life. Portraits and drawings reveal his love of family as his landscapes manifest an enjoyment of familiar terrains. However, events such as the death of his friend Elsheimer in Rome, the sack of Mantua, where he had been happy, and particularly the untimely deaths of his first wife and his brilliant brother Philip made heavy demands on his spirit.

"Rubens è un italiano," wrote Bernard Berenson. Certainly Rubens knew Italy as few men from the North have known it. He had made his way first to Venice, her great age of painting only just past, and he was frequently to revisit that city. The Veneto, Lombardy, and Emilia were all within easy riding distance of Mantua, where he soon settled in the service of the Duke Gonzaga and where the Gonzagas held the largest art collections in Italy outside the Vatican; besides antiquities, the collections included masterpieces of every Renaissance school. Within a few months of his arrival, Rubens had his first look at the Medici collections and within a year reached Rome. By the age of 27 he had been to Genoa and Spain as well. In the service of the Gonzagas he had unsurpassed opportunities to study the entire scope of Renaissance achievement *in situ originale*, and by energetic copying he made the most profitable use of his sightseeing. Within five years of crossing the Alps he could pen a letter like a man Tuscan born; and of the six languages he came to speak and write with ease, Italian remained his favorite for his vast correspondence with patrons, diplomats, and scholars. Italy to him was both the ancient and eternal home of all the arts of civilization. To the palatial house which he built for himself and which rapidly became a famous sight far beyond Antwerp, he added a domestic pantheon to show his statuary, cameos, coins, and jewels — a hoard of antiquities so renowned that the Duke of Buckingham was importunate in his greed to acquire them for York House; to ever-higher bids from London, Rubens at length felt himself forced diplomatically to accede.

Whatever survived of the ancient world was to Rubens more precious than a mere collector's piece or a curiosity to invite learned exchanges with the antiquary Nicolas Claude Fabri de

Peiresc. Rubens was steeped in classical literature and inspired by Renaissance art; he utilized in his painting works from every era and endowed them with rich contemporary significance. The pen drawing *Hercules and the Nemaean Lion* (ca. 1612; Brussels, private coll.) is developed from an antique sarcophagus fragment (Cambridge, Eng., private coll.); Pordenone's mounted standard-bearer (16th cent.) frescoed in Cremona Cathedral is echoed in reverse by the corresponding figure in Rubens's *Landscape with St. George*; the compositions of two contemporaneous Roman altarpieces, F. Zuccari's (Zuccaro) in the Gesù and Pomarancio's in SS. Nereo e Achilleo, were utilized by Rubens in his final designs for the Chiesa Nuova.

So imbued was Rubens with the magic of Italy that his allegiance to the lands of his birth and upbringing is occasionally overlooked. His youthful copies of northern prints were followed in the dozen years after his return from Italy by painted copies of portraits by Holbein, Massys, Jan Cornelisz. Vermeyen, and Hans Maler; he continued to draw from or to work over the drawings of Maerten van Heemskerck, Michiel Coxie, and Lucas van Leyden. The group of peasants on the wooded bank in the *Landscape with St. George* reflects Pieter Bruegel's *Sermon of John the Baptist* (1566; Budapest, Mus. of Fine Arts) as much as Polidoro da Caravaggio's *Procession to Calvary*. In *Rubens and Helena Fourment Walking in Their Garden* (ca. 1631; Munich, Alte Pin.), the architecture of the garden pavilion is a reminder that Rubens published *I Palazzi di Genova*; but the old servant who stands by the pavilion, and especially the pen drawing for her (Berlin, Kupferstichkabinett), is a tribute to Bruegel's "naer het leven" studies. Twenty years earlier, Rubens's pen drawing for the *Christ Child Carried by St. Christopher* (Br. Mus.) shows his interest in Dürer's design as well as in Elsheimer's chiaroscuro, to dramatize a figure whose gigantic strength derives from the Farnese *Hercules*. This early pen drawing indicates its antecedents in Dürer and Elsheimer even more clearly than does the contract *modello* (Munich, Alte Pin.) painted for the outside wings of the Antwerp *Raising of the Cross* (1610; PL. 327). Such complexity of inspiration is characteristic of Rubens. In northern art, monumental use of the human figure had appeared in stained glass and tapestry; Rubens's Antwerp triptychs attempted to provide some equivalent to the scale and grandeur of High Renaissance frescoes. Both his use of oak panels prepared with shining fields of gesso (to enhance the luminosity of such works as the *Musicant Angels*, ca. 1614) and his depiction of simulated statues in grisaille on the outside of the organ shutters (Vaduz, Liechtenstein Coll.) follow on an increased scale established Antwerp practice. This work was in contrast to the optically very different manner of glaze paintings over *bolo bruno-rosso*, which Rubens had trained himself to use after the Venetian fashion. He was to use it again, before he finally lightened his palette, after his second visit, in 1628, to see the Titians in the Escorial.

Rubens's Italian years were the essential formative experience of his career. Titian remained his greatest love, from the period of his early careful drawings of Titian's *Sacrifice of Isaac* (Rubens copy ca. 1601, Vienna, Albertina) to the time of his brilliantly free renderings of Titian's two Bacchanals (Rubens copies, ca. 1638, Stockholm, Nationalmus.), which he must also have copied 30 years earlier in Rome. At first he grasped Titian's outer forms only, reaching their inner meaning later as his more mature understanding developed, by about 1628–29. Also important in Rubens's development was Tintoretto, with his dramatic illuminations, jagged brushwork, and daring foreshortenings (e.g., Rubens's *Transfiguration* for SS. Trinità, Mantua; now Nancy, Mus. B.A.). Tintoretto evoked an immediate response. But his lasting importance was in concepts — Rubens repeatedly adapted the flying figure in Tintoretto's *Miracle of St. Mark* even as late as his own *Blessing of the Reign of James I* (1634; Whitehall, Banqueting House) — and in the rapid sketching of ideas directly in oils; Rubens had been aware of this latter practice of the Tintoretto family shop since 1600. Paolo Veronese, with his scenographic taste and love of opulent materials, also produced an immediate reaction (e.g., Rubens's *svizzeri* in the arcades flanking *The Gonzaga Family in Adoration of the Trinity*; Mantua, Palazzo Ducale). Rubens was drawn to the steep perspectives of Veronese's ceilings and to his skill in combining figures with architecture (e.g., Veronese's *Esther before Ahasuerus*; Venice, S. Sebastiano). He reinterpreted these effects for the Antwerp Jesuits and a decade later for Charles I in Whitehall.

Also of decisive significance to Rubens in evolving his own method of oil sketching and in presenting painted rather than drawn *modelli* were the examples offered by Polidoro da Caravaggio, Federico Barocci, and Il Cigoli (L. Cardi). These three masters were important to Rubens in other ways as well. Polidoro, accepted by the 17th century as an authority nearly equal to Raphael on decoration *all'antica*, frescoed the façade of the Palazzo Maschero d'Oro; Rubens's copies of the façade still survive, and Polidoro's decorative system was later reflected on the outside of Rubens's own house in Antwerp. Barocci, Rubens's senior contemporary, probably met the younger man first through Vaenius; very likely Rubens had become familiar with two of Barocci's altarpieces while working for the Chiesa Nuova. Barocci's formula for representing flesh by juxtaposition of local colors, warm and cool, was tried by Rubens in such immediately post-Italian works as his *Annunciation* (Vienna, Kunsthist. Mus.); the procedure was retained until Rubens evolved his own more vibrant method of applying flesh tone over a striping of charcoal and gum that was spread in broad diagonal strokes on a gesso-prepared panel. Barocci's peculiar sensibility to trees and wooded banks affected Rubens through a long stretch of his career, interpenetrating his otherwise faithful response to Titian in the drawing done from Barocci's *Penitent St. Jerome* (Rubens version, Haarlem, Teylers Mus.); it persists even in the grisaille *modello* (formerly London, Morris Coll.) painted to instruct Paulus Pontius in engraving *The Ascent to Calvary* in 1631–32. Rubens's strikingly close approximation to Barocci's pen-and-wash style for the composition trials (1613–14) of the wings for the Antwerp *Descent from the Cross* suggests strongly that Rubens had acquired Barocci drawings when the latter died in 1612; this may have been accomplished through the agents whom Rubens maintained in Italy for copying and buying works of art (according to Padre Sebastiano Resta and others).

In similar circumstances Rubens undoubtedly acquired Cigoli drawings. Cigoli's *Deposition* comprised part of a compound influence (that also included Barocci's *Deposition*, Daniele da Volterra's, and more remotely Raphael's) at work on Rubens's treatment of the theme for the Antwerp Cathedral. Among other instances of Rubens's development of Cigoli's compositional ideas are his *Ecce homo* (Leningrad, The Hermitage) and *The Last Supper* (Il Cenacolo; Brera) of 1632. In this last, an altarpiece for St-Rombaut in Malines, Rubens painted a disciple muffled in drapery but recognizably posed like the *spadario* in Cigoli's *The Calling of St. Matthew*; a sheet penned with trials for a Last Supper (ca. 1602; Derbyshire, Trustees of the Chatsworth Settlement) shows that Rubens must have studied the Cigoli painting in S. Luigi dei Francesi.

His attested admiration for Caravaggio (q.v.; Sandrart, 1675–79) was limited to figures and compositions and not to the working method, which he found antipathetically slow. The *Supper at Emmaus* (recorded by Isaac van Swanenburg's engraving of 1611), in which Caravaggio's ideas are fused with Titian's version (then in the Gonzaga collections in Mantua) is an example of this. Another example is the brilliant sequence of developments behind Rubens's Chiesa Nuova *Entombment of Christ* (1613–15) based on Caravaggio's *Entombment* (Rome, Vat. Mus.); it started with a free copy (ca. 1612; Ottawa, Nat. Gall.) made on the basis of a *ricordo* done in Rome and ending with a fully independent *modello* in which, characteristically, the iconography is simplified. Movement of the greatest complexity is infused in the Rubens version, whereas in Caravaggio all had been oppressively airless and motionless.

Rubens's emphatic chiaroscuro and natural colors, often attributed to the influence of Caravaggio, emerge rather from Rubens's study of the 16th-century Venetians and the Carraccis (q.v.), to whom the Venetians owed so much. Rubens must have noted this family's achievement on his first journey south from Mantua to Rome, at the very least because Cardinal

Montalto had been legate in their city. But the Carracci frescoes of the Farnese Gallery were to be of even more importance to Rubens than those of Magnani Palace. He not only copied in the Roman palace; he must have had access to Annibale Carracci's working methods — drawing from life on a bold scale in chalks both as a salutary exercise and to clarify every posture and gesture in his composition trials before the definitive design was resolved for the cartoon. From Rubens's life studies for the *Raising of the Cross* in Sta Croce in Gerusalemme onward — and there are handsome examples in connection with the altarpieces for the Jesuit church, the Job triptych, and his second *Raising of the Cross* in Antwerp — one can see what profit he took from the example of Annibale at work. The active admiration shared by Rubens and Bernini for Annibale's boldness and vitality as a draftsman is the fundamental premise of the baroque style, in both a physical and spiritual sense. Annibale, as the heir to Raphael in his vitality and the humanity of his classicism, had important benefits to offer one so penetratingly observant as Rubens, who from his early days was interested in heading a great studio organization.

Also through the art of Annibale, Rubens was able to digest the superhuman suggestions left by Michelangelo in the Sistine Chapel. The morphology of Rubens's superficially faithful transcriptions (Br. Mus.) from the *ignudi* confirms this view. In the *Baptism* for SS. Trinità in Mantua, Rubens set out to challenge comparison with Michelangelo as a painter. But his obsession with Michelangelo had less to do with painting than with the Neo-Hellenistic treatment of muscular tensions and interactions in Michelangelo's sculpture; exceptions to this are Michelangelo's lunette scene of the Brazen Serpent, which Rubens copied (Br. Mus.), and the Adam figure as well as the general emotion and movement on Michelangelo's *Last Judgment* wall. Rubens shared Michelangelo's passion for the *Laocoön* and for the Belvedere torso; his *Rape of Ganymede* (ca. 1612; Vienna, Coll. Schwarzenberg) demonstrates his power to "carve" in paint a new son for Laocoön. By drawing Hellenistic, Roman, and High Renaissance sculpture from many viewpoints, he shaped his plastic sense.

Rubens also admired, with discrimination, some who admired Michelangelo. He reworked, "pour échauffer son génie" (Mariette, 1851–60), drawings by Francesco Salviati (Angers, Mus. Pincé; Louvre); and in his *Flagellation* for St. Paul's, Antwerp, he used a side view of Jacopo Sansovino's *Christ in Limbo*, the latter a development of Michelangelo's most potentially mannerist work in S. Maria sopra Minerva; the Michelangelo painting itself was the inspiration of Rubens's *Christ* for the Duke of Lerma.

For the more than thirty years of his full artistic maturity Rubens kept for reference his copies of Michelangelo, of Leonardo (Rubens copy, IX, PL. 119), of the Roman works of Raphael, of Andrea del Sarto in the Florentine Cloister of the Scalzi (I, PLS. 257, 258), and of the cupola and altarpiece designs of Correggio. Also of intense interest to him, particularly during his Italian years, were those whom he saw as his forerunners in their efforts to bring about the marriage of Florentine-Roman *disegno* and Venetian *colore*. These artists were Tintoretto, Giuseppe (Porta) Salviati, and, in the context of heroic presence and action visualized in Venetian terms, Pordenone at Treviso.

Rubens's interest in his great predecessors at the Mantuan court was more than respectful. The Chatsworth Sketchbook of his assistant Anton van Dyck suggests that Rubens had a set of Mantegna engravings from which he had copied figures during his youth in Antwerp. Copies of Mantegna's *The Triumph of Caesar* (Hampton Court, Royal Colls.) were in his inventory in 1640. From this frieze he painted an evocation (London, Nat. Gall.), introducing elements from Giulio Romano, an admirer of Mantegna. Not surprisingly, Rubens selected for the background to a group portrait of himself, his brother, and their friends (Munich, Treuhandverwaltung) the same view of the lake in Mantua, showing the Ponte di S. Giorgio, that Mantegna had chosen for *The Death of the Virgin*. Rubens reveled in Giulio Romano's productivity as a decorator. In Mantua he reworked copies of Giulio's *Deaths of the Ovidian Heroes*; and at least one of these (Paris, Coll. Lugt) he recopied

about 30 years later, more freely and entirely by his own pen and brush (*Hylas and the Nymphs*, Cambridge, priv. coll.), having meanwhile penned variants of some of the nymphs on another sheet (Paris, Coll. Lugt). His *Birth of Venus* (oil sketch, Brussels, Mus. Royaux B.A.) for the Torre de la Parada incorporates the putto inspired by Giulio with the Venus deriving from Giulio's ceiling design for the Palazzo del Te.

As an artist of immensely creative eclecticism, Rubens was able to learn from the designs of minor as well as major men. His first *Raising of the Cross* (for Sta Croce in Gerusalemme, Rome) is based on the engraved design of C. Swartz, another northerner who made his way to Venice. Drawings in his collection which he repaired more or less extensively include Zuccari's drawing for the *Christ and the Samaritan Woman* in S. Francesco della Vigna, Venice (Lulworth, Eng., Weld Coll.), Salviati's for the altar of S. Maria Gloriosa dei Frari in Venice (Paris, Coll. Lugt), and one attributed to Aert van Leyden (Leningrad, The Hermitage), besides his own copy from the Farnese Gallery cove. These repairs range widely over his career.

The scope of Rubens's artistic interests was exceptional. Nothing escaped his notice, and visual knowledge was valued for its own sake. To supplement his graphic material, he and his principal assistant Van Dyck painted a stock of expressive head studies for later use in crowded compositions, a provision in which they followed the practice of Frans Floris de Vriendt, who instructed his pupils in this manner. However, these materials could not have been put to full use without the astonishing powers that Rubens developed to sketch directly in paint (from 1605 on) and to organize the production of a studio of painters and engravers (from 1609 on). The sketches were done on small panels, except for a few in the Italian period that were painted on canvas and an occasional later one painted on paper. They were always produced at great speed with a special quick-drying oil that was developed in the Antwerp studio. The sketches vary in degree of color and finish, depending upon whether they were Rubens's first thoughts (e.g., grisailles for the ceiling compartments of the Jesuit church in Antwerp, now in London, Dulwich College; Oxford, Ashmolean Mus.; Rotterdam, Mus. Boymans-Van Beuningen); or instructions to assistants (e.g., colored sketches for the same church), to silversmiths (e.g., London, Nat. Gall.), or, most precisely demanding of all, to engravers (e.g., Leningrad, The Hermitage); or whether they were contract models to gain the approval of clients (e.g., *The Descent from the Cross*, London, Courtauld Inst. Galls.). In every case they can be reckoned small works in size only. Without them the magnitude of Rubens's achievement is inconceivable. At neither the beginning nor the end of his career, however, did the use of oil sketches preclude composition trials on paper in the more traditional media of ink and chalks or *gouache*, whether or not these were in conjunction with oil sketches.

Among painters, Rubens was the greatest impresario, along with Raphael, coaxing and coordinating major as well as minor talents into coherent productions within his own style. This is exemplified by the large composition *Christ in the House of Simon* (ca. 1618; Leningrad, The Hermitage). The figure arrangement of Ruben's preparatory oil sketch (Vienna, Ak. der Bildenden K.) was modified by at least one head study (Berlin, Staat. Mus.) painted by Van Dyck from the model. Van Dyck was responsible for all five figures in the right-hand group of the finished work. That the figures seated on the left were painted by Jacob Jordaens can be no less well established. Confirmation comes from the *ricordo* in colored chalks (Leningrad, The Hermitage), always attributed to Jordaens; in this drawing only those figures painted by Van Dyck and the two servants standing at the back differ from the same figures in the final painting, to which Rubens himself can only have given a few approving touches. Yet at a reasonable distance it passes as the work of one hand as well as of one imagination. The seeming irreconciliability of styles between Van Dyck and Jordaens is marked sensationally by their respective altarpieces of 1628 for the Antwerp Augustinians.

On his return to Antwerp in 1609, Rubens's success and

the distinction of his personality attracted pupils long before Van Dyck or Jordaens came into his orbit. Relieved of the obligation to live at the Brussels court, he was also exempt from guild regulations and so became free to engage pupils or collaborators without having them enrolled. By 1611 he wrote that he had refused over 100 applicants. As his international reputation grew, in part through careful organization of printmaking to advertise his designs, numerous large-scale works issued from his house in Antwerp. According to the price and client, these works might be generally retouched by Rubens, or only in certain areas, or not at all. Of the *Judgment of Solomon* (Copenhagen, Nationalmus.) Rubens wrote: "A hunt of men on horseback and lions, begun by one of my pupils, after one that I made for His Most Serene Highness of Bavaria, but all retouched by my hand 8 × 11 ft." (letter of Apr. 28, 1618, to Dudley Carleton). For the *Assumption* (ca. 1625–27) for the Heiligkreuzkirche, Augsburg, Rubens painted in preparation a double study of two Apostles' heads already composed expressively in light and shade (Cheshire, Eng., Capesthorne Hall).

There are also works of collaboration between Rubens and certain specialists: "A Prometheus bound on Mt. Caucasus, with an eagle which pecks his liver. Original, by my hand, and the eagle done by Snyders." (The large canvas, ca. 1612, now Philadelphia, Mus. of Art; Frans Snyders' drawing, Br. Mus.) In *Adam and Eve in Paradise* (The Hague, Mauritshuis) Jan Brueghel did the flowers, landscape, and animals, while Rubens did one or more human figures; the same arrangement was followed in *Noli me tangere* (San Francisco, De Young Mus.) and *Diana Resting after the Chase* (Schleissheim, Germany, Schloss). Jan Wildens (1586–1653) did the river landscape and *staffage* in *Latona and the Frogs* (Munich, Alte Pin.); Paul de Vos painted the animals in *The Bear Hunt* (Raleigh, North Carolina Mus. of Art); and Cornelis Saftleven, the Rotterdam landscapist who visited Antwerp in 1631, painted some small works with Rubens.

In impatience or to please his fancy Rubens sometimes inserted whole figures or groups into what are otherwise largely school works — for example, the women and children at the right in *The Obsequies of the Consul Decius Mus* (Vaduz, Liechtenstein Coll.), or the red fox slinking away in *The Wolf and Fox Hunt* (Met. Mus.).

After Rubens's prime originals, usually painted on panels (if in Antwerp), a number of secondary canvas versions exist of the Bacchic scenes, hunts, and other secular subjects in vogue, the best of which were usually retouched by Rubens. But in every period Rubens painted some virtual replicas. The *Hero and Leander* (ca. 1606; New Haven, Yale Univ. Art Gall.) on a bolus ground was repeated with a few compositional variants on another canvas with a light ground (ca. 1612; Dresden, Gemäldegal.). The *Return from the Flight into Egypt* for Archduke Albert's chapel in Sta Croce in Gerusalemme, Rome (ca. 1616; Hartford, Conn., Wadsworth Atheneum), was repeated in a much more Venetian technique perhaps 10 years later for a private client (Norfolk, Holkham Hall, Earl of Leicester Coll.). There is an autograph reduction (Williamstown, Mass., Clark Art Inst.) of the composition on the outside of the S. Ildefonso altar (Vienna, Kunsthist. Mus.). With notable variations of background there are two more or less contemporaneous autographs of *The Garden of Love* — one on canvas (PL. 334) and one on panel (Buckinghamshire, Waddesdon Manor, Nat. Trust).

The repetition of the *Return from the Flight into Egypt* may have been commissioned on the strength of the Lucas Vorsterman engraving of the original design. At Rubens's order the design was redrawn for Vorsterman in a special model by Van Dyck (Louvre). Rubens attached much importance to the circulation of prints as a means of direct income, advertisement, and protection against plagiarism in an age of insecure copyright. As Sir Joshua Reynolds was the first to appreciate, Rubens's triumph was the extent to which he was able to have a richly colored and painterly achievement successfully transposed into linear black and white. Rubens's exacting demands in this field, as well as Vorsterman's own temperament, must

have contributed to the latter's breakdown in 1620. No replacement of his quality as an engraver could be found until Rubens, after his diplomatic voyages, engaged Vorsterman's own star pupil, Paulus Pontius. The finest collective production of Rubens's cadre of engravers is the 1638 series *Busts of Emperors and Philosophers*. This was achieved because Rubens found time to provide special *modelli*; without *modelli* the difficulties of retaining the character of forms and movement on a reduced scale and of matching the printed line to Rubens's mature brushwork tended to defeat engravers. Rubens also employed one first-rate woodcutter, Christoffel Jegher, and is himself credited with one etching, the *St. Catherine* (corrected proof, Met. Mus.). His sensitivity to the individual requirements of the graphic processes is illustrated by the *modelli* (Met. Mus.) drawn to reproduce *The Garden of Love* (PL. 334); his penwork at the left shows that he originally had copper engraving in mind, shifting in the course of work to a broader stroke perfectly adapted to the requirements of Jegher.

Demanding six months' notice, Rubens supplied the Plantin Press with many designs for title pages and book illustrations. His own publications, had time permitted, would have been augmented. Some illustrations for his Anatomy Book were published posthumously, engraved by Pontius for the *Livre à Dessiner* (Antwerp, 1649); these drawings survive (formerly London, H. M. Calmann Coll.; Amsterdam, Coll. v. Regteren Altena), as well as one that was not engraved (Derbyshire, Trustees of the Chatsworth Settlement). Fragments probably intended for his Architecture Book survive (Leningrad, The Hermitage). His essay *De Imitatione (antiquarum) Statuarum* (reproduced by R. de Piles) was almost certainly the only part of his famous notebook (most of which burned in Boulle's atelier, Paris, 1720) that was ready for the press. But two late-17th-century transcripts of considerable parts of this book (MS de Ganay, used by C. A. Jombert, *Théorie de la Figure Humaine*, Paris, 1773; MS Marsden, unpublished), plus some original pages, indicate Rubens's further interests: the Cabala, illustrating Vergil, the Pythagorean structure underlying male and female forms, and a scale of beautiful attributes.

SOURCES. Vita Petri Pauli Rubenii, ed. F. de Reiffenberg, Nouvelles recherches sur Pierre Paul Rubens, Brussels, 1837; G. Mancini, Considerazioni sulla pittura (ed. A. Marucchi and L. Salerno), 2 vols., Rome, 1956–57; G. Baglione, Le Vite de' pittori, scultori, et architecti, Rome, 1642; F. Pacheco, Arte de la pintura (ed. F. J. Sanchez Cantón), Madrid, 1956; G. P. Bellori, Le Vite de' pittori, scultori ed architetti moderni, Rome, 1672; J. von Sandrart, Academie der Bau-, Bild- und Mahlerey-Künste, 2 vols., Nürnberg, 1675–79; R. de Piles, Abrégé de la vie des peintres, Paris, 1699; R. de Piles, Cours de peinture par principes, Paris, 1708; P.-J. Mariette, Abecedario (ed. P. de Chennevières and A. de Montaiglon), 6 vols., Paris, 1851–60; P. Rombouts and T. van Lerius, De Liggeren en andere historische archiven der Antwerpsche Sint Lucasgilde, 2 vols., Antwerp, 1872–76; M. Rooses and C. Ruelens, ed., Codex Diplomaticus Rubenianus, 6 vols., Antwerp, 1887–1909; J. Denucé, De Antwerpsche 'Konstkamers', Antwerp, 1932; J. Denucé, Na Peter Pauwel Rubens, Antwerp, 1949; M. de Maeyer, Albrecht en Isabella en de schilderkunst, Brussels, 1955; R. S. Magurn, ed., The Letters of Peter Paul Rubens, Cambridge, Mass., 1955; F. Mols, MSS. 21740, 5722–30, Bib. royale, Brussels.

BIBLIOG. P. Arents, Geschriften van en over Rubens, Antwerp, 1940; M. V. Dobroklonsky, Risunki Rubensa (Drawings by Rubens), Leningrad, 1940 (cat.); G. Glück, Rubens as a Portrait Painter, BM, LXXVI, 1940, pp. 172–84; C. Norris, Rubens before Italy, BM, LXXVI, 1940, pp. 184–94; J. Q. van Regteren Altena, Rubens as a Draughtsman, BM, LXXVI, 1940, pp. 194–200; F. van den Wijngaert, Inventaris der Rubeniaansche Prentkunst, Antwerp, 1940; H. F. Bouchery and F. van den Wijngaert, P. P. Rubens en het Plantijnsche Huis, Antwerp, 1941; H. G. Evers, Peter Paul Rubens, Munich, 1942; L. van Puyvelde, A Landscape by Rubens, BM, LXXVIII, 1942, pp. 188–91; P. Arents, Rubens-bibliographie, Brussels, 1943; H. G. Evers, Rubens und seine Werk: Neue Forschungen, Brussels, 1943; F. Lugt, Rubens and Stimmer, AQ. VI, 1943, pp. 99–115; W. Stechow, Two 17th Century Flemish Masterpieces, AQ, VII, 1944, pp. 296–99; G. Glück, Die Landschaften von Peter Paul Rubens, Vienna, 1945; M. de Maeyer, Rubens' Terugkeer uit Italie naar Antwerpen, Gentse Bijdragen tot de Kunstgeschiedenis, XI, 1945–48, pp. 147–65; L. R. Lind, The Latin Life of Peter Paul Rubens by His Nephew Philip: A Translation, AQ, IX, 1946, pp. 37–44; N. MacLaren, Rubens: The Château de Steen, London, 1946; W. R. Valentiner, Rubens Paintings in America, AQ, IX, 1946, pp. 153–68; O. Bock von Wülfingen, Rubens in der deutschen Kunstbetrachtung, Berlin, 1947; F. Clijmans, The Reconstruction of the House and Studio of Rubens, Antwerp, 1947; J. de Coo, Rubens-gids voor de Antwerpse kerken, Antwerp, 1947; J. A. Goris and J. S. Held, Rubens in America, New York, 1947; J. S. Held, Rubens and Virgil: A Self-criticism, AB, XXIX, 1947, pp. 125–28; L. van Puyvelde, The Sketches of Rubens (trans.

E. Winkworth), London, 1947; C. van Herck and A. Jansen, Inventaris van de tekeningen bewaard op het Archief van de Sint Caroluskerk te Antwerpen, Tijdschrift voor Geschiedenis en Folklore, XI, 1948, pp. 45–91; C. Norris, Rubens and the Great Cameo, Phoenix, III, 1948, pp. 178–88; W. Schoene, Die Leda von Michelangelo und Rubens, Kunst, I, 1948, pp. 30–35; P. Arents, Pompa Introitus Ferdinandi, De Gulden Passer, XXVII, 1949, pp. 81–348, XXVIII, 1950, pp. 147–48; M. V. Dobroklonsky, Coronation of the Madonna (in Rus.), Hermitage Rec. de trav., III, 1949, pp. 17–23; G. C. Grimm, Architectural Motifs in Rubens, Paintings and Their Source (in Rus.), Hermitage Rec. de trav., III, 1949, pp. 61–71; T. D. Kamenskaya, The Repercussions of Rubens on French Drawings of the 17th and 18th Centuries (in Rus.), Hermitage Rec. de trav., III, 1949, pp. 113–40; F. Lugt, Inventaire général des dessins des écoles du Nord: Ecole flamande, I, Paris, 1949; E. G. Lysenkov, Rubens' Illustrations for Aguilonius' Optica (in Rus.), Hermitage Rec. de trav., III, 1949, pp. 49–60; D. A. Schmidt, Rubens' Sketches for the Descent from the Cross (in Rus.), Hermitage Rec. de trav., III, 1949, pp. 25–32; V. K. Stegman-Haeva, Rubens' Influence on Ivory Carving (in Rus.), Hermitage Rec. de trav., III, 1949, pp. 101–12; L. Burchard, ed., Peter Paul Rubens Kt., London, 1950 (cat.); J. C. Burckhardt, Recollections of Rubens (ed. H. Gerson, trans. M. Hottinger and others), New York, 1950; J. C. van Gelder, Rubens in Holland in de zeventiende eeuw, NedKhJb, III, 1950–51, pp. 102–50; H. Olsen, Rubens og Cigoli, Kunstmuseets Arskrift, XXXVII, 1950, pp. 58–73; L. Burchard, ed., A Loan Exhibition of Rubens, New York, 1951 (cat.); C. Norris, Rubens in Retrospect, BM, XCIII, 1951, pp. 4–11; L. van Puyvelde, Rubens, Paris, Brussels, 1952; F. Baudouin, Nota's bij de Tentoonstelling Schetsen en Tekeningen van P. P. Rubens, B. Mus. Royaux des beaux-arts, II, 1953, pp. 46–54; L. Burchard, Rubens' Feast of Herod at Port Sunlight, BM, XCV, 1953, pp. 383–87; H. Delasalle, Du Luxembourg au Louvre: la Galérie Médicis, RArts, III, 1953, pp. 203–08; E. Haverkamp-Begemann, ed., Olieverfschetsen van Rubens, Rotterdam, 1953 (cat.); J. S. Held, The Authorship of Three Paintings in Mons, B. Mus. Royaux des beaux-arts, II, 1953, pp. 99–115; J. S. Held, Rubens-Esquisses-Dessins: Musée d'Art Ancien, Arts plastiques, VI, 1953, pp. 107–16; M. Jaffé, Rubens' Portrait of Rogier Clarisse, BM, XCV, 1953, pp. 387–90; M. Jaffé, Rubens' Sketching in Paint, AN, LII, 3, 1953, pp. 34–37, 64–67; M. Jaffé, The Sketch of St. Gregory Nazianzenus by Rubens, Gall. Notes (Buffalo), XVII, 1953, pp. 2–6; M. Jaffé, Two Rubens Drawings Rediscovered, AQ, XVI, 1953, pp. 131–36; C. Norris, The St. Jerome from Sanssouci, BM, XCV, 1953, pp. 391–93; J. Q. van Regteren Altena, Rubens en de Galerie d'Ulysse, B. Rijksmuseum, I, 1953, pp. 8–13; Royal Academy, Flemish Art, London, 1953 (cat.); A. Seilern, An Entombment by Rubens, BM, XCV, 1953, pp. 380–83; O. Benesch, Beiträge zum Werk Rubens, Alte und Neue Kunst, III, 1954, pp. 8–19; V. H. Elbern, P. P. Rubens: Triumph der Eucharistie, Wandteppiche aus dem Kölner, Dom Essen, 1954 (cat.; rev. by M. Jaffé, BM, XCVIII, 1956, p. 133); E. Haverkamp-Begemann, Rubens Schetsen, B. Mus. Boymans, V, 1954, pp. 1–22; R.-A. d'Hulst, De Morenkoppen, B. Mus. Royaux des beaux-arts, III, 1954, pp. 117–21; J. Jacob, A Holy Family and Other Related Pictures by P. P. Rubens, Jb. Koningklijk Mus. voor Schone Kunsten Antwerpen, 1954–60, pp. 5–16; M. Jaffé, Rubens and the Influence of Italy, The Listener, LI, 1954, pp. 135–37; M. Jaffé, Rubens at Rotterdam, BM, XCVI, 1954, pp. 53–60; M. Jaffé, Some Unpublished Head Studies by P. P. Rubens, BM, XCVI, 1954, pp. 302–07; A. Scharf, Autour de Rubens au Musée des Beaux-Arts de Poitiers, Soc. des Amis des Mus. de Poitiers, I, 1954, pp. 22–27; D. Sutton, Flemish Painting at the Royal Academy, Arts plastiques, VI, 6, 1954, pp. 1–71; P. Bjurström, Rubens' St. George and the Dragon, AQ, XVIII, 1955, pp. 27–43; M. Jaffé, Rubens en de Leeuwenkuil, B. Rijsmuseum, III, 1955, pp. 59–67; H. Kauffmann, P. P. Rubens im Lichte seiner Selbstbekenntnisse, Wallraf-Richartz Jhb., XVII, 1955, pp. 181–88; A. Seilern, Flemish Paintings and Drawings at 56 Princes Gate, London, 1955; O. Benesch, Die Genesis einer Altarbildkomposition von Rubens, B. Mus. Royaux des beaux-arts, V, 1956, pp. 35–40; L. Burchard and R.-A. d'Hulst, Tekeningen van P. P. Rubens, Antwerp, 1956 (cat.); J. S. Held, Drawings and Oil-sketches by Rubens from American Collections, BM, XCVIII, 1956, pp. 123–24; M. Jaffé, Rubens' Drawings at Antwerp, BM, XCVIII, 1956, pp. 314–21; A. Mongan, Drawings and Oil-sketches by Rubens from American Collections, Cambridge, Mass., 1956 (cat.); A. E. Popham, Rubens and Salviati, BM, XCVIII, 1956, p. 417; W. Wagner, Handzeichnungen von P. P. Rubens, Kchr., IX, 1956, pp. 323–24; L. Bergström, Osias Beert the Elder as a Collaborator of Rubens, BM, XCIX, 1957, pp. 120–24; E. Haverkamp-Begemann, De Kronik van Maria door Rubens, B. Mus. Boymans, VIII, 1957, pp. 82–90; J. S. Held, Comments on Rubens' Beginnings, Misc. D. Roggen, Antwerp, 1957, pp. 125–36; M. Jaffé, Current and Forthcoming Exhibitions: The Agnew Exhibition of Old Masters, BM, XCIX, 1957, p. 432; M. Jaffé, The Interest of Rubens in Annibale and Agostino Carracci: Further Notes, BM, XCIX, 1957, pp. 374–79; M. Jaffé, Painting from Irish Collections, BM, XCIX, 1957, pp. 275–77; M. Jaffé, A Sheet of Drawings from Rubens' Second Roman Period and His Early Style as a Landscape Draughtsman, Oud-Holland, LXXII, 1957, pp. 1–19; Herinneringen aan P. P. Rubens, Antwerp, 1958 (cat.); M. Jaffé, Un chef-d'œuvre mieux connu, L'Oeil, 43–44, 1958, pp. 14–80; M. Jaffé, Review of Flemish Art in Spanish Collections, BM, C, 1958, pp. 366–67; M. Jaffé, Rubens in Italy: Rediscovered Works, BM, C, 1958, pp. 411–23; M. Jaffé, Rubens' Christ on the Cross, BM, C, 1958, pp. 21–24; M. Jaffé, Rubens' Drawings after 16th Century Northern Masters: Some Additions, AQ, XXI, 1958, pp. 401–06; O. Millar, Rubens: The Whitehall Ceiling, London, 1958; J. Bruyn, Rubens' schets voor de Kruisdraging, B. Rijksmuseum, VI, 1959, pp. 3–9; J. S. Held, Rubens: Selected Drawings, 2 vols., London, 1959 (rev. by J. Müller Hofstede, Kchr., XV, 1962, pp. 93–107, 129–37); L. van Puyvelde, Les Saint Ignace et Saint François Xavier de Rubens, GBA, LIII, 1959, pp. 225–36; H. S. Francis, Diana and Her Nymphs Departing for the Chase, B. Cleve. Mus. of Art, XLVII, 1960, pp. 19–27; J. S. Held, Rubens' Designs for Sepulchral Monuments, AQ, XXIII, 1960,

pp. 247–70; M. Jaffé, The Union of Earth and Water Revived for the Fitzwilliam, BM, CII, 1960, pp. 448–51; K. Fremantle, Themes from Ripa and Rubens in the Royal Palace of Amsterdam, BM, CIII, 1961, pp. 258–64; M. Jaffé, The Companion to Rubens' Portrait of Rogier Clarisse, BM, CIII, 1961, pp. 4–6; M. Jaffé, The Deceased Young Duke of Mantua's Brother, BM, CIII, 1961, pp. 374–78; M. Jaffé, "The Return from the Flight into Egypt" by Peter Paul Rubens, B. Wadsworth Atheneum, 5th ser., VIII, 1961, pp. 10–26; Oil Sketches and Smaller Pictures by Sir Peter Paul Rubens, London, 1961 (cat.); C. Parkhurst, Aguilonius' Optic and Rubens' Color, NedKhJb, XII, 1961, pp. 35–49; L. van Puyvelde, Projets de Rubens et de van Dyck pour les tapissiers, GBA, LVII, 1961, pp. 143–54; G. W. G. Agnew, Artist to Artist, King's Lynn, 1962 (cat.); F. Baudouin, ed., Rubens diplomate, Antwerp, 1962 (cat.); P. Coremans and others, La descente de croix de Rubens: Etude préalable au traitement, B. Inst. royal du patrimoine artistique, V, 1962, pp. 6–187; M. Jaffé, Rubens' Portrait of Father Ruzzola, BM, CIV, 1962, pp. 389–90; J. Müller Hofstede, Zur Antwerpener Frühzeit von Peter Paul Rubens, MJhb, 3d ser., XIII, 1962, pp. 179–215; J. Müller Hofstede, Zur frühen Bildnismalerei von Peter Paul Rubens, Pantheon, XX, 1962, pp. 279–90; L. van Puyvelde, La Salle des Etats à Anvers, Louvain, Paris, 1962; M. Röthlisberger, An "Ecce Homo" by Rubens, BM, CIV, 1962, pp. 389–90; L. Burchard and R.-A. d'Hulst, Rubens Drawings, 2 vols., Brussels, 1963 (bibliog.); J. Hayes, Gainsborough and Rubens, Apollo, N.S., LXXVIII, 1963, pp. 89–97; J. S. Held, Prometheus Bound, B. Phila. Mus., LIX, 279, 1963, pp. 16–32; M. Jaffé, P. P. Rubens and the Oratorian Fathers, Proporzioni, IV, 1963, pp. 1–56; M. J. Lewine, The Source of Rubens' Miracles of St. Ignatius, AB, XLV, 1963, pp. 143–47; V. H. Miesel, Rubens' Study Drawings after Ancient Sculpture, GBA, LXI, 1963, pp. 311–26; A. P. de Mirimonde, La musique dans les œuvres flamandes du XVIIᵉ siècle au Louvre, Rev. du Louvre, XIII, 1963, pp. 168–73; B. Teyssèdre, Une collection française de Rubens au XVIIᵉ siècle: Le cabinet du Duc de Richelieu décrit par Roger de Piles (1676–81), GBA, LXII, 1963, pp. 241–300.

Michael JAFFÉ

Illustrations: PLS. 325–335.

RUBLËV, ANDREI.

RUBLËV, ANDREI. Old-Russian painter, representative of the Moscow school (b. between 1360 and 1370; d. ca. 1430). There is little reliable information about Rublëv's life. He was a monk in the Trinity-St. Sergius Monastery founded near Moscow by St. Sergius of Radonezh (d. ca. 1392), and it was in this simple community, for which Sergius's teaching on man's exalted moral predestination constituted the supreme vital principle, that Rublëv received his artistic training. It would seem that his principal teacher was Prochor of Gorodets, who was an exponent of the Byzantinizing tendency in Muscovite painting at the end of the 14th century.

The earliest of Rublëv's surviving works are the frescoes on the altar pillars of the Cathedral of the Dormition in Zvenigorod, most probably executed about 1400. Representing St. Florus (whose head is lost) and St. Laurus (PL. 338), who were honored in old Russia as the patron saints of cavalrymen and horse breeders, these frescoes show an undeniable familiarity with the work of the illustrious Theophanes the Greek, who had come to Moscow in the early 1390s. The contour of the head of St. Laurus is traced in easy-flowing curves, creating an almost symmetrical silhouette; the face is painted with steady, even brush strokes, endowing the figure with a particular firmness and serenity.

According to the chronicles, in 1405 Rublëv, Prochor of Gorodets, and Theophanes the Greek worked together in the Cathedral of the Annunciation in Moscow, where they painted not only the walls of the church but also the iconostasis; this was later transferred to the new structure erected in 1484 on the site of the old Cathedral of the Annunciation, which had been destroyed. Theophanes and his apprentices did the icons for the Deësis tier of the iconostasis, while Prochor of Gorodets and Rublëv were responsible for the icons in the festival tier. To Rublëv may be attributed the icons of the Annunciation (PL. 338), the Nativity, the Presentation in the Temple, the Baptism, the Raising of Lazarus, the Entry into Jerusalem, and the Transfiguration, all of which are outstanding for their exceptionally rhythmical composition and for the rare beauty of their vivid coloring. The iconostasis of the Cathedral of the Annunciation, with its towering Deësis figures and numerous festivals, can be considered a prototype of the tall, classic old-Russian iconostasis. This was unknown to the Byzantines, who used a lower type with only three rows of icons: the local tier, the Deësis with its half-length figures, and the festival tier. Through the multiplication of the rows of icons and the increased size of the festival tier the Russian iconostasis acquired an extraordinary monumentality and became an indispensable element of church interior decoration.

Collaboration with Theophanes the Greek undoubtedly stimulated Rublĕv's artistic gifts, but by temperament the two men were fundamentally unlike. Theophanes's passionate, tormented, restless figures remained alien to Rublĕv, whose aim was quite different. Rublĕv strove for a particular limpidity and purity of expression and for a harmonious balance between spiritual content and corporeal form. He was not bound by tradition: the Deësis with half-length figures that he created for the Cathedral of the Nativity of the Virgin in the Savvino-Storozhevsk Monastery near Zvenigorod bears ample witness to this. Three of its icons, now preserved in the Tretyakov Gallery in Moscow (XIII, PL. 72), and painted most probably around 1406–07, are striking for the translucence of their figures and the superb beauty of their cool, light hues. The blues, pinks, pale mauves, and cherry colors blend so skillfully with the gold of the background that the effect is one of perfect harmony.

Rublĕv next painted the frescoes in the Cathedral of the Dormition in Vladimir (PL. 339), where, according to the chronicles, he worked in 1408 in association with Daniel (Daniil) Chorny. Twenty years later, the two masters again worked together in the Trinity-St. Sergius Monastery. It seems that they had become close friends, for in the ancient sources we find them referred to as "companions" and "partners in penitence," and there is every reason to believe that they belonged to the same artists' work group, which enjoyed wide renown and received a constant stream of commissions. Of the once extensive murals in the Cathedral of the Dormition there now remains only the one on the west wall, showing fragments of a large, multifigured Last Judgment. The artists were eminently successful in relating the painting to the architectural background: the mural follows the two-dimensional rhythm of the wall and can be said to be architectonic in the best sense of the word. Two distinct styles are clearly apparent in this surviving fragment, substantiating the chronicler's mention that two masters had been at work here. To Rublĕv, the younger of the two, may be attributed the Christ among the seraphim, the apostles and angels (PL. 339), the Hetimasia with SS. Peter and Paul and the figures of the trumpeting angels, St. Onuphrius, St. Anthony the Great, the half-length figures of the Prophet Isaiah, David, and others. Compared to the freer and more pictorial style of Daniel, which still closely adheres to 14th-century traditions, Rublĕv's design is much more rigorous and precise and already tends toward an iconographic treatment of forms. Avoiding bold, asymmetrical compositions, he shows a marked partiality for flowing curves; his favorite form is the circle because of its simplicity and repose, and it is in fact to the circle that he most often assimilates the contour of the head. The faces in his frescoes are particularly expressive, marked as they are by a rare softness and purity.

Following the practice current in Russia at the time, Rublĕv and Daniel painted not only the walls of the Cathedral but also the iconostasis (the restored icons of which are in the Russian Museum in Leningrad and in the Tretyakov Gallery in Moscow). This iconostasis is the largest of all such works surviving today; the monumental icons of the Deësis tier are just over 10 ft. high and constitute a grandiose composition. The towering figures, facing the center, are clearly delineated against the gold background. The rhomboid shape of the figures, which is widest at the waist and taper toward the head and feet, is a striking characteristic of Rublĕv's work. Hardly touching the ground, their bodies concealed by ample, free-flowing garments, the figures thus acquire an incredible lightness. The exquisite coloring of the Deësis icons, conceived as a unified scheme with the paint applied in large, unbroken surfaces, also demonstrates Rublĕv's close association with these icons. The best of them — the Christ, John the Baptist, the apostles Peter and Paul — are by the master's own hand, as is also the Ascension in the festival tier.

Rublĕv's masterpiece is the famous icon of the Trinity, now in the Tretyakov Gallery in Moscow (PL. 336). According to ancient sources, Rublĕv dedicated this icon to the memory of St. Sergius of Radonezh. In all probability it was painted in 1411, the year when a wooden church was erected on the site of Sergius's grave in Moscow. The wooden church was dedicated to the Trinity, as was the limestone cathedral built to replace it in 1423–24. Although a number of researchers are inclined to connect Rublĕv's icon with this stone cathedral and to assign it to the mid-1420s, stylistic considerations make so late a dating implausible. The profound symbolism of Rublĕv's Trinity icon, the intense spirituality and enchanting grace of the angels, and the perfection of the composition with its subtle circular rhythm all combine to make this icon an authentic masterpiece of old-Russian painting.

Rublĕv spent his mature years in the Andronikov Monastery in Moscow, which now houses the museum named after him. There he executed the murals of the Church of the Saviour (which have not survived), and he was also buried there. The historian Pakhomii Logofet records that shortly before his death in 1427, Nikon, the Father Superior of the Trinity-St. Sergius Monastery, had asked Daniel and Rublĕv to do the murals of the new Trinity Cathedral. Feeling that his days were numbered, he hurried the painters to finish their work, and the same Pakhomii asserts that other masters worked along with Daniel and Rublĕv to fulfill Nikon's commission. The iconostasis, which, like the iconostasis of the Cathedral of the Dormition, has a tier of prophets, presents a startling variety of painting styles, thus fully confirming Pakhomii's assertion. Indeed, this work was the result of the combined efforts of a large artel, composed of master artists of both the older and the younger generation. Rublĕv himself painted only three of the icons: the Baptism, the archangel Gabriel, and the apostle Paul. Of the various other icons linked with his name, the ones that exhibit the closest kinship with his style are the Saviour (PL. 337), the Christ in Glory, and the half-figure of the Pantocrator, all in the Tretyakov Gallery, and the icon of Our Lady of Vladimir, preserved in the Vladimir museum.

Rublĕv's work was to have a lasting influence on the development of old-Russian painting. The many specifically Russian traits of his icons and frescoes were a novel feature. They brought about, if not a total break with Byzantine tradition, at least a thoroughgoing creative reinterpretation of it. Intellectually Rublĕv, who lived at a time of national rebirth, was most attracted by an image that represented man as kindhearted, active, and ready to come to the aid of his fellow men. It was this ideal type that the artist depicted in the shape of angels, saints, and sages: to him they were the incarnations of lofty ideas. He succeeded in embodying in these figures the innocent beauty of youth, the resolute strength of maturity, and the noble wisdom of old age, while at the same time consciously avoiding Byzantine sternness and austerity. Behind Byzantine iconographic types he perceived the classical elegance, spirituality and clarity of conception, devoid of any embellishments and compelling in their noble and austere simplicity. Because of his creative interpretation of the Byzantine tradition, Rublĕv was able to go beyond it. For the nervous, colorful modeling of the Byzantines, Rublĕv substituted smooth expanses of sustained color; for their vibrant outline, a simple and sparing contour, which clearly delineated the figures; for the involved Byzantine scheme of highlights, a neat graphic treatment. Rublĕv took his colors not from the traditional color canons but from the surrounding Russian landscape, to the beauty of which he was keenly sensitive. Through these admirable colors and the wonderful rhythm of his lines Rublĕv gave poetic expression to his inner world of feeling and experience, the world of a deeply contemplative painter whose art marks one of the high points in the history of old-Russian painting.

BIBLIOG. M. and V. Uspenskie, Zametki o drevne-russkom ikonopisanii (Notes on Ancient Russian Iconography), St. Petersburg, 1901; N. Likhachev, Manera pis'ma Andreia Rubleva (The Style of Andrei Rublĕv), St. Petersburg, 1907; N. Protasov, Freski na altarnykh stolbakh Uspenskogo sobora v Zvenigorode (Frescoes on the East Pilasters of the Altar of the Cathedral of the Dormition at Zvenigorod), Svetil'nik, 1915, 9–12, pp. 26–48; N. Punin, Andrei Rublev, Apollon, 1915, 2, pp. 1–23; M. Alpatov, La Trinité dans l'art byzantin et l'icone de Roublev, Echos d'Orient, 146, 1926, pp. 150–57; I. Grabar', Andrei Rublev: Ocherk tvorchestva khudozhnika po dannym restavratsionnych rabot 1918–1925 godov (Andrei Rublěv: Essay on the Artist's Activity according to Data Provided by the Restorations of 1918–25), Vosprosy Restavratsii, I, 1926, pp. 7–112; V. Lazarev, O metode raboty v rublevskoi masterskoi (The Method of Work in Rublěv's Studio), Doklady i soobshcheniia filologicheskogo fakul'teta Moskovskogo Gos. Univ., I, 1946, pp. 60–66; L. Ouspensky and W. Lossky, Der Sinn der Ikonen, Bern, Olten, 1952, pp. 201–07; N. Demina, Poeziia zhivopisi Andreia Rubleva (Poetry of Andrei Rublěv's Painting), V zashchitu mira, 41, 1954, pp. 102–06; V. Lazarev, Andrei Rublev i ego shkola (Andrei Rublev and His School), Istoriia russkogo iskusstva (History of Russian Art), III, Moscow, 1955, pp. 102–86; V. Antonova, O pervonachal'nom meste "Troitsy" Andreia Rubleva (The Place of Origin of Andrei Rublěv's "Trinity"), Gos. Tret'iakovskaia Gal. materialy i issledovaniia, I, 1956, pp. 21–43; N. Demina, Cherty geroicheskoi deistvitel'nosti XIV–XV vekov v obrazakh liudei Rubleva i khudozhnikov ego kruga (Elements of Heroic Reality of the 14th–15th Century in the Images of Rublěv and the Painters of His Circle), Trudy otdela drevnerusskoi literatury Inst. russkoi literatury, XII, 1956, pp. 312–24; J. Lebedeva, K voprosu o rannem tvorchestve Rubleva (Problem of the Early Works of Rublěv), Iskusstvo, 1957, 4, pp. 66–69; M. Alpatov, Andrej Roublev e l'arte bizantina, L'Arte, LVII, 1958, pp. 251–78; M. Alpatov, Ikona "Sreteniia" iz ikonostasa Troitskogo sobora Troitse-Sergievoi Lavry (The Icon of the Presentation in the Temple from the Iconostasis of the Cathedral of the Trinity in the Troitse-Sergievoi Monastery), Trudy otdela drevnerusskoi literatury Inst. russkoi literatury, XIV, 1958, pp. 557–64; M. Alpatov, La valeur classique de Roublev, Comm, IX, 1958, pp. 25–37; N. Kazakova, Svedeniia ob ikonakh Rublev, nakhodivshikhsia v Volokolamskom monastyre v XVI veke (Notes on Rublěv's Icons Found in the Monastery of Volokolamsk in the 16th Century), Trudy otdela drevnerusskoi literatury Inst. russkoi literatury, XIV, 1958, pp. 310–11; M. Alpatov, Andrei Rublev, Moscow, 1959; V. Lazarev, La Trinité d'André Roublev, GBA, LIV, 1959, pp. 289–300; N. Demina, Freski Andreia Rubleva vo Vladimire (Frescoes of Andrei Rublěv at Vladimir), Dekorativnoe iskusstvo, 1960, 8, pp. 5–9; M. Il'in, Iz istorii moskovskoi arkhitektury vremeni Andrei Rubleva (History of Moscow Architecture at the Time of Andrei Rublěv), Voprosy istorii, 1960; Vystavka, posviashchennaia shestisotletnemy iubileiu Andrei Rublev (Exhibition Dedicated to the 6th Centenary of Andrei Rublěv), Moscow, 1960 (cat.); J. Blankoff, André Roubliov et l'art de la Russie ancienne, Rev. Univ. de Bruxelles, N.S., XIV, 1961–62, pp. 204–27 (bibliog.); J. Keim, André Roublev, Jardin de l'art, 77, 1961, pp. 40–47; J. Keim, André Roublev: Le maître de l'icone russe, Critique, XVII, 1961, pp. 226–48; K. Onasch, Ikonen, Berlin, 1961, pp. 19–22, pls. 95–104; M. Tikhomirov, Andrei Rublev i ego epokha (Andrei Rublěv and His Era), Voprosy istorii, 1961, 1, pp. 3–17; J. Lebedeva, Andrej Rubljow, Dresden, 1962; K. Onasch, Das Problem des Lichtes in der Ikonenmalerei Andrej Rublevs, Berlin, 1962.

Victor LAZAREV

Illustrations: PLS. 336–339.

RUGS. See TAPESTRY AND CARPETS.

RUISDAEL (RUYSDAEL), SALOMON AND JACOB VAN. Members of a family of Dutch landscape painters of the 17th century whose original name, De Goyer (or De Gooyer), was changed to Ruysdael, a name probably derived from the Castle of Ruysendael or Ruysdael near Blaricum, where the family originally lived. Salomon van Ruysdael was the son of Jacob Jansz. de Goyer, a wealthy burgher of Naarden, and Jacob van Ruisdael was the son of Salomon's brother Izaäck, a Haarlem ebonist and art dealer. Jacob has sometimes been confused with his cousin, Salomon's son, whose name was also Jacob, and who was a painter of lesser repute.

SUMMARY. Salomon van Ruysdael (col. 609). Jacob van Ruisdael (col. 611).

SALOMON VAN RUYSDAEL. Salomon was born at Naarden, probably within the years 1600–1602. In 1623 he was enrolled (as Salomon de Gooyer) as a master painter in the painters' guild of Haarlem, and in a publication on Haarlem dating from 1628 he was already praised as a landscape painter. He remained throughout his life in Haarlem, where he was held in high esteem as a burgher and played a predominant part in the guild. He was buried in Haarlem on Nov. 3, 1670. He usually spelled his name Ruysdael or Ruijsdael (never Ruisdael as his nephew Jacob did), but during the years 1628–31 he signed his name Ruyesdael. Later he sometimes signed his work with the monogram SVR.

Owing to a long series of dated works Salomon's evolution can be quite easily followed. The artistic environment of his formative years was that of the Haarlem landscape painters, who in the second and third decades of the 17th century played an important part in the development of realism in Dutch landscape painting through their growing interest in the surrounding countryside (see BAROQUE ART).

Two leading painters of this group so clearly influenced Ruysdael's early work that, although there are no documents mentioning his teachers, it can be assumed that he was their apprentice. The first was Esaias van de Velde (ca. 1590–1630), who about 1616 was the teacher of Jan van Goyen (q.v.) in Haarlem. Although Ruysdael yielded much less to his influence than Jan van Goyen did, he may well have been his apprentice during the years prior to 1618, when Esaias van de Velde left Haarlem to settle in The Hague. The second painter was Pieter de Molijn (1595–1661), who in 1616 entered the Haarlem guild and after 1618 seems to have succeeded Esaias van de Velde as the leading Haarlem landscape painter. It is very possible that Ruysdael finished his training in Pieter de Molijn's studio before he established himself as an independent painter.

The earliest known work by Salomon van Ruysdael, an elaborate picture of a horse market in a Dutch village, is dated 1626 and still shows much affinity with Esaias van de Velde's work. It was followed in 1627 by some winter scenes with figures on the ice (Vienna, Kunsthist. Mus.), a traditional subject in Flemish and Dutch art but here treated in a more modern fashion than, for instance, in Jan van Goyen's contemporaneous work. The theme is simplified, and stress is placed more on the landscape and less on the human action that takes place in it. Just at this time there arose what is known in the history of Dutch painting as the new Haarlem landscape style. This new conception, with its preference for simple motifs from the sand dune area near Haarlem, was introduced by Pieter de Molijn in his paintings and etchings of 1628. The human figure, which before then had always been the center of attention, conferring an anecdotal character on the composition, is now subordinated to the purely scenic data, with rural houses, huts, and fences in a wood silhouetted against a rising glow from the dune lands. A marked diagonal composition dominates the picture, as well as a prevailing use of brown, straw-colored, and gray-green hues. This new type of dune landscape with its authentically domestic character was immediately adopted by other painters. Along with Pieter de Molijn, Jan van Goyen and Salomon van Ruysdael were the chief exponents of this important innovation. Pieter de Molijn's influence was strongest in the years up to 1630. A further development gave rise to a landscape art that, while retaining the diagonal composition, gained in space and clarity through a greater sense of distance and a wider perspective. It is probable that the influence of Adam Elsheimer (1578–1620), which largely dominated the popular art of engraving, also greatly contributed to this spatialization of perspective, in which the outlines of the closely adjoining, rounded trees receding into the distance play an important part.

Among other themes, Ruysdael favored the traditional motifs of the cart track leading past a village or a stop near a country inn, an example of which is the landscape in Berlin dating from 1631 (PL. 340). Later he often repeated such motifs, as in the picture of 1660 in the Rijksmuseum, Amsterdam. For Ruysdael the stop at an inn always remained essentially a landscape, whereas his fellow townsman Isaac van Ostade (1621–49) treated this motif in the manner of a genre painter. A comparison of Ruysdael's two paintings of 1631 and 1660 clearly shows what profound changes his style underwent. In his early work the forms are compact, the outlines are tight, and the prevailing tones are brown, green, and gray. Later, the forms gradually grow looser and the elements more casually distributed. The composition is more open and vivid, the trees stand out against the sky like fine lace, and the colors become brighter and more effective, with a more natural deep green in the trees and with reddish or light rosy clouds against the pale blue sky.

Another motif that became classic with Ruysdael is the riverscape (PL. 341), which appeared about 1630 and initially showed the same strictly diagonal composition as the dune landscape. There are obvious affinities between Ruysdael's river paintings and the approximately contemporaneous work of Jan van Goyen, whose evolution, then as well as before 1630, ran mostly parallel to Ruysdael's. It is difficult to ascertain which of the two was the giver and which the taker. A comparison of their dated works suggests that the influence was mutual. When superficially viewed their paintings show striking similarities. There is, however, an important difference. Generally speaking, Jan van Goyen's work is more dashingly conceived, with greater technical facility and more temperament, while Ruysdael's work is more sober, more earnest, and more meticulously painted. In the figures he is weaker than Jan van Goyen, but, especially in his later work, he is often more monumental in his general composition. His colors are more vivid and varied than those of his generally monotonous colleague, who was above all a draftsman. It is without doubt a telling fact that numerous brilliant drawings by Jan van Goyen have been acknowledged, while agreement has not yet been reached on the attribution of a relatively small number of drawings to Salomon van Ruysdael.

After the 1640s, when Ruysdael's art reached full maturity, his work is characterized by rich colors and vivid, open composition. By this time Jan van Goyen's and Ruysdael's ways had parted, and in some respects Ruysdael's painting was now closer to the art of his nephew Jacob, who was at the very outset of his career. This can be seen from, among other things, the care with which — perhaps following like Jacob the example of Cornelis Hendricksz. Vroom — he began analyzing trees, which he had earlier treated merely as a decorative mass. A good example of his art during this period is the river landscape dating from 1647 (Brussels, Mus. Royaux des Beaux-Arts). The motionless surface of the water in the flat Dutch countryside, with a wide horizon below a high cloudy sky and the ferryboat in the foreground near a bank lined with tall trees, became one of Ruysdael's favorite subjects. It was well suited to that mastery in the depiction of light and atmosphere for which he is chiefly famous. He knew how to express in a convincing way the poetry of this typical Dutch scene.

About 1653 winter landscapes also reappeared in his works (VI, PL. 72). In these, as well as in the river landscapes, there are often architectural elements based on existing buildings. Obviously Ruysdael, who is generally supposed to have undertaken no travels abroad, visited many parts of his own country, especially along the rivers. The noteworthy buildings or ruins that he saw on his trips are often easily recognizable in his paintings, but sometimes he takes great liberties in rendering the geographical situation, so that the paintings are not merely topographical (Houbraken, 1721). In a winter landscape dating from 1661 (Stechow, 1938, pl. 27) a view near Amsterdam has been recognized. Also, it was probably during his later years that he executed the large undated paintings of river mouths with sailing craft in calm weather (a genre in which Jan van Goyen had preceded him), as well as a small number of still lifes with dead game, a rather unexpected addition to his otherwise homogeneous repertoire.

JACOB VAN RUISDAEL. Jacob was born in Haarlem in 1628 or 1629. This supposition is based on a document concerning expert advice given by him in 1661, when his age was stated as thirty-two. When he entered the Haarlem painters' guild in 1648, he must have been nearly twenty. In June, 1657, according to documents that concern his joining of the Reformed Church, he was living in Amsterdam. In 1659 he acquired citizenship in Amsterdam and stayed there until his death. In October, 1676, he was proclaimed doctor of medicine at Caen in France, whereupon his name was entered in the "Series Nominum Doctorum" in Amsterdam, and he seems also to have practiced this profession with success. He died a bachelor, presumably in Amsterdam, and was buried in Haarlem on Mar. 14, 1682. It was long believed that he ended his days poor and insane in the Haarlem workhouse, but this was actually the lot of his cousin and namesake, the son of Salomon van Ruysdael, with whom he has often been confused. Jacob always spelled his name Ruisdael, and wherever his work bears the form Ruysdael the signature must be attributed to another hand. He also often signed with the monogram JvR.

No facts are known about Jacob van Ruisdael's apprenticeship. His father, Izaäck de Goyer (later changed to Ruysdael), was an ebonist and art dealer in Haarlem. It seems certain that he also painted but it has not yet been possible to ascribe any paintings to him conclusively. In all likelihood Jacob received his first lessons from him. Otherwise it appears that he was trained and guided by his uncle Salomon, who emerged in the 1640s as an outstanding, if not the most important, landscape painter in Haarlem. Ruisdael was already creating masterpieces of rare perfection at such an early age that this precocious maturity would seem inconceivable if his own dating did not preclude all doubts. The problem of chronology arises in connection with the works of his great classical period, after he settled in Amsterdam, when he dated only a few paintings. Therefore, the dating of his most famous works is mere guesswork, and opinions on the subject differ widely. From 1646 until his Amsterdam period he often dated his work, so that it is generally possible to place his early undated paintings by comparison. An example of this is the small dune landscape in the Rijksmuseum in Amsterdam, which was probably painted between 1647 and 1649. In those years he also did a number of drawings and etchings of stunted oak trees. One of the most famous etchings, *The Cornfield* (Paris, Petit-Palais, Coll. Dutuit), is one of the masterpieces of 17th-century Dutch engraving.

In his youth Ruisdael was greatly influenced by his fellow townsman Cornelis Hendricksz. Vroom (1590/91–1661). Ruisdael shared Vroom's predilection for trees, not merely as a decorative conventionalized element of composition but also as an individual phenomenon deserving careful elaboration. One of the most obvious characteristics of his earlier work is the curiosity with which he analyzed the form and color of trees and his faculty for rendering them lifelike. This attitude toward nature was new, and Ruisdael was one of its greatest exponents. The previous generation (e.g., Pieter de Molijn, Jan van Goyen, and Salomon van Ruysdael) had, it is true, already liberated landscape from traditional academic formulas and introduced in their works the simple realism of the Dutch canals and dune lands; but there remained a tendency toward a decorative interpretation of nature, and the motifs resulting from the academic tradition had not been quite forgotten. Ruisdael now became the leader of the younger generation, which definitively broke with these last vestiges of manneristic stylization, replacing it with a new realism and feeling for nature. Later, Vroom in his turn underwent the influence of young Ruisdael, together with many others.

Besides the particular attention paid to trees there was also another element in this significant renewal: the artist's feeling for nature came to be revealed in the whole of the landscape he painted. Ruisdael rendered nature in a direct, one might almost say an unselective, way. This can clearly be seen in the dune landscape mentioned above. The scene, with the dune path meandering near the low oak grove, is a fragment of the landscape, apparently randomly chosen, as it appeared to the painter on his travels. Its character of "seen" reality (as opposed to "imagined" reality) gives this landscape a new vividness and life.

Before he moved to Amsterdam, in about 1650, Ruisdael undertook a journey to Bentheim in Germany, just across the Dutch border, probably accompanied by Claes (Nicolaes) Pietersz. Berchem (1620–83), a close friend who sometimes painted the figures in his landscapes. On this trip, which took him through Gelderland and perhaps also through the district of Cleve, he saw hilly countrysides, with huge forests and turbulent mountain streams, picturesque water mills, half-timbered houses, and impressive castles. He subsequently elaborated all these motifs in four etchings, which were his final productions as an engraver, and in numerous paintings. The intimate and incidental character of his earliest landscapes was now replaced by an increasing monumentality, a deliberate structure, in which light and shade, masses, and space reached a classical equilibrium, an ideal harmony. But the realistic elaboration of the elements with which he composed his paintings still commanded his attention; in this respect he remained true to his old ambitions. The large landscape with the Castle of Bentheim of 1653 (Rosenberg, 1928, fig. 18) is not the first (which dates from 1651) but is surely the most impressive evidence concerning this trip. A comparison with the site, which still exists, shows that Ruisdael has subjected the view of the castle to the caprices of his imagination, exaggerating the height of the hill in order to achieve a romantic effect.

Possibly soon after settling down in Amsterdam Ruisdael painted *The Morass* (Leningrad, The Hermitage), an undated work in which gnarled oaks rise above a reedless expanse of water. This is merely one example from a long series of forest landscapes, which served as models for much later painters — for instance, in France and the Netherlands in the 19th century.

During this first period in Amsterdam Ruisdael's relationship with Meindert Hobbema (1638–1709; q.v.) began. For some years before 1660 Hobbema was Ruisdael's apprentice and journeyman, and subsequently they always remained on friendly terms. After 1660 the younger artist continued to imitate Ruisdael's art and more than once painted the same landscape motifs as his master; but he confined himself primarily to wooded landscapes, farms surrounded by many trees, and water mills, whereas Ruisdael was developing great versatility in his choice of subjects. It seems that Ruisdael's large waterfalls in rocky mountain settings (PL. 342) were very popular. Most of them probably date from the 1660s and show an obvious affinity with the torrents and mountains painted in approximately the same period by his fellow townsman Allart van Everdingen (1621–75). It is generally accepted that Allart van Everdingen introduced this type of landscape after his Scandinavian journey early in the 1640s and that Ruisdael more or less followed his example, stimulated by the success that these landscapes achieved. Allart van Everdingen stressed the Scandinavian elements in his compositions, introducing log cabins, for example. Ruisdael replaced these with his German travel recollections and succeeded in making his subjects more dramatic. *The Waterfall* (Brunswick, Germany, Herzog-Anton-Ulrich-Mus.) is an example of this type of landscape, which with his forest landscapes makes him, to a certain extent, a forerunner of the romantic painters of the 19th century.

Among Ruisdael's romantic and lyrical landscapes, the so-called *Jewish Cemetery* occupies a place apart. Of the two versions in Detroit (Institute of Arts) and Dresden, the latter is especially well-known (PL. 343). This work delighted Goethe, who recognized its poetic qualities, full of the symbolism of life's transience. In fact, this composition, with its dramatic light effects, is regarded as one of the most beautiful of Ruisdael's landscapes. The question of the date of this painting and the reason for its unusual conception has been debated at great length, but the extremely divergent suggestions are all inconclusive. The tombs, which are placed in an imaginary setting, have been identified as some of the oldest extant tombs in the Portuguese Jewish burial ground at Ouderkerk, near Amsterdam. They are exact reproductions of one of the two drawings that Ruisdael did on the spot and that were printed by Abraham Bloteling in 1670. Perhaps these drawings were made early in the 1660s, when Ruisdael was interested in the topography of Amsterdam and drew a number of pictures of the old ramparts, which were demolished in those years because of the town's rapid expansion.

The early dune landscapes and sylvan scenes, so intimate in character, and the impressive landscapes that Ruisdael painted after his travels abroad had one thing in common notwithstanding their diversity: his great interest in trees. But Ruisdael's repertoire also included quite different motifs: stormy seascapes with sailing ships, Dutch winter landscapes such as the one in Amsterdam (IX, PL. 14), beach landscapes, wide panoramas of the flat Dutch countryside, and views of towns. *The Shore at Egmond-aan-Zee* (PL. 343) was probably painted in the 1670s judging by the clothes of the figures, which are generally supposed to have been painted by someone else, as was probably often the case with Ruisdael's paintings. He painted Egmond more than once. Views of this small town on the North Sea are already found among his earliest paintings.

The ruins of the old castle called "Slot op de Hoef" in the Egmond area are to be seen in a number of splendid drawings as well as in several paintings. There is some kinship between the composition of the beach landscapes and the famous *Mill at Wijk bij Duurstede* (PL. 344), a Dutch riverscape that is conceived in a spirit totally different from that of his uncle Salomon's friendly and intimate riverscapes; for Jacob gave a heroic quality to the mills, stressing their obstinate steadfastness in wind and weather.

In Ruisdael's town pictures, topographical peculiarities and the clothing of the figures often help in the general dating. Thus there are a number of closely related views of the dam of Amsterdam, which Ruisdael probably painted in the 1670s. But the city of Amsterdam had already fascinated him much earlier. The view of the Buiten-Amstel (Budapest, Mus. of Fine Arts) was probably painted before 1661, and about 1665 he painted a view across the Damrak toward the harbor on the Ij, probably from the roof of the new town hall near the dam (Bowood, England, Marquess of Lansdowne Coll.). This painting, for which Ruisdael made a sketch on the spot (Amsterdam, Rijksmus., Prentenkabinet), shows the town in a wide panorama from a high vantage point. It can therefore be considered as a counterpart of one of the numerous panoramas of the Haarlem area that Ruisdael probably began to paint at the same time. These panoramas, in which he was perhaps inspired by the work of his fellow townsman Philips de Koninck (1619-88), include the views from the top of the dunes near Overveen and over the flat country with the famous linen-bleaching works toward the town of Haarlem and the Cathedral of St. Bavo. These extensive views, below a high cloudy sky through which the sun breaks here and there, throwing streaks of light over the countryside and the town, are among Ruisdael's undisputed masterpieces. Despite the spaciousness they convey their dimensions are actually quite limited, and they are in fact painted in a more subtle style then Ruisdael generally used, yet with rich colors to suggest, for example, the play of sunlight on red roofs.

With a few variations Ruisdael often painted the view toward Haarlem, of which there is a fine example in The Hague (PL. 344). Although the painter, according to an inventory of 1669, already had this subject in his repertoire before that period, it is fairly certain that some versions were painted much later. This assumption is supported by the painting in the Staatliche Museen, Berlin, which is closely related to the above-mentioned picture in The Hague. The Berlin *View of Haarlem* seems above all to be the counterpart of the *View on the Amstel near Amsterdam* (Cambridge, England, Fitzwilliam Mus.), or perhaps of another version of this picture. The *View on the Amstel* has dimensions similar to those of the Berlin *View of Haarlem* and is also a panorama seen from above, while the two paintings also show striking similarities in the composition of the foreground and the treatment of the sporadic sunlight. The *View on the Amstel* can, on the basis of topographic peculiarities, be dated with certainty after 1675, which means that the Berlin *View of Haarlem* must also be among Ruisdael's last works. It is above all these panoramic paintings that have earned the painter the title of "portraitiste de la Hollande," as he was called nearly a century ago by Eugène Fromentin.

BIBLIOG. *Salomon*: R. Grosse, Die holländische Landschaftskunst 1600–1650, Berlin, Leipzig, 1925, pp. 79–87; H. F. Wijnman, Het leven der Ruysdaels (I), Oud Holland, XLIX, 1932, pp. 49–60; K. E. Simon, ThB, s.v.; W. Stechow, Die "Pellekussenpoort" bei Utrecht auf Bildern von J. van Goyen und S. van Ruysdael, Oud Holland, LV, 1938, pp. 202–08; W. Stechow, Salomon van Ruysdael, Berlin, 1938; A River Landscape by Salomon van Ruysdael, B. Minneapolis Inst. of Arts, XXXV, 1946, pp. 4–7; W. Stechow, Het vroegst bekende werk van Salomon van Ruysdael, Kunsthist. Meded., II, 1947, pp. 36–40; H. C. de Bruyn, Jr., "Out poortie tot Uytregt": Thema met variaties op een architectonisch motief in landschappen van Salomon van Ruysdael en Jan van Goyen, Op de Uitkijk, Wageningen, 1958–59, p. 269; J. W. Niemeijer, Het topografisch element in enkele riviergezichten van Salomon van Ruysdael nader beschouwd, Oud Holland, LXXIV, 1959, pp. 51–56; H. J. J. Scholtens, Salomon van Ruysdael in de contreien van Holland's landengte, Oud Holland, LXXVII, 1962, pp. 1–11. *Jacob*: A. Houbraken, De Groote Schouburgh der Nederlantsche Kunstschilders en Schilderessen, III, Amsterdam, 1721, p. 65; J. W. Goethe, Ruisdael als Dichter, Morgenblatt für gebildete Stände, 107, May 3, 1816 [repr. in J. W. Goethe, Schriften zur Kunst (ed. E. Beutler), Zurich, 1954.

pp. 670–76]; E. Fromentin, Les maîtres d'autrefois, Paris, 1876, pp. 243–59 (Eng. trans., A. Boyle, New York, 1948, pp. 136–46); E. Dutuit, Manuel de l'amateur d'estampes, VI, Paris, London, 1885, pp. 275–84; C. Hofstede de Groot, Beschreibendes und kritisches Verzeichnis der Werke der hervoragendsten holländischen Maler des XVII. Jahrhunderts, IV, Esslingen a.N., 1911 (Eng. trans., IV, London, 1912); W. A. Bradley, The Etchings of Jacob Ruysdael, Print Collector's Q., VII, 1917, pp. 153–74; W. R. Valentiner, The Cemetery by Jacob van Ruysdael, B. Detroit Inst. of Arts, VII, 1926, pp. 55–58; J. Rosenberg, Jacob van Ruisdael, Berlin, 1928; J. Zwarts, Het motief van Jacob van Ruisdael's "Jodenkerkhof," Oud Jb, VIII, 1928, pp. 232–49; K. E. Simon, Jacob van Ruisdael, Berlin, Lankwitz, 1930; H. F. Wijnman, Het leven der Ruysdaels, Oud Holland, XLIX, 1932, pp. 49–60, 173–81, 258–75 (rev. by J. Rosenberg, ZfKg, II, 1933, pp. 237–38); H. Gerson, The Development of Ruisdael, BM, LXV, 1934, pp. 76–80; K. E. Simon, ThB, s.v.; K. E. Simon, Wann hat Ruisdael die Bilder des Judenfriedhofs gemalt?, Festschrift zum 70. Geburtstag von Adolph Goldschmidt, Berlin, 1935, pp. 158–63; K. E. Simon, Ruisdael aanschouwt Amsterdam, Historia, V, 1939, pp. 23–25; W. Martin, De Hollandsche schilderkunst in de 17. eeuw, 2d ed., II, Amsterdam, 1942, pp. 293–310; W. F. H. Oldewelt, Jacob Ruisdael en zijn Damgezichten, Amsterdamsche Archiefvondsten, Amsterdam, 1942, p. 163; D. C. Rich, Two Great Romantic Landscapes, B. Art Inst. of Chicago, XLIII, 1948, pp. 20–22; L. J. Roggeveen, Een gezicht op het Damrak van Jacob van Ruisdael, Phoenix, III, 1948, pp. 91–94; E. Smith, An Early Landscape by Ruisdael, B. Currier Gall. of Art, Dec. 1950, pp. 1–4; H. Hijmans, Wijk bij Duurstede, Rotterdam, The Hague, 1951; A. Trèves, Le moulin de Ruysdael, Le Peintre, 18, 1951, p. 5; H. Rosenau, The Dates of Jacob van Ruisdael's "Jewish Cemeteries," Oud Holland, LXXIII, 1958, pp. 241–42; J. Rosenberg, A Seascape by Jacob van Ruisdael, BMFA, LVI, 1958, pp. 144–46; F. Stampfli, An Early Drawing by Jacob van Ruisdael, AQ, XXII, 1959, pp. 160–63; N. MacLaren, The Dutch School (Nat. Gall. Cat.), London, 1960, pp. 353–71.

C. J. DE BRUYN KOPS

Illustrations: PLS. 340–344.

RUSSIAN ART. See BYZANTINE ART; SIBERIAN CULTURES; SLAVIC ART; UNION OF SOVIET SOCIALIST REPUBLICS; UNION OF SOVIET SOCIALIST REPUBLICS: MODERN MOVEMENTS.

RYDER, ALBERT PINKHAM. American painter (b. New Bedford, Mass., Mar. 19, 1847; d. Elmhurst, N.Y., Mar. 28, 1917). Descended on the paternal and maternal sides from old Cape Cod families, many of whom had followed the sea, Ryder was brought up in New Bedford, then the world's greatest whaling port; from childhood the sea played a large part in his consciousness. His education ended with grammar school, owing to oversensitive eyes. Without having any regular art instruction, he began painting landscapes outdoors. About 1870 he settled permanently in New York. For four years he studied at the National Academy of Design, with informal teaching by the portraitist William E. Marshall. Ryder's early paintings, first exhibited in 1873, were small landscapes, usually with figures or cattle: reminiscences of the New England country, marked by visionary poetry, childlike simplicity of style, and a highly personal sense of form and color.

In 1877 he made his first visit abroad, spending a month in London. In the summer of 1882 he toured the English cathedral towns, and then, with two friends, visited France, Spain (with a trip to Tangier), Italy, and Switzerland. Two more visits, in 1887 and 1896, were primarily sea voyages, with only two weeks in London each time. Thus his total foreign experience was much less than most of his American contemporaries'.

About 1880 Ryder embarked on imaginative subjects, drawn from the Bible, classical mythology, and the poetry of the English-speaking world — the early ballads, Chaucer, Shakespeare (his favorite poet), and the 19th-century romantics, Coleridge, Byron, Campbell, Moore, Poe, and Tennyson. Wagner's operas inspired two of his finest paintings, *Siegfried and the Rhine Maidens* (I, PL. 109) and *The Flying Dutchman* (Washington, D.C., Nat. Coll. of Fine Arts). These imaginative works were not "literary" in the usual sense; they were pictorial dramas based on great themes, but changed into intensely personal conceptions. In all of them nature played an essential role. The sea haunted him all his life, in his recurring image of a lonely ship sailing moonlit waters. But his principal works, such as *Macbeth and the Witches* and *Resurrection* (both, Washington, D.C., Phillips Coll.), *Christ Appearing to Mary* and *Jonah*

(both, Washington, D.C., Nat. Coll. of Fine Arts), *The Temple of the Mind* (Buffalo, N.Y., Albright-Knox Art Gall.), *The Story of the Cross* (Glen Head, L.I., N.Y., Guennol Coll.), *Constance* (Boston, Mus. of Fine Arts), *The Race Track* (Cleve. Mus.), and *The Forest of Arden* (Met. Mus.), were more than simple nature poems; their central themes were human or often superhuman, for Ryder's art was fundamentally religious. He was a mystic who transformed the external world into pure subjective imagery. Never confined to literal naturalism, he used nature more freely than any other 19th-century American artist. His instinct for design, the richness of his forms, and his sense of rhythmic movement made him one of the purest plastic creators of his time. Though without the tremendous range of a Delacroix, he was a true if belated son of the romantic movement.

As a person, Ryder was completely unworldly. He cared nothing for success or money, he never married, and in later life he became a recluse.

Ryder worked for years over his pictures, and his lifework totaled only about 165 paintings. Because of his inadequate technical knowledge, many of his pictures have deteriorated physically. He has been extensively forged, and the false works outnumber the genuine about five to one.

The largest groups of his works are in the Metropolitan Museum and the Brooklyn Museum in New York and in the Phillips Collection and the National Collection of Fine Arts in Washington.

BIBLIOG. F. F. Sherman, Albert Pinkham Ryder, New York, 1920; L. Goodrich, Albert P. Ryder, New York, 1959; Corcoran Gallery of Art, Albert Pinkham Ryder, Washington, D.C., 1961 (cat.; text by L. Goodrich).

Lloyd GOODRICH

SAARINEN, ELIEL AND EERO. Finnish-American planners, architects, and industrial designers (Eliel, b. 1873, Rantasalmi, Finland; d. 1950, Bloomfield Hills, Mich.; his son, Eero, b. 1910, Kirkkonummi, Finland; d. 1961, Bloomfield Hills, Mich.).

After studying painting and architecture in Helsinki (1893–97), Eliel began architectural practice in 1896 with H. Gesellius and A. E. Lindgren. His designs for the Finnish Pavilion (1899–1900) at the Paris Exposition, the National Museum (1902) in Helsinki, and the Helsinki Central Station established his European reputation. The station, for which he won the commission in a competition in 1904, was constructed between 1910 and 1914 but was not used until after World War I. With its conspicuous tower, the structure is a landmark in the hub of the city. Immense arches usher travelers into huge vaulted spaces bounded by clean surfaces trimmed with restrained abstract decoration, prophetic of American practice in civic architecture of the 1930s. Antitraditional, yet monumental, the train station is one of the best early-20th-century attempts to establish forms appropriate to the new century; thus it bears ideological links with the contemporaneous work of the Dutch architect H. P. Berlage, the Austrians Joseph Olbrich and Otto Wagner, and the German Peter Behrens. The formal freshness of Saarinen's design can be appreciated by comparing it with the historicizing approach to the same problem in the Romanized Pennsylvania Station (1906–10) in New York by McKim, Mead & White (q.v.).

Eliel became known in the United States through his second-prize-winning design in the Chicago *Tribune* competition of 1922. With its elegant set-back outline and crisp, simplified detail, it seemed remarkably fresh compared with the Gothicized project designed and executed by the Americans John Mead Howells and Raymond M. Hood. Although Saarinen's design was not realized he won a moral victory and wide acclaim; his composition greatly influenced subsequent American skyscraper design and won praise from the early skyscraper master Louis Sullivan.

After emigrating to the United States with his family in 1922 Eliel designed several stylistically conservative but humanistically rich environments, such as the Cranbrook School for Boys (1926–30) and the Cranbrook Academy of Art (1926–31), both in Bloomfield Hills, Mich. His later works, done in collaboration with Eero, were oriented more toward the "international style." Kleinhans Music Hall (1938) in Buffalo is geometrically purer and structurally more expressive than Eliel's early works. The Tabernacle Church of Christ (1940–42) in Columbus, Ind., a large complex of vertical and horizontal blocks that intersect around a tower and a water pool, is similar to the Hilversum (Netherlands) Town Hall, designed and built during the 1920s by the Dutch architect Dudok. He was also designer of the similar, though smaller, Christ Lutheran Church in Minneapolis, Minn. (I, PL. 95).

Eero studied sculpture in Paris (1930–31) and architecture at Yale (B.F.A., 1934) and worked in his father's office from 1936 to 1950, when he formed Eero Saarinen and Associates, which he headed until his death. The younger Saarinen first gained recognition in 1948, when he won the competition for the Jefferson National Expansion Memorial (completed 1965) in St. Louis, Mo., with a design conspicuous for its enormous stainless-steel arch. He designed the large-scale General Motors Technical Institute (I, PL. 94; IV, PL. 198), an industrial campus organized along the classical lines of Mies van der Rohe's Illinois Institute of Technology campus (X, PL. 59) in Chicago. With the Massachusetts Institute of Technology Auditorium and Chapel (1953–56), Cambridge, Mass., the younger Saarinen developed the first major shell construction in the United States. Also famous as a designer of industrially produced furniture (I, PL. 135; VIII, PL. 51), he gained world-wide attention as an architect with his designs for the United States Embassy buildings in Oslo (1955–59) and London (1955–60). His ingenuity in structural engineering became apparent in the reinforced-concrete Ingalls Hockey Rink (XIII, PL. 229) at Yale University, and the Trans World Airlines Flight Center (XI, PL. 398) at Kennedy International Airport, New York City.

But it was not until the end of his life, with the design of Dulles International Airport (1958–62; XIII, PL. 229) at Chantilly, Va., that Eero achieved an indisputably high level of architectural performance. The first facility organized specifically for jet travel, this airport serving Washington, D.C., marks a radical departure from the conventional terminal. It is designed for maximum ground efficiency, enabling travelers to filter from private or public transportation into an enormous space, defined by concrete piers that support a canopy slung between them, visually reminiscent of the roof of Le Corbusier's chapel at Ronchamp, France (I, PL. 381). After the ticket, baggage, and customs formalities, the passenger is whisked in a mobile lounge to the aircraft waiting some distance away; maximum efficiency is maintained by separating passenger and aircraft handling. From its imposing over-all form down to its most trivial details, the airport forms an environment that is controlled, yet expressive of its dynamic function. A symbolic gateway to the United States, Dulles Airport is a highly successful fusion of modern technology and monumentality, a form as appropriate to its task as the equally successful Helsinki Central Station; and both are of the highest quality for their periods.

The Saarinens were among the many Europeans who not only enriched the physical environment of their adopted country but also made important contributions to Western architecture from their home base in the United States.

WRITINGS. Eliel Saarinen, The City: Its Growth. Its Decay. Its Future, New York, 1943; Eliel Saarinen, Search For Form, New York, 1948.

BIBLIOG. A. Christ-Janer, Eliel Saarinen, Chicago, 1948; A. B. Saarinen, ed., Eero Saarinen on His Work, New Haven, 1962; A. Temko, Eero Saarinen, New York, 1962.

Theodore M. BROWN

SAENREDAM, PIETER JANSZOON. Dutch painter of architectural subjects (b. Assendelft, June 9, 1597; buried Haarlem, May 31, 1665). Saenredam studied with his father, the engraver Jan Pietersz. Saenredam (d. 1607), and with Frans Pietersz. de Grebber, who was his teacher from 1612 to 1622. He entered the Haarlem artists' guild in 1623, served as one of its officers in 1635 and 1640, and was elected dean in 1642. He married

in 1638 but remained childless; his wife died before 1651. Saenredam seems to have traveled a great deal and on the evidence of his works was repeatedly in Utrecht and Alkmaar, as well as in Rhenen, Amsterdam, and 's Hertogenbosch.

Painting architectural scenes was a specialty that had been developed before Pieter Saenredam's work in this field. In contrast to his forerunners, however, Saenredam invariably portrayed existing buildings, especially churches. Examples of such paintings are The Odulphuskerk in Assendelft (Amsterdam, Rijksmus.), The Mariakerk in Utrecht (Rotterdam, Mus. Boymans–Van Beuningen), and The Nieuwe Kerk at Haarlem (Budapest, Mus. of Fine Arts). Occasionally he depicted town halls and other secular structures. He also drew the sky lines of Dutch towns and made topographic drawings that were engraved and used for book illustrations.

Saenredam's art is distinguished by linear accuracy and skillful perspective; it is saved from dryness or pedantry by the artist's innate feeling for delicate patterns of light and a subtle compositional balance. He constantly found new ways of suggesting the quiet beauty of whitewashed Dutch churches, with their arches and vaults flooded with a clear light from large windows (V, PL. 307; XI, PL. 451). Saenredam generally prepared his paintings with painstaking drawings, bearing pertinent information that often included the date on which they were drawn. Unlike the painters of church interiors of the second half of the 17th century, such as E. de Witte, Saenredam used simple color schemes, with little more than gray-blue, brown, or black added to the prevailing white or ivory tones. Figures are used sparingly in his pictures; occasionally the figures seem to have been painted by other artists.

His art is memorable not only for its engaging modesty and purity of color and form; it is also of considerable archaeological importance since many buildings drawn and painted by him are no longer extant, such as the Mariakerk in Utrecht or the old town halls of Amsterdam, Haarlem, and 's Hertogenbosch.

BIBLIOG. P. T. A. Swillens, Pieter Janszoon Saenredam, Amsterdam, 1935.

Julius S. HELD

SAFAVID ART. The Safavid dynasty, of Turkish origin, has been considered the national Persian dynasty of the modern age. Because its founder, Shah Ismā'īl, was crowned while Iran was still under the sway of the Turks and Mongols and because of a period of regency in its closing years, the dynasty has been difficult to date exactly; however, it is generally considered to have lasted from 1502 to 1736. Under Ismā'īl's rule the Shiite doctrine (see ISLAM), which was to become the predominant form of Mohammedanism in Persian Islam, was imposed as the state religion. The dynasty's long duration and the consequent consolidation of its religious and cultural aspects contributed to reinforcing this tradition. The artistic production of these two centuries was, once again, completely Iranian (see IRAN). The only innovation is to be found in attempts at town planning (q.v.), of which there is still evidence, but a new nobility of style is to be found in miniatures, fabrics, and carpets.

SUMMARY. General characteristics (col. 618). Architecture (col. 619). Painting and miniatures (col. 625). Decorative arts (col. 628).

GENERAL CHARACTERISTICS. The 16th and 17th centuries occupy a special place in the history of Iran. Modern criticism has shown the inconsistency of the old theory according to which the Safavid dynasty played the leading role in a conscious renaissance of Iranian nationalism after the country's subjection to "foreign" dynasties for many centuries. The Safavids, whom V. Minorsky (1956) considers as representatives of a "second westward-moving Turkoman wave," were no less Turkish than the Seljuks and Timurids, both ethnically and in their social structure and organization, while their religious thought was also closely allied to similar movements in the Turkoman world (in Western Asia and Anatolia). The Safavids were part of the same medieval and feudal Turko-Iranian cultural tradition, dominated by the Persian spirit in every field, as the Seljuks, Ilkhanids, and Timurids, to whose heritage they succeeded without any break in continuity. The Safavid state was, however, more strongly centralized in its administration, and several economic successes, achieved especially in the period of Shah 'Abbās I (1587–1629), improved, even if only temporarily, the general situation in Iran.

From this point of view Safavid building technique achieved a real "Iranian synthesis," completely harmonizing the canons of the Timurid east (Khorasan and Transoxiana) with those deriving from the "western tradition" (from Isfahan). From the latter came the plan of the four-liwan mosque, which was unknown in Khorasan until an architect from Shiraz built the Jauhar Shād of Meshed (Mashhad) in the reign of Shah Rukh. In western Iran the liwan was conceived, however, merely as an entrance chamber to the domed sanctuary. The feature

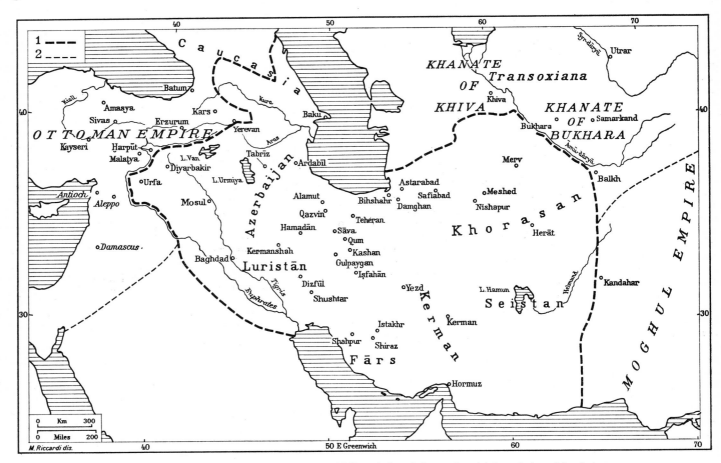

Boundaries of the Safavid empire about 1512. Key: (1) Boundaries of the empire; (2) boundaries of bordering states.

Beginning in the 16th century the artistic culture of Iran entered a new period of splendor, though it was only partial and, if possible, even more aristocratic in nature than the preceding periods. Safavid Persia was in contact with the other countries of the Near East and also with Europe. Political rivalry with the Ottomans (see OTTOMAN SCHOOLS) did not prevent Persian culture from continuing to exert its old fascination on the Turks, but this phenomenon was more marked in the literary than in the artistic sphere. In the East the "Persian style" remained an essential element of the artistic culture of Moghul India (see MOGHUL SCHOOL), which, however, even within the limits of this style, experimented more boldly than Iran. A similar tendency was also to be found in literature. Also, for the first time in many centuries, relations with Central Asia suffered an appreciable decline during this period; yet the Uzbek culture, deriving from the Timurid tradition (see TIMURID ART), completely identical with that which formed the basis of Safavid culture, was merely an internal feature of the Iranian culture of the 16th and 17th centuries and presented only regional stylistic variations.

ARCHITECTURE. The religious architecture of Iran of the 16th and 17th centuries was dominated by the old but still vital canons of large buildings with a central plan and of mosques and madrasahs with four liwans.

that inspired the Safavid architects, who carried to extremes a tendency typical of eastern Iran, was the accentuation of the monumental function of the liwan, expanding and magnifying its proportions at the same time as its verticality was emphasized by gradually narrowing it toward the top. In Khorasan the liwan had, in fact, completely overshadowed the dome, and this local style survived through inertia, in isolated instances, into the 17th century, under the new dynasty. Examples are the liwan of the tomb of Sheik Qutb ad-Dīn Ḥaidar, Turbat-i-Ḥaidarīya, commissioned by Shah Ṣafī (1629–42), and especially the Muṣallā of Meshed (1676–77; PL. 345), of the reign of Shah Sulaymān (PL. 345), where the designer Ḥājjī Shujā', although from Isfahan, aimed solely at creating a liwan impressive for its height and depth, flanked by two more modest domed chambers in the Turkistan style. In most cases, however, the western style acted as a corrective, and the central building emerged from the surrounding architectural mass like a prism or cylinder surmounted by a dome, which was clearly differentiated from its Seljuk prototypes by its more marked vertical thrust (for example, the contemporaneous tomb of Sheik Ji-brā'īl near Ardebil, beginning of the 16th century; Khwāja Rabī' near Meshed, 1622; the Mausoleum of Bābā Rukn al-Dīn in Isfahan, 1629; the shrine of Qadamgāh near Nishapur; the Imāmzāda Hifdātān in Gulpaigān) and sometimes by a well-conceived insertion, in the very mass of the building, of a base consisting of an octagonal section with arches (for example, at Isfahan in the Masjid-i-Shāh, the Masjid-i-Shaykh Luṭfullāh, and the Imāmzāda Ismāʿīl). In the constructional technique of these domes, in isolated buildings with a central plan and in mosques, Transoxianic elements were again included. The dome, which in its typical shape was narrow at the top and slightly swollen in the lower part, in fact contained another dome, both resting on the high, solid cylindrical drums that, even as early as the Transoxianic architecture of the 15th century, had completed the transition from a square ground plan to a circular plan of support. This transition was achieved by the progressive reduplication of the sides of the intermediary forms.

Although an Ilkhanid prototype of this technique was clearly apparent in the khankah of ʿAlā ad-Daula Simnānī in Safiabad near Simnan, the technique was subsequently found almost exclusively in Central Asia and particularly in Samarkand, in the architecture of the Shāh-i-Zind mausoleums (XIV, PL. 69). But the typical elements of Timurid funerary architecture were used by Ṣafavid architects in the classic monumental context of the mosque and madrasah. Inside, false ribs, which served merely to emphasize the decorative rhythm, masked the building process; outside, the architectural composition of the large mosques and madrasahs was completed by a great number of minarets, again decorative, set at the corners of the buildings and along the sides of the liwans. On the minarets, accentuating their verticality in a completely different way from that of the old progressive narrowing of the construction, slim little towers crowned with tiny cupolas rose on small balconies, resting on a corona of stalactites. The decoration in kashi completely covered the walls, vaults, and domes, and the blue that predominated in the 15th century gave place to a wider range of colors. The stalactites had completely lost their functional character and were often multiplied excessively, as in the large western liwan of the Masjid-i-Jāmiʿ in Isfahan.

In architectural decoration great importance was given to calligraphy (PLS. 346, 347; VII, PL. 409), which was transformed into an art of monumental inscription, a development of particular artistic merit in the art of kashi. Its chief exponent was a certain Muḥammad Riẓā-i-Imāmī of Isfahan (1629–30), who worked in Qum, Qazvin, and above all, between 1673 and 1677, in Meshed. It would seem that members of his family practiced this art throughout the entire Safavid period.

Civil architecture followed the classic forms, and attempts at town planning acquired a new importance. Nothing is known, however, about the possible and plausible precedents of these attempts, and so-called Safavid "urban planning" often seems, on further examination, to be merely a particularly grandiose expression of the ideals of an aristocratic mentality that was attracted by garden architecture and open spaces medievally conceived as courses for aristocratic games. At Qazvin almost every trace of the great public works of Ṭahmāsp I (1524–76) has disappeared, so that the most extensive town planning that survives from the Safavid period is that executed by ʿAbbās I in his capital, Isfahan. In the center of the town the rectangular Maidan-i-Shāh, over 1,600 ft. long, became a polo field. Not far away a broad tree-lined avenue, the Chahār Bāgh, was constructed, crossing the maze of muddy alleys in a straight line for 2 miles and extending beyond the Zayinda River over a magnificent bridge leading to the gardens of the southern suburbs. The square and the avenue were almost casually superimposed on the old town, rather than being integrated into its plan, and even the four large buildings (see IRAN, col. 244) symmetrically designed at the center of each of the four sides of the Maidan-i-Shāh seem inspired by principles far removed from those of town planning. Instead of constituting the necessary monumental buttresses of the large open space, their fragile miniature architecture vanishes in it; and instead of firmly delineating the space, they make its limits uncertain.

Another important example of Iranian town planning of this period, the Rigistan in Samarkand (FIG. 622), has more solid and monumental qualities. Overlooking a square, set in the highest part of the town, are the façades of three madrasahs flanked by enormous minarets. The Shīr Dār and the Ṭila Kārī madrasahs are variants of the Timurid madrasah of Ulugh-Beg, which faces the Shīr Dār across the square. Whereas in the Maidan-i-Shāh in Isfahan a light blue predominates in the majolica decoration of the square, here splashes of orange and yellow accentuate the rhythm of the space, marked by three enormous arches. Although the Shīr Dār Madrasah, designed by the architect ʿAbd al-Jagbar between 1619 and 1636, is a copy of the Ulugh-Beg, its kashi decoration is much more barbaric in its opulence and variety — despite the predominance of the Iranian motif of the lion and the sun with a human face — than the restrained decoration of the Timurid madrasah. The Ṭila Kārī Madrasah, which was begun in 1646 and served as the Masjid-i-Jāmiʿ of Samarkand, has a façade in Bukhara style, based on a double line of arches flanking the doorway on both sides.

A similar attempt at monumental layout of the town center is found at Bukhara. There, opposite the Masjid-i-Kalān (early

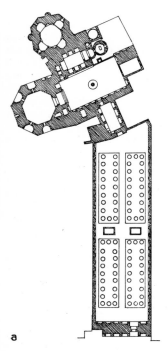
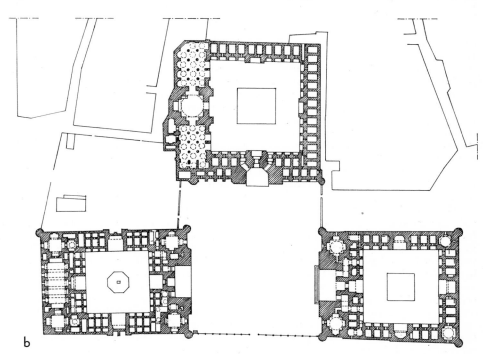

Monumental complexes of the Safavid period. (*a*) Ardebil, the sanctuary, plan; (*b*) Samarkand, the Rigistan, plan (*from Veimarn and Kolpickov, 1961*).

16th cent.), of the classic four-liwan type, is the Mīr-i-Arāb Madrasah (1530–36), with its large doorway in Timurid style, vertically flanked by two rows of niches. Inside, the decoration of the domes in this madrasah assumed new and original characteristics, which were then repeated in other Bukhara buildings of the 16th century (the Kukeltash Madrasah, the Char-Bakr complex, and the Ṭāq-i-Zargarān in the bazaar) and 17th century (Madrasah of 'Abd al-Azīz).

Another interesting monumental ensemble of the Safavid period is the sanctuary of Sheik-Ṣafī in Ardebil (FIG. 621), with its series of courtyards leading to a group of domed polyhedral buildings. The main entrance leads into a large courtyard with a garden, from which a gallery runs into a second inner courtyard onto which open the burial chamber, a large prayer hall, and a mosque with a roof supported by 16 wooden columns, following an architectural plan that came back into fashion at this time.

In Meshed, according to the travel journals of Chardin (1711), Shah 'Abbās I was responsible for many new developments in the sanctuary of Imam 'Ali al-Rizā. He widened the courtyard so that the liwan of Mīr 'Alī Shīr Nawā'ī, formerly in a corner, stood in the center of the boundary wall of the new courtyard, and then built another liwan opposite. He also constructed an avenue from the west gate of the city to the east gate so that in approaching the sanctuary from either direction one passed under a liwan. In addition he created basins and qanats, built a canal into the city, and had a great basin excavated in the middle of the courtyard, from which water flowed toward the eastern avenue. It is not possible, however, to attribute to 'Abbās I the present layout of the sanctuary, which includes many fortuitous superimpositions of works from different periods.

The Safavids also turned their attention to another monumental group of buildings: the sanctuary of Nūr ad-Dīn Ni'mat Allāh at Mahan near Kerman. This has a series of courtyards, two of which have been attributed to 'Abbās I, despite the fact that many of the elements are roughly built of earth. Apart from the nucleus, which dates from the 15th century, the sanctuary's present form derives mainly from the 18th-century Qajar period, as does the great sanctuary in Qum. More worthy of note are the great public works of the Safavid period undertaken in Kerman by the governor and town planner Ganj 'Ali Khān (mosque, baths, bazaar, caravanserai, and madrasah with unusual kashi decoration).

Other notable public works of the Safavid period are the bridges, especially those in Isfahan over the Zayinda River: the bridge of Allāhvardī Khān (1598), with a double row of arches, its rhythm marked by tower-shaped projections; the bridge and aqueduct of Chūbī (1611); and the Khāju bridge of 'Abbās II (1643), also of two stories, which serves as a dam, following an old Iranian architectural tradition dating from the Sassanian period (see SASSANIAN ART). There is also the dam commissioned by 'Abbās I in Qumrud near Kashan. The roads no longer exist, but innumerable caravanserais scattered throughout the country attest to 'Abbās I's desire for a reliable system of communications. Finally, one should mention the ramparts that still surround many old Persian cities, especially the citadel of Bam and the remains of the walls of Yezd.

Few traces remain of the building activity of the first Safavid ruler, Ismā'īl 'Ādilshāh (1500–24). The two great palaces that Ismā'īl built at Khoi and Qazvin have disappeared; the one at Qazvin was last seen in 1681, and even then it may have been only the modifications made by Ismā'īl's successor, Ṭahmāsp, that were seen. The only remaining examples from which to judge the work of the first Safavid ruler are a few religious monuments of little significance, such as the tomb of Sheik Jibrā'īl in Ardebil and the Khātūn Qiyāmat and Bībī Dukhtarān mausoleums in Shiraz, which have a central plan and show no great originality. There are, however, superb examples of kashi decoration, still restrained and harmonious in its richness, at Sava on the mihrab of the Masjid-i-Jāmi' (PL. 347), where the big liwan is also Safavid, and that of the Masjid-i-Maidan, and especially in Isfahan on the portals of the Hārūn-i-Vilāyat (1513) and the Mosque of 'Ali (1521).

It is known that the architects of Ṭahmāsp I worked in the sanctuaries of Ardebil and of Meshed; in the latter a gold minaret was constructed in the northern corner of the "old court." But this sovereign's architects worked mostly in the new capital of Qazvin, which had displaced Tabriz under Ṭahmāsp's rule. Here he commissioned a "Turkish" architect (probably from Azerbaijan) to build a large palace with seven portals, which was rebuilt by 'Abbās I. It must have been a very impressive building, judging by the one remaining gate, the so-called 'Ālī Qāpū, an enormous liwan flanked by two short secondary wings, which may have opened onto a "square of the shah" used as a polo field, like the Maidan-i-Shāh in Isfahan. In Qazvin there were also royal gardens and a sort of guest house for important visitors, with at least 250 rooms. In addition the Chihīl Sutūn survives, if this can still be called Safavid after the restorations undertaken by the Qajar governor Sa'd al-Salṭāna at the end of the 19th century; it is a large pavilion with two stories, the first surrounded by an arcade, the second by a balcony supported by wooden pillars. In 1955 important fragments of pictorial decorations were discovered there. Among Ṭahmāsp's public works in Isfahan were an aqueduct; a great wooden talār, now destroyed, which was, according to Chardin (1711), a pavilion without walls and with a ceiling supported by wooden columns, finely decorated and covered, like the ceiling, with gold leaf; the fine portals of the Qutbiya mosque (1543) and of the Pīrpīnādūz mosque (Masjid-i-Jaubara) — both now in the garden of the Isfahan Chihīl Sutūn — decorated with the last examples of kashi work in the history of Iranian art; and dating from the same year, 1543, the Mosque of Dū'l-fiqār.

In addition to some highly original architectural innovations such as the pentagonal Mausoleum of Bābā Rukn al-Dīn, Isfahan has some notable examples of religious architecture from the period of Shah 'Abbās I: the Masjid-i-Surkhī, the Masjid-i-Maqsūd Beg, the Madrasah of Mullā 'Abdullāh, and the Masjid-i-Shāh (PL. 345; FIG. 625), which gives an impressive sense of fragile, unbounded vastness deriving from the broad blue expanse of its vaults. The elements of civil architecture introduced or established at this time show a greater originality; for example, in interior architectural decoration, there are the niches of painted stucco in the palace of 'Ālī Qāpū. The popularity of such niches later, under Shah Ṣafī (1629–42), is apparent in his alterations of the 14th-century Ardebil sanctuary of Sheik Ṣafī. For a long time the cruciform plan of the country villas enjoyed a similar popularity; examples are the villa of Safiabad that Shah Ṣafī built near Bihshahr in Mazanderan, greatly altered today, and masterpieces such as the villa of Bayramabad near Kerman, dating from the end of the 17th century.

Generally speaking, the civil architecture under 'Abbās I and his successors, especially 'Abbās II and Sulaymān, was governed by the same styles; at least it is difficult to distinguish the work of the builders from that of the restorers. This civil architecture is a garden architecture, with many loggias and balconies. In some cases the loggia may be square and enhance the façade forming the chief entrance to the pavilion, as in the Chihīl Sutūn in Isfahan, which has a single story and a flat roof resting directly on high wooden pillars, arranged in triple rows (1590? with restorations by 'Abbās II). The ceiling is coffered and richly decorated, while the columns of the loggia are reflected in the ornamental lake that lies in front of it, designed to enhance not only the landscape effect but also the proportions of the building. In the large six-story palace of 'Ālī Qāpū, dating from the beginning of the 17th century, the loggia with wooden pillars occupies the upper part of the building. The round balcony that surrounds it continued to predominate as a feature of the hunting pavilions of the following centuries, while the simpler flat-roofed liwan supported by two wooden columns — first introduced in the rear façade of the Chihīl Sutūn and firmly established by the Tālār Ashraf of Sulaymān (1669) — was to remain a classic feature of the large state pavilions of the Persian court until the end of the 19th century (see QAJAR SCHOOL).

In Isfahan the Hasht Bihisht of Shah Sulaymān (1669; FIG. 626) is, despite its alterations, a fine example of civil architecture. Finally, in the Isfahan architecture of Shah Sultān

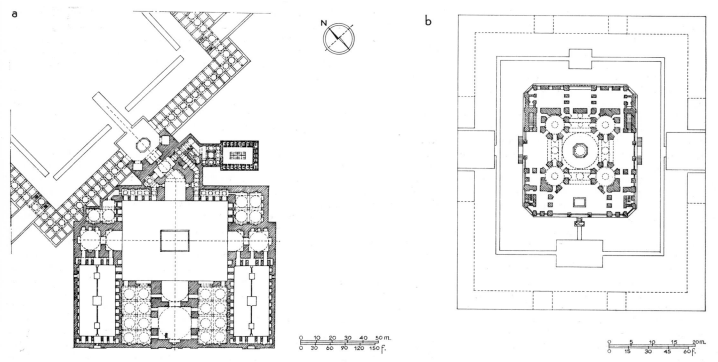

Isfahan. (*a*) The Masjid-i-Shah, plan; (*b*) the Hasht Bihisht pavilion, plan (*from SPA II, figs. 419 and 421*).

Ḥusayn (1694–1722), the style is strictly and correctly academic; examples are the madrasahs of Chahār Bāgh (or Mādar-i-Shāh; 1706) and of Shamsābād (1713–14) and the Mosque of ʿAlī-qulī Āqā. Mention should be made of the attempts made by ʿAbbās I in 1606 to adapt Iranian architecture to the religious needs of the Armenian community at Julfa, outside Istanbul (see IRAN, col. 245), which was granted many churches by royal favor. In Meshed the chief Safavid benefactors of the sanctuary after ʿAbbās I were ʿAbbās II — who built the northern liwan and the tomb of Allāhvardī Khān, as well as the subsidiary sanctuary of Qadamgāh (1643–44) on the Nishapur-Meshed road, about 17 miles east of Nishapur — and Sulaymān, who promoted extensive restoration work after the 1673 earthquake, chiefly on the dome of the mausoleum, the Jauhar Shād Mosque (1676–77), and the Madrasah-i-Dudar (1677–78). This ruler also had new buildings constructed within the sacred precinct: the Pā'in-Pā Madrasah (1676–77), the Parīzād Madrasah, the Dār al-Ziyārāt caravanserai, and the caravanserai of Shah Allāhvardī Khān (1680–81); but the Safavid works constructed outside the sacred precinct are more notable. Among these are the Masjid-i-Shāh, the Jauhar Shād Mosque mentioned above, and especially the Mausoleum of Khwāja Rabīʿ (1622; restored in 1672 and 1707), with a domed central plan and an octagonal exterior with niches finely decorated in kashi. This is the prototype of a style of architecture that spread throughout the East as far as the Tāj Mahal of Agra (see MOGHUL SCHOOL).

PAINTING AND MINIATURES. Inside their palaces the Safavids alternated pictorial decoration with the traditional decoration in kashi or ceramics. In the frescoes and pictorial decorations of the palaces, however, as far as can be judged from the few remaining fragments, the Safavid artists seem far from a full understanding of the characteristics and aims of monumental wall painting, some examples of which were executed by miniaturists. From the descriptions of Western travelers it is known that there once existed battle scenes in Shiraz showing the capture of Hormuz from the Portuguese, as well as erotic scenes in Julfa and pastoral and fishing scenes in the Hazār Jarīb palace in Isfahan. Western influence in this field is documented by Thomas Herbert (1634) and García de Silva y Figueroa (1667), and Pietro della Valle describes in detail the paintings of the palace of Ashraf and those of the ʿĀlī Qāpū. The remains of these paintings, together with those of the

Chihīl Sutūn in Isfahan (much restored), the Chihīl Sutūn in Qazvin, and some rooms of the Ardebil sanctuary, give an idea of the purely decorative nature of these compositions, which depict youths and maidens and minstrels, round-faced and almond-eyed, with goblets of wine and musical instruments, against a background of gardens.

The town of Herat was the great Iranian miniature-painting center of the Timurid period (see MINIATURES AND ILLUMINATION), but in the 16th century, after its capture by the Safavids, the leading artists emigrated, some to India and some to the Safavid capital, Tabriz, or the Shaybanid capital, Bukhara. In the evolution of 16th-century Central Asian miniature painting two main tendencies, not unrelated, can be distinguished. The first represents a continuation of the Herat school; its chief representative is Maḥmūd Muzāhib, who, after working at the court of Ḥusayn Bayqarā, executed equally skillful works at the court of the Shaybanid ʿAbd al-ʿAzīz. The other trend is an outgrowth of local tendencies.

One of the main innovations of the miniaturists of Bukhara was the introduction of plant and animal motifs in the margins of the miniatures (*Būstān* of Saʿdi, done by Sulṭān ʿAlī Mash-hadī, d. 1519). Among the outstanding exponents of the Bukhara school were ʿAbdullāh Muzāhib, also known as Mīr Muṣawvir; the anonymous miniaturist of the *Fatḥ-nama* (1506–07) of Shaybānī Khān; the miniaturist of the works of Mīr ʿAlī Shīr Nawā'ī (1521–22; Leningrad, State Lib.); and above all Muḥammad Murād of Samarkand. The latter executed the 115 illustrations of a *Shāh-nama* produced in 1556 for the prince of Khiva, and in his miniatures the stylistic features of the Central Asian school are most clearly evident. In these miniatures, which usually run vertically, dramatic scenes (battles, duels, killings, tortures) prevail over lyrical or courtly ones. The artist diverged in his compositions from the traditional style of the "carpet" miniature, with its numerous figures and details, drawing only what was actually meant to illustrate the text and setting some large figures against a neutral purplish-blue background. The landscape was never permitted to become an emotionally independent element. The expression is compact and concrete, as are the colors, which, despite occasional bold touches, are characterized by a certain austerity resulting from the gray-lilac tones. In comparison with the Timurid traditions, this artist's miniatures drew less on legend for their subjects and were less opulent but were richer in human interest. The Central Asian style differed in this period from the "internal" Iranian style (which was more truly Safavid) in that it derived from less refined and less courtly circles. In the following century the masterpiece of Central Asian miniature painting was the *Ẓafar-nāma* of Sharīf ad-Dīn 'Alī Yazdī, dating from 1628 and preserved in Tashkent. The 12 large miniatures, the work of a Samarkand master, are authentic battle pictures full of fierce details.

The other chief miniature center of the period was Tabriz, where, in 1522, Shah Ismā'īl appointed the famous Bihzād (q.v.) director of his library. Bihzād was succeeded in this post by Sulṭān Muḥammad, probably under Shah Ṭahmāsp. Although not enough is known yet about the Tabriz school to trace its history, it is clear that it represents the mature production of the Bizhād style: skillful representation of the movements, attitudes, and gestures of the figures, with an interest in details, landscapes, and architectural interiors. The Tabriz miniatures exploit to the full all the resources of the color scale; the compositions, complex and full of figures, fill the space (VIII, PL. 143).

The characteristic features of the school can be seen in the illustrations of a manuscript of the *Khamsa* of Niẓāmī of 1539–43 (VII, PL. 410), executed by Āqā Mīrak of Isfahan, his pupil Sulṭān Muḥammad, and the Tabriz artists Mīr Sayyid 'Alī (q.v.), Mīrzā 'Alī, and Muẓaffar 'Alī. One of the best miniatures by Āqā Mīrak is that of Anūshirvān listening to the owls' conversation, where realism, although present, is completely subordinated to the world of fable. The Shah and his vizier are shown approaching the ruins of a palace; the magical atmosphere is not broken by the semirealistic detail of the two small figures cutting wood and the woolly donkey grazing. Taken as a whole the illustration is far from expressing the epic tragedy of the corresponding passage in Niẓāmī. A miniature by Mīr Sayyid 'Alī shows Majnūn being led in chains to Laylā's pavilion, but the dramatic impulse is lost before the spectacle of Laylā's beauty. Here the subject does not matter and is treated with indifference. In another miniature by Mīr Sayyid 'Alī, Khusrau, full of nostalgia for Shīrīn, is supposed to be consoling himself by listening with his courtiers to the spellbinding singer Bārbad. The latter, however, is anything but the focal point of a composition crowded with figures, all of whom are going about their own business merely in order to supply an extra detail for the miniaturist's fancy.

The most typical representative of the Tabriz school (and the most painstaking painter of realistic natural details used as a pretext for decoration) is Sulṭān Muḥammad, who was master of painting at Ṭahmāsp's court, director of the library, and a designer of carpets. The historian Iskandar Monshī considered him the equal of Bihzād in artistic skill as well as in universal popularity. Among the best of his few extant signed works are a Khusrau and Shīrīn illustration and a miniature showing a royal hunt, executed in 1540 in a Jāmī manuscript (Leningrad, State Lib.). Full of lively details, the miniature shows huntsmen, courtiers, horses, camels, and gazelles moving harmoniously and gracefully against a background of blue sky and green-gold countryside. Sulṭān Muḥammad aimed at more complex effects in his illustrations for the *Dīvān* of Ḥāfiz (Paris, Coll. Louis Cartier). This joyful orgy scene, intoxicating the angels on the palace roof and the men below, is a pictorial representation of the mystical ideals of esoteric impiety, making use of all the "realistic" fantasy of the Tabriz school and revealing the full decorative potentialities of an almost naturalistic imagination. As an example of Sulṭān Muḥammad's interest in depicting isolated figures, one may mention the miniature of a young man, also in Leningrad (State Lib.), attributed to him.

Among the miniaturists of secondary importance in Tabriz were Shaykh Zādā, whose works are in Paris (Coll. Louis Cartier; Bib. Nat.) and New York (Met. Mus.); Khwāja 'Abd al-'Azīz, with a portrait of a prince preserved in the Topkapı Saray, Istanbul; Shāh Muḥammad, with two miniatures in Istanbul and a portrait in Boston; Mīr Naqqāsh, Sulṭān Muḥammad's successor and director of the library; and Shaykh Muḥammad of Shiraz, who was still living under Shah 'Abbās. From Tabriz, whose last great painter was Ustād Muḥammadī (Muḥammadī Beg), active about 1584, the Persian style once more radiated eastward and westward; Mīr Sayyid 'Alī and 'Abdu'ṣ-Ṣamad (qq.v.) both emigrated to India; and both Shāh Qilī, a pupil of Āqā Mīrak, and Valī Jān of Tabriz, who was still active in 1601, emigrated to Turkey.

At the end of the 17th century, with the transfer of the capital there, Isfahan became the painting center of the country. While the local school of miniature painting in Shiraz wearily repeated the motifs of Tabriz, the Isfahan school, although it continued to respect the traditional principles, was receptive to new experiments and began to adopt the first Western ideas, which had penetrated into the country chiefly through engravings. This superficial influence was often confined to the casual adoption of isolated elements and perhaps new subjects, but nonetheless it helped to free painting from the art of manuscript decoration, transforming miniature painting into an independent art. Introducing new and previously unknown features into their illustrations, artists gradually abandoned the classic decorative tradition although continuing to paint miniatures on separate sheets. Narrative compositions became fewer and portraits more numerous. These, it is true, were merely enlarged miniature figures, but in them the artist was attracted by what the old miniaturists had ignored — by line rather than composition and by drawing rather than color. The basic characteristic of the Isfahan school is an interest almost entirely concentrated on the movement of the figures, which esthetically takes the form of sinuous arabesques linking all the elements of the subjects.

The foremost artist of this school was the court painter Riẓā-i-'Abbāsī (q.v.; PL. 351), of all Persian painters the most observant of nature and of human types, although still respecting the traditional principles. Other leading representatives of the Isfahan school were 'Alī Aṣghar, Mīr Zayn al-'Ābidīn, and Maulānā Ḥasan of Baghdad. In the works of the painters of the succeeding generations, however, all semblance of balance was lost, as witness the banality of the miniatures of Muḥammad Zamān, whom Shah 'Abbās II sent to study in Rome and who worked on a *Shāh-nāma* (Dublin, Chester Beatty Lib.) and on a Niẓāmī manuscript of 1675 (New York, Pierpont Morgan Lib., Ms. M469).

It may never be possible to establish the Safavid antecedents of a popular school of painting, for which extensive documentation has become available only in the last two centuries. Popular taste in art, however, like that in literature, must be closely connected with elements of a religious nature, and in the Safavid period there was a popular diffusion of Shiite theological doctrines, the most striking and the most susceptible to emotional interpretation in Moslem sacred history. The "sacred" frescoes of the Imāmzāda Zayd in Isfahan, representing scenes from the Passion of Ḥusayn and commissioned by Sulaymān in 1685–86, are among the few surviving works that bear witness to this development in the visual arts. They are far removed from any courtly atmosphere and, in some ways, come close to European sensibility, at least on the level of popular inspiration if not on that of a broad and conscious artistic purpose. Only in the style of the costumes depicted is there a faint echo in these works of the atmosphere of the Safavid courts.

DECORATIVE ARTS. In ceramics, the motifs and techniques of the preceding periods continued with little change. Ceramic tiles (kashi; PL. 346) were produced especially in Tabriz and in Samarkand. Other types of ceramics of this period were the Kubachi ware (PL. 350); the blue-and-white and the polychrome wares of Kerman, with designs that recall contemporaneous miniatures; and the interesting bottles and flasks produced in Isfahan (see CERAMICS, cols. 254–55).

Minor arts of the Safavid period also include glassmaking (see GLASS, col. 378) and metalwork (PLS. 352, 353). In gold- and silverwork Safavid Iran specialized in the production of swords and daggers (VI, PL. 281) and of gold vessels such as bowls and jugs, often set with precious stones (see GOLD- AND SILVERWORK). The art of manuscript binding made marked technical progress during the Safavid period; modestly decorated leather bindings yielded, perhaps under the influence of Chinese methods, to pasteboard bindings with increasingly elaborate lacquer ornamentation (one of the oldest of these bindings bears the date 1557). From manuscript bindings this technique spread widely until, in the last centuries of Safavid rule, it became the most characteristic Persian decorative technique and was even adopted for the decoration, chiefly floral, of the wooden doors of Persian houses.

Textiles were greatly developed during the Safavid period (PLS. 348, 354; XIV, PL. 17; see also TEXTILES, EMBROIDERY, AND LACE). Isfahan, Kashan, and Yezd produced silks, and Isfahan and Yezd, satin; Kashan was famous for its brocades. Persian materials were exported to Europe, especially to eastern Europe, which then had no high-grade textile industry of its own. They were sent particularly to the Russian market, where they were known as "kizilbashes," from the designation applied to certain Turko-Persian merchant communities or tribes. In the Armory Palace (Oruzheinaya Palata), or Hall of Arms, in the Kremlin in Moscow there is a Persian cloth with the Christian symbol of St. Mark's lion; and in the same museum a masterpiece of Alexander fighting the dragon, embroidered in red on a blue background, is preserved. Persian cloths in the 17th century often had a floral decoration on a light background. The old geometric motifs gave way to the depiction of pseudorealistic scenes full of human figures. In addition to a strongly discernible Chinese influence in the textiles of this period, there are close affinities to the painting of Riżā-i-'Abbāsī. During the reign of Shah 'Abbās I there were some remarkable cloths signed by the famous Ghiyāth ud-Dīn 'Alī: one showing Shīrīn bathing and many with scenes of Laylā and Majnūn. Other well-known weavers were Ghiyāth ud-Dīn 'Alī's son, Mu'izz ud-Dīn, and 'Amal-i-Ḥusayn.

Carpets (see TAPESTRY AND CARPETS) occupy the major position in the textile field, with the major centers of weaving in Kerman, Kashan, Shiraz, Yezd, and Isfahan. There was a great variety of types, such as the "hunting carpet" (XIII, PL. 424), the "animal carpet" (XIII, PL. 425), the "garden carpet" (PL. 354), and the "flower-vase carpet." The Safavid carpet from the interior of Iran indulged almost everywhere in gaudy, sinuous, and overlavish decoration, full of a conventional realism that increasingly broke down the old stylized geometric motifs, though the latter continued to be used by the nomads of outer Iran. In Central Asia, Turkoman carpets (commonly but erroneously called Bukhara carpets) became very famous. Although each tribe had a style of its own, all Turkoman carpets had in common a deep red background, sometimes almost blackish, sharply punctuated by stylized motifs in blue, green, orange-yellow, or white. Tekke, Salur, and Saryk carpets were of this style, while in the Yomud, Ersari, and Chaudor carpets, rhomboidal and serrated designs and anchor-shaped, floral, and animal motifs predominated. The Asmolduk carpets of the 18th century had graceful stylized birds, and in the Yomud and Chaudor carpets large patches of green, blue, and white punctuated the brick-red background. The multicolored Herat carpets also had floral and geometric designs, while Afghanistan produced thick woolen carpets in clear colors, usually with polygonal decorations on a dark cherry-red background. There were other carpet-weaving centers in Azerbaijan. The southern Azerbaijan carpet (Tabriz) often had animal and hunting motifs and was similar to the Iranian carpet proper. A superb example is the huge carpet restored by Shah Ṣafī (London, Vict. and Alb. Mus.), which was woven for the Ardebil sanctuary in 1539, with motifs that repeat those of the majolica decorations of the mosque (XIII, PL. 423): in the center of a rich, multicolored floral decoration on a blue background, there is a gold star-shaped medallion with rays and two chandeliers set lengthwise. Northern Azerbaijan produced the Shirvan and Kuba carpets, with geometric and floral designs, as well as stylized animals, blue and emerald-green in color; the luminous Gangia carpet with geometric patterns on a red, blue, or green background; and the Karabagh carpet with a garden motif on a dark-red, dark-blue, or green background. In the 18th century the almond-tree motif predominated in this area.

BIBLIOG. In Persian: İgen Mītūḥ, Riżā-i 'Abbāsī, Kāve, II, 23, Berlin, 1335-36, A.H. (1900), pp. 5–7; Ṭāhirzāda-i-Bihzād, Sharḥ-i ḥāl-i Āqā Mīrak (Notes on Āqā Mīrak), Sūdmand, I, 1305–07 A.H. (1926–29), p. 447; Naṣrullāh Falsafī, Taṣvīr-i ḥaqīqī-i du pādshāh-i ṣafawī (True Portrait of Two Safavid Sovereigns), Ta'līm u tarbīyat, IV, 1313, A.H. (1934–35), pp. 577–82; Isà Bihnām, Naqqashī dar 'aṣr-i ṣafawī (Painting in the Safavid Period), Armaghān, 17, 1315 A.H. (1936–37), pp. 100–03; Aḥmad Suhailī Khwānsārī, Maulānā 'Alī Riżā-i 'Abbāsī va Āqā Riżā-i Muṣavvir (Maulānā 'Alī Riżā-i 'Abbāsī and Āqā Riżā the Painter), Armaghān, 17, 1315 A.H. (1936–37), pp. 197–204; İgen Mītūḥ, Riżā-i 'Abbāsī, Rūzigār-i nau, II, 2, 1942–43, pp. 2–8; Isà Bihnām, 'Alī Riżā-i 'Abbāsī, Rāh-i nau, II, 1944–45, pp. 168–69; Mahdī Bahrāmī, Riżā-i 'Abbāsī, naqqāsh-i ma'rūf (Riżā-i 'Abbāsī the Famous Painter), Āyanda, III, 1323–24 A.H. (1944–46), pp. 617–21; Zahrā Dā'izāda, 'Alī Riżā va Riżā-i 'Abbāsī, Ruzigar-i nau, IV, 5, 1945, pp. 68–71; 'Abbās Iqbāl, 'Alī Riżā-i 'Abbāsī-i Khushnivīs va Riżā-i 'Abbāsī-i naqqāsh ('Alī Riżā-i 'Abbāsī the Calligrapher and Riżā 'Abbāsī the Painter), Yādigār, II, 10, 1325 A.H. (1946), pp. 37–57; Izà Bihnām, Yakī az kārhā-i Riżā 'Abbāsī dar mūza-i sanāyi'-i sharqī da Moskou (A work of Riżā 'Abbāsī in the Museum of Eastern Art at Moscow), Payām-i nau, IV, 2–3, 1937 A.H. (1948), pp. 162–65; Mahdī Bayānī, Du taṣvīr az salāṭīn-i ṣafavī (Two Portraits of Safavid Sovereigns), Yādigār, V, 8–9, 1328 A.H. (1949), pp. 82–84; Ṣadrā Ṣadr, Ustād Riżā 'Abbāsī, Farhang-i jahān, I 1, 1332 A.H. (1953–54), pp. 6–12; Isà Bihnām, Dar bāra-i Riżā 'Abbāsī (On Riżā 'Abbāsī), Naqsh u nigār, 2, 1334, A.H. (1955), pp. 17–22; Muḥammad 'Abdullāh Changhatā'ī, Āqā Riżā-i Muṣavvir (Āqā Riżā the Painter), Hilāl, 4, 1956, pp. 46–50; 'Alī Aṣghar Ḥikmat, Ṣafḥa'ī az ta' rīh-i ravābiṭ-i Īrān u Hind: taṣvīrī as shāh-i 'Abbās-i kabīr (A Page in the Relations between Iran and India: A Portrait of Shah 'Abbās the Great), Nashrīya-i vizārat-i umūr-khwārīja, II, 6, 1959–60, pp. 22–29. In other languages: T. Herbert, A Description of the Persian Monarchy..., London, 1634 (reissued, W. Foster, ed., Thomas Herbert, Travels in Persia, 1627–1629, London, 1928); García de Silva Figueroa, L'Ambassade de Don Garcias de Silva Figueroa en Perse..., Paris, 1667; J. Chardin, Voyages en Perse et autres lieux de l'Orient, Amsterdam, 1711 (abridged ed., P. Sykes, ed., Sir John Chardin's Travels in Persia, London, 1927); J. Daridan and S. Stelling-Michaud, La peinture séfévide d'Ispahan, Paris, 1930; S. Katchadourian, Persian Fresco Paintings, New York, 1932; SPA, II–III, passim; M. Aga-Oglu, Ṣafawid Rugs and Textiles, New York, 1941; G. D. Guest, Shiraz Painting in the 16th century, Washington, 1949; V. Minorsky, Iran Islamico, Le Civiltà dell'oriente, I, Rome, 1956; I. Stchoukine, Les peintures des manuscrits safavis de 1502 à 1587, Paris, 1959; B. V. Veimarn and I. D. Kolpichkov, ed., Vseobshchaia istoriia iskusstv (Universal History of Art), II, Moscow, 1961, pp. 93–104, 118–25, 147–50; E. J. Grube, ed., Muslim Miniature Paintings from the XIII to XIX Century, Venice, 1962, pp. 79–90, 109–38 (cat.; bibliog.); U. Monneret de Villard, Arte cristiana e musulmana del Vicino Oriente, Le civiltà dell'oriente, IV, Rome, 1962, pp. 456–54.

Gian Roberto SCARCIA

Illustrations: PLS. 345–354; 3 figs. in text.

SAHARAN BERBER CULTURES.

The Sahara zone has for thousands of years represented an area of transition between fundamentally different cultural provinces, from the Nile Valley to the Atlantic Ocean along the east–west axis and from the shores of the Mediterranean Sea to the Niger region of the Sudan along the north–south axis. It is to its constant function as a link between these spheres that it owes the multiplicity of influences still apparent today in the cultures of its inhabitants, who are of predominantly Berber stock, as well as the individual stamp of those cultures, which are influenced by environmental conditions entirely different from those of the surrounding areas. Although the settled Berbers of Mediterranean Africa have largely been assimilated to Arab civilization and have adopted Islamic forms of art and architecture (see ISLAM), and although the non-Berber peoples of the eastern Sahara (the Tibbu, Daza, Bideyat, and related peoples) have developed no noteworthy artistic production, the nomads of the western Sahara have succeeded in creating interesting traditions of style and expression, overcoming the obstacles of Islamic aniconism and of extreme poverty of resources.

This article deals with the arts of the Mauritanians, the Tuareg, and the Bororo Peul, the only Saharan peoples with characteristic art products.

SUMMARY. Introduction (col. 630). Influence of rock art on contemporary artistic production (col. 632). Architectural remains of the pre-Islamic period (col. 633). Islamic and magical influences (col. 634). Tribal arts (col. 635): The Mauritanians: a. Crafts; b. Mural decorations of Walata; The Tuareg; The Bororo Peul.

INTRODUCTION. The western Sahara comprises some 1,660,000 sq. mi. of desert, bordered on the north by a steppe zone, varying in width from nearly 200 to 400 mi., and on the south by a transitional zone that starts from Nouakchott in Mauritania and has its eastern border at Fada in Ennedi

(Chad). This southern zone marks the end of a region of sparse scrub, of "pastures" of *had* and alfalfa, and the beginning of the *kram-kram* fields (*Cenchrus biflorus*), doom palms, gum acacias, and baobabs. In other words, this is the *bled es-Sudan* of the Arab geographers and the zone called *sahélienne*, from *sahel* ("shore"), by the botanist Auguste Chevalier. It marks the beginning of intensive life in a region of dense population, on the Saharan scale, which absorbs more than 90 per cent of the great nomadic peoples, namely, from west to east, the Mauritanians, the Tuareg, and the Tibbu.

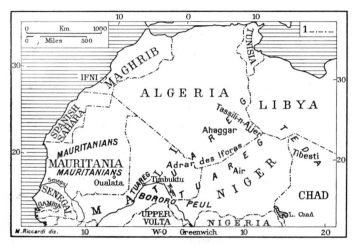

Distribution of the chief art-producing ethnic groups in the area of the Saharan Berber cultures (names of the peoples in heavy capitals). *Key:* (1) Modern political boundaries.

The Sahara may be likened to a sea, with ports established at the north and south of the "sahelian" or transitional zones. These ports, like all other ports, are points of arrival and departure, markets, and meeting places, from which radiates an economic life as well as a political and spiritual life, every port being the terminal or relay point of the Mediterranean civilization in the north and the Negro African culture in the south.

The study of techniques, one of the criteria used by ethnologists to define levels of culture, together with linguistics, anthropology, and material culture, makes it possible to determine the trade currents between these ports, the main axes of conquests and migrations, the phenomena of ethnic interpenetration between Arab Berbers and Negro Africans, and the phenomena of acculturation between technically primitive and developed cultures. Such a study reveals the presence of two worlds in the Sahara, one in the west, familiar with weaving (the Mauritanians), and the other in the east, which is unacquainted with weaving but whose metalwork makes use of the lost-wax casting process (the Tuareg of the Azauak and Air regions).

Throughout these territories, pottery utilizes the Negro African coil technique, without a potter's wheel. The techniques of weaving reached the Mauritanians from the Bedouins of southern Morocco. The Mauritanian goldsmiths may have borrowed their techniques from the early goldworkers in the old Ghana empire, as well as from the Wolof and Songhai, the carriers of the techniques of the Baule or Ashanti, the gold diggers of the Gulf of Guinea. Brassware, which is rare, and embroidery are Moroccan in origin, whereas jewelry, amulets, and shell work are Negro. Certain house-building techniques at Tichitt and Chinguetti are clearly Berber and can also be found among the walled villages of the Moroccan Sous. But the decoration of the houses in Walata (Oualata) is either an adaptation of leatherwork technique — on a wall scale — or an interpretation of Mongolian silks imported by pilgrims from some famous pilgrimage, such as that of Kankan Musa in the 14th century; or it may even be the product of a fertility cult practiced by Negro Saharans of the shepherd

period. The influence of India is apparent in the numerous agate pendants — the Mauritanian *khurb* or Tuareg *cherot*. The copper, iron, and brass locks may well be of Chinese inspiration.

These are only some of the essential features of the astonishing history of Saharan techniques, with their Mediterranean, Phoenician, Egyptian, Jewish, Arab Berber, and Negro African sources and their further borrowings from the very heart of the highly developed culture of white Africa (Pharaonic empire) and from Negro Africa (Ife, Benin), as well as from the Middle East and Asia. The bearers of these influences were pilgrims, traders, or even warriors, following roads that were but a prolongation of the great world highways that make up the Silk Road.

The term "art" should be understood here in a functional sense, established by the social structure of the group, by economy, magic, and religion as much as by technical processes. Common aspirations and a universal esthetic language can be found in it — the Mauritanians' desire for embellishment, or the saying that the Tuareg women of the Ahaggar (Hoggar) Mountains quote, referring to their richly decorated *tesenit* baskets, designed to hold their nomad treasures: "Beautiful things must abide with beautiful things." But this is first and foremost a practical art that prays, implores, protects, asks something of God or the spirits, almost a prayer-wheel mechanism. The margin of individual freedom remains restricted, and the creative element is difficult to establish, although it is frequently stressed — in the manner of the craftsmen of ancient Greece — by an explosion of pride or joy in a signature: *aua nek inna Hunna* ("this is I named Hunna").

Between the two poles of the desert and Islam, art could be only an art of miniaturists, imported from the East, or else an art of carpet designing applied to leather, wood, and metal, an art of decoration, a minor art, since, in the words of Malraux, "it does not express man."

And yet, even amid the complexities of geometric decoration, and despite the constraint of an almost inhuman stylization, individual expression persists; but it has to be interpreted in the artist's personal world and with his own vocabulary. These men, through the Tuareg *enaden* or Mauritanian *malemin* (artisans), tell us their story, albeit in a somewhat hermetic language. They tell of wells, of herds, of gazelles, of their poorly furnished houses, of God, and above all of the *jinnūn* or "the folk of the empty spaces," the "sons of the devil," the evil eye, scorpions and vipers, thirst and sandstorms. It would be merely an art of fear, the cries of alarm of a threatened civilization incapable of defending itself, if at the same time it did not reveal a positive human challenge to the forces of nature. It has been said that one of the most widespread beliefs among primitive populations is the conviction that an aim can be achieved by imitating the desired event. But to this imitative magic should be added the concept of a personification of nature, of the mastering of superior and rather terrifying forces of a human nature accessible to symbolic rites similar to acts of faith, as moving as prayers written in threads of wool on a carpet or engraved with a burin on copper or silver.

This protective art, at this particular cultural stage, is closer to conquest than to submission. Thanks to his amulets painted on his traveling bags, to the theme of the "good eye," so frequent in the decoration of weapons, jewels, and ornaments, the nomad finally believes in the taming of winds, of paths and wells, in an understanding with gazelles, ostriches, bustards, and guinea fowl. He feels released from part of his fears, the master of the desert and of his own road. The rest is in the hands of God. "God does everything, and we weigh nothing in His hand" says Islam.

INFLUENCE OF ROCK ART ON CONTEMPORARY ARTISTIC PRODUCTION. Examples of rock art are to be found throughout the western Sahara (see PALEO-AFRICAN CULTURES; PREHISTORY). They include representations of wild animals dating from the hunting period (ca. 5000 B.C.) and of domestic animals during the succeeding pastoral period. The later paintings of horse chariots are connected with the warlike Garamantic peoples mentioned by Herodotus, while the final cameline phase testifies to the introduction of the dromedary in the Sahara in the first centuries of the Christian Era. With some exceptions (e.g., the paintings of Wadi Mertutek in the Ahaggar Mountains), the representation in this rock art is clumsy. During the cameline period it became increasingly governed by geometric symbolism.

Both the Mauritanians and the Tuareg knew and still know the art of the pre-cameline peoples. Travelers still engrave their names, a love message, or even some insult or ribald comment next to the Garamantes' chariots, or beside the bovids, elephants, and giraffes of a watered, populated Sahara. They know where to find the halting places of the Adrar region in Mauritania, those of the Tamesnar, the Ahaggar, the Tassili-n-Ajjer (Azger), the Tibesti, the Erdi, and the Borku. Sometimes they fear these sites because of the presence of the "folk of the empty spaces" or of some other spirit or malignant power; sometimes they use them as a place of worship, but for cults of a pre-Islamic or a Negro character, such as the phallic cult recorded by many travelers in the Ahaggar and the Adrar des Iforas. The *tibardin*, or Tuareg idols, may well belong to similar beliefs.

The Tuareg, the Mauritanians, and the Tibbu do not seem to have been in any way inspired by these rock paintings. The naturalistic art of the ancient shepherds, of the "cowmen," as they scornfully call them, belongs to a world far removed from theirs. It shows a way of life they do not value, in a country which they no longer recognize or which has receded more than 1,000 mi. toward the south. Neither their social organization nor their religion is in tune with these "fetishistic" customs. Their pictorial idiom has in fact little use for a direct representation of nature. They are turned toward other realities: spirits, good or bad influences, God. Their Islamic faith makes them aspire to an art of disembodied formulas. Their decorative arts, such as leatherwork, therefore have no connection with the rock paintings, except for the geometric symbolism of the cameline period, a symbolism that is a universal form of expression in primitive art.

Although the rock paintings seem to have left no sequel in present-day Saharan arts, the same is not true of the rock engravings of footprints, such as those found in 1961 near Ideles and Hirafok. They represent sandals as well as footprints of cattle, gazelles, and crows and are very meticulously incised, hollowed out, or hammered. To the prehistoric hunter, the representation of footprints undoubtedly had magical and symbolic connotations (see PREHISTORY), and for the modern nomads of the Sahara — hunters, shepherds, and travelers — desert tracks have retained much of this significance. For example, the nomads of a very ancient tribe, the Nemadi, draw such signs as "the track of the serpent" at night for divine protection against snakes. The representation of footprints is connected with the "part-for-the-whole" symbolism that is common in Saharan art. The Tuareg, for example, represent the fish by its scales or the guinea hen by stylized feathers. Footprint motifs are discernible in many leather, wood, and metal objects made by the Mauritanians and Tuareg. The motifs are sometimes engraved with a burin or an iron tool (poker work); they may be painted with a reed pen or obtained by embossing leather or stamping metal; they may be punched or cut out with the point of a knife. They are usually in the center of the decoration or form part of the general design and are always identifiable, recognized, indicated, and named by the Mauritanians and Tuareg.

ARCHITECTURAL REMAINS OF THE PRE-ISLAMIC PERIOD. Today, throughout North Africa, especially in the cities, architecture of Islamic derivation prevails, but in the rural and interior areas types of dwellings and structures of the original Berber or Sahara cultures are still used. In the Tibesti region, as well as in central Morocco and the Atlas Mountains region, the Berber house is still found, built of stones held together with lime mortar. There is an outside staircase; the ground floor serves as a stable, the first floor as the family residence, and the second floor as a granary.

Sometimes these houses have undergone architectural variation, acquiring the appearance of small forts: in this case they are used as storehouses. Houses of this type are found in the middle Atlas region, where they are called *tirremt* in southern Morocco, in the Aurès Mountains, and in southern Tunisia. Other constructions that go back to the aboriginal cultures are the artificial caves with countless recesses serving as rooms, which are numerous, for example, at Taza in Morocco; and the *gurbi*, the dwellings of seminomadic tribes, consisting of a single windowless room made of stone, dried mud, or boughs. Similarities have been observed between these *gurbi* and the foundations of neolithic huts.

Throughout the area there are many ruins of monuments of various types, undoubtedly dating back to the pre-Islamic period and, in many cases, displaying Roman influences, such as the ruins in the small village of Iherir, in the Tassili-n-Ajjer (Perret, 1936).

Funerary mounds are common; they consist of heaps of pebbles and stones of varying shapes and sizes and are usually set on heights, either singly or in dense groups. In the El Agial wadi, near Germa, where 60,000 have been counted, they form the largest necropolis of the ancient world. Their distribution testifies to the existence of a nomadic form of life. Generally they are large monuments requiring considerable constructive effort, especially as the necessary materials often had to be brought from a great distance. Eight main types have been identified in the central Sahara, but they have not yet been studied systematically from the standpoint of chronology, typology, and distribution.

Other monuments, found throughout the Ahaggar, in the Tassili-n-Ajjer, the Adrar des Iforas, and the Air region, are stone circles, regularly arranged in one or two rows, and reaching a considerable diameter, sometimes up to about 40 ft. These isolated monuments, whose stones are set deep in the ground, are still a mystery; according to Frobenius (1916), they are funeral monuments, according to Gautier (1928, 1934), their purpose was connected with sacrifice, while Kilian (1929) relates them to festivals and Lhote (1955) to religion.

Among the Tuareg, upright stones, which are numerous throughout the central Sahara, are objects of worship; the Iherga center on the upper I-n-Daladj, with its many steles bearing Libyan Berber inscriptions, is famous. The inscriptions are probably later in date than the actual steles.

ISLAMIC AND MAGICAL INFLUENCES. The *kitaba* and *simiya* sciences of magical letters and numbers are well known to the marabouts. They use them to compose Koranic amulets (called *kitaba* among the Tuareg), safety talismans, the names of Allah written in numbers on rings and pendants, on paper to be placed in small leather bags, or on small Koranic tablets. Each letter possesses a divine character corresponding to one of the 28 lunar houses. The Mauritanians, especially, use letters as ornamental motifs for the *faro* and the *ghlaf* (sheep- and lambskin rugs), and on gourds, wooden bowls, jewels, locks, and even on the walls of Walata. These letters are used in their isolated or initial form. The Arabic character for five (ه) appears frequently in ornaments as the symbol of the hand of Fāṭima, the symbol of the five blessed persons (Mohammed, Alī, Fāṭima, Ḥasan, and Ḥusayn), or as the symbol of Providence, the Law, and religion. On crosses and sometimes on *tassufra* (leather bags), the number appears under many different aspects: worked with silver beads or dots, in cruciform motifs, in pentagrams and five-pointed stars, in a double cross transformed into a double square (the eight-pointed star with the ends of the points joined by lines; PL. 355). This double cross of the Trarza is also used in an ornamental motif on Mauritanian bowls called the "gourd amulet" (PL. 360).

Magical influences often mingle with Islamic influences. Magic and religion are in fact closely associated in primitive societies, and Islam is a complaisant carrier of gnostic, Hebrew, Babylonian, and Assyrian magic. The nomads, a people more intuitive than logical, are incapable of discriminating between magic and religion; the mere thought would entail, in their eyes, some punishment from the spirits.

The fear of the evil eye, so frequent among the Berbers, appears in the triangle motif (the stylized eye). Herber (1950) points out the theme of the triangle in Morocco, as well as the example of the great *khamsa*, the heavy breast pendant of the prostitutes of the Dra Valley. Among the Tuareg, similar examples are the large breast pendant called *teraut* in the Ahaggar and *cherot* in the Air and the leather triangles trimmed with green that decorate the fringes of the *tassufra* and, also in the Air, the saddle cushions (PL. 362).

The evil eye is combatted with the representation of the "good eye," which is an extremely common ornamental element. It can also be counteracted by the glitter of mirrors, glass, and jewels and by the influence of the cross (a frequent motif among the Tuareg), whose arms disperse the malignant fluid to the four cardinal points. Finally there are all the Koranic amulets which are carried in small leather or silver containers and consist of texts written by the marabouts.

Magical powers are attributed to various metals and stones. Copper and brass, for example, neutralize the influence of iron, which is an impure metal. They also have protective powers in battle, as well as against rheumatism and ankle sprains when worn in the form of toe rings and anklets. Carnelian or agate coagulates the blood of wounds and protects from miscarriages, while amber has prophylactic virtues. Silver is a pure metal, authorized by the Prophet, whereas gold is feared and seldom worn by the Tuareg, although it forms part of the dowry of the Mauritanian women.

TRIBAL ARTS. Saharan arts, whether Peul, Tuareg, or Mauritanian, are primarily graphic arts of an abstract, geometric character. They have been influenced by numerous factors such as religion, magic, social milieu, way of life, history, and crafts. The tools used in nomad countries are necessarily rudimentary, and in the Sahara they are often archaic. There are, of course, variations in the technical skill, ingenuity, and inventiveness of the craftsmen. However, the general use of a reed pen or a goat-hair brush, a padded stick, the palm of the hand, the fingers, the point of a knife for excising leather, and very often the ruler and compass of the shoemaker or the smith in itself determines a certain rhythm, a resemblance between the Mauritanian and Tuareg styles. The colors, too, underline the technical uniformity of Saharan arts. They include the primary colors, with a preference for red, and are used in flat tones — the classic method of popular arts. In most compositions there is a dominating background color: red, then, in order of importance, yellow, green, and black (among the Tuareg), always in pure tones.

These arts bear the mark of a caste, that of the artisans, who are technicians as well as magicians. However, this is not an absolute rule, and many noblewomen or women of lower class do leather- and basketwork. Sometimes noblewomen summon artisans' wives and give them precise instructions for the decoration of a mat or a *tassufra*. Art, in its European sense, is not without influence in the Sahara; poetry, music, the quality of a weapon, the color of a saddle or a carpet, the value of a mehari are the themes of animated discussions and form part of education, social position, and a keenly felt notion of prestige.

The history of Saharan arts is a complicated one. It is concerned with Morocco and Lybia and therefore with Arabs, Berbers, possibly Jews, but predominantly with Negroes. The study of certain tribal genealogies clearly shows the complexity, and to some extent the futility, of the problem. For the Mauritanians, the Tuareg, and the Peul each have their own esthetic, which is neither Arabic, Berber, nor Negro, neither noble, vassal, nor captive, but has its individual character within the ethnic group. It documents an ancient culture, perfectly suited to its environment, whose widely varying elements were absorbed so long ago that it is hard to say which are Negro, Arab, or Berber. Despite the uniformity of the physical environment and the way of life and the consequently similar economic needs, each people seems to have retained sharply marked differences. Thus the Bororo Peul, who live in close contact with the Aulliminden Tuareg, have remained, within the same territory, a quite distinct ethnic group.

The Mauritanians. a. Crafts. The population of Mauritania, numbering a little over half a million, is settled in a region extending over about 1,250 mi. from north to south, between Morocco and Senegal. It is a population composed of Arab Berbers and Negro Africans; Hassan, the descendants of the Beni Hassan, who invaded Mauritania in the 15th and 16th centuries; Tolba or Zawiya (maraboutic tribes, often of Berber origin); and tributary tribes such as the Zenaga and Haratin (freedmen, former captives of Negro ancestry, artisans, and slaves). Techniques have undergone no deep modifications. On the other hand, the markets have shrunk and changed, and there is increasing competition from manufactured goods. As a result the production of handmade leather, metal, and wooden objects is declining. Social structures are changing, especially where the artisan and Haratin or slave classes are concerned. The classic phenomenon of detribalization is gradually overtaking the Saharan nomads.

The predominance of livestock raising in Mauritania has created a nomadic, pastoral civilization, where leatherwork is the chief artistic production. The most elaborate examples of this work are the *tassufra*, or traveling bags. They are generally made of five sheepskins and are about 40–50 in. long and 22–23 in. wide. In the west of the region they have a colored background, which is obtained by spreading on the color with the palm of the hand. The thick lines that form the framework of the decoration are painted with the finger or a small leather or rag pad on the end of a small stick. The more delicate lines are obtained by means of two brushes, the first a small twig with strong fibers and the second made of goat hair. There are two different types of decoration, one painted and the other tooled, which are executed by two different women belonging to the artisans' caste. Many other kinds of bags are also made; handbags, bags for grain, sugar, tea, etc. The cushions (for example, those from Boutilimit), the women's traveling bags, or *tiziaten*, the baskets for tea utensils, or *kuntié*, the *faro* and *ghlaf* (sheepskin rugs), and the sandals are also interesting for their decoration.

Mauritanian metalwork, as the long-established presence of these crafts in the Moroccan Sous would suggest, is clearly of Arab derivation, and is possibly influenced by Jewish techniques. Products of this craft include such objects as shoemakers' knives, locks, anklets, bracelets, daggers (rare), caskets and chests, and teapots. The shoemakers' knives (*ammas*) are "protected" by small shields or "knife amulets," soldered at the base of the blade. One engraved plate is often made of brass, the other of copper, a combination of metals that destroys the malignant influence of the iron. Mauritanian locks (*egfal*; PL. 358) are more complicated than those of the Tuareg. To the usual system of rod and spring is added a screwing device for fastening. As usual the iron framework of the lock is covered with small plates of copper and brass occasionally inlaid with silver. Anklets are made of silver or copper. When they are well decorated — e.g., the Boutilimit anklets (PLS. 355, 358) — the craftsman signs them, or rather, he adds the mark or brand of his family, if not that of his tribe. This ownership brand is the same for his tools and his cattle. A frequent motif is that of the *waw* (و; a fertility symbol) with circles containing either a cross or a dot, which serves to protect the foot against rheumatism, thorn pricks, scorpion or tarantula stings, adder bites, and the like. The caskets and chests are rather roughly made of small boards of false ebony. But on these boards the craftsman inlays silver *waw* motifs and applies fine sheets of silver, which are either pierced or engraved. The motif of the Trarza cross is also frequently used. The workshops of Méderdra produce chests with decorations cut from sheet iron (PL. 356).

Wood carving is limited to the decoration of baggage carriers (for the *tiziaten*), bowls, milk containers, small mortars, sandals, ladles, and spoons. The baggage carriers are flexibly constructed and consist of a frame with four legs, bound with leather thongs and strengthened with transverse wooden struts. Only the legs are carved; they recall the decorations of cedar doors and ceilings in Morocco (PL. 356). Bowls are frequently made of a hard wood called *adress* by the Mauritanians (*Balsamodendron africanum*); containers are made of a softer wood called *turja* (*Calotropis procera*). The decoration of the *adress* bowl is usually first cut into the bowl with a gouge and chisel; then the surface of the bowl is planed down around the motif in order to make it stand out in relief. The classic "gourd amulet" ornamentation of these bowls consists of two motifs: a fret pattern and a Trarza cross (PL. 360). The second is set off by five dots, five being the number that symbolizes, among other things, Fāṭima's hand and the five blessed persons (see above). The milk containers and mortars are more soberly executed. The soft *turja* wood lends itself to gouging and poker-work decoration, and broad surfaces are also painted in red, yellow, and sometimes mauve. The same techniques are used for wooden sandals.

b. Mural decorations of Walata. Walata (Oualata) was apparently founded at the end of the 11th century, under the name of Biru, by fugitives from Ghana, the ancient gold capital. It was an active and influential town, a commercial center, a crossroads for caravans between Morocco, Senegal, and Sudan, and a well-known center for Islamic studies. Then the advent of the motorized age marked the end of the great caravans and of the town's prosperity.

In this poor and austere milieu are to be found some extraordinary mural decorations (PL. 357). Their graphic style has no equivalent anywhere in Morocco, Mali, or Senegal. Only at Nema, which came under the influence of the Walati at the beginning of the 20th century, is anything similar to be found. They were executed with the fingers in red on a background of brilliant white chalk, the whole composition standing out against the ocher façades. Several hypotheses about these decorations have been advanced. One is that the art must have originated in Iraq and been introduced into Mauritania by the Mehajib, a group whose origin can be traced to Baghdad. Another hypothesis is that the famous pilgrimage undertaken in 1324 by Mansa Musa, the emperor of Mali, resulted in the copying of textile motifs. A chronicle of the time, in fact, mentions that the caravan brought back, among other things, a load of "700 pieces of Mongolian cloth."

The artisans of Walata have a complete terminology for the main motifs of these decorations, which reveal a familiar symbolism, linked to the fertility cult through motifs of a sexual nature, such as those of the virgin, the baby girl, the young woman, the woman with long braids, the mature woman, and the mother of the hips (FIG. 637). With these motifs the male element is always discreetly associated, transposed into

Ornamental wall motifs from Walata: (1) *arba* (virgin); (2) *tfaila* (baby girl); (3) *mra sghira* (young woman, 20 years); (4) *m'soulfa* (woman with long braids, 30 years); (5) *mra Kbira* (mature woman, 40 years); (6) *um lehregfat* (mother of the hips); (7) *aroueguij* (the people); (8) *ratmé* (corner).

graphic signs named the people and the small man; small niches with phallic decorations are also found. These themes would appear to derive from Negro African magical practices intended to stimulate the wife's fertility and ensure numerous descendants for each house.

A final hypothesis is that these mural decorations are hardly more than a century old. And in fact, the great Arab travelers of the 12th and 14th centuries never mentioned them, even though they are extremely striking. According to this theory,

they are based on the art of leatherwork, on the decoration of the *tassufra*, and the tea and rice bags and cushions, enlarged to the scale of a house. This would mean that the miniature style, executed with a reed pen, the finger, or a pad, has been enlarged, adapted to the wall, and simplified into broad lines. The terminology of these signs and motifs would then merely have a reference value for the artisans. However, even in this case, leather being a vehicle for sexual symbolism, the explanation of the motifs through terminology would remain equally plausible.

An interesting and original pottery is produced in Walata (PL. 363), but most of its motifs bear little relation to those of the wall decorations.

The Tuareg. This people, widely disseminated over the Sahara, is divided into six groups, covering the Tassili-n-Ajjer and Ahaggar massifs to the north and extending approximately 300 mi. beyond the loop of the Niger. The Tuareg number about 300,000. The Kel Ahaggar, or Ihagarren, and the Kel Ajjer represent only 2 per cent of this population; the great mass of the Tuareg people is settled in the "sahelian" savanna, which is particularly suited to the raising of cattle, their main resource. Bearers of traditions that probably go back to the Garamantes, they are now subject to the influences of political and economic changes and the presence of the oil industry. In an insidious but irresistible way, a shift is slowly taking place toward a technical civilization, whose materials are enamel and plastic, salvaged tires, barrels and cans, and tent cloth — a shanty-town civilization that is spreading among the nomads of the desert and rapidly causing the disintegration of their traditional cultures.

For leatherwork the Tuareg use tools and techniques similar to those of the Mauritanians, with, however, a few local differences. The dyes are less influenced by European products, although bags of aniline powder are common in the southern markets (Gao, Tahua, Maradi, Zinder, Agadès) as well as in the north [Tamanrasset, In Salah, Wargla (Ouargla), Tuggurt, Gat, Gadāmes]. The usual techniques of decoration are excision, appliqué work, braiding, and pierced or tooled bands, rather than designs executed with pen or brush. The latter designs are found, however, under Mauritanian influence, in the regions of Timbuktu, Gundam (Goundam), Gurma, Rharus, and Adrar des Iforas, which are zones of contact between the Tuareg and the Mauritanians. A common color is one known as Kano green, which the Tuareg call *amazer* or *idaline*, or, borrowing the Hausa word, *kurino*.

The women's bags (*taseïhat*; PL. 361), the saddle cushions known as *adafor*, and other leather articles reveal different styles. Among the Icherifen of Gao one often finds decorations of leather patchwork, which are then embroidered in the style of Timbuktu. Among the Aulliminden of the west and east, the bags are larger and decorated with many fringes and triangular pendants with numerous appliqués. As usual, the predominant colors are red and green. Among the Tuareg of the Air, Hansa influences are particularly apparent in the leather saddle cushions, which are black in the center while the extremity, widening out like a fishtail, is covered with green triangles on a red background, the whole design being boldly embroidered with red circles (PL. 362). The sandals lend themselves by their shape and surface to interesting decorations. The broader sandals, reserved for the chief or for gifts, come from Filingué to the west of Tahua. The decorative themes are geometric, with, however, the appearance of the lizard — not the *dob*, a motif current among the Tuareg of the Tassili, but the *marguia* of the Hausa. On saddles, in particular the Agadès saddles, the *amanzar* technique is used, consisting in the application of metal leaf (sometimes silver but mostly aluminum) on the back of the cantle. The metal is decorated with red and green triangles and with embroideries.

Metalwork is on the whole a recent art, introduced by captive artisans: it is a Negro art in its techniques, even though among the Tuareg numerous smiths are Arab Berbers. It is possible, however, that the ancient Jewish peoples of the Tuat bequeathed them some of their techniques.

The decoration of pendants (*shira*) is simply repoussé work effected with a punch. All the interest lies in the triangular shape — against the evil eye — and the contents (when the pendants are not filled with sand), consisting of a text from the Koran or some magic formula slipped in by the marabout, or *aneslem*.

Although the tea ceremony is of recent importation among the Tuareg, from a social point of view it has acquired the importance of a rite. This is why the sugar hammer and tongs or scissors are never purely functional objects. They are always decorated like jewelry with engraved designs and add to the prestige of the tent. The *tafadist* hammer is of brass cast by the lost-wax process on an iron rod. The principle is the same as that used for shields or dagger amulets (*takuba*). A small disk of red copper is soldered to the upper part of the handle, while the bottom ends in a head of solid silver, cut in facets, identical with the heads of Tuareg bracelets, or even of certain earrings.

Wood is a rather rare material among the Tuareg. This is why such objects as wooden bedsteads, tent pegs, and plates are generally repaired and handed down from one generation to another. Wooden articles are decorated with appliqué copper and small inlaid strips of silver. Such decoration is used, for example, for the woman's palanquin (*ekhaui*) of the Adrar des Iforas, for the pommels of litters (*tandawin*), and for the lateral supports of cushions (*itar' alaten*). Among the Tuareg of the River (Tinqurriquif), the boards of the beds (*assekbel* or *asegagu*) are engraved with a burin, like a piece of metal. The Tinqurriquif also carve their cushion stands and baggage carriers (*aguet*), their entrance posts (*iguetten*), and their gourd holders (*tizikant*). Wooden pots (*aylal*) belong to nomad art and are gradually being replaced by gourds or by glazed bowls of European origin. For ladles (*ammola*) and spoons (*tisokalin*), as for butter dishes and mortars, the most frequent decorative technique is either poker work or engraving with a burin or a punch.

Basketwork is an authentically Tuareg art and includes three types of mats: (1) screen mats (*issaber, assaber, chetek,* or *tadeint*); (2) prayer mats (*taussit*); (3) bed mats (*asserir*). The first form the wall elements of the tent, the equivalent of a screen that is drawn or closed according to the hours of the day, the movements of the wind, the position of the sun, and the temperature. They are therefore an essential part of the tent furnishings. The *taussit* covers the Tuareg bed and is also used as a prayer mat. The *asserir*, a coarser type of mat, is spread directly over the cross boards of the bed. The materials are different in each case: bundles of *Panicum turgidum* for the screen mats, *afazo* splints for the prayer mats, and bundles of *atawas* for the *asserir*. With the exception of the *asserir*, these mats are delicately decorated with narrow punched strips of leather, in black, red, or green. The main motifs suggest the turtledove (*tedebert*), ears (*tamezurk*) along the edge of the mat, tile flooring or a chessboard (*amareida*), fingers (*ideuan*), fingers tracing a game of divination on the sand, called, by analogy, *idjehan*, laughter (*tadasark*), and the six-pointed star of David (*atri*).

The Bororo Peul. In the Azauak and Air territories, the ethnic groups that seem to have the strongest social cohesion are the Bororo Peul. They practice endogamy and have their own Peul language; in religion, although they call themselves Moslems, they preserve such strong pre-Islamic traditions that even the Tuareg, who are far from orthodox, consider them "rejected by God." All their ornaments — earrings, necklaces, belts, and baldrics — are loaded with amulets: carnivores' claws and fangs, hyena manes, cow-hair. Magic plays an important role in their lives.

These prosperous cattle owners — they are richer than the Tuareg — have no desire for possessions and live in camps that are mere thornbush enclosures. Property would be only a hindrance to such nomadic cattle raisers. They know that after four or nine days, according to the seasons, the pasture is exhausted and it is necessary to leave.

All their material goods are Hausa or Tuareg, except for a few objects, such as amulets, feathered hats, young girls'

anklets, ceremonial axes, bark carpets, two types of ropes, butter churns, and gourds in the shape of a bottle, with very narrow necks plaited with doom fibers. Their only notable crafts are the engraving or painting of gourds, embroidery on dancing costumes for the *gerawol* feast, and face painting of a ceremonial nature. Usually the gourds are purchased in markets and decorated by sedentary artisans or by Peul captives, the *machudos*, who can become weavers, smiths, or farmers provided they give half their profits or produce to their master. But in some cases the young girls or women of the noble class engrave highly stylized designs with a punch. This is an authentic Bororo Peul style, called *kettul* after the technique. Another type of decoration is achieved by grating down the rind of the gourds on the large surfaces, sometimes in the shape of an elongated triangle, to give the material a different texture, and then painting suns at the ends, with the finger dipped in whitewash.

BIBLIOG. L. Frobenius, Kleinafrikanische Grabbau, Prähistorische Z., VIII, 1916, pp. 1–84 at 14; R. Chudeau, Les monuments lithiques du Sahara, L'Anthropologie, XXX, 1920, pp. 111–14; J. Gabus, Note sur les coutumes des Toubous du Nord: Fractions nomades du Tibesti et fractions sédentaires des oasis du Kaouary, B. Comité d'ét. h. et sc. de l'Afrique Occidentale Fr., IX, 1926, pp. 131–52; E. F. Gautier, Le Sahara, Paris, 1928; C. Kilian, Quelques observations et découvertes de ma mission 1927–1928 aux confins Imouhar-Teda dans le Sahara Central, CRAI, 1929, pp. 318–25; H. Terrasse, Notes sur l'origine des bijoux du sud marocain, Hesperis, XI, 1930, pp. 125–30; M. Ardant du Picq, Etude historique et ethnographique sur les Dyerma, B. Comité d'ét. h. et sc. de l'Afrique Occidentale Fr., XIV, 1931, pp. 477–704; F. Benoit, C. Begouen and L. Begouen, Les tumuli du Hoggar (Tedefest): Note préliminaire, Actes XVᵉ Cong. int. d'Anthr. et d'Archéol. préhistoriques, II, Paris, 1931, pp. 213–19; D. Brosset, Les Nemadi: Monographie d'une tribu artificielle des confins sud ou Sahara occidental, Renseignements Coloniaux, IX, 1932, pp. 337–46; O. Durand, Les industries locales au Fouta, B. Comité d'ét. h. et sc. de l'Afrique Occidentale Fr., XV, 1932, pp. 42–71; E. F. Gautier, Rapport sur la mission Gautier-Reygasse de 1934, CRAI, 1934, pp. 149–59; C. Kilian, L'art des Touareg, La Renaissance, XVII, 1934, pp. 147–55; R. Perret, Recherches archéologiques et ethnographiques au Tassili des Ajjers, JSA, VI, 1, 1936, pp. 41–64; L. Tauxier, Moeurs et histoire des Peuls, Paris, 1937; C. G. Feilberg, La tente noire: Contribution ethnographique à l'histoire culturelle des nomades, Copenhagen, 1944; B. Appia-Dabit, Notes sur quelques bijoux sénégalais, BIFAN, V, 1947, pp. 27–32; G. Balandier and P. Mercier, Les outils du forgeron maure, NIFAN, XXXIII, 1, 1947, pp. 8–11; Galerie de l'Orfèvrerie Christofle, Bijoux berbères du Maroc, Paris, 1947 (cat.); H. Lhote, La poterie dans l'Ahaggar: Contribution à l'étude des Touaregs, Trav. Inst. de recherches sahariennes, IV, 1947, pp. 1–10; J. Gabus, Organisation et premiers résultats de la Mission Ethnographique chez les Touaregs soudanais 1946–1947, Acta Tropica, V, 1948, pp. 1–56; R. Mauny, Le judaïsme, les juifs et l'Afrique occidentale, BIFAN, XI, 1949, pp. 354–78; Soeur Pauline-Marie, Le tissage dans la vie féminine au Mzab, B. Soc. neuchâteloise de Géog., LV, 1949–51, pp. 15–30; G. J. Duchemin, A propos des décorations murales des habitations de Oualata (Mauritanie), BIFAN, XII, 1950, pp. 1095–1110; J. Herber, Influence de la bijouterie soudanaise sur la bijouterie marocaine, Hesperis, 1950, pp. 5–10; H. Lhote, Contribution à l'étude des Touaregs: les sandales, Contribution à l'étude de l'Air, Mém. IFAM, 10, 1950, pp. 512–33; H. Lhote, La technique de la poterie à Agadez, Contribution à l'étude de l'Air, Mém. IFAN, 10, 1950, pp. 507–12; M. Reygasse, Monuments funéraires pré-islamiques de l'Afrique du Nord, Paris, 1950; J. Gabus, Contribution à l'étude des Nemadi, chasseurs archaiques du Djouf, B. Soc. suisse d'anthr. et d'ethn., XXVIII, 1951–52, pp. 49–83; J. Gabus, Les sources magico-religieuses de l'art maure, Rapport Mus. et Bib. de la Ville de Neuchâtel, 1951, pp. 1–21; H. Lhote, Les boîtes moulées en peau du Soudan, dites "baba," BIFAN, XIV, 1952, pp. 919–55; J. Besancenot, Bijoux arabes et berbères du Maroc, Casablanca, 1953; P. Dubié, La vie matérielle des Maures, Mém. IFAN, Mél. ethn., 23, 1953, pp. 110–252; T. Monod, Sur quelques graffiti sahariens modernes, NIFAN, LVII, 1, 1953, pp. 8–9; R. Mauny, Une enigme non résolue: origine et symbolique de la croix d'Agadès, NIFAN, LXIII, 7, 1954, pp. 70–79; J. Schacht, Sur la diffusion des formes d'architecture musulmane à travers le Sahara, Trav. Inst. de recherches sahariennes, XI, 1954, pp. 11–27; L. Zöhrer, Ritter der Sahara, Vienna, 1954; C. Béart, Jeaux et jouets de l'Ouest africain (Mém. IFAM, 42), 2 vols., Dakar, 1955; C. Blanguernon, Le Hoggar, Paris, 1955; H. Lhote, Les Touaregs du Hoggar, 2d ed., Paris, 1955; R. Mauny, Notes d'histoire et d'archéologie sur Azougui, Chinguetti et Ouadane, BIFAN, XVII, 1955, pp. 142–62; T. Monod, Sur la forme de la théière traditionnelle, NIFAN, LXVII, 7, 1955, pp. 71–72; Y. Urvoy, L'art dans le Territoire du Niger (Et. nigériennes, II), Dakar, 1955; H. Brandt, Nomades du soleil, Lausanne, 1956; R. Capot-Rey, Greniers domestiques et greniers fortifiés au Sahara: le cas de Gourara, Trav. Inst. de recherches sahariennes, XIV, 1956, pp. 139–58; C. Jest, Decoration des calebasses foulbées, NIFAN, LXXII, 10, 1956, pp. 113–16; J. Chapelle, Nomades noirs du Sahara, Paris, 1957; O. du Puigaudeau, Contribution à l'étude du symbolisme dans le décor mural et l'artisanat de Walâta, BIFAN, XIX, 1957, pp. 137–83; J. Gabus, Au Sahara: arts et symboles, Neuchâtel, 1958; B. Blaudin de Thé, Essai de bibliographie du Sahara français et des régions avoisinantes, 2d ed., Paris, 1960.

Jean GABUS

Illustrations: PLS. 355–364; 2 figs. in text.

SAINTS, ICONOGRAPHY OF. The veneration of saints, which spread with Christianity throughout Europe and the Byzantine world, resulted in the development of a specific iconography in the visual arts that often influenced religious architecture. Only a general treatment of the subject is possible here because of the magnitude and complexity of this iconography, which reflects variations in the attitude of the Church, in historical trends, and in popular beliefs and observances. (See also BIBLICAL SUBJECTS, ESCHATOLOGY, IMAGES AND ICONOCLASM, and SYMBOLISM AND ALLEGORY.)

SUMMARY. Introduction (col. 641). Attributes and symbols (col. 643). Iconographic development (col. 644): *Fourth to seventh centuries; Posticonoclastic period: a. Byzantine art; b. Western art; End of the medieval era to the present. Iconography of selected saints* (col. 659).

INTRODUCTION. In ancient times persons who distinguished themselves by conduct that was exceptionally pious or virtuous according to contemporaneous moral standards were regarded as holy (Lat., *sanctus*; Gr., ῞αγιος) and worthy of respect and emulation. In the Christian context, such persons are called saints and, after death, may be officially recognized by the Church for their holiness and commended as exemplars for the faithful.

In the early years of the Church canonization (the official proclamation of sainthood) could be granted by acclamation by the people (the so-called "vindicatio," probably the subject of a scene in a panel of the wooden portal of S. Sabina, Rome); later it became the prerogative of the bishop within his diocese, and finally could be conferred only by the Pope after the prescribed canonization process. The appellation "saint" was not used by the Church until the 5th century.

Foremost in the list of the saints is the Virgin Mary (venerated as the Theotokos, or God-bearer, by the Orthodox after the Council of Ephesus in 431 and, more simply, as St. Mary by the Monophysites). John the Baptist, called the Prodromos, or precursor, by the Byzantines, and a wide range of people from the Old and New Testaments are also venerated as saints. Adam and Eve, the patriarchs, the prophets, and the kings of Israel are numbered among the saints. New Testament saints include Joseph, the husband of Mary; Anna and Joachim, her parents; Elizabeth and Zacharias, the parents of John the Baptist; the Apostles and St. Paul; the Evangelists, of whom Luke, Matthew, and Mark were disciples of the Apostles; the Holy Innocents; and Stephen, the protomartyr. The Church has included the angels among the saints from its early centuries; angels have the task of defending rather than interceding for man, and, in relation to the Divinity, they serve as messengers and adorers.

From the beginning the Church fostered devotion to the saints by recording their names in special calendars and noting their *dies natalis* (anniversary of death, i.e., heavenly birthday) and places of burial. These calendars (e.g., the Roman *Depositio martyrum* and *Depositio episcoporum*, the Roman Calendar of 354, the Calendar of Carthage of the 6th cent.), at first of limited local interest, later acquired greater importance and were the forerunners of the early martyrologies, in which brief biographical sketches that were not always authenticated appeared next to the name of the saint. These so-called "historical" martyrologies were revised early in the 8th century by the Venerable Bede. A historical martyrology (875) by Usuard of St-Germain-des-Prés was used as the basis of the important revision, the *Martyrologium Romanum* (1584), that was officially adopted by the Catholic Church.

The Menaion, synaxarion, and menologion of the Byzantine Church correspond to the calendars and martyrologies of the Latin Church. The Menaion is a collection of 12 liturgical books, one for each month of the year; in them, each day of the month commemorates a saint, whose name is followed by a brief office and prayer and a biographical note. The synaxarion does not follow the order of the Menaion, and lists only selected saints. A complete catalogue of all the saints of the year is contained in the menologion. The last two were often illustrated, as was the Menologion of Basil II of the 10th century

(II, PL. 447; VII, PL. 220; X, PL. 69); later the texts were replaced by simple schematic illustrations, as in 12 icons in the Monastery of St. Catherine on Mount Sinai, in some Russian icons, and in the monastery church of Dečani in Yugoslavia.

The first and most important literary sources of the iconography of saints are the Old and New Testaments and the Apocrypha. Next in importance and more reliable than the Apocrypha are the writings of the jurisconsults, imperial edicts, and passages from the Church Fathers. Other extensive literary sources are the Acta and the Passiones, which are the most important, followed by the Lives of the Confessors, the Homilies, the Panegyrics, and others.

Originally, the Acta were copies of official reports of martyrs' trials, recorded by one or more notaries, as was the custom (in the Rossano Codex a notary with tablet and stylus is depicted in a scene with Pilate; X, PL. 67). After the Edict of Diocletian ordering the destruction of holy books and vessels, many of these texts were lost; some were later reconstructed on the basis of oral tradition (e.g., the Acta of SS. Paul and Thecla) and substantially altered by the introduction of wholly fictitious elements.

Although these Acta, at least in their unabridged versions, soon ceased to be officially recognized, they continued to be read for purposes of edification during the following centuries. Excerpts from them were printed in devotional books; they served chiefly as the oral reading matter required as an accompaniment to meals in monasteries and convents and were known generically as comes and legenda. Fantastic tales and hearsay reports permeated these legenda, which were widely circulated especially in the late Middle Ages, when the new preaching orders (Franciscans and Dominicans) used them for the *exempla* that formed the basis of their sermons exhorting the faithful to lead edifying lives. This was the origin of such late-medieval hagiographic texts as the *Speculum majus* (1264) of Vincent of Beauvais and the *Legendarium* (1348) by Pietro Calò. The best-known of these texts was the *Legenda aurea* (*Golden Legend*; 1298) by Jacobus de Voragine. Because of these accounts the word "legend" came to mean falsified fact, a meaning that it had not had in the Middle Ages. In the 9th century the angels, especially St. Michael, began to play an important role in legends (the earliest sources of the iconography of angels are the Old and New Testaments and the writings of the Church Fathers).

Legends were a basic material in the creation of the iconography of saints. Artists, particularly in the Latin Church, drew on them profusely, especially with the emergence of the Romanesque style. The legends, formed over the centuries, had different origins. Some were derived from so-called "verbal imitation," according to which the story of the main dramatic episode of the saint's life was based on the literal meaning of his name; for example, St. Christopher (Gr., "Christ-bearer") is reputed to have crossed a river with the Christ Child on his back (cf. PL. 378), and St. Hippolytus (Gr., "rent by horses") is believed to have been tied to four horses and torn asunder. Other legends were the result of a confusion of the literal and the figurative. For example, saints were described as soldiers because the epithet "soldier of Christ" was frequently applied to the martyrs (cf. portrayals of St. Demetrius in late Byzantine art). Sometimes the representation gave rise to the legend. Thus the golden collars worn by St. Sergius and St. Bacchus as members of the imperial guard (PL. 367) were transformed in popular accounts into the heavy chains by which they were dragged through the streets of Constantinople before their death.

In some cases the same type of legend was indiscriminately applied to members of a particular category of saints. For example, use of temptation scenes became customary in the depiction of anchorites such as St. Anthony Abbot (PL. 372); martyrs were represented standing before their judges, as in portrayals of Catherine of Alexandria (PL. 367); in representations of bishops and founders of religious orders the wonders associated with their lives were included, as in depictions of St. Benedict (PL. 178) and in scenes from the life of St. Nicholas of Tolentino in the Church of S. Nicola in Tolentino (14th cent.). In representations of the first bishops, artists depicted their struggle against paganism in their dioceses, which was symbolized by a dragon or monster (e.g., frescoes of scenes from the life of St. Sylvester I, Church of S. Silvestro, Tivoli). In depictions of hermits, their power to tame animals was illustrated (e.g., St. Jerome and the lion; PL. 37; I, PL. 311; IV, PLS. 42, 43; IX, PL. 115). Representations of virgins and martyrs who were killed in Roman amphitheaters dramatized their power to turn ferocious beasts into meek ones.

Among the litanies or invocations recited by Christians since earliest times appear those addressed to the saints, invoking their intercession. One of the first lists of saints in the form of a litany is to be found in the martyrology of Gregory the Great (6th cent.); another longer one is included in the Stowe Missal (8th cent.; Dublin, Royal Irish Academy, Ms. D. 2), and other lists appear on ivory triptychs (e.g., 12th-cent. triptychs in Vat. Mus. and Mus. di Palazzo Venezia in Rome; the Harbaville triptych, XIII, PL. 342). From these litanies and from such other evidence as the prayers of the offertory of the Mass, it is clear that in the early days of the Church a hierarchical order had been established among the saints, who were often invoked collectively. Heading this hierarchy were the angels (with Michael and Gabriel cited separately), followed by the Virgin (who might take precedence, as in the Stowe Missal). In the Eastern Church John the Baptist follows; in the Latin Church, St. Peter. The next rank is variously assigned to the patriarchs, the prophets, and the Apostles, among whom Paul was sometimes included. The Evangelists follow as a group. Next come martyrs, virgins, holy women, confessors, hermits, and monks; added to the list in a later period were the Doctors of the Church (that is, those whose writings contributed to the establishment of the fundamental principles of Christian doctrine) and the popes. Each of these groups is followed by a list of names that often reflects, in order of precedence, the special veneration accorded to local saints; there is also an invocation of all the saints to whom a date in the liturgical calendar has been assigned. The hierarchy of saints established in these invocations was often reflected in the decoration of religious buildings, in which a fixed iconography distinguishes each group.

ATTRIBUTES AND SYMBOLS. During the early centuries of the Christian Era, artists generally placed the saint's name next to his image in order to distinguish one saint from another. As early as the 4th century, differences in physiognomy began to appear in representations, and once established, they remained the same, with rare exceptions, throughout the Middle Ages and even later.

So that the uneducated might be able to identify the saints depicted in religious art, it became customary to use conventional symbols or attributes to distinguish their identities as individuals or as members of a group. Among the generic attributes is the round halo or aureole around the head. In late-antique art this was reserved for emperors; it can be seen in the Missorium of Theodosius (II, PL. 487), in the 6th-century mosaic portraits of Theodora and Justinian in S. Vitale in Ravenna (II, PL. 440, IV, PL. 18), and as late as the 11th–12th century in the representations of the Macedonian emperors in Hagia Sophia in Istanbul (II, PL. 448; X, PL. 185). Later a square halo was used to distinguish living persons (e.g., Pope Paschal I in the apse mosaic in S. Prassede, Rome; X, PL. 182).

Clothing also served to identify the saints: prophets and Apostles were almost always depicted wearing the chlamys and pallium; hermits and anchorites appeared in long robes; soldier-saints wore breastplate and short cloak. As the monastic orders became more numerous, especially in the Romanesque and Gothic periods, the habit of the order was used to identify monks who were saints, while the insignia of office distinguished saints who were Church dignitaries (the pope's tiara; the bishop's miter and crozier; cf. PL. 374). Saints who were kings were depicted wearing crowns, which can also be seen in representations of Old Testament kings (e.g., Solomon, David; II, PLS. 295, 296).

From the first centuries it became customary for artists to identify saints by depicting them with generic attributes that indicate the nature of the saint's activity during his lifetime. Thus prophets, Apostles, Evangelists, and the Fathers and Doctors of the Church are often shown holding a scroll or book (St. Thomas Aquinas, PL. 375); soldier-saints carry a sword or lance (St. Demetrius, St. Theodore Stratelates, III, PL. 457); pilgrim saints are shown with a staff and broad-brimmed hat (St. Roch, XIV, PL. 89) and sometimes a shell; hermits carry the T-shaped staff (St. Anthony Abbot; PL. 372). The attribute is sometimes a symbol, as the Cross, which, when represented with St. Peter (II, PLS. 188, 469; IX, PL. 346) and St. Andrew (II, PLS. 168, 191; IV, PL. 52; VIII, PL. 219) refers not only to the Passion of Christ but also to the crucifixion of these saints themselves. Except for some rare instances, it was the generic attribute that was retained in Byzantine art. The personal attribute is typical of Western art.

The personal attribute may refer to an important episode in the saint's life (e.g., St. Peter's keys, which symbolize the authority to loose and bind conferred on him by Christ, PL. 237; IV, PL. 300; St. Helena's cross, which recalls the finding of the Cross of Christ, XIV, PL. 29). The attribute may indicate the instrument of martyrdom (the gridiron for St. Lawrence, IV, PL. 106; the sword for St. Paul, IX, PLS. 299, 342; the wheel for St. Catherine, IX, PL. 301; bow and arrows for St. Sebastian, PL. 367; II, PL. 328). It may also derive from the saint's name, as the lamb for St. Agnes, and the figure of the Christ Child on the shoulders of St. Christopher; or it may refer to the saint's profession (a jar of unguent and a scapular for SS. Cosmas and Damian, physicians). Although some of these personal attributes appeared as early as the 5th and 6th centuries, they came into wide use only toward the end of the Romanesque period and were even more widely diffused in the Gothic age.

The custom of considering the saint as a patron and depicting him with his hand on the shoulder of his protégé dates from the first centuries after the reign of Constantine (fresco, *Madonna and Child with the Donatrix Turtura*, in the Catacomb of Commodilla, Rome, 6th cent.; St. Demetrius, X, PL. 181). In connection with the veneration of patron saints in the Latin Church, numerous votive images had appeared on church walls as early as pre-Romanesque times and became even more widespread with the Romanesque period, when nations, cities, congregations, and individuals placed themselves under the protection of saints.

During the 14th century the patron saint's power to protect from evil was construed in an almost apotropaic sense and was extended to include other powers: guarding against illness (St. Roch is invoked by the plague-stricken) and bad weather (St. Barbara protects against thunderstorms) and protecting animals (St. Anthony Abbot is their patron). The gigantic figures of St. Christopher on the façades of churches in Alpine regions have the same apotropaic and tutelary significance.

About the same time confraternities, associations, and social classes designated their patron saints (St. Ursula was named patroness of virgins; St. George, of knights; St. Nicholas of Myra, of sailors). For each of these patrons an iconography of specific attributes was established (e.g., St. Joseph, patron of carpenters, is depicted holding a carpenter's plane). The angels were considered guardians of individuals and protectors of churches. The seven churches mentioned in the Apocalypse (1: 17) were protected by angels and are so pictured in Mozarabic art (q.v., esp. col. 370; PL. 207). According to the *Stromateis* of Clement of Alexandria (VI, XVII, 157, 4), the angels are the patrons of the nations. Among the Byzantines, the protection of the army (and of knights) and the defense of city walls were entrusted to the archangels (Istanbul was protected by the Archangel Gabriel). Every person had a guardian angel (devotion to the guardian angel became widespread in the Latin Church after the Counter Reformation). The angels also protected against storms and other phenomena of nature.

ICONOGRAPHIC DEVELOPMENT. *Fourth to seventh centuries.* During the first three centuries of the Christian Era, religious persecutions had impeded the formation and diffusion of an iconography of saints. The only image represented in the catacombs and on sarcophagi was the anonymous orant derived from classical tradition, who symbolized in the new religion the soul freed from the bonds of the body, preparing to rejoice in divine glory. The orant inspired the earliest known portrayal of martyrs (12 figures in the dome of the 4th-century Church of St. George in Salonika, built by Galerius and converted into a church by Theodosius I). Represented frontally with bared head and arms extended in the ritual gesture of prayer (Tertullian, *Apologeticus*, 30), they are depicted against an architectural background that unfolds in trilobed bemas (II, PL. 438; IX, PL. 62); they surround the figure of Christ borne by angels at the center of the dome. Although the facial characteristics are differentiated, they do not serve to identify the martyrs, whose garments indicate the group to which they belonged and whose names are inscribed in large letters next to each figure. Similar figures probably dominated the apses of the martyria (Grabar, 1946), as is suggested by the figure of St. Apollinaris in the Church of S. Apollinare in Classe, Ravenna (6th cent.) and by that of an unidentified saint in Abu Girga in Epypt (Grabar, 1946, pl. 60). Although it appeared much later, another proof of this theory can be found in the Menologion of Basil II (10th cent.), in which the figure of the praying martyr recurs persistently and, like those in the dome of St. George in Salonika, stands out against an architectural background.

Contemporaneously there developed another typical image of the martyr, one that was especially popular in the Latin Church and was usually found together with the figure of Christ. It was derived from the classical figure of the winner of the circus games, and it exists in different versions. The first version shows the martyr with the crown of victory in his hand, which is outstretched toward a figure of Christ (Baptistery of S. Giovanni in Fonte, Naples, 5th cent.; S. Apollinare in Classe, Ravenna, 6th cent.; domes of the baptisteries in Ravenna, 5th and 6th cent.). The second shows the martyr being crowned by the hand of God the Father (S. Vitale, Ravenna, 6th cent.), just as the victorious athlete of classical antiquity was crowned by Tyche. Another figure derived from classical art is the bust of the martyr wearing the crown of victory, as depicted in the Chapel of S. Vittore in Ciel d'Oro in S. Ambrogio in Milan (5th cent.) and in simple medallions and clipei (in S. Vitale and in the chapel of the Archbishop's Palace, both Ravenna, 6th cent.).

A typically Christian iconography, probably of Eastern origin and constantly evident in Byzantine art even after the iconoclastic conflict, was the image of the martyr, who, like Christ, carries the cross, as in representations of St. Lawrence (so-called "Mausoleum of Galla Placidia," Ravenna, 5th cent.), St. Victor (Chapel of S. Vittore in Ciel d'Oro, S. Ambrogio, Milan), and St. Peter (Tempietto del Clitunno, near Trevi, 6th cent.). A symbolic identification of the martyr with the cross can be seen on small encolpia and pectoral crosses, largely of Eastern origin, in which the martyr is represented on the cross (encolpion of St. George and St. Theodore; Coll. P. Cellini, Rome).

Another type of portrayal is biographical and relates an episode of the martyr's life, exalting his martyrdom. Although documents indicate that this type of representation existed in martyria, none is extant. However, some devotional objects provide additional evidence. On a medal of St. Lawrence (Vat. Mus.) the saint appears in front of a martyrion dedicated to him; on the reverse the scene of his death on the gridiron is clearly depicted. On a pyxis of Coptic origin (Br. Mus.), which can be dated to the 6th century, is represented the torture of St. Menas before the judge who condemned him and the figure of Christ praying in front of the saint's martyrion. The iconographic sources of these scenes are presumably the Passiones and the Acta. From them also derive the two representations of St. Thecla (her conversion by St. Paul at Iconium and her torture) that were crudely painted in the cupola of a funerary chapel at El Bagawat in Egypt in the 6th century. The first complete martyrdom still extant is that in the chapel attached to S. Maria Antiqua, in which scenes based on the Acta of SS. Julita and Quiricus (8th cent.) are represented.

A third type of portrayal probably developed very early;

it was votive or commemorative and was offered by one of the faithful. An example is in the Catacomb of Domitilla (4th cent.) in Rome, where St. Petronilla is depicted escorting a protégé into Paradise. There the figure of the saint is shown in the role of intercessor, as in one of the lost mosaics of the Church of St. Demetrius in Salonika, in which the saint, to whom a mother held out her baby, addressed the Virgin, who in turn addressed Christ; this was the order of intercession established by Church doctrine. In these scenes the saint is not represented frontally but is seen in profile, in a pose that was for centuries to signify the act of intercession. Other mosaics in St. Demetrius in Salonika, all of which are votive panels offered by the faithful, present the saint in the role of patron: a 7th-century panel has a frontal view of Demetrius placing his hands on the shoulders of his protégés, Leontius and Bishop John (just as Christ places his hands on the shoulders of St. Menas in a 6th-century icon in the Louvre from the Monastery of St. Catherine on Mt. Sinai). This type of representation developed into the icon, a frontal image of a saint painted on wood (PLS. 373, 379) that had thaumaturgical value for the faithful; icons were not necessarily housed in a church, and eventually they were venerated as objects holy in themselves, rather than as mediums of worship, and thus they became one of the main causes of the iconoclastic conflict.

After the early representations of the martyrs appeared those of the confessors, beginning with a series of depictions of anchorites and hermits clothed in long gowns, their heads covered by cowls (Rabula Gospels, 6th cent.; Florence, Bib. Laurenziana, Plut. I, cod. 56); among these the stylite saints can be recognized (medallion of St. Simeon Stylites, 4th cent.; Grabar, 1943–46, pl. 63) in half figures on columns, in the posture of orants, with arms open, Western fashion, or with palms turned outward and held against the breast in the Byzantine manner. After the 5th century there also appeared representations of popes and bishops in ecclesiastical garments, with chasuble and stole over the amice. These were assigned the last hierarchic place in the apse (usually preceded by angels and the Apostles), as in the 6th-century mosaics in SS. Cosma e Damiano in Rome and in those of the same period in the Basilica in Poreč, Yugoslavia (VII, PL. 266), and in S. Vitale, Ravenna. Less common are the figures of soldier-saints with lance and shield, probably of Coptic origin, which appear in great numbers in the chapels of Bawit, Egypt (III, PL. 454); their iconography was perhaps derived from the steles of the Thracian knights.

In the Early Christian communities virgins and especially holy women had the function of teaching catechumens and assisting the presbyters as deaconesses. In most cases they belonged to the category of martyrs and are represented as such, but they are always depicted with head covered, in accordance with the custom of the period and St. Paul's admonitions (I Corinthians, 11). Such a woman instructing a catechumen has been discerned by De Rossi (1894) on the sarcophagus of the Arieti (Vat. Mus.) in the seated, heavily veiled figure on the left who holds an open book. Another example is the figure of St. Petronilla in the Catacomb of Domitilla in Rome, beside whom the artist sketched a capsa with several scrolls. The virgins in a mosaic in S. Apollinare Nuovo in Ravenna (6th cent.; PL. 366) are lightly veiled. The holy women and virgins depicted in the chapel of the Archbishop's Palace in Ravenna and in S. Prassede in Rome are shown wearing veils or mantles. The slab portraying St. Agnes in the Basilica of S. Agnese in Rome (4th cent.) is an exception. Later, virgins were often depicted in crowns and regal garments (St. Agnes, X, PL. 181).

The Apostles were among the first saints depicted as a distinct group, and they appear in Christian art even before the Edict of Milan. The earliest examples are in the catacombs and on sarcophagi, gilded glass, medallions, and liturgical objects (PL. 365). With Matthias in the place of Judas, who was often depicted hanged (lipsanotheca, 4th cent.; Brescia, Mus. Cristiano), the Apostles numbered 12. Frequently Matthias was replaced by St. Paul, Apostle of the Gentiles, as in the domes of the baptisteries in Ravenna (5th–6th cent.). The number of the Apostles was sometimes increased to 14 to include the

Evangelists Luke and Matthew, disciples of the Apostles; at times Barnabas, St. Paul's companion in Cyprus, was also included. In the sarcophagus of Sextus Petronius Probus and his wife Anicia (4th–5th cent.; Vat. Grottoes), the Apostles number 22. Only three of the Apostles were depicted with distinctive physical traits: St. Peter had a thick head of hair and a short white beard; St. Paul was bald with a thin face and a long, tapered black beard (Rome, S. Costanza, 4th cent.); St. Andrew had chestnut or white wavy hair and beard (Ravenna, S. Apollinare Nuovo, 6th cent.). Iconographically they were all modeled on the type of the ancient philosopher (cf. IX, PL. 84): they might or might not have beards (St. John was generally beardless, as St. Thomas and St. Philip often were); they were almost always barefoot. Rarely, they held the martyr's crown; and more frequently they carried a scroll or book (those held by the Evangelists were often open). St. Peter was generally depicted holding keys (Ravenna, Baptistery of the Arians, 6th cent.). In representations of the Apostles with Christ, Peter and Paul had the places of honor; in the earliest portrayals Paul was generally on the right and Peter on the left, but later the positions were reversed. No hierarchy was established for the other Apostles. The mission of the Apostles — one of the most popular themes in Early Christian art — is represented in the Cubiculum of Ampliatus (2d–3d cent.) in the Catacomb of Domitilla in Rome and on many 4th-century sarcophagi (e.g., the sarcophagus formerly called "of Stilicho," IX, PL. 64). In the 4th century the same theme was used on a larger scale in the Catacomb of Domitilla and in the apse of the Chapel of St. Aquilinus in S. Lorenzo in Milan (IX, PL. 74). In the apse of S. Pudenziana in Rome (early 5th cent.) the Apostles are portrayed in a group with other figures, symbolizing the Church Triumphant or the Heavenly Jerusalem. In the dome of the Baptistery of the Orthodox in Ravenna towering figures of the Apostles surround the scene of the Baptism of Christ (IX, PL. 72). In a fragment of a prince's sarcophagus (4th cent.; Istanbul, Archaeol. Mus.) they flank the Cross.

The Apostles naturally have an important place in scenes of Christ's public life; the number of Apostles depicted depends on the scene. For example, in mosaics in S. Apollinare Nuovo in Ravenna (in which St. Andrew and St. Peter are clearly recognizable by the characteristics indicated earlier) 11 Apostles are depicted in the scene in the Garden of Gethsemane. There are 11 also in the representation of the Communion in the Rabula Gospels. The number varies, too, in the Sinope Codex (Paris, Bib. Nat., Suppl. gr. 1286), and on a small ivory casket (Br. Mus.), both executed in the 6th century. The scene of the Last Supper in the Rossano Codex (Codex purpureus rossanensis; Rossano, Italy, Mus. Arcivescovile) depicts 12 Apostles at the moment when Judas dips his hand into the dish. In the same codex the Communion scene is depicted on two pages, as the Eucharist is represented under two species; there are 6 Apostles on each page, and Christ is depicted twice. The same scene is portrayed on the 6th-century Riba paten (Washington, D.C., Dumbarton Oaks Coll.) and the paten from Stuma (IX, PL. 162); it perhaps also appeared in the apse of the Church of the Holy Apostles (destroyed) in Istanbul. In the Rabula Gospels (fol. 1a), an unusual scene represents 11 Apostles choosing between two candidates for the place of Judas.

The Apostles Peter and Paul are often portrayed together, especially in Western religious art. Their busts in profile appear on a 3d-century bronze medallion (Vat. Lib.) and on a gilded glass (Vat. Mus.). They flank Christ in the scene of the Traditio Legis ("Delivery of the New Law") in one of the apses of S. Costanza in Rome (4th cent.), where the word "legem" on the scroll has been replaced by the word "pacem" in view of the funerary character of the monument, which was originally the mausoleum of Constantina and was later transformed into a church. This representation, almost certainly of Western origin (probably modeled on a sculpture on the Arch of Constantine), is an explicit declaration of the primacy of Peter as head of the Church by divine election. The earliest Roman calendars indicate the anniversary of the Cathedra Petri. There are a few rare depictions of St. Paul receiving the law on some sarcophagi in Ravenna (cf. G. de Francovich, *Felix Ravenna*,

No. 26, 1958). Scenes from the lives of the two Apostles also were represented. On the sarcophagus of Junius Bassus (II, PL. 282) they appear in separate scenes being led to their martyrdom, and on the Rinaldo sarcophagus they appear together with Christ (IX, PL. 65). The cock appears in numerous representations of Peter's denial of Christ, as in S. Apollinare Nuovo in Ravenna, on one of the columns of the ciborium in S. Marco, and on the lipsanotheca in Brescia (Mus. Cristiano). The image of St. Peter in a boat, which symbolized the Church, was probably used frequently, as in a 4th-century bronze liturgical lamp (Florence, Mus. Archaeol.), on which he is depicted with St. Paul. Scenes from St. Paul's life, including the shipwreck off Malta and the miracle of the serpent, are carved on an ivory diptych (Florence, Mus. Naz.).

As early as the end of the 4th century and the beginning of the 5th, the Apostles were represented by symbols. They are symbolized by 12 white doves in the Albenga baptistery (5th–6th cent.); they appear as lambs in the lower band of mosaics in the apse of SS. Cosma e Damiano (IX, PL. 75) and in S. Prassede (X, PL. 182), both in Rome. Many churches had 12 pillars to symbolize the Apostles, thus concretizing the frequently employed literary image describing them as "pillars of the church."

Mark, John, Luke, and Matthew, as Evangelists, had to be distinguished from the Apostles. The Fathers of the Church saw them foreshadowed in the four tetramorphic creatures of Ezekiel's vision (Ezekiel, 1: 6), which correspond to those in the vision of John (Apocalypse, 4: 7–8). According to the description in the later text, each has a distinctive physiognomy (a bull, an eagle, a lion, a man) and six wings (the number of wings varies; often only two are represented). In the Latin Church portrayals of them followed John's description, with the exception that only their heads and shoulders were shown, as on the triumphal arch in S. Maria Maggiore in Rome (II, PL. 283), in the vault of the Baptistery of S. Giovanni in Fonte in Naples (IX, PL. 61), in the apse of S. Pudenziana (beginning of the 5th cent.) on the triumphal arch of S. Paolo fuori le Mura in Rome (5th cent.), in the vault of the so-called "Mausoleum of Galla Placidia" (5th cent.) and on the triumphal arch of S. Apollinare in Classe (X, PL. 181), both in Ravenna, in the apse of Hosios David in Salonika (5th cent.), and in the vault of the chapel in the Archbishop's Palace in Ravenna. In order to make the symbolism clearer, artists sometimes represented these figures holding a scroll or a book (the Gospel). In S. Vitale in Ravenna (6th cent.) the Evangelist's symbol is depicted above the representation of his seated figure.

Eastern art represented the Evangelists as human figures, without symbols; they are shown in this manner on the "throne of Maximian" in Ravenna (V, PL. 432) and in the Rabula Gospels, in which they are depicted beside St. John the Baptist with books in their hands. In Early Christian art the Evangelists were sometimes symbolized by the four rivers of Paradise, as on the Rinaldo sarcophagus in Ravenna Cathedral.

Except for the Virgin, almost all the saints of the New Testament were depicted in a historical context (see BIBLICAL SUBJECTS). After the Council of Ephesus (431), the figure of the Virgin enthroned dominated church apses; she was represented with the Christ Child on her lap (X, PLS. 182, 185). Mary is the only saint who was depicted being escorted by the heavenly host of angels (Rome, S. Maria Maggiore, 5th cent.; Ravenna, S. Apollinare Nuovo, 6th cent.), and who precedes them in the celestial hierarchy (see CHRISTIANITY, col. 602).

In Early Christian art the figure of John the Baptist was almost always clothed in a sheepskin that recalled his life in the desert. Thus, with a sheepskin over his tunic and a clipeus with an image of the Lamb of God in his hand, John the Baptist appears in the center of the "throne of Maximian" (PL. 365). The saint is rarely portrayed alone; he most often appears in the scene of the Baptism of Christ, which was frequently represented in catacombs and on sarcophagi even before the reign of Constantine and which was later used in baptisteries (e.g., Ravenna), where he is generally depicted in a sheepskin, pouring the baptismal water on Christ's head. The same scene on the cover of the reliquary casket of the Sancta Sanctorum (6th cent.;

probably of Syrian origin; Vat. Mus.) shows him clad in tunic and pallium.

Among the saints of the New Testament, St. Joseph almost always appears in the scene of his dream. He holds a carpenter's saw in the Nativity scene on a 5th-century ivory diptych (Milan, Cath. Treas.). The Magi wear Phrygian caps and Persian costumes, as in the ambo from Salonika (4th–5th cent.; Istanbul, Archaeol. Mus.) and in the nave of S. Apollinare Nuovo in Ravenna. The Holy Innocents are depicted only in scenes of their massacre. Lazarus, Martha, and Mary generally are portrayed in a scene in which Lazarus, wrapped in his shroud, looks out from the edge of his grave (lipsanotheca, Brescia, Mus. Cristiano).

The earliest representations of the Old Testament saints are found in the catacombs (Noah leaving the ark, Daniel in the lions' den, and the deliverance of Jonah) and on sarcophagi (Moses drawing water from the rock). Scenes with personages from the Old Testament were important in the illustrations of the parallels between the Old and New Testaments (*concordia veteris et novi testamenti*). The Rabula Gospels and Rossano Codex (Rossano, Mus. Arcivescovile) indicate that in the Eastern Church these parallels were illustrated in manuscripts not in two scenes but in single scenes in which the figures of the prophets emerge from tribunes on which their prophecies are inscribed; a New Testament scene at the top or middle of the page illustrates the fulfillment of these prophecies. Other favorite Old Testament subjects in Early Christian art in the East were scenes from the life of Joseph ("throne of Maximian," Ravenna, Mus. Arcivescovile) and, later, scenes from the life of David (7th-cent. silver dishes in Nicosia, Cyprus Mus., and Met. Mus.; VII, PL. 312).

Representations of angels generally were derived from the genii and winged victories of classical art. Always depicted as youthful and beautiful, these androgynous figures were generally represented clad in a white tunic or pallium, with head bound by an infula and feet bare or lightly sandaled. Wings and aureoles appeared in depictions of angels only after the 5th century (IX, PL. 75). In the earliest portrayals their flesh is tinged with red (Rome, S. Maria Maggiore, triumphal arch) and they are sometimes clothed in red (Ravenna, S. Apollinare Nuovo, 500–26; Kirschbaum, 1940). In his *Carmen Paschale* (I, v, 328) Sedulius declared: "Flammens aspectu niveo preclarus anuctu." However, this manner of representation was explicitly condemned by the Second Council of Nicaea, and it is known from the acts of this council that one bishop was particularly zealous in fostering the notion of angels dressed in white rather than red. Angels precede the saints hierarchically in liturgical representations; they flank the thrones of Christ and the Virgin (Ravenna, S. Apollinare Nuovo, S. Vitale; Poreč, Basilica) and appear beside the Cross (paten, 6th cent., Leningrad, The Hermitage). In these scenes they are often depicted holding a long staff or, rarely, a thurible (as at Bawit, III, PL. 454) or sphere (as in the Church of the Panagia Angeloktistos at Kition, Cyprus; 6th–7th cent.).

In scenes from the Old and New Testaments (nave and triumphal arch of S. Maria Maggiore, Rome, 5th cent.) they usually appear as messengers of God; in the scene of the visitation of Abraham they number three, symbolizing the Trinity (Rome, S. Maria Maggiore; Ravenna, S. Vitale). At times, when the Scriptures have specifically identified them, their names appear next to their images (e.g., Gabriel in representations of the Annunciation). In other representations the angels were identified only infrequently, as in a painting in the apse of the church of Deir el-Suryani in Egypt and in representations of them as protectors of churches (e.g., sculptures on the portal of Church I at Alahan Monastir).

In laudatory representations, angels in flight (child's sarcophagus, 4th cent., II, PL. 468; mosaics in Ravenna, S. Vitale) and angels as caryatids (Ravenna, chapel of the Archbishop's Palace and vault of the presbytery of S. Vitale, 6th cent.) carry crowns or clipei inscribed with the Cross, the monogram of Christ, the Lamb of God, or the bust of the Pantocrator.

As protectors, they are portrayed in warriors' garments. In other representations, angels assume the attire of court dignitaries — dalmatic, tunicle, an silk chlamys — as in S. Vitale in Ravenna, where they guard the bema; they also have the function of indicating to the faithful that the sacrifice carried out on the altar is transported *in sublime altare* (that is, to the heavenly Altar) by *manus sancti angeli tui* (the hands of Thy holy angel). In the same mosaic in S. Vitale the archangel holds a labarum on which the word Ἅγιος appears three times (recalling the Trisagion of the Eastern Mass). The archangels in Ravenna had parallels in the Church of the Dormition (destroyed) in Nicaea in four angelic figures garbed in the heavy embroidered loros (imperial and senatorial garment derived from the Romans, which in the Eastern Church seems to symbolize the Resurrection (the figures have been variously dated but are probably of the late 6th cent.).

The cherubim, at times confused with the seraphim, have a special iconography. Identified with the beings who attend the throne of the Lord in the vision of Ezekiel, they are represented as tetramorphs (with the heads of a bull, an eagle, a lion, and an angel) with four wings covered with eyes, moving on wheels of fire. Representations of such figures can be seen on the architrave of Church I of Alahan Monastir, in the scene of the Ascension in the Rabula Gospels, on the columns of the baldacchino above the high altar of S. Marco in Venice, in some late copies of the Cosmas Indicopleustes, and in the apses of Romanesque churches in Catalonia. These figures, which were widely used in the art of the Eastern Church, probably cannot be identified with the Evangelists as they were in the same period in the art of the Latin Church.

The Apocalypse and — to a greater extent — Ezekiel indicate that the angels are to have an important role in the Last Judgment. In Western art, the angel of the Last Judgment (not clearly identified) was represented for the first time in S. Apollinare in Classe, in Ravenna, where its reddish aspect is contrasted with that of a blue-toned angel who represents the devil. Trumpets are the distinctive attributes of angels in this context, as in the Church of S. Michele in Affricisco (destroyed), in Ravenna. Those depicted on the triumphal arch of the Church of S. Paolo fuori le Mura in Rome carry long rods that recall Charon's staff. The archangel Michael is often depicted in the act of transfixing the devil (e.g., 5th- or 6th-cent. ivory, Br. Mus.). Later the treatment of the Last Judgment became much more complex (see ESCHATOLOGY). The motif of the angel-psychopomp and angel-psychagogue who conduct souls to the hereafter is derived from a combination of classical and Egyptian themes, along with subjects suggested to the Apocalypse, which assigns to the good angels, led by St. Michael, the task of driving the wicked angels into Hell and reserves for the angels a special role in the Last Judgment.

Posticonoclastic period. a. Byzantine art. During the 8th century the iconoclastic movement strongly affected the development of representational art in the Byzantine world. The movement was opposed by the Latin Church and by monks, who, in remote monasteries on the heights of Mt. Sinai and in Cappadocia, strove to keep iconographic traditions alive. Not until the second half of the 9th century and the end of the iconoclastic conflict did images reappear in churches, where they often replaced the aniconic decoration that had been used during the iconoclastic period. These images were based on earlier pictorial schemes, a few of which had probably been preserved in illuminated manuscripts and liturgical objects such as ampullae and pyxes.

Once again the saints were represented next to the figures of Christ and the Virgin on the walls of churches, on the iconostases, on icons, in manuscripts, and on every kind of devotional object. At first the links with preiconoclastic figures were evident, as in the figures of bishops on the wall of the nave of Hagia Sophia in Istanbul and in miniatures illustrating the Homilies of St. Gregory Nazianzen (II, PL. 480). However, these posticonoclastic expressions are pervaded by an intensified spirituality; the golden background on which the figures were always portrayed suggests the immutability of eternity in the midst of a transitory world. The faces are alike, but idealized personal features are represented (e.g., various portrayals of

St. John Chrysostom in manuscripts and in churches: II, PL. 457; X, PL. 184; XIII, PL. 64). Only rarely were the saints depicted in Byzantine art with the personal attributes that were common in contemporaneous religious art in the Western Church. They were identified in the art of the Eastern Church by their names written in large letters next to their figures; they have a nimbus, and they carry small crosses, books with precious bindings, or scrolls. Only the Evangelists were represented seated; they were depicted in small studies and were never shown with their symbols. Clothing was commonly used to distinguish different categories of saints: prophets, patriarchs, and Apostles were represented in tunic and pallium as in Early Christian times, but these were almost always bicolor; deacons were depicted in heavy mantles fixed by large brooches and wearing small hats. Fathers and Doctors of the Church as well as bishops were depicted in their ecclesiastical garb (tunic, chasuble, and stole with crosses), while monks and hermits were clad in long habits and cowls. The kings of the Old Testament, Christian emperors, and martyrs who were officials of the Roman Empire were portrayed in the court costumes of the period. When the saints were represented as soldiers, they were shown in military garb: breastplate, short pleated tunic, sagum, and knee-high red leather boots; the same costume was worn by the emperor when celebrating a triumph, as in the portrait of the ruler in the Psalter of Basil II (Venice, Bib. Marciana; Ms. gr. Z 17.421). Only kings and emperors were represented with crowns. Daniel was often represented in Persian costume (e.g., in the Pala d'Oro in S. Marco, Venice; IV, PL. 405).

The angels were especially revered by the Byzantines, and there were many representations of the archangels, whose attire varies according to their function. When depicted next to God as members of the heavenly hierarchy, they wear courtly clothing (as in Hosios David in Greece). When they are fulfilling a liturgical function, their garb is the same but in their hands they carry the labarum with the Trisagion. As protectors of the army they wear military dress, with shield, lance, and sword; as messengers of God they appear in the tunic and pallium common to all angels. The cherubim and seraphim are the only other types of angels represented in Byzantine art of this period. They are not clearly distinguishable but may be identified with winged tetramorphous figures similar to those mentioned above.

Just as the cermonial costumes of the court were the pattern for the clothing of some groups of saints, so the hierarchy of the court officials under the emperors suggested the hierarchy of the saints under God as illustrated in the churches (which in sermons of the time were often compared to the imperial palace). Representations of the Virgin were placed in the semidome of the main apse beyond the bema (almost all posticonoclastic churches were built on an inscribed-cross plan); Mary was depicted as the Theotokos with the Christ Child either on her knees or in her arms (as in Hagia Sophia in Istanbul, II, PL. 448, and in Hosios Loukas in Greece, X, PL. 185). Other saints were depicted in the naos. Around the bust of the Pantocrator that dominated the dome a circle of archangels (as the emperor's personal servants) was represented with labarums and spheres (Hosios Loukas, Phocis; St. Sophia, Kiev); in the drum prophets, patriarchs, and kings were represented (as the senators); in the squinches or pendentives the Evangelists (as the scribes) sometimes were depicted; and the martyrs and confessors were represented on the walls. Never before in Christian art (not even in the Latin Church) had such a great number of saints been depicted in a church. They are all standing as if they were in the imperial consistorium, where only the emperor could remain seated. Interspersed among the figures are scenes from the life of Christ and the Virgin (Daphne, Greece). The episodes from the life of Christ (not always depicted in the same manner and location) were chosen from among the feasts of the Byzantine calendar; scenes from the life of the Virgin were inspired by the Protoevangelium of St. James (the Dormition of the Virgin was always depicted on an interior wall adjoining the narthex). Both cycles, which were designed as visual refutations of the Arian heresy, seem to be a demonstration of the fulfillment of the Redemption, in which the Mother of God had such an important role (the denial of her divine maternity by Arius had caused severe religious and political conflict in the Byzantine Empire of the preceding centuries). In the Christological cycle John the Baptist and the Apostles are second to Christ in importance, and in the Mariological cycle Joachim and Anna figure prominently next to Mary (II, PLS. 449, 450).

A hierarchical order more or less similar to that used in the churches can be seen in the icons on the iconostasis and staurotheke (reliquary of the Cross) such as that in the Cathedral of Limburg an der Lahn. It is also evident in the Pala d'Oro of S. Marco in Venice and in some ivory triptychs in Rome (Mus. di Palazzo Venezia). In these works appears the Deësis, that is, the representation of the Virgin and John the Baptist as intercessors with Christ (II, PL. 455; VIII, PL. 174). On that side of the staurotheke on which the relic of the Cross was displayed, Constantine and his mother Helena were generally depicted. No scenes of the lives of the martyrs and confessors have survived in monumental art, except in some monastic complexes such as the rock-cut churches in Cappadocia. Such scenes probably existed in churches, as in the Nea of Basil I (Theotokos Pharos) in Constantinople, where there were scenes of the lives of the martyrs on the vaults.

Scenes from the lives of the saints appeared in illuminated manuscripts, especially in menologia (e.g., Menologion of Basil II, Vat. Lib., Cod. gr. 1613), in which the scene of martyrdom or death, the depositio, or the translatio was depicted.

Depictions of scenes from the lives of saints were used more prominently in Western churches decorated by Byzantine artists (e.g., at Cefalù and Monreale and the Cappella Palatina in Palermo), for the didactic value of painting was stressed in the West by theologians and by the Pope. Old Testament scenes were included in these representations (as at Monreale; II, PL. 286). In the Church of Sant'Angelo in Formis near Capua, where the frescoes were painted by local artists following the example furnished by artists called to Montecassino by Abbot Desiderius, the theme of the parallels between the Old and New Testaments was used (in these frescoes a prophet, with an open scroll on which his prophecy is inscribed, contemplates the scenes painted above his head of the life of Christ, whose advent he had foretold). That this custom, of Eastern origin, was continued in Byzantine miniatures is confirmed by a miniature of the Ascension (Paris, Bib. Nat., Cod. gr. 1208, fol. 3v).

While the canonic order of preceding centuries was preserved, popular and monastic traditions contributed a number of new themes drawn extensively from apocryphal writings. There was a transition from the hieratic immobility of the middle Byzantine period to a spirited and free movement (particularly evident in Macedonian churches) enlivened by colors, and there was a variety of costumes often copied from clothing of the period. Complete cycles of lives of the saints were added to the Christological cycle (generally in the narthex, as in the monastery church of Dečani, XIII, PL. 54). The representation of the Communion of the Apostles was changed to depict Christ in ecclesiastical garb taking part in a celestial liturgy while the angels, in the white tunics of deacons, serve at the rite; in scenes of the Dormition of the Virgin, the Apostles appeared in everincreasing numbers (Gračanica, Péc, Dečani). In the apse prophets, patriarchs, bishops, kings, and Doctors of the Church, enveloped in large copes, were depicted (II, PLS. 452, 457), often in double file and bowing to the figure of God, while the images of stylites on pillars at the sides of the bema were reminiscent of torches casting their light on the scene.

Increasingly icons were used in private as well as public worship. Often the image of the saint was framed by biographical scenes (cf. icon of St. Theodore Stratelates, PL. 373). Even the Menaion and menologion came to consist entirely of pictures (menologia painted on the walls of the Monastery of St. Catherine on Mt. Sinai and on the walls of the monastery church of Dečani). Icons for popular use were produced in great quantity by the Cretan-Byzantine school (q.v.) and the Russian school, which continued until the 18th century. The archangel Michael was the subject of countless icons, as were the three angels symbolizing the Trinity in portrayals of Abraham. Choirs of angels were represented in multicolored robes surrounding Christ (IV, PL. 47). Cherubim depicted as bodiless, winged infants were probably of Western derivation.

b. Western art. The political upheaval in western Europe during the barbarian invasions checked the development of the iconography of saints. The iconography of the Evangelists seems to be the only one to have survived in illuminated manuscripts, which were often copies of earlier texts. For example, the Evangelists sometimes depicted with their symbols recall those in S. Vitale, Ravenna. Similar figures, interpreted in a more decorative style, are to be found in Hiberno-Saxon art (see ANGLO-SAXON AND IRISH ART; MINIATURES AND ILLUMINATION), in which the symbols of the Evangelists appear with or without books [Book of Kells, Dublin, Trinity College, Ms. 58 (A.I.6)].

Some frescoes of scenes from the lives of the saints appeared in small churches and oratories, as in the Church of S. Procolo in Naturno, near Bolzano, where fragments of scenes from the life of St. Paul (8th cent.) are preserved. In the Sacramentary of Gellone (Paris, Bib. Nat., Ms. lat. 12048) the symbols of the Evangelists are anthropomorphous; this iconography was later used extensively in Mozarabic art (q.v.) and influenced Romanesque art (q.v.), particularly in Spain, and Gothic art (q.v.). In Merovingian art representations of Daniel in the lions' den appear frequently on fibulas. The Lombards' crude Altar of Ratchis (7th cent.) shows six-winged cherubim with human faces (XI, PL. 326) and a representation of the Visitation; in the scene of the Adoration of the Magi, what is probably the figure of the prophet Balaam behind Mary's throne in later iconography became the figure of Joseph.

In the second half of the 8th century, Byzantine iconoclasm threatened to disrupt the continuity of Western art. But the Pope and the emperor Charlemagne defended the use of figural representation, which then spread to the barbarian tribes settled in central Europe (see CAROLINGIAN ART). The few surviving examples of the iconography of this period are based on earlier works, but they were often developed in a new manner. In a painting in the crypt of St-Germain in Auxerre of scenes from the life of St. Stephen, the first scene shows the saint in the traditional posture of prayer, but the second, the scene of the stoning, is imbued with a new sense of humanity, for both invocation and offering are suggested in the saint's attitude as he leans toward the outstretched hand of God (III, PL. 54). Another illustration of this new treatment is the procession of martyrs and virgins depicted in the crypt of S. Maximin in Trier (III, PL. 54); each of the figures carries a palm (probably derived from classical representations of Tyche; cf. VII, PL. 157) instead of the crown that is carried in similar processions depicted in S. Apollinare Nuovo in Ravenna. In the Crucifixion scene in the same crypt, the figure of St. John the Evangelist appears at the foot of the Cross, his grief-stricken face resting on his left palm (the pose derives perhaps from that of a Byzantine figure of which there is evidence in later examples). In a chapel at San Vincenzo al Volturno (9th cent.), near Montecassino, the scene of the martyrdom of St. Lawrence recalls that on the medal in the Vatican Museums, and the crowned saints in procession are similar to the figure of the martyr in the apse of S. Agnese in Rome, where, for the first time, a saint who was not a queen was depicted wearing a crown (adapting the traditional theme of the coronation of the martyr, the artist depicted the martyr as already possessing the crown as an attribute).

Illumination provides additional iconographic evidence. Among the rare surviving examples of historical scenes there is a page with scenes from the life of St. Paul and another with scenes from the life of St. Jerome in the Moutier-Grandval Bible (9th cent.; Br. Mus., Add. Ms. 10546), in which the series of narrative pictures appears on three horizontal sections of a page. The most complete cycle of scenes from a saint's life is that of St. Ambrose on the golden altar by Wolvinius in Milan Cathedral. Evidence of the existence of icons depicting saints is provided by a miniature in the Lorsch Sacramentary (Chantilly, Mus. Condé, Ms. 1447), in which icons of Abraham, David, and Jechoniah are carried in triumph by the crowd.

Although few portrayals of martyrs and confessors were executed during this period, the Evangelists were frequently represented. Often their figures appear with their symbols, as in S. Vitale in Ravenna, but it was customary also to depict them as zoomorphous creatures; sometimes only their heads were portrayed. In the Moutier-Grandval Bible the illuminator arranged the three or four symbols (depending on the number of canon tables included) with an unfurled scroll or an open book between them.

The Apostles (12, including St. Paul) generally are depicted on the ivory covers of codices in such traditional scenes as Pentecost and the Ascension. The images of Peter and Paul follow the traditional iconography. Angels, too, appear in scenes from the life of Christ; they are prominent in the Utrecht Psalter (III, PL. 58; IV, PL. 231), as are personages from the Old Testament.

With the collapse of the Carolingian empire and the establishment of the Ottonian dynasty, art, while still courtly in character, was enriched by new themes that clearly revealed an intensification of the devotion to saints. The Fathers of the Church, who were especially honored for their learning, and the founders of monastic orders were exalted among the saints. Evidence of this growing cult, which was centered in the monasteries, is provided by the so-called "dedicatory pictures" of codices, in which the amanuensis offers the codex transcribed by him to a saint, either directly or through a superior (cf. X, PL. 464). The most common iconography of this scene comes from the Missorium of Theodosius, 4th cent.; Madrid, Real Academia de la Historia). The dedication that had been directly addressed to Christ in the Early Christian era (e.g., in S. Vitale in Ravenna) was then addressed to the saint, who, it might be said, substituted for Christ. The same scene is repeated in the Gero Codex (Darmstadt, Landesbib., Ms. 1948), where the manuscript is offered by Aunus to St. Peter, who wears sacerdotal garments (chasuble and stole). For the first time in the Gospels from the Abbey of Poussay (Paris, Bib. Nat., Ms. lat. 10514, fol. 30) the scribe is represented with two angels as he offers his book to Christ. In these dedicatory pages, the figures of saints are often notably larger than the figures of the donors (as in the Missorium of Theodosius). As time passed this difference became more marked, and there evolved a new perspective, determined by religious and moral criteria, that strongly influenced the art of the Romanesque period.

Ottonian artists, free from traditional rules, invented new forms for ancient subjects. Their imaginative genius can be seen throughout their art; old themes were interpreted in an almost completely original manner. Although the treatment was sometimes extremely daring, it was always characterized by a strong classical feeling. Even the costumes remained traditional; Christ, the Apostles, Evangelists, angels, and sometimes even John the Baptist were depicted wearing tunic and pallium (rarely the dalmatic) and were thereby distinguished from court personages and the populace, who were portrayed in contemporaneous clothing. Also represented in contemporaneous dress are four of the stucco figures of virgin martyrs in S. Maria in Valle (the so-called "Tempietto") in Cividale del Friuli (10–11th cent.; XI, PL. 324). The figures hold crowns, in accordance with Early Christian tradition, although they wear them, too. The same iconography is evident in frescoes of female saints in the apse of S. Sebastiano al Palatino in Rome (10th cent.).

In general, these figures did not follow existing models, except for St. Peter and St. Paul (as in the Book of Pericopes of Henry II, Munich, Bayerische Staatsbib., Clm. 4452 and in an epistolary, Cologne, Cath. Lib., Cod. 143), and even these were not always true to type. The names of the saints depicted are not always indicated as they had been in Byzantine art, because at that time they simply illustrated the *titula* of the church or of the page of the codex. Among the Evangelists, St. Mark sometimes appeared in chasuble and stole (Paris, Bib. Nat., nouv. acq. 2196); this costume was also used by Ottonian artists for those few saints who were represented on full pages of manuscripts. Notable among the other saints are Gregory, who was represented with a dove at his ear (*Registrum Gregorii*, ca. 983, Trier, Stadtbib.), and Jerome (Milan, Bib. Ambrosiana, Ms. C. 53 Sup.; Bible frontispiece, Paris, Bib. Nat., Ms. fr. 166). The scribes beside them indicate their status as Church Fathers or Doctors. Scenes of martyrdom and episodes from the lives of the saints are rarely found. The traditional representation of St. Lawrence on the gridiron is occasionally seen, and the scene depicting St. Martin and the beggar makes its first appearance. David seems to have been the only Biblical character represented; he was clad in royal robes and shown with his harp, according to the tradition of the Carolingian court.

Except for a few six-winged cherubim, the figures and costumes of angels were not differentiated and their rank was not indicated. They were generally represented as much larger than human figures (manuscripts of the Reichenau school). The angel psychagogue appears carrying souls to the bosom of Abraham (Codex Aureus Epternacensis, Nürnberg, Germanisches Nat.-Mus., deaths of David and Lazarus). The avenging angels, with St. Michael defeating the devil, are depicted in a fresco of the Last Judgment in Burgfelden (11th cent.); this was to become a basic theme on the tympanums of Romanesque portals.

Beginning with the 10th century, sacred images acquired a new significance as the Church defined their cult as a form of veneration rather than worship. The veneration of relics continued in great favor as many churches became the goal of pilgrimages and saints' remains were transferred from one place to another (such *translationes* were depicted on capitals in the church at Saint-Benoît-sur-Loire and in the crypt of the Abbey church at Vézelay). However, devotional fervor was concentrated on the rapidly multiplying painted and sculptural images of the saints. This was evident in the growing tendency to create reliquaries in human form (e.g., reliquary statue of Ste Foy, X, PL. 473; bust reliquaries of St. Maurice and St. Candidus in the Abbey of Saint-Maurice, in Switzerland) and to decorate others with scenes from the lives of saints (reliquary of St. Hadelin, ca. 1190, Church of St-Martin in Visé, near Liège; reliquary of S. Millàn, 11th cent.; Madrid, Mus. Arqueol. Nac.). Such scenes also decorated sarcophagi.

While in the Early Christian period the saint's martyrdom had been emphasized as a parallel with Christ's death, in this period it was the saint's whole life in imitation of Christ that served as an inspiring example to the faithful. Visions and presages were represented in scenes of the saint's birth; his childhood was depicted in edifying terms (as in miniatures illustrating the life of St. Benedict; Vat. Lib., Cod. lat. 1202). Later scenes included temptations (PL. 247), miracles (PLS. 276, 369), sermons (St. Fulbert preaching and the scene before the judge, Chartres Cath., Ms. 104, ca. 1028; altar frontals with stories of St. Margaret, Vich, Spain, Mus. Episcopal), suffering (scenes from the life of St. Andrew) and death by torture (martyrdom of St. Vincent, Church of S. Vincenzo, Galliano; death of St. Thomas à Becket, 12th cent., S. María, Tarrasa, Spain), and peaceful death, with the angel carrying the soul to heaven or to Abraham's bosom. These stories, narrated with spontaneity as well as a new sense of drama and humanity, and extensively illustrated, often on full pages, in illuminations of texts, became a valuable instrument in the Church's attempt to lead men to God.

Scenes from the lives of the saints were subordinated to the Christological and Mariological cycles and were always placed somewhere between two imposing representations of Christ: the by-then usual portrayal of the apocalyptic Christ in the tympanum of the church portal and the representation of Christ in Glory or in Majesty in the apse (VIII, PL. 177). The place allotted to representations of the lives of the saints might be the lower zone of the apse (as in S. Vincenzo, Galliano), the upper zone of the walls of the nave (as in S. Pietro al Monte, Civate, near Como), chapels (S. Pudenziana, Rome), or following the Carolingian and Ottonian traditions, the crypt (parish church, Barzé-la-Ville, Saône-et-Loire). Often, especially in Spain, these scenes were painted on wooden frontals (PL. 369; frontals with scenes from the life of S. Cebrián, Vich, Spain, Mus. Episcopal; others with scenes from the life of St. Eugenia, Paris, Mus. des Arts Décoratifs), while in Italy there was a preference for dossals with the image of the saint painted at the center and scenes from his life on the sides (an iconography

probably derived from Byzantine icons). Scenes from the lives of saints also began to appear in monumental sculpture and can be found on the lateral portals of churches (scenes from the life of St. Stephen, lateral portal of the Cathedral of Cahors, ca. 1150). Often the figure of the titular saint of a church or the image of a local patron was introduced into a scene with which he was not directly connected.

Personifications of virtues are shown with the saints even out of biographical context; opposite personifications of the vices also appear in many such representations. Thus the life of the saint was illustrated in pictures of broad allegorical significance in which the saint was the bridge between the human and the divine. It is in this concept that the Romanesque and the Byzantine styles differ, for in posticonoclastic Byzantine art the saints were always depicted as superhuman beings, isolated in celestial glory.

In addition to the scenes from the lives of the saints depicted in determined zones of pictorial decoration, numerous devotional images were collocated within the church. Sculptural images (perhaps derived from reliquary statues) were placed on altars; devotional images were painted in various areas of the church, even on piers. These representations were frontal views of the saint enthroned or standing, but never in the posture of prayer. If the image was a votive one, the donor, on a much smaller scale, was depicted kneeling at the saint's feet. Often the name of the saint appeared written next to the image; however, attributes were used increasingly, especially in sculptural representations.

In the iconography of this period the Twelve Apostles were depicted in the apse or on church façades in the architrave of portals, where they might be related to such scenes as the Ascension and Pentecost on the tympanum (cf. PLS. 237, 242). They appear also in scenes of the Last Supper. Elsewhere, as in the Church of St-Gilles in Saint-Gilles-du-Gard, figures of the Apostles flank the portals (PL. 246). In church interiors representations of the Apostles are grouped at the base of the apse singly or in pairs (an iconography probably drawn from Early Christian sarcophagi) in increasingly animated portrayals. In large Crucifixions and Depositions (frequently sculptural; PL. 258), St. John the Evangelist is represented at the right of the Cross. The Apostles were always depicted as part of the Christological cycles, which came to be more freely conceived. St. Peter was depicted with the keys (PL. 237); St. Paul was sometimes represented with the sword (Maguelone, Cathedral). The attributes that were created for the other Apostles did not remain constant. At times St. Peter and St. Paul were depicted in such allegorical scenes as that at the mill where the Apostles grind the grain to obtain the flour of the Gospels.

The Evangelists were generally represented in human form (PL. 262), although in Spain, then still under the influence of Mozarabic art, they were depicted as anthropomorphous figures (Pantéon de los Reyes, Cathedral of León, 12th cent.). The tetramorph, with the eagle serving as lectern, can be seen in Italian ambos (VIII, PL. 181). The figure of John the Baptist was less importantly placed than in Byzantine churches and was rarely depicted alone, while that of St. Joseph appeared with increasing frequency in scenes with the Christ Child drawn from the apocryphal gospels and in the dream scene (Gabriel is sometimes shown pulling his beard, as in a capital in the Church of Notre-Dame-du-Port in Clermont-Ferrand). The Magi were represented wearing crowns instead of Phrygian caps and were called kings; their number was fixed at the canonical three.

Among the personages of the Old Testament, Solomon and the Queen of Sheba were frequently represented in the sculptures of this period (statues from the portal of Notre-Dame in Corbeil, 12th cent.; Louvre). The Elders of the Apocalypse were depicted wearing crowns and appear in the arches of portals with musical instruments in their hands.

Martyrs and confessors were portrayed in many different ways, often dressed in the clothing of the period. They were depicted with monks' tonsures, kings' crowns (reliquary statue of Ste Foy, Church of Ste-Foy, Conques), and the miters and croziers of bishops; they were shown seated on thrones or faldstools; female saints were often portrayed wearing the wimples fashionable at the time, and virgin saints were clad in royal attire. Constantine I (whom popular tradition acclaimed as a saint) was often represented on horseback, especially in northern France.

Representations of angels were numerous, and their hierarchical rank and costumes generally were not differentiated. In apocalyptic scenes, in which Michael is the central figure, angels were given the most prominent roles (PL. 275; as also at the Abbey church of St-Pierre in Moissac and the Cathedral of St-Lasare in Autun). In the Church of Ste Foy in Conques the angels hold placards inscribed with the name of the virtues. In scenes of the Last Judgment in the apses, Michael and Gabriel often hold a labarum or scroll with inscriptions (PL. 254). Gabriel appears in Annunciation scenes; these were often executed on the exterior of the church, sometimes on capitals, as in the lateral portals of Verona Cathedral; Raphael was represented with Tobias. Cherubim were depicted with human heads and six wings covered with eyes (wall paintings from S. María in Esterri de Aneu, Barcelona, Mus. de Bellas Artes de Cataluña); they were represented as tetramorphous creatures on the reliquary of St. Maurice (see above). At that time the first musician angels appeared, heralding the Gothic iconography.

With the spread of the Gothic style and the diffusion of the Franciscan and Dominican preaching orders, religious teaching emphasized the theme of grace. Consequently the role of the saint as intercessor, advocate, and patron became more important. Images of saints were widely displayed on the façades of churches; on the main portals they were placed according to a determined hierarchy. At the base were represented Biblical personages (statues on the columns of the portals); above them, in the architrave, the Apostles were shown; the pyramidal composition closed with Christ in Majesty in the tympanum. As in Early Christian art, the figures thus symbolized the passage from the Old to the New Testament, but the emphasis was now on the Redemption theme, in which the saints had important roles. Scenes from the lives of the saints, especially from the life of the Virgin, were placed on the lateral portals (as in St-Denis). Saints were represented in groups: martyrs and confessors (as on the south façade of Chartres Cathedral; VI, PL. 343) or doctors, martyrs, and confessors (central portal of Notre-Dame in Paris). The king-saints, patrons of the conversion of the pagans and symbols of the mission entrusted by God to sovereigns, were represented in allegorical scenes. The baptism of Clovis I was depicted on the north façade of Reims Cathedral, at the center of a row of statues of the kings of France. In the Abbey church of St-Denis scenes from the life of Dagobert I were represented in a sort of tympanum on the ruler's tomb.

Within the churches, scenes from the lives of saints were painted in place of the Christological cycle. Freely conceived and imaginatively interpreted, these scenes unfold along the naves, glow in the glass windows, and completely cover walls of chapels and vaults (e.g., Assisi, S. Francesco; I, PL. 386). Altar dossals were gradually replaced by triptychs and polyptychs, in which rows of saints, often in three-quarter view, look toward Christ or the Virgin and Child. The angels played a prominent part in this iconography. They appear everywhere, dressed in multicolored garments patterned on contemporary female costumes, crowned with roses, holding musical instruments (VI, PL. 346), candelabra (VI, PL. 354), and flowers.

The sarcophagi of the dead often were decorated with the figures of patron saints, as were the 14th-century tombs of Alberto della Scala (Verona, S. Maria Antica) and Guglielmo di Castelbarco (Verona, S. Anastasia). At the same time devotional statues of saints came to be placed not only on church altars but also in shrines on public squares, along roads, and at street corners; images and statuettes were placed in the home. (see DEVOTIONAL OBJECTS AND IMAGES, POPULAR). These were gentle and sweet figures, very different from the lively and sometimes violent representations of Romanesque art, designed to inspire the type of devotion that the Church wished to foster in the faithful.

Artists of the late Gothic period depicted the saints as contemporary courtiers, as did Pisanello in scenes from the legend of St. George (XI, PL. 177) and from the life of St. Eustace (PL. 373) and Gentile da Fabriano in the Adoration of the Magi (VI, PLS. 84, 85).

Fernanda de' MAFFEI

End of the medieval era to the present. At the end of the Middle Ages, political and social developments and the subsequent expansion of trade contributed to a change in devotional images. A wealth of new subjects was introduced, and the images became widely popular in homes. Artists continued to paint frescoes of the great narrative cycles, especially the cycle of St. Benedict (frescoes in the Chiostro degli Aranci, 1436–39, in the Badia in Florence; frescoes by Signorelli in the Abbey of Monte Oliveto Maggiore; XIII, PL. 35). Increased religious fervor brought about a great increase in the production of devotional and votive images painted on wood panels. The dossal was replaced by the altarpiece, which was frequently dedicated to the patron saint of the donor, who appeared in the scene as the votary, without an aureole. The altarpiece also might show a group of saints gathered around the Virgin and Child (I, PL. 262). The rich and varied themes were treated in the characteristic style of the religious art of the early Renaissance (q.v.). Sacred scenes were superimposed on landscape backgrounds, in which the artists depicted episodes, even genre scenes, not all related to the subject.

Throughout the 15th century the figures of saints were characterized by calm dignity; violent scenes of martyrdom and death were rare, although attributes were widely used. Occasionally the taste for classical antiquity led to iconographic changes; thus, in the St. James cycle painted by Mantegna in Padua (PL. 140), the artist placed the figure of the saint in a classical architectural setting. With Michelangelo the classical development of iconography reached a peak, as in *The Last Judgment* and the *Conversion of St. Paul*, in which he limited hagiographic details to a minimum and transformed saints into the nude Titans of antiquity (IX, PL. 537). The panegyric style of medieval hagiography disappeared in the artist's effort to bring to life the human figure in its heroic isolation.

The Counter Reformation (see REFORMATION AND COUNTER REFORMATION) based its revision of religious art on a rigorous trend toward the essential, but the attempts to transform the heroic figure into a devotional image were not successful. The earliest examples of the new iconography reflected unsure and contradictory trends. The artistic requirements of the Church were elucidated in numerous publications that established the details of sacred iconography on the basis of undisputed hagiographic fact. Esthetic and ornamental considerations did not suffice to justify a work of art. For the Church, religious art was to acquire the specific function of a weapon to be used in the battle to defend Catholic institutions. The basic purpose of sacred art was to inspire faith, and accordingly, it did away with all elements that did not serve that purpose. Furthermore, to be effective as propaganda it had to be immediately comprehensible, so artists returned to the simplicity of early Christianity.

This revival was favored by the discovery in 1578 of the Catacomb of the Jordani, erroneously believed at the time to be the Catacomb of Priscilla. Cardinal Cesare Baronius considered the event a miracle and decided that the Early Christian iconography was an ideal interpretation of the religious values that should be reflected in sacred images. In his *Annales ecclesiastici* (Rome, 1588–1607), and his revision of the Roman martyrology, Baronius provided the means for rigidly controlling pictorial representation. Thus, while one current of religious art fostered the execution of works that were pure, abstract, and timeless idealizations, the other was influenced by the historical erudition of the *Annales* (cf. Barocci's *Martyrdom of S. Vitale* in the Brera and Domenichino's *Flagellation of S. Andrew* in the Oratory of S. Andrea al Celio, Rome). Further contributions to the iconography of saints were Antonio Bosio's *Roma sotterranea*, published posthumously by Giovanni Severani (Rome, 1632), which presented the pictorial subject matter of Early Christian and Byzantine art, and the Jesuit Jean de Bolland's *Acta Sanctorum* (1643), a comprehensive and historically reliable source of the lives of the saints.

The martyrdom theme, a controversial issue during the Counter Reformation, served a specific purpose in the training of missionaries; as early as the end of the 16th century it had, in fact, been an extremely popular subject for painting and remained so throughout the 17th century, when cycles of paintings of the lives and deaths of the saints were characterized by a ferocious interest in horrifying detail. Most of these were executed in Rome, the training center for the future martyrs of the Counter Reformation. In the Church of S. Stefano Rotondo Niccolò Circignani collaborated on a grandiose martyrology (XI, PL. 452); the same artist painted scenes of the English martyrs in the Church of St. Thomas of Canterbury in the English College, Rome (paintings destroyed in 1800; known from drawings by Giovanni Battista de Cavalieri). Other martyr cycles were executed in the churches of S. Apollinare, S. Andrea al Quirinale, and S. Vitale — all in Rome.

In the face of iconoclastic opposition and Protestant scorn, the cult of images in Catholic countries assumed more imposing proportions each year. Little-known martyrs such as SS. Severo, Severiano, Carpofaro, Vittorino, Praxedis, Pudentiana, Petronilla, and Agnes were exalted. In many cases artists chose to follow the directives of priests in their paintings rather than risk falling into error and compromising the devotional value of the work and its acceptance by the authorities. These priestly directives served to modify existing iconography and create new subjects for sacred images, with the purpose of exalting whatever was belittled in Protestant countries.

While St. Robert Bellarmine was engaged in refuting Calvin's doctrines, artists were representing scenes of religious ecstasy (PL. 376). The new mystical current within the Church during the Counter Reformation produced works such as Bernini's *Ecstasy of St. Theresa* (II, PL. 273). In the 18th century the portrayal of saints followed the models proposed in the hagiographic literature of the Counter Reformation and remained independent of other trends in painting.

Neoclassicism was predominantly nonreligious; the great artists of the movement, including those closest to the Catholic Church, such as Canova, rarely represented saints, preferring allegorical personifications that permitted greater freedom of conception, according to a fundamentally pagan ideal. This stylistic break in the production of devotional art had an adverse effect on the iconographic patrimony so jealously preserved and classified by the Catholic Church.

In the 19th century representations of saints — and all religious art — in spite of the efforts of the Nazarenes and the *puristi* (see PRE-RAPHAELITISM AND RELATED MOVEMENTS; cf. PL. 368), showed a dreary poverty of inspiration, as is evident in Thorvaldsen's cold and measured academicism (the *Twelve Apostles* in the Vor Frue Kirke in Copenhagen), Domenico Morelli's works, Puvis de Chavannes' scenes from the life of St. Geneviève in the Panthéon in Paris, and the scenes from the life of Joseph of Arimathea painted by the Nazarenes (Berlin, Staat. Mus.).

The iconography of the saints in the 20th century continued to stress the role of the saint as intercessor. The saints were represented with their attributes, and the images followed the established iconography, often in a somewhat stylized manner that is reminiscent of Byzantine art. Traditional iconographic forms, with interesting local variations, appeared in popular religious art (PL 380).

Piero M. CAPPONI

ICONOGRAPHY OF SELECTED SAINTS. The following list is not intended to be comprehensive; it is, rather, a selection of some of the best-known and most frequently represented saints, with their principal attributes and the manner in which they generally are depicted in Christian art. For more exhaustive information on the iconography of saints, the reader is referred to the bibliography of this article, and especially to Ferguson (1959) and Roeder (1955).

Agatha, virgin martyr. Patroness of bell founders, jewelers, children's nurses, shepherdesses, and weavers, also of Catania, which she protects from Etna's eruptions; invoked against earthquake, fire, lightning, storm, sterility, wolves, and diseases of the breast. Depicted carrying the palm of victory and a dish bearing two female breasts, an allusion to her martyrdom; sometimes appears covering her shorn breasts, or with the pincers or shears, instruments of her torture (IX, PL. 302; XIV, PL. 56); generally wears a long veil, the relic of the saint that miraculously saved Catania from Etna's fury; also appears crowned (XI, PL. 327).

Agnes, virgin martyr. Patroness of betrothed couples, gardeners, and maidens; invoked in defense of chastity. Depicted with a lamb and a palm (X, PL. 181; XIV, PL. 105), often with the long hair that covered her nudity; sometimes represented with a sword in her throat or amid flames (II, PL. 167).

Ambrose, Bishop of Milan, Doctor of the Church. Patron of beekeepers, domestic animals, geese, and wax refiners. Often shown with a beehive, referring to a legendary appearance of a swarm of bees that alighted on his mouth, foretelling his future eloquence; represented in bishop's vestments, with miter and crozier and a book. Appears sometimes with a scourge that recalls his role in driving the Arians out of Italy.

Andrew, Apostle. Patron of Scotland and of fishermen, fishmongers, and sailors; invoked against gout and stiff neck. Generally depicted as an old man with an X-shaped cross, the instrument of his martyrdom (II, PLS. 168, 191; VIII, PL. 219; earliest representations show a straight or a Y-shaped cross, IV, PL. 52); also sometimes appears with fish or a fishing net, with a rope, or on a ship.

Anne (Anna), mother of Virgin Mary. Appears in scenes from the life of the Virgin, such as the Birth of the Virgin and the Presentation of Mary in the Temple, and the Meeting with Joachim at the Golden Gate; shown teaching Mary to read or embroider (XI, PL. 453), and often with the Virgin and Christ Child (PL. 77; III, PL. 38; IX, PLS. 122, 123, 341).

Anthony Abbot. Patron of basketmakers; invoked against erysipelas. Usually depicted as an old man in monk's robes with a T-shaped staff (originally signifying a theta for *Theos*) and a bell (PL. 372; IX, PL. 182; XI, PL. 176); sometimes shown in his struggles with temptations (XIV, PL. 55), or with a hog symbolizing the demon of sensuality that he overcame; also depicted with St. Paul the Hermit, with a centaur and satyr, or making baskets.

Anthony of Padua, Franciscan. Invoked for recovery of lost property. Depicted in Franciscan robe (XIV, PL. 89), often bearing lily and book, with Christ Child resting on book; also shown preaching to fishes or carrying the Sacrament, with an ass kneeling before him (recalling a legend that the ass, at his prayer, left the stable to adore Christ in the Eucharist in refutation of a heretic's unbelief); sometimes shown in scene of dead miser's heart being found in money chest, or healing a young man's foot (XI, PL. 94).

Augustine, Bishop of Hippo and Father of the Latin Church. Usually depicted in episcopal robes (PL. 32; II, PL. 328; IV, PL. 52; X, PL. 475), often writing in his study (PL. 32); shown with the Virgin and the Trinity, or with the three Doctors of the Latin Church (X, PL. 475), or with a vision of St. Jerome, or with his book held by an eagle symbolizing St. John the Evangelist, or as a penitent (XIII, PL. 147); his special attribute is a flaming heart, sometimes pierced by an arrow; frequently represented with a child who holds the spoon with which he tried to empty the sea into a hole in the sand, and who answered Augustine that this task was no more impossible of fulfillment than the Saint's attempt to explain divine mysteries (X, PL. 475); may also appear as a young layman with St. Monica, his mother, or being instructed or baptized by St. Ambrose.

Barbara, virgin martyr, one of the Fourteen Holy Helpers (auxiliary saints, or saints of healing). Patroness of architects, builders, artillerymen, firemen; invoked against thunderstorms and fire. Shown as a princess with palm and tower (II, PL. 244; V, PL. 220), sometimes bearing chalice and Host or with a sword (II, PL. 244); also represented in scenes of her martyrdom (VI, PL. 375).

Bartholomew, Apostle. Patron of Florentine salt and cheese merchants, also of bookbinders, butchers, grain merchants, dyers, glovers, furriers, leatherworkers, plasterers, shoemakers, tailors, and vineyards; invoked against nervous diseases and twitching. Shown bearded, middle-aged, or venerable (XIV, PL. 430), with book and knife (PL. 368), often carrying over one arm his flayed skin, indicating the manner of his martyrdom; also depicted being crucified (II, PL. 192).

Benedict, Abbot, founder of Benedictines and father of Western monasticism. Patron of coppersmiths and school children; invoked against fever, gallstones, nettle rash, poison, and witchcraft, also by servants who have broken their master's possessions, and by the dying. Usually shown as venerable figure with flowing beard, dressed in abbot's cowled robe (PLS. 178, 376; I, PL. 240; XI, PL. 303); often holding the book of his rule; attributes include a serpent and broken cup (recalling the miracle of the breaking of a poisoned cup of wine offered him by a rebellious monk), a raven (fed by him as a hermit at Subiaco), a broken tray (miraculously mended by him), and a dove (representing the soul of his sister, St. Scholastica, which he saw ascending to heaven); often represented in holy converse with his sister, or with his disciples Maurus and Placidus in the scene in which Maurus walks on water at his command to rescue Placidus from drowning; also shown having a heavenly vision (PL. 178).

Bernard, founder of the Cistercians, Abbot of Clairvaux, and Doctor of the Church. Patron of beekeepers and wax melters. Depicted in white Cistercian habit (IX, PL. 147; XIII, PL. 147), with book or writing, often with the Virgin (VIII, PL. 209; IX, PL. 149; XI, PL. 111); may be shown with instruments of the Passion to represent his mystical *Meditations*; with three miters at his feet, representing the bishoprics he refused; trampling a chained demon to represent his defeat of heresy; with a beehive, symbolizing his eloquence; being embraced by Christ from the Cross (XIII, PL. 147).

Bernardino of Siena, Franciscan, founder of the cult of the Holy Name. Patron of wool weavers; invoked against diseases of chest and lungs. Depicted as Franciscan (bearded in El Greco's painting) bearing IHS emblem (IV, PL. 401; IX, PL. 210) often with miters (or green mounds representing them) at his feet, in token of the bishoprics he refused.

Blaise, physician, Bishop of Sebaste (Armenia), one of the Fourteen Holy Helpers. Patron of physicians, candlemakers, wool carders, and wild animals; invoked against diseases of the throat and diseases of cattle. Represented as a bearded, venerable bishop, holding an iron comb (instrument of his martyrdom) and two candles representing his healing of the sick; often shown in cave with wild animals, blessing birds, rescuing poor woman's pig from wolf, or saving life of boy choking on a fish bone.

Catherine of Alexandria, virgin martyr, one of the Fourteen Holy Helpers. Patroness of young women, wheelwrights, attorneys, philosophers, scholars, students, spinsters, saddlers, and ropemakers. Depicted as a well-born maiden with book and spiked wheel (referring to her torture, PL. 40; II, PL. 243; IX, PL. 301; XIV, PL. 88); may wear a crown or carry a palm or sword (IV, PL. 284; VI, PL. 86); often shown being beheaded or carrying her head on a dish, and frequently in the scene of her mystic marriage to Christ, who is commonly shown as a child (PL. 64; III, PL. 466; VIII, PLS. 188, 215).

Catherine of Siena, Dominican tertiary. Patron of Italy. Depicted in the black-and-white habit of the Dominican Order, with stigmata, lily (PL. 375), and book (PLS. 63, 86), sometimes holds a crucifix and lily (VIII, PL. 196); appears carrying a rosary or wearing a crown of thorns; sometimes shown with a heart on a book, with a heart at her feet, or with heart, skull, book, and lily. Depicted receiving the stigmata (PL. 63), in ecstasy (II, PL. 165), being crowned by angels with three crowns, disputing with philosophers as she marks off the points of her argument on her fingers (IX, PL. 378), and giving clothes to a beggar, who is really Christ. Like Catherine of Alexandria, she is also depicted celebrating her mystic marriage with the Christ Child.

Cecilia, virgin martyr. Patron of musicians, reputed to have heard heavenly music during her lifetime. Her special attribute is the organ, which she is said to have invented (PL. 367); also shown with such other musical instruments as the viol and harp; sometimes represented with crown and palm, converting her husband Valerian (IV, PL. 105), or with a crown of red and white roses on her head. Three wounds in her throat refer to her martyrdom and the attempts of an executioner to behead her.

Christopher, legendary martyr, one of the Fourteen Holy Helpers. Patron of travelers, sailors, and navigators; invoked against storms and for a safe journey. Most commonly represented as a large, powerful man bearing the Christ Child on his shoulders across a turbulent stream (PLS. 33, 378; IV, PL. 423); usually has a flowering staff in his hands; shown in less common representations being baptized by a hermit, meeting the devil on horseback, being beheaded, being shot at with arrows that turn on his executioners, and standing at a watermill.

Clare of Assisi, disciple of St. Francis and foundress of the Order of the Poor Clares. Depicted in the gray tunic and black veil of her order, carrying a monstrance (V, PL. 359) with which she drove away a horde of Saracens besieging her convent, an event also recalled in representations of Clare trampling a turban, which she transfixes with a crucifix, and with a scimitar under her feet; also shown with a cross and book (PL. 375), a flaming horn, a vase, and a lily or rosary; frequently appears in scenes with St. Francis, and sometimes with a dove hovering above her; sometimes is depicted being crowned by Christ and the Virgin.

Clement, early Bishop of Rome. Depicted with an anchor and fishes, in reference to his martyrdom when after his persecutors tied an anchor around his neck and threw him into the sea, the waters receded in answer to the prayers of his followers, revealing a small temple in which lay the saint's body; also derived from this legend are his other attributes, the lamb who led him to the place where Clement caused a miraculous fountain of fresh water to spring up,

the fountain itself, and a millstone (in place of the anchor). Depicted in papal attire with the keys, with a book, and sometimes, in the scene of the discovery of his body under the sea (PL. 369).

Cosmas and Damian. Patrons of physicians and surgeons, barbers and apothecaries; adopted as patrons of the Medicis. Always depicted together (IX, PL. 62), generally in the long red gown and cap of the physician, holding a surgical instrument or a mortar and pestle and a box of ointment, or holding the rod of Aesculapius; also shown in scenes of their martyrdom: in a furnace, cast into the sea and rescued by angels, crucified and shot with arrows, or beheaded (I, PL. 273).

Denis, 3d-century Bishop of Paris, whose attributes have become confused with those of Dionysus (Denis) the Areopagite (1st cent.). Patron of Paris; protects against frenzy, headache, and strife. Depicted as a bishop carrying his own head on a book; also shown catching his own head at his execution, being beheaded with the deacons Eleutherius and Rusticus, and receiving the Eucharist from Christ in prison (V, PL. 382); sometimes represented enthroned with SS. Peter, Paul, and Ecclesia, or as a bearded figure with a book.

Dominic, founder of the Dominican Order (Order of Preachers). Represented in the black-and-white habit of his order, with the rosary, a devotion instituted by him (XIV, PL. 59) (he is often shown receiving it directly from the hands of the Virgin), and a star on his breast or over his head, alluding to the legendary one that appeared on his forehead at birth. His special attribute is a dog with a torch in its mouth, recalling a dream of Dominic's mother and symbolizing the perseverance of Dominic and his followers in spreading the Gospel; a loaf of bread refers to the miraculous appearance of angels with bread at Dominic's monastery (X, PL. 326); also depicted with lily and book (VI, PL. 83; VIII, PL. 183), standing atop the terrestrial globe, receiving a sword and book from SS. Peter and Paul, with star, crucifix, and church, with Reginald of St. Giles anointed in his illness by the Virgin in answer to Dominic's prayers, with the devil as a monkey snuffing the saint's candle. Representations of Dominic with Francis of Assisi are common, and it is usual for the Franciscans to include an image of Dominic in their churches; the Dominicans do the same with likenesses of St. Francis.

Dorothy, virgin martyr. Patron of brewers, brides, florists, gardeners, midwives, and newly wedded couples. Usually depicted as a maiden with a basket of fruit and flowers (VIII, PL. 219), or with an angel holding three roses and three apples; sometimes also represented crowned, with palm, and surrounded by stars; shown veiled, holding apples from Paradise on a branch, with flowers in her lap (IX, PL. 193), or with the Christ Child; sometimes shown crowned with flowers, kneeling before her executioner or tied to a stake.

Elizabeth, mother of John the Baptist. Frequently shown as an elderly woman with Zacharias in scenes of the Visitation and the Birth of John the Baptist (V, PL. 367).

Elizabeth, queen of Hungary, Franciscan tertiary. Patron of bakers, beggars, lacemakers, and those who do good works; invoked against toothache. Most commonly represented as a queen surrounded by beggars, to whom she gives food or clothing, or with a beggar sheltered under her cloak; also shown carrying a pitcher and loaf (VII, PL. 93); or with loaf and fishes; crowned or with three crowns at her feet. Sometimes depicted in the Franciscan habit kneeling before St. Francis or before a bishop who hands a palm, while St. Francis, holding shears, looks on. When portrayed with bread that turns into roses in her lap, she is sometimes confused with the lesser-known St. Elizabeth of Portugal, who shares that attribute.

Eustace. Patron of hunters. Generally represented as a knight (XI, PL. 182) or soldier on horseback; special attribute is the stag with a cross between its horns; depicted with his hounds at the hunt, blowing a hunting horn; shown in representations of his martyrdom being burnt inside a huge brass bull; occasionally depicted as a Roman soldier with his two sons.

Faith (Foi), virgin martyr. Depicted as a maiden with sword and gridiron; also shown crowned and seated with book, gridiron, and bundle of rods; sometimes appears being beheaded (XIII, PL. 177).

Fina (Serafina). Represented as a maiden holding a bunch of flowers, with the town of S. Gimignano; most common attributes are a rat, recalling those that attacked her as she lay suffering, and white violets, which were found on the pallet where she had lain. Also depicted lying on her pallet attended by a nurse, or with St. Gregory the Great, who appears to her (VI, PL. 179).

Florian. Patron of upper Austria and Poland, and of brewers, coopers, chimney-sweeps, and soapmakers; protects against fire, bad harvests, battles, flood, and storm. Generally shown as a young man, sometimes in the armor of a Roman soldier, pouring water on a burning house, church, or city; also depicted with a millstone around his neck (I, PL. 62); leaning on a millstone while extinguishing a fire; lying dead on a millstone and guarded by an eagle; sometimes shown being beaten; also with hat and staff, or a sword (IV, PL. 7).

Francis of Assisi, founder of the Franciscan Order. Patron of animals and animal welfare societies. Almost always shown as a small, bearded man in the dark brown robes of his order (III, PLS. 81, 84; IV, PL. 233; VI, PLS. 180, 185); depicted with the marks of the stigmata on his body (I, PL. 143; III, PL. 328; IV, PL. 239; VIII, PL. 181). His principal attributes are the lily, skull, crucifix, wolf, and lamb. Also depicted meditating (XIV, PL. 484), preaching to the birds, surrounded by animals, walking through fire before a Caliph, being tempted (II, PL. 208), crowned with thorns, witness to an apparition of the Virgin, in ecstasy (II, PLS. 188, 253), or receiving the stigmata (PL. 41; IV, PL. 234; VI, PL. 198). Shown as a young layman giving his cloak to a poor man (VI, PL. 196) or stripping himself of his clothes before his father (VI, PL. 207). His symbolic marriage to poverty (XIII, PL. 344) and his receiving the Christ Child from the hands of Mary are frequently represented. Appears in scenes with St. Clare, investing her as a novice and as she attends his funeral; shown with St. Dominic (see above), and as the Pope dreams of the two saints holding up the Lateran; depicted receiving his Rule from the Pope (XI, PL. 89) and at his death (PL. 330).

Francis of Sales, Bishop of Geneva, Doctor of the Church. Patron of journalists. Depicted as a 17th-century Franciscan bishop, often in the purple bishop's cassock, with a bald head and a long beard, holding a book or sometimes a picture of the Virgin. Also shown with a pierced heart surrounded by a crown of thorns, with a cross in glory above him.

Francis Xavier, Jesuit missionary. Depicted as a young bearded Jesuit with torch, flame, cross, and lily; shown holding a cross, with St. Ignatius Loyola, with the Virgin appearing to him, dying on straw, while angels hold a crucifix and lily; shown kneeling before a vine in which the figure of Christ crucified appears; sometimes depicted preaching to, healing, or baptizing Indians.

George. Patron of England and of Venice and Ferrara, of cavalrymen, soldiers, and armorers. Represented as a young knight in fine armor (PL. 505) with banner or shield emblazoned with a red cross (IV, PL. 241); usually shown killing the dragon to save the princess (who sometimes has the attributes of St. Margaret) (PLS. 42, 373, 380; II, PL. 254; III, PL. 70; IV, PLS. 242, 427; V, PL. 389; VI, PLS. 133, 351; X, PL. 327; XIII, PL. 66; XIV, PLS. 202, 375); princess sometimes shown leading the docile dragon in the presence of the saint; may be shown with a broken lance; depicted in the robes of the Order of the Garter or with St. Demetrius; shown being burned inside a brazen bull, dragged by horses, or beheaded (I, PL. 69).

Gregory the Great. Pope, Doctor, and one of the four Fathers of the Latin Church. Patron of the fringe makers, masons, musicians, scholars, singers, students, and teachers; invoked against gout, plague, and sterility. As a pope, shown in papal attire (PL. 278) with a book (PL. 218) and with a dove at his ear (IV, PL. 229; X, PL. 475), or with tiara, book, and ceremonial papal canopy or umbrella over his head; sometimes with the bull of St. Luke supporting his book; shown carrying a church; depicted celebrating Mass while souls are released from purgatory through his intercession; appears with St. Fina (see above) or as a monk declining the papal tiara. As a Doctor of the Church, shown at his desk with pen and book and with the papal insignia nearby; appears in these representations with dove and sometimes a peacock.

Helena. Patroness of dyers, nail makers, and needlemakers; invoked against fire and thunder. Depicted in royal attire and crowned (XIV, PL. 29); attributes are a large cross and nails; sometimes shown with a model of the Holy Sepulcher in her hands; frequently appears in the scene of her vision of the True Cross and of her discovery of the Cross; also represented with her son Constantine or as a crowned personage giving a letter to a messenger.

Ignatius Loyola, founder of the Society of Jesus. Depicted as a bearded Jesuit with the book of his rule, kneeling before Christ. Often appears with Christ (II, PL. 172) and with other Jesuit saints; usually bears the IHS emblem on his breast; sometimes depicted with his heart pierced by three nails; also shown performing miracles (PL. 377).

James the Greater, Apostle. Patron saint of Spain, where he is venerated at Compostela, and of pilgrims and furriers. Most often (and especially in Italian art) depicted as a young man (XIV, PL. 106), pilgrim with staff, hat (XI, PL. 182), wallet, and cockleshell; sometimes (as in Spanish art) shown on horseback, carrying a banner (XIV, PL. 63). As an Apostle, he carries a scroll with his text testifying to the Incarnation written on it; also depicted exorcising demons (IX, PL. 258).

Jerome. Doctor and Father of the Latin Church. Usually depicted with a lion (PL. 86; I, PLS. 236, 237; IX, PL. 115), which in some representations becomes a domestic cat; sometimes shown extracting a thorn from the lion's paw; usually shown as an old man, often as a hermit in the wilderness (PL. 372; I, PL. 314; IV, PL. 42; VIII, PL. 199), praying, or writing (XIII, PL. 284), with a crucifix, skull, and owl (IX, PL. 94). Sometimes represented in cardinal's robes (PL. 37),

or with a cardinal's hat nearby, reading or writing in his study (I, PL. 311; XIV, PL. 105); also represented with SS. Paula and Eustochium.

Joan of Arc. Patron of France. Generally depicted dressed in armor (PL. 373), with long flowing hair, or in simple female dress carrying a sword; often shown with lilies symbolizing both purity and France.

John the Baptist. Patron of the city of Florence, of farriers and tailors. His principal attribute is the lamb (II, PL. 318; XIV, PL. 484); often carries a cross made of reeds, or a banner emblazoned with a cross, or a scroll with "Ecce Agnus Dei" written on it (IV, PL. 52; IX, PL. 210). Depicted as a child (PLS. 65, 378) or a bearded prophet dressed in animal skin (PL. 365; IV, PL. 239); often represented in scenes of the Baptism of Christ (II, PL. 204; III, PL. 84) and of his beheading (II, PL. 236).

John, Evangelist. Patron of art dealers, craftsmen and dealers in the printing and publishing trades, engravers and lithographers, papermakers, sculptors, and writers. His attributes are the eagle and the book (PL. 370; IV, PLS. 7, 240, 300; VI, PL. 171); usually represented as a handsome young man in scenes from the Gospel (VI, PL. 208), especially those of the Last Supper, Crucifixion, and Descent from the Cross; occasionally shown with a caldron of oil or a cup and snake in reference to attempts on his life.

Joseph. Protector of carpenters, confectioners, the dying, engineers, the family, married couples, house hunters, pioneers, and travelers; invoked in doubt, hesitation, or when looking for a house. Shown with the Christ Child (PL. 378; IX, PL. 210), usually with a flowering staff and the lily; also depicted with carpenter's tools (PL. 380; II, PL. 185; VI, PL. 66), in scenes of the Presentation, and with two doves in a basket.

Jude, Apostle. Invoked in desperate situations. Shown with a lance or halberd, instrument of his martyrdom; also depicted holding a saw, a book, a scroll, or a carpenter's rule.

Lawrence. Patron of brewers, confectioners, cooks, cutlers and armorers, schoolboys, students, washerwomen, and glaziers. Depicted with the gridiron, on which he was martyred (IV, PL. 106); also shown carrying a palm and book. Generally appears in deacon's robes (PL. 368; X, PL. 477); may carry a plate or bag of coins representing the Church's treasure that he distributed to the poor (I, PL. 270); occasionally shown carrying a censer or a cross, and sometimes appears in a tunic covered with flames; also shown with Pope Sixtus II, whom he followed to martyrdom (X, PL. 474).

Louis IX. King of France and Franciscan Tertiary. Depicted with the fleur-de-lis, the crown of thorns, a cross, a kingly crown, and a sword (VI, PL. 316).

Louis of Toulouse, Bishop of Toulouse. Depicted as a bishop with the Franciscan habit under his cope, which is decorated with fleur-de-lis (PL. 538; IX, PL. 336); fleur-de-lis may also appear on his crozier; sometimes with crown that he renounced at his feet; occasionally three crowns are shown.

Lucy, virgin martyr. Patron of cutlers, glaziers, notaries, peddlers, saddlers, servant girls, scribes, tailors, and weavers; invoked against blindness, fire, infection, hemorrhage, and sore throat (PL. 40). Eyes are her special attribute; shown carrying eyes (IV, PL. 7), sometimes on a plate (IV, PL. 235); often appears with a lamp, symbolizing divine light and wisdom, and a sword; represented with a dagger or a wound in her neck (I, PL. 73; IV, PL. 234), in reference to her martyrdom, or with a flaming horn.

Luke, Apostle. Patron of butchers, bookbinders, physicians, painters, sculptors, goldsmiths, surgeons, and notaries. Depicted with a winged bull and a scroll or book (PLS. 30, 370; X, PL. 199; XIV, PL. 82); often represented painting or holding a portrait of Mary (IV, PL. 272; V, PL. 290); sometimes shown in physician's cap and gown.

Margaret. Protectress of women (especially maidens), nurses, and peasants; invoked in childbirth and against barrenness or lack of milk. Shown with a dragon, which she tramples or leads on a chain; often holds a cross and the crown and palm of martyrdom; rarely, is identified with the princess for whom St. George slays the dragon.

Mark, Apostle, Evangelist. Patron of Venice, of glaziers and notaries; invoked by captives. His particular attribute, in addition to the book (II, PL. 244; VIII, PL. 86) or scroll of the Evangelists, is the winged lion (PL. 370; I, PL. 282; IV, PL. 246).

Martha. Patron of housewives and innkeepers. Generally depicted as a housewife with a ladle in her hand or with a large bunch of keys hanging from her belt. The aspergillum is another of her attributes, and appears together with the dragon, which she overcame with holy water (XIV, PL. 482). Also appears with Mary, Lazarus, or Mary Magdalene in scenes from the Gospel. Sometimes represented weeping (V, PL. 376), with Mary and Lazarus in a boat crossing the sea to Marseilles, and in scenes of her martyrdom (XI, PL. 452).

Martin of Tours. Patron of armorers, beggars, cavalry, coopers, domestic animals, girdlers, glovers, horses and horsemen, millers, innkeepers, tailors, wine-merchants, and wool weavers; invoked against drunkenness, storms, and ulcers. Usually shown in soldier's garb, on horseback, dividing his cloak with his sword to give half to a beggar (PL. 380; II, PL. 246; IV, PL. 307; V, PL. 353; VI, PL. 360; VIII, PL. 181). The beggar as his attribute (and sometimes a goose) appears in depictions of him as a bishop (II, PL. 240; VI, PL. 343).

Mary Magdalene. Attributes are flowing hair (XI, PL. 361) and a jar of ointment (PLS. 38, 40, 99); depicted in scenes from the Gospels, most frequently anointing the feet of Jesus, clinging to the foot of the Cross, in the Deposition and the Noli Mi Tangere (PL. 94), and sometimes as an aged penitent (III, PL. 211); also shown being carried by angels and in scenes of the voyage to Marseilles with Martha and Lazarus.

Matthew, Apostle and Evangelist. Patron of bankers and tax collectors. The angel is his special attribute and appears together with the Evangelist's book or scroll (PL. 370; III, PL. 84; IV, PLS. 106, 159; V, PL. 360; VI, PLS. 175, 216; IX, PL. 529; X, PLS. 70, 394; XIV, PL. 82); usually depicted long-haired and bearded; sometimes shown with bags of coins, in reference to his profession (III, PL. 41), or with an ax, the instrument of his martyrdom; also represented being put to death by the sword (III, PL. 37).

Maurice, Captain of the Theban Legion. Patron of armies, armorers, infantry, hatters, and knife grinders; invoked against demoniac possession, enemies of religion, and gout. Depicted as a Moorish warrior in armor (VII, PL. 90); carrying a lance and with a trefoil cross on his shield or banner; often shown with his legion (VI, PL. 459); may carry a banner with seven stars or a rampant lion, or a sword with a crown of thorns on its hilt.

Monica. Depicted as a mother, in widow's clothing or nun's habit (XIII, PL. 148) with her son Augustine; also shown holding a tablet with the emblem IHS.

Nicholas of Myra (or Bari), Bishop of Myra. Patron of Russia and of children, bankers, captives, pawnbrokers, and sailors. Depicted in bishop's robes (IV, PL. 106); his attribute is the three purses or gold balls (I, PL. 267; VI, PL. 86) that recall his works of charity; often depicted with an anchor or ship (IX, PL. 202) and sometimes with a small child or children (VIII, PL. 216).

Nicholas of Tolentino, Augustinian monk. Invoked against plague and shipwreck. Generally depicted in the black robes of the Augustinian Order; his attributes are the star, book, and lily; star usually appears on his breast, but may take the form of a starfish which he carries on a dish. His intercession against the plague is symbolized by his interception of arrows from heaven as he stands with the city of Pisa or of Empoli at his feet.

Patrick, Bishop. Patron saint of Ireland. Depicted in bishop's robes; his special attribute is the snake, many of which are shown at his feet or twined around his crozier; often holds a shamrock or pen and book.

Paul, Apostle. Patron of missionaries and ropemakers; invoked against snakebite. His attributes are the sword (XIV, PL. 205) and the book (IX, PL. 342; XI, PL. 327); usually depicted bald and bearded (II, PL. 484; III, PL. 61), writing, reading, or preaching. Often appears in scenes of his conversion (III, PL. 34; IX, PLS. 299, 537; XIII, PL. 35) or execution; shown being let down from the walls of Damascus in a basket (III, PL. 57), making tents, or meeting with St. Peter (PL. 81; II, PL. 187).

Peter of Alexandria, Patriarch of Alexandria. Patron of Siena. Depicted as a bishop enthroned between angels, often holding the city of Siena, wearing the tiara instead of the miter.

Peter, Apostle. Patron of bankers, bridgebuilders, butchers, carpenters, clockmakers, fishermen, fishmongers, glaziers, masons, netmakers, potters, stationers, and shipwrights; protects against fever, foot troubles, frenzy, snakebite, and wolves, and invoked for a long life. Principal attribute is the key (PLS. 237, 246; IV, PL. 300; XI, PL. 113; XIV, PLS. 342, 430); also shown with fish or a fishing net (XIV, PL. 429), with a cock, or with a cross (II, PL. 469), depicted as a robust middle-aged (PL. 81; II, PL. 483; VI, PL. 181; IX, PLS. 93, 374) or elderly person (II, PL. 168); often wears a bright yellow mantle that symbolizes revealed faith (I, PL. 263); appears in scenes of his crucifixion (II, PL. 188; IX, PL. 346).

Peter, martyr. Patron of inquisitors and midwives. Represented in the black-and-white Dominican habit with a wound (V, PL. 358) or knife in his head; often carries the palm and occasionally appears with knife in his shoulder.

Petronius, Bishop of Bologna. Shown in bishop's robes (VIII, PL. 219) with the miter on his head and the city of Bologna in his hands (PL. 374; IV, PL. 7); also represented between SS. Cosmas and Damian.

Philip, Apostle. Patron of hatters and pastrycooks. Usually represented as an old man; attribute is a tall cross, instrument of his

martyrdom (V, PL. 407; IX, PLS. 147, 148); also shown with loaves and fishes, with loaves and a book (XIII, PL. 54), or with a snake or dragon (IX, PL. 147).

Remigius (Remi), Bishop of Reims. Shown as a bishop holding holy oils; often depicted with Clovis, whom he baptized and anointed.

Roch. Protects against the plague. Depicted in pilgrim's garb (III, PL. 149), with cockleshell, wallet, and staff, and shown with one leg bared to reveal a plague spot (XI, PL. 46; XIV, PL. 89); often accompanied by a dog (XI, PL. 46).

Romuald, Founder of the Camaldolese Order. Depicted as an old man in the white robes of his order (I, PL. 240); most common attribute is the ladder by which his monks ascend into heaven; sometimes shown having a vision of monks rising to heaven without the ladder (VIII, PL. 220); occasionally depicted enthroned with a candle (XIV, PL. 104), a book (IX, PL. 201), or a model of his monastery; sometimes depicted trampling the devil underfoot.

Rose of Lima, Dominican tertiary. Patron of South America and the Philippines. Principal attribute is the rose; shown in the habit of the Dominican Order, crowned with roses, holding an anchor, or with a city surrounded by waves; sometimes depicted with the Christ Child, who accepts a rose from her, or who appears in a rose that she holds.

Scholastica, Benedictine Abbess, Patron of Montecassino and all Cassinese communities. Depicted in the habit of a Benedictine nun with her brother, St. Benedict; represented holding a lily or crucifix, with a dove that refers to Benedict's vision of her soul ascending into heaven.

Sebastian. Patron of armorers, bookbinders, burial societies, arrowsmiths, corn chandlers, gardeners, ironmongers, lead founders, needlemakers, potters, racket makers, stonemasons; invoked against cattle pest, epilepsy, enemies of religion, plague, and by the dying. Attribute is the arrow; almost always depicted as a young man whose naked body is transfixed by arrows (PLS. 535; I, PL. 316; II, PLS. 272, 328; III, PL. 148; IV, PL. 270; V, PLS. 357, 386; VI, PL. 458; VII, PL. 87; IX, PLS. 92, 325; XI, PLS. 113, 115, 182, 362; XIV, PL. 95); occasionally appears holding the arrows (PL. 367).

Simon, Apostle. Attribute is the saw; generally depicted as a middle-aged man; may also be seen with a cross or a book.

Stephen, protomartyr. Depicted as a deacon (III, PLS. 21, 75) with the stone as his attribute, recalling his martyrdom by stoning (I, PL. 270; III, PL. 54); stone may appear on a book, at his feet, in his hand, or on his head (V, PL. 365; VI, PL. 205; XI, PL. 48); often appears with St. Lawrence; also depicted preaching (III, PL. 75) and with palm (V, PL. 360; XI, PL. 48) and book.

Sylvester, Pope. Depicted in papal attire (PL. 374); his special attribute is the bull; sometimes shown with a dragon (VIII, PL. 193); appears in scenes with the emperor Constantine.

Thecla, virgin martyr. Patroness of Este and Milan. Depicted with serpent as her attribute; usually represented as a maiden in a dungeon surrounded by serpents or in a dark mantle holding the palm; sometimes appears with lions or other wild beasts.

Theresa of Avila, Carmelite Abbess. Patroness of lacemakers; invoked by those in need of grace. Represented as a Carmelite nun; shown with her heart pierced by an arrow borne by an angel (II, PL. 273); appears with Christ and a cross; sometimes shown with IHS emblem on her heart; may be shown with pen and book.

Thomas, Apostle. Patron of architects, builders, carpenters, masons, geometricians, and theologians. Attribute is the carpenter's rule or square; also depicted in scenes from the Gospels, including that in which he touches Christ's wounds; shown with other Apostles (II, PL. 280).

Thomas Aquinas, Doctor of the Church. Patron of booksellers, Catholic universities, pencilmakers, scholars, and students; invoked for chastity and learning, against storm and lightning. Usual attributes are the ox, which refers to his nickname, the star (or sun), which appears on his breast, and the chalice, which alludes to his writings on the Eucharist; depicted as a heavy-set man in the Dominican habit (PL. 375; IV, PL. 211; XIII, PL. 344); often appears with book or books from which come rays of light; sometimes shown with St. Bonaventure.

Thomas à Becket. Depicted in archbishop's vestments, generally at the altar. Shown in the scene of his death at the hands of three knights; appears alone with a sword in his head.

Thomas More. Depicted in scholar's cap, fur-trimmed robe, and the chain of the Chancellor of England. Sometimes shown with the chalice, Host, and papal insignia nearby.

Ursula, virgin martyr. Patroness of maidens, drapers, and teachers; invoked for chastity, and holy wedlock, and against the plague. The arrow is her attribute and recalls her martyrdom (IX, PL. 461). She is generally represented as a crowned princess (III, PL. 73) holding an arrow, often surrounded by her handmaids (PL. 369; IX, PL. 179). Also shown in scenes from her life (III, PL. 78; VI, PL. 361; XIV, PL. 107), with Conon, her betrothed, and their attendants.

She may also hold the pilgrim's staff surmounted by a banner (IX PL. 205).

Veronica. Patroness of linen-drapers and washerwomen. The veil on which the face of Christ appears is her attribute; generally shown in scenes of Christ's Passion (cf. XIII, PL. 142).

Vincent. Patron of bakers, roof makers, sailors, schoolgirls, and vine dressers. Represented as a young man in deacon's robes (XI, PL. 182); his special attribute is the raven, linked to legendary events in the life of the saint. Also appears with attributes alluding to his martyrdom: millstone, whip, iron hooks, gridiron with spikes, and chains.

Zacharias. Depicted as an old man with a censer, and in scenes of the birth and childhood of John the Baptist (XI, PL. 49).

Zeno, Bishop of Verona. Patron saint of Verona; protects children learning to speak and walk. Depicted in bishop's robes with a fish hanging from his crozier, or holding a book (X, PL. 182).

Zenobius, Bishop of Florence. Invoked against headache. Depicted as a bishop (IV, PL. 233; VI, PL. 181) with a dead or living child (VI, PL. 176) and sometimes with a flowering tree, both references to his power to restore life (II, PL. 332); often represented with the city of Florence in the background or with the Florentine lily on his cope (IX, PL. 147).

BIBLIOG. *General Works*: PL; A. Springer, Ikonographische Studien, Mit. der K. K. Zentralcommission zur Erforschung u. Erhaltung der Baudenkmale, V, 1860, sp. 29ff; G. B. de Rossi, La Roma Sotterranea Cristiana, 6 vols., Rome, 1864–77; C. Cahier, Caractéristiques des SS. dans l'Art Populaire, Enumérées et Expliquées, 2 vols., Paris, 1867; F. Kraus, Real-Encyklopädie der Christlichen Alterthumer, 2 vols., Freiburg im Breisgau, St. Louis, Mo., 1882–86; A. Didron, Christian Iconography, 2 vols., London, 1886; X. Barbier de Montault, Traité d'Iconographie Chrétienne, 2 vols., Paris, 1890; C. Rohault de Fleury, G. Rohault de Fleury, Archéologie Chrétienne, les SS. de la Messe et leurs Monuments, 10 vols., Paris, 1893–1900; H. Detzel, Christliche Ikonographie, 2 vols., Freiburg im Breisgau, St. Louis, Mo., 1894–96; A. B. Jameson, Sacred and Legendary Art, 2 vols., London, 1896; H. Delehaye, Les Légendes Hagiographiques, Brussels, 1905 (4th ed., 1955); H. Gregoire, Saints Jumeaux et Dieux Cavaliers, Etude Hagiographique, Paris, 1905; H. Delehaye, Les Légendes Greques des Saints Militaires, Paris, 1909; M. Liefmann, Kunst und Heilige, Ein Ikonographisches Handbuch zur Erklärung der Werke der Italienischen und Deutschen Kunst, Jena, 1912; E. Mâle, La Part de Suger dans le Création de l'Iconographie du Moyen Age, Rev. de l'Art Ancien et Mod., XXXV, 1914, p. 91ff.; G. Millet, Recherches sur l'Iconographie de l'Evangile aux XIV, XV, et XVI Siècles, 2 vols., Paris, 1916; Index of Christian Art, Princeton, N.J., 1917; E. Mâle, L'Art Allemand et l'Art Français du Moyen Age, Paris, 1917 (4th ed., 1923); W. Molsdorf, Führer Durch den Symbolischen und Typologischen Bilderkreis der Christlichen Kunst des Mittelalters, Leipzig, 1920; Mâle, I; F. G. Holweck, Biographical Dictionary of the Saints, 2 vols., New York, 1924; L. Menzies, The Saints in Italy, London, 1924; M. C. de Ganay, Comment Représenter les Saints Dominicains, Autun, 1926; K. Künstle, Ikonographie der Christlichen Kunst, 2 vols., Freiburg im Breisgau, 1926–28; W. Molsdorf, Christliche Symbolik der Mittelalterlichen Kunst, Leipzig, 1926; E. Mâle, Art et Artistes du Moyen Age, Paris, 1927; L. Bréhier, L'Art Chrétien, son Développement Iconographique des Origines à nos Jours, 2d ed., Paris, 1928; E. Ricci, Mille Santi nell'Arte, Milan, 1931; F. Borromeo, De Pictura Sacra, Sora, 1932; C. Smits, De Iconographie van de Nederlandsche Primitieven, Amsterdam, 1933; J. M. B. Clauss, Die Heiligen des Elsass in Ihrem Leben, Ihrer Verehrung und Ihrer Darstellung in der Kunst, Düsseldorf, 1935; G. de Jerphanion, La Voix des Monuments, Notes et Etudes d'Archéologie Chrétienne, Rome, 1938; N.S.; V. L. Kennedy, The Saints of the Canon of the Mass, Vatican, 1938; B. Knipping, De Iconographie van de Contrareformatie in de Nederlanden, 2 vols., Hilversum, 1939–40; M. Praz, Studies in Seventeenth Century Imagery, 2 vols., London, 1939; Jacobus de Voragine, The Golden Legend of Jacobus de Voragine, 2 vols., London, New York, 1941; J. Braun, Tracht und Attribute der Heiligen in der Deutschen Kunst, Stuttgart, 1943, 1964; O. A. Nygren, Helgonen i Finlands Medeltidkonst, en Ikonografisk Studie, Helsingfors, 1945; A. Grabar, Martyrium, Recherches sur le culte des reliques et l'art chrétien antique, 3 vols., Paris, 1946; J. J. M. Timmers, Symboliek en Iconographie der Christlijke Kunst, Roermond-Maaseik, 1947; F. Antal, Florentine Painting and Its Social Background, London, 1948; J. Ferrando Roig, Iconografía de los Santos, Barcelona, 1950; G. Bettoli, L'arte a Servizio del Culto dei Santi, Arte Cristiana, XXXIX, 1952, pp. 172–79; J. Ferrando Roig, Arte Religioso Actual en Cataluña, Barcelona, 1952; G. Kaftal, Iconography of the Saints in Tuscan Painting, Florence, 1952; H. Lützeler, The Saints, Freiburg im Breisgau, 1955; L. Réau, Iconographie de l'Art Chrétien, 3 vols. in 6, Paris, 1955–59; H. Roeder, Saints and Their Attributes, London, New York, Toronto, 1955; A Pigler, Barock-Themen, 2 vols., Budapest, 1956; L. Behling, Die Pflanze in der Mittelalterlichen Tafelmalerei, Weimer, 1957; L. Böer, ed., Lexikon der Marienkunde, fasc. 1–6, Regensburg, 1957–65; Y. Hirn, The Sacred Shrine, a study of the Poetry and Art of the Catholic Church, Boston, 1957; F. Zeri, Pittura e controriforma, Turin, 1957; E. Mâle, The Gothic Image, New York, 1958; E. Mâle, Religious Art from the Twelfth to the Eighteenth Century, New York, 2d ed., 1958; E. Mâle, Les Saints Compagnons du Christ, Paris, 1958; H. Schrade, Vor- und Frühromanische Malerei, die Karolingische, Ottonische und Frühsalische Zeit, Cologne, 1958; H. Aurenhammer, Lexikon der Christlichen Ikonographie, vols. 1–4, Vienna, 1959–65; G. W. Ferguson, Signs and Symbols in Christian Art, New York, 1959; C. Ihm, Die Programme der Cristlichen Apsismalerei vom Vierten Jahrhundert bis zur Mitte des Achten Jahrhunderts, Wiesbaden, 1960; C. Emond, L'Iconographie Carmélitaine dans les Anciens Pays-Bas Méridionaux, Mem. d'Acad. Royale de Belgique, Classe des Beaux-Arts (2), tome 12, fasc. 5, 1961; M. L.-H. Grondijs, Croyances, Doctrines et Iconographie de la Liturgie Céleste, Mél, LXXIV, 1962, pp. 665–703; H. Buchtal, Some Notes on Byzantine Hagiographical Portraiture, GBA, LXII, 1963, pp. 81–90; H. Schrade, Die Romanische Malerei, Ihre Maiestas, Cologne, 1963; D. Attwater, The Penguin Dictionary of Saints, Baltimore, 1965; G. Kaftal, Iconography of the Saints in Central and South Italian Painting, Florence, 1965; G. Schiller, Ikonographie der Christlichen Kunst, vol. 1, Guterslöh, 1965.

Special Iconography. Apostles: R. A. Lipsius, Die Apokryphen Apostelgeschichten und Apostellegenden, 2 vols. in 3, Braunschweig, 1883–87; J. Ficker, Die Darstellung der Apostel in der Altchristlichen Kunst, Leipzig, 1887; R. A. Lipsius, Die Apokryphen Apostelgeschichte und Apostellegenden, Ergänzungsheft, Braunschweig, 1890; R. A. Lipsius, M. Bonnet, Acta Apostolorum Apocrypha, 2 vols., Leipzig, 1898–1903; J. E. Weis-Liebardorf, Christus und Apostelbilder, Einfluss der Apokryphen auf die Ältesten Kunsttypen, Freiburg im Breisgau, 1902; G. de Jerphanion, Quels Sont les Douze Apôtres dans l'Iconographie Chrétienne? Recherches de Science Religieuse, X, 1920, pp. 358–67; P. Lutze, Darstellung der Rede in der Deutschen Bildenden Kunst des Mittelalters Gezeigt an Propheten und Aposteln, Berlin, 1935; F. M. Godfrey, Christ and the Apostles, the Changing Forms of Religious Imagery, London, New York, 1957; M. Sotomayor, Über der Herkunft der "Traditio Legis," RQ, LVI, 1961, pp. 215–30; M. Sotomayor, S. Pedro en la Iconografía Paleocristiana, Granada, 1962. *Evangelists*: T. Zahn, Die Tiersymbole der Evangelisten, Forschung zur Geschichte des Neutestamentlichen Kanons und der Altkirchlichen Literatur, II, Erlangen, 1883, pp. 257–75; N. R. E. Bell, Lives and Legends of the Evangelists, Apostles, and Other Early Saints, London, 1901; F. Saxl, Frühes Christentum und Spätes Heidentum in Ihren Künstlerischen Ausdruckformen, Wiener Jhb. f. Kg., XVI, Band II, 1923, pp. 63–121; A. M. Friend, The Portrait of the Evangelists in Greek and Latin Manuscripts, Art Studies, V, 1927, pp. 115–47; E. Schlee, Die Ikonographie der Paradiesesflüsse, Leipzig, 1937; W. Weisbach, Les Images des Evangelistes dans l'Evangélaire d'Othon III et leurs Rapports avec l'Antiquité, GBA, XXI, 1939, pp. 131–52; R. Crozet, Les Premiers Représentations Antropo-Zoomorphiques des Evangelistes, VIe–IXe Siècles, Etudes Mérovingiennes, Actes des Journées de Poitiers, 1er–3 May 1952, Paris, 1953, pp. 53–63; R. Crozet, Les Représentations Antropo-Zoomorphiques des Evangelistes dans l'Enluminure et dans le Peinture Murale aux Epoques Carolingienne et Romane, Cah. de Civ. Med., X^{e}–XIIe Siècles, I, 1958, pp. 182–87; R. Crozet, Les Quatre Evangelistes et leurs Symboles, Assimilations et Adaptations, Cah. Technique de l'Art, IVe, 1962, pp. 5–26. *Angels*: O. Wulff, Cherubim, Throne und Seraphim, Ikonographie der Ersten Engelshierarchie in der Christlichen Kunst, Altenburg, 1894; G. Stuhlfauth, Die Engel in der Altchristlichen Kunst, Freiburg in Breisgau, 1897; C. E. (Clement) Waters, Angels in Art, London, 1898; H. Mendelsohn, Die Engel in der Bildenden Kunst, Ein Beitrag zur Kunstgeschichte der Gotik und der Renaissance, Berlin, 1907; K. Felis, Die Niken und die Engel in Altchristlicher Kunst, RQ, XXVI, 1912, pp. 3–25; G. Fogolari, Le Gerarchie Angeliche negli Affreschi Scoperti agli Eremitani di Padova, BArte, 3, XXVI, 1932–33, pp. 81–89; G. de Jerphanion, L'Origine Copte du Type de Saint Michel Debout sur le Dragon, CRAI, 1938, pp. 367–81; E. Kirschbaum, L'Angelo Rosso e l'Angelo Turchino, RACr, XVII, 1940, pp. 209–48; J. Villette, L'Ange dans l'Art d'Occident du XIIième au XVIième Siècle, France, Italie, Flandre, Allemagne, Paris, 1940; R. P. Regamey, Anges, Paris, 1946; H. W. Hegemann, Der Engel in der Deutschen Kunst, Munich, 1950; J. Daniélou, Les Anges et leur Mission d'après les Pères de l'Eglise, 2d ed., Paris, 1953; E. Peterson, Das Buch von den Engeln, 2d ed., Munich, 1955; C. D. Müller, Die Engellehre der Koptischen Kirche, Wiesbaden, 1959; R. Hammerstein, Die Musik der Engel, Bern, Munich, 1962. *Doctors of the Church*: X. Barbier de Montault, Le Culte des Docteurs de l'Eglise à Rome, Rev. de l'Art Chrétien, XLI, 1891, pp. 275–90; 498–505. *Individual saints. St. Agnes*: P. Franchi de' Cavalieri, St. Agnese nella Tradizione e nella Leggenda, Rome, 1899; T. Shearman, The Veneration of St. Agnes, Sydney, 1904; G. Ring, Die Gruppe der Heiligen Agnes, Oud Holland, LVI, 1939, pp. 26–47; A. Ferrua, Sant'Agnese e l'Agnello, La Civiltà Cattolica, Q. 2606, 1959, pp. 141–90. *St. Alexis*: F. G. Pariset, L'Image de S. Alexis de Georges De La Tour, GBA, XX, 1938, pp. 63–66. *St. Ambrose*: F. Wieland, Zur Ikonographie des Hl. Ambrosius, RQ, XXIII, 1909, pp. 132–35; F. H. Dudden, The Life and Times of Saint Ambrose, 2 vols., Oxford, 1935. *St. Andrew the Apostle*: M. Fransolet, Le St. André de François Duquesnoy à la Basilique de St.-Pierre au Vatican, B. de l'Inst. Historique Belge de Rome, XIII, 1933, pp. 227–86; E. Mâle, Histoire et Légende de l'Apôtre S. André dans l'Art, Rev. des Deux Mondes, V, 1951, pp. 412–20. *St. Anne*: C. Vincens, De l'Iconographie de St. Anne et de la Vierge Marie, à propos d'une Statue du XVe Siècle, Marseilles, 1893; M. V. Ronan, St. Anne, Her Cult and Her Shrines, New York, 1927; B. Kleinschmidt, Die Heilige Anna, ihre Verehrung in Geschichte, K., und Volkstum, Düsseldorf, 1930. *St. Anthony Abbot*: R. Flahault, Le Culte de St. Antoine Ermite dans la Flandre Maritime, Dunkerque, 1898; L. Réau, Mathias Grünewald et le Retable de Colmar, Nancy, 1920; A. de Castro, Sant'Antonio nell'Arte, Leggenda e Poesia, Naples, 1932; C. D. Cuttler, The Temptations of St. Anthony in Art from Earliest Times to the First Quarter of the XVIth Century (New York Univ. Diss.), 1952. *St. Anthony of Padua*: C. de Mandanch, St. Antoine de Padove et l'Art Italien, Paris, 1899; P. Schlager, Der Heilige Antonius von Padua in Kunst und Legende, Munich-Gladbach, 1923; B. Kleinschmidt, Antonius von Padua in Leben und Kunst, Kulte und Volkstum, Düsseldorf, 1931. *St. Augustine*: J. Stiennon, L'Iconographie de St.-Augustin d'après Benozzo Gozzoli et les Croisiers de Huy, B. de l'Inst. Historique Belge de Rome, XXVII, 1952, pp. 235–48; L. Réau, L'Iconographie de St. Augustin, Actes du Cong. des Soc. Savantes, LXXIX, 1954, pp. 387–91. *St. Bartholomew*: E. Mâle, The Early Churches of Rome, London, 1960. *St. Benedict*: F. Cabrol, St. Benedict, London, 1934. *St. Carlo Borromeo*: San Carlo Borromeo, con introduzione di L. Ferretti, Rome, 1923; Mâle, IV; A. Pigler, Barock-Themen, 2 vols.,

Budapest, 1956. *St. Catherine of Siena*: J. Rodenberg, Die Hl. Katharina von Siena und ihre Darstellung in der Sienesischen Kunst, Bremen, 1910; L. Ferretti, S. Caterina da Siena, Rome, 1926; A. Masseron, St. Catherine de Sienne, Paris, 1934; G. Kaftal, St. Catherine in Tuscan Painting, Oxford, 1949. *St. Cecilia*: P. Benati, Santa Cecilia nella Leggenda e nell'Arte, Milan, 1928.

Attributes: F. C. Husenbeth, Emblems of Saints by Which They Are Distinguished in Works of Art, 3d ed., Norwich, 1882; A. Krücke, Der Nimbus und Verwandte Attribute in der Frühchristlichen Kunst, Strasbourg, 1905; J. Wilpert, Le Nimbe Carré, à propos d'un Momie Peinte du Mus. Egyptien au Vatican, Mél., XXVI, 1906, pp. 3–13; J. T. Perry, The Nimbus in Eastern Art, BM, XII, 1907–08, pp. 20–23, 95–96; E. A. Greene, Saints and Their Symbols, A Companion in the Churches and Picture Galleries of Europe, London, 1911; F. Brunswick, Heilige und Ihre Symbole in der Darstellenden Kunst, Rome, 1914; K. Fries, Die Attribute der Christlichen Heiligen, Leipzig, 1915; Maurice Drake, Wilfred Drake, Saints and Their Emblems, London, 1916; R. Pfleiderer, Die Attribute der Heiligen, Ulm, 1920; M. E. Tabor, The Saints in Art with Their Attributes and Symbols Alphabetically Arranged, 3d ed., London, 1924; A. De Bles, How to Distinguish the Saints in Art by Their Costumes, Symbols and Attributes, New York, 1925; H. Delehaye, Les Caractéristiques des Saints dans l'Art, Le Correspondant, CCLXXVII, 1928, pp. 481–500; E. Schäfer, Die Heiligen mit dem Kreuz in der Altchristlichen Kunst, RQ, XLIV, 1936, pp. 67–104; G. de Jerphanion, Les Caractéristiques et les Attributs des Saints dans la Peinture Cappadocienne, Analecta Bollandiana, LV, 1937, pp. 1–28; J. Braun, Tracht und Attribute der Heiligen in der Deutschen Kunst, Stuttgart, 1943; O. Brendel, Origin and Meaning of the "Mandorla," GBA, XXV, 1944, pp. 5–24; R. L. P. Milburn, Saints and Their Emblems in English Churches, London, 1949; A. Grabar, Le Trône des Martyrs, CahA, VI, 1952, pp. 31–41; H. Roeder, Saints and Their Attributes, London, 1955; E. Coche de la Ferté, Palma et Laurus, Jhb. der Berl. Mus., III, 1961, pp. 134–47; M. Collinet-Guérin, Histoire du Nimbe des Origines aux Temps Modernes, Paris, 1961.

Patronage: L. Broc de Segange, Les Saints Patrons des Corporations et Protecteurs Spécialement Invoqués dans les Maladies et dans les Circonstances Cretiques de la Vie, 2 vols., Paris, 1887; D. Kerler, Die Patronate der Heiligen, Ulm, 1905; W. Deinhardt, Frühmittelalterliche Kirchenpatrozinien in Franken (Studien zur Frühgeschichte der Diözesen Bamberg und Würzburg), Nürnberg, 1933; J. Seguin, En Basse-Normandie, Saints Guérisseurs, Saints Imaginaires et Dévotions Populaires, 2d ed., Avranches, 1944; J. Stany-Gauthier, Les Saints Bretons Protecteurs des Récoltes et des Jardins, Arts et Traditions Populaires, I, 1953, pp. 307–21; M. Leproux, Dévotions et Saints Guérisseurs (Contributions au Folklore Charentais: Angoumois, Aunis, Saintonge) Paris, 1957.

* *

Illustrations: PLS. 365–380.

SALVADOR, EL.

SALVADOR, EL. The Republic of El Salvador (República de El Salvador), independent of Spain since 1821, is bounded by the Pacific Ocean on the south and borders on Guatemala on the west and on the Republic of Honduras on the north and east. When the Spaniards reached the territory of what is now El Salvador, they found two native provinces: Cuscatlán in the west and Chaparrastique in the east, separated by the Lempa River. However, some of the old cultural elements of the eastern province penetrated to the western centers, and the western culture, at least in its final phase, was widely diffused in the eastern part of the country. From the 16th to the 18th century, the country was under the Spanish influence, especially in religious architecture; it became open to international cultural influences from the 19th century on.

SUMMARY. Pre-Columbian periods (col. 669): *Western province; Eastern province.* Colonial and modern periods (col. 673).

PRE-COLUMBIAN PERIODS. *Western province.* Throughout the province of Cuscatlán are raised-mound dwelling, burial, and ceremonial sites with ball courts. The common types of construction consist of squared stone fitted in adobe mortar, as seen in Opico; stone and masonry, mortar fitted and faced on both wall and floor surfaces, as in Campana-San Andrés and Tazumal; blocks of talpatate, a yellowish-white stone with a pumice conglomerate, as in, for example, Santa Emilia; and roughly cut slabs of volcanic stone covering boulder and adobe cores, found at sites in the vicinity of Lake Guija.

At the Campana-San Andrés and Tazumal sites there is evidence of rebuilding; remains of the earliest period are characterized by finer materials and workmanship and some of the façades are painted white. The enormous, steeply battered bases of the principal platform mounds, which are surrounded by smaller ones, the terraces, and the balustraded stairs are executed with an austere simplicity

that suggests close cultural connections with the Esperanza phase of the classic period of Kaminaljuyú, Guatemala, and the Toltec culture in the Valley of Mexico. Other distinctive features of these sites are, at Tazumal, a plaza enclosed by stepped walls in the interior of the upper main platform, and, at Campana-San Andrés, cornices used to decorate terrace edges (from the second period).

Ancient monumental sculpture is limited to the west. Only one stele is known, the so-called "Tazumal Virgin," which represents a human figure in ceremonial regalia wearing a headdress depicting the face of the Mexican rain-god, Tlaloc, and holding a bar in one

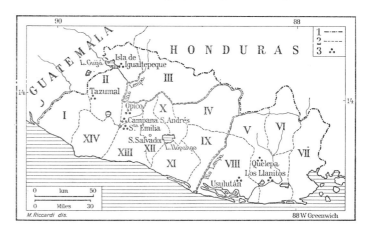

El Salvador, principal archaeological and modern centers. *Key:* (1) Modern national boundaries; (2) internal department boundaries. Departments: I Ahuachapán; II Santa Ana; III Chalatenango; IV Cabañas; V San Miguel; VI Morazán; VII La Unión; VIII Usulután; IX San Vicente; X Cuscatlán; XI La Paz; XII San Salvador; XIII La Libertad; XIV Sonsonate; (3) archaeological sites.

hand. Incised glyphlike forms appear on the sides but the back is not worked. The carving lacks depth and the hieroglyphs do not resemble any known type. Two Chac-Mool figures of a type that is generally associated with the Mexican plateau and Yucatán, but that has been found as far east as Costa Rica, and a so-called "standard bearer" figure exist.

In the departments of Santa Ana and Ahuachapán, large jaguar heads carved on boulders are characterized by protruding canine teeth and heart-shaped ears. Techniques of sculpture vary from in the round to incision and high and low bas-reliefs. The closest parallel of this group of sculptures, considered as a complex, occurs on the Pacific slope of Guatemala.

In the northern portions of both eastern and western El Salvador, but more commonly in the east, are found caves with painted pictographs and petroglyphs carved on boulders, occasionally with paint on the carvings. The west has two styles of petroglyphs: those executed with fine double lines, and a single line style. Igualtepeque Island in Lake Guija is noted for the first type. Here more than 200 geometric and conventionalized animal and human figures are incised on boulders. Single line petroglyphs of human beings with a ceremonial bar occur at Las Victorias. The technique recalls that of the Tazumal stele.

Among the other artistic manifestations associated with the west are supposedly "archaic" small but massively shaped animals and men with limbs carved on the body in relief; crude monkeys sitting on human backs or eating; seated figures with prominent, stylized spines, upturned faces, and closed eyes reminiscent of "sukia" representations from eastern Central America (the name "sukia" is derived from the Misquito Indian term for medicine man); tenoned animal, parrot, or serpent heads; mace heads that are circular or star-shaped or have a face carved in relief; occasional jades cut with Maya motifs; Totonac elements such as three-pointed stones decorated with masklike faces; flat heads (*hachas*) with scale motifs down the back; and ceremonial yokes.

In the potter's art these cultures found a significant means of expression. Mexican influences continued to predominate, principally in the west, where the "archaic" period is more ancient. This period is represented by highly stylized figurines, solid or hollow, with plump torsos, tapering limbs, and shallowly modeled heads. They can be divided into eight different groups depending on how the eyes are depicted. Hands and feet take the shape of knobs or are pinched front and back for standing. Features and ornaments are represented by grooving and the addition of buttons and fillets. Occasionally the modeled surface is painted. Globular vessels, with or without lugs, spouts, and tripod supports, sometimes modified into faces or feet, are decorated with incised geometric designs or with motifs in panels between the handles.

Totonac-like pottery is distinguished by cylindrical or bell-shaped legs with attached heads, often with painted eyeballs.

A style that developed in western El Salvador but was influenced by Mexican currents can be seen in the so-called "plumbate" ware. This ware is composed of hard, well-fired bistred clay ranging in color from steel gray to orange-brown. Basic forms are subglobular, tall-necked, and pear-shaped, executed with or without a ring base or bulbous or effigy supports. Decoration consists of incising, representations of Tlaloc and bearded faces, and animal effigies modeled with details on the vessel body. "Plumbate" ware belongs to the late or Pipil period and is the most widely diffused of any Central American ceramic style.

There are many indications of Aztec influence, for which possibly the Pipil Indians were responsible. These include unpainted, bottle-shape, rim base vases with a Tlaloc face modeled on the front and a loop handle at the rear (early examples are unpainted, later ones are tinted blue); unpainted shallow-dish incense burners with cylindrical handles ending in a serpent's head either modeled in one piece or built up with fillets and nodules; broad, hollow, open-base clay frogs, sometimes painted with black pigment; and large incense burners with the figure of a seated priest, modeled in the round, wearing an animal headdress and the flayed skin of the dead, which distinguishes the Xipe cult.

Mayoid and Naturalistic Ulúa polychrome ware appears at a late period throughout El Salvador. Two common forms are cylindrical vessels on short tripods and wide-mouthed bowls, both comparable to Honduran forms. Legless cylindrical vessels and wide-mouthed bowls decorated with painted bands or panels of stylized hieroglyphs, often in the form of faces with appendages and combined with realistic figures of men in ceremonial dress, and small unpainted clay bottles stamped with elaborate scenes of Maya priests recall forms found in Copán, Honduras, and highland Guatemala. Manifestations of this ware extend east of the Lempa River, but in this area there is a degeneration in the painting techniques.

Despite the important and evident contributions of foreign cultures to the ceramic art of El Salvador, local inspiration is apparent in the color and design of certain wares. Red on gray grounds and purple and red on orange grounds in geometric designs in curvilinear patterns and in panels are associated with the western section of the country.

Another local development is seen in scraped-slip pottery. This is named for the curvilinear designs produced by scraping off parts of the white slip either with the fingers or with a widely separated brush. Common forms are highly polished bichrome or polychrome bowls and jars. This ware appears early at Tazumal and was known at Lake Yojoa, Honduras, and Kaminaljuyú, Guatemala, during the Esperanza phase.

Examples from the late "archaic" period can also be found in the east and consist largely of handmade and mold-made figurines.

Eastern Province. Dirt and stone mounds, sometimes grouped around a small plaza, are typical of eastern El Salvador, but ceremonial centers with ball courts are rare and seem limited to the departments of Usulután and San Miguel. Fortified sites with stone mounds and low stone walls are peculiar to the northeast. Little excavation has been carried out in the east, but at least one location, Los Llanitos, has yielded evidence of constructions of pumice blocks joined with adobe mortar and the use of buttresslike elements.

East of the Lempa River, grinding stones with projecting animal heads and jadeite ax-gods recall artifacts from northeastern Honduras and Costa Rica. Small green stone images of human beings and gross animals with limbs and features in low relief extend into the western highlands of Honduras. Flat heads (*hachas*) are sometimes found; animal heads decorated with geometric motifs and mushroom-shaped stones of unknown use are also present.

The brilliant hues and, in particular, the effigy shapes of the Las Vegas polychrome ware seen in central Honduras reappear in El Salvador, mainly in the east. This pottery has often been mistermed Nicoya polychrome. Although the Salvadoran specimens have definite affinities to this group, they should be classified with Las Vegas ware and not with Costa Rican ceramics.

Among the colors associated with eastern ceramics are purple, orange, and black on gray grounds and purple-red and brown on cream grounds — seldom seen outside of El Salvador. Monochrome red and brown wares are common. Characteristic forms have spouts and bulbous and ring supports. Storage jars are often decorated with nodules, loop handles, and outcurving necks. In effigy vessels with modeled features, the head is generally placed on the vessel neck, as in the red-on-orange style of Quelepa.

Also present in the east are handmade figurines reminiscent

of Honduran Playa de los Muertos types, grotesque monkey heads with crowns, crude so-called "pensamiento" figures resting their heads on one hand (similar to "sukia" figures), and hollow figurines and whistles.

Usulután ceramics are contemporary with the oldest "archaic" types of the west. Associated with the east, but spread throughout the country into highland Guatemala and Honduras, this ware is characterized by bowl shapes, by occasionally spouted and effigy forms, bulbous and conical legs, painted parallel-line designs, thickened lips, and offset rims. Usulután technique and patterns appear in early phase polychrome pottery from Tazumal. Effigy ware representing animals or men with arms and heads protruding in characteristic positions and vessel necks adorned with modeled heads have often been considered "archaic." However, in this author's opinion, the influence of effigy styles associated with the monochrome non-Meso-American wares of Central America is evident here. The Salvadoran type is a local interpretation of those styles.

Also typical of the east are globular vessels with two loop handles with raised nubbins suggestive of forms associated with highland Honduras. Decorative motifs are characteristic of eastern El Salvador, however, and consist of panels or bands of geometric designs in red tones.

Vessels in shoe forms and modeled alligator ware are found on the Pacific littoral from Nicoya Peninsula in Costa Rica up to the Lempa River.

The influence of Mexican cultures in the artistic development of the Isthmian area is perhaps more obvious in El Salvador than in any other part of Central America. A stratum of early or "archaic" art seems to be common to the Valley of Mexico and much of this country. Artifacts associated with the region of Veracruz and the Tenochtitlán dwelling of Montezuma add archaeological evidence to historical documentation concerning the Aztec emperor Ahuitzotl's attempt to spy out the land in preparation for enlarging his empire.

With the exception of a small area in the east, all of El Salvador was culturally Meso-American (see MIDDLE AMERICAN PROTOHISTORY) at the time of the arrival of the Spaniards and showed signs of persistent and lengthy occupation by Mexican peoples. These links with Mexican culture are apparent in the diversity of pottery styles; in the distinctive "plumbate" ware; in religious motifs, such as Xipe and Tlaloc; in large-based, steeply battered, terraced platform mounds; and in stonework. Mayan influence came into El Salvador from highland Guatemala, Copán, and the Ulúa River drainage. It was relatively late and degenerated east of the Lempa. Relationships with non-Meso-America can be noted particularly in the east, for example in jadeite ax-gods, modeled alligator ware, and vessels in shoe forms.

Despite this marked evidence of foreign cultures, El Salvador developed its own art styles, especially in ceramics. Painted linear and geometric patterns characterized local Salvadoran pottery, from the early Usulután ware to the red-on-orange of Quelepa and the scraped-slip pottery of Tazumal. Purple paint and a gray ground are other distinctive features. Some of these wares were important items of exchange with Guatemala and Honduras and are associated with the early horizons in both these countries.

BIBLIOG. *a. General*: Relación breve y verdadera de algunas cosas de las muchas que sucedieron al fray Alonso Ponce en las provincias de Nueva España . . . escrita por dos religiosos, 2 vols., Madrid, 1873; H. J. Spinden, Notes on the Archaeology of Salvador, AmA, N.S., XVII, 1915, pp. 446–91; Colección de documentos importantes relativos a la República de El Salvador, San Salvador, 1921; P. de Alvarado, An Account of the Conquest of Guatemala in 1524 (ed. S. J. Mackie), New York, 1924; S. K. Lothrop, The Museum Central American Expedition, Indian Notes, Heye Foundation, IV, 1, 1927, pp. 12–33; S. K. Lothrop, Pottery Types and Their Sequence in El Salvador, Indian Notes, Heye Foundation, I, 1927, pp. 165–220; J. M. Longyear III and S. H. Boggs, Archaeological Investigations in El Salvador (Peabody Mus. Mem., IX, 2), Cambridge, Mass., 1944; W. Haberland, Ceramic Sequences in El Salvador, AmAnt, XXVI, 1960, pp. 21–29. *b. Western El Salvador*: W. Lehmann, Ergebnisse einer Forschungsreise in Mittel-Amerika und Mexico, 1907–1909, ZfE, XLII, 1910, pp. 687–749; P. Henning, La arqueología mexicana como norma para el estudio de las antigüedades Nahoa-Pipiles: El Xipe del Tazumal de Chalchuapa, Departamento de Santa Ana, República de El Salvador (Disertaciones científicas de autores alemanes en México, IV), Mexico City, 1918; J. Lardé, Arqueología Cuzcatleca: Vestigios de una población pre-Máyica en el valle de San Salvador, San Salvador, 1924; J. Lardé, Región arqueologica de Chalchuapa, Revista de etn., y lingüística, I, 1926, pp. 163–173; S. K. Lothrop, The Southeastern Frontier of the Maya, AmA, N.S., XLI, 1939, pp. 42–54; J. M. Dimick, Notes on Excavations at Campana-San Andrés, El Salvador, Yb. Carnegie Inst. of Washington, XL, 1940–41, pp. 298–300; F. B. Richardson, Non-Maya Monumental Sculpture of Central America, in The Maya and Their Neighbors, New York, 1940, pp. 395–416; S. H. Boggs, Notas sobre las excavaciones en la Hacienda San Andrés, Departamento de La Libertad, Tzunpame, III, 1, 1943, pp. 104–25; S. H. Boggs, Observaciones respecto a la importancia de Tazumal en la prehistoria Salvadoreña, Tzunpame, III, 1, 1943, pp. 127–33; W. Haberland, A Pre-classic Complex of Western El Salvador, Proc. 32nd Int. Cong. of Americanists (1956), Copenhagen, 1958, pp. 485–90. *c. Eastern El Salvador*: A. Peccorini, Ruinas de

Quelepa, Rev. de etn., arqueol. y lingüística, I, 1926, pp. 249–50; A. E. Sol, Informe del director de Departamento de Historia sobre las ruinas de Quelepa, Rev. El Salvador Departamento de H., I, 2, 1929, pp. 37–39; W. Haberland, On Human Figurines from San Marcos Lempa, El Salvador, El México antiguo, IX, 1959, pp. 509–24.

Doris STONE

COLONIAL AND MODERN PERIODS. The Spanish occupation, which began in the first half of the 16th century, brought about the diffusion of Spanish colonial architectural forms throughout the country. More original expressions were realized in the sphere of the baroque style. The country remained subject to Spain until the beginning of the 19th century, when it achieved independence. Subsequently, many buildings of an official nature were constructed. Through close trade relations with Europe and North America, the country was exposed to the European styles of the 19th and 20th centuries, and, more recently, to international architectural forms.

There are very few surviving examples of the colonial architecture of the Spanish period. Even the oldest city, San Salvador, the capital, which was founded in 1525 by Pedro de Alvarado and repeatedly destroyed by earthquakes, preserves the old street layout only in part, and its buildings have been reconstructed several times. It is now essentially modern in appearance, with broad, straight streets, large parks, and rationally distributed buildings. Among the outstanding edifices are the Cathedral, Presidential Palace, National Palace, Teachers College, Polytechnic Institute, Rosales Hospital, National Theater, and Academy of Sciences and Letters. Many government and administrative buildings, schools, hospitals, hotels, banks, and business buildings are in the latest international style, as well as a large number of apartment buildings in the outlying districts. New residential centers have sprung up recently in the suburbs. The National Museum and the National Institute, which has a small collection, are located here.

San Miguel, in eastern El Salvador, was founded near a destroyed Indian city in 1530, with a regular checkerboard plan. In the following centuries it was enhanced by fine buildings in the colonial baroque style, of which some interesting examples of religious architecture survive. The High Court building and the city hall are noteworthy. Recent constructions, such as the Central Hospital, schools, hotels, and many private buildings and dwellings, are in the international style.

Francesco NEGRI ARNOLDI

BIBLIOG. P. Torres Lanzas, Relación descriptiva de los mapas, planos, etc. de la audiencia y capitanía general de Guatemala . . . existentes en el Archivo general de Indias, Madrid, 1903; L. A. Ward, Libro azul de El Salvador: Historia y descripción, San Salvador, 1916; M. Arguello, El Salvador: Tourist's Guide, San Salvador, 1928; A. Guerra Trigueiros, The Colonial Churches of El Salvador, B. Pan-Am. Union, LXXII, 1938, pp. 271–79; D. Angulo Iñiguez, Historia del arte hispanoamericana, III, Barcelona, 1956, pp. 62–74; J. Sanz y Díaz, Pintores Salvadoreños contemporáneos, Ars, 8, 1957, pp. 53–69.

* *

Illustration: 1 fig. in text.

SAMANID ART.

The artistic culture that flourished in Transoxiana (western Turkistan) and Khorasan in the 9th and 10th centuries under the Samanid dynasty represents one of the fundamental aspects, as yet insufficiently explored and clarified, of medieval Islamic civilization (see ISLAM). Samanid art follows directly in the Iranian artistic tradition, of which it represents a consistent and unique development. Originating in areas that were exposed to manifold influences (such as those from the steppe) and were traversed by the great Central Asian caravan trails, Samanid art absorbed and recast these various stimuli in an integrated artistic style flourishing under the enlivening impetus of international Arab culture. Its contribution to the history of Islamic Iranian art was therefore to be of fundamental importance, constituting the point of departure for the great works of Ghaznevid art (q.v.) and subsequently of Seljuk art (q.v.).

SUMMARY. Historical background (col. 673). City planning (col. 675). Architecture (col. 675). Architectural decoration (col. 677). Painting (col. 678). Ceramics (col. 678). Decorative arts (col. 680): *Metalwork; Glass; Textiles.*

HISTORICAL BACKGROUND. The Samanid dynasty (874–999), which arose in eastern Khorasan, took its name from Sāmānkhudā — that is, the "lord of Sāmān" (a village in the Balkh

region), who was a member of the ancient Iranian landed nobility claiming descent from the famous Sassanian king Bahrām Chūbīn (see SASSANIAN ART). Under the protection of the Arab governor of Khorasan, Asad ibn-'Abdullāh al-Qushayrī, who died in 758, Sāmān was converted from Zoroastrianism to Islam. His descendants enjoyed the favor of the caliphs of Baghdad, so that by 874, through investiture or conquests, they ruled all of Transoxiana and Khorasan, and in the first half of the 10th century, with the title of emir and acknowledging the jurisdiction of the caliphs in name only, they

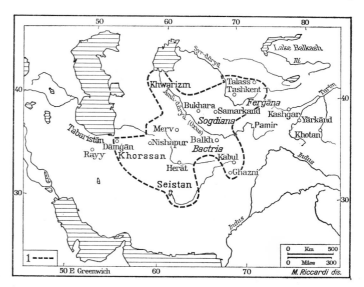

Area under Samanid rule in the 10th century. Key: (1) Borders of the emirate.

ruled over an immense territory that included, besides all of Turkistan, almost all of what is today Afghanistan and a large part of eastern Iran.

With the lessening of the caliphs' power, the 9th and 10th centuries represent a period of capital importance for Iran, not only from a political, economical, and social point of view but also in terms of the history of art and culture. In fact, after the serious crisis following on the Arab invasion, the landed nobility, represented by the *dihqān*, or feudal lords, gradually returned to power in eastern Iran, bringing about, with the decline of Baghdad, the emergence of several independent principalities, the most important of which was that ruled by the Samanids. Economically the period represents a moment of great prosperity, accompanied (at least among the Iranian people) by undeniable social progress. The 9th and 10th centuries mark, moreover, the point at which the entire Islamic world, from the Atlantic Ocean to the Indus, enjoyed its greatest cultural enrichment.

The principal center of the Iranian "rebirth" — aristocratic in character and neither popular nor, in the modern sense of the term, nationalistic — was the brilliant court of the Samanids, which numbered among its rulers great art patrons and refined connoisseurs, notably the emirs Ismā'īl (892–907), Naṣr II ibn-Ahmad (913–42), and Nūḥ II ibn-Naṣr (943–54), who turned Bukhara and Samarkand into famous cultural centers of the Iranian world. They lent great impulse to the establishment of New Persian as the administrative and cultural language, furthering, among other things, the collecting of ancient Iranian tales and legends. Famous writers and artists flocked to their court, especially Persian-language poets, including Rūdagī (914–43), Daqiqi, and the great Firdausī (940–1029), whose *Shāh-nāma* was begun at the court of the Samanid Nuḥ II ibn-Mansūr (976–97) and completed at the court of Maḥmūd the Ghaznevid (998–1030).

The art forms of the period were thus aristocratic in origin; nevertheless they depended (at least in many of their manifestations) on a practically uninterrupted tradition. For example, in the Samanid period idols were still preserved on the doors of castles belonging to the feudal lords, and similar figures, although with mutilated heads, were to be found on the doors of the chief mosques; there was still a castle in the 12th century whose gate was adorned with an idol. Narshakhī, the historian of Bukhara, who was active about the middle of the 10th century, reported that even in his day an immense number of idols were sold in the Makh-ruz bazaar of Bukhara. Also of interest is the account given by Ibn-Ḥawqal (10th cent.), who recalls that statues of horses, oxen, camels, and wild animals were set up in the squares of Samarkand, heraldically counterrampant or fighting, in keeping with ancient iconographic tradition.

CITY PLANNING. According to a reconstruction outlined by Barthold (1958), the typical medieval Islamic city of Central Asia was composed of three main parts: a defensive center (arg or kuhandiz), a municipal center (shahristān), and the "suburb." According to some studies, this system arose in the 6th and 7th centuries, beginning with the castle of the feudal lord, which constituted the arg, around which were added the shahristān, containing the artisan and commercial quarters and the administrative offices; in the 9th and 10th centuries the "suburb," or rabaḍ, developed, and all the most important activities of the city were transferred there. Such a reconstruction, however, does not correspond to historical fact, as archaeological research is making clear. It must be remembered that the Arab invasion had wreaked havoc throughout the country and that in the 7th century most of the cities were abandoned; when they were rebuilt, several centuries later, many of them occupied a different site from the former city. In these new centers of habitation the ribāṭ, or fortress of the "defenders of the faith," built by the Arabs, occupied an important place. At Merv (mod. Mary), the arg-shahristān-rabaḍ plan no longer held: in the 10th century the true city — the prosperous Merv, "mother of all the cities of Khorasan," according to the description of al-Muqaddasī — was the rabaḍ; the arg was reduced to a watermelon plantation, and the shahristān was almost completely abandoned. At Nishapur, which was built on such a plan, the administrative center and the commercial life of the city were in the rabaḍ. At Herat, the seat of government lay a mile west of the actual city. It must be remembered, moreover, that in the 9th and 10th centuries a sharp distinction was not drawn between the shahristān and the rabaḍ. The latter, when it existed, was not, as has been seen, a true suburb but part of the city itself, often set within the city walls, as at Samarkand.

The cities of this period, therefore, cannot be classified in terms of one single type but differ in accordance with various historical, political, topographic, economic, and social factors. It is possible, however, to discern an over-all consistency in the principles of city planning, resulting from a certain similarity in the economic and social progress that brought about the rise and growth of these centers of habitation. The focal points of the cities were the market places, surrounded by the shops of artisans and merchants; nearby were the caravanserais. The main streets of the city, often laid out in a uniform network, centered on these squares. The number of main streets varied (Nishapur has more than 50); they were often broad and well constructed, and almost all of them were paved in stone, as at Bukhara and Samarkand. Next to the market place was situated the most important building of the city, the mosque. The administrative buildings were usually, though not always, located on another square.

ARCHITECTURE. In the pre-Islamic period the basic type of monumental architecture was represented by the castle of the feudal lord; this limited typology was later extended, and documentary sources mention the building of mosques, madrasahs, markets, caravanserais, palaces, and mausoleums. However, the only known examples of 9th- and 10th-century architecture, besides the famous mausoleum of Ismā'īl (see below), are a number of castles described by archaeologists from the U.S.S.R.

These castles, generally two stories high and made of pressed mud and unbaked bricks, are square and consist of a high, sloping foundation upon which an elevation is raised whose walls are broken up into a series of adjoining semicircular bastions, spanned at the top by niches supporting a parapet. There seems to have been only one entrance. The rooms are laid out in accordance with the principle of axial symmetry. One of the commonest types of floor plan has a two-story cruciform room in the center, with vaulted wings and a dome resting on squinches over the crossing. This layout, typical of ancient Iranian tradition, remained characteristic of the Khorasan province, from whence it was to spread to the rest of Persia. A similar cruciform plan is to be found in various Ghaznevid castles of Lashkari Bazaar in Afghanistan. Among the castles and fortresses of southern Turkistan are, in the Merv region, those of Gyaur Kale near Merv (FIG. 676), Haram, Akhuili-Koshuk (FIG. 676), and Sulu Koshuk, all of the 9th century; and in Khwarizm (q.v.), those of Naib Kale and Buran

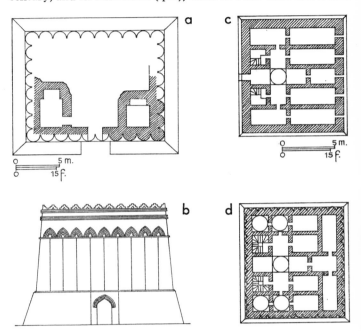

Gyaur Kale, castle: (a) schematic plan; (b) reconstruction of the façade. Akhuili-Koshuk, castle: (c) plan of first floor; (d) plan of second floor (from G. A. Pugachenkova, 1958).

Kale, dating from the 10th and 11th centuries. This type of building, which probably developed during the 6th and 7th centuries, was to continue up to the 12th century (Kavat Kale, 12th–13th cent.). A notable example is the superb Ribaṭ-i-Malik in Uzbekistan, an imposing structure of fired brick, dating from just after the middle of the 11th century. An interesting picture of a fortified castle, which, together with the Ribaṭ-i-Malik, helps to give an idea of how these castles must have looked, is to be found on a celebrated plate in The Hermitage in Leningrad, dating perhaps from the 8th century.

The mausoleum of Ismā'īl the Samanid (PLS. 381, 382; FIG. 677) was built at Bukhara before 907. It is a construction of fired brick in the form of a square room with four doors and is surmounted by a dome. An octagon, composed of arches and opening out into windowless niches at the four corners, rests on the quadrilateral base; the dome is joined to the octagon by means of a narrow 16-sided fascia, 8 sides of which rest on 8 small columns flanking the corner niches. The octagon is masked on the outside by a gallery of arched windows, surmounted at the four corners by four small domes that frame the large central dome. The corners of the building below the gallery are resolved into round pilasters. This type of tomb, from which one of the basic types of Moslem mausoleum originates, is clearly derived from Sassanian models. An immediate precursor may be seen in a building of Hazara whose purpose is uncertain,

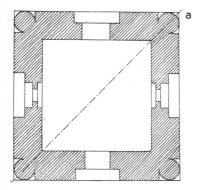
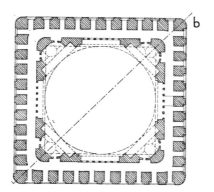

Bukhara, Uzbekistan, mausoleum of Isma'il the Samanid. (a) Ground-floor plan; (b) upper gallery; (c) vertical section (from SPA, II).

though it was possibly a mosque, dating from the 8th or 9th century. It, too, is a square building, the central part of which contains a room set off by four massive round pillars supporting ogee arches. The room is covered by a dome connected by squinches set around the base. The central room is closed in by four vaulted ambulatories bearing small domes at the corners — a construction that stems directly from the Sassanian chahār ṭāq (see IRAN, col. 215), such as the one at Farrashband in Fars.

The gallery of the mausoleum of Ismā'īl, with its four small domes, obviously stems from buildings of the fire-altar and Hazara types; the upper gallery remained typical of northeastern Iran for centuries, and together with the feature of the small corner domes, was to reappear in Moghul Indian architecture (see MOGHUL SCHOOL). The round corner pilasters, which trace their origin from the fortified castles mentioned above, are typical of Turkistan architecture and eventually influenced the funerary buildings of northern Iran.

ARCHITECTURAL DECORATION. The decoration of the mausoleum of Ismā'īl, which is realized in fired brick, with various elements in terra cotta, constitutes the most original aspect of the building and merits separate consideration. The mausoleum is perhaps the oldest known example of this kind of decoration, which was later used extensively by the Ghaznevids (VI, PL. 162) and the Seljuks (PL. 542), who spread it throughout Iran. The practice of arranging bricks to form patterns was already familiar to the Iranian world, but only in a structural use, since the pattern was hidden beneath the plaster facing. In the Ismā'īl tomb, however, the structural and functional qualities and characteristics of brick have been exploited for decorative and ornamental effect. The influence of ornamental models derived from wickerwork and from wood inlay is perhaps admissible, but it must be noted that in this monument the decoration is not superimposed on the wall but is an integral part of it, showing the extraordinary craftsmanship of the Samanid builders, who, however, still remained faithful to the traditional and typical Iranian fondness for superimposed wall ornament.

The decorative patterns achieved by playing upon the various possibilities of fixing the bricks together are highly varied but reveal admirable coherence; the bricks are arranged in accordance with refined principles of design. The fired bricks are used together with a number of prefabricated elements (also of Sassanian origin), such as the disks in the spandrels of the arches around the interior of the octagon, the square panels adorning the portals, the great strings of "pearls," and the stucco incrustations on the inner surfaces of the niched squinches. Although the brickwork decoration tends to give the impression of perforated fretwork, this never interferes with or impairs the architectural essence of the building.

The Nishapur excavations are still too little known for the buildings ascribed to the Samanid period to be properly evaluated; even so, an idea of the architectural decoration may be gained from some stucco decorations, dating with certainty from the second half of the 10th century, that formed the socle of a liwan excavated by the American expedition at Sabr Pushan.

The panels are decorated with a series of large multilobed rosettes, richly embellished with whorls of palmettes, split palmettes, and small rosettes, originally painted in yellow, black, white, red, and blue. It is interesting to note the presence of the animal style of ancient Iranian tradition in several of the large rosettes, where the palmettes hang from the beaks of highly schematic birds' heads. The ornaments are two-dimensional; only a few of the minor details are modeled in relief. A number of stucco fragments from a mosque discovered at Tepe Madrasah, at Nishapur, may be ascribed to this same period. Both groups of stuccoes are comparable to the stuccoes from the Masjid-i-Jāmi' at Nayin, dating from the beginning of the 10th century, although these latter show a much higher degree of schematization.

Samanid wood sculpture is known only from a few examples in poor reproductions. They include a wooden column and three wooden panels from Oburdan in Tadzhikistan, now divided between the Tashkent and Samarkand museums, and a column from Kurut similar in style to the stuccoes of the Masjid-i-Jāmi' at Nayin, though dating apparently from a slightly later period.

PAINTING. Practically nothing is known of Samanid painting, except for a few fragments of wall paintings excavated by the American expedition at Nishapur. Worthy of note is the almost life-size image of a falconer on horseback, riding a horse at a "flying gallop," in keeping with modes derived from Sassanian tradition. The falconer is dressed in Iranian costume, though several details reveal an influence from the steppe, such as the high boots and the three long sword straps hanging in Turkic fashion from his belt. The pictorial fragment of Nishapur is related not only to the painting of Samarra, which has a marked Persian cast, but also to the slightly later painting from the first Ghaznevid period discovered at Lashkari Bazaar in Afghanistan (see AFGHANISTAN and GHAZNEVID ART). The paintings of Nishapur and Lashkari Bazaar seem to have sprung from the same stylistic roots, aside from the motifs common to all Central Asian art.

Nothing remains of Samanid miniatures, though it is perhaps possible to gain an idea of them, not only from the Manichaean miniatures familiar through the early-9th-century fragments found in Central Asia (see MANICHAEAN ART, cols. 439–41, PLS. 281, 282, 284, 287), but also from the miniatures in the Andarz-nāma manuscript completed at Gurgan (mod. Asterabad) in 1090 (Cincinnati, Art Mus., Ms. 1954.112), which reveals the presence of a conservative stream of provincial art in the Sassanian tradition. It is interesting to note the striking stylistic similarity between several of the Andarz-nāma miniatures and the painted figures on a typical variety of 10th-century Nishapur pottery. No trace remains (except in literary sources) of works by the Chinese painters summoned to the Samanid court by Naṣr II ibn Ahmad to illustrate Rūdagī's Persian version of the Kalīla u Dimna.

CERAMICS. The most complete documentation of Samanid art is to be found in its ceramics (q.v., col. 251). Aside from those pieces influenced by Chinese T'ang ware (which is not dissimilar to Mesopotamian pottery) there is a typical Samanid ware that probably attained the highest degree of originality, combined with great formal refinement, to be found in Persian ceramics or even in the entire body of Islamic ceramics. It makes use of a rather limited variety of ornamental devices, most of them common to the rest of Islam; but in the application of decoration under the glazing it adopts a technique peculiar to the ware of Transoxiana (PLS. 383, 385, 386). This technique consists in mixing the metal oxides used for coloring with a fine clay slip; this prevents the colors from blurring or fading when the lead glazing substances are exposed to heat.

This ware, originating in Transoxiana in the 9th century, enjoyed vast popularity throughout all the eastern provinces of Persia, and exported pieces have been found as far east as Sind (Brahmanabad and Bamfore) and Swat and as far west as Susa. It gave rise to numerous local imitations, as in Afghanistan and Seistan, and was being produced at least as late as the end of the 11th century and the beginning of the 12th. It was first discovered in large quantities in the early 20th century, at Afrasiyab near Samarkand (which has given its name to this type of ceramics) and at Nogai Kurgan near Tashkent; later it was found in excavations conducted by Soviet archaeologists in Central Asia and by American archaeologists in Nishapur (PL. 384). The material as a whole still awaits scientific classification. Wilkinson (1960) suggests that the principal manufacturing centers, besides Samarkand in Sogdiana, may have been Nishapur and Merv in Khorasan.

The colors generally used for the background are cream-white, black, and red; the colors used in the painted decorations include also green, yellow, ocher, salmon-pink, and various shades of brown. The best-known and most refined pottery of this Samarkand type is that bearing large inscriptions in Kufic or in "ceramic cursive," painted in black on a white background which Lane (1947) believes may be classed among the most ancient ware. Besides these epigraphic or pseudoepigraphic designs, which usually occupy only part of the available surface and constitute the only decoration, extensive use was also made of palmettes, split palmettes, and flowers. Motifs were often copied from textiles — roundels, rosettes, small hearts, peacock-tail "eyes"; and there are geometric motifs, often separated by dotted bands, in which the influence of the textiles of the Turkic nomads has been detected.

In Transoxianic decoration the human figure never appears, and animal forms are restricted to a small bird, highly stylized and often incorporated into a design of epigraphic origin.

Khorasan ware, known primarily from material excavated at Nishapur, includes a number of types also to be found in Transoxiana, as well as some that are unique. Among the latter is a type whose ornamentation includes figural representations, characteristic both in their style and in the colors employed: black for outlining the figures, green, bright mustard-yellow, and various shades of manganese brown. The faces of the human figures often resemble those to be found on late Mesopotamian glazed pottery and even more those in the *Andarz-nāma* manuscript mentioned above. Among the typical examples of this type of pottery are the bowl in Teheran (Archaeol. Mus.) and the bowl with a standing figure (III, PL. 141). The figures stand forth against a background abounding in animals, flowers, palmettes, and inscriptions.

Khorasan is also the birthplace of a type of ceramics (decorated with large animal figures, often shown fighting) of outstanding stylistic quality, which seems (from certain dynamic and distorted schematizations) to have been influenced by the animal art of the steppe. Also worthy of note are the various "local" derivatives of Nishapur ceramics, such as the pottery of Sari, characterized by large, crested birds, painted mostly in black and ocher, with touches of white and green.

Khwarizm pottery of the 9th and 10th centuries also seems to have distinctive characteristics, at least to judge from the available material, which seems to compare with certain Khorasan types.

In both Transoxiana and Khorasan a pottery is found, painted in light brown or greenish-yellow, which, because of the choice of colors and the figural motifs, may be considered an imitation of late-Mesopotamian metal-glazed painted pottery.

DECORATIVE ARTS. *Metalwork*. Writing at the end of the 10th century, al-Muqaddasī named as important centers for metalwork Bukhara and Samarkand in Transoxiana and Merv in Khorasan (M. J. de Goeje, ed., *Biblioteca graphorum arabicorum . . . , auctore al-Mokkadasi*, Leiden, 1877). The fame of Khorasan metalwork (VIII, PL. 152), especially in the succeeding period, is indicated by the numerous articles signed by artists from Merv, Nishapur, Herat, and Isfarayin. Unfortunately, few objects have survived from the Samanid period.

Two beautiful silver ewers (Leningrad, The Hermitage), with spherical body and long neck in the shape of a truncated cone and bearing a Kufic inscription around the base, may perhaps be ascribed to Samanid art. One of the ewers, decorated with embossed work and incisions, is embellished with birds holding a ribbon in their beaks, framed by plaited medallions; on the neck of the other ewer there are peacocks and griffins set into square panels, and on the body, birds represented in relief framed by whorls of palmettes and split palmettes. The designs are of Sassanian type and style. The large octagonal plate in Berlin (Staat. Mus.), decorated with senmurvs (imaginary winged animals) set into medallions and dating perhaps from the 10th century, almost surely belongs to this same artistic environment, though it could also have been produced in one of the workshops south of the Caspian Sea. A pear-shaped bronze ewer in the Herat Museum, with a brief inscription in inlaid-silver Kufic characters, is dated by Ettinghausen (1957) to the end of the 10th century; it is one of the oldest surviving examples of this technique in Islamic Iran. The form is in the Sassanian tradition and is in all respects comparable to numerous other examples preserved in museums. Again according to Ettinghausen, several large round bronze bowls with incised decorations may be placed in either a Samanid or a Ghaznevid setting; for example, the bowls preserved by the Kevorkian Foundation in New York, in the Ettinghausen Collection in Washington, D.C., and in the Kabul Museum. These in turn are related to the bowl decorated with the figure of a horseman in the Sassanian tradition, signed by an artist from Seistan, Abū Naṣr Muhammad ibn-Aḥmad (London, Sydney Burney Coll.); it dates from the end of the 10th century. Also dating probably from the end of the 10th century or the beginning of the 11th is a small cylindrical bronze pail discovered at Merv, now in the Ashkhabad Museum; its restrained and elegant decoration, consisting of two delicate Kufic inscriptions around the top and bottom and small bosses along the sides, resembles, in its taste, some epigraphically decorated pottery.

Glass. The large quantity of glass discovered in the Nishapur excavations has not yet been made public; but several pieces are known that can be dated with some certainty to about the middle of the 10th century. An example is an elegant ewer with spherical body and truncated-cone neck, similar in form to the silver ewers in The Hermitage; the body has incised decorations consisting of three medallions, two of them containing a bird and the third a lion. This ewer is in every respect comparable to the one in the Buckley Collection of the Victoria and Albert Museum. Of more or less this same period are a drinking glass decorated with birds, and a cylindrical bottle with geometric ornamentation, this latter of a widely diffused type.

Also dating from the 10th century is a turquoise-blue bowl of glass paste (VI, PL. 224), on the bottom of which the Kufic inscription in relief, "Khorasan," indicates its place of origin. It is delicately decorated with figures of crouching animals, represented in relief with incised details.

Textiles. Except for several examples of the *tiraz* (cloth strip used to decorate the sleeve) from Merv and Nishapur, stylistically similar to those from other provinces of Islam, nothing remains of the vast production of the textile workshops of Transoxiana and Khorasan (see TEXTILES, EMBROIDERY, AND LACE), highly renowned through literary references, except the celebrated silk and cotton fragment known as the "Sudarium of St. Josse" (I, PL. 7). The cloth is decorated with facing elephants set off by borders of Kufic characters and rows of Bactrian camels. It is inscribed to Abū Manṣūr Bukhtakīn, a high official of the Samanid court who was put to death by 'Abd-al-Malik ibn-Nūh in 960. The fabric may almost certainly be considered the product of a Khorasan workshop. Although the figures are rather stiff and schematized, Sassanian models have been closely adhered to, both in the general composition and in the individual motifs. The same is true of other fragments of 10th-century Samanid fabrics, for example, those ascribable to Buyid art that were discovered in the burial ground of Bībī Shahr Bānū near Rayy (Rhages), dating from the end of the 10th century or the beginning of the 11th, and are preserved in the Cleveland Museum of Art and the Textile Museum of Washington, D.C.

BIBLIOG. *General*: G. Le Strange, The Lands of the Eastern Caliphate, Cambridge, 1905; E. Bertel's, Persidskaia poesiia v Bukara x vek. (Persian Poetry in 10th Century Bokhara), Moscow, Leningrad, 1935; J. M. Upton, The Persian Expedition 1934-1935: Excavations at Nīshāpūr, BMMA, XXXI, 1936, pp. 176-80; C. K. Wilkinson, W. Hauser, and J. M. Upton, The Iranian Expedition, 1936: The Excavations at Nīshāpūr, BMMA, XXXII, 9, sup., 1937, pp. 3-39; C. K. Wilkinson, W. Hauser, and J. M. Upton, The Iranian Expedition, 1937: The Museum's Excavations at Nīshāpūr, BMMA, XXXIII, 11, sup., 1938, pp. 3-23; W. Hauser and C. K. Wilkinson, The Iranian Expedition, 1938-1940, BMMA, XXXVII, 1942, pp. 82-119; R. N. Frye, The Samanids: A Little Known Dynasty, Muslim World, XXXIV, 1944, pp. 40-45; B. Spuler, Iran in frühislamischer Zeit, Wiesbaden, 1952, pp. 76-90, 273-87; D. Barrett, The Islamic Art of Persia, in A. J. Arberry, ed., The Legacy of Persia, Oxford, 1953, pp. 116-20; R. N. Frye, The History of Bukhara: Translated from a Persian Abridgment of the Arabic Original by Narshakhī, Cambridge, Mass., 1954 (Addenda et Corrigenda HJAS, XIX, 1956, pp. 122-25); R. N. Frye, Notes on the Renaissance of the 10th and 11th Centuries in Eastern Iran, CAJ, I, 1955, pp. 137-43; M. Bussagli, ed., Arte iranica, Rome, 1956 (cat.); E. Kühnel, Die Kunst Persiens unter den Buyden, ZMG, CVI, 1956, pp. 78-92; V. Barthol'd, Turkestan down to the Mongol Invasion, 2d ed., London, 1958; M. S. Dimand, A Handbook of Muhammadan Art, 3d ed., New York, 1958; A. Bausani, Letteratura Neopersiana in A. Pagliaro and A. Bausani, Storia della letteratura persiana, Milan, 1960, pp. 159-69; R. Ghirshman, ed., Sept mille ans d'art en Iran, Paris, 1961 (cat.).

Painting and illumination: R. N. Frye, The Andarz Nāme of Kāyūs b. Iskandar b. Kāpūs b. Vušmgīr, Serta Cantabrigiensia, Cambridge, Wiesbaden, 1954, pp. 7-21; B. Gray, Persian Painting, Geneva, 1961, pp. 11-18.

Architecture and town planning: E. Cohn-Wiener, Turan: Islamische Baukunst in Mittelasien, Berlin, 1930, pls. I-II; L. Rempel, The Mausoleum of Isma'il the Samanid, B. Am. Inst. for Persian Art and Archaeol., IV, 1936, pp. 198-209; E. Schroeder, SPA, I, pp. 945-50; A. U. Pope, SPA, II, pp. 1267-68; S. P. Tolstov, Po sledam drevneikhorezmskoi tsivilizatsii (On the Track of the Ancient Civilization of Khwarizm), Moscow, 1948; V. A. Nil'sen, Mechet' Diggaru v selenie Hazara: Arkhitekturna-arkheologicheskaia ocherk (The Diggaru Mosque in the Village of Hazara: Architectural and Archaeological Essay), Trudy Inst. istorii i arkheol. Akad. nauk Uzbekskoi SSR, VII, 1955, pp. 61-75; G. A. Pugachenkova, Puti razvitiia arkhitekturi iuzhnogo Turkmenistana pory rabovladeniia i feodalisma (The Development of Architecture in Turkmenistan in the Period of Slavery and Feudalism), Trudy iuzhnoturkmenistanskoi arkheologicheskoi kompleksnoi ekspeditsii, VI, Moscow, 1958, pp. 118-87; Y. Yaralov, Architectural Monuments in Middle Asia of the 8th-12th Centuries, 1st Int. Cong. of Turkish Art (1959): Communications, Ankara, 1961, pp. 364-70.

Ceramics: R. L. Hobson, British Museum: A Guide to the Islamic Pottery of the Near East, London, 1932, pp. 21-23; K. Erdmann, Cermiche di Afrasiab, Faenza, XXV, 1937, pp. 125-37; S. Flury, The Ornamental Kufic Inscriptions on Pottery, SPA, II, pp. 1743-69; K. Erdmann, Die Keramik von Afrasiab, Berichte aus den persischen Kunstsammlungen, LXIII, 1942, pp. 18-28; K. Erdmann, Afrasiab Ceramic Wares, B. Iranian Inst., VI, 1946, pp. 102-10; A. Lane, Early Islamic Pottery, London, 1947, pp. 17-19; O. G. Bol'zhakov, Arabskie nadpisi na polivnoie keramika Srednei Asii (Arabic Inscriptions on Glazed Ceramics of Central Asia), Epigrafia Vostoka, XII, 1958, pp. 23-38; N. N. Vakturskaia, Khronologicheskaia klassifikatsiia srednevekovoi keramiki Khorezma (Chronological Classification of the Medieval Ceramics of Kkwarizm), Trudy khorezmskoi arkheologo-etnograficheskoi ekspeditsii, IV, Moscow, 1959, pp. 268-300; C. K. Wilkinson, The Kilus of Nishapur, BMMA, N.S., XVII, 1959, pp. 235-40; K. Erdmann, Eine neue Gattung persischer Keramik, Pantheon, XVIII, 1960, pp. 161-65; C. K. Wilkinson, The Glazed Pottery of Nishapur and Samarkand, BMMA, N.S., XVIII, 1960, pp. 102-15; K. Erdmann, Keramische Erwenkungen der islamischen Abteilung, 1958-1960, Berliner Museen, X, 1961, pp. 6-15.

Metalwork: Y. I. Smirnov, Vostochnoe serebro (Eastern Silver), Saint Petersburg, 1909; J. Orbeli, Sasanian and Early Islamic Metalwork, SPA, I, pp. 716-70; J. Sauvaget, Remarques sur les monuments omeyyades, II: Argenterie Sassanide, JA, CCXXXII, 1940-41, pp. 19-57; M. S. Dimand, A Review of Sasanian and Islamic Metalwork in a Survey of Persian Art, Ars Islamica, VIII, 1942, pp. 192-214; D. Barrett, Islamic Metalwork in the British Museum, London, 1949; J. Sauvaget, Une représentation de la citadelle seljoukide de Merv, Ars Islamica, XV-XVI, 1951, pp. 128-32;

R. Ettinghausen, The "Wade Cup" in the Cleveland Museum of Art: Its Origin and Decorations, Ars Orientalis, II, 1957, pp. 327-66; R. H. Pinder-Wilson, An Islamic Ewer in Sassanian Style, BMQ, XXII, 1959, pp. 89-92.

Textiles, wood carving, glass: J. H. Schmidt, Persian Silks of the Early Middle Ages, LVII, 1930, pp. 284-94; B. Deniké, Quelques monuments de bois sculpté en Turkestan occidental, Ars Islamica, II, 1935, pp. 69-83; C. K. Wilkinson, Water Ice and Glass, BMMA, N.S., I, 1943, pp. 175-83; R. B. Serjeant, Material for a History of Islamic Textiles up to the Mongol Conquest, Ars Islamica, XI-XII, 1946, pp. 111-30; G. Wiet, Soieries persanes (Mem. Inst. d'Egypte, LII), Cairo, 1947; D. G. Shepherd and W. B. Henning, Zandanījī Identified, Aus der Welt der islamischen Kunst: Festschrift für E. Kühnel, Berlin, 1959, pp. 15-40.

Umberto SCERRATO

Illustrations: PLS. 381-386; 3 figs. in text.

SANGALLO. Most prominent among the clan of Florentine artists known by the name of Sangallo (because they lived near the Porta S. Gallo in Florence) were the architects Giuliano, Antonio the Elder, and Antonio the Younger. The Sangallos, comprising members of the Giamberti and Cordiani families, were active for approximately 100 years, starting with the last decades of the 15th century. The frequent mention of "il Sangallo" by such authors as Carducci and D'Annunzio refers to Antonio the Younger, whose reputation was greatly enlarged — often at the expense of the other Sangallos — by these writers because (apart from discussions of his artistic merits) of his interesting personality and his connections with well-known figures and events of the Renaissance courts, which were favorite literary subjects of the Italian romantic period.

The head of the Sangallo clan was Francesco Giamberti, a *legnaiuolo* (worker in wood). Therefore, according to the occupational nomenclature of the mid-15th century, he was a craftsman who specialized in intaglio, intarsia (in which he made some remarkable experiments in perspective effects), and in the making of furniture, architectural frames, and architectural models. This last activity was also the starting point in the art of building for many of his followers, among them such gifted architects as Giuliano da Maiano. Francesco attended the court of the Medicis, where he performed as a musician. A decisive turn in the fortunes of his family occurred when he was made responsible for the secret upbringing of the natural posthumous son of "il bel Giulio," Giuliano de Medici (brother of Lorenzo the Magnificent), who was assassinated in the Pazzi conspiracy. The boy, Giulio, later became Pope Clement VII; it is possible that he was born to one of the women of Francesco's family.

Critical judgment of the Sangallos has rarely gone beyond a general appreciation of them as excellent builders and clever engineers, the characterization emphasized by Vasari, who knew Antonio the Younger and obtained his information on Giuliano and Antonio the Elder from Francesco, son of Giuliano. There was a surge of interest in the graphic work of Giuliano in Germany at the beginning of the 20th century, at a time when classical scholarship was directed toward the Italian Renaissance by the work of J. C. Burckhardt, who collected the drawings of Giuliano and assembled them in two volumes. These prompted documentary research by C. von Fabriczy (1902) and two monographs treating the Sangallo clan collectively, one by G. Clausse (1900-02) and one by G. K. Loukomski (1934), both based on biographical elements.

It can therefore be said that, apart from Giuliano, who has been the subject of a few analytical studies, no truly critical evaluation of the Sangallos has been formulated. An approximate valuation of their work can, however, be derived from a number of scholarly and historical sources.

SUMMARY. Giuliano (col. 682). Antonio the Elder (col. 686). Antonio the Younger (col. 688). The "setta sangallesca" (col. 690).

GIULIANO. The son of Francesco, Giuliano was born in about 1443 and died in 1516. (There is some question as to the exact date of his birth; the lack of an entry for him and for another son, Antonio, in the land registry of 1451 could be explained by the fact that neither of the boys then lived in Francesco's house, possibly because they were not his real sons.) Giuliano received his earliest training in the arts from Francesco di Giovanni, known as Il Francione, a more active teacher in the field than the boy's father; little is known of him save that he was an intarsist and a military engineer of no great renown. Teacher and pupil were associated in Rome with other Florentines and the group of Lombard builders who were engaged in drawing up plans for the renewal of Rome sponsored by Pope Nicholas V at the instigation of Leon Battista Alberti and under the direction of Bernardo Rossellino (q.v.), who also began his career as a Florentine *legnaiuolo*. According to autobiographical data Giuliano is known to have participated from 1465 in the work in progress during the pontificate of Paul II. The projects of the group, based on a delicate interpretation of the more complex and magnificent aspects of Roman imperial architecture, continued quietly under the pontificate of Sixtus IV. Very few examples of this architecture have survived, but it may be possible to distinguish a few that could be attributed exclusively to Giuliano. (This has been attempted by P. Tomei.) At the same time Giuliano surveyed and studied the ancient monuments; these studies are documented by a volume of drawings in the Vatican Library (Cod. Barb. lat. 4424) and by a sketchbook in the Biblioteca Comunale of Siena. This evidence indicates that he devoted himself more to a visual and pictorial examination of the external aspects of these monuments than to a study of their forms, proportions, or principles.

Giuliano began his activity in Florence in about 1470 — at a relatively early age for an architect — under the patronage of the Medicis; it is possible that examples of his work from this early period may exist in Florence. Two possibilities have been suggested by P. Sanpaolesi: the Palazzetto Cocchi in Piazza Sta Croce (ca. 1469–74), and the small palace of Bartolomeo Scala (later incorporated into the Palazzo della Gherardesca), for which the earliest plausible date can be set shortly after 1472.

In these and in his other works Giuliano attempted to establish in Florence the complex style reminiscent of ancient architecture that had already been introduced by Alberti in the Palazzo Rucellai. Influences of a composite Lombard culture can be detected in the square double-light windows of the original design for the courtyard of the Palazzetto Scala; and technical methods derived from ancient Roman architecture, such as ceilings of poured concrete, can be seen in the Villa di Poggio a Caiano (PL. 387; FIG. 683; I, PL. 305), commissioned by Lorenzo the Magnificent. The plan of this villa centers around a large barrel-vaulted hall, a design inspired by the ancient thermae, and the whole structure rests on a platform above a portico as did the villas and temples of antiquity.

The portico reflects a return to the complex but logical architecture of ancient tradition; but the pronaos, although

strictly classical in form, is more linear in feeling, in the local Tuscan tradition which still followed the Brunelleschian idiom. There are, however, some subtle variations of the traditional style; certain perspective effects, such as the placement of the pronaos, which appears to project from the façade, are emphasized in the unusual design of the outside stairways (VIII, PL. 428). A free and picturesque spatial concept is evident in the exterior projection of the villa itself, specifically in the basement portico surmounted by a terrace, and in the careful integration of the villa into the surrounding landscape. This villa is in perfect harmony with the contemporary culture as exemplified by the Italian and Latin poetry of Politian and the painting of Botticelli.

Although his preferences certainly lay in that direction, Giuliano Sangallo was later obliged to limit the classicizing tone of his idiom, at least in its most obvious expression, probably because of environmental demands. The atrium of S. Maria Maddalena dei Pazzi (PL. 387) combines a decorative scheme on a strictly linear basis (a development derived from the Pazzi chapel) with ancient idioms, in the motif of the quadriporticus and in the bizarre form of Doric capitals copied faithfully from an ancient one excavated shortly before the church was built. The interior developed effects based on light and spatial depth (although this is not so evident today).

The dialectic framework within which Giuliano's creative imagination worked provides a logical explanation of the nature of the other structure he built during his long period of activity in and around Florence — the Church of S. Maria delle Carceri in Prato (PL. 388; FIG. 684) founded in 1484. This church,

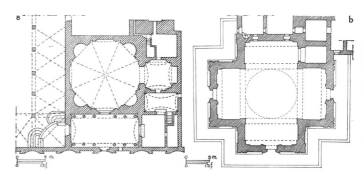

Giuliano da Sangallo: (a) Florence, Sto Spirito, sacristy, plan (*from E. Lundberg, Arkitekturens formspråk, 1420–1620, Stockholm, 1954*); (b) Prato, S. Maria delle Carceri, plan (*from G. Clausse, 1900–02*).

in the form of a Greek cross, is derived from Brunelleschi models, especially in the interior. (A freer interpretation of Brunelleschi's schemes could be seen in the apse section of S. Felice, in Florence, but it is not known if it was designed prior to S. Maria delle Carceri or if, indeed, it was the work of Giuliano at all.) For the façade of S. Maria delle Carceri Giuliano attempted to create a marble inlay in order to resolve the problem of facing (a problem left unsolved by Brunelleschi). The church of the Convent of S. Gallo, in Florence (ca. 1488, destroyed 1524), with a nave flanked by lateral chapels, was the prototype for many other buildings. The sacristy of the Church of Sto Spirito (PL. 6; FIG. 684) begun in 1489, reproduces the form of an ancient tomb; the interior is organized within a linear framework, essentially decorative in character. The model for Palazzo Strozzi (1489) and the Palazzo Gondi (PL. 388), begun in 1490, are even more in the tradition of the Medici palace, although they are more refined in their execution.

Giuliano was also a sculptor. In 1486 he designed the Sassetti tombs in the Sassetti Chapel in Sta Trinita; later he carved at least a portion of the fireplace in the Palazzo Gondi. In his ornamentation he availed himself of a freedom of movement derived from the school of Donatello and of the pictorial quality evident in the contemporary work of Verrocchio. He introduced into the architectural repertory an element, derived from Donatello, that was to have a widespread use — the spool baluster. (In the base of Donatello's *Il Marzocco*, this was

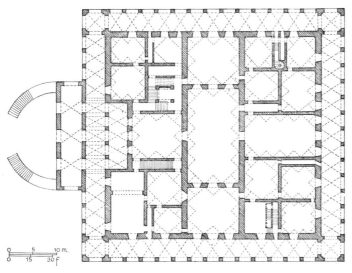

Giuliano da Sangallo, Villa di Poggio a Caiano, plan.

formed by two vase-shaped balusters placed one above the other, mouth to mouth.) Giuliano used this type of baluster in the parapet balustrade at Poggio a Caiano and in the staircase of the Palazzo Gondi.

When Giuliano was free from outside influences, he further developed the same spatial concepts that he used at Poggio a Caiano — for example, in the designs for a projected royal palace in Naples submitted to Ferdinand I in 1488. For the Naples design he drew inspiration from the spatial concepts of the great Roman baths. In his own house (in the Borgo Pinti in Florence) he repeated the forms of Poggio a Caiano. In Savona he built a palace for Cardinal Giuliano della Rovere, with whom he had maintained a close relationship from the time of his first Roman stay during the pontificate of Sixtus IV (also a member of the Della Rovere family) and for whom he worked at various times in Rome. The façade of this palace, with three superimposed orders, still survives. Giuliano's advanced architectural ideas, even if limited to the Florentine milieu, explain the enmity of the conservative Giuliano da Maiano, who, in comparison, must have appeared somewhat backward in point of view.

A measure of credit must be given to Giuliano da Sangallo for his work in military architecture. After very brief experience in this field, he abandoned the traditional circular towers and created the polygonal bastion in order to extend the range of firepower, as in the fortress and fortifications of Poggio Imperiale, near Poggibonsi (1488), which became the archetype of later permanent fortifications such as the fortress of Borgo San Sepolcro [with certain stylistic details derived from Francesco di Giorgio (q.v.)] built in 1500, the Arezzo fortress (1502), and the small fort of Nettuno (also built in 1502).

The fall of the Medicis and the crises that shook the Florentine state in the last decade of the 15th century deprived Giuliano of the favorable working conditions he had hitherto enjoyed. A typical example of the tendencies of this period can be seen in the architectural construction of the Gondi Chapel in S. Maria Novella in Florence, where the classical plan of the triumphal arch assumes fantastic proportions, and the use of colored materials gives it a grim, restless character.

The mounting crises left their mark on the expressive quality of Giuliano's work when he went to Rome after the election to the papacy of Giuliano della Rovere (Julius II) in 1503. He hoped to obtain important commissions, but to his intense disappointment, he received very few. Bramante (q.v.) had achieved a far more synthesized and grandiose concept of space, based on his superior knowledge of Roman imperial architecture; Michelangelo and Raphael (qq.v.), who were both present in Rome, competed in the creating of a climate of courtly classical solemnity with which Giuliano was unable to keep pace, in spite of his friendship and close contact with these and other artists. This is evident in his design project for the loggia of the papal musicians for the new St. Peter's (Florence, Uffizi, Gabinetto dei Disegni e Stampe).

Giuliano was again disappointed when he went to Rome in 1513. This time his hopes had been aroused by the election of Leo X (son of Lorenzo the Magnificent) to the papal throne, but no new projects resulted for the artist. Only his designs for the projected papal palace in Piazza Navona in Rome (1513; Florence, Uffizi, Gabinetto dei Disegni e Stampe) show an unusual sense of synthesis and of classically sculptural accents within a traditional framework. (This traditionalism was observed even more strictly in another design for a palace for the Medicis in Florence.) The projects for St. Peter's, where Giuliano was director of works for a year and a half (together with Bramante and, later, Raphael and Fra Giovanni Giocondo), although they adopt certain details of Bramante's idiom, pedantically break them down in an unrelated series of repetitions of limited scope.

A final flash of unsuspected artistic and imaginative vitality appeared in the numerous designs for the façade of S. Lorenzo in Florence, which Giuliano prepared for the competition of 1515. These designs, together with several sketches in the manner of Raphael, reveal a number of highly pictorial and picturesque solutions for a framework of rhythmically varied, restless forms filled with figural motifs. These exerted a decisive influence on Michelangelo's first architectural attempts.

The psychological conflict evident in Giuliano's work is not unique in his time; his personal and artistic problems, like those of Filippino Lippi, Botticelli, and Piero di Cosimo, must be regarded as part of a crisis of the early Renaissance, which furnished many direct antecedents for similar mannerist phenomena.

ANTONIO THE ELDER. Ten years younger than his brother Giuliano, Antonio da Sangallo the Elder was born about 1453; he died in 1534. Although he is one of the three major figures of his family, he is the least renowned because, coming as he did between Giuliano and his nephew Antonio the Younger, he was overshadowed by them. From sources and documentary evidence it appears that Antonio the Elder was primarily engaged in engineering activities, especially as a military architect, although he undoubtedly kept up, in partnership with his brother, the family carpentry and cabinetmaking workshop. Some of the several crucifixes he carved have survived; but accurate and scholarly research on his creative work has not been undertaken. Nevertheless, from the mass of available evidence it appears that his artistry, based more on intuitive gifts than on training, had strong individual qualities. This is evident in a group of works from his mature period (after the death of Giuliano) which confirm the belief that Antonio was able to achieve independence as an architect only in this late period. It would be very useful to be able to assess his abilities in the earlier periods, especially in the last decade of the 15th century, because after having carefully investigated the more solid and massive aspects of ancient Italic architecture and the Roman system of arches incorporated into orders he may have played an important part in the preparation for the classicizing architecture of Bramante and Raphael. Until further research is undertaken, however, this must remain a supposition. Antonio the Elder's best-known and most documented work is the Church of S. Biagio (PL. 389; FIG. 686; III, PL. 390), near Montepulciano, which repeats the Greek-cross form of S. Maria delle Carceri in Prato, but with a spatial design and a style reflecting his

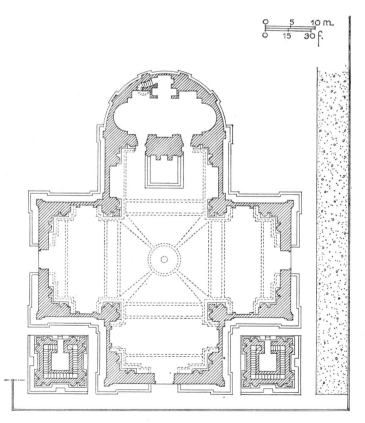

Antonio da Sangallo the Elder, Montepulciano, S. Biagio, plan (from A Schiavo, B. del Centro di S. di Storia dell'Arch., no. 6, 1952).

experience and the maturity gained in Rome in the workshops of St. Peter's under the influence of Bramante and Raphael. It is possible that Antonio the Younger may have executed some of the designs for S. Biagio, since the construction went on until 1529 and was then left unfinished. In this church there are a number of departures from the simple Greek-cross plan, such as the two campaniles near the base of the cross and the apselike sacristy at the head. In the interior an ostentatious framework of massive unadorned classicizing structural members of travertine extends, with an appearance of unshakable solidity, to the dome as the crowing point of the whole complex. In the choice and the harsh treatment of the stone, in the systematic adoption of the Doric and Tuscan orders, in the extreme simplicity of the ornamentation, and in certain proportional relationships an instinctive harmony with the dark world of the Etruscans seems to emerge. The classicizing style does not seem to have been employed for its formal values for the sake of optimistic contemplation, but rather for its power to emphasize the cohesiveness of the material. This same quality of powerful unity is also revealed in (among many other examples) the trapezoidal door with a lugged frame at the tip of the main bastion of the fortress at Poggio Imperiale (designed by Giuliano with the collaboration of Antonio), which can be ascribed to Antonio. The lugged doorframe, which was used with great success by Antonio the Younger, originated with Antonio the Elder, who employed it frequently in civil architecture. The Etruscanizing tendency appears as early as 1506 in the addition of the low and dark lateral aisles to the Church of the SS. Annunziata in Arezzo, to which Antonio also added an imposing vestibule. It is also evident in his last work, the project for the remodeling of the Church of S. Agostino in Colle Val d'Elsa (design dated 1521, but not carried out by him), in which he filled the original nave with arches and barrel vaults, creating the impression of an unending succession of sculptural elements and emphasizing the rows of thickset columns.

The old fortress in Leghorn (1515), although well documented, is of lesser significance. Consistency and a process of elimination demand that to this group of late buildings there should be added the large number of palaces in Montepulciano, including the complex and massive Palazzo Tarugi (PL. 390) and the Contucci, Cervini (PL. 389), and Del Pecora (Cocconi) palaces. In these may be found combinations of superimposed orders of Roman derivation, but in an unusual arrangement, with simple ground floor windows having corbeled frames (in the tradition of Michelozzo), those above surmounted by a pediment of Raphaelesque design, and a new type, a combination of the first two, with the pediment resting on corbels above the rectangular opening. This last type was later much used by Antonio the Younger and met with very wide favor. Classicizing projecting ashlar masses such as those used by Bramante and the more picturesque ones favored by Raphael also appear in the Montepulciano palaces. A splendid example of a complete design, which is also noteworthy for its positioning in the surrounding space, is the palace of Cardinal Del Monte (later Pope Julius III), now the Palazzo Comunale, in Monte San Savino. It belongs to the same group of palaces which can be ascribed to Antonio the Elder's late period, which began with S. Biagio in Montepulciano.

The significant features of these designs is the search for structural strength and a great freedom in the combination of forms — solutions and proportions which went beyond the logic required by the classicizing style and the prevailing tendencies of the period, toward an elaboration and refinement of the formulas of the established stylistic canons.

In 1507 Antonio the Elder collaborated with a number of other architects in the building of the catwalk of the dome in the Cathedral of Florence; in 1517 he designed, in partnership with Baccio d'Agnolo, the portico of the Piazza dell'Annunziata as a copy of the portico of the Ospedale degli Innocenti; but he created few important works in either Florence or Rome. Evidently he was rejected by those circles whose stylistic idiom was different from his. His important work lies mainly in the provinces, in what might be termed "neutral" zones lacking in strong local traditions. The perimetral structures of Civita Castellana (FIG. 688), begun in 1494, have been attributed to Antonio the Elder. If it is his work, he developed the new proportions of elevation introduced by Giuliano at Poggio Imperiale; and if the central court with a double portico can also be attributed to Antonio, as sanctioned by tradition and by logic (based on the fact that the vaults of the lower portico bear painted decorations showing the emblems of the Borgias), its classicizing design of two orders of arches framed by pilasters and trabeation could represent an attempt to reach a structural

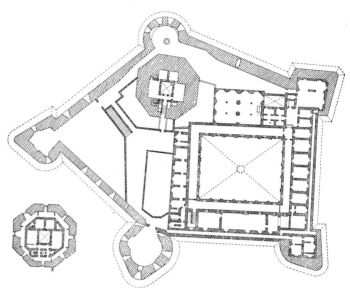

Civita Castellana, plan of the fortress and (lower left) of the keep, with the part projected by Antonio da Sangallo the Elder indicated by hatching (from Palladio, IX, 1959).

solution beyond the superficial and tenuous derivations from ancient prototypes fashionable in Rome before Bramante. This would make tenable a hypothesis whereby Antonio the Elder, who went to Rome for the first time in 1490, may have influenced Bramante to adopt a more proportioned, organic, and restrained style together with an interpretation of the styles of antiquity hitherto unknown. Nor did Antonio's basic artistic strength fail to influence Michelangelo in the designs for the Medici library and chapel (I, PL. 381; IV, PL. 459) near S. Lorenzo, in Florence, as evidenced by certain specific details.

ANTONIO THE YOUNGER. Antonio the Younger was the son of the sister of Antonio the Elder and Bartolomeo Cordiani. He was born in 1483 and was trained in architecture by his uncles; he worked in the Sangallo enterprise, which he later enlarged and reorganized. The main activity of the workshop was building, but it also handled the preparation of plans and projects and was able to offer its services, based on the technical experience of several generations, for the solution of problems ranging from woodworking to hydraulics and ballistics. Moreover, the Sangallos closely followed every new cultural development. Through their activities the leading members of the clan not only maintained working relationships with the great men and the cultural circles of their times, but their position, socially, culturally, and financially (especially in the case of Antonio the Younger), was a very high one. Visible evidence of this can be found in the magnificent houses they built for themselves both in Florence and in Rome. The Sangallos are typical examples of the high esteem in which artists were held during the Renaissance.

Antonio the Younger was taken to Rome in 1503 by Giuliano on the occasion of the election of Pope Julius II. He remained there for almost his entire life (he died in 1546) as adviser and confidant of several popes, among whom were Leo X and Clement VII, both of the Medici family. He received a great many commissions, even from private persons, some in distant places. Owing to the organization of his studio and the cooperation of the members of his family he was able to execute them. Some of these commissions concerned the most important projects of the time, such as the continuation of the building of St. Peter's, for which he was appointed Master of Works in 1520, succeeding Raphael (whose collaborator he had been since 1516), and was reconfirmed in this position in 1538. He also built the Palazzo Farnese (PL. 56) in Rome and the fortifications of the city. In his execution of these commissions he showed facility in the instinctive blending of technical and formal solutions. He was responsible for the diffusion throughout much of Italy of the spiritual balance represented by Rome as a dynamic cultural center, and he remained faithful to this ideal, as had his uncles (though not to the point of appearing to have been superseded, as did Giuliano), resisting the pressures of mannerism until the advent of the Michelangelesque revolution.

The position of Antonio the Younger in the world of art is more that of a developer than of a creator; but his works often reached a measure of greatness, even though he generally concentrated on the visual and superficial aspects of construction. A typical product of his formalist spirit, which is also indicative of the limits of his artistic personality, can be seen in his project for St. Peter's, the model of which has survived (X, PL. 102). In this design individual forms of classicizing idiom are repeated interminably, and Bramante's original design is broken down into a series of recurrent variations.

The building of the Palazzo Farnese went forward very slowly; it was not finished by Antonio. (Michelangelo, on order of Paul III, synthesized by means of the cornice the huge mass of the palace.) The most successful portions of the design are the courtyard, in which is used the system of superimposed arcades within an arch-and-pier frame (an architectural device, then greatly admired, derived from the Theater of Marcellus and the Colosseum), and the vestibule (PL. 55), divided into three aisles by columns. In the vestibule Antonio carried out a project close to Giuliano's heart when he used a part of his uncle's design for a royal palace in Naples. Antonio the Younger endowed the Palazzo Farnese with a rich and dynamic appearance by means of the modulation of the members and niches. The avoidance of unnecessary ornamentation, the clarity of expression, and the desire for simplicity are evidence of a Florentine spirit, which is also seen in other typical details of the exterior, such as the placing of simple unadorned windows on the ground floor, in accordance with 15th-century tradition, and in the rejection of the projecting members made fashionable in Rome by Raphael. Indeed, Antonio the Younger might be said to have created in such works as the Palazzo Baldassini (PL. 390) a prototype for bourgeois and aristocratic private houses in Rome that remained standard until the beginning of the 20th century.

In other lively returns to the idiom of 15th-century Florence, Antonio created the delicate ground floor of S. Maria di Loreto (in Trajan's Forum in Rome, 1507; FIG. 690), so reminiscent of the style of Giuliano, and in the atrium and sacristy of the church of the Abbey of Montecassino. Influences of his other uncle, Antonio the Elder, are evident in the composition of the Palazzo Baldassini and in the use, which later became very widespread, of sections of rusticated ashlar and rows of lugs on the corners or surrounding the doorways of civic buildings with plain volumetric surfaces, as in the Palazzetto Le Roy (Piccola Farnesina; now Mus. Barracco) in Rome. The external simplifications he employed in this palace serve admirably to emphasize the aristocratic and Humanistic tone of the courtyard and the interiors. As his style developed, Antonio tended more and more to simplify his spatial syntheses, as in the façade of the Mint, now the Palazzo del Banco di Sto Spirito (1523–24; PL. 390), and in several church interiors. The interior of S. Maria di Monserrato (1518) and of Sto Spirito in Sassia (1538–44; FIG. 690), both in Rome, repeat the plan of a nave flanked by lateral chapels opening within the frame of the arches. The same plan is found in the Chapel of the Sacrament (ca. 1517) of the Cathedral of Foligno, in the Chapel of Cardinal

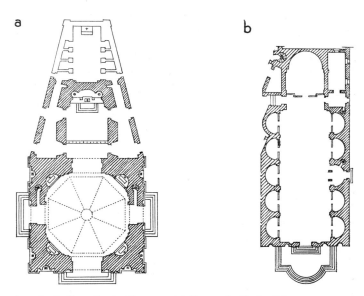

Antonio da Sangallo the Younger: (*a*) Rome, S. Maria di Loreto, plan of the ground floor (*from G. Clausse, 1900–02*); (*b*) Rome, Sto Spirito in Sassia (*from G. Giovannoni, 1935*).

Alborense (ca. 1520), in S. Giacomo degli Spagnoli, Rome, and in the Sala Regia (ca. 1537; IX, PL. 294) and the Pauline Chapel in the Vatican.

Antonio the Younger's fortifications, particularly the Forte Michelangelo at Civitavecchia, the Fortress of Caprarola (built in 1515, but later transformed into a villa by Vignola), the Fortezza da Basso in Florence (1534–37), and the Ancona fortress (1537), represent a utilitarian and functional plan of bastions and curtain walls that employs the harmonious development of geometric patterns. The Pozzo di San Patrizio, in Orvieto, resolves an even more complex engineering problem with the clarity and grace of a delicate witticism.

The works of Antonio the Younger, after his death in 1546, have been the subject of considerable research, rendered possible by the great mass of material available in his working papers, which survived almost complete (about 1000 items) in the collection of drawings in the Gabinetto dei Disegni e Stampe of the Uffizi in Florence (IV, PL. 187). The attributions have been made mostly on the basis of the handwriting of the notes (although the work was done cooperatively, as in a modern architect's studio) — obviously an unreliable source. Later studies have benefited from a comprehensive collection of data and of relative analyses of them by G. Giovannoni, who has resolved many problems and has indicated new fields for research. Giovannoni's work suggests, but does not explicitly state, a positive judgment on the artist, and it points up the need for an accurate revision and a careful study of the several monuments.

THE "SETTA SANGALLESCA." Among the numerous other members of the Sangallo clan who collaborated to a greater or lesser extent in the family enterprise and formed what Vasari termed (in referring somewhat acidly to the discussions on St. Peter's in Rome) the "setta sangallesca" (Sangallic sect) are the brothers Bastiano (known as Aristotile) and Giovan Francesco, sons of a sister of Giuliano; Battista, called Il Gobbo ("the hunchback"), a brother of Antonio the Younger; and the outstanding son of Giuliano, Francesco (known as Il Margotta), who was born in 1494 and lived until 1576. It was he who collected and preserved the family papers.

Francesco's activity was primarily in the field of sculpture, although his position reflects that of his family. He resembles his father in that he was in some ways behind the times in his application of an analytical realism to the grandiose and agitated designs current in the early years of the 16th century. This could be very effective, however, as in the tomb of Bishop Marzi-Medici (1546) in the Church of the SS. Annunziata in Florence and in the tomb of Bishop Bonafede (1550) in the Certosa di Val d'Ema, near Florence. In his personal style Francesco differed from his companions and collaborators, such as Andrea Sansovino (q.v.) and Niccolò Tribolo, in his insistence upon analytical modulations and in the streak of decadent restlessness reminiscent of certain late stylistic elements in his father's work; he entered, at least in spirit, into the mannerist current that was felt in Florence sooner and more violently than anywhere else.

SOURCES AND DOCUMENTS. Vasari, IV, pp. 267–91, V, pp. 447–73; C. Fea, Notizie intorno a Raffaello Sanzio... Giuliano da San Gallo..., Rome, 1822; J. W. Gaye, Carteggio inedito d'artisti, 3 vols., Florence, 1839–40; A. Poliziano, La congiura dei Pazzi (ed. A. Bonucci), Florence, 1847 (2d ed., 1856; 3d ed., 1895); C. Ravioli, Notizie sui lavori di architettura militare... da San Gallo, Rome, 1863; C. Ravioli, Nuove dichiarazioni sopra i Sangallo, Il Buonarroti, 3d ser., I, 1882–4, pp. 146–57; E. Müntz, Les arts à la cour des Papes, Rome, 1884; H. von Geymüller, Documents inédits de la famille des Sangallo, MAF, XLV, 1885, pp. 222–52.

BIBLIOG. a. General: J. Burckhardt, Der Cicerone, Basel, 1855 (new ed., Leipzig, 1925; Eng. trans., Mrs. A. H. Clough, London, 1908); C. M. Stegmann and H. von Geymüller, Die Architektur der Renaissance in Toscana, 11 vols., Munich, 1885–1908; E. Müntz, Histoire de l'art pendant la Renaissance, 3 vols., Paris, 1889–95; G. Clausse, Les San Gallo, 3 vols., Paris, 1900–02 (rev. by C. von Fabriczy, RepfKw, XXVII, 1904, pp. 73–78); Michel, III, 2, pp. 499–502, IV, 1, 39–40, 47–48; Venturi, VIII, 1, pp. 438–74, X, 1, pp. 243–59, XI, 1, pp. 469–685; G. K. Loukomski, Les San Gallo, Paris, 1934; L. H. Heydenreich, ThB, s.v. (full bibliog.). b. Giuliano: C. von Fabriczy, Giulianos da Sangallo figürliche Kompositionen, JhbPreuss-KSamml, XXIII, 1902, pp. 197–204; C. von Fabriczy, Die Handzeichnungen Giulianos da Sangallo, Stuttgart, 1902; R. Falb, Il taccuino senese di Giuliano da Sangallo, Siena, 1902; C. Hülsen, Il libro di Giuliano da Sangallo, Leipzig, 1910; P. Tomei, La palazzina di Giuliano della Rovere ai SS. Apostoli, Rome, 1937; G. Marchini, Il Cronaca, RArte, XXIII, 1941, pp. 99–136; L. Bianchi, La villa papale della Magliana, Rome, 1942; G. Marchini, Giuliano da Sangallo, Florence, 1942; P. Tomei, L'architettura del '400 a Roma, Rome, 1942; P. Sanpaolesi, Le prospettive architettoniche di Urbino, di Filadelfia e di Berlino, BArte, XXXIV, 1949, pp. 322–37; G. Marchini, Aggiunte a Giuliano da Sangallo, Comm, I, 1950, pp. 34–38; B. Degenhart, Dante, Leonardo und Sangallo, Römische Jhb. für Kg., VII, 1955, pp. 101–292 (problem of drawings); G. Marchini, Quattro piante per il S. Pietro di Roma, BArte, XLI, 1956, pp. 313–17; P. G. Hamberg, The Villa of Lorenzo il Magnifico at Poggio a Caiano and the Origin of Palladianism, Figura, N.S., I (Idea and Form), 1959, pp. 76–87. c. Antonio the Elder: A. Lambert, Madonna di S. Biagio près Montepulciano, Stuttgart, 1884; A. Sacchetti Sassetti, Antonio Sangallo e i lavori delle Marmore, Rome, 1958; F. Sanguinetti, La fortezza di Civita Castellana e il suo restauro, Palladio, N.S., IX, 1959, pp. 84–92. d. Antonio the Younger: A. Bertolotti, Documenti inediti su Antonio da Sangallo, Rome, 1885; K. Frey, Studien zu Michelangelo Buonarroti und zur Kunst seiner Zeit, JhbPreussKSamml, XXX, 1909, app., pp. 103–80 at 167; E. Scaccia Scarafoni, L'atrio della chiesa di Montecassino, BArte, N.S., XII, 1932, pp. 22–33; G. Giovannoni, Saggi sull'architettura del Rinascimento, 2d ed., Milan, 1935; A. Nava, Sui disegni architettonici per S. Giovanni dei Fiorentini in Roma, CrArte, I, 1935–36, pp. 102–08; G. Giovannoni, Lo studio civile di Antonio da Sangallo il giovane, Palladio, I, 1937, pp. 173–79; G. Giovannoni, Progetti sangalleschi per il S. Marco di Firenze, Atti I Cong. naz. Storia dell'arch. (1936), Florence, 1938, pp. 231–35; E. Scaccia Scarafoni, Architetture cinquecentesche in Montecassino, BArte, XXXII, 1938, pp. 9–23; P. Gazzola, Un disegno sangallesco inedito per la basilica vaticana, Palladio, VI, 1942, p. 32 ff.; H. Siebenhüner, Der Palazzo Farnese in Rom, Wallraf-Richartz Jhb., XIV, 1952, pp. 144–64; B. Degenhart, Dante, Leonardo und Sangallo, Römische Jhb. für Kg., VII, 1955, pp. 101–292 at 273; W. Lotz, Die ovalen Kirchenraume des Cinquecento, Römische Jhb. für Kg., VII, 1955, pp. 7–99 at 21; H. Siebenhüner, S. Giovanni dei Fiorentini in Rom, Kunstgeschichtl. S. für H. Kauffmann, Berlin, 1956, pp. 172–91; E. Rufini, S. Giovanni dei Fiorentini, Rome, 1957; G. Giovannoni, Antonio da Sangallo il Giovane, 2 vols., Rome, 1959; E. Battisti, Disegni cinquecenteschi per S. Giovanni dei Fiorentini, Saggi di storia dell'arch. in onore di V. Fasolo, Rome, 1961, pp. 185–94; E. Scaccia Scarafoni, Ancora del Sangallo a Montecassino, BArte, XLVII, 1962, pp. 69–74. e. Other Sangallos: U. Middeldorf, Portraits by Francesco da Sangallo, AQ, I, 1938, pp. 109–38; P. G. Hamberg, Giovan Battista da Sangallo detto il Gobbo e Vitruvio, Palladio, N.S., VIII, 1958, pp. 15–21; O. Fasolo, Contributo ad Antonio e Giovan Battista da Sangallo: La Rocca di Montefiascone, Saggi di storia dell'arch. in onore di V. Fasolo, Rome, 1961, pp. 159–68.

Giuseppe MARCHINI

Illustrations: PLS. 387–390; 5 figs. in text.

SANMICHELI, MICHELE. Italian architect (b. Verona, 1484; d. 1559). The descendant of a long line of Lombard stonecutters, Sanmicheli went to Rome at the age of sixteen, and received his training in the circle of papal architects that had formed around Bramante and Giuliano da Sangallo. This enabled him to collaborate with Antonio da Sangallo the Younger

and to combine the styles of Raphael and Michelangelo in his first works, executed in Orvieto and Montefiascone between 1509 and 1527. While the Palazzo Pompei (VIII, FIG. 417) and Palazzo Canossa in Verona (PL. 391; FIG. 692) are in the classical style, Sanmicheli's Palazzo Bevilacqua (PL. 92; FIG. 695) is in the mannerist style and even anticipates post-Michelangelesque themes. The author of works based directly on archaeological models, such as the doorway of his own home in Verona, he nevertheless proved himself a strikingly original artist in the semicircular chancel screen of the Verona Cathedral (PL. 394) and in the Porta Palio (PL. 393). He could be ponderous and monumental in a truly Roman way, as in the Porta Nuova (PL. 392; FIG. 696) or, by contrast, ethereal and metaphysical, as in the Pellegrini Chapel (FIG. 695). He had the broad architectural vision of a town planner, but at the same time the Church of the Madonna di Campagna (FIG. 697) and the *tempietto* of the Lazzaretto (PL. 394; FIG. 692) show his interest in isolated, independently centered buildings. He has been

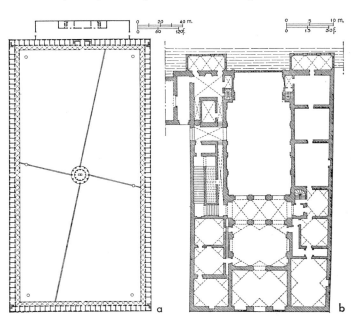

Secular buildings, Verona. (a) Lazzaretto; (b) Palazzo Canossa, plan of the ground floor (*after Ronzani-Luciolli, 1823*).

variously described as "a Venetian influenced by Tuscany," as "a Tuscan softened by a Venetian pictorial sense," and even as a "Tusco-Roman." Sanmicheli seems a complex and obscure figure whose place in art history has not been established by criticism and whose art accordingly appears to consist, in the opinion of Fiocco (in *Michele Sanmicheli*, 1960), "often more in compromise than in substance."

The copious literature devoted to Sanmicheli shows that an understanding of this architect has been constantly hindered by two difficulties. The first, one of methodology, arises from a desire to distinguish between the "pure" works and the prosaic, scholarly ones of his vast productive cycle, to separate the genuine creative productions from the long series of dull professional jobs: a fruitless attempt, particularly because it is based on considerations of style alone. The second obstacle lies in the habit of making an extrinsic comparison between the architecture of Sanmicheli and that of Palladio, whose work was separated, in time, from that of Sanmicheli by a generation and executed in an atmosphere free of the psychotic terror caused by the Sack of Rome (1527) and in a district which, although geographically near, was far removed from Sanmicheli's in terms of intellectual vitality, architectural content, and formal approach. Beside Palladio, who was lyrical, elegiac, and uncommitted to any particular artistic position, Sanmicheli must appear to be a learned engineer but not a Humanist, a man of cultural rather than of poetic inclinations.

Sanmicheli's artistic personality cannot be pieced together from an analysis of his buildings, since the undercurrent of mannerism which runs through them is too changing and ambiguous to serve as a basis for a sustained study. Neither is it enough to cite his acquaintance with Antonio da Sangallo in order to explain his ideas, since these involve a far broader creative vision, a coherence originating in and conditioned by large-scale territorial planning. More than an architect, Sanmicheli was an urbanist or, rather, a town planner in the modern sense — that is to say, one whose vocational instinct teaches him to go beyond the isolated building, the street, and the square, and to transcend even the closed mass of the town itself to take in the surrounding landscape as well. He is an anomalous figure, and consequently, as a rule, misunderstood.

As is well known, the town planner's vocation has been up to the present more a subject for reportage than for art history. The critical fortunes of Sanmicheli cannot be compared to those of a Biagio Rossetti, whose work, apart from his town planning in Ferrara, was not understood for centuries. Nevertheless, despite the prominent position accorded Sanmicheli in critical works since Vasari's time, the separation of his career into that of military engineer and that of civil architect has never been fully overcome, and as a result of this distinction an interpretation of Sanmicheli as a regional planner has never been realized. Ronzani and Luciolli (1823) and Da Lisca (1916) have described the engineer but not the artist; from Venturi to Fiocco, art historians have examined his buildings — palaces, churches, and gateways — but considered in themselves and not in their relation to urban thinking or to the fortifications as a whole, which are tacitly considered to be of only secondary importance from the point of view of artistic expression. Langenskiöld, in his valuable monograph (1938), dealt equally with both fields of Sanmicheli's activity, but without integrating and combining the two.

From 1525, when he inspected the fortresses of the papal states (Imola, Faenza, Forlì, Cesena, Rimini, Cervia, Ravenna, Parma) with Antonio da Sangallo, Sanmicheli's entire architectural activity developed against the background of military engineering, which, with the passage of time, acquired an increasingly coherent urbanistic character. It is natural to suppose that in his youth Sanmicheli devoted some study to this branch of the profession, drawing on the experience of Taccola, Francesco di Giorgio, and Fra Giovanni Giocondo. From the fortifications of Legnago, Alessandria, Vigevano, Brescia, and Bergamo, to the defensive walls of Verona (erected over a period of decades); from the splendid fortress of S. Andrea opposite the Lido of Venice to the grandiose military structures in Dalmatia and the Venetian Levant, in Zadar (Zara), Šibenik (Sebenico), Corfu, Napoli di Romania, Cyprus, and especially on the island of Crete; from the fortifications in Orzinuovi (FIG. 696) to those in Padua and Peschiera, Sanmicheli was engaged primarily in the construction of walls, embankments, ramparts, gates, channels, and glacis. The fortifications works that Sanmicheli undertook for Venice were executed without any technical theories but with a spontaneous adherence to the nature of the site, the character of the landscape, the topographical peculiarities and the urban conditions, and with a creative insight that transforms the military structure into a factor that both humanizes the countryside and animates the town. This is shown by the numerous letters and reports that Sanmicheli wrote during his inspection trips; the brief comments and rapid observations in his reports on the progress of work show an exceptional sensitivity in appreciating the inner laws of the urban structures of Chioggia, Venice, and Padua. In his plans the military buildings of these cities acquire the function of a natural protective shell and of an incentive to the growth of the cities.

This explains why Sanmicheli's fortifications are architecturally valid centuries after their original function has become obsolete. They follow the form of what they enclose with elastic flexibility, give an outline to a shapeless island, as at S. Andrea, and adapt themselves to the topography of the site. The very fact that Sanmicheli was not the inventor of the polygonal fortress, as Vasari (1550) claimed, seems to be in character with one who was not a theorist, a formulator of dogmatic defensive systems, or a mere technician, but rather a town planner or landscape architect. The mainspring of Sanmicheli's creativity lies in his understanding of the preexisting geographical and social conditions.

It is this particular interest of his which also offers the key to understanding his architectural work and to identifying its unifying principle. There can be no doubt that Sanmicheli falls within the framework of mannerism and even, in some ways, anticipates its maturity. But, unlike the major artists who were his contemporaries, he became a mannerist through his practical experience rather than through his cultural experience. The deformation of academic prototypes and the freedom from classical norms and from rigid perspective compositions that are characteristic of his work were born not of tragic religious torments, violent introspection, or intellectual strainings, but rather of a flexible, questioning vision of reality acquired through the very process of planning. In military architecture, as Argan (1956) has written, "space was not an a priori geometric construction, but simply the datum of a problem. It was no longer thought of in terms of a constant system of proportions, but as a complex of objective circumstances: it was first of all the land, the variations in the level of the terrain, a question of access and cover, of the possibilities of movement and maneuver. The new methods of warfare had by then outdated the closed plan, which was still linked to the plan of the ideal city; consequently, the defensive system of the towns was gradually extended into the surrounding countryside taking in the nearby villages, the road network, watercourses, and natural features of the terrain."

Sanmicheli's artistic frame of reference, which was always based on this dynamic point of view of space, included the classical sources, the various trends of the 16th century, the Venetian artistic culture, and the Hellenistic ideas acquired during his travels in the East. Together they formed the premises of a syncretic artistic impulse whose humanism, not being of learned or literary origin, rejected simplifying choices and reveled in encyclopedic borrowing. In other artists, even in the mannerist period, such catholic borrowing would imply eclecticism; but all Sanmicheli's cultural ramifications begin and end in an urbanistic conception of architecture and thus achieve coherence on a level that transcends mere stylistic considerations. It is possible to verify this even in the most cursory survey of his main works.

The records of Sanmicheli's artistic activity are still full of gaps. Of the period that precedes his return to Verona, in 1527, there remain some works that cannot be attributed to him with any certainty, such as, in Orvieto, the cusps and tympanum of the façade of the Cathedral, perhaps the altar of the Magi, the Petrucci Chapel in S. Domenico, and the Palazzo Petrucci; and in Montefiascone, the crypt of the Cathedral of S. Margherita and some parts of the upper church. The sources of Sanmicheli's artistic expression are all represented: Bramante in the clear spatial structure of the crypt with its ambulatory; Sangallo and Raphael in the octagonal underground chamber of the Petrucci Chapel and in the Palazzo Petrucci, where, however, numerous suggestions of Michelangelo are to be found, especially in the heavy modillions of the doorways; and, if the Cathedral spires and the altar of the Magi are by him, it is clear that he accepted, as another source of expression, late Gothic themes, which are transformed by the intricate decoration into baroque-style effects. Some authorities see occasional signs of imitation of Venetian art in this ideal linking of Gothic and baroque.

After the Sack of Rome, at the age of forty-three, Sanmicheli returned to Verona. The Palazzo Pompei (VIII, FIG. 417) and the Palazzo Canossa (PL. 391; FIG. 692) recall the schemes of Bramante and Raphael. In the courtyard of the former he stressed the diaphanous character of the disjointed, superimposed orders; in the latter he designed a residential structure of four floors, whose façade is not very successful. Shortly afterward he erected the Pellegrini Chapel (FIG. 695) and the Palazzo Bevilacqua (FIG. 695; PL. 92). Here he made a complete break with the past. In the palace, the framework loses its

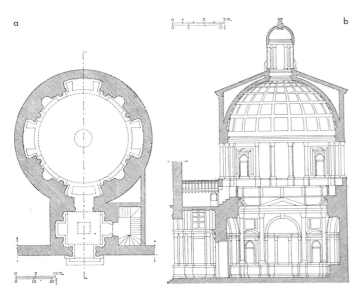

Verona, Pellegrini Chapel, Church of S. Bernardino. (*a*) Plan; (*b*) section (*after Ronzani-Luciolli, 1823*).

function of defining the static or spatial relationships; the alternation of apertures of different height and execution deliberately complicates the structure of the whole; the columns with their spiral strigils seem designed to emphasize the relationship between the sculptural values and the light. In the chapel, a metaphysical atmosphere pervades the dome, widened beyond the cylinder of the chapel. Although this atmosphere is faintly reminiscent of Raphael, it is more a result of a rebellion against all the traditional forms and of a breaking down of strict syntactic links, a tendency that reaches a state of ferment in the upper fascia of the Palazzo Bevilacqua. These two buildings date from roughly 1530 and reveal Sanmicheli's delayed, almost traumatic reaction to the Sack of Rome.

The three palaces in Verona seem to reflect the various stages of Sanmicheli's youth, and dramatically mark its end. The buildings are a reworking of the styles of Bramante, Raphael, Sangallo, Giulio Romano, Sansovino, and Michelangelo, but conceived as if the artist were in a tormented state. They reinterpret the ancient monuments of the city, from the Porta dei Borsari to the Arco dei Gavi and the Porta dei Leoni, progressively distorting the monuments' rational designs by an emphasis on sculptural decoration and chromatic density. Nothing remains of that sense of self-assurance that characterized the styles of ancient and Renaissance artists. In Sanmicheli's home in Verona, the doorway is a faithful copy of the 4th-century doorway of S. Salvatore in Spoleto. This illustrates how Sanmicheli's only way of surviving his stylistic crisis was to take refuge amid the ruins of an earlier date, to reinstate, in a visionary form, a late Roman repertory that was both severe and capricious, a classicism that was "more external gesture and expression than substance and structure" (Argan, 1956).

After this period of upheaval, Sanmicheli continued his artistic activities in a twofold direction; on the one hand, he regained his confidence by studying and then integrating into his work various elements of the Roman heritage, as in his massive Porta Nuova (PL. 392); on the other, he allowed himself flights of fancy as in the semicircular chancel screen of the Cathedral (PL. 394), which in an ellipsoid sweep changes the spatial direction of the church interior, and breaks up the space with the superb linear rhythms of its suspended Ionic colonnade. These two are simultaneous impulses (ca. 1535) and only apparently antithetic since both are characterized by a desire to overcome his preceding crisis. The lyrical element triumphed over the ponderous features of the Porta Nuova, and resulted five years later in the lightened design of the fortress of S. Andrea in Venice. Here the great impact of the setting compensates for the formal disintegration and stimulates the artist's creativity once more. The serriform ramparts in S. Andrea (also used in Legnago) are well suited to the outline of the island. The low encircling wall dominated by the keep contains and embraces the land rising from the water in the same way that the semicircular chancel screen of the Cathedral in Verona surrounds and compresses the space of the presbytery and of the apse. In S. Andrea the distinction between military and civil architecture is finally overcome: the two disciplines become joined and identified in the process of town planning.

While the fortified wall of Orzinuovi (FIG. 696) forms an enclosure that might well contain an ideal Renaissance city, the ramparts of Verona are far from such geometrical simplifications. The town complex has a dynamic layout that Sanmicheli, far from disrupting, favored in his empiric plan of the walls and ramparts with their tenailles and swallowtails, superbly cast in acute angles and molded to follow the valleys and protect the hills, to "cannonade and thunder" in all directions, but

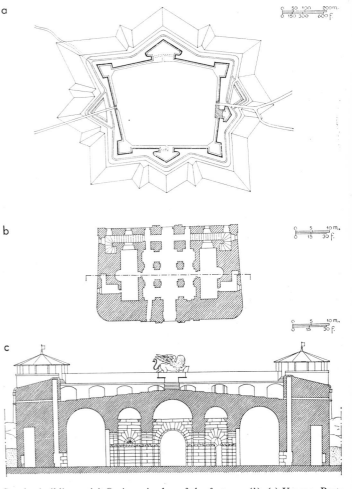

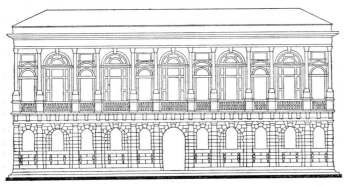

Verona, Palazzo Bevilacqua, façade (*after Ronzani-Luciolli, 1823*).

Secular buildings. (*a*) Orzinuovi, plan of the fortress; (*b*), (*c*) Verona, Porta Nuova, plan and longitudinal section (*after Ronzani-Luciolli, 1823*).

designed also to encourage a dialogue between the city and the surrounding countryside. He insisted on the rights of social life above those of military defense, and thus expanded or molded the outline of these defenses to define the limits of growth of the town and its road network. When in 1535 the Venetian Senate engaged him to demilitarize the citadel built by Gian Galeazzo Visconti in Verona and to "lay out the streets on the aforesaid site, making them lead to the street of Porta Nuova and to the other main streets that they may be of greater convenience and ornament to the aforesaid city, dividing the houses and the land in as many parts as shall seem best to him and shall be to the Signoria's greatest advantage," he outlined what was in every sense a town plan, shaping the city with a foresight that was to remain valid until the beginning of the 20th century.

Even the architectural variety of the gateways, all incorporating the old lateral towers and thus forming an organic part of the walls, is governed by three different factors: the city road system, the linking with internal traffic, and, principally, their civic function. From the Porta S. Giorgio, built before 1527 but designed by Sanmicheli, to the Porta Nuova, executed between 1533 and 1540 (PL. 392; FIG. 696) and altered in the middle of the 19th century, from the Porta S. Zeno of 1541 (PL. 393) to the Porta Palio begun in 1546 and still unfinished in 1557 (PL. 393), a whole hierarchy of values can be traced. This cannot be ascribed only to fanciful choice or to a cultural process that tends to go back from rustic Roman to archaic Doric, but depends also, and above all, on Sanmicheli's intention of polarizing the road network of the internal and external communications and of reflecting, through his careful planning of the architectural elements, the various social and environmental pressures of the suburbs growing up on the outskirts. Goethe, with his critical genius, understood this intention.

The Porta Palio constitutes the masterpiece both of Sanmicheli's military art and of his architecture, since its style shows his awareness of the civic role that it held as the end point of the axis starting in the Piazza delle Erbe. The name itself (palio, or banner) is a reminder that it acted as a passageway for races and processions, that is, it was linked in the popular imagination to traditions and peaceful customs and therefore could not have the rugged, severe appearance of the Porta Nuova or the funereal quality of the Porta S. Zeno. Ten years of hard work guaranteed its Greek perfection, both on the side facing the city, with its five barrel vaults separated by twin columns and ashlar pillars and joined to the trabeation by typical roughhewn protruding keystones, and on the more elaborate external side, where columns and fluted Doric pillars stand out on the horizontal ashlar work of the wall which is hollowed out by rectangular niches. The different modeling of the two façades and of the openings is to be explained partly by the varying intensity of the light that makes them vibrate, but mainly by the organic interpretation of the gateway in the continuous whole of the fortified wall. On the inside its proud, unadorned order emphasizes the enclosing of the urban space; from the outside the gate seems to break up the wall to emphasize the entry into the city. The central part of the gateway completes the defensive structure, with its monumental rooms for the garrison and emplacements for artillery, in a dazzling Piranesian vision of arches, vaults, and stairways seen in perspective.

On the right bank of the Adige, a few miles from Verona, the imposing complex of the Lazzaretto (FIG. 692), begun in 1548, bears witness to the city's concern with social services, and is also particularly indicative of Sanmicheli's artistic procedure. He started with classical schemes: an enormous rectangle, with a portico, whose sides measure 263 × 129 yards, is formed by 152 cells placed around the entire perimeter; in the center is a domed *tempietto* with a double order of Tuscan columns (PL. 394). The area, however, had to be divided in both directions to segregate the four wards for people in quarantine, and thus two high walls are obliquely aligned to the sides of the rectangle and cross the immense courtyard, penetrating the chapel with pilasters inserted into the circle of the columns. The *tempietto*, inspired by Bramante's prototype of S. Pietro in Montorio, breaks down the isolating factor, merges with the dividing partitions, and becomes the pivot of a rotating spatial composition.

The unfinished façade of S. Maria in Organo, which recalls the delicate working of the semicircular chancel screen, the austere Palazzo degli Honorij (later known as Guastaverza and now as Malfatti), the cupola of S. Giorgio in Braida (FIG. 697), and the campanile of the Cathedral complete the series of Sanmicheli's works in Verona. They are characterized by a slight slackening in imaginative originality, owing somewhat to the increasing part taken by the assistants on whom Sanmicheli, overburdened by commissions, was obliged to rely.

A more lively creative tension is present in his Venetian works: in the vertical articulations of the Palazzo Cornaro-Mocenigo, which blend the spirit of the local styles with undertones of Serlio; and even more in the rhythmic opulence of the Palazzo Grimani (PL. 393; VIII, FIG. 426), an interweaving of proportional modulations in which the sculptural elements of the Roman triumphal arches are absorbed and transformed in terms of color, their density being intensified in the magnificent atrium. Also worthy of mention are the Palazzo Roncale in Rovigo, the Porta S. Andrea and the Porta S. Giorgio in Orzinuovi, and the villas, particularly the Soranza in Treville di Castelfranco Veneto. The Church of the Madonna di Campagna (FIG. 697) was begun after the master's death, and so falls into the category of works by the flourishing school of

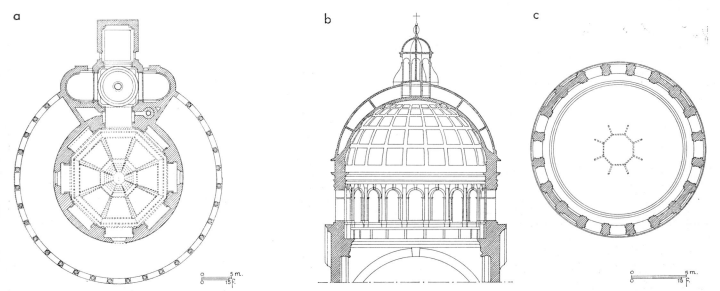

a   b   c

Religious buildings, Verona. (a) Madonna di Campagna, plan; (b), (c) S. Giorgio in Braida, section and plan of the dome (*after Ronzani-Luciolli, 1823*).

Sanmicheli, which included his nephew Gian Girolamo, Domenico Curtoni, Alessandro Pompei, and Adriano Cristofali, and left its imprint on the appearance of Verona in the following centuries.

Sanmicheli could not pass on to his immediate or distant pupils that particular mannerist quality formed by the dramatic experiences of the Sack of Rome, nor the troubled and visionary interpretation of the past that seems like a prelude to Piranesi's architectural elevations. But he did bequeath the habit of architectural syncretism, based on observation of the actual conditions of the landscape and of urban complexes. For many years the military works executed by his disciples were to reflect his sensitivity and to follow his procedures, stamping a very extensive area with their master's seal. By his humanizing effects on the countryside, his ability to plan on a regional scale, and his tendency to break up buildings in order to permeate them with an urban form, Sanmicheli bridges the gap that separates the classical world from the open conditions of the modern age.

SOURCES. V. Joppi, Discorso di Michiel da Sanmichiel circa il fortificar la città di Udine ed altri luoghi della Patria del Friuli, diretto al Doge di Venezia Pietro Lando (1543), Arch. storico it., N.S., XIV, 2, 1861, pp. 28–32; V. Joppi, Informazione fatta assieme al Colonnello Antonio da Castello sui ripari da farsi al Tagliamento, datata da Osoppo 20 Aprile 1543, Udine, 1865; G. Vasari, Le Vite, Florence, 1550; A. Palladio, I quattro libri dell'Architettura, IV, Venice, 1570, p. 64; S. Maffei, Verona illustrata, II, 4, pp. 393–94, III, 4, pp. 150–71, 5, p. 199, Verona, 1732; A. Pompei, Li cinque ordini dell'architettura civile di Michel Sanmicheli rilevati dalle sue Fabbriche, e descritti e pubblicati con quelli di Vitruvio, Alberti, Palladio, Scamozzi, Serlio e Vignola, Verona, 1735; G. Fracastoro, Lettere, Padua, 1739, pp. 100, 102–04; T. Temanza, Vite dei più celebri architetti e scultori veneziani che fiorirono nel secolo decimosesto, Venice, 1778, pp. 151–97; F. Milizia, Memorie degli architetti antichi e moderni, I, Bassano, 1785, pp. 178–87; F. Milizia, Principj di architettura civile, Bassano, 1785; F. Milizia, Dizionario delle belle arti del Disegno, Bassano, 1787; F. Albertolli, Porte di città e fortezze, depositi sepolcrali ed altre principali fabbriche pubbliche e private di Michele Sanmichele Veronese, Milan, 1815; G. Bottari, Raccolta di lettere sulla pittura, scultura e architettura scritte dai più celebri personaggi dei secoli XV, XVI e XVII, 2d ed., 8 vols., Milan, 1822–25; F. Ronzani and G. Luciolli, Le fabbriche civili ecclesiastiche e militari di Michele Sanmicheli, Verona, 1823; A. C. Quatremère de Quincy, Histoire de la vie et des ouvrages de plus célèbres architectes du XVIᵉ siècle jusqu'à la fin du XVIIᵉ, I, Paris, 1830, pp. 155–77; C. Ravioli, Intorno alla relazione delle rocche di Romagna pontificia fatta nel 1526 da Antonio Picconi da San Gallo e da Michele Sanmicheli, Giorn. Arcadico di sc., lettere ed arti, CXXXVII, 1854, pp. 126–39; Vasari, VI, 1881, pp. 341–77.

BIBLIOG. For a comprehensive annotated bibliog. (including sources) prior to 1960, see N. Carboneri, Bibliografia ragionata su Michele Sanmicheli, in Michele Sanmicheli: Studi raccolti..., Verona, 1960, pp. 195–296. See also: E. Rocchi, Le fonti storiche dell'architettura militare, Rome, 1908, pp. 267–68, 283, 284–91, 301; G. Ludwig, Archivalische Beiträge zur Geschichte der venezianischen Kunst, Berlin, 1911, p. 50; A. Avena, La paternità del Campanile del Duomo di Verona: Commento a una pagina del Vasari, Madonna Verona, VIII, 1913, pp. 52–54; G. Da Re, La Cappella Pellegrini di S. Bernardino, Verona, 1914; G. Fiocco, Introduzione, note e bibliografia alla Vita di Frà Giocondo e d'altri veronesi di Giorgio Vasari, Florence, 1915; A. Da Lisca, La fortificazione di Verona dai tempi romani al 1866, Verona, 1916, pp. 115–16; G. Da Re, Nuovi documenti sanmicheliani, Madonna Verona, XIII, 1919, pp. 1–23; G. C. Argan, Sebastiano Serlio, L'Arte, XXXV, 1932, pp. 183–99; A. Venè, Il Lazzaretto vecchio di Verona, Dedalo, XII, 1932, pp. 253–59; G. K. Loukomski, I maestri dell'architettura classica da Vitruvio allo Scamozzi, Milan, 1933, pp. 355–58; O. Pellegrini, La scuola sanmicheliana a Verona, B. Soc. lett. di Verona, V–VI, 1933, pp. 156–62; R. Brenzoni, Michele Sanmicheli e la sua sepoltura in S. Tommaso di Verona, Arch. veneto, XVII, 1935, pp. 260–76; ThB, s.v.; G. Gronau, Documenti artisti urbinati, Florence, 1936; R. Brenzoni, Il Palazzo Sanmicheliano degli Honorij in Piazza Bra di Verona, RArte, XIX, 1937, pp. 57–69; G. Zorzi, Contributo alla storia dell'arte vicentina nei secoli XV e XVI: Il preclassicismo e i prepalladiani, Misc. S. e mem. della R. Deputazione di Storia patria per le Venezie, III, 1937, pp. 17–52; E. Langenskiöld, Michele Sanmicheli: The Architect of Verona, Upsala, 1938 (reviewed by W. Lotz, ZfKg, IX, 1940, pp. 220–23); I. Marinelli, Le antiche fortezze di Romagna, Imola, 1938; N. Pevsner, An Outline of European Architecture, Harmondsworth, 1943 (6th ed., 1960); G. Silvestri, Il Palladio in casa del Sanmicheli, Le tre Venezie, 1943, pp. 323–28; E. Tietze-Conrat, The Iconography of Michele Sanmicheli, GBA, XXIX, 1946, pp. 378–82; S. Bettini, La critica dell'architettura e l'arte del Palladio, Arte veneta, III, 1949, pp. 55–69; R. Wittkower, Architectural Principles in the Age of Humanism, London, 1949, pp. 69–70, 75 (3d ed., 1962); F. Pellegrini, Il Lazzaretto di Verona, Verona, 1950; E. Striglio, Relazione sul progetto dei lavori di consolidamento e di ripristino della Chiesa cattedrale di S. Margherita di Montefiascone, Viterbo, 1954; P. P. Brugnoli, La Cattedrale, Verona, 1955; G. C. Argan, L'importanza del Sanmicheli nella formazione del Palladio, Venezia e l'Europa (Atti XVIII Cong. int. di Storia dell'Arte, 1955), Venice, 1956, pp. 387–89; R. Brenzoni, La sanmicheliana Cappella Pellegrini in San Bernardino di Verona, Atti Ist. veneto di sc., lettere ed arti, CXV, 1956–57, pp. 119–31; R. Brenzoni, La Loggia del Consiglio Veronese, Atti Ist. veneto di sc., lettere ed arti, CXVI, 1957–

58, pp. 269–307 at 287; F. Mancini, Le rocche di Romagna, Bologna, 1958 (cat.); L. Puppi, Michele Sanmicheli a Vicenza, Vita veronese, XI, 1958, pp. 449–53; P. Gazzola, Appunti per quattro lezioni su Michele Sanmicheli, B. Centro int. di s. d'arch. Andrea Palladio, I, 1959, pp. 24–26; P. Gazzola, Un grande architetto: il Sanmicheli, Le vie d'Italia, LXV, 1959, pp. 1173–80; G. Giovannoni, Antonio da Sangallo il giovane, 2 vols., Rome, 1959; M. Maimeri, Cronologia sanmicheliana: Nel quarto centenario della morte, Vita veronese, XII, 1959, pp. 109–13; M. Maimeri, Onoranze al Sanmicheli, Vita veronese, XII, 1959, pp. 135–37; M. Maimeri, Sommario di bibliografia sanmicheliana, Vita veronese, XII, 1959, sp. no., pp. 91–97; L. Puppi, L'architettura civile, Vita veronese, XII, 1959, sp. no., pp. 49–76; C. Semenzato, Classicità e classicismo di Michele Sanmicheli, Vita veronese, XII, 1959, sp. no., pp. 3–7; B. Zevi, Sanmicheli: Attualità del suo insegnamento sincretico, L'Architettura, V, 1959, pp. 294–95; G. Zorzi, Preoccupazioni cinquecentesche per l'interramento di Venezia e della Laguna e alcune proposte di Michele Sanmicheli, Atti Ist. veneto di sc., lettere ed arti, CXVIII, 1959–60, pp. 163–210; R. Brenzoni, I Sanmicheli: Maestri, architetti e scultori del XV e XVI secolo oriundi di Porlezza di Valsolda, Arte lombarda, V, 1960, pp. 57–65; P. Gazzola, Michele Sanmicheli, Venice, 1960 (cat.); Michele Sanmicheli: Studi raccolti..., Verona, 1960 (articles by G. Fiocco and others); M. Kahnemann Mangione, La tomba Petrucci di Michele Sanmicheli in San Domenico d'Orvieto, Arte veneta, XV, 1961, pp. 59–76; E. Miozzi, Il forte di S. Andrea del Sanmicheli e il ponte di S. Nicolò del Malacreda in parte già crollati ed oramai prossimi alla completa rovina, Rapporti preliminari Ist. veneto di sc., lettere ed arti, I, 1961, pp. 201–36.

Bruno ZEVI

Illustrations: PLS. 391–394; 5 figs. in text.

SANSOVINO, ANDREA AND JACOPO. Andrea Sansovino (Andrea Contucci), sculptor and architect, was born in Monte San Savino about 1460 and died there in 1529. Andrea's pupil Jacopo (Tatti) Sansovino, who was born at Caprese, near Florence, in 1486 and died in Venice in 1570, adopted the name of his teacher and his professions of sculpture and architecture. Both Andrea and Jacopo received a Florentine training but became known for their work away from Florence.

After apprenticeship with Antonio Pollaiuolo and work with Bertoldo di Giovanni and Giuliano da Sangallo, Andrea began his independent career in 1491 when he was sent by Lorenzo de' Medici to King John II of Portugal, where he remained until 1501 except for activity in 1493–96 on the Baptistery in Florence. For the next dozen years Andrea traveled between Florence and Rome and, in addition, made the Baptistery font at Volterra (1502) and a *Madonna* and a *John the Baptist* for the Cathedral of Genoa (1503–04). His *Christ and St. John* for the Baptistery in Florence, commissioned in 1502, was finished some years later; his work in Rome ranged from the tombs (1505–09) of cardinals Ascanio Sforza (IV, PL. 455) and Girolamo Basso della Rovere in S. Maria del Popolo to the *Madonna, Child and St. Anne* (1512) in S. Agostino. Andrea's later years were centered about his major monument, the elaborate Sanctuary of the Holy House in the Basilica of Loreto. Designated Capomaestro for the sculpture and architecture of Loreto by Leo X in 1512, he only finally left there in 1527. While much of the complex program of the shrine was executed by pupils, such reliefs by Andrea as the *Annunciation* (PL. 58) reveal an artistic attitude still in harmony with the more conservative sculpture of later years of the 15th century in Florence; the forms are more ample, ornamental flourishes are multiplied, yet the same impression of a competent, dignified narration is given. In a period dominated by artistic giants, Andrea's stature is modest; yet as a serious craftsman and teacher he played a part in carrying forward a substantial artistic heritage.

A more dramatic development is found in the work of Jacopo Sansovino, who followed Andrea to Rome about 1503 and began to extend his Tuscan training by making restorations of ancient sculpture and by studying modern and ancient monuments. These various influences are apparent in his earlier works in Florence (1511–17) and again in Rome (1518–27). Andrea's influence is recalled especially in Jacopo's *Madonna del Parto* (Rome, S. Agostino, 1519) and in his work on the Michiel tomb (Rome, S. Marcello, 1519; VIII, PL. 206), while both Michelangelo and ancient prototypes are reflected in the *Bacchus* (Florence, Mus. Naz., 1514; III, PL. 391). Jacopo's potential is suggested in the vitality and assurance of the *Bacchus* and the spare dignity of his *St. James* (Rome, S. Maria di Monserrato, 1520); it was fully realized when, after the Sack of Rome in

1527, he moved to Venice. In the succeeding years Jacopo became a leading figure there, the friend of Titian (q.v.) and of Pietro Aretino and the creator of sculpture and architecture whose quality and extent creates much of the effect of Venice today.

The wide range of Jacopo's buildings includes the Palazzo della Zecca (1536), the Palazzo Corner (now Ca' Grande, 1533), S. Francesco delle Vigne (1534), the Libreria Vecchia di S. Marco (1537–54), the Loggetta (1537–40; PLS. 56, 59), and the Scuola Nuova di S. Maria Valverde della Misericordia (1532–63). His sculpture provides even sharper contrasts: from the colossal figures of the Scala dei Giganti (Doges' Palace courtyard, 1554; VIII, PL. 198) to the fluent decorative reliefs of the Loggetta. Appointed Protomaestro of St. Mark's in 1529, Jacopo crowned his activities there with the bronze sacristy doors (1563; VIII, PL. 214), which form a virtual summary of his entire career, fusing Tuscan and Roman sources in a new, independent style characterized by a combination of strength and elegance and a feeling for pictorial effects of light and shade, color and atmosphere. In Venice Jacopo trained a host of younger artists, among them Alessandro Vittoria and Danese Cattaneo.

Bibliog. P. Schönfeld, Andrea Sansovino und seine Schule, Stuttgart, 1881; L. Pittoni, Jacopo Sansovino, scultore, Venice, 1909; G. Lorenzetti, Jacopo Sansovino, Venice, 1910; G. H. Huntley, Andrea Sansovino, Cambridge, Mass., 1935; R. Gallo, Contributi su Jacopo Sansovino, Saggi e memorie, I, 1957, pp. 81–107.

Eleanor D. Barton

SARGENT, John Singer. American portrait painter and muralist (b. Florence, Jan. 12, 1856; d. London, Apr. 15, 1925). Born abroad of American parents, Sargent commenced his formal art training at the Accademia di Belle Arti in Florence (1870–73) and was then encouraged to continue his studies in Paris under Charles Auguste Emile Durand (1837–1917), a brilliant and fashionable portrait painter who styled himself "Carolus-Duran." Between the time of his entry into the Carolus-Duran studio in 1874 and the submission of his first award-winning painting, *The Oyster Gatherers of Cancale*, to the Salon of 1878 (Washington, D.C., Corcoran Gall. of Art), Sargent absorbed the salient qualities of Carolus-Duran's technique. Founded upon the study of realist painters, especially Velázquez and Courbet, and influenced by the work of Manet, this technique called for a disciplined eye, permitting the artist to approximate with great accuracy any given set of values existing in nature, and encouraged economy of means and spontaneity of execution. This approach to painting was the basis of Sargent's bravura style, which culminated in 1900 in *The Wyndham Sisters* (New York, Met. Mus.).

Sargent continued to advance his position in the Paris art world through a series of increasingly daring submissions to the Salons. His *Portrait of Carolus-Duran* (Williamstown, Mass., Sterling and Francine Clark Art Inst.), sent to the Salon of 1879, was acclaimed by the public and the press. His large, theatrical genre subject, *El Jaleo* (Boston, Isabella Stewart Gardner Mus.) was bought by a New York dealer from the Salon of 1882; and the following year Sargent exhibited his dramatic *Daughters of Edward D. Boit* (Boston, Mus. of Fine Arts), which became the sensation of the exhibition. But his most ambitious subject, *Portrait of Madame X* (I, PL. 108), brought disaster upon Sargent's career in Paris. In this painting he created a symbol of worldly elegance while remaining faithful to an objective representation of a notorious professional beauty. It was received at the Salon of 1884 with an outburst of public indignation and derision. The portrait was regarded as a shameless revelation of unpleasant fact, and only a few critics saw the modernity implicit in its startling realism.

Unable to support himself in Paris, Sargent transferred his studio to London in 1885, eventually taking over Whistler's house in the Chelsea section. While gathering commissions for portraits, he began to explore the art of plein-air landscape painting. During the summers of 1885 to 1889 he stayed in rural Worcestershire with a group of American painters, including Edwin Austin Abbey (1852–1911). There he painted *Carnation, Lily, Lily, Rose* (London, Tate Gall.) a remarkably accurate,

though labored, treatment of the elusive effects of twilight. A large body of rapidly executed landscape studies from this period attests to his admiration for the works of Claude Monet (1840–1926), with whom Sargent formed a lifelong friendship. By 1890 he had become securely established as a portrait painter in England as well as in the United States. Through his friend the architect Charles Follen McKim (1847–1909) Sargent obtained a commision to create a set of mural decorations for the Boston Public Library, a project that absorbed a large portion of his creative energies over a span of 26 years until its completion in 1916.

After about 1900, however, Sargent began to manifest growing dissatisfaction with portraiture. By 1907, having produced nearly four hundred portraits, he had declared his intention to abandon the profession, of which he had wearied. Nevertheless, the last 25 years of his life saw a prodigious outpouring of landscape and genre subjects. His water colors of this period take their place with those of Winslow Homer (1836–1910) in brilliance and mastery of execution.

Sargent's art has been criticized for concentrating on a purely objective view of the world — the surface rather than the substance of things. Few artists, however, have combined such direct and accurate vision with the powerful bravura technique that Sargent possessed; and in this respect his art yields lasting pleasure.

Bibliog. *General*: W. H. Downes, John S. Sargent, His Life and Work, Boston, 1925; E. E. Charteris, John Sargent, New York, 1927; C. M. Mount, John Singer Sargent, a Biography, New York, 1955, London, 1957; D. F. Hoopes, The Private World of John S. Sargent, New York, 1966. *Catalogues*: Catalogue of the Memorial Exhibition of the Works of the Late John Singer Sargent, Mus. of Fine Arts, Boston, 1925; Memorial Exhibition of the Work of John Singer Sargent, Met. Mus., New York, 1926; Sargent Memorial Exhibition, Royal Acad. of Arts, London, 1926; Sargent, Whistler and Mary Cassatt (introd., F. A. Sweet), Art Inst., Chicago, 1954; A Centennial Exhibition: Sargent's Boston (introd., D. McKibbin), Mus. of Fine Arts, Boston, 1956; The Private World of John Singer Sargent (introd., D. F. Hoopes), Corcoran Gall. of Art, Washington, D.C., 1964.

Donelson F. Hoopes

SARTO, ANDREA DEL. See ANDREA DEL SARTO.

SASSANIAN ART. The Sassanian dynasty, named after Sāsān, lord of Persia and high priest of the temple of Anāhitā in Istakhr, ruled Iran from the 3d to the 7th century of our era and constituted the last great Iranian empire before the Moslem conquest. It was founded in 226 by Ardashir I, following his defeat of the last Parthian king, Artabanus V. Politically and ideologically, the Sassanian era represented the Iranian national revolt against the Parthians (see PARTHIAN ART), who were considered usurpers, and its aim was the restoration of the Achaemenid Empire (see IRANIAN PRE-SASSANIAN ART CULTURES). Naturally, this aim was reflected also in the art of the era: Sassanian art was essentially aulic, and it was determined to assert its links with Achaemenid artistic traditions. At the same time, however, it could not help continuing, at least at the beginning, the Parthian culture — the more so because the latter in its last phases had become wholly Iranian in character. Actually, Sassanian art was the final phase of a gigantic artistic development that had started in the Mesopotamian and Iranian area some four thousand years earlier.

Summary. Architecture (col. 702): *General considerations; City planning; Monumental types; Public works; Religious architecture; Architectural decoration.* Sculpture (col. 714). Painting and mosaics (col. 719). Metalwork (col. 721). Gems and glyptics (col. 723). Coins (col. 724). Ceramics and glass (col. 725). Textiles (col. 725). The diffusion of Sassanian art (col. 727).

Architecture. *General considerations.* The earliest monuments that may be attributed to the Sassanians are the castle called Qal'a-i-Dukhtar and the palace of Ardashir at Firuzabad, both in Fars. Although these monuments and subsequent ones are known, scholars have not been able to trace an organic historical development of Sassanian architecture. The monuments have as yet been little studied and thus are more famous than familiar; they are scattered over an immense area, they differ from one another in many respects — some, indeed, are unique structures — and they offer great dissimilarities in basic elements, probably dictated by local traditions about which little or nothing is known. Finally, the chronology of Sassanian monuments, with the exception of a few, is far from certain.

In addition to local traditions, Parthian architecture must have been responsible for a great many of the Sassanian architectural characteristics. However, comparisons between the two must be viewed with caution, since there exists no direct evidence for Parthian architecture on Sassanian soil; with the exception of the palace at Kuh-i-Khwaja in Seistan, Parthian monuments lie either outside Iranian territory — Ashur (Assur), Hatra — or in the ever-changing cultural sphere of outer Iran, for example, Nysa. Nevertheless, Sassanian architecture owes one of its essential features to the Parthians: the liwan, a vaulted room closed on three sides and completely open on the fourth. Many of the Greek motifs employed by the Sassanians were also acquired through the Parthians. The adoption of such Achaemenid features as the "Egyptian gorge" (or "Egyptian grooving") at Firuzabad or the corbels at Bishapur, Fars, was self-conscious as well as sporadic; other Achaemenid elements, such as the artificial terrace of the Qasr-i-Shirin, possessed a valid, fundamental significance. A strong influence of Roman culture made itself felt in the construction of public works, especially bridges and dams.

The building material used in western Iran was stone rubble, which was bonded with a chalky mortar, and in Mesopo-tamia and Seistan, baked, or sometimes unbaked, bricks. Stone blocks were used to some extent, notably in the fire temple and the "Stone Palace" (Palace B) at Bishapur, and in the Ṭāq-i-Girrā and at Paikuli in the Zagros Mountains.

A distinctive characteristic of all Sassanian architecture was the preference for either barrel vaults or vaults with a parabolic cross section (PL. 397). Other typical features were the vault resting on semidomes, which may be considered a Sassanian invention, and the square room surmounted by a dome that was set on corner squinches. The liwan, unlike the liwan in Parthian buildings, was conceived not as a room in itself but rather as the huge entrance hall to the domed square room.

The principle of symmetry among the various parts of a building, easily discernible in the plans, was widespread; at the same time, elevations were kept in a graded order of dimensions corresponding to the functions of the different parts of the building (i.e., the public reception rooms were taller, the private quarters lower).

The unique characteristic of Sassanian architecture, expressed in all its finest examples, was, however, its compelling concept of space. Space was distinct, that is, described by the walls. The interplay of forces that constitutes the static balance was always clearly apparent, not concealed within the structure or relegated to the outside. In this respect, Sassanian architecture was the exact antithesis of Roman architecture, which was engaged in the search for an illusory and dynamic space.

The use of columns must have been known to Sassanian architecture, judging from the marble capitals in Byzantine style that were discovered at the Ṭāq-i-Bustān and at Bisutun and Isfahan.

Principal centers of the Sassanian empire. *Key:* (1) Boundaries of the empire; (2) Sassanian rock reliefs; (3) remains of other Sassanian monuments.

City planning. Very little is known about Sassanian city planning. Firuzabad, which was founded by Ardashir I (ca. 226–41) and named Gur, was built on a perfectly circular plan, modeled after the Parthian city of Darabjird. This type of city plan was originally derived from an ancient Assyrian tradition and had been adopted by the Parthians for their military encampments. When Shāpur I (241–72), however, built the city of Bishapur, he fashioned it on the Hippodamian plan (see HIPPODAMOS), giving it a gridiron type of layout and dividing it into various sectors. Many other Sassanian cities are known from documentary sources, but most of them have never been located. A number of them were built and populated by Roman prisoners, and since they were based on the plan of a Roman military camp, they had a rectangular outline. Examples are Jundi Shapur, between Dizful and Shushtar in Khuzistan, built during the reign of Shāpur I, and the city-fortress known as Ivan-i-Karkha in the same region near Susa, dating from the time of Shāpur II (309–79). When Khusrau I (531–79) conquered Antioch in 540, he transplanted the inhabitants to Babylonia, where he forced them to reconstruct a city like the one they had left.

Monumental types. The palace at Firuzabad (FIG. 705), erected by Ardashir I, was built on a rectangular plan, with considerably elongated sides in the north–south direction. The façade of the short northern end was dominated by a large liwan, as high as the building to which it was the monumental entrance hall. To the right and left of the liwan, two pairs of vaulted rooms were set at right angles to the longitudinal axis of the building. The liwan led into a square, domed room, which communicated through narrow passageways on the right and left with two other identical rooms. Another passageway

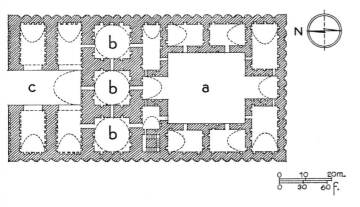

Firuzabad, plan of the palace of Ardashir I. (*a*) Courtyard of the living quarters; (*b*) public reception rooms; (*c*) liwan (*from SPA, I, fig. 150*).

led from the middle room through a central liwan into a square court, on the opposite side of which was another liwan. Oblong rooms with narrow entrances were set around all sides of the court. The rigid symmetrical layout of the building is hence very plain. On the façade, the wide liwan opening was framed on either side by two orders of niches; the outer wall surfaces of the other three sides of the palace were broken up into salients and reentrants joined above the arches.

One of the most remarkable monumental structures, the Qal'a-i-Dukhtar — which R. Ghirshman (Firuzabad, *BIFAO*, XLVI, 1947, p. 26) considers earlier, if only by a few years, than the palace of Ardashir described above — was set like an aerie on a high rocky spur just before the Tang-i-Ab gorge opens into the Firuzabad plain. Fortified by a system of ramparts that sloped down the mountainside and barricaded the valley, the construction was composed of three parts which were placed on different levels and were enclosed by a single circuit of wall. The highest part of this wall was reinforced by an enormous semicircular, embattled tower. On the lowest level was a courtyard, into either side of which two large square towers protruded. Within each tower, a staircase wound upward around a central

column, leading to a courtyard on the second level; three liwans opened onto this court on its far side. Flights of stairs, or perhaps ramps, led up to the third level, which comprised an open space or terrace; at its center can still be seen a rectangle paved with flagstones, which may be the remains of a throne. The terrace was dominated by a majestic liwan, from which a wide, vaulted passageway led into a square room surmounted by a dome on squinches. Other rooms, set between the nucleus of the complex and the encircling wall, were reached by means of two open passageways along the sides of the liwan. In one of the rooms on the south side, a spiral staircase led up to the base of the dome. The only trace of stuccowork that has survived is the decoration around one of the niches that embellished the liwan — an "Egyptian-gorge" type cornice copied from Persepolitan models. The entire encircling wall, which was provided with balistrarias, was broken up into salients and reentrants, as in the Firuzabad palace. The structure has all the characteristics of a fortress and, with its defensive wall system, resembles the one Shāpur I erected at the entrance of the Bishapur valley. Here, however, the liwan on the highest level served as the entrance hall into the domed room; that is, the building contained the architectural arrangement typical of the ceremonial areas of Sassanian palaces, so that on special occasions that part of the fortress could also be used to receive the ruler. It is quite probable that the arrangement of an edifice on three levels held some symbolic magical or religious significance.

The palace chronologically nearest to the one at Firuzabad was the palace of Shāpur I, or Palace A, at Bishapur (FIG. 706). It has been excavated only partially, the known part consisting of an official ceremonial area; the private apartments must have been located elsewhere. A triple liwan remains, very much reworked, similar to the Parthian triple liwans at Hatra (XI, FIG. 111). Next to it stood a building enclosed by a high wall with a passageway running around all four sides. Ghirshman (1938), who unearthed it, thinks it must have been a large square hall covered by a dome, with four large liwans facing

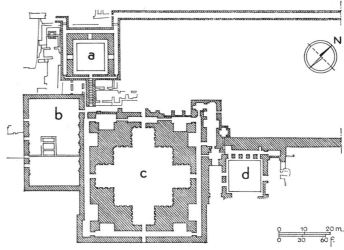

Bishapur, plan of the palace of Shāpur I (Palace A). (*a*) Fire temple; (*b*) courtyard with mosaic pavement; (*c*) square hall (or court) with four liwans; (*d*) triple liwan with mosaics (*from Ghirshman, 1956*).

each other in cruciform fashion. Considering the size of the central quadrangle, each side of which measures 72 ft., Godard (1938) doubts that such a vast space could have been covered by a dome and believes, instead, that it must have been an open court with a liwan on each side. Whatever the case may be, a ground plan of this sort must be linked with the Parthian palaces of Nysa and Ashur, which were, in fact, built around a court with four liwans. The walls around the hall — or court — were divided into a series of niches decorated with stuccowork.

Although it was built much later, perhaps during the reign

of Bahrām V Gūr (420–40), the palace at Sarvistan, in Fars (FIG. 707), had a ground plan closer to that of the Firuzabad palace than to the one of Shāpur's palace. At Sarvistan, the principle of a graded order of dimensions was observed; however, the rooms were not disposed symmetrically. The façade

rose rectangular piers. These piers terminated in squinches, which supported the semidomes that spanned the area between the piers. This construction left a narrow passageway close to the wall, which had no practical function, but served rather to expand the room by setting up a distinction between the struc-

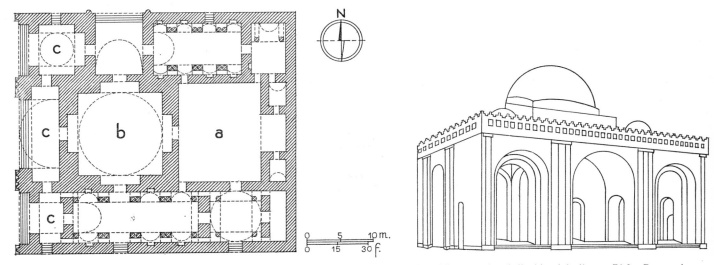

Sarvistan, palace of Bahrām V. *Left*: Plan. (*a*) Courtyard in the living quarters; (*b*) public reception hall; (*c*) triple liwan. *Right*: Perspective reconstruction of the façade (*redrawn from SPA, I, figs. 142, 151*).

had three liwans, in keeping with the Parthian pattern. Noteworthy are two long rooms whose roofs were formed by a combination of barrel vaults and semidomes. In front of the walls on the long sides stood pairs of round, squat, coupled pillars, which were joined to the wall by arches and from which

tures that bore the weight and those which defined the enclosed space. This architectural type, which may be found throughout Mesopotamia, has been claimed to be an original Sassanian invention; nevertheless, some authorities have related it to the Western architectural type of the basilica.

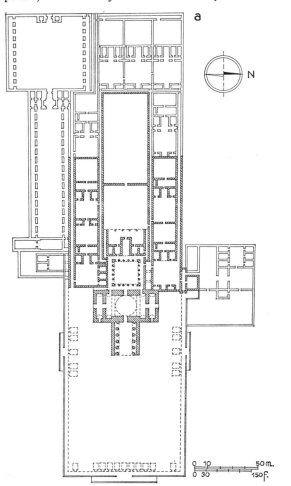

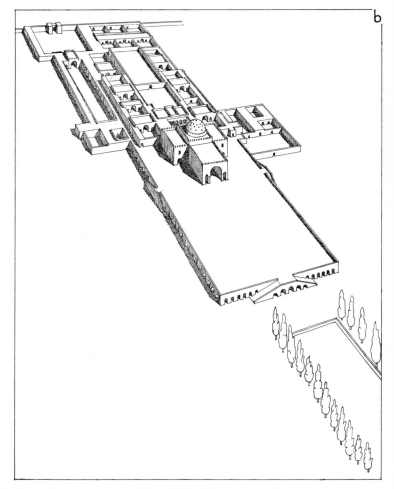

Qaṣr-i-Shīrīn, 'Imārat-i-Khusrau. (*a*) Plan; (*b*) Perspective reconstruction (*from SPA, I, figs. 153, 154*).

Within the city-fortress founded by Shāpur II after the destruction of Susa, following the Christian revolt, stands the ruin known as Ivan-i-Karkha, the date of which had remained dubious until Ghirshman made preliminary excavations in 1950; this made it possible to date it from the 4th century. It had been part of the royal quarters, which comprised various buildings scattered about the gardens. The structure consisted of two corridors about 100 ft. long that flanked a square room with a dome. To cover the extremely long corridors, transverse arches were spaced along them and connected by barrel vaults set at right angles to the arches. This device also made it possible to obtain good lighting — without endangering the structural equilibrium of the building — through wide window openings along the walls. It appears that this system had its precedent in the Parthian palace of Kuh-i-Khwaja in Seistan. However, the plan of Ivan-i-Karkha is found not only on Iranian territory; almost identical plans were adopted in — and, in fact, seem to have been typical of — the hot-springs regions of Asia Minor.

An imposing group of practically unexplored ruins is the one known as the Qaṣr-i-Shīrīn, in Kurdistan, which is thought by some to have been the residence of Shīrīn, the Christian bride of Khusrau II (590-628). The entire complex was destroyed by Emperor Heraclius in 628. Prominent among these ruins is the 'Imārat-i-Khusrau (FIG. 707), a stately palace built, like Achaemenid residences, on an immense terrace reached by flights of stairs. Its plan is very uncertain, but it seems that the principles of symmetry and the graded differentiation of dimensions were observed. From the palace proper an edifice protruded that, according to the most recent reconstruction, was divided into "nave and aisles" by two rows of immense columns; its façade took the form of a wide liwan flanked by two small ones, a pattern similar to the ones found in Palace II at Kish (FIG. 711) in Mesopotamia and at Damghan (FIG. 710) in northern Iran and going back to the original west Parthian model, the palace of Hatra. The great liwan led directly into the rectangular throne room.

The palace known as Haush Qurī, some three miles south of the 'Imārat and joined to it by a *paradeisos*, seems to have been based on the same plan.

Very little is known about the third large group of buildings in the same area, known as the Chahār Qāpū ("four doors"), taking its name from the most striking ruin in the group. This was a large square structure with a door on each side, covered by a wide dome and perhaps encircled by a vaulted passageway. Sarre and Herzfeld (1910) think it may have been a fire sanctuary; other authorities, such as Godard (1938), believe it was a throne room. It was situated on the far side of a wide courtyard, around which were laid out the living quarters, or *bayts*, dwellings similar to the ones found in the 'Imārat-i-Khusrau.

The most famous Sassanian monument is undoubtedly the imposing Tāq-i-Kisrā at Ctesiphon (PL. 397; FIG. 713). Its dates, like those of the other monuments, are uncertain; E. Herzfeld (*Archaeological History of Iran*, London, 1935, p. 94) is inclined to attribute it to Shāpur I (241–72), but others prefer the traditional attribution to Khusrau I Anūshirvān (531–79). The building, whose large and distinctive façade was still intact in 1888, is now reduced to little more than the huge liwan and the south part of the façade. The liwan, with a span of almost 84 ft., is the largest one known. Its vault has the typical parabolic cross section; however, it did not lead into a domed room, and in this respect it appears closer to Parthian structures.

On the road between Baghdad and Kermanshah stands the monument known as the Tāq-i-Girrā, the purpose of which is rather obscure; perhaps it was a royal stopping place. Constructed of ashlar, the ruin consists of a liwan, in which Greek forms of decoration are apparent, and is obviously related to the Parthian monuments of Hatra. Its dates have been debated at length, but it is probably to be attributed to the reign of one of the first Sassanian kings, perhaps Shāpur I.

Private dwellings were built according to the plan adopted for the living quarters of the palaces; that is, they were fundamentally variations of the *bayt* type, consisting either of one liwan bordered by two rooms and opening onto a court or of

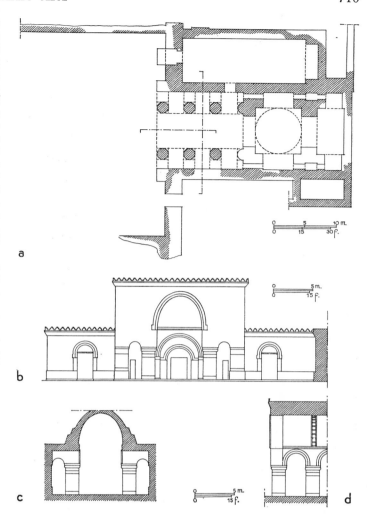

Damghan, Sassanian building. (*a*) Plan; (*b*) reconstruction of the façade; (*c*) cross section; (*d*) partial longitudinal section of the liwan (*from SPA, I, figs. 166, 167*).

two liwans, again between two rooms each, facing one another across the court. The houses excavated at Ctesiphon, of a rather late period, were more complex but were basically derived from this liwan-type arrangement. As many as three, and perhaps even four, liwans were set around the court of a house at El Ma'arid, which is reminiscent of the four-liwan Parthian plan at Ashur. When a house had several liwans around its court, the liwans were arranged in order of importance, the most important one, which was much more richly decorated than the others, being placed across from the main entrance.

Palaces I and II at Kish (FIG. 711) must also be considered private habitations, although they are closer to court architecture. The liwan of Palace II is divided into three aisles by a double row of columns with capitals of direct Western derivation; at the end of the liwan a room with an apse was substituted for the domed room, a design obviously borrowed from Roman models.

Public works. Many public works, especially roads and drainage systems, were constructed during the Sassanian period. Among the most famous was the water-control and drainage system in the Shushtar area. In these works, the signs of Roman workmanship are plainly visible. Shāpur I, after conquering the Romans at Edessa in 260, employed countless numbers of Roman prisoners in the construction of bridges and dams in the Khuzistan province, particularly at Shushtar.

The bridge-dam known as the Band-i-Qayṣar ("the emperor's bridge") — because it was built by Valerian's defeated troops — is in this area. It was constructed in an irregular zigzag line,

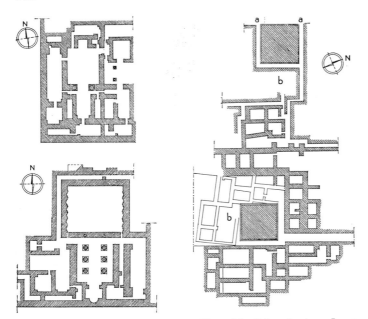

Kish, principal Sassanian monuments. *Upper left*: Palace I, plan. *Lower left*: Palace II, plan. *Right*: Group of buildings east of the palaces: (a) entrances; (b) brick platforms (*from SPA, I, figs. 169, 174*).

since its foundations were sunk into the outcroppings of rock across the river bed. The Band-i-Qayṣar was built of precisely dressed ashlar blocks bonded with mortar. Along the top of the dam, massive piers were erected to support the arches of the bridge proper, over which ran a spacious road. Typical of the bridge's Roman construction were the stoneworking technique and the small arch that was set over each pier for supplementary support; during the great floods, it also served to reduce the pressure of the water by helping the downward flow. Of a similar type was the Dizful bridge-dam, also built by Roman prisoners under Shāpur I.

Religious architecture. Fire, the symbol of Ahura Mazda, was the object of supreme worship during the Sassanian era, which had made Mazdaism or, as has also been claimed, its reformed version, Zoroastrianism, its official state religion. Of the many temples, which were located especially in the highland regions, there remain today only about 50 structures that may be related to the fire cult, most of them in the western part of the country, particularly in Fars. Only in a few cases is it possible to propose dates, even tentative ones, since archaeological study of these monuments is still in an early stage. The structures reveal an essential unity of architectural types, though their particular forms may vary considerably.

The sacred fire was kept burning in a temple called the *ātashgāh* ("place where there is fire"), which was enclosed and inaccessible to the multitude of the faithful; during ceremonies, another fire was lighted and exposed in a sort of pavilion, or kiosk, open on all four sides and called, therefore, *chahār ṭāq*, "four gates."

In the excavations at Tang-i-Chak Chak in Laristan (1957) and Kunar Siah in Fars (1959-61), two fire sanctuaries were brought to light, each including both temple and pavilion that clearly reveal their combined function. At the former site, the two main buildings are in quite good condition, whereas the appendages, which are appreciable in the Kunar Siah sanctuary, have been almost completely destroyed.

The *ātashgāh*, as a rule, was a square structure covered by a dome set on corner squinches and had a single entrance. The *chahār ṭāq* had the form of a dome resting on four arches that were supported by pillars or piers — for example, the *chahār ṭāq* of the Tang-i-Chak Chak sanctuary; but perhaps more common was the type that was surrounded by an enclosed passageway that had an opening on each side — like the one at Kunar Siah.

This plan, though either more simplified or more elaborate, may be found in various other sanctuaries. At Atashkuh, south of Qum, there are the remains of a *chahār ṭāq* whose dome rested on four piers with heart-shaped cross sections; opposite one of its entrances stood two small symmetrical rooms joined by a liwan, one of them clearly the *ātashgāh*, the other the priest's quarters or a storeroom. In the *chahār ṭāq* called the Khurmā Yak, near Farrashband in Fars, the encircling passageway was extended to form a corridor that led to an oblong structure divided into three rooms. Another *chahār ṭāq* near Farrashband, at Tall-i-Jangi, was connected by two projecting walls to two pairs of rooms. Here, too, the *chahār ṭāq* was surrounded by a passageway, but boasted the special feature of a small dome over each corner of that passageway. (For Kunar Siah, Khurmā Yak, and Tall-i-Jangi see ZOROASTRIANISM, text figures.) The structural device of small corner domes seems to have been copied, though in a more striking variation, in a building portrayed on a famous post-Sassanian bronze salver in Berlin (Staat. Mus.), and it was reinterpreted at the beginning of the 10th century in the mausoleum of Ismā'il the Samanid (see SAMANID ART) in Bukhara, Uzbek S.S.R. (PL. 382). The fire sanctuary at Takht-i-Sulaymān in Azerbaijan, a tetrapylon with a passageway around it, appears to be a 6th-century Sassanian reconstruction of an earlier edifice. The structure at Hazara, Transoxiana, which Russian scholars have dated from the 10th century, obviously represents a survival of the Sassanian *chahār ṭāq* style.

The architectural plan of a tetrapylon with a surrounding passageway had already appeared in the fire sanctuary of the Kuh-i-Khwaja palace, which Herzfeld (1941) ascribes to the Parthian period (ca. 1st century A.D.), and in its simplest form — a square chamber isolated by a passageway — dates back to the prototypes from which the temple at Hatra was derived. In that form, the plan was adopted again at Bishapur about the middle of the 3d century, in the fire temple adjoining the Palace of Shāpur I. This temple, which was perhaps dedicated to Anāhita, the goddess of fertility and water whose cult incorporated the worship of fire, was built of scrupulously dressed stone blocks, following a Roman technique. The structure was half underground and consisted of a square room with four openings, surrounded by an exceptionally narrow passageway (which some authorities see as an element borrowed from Babylonian temple architecture). The passageway was covered by horizontal wooden beams resting on corbels with taurine protomas copied from Achaemenid models.

In Khorasan, there are remains of a unique building known as the Bāz-i-Hūr. Rectangular on the outside, its inner chamber was square and was surmounted by a dome supported not by squinches but by wooden beams thrown across the corners. Four large vaulted openings were cut into each side of the chamber, giving it the appearance of a cross-shaped hall. On the two short sides of the structure, within the massive walls, were two narrow, disconnected passageways, one of which turned at a right angle into the entrance side of the building. Godard (1938), who dates the edifice from the 3d century, questions the possibility of its being a fire temple.

Among noteworthy *chahār ṭāqs* without covered passageways are those at Naysar — perhaps one of the oldest — and Natanz in central Iran and at Dara Bagh, Kiratah, Bala Dih, and Naudaran in Fars. Two of the several *chahār ṭāqs* near Farrashband were rectangular on the outside, whereas the central chamber was square, since one of its sides was adjoined by a liwanlike structure. There is some question as to whether the Chahār Qāpū of the Qaṣr-i-Shīrīn did or did not have a passageway around it; in fact, some authorities are convinced that it cannot have been a sanctuary at all. In the center of the ancient city of Firuzabad there is a ruined tower that once had a flight of stairs winding around it to the top, where apparently there was a shrine for displaying the fire. About 300 ft. to the northeast there is another ruin, the Takht-i-Nishīn, which once consisted of a large raised terrace upon which a square base of ashlar blocks was set. The imposts of four pillars on this base, marking the outlines of a central room, may be recognized as the vestiges of an enormous *chahār ṭāq*.

The fire sanctuary of the Qal'a-i-Dukhtar near Qum had an unusual plan: it consisted of a square pavilion completely open on two adjoining sides, where the fire was displayed during ceremonies; at other times, the fire was kept in a closed chamber set against one wall, which was approached through an L-shaped passage.

Of considerable interest are, lastly, a number of sanctuaries that were set up as beacons on elevated places, such as the ones at Takht-i-Rustam and Takht-i-Kayka'us near Teheran. The *chahār ṭāq* has disappeared from both, but the enclosure where the fire was kept, quite some distance away, may still be seen. A small fire shrine on a mountaintop near Shahristanak in Mazanderan, which M. Siroux (Le Ḳal'è Dukhtar de Sharestānek, *Athar-é Iran*, III, 1938, pp. 123-32) dates from the end of the Sassanian period, consisted of two barrel-vaulted rooms set side by side and preceded by a vestibule whose entrance was off center.

Aside from Kuh-i-Khwaja, other interesting fire sanctuaries in Seistan are the little-known shrines at Karku and Ram Shahristan.

A number of fire altars dedicated to worship during public ceremonies were erected in the open air, such as the twin altars at Naqsh-i-Rustam near Istakhr, the altar at Harsin, Luristan, which was found attached to an uncompleted shrine, and probably the altar at Qalaban' in Tabaristan. The altar at Qanat-i-Bagh, in Fars, resembles the altars shown on coins (III, PL. 399; XIV, PL. 477), consisting of a square pillar topped by a graded, or stepped, mensa.

Mention must be made here of the Christian churches that were built during the Sassanian period and are known through the examples to be found in Mesopotamia. Although they are not of high quality, in terms of typology they are quite unusual and offer a rich field for study. The oldest churches, built of unbaked brick, are those found at Ctesiphon (FIG. 713). These churches took as their model a type of columned hall similar to the oblong rooms in the palace of Bahrām V at Sarvistan, as has been pointed out by Monneret de Villard (1940), who, together with Reuther (1938), denies the possibility of their derivation from the plan of the Western basilica.

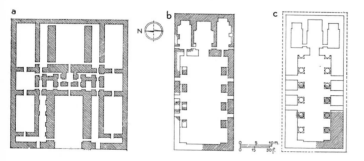

Ctesiphon, buildings of the Sassanian period. (*a*) Ṭāq-i-Kisrā; (*b*, *c*) Christian church, (*left*) plan of the lower floor, (*right*) plan of the upper floor (*from SPA, I, figs. 155, 162*).

Characteristic of these hall churches is the fact that the entrances were set along the sides, which in Monneret de Villard's opinion represents a continuation of the Babylonian type of broad-cella temple (IX, FIG. 781). Another feature of the Mesopotamian churches was the chancel that was broken up into three oblong, windowless rooms connected by several corridors, an arrangement that has been ascribed to Nestorian art (q.v.). In Syria, hall-type churches with side entrances were apparently extant as early as the end of the 4th century. An element of Western influence is noticeable in Church XI at Hira, for example, the main body of which was divided into three naves; however, the side entrances were still retained here. The churches in the Tur 'Abdin, the mountainous region of northern Mesopotamia, were vaulted, perhaps even surmounted by a dome, and represented a special type. Many of them, being modeled after the basilica of the West, had semicircular apses, while the hall-type plan was preserved in each case.

Architectural decoration. The walls of Sassanian buildings were covered with highly distinctive decorations. Most façade elements were taken from Hellenistic sources through the intermediary of Parthian art but were reinterpreted in a completely Iranian spirit. The decoration was applied to the wall surface in a veneerlike layer, which in no way reflected the underlying structure of the building but, rather, treated the expanse of the wall pictorially, in accordance with the practices of Eastern art.

The façade of the Firuzabad palace, with its huge liwan in the center and the spread of tall and short niches on either side, was derived from the façade of the Parthian palace at Ashur. The façade decoration on the palace at Sarvistan was also inherited from Parthian traditions, but it was more directly modeled on the prototypes at Hatra (XI, FIG. 112). A similar pattern was followed in the Ṭāq-i-Kisrā. Its colossal façade of niches and arches (PL. 397) resembles very much the *frons scaenae* of ancient theaters, to which it is undoubtedly related. However, it assumed its own character by the alteration of the classical relationship between the diameter and the height of a column, by the juxtaposition of large and small elements, and by the violation of that other basic principle of classical architecture, the vertical alignment of axes.

Interior ornamentation at Firuzabad was very restrained; the only decoration in the palace was the stucco cornices of the "Egyptian-gorge" type over the doors, which were imitations of Persepolitan models, as were their counterparts in the palace of Shāpur I at Bishapur and in the fortress of Qal'a-i-Dukhtar near Firuzabad.

Although little has remained *in situ*, it is known from archaeological findings that great importance was given to decoration in stucco, both sculptured and shaped in molds; the latter technique boasted a long tradition in the Mesopotamian region; it had certainly been practiced during the time of the Seleucid Empire (4th–3d cent. B.C.) and was widespread also during the Parthian period (see STUCCO). Sassanian patterns were composed of geometric and plant designs (PL. 399), as well as figural designs including a vast assortment of animals. Together with motifs borrowed from Hellenistic models, there existed an immensely rich repertory of patterns; these were either spread over the entire wall surface or set within geometric designs. A characteristic motif, which appeared at least as early as the 5th century, was that of floating ribbons, frequently tied around the necks of animals; human busts were also popular and were often set in medallions, or roundels.

The problem of dating the stuccoes has still not been adequately solved; yet a certain stylistic evolution may be observed in the progressive tendency toward stylization of forms, with the modeled surface eventually being reduced to only two planes.

Decoration in stone, although less frequent, was also used by the Sassanians, as is evident from such examples as the footing of the "Stone Palace" in Bishapur — a carry-over from Parthian tradition; the bull's-head corbels of the fire temple at Bishapur; the votive monument, But-Khāna, at Paikuli; and the capitals in Byzantine style found at Isfahan, Bisutun, and near the Ṭāq-i-Bustān.

SCULPTURE. Sassanian stone sculpture is known almost exclusively through a series of large, impressive rock reliefs, some thirty altogether, most of them located in Fars. One is in the region of Khuzistan, at Khang-i-Nauruzi, another at Shapur (anc. Salmas), northwest of Lake Urmia in Azerbaijan, and lastly, a small but important group, the Ṭāq-i-Bustān (PLS. 398, 401). Sculpture in the round was apparently known, judging from a few remains: a Syrian-style monument in honor of Shāpur I, at Bishapur, which — according to an inscription — was once adorned by a statue; the fragments of a colossal statue of the same king, located in a cave outside Bishapur; and a severely mutilated statue at the Ṭāq-i-Bustān. But rock reliefs were undoubtedly much more congenial to the spirit of Iranian art as the continuation of an ancient Eastern tradition that had flourished in Mesopotamia as early as the middle of the 3d century B.C.

Sassanian rock sculpture preserved the magical and religious values that had been the essence of this form of art since its ancient beginnings, even though these values were partially distorted under the Sassanians, as their sculpture lacked the essential quality of inaccessibility still inherent in Achaemenid reliefs. The magicoreligious, and even propagandistic, significance of the Sassanian reliefs is further confirmed by the fact that they were almost all sculptured in the native region of the dynasty, Persis, largely the modern Fars, which had also been a stronghold of the Achaemenids. In this way, the Sassanians meant to establish the legitimacy of their reign as the heirs to Achaemenid traditions and as the restorers of their forebears' "world kingdom." Such ambitions are well documented by the reliefs carved at the bases of the cliffs at Naqsh-i-Rustam, near Persepolis, the upper parts of which contained the tomb of the Achaemenid kings (IV, PL. 457; VIII, PL. 136).

Although a number of non-Iranian influences may be discerned in Sassanian reliefs, they still lie completely within the Eastern artistic tradition, even where those other influences are prevalent, as, for example, in the reliefs of Shāpur I at Bishapur, Naqsh-i-Rustam, and Darab (anc. Davabjird). Because their meaning was symbolic, the scenes depicted in these reliefs lack any specific historical characterization. This is true even in those instances where the historical reference is clear, as in the series of scenes showing the defeat of the Romans, since basically these scenes are but symbolic representations of the triumph of good over evil. Such an approach also explains the absence of any reference to landscape and the lack of any attempt at portraiture; even the kings may be identified only by the shape of their crowns (which has frequently caused conflicting attributions) or, in some rare instances, by accompanying inscriptions.

The subject matter of the reliefs was rather unvaried and always aimed at glorifying the divine aspect of the king, who was invested with power by Ahura Mazda and, like the god, engaged in a victorious struggle against evil. Most of the reliefs represented investiture scenes, in which also the downfall of the enemy was celebrated, triumphs, scenes showing the king defending the members of his household, the king enthroned, and royal hunts. Whatever the subject, the scene always has a decidedly rigid ceremonial character; there is never any true dramatic action. Typical are the composite, generally heraldic, and almost always strictly symmetrical arrangements of the figures, as well as the gigantic size of the king's figure, which towers above all the others, sometimes even over that of a deity in the scene.

The earliest known Sassanian rock carvings are those at Firuzabad, attributed to the beginning of Ardashir I's reign and still bound to the conventions of Parthian art. The relief itself is very low, the details are rendered by means of fine incisions, and the forms are heavy and massive but not without a certain vigor. One relief, carved on a rock wall at the Tang-i-Ab gorge near the Firuzabad plain, consists of three separate dueling scenes that express vividly the Iranian concept of battle as a series of individual engagements. In one scene, Ardashir is shown on horseback, launched in the characteristic "flying gallop," having overthrown his adversary, the last Arsacid king, Artabanus V; in the second, the Arsacid vizier is represented falling before the attack of Ardashir's son, Shāpur I, while the last scene shows the combat between two soldiers.

Another, slightly higher relief in the same gorge represents the investiture of Ardashir by the god Ahura Mazda, who is seen handing the King the symbol of power — a diadem with floating ribbons — as the royal retinue looks on. Placed between the two standing figures is a small altar, an iconographic element that was not to reappear in any subsequent reliefs portraying the investiture of a king.

More body was given the figures in the investiture scene of Ardashir at Naqsh-i-Rajab, near Istakhr, while the same type of scene at Naqsh-i-Rustam was carved in very high relief; the latter is also the first of a series of investiture scenes on horseback, a theme that was to last throughout the remainder of the 3d century. Both Ardashir and Ahura Mazda are shown sitting on their horses in a stiff heraldic pose. Under the hoofs of one horse lies the body of Ahriman, the personification of evil, and under the hoofs of the other, Artabanus V. The motif of an enemy's trampled body was to become typical and one of the most popular.

The relief at Shapur in Azerbaijan, in which the king, portrayed on horseback, receives the homage of the conquered Armenians, has been attributed to Ardashir as well as to Bahrām II (276–93).

The development toward extremely high relief with rounded and massive forms, which began with the investiture scene at Naqsh-i-Rustam described above, was to persist during the following period. This process has been ascribed to an Eastern influence derived from Greco-Indian traditions, but it was more likely due to frequent encounters with the Western world, as seems evidenced by the reliefs of Ardashir's son, Shāpur I. The King's victorious military exploits against the Romans, specifically his subjugation of Gordianus III, the surrender of Philip the Arabian, and the disastrous defeat suffered by the Romans at Edessa, in which Emperor Valerian himself was captured by the Persians, were undoubtedly the most decisive and most symbolic events of Shāpur's reign. The Great King not only recorded them in a lengthy trilingual inscription — known as the *Res gestae divi Saporis* — on the Achaemenid monument at Naqsh-i-Rustam, the Ka'ba-i-Zardusht, but also had them documented in a series of five monumental rock reliefs in Fars. Three of them are located near Bishapur, one at Darab, and a fifth at Naqsh-i-Rustam, this last one being placed, by no means unintentionally, beneath the tomb of Darius the Great (VIII, PL. 136). In most of them the influence of Roman historical bas-reliefs and the active participation of Western artists in their execution are obvious.

Before the discovery of the *Res gestae* in the 1930s, these reliefs were generally interpreted as commemorating the defeat of Valerian; then, after a partial reexamination by G. Pugliese Carratelli (*La Parola del Passato*, II, Naples, 1947, pp. 209–39), Macdermot (1954) offered a new and convincing explanation of the events they represent; they appear to deal not only with Valerian, but with his ill-fated predecessors as well.

The triumph on one of the reliefs at Bishapur was conceived in typically Iranian fashion, that is, coupled with an investiture scene on horseback; it must be considered the oldest relief of the series, perhaps dating from not much later than 244. Trampled beneath Ahura Mazda's horse is the body of Ahriman, while Shāpur, who is receiving the symbol of power, crushes the body of Gordianus III beneath his horse; between the horses, Philip the Arabian kneels in the act of surrender. The work is of high artistic quality and achieves an intensely dramatic effect.

Shāpur's victories over the three emperors are synthesized in the center panel of an enormous relief carved into a natural recess of the rock. In the four horizontal registers that flank the main panel, the Persian army is shown on one side, and on the other, the conquered army bearing the spoils. The influence of Roman historical bas-reliefs is unmistakable. The models were obviously the spiral friezes on the columns of Trajan (XIII, PL. 109) and, even more so, of Marcus Aurelius in Rome, but in several details, the Sassanian reliefs show a surprising similarity to some of the reliefs on the Arch of Septimius Severus in Rome, and in other details anticipated certain elements that were to appear on the Arch of Galerius in Salonika. As has been stated, however, there is a very profound difference in concept.

The Iranian concept of symbolism is even more marked in the third relief at Bishapur, yet it, too, falls within the tradition of Roman historical reliefs, with its episode of the threefold triumph placed at the center and flanked by two series of panels arranged on two levels; again, the representation is static and devoid of all emotional content.

A variant form of the triumph motif is the subject of the relief at Darab, which shows the standing figures of two living Roman emperors. The composition of this relief was probably based on an allocution scene, and the attempt to treat the scene spatially is evident, though it remained little more than an intention.

The fifth triumph relief, the one below the tomb of Darius I at Naqsh-i-Rustam, is perhaps the most famous. In it the arrangement of the central panel of the third relief at Bishapur is repeated in inverse order, with the figure of Gordianus missing.

A relief of outstanding quality, portraying Shāpur on horseback accompanied by a group of dignitaries, is the one at Naqsh-i-Rajab. Remarkable is the figure of the King, who is seated on his horse in a typical pose, with his head and chest in full front view.

Relief sculpture reached its zenith under Bahrām I (273–76), the son of Shāpur I, who was responsible for a fine investiture scene at Bishapur, in which the forms have lost all stiffness and the workmanship is both elaborate and vigorous.

The quality of relief sculpture remained at a high level under the reign of his successor, Bahrām II, who often had portraits of himself and his family executed on reliefs and coins. Under his rule, the repertory of motifs was also enlarged. A very high relief of Naqsh-i-Rustam, one of the finest products of Sassanian art, is imposingly monumental in character. The King is shown standing with his body in front view, but his head in profile, and his hands resting on his sword in the act of receiving the homage of the court. Two other sculptures in the same place, carved in very high and massive relief, show the same king in dueling scenes on horseback (PL. 400); one of the scenes, executed in two registers, has also been ascribed to Bahrām IV (388–99). In an admirable relief at Sar-Mashhed, Bahrām II is shown fighting two lions in the presence of his wife and children. He also appears in two reliefs at Barm-i-Dilak; in the large one, he and the queen are shown standing side by side, and in the smaller one, he is depicted offering a sacrifice to the fire. At Guyum, Bahrām II seems to be portrayed in the guise of an orant. At Naqsh-i-Bahram, he is shown in front view, seated on the throne, as he receives the homage of dignitaries. Interesting is the rather awkward motif of the seated figure, which appeared here for the first time in Sassanian relief work but which had become very popular in eastern Iran, where it was derived from Parthian sources.

A sculpture at Bishapur, ascribed to Bahrām II, portrays the King on horseback as the conqueror of the Arabs; this is a smaller version of the scheme employed in the large triumph of Shāpur I at the same place.

That relief sculpture had sunk to a low level and become rather dull and conventional is evident in the investiture scene with standing figures at Naqsh-i-Rustam, showing Narsah (293–302), another of Shāpur's sons, receiving the emblems of power from Anāhitā (PL. 401).

Another relief at Naqsh-i-Rustam, depicting Ormizd II (302–09; PL. 400) engaged in a dueling scene, follows the layout in the Ardashir dueling episodes at Firuzabad. The last relief in chronological order at Naqsh-i-Rustam (unfortunately severely damaged), which shows a king full face seated on a throne, is attributed to the reign of Ormizd II's successor, Shāpur II, as is another one in Bishapur with a triumph motif. In the latter there is a return to the representation in two registers; on the left in both registers are the Persians, and on the right, the prisoners in chains. All figures are shown with their bodies in front view and their heads in profile. In the center Shāpur II is seen in full front view seated on the throne. The relief has generally been interpreted as a triumph over the Indians; Ghirshman (1962) maintains, however, that it represents the conquest of the Kushans (see KUSHAN ART). The figures in this relief, which is not very high, have a rather bloated appearance and their clothes are rendered stiffly and conventionally.

The reliefs that have survived from the end of the 4th century are located in Kurdistan, at the site called the Ṭāq-i-Bustān. Along the shores of an artificial lake, where fragments of sculptural work were found, reliefs were carved in caves of different sizes and in a rock face nearby. The latter relief shows the investiture of Ardashir II (PL. 401), who receives the ring from Ahura Mazda; both are portrayed trampling the body of a conquered enemy underfoot, while the god Mithras is shown standing behind the king. A few years after he had been called to the throne, Ardashir II was overthrown by a conspiracy of nobles and replaced by Shāpur III (383–88), who had himself portrayed with his father, Shāpur II, in the smaller one of the Ṭāq-i-Bustān caves.

The last known reliefs of the Sassanian dynasty are those in the large cave of the Ṭāq-i-Bustān (PL. 398), next to the cave with the Shāpur III reliefs. There is some disagreement as to their dates: the common ascription is to Khusrau II (590–628), but Erdmann (1937) suggests they be ascribed to Firūz II (459–84); however, judging by the type of crown, the first ascription would seem more correct.

The front of the cave, which is practically a liwan, is treated architecturally and is evidently based on the Roman triumphal arch, although the Western elements in it exist side by side with traditional Iranian ones. The rear wall of the cave is divided into two zones. The upper zone contains an investiture scene with Khusrau in the middle receiving the ribboned crown from Ahura Mazda; to the right of the king is the goddess Anāhitā, who also holds out a crown tied with long, heavy ribbons. These three rigidly frontal figures are placed on three small pedestals; the only movement is the awkward crook of their arms. Beneath this lunette-shaped zone is an imposing high relief, almost in the round, of a man on horseback, generally considered to represent Khusrau II riding his horse, Shabdiz. The Monarch wears the heavy coat of mail of the Iranian knights, and his head is completely hidden by a helmet. The horse is caparisoned with heavy armor that covers its whole front.

The two large bas-reliefs on the side walls of the liwan, showing two royal hunting parties — one them in a *paradeisos* — are also interesting. The episodes are represented in typically Eastern fashion, with the figures superimposed, of various sizes, and spread over the entire area. Perspective is ignored, and the figure of the king not only towers, as usual, over all the others, but also appears several times, in keeping with the norms of continuous narrative representation. As Herzfeld (1928) has pointed out, and as the fragment of a fresco with hunting scenes at Susa would seem to substantiate, the reliefs must have been derived from pictorial models; if so, they give some idea of what Iranian painting was like, at least in terms of composition, at the beginning of the 7th century.

A stag hunt is depicted on the right wall of the cave, while a turbulent boar hunt is spread over the left one. The episodes in the latter unfold within a boggy tract of marshland scattered with pools and patches of reeds. The king and his retinue carry on the hunt from large boats, assisted by beaters riding on elephants and accompanied by numerous musicians, especially harp players. The careful execution and the particular attention to detail in rendering the animals, which are of a force and vigor that reflect the great Mesopotamian tradition of animal representations, are remarkable. The boar-hunt relief is the only one known in which landscape is suggested, probably because the cartoon was originally derived from a painting. Pictorial sources were also responsible for the interest in picturesque detail and the fondness for narrating and minutely describing scenes and characters, which virtually constitute the beauty of these large compositions that are virtually frescoes in stone.

Considering the entire complex of Sassanian rock sculptures, a certain stylistic rise and decline becomes apparent: from the flat forms of the early reliefs founded on the Parthian tradition, the art turned to the more sophisticated and — owing to Western influence — more rounded forms that appeared during the period of Shāpur I, culminating in the dramatic investiture scene of Bahrām I at Bishapur, then retrogressed to uninspired and trite forms under Narsah, and finally returned to the absolutely nonclassical style evident in the reliefs of Khusrau II.

From the outset, one of the most striking characteristics of Sassanian relief work was the stylistic convention of showing figures in profile or, rather, partial profile, since the body was generally shown in front view and only the head was in profile. This does not represent a return to Achaemenid tradition, as has sometimes been claimed, but rather the persistence, or perhaps merely the continuation, of the Greco-Oriental style that had emerged about the 1st century of our era; a typical example of that style may be found in the reliefs on the tomb of Antiochos I Commagene (69–34 B.C.). The profile view appears most natural in the scenes of action, but it was also adopted for ceremonial scenes. In addition to the profile view, there was a marked interest in three-quarter and in front views. The latter, probably of Parthian origin, appears in the scenes showing a monarch enthroned with the court paying homage. After the 4th century, the tendency toward this frontal view grew increasingly popular, becoming the prescribed practice in the motif of the "*divina maiestas*": Shāpur II is portrayed in this way in his two known reliefs and Khusrau II in his investiture scene at the Ṭāq-i-Bustān.

The stylistic convention of showing the head in three-quarter profile, almost full face, and the body frontally, as in the investiture scene of Ardashir II (PL. 401) and in the relief of Shāpur III at the Ṭāq-i-Bustān, is certainly to be attributed to Hellenistic influences, probably introduced through contacts with eastern Iran.

Thus, even though Sassanian rock sculpture originated in typically Eastern themes and remained Eastern in spirit and subject matter, in some of its modes of expression and some of its basic stylistic conventions, it may be considered, as Will (1962) suggests, one of the "non-Mediterranean descendants of Greek art" that Schlumberger (1960) mapped out.

The stone busts at Paikuli, which are really only symbolic portraits, may be briefly mentioned here as well as the huge statue of Shāpur I at Bishapur, with its full-bodied and vigorous forms and the characteristic stylization of the clinging garments. A small stone head, of particularly massive structure (Berlin, Staat. Mus.), is perhaps to be ascribed to Narsah.

Figural sculpture in stucco was employed primarily as decoration for interiors. This decoration was richly colored and constituted an art form halfway between painting and relief. Good examples of such sculpture are the panels with boar-hunting scenes from Shahar Turkhan, near Rhages (anc. Rayy), now in Philadelphia (Mus. of Art), which probably date from the time of Khusrau II. Several other panels deserve mention; for instance, those from Damghan: one, showing a stag drinking at a spring, also in the Philadelphia museum, and others in Teheran (Archaeol. Mus.); several with animals, from Um Za'atir, near Ctesiphon, now in Berlin (Staat. Mus.); and the fine horse's head (XIII, PL. 272) and the figure of a horse, probably originally with rider, from Nizamabad, also in Berlin (Staat. Mus.). Several male heads, one of them attributed to Kavādh I, and now in Chicago (Art Inst.), are of remarkable vigor.

PAINTING AND MOSAICS. Unfortunately, almost nothing is known about Sassanian painting. Miniatures were apparently very highly regarded, chiefly owing to Mani (216/17–77), who was a painter himself and who considered them particularly important for the propagation of his religious doctrines (see MANICHAEAN ART). The contents of one of his illuminated manuscripts are known indirectly through the confutation of his theories by St. Ephraem Syrus (4th cent.). Some idea of Manichaean painting can nevertheless be gained from the Central Asian paintings that were discovered about the beginning of the 20th century. Ancient sources reveal, moreover, that an album of miniatures existed in which all the Sassanian kings were portrayed; al-Mas'ūdī had seen it as late as the 10th century and Ḥamza al-Iṣfahānī used it as a reference.

Wall painting seems to have been particularly popular among the Sassanians, especially from the 4th century on. Evidence of its existence at the time of Shāpur II is provided by Ammianus Marcellinus (4th cent.), who mentions (*Rerum gestarum libri qui supersunt*, XXIV, 6, 3) the favorite subjects of Sassanian wall painting: hunting and battle scenes like those he had seen in the halls of a royal palace near Seleucia. Nothing has survived except scant archaeological evidence, which is still little known. The fragment of a large fresco with a hunting scene at Susa may be dated from the first half of the 4th century. It shows two men on horseback and a pack of wild boars and antelopes running at a "flying gallop," as in the great hunting scenes of the Ṭāq-i-Bustān; the figures are outlined in black, the colors are flat, without chiaroscuro, and there is no perspective rendering. A fresco at Dura-Europos, showing knights in combat, of which little more remains than the outlines, is perhaps earlier, dating from the reign of Shāpur I. This fresco

was composed of disconnected sections depicting individual battle scenes unrelated to one another except in their subject matter. Several fragments discovered at Ivan-i-Karkha and in very poor condition (*in situ*) are almost certainly to be attributed to the reign of Shāpur II; a few other fragments have come to light at El Ma'arid and Damghan during the excavations of Ctesiphon.

The Islamic period has provided some literary evidence for Sassanian painting, such as that offered by al-Ṭabarī (9th cent.), who mentions a large wall painting showing Bahrām V Gūr (420–40) in a hunting scene. Fire temples also seem to have been decorated with paintings, at least according to al-Mas'ūdī. Some idea of Iranian painting during the 7th century can be gained from a few remnants of wall paintings found in Afghanistan (q.v.), at Bamian, at Dukhtar-i-Noshirwan — an audience scene, unfortunately severely damaged — and at Fondukistan; these paintings were greatly influenced by Central Asian art (see INDO-IRANIAN ART; SOGDIANA).

With respect to mosaics, too, there is more literary than archaeological evidence (see MOSAICS). Following a Byzantine fashion, the upper parts of walls were covered with mosaics, at least in the 6th century, while the lower parts were decorated with marble or stucco. The throne room of Khusrau I was adorned with a large mosaic depicting the siege of Antioch by the Persians. The mosaic was probably executed by Antiochian workmen transported to Ctesiphon by Khusrau, like the mosaics that, according to al-Mas'ūdī, embellished the houses of the new city Khusrau built near Ctesiphon, named Beh-az Ankia-Khusrau ("the city of Khusrau more beautiful than Antioch").

The only extant remains of wall mosaics are the tesserae recovered at Ctesiphon; however, there are important remains of floor mosaics, which were uncovered at Bishapur at the beginning of World War II. They decorated the main floor area of the triple liwan next to the large cruciform room, and the court to the west of the same room (FIG. 706). They may be dated to the time of Shāpur I (3d cent.) and were probably executed by Antiochian artisans. Their technique and style are fundamentally Roman, as is their subject matter, the latter having much in common with North African and Antiochian art, from which the cartoons were most certainly derived. Decidedly Iranian in spirit, however, are the general decorative layout and the particular way in which the source models have been interpreted, combined with the introduction of a number of conventional figural devices, such as the draperies that fall in billowing folds to the floor.

Floor mosaics, as is well known, were common throughout the Greco-Roman world, and it was a general practice to place the main subject of the decoration in the center of the mosaic; in contrast, the decoration of the Bishapur mosaics was confined to a wide border around the edge, while the center was apparently inlaid with stone slabs, probably arranged in a geometric pattern imitating a large carpet. In the liwan, the mosaics were laid along the two longer sides, with the figures set into panels of various sizes. The larger panels contained standing or sitting women, dancers, musicians, and courtesans (X, PL. 177; now in Teheran, Archaeol. Mus.), while the smaller, oblong ones with which they alternated contained series of heads.

Most of the heavy, fleshy female figures are shown draped only in a light veil thrown over the left shoulder, but others are wearing long garments, with or without sleeves and usually completed by a veil thrown over the left shoulder, a costume similar to the dress of Roman women and apparently a privilege of the ladies of the court. The oblong panels are decorated with a series of heads facing almost entirely front and shown without necks, in keeping with an ancient Iranian tradition that the Parthians had transmitted to Greco-Roman art. Ghirshman (1956) has suggested that these figures may represent the members of the court who entertained the prince. This is a plausible interpretation, and to a certain extent it would explain why the figures are set around the room in an arrangement that seems to reflect a ceremonial order.

Of the mosaics in the court, only a few fragments have survived: in one of them part of a nude female figure may be made out, and another one shows a winged male genie wearing a tunic, a small cape, and the typical Phrygian cap. Other fragments would seem to indicate that the latter was balanced, in the Greek fashion, by another similar figure.

METALWORK. During the Sassanian period, metalwork flourished and enjoyed a vast popularity that was to extend beyond the limits of the empire. Silver was the most commonly used metal, but gold and bronze were also employed. Most of the objects that have survived were found in the U.S.S.R. The richest collection of them is preserved in The Hermitage in Leningrad (see GOLD- AND SILVERWORK; METALWORK).

The most popular shapes included the large round plate, the round or elongated lobed bowl, the oval pitcher with a wide trumpet-shaped foot, and the pear-shaped vase with a wide, flaring neck (PLS. 396, 402–04, 407; VI, PL. 256).

The decoration was executed in various ways: the objects were hammered or beaten, engraved, and also cast. A special technique was often used on silver vessels; small repoussé plaques were embossed or chased separately and then applied to the dish. The silver was often gilded and nielloed.

The subjects most often portrayed on silver dishes included royal hunts, investiture scenes, the king enthroned or banqueting, dancers, and scenes of a religious character. There is also a group of cups whose decoration consists of a small central medallion with a portrait bust of some high dignitary, sometimes framed by a halo of delicate rays. They were probably religious vessels. Motifs of both real and imaginary animals also frequently recur in the decoration.

The chronological and stylistic classification of Sassanian metal objects still presents numerous problems. The kings portrayed on many of them, it is true, wear their distinctive crowns, which, by comparison with the likenesses on coins, should make it possible to establish sufficiently accurate dates; nevertheless, the vagueness in the representation of the attributes has resulted in considerable discrepancy between the dates put forth by various authorities. Further complications are introduced by the fact that many of these objects were widely imitated in various periods, and often in workshops outside Iran. In fact, the imitations continued to be produced long after the downfall of the Sassanian dynasty, and several types seem to have been produced at least up to the 11th century.

No attempt has been made to correlate all the products that have been found scattered over so enormous an area. Scholars in the U.S.S.R. have proposed, with good reason, that all this material be reclassified, with a view to defining regional characteristics more clearly; they have suggested that the term "Sassanian" be limited to those products which originated in Persia. These authorities are now ascribing the many pieces found in the U.S.S.R. to those artistic centers which new research has identified more specifically, such as Khwarizm, Sogdiana (qq.v.), and Caucasia.

By analyzing the group of bowls with hunting scenes and using the types of crowns as his basis, Erdmann (1936) has attempted to establish an absolute chronology and to trace a constant stylistic evolution in Sassanian toreutics. According to his findings, decoration in high relief was characteristic of the works produced up to the middle of the 5th century; after that date, during the 6th and 7th centuries, the relief became gradually lower and flatter, to be ultimately replaced by engraved designs set in wide, deeply grooved borders.

Nevertheless, the hypothesis of a consistent stylistic development cannot be accepted without reservation; on the contrary, it seems that from the very beginning, and certainly as early as the 4th century, there was a variety of styles. This becomes clear when approximately contemporaneous works are compared, for example, several of the shallow silver dishes or bowls generally attributed to the period of Shāpur II (309–79): there is one showing a lion hunt and another, a fragment, showing an ibex hunt (both, Leningrad, The Hermitage); one with a boar hunt (Washington, D.C., Freer Gall.); and a fourth with a stag hunt (London, Br. Mus.; PL. 402). To these may be added a bowl, dating from the time of Shāpur III (or Shāpur I, according to Erdmann), on which the king is shown on foot,

killing a lion (The Hermitage). Common to them all is the technique of applied repoussé sections, but stylistically the reliefs differ considerably, even though in all five pieces the surface is conceived as a unified whole. Of particularly dramatic effect is the dish at The Hermitage showing the lion hunt, whereas the stag hunt in the British Museum is more decorative in concept. The four dishes attributed to Shāpur II are devoid of any reference to landscape, while on the one ascribed to Shāpur III there is a suggestion of landscape in the lower part of the rim, in the form of three stylized mountains, a symbolic motif that was to enjoy great popularity and become typically Sassanian. The representation of landscape appears in more developed form on a beautiful cup in Teheran (Archaeol. Mus.), which is generally dated from the 4th century but, according to Göbl (1962), should be ascribed to the reign of Ormizd I (271–73).

A person of high rank is shown hunting with a snare on a cast-silver dish from Krasnaya Polyana (Sukhumi, Abkhazia State Mus.), which archeologists in the U.S.S.R. have recently published as the product of a Caucasian workshop but which is unquestionably Sassanian; if it dates from the 3d century, as Fajans (1957) has suggested, it would be one of the oldest known examples, together with the silver bowl showing the figure of Narsah (293–302; Teheran, Foroughi Coll.).

A handsome plate representing a king on horseback chasing a herd of wild goats (PL. 407) is attributed to Fīrūz II (457–84/85). A valuable silver dish (Paris, Cabinet des Médailles), commonly attributed to Khusrau II (590–628) but ascribed by Erdmann to Fīrūz II, is decorated with an animated hunting scene, which Herzfeld (1928) compares to the pictorial style of the Ṭāq-i-Bustān reliefs of hunting scenes. Also to be noted on this plate is the rather uninspired representation of landscape.

A certain heaviness is apparent in the scene on another plate in The Hermitage, attributed, though not unanimously, to the reign of Khusrau II. The figure of the standing king shooting arrows at a herd of wild goats certainly belongs to the same stylistic tradition as the investiture scenes at Ṭāq-i-Bustān, and it varies considerably from the similar but unquestionably better-balanced scene representing Shāpur III killing the lion.

The Sassanian tradition was pursued by several workshops in the mountainous regions south of the Caspian Sea, where for a certain period a number of semi-independent kingdoms, which had not fallen to Islam, continued to exist.

Among the subjects that appeared on Sassanian silver, there were also scenes of a ceremonial nature, all of them, however, dating from the last period of the dynasty; also very late are several cups showing a king banqueting, and various plates with religious subjects, such as the plate depicting a ritual, perhaps in honor of Anāhitā (Paris, Bib. Nat.), and the one showing the moon chariot (III, PL. 490). The plate showing a fortress encircled by mounted soldiers (The Hermitage) has even been considered a Seljuk product (see SELJUK ART) dating from the middle of the 12th century; but it is unquestionably earlier, in any case not later then the 7th or 8th century.

Several table articles with figures of dancers and musicians show Greco-Byzantine influences. Particularly interesting are a few round, deep bowls recently discovered in a small tomb in Mazanderan and published by Ghirshman (1957), who dates them from sometime after the beginning of the 6th century. The cups are of cast silver, decorated with separate sections in very low relief, each section containing a female figure set in a frame of grapevines curved into an arch (PL. 408).

Many works of silver are decorated with various kinds of animals, but only a few of these objects may be considered as truly belonging to the Sassanian period. Among them are several plates decorated with birds set in medallions, or roundels, such as one in The Hermitage and another, from Mazanderan, in Teheran (VI, PL. 256). A cast-silver plate showing a wolf-like animal (PL. 408) is probably Sassanian, though many authorities believe it to be much later.

Oval, boat-shaped basins with repoussé decoration, most of them dating probably from the 6th or 7th century, are typical (Beirut, Kettaneh Coll.; Teheran, Foroughi Coll.; Basel, E.

Borowski Coll.), with dancing girls, birds, felines, imaginary animals, and other motifs. Two other examples are in cast silver: one, in Baltimore (Walters Art Gall.), portrays an enthroned king with dancers; the other, in Moscow (Historical Mus.), shows two facing peacocks on either side of an altar. Particularly interesting is the iconography of the two birds; their bodies consist of fish combined with human and animal heads, forming true grylli.

A large assortment of gilded silver pitchers with oval or pear-shaped bodies are late Sassanian, such as the famous one in Paris (Cabinet des Médailles), its body decorated with two Trees of Life alternated with two pairs of rampant crossed lions, their bodies in profile and their geometrically stylized heads facing out, a motif that was also typical of Greco-Bactrian works. A number of elegant vessels, their bodies decorated with two large roundels containing stags or senmurvs, also date from the 6th or 7th century. Of considerable interest are several bottles with high cylindrical necks and oval bodies embellished with the roundel motif, for example, the one in the Kettaneh Collection, dating from the 7th century. Several pear-shaped vases with low, wide necks and bodies adorned with designs copied from textiles have been similarly dated. Another large vase in The Hermitage is decorated with two large roundels, each containing an eagle with a fawn in its claws, a motif that appears frequently, as, for example, on a beautiful cup discovered at Ufa in Bashkiria and on a handsome gold vessel in the famous treasure found at Nagy-Szent-Miklós, Hungary (now Sânnicolaul Mare, Romania), the work of Turkish artists of the 8th or 9th century (Vienna, Kunsthist. Mus.).

No exact dates have been established for a series of silver repoussé sculptures of animals or parts of animals, such as the fine horse's head (Louvre) that was perhaps originally a part of a throne and is dated by some authorities to the 5th century; an askos in the shape of a horse (New York, D. Selikowitz Coll.); and a rhyton in the shape of a horse's head (Cincinnati, Art Mus.), which is remarkable for the exquisite realism of its style and is dated by Ghirshman to the 6th or 7th century.

Most of the bronzes that have been preserved are very late; however, the Sassanian style persisted long after the fall of the dynasty and is thus strikingly apparent in post-Sassanian (PL. 410) and proto-Islamic bronzes. Among the few that may be dated with certainty to the 5th–6th century is the magnificent oval pitcher in New York (Met. Mus.). The same elegance of form that distinguishes the silver and bronze vessels was also adopted for the objects made of gold, some excellent examples of which are preserved in The Hermitage (e.g., an elongated, multilobed cup and a lidded jar).

Only a few metal objects with cloisonné decoration (see ENAMELS) have come to light within the borders of the Iranian empire; nevertheless, it is possible to obtain a sufficiently clear impression of Sassanian cloisonné work from a number of objects of outstanding quality discovered in the surrounding areas and in Europe. Most of these works were probably produced by or for barbarian nomad populations but in workshops strongly influenced by Iran. One of the oldest known pieces, which may be dated from the 3d–5th century, is a square gold buckle ornamented with mounted hyacinths (Wiesbaden, Städt. Mus.). It was discovered in a Germanic tomb, together with a coin of the Roman emperor Valens (364–78); on its back, engraved in Pahlavi, is the Iranian name of its owner, one Ardashir. A multilobed gold buckle decorated with carnelians (Teheran, Coll. Gen. M. H. Firouz) would seem to be contemporaneous with it or slightly older. Another object, which may be dated to the 4th century, came from Susa: a rock crystal engraved and set in an oval frame, with S-shaped cavities that were originally filled with some kind of inlay (Louvre). Lastly, mention should be made of the beautiful gold cups from the treasure of Petrossa in Romania, with decorations in enamel, glass paste, and rock crystal.

GEMS AND GLYPTICS. An example of the Sassanian type of glyptics is the plate called the "Cup of Khusrau" (PL. 395). This work may also be considered cloisonné, for the plate is formed of a network of thin gold circlets, diminishing in size from the outside to the center; the circlets are inlaid with white and red glass disks that are decorated with carved rosettes, and the interstices are filled with green lozenges. This decoration forms a kind of halo around a large central medallion of rock crystal engraved with the figure of an enthroned Sassanian king: Khusrau II or Khusrau I, or even the latter's father, Kavādh I. Aside from the dishes mentioned above, there are only a few other objects employing rock crystal (see GEMS AND GLYPTICS) — always a highly valued material in the East — that may be said to date from the Sassanian period: a broad-brimmed dish decorated with a carved ring of palmettes (Venice, Treas. of S. Marco), and a goblet with stylized plant motifs in a private collection (Ghirshman, 1954, pl. 46a). Of much later date, perhaps already Islamic, though Sassanian in tradition, is a sardonyx vase preserved in the Palazzo Pitti in Florence.

Cameos are scarce. A famous piece is the sardonyx carved in three layers showing a duel on horseback between a Sassanian king and a Roman emperor, thought to be Shāpūr I capturing Valerian (Paris, Cabinet des Médailles). Another cameo, which was perhaps used as a seal, is engraved with a portrait of Kavādh I (PL. 525, no. 10). A sardonyx fragment (Paris, Cabinet des Médailles) probably represents Ardashir I taming a bull.

There is a rich collection of Sassanian seals (q.v.). They are of two types: flat ones, to be mounted on rings, and rounded ones with a hole through them, to be worn around the neck. The variety of semiprecious stones used for them is immense. The seals offer a wide iconographic range of royal portraits and those of dignitaries, which are often accompanied by an inscription giving title or name (PL. 525, no. 12); less common are female portraits and the images or symbols of divinities. But investiture scenes, triumphs, hunts (PL. 525, no. 13), banquets, zoomachies, imaginary animals, and grylli were also frequently represented, and seals bearing monograms were characteristic and probably endowed with magical power.

COINS. Sassanian coins, which were first systematically catalogued by Paruck (1924) and which are now being methodically reclassified by Göbl (1954), are decidedly Eastern in type, that is, free from all Greek influence (see COINS AND MEDALS).

The obverse of the most common variety of coins shows the bust of the king in profile; he wears a crown and is richly attired (III, PL. 399); full-face portraits are rare. On one coin (Paris, Cabinet des Médailles) — remarkable in that the king alone was usually portrayed on coins — Bahrām (Varahran) II's profile is shown beside that of his wife, with the small profile of their son facing them. The obverse of the coins minted by Jāmāsp (496–99) is unique, with a stylized investiture scene, in which the king's head in profile is accompanied by the small figure of a divinity handing him the crown. The reverse of most coins shows a fire altar, usually with an acolyte on either side (III, PL. 399, no. 12; XIV, PL. 477). Beginning with Ormizd II (302–09), the bust of a divinity, which in some instances may be identified as Ahura Mazda, appears amid the flames. As early as Bahrām II (276–93), or perhaps even earlier, the reverse also occasionally depicted an investiture, but sometimes the king alone is shown holding the crown in his hand. On the reverse of coins minted by Khusrau II (590–628) there is the bust in full face of a divinity crowned in flames (III, PL. 399, no. 4).

The coins are very thin silver or gold disks and characteristically have a border encircling the figures on both the obverse and reverse sides, which, starting with Shāpur III (383–88), grew progressively wider and was partially occupied by the upper part of the crown and by various symbols. The crowns, whose symbolic and religious connotations are always clear, are especially important because, varying as they do from king to king, they constitute an extremely useful guide — and often the only one — to the chronology of Sassanian art. The coinage, on the whole, affords a rather monotonous artistic expression; nevertheless, some variations can be observed. With Ardashir I (ca. 224–41) it reflected the influence of the Parthian coins of Mithradates II (ca. 124–87 B.C.), but the somewhat abstract style was mingled with a more natural one, owing perhaps to the influence of Western engravers. The naturalistic style continued under Ardashir's successor, Shāpur I, and, with an occasional lapse into stiffer and more conventional forms, became characteristic of most of the 4th century, during which coinmaking as an art remained on a rather high level. Then, during the 5th and 6th centuries and until the end of the dynasty, the designs on coins became increasingly linear and abstract. There were coinages of vigorous beauty, such as several of Khusrau II; but on the whole, the figures grew increasingly rigid and coarse.

CERAMICS AND GLASS. Very little is known about Sassanian ceramics, and they are often confused with Parthian products (see CERAMICS). They were certainly not of such outstanding quality as to bear comparison with the great Iranian tradition of earthenware (see ASIATIC PROTOHISTORY; IRANIAN PRE-SASSANIAN ART CULTURES). The forms are heavy and coarse, showing only faint traces of classical influence. Large globular jars and flasks were extremely popular, but somewhat elongated forms also existed. The decoration was often in relief — molded or applied in barbotine — or was stamped or incised. A heavy, thick glaze of turquoise or blue was characteristic (III, PL. 139).

The art of glassmaking (see GLASS) was probably introduced into Iran from the Mediterranean area, where the famous workshops of Alexandria and Syria were active. Iran in turn then transmitted it to the Far East. There are still few objects that can be attributed with certainty to Sassanian culture; among them are several cups of molded glass trimmed with small disks, probably of Syrian inspiration; most of them were found at Gilan, south of the Caspian Sea, but one fragment of such a cup was uncovered at Ctesiphon by the German and American expeditions (EAA, s.v. Ctesifonte, II, 1959). A famous piece of glassware of the same kind is preserved in the Shōsōin of the Tōdaiji Temple in Nara, Japan. Several other examples were found in Japan as burial accessories, evidently objects that had been imported through Chinese or Korean merchants. A cup in Berlin (Staat. Mus.), with separately molded and applied decoration in the form of disks decorated with hippogriffs, and a vase with plain disks in Teheran (Foroughi Coll.; PL. 409) date from the 6th–7th century. Similar in style is a beautiful blue-glass goblet with circles in relief in the Shōsōin in Nara. This treasury also contains a handsome blown-glass piece, similar in form to such pear-shaped metal jars as the one excavated at Susa, now preserved in Teheran (Archaeol. Mus.). An elegant oval dish of yellow glass, with handles and spiral decoration in relief, is also in the Foroughi Collection (PL. 409).

TEXTILES. Sassanian textiles were well known throughout Eurasia and were largely responsible for carrying most of the decorative motifs of Sassanian art beyond the borders of Iran (see TEXTILES, EMBROIDERY, AND LACE).

The importation of both raw and finished silk from China over the famous Central Asian caravan route was one of the most important factors in the trade that represented one of Iran's great sources of wealth; it was also the principal reason for the unceasing conflict between Persia and the Roman Empire. When, during the 3d and 4th centuries, the importation of finished textile goods from China had ceased or greatly diminished — even though China still supplied raw silk, on which it held a monopoly — a flourishing textile industry grew up in Persia. Strongly encouraged by Shāpur I, this industry generally employed Syrian workers, and especially Antiochian craftsmen, who by that time had attained a high degree of proficiency.

The most important textile centers were Susa, Shushtar, and Jundi Shapur in Khuzistan, but there were others in Gilan, in Khorasan, in Transoxiana, and along the Silk Route itself that followed Iranian models, although with some originality.

Few Sassanian textiles are known today and none of them have been found within Iranian territories. Most of the examples in museums — generally small fragments — come from the treasuries of various European abbeys and cathedrals, where they had been brought by pilgrims as precious protective wrappings for the relics collected in the sanctuaries of the East. Several fragments were discovered during excavations in Central Asia; a rather large piece bearing an inscription in Sogdianian, now in Huy, Belgium (Collegiate Church of Notre-Dame), has been identified as stemming from Transoxiana. Several fragments of outstanding quality are also preserved in various Japanese temples.

The most common and characteristic pattern consists of a series of medallions, or roundels, adjoined or separate, with frames of leaves or "pearls"; enclosed in the roundels are the figures of animals — either a single animal or, often, two facing a Tree of Life — or symbolic hunting scenes of heraldic design, presumably depicting the exploits of Bahrām V Gūr, or large flowers and palmettes. Another common pattern consists of figures set in a network or grid, but it is not unusual to find the same figures without the separating framework. Both patterns are of ancient tradition.

Various attempts have been made to attribute the extant fragments of Sassanian fabrics to the textile centers mentioned in literary sources, but these attributions are to be accepted with caution.

The typical medallion pattern appears in two fragments of silk, one in Paris (PL. 406) and the other in London (Vict. and Alb.); they are in two shades of green with large senmurvs set in "pearled" roundels. There are two other beautiful examples, similarly decorated with animals in green, white, red, and purple on a dark-blue background; one of them is in Paris (Mus. des Arts Décoratifs), and the other in Florence (Mus. Naz.). This pattern is exactly the same as the one which appears on the robes of Khusrau in the boar-hunting scene at the Ṭāq-i-Bustān. A fragment in Berlin (Staat. Mus.), made of wool, has birds with fluttering ribbons around their necks. Two pieces of silk with a brightly colored bird motif are in the Vatican; one of them is in white, green, and black, and the other in white, red, and blue (PL. 405). Two other fragments are of a particularly individual design (New Delhi, Nat. Mus.): one, discovered and published by A. Stein (Innermost Asia, Oxford, 1928), shows a boar's head framed by the pearl motif in black on a background of brownish-yellow and has much in common with paintings found in Afghanistan (Bamian, Group D) and Central Asia (such as Kizil and Turfan; see ASIA, CENTRAL); the other one, from Astana, has the typical Central Asian motif of a palmette growing out of a Tree of Life.

The rectangular grid pattern is very well exemplified by two fragments in which ducks and roosters alternate with small fan-shaped palmettes (Berlin, Staat. Mus.); one fragment (Leningrad, The Hermitage) has large crouching goats, and another (Berlin, Staat. Mus.), pink, purplish-red, and white flowers set within the grid pattern.

Also very common is a pattern in which the figures are set in rows without any network divisions, as in the famous fabric in which bejeweled blue rams are set against a white background (Lyons, Mus. Historique des Tissus). The pattern of animals without geometric network, which reappeared in the Ṭāq-i-Bustān reliefs, dates back to an ancient tradition, as is attested by an Achaemenid gold plaque in the Oxus Treasure (Br. Mus.), which shows a person wearing trousers decorated with small geese. A pattern of heart-shaped leaves, characteristic of the late Sassanian period, is found on a piece of silk with white, blue, and red designs on a red background (Louvre).

Of the magnificent, heavily embroidered royal fabrics, studded with pearls and precious stones, nothing has survived; they are known only through various literary references and the investiture scene at the Ṭāq-i-Bustān, in which Khusrau II is dressed in an imperial cloak that resembles the one described in legend, woven in gold thread and studded with pearls and rubies (PL. 398). The robes shown on a statue from Fondukistan, the so-called "Buddha adorned" (VIII, PL. 11), were undoubtedly made of a material of this kind. Slightly more is known about tapestry, from a late-Sassanian fragment in red, pink, white, and blue showing a rooster set in a roundel (The Hermitage), and from another one in which a white ibex is shown against a red background, possibly dating from the 6th or 7th century (New Haven, Yale Univ. Art. Gall.).

Generally speaking, Sassanian textiles, although influenced by earlier prototypes, possessed an unmistakable quality of their own and were refined and elegant; they were immensely popular and widely imitated.

The colors, which were rather restrained and limited in range at the beginning, were gradually enriched, owing, it would seem, to Syrian influences.

Nothing is known about Sassanian carpets except for some references in literary sources and a few representations on the Ṭāq-i-Bustān reliefs and in Central Asian paintings, which show the patterns to be essentially the same as those used for other fabrics.

The carpets that adorned the royal palaces were often decorated with subjects suited to the various events occurring at court and in the life of the king and had symbolic significance. The carpet representing the four seasons, which decorated Khusrau II's throne room, was famous; it was woven of gold and silver silk threads and bordered with emeralds and with flowers embroidered in many-colored precious stones. A large carpet mentioned by Baalamī, representing springtime in flower, covered the floor of another hall in the palace, where the king banqueted in winter (see TAPESTRY AND CARPETS).

THE DIFFUSION OF SASSANIAN ART. The tendency to diffuse, ever a characteristic of Iranian cultures, took on vast proportions during the Sassanian period, whose art was marked by a vitality that was to go far beyond the territorial and chronological limits within which it had developed. Sassanian art was carried over an immense territory stretching from the Far East to the shores of the Atlantic and played a foremost role in the formation of both European and Asiatic medieval art. A vast assortment of motifs and iconographic types, of architectural plans, and of esthetic concepts was to radiate outward from Iran, either through direct contact or through the channels of commerce and trade.

Byzantine art drew lavishly from it. Countless Byzantine reliefs were inspired by Sassanian models, such as the zoomachies in Istanbul (Archaeol. Mus.) and Athens (II, PL. 436), the relief with lions facing a Tree of Life in Heraklion (Archaeol. Mus.), and the mosaics with senmurvs in the Church of Panagia Angeloktistos on the island of Cyprus. Certain aspects of Byzantine architecture would be inexplicable without reference to Iranian influences.

Nomad tribes were dazzled by the quality and richness of Sassanian products; Sassanian models and designs appeared as far away as central and western Europe, where goldsmiths and silversmiths continued to copy them, as is abundantly evidenced by the works of the Vandals, the Goths, the Lombards, and the Merovingians. Turkish nomads carried with them and, under Iranian influence, executed exquisite articles in gold and silver, which were found in large quantities in the various treasures discovered in the Balkans. The rock reliefs at Madara in Bulgaria (XIII, PL. 45) are in the great Iranian tradition.

Sassanian architectural prototypes also were followed in the West, not only in Byzantium and in the palace at Aboba (mod. Pliska) in Bulgaria — which is copied from the palaces at Firuzabad and Sarvistan — but even as far west as France: the late-8th-century oratory built by Bishop Theodulf, at Germigny-des-Prés near Orléans, was partly derived from Sassanian models and is decorated with mosaics representing a Tree of Life closely resembling the ones shown at the entrance of the large cave of the Ṭāq-i-Bustān, and the 10th–11th-century Church of St-Philibert at Tournus recalls the imperial palace at Ivan-i-Karkha.

The bas-reliefs on many of the barbarian sarcophagi in France and Spain were inspired by Sassanian textile motifs. Sassanian-type stuccoes adorned the 7th-century tomb of Abbess Agilberta in the crypt of the Abbey of Jouarre, and some of the pre-Romanesque and Romanesque sculpture in France and Italy may have been inspired by Sassanian art. In the Campania of Italy, the beautiful marble screens in the oratory of S. Aspreno in Naples and the famous bas-relief screens and panels from the Cathedral of Sorrento (Sorrento, Mus. Correale di Terranova) have been claimed to be of Sassanian inspiration.

The patterns of the marble pavement of the Baptistery in Florence appear to have been derived from Sassanian textiles.

The great influence Sassanian models exerted on the manufacture of Egyptian and Syrian textiles was convincingly illustrated by Pfister (1932) and need only be mentioned here.

The diffusion of Iranian religious and esthetic thought into India, Afghanistan, and Central Asia was of enormous importance and gave rise to an art of a distinct Iranian cast that flourished in the rich oases of Central Asia; it is sufficient to mention here the centers of Kucha, Tumshuk, and Turfan, which transmitted this art to China. It enjoyed immense favor during the T'ang dynasty, which was responsible for its introduction into Korea and Japan.

Islam (q.v.), however, was the true heir to Sassanian art, whose concepts it was to assimilate, at the same time instilling fresh life and renewed vigor into the ancient esthetic and iconographic formulas. Owing to a favorable combination of historical and environmental circumstances, the art of Iranian Islam was to acquire a distinct and unmistakable quality of its own, and through it, Sassanian art was to continue to cast its spell over the peoples and cultures with which Islam maintained or reestablished contact in the course of its long history.

BIBLIOG. *General works*: U. Monneret de Villard, Il problema dell'arte sāsānide, Art S., V, 1927, pp. 57–63; E. Herzfeld, ed., Iranische Denkmäler, I, 4 vols., Berlin, 1932–33; P. Ackerman, Some Indo-Iranian Motifs in Sasanian Art, Indian Art and Letters, XI, 1937, pp. 35–42; K. Erdmann, Zur Chronologie der sasanidischen Kunst, Forsch. und Fortschritte, 1937, pp. 169–70; J. Sauvaget, Remarques sur l'art sassanide, Rev. des ét. islamiques, XIV, 1938, pp. 113–31; E. Herzfeld, Iran in the Ancient East, London, New York, 1941; A. Christensen, L'Iran sous les Sassanides, 2d ed., Copenhagen, Paris, 1944; K. Erdmann, Neue Forschungen zur Entwicklung der sasanidischen Krone, Forsch. und Fortschritte, XXIV, 1948, pp. 253–56; K. Erdmann, Lückenforschung im iranischen Kunstkreis, Kunst des Orients, I, 1950, pp. 20–36; K. Erdmann, Die universalgeschichtliche Stellung der sasanidischen Kunst, Saeculum, I, 1950, pp. 508–34, K. Erdmann, Die Entwicklung der sasanidischen Krone, Ars Islamica, XV–XVI, 1951, pp. 87–121; A. Jäger, Das Bild der sasanidischen Königskrone, Berliner numismatische Z., V, 1952, pp. 252–54; K. Erdmann, Die Kunst Irans zur Zeit der Sasaniden, Berlin, 1953; R. Ghirshman, Iran: From the Earliest Times to the Islamic Conquest, Harmondsworth, 1954; U. Monneret de Villard, L'arte iranica, Verona, 1954; M. Bussagli, Arte iranica, Rome, 1955 (cat.); H. H. von der Osten, Die Welt der Perser, Stuttgart, 1956; L. Vanden Berghe, Archéologie de l'Iran ancien, Leiden, 1959; A. Mongait, Archaeology in the U.S.S.R. (trans. D. Skvirsky), Moscow, 1959; R. Ghirshman, Sept mille ans d'art en Iran, Paris, 1961 (cat.); R. Ghirshman, Parthians and Sassanians, London, 1962; A. Godard, L'art de l'Iran, Paris, 1962.

Architecture: E. Herzfeld, Paikuli, 2 vols., Berlin, 1924; F. Wachtsmuth, Der Raum, I: Raumschöpfungen in der Kunst Vorderasiens, Marburg, 1929; O. Reuther, ed., Die Ausgrabungen der deutschen Ktesiphon Expedition im Winter 1928/29, Berlin, 1930; E. Kühnel, Die Ausgrabungen der zweiten Ktesiphon Expedition 1931/32, Berlin, 1933; A. U. Pope, A Sasanian Garden Palace, AB, XV, 1933, pp. 75–85; J. H. Schmidt, L'expédition de Ctésiphon en 1931–1932, Syria, XV, 1934, pp. 1–23; G. Salles and R. Ghirshman, Fouilles de Chapour, RAA, X, 1936, pp. 117–29; R. Ghirshman, Fouilles de Chapour: Deuxième campagne, 1936/37, RAA, XII, 1938, pp. 12–19; A. Godard, Les monuments du feu, Āthār-e Irān, III, 1938, pp. 7–79; O. Reuther, Sasanian Architecture, SPA, I, pp. 579–84; L. C. Watelin, The Sasanian Building near Kish, SPA, I, pp. 584–92; U. Monneret de Villard, Le chiese della Mesopotamia, Rome, 1940; K. Erdmann, Das iranische Feuerheiligtum, Leipzig, 1941; K. Erdmann, Feuerheiligtum-Kreuzkuppelkirche, Spätantike und Byzanz, I, 1941, pp. 53–70; R. Ghirshman, Cinq campagnes de fouilles de Suse (1946–1951), Rev. d'assyriologie, XLVI, 1952, pp. 1–18; H. Lacoste, L'art de Ctésiphon, Sumer, X, 1954, pp. 3–22; R. Ghirshman, Bîchâpour, II: Les mosaïques sassanides, Paris, 1956; G. A. Pugachenkova, Puti razvitiia arkhitektury iuzhnogo Turkmenistana pory rabovladeniia i feodalizma (Lines of Development of Southern Turkmenistan Architecture in the Era of Slavery and Feudalism), Moscow, 1958; L. Vanden Berghe, Récentes découvertes de monuments sassanides dans le Fars, Iranica antiqua, I, 1961, pp. 163–98.

Sculpture: F. Sarre and E. Herzfeld, Iranische Felsreliefs, Berlin, 1910; E. Herzfeld, Am Tor von Asien, Berlin, 1920; E. Herzfeld, La sculpture rupestre de la Perse sassanide, RAA, V, 1928, pp. 129–42; N. C. Debevoise, A Portrait of Kobad I, B. Art Inst. of Chicago, XXIV, 1930, p. 10; M. S. Dimand, Sasanian Wall Decoration in Stucco, BMMA, XXVI, 1931, pp. 193–95; K. Erdmann, Das Datum des Ṭak-i Bustān, Ars Islamica, IV, 1937, pp. 79–97; H. G. Farmer, Instruments of Music on the Ṭāq-i Bustān Bas-reliefs, JRAS, 1938, pp. 397–412; E. Herzfeld, Khusrau Parwēz und der Ṭaq-i Vostan, Archaeol. Mitt. aus Iran, IX, 1938, pp. 91–158; J. Baltrusaitis, Sasanian Stucco, A: Ornamental, SPA, I, pp. 601–30; A. U. Pope, Sasanian Stucco, B: Figural, SPA, I, pp. 631–45; F. Sarre, Sasanian Stone Sculpture, SPA, I, pp. 593–600; K. Erdmann, Zur Deutung der iranischen Felsreliefs, Forsch. und Fortschritte, XVIII, 1942, pp. 209–11; K. Erdmann, Sasanidische Felsreliefs, Römische Historienreliefs, Antike und Abendland, III, 1948, pp. 75–87; K. Erdmann, Die sasanidischen Felsreliefs von Barm-i Dilak, ZMG, XCIX, 1949, pp. 50–57; R. Ghirshman, Notes iraniennes, III:

A propos des bas-reliefs rupestres sassanides, AAs, XIII, 1950, pp. 86–98; H. Lenzen, Zur relativen Chronologie der sasanidischen Stuckarbeiten, AAnz, 1952, cols., 188–221; B. C. Macdermot, Roman Emperors in the Sasanian Reliefs, JRS, XLIV, 1954, pp. 76–78; D. Schlumberger, Les descendants non-méditerranéens de l'art grec, Syria, XXXVII, 1960, pp. 131–66, 253–319; E. Will, L'art sassanide et ses prédécesseurs, Syria, XXXIX, 1962, pp. 45–63.

Painting and mosaic: U. Monneret de Villard, Arte manichea, Rend. Ist. lombardo di sc. e lettere, LVI, 1923, pp. 971–84; H. Herzfeld, Die Malereien von Samarra, Berlin, 1927; R. Ghirshman, Bîchâpour, II: Les mosaïques sassanides, Paris, 1956.

Metalwork: A. Odobesco, Le trésor de Pétrossa, 3 vols., Paris, 1889–1900; Y. I. Smirnov, Vostochnoe serebro (Eastern Silver), St. Petersburg, 1909; E. Herzfeld, Der Thron des Khosrō, JhbPreussKSamml, XLI, 1920, pp. 1–24, 103–47; O. M. Dalton, The Treasure of the Oxus, 2d ed., London, 1926; F. Sarre, Bronzeplastik in Vogelform, JhbPreussKSamml, LI, 1930, pp. 159–64; L. Bachhofer, Sasanidische Jadgschalen, Pantheon, XII, 1933, pp. 62–66; K. Otto-Dorn, Das sasanidische Silbergeschirr und seine Sinnbilder, Vienna, 1933; M. S. Dimand, A Sasanian Silver Dish, BMMA, XXIX, 1934, pp. 74–77; I. A. Orbeli and K. V. Trever, Sasanidskii metali: khudozhestvennye predmety iz zolota, serebra i bronzy (Sasanian Metalwork: Objects in Gold, Silver and Bronze), Moscow, Leningrad, 1935; K. Erdmann, Die sasanidischen Jagdschalen, JhbPreussKSamml, LVII, 1936, pp. 193–232; K. V. Trever, Novye sasanidskie blyuda Ermitazha (New Sasanian Dishes of the Hermitage), Moscow, Leningrad, 1937; K. Erdmann, Eine unbekannte sasanidische Jahdschale, JhbPreussKSamml,LIX, 1938, pp. 209–17; P. Ackermann, Sasanian Jewelry, SPA, I, pp. 771–78; E. Margulies, Cloisonné Enamel, SPA, I, pp. 779–83; I. A. Orbeli, Sasanian and Early Islamic Metalwork, SPA, I, pp. 716–70; J. Sauvaget, Remarques sur l'argenterie sassanide, II: Argenterie sassanide, JA, CCXXXII, 1940–41, pp. 19–57; M. S. Dimand, A Review of Sasanian and Islamic Metalwork: A Survey of Persian Art, Ars Islamica, VIII, 1941, pp. 192–214; R. Ghirshman, Notes iraniennes, I: Un plat d'argent doré, AAs, X, 1947, pp. 89–99; A. P. Smirnov, Novyi sasanidskii zolotoi sosud uz Molotovskoi oblasti (A New Sassanide Gold Vessel from the Molotov Region), KS, XIV, 1947, pp. 40–48; O. N. Bader, A Sasanian Vessel from Kungur, Ars Islamica, XV–XVI, 1951, pp. 139–42; A. Alföldi, Etudes sur le trésor de Nagyszentmiklos, II: Le motif du rapt de Ganymède par l'aigle sur les vases en or 2 et 7 du trésor, CahA, VII, 1952, pp. 43–53; A. N. Melikhov, Serebriannoe blyudo iz Krasnoi Polyany (A Silver Dish from Krasnaya Polyana), KS, XLIII, 1952, pp. 44–79; R. Ghirshman, Notes iraniennes, V: Scènes de banquet sur l'argenterie sassanide, AAs, XVIII, 1955, pp. 4–19; A. Parrot, Acquisitions et inédits du Musée du Louvre, 3: Bronzes iraniens, Buste de roi sassanide, Syria, XXX, 1953, pp. 5–9; J. David-Weill, Têtes de chevaux sassanides, RArts, IV, 1954, pp. 157–64; R. Ghirshman, Notes iraniennes, VI: Une coupe sassanide à scène de chasse, AAs, XVIII, 1955, pp. 4–19; A. Parrot, Bronze royal sassanide, Syria, XXXII, 1955, pp. 308–09; S. Fajans, Recent Russian Literature on Newly Found Middle Eastern Metal Vessels, Ars Orientalis, II, 1957, pp. 55–76; R. Ghirshman, Argenterie d'un seigneur sassanide, Ars Orientalis, II, 1957, pp. 77–82; C. Amiranachvili, Une coupe en argent du début de l'époque sassanide provenant des fouilles de Armasiskhevi (Georgie), RSO, XXXV, 1959, pp. 149–62; M. S. Dimand, A Group of Sasanian Silver Bowls, Aus der Welt der islamischen Kunst: Festschrift Ernst Kühnel, Berlin, 1959, pp. 9–14; W. B. Henning, A Sassanian Silver Bowl from Georgia, BSOAS, XXIV, 1961, pp. 253–56.

Seals: P. Casanova, Sceaux sassanides, Rev. d'assyriologie, XXII, 1925, pp. 135–40; C. Wilkinson, Notes on the Sasanian Seals Found at Kasr-i Abu Naṣr, BMMA, XXXI, 1936, pp. 180–82; P. Ackerman, Sasanian Seals, SPA, I, pp. 784–815; R. Cotteviellle-Giraudet, Coupes et camées sassanides du Cabinet de France, RAA, XII, 1938, pp. 52–64.

Numismatics: F. D. J. Paruck, Sasanian Coins, Bombay, 1924; E. Herzfeld, Kushano-Sasanian Coins (Mem. Archaeol. Survey of India, XXXVIII), Delhi, 1930; J. de Morgan, Numismatique de la Perse antique, III: Dynastie sassanide, Paris, 1933, pp. 543–738; J. Walker, Catalogue of Arab-Sassanian Coins, London, 1941; R. Göbl, Sasanidischen Münzstudien, Mitt. ö. numismatischen Gesellschaft, VII, 1951–52, pp. 112–14, 133–35, 138–40; R. Göbl, Stand und Aufgaben der sassanidischen Numismatik, La nouvelle Clio, IV, 1952, pp. 360–68; R. Göbl, Aufbau der Münzprägung, in F. Altheim, Ein asiatischer Staat, I, Wiesbaden, 1954, pp. 51–128; R. Göbl, Die Mün- zen der Sasaniden im Königlichen Münzkabinett, The Hague, 1962.

Ceramics and glass: M. Pézard, La céramique archaïque de l'Islam et ses origines, Paris, 1920; O. H. W. Puttrich-Reignard, Die Glasfunde von Ktesiphon, Kiel, 1934; R. Ettinghausen, Sasanian Pottery, SPA, I, pp. 664–80; S. Fukai, On Two Cut Glasses Treasured Up in the Shôsôin Repository, Kokka, 812, 1959, pp. 1, 3–12 (in Jap., Eng. summary).

Textiles: R. Pfister, Gobelins sassanides du Musée de Lyon, RAA, VI, 1929–30, pp. 1–23; R. Pfister, Les premières soies sassanides, Etudes d'orientalisme... R. Linossier, II, Paris, 1932 pp. 461–79; R. Pfister, Le rayonnement de l'art textile sassanide, L'art vivant, VIII, 1932, pp. 83–84; L. Ashton, A New Group of Sasanian Textiles, BM, LXVI, 1935, pp. 26–30; O. von Falke, Kunstgeschichte der Seidenweberei, 3d ed., Berlin, 1936; C. J. Lamm, Cotton in Mediaeval Textiles of the Near East, Paris, 1937; P. Ackerman, Textiles through the Sasanian Period (with a Catalogue of Sasanian Silks), SPA, I, pp. 691–715; R. Pfister, Coqs sassanides, RAA, XII, 1938, pp. 40–47; G. Wiet, Soieries persanes, Mém. Inst. d'Egypte, LII, 1948, pp. 1–251; D. G. Shepherd and W. B. Henning, Zandanījī Identified, Aus der Welt der islamischen Kunst: Festschrift Ernst Kühnel, Berlin, 1959, pp. 15–40.

Influence: U. Monneret de Villard, Le transenne di Sant'Aspreno e le stoffe alessandrine, Aegyptus, IV, 1923, pp. 64–71; T. W. Arnold, Survivals of Sasanian and Manichaean Art in Persian Painting, Oxford, 1924; A. von Le Coq, Bilderatlas zur Kunst und Kulturgeschichte Mittelasiens, Berlin, 1925; U. Monneret de Villard, Amboni copti e amboni campani, Aegyptus, VIII, 1927, pp. 258–62; E. Mâle, L'art religieux du XIIᵉ siècle en France, 4th ed., Paris, 1931; M. T. Tozzi, Sculture medievali dell'Antico Duomo di Sorrento, Rome, 1931; Y. Harada, The Interchange of Eastern and Western Cultures as Evidenced in the Shôsôin Treasures, Mem. Research Dept. of the Toyo Bunko, XI, 1939, pp. 55–78; W. F. Volbach, Oriental Influence in the Animal Sculpture in Campania, AB, XXIV, 1942, pp. 172–80; M. Bussagli, L'influsso classico ed iranico nell'arte dell'Asia Centrale, RIASA, N.S., II, 1952, pp. 171–262; D. Talbot Rice, Persia and Byzantium, in A. J. Arberry, ed., The Legacy of Persia, Oxford, 1953, pp. 39–59; W. R. Valentiner, The Relief from Aversa, AQ, XVI, 1953, pp. 181–92; M. N. D'iakonov, Rospisi Piandzhikenta i zhivopis' Srednei Azii (The Wall Paintings of Piandjikent and Central Asian Painting), in Zhivopis' drevnego Piandzhikenta (Painting of Ancient Piandjikent), Moscow, 1954; J. Ebersolt, Orient et Occident: Recherches sur les influences byzantines et orientales en France avant et pendant les Croisades, 2d ed., Paris, 1954; B. Gyllensvärd, T'ang Gold and Silver, BMFEA, XXIX, 1957, pp. 1–230. See also the bibliogs. for IRAN; IRANIAN PRE-SASSANIAN ART CULTURES.

Umberto SCERRATO

Illustrations: PLS. 395–410; 8 figs. in text.

SASSETTA.

Stefano di Giovanni (b. Siena?, 1392?; d. 1450), the greatest painter of the Quattrocento Sienese school, is usually known as Sassetta, a name for which there is no contemporaneous evidence (he always signed his works Stefano di Giovanni) but which seems to have been established in the 18th century. Although his father was from Cortona, Sassetta may have been born in Siena, possibly in 1392 (on the basis of the interpretation of a document) but more likely toward the very end of the century or even after 1400. Nothing is known of his activity until 1426, the date of his first documented work, a polyptych for the Arte della Lana guild at Siena, probably painted between 1423 and 1426, which survives only in fragments, most of which are in the Pinacoteca Nazionale of Siena.

One of Sassetta's masterpieces, the *Madonna della Neve* altarpiece (Florence, Coll. Contini Bonacossi), at one time in the Cathedral of Siena, dates from 1430–32; the fragments of a crucifix for the Church of S. Martino (Siena, Coll. Chigi-Saracini) from 1433; and the polyptych for the Church of S. Francesco at Cortona (Mus. Diocesano) from between 1433 and 1437. In 1437 he also began his most ambitious and complex work, the two-sided altarpiece for the high altar of the Church of S. Francesco at Sansepolcro, which he contracted to paint in that year and delivered in 1444. The main panel of the front of the altarpiece, representing the Madonna enthroned between St. Anthony of Padua and John the Evangelist, is in the Louvre; the back panel with St. Francis in ecstasy, John the Baptist, and Blessed Ranieri, is in the collection of the Berenson Foundation at I Tatti, near Florence; of the eight panels with scenes from the life of St. Francis that flanked the back of the altarpiece, seven are in London (Nat. Gall.) and one is in Chantilly (Mus. Condé); and some of the predella panels are scattered among various collections. Sassetta's last work, commissioned in 1437 but probably not begun until the completion of the Sansepolcro altarpiece, was the fresco decoration of the Porta Romana at Siena, left incomplete at the artist's death in the spring of 1450.

Sassetta's surviving works — which include minor paintings, such as the *Madonna of the Cherries* in Grosseto Cathedral, another *Madonna* in Florence (Coll. Carli), the Chigi-Saracini *Adoration of the Magi* (fragment in New York, Griggs Coll.), and some controversial predella fragments — are few. On the basis of this small surviving production it may be argued that Sassetta was born in the first years of the 15th century rather than in the last decade of the 14th. Nothing is known of his training as a painter, but his earliest works are executed in the tradition of Sienese painting of the 14th century, a style composed of a lively palette, rich decoration, a highly elegant sense of line (recalling Simone Martini, Ambrogio Lorenzetti, and Gentile da Fabriano), and a preference for gold backgrounds, except in small predella panels and minor scenes. Sassetta did not therefore participate in Gothic trends but, instead, tried with great success to transform the traditional vocabulary of Sienese Gothic painting into the new Renaissance idiom by studying the major contemporary Florentine artists. He must have been familiar with the innovations of Masolino, Masaccio, Ghiberti, Angelico, and others. In works such as the Contini Bonacossi altarpiece a new sense of space is clearly apparent and the figures are disposed with a coherent relationship to each other. Especially in the stories of the predella (the Pope's dream, the foundation of S. Maria Maggiore in Rome, etc.) a real world is vividly depicted, and the landscape and figures are studies from life. This is also evident in the stories of St. Francis from the Sansepolcro altarpiece, combined with an elegance of form and narrative rhythm which were thought by Berenson to have derived from the Limbourg brothers. The magic of Sassetta's art lies in this poetical transformation of reality into an enchanted world, still belonging to the International Gothic style but showing a freshness and understanding of the new problems set by the Florentine Renaissance generation that makes him a "modern" artist and a new interpreter of the Sienese tradition.

Mention should be made of the still unresolved problem connected with Sassetta's *œuvre*. At least three important works are no longer regarded as Sassetta's production: a triptych with the Madonna Enthroned and SS. Jerome and Ambrose in the Church of the Osservanza, outside Siena; a panel with the Nativity in the Museo d'Arte Sacra of Asciano; and various panels, which formed part of an altarpiece dedicated to St. Anthony Abbot, in a number of public and private collections in Europe and America. Some critics relate these works to the circle of Sassetta — either executed in his studio or by some immediate assistant. They are generally known as the works of a so-called "Master of the Osservanza," an artist who was active at the same time as Sassetta and who was influenced by him. On the other hand, Brandi (1949) regards them as the work of the young Sano di Pietro, but the whole question is still far from being conclusively resolved.

BIBLIOG. B. Berenson, A Sienese Painter of the Franciscan Legend, London, 1909; B. Berenson, Pitture Italiane del Rinascimento, Milan, 1936; J. Pope-Hennessy, Sassetta, London, 1939; B. Berenson, Sassetta, Florence, 1947; A. Graziani, Il Maestro dell'Osservanza, Proporzioni, II, 1948; C. Brandi, Quattrocentisti senesi, Milan, 1949; E. Carli, Sassetta e il Maestro dell'Osservanza, Milan, 1957 (with full bibliog.).

Marco CHIARINI

SCAMOZZI, VINCENZO. Italian architect and theorist (b. Vicenza, 1552; d. Venice, Aug. 7, 1616). His style was formed by the study of Sebastiano Serlio, Sansovino (qq.v.), and, above all, Palladio (q.v.), two of whose major works in Vicenza, the Teatro Olimpico (PL. 425; XI, PL. 36) and the villa called "La Rotonda" (XI, PL. 31), and one in Venice, S. Giorgio Maggiore (PL. 49), he completed after Palladio's death in 1580. The influence from Serlio probably came through Vincenzo's father, Giovanni Domenico Scamozzi (ca. 1526–82), who was the editor of the 1584 complete edition of Serlio. (Recent attempts to give most of the credit to Vincenzo seem ill-founded.) Sansovino's influence depends mainly on the fact that Scamozzi's major work, the Procuratie Nuove (VIII, PL. 214) in the Piazza di S. Marco, Venice, was designed to range with Sansovino's Libreria Vecchia, parts of which were actually completed by Scamozzi (designs for both, 1582; the Procuratie begun in 1583 and the definitive model approved in 1596 and 1597). In his *Idea* Scamozzi claims to have used an architectural treatise by Sansovino, now lost. The final element in the formation of Scamozzi's style came from his study of Roman antiquities during his three or four visits to Rome — the first from 1578 to 1580 — after which he published two engravings, of the Baths of Caracalla and Diocletian (1580), and his *Discorsi* (1582).

Among the most important of Scamozzi's original works, all very clearly influenced by Palladio, are the Villa Pisani at Lonigo, designed in 1576, the Villa Verlato at Villaverla (1574, enlarged 1590–1615), and the Villa Dondi dell'Orologio (FIG. 99), designed in 1597 for Niccolò Molini. Inigo Jones (q.v.), the great English Palladian, derived several features from Scamozzi's villas, but had a low opinion of him when they met in Venice in 1614: "this secret Scamozio being purblind under stoode nott."

The 1569 project (not executed) for Palazzo Godi and the palazzo for Francesco Trissino near the Cathedral in Vicenza (begun in 1577) are also closely based on Palladio, but Scamozzi's beautiful Theater at Sabbioneta (IV, PL. 188), built for Vespasiano Gonzaga in 1588–89, is less fanatically antique. In 1593 he was present at the foundation of the nonagonal fortress-city of Palmanova in Venezia Giulia, but little of what was actually built can be attributed to him.

Scamozzi traveled widely, especially in 1599 and 1600, when he went to Poland and came back through Germany to Paris, returning to Venice through Nancy. During this trip he kept a diary in which are to be found some interesting remarks on both Gothic and other buildings. In 1604 he went to Salzburg at the request of the archbishop to design a cathedral and a palace. Drawings were made in 1606–07 but the project was not executed; the present Cathedral was built between 1611 and ca. 1628. However, the original design was influential in the development of Salzburg architecture (see R. Donin, *Vincenzo Scamozzi und der Einfluss Venedigs...*, Innsbruck, 1948).

Far and away the most important of Scamozzi's writings is his large and turgid treatise *L'Idea della Architettura Universale...*, Venice, 1615, even though it contains only six of the proposed ten Books. It includes a good deal of autobiography as well as lengthy expositions of theory, the most important being Book VI on the Orders. Translations into Dutch, German, English, and French soon appeared. Among Scamozzi's other writings are the *Discorsi sopra le antichità di Roma*, Venice, 1582 and 1583 (in imitation of Palladio's guidebook) and his travel diary, recently published as *Taccuino di viaggio da Parigi a Venezia (14 marzo–11 maggio 1600)*, ed. F. Barbieri, Venice, 1959.

BIBLIOG. L. Roncone, Lettera a Francesco Senese, preface to the 1584 complete edition of Serlio, Venice, 1584 (and later eds.); T. Buzzi, il "Teatro all'Antica" di Vincenzo Scamozzi in Sabbioneta, Dedalo, VIII, 1927–28, pp. 488–524; F. Barbieri, V. Scamozzi, Vicenza, 1952; Schlosser, pp. 415 ff.; G. Zorzi, La Giovinezza di Vincenzo Scamozzi secondo nuovi documenti, Arte Veneta, X, 1956, pp. 119–32, XI, 1957, pp. 119–28.

Peter MURRAY

SCANDINAVIAN ART. Scandinavia, the ancient name of the country of the Norsemen and the linguistic designation for the aggregate of countries in which a derivative of Old Norse is spoken today, comprises modern Sweden, Norway, Denmark, and Iceland. Finland, a separate historicogeographic entity in which Finnic, a non-Germanic language, is spoken, was under Swedish domination during the early centuries of its development and, for the purposes of this examination, may be considered part of the same cultural complex. A treatment of the art and culture of these various countries can be found in the separate articles for each (see DENMARK; FINLAND; ICELAND; NORWAY; SWEDEN), and additional material is included in the articles on the minor arts such as FURNITURE, GLASS, METALWORK, and TEXTILES, EMBROIDERY, AND LACE, as well as in the articles on major European art periods and styles. Only certain of the more significant and widespread artistic manifestations are therefore dealt with in this survey.

SUMMARY. Prehistory and protohistory (col. 732). The Middle Ages (col. 734). *Development of ornament; Architecture and sculpture.* The castles of the 16th–18th centuries (col. 741). Folk art (col. 741). Modern architecture and town planning (col. 742). Industrial design (col. 743).

PREHISTORY AND PROTOHISTORY (see also EUROPEAN PROTOHISTORY; PREHISTORY). As the polar cap of the Würm glacier receded, mesolithic peoples from the area that is now northern Germany moved into the forests and tundra of what is modern Scandinavia. These earliest Scandinavian cultures developed, between 8000 and 1000 B.C., definitive rock art forms, of which a number of examples remain. It is possible to trace the development of this art — from its earliest, naturalistic phase (beginning ca. 6000 B.C.; V, PL. 151; XI, FIG. 605) through a period of seminaturalism (from ca. 3000 B.C.) to the consummation of an art that, while still figural, was highly imaginative and schematic (beginning ca. 2000 B.C.) — in the rock engravings that have been discovered from this period, especially fine examples of which remain in Skjomen and Leiknes, Norway (XI, PLS. 290, 291). Although engravings constitute the greater part of what remains of this rock art, a number of paintings from the mesolithic era have been found in Norway and Sweden, whose stylistic evolution follows closely the phases of the petroglyphs.

During the late Neolithic period the tradition of rock paintings and engravings of animals was carried on by the hunting cultures of northern Scandinavia. Two distinct styles — naturalistic depictions and schematic ones — had by this time emerged and existed collaterally, although the former, the older of the two, was used most extensively in Norway. Human beings, birds, and trees, as well as animals, have been identified in the more stylized rock art of this age. A number of examples of chattel art from the late Neolithic era have also been found in northern Scandinavia. Knives and hatchets with carved animal heads for handles (V, PL. 152) were part of the same artistic tradition as the rock art of the period.

An independent line of development dating from a somewhat earlier period occurred in southern Scandinavia. The unpolished pottery of the Ertebølle culture (III, FIG. 197) set this art apart from the mesolithic tradition to which it belonged in date. It was replaced by a new style of pottery at about the time of the first agricultural development. Although found mainly in northern Germany and Poland, funnel beakers, the chief output of this style, were produced on the tip of the Scandinavian peninsula as well and are presumed to date from slightly before 2500 B.C. The so-called "combed pottery" (with allover decoration incised with a comblike instrument; *Kammkeramik*; V, PL. 152) appears to have been indigenous to Finland.

The second phase of the Bronze Age produced in Scandinavia an exceptionally delicate and intricate style of metalwork (V, PL. 169). A flowing decorative pattern, consisting primarily of spiral motifs (V, PL. 166), adorned metallic belt bosses and buckles and the surfaces of axes; a concentric-circle motif later replaced the spiral. Heavier gold- and bronzework — goblets, massive jewelry, trumpets — was produced in Denmark, where the precious materials were more easily obtained from southern lands. No bronzes of high artistic value were produced in Finland. A new style of decoration for ornaments and domestic utensils was developed at the end of the Bronze Age and, although characteristic of Scandinavia in general, was found especially in Norway. It was distinguished by cast ornaments inlaid with a darker substance, most often resin, which replaced the common spiral and circle motifs with stars and scallops or bands of various shapes.

Nordic artistic production during the last part of the early Iron Age has been linked with the coeval Hallstatt sculpture of Continental Europe. Numerous small bronze figures, possibly crafted as sacrificial offerings, and other artifacts in bronze have been found in Norway and especially in Denmark. The sculpture from the Fårdel site in northern Jutland is particularly fine (V, PL. 178). Suggestions of Etruscan and central-European features can be seen in certain Scandinavian bronzes.

Rock engravings continued to be produced in southern and central Scandinavia during the Hallstatt epoch. The most common representations — ships, wheels, weapons, tools, battle scenes, and scenes depicting plowing, as well as animals (both hunted and domesticated) — are a veritable pictorial history of the evolution of a more advanced culture during the metal age. Intimately connected with the petroglyphs of the Hallstatt period are the engraved decorations of razor blades of the same time. Such blades were most often engraved with figural patterns, decorative motifs such as garlands, and simple representations of ships, frequently contained within a pair of animal heads.

The art of the La Tène epoch of the late Iron Age, although it had little impact in the northern countries during its early stages, strongly influenced Scandinavian production in its final phase. Some outstanding examples of the La Tène style, including two typically Celtic chariots with remarkable laminated bronzework and the famous Gundestrup silver caldron (III, PL. 118; V, PL. 184), have been found in Denmark. This style incorporated a variety of motifs, including human and animal figures; but in Finland the native decorative motifs from the La Tène period are nearly all geometric.

* *

THE MIDDLE AGES. *Development of ornament.* The Scandinavian countries, having remained free of any profound Christian influences longer than most European countries, experienced a transitional period that merits special treatment. After making notable contributions to pre-Christian art (see EUROPE, BARBARIAN), the Nordic cultures continued their older traditions and accepted impulses from more Christianized Continental and Insular sources only reluctantly.

The vigorous growth of Germanic art during the 6th and 7th centuries expressed itself in a characteristic pictorial art and especially in zoomorphic ornamentation. Within a vast area extending from Italy in the south and Hungary in the southeast to England in the west and the Scandinavian countries in the north, these phenomena have been studied both in their diversity and in their dependence on the great universal currents within art, which showed an increasing Christian influence.

In the 8th century Scandinavia produced a beautiful zoomorphic style — Salin's Style III (see V, cols 163–72). The animal bodies bend in soft, ribbonlike interlacing loops, gradually narrowing and then widening; the rhythmically recurring swellings dissolve into narrower interlacing bands that twine in curves around the main theme to form a rich and vivid ornamentation of great beauty and perfection, as, for instance, in the large gilt fibula from Othem on the island of Gotland (X, PL. 438). In over-all conception this style had much in common with contemporaneous Hiberno-Saxon art (see ANGLO-SAXON AND IRISH ART). The Lindisfarne Gospels (I, PL. 280), for instance, contain many details that constitute direct parallels. Even the common trumpet patterns in Insular manuscripts, with their rhythmically swelling lines, their discontinuous strokes, and their vignetting, reveal traits of the same style.

During the second half of the 8th century this exuberant ornamentation adopted more realistic bird figures and quadrupeds, which, nevertheless, still fitted into the rhythmic convolutions of the style. These representations seem to dissolve into a beautiful pattern of ornamental curves on a sword hilt from Stora Ihre, Gotland, for instance, and on the harness mounts from Broa, Gotland (PL. 411). These fittings also include other animal figures of entirely different appearance, those known in the literature as "gripping beasts," which were at first regarded as a new trend in Scandinavian art from about 800 and were thought to have originated from Continental Carolingian art. This assumption is now being abandoned, especially since Almgren (1955) published an interesting paper that seems to prove that the gripping beasts were nothing more than a new variation on the ancient theme. Almgren's procedure, based on analysis of the compositional scheme, showed that the Scandinavian artistic styles of about 800, however diverse they occasionally appear, were characterized by a limited number of curves or curved figures. The gripping beasts, which were typical of much of the art of the 9th century, thus appear to go back to the tradition of the last decades of the 8th century, a probability that also answers the question of their international ties: it was no doubt the contact with the British Isles that had proved particularly fertile.

A great wealth of material exemplifying the luxuriance of 9th-century Scandinavian art is included in one single find — the famous ship burial at Oseberg, Norway, where among other things the well-preserved wood carvings and textiles are of inestimable value (PL. 413; IV, PL. 176; V, PL. 340; see ARCHAEOLOGY, col. 568; DEMONOLOGY, col. 322). In a penetrating monograph Shetelig (1920) divided the rich material into separate schools to which he gave names — the schools of the "Ship Artist," of the "Scholar," of the "Baroque Artist," and of the "Eclectic," representing practically all varieties of 9th-century art. The ancient traditions are most noticeable in the work of the "Ship Artist" school and the "Scholar" school, in which it is particularly easy to trace the Insular influence. On the so-called "Carolingian" animal's-head post, also from Oseberg, there are many gripping beasts, while below the geometric frame- and latticework on sleighs (XIV, PL. 296) a teeming animal world has been carved into the wood, seemingly without rules or inhibitions. Investigation has revealed, however, the same consistency and perfection as in contemporaneous metal art.

As early as the Oseberg ship burial one can trace the tendencies that were to transform the gripping beasts into the distorted reptiles (*Kringeldjur*) with large full-faced heads that marked the second half of the 9th century and a large part of the 10th. *Kringeldjur*, masks, and various interlacing reptiles were stylistic components that for a time became characteristic of Scandinavian art. Some of these were no doubt derived from ancient indigenous traditions, but certainly many impulses came from the west as well. This was a natural consequence of closer contacts with Insular art from the middle of the 9th century; in this connection valuable information can be drawn from the material remaining in the former Norse settlements on the Scottish islands and in Scotland, Northumberland, and Ireland.

It was surely Insular art, too, that gave rise to the magnificent flowering of Scandinavian filigree art during the second half of the 9th century and the 10th century. Both technique and choice of motifs show the influence of Christian handicrafts in England and Ireland. Several of the products, such as ring-shaped brooches and pins, round filigree brooches, and three-lobed brooches, bear such a close resemblance to the models that it is difficult to determine their origin. It can be taken for granted that there were workshops in Northumberland and Scotland that supplied the Scandinavian market and that Scandinavian workshops also were making similar products.

The Scandinavian silver and gold treasures from the Viking period include several exquisite examples of the goldsmith's art, especially the gold treasures found at Rød and at Hon in Norway. The Hon treasure includes a three-lobed gold buckle (PL. 412), its surface covered with abundant acanthus ornamentation, which differs strikingly from what was customary in Scandinavia. Generally speaking, plant ornamentation was never popular in Norse art, so there must have been specific reasons for its sudden sporadic appearance about the middle of the 9th century. The explanation was surely the viking raids, and it may even be postulated that the first Scandinavian contact with plant ornamentation took place in 853, when a viking fleet sacked the town of Tours in France. It is indeed beyond question that the plant ornamentation adopted by the Scandinavian countries was mainly of the kind that distinguished the Tours school of painting during the second quarter of the 9th century.

The acanthus ornamentation on the Hon buckle is, however, somewhat more developed than that of the Tours school and is rather reminiscent of Continental work from about 870 — for instance, the cover of the Book of Lindau (I, PL. 287). There can, in fact, be no doubt that the Hon buckle is a genuine Carolingian art product. From the middle of the 9th century and well into the 10th, Scandinavian craftsmen worked with models of this sort. Particularly in metal art, this evolution can be followed step by step, as the Carolingian plant ornamentation was gradually deformed, becoming more and more geometric and zoomorphic until it finally merged with the indigenous zoomorphic ornamentation. The numerous trilobate brooches scattered throughout Scandinavia reflect this transformation.

More than anything else this evolution testifies eloquently to the Scandinavians' tenacious adherence to old traditions and to the considerable force and attraction that the ancient zoomorphic ornamentation still exerted. The Scandinavian styles of the 10th century clearly confirm this. The gripping beasts of the 9th century live on, sometimes transformed into elaborately coiled *Kringeldjur*. The more realistic animal figures of the 8th century, too, are encountered again, but in a clearer and

less interlaced form than before. The undulating ribbon-shaped animals, which constituted through the centuries a fundamental theme of Scandinavian art, also survive. A common 10th-century design of the ribbon-shaped animals, as well as the typical animal heads executed chiefly as sculpture in the round — masks, bird figures, etc. — can be found in the decorations on Danish saddle bows from this period.

To this period also belongs one of the largest, most outstanding monuments of Scandinavian art of the Viking era — the large runic stone from Jelling, Denmark (PL. 414; see PRE-ROMANESQUE, col. 681). On one side it has the figure of Christ, on the other, the figure of a lion, both surrounded by ribbon loops, in plant form around Christ and in snake form around the lion. This monument is a good example of Scandinavian art of the end of the pagan era; the stone's Christ clearly announces the coming of Christianity. It is likely that the Scandinavian author of this monument learned much from the contemporaneous art of the British Isles, since nearly all the characteristic components of its style and details have equivalents in that art. The same observation can be made of metalwork, stone sculpture, and miniatures (see PRE-ROMANESQUE ART, especially col. 680–81).

This same influence emerges clearly also from a study of 11th-century Scandinavian art (XI, PL. 328). Illustrative of this period are the reliquary in Cammin, Poland, and the one in Bamberg, Germany (see PRE-ROMANESQUE, col. 681). Despite their present locations, their Scandinavian origin can scarcely be questioned. In general character, the birds and quadrupeds are definitely Scandinavian, but they are detached and surrounded by loops and ribbons resembling those found in Insular manuscripts from the second half of the 10th century and somewhat later. The plant ornamentation on the two reliquaries seems to have the same origin. Bronze weather vanes from the 11th century — two from Sweden and one from Norway — are adorned with animal figures and pampres of the same kind (see PRE-ROMANESQUE, col. 682; XIV, PL. 463). Akin to these are the many runic stones that are such a characteristic feature not only of Scandinavian 11th-century art but also of the landscape of central Sweden, which abounds in runic monuments (PL. 414).

All these pieces show great elegance of line. They are ornamental in the truest sense of the word, with motifs including dragons pulled into ribbon shapes, snakes, palms, distorted plant ornament, and vines of conventionalized geometric form. Realistic human or animal figures occur seldom; however, a cross with equal arms often plays an important part. This is the Christian cross, and the Christian meaning of the symbol can occasionally be gleaned from the inscriptions. The reasons for its appearance are evident, for during the first half of the 11th century, Christian England was occupied by the Danes, resulting in a strong Christian influence that spread to the other Scandinavian countries. English miniature art from this period shows many ornamental components that reappear on Scandinavian runic stones and other monuments, and it seems clear that it was the English stylistic details that influenced the Scandinavian ones.

It would be a mistake to regard the beautiful carved porch of the church at Urnes as an example of pagan art. On the contrary, it is not merely an outstanding example of Scandinavian wood carving — with its unique keyhole-shaped portal, corner posts, and highly ornamented wall boards (X, PL. 438) — but also a great Christian monument. In Christian England and Ireland, churches were embellished in the same fashion, although there stone was used instead of wood.

The ornamental style of the period of transition, with its pagan traditions and its Christian features, put its stamp on Scandinavian art for a long time, even after the final victory of Christianity. Old styles lingered in church decoration almost until the 13th century. The Norwegian wooden stave churches are outstanding examples of the strength of tradition, as are the many good examples in Sweden (PLS. 233, 415; see below, *Architecture*). The past also makes itself felt in the form of a tendril that borrowed its flexible curves and thin twining leaves from the ribbonlike pagan animal with its coiling extremities, or in a grotesque animal head that is not the tame kind known from Romanesque art (q.v.) but reflects a savage beast from the heathen past. A splendid illustration of this mixture of old and new, of paganism, transition, and Christianity, is the sepulchral monument from Botkyrka, Sweden, which probably dates from the middle of the 12th century (PL. 415).

The art of the transitional period is not only reflected in large monuments but is perhaps more truly represented in the minor arts, of which many works survive in the Scandinavian countries (e.g., the Baldishoel Tapestry, PL. 415). There are several hundred silver treasures from the 11th and 12th centuries, containing great quantities of jewelry (see PRE-ROMANESQUE, col. 683). These also include many objects of Christian origin such as crosses and reliquaries, showing definite affinity to the Christian art of the time (see ROMANESQUE, col. 464). During the 11th century, and in Finland even during the 12th, the pagan habit continued of placing gifts, sometimes of great value, in tombs. However, this abundant and valuable material is still awaiting art-historical evaluation.

Besides the connections with Christian art in England in this transitional period, certain contacts with countries to the east can be traced, especially in Finnish works. Certain plant motifs (palms, rosettes, truncated pampres), as well as realistic bird figures and quadrupeds, belong to the eastern European tradition; and several of the Christian crucifixes included in the Scandinavian finds seem to stem from the Byzantine world. Crucifixes of this type, as well as fluted silver bowls and other objects, were widely imitated in Scandinavia.

BIBLIOG. B. Salin, Die altgermanische Tierornamentik, Stockholm, 1904 (2d ed., 1935); H. Shetelig, Urnesgruppen, Aarsberetning for Foreningen til norske fortidsminnesmerkers bevaring, 1909, pp. 75–107; T. J. Arne, La Suède et l'Orient, Uppsala, 1914; H. Shetelig, Oseberg-fundet, III, Kristiania, 1920; J. Brøndsted, Early English Ornament, London, Copenhagen, 1924; C. A. Nordman, Karelska järnälderstudier, Helsinki, 1924; S. Grieg, Vikingetidens skattefund, Univ. oldsaksamling skrifter, II, Oslo, 1929, pp. 177–311; S. Lindqvist, Yngre vikingastilar, in H. Shetelig., ed., Kunst (Nordisk kultur, XXVII), Stockholm, 1931, pp. 144–79; C. R. af Ugglas, Gotlandisch oder deutsch: Ein Silberkruzifix von Valdemarstågets tid, Stockholm, 1936; H. Arbman, Schweden und das karolingische Reich, Stockholm, 1937; N. Åberg, Keltiska och orientaliska stilinflytelser i vikingatidens nordiska konst, Stockholm, 1941; J.-E. Forssander, Irland-Oseberg, Medd. från Lunds univ. historiska mus., 1942–43, pp. 294–404; R. Skovmand, De danske Skattefund fra Vikingetiden og den aeldste Middelalder indtil omkring 1150, Aarbøger for nordisk oldkyndighed og historie, 1942, pp. 1–275; C. A. Nordman, Gotlandisch oder deutsch: Ein Silberkruzifix von Halikko im eigentlichen Finnland, ActaA, XV, 1944, pp. 29–62; M. Stenberger, Die Schatzfunde Gotlands der Wikingerzeit, 2 vols., Lund, Uppsala, 1947–58; W. Holmqvist, Sigtunamästaren och hans krets, Situne Dei, VII, 1948; S. Lindqvist, Osebergsmästarna, Tor, 1948, pp. 9–28; H. Shetelig, The Norse Style of Ornamentation in the Viking Settlements, ActaA, XIX, 1948, pp. 69–113; T. D. Kendrick, Late Saxon and Viking Art, London, 1949; H. Shetelig, Classical Impulses in Scandinavian Art from the Migration Period to the Viking Age, Oslo, Cambridge, Mass., 1949; W. Holmqvist, Viking Art in the 11th Century, ActaA, XXII, 1951, pp. 1–56; E. M. Kivikoski, Die Eisenzeit Finnlands, II, Helsinki, 1951; A. Bugge, Norwegian Stave Churches (trans. R. Christophersen), Oslo, 1953; B. Almgren, Bronsnycklar och djurornamentik, 2 vols., Uppsala, 1955; O. H. Moe, Urnes and the British Isles, ActaA, XXVI, 1955, pp. 1–30; E. C. G. Oxenstierna, Die Nordgermanen, Stuttgart, 1957; H. Arbman, Skandinavisches Handwerk in Russland zur Wikingerzeit, Medd. fran Lunds univ. historiska mus., 1959, pp. 110–35; W. Holmqvist, The Silver Pin from Sylloda, Suomen Mus., LXVI, 1959, pp. 34–63; W. Holmqvist, The Dancing Gods, ActaA, XXXI, 1960, pp. 101–27; W. Holmqvist, Sydskandinavisk stil, Fornvännen, LV, 1960, pp. 135–41.

Wilhelm HOLMQVIST

Architecture and sculpture (see also GOTHIC ART; ROMANESQUE ART). As already mentioned, Christianity did not gain a footing in Scandinavia until the late Middle Ages. Gamla (Old) Uppsala, the last stronghold of paganism in Sweden, was not conquered until about 1130; Christianity was not truly assimilated by Finland until about 1200; and although Denmark became officially Christian with the baptism of King Harald in 950, its complete conversion was not achieved until a century later. The foreign religion brought with it foreign art forms, which were gradually assimilated by the native art traditions. The finished product of this amalgamation, Scandinavian Romanesque, was, in spite of its obvious debt to the art of Lombardy, western Germany, southern France, Normandy, and England, perhaps the most truly unique and indigenous of all medieval art styles.

The first churches, the so-called "stave churches," were constructed upon piles driven into the ground and built of forked, interlocking logs, most often of oak (see NORWAY, col. 721). Probably modeled initially after pagan houses and temples, stave churches were later diversified to include many types of construction — from the simple single-aisled structure to the basilican form, with ranges of wood posts and extensive decorative features borrowed from Romanesque stone architecture. An example of the former type has been reconstructed in Denmark from the remains of a small stave church built in Jelling, Jutland, by King Harald, and is believed to be typical of the churches built in Scandinavia in this early Christian period (last half of the 10th century). Only fragments of stave churches have been found in Denmark, but important remains have been discovered in Sweden, at Lund, Skåne, from which a reconstruction has been made. The original church was about twice as large as the one in Jelling, and although the native stave techniques were retained, influences from Continental stone churches are obvious in the construction and decoration.

Stave churches continued to be constructed in Norway long after they had been replaced by stone elsewhere in Scandinavia, and it is there, consequently, that they reached their fullest development. About twenty-five have been preserved. The one in Urnes (PL. 233), with a small rectangular nave and a projecting straight-ended choir, is representative of the Jelling type of stave-church construction, but the style of its carved ornamentation (see above) demonstrates the builder's attempt to approach stone architecture. Norwegian stave churches of the 12th and 13th centuries are generally of basilican size and plan, and often show such features as towers, dragon heads on ridge poles, and tarred shingled walls. The portals of these later churches were usually elaborately carved with both native zoomorphic motifs and adopted Romanesque elements.

The first stone churches date from the early 11th century, when the Danes began to use travertine, but stone construction did not become common in Scandinavia until the 12th century and did not, in fact, reach Finland until the 13th. The earliest stone churches show both Continental and English influences, explained by the strong German and English missionary centers that existed at the time in Norway and Sweden and by the fact that until 1103 Scandinavia belonged to the archdiocese of Hamburg-Bremen.

The first cathedral of Lund (Malmöhus, Sweden), erected about 1080 by King Canute on the site where the slightly later cathedral still stands, was probably of the Anglo-Saxon type with no side aisles and with transept and choir terminating in semicircular apses, like most Norwegian Romanesque churches. The foundations of the original church are preserved in the enormous crypt under the entire east end of the later building (begun ca. 1103). This later cathedral is an outstanding example of a mélange of styles. The *Westwerk* was part of its original plan, but the two west towers were not actually constructed until the beginning of the 13th century. The façade has since been altered; the most recent architectural work on the structure dates from the beginning of the 19th century. The plan of the church reveals influences from Flanders and Normandy, but it has been hypothesized from the quality of the sculpture adorning capitals, moldings, and portals that the builders were from Lombardy. The later ornamental work, executed under a different architect, is of a more classical style and shows obvious Byzantine features (see SWEDEN). Lund Cathedral is especially important for the influence it exerted in southern Sweden, Gotland, and Denmark. The Cathedral of Viborg (Jutland), for example, owes a great debt to the one in Lund. Ribe Cathedral (Jutland; PL. 233), known especially for its huge domical vault over the crossing, shows an unmistakable Rhenish influence, and other churches of this time (e.g., the brick and granite Cathedral of Roskilde, Zealand) demonstrate certain architectural alliances with the Rheno-Lombardic Romanesque.

The unique round churches, found chiefly in Denmark, can be seen also in parts of Sweden and occasionally in Norway (e.g., Tønsberg). Especially famous are the four on the island of Bornholm in Denmark, of which the one at Østerlars is the best preserved. It is particularly interesting for its huge central pillar containing a chapel. The other Bornholm round churches are those of Nylars, Ny, and Ols (PL. 416). Many of these stone or brick structures have enormously high conical roofs of timber; that of Ols is 50 ft. high. These churches often also served as strongholds or fortress chapels — e.g., the church of Bjernede (Zealand), the Ols church with its embrasures, and the Nylars church with its watchman's gallery.

Contemporaneously with these developments in ecclesiastical architecture, the Romanesque style appeared in castles and fortresses. With the introduction of new masonry techniques at the beginning of the 11th century, stone fortifications and fortress towers came to supplement stone embankments and wooden entrenchments. As early as the 13th century, several towered fortresses were replaced by an encircling wall with towers and a palace, while in Stockholm the old tower was preserved inside the new walls. Several excellent examples of late-13th-century castles surrounded by rings of turreted fortifications exist in Finland.

Such elements as ribbed vaulting and the pointed arch, introduced by the Benedictine and Cistercian monks in the second half of the 12th century along with the masonry techniques of Burgundy, were used in Scandinavian construction considerably before a true Gothic art was established in this area in about the last half of the 13th century. Examples of this hybrid style can be found throughout Scandinavia. For instance, the exterior of Trondheim Cathedral in northern Norway, originally planned in the middle of the 12th century as a church of the Anglo-Norman type, is unmistakably Romanesque; inside, however, pointed arches were used in the ribbed vaulting. Other Gothic features were incorporated when the Archbishop of Trondheim, upon returning from England in 1183, altered the plans of the building to incorporate, among other features, a large octagonal chapel at the east end of the preexisting choir. The original single-aisled choir was converted at the beginning of the 13th century into one of the three-aisled English type, and a High Gothic nave was begun in 1248. Changes in and additions to the Cathedral did not finally cease until about 1320 (see GOTHIC ART, cols. 525–26; NORWAY, col. 722). The Abbey church of Varnhem in Sweden, founded in 1150 by monks from Alvastra (the site of the first Cistercian abbey in Sweden), was modeled on the Abbey church of Clairvaux, but the Gothic style was not consistently carried through in its execution. There are many other examples of quasi-Gothic Scandinavian churches, either originally Romanesque with later Gothic changes and additions or entirely constructed in a transitional style. These churches influenced later ones almost as much as direct Gothic importations did.

The best example of English-influenced Gothic in Sweden is the Cathedral of Linköping, begun in 1230 and completed a century later (VI, PL. 330). Although the first parts of this church to be erected, the choir and the transept, demonstrate the Rhenish transitional style, all later construction bears the English stamp, and the clustered piers supporting the vaults on the west side were in fact executed by English stonemasons (see GOTHIC ART, col. 526). English influence in Denmark can be seen in the Church of St. Canute (St. Knud) in Odense, completed in 1301. Little noteworthy Danish architecture was produced, however, in the Gothic period, during which Denmark was strongly overshadowed by the newly powerful cities of the Hanseatic League. The Orthodox part of eastern Finland produced only wooden Byzantine churches, although the rest of Finland was one of the most prolific areas of Gothic architecture in Scandinavia. The principal Gothic monument in Finland is the Cathedral of Turku, which was not finished until the 15th century.

The French Gothic influence was especially strongly felt in Sweden. The brick Cathedral of Strängnäs was evidently patterned in plan and detail after that of Poitiers. The foremost example of French High Gothic in Norway was the Church of the Apostles, no longer extant, in Bergen; in its plan it resembled Ste-Chapelle in Paris. Although a great number of cathedrals were influenced by the French, the Cathedral of Roskilde in Denmark is the only Scandinavian church to demonstrate a wholly French Gothic plan and interior.

At the end of the Scandinavian Middle Ages many Gothic churches were remodeled in part: large choirs and chapels were added to a number of structures, as well as high steeples on the cathedrals in the Swedish cities of Strängnäs, Västerås, and Stockholm and in Turku, Finland; and the wooden roofs of many churches in central Sweden were given ribbed vaulting in star-shaped patterns.

As in architecture, the barbarian style persisted in Scandinavian sculpture long after it adopted Christian content; much work produced in the 12th and 13th centuries combined zoomorphic ornament with one or several styles of Romanesque. Scandinavia came in contact with Continental sculpture through the stoneworkers who were employed in the great church-building enterprises, and the rapid development of monumental figure sculpture that occurred in the north during this period was an echo of what had taken place in Continental Europe slightly earlier.

The Cathedral of Lund, which had such a tremendous influence on Romanesque architecture in Scandinavia (see above) is also an especially good example of adopted Lombard and Byzantine sculptural forms that similarly had great influence on native production (see SWEDEN). The tympanum relief of the Descent from the Cross on the south portal of Ribe Cathedral reveals in style and iconography definite influences from Spain and Italy. The influence of these great cathedrals can be seen also in the simpler styles of sculptors with their roots more firmly in the Scandinavian tradition. Baptismal fonts carved in relief were produced especially in Gotland and exported to the Baltic area, largely to Skåne and Jutland, where they were extensively copied. Most sculpture from the workshops of Gotland is somewhat Byzantine in style (see SWEDEN), whereas in Norway and western Sweden, fonts were generally of the Anglo-Saxon type. English-influenced reliefs tended, however, to be rather crude in contrast with, for example, the marble head (ca. 1120) in the Monastery of Munkeliv outside Bergen.

The best examples of wood sculpture from this period are the decorations from the stave churches (PL. 415). The carved wall boards from the Urnes stave church (PL. 233) show the ancient Scandinavian zoomorphic style at its most distinguished. The narrow portals of Norwegian stave churches are commonly decorated with a wide, symmetrically composed framework of lavish calligraphic patterns. The motifs are generally those of zoomorphic Style III (see EUROPE, BARBARIAN) combined with foliage and palmette borders originating in Continental Romanesque. Intricate animal decoration was also used in the several unique house-shaped reliquaries that remain from this period, with designs of walrus tusk and elk antler set in a framework of gilded bronze.

The French-influenced sculptures from the end of the 12th and the beginning of the 13th century are especially noteworthy. The Virgin from Viklau, Gotland, is so much akin to the Virgin of the Royal Portal of Chartres that it was long believed to be a French import. The most common Virgin type, however, shows western German elements, although English influences can also be seen in a number of Virgins from Norway and Sweden. Wooden crucifixes of Romanesque style were also executed in Scandinavia, the most exceptional of which — a noble image, modeled in classical harmony — is in Skåne, Sweden (1160). The style of crucifixes varies from archaically severe, rigorously frontal images of Christ to a softer, more expressive modeling, reflecting the Rhenish style. Saints' images also exist, especially of the Scandinavian St. Olaf. Late forms were particularly influenced by close contact with art centers in England and Germany. In general during this later period English workshops were most influential in Norway and Stockholm; Rhenish centers in Denmark; and Westphalian and Saxon workshops in Gotland.

By and large, French Gothic sculpture was the greatest influence on Scandinavian Gothic production, and the wood sculpture of the so-called "Bunge Master" (see SWEDEN), who was active about 1300 in Gotland, was executed in a style closely approaching French High Gothic. Gothic sculpture throve especially on Gotland, where several outstanding workshops flourished during the 14th century. In Norway the

English influence is apparent in some of the wood sculpture and can also be seen in the stone heads from the Cathedral of Trondheim; but later sculpture from Trondheim, whose west façade has perhaps the finest Gothic stone sculpture in Scandinavia, reveals strictly French influences, and a number of Swedish Gothic works are thought to have been executed by French sculptors. During the second half of the 14th century, however, German influences predominated in Scandinavian sculpture, as demonstrated in the wood reliefs on the choir stalls of the cathedrals of Lund and Roskilde. At this time Vadstena (Östergötland) became an important northern art center, and fine Gothic sculpture can be found there.

THE CASTLES OF THE 16TH–18TH CENTURIES. The same borrowing from the Continent that had characterized the development of medieval art styles in the northern countries occurred in Scandinavia during the 16th–18th centuries. The stimulus of Italian art was transmitted to the Baltic through Germany, Flanders, and France, with the expanding power of the Hanseatic League forming a strong link between Scandinavia and northern Germany. The Reformation was a turning point: kings and princes became the chief patrons of an art devoted chiefly to castles and fortresses; religious architecture, painting, and sculpture declined significantly; and the Gothic style, looked upon as a vehicle of Catholicism, was rejected.

Although the decoration (ca. 1550) on the gables of the Castle of Hesselagergård shows Italian influences, it was not until the end of the 16th century that art in Denmark became truly aware of the Renaissance. Kronborg Castle at Helsingør (Elsinore; completed ca. 1583) was designed by two Flemish architects, and although it demonstrates certain universal Renaissance principles such as symmetry, it is naturally of the Dutch style rather than the Italian. A number of other late-16th- and early-17th-century castles in Denmark also reveal this mixed style (see DENMARK). The Castle of Frederiksborg, built in the 18th century for Frederik IV, is Italianate in design and construction. Under Frederik's son, Christian VI, Nikolas Eigtved, whose work more closely approached true baroque, built the Castle of Christianborg. Eigtved was also responsible for the layout of Amalienborg, a new quarter of Copenhagen, which is an excellent example of rational mid-18th-century city planning (see DENMARK).

In Sweden, Renaissance art arrived in a purer form about a generation after it had reached Denmark. Foreign craftsmen, primarily from Flanders, were frequently brought in to direct the construction of the large palace-fortresses built for royalty and the nobility. The door and the well of the Castle of Kalmar, designed about 1570 by Dominikus Parr (Pahr), a Frenchman who had studied in northern Germany, were stylistically more French than Italian; the doors of the Castle of Vadstena (Östergötland), executed by the Italian sculptor Pietro della Rocca in the 1590s, were completely Italian in style, but since they represented the earliest Renaissance style, they were shortly outmoded.

In Norway major post-Reformation monuments are the 17th-century fortresses of Christiansten, Frederiksten, Frederikstad, and Kongsvinger. The 18th century, during which Norway was fighting for political independence, was less artistically productive.

It is notable that for the most part only castles and manor houses reflected the new style. Small buildings continued to be erected according to medieval plans and construction techniques; some 16th- and 17th-century timber storehouses from the Lake Siljan region (PL. 416) resemble quite closely the earliest medieval farmhouses (see also SWEDEN).

FOLK ART. Folk art (q.v.) constitutes an important feature of Scandinavian culture even into the 20th century. The repertory of early folk-art forms and motifs drew heavily on the store of Germanic zoomorphic representations, a style that had never really died out but had been enriched and sometimes completely altered by successive adaptations of Continental decorative styles. Any or all of the major European motifs and forms, from Gothic through rococo, were at times incorporated into Scandinavian folk production. High quality and great individuality of character were attained in four major areas of Scandinavian folk art: carving in wood and other materials, painted decoration of walls and furniture (particularly rosemaling), metalwork, and textiles; and such mediums as vehicles, glass, ceramics (III, PL. 164), and costume (qq.v.) also reflected folk design.

Woodcarving was the chief medium of decoration for architectural elements, furniture, household articles (q.v.), and utensils and tools (q.v.; V, PL. 343). Depending on the article being produced, woodcarving was often combined with some other craft. An 18th-century Swedish jack plane was made of iron and carved wood, and a pair of sheath knives of birch bark and metal were produced in Finland in 1892 (XIV, PLS. 281, 282). Some furniture was unadorned except for carving and turning (V, PLS. 340, 341), while other articles combined carving and painting (V, PLS. 335, 342; VII, PL. 346). Woodcarving was extremely popular all over Scandinavia until the 18th century, when it was partially supplanted by painting. The dominant motifs were abstract, both curvilinear and geometric, although Danish designs tended to incorporate human figures, animals, birds, and flowers. The Laplanders were particularly skilled at carving horn and bone with delicately incised geometric designs. From Finland come beautifully crafted kanteles, the ancient musical instruments used to accompany runic songs. Other types of Scandinavian instruments were also carved with folk motifs.

Although early folk painting existed, the technique of rosemaling (polychrome painting used to decorate any smooth wooden surface, usually in designs of botanical origin) was not employed extensively until the 18th century. The designs and bright colors of rosemaling (V, PLS. 335, 342) set it apart from the folk painting of northern Continental Europe.

The vocabulary of woodcarving was applied to the techniques of metalwork; tools, utensils, and common household objects (XIV, PLS. 281, 282) are often as highly ornamented as jewelry of gold and silver.

The textile arts comprise a large and significant part of the folk-art output of Scandinavia. Woven and embroidered fabrics were used for interior decoration as well as for clothing and were sometimes very rich, incorporating precious stones and metal beads or threads. Although the especially fine Swedish tapestries were exported to the other Scandinavian countries, each area had its own characteristic textile production. A kind of openwork embroidery called "hedebo" was popular in Denmark; the tufted, patterned ryijy cloth was peculiar to Finland; and in Lapland decorated clothing is made of reindeer skin.

There are many public folk-art collections in Scandinavia; especially noteworthy are the fine open-air museums located in a number of the larger cities. The Norsk Folkemuseum in Oslo, with its excellent collections of furniture, tapestries, and religious objects, and the Skansen Museum in Stockholm, the largest open-air museum of its kind in the world, are particularly well known.

MODERN ARCHITECTURE AND TOWN PLANNING. The Stockholm Exposition of 1930 is frequently cited as the event that marks the beginning of modern architecture in Scandinavia. The extensive construction done by the noted Swedish architect Gunnar Asplund for this exposition challenged the reactionary academic movement of the time and favored new and inventive forms and materials (see SWEDEN). The Finn, Eliel Saarinen (q.v.), was probably the first modern Scandinavian architect of international significance, although his earliest buildings have been held to demonstrate national romanticism more than modern trends. In 1922 he emigrated to the United States, where both his works — many designed in collaboration with his son Eero (see below, Industrial design) — and his teaching exerted an important influence on American architectural design. The emergence in the late 1920s of Saarinen's fellow-countryman Alvar Aalto (q.v.; I, PLS. 1–3; V, PL. 118, FIG. 240) confirmed the secure establishment of a truly modern architecture in Scandinavia. Aalto, too, built, exhibited, and taught in the United States (where his work won enthusiastic recognition from Frank Lloyd Wright). The achievements of these two outstanding architects dominate the architecture of modern Scandinavia, but other noteworthy architects can be cited as well, among them the Danes P. V. Jensen Klint (V, PL. 108) and Arne Jacobsen, whose designs for public buildings (V, PLS. 111, 114, FIG. 247) are world-famous. Sweden, too, has produced modern architects of the first rank (V, PLS. 113, 114, FIG. 241). Modern Scandinavian architecture is distinguished for its radical functionalism, adhering tenaciously to Louis Sullivan's credo, "form follows function"; and for the effect of airy lightness it has achieved by the use of light colors and modern structural materials such as glass (see EUROPEAN MODERN MOVEMENTS, cols. 226, 240–41, 243–44, 246).

Town planning (q.v.) in 20th-century Scandinavia came into being less as a result of the new movement in architecture than as a reaction to the problems of urban development that followed the Industrial Revolution; but it soon called into play and gave new scope to Scandinavian architectural talent. The so-called "City Beautiful" era in the United States had a strong parallel in the Nordic lands. The concepts of regionalism and zoning began to find application in the 1930s; Stockholm (XIV, PLS. 139, 141, 159, 176) and Copenhagen (XIV, PLS. 141, 160, 177) led the way. In 1945 the general layout of Stockholm was placed under study, and in 1948 a new law on town planning was passed. Elsewhere in Scandinavia similar studies were made and legislative measures taken. Swedish housing and commercial developments, such as those designed by Swen Backström and Leif Reinius (V, PL. 113, FIG. 247; XIV, PL. 158), are outstanding.

INDUSTRIAL DESIGN. Modern Scandinavian industrial design (q.v.) has concentrated on beautifying objects of everyday use. As in architecture, functionality is its distinctive feature. Scandinavian designers have been particularly successful in adapting their art to the technical and social requirements of the day without esthetic compromise, so that Scandinavian design has everywhere become synonymous with quality and beauty.

Scandinavian industrial arts tend to the use of natural wood, ceramics, and glass, although metal and plastic are also employed. Furniture and household objects (qq.v.) have been particularly responsible for Scandinavia's reputation in this sphere. The architects Alvar Aalto (VIII, PL. 50) and Arne Jacobsen (V, PL. 456) are also outstanding designers of furniture. Finnish-born Eero Saarinen, an architect-planner-designer like his father Eliel (see above, *Architecture*), created distinguished American furniture (VIII, PL. 51); some of his work was done in Scandinavia also, and much of his American work found its way there. To this list could be added many other artists whose works reflect, with great originality, a peculiarly Scandinavian interpretation of modern design (V, PL. 457).

Many designers of furniture have also used their talents to create household objects of great beauty and utility. Fine work in cutlery (especially in stainless steel; VII, PL. 325), other kitchen implements (VIII, PLS. 54, 57), and tea and coffee services exemplifies contemporary Scandinavian design.

Glassware, both functional (VI, PL. 239) and purely decorative, is another specialty of modern Scandinavia. The chief production center is the Swedish city of Orrefors (VII, PLS. 323, 325). Much of the Swedish glass of the mid-20th century is tinted one or more colors or smoked. It ranges from extremely heavy to fragile and is usually perfectly symmetrical; often it is engraved with complex delicate motifs, generally nonfigural. Finnish glass (VII, PL. 316) is entirely different in character. Its shapes and decorative motifs are frequently derived from nature; it tends to be asymmetrical and is either sparsely engraved or coarsely incised. It sometimes contains white or opalescent layers (see also GLASS, cols. 394–95).

Porcelain, ceramics, and enameled cast-iron objects, sometimes decorated with folk motifs, reflect the heritage of Scandinavia applied to modern design. Tools, utensils, and machines have also benefited from Scandinavian industrial design, so that door handles, adding machines, and even heating apparatus have gained new dignity from their extra-utilitarian beauty.

The textile arts, important throughout the cultural history of Scandinavia, have particularly flourished in the present century. Highly original rugs, curtains, tablecloths and mats, and fabrics for clothing and upholstery have been produced on a large scale in all the Scandinavian countries. Most of these fabrics are colorful and somewhat abstract in pattern or design. Fabrics from Finland and from Sweden are especially noteworthy and are exported all over the world.

BIBLIOG. See bibliogs. for DENMARK; FINLAND; ICELAND; NORWAY; SWEDEN. See also: S. H. Müller, Nordens Billedkunst, Copenhagen, 1905; C. Holme, Peasant Art in Sweden, Lapland and Iceland, London, 1910; J. Roosval, Die Kirchen Gotlands, Leipzig, 1912; A. Lindblom, La peinture gothique en Suède et en Norvège, Stockholm, 1916; A. L. Romdahl, Gammal konst, Stockholm, 1916; H. Aal et al., Kunst og haandverk, Kristiania, 1918; J. P. Thiis, Samlede avhandlinger om nordisk kunst, Kristiania, 1920; C. Laurin, E. Hannover and J. P. Thiis, Scandinavian Art, New York, 1922; A. Lindblom, Caractères nationaux dans la sculpture suédoise au moyen âge, Actes XIᵉ Cong. int. d'h. de l'art (1921), III, Paris, 1924, pp. 479–84; P. Lespinasse, Les artistes français en Scandinavie, Paris, 1929; H. Shetelig., ed., Kunst (Nordisk kultur, XXVII), Stockholm, 1931; Actes XIIIᵉ Cong. int. d'h. de l'art, Stockholm, 1933; R. Krarup, Nyervervede textiler, Det danske kunstindustrimuseums virksomhed, 1949–54, pp. 61–75; G. Serner, ed., Treasures of Swedish Art from Earliest Times to the Beginning of the 13th Century, Stockholm, 1950; E. S. de Mare, Scandinavia, London, 1952; A. Bugge, Norwegian Stave Churches (trans. R. Christophersen), Oslo, 1953; A. Lindblom, Björsätermalningarna, Stockholm, 1953; R. Hauglid and L. Grodecki, Norway: Paintings from the Stave Churches, Greenwich, Conn., 1955; T. Paulsson, Scandinavian Architecture, London, 1958; H. Engelstad, Norwegian Tapestries: A Viking Visit, AN, LVIII, 6, 1959, pp. 32–35; A. Andersson, Two 14th Century Calvary Groups in West Sweden, The Connoisseur, CXLV, 1960, pp. 90–95; R. Krarup, Textilsamlingens vaekst, Copenhagen, 1960; F. Malusardi, Vicende dell'urbanistica svedese, Q. Soc. generale immobiliare, 13, 1960, pp. 3–32; W. D. Simpson, The Castle of Bergen and the Bishop's Palace at Kirkwall, Edinburgh, London, 1961; C. Stewart, The Round Churches of Bornholm, J. Royal Inst., LXVIII, 1961, pp. 539–42; A. Tuulse, Katolskt och protestantiskt i Sveriges och Danmarks kyrkomålningar, Fornvännen, LVI, 1961, pp. 271–88; I. Rácz and R. Pylkkänen, Art Treasures of Medieval Finland, London, 1962.

* *

Illustrations: PLS. 411–416; 1 fig. in text.

SCENOGRAPHY.

The term "scenography" is here understood as denoting that aggregate of pictorial and plastic elements which in the theater contribute to the realistic, ideal, or symbolic reconstruction of the setting of the action represented: in sum, everything that constitutes the visual and pictorial part of the spectacle, with the exception of the physical presences of the actors. In this sense scenography includes particular technical effects such as real or artificial illumination, which are not separable from the illusion of lighting achieved by painting; the actual changes of scenery in full view of the audience as elements of rhythm and theatrical effect; and even the actors' costumes, whose styles and colors enliven and modify the stage picture. In a broader sense, scenography covers the whole range of properties and decorations employed during certain festivals and anniversaries to lend a particular aspect to an open place in city or country or to the interior of a building. In such cases the dramatic action of the celebration, with its precise regulation of masses and their movements, and its historical, allegorical, and religious content, depends on this "extratheatrical" scenography to theatricize the site selected.

SUMMARY. Introduction (col. 744). The West (col. 748): *Classical antiquity; The Middle Ages: a. Byzantium; b. Western Europe. The secular mise en scène of the 14th–16th centuries: the neutral stage and the traveling play; Perspective scenography in Italy; Changeable scenery and perspective illusionism in Italy; Spread of perspective scenery in Europe; Angular perspective and the rococo picture stage; From neoclassicism to naturalism; The 20th century; From neorealism to Brecht's didactic epic drama.* The East (col. 787): *China; Japan; Other areas.*

INTRODUCTION. Scenography is an ephemeral art. Its first and fundamental characteristic is evanescence: it begins and ends with the show. Although, like every other art, it obeys definite laws of taste, often exaggerating the style of its own period just because of its impermanent and ephemeral nature, it leaves no documents addressed to the student. Another characteristic of scenography is that in its modern development it employs numerous techniques and various artistic means, borrowing from all the figural arts and the mechanical arts as well, to fortify stagecraft, that is, the ensemble of technical means involved in the realization of a stage set. Thus, unitary as the initial concept may be in scenography, in the course of its practical realization the scenographer finds himself directing a complex workshop and using means — such as movement, to name but one — quite uncommon in art.

Few human endeavors show such changing characteristics and functions over the course of time. The history of scenography is linked with the history of dramatic representation, the roots of which are found in primitive rites of a sacral character. The only, or at least the most conspicuous, visual aspect of ancient collective rites that can be reconstructed (and is still encountered among primitive peoples) is costume, which is sometimes accompanied by a genuinely artistic accessory, as in the case of the mask. In their very nature these rites, though they do not exclude such theatrical elements as the dance, the dramatic recitation, the chorus, music and song (and, as has been said, the rudiments of costume), have absolutely no need of scenography: because of their sacral character and the identification of actors with the mythical beings they represent, the sophisticated notion of scenic fiction is alien to these ceremonies.

The ritual performances of primitive peoples do not require the reconstruction of a setting inasmuch as the dramatic action does not simulate but is the mythical action it represents. This holds true for ostensibly secular performances that recall hunting and fighting scenes, but there too it would be difficult not to see links with mythical elements. Even in complex spectacles such as the annual ceremony of the Algonquian Lenape in honor of their supreme being or those of the Pueblo Indians of New Mexico and Arizona, in which the masked figure (kachina) impersonating the spirit of a messenger of the gods is much in evidence, no attempt is made to reconstruct a setting, whether the ceremony takes place outdoors or in the special ceremonial chamber (e.g., the kiva of the Pueblo Indians). The same can be said of all the dramatic spectacles of primitive tribes in America, Africa, and Oceania as well as of those of the shaman type in Asia (see SHAMANISM).

Again in connection with the prevailing popular religious ceremonies of Western Europe in antiquity and the early Middle Ages one must speak of decoration rather than scenography. At the same time it should be borne in mind that the particular arrangement of an altar, the rudimentary directing of processional groups, and the ornamentation of the holy route were seeds of the extratheatrical outdoor scenography that, developing during the late Middle Ages and the Renaissance and reaching its apex in the baroque period, was closely related to theatrical scenography in a sort of osmosis, for scenographic elements flowed from church to piazza, to theater, and back, along with the very life of the spectacle.

When the dramatic performance began to draw upon history, communal activities, and daily life for material and the characters began to assume individual identities, the need arose for the scenic environment. In the West this started with the Greek theater, and it was in the Greek theater that the modern concept of scenography was born. The very word "scenography," that is, the painting and decoration of the Greek skene (Lat., scaena), is a direct reference to the place and the culture in which this art originated and developed into an independent form of expression. Moreover, from the very beginning the concept of scenography has been closely connected with the representation — even if illusory — of space or, rather, of a space. Since the concept of optics and the concept of perspective blended and came to be seen as identical in the ancient world, Vitruvius uses the word scenographia to indicate the rules for representing the third dimension on a plane. For the most part, ancient stage decoration was painted, except for fixed structures, such as the scenic façade, which formed part of the architecture of the theater; however, it was the kind of painting that was not limited to the theater in its application but had an important influence on the decoration of interiors. But whichever tendency has predominated in scenography — whether the three-dimensional architectural style of the Middle Ages and the early Renaissance, the baroque mixture of painting and building, or the pure painting used for the settings of shows of this century — its basic function has always been representing a space. And of course as the notion of space has changed, the conception of scenography has changed with it.

In the history of scenography in Western Europe during the medieval and modern periods two salient facts must not be lost sight of. First, this art is always in rapport with literature and the drama, upon which it is premised, and with the figural arts, which shape its means of expression: these are the two poles that it swings between, reflecting their quality and their predilections — sometimes closer to the one, sometimes to the other. Second, not to be overlooked are the close ties between the spectacle and its organizers — that is to say, those religious, social, and political functions which so effective a medium of communication as the theater, of necessity, assumed during certain epochs. The interdependence with literature and drama is too apparent to require explanation. As for art, the interdependence stems from the fact that scenography is the visualization and practical representation of a space and hence falls within the orbit of the figural arts. Indeed, long before scenography became an autonomous profession it was the painters, the sculptors, and the architects of the early communal centers, and later of the Renaissance courts, who took charge of the staging of theatrical displays.

The close connection between scenic and figural art is exemplified by the parallelism of the multiple setting in medieval painting and medieval theater: just as within the framework of a 14th-century fresco or panel various episodes are represented, so on a single stage the separate phases of the action were accommodated by the several luoghi deputati, "mansions," or "houses" (FIG. 757; PL. 419), as these were most commonly called. Similarly, when, in the Renaissance, the ideal of a unitary space scientifically governed by the laws of perspective asserted itself, scenography conformed after a certain time lag. Inquiry into the causes of the lag throws light, in turn, on the relation between dramatic text and scenery. In the figural arts the idea of a unitary perspective space prevailed as early as the third decade of the 15th century in Florence and by about the middle of the century in all Italy. In scenic design, however, it was not adopted until the beginning of the 16th century because plays of the medieval type, which continued to be performed throughout the 15th century, influenced the mise en scène. Meanwhile, the revival of interest in the classical theater and the first performances of Greek and Roman comedies (PL. 423) by the academies rendered newly current, at the end of the 15th and the beginning of the 16th century, the famous Aristotelian unities of time, place, and action.

It was in this period that scenography, until then largely empirical, became — like all Renaissance art — the object of elaborate theoretical considerations, and for the first time the need was felt for codification of its rules in treatises (q.v.). Connections were established on the one hand with Aristotelian poetics and on the other with 15th-century theories of perspective. The remarkable interpretation by Renaissance artists of the staging of antiquity was summed up (1545) by Sebastiano Serlio (q.v.), who divided Greek scenes into three kinds — tragic, comic, and satyric — corresponding to the three theatrical genres and each requiring a particular type of decoration. But the decidedly new element — and one that reflects the ideal of the constant setting characteristic of the Renaissance — is the change from the ancients' painting of scenes on periaktoi (confused references to which are found in Vitruvius; see below) to an actual structure, enclosed within the rays of the optical pyramid, that reproduces the setting of the action with three-sided constructions in wood and cloth, in rigorously central perspective. From this the general observation can be drawn that scenography, with rare exceptions, is always affected by the three major arts and is, as Kernodle (1944) affirms, highly receptive to their influence.

From the 16th century on, every treatise on painting and perspective had a chapter devoted to the art of building scenery, and gradually perspective scenery *à l'italienne* conquered the stages of the whole of Europe. It was at the same time — that is, from the beginning of the 16th century — that the art of scenography expanded to include the architecture of the entire theatrical structure and that concepts of scenic space, of its perspective realization, and of its visual relation to the spectator gave rise to and molded the structure of the modern theater.

At the end of the 16th century the principle of a unified and constant setting so favored in the Renaissance definitely lost its hold, and at once scenography shifted its aims. It became spectacular and dynamic, and the change of scene in full view of the audience added a new and exciting element. This brought about a rapid increase in technical contrivances, which by the time of Sabbatini's *Pratica* (1638) seem remarkably numerous compared to the modest repertory of devices listed by Serlio. The relative scarcity of documents about the machines and devices used by the great scenographers of the 17th century can be attributed to the strict secrecy maintained in this highly specialized and competitive profession. It was in the 17th century, in fact, that scenography became an activity so vast and complex as to demand total absorption, and the painter or architect who occasionally staged a production was supplanted by the professional scenographer. Within the profession itself arose individual forms of specialization: the architect-inventor of stage machinery, who was the real creator of the spectacle, and the set painter, who carried out the designs for stage sets. Moreover, in the theorizing about stage design the doctrinaire rigidity of the Renaissance evaporated. In the treatises of the baroque period there are indications of definite stylistic preferences (e.g., Ferdinando Galli Bibiena's emphasis on the angular set shows a taste for the illusionistic spatial effects typical of baroque art), but there is no conceptualization of the art. In short, the writing of treatises withered into the drawing up of rules and practical expedients for the fabrication of sets and the shifting of scenery.

Perhaps this can be considered the high point of European scenography. Humanistic interest in the reconstruction of the ancient theater has dwindled, society has changed, and the absolute monarchy dominates the political scene. Official art is completely committed to depicting and glorifying the figure of the prince or the dominant authority of the Catholic Church, issuing undaunted from its long struggle with the forces of the Reformation. Representational art is permeated by a predilection for the open space, dynamic and exalting, and with subtle rhetorical intent the masses are drawn, by means of an art infused with seductive sensuality, to worship the spectacle of political power and celestial glory. The theater has given up the closed gardens of classical drama and, along with them, the tyrannical unities. A new genre triumphs everywhere and is acclaimed by gentleman and commoner alike: the opera, with its fantastic or pathetic libretto, its display of vocal virtuosity, and, most important, its exploitation of the stunning resources of a scenography left to its own devices and no longer tied down by the text. The opera of the 17th century is dominated by its visual components — by machines that open cloud-filled skies and cause the stars to rise and set; by changes of scene in full view of the audience; and by the splendid costuming of throngs of dancers. It is interesting to note in this connection that on the printed librettos prepared for the premieres, the scenographer's name, an assured drawing card, always appears, while the composer's name is often absent. In the great court spectacles of Vienna and Paris the reigning dynasties had their own splendor mirrored in the splendor of the settings, so that the reality evoked by the scenery was a kind of projection of the select and hyperbolical world in which moved — or so he wished his subjects to believe — the absolute prince.

Clearly, baroque scenography, which reached out from the theater to the tourney, to the public display, to the pyrotechnic spectacle, and back, ultimately becoming in a real sense a civic enterprise, reflected ideals completely different from those of Renaissance scenography and served much broader functions. In this way the concept of scenography changed in actual practice. It was to change even more through the neoclassic reaction of the 18th century — in theory as well (Algarotti, 1763; Milizia, 1771) — taking a polemical position toward the *mise en scène* of the 17th and the first half of the 18th century: implausible stage machinery was rejected in favor of a more rigorous realism already colored by archaeological study of the theater and by the new classical scholarship on the scenic environment. Romanticism turned this trend in the direction of nationalism, and in the theater even the Middle Ages were reconstructed with patriotic fervor. But this very passion for re-creating the past ultimately curtailed the artistic freedom of the stage designer and prepared the way for a new concept of scenography that subordinated it to the text and tied it down to the academic reconstruction of sites and costumes. Some late-19th-century opera scenography is typical of this tendency.

Toward the end of the 19th century began a splendid new period, rich in activity and in revolutionary innovation: from the theater of Antoine, with the stark, bare stages of his extreme realism, to the abstract constructions of Adolphe Appia and Edward Gordon Craig, to the infiltration of the stage, before and after World War I, by the great experiments in painting of the French Fauves and of the cubists and then of the futurist, expressionist, and constructivist movements.

The cropping up of experimental theaters all over Europe, the revival of the outdoor performance, the very fruitful involvement of painters in the world of the theater that marked the first two decades of the present century, together with the new prominence of the stage director, who tended increasingly to take the entire production into his own hands, expressing his own personality through his interpretation of the play — all this enriched and revolutionized scenography. Concurrently, the instruments that rapid technical progress placed in the hands of scenographers (foremost among them electricity for lighting and power) advanced stagecraft to the point where it was completely transformed. The first half of the present century, a period in which interest in the theater has been at a peak, has been characterized by not one but many different conceptions of scenography. All are related to similar conceptions of the drama and the theater itself, and all reflect the new tendencies in the visual arts, from the theater of the Russian ballet, all color and nuance, to the constructivist theater, all plastic form and mass. They reflect the diverse esthetics encountered in the figural arts and in architecture, from the Fauves to the cubists, from Klee to Mondrian, from the futurists to the expressionists. They reflect, too, particular political and social ideals in a world which is divided between fascism, socialism, and capitalism and which, as always, lays bare in the theater, and hence in scenography, its social structure.

Alessandro MARABOTTINI MARABOTTI

THE WEST. *Classical antiquity.* Aristotle, in a grammatically corrupt passage of the *Poetics* (49a. 19–20), credits Sophocles with the introduction of scene painting (*skenographia*) in the Greek theater. The statement, which may be a later interpolation, does not conflict with the testimony of Vitruvius (*De architectura*, VII, Pref. 11), who gives us the name of the first Greek scene painter (*skenographos*) and claims that he worked for Aeschylus. According to this source, Agatharchus of Samos fashioned a setting (*scaenam fecit*) when Aeschylus was producing a tragedy (*Aeschylo docente tragoediam*) in Athens. Since Sophocles made his first public appearance as a dramatist in 468 B.C. (Plutarch, *Cimon*, VIII), and Aeschylus produced his last Athenian trilogy, the *Oresteia*, in 458, the careers of the two tragic poets overlapped, and the statements of Aristotle and Vitruvius can be reconciled. During the decade 468–458 Sophocles seems to have begun to experiment with some form of scene painting, and during the same period Agatharchus designed a setting for Aeschylus. However, the anonymous *Vita* of Aeschylus gives him full credit for having introduced stage decoration: "Aeschylus was the first to decorate the *skene* and to delight the eyes of the spectators with the splendor of paintings and machines, altars, tombs, trumpets, spirits, and Furies."

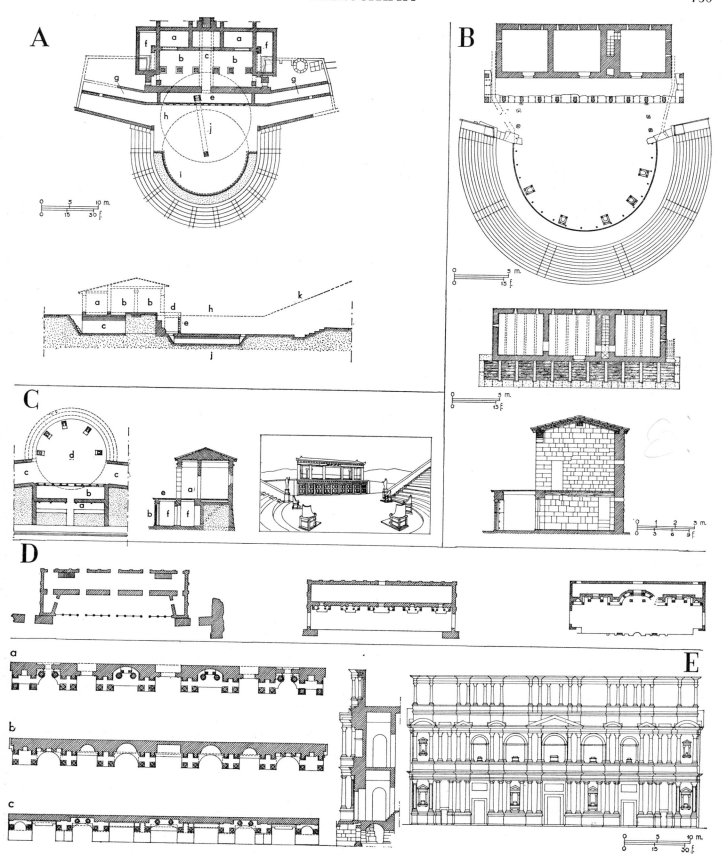

Theaters of the Greek and Roman periods. (*A*) Theater of Eretria, beginning of the 4th century B.C. and ca. 300 B.C. *Above*: Plan. *Below*: Section: (*a*) Scene building in the earlier phase; (*b*) scene building in the later phase; (*c*) vault under scene building; (*d*) logeion; (*e*) proscenium (*proskenion*); (*f*) parascenium (*paraskenion*) in the earlier phase; (*g*) parascenium in the later phase; (*h*) level of orchestra in the earlier phase; (*i*) level of orchestra in the later phase; (*j*) passage under orchestra; (*k*) level of the auditorium in the earlier phase (*from Bieber, 1961*). (*B*) Theater of Priene, Hellenistic period, in the earliest phase. *Above*: Reconstructed plan. *Center*: Plan of upper story of scene building. *Below*: West side of scene building (*from Bieber, 1961*). (*C*) Theater of Oropos, Hellenistic period. *Left*: Plan. *Center*: Section. *Right*: Reconstruction: (*a*) Part behind stage; (*b*) proscenium; (*c*) parodos; (*d*) orchestra; (*e*) logeion; (*f*) hyposcenium (*hyposkenion*; *from Bieber, 1961*). (*D*) Large theater of Pompeii, plan of stage in three successive phases. *Left*: 3d, or (more probably) 2d cent. B.C. *Center*: shortly after 80 B.C. *Right*: Augustan Age (*from L. Crema, L'architettura romana, Turin, 1959*). (*E*) Theater of Ephesus, A.D. 66, perhaps with 3d-cent. reworking. *Left*: Plans: (*a*) 1st level; (*b*) 2d level; (*c*) 3d level. *Center*: Section. *Right*: Façade (*from H. Hörmann, JdI, XXXVIII–XXXIX, 1923–24*).

The question of priority is of lesser importance than the nature of the invention. Fortunately, Vitruvius volunteers additional information at this point, when he tells us that Agatharchus wrote a treatise (*commentarium*) about the set he had designed for Aeschylus. This prompted Anaxagoras and Democritus to write on the same topic, namely, the use of perspective in scene design. That Agatharchus had already discovered the principle of perspective with a central vanishing point becomes obvious when we read Vitruvius's definition of scenography. It implies, he writes (I, 2, 2), "the shading of the frontal parts and receding sides whereby all lines are related to the center of the circle" (*Scaenographia est frontis et laterum abscendentium adumbratio ad circinique centrum omnium linearum responsus*). From Plutarch (*Pericles*, XIII) we learn that Agatharchus was a facile craftsman, who, in contrast to his great competitor Zeuxis, did not strive to work for eternity but was resigned to the ephemeral nature of his painting. Alcibiades once literally forced him to paint the inside walls of his house (Plutarch, *Alcibiades*, XVI), and this kind of fresco wall decoration may be the ancestor of the ornate wall paintings that archaeologists uncovered in the private houses and the public theaters of the age of the Flavian emperors. At any rate, with Agatharchus a certain amount of illusion based upon the technique of foreshortening must have entered the Athenian theater. This trend continued, and in the last third of the 5th century, the great period of Euripidean and Sophoclean creativity, we hear of the work of the scene painter Apollodorus, who increased the illusion by the skillful use of gradation of color and shading, evidently chiaroscuro effects, which earned him the nickname "shadow painter" (*skiagraphos*).

According to Vitruvius (V, 6, 9), the Greeks knew three types of scenery in their theaters: the *genus tragicum*, exhibiting columns, pediments, statuary, and other royal appurtenances; the *genus comicum* (for the plays of Aristophanes, for example), showing dwellings of ordinary citizens with balconies and windows; and the *genus satyricum*, marked by the presence of trees, caves, mountains, and various rustic objects on the stage.

The Greek theater, even of the archaic and pre-Periclean periods, is unthinkable without the employment of set pieces, such as altars, tombs, rocks, and tents. Once a wooden stage building (*skene*) was erected in the Athenian theater of Dionysus Eleuthereus (468–458 B.C), the scene designer, in the person of Agatharchus, made his entrance and drew his foreshortened images on screens or panels (*pinakes*) that were mounted against the front wall of the *skene*. The "set" could be changed by changing the *pinakes*. Later, the two-storied structures of the Hellenistic theaters offered additional display spaces for the mounting of *pinakes* between the columns of the *proskenion* and in the thyromata openings of the *episkenion*.

During the Hellenistic period another scenic device established itself as a convention in the Greek theater, the *periaktoi;* these were triangular wooden prisms, each face of the three-sided machine carrying a different decoration, painted on panels which Pollux called *katablemata*. By the revolving of the *periaktoi* a scene shift could be indicated (cf. Vitruvius V, 6, 8).

The modest wooden stages for the original productions of the plays of Plautus and Terence had no need for the services of a scene designer. The plays were given on a platform stage backed by a curtain or wall on which the entrances to the various houses were marked either by slits in the curtain or by practicable doors in the wall. For the rest, the dramatist's lines localized the play. Eventually the wall in the rear developed into a highly decorative *scaenae frons*. This phase was reached about 99 B.C., when Claudius Pulcher erected a stunning stage wall in his temporary wooden theater (Pliny, *Natural History* XXXV, 23). We do not know the name of the artist who decorated this *scaenae frons*, but the painting was executed in an extremely illusionistic style so that even the birds were deceived and tried to perch on the "tile" roof, which was actually painted on a flat vertical surface.

In Augustan times fresco painting went through a period of decadence. At least Vitruvius (VII, 5) thought so and mentioned the case of the painter Apaturius, who designed a *scaenae frons* that violated, in purely painterly terms, the laws of gravity.

While the audience was willing to accept this fanciful style, Apaturius was censured for his mannerism by a mathematician, who forced him to alter the design and to make it conform to reality. Vitruvius could only wish that more scientists would speak up and "reform the current trend of folly and mistaken practices in fresco painting." To what extent this complaint also applied to theatrical scenery is a matter of conjecture.

The elder Pliny, to whom we owe the reference to the theater of Claudius Pulcher, also informs us (XXXIV, 36) about the next phase in the development of the Roman stage, when the *scaenae frons* assumed an architectural and sculptured character and the architects used columns, pilasters, niches, and statues as primary structural elements (PL. 418, below). Pompeian wall paintings still preserve for us the highly decorative appearance that the Roman *scaenae frons* must have displayed at the time when Seneca wrote his tragedies (PL. 418, above).

A. M. NAGLER

The Middle Ages. a. Byzantium. Owing to the destruction of pictorial and literary documents — especially during the iconoclastic struggle, in the sack of 1204, and in the subsequent periods of foreign domination — attempts to reconstruct the history of the theater and related spectacles in Byzantium must remain fragmentary and problematic despite the richness and variety suggested by the surviving evidence. In late antiquity the state ceremonial of Rome, which had long incorporated such formal episodes as the *acclamationes* and *adventus* (receptions), underwent a great elaboration in accordance with the enhanced sense of imperial majesty. The details of the later imperial ceremonial of Byzantium, closely intertwined with the magnificent ritual of the church, may be gleaned from *De cerimoniis* (ca. 953), a book by the scholarly emperor Constantine VII Porphyrogenitus; in addition to the complicated etiquette required within the Great Palace, Constantine records the solemn processions that passed through the streets of Constantinople on feast days throughout the year. Documentation of the pomp and splendor of church ritual, which increased *pari passu* with that of the state, and of the fixity of established ceremonial is provided by the great murals and mosaics of the time, for example, the procession of the virgins and martyrs in Ravenna (PL. 366; III, PL. 301; XIII, PL. 107).

The imperial throne room of Constantine housed an assortment of ingenious mechanical devices designed to overawe visitors; the comments of the western ambassador Liutprand of Cremona (ca. 920–72) reveal the effectiveness of these devices. On a lower level, the Roman custom of providing mass spectacles for the populace persisted in the hippodrome, which attracted the passionate support of officially recognized factions. As for the theater proper, it is known that despite church opposition the eastern capital boasted at least four devoted to light entertainment. Roman mime lived on in Constantinople and catered to a broadly based audience, though the upper classes seem to have preferred a kind of ballet-pantomime that was performed in the Great Theater. Unfortunately, since not a single text of these secular plays has survived, no concrete idea can be formed of the *mise en scène*. Costume is less obscure; the garb of the individual performer is illustrated by such miniatures of the period as that in a codex in Paris (Bib. Nat., Ms. gr. 74) depicting the Washing of the Feet, with Christ wearing a dalmatic and the apostles in a circle around him dressed as mimes and jugglers.

On the sacred drama our information is more substantial, for a number of texts of plays on Christian subjects have been recovered. The least interesting in this context, since they were never intended for public performance and hence seem to have had no influence on the development of the Byzantine stage itself, is a series of purely literary plays. Typical of these curious works is the *Christos Paschon*, a Passion play probably dating from the 11th or 12th century, and composed according to the cento method.

Owing to the researches of La Piana (1912, 1936), a kind of rudimentary liturgical drama has been identified in the preiconoclastic period (7th–8th cent.) and a number of texts pieced together. It seems that these "dramatic homilies" or sermons in dialogue were commonly performed in churches, only a minimum of action and stage properties being required. By the mid-Byzantine period, however, a full-fledged liturgical drama had evolved in the Byzantine Empire. This drama is known principally from a detailed scenario in ten scenes written in Cyprus in the 13th century, but probably incorporating older material. The actors apparently made their entrances and exits through a curtain (*siparium*) parted in the middle, as depicted in 12th-century miniatures (Bréhier, 1921). At least one side of the stage was devoted to a "house," a structure which could variously represent the Sepulcher of Lazarus, the Temple, and other locales. The stage properties required for some of the scenes were fairly extensive, and machinery must have been employed for rolling the stone away from the entrance to the Sepulcher.

Wayne DYNES

b. *Western Europe.* Concurrent with this Byzantine dramatic literature was the development of the liturgical drama in Europe. Organized by the chapter, under the direction of the bishop or abbot, as an edifying diversion for the *schola cantorum* and the religious community, it was soon inserted into the rite of the mass, being interpreted by the clergy only (deacons, sub-deacons, and clerks). The setting was the church, by its very purpose mystically receptive to the evocative representation of a dramatic action whose content was drawn not from human experience or from sacred history but straight from the divine mystery. Thus not faith alone but initiation was the key to this privileged spectacle, in Latin, which the crowd of the faithful witnessed with the same reverent detachment and the same acceptance based on faith that they accorded the rite of mass. Secure in the mystical assumptions of the service, the dramatic "office" required no other setting, language, decoration, or convention than the symbolic ritual worked out through the centuries. Between the 11th and the 12th century, before the *ludus* became independent of the mass, to merge with other symbolic-religious functions, this choreographic ritual presentation was already fixed, through precise, more or less unchanging and unchangeable directions and through the universal observance of the Gallicanized Roman rite, which, as Bishop Æthelwold's description in the *Regularis Concordia* (965–75) indicates, was in practice almost invariable and valid throughout Christian Europe.

The church by its nature provides for the two sites required for the two phases of the action. The high altar was the place assigned to the main action — the dialogue between the Angel and the Marys (PL. 419); between Christ and his Mother; between the Virgin and the shepherds — which unfolded around the apse and extended as far as the threshold of the presbytery and the ambos. The choir, or *schola cantorum*, and the nave were used for group action, that is, the movements of the choirboys, monks, and clerks who introduced, accompanied, and concluded the whole *repraesentatio*. This left the two aisles and the *matroneum* (section reserved for women), when there was one, to accommodate the faithful.

The principal characters, as well as the choir, made their entrance in procession, and then took their places, moving only as the action required. The procession started from the sacristy or the cloister or the chapter house, or, if necessary, from the bishop's dwelling. The sacristy served as a dressing room, and it also accommodated the decorations and vestments needed for the *repraesentatio*. After the 12th century, the texts of the *ludi* began to be enriched by extraneous and picturesque elements (including dialogues in the vernacular), revealing, together with a greater dramatic interest, an evident striving after a universally comprehensible idiom; at the same time secular items were added to vestments and decorations for purposes of characterization, and the action invaded part of the nave. The angels still wore the dalmatic or the alb, but now these were supplemented *cum alis et libris*; the Marys wore ordinary feminine garb instead of mantles and copes; Herod and his *capellanus* (military attendant) appeared *vilissimi strictis et infulis*. The Church purchased masks beards, and wigs

(for the lions in the Beauvais *Daniel*; for the devil in the *Passion* of Benediktbeuern).

From the sacristy came tapestries, draperies, standards, parchment scrolls, the candles symbolizing the stars of the Magi and the celestial lightning; and even the unconsecrated wafers which, thrown from above to rain upon the faithful, symbolized the manna in the desert (*Ordo Prophetarum* of Padua).

For the high altar — which, with its curtain enclosing the ciborium, permitted the angels to unveil the Holy Sepulcher (*Quem quaeritis*), or the *obstetrices* (midwives) to open the manger to show Jesus to the Magi (*Officium Stellae*) — was substituted a real *monumentum*, that is, a provisional sepulcher built for the Easter services (PL. 419), or an icon with the Virgin and Child (*Officium Pastorum*, version from Padua).

After the 12th century the growing stress on secular topical references and individual characterization in the spectacles made them incompatible with liturgical rite even though they stayed within the bounds of decorum, and they were made separate from religious services. From the clergy, the organizational monopoly of dramatic performances passed to the religious and lay confraternities and the craft guilds, but the church continued to be one of the places devoted to the drama, especially in Umbria and Tuscany and in certain German-speaking centers, such as Bolzano and Vienna; elsewhere the churchyard was preferred. Unfortunately, little has come down to us from this period (i.e., from the close of the 13th to the opening of the 15th cent.). Detailed information begins to be available (more through rubrics than through illustrations) when, on the eve of modern times, the sacred *mise en scène* parts company with the universal and uniform language originally imposed by the liturgical discipline. Even within the general outlines of the recurrent types of scenery several regional tendencies can be distinguished: there now converge in the organization of the spectacle — from the literary origin of the texts to the artistic and craft tradition involved in the actual creation of the set — recognizable and diverse influences stemming from the political regime and the economic system.

In Italy only in the case of the Umbrian *laudi* — which the lay confraternities of the *Laudesi* had developed independently of the liturgical drama, and which had taken root all over the peninsula starting with the 13th century — is it possible to reconstruct, albeit roughly, the stage setting. The clues are to be found in the stage directions in the texts, corroborated by the actors' attendance records.

The performance took place in the oratory (a chapel of the church) or an ordinary house, or, more rarely, in the churchyard or in the square. Thus the atmosphere was still suggestive of the religious ceremony, but the remote liturgical symbolism was replaced by a simple, almost abject, language expressing the penitential spirit of its origins and aimed primarily at providing for direct comprehension of the action and the humble collective participation of the whole confraternity in the form of a chorus. More convincing than the theory of Galante Garrone (1935) that the single scene of action was a kind of "mount" (a multiple stage in several levels, painted to represent a mountain) is the hypothesis that it was an extremely simple platform but elevated to permit visibility by the entire assembly. The monodic *laudi* and the earliest *laudi* in dialogue form probably did not require special scenery, the still rudimentary action being still adequately supported by a few eloquent symbols of the faith: the cross, the image of the Virgin, the thurible, and the lighted candle.

At the end of the 13th century, as the *laudi* in dialogue form developed into dramatic presentations, the platform became a permanent stage with a few *luoghi deputati* to indicate continuous action. At one end was the gate of Paradise, at the other the pit of Hell; between the two places was a painted backcloth mounted on a roller (neutral "curtains," decorated with scenes) or a practicable (the "trasanda," or wooden hut, for the Nativity, the "mount" for the Transfiguration, the "heaven" with Christ and God the Father in a glory). The principal actors mounted the platform in turn. The chorus, which surrounded the stage, narrated the antecedent action and offstage events, connected the actions of the protagonists, or commented on them and, while describing the stage decorations, pointed out the *luoghi deputati* and explained their conventional significance. Of extreme importance in so bare and austere a framework was the function of the costumes: they were sharply typified (by wigs, masks, and symbols) and were patterned, without regard for anachronism, on canonical vestments and contemporary apparel.

It is difficult to establish whether this type of rudimentary, rather primitive, *mise en scène* had counterparts in contemporaneous religious drama elsewhere in Europe. Certainly in as early a work as *Le Mystère d'Adam* of Tours (12th cent.) the stage directions appear to call for "painted canvases" and for the presence of the gate of Paradise and the mouth of Hell. The *Praesentatio Virginis* of Philippe de Mézières (14th cent.) distinctly provided for the construction of two raised platforms. But these plays are both still semiliturgical and do not warrant the making of generalizations.

Along with the *laudi* other forms of religious drama were developing in various Italian towns, influenced both by the *laudi* themselves and by the older tradition of liturgical drama. Thus evolved a civic and collective drama that was less subject to religious control than that of other European countries. Its stage, which is known to us in detail only from the 15th century, tended to be more original and somewhat more improvisatory than elsewhere, but except for the *ingegni* (machines) it did not differ essentially from the over-all European standard of the time. As has been indicated, this development of the drama took two main directions: the traveling play and the play with a fixed place of presentation, indoor or outdoor. In time both were enriched with more magnificent appurtenances and decorations and enjoyed the collaboration of such famous artists as Filippo Brunelleschi, Francesco del Cossa, Jean Fouquet (qq.v.), Hubert Cailleau (PL. 419), Karel van Mander, Giulio Mazzoni, Vigil Raber, Wilhelm Rollinger, Nicoletto Segna, and Trullo (Giovanni Bianchini).

The various kinds of permanent stage settings can be divided into four basic types deriving their designations not only from their plan and structure but also from the place of their widest diffusion: the "flat" stage after the French style, the "volumetric" or "cubic" stage after the German, the English theater in the round, and the Florentine "machine" stage. The first two — these designations notwithstanding — were fairly common almost everywhere; the other two were almost exclusively found in Great Britain and Italy, respectively. Only the English theaters in the round were stable in form from the beginning.

The common denominator was the *luogo deputato*, namely, the place in which the actor was stationed waiting for his entrance, from which each individual action began, to end in the collective action that took place on the unlocalized acting space at the center of the theater or on the forward part of the stage — but always in direct contact with the audience. This structure could be placed at any point on the stage so long as it was conventionally identifiable as the locality it represented (the sea, a street, the garden of Gethsemane). For the most part, however, it had the appearance of a house (hence the terms "mansion," *guérite*, *Haus*, "house," etc.) — that is, it was a small booth patterned on contemporary Romanesque and Gothic paintings; open on its four sides and equipped with sliding curtains, it could, by the use of a few properties, indicate in turn Mary's house, the Temple of Jerusalem, Herod's palace, and Lazarus's abode. The only indispensable and permanent locales were Paradise (a two-level booth, the upper part of which was the celestial "wheel") and Hell (an ogress with mobile jaws, sometimes surmounted by the towers of the city of Dis). The mansion is the characteristic element par excellence of medieval *mise en scène*; neutral without being impersonal, extremely adaptable and maneuverable, it satisfies all the demands of dramatic action that must unfold without interruption and hence require a multiple, simultaneous, and conventionalized setting.

On the juxtaposed set in the French style, all the mansions were placed one next to the other on a single stage along one horizontal line (whence the term "flat" stage). The audience was seated on tiers of seats directly in front of the stage or stood up in the large space between the stage and the seating arrangements that was reserved in part for the less wealthy spectators and in part for the dramatic action.

In the arrangement in the German style each had its own platform visible from all four sides (whence the terms "volumetric" and "cubic"). All the platforms were arranged in an open area — public square, market, or cloister — in a definite order, proceeding from Hell to Paradise and from Paradise to the Cross (FIG. 757). Here too the audience sat on tiers of seats or grandstands running along two or more sides of the square; otherwise they stood in the "parterre."

Likewise in the English circular theaters, exemplified by the Cornish "mounds" (*Plen an Gwary*; FIG. 757), the mansions were mounted on individual platforms. The large circular clearing was bounded by a hill which had been terraced to provide seats for the audience and was protected by a moat on the outside. On the hill, at prearranged intervals, the separate stations were arranged, as follows: to the east, Heaven; to the northeast, the mouth of Hell; to the west, the powerful of the earth; to the north, the pagans, magicians, and outlaws. Again, the action started from the mansion and came to a close in the clearing, in the middle of which there was sometimes a larger platform with the lower part open for visibility (*The Castle of Perseverance*, ca. 1425), or equipped with a device perhaps communicating with a small underground passage for the sudden appearance of characters (e.g., Eve in the scene of the creation of woman).

In all three forms of staging — the so-called "French," "German," and "English" — there are apparent, in addition to the principle of multiple and simultaneously represented settings, two other organic constituents of the medieval concept: first, the mingling of spectators and spectacle; second, the coexistence in a single spectacle of two types of action, one on a raised level, taking place in the mansions, and the other, the central events, unfolding on the level of the ground.

The Florentine *ingegno*, brought to perfection by Filippo Brunelleschi and Il Cecca (Francesco d'Angelo) — which can in fact be documented just about everywhere in Italy — is a notably different matter from the forms just described. It was not so much a stage as a monumental machine for depicting sacred subjects, generally placed in the nave of a church and involving two levels. On a lower platform raised above the floor were two mansions in the traditional sense: the dwelling of Mary (Annunciation; Assumption), or the city of Jerusalem, and the Mount of Olives (Ascension). On the second level, just below the beams of the church, which represented heaven, were God the Father and the angels in glories. The descriptions that have come down to us suggest, here too, a diversity of forms. There was Brunelleschi's large hemisphere; there were the traditional painted concentric "wheels" of the glories expanded to gigantic dimensions; and finally, as Molinari (1961) has suggested, there was probably a half-cone formed by concentric sloping tiers supporting the divine throne at the top. Mechanical devices and lighting techniques made it possible for the apparatus as a whole to revolve in one direction, while its separate parts moved independently, so that startling effects of noctural lights and celestial splendor were produced.

Even in the other traditional types of religious *mise en scène*, stagecraft had achieved such an impressive technical level and range that it was possible to simulate meteorological phenomena such as rain, wind, thunder and lightning, to lend naturalism to depictions of navigation, martyrdom, and so on, and to portray such supernatural events as apparitions, disappearances, flights through the air. In a sense, in view of the nonrealistic, generalized character of medieval scenery even when it was highly stylized and even sumptuous, one almost has the impression that it was really the technical stage effects, together with the costumes, that constituted its most distinctive aspect.

The costumes of the later *sacre rappresentazioni*, like those in the *laudi* of the early Middle Ages, had a twofold orientation — toward the stylized symbol and toward the naturalistic characterization: the utmost in verisimilitude for the daily realities (for the medieval spectator, the drama of divinity was ever-present); the symbols of perfect beauty for the celestial kingdom; and grotesque images of violence and even horror for the lower world of demons, sorcerers, and sinners. Generally speaking, the average costume was the normal, easily identifiable garb of the different classes, trades, and professions. The costumes for the Divinity and the celestial hierarchy were ecclesiastical vestments; the traditional iconography of monsters inspired the costumes for the inhabitants of hell. The striking colors, the use of beards, wigs, demon and angel masks, plus the skillful use of highly idealized and stylized make-up completed the effect and gave point to the argument.

In the itinerant religious drama the machine for scriptural scenes and the stage cart served the purpose of the mansions. All the devotional processions contained elements of spectacle, whether in the street decorations or in the prescribed attire (uniforms of the confraternities, guilds, and magistrates, and clergy), but most pertinent to the present discussion are the dramatic or semidramatic processions organized generally for Holy Week and for the festivals of Corpus Christi, the Ascension, and Pentecost. These processions were merely mimetic and plastic rather than dramatic in character when the pageant wagons displayed only sculptured representations and great *tableaux vivants*, as did the *nuvole* (clouds) and *edifici* (edifices) in the procession of S. Giovanni in Florence, the *Ceri* in Gubbio, the *Casazze* in Genoa, the *Graouilly* (or *Grauli*) in Metz, the *Grands Gueules* in Lyons and Poitiers, the carts of the early Spanish *entremeses*, and the *Figuren* in the German *Prozessionsspiele*.

However, along with these hybrid forms there existed — and in Spain lasted through the 17th century — a type of regularly acted dramatic presentations divided into days and stations, in which the actors performed in public on perambulatory stages. Such were the pageant carts ("pageants") of the English mystery plays and those of the Spanish *autos sacramentales* (FIG. 757).

The company moved across the city with the entire stage and stopped to perform the mystery play at predetermined points (public squares, courtyards, etc.). Elsewhere the stations were permanent, and the actors moved from one to another in procession until they had completed the cycle. This was the procedure in the German *Standortspiele* and in the Italian Holy Week processions, of which traces remain in the Easter celebrations at Sezze Romano, Grassina, Sordevolo, and other places.

The decorations of the stage wagons were based on the same iconography as the *mise en scène* of the permanent stages, except as exigencies of transportation and the building of separate and independent mansions visible from every part of the audience required changes. In the first Spanish *autos sacramentales* every unit had three wagons: a center one (*carrillo*), long, narrow, and completely bare, which served as the actual stage, and two others (*medios carros*), which carried the mansions and were hooked onto the ends of the *carrillo* when the performance started. Later, stages (*tablados*) were built in permanent form, at various points in the city, the scene wagons (two or four, as required) remaining perambulatory.

The number, kind, and splendor of the wagons in the various representations depended of course on the available economic resources and on the artistic level of the audience. In Florence some of the *nuvole* and *edifici* were designed by Brunelleschi, while others were created by Francesco Granacci and Il Cecca. In Madrid, Baccio del Bianco and Cosimo Lotti designed wagons for the *autos sacramentales*. In England, where the court did not interfere with the organization of these processional plays, and each guild was completely responsible for the preparation of the wagon assigned to it, the pageant wagons seem to have been cruder and more generalized.

The secular mise en scène in the 14–16th centuries: the neutral stage and the traveling play. The rudimentary staging of the

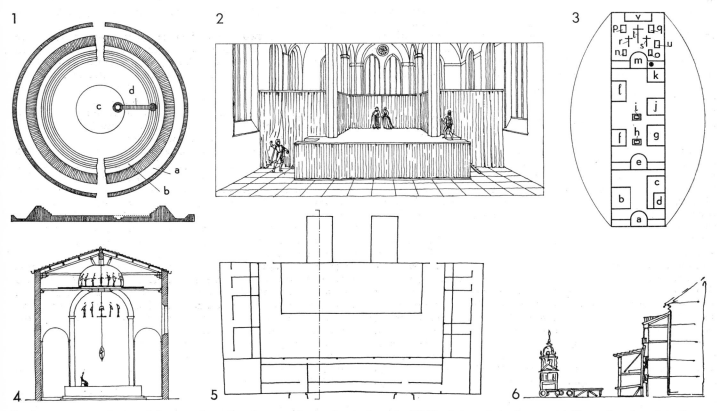

Scenic arrangements for sacred drama performed outdoors and in the church, from the Middle Ages to the 17th cent.: (1) Plan and section of the Perran Round in Cornwall: (*a*) Outer moat; (*b*) tiered embankment for audience; (*c*) stage; (*d*) underground passage with trapdoor for appearance of characters (*from W. Borlase, The Natural History of Cornwall, 1758*); (2) schematic drawing of the stage of the Meistersinger in the Church of St. Martha in Nürnberg, late 15th–early 16th cent. (*from the reconstruction by A. Köster*); (3) reconstruction of the plan for the mansions in the medieval Passion Play in the square of Donaueschingen: (*a*) First gate; (*b*) Hell; (*c*) Garden of Gethsemane; (*d*) Mount of Olives; (*e*) second gate; (*f*) Herod; (*g*) Pilate; (*h*) column of the flagellation; (*i*) column of the cock; (*j*) Caiaphas; (*k*) St. Anne; (*l*) The Last Supper; (*m*) third gate; (*n, o, p, q*) tombs; (*r, s*) thieves' crosses; (*t*) Christ's Cross; (*u*) Holy Sepulcher; (*v*) Paradise (*from ms. of the second half of 15th cent. in the Hofbibliothek of Donaueschingen*); (4) section of the Church of S. Felice, Florence, with schematic reconstruction of Brunelleschi's machine for the *sacra rappresentazione* of the Annunciation (*from Molinari, 1961*); (5, 6) plan and section of devices, stage, and tribunes for *autos sacramentales* performed in the Plaza Mayor, Madrid, 1644.

secular drama in the early Middle Ages had little to offer compared to the mystical spell cast by the liturgical drama. For the lay world the theater consisted of the banquet pantomime, carnival buffoonery, entertainments at fairs, and folk festivals. One or another of these might be fitted indiscriminately into the celebration of festive occasions or of the immovable feasts, and their rudimentary and generalized trappings — tapestries, draperies, trophies, floral arrangements, greenery, and lights — were interchangeable.

The garb of the players partook of the nature of costume, but not so much from the deliberately fantastic transposition of styles as from the meaningful allusiveness of the accessories and of the attributes of the various professions, in which a magnified and distorted picture of the daily life of a society in ferment was reflected.

Religion was still the driving force of such obscure popular representations as the *libertas Decembrica*, the *Ludus Carnelevariis*, and the *Cornomannia*. The holidays granted the lower clergy became the occasion for licentious revelry; the folk and the sacred festival were commingled, and the latter was contaminated by pagan elements carried over from early propitiation rites. Irreverence degenerated into sacrilege, and the procession was swept up in a kind of collective madness against which neither the church nor its consecrated symbols of ecclesiastical dignity was proof.

In palace and castle the strolling player performed on a small podium or any spot in the center of the hall, surrounded by invited guests. Sole protagonist of this dubious theatrical presentation, he interpreted all the roles and played all the parts with the help of a few easily recognizable accessories. The first and only comic mask of the Middle Ages, he was invariably clad in the madman's cruel, stark uniform: bicolored tights, jagged sleeves and doublet, pointed hood with ass's ears, bells jingling on his feet, collar, and hood, with the obscene scepter of folly in his hand.

The neutral stage, bare of any representational element to set the scene, was for centuries the common denominator of the secular *mise en scène* in Europe. The first representational elements appear rather in the *tableaux vivants* and short pantomimes (*entremets*) of the allegorical *carri* (PL. 421) that, from the second half of the 14th century, were brought into halls during banquets or formed part of the official processions — royal entries, weddings (PL. 421), baptisms, accessions — in which the court appeared in public and princely authority and patrician privilege were thus celebrated in the presence of the whole community.

Here, as in the street theaters and arches adorning the route of the procession, the representational art was appropriate to the content of the pantomime or brief recitation and clarified its purpose. The subject matter was drawn from current events, history, and the literature of chivalry and love. The images (towers, castles, giants and animals, celestial knights and infernal monsters, coats of arms and trophies) evoked a heroic and mysterious world whose metaphor was understood by all. This was a language articulated similarly, except for differences in allusions, all over Europe — in the French *entremets*, the Portuguese *momos*, the English pageant, the Italian *trionfo*, the Spanish *entremés*, and the Venetian *momario*. So consistent and so independent was this expression that it suggests not so much reciprocal influences, which may indeed have existed, as a fundamental correspondence of situations and interests.

These celebrations excepted, the public stage of the *bourgeoisie* remained faithful, as has been said, to the functional adaptability and impersonality of the neutral stage. The earliest iconographical evidence that has come down to us shows a raised platform with a curtain that can be opened in the center at the back or, at most, with a tiny room formed by curtains hung on four supporting poles (PL. 420). Except for differences in the kinds of curtains and the addition of all-purpose elements (e.g., the two side *guérites* appearing in certain illustrations of French farces), and of symbolic and grotesque motifs (*soties*, *Fastnachtspiele*), this scenic arrangement prevailed everywhere in Europe — in Spain, France, Austria, Germany, the Low Countries (kermesses), Great Britain, and Italy (early presentations of the *commedia dell'arte*) — until the beginning of the 16th century, and even later.

In the 16th century, when an organic dramatic repertory had grown out of the welter of literary forms of the medieval festival, and theatrical activity was solidly based on well-established permanent companies, the neutral stage developed further, and recognizable national types emerged. However, what was common to all was the intentionally generalized character of the setting, which (except in the case of the Italian perspective set) marked all phases of the gradual evolution from the medieval tent to structures susceptible of easy transformation. The stage of the German Meistersinger, the ornate temporary stages of the Dutch Rederyker Kamers, or Chambers of Rhetoric (PL. 428), the Elizabethan stage (PL. 425), and the settings of the Spanish *corrales* are the commonest and most organic prototypes of this kind of *mise en scène*, which was developed under the differing auspices of the polished amateur productions and the professional theater.

The stage of the famous Meistersinger of Nürnberg directed by Hans Sachs, whether in the reconstruction by Max Hermann or by Albert Köster (FIG. 757), still comes closest to being the paradigm of the medieval neutral setting. The stage consisted of a long podium, over a yard from the ground, accessible by means of a ladder visible at each end. The back of the podium was marked off by an arrangement of hangings that receded to form a kind of alcove, or small rectangular room.

On the temporary stages that the Dutch Rederykers erected in squares for their great annual celebrations, the canopy was supported, or sometimes replaced, by large, beautifully decorated wooden structures with excellent architectural lines. The types varied: sometimes the stage had a spacious but simple rectangular setting consisting of a *frons* with three doors or, better, three arches crowned by an architrave or spandrel (Louvain, PL. 428; Amsterdam, 1609). Elsewhere the setting was elaborated into massive constructions of several levels recalling magnificent structures of the Roman *frons scaenae* (Ghent, 1539; Antwerp, 1561).

Unlike these two types of stage setting, which still have the provisional character of a decorative superstructure, both the Elizabethan theater and the Spanish *corrales* derive their stage directly from the traditional local architecture, arriving by similar paths at different solutions. They are both large courtyard theaters with the seating space located in wooden galleries or in wall boxes completely surrounding the vast central court (*corral*); in both the stage is formed by separating a whole section of the boxes from the rest.

In the Elizabethan theaters, which had by the last two decades of the 16th century acquired a distinctive architectural style (different from that of other English buildings), the section reserved for the stage was called the tiring house. This section had two or more stories where the actors who were not on stage, the orchestra (generally placed on the highest gallery in full view of the audience), the properties and costumes, and even some privileged spectators were accommodated. The first and second levels could also serve as stage space, forming an inner stage and an upper stage, respectively. The inner stage was a large central recess, where the players performed, flanked by two practicable doors for the actors' entrances and exits. However, most of the action took place on the outer stage, a large raised platform that extended into the center of the yard. It was square or polygonal, with a trapdoor in the floor, and absolutely bare of any descriptive or illusionistic scenographic element. A large canopy placed on top of the tiring house, or resting on pilasters or columns in front of it, covered the whole or part of the stage (PL. 425).

The architecture of Spanish theaters adhered to the styles of ordinary buildings for a longer period. The stage, set up along one of the short sides of the *corral*, never assumed the proportions of an architectural unit, remaining a generalized, if not completely indeterminate, scenic superstructure. Between the pillars supporting the balconies were curtains that could be drawn, forming the neutral background; the pillars could be transformed by decorated canvas curtains depicting scenery (trees, columns, rocks, etc.). The first balcony was the real theater, that is, the stage, in the sense of a place from which the actors emerge; the second balcony, *lo alto del teatro*, corresponding to an "attic," formed an upper stage; a possible third balcony, equipped for the same purposes, was referred to as the *segundo alto*. The action took place on the spacious platform that protruded deep into the *corral*. A drop curtain was lowered at the beginning of the performance and remained so throughout, as was the fashion in contemporary European productions.

Perspective scenography in Italy. While out of the diversified European traditions there was developing, under the two distinct influences of the public theater and the court show, an ingenious, adaptable, but representationally limited *mise en scène*, in Italy the more challenging project of perspective scenery was in process from the beginning of the 16th century. Even though Humanism, which was one of the factors that gave rise to the new trend in stage design, had been deeply influencing all Italian art and culture for more than a century, during almost the whole 15th century the theater did not differ in any essential way from that of the rest of Europe except for the frequency of large official spectacles sponsored by the political and economic organizations formed all over the peninsula during the period of the *signorie*.

Toward the middle of the century, when the Italian princes, having consolidated their territorial gains, embarked on an extensive program of official entertainment, the autonomy enjoyed by theaters in other countries (despite the fetters of "patents" and "privileges") disappeared. The court took the place of the municipal authorities, controlling public spectacles either directly through its agencies or indirectly through patronage, eventually becoming the sole arbiter, even when the citizens' participation in financing and organization gave the impression of free enterprise.

In contrast to the public celebrations, which took the usual forms of the official processions (entries, funerals, baptisms), tourneys, and religious processions, there were the private festivities held within the palace walls for the members of the court and their guests. Of these, dramatic performances were only one category: perhaps the most refined, they certainly were not more popular than banquets, balls, and vocal concerts.

Thus 15th-century scenography arises, properly speaking, not as stage décor but as the framework of court festivities, and takes on their sumptuous character. Staging of this type also suited the performance patterned on the simple banquet intermezzo, as well as the more evolved performance on the lines of the eclogue and the farce, drawing on the more showy and adaptable elements of the medieval *mise on scène* as needed. These were operatic compositions abounding in personal and topical allusions, performed without interruption, and devoid of effective dramatic progression; the action, a compound of dancing, combats, and pantomime, often occupied the whole room and opened and closed with a procession. This type of performance required not mansions or a raised stage but allegorical floats and the allusive representations of the *entremets* and the pageant. The spirit of the decoration changed and was now permeated by classical references and mythological subjects. The *ingegno* of the medieval Paradise became the throne of Olympus; Hades replaced Hell; and the sky with its planets the celestial spheres. The type of decoration also changed, faithfully following Renaissance models — as did the structure of the carts and the machines, the taste in costumes, and the use of masks and make-up — to symbolize, in the spirit of the time, the rediscovery of an earthly *humanitas*.

In Naples, Costanzo de Moris and Carluccio da Padova built a practicable temple on 20 columns for the *Presa di Granata* of Jacopo Sannazzaro (1492). In Milan, Leonardo da Vinci (q.v.) introduced into an exquisite Renaissance setting (leafy arches, damasks, draperies) machines of the medieval type, magnifying them and transforming the separate *luoghi deputati* into enormous autommomous mechanical stages far removed from their models in purpose and meaning: the heaven of the *Festa del Paradiso* (1490), the Hades of *L'Orfeo* (1490–95), and the shining "star" of the *Danae* (1496). In Mantua (1501) a huge

allegorical machine (*Grotta della fortuna*) served as the *luogo deputato* for five classical comedies in a setting adorned by the great series of paintings *The Triumph of Caesar* (PL. 32; VII, PL. 268) by Andrea Mantegna (q.v.). Leonardo's settings and the Mantuan scenic apparatus are the apogee of this type of *mise en scène*, a compromise between the persisting medieval stagecraft and the irrepressible thrust toward modern decoration.

Elsewhere, in the meantime, another type of *mise en scène* was taking form, which while borrowing certain ideas and devices from the medieval multiple setting derived its particular coloration from very different cultural and intellectual premises. The classical repertory (especially Plautus and Terence) and Vitruvius's chapters on the theater were in the public domain in Italy starting from the middle of the 15th century; and the Humanist academies had undoubtedly practiced reading the Latin texts aloud in groups even before the authorized performances took place, at the Medici Palace in Florence (1476) and in the circle of Francesco della Rovere (Sixtus IV) and Cardinal Riario at the pontifical court in Rome (1478–86). Any attempt to form an accurate picture of these productions on the basis of obscure references by contemporary chroniclers must be arbitrary. The Terentian stage itself, which was used for performances in the academies not only in Italy but also in France (PL. 423) and in Germany, and which on the basis of contemporary illustrated editions has been reconstructed as a kind of *scaenae frons* formed by small juxtaposed arches enclosed by curtains, is still the subject of controversy.

On the other hand, a much more definite picture emerges in the descriptions of the contemporary diarists of that "Ferrarese city" which, between 1486 and 1502, was used as a setting for performances of classical or pseudoclassical texts at the court of the D'Estes: "In front of the tiers of steps," wrote Isabella d'Este to her husband in 1502, "there is built a wooden wall surmounted by battlements, like a city wall, and as tall as a man; above it are the houses of the plays, which are six and not set farther forward than usual." Contrary to the opinion of Herrmann (1914) and others, the scene was probably not a medieval street extending into stage depth but a series of "houses" aligned in a single row like the mansions of the medieval multiple setting in the French style; that is to say, it was the same kind of stage as the arrangement used for the religious plays presented in Ferrara during the same period and described by the same diarists; the street could be identified with the proscenium, and the walls of the city with the proscenium podium. Perhaps the form, or rather the purpose, of the "houses" was different; most striking was the clear intent to abandon the multiple setting and the striving for unity of place apparent in the evocation of the city as a whole.

Six years later the chronicles of Ferrara record the first official description of a perspective setting, painted by Pellegrino da Udine for the first play from the pen of Lodovico Ariosto, *La Cassaria*. Even without entering into the controversial question of the painted panels of Urbino executed in the circle of Piero della Francesca (q.v.) and Giuliano da Sangallo, which have been recognized as the 15th-century patterns for the tragic and the comic stage set, it is clear that this scenic achievement of Pellegrino da Udine was not born *ex abrupto*. Rather, he made tangible an existent trend in form that had been fully worked out in theory within the academies and had already been given expression in the great representational art of the time.

What had apparently been missing in all the previous theatrical forms based on dialogue and chorus was the dramatic premise that would also revolutionize the *mise en scène*. The so-termed "regular" comedy and the new forms of the tragedy and the pastoral introduced through the works of Ariosto and G. B. Giraldi (Cinzio), respectively, into the court and the *Studio* of Ferrara were to provide the occasion as well as the material required for such a radical change.

The process was gradual, involving every aspect of dramatic presentation, and in the course of a thirty-year period led to a completely different concept of the theater. In the first place, the performance, while remaining within the sphere of the celebration, began to stand out and be distinct from it. A more organic and complex form of drama called for a regular company, a stage functionally suited to the new text, and a separate base for the performance. The amateur court company was reinforced constantly by professional performers until, in the last half of the century, it was supplanted by the *compagnie dell'arte*, companies of actors recognized not only as interpreters of improvised plays but as accredited representatives of the profession.

The tendency was toward permanent housing for the drama, and here again figures the name of Ariosto, who organized at the court of Ferrara the first permanent court theater of which there is record (1531). Whether temporary or permanent, the theaters, all of which had raised stages and tiered seats, were of three basic types: (1) with only one sector facing the proscenium; (2) with long tiers of seats running along two or three sides of the hall, surrounding an orchestra reserved for the prince's box or for ballet dancing and tournaments; and (3) with a pseudo-classical semicircular cavea. The stage setting featured geometrical perspective with a single central vanishing point. This is the theater par excellence, developed by the keenest and most learned theoreticians and the most exciting and original artists. It represents the coherent sum of seemingly contradictory postulates, creating out of the three rigid academic types of theatrical setting (tragic, comic, and satyric; III, PL. 204) the ideal background for the new Renaissance drama. As a first step, the tragic and comic scenes were combined into a single type of stage picture, the *prospettiva urbano*, including all the elements of traditional scenery: the piazza with its temples, arches, palaces, and the market with its shops and taverns. The setting for the satyric play, however, remained independent except that it is likely to be confused with settings having decorations from nature, based on plants and floral festoons. The urban scene especially was a type at once both multiple and unitary, since it remained one and fixed throughout the play (and sometimes through several different plays) and yet included, however unified the view as a whole may be, several different places: a street, a house, a piazza, and even an interior, suggested by a character talking through a window. It was a "generic," or generalized, setting because it was conceived in terms of the genus drama and not in terms of the subject matter of a particular drama. And so it remained, even when it served the festive purpose of a celebration and reproduced on the stage the most important monuments of a city (Venice, Rome, Florence), copying them directly from reality and aligning them on the two diagonals of the centralized perspective with no concern for topographical accuracy (PL. 422). The scene was both illusionistic and realistic, since the reality it reconstructed was conceptual rather than historical or illustrative. In fact, the aim was to create around the physical action of the players, not a particular place, but a real space, or rather the illusion of a real space.

From the perspective scenery of Pellegrino da Udine (1508) to the second book (1545) of Serlio's *Architettura*, in which he lucidly presents the theoretical premises and practical experience of earlier stage designers, the history of perspective scenery is filled with the names of the most renowned figures in the art of the Renaissance (q.v.): Gerolamo Genga (Cardinal Bibbiena's *La Calandria* in Urbino, 1513), Baldassare Peruzzi (q.v.; PLS. 422, 431; *La Calandria* in Rome, 1514); Raphael (Ariosto's *I Suppositi*, Rome, 1519), Andrea del Sarto (Machiavelli's *La Mandragola*, 1521, and *Clizia*, 1526, Florence), Bastiano da Sangallo (Lorenzo de' Medici's *L'Aridosia*, Florence, 1536), in addition to Giulio Romano, Serlio, and others.

During this period the iconography and the technical side of stagecraft also changed radically; while the different phases of the evolution elude us, its broad outlines can be discerned in the statements of Serlio and Vasari. In the first phase spatial depth was entirely illusionistic *immaginata sopra le mura piane* ("imagined on flat walls"), that is, the scene was painted on a backdrop and completed on two large wings in the foreground, which were either painted (Pellegrino da Udine) or worked in relief (Genga).

In Peruzzi's two sketches for the *Bacchides* (Rome, 1531), which in any case can be taken as a *terminus post quem*, the ground plan (*piantazione*) already seems to have progressed in the direction of the stage picture that Serlio described as *materiale*, and that Vasari affirms was introduced by Peruzzi himself at some time between 1514 and 1531. The *Bacchides* sketches (preserved in the Uffizi), one a plan and the other an elevation, show a perspective setting developed by a series of angle wings spaced at regular intervals, set up with one frame of the wing placed frontally and the other at an angle, along diagonal axes that break in the middle and narrow toward the back. The stage floor is sloped and divided into two zones. The first zone, which includes the proscenium and the first two "houses," corresponds to the piazza and is the actual site of the dramatic action, which takes place along the whole width of the stage. The second zone, considerably narrower, creates the illusion of a distant street which is depicted on the backdrop and on several much smaller, impracticable wings. Notwithstanding the presence of the street on the backdrop, the problem of stage depth is here dealt with on the logical, not the imaginary, level of a real and limited space.

In the years between 1550 and 1565, perspective iconography took a further step when the artists in Vasari's circle in Florence no longer modeled their scenes on Peruzzi's piazza, organized in two depth planes, but created a continuous perspective by placing all the wings along two unbroken diagonals. In the first place, the innovation affected the appearance of the setting, changing the piazza into a wide street in the very far distance and giving the real space an expressly illusionistic depth. Furthermore, since the available acting space now extended from the proscenium to a larger section of the stage slope, as far as the third "house" (G. B. Cini, *Descrizione degli Intermezzi alla Cofanaria*, 1565), the action started to move toward the inner part of the stage and develop in depth.

Between the stage and the orchestra we now have the insertion of the *prospetto scenico*, the imaginary fourth wall of the auditorium, which separates the audience from the action, illusion from reality, and coordinates and sharpens the stage picture by enclosing it within a framework. As yet limited to a wooden partition, the *prospetto scenico* had not assumed the stability of an architectural structure, but as a logical solution, inobtrusive and independent from the representational point of view, it had already replaced the elementary Serlian scenic frame formed by merely connecting the two proscenium "houses" with a simple decorative festoon.

The time was ripe for illusionism, and theatrical techniques had perfected means previously unimaginable to achieve it. The court show, for its part, had developed two special kinds of presentation, the *intermedio* and the *abbatimento*, which at their apogee found in the marvelous illusionistic inventions of the new stagecraft their ideal scenic idiom. The *intermedio* — originally introduced into dramatic presentations to provide light entertainment during intermissions, thus permitting the play to be interrupted while preserving a semblance of continuity (in deference to the three unities) — had for a long time been ramifying as to subject matter and intent, to the point of becoming a show within a show. The type known as the *intermedio* (or *intermezzo*) *apparente* had musical accompaniment, lavish costumes, and sometimes even floats and machines. As early as 1539, Bastiano da Sangallo seems to have sensed the importance of these interludes: in the course of the performance of *Il Commodo* as part of the festivities for the wedding of Cosimo I, he transferred two of the *intermezzi* (*The Sirens* and *Silenus*) from the stage to the foot of the proscenium, which was decorated to represent the Arno. In 1567, still in Florence, for the performance of *I Fabii* following the baptism of Eleanora de' Medici, Baldassare (Lanci) da Urbino mounted frames covered with painted cloth on revolving prisms (*periaktoi*), and for the fourth act the scene, depicting Florence, changed in sight of the audience — Canto della Paglia taking the place of Piazza della Signoria.

In 1585 during the performance of the great musical intermezzi of *L'Amico fido* staged by Bernardo Buontalenti (IV, PL. 187) in the new permanent hall in the Uffizi, while the Florentine décor of the play remained the same, the setting changed for each intermezzo, and the intermezzi were also embellished by spectacle-creating machines that crossed the stage in every direction, from side to side and from top to bottom. In such splendor the Italian theater made its start toward the new drama with music.

By diverse paths the *abbattimento cavalleresco*, or knightly mock combat, had also arrived at scene changing and the marvelous techniques employing machines for surprise effects. As early as the 15th century, they had initiated not only a choreographic but a dramatic form as a result of the pageant-contests on a given subject, which called for allegoric or symbolic floats and appropriate costumes. In 1561 the presentation in Ferrara of the *Castello di Gorgoferusa*, in the ducal courtyard, to celebrate the appointment of Luigi d'Este as cardinal suddenly presents an absolutely new but organically defined form of *abbattimento*. All the characteristics of the baroque knightly festival are already present and are coordinated in a brilliant choreography: the dramatized allegoric introduction, the prearranged battle, the knights' appearance on the machines and floats, plus the arrangement of the theater with a raised stage and tiered seating.

Actually what was created in this case was not so much a scenographic stage picture as an enormous theater machine with a décor that drew upon all the traditional forms of staging, public and theatrical: the *castello*, consisting of several levels of practicable scaffolding; the false façade; perspective; pyrotechnic effects. But the most stupendous innovation was the change of scene *à vista*, which at the end of the representation, amid exploding fireworks, transformed the castle, the site of the combat, into a gigantic "triumphal" rock. In the course of the introduction to the *Tempio d'Amore* tournament of 1565 at Ferrara several scenic elements mounted on *periaktoi* changed, showing now a temple, now a rocky coast. In the *Isola Beata* (1569; Pasi da Carpi and Pirro Ligorio, architects) the stage was situated on a large artificial island in the city moat and was transformed, again by means of pyrotechnic art, from an enchanted fortress to a palace of delights.

From Ferrara this genre quickly spread over the whole peninsula, and the next century brought it to the point of perfect organization (PL. 432), with theatrical edifices and stage scenery shaped into a distinctive type, which in certain respects influenced the staging of regular dramatic and musical plays.

Costume played an extremely important part in the gradual evolution of 16th-century stage design (PLS. 421, 424, 427) as drama moved from the reason and balance of the Renaissance to prebaroque illusionistic exuberance. From the medieval stage 15th- and 16th-century costumes had inherited certain characteristics: (1) the anachronistic use of contemporary clothes, as well as the ability to make them dramatic simply by the mere accentuation of the decorative element and by the use of precious and gaudy fabrics; (2) the tendency to conventionalize the garments of supernatural characters, stylizing them according to certain esthetic principles and symbols or distorting them through grotesquely realistic characterization.

To this the Renaissance added an interest in history and documentation that eventually produced three basic types: costumes patterned completely on the wardrobe of contemporary nobility, and used for comedies of all periods and places, without concession to historical or social accuracy; costumes *all'antica*, reserved for tragedies (as well as triumphal processions and corteges), in which the long garment of high-ranking personages outnumbered tights and cloaks and in which the decoration was based on the classical motifs of ancient monuments (frets, swastikas, imitation armor, and knee-length tunics); and finally the fantastic costumes used for ballet, Moorish dances, exhibition tournaments, pastorals, and intermezzi. In this last type, contemporary fashion is transformed to the point of being unrecognizable by the extravagance of the styles, the ornateness of the ornament, and the use of exotic motifs inspired by the discovery of new worlds. Contrasting with this type of costume, inconceivable away from the luxurious milieu of the court theater, is the costume of the *commedia dell'arte* (PL. 510), that improvised, lively, dramatic phenomenon born and nurtured in the piazza or the chamber theater.

The professional company, a complex institution, supplanted both the court and the public theater, serving as a link between these two widely separated worlds. Through the former it became acquainted with the court repertory, which it popularized through a skillful use of improvisation enlivened by vitalizing,

if less refined, topical allusions. The court also taught the importance of trained actors (for notwithstanding appearances, the players in improvised performances were trained) and the value of the stimulus of stage settings — which, however, were reduced to a number of conventional types, of dimensions that facilitated their transportation from city to city. The repertory of sets was modest: a street on a central axis with a few "houses" arranged on diagonals on two sides of the small platform; on the backdrop the *prospettiva* (stage picture) showing a piazza, a palace, a mountain or a forest (PL. 429). All that was needed to turn a "house" into a prison, or a tavern into a brothel, was the addition of a window grating or the removal of a sign.

The less prosperous companies managed with one painted backdrop (perhaps even in perspective) significantly similar to the former neutral curtain of medieval farces. The list of properties tells the actor-manager what fittings he has to provide for each performance: "Trumpets, drums, three suits of armor, one ugly suit of armor, two slaves' costumes. Costumes for the Magician and the Devil" (*Scenari per Istrioni*, 17th-cent. mss., Bib. Corsiniana, Rome).

Costume, an indispensable adjunct to this simple and ingenious setup, revealed, even more than the scenery, its mixed origin. The court repertory had indicated and then imposed the principal basic roles (elders, servants, lovers, the tyrant, the nurse) and had also established costumes for the characters named. The piazza supplied, from life, the middle- and lower-class types, which were branded by the unmistakable characterizations of the "masks" (PLS. 429, 434): Pantalone and the Doctor, the two old men; Harlequin and Brighella, the two servants. To these were added in the course of time a variety of roles not masked but easily recognizable: Corallina, the Captain, Mezzetino, Scapino, Scaramouche, and others. The costume became the uniform of the personage, set in a universal pattern, which is at the same time a stylization of regional fashion and professional attire and a garment functionally adapted to the technique of the *commedia dell'arte*, in which the gesture — that is, dexterity in patomime and acrobatic agility — takes precedence over the word.

Changeable scenery and perspective illusionism in Italy. Baroque scenography was, then, ushered in by the scene changing and perspective illusionism which developed in Italy through the functioning of the new kinds of spectacle that burgeoned at the beginning of the 17th century out of the promise of the late 16th century. Moreover, the success of this new style coincided with a change in the economic and political conditions of Italian society, which proved to be decisive.

Italy had not been spared the effects of the Counter Reformation and the wars for hegemony that had cast a shadow over the whole continent. On all sides, in the principalities, the patrician class was growing more independent, claiming public office, assuming the administration, if not the government, of the country and changing what had hitherto been court politics into a real and authentic oligarchic diplomacy extending to the level of international affairs. The burden of official entertainment, with its complicated public and private ceremonial, fell on individual families, who, even if wealthy, found it difficult to maintain the spectacle on the grand scale that the court treasuries had previously made possible. Thus arose the twofold theatrical organization that obtained throughout the 17th and 18th centuries in Italy: the financing of public theaters was shared by the literary-"knightly" academies and the aristocracy, but on a commercial basis.

Beginning in 1637, the year when the first opera season was inaugurated at the Teatro di San Cassiano in Venice, the new public theaters were for the most part opera houses, since opera, being the latest fashion, assured both large audiences and a return on capital. However, the academies continued to present, without charge, the traditional courtly dramas with less appeal to the general public. At the same time they also assumed the monopoly of the *festa cavalleresca* and the *abbattimento*, that is, of the other typical 17th-century spectacle, which, together with the musical drama and the ballet, was responsible for the technical innovations of the baroque *mise en scène*.

Between the Florentine festivals of 1585 and 1589 and the Ferrari-Manelli *Andromeda*, performed in Venice in 1637, there was a long and complex formative period dominated by the decisive modernizing influence of the experiments of the Florentine school — Bernardo Buontalenti, Alfonso Parigi, Giulio Parigi (PL. 427), Baccio del Bianco, Cosimo Lotti, and Ferdinando Tacca — and the Ferrara group — G. B. Aleotti, Alfonso Rivarola (Chenda), and Francesco Guitti.

The Florentine school, involved in the court life of the Medici and the Accademia degl'Immobili, drew upon a hybrid repertory made up of intermezzi, ballets, nocturnal revelry, and jousts, all preceded by a vocal introduction and accompanied by enthralling changes of scene *à vista* and the surprise effects of theater machines. Iconographically the stage maintained an architectural severity that Florentine tradition never renounced: the street-and-piazza of the Vasarian phase gave way definitively to the continuous perspective view with central axis and single vanishing point located beyond the wall of the stage but not beyond the horizon line. The spectator was still within the boundaries of a limited distance — illusive but not illusionistic — measurable on the basis of a real proportion. The wings no longer changed by revolving units on *periaktoi* but were slid on fixed grooves by manual traction.

The school of Ferrara produced almost exclusively outdoor and indoor tourneys with introductions, drawing on an iconographic repertory less complex stylistically than that of the Florentines. Nevertheless they excelled in stage engineering and achieved miraculous effects. But their greatest contribution was made in the field of theatrical architecture, which certainly owes to Aleotti and his successors several fundamental innovations, among them the architectural scenic façade, the placing of the orchestra in front of the proscenium, and the arrangement of the auditorium into separate small boxes.

In 1637 the Venetian school began to assert itself alongside the Florentine and the Ferrarese, not so much on the level of artistic originality as of the professional organization that turned the scenographic enterprise from a patrician pastime into public theater with regular daily performances of normal proportions and normal costs. Except for Giuseppe Alabardi, a Venetian, the first important scenic designers working on Venetian stages came from the mainland: Chenda (Alfonso Rivarola) from Ferrara and Giovanni Burnacini and Giacomo Torelli (PL. 435), the real originators of the new school of the Marches — if we reexamine the real importance of Nicolò Sabbatini and his *Pratica* (1638). In the middle of the century these artists introduced the second phase of baroque stage design, beginning the unrepeatable adventure of illusionistic perspective with the vanishing point at infinity (*all'infinito*). All Italy, including the provinces, was now involved. The dramatic genres were defined, and the theatrical season and the dramatic repertory became regularized. Public theater auditoriums acquired a functional organic pattern: orchestra, boxes, and orchestra pit.

The stage was organized on three levels: understage pit; stage floor; and stage gallery. Stage machinery was completely hidden by the architectural set and its smooth functioning assured by perfect mechanical dumbwaiters going to the very top. Sometime between 1600 and 1642 the ground plan with angle wings (one frontal and the other oblique) disappeared and perspective began to be created graphically by a symmetrical series of numerous flat wings (PL. 431). Torelli appears to have introduced, in the Teatro Novissimo in Venice, the technique of making simultaneous scene changes by connecting all the wings to a single mechanism beneath the stage — the origin of the traditional system of pulleys and counterweights still in existence.

Perspective was still centralized, with a single vanishing point at infinity, giving the effect of interminable distance in which the eye loses itself. It became a kind of spatial extravaganza. But to Ludovico Burnacini (1636–1707; PLS. 434, 435), who at an early age had gone to work in the Viennese court with his father, Giovanni, it presented no problems of verisimilitude or visual rationality: depending on the compelling effect of symmetrical repetition, he immersed his structures in a boundless space in which all architectonic obligations disappeared. This disintegrative process was accompanied by a striving for endlessly elaborated decoration: the static unity of separate architectural elements was transformed into symbolic compositions or anthropomorphic structures typical of northern fantasy (PL. 435). On the other hand, Torelli, who emigrated to the French court in 1645, was influenced by French classicism, which, while curbing the free expression of his artistic imagination, fostered the development of his gift for architectural structure. Hence his interest in resolving logically the connection between the perspective created by a succession of side wings and the vanishing point at infinity painted on the backcloth. For this, an architectural transept (arch, terrace, or portal) was inserted at the back of the stage, between the two diagonal axes, which without breaking up the composition established the continuity of the foreshortening even when it interrupted and divided it into two superimposed levels or into several paths all moving together toward infinity, tending toward a single imaginary and invisible focus (PL. 435).

It may well be asked how there can be any harmony of proportion or visual concordance between this phantasmagoric stage frame and the dramatic action for which it was intended. By now scenography had become autonomous. It drew on the fantastic, historical, exotic, and erotic subjects of the librettos and introductions for inspiration and freely elaborated these themes, unconcerned with verisimilitude or functionality, in a quest for visual dynamism and "wonder" as ends in themselves, unrelated to the unity and coherence of the representation as a whole. What mattered was the spectacle, in and for itself — immediate visual delight, instantaneous emotion, and a contagious collective illusion.

As a matter of fact, in this period the only type of spectacle whose scenery corresponded to its form and content — the *abbattimento cavalleresco* — was disappearing. The opera and the ballet had no difficulty in adapting to the baroque trend, and even the drama, which all during this half-century had somehow maintained the principle of unity of place, conformed. The single permanent set (an urban perspective scene for tragedy and comedy; a sylvan perspective scene, with or without a seascape, for the pastoral) was succeeded by the regular repertory of changeable scenes patterned on those used for the opera (a nobleman's dwelling, a jail, a forest, etc.).

The plays given in Jesuit colleges played a greater part in the modernization of theatrical forms than did those of the academies. In the hands of the teacher of rhetoric, the Jesuit theater became an extremely effective instrument in the education of young noblemen, instilling the fear of God and training them in the spiritual and social self-control essential to public life. The repertory was brought up to date and included intermezzi, ballets, and dramas with music; tragedies were patterned on the religious plays, and the religious plays used the themes of the literature of chivalry and *Ecclesia triumphans*. The *mise en scène*, within the limits of a didactic symbolism, took to strong colors, capable of making a violent impact on the spectator. Every college boasted of a temporary or permanent theater (PL. 436), a well-stocked wardrobe, and a supply of scenery and machines hardly inferior to those of the public theaters. As early as 1586 the *Ratio studiorum* had sanctioned this activity in all its aspects, converting it into a regular academic discipline and making it valid and permanent wherever in Europe Jesuit colleges would be established.

Spread of perspective scenery in Europe. It was in this developed and spectacular form that perspective scenery spread and became established throughout Europe toward the middle of the 17th century, adapting itself in various ways to local traditions.

In France, where the influence of the Italian style was strongly felt as early as the 16th century, especially in court circles (PL. 436), perspective scenery remained rather uncommon, being produced almost exclusively by Italians (Andrea Nannoccio, Lyons, 1548; Cosimo Ruggieri, Nantes, 1596) for official celebrations. Even after 1645, when Torrelli ushered in that long-lived and fertile school of perspective stage design that was to include such illustrious figures as Gaspare Vigarani, Gian Lorenzo Bernini (q.v.), Carlo Vigarani, and Niccolò Servandoni, perspective scenery continued to be used only for the so-called "nonlegitimate" genres: the *ballets de cours* (PL. 426), the *pastiches*, and the *tragédies lyriques* performed at court; and the famous *pièces à machines* produced (1647-71) by George Buffequin and Prat at the Théâtre du Marais before a sophisticated aristocratic audience.

In 1671, with the inauguration of the Académie Royale des Opéras, directed by J. B. Lully (or Lulli) and Carlo Vigarani, the sphere of influence of illusionism widened, but a new element was already discernible in the local trend. Carlo Vigarani, who was himself a follower of Torelli, and used his compositional pattern, modified the perspective foreshortening so that it did not extend into infinity but opened into wide, luminous landscapes or the monumental stateliness of an architectural backdrop.

With Jean Bérain (1637-1711; PL. 436) succeeding Carlo Vigarani in 1680, the French tradition was reinforced and its style clarified. A diminution of interest in perspective was compensated for by decorative invention of the most sumptuous order and by an anticipation of a pictorial (or picturesque) stage setting in terms of a stage space developed in breadth rather than in depth, but still the ideal arena for the most daring stage machinery. Successively, M. A. Slodtz, C. M. A. Challe, Boucher (q.v.), P. A. Paris, J. B. Boquet, and J. S. Berthélemy took charge of the *menus plaisirs* and the ateliers of the Opéra, carrying on the traditions of operatic staging, save for the break caused by the French Revolution, up to the neoclassic period.

The *mise en scène* of the prose drama, which in the second half of the century is adorned with the names of Corneille, Racine, and Molière, adopted the single scene of the classical tradition. The transition from the simultaneous setting still in use on the old stage of the Hôtel de Bourgogne (now presenting secular performances) to the large, generalized architectural structure known as the *palais à volonté* was not without conflict. At the beginning of the century farce was still performed in a standard setting, a refined version of the medieval neutral stage: an architectural stage façade, with a portal instead of a curtain in the center, and an ample *guérite* with door and windows at either side, as seen in a much reproduced engraving of about 1630 by Abraham Bosse. For comedies, the setting, as shown in the frontispiece of Scudéry's *Comédie des comédiens* of 1635, was a *carrefour*, a modest copy of the urban scene *à l'italienne*. Soon after this, the theater passed definitely into the hands of the Comédiens du Roi, and farces were replaced by a repertory on a higher level, with tragedies predominating. This is the period covered by the *Mémoire de Mahelot*, a kind of production book, or work journal, of the company, containing, *inter alia*, a large group of drawings (PL. 429), and by Laurent. They are sketches of multiple settings in which scenic sites of diverse character appear simultaneously but are no longer juxtaposed, as were the medieval mansions; they are arranged on the stage one behind the other according to the principle of the perspective ground plan. Doubtless a knowledge of the works of Serlio and Vitruvius, by then widespread in France, was at the root of this artistic compromise, but in its execution the less authoritative but more immediate and practical influence of the heterogeneous equipment of the Italian *compagnie dell'arte*, who were often guests in this very theater, should not be overlooked.

The innovating intent of Mahelot's miniatures is apparent, but it did not get far, for from the notes of his successor, Michel Laurent (1673-78), emerges clearly the new type of single scene which is influenced by the fresh offensive of academic classicism and which partly accepts and partly rejects the old classifications of Serlio: a *carrefour* and a *chambre* closed on three sides for the comedy, and a *palais à volonté* for tragedy. The stage space once again develops in breadth, and the neutral but not general setting adaptable to any dramatic work rejects the aim of visual satisfaction in favor of concentrating the attention of the spectator on the only valid element of the play, the text — that is, the word, the poetry.

In Great Britain changeable perspective scenery appeared at the beginning of the 17th century in the Florentine styles of the two Parigis as they influenced Inigo Jones (q.v.; PL. 430), and it was widely used in the sumptuous staging of the court masques (VIII, PL. 342). But the general urban public did not have the opportunity to enjoy this type of setting until after the Restoration (1660), when the Drury Lane Theatre and the Duke's House (Lincoln's Inn Fields Theatre), two houses protected by royal patent, were reopened for regular performances as a result of the efforts, respectively, of Thomas Killigrew and Sir William Davenant. Killigrew remained faithful to the staging of the Caroline period. But Davenant, whose *Siege of Rhodes* had already had a successful private performance with the collaboration of John Webb (1611-72), preferred the new style. However, just as the neutral stage with tapestries at Drury Lane had by now very little in common with the settings of the Elizabethan permanent stage, so the new settings by Webb (*The Siege of Rhodes*, Rutland House, 1656; PL. 430; *The Tragedy of Mustapha*, Whitehall, 1666) reveal a basic disenchantment with the illusionistic possibilities of perspective scenery as applied to the narrow space of a public stage. Only the front part of the stage had a permanent ground plan, which was bilateral and symmetrical (with three or four wings on each side); the back was closed off by a large nonperspective backcloth decorated with a large representation illustrating the events of the act under way.

The legitimate playhouse in England was developing its own type of *mise en scène*, based on the successive scene changes but free from the problems of symmetry of the perspective set and ready for the type of closed space foreshadowing the *parapettata* that characterized 18th-century staging (*The Empress of Morocco*, Duke's Theatre, 1673). Besides, even when the importation of Italian opera at the beginning of the 18th century together with the traditional staging of "operas" and pantomimes (John Gay, John Rich, David Garrick) reopened the question of open perspective scenery, the new English stage-designers (James Thornhill 1675-1734; John Devoto, fl. 1708-44; G. Laurent, 1710-65) preferred the moderate and pleasing style of the neighboring French school to the cumbersome machines of the Italian masters, who followed the Galli Bibiena tradition.

In other parts of Europe perspective scenery was assimilated with less originality. In Spain the Italian tradition — Cosimo Lotti was active there between 1618 and 1650, Baccio del Bianco between 1650 and 1656, and Francesco Rizzi lived there until 1685 — remained for a long time restricted to the court circles of the Buen Retiro, the Prado, and the Zarzuela. The religious play and the public spectacle remained firmly attached to the large itinerant *carros* of the *autos sacramentales*, and the neutral or generalized stage of the *corrales*. In the Slavic countries, which were just on the threshold of European civilization, and in the Low Countries, perspective scenery succeeded the large temporary constructions of the Rederykers, which were evidently influenced by Renaissance classicism. The vehicle of this transition was the interesting semipermanent scenery of the Schouburg in Amsterdam (1638), a compromise between a large triumphal arch and a platform for the *landjuweel* (dramatic contest), which was replaced in 1665, through the influence of the Humanist theologian Gerhard Jan Voss, by a normal set *à l'italienne*.

The area in which Italian theater hands found most employment was the region that comprises Germany, Austria, and their neighbors. The Thirty Years' War had definitively undermined, all over northern Europe, the amateur- and artisan-based organization of the Meistersinger. The *bourgeoisie*, exhausted by the struggle, had relinquished its hold, and dramatic activity gravitated to three different centers: the fairs, resort of the companies of local and foreign strolling players; the scholastic theaters (especially of the Jesuit colleges); and the courts.

During the whole first half of the century the liveliest and best-informed milieu was the Jesuit college. A stable force in the ordinary life of a society still in the process of formation, it had at its disposal a program of work and a technique for its execution that had already been tested by experience. In the case of the theater, it was the great channel that, after the uncertain beginnings of the 16th century, carried illusionistic scenery with all its advantages and all its limitations to the northern part of Europe. The Jesuit college accustomed the privileged classes to this type of scenography, cultivating in their high-born pupils a taste for it and for the type of entertainment that went with it; thence it was transmitted to the court theaters, when the court claimed the right to monopolize the theatrical spectacle and college plays once again became a normal scholastic exercise.

At this point there was a repetition, although on different historical and cultural bases, of what had happened in the Italian courts of the Renaissance. Under the decentralizing impulse of the new political settlement, which made the Empire an aggregate of federated states, the German courts multiplied and became independent. Conspicuous artistic consumption became the measure of the importance of a house; the spectacle was identified with celebration and competition became a contest in prodigality. Every court had a permanent theater, and every theater had a large staff, with foreign artists, especially Italians, predominating (G. Arcimboldi, N. Gallizia, the elder and the younger Burnacini, the Mauro family, Francesco Santurini, T. Giasti, etc.). Native competition was negligible, there being only two important artists: Joseph Furttenbach (1591–1667) and Johann Oswald Harms (1643–1708; PL. 430). The renown of Furttenbach, a pupil of Giulio Parigi in Florence (1621) and later active as architect and scenic designer in Ulm, is especially linked to his treatise *Architectura recreationis* (Augsburg, 1640), a work comparable in influence and importance to Sabbatini's *Pratica*. Harms, whose style had also been shaped by the Italian school through the influence of Ludovico Burnacini, later adopted an independent position. While continuing to employ the Italian stage set, he established his own iconographic content, tending toward what might be termed a documentary approach, at times drawing inspiration with great imaginativeness from the new fashion of Oriental exoticism but more often using the local landscape: stormy seas, leafy woods, Low German villages.

Angular perspective and the rococo picture stage. While the various European styles were developing along the lines of centralized perspective, in Italy as early as the last years of the 17th century a revolutionary movement was afoot which upset the optical principle and the illusionistic character of the baroque *mise en scène* without changing its esthetic aims. The too insistent symmetry of perspective sets with the vanishing point at infinity had made any further development of the centralized perspective impossible and made imperative a break with traditional schemes. Only by introducing a plurality of visual axes and multiplying the vanishing points could perspective stage design continue to be used.

The new trend, absorbed from the Galli Bibiena family at the end of the 17th and perfected during the 18th century, was with reason identified with their name and their work (PLS. 438, 439; VIII, PL. 106). But it was also the felicitous conclusion of an evolution in form that had taken place in the field of fresco painting as a result of the efforts of the ingenious Bolognese *quadraturisti* (painters of illusionistic architectural works; see PERSPECTIVISTS), among them Dentone, A. Mitelli, A. M. Colonna, Baldassare Bianchi and G. G. Monti, whose discoveries had been transmitted to stage designers — in precisely what terms and to what degree is not known, because of the lack of iconographic documentation. Ercole Rivani and M. Chiarini (1652–1730; PL. 439) are the last artists known by name before Ferdinando (1657–1743) and Francesco (1659–1739) Galli Bibiena emerge; and there is no doubt that they were their direct forerunners in the art of stage design.

The period of the angular view (*scena per angolo*), painted architectural scenery, and diagonal or oblique perspective had begun. These three self-explanatory formulas form the basis of the whole new system and its infinite variations. The center of the composition is transferred from the central vanishing point (an imaginary, invisible point on the backdrop) to the corner of a three-dimensional piece of architecture in the foreground, from which many perspective axes radiate toward the two vanishing points lateral to the stage picture. The new possibilities of dynamic richness are unlimited; the eye can move in two directions. In each of these paths into space, cut-out architectural representations on flats are set up, one after another, defining through their cornices the foreshortening of the perspective. Thus it seems to continue, with first one and then another flat repeating the effect, prolonging the illusion into infinity.

On the other hand, the use of large machines, while not altogether ceasing, declined. Scenography had by now broken away from the area of the practicable and from the content of the play; the backdrops were anachronistic and marvelous, *tours de force* that were ends in themselves; they reach the acme of self-sufficiency in the ocular spectacles of Giovanni Niccolò Servandoni, without music or human action, given in the Tuileries (1738–58).

The new asymmetric (*eccentrica*) style prevailed almost without a break throughout the 18th century, ultimately, in roundabout ways, rejoining — but with its essential elements distorted — the current of neoclassicism. However, as early as the mid-century, when the Galli Bibiena influence was in full sway through the works of Giuseppe (1696–1756; PL. 439), Antonio (1700–74; VIII, PL. 106), Carlo (1728–87) and Giovanni Maria (1739–69), the European *mise en scène* was again in a critical situation. This, on the whole, was connected with the appearance of the new picture stage, which in the rococo temper was preferred to the perspective set and which only in the Italian school, whether at home or abroad, took on the flavor of a reactionary change; elsewhere, for example, in France and in England, it was no more than a confirmation of directions that had already been taken.

Diverse cultural and artistic factors are involved in this many-faceted but not necessarily controversial process. On the one hand, there is the arresting reaffirmation of classical thought, which tends to reeducate taste toward greater severity in composition; on the other hand, there is the revival in the visual arts of the classical taste for ruins, the achievement of aerial perspective, and the less important use of decoration for its own sake.

In scenography the transition is not clearly defined: the two tendencies — perspective-architectural and pictorial-decorative, they can be termed — coexist and often complement rather than contrast with each other. Further, the exuberance of the perspective effects is reorganized in the striving for a space that is not closed but well defined and, most important, no longer broken up in a virtuosic manipulation of distances. The foreshortening gives way to new rhythms of composition, semicircular and curvilinear, that enlarge and at the same time reconstruct the composition, keeping it from going out of bounds; the angular view is replaced by a simple diagonal, and the backdrop is enlivened by suggestions of landscapes.

In the case of the picture stage the whole composition is based on the backdrop with special concern for the pictorial element but not abjuring perspective means (a large cornice at the proscenium arch in the foreground and a few architectural side or back wings), thus providing structural stability which is general and not limiting.

The cleavage between the two trends was not absolute; they interacted continuously in a variety of ways, finally producing the hybrid type of scenography that reigned throughout Europe at the end of the century, comprising pre-neoclassic architecture and preromantic landscapes. Between the excellent but isolated pioneer work of Filippo Juvara (q.v.; PL. 437) and the "romanticism" of Philippe Jacques de Loutherbourg (1740–1812; PL. 440) there is, from the second half of the century, a long list of artists worthy of mention: Pietro Righini (1683–1742), who should be included among the precursors; the painters of the Venetian school, whose occasional stage designs had great influence (Marco Ricci, Bernardo Bellotto, Giovanni Battista Crosato, Giovanni Francesco Costa, the Valeriani); the Piedmontese family of the Galliari (PL. 439), in whose work all the various impulses generated in Italy in the first half of the century came to fruition. Then there were the Fossatis and the Sacchettis, active in Venice at the turn of the century; Mozart's stage designer in Venice, Josef Platzer (1750–1806), who served as a link between the Italian tradition and the new Austrian school; the Quaglio family, which worked in Munich and Mannheim; John Devoto (fl. 1708–44), who was torn between the Bibienesque architectural style and the French decorative pictorial style; Pierre Adrien Paris (1745–1819), a preromantic landscape painter fascinated by archaeology, Jean Louis Desprez (1743–1804), creator of the famous scenery for the Drottningholm Theater, outside Stockholm, which was a compromise between the charm of the late baroque and the apparent need for a historicizing background.

From neoclassicism to naturalism. While the last declining forms of baroque and rococo alternated on the opera stages of Europe, the 18th-century theater found elsewhere the sources of a genuine revival. This time the impetus came from outside the superseded Italian tradition and, significantly, outside the opera stage. It was an intellectual rather than an artistic reaction, and it was basic even though it involved the aims of the spectacle rather than the achievement of a new artistic idiom. The *Sturm und Drang* movements in Germany (1770–80) and the theatrical circles of the Enlightenment were the focal points of this ideological movement.

In Germany opposition to the overloaded baroque stage set had started as early as the middle of the 18th century with the polemics of the actress-manager Karoline Neuber, popularly called "Die Neuberin," and the scholar-playwright J. C. Gottsched. In fact, here more than elsewhere the outdated taste for perspective scenery and violent stage effects had run riot even on the traveling stages of the regular theater and had been taken over by the companies of the *Haupt- und Staatsaktionen* for obvious reasons. Aimed at satisfying the taste and curiosity of the middle and lower classes, this particular kind of theatrical hodge-podge, which became current in the second half of the 17th century, had automatically substituted a showy but rudimentary set patterned on that of the court opera or of the Jesuit college play for the neutral set of the Englische Komödianten or the generalized setting of the *commedia dell'arte*. After the attempt of Frau Neuber and her husband to restore a sense of decorum to stage design (with costumes by Von König and scenery by G. H. Koch) and Hans Konrad Ekhof's successful efforts in the same direction, came the demand of the *Sturm und Drang* for "a historically accurate setting, for a dynamic and realistic text." Unfortunately, once again more is known about the aims of theater men (F. L. Schröder, J. Brockman, A. W. Iffland) than about the execution of the new equipment in the ateliers commissioned to make it. The "historically accurate, true-to-life, and functional setting" is still as far off as it was from the contemporary French stage designers, despite the opposition of theoreticians (e.g., Diderot, Voltaire) and playwright-directors (e.g., Beaumarchais), both to illusionistic perspective and to the neutral permanent *palais à volonté*.

The one positive — if only partial — achievement of these years was made in the field of costume design. With the "golden" balance of setting and costume which established itself naturally in the Renaissance upset, baroque costume had become an independent element, a completely autonomous means to the spectacular and the astonishing with very little relation to the geometrical dimensions of the setting or the historical and poetic content of the text and music. Rather, setting and text had as a common esthetic basis the quest for spectacular stage effects, extravagance in decoration, and an anachronistic exuberance in fashion — and in this sharing an artistic unity and visual satisfaction were recovered.

In the next century, form deteriorated further with the increasingly widespread and uncritical acceptance of the practice of using on the stage, along with regular costumes, clothes from the gala wardrobes of aristocratic patrons. Reform made some headway in two areas, the ballet and the play. In the ballet the lead was taken by J. G. Noverre and the costumist L. R. Boquet, who in time succeeded in abolishing the *paniers*, the *tonnelets*, the high-heeled pumps, the plumed crests, and masks. Greater opposition was met with in the playhouse, but progress was made simultaneously in various places: in London, with Charles Macklin, David Garrick and J. P. Kemble; in Germany, with Ekhof and Gottfried; in Paris on the stage of the Comédie Française and the Opéra Comique, with Mlle. Clairon, Lekain (Henri Louis Cain), and Marie Favart, supported by the authoritative voices of Marmontel, Diderot, and Voltaire. At the beginning, it had been a case of anachronism within anachronism, for only a few of the main actors wore costumes that were historically more or less authentic; the rest of the company continued to appear in lavish, opulent, heavily ornamented 18th-century garments.

Despite the modesty of the results achieved, the *mise en scène* had made an advance in several essentials: critical attitude had changed and the standards of scenography had matured, so that the balance sheet for the century showed progress as it came to a close, with the authoritative emergence of neoclassicism and its leveling action. The neoclassic influence reached the theater by way of theoreticians — Count Francesco Algarotti, Francesco Milizia, Karl Friedrich Schinkel (q.v.; PL. 440) — whose principles were modified in practice, through the mediation of current fashion, into clearly compromising attitudes.

The guiding principles of the new *mise en scène* were such as to completely undermine all previous attitudes. They called for a unified conception of the spectacle, which was entrusted to the playwright, the chief actor, and the director of the orchestra; historical fidelity and respect for style in architectural reconstruction; and verisimilitude and strict adherence to fact in depicting nature.

This self-reappraisal by the theater was based on the premise that the function of the setting was to create a background and not to become part of the poetic content of the text or the dynamics of the action. This was in clear opposition to illusionism as an end in itself, and it aimed at reevaluating the means of creating illusion through reasoned use and control. But the insistence of theoreticians and the automatic acceptance of artists, who adjusted themselves only too easily to the superficial aspects of the system, once again diverted the *mise en scène* toward a generality without character, though exquisite in style. The historical style became identified with the idealized reconstruction of Greco-Roman architecture, an imperfectible model and as such the series of iconographic formulas as conventional as those of the baroque and the rococo. The outdoor scenes became broad landscapes, fit settings for the scattered elements of reconstructed classic architecture that no longer had anything in common with the motifs introduced by the classical taste for ruins.

In practical application, this process, revolutionary in theory, turned out to be no more than a refurbishing of earlier forms. New iconographic themes were grafted on graphic and structural models of the perspective tradition or on the landscape compositions of the picture stage, both of which were purged of all decorative superstructure, of all dynamic or dramatic emphasis. The play of colors was attenuated, color gave place to tone and forms became slight, neat, almost fragile in the cold rays of oblique lighting.

The repertory of stage equipment, especially in legitimate theaters, was brought up to date by replacing some of the traditional elements (e.g., the entrance hall, the magnificent portal) with others better attuned to the new archaeological backgrounds and the new nostalgia for nature. There appeared monumental palaces, forums, hippodromes, Gothic castles, military encampments, rustic interiors and exteriors, remote places, and dungeons with huge underground vaults. The *chambre* and the *palais à volonté*, like the aristocratic and the middle-class interior, changed their fittings (painted or practicable), acquiring Empire furniture and Pompeian hangings.

In an attempt to escape from the undisciplined baroque, other, even more restrictive patterns were adopted, based on the rational imperative that denied the advantage of imaginative transfiguration. But even this attitude found values of poetic emotion, provided that the rational reconstruction yielded to the nostalgic evocation of distant times and places. And in this emotion — more often than later critics are willing to admit — scenography rediscovered a spur to poetic inspiration and artistic creation, while between the form and content of the play the harmony and its framework is, once again in a roundabout way, reestablished. Cases in point are the French productions of Talma at the Théâtre Français, in which the indirect participation of David and Ingres cut deeper than the routine professional activity of I. E. M. Degotti and J. B. Isabey at the Opéra. There were also, in other Parisian theaters, the excellent sets of J. P. Alaux, Adam, and Moench, worthy complements to the operas of Gluck (d. 1787), Spontini (PL. 440), and Méhul. There were also Goethe's systematic efforts in his second Weimar period, when he finally found his ideal stager in F. Beuther (1776–1856), after having tried the extemporaneous staging of

G. M. Kraus (1737–1806), C. Heideloff (1770–1814), and H. H. Meyer (1760–1832).

Active in Vienna were J. Platzer and A. de Pian (1784–1851), and in Munich and Mannheim the Quaglios. In Berlin's Neues Schauspielhaus (1818–1824), Schinkel, the most intransigent of the neoclassicists, mounted the works of Schiller, Goethe, Spontini, and even Mozart (*La Clemenza di Tito*) on a bare stage where all the action took place on the proscenium, the scenery being reduced to a two-dimensional picture: a large neoclassic or Neo-Gothic backdrop framed in a painted neutral proscenium arch. In Italy it is the authoritative tradition of the Teatro alla Scala (PL. 440), supported by the Accademia di Belle Arti (Palazzo di Brera, Milan), the only still productive and original force in the country, which stands out through the distinguished work of Paolo Landriani, Pietro Gonzaga, Giovanni Perego, and Giorgio Fuentes.

From this promising basis, 19th-century scenography began to make its way toward the modern conception of the spectacle, passing through trial stages that from time to time assumed the assurance of truth attained. From that period to the present, the history of the *mise en scène* is a history of reactions and polemics. The orderly evolution, over a period of three centuries, of the perspective tradition, which pushed forward from the Peruzzian piazza, through the Galli Bibienas' illusionism, to neoclassic formalism, is no longer conceivable in the churning contemporary world where a battle of ideas always precedes innovation in form, so that thesis sometimes becomes antithesis even before it has found its proper application.

The second phase of this chain reaction was dedicated to romanticism, which rebelled against neoclassicism, rejecting objective, rationalistic imitation, opposing the imposition of one unalterable truth in favor of individual truths and in favor of a revitalization of history through the artist's subjective interpretation. "Créer un théâtre... national par l'histoire, populaire par la verité, humain, naturel, universel par la passion," was the cry of Victor Hugo: every element of the performance is to be subordinated to these ends. Again the abolition of the three unities and the necessity of successive changes of scene become live issues: the neoclassic principle of naturalistic verisimilitude and historical accuracy persist, but they are applied in terms of the new credo of freedom of interpretation and the autonomy of the individual imagination.

The historical horizon widens beyond classical times to embrace every culture and every epoch of the human past. Historical inquiry becomes archaeological research, and is concerned with scenery as well as costume; the study of styles is intermingled with the study of milieus and with exotic imaginings. At long last, scenographic imagery is in harmony with the poetic or musical rhythm of the text — a dramatic rhythm in which grandeur is dominant. Every scenic element enlarges and becomes more evocative: imposing Gothic architecture, wild landscapes, luxuriant gardens, measureless caverns, or airy rustic haunts. Compositional schemes and techniques of stagecraft change: the stage is divided into paths and sectors traversing lengthwise the entire floor; scenery is practically limited to the backdrop, while the action takes place on the whole stage, toward the proscenium, within a zone almost always clearly bounded by scenic elements (architectural or natural) so placed as to create a definite foreground. It is in a measure a return to the rococo picture stage, or, rather, to the basic scheme of Schinkel, but changed and, above all, more flexible by virtue of being executed with a new sensitivity, altogether concentrated on pictorial effect and luminosity. Everything is used in profusion — color, illustration (the furniture is extraordinarily rich and varied, even though most of it is painted), atmospheric play of light, and varied costume.

What has been said is applicable, by and large, to Europe as a whole, with due allowance for variations in quality according to the imaginativeness, originality, and skill in execution of the individual artist. In Paris the leader was P. L. C. Cicéri (1782–1868), who along with C. A. Cambon, Léon Feuchères, and E. D. J. Despléchin and the costumers Louis Boulanger, E. L. Lami, and Garnerey met all the needs of the Opéra, the Comédie, the Odéon, the Théâtre Historique, and all the other theaters in which the romantics took their stand. Working in London, at Drury Lane, were William Capon (1737–1827) and Thomas Greenwood, with M. Phillips and Pugh, under the direction of J. P. Kemble and Sarah Siddons, together with the costumers Johnston, Gay, and Miss Rein. Then came the Grieves and the elder Telbin (1815–73), who were active in the major theaters of the city, especially Covent Garden. In Vienna worked Antonio de Pian (1784–1851), whose eclecticism was redeemed by an inspired imagination, and Hermann Neefe, who was also active in Mannheim and Brunswick. Simon Quaglio (1795–1878), the most prolific of the family, worked in Munich, where he staged Schiller and Victor Hugo as well as Weber and Wagner. In Milan Alessandro Sanquirico (1777–1849; PL. 440), in Venice Francesco Bagnara (1784–1866), and in Naples Antonio Niccolini (1772–1850; XIII, PL. 258), all artists of vigorous temperament, trained on the opera stage to an understanding of stage depth as dramatic space not so much in practicable terms as in terms of being the place for monumental pictorial representations of striking effect.

Judged by its most gifted exponents, romantic scenography appears as a forward-moving phase rounding off the achievements of neoclassicism by carrying it on to the level of psychological characterization as applied to background and costume. But it cannot be denied that there was an implicit tolerance of artistic exaggeration and an overindulgence in emotion in the name of individualism, imagination, and sentiment. Moreover, the taste for evocative effects continually triumphed over the goal of creating a background, and in the exuberance of artistic expression the voice of critical self-control was extinguished. On

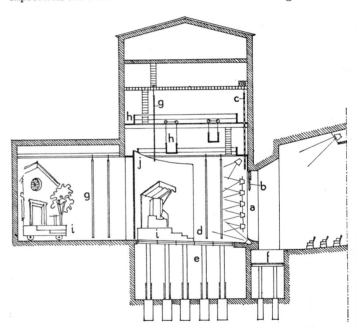

Schematic section of modern theater stage: (*a*) Proscenium; (*b*) curtain and proscenium arch; (*c*) asbestos curtain; (*d*) stage level; (*e*) below stage, with elements that can be raised, trapdoors, and so on; (*f*) orchestra pit; (*g*) sliding and drop curtains; (*h*) fixed and movable catwalks; (*i*) practicable and movable elements; and (*j*) backdrop.

the other hand, there were the handicaps of a decline in the economy and a system of theatrical production under which private impresarios had to carry almost the whole burden, without the aid of state subsidies or patronage. Few theaters had at their disposal complete and adequate staffs, so that the hiring of sets and costumes increased and the *case d'arte* and scenography workshops grew more important, with several scenographers collaborating and dividing the work on the basis of individual specialization (landscape, architecture, figures, etc.). Thus, from the initial enthusiasm that aimed at making every play a historical reconstruction there was a regression to the wholesale fabrication of period settings, replacing formal perspective scenery. Once more stage design fell into superficiality and carelessness.

The crisis through which scenography passed in Europe and elsewhere after the second half of the 19th century, called the "crisis of realism" by contemporary critics, was a general social phenomenon rather than merely an artistic one. Of this crisis, realism (q.v.), which was a valid movement as a coherent expression of a coherent society, was only one aspect, although dangerously prolonged in the theater beyond the chronological limits of the movement as a whole. The deadlock in scenography was brought about by the system of group production, mass fabrication of sets, and the continued lax practice of using rented scenery and costumes.

After all, the generalized character of much of stage design in the period preceding neoclassicism, from the abstractly indeterminate medieval multiple setting to the baroque machines for surprise effects, was automatically justified by the prevailing historico-esthetic assumptions — or by the complete lack of them. But after such insistent exhortations to verisimilitude and historical authenticity generalized staging becomes reprehensible license.

Not even realism escaped the snare, however violently opposed it was to arbitrary and excessive application of the romantic cult of the individual. In fact it accepted the current system of production as being the most comprehensive and exploited it as far as possible. The affirmation of the new tendency was a long and involved process that had begun as early as the middle of the 19th century, at the peak of romanticism, and had captured the English stage in the sober form to be known later as historical realism, with W. C. Macready's moderate experiments and the more decisive statements of Samuel Phelps and Charles Kean. Working in the period between 1840 and 1867, Charles, the disciplined heir of the undisciplined Edmund Kean, enjoyed the collaboration of such experts in other fields as E. W. Godwin and G. Sharp, as well as of the leading contemporary English stage designers, from the Grieves to W. Telbin, H. Emden, and F. G. Fenton. He employed the complicated *mise en scène* of the pantomine in mounting regular plays, making wide use of practicables, bridges, turrets, ramps, balconies, virtuoso lighting, and a great variety of meteorological and supernatural scenic effects. He rigorously supervised the activity of consultants as well as of stage technicians and imposed upon the actors a discipline of strenuous rehearsals and group work. But the repertory still favored traditional classical works and historical costume plays, turning stage design toward the reconstruction of styles and an imaginative, if not fantastic, transfiguration of iconographic forms.

The alarming platform inaugurated by Gustave Courbet (q.v.) in 1852 ("Je suis un realiste — faire vrai, ce n'est rien — c'est faire laid, qu'il faut") finds no echo in the theater. Even the unexceptionable Meiningen players (PL. 441), who influenced staging throughout the north of Europe, still confined themselves to the classical repertory (Shakespeare, Schiller, Wagner) and to minute, meticulous, costly and dull historical reconstruction. In addition to having the benefit of Kean's experience, they had all the advantages that accrue from being a court company with a duke (George II, Duke of Saxe-Meiningen) as actor-manager: time, means, and opportunity as well as the benefit of the constant collaboration assured by the quasi-military authority of the Duke and the guidance of such genuinely talented artists as H. G. von Bülow (musical director), F. M. von Bodenstedt (poet and writer), and Ludwig Chronegk (producer). The Duke himself designed most of the scenery and costumes, which were executed by his adviser, Max Brückner, codirector of the large workshop that outfitted the major German theaters of the period.

Order, discipline, and accuracy were the keynotes of realism in theory and practice. Realistic precision of performance was achieved by serious group study of the script under the guidance of the actor-manager, who had the responsibility and the independence of a director, to say nothing of the forlorn hope of suppressing or curbing individual interpretations in favor of ensemble acting. The documentary reconstruction of settings, richer in detail than in emotion, had not yet succeeded in freeing

itself from the hold of pictorialism, but it did introduce the idea of real space, of practicable interiors with more than one story, solid constructions, real furniture, and real objects. Stagecraft was brought up to date, and exploited the latest discoveries that an advancing science had put at its disposal — hydraulic power (for raising bridges) and electricity (for projections and rheostat-controlled lighting effects).

Following Wagner's essays in the psychoepical drama (PL. 440), which were not very felicitously staged (Paul Joukowsky, Max Brückner, Angelo II Quaglio), and after the interesting experiments of Otto Devrient, who succeeded in mounting Goethe's *Faust* on a medieval multiple stage divided into three planes (Weimar, 1878), the new school reached its apogee with the intransigent battle cry of naturalism and realism: "Faire vrai, . . . faire laid." Stage design lost all vitality and turned into a mechanical furnishing of the stage; historical reconstruction became at best arid research, in which detail was used for the sake of detail. In this excess of particulars, the historical intent became vague and confused: the result was not the creation of a setting but the photographic reproduction of reality.

In this general direction moved the Théâtre Libre of Antoine (Paris, 1887–96), the Freie Bühne of Otto Brahm and Gerhart Hauptmann (Berlin, 1889–1901), the English naturalism of Sir Henry Irving and Sir Beerbohm Tree (scenic designers, J. C. Barker and Hawes Craven); Russian naturalism in the Maly Theater, dominated by Aleksandr Ostrovski; and Italian realism, at its best in the opera, from Verdi to Mascagni, and in the large private scenographic workshops directed by Carlo Ferrario (1833–1907), Alessandro Bazzani (1846–1911), and Antonio Rovescalli (1864–1936). Among all the dedicated professionals of the time, committed to genuinely high standards, it can be said only of Antoine that his settings, in the Théâtre Libre (PL. 441) and elsewhere, had — in their telling sense of proportion and careful selection and harmonious arrangement of relevant details — the unmistakable stamp of high artistic quality. The scenographers working with him were Ménessier, Cornil, Lucien Jusseaume, Emile Bertin, and Eugène Ronsin.

This type of naturalistic scenography easily degenerated into dull and conventional routine; hence by the end of the century a violent reaction set in within the ranks of the movement itself. A stand was taken by theater people against documentary plays completely devoid of emotional impact, but not against historical and natural data and their reproduction. In such circumstances bringing theatricality back into the *mise en scène* had to be accomplished through compromise, in which the deciding element could only be taste. The Moscow Art Theater (1898) under K. S. Stanislavsky (PL. 441) and V. I. Nemirovich-Danchenko stressed historical reconstruction, — but pondered and experimented with during the intensive and nerve-wracking preparation on the stage itself; here the *mise en scène* makes the transition from exterior to interior naturalism, and scenery and costume are transformed from a cumbersome framework into a technical means that helps the actor in the difficult process of isolation and concentration which is one of the props of the "method."

In Paris the symbolist Paul Fort vainly advocated a return to the formalistic and decorative *théâtre de poésie*; the Théâtre des Arts, which he founded, was short-lived (1890–93) despite the contributions of such artists as Pierre Bonnard and Henri de Toulouse-Lautrec (qq.v.) and Maurice Denis. Antoine himself aims at a new kind of simplified and colorful historical setting. But the "melodramatic realism" of Sarah Bernhardt and Paul Mounet-Sully prevailed: they encumbered the stage with draperies, furniture, rugs, and esthetic objects (PL. 441). At the Oeuvre theater, A. M. Lugné-Poe stripped the setting following his antiscenography theory compounded of an ironic disdain of furniture in general and a deep concern with immediacy of expression. After her first period of purely conventional theater, Eleonora Duse explored Lugné-Poe's "pure" staging, shifted Gabriele d'Annunzio's decadent literary formalism, and turned in her last years to the daring and ambiguous avant-garde experiments of Edward Gordon Craig.

Trained to a disciplined professional attitude, the same scenographers are found working for directors of different schools:

Eugène Ronsin (1867–1938) with Sarah Bernhardt, Antoine, and Lugné-Poe; Rovescalli with Duse, Coquelin, and La Scala; V. A. Simov and Mstislav Dobuzhinski with the Moscow Art Theater (PL. 441) and the Komisarjevskaya theater; Henry Emden (1852–1938) and Attilio Comelli (1858–1925) with Charles Kean and also with the brilliant Savoy operas as well as the equestrian drama that held sway on the London stages of the period.

The 20th century. However laudable the endeavors of the realists at the end of the 19th century, they were not so authoritative or radical as to change the traditional type of staging, or to reform the increasingly retrograde routine of the "art houses." The new cycle introduced by neoclassicism was blocked by its own excesses, and only a radical break could reestablish the conditions required for a dynamic and vital change. Once the inadequacy of mere correspondence between the iconography of the stage setting and the historical and social background of the text became apparent the problem had to be attacked from another angle, and the directions the antirealist reform would take were clear from the very beginning: first, the shifting of attention from the written text to the acted text, that is, to scenic action and the physical persons of the actors; second, the execution of the setting on the plane of allusive, imaginative abstraction rather than descriptive naturalism. All the revolutionary artistic theories of the beginning of the 20th century tend, by different and often contradictory routes, toward a common goal: to re-create the "theatrical convention" as against documentary conventionalism, to define a "preestablished" language, a "fiction" that is frankly fictional and as such automatically restores the emotional complicity of actor and audience.

These ideas were already evident in writings of Adolphe Appia (1862–1928) and Edward Gordon Craig (1872–1966) at the end of the 19th century, but their theoretical and polemical work begun at this time did not bear fruit and win official recognition until after World War I, when they had both been superseded by a younger generation. Appia published his major writings on the theory of the art of the theater in 1895 (*La mise en scène du drame Wagnérien*) and 1899 (*Die Musik und die Inszenierung*), but his actual executions (*Orfeo ed Euridice* mounted at Emile Jaques-Dalcroze's school of eurythmics, Hellerau, near Dresden, 1911; *Tristan und Isolde* at La Scala in Milan, 1924; etc.) did not go beyond the stage of experiment. Craig published *The Art of the Theatre* in 1905, yet he carried on most of his activity as director and scenic designer without applying his own theories, outside of emphasizing extreme simplification. The difficulties with Duse about his Florence production of *Rosmersholm* (1906) and with the Moscow Art Theater about his *Hamlet* (1910–11) were counteracted only slightly by the production of Ibsen's *Kongsemnerne* (*The Pretenders*) in Copenhagen (1926).

Though temperamentally different, the two artists pursued a similar aim (Craig was strongly influenced by Appia): the creation of a plastic three-dimensional set stripped of all descriptive and pictorial elements, conceived in terms of the physical presence of the actor rather than his expressiveness. For Appia (PL. 442) the actor was the absolute measure of the play, being the obligatory link between author and director, text and action, stage space and the "living scene." When he moves he coordinates and galvanizes all the elements of the play; and the stage organized in terms of such movement is cleared of any suggestion of a specific background, becoming a graceful complex of flights of steps, terraces, columns, and plastic forms. This plastic set, in turn, placed in the inert stage space bounded by neutral backdrops, divides it into the three dimensions of height, breadth, and depth, and transforms it into a complex "rhythmic space." With the pictorial element eliminated, lighting has the function of providing color and atmosphere as well as the "poetic and emotional space," which only through the functional movements of the actor are transfigured into "living space." The director's is the coordinating intelligence that conceives, guides, and executes each phase of this creative process.

Edward Gordon Craig turns the actor into a supermarionette (*Übermarionette*) and the director into a *deus ex machina*.

The plastic set is developed vertically, the plastic elements are reduced, and all reliance is placed on a system of combinable panels (a "thousand scenes in one"), which can be composed in a variety of ways and, with the help of lighting effects, can solve any problems of representation, creating the illusion of stage depth and dramatic atmosphere. The Abbey Theatre in Dublin (1911) and the Festival Theatre in Cambridge (1926) adopted this type of set, but it was never really perfected.

In reaction to the reform movement toward the plastic and three-dimensional movement a successful new movement favoring pictorial staging was initiated, rejecting the extreme and impersonal severity of Appia's mystical space and advocating descriptive, atmospheric, but not conventional naturalism. The German school and the new Russian group were the most original and influential forces tending in this direction.

In Germany the reform was introduced by the Künstler Theater of Munich (1907) directed by Georg Fuchs, with Fritz Erler (1868–1940) and H. B. Wieland as scenographers. Synthetic and rational, the Reliefbühne solved all stage problems within the limits permitted by a permanent antitraditional ground plan: a rigid geometric frontispiece which framed the stage picture; two practicable and transformable proscenium turrets at the sides; a large platform that could be moved sidewise; and a large backdrop slightly behind. On this were painted a very few telling and essential elements, and it served as a background to the plastic figure of the actor, whose entire performance was carried out on the proscenium, where he provided the "relief," the other term of the equation.

In Russia the reaction was shaped by two different influences, the "conventional theater" and the folk symbolism of the Mir Isskustva group (after Diaghilev's review), identifiable, from the theatrical point of view, with the epoch-making Ballets Russes (1908–29). Although the two shared a taste for highly refined pictorial stylization, they did not have the same vitality or, which was more important, the same working conditions. The "conventional theater" went against the current and worked in opposition to a milieu that accepted the Stanislavsky methods as gospel without ever advancing completely past the experimental stage, despite the remarkable gifts of such scenographers as Y. P. (Georges) Annenkov, N. Ulanov, and V. E. Egorov and the important contributions of such directors as Meyerhold and Evreinov (First Studio of the Art Theatre, 1905–09; Old Theatre, 1907–08; the Komisarjevskaya theater, 1909–14; The Distorting Mirror, 1910–17). It used a formalistic type of *mise en scène*, in which the fittings were reduced to the essential minimum but were taken pains with to the point of decadent refinement: draperies, monochromatic panorama, exquisite furniture, and symbolic elements painted or embroidered in stylized figures, and, dominating all, the "psychological timbre" of the colors.

The Ballets Russes, on the other hand, worked on a professional level, and in Paris, the most receptive and unprejudiced milieu of the time. The set was adapted to the requirements of the ballet, consisting of a large painted backdrop related to the proscenium by a few scenic units (wings, flats) and leaving the stage floor free for the movements of the dancers. In the hands of the most interesting painters of the period, the backdrop acquires the value of an extraordinary picture. First the painters, Alexandre Benois, Léon Bakst (PL. 442), Michael Larionov, Nicholas Roerich, and Nathalie Gontcharova, came from the Mir Isskustva (1908–14), refined interpreters of Slavic barbarian iconography in an Occidental style; they created enormous panels in which the clamorous aggressiveness of the color was sharply set in vigorous design. Later, after the war had driven the group from Paris, there was a fresh and continuous flow of all the streams of avant-garde painting, from futurism to cubism and from constructivism to expressionism, in the exciting work that bore the signatures of J. M. Sert and of André Derain, Pablo Picasso (PL. 443), Henri Matisse, Georges Braque, Joan Miró, Antoine Pevsner, Giorgio de Chirico, and Georges Rouault (qq.v.). The stage of the Ballets Russes was the channel through which the routinized technique of the *mise en scène*, deteriorated by a century of management by artisans, was infused with the life blood of great painting and artistic commitment.

The credit for this enormous contribution to raising the style and technique of stage design to another plane goes to the *peintres-décorateurs* working in the milieu of the Ballets Russes and elsewhere — witness Jacques Rouché's Théâtre des Arts, with Jacques Drésa, Maxime Dethomas, and J. Edouard Vuillard (q.v.); and certain essential experiments by Max Reinhardt with Edvard Munch (q.v.), Adolf von Menzel, and Max Kruse. Their participation was extremely valuable and important despite the harmful effect their "artistic" intolerance and individualism might have had on a collective enterprise such as a theatrical production; and despite their jeopardizing of scenography (which is based on a three-dimensional space for dynamic action) by their preference for painting, with its static two-dimensional space.

The years immediately preceding the war saw the founding and first phase of three other important movements: futurism (see CUBISM AND FUTURISM), expressionism (q.v.), and constructivism (see NONOBJECTIVE ART). These literary and artistic movements elaborated their basic ideas and esthetic theories outside the theater, to which they later came as to an altogether necessary development. Their challenging stand was a new approach to scenography: a stage was no longer only a "setting space," where movement and action took place, but a person stage, itself an active participant in the action, as a dynamic element, an overt and compelling expression of a mood, and as an abstract symbolizing of a concrete and mechanical reality.

With the two manifestos of the *Varietà* (1913) and Synthetic Theatre (1915) futurism takes its place on the international stage with much exhibitionistic clamor, claiming to be *sintetico, atecnico, dinamico-simultaneo, autonomo-alogico-irreale*. But the first Italian embodiments of these principles (Berti-Masi, De Angelis, Zoncada, and Domenico Tumiati companies) turned out merely to be very short and very sketchy; while the abolition of the "mechanical splendor" of the scenery was achieved by a banal use of hired fittings carelessly camouflaged.

After the war futurism achieved a more coherent and natural expression of its unorthodox principles in the staging of ballets and pantomimes, winning deserved acclaim in countries outside Italy. It was the period of the experiments of the Teatro del Colore (1920), the Teatro degli Independenti (1922–31), the Viennese Keinz-Bühne, the Prague Osvobozené Divadlo as well as Art et Action and the Théâtre de la Pantomime Futuriste (Paris, 1927–28). In 1924 the new *Manifesto dell'Atmosfera Scenica Futurista* reaffirmed the threefold principle of the synthesizing, plastic, and dynamic stage set. Enrico Prampolini (1894–1956; PL. 444) and Fortunato Depero were the most ingenious in applying it; Anton Giulio Bragaglia (1890–1960) was its most erratic and picaresque popularizer. Wholly rejecting tradition, whether pictorial, architectural, illustrative, or symbolic, the manifesto calls for an abstract set which is "four-dimensional," the fourth dimension being provided by motion — motion that animates, colors, and evokes all the mysterious possibilities of the stage space by means of mechanical devices and lighting effects. But the system, effective as it might be considered in terms of a hypothetical futuristic theater where only objects and sounds have a role, immediately resorted to traditional means (even if utilized in antitraditional ways) as soon as a flesh-and-blood actor made his entrance. Everything was then conceived in relation to the actor's presence, and the composition once again became the abstract architecture of "polydimensional volumes" or "spatial planes," that is, plastic units or painted surfaces placed in space according to a distorted perspective related to the animating motion of lights rather than to spatial depth.

An opposite direction, intensely subjective, was taken by expressionism, the formulation of whose scenographic principles (*Manifesto of the Tribune*, Berlin, 1919) clearly was made to wait upon the production of plays. Splendidly represented by Oskar Kokoschka (q.v.; PL. 445), Marc Chagall (q.v.), Emil Pirchan (1884–1957), César Klein (1876–1954), Otto Reigbert (1890–1957), and Adolf Mahnke (1891–1945), expressionism dominated the *mise en scène* of Germany and northern Europe, continuing to be influential as a determinant of style and taste long beyond the chronological limits of the movement as such.

Expressionism in the *mise en scène*, as elsewhere, took many different forms, although certain general principles were held in common. Given a conviction of the absolute primacy of the text, as a passionate metaphysical or a sociopolitical affirmation of the human condition, every element of the spectacle had to be coordinated to express its theme. The acting, antinaturalistic, was spasmodically emphasized by gesture and pause, by word and silence. The setting became an indispensable visual complement, heightening the effect of the actor's words and pointing up the thesis of the play. Introspective concentration was the method and subjective distortion the means for achieving the final result. Used to this end, all formulas, all forms of expression, all techniques were equally valid: exaggerated coloring, subdued monochromatic schemes, plastic distortion, asymmetric perspective, absolute symmetry, intricacy of form, grim bareness. The important thing was that the key sign, which might be emphasized by extreme simplification or by insistent repetition, the two expressionistic methods par excellence, be transformed into an eloquent symbol of the human situation at that moment being dramatized on the stage.

Constructivism goes back to futurism's principles of rhythm and dynamics, which became familiar through the paintings of the cubist-futurist school. It was in 1913, with Mayakovsky participating, that the performances organized by the First Futurist Theatre in the World took place in St. Petersburg, the same year that saw the start of the constructivist movement. Abstractionism and dynamism were here anchored in an original way, by means of symbols, to reality rather than to matter. For constructivism the entire stage space was really practicable in all directions. From floor to ceiling there existed an infinite number of potential levels of action, which the scenographer could delimit with terraces, slides, and tiers of steps and platforms held up by metallic supports, tubes, bars, and crossbars. On each level the player's action, the lighting effects, or the spectator's stimulated fancy could create, suggest, or imagine an action or a movement. Again the supporting structure was a rhythmic and dynamic element, transformed into a symbolical-realistic medium deliberately declaring the material of which it was made (wood, iron, textile, paper) as an explicit allusion to the mechanical and materialistic civilization that produced it. This was the "new technical constructivism" (1920–34) of Aleksandr Rodchenko, Vladimir Tatlin, Lyubov Popova, J. V. Rabinovich, and Aleksandra Exter; it is seen in the theater of V. E. Meyerhold (PL. 445), Vladimir Mayakovsky, and Aleksandr Taïrov.

Dada, in the beginning a literary movement, has a distinct place in the history of the spectacle, but one that is difficult to define because of the intentional confusion inherent in its activities, among which the performance, the exhibition, the entertainment were prominent. In the Dadaist spectacles of the years 1916–23, produced with the aim of creating scandal and using the *idée fixe* as a touchstone, the Dadaists pushed the boundaries of all styles in all directions, finally overstepping the limits of good taste. Yet the famous soirées in Zurich and Paris and the absurd "Dada balls" (the *Noir Cacadou* was danced by five people with their heads thrust into stovepipes) are still remembered because of their revolutionary impact and the furious controversy they provoked. However, the most important contributions were made in the Slavic countries through the transitory but interesting experiments of such scenic artists as G. B. Jakulov and Tatlin and the work of Taïrov (*Princess Brambilla*, 1920), J. Masek, Vlasta Burian, and Jiří Frejka as directors.

In 1924, with the emergence of surrealism (q.v.), the polemical assault on traditional staging was reactivated. What these new iconoclasts aimed at undermining was not so much the objective image of forms as the logical relation that bound them to the apparence of reality — this in the name of a higher reality hovering in a secret cosmos, impervious to reason and accessible only to the automatic working of the subconscious. Once again the scenographer was obliged to express himself through symbols and he chose the symbols suggested by the text but directly from the realm of physiology and nature. He respected the image, but broke up its traditional elements (form, color, weight, measure, volume, and position) and recomposed them artistically in an alogical arrangement, in disturbing, absurdly anthropomorphic configurations, free of any concern for the esthetic or the moral. A second manifesto (1930) relieved the artist even of the obligation to communicate with the spectator. In this way the path to paradox was opened, a dangerous invitation to egocentrism, which, when not redeemed by the delirious chromatic richness of a Leslie Hurry, the irresistible metaphysical irony of an Alberto Savinio, or the rarefied intelligence of a Pavel Tchelitchev, can easily stray into the gay irrelevance of Salvador Dali (q.v.; PL. 447) or the cold, detached preciosity of Fabrizio Clerici and Jean Dubuffet.

From neorealism to Brecht's didactic epic drama. While "ideological" (*à thèse*) scenography shifted hazardously from one credo to another in the wake of the visual arts, the professional theater maintained an independent position, proceeding in a course parallel to that of the great contemporary movements, sometimes becoming genuinely involved but, in the happier instances, simply drawing upon them in accordance with its needs. Once the principles fought for in the early 20th century were accepted, at least in theory — the coordinating role of the stage director; the plastic and dynamic concept of the actor; the function of the stage set as establishing the background, the emotional tone, and the illusion; the indissolubility of the connection between scenery and costume — the director, using his own judgment, could choose from an unlimited number of styles and solutions expressing the attitudes and aspirations of the human condition. Stagecraft and lighting techniques advanced *pari passu* with artistic clarification, and during the two decades between the wars, European and non-European theaters, participating in various ways in all the cultural innovations affecting the *mise en scène*, brought forth the most interesting figures in modern stage production.

Max Reinhardt (1873–1943) is the prototype of the eclectic and somewhat histrionic superdirector. Starting as an actor in the realistic experiments of the Deutsches Theater (under Otto Brahm), he turned to directing, at the beginning (1906–08) adopting an anticonformist pictorial style, making use of the impressionistic and expressionistic creations of Karl Walser, Edvard Munch, Ludwig von Hofmann, and A. von Menzel. At the same time, in collaboration with Alfred Roller (1909), he experimented with the plastic three-dimensional set and avant-garde stagecraft, of which he remained an adherent in his own particularly vital and characteristic versatility and enthusiasm. To this style he remained faithful even in mounting gigantic spectacular productions (*Ein Sommernachtstraum, Das Mirakel, Dantons Tod*), transforming the mystical sets inspired by Appia into sturdy structures capable of supporting any superstructure — pictorial, decorative, symbolic, or even realistic — required by the play. Thus in the coherence of Reinhardt's "romantic baroque" were the disparate tendencies represented by his successive collaborators, Ernst Stern, Oskar Strnad, Emil Orlik, Edward Suhr, Oskar Laske, Traugot-Miller.

In Berlin in the 1920s Erwin Piscator (1893–1966) kept his political theater within the framework of expressionism and constructivism, but he sharply stylized both the plastic (Mohaly-Nagy) and the pictorial (O. Reigbert, G. Grosz, E. Suhr, and Traugot-Miller) elements. He modulated the passionate color and attacked constructivist mechanicalness, integrating the two by means of the most unexpected and advanced scenic innovations: films, multiple scenes, revolving stages, elevators, transparent screens, and striking lighting effects. The Czech and Polish directors V. Burian, K. H. Hilar, J. Frejka, L. Schiller, and J. Osterwa adopted tendentious positions even though they nonchalantly passed from expressionism to realistic constructivism, from the most ornate symbolism to a bare plastic monumental set. They were assisted by such outstanding scenographers as Vlastislav Hofman, Bedřich Feuerstein, Wincenty Drabnik, and Władysław Daszewski.

In Paris, however, the directors of the Cartel, following the example of Jacques Copeau, freed the *mise en scène* from the tyranny of categorical principles. Copeau gradually gave up the excessive exploitation of scenic inventions and finally perfected his ideal of a purely structural functionalism in the permanent architectural set on the stage of the Théâtre du Vieux-Colombier (PL. 446). The directors of the Cartel reestablished the tradition of professional cooperation between the artistically committed director and scenographer, which gave rise to such unforgettable paired names as Copeau-Dasté, Dullin-Hugo, Dullin-Barsacq, and Jouvet-Bérard. In other cases, directors performed both functions, as was true more often than not of Gaston Baty and Georges Pitoëff.

In Italy professionalism in scenography came relatively late. The large outdoor spectacles organized by the Istituto Nazionale del Dramma Antico and by the summer festivals (Verona and Venice) called upon architects of the new generation — Duilio Cambellotti (PL. 445), Ettore Fagiuoli, Pietro Aschieri, Virgilio Marchi and Pino Casarini — for the staging of their productions. The Maggio Musicale Fiorentino, the festival of Venice, and later the Teatro alla Scala in Milan turned to painters [De Chirico, Filippo De Pisis, Carlo Carrà, Mario Sironi, Felice Casorati, Gino Severini (q.v.), and Mario Mafai], thereby involving all the artistic tendencies that had held sway in Italy from the opening of the 20th century in an enterprise that was relatively transitory but crucial for the advance of stage design.

Starting with the period immediately preceding World War I, scenography in the United States was also seeking an idiom of its own and a national tradition. Just before the war Walter Gropius (q.v.) and Norman Bel Geddes (1893–1958) presented an extremely mechanized and versatile set in the spirit of Appia and constructivism. Both types of stage design had been reworked by the Bauhaus group but were visualized on a scale so gigantic as to be incapable of realization. In fact, both Gropius's plans for the *Totaltheater* (FIG. 783) — a superrationalized synthesis of the three traditional forms of auditorium, with a raised stage in the center of the auditorium, on which cinema screens could be used — and Bel Geddes' projects for a "total stage," consisting of a multiform mechanical stage that could be changed in full view of the audience, have remained unrealized.

The theories of Appia and Craig are also the basis of the reform of staging carried out by the "little theaters" in New York,

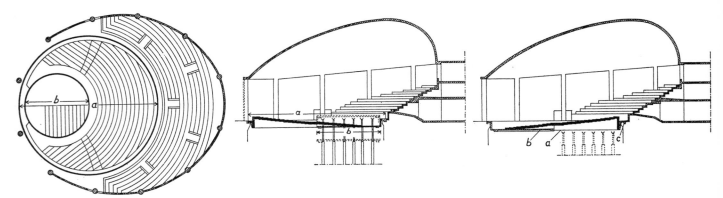

Project for *Totaltheater* (architect, W. Gropius). *Left*: Plan: (*a*) Rotating area; (*b*) raisable area. *Center, and right*: Longitudinal sections with the stage in two different positions.

which were searching for a new kind of epic drama that would reproduce and clarify contemporary life in all its immediacy. The lesson they learned was the absolute necessity of simplification — beyond the sacred impersonality of the Appian mystique and receptive to all contemporary stylistic currents. From this emerged a kind of basic scenic idiom adjusted to a repertory that was programmatic without being circumscribed.

Robert Edmond Jones (1887–1954), properly considered the originator of the American school, a founding member both of the Provincetown Players (1915–29) and of the Washington Square Players (1914–18), which later became the Theatre Guild (founded 1918), and Lee Simonson (b. 1888), who was connected with the most important period of the Theatre Guild, were both masters of this art of eloquent simplification. Jones was still under the influence of an illustrative style and was inclined to make use of atmospheric lighting and the play of shadows. Lee Simonson was more radical in his opposition to the illustrative approach, and, introducing a variety of themes and ideas, achieved an exceptional degree of emotional intensity and intellectual unity in a bare, three-dimensional scenic space of many levels, animated by an extraordinarily modern sense of rhythm. Theirs was a scenic idiom that can be characterized as coherent rather than univocal, as was true also of the other stage designers — Boris Aronson, Theodore Komisarjevsky, Mordecai Gorelik, Jo Mielziner (PL. 447), Donald Oenslager, Raymond Sovey, Cleon Throckmorton — who, like Simonson, worked for the Theatre Guild and later for the more tendentious Group Theatre (1931–41), directed by Harold Clurman and Lee Strasberg, and who from here shifted their activities to Broadway. Meanwhile the short-lived but interesting experiment of the Federal Theatre (1935–39) introduced on the plane of organized dissemination of ideas and information the vanguard methods of Howard Bay, Manuel Essman, John Pratt, and others.

These artists, very different in training and temperament, often produced extremely personal solutions, widely varied, to the problems of the stage set. But they had in common a professional attitude vis-à-vis esthetic theory and the revaluation of reality, however transfigured by art. On the one hand, they had an open mind toward any means of expression, maintaining that scenography is — although on a high level — a craft. They called for the greatest possible latitude in the choice of styles within a theatrical organism where the danger of routine eclecticism is avoided by the director, who is responsible, through his critical intervention, for the unity and character of the production.

On the other hand, they sought a more rational relationship between reality and artistic expression. For example, according to Wolfgang Roth, the play is not a substitute for reality but an art form in which a stage should create an effect rather than an illusion. "Effect" here means a fiction which is intentionally fictional, that is, a "theatrical convention." Included in this convention is the neorealist process of "paring down," which is not a rejection or distortion of the real appearance of things but the selecting, isolating, and emphasizing of them until they become symbols of themselves. This is a reversal that, going back to a new, ingenious, highly refined professionalism and a new humanism whose object is reality, characterizes scenography, not only in America and in Europe but elsewhere, particularly after World War II. But it is not the 19th-century subservience to the contingent and sensory "reality," opposed to the excesses of romantic individualism in the name of the immutable and perfect mechanism of the scientific process. It is not, in other words, the traditional realism unsuccessfully propounded by the regressive totalitarian regimes during the period between the two wars. It is rather the affirmation of the human condition seen in its historical setting, the sum of all experience, social and cultural as well as artistic. As a matter of fact, even though early-20th-century esthetic theories verbally rejected reality and traditional logic, they had the same aims as those which accepted them — that of idealizing human experience by transposing it into rigorous forms. In this sense any stylization can be appropriately used for the staging of neorealistic drama. Was this a victory or a compromise — a drying up of inventiveness or the adjustment

of a profession to the group collaboration its nature makes inevitable?

For Bertolt Brecht (1898–1956), a uniquely authoritative voice of dissent, the theater's deficiencies went deeper and were inherent in the very roots of the system. According to him, for more than a century the esthetic of the theater had striven to no purpose to fashion a method of achieving perfect illusion and empathy through the emotional and intellectual transformation of the actor into the character and of the spectator into the actor. In the philosophy of Brecht's epic theater, already defined in the polemical statements of *Versuche 1* (1930), this principle of empathy and participation constitutes the fundamental error. For it deprives the individual — be he actor or spectator — of his lucidity, and consequently of comprehension, judgment, and choice. All the trends in scenography of the previous sixty years, from Wagner to Reinhardt and from Appia to surrealism, were again open to question. All their gains in style and content were distorted in terms of this new kind of theater, which drew its poetry directly from daily life and from history, and found its own ideological validity in the capacity for lucid and rational examination, understanding, and judgment of every human or historical situation presented to it. This epic-didactic theater is based on the concept of *Verfremdung* ("alienation" or "estrangement"), which confronts the actor as conscious judge with the text and the spectator as conscious judge with the performance.

The *mise en scène* is only one aspect of this process. The spectator must always be aware that he is seated in a theater and that before him is being enacted a fiction studied and prepared in advance. The stage set must be so constructed and lighted as to make the conventionality of the fiction apparent, so that the spectator understands and recognizes the intentions of the stage director and the scenographer, as well as the effort expended in realizing them.

Just as Brecht demands the actor's "estrangement" from the character, so he demands that the scenery be "estranged" from stage effect (PL. 446). In the contemporary esthetic every element of the *mise en scène* contributes to the creation of a total illusion, and that they may all be so harmonized as to fuse, in order not to distract the spectator, the alert stage director is the agent of this fusion. In Brecht's esthetic all the elements of the *mise en scène* work together but do not fuse: each retains its own identity and is "estranged" from the others. The director becomes the mind that chooses, weighs, and coordinates all the elements, keeping them separate from one another.

The means that Brecht used to achieve this "estrangement" and to create the appropriate historical and psychological background comprise all the methods developed by stagecraft over the ages — any form, technique, illustration, or lighting effect is used so long as it does not conflict with the basic concept of reality and human history and so long as it does not impinge upon the didactic function for the sake of theatricality. Applying these theories, Otto Reigbert, Theo Otto, and Caspar Neher achieved superlative results. Their style can be defined as a kind of materialistic symbolism halfway between symbolism and naturalism with constructivistic insistence on authentic materials for the objects on the stage (i.e., iron for iron objects, cloth for cloth objects). Brecht chose his objects and his subjects from the natural world, but object and background were charged with symbolism, and the choice of didactic and artistic techniques was governed by their relevance to his purpose.

"Separate the songs from the rest," was Brecht's order. Each element is separated from the others and aimed at the audience. In order to sharpen the situation any means is acceptable — a musical note, an allusive song, slogans on posters, written messages or photographs flashed on a screen, realistic touches, symbolic elements, masks, puppets made up as characters, actors made up as puppets, painted scenery, Elizabethan devices, and practicables. Over all this, clearly visible devices shed a glaring light completely devoid of atmospheric effect like the light used for a boxing ring, in order that the spectator may not miss a single move in the contest.

In the theatrical convention that has come to be known as the theater of the absurd, the effect of "alienation" (which

the theater of Brecht, because of the brilliance of its characterization, was not wholly successful in achieving) is sought through
other means. This contemporary phase takes its place in the
long tradition of "non-sense" that has been traced from the
mime of antiquity through the entire history of the spectacle.
Closely related to the surrealist trend, it confronts the spectator
with characters and situations whose incomprehensibility prevents identification and precludes illusion. All the elements
of stagecraft, including scenography, are subordinated in the
theater of the absurd to the creation of an esthetic experience
that embodies a truth beyond the power of rational representation to convey.

                                                    Elena POVOLEDO

THE EAST. *China.* The stage of the Chinese classical theater,
Ching hsi, which has its origins in the unexplored past, is a
bare raised platform from which the actors re-create the play
through song and recitation accompanied by highly conventionalized gestures and a minimum of properties. A hanging
curtain at the rear of the stage, a carpet on the floor, and plain
wooden chairs and tables constitute the basic stage accessories.
The lavish costumes, colorful make-up, and elaborate headdresses worn by the actors provide dramatic contrast to the
severity of the stage setting and draw the entire attention of
the audience to the actors themselves. Custom strictly dictates
the handling of the stage properties and the dress of the
characters, and the conventions of the theater are universally
understood by the audience.

The orchestra is on the stage, generally seated to the
audience's right. The members of the orchestra come and
go during the performance and wear costumes of their own
choice. Stage assistants, also informally clad, move about the
stage in leisurely fashion during the play. The relaxed movements of the musicians and stage assistants contrast sharply
with the rigid formality of the acting.

There are four principal groups of actors in the classical
plays: the *sheng* are the male heroes, who wear no painted
make-up but generally have beards entirely covering their
mouths; the *tan* are the women's roles, most often taken by
female impersonators, whose elaborate headdresses and colorful
costumes brighten the bare stage; the *ching* are warriors, bandits,
evil ministers, or upright judges, whose boldly painted faces
(PL. 450) and imperious strutting combine to present a picture
of great power; the *ch'ou* is the clown or comic actor, the great
mime and acrobat of the play, made up invariably with patches
of white paint around his eyes and nose, and sometimes black
superimposed upon the white.

Every role has its own type of costume, so that a scholar,
general, or emperor is immediately recognizable as such. The
costumes are often of richly embroidered silks, lavishly decorated.
Little attention is paid to historical accuracy, however, and
even costumes that bear some resemblance to those actually
worn in the period represented are greatly exaggerated versions
of the authentic dress of the time. Different colors indicate
different ranks, and color also indicates something of the personality of the wearer. Good characters of high rank, for
example, wear red, while aggressive ones wear black. Decorative
motifs on the costumes or headdress may indicate longevity,
happiness, or wisdom.

The stylized gestures of the actors convey a wealth of
meaning. The way a *tan* actor moves his long, sweeping sleeves
may provide a signal to the orchestra that he is about to begin
his speech or song. It may, on the other hand, indicate that
the character is worried, has made a decision, is angry, does
not wish to listen to another character's explanations, is sum-
moning someone, is looking into the distance, is particularly
happy, or is, perhaps, feeling lost and helpless. These and
many other gestures performed by the *tan* and other actors
with their sleeves are all exactly prescribed. Similarly, the
seven principal gestures made with the hands, plus the twenty
different methods of pointing, are all movements learned by
the actors during years of rigid training. There are also prescribed
ways to walk and run, depending on the costume, character,
and events in the play. False feet are sometimes worn by

female impersonators in an attempt to simulate the bound
feet of Chinese women in premodern times.

The actors often carry weapons which they use in acrobatic
battles on stage. Pikes, spear-shaped blades, scimitars, and
two-edged swords are used to accompany martial dances in
the war plays. One of the most common properties is the
ma pien, a riding switch with a loop on one end and four colored
silk tassels. Through conventional gestures with the *ma pien*
an actor can indicate that he is riding, dismounting from,
backing, or tethering his horse. Characters portraying nuns,
priests, or Taoist magicians carry a long plume of white horsehair
mounted on a handle. Black silk flags carried by a group of
four actors indicate a storm; a pair of the same flags held
horizontally to the side by one actor while another runs between
them represents progress of the latter in a chariot or wagon.
A crimson-bordered white banner represents a military decree,
and a banner embroidered in crimson and gold held by an
attendant over the head of an actor indicates that the actor
is leading an army. A group of four men carrying flags represents an army. Another type of flag denotes water — a
sea or a river or a spring. To indicate a city wall, attendants
hold up between two bamboo poles a dark blue cloth carrying
a design of bricks.

The table and chairs that are among the fundamental properties
have many "scenographic" uses. Two stacked tables with a
chair on top represent a city tower. A chair may serve as an
official seat for a high dignitary or as a bench beside a rural
cottage. Variously arranged, chairs and tables can represent
a prison, a gate, a loom, a well, a precipice, a high mountain.
An embroidered satin curtain on bamboo poles signifies a
bed or canopy, while lanterns carried on poles indicate nightfall.
An actor carrying a light wooden pole is recognized as being
aboard a boat.

Japan. Discussion of the classical theater of Japan must
distinguish between No, Kabuki, and Bunraku (puppet theater)
— art forms which themselves developed from the earlier
Sarugaku and Bugaku (PL. 448; VIII, PL. 278). Despite the
borrowings of Kabuki and Bunraku from No and from each
other, the three types of theater have their own characteristic
features.

The No plays (PL. 449) are performed on a stage of highly
polished cypress wood. The main stage is approximately 18 ft.
square and is covered by a wooden roof resembling that of a
Japanese shrine, supported by four pillars; the stage is open
on three sides. The back wall is painted with a picture of a
spreading pine tree. The backstage, an area about 9 ft. wide,
is used by the four members of the orchestra. A space about
3 ft. wide to the audience's right of the stage accommodates
the chorus of six to eight men. Leading from the left end of
the backstage to the actors' dressing room is a long railed
passageway, or bridge (*hashigakari*). The *kôken,* or helper,
sits in the left-hand corner of the backstage, ready to assist
the main actor, or *shite,* in adjusting or changing his costume.
When the *shite* is seated in this corner of the stage, he is supposed
to be invisible.

At the beginning of the performance, the members of the
orchestra enter from the dressing room, through a satin curtain
of black, yellow, red, green, and white vertical stripes, and
across the bridge. The *waki,* or player of the second role,
and the *shite* also enter through this curtain and along the
bridge.

When the *shite* enters, he generally pauses and begins his
performance at the stage pillar closest to the bridge. The
forward pillar on the audience's left is the center of his performance; the forward pillar on the right marks the point to
which the *waki* retires when he has finished performing. No
use is made of lighting effects.

The actors in the No do not wear make-up. The *shite*
generally wears a mask, which he may change if a transformation is involved in the plot. The *shite-zure,* or assistant *shite,*
is masked when playing a woman. These masks are themselves
works of art and are prized possessions of the various theatrical
troupes (IX, PL. 362). There are masks for every type of

character found in the plays — for young women, middle-aged women, old women, vindictive women, for young men, old men of gentle, disgruntled, plebeian, smiling, terrified, outlandish, or divine mien, for young court nobles, warriors, Buddhists. There are masks for old and young blind men, these being sometimes used for supernatural beings, and for monstrous divinities (see also JAPANESE ART; MASKS).

All the actors wear costumes which are stylized versions of Japanese clothing of the 15th century. The outer garments worn by beautiful women and heavenly spirits are particularly magnificent examples of the silk weaver's art. Humble characters are appropriately clad in simple costume, hunters donning a feather apron, fishermen or boatmen wearing hemp aprons.

The actors may wear wigs of black, red, or white hair, short or long. The wig for an actor playing a woman has the hair neatly parted and tightly drawn back into a bun, and kept in place by a hair band. Wigs for older persons are white and styled to suit the character portrayed. Red wigs are used for lions and orangutans. Various types of headgear appropriate to priests, noblemen, and other dignitaries are worn.

Simple articles are carried to symbolize actions in the play. Folding fans may represent swords, arrows, writing brushes, winecups. A round fan can signify either a Chinese person or a hobgoblin. A madwoman always carries bamboo grass. Beads, canes, brooms, fishing rods, bamboo sticks, rakes, flowering grasses, torches, knapsacks, and fagots are among the other objects carried on by the actors.

The stage of the Nō theater is almost completely bare. The only properties used are frames of bamboo or wood wrapped with cloth strips shaped to suggest a boat, cart, bell, tombstone, house, well, pine tree, or other scenic object. Occasionally a small tree or bush is brought onstage in such a frame.

In contrast to the marked severity of the Nō stage, the sets of the Kabuki theater may be extraordinarily complicated and elaborate. The entire interior of a house, with sliding doors, screens, and furnishings of various sorts, may occupy the right half of the stage, while the left half may depict a similarly detailed outdoor scene. In modern times, the stage of the Kabuki theater is built with the conventional proscenium, and a curtain is drawn between plays or scenes. A bridge runs from the stage back through the left-hand side of the audience, providing the setting for dramatic exits and entrances. A narrower bridge parallels it on the opposite side of the theater. Many Kabuki plays are borrowed from the Nō (PL. 449), but these are remarkably transformed by the use of brightly colored backdrops and stage properties and the addition of elaborately costumed characters. As in the Nō plays, women's parts are taken by men.

Rapid shifts of scene are made possible in the Kabuki theater by the use of the revolving stage, a Japanese invention of the 18th century. There are also movable platforms by which characters are raised to the stage from below. Attendants clad in black, their faces covered with black hoods, assist on stage during the performance and act as prompters. Additional help is provided by kōken, clad in traditional Japanese mens' garments.

Lavish make-up, elaborate wigs, and colorful costumes characterize the Kabuki theater. Musicians are often seated on the stage, their number varying with the type of play. In dramas adopted from Bunraku, chanters deliver the narrative. Costume and make-up may be realistic or fantastic, contemporary or reminiscent of the Nō. Dramatic lighting heightens the excitement engendered by the more thrilling scenes.

In Bunraku, the puppet theater, the setting — a realistic portrayal of a landscape or interior — is generally painted on a backdrop. If the characters are to travel, the backdrop is painted with a series of vertical landscape panels that are moved laterally while the puppets themselves remain in one place. For interior scenes, the gate and the framework of a house, and generally one of its rooms, are depicted on the backdrop. A garden and nearby building may also be shown. Usually there is a doorway at the center rear of the stage to permit dramatic exits.

Whenever possible, furnishings are painted on the backdrop to afford the three men operating each of the main characters the greatest possible freedom of movement. The manipulators of the puppets generally handle the few properties necessary to the action; these are disproportionately large. The operator inserts his hand into the puppet's sleeve and holds, for example, a sword, lantern, or broom. However, in certain plays specially formed hands are used that enable the puppets to play an instrument or grasp a brush, fan, or drumstick. Some of the puppets' hands can move at the joints. There are also various types of legs, some of which bend at the knees. Until recent times, when a movable stand was introduced, props were held in place by the manipulators until they were called for in the action.

The typical Bunraku stage is 36 ft. wide, 25 ft. deep, and 15 ft. high. There are three raised partitions of different heights across the width of the stage in front of trenchlike passages in which the operators work. The partitions conceal part of the body of the operators and also provide the ground level on which the puppets walk. The puppets enter from the (audience's) left. To the right of the audience, on the same level, sits the chanter, who recites the entire play and, enthroned on high cushions before an elaborate stand, vividly interprets by his countenance and bearing the dialogue of each of the characters: his impassioned expressions and profuse weeping or laughter often attract the attention of the audience. To his left sits the samisen player, whose music provides the cues for the chanter and puppeteers. The chanter and samisen player are sitting on a revolving dais which is turned around as each scene is completed to reveal the pair who will carry on the next scene.

The main operator, who handles the body and right arm of the puppet and manipulates the eyes and mouth, wears a brightly colored, stiff jacket over his kimono. His face is uncovered; the other two operators generally wear black and are hooded. Secondary characters are manipulated by one operator, dressed in black.

The puppets are two-thirds life size. Male characters are larger than female. The heads are disproportionately small for the bodies. Female dolls generally do not have feet, their kimonos reaching to the ground level. There are different heads for the various types of characters. In some cases, the head is changed in the course of a play when a character's personality or position in life is markedly altered. It is possible to move the eyes, eyebrows, and mouth of some of the male heads. The greatest variety of facial expression is possible for villains and comics.

Marleigh RYAN

Other areas. Although the history of scenography seems in the telling to be made up of an overwhelming number of developments in different directions taking place in different countries, the evolution of the stage all over the world can in fact be seen as falling into a relatively simple pattern (Southern, 1961). As the coverage of the present article indicates, the phase of the scenic stage is almost exclusively exemplified by the theater of Europe and America and the Kabuki theater of Japan. However, since there is much in the nonscenic theater of other Eastern regions that is pertinent to the subject of scenography, a list of works relating to the theater of these regions has been included in the bibliography. It should be added that they represent a study which is still in its beginnings.

* *

SOURCES. S. Serlio, Il libro secondo di prospettiva, Paris, 1545; Vasari; N. Sabbatini, Pratica di fabricar scene, e machine ne' Teatri, Ravenna, 1638; C. Malvasia, Felsina Pittrice, Bologna, 1678; F. Baldinucci, Notizie de' professori del disegno, 6 vols., Florence, 1681–1728 (2d ed., D. M. Manni, 10 vols., 1767–74); P. A. Orlandi, Abecedario pittorico, Bologna, 1704; A.-F. Frézier and J.-C. Perrinet d'Orval, Traité des feux d'artifice pour les spectacles, Paris, 1707; G. C. Zanotti, Storia dell'Accademia Clementina in Bologna, 2 vols., Bologna, 1739; F. Galli Bibiena, Direzioni della prospettiva teorica, Bologna, 1753. See also G. Baldini, Libro de' fuochi artificiati (Mss. Arch. di Stato di Modena), and the numerous contemporaneous published works containing descriptions of festivities, triumphal entries, funerals, and other public and court functions, as well as paintings and drawings depicting these activities.

BIBLIOG. *Classical antiquity*: E. R. Fiechter, Die baugeschichtliche Entwicklung des antiken Theaters, Munich, 1914; J. T. Allen, The Greek Theater of the 5th Century B.C., Berkeley, 1920; M. Bieber, Die Denkmäler zum Theaterwesen im Altertum, Berlin, 1920; J. T. Allen, Stage Antiquities of the Greeks and Romans and Their Influence, New York, 1927; H. Bulle, Untersuchungen an griechischen Theatern, Munich, 1928; G. Libertini, Il teatro antico e la sua evoluzione, Catania, 1933; A. M. G. Little, Scaenografia and Perspective, AB, XVIII, 1936, pp. 407–18; A. M. G. Little, Perspective and Scene Painting, AB, XIX, 1937, pp. 485–95; T. Musenides, Aischylos und sein Theater, Berlin, 1937; G. M. A. Richter, Perspective, Scritti in onore di B. Nogara, Vatican City, 1937, pp. 381–88; A. W. Pickard-Cambridge, The Theatre of Dionysus in Athens, Oxford, 1946; C. Anti, Teatri greci arcaici, Padua, 1947; K. Reinhardt, Aischylos als Regisseur und Theologe, Bern, 1949; A. W. Pickard-Cambridge, The Dramatic Festivals of Athens, Oxford, 1953; H. Kenner, Das Theater und der Realismus in der griechischen Kunst, Vienna, 1954; W. Beare, The Roman Stage, 2d ed., London, 1955; T. B. L. Webster, Greek Theatre Production, London, 1956; J. A. Hanson, Roman Theater-Temples, Princeton, 1959; M. Bieber, The History of the Greek and Roman Theater, 2d ed., Princeton, 1961; P. D. Arnott, Greek Scenic Conventions in the 5th Century B.C., Oxford, 1962.

Middle Ages. a. Byzantium: H. Reich, Der Mimus, Berlin, 1903; G. La Piana, Le rappresentazioni sacre nella letteratura bizantina dalle origini al secolo IX, Grottaferrata, 1912; L. Bréhier, Les miniatures des homélies du moine Jacques et le théâtre religieux de Byzance, Paris, 1921; A. Vogt, Etudes sur le théâtre byzantin, Byzantion, V, 1931, pp. 37–74; A. Vogt, Le théâtre à Byzance et dans l'Empire du IVe au XIIIe siècle, I: Le théâtre profane, Rev. des questions historiques, XIX, 1931, pp. 257–96; G. La Piana, The Byzantine Theater, Speculum, XI, 1936, pp. 171–211; A. C. Mahr, The Cyprus Passion Cycle, Notre Dame, Ind., 1947. *b. The Latin West*: A. D'Ancona, Origini del teatro italiano, 2d ed., Turin, 1891; E. K. Chambers, The Medieval Stage, Oxford, 1903; J. S. Tunison, Dramatic Traditions of the Dark Ages, Chicago, 1907; D. C. Stuart, Stage Decoration in France in the Middle Ages, New York, 1910; Mâle, II–III; A. Nicoll, Masks, Mimes and Miracles: Studies in the Popular Theatre, New York, 1931; K. Young, The Drama of the Medieval Church, 2 vols., Oxford, 1933; V. Galante Garrone, L'apparato scenico del dramma sacro in Italia, Turin, 1935; A. Rapp, Studien über den Zusammenhang des geistlichen Theaters mit der bildenden Kunst im ausgehenden Mittelalter, Kallmünz, 1936; A. Rava, Teatro medievale, Rome, 1940; H. C. Gardiner, Mysteries' End: The Last Days of the Medieval Stage, New Haven, 1946; E. H. Kantorowicz, Laudes Regiae, Berkeley, 1946; G. Cohen, Le théâtre en France au moyen âge, 2d ed., Paris, 1948; G. Cohen, Histoire de la mise en scène dans le théâtre religieux français du moyen âge, 2d ed., Paris, 1951; C. J. Stratman, Bibliography of Medieval Drama, Berkeley, Los Angeles, 1954; H. Craig, English Religious Drama of the Middle Ages, Oxford, 1955; B. Hunningher, The Origins of the Theater, The Hague, 1955; G. Cohen, Etudes d'histoire du théâtre en France au moyen âge et à la Renaissance, Paris, 1956; R. Southern, The Medieval Theatre in the Round, London, 1957; R. B. Donovan, The Liturgical Drama in Medieval Spain, Toronto, 1958; J. Frappier, Le théâtre profane en France au moyen âge, Paris, 1959; M. F. McKean, The Interplay of Realistic and Flamboyant Art Elements in the French Mystères, Washington, 1959; S. Corbin, La déposition liturgique du Christ au vendredi saint, Paris, 1960; E. Franceschini, Teatro latino medievale, Milan, 1960; E. Prosser, Drama and Religion in the English Mystery Plays: A Reevaluation, Stanford, Calif., 1961; A. Williams, The Drama of Medieval England, East Lansing, Mich., 1961; O. Pächt, The Rise of Pictorial Narrative in 12th-Century England, Oxford, 1962; C. Heitz, Recherches sur les rapports entre architecture et liturgie à l'époque carolingienne, Paris, 1963; W. F. Michael, Frühformen der deutschen Bühne, Berlin, 1963.

The modern West: F. Algarotti, Saggio sopra l'opera in musica, Leghorn, 1763; F. Milizia, Discorso sul teatro formale e materiale, Rome, 1771; S. Arteaga, Le rivoluzioni del teatro musicale italiano, 2d ed., 3 vols., Venice, 1785; E. Morice, La mise en scène depuis les Mystères jusqu'au Cid, Rev. de Paris, XXII, 1835, pp. 5–40, XXIII, 1835, pp. 73–107; P. Lacroix, Ballets et mascarades de cour, de Henri III à Louis XIV, 6 vols., Geneva, 1868–70; L. Celler, Les décors, les costumes et la mise en scène au XVIIe siècle, Paris, 1869; L. Josephson, Våra teaterförhallånden, Stockholm, 1870; R. Genée, Lehr- und Wanderjahre des deutschen Schauspiels vom Beginn der Reformation bis zur Mitte des 18. Jahrhunderts, Berlin, 1882; L. Becq de Fouquières, L'art de la mise en scène, Paris, 1884; F. T. Hedberg, Svenska skådespelare, Stockholm, 1884; C. Gurlitt, Geschichte des Barockstiles des Rococo und des Klassizismus, 3 vols., Stuttgart, 1887–89; P. Morozov, Istoriia russkogo teatra do poloviny XVIII stoletiia (History of the Russian Theater to the Middle of the 18th Century), St. Petersburg, 1889; B. Scholdström, Brokiga bilder, Stockholm, 1892; C. G. Bapst, Essai sur l'histoire du théâtre, Paris, 1893; E. Flechsig, Die Dekorationen der modernen Bühne in Italien von den Anfängen bis zum Schluss des 16. Jahrhunderts, Dresden, 1894; H. A. Evans, English Masques, London, 1897; A. von Weilen et al., Die Theater Wiens, 4 vols. in 6, Vienna, 1899–1909; G. Ferrari, Scenografia, Milan, 1902; A. Antoine, Causerie sur la mise en scène, Rev. de Paris, X, 2, 1903, pp. 596–612; C. H. Kaulfluss-Diesch, Die Inszenierung des deutschen Dramas an der Wende des 16. und 17. Jahrhunderts, Leipzig, 1905; E. Rigal, La mise en scène dans les tragedies du XVIe siècle, Rev. d'h. littéraire de la France, XII, 1905, pp. 1–50, 203–26; L. V. Gofflot, Le Théâtre au Collège, Paris, 1907; E. V. Albright, The Shakespearian Stage, New York, 1909; F. Erler, Ausstellung der Bühnenentwürfe, Munich, 1909; G. Fuchs, Die Revolution des Theaters, Munich, 1909; J. Rouché, L'art théâtral moderne, Paris, 1910; E. G. Craig, On the Art of the Theatre, Chicago, 1911 (repr. New York, 1925); W. J. Henderson, Some Forerunners of Italian Opera, London, 1911; J. Mauermann, Die Bühnenanweisungen im deutschen Drama bis 1700, Berlin, 1911; E. G. Craig, Towards a New Theatre, London, New York, 1913; H. Prunières, Le ballet de cour en France avant Benserade et Lully, Paris, 1913; H. Prunières, L'opera italien en France avant Lulli, Paris, 1913; S. Cheney, The New Movement in the Theatre, New York, 1914; M. Herrmann, Forschungen zur deutschen Theatergeschichte des Mittelalters und der Renaissance, Berlin, 1914 (2d ed., 2 vols., Dresden, 1955); C. Ricci, I Bibiena, Milan, 1915; A. Bakshy, The Path of the Modern Russian Stage, London, 1916; C. Hagemann, Moderne Bühnenkunst, 2 vols., Berlin, 1916–18; W. Widmann, Theater und Revolution, Berlin, 1920; A. Appia, L'œuvre d'art vivant, Geneva, 1921 (Eng. trans., H. D. Albright, Coral Gables, Fla., 1960); M. von Böhn, Rokoko: Frankreich im 18. Jahrhundert, Berlin, 1921; K. Macgowan, Theatre of Tomorrow, New York, 1921; C. Hagemann, Die Kunst der Bühne, Stuttgart, 1922; L. B. Campbell, Scenes and Machines on the English Stage during the Renaissance, London, 1923; E. K. Chambers, The Elizabethan Stage, III, London, 1923; O. Fischel, Das moderne Bühnenbild, Berlin, 1923; J. Muñoz Morillejo, Escenografia española, Madrid, 1923; J. W. F. Werumeus Buring, Het Tooneeldecor, Rotterdam, 1923; J. Gregor, Wiener szenische Kunst, 2 vols., Vienna, 1924–25; P. Markov, Noveishie teatral'nye techeniia (The Most Modern Trends in the Theater), Moscow, 1924; P. Simpson and C. F. Bell, ed., Designs by Inigo Jones for Masques and Plays at Court, Oxford, 1924; A. Boll, Du décor du théâtre, Paris, 1925; B. Diebold, Anarchie im Drama, Frankfurt am Main, 1925; A. Winds, Geschichte der Regie, Stuttgart, 1925; P. Zucker, Die Theaterdekoration des Barock, Berlin, 1925; P. Zucker, Die Theaterdekoration des Klassizismus, Berlin, 1925; A. G. Bragaglia, Del teatro teatrale, Rome, 1926; A. G. Bragaglia, La maschera mobile, Rome, 1926; J. Gregor, ed., Denkmäler des Theaters, 12 vols., Munich, 1926–30 (Eng. trans., Monumenta scenica, 12 vols., London, Vienna, 1926–30; N.S., I, Berkeley, 1954); G. Gori, Scenografia, Rome, 1927; A. Nicoll, The Development of the Theatre, London, New York, 1927 (4th ed., 1958); G. Sheringham and J. Laver, Design in the Theatre, London, 1927; V. Svietlov et al., Bakst, New York, 1927; E. Welsford, The Court Masque, London, 1927; S. Cheney, Stage Decoration, New York, London, 1928; J. Gregor and R. Fülöp-Miller, Das russische Theaters, Vienna, 1928; A. Appia, Ier septembre 1862–29 février 1928, Zurich, 1929; O. S. Coad and E. Mims, The American Stage, New Haven, 1929; W. R. Fürst and S. J. Hume, 20th Century Stage Decoration, 2 vols., London, New York, 1929; R. Cogniat, Décors de théâtre, Paris, 1930; V. Mariani, Storia della scenografia italiana, Florence, 1930; G. Mourey, Le livre des fêtes françaises, Paris, 1930; C. Ricci, La scenografia italiana, Milan, 1930; R. Stumpfl, Die Bühnenmöglichkeiten im 16. Jahrhundert, Z. für d. Philologie, LV, 1930, pp. 49–78; F. Biach-Schiffmann, Giovanni und Ludovico Burnacini: Theater und Feste am Wiener Hofe, Vienna, 1931; V. E. D'Amico, Theater Art, Peoria, Ill., 1931; N. Gourfinkel, Théâtre russe contemporain, Paris, 1931; J. Gregor and R. Fülöp-Miller, Das amerikanische Theater und Kino, Zurich, Vienna, 1931; L. Moussinac, Tendances nouvelles du théâtre, Paris, 1931 (Eng. trans., London, 1931); H. Prunières, Cavalli et l'opera venitien au XVIIe siècle, Paris, 1931; G. Baty, Vie de l'art théâtral des origines à nos jours, Paris, 1932; E. Boswell, The Restoration Court Stage, London, 1932; M. C. Bradbrook, Elizabethan Stage Conditions, Cambridge, 1932; L. Simonson, The Stage is Set, New York, 1932; J. Gregor, Weltgeschichte des Theaters, Zurich, 1933; S. W. Holsboer, Histoire de la mise en scène dans le théâtre français de 1600 à 1657, Paris, 1933; T. Komisarjevsky and L. Simonson, Settings and Costumes of the Modern Stage, London, New York, 1933; O. H. S. Messel, Stage Designs and Costumes, London, 1933; G. Schöne, Die Entwicklung der Perspektivbühne von Serlio bis Galli-Bibiena nach der Perspektivbüchern, Leipzig, 1933; L. Simonson, ed., Theatre Art, New York, 1934 (cat.); H. H. Borcherdt, Das europäische Theater im Mittelalter und in der Renaissance, Leipzig, 1935; M. C. Linthicum, Costume in the Drama of Shakespeare and His Contemporaries, Oxford, 1936; D. M. Oenslager, Scenery: Then and Now, New York, 1936; A. Nicoll, Stuart Masques and the Renaissance Stage, London, 1937; M. A. Allevy, La mise en scène en France dans la première moitié du XIXe siècle, Paris, 1938; A. de Angelis, Scenografi italiani di ieri e di oggi, Rome, 1938; H. Burris-Meyer and E. C. Cole, Scenery for the Theatre, Boston, 1938; H. Tintelnot, Barocktheater und barocke Kunst, Berlin, 1939; G. Freedley, ed., Theatrical Designs, 3 vols., New York, 1940; E. Grönewold, Garten- und Landschaftsgestaltung auf der Bühne im 16. und 17. Jahrhundert, Berlin, 1940; R. Myerscough-Walker, Stage and Film Décor, New York, London, 1940; A. Nicoll, A History of Restoration Drama, 1660–1700, London, 1940; R. E. Jones, Dramatic Imagination, New York, 1941; A. Boll, La mise en scène contemporaine: Son évolution, Paris, 1944; G. R. Kernodle, From Art to Theatre, Chicago, 1944; C. Niessen, Die deutsche Oper der Gegenwart, Regensburg, 1944; A. Beijer, 16th–18th Century Theatrical Designs at the National Museum, Stockholm, GBA, XXVIII, 1945, pp. 213–36; A. H. Mayor, The Bibiena Family, New York, 1945; G. Amberg, Art in Modern Ballet, New York, 1946; G. M. Bergman, Regi och spelstil under Gustaf Lagerbjelkes tid vid Kungl. teatern, Stockholm, 1946; E. Pirchan, Bühnenmalerei, Vienna, 1946; M. Gorelik, New Theatre for Old, New York, 1947; P. Blanchard, Histoire de la mise en scène, Paris, 1948; H. Kindermann, Theatergeschichte der Goethezeit, Vienna, 1948; L. Moussinac, Traité de la mise en scène, Paris, 1948; A. St. H. Brock, A History of Fireworks, London, 1949; E. Pirchan, 2000 Jahre Bühnenbild, Vienna, 1949; A. N. Vardac, Stage to Screen, Cambridge, 1949; J. Scholz, Baroque and Romantic Stage Design, New York, 1950; L. Simonson, The Art of Scenic Design, New York, 1950; P. Fechter, Die grosse Zeit des deutschen Theaters, Gütersloh, 1951; J. Laver, Drama: Its Costume and Decor, New York, 1951; A. M. Nagler, Sources of Theatrical History, New York, 1952; R. Southern, Changeable Scenery, London, 1952; R. Altman et al., Theatre Pictorial, Berkeley, Los Angeles, 1953; N. Decugis and S. Reymond, Le décor de théâtre en France du moyen âge à 1925, Paris, 1953; H. Philippi, Stagecraft and Scene Design, Boston, 1953; R. Southern, The Open Stage, London, 1953; S. d'Amico, Mettere in scena, Florence, 1954; A. H. Mayor et al., Tempi e aspetti della scenografia, Turin, 1954; R. Cogniat, Les décorateurs de théâtre, Paris, 1955; W. H. Rohmstöck, Bühnenbild und Szene im 20. Jahrhundert, Nürnberg, 1955; O. Schuberth, Das Bühnenbild, Munich, 1955; P. Toschi, Le origini del teatro italiano, Turin, 1955; G. Védier, Origine et évolution de la dramaturgie néo-classique, Paris, 1955; J. Gassner, Form and Idea in the Modern Theatre, New York, 1956; R. Hainaux, ed., Stage Design Throughout the World since 1935, New York, 1956; R. Jacquot, ed., Les fêtes de la Renaissance, 2 vols., Paris, 1956–60; H. Leclerc, Scénographie et architecture théâtrale en Angleterre, Rev. de l'h. du théâtre, VIII, 1956, pp. 22–44; S. Melchinger, Modernes Welttheater, Bremen, 1956; S. Melchinger, Theater der Gegenwart, Frankfurt am Main, 1956; N. A. Gorchakov, The Theatre in Soviet Russia, New York, 1957; T. E. Lawrenson, The French Stage in the 17th Century, Manchester, 1957; L. Moussinac, Le théâtre des origines à nos jours, Paris, 1957; A. M. Nagler, Shakespeare's Stage, New Haven, 1958; A. Nicoll et al., ed., The Renaissance Stage: Documents of Serlio, Sabbattini and Furttenbach, Coral Gables, Fla., 1958; H. A. Frenzel, Brandenburg-preussische Schlosstheater, Berlin, 1959; G. Fuchs, Revolution in the Theatre: Conclusions Concerning the Munich Artists' Theatre, Ithaca, 1959; G. Wickham, Early English Stages: 1300 to 1660, 2 vols., London, New York, 1959–63; F. A. Yates, The Valois Tapestries, London, 1959; S. W. Holsboer, L'histoire de la mise en scène dans le théâtre français à Paris de 1600 à 1673, Paris, 1960; G. Marchiori, Momenti e aspetti della messinscena, Milan, 1960; P. Moisy, Eglises et théâtres, Rev. de l'h. du théâtre, XII, 1960, pp. 103–17; G. Schöne, Barockes Feuerwerkstheater, Maske und Kothurn, VI, 1960, pp. 351–62; R. Smith, Three Modern Theatres, London, 1960; W. L. Wiley, The Early Public Theatre in France, Cambridge, Mass., 1960; P. Bjurström, Giacomo Torelli and Baroque Stage Design, Stockholm, 1961; B. T. Mazzarotto, Le feste veneziane, Florence, 1961; C. Molinari, Spettacoli fiorentini del Quattrocento, Venice, 1961; O. Schlemmer, L. Moholy-Nagy and F. Molnar, The Theater of the Bauhaus (trans. A. S. Wenzinger), Middletown, Conn., 1961; R. Southern, The Seven Ages of the Theatre, New York, 1961; F. Hadamowsky, Die Familie Galli-Bibiena in Wien, Vienna, 1962; B. Mello, Trattato di scenotecnica, Milan, 1962; M. Ferrero Viale, La scenografia del Settecento e i fratelli Galliari, Turin, 1963; M. M. McGowan, L'art du ballet de cour en France, 1581–1643, Paris, 1963; R. Hainaux, ed., Le décor de théâtre dans le monde depuis 1950, Brussels, 1964; (Eng. trans., Stage Design Throughout the World since 1950, New York, 1924); R. Jacquot, ed., Le Lieu théâtral à la Renaissance, Paris, 1964; F. Mancini, Scenografia napoletana dell'età barocca, Naples, 1964; A. M. Nagler, Theatre Festivals of the Medici, 1539–1637, New Haven, 1964; E. Schepelmann-Rieder, Emil Pirchan und das expressionistische Bühnenbild, Vienna, 1964; J. Willet, ed. and trans., Brecht on Theatre: the Development of an Aesthetic, New York, 1964. See also the many periodicals dedicated to this subject and to the history of the theater in general.

The East: a. China: Wu Mei, Chung-kuo hsi ch'ü kai lun (Essay on the Chinese Theater), Shanghai, 1926; L. C. Arlington, The Chinese Drama from the Earliest Times until Today, Shanghai, 1930; Tsian Un-kai, Le K'ouen Kiu: Le théâtre chinois ancien, Paris, 1933; C. S. L. Zung (Hsiu-ling Ch'êng), Secrets of the Chinese Drama, Shanghai, 1937; Tchiao Tch'eng-tchih, Le théâtre chinois d'aujourd'hui, Paris, 1938; J. Chen, The Chinese Theatre, London, 1949; Chou I-pai, Chung-kuo hsi chu shih (History of Chinese Theater), 3 vols., Shanghai, 1953; A. C. Scott; The Classical Theatre of China, London, 1957. *b. Japan*: O. Edwards, Japanese Theatres, Tr. and Proc. of the Japan Soc., London, V, 1902, pp. 141–64; A. Waley, The Nō Plays of Japan, New York, 1922 (repr. London, 1950; New York, 1957); Z. Kincaid, Kabuki: The Popular Stage of Japan, London, 1925; C. Glaser, Japanisches Theater, Berlin, 1930; S. Kawatake, Kabuki-shi no kenkyū (Studies in the History of Kabuki), Tokyo, 1943; N. Peri, Le Nō, Tokyo, 1944; Z. Toki, Japanese Nō Plays, Tokyo, 1954; E. Ernst, The Kabuki Theatre, New York, 1956; P. Arnold, Le théâtre japonais, Paris, 1957; A. C. Scott, The Kabuki Theatre of Japan, London, 1957; P. G. O'Neill, Early Nō Drama, London, 1958; R. Tanaka, Kabuki Stage Designs, Tokyo, 1958; S. Kawatake, Nihon engeki venshi (Complete History of Japanese Theater), Tokyo, 1959; F. Bowers, Japanese Theatre, New York, 1960; S. Kawatake, ed., Engeki hyakka dai-jiten (Encyclopedia of the Theater), Tokyo, 1960; D. Keene, Bunraku, Tokyo, 1965. *c. Other areas*: A. Leclère, Le théâtre cambodgien, Paris, 1911; B. Laufer, Oriental Theatricals, Chicago, 1923; H. I. Woolf, Three Tibetan Mysteries, London, 1934; A. Meerwarth, Les Kathākalis du Malabar, J. asiatique, CCIX, 1926, pp. 193–284; Prince Bridhyakorn and Dhanit Yupho, The Khon, Bangkok, 1934; B. de Zoete and W. Spies, Dance and Drama in Bali, London, 1938; P. H. Hiss, Bali, New York, 1941; M. H. Duncan, Harvest Festival Dramas of Tibet, Alexandria, Va., 1955; K. Bharatha Iyer, Kathakali, London, 1955; Kathakali: Theatre of Imagination, Mārg, X, 1, 1957, pp. 1–56; A. Waley, The Green Bower Collection, O. Art, N.S., III, 1957, pp. 50–54, 107–10; B. de Zoete, Dance and Magic Drama in Ceylon, London, 1957; J. Auboyer et al., Les théâtres d'Asie, Paris, 1961; B. Gargi, Theatre in India, New York, 1962.

Illustrations: PLS. 417–450; 4 figs. in text.

* *

SCHINKEL, KARL FRIEDRICH. German architect (b. Neuruppin, Germany, Mar. 13, 1781; d. Berlin, Oct. 9, 1841). Schinkel was one of the greatest architects of the first half of the 19th century, rivaled only by his older contemporary, Sir John Soane (1753–1837). His architectural career began effectively only in 1815, when he was named State Architect of Prussia by Friedrich Wilhelm III, but he already had a reputation as a stage designer and painter (PL. 440). A master

of the programmatic Greek revival (see ANTIQUE REVIVAL; NEOCLASSIC STYLES), he provided Berlin with a series of prominent public buildings, beginning with the Neue Wache in the Unter den Linden (VI, PL. 157). There followed the Cathedral (1817–22) beside the Royal Palace, long since destroyed; the Schauspielhaus (1819–21), in which Schinkel's characteristic "pilastrade" motif, reducing walls to a grid of small Grecian antae linked by architraves, was even more prominent than the Ionic portico; and the Altes Museum (1824–28), a long Ionic stoa fronting a two-story building organized around a domed *pièce centrale* in the manner of the French architect J. N. L. Durand (1760–1834). The functional organization of these buildings was as notable as the severe refinement of the detailing, as was true of other more modest works of the 1820s. But Schinkel had long been fascinated by the Gothic as well as the Grecian and often supplied alternative Gothic designs, especially for churches. Between 1819 and 1821 he completed the War Memorial on the Kreuzberg of Berlin in Gothic style, and as evidence of his "modernism," executed it entirely in cast iron. The large warehouses (Packhofgebäude, 1828–33) formerly behind the Altes Museum illustrated his ability as a functional designer of semi-industrial buildings.

Although Schinkel built in various parts of Germany at one time or another, his later career is especially associated with Potsdam, where he worked in close association with the architecturally minded crown prince who became King Wilhelm IV in 1840, the year before Schinkel's death. The Prince's own house, Charlottenhof, remodeled from 1826 on, is Grecian, with formal terraces and a romantic garden setting carried out in collaboration with the garden designer P. J. Lenné (1789–1866). Schloss Glienecke, also begun in 1826, for Prince Karl of Prussia, is simpler and more original, with an asymmetrical layout. Schinkel's interest in asymmetry and the incorporation of voids in architectural composition is especially notable in the Charlottenhof Court Gardener's House of 1829–31. Here, as in many of his later works, the stylistic references are Italian rather than Grecian or Gothic. This Italian influence, more severely disciplined, appeared also in such once-prominent works in Berlin as the Feilner house of 1829 and the Palas Redern of 1832–33. Nor was this the extent of his eclectic interests: Schloss Babelsberg, begun in 1835 for the Crown Prince's brother, later Emperor Wilhelm I, was castellated, rather in the contemporary or slightly earlier English style of Benjamin Wyatt and John Nash (q.v.).

After Schinkel's death a group of Prussian architects, the ablest of them Ludwig Persius (1803–45), continued his personal tradition, emphasizing the more romantic aspects of his style but maintaining a good deal of the restraint and elegance of his detailing. In addition to setting the pace for mid-century architecture in Germany, Schinkel influenced other northern European countries, for instance, he was largely responsible for the design of Oslo University, built 1841–51 by C. H. Grosch (1801–65).

PARTIAL LIST OF WORKS. *a. Paintings*: Mittelaltliche Stadt am Wasser, 1813. — Heilige See bei Potsdam, 1815. — *b. Stage designs*: Zauberflöte, 1815. — Alceste, 1817. — *c. Buildings*: Schloss Humboldt, Tegel, 1822. — Behrend house, Charlottenburg, 1822. — Singakademie, Berlin, 1822. — Zivilkasino, Potsdam, 1823. — Lighthouse, Arkona, 1825. — Werderkirche, Berlin, 1825. — Schloss Neu-Hardenburg, c. 1825. — Palas Prinz Karl, Berlin, 1827. — Nikolaikirche, Potsdam, 1829–37 (completed in 1843 by Persius). — Bauakademie, Berlin, 1832–35. — Hauptwache, Dresden, ca. 1835. — Observatory, Berlin, 1835–36.

BIBLIOG. C. F. Schinkel, Sammlung architektonischer Enkwürfe, Berlin, 1819–40; A. Grisebach, Karl Friedrich Schinkel, Leipzig, 1924; P. O. Rave et al., Karl Friedrich Schinkel Lebenswerk, I, Berlin, 1931; ThB, XXX, 1936, s.v.

Henry-Russell HITCHCOCK

SCHONGAUER, MARTIN. German painter, draftsman, and engraver (b. Colmar, ca. 1450; d. Breisach, Feb. 2, 1491). Schongauer was one of the greatest German painters and the most important draftsman and copperplate engraver before

Dürer. He was the son of a goldsmith, Caspar Schongauer, who moved from Augsburg to Colmar on the Upper Rhine in 1440 at the latest. The Schongauers were descended from an old patrician family in Augsburg, and for a long time occupied, besides other important posts, the office of burgrave, which was conferred by the bishop.

Martin had three brothers who became goldsmiths, and a fourth brother, Ludwig, who became a painter. Martin was sent to the university in Leipzig in 1465, probably to study for the priesthood. But he soon must have turned to painting. He certainly learned to draw and make copper engravings very early in his father's workshop. Later, Martin is mentioned several times in the Colmar tax register as a householder. In 1488 he left money to the Church of St-Martin in Colmar for the celebration of an annual memorial mass for his family. A year later he became a citizen of Breisach and painted the great *Last Judgment* frescoes in the Cathedral (PL. 453). He died in 1491, probably of the plague that was then raging in the Upper Rhine.

One of the most important documents concerning the master is a portrait of Schongauer in Munich (Alte Pin.) with a label attached to the back of it. The portrait, by Burgkmair, is dated 1483, and the label contains important information about Schongauer's life. Schongauer appears to be between thirty and thirty-five years old in the painting. Since the date on the painting was wrongly read as 1453, Schongauer's birth date was hotly disputed for a long time. Buchner (1941) and Stange (1955) supposed that he was born between 1425 and 1430, and they ascribed to him several pictures from this alleged early period, particularly the *Beheading of John the Baptist* (Munich, Alte Pin.), as well as the Stauffenberg Altar and the Bergheimer Predella (both, Colmar, Mus. d'Unterlinden). These attributions have been rejected by recent critics. The works in question are actually a typical expression of the stage of Alsatian painting immediately before Schongauer's time. Dürer owned many drawings by Schongauer. The most important evidence for Schongauer's birth date is a note by Dürer on one of the master's drawings, now lost: "Handsome Martin drew this in 1470. A year when he was an apprentice" (*Diesz hat der Hübsch Martin gerissen [gezeichnet] im 1470 jar [jahr], da er junger gesell was*). If this is taken to mean a young man of about twenty, he must have been born about 1450.

Dürer, whose youthful works were much influenced by Schongauer and who probably knew the master's work better than any of his contemporaries, had precise information about the circumstances of Schongauer's life. Dürer went to Colmar in 1492, principally to make Schongauer's acquaintance, but since the master had just died Dürer met only Schongauer's brothers. Dürer's evidence coincides with the facts, for no single work authenticated as Schongauer's could date from much before 1470. According to Lehrs (1925), no engraving by the master can be authenticated before 1465. Thus, for example, the Master of the Banderoles, who was active until 1467, copied numerous engravings by Master E.S., among others, but not a single one by Schongauer, clearly because they did not yet exist. This is confirmed by the newly compiled collection of Schongauer's drawings by Winzinger (1962). Three drawings carry the date 1469, and one is dated 1470. A comparison with his later production shows that these are clearly youthful works; the limited command of technique is what would be expected of someone about twenty years old.

In copper engraving, especially, Schongauer continued the old traditions of the Upper Rhine (e.g., Master E.S. and the Master of the Playing Cards). But his descent from the older Alsatian tradition (Caspar Isenmann) was less decisive for his artistic development than his response to Rogier van der Weyden's art. One of Schongauer's drawings of 1469, *Christ in Glory* (PL. 454), is closely related to the Christ of Weyden's *Last Judgment* in Beaune (XIV, PL. 414). This influence is also seen in the Breisach frescoes. Schongauer was evidently familiar with the art of Dirk Bouts and Hugo van der Goes. Vasari even mistakenly took him for a Flemish artist, and in the second edition of the *Vite* referred to Schongauer as Martin of Antwerp and as Martin of Holland. In 1565 Lambert Lombard informed Vasari that "Rogiero" had been "suo [Schon-

gauer's] maestro," but as Weyden died in 1464, Schongauer probably never met him. However, it is possible that he visited Weyden's flourishing workshop in Brussels after Weyden's death. A contact with Italian art is scarcely imaginable, although the newly discovered drawing, *Crossbowman* (Br. Mus.; Winzinger, 1962, pp. 35–36), with the movement of its images freely extended in space, makes it possible to suppose that there was such an encounter. The countless Moors' heads among his drawings, as well as certain details such as exotic dragon trees and lizards, suggest the hypothesis that Schongauer was also in Spain.

Although very few of Schongauer's original paintings have survived, he was famous principally as a painter. Known as Martin Schön, Hübsch Martin, Bel Martino, Martinus Bellus, and Beau Martin, he was celebrated throughout the centuries as *pictorum gloria*. More important, however, were his copper engravings, which strongly influenced the style of the succeeding generation. Schongauer had a decisive influence on the youthful Dürer. Everything that Schongauer achieved artistically, especially his entirely new style of drawing, became young Dürer's spiritual legacy, and his stormy and supremely gifted early development is inconceivable without this inheritance from Schongauer. In its Swabian caution, however, Schongauer's art does not have the passionate excitement that almost always characterizes Dürer's early work. Schongauer had a high concept of the dignity of man; his work reveals a simple sense of calm beauty and a conscious striving after an ideal image of man that is in contrast to the often agitated, overexcited figures of German late Gothic art.

By far the most important of Schongauer's paintings is a large panel, the *Virgin in the Rose Bower* in Colmar (1473; PL. 451; VI, PL. 135). The panel has been cut down; an early, much reduced copy in Boston (Isabella Stewart Gardner Mus.) gives an idea of its original state (Martin, 1959). Also in Colmar (Mus. d'Unterlinden) is the Orliac Altar, named after the donor, Jean d'Orliac. The outer wing depicts the *Annunciation*; the inner wing portrays the *Adoration of the Child* and *St. Anthony and Donor*. There also exist three small panels: *Holy Family* (Vienna, Kunsthist. Mus.), *Nativity* (VI, PL. 131), and *Adoration of the Shepherds* (PL. 452). The small panel of the *Virgin in the Window Crowned by Angels* (present location unknown) is a work of uncertain authenticity. The *Portrait of a Young Woman* in Kreuzlingen, Switzerland (Kister Coll.), which was ascribed to the master by Bauch in 1959, can very probably be considered Schongauer's work; this important discovery gives a substantially broader idea of his art. His limited production of paintings concludes with the monumental *Last Judgment* frescoes in Breisach (1489–91; PL. 453), rediscovered in 1931. On the west wall is *Christ in Judgment*, on the north wall the damned are depicted, and on the south wall the blessed are portrayed.

The high altar from the Dominican church in Colmar (now in Colmar, Mus. d'Unterlinden), which Flechsig (1951), for example, has considered to be a work by Schongauer, must, because of numerous weaknesses in the execution, be regarded as a work from Schongauer's workshop. The high altar (ca. 1475) consists of 24 panels: the 8 inner ones depict the *Hunt for the Unicorn*, the *Coronation of the Virgin*, the *Visitation*, and scenes from the Infancy of Christ; the 16 inner panels portray scenes from the Life of Christ from the Passion to the Resurrection up to the Pentecost.

Schongauer's drawings, according to the newest compilation by Winzinger (1962), consist of 52 originals and about the same number of copies of lost drawings by the master. Some of these are small half-length pen portraits that were once part of a book of patterns. Among the drawings are several realistic representations of Oriental heads. The original drawings, which are equal in quality to similar drawings by the early Netherlandish artists, are chiefly in Berlin (Mus. Dahlem, Kupferstichkabinett), Dresden (Kupferstichkabinett), Copenhagen (Statens Mus. for Kunst), Florence (Uffizi), London (Br. Mus.), and Paris (Louvre; e.g., PL. 454).

The most important part of Schongauer's production consists of 115 copper engravings that are among the most perfect works of graphic art of all time. They were diffused throughout Europe while the master was still alive and were used as models in all the workshops of the time. The most important artists were inspired by them. The youthful Michelangelo, when he was a pupil of Ghirlandajo, was so fascinated by Schongauer's large engraving of *The Temptation of St. Anthony* (B. 47; IV, PL. 427) that he copied it in 1488 (Vasari, v, p. 398) in a painting that perhaps can be identified with one that was recently discovered in London. His engravings were often copied by Italian engravers, for example, Nicoletto da Modena (Nicola Rosex).

All the engravings carry his signature, consisting of an M and an S between which there is a small cross with an ornament in the shape of a half-moon. Religious subjects predominate among these engravings. A few ornamental prints and many details in his engravings, as well as the engraved *Pedum* (B. 106) and an especially beautiful *Censer* (B. 107), reveal a connection with the goldsmith's trade. All the engravings are undated, but they begin about 1470. Many scholars have endeavored to put the engravings in chronological order. Eleven early engravings can be grouped with certainty because they carry an older signature in which the two sides of the initial M are perpendicular; later the sides are more oblique. The ascription of a very large incomplete engraving, the *Battle of St. Jacob against the Moors* (B. 53), is disputed, but it is very probably the work of assistants.

Schongauer, like Master E.S., created several series of engravings: the Life of the Virgin (4 sheets; B. 4, 6, 7, 33; PL. 454), the Passion of Christ (12 sheets; B. 9–20), the Apostles (12 sheets; B. 34–45), the Wise and Foolish Virgins (10 sheets; B. 77–86), Evangelists' symbols (4 sheets; B. 73–76), pattern sheets for coats of arms (10 sheets; B. 96–105), and material for ornamental details (9 sheets; B. 108–16).

Among the single sheets the most important are *Man of Sorrows with the Virgin and St. John* (B. 69), *Temptation of St. Anthony* (B. 47; IV, PL. 427), *Christ Bearing the Cross* (B. 21), *St. Sebastian* (B. 59), the *Censer* (B. 107), and the *Pedum* (B. 106).

The sheets with secular subjects are *Peasants Going to Market* (B. 88), *Goldsmith Apprentices Fighting* (B. 91), *Miller with She-ass* (B. 89), *Two Moors in Conversation* (B. 90), *Family of Pigs* (B. 95), *Stag and Hind* (B. 94), *Fabulous Animal (Griffin)* (B. 93), and *Elephant* (B. 92).

Bibliog. Vasari; J. A. von Bartsch, Le peintre-graveur, 21 vols., Vienna, 1803–21; M. J. Friedländer, Martin Schongauer, Leipzig, 1922 (prior bibliog.); J. Rosenberg, ed., Martin Schongauer Handzeichnungen, Munich, 1923; M. Lehrs, Katalog der Kupferstiche Martin Schongauers, Vienna, 1925 (basic cat. of engravings); M. Geisberg, Die Geschichte der deutschen Graphik vor Dürer, Berlin, 1939; E. Buchner, Martin Schongauer als Maler, Berlin, 1941; U. Middeldorf, Martin Schongauer klassischer Stil, D. Beiträge zur geistigen Überlieferung, I, 1947, pp. 94–114; J. Baum, Martin Schongauer, Vienna, 1948; E. Flechsig, Martin Schongauer, Strasbourg, 1951; A. Stange, Deutsche Malerei der Gotik, VII, Munich, 1955; K. Bauch, Bildnisse Martin Schongauers, S. zur Kunst des Oberrheins: Festschrift für W. Noack, Konstanz, Freiburg im Breisgau, 1959, pp. 73–81; L. Fischel, Zu Schongauers "Hl. Antonius," S. zur Kunst des Oberrheins: Festschrift für W. Noack, Konstanz, Freiburg im Breisgau, 1959, pp. 92–98; K. Martin, Zur "Madonna im Rosenhag" im Isabella Stewart Gardner Museum in Boston, S. zur Kunst des Oberrheins: Festschrift für W. Noack, Konstanz, Freiburg im Breisgau, 1959, pp. 83–91; F. Winzinger, Die Zeichnungen Martin Schongauers, Berlin, 1962 (bibliog.).

Franz WINZINGER

Illustrations: PLS. 451–454.

SCIENTIFIC AND MECHANICAL WORKS.

Science and technology have furnished, throughout the centuries, means, as well as sources of inspiration, for works of artistic interest. The interdependence of science and art is shown historically by the continual exchanges between the two spheres, independent but always intercommunicating. Because science, however, ever since antiquity, had been conceived as comprising only abstract knowledge or pure theory, for many centuries artists and artisans tended to monopolize the empirical and instrumental aspects of technology, which only in modern times came to be

thought of as an essential, inseparable, and fundamental basis of science. This article treats of three aspects of the problem: the technoscientific foundations of the visual arts; the typology of scientific and mechanical products of artistic interest; and the art forms, mostly graphic, of scientific illustration.

SUMMARY. Art and science (col. 798); Scientific and technical foundations of artistic activity (col. 802); Scientific and mechanical objects of artistic interest: function, form, and ornamentation (col. 804); Scientific illustration (col. 807).

ART AND SCIENCE. In specific historical contexts, art and science may assume various relationships of subordination or of equality. The subordination of art to science occurs when the artist, whether from conviction or in accordance with the conditions of a commission, uses the operative processes of his own art (literary, visual, or even musical) as so many means of scientific research or as means for placing before the layman the results of scientific research in his field of activity. An example of a theory of art in which art is conceived as an instrument of scientific research is Leonardo da Vinci's *Treatise on Painting*, in which pictorial art is conceived and studied as an instrument for the scientific study of nature. An example of art (literature) conceived and executed as an instrument of scientific analysis (biologicosociological) is the "naturalistic" novel of the 19th century, the most perfect representative of which is the Rougon-Macquart cycle, in which Emile Zola used the novel as an instrument of scientific research for the study of the mechanisms and effects of heredity and of the evolution of French society at a given period. Examples of art conceived and practiced as an exposition of scientific knowledge, with the aim of making it accessible to those who lacked sufficient knowledge to understand it in its pure form — in other words, examples of what might be called intentional esthetic mediation of scientific knowledge — are the didactic art of all periods.

The concept of art as allegory, the oldest theoretical expression of which is the Aristotelian theory of metaphor enunciated in the *Poetics* and in the *Rhetoric*, is another fundamental example of art used for the transmission of scientific knowledge (or of moral teaching) through its transformation into poetic, figurative, or architectural forms (see SYMBOLISM AND ALLEGORY). The doctrine of allegory as intentional esthetic transmission of scientific knowledge did not end with the Middle Ages but continued in various historical and cultural contexts; it represents the most complete example of the subordination of art to science, investing now the creative moment, now the critical-interpretative moment, sometimes both. When allegory, insofar as it considers art a means of transmitting scientific knowledge, involves only the critical-interpretative moment, it can refer also to works in whose origin the subordination of art to science (at least as conceived by allegorizing interpreters) has no part. Examples of allegorical interpretation of this sort first appeared in late antiquity and became more frequent in the Middle Ages, especially after the treatise of Prudentius, *De continentia vergiliana*, which founded a tradition that was to culminate in the *Commentum super sex libros Aeneidis Virgilii* by Bernardus Silvestris. In the 20th century, psychoanalytical interpretation, the prototype of which is Sigmund Freud's analysis of Leonardo's painting (*Eine Kindheitserinnerung des Leonardo da Vinci*, Leipzig, 1910), is an example of this manner of conceiving the relationship between science and art as a subordination to science, not so much of the creative artistic process as of the exegetical process of evaluating art works. The influence of this attitude within a certain cultural context cannot fail, moreover, to affect the work of the artist who conceives his art as esthetic transmission of science (or of what, in his culture, is considered to be science).

The art-science relationship may also take the form of subordination of science to art. The supremacy of art over science is, in fact, to be seen whenever the practical processes and results of scientific research are carried over into the artistic process and used as instruments within it. Examples of the instrumental use of the results of science for artistic purposes may be seen in Italian painting of the 15th century, insofar as it is closely linked with the study of optics (see OPTICAL CONCEPTS) and descriptive geometry (see PROPORTION), and in the theoretical treatises that accompany it, as well as in the success of the perspectivists (q.v.).

It is, moreover, difficult to determine the dividing line between the use of science as an intrinsic component of the operative process in art, considered as a subservience of science to art, and the state of equality in which art, in using scientific methods or in taking scientific results as the subject of its own esthetic treatment, contributes directly, without falling under the domination of science, to the progress of science itself. Equality of this sort is always present in architecture (q.v.), because of the aims this art sets itself, the techniques it employs, and the materials it uses; and it is to be found also in literature and in painting. In Goethe's narrative and poetic works, the equality of art and science is seen in the verses brought together under the title "Gott und Welt," among them the famous poems entitled "Metamorphose der Pflanzen" (Metamorphoses of the Plants) and "Metamorphose der Tieren" (Metamorphoses of the Animals), in which Goethe transposes into poetry the methods and conclusions of his natural-science research; while in the novel *Die Wahlverwandshaften* (Elective Affinities), he uses the technique of the narrative to study the psychology of love and human destiny according to the principles and methodology applied by him in his studies of mineralogy and crystallography. Even his studies on color theory were pursued in terms of poetics; whereas Schelling, who agreed with Goethe's scientific concept of the origin of color in the contrast of light and shade, used it as a basis for the critical appreciation of painting.

An equality wherein painting takes advantage of mathematical processes without either subordination or predominance is to be found in the 20th century in abstract geometric art and its various ramifications.

Not to be included in any of these categories is the use of art processes and techniques in the illustration of physical, chemical, and medical theories (as in the medieval treatises on medicine and hydrotherapy, in bestiaries, herbals, and lapidariums; or in the drawings done by Goethe to illustrate his theories mentioned above) and in the graphic execution of geographic and astronomical works and the like. In these and similar cases, art, even when it attains a high level of perfection, performs only an illustrative function, and its relation to science remains external so far as its creative processes and its choices in taste are concerned.

Rosario ASSUNTO

Theoretical science, based on pure knowledge, and applied science or technology, based on experimentation, application, and production, were for centuries considered two separate worlds and thus came to be actual opponents, both socially and intrinsically as values. Theoretical science took its place among what the Middle Ages called the "liberal arts," while applied science was included among the "mechanical arts." The very term "art" (Lat. *ars*, Gr. τέχνη) originally signified "operating rules," in other words, techniques, as applied to any kind of human operation or production. There was, then, a sharp division between scientists and technicians: the scientists took no heed of experiment, of application, of creation that implied manual work. The *Homo sapiens* was very careful to remain apart and to rise above the *Homo faber*. Artists, on the other hand, belonged to the category of "mechanicians" and, on their side, did not theorize their own experiences, limiting themselves, at least until the Renaissance, to accumulating manual working practice.

This antithesis between science and art, between theory and practice, is very clear in Aristotle, who, conceiving science as a form of disinterested research and contemplation of truth, excluded "mechanical workers" from the category of citizens, distinguishing them from slaves only as they ministered to the needs of many persons whereas slaves busied themselves with a single individual. In this way the difference between slaves and freemen tended to take shape in the opposition of science and "mechanics," of rational knowledge and knowledge as put into practice and therefore immersed in the world of tangible and material objects. For many centuries the contempt felt for those who practiced a manual activity was brought to bear on the activities themselves, which were thus taken as the lowest in the scale of social values and were excluded from any scale of cultural values (see HANDICRAFTS). In the Middle Ages also, science was conceived as theology, philosophy, and meditation. In the castles and in the monasteries the spirit of the medieval encyclopedia was exemplified in the scientific collections: minerals, animals, plants, and curiosities were systematically classified according to rigid hierarchical systems (see MUSEUMS AND COLLECTIONS). Although the spirit of observation and ability in the mechanical arts were strong, craftsmanship and technical activity, which were limited to the craftsman, found expression only in pratical handbooks, which never rose to the level of theory.

*

Between 1400 and 1700, long before the Industrial Revolution, a deep ideological transformation in European culture went hand in hand with the first technical developments and the steady rise in importance of the machine. In the writings of the artists and experimenters of the 15th century and in the treatises on mine engineering, nautical arts, ballistics, and the art of fortification written a century later, there arose a new concept of labor, of the cultural function of the mechanical arts, and of the cognitive significance of artificial processes for the transformation of nature. In the world of philosophy, a new evaluation of the arts arose in the 17th century: culture was no longer seen as coinciding exclusively with the field of the liberal arts, and the ancient concept of science as research, as an occupation separate from the provision of the necessities of life, was abandoned.

A new concept was thus slowly making headway in the philosophic, artistic, and scientific world. In the writings of the French potter Bernard Palissy and of the English compass maker Robert Norman, as in the works of authors in the great humanistic tradition such as Rabelais, Andreas Vesalius, and Juan Luis Vives, there are a series of common themes: the processes adopted by artists and craftsmen, by engineers and technicians, have a value of their own as pursuit of knowledge; these processes acquire the dignity of cultural facts, and "cultivated" men must abandon their traditional contempt for manual practice and operations, their rhetorical or "contemplative" concept of learning, and turn to the actual observation and study of applied techniques and arts. It was not a question merely of recognizing the dignity of the arts or of trying to include them in a program of complete education directed toward the formation of a new type of gentleman. In the authors mentioned (whose works were published between 1530 and 1580) there was an explicit declaration that was destined to echo far and wide: certain processes adopted by man for making practical objects or for building machines, for modifying or transforming nature through manual labor, are more helpful toward the knowledge of natural realities than those intellectual constructions and philosophic systems that end by preventing or limiting the actual exploration by man of the world of nature.

This revolutionary evaluation of the mechanical arts and the recognition of the debt of science to them — a recognition found in the works of Bacon, Descartes, Harvey, Galileo, and Boyle — implied, in the last analysis, a rejection of the Aristotelian concept of science as disinterested research and mediation of truth that was not without effect on ethics and politics. The traditional hostility toward the mechanical arts survived through the 17th century and even later, as is apparent from the indignation aroused among the French Jesuits by the many technical passages in Diderot's *Encyclopédie*. In arguing against the Aristotelian concept of science, defending the dignity of the mechanical arts, and rejecting the idea of nature as a rigid hierarchy of forms, Palissy and Georgius Agricola (Georg Bauer), Vives and Vesalius, like Bacon and Boyle later, were in fact contributing to the destruction of a venerably old vision of the world.

At the same time, artists and craftsmen who had come in contact with Humanistic circles and the heritage of the classical world were seeking answers to their queries in the works of Euclid, Archimedes, Vitruvius, and Eronius. The literature of the 15th and 16th centuries is extraordinarily rich in technical treatises that contributed decisively to the establishment of contact between scientific learning and technical or crafts knowledge and had a determining effect on the birth of cooperation between scientists and technicians and between science and industry. To this literature produced by artists, engineers, and superior artisans belong the writings of Brunelleschi, Ghiberti, Piero della Francesca, Leonardo, Cellini (qq.v.), and Giovanni Paolo Lomazzo, Konrad Keyser's treatise on war machines (1366–1405), the technical treatises of Niccolò Tartaglia (Nicola Fontana; 1420) and Mariano (1483), the works on architecture of Alberti, Filarete (I, PL. 406; III, PL. 484), Francesco di Giorgio, and Palladio (qq.v.), Roberto Valturius's *De re militari* (1472; repr. Verona 1483 and four times in Paris between 1532 and 1555), the two treatises by Dürer (q.v.) on descriptive geometry and fortifications (1525, 1527), Vanoccio Biringuccio's *Pirotechnia* (1540; later published in two Latin, three French, and four Italian editions), Niccolò Tartaglia's work on ballistics (1537), the two treatises on mining engineering by Georgius Agricola (1546, 1556), the *Theatrum instrumentorum* by Jacques Besson (1569; later translated into various languages), Guidobaldo del Monte's *Mechanicorum libri* (1577), Agostino Ramelli's *Le diverse et artificiose machine* (1588; PL. 476; II, PL. 73), Simon Stevin's three books on mechanics (1586; translated into French from the Flemish in 1634), Bounaiuto Lorini's work on fortifications (1596), the treatises on the art of navigation by William Barlowe (1597), Thomas Harriot (1594), and Robert Hues (1599), the writings, already mentioned, of Bernard Palissy, and Robert Norman's work on the declination of the magnetic needle (1581).

Parallel to this huge output there was a significant renewed interest in the mathematical and technical works of classical antiquity: the first printed edition of Euclid appeared in Venice in 1482; Francesco Maurolico (1494–1575) published Latin editions of Archimedes, Apollonius, and Diophantus; and Federico Commandino (1509–75) published Euclid, Apollonius, Pappus, Eronius, Archimedes, and Aristarchus. After the beginning of the 16th century the commentaries became increasingly more elaborate and organic; new notions were introduced, and often there was a real integration of the texts. Many translations from the classics were explicitly directed toward artisans: Jean Martin, the French translator of Vitruvius (1547), wrote "for workers and other people who do not understand Latin"; Walther Rivius, or Ryff, in his presentation of the same text in German (1540), addressed himself to "the artisans and goldsmiths, architects and weavers." The numerous commentaries on Vitruvius offer a clear example of the importance and significance of these new presentations of the classical authors. From Philander (1541) to Daniele Barbaro (1556), these commentaries assumed the character of real encyclopedias. Barbaro, who made use of Palladio's collaboration, knew a number of the principal texts on 16th-century techniques, including the *Arte de Navegar* of Pedro de Medina, Dürer's treatises on proportion and on the use of the compass, Commandino's *Commentaries on Ptolemy*, and Sebastian Münster's *Compositio horologiorum*.

It was no accident that Alberti (q.v.), the 15th-century Humanist, was the initiator of that scientific concept of art which saw in mathematics (the theory of proportion and that of perspective) the most propitious ground for work in common between painters and scientists. For Alberti, painting was science and so was the perspective vision on which it is founded and which is specific to painters. On the other hand, in the architect's work occurs the fusion of "reason," "rule," and "labor," and the eulogy of the architect-engineer was soon applied to the technology that could transform mountains, divert rivers, and open to all the peoples of the earth new roads and new communications. Like Alberti, Piero della Francesca (q.v.) insisted, in his *De prospettiva pingendi*, on the necessity

of "science" and "geometry" and protested against the prejudice shown by many painters against the science of perspective.

Well before the figure of the artist came to be identified with that of the "genius," the fusion of technical and scientific activity, of manual work and theory, had taken place in the Florentine workshops. Some of these turned into true industrial laboratories, at least during the execution of certain tasks. It was here, and not in the schools, that painters and sculptors, engineers and technicians and machine builders were formed. Here were taught — besides the art of carving stones and of casting bronze, besides painting and sculpture — the rudiments of anatomy and optics, mathematics, perspective, and geometry; and here were planned the building of domes and the digging of canals. The empirical knowledge of men "without letters" like Leonardo and Brunelleschi (qq.v.) had, as a background, this sort of milieu. The friendship and collaboration among the "engineer" Brunelleschi, the man of letters and mathematician Alberti, and Paolo del Pozzo Toscanelli, the "new Archimedes," can be taken as a symbol of that fruitful period of Italian culture which reached out simultaneously to the world of letters and that of men of action, of artists and craftsmen and technicians.

If Leonardo is seen within this context, his figure as a "technician" and "machine builder" acquires a more precise significance and truer dimensions. It is precisely out of his artisan's familiarity with the properties of all sorts of materials and the possibilities of working on them that Leonardo drew his conviction, which never faltered, that it was necessary to ally theoretical knowledge with practical work and experience. Far more than the so-called philosophical themes or the physics of Leonardo, the mechanical and anatomical drawings (PL. 467; IV, PL. 268; XI, PLS. 344, 345) are worth returning to, from a purely technical point of view. In this field Leonardo contributed decisively to the invention of a precise method for the representation and description of reality. Here empiricism became practical experimentation, experience resulted in operative research. It should not be forgotten that the invention of this rigorous method of describing reality in nature, the creation of the great artists of the 15th century, has the same importance for descriptive science, as Erwin Panofsky (1954) has shown, as the effects of the telescope or the microscope in the 17th century, as witness Dürer's engravings (IV, PLS. 297, 301) and the anatomy plates that illustrate the work of Vesalius. This collaboration between scientific and technical learning that began to take root at the beginning of modern times is one of the crucial and essential aspects of the new culture.

Paolo Rossi

SCIENTIFIC AND TECHNICAL FOUNDATIONS OF ARTISTIC ACTIVITY. Science and its applications are essential components of the artistic process. Technical foundations, however modest or elementary, are necessary to enable the painter, the sculptor, and the architect to carry out their creations, however simple or primitive they may be. The artist discovers and develops for himself his own technique: he may extract his colors from the earth, from herb juices, or from minerals, he may adopt a traditional technique that has been taught him, but always he tends to modify and perfect it to suit his own individual mode of expression, using it as an instrument that must be conditioned by expression. From a technical or scientific discovery the artist is capable of drawing stylistic and expressive conclusions that may revolutionize a whole century's outlook. It is enough to remember the various improvements in mural painting and the technical innovations that constitute the main milestones in the evolution of ceramics and of engraving. One may say that each century, each phase of civilization, has its own technique, freely chosen and developed. Mosaics are characteristic of the Middle Ages, water colors and pastels of the 18th century, not because these techniques were discovered in those periods but because they were then chosen as best corresponding to the artistic ideals of the times (see TECHNIQUES).

The scientific basis of art rises to a level well above that of a mere technical instrument when art, in order to fulfill its object, takes advantage of more extended scientific knowledge, adopting, for example, scientific, optical, mathematical, geometrical, or philosophical principles as foundations for artistic form (see OPTICAL CONCEPTS; PERSPECTIVE; PROPORTION). Symbolism and allegory (q.v.) translate into images the concepts elaborated by theologians and philosophers, by men of letters and historians — concepts which form the science of a period and which art faithfully reflects and interprets. The most complex of techniques is that of the architect, because he must take into account statics and structural problems as well as functionality. An architect is always an engineer and cannot, for instance, build an auditorium without any knowledge of the scientific principles of acoustics.

Science stands to art in much the same relation as talent stands to genius, the two concepts being kept distinctly apart, as they are in treatises. To the identification of art and science brought about by the Renaissance was opposed a clear distinction in the 17th century, when Nicolas Poussin could declare that the object of art was delight, beauty without utility; in other words, the "genius" and the "idea" of the artist were considered superior to talent and technique, which were thus reduced to the status of mere executive instruments. But this solemn declaration so characteristic of the 17th century — in which art and science were separated historically, functionally, and socially — can be countered by the statement that while the art of the Renaissance presented itself as science, science itself (technology) had for thousands of years presented itself as art. Technology had, for millenniums, fulfilled the final ends that the 17th century considered peculiar to the arts: pleasure, play, surprising and pleasurable effects, useless beauty, as witness the automata (q.v.), whose tradition runs without interruption from antiquity to modern times, or the hydraulic musical and theatrical machines made with purely esthetic and hedonistic aims. Mechanical ingenuity became as whimsical as the artist's imagination, perhaps even more so, quite independent of the practical scientific applications and the specific requirements of theoretical science and civilized progress. On the other hand, if extreme cases are excluded, the logic of the scientist or the technician always possesses some of the imaginative genius of the artist, and every invention demands intuition, daring imagination, and genius; whereas the imagination of the artist always materializes in rational forms that have their own logic and technique.

It has even been stated, and with reason, that the great technical inventions start first as art and then become science, finding their practical application only when the most complex historical requirements permit it. Two examples will suffice: the printing press and the clock. Lewis Mumford (1952) maintains that printing could have been invented at any time during the 2,500 years preceding Johann Gutenberg, because its technical basis was already known. And when it did appear, it found application first in visual art (xylography) and only later in writing. As for the clock, it developed with monastic life but remained imprecise until the 16th century — that is, until the need arose in urban civilization for greater precision instead of the subjective and natural method of calculating time according to the phases of the day. Finally, it was only when, with Galileo (1581), scientific requirements demanded absolute exactitude in the measurement of time that the clock became an instrument of scientific precision. In other words, invention is free, on the one hand, and on the other is pressed by the necessity of application.

During the Renaissance, artists were veritable scientists, and as anatomists they were considerably more expert than the physicians (see HUMAN FIGURE); they knew perspective, and were mathematicians, engineers, and inventors. It is significant that Alberti (q.v.), while defining art as science on the one hand, on the other recognized beauty as a value in purely scientific processes and devices. Brunelleschi (q.v.) and Alberti, besides being architects, were also engineers and experts in mathematics, geometry, hydraulics, and various craft techniques. In the same way, later, Francesco di Giorgio, Buontalenti, Giambologna (qq.v.), and Niccolò Tribolo were not only architects and sculptors but also inventors of machines; and this tendency toward a universal culture comprising both art and science found its culmination in Leonardo da Vinci.

Mannerism (q.v.) was affected by the experimentalism and the scientific utopianism that characterized the age. Art sought new rules for beauty in the new cosmic theories. A similar parallel can be drawn between Caravaggio (q.v.) and Galileo, who both express, one in art and one in science, the return to nature and the reaction against tradition on which the new age was based. Although art and science were separated within the system of culture, ties between the two worlds were still apparent: Lodovico Cigoli (L. Cardi) painted the moon at the feet of the Virgin (Rome, S. Maria Maggiore) exactly as it had been observed by Galileo through his telescope (E. Panofsky, 1954), and Paolo Guidotti da Lucca, painter and inventor, is remembered as a pioneer of aeronautics.

Apart from the influence of scientific progress on human sensibility (sense of space and time sense) and on the psychological system, definite effects of science on art can be pointed out, such as the influence of Chevreuil's, Rood's, and Sutter's optical and physiological theories of color and vision on neoimpressionism (see IMPRESSIONISM, col. 854), that of psychoanalysis on surrealism, and that of Einstein's physics and of mechanization on cubism, futurism, and suprematism. Much of contemporary poetics, too, like that of the Renaissance, has its origins in scientific theories.

Technique itself, in its historical development, has moved from the level of craftsmanship to a scientific-industrial level. Craftsmanship, which was characterized by the use of elementary instruments intended to aid the hands (the artisan's most natural and primordial instruments) in their work, permitted the control of each single object produced and the guarantee of its quality but could not satisfy the demands of mass production on an industrial scale. These demands were satisfied not by art but by science, which supplied the most complex machines for mass production and for the new methods of reproducing reality, such as photography and cinematography (qq.v.), as well as for the reproduction of works of art (see REPRODUCTIONS).

As a result of this progressive separation of the individual artistic technique of craftsmanship from collective industrial science, the great rift between the worlds of art and science grew wider. It seemed as though the old distinction between art as "idea" and technique as "practice" and concrete realization had returned to life, as though an abyss had opened between beauty and functionalism, esthetics and usefulness, art and society, art and science. The bridging of this abyss is the story of the development of modern art and industrial design (q.v.).

Luigi SALERNO

SCIENTIFIC AND MECHANICAL OBJECTS OF ARTISTIC INTEREST: FUNCTION, FORM, AND ORNAMENTATION. Science has a cognitive aim and a practical one. When a craftsman or scientist creates a machine, as elementary as the wheel or as complex as the clock, it is the objective function that determines its form; this creative process is therefore the opposite of the artistic process. But since esthetic symbols are the expression of man, of his subjectivity and his humanity, scientific creation is never purely "objective," inhuman, or a result of functionality, because there is always an attempt at humanization. The created object has a logic of its own: its form is conditioned by its function. But man tries instinctively to make functional and artistic form coincide, for he is not content to produce mere utilitarian form. The proof of this is that the very consciousness of scientific progress, in periods of technological dominance, far from seeming entirely satisfactory, induces men to look back nostalgically to a "golden age" that preceded science (see PRIMITIVISM). On the other hand, while it is true that art has been fascinated by the sciences and, for example during the Renaissance, has sought scientific justification, in civilizations like the present one that are dominated by science and technology, industrial production in turn seeks an artistic justification in order to maintain contact with humanity and with human feelings.

Entire periods, such as the Middle Ages, were convinced that ornamentation added to the value of the material used. Thus beauty was added to usefulness and ornament to the object, increasing what was considered to be objective value. Scientific instruments, and in general all utilitarian objects, were ornamented. From the artistic point of view, therefore, these instruments cannot be classified purely as such, since the ornamentation was the work of goldsmiths, ebonists, engravers, painters, and other artist-craftsmen.

It has been said that function leads to form and partly conditions and determines it. This is true not only for architecture and furniture but even more for scientific objects and instruments (machines). But it took centuries (as with the clock) for form, function, and ornamentation to become integrated. The story of the clock shows how every kind of technique was applied to this instrument: that of the marble cutter and the painter called in to carve in bas-relief or paint the signs of the solar clock, that of the metalworker, the goldsmith, the sculptor, the ceramist, the cabinetmaker, and others. Moreover, not only the embellishments but also the scientific mechanisms (again, as with the clock) were frequently created by artists. When Leonardo drew a war machine, an insect, or a leaf (PL. 467; IV, PL. 268; IX, PL. 118) the picture inevitably had esthetic value; similarly, artists who made mechanisms of clocks, complex musical instruments, or hydraulic machines created forms of esthetic merit, sometimes even beyond the original intention (PLS. 460, 476). This is equally true of the mechanical parts of organs, carillons, automata, and the like, which were concealed in cases or receptacles whose function was purely esthetic and ornamental.

Among the objects most closely connected with the worlds of science and technology are the artisan's instruments themselves, which, in modern civilization, have been supplanted by ever more complicated machines: building instruments, those for the processing of metals and wood, of glass and ceramics, various types of looms for cloth weaving, and the like. These instruments were frequently decorated and ornate, revealing the pleasure taken by the maker in the form, sometimes very strange and curious because it was conditioned purely by the function (see UTENSILS AND TOOLS). To these instruments others should be added, such as scales (PL. 455), oil lamps, and stoves and such machines as the hydraulic saw drawn in the notebook of Villard de Honnecourt (ca. 1240; PL. 474), the printing press (PL. 466), and the lathe (PL. 466).

Geography and astronomy offered a broad, rich field from an artistic point of view. Maps (PL. 477; III, PLS. 491, 493–496, 499), plans, and globes (PL. 468; III, PL. 500) were the work of painters (see COSMOLOGY AND CARTOGRAPHY). The necessary instruments in this field were the astrolabe and the compass. The astrolabe (PL. 457; II, PLS. 28, 31) was already in use in ancient Greece; perfected by the Arabs, it survived until the 18th century. It was elaborately decorated and is one of the most remarkable examples of a scientific instrument of great precision presented as a work of art.

The most widely used instrument, and hence the most interesting for the evolution of its form and for the artistic importance it acquired, is the clock. Since ancient times there have been many types of sundial (the first timepiece, common to Egyptian, Babylonian, and American Indian cultures; PLS. 456, 458, 459, 461, 469, 470; II, PL. 27), such as the skaphe, or hemicycle (PL. 456; probably originated by Berossus, a Chaldean priest of the 3d century B.C.), the spider (a dial with lines like a spider web), the plinth (or lacunar), the *pelecinum* (a dial shaped like a double ax), the cone, the quiver, and the hollow conical spider (Vitruvius, *De architectura*, IX, viii, 1). The clepsydra using water existed in Egypt (the hourglass with sand seems to be of medieval origin) and according to Vitruvius (loc. cit., 2) was perfected by Ctesibius, an Alexandrian engineer of great fame in ancient times.

The most widespread medieval clocks were of the monumental sundial type. The oldest of these are in England, for example at Bewcastle and Kirkdale (PL. 456), and date from the 11th century. Perhaps the most beautiful such sundial is the one in the south transept of Chartres Cathedral, dating from about 1230. There were also pocket sundials (PLS. 458, 459, 470), made in great quantities in the 15th and 16th centuries at Nürnberg and Augsburg. Also in use were the mechanical water clocks derived from those made in Alexandria. The prototype of the clock with an action set in motion by weights (PL. 460) may have been one on the bell tower of a church in Verona. In Villard de Honnecourt's notebook there is a design for an apparatus that was to make the figure of an angel turn constantly toward the sun by means of a system of weights. The mechanical clock was invented about 1300, and the spring mechanism came into use in the courts of the 15th century. The principal makers were Erhard Etzlaub, Georg Hartman, Georg Reimann or Reinmann, and Christian Heiden in Nürnberg and Christoph Schissler in Augsburg.

Three types of clock had thus evolved: the ecclesiastical clock (for churches and monasteries), the private clock (for princes' palaces), and the town clock (a mechanical clock connected with bells). In form the clock might be monumental (specifically architectural), or portable (suitable for interior decoration), or miniature (used as a piece of jewelry). The last type (PL. 464) became a French specialty. At first these were oval or octagonal in shape, later circular; they were made of silver, of copper with niello work or engraving, or sometimes of rock crystal, later of silver or gold with enamel ornamentation. Among the 16th-century artists who made designs for French clocks were Etienne Delaune, Theodor de Bry, and Pierre Woeiriot. In the 17th century, with the clocks of Abraham Hecken (or Heeck) and Philippe Millot and, under Louis XIII, those of Claude Rivard, ornamentation grew richer; and this trend continued under Louis XIV, with Daniel Maret, Paul Decker, and the Gribelins.

Table clocks (PL. 463) were of German origin and were widely used in the 16th century; they were rectangular or cylindrical and were made of bronze or brass with engraved designs. The main centers of production were again Augsburg (with artists such as Johann Paul Pflege, Caspar Lengenbücher, Jeremias Metzger or Metsker, Wenzel Jamnitzer, and Nikolaus Plankh) and Nürnberg (Paul Schuster). Other centers were Munich (Benedickt Fürstenfelder) and Vienna.

Clocks were adapted to the various styles that succeeded one another from late baroque times to the 19th century. Under Louis XIV beautiful mantel and pedestal clocks were produced by craftsmen such as André Boulle and Filippo Caffieri. In the Louis XV period the pendulum clock with bronze ornamentation was in wide use and remained so throughout the Empire period (PL. 465). Precious marbles, ebony, porcelain, tortoise shell, gilt bronze, gold, and silver were among the materials used. In the 19th century no new type worthy of the tradition was created, and with the approach of the 20th century the clock gradually lost its esthetic appeal.

Typical of the clock was the distinction made between the mechanism and the case which was to conceal it and was its esthetic envelope. The scientific appliance, the mechanism, was independent of the appearance given it by artists and imposed only a minimum conditioning of form.

Other instruments of mensuration whose esthetic effect was taken into particular consideration were barometers and thermometers (PLS. 471, 473). The barometer, invented by E. Torricelli and perfected by Blaise Pascal, was widely used in the 19th century as a decorative object. The weathercock for meteorological forecasts was of ancient use in connection with the observation of atmospheric phenomena. In the 1st century B.C., Andronikos of Kyrrhos constructed at Athens a water clock known as the "Tower of the Winds"; it was octagonal, and on it was placed a pivoting triton that gave the direction of the winds, represented on the fascia, or relief, under the roof. This instrument, too, was widely used and elaborated during the Middle Ages. Optical instruments such as the telescope and the microscope were also decorated (PLS. 471, 472).

Architecture and engineering deserve a history of their own and much longer treatment. It will suffice here to refer to the work on the problems of statics (see STRUCTURAL TYPES AND METHODS) and acoustics (q.v.) and to mention such specific fields as installations for irrigation through screw pumps as in Egypt, heating installations (already perfected in ancient Rome), and the various types of stove derived from them. Moreover, architects studied hydraulic problems: the canalizing of water, the raising of its level, its exploitation as energy, and the like (PLS. 474, 476). The fountains of the 16th century, with their splendid play of water, reveal remarkable technical progress. Many architects, like Francesco di Giorgio, were also engineers, urbanists, cannon and war-machine builders, and constructors of weight-lifting machines and scaffolding for building.

Ships and many other ancient vehicles possess interesting contrivances such as, for example, the pivoting platforms on rollers or balls of the ships of Nemi, cylinder pumps, and the anchor with a movable stock. But this is to enter the field of machinery.

Concerning war machines (see ARMS AND ARMOR), Flavius Vegetius (4th century) left a treatise in which are described such military contrivances as catapults and crossbows. With the invention of gunpowder the art of war became more complex, and architect-engineers studied cannon, armored cars, fortifications, and other weapons (IV, PL. 268; IX, PL. 118).

Ctesibius, whose machines exploited the physical principles of air and water, invented, besides the water clock already mentioned, a water organ, a compressed-air pump, and various war machines. He also built automata: little figures that drank and moved, birds that sang, and the like, which excited the greatest admiration.

In the 16th century a veritable cult of the machine developed. The principle of the exploitation of natural elements as sources of energy was adopted for impressive artistic creations by architects and scenographers. Water, pyrotechnical, and air displays were executed on a huge scale; in gardens and villas appeared majestic organs that produced music through the pressure of water and air. Various pyrotechnical machines are described by G. B. della Porta in his *Magia naturalis* of 1538. In the same century, too, there arose the virtuosi, that is, dilettantes in art and science. The increase in demand and hence in production led craftsmanship in the direction of industrialization, and science helped strengthen it technically. Many *studioli*, or *Wunderkammern*, in which princes delighted in alchemy and other scientific experiments, were laboratories for industrial research.

An important consequence of scientific discovery that reached a peak in the 18th century was the mechanical production of objects of common use. The mass-produced object obtained mechanically with molds imitated the handmade product without equaling it in quality. In the 19th century the great inventions in the field of transportation, such as the steamship and the steam engine, and later the automobile and the airplane, revolutionized civilization. In the same way the discovery of new sources of energy opened up new prospects, and new objects, instruments, machines, and vehicles came into use. At first an attempt was made to reconcile with the ornamental tradition the new forms determined by the various functions; machines took on shapes and ornamentation that belonged to the traditional arts. The history of the progressive liberation from the tyranny of style and from the artisan and academic concept of ornamentation, with the identification of form, function, and esthetic value, constitutes the most important chapter in the development of modern art and of industrial design (q.v.).

* *

SCIENTIFIC ILLUSTRATION. Illustrations are used in science for the representation of objects as well as of ideas and concepts. For the latter the best means of reproduction is the sketch based on description or imagination. In mathematics, physics, chemistry, and crystallography more or less detailed sketches abstract what is relevant, disregarding realistic detail. A greater perfection in detail, but of a more symbolic than realistic nature, is aimed at in astronomical charts and in maps, as well as in technical construction designs. Perfection in detail is demanded of those illustrations which, in lieu of the object itself, are used for further research work (documentary-descriptive illustration). They are used mainly in the descriptive branches of natural sciences such as mineralogy, geology, botany (PLS. 474, 479), and zoology (PLS. 474, 480), in medicine (PLS. 474, 475, 478), in geography and ethnology, and in other similar sciences.

The first substitute for the object of research work is the three-dimensional reproduction conformable to nature. It plays an important part in all sciences, beginning with the stereometric structures of mathematicians and crystallographers. The planisphere, the globe, and the orrery (PL. 468) are examples taken from the field of astronomy; physical scientists have built atom models, geographers use the globe and morphologic reliefs, military men use sand tables, botanists use glass or wax models of flowers and plants, zoologists and paleontologists use animal models, ethnologists and prehistorians use wax dolls, casts, and reconstructions in space, and architects and technicians use scale models (q.v.). The high cost of production and reproduction limits the use of models considerably. But the scientist can easily produce a sketch or diagram for teaching purposes, and in fact, documentary illustration requires more competence in the matter than skill in drawing, especially where smaller objects are concerned. The preeminence of the diagram is due to its almost unlimited reproducibility; it can be made available to all, together with the text.

Pen or pencil drawings are well adapted to scientific illustration, where precision is important; for their reproduction, the linear graphic techniques (woodcut and engraving, copperplate engraving, etching, and lithography) are the most appropriate. For microscopic and similar small objects only these methods can be used; for larger objects such processes as aquatint, mezzotint, and halftone engraving are also suitable. The collotype, the most perfect reproduction technique, is rarely used because of its high cost. Only transparent colors can be used (water color or gouache, no oil color), in order not to obscure the drawing. Until far into the 19th century colors were generally applied direct or with stencils (hand coloring), but sometimes, in the second half of the 18th century and the first half of the 19th, with the so-called English colorprint process (in which a print from a single plate was treated with several colors). With the perfecting of modern colorprinting processes, both these were completely abandoned. At first colored lithography, often with eight or more plates, prevailed; but by the second half of the 20th century the four-color process was almost the only one used.

The scientific illustration, especially the documentary illustration, differs from any purely artistic realism or verism in two ways. First, the clarity and exactitude both of the whole and of the detail must always prevail over esthetic demands or desires. Thus, for example, foreshortening and overlapping must be avoided, shadows must be lightened, and sometimes even an unnatural position or disposition of an object may become necessary if it is the only way every detail can be seen. Furthermore, scientific illustration must reproduce not an individual exemplar, with characteristics that may be coincidental, but the prototype (species or variety) and must therefore generalize or idealize. Sometimes it must even combine successive stages of development in one illustration, as is often the case in botany. Thus it differs fundamentally from the purely artistic still life or animal picture. A certain *rapprochement* can be traced, however, inasmuch as in reproductions of larger animals, their characteristic attitudes, whether standing or in movement, must be true to nature.

From a historical point of view the documentary illustration is far more recent than the diagram, because its need was felt only when the number of research workers as well as research objects increased. In classical antiquity as well as during the Middle Ages their number was so trifling that teaching was based mostly on oral methods. The illustrations needed to make the subject understood — schemata, or *diagraphai*, as Aristotle calls them — were drawn in the sand or on the wall, undoubtedly only the barest outlines or diagrams. During the reign of Augustus, at the latest, detailed and faithful reproductions made by artists must have existed. Bethe (1945) is of the opinion that these didactic illustrations were at first distributed on their own merits, on single plates or as a picture series without text or with very brief commentaries, and that it was only at a later stage that they were combined with relevant text to make the first textbook. In poetry the process may have been reversed, but where natural-science illustrations are concerned, Bethe's thesis is most probable. His most impressive argument is the copy of the Dioscorides manuscript of Anicia Juliana (Vienna, Nationalbibliothek, Cod. Vindob. med. gr. 1) made in Byzantium in A.D. 512, the most important element of which comprises nearly 400 drawings of plants, each covering a whole page, accompanied by a text taken from the *De materia medica* of Dioscorides. The more ancient group of drawings probably goes back to the picture book of Crateuas (beginning of the 1st cent. B.C.) mentioned by Pliny (*Naturalis historia*, XXV, 4); the more recent group seems to have been compiled in A.D. 200 for an edition of Galen. The codex furthermore contains 48 pictures of birds, 24 of them on a single plate, illustrating a paraphrase of an *Ornithiaka* by a certain Dionysios of Philadelphia. That these illustrations, too, were created independently of the text can be established by the fact that some of the birds illustrated are not mentioned in the text; the sequence, too, is different in both groups. The statement by Byvanck (1949) that the illustrations in an edition of the Latin translation of the *Phaenomena* of Aratus can be traced back to a celestial globe also points to similar conclusions. In medicine numerous examples corroborate Bethe's thesis. Pictures of bloodletting, cauterization (PL. 474), and urine analysis, skeletons and the seat of entrails, skinned figures for the study of muscles and nerves (PLS. 475, 477; VII, PLS. 384, 387) wandered, individually or in series, from one text to the other, like the pictures of the zodiac in astronomy. The commentary of Apollonius of Citium on Hippocrates's work on the joints is illustrated with pictures of the old Hippocratic school, as is the work on the art of bandaging by Soranus of Ephesus (A.D. 90–150), which seems to have been written as a commentary for an existing series of pictures (both works, Florence, Bib. Laurenziana, Cod. Plut. LXXIV, 7). The 16 positions of the fetus in the gynecological work by Soranus (several copies, among the earliest being that in Brussels, Bib. Royale, Cod. 3714, ca. 900) are said to have been drawn by the midwife Olympias for Cleopatra a hundred years before Soranus used them (Sudhoff, 1907, 1929).

These old illustrations still show, in copies of the middle as well as late Byzantine "renaissance," a faithful reproduction of nature comparable to that of the Hellenistic paintings at Pompeii and elsewhere. The expressiveness of Greek art was so powerful that it was preserved unadulterated in Islamic art, especially in Syria and Mesopotamia, until the Mongol invasion in the 13th century (e.g., the *Kitāb al-baiṭāra*, a 1209 Arabic version of the Greek *Hippiatrica*; Cairo, Nat. Lib., Cod. med. VIII), although here, naturally, the Oriental tendency to the decorative and the fabulous can be felt more strongly (Weitzmann, 1952). In the famed Arabic version of Dioscorides's *De materia medica* of 1224 (Istanbul, formerly St. Sophia, now Topkapı Saray, Cod. 2147), which, besides good pictures of plants, contains rich narrative figural decoration, the composition is limited to a few variants clearly traceable to Greek sources; and the Greco-Oriental picture cycle of the *Physiologus* (Milan, Bib. Ambrosiana, Cod. E. 16) likewise shows the Greek influence (Gengaro, 1958).

In the West, on the other hand, because of Christian transcendence combined with Celtic-German ornamentation, the study of nature came to a pause for almost a thousand years. The pictures of plants, animals, and people that continued to be copied from available models therefore are much more stylized, drawn in a more linear manner than in the Moslem world, and in the end deformed beyond recognition. Only twice was this process interrupted, not so much because of personal study of nature but because of a reversion to better models: first during the Carolingian period, and again in the period beginning about 1200, when the models originated in the Norman Kingdom of the Two Sicilies (southern Italy and Sicily), where Byzantine and Islamic artistic influences

mingled with the *dolce stil novo* of the early Gothic period to create a new style. Characteristic of that period is, in addition, a turning to the antique, perhaps of urban Roman origin, that can be traced above all in sculpture. Its most important creations in the field of natural-science illustrations are the *Liber de simplici medicine* (known from its opening words as the *Circa instans*) by Matthaeus Platearius, the chief pharmaceutical work of the medical school of Salerno (Schuster, 1926), and the treatise on falconry, *De arte venandi cum avibus* of the Hohenstaufen emperor Frederick II. As his author's copy was lost in 1248 in Parma, his own contribution to the illustrations remains obscure. In the new copy compiled 1258/66 for his son Manfred (Rome, Vat. Lib., Cod. Vat. pal. lat. 1071), the animal pictures and hunting scenes distinctly show Byzantine and Islamic origins (Volbach, 1939). The assumption that new illustrations from nature had been made is unnecessary; even in the manner in which individual figures are grouped together is in accordance with exact models. Doubtless the imperial client, being familiar with the subject and knowing what was important, chose the models; according to reports of Arabic writers, Roger II (1095–1154) had once sent out emissaries to look for the best models. The close contacts between the East and the West created by the Crusades were particularly important in this respect. Mosaics, frescoes, and Gobelin tapestries especially were influenced in a decisive manner. The destruction of the Arab and Byzantine culture by the Turks interrupted this relationship and prevented the study of Chinese art, which had become known through the Mongolian invasion and which was distinguished, especially in Persia and India, by a realism that often preceded Western civilization by generations.

The Occident sought its way toward true-to-life representation on the basis of models of classical antiquity and at first, therefore, tried to achieve a correct perspective reproduction of space and of the human body. Animal and plant reproductions remained, for the time, under the influence of court art. Thus Gérard of Orléans (d. 1371) decorated Vaudreuil for John II ("the Good") with animal and hunting scenes, and Charles V had a hall of the Louvre decorated with birds and other animals in 1366. The Palace of the Popes in Avignon, too, was decorated during this period in the same manner. The actual place of origin of this fashion is indicated by the designation *ouvrages de Lombardie* used for this kind of decoration. Book illustrations, too, bear witness to this; in Lombard manuscripts, genre paintings and lifelike animal pictures can be found at an early stage — e.g., a manuscript of Pliny's *Naturalis historia* (Milan, Bib. Ambrosiana, Cod. E. 24), a *Circa instans* manuscript in Florence (Bib. Naz., Cod. pal. 586), a similar encyclopedia of natural science, the *Historia plantarum*, in Rome (PL. 474), and the so-called *Taccuinum sanitatis* manuscripts (Berti-Toesca, 1936). Also important in this connection is the sketchbook of the architect of the Milan Cathedral, Giovannino de' Grassi (d. 1398), and his son Salomone (Bergamo, Bib. Civ., Cod. Δ VII 14) and similar pattern books from northern Italy in Rome, Venice, and New York (Pierpont Morgan Lib., from the C. Fairfax Murray Coll.; reprod. privately for Murray Coll., London, 1910); these are a milestone in animal paintings, revealing the conflicting influences of tradition and the study of nature. The *Herbarium* executed in the 14th century, perhaps for Francesco da Carrara in Padua (PL. 479), which was used as a model for the famous plant illustrations of Andrea Amadio in the Codex Rinio (Venice, Bib. Marciana, Cod. lat. clm. VI, 59), is of the same importance. Court realism reached its peak with Pisanello (q.v.) and his Burgundian contemporaries André Beauneveau, Pol Limbourg (qq.v.), and Jacquemart de Hesdin. With them a synthesis was achieved in the late Gothic style between the medieval representation of nature, with its fixed formal repertory, and the free sketch of the Renaissance.

In specialized books dealing with natural science there was for long no sign of any actual study of nature. Pictures as well as text in herbals and bestiaries, in encyclopedias, and even in medical textbooks were slavishly copied from available models. Even the invention of typography can be said to have at first delayed rather than accelerated the development of illustration. As the first printers were mainly concerned with low production costs, they retained old models and haphazardly copied figures that their contemporaries had created for other purposes. Furthermore, these illustrations were reproduced at first with rather primitive woodcuts and by workmen who were incapable of altering the disposition competently, let alone rearranging individual figures in correct perspective. The most important printed books from the point of view of illustrations are the herbarium of Pseudo-Apulejus, or Apuleius Barbarus, found at the Abbey of Monte Cassino (Cod. Cassinensis 97) and published in Rome ca. 1481 by Johannes Philippus de Lignamine (Hinger, 1935); the *Herbarius* of 1484, published at Mainz by P. Schöffer; the *Gart der gesundheit*, Mainz, 1485, with over 350 illustrations (Schreiber, 1924), and the *Hortus sanitatis*, published by Jakob Meydenbach at Mainz in 1491, with nearly 1,100 illustrations. Only in the *Gart der Gesundheit* are there a number of pictures of plants newly drawn from nature (by Erhard Reuwich). Similarly, the first medical illustrations were taken from old manuscripts, e.g., Johannes de Ketham's *Fasciculus medicinae* (Venice, 1491, 1493; facsimiles 1924, 1925) in the *Buch der Cirurgia* by Hieronymus Brunschwig (Strasbourg, 1497) and the *Antropologium* by Magnus Hundt (Leipzig, 1501). Even Jacopo Berengario da Carpi, the greatest anatomist before Andreas Vesalius, could only partially free himself from tradition in his *Commentaria super anatomia Mundini* (Bologna, 1521).

While representational art for generations had been based on the direct study of nature, natural science had remained a philological science. For this reason even the outstanding discoveries of Leonardo da Vinci (q.v.) were not understood or appreciated — neither his manner of painting landscapes nor his anatomical and morphological studies (Huard and Grmek, 1962). It was only in 1530/40 that a change in this field could be clearly noted in illustrations. This revival in botany and zoology can be traced back to the genius and the example of Dürer (q.v.). In the *Herbarum vivae eicones* by Otto Brunfels (Strasbourg, 1530–32), the illustrations by Hans Weiditz still showed the lack of professional advice and assistance and reproduced plants with all their individual contingencies and defects. It was only in the *Neu Kreüterbuch* by Leonhart Fuchs (Basel, 1542–43) that, in close collaboration with the artists Albrecht Meyer and Heinrich Füllmaurer as designers and Veit Rudolf Specklin as woodcutter, the first real botanical representations of plants were achieved, because Fuchs had insisted on illustrating in these pictures the complete life story of the plant from the bud to the fruit (Sprague and Nelmes, 1928–31). In Basel, too, Johannes Oporinus published the first anatomical illustrations that were completely based on post-mortem study, in the *De humani corporis fabrica* of Vesalius (PL. 475), illustrated by Titian's follower, Jan Steven van Calcar, from indications or models by Vesalius (Saunders and O'Malley, 1950). A decade later the revival of zoological illustration began in the animal books of Conrad Gesner (*Historia animalium*, Zurich, 1551–87). In 1553 and 1555 Pierre Belon's books on fishes and birds, with illustrations by Pierre Gourdelle, were published in Paris (*Histoire de la nature des oyseaux*; *Histoire naturelle des étranges poissons marines*; *La nature et diversité des poissons*); and in 1554 Ippolito Salviani's *Aquatilium animalium historiae*, with copperplate engravings by Antonio Lafreri, or Lanfrerius. However, it was only in the 17th century, in Ulisse Aldrovandi's *Ornithologiae* (Bologna, 1600–09), that illustrations of the same value and standard as those by Fuchs and Vesalius were achieved in woodcuts by Cristoforo Coriolano, from sketches by Lorenzo Bennini, Cornelius Swint, and Giacomo Ligozzi (PL. 480).

During this period the art of book illustration was transformed by the transition from wood engravings to copperplate engravings and etchings. The latter methods were more adequate because of the greater possibilities they afforded for reproducing detail in the documentary and descriptive pictures that were required by the natural-history texts of the following centuries in order to capture the incredible abundance of newly discovered objects. At first the picture plates and series of engravings were extensively used for other purposes and interests, especially by the applied arts, which increased the number of motifs by introducing colorful and exotic plants and animals, as did the desire of princes and rich merchants to publicize their gardens, menageries, and natural-history collections with expensive illustrations. The flower illustrations of Basilius Besler in his *Hortus eystettensis* were published in 1613; the pictures of oranges in the *Hesperides* by Giovanni Battista Ferrari in 1646, Johann Christoph Volckamer's *Nürnbergische Hesperides* in 1708–14, and Jakob Breyne's *Exoticarum aliarumque plantarum centuria prima* in 1678. There were also numerous illuminated manuscripts, such as the *Simulacrum scenographicum horti Itzsteinensis*, 1651–67 (London, Vict. and Alb., Ms 9774/75) by the painter Johann Walther from Strasbourg. In the 18th century, owing to the development and diffusion of science, purely scientific viewpoints began to prevail more and more. This was due also to the influence of certain research workers who had enough talent to illustrate their works themselves, such as Paolo Boccone, Charles Plumier, Mark Catesby, Johann Dillenius (or Dillen), and George Eberhardt Rumpf. Because famous artists became familiar with science, a new manner of representation was created, which, although not completely independent of contemporaneous art, was markedly sober and unadorned.

In France the *Collection des vélins* started by Gaston d'Orléans in the royal library became a reservoir of natural-history paintings. Until the Revolution the *peintres du roi* Nicolas Robert, Jean Joubert, Claude Aubriet, Madeleine Basseporte, and Gerardus van Spaendonck contributed to it. The latter transferred it to the Jardin des Plantes, where it remained for almost two centuries. Similar comprehensive collections were started in Amsterdam, Berlin, Dresden, Turin, and Vienna. In Germany, Nürnberg was for a long time — thanks to the activity of a successful doctor, Christoph Jakob Trew — the center of natural-science illustration, followed by Vienna, where Nikolaus Joseph von Jacquin produced a great number of important botanical picture plates.

In England the initiative came from Hans Sloane and Joseph Banks. George Dionysius Ehret, John Miller, the brothers Ferdinand and Franz Bauer and John and Charles M. Curtis, William Hooker, Sydenham T. Edwards, and James Sowerby were painters of botanical subjects; and John Sibthorp's *Flora graeca* (1806–40), William Curtis's *Flora londinensis* (1777–98), A. B. Lambert's *Description of the Genus Pinus* (1803), and Robert Thornton's *Temple of Flora* (1799–1807), all published in London, are masterpieces. Botanical illustration, however, reached its peak in France in the late 18th and early 19th centuries with Pierre Joseph Redouté, Antoine Biteau, Pierre Jean François Turpin, and Pancrace Bessa. Other important works of their time include the new editions of Henri L. Duhamel-Dumonceau's *Arbres et arbustes* (Paris, 1800–19) and *Arbres fruitiers* (Paris, 1807), the *Voyages aux régions équinoxiales* by Alexander von Humboldt and Aimé Jacques Bonpland, and the travel books of Louis Claude de Saulces de Freycinet, Jules S. Dumont d'Urville, and Louis M. A. Dupetit-Thouars (the expeditions to Egypt, the Peloponnesus, Tunis, Algiers, etc.). These works made extensive use of the monotype color print, with which Redouté became acquainted in 1790 in England and which was greatly improved by him and in the printing houses of Langlois, N. Rémond, Bougeard, and others (Blunt, 1950; Sitwell and Blunt, 1956).

In the 18th century and at the beginning of the 19th, zoological illustration also produced numerous and colorful picture plates, although only the representation of smaller subjects was completely satisfactory. Thus the pictures of butterflies by Maria Sibylla Merian, Franz Rösel von Rosenhof, René Antoine Ferchault de Réaumur, Jakob Huebner, Jan Christiaen Sepp; the beetles drawn by Thomas Martyn, Moses Harris, Edward Donovan, Jean Baptiste Audebert, Johann Rudolph Schellenberg, and Jakob Sturm; the shells by Nicolaus Georg Geve, Franz Michael Regenfuss, and James Sowerby and his son; and the ichthyological illustrations in the works of Markus E. Bloch, Georges Léopold Cuvier and Achille Valenciennes, Karl Siebold, Pieter Bleeker, and Louis Agassiz are to this day unexcelled. The reproduction of larger vertebrates, however, as in the books on mammals by Johann Christian von Schreber (1774–1855) and Etienne Geoffroy Saint-Hilaire (1824–42), in spite of precision in details and harmonious colors, are as stiff and unnatural as the bird pictures of Johann Leonhard Frisch, George Edwards, François Martinet, Jacques Barraband, Henriette Gertruide Knip, and their contemporaries.

It was only later in the 19th century that, under the guidance of gifted research workers like Hermann Schlegel, William Swainson, and William Jardine, the faithful reproduction of the natural positions of animals at rest or in movement that had been aimed at by Audubon (q.v.; I, PL. 106) and Johann Friedrich Naumann was achieved. Edward Lear, Joseph Wolf, Joseph Smit, and Benjamin Waterhouse Hawkins were the forerunners in this field, followed by Paul Oudart, John Charles Werner, and Nicolas II Huet in France and Michael Schmidt, Wilhelm Hartmann, Wilhelm Kuhnert, and others in Germany. The reptile illustrations by George Ford, Jacob Green, and Ferdinand Sordelli are remarkably lifelike; and ornithological illustrations became a succession of masterpieces. In England these were due to the talent of John Gerrard Keulemans, Henrik Grønvold (a Dane who worked in England), Archibald Thorburn, G. E. Lodge, Roland Green, and Peter Scott; in America to Allan Brooks, Louis Agassiz Fuertes, and George M. Sutton; in Scandinavia to Bruno Anders Liljefors, Johannes Larsen, Gerhard Heilmann, and Gustaf Swenander; in Holland to M. A. Koekkoek and many others. The work of most of these artists extended into the 20th century.

The personal contribution of research workers to illustrations in bacteriology, anatomy, and histology is even greater than in zoology and botany because schematization, abstraction, and interpretation of the visual object — especially if it is of microscopic dimensions — are often vital for comprehension.

The first period, still entirely dominated by technical difficulties pertaining to optics and optical equipment, extends from the pioneers such as Anton van Leeuwenhoek, Jan Swammerdam, Marcello Malpighi, and Robert Hooke to the colored engravings of Heinrich von Gleichen-Russwurm and Ledermüller, who still took subjects from the three kingdoms of nature indiscriminately. An important change dates from the introduction of dyeing methods to reveal tissue structure clearly. As this happened almost at the same time as the perfecting of the color print, the multicolor copperplate print, and chromolithography, medical and especially pathological and anatomical illustrations became increasingly colorful. The culminating achievements of this development were the volumes on skin diseases by Jean Louis Alibert (1806), Pierre Louis Cazenave (1845), and Pierre François Rayer (1839/41); the editions of *Anatomie pathologique du corps humain* by Jean Cruveilhier (1829–42) and Hermann Lebert (1857); and the *Selecta praxis medico-chirurgica* (1851) by Alexandre Auvert.

Even today drawing remains indispensable for scientific illustration (PL. 478), but its range of application has been considerably reduced since the invention of photography. However, the fact that photography reproduces with the same emphasis the essential and the unessential details and has no ability to generalize or to abstract militates against its eventual monopoly of this field.

Claus Nissen

BIBLIOG. *General*: G. Cosci, Della meccanica nelle arti del bello, Florence, 1858; L. Figuier, Les merveilles de la science..., 4 vols., Paris, 1867–70; F. Faideau, La science curieuse et amusante, Paris, 1902; J. von Schlosser, Die Kunst- und Wunderkammern der Spätrenaissance, Leipzig, 1908; C. Hülsen, Der Liber instrumentorum des Giovanni Fontana, Festgabe für Hugo Blümner, Zurich, 1914, pp. 507–15; John Crerar Library, A List of Books on the History of Industry and Industrial Arts, Chicago, 1915; E. Kris, Georg Holfnagel und der wissenschaftliche Naturalismus, Festschrift für Julius Schlosser, Zurich, 1927, pp. 243–53; H. W. Van Loon, Man the Miracle Maker, New York, 1928; G. Boffito, Gli strumenti della scienza e la scienza degli strumenti, Florence, 1929; F. Savorgnan di Brazza, Un inventore dalmata del Cinquecento, Arch. storico per la Dalmazia, XIII, 1932, pp. 55–73; G. Volpe, Medioevo italiano, 2d ed., Florence, 1933; L. Mumford, Technics and Civilization, New York, London, 1934; G. B. Manieri, Dizionario cronologico d'invenzioni e scoperte, L'Aquila, 1935; C. L. Ragghianti, L'arte e il macchinismo, CrArte, I, 1935–36, pp. 297–99; N. Pevsner, Pioneers of the Modern Movement from William Morris to Walter Gropius, London, 1936 (3d ed., Harmondsworth, 1940); A. Lotz, Das Feuerwerk, Leipzig,

1940; F. Savorgnan di Brazza, Da Leonardo a Marconi, 4th ed., Milan, 1940; A. Gabrielli, L'uomo questo grande artefice, Milan, 1941; M. Goretti, Poesia e macchina, Bologna, 1942; W. E. Houghton, The English Virtuoso in the 17th Century, J. H. of Ideas, III, 1942, pp. 51–73, 190–219; V. Ronchi, Galileo e il cannocchiale, Udine, 1942; F. Tajani, Le grandi invenzioni, Milan, 1944; A. Uccelli, ed., Storia della tecnica dal Medioevo ai nostri giorni, Milan, 1944; W. B. Honey, Science and the Creative Arts, London, 1945; R. Todd, Tracks in the Snow, London, 1947; W. C. Dampier, History of Science, 4th ed., London, 1948; S. Giedion, Mechanization Takes Command, New York, London, 1948; F. H. Taylor, The Taste of Angels, Boston, 1948; J. S. Ackermann, Ars sine scientia est nihil: Gothic Theory of Architecture at the Cathedral of Milan, AB, XXXI, 1949, pp. 84–111; H. Dingle, Science and Literary Criticism, London, 1949; M. C. Johnson, Art and Scientific Thought, New York, 1949; A. D. Stokes, Art and Science, London, 1949; Museo di storia della scienza, Prima Esposizione nazionale di storia delle scienze (1929), Florence, 1952; L. Mumford, Art and Technics, New York, London, 1952; M. Buccar, Grandes inventions, Paris, 1953; H. Heydenreich, La dessin scientifique de Léonard, Les arts plastiques, VI, 1953, pp. 11–26; G. Canestrini, Il Quattrocento e le macchine, Civiltà delle macchine, II, 3, 1954, pp. 16–18; P. Pagnini and M. L. Bonelli, ed., Catalogo degli strumenti del Museo di storia della scienza, Florence, 1954; E. Panofsky, Galileo as Critic of the Arts, The Hague, 1954; F. Pannaria, Arte e scienza, Comm, V, 1954, pp. 3–13; C. J. Singer et al., ed., A History of Technology, 5 vols., Oxford, 1954–59; J. Le Goff, Les intellectuels au moyen âge, Paris, 1955; P. Portoghesi, I disegni tecnici di Leonardo, Civiltà delle macchine, III, 1, 1955, pp. 30–48; G. Sarton, The Appreciation of Ancient and Medieval Science during the Renaissance, Philadelphia, 1955; F. Valori, Trenta secoli di invenzioni, dalla scienza antica alla bomba atomica, Genoa, 1955; P. Rossi, Sulla valutazione delle arti meccaniche nei secoli XVI e XVII, Riv. critica di storia della filosofia, XI, 1956, pp. 126–48; I. Toesca, Un codice del Valturio, Paragone, VII, 77, 1956, pp. 55–56; R. De Benedetti, Invenzioni nella storia della civiltà, Rome, 1957; J. D. Bernal, Science in History, London, 1957; C. Singer, The Confluence of Humanism, Anatomy and Art, in D. J. Gordon, ed., Fritz Saxl, London, 1957, pp. 261–69; Brockhaus der Naturwissenschaften und der Technik, 4th ed., Wiesbaden, 1958; J. Gimpel, Les batisseurs de cathédrales, Paris, 1959 (Eng. trans., C. F. Barnes, New York, 1960); A. Guzzo, ed., Arte e scienza, Florence, 1959; P. Barocchi, ed., Trattati d'arte del Cinquecento, 3 vols., Bari, 1960–62; R. Borsari, Arte e scienza, Atti VIII Conv. naz. artisti, critici e studiosi d'arte (1959), Bologna, 1960, pp. 21–24; C. Genovese, Le arti figurative e le ricerche della psicologia sperimentale, Atti VIII Conv. naz. artisti, critici e studiosi d'arte (1959), Bologna, 1960, pp. 25–28; M. Praz, Bellezza e bizzarria, Milan, 1960; R. Assunto, La critica d'arte nel pensiero medievale, Milan, 1961; R. Hönigswald, Wissenschaft und Kunst, Stuttgart, 1961; A. von Muralt, Versuch einer Bewertung der Rolle der Naturwissenschaften und Medizin in der Renaissance, Festschrift H. R. Hahnloser, Basel, Stuttgart, 1961, pp. 373–81; H. H. Rhys, ed., 17th Century Science and Art, Princeton, 1961; E. Battisti, Antirinascimento, Milan, 1962; L. Salerno, Arte, scienza e collezioni nel manierismo, Scritti in onore di Mario Salmi, III, Rome, 1963, pp. 193–214.

Scientific representation and illustration: H. Schlegel, Verhandeling over de vereischten van natuurkundige afbeeldingen, Verh. Teyler's tweede genootschap, XXIV, 1849, pp. 1–86; L. Choulant, Geschichte und Bibliographie der anatomischen Abbildung, Leipzig, 1852 (Eng. trans., M. Frank, History and Bibliography of Anatomic Illustration, Chicago, 1920; 2d ed., New York, 1945); L. C. Treviranus, Die Anwendung des Holzschnittes zur bildlichen Darstellung der Pflanzen, Leipzig, 1855 (2d ed., Utrecht, 1948); L. Choulant, Graphische Inkunabeln für Naturgeschichte und Medizin, Leipzig, 1858 (2d ed., Leipzig, 1924); J. von Schlosser, Ein venezianisches Bilderbuch und die höfische Kunst des 14. Jahrhunderts, JhbKhSammlWien, XVI, 1895, pp. 144–230; H. Schöne, ed., Apollonios von Kitium: Illustrierter Kommentar zu der Hippokratischen Schrift περὶ ἄρθρων, Leipzig, 1896; M. Wellmann, Krateuas (Abh. Gesellschaft der Wissenschaften zu Göttingen, Philol.-historische Klasse, N.S., II, 1), Berlin, 1897; G. Thiele, Antike Himmelsbilder, Berlin, 1898; J. von Schlosser, Zur Kenntnis der künstlerischen Überlieferung des späten Mittelalters, JhbKhSammlWien, XXIII, 1902–03, pp. 279–338; J. Chiapusso-Voli, Appunti intorno alla Iconografia Taurinensis 1752–1868, Malpighia, XVIII, 1904, pp. 293–343; K. Sudhoff, Tradition und Naturbeobachtung in den illustrierten medizinischer Handschriften und Frühdrucke, Leipzig, 1907; K. Sudhoff, Ein Beitrag zur Geschichte der Anatomie im Mittelalter, Leipzig, 1908; F. Weindler, Geschichte der gynäkologisch-anatomischen Abbildung, Dresden, 1908; S. Killermann, Dürers Pflanzen- und Tierzeichnungen in ihrer Bedeutung für die Naturgeschichte, Strasbourg, 1910; O. Mattirolo, I vegetali nell'arte degli antichi e dei primitivi, Turin, 1911; A. Arber, Herbals: Their Origin and Evolution 1470–1670, Cambridge, 1912 (2d ed., 1938; 3d ed., 1953); J. de M. Johnson, A Botanical Papyrus with Illustrations, Arch. Geschichte der Naturwissenschaft und Technik, IV, 1912, pp. 403–08; P. Toesca, La pittura e la miniatura nella Lombardia, Milan, 1912; A. Hauber, Planetenkinderbilder und Sternbilder, Strasbourg, 1916; F. H. Garrison and E. C. Streeter, Sculpture and Painting as Modes of Anatomical Illustration, Ann. Medical H., II, 1919, pp. 305–29; F. Bruns, Die Zeichenkunst im Dienst der beschreibenden Naturwissenschaft, Jena, 1922; E. S. Rohde, The Old English Herbals, London, New York, 1922; G. B. de Toni, Le piante e gli animali in Leonardo da Vinci (Pubbl. Ist. S. Vinciani, IV), Rome, 1922; O. H. Giglioli, Giacomo Ligozzi: Disegnatore e pittore di piante e di animali, Dedalo, IV, 1923–24, pp. 554–70; B. D. Jackson, Botanical Illustration from the Invention of Printing to the Present Day, J. Royal Horticultural Soc., XLIX, 1924, pp. 167–77; W. L. Schreiber, ed., Garten der Gesundheit (1485), Munich, 1924; E. Goldschmid, Entwicklung und Bibliographie der pathologisch-anatomischen Abbildung, Leipzig, 1925; R. T. Gunther, ed., The Herbal of Apulejus Barbarus (Cod. Bodley 130), Oxford, 1925; A. C. Klebs, A Catalogue of Early Herbals, Lugano, 1925; W. L. Schreiber, Die Kräuterbücher des 15. und 16. Jahrhunderts, Munich, 1925; L. Bultingaire, L'art au Jardin des Plantes, Arch. Mus. nat. H. naturelle, I, 1926, pp. 129–49, III, 1928, pp. 19–36, VI, 1930, pp. 49–

56, XII, 1935, pp. 665–78; Van Marle, XII; J. Schuster, Secreta Salernitana und Garten der Gesundheit, Mittelalterliche Handschriften (Dedering-Festgabe), Leipzig, 1926, pp. 203–37; E. Howald and H. E. Sigerist, ed., Pseudo-apulei Herbarius, Leipzig, 1927; C. Singer, The Herbal in Antiquity and Its Transformation to Later Ages, Hellenic S., XLVII, 1927, pp. 1–52; M. R. James, The Bestiary: Being a Reproduction in Full of Ms. Ii.4.26 in the University Library, Cambridge, 1928; T. A. Sprague and E. Nelmes, The Herbal of Leonhard Fuchs, J. Linnaean Soc., XLVIII, 1928–31, pp. 545–642; H. Fischer, Mittelalterliche Pflanzenkunde, Munich, 1929; W. Konstantinowa, Ein englisches Bestiar des 12. Jahrhunderts, Berlin, 1929; K. Sudhoff, Biologie und Medizin im Wandel der Zeiten, samt ihrem Niederschlag in Bild und Schrift, Aus Wissenschaft und Antiquariat: Festschrift G. Fock, Leipzig, 1929, pp. 105–50; M. Wellmann, Der Physiologus, Leipzig, 1930; F. H. Garrison, Herbals and Bestiaries, B. N.Y. Acad. of Medicine, N.S., VII, 1931, pp. 891–904; M. R. James, The Bestiary, History, N.S., XVI, 1931, pp. 1–11; R. van Marle, L'iconographie de l'art profane au moyen âge et à la Renaissance, 2 vols., The Hague, 1931–32; F. M. G. de Feyfer, Jan Steven van Calcar (Joannes Stephanus), 1499–1546, Nederlandsche tijdschrift voor geneeskunde, LXXVII, 1933, pp. 3562–79; G. Sutton, Fifty Years of Progress in American Bird Art, Fifty Years' Progress of American Ornithology 1883–1933, Lancaster, Pa., 1933, pp. 181–97; R. T. Gunther, ed., The Greek Herbal of Dioscorides, Oxford, 1934; P. Leemann-van Elck, Der Buchschmuck in Conrad Gessners naturgeschichtlichen Werken, Zurich, 1934; A. Morassi, Storia della pittura nella Venezia Tridentina, Rome, 1934; Dioscorides, De materia medica libri VII: Acc. Nicandri et Euteusi opuscula medica (Cod. 652 Pierpont Morgan Lib.), 2 vols., Paris, 1935; P. W. Hinger, ed., The Herbal of Pseudo-Apulejus from the 9th Century Manuscript in the Abbey of Monte Cassino (Cod. Cass. 97), together with the First Printed Edition, Leiden, 1935; J. F. Mueller, A Manual of Drawing for Science Students, New York, 1935; E. Berti-Toesca, ed., Taccuinum Sanitatis della Biblioteca di Parigi, Bergamo, 1936; P. Buberl, Die antiken Grundlagen der Miniaturen des Wiener Dioskurideskodex, JdI, LI, 1936, pp. 114–36; W. Gundel, Dekane und Dekansternbilder (S. Bib. Warburg, XIX), Hamburg, 1936; W. Rytz, Pflanzenaquarelle des Hans Weiditz aus dem Jahre 1529, Bern, 1936; P. Buberl, Der Wiener Dioskurides und die Wiener Genesis, Leipzig, 1937; H. Röttinger, Hans Weiditz, Elsasslothringisches Jhb., XVI, 1937, pp. 75–125; J. Anker, Bird Books and Bird Art, Copenhagen, 1938; G. Dunthorne, Flower and Fruit Prints in the 18th and Early 19th Centuries, Washington, 1938; J. L. Ridgway, Scientific Illustration, Stanford, Calif., 1938; A. van Schendel, Le dessin en Lombardie jusqu'à la fin du XVᵉ siècle, Brussels, 1938; J. C. Webster, The Labors of the Months in Antique and Mediaeval Art to the End of the 12th Century, Chicago, Princeton, 1938; H. Wegener, Die wichtigsten naturwissenschaftlichen Bilderhandschriften nach 1500 in der Preussischen Staatsbibliothek, Zentralblatt für Bibliothekswesen, LV, 1938, pp. 109–20; A. Baldacci, Le piante in Leonardo da Vinci, Racc. Vinciana, XVI, 1939, pp. 67–84; E. Bethe, Antike Vogelbilder, Die Antike, XV, 1939, pp. 323–37; S. Piantanida and C. Baroni, Leonardo da Vinci, Milan, 1939; W. F. Volbach, Le miniature del Cod. Vat. pal. 1071 "De arte venandi cum avibus," RendPontAcc, 3d Ser., XV, 1939, pp. 145–74; H. Buchthal, Hellenistic Miniatures in Early Islamic Manuscripts, Ars Islamica, VII, 1940, pp. 125–34; C. D. Clarke, Illustration, Baltimore, Md., 1940; L. Serra and S. Baglioni, ed., Taccuinum Sanitatis della Biblioteca Casanatense, Cod. 4182, Rome, 1940; W. Neuss, Eine karolingische Kopie antiker Sternzeichen-Bilder in Cod. 3307 der Biblioteca Nacional zu Madrid, Z. d. Vereins für Kw., VIII, 1941, pp. 113–40; H. Buchthal, Early Islamic Miniatures from Bagdad, J. Walters Art Gall., V, 1942, pp. 19–39; S. A. Ives and H. Lehmann-Haupt, An English 13th Century Bestiary, New York, 1942; O. Benesch, Leonardo da Vinci and the Beginnings of Scientific Drawing, Am. Scientist, XXXI, 1943, pp. 311–28; C. Nissen, Die naturwissenschaftliche Abbildung, Gutenberg-Jhb., XIX–XXIV, 1944–49, pp. 249–66; E. Bethe, Buch und Bild im Altertum, Leipzig, 1945; C. Léger, Rédoute et son temps, Paris, 1945; G. E. Lodge, Memoirs of an Artist Naturalist, London, 1946; K. Weitzmann, Illustrations in Roll and Codex, Princeton, 1947; A. W. Byvanck, De Platen in de Aratea van Hugo de Groot, Meded. Koninklijke Akad. van Wetenschappen, Afdeeling letterkunde, N.S., XII, 1949, pp. 169–235; W. Kuhl, Das wissenschaftliche Zeichen in Biologie und Medizin, Frankfurt am Main, 1949; W. Schäfer, Das wissenschaftliche Tierbild, Frankfurt am Main, 1949; L. Bartning, Blumenzeichnen-Blumenmalen, Ravensburg, 1950; W. Blunt, The Art of Botanical Illustration, London, 1950; O. Pächt, Early Italian Nature Studies and the Early Calendar Landscape, Warburg, XIII, 1950, pp. 13–47; J. B. de C. M. Saunders and C. D. O'Malley, ed., Illustrations from the Works of Andreas Vesalius, Cleveland, Ohio, 1950; A. Grabar, Le succès des arts orientaux à la cour byzantine sous les Macédoniens, MJhb, 3d Ser., II, 1951, pp. 32–60; C. Nissen, Die botanische Buchillustration, Stuttgart, 1951; C. Nissen, Schöne Fischbücher, Stuttgart, 1951; A. T. H. Robb-Smith, Zoological Illustration, Oxford, 1951; K. Weitzmann, The Greek Sources of Islamic Scientific Illustrations, Archaeologica Orientalia in memoriam Ernst Herzfeld, Locust Valley, N.Y., 1952, pp. 244–66; C. Nissen, Die illustrierten Vögelbücher, Stuttgart, 1953; S. Sitwell, H. Buchanan, and J. Fisher, Fine Bird Books 1700–1900, London, New York, 1953; R. B. T. Kelly, Bird Life and the Painter, London, New York, 1955; H. Buchthal, The Beginning of Manuscript Illumination in Norman Sicily, BSR, XXIV, 1956, pp. 78–85; S. Sitwell and W. Blunt, Great Flower Books 1700–1900, London, 1956; L. Premuda, Storia dell'iconografia anatomica, Milan, 1957; R. Ronsil, L'art français dans le livre d'oiseaux, Mém. Mus. nat. H. naturelle, N.S., A (Zool.), XV, 1957, pp. 1–131; K. Weitzmann, Narration in Ancient Art, AJA, LXI, 1957, pp. 83–91; M. L. Gengaro, A proposito delle inedite illustrazioni del Physiologus greco della Biblioteca Ambrosiana, Arte lombarda, III, 1958, pp. 19–27; M. C. McLarty, Illustrating Medicine and Surgery, Edinburgh, Baltimore, Md., 1960; G. Lapage, Art and the Scientist, Bristol, Baltimore, Md., 1961; P. Huard and M. D. Grmek, ed., Leonardo da Vinci: Dessins scientifiques et techniques, Paris, 1962.

Illustrations: PLS. 455–480.

* *

SCOREL, JAN VAN (also spelled Schorel, Schoorel, and Schoorl, and Latinized as Scorelius). Dutch painter, architect, engineer, and Humanist (b. Schoorl, near Alkmaar, Holland, Aug. 1, 1495; d. Utrecht, Dec. 6, 1562). Scorel holds a place of great importance in Dutch painting, because his works form a significant link between the still medieval productions of most of his predecessors in Holland and the Dutch paintings of the later 16th century, which revealed the new forms and feeling of the northern Renaissance (see FLEMISH AND DUTCH ART).

Scorel was the natural son of a priest. He attended the Latin School at Alkmaar and studied painting there with Cornelis Buys. At the age of seventeen he transferred to Amsterdam and became the pupil of Jacob Cornelisz. van Oostsanen. About 1518 he went to Utrecht, where Jan Gossaert (q.v.) held an important post as court painter. He seems to have stayed only a short time there, however, soon setting out on a long journey, which determined and influenced his entire career. Traveling through Speyer, Strasbourg, and Basel, he arrived at Nürnberg, where he is reputed to have studied briefly with Albrecht Dürer. He then went to Carinthia, where he attracted an important patron, Count Cristoforo Frangipani, who gave him his first important commission, the painting of a triptych, now in the church at Obervellach, Austria. This altarpiece of 1520 shows in the central panel the Holy Company, or family of Christ and the Virgin, with portraits of the Frangipani and Lang families. Even at this early age Scorel had achieved considerable technical ability, drawing figures well, composing groups in an able way, and already giving his portraits the direct and sober power for which he later became famous. In the fall of 1520 he went to Venice, where he joined a group of Dutch pilgrims sailing to the Holy Land, and then remained in Jerusalem until after Easter 1521. He later painted several group portraits of pilgrims to the Holy Land. On his return he visited Rhodes, then was again in Venice. From there he went to Rome, where he entered the service of the new pope, Adrian VI, who gave him a studio in the Vatican and sat to him for his portrait. Scorel profited by all the opportunities Rome offered to study the remains of classical antiquity and the works of Raphael and Michelangelo. Returning to the Netherlands, he became a canon in Utrecht, an office that necessitated his ordination as priest but required few ecclesiastical duties and provided him with an assured income for the rest of his life. Because of warfare in Utrecht he worked in Haarlem until 1529, when he resettled in Utrecht.

From then on he engaged in a lively career as a painter, constantly receiving commissions, many of which took him away from home for considerable periods of time. He also provided designs for the renovation of St. Mary's, his church in Utrecht, and supervised a number of important hydraulic-engineering projects. In 1540 he made a trip to France; ten years later he was one of the painters charged with the task of cleaning the Van Eyck altarpiece in Ghent (V, PLS. 215, 216; IX, PL. 11). Landscape was one of Scorel's specialties, and vistas of rocky cliffs and rich vegetation often form the background for his portraits and figure pieces (V, PL. 288).

BIBLIOG. G. J. Hoogewerff, Jan van Scorel, The Hague, 1923; Werken van Jan van Scorel, Utrecht, 1955 (cat.).

Margaretta M. SALINGER

SCOTLAND. See GREAT BRITAIN.

SCULPTURE. In a broad sense sculpture includes all representations in full relief, that is, in the round, and in partial relief (high and low relief, engraving, graffito, hollow relief) obtained by the carving or modeling of any material. The specific character of sculpture, above and beyond its tridimensionality, lies in the inseparability of the image it creates from the tangible solidity of the sculptured object in natural space, from the quality of the material and its volume, and from the various effects produced by the movement of shadows as a result of changing light. The word "sculpture," which is derived from the Latin verb *sculpere*, implies more specifically the idea of carving carried out on hard material by means of pointed and sharp tools (saws, chisels, punches, drills). The word "plastic," on the other hand, related to the Greek πλάσσω and its derivatives, is more properly applied to the working of malleable materials by the hand, either alone or assisted by tools (spatulas, modeling implements, burins) with the object of obtaining representations in relief, directly or indirectly (i.e., by subsequent procedures of casting metal in the form that has been modeled).

The extended use of the term "sculpture" to cover both these fundamental techniques is traditionally accepted, especially in certain modern languages (and, for practical reasons, is used in this article); for the same comprehensive sense other modern languages — for example, German (*die Plastik*) and Italian (*la plastica*) — favor the Greek derivative. Generally speaking, however, all objects produced through sculpture can be described as "plastic." Moreover, it should be noted that this word has in recent times been extended to painting and to the visual arts in general, since they too are the products of work carried out in material substance. The generalization of the word is also explained by the fact that painting can give the optical illusion of relief, so the relief value in sculpture, although realized in three dimensions, is perceived through effects of chiaroscuro, that is, of light and shade, and even of color, in images that are similar in type to those of painting.

The classifications of sculpture in current use, besides referring to the two fundamental processes of carving and modeling, also refer to material, dimensions, and the purpose or function for which the work was made. No hard and fast separation can be made even between the two basic processes; in fact, often the same piece is first carved and then modeled (see TECHNIQUES). Furthermore, generally speaking, the two processes have been known and used concurrently, depending on expediency, in every civilization in history. As for material, an initial, rough distinction should be made between sculptures in wood and stone, all of which are executed by carving, but usually with the help of a clay model, and sculptures in malleable materials (clay, wax, metal, etc.), which are mostly executed by modeling, generally followed by a process of either natural or artificial hardening (see CERAMICS; GLASS; STUCCO) or by casting in a firmer material (bronze, copper, silver, gold, etc.; see GOLD- AND SILVERWORK; METALWORK). Carved wooden sculptures are for the most part finished with a special surface treatment (varnish, patina, priming, polychromy, etc.); the same is true of other, similar techniques (see IVORY AND BONE CARVING). It should be added that applied sculpture — that is, sculpture as an applied art — can be the result of juxtaposition, as in the working of various parts of the same material (see BASKETRY) and in the combination of different materials (see ENAMELS; INLAY; MEDIA, COMPOSITE). In regard to size, no classification is possible: dimensions range from the greatest, in colossal sculptures and those intended for large-scale architectural decoration, to the most minute, in plaquettes, medals, coins (see COINS AND MEDALS), gems (see GEMS AND GLYPTICS), and jewels (see GOLD- AND SILVERWORK).

With reference to purpose or function, sculpture is seldom autonomous, serving as it generally does to decorate cities (see MONUMENTS), buildings (see ARCHITECTURE), objects (see, e.g., ARMS AND ARMOR; FURNITURE; HOUSEHOLD OBJECTS; LITURGICAL AND RITUAL OBJECTS; MUSICAL INSTRUMENTS), and persons (see COSTUME). However, the specific term "decorative sculpture" is applied to sculpture that serves a truly ornamental or integrating function in buildings or gardens; this is almost always the work of artisans. Plastic decoration can be superposed and attached to a building or object while preserving its autonomy of representation and even its separateness as an object, as in the case of statues and reliefs forming part of an architectural composition. Or it can be integrated with architectural elements, as in the case of the fluting of classical columns, the modeling of friezes, cornices, and bases, and the fashioning of capitals (see ORNAMENTATION) or with objects, as in the case of household articles in the shape of human figures, animals, and so on.

SUMMARY. General considerations (col. 818). Materials (col. 823). Processes (col. 824): *Polychromy*. Sculpture and architecture (col. 827). Sculpture and painting (col. 829). Applied sculpture (col. 831). Situation and setting: bases, niches, frames (col. 833). Conservation and restoration (col. 833). Imitations and reproductions (col. 835). Modern sculpture (col. 836).

GENERAL CONSIDERATIONS. There has been no scarcity of writing on the esthetics of architecture and painting (though in almost every case what is discussed is the poetics of a particular artistic current), but attempts to formulate a special esthetic for sculpture are rare. It cannot be said that there exists an exclusive order of visual values peculiar to sculpture, although in certain periods and cultures this art has been considered more capable than the others of the highest realization of esthetic values. Sculpture does not in fact have special visual problems of its own, and the values of beauty that it has pursued in the course of its history have not been essentially dissimilar to those of painting; even the debate over the superiority of the one art to the other concerns their respective technical possibilities in the attainment of a common end rather than the question of values.

In the esthetics of the Far East sculpture is considered subordinate to painting, the latter being compared to literary activity and regarded as more spiritual than sculpture, which is more closely tied to matter and to the procedures of the artisan. In Western esthetics, based on the idea of mimesis (q.v.), judgment has fluctuated between the two arts (tending in classical times to grant preeminence to sculpture), since it is acknowledged that sculpture has the merit of realizing things in relief, and painting that of realizing them in color; hence it is not unusual to find the surpassing worth of the one art and the other being alternatively affirmed by writers of the same time and culture. However, the esthetic end is the same in both cases, and the difference resides in the varying capacity of the technical medium involved to attain it fully.

Much has been written on the technique of sculpture. This in itself indicates, in the first place, that the specific difference in the techniques of sculpture and painting claims a preponderant and almost exclusive importance in the distinction between the two arts and, secondly, that the technique of sculpture, though related to that of various kinds of artisanship, claims a dignity that renders it worthy of theoretical treatment.

If it is not possible to establish an independent esthetic for sculpture, at least there is no lack of special works dealing not only with the techniques peculiar to it but also with its specific functions and with what might be termed the partial coincidence of the figural fields of sculpture and painting. It follows that the specific difference has been taking shape and becoming defined in the course of the historical development of the two arts, in ratio to the difference in their respective technical processes and functions. The distinction is not precise, to be sure, even in the classification of works: there are painted sculptures and sculptural paintings in mezzo-rilievo, with the two techniques clearly associated, and there are sculptures that imitate painting and, still more numerous, paintings that imitate sculpture, and there are cutout, free-standing paintings and sculptures developed on a surface to be affixed to a wall.

Aside from technique, the circumstances that have helped to establish the distinction between sculpture and the other figural arts, within the compass of their common visual intent, are: (1) duration; (2) greater cost of production; (3) the solidity, as an object, of the sculptured work; and (4) themes. Generally speaking, a sculpture is meant to last for a long time, longer than a painting — even, at least in theory, indefinitely; hence it is generally made of imperishable materials such as stone and metal, sometimes of precious stones and rare and precious metals. This characteristic of being long-lasting and almost eternal is the reason that sculpture in particular is entrusted with the preservation and handing down of images to which an ideal significance is attached: the dead whose memory is sacred to family or community; figures divine, sainted, and illustrious; and allegorical representations expressing concepts or at least ideal values that are commonly accepted. The permanence of esthetic values — for instance, of the various ideals of beauty — is also expressed by the long-lastingness of sculpture, which is considered an art almost outside time and scarcely affected by changes in fashion and taste. This enduring character is so much a part of sculpture that the visible marks of time are sometimes regarded as an integral element of the esthetic value and are even artificially obtained, the barely finished work being given the appearance of an antique through patination, abrasion, and even fractures, corrosions, and mutilations. From this view derives, for instance, the "torso," that is, the statue made without arms and legs, as if the mutilated statue was a "species" of the general type covered by the term "statue."

The durability of the sculptured work, no less than the esteem accruing to it from the cost of the materials and of working them, is the main reason for the slower rate of change of the themes, style, and techniques of this art as compared with painting. It is rarely that the thrust of an innovating movement is exerted through sculpture — unless such renewal, as in the early Renaissance and during the neoclassic phase, polemically proposes a return to antique or even archaic styles. Thus, though sculpture may seem on the whole to be firmly linked to history and consequently less open to experimentation, it is also the art that more than any other expresses the ideal values that are set in the past and in history, and so it stands — at least in its salient aspects — as the visual image of the sense, or consciousness, of history. The monument and the statue, the basic types of sculpture, respectively imply the idea of a memory handed down to serve as an example and of a simulacrum set up forever. Bound in, then, with the physical endurance of the work is the thought that sculpture essentially presents images associated with concepts or personages elevated to ideal or symbolic value, while painting is free to move without restriction in the realm of sensory and visual images. The necessity for sculpture to be enduring also favors the stabilization, or the gradualness of modification, of the technical process, in that they carry on an almost ritual tradition of the shaping and casting of images. Until the early years of the 20th century, the technical processes of carving, with its stages of boasting and finishing, modeling, casting, and embossing, had remained virtually unchanged except that they were gradually facilitated and accelerated by the use of modern equipment; only in contemporary sculpture have entirely new processes been devised — even if deriving, directly or indirectly, from industrial techniques (see EUROPEAN MODERN MOVEMENTS).

The question of costs, particularly in connection with monumental sculpture, is obviously related to duration, but it especially influences the social relation between artists and the commissioners of their works, limiting the latter to a sphere of rank or authority and very often putting the artists in direct contact with the government, the municipal authorities, and churches. Before long, the public destiny that is thus assigned to sculpture in some way directs its forms toward common ideals or interests, the stability and permanence of which are upheld and, as it were, almost demonstrated through the centuries-long duration of sculptured works: it is easy to see how the commemorative, rhetorical, and often regal style of monumental sculpture influences the plastic idiom of its customary and even its popular forms.

The most characteristic attribute of the plastic work of art is lent by its materiality as object. A sculpture is certainly a representation in the same way as a painting, just as a painting is an object in the same way as a statue or a relief, so that, strictly speaking, no theoretical distinction can be drawn between them. Nevertheless, it remains a fact that a sculptured image is far more intimately related to the stone or bronze of which it is made than a painted image to the physical character of the surface on which it is painted. In short, the reality of a painting as an object is merely the physical condition of the representation, whereas in sculpture the object maintains a reality and validity of its own, beyond the fact of being a representation. This distinction does not consist merely in the fact, otherwise not negligible, that a sculpture is available both to sight and to touch, and that the latter mode of perception sometimes contributes to the appreciation of its esthetic quality; rather, it

consists in the difference in the relation that the sculpture and the painting establish with their surroundings. The dimensions, the shape, and the lighting of the setting undoubtedly have an effect on the perception of a painting, but only in the sense of rendering it more or less clearly visible: in other words, there exist a point of view, a distance, and lighting conditions that bring out the qualities of the painting at their best, and all others (though some may serve the purpose of a close-up examination of details) must be considered inadequate. On the contrary, a sculpture can and should be looked at from many angles and in various degrees of light without any lessening, undermining, or alteration of esthetic value. It follows that the value of the plastic work is generally the sum of many aspects, of many distinct, successive moments of perception, and that consequently the mental process which establishes its value is more complex than, if not different in nature from, that performed in the case of a painting.

This observation, which is valid for sculpture in the round, applies equally to high and low relief, for clearly the change in point of view sets the relief forms in an ever-changing perspective, somehow anticipated by the artist. If, then, in one way, the very physical solidity of the sculptured object sets it like any other object palpably within the area of empirical experience and therefore assigns to it a character of materiality, which painting with its mode of representation more readily surmounts, in another way this very materiality of the object confers on the form a more intellectual character, setting it up as a value that transcends the fortuitousness of visual aspects and effects; thus sculpture tends to present the work as an object, perfected and idealized, rather than as the representation of an object. It is for this reason that, at least in the art of the West, sculpture has adopted as its basic motif the human figure (q.v.), as a chosen and favored natural form, and that the formal ideal of the beautiful tends to be identified with plastic rather than painted forms.

Moreover, while the painter determines directly, through chiaroscuro and color, the lighting of his picture, the sculptor must avail himself of actual light — capable, to be sure, of being elaborated through the revealing contact with the surface of the sculptured work — as a material component of his work. This relation, the result of atmospheric and light factors, is regulated by the artist through his arrangement of masses and volumes and his modeling and texturing of the surface. Structure, in establishing the distribution of the masses and the orientation of the planes, creates the premises for the major contrasts of light and shade and a kind of unitary base for the more changeable play of the light effects on the surface; it is through the greater or lesser depth of the modeling, the variously stressed movement of the planes, the continuous or interrupted development of the form, that the artist obtains light-and-shade effects that may range from the outright luministic contrasts of maximum dark and light to continuous gradation and to the most subtle effects of shading.

Clearly, then, whatever the artist's intention, the idea of a plastic form develops not as an entity in itself but as a kind of relation between the sculptured object and space (PL. 513) or, rather, as a relation that involves natural space in the artistic effect, transforming light and atmosphere into elements of form and even into the very substance of the work (PL. 522, above). Beyond these two degrees of relation, which could be defined as maximum and average, there is a third, minimal one that is the result of modeling as well as of other elements of surface treatment. As we know, both the roughly shaped block of stone and the cast bronze undergo a careful finishing process with sharp tools (e.g., burins, chisels), which defines the slightest movements of the planes and thus the most subtle vibrations of light; in Greek marble sculpture (PL. 515) the process of ganosis (γάνωσις) was associated with polychromy and also served to subtilize the play of light on the surface. With the same end in view, finer wood sculpture was often covered with thin canvas on which was spread a priming meant to receive the final modeling — the color and gilt. A further treatment of the surface is carried out by means of processes that render it glossy or dull (PL. 520), smooth or rough, and that are accomplished by mechanical means or through varnish and other substances (oil, wax, etc.) which are absorbed by the surface and affect its reflection of light. Polychromy, too, understood as integrating the plastic form and not as a superficial naturalistic imitation of nature, has the function, as will be seen later, of establishing a relation with the light of the surrounding space.

Especially in works that are meant to be viewed in the open, the sculptor also applies many optical corrections of the dimensions and proportions of the image (enlargement of the parts farther away from the viewing point, foreshortening, etc.) with the aim of correcting the "normal" relation between the sculpture and space or, more precisely, of engaging space in a different and special relation valid exclusively for the particular object (which is form as modeled material) and thus lifting it out of its natural context, or rather subordinating the context to the authority of the form. All this may account for another condition that almost invariably affects sculpture of classical origin: precisely because the sculptured image is a simulacrum, that is to say, repeats the physical characteristics of the figure, it is mimetic art par excellence; but the very fact that it possesses these characteristics and hence appears as the "double" of the figure, in a different material and spatial dimension, makes it "artificial" to the utmost degree — in other words, makes the form appear to spring from a metamorphosis wrought on the material by the "artifice" of the artist. That the artifice or technique of sculpture involves a kind of transubstantiation is demonstrated, besides, by the fact that in the classical cultures the form is not always conceived in the final material: first a sketch or even a finished figure is made in clay, and then this is transferred to marble or cast in bronze.

The inflexibility and almost ritualistic fixity of the techniques of sculpture constitute a limitation of its thematic scope — a limitation that, despite frequent attempts to overcome it, is made almost imperative by the social conditions that affect the work of the sculptor. The very slowness of the work restricts, especially within the framework of the classical poetics of mimesis, those possibilities for fluent, running narrative that painting so widely exploits. In classical art sculpture creates the image, or simulacrum, of the god: painting (or relief, which may be considered a kind of painting realized through the means of sculpture) tells his story, or myth. Not only this, but while painting seems to work its way down from ideas to things, in their multiplicity of configurations and variety of effects, sculpture seems to take the opposite path and to ascend from things to ideas. Thus the scope of visual experience seems far wider for painting and its techniques. Throughout its history, in the civilizations of the West as of the East, sculpture in the round has been restricted almost entirely to the sphere of the monument and the statue.

Monuments are generally made up of a group of statues or reliefs incorporated into an organic architectural structure; a statue is an isolated figure representing a god or, by analogy, an illustrious person — standing, sitting, or reclining, sometimes riding horseback — whose image is supposed to have an exemplary or symbolic value. With the expansion of the courtly, commemorative, and eulogistic character of sculpture, the statue-simulacrum gave rise to more general types, such as the portrait (full figure, bust, or head). In many instances statues are grouped together without monumental intent, simply for the purpose of composing a scene; cases in point are the *Laocoön* (PL. 130; VII, PL. 189), the "Farnese Bull" (PL. 121), the celebrated Romanesque *Deposition* in Tivoli (PL. 258), the Lamentations by Niccolò da Bari (dell'Arca; PL. 19) and Guido Mazzoni (VIII, PL. 200), the lively narrative representations of Antonio Begarelli, and, in a wider range of forms, the Neapolitan *presepi* (PL. 492) and folk art in general. The thematic limitations of sculpture — at least in its courtly and public aspects — have given rise to the distinctive field of "statuary," a special category, which, during the Renaissance, found such apologists as Alberti (1464) and Gaurico (1504), who not only refer to the "literary" type, so to speak, of the statue (such as the sermon and the eulogy) but also to the technical means of prolonging the life of the statue, to its placement, and so on.

A far broader range of themes, types, and technical variations characterizes the relief (PLS. 483, 492, 493, 501, 506–508, 514, 520). Examples include many animated narrative representations, either in a compartmental arrangement in series and with figures juxtaposed and distributed along successive bands as in archaic and medieval sculpture or with unitary perspective compositions, not infrequently approaching landscape, and vivid portrayals of settings and still life with striking effects of light as in the classical, Renaissance, and modern relief.

From a technical point of view, relief exploits a whole series of devices directed toward overcoming the limit imposed by the actual depth of the slab, sometimes using it to establish the background and at other times employing as background an intermediate plane between the projecting and the recessed parts, and taking full advantage of the receptivity of the form to light to obtain effects of diffused, shadowed, direct, or reflected light. Numerous, too, though less so than in painting, are illusionistic expedients: the flattened relief (*relievo schiacciato*, or *stiacciato*) of Donatello (PL. 506), which, in an apparent contradiction, makes use of an actual lessening of the relief to obtain a greater visual effect of projection and recession through a stronger contrast of light and shade; at many points this is accented by a sharp cavity (*sottosquadro*) which, transforming the line between certain relieved parts and the background into a great dark groove, suggests that a great distance separates the two levels. In terms of volume, relief ranges from the round, limited of course to a few projecting elements (PL. 508), to sheer graffito on the surface for the more distant images; hence the possibility, especially exploited in Hellenistic, Renaissance, and post-Renaissance sculpture, of achieving striking naturalistic effects comparable to those of landscape and still-life painting. Such effects are not (with certain exceptions, as in baroque sculpture) attainable by sculpture in the round because of the obvious contradiction, at least from the point of view of the mimetic esthetic, of representing shapes as motionless that in nature are in constant motion or subject to frequent changes of aspect. A special case is the *à jour*, or openwork, carving — seen chiefly in Byzantine decoration (capitals, grilles, etc.) — which virtually reduces sculpture to an alternating rhythm of full and empty spaces on the two-dimensional screen of the surface (see BYZANTINE ART).

From relief one must go on to consider those aspects of modeling which because of their materials and their applications break with the concept of sculpture that has so far been suggested — namely modeling in very low-cost materials, such as terra cotta, and the making of figures in soft wood and even dough, sugar, and so on. In this whole vast output, different in every culture, the thematic material is just as diverse, depending upon cult, tradition, and taste, which change from time to time and from place to place, and upon function, running the gamut from ex voto to musical instrument (PL. 521), from household object to toy. The fragility of the materials, together with the large consumption, fosters frequent changes in type and style; mass production and the low cost of manufacture facilitate diffusion even among the poorest classes. In clay sculpture the variety of types and styles is remarkable (PLS. 498, 499); many of these sculptured objects are products not only of popular but even of domestic craftsmanship. This explains why in this production, for example in the Middle American and South American cultures (especially the Mexican; PL. 497), the assessment of quality is not always connected with technical skill; rather it is associated with the gift for improvisation of the modelers who produced the images — sometimes in a spirit of playfulness. Thus it happens that these modelers successfully touch upon motifs generally avoided in courtly and official sculpture (e.g., caricature, the comic, and genre scenes), and this, together with the liveliness of their colors, brings them close to painting. Not infrequently the same qualities appear in small sculptures in bronze (PL. 502) and other metals (brass, lead, tin, etc.).

The modeling techniques, which in loftier and more courtly sculptures retain their purity, multiply at lower levels, down to the infinite forms of their artistic application in folk art.

From the strictly phenomenological point of view, all works that are the result, in their structure or decoration, of processes of modeling or carving — whether sarcophagi, urns, caskets, cases, arms, jewels, coins, medals, gems, engravings, vases, plates, cups, musical instruments, furniture, frames, etc. — must be considered sculpture. It is here that modeling is associated with the most varied substances — stones and metals of every kind, wood, stucco (PL. 519), ivory, leather, and other materials — and with the most varied processes — not only painting but enamel (PL. 505), glass, inlaid metal, gilt, and so on. Finally, the actuality of the sculpture as object offers possibilities for more numerous useful applications than painting, while the techniques of modeling and casting allow for rather extensive mass production, as is demonstrated (aside from the adoption of relief for objects, such as coins, intended for unlimited reproduction and circulation) by the great diffusion of ceramic sculpture, glyptics, and gold- and silverwork.

MATERIALS. There are virtually no limits to the choice of materials for sculpture. Besides clay — for which wax (PLS. 509, 516) and, in more recent times, plasticine, an oily substance that does not harden and become subject to cracks and fractures, are sometimes substituted in the first modeling stage — the typical materials of sculpture are stone in all its varieties, metal (preferably bronze), and wood. In addition to these basic materials, there are many others, each with its special techniques: ivory, bone, glass, crystal, stucco, leather, and so on. Often different materials are used in the same work: typical examples are archaic acroliths, images with bodies of wood and limbs and head of stone; the chryselephantine statues composed of wood, gold, ivory, and bronze, with eyes of enamel, glass paste, or semiprecious stones; Oriental wooden images with metal parts; baroque and rococo statues in which the figure and the clothes are made of different types of marble (PL. 488); and the bronze Islamic figures inlaid with gold and silver. In some cases (e.g., in rococo art) the combination of different materials achieves effects of optical illusion. Sometimes, also, the sculptured figures were intended from the start to be arrayed, usually for cult purposes, in armor or garments or jewels: the xoana of archaic Greece were statues of wood or stone that were adorned on the occasion of festivities, and similar creations are to be found among medieval and Renaissance sculptures of the West (e.g., votive statues of warriors dressed in the armor they wore in battle, images of Christ, of the Virgin Mary, and of saints clad in precious cloths and adorned with votive jewelry). There are examples, especially in the sculpture of primitive peoples and that of colonial Latin America, of sculptured figures to which hair, beard, and even human teeth are attached. When these are not defacements made by the faithful as a sign of devotion (which is what serves to indicate the character of idol that the sculptural object tends to assume in the cult) but are planned by the artist for esthetic effect, they prove once more the importance in sculpture of the physical palpability of the image as object and, consequently, its material character. In modern sculpture in fact, with the gradual decline of the human figure as the main theme, ever-increasing significance attaches to the character of the material, which in the end sometimes itself becomes the object, regarded as a nucleus and organism in space (PL. 522). The process of transposition from one material to another, which occurs in almost all phases of sculpture, emphasizes rather than diminishes the significance of the final material, making it, much more than a means toward or condition of executing the image, an essential component of the esthetic value; in other words, the material constitutes the substance of the form. It is thus clear why the material, precisely as such, poses a constant problem. Whether the artist intends to emphasize it or whether, instead, he strives like Michelangelo to "free" the form as an ideal image from the weight and physical reality of the material, there still exists between the two terms a dialectical relation that evolves throughout the working process. Just as there are periods when artists tend to make or leave evident the original composition of the material as a mass or block (PL. 511), and even its external or superficial character, so there are other times when they resort to materials extremely sensitive to light (PLS. 485, 486, 516) because of their whiteness (e.g., Parian marble) or their mirrorlike hardness (e.g., basalt), their rough opacity (e.g., granite; PL. 488), or their luminous porousness and permeability (e.g., sandstone), almost suggesting a refinement and sublimation of the material into another, more subtle one, so that its objective limitations are overcome and it is assimilated into light and space. It is no different with metal, which creates reflections of light that the artist can anticipate and control only within certain limits when forming the model in clay or plaster.

PROCESSES. Up to the 20th century and the beginnings of modern sculpture, the processes specific to sculpture had come down to us from remotest antiquity with only minor variations; they can be simply classified on the basis of materials: stone, metal, clay, and wood. In only a few periods are sculpture and painting assigned a common origin in drawing; in the majority of cases sculpture springs from the observation of the object in its physical reality and from the possibility of preserving its form by separating it from its original, perishable material and translating it into another that will presumably be everlasting. In prehistoric cultures the first sculptural activity arose perhaps as the adaptation of natural stone "block" (PL. 511) or of a natural friezelike formation with figures probably suggested by religious or magic impulses (PL. 481). This may have been the case with the earliest known sculpture, the nude female statuettes dating from the Aurignacian-Perigordian period (VII, PL. 351; IX, PL. 247; XI, PL. 257), the oldest of which are about 30,000 years old, and with the animal figures in profile shaped from the unevennesses in the surfaces of cave walls (see PREHISTORY). To judge from the persistence of the original characteristics of the stone surface despite the endeavors made to impose upon it the desired form, which often remained incomplete, it must have required a great deal of effort to overcome the resistance of the material, to splinter and partially smooth it, with only stone tools (perhaps also wooden ones) and clay or sand. But as early as the Upper Paleolithic — though probably not until the later Magdalenian phase — there is evidence (e.g., the figures of the cave of Tuc d'Audoubert; XI, PL. 259) of an assured and active imposition of form in the modeling of clay, in an advance that, spreading during the Neolithic, was to prevail also in the small figures in the round that carried on and developed the iconographic themes of paleolithic sculpture. On the other hand, in the aëneolithic cultures castings were already being made involving the following stages: shaping a figure in clay (the model), transforming the shape in relief, by means of a cast, into a hollow, or negative, form (the mold), pouring molten metal into the mold, and then possibly refining the positive of the metal object in the cold state.

The technique of stone carving generally, though not necessarily, comprises more stages: the shaping of a model (PL. 498, below) and the subsequent transposition into stone of the main outlines of the model (usually carried out by a specialized artisan), and the artist's final shaping by careful work with the chisel. The model, commonly of clay, may be more or less detailed and may come more or less close to the intended dimensions of the work in stone; the sculptor must, however, have very clearly in mind the image he wants to achieve and be able to anticipate the different effects that will arise from the transfer of his model from a soft, dull material such as clay to a hard, reflecting material such as white or colored stone. For this reason, the artists of old gave careful attention to the choice of the block, sometimes actually going to select it at the quarry as Michelangelo did. The rough first cutting, generally performed by a stonecutter using the old method of pointing (transferring from model to block, by means of sharp tools, the main projections and indentions), is followed by the work of cutting, which chisels the plastic work out of the whole and progresses up to the last refinements of modeling (PLS. 487, 507, 508) with less and less penetrating tools so as to avoid leaving the white marks ("pisti") made by the tools (unless intentional, as in the "non finito" sculptures of Michelangelo; PL. 517).

The tools most often used for this finishing are a kind of drill (bow drill, or "violino") and the rasp, both of which permit the execution of those parts connected to the block only by small struts without much danger of fracture. The finishing touches are then carried out by subjecting the marble to a greater or lesser degree of smoothing with fine rasps and rubbing with pumice or sand and by adding to the surface a transparent patina, generally made on an oil or wax base.

Similar finishing is necessary for bronze (PLS. 500, 502, 503), both to eliminate the dross and imperfections of the casting (e.g., the vents; see below) and to give the surface greater refinement of modeling. The casting technique has remained almost unchanged since earliest times except for mechanical improvements that have permitted the casting of larger and larger pieces and gradually reduced the risks of failure. An essential condition in casting is that the metal be melted to exactly the right degree of fluidity so that it may adhere to the mold in order to receive and set even the finest details of the model; this depends on the alloying of the metal and on its temperature and also on the distribution in the mold of an efficient system of vents to enable the metal to flow in and circulate and to provide for the escape of air and steam.

The most widespread casting method in sculpture is the lost-wax process. The first part of the procedure consists in covering a core of refractory clay with wax; a second, thick layer of clay is applied on the wax, which is thus held between the two clay masses. When the envelope thus obtained is brought to a high temperature, the wax melts and flows out of the appropriate vents. Into the thin, empty space left by the wax between the two clay masses is poured the molten alloy, which, cooling and hardening, forms the statue. The most commonly used bronze alloy is composed of copper, lead, and zinc: it forms, in the casting, a thin and uniform layer. Another process, more like the one used in industrial casting, is that known as the "sandbox" technique; it consists of juxtaposing a positive and a negative mold in such a way as to leave between them, without the intervention of wax, a thin cavity into which the molten alloy can be poured. This system, which permits many examples to be made without remodeling of the wax each time, is used especially for plaques and medals.

Other technical processes of metal sculpture are repoussé work and coinage. The repoussé technique consists in working sheet metal from the reverse side with graving tools, exploiting its ductility to create high and low relief, generally of small dimensions; it is largely employed in gold- and silverwork (q.v.). In archaic Greece and Etruria, however, large and even gigantic figures were realized through this technique: sheets of metal were embossed with hammers and then fastened together — the *sphyrelaton* (PL. 501; IX, PL. 503). Coinage is the impression on metal of a representation carved in negative on a mold of very hard metal (the die). This process is always used for currency; medals are often struck in the same way.

Terra cottas (PLS. 497–499, 521) are produced by firing an image modeled in clay. The technique is derived from methods common to the making of pottery and bricks. Terra cotta is often colored with substances that in a second firing are fused to the modeled form, covering it with a glassy layer.

The procedures in wood sculpture — for which hard, seasoned wood is generally used (sycamore in ancient Egypt, PL. 495; cypress and box in Greece; and most commonly walnut in the art of the West) — are not dissimilar to those used in stone sculpture. The trunk, having been hollowed out to reduce its weight and to remove the part most sensitive to humidity and temperature, is carved with chisels; but the surface is generally covered with a chalk priming (sometimes also with a layer of cloth) on which the actual modeling is done and to which gold or polychromy are often applied (PLS. 490, 496). The variations of the basic techniques are numerous, as is understandable, considering the variety of the materials that can be worked and the implements that can be used: saws, large and small chisels, drills, hand presses, oxyhydrogen flame, and so on.

Preliminary operations and others subsequent to the actual sculptural process determine, respectively, the structural form and the surface configuration of the work. The preliminary procedures are, for stone and wood sculpture, choosing the type of material and deciding on the dimensions and cut of the block or trunk; ascertaining its homogeneity (absence of cracks or veins in the marble, of knots or flaws in the wood); outlining the figure roughly in the block by transferring it from the sketch or model through the method of pointing; and boasting. For metal sculpture, especially for large works, the preliminary operations involve the construction of the inside armature and the preparation of the molds and apparatuses for casting. In addition to the final tooling that determines the character of the surface, the supplementary procedures include patination and polychromy. In the case of marble the patina is generally made of wax, oils, and other lubricants, which are melted into the outer surface of the stone, forming, so to speak, its skin; the patina of bronze, which is usually greenish or bluish green, imitates the natural oxidation of the metal. In both cases patination serves the purposes of simulating the action of time, atmospheric agents, and even of mineral salts on the material (as if the work had been long buried): it is an artificial aging that endows the work with a kind of imagined antiquity, as if to demonstrate by a supposed previous life its capacity to withstand the vicissitudes of history and the destructive action of natural agents.

Polychromy. The problem of polychromy is a complex one, varying greatly from period to period and culture to culture (see PLS. 484, 489, 490, 499, 509, 510). In almost all the ancient civilizations — Western, Eastern, African, and pre-Columbian — plastic form and color have been linked. Color is of course more often absent in metal sculpture, though, in a strict sense, coloristic elements can be said to include patina, the combination of different materials (inlay, enamels, etc.), and even certain kinds of finishing and chasing, which by simulating ornaments or details of clothing and hairdress produce on the surface frequencies of light different from those produced on the smoother surface of the modeled mass. Considering polychromy in the technical sense of the term — as a layer of various colors applied on the modeled form — there are two possibilities: either it represents the local color of the figure (complexion, hair, clothes, etc.) or it is independent of external reality and serves as a visual integration of the plastic work. Moreover, polychromy can be total or partial: it may be as slight as a few touches of color or gilt; it may be limited to certain parts, while the color of the material forms the uniform base (e.g., the English alabaster reliefs of the 13th and 14th cents.); or it may cover the whole surface and form the background as well (e.g., the glazed terra cottas of the Della Robbias; PL. 520). In the mimetic frame of reference polychromy would seem bound to overcome the limits of both painting and sculpture by effecting a synthesis, by adding color to relief. As a matter of fact, color applied as local color to a definite and unchanging shape can no longer suggest, as in painting, the mutability of the form with the changing of the light, nor can it fit as a chromatic variation into the scale of the chiaroscuric values established by the plastic modulation of the masses and planes. Inversely, introducing a constant color into that scale of values hinders the free development of the sculptural chiaroscuro and thus limits the range of possible relations between the plastic form and the surrounding space. Thus strictly naturalistic polychromy has no possibilities of development and, in fact, rapidly leads to commercial and popular art, in which, if it preserves any value at all, it is no longer that of perfect imitation but of a more or less pleasing naïve naturalism. A far greater value attaches to the polychromy of sculpture based on a nonnaturalistic esthetic, whether in the highly developed art of the Middle and Far East, or the art of the Middle American civilization, or the art of primitive peoples. Here polychromy may take on an essentially symbolic and sometimes a ritual significance concomitant with the symbology and ritual character of the forms (figures, gestures, attributes), thus contributing to the emancipation of the image from the "normal" relation between things and space and situating it in a dimension of its own as a nonnatural thing that is incapable of entering through a "normal" relation into a natural context. A third case, which is only seemingly intermediate between these two extremes, is that of an essentially naturalistic polychromy that does not repeat the local colors but, because of its aim, pertains instead to the esthetics of mimesis — for example, the polychromy of ancient sculpture, especially of the classical and Hellenistic periods, when its use must have been much more widespread than one might surmise on the basis of the few pieces that have survived with the original colors (the "whiteness" of ancient marble, which was to become an element of the esthetic of modern classicism, being actually a mere consequence of the disappearance of the original polychromy). Judging from what can still be seen, it must have been a partial polychromy of subdued tones not unlike but not identical with the natural colors of flesh, hair, and robes: a kind of polychromy that altered the natural relation between object and space just slightly, lessening the variations and thus suggesting around the image a rarefied space, which could actually be considered to integrate and complement it (generally represented in relief by a blue or purplish background). A similar process of association of chromatic with linear rhythm is to be found in early wood sculpture and in Far Eastern terra-cotta and glazed ware; while a seemingly opposite but essentially similar process, is based on a chromatic intensification, is seen in Romanesque and Gothic polychrome sculpture: in the large altarpieces a perfect accord is reached between painted panels and polychrome sculptures, even in terms of their plastic and chromatic qualities.

On the other hand, in early terra cotta (whether Etruscan or early medieval) polychromy has an essentially and primarily decorative function; it tends to be integrated into the plastic form, being realized as a genuine composition of colored masses or of colored planes distributed on various levels. The integrating and subordinate function of polychromy is typically demonstrated by the earlier Della Robbia glazed terra cottas, in which the figures, or rather the sculptured portions of them, are white, the background is blue, and the frames formed by garlands of flowers and leaves display only a few fundamental colors. The glossy whiteness of the more projecting parts clarifies the relief of planes and volumes, transposing the chiaroscuro into a wide scale of light — perhaps the indirect influence of Angelico (q.v.) — and hence determining the chromatic treatment of the parts that, according to an ideal perspective (historically explainable by the initial bond of the Della Robbia terra cottas with the architectural works of Brunelleschi) form the foreground (the frames and the garlands) and the background (the blue that suggests the sky).

An entirely different order of values characterizes mannerist and baroque polychromy, often limited to the use of marble mosaic and *pietra dura* inlay in the bases of statues but sometimes also extended to the figures, various parts (faces, clothes, ornaments) being differentiated by the color and character of the stone (PL. 488). This is in fact a new instance of symbolic transposition, no longer in the sense that to the different colors and characters of the stones different meanings are attached but in the sense that the various materials composing the object, while preserving their original specific difference, in undergoing the same selective process are transformed from fragile and perishable to hard and immutable.

The gradual disappearance of polychromy in the technical sense of the term is probably a consequence of the development of plastic modeling, which has gradually come to absorb the pictorial values formerly obtained through color; of the diffusion of bronze sculpture, which clearly does not lend itself to painting; and of the damage that color suffers from exposure to atmospheric agents. However, it has largely survived in wood sculpture — which has begun only in relatively recent times to appear without a coat of color — and in all forms of decoration, starting with terra cotta, ceramics, and porcelain (PL. 510). Color reappears in modern sculpture, in which it is no longer a complement of plastic form, but an independent element capable of being shaped and modeled so as to create masses, volumes, and planes of color. At first, the favorite medium for this integration of color with form was ceramics, but it is also often met with in plaster, wood, and colored metals.

SCULPTURE AND ARCHITECTURE. Sculpture has exercised a function of primary importance in architectural decoration,

but the line of demarcation between architectural and sculptural elements remains as uncertain as ever (PL. 518). A basic factor in the relation between the two arts is the essential similarity of their working methods. As Quatremère de Quincy put it (*Dictionnaire historique d'architecture*, 1832, s.v. Sculpture): "The works of sculpture present themselves to the eye only through the materials employed; architecture likewise becomes tangible only through the materials that it brings into play, so that, reduced to the simple idea of mechanical execution, the art of building can attain the realization of its concepts only by making use of most of the processes and practical means that it has in common with the art of the sculptor."

In the art of ancient Egypt and of the ancient East, large architectural elements were replaced by colossal statues or rows of statues (IV, PL. 356), which were sometimes produced in series; and there are types of architecture in which the exterior configuration (whether or not it corresponds to an internal structure) appears as a unitary and compact form — for example, the Egyptian pyramids (IV, PLS. 329, 332) and obelisks (IV, PL. 355) and the temples of pre-Columbian Mexico (X, PLS. 12, 31, 35, 37, 41), which could with as much justice be called either architecture or sculpture. No doubt it would be arbitrary to regard the pyramids as architecture just because they have a geometric form and to consider the Great Sphinx (IV, PL. 333) sculpture because of its human-animal form. Starting from these considerations, one could properly call a classic column and a Gothic pillar sculpture, in that they are made by methods that belong to sculpture. Nor is there any doubt that the art of the stonecutter belongs, if only at the artisan level, to the sphere of sculpture, and that works such as the Egyptian hypostyle halls (IV, PL. 358) and the Indian temples cut out of living rock (PL. 482) stand on the borderline between architecture and sculpture [Ajanta (II, PL. 381; VII, PLS. 140, 454, 455), Ellora (IV, PLS. 130, 171; VII, PLS. 468, 469), Elephanta (VII, PL. 467)]. In Hindu art the distinction disappears completely, as it had earlier in Egypt (e.g., Abu Simbel, IV, PL. 359): architecture entirely covered with sculptures and with only slight structural articulation can in fact be considered a huge mounting for the display of a figural arrangement, and since it is this display that conveys the religious function of the temple, it is hierophantic and can hardly be called decorative or ornamental.

Even in classical architecture, where the articulation of the supporting system is precise and complex, it would certainly be unfair not to consider the decorations as sculpture, even though they are fully part of the architectural context. The fluting of the columns, the bases, the capitals, the triglyphs, the friezes, and so on are not only essential elements of the framework and the structural articulation but also plastic forms carved in the stone, and each of them is the synthetic and schematic representation of a spatial value (PL. 518). To take as the line of demarcation the presence of figural elements — anthropomorphic, zoomorphic, or in plant form — would be equally arbitrary: without going back to the legendary origins of columns and the orders, it suffices to note how frequently statues fulfill supportive functions as pillars and columns (caryatids); how statues and statuary groups or reliefs placed in the architectural space defined by tympanums, friezes, and the like integrate it and really become part of it; how in Romanesque and Gothic architecture sculptures of high quality define the constructional and spatial values of the architectural surfaces and of the structural form of portals, piers, spires, and pinnacles, and, finally, how absolutely sculptural an element is the luxuriant architectural decoration of the baroque, as is stucco decoration, which is modeled as it is being applied to walls and vaults, its function being the definition of forms (PL. 519). In the same category must be placed the incised or relief inscriptions in stone or in metal common to all cultures, though they constitute a purely decorative element in terms of the architectural composition, as well as the statues and reliefs that, placed in prearranged spaces and frames, contribute to the spatial dynamics of the building itself and convey its religious or secular significance, even though intrinsically they are incontestably plastic, or sculptural, works.

Another, no less significant, type of indissoluble association of the two arts is represented by ciboria, ambos, grilles, pulpits, funerary monuments, and the like, which are aggregates of architectural and figural elements. The problem, however, does not consist in establishing where the boundary between architecture and sculpture occurs in a unitary work of art: the point is that many works securely recognizable as works of sculpture, with an absolute and hence autonomous esthetic quality, are also structurally related to the architecture — in other words, their plastic quality is justified within the scope of the spatial dynamics established by the architecture of the building in which they have been placed.

The range of phenomena classifiable under the head of the architecture-sculpture relation is such as to warrant the statement that plastic form is so often conditioned by architectural spatial dynamics that the latter can be considered a permanent — or virtually permanent — factor in the determination of plastic form; even when the relation is not objectively expressed, the plastic form bears a relation to an ideal architecture, as in the case of isolated statues having no original or ascribed significance in the architecture of an urban setting and having, precisely by virtue of this relation, the value of a monument. The *Marcus Aurelius* placed by Michelangelo in the Piazza del Campidoglio, Rome; the *Gattamelata* by Donatello, in Padua; the *Bartolommeo Colleoni* by Verrocchio, in Venice (XIV, PL. 359); and the "Quattro Mori," incorporating figures by Giovanni Bandini and Pietro Tacca, in Leghorn, are cases in point. Similarly, architectural elements such as the column may acquire, independently of the figure they bear, the value of statues, as is shown by Trajan's Column (X, PL. 152) and the Antonine Column, in Rome, and the column in the Place Vendôme, in Paris (X, PL. 153). Quatremère de Quincy went so far as to question whether the use of reliefs ever went beyond the sphere of architectural function, thus taking the position that the spatial illusionism of relief is no more than the continuation, development, or integration of architectonic spatial dynamics and is not the representation of natural, or empirical, space.

SCULPTURE AND PAINTING. At least a portion of the plastic expressions that occur outside the spatial relation, real or imaginary, of sculpture with architecture can be accounted for on the basis of the relation between sculpture and painting. If figural sculpture, as well as ornamental sculpture, is a function of architecture, it is so in that it expresses the "purpose" of the building, that is, it expresses through figures the religious, civil, ideological, or moral content or meaning attached to the building and thus acquires the value of an exemplary representation, or ecphrasis. But, since "historical" representation is traditionally proper to painting, it might logically be inferred that sculpture has generally been conceived as a middle ground between painting and architecture, almost a reduction of the open and free vision of the former to the closed, rigorous structural and spatial dynamics of the latter. In fact, between paintings placed in an architectural context and the context itself there is very often the plastic mediation of sculpture in the form of modeled and sometimes figural frames.

The relation between sculpture and painting may be variously approached: from the points of view of esthetic values, of the conceptual and executing processes, and of the search for style. It has been pointed out above that the aim of the two arts, understood as the pursuit of the ideal of the beautiful, is generally the same and has had the same development in the course of history: the beautiful in painting is no different from the beautiful in sculpture, even though some values within the realm of the beautiful are said to be more easily attainable through the technique of sculpture and others through the technique of painting. In connection with classical art, especially in the Renaissance, this concept was justified on the grounds that the ideal value of art resided in *disegno* as the formal conceptualization independent of any material or technique and thus anteceding the choice of the operation that translates the mental image into visible form. In actual fact, however, the plastic work (such as the painting) does not always seem to be connected with a conceptual drawing or design: in the archaic cultures of the Western world, in Oriental art, in the Middle American cultures, in Negro art, and in some modern trends, for instance,

the plastic work originates either as the elaboration of a certain type of image (e.g., the traditional figure of a divinity) or as the formal development of the very structure of a natural material (typical case, the earthenware jar). Even Michelangelo, who can be considered the supreme representative of the esthetic of *disegno*, upheld the necessity of seeing the statue in the block and freeing it by dint of "cutting away" — that is by removing the "excess," attacking it directly with chisel and mallet.

However, allowing the greater margin to exclusively plastic procedures, there are other processes of conceptualization of the image, in addition to *disegno*, that the two arts have in common, beginning with allegory and the translation of abstract ideas into visual images; and it must be noted that, because of the tradition of ideas connected with sculpture, this art yields forms which are in essence either completely or partially allegorical, in that they attach to the figure an ideal or universal significance. Also, the historicity attaching to and almost inherent in the image is an idea common to the two arts, though painting ranges over a vaster realm, which encompasses the vivid and almost flagrant representation of events, while sculpture, being less suited to representing events with immediacy, tends rather toward an exemplary or paradigmatical representation — or to the "judgment" in the eulogistic and commemorative form of the statue.

In Western cultures the relation of mutual dependence between architecture and sculpture prevailed almost until the 19th century — if we understand architecture, in its wider sense, as organized space, which would then include the open space of the urban setting and the park. It was only at the end of the 19th century that, on the one hand, architecture began to be reduced to its structural essentials, with the elimination of plastic decoration, and, on the other hand, sculpture started to become independent of architectural space, to renounce its ancient decorative function, and to venture into visual experiments necessarily related to those of painting. From the middle of the 19th century sculpture has tended to break the bonds of the traditional themes and forms: Barye (q.v.), following the paintings of Delacroix (q.v.), chose wild animals as his favorite subjects; Daumier (q.v.) ventured into the field, until his day virtually unexplored, of caricature and political satire; Rodin (q.v.), while retaining the monumental character of sculpture, sought to master the impressionists' vision of color and light; and Medardo Rosso, though eschewing statuesque and monumental themes, was engaged in the same quest (PL. 516). More and more frequently it happened that the best sculpture was being made by artists whose primary activity was painting and who were seeking to examine the structural dynamics of the plastic art. Among these artists, to cite only a few outstanding names, were Matisse, Modigliani, Picasso, Boccioni, and Max Ernst (qq.v.).

But there have been times when sculpture has been in the position of the vanguard and of breaking away from painting, and this has occurred whenever European art has taken as the objective of its explorations the conquest or reconquest of a solid plasticity of form. The sculpture of the Romanesque and Gothic periods was decidedly innovating as compared with the Byzantine pictorial tradition (even when it involved a return to antique forms — or rather precisely for this reason). In the early Renaissance the sculpture of Brunelleschi, of Nanni di Banco, and especially of Donatello was abreast and sometimes even ahead of the gradual liberation of the painterly vision from the mannered grace of late Gothic style, and their work established certain modes of plastic structure of forms that were to be accepted and developed by such painters as Andrea del Castagno, Filippo Lippi, Antonio Pollaiuolo (who was a sculptor as well as a painter), and, above all, Andrea Mantegna (qq.v.). In this period, when the supreme objective of art was plastic and structural concreteness of form, there were thus specific instances of the influence of sculpture upon painting, above all in the order of seeing, so that it may be said that the character of the art of the time even in painting was plastic or sculptural, or downright statuesque. In the 17th, the 18th, and especially the 19th century, however, the influences that affected the order of seeing proceeded from painting to sculpture, so that it can be said that the character of the sculpture of those periods was pictorial, and in some cases picturesque.

Yet there are sculptural works which, in their genesis and development, seem to be dependent neither on the structure-based spatial dynamics of architecture nor on the naturalistic — or, rather, the atmosphere-, color-, and light-based — spatial dynamics of painting; they seem, instead, to spring from the need to model or carve the material, giving it form and spatial dynamics (PL. 511). This was the typical case with the clay sculpture of ancient Mexico (especially of the western areas), where not only was the image of soft clay "invented" rather than modeled, but the images of the external world, with its boundless wealth of thematic possibilities, immediately and spontaneously became associated with traditional forms of objects, giving rise to vases, cups, plates, musical instruments, and other objects which were at the same time human or animal figures (PL. 521). Generally speaking, this is also the case with what is usually termed "small sculpture": figurines, and statuettes (both votive and other), small reliefs (e.g., plaques and plaquettes), coins, medals, and so on, made in a wide range of materials, including terra cotta, marble, bronze, gold and silver, wood, ivory, and bone (PLS. 485, 491, 493, 494, 495, 497, 500, 501, 502, 504; the Tanagra figurines, II, PL. 59; III, PL. 138). These may or may not be small-scale reproductions of large sculptures; in any event, there is realized in them a spatial dynamics that can be accounted for in relation neither to architectural nor to pictorial space, even though there undoubtedly exists a relation of scale, so to speak, between them and the objects to which they were sometimes added as ornaments (e.g., furniture, coffers, bookbindings, arms, cups, inkpots) or to which they are actually identical.

APPLIED SCULPTURE. As has been suggested previously, the corporeal reality of the sculptural work makes possible an almost unlimited range of applications, or secondary uses. Whereas painting, in its applications, generally remains distinct from the objects being added to or superposed on it, sculpture tends to become one with the object, that is, to be grafted directly onto the structural forms (PL. 521). Thus there is a great gamut of objects in which sculpture not only fills some parts with representation in relief but directly models the structural parts of the object itself: vases and cups whose stems, lugs, and handles are true sculptures; fountains of which all or almost all the parts are practically autonomous sculptural elements; shields covered with relief; swords with hilts in the form of figures; buckles, combs, jewelry, and so on, in which it is impossible to distinguish the structural configuration of the base from the plastic decoration.

In the furniture (q.v.) of various periods and cultures sculpture may be present as an added ornament (bronze appliqué; reliefs, mostly of alabaster or of *pietra dura* inlaid in wood; etc.), but the point may be reached — especially in the case of objects with a ritual or ceremonial function such as kings' and bishops' thrones — where the sculpture covers and determines the entire configuration of the object.

A typical application of sculpture that does not seem to be comprehended in the above-outlined relation between sculpture (as architectural ornament) and architecture is sculptured doors; in these, sculpture is sometimes subjected to subdivision into panels dictated by architectural considerations but more often takes shape entirely out of the imagination of the sculptor, who subordinates panels, coffers, compartments, and frames to the needs of the sequence of scenes, to the rhythm of the representation, and to the greater or lesser three-dimensional development of the representation itself. Other applications of sculpture are to be seen in that whole series of objects which, while presenting the appearance of sculptured works, fulfills a practical or ritual function — for example, choirs, wall and floor tombs, baptismal fonts, stoups, and confessionals. In these and similar objects sculpture certainly determines the entire configuration as a whole and in detail; yet it must conform to certain styles of presenting an image, stemming from the traditional types, from the purpose and function, and even from the accustomed appearance of the object. To cite a single example, the sculptural development of the figure of the deceased on a floor tomb is doubtless conditioned by traditional types and by its position, which allows it to be seen only from above, as well as by the practical necessity of having the relief so low as not to interfere with the utility of the floor. Similarly, in wall tombs the figure of the deceased lying on the sarcophagus is generally tilted forward so that it may be visible to those who view it frontally and from below.

Practical requirements and the exigencies of taste also determine other formal and structural types — for instance, the *à jour* relief of grilles and balustrades, the rather pronounced projection of stucco decoration, the sharply modeled projection of the high-placed Gothic gargoyles and the free and light-oriented modeling of garden statues. It is not rare for true genres to arise out of the various ways in which sculpture is applied: stylistically autonomous works of sculpture may be invested with a practical function, as are the candleholders in the form of angels (PL. 521) and the reliquary busts (PL. 379); the fashion of the grotesque and the monstrous (see MONSTROUS AND IMAGINARY SUBJECTS) is, in Western art, directly related to such functions as those of the Gothic gargoyles and of certain garden sculptures (e.g., the mannerist monsters in the park of the Palazzo Orsini at Bomarzo; X, PL. 137); certain distortions that have a stylistic value, as do rhythm and meter in poetry, have functional origins in the adaptation of the image to the structure of which it forms part, as in the figures in French Gothic portals.

The physical reality of the sculptured object has often suggested the idea of animating it: there are sculptures with flexible limbs that can be moved to different positions, and, reaching back to antiquity, there is a vast succession of automata (q.v.), that is, sculptures moved by hidden mechanisms, typical examples of which are the moving statues of the clocks in many cities of northern Europe, and the famous "Moors" that strike the hours in Piazza S. Marco in Venice (II, PL. 74).

The very techniques of sculpture have given rise to minor productions that cannot, except in the few cases of particularly refined elaborations, be strictly classified as sculpture but are unquestionably related to it. Death masks are the result of a method of preparing a mold through casting that is certainly a process typical of sculpture; and it cannot be denied that death masks have contributed to originating the type of the portrait in sculpture (see PORTRAITURE), as is clear from the *imagines maiorum* of the Republican age, which constitute the starting point of the great Roman tradition of portraiture. Moving back in time, it is seen that Egyptian, Mycenaean, Greco-Illyrian (e.g., finds at Trebenište), Etruscan, and other masks required a final process of chased repoussé work which securely classifies them as works of art (even though this application of sculpture is to be found only on the periphery of the Greek world). Mention must also be made of ritual and theatrical masks, the forms of which are connected with certain facial types and expressions as well as with the gestures of dancing and of the rites that were to be performed by the masked persons (see MASKS). Reliefs having the autonomous character of sculpture also appear as decoration on suits of armor, chiefly those for tournaments and parades (see ARMS AND ARMOR); in fact, suits of armor themselves should be considered works of sculpture, for they not only enclose the body to protect it but also shape it into forms that enhance in it its warlike strength. In the 17th and especially in the 18th century furniture was made which had the autonomous character of sculpture and which, precisely because of this, stands out from the traditional types: suffice it to mention the works of Filippo Parodi in Genoa and of Andrea Brustolon in Venice. In the field of gold- and silverwork (q.v.) and of ceramics (q.v.) the range of applications of sculpture becomes practically limitless.

A category apart that should be considered here because it comprises small objects for personal adornment and for household decoration, as well as statuettes, amulets, and small reliefs, is jade, a hard, translucent mineral, variously colored and veined. The working of this stone, which was particularly popular in China from the early dynasties up to the 19th century, was carried out by a reduction process employing abrasive powders (quartz, emery, etc.), the images for the most part being suggested to the artist by the form of the fragment of crude mineral or by direction of the spots and veins (PL. 491). Like processes, essentially similar to those for the working of precious stones, have been used, though less systematically and constantly, for quartz, rock crystal, and such; here too the formal and coloristic suggestions of the piece of material have been exploited, and the aim has been, above all, to conserve and to show to advantage, through shaping into human, animal, or flower form, the transparency and brilliance of the material, the play of shading, veining, and so on. Not unlike this, as a process, is the work of carving in semiprecious stones (PL. 491) and rock crystal (PL. 492) and the engraving of glass (q.v.) with the emery wheel (VI, PLS. 236, 238).

SITUATION AND SETTING: BASES, NICHES, FRAMES. The bases of sculptures in the round and the frames of reliefs are integrating elements of the artistic form of the work and contribute to the spatial definition of the image. In many cases the bases form an actual part of the sculptured works: they are modeled by the artist and carved or cast together with the figures. Besides the base that constitutes the direct support of the statue, there is almost always another larger and more elaborate one that serves as a link between the statue and the surface on which it stands or between the statue and the architecture; this base may be simply an architectural element, in the form of a plinth or the trunk of a column, but it may also bear figural or ornamental reliefs, inscriptions, or even other statues ideologically related, as a historical commentary or allegory, to the main figure. Besides being important as a part of the work or even as an independent work linked to the principal theme, the base serves to set the statue at the proper height and in the proper situation and thus constitutes a necessary condition for its being seen to advantage.

A niche is an architectural element cut into the thickness of the wall for the specific purpose of containing statues or busts. A niche may open into the surface of the wall without a frame or be framed (aedicule or tabernacle niche) between posts, frontons, or small columns (as in Orsanmichele, Florence; III, PL. 391; VI, PL. 175). In section a niche may be quadrangular, polygonal, or curved. If it is meant to hold a bust, it may be quadrangular, circular, or oval. As a typical element linking sculpture and architecture the niche draws the statue into the plane of the wall, at the same time creating a perspective background or an empty space corresponding to the relief of the sculptural form, even though it obviously prohibits an all-round view of the statue. In most cases the niche does not exclude, indeed it requires, the presence of a base, as is easy to understand when one remembers that the niche, acting as an intermediate element, links the statue to the architecture, at the same time isolating the work as an independent value, as if to separate its decorative function from its sculptural quality.

In most cases the frames of reliefs also form a connection between sculpture and architecture. They may have straight, curved, or mixtilinear outlines; mostly they consist of architectural moldings or decorative elements with motifs of garlands, candelabra, or grotesques, to which are often added, especially in Romanesque and Gothic art, figural elements of symbolic or allegorical significance. Besides affording a tie with the architecture, the frame, acting as a shortened perspective, establishes the spatial dynamics of the relief, being linked to the main lines of the composition and, above all, fixing the depth or plane of the representation itself. This plane may be the flat background on which the figures stand out in relief flush with the level of the frame (or, as often in Egyptian sculpture, rise from a hollow; PL. 506; IV, PL. 365) or else it may be a perspective plane intermediate between the relief parts that reach to and beyond the level of the frame and the parts in depth that are barely relieved or are simply drawn on the plane of the background (PLS. 507, 508).

CONSERVATION AND RESTORATION. Although sculpture is made to endure, it is subject to various kinds of deterioration: variously caused breaks, disintegration of materials, encrustation, rusting, and so on. Most of the antique sculptures found at the site of excavations are mutilated, and only in certain cases has it been possible to recover all the fragments necessary for a reliable, if not complete, reassembling of the original. When there are serious lacunae, the problem of reconstructing the details as well as the whole presents itself.

In the past, when interest in the apparent wholeness of the object predominated over concern for documented and rigorous reassembling (if almost always incomplete), the problem was empirically solved by the pure and simple substitution (often conjectural) for the missing parts of other sculptures by a contemporary artist in the style of the antique piece, disposed according to what was believed to have been the original plan of the work (see RESTORATION AND CONSERVATION). Reconstruction along these lines occurred during the Renaissance and, later, in the mannerist, baroque, and neoclassic periods, but it has been amply demonstrated that in general these approximate reconstructions and reassemblings agreed somewhat more with the style and the esthetic of the period when they were carried out than of the period when the work was conceived; in fact, in most cases, the reconstruction of the gestures was based rather on the probabilistic principle of the "natural" than on a rigorous study of the original form. This reached the point, as early as the Middle Ages, where antique pieces were often reworked even in the parts that had been preserved — either for practical reasons (e.g., to adapt antique pieces to modern purposes) or in accordance with a false stylistic criterion, which could consist in the adjustment of the antique to the contemporary ideal of form or, more often, in the adjustment of the piece to what the contemporary culture held to be the ideal style of classical art. There is no need to labor the arbitrariness of such procedures, which is also attributable to the fact that restoration was entrusted entirely to artists, without any control by students of antiquity: these restorers were not even (as in the case of painting) artisans but, because of the importance attached to objects from antiquity, very famous sculptors, [e.g., Giovanni Angelo Montorsoli in the 16th cent. and Antonio Canova (q.v.) at the beginning of the 19th cent.] with well-defined personalities and styles of their own, which often prevailed over that of the original.

The current consensus is that restoration is essentially scholarly work addressed to the recovery of the integral composition, even through the elimination of interpolations, and that as such it aims, above all, at the material conservation of the original parts; thus the restorer should not fill in lacunae or attempt reconstructions from imagination but should work in accordance with the directions and under the constant supervision of an art historian. Since it is often necessary, however, to link the fragments together on the basis of a mental image to make it possible for the viewer to "read" them, scientific restoration generally proceeds in the following stages: (a) systematic collection and study of all available fragments; (b) study of the materials, technique, and thematic and stylistic characteristics of the work, as well as of the materials, techniques, themes, and styles of the time and place to which it belongs, so as to place the object to be restored in its proper historical and stylistic setting; (c) systematic comparative examination of the figural and literary sources as well as of all the thematically, typologically, and stylistically similar representations and the ascertainment of their relative chronology; (d) theoretical reconstruction of the original in its most probable form, with reference not to the "natural" or to "common sense" but to the historical development of art; (e) the establishment of the position of the fragments within the whole; (f) the assembling of the fragments in the method best qualified to afford a "reading" of the preserved parts, differentiating the connecting elements by means of materials and modeling. In every case the processes of reinforcing and cleaning the original parts must be done with consideration for the antique modeling and patina as well as for the alterations that time has produced on the surface — except in the case of incrustations that seriously reduce the "legibility" of the work or of unskillful repainting such as is often found on wood sculpture. It must be borne in mind that, as has been indicated, the original patina and even certain mutilations and abrasions constitute a kind of desired, or at least anticipated, aging that suggests duration in time and a previously established relation between the sculptured work and the real space surrounding it, so that within limits the progressive accentuation of these marks can be taken as a development esthetically inherent in the work.

Especially subject to deterioration through the effects of atmospheric agents are sculptures exposed to the open air, particularly if they are made of soft or friable stone (e.g., the rich decorations of Romanesque and Gothic churches); wind, frost, rain, sharp changes in temperature, and the corrosive substances sometimes suspended in the atmosphere all cause damage. The acceleration of the process of disintegration, or at least of erosion, in recent times has given rise to far-reaching scientific research directed toward finding a way of effecting a deep-reaching reinforcement of the weakening materials by means of chemical solutions, mostly with a base of silicates or synthetic resins.

Bronze sculptures sometimes suffer from certain kinds of deterioration caused by the accumulation of corrosive substances on the surface or by actual impairments in the metal, which may produce cracks, fractures, perforations, and so on. For this kind of damage, generally more serious in works that have long been in contact with the ground, electrolytic processes are the chief remedial means.

IMITATIONS AND REPRODUCTIONS. The undeniably important role that mechanical operations play in sculpture apparently facilitates the reproduction, imitation, and falsification of works (see FALSIFICATION AND FORGERY; REPRODUCTIONS). A sculpture in stone is capable of being faithfully reproduced by the method of pointing, and a work that is cast can easily be produced in multiple from the same mold, using the same metal alloy. In any case, the casting process makes it possible to obtain repetitions that are accurate both in size and, to a lesser extent, in modeling. The facile repeatability of sculpture has promoted the spread of knowledge of the most celebrated works, which quickly attained (especially in the classical cultures) the status of archetypes, and from these proceeded numerous copies, often of high artistic quality (e.g., the Roman copies of Greek originals; PL. 512). Nor were marble copies of bronze originals — and vice versa — rare, although the reactions of the two materials to light are very different.

The criterion by which an original is distinguished from a copy ("originals" being understood to include replicas by the artist) is the direct intervention of the artistic creator in all, or at least in the final, stages of the operation, that is, in the refining of the modeling of the marble or in the trimming and last work of chiseling on the bronze. Regarded as replicas that are not by the artist are examples obtained from the original mold on which the work of finishing has not been carried out by the artistic creator; copies are the mechanical reproductions obtained from the cast. Although modern science has found reliable ways to establish the period during which the materials were worked, falsifying sculpture appears to be easier (and therefore more difficult to detect) than falsifying painting. (The carbon 14 test, based on measuring the loss of radioactivity with time, is valid only for minerals and vegetable matter, not for metals.) It is, in fact, possible to reproduce parts of an original sculpture by means of a mold, to cast an object in the same alloy as that of the antique work, and to obtain patinas and weathering in every respect similar to the antique by the use of chemical and electrolytic processes. However, the mechanicalism of the processes facilitates the detection of the forgery, whether obtained by mechanical processes or by simulation of style.

There is practically no limit to the range of ornamental copies of masterpieces of sculpture in materials, dimensions, and techniques different from those of the originals; and the stylistic quality of these reproductions swiftly degenerates as they become more common and completely commercial, like those carried out in ceramics, plaster, porcelain, and sundry metals in various periods, especially in the 19th century. However, there have been phases in which even the ornamental copy has had a certain esthetic interest: to cite only a few instances, the diffusion of the bronze sculpture of the Far East,

of the Renaissance bronze sculpture derived from the antique, and also of the copies of antique statuary in Wedgwood, Sèvres, and Capodimonte porcelain.

In the field of sculpture especially, and particularly in Western cultures, the formation of an artist's style has often come about through the study of antique exemplars: in Padua, in the 15th century, Francesco Squarcione owned a collection of ancient monuments (anticaglie) for study by young artists, and Bertoldo di Giovanni (q.v.), a disciple of Donatello, conducted the Medici school of sculpture in the Boboli Gardens. With the spread of the technique and use of plaster casts, these became the most common teaching material for training in sculpture and art in general, so that the academies of disegno, later known as academies of belle arti, often formed outstanding collections of casts (gipsoteche) whose importance for historical studies of antique art was considerable. Collections of casts remain an essential element for the study of antique art, especially when the original is lost or inaccessible. The possibility must not be dismissed that the practice of studying plaster casts, which translate the transparency of marble and the reflections of bronze into a tenuous and uniformly shaded chiaroscuro, has had an influence on the traditional and academic conception of classical sculpture and the abstractly classicizing style of certain periods in the history of art, neoclassicism in particular.

Graphic reproductions should be mentioned along with reproductions and copies in plastic form as factors in the spread of the knowledge of sculpture. Mostly in outline, and very popular in the 18th and the 19th century, these are remarkable especially for the efforts that the copyists made to render in simple linear contours the roundness of the form of the original. At the opposite extreme from this method of reproduction, which virtually eliminates the interplay of light and shadow in seeking the equivalent in pure graphic form of the pure plastic form, is the modern photographic reproduction, which, however, establishes one or several distinct points of view, often favoring sharp contrasts of light and shadow at the expense of the more subtle qualities of the modeling. The cast method remains widespread, however, also being used for scientific documentation. Modern techniques (applications of gelatin, resins, etc.) offer the possibility of making casts without in any way endangering the preservation of the work of art, even with respect to the most delicate patina.

MODERN SCULPTURE. The continuity of the technical tradition, the themes, and the celebrative and eulogistic function of sculpture was interrupted in the 19th century. The outward causes of the crisis were — besides the marked lack of middle-class society interest in the visual representation and monumental exaltation of their political and religious ideals — the new concept of history as objective research rather than as edifying instruction and, in consequence, the increasingly anachronistic nature of the celebrative and historical function of the monument. More direct causes, esthetic in character, were the gradual reduction of architecture to simple, unadorned structures, with explicit rejection of all plastic decoration, and the new theories and aims of visual experimentation in painting.

The beginning of the crisis of representation in sculpture coincided with the attempt of neoclassicism to reconstruct an idealized and suprahistorical classicism in place of the direct interpretation of historical classicism (see NEOCLASSIC STYLES). In this phase sculpture produced images that remained isolated in their reality as objects, establishing no relation to natural space or historical time. The crisis was intensified with romanticism (q.v.), which broke the bonds of the traditional themes and ideological content; this resulted on the one hand in a more or less realistic academicism that sought vainly to adjust stylistic forms of sculpture to a superficially modern content and on the other hand in the effort to reconcile with the classical heritage the new themes and visual possibilities that were being experimented with in painting. The "pictorial" phase of sculpture, directed toward realizing in marble, bronze, and materials even more light-sensitive and ductile (e.g., wax) the atmospheric and light effects of painting, soon brought about, as one trend, the attempt at a "modern" classicism such as that of Maillol and, as another, a direct involvement of sculpture in the visual experimentation of painting. It is undoubtedly significant that, from the end of the 19th century on, the most serious attempts at renewing and updating the plastic idiom of sculpture have been made by painters who have created works of sculpture in order to verify the sculptural and structural validity of their chromatic vision: without discussion of Gauguin and Bonnard or of the highly important sculptural activity of Degas (qq.v.), the arts of sculpture and painting, starting with the Fauves and, immediately afterwards, the cubists, appear like two complementary branches of research in form, pursuing the same ends. Matisse and Modigliani were sculptors, and among the cubists Picasso and Braque, to cite only the leading figures, created works of sculpture; the futurist Boccioni was also both a painter and a sculptor (see CUBISM AND FUTURISM). The themes of the plastic and of the pictorial search were identical: the relationship between form and space above and beyond the traditional concept of object and surroundings understood as separate entities. The first consequence was the displacement of the human figure as the fundamental and almost exclusive theme of sculpture: now that reality was regarded as the synthesis of object and space sculptors could turn to still life (q.v.) without running the risk of merely copying the real object, and they could even attempt interior and open-air effects without a feeling of inadequacy in dealing with the rendering of visual illusion. In the same way, the dynamic concept of form discredited the common characterization of sculpture as static in contradistinction to painting with its acknowledged power to represent motion.

Of even greater importance was the overturn of the traditional concept that sculpture was the elect form, almost a sublimation — through the choice of noble materials and superior technical processes — of the loftier forms of nature. Now, on the contrary, the technique of sculpture was thrown open to all materials and all procedures, not excluding (but rather preferring) the materials and techniques of modern production (PL. 522; I, PL. 132). Thus appeared the first sculptures made of concrete, steel, aluminum, glass, and so on; the use of plate, section iron, and metal wire; and the use of such means as oxyhydrogen flame welding and mechanical drills and chisels in the technical elaboration of works. The use of color, no longer regarded as an added element, was greatly expanded; it became an integral factor of form or, rather, a plastic form in itself.

A further step was the use of objects or fragments of objects from real life in a sculptural context. This undoubtedly had its origin in the cubist collage, which may be considered an ambivalent form, that is, both painting and sculpture. It was exactly in those terms that Picasso understood and developed the introduction of real objects into the plastic form. As early as 1912 Marcel Duchamp proposed the thesis of the "ready made," that is, of the object lifted from real life and raised, without any elaboration, by a mere act of judgment or attribution of value, to the plane of the esthetic. The esthetic value of the object, usually an object having a history of its own (e.g., a broken, discarded thing that has lost its original function), constitutes the fundamental motif of Dadaist and surrealist sculpture (see SURREALISM). At the opposite pole, the geometry or stereometry of the form is the basis of the constructivist sculptural explorations.

It is clear, in any case, that the esthetics of modern sculpture are tending toward the complete elimination of the traditional distinction between sculpture and painting, not only in plastic and visual results, but also in the technical procedures, which are now released from all restrictions of category. Even though there are still tendencies working to preserve a figural content in sculpture, however modernized, and others striving to obtain monumental effects of form from the new morphologies, and even to restore to sculpture its old celebrative and commemorative function through a new symbology, the predominant trend of modern experimentation can no longer be characterized

as a striving by sculpture toward its own exclusive ends; its trend is part of the contemporary artistic current, without regard to themes, materials, techniques, or values.

Giulio Carlo ARGAN

SOURCES: Theophilus Presbyter, Schedula diversarum artium, III, 12 (Eng. trans., C. R. Dodwell, London, New York, 1961); J. Le Bègue, Treatise (1431, Bib. Nat. Mss.; Eng. trans., Mrs. M. P. Merrifield, Original Treatises . . . on the Arts of Painting, I, London, 1849, pp. 1–320); C. Cennini, Il libro dell'arte, IV, 181 (on casting metal; Eng. trans., D. V. Thompson, 2 vols., New Haven, 1932–33); L. Ghiberti, I commentarii (ca. 1450; ed. J. von Schlosser, 2 vols., Berlin, 1912); L. B. Alberti, De statua (ca. 1464. ed. H. Janitschek, Albertis kleinere kunsttheoretische Schriften, Vienna; 1877, pp. 165–205); P. Gaurico, De sculptura, Florence, 1504; B. Cellini, Vita (ed. O. Bacci), Florence, 1901 (Eng. trans., J. A. Symonds, ed. J. Pope-Hennessy, New York, 1949); Vasari; B. Cellini, Trattato della scultura. Florence, 1568; J. de Arphe y Villaphane, De varia commensuración para la escultura y architectura, Seville, 1585 (6th ed., Madrid, 1773); D. de Villalta, De las estatuas antiguas, n.p., 1590; O. Boselli, Osservationi della scoltura antica, 17th cent. (see M. Piacentini, Le "Osservazioni della scoltura antica" di Orfeo Boselli: Un inedito trattato della teoria e la teoria della scoltura dal Rinascimento al Barocco, B. R. Ist. di archeol. e storia dell'arte, IX, 1939, pp. 5–35); T. Turquet de Mayerne, Pictoria, sculptoria et quae subalternarum artium (Ms. Sloane 2052, Br. Mus., 17th cent.; see E. Berger, Beiträge zur Entwicklungsgeschichte der Maltechnik, IV, Munich, 1901, pp. 92–410); F. Zuccaro, L'idea de' scultori, pittori e architetti, Turin, 1607; J. C. Boulenger, De pictura, plastica, statuaria libri duo, Lyon, 1627 (repr. in J. Gronovius, Thesaurus graecarum antiquitatum, IX, Leiden, 1701); G. B. Moroni, Le pompe della scultura, Ferrara, 1640: G. D. Ottonelli and P. Berettini da Cortona, Trattato della pittura e scultura, Florence, 1652; G. A. Borboni, Delle statue, Rome, 1661; F. Lemée, Traité des statues, 2 vols., Paris, 1688; G. de Boffrand, Description de ce qui a été pratiquée pour fondre en bronze d'un seul jet la figure équestre de Louis XIV . . . en 1699, Paris, 1743; L. Doissin, Sculptura, 2 vols., Paris, 1753; J. J. Winckelmann, Gedanken über die Nachahmung der griechischen Werke in der Malerei und Bildhauerkunst, Friedrichstadt. 1755; E. M. Falconet, Reflexion sur la sculpture, Paris, 1761; J. J. Winckelmann, Geschichte der Kunst des Altertums, 2 vols., Dresden, 1764; G. E. Lessing, Laokoon, Berlin, 1766 (Eng. trans., E. A. McCormick, Indianapolis. 1962); E. M. Falconet, Observations sur la statue de Marc-Aurèle, Amsterdam. 1771; J. G. Herder, Plastik, Riga, 1778 (ed. S. H. Begenau, Dresden, 1955); P. Zani, Enciclopedia metodica critico-ragionata delle belle arti, 8 vols., Parma, 1794 (2d ed., 28 vols., 1817–24); F. Carradori, Istruzione elementare per gli studiosi della scultura, Florence, 1802; J. Flaxman, Lectures on Sculpture, London, 1829.

BIBLIOG.: *Theory and technique*: H. Blümner, Technologie und Terminologie der Gewerbe und Künste bei den Griechen und Römern, 4 vols., Leipzig, 1875–87; A. Ricci, Manuale del marmista, 2d ed., Milan, 1895; H. Lüer, Technik der Bronzeplastik, Leipzig, 1902; A. Hildebrand, Das Problem der Form in der bildenden Kunst, 4th ed., Strasbourg, 1903; H. Lüer and M. Kreutz, Geschichte der Metallkunst, 2 vols., Stuttgart, 1904; G. Lehnert, Geschichte des Kunstgewerbes, 4 vols., Berlin, 1921–31; F. Schottmüller, Bronze Statuetten und Geräte, 2d ed., Berlin, 1921; A. Wildt, L'arte del marmo, 2d ed., Milan, 1922 (ed. U. Bernasconi, Milan, 1948); K. Kluge and K. Lehmann-Hartleben, Die antiken Grossbronzen, 3 vols., Berlin, 1927; H. T. Bossert, ed., Geschichte des Kunstgewerbes, 6 vols., Berlin, 1928–35; M. Guerrisi, Discorsi sulla scultura, Turin, 1930; S. Casson. The Technique of Early Greek Sculpture, Oxford, 1933; M. Hoffman, Sculpture Inside and Out, New York, 1939; B. Putnam, The Sculptor's Way, New York, 1939; B. Adriani, Problems of the Sculptor, New York, 1943; E. Murbach, Form und Material in der spätgotischen Plastik, Basel, 1943; L. Ashton, ed., Style in Sculpture, London, 1947; J. C. Rich, The Materials and Methods of Sculpture, New York, 1947; W. Zorach, Zorach Explains Sculpture, New York, 1947; C. D. Clarke, Metal Casting of Sculpture, Butler, Md., 1948; L. Slobodkin, Sculpture: Principles and Practice, Cleveland, Ohio, 1949; A. Toft, Modelling and Sculpture, 3d ed., New York, 1950; J. Struppeck, The Creation of Sculpture, New York, 1952; C. Bluemel, Greek Sculptors at Work, London, 1955; J. Chevalier, Sculpture sur bois, Paris, 1957; B. Laughton, Sculpture Display, Mus. J., LVII, 1957–58, pp. 277–82; F. Eliscu, Sculpture, London, 1959; V. Volavka, O soše úvod do historické technologie a teorie sochařstvi (History of the Technique and Theory of Sculpture), Prague, 1959; H. M. Percy, New Materials in Sculpture, London, 1962; K. Badt, Raumphantasien und Raumillusionen, Cologne, 1963; J. W. Mills, The Technique of Sculpture, London, 1965; B. S. Ridgway, Stone and Metal in Greek Sculpture, Archaeology, XIX, 1, Jan. 1966, pp. 31–42.

Sculpture and architecture and painting: G. Semper, Kleine Schriften, Berlin, Stuttgart, 1884; T. P. Bennett, The Relation of Sculpture to Architecture, Cambridge, Eng., 1916; A. E. Brinckmann, Plastik und Raum als Grundformen künstlerischer Gestaltung, Munich, 1922; W. R. Agard, The New Architectural Sculpture, New York, 1935; H. Appel, Plastik am Bau, Berlin, 1946; P. F. Damaz, Art in European Architecture, New York, 1956; P. Reuterswärd, Studien über Polychromie in der Plastik: Griechenland und Rom, Stockholm, 1960; U. Boeck, Plastik am Bau, Tübingen, 1961; W. C. Seitz, The Art of Assemblage (cat.), Garden City, N.Y., 1961; U. Lammert, Architektur und Plastik: Ein Beitrag zu ihrer Synthese, Berlin, 1962.

Iconography: J. J. Bernoulli, Römische Ikonographie, 2 vols., Stuttgart, 1882–94; A. Della Seta, Religion and Art (trans. M. C. Harrison), London, 1914; R. Delbrück, Spätantike Kaiserporträts, Berlin, 1933; H. P. L'Orange,

Studien zur Geschichte des spätantiken Porträts, Oslo, 1933; I. Dahl, Das barocke Reitermonument, Düsseldorf, 1935; H. P. L'Orange, Apotheosis in Ancient Portraiture, Oslo, Cambridge, Mass., 1947; W. R. Agard, Classical Myths in Sculpture, Madison, Wis., 1951; G. Hafner, Späthellenistische Bildnisplastik, Berlin, 1954; H. s'Jacob, Idealism and Realism: A Study in Sepulchral Symbolism, Leiden, 1954; K. Clark, The Nude: A Study in Ideal Form, New York, 1955; E. Buschor, Das Portrait: Bildniswege und Bildnisstufen in fünf Jahrtausenden, Munich, 1960; G. M. A. and I. A. Richter, Kouroi: Archaic Greek Youths, 2d ed., London, 1960; E. Panofsky, Funerary Sculpture, London, 1964; G. M. A. Richter, The Portraits of the Greeks, 3 vols., London, 1965.

History: a. *General works*: C. R. Post, A History of European and American Sculpture from the Early Christian Period to the Present Day, 2 vols., Cambridge Mass., 1921; G. H. Chase and C. R. Post, A History of Sculpture, New York, 1924; A. Malraux, Le musée imaginaire de la sculpture mondiale, 3 vols., Paris, 1952–54; E. H. Ramsden, Sculpture: Theme and Variations, London, 1953; H. Read, The Art of Sculpture, New York, 1956; F. Baumgart, Geschichte der abendländischen Plastik von den Anfängen bis zum Gegenwart, Cologne, 1957.

b. *Ancient Near East*: H. Fechheimer, Die Plastik der Ägypter, Berlin, 1923; H. G. Evers, Staat aus dem Stein, 2 vols., Munich, 1929; W. S. Smith, A History of Egyptian Painting and Sculpture in the Old Kingdom, 2d ed., Boston, 1949; B. Horneman, Types of Ancient Egyptian Statuary, 3 vols., Copenhagen, 1951–57; Brooklyn Inst. of Arts and Sciences, Brooklyn Mus., Egyptian Sculpture of the Late Period, New York, 1960; J. A. H. Potratz, Die menschliche Rundskulptur in der sumero-akkadischen Kunst, Istanbul, 1960; G. Garbini, Le origini della statuaria sumerica, Rome, 1962.

c. *Greece and Rome*: R. Kekulé von Stradonitz, ed., Die antiken Terrakotten, 4 vols. in 6, Berlin, Stuttgart, 1880–1911; C. Robert et al., Die antiken Sarcophagreliefs, Berlin, 1890 ff.; P. Arndt, Photographische Einzelaufnahme antiker Sculpturen, 17 vols., Munich, 1893–1947; A. C. L. Conze, ed., Die attischen Grabreliefs, 4 vols., Berlin, 1893–1922; A. Furtwängler, Masterpieces of Greek Sculpture (trans. and ed. E. Sellers), New York, 1895; E. Loewy, The Rendering of Nature in Early Greek Art (trans. J. Fothergill), London, 1907; H. Bulle, Der schöne Mensch in der bildenden Kunst des Altertums, 3d ed., Munich, 1922; E. Strong, La scultura romana, 2 vols., Florence, 1923–26; W. Lamb, Greek and Roman Bronzes, New York, 1929; C. Picard, Manuel d'archéologie grecque: La sculpture, 4 vols., Paris, 1935–54; E. Buschor, Die Plastik der Griechen, Berlin, 1936; P. H. von Blanckenhagen, Das Bild des Menschen in der römischen Kunst, Krefeld, 1948; G. Lippold, Die griechische Plastik, Munich, 1950; G. M. A. Richter, The Sculpture and Sculptors of the Greeks, 2d ed., New Haven, 1950; L. Alscher, Griechische Plastik, 4 vols., Berlin, 1954; M. Bieber, The Sculpture of the Hellenistic Age, 2d ed., New York, 1960; R. Carpenter, Greek Sculpture, Chicago, 1960; R. Lullies and M. Hirmer, Greek Sculpture (trans. M. Bullock), rev. ed., London, 1960; A. Hus, Recherches sur la statuaire en pierre étrusque archaïque, Paris, 1961; D. E. Strong, Roman Imperial Sculpture, London, 1961; E. Langlotz, Ancient Greek Sculpture of South Italy and Sicily, New York, 1965.

d. *Medieval and modern Europe*: A. E. Brinckmann, Barockskulptur, 2 vols., Berlin, 1919; A. E. Brinckmann, Barock-Bozzetti, 4 vols., Frankfurt am Main, 1923–25; A. K. Porter, Romanesque Sculpture of the Pilgrimage Roads, 10 vols., Boston, 1923; E. Panofsky, Die deutsche Plastik des elften bis dreizehnten Jahrhunderts, 2 vols., Munich, 1924; W. Pinder, Die deutsche Plastik von ausgehenden Mittelalter bis zum Ende der Renaissance, 2 vols., Potsdam, 1924–29; H. Jantzen, Deutsche Bildhauer des dreizehnten Jahrhunderts, Leipzig, 1925; G. Weise, Spanische Plastik aus sieben Jahrhunderten, 3 vols. in 5, Reutlingen, 1925–39; G. Delogu, Scultura italiana del seicento e del settecento, Florence, 1932; P. Vitry, La sculpture française classique de Jean Goujon à Rodin, Paris, 1934; L. Bréhier, La sculpture et les arts mineurs byzantins, Paris, 1936; J. de Borchgrave d'Altena, Œuvres de nos imagiers romans et gothiques: Sculpteurs, ivoiriers, orfèvres, fondeurs, 1025 à 1550, Brussels, 1944; M. Aubert, La sculpture française au moyen âge, Paris, 1947; R. dos Santos, A escultura em Portugal, Lisbon, 1948; V. Thorlacius-Ussing, ed., Danmarks billedhuggerkunst fra oldtid til nutid, Copenhagen, 1950; A. Feulner and T. Müller, Geschichte der deutschen Plastik, Munich, 1953; G. H. Crichton, Romanesque Sculpture in Italy, London, 1954; P. Francastel, ed., Les sculpteurs célèbres, Paris, 1954; J. Pope-Hennessy, Italian Gothic Sculpture, London, 1955; L. Stone, Sculpture in Britain: The Middle Ages, Harmondsworth, 1955; G. Weise, Spanische Plastik der Renaissance und des Frühbarock, Tübingen, 1956; G. Oprescu, Rumanian Sculpture, Bucharest, 1957; J. Pope-Hennessy, Italian Renaissance Sculpture, London, 1958; K. Lankheit, Florentinische Barockplastik, Munich, 1962; A. Grabar, Sculptures byzantines de Constantinople (IV–X siècle), Paris, 1963; J. Pope-Hennessy, Italian High Renaissance and Baroque Sculpture, 3 vols., London, 1963; W. Sauerländer, Skulptur des Mittelalters, Frankfurt am Main, 1963; G. Hubert, La sculpture dans l'Italie napoléonienne, Paris, 1964; M. Gómez Moreno, The Golden Age of Spanish Sculpture, London, 1964; M. Whinney, Sculpture in Britain, 1530–1830, Harmondsworth, 1964; C. Seymour, Sculpture in Italy, 1400–1500, Harmondsworth, 1964.

e. *Contemporary sculpture*: A. C. Ritchie, Sculpture of the Twentieth Century, New York, 1953; G. C. Argan, Studi e note, Rome, 1955; H. Schaefer-Simmern, Sculpture in Europe Today, Berkeley, Calif., 1955; W. Hofmann, Die Plastik des 20. Jahrhunderts, Frankfurt am Main, 1958; M. Seuphor, The Sculpture of This Century (trans. H. Chevalier), London, 1959; C. Giedion-Welcker, Contemporary Sculpture: An Evolution in Volume and Space, 2d ed., London, 1961 (bibliog.); E. Trier, Form and Space: The Sculpture of the Twentieth Century (trans. C. Ligota), London, 1961; R. Maillard (ed.), A Dictionary of Modern Sculpture (trans. B. Wadia), London, 1962; J. Selz, Modern Sculpture: Origins and Evolution (trans. A. Michelson), New York, 1963; H. Read, A Concise History of Modern Sculpture, London, 1964.

f. *Eastern civilizations*: E. Chavannes, Mission archéologique dans la Chine septentrionale, 5 vols., Paris, 1913–15; K. With, Buddhistische Plastik in Japan bis in den Beginn des 8. Jahrhunderts n. Chr., 3d ed., Vienna, 1922; L. Warner, Japanese Sculpture of the Suiko Period, Cleveland, 1923; O. Sirén, Chinese Sculpture from the Fifth to the Fourteenth Century, 4 vols., New York, 1929; S. Kramrisch, Indian Sculpture, London, New York, 1933; L. Warner, The Craft of the Japanese Sculptor, New York, 1936; L. Bachhofer, Early Indian Sculpture, 2 vols., New York, 1929; S. Kramrisch, Indian Sculpture, London, New York, 1933; L. Warner, The Craft of the Japanese Sculptor, New York, 1936; A. B. Griswold, Dated Buddha Images of Northern Siam, Ascona, 1957; L. Frédéric, Indian Temples and Sculpture, London, 1959; L. Warner, Japanese Sculpture of the Tempyo Period, 2 vols., Cambridge, Mass., 1959; W. Watson, Sculpture of Japan, London, 1959; H. Munsterberg, The Art of the Chinese Sculptor, Tokyo, Rutland, Vt., 1960; J. E. Kidder, ed., Masterpieces of Japanese Sculpture, Tokyo, Rutland, Vt., 1961; M. Giteau, Khmer Sculpture and the Ankor Civilisation, London, 1965.

g. *Primitive cultures*: C. Kjersmeier, Centres de style de la sculpture nègre africaine, 4 vols., Paris, 1935–38; P. Wingert, American Indian Sculpture: A Study of the Northwest Coast, New York, 1949; P. Wingert, The Sculpture of Negro Africa, New York, 1950; W. Fagg, The Sculpture of Africa, London, 1958; C. A. Schmitz, Oceanic Sculpture: Sculpture of Melanesia, London, 1962; M. Trowell, Classical African Sculpture, rev. ed., London, 1965; W. Fagg, Tribes and Forms in African Art, London, 1965.

* *

Illustrations: PLS. 481–522.

SCYTHIAN ART. See GRECO-BOSPORAN AND SCYTHIAN ART.

SEALS.

SEALS. The study of seals, or sphragistics (from the Greek σφραγίς, seal), must take into account their origin, dissemination, and evolution, their typology and iconography, their function, and, finally, their historical, social, and cultural significance. In the most ancient civilizations — those of Western Asia — seals were important as a means of authenticating and guaranteeing documents and as identification signs. These functions endured and expanded, so that seals came to be, on the one hand, an expression and validation of power and, on the other, instruments in private legal transactions. Artistically, their value resides essentially in the expressive, emblematic, or symbolic qualities of the images, some of which attain great esthetic distinction (see EMBLEMS AND INSIGNIA; SYMBOLISM AND ALLEGORY). Technically, seal cutting belongs partly in the realm of working hard stones and parallels the making of jewelry (see GOLD- AND SILVERWORK); iconographically, seals are in numerous ways linked with coins (see COINS AND MEDALS). It should be noted that the term "seal" may apply either to the matrix or to the impression made from it.

SUMMARY. Origin and development of seals in the civilizations of the ancient East (col. 840): *Mesopotamia; Protohistoric Iran; Indus Valley civilization; Egypt; Syria and Palestine, Anatolia, Cyprus; Achaemenid and Sassanian Persia; India*. Greek and Roman seals (col. 847). The great art of medieval seal cutting (col. 850). Traditions and decline of Western seal cutting in modern times (col. 853). Islamic seals (col. 854). Chinese seals (col. 855).

ORIGIN AND DEVELOPMENT OF SEALS IN THE CIVILIZATIONS OF THE ANCIENT EAST. The importance of the seal, from the beginnings of Sumerian and Egyptian culture until the fall of the Roman Empire, lies partly in its close kinship to writing. For the seal device was originally nothing other than a mark engraved on a stone that, on given occasions, became identical with the legal person of the owner. In the form of a royal or state seal, it became a symbol of power and, depending on the cultural level of the peoples and states it represented, a work of art. How highly prized as a work of art the seal was in antiquity may be gathered from an anecdote relating that the object Polycrates of Samos sacrificed to the gods as his most valuable possession was a seal ring fashioned by the sculptor Theodoros of Samos (Herodotus, III, 41).

Marie-Louise VOLLENWEIDER

The appearance of seals in ancient Western Asia is linked with the development of the urban civilizations that flourished, from the Neolithic epoch onward, along the banks of the great rivers. The emergence of the Sumerian city-states and of the two predynastic Egyptian kingdoms was accompanied by the initial formation of a social hierarchy that, in the absence of writing, employed seals as the surest means of establishing identity. The origin of seals is traceable to a technique widely disseminated in prehistoric times and which can to this day be encountered among primitive peoples: that of reproducing upon another material (most often clay) a given image that is considered, in some manner or other, to be a reflection of the owner's individuality.

Mesopotamia. It is characteristic of seal cutting in Mesopotamia, which is attested continuously from prehistoric times until the 1st millennium B.C., that its motifs were not subordinated to the repertory of forms of monumental art (PL. 523; III, PL. 487; VI, PL. 33; IX, PL. 496). Iconographic elements unknown to that art are often presented in the seals, whose variety probably reflects the changing political and social conditions of the region. The oldest stamp seals with a flat base (cachets) come from northern Mesopotamia (Tell Arpachiya, Tepe Gawra) and date back to the first half of the 4th millennium (Tell Halaf period). They bear crisscross patterns and the first sparse examples of animal motifs, which were to have a wide dissemination in later epochs. To the subsequent al-'Ubaid phase belong some six hundred seals and impressions from Tepe Gawra (levels XIX–XII), in which the human figure makes its first appearance in scenes featuring the hero as animal tamer. The rise of a great school of seal designing at Uruk (levels V–IV) coincides significantly with the architectural activity in the sacred precinct of E-anna in that city and may be regarded as a consequence of the high degree of prosperity attained by the Sumerian city-states. The Uruk period witnessed the invention of the cylinder seal, to which the Mesopotamian engravers brilliantly adapted a decoration consisting of continuous files of stepping animals, ordered with elegant variations: sometimes the animals are grouped in facing pairs; sometimes superposed rows advance in opposite directions. The modeling is of an admirable realism. The seal cutters also began to delineate actual scenes: religious ones with men beside sacred edifices; and battle scenes with prisoners, their arms behind their backs, dominated by the figure of the "priest-king," who is encountered again in the great monumental art of Uruk. At the same time there existed a more abstract vein of glyptic art, which was essentially decorative and favored symmetric and antithetical groupings of animals with linked tails and necks. Elements independent of the Uruk and other Sumerian schools appear in the seals of the Diyala region and in the Susian seals of the archaic period (Susa C a) and of the proto-Elamite period; in this last group the figures, projected in vigorous relief, give an extraordinary sense of movement (PL. 523).

A brief parenthesis, without significant sequel, is marked by the "brocade" pattern (IX, PL. 496), which made its appearance in the Diyala region in the period of transition between the predynastic and the archaic dynastic epochs and whose little-varying motifs and geometric filling elements testify to a pronounced horror vacui. In the "protodynastic" period (2700–2350) the naturalistic style reappeared, strengthened by a surer sense of space. Two phases have been distinguished. The first, illustrated by seals of the Diyala region and Fara, is characterized by pyramidal groupings in which a pair of crossed figures is flanked by other figures inclined toward a common apex and by those bizarre hybrid figures whose symbiotic sharing of limbs was originally dictated — as Frankfort saw — by the necessity of binding the various motifs into a homogeneous frieze. The second phase witnessed the spread of inscriptions on seals.

The use of inscriptions and an unfailing spatial sense mark Akkadian glyptic art (ca. 2350–2150), which is notable particularly for its wealth of religious, mythic, and cultic scenes and for a characterization of the principal divinities that reveals a progressive elaboration of the pantheon under the influence of the Semitic population then in power. Of the exuberant diversity of Akkadian seals, those of the Neo-Sumerian period (2050–1950) show but a pallid reflection. The dominance of inscription over representation went hand in hand with the devitalization of personages and of scenes, which with monotonous regularity depict the presentation to a god of a worshiper, or of an offering, by a subsidiary deity. The decline of Mesopotamian seal engraving was not arrested in the period of the 1st dynasty of Babylon, whose glyptic art was frigidly courtly in its themes, but partly redeemed by violent baroque effects of light and shade, especially in the closely pleated feminine garments. Even these chiaroscuro elements, which confer value on certain seals of Hammurabi's age, are absent from Kassite seals, in which a single divinity stands next to an inscription that fills the whole field of the seal. Some of the Kassite examples, however, show new features deriving from the Middle Assyrian school, which flourished at the same time in northern Mesopotamia. This school, prolonged in the Neo-Assyrian production of the first centuries of the 1st millennium, represented the last great tradition of seal cutting in Mesopotamia. New life was given the ancient, now depleted repertory, without repudiation of its principal motifs, by the introduction of fresh iconographic elements drawn from the vast fund of Syrian and Mitannian themes (see below). Animal combats, heroes and divinities struggling with monsters, and religious scenes beside the sacred tree reappeared. An airy freedom animates these mythical and feral combats, in which picturesque and vibrant effects of light and shade were obtained by use of the drill. The danger inherent in this superabundant production, which was not to be without influence on Near Eastern seal engraving of the 1st millennium, was a preciosity sometimes bordering on ornamental calligraphism.

Anna Maria BISI

Protohistoric Iran. The oldest Iranian examples of stones engraved as seals go back to the early Chalcolithic period and hence antedate Mesopotamian examples. The material used is very varied: limestone of different colors, marble, alabaster, and occasionally rock crystal. The forms are of the simplest: conical or pyramidal. Of somewhat later date are two kinds of stamp seal found at Tepe Giyan, Tepe Hissar, and Susa: one dome-shaped, engraved on the flat surface, and bored from side to side; the other in the form of a button with a shank pierced by a hole. During the middle Chalcolithic period stamp seals were gradually replaced in many localities by cylinder seals, which differed greatly in style and subject. A large number of the seals must have had apotropaic functions, for they favor motifs clearly referring to divine power and the fertility of the earth — trees, mountains, various horned animals, felines, eagles, and snakes. Anthropomorphic divinities are relatively rare, with a few exceptions such as the Twins, the moon god, Gayūmarth, and the hero who subdues wild beasts. Often the other divinities, especially those of the underworld, were represented by means of animal avatars, particularly after the Akkadian conquest of Elam.

During the Akkadian period the seals of Susa came to conform entirely to Mesopotamian tastes, so much so that they can be differentiated from Mesopotamian seals only by the most minute analysis of details. Some majolica cylinder seals from Susa, with horned figures, appear to be linked with the barbarian style of the Guti, who overthrew the Akkad dynasty in 2150. Elamite cylinder seals of the first half of the 2d millennium found at Susa and Chuga Zanbil are very similar to Mesopotamian examples of the contemporaneous Old Babylonian empire. The seals of the middle Elamite period (ca. 1500–1000) are for the most part of colored stones and bear precise designs, often obtained with a fine drill. Many of the seals from Chuga Zanbil are probably of the same period, but they are of glass or frit and show approximative and coarse engravings. Examples from the subsequent Neo-Elamite period present marked affinities with motifs characteristic of Luristan, notably the cross with branches inserted between the arms and the tree with five ball-tipped branches similar to the flowers of the date palm. The Luristan seals are either of the ring or stamp type, the latter often in the shape of birds, and all are invariably executed in bronze.

With the resurgence of the Babylonian empire, Elamite seals were adapted to Mesopotamian themes, but the superior energy and vitality they convey and the greater freedom of movement permeating their designs differentiate them from Babylonian seals, whose hieratic formalism might almost be taken as a prelude to the new wave of power incarnated by the Achaemenids.

Indus Valley civilization. The oldest Indian seals have been found at Harappa, Mohenjo-daro (PL. 523; II, PL. 18; VIII, PL. 69), and some minor centers of the Indus Valley, such as Jhukar and Chanhu-daro. The typical seals from the Harappa-culture levels are square (each side measuring 2–4 cm.), have a perforated projection in back, and are cut from a block of steatite softened before engraving and afterward coated with an alkaline substance. The most recurrent figure engraved on the seals is the one-horned bull, almost always facing a strange object identified as a "standard" or a "sacred manger." Above the figures appear inscriptions, so far undeciphered notwithstanding many attempts by various scholars. Since all the inscriptions differ from one another, they can have no reference to the recurrent animal figures; nor can they be apotropaic invocations, for such would demand constant repetition. These seals seem to date back to 2000–1900 B.C., while others, suggesting vague Mesopotamian influences in the figure of a being that subjugates tigers, on the pattern of the hero Gilgamesh, seem of slightly later date. It is interesting to note that, in contrast to the animal figures, which are of a superb realism and execution, the human ones are rather crude and approximative.

To the period of the invasions (ca. 1800) belong some compartmented copper seals from Shahi Tump, closely related to some specimens found in Iran, at Hissar III and Anau III.

Bianca Maria ALFIERI

Egypt. While in other regions of the eastern Mediterranean seals were produced before the invention of writing, in the Nile Valley they had from the beginning an eminently epigraphic character. According to the most generally accepted hypothesis, the cylinder-shaped seal perforated along its axis, known in Egypt from the predynastic period onward, is of Mesopotamian origin; indeed a Gerzean grave of Naga ed Deir yielded a cylinder seal which can be securely attributed to the Mesopotamian production of the Jamdat Naṣr period (1st half of 3d millennium) and testifies to the artistic exchanges that seem to have existed between the two regions in the predynastic period. But even if the cylinder is of foreign origin, the Egyptians used the seal of Mesopotamian type with notable freedom. Among the rare specimens with a decoration of figures composing a scene are an impression depicting the hunt of Udimu and another from the tomb of Hemaka or, according to a more recent interpretation, Udimu, showing this pharaoh engaged in the ritual race of the Sed, the jubilee festival. The majority of impressions on jar sealings of the Thinite period bear long single or double rows of rectangular frames, or *serekh*s, in which the Horus nams of the pharaoh is inscribed, his other titles appearing in between. This type of decoration, already found on impressions from tombs of the 1st dynasty, such as that of Nithotep (Neith-hetep) at Naqada, is genuinely Egyptian in spirit and is akin to that of contemporaneous steles from Abydos. From the time of the Middle Kingdom onward, the cylinder, which was better adapted for sealing clay tablets than papyrus documents, was gradually replaced by the stamp seal in the form of a scarab (PL. 524; see GEMS AND GLYPTICS). Although cylinders of the 12th dynasty have been found in the Fayum district, the use of this form became increasingly rare, and there is reason to suppose that the few cylinders of the 18th dynasty, like those of blue faïence produced during the brief archaistic renaissance of the Saite period, were used exclusively as amulets.

Syria and Palestine, Anatolia, Cyprus. The seal production of the other regions of ancient Western Asia revolved in the Mesopotamian orbit and echoed its principal motifs, sometimes misapprehending them, sometimes adding original elements. Although the production of the oldest Syrian workshops is characterized by imitation of Mesopotamian seals, the Syrian repertory of the 3d millennium, with its animal friezes of Elamite derivation, shows local decorative features such as the circle with the dot in the center and the herringbone band separating the two registers of the seal — a forerunner of the braidlike guilloche widely employed in Syrian seals of the following millennium.

The beginning of the 2d millennium saw the rise of local schools (PL. 524). In Anatolia the impressions found in the Old Assyrian settlement of Kanesh in Cappadocia offer Mesopotamian motifs accompanied by original ones reflecting local beliefs: the weather god, the goddess who opens her robe, revealing herself nude, and chariot scenes. In the northwest of Mesopotamia another school of seal engraving arose, that of Nuzi, in which Mesopotamian motifs are found beside others of Indo-European origin; among the latter is the so-called "pillar of heaven," surmounted by a winged disk — this last probably introduced from Egypt during the period of hegemony in Syria of the pharaohs of the 12th dynasty. That the rise of the Nuzi school coincided with the diffusion of the Hurrian ethnic element, dominant in the Mitannian state, does not imply a close dependence on Mitanni, for specimens of Nuzi glyptic art are not limited to the Mitannian area of influence but are found throughout Western Asia.

Whereas Frankfort made foreign influences — Egyptian, Mesopotamian, and Aegean — the basis of his classification of Syrian glyptics of the 2d millennium into three groups, the idea is now gaining acceptance that the determinant factor in the diversity of themes was the geographical dispersion of the local schools of seal cutting. Beginning with the period of the 1st Babylonian dynasty, there occurred — alongside work in the traditional Mesopotamian court taste — the production of provincial schools, marked by less iconographic homogeneity and differentiated either iconographically or stylistically from Old Babylonian production; in these seals the ornamental elements tend to be separated from the main figures and to form self-contained friezes, while an increased illusionistic sensibility created softer reliefs and more graduated planes than in Old Babylonian seal engraving, heir to the Neo-Sumerian court tradition that was attentive to formal values. A product of this progressive detachment from the Mesopotamian heritage is precisely the afore-mentioned glyptic art of Nuzi, characterized by the use of the drill and an extreme decorative virtuosity, which reduced figures to pure arabesques.

Egyptian influence, which had prevailed in Palestine since the 3d millennium and then in the Hyksos period, was again preponderant at the beginning of the Iron Age; it was under this influence that the transition from the cylinder seal to a stamp seal of the Nilotic scarab type was accomplished. The iconographic repertory of these stamp seals, which fit into the framework of Phoenician and Israelite production, is very meager, gathering together motifs of various origins (VIII, PL. 332). Besides the personages combating wild beasts, of ancient Mesopotamian derivation, it includes winged scarabs, sphinxes and griffins, and Egyptian and Egyptianizing divinities, often accompanied by the name of the owner of the seal (PL. 524).

Finally, a brief mention must be made of Cypriote seals belonging to the second half of the 2d millennium. They were fashioned after Syrian and Mitannian models, but show original motifs (e.g., elegantly schematized limbs) and notable Aegean influences.

Anna Maria BISI

Achaemenid and Sassanian Persia. The very numerous Achaemenid seals (PL. 525), though not original in form or material, present some variations from Neo-Babylonian ones. The stamps are conoid or scaraboid — the latter form quite foreign to Neo-Babylonian glyptics, although it was sometimes used in Syria and Palestine in imitation of Egyptian models. While the cylinders generally present scenes of religious significance, the stamps tend to treat lowlier subjects: private individuals, fabulous monsters, combats of hunters with their quarries, and running animals. The animals are drawn with extraordinary precision of detail and energy of movement; the human figures, less frequent, are decidedly inferior.

The images on Achaemenid seals are rich in religious and mythic symbolism. The worshiper in adoration before an altar bearing emblems of deities occurs on both cylinders and stamps. The winged disk, symbol of Ahura Mazda, always appears in the upper part of the design in religious scenes. The numerous hunting scenes have an astral significance: the sky-sun god, the most important deity in the Iranian pantheon, is a hunter — he "hunts" the constellations, compelling them to follow one another in their appointed course. The wild boar, among the most often represented of the more common beasts of prey, is winter, which the sun has to vanquish to bring back the season of fruits; the stag evokes the passing of winter; the lion is summer. The bull is often an incarnation of the great sun god, and taurine protomas are sometimes shown disposed in a *triśūla*, or trident, pattern. The moon is represented by the bearded god Māh, his head often bearing the serrated crown characteristic of Iranian sovereigns, his body in the shape of an ox or a scorpion, in reference to the position of Scorpio at full moon. Some figures from the Egyptian or Assyrian iconographic repertory (the god Bes, the winged bulls with human heads), which were certainly employed by the Achaemenid seal cutters without any real understanding of their significance, always have an apotropaic function.

It has often been maintained that certain peculiarities of Achaemenid seals, such as the characteristic handling of folds in the long imperial garments and the elegance of movement of the animal figures, are due to Greek engravers. Many seals have in fact been classified as "Greco-Persian." But with regard to the stylization of garments, a fragment of sculpture from Pasargadae proves that such stylization was already known in Cyrus's time, and hence might have been transmitted by the Persians to the Greeks. Moreover, although the possibility cannot be excluded that the Achaemenids, with their innate eclecticism, learned some techniques from Greek artists, it must not be forgotten that the ability to delineate animals represents for Iran not an innovation but rather the culmination of a tradition reaching back to prehistoric times.

It is still difficult to identify with any certainty the seals of the Parthian and Seleucid periods, both because of the relative scarcity of the finds and because the Parthian Arsacids often handed down the best Achaemenid and Seleucid seals from one generation to the next, either engraving them anew or cutting them up into beads. For their original seals the Parthians seem to have used the same materials as the Achaemenids, and the same forms, with a marked preference for the stamp seal. In fact, the cylinder disappeared almost entirely, probably, among other reasons, because of the now frequent use of parchment and papyrus, to which cone seals applied to bullae were better adapted. Engraved seal stones for rings, in the current Greco-Roman style, were rather common. Greek influence was strong in parts of Mesopotamia, but there was no lack of craftsmen of great originality and skill, who transmitted their art to the succeeding Sassanians. Among the most common subjects were busts of various kinds, possibly of sovereigns or of the owner of the seal, horsemen, hunting scenes, the customary Iranian repertory of real and imaginary animals, plants, and scenes of a religious character. The most clearly Greco-Roman motifs are insects and such deities as Eros, Artemis, and Helios.

During the Sassanian period seals played a role of major importance (PL. 525). The most widely used materials were carnelian, chalcedony, agate, and jasper; less commonly used were lapis lazuli, amethyst, topaz, and hematite. Al-Mas'ūdī describes a seal of Khusrau II (590–628) with the likeness of the king engraved on a ruby, together with his titles, and he adds that the sovereign used nine different seals for his letters and various diplomas. A full-length portrait on an onyx presents Bahrām IV (388–99) in the same pose as in the great rock reliefs, with a vanquished foe prostrate underfoot. The abundance of portraits with names of officials, priests, and members

of the court that have come down to us suggests that each one of these had his own personal seal. From a passage in the *Shāh-nāma* of Firdausi it can be deduced, moreover, that members of the court also received the royal seal, perhaps as a mark of favor or, if they were sent to distant posts, as confirmation of their authority. The portraits are almost always executed in profile, but full-faced representations are not lacking. Virtually absent in the portrait seals are apotropaic elements; an exception is the above-mentioned seal of Bahrām IV, which repeats an old Egyptian and Near Eastern theme.

In other types of seals, however, the owners invoked divine protection with representations of deities or of their avatars or symbols: the fire altar, the portal of heaven, and the splayed hand, emblem of the sky god and also of Anāhitā, especially when combined with a lotus flower. It is also possible that the fire altar had specific reference to Ahura Mazda, and the recumbent stag might represent the moon or Verethraghna. The peacock, the dog, the dove, and perhaps the eagle also conceivably represent Anāhitā, while the lion, the griffin, the horse, and the hippogriff — solar symbols — may represent Mithras or another solar deity, as may also the swastika, the spiral rosette, and the trident. Sometimes the animals are combined in complex forms that always have an astral significance; thus the triple-ray pattern in which the protomas of three animals seem to follow a rotating movement is connected with the sun, rising, at its zenith, and setting.

India. Seals of the historical era have been found in various places. In the Bhir Mound — as the first of the successive sites of the ancient city of Taxila (in West Pakistan) is known — at a level of the 4th or 3d century B.C., a black stone scaraboid and a terra-cotta sealing came to light, both with designs of a lion couchant and in the field, respectively, a *nandipada* (a tripronged design; lit., the foot or trace of Nandi, Śiva's bull) and a bird. At nearby Sirkap, the site of the Scytho-Parthian Taxila, were found two seals, one of glass with the figure of a lion, the other of carnelian mounted in gold, with the figures of Eros and Psyche with a cupid, clearly of Western derivation.

From Kumrahar, near Pataliputra (mod. Patna), come 20 sealings and matrixes, most of them round, some with inscriptions in Gupta characters or Prakrit. They date as far back as the 3d century B.C., but the majority are of the Gupta period. The rather crude engravings generally represent religious symbols: *triśūlas*, or tridents, wheels, conches, and swastikas.

Some two hundred sealings and matrixes of various forms and designs were recovered at Bhita, near Allahabad, a city that has been identified both as Bhitthaya-Pattana, which flourished in the time of Mahāvīra, the founder of Jainism, and as Vicchi or Vicchirama. They seem to have belonged to temples, governors of the region, officials, and the like. With the single exception of a Persian fire altar, the religious ones have Śaiva or Vaishnava symbols: among the first, the linga (phallic symbol of Śiva), the trident combined with a battle-ax, the *nandipada*, and the bull, often with a disk between the horns, as on some Andhra coins; among the second, Lakṣmī with the lotus flower and the elephants, conch shells, and wheels. A number of seals with standard symbols such as the bull and the wheel belong to private individuals; others carry geographical names. All these seals are of different periods, ranging between the 4th or 3d century B.C. and the 9th or 10th century of our era. The majority are of the imperial Gupta period, with inscriptions in Sanskrit. The pre-Gupta ones have inscriptions in Prakrit or in mixed Sanskrit.

At Basarh, near Muzaffarpur, an important center of the Gupta period, perhaps identifiable with Vaisali, capital of the Licchavis, were found a large number of clay sealings, generally unbaked, which had been affixed to strings tied around letters or other documents. The inscriptions, in Gupta characters, have by and large been deciphered. Presumably of the 4th or 5th century of our era, the seals reproduce the usual sacred animals, anthropomorphic deities, wheels, conches, and trees, but the most common emblems are two human feet (*pāduka*) and a flower pot (*kalaśa*).

From Kula Dheri, near Charsadda, in West Pakistan, come

a certain number of terra-cotta seals presumably used as countersigns and attributable to the Śaka, Kushan, and Gupta periods. At Paharpur, in East Pakistan, were found some interesting terra-cotta sealings with the effigy of Tārā.

A considerable number of terra-cotta seals and seal impressions came to light in the Visakhapatnam district northeast of Madras, near the village of Sankaram, among the Buddhist remains of the Bhojannakonda hills, which date from the 6th and 7th centuries. Their very simple designs represent stupas, dagobas, and probably worshipers.

Some clay sealings found at Kasia, in the Gorakhpur district, bear on the question whether this city is to be identified with Kusinagara, where it is said the Buddha died, for they carry legends, of the Gupta period and later, referring to the Monastery of the Great Decease (*Mahāparinirvāṇa*), and several show a coffin between two sal trees. Other sealings present what is probably the effigy of the goddess Hāritī and her children; still others, Buddhist creed formulas in late medieval script. In general the designs are of rather coarse quality.

At Besnagar, near Bhilsa, in the former state of Gwalior, some thirty red and black sealings of unbaked clay were found, round or oval in shape, with designs of bulls, elephants, and flowers, and often with illegible inscriptions; they are of the 8th–9th century of our era.

Excavations at Nalanda (state of Bihar) yielded clay sealings and plaques with the names of persons, references to the community of monks of the great Vihara of Nalanda, and formulas of the Mahayana Buddhist creed. On the back there are often impressions of palm-leaf fiber and string, traces of the documents to which the sealings must have been affixed. They would seem to belong to the 9th–10th century.

The Pearse Collection in the Indian Museum of Calcutta contains a number of seals of the Kushan period, some with inscriptions in Kharoshthi characters and figures of horses, winged monsters, bulls, and astral symbols, among them Sagittarius. Two Śaka seals present interesting scenes: a vassal offering a torque to an enthroned ruler and a warrior spearing a foe. The Gupta examples, notably inferior in execution, bear simple inscriptions or figures of animals, such as the lion and the *makara* (an aquatic monster), fire altars, and heads of sovereigns with long earrings; they must be of the 6th–7th century.

Bianca Maria ALFIERI

GREEK AND ROMAN SEALS. From the very beginning Cretan and Greek seals (PLS. 526, 527; see also IV, PL. 66; VI, PLS. 34–38) displayed far greater freedom of expression than Oriental ones. What is striking in these seals is a particular delight in figural representation, which allowed a subject taken from life and reproduced with the greatest possible fidelity — a tree, a plant, a worker at his task — to become a mark of identification. By contrast with Eastern examples the stones lack a magical or religious quality; and the official or ruler's seal is less unmistakable, less readily identifiable. The Cretans were disinclined to emphasize such a function, and it is not clearly recognizable even in the two clay impressions found in the "Hieroglyph Deposit" at Knossos in which Evans saw the representations of a king and his son (Kenna, 1960, p. 40, figs. 58–59). Perhaps the seals with effigies of lions found at Mycenae (Furtwängler, *AG*, pl. III, 46–47) may be identified as those of rulers, since these animals also appear on the gate of the north wall of the citadel.

After the decline of the Cretan and Mycenaean culture the seal lost its value and significance as a work of art and as a symbol of legal action. Not until the 8th and 7th centuries B.C. did the rise of the Greek city-states, the growth of commercial intercourse and friendly ties among them, and the increasing power of the noble families cause a revival in the use of seals. The importance of the official seal image increased from the moment that, stamped upon silver and gold, it could be widely disseminated as a coin type and as a symbol of a city's economic stability (see G. Macdonald, *Coin Types*, Glasgow, 1905, pp. 60 ff.). Images on some gems show a similarity to coin types so close as to argue an immediate connection

between them. To give only a few examples: the sphinx on the coins of Chios and the he-goat on those of Aenos (mod. Enez) are repeated on scaraboids in the British Museum; the sow on the coins of the Ionian Revolt reappears on a scarab in a private collection; the leaping horse of Thessalian coins is duplicated on a scaraboid set in a gold ring of the first half of the 5th century B.C. in the Remund Collection in Zurich and on a scaraboid of the second half of the 5th century in the British Museum; the cow with calf on the coins of Euboea appears again on a stone in The Hermitage in Leningrad, and the owl and Athena on a scarab also in The Hermitage.

The owl, in particular, appears everywhere as the vouching symbol of the city of Athens: for example, on the lead tesserae presented by the prytanes when drawing their salaries. The literature of the 5th century B.C. is informative in regard to the use of seals in Athens. But even here it is not always easy to determine for what purpose the official seal in custody of the chief prytanis was reserved, and for which transactions the private seals of the high officials were used. A commission representing the gerusia, for example, doubtless employed the state seal. Likewise, state property and confiscated goods, state slaves and sacrificial animals, were marked with the official stamp or seal. On the other hand, functionaries, judges, and priests could use their own seals for public matters falling under their personal jurisdiction.

Under Alexander the Great and the Diadochi particular importance also came to be attached to the seal of the monarch, who disposed of the right of mintage. Unfortunately the written sources give information only about the seal image of the Seleucids, apparently an anchor — an allusion to the mythical role of the anchor in the life of Seleucus (Appian, *Romaïka*, XI, 56). The seal image of Alexander is unknown. But that portraits of him engraved on gems existed in his lifetime may be gathered from Pliny (*Naturalis historia*, XXXVII, 8), who relates that Alexander did not allow anyone but Pyrgoteles to cut his likeness on emeralds. It cannot be proved, however, that these emeralds were used for sealing purposes. Yet, since in ancient Egypt the king lent out his seal, it may be assumed that Lysimachus and Ptolemy I Soter, for example, possessed such gem portraits of Alexander and, when they became kings, had them copied by their diesinkers. It is a fact that the portrait was one of the most popular motifs of glyptic art in the Hellenistic period (PL. 528), and since various portraits (e.g., of Ptolemy III and, probably, of Ptolemy V) appear on gold rings of a type known from the time of the New Kingdom these, too, may be taken to have served as official state seals. That the Ptolemies actually used their own likenesses as seals is confirmed by a depot, found at Edfu, of about three hundred seal impressions that show portraits from Ptolemy I Soter to Cleopatra (Milne, 1916, pp. 87 ff.). Since different seal images of the same king have survived in many instances, it is to be inferred not only that the king used several seals but that authorized persons could seal with his portrait. The large silver and bronze rings with Ptolemaic portraits that have come down to us must also have had their function, possibly that of sealing and marking goods and amphoras from the royal holdings. During the excavations at Windisch (anc. Vindonissa) in 1959 (*Jahresbericht der Gesellschaft Pro Vindonissa*, 1959–60, p. 36), the likeness of a Pontic king was found on an earthenware shard from an early imperial amphora.

In republican Rome the predilection for portrait seals (PL. 528) was strengthened, especially among members of the ruling families, by the particular reverence in which the images of ancestors were held. According to Valerius Maximus (III, 5, 1), Cn. Cornelius Scipio, son of Scipio Africanus the Elder, wore a likeness of his father in his ring; and in 63 B.C. the Catilinarian P. Cornelius Lentulus Sura sealed a letter to the Allobroges with the likeness of his grandfather. Thus the likenesses of forebears were used at least as far back as the 2d century B.C. and became the seals of magistrates — in Rome substitutes for the official state seal. In the 1st century B.C. the annually replaced mintmasters, too, generally gave prominence to family portraits. Families descended from the archaic kings, such as the Marcii, the Titurii, and the Vettii, displayed the likenesses of their ancestors. Brutus may have owned a seal with the portrait of his ancestor the tyrannicide, which he had likewise applied to coins. Caesar wore a representation of his mythical ancestress the Julian Venus in a ring and had it reproduced on coins. That it was but a short step from veneration of the dead hero to veneration of the living one is shown not only by the coin types of 50–30 B.C. but also by many stylistically related gems and, above all, by the glass pastes, which testify to a mass diffusion.

Augustus's decision to have his own likeness engraved on the state seal accordingly had its antecedents in Rome itself, and, at the same time, in the Hellenistic monarchies, in particular the Ptolemaic; in fact, this step was prepared for by his earlier use of the likeness of Alexander. Although the reason adduced by Pliny for the adoption of Alexander's likeness is simply that the previously employed image of the sphinx was detested because it was associated with exactions of money, political events, too, may have motivated it. After the defeat of Mark Antony and Cleopatra, Octavian remained for a time in Alexandria and revived the memory of the great king, whose likeness on his papers and proclamations must have signified, above all for the East, a renewal of the universal Greek monarchy. The seal with his own likeness then marked his claim to world dominion, especially when he obtained the honorific title of Augustus — "the Exalted" — in 27 B.C. This seal portrait gains added importance as the work of Dioskourides, known both from the literature and from signed gems (see VI, PL. 38).

The likeness of Augustus, used on the seals of his successors, became the symbol of the Roman Empire and of imperial power. It is revealing that in the crisis of A.D. 68–69 Galba, of the gens of the Sulpicii, made his own blazon — allegedly a dog couchant — into the state symbol, in the manner of the patrician families of the 1st century B.C. Vespasian then reverted to the seal of Augustus, which was probably still in use in the time of Dio Cassius, that is, of the Severi. A change must have occurred in the revolutionary period of the 3d century, but no information about that exists. Gem portraits became more frequent again in the time of Constantine. A large blue sapphire, once owned by Prince Trivulzio (Furtwängler, *AG*, III, p. 364, fig. 198), represents Constantius II on a boar hunt. Bearing the inscription "Constantius Aug" above and the figure of the city goddess Caesarea, with the corresponding identification, underneath, it may have originated in the imperial workshop and been given to the city in question. By the time of the early imperial period the possession of a ring with the imperial likeness was regarded as a privilege. Under Claudius the owners of such rings had personal access to the emperor (Pliny, op. cit., XXXIII, 41). In the Constantinian period petitions accompanied by the imperial gem portrait had precedence over others.

That portrait seals were still used as state seals in late antiquity may be deduced from the surviving seals of barbarian kings (e.g., Childeric, Alaric II, and Theodoric the Great), which no doubt merely imitate the imperial portrait seals. In their disjointed style they proclaim the end of an era; yet it was through them that the royal portrait as an earmark of the state seal was transmitted to the Middle Ages.

From an art-historical point of view private seals are closely related to contemporaneous royal and state seals, as can be seen especially from Egyptian and Eastern examples; or else they are the outcome of a centuries-old tradition of workmanship, which, in turn, is connected with the engraving of coins — a connection exemplified by the Italic stones of the 2d–1st century B.C. with symbols and inscriptions testifying to ownership.

In Greece and Rome all household goods, even larders, were stamped and sealed as a precaution against thievery. For reasons of security, documents, testaments, commercial contracts, and letters, whether written on wax tablets or rolls of papyrus, were also sealed; they were bound with a string whose ends were fastened with lumps of wax or clay, which received a seal impression. At the same time the seal became a means of recognition and as such played a central role, for example, in Sophocles' *Electra* (see V. E. G. Kenna, "The Return of Orestes," *JHS*, 1961, pp. 99 ff.). A similar function is attributable to the seal image (designated in Latin by the nearly equivalent terms *anulus* and *symbolus*) in the application of the ancient laws of hospitality. The seal could also be displayed, as it is in Plautus's *Bacchides* (329 f.), for purposes of collecting a debt, or it could represent the deposition of a witness in the authentication of documents.

The widespread wearing of signet rings by the common people in antiquity is attested not only by the surviving clay impressions (*NSc*, 1883, pp. 288–314, pls. VII–XV) but also by numerous bronze and iron rings as well as little ring stones. Among the subjects depicted are divinities or simply their symbols — the caduceus, lightning, or the thyrsus; animals — bulls, cows, lions, birds; and actors (or simply their masks), moneychangers, fishermen, and shepherds in the exercise of their calling.

Marie-Louise VOLLENWEIDER

THE GREAT ART OF MEDIEVAL SEAL CUTTING. In the Middle Ages as in antiquity, the seal was the most effective means of validating and authenticating documents, often wholly replacing autograph subscriptions and signatures at the bottom. At first used only by sovereigns, princes, feudal lords, and ecclesiastic authorities (PL. 529), it was adopted in the second half of the 12th century and in the early 13th century by towns, nobles, professional colleges, corporations of artisans and tradesmen, and the like (PL. 530). An indication of the importance of seals in the Middle Ages is that their use was regulated by certain standards and laws and that sovereigns and popes entrusted their custody to high functionaries.

As mentioned previously, the term "seal" can refer both to the matrix or die — that is, the engraved "negative" — and to the positive imprint, generally of wax, obtained by pressing the matrix on suitable material. In medieval as in modern times, the matrix was commonly made of metal, most often bronze; gold and silver were rarely used. The matrix came to assume ever larger dimensions, reaching a diameter of 10 cm. and over. Sometimes it consisted of a metal cylinder engraved with a larger seal at one end, a smaller seal, or "counterseal," at the other. The secretum, the private seal of the prince or prelate, was usually a carnelian, a ring, or a tiny matrix of silver or gold worn hanging from a small chain. The most peculiar example of the secretum is the key-seal. Rings with a revolving matrix engraved on both faces also occur. A number of handles for seals have come down to us, made of ivory, gold, coral, and rare stones and carved with a variety of representations.

There are two kinds of medieval seal impressions: affixed and pendant. The first, applied to the document itself, are of wax pressed under the action of heat with a matrix. The second, suspended from the document by a hemp or silk cord or by a parchment or paper strip, are of wax or metal. Most commonly the seals are round, vesica-shaped (pointed oval), or oval; the shield form occurs rather often, the octagon rarely. The fragility and preciousness of the wax impressions made it necessary to protect them with cloth bags or, more often, with sheaths of hollowed wood or metal, sometimes embossed or engraved. The rare metallic seal impressions, known as bullae, were utilized particularly by the Church (PL. 532). The image was impressed on the metal, generally lead, by means of large pincers; in the papal chancellery a large press was used. Byzantine seals are characteristically suspended lead bullae with two engraved faces.

Within the vast iconographical range covered by the seals of west-central Europe, the following types of images and devices may be distinguished: portraits; sacred and profane figures; hagiographic, mythological, and other kinds of scenes; views of churches, castles, and cities; heraldic devices; emblems (symbols of office, of a craft or trade, and other allegories); canting devices, or rebuses, suggesting a name pictorially; animals and plants, decorative rather than heraldic or emblematic; letters, initials, and monograms, pertaining to the degree or function of the person or institution that used them; and "classical" subjects (mythological deities or symbols on ancient gems or on imitations made in the Middle Ages and the Renaissance).

The inscriptions, which are almost always related to the image, proclaim the name and title of the personage or the name of the diocese, monastery, city, or building. They may include verses, mottoes, or invocations. As a rule, they are in Latin in west-central Europe and Greek in the Byzantine area (which took in certain Italian regions: Sicily, southern Italy, Sardinia) and, in some instances, bilingual.

The sacred images of the Latin territories are substantially different from the Byzantine images. The figure of the Eternal Father is very rare, and when it occurs He is represented enthroned and blessing, or seated on clouds, or standing and holding the crucified Christ. The Saviour is represented most often as a child in the lap of His Mother; usually one hand blesses and the other holds the globe. In the rarer instances when He is pictured as an adult He is shown standing and blessing, seated on the tomb or rising from it for the Resurrection, or else crucified. Crucified, He appears prevalently on the seals of the Carmelites and brotherhoods, churches, and monasteries with names referring to the Cross. He is depicted lying in the Holy Sepulcher on the bullae of some patriarchs of Jerusalem from the 13th and 14th centuries and on the lead bullae of the Order of St. John of Jerusalem from the 12th century to our day. Occasionally the figure of Christ is rendered in the taste of the Roman imperial medallions: bust in profile, with a mantle similar to a toga, folds gathered on the shoulder by a fibula, the hair bound by a laurel wreath with dangling ribbons; a noteworthy example is the seal of Bernard of Parma (Br. Mus., no. 22,192), dated 1265 and bearing the legend "Michi credite" — "Believe me." One of the most common seal devices consists of a motto or an invocation to the Saviour or to the Virgin, in which the letters are disposed around a cross or arranged in the form of a cross.

Devotion to the Virgin, profound and widespread in the Middle Ages, is often reflected in the seals. Marian iconography is very rich, and among the most widely explored themes are those of the Mother of God, generally seated with the little Jesus on her lap or on her arm or, sometimes, nursing him, and of the so-called "Virgin of Mercy," who spreads her mantle over a city, a church, a castle, or a group of worshipers; both themes are abundantly exemplified in the field of painting and probably derive from it. Other Marian motifs are the crowned Virgin and the Virgin in glory, upon clouds. Angels are depicted in the act of adoration beside Christ or the Virgin, or in flight around the risen Christ, or in scenes of the Assumption. The heads of the apostles Peter and Paul countersign the bullae of the pope, and only exceptionally other seals. But a survey, however summary, of the vast iconography of the saints (q.v.) cannot be undertaken in this article.

The so-called "portrait seals" began to occur with a certain frequency from the 11th century onward and were widespread until the 14th century. The oldest examples are almost always round and display the head or bust of the owner or else show him full length. Busts became rarer in the course of the 12th century, while full-length figures, seated or standing, came into their own in the 11th century and gained wide dissemination in the following century.

Equestrian seals, that is, with a personage on horseback, were almost exclusively reserved for lay personalities. Sovereigns, princes, nobles, and knights are depicted on horseback and in armor. The horse advances sometimes at a walk, more often at a trot or gallop. The rider brandishes a sword or holds a lance at rest. His left hand supports a shield upon which the heraldic insignia of the family or the state are reproduced; these insignia are sometimes repeated on the cuirass of the warrior and on the saddlecloth of the mount, as they were in reality. The counts palatine of Lomello are always pictured in the act of brandishing a battle-ax (PL. 529); depictions of knights brandishing a mace are rare. Sometimes the riders are shown in hunting apparel, generally holding a falcon with the gloved right hand and the reins with the left. Ladies, too, may be represented on horseback and in hunting dress. Saints occasionally appear on horseback, with or without armor and with aureoled heads. Queens and great ladies are often shown crowned, seated on thrones or standing, or in architectural

niches with pinnacles (PL. 530). These different types of representations were often inspired either by examples of the ancient and classical world or by the contemporary taste for images modeled in various metals, in the form of medallions, plaquettes, and so forth (see COINS AND MEDALS).

Representations of buildings include churches, monasteries, castles, and entire cities (PL. 530). Ecclesiastic matrices sometimes bear schematic representations of places of worship. In the seals of the communes it is not rare to see a fortified city or battlemented walls and towers, symbols of acquired autonomy (before the Peace of Constance, which granted independence to the Lombard cities and other communes of the Holy Roman Empire in the late 12th century, they were not allowed to erect fortifications). In the seals of feudal lords the images of castles or towers constituted the insignia of ownership of the castrum as the center of the feudal territory and the symbol of jurisdiction and other powers. In Savoy in the 13th century seals with castles were used; the allusion here, however, was to the office of castellan. The castles found on later seals were no longer feudal symbols but references to family names such as Castell, Castelacre, Castellani, and Castillon (these are canting arms, for which see below).

"Heraldic" seals, bearing the coat of arms of the owner, belong to the province of heraldry (see EMBLEMS AND INSIGNIA) rather than of seals, but they must be mentioned here because of their relevance to the subject. In the 12th and 13th centuries scutiform seals, obviously the best shape to accommodate a heraldic shield, were rather frequent; nonetheless, until the 15th century, the majority were round. Subsequently the oval form prevailed. The chief heraldic figures are the eagle and the lion. The eagle, nearly always shown with spread wings, symbolizes either feudal tenure conferred by the Empire or adherence to the Ghibelline faction; however, there is no want of arbitrary adoptions of such a symbol. Eagles are more frequent on the seals of northern Italy, because it was there that the dominion, or at least the influence, of the Empire lasted longest and the Ghibelline movement was most developed. The so-called "evangelical" eagle with a halo on its head (in contrast to the imperial eagle, which wears a crown), folded wings, and claws placed on the Gospel also occurs. The Guelphs adopted the "inverted" eagle with its head turned in the opposite direction from the imperial eagle and feet sometimes resting on a slain dragon to symbolize the Guelph victories over the Empire. The lion, symbol of force, sovereignty, and loyalty, is generally depicted rampant; sometimes it holds a sword in its right paw.

Churchmen did not adopt armorial bearings on seals until at least a century after the nobility, that is, not until the second half of the 13th century. The owner's shield, or that of his family, was often flanked by one bearing the insignia of a diocese or a religious order or some other ecclesiastic institution. At first the religious insignia consisted of sacred symbols such as the Agnus Dei, the haloed dove of the Holy Ghost, and the variously shaped crosses peculiar to the different religious orders, but in a later phase these became true armorial bearings. Insignia of rank were added to the clerical shield from the 15th century onward. Heraldic seals were often adopted by universities, colleges of professional men, guilds of artisans and tradesmen, and towns.

The forms of the shields are varied, but at first the so-called "Samnite" form prevailed: rounded or pointed at the bottom or triangular with rounded sides. In the 15th century the "jousting" shield, somewhat asymmetric and provided with a lateral notch to rest the lance, became widespread, especially in Germany and Italy. In Italy the shield with bucranium ornamentation was widely used and became the characteristic Italian shield of the Renaissance. From the 16th century onward the oval shield became dominant. Sometimes molded, it was framed by a baroque cartouche with strapwork and fanciful ornaments.

The term "canting seals" designates those with rebuses, or representations clearly alluding to a family name, a local name, an art, or a profession (IV, PL. 399). Later the canting devices, whose use is very ancient, became true armorial bearings. Some of them are obvious, others obscure; many are composite, with two or more figures, only one of them canting. Innumerable examples can be given: the fish in a burn of Simon Fishburn, the trees of Orchard, the three bells of Thelemann Klocke, the sheaves of oats of the counts of Candavène, the stairs of the Scaligeri of Verona, the flower of the city of Florence, the three iron hats of Landshut, the deer in a by, or park, of Derby, the ox passing a ford on the seal of a mayor of Oxford (here it must be noted that, as often as not, the rebuses are based on false etymologies), the hand holding a cup of Thomas the Vintner, the shuttle and three spindles of a weavers' company, and the open shears of a fraternity of tailors.

Animals, plants, and flowers appear on seals as heraldic or symbolic figures, but often their function is merely decorative. The theme of two birds, generally doves, drinking from a cup or a fountain, goes back to Early Christian monuments; churchmen sometimes used it as a eucharistic symbol, and laymen copied it. From this theme derive the motifs of peacocks beside a fountain or a well and, in some instances, hawks and other birds beside a tree, a shrub, or a stylized flower. Such compositions, originally allegorical (see SYMBOLISM AND ALLEGORY), at a given point became purely ornamental. The eagle attacking the fox, seen on some private seals as well as on civic tokens, symbolizes the triumph of justice over fraud. The significance of the stag is not so clear, but the allusion must originally have been a religious one. The function of plants and flowers seems more often decorative than symbolic, and allusions, where they exist, are difficult to interpret.

Giacomo BASCAPÈ

TRADITIONS AND DECLINE OF WESTERN SEAL CUTTING IN MODERN TIMES. In the 15th and 16th centuries engraved stones (see GEMS AND GLYPTICS) won great vogue as private seals, or secreta, for personal correspondence; they were used only exceptionally for official documents. In the High Renaissance blazons and allegories became prevalent, and the baroque period saw a veritable triumph of the heraldic genre, which was already gaining dominance at the end of the 16th century, with the diminishing use of figures (PLS. 531, 533).

In the 15th century direct engraving was replaced by a technique of casting and of punching the legend. Renaissance seals, despite such mechanization, attained the highest artistic value. The exacting work was undertaken by illustrious goldsmiths, among them Lautizio Rotelli and Benvenuto Cellini. Cellini executed seals for Cardinal Ippolito d'Este (PL. 533) and for Cardinal Ercole Gonzaga and described the technique in the chapter "on cardinals' seals" in one of his treatises. In the Renaissance and the baroque period Italy's supremacy in the field was absolute.

A whole series of wax impressions submitted as samples document the activity of Roman engravers in the 17th and 18th centuries — the Hamerani, the Travani, the Astesani, Giovanni Borghini, Antonio Pilaia, and Gaetano Savò (or Sevò), who under Innocent XIII and Benedict XIII was honored with the title "seal cutter of the Holy Palace."

By the late 18th century the evolution of the seal had come to a virtual end. While sealing was securely established for the ratification of laws and decrees of state, the importance of seals as personal distinguishing marks gradually lessened. Their personal use — often with a solely decorative purpose — still continued in the early 19th century, in forms strongly reminiscent of the medals and cameos of the ancient classical world. In France, during the Napoleonic reign the fashion of the portrait seal was fully restored, with works of the highest finish that approach the perfection of certain engraved gems (see GEMS AND GLYPTICS). Later in the 19th century, in Victorian England, the seal with intertwined initials, often ingeniously and delicately designed, came into use. The 19th-century seal dies, nearly always made of more or less precious metal, are frequently decorative objects in their own right, the handle often assuming the form of a small bust or something else quite unrelated to the seal itself and purely ornamental in function. In more recent times the use of seals to close private correspondence and packages has almost disappeared, and is confined to firms and societies that wish to distinguish their products with an unmistakable identifying mark and at the same time guarantee their integrity when, for example, they are mailed.

* *

ISLAMIC SEALS. The oldest Islamic seal known is the one that belonged to the conqueror and first Arabian governor of Egypt, 'Amr ibn-al-'Āṣ. It bears the design of a bull, despite the rigorous Moslem prohibition against the representation of living beings. Other seals from Egypt, Syria, and Asia Minor also sometimes present images of animals, horsemen, and even Christian saints, with bilingual inscriptions in Greek and Arabic characters, doubtless under the influence of local usage. Later, however, with few exceptions, Arabian seals bore only the name of the owner and some expression of faith or trust in God.

Both the matrix and the seal impression were called in Arabic khātam, a word actually designating any object on which an inscription is engraved. According to Moslem tradition the Prophet, too, had a silver khātam or signet ring, with the simple text "Muḥammad rasūl [messenger] Allāh." He adopted it in the 7th year of the Hegira, as a substitute for a previous seal made of gold, very common in pre-Islamic Arabia, when he forbade the use of this metal, as well as of silk and brocade.

The most common types of matrices were the signet ring and the seal mounted on a handle and worn hanging from the neck or carried in a breast pocket. The great dignitaries employed a muhrdār, a seal bearer or keeper, who carried the seal on his person in a small bag; in Persia the seal was kept in a casket and the muhrdār was the one who affixed it to documents. The signet rings were commonly of silver or copper with a precious or semiprecious stone: turquoise, carnelian, garnet, black agate, or coral. The turquoises were sometimes cut as amulets to be worn around the neck and were engraved with inscriptions inlaid in gold.

The impressions were usually of lead, of karkas (or qarqas, a particular kind of clay), or of red wax when the climate permitted. They were commonly oval, but rectangular, hexagonal, and octagonal ones also occur. The lead seals or bullae had a double face, like the Byzantine bullae; bored lengthwise, they were attached to the document by means of strings. Sometimes the bullae were of silver, more rarely of gold.

The use of seals was widespread among the Turks. It seems that in Constantinople there existed a corporation of engravers, rigorously selected, who resided in a special quarter of the bazaar and dedicated themselves exclusively to the engraving of seals, which the law required to be all different from one another. The first sultans adopted silver seals with inscriptions engraved on red hematite. Later three different seals, consisting of emeralds set in gold, served the various requirements of the court; one was reserved for the harem.

A characteristic peculiar to Ottoman imperial seals was the tughra, a kind of calligraphic flourish which appeared beside the signature of the sultan, his titles, and the religious legend. One theory is that it was derived from the imprint of a hand and used as a substitute for the signature of the first Turkish sovereigns because they were illiterate. The best-known Ottoman seal is the one that belonged to Sultan Mustafa II and was in the possession of his grand vizier Elmas Mehmet Pasha when he died at the Battle of Senta in 1697.

The seals of the shahs of Persia, like those of the Turkish sultans, were of various types: some, of large format, were reserved for official documents; others, of small dimensions, served to seal documents of lesser account. In each case they were simply engraved with the name of the sovereign, which was scraped off at his death and replaced by that of his successor. The larger seals sometimes bore the names of the 12 Shiite imams or a verse from the Koran. The seals were in the stamp or ring form and were fashioned with a drill and a small emery wheel.

The Moghul emperors of India had many personal seals, for the most varied uses. Akbar adopted, for correspondence with foreign rulers, a round seal with his name and that of his predecessors back to Tīmūr Lenk (Tamerlane). For internal affairs he employed a simpler seal, with his name alone; for judicial acts he used a lozenge-shaped seal with verses exalting justice; finally, for papers concerning the harem, he had a smaller seal made of zinc. Many dignitaries of the court had personal seals, often with florid inscriptions. In the 18th and 19th centuries in India English functionaries, too, had seals made, with their names in Arabic characters.

The Sa'adid and 'Alawid sovereigns of Morocco used seals, mostly round or oval, only to authenticate official documents, as did the Ommiad caliphs of Mohammedan Spain, the texts of whose seals were recorded by the chroniclers.

Islamic seal cutting reached its peak in the 16th and 17th centuries; in the following century it began to decline, and vanished altogether in the late 19th century.

Bianca Maria ALFIERI

CHINESE SEALS. The use of seals in China is of ancient date (PL. 534). The historiographer Ma Tuan-lin, who lived toward the end of the Sung dynasty, in the 13th century, asserts in his *Wên-hsien t'ung-k'ao* that before the end of the Three Dynasties (Hsia, Shang, and Chou) seals did not exist — an assertion contradicted by the inscriptions found on pottery of the Chou dynasty, made with stamps including one to four ideograms. The seal serving to authenticate official acts seems to have made its appearance in the Ch'in dynasty, when Shih Huang-ti first adopted a great seal with eight ideograms, which was to remain until after the fall of this dynasty the symbol of imperial authority. With the succeeding Han dynasty (206 B.C.–A.D. 221) the seal on clay began to be used also by private individuals as a practical means of authenticating documents. Seal production gradually became a refined art, and seal matrices of jade, gold, silver, and sometimes of ivory or rhinoceros horn were made. The characters on the stamping surface were always incised. Not until A.D. 500 are the first seals with characters cut in relief encountered. The matrices assumed a great variety of forms, representing tigers, tortoises, bears, dragons, and other animals. They were generally inked with a special red paste.

The Taoists used wooden seals several inches wide to stamp magic or apotropaic formulas. The Chinese name for seal is *yin*, indicated by the same ideogram that subsequently came to signify "printing"; and, in point of fact, these impressions of large Taoist seals are considered a transitional form to the first xylographic blocks that, in China, preceded the invention of printing.

It was during the Sung dynasty (960–1279) that seals had their widest dissemination — and no longer for solely practical purposes. The number of private seals increased by comparison with official ones, and painters began to apply seals with their own names to their works; shortly afterward collectors, too, applied their seals to the paintings, and in this manner a series of seals on a painting guaranteed its authenticity and documented its transmission from collector to collector. Under the Sungs, with the burgeoning of interest in ancient objects and the spread of the taste for collecting, came the publication of the first collection of seal impressions, the *Hsüan-ho yin-pu* (in four parts). Thus, aside from their importance as a means of authentication (of documents or paintings), seals acquired value as art objects in their own right — a double value if the matrix is regarded as a superior expression of specialized craftsmanship and if the impression left by it on paper and silk is taken into account.

Lionello LANCIOTTI

BIBLIOG. *Ancient Near East: a. General*: J. Ménant, Les pierres gravées de Haute Asie: Recherches sur la glyptique orientale, 2 vols., Paris, 1883–86; J. Ménant, Collection de Clercq, I: Cylindres orientaux, Paris, 1888; H. Carnegie, Catalogue of the Collection of Antique Gems Formed by James Ninth Earl of Southesk, London, 1908; L. Delaporte, Catalogue du Musée Guimet: Cylindres orientaux, Paris, 1909; L. Delaporte, Catalogue des cylindres orientaux … de la Bibliothèque Nationale, Paris, 1910; W. H. Ward, The Seal Cylinders of Western Asia, Washington, 1910; L. Speelers, Catalogue des intailles et empreintes orientales des Musées Royaux du Cinquantenaire, Brussels, 1917 (Sup., Brussels, 1943); L. Delaporte, Catalogue des cylindres, cachets et pierres gravées de style oriental du Musée du Louvre, 2 vols., Paris, 1920–23; O. Weber, Altorientalische Siegelbilder, Leipzig, 1920; G. Contenau, Manuel d'archéologie orientale, 4 vols., Paris, 1927–47; H. H. von der Osten, Ancient Oriental Seals in the Collection of Mr. Edward T. Newell, Chicago, 1934; H. H. von der Osten, Ancient Oriental Seals in the Collection of Mrs. Agnes Baldwin Brett, Chicago, 1936; H. Frankfort, Cylinder Seals, London, 1939; E. D. van Buren, The Cylinder Seals of the Pontifical Biblical Institute, Rome, 1940; G. A. Eisen, Ancient Oriental Cylinder and Other Seals, Chicago, 1940; A. Moortgat, Vorderasiatische Rollsiegel, Berlin, 1940; E. Borowski, Cylindres et cachets orientaux conservés dans les collections suisses, I, Ascona, 1947; E. Porada, Corpus of Ancient Near Eastern Seals: The Collection of the Pierpont Morgan Library, New York, 1948; A. N. Zadoks-Josephus-Jitta, Catalogue sommaire des cylindres orientaux au Cabinet Royal des Médailles à la Haye, The Hague,

1952; U. Moortgat-Correns, Altorientalische Rollsiegel in der Staatlichen Münzsammlung Münchens, MJhb, 3d ser., VI, 1955, pp. 7-27; H. H. von der Osten, Altorientalische Siegelsteine der Sammlung Hans Silvius von Aulock, Uppsala, 1957; E. D. van Buren, Catalogue of the Ugo Sissa Collection, Rome, 1959; J. M. Munn-Rankin, Ancient Near Eastern Seals in the Fitzwilliam Museum, Cambridge, Iraq, XXI, 1959, pp. 20–57; D. J. Wiseman, Cylinder Seals of Western Asia, London, 1959; O. E. Ravn, A Catalogue of Oriental Cylinder Seals and Impressions in the Danish National Museum, Copenhagen, 1960.

b. Mesopotamia: P. Amiet, La glyptique mésopotamienne archaïque, Paris, 1961 (full bibliog.) is fundamental. See also: A. Moortgat, Assyrische Glyptik des 13. Jahrhunderts, ZfAssyr, N.S., XIII, 1942, pp. 50–88; A. Moortgat, Assyrische Glyptik des 12. Jahrhunderts, ZfAssyr, N.S., XIV, 1944, pp. 23–44; F. Basmachi, Cylinder Seals, Sumer, II, 1946, pp. 156–64; E. Porada, Suggestions for the Classification of Neo-Babylonian Cylinder Seals, Orientalia, XVI, 1947, pp. 145–65; E. D. van Buren, The Esoteric Significance of Kassite Glyptic Art, Orientalia, XVI, 1954, pp. 1–39; B. Parker, Excavations at Nimrud 1949–1953: Seals and Seal Impressions, Iraq, XVII, 1955, pp. 93–125; T. Beran, Assyrische Glyptik des 14. Jahrhunderts, ZfAssyr, N.S., XVIII, 1957, pp. 141–215; T. Beran, Die Babylonische Glyptik der Kassitenzeit, AfO, XVIII, 1958, pp. 255–78; W. Nagel, Glyptische Probleme der Larsa-Zeit, AfO, XVIII, 1958, pp. 319–27; P. Amiet, La glyptique de Mari à l'époque du Palais: Note additionelle, Syria, XXXVIII, 1961, pp. 1–6; R. M. Boehmer, Falschungen-Repliken-Originale: Ein Beitrag zur mesopotamischen Glyptik des dritten Jahrtausends, BJVF, I, 1961, pp. 201–10; J. R. Kupper, L'iconographie du dieu Amurru dans la glyptique de la Ier dynastie babylonienne, Brussels, 1961; B. Parker, Seals and Seal Impressions from the Nimrud Excavations, 1955–1958, Iraq, XXIV, 1962, pp. 26–40; D. J. Wiseman, Catalogue of the Western Asiatic Seals in the British Museum, I, London, 1962; W. Nagel, Datierte Glyptik aus Altvorderasien, AfO, XX, 1963, pp. 125–40; E. Strommenger, Five Thousand Years of the Art of Mesopotamia, New York, 1964.

c. Egypt: W. M. Flinders Petrie, The Royal Tombs of the First Dynasty, I, London, 1900, pls. XVIII–XXIX, II, London, 1901, pls. XXIII–XXIV; P. E. Newberry, Scarab Shaped Seals, London, 1907; G. A. Reisner and A. C. Mace, The Early Dynastic Cemeteries of Naga ed-Der, 2 vols., Leipzig, 1908–09; R. Weill, Les origines de l'Egypte pharaonique: Les IIe et IIIe dynasties égyptiennes, Paris, 1908, ch. 2–3; H. R. Hall, Catalogue of Egyptian Scarabs … in the British Museum, I: Royal Scarabs, London, 1913; W. M. Flinders Petrie, Buttons and Design Scarabs, London, 1925; J. Vandier, Manuel d'archéologie égyptienne, I, 1–2, Paris, 1952, passim; W. B. Emery, Archaic Egypt, Harmondsworth, 1961; H. Goedicke, Die Siegelzylinder von Pepi I., Mitt. d. archäol. Inst. Kairo Abteilung, XVII, 1961, pp. 69–90; P. Kaplony, Die Inschriften der ägyptischen Frühzeit, 3 vols., Wiesbaden, 1963.

d. Relations between Egypt and Mesopotamia: W. B. Emery, A Cylinder Seal of the Uruk Period, AnnSAntEg, XLVII, 1947, pp. 147–50; H. J. Kantor, Further Evidence for Early Mesopotamian Relations with Egypt, JNES, XI, 1952, pp. 239–50; H. Frankfort, The Birth of Civilization in the Near East, 4th ed., London, 1959; R. Weill, Recherches sur la Ier dynastie et les temps prépharaoniques, II, Cairo, 1961, pp. 283–356.

e. Syria, Palestine, Anatolia, Cyprus: A. Palma di Cesnola, Salaminia (Cyprus), 2d ed., London, 1884, D. G. Hogarth, Hittite Seals, Oxford, 1920; D. Diringer, Le iscrizioni antico-ebraiche palestinesi, Florence, 1934; A. Rowe, A Catalogue of Egyptian Scarabs … in the Palestine Archaeological Museum, Cairo, 1936; J. Nougayrol, Cylindres-sceaux et empreintes de cylindres trouvées en Palestine au cours de fouilles régulières, Paris, 1939; H. G. Güterbock, Siegel aus Boghazköy, 2 vols., Berlin, 1940–42; E. Porada, Cylinder Seals of the Late Cypriote Bronze Age, AJA, LII, 1948, pp. 178–98; B. Parker, Cylinder Seals from Palestine, Iraq, XI, 1949, pp. 1–43; A. Reifenberg, Ancient Hebrew Seals, London, 1950; A. Parrot, Cylindre hittite nouvellement acquis, Syria, XXVIII, 1951, pp. 180–90; N. Özgüz, Vorbericht über die Siegel und Siegelabdrücke der Kültepe-Grabung 1950, Belleten, XVII, 1953, pp. 119–27; U. Moortgat-Correns, Neue Anhaltspunkte zur zeitlichen Ordnung syrischer Glyptik, ZfAssyr, N.S., XVII, 1955, pp. 88–101; M. W. Prausnitz, Earliest Palestinian Seal Impressions, Israel Exploration J., V, 1955, pp. 190–93; H. Seyrig, Antiquités syriennes, Syria, XXXII, 1955, pp. 29–48; J. L. Benson, Aegean and Near Eastern Seal-impressions from Cyprus, The Aegean and the Near East, New York, 1956, pp. 59–79; O. Masson, Cylindres et cachets chypriots, BCH, LXXXI, 1957, pp. 6–37; E. Porada, Syrian Seal Impressions on Tablets Dated in the Time of Hammurabi and Samsu-iluna, JNES, XVI, 1957, pp. 192–97; V. Nagel and E. Strommenger, Alalaḫ und Siegelkunst, J. Cuneiform S., XII, 1958, pp. 109–23; N. Özgüz, Die Siegel der Schicht I-b im Kārum Kaniš von Kültepe, Belleten, XXIII, 1958, pp. 13–19; T. Beran, Stempelsiegel und gesiegelte Bullen, Mitt. d. Orientgesellschaft, XCIII, 1962, pp. 59–68; P. Matthiae, Ars syra, Rome, 1962; G. E. Wright, Selected Seals from the Excavations at Balāṭah (Shechem), BAmSOR, CLXVII, 1962, pp. 5–13; P. Amiet, La glyptique syrienne archaïque, Syria, XL, 1963, pp. 57–83.

f. Achaemenid, Parthian, and Sassanian Iran: E. Maximova, Griechischpersische Kleinkust in Kleinasien nach der Perserkriegen, AAnz, 1928, cols. 647–78; H. H. von der Osten, The Ancient Seals from the Near East in the Metropolitan Museum, AB, XIII, 1931, pp. 221–41; N. C. Debevoise, The Essential Characteristics of Parthian and Sasanian Glyptic Art, Berytus, I, 1934, pp. 12–18; M. Rutten, P. Ackerman, J. Gadd, R. S. Cooke, and N. C. Debevoise, SPA, I, pp. 289–98, 383–96, 471–74, 784–815; G. M. A. Richter, Late Achaemenian or Graeco-Persian Gems, Commemorative Studies in Honor of T. L. Shear (Hesperia, sup., VIII), Princeton, 1949, pp. 291–98; H. Seyrig, Cachets achéménides, Archaeologia Orientalia in memorian E. Herzfeld, Locust Valley, N.Y., 1952, pp. 195–202; J. M. Unvala, Sassanian Seals and Sassanian Monograms, M. P. Kharegat Memorial Volume, I, Bombay, 1953, pp. 44–74; L. Vanden Berghe, Archéologie de l'Iran ancien, Leiden, 1959, passim; E. Porada, Alt-Iran, Baden-Baden, 1962, passim; E. Porada, The Art of Iran, New York, 1965, passim.

India: T. Bloch, Excavation at Basarh, Ann. Rep. Archaeol. Survey of India, 1903–04, pp. 81–122; J. P. Vogel, Excavations at Kasiā, Ann. Rep. Archaeol. Survey of India, 1905–06, pp. 61–85; A. Rea, A Buddhist Monastery on the Śankaram Hills, Vizagapatam District, Ann. Rep. Archaeol. Survey of India, 1907–08, pp. 149–80; J. H. Marshall, Excavations at Sahēṭh-Mahēṭh, Ann. Rep. Archaeol. Survey of India, 1910–11, pp. 1–24; J. H. Marshall, Excavations at Bhīṭa, Ann. Rep. Archaeol. Survey of India, 1911–12, pp. 29–94; H. Śastri, Excavations at Kasiā, Ann. Rep. Archaeol. Survey of India, 1911–12, pp. 134–40; D. B. Spooner, Mr. Ratan Tata's Excavations at Palatiputra: List of Seals Found at Kumrahar, Ann. Rep. Archaeol. Survey of India, 1912–13, pp. 53–86; D. B. Spooner, Excavations at Basarh, Ann. Rep. Archaeol. Survey of India, 1913–14, pp. 98–186; D. R. Bhandarkar, Excavations at Besnagar, Ann. Rep. Archaeol. Survey of India, 1914–15, pp. 66–88; J. H. Marshall, Excavations at Taxila, Ann. Rep. Archaeol. Survey of India, 1914–15, pp. 1–35, 1924–25, pp. 48–50; J. H. Marshall, Harappa and Mohenjo-daro, Ann. Rep. Archaeol. Survey of India, 1923–24, pp. 48–54; J. H. Marshall, Mohenjo-daro, Ann. Rep. Archaeol. Survey of India, 1925–26, pp. 51–97; Rai Bahadur Ramaprasad Chand, Indian Museum, Calcutta: Pearse Collection of Gems, Ann. Rep. Archaeol. Survey of India, 1928–29, pp. 131–39; G. H. Chandra and K. N. Dikshit, Excavations at Paharpur, Ann. Rep. Archaeol. Survey of India, 1930–34, pp. 113–28; J. H. Marshall, Mohenjo-daro and the Indus Civilisation, 3 vols., London, 1931; G. H. Chandra, Excavations at Nalanda, Ann. Rep. Archaeol. Survey of India, 1934–35, pp. 38–40; E. Mackay, Early Indus Civilisations, London, 1948; S. Piggott, Prehistoric India, Harmondsworth, 1950; R. E. M. Wheeler, The Indus Civilisation, London, 1953 (2d ed., 1960); J. N. Banerjea, The Development of Hindu Iconography, Calcutta, 1956, pp. 158–202; D. H. Gordon, The Prehistoric Background of Indian Culture, Bombay, 1958 (2d ed., 1960).

Antiquity: *a. General*: J. Diehl, Sphragis: Eine semasiologische Nachlese, Giessen, 1938. *b. Minoan and Greek cultures*: R. Y. Bonner, The Use and Effect of Attic Seals, Classical Philology, III, 1908, pp. 399–407; F. Matz, Die frühkretischen Siegel, Berlin, 1928; H. Biesantz, Kretisch-mykenische Siegelbilder, Marburg, 1954; A. Xénaki-Sakellariou, Les cachets minoens de la collection Giamalakis, Paris, 1958; V. E. G. Kenna, Cretan Seals, Oxford, 1960; A. Sakellariou, Die minoischen und mykenischen Siegel des National-museums in Athen, Berlin, 1964. *c. Hellenism*: J. G. Milne, Ptolemaic Seal Impressions, JHS, XXXVI, 1916, pp. 87–101. *d. Rome*: A. Blanchet and E. Pottier, DA, s.v. Sigillum; V. Chapot, DA, s.v. Signum; L. Wenger, RE, s.v. Signum; L. Wenger, Die Quellen des römischen Rechtes, Vienna, 1953, pp. 129–49; P. E. Schramm, Herrschaftszeichen und Staatssymbolik, I, Stuttgart, 1954, pp. 213–32; M. L. Vollenweider, Verwendung und Bedeutung der Porträtgemmen in der römischen Republik, Mus. Helveticum, XII, 1955, pp. 96–111; H. U. Instinsky, Die Siegel des Kaisers Augustus (D. Beiträge zur Altertumswissenschaft, XVI), Baden-Baden, 1962; M. L. Vollenweider, Die Steinschneidekunst und ihre Künstler in der spätrepublikanischen und augusteischen Zeit, Baden-Baden, 1963; M. L. Vollenweider, Die Gemmenporträts der römischen Republik (in preparation).

Medieval and modern Europe: H. Grotefend, Über Sphragistik, Breslau, 1875; G. Schlumberger, Sigillographie de l'empire byzantine, Paris, 1884; W. de Gray Birch, Catalogue of Seals of The British Museum, 6 vols., London, 1887–1900; G. A. Seyler, Geschichte der Siegel, Leipzig, 1894; J. Pflugk-Harttung, Die Bullen der Päpste bis zum Ende des 12. Jahrhunderts, Gotha, 1901; G. Pedrick, Monastic Seals of the 13th Century, London, 1902; J. H. Bloom, English Seals, London, 1906; T. Ilgen, Sphragistik, Leipzig, 1906; W. de Gray Birch, Seals, London, New York, 1907; O. Posse, Die Siegel der deutschen Kaiser und Könige, 5 vols., Dresden, 1909–13; C. Serafini, Le monete e le bolle plumbee pontificie del Medagliere Vaticano, 4 vols., Milan, 1910–28; J. Roman, Manuel de sigillographie française, Paris, 1912; W. Ewald, Siegelkunde, Munich, 1914; C. H. Hunter Blair, A Note upon Medieval Seals with Special Reference to those in Durham Treasury, Soc. of Antiquaries of Newcastle-upon-Tyne, Archaeologia Aeliana, series III, XVII, 1920, pp. 244–313; J. Ebersolt, Catalogue des sceaux byzantins, Paris, 1922; E. Freiherr von Berchem, Siegel, 2d ed., Berlin, 1923; C. Brinchmann, Norske Konge-Sigiller og andre Fyrste-Sigiller fra Middelalderen, Oslo, 1924; N. A. Mouchmov, Numismatique et sigillographie bulgare, Sofia, 1924; A. Giry, Manuel de diplomatique, 2d ed., Paris, 1925, pp. 622–57; E. Re, Stemmi e sigilli romani del Seicento e del Settecento, Dedalo, VI, 1925–26, pp. 598–613; P. Kletter, Die Kunst im österreichischen Siegel, Vienna, 1927; V. Laurent, Bulletin de sigillographie byzantine, Byzantion, V, 1929–30, pp. 571–654; E. J. King, The Seals of the Order of St. John of Jerusalem, London, 1932; M. Tourneur-Nicodème, Bibliographie générale de la sigillographie, Besançon, 1933 (sup., Arch., bib. et mus. de Belgique, XXX, 1959, pp. 127–96); H. Fleetwood, Svenska medeltida Kungasigill, 3 vols., Stockholm, 1936–47; H. Brugmans and K. Heeringa, ed., Corpus sigillorum neerlandicorum, 3 vols., The Hague, 1937–40; H. Jenkinson, The Study of English Seals, J. Br. Archaeol. Assoc., 3d ser., I, 1937, pp. 93–125; W. Erben, Kaiserbullen und Papstbullen, Weimar, 1938; G. Schlumberger, F. Chalandon, and A. Blanchet, Sigillographie de l'Orient latin, Paris, 1943; P.-B. Grandjean, Dansk Sigillografi, Copenhagen, 1944; C. Braibant et al., L'art et la vie au moyen âge à travers les blasons et les sceaux, Paris, 1950 (cat.); M. Gumowski, Pieczęcie Książąt pomorskich (Seals of Pomeranian Princes), Toruń, 1950; L. Rouvier, Les sceaux de la grande chancellerie de France de 458 à nos jours, 2d ed., Marseille, 1950; V. Laurent, La collection V. Orghidan: Documents de sigillographie byzantine, Paris, 1952; A. B. Tonnochy, Catalogue of British Seal-dies in the British Museum, London, 1952; F. Gall, Zur Geschichte des österreichischen Sphragistik, Jhb. f. Landeskunde von Niederösterreich, N.S., XXXI, 1953, pp. 180–86; G. C. Bascapè, La sigillografia in Italia: Notizia e saggio bibliografico, Archivi, 2d ser., XXI, 1954, pp. 191–243; G. C. Bascapè, Lineamenti di sigillografia ecclesiastica, Scritti in memoria di A.

Visconti, Milan, 1955, pp. 53–144; R. Gandilhon, Bibliographie de la sigillographie française, Paris, 1955; L. Sandri, La "Sigillografia Universale" di Anton Stefano Cartari: Contributo agli studi di sigillografia nel secolo XVII, Rass. arch. di Stato, XV, 1955, pp. 141–88; G. C. Bascapè, Sfragistica dell'Italia bizantina, Corsi d'arte e di cultura bizantina, II, Ravenna, 1956, pp. 5–21; G. C. Bascapè, Sigilli universitari italiani, S. in memoria di A. Mercati, Milan, 1956, pp. 41–71; J. M. Alvarez Cervela, Signos y firmas reales, Santiago de Compostela, 1957; G. C. Bascapè, I sigilli delle signorie e dei principati, S. in onore di C. Castiglioni, Milan, 1957, pp. 47–82; G. C. Bascapè, Le raccolte di sigilli: Questioni di metodo per l'ordinamento, per la classificazione, per i cataloghi, Rass. arch. di Stato, XVIII, 1958, pp. 324–48; E. Vîrtosu, Glose sigilografice, S. şi cercetări de numismatică, II, 1958, pp. 419–37; G. C. Bascapè, Sigilli di collegi e di corporazioni, S. in onore di R. Filangeri, I, Naples, 1959, pp. 145–59; G. Galavaris, Seals of the Byzantine Empire, Archaeology, XII, 1959, pp. 264–70; E. Vîrtosu, Note şi discutii sigilografice, S. şi cercetări de numismatică, III, 1959–60, pp. 519–39; M.-E. Gaderer, Die Siegel der steirischen Adelsgeschlechter bis 1300, Graz, 1960; T. Gerasimov, Sceaux bulgares en or des XIIIᵉ et XIVᵉ siècles, Byzantinoslavica, XXI, 1960, pp. 62–74; C. Lapaire, La pénétration de la Renaissance en Suisse, étudiée d'après les sceaux, ZfSAKg, XX, 1960, pp. 125–38; V. Laurent, Le corpus des sceaux de l'empire byzantin; Plan, situation et travaux, Akten 11. int. Byzantinkongress (1958), Munich, 1960, pp. 302–07; G. C. Bascapè, L'arte del sigillo nel Medioevo e nel Rinascimento, L'arte, LX, 1961, pp. 1–23; J. Déer, Die Siegel Kaiser Friedrichs I. und Heinrichs VI. in der Kunst und Politik ihrer Zeit, Festschrift H. R. Hahnloser, Basel, Stuttgart, 1961, pp. 47–102.

Islam: C. G. von Murr, Drey Abhandlungen von der Geschichte der Araber, Nürnberg, 1770, pp. 85–102; J. Chardin, Voyages en Perse (ed. L. Langlès), Paris, 1811, IV, p. 143, V, pp. 451–63; J. Reinaud, Monuments arabes, persanes et turcs, I–II, Paris, 1828; C. White, Three Years in Constantinople, III, London, 1845, pp. 147–58; J. von Hammer-Purgstall, Abhandlung über die Siegel der Araber, Perser und Türken, Vienna, 1850; E. Lane, Manners and Customs of the Modern Egyptians, 5th ed., London, 1860, p. 31; G. Ztickel, Zur orientalistischen Sphragistik, ZMG, XX, 1866, pp. 336–76; Abū'l-Faḍl 'Allāmī, Ā'in-i Akbarī (The Institutes of Akbar; trans. H. Blochmann), I, Calcutta, 1873, pp. 45, 52, 263–64; Abū'l-Ḥasan 'Alī ibn al-Ḥusayn al Mas'ūdī, Kitāb al-tanbīh wa'l-išrāf (Book of Admonition and Revision), ed. M.-J. de Goeje, Leiden, 1894 (Fr. trans., A. Carra de Vaux, Paris, 1896); D. H. Müller, Südarabische Alterthümer, Vienna, 1899, pp. 52–57; Halil Edhem, A Catalogue of Arabic, Arabic-Byzantine and Ottoman Lead Seals in the Imperial Ottoman Museum (in Turkish), Istanbul, 1904; J. Allan, E. of Islam, s.v. khātam; T. J. Meek, Ancient Oriental Seals in the Royal Ontario Museum, Berytus, VIII, 1943–44, pp. 1–16; H. L. Rabino di Borgomale, La sigillographie iranienne moderne, J. asiatique, CCXXXIX, 1951, pp. 193–203; A. Grohmann, Ein Beitrag zur arabischen Sphragistik, Archaeologia Orientalia in memoriam E. Herzfeld, Locust Valley, N.Y., 1952, pp. 134–38; G. Fehér, Les cachets et anneaux sigillaires à inscription turque du Musée national hongrois, Folia archaeol., XI, 1959, pp. 187–96.

China: P. Daudin, Sigillographie sino-annamite, Saigon, 1937; V. Contag and Wang Chi-ch'üan, Maler- und Sammler-Stempel aus der Ming und Ch'ing Zeit, Shangai, 1940; R. Kelling, Chinesische Stempel, Buch und Schrift, N.S., III, 1940, pp. 1–57; Yeh Ch'iu-yuan, The Lore of Chinese Seals, Tien Hsia Monthly, X, 1940, pp. 9–22; R. H. van Gulik, Chinese Pictorial Art as Viewed by the Connoisseur, Rome, 1958.

* *

Illustrations: PLS. 523–534.

SEBASTIANO DEL PIOMBO.

SEBASTIANO DEL PIOMBO. Italian painter (b. Venice, ca. 1485, d. Rome, June 21, 1547). Sebastiano was called "del Piombo" after his appointment as *Piombatore Papale* (keeper of the papal seals) in 1531. Although his family name, known from documents, was Luciani, he appears in Vasari's *Vite* simply as "Sebastiano Viniziano."

About 1500 Sebastiano turned from his early vocation, music, to painting, first in the workshop of Giovanni Bellini, then in that of Giorgione, with whom he remained closely associated until the latter's death in 1510. Early in 1511 Sebastiano was invited by Agostino Chigi to paint a series of mythological frescoes in the Farnesina, and from then on Rome was the center of his activity. During the early Roman years Sebastiano was on friendly terms with Raphael, but, as Sebastiano's letters to Michelangelo indicate, the friendship turned to animosity by 1515/16. At this time Sebastiano became closely connected with Michelangelo, with whom he remained on intimate terms until the early 1530s. This relationship is documented both by a rich correspondence and by Sebastiano's own work. The decoration of the Borgherini Chapel in S. Pietro in Montorio (begun 1516; PL. 537) reveals that Sebastiano was already one of Michelangelo's followers, while the *Raising of Lazarus*, commissioned by Cardinal Giulio de' Medici in the same year (PL. 537), shows Sebastiano's intention of rivaling Raphael, from whom the same patron had commissioned the *Transfiguration*. Despite Sebastiano's success in this enterprise and Michelangelo's intercession, Sebastiano was unable to obtain the Vatican commissions left incomplete on Raphael's death. Around 1520 Sebastiano painted a series of altarpieces: the *Martyrdom of St. Agatha* (1520, Florence, Pitti), the *Visitation* (1521, PL. 540), the *Holy Family*, known as *La Madonna del Velo* (PL. 540), and the beautiful *Pietà* in Viterbo (PL. 75). Outstanding among his portraits during the 1520s are *Andrea Doria* (1526, PL. 536) and *Pope Clement VII* (1526, PL. 540).

After the Sack of Rome (1527) Sebastiano returned briefly in 1528–29 to his native city, where he renewed friendships with Aretino, Sansovino, and Titian, received a commission from Patriarch Grimani of Aquileia for a *Christ Bearing the Cross* (Budapest, Mus. of Fine Arts), and came into contact with Isabella d'Este. On his return to Rome early in 1529, Sebastiano became friendly with Benvenuto Cellini, as the latter reports, and with Giovanni Gaddi, Annibale Caro, and other literary figures. After 1531, when he obtained the post of *Piombatore Papale*, his production of large-scale works was greatly curtailed. However, he continued his production as a portraitist throughout the 1530s. Sebastiano painted a portrait of the beautiful Giulia Gonzaga for Ippolito de' Medici, Cardinal Pole (Leningrad, The Hermitage), and, according to Vasari, Vittoria Colonna (perhaps the one formerly in Barcelona, Cambò Coll.).

In 1536 Sebastiano purchased a house in Rome. Here he lived with his two illegitimate sons Luciano and Giulio until his death.

Since there exists neither a signed nor a securely documented work of Sebastiano's Venetian period, our knowledge of his early works results entirely from the painstaking critical efforts of recent years. The most reliable point of departure is the statement in the second edition of Vasari's *Vite* (v, p. 566) that the altarpiece depicting St. John Chrysostom and saints (Venice, S. Giovanni Crisostomo) was not, as he had previously supposed in 1550, the work of Giorgione but of Sebastiano. There is no longer any doubt that the somewhat earlier organ shutters of S. Bartolomeo a Rialto, Venice, representing SS. Louis and Sinibald on one side (PL. 538) and SS. Bartholomew and Sebastian on the other, are by Sebastiano, as are the paintings with half-length figures, such as the portrait of a young woman (Budapest, Mus. of Fine Arts), *Salome* (1510; London, Nat. Gall.), and the portrait of a young woman as Mary Magdalene (Washington, D.C., Nat. Gall., Kress Coll.), as well as the *Sacra Conversazione* (formerly, Duke of Cumberland Coll.) and the *Judgment of Solomon* (Dorsetshire, Eng., Kingston Lacy, Bankes Coll.). In all probability, two more paintings with half-length figures, the *Madonna with St. Catherine and John the Baptist* (Venice, Accademia) and the *Holy Family with SS. Catherine and Sebastian and Donor* (PL. 535), also belong to this group. These pictures clearly demonstrate that Sebastiano was not a pupil of Cima da Conegliano, that he in fact received his early training in the workshop of Giovanni Bellini, and that despite the constant presence of a more or less intensely Giorgionesque component, Sebastiano's personal style was fundamentally antithetical to that of Giorgione even at this early period. In such works as the organ shutters of S. Bartolomeo a Rialto a mixture of new and traditional elements is apparent: the calm dignity, the relationship between niche and figure, and the tonality evident in the painting of St. Louis are still in the Bellini tradition, while SS. Sebastian and Bartholomew, with their pathos of expression, movement, vestments, and more energetic *contrapposto*, foreshadow the *maniera grande* of Rome. The composition of the S. Giovanni Crisostomo altarpiece represents an elaboration of the *sacra conversazione* type, departing from the earlier examples in the disposition of the figures, here freely disposed around St. John Chrysostom (who is no longer frontally posed), in the orchestration of color, and in the expressive solemnity of the flanking portico. The half-length figures, such as those of Salome and Mary Magdalene, are permeated with a sense of the calculated dramatic moment revealed in the accentuation of contrasting volumes, in the sharp-edged drapery folds, and in the chill sentiment. They mark the liberation — both internal and external — from the Giorgionesque spirit, the beginning of a more nearly central-Italian conception of style, which although not yet entirely absorbed (and hence susceptible of crises) was highly individual.

Sebastiano's Roman period began with the eight lunettes of mythological subjects from the *Metamorphoses* of Ovid, painted for Agostino Chigi in the Farnesina, which must have been completed at the end of 1511, since they are mentioned in Blosio Palladio's poem *Suburbanum Agustini Chisii*, dated Jan. 27, 1512. Sebastiano's lunettes suffer by comparison with the adjacent works of Raphael and Peruzzi. The fresco technique, unknown to Sebastiano until then, seems to have affected the formal and coloristic qualities of the lunettes because of the attempt to continue with oil-painting effects, and it also appears to have hampered his powers of poetic invention, completely inhibiting any narrative fluency. Even the simple decorative accord between pictorial forms and their size has been disrupted. The unassimilated example of Michelangelo's Sistine Chapel ceiling proved dangerous to Sebastiano, whose figural compositions during his early Roman years reflect his struggles with it; even an easel painting such as the *Death of Adonis* (PL. 537) betrays this struggle, in spite of Sebastiano's attempt to compensate for the excessive formalism by the use of landscape and chromatic orchestration. But when, during this period, Sebastiano turned to portrait painting, all constraint disappeared. In this field the transition from the early Venetian period to the late Roman Renaissance was smooth: the warm tonal color and the sensual rendering of material remained, and Giorgionesque motifs (parapet, three-quarter pose, suggestions of landscape) were united to an increased plasticity and firmness of composition, expressive of a heightened sense of the dignity of the image. These characteristics developed gradually in two portraits of young women (*La Fornarina*, 1512, Uffizi, and *Dorothea*, ca. 1512, Berlin, Mus. Dahlem), the *Young Violinist* (which bears the date of 1518, but is a work of 1515; Paris, Baron G. de Rothschild), *Cardinal Ferry Carondelet with His Secretaries* (Lugano, Thyssen-Bornemisza Coll.), *Portrait of a Young Man* (Budapest, Mus. of Fine Arts), *Cardinal Antonio Ciocchi del Monte Sansovino* (Dublin, Nat. Gall. of Ireland), *Portrait of a Monk* (Rome, private coll.; Pallucchini, 1944, pl. 32), and *Man in Armor* (Hartford, Conn., Wadsworth Atheneum; ibid., pl. 33). A number of these portraits were long attributed to Raphael, and it should be noted that the influences between the two artists were surely reciprocal. If Raphael introduced Sebastiano to the "new style" of Rome, Sebastiano suggested a new range of Venetian chromatic possibilities to Raphael.

The Farnesina cycle was followed after 1516 by the *Deposition* (Leningrad, The Hermitage) and the frescoes of the Borgherini Chapel in S. Pietro in Montorio in Rome, representing the *Transfiguration* and the *Flagellation* (PL. 537), works that mark the beginning of Sebastiano's Michelangelesque period. In the Hermitage painting the influence of Michelangelo is still tangential, apparent only in the solidity and sobriety of the composition, but in the Borgherini Chapel frescoes it assumes an entirely new intensity. It can be presumed, on the basis of Vasari's *Vite* (v, p. 569) and Sebastiano's correspondence with Michelangelo (Frey, 1899, nos. XXIII, XXV), that Michelangelo's personal participation in these projects did not extend to a design of the whole, but consisted in supplying sketches of details (such as the figure of Christ and perhaps the two flagellators in the *Flagellation*), a form of collaboration that indeed afforded Sebastiano a wide scope for independent solutions. That Michelangelo intervened in the design of the *Transfiguration* lunette, which was created first, is unthinkable. The Christ is in fact reminiscent of Early Christian mosaics, and Moses, Elijah, and the Apostles reveal only a sporadic and unspecifiable relationship to the figures of Michelangelo. The two prophets above the arch, however, reflect the direct inspiration of the Sistine Chapel. While there is a disunity in the upper area, evident even in the handling of the color (because it is in fresco), the *Flagellation* (in oil) is free from this defect. The architectural setting, the masterly compositional rhythm (in which the light plays a decisive part), the grandiose proportions and articulation of the image of Christ, and the restrained pathos impart to this scene a classical character never again achieved by Sebastiano.

The *Raising of Lazarus* (PL. 537), commissioned for the Cathedral of Narbonne late in 1516, was completed by the end of 1518. According to Vasari (v, p. 570), the painting was carried out "sotto ordine e disegno" of Michelangelo; however, neither the surviving drawings (Br. Mus.; Bayonne, Mus. Bonnat) nor the painting itself reveals any more than a simple use of the Sistine Chapel models. The rich vocabulary of borrowed motifs enlarges the expressive range of the composition: the great figure of Lazarus attains the full stature of *terribilità*, although the figure of Christ is not entirely free of rhetoric. The picture lacks organic unity, but the color orchestration and the chiaroscural fusion of figures and landscape compensate for it.

To this same period belongs the *Pietà* in Viterbo (PL. 75); nowhere else does the artist achieve such a happy fusion of his innate Venetian colorism and the Tuscan-Roman grand manner. The relation of figural conception to theme in the identification of Mary's sorrow with the night landscape is unrivaled. Here, too, Sebastiano made use of a Michelangelesque idea, still recognizable in a drawing from Michelangelo's workshop (Vienna, Albertina; cf. A. Stix and L. Fröhlich, *Kat. der Albertina*, III, no. 134), but the genuine expressive power of the image testifies to the autonomy of execution. The *Martyrdom of St. Agatha* (Florence, Pitti) is dated 1520; the colorful and dignified *Visitation*, painted for Francis I (PL. 540), is from 1521; the *Madonna and Child* (Burgos, Cath.) is a slightly later work. In the decade between 1520 and 1530 Sebastiano was at the height of his powers as a portrait painter. Even though his activity was entirely autonomous, these paintings too reveal Michelangelo's influence in the grandeur, the plastic solidity, and the energy of composition. The authoritarian attitudes and poses of the sharply defined personalities, however, are new and are not to be found in Sebastiano's Roman portraits painted before 1516. Sebastiano's psychological insight is apparent in works such as the two portraits of a man, one of which is known as *Columbus* (both, Met. Mus.), *Portrait of a Humanist* (Washington, D.C., Nat. Gall., Kress Coll.), *Portrait of Anton Francesco degli Albizzi* (Houston, Texas, Mus. of Fine Arts, Kress Coll.), *Portrait of a Lady* (formerly, Barcelona, Coll. Cambò), *Portrait of Pietro Aretino* (Arezzo, Pal. del Comune), and most extraordinarily in the great portrait of *Andrea Doria* (1526, PL. 536), in the three-quarter-length *Pope Clement VII* (PL. 540) of the same year, and in the *Portrait of Baccio Valori* (1530/31, Florence, Pitti).

Sebastiano's dwindling production after 1531 was attributed by Vasari as the consequence of his having received the post of *Piombatore Papale*, but other documents suggest more profound reasons than those indicated by Vasari. After the Sack of Rome the artist consciously shared in the general spiritual crisis of the time. In a letter of Feb. 24, 1531, to Michelangelo (Milanesi, 1890, p. 38) he observes, "Ancora non mi par esser quel Bastiano che io era inanti el sacco...." Works such as the *Christ Bearing the Cross* (PL. 540; other versions in Budapest, Mus. of Fine Arts; Leningrad, The Hermitage) and the *Christ in Limbo* (PL. 539) reveal an anticlassical spirit not only in their compositional structure but particularly in their weighty and expressive gravity, supported by the action of color and light. These subjects were commissioned in Spain, as was the *Pietà* of 1539 in Ubeda (Church of El Salvador), for which Michelangelo was once again the spiritual father (cf. the torso by Michelangelo, Florence, Casa Buonarroti, no. 69 F, and Sebastiano's drawing inspired by it, Louvre, Cabinet des Dessins, no. 125).

Sebastiano also asked Michelangelo's help in connection with the monumental *Birth of the Virgin* in S. Maria del Popolo, Rome, begun in 1532. In a letter he explains what he requires: "...facto grosso modo a me mi basta solamente chiarirmi come la intenderesti vui circha l'inventione" (Milanesi, 1890, p. 88). The direct presence of the Florentine is not, however, perceptible in the picture. A superficial Michelangelesque influence may be seen in the upper section, in particular in the God the Father and angels, and it was no accident that this part remained incomplete at the artist's death (it was finished by Francesco Salviati in 1554). The great picture of the *Visita-*

tion for the choir of S. Maria della Pace, Rome, was also left unfinished at Sebastiano's death, but even the remaining fragments (Northumberland, Eng., Alnwick Castle; a 16th-cent. Dutch engraving shows its composition) reveal how labored the pictorial process had become.

In portraiture, however, Sebastiano retained his creative powers even in the late period, a fact that may be presumed from the number of his commissions rather than from the surviving works. The appearance of the much-praised portrait of Giulia Gonzaga can only be partially deduced from the portrait in Kiel, Germany (Martius Coll.), from a number of reduced copies and variants, and from the well-preserved female portrait at Longford Castle (Salisbury, Wiltshire, Eng.) that, judging from its courtly character, perhaps also should be considered a portrait of Giulia. Of the male portraits of high rank of this period only the one of Cardinal Pole in Leningrad (The Hermitage) has been preserved; it is in every way inferior to the intense and powerful portrait of Pope Clement VII of 1526.

The critical regard for Sebastiano's art has remained constant over the centuries, even though some scholars, such as H. Thode (*Michelangelo und das Ende der Renaissance*, 3 vols. in 4, Berlin, 1902–13), by placing too much emphasis on Vasari's report of Michelangelo's collaboration, have classified him as an eclectic. More recent studies — by Gombosi (ThB), Pallucchini (1944), and Dussler (1942) — have tended to interpret the artist historically and stylistically in the light of mannerism. Although Berenson (1903) successfully isolated the corpus of Sebastiano's drawings from that of Michelangelo's, the problem has recently been reopened by Wilde (1953), who attributes some drawings of Sebastiano to Michelangelo.

BIBLIOG. Vasari, V, pp. 565–86; G. Milanesi, Les correspondents de Michel-Ange, I: Sebastiano del Piombo, Paris, 1890; F. Propping, Die künstlerische Laufbahn des Sebastiano del Piombo bis zum Tode Raphaels, Leipzig, 1892; K. Frey, ed., Sammlung ausgewählter Briefe an Michelagniolo, Berlin, 1899; F. Wickhoff, Über einige italienische Zeichnungen im British Museum, JhbPreussKSamml, XX, 1899, pp. 202–15; B. Berenson, The Drawings of the Florentine Masters, London, 1903 (2d ed., 3 vols., Chicago, 1938); E. A. Benkard, Die venezianische Frühzeit des Sebastiano del Piombo, Frankfurt am Main, 1907; P. d'Achiardi, Sebastiano del Piombo, Rome, 1908; G. Bernardini, Sebastiano del Piombo, Bergamo, 1908; L. Venturi, Giorgione e il Giorgionismo, Milan, 1913; H. Voss, Die Malerei der Spätrenaissance in Rom und Florenz, 2 vols., Berlin, 1920; E. Panofsky, Die Pietà in Ubeda, Festschrift f. J. von Schlosser, Vienna, 1927, pp. 150–61; B. Berenson, Italian Pictures of the Renaissance, Oxford, 1932 (2d ed., 2 vols., London, 1957); G. Gombosi, ThB, s.v. Piombo; O. Fischel, A New Approach to Sebastiano del Piombo as a Draughtsman, Old Master Drawings, XIV, 1939–40, pp. 21–33; L. Dussler, Sebastiano del Piombo, Basel, 1942; R. Pallucchini, Sebastiano Viniziano, Milan, 1944 (bibliog.); I. Fenyö, Der kreuztragende Christus Sebastiano del Piombos in Budapest, Acta h. artium, I, 1953, pp. 151–63; J. Wilde, Italian Drawings in the Department of Prints and Drawings in the British Museum: Michelangelo and His Studio, London, 1953; E. Tietze-Conrat, Il "Cristo portacroce" di Sebastiano del Piombo, CXXIII, 1956, pp. 99–104; R. Salvini, Note sui ritratti Sebastianeschi di Clemente VII, Emporium, CXXIX, 1959, pp. 147–52; J. Bean, Les dessins italiens de la Collection Bonnat, Paris, 1960, no. 65; E. Larsen, A Contribution to Sebastiano del Piombo's Changing Conception of "Christ Carrying the Cross," L'arte, N.S., XXV, 1960, pp. 209–15; A. Perrig, Bemerkungen zur Genesis von Sebastiano del Piombos Auferweckung Lazari in der National Gallery in London, Wallraf-Richartz Jhb., XXII, 1960, pp. 173–94; A. Perrig, Michelangelo Buonarrotis letzte Pietà-Idee, Bern, 1960, pp. 134–74; L. Baldass, Zur Erforschung des "Giorgionismo" bei den Generationsgenossen Tizians, JhbKhSammlWien, LVII, 1961, pp. 69–88; S. I. Freedberg, Painting of the High Renaissance in Rome and Florence, I, Cambridge, Mass., 1961, pp. 370–97; C. Gilbert, A Sarasota Note Book, II: A "New" Work by Sebastiano del Piombo and an Offer by Michelangelo, Arte veneta, XV, 1961, pp. 38–42; M. Hirst, The Chigi Chapel in S. Maria della Pace, Warburg, XXIV, 1961, pp. 161–85; J. Shearman, The Chigi Chapel in S. Maria del Popolo, Warburg, XXIV, 1961, pp. 129–60; P. Pouncey and J. A. Gere, Italian Drawings in the Department of Prints and Drawings in the British Museum: Raphael and His Circle, London, 1962, pp. 165–69.

Luitpold DUSSLER

Illustrations: PLS. 535–540.

SECULAR SUBJECTS. See GENRE AND SECULAR SUBJECTS.

SEGHERS, HERCULES PIETERSZ. (also spelled, by the artist himself, Herkeles Segers). Dutch painter and engraver who specialized in landscape (b. probably in Haarlem, 1589/90;

last mentioned January, 1633). Only a few facts about the life of Hercules Seghers are certain, but there are many questionable assumptions. There is no record of his having begun to study art in Haarlem, where he was probably born. He is known, however, to have been the pupil of the Flemish landscape painter Gillis van Coninxloo, who had moved from Antwerp to Amsterdam in 1585, and many traces of the style of this artist are to be found in Seghers' work. When Coninxloo died in Amsterdam in 1607, Seghers bought, at the sale of his estate, prints and drawings by various artists and an oil painting in a gold frame by his late master, referred to as a "rocky landscape," a description that could be applied to the majority of Seghers' own works (see II, PL. 214; V, PL. 310). Other later records of his sales of pictures indicate that he was a dealer as well as an artist. Not many years after Coninxloo's death Seghers returned to Haarlem, where by 1612 he had become a member of the painters' guild. By the end of 1614 he was back in Amsterdam; and there, early in the following year, he married and subsequently bought a house. In May, 1631, there is mention of his being in Utrecht; when last heard of, in 1633, he was living in The Hague.

Only four or five paintings bearing Seghers' signature have survived, none of them dated. On the basis of these, however, and a number of engravings, a considerable body of work has been ascribed to him, largely through the efforts of the German scholar Wilhelm von Bode (1845–1929). His style is characterized by originality and by a peculiar combination of compositional breadth and meticulous granular detail. In attempting to account for this style, scholars have postulated a trip to Italy during the artist's youth and have assumed that he came in contact there, between 1607 and 1612, with the German landscape painter Adam Elsheimer (1574 or 1578–1620). It has also been suggested that more than two decades later he traveled in the Alps. In any case a view of Brussels by Seghers (Cologne, Wallraf-Richartz-Mus.), with both artist and subject correctly given in an early inventory, proves that he certainly traveled to the southern Netherlands and saw the stern and imposing mountains of Ardennes. There are clear relationships between the work of Rembrandt and that of Seghers, and certain pictures have at different times been attributed to each. At least eight paintings by Seghers belonged to the collection of works of art formed by Rembrandt, who seems also to have borrowed motifs from the older artist. Seghers' landscapes are grand and awe-inspiring, and in them his imagination transforms nature into epic poetry. His accomplishments in the field of etching have earned him an important place in the history of engraving (IV, PL. 435). He experimented boldly with techniques, and his skill equaled the majesty of his conception.

BIBLIOG. ThB, XXX, Leipzig, 1936, s.v.; L. C. Collins, Hercules Seghers, Chicago, 1953; N. Maclaren, The Dutch School (Nat. Gal. Catalogues), London, 1960, p. 391 ff.

Margaretta M. SALINGER

SELJUK ART. The Seljuk period in the history of art and architecture may be said to comprise not only the years during which that dynasty and its feudatories held sway in Iran and Anatolia but also the periods of disintegration that followed immediately upon its extinction. Thus in Iran it extends for about two centuries, from the Seljuk conquest in the second quarter of the 11th century to the establishment of the Ilkhan dominion (see ILKHAN ART) in the second quarter of the 13th. In Anatolia it may be considered as beginning with the establishment of the separate Sultanate of Rum (1078); although the dynasty as such came to an end about 1308, it was continued through the 14th century in the various beylics or principalities into which the country was divided. The most important of these — that of Karaman — was finally annexed by the Ottoman Sultan Mehmet II in 1472 (see OTTOMAN SCHOOLS).

The artistic production of Seljuk Persia was of fundamental importance in the formative process and final shaping of the classic patterns of Islamic art in that country, as well as in those countries where it made its influence felt more or less directly (see ISLAM). The stylistic innovations introduced by the Iranian architects of this period were, in fact, to have vast repercussions, from India (Quṭb Minār of Delhi; see INDIAN ART; INDO-MOSLEM SCHOOLS) to Asia Minor. The brilliant imagination of the artists made full use of the widest possible range of ornamental elements, in a truly remarkable decorative equilibrium, applied to many categories of objects, from textiles to ceramics, ivory, and metals, with distinctive features peculiar to each region.

SUMMARY. Historical background (col. 864). Architecture (col. 866): *Iran; Anatolia.* Decorative arts (col. 875): *Ceramics; Miniatures; Textiles; Metalwork; Ivories.* Conclusion (col. 879).

HISTORICAL BACKGROUND. At the beginning of the 11th century the Turks (see TURKIC ART) started to cross in great numbers, for the first time, the northeastern borders of the Islamic world (see ISLAM), becoming the initiators of the momentous events that were to weigh so heavily on the history of West Asia as well as that of Europe. The eastern Arab world — that is, the Abbasside Caliphate (see ABBASSIDE ART) — was at the time in full decline as a state organization and political body. Small local dynasties sprang up within its boundaries, linked to the Caliphate only by nominal ties of vassalship, while non-Arab adherents to Islam steadily penetrated the ruling classes. Arab supremacy, once political and military, shifted to the cultural level: the essence of the unitary veneer of this vast world, which from the eastern Mediterranean stretched as far as Transoxiana, rested by then almost exclusively upon the common Islamic faith.

Until the end of the 10th century the Iranian dynasty of the Samanids (see SAMANID ART), who were also nominally subject to the Caliph of Baghdad but in fact were independent rulers of Transoxiana, had represented an active barrier against the infiltration of Turkic nomads bearing down toward the west. As far back as the 9th century, spearheads of these peoples had found their way into the organizational structure of the caliphate as bodyguards and mercenaries, but, at the time of the Samanids' fall in 996, these turbulent masses, led by valiant chiefs, introduced the Turkic element into regions whose ancient tradition was Iranian notwithstanding their conversion to Islam.

The Seljuks were a clan of the Oghuz Turks (Ar., Ghuz), who derived their name from Seljūq (or Seljūk), one of their Chieftains, who died in 1009 or 1010 on the Amu Darya (Oxus). The original seats of the Oghuz were probably located between Lake Balkhash and Lake Aral, perhaps even farther to the east. After their conversion to Islam the Seljuks detached themselves from the main body of the Oghuz, placed themselves at the service of the Samanids, and settled on the outskirts of Samarkand. According to Rossi (1956), whose source is the Persian historian Gardīzī (11th cent.), in 1025 the Seljuks were granted permission by Mahmūd of Ghazni (see GHAZNEVID ART) to cross the Amu Darya and settle at Sarakhs in Khorasan. This first settlement formed the nucleus of the Seljuk princedom that was to become, in the course of about half a century, a unified though short-lived empire. This empire gradually extended to cover a wide belt of territory until it included almost all of Asia Minor, and brought about ethnic and linguistic changes in many regions. From then on Anatolia was thoroughly and definitely Turkicized; notable changes took place also in western Azerbaijan, but Persia proper reacted in the opposite way by absorbing and Iranizing the invaders.

By 1040 masters of the whole of Khorasan, the Seljuks turned to central Persia, where Rayy (Rhages) and Isfahan fell into their hands. In 1055 their leader Tughril was in Baghdad, where he received the title of Sultan from the Caliph 'Abdullah al-Qā'im and thus became the "arm" of the supreme Islamic magistracy. Alp Arslān (1063–72), Tughril's nephew and successor, occupied Azerbaijan, northern Mesopotamia, and Syria, achieving a victory at Malazkirt (Manzikert) in 1071 over the Byzantine Emperor Romanus IV Diogenes and thus opening the road to Seljuk penetration into Anatolia (see BYZAN-

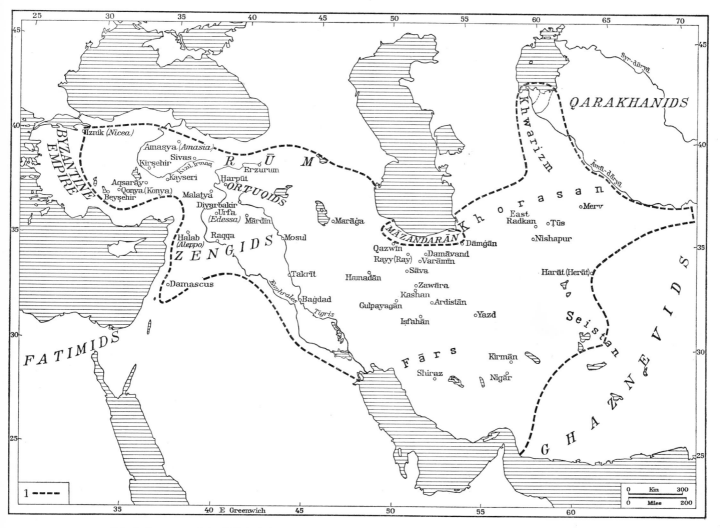

Principal centers of the Seljuk Sultanate. (1) Boundaries of the Sultanate at the end of the 11th century.

TINE ART, cols. 784–85). Alp Arslān was succeeded by his son Malikshāh (1072–92), who retained as vizier his father's former adviser, the learned Persian Niẓām al-Mulk — a great statesman, able politician, and representative of the Persian ruling class. But despite the splendid outward appearances, the bases for eventual disintegration were inherent in the fact that these nomads lacked the concept of nationhood and government and considered the conquered territories the personal property of the khan's family.

The dynasty known as the Great Seljuks (to distinguish it from the other Seljuk kingdoms) continued to rule in Khorasan and in Transoxiana, coming to an end with the death of Sanjar in 1157. After that date these territories were ruled by a rival Turkish dynasty, the Khwarizmshāhs, until they succumbed before the onslaught of the Mongols in 1235. In Asia Minor, the Seljuk Sultanate of Rum (the Arabs called Byzantine Anatolia "the land of the Romans") lasted until about 1308 (its capital at first was Iznik, anc. Nicaea — from 1078 to 1097 — and later Konya, anc. Iconium), though under a form of vassalage after the Mongol conquest in 1243 (see ILKHAN ART). With the extinction of the dynasty the unity of the Sultanate of Rum broke down, and the power passed into the hands of a number of independent beys. Another Turkoman dominion, resulting from the conquest of Anatolia, was that of the Ortuqids of Diyarbakir (anc. Amida); their art, not yet exhaustively analyzed, seems to have developed features worthy of greater attention. The historical background outlined appears far from favorable to artistic development; yet this period is outstanding for its superb achievements in all artistic fields.

ARCHITECTURE. *Iran.* Despite the introduction of a new ethnic element, which, moreover, constituted the class in power, architecture in Persia during the Seljuk period continued without interruption the history of Iranian architecture. Some problems stand out, such as the adoption of the double dome and certain aspects of architectural decoration and building methods; on the whole, however, the plans and characteristics of the structures built at that time, though partly conditioned by new and different functions, remained essentially Iranian and based on ancient tradition. In the period between the Arab invasion and the advent of the Seljuks, with the exception of a few mosques of the Arab type (such as the Tārīkh Khāna of Damghan and the Masjid-i-Jāmi' of Nayin), architecture, religious and other, made use of ancient forms such as the *chahār ṭāq*, or fire temple. This fire temple, derived from the Sassanians (see SASSANIAN ART), with a dome resting on four columns joined by arches, was to be the point of departure for the pavilion mosques, generally preferred in the western regions. The Parthians (see PARTHIAN ART) are said to have introduced the liwan into Mesopotamia from its land of origin, Khorasan, where preference was given to the type of mosque composed almost solely of a liwan containing a mihrab (niche) and preceded by a courtyard encircled by a low wall, like the small mosques discovered by Godard (1962) at Bamian. The southern regions, however, tended to adopt a vaulted gallery with a central dome, similar to the Sassanian structure at Ivan-i-Karkha. But preference for a certain type of structure was not limited by strict regional boundaries; when the architects of the Seljuk period were faced with the need for new constructions, they found examples of Moslem religious buildings that followed both ancient plans.

These architects were almost certainly Iranian, in view of the differences in class and duties between subjects and conquerors (the latter kept almost exclusively for themselves the organization of the military machine, while the bureaucracy of the country and the artisan and peasant classes remained fundamentally Iranian). They are to be credited with the ultimate and most complex achievement of the characteristic Iranian mosque: this originated from the juxtaposition of the mosque having a domed pavilion or the sanctuary having one liwan with the courtyard having four liwans, derived, in all likelihood, from the typical Khorasan dwelling. The result was the large structure known as a madrasah-mosque, perhaps built in order to vie with the spacious caliphal mosques by taking advantage of typically national features; it took shape in the region of Isfahan, and the earliest example of it would seem to be the Masjid-i-Jāmiʿ of Zavara (FIG. 867). Godard (1962) maintains that the builders of the Masjid-i-Jāmiʿ of Isfahan (PL. 549), the most splendid architectural achievement of the Great Seljuks, used as a model, when erecting its spacious courtyard with four liwans, the Madrasah of Kharjird (FIG. 867) built by order

formed the zone of transition to the circular base of the dome, constituting the drum. The dome was double for reasons of internal space and external form; the inner dome was hemispherical, while the outer one had a slightly pointed ovoid shape (Monneret de Villard, 1962, p. 497). The Seljuk structural solutions with regard to the dome were to be the point of departure for all future Iranian architecture, especially for that of the Timurid period (see TIMURID ART). The outstanding Seljuk achievement in this field is perhaps the dome of the Masjid-i-Jāmiʿ of Isfahan (FIG. 868; VIII, PL. 160), dating from 1092 and described by Schroeder (1938, p. 1009) as "powerful in its inspiration, subtle in its mathematical calculations, impeccable in its mechanics."

To complete the structure of the four-liwan type of mosque, a new type of minaret was introduced, consisting of a tall tapering cylindrical body resting on a square base. Examples of this type appeared as far back as the beginning of the 11th century, sometimes with an octagonal or even star-shaped base. It was widely adopted, however, only in the 12th century, when the unplastered brick ornamentation laid in geometric patterns greatly enhanced its beauty and impressiveness. Particularly noteworthy are the minarets of Damghan (1026–30

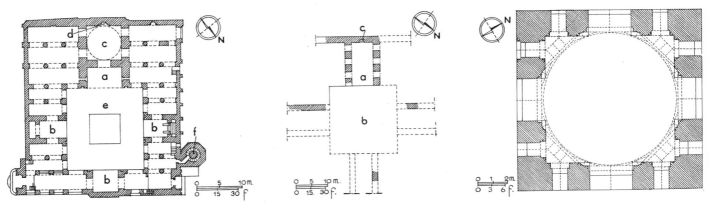

Left: Zavara, Masjid-i-Jāmiʿ, plan: (a) Principal liwan; (b) secondary liwans; (c) dome; (d) mihrab; (e) courtyard; (f) minaret. Center: Kharjird, Niẓāmiya madrasah, plan: (a) Liwan; (b) courtyard; (c) mihrab (from Godard, 1962). Right: Isfahan, Masjid-i-Jāmiʿ, domed room of the Seljuk period (from SPA, vol. II).

of the vizier Niẓām al-Mulk. One of the liwans serves as the entrance; the one axial to the first, followed by the domed hall containing the mihrab, represents the sanctuary. Another example of a Seljuk mosque based on a courtyard with four liwans is the Masjid-i-Jāmiʿ of Ardistan, built about 1158 on the remains of a previous domed sanctuary; this was redecorated and completed by a courtyard having four liwans, of which the southern one is the most remarkable (PLS. 545, 546). The original plan of the mosque in Herat, of a slightly later date (beginning of the 13th cent.), included passageways encircling the liwans, as in the Parthian palace of Ashur (Assur). In the Masjid-i-Jāmiʿ of Qazvin (beginning of the 12th cent.), a large liwan precedes the domed sanctuary, which recalls the plan of the audience halls of Sassanian palaces. These two mosques give further indication of the uninterrupted application of national Iranian traditions in the architectural field.

As already mentioned, the adoption of the double dome presents a problem. Some scholars — among them Monneret de Villard (1962) — have been led to seek its origin in certain Buddhist stupas of Central Asia (see ASIA, CENTRAL). However, it must not be forgotten in this connection that the architecture of Central Asia also availed itself of rock structures and that, furthermore, the static requirements of the two countries differed widely, inasmuch as the building materials employed in Central Asia were inferior to the perfect baked bricks of Iran. At any rate, the Seljuks lavished particular care on the double dome, and they devised for it a new type of support, the trefoil, composed of two lateral lanceolate lobes on which rests the impost of a third. The lateral galleries that bore part of the weight of the Sassanian domes were abolished and replaced, above the level of the squinches, by a series of 16 arches that

FIG. 869); of Zavara (1068); of the Chihil Dukhtarān in Isfahan (1107–08); and the later one of Jar Kurgan, whose body, instead of having a smooth surface, is made up of a number of close-fitting half cylinders surrounding the shaft and joined at the top by a series of small arches.

Another type of building bound to the religious and spiritual life of Islam is the already-mentioned madrasah. Originally this was a school for the teaching of religion and for the reading and exegesis of the Koran in the eastern regions of Iran, especially in Khorasan. About the 5th century of the Hegira — mainly on the initiative of Niẓām al-Mulk — the madrasah expanded beyond the sphere of teaching and became an outright instrument of political and religious propaganda. It spread throughout the various regions of the Seljuk empire and naturally took with it its characteristic architectural form based on the courtyard with four liwans, typical of its country of origin. One of the most famous is the Niẓāmiya of Baghdad, built by order of the Grand Vizier for the jurist Shīrāzī, who began his lectures there in 1067. Niẓām al-Mulk had other madrasahs built in Nishapur, Isfahan, Balkh, Basra, and elsewhere. The oldest example of this type of structure is the Niẓāmiya of Kharjird, undoubtedly built before 1067, as shown by an inscription. It has four liwans placed axially around a rectangular courtyard, the qibla (the one oriented toward Mecca) being the largest. At the corners of the courtyard were the lecture halls and residential and service quarters.

Funerary monuments of the Seljuk period are perhaps structurally the furthest removed from the Iranian tradition, although there are examples in Persian territory previous to the advent of the dynasty — the tomb towers with a circular plan, covered by a dome hidden on the outside by a pyramidal or conical

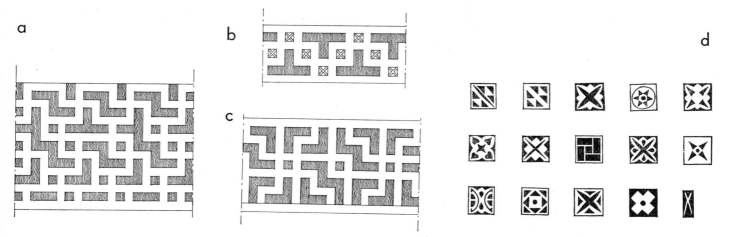

Types of Seljuk architectural decoration. (*a, b, c*) Ornamental motifs in brick: (*a*) Sangbast, minaret; (*b*) Damghan, minaret of Chihīl Dukhtarān; (*c*) Damghan, tomb tower of Pīr-i-'Ālamdār; (*d*) Isfahan, Masjid-i-Jāmi', large domed hall, wall panels of stucco (*from SPA, vol. II*).

roof. Sometimes the cylindrical body is strengthened externally by buttresses or abutments of triangular section, as in the Gunbad-i-Qābūs near Gurgan (PL. 544; FIG. 869), built in the very first years of the 11th century, or by semicircular buttresses, as in the later tower of East Radkan — similar in this to the minaret of Jar Kurgan — which imitates the structure of the Ribāt-i-Malik near Bukhara, built prior to 1078. This type of structure is to be found in other defensive works in Khwarizm (q.v.), which would seem to imply that it was imported from Central Asia (Monneret de Villard, 1962, pp. 496–97). The conical or pyramidal roof that covers the dome has, in fact, often been interpreted as a version of the canopy of the nomads' tent. During the years 1015–25, that is to say, before the Seljuks had completely asserted their rule, were built the perfectly circular mortuary towers of Lajim, Resget, and West Radkan. They were the burial places of some members of a local Iranian ruling family; all were located in the same region and were adorned with Kufic and Pahlavi inscriptions. In this case, also, therefore, the Turkish innovation is not easy to assess. In the central regions the tomb tower acquired a different plan: octagonal, as in the Gunbad-i-'Alī of Abarquh (1056), or decagonal, as in the Mausoleum of Mu'mina Khātūn of Nakhichevan (FIG. 869), which was built, however, in 1186–87. In western Persia, Maragha offers a splendid example of a tomb tower with a rectangular plan: the Gunbad-i-Surkh (Red Tomb; FIG. 869), which an inscription dates to 1147–48; it contained at one time the remains of 'Abd-al-'Azīz, perhaps a prince of the local Kurdish dynasty. The Red Tomb, remarkable for the harmony and elegance of its structure and of the red-brick decoration, also offers what may be the first instance of ornamentation in colored enamels: the red of the unplastered brick is subtly enhanced by touches of turquoise-colored enamel. According to Godard (1962), the first attempts at colored architectural decoration — which was later to have such success —

are to be found in the Gunbad-i-Khākī of the Masjid-i-Jāmi' in Isfahan, dating from about 1088, where the inside of certain niches is decorated with stalactites in materials of different colors (gray stone, black stone, natural brick, etc.). The funerary-tower structure did not bring about the disappearance of the earlier type of tomb with a rectangular, domed chamber and axial doors or with an upper gallery, to be found also in the Samanid period (see SAMANID ART); a typical example is the Mausoleum of Ismā'īl the Samanid at Bukhara (PLS. 381, 382). But this type of tomb was usually reserved for distinguished religious personalities, while the tomb tower was preferred for members of the princely families; the only known exception is the Mausoleum of Sultan Sanjar (d. 1157) near Merv, roofed with a double dome.

It is to be assumed that, simultaneously with buildings intended for religious purposes (of which a considerable number have been preserved), secular architecture must also have developed; among the few surviving traces are the ruins of a bridge in Tus and of baths at Nigar. The Persian secular structure of the Seljuk period on which most information is available is the caravanserai. Like the madrasah, it represents an application, on a larger scale, of the courtyard with four liwans. Leaving aside the minor caravanserais and those of the cold mountain regions (which were entirely covered and had a central dome), the monumental caravanserais were always composed of a spacious courtyard with four liwans, placed at the end of the normal axes; the one through which access was gained was in some cases surmounted by a dome and had lateral galleries and shops disposed on one or sometimes two levels.

In summary, it may be said that the Seljuk period represented for Persian architecture a sort of balance that comprised the Iranian structural experiences of past centuries and fixed for the future the new patterns. The characteristic feature of the buildings of this period is the use of unplastered brick,

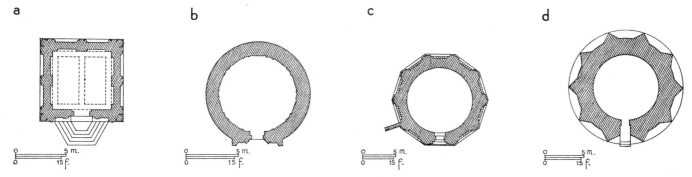

Seljuk funerary monuments in Iranian territory, plans. Maragha: (*a*) Gunbad-i-Surkh (the Red Tomb); (*b*) tomb tower with a circular plan. (*c*) Nakhichevan, Mausoleum of Mu'mina Khātūn. (*d*) Gunbad-i-Qābūs, tomb tower (*from Godard, 1962*).

in the utilization of which Iranian architects displayed skill and sensitivity. The earlier use of stucco facings on the outer walls as well as on the inside (to conceal the inferiority of the building materials) was discontinued, although it was to reappear later. The use of stucco was for a time limited to certain parts, such as the mihrab and the cornices. It has been stated that plaster is an architectural disguise; in the architecture of the Seljuk period, on the contrary, the supporting elements remained visible, as if transferred to the surfaces. The surfaces themselves were transformed into decorative features by the elegant placement of bricks of excellent quality to form geometric patterns, in accordance with a rigorous style that is admirably suited to the outlines of the buildings. The basic style also revealed a striking inventive fertility in the designs and in the pleasing, minute play of light and shape in the more or less projecting lacelike pattern of the bricks themselves; and all this was sustained by a truly amazing technical ability. From the Mausoleum of Ismā'īl to Ghaznevid architecture (see GHAZNEVID ART) to the superb Seljuk creations, the line of development followed by this technique is far from obvious, but the unequaled beauty of the perfect geometry of volume and surface endures. Its influence is still strongly felt; the modern Iranian architects who built the Mausoleum of Avicenna at Hamadan in 1952 adopted, in a modern interpretation, the forms of the Gunbad-i-Qābūs.

Outside Iranian territory, the regions bound in one way or another to the empire of the Great Seljuks continued to exist as Seljuk domains for some time even after the death of Sanjar. They developed an architectural style peculiar to themselves, which in part absorbed the trends coming from the more easterly regions and in part retained the forms and methods of previous centuries. The courtyard with four liwans was widely accepted in Syria and Mesopotamia; it became a normal element, here as in all Islamic countries, of the madrasah and the caravanserai, while the plan of the mosques presented special aspects. The mosque built by Nūr ad-Dīn in Mosul, from the 12th century, seems to have had — as far as can be judged on the basis of the few sections that remain from this period — a chessboard plan with the squares covered alternately with a dome or a barrel vault. The Ulu Cami of Diyarbakir, in Ortuqid territory, comprised three arcades, parallel to the qibla wall and cut through the center by a transept higher than the rest of the building. The entire structure was covered by a closing roof on trusses. Other structures (e.g., the mosque of Mayyafariqin) had aisles covered by a barrel vault resting on pilasters, while the central nave in front of the mihrab was replaced by a domed square hall. The building material utilized was for the most part ashlar, placed in regular bands, dressed and laid with great skill.

In Mesopotamia the minaret was of the type with a tall cylindrical body and brings to mind the Persian ones, not only by its shape but also in the ornamentation of unplastered brick placed so as to form decorative designs. The base was sometimes square, as in the minaret of the Jāmi' al-Kabīr in Mosul (I, PL. 6), and sometimes octagonal, as in the Sahaga minaret of Erbil (1190–1232). Minarets with an octagonal body are to be seen in the Qal'a of Mosul and at Balis (1192–1218). Mortuary monuments also reveal the same attitude with regard to Iranian creations: the structure known as the Tomb of Zubayda, not far from Baghdad, displays an octagonal plan, with a high dome covered on the outside by a pyramidal turret with stalactites. The Mausoleum of the Imam Yaḥyā in Mosul (second quarter of the 13th cent.) comprises a cubical base on which stands a domed octagonal body with the usual pyramidal roof (Monneret de Villard, 1962, pp. 498–99).

The scarce remains of Mesopotamian secular architecture of the Ortuqid period show it to have been particularly sensitive to the charm of decoration, as proved by the surviving ornamental parts of the liwan in the Qal'a of Baghdad and by the bands with inscriptions and animal figures on the powerful bastions added to the ancient walls of Constantius II at Diyarbakir.

Anatolia. The Seljuk Sultanate of Rum broke its bonds — nominal as they were — with the Great Seljuks during the reign of Mas'ūd I (1116–56), and Anatolia then enjoyed the utmost autonomy until, after the year 1246, it had to submit to the authority of the Mongols of Persia (see ILKHAN ART). With the death of Mas'ūd III (1308) the unity of Anatolia came to an end, and it disintegrated into a number of independent principalities. The Seljuks of Anatolia had been great builders throughout their history, and the beys who succeeded them — outstanding among them the lords of Karaman — inherited their tradition. The Seljuk architecture of Anatolia is immediately striking for its substantial difference from the Iranian: the use of different building materials resulted in a considerable change in the esthetics of the structures. Bricks were replaced by ashlar, and frequent use was made of wood for the interiors and, later, of marble for wall facings: this brought about the gradual disappearance of that fantastic aspect typical of eastern Islamic architecture. Furthermore, the different climate of the country explains the modifications made in the open-courtyard Iranian structures; here the courtyards were enclosed and frequently covered by a flat roof. More than any of the other regions conquered by the Turkish peoples, Anatolia submitted completely to the taste and usage of the invaders and became thoroughly Turkicized, even from an ethnic point of view. The austerity of the rulers, at least the earlier ones, gave considerable impulse to religious rather than secular architecture; but religious and secular buildings stemmed from the same structural bases, although great variety eventually developed in the materials, the dimensions, and the decoration.

The early Moslem mosque (with a flat roof supported by arches resting on pilasters and with the central span wider than the others) was adopted by the Seljuks of Anatolia, who closed the previously open façade; this type of mosque was called *ulu cami* (Ar., *masjid-i-jāmi'*). The flat covering of clay slabs resting on horizontal wood rafters was supported in the earlier structures by columns also made of wood; the use of wood was continued even in the later period, simultaneously with buildings in which stone was used for supports and arches. At times a part of the roof over the central aisle was left open to correspond to an ablution fountain (*ṣadirvan*) below, as in the Ulu Cami of Erzurum (1179). In some cases, as in the Eşrefoğlu Cami of Beyşehir of a later date, the position of the mihrab is emphasized by a dome pierced with a window oriented toward Mecca. In the Ulu Cami of Kayseri (ca. 1140), the axis of the mihrab is further marked by two domes, one of them with a wide central opening; in the Iplıkçi Mosque, in Konya (FIG. 873), there are three domes. The Mosque of 'Alā ud-Dīn in Konya, built between 1156 and 1220 at the time of Kilij Arslān (Kılıçarslan) II, displays, particularly in the turbeh (Turk., *türbe*, mausoleum) of the founder, characteristic features of Seljuk architecture in the dome resting on a series of corbeled triangular slabs and hidden externally by the typical conical roof. In the Loğ Minare Cami (Mosque of the Spiral Minaret) in Amasya (1237–47) and in the Hacı Kılıç Cami in Kayseri (1250) it is possible to trace further phases of development of the Seljuk mosque in Anatolia: a reduction in the number of supporting pilasters and a widening of the central aisle, in accordance with a procedure already applied in 1229 in the Ulu Cami of Divriği, the most monumental of the period, built entirely of stone, to which was added a hospital that repeated its plan with the barrel-vaulted central aisle (FIG. 873).

Other structures, such as the Arapzade of Karaman, built of stone (1374–1420), and the Ulu Cami of Artuk, are wider than they are deep, with broad ovoid domes supported by pendentives. In the course of the 14th century a porch was added to the façade, as in the Akçasar Mosque of Karaman and in the Ulu Cami of Birgi; later this took the form of a sort of internal courtyard, as in the Mosque of Isa Bey at Aya Soluk (anc. Ephesus). The Davgandos Mosque at Karaman shows yet another plan: a large, square, domed hall and a porch on the façade with three minor domes (FIG. 873).

The mosques of Anatolia are not derived from Persian models, although they reveal some features of Abbasside architecture (see ABBASSIDE ART), as in the Ulu Cami of Sivas (11th cent.; FIG. 873); closer study might lead to the discovery of some forms derived from the Christian architecture of Syria (q.v.). The madrasahs, however, repeat the basic structure of

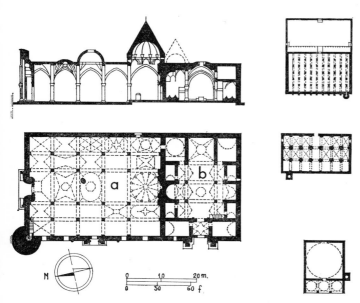

Seljuk mosques in Turkey. *Left*: Divriği, section and plan of the monumental complex: (*a*) Ulu Cami; (*b*) hospital. *Right, above*: Sivas, Ulu Cami, plan; *center*: Konya, Iplıkçi Mosque, plan; *below*: Karaman, Davgandos Mosque, plan (*from B. Ünsal, 1959*).

the Iranian ones with, in some cases, a variant typical of Anatolia, where climatic conditions led to the roofing of the previously open courtyard (a flat roof was used with, occasionally, a central dome); a small mosque containing the mausoleum of the founder was also added at times. The Madrasah of Yağı Basan in Niksar, one of the earliest, apparently dates from 1157; it has a lateral entrance, a double liwan, and a central dome. The Sırçalı Madrasah of Konya (1243) is open, while the Büyük Karatay (1251) has a courtyard covered by a wide dome pierced with a window. Also in Konya is the Ince Minare Madrasah (1258; FIG. 873), which owes its name to the minaret (with tall cylindrical body and semicircular buttresses) of a previous *mescit* (prayer hall), which it incorporated; the Büyük Karatay clearly served as a model for the transition from the base to the 20-sided polygon on which the dome rests, by means of groups of four triangular corner corbels. A beautiful decoration of unplastered brick graces this building, which reveals great maturity in the absolute symmetry of the construction.

In Sivas, the second capital, the Şifaiye Madrasah (Daruşşifa), comprising a medical school and hospital, is shaped like a double madrasah (1217). Worthy of particular attention also are the Çifte Minare Madrasah (1271–1322) and the Gök (blue)

Madrasah (the name is derived from the blue tiles with which it was decorated), contemporaneous with and similar to each other, with arched porticoes enclosing the courtyard. Apart from other examples to be found in Kayseri and Amasya, mention should be made of the Hatuniye Madrasah at Erzurum (1253), in which the two-storied porticoes surrounding the courtyard are interrupted by four liwans, two minarets at the sides of the portal, and a turbeh placed after the liwan at the far end of the main axis. At the time of the beys, the same plans were used with few variants: the Ak Madrasah of Niğde (1409), symmetrical and two-storied, has an arched veranda flanking the portal of the façade at second-floor level.

The structure of the tomb towers brings to mind some aspects of the Iranian ones, such as the circular or polygonal body joined to the square base by means of triangular supports. The covering is a dome with an external conical roof. Here again the use of stone results in a different decoration in the form of relief. Worthy of mention are the primitive octagonal Turbeh of Halife Gazi in Amasya (1146) and the Mausoleum of Melik Gazi in Kırşehir (1250; FIG. 873), in which the conical roof is joined to the octagonal body by triangular projecting surfaces turned downward, a motif that is repeated inversely to join the polygonal body to the square foundation. The Döner Kümbet in Kayseri (ca. 1275) is based instead on a dodecagonal plan and is adorned by blind arcading, in accordance with forms that are repeated more elaborately in the Mausoleum of Hudabend Khātūn in Niğde (1312). The Mausoleum of Sheik Hasan Bey in Sivas (1340) has a circular plan and brick decoration, while the Mausoleum of Emir Bayındır (1491) has external open arcades.

It must be noted first of all that examples of secular architecture are much more numerous in Anatolia than in Persia. A structure typical of the commercial organization of Islamic countries is the caravanserai, or han (Ar., *khān*), erected in the cities as well as on the main trade routes at intervals of one day's travel. The han was usually rectangular in plan; its entrance gate or portal opened onto a large hall with a flat roof supported by columns, around which ran corridors with rooms for lodging and business transactions. In the larger caravanserais the portal led through an open courtyard to a large vaulted hall whose dome was pierced with a central window for light and ventilation. The walls were often of rubble masonry, with the façade, pilasters, and arches faced with ashlar. Many of these hans have survived, among them the Sultan Han (1236) on the Kayseri-Silvas road and another of the same name on the road between Konya and Aksaray (1229; VIII, PL. 161); both have a small *mescit* at the center of the courtyard, while in the Sarı Han (near Avanos) the small *mescit* is placed immediately above the portal. The Yeni Han (built after 1317), on the Tokat-Sivas road, with its double row of shops at the sides of the central passage, appears as the prototype of the later Ottoman hans (see OTTOMAN SCHOOLS).

Just as town planning, perhaps influenced by the oasiscities of central Asia, always involved vast gardens and green spaces, so the Seljuk palace (serai) of Asia Minor comprised, like the later Ottoman palaces, a certain number of detached pavilions made of wood or bricks, encircled by a wall and distributed over a series of courts and gardens. No Seljuk palace survives; only the ruins of that of 'Alā ud-Dīn Kaykūbad in Beyşehir, excavated in 1949, give an idea of the materials used and of the style of these palaces. The picture is completed by miniatures of the Ottoman period, which depict a type of structure that must have persisted with few modifications; these concern mostly the decoration, which was undoubtedly more lavish and elaborate in the later period.

Seljuk Anatolia also built public baths in great number; a Roman origin was often erroneously attributed to them, as with the more ancient baths of Damascus. Only the hypocausts were retained from the thermal baths of the classical period, while the plan was based on an octagon, four sides of which opened into liwans; the actual waterworks did not provide for bathing pools, which were used only in the larger establishments or for therapeutic purposes. The outstanding examples of these structures are the baths of Sultan Humam in Konya,

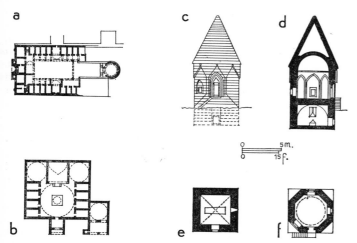

Left: Madrasahs of the Seljuk period: (*a*) Erzurum, Çifte Winare; (*b*) Konya, Ince Minare. *Right*: Kırşehir, Mausoleum of Melik Gazi: (*c*) façade; (*d*) section; (*e*) plan of the basement; (*f*) plan of the upper chamber (*from B. Ünsal, 1959*).

with separate buildings for men and women; the Kaplıca of Ilgın (1236); the baths of Ābid Çelebi (1283–1338); and the Meram Hamam (1423). The last is the only one still standing of those built under the rule of the beys of Karaman. In connection with the baths, mention should also be made of the fountains, which, however, did not reach at this time the monumental importance they were to acquire in the Ottoman period.

Despite the fact that the architectural patterns appear at first glance to be more or less similar, there is considerable difference between the Seljuk architecture of Persia and that of Mesopotamia and Anatolia. The esthetic vision of Persia, inseparable from a sustained lyricism and from the fantastic perception of things, was supported by the decorative use of brick (PL. 542) and by its color and that of the ceramic facings. The architecture of Anatolia has a less formal appearance (primarily because of the materials used), is of more modest proportions, and rationalizes the use of the decorative elements. Finally, the ornamental repertory, though rich, is far less impressive, and it avails itself — in addition to the typical motifs of Islamic decoration — of elements drawn from the most ancient local traditions, sometimes more reminiscent even of the tribal and totemic legacy.

DECORATIVE ARTS. *Ceramics.* Some time after the advent of the Seljuks (though comparatively late with respect to the development of other artistic activities), various types of ceramics appeared in Persia, produced in certain centers of major importance (Rayy and Kashan in Iran and Raqqa, or Rakka, in Mesopotamia) and perhaps some minor ones that derived their techniques and patterns from the principal centers (see CERAMICS, cols. 251–53). The salient characteristic of the Seljuk production is the use of a white paste, obtained by mixing 10 parts pulverized quartz, 1 part glass paste (alkaline earth with a quartz and potassium base), and 1 part fine white clay. The advantages inherent in the use of this mixture — body and glaze, composed basically of the same substance, blended extremely well in firing and thus slip became superfluous — have been exhaustively pointed out by Lane (1958), but esthetic considerations also enter in. For over two centuries specimens of Chinese pottery had found their way into the western regions (the excavations carried out at Samarra have brought to light a number of pieces); and it was in this period that a large-scale attempt was first made to reproduce Chinese monochrome ceramics with their fine decoration carved under the glaze. The paste used in Iran was soft, the glazing transparent (though it could be dulled by the addition of tin), usually colorless, and fragile. Ceramics of this type came almost exclusively from Rayy (PL. 551; VIII, PL. 154). About the 12th century some pieces appeared in which the body was decorated with openwork and the openings filled with a transparent glaze in an attempt to achieve a lighter effect. Toward the middle of the same century, the glazing was colored, usually in turquoise or dark blue. The overglaze designs eventually gave rise to a sort of low relief, which later led to the use of inset ornamental pieces and finally to molded decoration.

With the adoption of polychrome glazing, a step was taken toward the *lakabi* (painting) technique. The designs were carved on the body of the vessel so as to leave small grooves into which the glazes of various colors (blue, yellow, red, and green) were permitted to run; the designs were always comparatively simple because of the difficulty of this technique. This type of pottery was rather rare; it was perhaps produced at Kashan, although somewhat coarser pieces seem to have originated from Raqqa. At this time technical problems arose that led to the creation of the so-called "silhouette" wares, in which the figures were laid on in thick black slip or cut into it; the entire surface was then given an ivory or turquoise overglaze (III, PL. 141).

Luster-painted ceramics also made their appearance in the 12th century; it is difficult to assess the part played by Persia in the invention of this technique. The earliest examples seem to have originated in Mesopotamia and, later, Egypt, and the technique was already quite advanced when it first appeared in Persia. A certain amount of tin, added to the glaze, dulled the enamels, which took on their characteristic metallic aspect, after

firing, from the mixture of silver oxide and copper oxide. Two stylistic trends, associated with Rayy and with Kashan, can be differentiated. In the first, the luster-painted background bears figures of horsemen, birds, and musicians, surrounded by stylized decoration of spiraling plants; this secondary decoration eventually gained in importance until the human and animal figures were reduced to small recurrent motifs within the plant motifs. In the ceramics of Kashan — which was later to become so famous for its tiles — human figures were often set against a landscape, either summary or symbolical, represented by a tree and by stylized secondary motifs. There is either a single figure — later symmetrically multiplied — or a pair, sitting in the typical squatting position of conversation; the elongated eyes are enhanced by the dark curve of the eyebrows. In certain aspects this type of ceramics poses the problem of a possible derivation from the paintings of Central Asia, and one may well wonder whether it does not incorporate some echoes of Manichaean miniatures (see ASIA, CENTRAL, col. 827 ff.; MANICHAEAN ART). Raqqa produced wide vessels bearing relief decorations and further ornamented with inscriptions and Seljuk arabesques (III, PL. 140); these pieces are slightly coarser than the Persian ones in materials and technique.

The last quarter of the 12th century saw the creation of the splendid and elaborate *mīnā'ī* (enamel) ceramics, produced by means of a double-firing technique to set the varnishes over the enamel; the earliest examples seem to be the most elaborate. This type of ware, which originated in Rayy, Kashan, and perhaps Sava (VIII, PL. 153), displays ornamentation similar to the luster-painted ware of Kashan; occasionally, however, it also bore small compositions depicting battle scenes or episodes drawn from the *Shāh-nāma*, probably created by individual artists in accordance with patterns closely resembling those of contemporaneous miniatures.

Considerable technical progress was made in the last years of the 12th century, and the first examples of the *lajvardina* (blue) ceramics (so called from the color of the glaze applied) may well date from that period. While the Mongols invaded Persia, the Seljuks of Rum continued their domination over Asia Minor; a few doubtful fragments have been obtained from the excavations made, but the monuments of Konya and Sivas and many others sometimes show sections covered with glazed tiles of a vigorous style. These are decorated with animal motifs — outstanding among them the double-headed eagle, the emblem of the Seljuks of Rum — and were produced in the centers, perhaps active from the time of the Seljuk domination, that were to become the pride of Turkish pottery in the Ottoman period.

Miniatures. Seljuk miniatures, of which few traces remain because of the widespread destruction by the Mongol invasions, must also have been extremely ornate, like other art forms of this period, and certainly must have displayed features similar to pottery painting. It was at this time that the poet Nizāmī composed the *Khamsa*, which was to acquire in subsequent periods such wide renown; it is easy to imagine how even then it must have deeply stirred the interest of artists. A goblet now in Washington, D.C. (Freer Gall. of Art), portrays an episode drawn from a story by Firdausī; it is illustrated in successive scenes disposed on three levels, all showing a certain lack of detail. One may well wonder whether the pattern of composition was not drawn from contemporary miniatures. The persistence of the Hellenistic cultural tradition in Mesopotamia resulted in the production of copies of the manuscripts of Dioscorides and Galen. The Galen manuscript in Vienna (Nationalbib., A.F. 10) may well serve as an example, and its miniatures, depicting richly colored monumental scenes, still reveal Sassanian echoes (see SASSANIAN ART). According to Gray (1961), the frontispiece of this copy has the same origin as the frontispieces of the *Kitāb al-Aghānī*, an anthology of Arabian verse in many volumes, of which two are preserved in Istanbul (Feyzulah Lib., nos. 1565, 1566) and four in Cairo (Egyptian Lib., *adab* No. 579), copied for Badr ad-Dīn Lu'lu', an Armenian slave who became regent of Mosul and, in 1233, its ruler. The beginning of the 12th century is the probable approximate date of the *Warka u Gulshah* manuscript (Istanbul, Topkapı Saray Lib., Hazine 841), in which the Iraqi school appears very close, in composition and vivacity of color, to the figures of Seljuk ceramics; this hypothesis is borne out by the Persian origin of the poem and of the calligrapher himself.

A *Mufīd al-Khāss* of Abū-Bakr ibn-Zakariyyā al-Rāzī (1200) preserved in the library of the shrine at Mashhad (Meshed), its fine and graceful colored drawings illustrating some medicinal plants, shows traces of Sassanian heraldic compositions (see SASSANIAN ART), on a more minute scale, in the pairs of confronted animals in naturalistically free, easy poses at the foot of a tree. Two 13th-century copies of the *Kalīla u Dimna*, one in Worcester, Mass. (Art Mus.), the other in Paris (Bib. Nat., nos. 3465, 3467), reveal a rather different style in the animal scenes: in the first, they are composed in a more mature and elegant design; those of the second show — their small dimensions notwithstanding — a more cursory style, expressed in rather vivacious color drawings. A page of the Koran, now in the Teheran National Museum (11th–12th cent.), is a further example of the highly decorative use of Kufic script; the miniatures, whose schemes also are purely decorative, are used to subdivide the inscriptions and bring them into relief. The same applies to some pages of the Koran (1036) in the British Museum (Add. Ms. 7214).

Textiles. Except for pottery, which has always been the object of more sustained interest and careful study on the part of scholars, the various forms of artistic production of this period are still far from presenting a well-defined and clear picture, mainly owing to their great richness and complexity. As with the art of miniature, which has been briefly outlined above, a definite orientation in the field of textiles is almost impossible (see TEXTILES, EMBROIDERY, AND LACE). Stylistic differences testify to various origins: as many as 12 classifications have been made. A careful comparative study of the different art forms, so as to establish satisfactorily the characteristics of the styles related to the various centers or regions, would be of great interest and usefulness, since today, unfortunately, apart from the help supplied by the collation of inscriptions, hypothesis and intuition still prevail in this field. It seems that silk was introduced from China into Iran during the Parthian period, was already being produced under the Sassanians, and was woven extensively throughout Persia from the beginning of the Islamic period. The technical ability on the whole is remarkable and was applied to the production of various types of fabric (twills, satins, and brocades) decorated with considerable iconographic variety. The earliest fabrics reveal a certain sensitivity in the matching of a few colors placed in bands, with transverse borders formed by elegant inscriptions. They display a striking sobriety and grace, as in the silk fragment of the 11th century, woven in purple, red, and gray bands, now in Washington, D.C. (Textile Mus., T.M. 3.200). There is also a wide repertory comprising figurations of mythical animals, examples of which are to be found in the Textile Museum; these figures are placed in rows or inside medallions and lozenges or are scattered freely over a leafy background, which at times constitutes the sole decoration of the entire surface. A textile fragment in New Haven (Yale Univ. Art Gall., Moore Memorial Coll., No. 1937.4609) portrays a pair of youths crouched at the foot of a tree, within a lanceolate frame; this composition suggests a close relation with the iconography of the Kashan ceramics. Worthy of mention are the extremely successful representation of the Sun's horses and a type of figuration, often repeated, representing a double-headed eagle carrying off a crowned figure and two roebucks.

Metalwork. During the Seljuk period metalwork was particularly widespread and flourishing; it always attained an extremely high level of workmanship, which set for itself, perhaps, specifically artistic aims. These aims were often achieved, as is proved by the fact that a great number of pieces, especially those from the Khorasan centers, bear the date and the signature, or signatures, of the casters, engravers, and skilled workers who executed them.

Bronze was by far the most widely used metal during the 11th and 12th centuries (brass being a later addition). It was cast, engraved, sometimes inlaid with silver or copper or executed in openwork, and in some cases even graced with enamel decorations. In northeastern Persia, the aspect of the bronzes varied depending on the shiny patina applied to them, which could be either reddish brown or dark green. The objects decorated with silver or copper inlay had for the most part a lighter-colored patina. A wide range of objects was produced at the time, often imitating ancient traditional models: engraved or openwork perfume burners (PL. 552), usually in the shape of animals (birds or lions); pestles; mirrors; candlesticks; pitchers that recall the pear-shaped outline of Sassanian examples (whereas the animal-shaped perfume burners or vases seem to be connected with the remote tradition of the monster-shaped rhytons of the highlands). The decorative features included inscriptions in Kufic or Naskhi script, animals against a background of foliated arabesques, and medallions engraved with harpies and griffins.

Among the numerous examples of high-quality Seljuk metalwork are a bronze dish (Vict. and Alb.) engraved, in a sober but vigorous style, with the figure of a fantastic animal encircled by an inscription in Kufic characters; and a bronze incense burner in the shape of a stylized lion, in engraved openwork with copper insets (VIII, PL. 152). Both these objects date from the 12th century. The Hermitage also houses two remarkable pieces from Khorasan with copper insets. The first is a box, dated 1148, with inlaid inscriptions in silver and copper and small engraved figures of birds and foliage; it is probably the earliest dated damascened piece. The other Hermitage piece is the kettle from the Bobrinsky Collection; an inscription states that it was executed in Herat in 1163, and it bears the names of the caster, the author of the insets, and the merchant for whom it was made. The decorative insets represent festive, court, and hunting scenes; the Naskhi inscriptions follow a characteristic fashion, with the vertical strokes of the letters topped by small human heads. Many other pieces signed by artisans of Khorasan prove how flourishing and well organized was this form of craftsmanship in the region. No traces of monumental sculpture in the round are available except for a few statuettes.

Finally, particular mention should be made of a dish (The Hermitage) which, though not of the highest quality, is especially interesting from an iconographic point of view: it depicts a scene identified by Sauvaget (1951) as the one where proof is given, before the citadel of Merv, of the execution of two Ismailians who had hatched a plot against Sultan Sanjar in 1154. The Sultan himself is said to be portrayed there, certainly not with the aim of producing a realistic portrait but rather of representing some typical details of the costume of that time. Assuming that the identification of the scene is correct — other scholars deem it to belong instead to the late Sassanian period (see SASSANIAN ART) and to be dated no later than the 9th–10th century — this would be a comparatively rare case in Islamic iconography, since the scene would then represent a well-attested historical episode, which, according to Sauvaget, can be pinpointed by reference to the architectural forms and to details of Turkish military costume. The dish was almost certainly made in the region, inasmuch as it seems to indicate the artist's direct knowledge of the citadel mentioned above.

In northwestern Iran the production included bell-shaped candlesticks (VIII, PL. 156) and grooved metalware reminiscent of the embossed work of the Achaemenid and Sassanian periods (see IRANIAN PRE-SASSANIAN ART CULTURES; SASSANIAN ART); some pitchers are particularly noteworthy. Precious metals were never so widespread as bronze; some of the most representative objects are now in collections in the U.S.S.R. or in Berlin (Staat. Mus.), while in Boston the most beautiful and famous piece of all Islamic metalwork is preserved: the silver salver of Sultan Alp Arslān (VI, PL. 280). A large Kufic inscription states that it was made for that ruler by Ḥasan al-Kāshānī in 1066. The decoration, in which the inscriptions themselves play a large part, consists further of two lunettes engraved with leaf motifs, against which stand out some elegant small figures of animals, remarkably lively though stylized.

The style of Seljuk metalwork is always incisive, swift, and exuberant, with little attention to detail. Anatolia and Mesopotamia, on the other hand, more strictly bound to formalism, made great use of decorative inscriptions. Extensive use was also made of engraved designs, of insets, and of multilobed medallions enclosing scenes with human figures. Mention should be made of the ewer from the Blacas Collection in the British Museum, dated 1232 and signed by Shujā' ibn-Man'a, of Mosul, where a high level of craftsmanship persisted into the Ilkhan period (VIII, PL. 159). Mesopotamia also seems to have used enamel decoration on bronze; a striking (and almost the only) example is the dish made for the Ortuqid ruler Daūd ibn-Suqmān during the first half of the 12th century and adorned with enameled medallions, of which the central one depicts the apotheosis of Alexander (IV, PL. 408).

Ivories. Monneret de Villard (1962) assigns to the 12th-century production of Mesopotamia or western Persia some ivory objects previously attributed to various other regions. These comprise almost exclusively caskets decorated with vividly colored scenes of horsemen, falconers, and hunters — one of which is in the Vatican (Treas. of the Sancta Sanctorum) — and a series of combs (many in Br. Mus.) ornamented with brightly colored animals and human figures whose features are distinctly Mongolian. Also ascribed to the Seljuks are an elephant — now in Florence (Mus. Naz.) — and a small head, perhaps a doll or an amulet (Br. Mus.); the surface is not modeled, and the essential features are indicated by a sharp groove.

CONCLUSION. The Seljuk period was undoubtedly one of the most intensely creative in the history of the Islamic world; it displays splendid achievements in every artistic field, with various subtle differences in style from one region to the next, differences that still pose many problems which are unsolved or for which only unsatisfactory solutions have been offered. In the field of architecture, brick was put to a decorative use; attempts were made to insert colored elements, especially in Anatolia, where this technique was more developed and elaborate; stucco was arranged — in a fashion that has not died out — in fantastic leaf motifs, as at Qazvin in the interiors of the Masjid-i-Jāmi' and the Ḥaydariya. Certain elements of decorative plant motifs, such as the palmette and the rosette, gradually disappeared and made room for the wider use of acanthus scrolls, lotus flowers, and particularly the vine leaf.

The style of animal figures often preserved the Sassanian heraldic trends; arabesques, revealing a subtle instinctive feeling for proportion, might appear at first glance to be set within fixed schemes but were in fact always varied, endowed with a rhythm by turns relaxed and turbulent, and were often combined with geometric patterns usually based on the eight-pointed star. The human figure was far from neglected: it sometimes stood out freely on its own in the decoration of ceramics, sometimes was enclosed within medallions of many shapes on the surface of metal objects. Single or paired, portrayed in varied postures, it played its role in all art forms, often inserted within the schemes of geometric decoration in poses such as those which can be seen on ceramics, as in a stucco panel from Rayy (PL. 550). Another of these panels, now in Philadelphia (Univ. Mus.), bears an inscription in the name of Tughril Beg II (1195), accompanied by a scene that depicts a ruler on his throne and stands out against a background entirely covered with geometric and floral motifs.

BIBLIOG. See generally K. A. C. Creswell, A Bibliography of the Architecture, Arts and Crafts of Islam, London, 1961. See also: C. A. Barbier de Meynard, ed., Dictionnaire géographique, historique et littéraire de la Perse, extrait du Mo'djem el-Bouldan de Yakout, Paris, 1861; F. Sarre, Denkmäler persischer Baukunst, 2 vols., Berlin, 1901–10; G. Le Strange, The Lands of the Eastern Caliphate, Cambridge, 1905; F. Sarre, Seldschukische Kleinkunst, Leipzig, 1909; M. van Berchem, E. de l'Islam, I, Paris, Leiden, 1913, pp. 429–31, s.v. Architecture; J. Laurent, Byzance et les Seljoucides, Nancy, 1913; E. Diez, Khurasanische Baudenkmäler, Berlin, 1918; G. Migeon, Les arts du tissu, Paris, 1929; A. T. Wilson, A Bibliography of Persia, Oxford, 1930; R. M. Riefstahl, Turkish Architecture in South Western Anatolia, Cambridge, 1931; A. Godard, Les monuments de Maragha, Paris, 1934; A. Gabriel, Le Masdjid-i-Djum'a d'Isfahan, Ars Islamica, II, 1935, pp. 7–44; H. C. Hollis, A Unique Seljūk Bronze, Ars Islamica, II, 1935, pp. 231–35; J. H. Schmidt, Persische Seidenstoffe der Seldjūkenzeit, Ars Islamica, II, 1935, pp. 84–90; A. Godard, Abarkuh, Āthār-e Īrān, I, 1936, pp. 47–72; A. Godard, Notes complementaires sur les tombeaux de Marāghe, Āthār-e Īrān, I, 1936, pp. 125–60; A. Godard, Les tours de Ladjim et de Resget, Āthār-e Īrān, I, 1936, pp. 109–21; Ḥudūd al-'Alām, The Regions of the World: A Persian Geography, 372 A.H. (982 A.D., ed. V. Minorsky), London, 1937; E. Diez, Islamic Architecture: Principles and Types, SPA, II, pp. 916–29; S. Flury, Calligraphy: Ornamental Kūfic Inscriptions on Pottery, SPA, II, pp. 1743–70; V. A. Kratohkovskaya, Calligraphy: Ornamental Nashkī Inscriptions, SPA, II, pp. 1770–85; A. U. Pope, Ceramic Art of Islamic Times: The History, SPA, II, pp. 1446–1666; E. Schroeder, Islamic Architecture: Seljūq Period, SPA, II, pp. 981–1045; E. Schroeder, Islamic Architecture: Standing Monuments of the First Period, SPA, II, pp. 916–30; P. Ackerman, Bone and Ivory Carving, SPA, III, pp. 2659–64; P. Ackerman, Textiles of the Islamic Period, SPA, III, pp. 1995–2162; R. Harari, Metalwork after the Early Islamic Period, SPA, III, pp. 2466–2529; U. Monneret de Villard, The Relation of Manichean Art to Iranian Art, SPA, III, pp. 1820–29; A. U. Pope and P. Ackerman, A Survey of Persian Ornament: The Seljūq Period, SPA, III, pp. 2726–38; G. Wiet, La valeur décorative de l'alphabet arabe, Arts et métiers graphiques, Paris, 1949, pp. 9–14; A. Godard, L'origine de la madrasa, de la mosquée et du caravansérail à quatre īwāns, Ars Islamica, XV, 1951, pp. 1–9; J. Sauvaget, Une représentation de la citadelle seljouqide de Merv, Ars Islamica, XV, 1951, pp. 128–30; B. Farès, Essai sur l'esprit de la décoration islamique, Cairo, 1952; D. Barrett, Islamic Art of Persia, in A. J. Arberry, ed., The Legacy of Persia, Oxford, 1953, pp. 116–48; H. Goetz, Persia and India after the Conquest of Mahmūd, in A. J. Arberry, ed., The Legacy of Persia, Oxford, 1953, pp. 89–116; U. Monneret de Villard, L'arte iranica, Verona, 1954; A. Lane, Victoria and Albert Museum: Turkish Pottery, London, 1955; M. Bussagli, L'arte iranica, Milan, 1956 (cat.); V. Mnorsky, Iran islamico, Le civiltà dell'Oriente, I, Rome, 1956, pp. 459–515; E. Rossi, I Turchi, La civiltà dell'Oriente, I, Rome, 1956, pp. 515–83; F. Gabrieli, Gli Arabi, Florence, 1957; A. Lane, Victoria and Albert Museum: Mediaeval Near Eastern Pottery, London, 1957; W. Barthold, Turkestan down to the Mongol Invasion, 2d ed., London, 1958; A. Lane, Early Islamic Pottery, 4th ed., London, 1958; K. Otto Dorn, Seldschukische Holzsäulen-moscheen in Kleinasien, Aus der Welt des islamischen Kunst: Festschrift für E. Kühnel, Berlin, 1959, pp. 59–88; B. Ünsal, Turkish Islamic Architecture in Seljuk and Ottoman Times, 1071–1923, London, 1959; B. Gray, Persian Painting, Geneva, 1961; Tamara Talbot Rice, The Seljuks in Asia Minor, London, New York, 1961; A. Godard, L'art de l'Iran, Paris, 1962; U. Monneret de Villard, Arte cristiana e musulmana del vicino Oriente, Le civiltà dell'Oriente, IV, Rome, 1962, pp. 453–655; D. Hill and O. Grabar, Islamic Architecture and its Decoration (800–1500), London, 1965; W. Lillys, R. Reiff, and E. Esin, Oriental Miniatures, London, 1965; David Talbot Rice, Islamic Art, London, 1965.

Margherita ALOSI CATELLI

Illustrations: PLS. 541–553; 6 figs. in text.

SERLIO, SEBASTIANO. Italian architect and theorist (b. Bologna, Sept. 6, 1475; d. Fontainebleau, 1554 or, less probably, 1555). Serlio began his career as a perspective painter (see PERSPECTIVISTS), and it was his interest in perspective that led him to study under Baldassare Peruzzi in Rome. Although Peruzzi was the younger, Serlio seems to have remained under his guidance from about 1514 until the Sack of Rome in 1527, when Serlio fled to Venice. Peruzzi later bequeathed his own drawings and probably some by Bramante to Serlio, who acknowledged their importance in his treatise.

By Apr. 1, 1528, Serlio was in Venice. He worked in the Veneto for at least nine years, but no buildings by him survive from this period. It was not until 1537, when he was over sixty, that Serlio emerged as a major figure with the publication of a prospectus for a treatise on architecture in seven books, the fourth of which was published simultaneously under the title *Regole generali di architet(t)ura*. Book IV was soon reprinted and even translated as though it were a complete work; a Flemish translation (Antwerp, 1539) appeared before the publication of Book III (Venice, 1540). Book III is especially important because it deals with the antiquities of Rome and includes information about works by Bramante and Peruzzi (qq.v.) found in no other source.

Serlio dedicated Book III to the French king, Francis I, who invited him to France in 1541 and on December 27 of the same year appointed him Painter and Architect in Ordinary. Serlio spent the rest of his life in France, although he fell somewhat out of favor after the death of Francis I in 1547. Books I and II, on geometry and perspective (see III, PL. 204), were published together in France in 1545, followed in 1547 by Book V, on churches. In 1551 a book on elaborate doorways, reflecting the exuberance of northern taste, was published as a *Libro Extraordinario*. This is not part of the original treatise, although it has often been confused with Book VI, which exists in manuscript in the Staatsbibliothek, Munich, and at Columbia University, New York, and deals with types of houses. Serlio's Book VII was published posthumously in Frankfurt in 1575. Yet another manuscript, for a projected eighth book, is also in Munich.

All through the 16th and 17th centuries there appeared reprints (e.g., complete ed., Venice, 1566, 1584) and translations in most European languages, including an English version of 1611, so that Serlio's treatise exerted incalculable influence. The immense popularity of the treatise arose from the fact that it was the first practical handbook on architecture, as distinct from the editions of Vitruvius or Alberti's *De re aedificatoria*, which was in effect a modern version of Vitruvius. Serlio seems to have invented the illustrated handbook, since he realized that the best means of conveying information to patron, amateur, or master craftsman is by a clear diagram with a short explanatory text, rather than by a long disquisition without illustrations. In Book IV, for example, his woodcuts and text reduce the classical orders, which are the basis of all Renaissance architecture, to a series of easily copied schemata. Later treatises by Vignola or Palladio (qq.v.) are more scholarly and give more accurate details, but the very simplicity of Serlio appealed to English, French, and Flemish master masons. At the same time, the *Libro Extraordinario* shows how Serlio's own tastes were modified by contact with the less refined forms that were current in France.

During his years in France, Serlio seems to have been active mainly as a theorist. However, two surviving works are associated with him: a doorway from the no-longer-extant house of the Cardinal of Ferrara in Place Général-de-Gaulle in Fontainebleau and the château at Ancy-le-Franc in Burgundy. Serlio's original designs for the château were altered during construction and later, but it was probably he who replaced the Italian flat roof with the high-pitched roof that served as a model for later French châteaux.

BIBLIOG. G. C. Argan, Sebastiano Serlio, L'Arte, N.S., III, 1932, pp. 183–99; W. B. Dinsmoor, The Literary Remains of Sebastiano Serlio, AB, XXIV, 1942, pp. 55–91, 115–54; A. F. Blunt, Art and Architecture in France, 1500–1700, Harmondsworth, 1954, pp. 44–50; Schlosser, pp. 406–09, 418–20; S. Serlio, Tutte l'opere d'architettura e prospettiva (facsimile of 1619 ed.), Ridgewood, N. J., 1964.

Peter MURRAY

SESSHŪ. Japanese painter (1420–1506), the greatest master of ink painting (*suiboku*) in the history of Japanese art (q.v.). The events of the early years of Sesshū's life are still uncertain, but it is generally accepted that he was born in Akahama in the province of Bitchū (mod. Okayama prefecture), probably into the Oda family. If, as seems likely, he was taken about 1430 to the Shōkokuji in Kyoto, he must have studied at that monastery with Shunrin Shūtō, a famous Zen master, and with Shūbun, the first important Japanese painter of monochrome landscapes, both of whom lived there at the time. Sesshū is believed to have moved to the province of Suō (mod. Yamaguchi prefecture) before the year 1464, since in that year a distinguished Zen monk who was a good friend of his is known to have visited his atelier there, which was called Unkoku-an. He was then known as Unkoku Tōyō, and his works of this period are signed Tōyō.

About 1466 the artist acquired a work of calligraphy by a famous Zen monk of the Yüan dynasty that included two characters reading "Sesshū"; he adopted and thenceforth used this as his name. Later he was often called Sesshū Tōyō.

In 1467, as a member of the trade mission to China organized by his patrons, the Ōuchi family, Sesshū set forth for China, at that time ruled by the Ming dynasty; he arrived there in 1468. (From the same year dates the first appearance of the signature Sesshū.) He landed at Ningpo (mod. Ninghsien), where he was given an honorary title in the monastery of T'ien-t'ung-shan (Sino-Jap., Tendōzan). As yet conjectural are a trip he may have taken during that year through the province of Shantung to Peking and his supposed study of painting under Li Tsai and Chang Yu-shêng, both Chinese painters of the time. He must have seen the works of Ma Yüan and Hsia Kuei (qq.v.) and been struck by the natural beauties of China, which he considered his true source of inspiration. In any case, he formed so individual a style and acquired such skill that his name probably reached the emperor, for there is evidence that he was commissioned to execute mural paintings in the ceremonial hall of the Imperial Palace in Peking.

Sesshū is believed to have left Peking in February, 1469, and to have sailed from Ningpo in June of that year for Japan, where he once more took up residence in Yamaguchi. Before 1476 he moved to the province of Bungo (Oita prefecture), where he built a studio, Tenkai Zuga-rō ("Heaven-created Painting Pavilion"); after that date he traveled for a period. In 1486 he is known to have returned to Yamaguchi. Whether in fact he later moved, as some scholars hold, to the province of Iwami (mod. Shimane prefecture) and finally to the Temple of Taikian, near the town of Iwami-Masuda (Yamaguchi prefecture), is not clear. The place of his death is uncertain (as is the site of his burial, a number of temples claiming the honor).

Sesshū's fame in his own time and the influence his work exerted on contemporaneous and subsequent painting were extraordinary, and he may without hesitation be called the greatest Japanese painter as well as the foremost exponent of *sumi-e*, or *suiboku-ga* (painting in India ink). Technically his works are distinguished by a heavy line and strong contrasts in chiaroscuro, and they are invested with a detached and serene love of nature. His style is completely different from that of the *sansui* (landscape) painting in vogue during the Muromachi period. In fact, while most of the *sumi* (*suiboku*) painters imitated the style brought from China, Sesshū, who had evolved his style in China through the direct observation of nature, was inspired to create something new and original that defied imitation.

A large body of works is associated with the name of Sesshū, but the attribution of many of them is still doubtful. Conspicuous among his authenticated works for stylistic perfection are the *Four Seasons Landscape* in the National Museum in Tokyo; the "long scroll" landscape in the Mōri Collection (Yamaguchi prefecture); the "short scroll" landscape in the Asano Collection (Odawara); the *Ama-no-Hashidate* in the National Museum in Kyoto (formerly in the Yamanouchi Coll.; PL. 556); the *haboku sansui* (landscape in ink-splash technique) in the National Museum in Tokyo; the *Autumn Landscape* (PL. 555) and the *Winter Landscape* (VIII, PL. 307) in the same museum, which originally formed part of a Four Seasons series; the bird and flower screens in the Kosaka Collection (Tokyo); the Ishibashi *Four Seasons Landscape* in Tokyo; and the portrait of Masuda Kanetaka in the Masuda Collection (Tokyo).

The most famous of these is the landscape in the Mōri Collection, known as the *sansui chōkan* (long scroll landscape) to distinguish it from the *sansui shōkan* (short scroll landscape) in the Asano Collection. The work, which is almost 50 ft. long, depicts the changing seasons, moving along (right to left) from a spring to a winter scene. Probably dating from the year 1486, when the artist was past the age of sixty-five, it affords a true measure of his genius. Although painted after the Chinese manner, it is completely in his own personal style, free of any taint of imitation; it is striking in the vigor and confidence of the brushwork and the variety of the composition. The lines are often heavy and angular and the forms, especially in the case of the buildings, highly abstract.

A work in which these characteristics are even more fully apparent is the above-mentioned *Winter Landscape*. Strong, vigorous strokes outline the shapes of trees and rocks, and the bare branches stand out with extraordinary boldness. These dense, expressive contours — now dark, now light, now fine, now heavy — are offset by the open areas of the sky and the hills on the left, which seem virtually bare. The tiny structure visible in the middle ground of the painting is rendered by a few essential lines, and in the foreground a human figure can be discerned ascending a flight of steps that disappears behind the hills. In the flattening of three-dimensional space and the emphasis on angular linear patterns Sesshū here shows himself to be far removed from the style of his first teacher, Shūbun, who emulated the misty, mysterious depths of Chinese painting.

A completely different aspect of Sesshū's genius is revealed by the *haboku sansui* in the National Museum in Tokyo. Painted in 1495, near the end of the artist's life, as a tribute to his pupil Sōen, it, unlike the landscape scroll in the Mōri Collection, is highly abstract; it brings to mind the style of the Chinese painter Ying Yü-chien of the Southern Sung dynasty. The technique employed — dark ink splashed over light, still-wet ink, creating a soft, fused effect (cf. PL. 554) — is that prescribed by the principles of Zen doctrine, according to which, revelation (*satori*) is as sudden as a flash of lightning; this is what Sesshū tried to convey. The work is so abstract that at first glance all that seems perceptible is ink spots splashed on a sheet of paper; closer scrutiny reveals the presence of a rocky mountain with shrubs and trees, a small building, and the delicate outline of a boat with minute human figures. Much of the surface area was intentionally left empty because only thus could the artist bring about a harmonious relation between the gray and the heavy black splashes of ink and the pure white: from this sparseness the picture gains in expressive power.

All Sesshū's paintings bear the mark of his love of nature, the strength of which enabled him to seize upon its inner essence. The trait is perhaps nowhere better shown than in the *kakemono* (vertical scroll) depicting Ama-no-Hashidate, a site not far from Tokyo, traditionally esteemed as affording one of the three most beautiful panoramic views in Japan (PL. 556). This is not merely a painting of an idealized landscape in the Chinese style; it is the artistic rendering of an actual scene along the coast of the Sea of Japan. The prospect is of a deep inlet: from one side a sandy point of land extends into the center of the picture, almost meeting a rocky promontory jutting out from the other side; in the distance there rises, from a wooded shore dotted with houses, a chain of mountains studded with Buddhist monasteries and Shinto shrines.

Sesshū drew upon a vast repertory of themes; portraiture, too, found effective expression through his brush. Particularly noteworthy is the above-mentioned portrait of Masuda Kanetaka, painted in 1479, in which the artist shows his dexterity in the traditional style of Japanese painting (see TOSA SCHOOL). On the other hand, the bird and flower screens in the Kosaka Collection are examples of a less traditional type; since they are known to have been painted about 1483, they are useful in establishing the chronology of this genre.

Undoubtedly one of Sesshū's greatest works is the *Daruma and Hui-K'o* (also known as the *Eka-dampi-zu*), preserved in the Sainenji (Aichi prefecture). In this painting Sesshū, working at the end of the 15th century (1496), made use in a fresh manner of the heavy line that had figured so largely in the style of the Buddhist artist Chōdensu (1352–1431), infusing new life into an old tradition.

Sesshū's genius as an artist, manifest in the chaste composition, the warm shades of black, and the genuinely intuitive appreciation of nature, freed *suiboku-ga* from the conventional and idealized forms of Chinese ink painting of the Sung and Yüan periods, creating a style of painting closer to the spirit of Japan and purely Japanese in its premises and objectives.

BIBLIOG. A. Morrison, The Painters of Japan, 2 vols., London, 1911; R. Fukui, Nihon suiboku-ga no genryū (Collection of Japanese Suiboku Paintings), Onshi Kyoto Hakubutsukan Kōen Shū, Kyoto, 1930; J. C. Covell, Under the Seal of Sesshū, New York, 1941; Pageant of Japanese Art, II, 2, Tokyo, 1952; Shin'ichi Tani and Seiroku Noma, Nippon bijutsu jiten (Dictionary of Japanese Art), Tokyo, 1952; H. P. Stern, New Sesshū Screens at the Freer Gallery, O. Art, N.S., I, 1955, pp. 54–56; N. Kumagai et al., A Survey of Studies on Sesshū, Museum (Tokyo), LXII, 1956, pp. 2–32; M. Takaaki, Sesshū: His Life and Art, Japan Q., III, 1956, pp. 460–67; E. Grilli, Sesshū Toyo (1420–1506), Tokyo, Rutland, Vt., 1957; S. Hasumi, Sesshū, Tokyo, 1958; I. Kondo and S. Noma, Masterpieces of Sesshū, Tokyo, 1958; N. Kumagai, Sesshū, Tokyo, 1958 (Jap. text, Eng. captions); R. Chiba, ed., Sesshū's Long Scroll: A Zen Landscape Journey, Tokyo, Rutland, Vt., 1959; S. Hasumi, The Study of Sesshū Tōyō, Tokyo, 1961 (Jap. text, Eng. summary).

Antonio PRIORI

Illustrations: PLS. 554–556.

SEURAT, GEORGES PIERRE. French painter, one of the major postimpressionists and leader of the neoimpressionist group. He was born in Paris on Dec. 2, 1859, the youngest child of Ernestine Faîvre and Antoine Seurat. Seurat's father, a bailiff, was a singular personality who was seldom at home and, because his brother and sister were much older, the young artist lived alone with his mother throughout most of his short life. In 1875 he entered the small municipal school of the sculptor Justin Lequien, and from about March, 1878, until November, 1879, he studied at the Ecole des Beaux-Arts, in the class of Henri Lehmann, a mediocre disciple of Ingres. He applied a remarkably precocious talent to the study of antique sculpture, Renaissance masters, and the drawings of Ingres, and at the same time he displayed a penetrating naturalism reminiscent of Holbein in his drawings from life. During a year's military service in Brest (from November, 1879, until November, 1880) he turned from traditional subjects toward naturalistic themes and after his return to Paris rapidly developed his mature drawing style. By 1882 he was master of the rich, velvety compositions in Conté crayon, whose unique qualities alone would have guaranteed him lasting fame.

Although Seurat matured first in drawing, he devoted himself equally to painting. Fascinated by scientific color theory from early youth, he had read by 1881 treatises on optical science by Chevreul, Helmholtz, and Rood and had studied the writings and paintings of Delacroix. In more than 80 paintings completed before his first major canvas, *Une Baignade, Asnières* (1883–84; VII, PLS. 436, 437), he explored landscape, first in the Barbizon tradition and then, by late 1882, in a mode closer to that of contemporary impressionism (q.v.). Seurat exhibited publicly in 1883, when the official Salon accepted his drawing *Aman-Jean*, but it was only in the spring of 1884, when *Une Baignade* became one of the chief attractions of the Groupe des Artistes Indépendants, that he drew some general notice. There he met Paul Signac (q.v.), and with Odilon Redon and others they founded the long-lived Société des Artistes Indépendants, which held its first exhibition in the fall of 1884. Also, neoimpressionism was born of the exchange of ideas between Seurat and Signac. Camille Pissarro, already a major impressionist, joined the younger artists late in 1885 and insisted upon their inclusion in the eighth and last impressionist exhibition in May, 1886. Seurat's *Sunday Afternoon on the Island of La Grande Jatte* (PL. 557; studies, IV, PL. 280; V, PL. 115; VII, PL. 440), the most discussed painting of the exhibition, brought him national prominence. Its regular, dotlike brush stroke was greeted as a scientific rationalization of impressionist technique and its stately geometry as a willful, classicizing paradigm of a favorite impressionist subject. The younger symbolist critics and poets, particularly Félix Fénéon, Gustave Kahn, Emile Verhaeren, and Paul Adam, rallied around Seurat and Signac. By the time of the exhibition of the Indépendants in the fall of 1886, the two young painters had been joined by other artists who took their lead to establish the neoimpressionist group, which dominated the Indépendants until well after Seurat's death. While Seurat, Signac, and the elder Pissarro (who later abandoned neoimpressionism) drew the most attention, other members of the group such as Henri-Edmond Cross, Charles Angrand, Lucien Pissarro, Maximilien Luce, and Albert Dubois-Pillet exhibited together and benefited from the friendly articles of the symbolist press, which made neoimpressionism the major radical movement between 1886 and 1890.

Seurat became known outside Paris through the articles of the symbolists and through exhibitions, especially in Brussels. The progressive Society of the Twenty, which included James Ensor and Félicien Rops, invited Seurat to their exhibitions in the spring of 1887, and with the inclusion of Théo van Rysselberghe, Alfred William Finch, Henri van de Velde, Anna Boch, and Georges Lemmen, Brussels soon became an important second center of neoimpressionism. So powerful was Seurat's artistic temperament and so indefatigable were Signac's proselytizing efforts that hardly a major artist escaped their influence. Gauguin, Van Gogh, and Toulouse-Lautrec, for example, each went through a neoimpressionist phase.

The pattern of Seurat's short career was established by 1886. His winters in Paris were devoted to drawing, which he considered as important as painting, and to the execution of a major mural-scale canvas. He spent most of his summers on the Channel coast, bringing back for completion in Paris a number of seascapes and seaport views, such as those of Grandcamp (1885), Honfleur (1886), Port-en-Bessin (1888), Crotoy (1889), and Gravelines (1890; IX, PL. 24). With Signac he frequented Parisian literary circles and also knew Charles Henry, a brilliant young esthetician whose quasi-scientific writings influenced both artists. Seurat was much taken by Henry's theories of the emotional character of linear directions and incorporated them into his later work. Contributing annually to the Indépendants exhibitions, he also maintained close contact with the symbolists, although his indrawn nature kept his Montmartre studio and his private life in relative secrecy. Then, causing shock to his friends, the apparently robust artist, just over thirty-one years old, died suddenly on Mar. 29, 1891, after a brief illness involving infectious angina. Only his death exposed his liaison with Madeleine Knobloch, the subject of his only large portrait, *Jeune Femme se Poudrant*. Two weeks later their thirteen-month-old son died of the same illness, and soon after the mother miscarried a second child. She went to Brussels in the same year and subsequently disappeared.

Given his short career, Seurat's output as a painter was prolific — 7 large and about 60 small canvases, as well as approximately 160 tiny wood panels. Mid-century naturalism was the source of his early style, both his palette and his subjects (e.g., *Casseurs de Pierre, Le Raincy*) reflecting the work of Millet and Corot (qq.v.). By 1883 his concern for color theory, united with a growing awareness of impressionist painting, led to a brighter palette in paintings celebrating industrial and picnic themes of the suburbs. *Une Baignade, Asnières*, completed in 1884, combines an impressionist theme with a geometric idealization reminiscent of Puvis de Chavannes. *La Grande Jatte*, finished two years later, is the first complete statement of neo-impressionism. Its precise brushwork and intense palette canonized the theory of "mélange optique," by which pure color-light is broken down to its constituent hues. Equally remarked at the time were the work's "primitive" qualities, its hieratic geometry (which was likened to Egyptian, Greek, Quattrocento, and even popular art, and which was in fact an outgrowth of Seurat's strong interest in all those styles) and its denial of the impressionists' concentration upon the hedonistic, fleeting moment. *La Grande Jatte*, however, was the last major effort of his early mature style. Thereafter he moved rapidly toward a linear-arabesque style, with more sprightly rhythms and a radical flatness. *Les Poseuses*, executed in 1887–88, was a deliberate modernization of a traditional theme (cf. study, PL. 558), and *La Parade* (PL. 560), of the same date, marked his exploration of the theories of Charles Henry, its horizontal and downward-moving lines and its somber tones embodying a mood of calmness and melancholy. His last major canvases, *Le Chahut* (PL. 560) and *The Circus* (PL. 559; unfinished at his death), are far removed from the stately grandeur of *La Grande Jatte*. There bouncing rhythms and a tendency toward caricature, manifestations of his fondness for the poster artist Jules Chéret, reflect the *fin-de-siècle* spirit of the 1890s.

Although in his lifetime Seurat was known exclusively for his painting, he is equally important for his drawings, which rank with the greatest in the French tradition. The author of about 485 known drawings, he achieved astonishing maturity in black and white by 1882. Molding his shadowy forms by rubbing a heavy-textured paper with the end of a Conté crayon, Seurat produced an impressive number of drawings, ranging from the classicizing *Le Nœud Noir* or *Au Concert Européen* (PL. 560) to the less well-known but equally numerous compositions of romantic and moody character such as *Paysans* (*Men before a Factory*) or *Le Pont-Levis* (*The Drawbridge*). His "tenebreuse" style was formed from a deep appreciation of Rembrandt, Goya, Millet, and Daumier. The works of the latter two also influenced his subject matter, for his early drawings often depict humble peasants at work and the urban poor. After 1886 his contact with the impressionists, especially Degas, helped to turn him toward *café-concerts* and sidewalk fairs.

Of nearly equal importance are his many landscapes, which are more varied but generally exhibit the same evolution. Among the finest are *Le Bec du Hoc, Grandcamp*; *The Asylum and the Lighthouse, Honfleur*; *Port-en-Bessin, un Dimanche*; and *The Channel at Gravelines, Evening*. Seldom showing people and eschewing the familiar scenes of traditional interest to tourists, these splendid seaport paintings breathe a highly personal air of penetrating melancholy.

The rich variety of Seurat's work is dominated by a rational, organizing mind. Unlike Monet he was not willing to rely almost exclusively on sensory perception and the immediate; instead, he stressed strong, often geometric surface patterns that embodied his concern for the permanent and the rationally known. Like Cézanne he pondered every stroke of crayon or brush, and in his works sensations are felt to be the point of departure for a highly conceptual art. His faith in rationalism and science reflects his desire to eliminate the accidental and the transitory, to express what he believed were universal laws of nature underlying mere appearances. Yet one has only to meditate before his moody twilight drawings, with their scumbled lines and Goyaesque intensity, to realize that a profound passion underlay his apparently calm exterior. Because of this deep-rooted creative ardor Seurat represents to the 20th century the spirit of Piero della Francesca, Raphael, and Poussin. "In Seurat," wrote Amédée Ozenfant, "we admire the perennial dryness of the great French tradition, that lucidity and polish of truly great things, that finely grained skin which imbues the rich underlying tissues." And his friend Gustave Kahn said of Seurat's art: "To transcribe in this way is to penetrate to the heart of meditation, to celebrate the cult of beauty and expression, to tremble with a suffocating emotion before reality and its power, to enjoy an almost total communion with the most intense sense of life."

SELECTED WORKS LIST. *Drawings: Le Marchand d'Oranges*, 1881 (Louvre). – *Le Labourage*, 1881 (Louvre). – *Le Pont-Levis*, 1882–84 (New York, Mr. and Mrs. S. Simon). – *Paysans*, 1882–83 (Louvre). – *La Mère de l'Artiste*, 1882–83 (New York, Met. Mus.). – *Le Nœud Noir*, 1882–83 (Paris, private coll.). – *Bords de Rivière*, 1883–86 (Winterthur, private coll.). – *Au Concert Européen*, 1886–87 (New York, Mus. of Mod. Art). – *A l'Eden-Concert*, 1887–88 (Laren, Netherlands, V. W. van Gogh Coll.). – *Paul Signac*, 1890 (Paris, private coll.). – *Deux Voiles*, 1890 (Paris, Mme J. Follain-Dinès).

Paintings: Casseurs de Pierre, Le Raincy, 1880–81 (Paris, private coll.). – *Maison dans les Arbres*, 1881 (Glasgow, Art Gall. and Mus.). – *Les Pêcheurs à la Ligne*, 1883 (Troyes, France, P. Lévy). – *Une Baignade, Asnières*, 1883–84 (London, Nat. Gall.). – *A Sunday Afternoon on the Island of La Grande Jatte*, 1884–86 (Chicago, Art. Inst.). – *Le Bec du Hoc, Grandcamp*, 1885 (London, Tate Gall.). – *The Bridge at Courbevoie*, 1886 (London, Courtauld Inst. Gall.). – *The Asylum and the Lighthouse, Honfleur*, 1886 (London, C. Beatty). – *Les Poseuses*, 1887–88 (Merion, Pa., Barnes Foundation). – *La Parade*, 1887–88 (New York, Met. Mus.). – *Port-en-Bessin, un Dimanche*, 1888 (Otterlo, Netherlands, Rijksmus. Kröller-Müller; other works depicting Port-en-Bessin in Minneapolis, Inst. of Arts, and St. Louis, City Art Mus.). – *Le Crotoy, Amont*, 1889 (R. H. Tannahill Coll.). – *Le Chahut*, 1889–90 (Otterlo, Rijksmus. Kröller-Müller). – *Jeune Femme se Poudrant*, 1889–90 (London, Tate Gall.). – *The Channel at Gravelines, Evening*, 1890 (New York, Mus. of Mod. Art). – *Le Cirque*, 1890–91 (Louvre).

BIBLIOG. J. Christophe, Georges Seurat, Les hommes d'aujourd'hui, VIII, 368, 1890; A. Alexandre et al., Georges Seurat, Brussels, ca. 1895; L. Cousturier, Seurat, Paris, 1921 (2d ed., 1926); W. Pach, Georges Seurat, New York, 1923; G. Coquiot, Seurat, Paris, 1924; E. Verhaeren, Sensations, Paris, 1927, pp. 195–203; G. Kahn, ed., Les dessins de Georges Seurat, 2 vols., Paris, 1928; D. C. Rich, Seurat and the Evolution of "La Grande Jatte," Chicago, 1935; R. Goldwater, Some Aspects of the Development of Seurat's Style, AB, XXIII, 1941, pp. 111–30; J. Rewald, Seurat, New York, 1943; F. Fénéon, Oeuvres, Paris, 1948; J. Rewald, Post-Impressionism from Van Gogh to Gauguin, New York, 1956; R. L. Herbert, Seurat in Chicago and New York, BM, C, 1958, pp. 146–53; H. Dorra and J. Rewald, Seurat, Paris, 1960 (bibliog.); C. M. de Hauke, Seurat et son œuvre, 2 vols., Paris, 1961; R. L. Herbert, ed., Seurat's Drawings, New York, 1963.

Robert L. HERBERT

Illustrations: PLS. 557–560.

SEVERINI, Gino. Modern Italian painter, one of the founders of futurism (b. Cortona, Apr. 7, 1883; d. Paris, Feb. 26, 1966). Late in 1899 Severini went to Rome, where he studied art informally while working at odd jobs. He met Umberto Boccioni (q.v.) in 1901 at the studio of Giacomo Balla (q.v.), with whom they both studied. After he moved to Paris in 1906 he pursued his way independently until, in 1910, he signed the two manifestoes of futurism (see CUBISM AND FUTURISM). For several years he was one of its major figures, especially important as the only futurist painter living in Paris. During World War I he began to move away from futurism, and by the early 1920s he had developed a classicizing style that was close in spirit to the contemporary work of Picasso, Gris, and the French Purists. He executed many major commissions, including frescoes in the churches of Semsales and La Roche in Switzerland (1926–27) and mosaics in the Palace of Art and the Palace of Justice in Milan (1933, 1939). He won important prizes at the Rome Quadriennale in 1935 and the Venice Biennale in 1950. Paris became his home in 1906, although he frequently visited Italy. His major paintings include *Le Bal Tabarin*, 1912 (New York, Mus. of Mod. Art); *14 July 1913* (Rome, Coll. N. Franchina); *Armored Train*, 1915 (New York, Mrs. C. J. Liebman Coll.); Composition *La*, 1917 (Milan, Coll. R. Jucker); *Still Life with Bread*, 1923 (Milan, Coll. F. Schettini); and *Rhythm of a Dancer*, 1953 (Milan, Coll. F. Schettini). Despite his return to the classical tradition after World War I and his subsequent change to an abstract manner reminiscent of futurism and cubism, Severini is still best known for his early futurist work. The major intermediary between his Italian colleagues and Parisian cubism, Severini created a personal idiom, less strident and polemic than that of his fellow futurists, more concerned with colors of luminous intensity controlled by a more sedate geometry.

WRITINGS. Du cubisme au classicisme, Paris, 1921; The Artist and Society, ed. B. Wall, London, 1946; Tutta la vita di un pittore, Cernusco sul Naviglio, Italy, 1946.

BIBLIOG. P. Courthion, Gino Severini, Milan, 1930; J. Maritain, Severini, Paris, 1930; J. Lassaigne, Les dessins de Severini, Paris, 1947; J. T. Soby and A. H. Barr, Jr., Twentieth-Century Italian Art, New York, 1949; G. Ballo, Modern Italian Painting, New York, 1956.

Robert L. HERBERT

SEX AND EROTICA. Sexual drive and imagination have always had a profound and direct connection with the arts. It can even be said that poetry and literature are universally inspired by the theme of love and provide the most suitable means of expression for narrating its "stories" and analyzing its emotions (dwelling chiefly, that is, on its psychological, idealistic, and social aspects), whereas the world of images represents the more sensual manifestations of love or alludes to them through sexual symbols. The significance of this sexual inspiration in artistic iconography transcends its original, and frequently intimate, connection with religious, mythological, and magical elements (see MYTH AND FABLE; MAGIC). It also transcends the conscious or unconscious psychological attitudes and impulses (see PSYCHOLOGY OF ART) and the descriptive or satirical representation of the customs of specific periods and civilizations (see COMIC ART AND CARICATURE; GENRE AND SECULAR SUBJECTS). Indeed, this inspiration has produced a thematic repertory of such variety that it merits special consideration. At the same time, however, it is obvious that one must take into consideration the mental and cultural levels of the various societies that have left works illustrating their concept of sex.

This article attempts to show that, at least in principle, there are two aspects of sexual representation. On the one hand there is the representation, the sphere of primitive naturalistic concepts, of sexual motifs connected with magicoreligious practices and beliefs or with speculations derived from them; in this sphere symbolism plays a large part (see SYMBOLISM AND ALLEGORY). On the other hand there are the phenomena of erotic indulgence that are of a more secular nature and char-

acterize more evolved and complex civilizations. The first aspect, appearing in the most remote regions of cultural experience, is found in many of the figural manifestations of antiquity and the Asiatic East, as well as in the folk art of the European world. Secular eroticism tended to establish itself in the sophisticated areas of Hellenism, modern Europe, and China. Obviously, it is difficult to make a clear distinction between the two forms of inspiration in the history of these iconographic traditions.

SUMMARY. Sexuality and art (col. 888). Sexual symbolism in prehistoric and primitive art (col. 889). Antiquity (col. 899): *Sexual art as an expression of the sacred; Erotic art.* The Christian West (col. 906): *Sexual motifs in medieval Europe; Erotic and "gallant" art in the modern world.* The East (col. 911): *Islam; India; China; Japan; Southeast Asia.*

SEXUALITY AND ART. Among the many theories advanced to explain the cause or causes of historical events and of political, social, and artistic revolutions, there is one (Klimkowsky, 1956) that considers the driving force of the great machine of history to be nothing more or less than the struggle between the masculine and feminine elements within the individual. Even the language of common sense speaks of "effeminate" or "manly" peoples, customs, and works, of "iron ages," of the century that knew the *douceur de vivre*, and uses similar expressions that show how instinctive this point of view is. But although the theory appears simple, it conceals several complications. The attempt to give it a scientific basis and to apply it to a multitude of individual facts destroys whatever was metaphorical and vaguely admissible in the judgment of common sense and may result in the error typical of all generalizations and classifications when they attempt to conform to criteria that will explain every aspect and fact. Admittedly, however, such factors as the form of objects, the elegance of furniture, and the cut of clothing in particular periods of a culture can be revealing. It is not fortuitous, for example, that the period in which women wore dresses leaving the bosom largely exposed was the one that produced the bulging Boulle furniture (VII, PL. 346); nor is it accidental that the feminization of men reached its culmination with the use of the wig, especially the powdered wig of the rococo period.

Others have explained revolutions in style by the theory that the artist springs from the union of an invader and a conquered woman. There is genetic evidence that in many species when a male from a northern environment unites with a female from southern regions there is a determined proportion of intermediate levels ("intergrades") among the offspring. In addition there is anthropological evidence that under particularly severe conditions the differentiation of the sexes by their more elementary and diverse functions is accentuated, while under milder circumstances less extreme sexual types survive.

In the light of this theory it has been maintained that the barbarian invasions infused new life into Western civilization, that the result can be seen in the widespread flowering of Romanesque architecture (see ROMANESQUE ART), and that the generations succeeding the period of crossbreeding between conqueror and conquered produced an intermediate, "artistic" sexual type that invented the Gothic (see GOTHIC ART). In the Romanesque period there seems to have been a prevalence of masculine elements. The arts were centered on architecture (a "masculine" art) and featured abstract tendencies (a "male" characteristic). The ideal woman was adolescent, with undeveloped breasts and slender hips; this suggests that man may have seen woman as an incomplete man. In Gothic art a mildness and softness completely unknown to the Romanesque prevailed. The images of Christ became sweeter, observation of nature was emphasized, and the treatment of decorative details became exquisite. For the first time trees appeared in landscape painting; and man assumed an attitude of chivalrous deference toward woman. Yet at the same time he tried to rebel against the excessive feminine element that he felt in himself. This is apparent from the misogynous satire of Jean de Meung and from the persecution of witches, as well as from similar echoes in philosophy and mysticism. During the Renaissance (q.v.) the excess of heterosexual elements in the two sexes subsided and a balance was reached. Man wanted to be Apollo and Hercules at the same time. The prevailing type of woman was no longer the young maiden but the adult woman. Fashion emphasized sex with the codpiece for men and the corselet to emphasize the abdomen for women (see COSTUME). Parallel phenomena in the history of ancient Greece, China, and other cultures seem to give substance to the law that at the beginning of a cultural period there appears a sexual type with obvious, clearly contrasting masculine and feminine characteristics.

The presence of the sexual element in works of art is frankly admitted by Kenneth Clark (1956, p. 344) when he asks: "Is there, after all, any reason why certain quasi-geometrical shapes should be satisfying except that they are simplified statements of the forms that please us in a woman's body? . . . This un-expected union of sex and geometry is a proof of how deeply the concept of the nude is linked with our most elementary notions of order and design." Today few people are aware that a peculiar psychological disposition in the Greeks was at the origin of the nude, which until recently was one of the corner-stones of Western art. Their penchant for nudity was an ex-pression of their sense of human completeness and thus con-tained an ethical as well as a physical aspect. Their deep awareness of what was implicit in physical beauty also saved them from the two evils of sensuality and estheticism. This inseparability of the physical and the psychological allowed them to give human form to abstract ideas and to create the statues of divinities that have obsessed the Western imagination for centuries. But in assuming new Christian erotic and ethical content, the nude ultimately ceased to be a vehicle for the expression of an idea and was reduced, in neoclassicism, to formally perfect, but too often empty, shells (see HUMAN FIGURE).

If, therefore, sexuality is omnipresent, even though in latent form or in forms sublimated by Greek art, one may ask where lies the point beyond which this inevitable element be-comes eroticism. According to the English philosopher S. Alex-ander, "if the nude is so treated that it raises in the spectator ideas or desires appropriate to the material subject, it is false art, and bad morals" (*Beauty and Other Forms of Value*, London, 1933, p. 127). But who can guarantee that even the least real-istic representations of the nude are not capable of arousing the spectator? Clark confesses that confronted by Matisse's *Blue Nude* (IX, PL. 387) he retreats in embarrassment, and that the *Torso* by Brancusi (q.v.) in Cleveland (Mus. of Art), which is a version of the feminine torso simplified to two low cylinders placed obliquely under a third cylinder, seems to him more disturbingly physical and less decent than the *Aphrodite of Knidos* (III, PL. 374). In opposition to Alexander's opinion, Clark (1956, p. 6) writes: "In the mixture of memories and sensations aroused by the nudes of Rubens or Renoir are many which are 'appropriate to the material subject.' And since these words of a famous philosopher are often quoted, it is necessary to labour the obvious and say that no nude, however abstract, should fail to arouse in the spectator some vestige of erotic feeling, even although it be only the faintest shadow — and if it does not do so, it is bad art and false morals." Current critical opinion tends toward that expressed by the novelist David Stacton (*Segaki*, London, 1958, p. 182), that "great art even when it seems erotic or shows us a nude, is never sexual" ("sexual" here being the equivalent of "pornographic").

Mario PRAZ

SEXUAL SYMBOLISM IN PREHISTORIC AND PRIMITIVE ART. It is well known that sexuality plays an important part in the cultural activities of peoples living outside the Christian West and its colonial territories. Some of the peoples of historical cultures derived from the common matrix of Near Eastern culture, however, as well as the Chinese, the Aztecs, and the Mayas, show little of note in this field. As regards Egyptian culture, an excess of scholarly prudishness seems to have prevented dis-closure of all the facts of the Egyptians' sexual life. Similarly the prejudices of the Spanish discoverers led to the disguising

of many of the sexual customs in Central America, particularly certain so-called "perversions." But the primitive peoples, at least prior to their exposure to missionaries, gave open ex-pression to their sexual instincts and desires in such arts as dancing, miming, drama, sculpture, painting, and drawing. This, however, is far from the pansexuality that J. Winthuis (1928) claimed to have discovered in New Britain, which would have reflected an abnormal mentality. The existence of such a highly involved system of sexual metaphors and symbols as he described (which recent investigations do not altogether confirm) would have to be regarded as an exceptional instance, even though somewhat similar manifestations are known to exist in Australia.

The early psychoanalytical studies of cultures conducted by Sigmund Freud were chiefly limited to Western civilization. In these studies Freud's pupil, Otto Rank, speaks of the dis-sociation — that is, the involution of the sexual instinct — revealed in the art of these cultures. Freud himself (1910) tried to present this regression in an almost tangible way. Although Rank (*Der Künstler*, Vienna, 1907, p. 36) defined art as merely an unsuccessful reproduction of dreams, ethnolo-gists have found only a few examples among primitive peoples to confirm this view.

Equally unreliable for an understanding of the art of prim-itive peoples is an insistence on the polarity — still widely accepted today — resulting from the cosmic and human image transmitted to us by the ancient Orient. The archaic commu-nities of the East, from which all agriculture and, therefore, all cultural systems superior to that of hunting peoples have ra-diated throughout the world, have left a legacy of a persistent and almost neurotic compulsion to consider only the two extremes of a cultural variation. In the ancient East there was a sharp contrast between the city dweller and the non-city dweller, heaven and earth, man and woman, the learned and the ignorant; and the tendency even today is still to see things in terms of good and evil, spirit and matter, and other similar polarities, regardless of the infinite number of intermediate values. Thus the classification of primitive sculpture into pairs of opposites such as ideoplastic and physicoplastic (M. Verworn, *Ideoplastische Kunst*, Jena, 1914, p. 5), imaginative and sensory (Kühn, 1923), or introvert and extrovert (Lem, 1948, to dis-tinguish the Sudanese style from the West African) leads to a denial of the innumerable intermediate forms.

Another question confronting ethnologists is the extent to which sexuality shapes culture (if at all) and particularly art. Basing his argument on an analysis of the sexual customs of the Babylonians, the Moors, the Greeks, and the Anglo-Saxons, Unwin (*Sexual Regulations and Human Behaviour*, 1933) tries to demonstrate that premarital chastity and sexual restraint through monogamy liberate intellectual and social energies and promote cultural development. There is, however, also eth-nological evidence to the contrary, supporting the opposite, popular view that sexual restraint is a sign of lowered vitality or is even a deterrent to cultural creativity. For example, if monogyny stimulates cultural progress, the hunting peoples who lived monogamously would presumably have emerged from their hunting and food-gathering type of culture into that of agriculture; and it was the polygamous Arabs who, in the Middle Ages, were the preservers of the Greek spirit and the natural sciences of antiquity.

The art of primitive peoples can scarcely be set in the con-text of these sociological factors. Any evolution is unmistak-ably a product of historical contact with a more developed culture. The lowest level of artistic development is illustrated by the hunting cultures still in existence, such as those of Tierra del Fuego, the Canadian and eastern Brazilian hunters, the Siriones, the Negritos of South Asia, and the African Pygmies. The Bushmen, who belong to the late Stone Age (and to its first high point in painting), as well as the Australian aborigines (with their neolithic influences and schematic rock paintings) show the same artistic liveliness as that which characterized the Aurignacian and the Gravettian peoples of Eurasia. Sculp-ture, however, is absent from both cultures. The Australian group, which has probably been more disrupted by subsequent cultures, shows the sexual element more clearly, as the Berndts (1951), among others, have demonstrated and as might be expected from the high sexuality of Australian myths and customs; whereas the animal images and hunting scenes in the rock paintings by the Bushman are as prudish as their mythology, the only erotic theme being the bull-eland dance.

The problem of whether the wish for procreation or for sexuality came first cannot be solved by the methods of the prehistorian or the ethnologist. However, it appears certain that purely erotic sexual images are extremely rare among primitive peoples of recent times: there is always a mythicoreligious background, a magicopropitiatory intention (for fertility or potency), or a magicodefensive purpose involved. Purely erotic sexual images, such as those of the pre-Columbian Mochica or Chimu ceramics from Peru (coitus positions and perversion; PL. 562), are completely foreign to the world of those American primitive peoples who had phallephoric dances, erotic and animal dances, phallic amulets, and the like, but only within the framework of magicoreligious rites. Even in the sculptures of copulating couples on village and men's houses, particularly in southeastern Asia and in the islands of the South Pacific — e.g., Melanesia (see MELANESIAN CULTURES) and New Zealand (PL. 562) — the magical intention cannot be disregarded.

In the conditions prevailing in Eurasia during the late Paleolithic era, which is known to have preceded the earliest Neolithic age in the area between the Balkan Peninsula and Iran, between Anatolia and Egypt, or between Jericho and Jarmo, one would expect to find real erotic images, both sculptured and engraved. However, not even these images can be unquestionably interpreted as purely sexual. The famous carving on bone from the cave of Isturitz (Basses-Pyrénées) of the Magdalenian period (R. de Saint-Périer, 1932) is clearly sexual, but there is an immediate magical explanation. On one side is a bison with steaming nostrils, rushing behind another bison, of which only the hindquarters are visible. This second bison has its tail raised and is clearly a female. The only perplexing feature is the two arrows in the body of the male bison. On the other side is an anthropomorph (a man?) behind a supine woman with pendulous breasts, shown as though he were about to approach her. Superficial interpretation readily found a sexual significance here. But the female also has an arrow in one of her thighs, and her back appears to be covered with horse hair or boar bristles. The parallelism of the two pictures is obvious. Scholars who pay greater attention to the arrow sign, which is apparently a magical element, may conclude that there is a curious affinity between the woman and game in hunting cultures, the "good behavior" of the woman being able to assure good hunting. Even pictures of ithyphallic men, of copulation, and the like cannot be compared with such purely sexual images as are found in modern pornographic drawings.

There is another equally interesting form of representation in early human art: sculpture. It is remarkable that, with few exceptions, the model is the female body. The oldest sculptures of the Paleolithic age (VII, PL. 351; IX, PL. 247; XI, PLS. 243, 244, 255, 257), with their accentuation of those parts of the woman's body associated with fertility (buttocks, trunk, breasts), unquestionably belong to hunting cultures. This contradicts the theory that such "realistic" sculpture, with its emphasis on the fertility element, is characteristic of agricultural peoples. It is difficult to establish whether in this sculpture the element of procreation dominates the purely erotic element in the ideal of beauty. The heavy-buttocked and thickset figures show no accentuated pregnancy, and there is no evidence that they were intended to represent a fertility deity. In hunting cultures, the hunt and sexuality are closely related, and it is more likely that the statuettes are connected with a magicosexual relationship between the female and the hunt, which is frequently found in Eurasia. It is possible that opulent women were regarded as favorable to the abundance of game. One should mention in this connection the "Lady of the Beasts" in the Hyperborean region (IV, PL. 217) and the more or less opulent female deities accompanied by animals in the Mediterranean and Oriental world of antiquity.

There is a line of steatopygous female statues from prehistoric Egypt that appears to have spread across northeastern Africa, Usukuma, Kinga, and into South Africa — probably with the penetration of the Khoisan race, who had a vestigial paleolithic culture and whose women, with their pronounced steatopygia, may have represented the ideal of the European Stone Age man. But a later migration of the eastern Mediterranean ideal of the "opulent female" within the framework of the Upper Nile cultures is also possible.

The transition from the concept of the steatopygous female as a magical symbol, an esthetic ideal, or a goddess (of animals, fertility, etc.), which probably originated in the eastern European Gravettian area, to neolithic female sculpture is represented by clay figures such as those found in Susa (PL. 561). There are also the statuettes from the early Tripolje settlement of Luka-Vrublevetskaya on the Dniester River (3000 to 2700 B.C.). Here 248 seated statuettes have been found, 60 of which contained wheat grains (emmer, or Triticum dicoccum) — that is, the basic food staple — mixed with the clay. It is possible that these statuettes were used as winter-solstice ceremonial figures for festivals in honor of the Earth Mother or grain virgins, but their use as fertility dolls in youth-initiation rites is more likely. There is a parallel, despite the geographic distance separating them, in the statuettes that are given to adolescent girls as fertility charms in matriarchal Bantu Africa.

The sculpture of all primitive peoples was derived from a tree trunk, stone sculpture being a relatively late creation of megalithic culture. Primitive sculpture was based on the principle of mass or block units: a long cylindrical body, arms joined to the trunk, short bent legs. The neck was a narrowed continuation of the trunk, and the whole was dominated by the head, which was disproportionately large, in spite of which the block unity was maintained. Masks also show the same principle, except that the costume covering the body replaces the wooden cylinder of the statue. Because of this, Von Sydow (1927) conceived the idea that figure sculpture was a narcissistic image of the phallus. It is also characteristic of real primitive sculpture to show no movement, only a statuesque repose. Any defensive movement of the arms or any forward-stepping motion of the feet is a stylistic break from the type form of the primitive style. It also appears to be established that only in the stylistic provinces "disturbed" by European influences are statuary compositions to be found. The true primitive sculpture (if such a thing exists) is a single autonomous statue (with the exception of caryatids, supports for chairs, and a few other objects).

In 1929 the term Pfahlplastik ("paliform sculpture") was coined for the figures carved by certain tribes of the African steppelands (Baumann, 1929). The statues are human figures roughly carved out of tree trunks, stakes, and the like, which are almost always worshiped as ancestor images, usually in couples of opposite sexes ("sex pairs"). The main area of their diffusion is the Sudan and East Africa. It is doubtful whether all these examples can be considered within a single definition; such a definition would be justified only if all this sculpture could be traced to the megalithic phallic menhirs (see below) that are numerous on the Gambia River, in Tondidarou, on the Niger, in southern Nigeria, and on the Cross River, as well as in southern Ethiopia. Undoubtedly they have some connection with these megalithic phallus statues; however, whether the whole of African sculpture can be ascribed to these megalithic "influences," which undoubtedly began at a rather late period in the northern half of Africa, is still an open question.

The main center of contemporary African sculpture is connected with the religious kingdoms and their court artists in Upper Guinea and in the southern Congo (q.v.). It is highly probable that in this area the simple paliform sculpture (which may be even older than the megalithic period), under the later influences of higher cultures, caused a flourishing of naturalistic round sculpture. If this is so, it is remarkable that African paliform sculpture presents hardly any overemphasis of the size of the head. This emphasis is found only in the sculpture of the East African tribal empires (Luba, Lunda, Congo, Yoruba-Benin, and Ashanti-Anyi).

The two-dimensional art of drawing and painting is first found in the Upper Paleolithic age, and has persisted in various forms and with various degrees of naturalism and abstraction among the hunting peoples of modern times (Bushmen, Australian aborigines, Eskimos, etc.). There seems to be little support for the theory (Von Sydow, 1927) that the graphic arts were derived from the decoration of the erogenous zones of the body. Admittedly, the hunter's nude body was used for experiments in art, as were the clay walls of peasant houses in later periods. But only rarely did this specifically involve the truly erogenetic zones such as the mons veneris, which was decorated with scarlike motifs in some areas of Melanesia and New Guinea, or the mouth, the tattooed outlining of which among the Ainu and Maori women has given rise to highly speculative theories.

The interpretation of the predominant colors used in primitive painting — red, white, and black — as menstrual blood, semen, and old age or death, respectively, may, in many cases, correspond to the symbolism of prehistoric peoples as well as to that of the culturally developed Bronze Age peoples. But there are remarkable deviations from this interpretation of colors. The Chokwe (Bajokwe) in Angola, for instance, identify red with man and, as in many Mediterranean areas, with death or danger; white is the color of the white earth (calcareous limestone), which is feminine and lunar, in other words healthful and health-giving.

A depth-psychology study of rock paintings, engravings, and even many wall paintings on houses that show no European influence might provide important information on the visual art of the nonwriting peoples. But the utmost caution is needed here. The archetypes of the collective unconscious that have been deduced by European medicine and psychology are drawn for the most part from the specifically European-determined portion of the early Oriental heritage of all developed cultures. Even if they are not demonstrably influenced by cabalistic, Talmudic, Gnostic, or mystical Buddhist literature, they cannot be proved to have existed in cultures that have preserved (from a time before the Neolithic age and before the archaic city cultures) the early Stone Age mentality. In the artistic imagery of the hunting peoples the uroborus, the "cross image," and the "world mountain" are nowhere to be found; bisexual cult idols, which might show the division of man and the universe, are also absent. The paleolithic rock paintings show little of the erotic symbolism that is so exuberantly developed in the neolithic and chalcolithic agricultural and urban societies.

Caution is also advisable in evaluating the content of the drawings of recent primitive peoples in sedentary agricultural societies, because sexual elements (the representation of coitus, perversions, etc.) may have been suppressed for various reasons. Formal treatment is much more important: for instance, the exaggeration of the genital parts, or even the multiplication of particularly significant parts of the body. Since it is not the resemblance but simply the enumeration of the most important features that is significant (the characteristic clothing, ornaments, beard, tattoos, sex characters, etc., of a tribe), these features are occasionally even shown beside the body in the drawing (Koch-Grünberg, 1909–10), just as, in some cultures, bones or vital organs inside the human or animal body are made visible (II, PL. 61; IV, PL. 451; IX, PL. 242). It is apparently characteristic of all so-called "primary" representations of human beings that they accentuate the hidden but important features, and the realistic portrait is undertaken only where peoples or groups already acquiring historical consciousness attempt the ultimate refinement of the memorial image. The Bakuba (Kuba) kings of the Congo, whose statues (II, PL. 113) have stood in European museums for several centuries, sought to leave to their posterity, which worships its dead rulers, some personal impression of themselves. Yet, with their stereotyped faces, they can be distinguished from one another only by the cult objects placed before them. In these images the sex organs are not especially prominent, unlike those ancestor images in which the genitalia were accentuated to recall their procreative potency. In images of Europeans made by Bakuba, however, the sex organs were shown through the tropical

clothing (Von den Steinen, 1894; Weule, 1908; Koch-Grünberg, 1909–10).

There is a certain connection between the graphic arts and body ornaments, in which erotic elements often appear. An example of such ornament is erotic tattooing, which in developed cultures is limited to certain classes such as sailors and criminals. It has not been conclusively proved that these tattooings originated in the period of the South Seas conquests in the 18th and 19th centuries, but it is known that they are not of Western inspiration. The early European body ornamentation (Picts, Scots, and Balkan peoples of the historical period) has nothing in common with such tattooing, but in this category of erotic symbolism could be included the original women's tattoos of the Berbers and the Bosnians, which show a great resemblance to Syrian and Arabian examples. The fattening of women in some initiation rites (in the "fatting houses" in southeastern Nigeria, for example) can be connected with the esthetic ideal of the opulent woman, which is undoubtedly rooted in the Hamitic-Semitic ethnic orbit. In tropical Africa the erotic ideal also has a magical background: it assures the fertility of women. It is still uncertain, however, whether the steatopygy of the Khoisan women in southwestern Africa is a heritage of the Stone Age hunting peoples.

There remains the question of the sexual principles underlying architecture, a subject treated by Von Sydow (1927). To those unfamiliar with the psychoanalytic treatment of cultural manifestations, this aspect may appear farfetched. Whereas a city is conceived as a female symbol, the house, contrary to Von Sydow's view and extending this sexual-symbolic logic, must be considered within two lines of development, depending on whether it is round or rectangular. Only the elements connected with the cylindrical-conical round house are male-determined; the rectangular construction represents the female concept. In the house with a conical roof, the biologically rooted phallicism is clear.

In China this idea has found surprising geometric expression in the connection of the male and female universal principles (yin-yang) in a female rectangular house (equivalent of yin) and a male round house (yang; cf. Baumann, 1955, p. 106). In the Chou period the male heaven (t'ien) was represented as a perforated jade disk; the symbol of its wife, the earth, (probably in the Han period) was the ts'ung, that is, a jade tube, rectangular on the outside and round on the inside, which represented the earth's conception organ, the vagina, as square, in contrast to the round symbol of heaven. The classic Eastern cultures mostly preserved the masculine principle, though mainly in religious architecture (the sexual significance of the frequent overtly phallic towers and minarets has often been recognized).

The abstract geometric designs of handicraft work are full of erotic symbols. From the woven ornaments of the South American Indians, Von den Steinen (1894) deduced that the lozenge symbolized the fish, which is beneficent for fertility, and that the triangle represented the vulva (mons veneris). Here as elsewhere, however, the symbols are polyvalent and change their content while still retaining their shape. Not all triangles are female symbols; if it points upward the triangle becomes a male symbol representing the distribution of the male pubic hair.

The widespread meaning of the cowrie shell (Cypraea moneta) as the vulva has lent the same significance to the decorative motif of the split oval. A Japanese neolithic clay sculpture of the Jōmon period, which is very similar in shape to the neolithic female figures of the Danube area, has a giant cowrie shell modeled on it (Singer, 1940). In Africa various customs reveal the cowrie's vulva symbolism (Jeffreys, 1940). For example, on the clay altar of Ewe erected to the wife, in the "place of the origin of humanity" (amedzowe) the husband puts the cowrie in the opening representing the vagina (Speiss, 1911). In northern Nigeria the use of the cowrie to ward off the evil eye (Meek, 1931) is connected with the belief that male or female genitals have this protective power. It is also possible that the use of cowries as eyes on cult statuettes has some significance in this context (cf. Schultze and Aigremont, 1909; Smith, 1919, p. 26; Gobert, 1951).

It would be impossible to mention all the implements that have sexual significance and symbolic meaning. Axes are male, hoes for working the fields female. Such attributions are understandable, since the ax was the tool used by primitive man for clearing forests, while the hoe was the implement of the female, who used it to loosen the earth in primitive agriculture. The stick, which sometimes replaces the hoe in Africa and which is used on the Bissagos (Bijagos) Islands, for instance, for sowing, may even have an ornamental engraving of two breasts and the mons veneris (Baumann, 1929).

The straight cudgel is regarded by the northwestern Australian Unambal as male, the split stick used by women for digging as female (Lommel, 1952). It is also understandable that jars and gourds, as products of female handicraft and as kitchen utensils, are usually symbols of fertility. Even the potter's wheel, although mostly used by men, is a symbol of procreation in India. Spears, arrows, battle-axes, stone axes, and the double axes of the ancient Aegean (which are also part of the cult of the Yoruba thunder god Shango) all appear in various places as phallic emblems. The drum symbolizes a mother's womb, the drumstick the phallus, and the drumming itself the sexual act. In Mozambique, the sex act is called "taking off the drumskin and getting into the drum" (*Anthropos*, 18/19, p. 81); and for the Shona in Rhodesia, the nailing or pegging of the drumskin has the same significance (Frobenius, 1932). On the Ivory Coast and in Togo, male and female drums are often used together and are frequently adorned with ornaments representing the genitalia.

The sexual symbolism of fire kindling and iron smelting is clearly recognizable in African art. The influences of Indian cosmogony, especially via the Eritrean area, in which everything is created through fire, can be recognized at an early date. A male (upright) bores into a female (prone), generating the essence of life, fire. The kings' official state fire, kindled by a couple who perform the sex act, is the life symbol of the consecrated kings and is generated at the time of their enthronement and put out at their death. The diffusion of the sexual symbolism of fire kindling in Africa is characteristic of the Upper Nile culture wave that moved from northeastern to southern Africa. In northwestern India the hole in the fire-drill block represents the yoni, and its significance corresponds to that of the swastika decoration stamped on the mons veneris of certain lead idols or face urns from Troy.

The modeling of the smelting furnace in the form of a woman, and of the bellows in that of a man, for instance among the Chokwe (Baumann, 1935), is a feature that became quite common in Africa, apparently with the diffusion of Iron Age culture. Smelting furnaces with clay breasts modeled on them can also be found among Sudanese tribes such as the Senufo; and bellows shaped like a man can be found on the lower Congo River.

Sexual plant symbolism is inexhaustible. The banana, for example, has a phallic significance, especially in the region of the former French Equatorial Africa and in Melanesia, and is often connected with circumcision and initiation rites. Mushrooms, pine cones, and manioc tubers all possess a similar significance in other areas.

Animals as sexual ornaments may vary in significance; they may appear as male, female, or even androgynous. One of the oldest erotic animal symbols is the fish (Kunike, 1912; Eisler, 1914; Tastevin, 1914). It is found as early as the Upper Paleolithic phallus-shaped perforated bone from Bruniquel, Tarn-et-Garonne (Breuil and Saint-Périer, 1927), and it persisted as an image of fertility, of the vulva, and of the phallus throughout antiquity, Judaism, Christianity, and the religions of India and China. The lizard, too, is sometimes phallic and at other times, like frogs and toads, symbolizes female fertility. In ancient Egypt the crocodile was called the phallus of the god Ra (Re); it is also found as a phallus between the sheatfish legs of the god-king or sea god Olokun of the Benin (Nigeria). The sexual symbolism of birds, like that of the snake and the lizard, is ambivalent.

The snake is a common phallus symbol in both art and mythology. A myth of the Nuforese in West New Guinea, in which the Nuri snake is killed by the closing of the two halves of a shell, signifies that the male is killed by the female (the vulva symbolism of the cowrie shell has already been discussed). This myth is the equivalent of the entry of the Maori hero Maui into the underworld of the Earth Mother Hine-Nui-Te-Po (PL. 562); the rocks close in on the hero and kill him (the Symplegades theme) or cut off his tail feathers if he flies in as a bird. In southern Nigeria Talbot (1923) found snails and turtles as female images and snakes as male symbols in several cults. On McCluer Gulf in West New Guinea, Röder (1959) found a rock image of a man with a snake-shaped phallus. The Benin statues of the sea god Olokun previously mentioned may show the phallus in the form of a snake instead of a crocodile.

Throughout West Africa the snake is the creature of procreation and birth. The Chokwe of Angola make clay or wooden statuettes of *salujinga*, the snake that begets children in women's wombs. In the cult of the Yoruba thunder god Shango, the phallus either is represented as a double ax (similar to the Cretan labrys) or is conceived as a snake. Among the Tem of northern Togo, iron snakes, which also appear as signs of lightning, are placed near images of copulating ancestor couples. Proof of the thesis that the phallus snake is an ancient Mediterranean-Oriental motif can be found in the use of the snake phallus as a defloration rod in ceremonies preceding hierogamy (Eisler, 1914); in the images on the bas-reliefs of Persepolis of leonine monsters with a tongue-flicking snake for a phallus; and in the great importance of the lingam surrounded by snakes in the south of India. The same phallic snake symbolism appears in the medieval representations of devils in Europe, in the cabalistic interpretation of circumcision, and in the phallic representations of the serpent in the Garden of Eden. In the ancient Judaic tradition Hawwāh (Eve) is the snake of Adam, and her menstruation results from copulation with a snake. In ancient Egypt the snake aspect of Amun as an ithyphallic god deserves mention. In pre-Islamic Arabia, too, the god Wass was simultaneously connected with a snake and love. Finally, the phallic component is also recognizable in the genesis of the Chinese dragon myth (the dragon being the royal *yang* symbol). As a winged male principle the dragon is intermediary between the winged phalluses of early Mediterranean symbolism and the Ungud snake (Ungud signifying primeval time) of northwestern Australia, with which the medicine man tries to identify himself. In his trance he sings to his penis in order to make it like an Ungud snake and then flies away with his alter ego, that is, with a snake similar to the Ungud, as soon as he has an erection (Lommel, 1952).

Santana Rodríguez found in Portugal an erotic tattooage of a snake wound around a woman's thighs, licking her genitals. This Iberian version of an old Mediterranean concept lacks any significance, however, and can in no sense be compared to the phallus snake that appears attacking a man's penis in a sculpture on Tami Island (northeastern New Guinea). In this carving two phallic elements meet in a meaningless way, and in this case an astrological significance of the snake phallus cannot be excluded. In illustrations of an astrological-medical scheme of the human body, to whose members planets and signs of the zodiac are assigned, the genitals are designated by the scorpion. But in the Mexican Borgia Codex in the Vatican (Vat. Borg. Mess. I) there is a similar image of a man in which, among the 20 signs of the universe corresponding to the individual parts of the body and having the significance of medical omens, a snake is assigned to the phallus. Because of the absence of connecting elements, it is difficult to demonstrate a relation between Eastern astrology, Tami, and Mexico. In Tami, however, the uroborus is also found as an alchemistic symbol in decorations, and according to E. Seler (*Commentarios al Codice Borgia*, Buenos Aires, 1963) there is evidence in the Borgia Codex that in Mexico the phallic snake appears in connection with a god (Tonacatecutli, lord of life and of numerous progeny) and a primal copulating couple in the same way as in the images of the serpent of the Garden of Eden or of the Tem group in northern Togo.

The lingam cults of India, with their connections with the snake cult, raise another problem: the role of the menhir as the most important element in the so-called "megalithic complex." This discussion is confined to the phallus-shaped menhir (PL. 562) as an aspect of the tall stone column (still preserved intact in the obelisks), excluding the smaller sculptural representations of the procreative organs used in phallus cults, although the two aspects must be considered closely related. The phallus-shaped perforation rods of the Upper Paleolithic age from Bruniquel and Gorge d'Enfer in France (Breuil and Saint-Périer, 1927) and the bone phalluses from Mézine in the Ukraine (Volkov, *Nouvelles découvertes dans la station paléolithique de Mézine*, Geneva, 1912), whose use is unknown, fall even further outside the framework of megalithic finds. Disregarding these examples, it is evident that the phallus-shaped menhir became widely diffused especially where the heaven-earth mythology (*hieros gamos*, the world or universal parent motif, etc.) was particularly developed. In Africa, for example, such menhirs are frequent in Gambia, the Republic of Mali (Tondidarou), southern Nigeria, northwestern Cameroon, and the Kenya-Ethiopia area (Baumann, 1955).

There can be scarcely any doubt that the phallic menhirs of Africa were in some way connected with those of the ancient Mediterranean area (extending from Brittany as far as Asia Minor and Canaan) and that one of their diffusion routes passes through Central Asia and another through India, extending eastward to Indonesia and Hawaii. The phallus cult that still persists in Japan fits well into this diffusion pattern; in the Mariana Islands (Tintian), phallic stones standing before a cave were worshiped.

Stone columns with clearly recognizable phallic characteristics are found in the early western European megalithic areas. They persisted as Hermes columns, often with only a head and genitals (according to Pausanias, the Hermes of Cyllene consisted simply of a phallus). The cult pole, often with jagged notches, is frequently found as a substitute for the phallic stone menhir. In East Asia the bifurcated pole is frequently a symbol of an ox as a sacrificial animal, but equally frequently the significance of a feminine symbol is assigned to it.

Phalluses of stone, clay, or wood of smaller size may have various functions. The most widespread is probably that of a defloration instrument during initiation rites. Such phalluses, of stone or even clay and with subincision markings (urethra cuts), have been found throughout Australia (Mjöberg, 1913). Another custom that has come down from archaic cultures to contemporary primitive peoples is the hanging of phalluses or the setting up of ithyphallic figures in the fields. In Upper Egypt this custom is perhaps directly derived from the ancient cult of the ithyphallic god Min. Phallic images have also been found in the yam fields of the Maori (Best, 1922) and in the rice fields of the Toradja and other ancient Indonesian peoples. The Ao Naga celebrate the construction of irrigation ditches with obscene songs, pseudo coitus, and phalloid decorations. In many places phallephoric mimed rituals were performed in order to increase the crop yields or to honor the dead, who were believed to control the growth of plants (Pechuë-Loesche, 1907; Koch-Grünberg, 1909-10). The famous phallephoric procession depicted on the inside of a bowl from Awatobi, an old settlement of the Hopi Pueblo (Berlin, Mus. für Völkerkunde) shows that such processions were performed in arid Arizona in order to bring rain.

Sexual themes are connected not only with plant growth but also with death. Thus themes of erotic union and perversion are to be found on graves and coffins, in cemeteries, and on the houses of the dead (among the Nias, Batak, Sumba, Toradja, and others), as well as on the erotic grave wares of ancient Peru and on Etruscan sarcophagi. With the widespread ritual obscenities in speech and song during burial and mourning ceremonies, they demonstrate the close connection between procreation and death among all living beings. There may also be the idea that the fire of the libido overcomes the coldness of death.

It is remarkable that this art culminates on the peripheral areas of developed cultures, especially where typical expressions of the so-called "megalithic" cultures are present. This is equally true of sexually apotropaic figures and of the represen-

tations of sexual union in the cults of fertility gods or of the union of the god of heaven with the earth goddess (*hieros gamos* in its pure form) shown on temples and men's houses as a prototype of earthly procreational activities. In India, the megalithic lingam as the phallus is united in Sivaistic Hinduism with the yoni as the vulva. The association of male and female procreative potency sometimes leads, as in the Tibetan Tantric Yab-Yum schema, to wild pictorial representations. The copulating figures on the Konyak Naga men's houses, like those on many Indian temples, seem to be mere portrayals of worldly lust.

Frobenius (1937) has presented some interesting parallels between certain coitus rock images of North Africa and those of Sweden. The paleolithic relief of Laussel (Aurignacian period; PL. 562) showing a man and woman copulating (?), lying with their heads in opposite directions, is particularly notable. Frobenius points out a specific parallel to this in paintings on the house of a priest in the region of the bend of the Niger River. There are also the antipodal ghost images of northern Asia (mirror images placed facing each other), which represent copulation and are supposed to bring numerous progeny and also fertility in nature. Such representations can in no way be regarded as bisexual. They simply represent a totally different copulation scheme, something similar to the protohistoric rock images of Rhodesia, the painted vessels of Elam, and the terra-cotta reliefs of Babylon. This scheme is also recognizable in the naturalistic coitus scenes of the "megalithic" cultures of contemporary primitive peoples.

Mythical and religious representations of bisexual beings (Baumann, 1955) such as those found in Africa and the South Seas (among the Senufo, Baule, Gere, Ekoi, Ibo, Yoruba, and Chokwe in Africa; the Nias in Indonesia; in New Ireland, in Melanesia — IX, PL. 448) are in some respects closely linked to the recent megalithic centers in the peripheral areas of the ancient classic cultures. It is certain that there is a historically determined connection between the concept of bisexual deities and the megalithic cultures. This subject, however, lies outside the scope of the present study.

The genitalia have an apotropaic significance in the whole ancient-culture area, and this has also penetrated among the so-called "primitive" populations that have been influenced by developed cultures. The use of the procreative organ as an element in a curse or an oath sets it on the level of a defensive object. Its use as an amulet to ward off the evil eye is also widespread, for example in Polynesia. Here a significant parallel is to be found in the eel-like tiki, which clearly personifies the defensive power of the phallus. Contemporary agricultural customs in Egypt (Hornblower, 1927) suggest that the god Min, probably the oldest Egyptian deity, who holds his phallus in his hand, is to be understood as making a defensive gesture rather than an autoerotic one, although the latter act is often mentioned in connection with the old Egyptian deities (for example, Atum). In the Museum für Völkerkunde in Berlin there is a wooden door from the tembe of the sultana of Buruku (Tanzania) with a sculpture of a figure repeating identically the gesture of Min.

So-called "image witchcraft," that is, the representation of objects in order to provoke in real life the condition portrayed by the image, produces sculptures of genitals in bronze, iron, clay, and wood that are then used not only for protection but also to cure sickness of these organs, as ex-votos, etc. Besides the sculptures with supposed curative powers in European Catholic countries, silver pudenda or copulating snakes are widely known, especially in southern India.

Female genitals are also frequently endowed with beneficial or protective powers. The vulva, like the phallus, may be worn as an amulet or may be carved on fruit trees, usually stylized as a lozenge, with the frequent addition of a clitoris. When the vulva is displayed, the heavenly raingiver is supposed to be stimulated and enemies lower their gaze in shame or are rendered helpless by its power. This is also the origin of the ritual nudity or denudation that is so widely diffused. The figures of women exposing themselves that are found on the gables of the men's houses in the Palau Islands, in Sepik, and elsewhere in Melanesia have very old prototypes, as Speiser (1927) and Frobenius (1937) have demonstrated; for example, in Tell Halaf there is a so-called "goddess" on the side of a jar, modeled with outspread legs.

The defensive nature of the exposed vulva is even clearer in Ireland in the Sheila-na-gig representations of women exposing themselves. They are clearly visible on medieval castles, and even over the doors of churches. In a church in Brittany is a beam with a carving very similar to a Sheila-na-gig, which readily recalls the well-known motif from the Irish Cuchulainn saga. In this legend the Irish queen bared her breasts and pudenda before the hero Cuchulainn (who had fallen into a berserk rage), thereby forcing him to lower his gaze and making it possible to put him into cold water (heat signifying libido).

In conclusion, it can be said that sexuality in the visual arts appeared most markedly at a relatively late stage, in the agricultural period of the societies that originated in the Neolithic age. Most authentic erotic sculpture can certainly be traced to the diffusion of the classic archaic cultures that penetrated the societies of the primitive peoples. The best examples of phallic monuments, of defensive gestures of the sexual type and corresponding apotropaic figures, of copulation scenes, and of bisexual sculptures are to be found especially in regions of recent megalithic influence. If sexual symbolism and ornamentation, which are similar to sexual metaphor and erotic miming, are traced far back in the history of mankind, it seems certain that sexual motifs entered the visual arts and became especially marked in the megalithic peripheral areas only with the appearance of the erotically characterized heaven-earth mythology of the classic archaic cultures.

Hermann BAUMANN

ANTIQUITY. Two currents should be distinguished in the study of sex and love in the visual arts of historic times. One is the persistence of magical rites, elements of the fertility cult, and, in general, religious ideas whose origin lies in aspects of primitive thought discussed in the preceding section. This heritage of the sacred character of nature was transmitted from prehistoric civilizations to the peoples of the ancient Orient and of the classical world; it continued to thrive throughout the entire antique period, especially among the rural populations. The other current of ideas is based on the representation of love and sex as ends in themselves, as, for example, in secular and genre works in which the magical character is absent.

In historical and artistic fact, these two main lines are not always distinct. For example, the rows of satyrs painted on archaic vases were derived from the cultural acts performed by initiates masquerading as quadrupeds. But in the scene of a satyr violating a nymph (PL. 563), the original idea of sacred union carried out to stimulate magically the productive forces of the earth is transformed into a creation of the erotic imagination. For reasons of methodology, the two trends will be considered separately but without ignoring their reciprocal influences.

Sexual art as an expression of the sacred. From the tradition of the female nude figure as a fertility symbol, dating from Paleolithic times (see above) and exalted in neolithic agricultural civilizations, is derived the well-known iconography of the Oriental goddess with her hands cupping her breasts seen in numerous terra-cotta statuettes and reliefs produced by the artisans of Mesopotamia and Syria-Palestine. One of the oldest and most important examples is a Babylonian female figure in the Louvre (PL. 561), depicted in a standing, frontal position, rigid and dignified; the bejeweled figure is a realistic nude with voluptuous curves, her sex strongly emphasized. The gesture of pressing or holding up the breasts with both hands (in other examples with only one hand, while the other is lowered and points to the sexual organ) signifies that this goddess was originally considered as mother and nurse. The latest examples of this type are a Punic figurine from Nora (6th cent.; Cagliari, Mus. Naz.) and a 6th-century limestone Cyprian sarcophagus from Amathus with four identical figures of the goddess carved in relief on the shorter sides (Met. Mus.; cf. also VII, PL. 31).

Because the goddess was believed to keep the dead alive and revive them, her image was placed in tombs. Statuettes with highly accentuated sexual organs, found in the Tophet (sanctuary of human sacrifices) in Carthage (Tunis, Mus. du Bardo), were products of Punic craftsmanship. Their presence in such a place may be explained by the concept that attributed to the image of the sexual organ the magical power of strengthening the effect of the sacrifice, which was carried out to further the material well-being of the state, primarily dependent on agricultural prosperity. A circumcised, and therefore Punic, terra-cotta phallus was found during the excavations at Tharros in Sardinia. Also from Tharros is a sandstone relief, now in the Museum of Cagliari, showing three nude female figures seen from the back, dancing around a cippus that seems to resemble in form the virile member. The dance is led by a priest holding a bull mask. Dancing in a circle was a magicoreligious ceremony intended to ward off sterility. The Punic sculptor clearly has been impressed by the lively and dynamic rhythms of Hellenistic art; this relief probably dates from the fourth or third century B.C.

Also part of the ancient Semitic cultural world was the custom of sacred prostitution that flourished in the shadows of the sanctuaries of female procreation divinities in Mesopotamia and Phoenicia and also in the West, at Mount Eryx in Sicily, in Punic Africa (Sicca Veneria, mod. Le Kef in Tunisia), and even in Greece at Corinth. Because of the lack of direct sources, however, the origin, characteristics, and extension of this rite, which was connected with the cult of the goddess Ishtar (Astarte) and other corresponding goddesses, remain somewhat obscure. Its manifestations in the visual arts are rare and unverifiable. The significance of the nude female funerary figurines found in Egypt is more obvious: they were representations of and substitutes for the concubines who were to cheer the nights of the deceased. Nor should a similar interpretation be excluded for the female "idols" in the Aegean, Sardinian, and Iberian tombs (see MEDITERRANEAN PROTOHISTORY, col. 657). In Cretan-Mycenean art (q.v.) the seminudity of the statuettes of the "goddess of the serpents" type (IV, PL. 55) has been interpreted as having a ritual meaning; a magical fluid that gave life to plants flowed from the naked breast of the goddess or her priestess. Nevertheless, the general diffusion of seminudity in works of art leads one rather to regard it as a product of secular fashion. At this point is should be mentioned that the tradition of the art of the Aegean world, and more generally that of the ancient Near East and the peripheral cultures of the central and western Mediterranean, almost always avoided the representation of total masculine nudity; in contrast, this was established and spread by Greek art, especially after the 6th century B.C.

In the Greece of historical times, a typical product of the current of magicoreligious traditions is the satyr Silenus, god of the earth and, according to myth, preeminently fecundating. In archaic art he was represented as a vigorous hybrid figure, ithyphallic, virile, bearded, and with a horse's tail, ears, and hoofs. This figure probably represented the remembrance, transformed by poetic and artistic imagination, of ancient masked rituals using the hides of animals to celebrate dances or sexual unions intended to cause fertility in the earth, in cattle, or in the women of the tribe, on the basis of the magical concept that "like acts upon like." The image of the satyr, therefore, was propitious to palingenesis, and for that reason there are processions of ithyphallic satyrs in the pictures on archaic vases placed in tombs. The same idea of magically promoting the fertility of the earth gave rise to the custom of placing in the fields, in tombs, at crossroads in the cities, and even in the houses, images of the Arcadian Hermes in the form of a small pilaster with sculptured indication of the phallus. The same can be said of the rustic images of Priapus, the great god of Lampsacus, guardian of vineyards and orchards, who was ritually represented with the sex organ emphasized in order to ward off evil spirits that might harm the harvest. In the wooden herms of Priapus this attribute was movable and had the practical function of acting as a scarecrow (see Horace, *Satires*, I, VIII). Indeed the apotropaic function of the phallus is universally demonstrated in Greek and Roman monuments. Large phalluses were carved in relief near the house doors (e.g., Delos, Pompeii, Leptis Magna); and an ithyphallic Silenus with kantharos (end of the archaic period, about 480 B.C.) was carved above a doorway in the bastions of Thasos: this was a cultural and propitiatory image that protected the entrance and assured the prosperity of the state. Two colossal phalluses placed on high pedestals decorated with reliefs are part of the Hellenistic choragic monuments of Karystios on Delos. Sometimes the isolated phallus was represented in mosaic, with or without the apotropaic eye, or mounted on the basins of oil lamps. In the Roman world this image is often found associated with bells and figures of pygmies. The ithyphallic pygmy, because of his grotesque appearance, and the tintinnabulum were prophylactic images and objects intended to ward off evil spirits (cf. VIII, PL. 239). A Priapus painted on the front wall of the vestibule in the House of the Vettii at Pompeii weighs his enormous phallus on a scale (thus comparing it, for its fertilizing function, with fruit, grain, and other vegetables that are sold by weight in the market place).

In the Greek world the phallus was the object of a cult. It is not known whether this cult existed before the development of the Dionysiac religion, but certainly the phallephoric procession in which an effigy of the phallus was carried and the rite of consecrating this effigy were both closely associated with the festivals of the god Dionysus as far back as the archaic period. Particularly famous were the Attic festivals that, apart from the carrying of the phallus on a cart, included parades of men with masks (some of them animal disguises), as well as bawdy songs and jokes. An idea of this sort of boisterous obscenity can be gained from Aristophanes' comedy *The Acharnians*. The entire Greek comic theater, including the folk farces called *phlyakes*, appears, throughout its centuries of existence, to be steeped in sexuality and eroticism. This is reflected in the ceramics of the time, particularly in the 4th-century vases called *phlyakikoi* because they were decorated with scenes inspired by these farces: humorous caricatures of erotic myths in which the actors, who impersonated gods and heroes, wore characteristic costumes with enormous sham phalluses and buttocks (PL. 417). A Hellenistic terra cotta in Mykonos (Archaeol. Mus.) shows a phallus on wheels ridden by a nude female figure; but the many representations in Attic ceramics from the end of the 6th century and the 5th century B.C. were already of this order. They showed images of women carrying the phalluses, sometimes animated with eyes (this too was an apotropaic feature), in positions which, going beyond inspiration deriving from the primitive religious trend, already tended toward decidedly secular erotic indulgence. In some of these pictures the juxtaposition or amalgamation of the penis with a winged creature (for example, the red-figure amphora in the Mus. du Pétit Palais, No. 307, by the Flying Angel Painter) probably traces its origin to animalistic sexual motifs inherent in primitive symbolism (see preceding section).

Fertility cults connected with the phallic images are known to have existed in ancient Italy. For example, at ancient Velia (or Elea), the image of the god known as Mutunus or Tutunus was crowned on certain days of the year by matrons wearing the archaic *toga praetexta*; the festival of Fascinus, guarded by the vestals along with other fetishes that were the penates of the Roman people, symbolized the fertilizing forces of the fields. In the same way, the Genius that was worshiped on the hearth of every home represented the virile potency of the master of the house. This latter concept is illustrated by the legend concerning King Servius Tullius, born of the maid Ocrisia, who had become pregnant by a phallus that had mysteriously emerged from the ashes in the hearth. Another celebration was the Liberalia, during which, as in Greece, the effigy of a phallus was paraded on a cart along country roads and, later, in the cities too. At Lavinium, after a bawdy antiphon, the phallus was solemnly erected in the square and crowned by a matron, with much pomp, *pro eventibus seminum*, that is, as an invocation of a good harvest. Another ancient Latin fertility god was Faunus, protector of cattle and shepherds, who was later identified with the Greek god Pan. During his

festival, the Lupercalia, his followers ran around the Palatine hill, clad only in goatskins, and, with whips cut from the hide of a goat that had just been sacrificed, whipped the women they met. This rite was of a sexual nature, since the women struck in this manner were supposed to become fertile.

The mystery religions that penetrated into the Roman world increased the importance attributed to sexual symbols, which were considered responsible for the periodic rebirth of plants, the multiplication of cattle, and the continuation of the generations. Almost all the titular divinities of these mystery religions — Dionysus, Isis, the Anatolian Great Mother Cybele, the Syrian goddess Atargatis, the virgin and mother Artemis of Ephesus — and all their initiation rites were of a sexual nature. The mystery cults were also responsible for the flourishing production of sacred images in which the superstitious masses saw the immediate magical remedy for patent and latent misfortunes.

As already mentioned, in the primitive religions, beginning with the agricultural cultures of the Neolithic period, there was a direct connection between the concept of generation and that of life and revival in the tomb, and the divinities of fertility were also therefore protectors of the dead. Indeed, phallic or erotic representations are to be found in Etruscan tombs; one thinks particularly of the Tomb of the Bulls at Tarquinia. Convincing proof of this concept is the presence, in tombs of the Roman period, of terra-cotta oil lamps decorated with molded figures of the phallus or of an erotic couple. The sexual image associated with the oil lamp increased the magical power of light as regenerator of the dead. One inscription defines the tomb as *mortis et vitai locus* (the place of death and of life). The idea of the infinite fertility of the earth had aroused in man the hope of drawing from the breast of the great universal Earth Mother a new vital and, therefore, sexual energy that would help him to survive death or be reborn.

Religious sexuality is apparent in two details of the most important and most discussed extant monument of Roman painting. In the frieze of the Villa of the Mysteries at Pompeii, a draped and kneeling woman is about to raise the veil covering the sacred liknon, or sieve (a basket used for winnowing grain), from which emerges the phallus. Here one is in the presence of a cultural act, a *hieros gamos*, a sacramental wedding between a mortal and a god; the union is symbolically achieved by the uncovering of the *vannus mystica*, in which Dionysus was traditionally born. Another group of figures in the same frieze represents the ceremony of ritual flogging. A young woman, scantily dressed and disheveled, seeks refuge in the lap of a nobly seated, draped, matronly figure (VII, PL. 203). In another scene the naked back of the initiate is exposed to the blows of a switch brandished by a nude and winged female figure (IV, PL. 168). The meaning of this scene may be explained by what is known about the Lupercalia, mentioned above. The painting dates from the Augustan Era, but its historical and artistic origin and its interpretation are unsolved problems. It is not impossible that the theme of the entire frieze is a premarital rite, perhaps connected with the Dionysiac mysteries, since the central figure is that of Dionysus.

Erotic art. In Greek mythology love is almost always violent. The gods take by brute force the nymphs, women, or young boys that attract them. Therefore in archaic art the representations of such love scenes show pursuit, abduction, or crude carnal violence. Peleus pursues Thetis, the Dioscuri pursue the daughters of Leucippus, Apollo pursues Daphne, Hades abducts Persephone, Zeus abducts the nymph Europa, Zeus abducts Ganymede, Boreas abducts Orithyia, Aurora abducts Cephalus, Aurora pursues Tithonus, Agamemnon tears Cassandra away from the sacred image and rapes her under the eyes of the goddess, satyrs trap maenads (PL. 563) or violate nymphs (PL. 564), and their lasciviousness is not even inhibited before the queen of the gods.

Sometimes this archaic love is cruel: the enchantress Circe changes her lovers into swine. Sometimes it is murderous: Achilles pursues the young Troilus and tears him to pieces because he has resisted; Artemis has Actaeon torn to pieces by dogs; and the sirens' song charms sailors, who throw themselves into the sea and drown trying to reach them. In some myths erotic violence rises to the level of real drama. King Oenomaus treacherously kills the suitors of his daughter Hippodamia and is finally killed himself by a candidate, Pelops, who is shrewder than he. The centaurs, at the wedding feast of their cousin, the king of the Lapiths, swoop down upon the women and children to violate them, under the influence of wine. The Lapiths resist, and in the bloody brawl that ensues the half-horse, half-human sons of Nephele have the worst of it. The greatest and most magnificent artistic expression of this myth is to be seen in the statuary group of the western pediment of the Temple of Zeus at Olympia (III, PL. 351; XI, PL. 75). Realistically, and in large plastic masses, it depicts the violent lechery of the monsters, gnashing their teeth in physical pain, clasping their prey, and too full of desire to let them go, notwithstanding the mortal blows of their adversaries. Hands clasp the breasts of the women, torn clothing reveals the desired flesh, hoofs and arms forcibly grasp the hips and thighs, and the veins of the equine stomachs swell from the effort.

The last of many episodes in the dense mythological web of Hercules is that concerning another erotic centaur, Nessus, who is shot by the hero because he had tried to violate the latter's wife, who in turn causes her husband's death in order to carry out the deceptive suggestion made by the dying centaur. Other myths in which love is interwoven with hate and death are those of Medea and Phaedra. The dramatic quality of violent eroticism reached its height in the myth of Penthesilea, queen of the Amazons. Mortally wounded by the hero Achilles, the virgin warrior falls in love with her enemy and dies in his arms (III, PL. 355). And sometimes love is even incestuous, as in the case of Oedipus or Myrrha.

Violence — a predominant element in mythical eroticism — is generally explained by the custom according to which the man carries off the woman he wants to marry, who usually belongs to another tribe (exogamy, found among modern primitive populations). In the light of this concept, two legends belonging to two peoples distant in time and space also acquire new meaning: one is the Ugaritic legend of King Keret, who, in order to marry the beautiful Huriya, presented himself at the head of an army on the borders of the realm of Pabil, the grandfather of the maiden, to conquer her by force of arms, without having asked for her hand in marriage; the other is the well-known Roman legend of the rape of the Sabines.

Parallel to these violent and dramatic mythical loves, one finds represented realistically in action the lasciviousness of the erotic couples in the reliefs and in archaic vase painting. Here the background is red, the men are black, and the women are white — colors mentioned in the preceding section; and there are nymphs and satyrs, satyrs and maenads (PL. 563), and simple mortals, in various positions but always in profile. The hetaira, the ephebus, and often the aulete are the protagonists of eroticism on the ceramics of the first half of the 5th century. Their presence enlivened the banquets and pleased their admirers. Here one is no longer in the world of mythology; the themes are developed as episodes of everyday life.

The acclamation *ho pais kalos* ("what a beautiful boy!"), which is frequently found on ancient cups, is a glorification of masculine homosexuality. The epithet *kalos* (beautiful) is also often added to names, but only to those of men. Similarly, the god Eros is represented as a winged youth. In a cup decorated by the Curtius Painter of about 450 B.C. (Rome, Mus. di Villa Giulia), a woman undresses before a man. In a redfigure cup attributed to the Kiss Painter, a young boy and girl are kissing (Met. Mus.). A red-figure fragment in the Louvre shows two lovers in bed; the language of love has become calm and pleasant, indeed almost bourgeois. A frequent theme is the passing of a purse from the hand of a man to the hand of a woman; in this case love becomes a commercial agreement. But sometimes the courtesan is slightly ennobled: in an alabastron by the Pan Painter, of about 470 B.C. (W. Berlin, Staat. Mus. in Charlottenburg, No. 2254), a hetaira is spinning as a client offers her a purse of money.

In the art of the classical period, at its height, even in the mythological scenes, love settles into an atmosphere that is almost idyllic and, later, even sentimental and languid. In the well-known hydria by the famous "mannerist," the Meidias Painter (q.v.), the rape of the daughters of Leucippus is relaxed and nondramatic (IX, PL. 439). Also in the erotic field, there are scenes by the same painter such as the Gardens of Aphrodite with the handsome Phaon (III, PL. 375), and wounded Adonis in the arms of Aphrodite in a grotto that is steeped in an atmosphere of quiet lasciviousness. From the same date (420–400 B.C.) there are scenes in the women's quarters and some of wedding preparations with draped women and ephebi-erotes. Eroticism is nobly restrained and far removed from the violent exuberance of the satyrs of archaic times. There are painters of the classical and Hellenistic periods who were authors of mythological pornography — Parrhasios, Aristeides, Pausias, Nikophanes, Ktesikles — but the form of such works is unknown. In the 6th and 5th centuries B.C. bronze mirrors were produced whose supports were formed by statuettes of nude women that should be interpreted as representing hetaraï or sacred prostitutes rather than Aphrodite. In the 4th century Praxiteles undressed Aphrodite. The statue at Knidus (III, PL. 374) was exhibited in an open niche in the midst of a luxuriant garden, harmonizing with the divine quality of the surrounding vegetation, which corresponds to the divine qualities of the goddess, whose nudity must therefore have still been of a fundamentally ritual nature. Even before Praxiteles, Skopas had created Pothos (XIII, PL. 42), a personification of the desire of love, in the form of a nude effeminate boy. From this same taste arose the winged hermaphrodite demon, whose figure recurs in the terra-cotta sculpture and ceramic painting of the period.

More or less aggressive and ardent eroticism prevailed once again in Hellenistic art: Pan, Daphne or Olympus, satyrs or Pan with bacchants or nymphs or hermaphrodites all reappeared (PL. 564). In this period erotic groups, or *symplegmata*, appeared in sculpture, wonderfully composed in a harmonious balance of dynamic plastic masses and light and shade effects. The group of "The Kiss," carved in relief on the Grimani Altar (Venice, Mus. Archeol.), was often copied by Renaissance artists, including Titian. The "bashful" Aphrodites are much less sacred and more human than the one at Knidos because their modesty (one hand on the breast, the other on the pubis) is nothing more than a gesture of refined coquetry on the part of a courtesan. In the Asiatic goddesses of fertility of the third and second millennia B.C., this gesture had been the expression of a fundamentally sacred sexuality. The most forceful aspect of the Hellenistic type of eroticism is the marble group of Aphrodite, Pan, and Eros in the National Museum in Athens, which was found at Delos in the building of the Poseidoniasts of Berytos (mod. Beirut). The goat-god is touching the nude goddess and she is threatening him with a sandal that she has in her hand; above, an Eros-putto acts as peacemaker and integrates the plastic unity of the group. Though Aphrodite threatens, she is smiling; she is provoking the desire of the already highly lascivious male. It would be inconceivable for the modern Western mentality to bestow a religious significance upon this work (which was, in fact, an ex-voto dedicated by a certain Dionysos, son of Zeno, toward the end of the 2d century B.C.) if the sacred legend were not known through the *Dionysiaca* of Nonnus. This legend is filled with erotic adventures connected with the founding of Berytos and the establishment of its cults. The last Hellenistic Aphrodite, the Callipygian Venus — in other words, she who is showing the charms of her uncovered buttocks (PL. 564) — poses in the same way as a courtesan at a banquet in classical art. This, then, is the point reached in the long story of sexuality in ancient Greek religion and art, a story that began with the steatopygous goddesses of small paleolithic statuary.

In the Roman world of the republican period public and private trends prevailed that were inspired explicitly — and often (as in respect to Hellenism) with polemical intent — by ideals of traditional simplicity, modesty, and close family ties. After a fashion, these ideals were symbolized and protected by the Venus Verticordia (whose counterpart was the Venus Erycine, patron of free love and courtesans). However, it is interesting to note that in the Italic and Roman family tradition women occupy a position of greater dignity and equality than in Greece, where they were confined to the women's quarters and never took part in banquets — except, of course, the hetaïraï. Perhaps this derived from an ancient Etruscan tradition that stressed the feminine element in society; there are echoes of this manner of thinking in the legends concerning the earliest days of Rome. Etruscan customs, largely documented in the paintings and funerary reliefs extant even in the archaic period (for example, in the banquet scenes), scandalized the Greeks, who could not understand the real significance of the explicit and social liberty of the Italic woman (cf. Athenaeus, *The Deipnosophists*, IV, 153d, XII, 517 ff.). Original Roman iconographic expressions of legalized love are found in the nuptial scenes carved in relief on the sarcophagi: they depict the *dextrarum iunctio*, the culminating point of the ceremony, when the bridesmaid, witness for the bride, solemnly unites the right hands of the couple. A similar concept, clearly derived from the Etruscan tradition, is the origin, at the height of the imperial period, of the representation on the lids of monumental sarcophagi of the couple stretched out as if at a banquet.

Triumphant Hellenism, imported into the Roman cultural world, brought a more pronounced artistic expression of eroticism and sex. Mythological scenes include Polyphemus and Galatea in Hellenistic-Roman wall paintings and reliefs; Ares and Aphrodite in the paintings of the cities in the area of Vesuvius (Naples, Mus. Naz.; here the god wears a soldier's helmet and caresses the breast of a courtesan); the fresco of ithyphallic Pan lifting the veil from a sleeping bacchant, seen from the back; the appearance, in more or less amorous guise, of Dionysus to Ariadne in paintings and sarcophagi; Pan and Hermaphroditus in paintings; Artemis descending toward the sleeping Endymion in paintings and reliefs; Leda and the swan in paintings; Eros and Psyche in paintings and on sarcophagi; and centaurs and Tritons abducting nymphs (the small statuary groups is the Vatican Museum conform to the spirit of the Hellenistic "rococo"). The accentuation of the erotic reached its peak in pornographic scenes of couples in figural works of the most varied types: wall paintings, oil lamps, engraved gems, vases (PL. 563), plates, appliqué work, etc.; all apparently derived from common archetypes, probably pictorial. Typical of the unequivocal secular purpose and function of erotic compositions is the presence of these painted pictures in the Lupanar of Pompeii. If to these archaeological data are added the literary sources — primarily the comedies of Plautus, the novel (in particular the *Satyricon* of Petronius), the epigrams of Catullus and Martial, and the satires of Juvenal — and some graffiti on the walls in Pompeii, an approximate idea can be gained of the environment of prostitutes, panders, and pederasts that formed the seething underworld of Roman society. In post-Pompeian paintings the most beautiful example, in which Venus triumphs, is the magnificent picture painted on a wall in the house of SS. Giovanni e Paolo in Rome (PL. 301). The image of the goddess is still in the Hellenistic tradition, but the composition, with the central figure much larger than the others, reveals the influence of the revolution in style that was to give birth to late Roman art. Among the last pornographic creations of antiquity is the white-agate cameo (Paris, Cab. Méd.) depicting the nude and ithyphallic Emperor Heliogabalus steering a biga drawn by naked women crawling on all fours like animals. The Greek inscription prays for victory for Epixenos — that is to say, the intruder, or foreigner. This epithet was given to Heliogabalus in allusion to the fact that he had introduced indecent Eastern customs, as substantiated by Lampridius in *Antoninus Heliogabalus* (*Historia Augusta*, 29); the representation is thus obviously satirical.

Clearly, the advent of Christianity signified a reaction to eroticism in customs, literature, and art. This reaction was not exclusively the consequence of the chastity and modesty established by the new faith; it also found favorable ground and wide acceptance in the severe Roman tradition that was reaffirmed — though polemically and negatively — by satire itself

and was encouraged, during the last centuries of the Empire, by the most elevated currents of pagan philosophical thought. An indication of the establishment of this reaction in the customs of late Roman society, independently of public or private attitudes to religion, may be recognized in the progressively increasing moralization of theatrical spectacles, especially the mime, which until that time had been a field for the easy exhibition and diffusion of "profane" sexuality. In the context of this trend can be placed a celebrated figural document of rare interest: the mosaic in the Roman villa of Casale, near Piazza Armerina, Sicily, dating from the 4th century, that depicts a troupe of young girls, mimes, or gymnasts whose nudity appears veiled by a two-piece covering of the breast and pubic area. This displays a prudishness that seems singularly modern and decidedly in contrast to the universal diffusion of the completely nude female in the monuments of the Hellenistic-Roman world.

Gennaro Pesce

THE CHRISTIAN WEST. The two main classifications continue: art from the erotic-magical sphere, probably connected with fertility rites that were progressively assimilated to witchcraft, and art portraying amorous scenes.

If it is true, as M. A. Murray has suggested (1921), that witchcraft is the continuation of a ritualistic structure from the Iron Age (additional evidence has been supplied by Runeberg, 1947), one should see in the witches' Sabbat (cf. IV, PL. 181), characterized by the coupling of nude young women with men masquerading as animals or demons, an exact parallel to the coupling of nymphs and satyrs on Greek vases. The attributing of a magical value to the round dance, which profane poetry of the time shows to be full of sexual allusions, is another continuing feature (cf. X, PL. 76).

The broom ridden by witches (the oldest representations are found in the Marienkirche in Gelnhausen on a capital of ca. 1210 and in the choir of the Cathedral of Schleswig, ca. 1280) is undoubtedly phallic (Troescher, 1953). The apotropaic value of the exposed genitalia, male or female, has been discussed in the preceding sections. On medieval castles, city gates, and even above church doors they are clearly to be seen. One might cite the "Putta di Modena" on the south façade of Modena Cathedral, the relief in the Castello Sforzesco in Milan that comes from the Porta Tosa, and the figures on the little church of S. Maria a Mare near Giulianova (14th cent.).

The "image witchcraft" extends beyond mere protection by the exposing of genitalia to the curing of maladies of these parts, and it is scarcely surprising to find images in European countries with supposedly curative powers or saints associated with fertility ceremonies. In France St. Guignolet or Guerlichon in the north and St. Foutin in the south might serve as examples. St. Leonard of Noblat, whose votive nail seems to have been in phallic form, is invoked in Bavaria for sufferers from syphilis and was throughout the Middle Ages a very popular saint. At Isemia in Italy there was until the 18th century a custom of offering an ex-voto in phallic form to St. Cosmas — together with St. Damian the patron of medical men — whose intercession was also sought on behalf of frustrated lovers (see Delaure, *Histoire des différents cultes*, II, 1882, p. 294). At Trani in Italy during the carnival a priapic figure was carried, called "il santo membro." It might also be added that the kermesse, a fair held in the northern countries on the annual feast of the patron saint, and other religious feasts soon became occasions for amorous excesses and license in general, and were to be so portrayed, particularly by the Flemish and Dutch painters (cf. II, PL. 357).

The phallic scenes in the famous Bayeux tapestry (11th cent.) have received no adequate interpretation; most likely they are of a sheerly secular character. Representations of amatory scenes in the medieval period would seem to be mainly confined to articles of value among the well-to-do, although the lovers on the façade of Fidenza Cathedral are an exception. This fairly mirrors the widespread poverty and also the great extent to which the graphic and sculptural artists worked for religious patrons and on religious themes. One may cite the silver plates in Leningrad (The Hermitage) and the ivory casket from Veroli (9th cent.?; Vict. and Alb.). Still later (13th cent.) is a gilt mirror in Frankfurt am Main (Städelsches Kunstinstitut) with two scenes of lovers on the handle and mounts.

Love stories were illustrated in frescoes (e.g., Camera del Podestà in the Pinacoteca, San Gimignano; fresco cycle in Castello Sforzesco, Milan) and especially in miniatures (many in Paris, Bib. Nat.). H. von Veldeke (*Eneide, die Bilder der Berliner Handschrift*, Leipzig, 1939) reproduces a 13th-century illustration from Book IV of Vergil's *Aeneid* showing Aeneas and Dido embracing on a bed. The stories of Boccaccio naturally provided many opportunities for this type of illustration; an example is a 15th-century miniature of the Lydian king Candaules exposing his sleeping wife to his favorite, Gyges (Paris, Bib. de l'Arsenal, Ms. Ars. 5193, fol. 78v.).

The complex of late-antique, northern barbarian, Byzantine, Eastern, and Mediterranean motifs and modes of representation became fused in the Middle Ages by the powerful focus of the Christian Church, which took note of the need for a synthesizing force, as reflected by Neoplatonism and the writings of St. Augustine. The struggle in the 6th, 7th, and 8th centuries between the iconic and aniconic schools of thought ended in the rehabilitation of images as a valid means of embodying the religious experience (see IMAGES AND ICONOCLASM) and, by *memoria rerum gestarum*, disposing the believer to action. In the words of Pope Adrian I, there was a necessity to *demonstrare invisibilia per visibilia*. This coincided with the intellectual vigor of centers in Spain and the artistic vitality and requirements of schools such as that of Saint-Denis under Abbot Suger, the ease of communication fostered by medieval pilgrim routes, and not least the challenge to security posed by the Islamic world.

It was in literature that the plastic and graphic arts found their wealth of allegorical themes in medieval times (see SYMBOLISM AND ALLEGORY). In the Apocalypse of St. John, in the bestiaries from the Alexandrian *Physiologus* on, in the *Psychomachia* of Prudentius, in the *Satyricon* of Martianus Capella, in the encyclopedic knowledge represented by the *Polyhistor* of Gaius Solinus (3d cent.), by the *Etymologiae* of Isidore of Seville, by the works of Honorius of Autun, Rabanus Maurus, Erigena, Bartholomaeus Anglicus, and Vincent of Beauvais — here was the source and explanation of the vast majority of medieval motifs and themes. To the predilection for allegory and the conviction that all activity was religious can be attributed the seeming incongruity of many of the medieval forms and subjects. It is perhaps a Middle Eastern vitality that was able to conjure up a myth for a moral and an evocation for an event, and certainly it is in Alexandria that the idealism of the Hellenic world and the realism of Syrian culture were fused in Christian art. Gregory the Great later marked out the middle path for the Church in describing the threefold meaning of Biblical history as literal, doctrinal, and moral.

In the light of such a synthesis must be viewed both the sentimental, well-nigh pagan excesses of sculpture and votive offerings already mentioned and the many traditional human archetypes and traits still visible in Christian art. The central place of candles, the idealization of the Virgin and the preoccupation with the Virgin Lactant theme, the sadistic portrayal of the martyrs and their tortures, the angels, even the Cross, can all be interpreted as a Christianizing of ancient symbols. They can also be seen in the light of the words of St. John, "And the Word was made flesh and dwelt among us, and we beheld his glory . . . ."

It is probably in the Middle East that the origin of the Fountain of Youth or Fountain of Life theme should be sought, as well as the probably related one of the public promiscuous bath — in both of which water stands as a regenerative element and source of vitality, and both of which lend themselves to illustration with mythological scenes. From the 14th century might be cited ivories in the Louvre with fountain scenes and the miniature *Trois commères aux bain*, of women bathing with a man eating between them (Paris, Bib. de l'Arsenal, Ms. Ars. 3525 fol. 86v.). A kindred spirit is present in a 15th-century Italian miniature of the Garden of Love (XIII, PL. 348); and

the fresco in the Castello della Manta in Piedmont has a beautiful example of a Fountain of Youth scene (VIII, PL. 427; also VI, PL. 64 for the Fountain of Life). Related, too, are the Fountains of Fertility composed of females pouring water from their breasts (cf. IX, PL. 315). Perhaps here may be mentioned the Garden of Delights theme, which could vary from the fairly academic theological 12th-century portrayal of heretics (VII, PL. 220) to the wild visions of Hieronymus Bosch at the end of the 15th century (II, PL. 316). In addition to personifications of sacred and profane love the allegory of the Castle of Love appears in the illuminations of Francesco da Barberini's *Documenti d'Amore* (Vatican Lib., Cod. Barb. 4016, 4017) and also on French Gothic ivories (Florence, Mus. Naz.; Venice, Mus. Correr). The illustrated manuscript *La Somme de Roi* (Paris, Bib. Mazarine) displays the same spiritualized hedonism as the portrayal of the Garden of Virtue. The *Triumph of Love* and *Venus and the Lovers* found on two Italian *desca da parto* from the early 15th century (PL. 566; XIII, PL. 348) might have lent themselves to erotic treatment, but the classical idealization appears to have remained paramount. In the early 15th century a fellow novice of Fra Angelico and Fra Bartolommeo (qq.v.), Antoninus, Archbishop of Florence, could denounce artists who were producing provocative religious representations made *non ex pulchritudine sed ex dispositione earum ut mulieres nudas et hujusmodi*. But though there is something of sensuous warmth in the representations of the early Renaissance, as well as increasing realism, especially in the north (cf. PL. 451; X, PLS. 245, 255), the frequent portrayal of the nude did not generally go beyond an incommunicable sexual characterization and could hardly be called erotic art.

It was in the 16th century that the erotic sentiment of Renaissance man began to blossom out fully in art. Nudity had been progressively freed of its medieval shameful connotations, from Maitani's Genesis figures on the façade of Orvieto Cathedral to the mythological figures of Piero di Cosimo and the Venus of Botticelli (q.v.; II, PL. 323). This paved the way for the *Sleeping Venus* of Giorgione (q.v.) and the *Venus of Urbino* (PL. 66) of Titian (q.v.). However, the reintegration of Renaissance man with his own physical aspect and with the natural world that surrounded him was assuredly a conscious and preconsidered one; the resulting ambivalence of the eroticism in art, as typified by Giorgione's *The Tempest* (VI, PLS. 186, 187) or Titian's *Sacred and Profane Love* (XIV, PL. 94; cf. PLS. 99, 102) and still present in some degree in his pictures of *Venus and the Organ Player* (Madrid, Prado, and W. Berlin, Staat. Mus. in Dahlem), is never henceforward entirely missing, even in the art of provoking lasciviousness such as that cultivated independently of the Church in the courts of Europe from the German mannerists on (cf. PLS. 567, 568).

This note of subterfuge in eroticism is perhaps another aspect of Schlegel's assertion that dynamic art must be related in some degree to ideas of religion or philosophy; indeed it was not merely because the Church was the greatest patron of art that those artists who devoted themselves to secular themes sooner or later found themselves dancing in the dark. It is this necessity for some sort of differentiation vis-à-vis the religious-philosophical trends that determines the path of erotic art. North or south of the Alps there remain two fruitful lines of recourse — to classical themes or to Biblical and allegorical motifs. By contrast, genre painting, so stimulatingly launched by Pieter Bruegel the Elder (q.v.) and reenhanced in the 17th century by gifted artists such as Adriaen Brouwer, Georges La Tour, the Le Nain brothers and, of course, Rembrandt (qq.v.), remained an apt purveyor of the gay and vulgar vitality of life in a highly artistic vein; but only with the "gallant" painters of France in the 18th century does the purely secular art become fused with the intentionally erotic — and then only for a limited span.

To return to the 16th century, the sensualism of the Venetian painters was not so exaggerated in the art of central Italy, where Neo-platonism and the idealistic abstraction of the preceding century did not permit the erotic element to be expressed with such violence. In spite of research by Freud (1910) connected with this subject, neither the paintings of Leonardo (q.v.) nor those of Michelangelo (q.v.) reveal any erotic atmosphere that is not on an ideal or abstract level. Nevertheless, the *Last Judgment* by Michelangelo came near to being destroyed on account of its nude figures, under the shadow of the Counter Reformation. If the paintings of Raphael (q.v., esp. col. 866) reveal a higher degree of sensuality and a participation in natural human relationships, this occurs either in an atmosphere of refined intellectualism that freezes any emotion — for example, his *Galatea* fresco (III, PL. 392) — or else within the framework of a detailed plan and a patron's requirements (e.g., the erotic scenes in the decoration of the bathroom of Cardinal Bibbiena in the Vatican).

It continued to be the classical themes that offered themselves best as an alibi for sensual pictures in spite of the fruitful impulse given by the rebellious Caravaggio (q.v.) toward genre subjects. The *Salamacis and Hermaphroditus* (Turin, Gall. Sabauda) by Francesco Albani might be cited, as well as the *Nymph and Satyrs with Putti* by Perino del Vaga (Br. Mus.), the scenes on the frescoed ceiling of the Palazzo Bindi-Sergardi in Siena by Domenico Beccafumi, and Bronzino's *Venus, Cupid, Folly, and Time* (IX, PL. 292). As the 16th century progressed the sexual undercurrent came more into the open with important painters such as Giulio Romano (q.v.; frescoes in the Sala di Psiche, of the Palazzo del Te in Mantua, PL. 82), Correggio (q.v.; *Leda and the Swan*, PL. 567; *The Rape of Ganymede*, III, PL. 476; *Jupiter and Antiope*, PL. 80), Tintoretto (q.v.; *Joseph and Potiphar's Wife*, XIV, PL. 81), and the Carraccis (especially Agostino's series of *lascivie*, PL. 568).

Reflecting many characteristics of the Italian mannerists but without their naïveté (cf. Andrea Meldolla's *Diana and Actaeon*, PL. 82) is the sensual but refined production of the French artists of the Fontainebleau school (PL. 103; V, PL. 392; IX, PL. 304). In Germany the onset of a more intense spiritual attitude to religion was combined with a revulsion against the sentimental and externalized piety of the south, and it is not mere coincidence that, for instance, the figures of Venus and Eve painted by Lucas Cranach the Elder (who was a firm upholder of Luther) are so similar, or that this iconoclastic reaction took place at the same time as obscene caricatures of monks began to spread. In the erotic and Boccaccioesque scenes by H. S. Behan, Matsys, and Cranach this trend toward social satire in northern Europe could have free play (for instance, with the theme of *The Ill-sorted Couple*), but the classical (cf. IV, PLS. 40, 44) and mythological themes were not neglected, or the traditional allegorical repertory of medieval themes (e.g., *The Fountain of Youth* by Lucas Cranach the Younger, W. Berlin, Staat. Mus. in Dahlem), or even characters from sacred history (e.g., *The Loves of Samuel* by Virgil Solis the Elder).

After the Council of Trent, labeled "the birthday of prudery," the ideas of the Counter Reformation restrained direct eroticism at least in official painting in Italy, although groups such at the Bamboccianti (q.v.; II, PL. 92) were continually courting indignation. In northern Europe during the 17th century the taste for erotic art became widespread, although mythological subjects still occupied a predominant position in the repertory of artists, inspiring Velázquez (q.v.; XIV, PL. 329), Nicolas Poussin (q.v.; *Sleeping Nymph surprised by Satyrs*, London, Nat. Gall.; *The Childhood of Bacchus*, II, PL. 199), Johann Liss (II, PL. 196), and Peter Paul Rubens (q.v.). Rubens's sensualism is present in almost all his works (II, PL. 195; VII, PL. 386) and reaches the outright erotic in paintings such as *The Feast of Venus* (Vienna, Kunsthist. Mus.) and the various scenes of pastoral gatherings, from which many engravings were made.

Engravings, which were in any case a more convenient medium for conveying the folkloristic traditions connected with sex and fertility, contained an increasing number of amorous allegorical subjects, freely illustrating the dissolute customs of the period. Printing aided the wide diffusion of these piquant representations, in the production of which many artists of varying talent took part. Hendrik Goltzius (q.v.) and Gerard de Jode deserve special mention, also Heinrich Aldegrever and, of course, Rembrandt (q.v.; *The Friar in the Cornfield, The French Bed, Joseph and Potiphar's Wife*), and others such as Adriaen van Ostade, Jan Steen (qq.v.), and Jan Molenaer, who worked as painters also and who introduced licentious scenes from everyday life.

Eroticism also marked the work of many 18th-century engravers and painters, among whom may be mentioned Thomas Lawrence, Thomas Rowlandson (qq.v.), F. Schall, P. A. Baudoin (PL. 570), Jean Raoux, and Félicien Rops, who was famous for his obscene series, *Les Sataniques*.

In France, in addition to the amorous activities of the pagan divinities and obscene illustrations for the fables of La Fontaine and the stories of Boccaccio, increasing use came to be made of the so-called "gallant" scenes, which with Francisco Goya and Antoine Watteau (qq.v.; *Le faux pas*, Louvre) came into the foremost rank of art, and which served as a convenient medium of François Boucher (q.v.; PL. 569; cf. also PL. 570; VII, PL. 388), author of a group of "gallant" paintings for the boudoir of Madame Pompadour, and Jean Honoré Fragonard (q.v.; *La Gimblette*, Paris, private coll.; *La chemise enlevée*, V, PL. 320; *The Swing*, V, PL. 372). These paintings and the engravings made from them gained widespread appreciation; however, political events at the end of the 18th century put an end to a type of genre painting that depended largely on the aristocratic and wealthy milieu.

Nevertheless, erotic sentiment that had been freely vented for two centuries did not disappear with the end of the rococo period but turned inward and continued to exert its power in the hinterland of the 19th-century artistic conscience. This period is typified by a sense of the morbid and by a repressed sexuality that manifested itself in new exotic themes and in the return to traditional subjects linked with eroticism, such as the bath and bathers (Théodore Chassériau, Ingres, Renoir, qq.v.; VIII, PLS. 71, 72, 75; XI, PLS. 114, 116, 118), the Roman orgy (cf. T. Couture, *A Roman Feast*, London, Wallace Coll.; *The Romans of the Decadence*, Louvre), and illustrations of episodes from classical mythology (Max Klinger) or of tales of chivalry (Henri Scheffer, Jean Jacques Henner, Ingres). Northern romanticism is pervaded with this form of unexpressed eroticism, which is present also in the numerous works of Prud'hon, Manet (qq.v.), and J. L. Gérome. The reaction to romantic morbidity expressed by the realism of Courbet (q.v.) is concretized in his naturalistic female nudes. In the second half of the century a free and less self-conscious erotic character is to be found in the social and political satires, in caricature (Paul Gavarni), and in blatantly obscene illustrations for books, newspapers, and magazines (Aubrey Beardsley, q.v.; Wilhelm von Kaulbach). The eroticism in certain works by Rodin (q.v.), such as *The Kiss* (PL. 186) and *Les Amies* (Louvre), can be considered a means to stylistic virtuosity as an end in itself.

At the beginning of the 20th century, the disintegration of naturalistic forms and their transformation into an abstraction of the represented object caused the disappearance of all erotic expression in figural art, even in those works in which some special form or sign clearly refers to sexual organs and functions. As a matter of fact, the analytical character of 20th-century formal tendencies refutes, as did the 15th century, any emotional suggestion, and the subject of a work, if any, is treated by means of lines, spaces, and colors that — in spite of Clark's assertion that a direct relationship exists between geometry and sex — preclude from the viewer all pleasing aspects of a reality that they are not intended to portray.

It is true, nevertheless, that the sexual theme sometimes acquires a universal and symbolical value when it rediscovers a clear, classical, and vital plenitude — for example, in the etchings of Picasso (q.v.) in the Vollard Suite (PL. 572) — or when it is introduced as a harsh denunciation of society, as in the expressionistic satire of a Grosz (PL 572) or a Maccari; to say nothing of the many sexual motifs that, according to psychoanalytical theories, appear in the work of the surrealists as elements arising out of the subconscious mind (see SURREALISM).

* *

The preceding section contains material contributed by Eugenio Battisti and Francesco Negri Arnoldi.

THE EAST. *Islam.* Erotic art depends to a large degree upon skill in representing the nude human body and its anatomical details. In those culture areas where religious convention or traditional taboos prevented the development of nude painting and sculpture, erotic representations did not reach an appreciable artistic level. The countries where Islam prevailed illustrate this point. Since orthodox Islam forbids the depicting of living beings, the drawing of even the draped human figure was frowned upon and that of the naked body was completely taboo. By contrast, Arabic literature abounds in books on carnal love, in which, for instance, the coital positions are described in great detail; and narrative literature in general often has highly realistic passages on heterosexual and homosexual intercourse. But the illustrations that accompany such texts are clumsy scribblings that are of importance only to the anthropologist. The shadow figures, too, that were used in Turkey and Egypt by itinerant folk singers for illustrating their stories, although not without a certain naïve charm, cannot claim artistic importance (see PUPPETS). In these shadow plays the erotic element is represented by an abnormally large, often movable phallus attached to the puppet of the comic hero Karagöz and by the bare breasts of his ladyloves; complete nudes are never depicted.

On the periphery of Islam, where less orthodox or even heretical Islamic sects held sway and where the influence of non-Islamic art could make itself felt, the orthodox taboos were not strictly observed. Especially in Iran miniature paintings of amorous couples are found, fully or partly dressed but in suggestive poses; their ingenuousness lends these pictures great charm. Chinese influence is noticeable in the details of the background but not in the drawing of the seminudes or in their poses. Neither is Chinese influence traceable in the erotic pictures of the heyday of Persian painting (15th–16th cent.; see SAFAVID ART; TIMURID ART), when trade with Ming China was flourishing; it would seem that Chinese censorship prevented Chinese erotic art (which developed greatly in the Ming period; see below, *China*) from being exported to the Middle East. In Persian painting, pictures of male homosexuality are of frequent occurrence, and medical works occasionally contain illustrated descriptions of bestiality.

After the Moslem conquest of India in the 12th century, these Iranian styles of painting were introduced there; modified by Indian elements, they gradually developed into the various Moghul schools (q.v.) of miniature painting. In the 18th and 19th centuries especially, Moslem painters in India tried their hand at erotic scenes. These pictures have the excellent coloring and loving care for detail that form the main attraction of Indo-Iranian (q.v.) painting, but the naked parts of the male and female anatomy are stiffly drawn, and one notices a marked reluctance to depict the genitalia; these are usually hidden or represented in a perfunctory manner. The most frequent positions are the woman sitting on the man's lap or reclining against a pillow with her legs raised. Sadistic traits and phenomena of perversion, although often mentioned in Arabic and Persian literature, are not portrayed in erotic art.

India. In Hinduism (q.v.) the veneration of the male and female genitalia as symbols of the divine creative force (respectively, lingam and yoni) played an important role. This religious significance of the sexual act explains the frequent occurrence of representations of the lingam and the yoni and of couples in amorous embrace on ancient Hindu temples and other monuments. The Sanskrit handbooks of love, such as the well-known *Kāmasūtra* by Vātsyāyana, gave detailed descriptions of the technique of love-making, including a great variety of coital positions. Since these books had a secular character, they did not, at first, exercise any influence on temple art.

Buddhism (q.v.), the other important Indian religious system, taught that sexual desire is one of the greatest obstacles to reaching enlightenment and attaining salvation; therefore in the oldest Buddhist art the erotic element is absent. It was Buddhist art, however, that fostered the evolution of the sculptured human nude or seminude body, and thus Buddhism paved the way for later religious and secular erotic art.

The human figures carved on the railing of the stupa at Bharhut (2d cent. B.C.) are rather clumsily executed (II, PL. 408), but the nudes of Sanchi show great technical progress (VII, PL. 441). Those of Nagarjunakonda (I, PL. 223; VII, PL. 392) have the same lithe grace as the nudes depicted in the murals of the Ajanta caves (ca. A.D. 200–600; I, PLS. 46–48). About this time, the artisan's handbooks, or Śilpaśāstras, formulated a definitive canon for the representation of the human body, including exact measurements for its component parts, the *tālamāna*; this canon ruled the Indian portrayal of the nude male and the nude female body throughout subsequent centuries.

The great flourishing of erotic art in the 7th and 8th centuries was brought about by the rise of Tantrism, a kind of sexual mysticism that spread like wildfire all over the Indian subcontinent; its origins probably lay outside India, partly in China, partly beyond the northwestern frontier. Both Hindu and Buddhist Tantrism teach that salvation can be reached by overcoming the sexual duality in oneself, thereby realizing the hermaphrodite nature of the godhead. This idea is clearly expressed in the great statue of Śiva in the rock temple of Ellora (7th cent.), in which he is shown as androgynous, his left half (with one feminine breast, and a hand holding a mirror) being female, the right half male. The central object of veneration in the temple is a lingam, and the nude female deities carved there often have a pronounced erotic character and emphasized genitalia. Tantrism teaches that the believer may merge the male and female elements in himself either by a process of intense meditation or by actual sexual intercourse with a woman, called his "energy," or shakti; hence Saivist Tantrism is also referred to as Shaktism. In Hindu Tantrism the prototype of the mystical union is the god Śiva embracing his spouse Pārvāti; in Buddhist Tantrism the mystical embrace is conceived as the union of gnosis (prajñā) and praxis (upāya) and is personified as a male and a femal edeity united in sexual intercourse. Thus almost every one of the myriad gods of the Mahayana pantheon is accompanied by a female counterpart.

These Tantric teachings, combined with the instructions about the art of making love contained in the *Kāmasūtra* and other ancient handbooks of physical love, resulted in the remarkable erotic sculpture of the temples at Khajuraho (10th–11th cent.; PLS. 518, 565; VII, PLS. 230, 393, 472, 473) and of the great Temple of the Sun at Konarak (13th cent.). On the reliefs decorating the walls of these temples are carved endless rows of amorous couples engaged in the act of love in all possible positions, often accompanied by female and male attendants who actively assist in the intercourse. These erotic reliefs are executed in a typical style that makes them remarkable works of art. There is a marked preference for standing coital positions — possibly owing to the artist's need to fill the oblong, vertical panels composing the reliefs. The women have large round breasts, narrow waists, and excessively broad and heavy hips but straight, rather spindly arms and legs.

In southern India Tantrism merged with local fertility cults of non-Aryan origin in which the Mother Goddess played a predominant role. Thus arose the cult of Durgā, also called Kālī, Gaurī, or Mahādevī, the awe-inspiring spouse of Śiva as all-devouring Divine Mother, more powerful than her husband. She is often represented in statues or pictures as a fearsome red or blue she-devil, dancing naked on the white body of her dead husband, dead but for his member in erection.

Tantrism spread northward to Nepal and Tibet (qq.v.), where one finds the well-known Lamaist statues and pictures of gods united in sexual embrace with their female counterparts, the so-called Yab-Yum (Father-Mother) images. On the paintings the sexual parts are usually invisible, but the bronze statues have carefully molded genitals, the male partner often being provided with a movable penis. One need not wonder, therefore, that Tibetan statues of this kind preserved in the palace of the Ming emperor in China were used for the sexual instruction of the young princes and princesses.

In the 12th century and after, the Moslem conquerors destroyed countless Hindu and Buddhist temples, and in India Buddhism never recovered from this catastrophe. But its teachings continued to prosper outside India, in Tibet, China,

Japan, and southeast Asia. In India itself the Tantric ideology lingered on in various Saivist sects, and the Vaishnava sect made the god Kṛṣṇa (Ang., Krishna), with his many ladyloves, into a symbol of *bhakti*, the divine love that hallows sexual intercourse. In secular erotic art, too, medieval Indian handbooks of love are often illustrated with the coital positions.

From the 17th to the 19th century several schools of Indian miniature painting developed, influenced by the Indo-Iranian schools yet having a character of their own. Many artists made Kṛṣṇa sporting with the milkmaids the subject of erotic paintings of a semireligious character. Kṛṣṇa and the girls are shown in various stages of undress but rarely completely naked, and the genitalia are usually hidden; the logical conclusion of the amorous play is often indicated by a bare leg or arm appearing from behind a bush. Secular painters depicted the coital positions of ancient handbooks of love in miniatures on paper and also on ivory plaques, evidently for the entertainment of householders and their womenfolk. The figures are shown in the nude, yet here, too, the genitalia are rarely shown. Some nudes are drawn remarkably well and are much closer to reality than those of the Moghul miniatures, which were bound by the rigid Indo-Iranian tradition. Artists of the northern schools also excelled in suggestive erotic paintings. In PL. 571 is shown an intimate scene in which the lover is loosening the cord of his mistress's trousers; such pictures have an artlessness that lends them a peculiar charm.

In northern India erotic sculpture almost ceased. In the south, however, it survived in brass and copper statues of gods and goddesses, cast according to the cire-perdue process. This art began in the 10th century and is still practiced today. In a southern Indian copper statue, dating from the 18th century, of Lakṣmī as goddess of fertility, stark naked, the measurements of the parts of the body correspond to those given in the ancient Śilpaśāstras.

China. At the beginning of our era there already existed in China detailed handbooks of sex written for the instruction of newly married couples, and literary evidence indicates that such handbooks were copiously illustrated with pictures of the coital positions. Such erotic pictures were, therefore, meant for sexual education. At the same time, however, erotic art meant for pleasure also existed. Historical records mention that one of the Han princes had the walls of his banquet hall painted with pictures of naked men and women engaged in sexual intercourse. Erotic representations were used also as amulets. Since the sexual act was deemed to represent the positive forces of life and light at their zenith, images of men and women locked in sexual embrace were supposed to ward off the evil forces of death and darkness; this seems to be the explanation of Han-dynasty roof tiles with sexual motifs.

Chinese religious beliefs have their roots in earliest antiquity, when Chinese society was organized on a matriarchal pattern; woman was considered as the Great Mother, nourishing not only her offspring but also her mate, who during coitus feeds on her inexhaustible vital force. Therefore the handbooks of sex from the beginning of our era stress that coitus strengthens the man both bodily and mentally. Later, Taoism taught that a man can even reach immortality by having sexual intercourse in a certain manner with numerous women, tapping their vital force. These ideas may well have reached India in the 6th and 7th centuries and may there have contributed to the rise of Tantrism (see above, *India*). In China itself this Taoist sexual mysticism has throughout the ages influenced erotic art, both directly and indirectly.

Until about A.D. 1200 the Chinese were remarkably free from inhibitions about sex. Notably during the T'ang dynasty (618–906), sexual matters were freely written about, and literary sources frequently mention erotic pictures. Since no actual examples of this erotic art survive, its artistic quality cannot be estimated. Literary evidence indicates that the male and female nude bodies were depicted in considerable detail and in full color. One source mentions such a picture by the well-known T'ang artist Chou Fang; it portrays a man copulating with a woman while two maidservants stand by. Nonerotic

T'ang paintings that survive in originals or copies show that the Confucian separation of the sexes was not carried out and that women were allowed to move about in public places, dressed in a manner that did not conceal their charms. Ladies wore long robes with a generous décolleté, and dancing girls performed half naked.

In the 13th century, however, Neo-Confucianism became more or less the state religion. This doctrine insisted on strict separation of the sexes, and it pronounced exposure of the body grossly indecent. The open bosom and neck of female dress were replaced by a high collar, and censorship bore down on secular and religious literature — the latter including both Tantric Buddhism and Taoist sexual mysticism. From then on a spirit of prudery prevailed, and erotic art was driven underground. Instead of the frank nudes of preceding centuries there developed a suggestive erotic art. Amorous couples were represented fully dressed and in apparently innocent attitudes, with only a small detail supplying the sexual element: the pair watches, for instance, two small copulating animals half hidden in a corner of the picture; or the lover assists his mistress to thread her needle — a well-known symbol of sexual intercourse. Pictures in which a lady displays her diminutive shoes were considered especially lascivious, for since the 7th century, when women had begun to bind their feet, these crippled feet had come to be considered the most intimate symbol of femininity, and as such, sexually much more exciting than exposed breasts or pubes.

It was only during the second half of the Ming period, from about 1570 to 1640, that the development of the color print gave a new impetus to erotic painting and occasioned a return to the uninhibited manner of the T'ang dynasty. Famous artists of that time, such as Ch'iu Ying and T'ang Yin, began to draw large pictures of completely naked men and women engaged in the sexual act and representing all the varied coital positions described in the ancient handbooks of sex. These highly realistic drawings were engraved on woodblocks by skilled artisans and struck off in various colors. Prominent scholars added poems and essays to these pictures in excellent calligraphy. Series of such pictures accompanied by explanatory texts were published in sumptuous albums, intended for private circulation among art lovers. The erotic album *Feng-liu-chüeh-ch'ang* (Summa Elegantia) consists of 24 color prints and was published in 1606. One picture, the twentieth of the series, bears the title *Afterward*; the man and woman have just risen from the couch, the woman is tying the cord of her skirt, and her lover is holding up her jacket for her to put on. The nudes in these albums are drawn so skillfully that one assumes that the artists often worked from live models. The genitalia are depicted accurately, and the facial expressions are cleverly rendered. Another erotic album is entitled *Hua-ying-chin-chên* (Variegated Battle Arrays of the Flowery Camp; see PL. 571). Contrary to the view expressed in some early Western books on China, the Chinese did kiss, as shown by a print in the *Hua-ying-chin-chên* album. Male homosexuality, although frequently mentioned in literature, especially that of the Ch'ing period, is not represented in classic erotic art, presumably because this practice was considered to lie outside the sphere of common sexual life. The background of these prints, too, is executed with painstaking care. The album *Chiang-nan-hsiao-hsia* (Whiling Away the Summer in Chiang-nan) is one of the last known specimens of this art; it dates from about 1640. Noteworthy are the bound feet of the woman and the loving care bestowed on portraying the furniture. These Ming albums represent the apex of Chinese erotic art, and they are also extremely important from the point of view of the anthropologist because of the sexual habits they reveal.

During the subsequent Ch'ing, or Manchu, dynasty (1644–1912) the censors had most of these albums destroyed, so those preserved are now items of the greatest rarity. Some of them must have circulated secretly during the first decades of the Ch'ing period, for their influence is clearly noticeable in later erotic art. Their designs can be recognized even in the pornographic pictures sold in the 19th and 20th centuries in China's port cities. The greater part of the erotic art of this modern period is but a clumsy echo of the Ming prints. Small porcelain statues and sexual representations on wine cups, snuff bottles, and the like evince a sly obscenity that is wholly lacking in older Chinese erotic art. It is worth mentioning, however, that this vulgar erotic art was used in the antiforeign campaigns conducted in southern China during the Opium War (1839–42); albums were put into circulation at that time depicting white men and women engaged in bestiality, sadism, pederasty, and other abnormal sexual activities.

Finally, mention must be made of the erotic "double folding fans." At first sight these seem to be folding fans of the ordinary type, with a landscape or flower painting on the obverse and a poem or essay on the back. However, every rib has a double strip of paper pasted on it that remains hidden if the fan is opened in the customary way, that is, from left to right; if one opens it from right to left, the reverse of each double strip becomes visible, and the strips together form an erotic picture.

Japan. In prehistoric times there existed in Japan an indigenous fertility cult that centered around veneration of the phallus; this cult has survived till the present day, for instance, in stones of phallic shape placed by the roadside. After the introduction of Chinese learning and Buddhism in the 4th century of our era, autochthonous elements merged with Sino-Indian Tantric teachings. The T'ang cult of the nude, however, never became popular in Japan; the Japanese viewed the naked body with religious awe, and its beauty was not appreciated. Esthetic and erotic interest concentrated on the long hair of a woman and her bare neck.

In the Heian period (794–1185) the Chinese handbooks of sex were introduced into Japan, but these were studied primarily as medical texts and therefore did not promote erotic art. Literature of that time, for instance the famous *roman de moeurs*, *Genji Monogatari* (The Tale of Prince Genji), abounds in descriptions of physical love, but in the illustrations the amorous couples appear fully dressed in the sumptuous ancient costumes. The only example of completely nude couples engaged in the sexual act is a *makemono* (horizontal picture roll) showing 16 couples in different positions and entitled *Kanjonomaki* (Scroll of the Initiation). The pictures are done in full colors, and each of them is accompanied by a brief Japanese text. This scroll is said to date from the 9th century, but the oldest copy known is one by the 13th-century painter Sumiyoshi Keion. Although the coital positions on this scroll are traceable to Chinese prototypes, the background is typically Japanese and the male and female organs are depicted as abnormally large — a feature that characterizes Japanese erotic art of the succeeding ages, and one that has not yet been satisfactorily explained. Some sources aver that the erotic scrolls served primarily for the instruction of newlywed couples or brides-to-be and that therefore the genitalia had to be abnormally large in order to enable the painter to depict in detail all physical phenomena connected with the sexual act; but this theory seems scarcely tenable.

During the Kamakura, Muromachi, and Momoyama periods (1185–1614) popular phallic art continued to flourish, but extant specimens of erotic painting and erotic sculpture are comparatively rare. The only erotic motif that was fairly common in both sculpture and painting was a Hindu one, namely, the "double Gaṇeśa," the Japanese Kangiten ("god of joy"); here Gaṇeśa is standing upright, linked in sexual embrace with his female counterpart, elephant-headed like himself. It would seem that the trunk of the Sino-Indian Gaṇeśa had strong phallic associations. Curious is the Kamakura statue of Benzaiten (Skr., Sarasvatī), the goddess of eloquence and wisdom; under her dress she has a realistically naked body carved from wood. Perhaps this statue figured in Tantric ablution rituals.

It was not until the Tokugawa (Edo) period (1615–1867) that erotic art developed fully, mainly owing to the introduction into Japan of Chinese color prints from the late Ming period and the subsequent technical progress of the Japanese woodcut. Hishikawa Moronobu and other early masters diligently studied the Ming erotic prints; Moronobu even published a Japanese version of the Ming album *Feng-liu-chüeh-ch'ang*. In

Moronobu's version of the Chinese original of the picture *Afterward* (PL. 571) the dress, hairstyle, and background were transformed in Japanese guise. The coital positions, too, of the early Japanese erotic prints were largely derived from Chinese sources, but the artistic treatment of these motifs was typically Japanese: the pairs were rarely shown completely naked because, as already remarked, the Japanese did not consider the naked body an esthetic or sexually attractive sight. Erotic interest was concentrated on the genitalia, always of abnormally large size and depicted in much greater detail than in the Chinese prints. As in the latter, the facial expressions cleverly render the emotions experienced by the couple. In these early erotic prints the women are sturdily built; they have round faces, large breasts, and heavy hips. Thereafter, however, with the flourishing of the Ukiyo-e (q.v.) school, one finds thin willowy women with oval faces, flat bosoms, and spindly arms and legs. The anatomical element is so much stressed that many of the erotic pictures and illustrated books resemble medical treatises in their details of various aspects of sexual intercourse. It should be noted that the Ukiyo-e artists also had little interest in the beauty of the nude body. Among the few exceptions are color prints of the naked fisherwomen of western Japan and a few bathroom scenes. Completely nude figures were utilized chiefly for achieving grotesque effects. Indeed, even erotic pictures must have been viewed with religious awe, since in Japan, as in China, such pictures were used as amulets; Japanese warriors put them in their helmets before going to the battlefield, and they were placed in storage boxes with books and clothes to prevent the goods from decaying. It was only after the Pacific war that the cult of the nude spread to Japan. Then nude sculpture and painting began to flourish, and there even developed a special branch of literature aptly called *nikutai-bungaku* ("literature of the flesh").

Southeast Asia. In those countries of southeast Asia in which Islam prevailed, erotic art did not develop. In Hindu-Buddhist areas, on the contrary, there was talented erotic painting and sculpture. This difference is demonstrated by the situation in Indonesia: on Islamic Java and Sumatra erotic art remained confined to phallic representations (notably in the puppets of the *wayang*, the popular shadow play); whereas on Bali and Lombok, where Tantrism remained influential, a well-developed erotic art came into being. In southeast Asia the normal supine position, with the man lying on top of the woman (predominant in China and Japan), is comparatively rare. The most common position is that of the woman reclining against a pillow with her legs raised and the man kneeling between. This position is frequently represented in Burmese erotic clay statues and also in Siamese erotic book illustrations and paintings on paper and cloth.

Robert H. van GULIK

BIBLIOG. *General*: C. G. Jung, Wandlungen und Symbole der Libido, Leipzig, 1912, 4th ed., Zurich, 1952 (Eng. trans., R. F. C. Hull, New York, 1956); G. Heard, Narcissus: An Anatomy of Clothes, London, 1924; M. J. Nicholson, Art and Sex, London, 1930; M. Mead, Sex and Temperament, New York, 1935; L. Goitein, Art and the Unconscious, New York, 1948; K. Clark, The Nude, New York, London, 1956; E. W. Klimkowsky, Geschlecht und Geschichte, Teufen A.R., 1956 (full bibliog.); H. Marcuse, Eros and Civilization, Boston, 1956; S. Freud, The Interpretation of Dreams, trans. J. Strachey, New York, 1959. See also the bibliog. for PSYCHOLOGY OF ART.

The primitive world: J. B. A. Raffenel, Voyage dans l'Afrique Occidentale, Paris, 1846; K. von den Steinen, Unter den Naturvölkern Zentral-Brasilien, Berlin, 1894; W. E. Gudgeon, Phallic Emblem from Atiu Island, JPS, XIII, 1904, pp. 210–12; W. Jochelson, The Koryak: Religion and Myths, New York, 1905; E. Pechuël-Loesche, Volkskunde von Loango, Stuttgart, 1907; K. Weule, Negerleben in Ostafrika, Leipzig, 1908 (Eng. trans., A. Verner, London, 1909); T. Koch-Grünberg, Zwei Jahre unter den Indianern: Reisen in Nordwest-Brasilien, 2 vols., Berlin, 1909–10; P. Schultze und S. Aigremont, Muschel und Schnecke als Symbole der Vulva, Anthropophiteia, VI, 1909, pp. 35–50; H. Ploss and B. Renz, Das Kind in Brauch und Sitte der Völker, 3d ed., 2 vols., Leipzig, 1911–12; C. Speiss, Zum Kultus und Zauberglauben der Evheer (Togo), BA, I, 1911, pp. 223–26; H. Kunike, Der Fisch als Fruchtbarkeitssymbol bei den Waldindianern Südamerikas, Anthropos, VIII, 1912, pp. 206–29; T. Volkow, Nouvelles découvertes dans la station paléolithique de Mézine (Ukraïne), Cong. int. d'anthr. et archéol. préhistoriques (XIV, Geneva), I, 1912, pp. 415–28; E. Mjöberg, Phalluskult unter den Ureinwohnern Australiens, Anthropos, IX, 1913, pp. 555–56; R. Eisler, Der Fisch als Sexualsymbol, Imago, III,

1914, pp. 165–96; C. Tastevin, Le poisson symbole de fécondité ou de fertilité chez les Indiens de l'Amérique du Sud, Anthropos, X, 1914, pp. 405–17; G. E. Smith, Evolution of the Dragon, London, 1919; F. Bieber, Kaffa, 2 vols., Münster i W., 1920–23; E. Best, Spiritual and Mental Concepts of the Maori, Wellington, N. Z., 1922; H. Kühn, Die Kunst der Primitiven, Munich, 1923; P. A. Talbot, Life in Southern Nigeria, London, 1923; H. Breuil and R. de Saint-Périer, Les poissons, les batraciens et les reptiles dans l'art quaternaire (Arch. de l'Inst. de Paléontologie Humaine, Mém., II), Paris, 1927; G. D. Hornblower, Further Notes on Phallism in Ancient Egypt, Man, XXVII, 1927, pp. 150–53; F. Speiser, Schlange, Phallus und Feuer in der Mythologie Australiens und Melanesiens, Verh. der naturforschender Gesellschaft, Basel, XXXVIII, 1927, pp. 219–54; E. von Sydow, Primitive Kunst und Psychoanalyse, Leipzig, 1927; J. Winthuis, Das Zweigeschlechterwesen bei den Zentralaustraliern und anderen Völkern, Leipzig, 1928; H. Baumann, Das afrikanische Kunstgewerbe, in H. T. Bossert, Geschichte des Kunstgewerbes, II, Berlin, 1929, pp. 63–104; R. Wilhelm and C. G. Jung, ed., Das Geheimnis der goldenen Blüte, Munich, 1929; C. K. Meek, Tribal Studies in Northern Nigeria, 2 vols., London, 1931; P. Daigre, Les Bandas de l'Oubangui-Chari (Afrique Equatoriale Française), Anthropos, XXVII, 1932, pp. 153–81; L. Frobenius, Erythräa, Berlin, 1932; R. de Saint-Périer, Deux œuvres d'art de la grotte d'Isturitz, L'Anthropologie, XLII, 1932, pp. 19–25; H. Baumann, Lunda, Berlin, 1935; L. Frobenius, Ekade Ektab: Die Felsbilder Fezzans, Leipzig, 1937; M. D. W. Jeffreys, The Cowrie Shell in British Cameroons, Man, XL, 1940, p. 63; K. Singer, Cowrie and Baubo in Early Japan, Man, XL, 1940, pp. 50–53; F. H. Lem, Sculptures soudanaises, Paris, 1948 (Eng. trans., Paris, 1949); R. M. and C. H. Berndt, Sexual Behaviour in Western Arnhem Land, New York, 1951; E. G. Gobert, La pudendum magique et les problèmes des cauris, La Rev. africaine, 426, 1951, pp. 5–62; L. F. Zotz, Idoles paléolithiques de l'Etre androgyne, B. Soc. préhistoire de France, XLVIII, 1951, pp. 335–40; A. Lommel, Die Unambal, Hamburg, 1952; E. W. Smith, African Symbolism, JRAI, LXXXII, 1952, pp. 13–37; H. Baumann, Das doppelte Geschlecht, Berlin, 1955; H. Melzian, Zum Festkalendar von Benin, in J. Lukas, Afrikanistische Studien, Hamburg, 1955, pp. 87–107; F. Hančar, Urgeschichte des Nahen Ostraumes, Saeculum, VII, 1956, pp. 136–67; J. Röder, Felsbilder und Vorgeschichte des MacCluer-Golfes, West-Neuguinea, Darmstadt, 1959; K. J. Narr, Weibliche Symbolplastik der älteren Steinzeit, Antaios, II, 1960–61, pp. 132–57.

Antiquity: F. Winter, Die Typen der figürlichen Terrakotten, 2 vols., Berlin, 1903; Pfuhl, III, indices, s.v. Pornographie; H. Licht, Die Erotik in der griechischen Kunst, Zürich, 1928; G. Furlani, La religione babilonese-assira, Bologna, 1929; F. Wirth, Römische Wandmalerei vom Untergang Pompejis bis am Ende des III. Jahrhunderts, Berlin, 1934; J. B. Pritchard, Palestinian Figurines, New Haven, 1943; R. Pettazzoni, La religione nella Grecia antica, Turin, 1953; J. Marcadé, Roma Amor, Geneva, 1961; J. Marcadé, Eros Kalos, Geneva, 1962; P. Grimal, L'amour à Rome, Paris, 1963; G. Säflund, Aphrodite Kallipygos, Stockholm, 1963.

The Christian West: H. Dollmayr, Lo stanzino da bagno del cardinale Bibbiena, Arch. storico dell'arte, III, 1890, pp. 272–80; E. Fuchs, L'élément érotique dans la caricature, Vienna, 1906; E. Fuchs, Die Frau in der Karikatur, Munich, 1906; A. Cabanés, Moeurs intimes du passé, 12 vols., Paris, 1908–36; E. Fuchs, Geschichte der erotischen Kunst, Stuttgart, 1908; G. J. Witkowski, L'art profane à l'Eglise, 2 vols., Paris, 1908; E. Fuchs, Illustrierte Sittengeschichte vom Mittelalter, 4 vols., Leipzig, 1909–10; S. Freud, Eine Kindheitserinnerung des Leonardo da Vinci, Leipzig, 1910 (Eng. trans., New York, 1916, repr. 1947); M. A. Murray, The Witch Cult in Western Europe, London, 1921; P. Negrier, Les bains à travers les âges, Paris, 1925; R. van Marle, L'iconographie de la décoration profane des demeures princières en France et en Italie, GBA, II, 1926, pp. 163–82, 249–74; RIDKg, s.v. Badezimmer; C. Baudouin, Psychanalyse de l'art, Paris, 1929; G. Antonucci, Temi fallici nell'iconografia medievale, Folklore italiano, VIII, 1933, pp. 61–67; I. Bloch, Ethnological and Cultural Studies of the Sex Life in England Illustrated as Revealed in its Erotic and Obscene Literature and Art, New York, 1934; G. Weise, Die geistige Welt der Gotik und ihre Bedeutung für Italien, Halle-Saale, 1939; E. de Bruyne, Etudes d'esthétique médiéval, II, Bruges, 1946; A. Runeberg, Witches, Demons and Fertility Magic: Analysis of Their Significance and Mutual Relations in West-European Folk Religion, Helsinki, 1947; R. Bernheimer, Wild Men in the Middle Ages, Cambridge, Mass., 1952; M. A. Murray, The God of the Witches, London, 1952; G. Troescher, Keltisch-germanische Götterbilder an Romanischen Kirchen, ZfKg, XVI, 1953, pp. 1–42; G. Widengren, Herleintracht und Mönchskutte, Clownhut und Derwischmütze: Ein Gesellschafts-. Religion- und Trachtgeschichtliche Studie, Orientalia Suecana, II, 2–4, 1953, pp. 41–111; W. Deonna, La femme aux seins jaillissants et l'enfant "mingens," Geneva, N.S., VI, 1958, pp. 239–96; M. Levy, The Naked and the Prude, The Studio, CLXII, 1961, pp. 12–15; E. Battisti, Antirinascimento, Milan, 1962, pp. 296–303 and passim.

The East: K. Shibui, Catalogue des estampes érotiques du Japon, Tokyo, 1926; H. Nishioka, History of Phallicism in Japan, Tokyo, 1950 (in Japanese); M.-P. Fouchet, L'art amoureux des Indes, Lausanne, 1957 (Eng. trans., London, 1959); J. Auboyer and E. Zannas, Khajuraho, The Hague, 1960; R. H. van Gulik, Sexual Life in Ancient China: A Preliminary Survey of Chinese Sex and Society from ca. 1500 B.C. till 1644 A.D., Leiden, 1961; Mulk Raj Anand, Kama Kala, New York, 1962; M. S. Randhawa, Kangra Paintings on Love, New Delhi, 1962; C. Grosbois, Shunga, New York, 1964. See also the bibliogs. for MINIATURES AND ILLUMINATION: *India, Islam.*

Illustrations: PLS. 561–572.

* *

SEZESSION. See EUROPEAN MODERN MOVEMENTS.

SHAHN, BEN. American painter and graphic artist (b. Lithuania, 1898). When Ben Shahn was eight years old, his family left Europe and settled in Brooklyn, N.Y. He worked as a commercial lithographer until 1930 while attending high school, university, and the National Academy of Design in New York. In 1925 and from 1927 to 1929 he traveled in Europe and North Africa. His first one-man show, consisting mainly of African subjects, was held in 1930.

In 1931–32 he produced 23 gouaches on the controversial Sacco and Vanzetti trial that exhibit a profound concern for social conditions and make full use of the contemporary visual language for propagandistic purposes. They are painted in emphatic patterns, with nervous and broken lines, and have an undercurrent of distortion and caricature. In 1933 Shahn's 15 paintings on the case of labor leader Thomas Mooney led to his employment by Diego Rivera to work on the frescoes (never completed) in Rockefeller Center, New York.

At this time Shahn began photographing New York street scenes, and he used many of these as subjects for paintings executed for the Federal Art Project of the Works Progress Administration. In 1934 his mural designs for Riker's Island Penitentiary, New York, were rejected by the city's Art Commission. In 1935–38 Shahn was employed by the Farm Security Administration as artist, designer, and photographer. He executed a large fresco (1937–38) for a Federal housing development in Roosevelt, N.J., where he took up permanent residence. He completed 13 large murals for the Bronx Post Office, N.Y. His sketches for mural treatment of the Four Freedoms for the St. Louis, Mo., Post Office were not accepted. In 1940 he won a competition for murals for the Social Security Building in Washington, D.C. During World War II Shahn designed posters for the Office of War Information.

Since the early 1940s Shahn has executed many commercial commissions for business concerns and magazines. He has been a visiting teacher at several universities and art schools, and in 1956–57 was Norton Professor at Harvard University, an appointment that led to his publication of *The Shape of Content.* His work was exhibited in London in 1947, he was given an award in 1954 by a São Paolo, Brazil, museum, and he was one of two American artists to be shown at the Venice Biennale in 1954.

In his art Shahn successfully joins clarity, persuasiveness, and personal expression (I, PL. 120; XI, PL. 446). He combines the unexpected directness of candid photographic vision with monumental form and a powerful personal symbolism in dealing with some of the most basic problems of the 20th century (labor movements, race relations, atomic warfare). He is interested in the emergence of intensely human expression within the confines of an industrial society. Mechanistic social forces mingle in his work with nature and memory. He often makes use of lettering and inscriptions. Technically, his uneven dry brush line, strong contrasts between positive and negative shapes and spaces, and subtle color modulations within firmly defined areas have had wide influence, particularly as regards serious commercial art.

BIBLIOG. *Writings of Shahn*: An Artist's Credo, College Art J., IX, 1, 1949, pp. 43–45; How an Artist looks at Aesthetics, J. of Aesthetics and Art Criticism, XIII, Sept., 1954, pp. 46–51; The Shape of Content, Cambridge, Mass., 1957.

Works on Shahn: J. D. Morse, Ben Shahn: An Interview, Mag. of Art, XXXVII, April, 1944, pp. 136–41; Ben Shahn, Mus. of Mod. Art B. 14, 4–5, 1947; J. T. Soby, Ben Shahn, West Drayton, Eng., 1947; T. B. Hess, Ben Shahn paints a picture, AN, XLVIII, May, 1949, pp. 20–22, 50–56; S. Rodman, Portrait of the Artist as an American; Ben Shahn: A Biography with Pictures, New York, 1951; J. T. Soby, Ben Shahn: His Graphic Art, New York, 1957.

Allen S. WELLER

PLATES

Pl. 1. F. Brunelleschi, Old Sacristy (completed 1428), S. Lorenzo, Florence, with sculptural decoration by Donatello.

Pl. 2. L. B. Alberti, S. Andrea, Mantua, Italy, crossing and apse (with late-18th-cent. decoration), from plans of 1470, built under the direction of L. Fancelli, 1472–94.

Pl. 3. Milan. *Above*: A. Filarete and Guiniforte Solari, Ospedale Maggiore (Albergo de' Poveri di Dio), 1456–65. *Below, left*: Michelozzo and others, Portinari Chapel (1462–68), S. Eustorgio. *Right*: Michelozzo, portal to Medici bank, 1456–64. Milan, Castello Sforzesco.

Pl. 4. *Above, left, and below*: Michelozzo, Palazzo Medici-Riccardi, Florence, exterior and courtyard, begun 1444. *Above, right*: Giuliano da Maiano, Palazzo Spannocchi, Siena, ca. 1473.

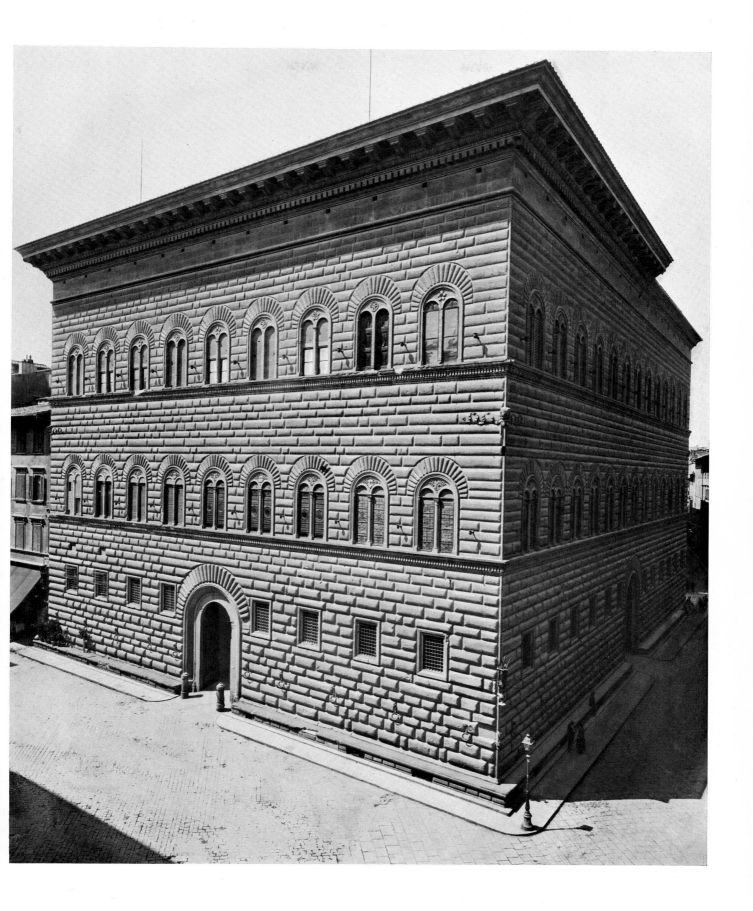

Pl. 5. Benedetto da Maiano and Il Cronaca (Simone del Pollaiuolo), Palazzo Strozzi, Florence, ca. 1490–1507.

Pl. 6. *Above*: Il Cronaca (Simone del Pollaiuolo), Palazzo Strozzi, Florence, courtyard, 1497–ca. 1507. *Below*: Giuliano da Sangallo, Sto Spirito, Florence, sacristy, 1489–92.

Pl. 7. Naples, Castel Nuovo, triumphal arch of Alfonso of Aragon, ca. 1454–67.

Pl. 8. Francesco di Giorgio (Martini), Church of the Madonna del Calcinaio, near Cortona, Italy, begun 1485.

Pl. 9. G. A. Amadeo, Cappella Colleoni, Bergamo, Italy, 1470–76.

Pl. 10. *Above*: Pavia, Italy, Certosa, façade, 1473–first half of 16th cent. *Below*: G. Battagio and G. A. Montanaro, S. Maria della Croce, near Crema, Italy, ca. 1490–1500.

Pl. 11. Venice. *Above*: M. Coducci and the Lombardo workshop, Palazzo Vendramin Calergi, ca. 1500–09. *Below, left*: M. Coducci, Palazzo Corner Spinelli, ca. 1500. *Right*: P. Lombardo, S. Maria dei Miracoli, 1481–89.

Pl. 12. *Above*: Ferrara, Italy, Palazzo dei Diamanti, designed by B. Rossetti, begun 1493. *Below*: Bologna, Italy, Palazzo Bevilacqua, second half of 15th cent. *Left*: Courtyard. *Right*: Façade.

Pl. 13. *Above*: Meo del Caprino, Cathedral, Turin, 1491–98. *Below*: Rome, S. Agostino, 1479–83. *Left*: Façade. *Right*: Interior (renovated by L. Vanvitelli, 1750).

Pl. 14. Rome. *Above*: Palazzo Venezia, ca. 1455. *Below*: Palazzo della Cancelleria (begun ca. 1485), courtyard.

Pl. 15. Donatello, David, ca. 1440. Bronze, ht., 5 ft., 2⁵/₈ in. Florence, Museo Nazionale.

Pl. 16. *Above, left*: Donatello and Michelozzo, tomb of the antipope John XXIII (Baldassare Coscia), ca. 1423–33. Florence, Baptistery. *Right*: Desiderio da Settignano, tomb of Carlo Marsuppini, ca. 1453. Florence, Sta Croce. *Below, left*: Mino da Fiesole, tomb of Count Hugo, ca. 1469–81. Florence, Church of the Badia. *Right*: A. Rossellino, tomb of the Cardinal of Portugal, begun 1461. Florence, S. Miniato al Monte.

Pl. 17. *Above, left*: A. Rossellino, Matteo Palmieri, 1468. Marble. Florence, Museo Nazionale. *Right*: Benedetto da Maiano, Filippo Strozzi, ca. 1491. Marble. Paris, Louvre. *Below, left*: F. Laurana, Battista Sforza, ca. 1473. Marble. *Right*: Desiderio da Settignano, Portrait of a Lady, after 1461. Marble. Last two, Florence, Museo Nazionale.

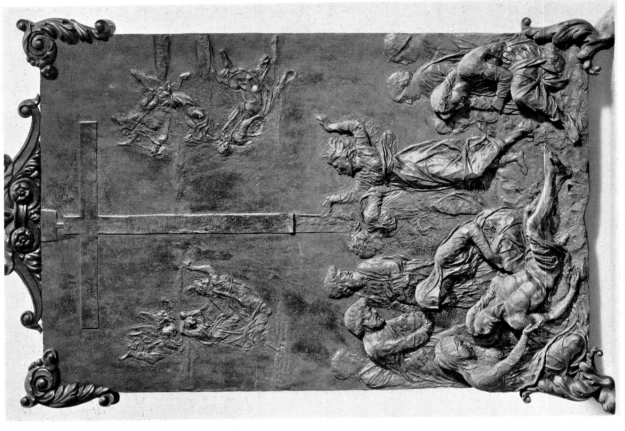

Pl. 18. *Left, above*: Agostino di Duccio, scene from the legend of St. Sigismund, originally part of an altar in the Tempio Malatestiano, Rimini, mid-15th cent. Marble. Milan, Castello Sforzesco. *Below*: Bertoldo di Giovanni (1420?–91), Battle Scene. Bronze, 16⁷/₈×39 in. Florence, Museo Nazionale. *Right*: Francesco di Giorgio (?), The Deposition, ca. 1475. Bronze, 33¹/₂×22¹/₂ in. Venice, S. Maria del Carmelo.

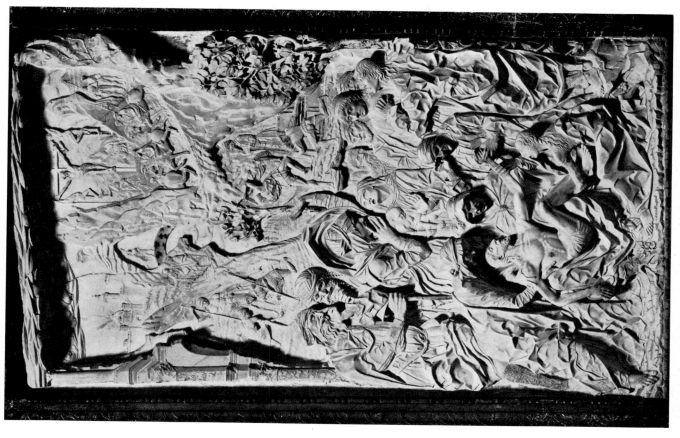

Pl. 19. The Lamentation. *Left, above*: By Niccolò da Bari (Niccolò dell'Arca), second half of 15th cent. Terra cotta. Bologna, S. Maria della Vita. *Below*: By Agostino dei Fonduti, 1483. Painted terra cotta. Milan, S. Maria presso S. Satiro. *Right*: By C. and A. Mantegazza, probably late 1480's. Marble, 6 ft., 5¹/₈ in. × 3 ft., 8¹/₈ in. Pavia, Certosa.

Pl. 20. G. A. Amadeo, tomb of Medea Colleoni (d. 1470). Marble. Bergamo, Italy, Cappella Colleoni.

Pl. 21. P. Lombardo, tomb of Antonio Roselli, completed 1467. Marble. Padua, S. Antonio.

Pl. 22. *Above*: A. Rizzo, Adam and Eve, second half of 15th cent. Marble; ht. of each, ca. 6 ft., 6 in. Venice, Doges' Palace. *Below*: A. Lombardo, The Miracle of the Newborn Child, ca. 1505. Marble. Padua, S. Antonio.

Pl. 23. Genoa, Cathedral (S. Lorenzo), Chapel of S. Giovanni Battista, ca. 1447–96.

Pl. 24. *Above*: C. Foppa (Il Caradosso), door of the tabernacle for St. Peter's chains, detail, 1477. Bronze; size of panel, 14⁵/₈×17³/₈ in. Rome, S. Pietro in Vincoli. *Below*: Rome, Vatican, Sistine Chapel, screen, ca. 1480.

Pl. 25. Masaccio, St. Peter Healing the Sick with His Shadow, detail, 1425–26. Fresco. Florence, S. Maria del Carmine, Brancacci Chapel.

Pl. 26. Piero della Francesca, The Madonna of Mercy, detail of central panel (XI, PL. 157) of a polyptych, commissioned 1445. Panel; full size, 4 ft., 4³/₄ in. × 2 ft., 11³/₄ in. Sansepolcro, Italy, Pinacoteca Comunale.

Pl. 27. *Above, left*: Paolo Uccello, portrait of Sir John Hawkwood, 1436. Fresco. Florence, Cathedral. *Right*: Andrea del Castagno, portrait of Boccaccio, ca. 1450, detail of frescoes from Villa Pandolfini. Florence, Cenacolo di S. Apollonia. *Below*: Domenico Veneziano, St. John in the Desert, from the predella of the Magnoli Altarpiece, ca. 1445–48. Panel, 11 1/8 × 12 3/4 in. Washington, D.C., National Gallery.

Pl. 28. *Above, left*: Fra Angelico, Virgin and Child with saints, detail of I, PL. 262, ca. 1437. Panel; full size, 5 ft., 11 in. × 6 ft., 7¹/₂ in. Florence, Museo di S. Marco. *Right*: A. Baldovinetti, Madonna and Child. Panel, 41×30 in. Paris, Louvre. *Below, left*: B. Gozzoli, The Damning of Cain, detail, ca. 1470. Fresco. Pisa, Camposanto. *Right*: S. Botticelli, Coronation of the Virgin, detail, 1488–89. Panel; full size, 12 ft., 5 in. × 8 ft., 3 in. Florence, Uffizi.

Pl. 29. *Above, left*: A. Pollaiuolo (attrib.), portrait. Panel, 18^{1}/$_{8}$×13^{3}/$_{8}$ in. Milan, Museo Poldi Pezzoli. *Right*: D. Ghirlandajo, portrait of Giovanna Tornabuoni, 1488. Panel, 30^{3}/$_{4}$×19^{3}/$_{8}$ in. Lugano, Switzerland, Thyssen-Bornemisza Coll. *Below, left*: Piero di Cosimo, portrait of Simonetta Vespucci. Panel, 22^{1}/$_{2}$×16^{1}/$_{2}$ in. Chantilly, France, Musée Condé. *Right*: Filippino Lippi, The Triumph of St. Thomas, detail, 1488–93. Fresco. Rome, S. Maria sopra Minerva, Carafa Chapel.

Pl. 30. *Above, left*: B. Bonfigli, Annunciation with St. Luke. Panel, 7 ft., 5³/₈ in. × 6 ft., 6³/₄ in. Perugia, Italy, Galleria Nazionale dell'Umbria. *Right*: Niccolò Alunno, Coronation of the Virgin with saints. Panel, 6 ft., 5 in. × 4 ft., 7 in. Foligno, Italy, S. Niccolò. *Below*: G. Boccati, Madonna and Child enthroned with angels, saints, and donors, known as the "Madonna del Pergolato," 1447. Panel, 8 ft., 5 in. × 10 ft., 3¹/₂ in. Perugia, Galleria Nazionale dell'Umbria.

Pl. 31. *Above, left*: Domenico di Bartolo, Madonna and Child with angels, 1433. Panel, 36⁵/₈×22⁷/₈ in. *Right*: Neroccio de' Landi, Madonna and Child with SS. John and Andrew, ca. 1496. Panel, 30³/₄×23⁵/₈ in. Both, Siena, Italy, Pinacoteca. *Below, left*: Matteo di Giovanni, Slaughter of the Innocents, 1491. Panel, 7 ft., 11 in. × 7 ft., 10¹/₂ in. Siena, S. Maria dei Servi. *Right*: Francesco di Giorgio, Adoration of the Shepherds, detail, last quarter of 15th cent. Panel; full size, 7 ft., 10 in. × 6 ft., 8 in. Siena, S. Domenico.

Pl. 32. *Above, left*: F. Squarcione, Madonna and Child. Panel, 31¹/₂×26 in. Berlin, Staatliche Museen. *Right*: N. Pizzolo, St. Augustine, detail of vault with the Fathers of the Church, ca. 1450. Fresco. Padua, Church of the Eremitani, Ovetari Chapel. *Below*: A. Mantegna, two scenes from The Triumph of Caesar, ca. 1486–92. Canvas; each, ca. 9×9 ft. Hampton Court, England, Royal Colls.

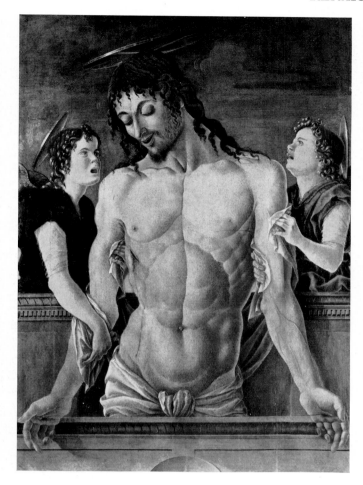

Pl. 33. *Above, left*: M. Zoppo, Dead Christ supported by two angels, ca. 1471. Panel, 40¹/₈×29¹/₈ in. Pesaro, Italy, Museo Civico. *Right*: G. Schiavone, Madonna and Child, ca. 1460. Panel, 28³/₈×24³/₈ in. Turin, Galleria Sabauda. *Below, left*: Bono da Ferrara, St. Christopher, ca. 1451. Fresco. Padua, Church of the Eremitani, Ovetari Chapel. *Right*: Galasso di Matteo Piva (?), Allegory of Autumn. Panel, 45¹/₄×28 in. Berlin, Staatliche Museen.

Pl. 34. *Above*: Pinturicchio and Antonio da Viterbo, Allegory of Astronomy, detail, 1492–94. Fresco. Rome, Vatican, Borgia Apartments, Sala delle Arti Liberali. *Below, left*: Perugino, Pietà with two saints. Detached fresco, 5 ft., 4 in. × 4 ft., 9 in. Spello, Italy, S. Maria Maggiore. *Right*: L. Signorelli, Holy Family. Panel, diam., 49 in. Florence, Uffizi.

Pl. 35. Filippo Lippi, Madonna and Child with angels and saints (Barbadori Altarpiece), detail, commissioned 1437. Panel; full size, 7 ft., 1¹/₂ in. × 8 ft. Paris, Louvre.

Pl. 36. C. Tura, Pietà, ca. 1468. Panel, 18⁷/₈×13 in. Venice, Museo Correr.

Pl. 37. *Above*: F. del Cossa, The Month of April, detail (cf. IV, PL. 2), ca. 1470. Fresco. Ferrara, Italy, Palazzo Schifanoia. *Below*: E. de' Roberti. *Left*: St. Jerome. Canvas, 8 ft., 8¹/₂ in. × 4 ft., 8 in. Ferrara, Pinacoteca. *Right*: SS. Apollonia and Michael. Panel; each, 10¹/₄×4³/₈ in. Paris, Louvre.

Pl. 38. *Left, above*: L. Costa, Madonna and Child with the Bentivoglio family, 1488. Canvas, 11 ft., 5³/₄ in. × 9 ft., 2¹/₄ in. *Below*: F. Francia, Madonna and Child with saints and angels, 1499. Panel, 10 ft., 6 in. × 9 ft., 2¹/₄ in. Both, Bologna, S. Giacomo Maggiore. *Right, above*: A. Aspertini, The Nativity with saints and donors. Panel, 7 ft., ⁵/₈ in. × 5 ft., 11⁵/₈ in. *Below*: T. Viti, Mary Magdalene, 1508. Panel, 6 ft., 3¹/₄ in. × 4 ft., 7¹/₈ in. Both, Bologna, Pinacoteca.

Pl. 39. Melozzo da Forlì, angel musician, fragment of the Ascension, from the apse of the Church of SS. Apostoli, Rome, ca. 1477–81. Fresco. Rome, Vatican Museums.

Pl. 40. *Above*: B. Zenale and B. Butinone, details of a polyptych, ca. 1485. *Left*: SS. Lucy, Catherine, and Mary Magdalene. *Right*: Madonna and Child enthroned, with angels. Panel; each panel, 6 ft., 6³/₈ in. × 3 ft., 5³/₈ in. Treviglio, Italy, S. Martino. *Below, left*: Bramantino, Crucifixion. Canvas, 12 ft., 2¹/₂ in. × 8 ft., 10¹/₄ in. Milan, Brera. *Right*: Il Bergognone (Ambrogio da Fossano), Annunciation, ca. 1500. Panel, 4 ft., 6³/₈ in. × 3 ft., 2¹/₄ in. Lodi, Italy, Church of the Incoronata.

Pl. 41. V. Foppa, St. Francis receiving the stigmata, part of a polyptych, 1478–81(?). Panel, 50³/₈×32¹/₄ in. Milan, Brera.

Pl. 42. C. Crivelli, St. George and the Dragon, after 1490. Panel, 11³/₈×8³/₈ in. London, National Gallery.

Pl. 43. Antonello da Messina, Portrait of a Man, 1476. Panel, 14³/₈ × 11 in. Turin, Museo Civico.

Pl. 44. Giovanni Bellini, The Feast of the Gods, 1514. Canvas, 5 ft., 7 in. × 6 ft., 2 in. Washington, D.C., National Gallery.

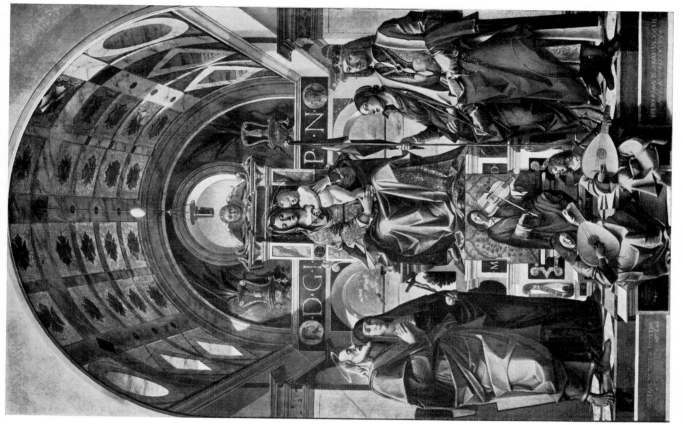

Pl. 45. *Left:* Alvise Vivarini and M. Basaiti, St. Ambrose enthroned, with other saints, ca. 1503. Panel, 16 ft., 5 in. × 8 ft., 2½ in. Venice, S. Maria Gloriosa dei Frari. *Right:* B. Montagna, Madonna and Child enthroned, with saints, 1499. Panel, 13 ft, 5½ in. × 8 ft, 6½ in. Milan, Brera.

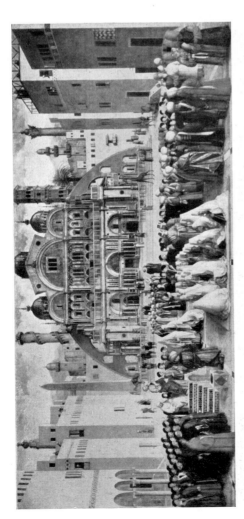

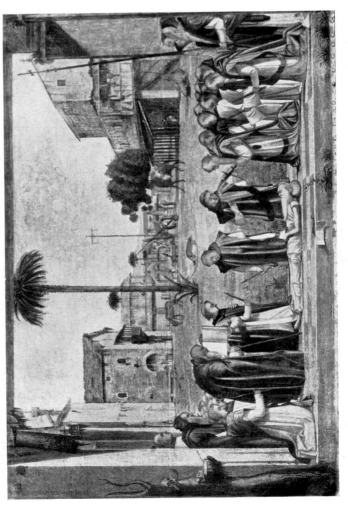

Pl. 46. *Left, above*: Gentile and Giovanni Bellini, St. Mark Preaching in Alexandria, ca. 1507. Canvas, 11 ft., 4 in. × 25 ft., 11 in. Milan, Brera. *Below*: V. Carpaccio, The Funeral of St. Jerome, 1502. Canvas, 4 ft., 8³/₄ in. × 6 ft., 10⁵/₈ in. Venice, Scuola di S. Giorgio degli Schiavoni. *Right, above*: Cima da Conegliano, Presentation of the Virgin in the Temple, ca. 1500. Panel, 3 ft., 5³/₈ in. × 4 ft., 9¹/₈ in. Dresden, Gemäldegalerie. *Below*: V. Catena, A Warrior Adoring the Infant Christ and the Virgin. Canvas, 5 ft., 1¹/₈ in. × 8 ft., 7³/₄ in. London, National Gallery.

Pl. 47. Bramante. *Left*: Milan, S. Maria presso S. Satiro, Baptistery, ca. 1480. *Right*: Abbiategrasso, Italy, Cathedral, great arch of façade, 1497.

Pl. 48. *Above, left*: Como, Italy, Cathedral (begun late 14th cent.), view with apse, 1513–19 (dome, 18th cent.). *Right*: Milan, S. Maria della Passione (begun 1482–85), lateral view with dome, completed 1530. *Below*: Lodi, Italy, Church of the Incoronata (begun 1488), view of loggia (renovated 1876).

Pl. 49. *Above*: A. Palladio, S. Giorgio Maggiore, Venice, 1566–1610 (completed by V. Scamozzi). *Below*: G. M. Falconetto, Loggia Corner (Cornaro), Padua, 1524.

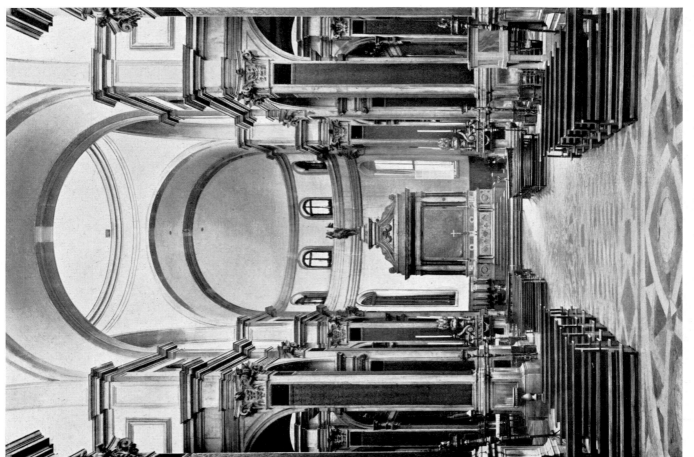

Pl. 50. *Left*: G. Spavento and T. Lombardo, S. Salvatore, Venice, 1506-34. *Right*: Padua, S. Giustina, 16th cent.

Pl. 51. *Left*: Rome, Villa Madama, view of loggia, with decoration by Giulio Romano and Giovanni da Udine, ca. 1520–23. (Cf. VIII, pl. 206.) *Right*: Todi, Italy, S. Maria della Consolazione, 1508–1607.

Pl. 52. B. Peruzzi, Palazzo Massimo alle Colonne, Rome, courtyard portico, 1532–36. (Cf. XI, PL. 121.)

Pl. 53. Giulio Romano. *Above*: Mantua, Italy, Palazzo Ducale, view of wings facing on the Cortile della Cavallerizza, completed by G. B. Bertani, ca. 1572. *Below*: Mantua, Palazzo del Te, ca. 1526–35. (Cf. VIII, PL. 428.) *Left*: Loggia. *Right*: Sala di Fetonte.

Pl. 54. Florence, Palazzo Guadagni, early 16th cent.

Pl. 55. *Above*: A. da Sangallo the Elder, S. Biagio, near Montepulciano, Italy, interior view, begun ca. 1518. *Below*: A. da Sangallo the Younger, vestibule of the Palazzo Farnese, Rome, begun ca. 1515.

Pl. 56. *Above*: A. da Sangallo the Younger, Palazzo Farnese, Rome, façade (completed by Michelangelo, ca. 1547). *Below*: J. Sansovino, Loggetta of the Campanile, Piazza S. Marco, Venice, 1537–45 (rebuilt early 20th cent.).

Pl. 57. *Above*: G. F. Rustici, John the Baptist disputing with a Levite and a Pharisee, 1506–11. Bronze. Florence, Baptistery, above north door. *Below, left*: G. A. Montorsoli, Scylla, from the Fountain of Neptune, 1557. Marble, ht., ca. 6 ft. Messina, Sicily, Museo Nazionale. *Right*: N. Tribolo, Fountain of the Labyrinth, ca. 1545. Marble and bronze. Florence, Villa della Petraia.

Pl. 58. A. Sansovino, The Annunciation, ca. 1523. Marble. Loreto, Italy, Sanctuary of the Holy House.

Pl. 59. *Left*: L. Lotti (Lorenzetto) after a design by Raphael, Jonah, 1519. Rome, S. Maria del Popolo, Chigi Chapel. *Right*: J. Sansovino, Madonna and Child with the Infant St. John, ca. 1540–45 (restored). Terra cotta, gilded and painted. Venice, Piazza S. Marco, Loggetta.

Pl. 60. Michelangelo, Dawn, detail of tomb of Lorenzo di Piero de' Medici, Duke of Urbino. Marble. Florence, S. Lorenzo, New Sacristy.

Pl. 61. Leonardo da Vinci, The Last Supper, 1495–97. Oil tempera on wall, 15 ft, 1⅛ in. × 28 ft, 10½ in. Milan, S. Maria delle Grazie, Refectory. (Cf. IX, pl. 125.)

Pl. 62. *Left*: B. Luini, Boy with a Puzzle. Panel, 16×13½ in. Peterborough, England, Elton Hall, Proby Coll. *Right*: A. de Predis, Girl with Cherries. Panel, 19¼×14⅞ in. New York, Metropolitan Museum.

Pl. 63. *Left*: Sodoma, St. Catherine swoons after receiving the stigmata, 1525–26. Fresco. Siena, S. Domenico. *Right*: Gaudenzio Ferrari, Nativity, 1513. Fresco. Varallo, Italy, S. Maria delle Grazie.

Pl. 64. Fra Bartolommeo, The Mystic Marriage of St. Catherine, 1512. Panel, 10 ft., 11³/₄ in. × 8 ft., 8¹/₂ in. Florence, Accademia.

Pl. 65. Raphael, Madonna and Child with the Infant St. John, known as "La Belle Jardinière," 1507. Panel, 48×31¹/₂ in. Paris, Louvre.

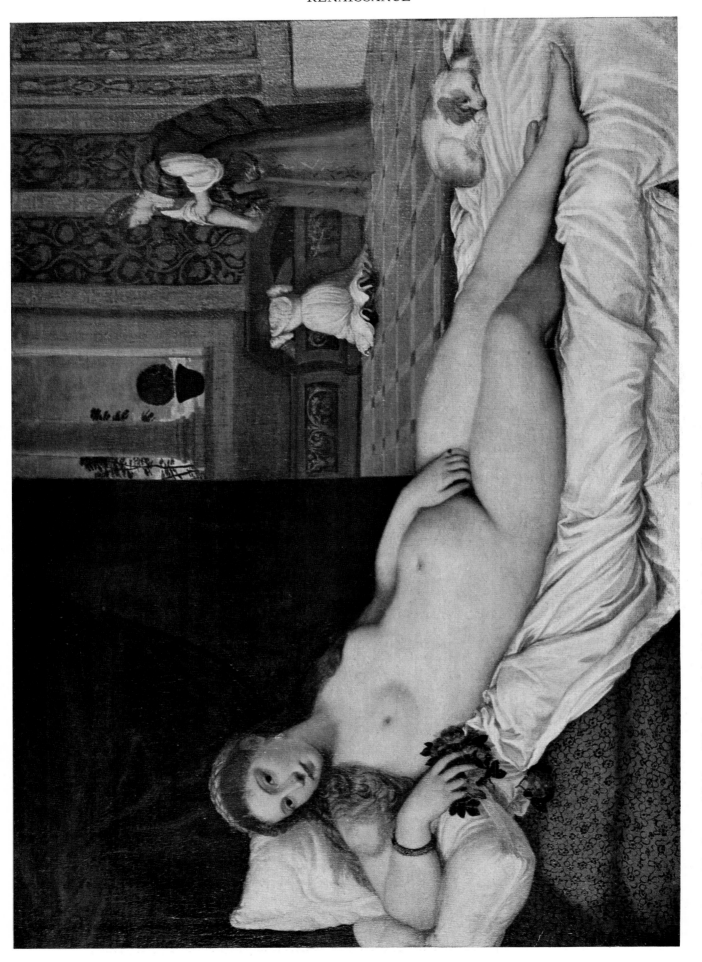

Pl. 66. Titian, The Venus of Urbino, 1538. Canvas, 3 ft, 11 in. × 5 ft, 5 in. Florence, Uffizi.

Pl. 67. *Left:* M. Albertinelli, Madonna and Child, 1500, central panel of a triptych. Panel, ca. 12 × 8 1/2 in. Milan, Museo Poldi Pezzoli. *Right:* Franciabigio, Madonna del Pozzo, ca. 1508. Panel, 41 3/4 × 31 7/8 in. Florence, Accademia.

Pl. 68. *Above*: Palma Vecchio, Reclining Venus, ca. 1517. Canvas, 3 ft., 8 in. × 6 ft., 1 in. Dresden, Gemäldegalerie. *Below*: Cariani (G. de' Busi), Madonna and Child with a donor, 1520. Canvas, 22×29 1/2 in. Bergamo, Italy, Accademia Carrara.

Pl. 69. Bonifazio Veronese, The Finding of Moses, detail. Canvas; full size, 5 ft., 9 in. × 11 ft., 4 in. Milan, Brera.

Pl. 70. G. G. Savoldo, Mary Magdalene approaching the Sepulcher. Canvas, 34×31¼ in. London, National Gallery.

Pl. 71. *Above, left*: Pordenone, The Lamentation, 1523. Fresco. *Right*: Il Romanino (G. Romani), Christ Crowned with Thorns, 1519–20. Fresco. Both, Cremona, Italy, Cathedral. *Below*: Moretto da Brescia, Elijah and the Angel, 1521–24. Canvas, 6 ft., 9 in. × 7 ft., 11 in. Brescia, Italy, S. Giovanni Evangelista.

Pl. 72. L. Lotto, Madonna and Child with saints, 1505–06. Panel, 5 ft., 9⅝ in. × 5 ft., 3¾ in. Santa Cristina, near Treviso, Italy, parish church.

Pl. 73. Dosso Dossi, Circe. Canvas, 5 ft., 9¹/₂ in. × 5 ft., 8¹/₂ in. Rome, Galleria Borghese.

Pl. 74. Michelangelo, *Ignudo*, detail of the Drunkenness of Noah, 1508–12. Fresco. Rome, Vatican, Sistine Chapel, ceiling.

Pl. 75. Sebastiano del Piombo, Pietà, ca. 1517. Panel, 8 ft., 10 in. × 7 ft., 4¹/₂ in. Viterbo, Italy, Museo Civico.

Pl. 76. Il Rosso, Portrait of a Young Man, ca. 1523. Panel, 47¼ × 33⅞ in. Naples, Museo di Capodimonte.

Pl. 77. *Above*: D. Beccafumi, Deucalion and Pyrrha. Panel, 20⁷/₈×52³/₄ in. Florence, Fondazione Horne. *Below, left*: Il Rosso, The Madonna and Child, St. Anne, and Infant St. John. Panel, 63³/₈×46¹/₈ in. Los Angeles, County Museum. *Right*: Pontormo, The Supper at Emmaus, 1525. Canvas, 7 ft., 6¹/₂ in. × 5 ft., 8⁷/₈ in. Florence, Uffizi.

Pl. 78. *Above, left*: G. Macchietti, The Baths of Pozzuoli, 1570–72. Slate, 46 1/8 × 39 3/8 in. *Right*: M. Cavalori, The Wool Factory, 1570–72. Canvas, 45 5/8 × 33 7/8 in. Both, Florence, Palazzo Vecchio, *studiolo* of Francesco I de' Medici. *Below*: G. Vasari, frescoes in the Sala degli Elementi, 1555. Florence, Palazzo Vecchio.

Pl. 79. Bronzino, The Deposition, detail, 1553 (artist's replica of original sent to France). Panel; full size, 7 ft., 11⅝ in. × 5 ft., 8½ in. Florence, Palazzo Vecchio, Chapel of Eleanor of Toledo.

Pl. 80. Correggio, Jupiter and Antiope, ca. 1525. Canvas, 6 ft., 2 $^3/_4$ in. × 4 ft., $^7/_8$ in. Paris, Louvre.

Pl. 81. *Above, left*: N. dell'Abate, The Martyrdom of SS. Peter and Paul, 1547. Panel, 11 ft., 10⁷/₈ in. × 6 ft., 6 in. Dresden, Gemäldegalerie. *Right*: Parmigianino, the so-called "Madonna dal Collo Lungo," ca. 1535. Panel, 7 ft., 1 in. × 4 ft., 4³/₈ in. Florence, Uffizi. *Below, left*: F. Primaticcio, study for a Bacchus. Pen, bistre, and white lead. Paris, École des Beaux-Arts. *Right*: F. Barocci, Rest on the Flight into Egypt, 1573. Canvas, 52³/₈×43³/₄ in. Rome, Vatican Museums.

Pl. 82. *Above*: Giulio Romano, The Marriage Feast of Cupid and Psyche, detail, 1528. Fresco. Mantua, Palazzo del Te. *Below*: A. Meldolla (Lo Schiavone), Diana and Actaeon. Panel, 13 3/4 × 32 5/8 in. Milan, Castello Sforzesco.

PI. 83. *Above, left*: J. Bassano, Annunciation to the Shepherds. Canvas, 38×31¹/₂ in. Rome, Accademia di S. Luca. *Right*: Palma Giovane, Senator Pasquale Cicogna attends Mass while Father Priamo Balbi administers the Sacrament to the pious women of the Hospice, 1585. Canvas, 11 ft., 9³/₄ in. × 8 ft., 7¹/₂ in. Venice, Oratorio dei Crociferi. *Below*: P. Veronese, The Family of Darius before Alexander. Canvas, 7 ft., 9 in. × 15 ft., 7 in. London, National Gallery.

Pl. 84. *Left:* B. Cellini, Narcissus, 1548. Marble. Florence, Museo Nazionale. *Center:* B. Bandinelli and G. Bandini, apostle on a choir screen, between 1547–72. Marble. Florence, Museo dell'Opera del Duomo. *Right:* Giambologna, Charity, from the Grimaldi Chapel, Genoa, ca. 1579–85. Bronze, ht., 5 ft., 8⁷/₈ in. Genoa, Palazzo dell'Università.

Pl. 85. *Left*: G. B. della Porta, Tomb of Vespasiano Gonzaga (d. 1591), with central statue by L. Leoni. Sabbioneta, Lombardy, the Incoronata. *Right*: D. Fontana, Tomb of Sixtus V, with Lombard and Flemish sculptures, 1585–90. Rome, S. Maria Maggiore.

Pl. 86. *Left*: A. Vittoria, St. Jerome, ca. 1565. Marble, ht. 6 ft., 3⅝ in. Venice, S. Maria Gloriosa dei Frari. *Right*: C. Mariani, St. Catherine of Siena, ca. 1600. Stucco. Rome, S. Bernardo alle Terme.

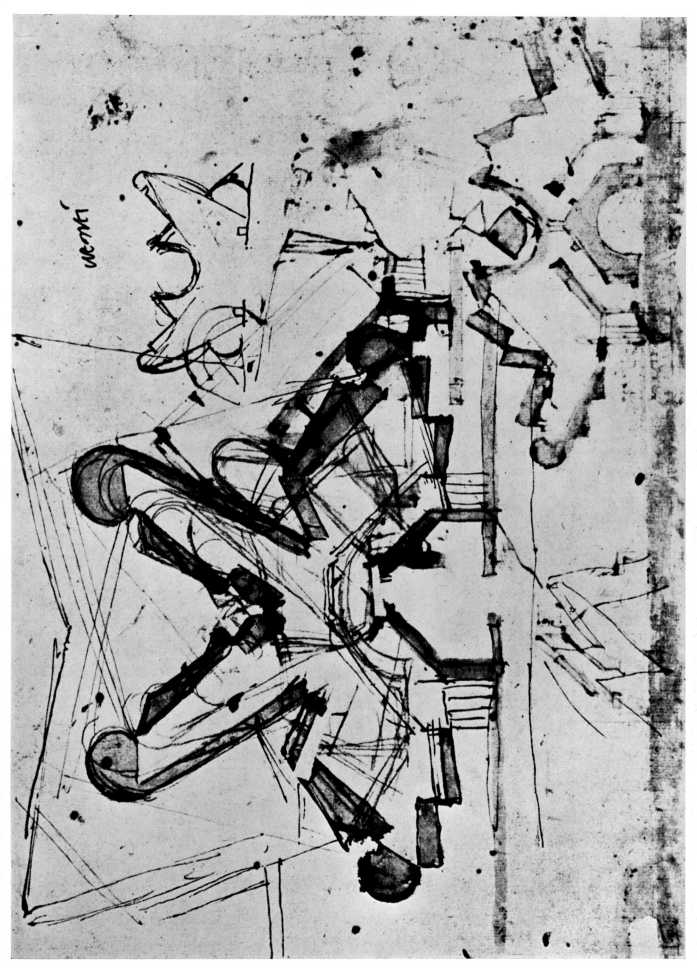

Pl. 87. Michelangelo, studies for the fortification of the Porta al Prato, Florence. Pen and wash with traces of sanguine, $11\frac{1}{4} \times 15\frac{5}{8}$ in. Florence, Casa Buonarroti.

Pl. 88. *Above*: B. Ammanati, Palazzo Pitti, Florence, courtyard, ca. 1558–70. *Below*: Pisa, S. Stefano dei Cavalieri, second half of 16th cent.

Pl. 89. Rome. *Above*: Vignola, Villa Giulia, 1551–53. *Below*: P. Ligorio, Casino of Pius IV, Vatican Gardens, 1558–62.

Pl. 90. Rome. *Above*: D. Fontana, Lateran Palace, Piazza S. Giovanni in Laterano, 1586–88. *Below, left*: Giacomo della Porta, S. Luigi dei Francesi, completed 1588. *Right*: M. Longhi the Elder, Altemps Chapel, S. Maria in Trastevere, ca. 1585.

Pl. 91. Milan. *Above*: G. Alessi, Palazzo Marino, courtyard, ca. 1553–60. *Below, left*: P. Tibaldi, S. Fedele, begun 1563 (completed by M. Bassi and F. M. Ricchino). *Right*: L. Leoni, Casa degli Omenoni, façade with sculptures by A. Abbondio, ca. 1573.

Pl. 92. *Above*: M. Sanmicheli, Palazzo Bevilacqua, Verona, 1530. *Below*: Vicenza, Palazzo Bonin (formerly Thiene),
courtyard, second half of 16th cent.

Pl. 93. Tintoretto, The Last Supper, 1576–81. Canvas, ht., ca. 17 ft., 9 in. Venice, Scuola di S. Rocco.

Pl. 94. Titian, "Noli me tangere." Canvas, 42 $^3/_4 \times 35^3/_4$ in. London, National Gallery.

Pl. 95. H. Memling, Portrait of a Man, ca. 1475. Panel, $10^{1}/_{4} \times 7^{1}/_{2}$ in. Venice, Accademia.

Pl. 96. D. Bouts, The Last Supper, central panel of a triptych, 1464–67. Panel, 5 ft., 11 in. × 4 ft., 11 in. Louvain, Belgium, Collegiate Church of St-Pierre.

Pl. 97. G. David, Crucifixion, ca. 1515 (?). Panel, 40¹/₈×35 in. Genoa, Palazzo Bianco.

Pl. 98. *Above, left*: Q. Massys (Metsys), Erasmus of Rotterdam, ca. 1517. Panel transferred to canvas, 23¼×18⅛ in. Rome, Galleria Nazionale. *Right*: F. Floris de Vriendt, Fall of the Rebel Angels, central panel of a triptych, 1554. Panel, 9 ft., 11¾ in. × 7 ft., 2⅝ in. Antwerp, Musée Royal des Beaux-Arts. *Below*: P. Bruegel the Elder, Summer, 1568. Pen drawing, 8⅝×11 in. Hamburg, Kunsthalle.

Pl. 99. *Above*: Cornelis II Floris de Vriendt, Town Hall, Antwerp, 1561–65. *Below, left*: Lieven de Key, Meat Market, Haarlem, Netherlands, 1602–03. *Right*: J. Dubroeucq, Mary Magdalene, ca. 1535–50. Mons, Belgium, Ste-Waudru.

Pl. 100. *Above*: Il Rosso and F. Primaticcio, fresco and stucco decoration, Gallery of Francis I in the Château at Fontainebleau, ca. 1533–44. *Below*: G. Pilon, The Deposition, ca. 1580–85. Bronze. Paris, Louvre.

Pl. 101. France. *Above*: Château of Azay-le-Rideau, begun 1518. *Below, left*: Château of Chambord, view of roof, begun 1519. *Right*: P. Delorme, façade elements from the Château of Anet, ca. 1547. Paris, École des Beaux-Arts, courtyard.

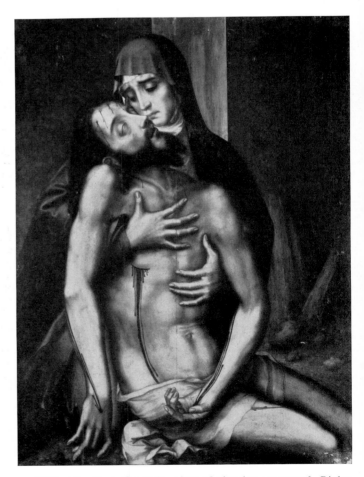

Pl. 102. Spain. *Above, left*: P. Machuca, Palace of Charles V (begun ca. 1526), Alhambra, Granada, view of circular courtyard. *Right*: A. Berruguete, Eve, detail of choir stall, 1539–48. Wood. Toledo, Cathedral. *Below, left*: P. Leoni, detail of the tomb of Charles V, 1593–98. Gilded bronze. El Escorial, near Madrid, church. *Right*: Luis de Morales (d. 1586), Pietà. Canvas, Madrid, Academia de S. Fernando.

Pl. 103. F. Clouet, Diane de Poitiers, third quarter of 16th cent. Panel, 36¹/₄×32 in. Washington, D.C., National Gallery.

Pl. 104. J. Gossaert (Mabuse), Neptune and Amphitrite, 1516. Panel, 6 ft., 2 in. × 4 ft., 1 in. Berlin, Staatliche Museen.

Pl. 105. W. Egckl, Antiquarium, Residenz, Munich, interior, begun 1569.

Pl. 106. *Left*: H. Gerhard, St. Michael, ca. 1588. Munich, St. Michael, façade. *Right, above*: N. M. Deutsch the Elder, Bathsheba in the Bath, 1517. Panel, $14^5/8 \times 11$ in. Basel, Kunstmuseum. *Below*: H. Burgkmair the Elder, Virgin and Child, 1509. Panel, $64^5/8 \times 39^3/8$ in. Nürnberg, Germany, Germanisches National-Museum.

Pl. 107. Engravings. *Left, above*: A. Durer, Apollo and Diana. *Below*: J. de' Barbari, Apollo and Diana. *Right, above*: A. Altdorfer, The Temptation of the Hermits, 1506. *Below*: H. Aldegrever, Hercules and Antaeus, 1550.

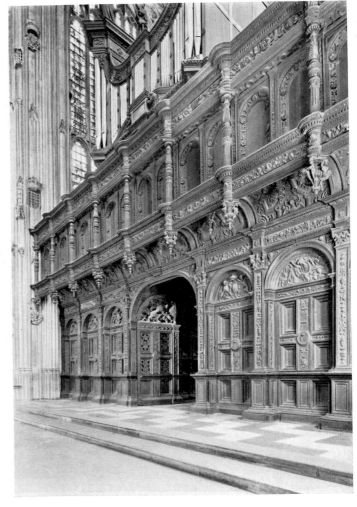

Pl. 108. England. *Above*: Hatfield House, Hertfordshire, 1607–11. *Below, left*: Marble chimney piece in the Long Gallery, Aston Hall, Birmingham, 1618–35. *Right*: Wooden organ screen (1533–35), King's College Chapel, Cambridge. (Copyright, *Country Life*.)

Pl. 109. A. Dürer, The Adoration of the Trinity, 1511. Panel, 4 ft., 5 in. × 4 ft., ¹/₂ in. Vienna, Kunsthistorisches Museum.

Pl. 110. H. Holbein the Younger, The Artist's Family, 1528 (or 1529?). Tempera on paper attached to panel, $30\,^1/_4 \times 25\,^1/_4$ in. Basel, Kunstmuseum.

Pl. 111. Helsingør (Elsinore), Denmark, Kronborg Castle, rebuilt according to designs by A. van Opbergen, ca. 1575–85 (restored).

Pl. 112. Moscow. *Above*: Aloisio (Alevisio Novi), Cathedral of the Archangel Michael, detail, begun 1505. *Below*: P. A. Solari (Solario) and M. Ruffo, Granovitaya Palace, 1487–91 (windows, 17th cent.).

Pl. 113. *Above, left*: The painter Sisley and his wife. Canvas, 42¹/₈ × 29¹/₂ in. Cologne, Wallraf-Richartz-Museum. *Right*: The painter Bazille. Canvas, 41³/₈ × 29¹/₈ in. Paris, Louvre. *Below*: Odalisque. Canvas, 27 × 48¹/₄ in. Washington, D.C., National Gallery.

Pl. 114. *Above*: Mme Charpentier and Her Children. Canvas, 5 ft., ¹/₂ in. × 6 ft., 2⁷/₈ in. New York, Metropolitan Museum. *Below, left*: La Fin du Déjeuner. Canvas, 39×32¹/₄ in. Frankfort on the Main, Städelsches Kunstinstitut. *Right*: After the Bath. Canvas, 45¹/₂×35 in. Winterthur, Switzerland, Georg Reinhart Coll.

Pl. 115. Le Bal à Bougival. Canvas, 5 ft., 10½ in. × 3 ft., 1¾ in. Boston, Museum of Fine Arts.

Pl. 116. Bathers. Canvas, 3 ft., 7¼ in. × 5 ft., 3 in. Paris, Louvre.

Pl. 117. *Left*: Victor Choquet. Canvas, 17³/₄×13³/₄ in. Cambridge, Mass., Fogg Art Museum. *Right*: Mme Charpentier. Canvas, 18¹/₈×15 in. Paris, Louvre.

Pl. 118. Sleeping Bather. Canvas, $31\frac{7}{8} \times 25\frac{5}{8}$ in. Winterthur, Switzerland, Oskar Reinhart Coll.

Pl. 119. The Tyrannicides, painting on an Attic lekythos of ca. 470 B.C., probably derived from the marble group by Kritios and Nesiotes (477–476 B.C.). Ht., 8½ in. (Cf. a Roman copy in marble, III, PL. 347.) Vienna, Kunsthistorisches Museum.

Pl. 120. Original and copy. *Left*: Caryatid of the Erechtheion, Acropolis, Athens, 421–406 B.C. *Right*: Roman copy, Hadrianic period. Hadrian's Villa, near Tivoli, Italy, Antiquarium.

Pl. 121. Derivations from a prototype, the Punishment of Dirce. *Above*: The so-called "Farnese Bull," 3d cent., probably a Roman copy of the group by Apollonios and Tau-
riskos of Tralles (late 2d cent. B.C.). Marble. Naples, Museo Nazionale. *Below*: Wall
painting in the House of the Vettii, Pompeii, 1st cent.

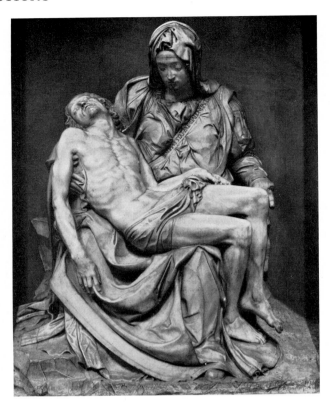

Pl. 122. *Above, left*: P. J. A. Bonacolsi called L'Antico (1460–1528), small-scale copy of the Apollo Belvedere (III, PL. 383). Bronze. Venice, Ca' d'Oro. *Right*: Nanni di Baccio Bigio (d. 1568), copy of Michelangelo's Pietà (IX, PL. 526). Marble. Florence, Sto Spirito. *Below*: B. Spranger (1546–1611), The Last Judgment, after Fra Angelico (I, PL. 261). Panel, Turin, Galleria Sabauda.

Pl. 123. Water-color rendering of a wall painting with Virgin and Child (3d cent.) in the Catacomb of Priscilla, Rome, executed on paper over a faint photographic image, by C. Tabanelli for J. Wilpert, *Die Malereien der Katacomben Roms*, Freiburg im Breisgau, 1903. (Cf. photographs of same catacomb, III, PLS. 93–95).

Pl. 124. Terra-cotta copy of a Chinese bronze vessel of the *kuang* type, with incrustations imitating patina. Rome, private coll. (Cf. an original of same type, Shang period, III, Pl. 222.)

Pl. 125. *Left*: P. P. Rubens, The Entombment of Christ, ca. 1613-15, after The Entombment by Caravaggio (Rome, Vatican Museums). Panel, 34³/₄×25³/₄ in. Ottawa, National Gallery of Canada. *Right*: Engraving of a ceiling fresco by Pietro da Cortona (II, Pl. 176), from G. Teti, *Aedes Barberinae*, 1642.

Pl. 126. Graphic reproduction of paintings. *Above*: Engraving of a fresco in the Camposanto, Pisa, from *Raccolta di pitture antiche*, Pisa, 1820. *Below*: Illustration of The Birth of the Virgin by Ghirlandajo (VI, PL. 184), from J. A. Crowe and G. B. Cavalcaselle, *A New History of Painting in Italy*, London, 1864–66.

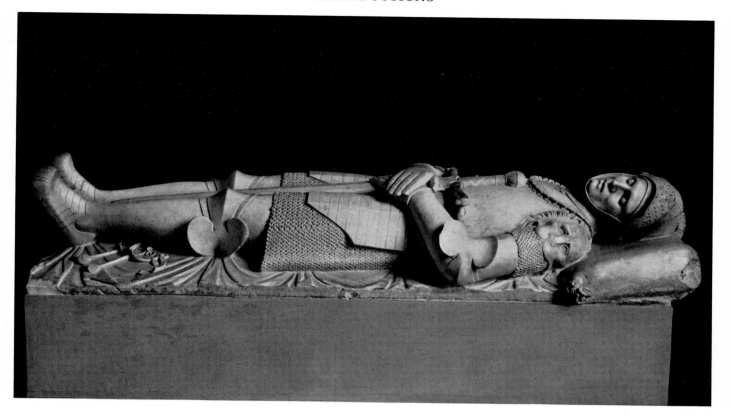

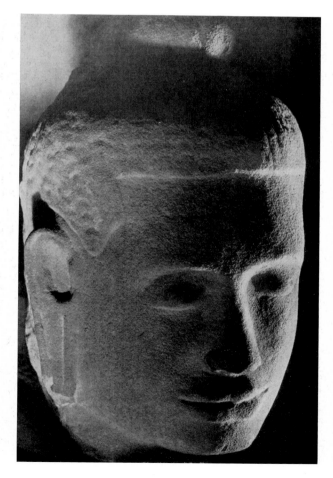

Pl. 127. Photographic reproduction of sculpture, exemplifying lighting effects. *Above*: T. Lombardo, effigy of Guido Guidarelli. Marble. Ravenna, Pinacoteca dell'Accademia di Belle Arti. *Below, left*: Head, Roman copy of a Hellenistic original (3d cent. B.C.). Marble. Rome, Museo Nazionale Romano. *Right*: Head of Buddha, Khmer period, 12th–13th cent. Stone. Prague, National Gallery.

Pl. 128. *Above*: Cast of a scene from Trajan's Column (X, PL. 152). Rome, Museo della Civiltà Romana. *Below*: Plastic reconstruction of St. Sophia, Kiev, in its 11th-century state. Kiev, St. Sophia.

Pl. 129. Ancient restorations utilizing clamps. *Left, above*: Bowl of Samarra ware, 4th millennium B.C., showing clamp holes remaining in modern restoration. Diam., 9³/₈ in. *Below*: Vase from Erech (Uruk), detail, 3d millennium B.C. Alabaster, diam. at rim, 14¹/₈ in. Both, Baghdad, Iraq Museum. *Right*: Attic amphora found with foot reattached, from Paestum, 530–510 B.C. Ht., 22⁷/₈ in. Paestum, Museo Archeologico.

Pl. 130. The Laocoön Group, Roman copy of a Greek original of ca. 50 B.C. Marble, ht., 7 ft., 11¼ in. Rome, Vatican Museums. *Left*: Former restoration by Montorsoli, 1532–33, and others. *Right*: Restoration by F. Magi, 1960.

Pl. 131. Rome, the Arch of Titus, ca. 82, restored and reintegrated with travertine by R. Stern and G. Valadier, 1820–21. *Left:* The monument as depicted in an aquatint by D. Havell, late 18th cent. *Right:* The present state.

Pl. 132. *Left, above:* Ruins, Temple of Zeus, Olympia, Greece, ca. 460 B.C. *Below:* Reconstitution according to A. J. Evans of the "Queen's Megaron," Palace of Knossos, Crete, 1700–1400 B.C. *Right:* Partial restoration, 1930, of the Temple of Vesta, Rome, 2d cent., extant parts reintegrated with travertine.

Pl. 133. Rome, campanile of S. Maria in Cosmedin, ca. 1200, before and after the restoration of 1958.

Pl. 134. Anagni, Italy, view showing demolition undertaken to reveal the complex of the Cathedral, 11th–12th cent., and adjacent buildings of the same period. (Photographed 1956, 1959.)

Pl. 135. Rome, cloister of S. Lorenzo fuori le Mura, ca. 1190, before and after the restoration of 1962.

Pl. 136. *Above*: Speyer, Germany, Cathedral, baptismal chapel, 11th cent., shown (*left*) with subsequent alterations including 19th–century decoration and (*right*) restored to its original form, 1957–61. *Below*: Grottaferrata, Italy, loggia of the Monastery, before and after the restoration of 1959.

Pl. 137. Discus thrower, detail of Etruscan wall painting, late 6th cent. B.C., detached and restored in 1958, from the Tomb of the Olympiad, Tarquinia, Italy. Tarquinia, Museo Nazionale.

Pl. 138. *Above*: Fragments from the west pediment of the Temple of Zeus, Olympia, Greece, ca. 460 B.C., assembled and mounted with supports. Marble. Olympia, Archaeological Museum. *Below*: Amazon, after an original attributed to Phidias, ca. 440 B.C. *Left*: The Mattei Amazon, Roman copy. Marble, ht., 6 ft., 11 in. Rome, Vatican Museums. *Right*: Restored cast of a head found at Hadrian's Villa (Rome, Museo Nazionale Romano), integrated with a cast of the Mattei Amazon. Rome, Università.

Pl. 139. F. Cozza, The Nativity, detail, ca. 1660–62. Fresco. *Above, and center*: Before restoration, photographed under normal and (*center*) raking light. *Below*: After restoration. (Cf. PL. 144.) Rome, Pantheon, Chapel of St. Joseph.

Pl. 140. A. Mantegna, Martyrdom of St. James, right side, 1454–57, bombed in 1944. Padua, Church of the Eremitani, Ovetari Chapel. *Left:* Initial recomposition with 1,800 recuperated fragments, based on photographs of the original. *Right:* The restored fresco, integrated with water color.

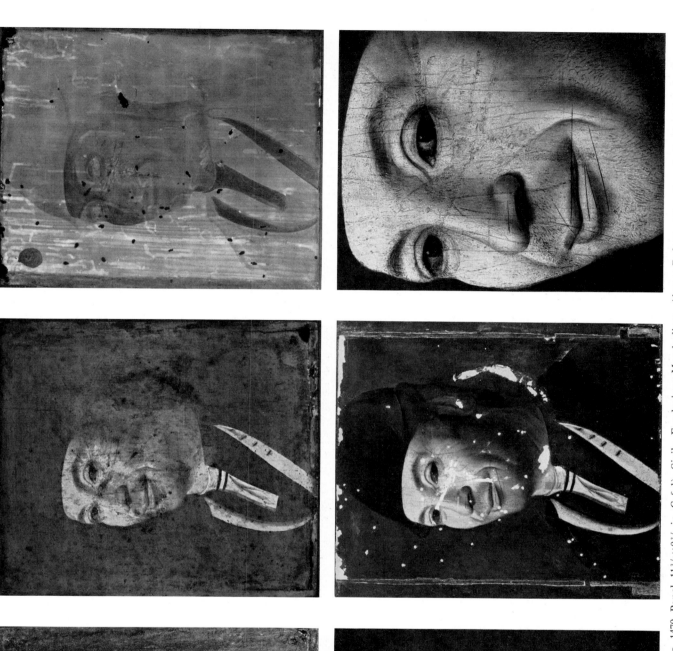

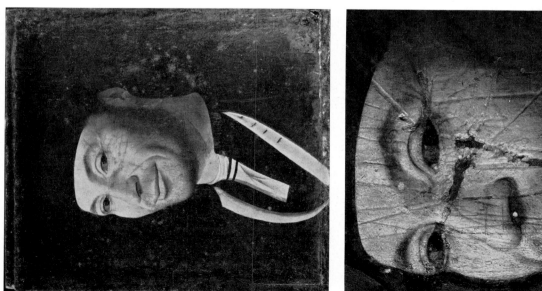

Pl. 141. Antonello da Messina, Portrait of a Man, ca. 1470. Panel, 11³/₄×9³/₄ in. Cefalù, Sicily. Fondazione Mandralisca. *Above:* Before restoration. *Left:* Photograph. *Center:* Ultraviolet photograph. *Right:* X-ray photograph (shadowgraph). *Below, left:* Detail of the stripped-down painting photographed under raking light. *Center:* The stripped-down painting, holes filled with stopping. *Right:* Completed restoration with water-color inpainting, detail.

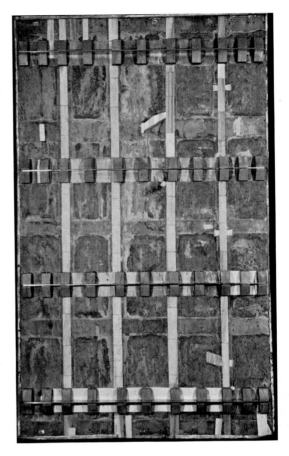

Pl. 142. Mechanical restraints. *Above, and below, left*: Back of panel (St. Clare and scenes of her life, 1283), showing original wooden cradling (*above, left*) and the steel and wood cradling applied in 1956 (*right*, detail *below, left*). Assisi, Italy, S. Chiara. *Below, right*: Back of panel in fragile state (Madonna della Clemenza, 8th cent.?), showing lightweight cradling of brass wire and Plexiglas applied with adhesive. Rome, S. Maria in Trastevere.

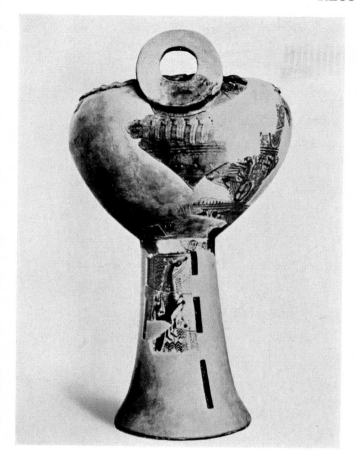

Pl. 143. *Left, and below*: Reconstitutions with minimal terra-cotta fragments. *Left*: Attic crater, Geometric period. Athens, National Museum. *Below*: Section of pedimental frieze, Temple of Athena, Syracuse, Sicily, early 6th cent. B.C. Syracuse, Museo Archeologico. *Right*: Fragment of bronze sheeting before and after treatment (mechanical cleaning and consolidation with metallic stucco), from Castel San Mariano, near Perugia, Italy, 6th cent. B.C. Perugia, Musei Civici.

Pl. 144. F. Cozza, The Nativity, ca. 1660–62, detail of fresco with section revealed by cleaning. (Cf. PL. 139.) Rome, Pantheon, Chapel of St. Joseph.

Pl. 145. *Above, left*: Lady Sarah Bunbury Sacrificing to the Graces. Canvas, 7 ft., 10¹/₈ in. × 4 ft., 11⁷/₈ in. Chicago, Art Institute. *Right*: Mrs. Carnac. Canvas, 7 ft., 8⁷/₈ in. × 4 ft., 9¹/₈ in. London, Wallace Coll. *Below*: Georgiana, Duchess of Devonshire, and her daughter. Canvas, 3 ft., 7³/₄ in. × 4 ft., 7⁷/₈ in. Derbyshire, England, Trustees of the Chatsworth Settlement.

Pl. 146. *Above, left*: Self-portrait. Canvas, 50×39³/₄ in. London, Royal Academy of Arts. *Right*: Mrs. Braddyll. Panel, 29¹/₄×24¹/₄ in. London, Wallace Coll. *Below, left*: The Infant Samuel. Canvas, 33³/₄×26³/₄ in. *Right*: The Age of Innocence. Canvas, 30×25 in. Last two, London, Tate Gallery.

Pl. 147. The Honorable Augustus Keppel. Canvas, 7 ft., 7³/₄ in. × 4 ft., 9¹/₂ in. London (Greenwich), National Maritime Museum.

Pl. 148. Kitty Fisher as Cleopatra. Canvas, 29^{7}/$_{8}$×24^{3}/$_{4}$ in. London, Kenwood, The Iveagh Bequest.

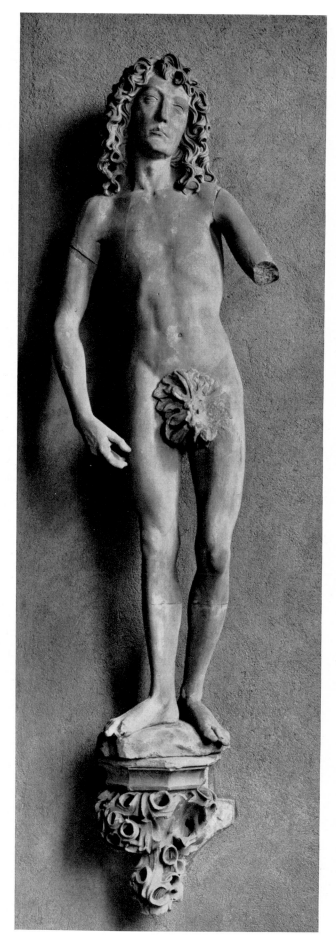
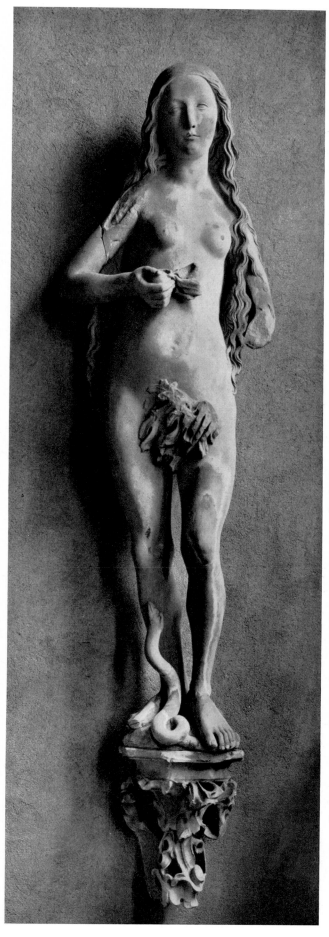

Pl. 149. Adam and Eve. Stone. Würzburg, Mainfränkisches Museum.

Pl. 150. Virgin and Child on a crescent moon, detail. Linden wood; full ht., 47⁵/₈ in. Berlin, Staatliche Museen.

Pl. 151. Hunchback with a bow. Miniature. Paris, Bibliothèque Nationale.

Pl. 152. *Above*: Old man resting under a tree. Miniature. Paris, Bibliothèque Nationale. *Below, left*: Man with a spindle. Miniature. Washington, D.C., Freer Gallery of Art. *Right*: Two lovers. Miniature. New York, Metropolitan Museum.

Pl. 153. John the Baptist. Panel, 21 1/4 × 12 1/4 in. Berlin, Staatliche Museen.

Pl. 154. *Above*: The Seizing of Christ and the Kiss of Judas, predella panel from S. Giovanni in Monte, Bologna. Panel, 13³/₄×46¹/₂ in. Dresden, Gemälde-galerie. *Below*: Detail of Pl. 156, The Madonna Enthroned.

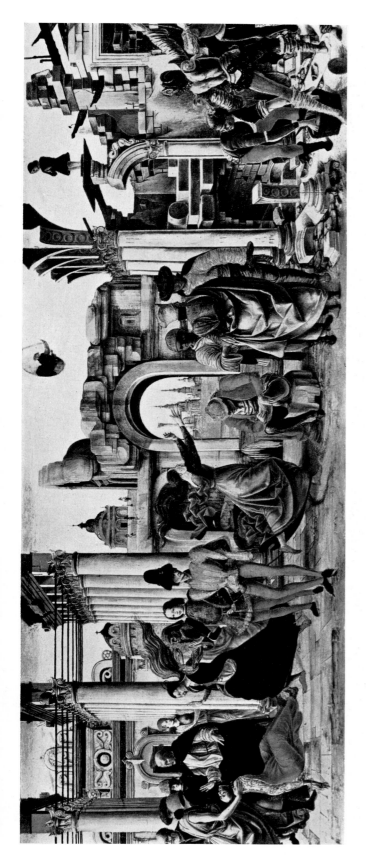

Pl. 155. Predella with scenes from the life of St. Vincent Ferrer, two details, from the Griffoni Altarpiece. Panel, ht., 10⅝ in. Rome, Vatican Museums.

Pl. 156. The Madonna Enthroned with four saints, altarpiece from S. Maria in Porto, Ravenna, Italy. Canvas, 10 ft., 7 in. × 7 ft., 10 1/2 in. (Cf. PL. 154.) Milan, Brera.

Pl. 157. *Above, left*: The Last Supper. Panel, 11³/₄×8¹/₄ in. London, National Gallery. *Right*: Pietà, part of a predella. Panel, 13¹/₂×12¹/₄ in. Liverpool, Walker Art Gallery. *Below*: The Israelites Gathering Manna. Panel transferred to canvas, 11³/₈×25 in. London, National Gallery.

Pl. 158. *Above*: Portraits of Giovanni II Bentivoglio and Ginevra Bentivoglio. Panel; each, 21¹/₈×15¹/₄ in. Washington, D.C., National Gallery. *Below, left*: Madonna and Child. Panel, 21¹/₈×14³/₈ in. Chicago, Art Institute. *Right*: Portrait of a Lady. Panel, 13¹/₄×10³/₄ in. (including frame). Philadelphia, Museum of Art, Johnson Coll.

Pl. 159. F. A. Maulbertsch, The Holy Family with saints, ca. 1755. Canvas, 50×35³/₈ in. Vienna Österreichische Galerie.

Pl. 160. N. de Largillière, portrait of the artist with his wife and daughter. Canvas, 4 ft., 10⅝ in. × 6 ft., 6¾ in. Paris, Louvre.

Pl. 161. J. B. Zimmermann, design for decoration of the Wieskirche, near Munich, detail of south side of chancel, 1748. Weilheim, Germany, Städtisches Museum.

Pl. 162. Paris. *Above*: G. G. Boffrand, Hôtel de Soubise, oval room, ca. 1735. *Below*: Hôtel de la Vrillière, *galerie dorée*, remodeled by F. A. Vassé, 1719.

Pl. 163. Potsdam, Sanssouci, library, with decorations by J. A. Nahl the Elder, 1746.

Pl. 164. J. M. Fischer, pilgrimage church, Zwiefalten, Germany, interior, with stuccowork by J. M. II Feichtmayr (Feuchtmayr) and frescoes by F. J. Spiegler, 1741–65.

Pl. 165. D. Zimmermann, Wieskirche, near Munich, interior, with decoration by J. B. Zimmermann, 1745–54.

Pl. 166. F. de Cuvilliés, the Amalienburg, in the Nymphenburg park, near Munich, 1734–39.

Pl. 167. Germany. *Left*: D. Zimmermann, pilgrimage church, Steinhausen, interior, with frescoes by J. B. Zimmermann, 1727–33. *Right*: Schloss Wilhelmstal (begun 1753), near Kassel, staircase (*Treppenhaus*), project by F. de Cuvilliés.

Pl. 168. Germany. *Left*: Birnau am Bodensee, pilgrimage church, interior, with stuccowork by J. A. Feichtmayr (Feuchtmayr) and frescoes by G. B. Göz, mid-18th cent. *Right*: Diessen, St. Maria, interior, with stuccowork by J. A. Feichtmayr and J. G. Üblhör and frescoes by J. G. Bergmüller, 1732–39.

Pl. 169. *Left*: Granada, Spain, the Cartuja, interior of the Sacristy, with stuccowork by L. de Arévalo, 1742–47. (Cf. XIII, pl. 291.) *Right*: Palermo, Sicily, Palazzo Bonagia, stair-case, by A. Giganti (1731–87).

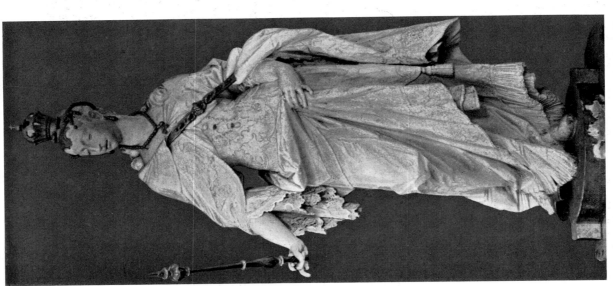

Pl. 170. *Left*: I. Günther, St. Kunigunde, 1762. Wood, with color and gilding; ht., 7 ft., 6½ in. Rott am Inn, Germany, former Benedictine monastery church. *Center*: Austrian school, Hunter, ca. 1750. Wood. London, Victoria and Albert Museum. *Right*: L. Mattielli, Boreas and Orithyia, between 1716 and 1731. Stone. Vienna, Schwarzenberg garden.

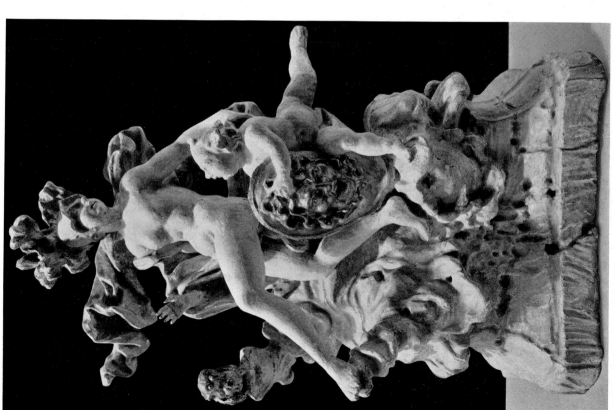

Pl. 171. *Left*: F. Dietz, Pallas Athene, 1768. Limewood painted white, partly gilded; ht., 13½ in. Nürnberg, Germanisches National-Museum. *Right*: E. M. Falconet, Madame de Pompadour as the Venus of the Doves, ca. 1763. Marble, ht., 29½ in. Washington, D.C., National Gallery.

Pl. 172. G. Serpotta, detail of stucco decoration, 1686–88 and 1717–18. Palermo, Sicily, Oratory of S. Zita.

Pl. 173. J. A. Feichtmayr (Feuchtmayr), The Virgin Immaculate, ca. 1760. Painted wood, ht., 5 ft., 3³/₄ in. Berlin, Staatliche Museen.

Pl. 174. J.-H. Fragonard, The Bathers, ca. 1765. Canvas, 25¹/₄ × 31¹/₂ in. Paris, Louvre.

Pl. 175. Engravings. *Left*: E. Fessard after A. de Saint-Aubin, The Foundlings' Chapel of Paris (decorated by C. J. Natoire), 1769. *Right*: N. Ponce (1746–1831) after P. A. Baudouin, L'Enlèvement Nocturne.

Pl. 176. *Above*: G. B. Piranesi, Gondola, 1744–45. Pen and brown ink and wash over black chalk sketch, 11⁵/₈×26⁷/₈ in. New York, Pierpont Morgan Library. *Below, left*: J.-H. Fragonard, Lit aux Amours. Pen and ink with water color, 18×12 in. Besançon, France, Musée des Beaux-Arts. *Right*: A. Pesne, Brandenburg landscape with cavaliers and ladies, ca. 1745 (?). Red chalk and gray color on grayish paper, 17⁵/₈×13³/₈ in. Berlin, Kupferstichkabinett.

Pl. 177. *Above*: J.-B. Pater, The Fair at Bezons, ca. 1733. Canvas, 3 ft., 6 in. × 4 ft., 8 in. New York, Metropolitan Museum. *Below, left*: F. Boucher, Venus commissions Vulcan to make arms for Aeneas, 1757. Gobelin tapestry. Paris, Mobilier National. *Right*: P. J. Sauvage (1744–1818), Venus and Cupid. Grisaille on canvas, 5 ft., 3 in. × 3 ft., 3³/₈ in. New York, Metropolitan Museum.

Pl. 178. *Above, left*: F. Solimena, The Fall of Simon Magus, 1690. Fresco. Naples, S. Paolo Maggiore, sacristy. *Right*: F. de Mura,
Vision of St. Benedict, 1740. Canvas, 6 ft., 8¼ in. × 4 ft., 2 in. *Below*: C. Giaquinto, Prophets, Heroines, and Sibyls, 1749.
Canvas, 15¾×38⅜ in. Last two, Naples, Museo di Capodimonte.

Pl. 179. *Above*: G. B. Pittoni, Hannibal's Oath. Canvas, 16¹/₈×28³/₈ in. Milan, Brera. *Below, left*: G. D. Tiepolo, The Golden Fleece, detail of ceiling, ca. 1764. Fresco. Madrid, Royal Palace. *Right*: F. or G. A. Guardi, Aurora. Ceiling canvas, 13 ft., 8⁵/₈ in. × 6 ft., 8³/₄ in. Venice, Palazzo Labia.

Pl. 180. *Above, left*: J. F. Oeben, secrétaire, Paris, ca. 1760. Wood with marquetry and ormolu, marble top. Munich, Residenz. *Right*: Porcelain fireplace with mirror, Vienna, ca. 1740. Vienna, Österreichisches Museum für Angewandte Kunst. *Below, left*: Wallpaper, from Palazzo Carminati (S. Stae), Venice, 18th cent. Venice, Ca' Rezzonico. *Right*: A. Bossi, detail of ceiling with gilded ornament on white ground and inset mirrors, 1741–45. Würzburg, Residenz, Spiegelkabinett.

Pl. 181. *Left, above*: Andirons, France, 18th cent. Gilded bronze. Versailles, Palace. *Center*: *Carnet de bal*, London (?), ca. 1750. Case of gold and precious stones, 2¹/₂×4¹/₂ in. Amsterdam, Rijksmuseum. *Below*: P. de Lamerie, tea caddy, London, 1747–48. Gilded silver, ht., 5¹/₄ in. London, Goldsmiths' Hall. *Right, above*: Porcelain clock, Strasbourg, mid-18th cent. Paris, Louvre. *Below*: Sedan chair of Maria Amalia of Bourbon, Naples, ca. 1750. Naples, Museo di Capodimonte.

Pl. 182. Porcelain. *Left*: F. A. Bustelli, Nymphenburg factory, ca. 1760. *Above*: Julia, one of a set of stage figures. Ht., ca. 7 in. *Below*: The Disturbed Sleeper. Both, Munich, Bayerisches Nationalmuseum. *Right, above*: J. J. Kändler, Meissen factory, Harlequin and Columbine Dancing, 1744. Ht., 8¹/₈ in. Amsterdam, Rijksmuseum. *Below*: Real Fabbrica, Naples, The Rape of Europa, 1771–1807. Naples, Museo di Capodimonte.

Pl. 183. G. B. Piazzetta, The Fortuneteller, detail, 1740. Canvas; full size, 5 ft., $\frac{1}{2}$ in. × 3 ft., 9 in. Venice, Accademia.

Pl. 184. G. B. Crosato, The Sacrifice of Iphigenia, ceiling of antechamber, detail, 1732. Fresco. Stupinigi, near Turin, hunting lodge.

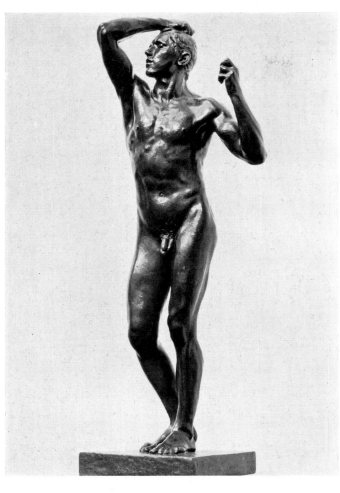
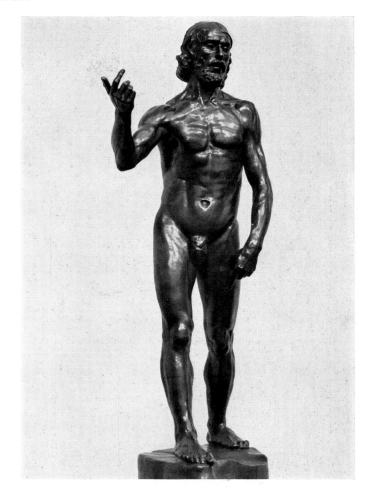

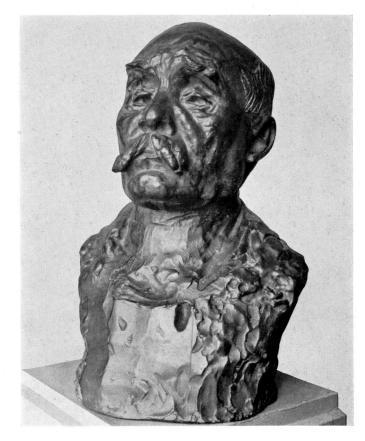

Pl. 185. *Above, left*: The Age of Bronze. Bronze, ht., 5 ft., 11¼ in. *Right*: St. John the Baptist. Bronze, ht., 6 ft., 6¾ in. *Below, left*:
Portrait of Balzac. Bronze; ht., excluding base, 12¼ in. All three, London, Tate Gallery. *Right*: Portrait of Clemenceau. Bronze,
ht., 18⅞ in. Paris, Musée Rodin.

Pl. 186. The Kiss. Marble, ht., 5 ft., 11³/₄ in. London, Tate Gallery.

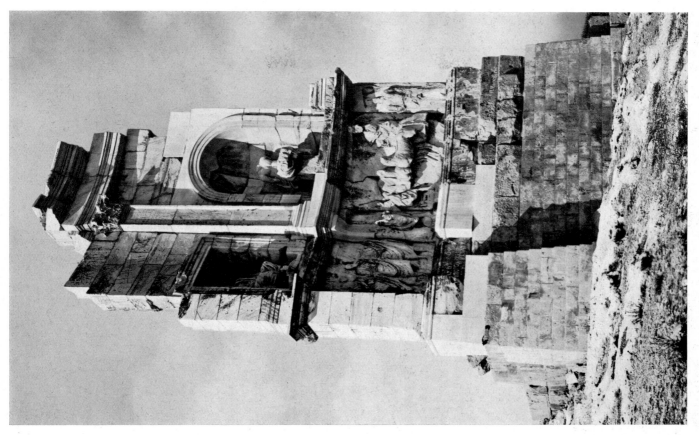

Pl. 187. Athens. *Left*: Arch or Gate of Hadrian, first half of 2d cent. *Right*: Monument of Philopappos, 114-16.

Pl. 188. Turkey. *Above*: Pergamum (mod. Bergama), sanctuary of Serapis, known as Kızıl Avlı or the Red Basilica, 2d cent. *Below*: Ephesus, theater, rebuilt in the Roman period.

Pl. 189. Turkey. *Above, left*: Ephesus, Temple of Hadrian, ca. 130, entrance. *Right*: Aizani (mod. Cavdarhisar), Temple of Zeus, ca. 125. *Below*: Gate of the agora, Miletus, ca. 170, reconstructed in the Staatliche Museen, Berlin.

Pl. 190. *Left*: Gerasa (mod. Jerash, Jordan), forum, 1st–2d cent. *Right*: Palmyra, Syria, monumental arch and great colonnade, 3d cent.

Pl. 191. *Left*: Palmyra, Syria, Temple of Bel, dedicated A.D. 32, interior view showing northwest angle and the seven columns. *Right*: Baalbek (Heliopolis), Lebanon, the round temple, 2d–3d cent.

Pl. 192. Baalbek (Heliopolis), Lebanon, general view.

Pl. 193. *Left*: Petra, Jordan, so-called "el-Khazna" ("The Treasury"), rock-cut façade of tomb, 1st–2d cent. *Right*: Hypogeum of Jarhai, from Palmyra, Syria, view with triclinium and funerary busts, 2d–3d cent. Damascus, National Museum.

Pl. 194. *Above, left*: Seated god, detail of Dionysiac cycle, first half of 2d cent. Marble. Athens, Theater of Dionysos, front of the Roman stage. *Right*: Arısteas and Papias, young centaur, first half of 2d cent. Marble, ht., 5 ft., 1³/₈ in. Rome, Capitoline Museum. *Below*: Relief with apotheosis of an emperor, probably Marcus Aurelius, fragment of a triumphal monument from Ephesus, second half of 2d cent. Marble, ht., 6 ft., 8³/₄ in. Vienna, Kunsthistorisches Museum.

Pl. 195. *Above*: Sarcophagus with architectural elements, front view showing married couple with attendants and the Dioscuri, 2d cent. Marble. Florence, Baptistery. *Below*: Sarcophagus with reclining couple and Amazonomachy, from Salonika, Greece, early 3d cent. Marble. Paris, Louvre.

Pl. 196. Syria. *Above*: Funerary reliefs from Palmyra, 2d–3d cent. Paris, Louvre. Stone, ht. (*right*), 21⁵/₈ in. *Below*: Sacrifice at the Fire Altar, wall painting from the Temple of Bel (or the Palmyrene Gods), Dura-Europos, 2d–3d cent., 34¹/₂×59 in. New Haven, Yale University Art Gallery.

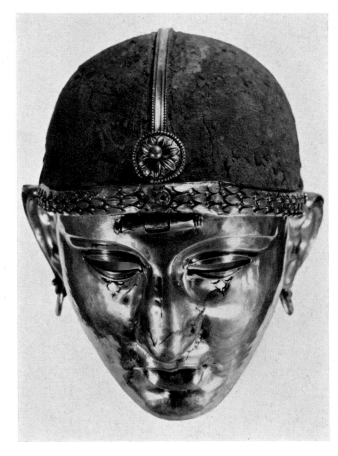

Pl. 197. *Above, left*: Head of a priest, so-called "Caesar," from Egypt. Stone, ht., 9½ in. Rome, Museo Barracco. *Right*: Parade helmet, from Emesa (mod. Homs, Syria), 1st cent. Iron with silver, ht., 9⅝ in. Damascus, National Museum. *Below, left*: Portrait of a young woman, from a mummy case, Fayum, Egypt, 3d cent. Encaustic on panel, 14½ × 8 in. Vienna, Kunsthistorisches Museum. *Right*: Portrait of the deceased, detail, Fayum, 160. Linen. Berlin, Staatliche Museen.

Pl. 198. Salonika, Greece, Triumphal Arch of Galerius, late 3d–early 4th cent., east side of south pier.

Pl. 199. Toulouse, France, St-Sernin, east view, late 11th cent. (crossing tower, 12th–13th cent.).

Pl. 200. France. *Above*: Nevers, St-Étienne, east view, second half of 11th cent. *Below, left*: Conques, Ste-Foy, nave, begun mid-11th cent. *Right*: Toulouse, St-Sernin, nave, second half of 11th–early 12th cent.

Pl. 201. France, abbey churches. *Above*: Beaulieu-sur-Dordogne, *chevet*, first half of 12th cent. *Below, left*: Jumièges, Notre-Dame, consecrated 1067. *Right*: Caen, La Trinité, second half of 11th cent. (tympanum, 19th cent.).

Pl. 202. France. *Left*: Paray-le-Monial, Sacré-Cœur (formerly Notre-Dame), late 11th–12th cent. *Right*: Poitiers, Notre-Dame-la-Grande, 11th–first half of 12th cent.

Pl. 203. Le Puy, France, Cathedral (11th–12th cent.), domical vaulting of the nave.

Pl. 204. Vézelay, France, Church of La Madeleine, nave, first half of 12th cent.

Pl. 205. France. *Left*: Saint-Martin-de-Boscherville, St-Georges, 12th–13th cent. *Right*: Lyon, St-Martin d'Ainay, consecrated 1107.

Pl. 206. Saint-Bertrand-de-Comminges, France, Cathedral cloister (12th–13th cent.), west gallery with pillar of the four Evangelists, early 12th cent.

Pl. 207. The Vision of St. John, Christ in Majesty with symbols of the Evangelists and 24 elders, from the "Apocalypse of Saint-Sever." (*Commentary on the Apocalypse* by Beatus of Liébana), painted in the Abbey of Saint-Sever, France, 11th cent. Illumination. Paris, Bibliothèque Nationale (Ms. lat. 8878, fol. 121v and 122).

Pl. 208. The Building of the Tower of Babel, scene in a fresco cycle, late 11th–early 12th cent. Saint-Savin-sur-Gartempe, France, Abbey church, nave.

Pl. 209. Spain. *Left*: San Salvador de Leyre, Navarra, monastery church (consecrated 1057), crypt, 9th cent. *Right*: San Pedro de Roda, Gerona, monastery church (consecrated 1022), piers of the nave.

Pl. 210. Cardona, Barcelona, Spain, Castle, S. Vicente (begun ca. 1020; consecrated 1040), crossing.

Pl. 211. Spain. *Above*: Ripoll, Gerona, Monastery of S. María, church, ca. 1020–32 (rebuilt 1886–93). *Below*: Frómista, Palencia, S. Martín, begun ca. 1066 (restored 19th cent.).

Pl. 212. Spain. *Above*: León, S. Isidoro. *Left*: Panteón de los Reyes, ca. 1054–67. *Right*: Nave, 1072–1101. *Below*: Jaca, Huesca, Cathedral (last half of 11th cent.), detail of lateral apse.

Pl. 213. Santiago de Compostela, La Coruña, Spain, Cathedral, south transept, ca. 1075–1122/24.

Pl. 214. Toro, Zamora, Spain, Colegiata de S. María la Mayor, view of crossing, ca. 1160–1240.

Pl. 215. *Left*: Spain. *Above*: Ávila, S. Vicente, 12th cent. and later (restored). *Below*: Segovia, S. Millán, 12th cent. *Right*: Coimbra, Portugal, Sé Velha or Old Cathedral, 12th cent., view of piers and gallery.

Pl. 216. Milan, Italy, S. Ambrogio, nave, begun 11th cent.

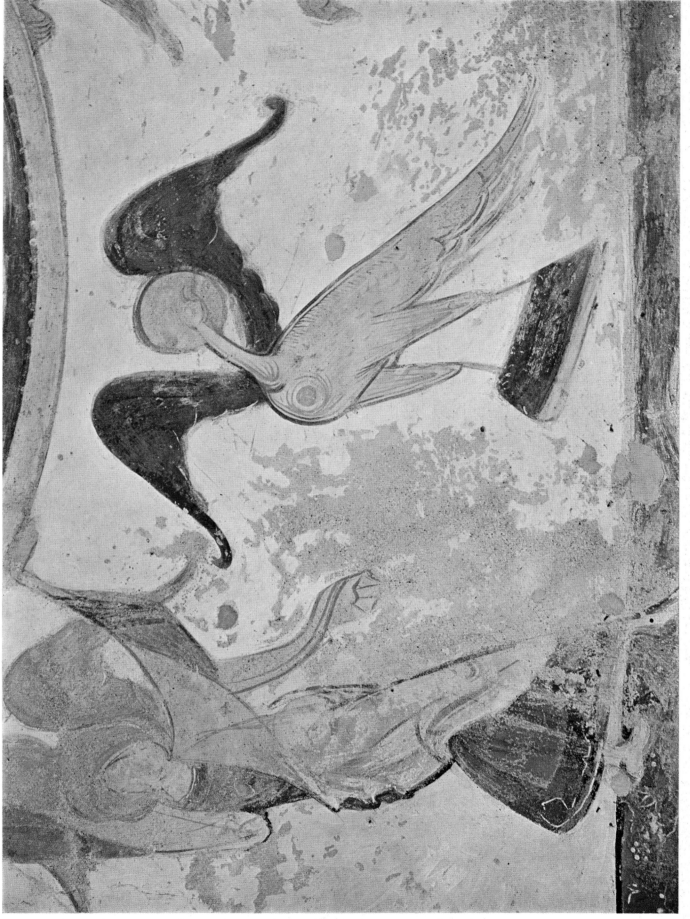

Pl. 217. The eagle, symbol of John the Evangelist, and angel, detail of fresco, 12th cent. Montoire-sur-le-Loir, France, Chapel of St-Gilles.

Pl. 218. St. Gregory, author page of the Letters of St. Gregory, from Saint-Amand-en-Pevèle, diocese of Tournai, second half of 12th cent. Illumination. Paris, Bibliothèque Nationale (Ms. lat. 2287, fol. 1v).

Pl. 219. Italy. *Above*: Como, S. Abbondio, consecrated 1095. *Below, left*: Pavia, S. Michele, 11th(?)–12th cent. *Right*: Modena, Cathedral, begun 1099 (rose window, 13th cent.; spire, 14th cent.).

Pl. 220. Italy. *Above, left*: Verona, S. Zeno, nave, 12th cent. *Right*: Parma, Baptistery, begun 1196. *Below*: Venice, S. Marco, begun ca. 1063.

Pl. 221. Italy. *Above*: Ancona, S. Ciriaco, 11th–13th cent. *Below, left*: Abbey church of S. Antimo (near Montalcino), nave, 12th cent. *Right*: Florence, S. Miniato al Monte, 11th–12th cent.

Pl. 222. Pisa, Italy. *Above*: Baptistery, Cathedral, and Campanile. *Below*: Cathedral (begun 1063). *Left*: Façade, 12th cent. *Right*: Nave, 11th–13th cent.

Pl. 223. Italy. *Above*: Troia, Cathedral, begun ca. 1093. *Below*: Bari, S. Nicola, begun ca. 1087, consecrated 1197.

Pl. 224. Italy. *Above*: Amalfi, Cathedral cloister, second half of 13th cent. *Below*: Monreale, Sicily, Cathedral, view of the apses, second half of 12th cent.

Pl. 225. Germany. *Above, left*: Speyer, Cathedral, nave, ca. 1030–1061 and ca. 1080–1106 (restored). *Right*: Mainz, Cathedral, east view, 11th–12th cent. *Below*: Maria Laach, Abbey church, 1093–1230.

Pl. 226. *Above, left*: Eberbach, Rheingau, Germany, former Cistercian Abbey church (consecrated 1186), nave. *Right*: Guebwiller, France, St-Léger (St. Leodegar), begun 1182. *Below, left*: Murbach, France, former Cistercian Abbey church, remaining east end, 12th cent. *Right*: Cologne, St. Gereon, east view, second half of 12th cent.

Pl. 227. Cologne, Germany, St. Aposteln (begun ca. 1020), nave, completed ca. 1219.

Pl. 228. Germany. *Above, left*: Cologne, Gross St. Martin, east view, late 12th–first half of 13th cent. *Right*: Limburg an der Lahn, Cathedral, (formerly Stiftskirche St. Georg), first half of 13th cent. *Below*: Worms, Cathedral, from northeast, 12th–first half of 13th cent.

Pl. 229. Worms, Germany, Cathedral, detail of the west end (cf. PL. 228).

Pl. 230. England. *Left*: Winchester, Cathedral (begun 1079), view of the transept and gallery. *Right*: Durham, Cathedral (1093 – ca. 1133), view of nave. (Cf. VI, pl. 425.)

Pl. 231. England. *Left*: Oxford, Cathedral, view of choir, second half of 12th cent. *Right*: Ely, Cathedral (begun ca. 1083), view of nave.

Pl. 232. Tewkesbury, England, Abbey church, late 11th–first half of 12th cent.

Pl. 233. Scandinavia. *Above*: Urnes, Norway, stave church, 11th–12th cent. *Below, left*: Ribe, Denmark, Cathedral, nave, 12th cent. *Right*: Kalundborg, Denmark, Cathedral, begun ca. 1170.

Pl. 234. *Above*: Loches, France, Castle, 11th–12th cent. and later. *Below*: Loarre, Huesca, Spain, Castle, late 11th–13th cent.

Pl. 235. *Above*: Ávila, Spain, section of the city walls, begun 1090. *Below, left*: Rochester, England, keep of the Castle, 12th cent. *Right*: Palermo, Sicily, La Zisa, 12th cent. (Photographed before World War II.)

Pl. 236. Toulouse, France, St-Sernin. *Left, above:* South portal (Porte Miégeville), detail with tympanum representing the Ascension, ca. 1100. *Below:* Bernard Gilduin, altar relief, detail, late 11th cent. Marble. *Right:* Bernard Gilduin, Christ in Majesty with symbols of the Evangelists, relief in the ambulatory, second half of 11th cent. Marble.

Pl. 237. Moissac, Tarn-et-Garonne, France, Abbey church of St-Pierre. *Left:* Portal with tympanum representing the Vision of St. John, first quarter of 12th cent. *Right:* Cloister, view showing corner pier with relief of St. Peter, ca. 1100.

Pl. 238. France. *Left, above*: *Trumeau* of ancient portal, showing the Sacrifice of Abraham, ca. 1140. Souillac, Lot, Abbey church. *Below*: *Trumeau* of south portal, showing interlaced animals and Jeremiah, Abbey church of St-Pierre, Moissac, 12th cent. *Above, right*: Relief with symbolic lion and ram, from St-Sernin, Toulouse, 12th cent. Marble, ht., 4 ft., 5 1/8 in. *Below*: Capital with the Wise and Foolish Virgins, detail, from the cloister of St-Étienne, Toulouse, 11th–12th cent. Last two, Toulouse, Musée des Augustins.

Pl. 239. Relief of the prophet Isaiah, fragment of original portal, now on reverse of façade, first half of
12th cent. Souillac, Lot, France, Abbey church. (Photographed from a cast.)

Pl. 240. France. *Left*: Capital with relief representing the Third Tone of Plain Song, from Abbey church, Cluny, choir, late 11th–early 12th cent. Cluny, Musée du Farinier. *Right, above*: Capital with relief showing the Vision of the Magi, 12th cent. Autun, Cathedral of St-Lazare, Cathedral museum. *Below*: Fragment of lintel with relief of Eve, from Cathedral of St-Lazare, Autun, 12th cent. Autun, Musée Rolin.

Pl. 241. Capital with the Adoration of the Magi, two details, 12th cent. Autun, France, Cathedral of St-Lazare.

Pl. 242. Tympanum with Pentecost scene, ca. 1130. Vézelay, France, Church of La Madeleine, west portal. (Photographed from a cast.)

Pl. 243. Annunciation to the Shepherds, detail of fresco, 12th cent. León, Spain, S. Isidoro, Panteón de los Reyes, vault.

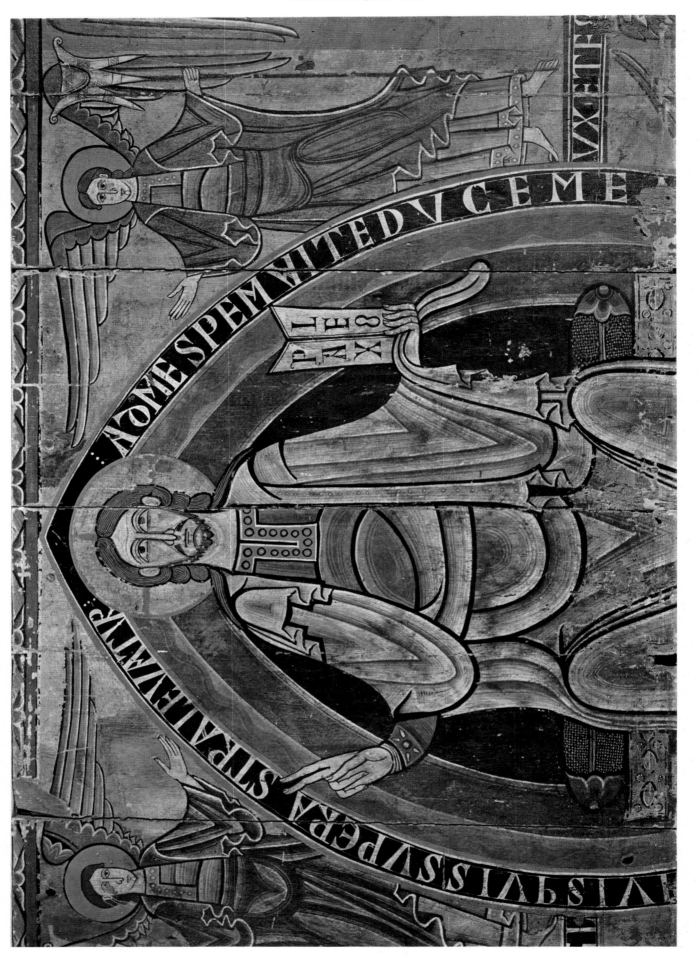

Pl. 244. The Pantocrator, detail of baldachin, from Ribas, Gerona, Spain, 12th cent. Panel. Vich, Spain, Museo Arqueológico Artístico Episcopal.

Pl. 245. Arles, France, St-Trophime, portal of the façade, ca. late 12th cent.

Pl. 246. France. *Above, and below, left*: Saint-Gilles-du-Gard, Church of St-Gilles, details of façade, 12th cent. *Above*: Cain and Abel. *Below, left*: SS. John and Peter, central portal. *Right*: Arles, St-Trophîme, pier of the cloister, representing the Journey to Emmaus, 12th cent.

Pl. 247. *Above, left*: Capital with the Temptation of Christ, 12th cent. Stone. Plaimpied, Cher, France, Abbey church, nave. *Above, right, and below*: Capitals (unfinished), 12th cent., found at Nazareth. Stone. Jerusalem, Museum of the Patriarchs (*above, right*); Nazareth, Franciscan monastery (*below*).

Pl. 248. Spain. *Above*: Sarcophagus of Alfonso Ansúrez, from Sahagún, Zamora, 1093. Stone. Madrid, Museo Arqueológico Nacional. *Below, left*: Capital, interior of S. Isidoro, León, second half of 11th cent. *Right*: Capital, lateral portal of the Cathedral, Jaca, Huesca, second half of 11th cent.

Pl. 249. Santiago de Compostela, Spain, Cathedral, Puerta de las Platerías, detail with King David, early 12th cent.

Pl. 250. Ripoll, Gerona, Spain, Monastery of S. María, portal of the church, second quarter of 12th cent. (?).

Pl. 251. Spain. *Left*: Sangüesa, Navarra, portal of S. María la Real, detail, mid-12th cent. *Right*: Monastery of S. Domingo de Silos, near Burgos, northeast angle of the cloister with relief of the Deposition, second half of 12th cent.

Pl. 252. B. Antelami, lunette and lintel of the south portal (called the "Door of Life"), 1204-08. Parma, Italy, Baptistery.

Pl. 253. The "Genesis of Gerona," detail of the cycle of Creation, Spain, first half of 12th cent. or earlier. Embroidery on wool. Gerona, Cathedral.

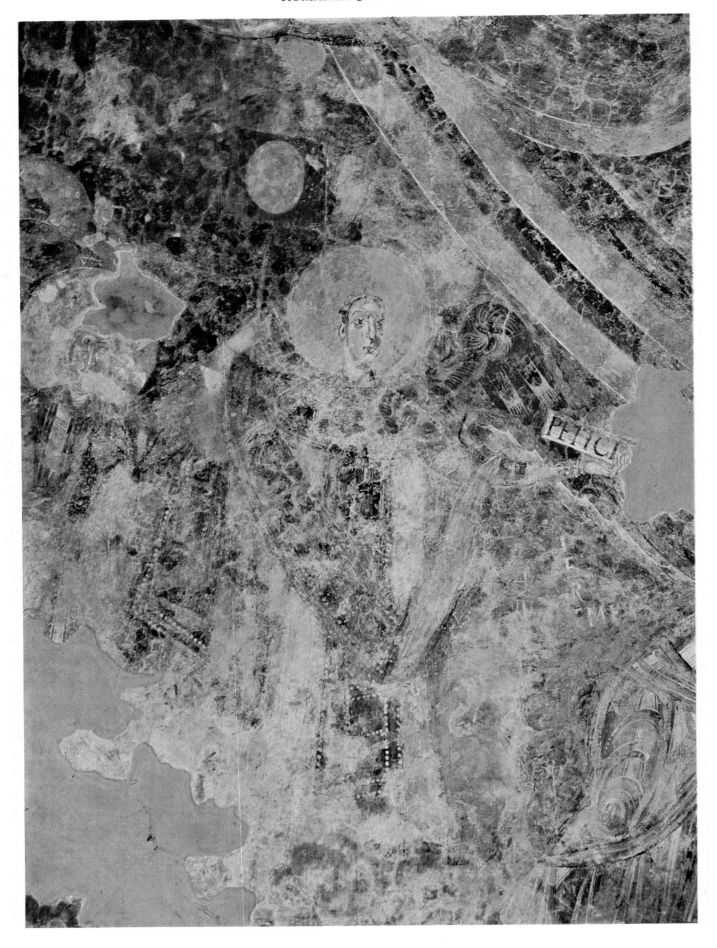

Pl. 254. The Archangel Michael, detail of fresco, early 11th cent. Galliano, Italy, S. Vincenzo, apse.

Pl. 255. Modena, Italy, Cathedral, reliefs, first half of 12th cent. *Above*: Truth tearing out the tongue of Falsehood, and (*at left*) Jacob and the Angel. *Below*: Wiligelmo da Modena, scenes from Genesis.

Pl. 256. Italy. *Above*: Martyrdom of St. Regulus of Lucca, lunette relief, 13th cent. Marble. Lucca, Cathedral, right portal of façade. *Below*: Labors of the Months, detail showing July, August, and September, 13th cent. Arezzo, Pieve di S. Maria, archivolt of main portal.

Pl. 257. Italy. *Above*: Maestro Roberto, scenes from the life of Moses, detail of baptismal font, second half of 12th cent. Marble. Lucca, S. Frediano. *Below*: Bonannus of Pisa, door panel (detail of III, PL. 12), 1186. Bronze. Monreale, Sicily, Cathedral.

Pl. 258. Descent from the Cross, first half of 13th cent. Wood. Tivoli, Italy, S. Lorenzo.

Pl. 259. Italy. *Above, left*: Sessa Aurunca, Cathedral, capital of the pulpit (VIII, PL. 175), detail, 13th cent. Marble. *Below*: Ravello, S. Pantaleone, pulpit by Niccolò di Bartolommeo da Foggia, detail, 1272. Marble and mosaic. *Right*: Cori, S. Maria della Pietà, Easter candlestick, early 12th cent. Marble.

Pl. 260. Troia, Italy, Cathedral, door of the façade, 1119. Bronze.

Pl. 261. Italy. *Above, left*: Bari, S. Nicola, episcopal chair (Throne of Elia), ca. 1098. Marble. *Right*: Cefalù, Sicily, Cathedral, capital, 12th cent. *Below*: Monreale, Sicily, cloister of the Cathedral, double capital, 12th cent.

Pl. 262. Germany. *Left, above*: Speyer, Cathedral, window, ca. 1100. *Below*: Bamberg, Cathedral, St. George Choir, reliefs of the choir screen with disputing prophets, ca. 1220–30. *Right*: Lectern with the Four Evangelists (restored), from the monastery at Alpirsbach, mid-12th cent. Wood. Freudenstadt, Stadtkirche.

Pl. 263. Pilate washing his hands, detail of fresco, second half of 11th cent. Sant'Angelo in Formis, near Capua, Italy, nave of the church.

Pl. 264. The Pantocrator surrounded by Old Testament scenes, second quarter of 13th cent. Fresco. Anagni, Italy, Cathedral, crypt vault.

Pl. 265. *Above*: Nativity, detail of bronze door from a Magdeburg foundry, third quarter of 12th cent. Novgorod, Russia, Cathedral of St. Sophia. *Below*: Group of slaves, detail of bronze door with scenes of St. Adalbert, 12th cent. Gniezno, Poland, Cathedral.

Pl. 266. England. *Above*: Archivolt and tympanum with Christ in Majesty, second half of 12th cent. Barfreston, Kent, church. *Below, left*: John the Evangelist, detail, from York, St. Mary's Abbey, ca. 1200. Stone. York, Yorkshire Museum. *Right*: Head of Christ, fragment of a Crucifixion, first half of 12th cent. Painted wood, ht., 6 in. South Cerney, Gloucester, church.

Pl. 267. Sweden, Skåne. *Above*: Baptismal font with the legend of St. Stanislaus, whole and detail, by the Magister Majestatis, ca. 1160. Sandstone. Tryde, church. *Below*: Baptismal font, ca. late 12th cent. Stone. Gumlösa, church.

Pl. 268. The Kiss of Judas, 12th cent. Fresco. Nohant-Vicq, Indre, France, St-Martin, choir.

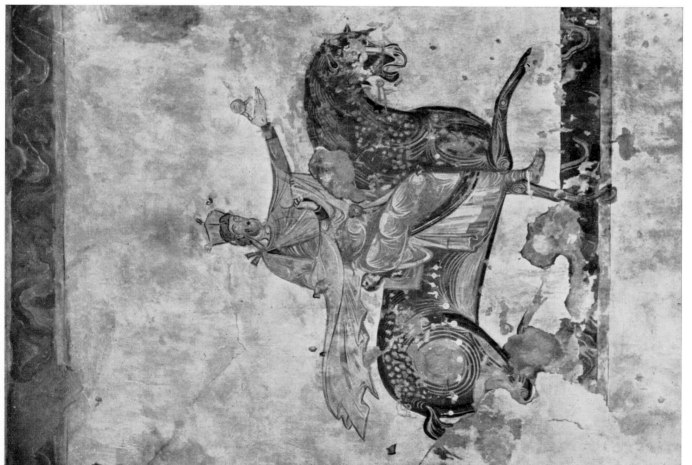

Pl. 269. France. *Left*: The Emperor Constantine on horseback, 12th cent. Fresco. Poitiers, Vienne, Baptistery of St-Jean. *Right*: David playing his harp, 12th cent. Fresco. Tavant, Indre-et-Loire, St-Nicolas, crypt.

Pl. 270. Adoration of the Magi and apostles, by the Master of Maderuelo, ca. 1123, from the central apse of S. María, Tahull, Lérida, Spain. Wall painting. Barcelona, Museo de Bellas Artes de Cataluña.

Pl. 271. Spain, Lérida. *Above, left*: Christ in Majesty, by the Master of Tahull, ca. 1123, from S. Clemente, Tahull. Wall painting. *Right*: The Virgin and St. John, by the Master of Urgel, 12th cent., from S. Pedro, Seo de Urgel. Wall painting. *Below*: Altar frontal of SS. Julita and Quiricus, from Durro, 12th cent. Panel. All, Barcelona, Museo de Bellas Artes de Cataluña.

Pl. 272. David and Goliath, by the Master of the Last Judgment, 12th cent., from S. María, Tahull, Lérida, Spain. Wall painting. Barcelona, Museo de Bellas Artes de Cataluña.

Pl. 273. Slaughter of the Innocents, panel of the so-called "Madonna of Constantinople," mid-13th cent. Carved and painted wood. Alatri, Italy, S. Maria Maggiore.

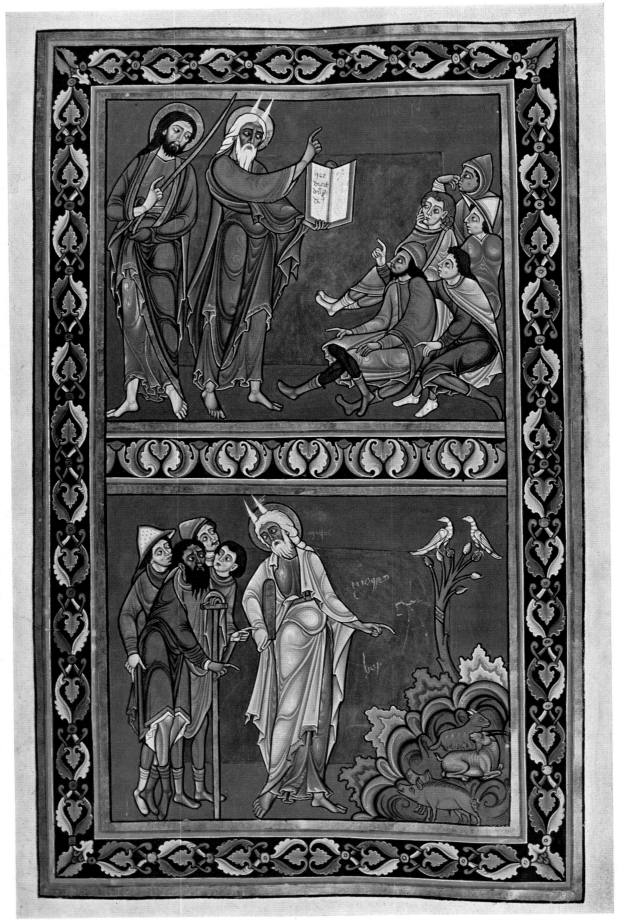

Pl. 274. The Bury Bible. Frontispiece of the Book of Deuteronomy, by Master Hugo, from the Abbey of Bury St. Edmunds, England, first half of 12th cent. Illumination. Cambridge, England, Corpus Christi College (Ms. 2, fol. 94r).

Pl. 275. Italy. *Above*: Apocalyptic scene with angels slaying the dragon, late 11th–12th cent. Fresco. Civate, near Como, S. Pietro al Monte. *Below*: The Deposition, ca. late 12th cent. Fresco. Aquileia, Cathedral, crypt.

Pl. 276. Italy. *Left, above:* Johannes, Stephanus, and Nicolaus, Elders of the Apocalypse, 11th cent. Fresco. Castel Sant'Elia, near Nepi, S. Elia, transept. *Below:* Translation of the Body of St. Clement, late 11th–early 12th cent. Fresco. Rome, S. Clemente, Lower Church, narthex. *Right:* Giunta Pisano, Crucifix, 13th cent. Panel, Assisi, S. Maria degli Angeli.

Pl. 277. Italy. Mosaics. *Left:* Biblical scenes, 13th cent. Florence, Baptistery, dome. *Right, above:* Personifications of Fortitude and Temperance, 12th cent. Venice, S. Marco, central dome. *Below:* Entry into Jerusalem, 12th cent. Palermo, Sicily, Cappella Palatina, south transept.

Pl. 278. *Above*: Christ in Majesty and saints, ca. 1170 (repainted 1875). Fresco. Schwarz-Rheindorf, Germany, Upper Church, apse and vaulting. *Below, left*: Christ and angels, ca. 1155–64 (repainted ca. 1900). Fresco. Regensburg, Germany, Cathedral, cloisters, Chapel of All Saints. *Right*: St. Gregory, first half of 12th cent. Fresco. Salzburg, Austria, Stift Nonnberg.

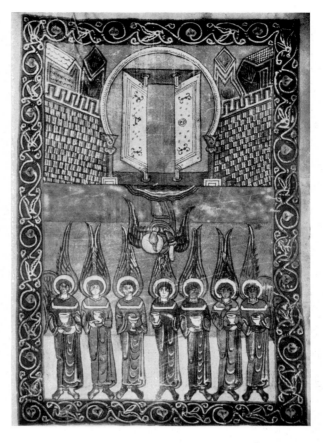

Pl. 279. Illuminations. *Above, left*: Psalter. Transport of the Ark and David with musicians, from the Abbey of Polirone, near Mantua, Italy, 12th–13th cent. Mantua, Biblioteca Comunale (Ms. C. III. 20, fol. 2r). *Right*: Beatus Apocalypse. Scene with seven angels leaving the temple, from San Millán de la Cogolla, Logroño, Spain, 11th cent. Madrid, Real Academia de la Historia (Ms. 33). *Below, left*: Book of Pericopes. Nativity, from Stift Nonnberg, Salzburg, ca. 1140. Munich, Bayerische Staatsbibliothek (Clm. 15903, fol. 9r). *Right*: Lambeth Bible. The Tree of Jesse, from Canterbury, ca. 1150. London, Lambeth Palace Library (Ms. 3, fol. 198r).

Pl. 280. *Above*: Shrine reliquary, ca. 1075. Silver repoussé with engraving and niello. Oviedo, Spain, Cathedral, Cámara Santa. *Below*: The Shrine of Charlemagne, detail showing the siege of Pamplona, 1215. Silver and copper. Aachen, Germany, Cathedral Treasury.

Pl. 281. Ivory. *Above, left*: Cross of Ferdinand I and Sancha, from S. Isidoro, León, Spain, 11th cent. Madrid, Museo Arqueológico Nacional. *Right*: Crozier head with New Testament scenes, Canterbury school, ca. 1180. W., 4³/₈ in. London, Victoria and Albert Museum. *Below, left*: Altarpiece, detail, 12th cent. Salerno, Italy, Cathedral. *Right*: Plaque with shepherds, lower Rhine region, 12th cent. Ht., 3¹/₄ in. Florence, Museo Nazionale.

Pl. 282. *Above*: Jeweled mountings. *Left*: Antique rock-crystal vase, from the treasury of the former Abbey at Saint-Denis, France, 12th cent. Paris, Louvre. *Right*: Chalice of Doña Urraca, with a late Roman onyx vessel, 11th cent. León, Spain, S. Isidoro. *Below*: Wilten chalice and paten with (*right*) inner side of paten, from the monastery of Wilten, Lower Saxony, ca. 1160–70. Silver, partly gilded; diam. of paten, ca. 9 in. Vienna, Kunsthistorisches Museum.

Pl. 283. Augustus, from Prima Porta, near Rome, probably after 13 B.C. Marble, ht., 6 ft., 8 in. Rome, Vatican Museums.

Pl. 284. Rome, remains of the Theater of Marcellus (superstructure, 16th cent.), dedicated 13 or 11 B.C., with (*at right*) columns of the Temple of Apollo Sosianus.

Pl. 285. *Left*: Vienne (anc. Vienna), Isère, France, Temple of Augustus and Livia, Augustan period (in part, older). *Right*: Pulj (anc. Pietas Julia), Yugoslavia, Arch of the Sergi (Porta Aurea), ca. late 1st cent. B.C.

Pl. 286. *Above*: Procession with priests and members of the family of Augustus, detail of the frieze of the Ara Pacis, Rome, 13–9 B.C. Marble. *Below, left*: Detail of frieze representing the construction of a city, from the Basilica Aemilia, probably 55–34 B.C. Marble. Rome, Antiquarium Forense. *Right*: Detail of altar with plane-tree branches and bucranium, found near the bridge of Sant'Angelo, Rome, 1st cent. Marble. Rome, Museo Nazionale Romano.

Pl. 287. *Left, above*: Cameo with Augustus and Roma, Augustan-Tiberian period. Chalcedony (in 17th-cent. enameled gold mounting), 4³/₈×4 in. Vienna, Kunsthistorisches Museum. *Below*: The "Paris cameo" (*grande camée de la Ste-Chapelle*), with members of the imperial family, Julio-Claudian period (?). Sardonyx, 12¹/₄×10¹/₂ in. Paris, Cabinet des Médailles. *Right, above*: Medallion with Augustus (obv.) and Diana (rv.), found at Pompeii, ca. A.D. 5. Gold, diam., 1¹/₄ in. Naples, Museo Nazionale. *Below*: Detail of crater with cupids fishing, from the Hildesheim Treasure, 1st cent. B.C. Silver; full ht., 14¹/₈ in. Berlin, Staatliche Museen.

Pl. 288. Rome. *Above*: "House of Livia," wall paintings in the so-called "tablinum," Augustan period (?). *Below, left*: Cryptoporticus of Nero, detail of stucco vault decoration, A.D. 54-64. *Right*: Domus Aurea (Golden House of Nero), detail of painted decoration, A.D. 64-69.

Pl. 289. *Left*: Nero (r. A.D. 54–68). Marble, ht., 12¹/₄ in. *Right*: Vespasian (r. A.D. 69–79). Marble, ht., 15³/₄ in. Both, Rome, Museo Nazionale Romano.

Pl. 290. Rome, Colosseum (Flavian Amphitheater), inaugurated A.D. 80.

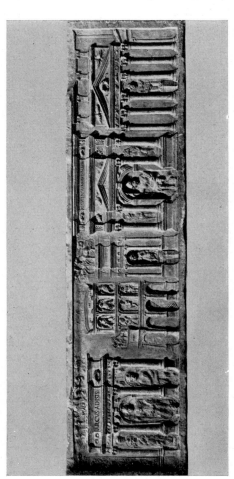

PL. 291. *Left, above*: Rome, detail of the Arch of Titus (PL. 131), last quarter of 1st cent. *Below*: Relief with monuments of Rome, from the tomb of the Haterii, near Rome, late 1st-early 2d cent. Marble, ht., 16¹/₂ in. Rome, Lateran Museums. *Right*: Hadrian's Villa, near Tivoli, ruins of the Great Baths, ca. 125-35.

Pl. 292. Rome. *Above*: Proclamation of the *Alimentatio Italiae*, reliefs on the Rostra balustrade ("Anaglypha Traiani") in the Roman Forum, ca. first half of 2d cent. Marble, w., 23 ft., 9 in. *Below*: Triumphal return of an emperor, panel of a frieze, ca. 111–14, later incorporated in the Arch of Constantine (inside central arch). Marble, ht., 9 ft., 9 in.

Pl. 293. Trajan conferring with a general, detail of Trajan's Column (X, PL. 152), Rome, 113. Marble.

Pl. 294. Rome. *Left:* The Pantheon, view of the portico, ca. 118–28. *Right:* Roman Forum, Temple of Antoninus and Faustina, portico, ca. 141 (with baroque church of S. Lorenzo in Miranda, constructed on site of cella).

Pl. 295. Dionysiac scene, from the House of Fabius Rufus, Pompeii, 1st cent. Glass, $9^{7}/_{8} \times 15^{3}/_{4}$ in. Naples, Museo Nazionale.

Pl. 296. Fragment of wall painting, from the Domus Transitoria, Rome, A.D. 54–64. Rome, Antiquarium Palatino.

Pl. 297. Portrait of a chief vestal (*virgo Vestalis maxima*), from the House of the Vestals, Roman Forum, 2d cent. Marble, ht., ca. 4 ft. Rome, Museo Nazionale Romano.

Pl. 298. *Left*: Sacrifice to Apollo, tondo from a monument of the Hadrianic period, reworked and incorporated in the north side of the Arch of Constantine, Rome. Marble, diam., 7 ft., ½ in. *Right*: Apotheosis of an empress (Sabina ?), from the so-called "Arch of Portugal" (demolished 1662), Rome, Hadrianic period. Marble, ht. 6 ft., 10½ in. Rome, Palazzo dei Conservatori.

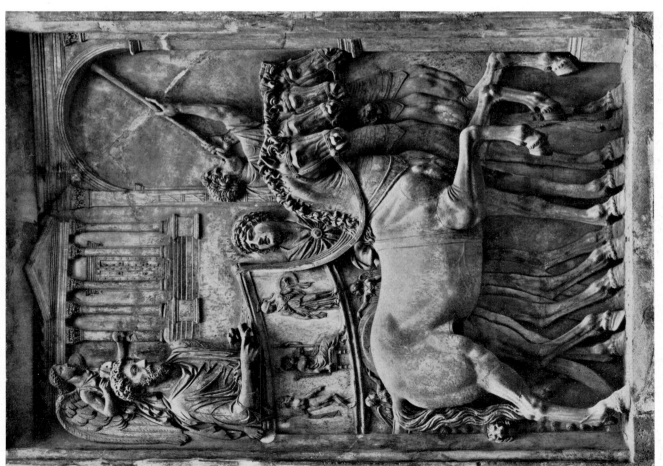

Pl. 299. *Left*: Marcus Aurelius in a quadriga, relief from a triumphal arch (?), ca. 176. Marble, ht. 10 ft., 7½ in. Rome, Palazzo dei Conservatori. *Right*: Roman soldiers and barbarian prisoners, detail of reliefs on the Column of Marcus Aurelius, Rome, completed ca. 193. Marble.

Pl. 300. *Above, left*: Sabina, wife of Hadrian, ca. 136–38. Marble, ht., 14⅛ in. *Right*: Lucius Verus, fragment of a relief, ca. 162. Marble, ht., 10⅝ in. Both, Rome, Museo Nazionale Romano. *Below, left*: Head, 2d cent., found in Athens. Marble, ht., 18⅞ in. Athens, National Museum. *Right*: Commodus as Hercules, last quarter of 2d cent. Marble, ht., 46½ in. Rome, Palazzo dei Conservatori.

Pl. 301. *Above*: Idyllic landscape, wall painting from the Villa dei Quintili on the Appian Way, near Rome, first half of 2d cent. Rome, Torlonia Coll. *Below*: Mythological scene, detail of wall painting in a Roman house under SS. Giovanni e Paolo, Rome, mid-2d–early 3d cent.

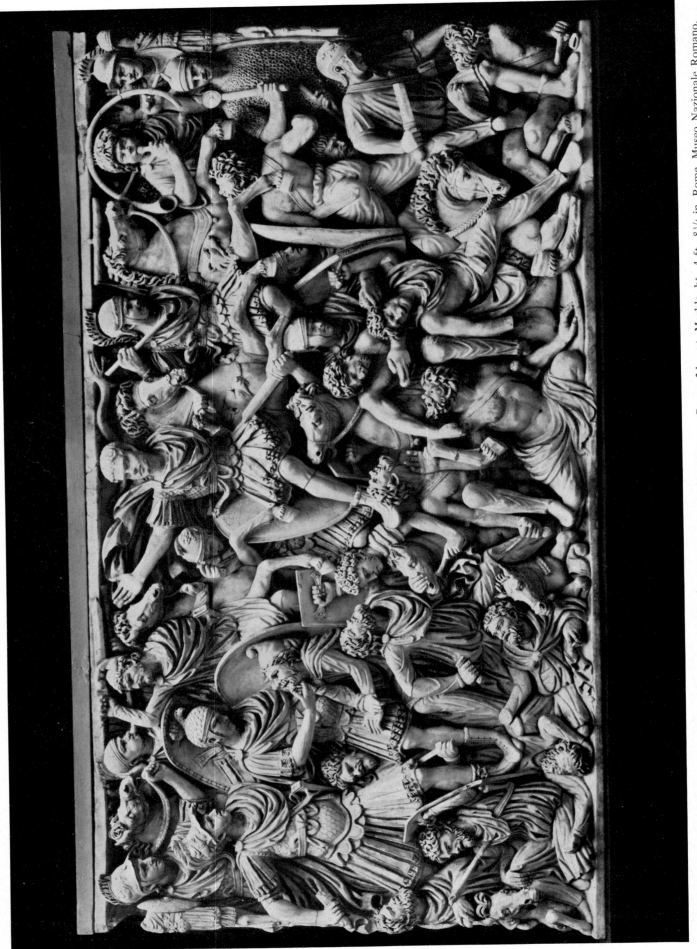

Pl. 302. Battle between Romans and barbarians, front panel of the so-called "Ludovisi sarcophagus," Rome, 3d cent. Marble, ht., 4 ft., 8¾ in. Rome, Museo Nazionale Romano.

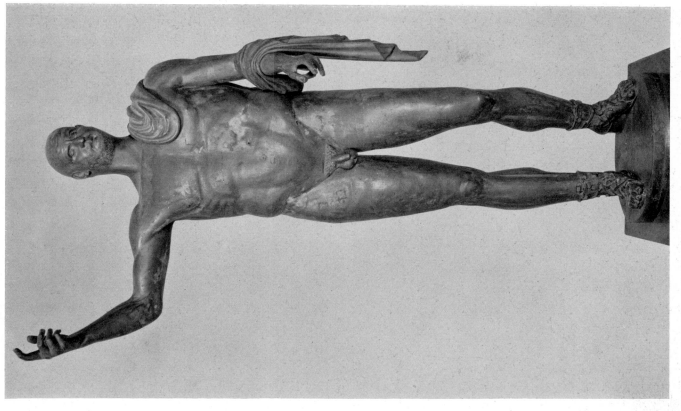

Pl. 303. *Left*: Sarcophagus (restored fragments) with young Gordianus III (?), the Genus Senatus, and philosophers, from Acilia, near Rome, ca. mid-3d cent. Marble, ht. of figures, ca. 4 ft. Rome, Museo Nazionale Romano. *Right*: Portrait statue of Trebonianus Gallus (r. 251-54). Bronze, ht. 7 ft, 11 in. New York, Metropolitan Museum.

Pl. 304. Rome, Roman Forum and the Palatine, view from the Capitoline.

Cet Oultremontain que tu veois
quau naturel Ie represente
des hommes surpasse les Loys
faisant vne estrange descente

De la Colomne de traIan
sans le detriment de sa vue
et dun grand serpent quil tua
à qui la force fut raue

la vraye Guide de Leltremontain icy portraict au naturel monstre lanticque et
moderne plan de la fabricque esleuee de Rome.

henry le Roy exc.

Pl. 305. F. Villamena (d. 1624), Foreign guide pointing out the monuments of Rome. Engraving, 14½×9¼ in.
Florence, Uffizi, Gabinetto dei Disegni e Stampe.

Pl. 306. H. van den Broeck (Arrigo Fiammingo), Resurrection, second half of 16th cent. Fresco. Rome, Vatican, Sistine Chapel.

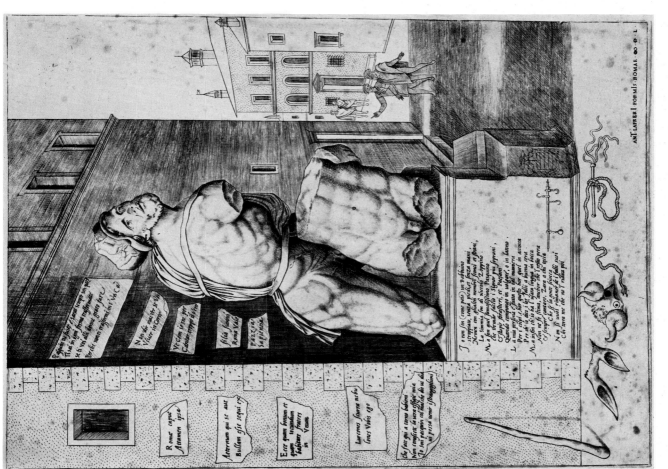

Pl. 307. *Left, and right, below:* N. Beatrizet (Beatricetto), engravings showing pasquinades alongside the ancient statues popularly called "Pasquino" (*left*) and "Marforio" (*below, right*), 16th cent. Both, Rome, Gabinetto Nazionale delle Stampe. *Right, above:* M. van Heemskerck, drawing of Roman remains, from the "Sketchbook," 1532–36. Rome, Museo di Palazzo Venezia.

Pl. 308. *Above*: G. B. Piranesi, section of wall enclosing the Piazza dei Cavalieri di Malta, Rome, second half of 18th cent. *Below, left*: Assembly of antique sculptured fragments. Rome, Palazzo Farnese. *Right*: H. Fuseli (J. H. Füssli), allegorical drawing with colossal foot and hand, ca. 1780. Red wash on paper, $16^3/_8 \times 14$ in. Zurich, Kunsthaus.

Pl. 309. *Above*: F. Zuccari, Taddeo Zuccari drawing the Laocoön, 16th cent. Pen and bistre with traces of black pencil, 7¹/₄×16³/₄ in. Florence, Uffizi, Gabinetto dei Disegni e Stampe. *Below*: J. Miel, Carnival in the Piazza Colonna, Rome, 17th cent. Canvas, 33³/₄×67⁵/₈ in. Hartford, Conn., Wadsworth Atheneum.

Pl. 310. *Above*: J. F. van Bloemen, Rome and the Alban Hills, seen from the Camilluccia, ca. 1740. Canvas, 6 ft., 7³/₄ in. × 8 ft., 1¹/₄ in. Rome, Società Montecatini. *Below*: H. Robert, The Porto di Ripetta at Rome, composite landscape, with the Pantheon, 1776. Canvas, 3 ft., 11 in. × 4 ft., 9 in. Paris, École des Beaux-Arts.

Pl. 311. *Above*: G. van Wittel (G. Vanvitelli, d. 1736), Trinità dei Monti. Canvas. Rome, Galleria Nazionale. *Below*: J.H.W. Tischbein, Goethe in the Campagna Romana, 1786–87. Canvas, 5 ft., 4 in. × 6 ft., 9 in. Frankfort on the Main, Städelsches Kunstinstitut.

Pl. 312. *Above*: F. Casanova (attrib.), Corsa dei Barberi, 18th cent. Pen and ink with wash and white, 13×18¹/₂ in. Warsaw, University Library. *Below*: B. Pinelli, Roman Carnival, Masque on Via del Babuino, 1834. Etching.

Pl. 313. E. Delacroix, Liberty Guiding the People, detail, 1830. Canvas; full size, 8 ft., 6³/₈ in. × 10 ft., 8 in. Paris, Louvre.

Pl. 314. T. Géricault, unfinished study for The Raft of the Medusa (VI, pl. 118), 1818. Canvas, 25⅝×32¾ in. Paris, Louvre.

Pl. 315. F. Goya, Gathering of Witches, ca. 1820–22. Mural transferred to canvas, 4 ft., 7 in. × 14 ft., 4¹/₂ in. Madrid, Prado.

Pl. 316. *Above, left*: G. B. Piranesi, etching from the prison series, 1760. *Right*: W. Blake, The Ancient of Days. Color over relief-etched print, 9¹/₈×6⁵/₈ in. Manchester, England, Whitworth Art Gallery. *Below*: G. Stubbs, White Horse Frightened by a Lion, 1770. Canvas, 40×50¹/₄ in. Liverpool, Walker Art Gallery.

Pl. 317. *Above*: J. Constable, The Marine Parade and Old Chain Pier, Brighton, 1824–27. Canvas, 4 ft., 2 in. × 6 ft., ³/₄ in.
Below: J. M. W. Turner, The Shipwreck, 1805. Canvas, 5 ft., 7¹/₂ in. × 7 ft., 11 in. Both, London, Tate Gallery.

Pl. 318. *Above*: C. D. Friedrich, Mountain Landscape with Rainbow, ca. 1809. Canvas, $27\,^1/_2 \times 40\,^1/_2$ in. Essen, Germany, Folkwang Museum. *Below*: P. O. Runge, Rest on the Flight into Egypt, ca. 1805. Canvas, $38\,^5/_8 \times 52$ in. Hamburg, Kunsthalle.

Pl. 319. *Above*: A. J. Gros, Napoleon on the Battlefield at Eylau, 1808. Canvas, 17 ft., 6 in. × 26 ft., 3 in. *Below*: A. L. Girodet-Trioson, The Burial of Atala, 1808. Canvas, 6 ft., 9½ in. × 9 ft., 4½ in. Both, Paris, Louvre.

Pl. 320. A. J. Gros, Napoleon at the Bridge of Arcole, 1796. Canvas, 28³/₈×23¹/₄ in. Paris, Louvre.

Pl. 321. *Above*: T. Rousseau, Springtime, ca. 1852. Panel, 16³/₈×25 in. *Below*: C. Troyon (1810–65), Stream in a Wood. Panel, 12³/₄×18³/₈ in. Both, Paris, Louvre.

Pl. 322. A. Fontanesi, Woman at the Spring, ca. 1865. Canvas, 20$^{1/2}$×28$^{3/4}$ in. Turin, Museo Civico.

Pl. 323. *Gopis* in an Arbor. W., 5 ft., 7 in. Calcutta, Asutosh Museum.

Pl. 324. A member of the Tagore family. Water color. Trivandrum, Kerala, India, Picture Gallery.

Pl. 325. Rubens and Isabella Brant, double portrait of the artist and his first wife in a honeysuckle bower. Canvas, 5 ft., 10 in.
× 4 ft., 5½ in. Munich, Alte Pinakothek.

Pl. 326. The Triptych of St. Ildefonsus, central panel. Panel, 11 ft., 6$^{1}/_{2}$ in. × 7 ft., 9 in. Vienna, Kunsthistorisches Museum.

Pl. 327. *Above, left*: The Lamentation over the Dead Christ. Canvas, 5 ft., 11 in. × 4 ft., 6 in. Rome, Galleria Borghese.
Right: The Raising of the Cross, central panel of a triptych. Panel, 15 ft., 2 in. × 11 ft., 2¹/₄ in. Antwerp,
Cathedral. *Below*: The Adoration of the Magi. Canvas, 11 ft., 4¹/₄ in. × 16 ft. Madrid, Prado.

Pl. 328. *Above*: Juno and Argus. Canvas, 8 ft., 2¹/₂ in. × 9 ft., 10 in. Cologne, Wallraf-Richartz-Museum. *Below*:
The Conversion of St. Bavo. Panel, 3 ft., 5¹/₂ in. × 5 ft., 5¹/₂ in. London, National Gallery.

Pl. 329. *Above*: The Flight into Egypt. Panel, 15³/₄×20⁷/₈ in. *Below*: Jupiter and Callisto. Panel, 4 ft., 1⁵/₈ in. × 6 ft., ¹/₂ in. Both, Kassel, Germany, Staatliche Kunstsammlungen.

Pl. 330. The Last Communion of St. Francis. Panel, 13 ft., 10 in. × 7 ft., 5 in. Antwerp, Musée Royal des Beaux-Arts.

Pl. 331. Peace and War, detail. Panel; full size, 6 ft., 6 in. × 9 ft., 9 in. London, National Gallery.

Pl. 332. Landscape with Rainbow. Panel, $37^{1}/_{4} \times 48^{1}/_{2}$ in. Munich, Alte Pinakothek.

Pl. 333. *Left*: The Adoration of the Magi. Panel, 14 ft., 8 in. × 11 ft. Antwerp, Musée Royal des Beaux-Arts. *Right*: The Martyrdom of St. Livinus. Canvas, 14 ft., 11 in. × 11 ft., 4¹/₂ in. Brussels, Musées Royaux des Beaux-Arts.

Pl. 334. *Above*: The Garden of Love. Canvas, 6 ft., 6 in. × 9 ft., 3¹/₂ in. Madrid, Prado. *Below*: The Horrors of War. Canvas, 6 ft., 9 in. × 11 ft., 4 in. Florence, Pitti.

Pl. 335. Achilles Dipped in the River Styx by Thetis. Panel, 17³/₈ × 15 in. Rotterdam, Museum Boymans - Van Beuningen.

Pl. 336. Icon of the Trinity, showing the Godhead incarnated. Panel, 4 ft., 8 in. × 3 ft., 9 in. Moscow, Tretyakov Gallery.

Pl. 337. The Saviour. Panel, 5 ft., 2¹/₄ in. × 3 ft., 5³/₄ in. Moscow, Tretyakov Gallery.

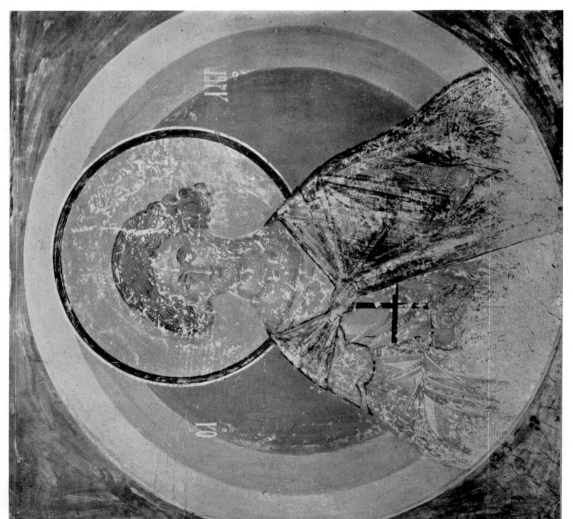

Pl. 338. *Left*: St. Laurus. Fresco. Zvenigorod, Cathedral of the Dormition. *Right*: The Annunciation. Panel, 31⁷/₈×24 in. Moscow, Cathedral of the Annunciation.

Pl. 339. Apostles and Angels. Fresco. Vladimir, Cathedral of the Dormition.

Pl. 340. S. van Ruysdael, Dutch Landscape. Panel, $26^3/_8 \times 41$ in. Berlin, Staatliche Museen.

Pl. 341. S. van Ruysdael, River Landscape. Canvas, 3 ft, 7^{1}/$_{4}$ in. × 4 ft., 11^{3}/$_{4}$ in. Amsterdam, Rijksmuseum.

RUISDAEL (RUYSDAEL)

Pl. 342. J. van Ruisdael, A Waterfall in a Rocky Landscape. Canvas, 38³/₄×33¹/₂ in. London, National Gallery.

Pl. 343. J. van Ruisdael. *Above*: The Jewish Cemetery. Canvas, 33 1/8 × 37 3/8 in. Dresden, Gemäldega-
lerie-Alte Meister. *Below*: The Shore at Egmond-aan-Zee. Canvas, 21 1/8 × 26 in. London,
National Gallery.

Pl. 344. J. van Ruisdael. *Above*: View of Haarlem. Canvas, 22×24³/₈ in. The Hague, Mauritshuis.
Below: The Mill at Wijk bij Duurstede. Canvas, 32⁵/₈×39³/₄ in. Amsterdam, Rijksmuseum.

Pl. 345. *Above*: Mashhad, Iran, the Muṣallā, 1676/77. *Below, left*: Isfahan, Iran, Masjid-i-Shāh, detail of arches, ca. 1611/12. *Right*: Isfahan, Masjid-i-Jāmiʿ, 12th–17th cent., arches of the southwest corner as reconstructed, 17th cent.

Pl. 346. Isfahan, Iran, Masjid-i-Shaykh Luṭfullāh, detail of kashi decoration, first quarter of 17th cent.

Pl. 347. Sava, Iran, Masjid-i-Jāmiʿ, mihrab, decorated with polychrome stucco relief, ca. 1512.

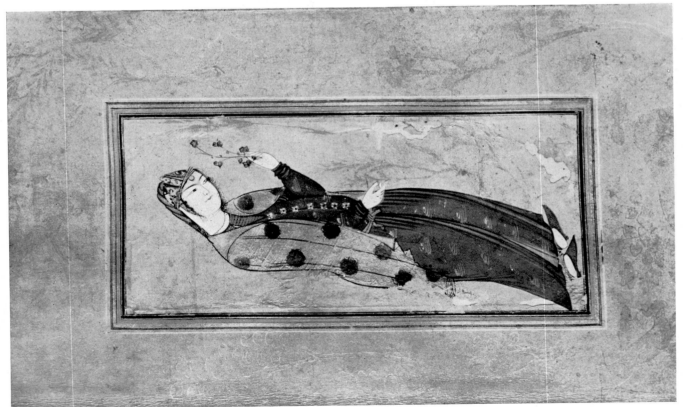

Pl. 348. *Left:* Illumination for a copy of Jāmī's *Yūsuf u Zulaykhā*, 16th cent. Venice, Biblioteca Marciana. *Right:* Yellow-ground figured silk enhanced with metal thread, inscribed with the name 'Abd-Allāh, early 17th cent. Ht. of repeat, 7 in. Cleveland, Museum of Art.

Pl. 349. *Left*: Muʿīn, drawing of a man leaning on a cushion, 1675/76. Pen, 6⁷/₈×3¹/₂ in. Teheran, Archaeological Museum. *Right*: Miniature with an alchemist or a magician, 18th cent. Gold and color on paper; full page, 10⁷/₈×8¹/₈ in. Seattle, Art Museum, Eugene Fuller Memorial Coll.

Pl. 350. *Above*: Incised bowl, 17th cent. Black-green jade, diam., 5⅝ in. Paris, Louvre. *Below*: Painted dish of Kubachi ware, 17th cent. Diam., 13⅝ in. New York, N. Heeramaneck Coll.

Pl. 351. Riẓā-i-ʿAbbāsī (attrib.), drawing with a man leaning on a long stick, 17th cent. Ht., 9¹/₂ in. Teheran, Archaeological Museum.

Pl. 352. Center boss of a withe and silk rondache, 17th cent. Engraved and inlaid steel, set with stones; diam., 22⁷/₈ in. Stockholm, Royal Armory.

Pl. 353. *Above*: Engraved bowl, executed by al-Imāmī of Aleppo, 1535–36. Tinned copper, diam., 13 3/4 in. New York, Metropolitan Museum. *Below, left*: Ewer with engraved arabesque ornamentation, ca. 17th cent. Brass, ht., 12 in. Edinburgh, Royal Scottish Museum. *Right*: Engraved candlestick, 1578. Brass, ht., 12 3/4 in. New York, Metropolitan Museum.

Pl. 354. *Above*: Polychrome silk velvet with white ground, 17th cent. Ht. of piece, 34⅝
in. Brussels, Musées Royaux d'Art et d'Histoire. *Below*: Portion of an incomplete "garden" carpet, from Kurdistan, 18th cent. Full size, 31 ft., 2 in. × 11 ft.,
8 in. London, Aberconway Coll.

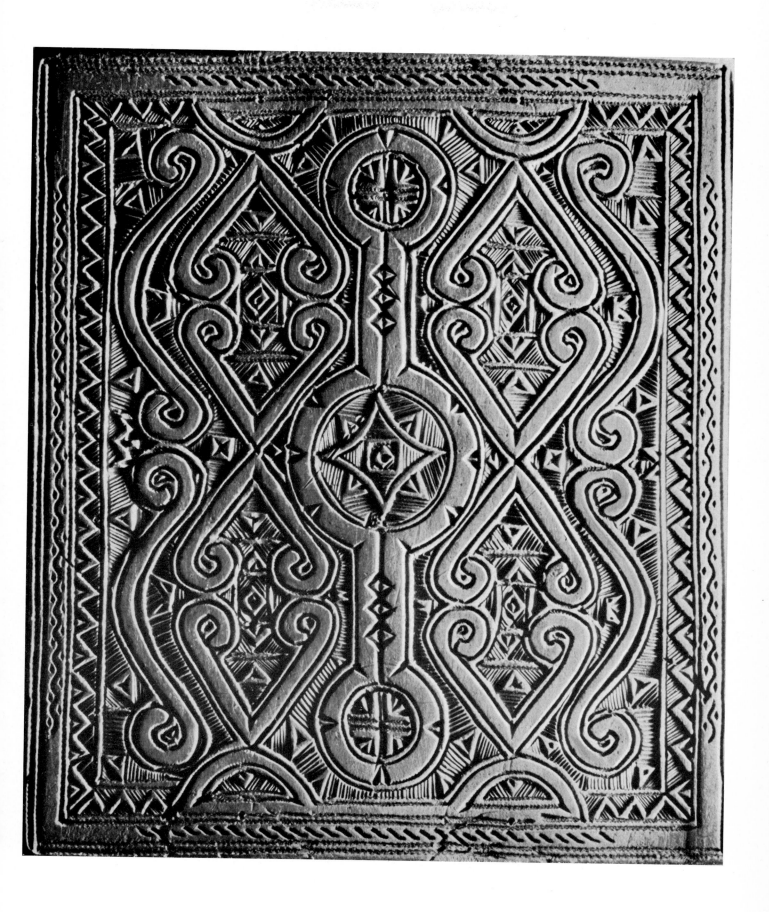

Pl. 355. Central plaque of an anklet (*khalkhel*), one of a pair, signed by Ahmed ould Moïlid, chief smith of Boutilimit, Mauritania, collected 1951. Hammered and chiseled silver, 2×1³/₄ in. Neuchâtel, Switzerland, Musée d'Ethnographie, Coll. J. Gabus.

Pl. 356. *Left*: Trarza baggage carrier (*amojar tiziaten*), detail of leg, Mauritania, collected 1954. Wood, w., 3 in. *Right*: Decoration on the cover of a tool chest (*sandong likbir*), from Méderdra, Mauritania, collected 1954. Sheet-iron appliqué on wood; size of cover, $20^7/_8 \times 11^3/_4$ in. Both, Neuchâtel, Switzerland, Musée d'Ethnographie, Coll. J. Gabus.

Pl. 357. Decoration on the wall of an interior court, Oualata, Mauritania.

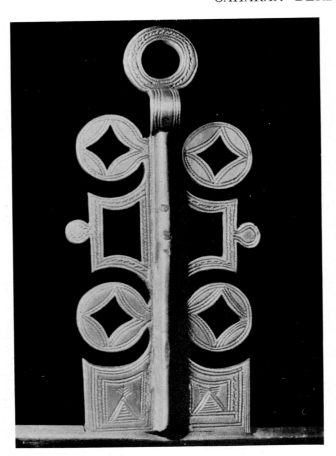

Pl. 358. *Above, left*: Fastening of a tool chest, from Méderdra, Mauritania, collected 1954. Iron with brass and copper, 4³/₈ × 1³/₄ in. *Right*: Side plaque of the anklet paired with that in PL. 355. Hammered and chiseled silver, ht., ca. 1 in. Both, Neuchâtel, Switzerland, Musée d'Ethnographie, Coll. J. Gabus. *Below*: Kabyle ornament, northern Algeria. Silver with inset red coral and enamel, l., ca. 12 in. Oxford, Pitt Rivers Museum.

Pl. 359. Tzul pottery with geometric decoration, Zerhoun massif, northern Morocco. Rabat, Musée des Arts Marocains.

Pl. 360. Utensils for milk or millet. *Above*: Antessar spoon (*tisokalin*) and bowl, from Timbuktu, collected 1960. Tamarisk wood, l. of spoon, 10³/₄ in. *Below*: Bowls decorated with the so-called "gourd amulet" motif in relief, from Méderdra, Mauritania, collected 1951. Wood, ht., 5⁷/₈ and 5¹/₂ in. All. Neuchâtel, Switzerland, Musée d'Ethnographie, Coll. J. Gabus.

Pl. 361. Tuareg women's bag (*taseīhat*), in the style of the Goundam–Timbuktu area, collected, 1948, in the nomad region near Gao, Mali. Painted and incised sheepskin, w., 33½ in. Neuchâtel, Switzerland, Musée d'Ethnographie, Coll. J. Gabus.

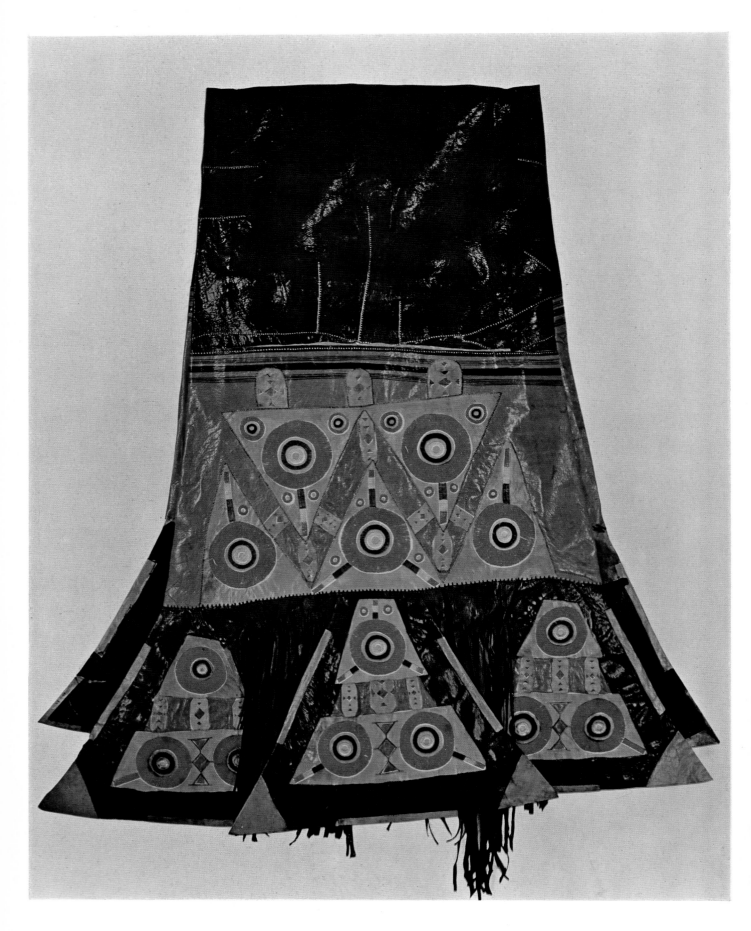

Pl. 362. Tuareg women's saddle pad (*adafor*), Air region, collected, 1948, at Agadès, Niger. Sheepskin, with leather appliqué and cotton embroidery; l., opened out, 6 ft., 8³/₄ in. Neuchâtel, Switzerland, Musée d'Ethnographie, Coll. J. Gabus.

Pl. 363. *Above*: Sarakole water jars, from Oualata, Mauritania. Pottery, ht., 9¹/₈ and 13³/₄ in. Neuchâtel, Switzerland, Musée d'Ethnographie, Coll. J. Gabus. *Below*: Berber vessel, consisting of five receptacles, from Algeria. Pottery, ht., 10⁷/₈ in. Hamburg, Museum für Völkerkunde.

Pl. 364. Kabyle camel-shaped figurine, from Tama Osht, northern Algeria. Pottery. Oxford, Pitt Rivers Museum.

Pl. 365. The Apostles, the Precursor. *Above, left*: Pyxis with the twelve apostles, 4th cent. Ivory, ht., 4³/₄ in., diam., 5³/₄ in. Berlin, Staatliche Museen. *Above, right*: John the Baptist, detail of the "throne of Maximian" (V, PL. 432). Ivory. Ravenna, Italy, Museo Arcivescovile. *Below*: The Last Supper, mid-14th cent. Fresco. Mistra, Greece, Peribleptos.

Pl. 366. Processions of saints. *Above*: The virgins, 6th cent., detail. Mosaic. Ravenna, Italy, S. Apollinare Nuovo. *Below*: Martyrs, 14th cent., detail. Fresco. Mistra, Greece, Brontochion, Church of the Afendiko.

SAINTS

Pl. 367. Martyrs. *Above, left* : St. Sergius, detail, 7th cent. Mosaic. Salonika, Greece, St. Demetrios. *Right* : St. Catherine before the judges, detail, from the Cathedral of Seo de Urgel, Spain, 13th cent. Fresco. Barcelona, Coll. Mateu. *Below, left* : J. Mates, St. Sebastian, ca. 1425. Panel, w., 3 ft., 3¹/₂ in. Barcelona, Museo de Bellas Artes de Cataluña. *Right* : Raphael, Ecstasy of St. Cecilia, 1514. Canvas, 7 ft., 2¹/₂ in. × 4 ft., 5¹/₂ in. Bologna, Pinacoteca.

Pl. 368. Scenes from legends. *Above, left*: Pietro da Cortona, Martyrdom of St. Lawrence, 1646. Canvas, w., 5 ft., 11 in. (upper part omitted). Rome, S. Lorenzo in Miranda. *Right*: G. B. Tiepolo, Martyrdom of St. Bartholomew, ca. 1721. Canvas, 5 ft., 5³/₄ in. × 4 ft., 6³/₄ in. Venice, S. Stae. *Below*: J. Duncan, St. Bride, 1913. Tempera on canvas, 3 ft., 11¹/₂ in. × 4 ft., 8¹/₂ in. Edinburgh, National Gallery of Scotland.

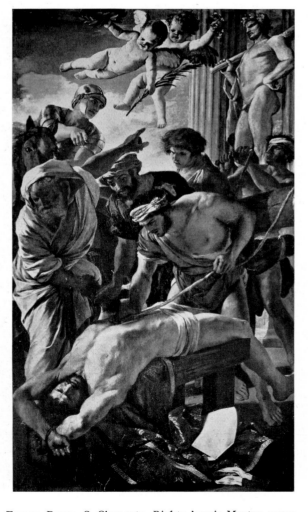

Pl. 369. Scenes from legends. *Above, left*: Miracle of St. Clement, ca. 1100. Fresco. Rome, S. Clemente. *Right*: Arguis Master, scene from the legend of St. Michael, with the defeat of Antichrist, 15th cent. Panel, $31^{1}/_{8} \times 31^{1}/_{2}$ in. Madrid, Prado. *Below, left*: H. Memling, Martyrdom of St. Ursula and Her Virgins, detail of shrine (IX, PL. 461), 1489. Painted wood. Bruges, Musée Memling. *Right*: N. Poussin, Martyrdom of St. Erasmus, ca. 1630. Canvas. Rome, Vatican Museums.

Pl. 370. The Evangelists. *Above, left*: St. Matthew, 14th cent. Mosaic. Salonika, Greece, Church of the Holy Apostles. *Right*: St. Mark, from the Ada Gospels, late 8th cent. Illumination. Trier, Germany, Stadtbibliothek. *Below, left*: Giovanni Pisano (or from his design), St. John, 1278–87 (?). Marble, ht., 5 ft., 7³/₄ in. Pisa, Italy, Baptistery. *Right*: A. Mantegna, St. Luke, central panel of a polyptych, 1453. Panel; size of polyptych, 5 ft., 9⁵/₈ in. × 7 ft., 6¹/₂ in. Milan, Brera.

Pl. 371. The Four Doctors of the Church. *Above*: Of the Eastern Church, perhaps from Mt. Athos, 16th–17th cent. Panel, ht., 12⅝ in. Rome, Vatican Museums. *Below*: Of the Western Church, by a follower of Giotto, ca. early 14th cent. Fresco. Assisi, Italy, S. Francesco, Upper Church.

Pl. 372. Hermits. *Above, left*: St. Simeon Stylites, from the Menologion of Basil II, late 10th cent. Illumination. Rome, Vatican Library (Cod. Vat. gr. 1613, fol. 2). *Right*: Master of the Osservanza (?), St. Anthony Abbot, mid-15th cent. Panel, 17³/₄×13³/₈ in. New York, R. Lehman Coll. *Below, left*: H. Bosch (ca. 1450–1516), Penitent St. Jerome, from the Retable of the Hermits. Panel, 34¹/₈×23⁵/₈ in. Venice, Doges' Palace. *Right*: Tintoretto, St. Mary of Egypt (Maria Aegyptica), 1583–87, detail. Canvas; full size, 16 ft., 5 in. × 6 ft., 11 in. Venice, Scuola di S. Rocco.

Pl. 373. Warriors, Knights. *Above, left*: St. Theodore Stratelates with scenes from his life, ca. 1500. Panel, 43¹/₄×27¹/₂ in. Novgorod, U.S.S.R., Museum of Art and History. *Right*: Pisanello, The Vision of St. Eustace, detail, ca. 1438 (?). Panel; full size, 21¹/₂×25³/₄ in. London, National Gallery. *Below, left*: J.A.D. Ingres, Joan of Arc at the Coronation of Charles VII, 1854. Canvas, 7 ft., 10¹/₂ in. × 5 ft., 10 in. Paris, Louvre. *Right*: A. Martini, St. George and the Dragon, ca. 1926. Terra cotta, ht., 32 in. Faenza, Italy, Museo Internazionale delle Ceramiche.

Pl. 374. Popes, Bishops. *Above, left*: St. Sylvester, 1340–60. Fresco. Mistra, Greece, Brontochion, Church of the Afendiko. *Right*: D. Bouts (ca. 1415–75), St. Hubert. Panel, $37 \times 22^{7}/_{8}$ in. Antwerp, Musée Royal des Beaux-Arts. *Below, left*: F. del Cossa, St. Petronius, 1473. Tarsia. Bologna, Italy, S. Petronio, choir. *Right*: H. Burgkmair the Elder (1473–1531), St. Ulrich. Panel, $41 \times 15^{3}/_{4}$ in. Berlin, Staatliche Museen.

Pl. 375. Monks, Nuns. *Above, left*: Cimabue, St. Francis, detail of III, PL. 328, ca. 1295. Fresco. Assisi, Italy, S. Francesco, Lower Church. *Right*: A. Vanni, St. Catherine of Siena, ca. 1385. Fresco. Siena, Italy, S. Domenico. *Below, left*: F. Traini, Apotheosis of St. Thomas Aquinas, mid-14th cent. Panel. Pisa, Italy, S. Caterina. *Right*: Alvise Vivarini (ca. 1444–1505), St. Clare, detail. Panel. Venice, Accademia.

Pl. 376. Monks. *Above, left*: Piero della Francesca, St. Benedict, from the polyptych of the Madonna of Mercy, commissioned 1445. Panel. Sansepolcro, Italy, Pinacoteca Comunale. *Right*: P. F. Mola (1612–66, version by another hand?), Ecstasy of St. Bruno. Canvas, 54³/₈ × 39³/₄ in. Rome, Galleria Doria Pamphili. *Below*: F. Pacheco (1564–1654), The Embarkment of St. Peter Nolasco. Canvas, 6 ft., 2³/₄ in. × 8 ft., 2¹/₂ in. Seville, Spain, Museo Provincial de Bellas Artes.

Pl. 377. Monks, Nuns. *Above, left*: F. Zurbarán, The Vision of Blessed Alonso Rodriguez, 1630. Canvas, 8 ft., 9 in. × 5 ft., 6 in. Madrid, Academia de S. Fernando. *Right*: P. P. Rubens, Miracle of St. Ignatius, 1619. Canvas, 13 ft., 1¹/₂ in. × 9 ft. Genoa, S. Ambrogio. *Below, left*: A. Cano with P. de Mena, St. Diego de Alcalá, detail, 1653–57. Polychromed wood; full ht., 6 ft., 6¹/₂ in. Granada, Spain, Palace of Charles V. *Right*: G. L. Bernini, tomb of Maria Raggi, detail, 1643. Gilded bronze. Rome, S. Maria sopra Minerva.

Pl. 378. Saints associated with the life of Christ. *Above*: J. Patinir (ca. 1480–1524), St. Christopher ferrying the Christ child. Panel, 3 ft., 3³/₈ in. × 4 ft., 11¹/₈ in. Escorial, near Madrid. *Below, left*: Raffaellino del Garbo (ca. 1466–1524), Madonna and Child with the Infant St. John. Panel, diam., 34¹/₄ in. Naples, Museo di Capodimonte. *Right*: F. de Herrera the Elder, St. Joseph with the Infant Christ, 1648, detail. Canvas. Madrid, Museo Lázaro Galdiano.

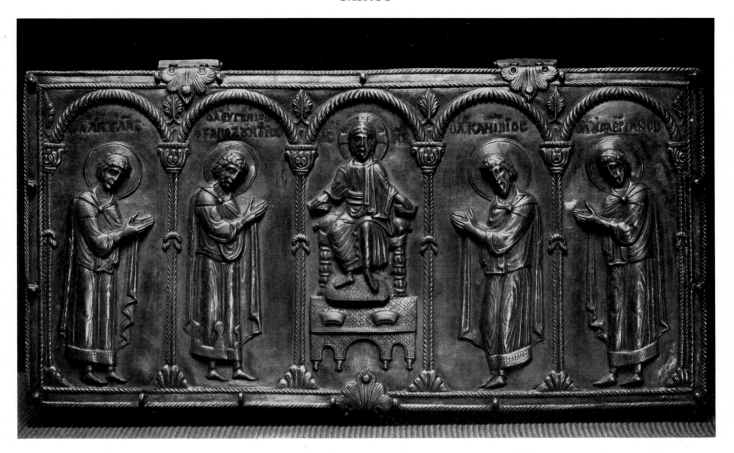

Pl. 379. *Above*: Reliquary of the four martyrs of Trebizond, 11th cent. Gilded silver. Venice, Treasury of S. Marco. *Below, left*: Reliquary of St. Baudime, Limoges workshop, 12th–13th cent. Enameled copper on oak. Saint-Nectaire, France, church. *Right*: Dmitry Prilutsky with scenes from his life, ascribed to Dionysius, late 15th cent. Oil on wood, 43 1/4 × 27 1/2 in. Vologda, U.S.S.R., Regional Museum of Local History.

Pl. 380. Popular art. *Above, left*: Woodcut with St. Francis Solano, missionary to America, issued in Barcelona, Spain, 18th cent. Barcelona, Archivo Histórico. *Right*: St. George and the Dragon, from Lithuania, late 19th cent. Painted wood, ht., 21⁵/₈ in. Paris, Musée de l'Homme. *Below, left*: Devotional print with St. Joseph and the young Christ, Japan. *Right*: *Santino* ("holy picture") with St. Martin and the beggar, Italy.

Pl. 381. Bukhara, Uzbek S.S.R., mausoleum of Ismā'īl the Samanid (d. 907), built of fired brick with carved terra-cotta ornament, detail of façade.

Pl. 382. Bukhara, Uzbek S.S.R., mausoleum of Ismāʿīl the Samanid (d. 907), two details.

Pl. 383. Bowl of Samarkand type, 9th–10th cent. Slip-painted pottery, purple-black on white; diam., 10 in. Oxford, Ashmolean Museum.

Pl. 384. Bowls of Samarkand type, from Nishapur, Iran, 9th–10th cent. Slip-painted pottery, purple-black on white; diam., 10³/₄ and (right) 9⁵/₈ in. Both, New York, Metropolitan Museum.

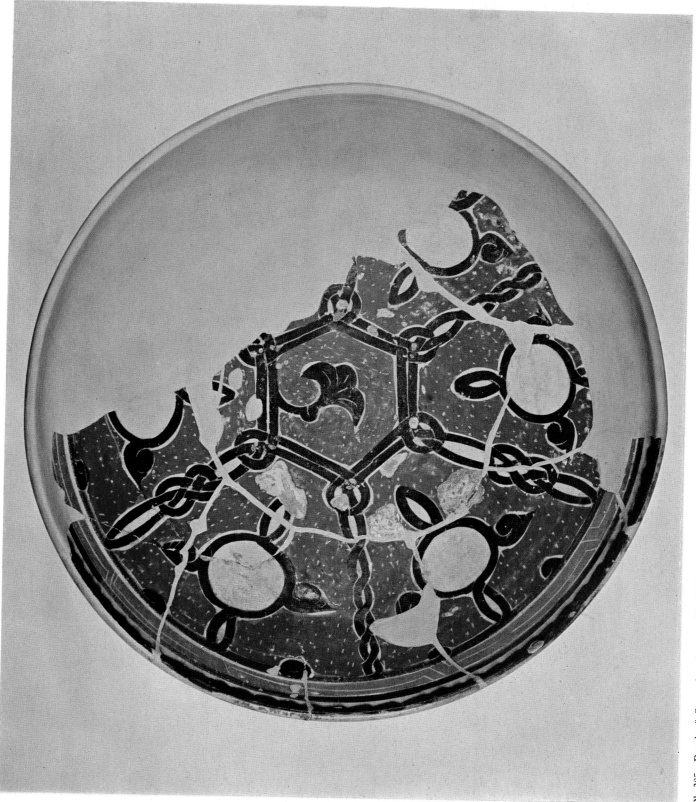

Pl. 385. Bowl of Samarkand type, 9th–10th cent. Slip-painted pottery, diam., 13³/₄ in. London, Victoria and Albert Museum.

Pl. 386. Deep bowl of Samarkand type, from Transoxiana, 10th cent. Slip-painted pottery, diam., 9⁷/₈ in. London, Victoria and Albert Museum.

Pl. 387. Giuliano da Sangallo. *Above*: Poggio a Caiano, near Florence, Villa. *Below*: Florence, S. Maria Maddalena dei Pazzi, cloister.

Pl. 388. Giuliano da Sangallo. *Left, and right, above:* Prato, Italy, S. Maria delle Carceri. *Below:* Florence, Palazzo Gondi, courtyard.

Pl. 389. Antonio da Sangallo the Elder. *Left*: Montepulciano, Italy, S. Biagio. *Right*: Montepulciano, Palazzo Cervini.

Pl. 390. *Above*: Antonio da Sangallo the Elder, Palazzo Tarugi, Montepulciano, Italy. *Below*: Antonio da Sangallo the Younger. *Left*: Rome, Palazzo Baldassini, stairway. *Right*: Rome, former Mint (Palazzo del Banco di Sto Spirito).

Pl. 391. Verona, Italy, Palazzo Canossa.

Pl. 392. Verona, Italy, Porta Nuova, inner façade.

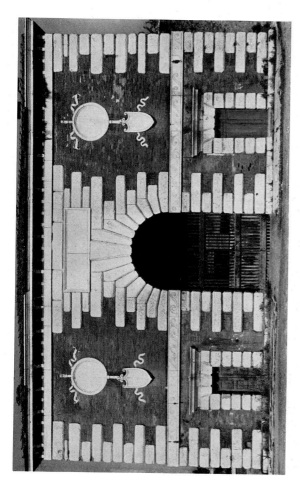

Pl. 393. *Left*: Verona, Italy. *Above*: Porta S. Zeno (attrib.), inner façade. *Below*: Porta Palio, outer façade. *Right*: Venice, Palazzo Grimani.

Pl. 394. *Above*: Verona, Italy, Cathedral, semicircular chancel screen. Marble. *Below*: *Tempietto* of the Lazzaretto, outside Verona.

Pl. 395. The so-called "Cup of Khusrau," 6th cent. Glass paste mounted in gold, center medallion of carved rock crystal; diam., 11 in. Paris, Cabinet des Médailles.

Pl. 396. Plate, with double-headed eagle, 6th cent. Silver, partly gilded; diam., 21 1/4 in. Geneva, N. Koutoulakis Coll.

Pl. 397. Ctesiphon, Iraq, Ṭāq-i-Kisrā, 3d or 6th cent. *Above*: Façade, photographed ca. 1880 (later virtually destroyed). *Below, left*: Interior of liwan vault. *Right*: South part of façade, rear view.

Pl. 398. Reliefs in the large cave of Ṭāq-i-Bustān, near Kermanshah, Iran, depicting the investiture of a king and the monarch on horseback, probably Khusrau II (590–628).

Pl. 399. Ornamental architectural panels with palmette motifs, from houses at Ctesiphon, Iraq, 6th cent. Stucco; ht. (*top to bottom*), 6¹/₂, 7¹/₂, 8¹/₂ in. New York, Metropolitan Museum.

Pl. 400. Rock reliefs of Naqsh-i-Rustam, near Persepolis, showing the king overthrowing an adversary. *Above*: Bahrām II (276–93).
Below: Ormizd II (302–09).

Pl. 401. Rock reliefs with investiture scenes. *Above*: Narsah (293–302), at Naqsh-i-Rustam, near Persepolis. *Below*: Ardashīr II (379–83), at Ṭāq-i-Bustān, near Kermanshah, Iran.

Pl. 402. *Above*: Vase, ca. 3d cent. (?). Repoussé and engraved silver, upper band of birds in niello (lower part restored); ht., 4 in. Basel, E. Borowski Coll. *Below*: Drinking bowl, with a king, probably Shāpur II, dispatching a stag, 4th cent. Silver with applied repoussé, engraved and partly gilded; diam., 7 in. London, British Museum.

Pl. 403. *Above*: Stemmed cup, from Mazanderan, Iran, 5th–6th cent. Silver and gold, ht., 3³/₄ in. Teheran, Archaeological Museum. *Below*: Oval dish, with ibex, 6th–7th cent. Silver. Beirut, Kettaneh Coll.

Pl. 404. *Left:* Oval dish, with wading bird, rosettes, and S motif, 6th–7th cent. Gilded silver, l., 8¼ in. *Right:* Vase, with cocks and birds, 6th cent. (?). Gilded silver, ht., 4¼ in. Both, Teheran, Foroughi Coll.

Pl. 405. Compound silk twill, fragment, with cocks, 5th–7th cent. (?). Ht. of roundel, 10½ in. Rome, Vatican Museums.

Pl. 406. Compound silk twill, with senmurv, detail of fragment, 6th–7th cent. Ht. of roundel, ca. 14^1/$_2$ in. Paris, Musée des Arts Décoratifs.

Pl. 407. Plate, depicting the king shooting ibexes with bow and arrow, probably Fīrūz II (457–84/5). Silver with applied repoussé, engraved and inlaid with niello; diam., 8⁵/₈ in. New York, Metropolitan Museum.

Pl. 408. *Above*: Bowl, with musicians in low relief, from Mazanderan, 5th–6th cent. Cast silver, engraved and inset with black stones; diam., 9¼ in. Teheran, Archaeological Museum. *Below*: Plate, with fantastic wolflike feline among lotus flowers, 6th–7th cent. Cast silver, engraved and partly gilded, with niello; diam., 9⅞ in. Paris, Cabinet des Médailles.

Pl. 409. Glass, 6th–7th cent. *Above*: Transparent yellow bowl, with spiral decoration in relief. Ht., 3³/₄ in. *Below*: Vase, from Luristan. Ht., 3¹/₈ in. Both, Teheran, Foroughi Coll.

Pl. 410. Post-Sassanian bronzes modeled on Sassanian prototypes. *Above*: Bird-shaped vessel, originally with copper inlay, 8th–9th cent. Ht., 13½ in. *Below*: Tray, ca. 8th cent. Diam., 25¼ in. Both, Berlin, Staatliche Museen.

Pl. 411. *Above*: Sword hilt, from Stora Ihre, Gotland, Sweden, ca. 800. Bronze, w., 4¹⁄₈ in. *Below, left and right*: Harness mounts, from Broa, Gotland, ca. 800. Gilded bronze; each, ca. 2×2¹⁄₄ in. All, Stockholm, Statens Historiska Museum.

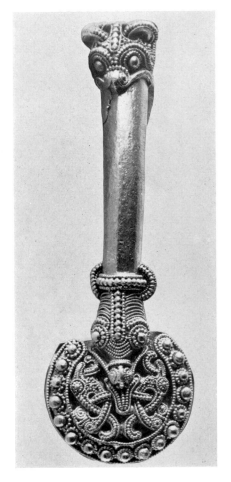

Pl. 412. *Left, and right, below:* Filigree work from Rød, Østfold, Norway, 10th cent. Gold. *Right, above:* Three-lobed buckle with acanthus decoration, from Hon, Buskerud, Norway, 9th cent. Gold. All, Oslo, Universitetets Oldsaksamling.

Pl. 413. The Oseberg burial ship, 9th cent., found in a mound at Oseberg, Norway. Oak with rails partly of beech wood, l., ca. 65 ft. Oslo, Viking Ship Museum.

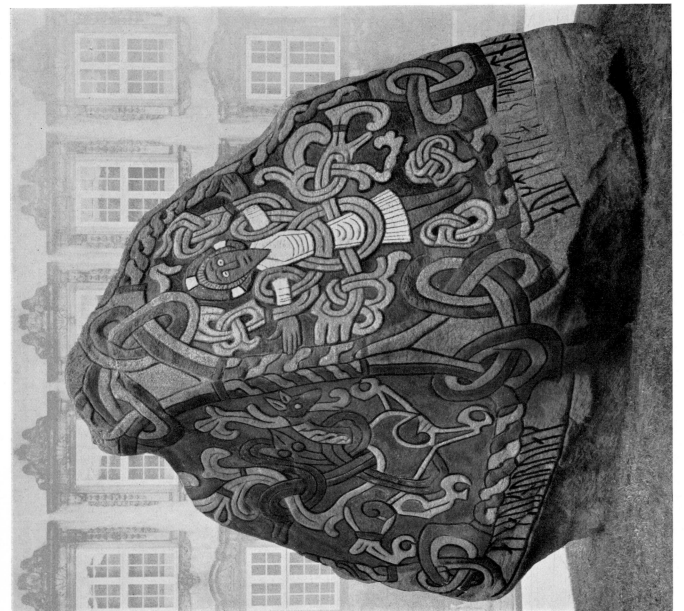

Pl. 414. *Left*: Runic stone, carved with an image of Christ, Jelling, Denmark, erected, ca. 940, by King Harald Bluetooth. (Presumed coloring restored.) *Right*: Runic stone, Sandby churchyard, Öland, Sweden, 11th cent. Limestone, ht., 5 ft., 5³/4 in.

Pl. 415. *Left*: Fragment of portal from the stave church at Hyllestad, Norway, 12th cent. Wood. Oslo, Universitetets Oldsaksamling. *Right, above*: Sepulchral monument, from Bot-kyrka, Sweden, 12th cent. Sandstone, l., 5 ft., 7 in. Stockholm, Statens Historiska Museum. *Below*: The Baldishoel Tapestry, fragment, Norway, ca. 1180, 6 ft., 6³/₄ in. × 3 ft., 11¹/₄ in. Oslo, Kunstindustrimuseet.

Pl. 416. *Above, left*: Bornholm, Denmark, Church of St. Ols, 12th cent. *Right*: Tapestry depicting the Adoration of the Magi, Norway, late 17th cent., 6 ft., 1 in. × 4 ft., 2 in. Oslo, Kunstindustrimuseet. *Below*: Timber storehouses from the Lake Siljan region, Dalecarlia, Sweden, 16th and 17th cent., now in the open-air section (Zorns Gammelgård) of the Zornmuseet in Mora.

Pl. 417. *Above*: Athens, Theater of Dionysos, rebuilt 4th cent. B.C., later additions. (Cf. plan, III, FIG. 667; II, PL. 52.) *Below*: The birth of Helen, scene from a farce (*phlyax*) showing Zeus breaking the egg of Leda. Vase painting, Apulia, 4th cent. B.C. (?). Bari Italy, Museo Archeologico.

Pl. 418. *Above*: Scene from *Iphigenia in Tauris* by Euripides. Wall painting, 1st cent., in the House of Pinarius Cerealis, Pompeii. *Below*: Sabrata, Libya, *frons scaenae* of the Roman theater, late 2d–early 3d cent. (reconstructed).

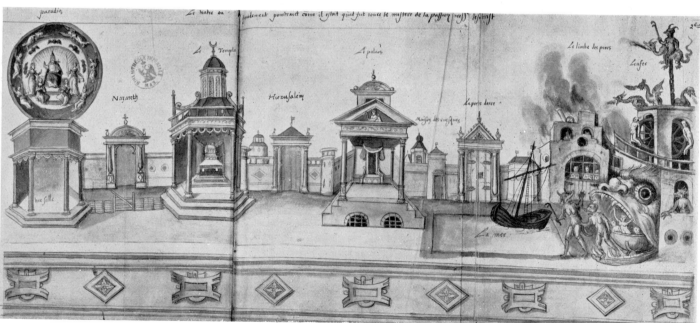

Pl. 419. Medieval religious drama. *Above, left*: The Three Marys discover the Empty Tomb. Illumination in an antiphonal of the Abbey of Saint-Gallen, Switzerland, 11th cent. *Right*: Loculus representing the Holy Sepulcher, 11th–12th cent., used for the enactment of Easter ceremonies until 1595. Aquileia, Italy, Cathedral. *Below*: Station stage for the mystery play at Valenciennes, France, showing the *mansions* for episodes in the life of Christ, Paradise, and the Mouth of Hell. Illumination by H. Cailleau, 1547. Paris, Bibliothèque Nationale (Ms. fr. 12536).

Pl. 420. *Above*: Strolling players on an outdoor platform. Colored drawing attributed to L. de Caullery (d. 1598). Cambrai, France, Bibliothèque Municipale (Ms. 126, fol. 53 r). *Below*: Herald, in a Shrove Tuesday play. Woodcut for *Spiel von der Kinderzucht* by J. Rasser, 1574, Ensisheim, Germany.

Pl. 421. *Above*: The Triumph of Time, with allegorical *carro*. Panel painting by J. del Sellaio. Florence, second half of 15th cent. Fiesole, Italy, Museo Bandini. *Below*: Masque celebrating the wedding of Sir Henry Unton (d. 1596). Panel painting, detail of a portrait of Sir Henry Unton with scenes of his career; full size, 2 ft., 4 in. × 5 ft., 2¹/₂ in. London, National Portrait Gallery.

Pl. 422. *Above*: B. Peruzzi, perspective studies of street scenes. Siena, Italy, Biblioteca Comunale (S. II. 4, carta 70). *Below*: B. Lancia, composite Florentine scene, perhaps a project for *La Vedova* by G. B. Cini, 1569. Colored pen drawing, 23 1/4 × 27 3/8 in. Florence, Uffizi, Gabinetto dei Disegni e Stampe.

Pl. 423. Medieval depiction of a Roman comedy, with actors costumed as jesters (upper scene). Illumination by the Master of the Duke of Bedford, frontispiece of *Térence des Ducs*, 15th cent. Paris, Bibliothèque de l'Arsenal (Ms. 664, fol. 1v).

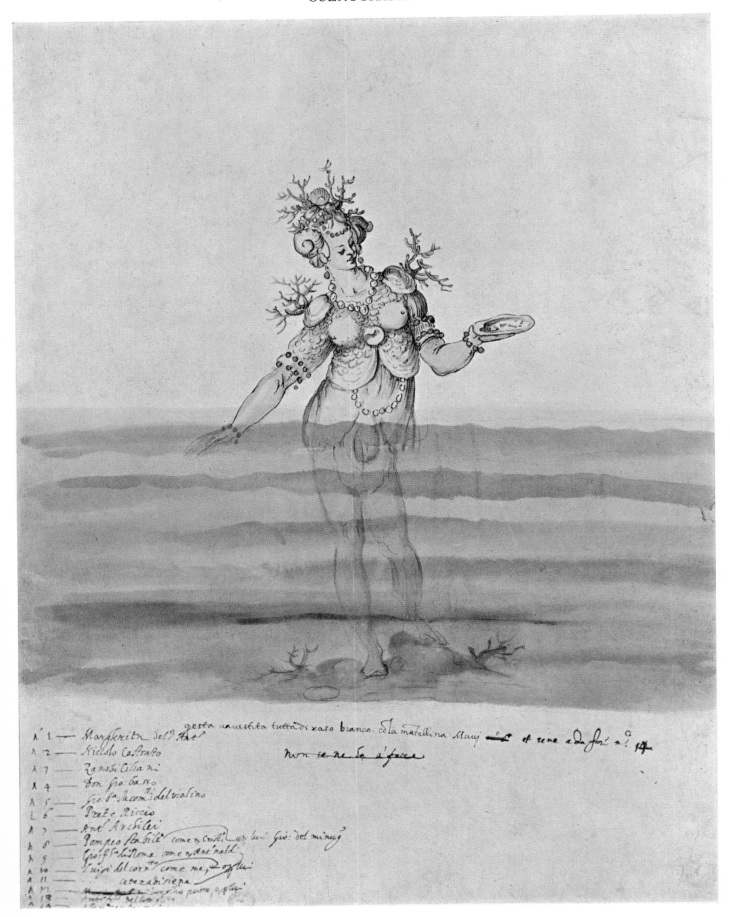

Pl. 424. B. Buontalenti, sketch with Amphitrite for *La Favola di Orione e Anfitrite,* third intermezzo of *La Pellegrina,* performed in Florence, 1589, for the marriage of Ferdinand I de' Medici and Cristina of Lorraine. Colored drawing. Florence, Biblioteca Nazionale.

Pl. 425. *Above*: A. Palladio, completed by V. Scamozzi, back wall of the stage of the Teatro Olimpico, Vicenza, Italy, 1580–85. (Cf. XI, PL. 36.) *Below*: The Globe Playhouse, London, 1599, stage and tiring house with adjacent galleries and pit, model reconstruction by J. C. Adams and I. Smith. Washington, D.C., Folger Shakespeare Library.

Pl. 426. Court ballet, *Ballet Comique de la Reine* by Baltazarini (Balthazar de Beaujoyeulx), performed in Paris, 1581. Engraving, from the libretto. Paris, Bibliothèque Nationale.

Pl. 427. First intermezzo of the ballet *La Liberazione di Tirreno*, stage design by G. Parigi, performed in the Sala delle Commedie (architect, B. Buontalenti, 1586), Palazzo degli Uffizi, Florence, 1616. Engraving by J. Callot. Florence, Uffizi, Gabinetto dei Disegni e Stampe.

Pl. 428. *Above*: The Judgment of Solomon, enacted in the Grande Place, Louvain, Belgium, in connection with the Om-
gang (historic procession of the city), 1594. Engraving after an ink drawing by G. Boonen in the Musée Communal,
Louvain. *Below*: Stage of the Theater on the Keizersgracht, Amsterdam. Engraving by S. Savery, 1658. Amsterdam,
Het Toneel Museum.

Pl. 429. *Above*: Scene from Italian *commedia dell'arte* with Scapino playing the guitar. Engraving. Bologna, Biblioteca Comunale dell'Archiginnasio. *Below*: L. Mahelot, multiple setting for *La Folie de Clidamant* by A. Hardy. Colored drawing from *Le Mémoire de Mahelot*, 1633–34. Paris, Bibliothèque Nationale.

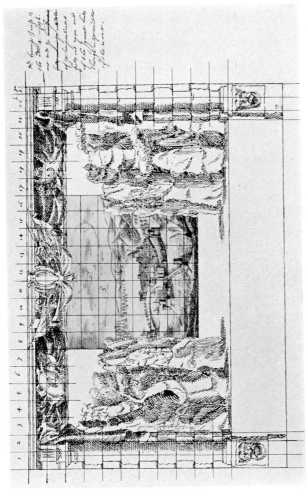

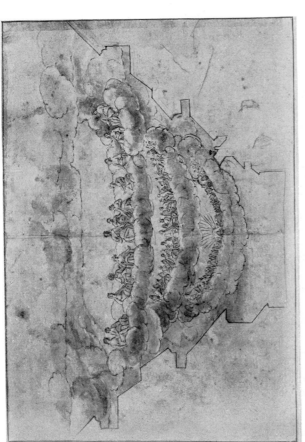

Pl. 430. *Above, left*: I. Jones, The Whole Heaven, sketch for the masque *Salamacida Spolia*, Scene V, presented in London, 1640. *Right*: J. Webb, scale drawing for *The Siege of Rhodes* by W. Davenant, showing the fixed side scenes with backdrop for Act I, Scene 1, 1656. Both, Derbyshire, England, Trustees of the Chatsworth Settlement. *Below*: J. O. Harms, design for *Heinrich der Löwe* by A. Steffani, presented in Hamburg, 1696. Brunswick, Germany, Herzog-Anton-Ulrich-Museum.

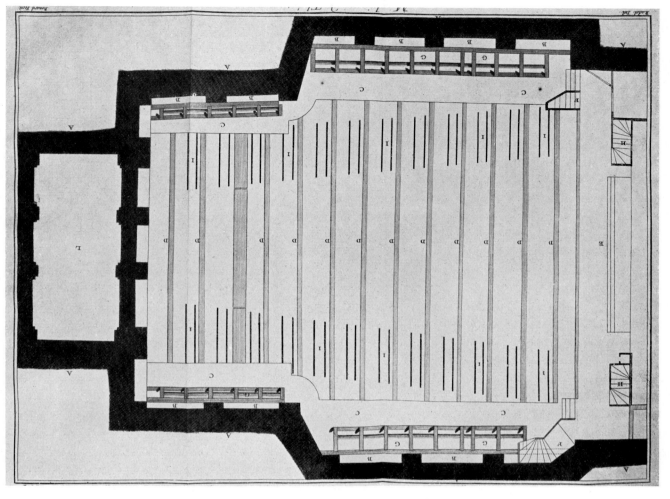

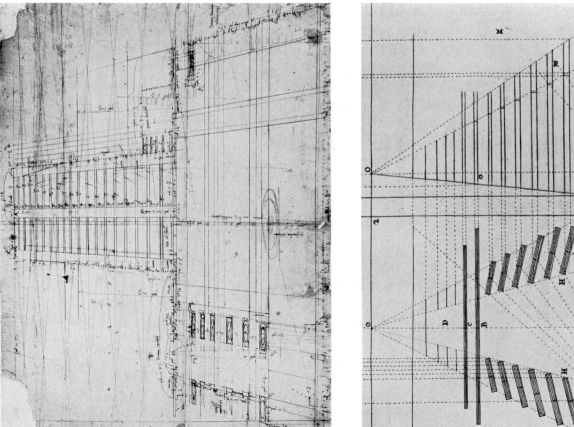

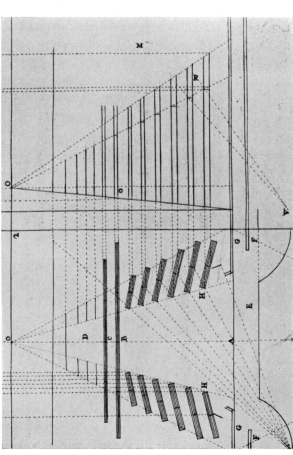

Pl. 431. Plans. *Left, above*: B. Peruzzi, scene for *La Calandria* by Cardinal Bibbiena, comprising a piazza with columns of a Temple of Apollo and a street lined with shops, 1520. Pen and red pencil, $24^3/_8 \times 32^7/_8$ in. Florence, Uffizi, Gabinetto dei Disegni e Stampe. *Below*: A. Pozzo, stage with oblique side flats (H), showing vanishing point (O) and lines of vision from the audience, ground plan and elevation, from *Prospettiva de' Pittori e architetti*, Rome, 1693. *Right*: Stage of the Palais Royal, Paris, from M. Radel, *Machines de Théâtre*, Paris, n.d. (after 1769).

Pl. 432. *Left, above*: Mock naval battle in Lake Maggiore, celebrating the marriage of Carlo Borromeo and Giovanna Odescalchi, 1677. Engraving. *Below*: L'Âge d'or, allegorical chariot de triomphe in the cortège celebrating the entry of Louis XIII into Paris, 1628, after the capture of La Rochelle. Paris, Bibliothèque Nationale, Cabinet des Estampes. *Right*: V. dal Re (d. 1762), construction for a pyrotechnic display at the Castel Nuovo, Naples. Engraving by G. Vasi.

Pl. 433. Temporary theater erected in Piazza Maggiore, Bologna, Italy, for a tournament in honor of Christina of Sweden, 1655. Miniature, from *Le Insignia degli Anziani del Comune*, Vol. VIII; $14^{1}/_{4} \times 22^{7}/_{8}$ in. Bologna, Archivio di Stato.

Pl. 434. *Above*: Entrée of the north and south winds in the ballet *La Primavera trionfante dell'Inverno*, performed at the court of the Duke of Savoy, Turin, Italy, 1657. Miniature. Turin, Biblioteca Nazionale. *Below*: L. Burnacini, harlequin costumes for court performance, Vienna, second half of 17th cent. Drawing with water color. Vienna, Nationalbibliothek.

Pl. 435. *Above*: L. Burnacini, the palace of Pluto for *Il Pomo d'oro* by M. A. Cesti, performed for the court in Vienna, 1667. Engraving. *Below*: G. Torelli (d. 1678), scene for *Il Trionfo della Continenza*. Drawing. Rome, Farnesina.

Pl. 436. *Above*: J. Bérain, décor for the ballet *Atys* by J. B. Lulli, Paris, 1676. Drawing attributed to J. Dolivar (1641–92), based on an engraving. Paris, Bibliothèque Nationale, Cabinet des Estampes. *Below*: Setting for the tragedies performed at the Jesuit theater, Rennes, Ille-et-Vilaine, France, ca. 1743. Engraving by Moreau and Cochin. Paris, Bibliothèque de l'Arsenal.

Pl. 437. F. Juvara, design, ca. 1711, for *Il Giunio Bruto* by Cesarini, Caldara, and Scarlatti. Drawing with water color. Vienna, Albertina.

Pl. 438. Francesco Galli Bibiena (1659–1739, attrib.), architectural setting for an oratorio (for performance in Vienna?). Drawing with tempera. Milan, Coll. Tordini.

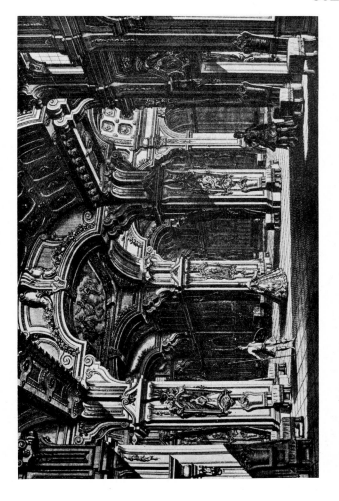

Pl. 439. *Above, left*: M. Chiarini, enclosed prison scene for *La Forza della Virtù* by C. F. Pollarolo, Bologna, 1694. Engraving. *Right*: G. Galli Bibiena, angle view into a palace hall, from *Architetture e Prospettive*, Augsburg, 1740–43. Engraving. *Below, left*: A. Jolli, project for a palace atrium with a long perspective. Colored drawing. Milan, Museo Teatrale alla Scala. *Right*: Fabrizio Galliari, landscape with background in contrasting scale, for *Nitteti* by I. J. Holzbauer, Turin, 1758. Pen and wash. Turin, Museo Civico.

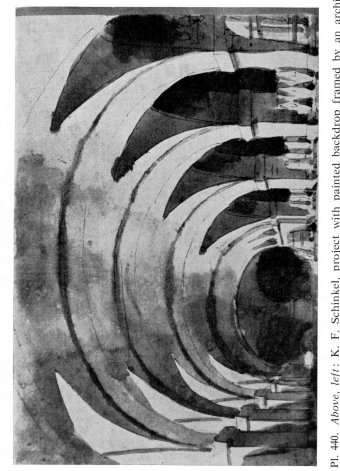

Pl. 440. *Above, left*: K. F. Schinkel, project with painted backdrop framed by an architectural interior, for the opera *Olimpia* by G. Spontini, Berlin, 1821. Engraving. *Right*: P. J. de Loutherbourg, model set for the pantomime *The Wonders of Derbyshire, or Harlequin on the Peak*, second half of 18th cent. London, Victoria and Albert Museum. *Below, left*: A. Sanquirico, sketch for the Teatro alla Scala, Milan, 1817. Pen and wash. Rome, private coll. *Right*: Depiction of a performance of Wagner's *Lohengrin*, Nationaltheater, Munich, 1867. Water color by M. Echter. Munich, Theater-Museum.

Pl. 441. Stage sets. *Above, left*: Dramatization of *La Fille Elisa* by E. and J. de Goncourt, performed at the Théâtre Libre of A. Antoine, Paris, 1890. *Right*: *Don Juan und Faust* by C. D. Grabbe, performed by the Meininger at the Herzogliches Hoftheater, Meiningen, Germany, 1897. *Below, left*: *La Città Morta* by G. d'Annunzio, performed by the company of Sarah Bernhardt at the Théâtre de la Renaissance, Paris, 1898. *Right*: *Provintsialka* by I. S. Turgenev, produced by Stanislavski at the Moscow Art Theater, 1912.

Pl. 442. *Above*: A. Appia, sketch for Klingsor's magic garden in Wagner's *Parsifal*, 1922. Drawing. Bern, Switzerland, Schweizerische Theater-Sammlung. *Below*: L. Bakst, design for *Le Martyre de Saint Sébastien* by G. d'Annunzio with music by Debussy, Théâtre du Châtelet, Paris, 1911.

Pl. 443. P. Picasso, sketch for *Pulcinella,* choreographed by L. Massine for the Diaghilev Ballets Russes, Paris, 1920.

Pl. 444. E. Prampolini, sketch for a Czech performance of *Il Tamburo di Fuoco* by F. T. Marinetti at the National Theater, Prague, 1933. Rome, Coll. A. Prampolini.

Pl. 445. *Above, left*: O. Kokoschka, set and costumes for his *Mörder Hoffnung der Frauen*, directed by H. George at the Neues Theater, Frankfort on the Main, Germany, 1920. *Below*: D. Cambellotti, set for the *Agamemnon* of Aeschylus, produced in the ancient Greek theater at Syracuse, Sicily, 1914. *Right*: V. Fedorov, scene in *Ryči, Kitay* ("Roar, China") by S. Tretyakov, produced by V. E. Meyerhold, Moscow, 1926.

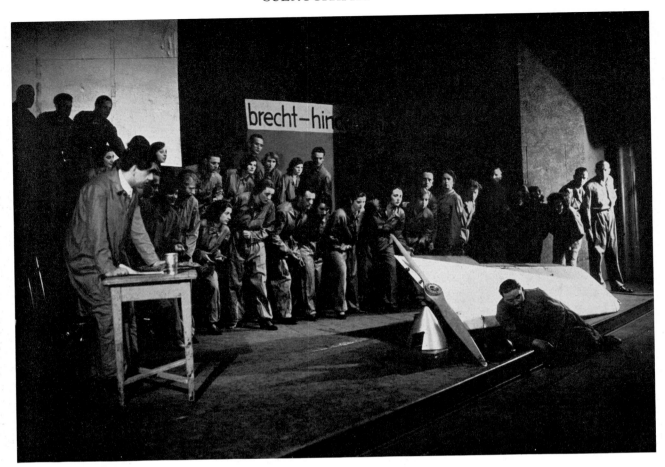

Pl. 446. *Above*: Performance by the Frankfurter Opernschule of *Das Badener Lehrstück vom Einverstandnis* by B. Brecht and P. Hindemith (composed 1929), in the Schauspielhaus, Frankfort on the Main, Germany. *Below*: Permanent set for the Théâtre du Vieux-Colombier, Paris, shown during a performance of *Le Viol de Lucrèce* by A. Obey, directed by M. Saint-Denis, 1930–31.

Pl. 447. *Above*: J. Mielziner, sketch for the musical play *Pipe Dream* by Rodgers and Hammerstein, Shubert Theater, New York, 1955. *Below*: S. Dali, design for the ballet *The Mad Tristan*, choreography by L. Massine for Ballet International, New York, 1944.

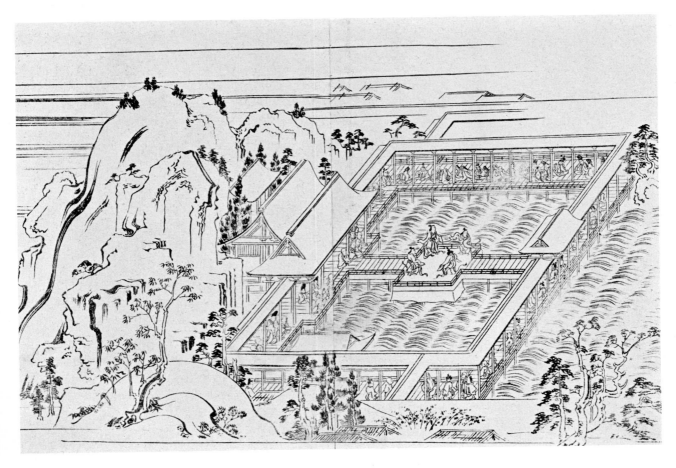

Pl. 448. Depictions of traditional Japanese performances. *Above*: Sarugaku. *Below*: Bugaku, executed in a court theater constructed over water. Woodcuts, 19th cent.

Pl. 449. Modern performances of Japanese No and Kabuki drama. *Above*: The company of the No Theater of Tokyo, at Venice, 1954. *Below*: The company of Azuma Kabuki, at Nervi, Italy, 1955.

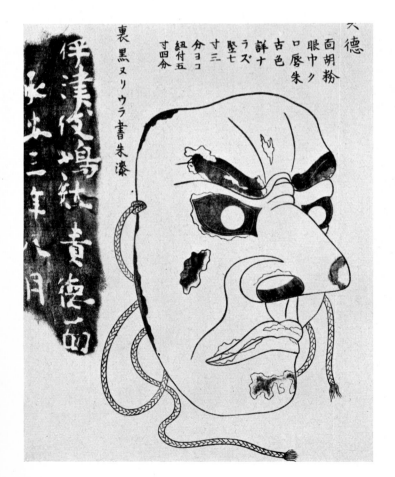

Pl. 450. *Above*: Chinese actors masked with cosmetics and paint. Lithograph, 20th cent. Vienna, Nationalbibliothek. *Below*: Japanese theatrical masks. Woodcuts, 19th cent.

Pl. 451. The Virgin in the Rose Bower, detail of VI, PL. 135. Panel. Colmar, France, St-Martin.

Pl. 452. The Adoration of the Shepherds. Panel, 14³/₄×11 in. Berlin, Staatliche Museen.

Pl. 453. The Last Judgment, two details. Fresco. Breisach, Germany, Cathedral.

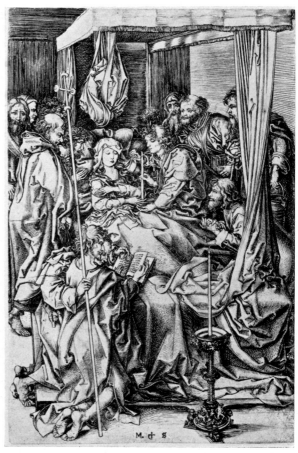

Pl. 454. *Above, left*: Christ in Glory. Pen drawing, 10¹/₄×7¹/₄ in. Paris, Louvre. *Right*: The Crowning with Thorns. Engraving, 6³/₈×4¹/₂ in. *Below, left*: The Entombment. Engraving, 6³/₈×4⁵/₈ in. *Right*: The Death of the Virgin. Engraving, 10×6⁵/₈ in.

Pl. 455. Weights and balances. *Left, above*: Egyptian weight of 100 beqa, inscribed "Herfu," ca. 2000 B.C. Green marble. London, University College, Department of Egyptology Museum. *Center*: Assyrian and Babylonian lion weights, 8th cent. B.C. Bronze. London, Science Museum. *Below*: Roman weight in the form of a pig, from Pompeii, lst cent. Bronze. Naples, Museo Nazionale. *Right, above*: Persian standard weight of $^1/_3$ Daric mina, inscribed in three languages, 521–486 B.C. Black basalt. London, British Museum. *Below*: Roman steelyard, from Pompeii, lst cent. Bronze. Naples, Museo Nazionale.

Pl. 456. Horologes. *Above, left*: Egyptian water clock, from Karnak, ca. 1415–1380 B.C. Alabaster. Cairo, Egyptian Museum. (Photographed from a cast.) *Right*: Sundial in the shape of a ham, marked with months of July and August, from Herculaneum, 1st cent. Bronze, originally silvered (gnomon broken); ht., 4⁵/₈ in. Naples, Museo Nazionale. *Below, left*: Hemicyclic dial, from Belo, Cádiz, Spain, Roman period. Marble. Madrid, Museo Arqueológico Nacional. *Right*: Saxon sundial on Kirkdale church, Yorkshire, England, ca. 1060. Stone, 22¹/₄×37¹/₂ in. (Cast, style missing.)

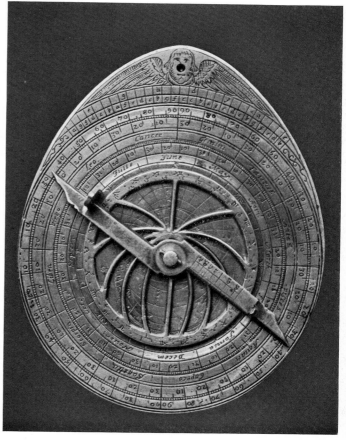

Pl. 457. Astrolabes. *Above, left*: Constructed by Ibrāhīm ibn-Sa'īd al-Anṣārī, Valencia, Spain, 1096. Metal, diam., 4³/₄ in. Rome, Osservatorio Astronomico. *Right*: School of Tunis (?), 14th cent. or later. Diam., 4³/₄ in. Tunis, Bardo. *Below, left*: Constructed by Gualterius Arsenius, third quarter of 16th cent. Brass, diam., 13³/₄ in. Florence, Museo di Storia della Scienza. *Right*: Constructed by R. Melbourne, 1631. London, Science Museum.

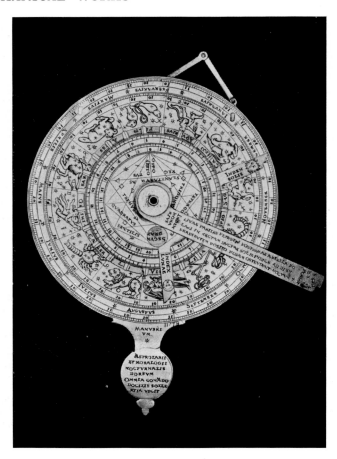

Pl. 458. *Left, above*: C. Schissler, tablet sundial and compass, Augsburg, 1566. Gilded and silvered brass. *Center*: J. Macarius of Mirandola (Modena), circumferentor or surveying circle, with fitting for tripod, 1676. Brass, diam. of disk, 12 in. Both, London, Science Museum. *Below*: E. Habermehl, graphometer with case, Prague. Diam., 9⁷/₈ in. Florence, Museo di Storia della Scienza. *Right, above*: C. Vopel, nocturnal and quadrant, Cologne, 1543. Gilded metal, diam., 5¹/₂ in. *Below*: D. Staphanus, portable column sundial, showing Italian hours adjusted for summer months, 1587. Ivory. Last two, London, Science Museum.

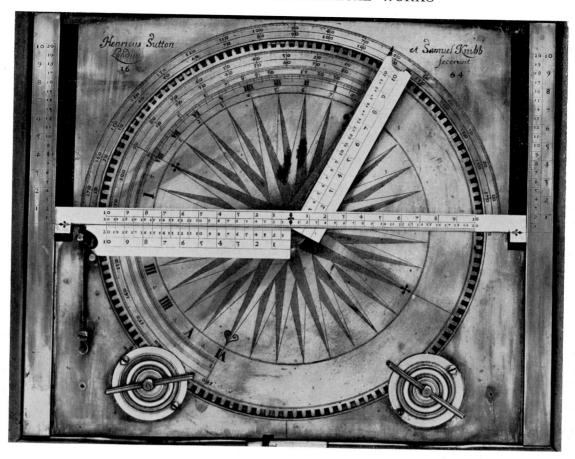

Pl. 459. *Above*: Samuel Morland's trigonometrical calculating machine, made by Sutton and Knibb, London, 1664. Brass, silvered on working surface; 12×12³/₄×2 in. London, Science Museum. *Below, left*: H. Koch, polyhedral sundial, Munich, 1578. Gilded brass, ht., 10¹/₄ in. Munich, Bayerisches Nationalmuseum. *Right*: Folding sundial with compass, Austria, 1451. Gilded brass, 3¹/₈×2¹/₄ in. Innsbruck, Tiroler Landesmuseum Ferdinandeum.

Pl. 460. Clocks. *Left*: Weight-driven, striking mechanisms. Forged iron. *Above*: From south Germany, 14th cent. Ht., 15³/₄ in. Würzburg, Germany, Mainfränkisches Museum. *Below*: From Dover Castle, England, late 16th cent. Ht., 35 in. London, Science Museum. *Right, above*: Clock of Philip the Good of Burgundy, Burgundian or lower-Rhenish, ca. 1430. Gilded bronze, ht., 18⁷/₈ in. Nürnberg, Germanisches National-Museum. *Below*: Italian monastic alarm clock, ca. 1500. Ht., ca. 10¹/₂ in. Bologna, Coll. A. Simoni.

Pl. 461. S. Bonsignori (?), polyhedral sundial, 17th cent. Painted paper and wood, ht., 8 1/4 in. Florence, Museo di Storia della Scienza.

Pl. 462. Cubic sundial, made in Florence, ca. 1560. Wood painted in distemper. London, Science Museum.

Pl. 463. *Above, left*: Camerini of Turin, chamber clock, 1656. Gilded copper. London, Science Museum. *Right*: B. Nusam, timepiece encased in leather and silver, London, ca. 1565. New York, Metropolitan Museum. *Below, left*: H. C. Schissler, universal clock with astrolabe and marine compass, 16th cent. Gilded brass, ht., 7^{7}/$_{8}$ in. Florence, Museo di Storia della Scienza. *Right*: Clock with sculptured figures, France, Louis XVI period. Bronze and gilding, ht., 14^{1}/$_{8}$ in. Paris, Musée des Arts Décoratifs.

Pl. 464. *Above*: Robin B. du Roy, gilded-bronze clock with sphinxes in white Vincennes porcelain, France, 1754. Paris, Louvre. *Below, left*: D. Ramsey, watch with case of Limoges enamel, England, ca. 1610–25. New York, Metropolitan Museum. *Right*: G. Seydell, brass verge watch with calendar dials, Germany, ca. 1660. Diam., 2¼ in. London, British Museum.

Pl. 465. *Left*: Clock, with rosewood marquetry by M. Carlin and gilded-bronze ornament by P. Gouthière, Louis XVI period. Ht., 7 ft., 4½ in. Paris, Louvre. *Right*: Long-case clock, with walnut veneer and marquetry of various woods, movement by W. Halstead, London, ca. 1720. Ht., 9 ft., 7½ in. London, Victoria and Albert Museum.

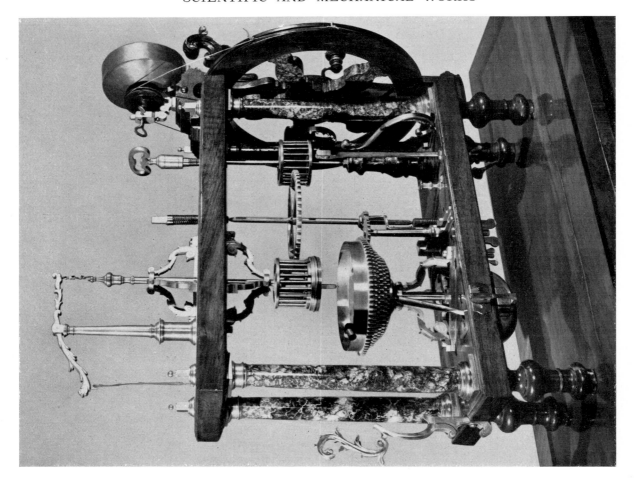

Pl. 466. *Left*: The Gutenberg printing press, 15th cent., reconstruction. Mainz, Germany, Gutenberg-Museum. *Right*: Frati's lathe for grinding lenses, Italy, 18th cent. Florence, Museo di Storia della Scienza.

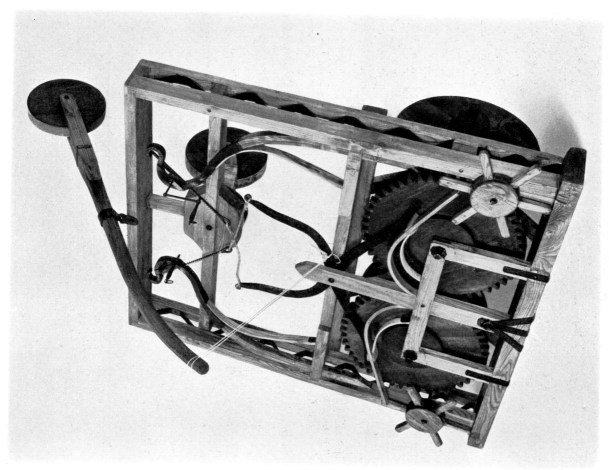

Pl. 467. Inventions of Leonardo da Vinci, models after his drawings (constructed 1952). *Left*: Self-propelled cart, after Cod. Atlanticus, fol. 296v-a (model by G. Canestrini). *Right*: Aerial screw, after Cod. B fol. 83v (model by A. M. Soldatini and V. Somenzi). Both, Milan, Museo Nazionale della Scienza e della Tecnica.

Pl. 468. *Above, left*: Florentine armillary sphere, inscribed "Hieronymus Camilli, Vulpariae Florentin," 1554. London, Science Museum. *Right*: German astronomical clock in the form of a celestial globe, ca. 1584. London, Victoria and Albert Museum. *Below, left*: A. Santucci dalle Pomarance, armillary sphere, made for Ferdinand I de' Medici (1588–93). Gilded wood. Florence, Museo di Storia della Scienza. *Right*: T. Wright, large orrery, 1733. London, Science Museum.

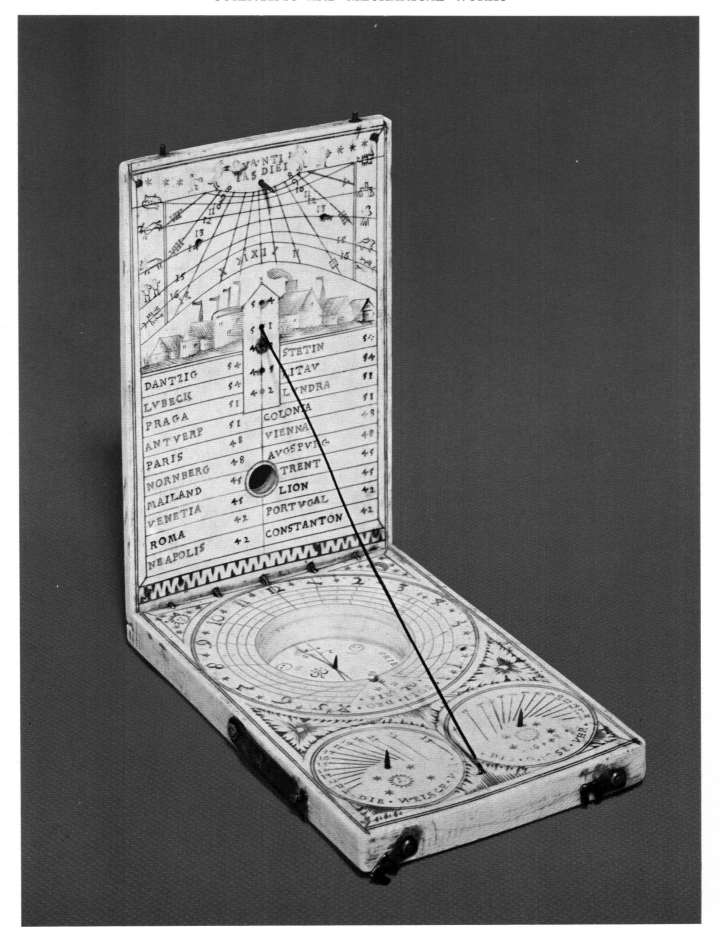

Pl. 469. Tablet sundial with compass, Germany, 1648. Engraved and colored ivory. London, Science Museum.

Pl. 470. *Above*: J. Martin, combination pocket sundial and perpetual calendar, Augsburg, late 17th cent. Gilded brass and steel; plate, 2³/₈ × 2³/₈ in. *Below*: Japanese bracket clock, with rotating dial showing old Japanese time system, early 19th cent. (?). Enameled brass, w., 5³/₈ in. Both, London, Science Museum.

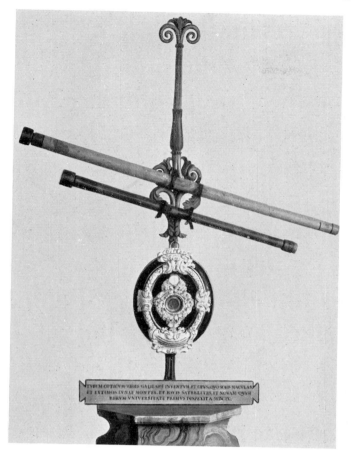

Pl. 471. *Above*: Galileo's telescopes and lens, early 17th cent., with later ivory mounting of lens (detail, *right*). L. of telescopes, 4 ft., 5¹/₂ in. and 3 ft., ¹/₄ in. *Below*: Thermometers of the Accademia del Cimento, Florence, 17th cent. Glass, ht., 41³/₄ in. (*left*) and 13³/₄ in. All, Florence, Museo di Storia della Scienza.

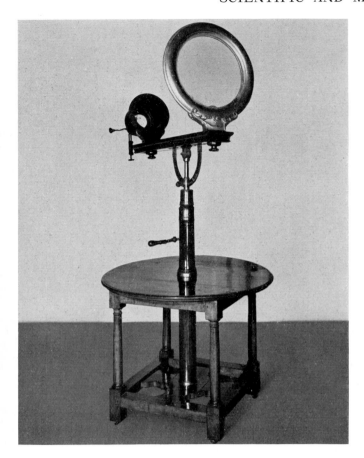

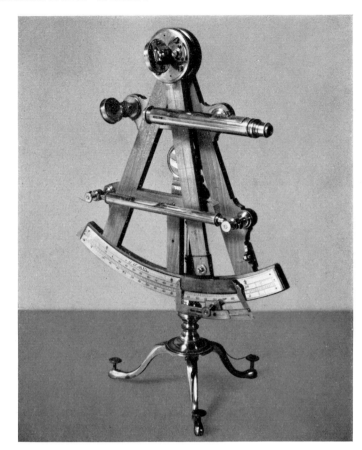

Pl. 472. *Above, left*: Burning glass by B. Bregans of Dresden, 1690, in a gilded wood mounting by F. Spighi, Italy, 1767. Diam. of lens, 17³/₄ in. Florence, Museo di Storia della Scienza. *Right*: G. F. Brander, reflecting octant, Augsburg, 1777. Wood and brass, ht., 21⁵/₈ in. Munich, Deutsches Museum. *Below, left*: The "New Universal" microscope of George Adams, example made for King George III, 1761, cased with beaten silver. Ht. of supporting column, ca. 13 in. London, Science Museum. *Right*: Aeolipile with spirit lamp. Copper. Florence, Museo di Storia della Scienza.

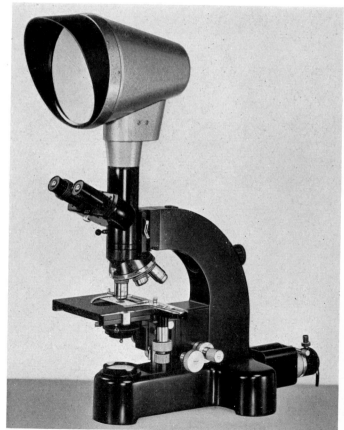

Pl. 473. *Above, left*: Working model of a Watt steam engine, bought in England, 1792. Bronze, iron, and wood; ht., ca. 6 ft. Munich, Deutsches Museum. *Right, two above*: Calculating machines, built by Sutton and Knibb, London, 1664 (*top*), and by Antonius Braun, 1727. Florence, Museo di Storia della Scienza (*top*), and Vienna, Kunsthistorisches Museum. *Below, left*: Barometer and thermometer, instruments by J. Ayscough, London, ca. 1755. Ht., 3 ft., 6 in. *Center*: Wheel barometer and thermometer, instruments by John Russell of Falkirk, Scotland, ca. 1800. Ht., 4 ft. Last two, London, Victoria and Albert Museum. *Right*: "Ortholux" microscope with viewer, manufactured by Leitz, Germany, 1964.

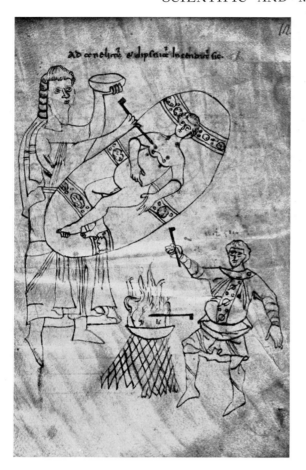

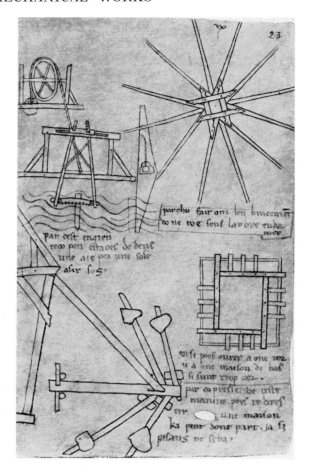

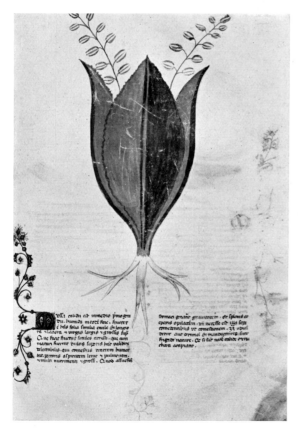

Pl. 474. *Above, left*: Cauterization as a cure for dyspnea, Cassinese school (?), Italy, 9th cent. Pen, with touches of red. Florence, Biblioteca Laurenziana (Ms. Plut. 73.41, fol. 122r). *Right*: Illustrations of machines in the textbook of Villard de Honnecourt, ca. 1235. Paris, Bibliothèque Nationale (Ms. 19093). *Below, left*: Giovannino de' Grassi (attrib.), "Mussa," in *Historia plantarum* (also called *Taccuinum sanitatis*, Ms. 459, fol. 172), north Italian, 14th cent. Illumination. *Right*: Beehives, in *Theatrum sanitatis* (Cod. 4182), Lombard school, 14–15th cent. Illumination. Last two, Rome, Biblioteca Casanatense.

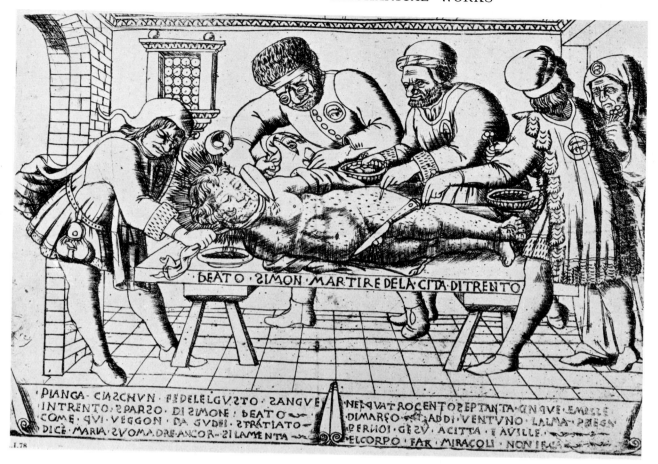

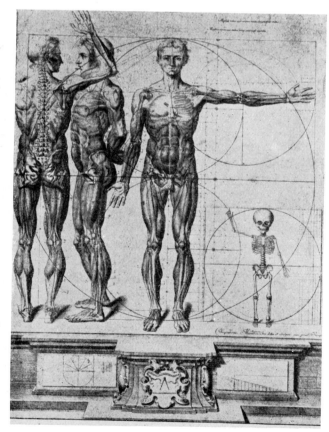

Pl. 475. *Above*: The Ritual Murder of St. Simon of Trent, depicted as a surgical operation. Florence (?), ca. 1475–85. Engraving. London, British Museum. *Below, left*: A. Vesalius, anatomical demonstration, title page of *De humani corporis fabrica*, Basel, 1543. *Right*: C. Martinez, anatomical and proportional studies, in *Nouvelles figures de proportions et d'anatomie...*, Paris, ca. 1689.

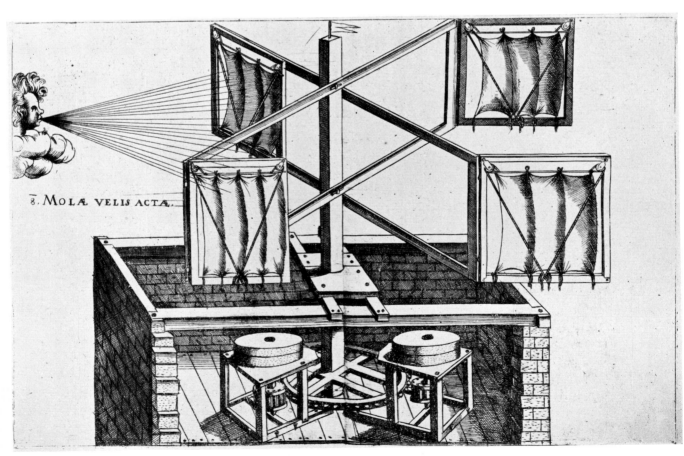

8. MOLÆ VELIS ACTA.

Pl. 476. *Above*: Pump and hoist, illustrations from A. Ramelli, *Le diverse et artificiose machine*, Paris, 1588. *Below*: Windmill, illustration from F. Veranzio, *Machinae novae*, 1595.

Pl. 477. *Above*: Map of the Moon, in J. Hevelius, *Selenographia*, 1647. *Below*: Illustration of bones and muscles in P. Mascagni, *Anatomia per uso degli studiosi di scoltura e pittura*, Florence, 1816.

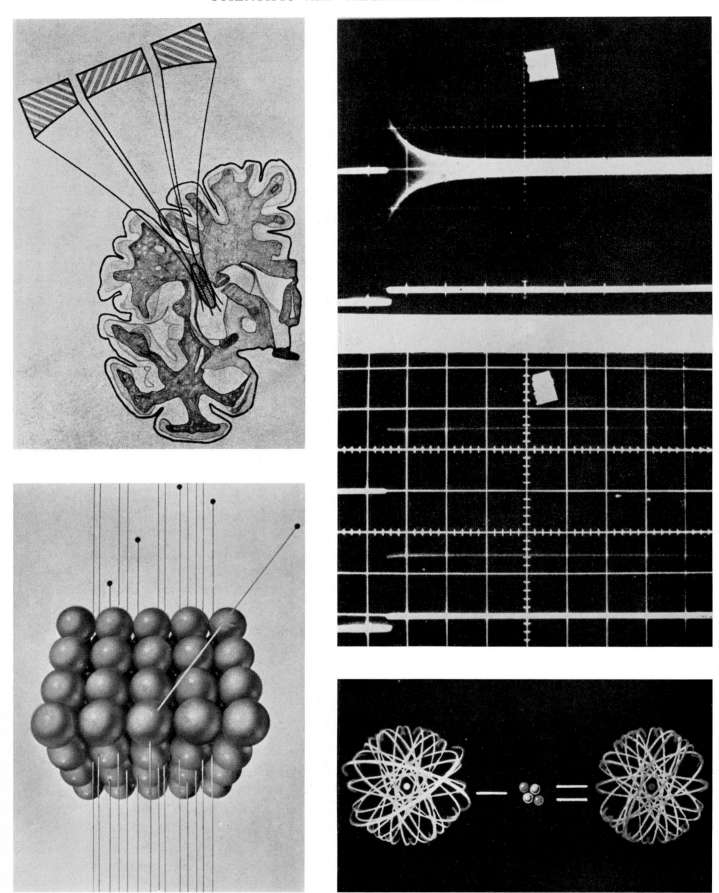

Pl. 478. Scientific illustration, technical and educational. *Above*: Diagram and two graphs for W. S. Fry, "Present and Future Applications of Ultrasonics in Biomedicine," *Proceedings of the Institute of Radio Engineers*, L, 1962, p. 1398. *Below*: Illustrations from H. Haber, *La Storia del nostro amico atomo, a cura di W. Disney*, Milan, 1956, p. 119.

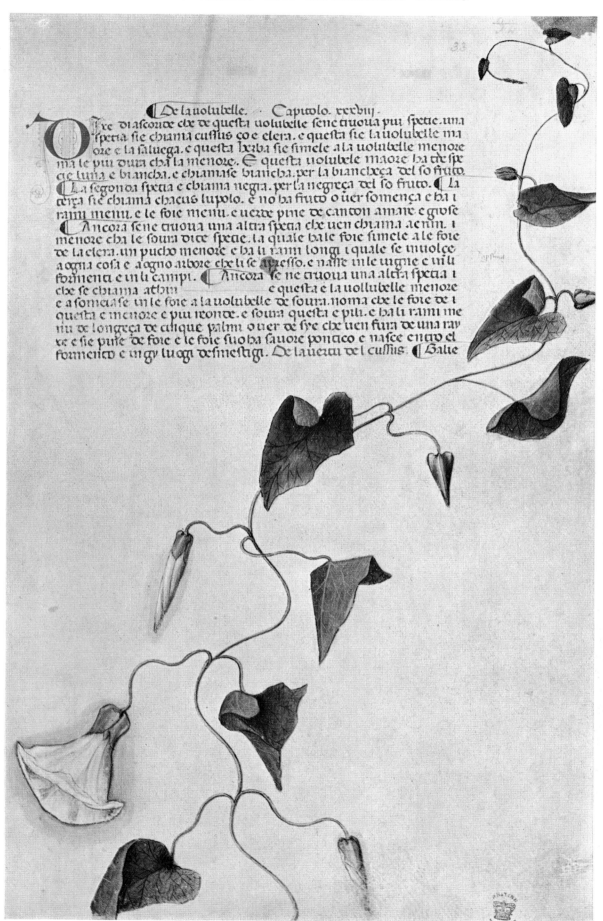

Pl. 479. Page with the convolvulus ("la volubelle"), in an Italian version of the *Herbarium* by Serapion the Younger, perhaps executed for Francesco il Giovane da Carrara at Padua, late 14th cent. London, British Museum (Ms. Egerton 2020, fol. 33).

Pl. 480. G. Ligozzi (1547–1626), Psittacus Ararauna, leaf from an album (no longer extant) executed for the Grand Duke of Tuscany. Tempera, $26^5/_8 \times 18^1/_8$ in. Florence, Uffizi, Gabinetto dei Disegni e Stampe.

Pl. 481. Sculptural effects in nature. Stalagmites in the Pech-Merle Cave, Lot, France, suggestive of the mammoths in prehistoric cave art.

Pl. 482. Sculpture in living rock. The Kṛṣṇa Govardhanadhara relief, north end, in the Five Pāṇḍava Cave, Mamallapuram, Madras, India, early 7th cent.

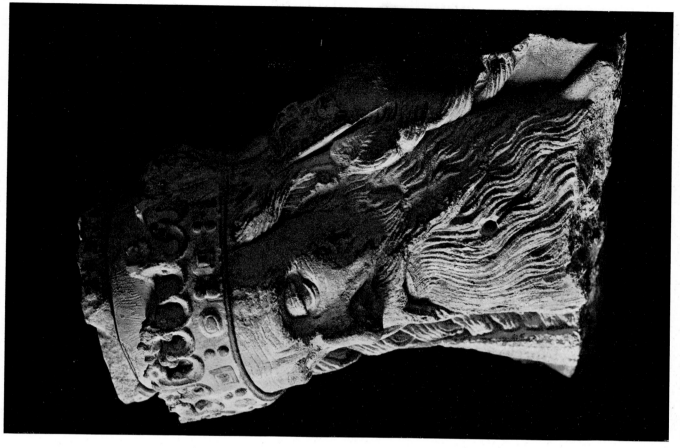

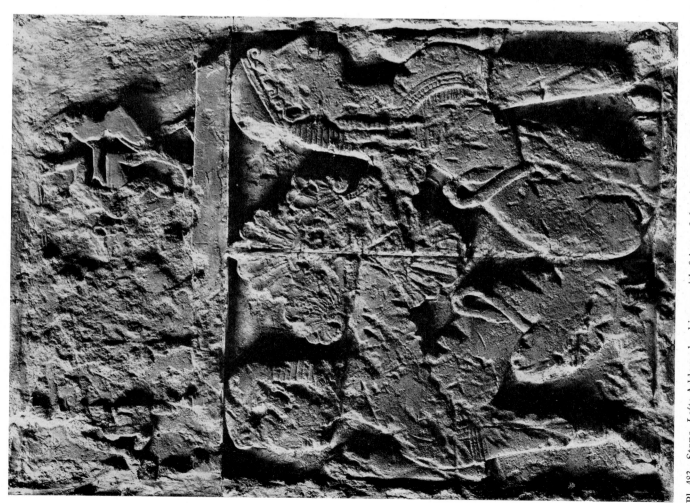

Pl. 483. Stone. *Left*: Addorsed sphinxes with frieze of dancing satyrs, flat relief from Caltagirone, Sicily, first half of 6th cent. B.C. Syracuse, Sicily, Museo Archeologico. *Right*: Head of God the Father, ca. 1480. Winchester, England, Cathedral, from the reredos.

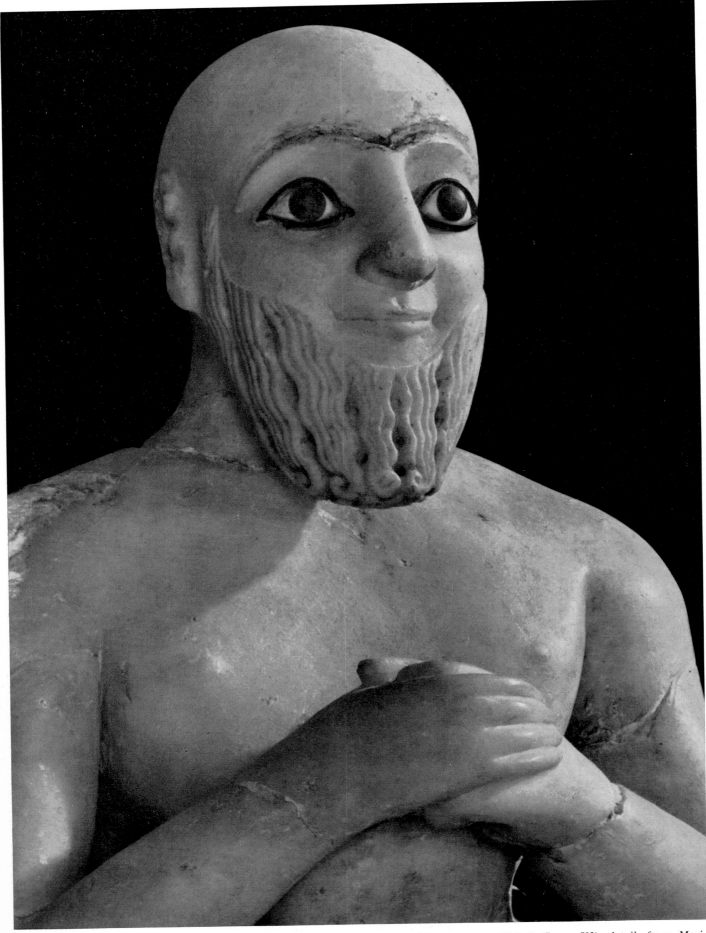

Pl. 484. Alabaster (with eyes of black stone, lapis lazuli, and mother-of-pearl). Statue of Ebih-il (I, PL. 503), detail, from Mari, Mesopotamia, first half of 3d millennium B.C. Paris, Louvre.

Pl. 485. Marble, elemental form. Cycladic statuette of a lyre or harp player, from Thera, Greece, ca. 2000 B.C. Ht., 6³/₄ in. Karlsruhe, Germany, Landesmuseum.

Pl. 486. Marble, refinement of modeling. Head of a goddess, from Chios, Greece, ca. 300 B.C. Ht., 14 1/8 in. Boston, Museum of Fine Arts.

Pl. 487. Marble, elaboration of technique. F. Queirolo, Allegory of Deception, mid-18th cent. Naples, S. Maria della Pietà dei Sangro.

Pl. 488. *Above, left*: Diorite. Statue of Gudea, from Lagash, Mesopotamia, second half of 3d millennium B.C. Paris, Louvre. *Right*: Red granite. Statue of the shipbuilder Bezmes, holding an ax, from a tomb near Giza, Egypt, 3d dynasty. Ht., 2 ft., 2 in. London, British Museum. *Below, left*: Porphyry. Bust from Athribis, Egypt, early 4th cent. Ht. of face, 6³/₄ in. Cairo, Egyptian Museum. *Right*: Varicolored marbles. Guglielmo della Porta, portrait of Paul III, ca. 1546. Naples, Museo di Capodimonte.

Pl. 489. Painted limestone (with rock-crystal eye). Head of Nefertiti, from Tell el 'Amarna, Egypt, first half of 14th cent. B.C. Ht., 19³/₄ in. Berlin, Staatliche Museen.

Pl. 490. Painted wood. The Virgin and Child, from Gerona, Spain, 12th cent. Barcelona, Museo de Bellas Artes de Cataluña.

Pl. 491. Gem stones. *Above*: Jade. Dragon of the Han dynasty (206 B.C.–A.D. 221), China. Singapore, Raffles Museum (on loan from S. T. Wang Coll.). *Below, left*: Jadeite. Olmec carving of a seated man, from El Tejar, Veracruz, Mexico, pre-Columbian period. Ht., 5¹/₂ in. Mexico City, Museo Nacional de Antropología. *Right*: Sardonyx. Florentine cameo, ca. 1500. Naples, Museo di Capodimonte.

Pl. 492. *Above*: Rock crystal. V. Belli, scenes from the life of Christ, panels of a casket executed for Pope Clement VII, 1537. Florence, Pitti, Museo degli Argenti. *Below*: Red coral. Nativity scene, Naples, 17th cent. Naples, Museo Nazionale di S. Martino.

Pl. 493. Ivory. *Above, left*: Assyrian female head, from Nimrud, 9th–8th cent. B.C. London, British Museum. *Right*: Vili trumpet, detail, from the Loango area, Congo (Brazzaville), 19th cent. Diam., 2¼ in.; full l., 20 in. Tervueren, Belgium, Musée Royal de l'Afrique Centrale. *Below, left*: French plaquette depicting a concert, first half of 14th cent. Ht., 3½ in. Paris, Musée de Cluny. *Right*: Moorish box, made in Zamora, Spain, for the caliph at Cordova, 946. Madrid, Museo Arqueológico Nacional.

Pl. 494. Wood, elemental form. Igorot *anito* (spirit) statues, from northern Luzon, Philippine Islands, collected 1887. Ht. without base, 23⅝ in. (*left*) and 20⅞ in. Madrid, Museo Etnológico y Antropológico.

Pl. 495. Wood, refinement of modeling. Statuette of an official (partially gilded), Egypt, 18th dynasty. Ht., 11³/₈ in. Berlin, Staatliche Museen.

Pl. 496. Wood, elaboration of technique. T. Riemenschneider and workshop, the Disputation of Christ in the Temple, predella panel from the Altar of the Virgin, 1505–10. Creglingen, Germany, Herrgottskirche.

Pl. 497. Uses of clay. *Above, left*: Baked clay. Neolithic head of the Lengyel culture. Piešťany, Czechoslovakia, Museum. *Right*: Burnished red clay. Colima warrior with sling and helmet, from Los Ortices, Colima, Mexico, pre-Columbian period. Ht., 16¹/₂ in. Mexico City, Coll. D. Olmedo Phillips. *Below, left*: Terra cotta. Hellenistic figurine, perhaps from Syracuse, Sicily, 3d cent. Ht., 14¹/₈ in. Syracuse, Museo Archeologico. *Right*: Glazed earthenware with traces of polychrome. Chinese *t'u-kuei* (so-called "earth spirit"), from a tomb of the T'ang dynasty (618–906). Ht., 13³/₄ in. Paris, Musée Guimet.

Pl. 498. Terra cotta. *Above, left*: Head of an Etruscan warrior, from Veii (mod. Veio, Italy), early 5th cent. B.C. Ht., 9 1/8 in. Rome, Museo di Villa Giulia. *Right*: Head of a girl, Roman, ca. A.D. 30. Ht., ca. 10 in. Berlin, Staatliche Museen. *Below*: Giambologna, sketch for the "Apennine" (VIII, PL. 430), second half of 16th cent. Florence, Museo Nazionale.

Pl. 499. Colored terra cotta. Antefix with female head, from Caere (mod. Cerveteri, Italy), late 6th cent. B.C. Ht., 10¹/₂ in. London, British Museum.

Pl. 500. Bronze. Statuette of a warrior, known as "Alexander the Great on Horseback," from Herculaneum (perhaps derived from the group of Alexander and his companions at the River Granikos, 334 B.C., by Lysippos). Ht., 19¼ in. Naples, Museo Nazionale.

Pl. 501. Sheet metal. *Above.* Bronze. *Left*: Etruscan *sphyrelaton*, bust of a woman, from Vulci, ca. 600 B.C. Ht., 13³/₈ in. London, British Museum. *Right*: Etruscan plaque with girl holding an alabastron, from Castel San Mariano, near Perugia, ca. 530–520 B.C. Ht., 18⁷/₈ in. Munich, Staatliche Antikensammlungen. *Below*: Gilded copper. Lombardian plaque showing King Agilulf and his retinue, 7th cent. Florence, Museo Nazionale.

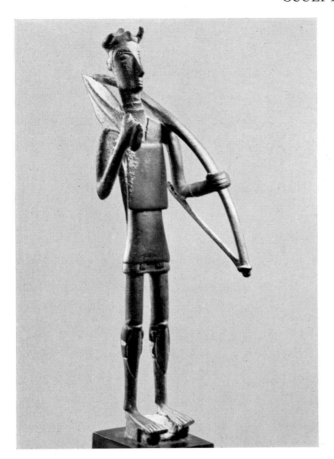

Pl. 502. Bronze, figurines. *Above, left*: Nuraghic armed warrior, found near Uta, Sardinia, 8th–6th cent. B.C. Ht., 9¹/₂ in. Cagliari, Sardinia, Museo Archeologico. *Right*: Kouros, from Samos, 6th cent. B.C. Ht., 9¹/₈ in. Berlin, Staatliche Museen. *Below, left*: Gallo-Roman statuette of a slave, from Reims, France, late 1st cent. Ht. with base, 8³/₈ in. Saint-Germain-en-Laye, France, Musée des Antiquités Nationales. *Right*: A. Briosco (Riccio, 1470–1532), Triton and Nereid. Florence, Museo Nazionale.

Pl. 503. Bronze. Hermes in Repose, Roman copy of a Hellenistic original, from Herculaneum. Ht., 41 3/8 in. Naples, Museo Nazionale.

Pl. 504. Precious metals. *Above, left*: Silver with sheet gold (on the head) and gold ornaments. Anatolian female statuette, from Hasanoglan, near Ankara, ca. 2000 B.C. Ht., 9³/₄ in. Ankara, Archaeological Museum. *Right*: Gold. Greco-Thracian rhyton, from Panagyurishte, Bulgaria, 4th cent. B.C. Ht., 5¹/₂ in. Plovdiv, Bulgaria, Archaeological Museum. *Below, left*: Gold. Quimbaya statuette, Colombia, pre-Columbian period. Ht., 8¹/₄ in. Madrid, Museo de América. *Right*: Silver. Reliquary of the Kushan king Kanishka, Gandhara, 1st–2d cent. Ht., 5¹/₈ in. Calcutta, Indian Museum.

Pl. 505. Gold with enamels. G. Loyet, Charles the Bold Presented by St. George, ca. 1471. Burnished gold with dull gold hair and parts of armor; flesh tints, dragon, cushion, and crest in enamel; reliquary with crystal; gilded-silver base, 20⅞×20⅞×13⅜ in. Liège, Belgium, Cathedral.

Pl. 506. Relief, degrees of projection. *Above, left*: Hollow relief. Young girl smelling a lotus flower, fragment of a mastaba, from Memphis, Egypt, ca. 2300 B.C. Limestone; ht. of figure, 47¹/₄ in. *Right*: Low relief. Votive stele, from Thasos, Greece, 6th cent. B.C. Marble, 9¹/₂×6³/₄ in. Both, Paris, Louvre. *Below*: Relief in multiple planes. Donatello (completed by collaborators), The Entombment, detail, ca. 1460–70. Bronze. Florence, S. Lorenzo.

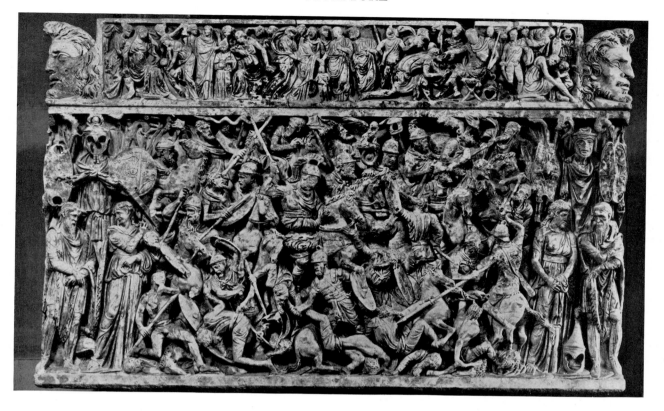

Pl. 507. *Above*: High relief. Sarcophagus with battle scene, found at Rome, last quarter of 2d cent. Marble. Rome, Museo Nazionale Romano. *Below*: Pictorial relief with *stiacciato* background. F. Laurana, The Bearing of the Cross, 1488. Marble. Avignon, France, St-Didier.

Pl. 508. High relief. G. B. Foggini and assistants, scene from the life of St. Andrea Corsini, 1685–87. Marble. Florence, S. Maria del Carmine.

Pl. 509. Colored wax. G. Zumbo, The Plague, second half of 17th cent. Florence, Museo di Storia della Scienza.

Pl. 510. Porcelain. Group of characters derived from *commedia dell'arte*, from Meissen, Germany, 18th cent. Ht., ca. 15 in. Rome, Palazzo dei Conservatori, Pinacoteca Capitolina.

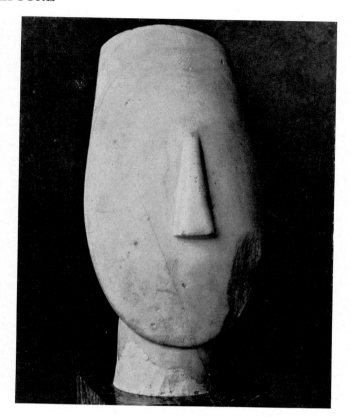

Pl. 511. Sculpture in the round, relation of form to the unworked material. *Above, left*: Head of a musk ox, from Le Fourneau du Diable, Dordogne, France, Upper Paleolithic period. Stone, ht., 10⅝ in. Saint-Germain-en-Laye, France, Musée des Antiquités Nationales. *Right*: Head of a Cycladic idol, from Amorgos, Greece, 2500–2000 B.C. Marble, ht., 10⅝ in. *Below, left*: Egyptian "block" statue, a Saite prince, 6th cent. B.C. *Right*: Kouros, from Aktion, Greece, Archaic period. Marble, ht., 39⅜ in. Last three, Paris, Louvre.

Pl. 512. Freestanding figure, naturalistic. Dancing maenad, Roman copy of an early Hellenistic original. Marble, ht., ca. 4 ft. Berlin, Staatliche Museen.

Pl. 513. Freestanding figure, conventionalized. J. Lipchitz, Sailor, 1914. Bronze, ht., 30 in. Buffalo, N. Y., Albright-
Knox Art Gallery.

Pl. 514. Treatment of surface, linear. Assyrian relief with winged genius before the sacred palm, from Nimrud, 9th cent. B.C. Gypsum, ht., 7 ft., 5³/₈ in. Paris, Louvre.

Pl. 515. Treatment of surface, modeled. Lapith woman, from the west pediment of the Temple of Zeus at Olympia, ca. 460 B.C. Marble. Olympia, Greece, Archaeological Museum.

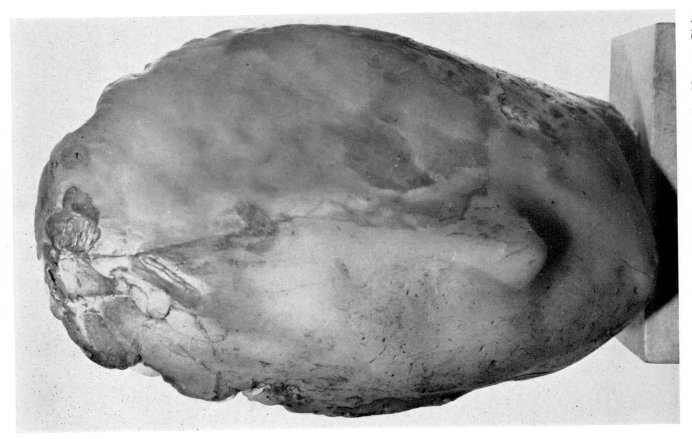

Pl. 516. Treatment of detail, stylized and minimized. *Left*: Roman head, a lady of the Flavian period. Marble, ht., 24¾ in. Rome, Capitoline Museum. *Right*: M. Rosso, Madame X, 1913. Wax. Venice, Galleria Internazionale d'Arte Moderna.

Pl. 517. Variation in finish. Michelangelo, The Deposition, detail of IX, pl. 526. Marble. Florence, Cathedral.

Pl. 518. Architectural sculpture. *Above, left*: Head of a caryatid (capital restored), from Delphi, ca. second half of 6th cent. B.C. Delphi, Greece, Archaeological Museum. *Right*: Portal of the Princes, detail, Bamberg Cathedral, Germany, second quarter of 13th cent. *Below, left*: Maya doorjamb, interior of Temple 22, Copán, Honduras, pre-Columbian period. *Right*: Detail of exterior decoration, Kaṇḍārya Mahādeva temple, Khajuraho, Madhya Pradesh, India, ca. 11th cent. (Cf. VII, PL. 473.)

Pl. 519. Architectural sculpture. A. Gherardi (called "Reatino"), Chapel of St. Cecilia, S. Carlo ai Catinari, Rome, ca. 1686.

Pl. 520. Uses of color. *Above, left*: Egyptian painted limestone relief, ca. 1300 B.C. Abydos, Egypt, Temple of Seti I, chapel of Osiris. *Right*: Roman polychrome mosaic relief, with Hermes, 1st cent. B.C. Naples, Museo Nazionale. *Below*: L. della Robbia, The Resurrection, glazed terra-cotta lunette, 1422. Florence, Cathedral, New Sacristy.

Pl. 521. Sculptured objects. *Above, left*: Zapotec funerary urn, from Oaxaca, Mexico, pre-Columbian period. Clay, ht., 13³/₄ in. Mexico City, Museo Nacional de Antropología. *Right*: Apulian askos, from Canosa, 2d cent. B.C. Taranto, Italy, Museo Nazionale. *Below, left*: Baule drum, Ivory Coast. Wood. Paris, Musée de l'Homme. *Center*: Head of a crosier, France, 11th–12th cent. Ivory. Florence, Museo Nazionale. *Right*: D. Beccafumi, candleholder in the form of an angel, ca. 1548–51. Bronze. Siena, Italy, Cathedral.

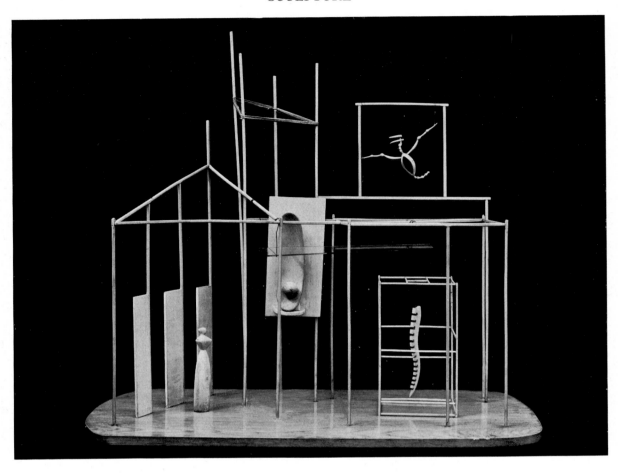

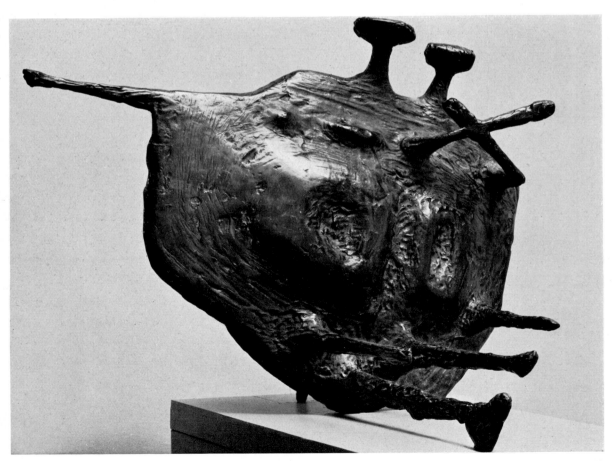

Pl. 522. Twentieth-century innovations, in media and in style. *Above*: A. Giacometti, The Palace at 4 A.M., 1932–33. Wood, glass, wire, and string; ht., 25 in. New York, Museum of Modern Art. *Below*: K. Armitage, Diarchy (small version), 1957. Bronze, 10×15 in. Property of the artist.

SEALS

Pl. 523. *1*: Proto-Elamite glass-paste cylinder and impression, with gazelles and antelopes, ca. late 4th millennium B.C. Ht., 4.9 cm. *2*: Proto-Elamite stone stamp and impression, depicting a lion (?), ca. late 4th millennium B.C. Ht., 4.1 cm. *3*: Steatite stamp with ibex, impression, from Mohenjo-daro, Pakistan, 3d–2d millennium B.C. *4*: Akkadian serpentine cylinder depicting the myth of Etana, impression, second half of 3d millennium B.C. Ht., 4.5 cm. *5*: Kassite sard cylinder with enthroned deity, impression, from Babylonia, mid-2d millennium B.C. Ht., 4.4 cm. *6*: Assyrian jasper cylinder (the seal of Nur-Adad) with winged figure and rampant winged bulls, impression, 8th–7th cent. B.C. Ht., 3.7 cm. *7–9*: Clay sealings with names of Hittite kings, from Hattushash (mod. Bogazköy, Turkey): 7: Urhi-Teshub (Mursilis III), ca. 1282–1275 B.C. Diam., 4.5 cm. 8: Suppiluliumas, ca. 1380–1340 B.C. Diam., 3.4 cm. 9: Muwatallis, ca. 1306–1282 B.C. Diam., 5.4 cm. *Location*: *1, 2, 5, 6*: London, British Museum; *3*: New Delhi, National Museum of India; *4*: Berlin, Staatliche Museen; *7–9*: Ankara, Archaeological Museum.

SEALS

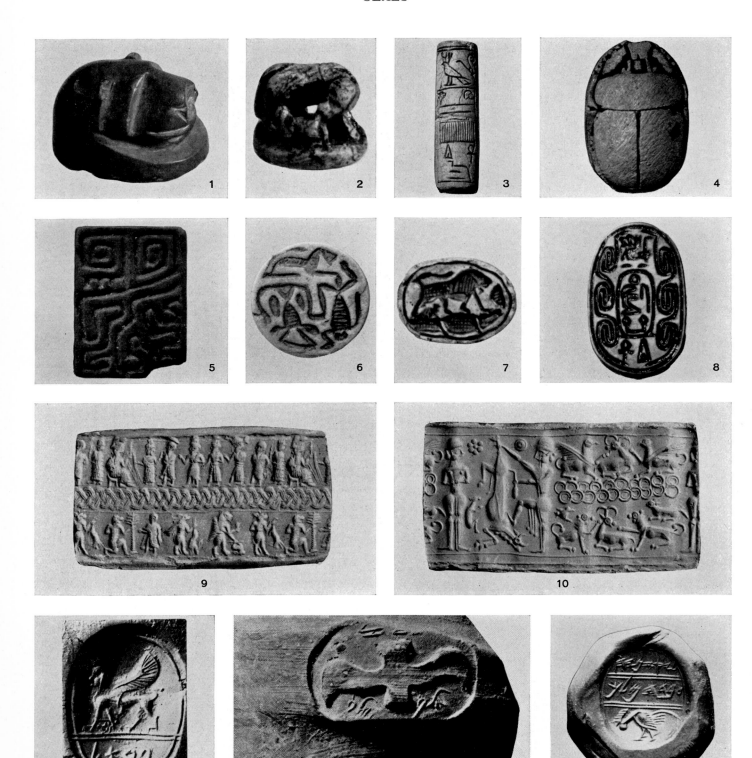

Pl. 524. *Top row*: Types of Egyptian seals. Glazed steatite. *1*: Stamp with feline head, First Intermediate Period. L., 2.1 cm. *2*: Stamp with animals, First Intermediate Period. Ht., 1.5 cm. *3*: Cylinder with cartouche, 13th dynasty. L., 1.9 cm. *4*: Scarab, from Lisht, 13th dynasty. L., 2.4 cm.; diam., 1.1 cm. *Second row*: Egyptian seal devices (showing undersides). *5*: Limestone button seal, First Intermediate Period, 3.8×2.7 cm. *6*: Bone button seal, First Intermediate Period. Diam., 2.5 cm. *7*: Glazed steatite scarab with lion and crocodile, Hyksos period. Diam., 2.5 cm. *8*: Jasper scarab with cartouche, 13th dynasty. L., 4.2 cm. *Third row*: *9*: Early Syrian cylinder with presentation to Ea (upper register), guilloche pattern, and Phoenician monsters, impression, 1900–1700 B.C. Ht., 2.8 cm. *10*: Late Syrian or Mitannian cylinder with nude goddess and animals, impression, ca. 1700–1200 B.C. Ht., 3.1 cm. *Bottom row*: Syro-Palestinian impressions. *11*: Quartzite scaraboid with cherub, found near Damascus, 8th cent. B.C., 15×7 mm. *12*: Stamp with winged scarab on a terra-cotta jar handle, 8th–7th cent. B.C., 3×2 cm. *13*: Onyx with fighting cock (seal of Jaazaniah), from Tell en-Nasbeh, ca. 600 B.C. Ht., 3 cm. *Location*: *1–8*: New York, Metropolitan Museum; *9*, *10*: Paris, Bibliothèque Nationale; *11*: Jerusalem, Israel, Reifenberg Coll.; *12*, *13*: Jerusalem, Jordan, Palestine Archaeological Museum.

Pl. 525. *Top three rows*: Achaemenid cylinder impressions, 6th–4th cent. B.C. *1*: Persian soldier attacking an infantryman, with winged sun disk. Chalcedony, ht., 3 cm. *2*: Māh the Moon God (?). Ht., 3 cm. *3*: Horseman spearing a lion, inscribed in Elamite. Chalcedony, ht., ca. 3 cm. *4*: Griffin attacking an ibex. Ht., ca. 2.5 cm. *5*: Encircled bust between sphinxes, with winged sun disk. Banded agate, ht., 2.4 cm. *6*: King before Ahura Mazda (*at left*) and Bes grasping stags, with sphinxes. Chalcedony, ht., 3 cm. *7*: Worship of divine emblems upon an altar (*at left*) and king subduing animals. Ht., ca. 3.2 cm. *8*: Symbolic boar hunt. Ht., ca. 2.5 cm. *9*: Subjugation of mythical creatures. Ht., ca. 4 cm. *Bottom row*: Sassanian seals and impressions. *10*: Portrait, probably Kavādh I (488–531). Carnelian, ca. 2.8×3.2 cm. *11*: Disk with Serpentarius surrounded by other constellations. Diam., ca. 3.8 cm. *12*: Portrait with the name of Bāfarrak, the Mūbadh of Mēshān (Basra), 5th cent. (?). Carnelian, ca. 4.2×4.9 cm. *13*: Hemisphere with hunting scene, 6th–7th cent. Agate, diam., ca. 2.9 cm. *Location*: *1, 3, 6, 7*: London, British Museum; *2, 4, 9*: Coll. of the late R. S. Cooke; *5*: Coll. of the late E. T. Newell; *8*: New York, Metropolitan Museum (on loan, Moore 104); *10, 13*: Paris, Bibliothèque Nationale; *11*: Boston, Museum of Fine Arts; *12*: Berlin, Staatliche Museen.

SEALS

Pl. 526. *Top row*: Cretan seals. *1–2*: Ivory stamp in the form of a perched owl, and device with papyrus buds, from the plain of Mesara (?), Middle Minoan. Ht., 1.6 cm. *3*: Yellow steatite prism bead, side showing a man with storage vessels, Early Minoan. L., 1.6 cm. *4–5*: Yellow steatite button seal, and device with an interlocking C-spiral design, from Knossos, Middle Minoan. Ht., 1.5 cm. *Center row*: *6*: Bezel of a gold ring with addorsed griffins, from Mycenae, 16th cent. B.C. Ht., ca. 1.7 cm. *7*: Steatite lenticular with stylized goat, Geometric period. Max. diam., 2.1 cm. *8*: Siculan gold signet ring with fish, from Pantalica, Sicily, 12th–11th cent. B.C. L. of signet, 1.3 cm. *Bottom row*: Greek steatite sealstones, Geometric period. *9*: With two human figures. Diam., 1.3 cm. *10*: With marine animals, 1.7×2.3 cm. *11*: Herakles wrestling Nereus (?). Diam., 1.9 cm. *Location*: *1–5, 9*: Oxford, Ashmolean Museum; *6*: Athens, National Museum; *7, 11*: London, British Museum; *8*: Syracuse, Sicily, Museo Archeologico; *10*: Paris, Cabinet des Médailles.

Pl. 527. *Above, left*: Etruscan scarab with man holding a branch, second half of 6th cent. B.C. Carnelian, 8×6 mm. Rome, Museo di Villa Giulia. *Right*: Greek scaraboid with woman at a fountain, early 5th cent. B.C. Green jasper, 1.4×1.1 cm. Berlin, Staatliche Museen. *Below*: Greek scaraboid with satyr and the name of Anakles, ca. 480–470 B.C. Black jasper, 1.65×1.2 cm. New York, Metropolitan Museum. (Cast.)

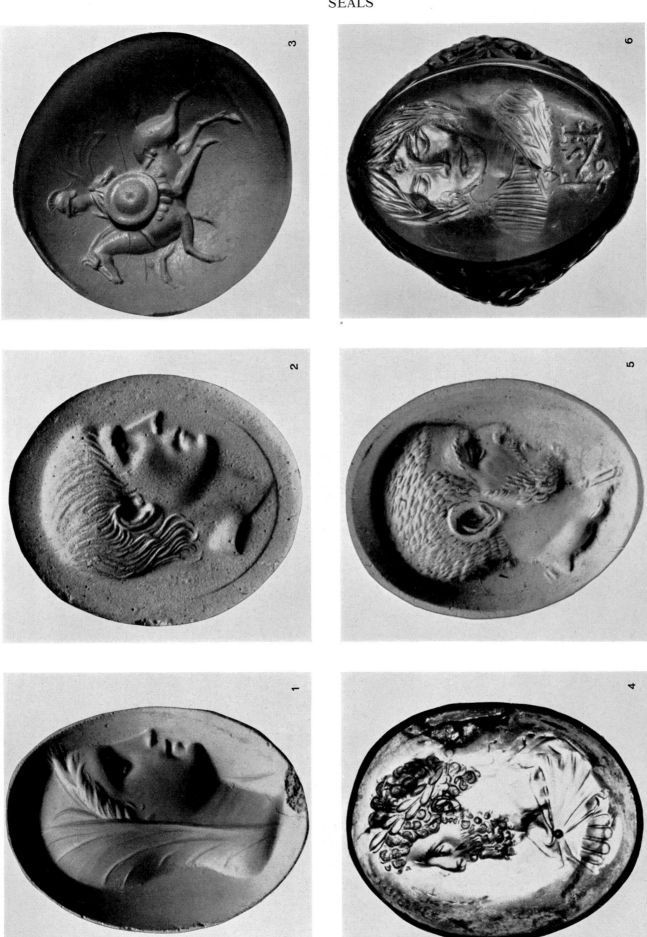

Pl. 528. *1:* Hellenistic carnelian with portrait of Arsinoë, ca. 270–250 B.C., 2.6×2 cm. London, British Museum. *2:* Roman bezel with portrait of Scipio Africanus the Elder, signed by Herakleidas, 2d cent. B.C. Gold, 2.8×2.2 cm. Naples, Museo Nazionale. *3:* Hellenistic-Roman sardonyx with galloping horseman, first half of 2d cent. B.C., 3.15×3 cm. Bern, Coll. Merz. *4:* Roman aquamarine with portrait of Commodus, A.D. 180–92, 3.1×2.5 cm. Paris, Cabinet des Médailles. *5:* Roman amethyst with portrait, 3d cent. Ht., 2 cm. Coll. Merz. *6:* Ring, so-called "seal of Theodoric," ca. 500 B.C. Amethyst, 2.2×1.65 cm. Bern, Coll. Merz. (*1–3, 5:* casts.) Copenhagen, Nationalmuseet.

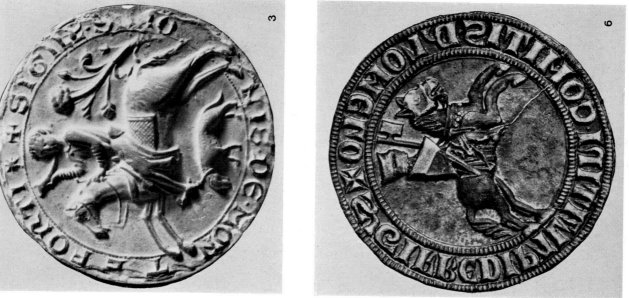

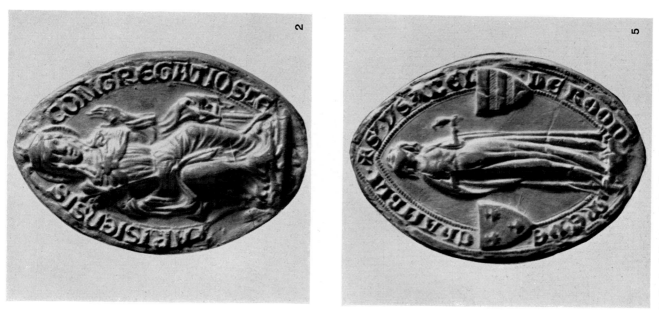

Pl. 529. *1–5*: Wax seals attached to documents in archives. *1*: Seal of Bertrand de Forcalquier, 1168. Diam., 5.8 cm. Bouches-du-Rhône, Archives Départementales. *2*: Seal of the Chapter of Notre Dame de Paris, 1222. Diam., 7 cm. *3*: Seal of Simon de Montfort, 1211. Diam., 7.5 cm. *4*: Seal of Louis, King of France, 1240. Diam., 8 cm. *5*: Seal of Isabelle de Rosny, 1294. Diam., 6 cm. Last four, Paris, Archives Nationales. *6*: Seal of Giffredo, count palatine of Lomello, Pavia, 1276. Bronze, diam., 6 cm. Rome, Museo di Palazzo Venezia. (Casts.)

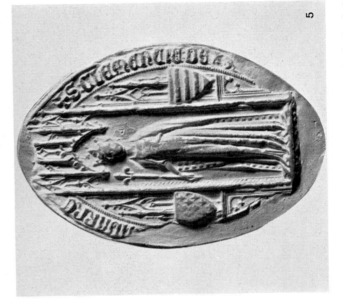

Pl. 530. Wax seals attached to documents in archives. *1*: Seal of the city of Lyons, 1271. Diam., 7 cm. *2*: Seal of the city of Bruges, 1281. Diam., 7.5 cm. *3*: Seal of the Sainte-Chapelle de Vincennes, 1406. Diam., 5.5 cm. *4*: Seal of Giovanni di Nicola, doctor of law, 14th cent. *5*: Seal of Clemence of Hungary, wife of Louis X, 1317. Diam., 9 cm. *6*: Seal of the Corporation des Poissoniers de Bruges, 1407. Diam., 5.3 cm. *Location: 1, 3, 5*: Paris, Archives Nationales; *2*: Rouen, Bibliothèque de la Ville; *4*: Siena, Palazzo Pubblico; *6*: Lille, Archives du Nord. (Casts.)

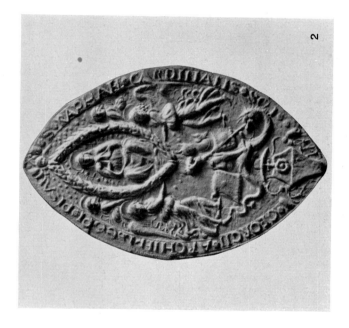

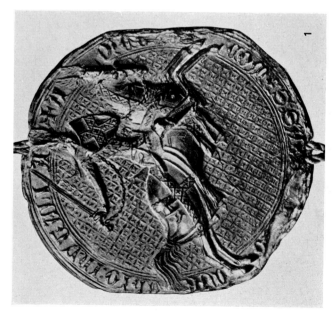

Pl. 531. *1*: Seal of Amadeus VI, Count of Savoy, 1370. Wax, 9.5 cm. Turin, Museo Civico, Medagliere. *2*: Pollaiuolo (attrib.), seal of Cardinal Rafaele Riario, Archbishop of Pisa, 1479–99. Bronze, 10×6.4 cm. (Plaster impression.) Rome, Museo di Palazzo Venezia. *3*: Seal of the city of Paris, 1412. Wax, 5.5 cm. (Terra-cotta cast of impression.) Paris, Archives Nationales. *4*: Imperial seal of Charles V of Spain, 1530. Wax seal in gold case with imperial coat of arms, diam., 9.8 cm. Florence, Archivio di Stato. *5*: Imperial seal of Philip II of Spain, 1555. Gold, diam., 11 cm. Rome, Archivio Vaticano. *6*: Seal of Sigismund III of Poland, 1587–1632. Paper.

Pl. 532. Papal bulla depicted in a painting by Colantonio, St. Jerome Extracting a Thorn from the Lion's Foot, mid-15th cent. Panel; full size, 4 ft., 1¼ in. × 4 ft., 11⅛ in. Naples, Museo e Gallerie Nazionali di Capodimonte.

SEALS

Pl. 533. *1*: Seal of Cardinal Marcello Crescenzi, 1542. Florence, Museo Nazionale. *2*: B. Cellini, seal of Cardinal Ippolito d'Este, 1540. Lead impression, 10.7×8.1 cm. Lyons, Musée des Beaux-Arts. *3*: Seal of Cardinal Filippo Sega, legate in France, 1591. *4*: Bulla of Urban VIII, 1623–44, with heads of SS. Peter and Paul. Lead, diam., 4.1 cm. *5*: Seal of Charles Emmanuel II of Savoy, 1743. Paper and wax, diam. of tondo, 4.7 cm. *6*: Seal of Angelo Durini, Archbishop of Ancyra (Ankara), nuncio in Poland, 1768. Paper, diam., 5.1 cm. *7*: Seal of Domenico Monti, Bishop of Anagni, 1750. Paper, 4.5×4 cm. Last five, Rome, Archivio Vaticano. *8*: Family coat of arms, wax impression, retouched and tinted, Italy, 19th cent. Rome, private coll.

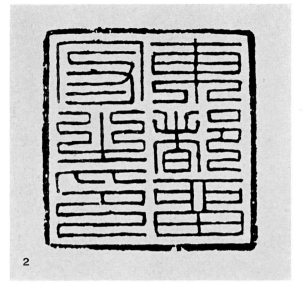

Pl. 534. *Above and center*: Chinese. *1*: An official seal of the Ch'in dynasty, imprint. *2*: Seal in ninefold script of the T'ang dynasty, imprint. *3, 4*: Ivory seal of the Ming emperor Hsien-tsung, 1467. Japan, Coll. Kawai Senro. *Below*: Japanese. *5*: Seal of the feudal lord Takeda Nobutora (1493–1573), with the character *nobu* and two tigers. Imprint. *6*: Seal of the general Oda Nobunaga (1534–82). Imprint.

Pl. 535. The Holy Family with SS. Catherine and Sebastian and donor. Canvas, 3 ft., $3^{1}/_{2}$ in. × 4 ft., $5^{1}/_{2}$ in. Paris, Louvre.

Pl. 536. Andrea Doria. Panel, 5 ft., × 3 ft., 5¹/₂ in. Rome, Galleria Doria Pamphili.

Pl. 537. *Above*: The Death of Adonis. Canvas, 6 ft., 2¹/₂ in. × 9 ft., 8 in. Florence, Uffizi. *Below, left*: The Raising of Lazarus. Canvas, transferred from panel; 12 ft., 6 in. × 9 ft., 6 in. London, National Gallery. *Right*: The Flagellation. Fresco. Rome, S. Pietro in Montorio, Borgherini Chapel.

Pl. 538. St. Louis of Toulouse (*left*) and St. Sinibald (*right*), originally on organ shutters. Canvas; each, 9 ft., 7³/₈ in. × 4 ft., 6 in. Venice, S. Bartolomeo a Rialto.

Pl. 539. Christ in Limbo. Canvas, transferred from panel; 7 ft., 5 in. × 3 ft., 9 in. Madrid, Prado.

Pl. 540. *Above, left*: The Holy Family, known as "La Madonna del Velo." Slate, 46¹/₂×34⁵/₈ in. Naples, Museo di Capodimonte. *Right*: The Visitation. Canvas, transferred from panel; 5 ft., 6 in. × 4 ft., 4 in. Paris, Louvre. *Below, left*: Christ Bearing the Cross. Canvas, 47⁵/₈×39³/₈ in. Madrid, Prado. *Right*: Pope Clement VII. Canvas, 4 ft., 9 in. × 3 ft., 3¹/₂ in. Naples, Museo di Capodimonte.

Pl. 541. Gulpaygan, Iran, Masjid-i-Jāmiʿ, view of portal, 1104/05–18.

Pl. 542. *Left*: Sava, Iran, Masjid-i-Jāmiʿ, minaret, 1110/11. *Right*: Damavand, Iran, polygonal tomb tower, 11th cent.

Pl. 543. Tomb tower, in the vicinity of Damghan, 11th cent.

Pl. 544. *Above*: Tomb tower called Gunbad-i-Qābūs, Gurgan, Iran, 1006/07. *Below*: Nayin, Iran, Ḥusayniya, 13th cent.

Pl. 545. *Above*: Ardistan, Iran, Masjid-i-Jāmi', detail of mihrab, ca. 1160. *Below*: Qazvin, Iran, Ḥaydariya, detail of interior, 11th–12th cent.

Pl. 546. *Above*: Zavara, near Ardistan, Iran, Masjid-i-Pā Minār, 11th cent. *Below*: Ardistan, Masjid-i-Jāmi', separation wall between the domed sanctuary and southwest liwan, showing stucco decoration in the liwan, 1158–60.

Pl. 547. Bowl with champlevé cream-colored glaze, from the Garrus region, Iran, second half of 12th cent. Diam., 12¼ in. London, Victoria and Albert Museum.

Pl. 548. Carved bowl with blue glaze, Iran, mid-12th cent. Diam., 7¼ in. London, Victoria and Albert Museum.

Pl. 549. Isfahan, Masjid-i-Jāmi', 11th–12th cent., interior details showing piers and decoration with inscriptions.

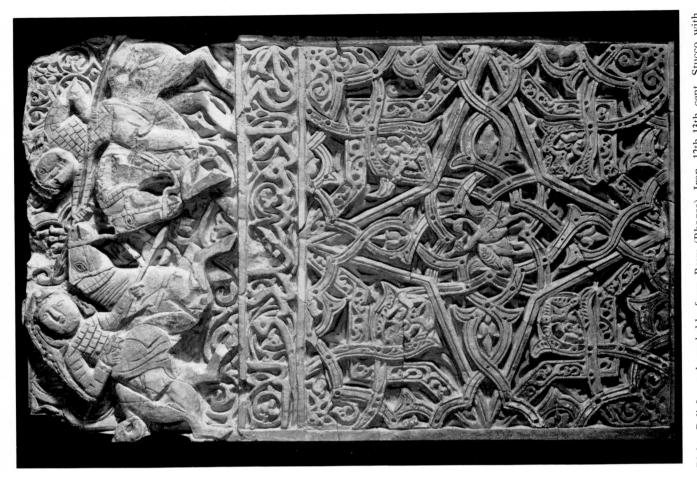

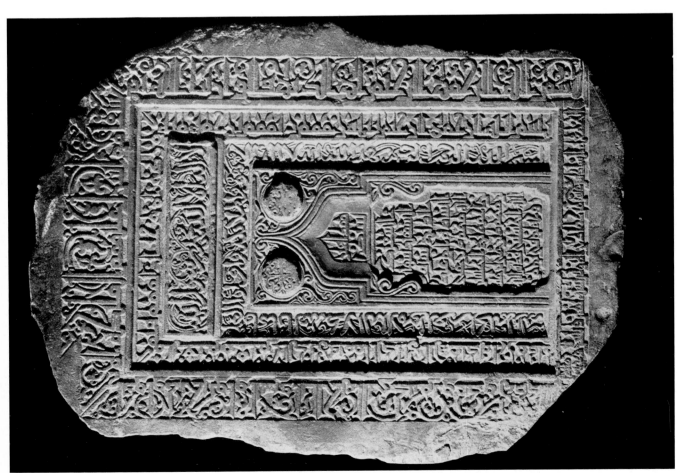

Pl. 550. *Left:* Fragment of a tombstone, representing a mihrab, 1143/44. Marble, ht., 26 in. *Right:* Relief panel, probably from Rayy (Rhages), Iran, 12th–13th cent. Stucco with traces of color, ht., 31½ in. Both, Seattle, Art Museum.

Pl. 551. *Left*: Bowl, depicting a prince hunting on horseback, from Rayy (Rhages), Iran, 11th–12th cent. Glazed pottery, diam., 7⁷/₈ in. *Right*: Bowl, from Gurgan, Iran, 13th cent. Blue and white faïence, diam., 12¹/₄ in. Both, Teheran, Archaeological Museum.

Pl. 552. *Above, left*: Bottle, from Gurgan, Iran, 12th cent. Pottery with gilded relief, ht., 12⅝ in. *Right*: Pitcher, from Gurgan, 13th cent. Lusterware, ht., 7⅛ in. *Below*: Openwork perfume burner, from Gurgan, 12th cent. Bronze, l., 11¾ in. All, Teheran, Archaeological Museum.

Pl. 553. Survival of Seljuk traditions after the Mongol conquest. Shams listening to the conversation of Shamat and the fairies, illumination in the *Kitāb-i-Samak ʿAyyār* by Ṣadaqa ibn-Abū'l-Qāsim Shīrāzī, from Shiraz, ca. 1330–40. Oxford, Bodleian Library (Ms. Ouseley 381, fol. 166 v).

Pl. 554. Landscape. Ink (*sumi*) on paper, 30³/₈×10⁵/₈ in.
Seattle, Art Museum, Eugene Fuller Memorial Coll.

Pl. 555. Autumn Landscape. Ink (*sumi*) on paper, 18¹/₄×11¹/₂ in. Tokyo, National Museum.

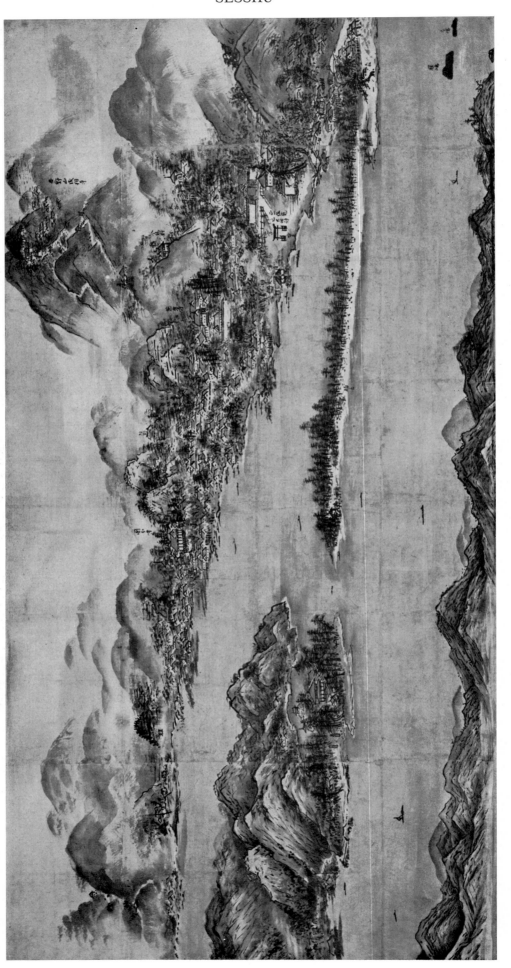

Pl. 556. Ama-no-Hashidate. Ink (*sumi*) on paper, 2 ft., 11¼ in. × 5 ft., 6½ in. Kyoto, National Museum.

Pl. 557. *Above*: Sunday Afternoon on the Island of La Grande Jatte. Canvas, 6 ft., 9 in. × 10 ft., ³/₈ in. Chicago, Art Institute. *Below*: The Bridge at Courbevoie. Canvas, 18×21¹/₂ in. London, Courtauld Institute Galleries.

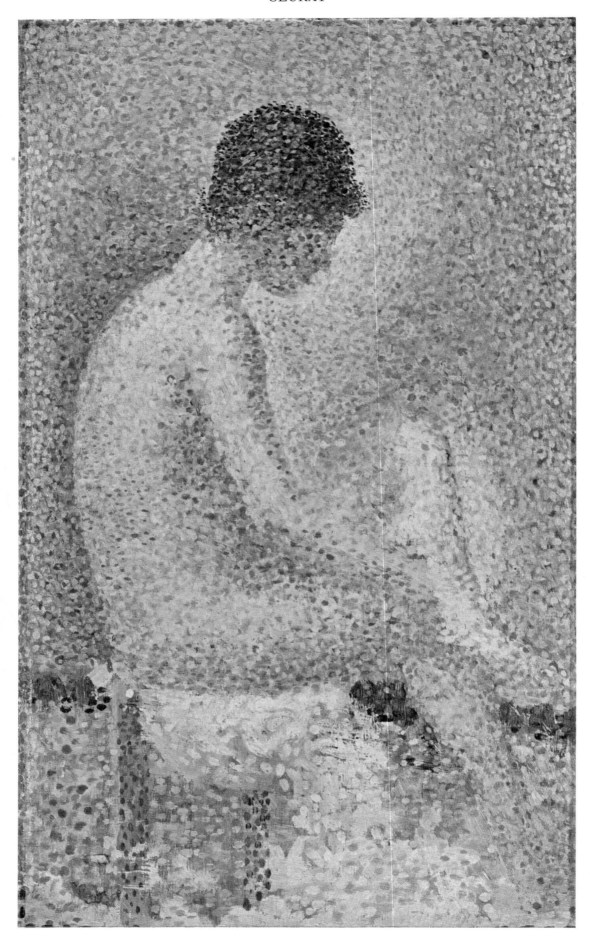

Pl. 558. Model in Profile, study for Les Poseuses. Panel, $9^7/_8 \times 6^1/_4$ in. Paris, Louvre.

Pl. 559. The Circus (unfinished). Canvas, ca. 6×5 ft. Paris, Louvre.

Pl. 560. *Above*: La Parade. Canvas, 39¹/₂×59¹/₄ in. New York, Metropolitan Museum. *Below, left*: Au Concert Européen. Conté crayon heightened with white, 12¹/₄×9³/₈ in. New York, Museum of Modern Art. *Right*: Le Chahut. Canvas, 5 ft., 6¹/₂ in. × 4 ft., 6³/₄ in. Otterlo, Netherlands, Rijksmuseum Kröller-Müller.

Pl. 561. Steatopygous female figurine, from Susa, late 2d millennium B.C. (?). Terra cotta, ht., 6³/₈ in. Paris, Louvre.

Pl. 562. *Above, left*: Rock relief representing birth or copulation (?), Laussel Shelter, Dordogne, France, Paleolithic period. Ht., 7⁷/₈ in. *Center and right*: Maori wall planks depicting (*center*) Maui's attempt to enter and slay the goddess of death, and (*right*) copulation, from New Zealand. *Below, left*: Pre-Columbian jar with erotic scene, in Mochica style, from Peru. Pottery. Last three, Hamburg, Museum für Völkerkunde. *Right*: Menhir, with supposed procreative or recreative symbolism, Filitosa, Corsica, Aëneolithic period.

Pl. 563. *Above*: Seilenos seizing a maenad, attributed to Makron, interior of an Attic kylix signed by the potter Hieron, 490 B.C. Full diam., 12³/₈ in. Paris, Louvre. *Below*: *Symplegma*, detail of an Arretine vase, Augustan age. Arezzo, Italy, Museo Archeologico.

Pl. 564. *Above, left*: Callipygian Venus, from the Domus Aurea, Roman copy (Hellenistic original, second half of 3d cent. B.C.). Marble, ht., 5 ft. Naples, Museo Nazionale. *Right*: Nymph struggling with satyr, Roman copy (Hellenistic-Alexandrine original, ca. 150 B.C.). Marble, ht., 22 1/2 in. Rome, Palazzo dei Conservatori, Museo Nuovo. *Below*: Sleeping hermaphrodite, Roman copy (Hellenistic original, ca. 160 B.C.). Marble, l., 4 ft., 10 in. Rome, Museo Nazionale Romano.

Pl. 565. *Mithuna* couple, detail of exterior decoration, Kaṇḍārya Mahādeva temple, Khajuraho, Madhya Pradesh, India, ca. 11th cent.

Pl. 566. Venus and the lovers, painted on a *desco da parto* ("birth tray," for gifts to the mother of a newborn child), northern Italy, first half of 15th cent. Wood, w., ca. 19 in. Paris, Louvre.

Pl. 567. *Above*: A. Altdorfer, Lot and His Daughters, 1537. Panel, 3 ft., 6 in. × 6 ft., 2 ½ in. Vienna, Kunsthistorisches Museum. *Below*: Correggio, Leda and the Swan, ca. 1530 (?). Canvas, 5 ft. × 6 ft., 3 ¼ in. Berlin, Staatliche Museen.

Pl. 568. *Above*: Agostino Carracci, Love in the Golden Age, one of the series of *lascivie*, 1588–89 (?). Canvas, 5 ft., 3 in. × 8 ft., 6³/₈ in. *Below, left*: H. von Aachen (1552–1615), Jupiter, Antiope, and Cupid. Copper, 12×8¹/₄ in. *Right*: J. Heintz the Elder (1564–1615), Venus and Adonis. Copper, 15³/₄×12¹/₄ in. All, Vienna, Kunsthistorisches Museum.

Pl. 569. *Above*: Rembrandt, Joseph and Potiphar's Wife, 1634. Etching, 3 1/2 × 4 1/2 in. *Below*: F. Boucher, Odalisque, 1743. Canvas, 20 7/8 × 25 5/8 in. Reims, France, Musée des Beaux-Arts (*dépôt de l'État*).

Pl. 570. *Above, left*: P. A. Baudouin (1723–69), Le Soir. Gouache, engraved by E. de Ghendt. *Right*: J.-H. Fragonard, The Love Letters, 1771. Canvas, 10 ft., 5¹/₄ in. × 7 ft., ⁵/₈ in. New York, Frick Coll. *Below, left*: F. Boucher (1703–70), Hercules and Omphale. Canvas, 35¹/₂×29¹/₈ in. Moscow, A. S. Pushkin Museum of Fine Arts. *Right*: F. Schall (1752–1825), Le Bât. Painting, engraved by J. Bonnefoy.

Pl. 571. *Above*: Hishikawa Moronobu, woodcut, from a Japanese version of the Chinese erotic album *Fêng-liu-chüeh-ch'ang* (pub. 1606). *Below, left*: Woodcut, detail, from the Chinese erotic album *Hua-ying-chin-chên*, late Ming period. *Right*: Miniature depicting a lover and his mistress, northern India, 18th cent. The Hague, R. H. van Gulik Coll.

Pl. 572. *Above*: G. Grosz, Dr. Benns Nachtcafé, 1918. Lithograph, 19³/₄×25⁵/₈ in. *Below*: P. Picasso, Sculptor and Model in Repose, 1933. Etching.